THE

CAMBRIDGE DICTIONARY OF CHRISTIANITY

The Cambridge Dictionary of Christianity is an authoritative reference guide that enables students, their teachers, Christian clergy, and general readers alike to reflect critically upon all aspects of Christianity from its origins to the present day. Written by a team of 828 scholars and practitioners from around the world, the volume reflects the plurality of Christianity throughout its history.

Key features of *The Cambridge Dictionary of Christianity*:

- Provides a survey of the history of Christianity in the world, on each continent, and in each nation
- Offers a presentation of the Christian beliefs and practices of all major Christian traditions
- Highlights the different understandings of Christian beliefs and practices in different historical, cultural, religious, denominational, and secular contexts
- Includes entries on methodology and the plurality of approaches that are used in the study of Christianity
- Respects each Christian tradition by providing self-presentations of Christianity in each country or Christian tradition
- Includes clusters of entries on beliefs and practices, each examining the understanding of a given Christian belief or practice in different historical and contemporary contexts
- Presents the relationship and interaction of Christianity with other religious traditions in the world
- Provides, on a Web site (http://hdl.handle.net/1803/3906), a full bibliography covering all topics discussed in the signed articles of this volume

Daniel Patte is Professor of Religious Studies and Professor of New Testament and Early Christianity at Vanderbilt University.

THE

CAMBRIDGE DICTIONARY OF CHRISTIANITY

Editor

DANIEL PATTE

Vanderbilt University

CAMBRIDGE UNIVERSITY PRESS
Cambridge, New York, Melbourne, Madrid, Cape Town, Singapore,
São Paulo, Delhi, Dubai, Tokyo, Mexico City

Cambridge University Press
32 Avenue of the Americas, New York, NY 10013-2473, USA

www.cambridge.org
Information on this title: www.cambridge.org/9780521527859

First published 2010

Printed in the United States of America

A catalog record for this publication is available from the British Library.

Library of Congress Cataloging in Publication data

The Cambridge dictionary of Christianity / edited by Daniel Patte.
p. cm.
ISBN 978-0-521-82096-7 (hardback) – ISBN 978-0-521-52785-9 (pbk.)
1. Christianity – Dictionaries. I. Patte, Daniel. II. Title: Dictionary of Christianity.
BR95.C24 2010
230.003 – dc22 2009019272

ISBN 978-0-521-82096-7 Hardback
ISBN 978-0-521-52785-9 Paperback

Additional resources for this publication at http://hdl.handle.net/1803/3906

CONTENTS

For a comprehensive bibliography, see http://hdl.handle.net/1803/3906.

EDITORIAL BOARD

AREA EDITORS AND ADVISORS

Jean-Noël Aletti, SJ, *Pontifical Biblical Institute, Rome, Italy*: Roman Catholicism

Ian Breward, *University of Melbourne, Australia*: Australasia; Australia and South Pacific

James P. Byrd, *Vanderbilt University, USA*: North America, History

Noriel Capulong, *Silliman University, Philippines*: Philippines

Elizabeth A. Clark, *Duke University, USA*: Women in the History of Christian Thought

Valentin Dedji, *St. Mark's Methodist Church, London, UK*: Western Africa (Francophone)

Beatriz de Vasconcellos Dias, *Comissão de Estudos de História da Igreja na América Latina e no Caribe (CEHILA), Brasil*: Brazil

Ramathate T. H. Dolamo, *UNISA, Pretoria, South Africa*: Southern Africa

Noel Leo Erskine, *Emory University, USA*: Caribbean Islands, Ethics, and Theology

George Thomas Kurian, *Reference Books, New York, USA*: Statistics (Christians in each nation)

Armando Lampe, *Comisión de Estudios de Historia de la Iglesia en Latinoamérica (CEHILA), Universidad de Quintana Roo, Mexico*: Caribbean Islands, History

Marjorie Lewis, *United Theological College of the West Indies; former General Secretary of the Jamaica Council of Churches (area editor following the untimely death of Lewin Williams)*: Jamaica and Jamaican Theology

Frank D. Macchia, *Vanguard University, USA*: Charismatic Movement and Pentecostalism

Fortunato Mallimaci, *Centro de Estudios e Investigaciones Laborales, Argentina*: Southern Latin America

Bonnie J. Miller-McLemore, *Vanderbilt University, USA*: Family and Children; Pastoral Theology

Nektarios Morrow, *Greek Orthodox Archdiocese of America*: Eastern Orthodoxy

Gerald O'Collins, SJ, *The Pontifical Gregorian University, Italy*: Roman Catholicism

Muriel Orevillo-Montenegro, *Silliman University, Philippines*: Philippines and Women in Asia

Peter Paris, *Princeton Theological Seminary, USA*: Poverty; Racism

Keith F. Pecklers, SJ, *Pontifical Gregorian University, Italy*: Roman Catholic Liturgy

Bishop Yeznik Petrossian, *Holy See of Etchmiadzin, Armenia*: Oriental Orthodoxy; Non-Chalcedonian Churches

María Alicia Puente Lutteroth, *Universidad Autónoma del Estado de Morelos, Mexico; Comisión de Estudios de Historia de la Iglesia en Latinoamérica (CEHILA), Mexico*: Mexico

Fernando F. Segovia, *Vanderbilt University, USA*: Latino/a Christianity and Theology

Karel Steenbrink, *Utrecht University, Netherlands*: Islam and Christianity

Elsa Tamez, *Universidad Bíblica Latinoamericana, Costa Rica; United Bible Societies, Colombia*: Central America and Latin American Theology

Archbishop Demetrios [Trakatellis], *Archbishop of America, Primate of the Greek (Eastern) Orthodox Church in America, USA*: Eastern Orthodoxy

Justin Ukpong, *Veritas University Abuja, Nigeria*: Western Africa (Anglophone)

Andrew Walls, *Centre for the Study of Christianity in the Non-Western World, University of Edinburgh, Scotland, and Akrofi Christaller Memorial Centre, Ghana*: Mission

Patricia A. Ward, *Vanderbilt University, USA*: Literature, the Bible, and Christianity

Paul Zamora, *Greek Orthodox, Archdiocese of America, USA*: Eastern Orthodoxy

CONTRIBUTORS

Rose Teteki Abbey, *Presbyterian Church, Ghana*: God, African View

K. C. Abraham, *Tainan Theological Seminary, India*: Eschatology and Apocalypticism in Asia; Liberation Theologies in Asia; Poverty, Asian View; Racism in Asia; South India, Church

David Tuesday Adamo, *Delta State University, Nigeria*: African Religion and Bible

LeRoy H. Aden, *Lutheran Theological Seminary, USA*: Compassion; Death, Bible, Patristic Views; Death, North American View

Efrain Agosto, *Hartford Theological Seminary, USA*: Jesus, Latino/a View; Philippians

Victor Aguilan, *Silliman University, Philippines*: Church and State in Philippines; Evangelicals/Evangelicalism in Philippines

Gillian T. W. Ahlgren, *Xavier University, USA*: Isabella I of Castille; Philip II; Teresa of Ávila

Charanjit Kaur AjitSingh, *England*: Sikhism

Dorothy B E A Akoto, *Trinity Theological Seminary, Ghana*: Ghana

Giuseppe Alberigo, *Università di Bologna, Italy*: Borromeo; Italy; RC in Italy

Daniel E. Albrecht, *Bethany University, USA*: Pentecostal Worship

Ruth Albrecht, *Universität Hamburg, Germany*: Pietism and Women

Daniel O. Aleshire, *Association of Theological Schools, USA*: Theological Education

Urs Altermatt, *Universität Freiburg, Germany*: Racism in Europe; Switzerland

Anand Amaladass, *Satya Nilayam, India*: Hinduism; Nobili

Michael Amaladoss, SJ, *Loyola College, India*: Uniqueness of Christ

James N. Amanze, *University of Botswana*: Anglicanism in Southern Africa

Lesley G. Anderson, *United Theological College, West Indies*: Christologies, Caribbean

Thomas C. Anderson, *Marquette University, USA*: I–Thou; Marcel

Victor Anderson, *Vanderbilt University, USA*: African American Theologies; Black Theology; Dewey; DuBois; Pragmatism; Racism; Thurman

Hope S. Antone, *Christian Conference of Asia, Hong Kong, China*: Family in Asia; Marriage in Asia; Women's Ordination in Asia

María Pilar Aquino, *University of San Diego, USA*: Feminist Theology, Latina

Paula Arai, *Louisiana State University, USA*: Shinto and Christianity

Victorio Araya Guillén, *Universidad de Costa Rica*: Anthropology, Latin American; God, Latin American View; Incarnation, Latin American View; Justice in Latin America; Preferential Option for the Poor

S. Wesley Ariarajah, *Drew University, USA*: Evangelicals/Evangelicalism in Asia; God, Asian View

Ellen T. Armour, *Vanderbilt University, USA*: Feminist Theology in North America; Postmodernism; Racism, Feminist View

Brett Gregory Armstrong, *Trevecca Nazarene University, USA*: Bancroft

Atsuhiro Asano, *Nihon University, Ochanomizu, Japan*: Galatians

Naim Stifan Ateek, *Sabeel Ecumenical Center, Israel*: Palestinian Liberation Theology

Mahmoud Ayoub, *Temple University, USA*; Muslim Views of Christianity

John Alembillah Azumah, *Director, Centre for Islamic Studies, London*: Church and State in Islamic Africa; Islam in Africa

Mercedes L. García Bachmann, *Instituto Superior Evangélico de Estudios Teológicos, Argentina*: Bible Interpretation in Latin America

Irena Backus, *Université de Genève, Switzerland*: Bolsec; Geneva, Calvin's

J. Wayne Baker, *University of Akron, USA*: Bullinger; Zwingli

Mieke Bal, *University of Amsterdam, Netherlands*: Deborah

Lewis V. Baldwin, *Vanderbilt University, USA*: Baker; Civil Rights; King, Martin Luther, Jr.; Malcolm X; National Baptist Convention, USA; Slavery through the Centuries; Slavery in North America; Southern Christian Leadership Conference; Spirituals; Turner

William Barbieri, *Catholic University of America, USA*: War

António Barbosa da Silva, *Universitetet i Oslo, Norway*: Cape Verde

David Basinger, *Roberts Wesleyan College, USA*: Philosophy of Religion; Predestination; Will

Bolaji Olukemi Bateye, *Obafemi Awolowo University, Nigeria*: Women's Practices in Africa

Oswald Bayer, *Universität Tübingen, Germany*: Justification, Western View; Lutheranism in Germany

Daniel H. Bays, *Calvin College, USA*: Chinese House Churches

Rosalie Beck, *Baylor University, USA*: Booth, C.; Booth, W.; Salvation Army; Women's Missionary Societies

Nancy Elizabeth Bedford, *Garrett-Evangelical Theological Seminary, USA*: Christologies, Latin American View; Latin American Theologies

Guy-Thomas Bedouelle, OP, *Université de Fribourg, Switzerland*: Devotio Moderna; Dominic; Dominican Order; Elisabeth of Hungary; Lefèvre D'Étaples

Chorbishop Seely Beggiani, *Our Lady of Lebanon Maronite Seminary, USA*: Antioch; Aphrahat; Maronite Church

Wolfgang Behringer, *Universität des Saarlandes, Germany*: Demonization; Devil; Witchcraft

Christopher M. Bellitto, *Kean University, USA*: Constantinople, Councils; Lateran Councils; Vatican I

Byard Bennett, *Grand Rapids Theological Seminary, USA*: Didymus

Harold V. Bennett, *Morehouse College, USA*: Deuteronomy

Teresa Berger, *Duke University, USA*: Women's Practices, History

Fr. Miguel A. Bernad, *Xavier University, Philippines*: RC in the Philippines

Henley Bernard, *United Theological College, West Indies, Jamaica*: Holy Spirit, Caribbean View

Alan E. Bernstein, *University of Arizona, USA*: Damnation; Death, European View; Eternity; Hell; Judgment; Purgatory

Jon L. Berquist, *Westminster John Knox Press, USA*: Ezekiel

Johannes Beutler, SJ, *Pontifico Instituto Biblico, Italy*: John, Epistles

Ana María Bidegain, *Member of the Editorial Board; Universidad Nacional de Colombia & Florida International University, USA*: Borda; Catholic Action; Catholic Action, Latin America; CELAM; Church and State in Colombia; Colombia; Contemplation; Feminist Theologies in Latin America; History of Christianity in Latin America; Mary in Latin America; Medellín; Protestantism in Colombia; Torres; Trujillo; Women's Religious Orders in Latin America

Matthew P. Binkewicz, *Hospice of the Finger Lakes, USA*: Dying, Care of the

Jennifer Bird, *Greensboro College, USA*: Church, Feminist View; Household Codes; Peter, 1 and 2

Joseph Blenkinsopp, *University of Notre Dame, USA*: Isaiah

Dmytro Bondarenko, *Economic and Social Research Council, Ukraine*: Orthodox Churches, Ukraine; Secularization and Orthodoxy

Paulo Bonfatti, *Juiz de Fora Federal University, Brasil*: Charismatics in Brazil

Riet en Pim Bons-Storm, *Rijksuniversiteit Groningen, Netherland*: Family in Western Europe

Jessica A. Boon, *Duke University, USA*: Angela of Foligno; Clare of Assisi; Clare of Montefalco; Jeanne of Jussie; John of Avila; Julian of Norwich; Kempe; Poor Clares

Marcus J. Borg, *Oregon State University, USA*: Jesus, Quest; Jesus Seminar

Mark Bosco, SJ, *Loyola University, Chicago, USA*: Greene

Peter C. Bouteneff, *St. Vladimir Orthodox Theological Seminary, USA*: Russian Orthodox Church

François Bovon, *Harvard Divinity School, USA*: Apocryphal Acts; Philip, Acts; Thomas, Acts

William D. Bowman, *Gettysburg College, USA*: Austria

Paul S. Boyer, *University of Wisconsin-Madison, USA*: Millennialism; Millennialism in North America

David Brakke, *Indiana University, USA*: Athanasius

Richard E. Brantley, *University of Florida, USA*: Romanticism

Marcus Braybrooke, *World Congress of Faiths, UK*: Baha'i: Christian View

Ian Breward, *University of Melbourne, Australia*: Anglicanism in South Pacific; Australia; Evangelicals in South Pacific; History of Christianity in South Pacific; Independent Churches in South Pacific; Mission in South Pacific; New Zealand; Protestantism in South Pacific

Ênio José da Costa Brito, *Pontifícia Universidade Católica de São Paulo, Brasil*: Slavery in Brazil

Jewel Spears Brooker, *Eckerd College, USA*: Eliot, T. S.

Johannes Brosseder, *Universität zu Köln, Germany*: RC and Lutheranism in Germany

Nicholas Canfield Read Brown, *Fuller Theological Seminary, USA*: Peace

Robert F. Brown, *University of Delaware, USA*: Schelling

Pamela K. Brubaker, *California Lutheran University, USA*: Poverty, Feminist View

Walter Brueggemann, *Columbia Theological Seminary, Atlanta, USA*: Psalms; Worship in Ancient Israel

Bishop Colin O. Buchanan, *Anglican Communion Institute, UK*: Anglican Communion; Anglican Worship; Forty-two Articles; Lambeth Conferences; Lambeth Quadrilateral; Thirty-nine Articles

Stanley M. Burgess, *Regent University, USA*: Charismatic Movement, History; Pentecostal Movement, History

Amy Nelson Burnett, *University of Nebraska, Lincoln, USA*: Bucer; Marburg Colloquy

J. Patout Burns, *Vanderbilt University, USA*: Cyprian

David B. Burrell CSC, *University of Notre Dame, USA*: Maimonides

David Buttrick, *Vanderbilt University, USA*: Preaching; Reformed Worship

James P. Byrd, *Vanderbilt University, USA*: Adams; Asbury; Hodge; Jefferson; Plymouth Brethren; United States; Williams

Lavinia Byrne, *West Nave House, UK*: Catherine of Sienna; Helena; Margaret of Scotland; Ward

Gerado Caetano, *Universidad de la República Uruguaya*: Church and State in Uruguay; RC in Uruguay; Uruguay

Marcos Caldas, *Universidade Federal Fluminense, Brasil*: Inquisition in Brazil; Religious Orders in Brazil

Alkiviadis Calivas, *Holy Cross School of Theology, USA*: Baptism, Orthodox View; Chrismation; Popular Practices in Orthodoxy

William J. Callahan, *University of Toronto, Canada*: RC in Spain; Spain

Salvatore Calomino, *University of Wisconsin, USA*: Barlaam and Josaphat

Euan K. Cameron, *Union Theological Seminary, New York, USA*: Waldenses

William S. Campbell, *University of Wales Lampeter, UK*: Käsemann

Marcelo Ayres Camurça, *Juiz de Fora Federal University, Brasil*: Popular Practices in Brazil

Daniel F. Caner, *University of Connecticut, USA*: Acoemetae; Circumcellions; Messalians

Paul E. Capetz, *United Theological Seminary of the Twin Cities, USA*: God, History

Carlos F. Cardoza-Orlandi, *Columbia Theological Seminary, New York, USA*: Mission in Caribbean; Valladolid

Patrick W. Carey, *Marquette University, USA*: Brownson; Hecker; Theological Education, RC View

Barbara Carvill, *Calvin College, USA*: German Literature

Hal Cauthron, *Southern Nazarene University, USA*: Nazarene, Church

Subhadra Mitra Channa, *University of Delhi, India*: Tribalism

Mark D. Chapman, *University of Oxford, UK*: History of Religion; Liberal Theology; Troeltsch

James H. Charlesworth, *Princeton Theological Seminary, USA*: Dead Sea Scrolls

Kenneth R. Chase, *Wheaton College, USA*: Violence

Chen Zemin, *Nanjing Union Theological Seminary, China*: Chinese Protestant Churches

Luciano Chianeque, *Seminário Emanuel Unido do Huambo, Angola*: Angola; Human Rights in Africa

Philip Chia Phin Yin, *Chung Chi College, Chinese University of Hong Kong, China*: Obadiah; Tobit

Francisca H. Chimhanda, *Congregatio Jesu, Zimbabwe*: Religious Orders in Africa

Daniel Chiquete, *Universität Hamburg, Germany*: Charismatics in Central America; Health, Healing, in Latin America; Holy Spirit, Latin American View

John T. Chirban, *Harvard University, USA*: Health, Healing, Orthodox View; Resurrection, Orthodox View

Soobin Choi, *Sogang University, Seoul, Korea*: Daoist Canon and Bible

Robert Choquette, *University of Ottawa, Canada*: Canada, Ryerson; Strachan; Taché

Mita Choudhury, *Vassar College, USA*: Arnauld, Jacqueline; Joncoux

Gerald Christianson, *Lutheran Theological Seminary, Gettysburg, USA*: Inner Mission; Wichern

John Chryssavgis, *Greek Orthodox Archdiocese of America, USA*: Ecology, Orthodox View

Sejong Chun, *Vanderbilt University, USA*: New Creation

Esther Chung-Kim, *Claremont School of Theology, USA*: Brenz; Hubmaier; Peasants' War

Charles M. A. Clark, *St. John's University, USA*: Poverty and RC

Elizabeth A. Clark, *Duke University, USA*: Asceticism; Historiography; Origenist Controversy; Virginity

Sathianathan Clarke, *Wesley Theological Seminary, USA*: Caste System; Dalit Theology

Fred Cloud, *American Baptist College, USA*: Prayer

John B. Cobb, Jr., *Claremont School of Theology, USA*: Hartshorne; Process Theology; Whitehead

W. Owen Cole, *Shap Working Party on World Religions and Education, UK*: Sikhism: Christian View; Sikh Scriptures

John A Coleman, SJ, *Loyola Marymount University, USA*: Global Ethics; Globalization

John J. Collins, *Yale University, USA*: Apocalypticism, Origins; Violence and the Bible

Sylvia Collins-Mayo, *Kingston University, UK*: Secularization and Desecularization

Paul K. Conkin, *Vanderbilt University, USA*: Darwinism; Edwards

Beth A. Conklin, *Vanderbilt University, USA*: Climate Change

Sean Connolly, *Queen's University, Belfast, UK*: Ireland

Demetrios J. Constantelos, *Richard Stockton College of New Jersey, USA*: Poverty, Orthodox View

Michael A. Conway, *Pontifical University, Ireland*: Blondel

Paula M. Cooey, *Macalester College, USA*: Body

Austin Cooper, OMI, *Catholic Theological College, Australia*: RC in South Pacific; Spirituality in South Pacific

Michael L. Cooper-White, *Gettysburg Seminary, USA*: Lutheran Churches, Evangelical Lutheran Church in America

Pamela Cooper-White, *Lutheran Theological Seminary, Philadelphia, USA*: Pastoral Theology

L. William Countryman, *Graduate Theological Union, USA*: Honor and Shame

Sérgio Coutinho, *Universidade Cátolica de Brasília, Brasil*: CEBs; Church in Brazil: Church and State in Brazil; RC in Brazil

Pamela Couture, *Saint Paul School of Theology, USA*: Family in North America

Shannon Craigo-Snell, *Yale University, USA*: Anthropology, Feminist View; Image of God, Feminist and Liberation Views

James L. Crenshaw, *Duke University, USA*: Covenant; Ecclesiastes; Joel; Prophecy; Proverbs; Sacrifice of Isaac; Wisdom of Ben Sira

David Crowner, *Lutheran Theological Seminary, Gettysburg, USA*: Inner Mission; Wichern

Humberto Horacio Cucchetti, *Centro de Estudios e Investigaciones Laborales, Buenos Aires, Argentina*: Church and State in Argentina

Lawrence S. Cunningham, *University of Notre Dame, USA*: Holiness

Elizabeth Mason Currier, *Trinity Evangelical Divinity School, USA*: Evangelicals; Evangelicals in North America; New Haven Theology

Emmanuel Cutrone, *University of Notre Dame, USA*: Ambrosian (Milanese) Rite

Mary L. Daniel, *University of Wisconsin, USA*: Portuguese Literature

David D. Daniels III, *McCormick Theological Seminary, USA*: Church of God in Christ

Robert Darden, *Baylor University, USA*: Gospel Music

Rolf Darge, *Katholisch-Theologische Fakultät der Universität Salzburg, Austria*: Suárez

Isaiah Dau, *Nairobi Pentecostal Bible College, Kenya*: Sudan

Jeffry C. Davis, *Wheaton College, USA*: Canaan; Elijah; Exile; Flood; Joseph, Husband of Mary; Joseph, Son of Jacob and Rachel; Noah; Samaria; Shepherd; Sodom; Star; Vine, Vineyard; Wilderness; Zion

Jane Dawson, *University of Edinburgh, UK*: Book of Common Order; Knox

Valentin Dedji, *St. Mark's Methodist Church, London, UK*: African Instituted Churches in Western Africa; Benin; Burkina Faso; Central African Republic; Chad; Gabon; Mission in Africa; Senegal; Togo

John W. de Gruchy, *University of Cape Town, South Africa*: Bonhoeffer; Democracy

Paul DeHart, *Vanderbilt Divinity School, USA*: Radical Orthodoxy

Wendy J. Deichmann Edwards, *United Theological Seminary, USA*: Shaw; Temperance; Willard

Miguel A. De La Torre, *Hope College, USA*: Latino/a Theologies

George E. Demacopoulos, *Fordham University, USA*: Mary, Theotokos

Thomas de Mayo, *J. Sargent Reynolds Community College, USA*: Angels

Leah DeVun, *Texas A&M University, USA*: Apocalypticism in Western History; Resurrection, Western View

Beatriz de Vasconcellos Dias, *CEHILA, Brasil*: RC in Brazil; Women's Religious Orders in Brazil

Dennis C. Dickerson, *Vanderbilt University, USA*: African American Churches; African American Holiness; African Methodist Episcopal Church; Allen; Payne

John M. Dillon, *Trinity College Dublin, Ireland*: Neoplatonism; Platonism

Luis Miguel Donatello, *Universidad de Buenos Aires, Argentina*: Angelelli; Argentina; Meinvielle; Moyano Llerena

Igor Dorfmann-Lazarev, *Centre d'Etudes ISTINA, France*: Armenia; Armenian Genocide; Gregory the Illuminator; Mashtots; Moses of Khoren; Nerses

Susanna Drake, *Duke University, USA*: Melania the Elder; Melania the Younger

Jonathan A. Draper, *University of KwaZulu-Natal, South Africa*: Colenso

Martin N. Dreher, *Universidade do Vale do Rio dos Sinos, Brasil*: Protestantism in Brazil

Otto Dreydoppel, Jr., *Moravian Theological Seminary, USA*: Bohemian Brethren; Comenius; Moravian Church; Moravian Worship; Zinzendorf

Angelyn Dries, OSF, *Saint Louis University, USA*: Maryknoll Missionaries

A. J. Droge, *University of Toronto, Canada*: Hellenistic Christian Self-definition

Francis X. D'Sa, SJ, *Bayerische Julius-Maximilians-Universität Würzburg, Germany*: Hinduism; Hindu Scriptures

Marilyn Dunn, *University of Glasgow, Scotland*: Benedict; Benedict, Rule of; Carthusian; Cistercian; Columba; Columbanus; Carta Caritatis; Iona; Monastic Rules; Regula Magistri

Nicole Wilkinson Duran, *Meadville Lombard Theological School, USA*: Eve; Herod; Herodians; Herodias; Judith; Mark; Miriam; Pilate; Salome; Tamar (Gen 38); Tamar (2 Sam 13); Tomb of Jesus; Tree of Life; Trial of Jesus; Zipporah

Rifaat Ebied, *University of Sydney, Australia*: Bar Hebraeus; Damian; Dionysius bar Salibi; Peter of Callinicus; Timothy II Aelurus; Tritheism

Mark J. Edwards, *Christ Church College, University of Oxford, UK*: Constantine; Eusebius of Caesarea

William H. Edwards, *University of South Australia*: Ancestors, Australian Aboriginal View; Anthropology, Australian Aboriginal View; Australian Aboriginal Traditions; Family, Australian View

Leonard H. Ehrlich, *University of Massachusetts, USA*: Jaspers

Nancy L. Eiesland, *Emory University, USA*: Disability

Martin Elbel, *Palacký University, Czech Republic*: Czech Republic; Slovak Republic

J. Harold Ellens, *University of Michigan, USA*: Ideological Studies; Ideology

Stephen Ellingson, *Hamilton College, USA*: Megachurches in North America

Marvin M. Ellison, *Bangor Theological Seminary, USA*: Family, Nonheterosexual

Robert Ellsberg, *Orbis Books, USA*: De Foucauld

Jean Bethke Elshtain, *University of Chicago, USA*: Addams

Eldon Jay Epp, *Case Western Reserve University and Harvard University, USA*: Junia

Peter C. Erb, *Wilfrid Laurier University in Waterloo, Canada*: Arndt; Boehme; Ephrata Cloister; Ephrata Community; Gladstone; Keble; Manning; Newman; Oxford Movement; Pusey; Schwenkfeld von Ossig; Ultramontanism; Wilberforce

Tassilo Erhardt, *Roosevelt Academy, The Netherlands*: Handel; Messiah, Handel's; Mozart; Palestrina

Maria Erling, *Lutheran Theological Seminary, Gettysburg, USA*: Lutheran Churches in USA; Muhlenberg

Noel Leo Erskine, *Emory University, USA*: Caribbean Islands, Theologies; Christologies, Caribbean View; God, Caribbean View; Gospel and Culture, Caribbean View; Justice, Caribbean View; Liberation Theologies, Caribbean View; Poverty, Caribbean View

Gillian R. Evans, *University of Cambridge, UK*: Bernard of Clairvaux; Anselm of Canterbury; Gregory I; Peter Lombard

Virginia Fabella, MM, *Institute of Formation and Religious Studies, Philippines*: Women's Religious Orders in Asia

Michael A. Fahey, SJ, *Marquette University, USA*: Baptism, RC View; RC in USA; Sacramental Theology; Sacraments in Western Churches

Edward Farley, *Vanderbilt University, USA*; Fundamentalism

Margaret A. Farley, *Yale Divinity School, USA*: Health, Healing, Feminist View; Health and Healing Theologies; Medical Ethics

Wendy Farley, *Emory University, USA*: Desire; Suffering

Robert Fastiggi, *Sacred Heart Major Seminary, USA*: Consecration; Holy Office; Ordination; Priesthood; Roman Catechism

Seena Fazel, *University of Oxford, UK*: Baha'i Faith, Baha'i Perspective

Duncan S. Ferguson, *Director, Committee on Higher Education, Presbyterian Church (USA); Eckerd College, USA*: Education as Christian Service; Educational Practices in USA; New Age Spirituality; Sunday School

Helwar Figueroa, *Florida International University, USA*: Church and State in Colombia

Paul Corby Finney, *University of Missouri, USA*: Jesus, Images of; Jesus, Images of, European View

Kyriaki Karidoyanes FitzGerald, *St. Catherine's Vision, USA*: Ecumenical Patriarchate; Laity, Orthodox View; Women's Ordination and the Orthodox Church

Thomas E. FitzGerald, *Holy Cross Greek Orthodox School of Theology, USA*: Ecumenical Patriarchate; Greek Orthodox Church in America; Orthodox Churches in USA

John R. Fitzmier, *Claremont School of Theology, USA*: Dwight

Marie Therese Flanagan, *Queen's University Belfast, UK*: Celtic Christianity

Sabina Flanagan, *University of Adelaide, Australia*: Gertrude; Hildegard of Bingen

Claude Flipo, SJ, *Centre Sèvre, France*: Ignatius of Loyola; Jesuits; Spiritual Exercises

Ronald B. Flowers, *Texas Christian University, USA*: Church and State in USA

Carole Fontaine, *Andover Newton Theological School, USA*: Bible Interpretation, Feminist View

David Ford, *St. Tikhons Theological Seminary, USA*: Marriage, Orthodox View; Martyrdom, Orthodox View; Saints; Saints, Devotion to, Orthodox View

Mary Ford, *St. Tikhons Theological Seminary, USA*: Marriage, Orthodox View; Martyrdom, Orthodox View; Saints; Saints, Devotion to, Orthodox View

Stephanie A. Ford, *Earlham School of Religion, USA*: Spirituality, North American View; Spirituality, Protestant View

Jim Forest, *Orthodox Peace Fellowship, USA*: Catholic Worker; Day

William Franke, *Vanderbilt University, USA*: Dante; Dionysius the Pseudo-Areopagite; Petrarch

Robert M. Franklin, *Emory University, USA*: Family, African American View

Ruth Franzén, *Uppsala University, Sweden*: Pietism in Scandinavia; Rouse

Edward H. Friedman, *Vanderbilt University, USA*: Spanish Literature

Samuel Frouisou, *Lutheran Church, Cameroon; University of Natal, South Africa*: Cameroon

Lorelei F. Fuchs, SA, *The Interchurch Center, New York, USA*: Dialogue, Ecumenical

Jojo M. Fung, SJ, *Arrupe House, Malaysia*: Shamanism

Inger Furseth, *KIFO Centre for Church Research, Norway*: Aarflot

Richard R. Gaillardetz, *University of Toledo, USA*: Laity

Brandon Gallaher, *University of Oxford, UK*: Florovsky

China Galland, *Graduate Theological Union, USA*: Black Madonna

Mark Galli, *"Christianity Today" Magazine, USA*: Mott

Ismael García, *Austin Presbyterian Theological Seminary, USA*: Justice, Latino/a View; Justification, Latino/a View; Kingdom of God, Latino/a View; Poverty Latino/a View

Tharscisse Gatwa, *Centre de Littérature Evangélique, Cameroon*: Rwanda

Jean-Marie Gaudeul, *Secrétariat pour les Relations avec l'Islam, France*: History of Christianity in North Africa; Islam in Western Europe

Luis María Gavilanes del Castillo, *Pontificia Universidad Católica, Ecuador*: CEBs; Church in Ecuador; Ecuador; Mercedes de Jesús; Miguel, Brother; Narcisa de Jesús; Proaño

Pavel L. Gavrilyuk, *University of St. Thomas, St. Paul, USA*: Patristic Thought

Volney P. Gay, *Vanderbilt University, USA*: Paradox

Metropolitan Athanasios Geevargis, *Syrian Orthodox Patriarchate, Antioch, Syria*: Syriac Orthodox Church

Kondothra M. George, *Orthodox Theological Seminary, India*: Malankara Orthodox Syrian Church

Mary Gerhart, *Hobart and William Smith Colleges, USA*: Analogical Imagination; Metaphor

Simon Gikandi, *Princeton University, USA*: African Literature (Anglophone)

Maurice Gilbert, SJ, *Pontificio Istituto Biblico, Italy*: Pontifical Biblical Commission

Michael J. Gillgannon, *Universidad Nacional de La Paz, Bolivia*: Bolivia

Verónica Giménez Beliveau, *Universidad de Buenos Aires, Argentina*: Bogarín Argaña; Church, Latin American View; Paraguay

Terryl Givens, *Richmond University, USA*: Latter-Day Saints; Mormon, Book of; Mormon Worship; Smith; Young

Beth Glazier-McDonald, *Centre College, USA*: Haggai; Malachi; Nahum; Zechariah

Philip Gleason, *University of Notre Dame, USA*: Carroll

Menghun Goh, *Vanderbilt University, USA*: Malaysia; Sung Shang-Jie

Brian Golding, *University of Southampton, UK*: Gilbert of Sempringham

Bishop Hilario M. Gomez, Jr., *National Council of Churches, Philippines*: Islam in Asia: The Philippines

Michelle A. Gonzalez, *Loyola Marymount University, USA*: Christologies, Latino/a; God, Latino/a View

Donald K. Gorrell, *United Theological Seminary, Dayton, USA*: Rauschenbusch; Social Gospel

Roy Gottfried, *Vanderbilt University, USA*: American Literature

Tamara Grdzelidze, *World Council of Churches, Switzerland*: Creation, Ecology, Orthodox View; Georgia; Orthodox Church of Georgia

Joel B. Green, *Asbury Theological Seminary, USA*: Cross and Crucifixion

Niels Henrik Gregersen, *University of Copenhagen, Denmark*: Science

Cristina Grenholm, *Member of the Editorial Board, Karlstad Universitët; Director, Theology and Ecumenical Relations, Church of Sweden*: Autonomy; Folk Churches; Heteronomy; Justification, Feminist View; Motherhood; Relationality; Spiritual Criticism; Sweden; Women's Ordination in Europe

Herbert Griffiths, *University of Leeds, UK*: Afro-Caribbean Christianity in UK

Eric W. Gritsch, *Lutheran Theological Seminary, USA*: Müntzer

Erich S. Gruen, *University of California, Berkeley, USA*: Diaspora

Christoffer H. Grundmann, *Valparaiso University, USA*: Health, Healing in the West; Hospitals and Healing

Paul H. Gundani, *UNISA, South Africa*: RC in Southern Africa; Zimbabwe

Jon P. Gunnemann, *Emory University, USA*: Marxism

Petre Guran, *Princeton University, USA*: Church and State in Eastern Europe; Olga; Vladimir

Vidar L. Haanes, *Det teologiske Menighetsfakultet, Norway*: Olaf

Jeremiah M. Hackett, *University of South Carolina, USA*: Bacon; Eckhart; Soul

Getatchew Haile, *Hill Monastic Manuscript Library, USA*: Ethiopia; Frumentius

Douglas John Hall, *McGill University, Canada*: Christologies, North American View; Eschatology and Apocalypticism, North American View; God, North American View; Gospel and Culture, North American View; Incarnation, North American View; Justification, North American View; Theologies as Human Undertaking, North Atlantic View

Nicholas Hammond, *University of Cambridge, UK*: Pascal

Daphne Hampson, *University of St. Andrews, UK*: Post-Christian Thought

Jehu J. Hanciles, *Fuller Seminary, USA*: Sierra Leone

Barry Hankins, *Baylor University, USA*: Southern Baptist Convention

Jennifer Haraguchi, *University of Chicago, USA*: Cereta

Stanley S. Harakas, *Holy Cross Greek Orthodox School of Theology, USA*: Ethics, Orthodox View; Justice, Orthodox View

Anthony John Harding, *University of Saskatchewan, Canada*: Coleridge

Conrad L. Harkins, OFM, *Franciscan Institute, USA*: Francis of Assisi; Franciscans

J. William Harmless, SJ, *Creighton University, USA*: Antony; *Apophthegmata Patrum*; Cassian; Evagrius of Pontus; Pachomius

Marjory Harper, *University of Aberdeen, Scotland*: Missions and Emigration/Colonization in North America

Amir Harrak, *University of Toronto, Canada:* Syria; Syriac Catholic Church

Joel F. Harrington, *Vanderbilt University, USA*: Marriage, in Western Churches

Mark W. Harris, *First Parish of Watertown, Mass., USA*: Racovian Catechism; Socinus; Unitarianism

Susan Ashbrook Harvey, *Brown University, USA*: Incense and Olfactory Experience in Worship

Van A. Harvey, *Stanford University, USA*: Bultmann; Demythologization; Feuerbach

R. Chris Hassel, Jr., *Vanderbilt University, USA*: Shakespeare

Jione Havea, *University of Melbourne, Australia*: Biblical Interpretation in Oceania

Daniel Hawk, *Ashland Theological Seminary, USA*: Joshua

Diana L. Hayes, *Georgetown University, USA*: Spirituality, African American; Womanist and African American Theologies

Leslie Hayes, *University of Toronto, Canada*: Women's Ordination, Earlier Periods

Priscilla Hayner, *International Center for Transitional Justice, USA*: Truth and Reconciliation Commissions

S. Mark Heim, *Andover Newton Theological School, USA*: Sacrifice

Simo Heininen, *University of Helsinki, Finland*: Agricola

Richard P. Heitzenrater, *Duke University, USA*: Wesley, John

Eila Helander, *Helsingfors Universitet, Finland*: Finland

David Hempton, *Harvard University, USA*: Methodism in UK

Scott H. Hendrix, *Princeton Theological Seminary, USA*: Luther; Schmalkaldic Articles

Jan-Olav Henriksen, *Det teologiske Menighetsfakultet, Norway*: Aulén; Creation Theology in Scandinavia; Existentialism and Christian Thought; Folk Churches; Lutheranism in the Nordic Countries

Gina Hens-Piazza, *Union Theological Seminary, USA*: Samuel, 1 and 2

Carter Heyward, *Episcopal Divinity School, USA*: Heterosexuality; Homosexuality; Sexuality

Nicholas J. Higham, *University of Manchester, UK*: Bede; Patrick

David Hilliard, *Flinders University, Australia*: Solomon Islands

Norman A. Hjelm, *Lutheran World Federation and Director of Faith and Order*: Ecumenical Movement; Edinburgh Conference, 1937; Faith and Order; Lutheran World Federation

Peter C. Hodgson, *Vanderbilt University, USA*: Baur; Eliot, George; Hegel; History as a Theological Concept; Liberalism in Theology

Arthur Holder, *Graduate Theological Union, USA*: Spirituality

M. Jan Holton, *Vanderbilt University, USA*: Families and Substitute Families in Squatter Camps

Dwight N. Hopkins, *University of Chicago, USA*: Anthropology, African American View; Anthropology, European-American View; Anthropology, Western View

Ronnie Po-chia Hsia, *Pennsylvania State University, USA*: Catholic Renewal; Mission, RC, in China; Trent, Council

Po-Ho Huang, *Dean, School of Theology, Chang Jung Christian University, Taiwan*: Taiwan

James Hudnut-Beumler, *Dean, Vanderbilt Divinity School, USA*: Church in North America; Economic Studies of Christianity in USA

Jennifer S. Hughes, *University of California, Riverside, USA*: Patronato/Padroado; Portuguese Conquests, Missions; Spanish Conquests, Missions

Leonard M. Hummel, *Lutheran Theological Seminary, Gettysburg, USA*: Pastoral Care

Mary E. Hunt, *Women's Alliance for Theology, Ethics and Ritual, USA*: Women's Ordination and RC

Laennec Hurbon, *Université Quisqueya de Port-au-Prince, Haiti*: Ancestors, Latin American and Caribbean View; Death, Caribbean View and Cult of the Dead; Dominican Republic; Guadeloupe; Haiti; Martinique; Vodou

Mark Hutchinson, *Southern Cross College, Australia*: Charismatics in Australasia; Charismatics in South Pacific; Incarnation, South Pacific View; Racism in South Pacific

Susan E. Hylen, *Vanderbilt University, USA*: NT Theology; Revelation

Mary Beth Ingham, CSJ, *Loyola Marymount University, USA*: Bonaventure; Duns Scotus; Olivi

H. Larry Ingle, *University of Tennessee, Chattanooga, USA*: Fox; Friends, Religious Society of; Grimké, Sarah and Angelina; Hick; Penn; Quaker Worship; Woolman

Dale T. Irvin, *New York Theological Seminary, USA*: History of World Christianity

Jon Isaak, *Mennonite Brethren Biblical Seminary, USA*: Hebrews

Paul John Isaak, *Wartburg Theological Seminary, USA*: Death, African View; Namibia

Ada María Isasi-Díaz, *Drew University, USA*: Feminist Theology, Mujerista

Hans Raun Iversen, *Københavns Universitet, Denmark*: Culture Christianity; Denmark; Grundtvig; Hemmingsen; Laity, Scandinavian View

Margaret C. Jacob, *University of California, Los Angeles, USA*: Freemasonry; Newton

Arthur James, *Gujranwala Theological Seminary; President, National Churches Council, Pakistan*: Pakistan

Maria Jansdotter-Samuelsson, *Karlstad Universitët, Sweden*: Ecology; Ecotheology

David Jasper, *University of Glasgow, UK*: Gadamer; Hermeneutics

Werner G. Jeanrond, *University of Lund, Sweden*: Love

Renée Jeffery, *LaTrobe University, Australia*: Arminianism; Grotius; Remonstrance

David Lyle Jeffrey, *Baylor University, USA*: Jesus Christ, Images of, in Literature

Theodore W. Jennings, Jr., *Chicago Theological Seminary, USA*: Justice, Western View; Law

David H. Jensen, *Austin Presbyterian Seminary, USA*: Labor

Robin Margaret Jensen, *Vanderbilt University, USA*: Arts

David Jobling, *St. Andrews College, Canada*: Bible Interpretation in North America

Dale A. Johnson, *Vanderbilt University, USA*: Civil Constitution of the Clergy; History of Christianity in Western Europe; Nonconformists; Nonconformity and Theological Education; Popular Christian Practices; Popular Christianity in North America

Elizabeth A. Johnson, *Fordham University, USA*: God, Feminist View; Incarnation, Feminist View; Mary; Saints, RC View

Maxwell E. Johnson, *University of Notre Dame, USA*: Worship in Early Christianity; Liturgies, History of

Sarah Johnson, *Duke University, USA*: Eddy; Jackson; Lee, Ann; McPherson; Palmer

Mark D. Johnston, *DePaul University, USA*: Llull

F. Stanley Jones, *California State University, Long Beach, USA*: Clementine Literature

James William Jones, *Rutgers University, USA*: Psychology

John R. Jones, *La Sierra University, USA*: Adventism; Branch Davidians; Seventh-day Adventist Worship; White

Alissa Jones Nelson, *University of St. Andrews, UK*: Prosperity Theology and Liberation Theology

Inge Jonsson, *University of Stockholm, Sweden*: Swedenborg

Jan Joosten, *Université des Sciences Humaines de Strasbourg, France*: Diatessaron

Elizabeth Judd, *Universidad Nacional Autónoma de México*: Asbaje y Ramírez; Garcés; Gómez Morín; Hidalgo y Costilla; Jesús, Felipe de; Llaguno Farías; Martínez; Méndez Arceo; Miranda y Gómez; Morelos y Pavón; Munguía; Palafox y Mendoza; Pro Juárez, Miguel; Quiroga; Sahagún; Thomson; Velázquez; Zumárraga

Mulambya Peggy Kabonde, *United Church of Zambia*: Water; Zambia

Robert Kaggwa, *Roehampton University, UK*: Kitagana; Luwum; Mukasa; Njangali; Uganda

Sylvester Kahakwa, *Tumaini University, Tanzania*: Ancestors, African View; Incarnation, African View; Justification, African View

Isaac Kalimi, *University of Chicago, USA*: Chronicles

Ogbu U. Kalu, *McCormick Presbyterian Seminary, USA*: Charismatic Movement, Studying; History of Christianity in Africa

Eunice Kamaara, *Moi University, Kenya*: Family in Eastern Africa

Wayne C. Kannaday, *Newberry College, USA*: Apologists; Clement of Alexandria; Scribes

Musimbi Kanyoro, *World YWCA, Switzerland*: Justice, African View; YMCA; YWCA

Veli-Matti Kärkkäinen, *Fuller Theological Seminary, USA*: Church; Church, Western View; Holy Spirit; Holy Spirit, European View; Holy Spirit, North American View; Inspiration

Frank Kaufmann, *Interreligious and International Federation for World Peace, USA*: Unification Church

Léon Nguapitshi Kayongo, *Université Simon Kimbangu, Democratic Republic of the Congo*: Kimbangu; Kimbanguism

Richard Kearney, *Boston College, USA*: Aesthetics; Ricoeur

Alice A. Keefe, *University of Wisconsin-Stevens Point, USA*: Hosea

Ralph Keen, *University of Iowa, USA*: More

Catherine Keller, *Drew University, USA*: Eschatology and Apocalypticism, Feminist

Anthony J. Kelly, CSsR, *Australian Catholic University, Australia*: Eschatology; Hope; Liguori

Karen Kennelly, CSJ, *St. Catherine College, USA*: Women's Orders in Europe and North America

Kathi Lynn Kern, *University of Kentucky, USA*: Anthony, Susan B.; Stanton

Fergus Kerr, OP, *University of Edinburgh, UK*: Aquinas; Thomism; Wittgenstein

Edward Kessler, *University of Cambridge, UK*: Israel; Judaism and Christianity, Jewish Views; Judaism and Christianity in Western Europe

George Kilcourse, *Bellarmine University, USA*: Merton

Heup Young Kim, *Kangnam University, Korea*: Ancestors, Asian View; Daoism, Neo-Confucianism, Christianity in Korea

Kim Sung-Hae, Sr., *Sogang University, Korea*: Daoism

Kim Yong-Bock, *Asia Pacific Graduate School for Study of Life, Korea*: Death, Asian View; Minjung Theology

Kim Yung Suk, *Virginia Union University, USA*: Korea, South

Richard King, *University of Glasgow, UK*: Religion

Thomas M. King, SJ, *Georgetown University, USA*: Teilhard de Chardin

Robert M. Kingdon, *University of Wisconsin-Madison, USA*: Beza; Farel; Marriage in Calvin's Geneva

Ross Kinsler, *Latin America Biblical University, Costa Rica*: Ministry/Ministries; Theological Education in Latin America

Hans G. Kippenberg, *Universität Erfurt, Germany*: Weber

Cheryl A. Kirk-Duggan, *Shaw Divinity School, USA*: Anthropology, Womanist View; Healing, African American View; Justice, Womanist View; Liberation Theologies, Womanist; Wells

Clifton Kirkpatrick, *President, World Alliance of Reformed Churches*: World Alliance of Reformed Churches

Leonid Kishkovsky, *Orthodox Church of America, USA*: Church, Orthodox View

Nadieszda Kizenko, *State University of New York, Albany, USA*: Russian Orthodox Church

Jeffrey Klaiber, SJ, *Pontifical Catholic University, Peru*: Human Rights in Latin America; Landázuri Ricketts, Juan; MacKay, John A.; Peru; RC in Peru; Rose, St., of Lima

Hans-Josef Klauck, *University of Chicago, USA*: Apocryphal Books of NT; Apocryphal Gospels; Ebionites, Gospel; Hebrews, Gospel; Nazarenes, Gospel; Peter, Gospel; Philip, Gospel; Thomas, Gospel; Thomas, Infancy Gospel; Truth, Gospel

Sidney Knight, *University of Peradenya, Sri Lanka*: Sri Lanka

Samuel Kobia, *General Secretary, World Council of Churches*: World Council of Churches

Robert Kolb, *Concordia Seminary, USA*: Augsburg Confession; Augsburg, Peace; Flacius; Gnesio-Lutherans

Karla Ann Koll, *Latin American Biblical University, Guatemala*: Guatemala

Heikki Kotila, *Helsingfors Universitet, Finland*: Thomas Mass

Donald Kraybill, *Elizabethtown College, USA*: Amish; Anabaptist; Brethren; Hutterites; Peace Movements; Radical Reformation

Philip D. W. Krey, *Lutheran Theological Seminary at Philadelphia, USA*: Nicholas of Lyra

Yves Krumenacker, *Université Jean Moulin, Institut Universitaire de France*: Chardon; Merici; Thérèse of Lisieux

Jeffrey Kah-Jin Kuan, *Pacific School of Religion, USA*: Bible Interpretation in Asia

Simanga R. Kumalo, *University of Natal, South Africa*: Church and State in South Africa

Peter Kuzmic, *Evangelical Theological Seminary, Croatia*: Charismatics and Pentecostals in Eastern Europe; Croatia; Mission in Eastern Europe

Simon Shui-Man Kwan, *Chinese University of Hong Kong, China*: Asian Theology; Confucianism in Hong Kong; Congress of Asian Theologians; Hong Kong; Programme for Theology and Cultures in Asia

Kwok Pui-lan, *Member of the Editorial Board; Episcopal Divinity School, USA*: Bible Interpretation by Asian Women; Chinese Women; Feminist Theology in Asia

André LaCocque, *Chicago Theological Seminary, USA*: Daniel; Esther; Genesis; Israel, People of; Jerusalem; Jonah; People of God; Promised Land; Song of Songs

Stephen E. Lahey, *University of Nebraska, Lincoln, USA*: Darby; Dispensationalism; Hus; Jerome of Prague; Pecock; Wyclif

John Tsz Pang Lai, *Chinese University of Hong Kong, China*: Chinese Literature

Emiel Lamberts, *Katholieke Universiteit Leuven, Belgium*: Belgium; Cardijn; Worker-Priests; Young Christian Workers

Armando Lampe, *Universidad de Quintana Roo, Mexico*: Caribbean Islands; Church and State in Cuba, Catholicism and Communism in Cuba; Cuba; Guyana; Jamaica; Rastafari; Trinidad and Tobago

Craig Lampe, *Bible Museum, USA*: Bible, English Translations

Beverly J. Lanzetta, *University of Arizona, USA*: Wisdom

Eve LaPlante, *American Society of Journalists and Authors, USA*: Hutchinson

Lizette Larson-Miller, *Church Divinity School of the Pacific, USA*: Burial; Dead, Prayers for; Laying on of Hands; Sick, Visitation and Anointing

Ariel Bybee Laughton, *Duke University, USA*: Marcella

Leonard Lawlor, *University of Memphis, USA*: Bergson; Berengarius of Tours; Phenomenology

Bentley Layton, *Yale University, USA*: Shenoute

Robin A. Leaver, *Rider University, USA*: Bach; Passions (Music)

Karen Lebacqz, *Pacific School of Religion, USA*: Bio-Medical Ethics; Justice, North American View

Archie Chi Chung Lee, *Member of the Editorial Board; Chung Chi College, Chinese University of Hong Kong, China*: Lamentations

Marilyn J. Legge, *University of Toronto, Canada*: Grace, Feminist View

Hervé LeGrand, *Institut Catholique de Paris, France*: RC in France

D. L. LeMahieu, *Lake Forest College, USA*: Paley

Raymond Lemieux, *Université Laval, Canada*: Guyard; Quebec

Bill J. Leonard, *Wake Forest University, USA*: Baptist Churches; Baptist Churches in North America; Baptist Worship

Ellen M. Leonard, CSJ, *University of Toronto, Canada*: Modernism, RC; Petre; Underhill; von Hügel

Outi Leppä, *University of Helsinki, Finland*: Colossians

Jean Lesaulnier, *Société des Amis de Port-Royal, France*: Arnauld, Antoine; Jansen; Jansenism

Nantawan Boonprasat Lewis, *Metropolitan State University, St. Paul, USA*: Thailand

Henrietta Leyser, *University of Oxford, UK*: Christina of Markyate

Alexei Lidov, *Research Center for Eastern Christian Culture, Moscow*: Hierotopy; Jesus Christ in Byzantine Iconography; Mary, Theotokos, in Byzantine Iconography

Bernard Lightman, *York University, Canada*: Huxley

Paul Chang-Ha Lim, *Vanderbilt University, USA*: Amyraut; Bunyan; Cyril of Jerusalem; John of the Cross; Kuyper; Las Casas, Bartolomé de; Laud

Carter Lindberg, *Boston University, USA*: Reformation

Mark R. Lindsay, *University of Melbourne, Australia*: Barmen Declaration; Barth, Karl; Church Struggle in Germany; Confession Church; Crisis Theology; Dialectical Theology; German Christians, Niemoller

James R. Linville, *University of Lethbridge, Canada*: Deuteronomistic History; Kings, 1–2

James C. Livingston, *College of William and Mary, USA*: Butler; Enlightenment; Enlightenment in North America; Möhler; Tyrrell

Ann Loades, *University of Durham, UK*: Feminist Theology in Western Europe; Sayers; Women's Christian Practices in the West

David Loades, *University of Sheffield, UK*: Elizabeth I; Foxe

Jean-Claude Loba-Mkole, *United Bible Societies, Kenya*: Bible Translations, History; Bokeleale; Congo, Democratic Republic of; Kimbangu; Malula

Lo Lung Kwong, *Chinese University of Hong Kong, China*: Ancestors in China

Wati Longchar, *Eastern Theological College, India*: Land and Indigenous Peoples' Views

Eleazar López, *Centro Nacional de Ayuda a Misiones Indígenas, Mexico*: Gospel and Culture, Mexican View

David W. Lotz, *Union Theological Seminary, USA*: Ritschl

Andrew Louth, *Durham University, UK*: Byzantine Theology; Cabasilas; Gregory Palamas; John of Damascus; Staniloae

Robin W. Lovin, *Southern Methodist University, USA*: Niebuhr, Reinhold; Political Studies; Political Theology; Social Ethics

William Luis, *Vanderbilt University, USA*: Caribbean Literature

Frank D. Macchia, *Vanguard University, USA*: Baptism in the Holy Spirit; Charismatics/Pentecostals in North America; Charismatics/Pentecostals in Europe; Health, Healing, Pentecostal/Charismatic View

Diarmaid N. J. MacCulloch, *University of Oxford, UK*: Common Prayer, Book of; Cranmer; Henry VIII; Mary Tudor

Kirk R. MacGregor, *Radford University, USA*: Word-Faith Movement

Marjory A. MacLean, *Depute Clerk, General Assembly, Church of Scotland*: Scotland, Church of

Donald MacLeod, *Free Church College, UK*: Scotland, Free Church; Westminster Catechisms and Confession

Tomas S. Maddela, *Saint Andrew's Seminary, Philippines*: Episcopal Church in Philippines

Inge Mager, *Universität Hamburg, Germany*: Germany; Mission in Germany; Theological Education in Germany; Women, Christian Practices in Germany

Laurenti Magesa, *Tangaza College, Kenya*: African Religion: Christian Perspective; Ethics, African View; Inculturation, Eastern African View; Tanzania

David G. Maillu, *Kenyata University, Kenya*: African Religion: African Religious Perspective

Fortunato Mallimaci, *Centro de Estudios e Investigaciones Laborales, Argentina*: Argentina

Philip Mamalakis, *Holy Cross Orthodox Seminary, USA*: Family, Orthodox View

Kä Mana, *Institut Supérieur de Pédagogie, Cameroon*: Gospel and Culture, African View; Prosperity Theology, African View

Ukachukwu Chris Manus, *Obafemi Awolowo University, Nigeria*: Bible Interpretation in Africa; Christologies in Africa; Health, Healing, African View

Herbert Robinson Marbury, *Vanderbilt University, USA*: Ezra and Nehemiah

Reuel Norman Marigza, *Silliman University, Philippines*: Philippines; United Church of Christ in the Philippines

Jacqueline Mariña, *Purdue University, USA*: Kant; Schleiermacher

Antti Marjanen, *University of Helsinki, Finland*: Judas, Gospel; Judas, Iscariot; Mary, Gospel; Mary, Magdalene; Pistis Sophia

Luiz C. L. Marques, *University of Bologna, Spain*: Arns; Câmara

Madipoane Masenya (ngwan'a Mphahlele), *University of South Africa, South Africa*: Feminist Theologies in Africa; Women's Practices in African Independent and Charismatic Churches

Caleb J. D. Maskell, *Yale Divinity School, USA*: Civil War, USA; Congregationalism; Franklin; Great Awakening; Revival, Revivalism; Whitefield

Steve Mason, *York University, Canada*: Hegesippus; Josephus

Thomas Massaro, SJ, *Weston Jesuit School of Theology, USA*: Baltimore, Councils; Christian Socialism; Social Encyclicals

Fernando Matamoros Ponce, *Benemérita Universidad Autónoma de Puebla, Mexico*: Popular Christian Practices in Mexico

András Máté-Tóth, *University of Szeged, Hungary*: Hungary

Odair Pedroso Mateus, *Ecumenical Institute, Switzerland*: Reformed Churches

Dinis Matsolo, *Secretary General, Christian Council of Mozambique*: Mozambique

Fumitaka Matsuoka, *Pacific School of Theology, USA*: Asian American Theology

John D'Arcy May, *University of Dublin, Ireland*: Buddhism: Christian Perspective; Buddhist Scriptures

Yelena Mazour-Matusevich, *University of Alaska, USA*: Gerson

Theodore Mbazumutima, *Carlile College, Kenya*: Burundi

John S. McClure, *Vanderbilt University, USA*: Reception Studies of Preaching

Christian McConnell, *Saint John's University, USA*: Liturgies, History of Worship in Early Christianity

Lee Martin McDonald, *Acadia Divinity College, Canada*: OT, Its Canonization

Gary B. McGee, *Assemblies of God Theological Seminary, USA*: Seymour

Thomas McGowan, *Diocese of Oakland, USA*: Cabrini

Alister E. McGrath, *University of Oxford, UK*: Incarnation, Western View; Protestantism

Richard J. McGregor, *Vanderbilt University, USA*: Myth

John A. McGuckin, *Columbia University, New York, USA*: Cyril of Alexandria; Iconography; Monasticism in the Byzantine Empire; Spirituality, Orthodox View; Transfiguration

Maud Burnett McInerney, *Haverford College, USA*: Joan of Arc; Virgin Martyrs

Elsie Anne McKee, *Princeton Theological Seminary, USA*: Calvin

Mary B. McKinley, *University of Virginia, USA*: Dentière

James F. McMillan, *University of Edinburgh, UK*: France; Lourdes

Ernan McMullin, *University of Notre Dame, USA*: Copernicus; Galilei, Galileo

Kathleen E. McVey, *Member of the Editorial Board; Princeton Theological Seminary, USA*: Bar Sauma; Bar Sauma of Nisibis; Church of the East or Assyrian Church; Ephesus, First Council of; History of Christianity in the Middle East; Jacob of Serug/Sarug; John of Ephesus; Melkites; Miaphysite; Monasticism, Russian; Monasticism, Syriac; Symeon; Synod of Jerusalem, 1672

M. Douglas Meeks, *Vanderbilt University, USA*: Economic Ethics; Economic Studies; Methodist Churches; Methodist Worship; Poverty, Protestant View; Wealth

Monica Jyotsna Melanchthon, *Gurukul Lutheran Theological College, India*: Grace, Asian View; Justification, Asian View; Women's Practices in Asia

Ilie Melniciuc-Puica, *University in Iasi, Romania*: Moldova Republic

Everett Mendoza, *Silliman University, Philippines*: Justice, Asian View

Raymond A. Mentzer, *University of Iowa, USA*: Bartholomew's Day; Camisards; Du Plessis-Mornay; Durand, Marie; Huguenots

William W. Menzies, *Assemblies of God Theological Seminary, USA*: Assemblies of God

Ina Merdjanova, *Sofia University, Bulgaria*: Albania; Bosnia-Herzegovina; Bulgaria; History of Christianity in the Balkans; Islam in Southeast Europe; Slovenia; Yugoslavia

Franziska Metzger, *Universität Freiburg, Germany*: Racism in Europe; Switzerland

Constant J. Mews, *Monash University, Australia*: Abelard; Rupert of Deutz; Scholasticism

Marvin Meyer, *Chapman University, USA*: Mithraism; Mystery Religions; Schweitzer

Carol Meyers, *Duke University, USA*: Exodus

Vasile Mihoc, *Member of the Editorial Board; Facultatea de Teologie Andrei Saguna, Romania*: Bible Interpretation in Eastern Orthodoxy; Romania; Romanian Orthodox Church; Theological Education in Eastern Europe

Gunner Bjerg Mikkelsen, *Aarhus Universitet, Denmark*: Mani, Manichaeism; Paulicians

Maria Inêz de Castro Millen, *Centro de Ensino Superior de Juiz de Fora, Brasil*: Women's Practices in Brazil

Clyde Lee Miller, *Stony Brook University, USA*: Nicholas of Cusa

Bonnie J. Miller-McLemore, *Vanderbilt University, USA*: Children; Family, Feminist View; Family for Western Churches

Alexander Mirkovic, *McNeese State University, USA*: Abgar

Paul Misner, *Marquette University, USA*: Christian Democratic Parties; Church and State in Europe: RC and Politics

Nozomu Miyahira, *Seinan Gakuin University, Japan*: Buraku Liberation; Japan; Kagawa; Kirishitans and Hidden Christians in Japan; Xavier

R. W. L. Moberly, *University of Durham, UK*: Abraham in Judaism, Christianity, and Islam

Gerald Moede, *Winchester Academy, USA*: Consultation on Church Union

Aloo Osotsi Mojola, *United Bible Society, Kenya*: Bible Translation in Africa

Sunanda Mongia, *Mahatma Gandhi Kashi Vidyapeeth University, India*: Indian Literature

Rebeca Montemayor, *Centro de Estudios Ecuménicos, Mexico*: Charismatics and Pentecostals in Mexico; Protestantism in Mexico; Women's Practices in Mexico

James Moore, *Open University, UK*: Creationism; Darwin; Evolution

Roger E. Moore, *Vanderbilt University, USA*: Blake; Milton

Craig E. Morrison O.Carm, *Pontifical Biblical Institute, Italy*: Bible, Early Translations; Bible, Manuscripts; Peshitta

Jeffry H. Morrison, *Regent University, USA*: Washington, George; Witherspoon

Keith Morrison, *Lincoln University, New Zealand*: Kingdom of God and Wilderness, Orthodox View

Wilson J. Moses, *Pennsylvania State University, USA*: Crummell; Douglass; Garvey; Washington, Booker T.

Tefetso Henry Mothibe, *National University of Lesotho*: Lesotho

Mokgethi Motlhabi, *University of South Africa, South Africa*: Dwane; Huddleston; Hurley; Mahabane; Mokone; Naude; South Africa

Fulata Moyo, *World Council of Churches; Coordinator, Circle of Concerned African Women Theologians, Malawi*: Holy Spirit in Africa; Spirituality, in Africa

Henry Mugabe, *Baptist Theological Seminary of Zimbabwe*: Protestantism in Southern Africa

Jesse Ndwiga Kanyua Mugambi, *Member of the Editorial Board; University of Nairobi, Kenya*: Anglicanism in Eastern and Western Africa; Berlin Conference;

Charismatic Movement in Southern Africa; Church, Ecclesiastical Structures; Culture and Christianity; Ecumenical Association of Third World Theologians; Kenya; Krapf; Liberia; Racism in Africa; Rebmann; Reconstruction, African Theologies of; Theological Education in Africa

Peggy Mulambya-Kabonde, *United Church of Zambia*: Water, African Perspective; Zambia

Robert Bruce Mullin, *General Theological Seminary of the Episcopal Church, USA*: Anglican Church in North America; Bushnell; Denominationalism

Pamela Mullins Reaves, *University of North Carolina, USA*: Perpetua and Felicitas

Saskia Murk Jansen, *Robinson College, UK*: Beguine Spirituality; Hadewijch; Marie D'Oignies; Mechtild of Magdeburg

Heleen L. Murre-Van den Berg, *Leiden University, Netherlands*: Islam in Lebanon; Jordan; Kazakhstan; Kyrgyzstan; Lebanon; Saudi Arabia; Turkey

Augustine Musopole, *Malawi Council of Churches*: Church and State in Central Africa; Eschatology and Apocalypticism, African View; Kingdom of God, African View; Millennialism, African View

Isaac M. T. Mwase, *Tuskegee University, USA*: Protestantism in Southern Africa

Philomena Mwaura, *Kenyatta University, Kenya*: African Instituted Churches in Eastern Africa; Charismatic Movement in Eastern Africa; Family in African Instituted Churches; Spirituality in African Instituted Churches

Cecilia Nahnfeldt, *Karlstads Universitët, Sweden*: Vocation

Anne Nasimiyu Wasike, *Kenyatta University, Kenya*: Christology, African View; Polygamy

Carmiña Navia Velasco, *Universidad del Valle, Colombia*: Latin American Literature (Spanish)

Thulani Ndlazi, *Church Land Program, South Africa*: Land, African View

Alexander Negrov, *St. Petersburg Christian University, Russia*: Protestantism in Russia

James B. Nelson, *United Theological Seminary of the Twin Cities, USA*: Alcoholics Anonymous

David G. Newcombe, *University of Cambridge, UK*: Hooper

Carol Newsom, *Emory University, USA*: Job

Helen J. Nicholson, *Cardiff University, UK*: Crusades; Hospitallers; Military Orders; Teutonic Knights

George W. E. Nickelsburg, *University of Iowa, USA*: Enoch; Essenes; Judaism, NT, and Early Christianity; Pharisees; Qumran; Sadducees

Tatyana Nikolskaya, *St. Petersburg Christian University, Russia*: Protestantism in Russia

Damayanthi M. A. Niles, *Eden Theological Seminary, USA*: Contextualization; Niles, D.T.; Thomas, M. M.

Bertil Nilsson, *Uppsala Universitët, Sweden*: Ansgar

Nyambura Njoroge, *World Council of Churches*: Sexuality, African View; Women's Ordination in Africa

Fidelis Nkomazana, *University of Botswana*: Botswana

Mary Beth Norton, *Cornell University, USA*: Witchcraft Trials in North America

Christian Nottmeier, *Evangelisches Institut für Kirchenrecht, Universität Potsdam, Germany*: Harnack

Sonene Nyawo, *Akrofi-Christaller Memorial Center, Swaziland*: Swaziland

Anthère Nzabatsinda, *Vanderbilt University, USA*: African Literature (Francophone)

Edward T. Oakes, SJ, *University of St. Mary of the Lake, USA*: von Balthasar

Gerald O'Collins, SJ, *Pontifical Gregorian University, Italy*: Biblical Theology; Redemption; Roman Catholic Church; Tradition, Post-Vatican II RC Perspective; Vatican Council II

Daniel O'Connell, *University of South Carolina, USA*: Mind

David W. Odell-Scott, *Kent State University, USA*: Metaphysics; Ockham

Mercy Amba Oduyoye, *Institute of Women, Religion and Culture, Ghana*: Theology as Human Undertaking: African Women Theologians Doing Theology

Kathleen O'Grady, *Concordia University, Canada*: Death, Western Feminist View

Oyeronke Olajubu, *University of Ilorin, Nigeria*: Church and State in Western Africa

Thomas O'Loughlin, *University of Wales Lampeter, UK*: Celtic Christianity

Dennis T. Olson, *Princeton Theological Seminary, USA*: Numbers

J. Steven O'Malley, *Asbury Theological Seminary, USA*: Bengel; Blumhardt; Francke; Holiness Movement; Labadists; Pietism; Spener

Cephas N. Omenyo, *Princeton Theological Seminary, USA*: Charismatics in Western Africa; Protestantism in Western Africa

Muriel Orevillo-Montenegro, *Silliman University, Philippines*: Christologies, Asian Women's Views

César Augusto Ornellas Ramos, *Uni LaSalle, Institutos Superiores de Ensigno Rio de Janeiro, Brasil*: RC in Brazil

Agbonkhianmeghe E. Orobator, SJ, *Hekima College, Jesuit School of Theology, Nairobi, Kenya*: RC in Western Africa

Kenan B. Osborne, OFM, *Franciscan School of Theology, Graduate Theological Union, USA*: Deacon, Diaconate

Carolyn Osiek, *Brite Divinity School, USA*: Acts of Martyrs; Basilina; Deaconess; Flavia Vitalia; Hermas, Shepherd of; Justina; Lampadion; Leta; Marthana; Olympias; Philemon; Phoebe; Sabiniana; Sophia, Second Phoebe

Javier Otaola Montagne, *Universidad Nacional Autónoma de México*: Educational Practices in Mexico; Eschatology and Apocalypticism in Mexico

Douglas F. Ottati, *Union Theological Seminary and Presbyterian School of Christian Education, USA*: Niebuhr, H. Richard

Anna May Say Pa, *Director, Association for Theological Education in South East Asia; Myanmar Institute of Christian Theology*: Myanmar (Burma)

Irina Paert, *University of Wales, Bangor, UK*: Eschatology and Apocalypticism, Orthodox European View; Old Believers

Jerry G. Pankhurst, *Wittenberg University, USA*: Belarus; Bulgaria

Aristotle Papanikolaou, *Fordham University, USA*: Apophaticism; Grace, Orthodox View; Incarnation, Orthodox View; Lossky; Trinity, Orthodox View

Samuele F. Pardini, *Vanderbilt University, USA*: Italian Literature

Stefano Parenti, *Pontificio Ateneo S. Anselmo, Italy*: Chrysostom, Liturgy; James, Liturgy; Mark, Liturgy; Sacramental Theology, Orthodox View; Sacraments, Orthodox View

Peter Paris, *Princeton Theological Seminary, USA*: Poverty, African American View

Sung Bae Park, *Stony Brook University, USA*: Buddhism: Buddhist Perspective

Cristián G. Parker, *Universidad de Santiago de Chile*: Charismatics in Chile; Chile; Church and State in Chile; RC in Chile; Syncretism

Raquel Pastor, *Universidad Nacional Autónoma de México*: Human Rights in Mexico; Lay Catholics in Mexico

Joseph Pathrapankal, CMI, *Dharmaram Vidya Kshetrom, India*: Malabar Christians

Daniel Patte, *General Editor; Vanderbilt University, USA*: Anger of God; Atonement; Authority; Beatitudes; Calendars; Catholicity; Christian; Conversion; Conviction; Discipleship; Dogma; Doubt; Easter; Eighteen Benedictions; Election; Esdras; Ethics; Faith; Fall; Grace, Western; Heresy; House Churches; Imitation of Christ; Immortality; James; John; John the Baptist; Jubilee, Year of; Judaizers; Kenosis; Kingdom of God in NT; Maccabees; Manassas; Mercy; Messiah; Moses; Mystery; Neighbor; New Covenant; Parable; Paul; Peter, Apocalypse of; Pilate, Acts of; Reception Studies of Scripture; Reductions; Romans; Salvation; Sanhedrin; Scriptural Criticism; Scripture; Semiotics; Sermon on the Mount; Servant or Slave; Son of God in NT; Son of Man; Synoptic Gospels; Temple; Twelve Apostles; Universalism

W. Brown Patterson, *University of the South, USA*: James I of England

Clive Pearson, *United Theological College, USA*: Christologies in South Pacific

Keith F. Pecklers, SJ, *Pontifical Gregorian University, Italy*: All Saints' Day; Compline; Culture and Worship; Divine Office; Eucharist Congresses; Eucharist Fast; Eucharistic Prayer; Eucharist in the West; Lauds; Liturgical Movement; Liturgy of the Hours; Mass, RC; Nuptial Mass; Requiem Mass; Vespers; Votive Mass

Nancy Cardoso Pereira, *Director, Comissão Pastoral da Terra, Brasil*: Land, Latin American View; Water

David Horace Perkins, *Vanderbilt University, USA*: Praise and Worship

Pheme Perkins, *Boston College, USA*: Ephesians; Jude; Peter

Edward N. Peters, *Sacred Heart Major Seminary, USA*: Codex Iuris Canonici; Excommunication; Latin, Ecclesiastical; Marriage Annulment in RC; Seal of Confession

Rebecca Todd Peters, *Elon University, USA*: Abortion; Birth Control; Pregnancy

Bishop Yeznik Petrossian, *Holy See of Etchmiadzin, Armenia*: Armenian Apostolic Church; Eucharist, Oriental Orthodox View; Oriental Orthodox Churches

Raymond Pfister, *European Institute for Conciliation and Reconciliation Studies, Birmingham, UK*: Gypsies, Charismatic

Peter C. Phan, *Georgetown University, USA*: Anthropology, Asian View; Christologies, Asian View; Dialogue, Interfaith; Incarnation, Asian View; Inculturation; Inculturation in Asia; Kingdom of God, Asian View; Mission, Western and Asian Views; Mission in Asia; Rahner; Vietnam

Isabel Apawo Phiri, *Member of the Editorial Board; University of KwaZulu-Natal, South Africa*: Circle of Concerned African Women Theologians; Education in Africa; Family, Southern African View; Health, Healing, African View: Dealing with AIDS; Inculturation, Central and Southern African Views; Malawi

William S. F. Pickering, *British Centre for Durkheimian Studies, UK*: Durkheim; Theodicy

Derrick G. Pitard, *Slippery Rock University, USA*: Lollardy

William Elvis Plata, *Universidad de San Buenaventura Bogotá, Colombia:* Acosta de Samper; RC in Colombia

Zlatko Plese, *University of North Carolina, Chapel Hill, USA*: Hermetic Writings

John Plummer, *Vanderbilt University, USA*: Chaucer; Donne; English Literature

James Newton Poling, *Garrett-Evangelical Theological Seminary, USA*: Abuse; Violence

Ronald Popivchak, *St. Peter and Paul Ukrainian Catholic Church, USA*: Dositheos; Mohila

Andrew Porter, *King's College London, UK*: Mission and Imperialism

Ute Possekel, *Center for Theological Inquiry, Princeton USA*: Bardaisan of Edessa; Edessa; Ephrem the Syrian; Eusebius of Emesa; Jacob of Edessa; Nisibis

James M. Powell, *Syracuse University, USA*: Averroes; Gennadios II; Innocent III; Louis IX; Urban II

Enos Das Pradhan, *General Secretary of the Church of North India*: North India, Church of

Devadasan Premnath, *St. Bernard's School of Theology, USA*: Amos; Micah

Jaime Adrían Prieto Valladares, *Universidad Bíblica Latinoamericana, Costa Rica*: Costa Rica; Protestantism in Central America

Anne Primavesi, *Centre for the Interdisciplinary Study of Religion, Birkbeck College, UK*: Ecofeminist Theology

Randall Prior, *Ormond College, Australia*: Holy Spirit, South Pacific View; Liberation Theologies, South Pacific

María Alicia Puente Lutteroth, *Universidad Autónoma del Estado de Morelos, Mexico*: Asbaje y Ramírez; Church and State in Mexico; Garcés; Gómez Morín; Hidalgo y Costilla; Jesús, Felipe de; Llaguno Farías; Martínez; Mary, Virgin of Guadalupe; Méndez Arceo; Méndez Medina; Mexico; Miranda y Gómez; Palafox y Mendoza

Eduardo Guzmão Quadros, *Universidade Estadual de Goiás, Brasil*: Protestantism in Brazil

Albert Rabil, Jr., *University of North Carolina, Chapel Hill, USA*: Erasmus; Humanism; Renaissance

Laurent William Ramambason, *Fiangonan'i Jesoa Kristy eto Madagasikara Ambatonakanga Faculty of Theology, Madagascar*: Anthropology, African View

Apolonio M. Ranche, *St. Andrew's Theological Seminary, Philippines*: Philippine Independent Church

Vololona Randriamanantena Andriamitandrina, *Église de Jésus-Christ, Madagascar*: Madagascar

Lawrence R. Rast, Jr., *Concordia Theological Seminary, USA*: Lutheran Church-Missouri Synod

Paul L. Redditt, *Georgetown College, USA*: Habakkuk; Zephaniah

Adele Reinhartz, *University of Ottawa, Canada*: Jesus, Images of, in Movies; John, Gospel

Rolf Rendtorff, *University of Heidelberg, Germany*: Leviticus

Pål Repstad, *Agder University College, Norway*: Norway

James N. Rhodes, *Saint Michael's College, USA*: Barnabas

John K. Riches, *University of Glasgow, UK*: Bible Interpretation, History of; Bible Interpretation in Western Europe

Joerg Rieger, *Southern Methodist University, USA*: Decolonizing Theology; Postmodernism and Liberation Theologies

Sharon H. Ringe, *Wesley Theological Seminary, USA*: Inclusive Language

Sandra Rios, *Florida International University*: Protestantism in Colombia

Tyler Roberts, *Grinnell College, USA*: Nietzsche

David M. Robinson, *Oregon State University, USA*: Emerson; Transcendentalism

James M. Robinson, *Claremont Graduate University, USA*: Q, Sayings Ascribed to Jesus

Joanne Maguire Robinson, *University of North Carolina at Charlotte, USA*: Porete

Richard A. H. Robinson, *University of Birmingham, UK*: Fátima; Father (Title); Portugal; RC in Portugal

Roy R. Robson, *University of the Sciences in Philadelphia, USA*: Avvakum; Boris and Gleb; Men, Alexander; Nikon; Russia; Sergius of Radonezh; Sorsky; Tikhon

Jack B. Rogers, *Moderator, General Assembly, Presbyterian Church (USA)*: Presbyterian Churches

Maria Roginska, *Polish Academy of Sciences, Poland*: Brest-Litovsk, Union of

Sidney Rooy, *Universidad Bíblica Latinoamericana, Costa Rica:* El Salvador; Honduras; Nicaragua; Panama; Protestantism in Latin America

Rev. Garnett Roper, *Sunday Herald, Jamaica*: Racism in Caribbean

Maria José Fontelas Rosado-Nunes, *Pontifícia Universidade Católica de São Paulo, Brasil*: Sexuality in Latin America

Andrew C. Ross, *University of Edinburgh, UK*: Livingston; Missions and Race

Stefan Rossbach, *University of Kent, UK*: Cold War

François Rossier, *International Marian Research Institute, USA*: Côte D'Ivoire

John D. Roth, *Goshen College, USA*: Mennonites; Mennonite Worship

John K. Roth, *Claremont McKenna College, USA*: Holocaust, Jewish; Judaism, Christian Views; Judaism and Christianity in North America

Phillip Rothwell, *Rutgers University, USA*: African Literature (Lusophone)

Richard E. Rubenstein, *George Mason University, USA*: Aristotle

Rosemary Radford Ruether, *Pacific School of Religion, USA*: Anti-Semitism; Patriarchy; Woman, Theological Views About

Markku Ruotsila, *University of Tampere, Finland*: Catholic Apostolic Church

John E. Rybolt, CM, *DePaul University, USA*: De Marillac; Paul, Vincent de

Risto Saarinen, *University of Helsinki, Finland*: Porvoo Declaration

John Saillant, *Western Michigan University, USA*: African American Literature; Haynes

Juan Sanchez, *Florida International University, USA*: Contemplation; Feminist Theology in Latin America; History of Christianity in Latin America

Wagner Lopes Sanchez, *São Luís College, Brasil*: RC in Brazil

Hugo N. Santos, *Instituto Universitario, Argentina*: Family, Latin American View

Gerhard Sauter, *Universität Bonn, Germany*: Revelation

Gloria L. Schaab, *Fordham University, USA*: God, Feminist View; Incarnation, Feminist View; Mary; Saints, Devotion to, in RC

Sandra M. Schneiders, IHM, *Jesuit School of Theology, USA*: Religious Life

Quentin J. Schultze, *Calvin College, USA*: Media; Media and Worship; Televangelism

Fernando F. Segovia, *Vanderbilt University, USA*: Biblical Interpretation, Latino/a

Turid Karlsen Seim, *University of Oslo, Norway*: Luke

Carsten Selch Jensen, *University of Copenhagen, Denmark*: Tausen

Alan P. F. Sell, *Union Theological Seminary, Wales, UK*: Locke

Frank C. Senn, *Immanuel Lutheran Church, Evanston, USA*: Communion; Lutheran Worship

Kent Davis Sensenig, *Fuller Theological Seminary, USA*: Pacifism

Damían Setton, *Centro de Estudios e Investigaciones Laborales, Argentina*: Paraguay; Protestantism in Argentina; RC in Argentina

Bal Krishna Sharma, *Nepal Theological College Kathmandu*: Nepal

Carolyn J. Sharp, *Yale Divinity School, USA*: Jeremiah

Thomas Sheehan, *Stanford University, USA*: Heidegger

N. Gerald Shenk, *Eastern Mennonite University, USA*: Reconciliation

Christian Sheppard, *University of Chicago, USA*: Symbolism

Charles Sherlock, *University of Melbourne, Australia*: God, Australian View; Gospel and Culture, Australian View; Justification, Australian View

Tabona Shoko, *University of Zimbabwe*: African Instituted Churches in Southern Africa; Church, African Instituted Churches' View

Walter B. Shurden, *Mercer University, USA*: Baptism, Protestant View

Marguerite Shuster, *Fuller Theological Seminary, USA*: Sin

B. Mark Sietsema, *Greek Orthodox Archdiocese of America, USA*: Patristic Thought, Orthodox View; Phyletism; Presanctified Liturgy

Batara Sihombing, *Abdi Sabda Theological Seminary, Indonesia*: Batak Churches

Neil Silberman, *Ename Center for Public Archaeology, Belgium*: David; Solomon

Clodomiro Siller, *Centro Nacional de Ayuda a Misiones Indígenas, Mexico*: Missions, RC, in Mexico

Samuel Silva-Gotay, *University of Puerto Rico*: Puerto Rico

Heikki Silvet, *Tartu Teoloogia Akadeemia Üliõpilaskond, Estonia*: Estonia

John K. Simmons, *Western Illinois University, USA*: Christian Science

Hagith Sivan, *University of Kansas, USA*: Ten Commandments

James C. Skedros, *Holy Cross Greek Orthodox School of Theology, USA*: Athos, Mount; Greece; Hesychasm; Macedonia; Macedonia, the Republic of; Orthodox Church in Greece

Abraham Smith, *Perkins School of Theology, USA*: Thessalonians, 1 and 2

Ashley A. Smith, *United Theological College, University of the West Indies, Jamaica*: Charismatics in Jamaica

Ted A. Smith, *Vanderbilt University, USA*: Blackwell, Antoinette Brown; Finney

Daud Soesilo, *United Bible Society, Timor Leste*: Timor Leste

Pia Søltoft, *Søren Kierkegaard Research Centre, Denmark*: Kierkegaard

Choan-Seng (C. S.) Song, *Pacific School of Religion, USA*: Spirituality, Asian View

Kathryn Spink, *Authorized Biographer, UK*: Taizé Community; Teresa of Calcutta

Bryan Spinks, *Yale University, USA*: Hooker

Eric O. Springsted, *President of the Simone Weil Society, USA*: Rationalism; Weil

Nicolas Standaert, *University of Leuven, Belgium*: Ricci

Brian Stanley, *University of Edinburgh, UK*: Baptist Missionary Society; Missions and Anti-slavery

Glen H.Stassen, *Fuller Theological Seminary, USA*: Militarism; Pacifism

Karel Steenbrink, *Utrecht University, Netherlands*: Indonesia; Islam; Islam in Indonesia; Qur'an

Stephen J. Stein, *Indiana University, USA*: Apocalypticism; Shaker

Andrea Sterk, *University of Florida, USA*: Diodore; John Chrysostom

Gregory E. Sterling, *University of Notre Dame, USA*: Philo

Columba Stewart, OSB, *St. John's Abbey, Minnesota, USA*: Benedictine Order; Cenobitic Monasticism; Eremetic Monasticism; Monastic Vow; Monasticism in the West

Jacques Stewart, *President, Fédération Protestante de France; President, Cimade*: Barot; Cimade; Protestantism in France; Refugees

Robert B. Stewart, *New Orleans Baptist Theological Seminary, USA*: Resurrection of Jesus

Cynthia Stokes Brown, *Dominican University of California, USA*: Clark, Septima Poinsette

Ken Stone, *Chicago Theological Seminary, USA*: Bible Interpretation, Queer

Anne Stott, *Open University, UK*: More, Hannah; Women's Practices in the UK

Elizabeth Stuart, *University of Winchester, UK*: Gay and Lesbian Theologies

Monya Stubbs, *Austin Presbyterian Theological Seminary, USA*: Indebtedness, Sense of; Lee, Jarena; Truth, Sojourner; Tubman

Marjorie Hewitt Suchocki, *Claremont School of Theology, USA*: Evil; Pluralism

David Kwang-sun Suh, *Ewha Womans University, Seoul, Korea*: Korea, North

Scott W. Sunquist, *Pittsburgh Theological Seminary, USA*: Ancestor Veneration, History

Keith Suter, *Wesley Mission, Sydney, Australia*: Justice, South Pacific View; Poverty, South Pacific View

Douglas Sweeney, *Trinity Evangelical Divinity School, USA*: Evangelicals; Evangelicals in North America; New Haven Theology

Charles H. Talbert, *Baylor University, USA*: Acts of the Apostles

Shawqi N. Talia, *Catholic University of America, USA*: Addai and Mari, Liturgy; Chaldean Catholic Church; Iran; Iraq

Elsa Tamez, *Universidad Bíblica Latinoamericana, Costa Rica*: Grace, Latin American View; James; Justification, Latin American View; Liberation and Theology; Oppression; Pastoral Epistles; Romero

Joseph B. Tamney, *Ball State University, USA*: Conservatism, Sociological Perspective

Jonathan Y. Tan, *Xavier University, USA*: Chinese Rites Controversy; Confucianism

Yak-Hwee Tan, *Trinity Theological College, Singapore*: Singapore

Kathryn Tanner, *University of Chicago, USA*: Creation; Culture and Theology

Feiya Tao, *Shanghai University, China*: Millennialism in China; Popular Christianity in China

Elizabeth S. Tapia, *Union Theological Seminary, Philippines; Drew University, USA*: Health, Healing, Asian View

Aquiline Tarimo, *Salvatorian Institute, Morogoro, Tanzania*: Poverty, African View

Claire Taylor, *University of Nottingham, UK*: Bogomilism; Cathars

Mark Lewis Taylor, *Princeton Theological Seminary, USA*: Civil Disobedience; Colonialism and Imperialism; Death Penalty; Ethos; Postcolonialism; Racism and North American White Churches

Bishop Abba Samuel Wolde Tekestebirhan, *Assistant to the Patriarch of the Ethiopian Orthodox Tewahedo Church, Addis Ababa, Ethiopia*: Ethiopian Orthodox Tewahedo Church

Eugene TeSelle, *Member of the Editorial Board; Vanderbilt University, USA*: Africa, Roman; Alexandria; Anger of God; Anointing; Anthropomorphisms; Apollinaris; Arianism; Atonement; Augustine; Basil of Caesarea; Basil, Rule of; Berlin Conference; Boethius; Canonization of the NT; Cappadocians; Carolingian Renaissance; Catechesis; Celibacy; Chalcedon, Council of; Christology: History in the West; Church and State; Church Discipline; City; Civil Religion; Clerical Garb; Conciliarism; Conscientious Objection;

Constance, Council; Constantine; Creeds; Dance; Donatism; Dualism; Easter; Election; Ephesus, Councils; Faith; Fall; *Filioque;* Florence, Council; Free Will; Freedom; Gallicanism; God, Names for; Grace, Western View; Great Schism; Gregory VII; Gregory Nazianzen; Gregory of Nyssa; Heidelberg Catechism; Heresy; Holy Roman Empire; House Churches; Human Rights; Iconoclasm; Ignatius of Antioch; Image of God; Immortality; Indulgence; Infallibility; Inquisition; Irenaeus; Irene; Joachim of Fiore; Julian the Apostate; Justin Martyr; Justinian/Justinian, Code of; Kenosis; Kingdom of God, Western View; Kingdom/Reign of Christ; Lay Piety Movement; Lamennais; Langton; Loisy; Macrina; Marcion; Marsilius; Martyrdom; Maximos the Confessor; Mercersburg Theology; Methodius of Olympus; Miracles; Monothelitism; Nantes, Edict of; Natural Law; Nestorius; Nicaea, Council; Omnipotence; Omnipresence; Omniscience; Ontological Argument; Ontology; Origen; Original Sin; Patristics; Paul of Samosata; Pelagius; Penance; Persecutions; Person; Philosophy; Pilgrim; Polity; Positive Theology, Positive Law, Positivism; Presence of Christ; Priscillianism; Property; Protestantism in Germany; Reason; Relics; Sanctification; Singing in Worship; Temple; Theodicy; Tertullian; Time; Trinity, Western View; Truth; Universalism; Universals; Universities; Vernacular; Word of God; World

M. Thomas Thangaraj, *Emory University, USA*: Holy Spirit, Asian View; Popular Christianity in Asia

David R. Thomas, *University of Birmingham, UK*: Islam in the Middle East

Andrew Thornley, *Pacific History Association, Australia*: Fiji

Scott Thumma, *Hartford Seminary, USA*: Internet Technology; Megachurches

Marcelo Timotheo da Costa, *Faculdade São Bento do Rio de Janeiro, Brasil*: Brazil; Human Rights in Brazil; Leme; Lima

George E. "Tink" Tinker, *Iliff School of Theology, USA*: Liberation Theology: A Native American Critical Perspective; Missionary Conquest in North America; Native American Traditions

Ola Tjørhom, *University of Agder, Kristiansand, Norway*: Apostolicity and Apostolic Succession

Karen Jo Torjesen, *Claremont Graduate University, USA*: Women's Ordination

Iain R. Torrance, *Princeton Theological Seminary, USA*: Severus, of Antioch

Fernando Torres-Londoño, *Pontifícia Universidade Católica de São Paulo, Brasil*: Missions, Catholic, in Brazil; RC in Brazil

Archbishop Demetrios [Trakatellis], *Greek Orthodox Church of America, USA*: Anthropology, Eastern Orthodox View; Divine Liturgy; Eastern Orthodox Churches; Greek Orthodox Church

Marit Trelstad, *Pacific Lutheran University, USA*: Christologies, Feminist and Womanist Views

Christine Trevett, *Cardiff University, Wales*: Montanism; Fell

Phyllis Trible, *Wake Forest University, USA*: Hagar; Isaac; Ishmael; Sarah

Johannes Tromp, *Leiden University, Netherlands*: Abraham, Testament of; Assumption of Moses; Baruch, Syriac Apocalypse of; Fourth Ezra; Isaiah,

Ascension of; Jubilees, Book of; Life of Adam and Eve; Pseudepigrapha of the Old Testament; Pseudo-Philo; Sibylline Oracles; Solomon, Odes of; Solomon, Psalms of; Testaments of the Twelve Patriarchs

Paul Turner, *North American Academy of Liturgy, USA*: Confirmation

Robert G. Tuttle, Jr., *Asbury Theological Seminary, Orlando, USA*: Evangelism/Evangelization

Archbishop Desmond Tutu, *Cape Town; Anglican Church of Southern Africa*: Reconciliation as a Christian Praxis

Peter Tyler, *Sarum College, UK*: Carmelites; Cloud of Unknowing; Luis of Granada; Molinos; Spirituality, RC Mystical

Anders Tyrberg, *Karlstads Universitët, Sweden*: Scandinavian Literature

Justin Ukpong, *Veritas University Abuja, Nigeria*: African Religion: Cultural Interactions; Nigeria

Javier Ulloa, *Seminario Bautista de México, Mexico*: Evangelicals/Evangelicalism in Mexico

Camillus Umoh, *Catholic Institute of West Africa, Nigeria*: *Ekandem*

Kristi Upson-Saia, *Occidental College, USA*: Eustochium; Paula

Martina Urban, *Vanderbilt University, USA*: Buber

Monica Uribe, *Universidad Iberoamericana, Mexico*: Anglicanism in Mexico; Church and State in Mexico; Orthodox Churches in Mexico; Religious Orders in Mexico

Elochukwu Eugene Uzukwu, CSSp., *Milltown Institute, Ireland*: Congo-Brazzaville; Exorcism; Health, Healing, African View; Inculturation, Western African View

Richard Vaggione, *Holy Cross Priory, Canada*: Arianism; Arius; Eunomius

Gabriel Vahanian, *University of Strasbourg, France*: Atheism; Death of God; God, Western Views; Iconoclasm; Technology; Tillich

Paul Valliere, *Butler University, USA*; Berdyaev; Bulgakov; Soloviev

T. J. Van Bavel, OSA, *Augustijns Historisch Instituut, Belgium*: Augustinian Hermits or Friars; Augustinian Rule; Religious Orders, History

Steven Vanderputten, *Ghent University, Belgium*: Charlemagne

Peter Van der Veer, *Utrecht University, The Netherlands*: Nationalism

Huub Van de Sandt, *Tilburg Theological Faculty, The Netherlands*: Didache

Louis Van Tongeren, *Tilburg Theological Faculty, The Netherlands*: Liturgical Year

Luke A. Veronis, *St. Vladimir's Orthodox Theological Seminary, USA*: Culture and Christianity, Orthodox View; Mission, Orthodox View

Noel Villalba, *United Church of Christ, Davao City, Philippines*: Human Rights, The Philippines

Ramón Vinke, *Rector, Universidad Simón Bolívar; Secretary for Ecumenism, Archdiocese of Caracas, Venezuela*: Venezuela

Tim Vivian, *California State University, Bakersfield, USA*: Syncletica

David Voas, *Institute for Social Change, University of Manchester, UK*: Jehovah's Witnesses; Russell

Elena Volkova, *Moscow State University, Russia*: Dostoevsky; Holy Fool; Russian Literature; Tolstoy

Katharina von Kellenbach, *St. Mary's College of Maryland, USA*: Family under Genocide and Wars; Forgiveness

Elina Vuola, *University of Helsinki, Finland*: Folk Churches in Nordic Countries

Timothy Wadkins, *Canisius College, USA*: Megachurches in El Salvador

Elaine M. Wainwright, *University of Auckland, New Zealand*: Feminist Theology in South Pacific; Matthew; Women's Practices in Australia

Randi Jones Walker, *Pacific School of Religion, USA*: United Church of Christ

Dewey D. Wallace, Jr., *George Washington University, USA*: Marprelate Tracts; Perkins; Puritans

Jerry Walls, *Asbury Seminary, USA*: Lewis, C. S.

Michael J. Walsh, *Heythrop College, UK*: Benedict XV; Boniface VII; John XXIII; John Paul II; Leo I; Leo XIII; Opus Dei; Paul VI; Pius IX; Pius X; Pius XI; Pius XII; Popes, RC; Siricius

Philip Walters, *Keston Institute, UK; Editor "Religion, State & Society"*: History of Christianity in Eastern Europe; Latvia; Lithuania

Janet Walton, *Union Theological Seminary, New York*: Hymn; Music in/as Worship; Women's Practices in USA

Jonathan L. Walton, *University of California, Riverside, USA*: Prosperity and Economic Empowerment Gospel, African American Churches

Wang Xiaochao, *Tsing Hua University, Beijing, China*: Church and State in China

Patricia A. Ward, *Vanderbilt University, USA*: Bossuet; Chateaubriand; Fénelon; French Literature; Guyon; Marguerite of Navarre; Maritain; Prayer of the Heart; Quietism

David Harrington Watt, *Temple University, USA*: Fosdick; Machen; Scopes Trial

Herold D. Weiss, *Saint Mary's College, USA*: Death, Latin American View

Laurence L. Welborn, *Fordham University, USA*: Corinthians, 1 and 2; History, Concepts of; Inculturation in the Greco-Roman World

Sharon D. Welch, *Meadville Lombard Theological School, USA*: Ethic of Risk and Womanist Ethics

Timothy Wengert, *Lutheran Theological Seminary, Philadelphia, USA*: Melanchthon

Traci C. West, *Drew School of Theology, USA*: Androcentrism; Sexism

Merold Westphal, *Fordham University, USA*: Levinas

David Wetherell, *Deakin University, Australia*: Papua New Guinea

Barbara Wheeler, *Auburn Theological Seminary, USA*: Theological Education, Concepts of; Theological Education in North America

Carolinne White, *University of Oxford, UK*: Friendship; Jerome; Martin of Tours; Paulinus

Jean-Paul Wiest, *Hong Kong University, China*: RC in China

Frans Wijsen, *Radboud University Nijmegen, The Netherlands*: Luxembourg; Netherlands

Terry L. Wilder, *Midwestern Baptist Theological Seminary, USA*: Apostle; Pseudonymity; Wisdom of Solomon

Felix Wilfred, *University of Madras, India*: Church, Asian View; Gospel and Culture, Asian View; India; Indian Christian Theologies; Theological Education in Asia

Rebecca Wilkin, *Indiana University, USA*: Descartes

Daniel H. Williams, *Baylor University, USA*: Ambrose; Tradition in NT and Early Church; Tradition and Reformation's Scripture Principle

D. Newell Williams, *Brite Divinity School, USA*: Campbell; Christian Church (Disciples of Christ); Restoration Movement; Stone

Michael A. Williams, *University of Washington, USA*: Gnosticism; John, Apocryphon of; Nag Hammadi

Vincent L. Wimbush, *Claremont Graduate University, USA*: African Americans and the Bible

Gabriele Winkler, *Universität Tübingen, Germany*: Basil, Liturgy

Anders Winroth, *Yale University, USA*: Canon Law; Gratian

Lauri Emílio Wirth, *Universidade Metodista de São Paulo, Brasil*: Protestantism in Brazil

James A. Wiseman, OSB, *The Catholic University of America, USA*: Mysticism; Ruusbroec

Ebba Witt-Brattström, *Södertörns högskola, Sweden*: Birgitta

Teofil Wojciechowski, *Jagiellonian University in Krakow, Poland*: Poland

John Wolffe, *The Open University, UK*: Evangelicals in UK; RC in UK; United Kingdom

Kenman L. Wong, *Seattle Pacific University, USA*: Business Ethics

Wong Wai Ching (Angela), *Chinese University of Hong Kong, China*: Cultural Studies; History of Christianity in Asia

Linda Woodhead, *Lancaster University, UK*: Sociological Studies

Wendy M. Wright, *Creighton University, USA*: Discipline (RC); Francis de Sales; Jane Frances de Chantal; Spirituality, RC View

Rose Wu, *Hong Kong Christian Institute, China*: Sexuality, Asian View

Keith E. Yandell, *University of Wisconsin-Madison, USA*: Hume; Natural Theology; Spinoza

Gale A. Yee, *Episcopal Divinity School, USA*: Judges; Ruth

Viktor Yelensky, *National Academy of Sciences of Ukraine*: Ukraine

Yeo Khiok-Khng, *Garrett Theological Seminary, USA; Peking University, China*: Confucian Classics and the Bible; Culture and Biblical Studies

Gustav K. K. Yeung, *Chinese University of Hong Kong, China*: Education in Asia

Angela Yiu, *Sophia University, Tokyo, Japan*: Japanese Literature

Amos Yong, *Regent University, USA*: Charismatic Movement in Asia

Yong Ting Jin, *Coordinator of Asian Women's Resource Centre, Kuala Lumpur, Malaysia*: Asian Women's Resource Centre

You Bin, *Central University of Nationalities in Beijing, China*: Chinese Ethnic Minorities

Youhanna Nessim Youssef, *Australian Catholic University, Australia*: Egypt; Coptic Orthodox Church

Eliana Yunes, *Pontifícia Universidade Católica do Rio de Janeiro, Brasil*: Brazilian Literature

Robert Michael Zaller, *Drexel University, USA*: Cromwell

Valarie H. Ziegler, *DePauw University, USA*: Howe

Barbara Brown Zikmund, *Doshisha University, Japan; Wesley Theological Seminary, USA*: Women's Ordination in North America

Joyce Ann Zimmerman, CPpS, *Institute for Liturgical Ministry, USA*: Blessing of Children; Blood; Bread as Symbol; Marriage, in Western Churches; Wine

Aurora Zlotnik, *Universidad Nacional Autónoma de México*: Popular Christian Practices in Mexico

Zhuo Xinping, *Chinese Academy of Social Sciences, China*: China

PREFACE

What is Christianity? This is the question that *The Cambridge Dictionary of Christianity* addresses. But do not look for the answer in an article entitled "Christianity." It is provided by the entire *Dictionary* in its more than 3,500 articles and entries.

Why is it necessary to devote an entire dictionary to this question? It is a matter not only of academic integrity, but also of ecumenical openness and sensitivity and of ethical accountability.

Academic integrity requires us to acknowledge that Christianity cannot be reduced to a set of correct beliefs, an orthodoxy*,[1] or a set of correct practices, an orthopraxy*. Indeed, churches often define themselves in this way, but in the process they exclude as heterodox or heretical* many believers who think of themselves as followers of Jesus Christ and thus as Christians. But an academic study of Christianity cannot exclude them. We must consider as Christians not only Roman Catholics (c1 billion in 2000) but also Protestants (c340 million), Eastern and Oriental Orthodox (c215 million), and Anglicans (c80 million), all of whom are in some ways heterodox, heretic, or schismatic from a Roman Catholic perspective. Furthermore, there is no reason to exclude the fastest-growing group, "independent Christians" (c385 million in 2000, projected to be c581 million by 2025), many of whom are Charismatic* and are found in the Two-thirds World. In addition, so-called marginal Christians (c26 million) must also be included.

As these approximate statistics (from *The World Christian Encyclopedia*, 2001)[2] dramatize, an academic study, in contrast to a confessional study, must begin with the broadest definition of Christianity: *a Christian is anyone who claims to be a follower of Jesus Christ.* In order to be academically responsible, a study of Christianity must account for the fact that, throughout its history, this religious movement has been highly diversified and remains so today.

The Cambridge Dictionary of Christianity includes articles on all sizable Christian churches, denominations, and movements. But in order to serve as an

[1] An asterisk (*) here and in the main body of the *Dictionary* indicates that a term so marked (or a related form thereof) refers to an entry in the *Dictionary*. In the case of a compound term or phrase, the asterisk specifies which of the terms is alphabetized.

[2] David B. Barrett, George T. Kurian, and Todd M. Johnson, *The World Christian Encyclopedia: A Comparative Survey of Churches and Religions in the Modern World, Vol. 1: The World by Countries: Religionists, Churches, Ministries*, 2d ed. (New York: Oxford University Press, 2001). Much of the statistical information in the *Dictionary* is taken from this encyclopedia. Following the advice of George T. Kurian, we urged the contributors of articles on Christianity in given nations to keep in mind that these statistics are often extrapolated from earlier data, and thus to check the statistics of *The World Christian Encyclopedia* against other sources, such as a recent census, when available.

authoritative reference guide that enables its users to reflect critically on all aspects of Christianity, it does not adopt a specific confessional perspective. No Christian tradition, however well established, should be viewed as a benchmark to determine what is or is not truly Christian.

This means, for example, that the *Dictionary* avoids the use of the qualifier "saint*" to designate any Christian believer as an "exemplary Christian." A "saint" beatified in one church may have been a persecutor of "heretics," members of another church who, in turn, view this beatified person as a "heretic"! Yet the term "saint" is so common in several traditions that it is impossible to eliminate its use completely. Thus two exceptions are made: first, the *Dictionary* keeps the appellation "saint" when it is part of the name of an institution, e.g. St. Andrew's Theological Seminary, or of a document, e.g. Liturgy of St. John Chrysostom; second, the appellation is maintained when the presentation of a topic requires it and makes clear that the person being referred to is a "saint" from the perspective of a particular church. Similarly, the *Dictionary* minimizes the use of the qualifier "heretic*," except when it is clear who considers a given person or group heretical; obviously the members of a church, e.g. the Waldenses*, do not think of themselves as heretics, even if they are seen as such by another church, e.g. the Roman Catholic Church – and this example can be reversed (to their dismay, Roman Catholics are viewed as heretics by many Christians of other churches).

In a more positive vein, the *Dictionary* adopts an approach marked by ecumenical openness and sensitivity. Since no confessional perspective is a benchmark, each Christian tradition, movement, or church presents its beliefs and practices from its own perspective, in the expectation that they will be considered by members of other Christian traditions and non-Christians with respect and that these presentations will foster genuine ecumenical and interfaith dialogue*.

In the quest for academic integrity and for ecumenical openness and sensitivity, the editorial board and the general editor, following the example of anthropologists and, more generally, of specialists in social and cultural studies, have sought to make the presentation of Christianity in the *Dictionary* ethically accountable. The general editor emphasized this point to each of the contributors from the outset. When presenting the beliefs and practices of others, especially those of people within other cultural contexts (e.g. members of an African Instituted Church), scholars are often tempted to portray them as inferior, uneducated, ignorant, or "subaltern" (Gayatri Spivak's term). The demeaning of others and their faith obviously occurs when one represents them as heretics, as members of a syncretistic* cult*, or the like; this amounts to "speaking to" them – teaching them what they *should* believe by dismissing what they *do* believe before even listening to them and trying to understand the religious and cultural "logic" of their beliefs and practices. But this ethically problematic attitude often takes more subtle forms. As Spivak points out, the superiors also commonly "speak for" the subalterns, demeaning them as people who are unable to express themselves appropriately, a common attitude toward members of what the superiors, explicitly or implicitly, view as inferior groups or cultures, e.g. Dalit*, tribal*, or mestizo*. How can scholars avoid these attitudes? As Spivak suggested, and as anthropologists and specialists of cultural studies regularly do, it is simply a matter of allowing others to speak for themselves. Then the appropriate role of scholars is to enter into dialogue with others, to listen to them, to learn from them; through their empathic presentations, scholars can foster further dialogue among their readers. In *The Cambridge Dictionary of Christianity*, people are allowed to speak for themselves, so that users of the *Dictionary* are exposed to the ideas of these Christian believers of other historical or present-day cultural contexts, and can learn from them.

Academic integrity, ecumenical openness and sensitivity, and ethical responsibility are thus tightly interwoven, for all are essential in a dictionary that offers, along with brief definitions of key terms, a concise and accurate presentation of the history of Christianity; an up-to-date overview of the status of Christianity in the world at the beginning of the 21st century; a sensitive presentation of churches, denominations, and groups; and well-balanced explanations of Christian theological concepts and religious and social practices.

ACADEMIC INQUIRIES: CHRISTIANITY THROUGHOUT HISTORY

As long recognized in other encyclopedic dictionaries, academic integrity requires that Christianity with its long history in many cultural, political, and religious contexts be presented in scores of articles by historians specializing in particular periods of Christianity in specific geographic areas. *The Cambridge Dictionary of Christianity* includes hundreds of such historical articles by leading scholars. The major articles about the history of Christianity are found in a "cluster" of 11 articles located under "History of Christianity":

History of World Christianity: A Survey

Followed by

History of Christianity in

Africa and North Africa	Asia	Europe: • Balkans • Eastern Europe • Western Europe	Latin America and the Caribbean Islands	Middle East	North America	South Pacific and Australia

These articles about the history of Christianity in regions or continents include cross-references to many of the articles about the history of Christianity in 134 nations – those nations with more than approximately 500,000 Christians. A perusal of these articles shows that some are much longer than others. This is by design. The length of an article on a given nation reflects the approximate number of Christians who reside in that country today. Thus a list of the longest "national articles" – those for nations with 10 million (M) Christians or more (according to *The World Christian Encyclopedia*, 2001), presented here in order of decreasing length – provides a snapshot of Christianity at the beginning of the 21st century.

Christians in the World				
United States 235.7 M	**Brazil 155.5 M**	**Mexico 95.2 M**	**China 89 M**	**Russia 84.3 M**
Philippines 68.1 M	**India 62.3 M**	**Germany 62 M**	**Nigeria 51.1 M**	**Democratic Republic of Congo 49.5 M**
United Kingdom 48.5 M	**Italy 47 M**	**Ukraine 41.9 M**	**France 41.8 M**	**Colombia 40 M**
Poland 38 M	**Spain 37.1 M**	**Ethiopia 36 M**	**Argentina 34 M**	**South Africa 33.6 M**
Indonesia 27.8 M	**Peru 25 M**	**Canada 24.7 M**	**Kenya 23.9 M**	**Venezuela 22.9 M**
Romania 19.8 M	**South Korea 19 M**	**Uganda 19 M**	**Tanzania 16.9 M**	**Australia 15 M**
Chile 13.6 M	**Netherlands 12.7 M**	**Ecuador 12.3 M**	**Angola 12 M**	**Ghana 11.2 M**
Guatemala 11.1 M	**Egypt 10.3 M**	**Greece 10 M**		

The distribution of Christians around the world in the early 21st century, compared with that at the beginning of the 20th century, is rather surprising. The often heard claim that the center of gravity of Christianity has shifted to the South is further confirmed by the location of the 95 nations with fewer than 10 million Christians; often these are nations with smaller overall populations but with a large percentage of Christians.

These 11 regional and 134 national historical articles in turn cross-reference hundreds of articles about men and women church leaders, their beliefs and practices, the documents they produced, and events emblematic of Christianity in given periods and geographic locations. These other historical articles have been written by scholars who are foremost in these fields, as their publications (listed in the Web-based bibliography) attest, and who graciously accepted our invitation to contribute to the *Dictionary.*

ACADEMIC INQUIRIES: CHRISTIANITY TODAY

The regional and national historical articles trace Christianity from its introduction in a geographic area until the early 21st century and have been prepared by scholars who have both a solid academic knowledge of the history and firsthand knowledge of early-21st-century Christianity in the given cultural contexts. The decision to elicit articles from such scholars was made during a weeklong meeting of the Editorial Board of *The Cambridge Dictionary of Christianity,* a senior editor at Cambridge University Press, and the general editor of the *Dictionary*. Academic integrity required that these articles be written by scholars who could identify with each cultural context.

Two centuries of scholarly research on historiography* and hermeneutics* have shown that historians cannot avoid cultural and religious pre-understandings in their studies. This means that no absolutely objective historical study is possible. Of course, accuracy about facts, events, dates, and the like is possible; the accuracy of factual information in the *Dictionary* has been confirmed by the best sources available and top scholars on each topic. But beyond the issue of accuracy, when preparing a report, a historian must make a choice between what is most significant, and should be included, and what is less significant, and could be omitted – an unavoidable choice for the historian, especially when composing a concise article, such as those in *The Cambridge Dictionary of Christianity.* Cultural and religious pre-understandings play a substantial role in such choices. As anthropologists have repeatedly exemplified, the description of the behavior or belief of people in a culture from an insider's perspective (an "emic" description) is quite different from the description from an outsider's perspective (an "etic" description). The general advantage of an insider's description is that it provides insights into aspects of a culture that outsiders often completely miss. This advantage is even greater in the study of Christianity in countries where mission and colonialism were (and often still are) closely associated, and where missionaries and their authoritative North Atlantic knowledge commonly silenced indigenous Christians as "subalterns" who were told what they should believe and experience. In such situations, a report written by a North Atlantic scholar of Christianity in a region of, e.g., Africa, Asia, or Latin America commonly either ignores "inculturated*" aspects of Christianity in the given cultural context or presents them as syncretistic* aberrations, because the form Christianity takes in that context is different from the Christianity in North Atlantic cultures, as if the latter were not inculturated. By contrast, insiders' descriptions clarify the distinctive features of Christianity in these countries.

Unlike strongly "West-centered" presentations of the history of Christianity – common until the late 20th century – formulated by scholars based exclusively in the academic institutions of Western Europe and North America, *The Cambridge Dictionary of Christianity* has benefited from the publication of scholarly studies of global Christianity, such as the nine-volume set of *The Cambridge History of Christianity* and the *History of the World Christian Movement* (Dale Irvin and Scott Sunquist), and, during the past generation, from the development around the world of research centers on local histories of Christianity. The members of the international Editorial Board of *The Cambridge Dictionary of Christianity* provided direct access to the work of these research centers.

Most of the articles on Christianity in the Latin American and Caribbean nations were written by members of CEHILA (Comisión de Estudios de Historia de la Iglesia en Latinoamérica), an organization of Latin American scholars devoted for more than 35 years to the study, from their insiders' perspectives, of the history of the church in all parts of the Latin American continent. These contributors were nominated and encouraged to write entries by two members of the Editorial Board: Enrique Dussel, who founded CEHILA in 1973, and Ana María Bidegain, one of its leaders. African scholars who wrote the articles on the history of Christianity in different parts of Africa were nominated by two members of the Editorial

Board. Jesse Ndwiga Kanyua Mugambi, who in 1992 founded Acton Publishers, a press in Kenya dedicated to African scholarship, readily drew up the list of articles needed for a balanced presentation of Christianity in Africa and nominated many authors for these, including authors of books published with Acton Publishers and African members of the Ecumenical* Association of Third World Theologians, the inaugural meeting of which he attended and facilitated at Dar es Salaam, Tanzania, in August 1976. In addition, Isabel Apawo Phiri, who coordinated the Circle* of Concerned African Women Theologians from 2002 to 2008, identified African scholars among the members of the Circle, as well as scholars in academic institutions in Southern Africa. Similarly, through their extensive scholarly networks, other members of the Editorial Board identified contributors for articles about the history of Christianity in other parts of the world: Asian scholars were identified by Kwok Pui-lan and Archie Chi Chung Lee, Eastern European and Middle East scholars by Vasile Mihoc and Kathleen E. McVey, and Western European and North American scholars by Cristina Grenholm and Eugene TeSelle.

ECUMENICAL INQUIRIES: CHRISTIAN CHURCHES, DENOMINATIONS, AND MOVEMENTS TODAY AND THROUGHOUT HISTORY

In addition to the historical entries, *The Cambridge Dictionary of Christianity* includes articles on all major Christian churches, denominations*, movements, groups, religious* orders, and parachurch* organizations. All of these "denominational articles," usually complemented by parallel historical articles (e.g. on nations), are written by insiders. In this case, the authors are not "cultural insiders" but "religious insiders," i.e. scholars whose voices are acknowledged as authoritative within their churches or groups and who agreed to write about their respective churches or groups for an academic audience. The list of "Churches* and Denominations" provides many relevant cross-references, ranging from Adventism* to Waldenses* and the Word*-Faith Movement.

A few examples will suffice to clarify the way churches and denominations are presented. Kimbanguism*, the theology and practices of the "Church of Jesus Christ on Earth by the Prophet Simon Kimbangu" (with c15 million members in Congo* DRC and Congo* Brazzaville), is presented by Professor Léon Nguapitshi Kayongo, a member of the Church who, after teaching in Switzerland, was called back to head the main Kimbanguist seminary in Congo; his article, which sketches the internal history of Kimbanguism, its main theological tenets, and its religious practices, is complemented by the historical articles by Jean-Claude Loba-Mkole (on Congo DRC) and Elochukwu Eugene Uzukwu (on Congo Brazzaville).

The much larger churches are presented in the same way, although often by groups of scholars. The Eastern Orthodox* churches are presented by Archbishop Demetrios (Trakatellis), while each autocephalous* Orthodox Church is presented by an Orthodox scholar teaching in one of the Orthodox seminaries or at other universities. Thus a cluster of entries on Eastern Orthodoxy includes, beyond the introductory entries:

			Orthodox Church, Eastern: In			
Georgia	Greece	Romania	Russia	Ukraine	Mexico	United States

Similarly, Bishop Yeznik Petrossian, head of the Armenian Apostolic Church, wrote the introductory entry for the cluster of entries on Oriental* Orthodox churches, and authorities from each of these churches wrote an article on each of them.

Orthodox Churches, Oriental				
Armenian Apostolic	**Coptic Orthodox**	**Ethiopian Orthodox Tewahedo**	**Malankara Orthodox Syrian**	**Syriac Orthodox Church, Universal**

All of these entries on Orthodoxy are complemented by the historical entries on Christianity in specific nations.

Similarly, the much larger Roman Catholic Church is presented by a group of insiders discussing various aspects of the Church: Jesuit scholars of the Pontifical Gregorian University (Rome), as well as members of other orders (e.g. Augustinian, Benedictine, Dominican, Franciscan, Sisters of the Immaculate Heart of Mary, Sisters of St. Joseph), each writing about her or his own order or related topics (e.g. monasticism*). In addition, it is important to recognize the contextualized character of the Roman Catholic Church in various nations. Thus there is a cluster of entries on "Roman Catholicism" in a sampling of geographic areas (all complemented by corresponding national entries), following the introductory entry, "The Roman Catholic Church and Its Theology."

Roman Catholicism in					
Southern Africa	**Western Africa**	**China**	**Philippines**	**France**	**Germany**
Italy	**Portugal**	**Spain**	**United Kingdom**	**Argentina**	**Brazil**
Chile	**Colombia**	**Mexico**	**Paraguay**	**Peru**	**Uruguay**
Canada	**United States**	**South Pacific and Australia**			

The presentations of Protestantism* and Anglicanism* similarly include articles related to diverse cultural and geographic locations. In each case, the articles are grouped in a cluster with an introductory entry by a respected voice in the tradition (for Protestantism Alister E. McGrath, who published *The Blackwell Companion to Protestantism*, and for Anglicanism Bishop Colin O. Buchanan, author of the *Historical Dictionary of Anglicanism*), followed by a sampling of contextualized manifestations of Protestantism and Anglicanism around the world (showing the growing importance and distinctive character of the churches in Africa, Asia, and Latin America in both traditions).

Regarding the highly decentralized Charismatic* and Pentecostal movements, the 15 entries of the cluster are introduced by a historical survey of these movements by Stanley M. Burgess (editor of the *Encyclopedia of Pentecostal and Charismatic Christianity*), preceded by a significant article by Ogbu U. Kalu (a Nigerian scholar, member of the Society for Pentecostal Studies, author of *African Pentecostalism*) on the study of these movements. In it Kalu outlines a critical method necessary for an academic study that would account for this complex and vibrant movement in Africa, Asia, and Latin America without denigrating its members, as proponents of classical North Atlantic methods tend to do. From this perspective, one can appreciate the "inculturated" character of the Charismatic Movement in 13 different contexts.

	Charismatic and Pentecostal Movements in					
Eastern Africa	**Southern Africa**	**Western Africa**	**Asia**	**Australasia**	**Eastern Europe**	**Western Europe**
Brazil	**Central America**	**Chile**	**Jamaica**	**Mexico**	**North America**	

All of these articles on churches, denominations, movements, groups, religious orders, and parachurch organizations (e.g. the Salvation* Army, YMCA*, YWCA*) and global church organizations (e.g. World* Council of Churches, by Samuel Kobia, its president; World Alliance of Reformed Churches, by Clifton Kirkpatrick, its president; and Lutheran World Federation, by Norman A. Hjelm, one of its leaders) show the differences among them with respect to theological issues and religious practices, as well as ethical issues.

CROSS-CULTURAL INQUIRIES: DYNAMICS OF CHRISTIAN THEOLOGIES AND PRACTICES

Together these academic and ecumenical inquiries exemplify and demonstrate that there exist several understandings of a given Christian theological concept (e.g. atonement*, Christ*), of a given Christian view of the religious life (e.g. conception of the church* and of ecclesiastical structures), and of a given Christian practice (e.g. conception of Christians' life in society, of ethics*, of justice*, of poverty*). Beyond these descriptions, the *Dictionary* clarifies the plurality of understandings of the main theological concepts and Christian practices, first by explaining why there is such a plurality.

The question "Why is there a plurality of understandings of any given theological concept or Christian practice?" reflects a longing for orthodoxy and/or for orthopraxy. It would be comforting to be able to identify a single, true understanding of a theological point or of what Christians should do in a specific situation. Yet throughout history and across denominations and cultures today, the plurality of understandings is simply a reality. Furthermore, it is hard to imagine that it could be otherwise when one recognizes that, implicitly or explicitly, each understanding of a given theological concept or of a Christian practice is the result of an interpretive process through which three variable components are interpreted in terms of each other: (1) a tradition or passage of Scripture that the interpreters view as authoritative (e.g. a biblical story, a creed, a teaching by Augustine); (2) certain religious experiences (or lack of such experiences) that the interpreters share with a community in a particular culture; and (3) pragmatic concerns that the interpreters have for people's needs in specific life contexts. The *Dictionary* presents many examples of each of these components, of the methodologies that have been devised by scholars to study them (see Methodologies for the Studies of Christianity, a list of relevant entries), and of the ways these three components interpret each other in the process of formulating particular understandings of given theological concepts and of Christian practices.

1. Scripture, Authoritative Tradition, and Believers' Lives. When they say that a text is Scripture – e.g. that the Gospel of Mark is Scripture – Christian believers mean that this text is a "Word-to-live-by." (The same is true of traditions* or other texts, e.g. creeds*, that Christians view as authoritative.) This means that the meaning of a scriptural text is not contained in the book; rather it is found in the way the book and its teaching interact with specific aspects of believers' lives. The common metaphors describing the Bible as Scripture – such as lamp to my feet, rule of the community (canon), good news, book of the covenant, prophecy (corrective lenses), empowering word, Holy Bible – refer to different ways in which believers relate a scriptural text to their lives (see Scripture). The recognition that Scripture is a Word-to-live-by for believers is the basis of a methodology for the critical study of the interpretations of Scripture by believers: scriptural criticism, itself based on a series of methodologies presented in the following articles and clusters:

	Scripture, Tradition, and Believers				
Scriptural Criticism	**Bible Interpretation Cluster** (in various religious and cultural contexts; 13 articles)	**Bible Translations Cluster**	**Hermeneutics** (and the numerous articles about various hermeneutic theories)	**Reception Studies of Preaching; Reception Studies of Scripture**	**Semiotics and the Study of Christianity**

Biblical scholars have long sought to clarify through the use of redaction* criticism and other methods (e.g. form criticism) the way in which biblical texts (e.g. the Gospel of Mark*) are themselves the product of the interpretation by the author of an authoritative tradition (e.g. about Jesus) as a Word-to-live-by for believers in a specific religious and sociopolitical life context (e.g. in the case of Mark, most likely the turbulent period of the Judean war against the Romans in the late 60s). The articles in *The Cambridge Dictionary of Christianity* about each of the books of the Bible and many other texts (e.g. Apocrypha*, Pseudepigrapha*, creeds) emphasize this aspect of biblical scholarship. These brief articles strive to show that each book was the product of the interpretation of a received tradition by a believer or a community in a specific context and, in addition, briefly mention how this book was received as a Word-to-live-by in later situations. (See all the articles on the books of the Bible, from Genesis to Revelation.)

2. Christian Religious Experiences, Their Theological Formulations, and Culture. The formulation of theological or ethical views by believers is based not only on their specific appropriation of authoritative traditions or scriptures, but also on their religious experiences (or lack of such experiences) and the positive or negative relation of these to the culture that believers share with a community. Thus various Christian religious experiences are presented in a series of articles and clusters:

	Christian Religious Experiences			
Worship Cluster (22 entries)	**Spirituality Cluster** (11 entries)	**Prayer** (and related entries)	**Mysticism; Monasticism Cluster** (7 entries)	**Charismatic and Pentecostal Movements Cluster** (15 entries)

These examples of Christian worship and religious experience illustrate the denominational differences among, e.g., Eastern Orthodox, Roman Catholics, Protestants, and Charismatics. They also illustrate how deeply "inculturated" Christian worship and religious experiences are. As can be expected, religious experiences are shaped by the Christian religious contexts in which they take place, e.g. a monastic community; the Roman Catholic Divine* Office; the Mass* with a large community; the Orthodox Divine* Liturgy; Protestant worship services; Charismatic services; revivalist* meetings; prayer meetings; or individual devotion, prayer, or contemplation. But they are shaped as well by broader religious and cultural contexts (including nonreligious, secularized contexts). As the 6 entries of the Inculturation Cluster and the 11 entries of the Popular Christian Practices Cluster show, Christianity and Christian religious experience have always been inculturated, whether in Palestinian Judaism as the earliest church was or, beginning with Paul*, in the Greco-Roman world, or throughout the centuries in all cultures of Africa, Asia, Australia, and Latin America, as well as of Eastern and Western Europe, in which Christianity was introduced at different times. Of course, Christianity distinguishes itself from existing religions (or secular cultures), rejecting them, often destroying their temples; but in each context, Christian religious experience and worship are nevertheless shaped by these existing religions. This is most apparent in the case of "accommodations" – e.g. when Christian worship is celebrated at the sacred places of an existing religion (e.g. see Mary, the Virgin, of Guadalupe; this was also the case for many European cathedrals) or when Christian worship is deliberately shaped by its secularized* culture (as in Thomas* Mass in Finland* and Scandinavia*). But this is also true when a Christian community so systematically rejects another religion (or secularized culture) that it becomes an inverted image of that religion, and indeed its mirror image (as happens with certain fundamentalist* communities). For Christians who forget or deny the inculturated character of their own religious experiences and worship – as Western Christians often do – those forms of Christian religious experience and worship that have been inculturated in other contexts are labeled syncretistic*. Yet for others, Christianity is necessarily deeply inculturated, because it is, by definition, "an incarnate faith" (see Incarnation Cluster; Popular Christian Practices Cluster: In Eastern Orthodoxy).

To clarify the characteristics of Christian religious experience, *The Cambridge Dictionary of Christianity* shows how Christianity is and was interrelated with other religions. Along with articles on specific religions (including those in the distant past), a series of clusters enhances these interrelations by including at minimum an article describing how Christianity is perceived from the perspective of the other religion (usually presented by a member of that religion) and an article describing how this other religion is perceived by Christians. The Judaism and Christianity Cluster seeks to reflect the long and often tragic interaction of Christianity with Judaism (including the Holocaust*); the Islam and Christianity Cluster provides, beyond a history of this relationship, eight entries on their interactions in different parts of Africa, Asia, Europe, and the Middle East.

	Religions and Christianity (in single entries or clusters)				
African Religion	**Ancestor Veneration**	**Australian Aboriginal Traditions**	**Baha'i**	**Buddhism**	**Civil Religion**
Confucianism	**Daoism**	**Freemasonry**	**Hellenistic Religious Traditions**	**Hinduism**	**Islam**
Judaism	**Mithraism**	**Mystery Religions**	**Native American Traditions**	**New Age Spirituality**	**Shamanism**
Shinto	**Sikhism**	**Vodou**			

In addition to having direct interactions with other religions, Christianity and Christian religious experiences are "inculturated" in their broader cultures, as the six entries of the Culture Cluster demonstrate. This becomes apparent both in the arts, especially in artistic "images of Jesus," and in literature. Thus in the Jesus, Images of, Cluster the *Dictionary* includes:

	Jesus, Images of, in			
Byzantine Iconography	**Latino/a Depictions**	**Literature**	**Movies**	**Western European Arts**

A greater diversity of contexts is emphasized in the articles on literature and Christianity in the following cultures (found under the culture's name) as well as in the many articles on the main authors discussed in these articles.

	Literature and Christianity (in the following cultures)				
African American	African-Anglophone	African-Francophone	African-Lusophone	American	Brazilian
Caribbean	Chinese	English	French	German	Indian
Italian	Japanese	Latin American	Portuguese	Russian	Scandinavian
Spanish					

The Cambridge Dictionary of Christianity also examines the ways in which these inculturated expressions of Christian religious experiences are studied and critically assessed. The most relevant methodological approaches are presented in the following articles (which refer to other articles):

	Methodologies			
Aesthetics and Theology	Hierotopy, the Creation of Christian Sacred Spaces	Iconography	Myth and the Study of Christianity	Philosophy and Christian Theology
Philosophy of Religion	Postmodernism and Theology	Religion as a Concept and Christianity	Structural Studies of Christianity	Symbolism

For Christian believers and theologians, doing theology involves making sense of their inculturated religious experiences in terms of the traditions and Scriptures they hold to be authoritative and, conversely, making sense of their particular way of relating these traditions and scriptures to their lives as a Word-to-live-by in terms of their religious experiences.

3. Contextual Concerns for People's Needs and Christian Ethics. For Christian believers, an inculturated theology that accounts for their religious experiences and for their appeals to authoritative traditions and Scripture still leaves out their daily life in socioeconomic and political contexts, where they and their neighbors* have concrete needs. Such pragmatic concerns also shape Christian believers' views of Scripture and traditions as well as their religious experiences and theological understandings, even as they more directly define their moral life and their ethics. Guided by the member of the Editorial Board who specializes in ethics, Beverly W. Harrison, *The Cambridge Dictionary of Christianity* addresses the ethical issues that Christian believers encounter in society and describes the ways in which Christians have sought to confront these issues.

Since morality is a matter of relationships with other people in life contexts, the Ethics and Christianity Cluster illustrates how Christian ethics is shaped in very different ways in distinctive religious and socioeconomic contexts and refers to entries and clusters of entries dealing with various relationships, such as the following (which in turn refer to other articles):

	Ethics			
Business Ethics	**Church and State Relations Cluster**	**Economy and Christianity Cluster**	**Family Cluster**	**Global Ethics**
Biomedical Ethics; Medical Ethics	**Political Studies of Christianity**	**Political Theology**	**Sexuality, Issues of, Cluster**	**Social Ethics**

The *Dictionary* describes the ways in which Christians in various contexts have sought to address ethical issues in each sector of life, emphasizing the plurality of perspectives on what many contemporary Christian theologians and ethicists view as crisis points, including the following:

	Ethical Issues			
Abortion	**Birth Control**	**Colonialism and Imperialism**	**Ecology Cluster**	**Oppression**
Patriarchalism	**Poverty Cluster**	**Racism Cluster, Slavery Cluster; Anti-Semitism**	**Refugees and Marginalized**	**War**

In its descriptive way, the *Dictionary* does not hide, and indeed exposes in the articles by scholars from many contexts around the world, that despite their ongoing concern for ethics and morality, Christians have been responsible for much historical and contemporary evil. Christians commonly condone and indeed promote systemic sin and systemic evil* – often doing so by passively participating in societies or cultures that contribute to them; decrying anti-Semitism only after it engendered the Holocaust*; decrying the Crusades* and the Inquisition*, yet constantly being on the watch for heretics* or marginalizing* members of other religions; decrying poverty* while not addressing the economic and colonialist issues in which cries for justice* are ignored; decrying oppression of all kinds, yet readily supporting states that do not respect human* rights or social institutions (including churches) that marginalize people on the basis of race, gender, sexual orientation, or (ability) disability*.

Various articles also discuss the ways in which these contextualized expressions of Christian practices are studied and critically assessed. In addition to entries on ethics, the most relevant methodological approaches are presented in the Anthropology Cluster (whose entries emphasize human limitations) and the articles on ideological* and sociological* studies of Christianity, as well as the entries on psychology*, science*, and technology*.

CONTEXTUAL CHRISTIAN THEOLOGIES AND PRACTICES

Through its academic, ecumenical, and cross-cultural inquiries into Christianity throughout history and across contemporary cultures, *The Cambridge Dictionary of Christianity* clarifies and illustrates by numerous examples that all Christian theologies – whether those of Origen*, Basil* of Caesarea, Thomas Aquinas*, Anselm* of Canterbury, Karl Barth*, or Georges Florovsky* – or all ethical teachings are as contextual as the contemporary theologies that readily identify themselves by their contexts, among which are the following:

		Contextual Theologies			
African American Theologies	**Asian Theology**	**Asian American Theologies**	**Black Theology**	**Buraku Liberation in Japan**	**Dalit Theology**
Decolonizing Theology	**Disability and Christianity**	**Feminist Theology Cluster**	**Gay and Lesbian Theologies**	**Indian Christian Theologies**	**Latin American Theologies**
Latino/a Theologies	**Liberation Theologies Cluster**	**Minjung Theology**	**Palestinian Theological Liberation**	**Reconstruction, African Theologies of**	

More generally, because each theological concept and each Christian practice is the result of the interpretation of authoritative traditions or Scriptures in terms of certain inculturated religious experiences and pragmatic concerns for people's needs in specific life contexts, it necessarily has several contextual definitions. For instance, as is well known, there are three different understandings of atonement, emphasizing (1) ransom and redemption from bondage or healing, (2) honor and juridical satisfaction, or (3) moral transformation. Each has been historically associated with distinct ecclesial and social contexts, while being solidly rooted in Scriptures and traditions, and associated with Christian religious experiences. Thus like many other works published since Gustaf Aulén's *Christus Victor: An Historical Study of the Three Main Types of the Idea of the Atonement* (1930; English, 1957), *The Cambridge Dictionary of Christianity* presents these three views of atonement, while emphasizing that, as contextual interpretations, they are equally legitimate. Christian theologians have a choice. Following the same principle, in its conceptual and practical articles the *Dictionary* presents a plurality of understandings of each theological concept or Christian practice (when this was not possible, rather than an article, there is a brief definition). Several contextual interpretations could usually be combined in a single article. Yet, in 44 cases, it soon became clear that the plurality of contextual interpretations required several authors from different contemporary contexts and thus a cluster of entries. None of the clusters pretend to be comprehensive; they simply provide a sampling of different (and often divergent) understandings from a diversity of historical and contemporary contexts (in the following tabulation, the number of contexts is given after the abbreviated title of each cluster).

	Clusters of Contextual Understandings of Theological Concepts or Christian Practices (with number of entries)			
Ancestor Veneration (6)	**Anthropology (theological) (10)**	**Apocalypticism (3)**	**Baptism (4)**	**Bible Interpretation (13)**
Bible Translations (4)	**Christologies (13)**	**Church, Concept of (13)**	**Church and State relations (17)**	**Death (8)**
Ecology (4)	**Educational Practices as Christian Practices (5)**	**Eschatology (6)**	**Ethics (4)**	**Eucharist (3)**
Family (15)	**God (12)**	**Gospel and Culture (8)**	**Grace of God (5)**	**Health, Healing (12)**
Holy Spirit (9)	**Human Rights (6)**	**Incarnation (9)**	**Justice (9)**	**Justification (9)**
Kingdom of God (6)	**Laity (6)**	**Land (4)**	**Marriage (6)**	**Mary, the Virgin (8)**
Millennialism (4)	**Mission (16)**	**Monasticism (7)**	**Poverty (9)**	**Racism (8)**
Sexuality (4)	**Slavery (4)**	**Spirituality (11)**	**Theological Education (9)**	**Tradition (4)**
Violence (3)	**Women's Christian Practices (11)**	**Women's Ordination (7)**		

THE CAMBRIDGE DICTIONARY OF CHRISTIANITY AS PEDAGOGICAL TOOL

The preceding table and the other tables in this Preface provide bird's-eye views of *some* aspects of the more than 3,500 articles and entries in this *Dictionary*, suggesting several of its possible pedagogical uses. It can be used for most courses dealing with Christianity, be they from a historical perspective or from a theological or ethical perspective; or be they courses on global Christianity, mission, comparative religion, or a specific theological topic.

As the general editor, I had access to the *Dictionary* (before copyediting began) for a full year prior to its publication as I was teaching in my own discipline – New Testament and early Christianity – courses on the Gospels and on Paul's letters, in which my students read relevant scholarly books on the topics at hand. During this last year, I also asked them to read, each time we encountered a theological term in the biblical text (e.g. faith*, sin*, atonement*, salvation*, evil*, kingdom*, discipleship*, mission*), the corresponding article or cluster of articles from the

Dictionary. With the plurality of contextual understandings of this theological concept before them, I asked them to tell me which of these understandings was closest to the one they presupposed in their initial reading of the biblical text and which was the closest to the one presupposed by the scholarly interpretation(s) they were studying. A debate over which understanding was the most appropriate and why ensued each time. Methodological issues were discussed (with the help of other articles from the *Dictionary*). When I forgot to provide the students with a relevant article (or cluster), they began asking for it. My classes had been transformed into laboratories for critical studies of the New Testament, as the students actively participated in the discussions with a clear vision that the choices of interpretation had important moral implications, and therefore that any biblical interpretation must be carefully assessed. Indeed, the *Dictionary* will now be a requirement for each of my courses.

Obviously, as the general editor who has read this volume at least three times, I am partial. Other teachers have other pedagogical goals, and the courses they teach cover very different topics related to Christianity. Yet as a dictionary, this volume is an extremely versatile tool, one that is also very helpful for personal use.

I myself have learned much from reading the *Dictionary*. The expertise of the 828 contributors and their insightful presentations are astounding. Dealing with so many contributors could have been drudgery. Instead, their gracious acceptance of an invitation to contribute articles, and their patience when I asked them to explain technical points that were foreign to me, an outsider to their fields, turned out to be a rewarding and enriching experience. I trust the readers of *The Cambridge Dictionary of Christianity* will have the same experience.

Daniel Patte
Editor
January 2010

ACKNOWLEDGMENTS

Obviously, a dictionary with more than 3,500 articles and entries and 828 contributors would not exist were it not for the help of many people. Retelling the story of how the *Dictionary* came into being is the most appropriate way of acknowledging and thanking all those who contributed to it.

When I was approached in July 2001 by Cambridge University Press to be the general editor of a dictionary that would provide a global presentation of Christianity, I was able to respond relatively quickly because I immediately received the support of several colleagues with whom I had the privilege to be associated in various ways: Cristina Grenholm, Eugene TeSelle, Jesse Ndwiga Kanyua Mugambi, Enrique Dussel, Archie Chi Chung Lee, and Vasile Mihoc, who were soon joined on the Editorial Board by Kwok Pui-lan, Kathleen E. McVey, and Beverly W. Harrison, and by Isabel Apawo Phiri and Ana María Bidegain.

Since 1998 Cristina Grenholm, Eugene TeSelle, and I had been involved in a program of the Society of Biblical Literature devoted to the study of the reception through the centuries of Paul's Epistle to the Romans*. It brought into dialogue (and still does) scholars from three main disciplines of the study of Christianity: New Testament studies, church history, and theology. The first years became an intense quest for a way of truly working together (rather than "across" disciplines) in a collective research project with equal contributions from everyone involved. When a methodological model emerged from these discussions, Cristina Grenholm and I formulated it and named it "scriptural criticism" in the "Overture" of *Reading Israel: Legitimacy and Plausibility of Divergent Interpretations* (2000; the first of a 10-volume series, Romans Through History and Cultures, T&T Clark/Continuum; with more than 100 contributors). From the perspective of this interdisciplinary scholarly model, in July 2001 I could readily envision the broad outlines of *The Cambridge Dictionary of Christianity* as a collective project in which writers representing all the disciplines involved in the study of Christianity would cooperate and support each other. Would Cristina Grenholm and Eugene TeSelle be interested in participating in such a project? They enthusiastically responded affirmatively.

Jesse Ndwiga Kanyua Mugambi and I met at an eye-opening "Conference on African Hermeneutics," a pan-African gathering of African theologians and biblical scholars in Hammanskraal, South Africa (1999), where he was the keynote speaker. We began to envision how to prolong this conference, contemplating a collective volume that would bring into dialogue African scholars and North Atlantic scholars. When I mentioned to him the possibility of *The Cambridge Dictionary of Christianity*, he quickly saw it as one way of bringing about what he had envisioned in Hammanskraal.

Archie Chi Chung Lee (Hong Kong), one of the associate editors of a *Global Bible Commentary* (then in progress; published in 2005), and Vasile Mihoc (Romania; a contributor to this commentary), as well as Enrique Dussel (Mexico; founder of CEHILA, who had been a visiting professor at Vanderbilt University), readily agreed to help develop *The Cambridge Dictionary of Christianity*. Similarly, although I had not had the privilege of working with them directly, Kwok Pui-lan and Kathleen E. McVey quickly responded positively and were soon joined by Beverly Harrison. With the support of these scholars, and knowing the range of their scholarship, I was able to accept the offer from Cambridge University Press to draft a formal proposal for such a dictionary. In October 2002, Jesse Mugambi joined me for several weeks at Vanderbilt University (where he was guest professor), helping me pull together this proposal, which was reviewed and revised by members of the Editorial Board.

Even though Cambridge University Press honored us by accepting the proposal, and I had started finalizing it following advice from formal reviewers, the question of the feasibility of this project remained an issue. Extraordinary and ongoing support from the chair of Vanderbilt's Department of Religious Studies, Volney Gay, and from the successive deans of the College of Arts and Science, Richard McCarty (now provost) and Carolyn Dever, made it feasible. A reduced teaching load for several years gave me the most precious of commodities: time. The Center for the Study of Religion and Culture at Vanderbilt (Volney Gay and Douglas Knight, directors) awarded a generous research conference grant to the project; this award was then complemented by a no less generous grant from the Louisville Institute and the Lilly Foundation. Money was available for a week-long meeting of the Editorial Board (Vanderbilt, July 2003) without which the implementation of the *Dictionary* would not have been possible.

The editorial meeting was preceded by much groundwork. A first draft of the head list of more than 2,000 articles and entries was prepared by Eugene TeSelle, then revised by the general editor and the other members of the editorial board. A Web site was created by Revelation Velunta (later updated by Yung Suk Kim) (http://www.vanderbilt.edu/AnS/religious_studies/CDC/) to make available the information about the *Dictionary* needed by the members of the editorial board, and subsequently by the growing number of area editors and advisors, and still later by the contributors around the world. By June 2003, the Web pages included tentative templates for 10 kinds of articles and the basic statistics about the number and type of Christians around the world (in order to determine the length of national entries). A large portfolio of about 200 pages was also prepared for the members of the Editorial Board. These would not have been ready on time without the help of Ph.D. candidates in the Graduate Department of Religion at Vanderbilt University, who greatly facilitated the Editorial Board meeting in all kinds of ways. Special thanks for their contributions to this vital first stage of the preparation of the *Dictionary* are due to Revelation Velunta, Monya Stubbs, James Metzger, Chul Heum Han, Ruben Munoz, and Yung Suk Kim.

Before the editorial meeting, we had an overall vision of the topics that were to be covered by the *Dictionary*. By the end of that meeting (July 2003), we had a detailed outline of the ways we wanted these topics to be presented. Each day we dealt with 2 of the 10 types of articles. While graduate students were taking minutes of the proceedings, nine members of the Editorial Board (Jesse Mugambi could not come a second time in less than a year; Justin Ukpong, Nigeria, an area editor for Western Africa, played an essential role in representing Africa), Andy Beck, humanities development editor of Cambridge University Press, and the general editor were joined by colleagues from Vanderbilt University who had agreed to contribute to the discussion of the articles related to their fields and what they needed to emphasize; some bravely sent (if they were out of town) or presented samples of articles that were deconstructed and reconstructed along with the drafts of the corresponding templates. Thus Victor Anderson (ethics), Lewis V. Baldwin (African American church history), James P. Byrd (US church history), Paul Conkin (US history), Dennis C. Dickerson (African American history), Edward Farley (theology), Joel F. Harrington (Reformation history), Peter C. Hodgson (theology), Leonard M. Hummel (pastoral care), Dale A. Johnson (church history), M. Douglas Meeks (Methodism, economics, and theology), Bonnie J. Miller-McLemore (pastoral care), and Patricia A. Ward (French literature) contributed most directly to the shaping of the *Dictionary*.

At this meeting, we decided that many of the topics should be insiders' presentations. The concept of "cluster of entries" was adopted, multiplying the number of articles. Essential topics were added (the head list of 2,000 articles grew to more than 3,500), including a series of entries on Christianity and literature (promoted by Patricia Ward, who became the area editor) and on Christianity and other religions. A new set of templates (50 of them!) had to be prepared. Yet it was necessary to maintain the maximum of 1 million words. Each article or entry was assigned a specific number of words; each was to be not only accurate but also concise. With all this, the envisioned number of contributors multiplied by four.

But the task I faced as general editor, while time-consuming, was never daunting, because help came in many ways. First, Eugene TeSelle, who had recently retired, drafted hundreds and hundreds of short entries defining technical terms in a few lines, or briefly identifying historical events or figures. (Most of the short entries without signatures were elaborated on the basis of these drafts as they were cross-referenced with longer signed articles.) He also wrote a large number of articles in his field (Western historical theology); he then reviewed with me the entire copyedited manuscript and was always ready to discuss editorial matters. Second, each of the members of the Editorial Board – joined by Isabel Apawo Phiri (Malawi and South Africa) and Ana María Bidegain (Colombia and Florida) – identified hundreds of specialized contributors. Yet authors in many areas still needed to be identified and the way to present certain issues still had to be clarified. Thirty area editors and advisors (see the list of their names and areas of expertise), each an authoritative voice in a specific field, stepped in, playing an essential role in helping us shape the *Dictionary* and identifying top scholars in their fields.

The Cambridge Dictionary of Christianity was becoming an actual possibility. Jennifer Bird and I drafted most of the additional templates needed for the clusters. Personal letters had to be sent to hundreds of nominated scholars, explaining to them what we were trying to accomplish with the *Dictionary*, who had nominated them, and what specifically we hoped they could contribute on the basis of their particular research or responsibilities. There were hundreds of letters to write. This process was begun by the graduate assistants who helped with the editorial meeting, but the bulk of the letter writing took place over several years with the help of Jason Jones, Sejong Chun, and Jennifer Bird. Without their help, this task would have been impossible. The gracious and often enthusiastic responses of most of the remarkable scholars to whom we wrote were overwhelming; and several who could not participate because of ill health or for other reasons nominated others. The names of the members of the Editorial Board and of the area editors or advisors clearly carried great weight among other scholars. Our conception of the *Dictionary* resonated well with the scholarship they had often developed over years of research.

Yet a steady flow of articles arriving from all over the world, often from contributors for whom English was not their mother tongue, needed to go through a first round of copyediting and to be collated with articles on similar topics. Articles also arrived in Spanish, French, Italian, German, and Polish; I wish to express my gratitude to Gloria Kinsler for her translation of four of the numerous Spanish articles, to William Franke for his translation of an Italian article, to Eugene TeSelle for his translation of a German article, and to Richard A. Rehl for his translation of a Polish article. I also express my gratitude to Kwok Pui-lan and Archie Chi Chung Lee, who reviewed all the transliterations from the Chinese. Ensuring that the articles were not too long was a constant struggle. Yes, in these concise articles and entries, we needed all the insightful information these specialists viewed as essential to each topic. But no, we could not go over the word limit calculated for the article; doing so for each article would mean going over the limit of the single-volume dictionary we envisioned. Jennifer Bird and I shared the task of copyediting and shortening articles during this round until she completed her Ph.D. and accepted a teaching position at Greensboro College.

Finally, I want to thank the very professional staff at Cambridge University Press who produced this volume, and especially Mary Becker, who during a second round of copyediting transformed this multi-voiced and multi-accented manuscript into a harmonious melody that Curious Georgia (Kwok Pui-lan's name for our ideal reader, a sharp undergraduate without any special knowledge of Christianity) would enjoy and fully appreciate.

In the meantime, Chul Heum Han, Rohun Park, Yung Suk Kim, Sejong Chun, Menghun Goh, and Sung Uk Lim also helped gather bibliographies (available on the Web) for most of the signed articles. And throughout these years, Betsy Cagle, the administrative assistant of the Department of Religious Studies, went out of her way to help produce this volume.

By naming all those who contributed for eight years to the production of this volume – I hope I did not exclude anyone – and by referring to the 30 area editors and advisors and the 828 contributors who are listed in the opening pages – I express how greatly I am indebted to each of them; without each of their contributions and help, the *Dictionary* would not be what it is. They have all my gratitude. Finally this volume would not exist if it were not for the patient support of Aline, my wife. Too many long walks were postponed or sacrificed because I needed to work on *The Cambridge Dictionary of Christianity*.

Daniel Patte
Editor
January 2010

ABBREVIATIONS

GENERAL ABBREVIATIONS

b	Born (b378)
BCE	Before the Common Era
c.	Century (20th c.)
c	Circa (c815)
CE	Common Era
d	Died (d1566)
Fr.	Father (a priest in the Roman Catholic Church)
Gk	Greek
HB	Hebrew Bible (as Jewish and Christian Scripture)
Heb	Hebrew
Lat	Latin
LXX	Septuagint
Msgr.	Monsignor, bishop
MT	Masoretic Text
NAB	The New American Bible (official translation of the Roman Catholic Church)
NRSV	The New Revised Standard Version
NT	New Testament (as Christian Scripture)
OT	Old Testament (as Christian Scripture)
par.	(after a reference to one of the Gospels): "and parallels passages in the other Gospels"
Sr.	Sister (a nun in the Roman Catholic Church)

ABBREVIATIONS OF BIBLICAL BOOKS

Hebrew Bible, Old Testament

Gen	Genesis
Exod	Exodus
Lev	Leviticus
Num	Numbers
Deut	Deuteronomy
Josh	Joshua
Judg	Judges
Ruth	Ruth
1–2 Sam	1–2 Samuel
1–2 Kgs	1–2 Kings
1–2 Chr	1–2 Chronicles
Ezra	Ezra
Neh	Nehemiah
Esth	Esther
Job	Job

Ps/Pss	Psalms
Prov	Proverbs
Eccl	Ecclesiastes (or Qoheleth)
Song	Song of Songs (Song of Solomon, or Canticles)
Isa	Isaiah
Jer	Jeremiah
Lam	Lamentations
Ezek	Ezekiel
Dan	Daniel
Hos	Hosea
Joel	Joel
Amos	Amos
Obad	Obadiah
Jonah	Jonah
Mic	Micah
Nah	Nahum
Hab	Habakkuk
Zeph	Zephaniah
Hag	Haggai
Zech	Zechariah
Ma	Malachi

New Testament

Matt	Matthew
Mark	Mark
Luke	Luke
John	John
Acts	Acts
Rom	Romans
1–2 Cor	1–2 Corinthians
Gal	Galatians
Eph	Ephesians
Phil	Philippians
Col	Colossians
1–2 Thess	1–2 Thessalonians
1–2 Tim	1–2 Timothy
Titus	Titus
Phlm	Philemon
Heb	Hebrews
Jas	James
1–2 Pet	1–2 Peter
1–2–3 John	1–2–3 John
Jude	Jude
Rev	Revelation

APOCRYPHA, SEPTUAGINT, AND OTHER ANCIENT TEXTS

1–2 Esd	1–2 Esdras
Jdt	Judith
1–2 Macc	1–2 Maccabees
3–4 Macc	3–4 Maccabees
Sir	Sirach/Ecclesiasticus

Tob	Tobit
Wis	Wisdom of Solomon
Adv. haer.	Irenaeus's *Adversus Haereses, Against Heresies*
De princ.	Origen's book, *De principiis* (On first principles)
Ep.	*Epistula,* Epistle (plural, *Epp. Epistulae,* Epistles), a common title referring to the letter(s) of the named author
Flacc.	Philo, *In Flaccum* (Flaccus)
Leg.	Philo, *Legum allegoria* (Allegorical interpretation)
Spec. leg.	Philo, *De specialibus legibus* (On special laws)
Orat.	Oration(s), a common title referring to the recorded sermons of the named author
Sent.	a common title referring to "Sentences" of the named author; e.g. Peter Lombard, *III Sent.,* d. 6 refer to Third Book of Sentences, distinction 6
Vat. Reg. Lat.	Latin Registry of the *Biblioteca Apostolica Vaticana*
Vis.	Vision, the different parts of the Shepherd of Hermas*

ROMAN CATHOLIC ORDERS

CM Congregation of Priests of the Mission (Vincentians or Lazarists)
CMI Carmelites of Mary Immaculate
CPPS Missionaries of the Precious Blood (Congregatio Missionariorum Pretiosissimi Sanguinis Domini Nostri Iesu Christi) and Sisters of the Most Precious Blood
CSC Congregation of the Holy Cross (Holy Cross Fathers)
CSJ Sisters of St. Joseph
CSSp Congregation of the Holy Spirit (Holy Ghost Fathers or Spiritans)
CSsR Congregation of the Most Holy Redeemer (Congregatio Sanctissimi Redemptoris) (Redemptorist)
IHM Sisters, Servants of the Immaculate Heart of Mary
MM Maryknoll Sisters
O.Carm. Carmelite (Order of Our Lady of Mt. Carmel)
OFM Order of Friars Minor (Franciscans)
OMI Oblates of Mary Immaculate (Missionary Oblates)
OP Order of Preachers (Ordo Praedicatorum) (Dominicans; also called "Blackfriars," especially in England)
OSA Order of St. Augustine (Augustinians)
OSB Order of Saint Benedict (Benedictines)
OSF Franciscan Brothers or Sisters
SA Society of the Atonement (Franciscan Sisters/Brothers of the Atonement)
SJ Society of Jesus (Societatis Iesu) (Jesuits)
SVD Society of the Divine Word (Verbites)

THE CAMBRIDGE DICTIONARY OF CHRISTIANITY

Aarflot, Berthe Canutte (1795–1859), author, speaker, leader, counselor. Born in Sunnmøre, Norway; married in 1817; six children. She wrote several collections of religious poetry, published in numerous editions, and a religious autobiography (1860); her collected writings were published in five volumes (1853–54, new ed. 1868–70). She was the best known woman in the Hauge Movement, a lay Pietist* movement led by Hans Nielsen Hauge (1771–1824). Her religious writings contributed to the diffusion of Pietism to a broader population and helped turn Pietism away from legalistic tendencies and more in the direction of Evangelicalism. She recruited her husband and turned her home into a religious and cultural center.

INGER FURSETH

Aaron, the older brother of Moses. Aaron speaks on Moses' behalf (Exod 4, 7, 8). When Moses is on Mount Sinai, Aaron yields to the people's request and makes the golden calf (Exod 32). The priesthood came to be limited to the descendants of Aaron, the first high priest; among them, a special role was assigned to the descendants of Zadok*. Hebrews* 5:4 emphasizes Aaron's calling by God, but his priesthood is superseded by that of Melchizedek*, who has no genealogy and foreshadows Christ, himself a descendant of Judah rather than of Aaron (Heb 7:11–14). Aaron later became a model for the Christian bishop*.

Abba, Amma, Aramaic terms for "father" and "mother." Jesus called God "Abba." Title of the male or female superior of a monastic* community.

Abbacy, the office, or term of office, of an abbot.

Abbess, Abbot, English designation (from Greek and Latin forms) for the female or male superior of a monastic* community. **See also BENEDICT, RULE OF; HIGUMEN.**

Abel, second son of Adam and Eve (Gen 4:1–16), killed by his brother Cain* because Abel's sacrifice as a shepherd was more satisfactory than that of Cain, a tiller of the soil. In the NT, Abel is the first of many righteous persons (Matt 23:35 = Luke 11:51; Heb 11:4); for the church, he foreshadows Christ or is the first citizen of the city* of God.

Abelard, Peter (1079–1142), philosopher, theologian, poet. Born in Brittany, Abelard studied logic in Anjou under Roscelin of Compiègne (d1120/25) and in Paris under William of Champeaux (d1122), and briefly theology in Laon under Anselm* (d1117). Abelard relates the controversy he provoked by arguing with teachers, and through his love affair with Heloise (1115–17), in his *Historia calamitatum* (1132/33). In his logical writings, Abelard promoted a nominalist* understanding of linguistic terms. After Heloise gave birth to Astrolabe and ostensibly secretly married Abelard, Abelard was castrated at her uncle's behest. While she became a nun at Argenteuil, Abelard became a monk at St. Denis and started writing about the Trinity*, combining his linguistic interests with an understanding of God as the supreme good glimpsed by prophets and philosophers alike. Having escaped from St. Denis (1122), he constructed an oratory dedicated to the Paraclete*, taken over by Heloise and her nuns in 1129. In the 1130s, he corresponded much with Heloise, while reestablishing himself as a teacher in Paris. He emphasized intention in his ethics and Christ's redeeming example in commenting on Paul (see Atonement #3). His theological writing was condemned at Soissons (1121) and Sens (1141) at the instigation of Bernard* of Clairvaux.

CONSTANT J. MEWS

Abercius (2nd c.), bishop of Hieropolis in Phrygia, whose epitaph, written in cryptic language, tells of his journey to Rome, as well as his travels through Syria as far as Nisibis*, with Paul as his companion, finding a faith shared with people everywhere.

Abgar, a historic ruler (13–50 CE) of Edessa*, a city-state between the Roman and Persian Empires. He allegedly wrote a letter inviting Jesus to continue his ministry in Mesopotamia. Eusebius* preserved Jesus' answer, promising an apostolic mission. Considered spurious in the West, the correspondence played a significant role in the East. The Syriac text *Doctrine* *of Addai** (c400) described the apostle Thaddeus's mission in Edessa. In the Syriac* and Armenian* churches, Thaddeus* (or Addai in Syriac) became the basis of apostolic succession, much as Peter did in Rome. The correspondence mentions a portrait of Jesus painted on Abgar's request. ALEXANDER MIRKOVIC

Abjuration, the formal renunciation of formerly held beliefs, usually under pressure. In Roman Catholic usage, the formal renunciation of heretical ideas, persons, or practices. Abjuration could also mean the renunciation of the "true faith" in order to avoid persecution, as the lapsed* did during the Decian* and other persecutions*. The term also refers to the renunciation of the devil* and the powers of evil as part of baptism* in the early church and today in some Protestant churches.

Ablution, ceremonial washing of the hands for purification, especially by the priest after celebrating Communion*.

Abortion refers to human action intentionally aimed at terminating a pregnancy*. Historically, women had three means of termination: intentional blows to the abdomen to induce miscarriage, the administration of an abortifacient herbal mixture, or surgical removal. Scripture does not directly address abortion, and Christian statements about it are fragmentary until the 19th c. They reflect concerns for the fetus's ontological* status, sexuality*, and the pregnant woman's health.

In the rare references in Scripture and tradition, the moral status of a fetus is different from that of an existing human. In Exod 21:22–23, the punishment for causing a woman to miscarry is a compensatory payment to the woman's husband for his lost "property." This was consonant with Greco-Roman attitudes. In medieval penitentials, the penance for abortion was similar to that for stealing an ox, rather than that for homicide. Furthermore, a distinction was made between "unformed" fetuses and "formed" fetuses believed to possess a "soul*." Abortion was usually condemned only after a fetus was formed (Augustine*, Aquinas*). Aquinas (following Aristotle) established this date as 40 days (for males) or 90 days (for females) after conception.

Attitudes toward abortion and birth* control were closely associated with attitudes toward sexual immorality. Poor women desiring abortion for economic reasons were considered less sinful than women attempting to conceal immoral sexual behavior. Until the 20th c., Christian theologians who believed procreation to be the unique purpose of sexuality* condemned abortion and birth control, which they associated with prostitutes and adulterers. Yet in popular practice, concerns for the pregnant woman's health and well-being (particularly in life-threatening situations) often moderated official attitudes.

While contemporary Christian debates about abortion continue to hinge on the question of "ensoulment" (when life begins), the debate broadened beyond the morality of abortion to its legality. Historically, access to abortifacients and women's control over revealing early pregnancies meant that many women obtained abortions within a certain veil of privacy. The medicalization of pregnancy, birth control, and abortion led to more public scrutiny of women's moral agency in reproductive decision making. Many mainline Protestant denominations in the USA (United Church of Christ, Presbyterian Church [USA], Methodist, Episcopal) affirm a woman's legal and moral right to make reproductive decisions. The Roman Catholic Church dropped the distinction between formed and unformed fetuses in 1869 (First Vatican* Council). In 1965 official Catholic teaching shifted the concern over abortion from the concealment of sexual sin to the protection of life. Regardless of official church positions, evidence indicates that Christian women obtain abortions at the same rate as women in the general population.

REBECCA TODD PETERS

Abraham (in Judaism, Christianity, and Islam). The significance of Abraham can perhaps be summed up by two statements in the Hebrew Scriptures. Abraham is the "friend of God" (Isa 41:8) and the "ancestor of a multitude of nations" (Gen 17:4). In fact, the world's two largest faiths, Christianity and Islam*, together with Judaism*, out of which they grew, are often called "the Abrahamic religions." Abraham is a foundational figure in all three. That he is the friend of God is cited with approval in the NT (Jas 2:23) and in Islam, where he is called Khalil Allah, "Friend of God."

The story of Abraham is told in Gen 12–25. What kind of material is this? First, these narratives were written many centuries later than the events they depict, whose setting appears to be the second millennium BCE. Even on the traditional assumption that Moses was the author, he would have been writing many generations later (Gen 15:13; 16:1–16 indicates a lengthy time between Abraham and the Exodus); thus, the earliest modern pentateuchal criticism in the 18th c. attempted to detect within Genesis the sources that Moses used. Since then, Gunkel, Van Seters, and Whybray have shown that, in all likelihood, the material was initially passed on orally and was subsequently written by several different hands, all long after the death of Moses, though dates and details cannot be established with precision.

Second, von Rad and Moberly have shown that the stories presuppose aspects of Israel's own history, which has been compressed into single episodes of depth and resonance, somewhat as the stories of Robin Hood compress the history and ideals of several centuries of English experience into a fixed cast of characters and a single historical context. The portrayal of Abraham is inseparable from the impact he continued to have in Israel.

The famous story of the near sacrifice of Isaac* (Gen 22:1–19; see Sacrifice of Isaac: The Aqedah) illustrates these points. Its distinctive character is marked by God's requirement that Abraham sacrifice his son, an action prohibited elsewhere (Jer 7:31). Yet God's requirement has clearly been interpreted with language that elsewhere characterizes Torah*: God's command is a *test* (Gen 22:1) whose purpose is to establish that Abraham *fears* God (22:12), terms that recur in a prime interpretation of the purpose of God's giving the Ten Commandments to Israel (Exod 20:20). Moreover, the site of the sacrifice is Moriah (Gen 22:2), elsewhere the site of the Jerusalem Temple (2 Chr 3:1); similarly the "mountain of YHWH" (Gen 22:14b) sounds like Jerusalem (Isa 2:3). This suggests that Abraham has been construed as a model for Israel's appropriate responsiveness to God; his costly relinquishment of Isaac interprets the meaning of Israel's Torah obedience and sacrificial worship.

The NT sees Abraham's action as that right responsiveness to God that Christians depict as faith* (Heb 11:17–19; Jas 2:18–24), as Paul*, Clement* of Rome, Ambrose*, and Augustine* also emphasize, though Paul distances Abraham's faith from Torah obedience (obeying the Law*; Gal 3; Rom 4).

The Qur'an* (37:83–113) sees Abraham as modeling surrender and obedience to God, Islam's key concept, and retells the story in a way that led Muslims to identify the son with Ishmael* and the place with Mecca.

Thus in each Abrahamic religion, Abraham has been understood according to the categories characteristic of that religion: Torah, faith, or surrender and obedience. Though it is sometimes proposed that Abraham could be an "ecumenical" or "normative" figure for the differing traditions (Kuschel), there simply is no "neutral" Abraham independent of the contours of each tradition (Levenson). Any attempt to reach behind Genesis to an "original" Abraham leads not to firm ground but only to unverifiable speculations. The significant Abraham is the Abraham of particular traditions.

R. W. L. MOBERLY

Abraham, Testament of, OT pseudepigraphon recording how Abraham* repeatedly manages to postpone the moment of his death, until he is finally outsmarted by God and the angels. In a sequence of heavenly journeys, Abraham is enlightened about humanity's sinfulness* and God's justice*, compassion*, and mercy*. Owing to unsolved text-critical problems, questions of date and provenance remain unanswered. **See also PSEUDEPIGRAPHA OF THE OLD TESTAMENT.**

JOHANNES TROMP

Abram (Heb "the father is exalted") was in Gen 12–25 the original name of Abraham*, "the father of a multitude" (Gen 17:5). The giving of a new name to the Patriarch as part of the covenant confirmed God's control even as it marked a new stage in Abraham's story.

Absalom, third son of David*. While he was attempting to usurp his father's throne, his long hair became entangled in an oak tree and he was killed by David's soldiers, despite David's instructions. David's mourning for Absalom became legendary (2 Sam 18:33–19:8).

Absolution, the remission of sins* by a priest or bishop on the basis of Christ's promise (John 20:23), especially in connection with penance*. Originally a prayer, it has been declaratory since the Fourth Lateran* Council.

Abstinence, refraining from certain things or actions (1) because they are regarded as sinful* or harmful, (2) as penance*, or (3) for the sake of self-discipline*. Fasting* is a refusal of food more complete than abstinence.

Abuse as Pastoral Care Issue. "Abuse" (from old English, French, and Latin) means to "abuse," i.e. "mis-use" or "mis-treat" someone or something so as to cause harm. In the legal area, "to abuse" means to mistreat persons in violation of their human* rights as defined by a particular culture*. In the moral sense, it means to threaten the life and health of someone in violation of religious law or tradition and to cause harm, including emotional trauma, physical injury, or death. In these definitions, "abuse" describes the attitude of the one abusing, i.e. intent to harm or reckless endangerment, as well as the consequences for the victim of abuse, the harm caused.

In theology, the word "abuse" became prominent (mid-20th c.) in the development of three theologies: Liberation* theologies arose from concern for the abuse of the poor through systemic violence (see Poverty Cluster); Black* and Womanist* theologies arose from concern for abuse during slavery* and afterward, especially the sexual abuse of female slaves, and ongoing racism*; Feminist* theologies arose from concern for the abuse of women in sexual and domestic violence. Biblically, these theologies consider the abuse and death of Jesus as an innocent victim to be the basis for Christian empathy for all victims of abuse.

Pastoral care theory gradually shifted because of these theological trends. Pastoral caregivers began to expand their horizon beyond individual sin* as the primary cause of all human suffering to include a focus on care for the victims of abusive agents and systems. Persons and families seek care from churches not only because of personal sin, but also because of oppression in the form of family* violence*, poverty, sexism*, racism, and other ideological* and socioeconomic systems.

Pastoral care practices shifted along with this change in theological perspective. Pastoral caregivers have to sort out the internal and external causes of human suffering. For victims, pastoral caregivers must develop a plan to cope with abusive systems, help victims to mourn the losses they have sustained because of abuse, and encourage them to reorganize a new life of liberation from abuse. This three-stage healing process is based on a model of empowerment of victims of abuse rather than of confession*, repentance*, and penance*, which were characteristic of previous models. For abusers, pastoral care requires sorting out the factors of sin, abusive attitudes, and behavior (inevitably part of persons' histories) and helping victims develop another way of relating to persons nonviolently. To exercise power over victims, abusers rely on deception, claim authority, and often maintain impunity afterward – issues difficult to resolve in pastoral care and counseling.

JAMES NEWTON POLING

Acacian Schism, the break of communion (see Schism) between Rome and Constantinople (482–519) because of the emperor Zeno's *Henoticon**. During this time, the popes became more independent of Constantinople, capital of the Byzantine Roman Empire; in 494 Gelasius differentiated the spiritual "authority" of the papacy and the temporal "power" of the Empire.

Accra Confession, a critique of the "neoliberal economics*" that has accompanied globalization*, issued by the World* Alliance of Reformed Churches in Accra, Ghana (2004), with statements beginning "We believe" and "We condemn" (cf. the Barmen Declaration). It condemns the spirit of competition, deregulation, and privatization that subordinates social obligations and the environment to capital accumulation and economic growth.

Acculturation, the process of adopting the behavior patterns of the culture in which one lives and/or the shared knowledge and values of a society; the assimilation of new ideas into one's culture; and ultimately, alienation from one's original culture (contrast with Inculturation).

Acoemetae (Lat "Sleepless Ones"), name given to a monastery outside Constantinople that specialized in perpetual doxology and prayer, a forerunner in the organized monastic performance of *laus perennis* (perpetual prayer). Perhaps inspired by Syrian models, it was founded c410 near the Euphrates by an itinerant monk, Alexander, who was banished as a Messalian* (427) because of his rigorous emphasis on prayer and poverty. Reformed under its third leader, Marcellus, the monastery provided rules and leaders for subsequent foundations (e.g. the Studios* Monastery) and became renowned for its library and staunch defense of the Council of Chalcedon*. DANIEL F. CANER

Acosta de Samper, Soledad (1833–1913, Colombia*), historian, novelist, journalist. She traveled extensively in Europe and the Americas while receiving a high level of education, especially for a woman of that time. An active and devoted Roman Catholic, she married José María Samper, a liberal politician, and had three daughters. One of the most important and prolific 19th-c. Colombian writers, she published travel journals, romantic novels, plays, cultural studies, critical literary essays, and biographies, as well as letters and articles for six magazines (each of which she edited for a time).

In all of her publications, she attempted to reconcile her Catholic faith with her quest for a more active role for women*.

WILLIAM ELVIS PLATA

Acts of the Apostles, Volume 2 of Luke-Acts, an anonymous narrative written post-70 and probably directed to Greek-speaking Christians throughout the Mediterranean world, telling of a Jewish sect's expansion from Jerusalem to Rome within the context of Roman imperial society (see Luke, Gospel of). Imperial values of order and stability, in a world with many ethnic, cultural, and religious differences, aimed to unite the world under one justice system. Religious traditions' fortunes depended on their compatibility with imperial norms.

The portrait of Acts' hero, Paul* (Acts 7:58–28:31), emerges in a period after his death when his legacy was contested. Was he a legitimate apostle, *the* apostle, or an apostle alongside the Twelve? Was he inferior or superior to them? Did Paul favor the established orders of society, like marriage, or was he a sexual ascetic who destabilized the social order? Did Paul renounce Judaism*, or was he a faithful Jew still? Acts portrays Paul as a faithful Jew, an apostle alongside but subordinate to Peter*, James*, and the Twelve*, who lived within the established social order, appealing to Roman justice and his Roman citizenship. He is depicted in a positive light to people with imperial values as a man of high status. He is a decisive man of action, with no mention being made of the letters he wrote.

Paul functioned as a model for Christians in his cordial relations with both Jewish and Gentile Christians, friendliness to authorities, willingness to appeal to Roman justice for protection, courage in the face of difficulty, and unwavering zeal for spreading the message of Christ to the ends of the earth.

Although split off from the Gospel of Luke when the fourfold collection of the Gospels was made, Acts joined the NT as the introduction to the "Apostles" section of the canon. Its story of the Twelve and Paul provided lenses for reading Paul's letters and the other epistles.

CHARLES H. TALBERT

Acts of Martyrs. This literary genre, highly popular in the 3rd and 4th c., was based on historical events, enhanced especially by christological typology*; it was intended to reinforce memory, to provide encouragement, and to facilitate spiritual formation.

The prototype was the account of the martyrdom of Eleazar and of the mother and her seven sons in 2 Macc 6–7, who withstood all threats and torture, and died bravely rather than allow themselves to be compromised by evil rulers. Some of the earliest Christian accounts were written in the style of simple courtroom trials (Justin*, c155; the Scillitan martyrs, 180). Others introduced the literary and theological embellishment that was to characterize later accounts (Polycarp*, c165; the martyrs of Lyon and Vienne, c170). The most popular 3rd-c. acts were those of Perpetua* and Felicitas in Carthage (c203) and of Cyprian* (257).

While according to more objective historical accounts most magistrates who tried Christians were not sadists, there are overtones in the martyr accounts of combating not political but demonic* power. The martyrs do battle with evil in the form of magistrates and opponents. Only the power of God, acting through the martyrs, can overcome such evil power. Family*, too, is sometimes part of the demonic power posed against them (e.g. Perpetua and Felicitas).

The power of God acting through martyrs is demonstrated in several ways. The process of martyrdom conforms to the Passion of Christ (the Christ typology, as is the case in the presentations of the martyrdom of Polycarp and of Blandina among the martyrs of Lyon). The power of the Holy* Spirit is demonstrated in prophecy and unusual courage (Perpetua and Felicitas). The courage of the martyrs often converts others on the spot (Perpetua and Felicitas, *2 Apology* of Justin). The beginnings of a cult of the martyrs can be seen in the gathering and preservation of Polycarp's remains. The serious question of perseverance is addressed; e.g. Quintus the Phrygian in the Acts of Polycarp at first puts himself forward, then apostasizes*; Blandina's mistress fears that her slave Blandina will not persevere, but she becomes the rallying point of the whole group.

By the 4th c., the cult of the martyrs was in full swing; every catacomb* in Rome had its own martyrs, and other martyrdom accounts were produced, becoming more and more legendary. While these later accounts were written in times of peace to entertain and edify, the earlier accounts were written while the possibility of violent death for the faith was still real. **See also MARTYRDOM.**

CAROLYN OSIEK

Acts of Philip. See PHILIP, ACTS OF.

Acts of Supremacy. See SUPREMACY, ACTS OF.

Adam and Eve (Heb for "man" and "life"), the first man and woman (Gen 2–3), thus the progenitors of the entire human race. Their eating of the fruit is said to have been the cause of later hardships (Gen 3:16–19) and of human sin* (Rom 5:12–14). Throughout Christian history, some emphasized that Eve, who alone had contact with the tempting serpent, was first led astray (1 Tim 2:14); yet even patriarchal interpretation affirmed that Adam, the decision maker, bore the chief responsibility. Both were affirmed to have been made in the image* of God (Gen 1:27), and Paul asserted that there is no difference between male and female "in Christ" (1 Cor 11:11–12; Gal 3:28). Later Adam was often viewed as foreshadowing Christ, and Eve as foreshadowing the church. Tatian* (late 2nd c.) was criticized for denying the salvation of Adam and Eve. During the Pelagian* controversy, it was debated whether their sin spread to others through imitation (Pelagianism) or through generation (see Original Sin). Since the Enlightenment*, many theologians have preferred to speak of "the first human beings," without proper names, and to ask what features of the human condition might give rise to sin.

Adams, John (1735–1826), second president of the USA. Adams initially considered going into the ministry, but instead studied law. He maintained lifelong beliefs in a ruling God, morality, and an afterlife of reward or punishment. For Adams, a Deist*, traditional Christianity perverted Jesus' moral teachings by turning them into confused doctrines about his divinity. Adams believed religion* was crucial because it reinforced the morality that a free nation required. He called the Bible "the most Republican Book in the World," containing "the most profound philosophy" and "the most perfect Morality" ever, and yet he felt that misinterpretations of Scripture* had created tyrants and inspired unjust wars. JAMES P. BYRD

Addai and Mari, Liturgy of, the liturgical rite of the Church* of the East (in classical Syriac) used by the Chaldean*, Syriac*, and Malabar* churches. It is linked to the apostolic age through the Syriac legend (c400) "Doctrine of Addai" (Addai is the Syriac name for Thaddeus, a 1st-c. disciple of the apostle Thomas*). Its independent prototype, as historical and liturgical evidence shows, is Edessan* (c120–30), not Antiochene* (as was believed), although it includes some Antiochene vestiges. The earliest commentaries are those of Aphrahat* (4th c.), Theodore* of Mopsuestia, and Narsai (5th c.). It was the uniform liturgy throughout Mesopotamia postulated by the Synod of Seleucia-Ctesiphon (410), yet was subjected to many reforms, especially that of Isho'yahb III (647–57).

The Liturgy of Addai and Mari is distinguished by its primitive constitution and austere simplicity. Three anaphoras* (eucharistic prayers) are conventionally celebrated: the Anaphora of the Apostles Addai and Mari; the Hallowing of Mar Nestorius*; and the Hallowing of Theodore of Mopsuestia. The ecclesiastical "menology" (liturgical calendar) has nine liturgical propers (texts changing from service to service).

Its liturgical cachet includes cantillation (intoned liturgical recitation), a solemn doxology, and incensation*. Its euchological hymnal, *To Thee, O Lord*, uniquely integrates what other churches call "the words of eucharistic institution" into successive hymns of thanksgiving and praise, and in the intercession that precedes the *epiclesis** – the prayer through which, from an Orthodox perspective, believers "ascend to" the consecration (a mysterious, eternal reality, the changing of the bread and the wine into the True Body and the True Blood of Christ, which Christ effected once and for all).

SHAWQI N. TALIA

Addams, Jane (1859–1935), US reformer, educator, pacifist, democratic theorist. A member of the first generation of college-educated women, Addams called women to lead meaningful lives based on a "certain renascence" of Christianity. Hull House, the pioneering settlement that she and a co-worker founded (1889), aimed at "mitigating" and "ameliorating" – Addams's terms – the social, economic, and political upheavals triggered by the arrival of millions of immigrants in the USA from 1880 to 1915. Based on hospitality*, charity*, and concern for the weak, poor, and stranger, Hull House was never denominational, yet a Christian undercurrent permeated its many activities, uniting women and men in a community life of service in a "congested immigrant quarter" in Chicago. Addams's loosely Quaker background helps to explain her later pacifism* as the stance most consistent with the teachings of Jesus, the great moral teacher. (Addams doubted the Incarnation.) For Addams, democracy encompasses social justice and civic peace, as well as individual rights, although she did not neglect ethical duties and obligations. Addams envisioned a providential role for the USA, as did Abraham Lincoln, who noted that "God's purposes are not our own," even for Americans, "the almost chosen people." However, Addams's sturdiest beliefs were in democracy, not in religious creeds. JEAN BETHKE ELSHTAIN

Adiaphora, Adiaphorists. Adiaphorists hold some things or actions to be indifferent (Gk *adiaphora*), neither good nor evil in themselves. During the Reformation, however, some held that in a situation of confession (*status* confessionis*), acts that would otherwise be indifferent might constitute an erroneous witness* to the gospel*. The Pietists* typically held, against other Lutherans, that worldly pleasures, especially dancing and the theater, were intrinsically sinful rather than indifferent.

Adivasis, "original dwellers of the land" in India*, about 60–70 million indigenous people belonging to some 635 ethnocultural minority communities, which have been neither annihilated nor integrated into Indian society; subaltern communities called "tribal*" by the Indian administration. Most Christians in India are either Dalits* or Adivasis.

Adjuration, an urgent demand to do or stop doing something, rendered more solemn by being coupled with the name of God, e.g. the high priest saying to Jesus, "I adjure you by the living God, tell us if you are the Christ, the Son of God" (Matt 26:23) (contrast with Abjuration).

Adoptianism, a form of Adoptionism*, advocated in Spain and France in the 8th c., which Charlemagne* rejected as a heresy*.

Adoptionism, the term given by historians to any view that Jesus was a human being who was adopted as the Son of God at his baptism (cf. Mark 1:11), perhaps even at his resurrection (cf. Rom 1:4). The alternative understanding is that Jesus is the incarnation* of the second person of the Trinity*. **See also CHRISTOLOGIES CLUSTER.**

Adoration, worship* of God; veneration* of saints and of earthly authorities.

Advent (from Lat for "coming"). In the Western Church, the period of four Sundays before Christmas* or, in the Eastern Church, the period of six weeks also called "Nativity Fast." The beginning of the church year, Advent is a time for commemorating Christ's "first coming" and anticipating his "second* coming." **See also LITURGICAL YEAR.**

Adventism (Lat *Adventus,* "coming; arrival"), a movement within Protestantism, arising particularly in mid-19th-c. North America, focusing on the imminent second coming of Jesus to destroy sin* and establish the everlasting Kingdom* of Heaven.

Emergence. Throughout its history, Christian thought has regularly included the prospect of the "second advent," i.e. Jesus' return to earth to establish the Kingdom* of God. This prospect has periodically erupted into renewed fervor in various Christian circles in connection with prophesied cataclysmic events or milestones. Such a resurgence marked the Second Great* Awakening, a revival in the northeastern USA and Great Britain in the 1800s. The emergence of this popular religious movement was based on Baptist and Methodist interpretations of the apocalyptic* books of Daniel* and Revelation*.

Central to the movement was William Miller* (1782–1849), a Baptist farmer and lay preacher in Low Hampton, New York. Miller and others calculated and preached Jesus' return in 1843–44 to as many as 100,000 followers from various Protestant denominations. When their strongest prediction failed to materialize, in the "great disappointment" of October 22, 1844, most of their adherents left the movement. A nucleus of "Millerites" convened in Albany, New York, in 1845 to reaffirm their faith in an imminent, personal return of Jesus – an enduring central element in Adventist thought and teaching.

From this experience, the Adventist movement has evolved into several denominational groups, including the Advent Christian Church, the Church of God General Conference, and the Church of God (Seventh Day). The largest denomination is the Seventh-day Adventist Church (North America, 0.9 million [M] members; and 11.9 M in 204 other countries, especially in Central and South America [4.2 M], Africa [4.2 M], and Asia [2.4 M]). Formative in the history of this denomination were the speaking and writing of Ellen White*, a youthful follower of Miller whose lifelong guidance regarding the church's teachings and organization derived from visionary experiences.

Adventists today embrace the core convictions of Christianity (although the nontrinitarian views of some early Adventists continue to be held by members of the Church of God General Conference). Characteristic beliefs, in addition to the emphasis on the second advent, typically include conditional immortality, according to which, at death, the individual abides in an unconscious condition until the eschatological resurrection. Most Adventists are Premillennialists*.

An early subcurrent within the Adventist movement was the observance of the seventh day of the week (Saturday) as symbolizing God's creatorship, the redemptive act at Calvary, and future re-creation. This Christian sabbatarian practice continues in the Church of God (Seventh Day) and the Seventh-day Adventist Church, and among non-Adventist Christians such as Seventh Day Baptists.

Seventh-day Adventist teachings uniquely emphasize a high-priestly ministry of Jesus in the heavenly sanctuary.

In keeping with their apocalyptic* heritage, Adventists tend to regard the world as declining spiritually. Their conviction concerning the "shortness of the time" (i.e. the end of time is near) translates into active evangelistic efforts to "warn" their fellow humans of all faiths about a soon-coming Judgment* and restoration of all things. While this has led to rapid membership growth, especially among Seventh-day Adventists, it has also in the past produced tension with fellow Christians. Recent decades have brought a more ecumenical spirit.

Adventists' pessimism regarding the fate of the present world does not deter them from engaging in social activism. Many early Millerites worked to end slavery* and, later, to foster educational programs for Americans of African descent. Liberation* theologians in South America recognize Seventh-day Adventist missionaries as their precursors in working on behalf of oppressed groups. Church-supported public health* programs and social work, as well as disaster relief and economic development projects, are common pursuits among Adventists in many countries. Church-affiliated educational institutions are disproportionately high among Adventists worldwide. These patterns derive from holistic attitudes that regard the human condition in its physical, mental, social, and spiritual dimensions as subject to the divine program of renewal already in this life.

Disagreements today focus more on the ordination of women* (favored in North America and Europe, opposed in South America, Africa, and the Confucian cultures).

Challenges. The Adventist experience sharpens the tension latent in all of Christianity, of living "between the times" – a challenge that grows with time. As Adventist groups move from sectarian to mainline church–type organizations, their eschatological thrust does not exempt them from the challenges of routinized corporate life. The question is then: how should the vitality of Millennialist fervor be transmuted into a more settled and mature spirituality? With the cultural diversity that accompanies mission outreach, Adventists are increasingly challenged to contextualize* thought and expression while maintaining essential unity in doctrine and polity worldwide. **See also SEVENTH-DAY ADVENTIST WORSHIP; WHITE, ELLEN GOULD.** JOHN R. JONES

Advowson, the authority of a bishop to appoint a member of the clergy to a parish; or the authority of a layperson to "present" the nominee for appointment. **See also PATRONAGE.**

Aesthetics and Theology. The relationship between Christian theology and aesthetics has been creatively re-explored by a number of contemporary thinkers. Whereas traditional philosophical approaches to theology tended to privilege Western notions of knowledge (epistemology*), being (ontology*), or the good (ethics*), aesthetics opens Western theology to a more accessible domain of imagination and poetics. Whereas doctrinal theory tended to hierarchize and exclude, aesthetic experience tends to traverse and translate.

Though beauty was always considered one of the transcendental properties, going back to Thomas Aquinas* and medieval Scholasticism*, it was most emphatically in the 20th c. that an aesthetic renewal of Christian theology came to fruition. This took various forms. Within Catholic thought, one finds Hans Urs von* Balthasar's theological readings of literary and artistic works and Umberto Eco's retrieval of Thomistic poetics, in the wake of James Joyce. Within Jewish thinking, one witnesses a revival of mystical, Hasidic, and Kabbalistic writings on symbol, dream, and fable in such influential authors as Martin Buber*, Gershom Scholem, and Ernst Bloch (where the influence of German romanticism is also evident). Within the Orthodox tradition, one finds the mystical strains of Dostoyevsky's* poetics mixing with the semiotic musings of Julia Kristeva on the Virgin Mary and the Song of Songs or of John Zizioulas on messianism and eschatology. Finally, within the Protestant tradition of Bultmann* and Ricoeur*, one sees a more hermeneutic retrieval of the hidden existential meanings behind the great symbols, myths, and metaphors of the Christian narrative.

But it is doubtless in the so-called religious turn in contemporary Continental thought that we find one of the most robust debates on the relationship between aesthetics and theology. Here we encounter a curious blend of the traditions of mystical and patristic theology with sophisticated phenomenological analyses of icons*, images, poems, paintings, and liturgical acts. Perhaps the most influential figures to date are French thinkers like Jean-Luc Marion, Jean-Louis Chrétien, and Jean-Yves Lacoste, who seek – after Heidegger* and Derrida – to retrieve an aesthetics of religious intuition and presence within the biblical and theological traditions. And in the English-speaking world, we might also mention the work of David Tracy, John Manoussakis, Kevin Hart, and Richard Kearney, thinkers who attempt to explore the possibilities of a new poetics of religion in a postmodern age.

Aesthetics provides an opening up of the question of God* from a common space of experience, prior to issues of denominational doctrine and dogma*, systematic speculation, or Church dogmatics. As such it proposes a quasi-universal space where the Divine may present itself to peoples of very different cultures and religions. Thus it offers an ethic of interconfessional hospitality that readily accommodates non-Western perceptions of God and the sacred. The emergence of important work in comparative theology – notably by Christian scholars in dialogue with Hinduism (Francis Clooney) or Buddhism (Joseph O'Leary) – is promising in this regard. Where the traditional approach to Christian theology was characterized by explicitly Western notions of metaphysics and epistemology, the approach of a new poetics of God is more open to peoples of diverse religious persuasions and cultures. Where dogma divides, art reconciles. **See also ARTS AND THEOLOGY; HIEROTOPY, THE CREATION OF CHRISTIAN SACRED SPACES.** RICHARD KEARNEY

Aeterni Patris. The encyclical of Leo* XIII (1879) encouraging the study of "Christian philosophy," specifically that of Thomas Aquinas*, but not to the exclusion of other Christian thinkers, many of whom are named with appreciation.

Africa, Roman. Christianity came to Carthage and its region during the 2nd c.; there are written records of the Scillitan martyrs (c180) and Perpetua* (203). When Christians in Rome were still using Greek, the African Church began using Latin in its liturgy and produced the Old* Latin translation of the Bible. Early major figures include Tertullian* (c197–c220); Cyprian*, who dealt with moral and ecclesial issues raised by the first major persecution (250–58); and Arnobius and Lactantius* (3rd c.). Donatism* grew out of the persecution under Diocletian (303–5), creating a schism (formally ended in 411). Augustine* had a major influence on the Western Church's understanding of the Trinity*, Christology*, evil*, and grace*. When the Vandals*, who were Arians*, invaded Africa (429), the Nicene Church continued, often under persecution. The reconquest of Africa under Justinian (534) brought the region back into contact with Constantinople; ironically, it became a center of opposition to the doctrinal policies of the emperors, first in the Three* Chapters controversy (543–53) and then in the monothelite* controversy (646–49). The Muslim Conquest (from 648) led to the end of the African Church, weakened by a succession of controversies. **See also HISTORY OF CHRISTIANITY CLUSTER: IN AFRICA: NORTH AFRICA.** EUGENE TESELLE

AFRICAN AMERICAN CLUSTER

African American Churches and Their Theologies

African American Holiness

African American Literature and Christianity

African Americans and the Bible

African American Theologies

African American Churches and Their Theologies. Neither formal confessional statements nor lengthy and learned treatises constituted the core of African American theologies. Rather the experience of slavery*, segregation, and other acts of involuntary servitude became the elements out of which black religious thought was forged. Although African Americans accepted Catholicism, joined various Protestant bodies, and developed their own separate denominations, the doctrines of these diverse religious organizations blended with foundational ideas that derived from their history as racially oppressed and economically marginalized peoples.

African Americans in the 18th to early 19th c. became Anglican, Dutch Reformed, Roman Catholic, Baptist, Methodist, Presbyterian, Congregational, and members of many other Christian movements. Each group promulgated particular doctrines that distinguished them from the others. Hence African American Baptists, like Euro-American Baptists, argued for immersion as the only mode of baptism*, just as African Methodists, like Wesleyan whites, stressed the sequential importance of salvation* and sanctification*. These allegiances, however, yielded to general Black theologies that transcended the denominational affiliations of African Americans.

Institutional Black religion before the Civil War existed mainly in the northeastern and midwestern areas of the USA. Though slavery had largely disappeared, African Americans in the North either had been slaves or experienced racial discrimination and violence outside of the South. Hence, their churches espoused liberationist* themes in their theological pronouncements. Henry Highland Garnet, a Presbyterian pastor in 1843, called on slaves to resist their masters and take their freedom. Frederick Douglass*, a onetime African* Methodist Episcopal (AME) Zion exhorter, similarly stressed the urgency of abolitionism. Christianity among slaves emphasized hermeneutic approaches to Scripture that affirmed the humanity of African Americans and expressed belief in divine deliverance from bondage.

The Civil War seemed a prophetic fulfillment as black chaplains served black troops in the Union army and black soldiers viewed their service as ordained by God. Theophilus G. Steward, an AME minister, best expressed the mindset of black church leaders who evangelized in the defeated Confederacy and collectively declared that "I seek my brethren." Some started churches and others simultaneously served as officeholders in Reconstruction governments. One AME congregation in Raleigh, North Carolina, explicitly espoused the freedom theme by calling itself the Lincoln Church because it possessed a statue of the martyred president and emancipator Abraham Lincoln. Black Millennialism* supplemented the liberationist thrust of black religious thinking in the late 19th c. The search for a glorious African past discovered in Scripture and biblical history provided evidence for contemporary claims of civic and human equality. These perspectives were persuasively presented in Benjamin T. Tanner's exploration *The Color of Solomon – What?* (1895), Henry M. Turner's declaration that "God is a Negro" (1898), and other Afrocentric texts.

Although 20th-c. African American churches pursued the salvation* of souls and developed Social* Gospel programs, black religious intellectuals mainly in the 1930s and 1940s in both campus and church settings articulated a theology that aimed morally to discredit legalized Jim Crow. Mordecai W. Johnson, Benjamin E. Mays, Howard Thurman*, William Stuart Nelson, George Kelsey, and other scholars advanced critiques arguing that racial segregation and discrimination were sinful and immoral. Their pastoral counterparts, William Holmes Borders, Archibald J. Carey, Jr., Vernon Johns, Adam Clayton Powell, Jr., and others in pulpits throughout the nation echoed the theme that US apartheid was morally wrong. Inspired by Mahatma Gandhi and the fight for India's independence from Great Britain, these black professors and preachers embraced *satyagraha*, or soul force, as a philosophical foundation for civil disobedience and nonviolent direct action. Martin Luther King*, Jr., James M. Lawson, and other activists in SCLC, CORE, SNCC, the NAACP and other groups drew from these ideas, and discredited and destroyed legalized racial segregation and discrimination. These African American Christian and Gandhian ideas, however, were engaged with the influential perspectives of the Nation of Islam, which rejected the "beloved community" as an objective for the civil rights movement and nonviolence as a tactic to achieve black equality.

The Black Theology Movement, which formally started in 1966 with the publication of James H. Cone's classic *Black Theology and Black Power*, challenged white churches and US society to recognize that authentic justice meant that the material condition of the disadvantaged had to be changed (see Black Theology). James Forman in *The Black Manifesto* of 1968 actually called on white churches to appropriate sizable sums to address the economic needs of impoverished poor and black communities.

DENNIS C. DICKERSON

African American Holiness emphasized the necessity of living a sinless life through the Holy* Spirit's empowerment – sanctification* being a "second blessing" occurring after salvation*. The Holiness Movement developed among black Christians (late 18th–early 19th c.) under the influence of Wesleyan theology (see Methodism Cluster: Methodist Churches and Their Theology). Richard Allen*, first bishop in the African* Methodist Episcopal Church (AME), alluded to this process in his autobiographical conversion narrative. Similarly, Jarena Lee*, whom Allen authorized to preach, discussed her anxious pursuit of sanctification and the holiness that proceeded from it. Holiness was also promoted by other 19th-c. black female preachers, including Sojourner* Truth, the abolitionist and women's rights advocate, and Amanda Berry Smith, an AME evangelist and transatlantic Holiness preacher (late 19th c.). The Zion Union Apostolic Church (1869) was the first organized group of Holiness blacks, but the movement occurred mainly within existing African American churches, including black Baptist churches. Other black ministers learned Holiness doctrine from predominantly white religious groups. William Seymour*, the movement's principal Pentecostal preacher, attended a Holiness Bible school and became affiliated with the Evening Light Saints.

Seymour started (1906) marathon worship services in Los Angeles, California, where pilgrims worldwide came to affirm their holiness and to receive the gift of glossolalia* (speaking in tongues). At Azusa* Street, Holiness blacks and whites experienced glossolalia and the Pentecostal fervor described in Acts 2, and Holiness ministers secured spiritual authority to establish innumerable new black and white denominations that institutionalized the Holiness Movement during the 20th c.

DENNIS C. DICKERSON

African American Literature and Christianity. The Bible was the subtext of most early African American literature (1760–1820). Early black authors were concerned about political and social events (especially slave* trade and slavery) in West Africa, England, and the Americas and also about 18th-c. theological debates, most significantly the Calvinist*–Arminian* controversy. Virtually all these authors were Calvinists, influenced by Jonathan Edwards* or the Countess of Huntingdon and her preachers, George Whitefield* and William Romaine. Africanist Calvinism was replaced by a free*-will Evangelicalism embodied in new black churches and denominations as well as in abolitionist literature (1820–65). Free-will Christianity (see Free Will, Freedom) provided metaphors and themes for uplift (1880–1920), Harlem Renaissance (1920–30), and civil* rights (1950–1970) literature. Beginning about 1960, black Christianity was criticized by the Nation of Islam. Today African American literary artists mine the Bible for language, but rarely delve into theological issues.

Early black authors chose Scriptures emphasizing divine providence* and God's care for the chosen people. Joseph* and the Israelites* in Egypt were prominent and Scriptures that corroborated the predestinarianism* of some West African religions and Islam. The Bible, for some, displaced the Qur'an as the archetypal sacred text, but some slaves practiced Islam in the New World. Africanist Calvinism was antislavery and pro-black. According to black Calvinists, God had ordained the slave trade and slavery much as he had commanded the Israelites' and Jesus' sufferings, but in the late 18th c. God's power and design were revealed in overruling the slavers' sins and inspiring the Christian North Atlantic world to eradicate the slave trade and slavery. Like Joseph in Gen 45:4–8, black Calvinists claimed insight into God's predestined design.

The birth of free-will Evangelicalism and the decline of Calvinism fostered another approach to Scripture, deeply felt, pointedly abolitionist, yet more humanist than theological. Antebellum blacks emphasized Jesus' benevolence and concern for the lowly and the Israelites' escape from Egyptian slavery. Evolving uses of Scripture are evident in changes in approaches to Exodus*. Black Calvinists had emphasized the continuity with the Joseph story and God's power over Pharaoh and the divine determination to display glory through the Egyptians' suffering and the Israelites' escape. Antebellum black Evangelicals streamlined Exodus into the escape of the Israelites. Modern black literature (since 1865) often displays either a Christian-humanist use of Scripture to criticize racism* or an anti-Christian hostility to a religion that supposedly encourages the lowly in society to be meek and patient. **See also ETHICS AND CHRISTIANITY CLUSTER: ETHIC OF RISK AND WOMANIST ETHICS.**

JOHN SAILLANT

African Americans and the Bible. See BIBLE INTERPRETATION CLUSTER: IN NORTH AMERICA: BY AFRICAN AMERICANS.

African American Theologies are as diverse as the histories and cultures that have produced them. "Under the bush arbor" meetings (outdoors worship services), slave* communities made sense of their oppression. In liturgies of praying, singing, admonishing, and preaching, they produced a slave theology. Among literate slaves and free persons, theology was usually biblical and evangelical. It emphasized conversion* and eschatological themes of freedom* and judgment*. It developed in journals, diaries, tracts, manifestos, and sermons that foregrounded divine justice* and liberation* for the oppressed and judgment against the evils of slavery. In historically black colleges and universities, academic theology was taught by New England educated whites whose theologies were biblical and evangelical. By the 20th c., African American theology was widely diffused among theological liberalism*, Boston Personalism, and the Social* Gospel. In the 1960s, during the Black Power Movement, a Black* theology of liberation emerged as a Northern urban reaction to white supremacy and the urban plight. While Process* theology has gained importance among some theologians, Black theology and its womanist* development remain a dominant influence in contemporary African American theological contexts. The best of contemporary constructive theology makes use of all these historical sources. **See also BLACK THEOLOGY; WOMANIST AND AFRICAN AMERICAN THEOLOGIES.**

VICTOR ANDERSON

African Christianity: Challenges. See THEOLOGICAL EDUCATION IN AFRICA: ISSUES IT FACES.

AFRICAN INSTITUTED CHURCHES CLUSTER

African Instituted Churches (AICs) in Central Africa

African Instituted Churches (AICs) in Eastern Africa

African Instituted Churches (AICs) in Southern Africa

African Instituted Churches (AICs) in West Africa

African Instituted Churches (AICs) in Central Africa. See KIMBANGUISM.

African Instituted Churches (AICs) in Eastern Africa date to the first decades of the 20th c., starting with the Nomiya Luo Mission in 1914. AICs are movements of renewal founded and led by charismatic men and women who derive their authority and legitimacy from their conviction of being called and guided by God. Varied in origin, history, theology, practice, and period of emergence, these Charismatic* churches are African responses to Christianity aimed at shaping Christian experience according to African cultures and under African leadership. Most numerous in Kenya – more than 6 million members in 700 denominations, 20% of Christians, but only 1.9% in Tanzania and 3.7% in Uganda – they draw the majority of their adherents from the rural and urban poor.

Despite their diversity, East African AICs have much in common in their theology and religious experience, which are contextual in nature – incorporating aspects of African culture and spirituality* – and rooted in the Bible following praxis-oriented interpretations. Like those of other churches, their theologies are centered on Christology*, pneumatology*, and ecclesiology*. AICs' practices include a strong missionary outreach across ethnic and national boundaries, a rigorous ethical code, concern for social and individual salvation revolving around healing rituals, a quest for holiness, a great sense of community, and innovative liturgy. They affirm women's leadership roles and a liberating experience of God for women, no longer fettered by limitations ascribed to them by culture, although women's functions are often limited to ceremonial roles as dictated by culture. AICs are liberating in that they provide their members with coping mechanisms to respond to the myriad challenges posed by a society in flux.

AICs' concern for holistic salvation* (or healing*) for both individual and society is a challenge for Western and African mainline churches with their emphasis on rationality, individualism, and a dualistic* conception of reality.

While traditional patterns of leadership tempered with borrowings from mainline church structures may promote church growth, and ensure group consolidation and means of solving conflicts, AICs are vulnerable to secessionist tendencies. Stress on pneumatic charismatic experiences has also rendered the movement vulnerable to numerous schisms. Though still vibrant, especially in rural and urban slums, AICs are threatened and challenged by the Western-influenced Charismatic churches and ministries that have invaded the religious landscape in Eastern Africa since the mid-1980s.

PHILOMENA N. MWAURA

African Instituted Churches (AICs) in Southern Africa. Since the 19th c., AICs have emerged from African initiatives fully or partially rooted in the Christian faith. They were founded by charismatic African leaders in a quest for independence from mainline churches, be it for political or racial, theological, or economic reasons. Scholars often refer to AICs as sectarian, separatist, heretical, or nativistic. Other scholars designate them as spiritual, Charismatic*, or Pentecostal* or by the names these churches use for themselves, such as Ethiopian, Zionist, and Apostolic. In 1995, South* Africa had more than 3,000 such churches, with an estimated 13 million adherents (a third of the population), the largest AIC being the Zion Christian Church. In addition to AICs that originated in South Africa, Zimbabwe* has sizable indigenous churches, especially the African Apostolic Church of Johane Maranke (almost 1 million members). In Botswana*, Zambia*, Malawi*, and Mozambique*, most AICs originated in South Africa and Zimbabwe. In both Zambia (less than 4% of the population) and Mozambique (c5% of the population), the numerous AICs are relatively small. But in Botswana, where AICs had become by 1995 the largest church group, and in Malawi (about 12% of the population), AICs have mushroomed at a tremendous rate since the 1970s, as they did in Southern Africa as a whole.

All the numerous and diverse AICs are "syncretistic*" (or, from another perspective, "inculturated*") and autonomous in relation to mission churches. They consider themselves Christians and view the OT and NT as normative and the main source of their teachings that most often bring together Christianity and African* Traditional Religion and culture.

The threefold thrust of AICs' theology is Christology*, pneumatology*, and ecclesiology*. Members confess the lordship of Jesus and how he meets African people at the point of their needs (often designating him by culture-loaded phrases like "our Ancestor*," the "African King," or "Healer of Heaven"). Their faith is centered on the Holy* Spirit; they practice prophetic healing* ministry and salvation because of their belief in evil powers and witchcraft. They operate as a community, where both women and men assume leadership roles. Their innovative liturgies combine African religious worldviews with

Christianity, involve singing, hand clapping, dancing, praying, and making pilgrimages to shrines. Various organizations of AICs give them a sense of belonging, even as individual AICs represent for Africans a "place to feel at home," unlike mainline Christianity, against which they protest. TABONA SHOKO

African Instituted Churches (AICs) in West Africa belong to the global Charismatic* Movement. West African countries, particularly Nigeria*, have witnessed a great proliferation of AICs.

The Liberian William Wade Harris (1825–1929) was one of the earliest West African Christian prophets. His prophetic visions and preaching date from 1913 in Côte* d'Ivoire and 1914 in the Gold Coast (Ghana*). The Harrist Church grew rapidly, Harris preaching and healing throughout the region. In Ghana, the first AIC (1918), Church of the Twelve Apostles, was started by Harris's converts Grace Tani and Kwesi John Nackabah; it had c200,000 adherents in 2000. The Harrist tradition motivated the emergence of several other churches in Côte d'Ivoire and Ghana.

In Western Nigeria, the Aladura Movement comprises a set of AICs of a common type but of diverse origins that arose among the Yoruba in 1918. The name "Aladura" (Yoruba for "one who prays") is the Nigerian equivalent of "Zionism" in South* Africa. Aladura churches initially emerged as prayer groups in "mission churches." They emphasize the power of God to protect, heal, and help believers in their lives; they view their leaders as prophets and practice Spirit possession in the forms of speaking in tongues* and visions as means of revelation; they stress personal holiness as the distinctive Christian style of life. "Holy water" and oil are extensively used as symbols of purification.

The Celestial Church of Christ (Église du Christianisme Céleste), founded in Porto-Novo (Dahomey, now Benin*) by Samuel Bilewu Joseph Oshoffa (1947), is the fastest-growing and most structured West African AIC, having increased from 254 to 2,316 parishes between 1976 and 1998.

AICs' theologies and practices are deeply rooted in the Bible, with a strong sense of Christology*, pneumatology*, and Mariology* (specifically in Celestial churches). Their self-reliant ecclesiology* is liberating because it empowers women* and has an African style of worship, including contextual liturgical and ritualistic practices. Their missionary visions transcend ethnic barriers. Socially, they excel in their holistic approach to human needs, making each individual believer a whole person fully integrated into a community. However, AICs are constantly threatened from within by power struggles for leadership and from without by confrontations with Western Charismatic and mission churches.

The AICs' ability to translate African spirituality and culture into a Christian ethos for underprivileged societies, where many struggle to find dignity and identity in the face of brutal exploitation, distinguishes them as a contextual Christianity that inaugurates what some call an "African Reformation." **See also NIGERIA.**

VALENTIN DEDJI

African Literature (Anglophone) and Christianity. In colonial Africa, Christianity and literacy went hand in hand. The Bible was most influential in shaping African literature, its language, and its form.

Writing in Anglophone Africa was almost always centered around the Christian mission and the Bible – the ur-text of translation and conversion. Missionaries created, structured, and controlled the institutions responsible for the emergence of a culture of letters and for the reduction of African languages into writing by translating the Bible into hundreds of African languages. In the colonial landscape, the Bible as the book of God became associated with the authority of writing; for many writers, it was the most powerful model of imaginative literature.

West African literature, e.g, has its roots in the Church Missionary Society at Abeokuta, where, beginning in the late 1840s, repatriated slaves led by Bishop Samuel Ajayi Crowther* produced primers and a translation of the Bible.

In Southern Africa, the elite writers were based at the Scottish mission at Lovedale and the French mission at Morija. Sol Plaatje, whose novel *Mhudi* was one of the first works of fiction in English, was initially a translator of the Bible at Kimberley. These writers' works echo the biblical stories and their cadences. Even works that barely mention the Bible, such as the allegorical narratives of the Yoruba writers Daniel Fagunwa and Amos Tutuola, reflect the allegorical and providential language of the OT or Bunyan's* *Pilgrim's Progress*. Works by harsh critics of the Christian mission – e.g. Ngugi wa Thiong'o's *The River Between* and *A Grain of Wheat* – draw their primary metaphors and themes from the Bible. Chinua Achebe's classic novel, *Things Fall Apart*, is perhaps more suffused with biblical idiom than any other work of African literature, even though it associates Christianity with colonialism. SIMON GIKANDI

African Literature (Francophone) and Christianity. With the Bible in one hand and a gun in the other, Europeans conquered African populations and proceeded to convert them, in the process changing not only their political and economic organizations, but also their traditional religious beliefs and practices. The introduction of writing, by Christian missionaries, in Francophone Africa affected the traditional oral literature (tales, epic, mythological, and panegyric narratives) and marked the beginnings of written literature in French.

Many of the Francophone writers depict Christianity as a theme of cultural and symbolic domination, a manifestation of mental alienation, a tool for European colonialism*, imperialism, and expansion. This critique appeared, e.g, in the novels of the Cameroonian Mongo Beti: *Le pauvre Christ de Bomba* (The poor Christ of Bomba, 1956). V. Y. Mudimbe from the Democratic Republic of Congo represented a similar critique in regard to Christian heritage. His novels *Entre les eaux* (1971; *Between Tides*, 1991) and *L'Écart* (1979; *The Rift*, 1993) illustrate a situation in which religion, politics, and intellectual divides of African ideas (including animism*, fetishism, and paganism*) are confronted by modernity that is carried through the written word and Christian teachings. Other writers underscored Africa's indebtedness to Christianity with regard to modernity, progress, and civilization. The Rwandan Alexis Kagame is an example. His *La Divine pastorale* (The divine pastoral, 1952) and *La Naissance de l'univers* (The birth of the universe, 1955) are biblical epic poems that draw on Rwandan pastoral poetry as they transpose biblical themes into African narratives: the hero they portray is God the creator surrounded by angels as taught in the Christian liturgy and the Bible.

While most African texts denounce the alienating effects linked to Christianity, a small portion of them point out the civilizing outcome of evangelization and praise the Africanization of the biblical teachings and symbols.

ANTHÈRE NZABATSINDA

African Literature (Lusophone) and Christianity. The first African texts written in Portuguese that overtly deal with Christianity are the letters of King Afonso of the Congo, sent to the kings of Portugal, Manuel I and João III (early 16th c.). Afonso, a devout convert to Christianity, was increasingly horrified by the discrepancy between Christian ideals and the slave-trading practices of the Portuguese priests sent to spread the gospel. In many ways, the tone of Afonso's texts is repeated throughout Lusophone African literary history by writers who highlight the hypocrisy of Catholic praxis in the Portuguese colonies. In 1940, the Portuguese dictator, Salazar, and the Vatican signed a concordat, effectively formalizing the Roman Catholic Church's support for Portuguese imperialism. Not surprisingly, the Church was disliked by those who struggled for independence, many of whom were part of the first generation of writers in the newly independent nations. Well-known examples include Agostinho Neto, the first president of Angola* and a formidable poet, and Amílcar Cabral, one of Lusophone Africa's most cultured intellectuals, who was assassinated shortly before the independence of Cape* Verde and Guinea-Bissau. Against this backdrop of distrust of the Catholic Church, Protestant missions had a key role, particularly in Mozambique* and Angola, in educating the future cultural and leadership elites. They undertook systematized research into local languages and translated the "Buku" (the Bible) into Bantu languages, rendering it both a literacy aid and a comprehensible instrument of proselytization. With regard to Christianity, modern Lusophone African literature generally follows two trends. Writers like the Angolan Pepetela and Abdulai Sila, from Guinea-Bissau, humorously attack the vestiges and resurgence of Christian hypocrisy in the equally hypocritical practices of malfunctioning Marxist states. Another current, led by the Angolan Ana Paula Tavares and the Mozambican Paulina Chiziane, owes a profound debt to the syncretic appropriation of Christianity by Lusophone Africa.

PHILLIP ROTHWELL

African Methodist Episcopal (AME) Church, though initiated in 1787 among African Americans in the newly organized Free African Society, bears the marks of Wesleyan theology and practice. The founder, Richard Allen* (1760–1831), a Delaware slave, embraced Christianity (1777) after hearing a Methodist circuit rider preach. Allen and other blacks adopted Methodism* and became enthusiastic practitioners and supporters. After his manumission from slavery (1783), he traveled and preached as a Methodist exhorter. Invited by St. George Church, Philadelphia, to minister to local blacks (1786), he drastically increased the number of black parishioners, making the dominant Wesleyan whites increasingly uncomfortable. The racial confrontation that moved Allen to establish a separate black congregation occurred either in 1787 or in the early 1790s (historians disagree). The dedication of Bethel African Methodist Episcopal Church (1794) showed that institutional independence would become a pattern among African American Christians.

Extemporaneous sermons stressing sanctification* and salvation*, enthusiastic singing, and emotional displays that gave evidence of deep spirituality characterized Wesleyan worship experiences within both urban congregations and rural camp* meetings. Exposed to this version of Methodism in the Delaware, Maryland, New Jersey, and Pennsylvania backcountry, Allen was dismayed that in Philadelphia and Baltimore Wesleyan whites had grown so formal that they showed the same signs of moribund Anglicanism from which John Wesley* had found escape. The rise of racial discrimination and equivocation on slavery* within Methodist institutions known for racial inclusiveness demonstrated, for Allen, a decline in the robust spirituality for which Methodists had been known. The creation of African Methodism became a twofold effort to renounce the racism* of Wesleyan whites and to associate blacks with a zealous Methodist evangelicalism.

This religious movement became institutionalized (1800–20) as Allen created an autonomous denomination through judicial enactment that included other congregations in Pennsylvania, Maryland, and New Jersey. Allen became the denomination's first bishop (1816). The AME Church spread throughout the non-slave areas of the USA and in Canada – with some inroads into Louisiana, Kentucky, Missouri, and (briefly) South Carolina. The denomination's defiance of Wesleyan whites added an emancipatory ethos* to its Methodist emphasis on evangelical preaching and saving the souls* of embattled free blacks and fugitives from slavery.

That day of "jubilee" seemed on the horizon as the nation moved toward civil war. Numerous AME Church ministers and members joined the Union army, some as chaplains who, during the Reconstruction period, pursued politics to safeguard the newly won rights of African Americans. They rapidly organized congregations throughout the former Confederacy. The denomination's membership rapidly grew to 400,000 by 1880. Already in Haiti* (1824), the AME Church expanded in the late 19th c. in the Caribbean – Dominican* Republic, British Guiana, Bermuda, and Cuba*. Bishop Henry M. Turner, a Civil War chaplain, Georgia legislator, and African emigrationist, took African Methodism to Liberia* and Sierra* Leone (1891) and to South* Africa (1896). Afrocentrism also affected the denomination's intellectual life. Three bishops, Benjamin W. Arnett, Benjamin T. Tanner, and Henry M. Turner, emphasized the African origins of Christianity, the color of Solomon, and the blackness of God.

During the 20th c., the massive migration of African Americans to Northern urban and industrial areas expanded denominational consciousness and participation in Social* Gospel ministries. Clergy such as Reverdy C. Ransom in Chicago and others in New York City inaugurated programs that addressed the effects of poverty*, unemployment, and various social pathologies. The civil* rights movement (1950s–1960s) laid the foundation for the activism of Rev. J. A. DeLaine of South Carolina and Rev. Oliver L. Brown of Kansas in a successful assault on public school segregation in the landmark *Brown* decision (1954). Moreover, the black power era gave birth to the Black* Theology Movement, which included such prominent proponents as James H. Cone, Cecil W. Cone, and Jacqueline Grant. They argued that God identified with the suffering and oppression of the disadvantaged and that Jesus Christ should be viewed as a liberator for the poor, persons of color, and women who battle gender bias. These theological explorations influenced the preaching and praxis of the AME Church and other religious bodies. Moreover, neo-Pentecostalism* (the Charismatic* Movement), which stressed the power and presence of the Holy* Spirit, motivated numerous pastors and parishioners to develop megachurches* in several US urban areas.

By 2000, the AME Church existed on four continents with 2.5 million members. Twenty bishops oversee 19 episcopal districts and an ecumenical office, and nine general officers administer the denominational departments. Expansion into new areas of Africa, which began during the 1990s, and growing pressure to include more persons outside the USA in denominational leadership represent unfinished tasks for the AME Church. **See also AFRICAN AMERICAN CLUSTER: CHURCHES AND THEIR THEOLOGIES** and **AFRICAN AMERICAN HOLINESS.** DENNIS C. DICKERSON

African Missions, Society of (Societas Missionum ad Afros, SMA), a community of Roman Catholic missionaries, founded in 1856, has some 1,800 priests, brothers, and lay missionaries in 16 countries, serving the people of Africa and those of African descent, seeking to witness to the gospel while preserving the culture of African people.

AFRICAN RELIGION AND CHRISTIANITY CLUSTER

African Religion and Christianity: An African Religious Perspective. From the perspective of practitioners of African Religion (also called African Traditional Religion), although there are different customary interpretations of and practices within it, one must speak of African Religion in the singular, in the same way that one speaks of Christianity in the singular, although there are many denominational and cultural interpretations of and practices within it.

African Religion is not a religion of the book. A religion of life into which one is born and in which generations after generations flourish, it is disseminated, exercised, and restored orally, along with all other aspects of African culture, philosophy, medicine, law, and history – although, in the same way that storytelling gave rise to African* literature, in Eastern Africa, African religious traditions are being gathered into what the compilers (led by David Maillu) call a sacred book, "The Ka, Holy Book of Neter" (the soul of God).

African Religion is founded on the belief that there is a Universal Force behind creation, as is the case in Christianity. Thus when one compares the African stories of the creation and the biblical story of creation one finds many similarities, though striking differences appear (see Present Cluster: Reading the Bible from an African Religious Perspective). Since practitioners of African Religion think of God primarily as "force" or "energy," conscious and purposeful, but not as a person, they find references to God as "Father" (or "Mother"), as in Christianity, surprising. Yet the most striking difference is that for African Religion there is no hell or heaven or paradise. African Religion does believe in the continuation of the human spirit after death. People are born innocent and sinless. Earthly sins are judged and punished during one's life. Thus practitioners of African Religion find it difficult to comprehend the Christian conception that humans are born with original* sin for which they have to repent, along with the other sins they commit, and this in order to be "saved" from eternal punishment* in hell* and granted eternal life in paradise* or heaven*. DAVID G. MAILLU

African Religion and Christianity: A Christian Perspective. As a distinctive way of viewing and structuring human relationships to sacred reality, African Religion is alive. Despite vigorous campaigns against it by Christianity, it survives on its own or underlies Christian religious beliefs and practices. This has been called "double or parallel religious consciousness," in which African Religion and Christianity exist side by side, externally as systems and in psyches as convictions*, without deep mutual contact. People draw spiritual sustenance from one or the other as the occasion demands.

God*, featuring prominently in Christian belief, is present in African religious perceptions, but ancestors* are most frequently venerated and addressed in prayer. They are the immediate actors in human affairs; God is appealed to when everything else fails. Although ancestral shrines have largely disappeared in compounds, they remain in many hearts. In the etiology of blessings, as in that of suffering, ancestors appear foremost in personal or social consciousness.

Whereas Christianity recruits adherents in various ways, African Religion does not proselytize. People are born into it and individuals are generally free to follow other religions, provided that these serve to increase personal and social life forces.

Apart from traditions and customs of the community handed down through the ancestors and inculcated at initiation and during other rites of passage, there is no codified religious doctrine as there is in Christianity. The domain of religion is life in its entirety; everything is sacred or has sacred implications.

Christianity and African Religion differ in their perception of "salvation*," humanity's ultimate goal. There is no single savior figure in African Religion, and Jesus of Christianity is best understood to be the original or proto-ancestor who brings physical healing and spiritual deliverance to humanity. Death* is a transformation whose final state depends on how one has lived on earth, as in certain forms of Christianity. To live on after death is in African Religion to become an ancestor.

Unlike Christianity, African Religion does not view suffering* as a manifestation of "evil" in abstract terms, but ultimately as a result of human agency, seen most vividly in the acts of witches*. Maintaining harmonious relationships with fellow human beings and the rest of creation is the most important ethical requirement, because not doing so risks disturbing good order and bringing down disaster (i.e. witchcraft). Morality and ethics* are communal, aiming at maximum attention to harmony. LAURENTI MAGESA

African Religion and Christianity: Cultural Interactions. The arrival of Christianity (with its texts: the Bible, hymn books, prayer books, and catechism books) in tropical Africa with Western missionaries brought the encounter of a powerful literary culture with an oral culture*. In the African mind, culture and religion are not separated. African people could have been absorbed by the new reality; yet they struggled to stay afloat as Africans, using four strategies.

1. Total Rejection of Christianity. A small number of Africans rejected Christianity, embracing reconstituted forms of African Religion. Their rituals include animal sacrifice and worship in the form of invocation of God, the divinities, and the ancestors*. Their theologians compile the scriptures of these religions, comprising prayers, songs, rites, and observances, collected orally from practitioners (see present cluster: An African Religious Perspective, Discussion of "The Ka, Holy Book of Neter"). Goddianism (Nigeria) and Afrikania (Ghana) are examples of reconstituted forms of African Religion.

Goddianism originated among the Igbo in Nigeria and is found in many parts of Africa (and also among Africans in Europe, Latin America, North America, and Asia). The name refers to the worship of God according to the beliefs and practices of African Religion. Goddianism originated in the context of political nationalist movements of resistance to colonial rule in Nigeria*. In 1949, the miners at the Enugu coal mine organized a demonstration to demand a pay raise. The colonial police killed nine demonstrators. As neither the Roman Catholic nor the Anglican Church in Enugu (led by white clergy) would permit the funeral service organized by the Miners' Union to be held on their premises, even though the dead were regular members of these churches, the Miners' Union held the funeral service in Aba, a nearby town, using traditional religious rites and songs, and invoking the ancestors, in defiance of the Christian churches' rejection of ancestor worship. A religious wing of one of the political parties became the National Church of Nigeria, renamed "Goddianism" in 1962 by its leader, Chief K. O. K. Onyioha.

Afrikania was founded in 1982 by Rev. Vincent Kwabena Dumuah, a former Roman Catholic priest of the Wasa Amanfi ethnic group in Ghana*. Dumuah defined Afrikania as a "refined African Religion." Emphasizing Afrocentrism, Afrikania asserts that to worship God authentically Africans must do so in their own way. After his ordination to the priesthood (1957), Dumuah studied at various universities in the USA (Ph.D. from Howard, 1971). After a successful career as a priest in Ghana, and a period of involvement in political activities, he left the Catholic Church and the priesthood (1982) and founded the Afrikania Mission, calling for a return to African beliefs, worship, and rituals.

2. Rejection of the Western Form of Christianity and Its Replacement by an African Form of Christianity. This is the strategy of the African* Instituted Churches. It originated when African Christians discovered in the Bible a Jesus somewhat different from that of the missionaries. In contrast to the missionaries' Jesus, who was interested only in the salvation* of souls*, they discovered a Jesus concerned about the material well-being of people: he healed the sick, fed the hungry, welcomed the outcast, and liberated the oppressed. They proclaimed this Jesus more relevant, focusing their ministry on the total well-being of people, materially and spiritually, communally and individually. They preached penance, fasting, confession of sins, and conversion of heart. They healed the sick and integrated politics, economics, and community, typically integrating African religious concerns into their teachings and practices.

3. "Syncretism" (in the Missiologist Sense). Africans who have accepted Christianity manage to stay religiously afloat by resorting to indigenous religious sacrifices and other rituals when their religious sensibilities are not satisfied in moments of crisis. This has continued in spite of persistent condemnation by the missionary churches, although syncretism* as a phenomenon is found throughout the history of the church and is often difficult to distinguish from "inculturation*."

4. "Inculturation." This has been a way of transforming missionary Christianity from within to make it adequately sensitive to African culture. The early Christian missionaries saw African Religion as incompatible with Christianity and did not allow any element of it in the church. However, African Christians found ways of circumventing this. Whenever they had a church assembly outside official church services and without a priest or minister, the songs they sang were not imported Western hymns but improvised and unwritten tunes that their local choirmasters, musicians, and group leaders composed from biblical texts or Christian teaching using indigenous music forbidden in the church. They carried this inculturated, grassroots Christianity to the marketplace and the fields. When this ongoing inculturation process was studied, African culture and African Religion came to be seen first as a preparation for the gospel (1970s, as Eusebius* and early Apologists* viewed Greek philosophy as preparing Hellenistic people to receive the gospel) and later as a veritable resource for Christian theology (from the 1980s).

Today, inculturation is a trademark of African Christianity as it seeks to develop an integrated African form of Christianity that would avoid the divided attitudes involved in syncretism and remain consonant with missionary Christianity.

JUSTIN UKPONG

African Religion and Christianity: Reading the Bible from an African Religious Perspective. To consider African Religion from the perspective of the Bible and to read the Bible from the perspective of African Religion is to continue a dialogue that started long ago. The people of ancient Israel did not live in isolation. They interacted with other nations, including ones in Africa (referred to as Cush in the HB). The question is: Are African religious traditions and the Bible exclusive of each other, as North Atlantic missionaries commonly viewed them? Or are they complementary in a quest for an African expression of Christianity that is necessary because, as Molefi Asante says, "If your God cannot speak to you in your language, then he is not your God"?

The existence of a creator* God* is taken for granted both in the Bible and in African Religion. In Gen 1:1 the creator God is called Elohim. Since in Semitic languages "El" generally refers to any god, "Elohim" means the sum total of the gods, or the supreme God, God of Gods. Beginning in Gen 2:4, God is called YHWH*, the name revealed to Moses (Exod 3:14; "I Am Who I Am," later abbreviated as "I Am"), possibly meaning the ever active God who was, is, and will be. In African Religion, the names of God are also important. For instance, among the Yoruba people of Nigeria, Olodumare is the supreme God, the God of Gods; Olorun refers to God as the owner of heaven; and Oluwa is the master.

In the Yoruba creation accounts, which are representative of African traditions, Olodumare created the earth in four days, then rested and worshipped on the fifth day, leaving to his deputy, Orisanla, the task of completing the creation by planting a primeval palm tree, silk, rubber, white wood, and dodo plants. After accomplishing this, Orisanla was assigned another job: molding human being from the dust of the earth. Then Olodumare, as the supreme God, gave it the breath of life. (In another version, Orisanla fails and is replaced by another deputy of Olodumare, but the tasks remain the same.)

The biblical and African views of God and creation are closely related. The main differences are as follows: in the African account, God has assistant(s) – thus humans have to interact with such intermediaries (e.g. ancestors*); there is no primeval chaos to overcome (in contrast to Gen 1:1) – evil powers are related to human agents (e.g. witches) and the evil spirits they manipulate; and the moon, sun, and stars are personified – a polytheistic perspective, although there is one supreme God.

In both the Bible and African Religion, religion is intricately related to all aspects of life, characterized by wholesome human relations, hospitality*, a sense of community life and of good human relations, respect for elders, a sense of the sacredness of life, and a sense of the power of language and thus of naming.

Two examples show what is at stake. Most commonly, North Atlantic missionaries demanded that, at baptism*, converts abandon their African "pagan" name and adopt a "Christian" name – usually a biblical name, which did not mean anything to them. Ironically, biblical names and African names have similar religious connotations. The most striking examples are theophoric names. The name Oluranti in Yoruba and Zachariah (the prophet's name) in Hebrew both mean "God remembers me" (see also 1 Chr 8:31, the name of the son of Gideon, Zecher, "remembrance"); in both cases, this name is a prayer that God should remember the one who bears the name and an expression of faith that God will do so. Similarly, the name Oluwayiopese in Yoruba and the place called YHWH-yireh in Hebrew (Gen 22:14) both mean "God will provide," an expression of faith that God will do so. The same can be said about Oluremilekun, "God comfort me," and its Hebrew equivalent Nahum (the prophet), "comfort, consolation [from God]"; or Olumayowa, "God will bring happiness," often abbreviated Ayo, "happiness," which corresponds to the Hebrew Asher (Gen 30:13). Likewise, there is a similarity among gratitude or praise names, such as Oluwatobi and Tobi (God is great; like the Hebrew Geuel, Num 13:15), Opeyeoluwa and Ope (God is praiseworthy), Olaoluwa (God's honor), Oluwatosin (God is worthy of worship), Modupe or Dupe (I give thanks), and Temitope (Mine is thanksgiving).

These and many other similarities, together with the recognition of sacred powers, lead Africans, in keeping with their traditional religious perspective, to see the Bible (as an object) and its words as having sacred power. Hence a growing number of African theologians and communities (including African* Instituted Churches) readily emphasize the continuity between "preparatory" African traditions and the Bible, developing "African interpretations" of the Bible. DAVID TUESDAY ADAMO

African Theologies. See RECONSTRUCTION, AFRICAN THEOLOGIES OF; THEOLOGICAL EDUCATION CLUSTER: IN AFRICA: ISSUES IT FACES; THEOLOGY AS HUMAN UNDERTAKING CLUSTER: AFRICAN WOMEN THEOLOGIANS DOING THEOLOGY BY MAKING CONNECTIONS.

Afrikania Mission, a movement founded in 1982 by Rev. Vincent Kwabena Dumuah to propagate a "refined African* Religion," based on the ideology of Afrocentrism. **See also AFRICAN RELIGION AND CHRISTIANITY CLUSTER: CULTURAL INTERACTIONS.**

Afro-Caribbean Christianity in the United Kingdom emerged in the 1950s owing to the arrival of immigrants from the West Indies. Not welcomed by the established denominations, they developed Afro-Caribbean congregations of a Pentecostal* or Charismatic* type, although Afro-Caribbean worshippers can also be found in the historic churches, including Seventh-day Adventist, Methodist, Baptist, Anglican, and Roman Catholic churches. In 2000 there were approximately 4,000 Afro-Caribbean congregations with more than 400,000 members in every major city in Britain. Afro-Caribbean churches have been the fastest growing in the UK, with some of the largest congregations nationally. In London more than 50% of all attendees at Sunday services are from the Black community. In 1984 the West Indian Evangelical Alliance (now African and Caribbean Evangelical Alliance) was established as a national umbrella organization for Black Majority churches in the UK.

Their worship style is distinctive. Guitars, drums, and keyboards enhance their weekly worship services, which usually include prayers, hymns, testimonies, Scripture readings, and preaching. Their services are strongly Bible centered. Their spontaneous and energetic preaching often calls for responses from the congregation such as "Amen" or "Praise the Lord." Each person in the worship service is encouraged by the leaders to fully participate. Twenty-first-century Afro-Caribbean Christianity goes beyond the confines of attending church worship; it encompasses reaching out to the local community. Many congregations that have their own building offer education and training to young people and adults, including nursery education, English classes, and basic computer training. Afro-Caribbean churches are also engaged in campaigns for social justice, and the advancement, development, and transformation of the wider community in Britain, as well as the promotion of unity, reconciliation, and understanding among the various cultural groups, local authority, government, voluntary agencies, and the wider church in the UK.

HERBERT GRIFFITHS

Afterlife. See ESCHATOLOGY CLUSTER; HEAVEN; HELL; IMMORTALITY.

Agape. Greek term for "love" in the LXX and the NT. At times, *agape* is opposed to *eros,* love as desire* (see Nygren), although love-desire for God is precisely the relation mystics* affirmed. *Agape* was also applied in the early church to the meal associated with the Eucharist* (hence "Love Feast"). **See also LOVE.**

Agapetai (also Gk *syneisaktoi;* Lat *subintroductae*), couples living together in chastity, in a spiritual relationship as a substitute for marriage*. The practice might be reflected in Paul, who says it is better for a man not to marry a virgin but to "keep her as his virgin" (1 Cor 7:36–38). Spiritual marriage was practiced for several centuries to show that ascetics* need not deny sexuality but could control it. Some virgins in fact became pregnant (Cyprian, *Ep.* 61), and there were prurient comments and suspicions. The practice was forbidden by 4th-c. councils, and John* Chrysostom attacked it in his writings.

Aglipay, Gregorio; Aglipayan Movement. See PHILIPPINE INDEPENDENT CHURCH.

Agnosticism, a term coined by Thomas Henry Huxley*, in contrast to atheism* and Gnosticism*, to denote the position that it is impossible to know, on the basis of generally accessible evidence, God and whether or not God exists. Agnosticism, similar to the position held by Hume* and Kant*, is compatible with a religious emphasis on faith* and revelation* in contrast to reason and experience.

Agnus Dei (Lat for "Lamb of God"), a liturgical address to Christ in the Latin liturgy, based on John 1:29, said or sung before Communion.

Agricola, Michael (c1507–57), Lutheran Reformer, bishop of Turku, founder of Finnish literature. Son of a Swedish-speaking peasant,

Agricola attended Luther's* and Melanchthon's* lectures in Wittenberg (1536–39), acted as headmaster of the school in Turku, then bishop (1554). A member of the Swedish peace delegation to Moscow, he died on the return trip.

He wrote the *ABC* book (*Abckiria*), the first book in the Finnish language, printed in Stockholm (1543), a primer for reading that also contains a catechism, based mainly on Luther's *Small Catechism*. His prayer book (1544) is the largest (more than 600 prayers) of the Reformation Era. Agricola translated the NT "partly from Greek and partly from Latin, German, and Swedish books" (as he said), the Psalter, and a selection of the OT prophets, wrote a Finnish manual, and translated a missal (from the Swedish Reformer Olavus Petri's works). Agricola was a widely read humanist, an admirer of Erasmus, and, as a Bible translator, a follower of Luther. SIMO HEININEN

Akron Architecture Plan, a church design featuring rooms opening onto the sanctuary, often a semicircular auditorium, with folding doors so that they can be enclosed for Sunday school classes or other meetings. **See also HIEROTOPY, THE CREATION OF CHRISTIAN SACRED SPACES.**

Alb, white linen garment worn by the minister during Mass, derived from the common Roman and Greek tunic. It was used in Christian worship for a long time before being viewed as a liturgical vestment*.

Albania. Since the proclamation of Kosovo's independence in 2008, Albania is the only European country with a Muslim majority (70%); it also includes Orthodox Christians (20%) and Roman Catholics (10%), whose history can be traced to early missions from Rome and Constantinople. Contrary to the situation in most Slavic nations, religion has not been a dominant factor in the Albanian nationalist project. Interfaith unions for the defense of autonomy have been common throughout Albanian history.

With the end of Communism (1990) and its restrictions on religious freedom (Albania was the only country where religion was completely banned, in 1967; it was proclaimed "atheistic" in 1976), religious communities attempted to reconstruct their institutions and religious life. Encountering serious resource problems, they depended heavily on foreign aid.

Because of the Communist oppression, no Albanian Orthodox was in a position to be elected as head of the Church; thus a Greek, Archbishop Anastasios Yannoulatos, was elected. His numerous charitable and social activities in the spheres of health* care, education*, culture, and environment on behalf of all people, regardless of their religious or ethnic background, are quelling the debates about his non-Albanian citizenship. Under his skillful leadership, a Holy Synod was created (1998) and the Albanian Orthodox Church has been on the rise.

The majority of the Roman Catholics live in the northwestern part of the country. Albania restored its diplomatic relations with the Vatican (1991); Pope John* Paul II ordained four new bishops in the Albanian Church (1993); and the Jesuits received permission to return to Albania. The Catholic community engaged in energetic charitable work and many religious, educational, and social activities under the leadership of Archbishop Rok Mirdita.

One of the main religious debates concerns the inter-Muslim relationship between the Sunni and the Bektashi community, a Sufi order, the majority of whose members value independence from the Sunni. According to the 1998 Constitution, all religions are equal, yet the four predominant religious communities enjoy a de facto privileged social status. The relations between the various religious communities are generally relaxed, a tolerance reflecting the long history of multiconfessionalism, the Albanians' traditional pragmatic attitude toward religion, and the considerable secularization* of society. **See also ISLAM AND CHRISTIANITY CLUSTER: IN EUROPE: SOUTHEAST EUROPE.**

Statistics: Population (2008): 3.6 million. Census on religion (1922): Christian, 30% (Orthodox, 20%; Roman Catholics, 10%); Sunni Muslims, 55%; Bektashi, 15%. The number of practicing believers is very low. (*Note*: The only existing data on religion are taken from the 1922 census, usually quoted owing to a lack of other sources, despite serious doubts about its present validity.)

INA MERDJANOVA

Albert the Great (Albertus Magnus) (1193 [or 1206]–1280), theologian, philosopher, scientist. He studied in Padua, entered the Dominican* order, studied theology in Cologne, and taught in Dominican houses in Germany. After teaching in Paris (c1240–48), where Thomas Aquinas* was one of his students, he returned to Cologne. In addition to writing on theological topics, introducing Aristotle's* ethics, metaphysics, and philosophical anthropology into Christian thought, he wrote commentaries on Dionysius* the Pseudo-Areopagite and Scripture. Appointed bishop of Regensburg, he resigned after two years (1262). He defended Aquinas against charges of heresy* (1277). His most direct influence can be found in the Neoplatonic* tendency of several German Dominicans, recognized as the "Albertist" school.

Albert of Prussia (1490–1568), the last grand master of the Teutonic* Knights, who in 1525 adopted the Lutheran faith, ended celibacy in the order, secularized the order's domains (East Prussia, Latvia, Estonia), and created the Duchy of Prussia. A member of the Hohenzollern family, he opened the way to the steady growth of its power in Germany.

Albigenses. See CATHARS, CATHARISM.

Alcoholics Anonymous (AA), a fellowship of recovering alcoholics helping each other stay sober and reaching out to other alcoholics, with more than 2 million members in 180 countries.

The movement began (1935) when "two hopeless drunks," Bill Wilson (a stock speculator) and Bob Smith (a surgeon), discovered they could find sobriety by sharing their stories of alcoholism with each other and reaching out to others caught in the addiction. The collective programmatic book *Alcoholics Anonymous* (the "Big Book") describes the illness of alcoholism and presents the "Twelve Steps" for recovery.

A lay-led coalition of autonomous local groups, with intermediate elected councils and a world headquarters (New York), AA supports itself through freewill contributions. Its spiritual program is not aligned with any particular religious group.

AA's core ideas are: the hopelessness of alcoholism; the necessity of radical ego deflation ("hitting bottom"); conversion from destructive self-centeredness to a joyful "recovering life" (though one is never "cured") through reliance on the "higher power" of one's own understanding; living sober one day at a time; regular participation in AA's spiritual fellowship of mutual support; and reaching out to those still suffering.

The founders discovered AA's core ideas in the work of psychologists and medical doctors (Carl Jung, William James, and William Silkworth) and, with Rev. Samuel Shoemaker, through involvement in the Oxford* Group (or Moral* Re-armament). This nondenominational, Evangelical movement calling for "moral and spiritual rearmament" shaped AA through its emphasis on intense fellowship, a merciful God, and the life-changing results of confession, conversion, and mission. Yet AA soon moved away from the Oxford Group's religious absolutism.

The understanding of alcoholism as a disease is a long-standing medical view (endorsed by leading 20th-c. medical associations), although its causes (genetic factors, the workings of the brain's neurotransmitters) are not yet fully understood. Yet according to the "Big Book," alcoholism is not simply an illness of the body; it is also a disease of the mind and spirit, marked by compulsive drinking, craving, denial, increasing physical tolerance to alcohol, and withdrawal symptoms. The first of the Twelve Steps describes the result: "We admitted we were powerless over alcohol – that our lives had become unmanageable."

AA considers the effects of alcoholism to be "sin*," but only when sin is understood to be a profound alienation from God, from the self, from others, and from the universe itself (rather than a moral failure) (for the view of "sin" as "disease," see Anthropology Cluster: In Eastern Orthodox Christian Theology; Atonement #1; Orthodox Churches, Eastern, Cluster: Introductory Entries). Because this addiction is so encompassing, AA believes that "sobriety" is always more than the cessation of drinking. It is the never-ending spiritual process of radical personality transformation through continuing reliance on God (as each one interprets the higher power), living with a relapse-prone disease but sober and grateful "one day at a time."

AA's Twelve Steps and its pattern of group meetings have been adapted for use with other substance addictions (e.g. narcotics and food) and with behavior addictions (e.g. emotions, gambling, and sex); it is also used by movements for the healing* and support of families and friends of addicted persons (see Abuse as Pastoral Care Issue). JAMES B. NELSON

Alcuin (c735/40–804). Born in Northumbria, educated in York in the tradition of Bede*, he became a key member of Charlemagne's* court. His works on the liberal arts helped to shape medieval education*; his scholarship on the text of the Bible and his adaptations of the Roman liturgy influenced later practice.

Alexander of Alexandria, bishop from 312 to his death in 328, when he was succeeded by

Athanasius*. His controversy with Arius*, one of his presbyters, whom he excommunicated, occasioned the Council of Nicaea* in 325.

Alexandria, Alexandrian Christianity and Its Theology. The city of Alexandria, at the mouth of the Nile, founded by Alexander the Great, became a major center of Greek learning and literature. Within its large Jewish community, the OT was translated into Greek (see Septuagint) and the Bible was interpreted along lines compatible with Greek philosophy (see Philo). The so-called Hellenists* in the early church were possibly influenced by this tradition.

When did Christianity come to Alexandria? It is uncertain, but the Alexandrian Church has been considered one of the apostolic churches because of its alleged founding by Mark*. By the 2nd c. it was a center of Gnosticism*; anti-Gnostic groups associated themselves with Rome and the incipient Catholic Church. Clement* of Alexandria and Origen* were influential throughout the Church. Two major doctrinal controversies, over the Trinity* and Christology*, originated in the city, exacerbated by rivalry between Alexandria, which developed the allegorical* interpretation of Scripture, and Antioch*, which adhered to a more literal and historical interpretation. After the Council of Chalcedon*, the bishops of Alexandria followed the Miaphysite*/Monophysite* doctrine, and any influence by the Empire in Constantinople came to an end with conquests by Persia (616) and the Arabs (642).

EUGENE TESELLE

Alienation, a loss of connection with one's self, property, fruit of labor, world, or God. Modern theology often speaks of sin* as alienation from God, self, and world. **See also HEGEL, GEORG WILHELM FRIEDRICH; MARXISM AND CHRISTIANITY; PSYCHOLOGY AND THEOLOGY.**

All Africa Conference of Churches (AACC) is an ecumenical fellowship of Christian churches in Africa, created in 1958, that accounts for more than 120 million Christian members of Protestant, Anglican, Orthodox, and African Instituted Churches across the continent.

Allegory, a method of interpretation developed among those who found the literal meaning of Homer or the Bible unsatisfactory and sought meanings more compatible with Platonist or Stoic philosophy. Philo* and Origen* were the chief allegorizers of the Jewish and Christian Scriptures. In contrast to typology* – which views biblical figures (David) or events (Exodus) as referring to other figures (Christ) or events (the cross) – allegorization seeks theological meanings or references to invisible realities (divine attributes; the heavenly Jerusalem). An analogue in modern critical study is the judgment that a biblical passage must be interpreted theologically rather than historically.

Alleluia (Heb "Praise the Lord"), an expression of praise in worship found in a number of Psalms* and adopted in Christian worship.

Allen, Richard (1760–1831),born into slavery in Philadelphia; sold as a child along with his family to a farmer in Delaware. Founder of the African Methodist Episcopal Church. Allen was converted to Methodism by a circuit rider (1777). After manumission from slavery (1783), he received the authority to preach as a Methodist exhorter. Allen and Absalom Jones, another black preacher, joined other former slaves and Quaker philanthropists to form the religious association Free African Society (1787), a mutual aid society for "free Africans and their descendants." Allen founded a more explicitly Methodist church for free Africans, the Bethel African Methodist Episcopal Church (1794), which became a denomination (1816). Allen was its first bishop. **See also AFRICAN METHODIST EPISCOPAL (AME) CHURCH; PROSPERITY AND ECONOMIC EMPOWERMENT GOSPEL AND AFRICAN AMERICAN CHURCHES.**

DENNIS C. DICKERSON

All Saints' Day, celebrated on November 1, is a day of remembrance of all the Christian saints*, both known and unknown. It originated in 609 with the consecration of the Pantheon by Pope Boniface IV, when the church at Rome chose to consecrate this 1st-c. temple dedicated to all the gods as a Christian basilica in honor of "Saint Mary and the martyrs" (*S. Mariae ad martyres*). An early example of non-Christian elements being incorporated into the church but with a new interpretation, All Saints' Day was originally celebrated on May 13. The feast was changed to November 1 when Pope Gregory III (d741) dedicated a chapel to "all the saints" in the Vatican basilica. Pope Gregory IV (d844) established it as a feast for the whole church.

All Saints' Day reminds Christians that they share in the wider communion* of saints, that they are intimately linked with their forebears in the faith, and that all Christians are called to sanctity in their own lives. The Litany of the

Saints often chanted on this day makes it evident: the names of saints are invoked as the assembly responds, "Pray for us." Recent developments in liturgical inculturation* (especially in Africa and Asia) draw attention to the importance of the communion of saints through reverence paid to the community's ancestors* during Christian worship. This is particularly evident in the "Roman Rite for the Dioceses of Zaire" (or "Congolese* Rite," approved in 1988), which always begins with the Litany of the Saints in the entrance procession.

KEITH F. PECKLERS, SJ

All Souls' Day, a Roman Catholic feast day, November 2, during which the church on earth prays for the souls of those in purgatory*.

Almsgiving (Gk *eleemosyne*), offering of assistance to the poor, motivated by mercy or pity. It has been regarded as essential for gaining forgiveness* and salvation* from God or as a service in response to salvation and grace – according to interpretations of NT texts (e.g. Matt 6:2–4).

Alpha and Omega, the first and last letters of the Greek alphabet, used with reference to God (Rev 1:8; 11; 21:6) and to Christ (21:13) to denote "the first and the last" (Isa 48:12), the source prior to, and the goal beyond, the cosmos.

Alphonsus Liguori. See LIGUORI, ALPHONSUS.

Altar, the place of offering sacrifice* in ancient Israel. When the death of Christ was interpreted as a sacrifice, the altar was replaced by the cross (Heb 13:10–13); the "temple made with hands" was superseded (Mark 14:58, Heb 9:24), because worship of God was not limited by place (Rom 12:1, John 4:24, Col 3:1–3). In the 2nd c., Christians began to speak of the Communion table as an altar and the presbyters* as priests*.

Alternative Trading, direct contact between producers and consumers on a nonprofit or cooperative basis, bypassing commercial intermediaries. Organizations are now linked through the International Federation for Alternative Trade and the Fair Trade Federation. Although alternative trading represents only a small portion of global trade, it demonstrates solidarity on a worldwide scale, building experience in nonexploitative forms of trade and showing their economic viability.

The Mennonite Central Committee organized SelfHelp Crafts (1946), now called Ten Thousand Villages (since 1996). In addition to marketing, it sends volunteers to more than 50 countries to assist with agriculture, community development, health and nutrition, education, peace work, and crisis intervention. Similarly, the Church of the Brethren organized SERRV (in 1949) to assist in the economic recovery of refugees* and now also emphasizes the importing of crafts to provide income opportunities for people in the Third World.

A number of religious and nonreligious organizations market specific products (shade-grown coffee and nuts, organic foods) in ways that promote sustainable practices and return the profits to the workers themselves.

Ambrose, Aurelius (c338–97). Born into Roman high society, trained in law, and appointed provincial governor, Ambrose found himself elected bishop of Milan (374), though he had not been baptized, when he entered the basilica to quell disturbances over the succession of the Arian* bishop, Auxentius. Within a week, Ambrose was baptized and hurried through ranks of the clergy.

As bishop, Ambrose first ostensibly followed Valentinian I's neutral policies, preserving an uneasy peace between Arians and Nicaeans*. But by 378, in *De fide* he openly defended the Nicene faith and won the Emperor Gratian's support just before the Council of Aquileia convened (381). Yet Ambrose's *On the Holy Spirit* and *On the Incarnation of the Lord* (381/82) still debated with Homoian* opponents.

Ambrose's many exegetical works, on OT figures and books (e.g. *On Joseph, On the Patriarchs, Isaiah*, the *Hexaemeron*) and one NT book (*Luke*), followed Philo*, Origen*, and Basil* of Caesarea by affirming multiple meanings and demonstrating a preference for the allegorical*. Most of his works – dogmatic, ascetic, and exegetical – were sermons that Ambrose later edited for publication.

A master at orchestrating social and political resources, Ambrose effectively championed Nicene Christianity against opponents, including emperors (especially Theodosius*). His deep piety and influential commitment to ascetic* celibacy for men and women are exhibited in his many letters, three funeral orations, and a few hymns (among the oldest to survive in the West).

DANIEL H. WILLIAMS

Ambrosian (Milanese) Rite, the liturgical rite of Milan and environs, is one of the few surviving non-Roman rites in the Catholic Latin liturgical family. Named for Ambrose*, the liturgy of Milan already had its own history when he introduced the Eastern practice of antiphonal singing of psalms and composed hymns. The rite developed from its indigenous roots and was influenced by the Roman Rite, the Eastern Church, and later an interplay with the Gallican* liturgy. The church of Milan successfully resisted several Roman attempts to suppress the rite completely. The Divine Office* of the Western Church, Mass*, and other rituals have been reformed in accord with the principles of Vatican* II.

The Ambrosian euchological* prayers often have a poetic literary style, distinct from the formal juridical language of the Roman Rite. Advent* lasts for six weeks. There is no Ash* Wednesday because Lent* begins on Sunday. The Sundays of Lent are named for the Scripture readings: Palm Sunday is "Sunday of Olives."

The Ambrosian Mass differs from the Roman Mass in the following ways: The offertory has no washing of the hands; the creed is said before the prayers over the gifts; there is a "proper" (adapted for the day) preface for each Mass; the eucharistic* prayer is a variant of the Roman canon; the fraction comes before the Our Father.

The revised Divine Office blends psalmody, readings, poetry, euchology, and song. Vespers opens with a procession, lighting of the candles, the use of incense, and the singing of hymns. This *lucinarium* (service of light) is the sole surviving example of a once almost universal practice in the early church (related to Jewish practices).

Recent liturgical reforms of the Divine Office, the Mass, and the ritual demonstrate the vitality of a rite that can claim an authenticity and legitimacy as strong as that of the Roman Rite.

EMMANUEL CUTRONE

Ambrosiaster, a name coined to refer to the author of the first Latin commentary on all of the Pauline Epistles, written in Rome during the pontificate of Damasus (366–84), wrongly attributed to Ambrose*. The same unknown author also wrote *Questions on the Old and New Testaments,* wrongly attributed to Augustine*.

Amen (Heb "truly," "let it be so"; connotes faithfulness*), a declaration used by Jews and then Christians to express agreement and faithful participation at the end of a prayer or a statement.

American Baptist Churches. See BAPTIST CHURCHES CLUSTER: IN NORTH AMERICA.

American Bible Society, nonprofit, interconfessional organization founded in 1816. Disclaiming any ecclesial function and claiming to avoid endorsing or advocating any doctrinal positions, it focuses on the translation and publication of Bibles and their distribution to as many people as possible. It is committed to making the Bible available to every person in a language and format (including that of media and communication technology) that each can understand and afford, "so all people may experience its life-changing message."

American Council of Christian Churches, fundamentalist* multidenominational organization in the USA founded (1941) in opposition to the Federal Council of Churches (now National* Council of Churches) that remained small in comparison with the National* Association of Evangelicals.

American Literature and Christianity. With the settlement of the North American continent, the connection between the new land and the promised one in Scripture* grounded much of early American literature in the Bible. Early works, such as the poems of Anne Bradstreet (1612–72) and Edward Taylor (1642–1729), were characterized by religious imagery and concerns. The model of self-examination and questions of divine judgment* in the writings of Cotton Mather (1663–1728) had a long-standing influence on American letters. Tracts and sermons expressly concerned with matters of belief, such as those of Jonathan Edwards* (1703–58) on predestination*, were widely influential in the New World. Even the claims for independence and self-government were sustained by a connection with religion, most notably in the references to God in the Declaration of Independence. Nathaniel Hawthorne (1804–64) returned to Puritan* concerns about election* in his brooding works set in New England, while his contemporary Herman Melville combined Miltonic* imagery and Calvinist* doctrine in the figure of Ahab in *Moby Dick* (1851). Responding to the challenge of the institution of slavery*, abolitionist sentiments found expression in the language of Christian sacrifice and redemption*, while slaveholders maintained that their rights of domination were founded in the Bible. Lincoln clearly drew on the Bible for both the language and the ethics of his most famous speeches.

The view of religious justice regarding slavery could be seen in the broad appeal of Harriet Beecher Stowe's* *Uncle Tom's Cabin* (1852). Increasingly, there were challenges to Calvinist doctrine; Emily Dickinson (1830–86) displayed such questions in many of her nearly 1,800 poems. A renewed revivalist religious fervor later yielded the most popular novel of the postwar years, *Ben Hur* (1880), historically set in Palestine of the Crucifixion, by Lew Wallace (a Union general in the war); this fictional account of an encounter with Jesus spawned many imitators. At the end of the 19th c., the influence of religion on letters was split between a view of piety in conflict with the material world, such as found in Harold Frederic's *The Damnation of Theron Ware* (1896), and the Social* Gospel concerned with the treatment of a growing society's poor, such as *In His Steps* (1896), by Charles M. Sheldon.

With the 20th c., realism and naturalism made their mark on the use of religious themes. Sinclair Lewis's *Elmer Gantry* (1927) explored a realistic and psychological approach to the figure of the tempted cleric. Ernest Hemingway (1899–1961) drew protagonists with a studied agnosticism* (although the author was willing to use a phrase from Ecclesiastes* as a title, *The Sun also Rises*). Robert Frost (1874–1962) intermittently used imagery from the Bible, although his imaginative thinking was often a challenge to orthodoxy. William Faulkner (1897–1962), of the deep Bible-based culture of the South, made use of biblical notions in the title of a work like *Absalom, Absalom* and through a Christlike figure, Ike McCaslin, who appears in several novels. Flannery O'Connor (1925–64), a religious anomaly as a Southern Catholic, was deeply engaged in biblical themes and religious questions in novels that sketched a Southern Gothic. Modern poetry, such as that of Robert Lowell (1917–77) and Sylvia Plath (1932–63), engages a confessional mode that owes its focus, if not necessarily its vocabulary or imagery, to the sense of self-examination found in traditional religious Christian models. Some contemporary poets, notably Mark Jarman (1952–), make direct and meaningful use of biblical themes. Current and extensive sales of popular novels based on the Apocalypse* (the *Left Behind* series) demonstrate the long intertwining of Christianity, the Bible, and popular literature in the USA. ROY GOTTFRIED

Amish (the) took their name from Jakob Ammann, a Swiss Anabaptist* leader who called for change, renewal, and greater purity in the church. They separated from Swiss Anabaptists (1693) before migrating to North America (18th c.). Living alongside non-Amish neighbors in small villages and farms in Ontario and 27 US states, they grew from about 5,000 (1900) to nearly 230,000 (2008).

Amish subgroups follow distinctive cultural patterns but most have the following in common: horse-and-buggy transportation, the use of horses for field work, plain dress, a beard (without mustache) for men, a prayer cap for women, a German or Swiss dialect, worship in homes, private schooling, the rejection of public utility electricity, and a taboo on television and computer ownership. Beyond this, the 1,800 local congregations (2008) interpret their own rules of behavior. Though fewer than 50% are farmers, Amish remain rural, working in Amish-owned shops, small businesses, and industries, and sometimes in outside-owned factories.

The community's welfare takes precedence over individual choice; members are expected to yield to the collective wisdom of the church, viewed as a redemptive community apart from the broader culture. Separation from the world is a key religious principle, encouraging Amish to avoid many of the values and practices of the larger society. DONALD KRAYBILL

Amos, Book of, the first extensive collection of recorded prophecies associated with a prophet, in response to the context and issues of Israel and Judah in the 8th c. BCE, consisting primarily of judgment speeches aimed at targeted groups (1:1–2:3, foreign nations, 2:4–6:14, various groups within Judah and Israel) and vision reports (7–9), all shaped over a long period of time.

The 8th-c. oracles of Amos address with passion and specificity why the plight of the poor* deteriorated at a time when Israel and Judah enjoyed economic growth and prosperity under Jeroboam II in the north and Uzziah in the south. Amos uses the ancient tradition of the Day of YHWH in a way that shatters popular expectations. In popular belief, YHWH's coming meant deliverance for Israel. But for Amos, the purpose of YHWH's coming is not to rescue but to punish Israel. Acknowledging God's sovereignty involves doing what God desires. The policies and practices of Israelite leadership are taking the nation on a disastrous path.

Therefore, judgment is inevitable. The key issue is establishing justice*. Without a commitment to justice, religious observances are meaningless.

Amos's critique of social injustice is grounded in the reality of the suffering of the poor majority. Does every member of the community have just and equitable access to the economic base? Striving toward human liberation* entails struggle against oppression* and injustice.

DEVADASAN PREMNATH

Amyraut, Moïse (1596–1644), French moderate Calvinist theologian. After studying law at Poitiers and theology at the Protestant Academy of Saumur, Amyraut was ordained (1626), became pastor in Saumur, and taught theology at the Academy (principal from 1641).

His brief *Traité de la prédestination** catapulted Amyraut into the center of controversy over universal grace* and the extent of atonement*. Amyraut formulated a moderate Calvinist view, equidistant between hyper-Calvinism (and the counter-Remonstrants*) and Arminianism*.

Tried for heresy because of his hypothetical universalism* (Synod of Alençon, 1637), he was acquitted. His *La Morale chrétienne*, posthumously published in 1652, is a key early text in Calvinist social ethic. PAUL CHANG-HA LIM

Anabaptist Movement (the) emerged in 1525 in Switzerland when a group of young adults baptized each other in a private home – an outrageous act of defiance against the Protestant Reformation*. These young Reformers were nicknamed "Anabaptists" (rebaptizers) by their opponents, because they had already been baptized as infants. Other clusters of Anabaptists soon emerged in South Germany, Austria, North Germany, and the Netherlands.

Today the word "Anabaptist" may refer to (1) these early Radical Reformers, (2) their theological heritage, or (3) members of contemporary churches, heirs of these Radical Reformers.

1. The Radical Reformers called for a cleaner break from Catholic traditions and a sharper separation of church* and state (anticipating the modern understandings of this separation). Apart from arguing that only adults who had made a voluntary decision to follow Jesus should be baptized, they raised questions about the Mass*, scorned the use of images, and criticized the morality of church officials. The Anabaptists' refusal to baptize infants (see Baptism Cluster), swear oaths of allegiance, and obey established tradition outraged both political and religious authorities. Declared heretics, thousands were cruelly killed (see the 1,200-Page *Martyrs Mirror*). Propelled by persecution and missionary zeal, the movement mushroomed throughout Europe. Anabaptists found refuge in Moravia, Alsace, the Palatinate, the Netherlands, Poland, and eventually the Ukraine and North America.

   Early Anabaptism attracted people with diverse backgrounds, including peasants, scholars, and mystics. Some expected Christ's quick return and the end of the world, others not. Some were pacifists*, others anarchists willing to use violence. By 1550, many of the views held by contemporary Anabaptist communities began to solidify.
2. Most Anabaptists accepted the historic creeds*; they, like other Protestant Reformers, emphasized salvation by grace* through faith*, the priesthood* of all believers, and the ultimate authority of Scripture* and the Holy Spirit over that of government and church officials. They had only one sacrament*: the gathered church – a covenant* community with the authority to make binding moral decisions that were ratified in heaven (based on Matt 18). Underscoring the role of the Holy Spirit in interpreting Scripture, they emphasized orthopraxis* rather than orthodox doctrine and the authority of Christ's teaching for daily living, especially the Sermon on the Mount – thus their rejection of swearing oaths and of violence (see Peace Movements).
3. The heirs of the early Anabaptists eventually formed churches with different names in numerous countries. In North America, Anabaptists are found in four church groups: Hutterite*, Mennonite*, Amish*, and Brethren*. DONALD KRAYBILL

Analogical Imagination. This term was first used by David Tracy (1981) as a complex strategy for enabling, encouraging, and augmenting a pluralist understanding of religions. His book *The Analogical Imagination: Christian Theology and the Culture of Pluralism* asks: What kind of public articulation and argument regarding religious meaning and truth is possible in a culture of religious pluralism? How can we best understand what it means to be authentically religious in this context? These questions arise in three public spheres – society, the academy, and the religious community – each with its own criteria and demands for appropriateness. In each case, neither resorting to superficial generalities nor privatizing religious beliefs and language is adequate for addressing these questions; the analogical imagination constitutes a suggestive alternative.

The analogical imagination is neither univocal nor equivocal. Instead, it is practiced in order to understand and negotiate similarities and differences. So informed, our conversations with other religions allow us not only to recognize the other as other and the different as different but also to recognize the other and the different as *possible*.

Tracy's principal resource is a shared notion of "classic." A classic (text, person, event) confronts and challenges one's ordinary way of thinking, discloses something genuinely new, and demands that one risk an interpretation. Religious classics (see Scripture), like artistic, musical, and literary classics, lead to an intensification and transformation of ordinary life experience. As Tracy underscores, in the classics' attempt to speak of limit-experiences, one is "caught up in some disclosure of the whole by the whole," or one senses judgment and healing upon an experience of "finitude and estrangement" from the "powers of the whole." The realities (God, self, world) give rise to both negations and affirmations of particular interpretations of the whole. For the analogical imagination, a classic both manifests and proclaims "the radical and gracious mystery* at the heart of human existence."

Christian theology focuses on the meaning and truth of the classic event of Jesus* Christ* as it is creatively manifested, proclaimed, and performed in the contemporary situation. The dissimilarity as well as the similarity-in-difference of the other is primary in critical reflection, argument, and prophetic action. The analogical imagination corrects the shortcomings of both literal* understanding and uncritical pluralism. It searches for coherence and truth within the Christian vision as a whole and in relation to the whole. MARY GERHART

Analogy, a description of God using terms derived from finite things, with the awareness that God is not totally *like* or totally *unlike* finite things. Analogical terms are applied to God "properly," not merely metaphorically*. Chief among these, says Thomas* Aquinas, are the "absolute perfections," whose definition does not imply any limitation and whose highest, original, and most proper application is to God. Since "being," "wisdom," and "goodness" are derived from God, their true meaning is found in God; yet since their meaning in human language is derived from finite things, we cannot fully understand their "mode of signification" when applied to God.

Anamnesis (Gk "remembrance"), in liturgy, remembrance of Christ's death (cf. 1 Cor 11:25) in the eucharistic* service by reading the words of institution or including them in the prayer.

Anaphora (from the Gk for "carrying up"), the chief eucharistic* prayer. In the early church, the sanctification of bread* and wine* by blessing God, a function later filled by the words of institution* and the *epiclesis**. Orthodox churches often designate the entire liturgy by reference to its central part, the anaphora (e.g. the Anaphora [Liturgy] of St. Basil*).

Anathema (Gk translation of Heb *herem*), originally, "devotion to God" by being destroyed (cf. Josh 1–12); subsequently, separation from the community (cf. 1 Cor 16:22; Gal 1:8–9). Starting in the 4th c., church councils pronounced anathema on those who were declared heretics*.

ANCESTOR VENERATION AND CHRISTIANITY CLUSTER

1) *Introductory Entry*

Ancestor Veneration and Christianity: Overview

2) *A Sampling of Contextual Views and Practices*

Ancestor Veneration and Christianity in Aboriginal Australia
Ancestor Veneration and Christianity in Africa
Ancestor Veneration and Christianity in Asia
Ancestor Veneration and Christianity in China
Ancestor Veneration and Christianity in Latin America and the Caribbean

1) Introductory Entry

Ancestor Veneration and Christianity: Overview. Ancestor veneration*, honoring the departed, must be distinguished from ancestor cult or worship* with specific rituals for caring for the dead. For many in East Asia, ancestors live in a spirit realm and have the power to help the living or, more often, to harm those who do not maintain their filial duties. Children, generally first sons, must honor the ancestors by providing gifts, burning joss sticks, and maintaining the burial site. In Africa, practices vary. In some regions, only special people "become" ancestors, who must be honored by the whole family. African ancestors also communicate with the living, but they are more likely to bless than to harm.

Ancestor veneration was common among the early Israelite tribes, in ancient China (from before 1500 BCE) and India, in Roman times, among Celtic and other European tribes, in Africa, and among the Inca and other Native American nations.

The Decalogue commands one to honor living parents, but Israelites like other ancient middle easterners honored departed ancestors. Early Christian practices of honoring the Christian dead – often martyrs* – developed into a cult of saints* that paralleled practices in Africa, Asia, and Latin America. When Roman Catholic missionaries followed Portuguese and Spanish expansion, the devotion to saints and ancestors was a point of dialogue. In China*, Vietnam*, and Japan*, both Christian and Asian practices were adapted. Ancestors were honored but not worshipped; they were remembered and given gifts of remembrance but not fed or paid, as was often the custom. This accommodating practice brought about the Chinese* rites controversy, resolved by the proscriptions of Pope Clement XI (1715) and Pope Benedict XIV (1742), which greatly reduced the development of Christianity in East Asia.

In Africa, ancestor veneration is not so much a matter of cultic worship as it is an ongoing communication and participation of the deceased with the family – one of the central beliefs of African* Religion. Christianity has commonly developed in Africa as a continuation and renewal of traditional African religious practices and beliefs; local Christian practices at times incorporated ancestors and at other times rejected them as evil powers (calling them "demons").

In Latin America, the Roman Catholic veneration of the saints adapted well both to the indigenous practices of ancestor veneration and to the African practices that accompanied slaves. In Latin America, but also in Asia (the Chinese Qing Ming Festival), Europe (Celtic* Christianity), and elsewhere (All* Saints' Day), there is a special time of the year to honor ancestors. Christian practices travel the thin line dividing worship of the dead and respect and thanksgiving for saints who preceded us (Heb 11).

SCOTT W. SUNQUIST

---

2) A Sampling of Contextual Views and Practices

Ancestor Veneration and Christianity in Aboriginal Australia. The worldview of Australian* Aborigines, encapsulated in the concept of the Dreaming (*tjukurpa*), does not involve the veneration of ancestors, strictly speaking. Although there is a sense in which the Dreaming is conceived of as belonging to a past era, it is also a present reality – the *everywhen* (the anthropologist W. E. H. Stanner's description). People in each generation live out the activities of the Dreaming as they participate in daily tasks and ritual life.

In Aboriginal societies, ancestor spirit beings are celebrated rather than human ancestors. Genealogies are not recorded, and relationship terms do not extend beyond grandparents. The spirit* *kurunpa* of deceased ancestors returns to the Dreaming spirit realm from which new persons are conceived (see Anthropology Cluster: Australian Aboriginal Theological Issues).

Reflecting an egalitarianism ethos, Aboriginal languages have no concepts for worship or veneration, but rather terms implying respect (*walkuni*) based on relationship (*walytja*). Aboriginal children, inculturated into the pattern of life enshrined in the Dreaming, are taught through example and story the expected behaviors based on relationship to others. A youth gives special respect to his mother's brother, who has an important role in his initiation.

When Christianity was introduced, Pitjantjatjara Christians were left on their own to relate the Dreaming traditions, as well as traditional forms of art and ritual, to Christian concepts of creation* and salvation*. The Aboriginal emphasis on relationships found resonance with the Christian concept of God as father* and Jesus as elder brother. Pitjantjatjara Christians emphasize the concept of belonging to a family*, referring to themselves as *Jesuku walytja*, relatives of Jesus. Since the Pitjantjatjara word *tjukurpa* is translated as both "dreaming" and "word," the translation of "The Word was God" links the traditional concept of the Dreaming with the introduced Christian concept of God.

The Dreaming stories provided the model for all aspects of life, including change. Thus dreams were significant in validating changes in mortuary rites when Christian burials replaced traditional practices in the 1970s. Previous fears of molestation by the spirit of the dead were replaced by a sense of hope in resurrection. **See also ANTHROPOLOGY CLUSTER: AUSTRALIAN ABORIGINAL THEOLOGICAL ISSUES; AUSTRALIAN ABORIGINAL TRADITIONS AND CHRISTIANITY; HEALTH, HEALING, AND CHRISTIANITY CLUSTER: IN AUSTRALIAN ABORIGINAL SOCIETIES.**

WILLIAM H. EDWARDS

Ancestor Veneration and Christianity in Africa. For Africans, ancestor veneration is an integral part of the ongoing relationship between ancestors and their descendants. As Mbiti underscored, theology that interprets African Christians' experience of God must include a theology of ancestors, "the living dead," whom one can call "parents who are resting."

Ancestors are past and present, active and not passive. Continuous communication between ancestors and their descendants is the sphere of ancestor veneration with roots in the conviction that the deep communion among family members is not broken by death.

Are ancestors venerated or worshipped? For the sociologist Herbert Spencer (1885), Africans "worship" their ancestors out of "fear" of them. Some theologians simply adopt this theory, although African scholars refuted it by emphasizing that for Africans (1) one does not worship out of fear, but out of love and respect; worshipping is adoring and honoring God; (2) the relationship between Africans and their ancestors is *pietas*, "reverence" (for Driberg), or "communion" (for Kenyatta and Rwehumbiza); (3) ancestral veneration is the descendants' expression of filial respect (Exod 20:12) beyond physical death; (4) ancestors are human beings in a parental role (thus with more power and knowledge than the descendants) but are not divinities to be worshipped; and (5) as the vernacular vocabulary shows, invocations and offerings to the departed are symbolic expressions of filial love and communion, not worship.

The proper question is therefore: Is ancestor *veneration* acceptable from a Christian point of view? Most missionaries and theologians, especially in the past, declared that ancestors (along with all spirits) are agents of Satan; their veneration should be eradicated. Consequently, Bibles in African vernaculars often translate "evil spirit" and "demon" by the vernacular word for "ancestor"! Debates of these views contribute to a better understanding of African worship of God. As in all other cultural and religious contexts, when Christianity is experienced by Africans within their frames of reference, it is "as if African Religion said a big YES to the gospel of Jesus Christ" (as Moila says). Without ancestor veneration, Christian faith and theology in Africa would have a hard time justifying its beliefs, as Roman Catholics and Lutherans have started to acknowledge. Thus a Lutheran World Federation consultation (Berlin 2006) called for the incorporation of some forms of ancestor veneration into a better understanding of Christian faith in Africa. Since Africans understand salvation* to be holistic (encompassing the whole community), salvation concerns the living, the departed, and the not yet born. Could not ancestor veneration (as a communion of saints) be an integral part of a holistic Christian conception of salvation?

SYLVESTER KAHAKWA

Ancestor Veneration and Christianity in Asia. Ancestor veneration has been and remains a significant cultural concern for Christians in Asia. The term "veneration" is used to differentiate this core cultural practice focusing on the attitude of reverence from ancestor "worship," which is theologically problematic (idolatry*). Ancestor veneration was a crucial societal ritual to uphold patrilineal (agnatic) solidarity among family members by the commemoration of common parents so as to achieve harmony in society as a whole. In East Asia, it incorporated features of neo-Confucian* thought such as the virtue of filial piety (cf. "Honor thy Father and thy Mother").

Violent persecutions against Roman Catholics took place in Korea* (about 10,000 martyred during 1791–1866) because their rejection of ancestor veneration was viewed as a subversive act that destroyed this backbone of society and so threatened the stability of the nation. Today, many in various denominations acknowledge that the crude dismissal of ancestor veneration as idolatry or superstition was a missiological mistake based on prejudice and ignorance about indigenous cultures and cultural imperialism by Western missionaries and their churches.

Since the Second Vatican Council, Roman Catholic churches in Asia have actively affirmed their appreciation of ancestor veneration through the theology of inculturation*. Although Protestant churches continue to frown on the use of ancestor tablets, food, incense, bowing, and the prayer for the dead, there is a growing trend toward a sympathetic reappreciation and constructive contextualization. Some argue that the Korean Protestant Church's clear break from ancestor veneration made possible its extraordinary growth by promoting a clear Christian identity. In fact, Korean Protestant Christians observe quite faithfully this filial duty toward their deceased family members, though in various Christianized forms.

Many viewed ancestor veneration as an issue of "Christ and culture" (see Niebuhr*, H. Richard; Culture Cluster: Culture and Christianity). However, a deeper issue is soteriological. Ancestor veneration calls for a collective soteriology* related to the holistic notion of community. In the neo-Confucian vision of anthropocosmic community, ancestors (past), the living (present), and descendants (future) are always interrelated in a holistic community. Ancestor veneration signifies a ritualistic enactment of this transtemporal vision where past, present, and future members of the community come together (cf. the communion* of saints*). From this vantage point, a present-oriented, individual salvation* is partial and incomplete. Ancestor veneration calls Christians to an enlarged theological vision of salvation, as a holistic, community salvation encompassing the deceased and the not yet born in the communion of saints. HEUP YOUNG KIM

Ancestor Veneration and Christianity in China. The dispute over the veneration of ancestors in China expressed itself in the rites controversy (1615–1742). The main questions were: Are Christian converts permitted to continue practicing the ancestral cult and the veneration of Confucius? Is the rite religious in nature, as diffuse religion (Yang)? Or is it a cultural activity expressing filial piety, integrating the community, and enhancing morality in society and ethnic identity?

Pope Benedict XIV's bull* (1742), *Ex Quo Singulari*, condemned the Chinese rites and imposed an oath on all Catholic missionaries in China to oppose them. Pope Pius XII in 1939 reversed the 1742 decision, authorizing Christians to take part in ceremonies honoring Confucius and ancestors.

Most of the participants in the three conferences of the Protestant missionaries of China (1877, 1890, 1907) condemned Chinese ancestral veneration/worship as an act of idolatry. However, it was also suggested that missionaries should learn how to differentiate the religious and non-religious elements involved in the rite and the connection of the rite with ethnic identity.

The debate among missionaries was also reflected among Chinese converts. The requirement to destroy the family ancestor tablets as a prerequisite for baptism had attracted attention, strong reaction, and persecution from Chinese society. Many of its anti-Christian publications condemn Christianity as an immoral religion because it does not honor parents and ancestors.

Although the understanding of the rite as an expression of filial piety was accepted by some Chinese Christians, the stance of missionaries that the rite is heretic* idolatry still prevails among many. Yet surveys conducted in Hong Kong and Taiwan in the 1980s reveal that most Chinese who participated in ancestral veneration/worship were motivated not by religious concern but rather by filial piety and social and moral reasons.

LO LUNG KWONG

Ancestor Veneration and Christianity in Latin America and the Caribbean. Wherever slavery* existed in the Americas, slaves invested with their own views the Christianity that was imposed on them and transformed it into an instrument of liberation* and a framework in which they could express their human rights. The practitioners of Candomblé and Umbanda in Brazil* and of Santeria in Cuba* do not feel any contradiction in identifying themselves as Catholics, while also worshipping African divinities through their veneration of the Virgin* and the saints*. Black communities had great difficulty abandoning entirely the memory of their origins, even as they made themselves at home in Christianity. In Venezuela*, the veneration of María Lionza is a good example of the veneration of ancestors that combines features of Christianity (devotion to the Virgin) with a rich mythology combining Amerindian and African ritual elements – beliefs in protective spirits (associated with rivers and mountains), spirit possession, and ecstatic experiences – and Spiritism* as the veneration of the ancestors' spirits.

The veneration of ancestors is even more central for the Garífuna, also called Black Caribs – people of African and Amerindian origin who live in the Atlantic coastal regions of Central America, from Belize to Nicaragua. The veneration of ancestors, which guarantees the success of healing* practices, takes the form of dances, songs, and festivities aimed at enticing the spirits of the ancestors to protect the community. Similarly, Mahikari, a movement with Japanese origins, was very successful during the 1980s in the French West Indies, in Puerto Rico, and somewhat in the Dominican* Republic, because its principal objective was to revitalize the belief in the ancestors, who, if they are properly acknowledged, are supposed to guarantee the believer's protection, while misfortune will befall believers and their community if they forget the ancestors. **See also DEATH, CHRISTIAN VIEWS OF, CLUSTER: IN THE CARIBBEAN AND THE CULT OF THE DEAD.**

LAËNNEC HURBON

Anchorite Life, withdrawal from the world (Gk *anachorein*) for contemplation and prayer. The term came to be applied specifically to persons (anchorites and anchoresses) enclosed in individual cells.

Andrew, Acts of. See APOCRYPHA CLUSTER: APOCRYPHAL ACTS OF APOSTLES.

Androcentrism, male-centered language, traditions, and practices. In the official teachings of most Christian traditions, maleness exclusively symbolizes the gender of God. Male characters in Scripture carry the most authority. Male authors of theology are considered the classical interpreters of Christian faith. The preaching and leadership style of ordained men set the standards. In the late 20th c., Christian feminist* scholars and church leaders vigorously challenged these assertions.

Androcentrism reinforces patriarchy* and provides its moral underpinning. In Christian patriarchal beliefs, the "headship" of the husband requires obedience to his power and authority. Maleness, not behavior or moral quality, entitles the husband to assume this role. He may physically assault his wife, sexually abuse his daughter, or do neither, but the recognition of a heterosexual male as the head upholds the definition of a patriarchal Christian family.

Cultural factors such as racial or ethnic identity and racism* inform the expression of Christian androcentrism. In the USA, for example, the prevalence of white supremacy has meant that white maleness is assumed to be most appropriate for images of God and Jesus* in artistic or media representations, for authoritative Christian theologians, and for model heads of Christian families. **See also SEXISM AND CHRISTIANITY.** TRACI C. WEST

Angela of Foligno (1248–1307). Visionary* mystic devoted to Jesus' humanity, she is known for her screams and trances in imitation* of Christ and Francis* during her mystical experiences. She was born in Foligno (near Assisi) and eventually married (1270?); following the death of her family members (1288?), she professed in the Third Order of St. Clare* (1291). In her *Memoriale,* dictated to and edited by "Brother A" (1292–96), Angela depicts a 30-step conversion and mystical process. In *Instructions* (c1300), she describes her interaction with Spiritual Franciscans* and Ubertino da Casale* as their "spiritual mother," as Lachance documents. Angela records repeated visionary experiences of Christ's human body, especially during his Passion, which resulted from intense meditation on the life and death of Christ. She experienced both extreme sweetness and severe suffering during her interactions with God, but focused her devotional practice on surpassing the sufferings of Christ, seeking extreme ways to chastise her body and wishing for a terrible death. Despite her emphasis on the body and emotions, which leads scholars to classify her as a cataphatic* mystic*, Angela ends the *Memoriale* by describing mystical experiences that alternate between the darkness of negative theology and the intense physicality of Passion mysticism.

JESSICA A. BOON

Angelelli, Bishop Enrique (1923–76), general vicar of Cordoba, then bishop of the Rioja, Argentina. He enrolled in the Catholic Integrist* Movement and eventually became an adviser of the Young* Christian Workers and of the comparable movement among students. He attended Vatican* II; becoming one of its champions, he led polemics against the Argentine Catholic hierarchy. As a result, he temporarily lost his leadership position in the Church. But once he was installed as bishop of La Rioja (1968), he strongly promoted the option* for the poor, thus confronting the military governments. After several threats, he died in an "accident" shortly after the 1976 coup d'état.

LUIS MIGUEL DONATELLO

Angels (Gk *angelos,* "messenger"), spiritual beings that serve God. Early Christianity inherited the long-evolving Jewish views of spirits, primarily from the intertestamental period (see Enoch, Books of). In Scripture, angels serve in the court of God as adversaries or challengers of human beings and as messengers. The devil* and his rebellious angels are said to have fallen from heaven*, becoming demons.

Angels mediate between God and humanity. They announce important events such as the Incarnation* (Matt 1:20–21; Luke 1:26–38) and the birth of Jesus (Luke 2:8–14). The 5th-c. Neoplatonic work of Dionysius* the Pseudo-Areopagite posits nine orders of angels, in three groups of three: seraphim, cherubim, thrones; dominions, virtues, powers; and principalities, archangels, and angels. Each order passes divine truths to the orders beneath; the final two orders, archangels and angels, relay messages to human beings. Contemplation of the angelic hierarchy serves as a ladder leading from human concerns to union with the Divine.

Most theological traditions consider angels to be an order of being distinct from human souls*. The Scholastic theologians (see Scholasticism) of the High Middle Ages explored questions of angelic nature and psychology. They argued that angels were naturally bodiless, although they could assume bodies in order to interact with human beings. Angelic perception was defined as intellectual, directly apprehending spiritual, not sensory, truths. The persevering angels had possessed free will* in choosing whether to rebel but were now confirmed as wholly good. These treatments were concerned with integrating angels into Aristotelian* understandings of the cosmos and remained largely unchanged into the early modern period.

Portrayals of angels often reflect their characteristic benevolence. "Guardian" angels serve as protectors of human beings and their communities, especially in depictions of children and in children's literature. As symbols of the afterlife, angels appear in memorial artwork (including at the site of Ground Zero, where the World Trade Center once stood in New York). Likewise, angels protect human souls from demons at death or at Judgment*, reflecting the human need for defense against hostile forces. Archangel Michael's expulsion of the devil from heaven (Rev 12:7–12) is one example of such contests between angels and demons. These many understandings of angels demonstrate their ongoing power as symbols of communication between the earthly and spiritual worlds. THOMAS DE MAYO

Anger or Wrath of God. Anger or wrath is an emotion often ascribed to God* in the Bible, as God's reaction to human sin*, especially disobedience to God's commands or neglect of God's promises. God is ready to destroy Israel (Exod 32:10) but is dissuaded from doing so by Moses, so that God "repents" of the evil that had been intended (Exod 32:14).

Wrath is often attributed to the "God of the Old Testament" and love or forgiveness to the "God of the New Testament." But the NT also speaks of God's wrath against sin, both in the present (Rom 1:18; 1 Thess 2:16) and at the time of Judgment* (1 Thess 1:10; Rom 2:5; Rev 6:16–17).

In Greco-Roman culture, anger (Gk *thumos;* Lat *ira*) was one of the natural inclinations of the soul*. "Be angry but do not sin; do not let the sun go down on your wrath," says Eph 4:26, probably following the Stoic view that anger hardens into hatred. Forgiveness has been described as the limiting of anger or resentment, the forswearing of revenge.

Questions were often raised about biblical passages that spoke of God's wrath, on at least two grounds. Morally and psychologically, it suggested a deity without reflectiveness or self-control, displaying some of the worst features of human beings. Metaphysically, theologians traditionally asserted that God is "impassible," not affected by events in the world (see Impassibility). On this theory, God's wrath had to be explained away as merely a human way of speaking; the effects of God's actions had to be described by a metaphor drawn from human experience. Modern theologians have been more willing than their predecessors to ascribe feelings and emotions to God (see Anthropomorphisms).

At one point, however, God's judgment and wrath against sin were given a central place in traditional theology. One classic answer to the question of why God became incarnate and suffered on the cross has been that the cross was morally necessary for satisfaction* (see Atonement #2). Especially as Calvin* stated it, the wrath of God the Father was satisfied, absorbed, or canceled by the death of Christ the Son; only then could sinful human beings be justified. This interpretation of atonement has been criticized, however, for giving free rein to the human desire for vengeance and projecting on God a kind of "divine child abuse." This stern justice* is often replaced in modern theology by an emphasis on divine forbearance and forgiveness.

In the understanding of atonement as redemption (see Atonement #1) – emphasized in Eastern Orthodox churches, Liberation theologies, and many non-Western Charismatic churches – the wrath of God is not something to be appeased. Indeed, it is directed not so much against guilty individuals as against the injustices and evil powers that oppress and keep all humans in bondage whom God wants to redeem – and eventually against individuals who promote such injustices. God's wrath is for the sake of liberation*. To speak of the wrath of God and of the Judgment* is primarily to say, "Not all is well in the world; God's interventions are needed," and in fact God does intervene and will intervene decisively in the future (the present and future wrathful judgment; cf. John 3:17–21) to bring about the "new* creation" in which God's justice and love will prevail. **See also ORTHODOX CHURCHES, EASTERN, CLUSTER: INTRODUCTORY ENTRIES.**

EUGENE TESELLE and DANIEL PATTE

ANGLICANISM CLUSTER

1) *Introductory Entries*

Anglicanism: Anglican Communion and Its Theology

Anglicanism: Anglican Worship and Liturgies

2) *A Sampling of Contextual Views and Practices*

Anglicanism in Africa: Eastern and Western Africa

Anglicanism in Africa: Southern Africa

Anglicanism in Asia: Episcopal Church in the Philippines

Anglicanism in Asia: India

Anglicanism in Australia and the South Pacific

Anglicanism in Europe: The United Kingdom
Anglicanism in Latin America: Mexico
Anglicanism in North America

1) Introductory Entries

Anglicanism: Anglican Communion and Its Theology. The Anglican Communion is a fellowship of autonomous provinces* (or churches), each springing from the 16th-c. Reformation* in England and Ireland, and each declaring itself in communion with the See* of Canterbury. In 2000 the total membership was between 70 and 90 million in 38 provinces – including four churches from the Indian subcontinent (originally formed by a union of Anglicans with non-Episcopal churches, but invited "back" into the Communion) – and some individual extraprovincial dioceses* under the metropolitical care of the archbishop* of Canterbury. Each church maintains the threefold order of ministers (bishop*, presbyter*, deacon*), derived from the English and Irish bishops of the Reformation, who traced their origins to early Christianity. Some churches or provinces prefer the title "Episcopal" to "Anglican."

The role of the archbishop of Canterbury has been decisive in forming and strengthening the bonds between these churches. Though the archbishop has no "primatial" or similar powers, he presides over the formally constituted Anglican Consultative Council (formed 1971) and convenes the regular meeting of primates*, and the once-per-decade Lambeth* Conferences have sprung from the personal initiative of successive archbishops.

The Church of England gained a distinct identity during the 16th-c. Reformation. After King Henry* VIII's largely political severance from Rome, Edward VI's reign (1547–53) ushered in a radical doctrinal change that has determined much of the character of the Church of England and Anglicanism since.

While Reformation church leaders conserved inherited church structures (which gave them their positions), they nevertheless propounded the supreme authority of the Scriptures* over any historic traditions. This was exemplified in the early restoration of the Communion cup to the people, in accordance with Jesus' instructions, countering the Roman Catholic withdrawal of it nearly three centuries earlier. Scriptural authority was given formal shape in Article 8 of the Thirty-nine* Articles of 1571: the creeds themselves were to be received and believed, not because they stemmed from ecumenical* councils and had been universally believed for 1,000 years, but because they could be "proved by most sure warrants of holy Scripture." This supremacy of Scripture* (amply reinforced in, e.g., the ordination rites of 1550 and 1552) placed the Church of England firmly on the Protestant side of the divide throughout Western Europe.

In the 16th c., the Thirty-nine Articles of Religion (1571), the Book of Common* Prayer, and the Ordinal* helped to define what the supremacy of Scripture meant in practice. The Prayer Book, enforced by successive Acts of Uniformity (1549, 1552, 1559), gave a fixed scriptural shape and content to worship, not only enshrining vernacular* language and a "receptionist" doctrine of the Eucharist*, but also excluding the intercession of the saints*, petitions for the departed, private masses*, mass vestments, and much of the previous ceremonial. The Articles established a normative Anglican position in relation to most historic doctrines of the church, with particular focus on Reformation divisions and asserting reformed doctrines of justification* and the sacraments*. It is uncertain to what extent the Articles gave the Church of England a confessional basis. The Ordinal retained the historic threefold orders of ordained ministry, thereby sustaining episcopacy* in the Reformed Church and re-creating a pastoral role for ministers that was shaped by the knowledge of Scripture and to which administering the Word with the sacraments was a normal accompaniment.

Until 1975 English ministers assented to the Articles, Prayer Book, and Ordinal as expressing their own beliefs and as "agreeable to the Word of God," at ordination and at their licensing to new appointments. Since 1975 the Declaration of Assent has declared, "My belief in the faith which is revealed in the Holy Scriptures and set forth in the catholic creeds and to which the historic formularies of the Church of England bear witness....' Thus the Articles, Prayer Book, and Ordinal have become historic witnesses to Anglican belief rather than the basis of the subscribing ministers' own living faith. Anglicanism lives by a corporate life as well as by the confession of a creed.

In 1689, the Episcopal Church of Scotland took on an independent life, leading to constitutionally autonomous provinces throughout the world, often corresponding to national political boundaries. The second of these was the Protestant Episcopal Church in the USA (1785), where the Thirty-nine Articles were entrenched, but in a slightly reduced form (e.g. excising all reference to royal supremacy). Later provinces have referred to secondary standards in different ways: first to the creeds* (at least the Apostles'* Creed and the Nicene* Creed), then to the Articles, Prayer Book, and Ordinal, while still retaining the power to revise their text or alter their status. The rise of Anglo-Catholicism in the 19th c. somewhat affected the view of these reforms, as this strand of Anglicans stressed the doctrines of episcopacy and the sacraments*, played down the role of the Articles, and emphasized the early fathers and the traditions of the church. These shifts are sometimes embodied in the formularies of provinces that took their origin from evangelism and church-planting affected by Anglo-Catholic missionaries.

The independence of the 38 autonomous provinces has always carried a threat of divergence, division, and even schism among them. However, other forces have exerted pressure on them to profess the same faith and strengthen common bonds. Thus the first Lambeth* Conference (1867), precipitated by the threat of schism in South* Africa (see Colenso, John William), began a mutual bonding. The third Lambeth Conference (1888) affirmed a common Anglican stance in the "Lambeth* Quadrilateral" as the minimum standard Anglicans held when entering a corporate union with another ecclesiastical body.

In addition to these conferences, more specialized commissions have worked at retaining common doctrinal standards during liturgical experimentation, internal doctrinal divisions, and tension between provinces and in a changing ecumenical context. The following are examples of such spheres of work:

1. International bodies working jointly with comparable bodies of other world denominations to clarify and demonstrate as far as possible what doctrinal positions they hold in common. Foremost have been the Anglican-Roman Catholic International Commission (1970–82; 1983–2005), the Anglican–Orthodox conversations, various Anglican–Lutheran conversations drawn together in 2000 as the Anglican-Lutheran International Working Group, and conversations since 1979 with the World* Reformed Alliance (leading to the report *God's Reign and Our Unity*, 1984).
2. The Anglican Communion's own commission, the Inter-Anglican Theological and Doctrinal Commission. This produced a report in 1986, *For the Sake of the Kingdom*. Then, reconstituted and renamed the "Eames Commission," it produced the Virginia Report on the nature of the Anglican Communion (1997), a major resource for the 1998 Lambeth Conference. It was reconstituted under its original title after 1998.
3. Further common declarations of faith and life have been proposed to the member churches of the Anglican Communion. After the consecration of a homosexually* active bishop in the USA in 2003, an action that threatened to divide the Communion irreparably, the Lambeth Commission on Communion was established, and its report, *The Windsor Report* (2004), proposed an "Anglican Covenant," creating a bond among the 38 provinces, each voluntarily pledging itself to the others on the basis of a common document. The draft was more than 2,000 words long, with detailed clauses on

relationships and mutual commitment, making a strong ecclesiological statement. Its future in the Communion is not yet clarified.

There remains some truth in the conventional aphorism that the Anglican churches are strong on central doctrines, weak on discipline, and totally indistinct at the boundaries.

BISHOP COLIN O. BUCHANAN

Anglicanism: Anglican Worship and Liturgies. The first Church of England Book of Common* Prayer (the 1549 BCP), after minor revisions until 1662 (the 1662 BCP), remained so uniform that as late as 1908 the Lambeth* Conference passed resolutions about it (and about its revision) as though there were but a single Prayer Book throughout the whole Anglican Communion. There was an American BCP, with a slightly revised Communion service, a "Scottish Communion Office," and a Church of Ireland BCP, very close to the 1662 BCP. Yet the presupposition of a single Prayer Book and a single Anglican liturgical ethos remained virtually intact. Further revised Prayer Books (e.g. in Scotland and Canada, early 20th c.) and the compilation of new provincial or diocesan eucharistic rites (e.g. in Zanzibar, South Africa, and Sri Lanka) may have hinted at the likely end of "uniformity," but the long reign of the 1662 BCP was only marginally disturbed. The 1948 Lambeth Conference, ignoring recensions, still believed that "the" Prayer Book continued to serve as a great bond of unity of the whole Communion and any revisions should be done with great care for that unity.

From 1950 onward, the dominance of the 1662 BCP began to decline. The 1958 Lambeth Conference agreed on principles for liturgical revision; various churches (e.g. in England and the USA) changed their canons* to allow experimental alternative rites to exist alongside the authorized texts; rubrics were loosened to allow for more freedom within the rites; and the active participation of the people was encouraged by responsive and congregational material, the greeting of peace, and a growing eucharistic ethos. The Continental Liturgical* Movement had contributed to this, as had the Roman Catholic Second Vatican Council (1962–65). A far-reaching further change came when, between 1967 and 1970, the whole culture of addressing God as "thou" in English-language liturgy began to collapse. Addressing God as "you" ushered in a completely new language of prayer, often differing among provinces, but always in tangible discontinuity with the culture of the 1662 BCP. Experimental booklets flourished for a generation; Lambeth Conferences and the International Anglican Liturgical Consultations encouraged local inculturation*, but after 1979 provinces began to return to official (often hardback) books. These gave congregations a great choice of material and scope for creativity within a given liturgical framework, but the sheer variety meant that a common Anglican ethos, let alone a clear dynastic descent from the 1662 BCP, became ever harder to discern. BISHOP COLIN O. BUCHANAN

---

2) A Sampling of Contextual Views and Practices

Anglicanism in Africa: Eastern and Western Africa. In Eastern Africa today, there are six Anglican provinces: Kenya*, Uganda*, Tanzania*, Sudan*, Rwanda*, and Burundi*. These provinces are held together by historical events that brought the entire region under the British imperial sphere of influence after World War I. Although French was the imperial language in Rwanda, Burundi, and Eastern Congo during the colonial period, Kiswahili became the medium of communication in trade and culture from the Indian Ocean to the Atlantic. These six provinces began as one missionary outpost under the jurisdiction of the archbishop of Canterbury. Over time, African clergy were trained, some of whom were consecrated as bishops and a few enthroned as archbishops. The Conference of Anglican Provinces in Africa brings together all the Anglican provinces of Africa into a consultative forum, with its secretariat in Nairobi, Kenya.

1. Anglican Christianity in Eastern Africa. The establishment of Anglican Christianity in this region can be traced to 1844, when the German missionary Dr. Johann Ludwig Krapf* was sent from Ethiopia* to open a new initiative for the evangelization of local peoples, having failed to win converts among the Oromo of Southern Ethiopia. He was joined in 1846 by another German, Johnnes Rebmann*. The two missionaries established a mission station at Rabai, a few miles inland from the coastal town of Mombasa.

Christianity had not been established earlier, because the east coast of Africa was dotted with Arab settlements – trading outposts – that had been present since the 7th c. and had remained distinct from the local African populations farther inland. Although the Portuguese had arrived in 1498 (Vasco da Gama visited Mombasa en route to India) and settled at Mombasa and Malindi during the 16th and 17th c., they were interested more in trade (or plunder) than in Christian mission and had been driven out of East Africa by the Arabs (1693), who established a sultanate until the colonization of East Africa by Britain (late 19th c.).

David Livingstone* (1812–73), coming from the south into Central Africa, made a name for himself when he campaigned for "legitimate commerce" (cash-crop agriculture) under British rule in opposition to "illegitimate commerce" in slaves under Arab control. The Christian missionary enterprise, as envisaged by Livingstone, was to lead tropical Africa along the path of this new economy, in which Africans would produce raw materials for factories in Britain and consume manufactured goods from British industrial centers such as London, Birmingham, Manchester, Bristol, and Liverpool. For this purpose, Anglican mission stations became the nuclei for the new African elite – complete with schools, dispensaries, vocational training centers, chapels, and catechism classes.

The modern Christian missionary enterprise in tropical Africa became intertwined with the European "scramble for the African continent" after the Berlin* Conference in 1885, where Livingstone's memory was misused. The Germans exerted their influence in Tanganyika (now the main part of Tanzania), while the British dominated Kenya and Uganda. The Belgians had the Congo* Basin as their sphere of imperial influence, particularly under the rule of King Leopold II. Uganda became a theater of absurd competition between the British Anglicans, French Catholics, Arab Muslims, and traditional Africans.

2. Anglican Christianity in Western Africa. Anglican Christianity was introduced earlier in Western than in Eastern Africa, namely in 1752 in Ghana* by missionaries from England. Eventually, Anglican Christianity was spread across the British colonies of Western Africa (now Ghana, Nigeria*, Sierra* Leone, and Gambia), primarily through the work of the Church Missionary Society, with the missionaries Henry Townsend and Samuel Ajayi Crowther* (a former slave) arriving in Nigeria from Sierra Leone in 1842. Crowther was consecrated bishop of Lagos (1864) – the first African bishop – at a time when the Anglican mission was in its infancy in East Africa.

The Church of the Province of West Africa was formed in 1951, which at that time included the dioceses of Ghana, Nigeria, and Sierra Leone. In 1979 the Diocese of Nigeria became a separate province; it is the largest Anglican province in Africa, with its head office in Lagos. The other dioceses within the province of West Africa remained under the See of Accra, and to it were added the Diocese of Liberia* (1982), followed by the Diocese of Gambia (1985). The province supports four theological seminaries (two in Ghana, one in Liberia, and one in Sierra Leone) and a lay training center in Ghana.

Cameroon* became a missionary diocese in 2003. But Ghana, together with 8 of the 15 dioceses in the Church of the Province of West Africa, is in the process of becoming an autonomous province in accordance with the requirements and guidelines of the Anglican Communion.

3. Anglican Christianity and the Multilingual and Multicultural Situation in Eastern and Western Africa. English is the official language and the medium of instruction within institutions of higher learning in Kenya, Uganda, and Tanzania, as well as in the Anglican provinces of West Africa and Nigeria. French enjoys a similar status in Rwanda and Burundi. Arabic is the official language in Sudan, although English is taught and used, particularly in South Sudan. Kiswahili is the common language used for commerce in Eastern and Southern Africa from the Indian Ocean to the Atlantic, transcending these imperial languages (see Krapf, Johann Ludwig). In addition, hundreds of African languages are spoken in these regions. Throughout tropical Africa, the Bible is available in African languages, and the liturgy is conducted in these languages. Pastoral and theological training is conducted mainly in the respective foreign languages (English, French, and Arabic), while the pastors are expected to serve their congregations in the respective African languages. The exception is in urban centers, where the multiethnic congregations of the schooled elite have to use foreign languages for convenience, relevance, and applicability. One of the greatest challenges for theological and pastoral training in tropical Africa and elsewhere on this continent is to ensure that the language of liturgy in the congregations is also the language of training and ordination. Christianity will not become fully rooted in African cultures until theological articulations and liturgical expressions are conducted in the languages used by the congregations and in training.

4. Anglican Christianity in Eastern and Western Africa and Its Theological Perspectives. Most of Eastern and Western Africa was introduced to Anglicanism through the Church Missionary Society (CMS), an agency that was from the beginning closely associated with the 19th-c. Evangelical* revivals* in Britain. Since the late 1920s, the East African Revival Movement has become widespread throughout the region, which has led to a great extension of the Anglican Church in Eastern Africa, even though part of this movement separated from the Anglican Communion. Yet in the coastal region of Tanzania and in Zanzibar, Anglicanism was brought by missionaries under the auspices of the Universities' Mission to Central Africa, an agency that was largely Anglo-Catholic, i.e. a mission society operated by the High Church faction of the Anglican Church. Thus Anglicanism in Tanzania has both Anglo-Catholic and Evangelical expressions in liturgy and ritual. Since the 1960s, there have been efforts to harmonize both strands of Anglicanism. The CMS has recently reconstituted itself into autonomous but related fraternal agencies, freeing the British "parent" society from the burden of funding missionary outreach outside of Britain. The implications of this shift are profound, anticipating the possibility of the re-evangelization of Europe and North America by the mission agencies from Africa and Asia, where Anglicanism is more dynamic and vibrant.

In Western Africa, Anglicanism is more homogeneous, as the constitution of the Church of the Province of West Africa (1951) shows. Its Article I states, "In conformity with Christian principles, the Church of this Province proclaims that all men have equal rights, value and dignity in the sight of God and while mindful to provide for the special needs of different people committed to its charge, it shall not allow any discrimination in the membership and government of the Church." The constitution further indicates that the primary mission of the province is to witness for Jesus Christ through its life and work in all aspects of the lives of people in the various countries, in order to achieve the abundant and holistic life envisaged in the gospel. The method of achieving this mission is evangelism* through teaching, preaching, and other pastoral services. The chief objective is to bring into submission to Jesus Christ the members of the church and those with whom they come into contact. That includes proclamation of the gospel, living a common life, and striving to create a just and fair society, through evangelistic, educational, agricultural, medical, and pastoral programs.

The core of the teaching of the Church of the Province of West Africa is the life and resurrection of Jesus Christ, as

Anglicanism in Africa

reflected in its catechism*, which includes the following articles:

> – Jesus Christ is fully human and fully God. He died and was resurrected from the dead. – Jesus provides the way of eternal life for those who believe. – The Old and New Testaments of the Bible were written by people "under the inspiration of the Holy Spirit". The Apocrypha are additional books that are used in Christian worship, but not for the formation of doctrine. – The two great and necessary sacraments are Holy Baptism* and Holy Eucharist*. – Other sacramental rites are confirmation*, ordination*, marriage*, reconciliation* of a penitent, and unction*. – Belief in heaven, hell, and Jesus' return in glory.

The threefold sources of authority in Anglicanism are Scripture*, tradition*, and reason*. These three sources uphold and critique each other in a dynamic way. This balanced perspective is traced to the work of Richard Hooker*, a 16th-c. apologist, for whom Scripture is the primary means of arriving at doctrine and things stated plainly in Scripture are accepted as true. Issues that are ambiguous are clarified by tradition*, which is checked by reason*

5. Anglican Christianity in Africa and the Anglican Communion. A rather unique and awkward situation emerged after the 1998 Lambeth Conference, in which some of the bishops in this region were invited to exercise jurisdiction over priests in North America who could not bear canonical obedience to the bishops in their respective parishes. This oddity was the result of the failure of the Lambeth Conference and the Anglican Consultative Council to reach consensus on matters of marriage and sexuality. The fact of African bishops having jurisdiction over priests in North America has opened new questions concerning the polity* and hierarchical structure of the Anglican Communion. During the colonial period, it was considered "normal" for bishops to have jurisdiction over priests in another region. With the shift in the numerical strength of Anglicanism from the North Atlantic to Africa, it is likely that more African bishops will have jurisdiction over priests in North America, Britain, Europe, Australia, and New Zealand.

The Anglican Communion holds together all the Anglican provinces worldwide, with between 70 and 90 million members. One of the unresolved questions is: What do Anglicans from various cultures and nations have in common other than an imperial history? The Anglican Consultative Council is mandated to deliberate this issue, while the Lambeth Conference symbolically and ritually convenes every 10 years to reaffirm Anglican unity. The crisis in the Lambeth Conferences of 1998 and 2008 over marriage* and sexuality* is one manifestation of the difficulty of affirming one faith in Jesus Christ in the context of diverse cultural identities. During his term as honorary general secretary of the Church Missionary Society (1841–73), Henry Venn formulated the goal of Christian missionary outreach as the establishment of self-governing, self-supporting, and self-propagating churches abroad. In practice, the relationship between the older and the younger provinces of the Anglican Communion has tended to be that of tutelage and condescension, with the older ones claiming more power and authority on the basis of wealth and history rather than of doctrinal and scriptural authenticity. The symptoms of this unhealthy relationship became manifest in the Lambeth Conferences of 1998 and 2008, although the issue has simmered since the first Lambeth Conference (1867; see Colenso, John William).

The 20th-c. ecumenical* movement was intended to affirm the one faith as bequeathed to the church through the Apostles' and the Nicene Creeds. Yet in the early 21st c., the World* Council of Churches has been overshadowed by the "World Christian Communions" (international organizations of churches of the same tradition or confession), of which the Anglican Communion is a prominent example. Should Christians across cultures affirm their denominational allegiance or their Christian unity? While Christian doctrine teaches us to uphold Christian unity, denominational history demands that we choose denominational allegiance, irrespective of the scandalous consequences for Christian mission. Anglicanism in Eastern and Western Africa is an interesting illustration of these tensions over doctrine, ecclesial structure, biblical hermeneutics, and theological reflection.

JESSE NDWIGA KANYUA MUGAMBI

Anglicanism in Africa: Southern Africa. The Church of the Province of Southern Africa, a part of the Anglican Communion, comprises dioceses in Angola*, Lesotho*, Mozambique*, Namibia*, Saint Helena, South* Africa, and Swaziland*, and is predominantly of High Church tradition. It is the most liberal province on matters pertaining to women's* ordination and homosexuality*. The primate is the archbishop of Cape Town.

Although the roots of Anglicanism in Southern Africa can be traced back to the 17th c., the Anglican Church's official establishment began with the appointment of Robert Gray as the first bishop in Cape Town (1848). He laid solid foundations for the expansion of the Church from Cape Town to Natal (1853), Orange Free State and Transvaal (1863), then to Lesotho (1876), Swaziland, Zimbabwe (1891), Mozambique (1893), Angola, Namibia, and Botswana.

Throughout its history, Anglicanism upheld the policy of equality of races. During the apartheid* era, the Anglican Church played a pivotal role in the struggle against apartheid, following the leadership of Bishops Geoffrey Clayton, Ambrose Reeves, and Trevor Huddleston and Archbishop Desmond Tutu. The Anglican Church has also contributed to the socioeconomic development of the people through the establishment of schools, colleges, and clinics.

The Church takes into account the importance of African culture in worship, church practice, spirituality, and church polity*. The 1986 election of Bishop Tutu as the archbishop of the province, the first black African in this position, was the culmination of many years of the Africanization of the Church in rank and file. As archbishop, he was able to speak with great authority on behalf of the churches not only in Southern Africa but in Africa as a whole.

JAMES N. AMANZE

Anglicanism in Asia: Episcopal Church in the Philippines. The Episcopal Church in the Philippines is a province of the Worldwide Anglican Communion. It upholds and safeguards the historic faith and order as contained in the Book of Common Prayer. Established as a missionary district of the Protestant Episcopal Church in the USA with Charles Henry Brent as its first bishop (1901), it was renamed the Philippine Episcopal Church (1937), became a missionary diocese (1965), but remained under the wing of the Protestant Episcopal Church in the USA. It named its first Filipino bishop, Benito Cabanban (1967); three dioceses were formed (1971), and it became an autonomous province of the Anglican Communion (1990), officially called the Episcopal Church in the Philippines. By 2000 it had six dioceses (about 120,000 members), with a mission statement declaring that the Church exists to promote with integrity the fulfillment of God's mission in this world by proclaiming the good news of the Kingdom of God, both by baptizing, teaching, and nurturing new believers and by responding to human needs with loving service, seeking to transform unjust structures of society, and safeguarding the integrity of God's creation. **See also PHILIPPINE INDEPENDENT CHURCH; PHILIPPINES.**

TOMAS S. MADDELA

Anglicanism in Asia: India. See NORTH INDIA, CHURCH OF; SOUTH INDIA, CHURCH OF.

Anglicanism in Australia and the South Pacific. The largest denomination in Australia* until recently, Anglicanism reflected the status, imperial vision, and differences of the parent body. The presence of the Anglican Church moved beyond convict chaplaincy to become an important influence in a free nation. The early establishment of a synodal polity* enabled dioceses to interact fruitfully with a democratic community in which there was no established church or religious tests, but significant financial aid for stipends, buildings, and education. Though that had ended by 1900, Anglicans made major contributions to the construction of a Christian society, despite secular crosscurrents. Many believed that God ordained Australia to Christianize the peoples of the north. With a few exceptions, Anglicans believed Aborigines were a dying race; they did little to remedy manifest injustice and devoted few resources to evangelization until the early 1900s. In Papua, however, the work of Anglican missions led to a strong church by the time of Papua's independence (1976). Anglican bishops and clergy significantly shaped public opinion, upheld the British heritage, and offered care for the needy and isolated through the Brotherhood of St Laurence and the Bush Brotherhoods. Women played almost no part in governance until the late 20th c. A long struggle led to women's* ordination to the priesthood (1992) and women's consecration as bishops (2008). Gradually an Aboriginal Church also emerged; its first bishop was consecrated in 1985. Torres Strait Islanders had been ordained in the 1920s.

Traditional religious and social priorities were increasingly questioned starting in the 1960s. The vision of a multicultural society emerged in response to massive immigration that began in 1945. The White Australia Policy was dismantled. Now Anglicans are adjusting to the substantial presence of other world religions, at the same time that their own institutional strength is in decline. International involvement, liturgical renewal, and an increasingly important General Synod have not overcome divisions between Sydney Evangelicals and other dioceses, but Anglicans still make a vital contribution to Christian witness. IAN BREWARD

Anglicanism in Europe: The United Kingdom. See PRESENT CLUSTER: ANGLICAN COMMUNION AND ITS THEOLOGY; UNITED KINGDOM.

Anglicanism in Latin America: Mexico. In the mid-19th c., new indigenous religious movements developed with Protestant influence, among them the Church of the Militant Jesus in the Land (Iglesia de Jesús Militante en la Tierra), known in short as the Church of Jesus. This occurred while the migration of Europeans and North Americans to Mexico aided the development of the Episcopal Church (of the United States), including the creation of an Episcopal missionary diocese. In 1904 the (Episcopal) Missionary District for Mexico was established. In 1906 the Church of Jesus, which viewed itself as the Mexican Episcopal Church, asked for admission to the Missionary District, uniting the English- and Spanish-speaking Episcopalians. In 1958 the (Episcopal) Diocese of Mexico was created. As its legal existence was recognized by the government, the Episcopal Church took the name Anglican Church of Mexico, which since 1995 has been an autonomous province of the Anglican Communion. MONICA URIBE

Anglicanism in North America. A number of churches trace their origins from the transplanting of the Church of England into North America, but the two principal ones are the Episcopal Church and the Anglican Church of Canada. Anglicanism permanently entered what is now the USA in 1607 and during the colonial period was legally established in all or part of six colonies. After the American Revolution, the Episcopal Church organized itself, secured bishops (absent during the colonial period), and modified the Book of Common* Prayer. The Church is governed by a general convention consisting of a house of deputies (clergy and laity) and a house of bishops.

Anglicanism was introduced in Canada* in 1713. In 1787 Charles Inglis was appointed bishop of British North America by the British crown. Until the mid-19th c., Canadian Anglicans viewed their church as an extension of the Church of England and as legally established (though this claim was contested). During the late 19th c., the Church became increasingly self-governing.

Both churches over the years have adapted to changes in theology and practice, and these changes have in turn led to splinter groups. In the mid-19th c., US Episcopalians (and to a lesser extent Canadian Anglicans) responded favorably to the catholicizing principles associated with the Oxford* Movement. In protest, a number of congregations broke away to form the Reformed Episcopal Church (1873). In the late 20th c., both churches moved in a liberal direction concerning Prayer Book revision (USA, 1979; Canada, 1988), the ordination* of women (Canada, 1975; USA, 1976), and the full inclusion of gay and lesbian persons (see Homosexuality). This movement resulted in a number of conservative splinter groups, and at present threatens an even greater division both within the two churches and in the relationship of the two churches to the wider Anglican Communion. **See also** CANADA; UNITED STATES.

ROBERT BRUCE MULLIN

Angola. Christianity arrived in what is now Angola with Portuguese colonization; as elsewhere in Africa, the appropriation of natural resources and land was justified by the threefold project of Christianization, civilization, and commerce. The Portuguese *assimilado* system (even worse than the South* African apartheid) divided the African population into *indigenas* and *assimilados* ("second-class whites," speaking and reading Portuguese and adopting a Portuguese way of life). The church (90% of the population is nominally Christian) has emerged through centuries of this harsh colonialism and decades of brutal civil war into a new freedom and a great opportunity to serve society.

The first Portuguese settlers arrived in Soyo (1482, at the estuary of the river Congo, now a rich oil field), followed by Roman Catholic missionaries (1491) while the kingdom of Congo was under the rule of King Nzinga-a-Nkuvu (1491–1506), who converted (baptized João 1) and with his successor, Afonso 1 (1506–42), established the Roman Catholic Church in the capital, Mbanza (renamed São Salvador, in the north of present-day Angola) (see Congo, Democratic Republic of). Christianity also spread farther south among the Kimbundu people in the kingdom of Ngola (including the region from Luanda to the Malanje highland in the east). (The name "Angola" is derived from the royal title "Ngola.") But the spread of the Roman Catholic Church was halted and soon declined owing first to the slave* trade that poisoned the Angolan soil in the 15th–16th c. and later to the rubber trade, which totally disrupted the lives of Angolans: all the men were forced to travel with long caravans to carry rubber from deep inland to the coast, while women remained in the villages to work in the fields and grow food for their families.

The planting of Christianity in Angola in the last quarter of the 19th century coincided with the scramble for Africa (see Berlin Conference), as European powers clashed at the estuary of the Congo River. Rivalries between French and Portuguese missionaries impeded the work of Catholic missions. Religious tensions between British Protestant and Portuguese Catholic missionaries were exacerbated by the colonial rivalries between Portugal and Great Britain. In the south (border of Angola with Southwestern Africa, now Namibia*), the tensions between Lutheran and Catholic missions reflected the conflict between Germany and Portugal. In addition, the African kings and chiefs, although they did not control vast territories, wielded sufficient power to permit or impede the establishment of missions in their areas. In the late 19th c., the king of the Congo exercised strong power over the Catholic and Protestant churches in the north; in the center of the country, the Ovimbundu Confederation, although decentralized, supported the church through strong kings such as Ekuikui II of Bailundo and Ndunduma of Bié; in the south, the Kwanyama kings frustrated the Catholic missionary efforts for many years.

The church was nevertheless planted in a social soil that varied according to the various ethnolinguistic groups. In the north, the Congo/Bakongo ethnolinguistic groups (13% of the population) were the first to be Christianized, and both Catholic and Protestant churches were established in their ancient capital, Mbanza. Immediately to their south, the Kimbundu/Mbundu ethnolinguistic groups (25% of the population) were largely "assimilated," long associated with the Portuguese colonial rule, and thus largely Catholics. The Umbundu/Ovimbundu ethnolinguistic group, the largest group (37% of the population), which spread from the central highlands (Huambo, Benguela, and Bié) to every province of Angola, was fertile soil for the planting of the church because of its homogeneity and because the people lived in large villages. It is among Umbundu that Christianity has been most in contact with African* Religion, because the Umbundu kings were high priests for their peoples (the spirits of the king's ancestors* were the principal communal religious authorities). Smaller ethnolinguistic groups (22% of the population, including the Ganguela, 7%) have distinctive characteristics and ways of relating to Christianity.

The Catholic Church, closely associated with Portugal, largely promoted "assimilation" (*assimilado*) until the country's independence (1975), although individual Angolan Catholic priests took the side of the liberation movements during the long war of independence (starting in 1961) and were imprisoned along with ABCFM (Congregational), Baptist, and Methodist missionaries while numerous Angolan pastors and teachers were killed by Portuguese soldiers (all Protestants were suspected of being revolutionaries). With the new secular constitution (and ongoing civil disturbance), the Catholic Church (now promoting an "authentically African" church) lost its privileged status despite its size, becoming one of the officially approved churches – beside diverse Protestant churches, Pentecostal and Charismatic churches, and African* Instituted Churches, including Kimbanguist* and Tokoist churches.

When missionaries arrived in the 1870s and 1880s, they dismissed the African* Religion as superstition because it lacked the main features of the Western religion: doctrinal statements, ecclesiastical structures, and scriptures. For a long time, Christianity remained the "whites' religion." However, by learning local languages and working with local people, missionaries entered the world of African Religion. Recognizing that African deities were not inconsistent with the Christian view of God, they employed the names for God in common use in each ethnolinguistic group: especially Nzambi (Kikongo, Kimbundu, and Chokwe), Suku (Umbundu), Kalunga (Ambo), Nzambi-Kalunga (Herero), and Iluku (Nyaneka-Humbe). In each case God can be described in Christian theological terms (omnipotent, omniscient, and omnipresent) but is best understood by entrance into the world of African Religion through its proverbs regarding God and the various rituals in response to the actions of the spirits (see God, Christian Views of, Cluster: In Africa; God, Christian Views of, Cluster: Names for God in the Bible and Church Tradition). This Africanization of Christianity also needs to account for the importance in African Religion of the *kimbanda*, healer or exorcist* who invokes the protection of benevolent spirits or exorcizes evil spirits. It is common for a well-educated person to go to church on Sunday and to the *kimbanda* when he or she wants, for instance, a professional promotion. Thus it is not surprising that with emphasis on healing and exorcism and on the prosperity* gospel, the Christian Charismatic* Movement progresses rapidly. But despite everything befalling the churches in Angola, the Church of Jesus Christ is one, with two natures: divine and human; the body of Christ that announces the coming of the Kingdom* of God and an African people or community.

Statistics: Population (2000): 12.8 million (M). Christians, 12.1 M, 94% (Roman Catholics, 8 M; Protestants, 2 M; members of African Instituted Churches and other independents, 0.9 M); African Religionists, 0.6 M, 5% (though many Christians also practice African Religion), nonreligious, 0.12 M, 1.0%. (Based on *World Christian Encyclopedia*, 2001.)

LUCIANO CHIANEQUE

Anhypostasia, in Christology*, Christ's lack of independent human life. **See also** ENHYPOSTASIA.

Animism, a belief that some or all inanimate things and natural phenomena – things that are independent of human life yet have an impact on it – have life, consciousness, or intention, and thus must be propitiated*, prayed to, or outwitted.

Annulment. See MARRIAGE, THEOLOGY AND PRACTICE OF, CLUSTER: IN WESTERN CHURCHES: MARRIAGE ANNULMENT IN THE ROMAN CATHOLIC CHURCH.

Annunciation, the angel Gabriel's* announcement to Mary* (Luke 1:26–38); also, the feast day (March 25) commemorating it, nine months before Christmas*.

Anointing, the application of oil for the consecration of kings in ancient Israel; the practice was later extended to the high priest. The hoped-for deliverer of Israel was called the Anointed or Messiah (Gk *Christos*); Jesus was given this title, and he is sometimes said to have been anointed by the Holy Spirit (Luke 4:18; Acts 4:27, 10:38; Heb 1:9).

In the NT there is mention of anointing the sick to heal body and soul (Mark 6:13, Jas 5:14–15); this did not become an ecclesial ritual for several centuries (ultimately becoming "final unction"; see Sick, Visitation and Anointing of). The church also began (late 2nd c.) to anoint with oil in connection with baptism*, as a sign of the imparting of the Holy* Spirit. After confirmation* was differentiated from baptism in the Western Church, the "oil of catechumens" was applied before baptism, and "chrism*" immediately following baptism (also in confirmation and ordination).

The anointing of rulers is found in Byzantium*, in Visigoth Spain*, and in Ireland*, where it is linked with the claims of the O'Neill kings to rule large areas of the island. When the pope replaced the Merovingian with the Carolingian* dynasty (751), Pippin* was anointed by the Frankish bishops. From then on, the popes appropriated the power to anoint rulers, thereby building alliances and creating new obligations on the part of rulers. Anointing, by giving rulers a sacral status, encouraged them to interfere in the affairs of the church. As a counterbalance, bishops were anointed at ordination* (beginning 9th c.).

The churches of the Reformation criticized the practice of anointing as superstitious; the anointing of the sick had originally been used to speed recovery, not in the context of last rites. Rulers continued to be anointed, however, in several countries of the Reformation (England*, Denmark*, and Sweden*). The Oxford* Movement led to the revival of anointing in the Anglican Communion, first informally and then, by vote of the bishops of each national church, as part of the official ceremonies, usually optional. In contemporary cultures where the use of oils on the body is common, anointing has become more readily accepted in Protestant and Anglican worship and pastoral care.

EUGENE TESELLE

Anomoians. See HOMOOUSIANS, HOMOIOUSIANS, HOMOIANS, ANOMOIANS.

Anonymous Christians, Karl Rahner's* designation for persons who, without having heard the Christian message, have responded to the grace* of God and thus are Christians in fact but not in name. **See also UNIQUENESS OF CHRIST.**

Anselm of Canterbury (c1033–1109), theologian, abbot of Bec, archbishop of Canterbury; born in Aosta in Lombardy. He traveled as a wandering student throughout France (1056–59), arriving eventually at the monastic school at Bec where Lanfranc was teaching. After some uncertainty, he became a monk at Bec (1060) and then prior (1063), taking over the school from Lanfranc. He became abbot of Bec (1078) and then archbishop of Canterbury (1093).

His time as archbishop was marked by painful disputes with successive kings of England during a period when the respective jurisdictions of church and state were being redefined. Twice he went into exile (1098 and 1103–7) to seek papal support for his attempts to defend the rights of the church. In 1098 he was asked by Pope Urban II at the Council of Bari to resolve the disagreements that underlay the schism of 1054 between Greek and Latin Christians. He continued to live the simple life of a monk to the extent that he could, in the community of St. Augustine at Canterbury and was still active as a theologian at the end of his life, eager to live long enough to solve the problem of the origin of the soul*.

Anselm lived during the earliest days of the emergence of the types of schools that were to evolve in a century into the first universities, but he remained primarily a monastic scholar. He was drawn into controversy about the Trinity* and the Incarnation* by Roscelin of Compiègne and about the relationship of church* and state by his quarrels with the English kings. But he preferred the quiet process of teaching and writing about a series of major theological issues.

Anselm is best known for his formulation of the ontological argument for the existence of God* (Chapter 2 of the *Proslogion,* 1077–78) and for his book *Why God Became Man (*Cur Deus homo, 1094–98), but he covered most of the topics of Christian theology, from the nature of God to the Trinity, Incarnation, and redemption*, to the relationship of human free will* to divine foreknowledge, predestination* and grace*, and the sacraments. Anselm also wrote a groundbreaking series of prayers and meditations for private devotional use.

Anselm's approach was essentially Platonic*, although he had a knowledge of Aristotelian* logic, which was then becoming fashionable. His leading idea was that reasoning was capable of showing the truth of orthodox Christian belief, so that faith* need never be in tension with reason*. Anselm's motto was "faith seeking understanding" (*fides quaerens intellectum*).

GILLIAN R. EVANS

Ansgar (c801–65), "Apostle of the North," (arch)bishop, saint; a Benedictine* monk, first in Corbie, France, then (from 815) in Corvey, Germany, where he taught. Emperor Louis* I, the Pious, sent Ansgar as a missionary to Hedeby, Denmark* (826–28); he became the first missionary in Sweden* (829–30) in the commercial town of Birka. The leader of the Nordic mission as bishop (831), then archbishop, of Hamburg-Bremen (848), he made a second visit to Birka and Denmark (851–52). An ascetic* monk, according to *The Life of Ansgar* (*Vita Ansgarii*) by Archbishop Rimbert, his successor, he was also a purposeful church politician.

BERTIL NILSSON

Anthem, Anglicized form of "antiphon"*; more generally, choral music used in worship.

Anthony, Susan B. (1820–1906), suffragist, abolitionist, temperance* advocate, longtime president of the National American Woman Suffrage Association.

Born in Adams, Massachusetts, and raised in the Quaker faith, Anthony believed in the "inner light," and that through quiet and careful listening, an individual could have a direct experience of God's message (see Quaker Worship). Aspects of Quakerism, especially its critique of church hierarchy and of an elevated clergy, informed Anthony's women's rights perspective throughout her career as a reformer (see Friends, Religious Society of). She decried the hypocrisy she witnessed among clergy who tolerated merchants of alcohol within their congregations or failed to endorse women's equality.

Believing that women's political liberty must precede their religious emancipation, Anthony declined to participate in Elizabeth Cady Stanton's* radical project, *The Woman's Bible* (1895), a feminist interpretation of Scripture. Yet Anthony defended Stanton publicly, when *The Woman's Bible* came under attack by reformers and Christian clergy. As she aged, Anthony became increasingly skeptical of all religious traditions, joining at age 73 the Rochester, New York, Unitarian* Church. Her primary spiritual commitment was to "convert" women to the suffrage cause. She championed religious tolerance and endeavored to create a broad-based suffrage movement in which agnostics, evangelicals, Catholics, and Jews were all welcome.

KATHI LYNN KERN

Anthony the Great (254–356). See ANTONY.

ANTHROPOLOGY CLUSTER

1) *Introductory Entries*

Anthropology in Eastern Orthodox Christian Theology

Anthropology in Western Christian Theology

2) *A Sampling of Contextual Views and Practices*

Anthropology: African American Theological Issues

Anthropology: African Theological Issues

Anthropology: Asian Theological Issues

Anthropology: Australian Aboriginal Theological Issues

Anthropology: European-American Theological Issues

Anthropology: Feminist Theological Issues

Anthropology: Latin American Theological Issues

Anthropology: Womanist Theological Issues

---

1) Introductory Entries

Anthropology in Eastern Orthodox Christian Theology. The Orthodox understanding of the human condition differs markedly from Western conceptions (including the Western emphasis on atonement* and justification*). The salvific effects of the Incarnation* extend not just to fallen humanity, but also to the entire cosmos. Original* sin is not understood as sharing in the guilt of Adam's fall but as the inheritance of his corrupted mortal nature. Humans are seen more as victims of the devil's deception than as criminals to be condemned by divine justice. Death* is understood not as God's curse on the creation, but as God's enemy and the inevitable consequence of separation from life with God. Sin* is viewed in terms of a disease of the soul more than as individual acts of lawbreaking. The human person is regarded as a psychosomatic unity that sin afflicts in its entirety, leading to all the sufferings of soul* and body of the present life.

Orthodox theology is markedly apophatic* in character, starting from the premise that human words and concepts are inadequate for conceiving of God, who in essence is unknowable. The idea of a *mysterion* (Gk "mystery*") is quintessentially Orthodox: the Trinity*, the Incarnation*, the Church* and its sacraments* are all referred to as "mysteries," which cannot be grasped intellectually and yet may be known through personal participation. Humanity can experience God in God's uncreated energies, attributes of divinity in which humans participate by the cooperation of their free will with God's energies. God is known always as *philanthropos*, "loving humankind." Responding fully to divine love leads a person to union with God, known as *theosis**.

Salvation* is thus defined not merely as forgiveness*, but even more as liberation* of the human mind from delusion and the renewal of human nature by union with the God-man Christ, whose healing presence is experienced through the Church and its sacramental mysteries*. These include baptism*, chrismation*, Communion*, confession*, unction*, matrimony*, and ordination*. The Divine* Liturgy is the high point of sacramental life. **See also ORTHODOX CHURCHES, EASTERN, CLUSTER: INTRODUCTORY ENTRIES.**

ARCHBISHOP DEMETRIOS (TRAKATELLIS)

Anthropology in Western Christian Theology. Theological anthropology is the study of human beings in conversation with a particular religious tradition. In Christian theology, anthropology concerns such issues as the origin of humanity; human ontological constitution, body* and spirit* (soul*, reason*); sin*; evil* and oppression; grace* and redemption* or liberation* – all as related to God.

European Christian theological anthropology begins with the Bible, as a plan according to which God creates human beings in a balanced and equal relationship within the self, with the neighbor, and toward nature. Decisively, human purpose is contingent on following God's supreme intent for human history. However, humans chose to "fall" by seeking to know all that God knew (see Fall). This disruption in the divine goal led to hierarchy, gender antagonism, anxiety, oppression* and exploitation, the destruction of nature, and human estrangement from God. God remained faithful to the sovereign plan by sending Jesus to save humanity's body and spirit, men and women. Through Jesus, God's intent becomes equality, liberation*, and just relations among beings, especially the marginalized.

The Roman Catholic Church (from the early church to the 16th c.) and the Protestant Reformation (16th c.) espoused a salvation* history, with humans fitting into God's plan. Drawing more on Greek philosophy, Roman Catholic scholastic* theology separated the spirit from the body of the human person. Yet it also pointed to community, in contrast to the advocacy of individual direct connection to God prevalent in mainline "orthodox" Protestant Churches. The latter fostered a theological anthropology of individualism and capitalism. The stirring of capitalist individualism and freedom of individual wealth owners versus the rigid hierarchy of feudal landlords helped set the conditions for the respective Protestant versus Roman Catholic debates over the definition of humanity.

Roman Catholic scholastic and orthodox Protestant theological anthropologies taught the supremacy of divine salvation history and God's preordained purpose for humanity. The European Enlightenment* (late 17th and 18th c.) produced a radical shift of focus, away from God toward humanity. Reason*, scientific discoveries, global voyages, and the consolidation of capitalism accented the power and freedom of humans. God's supremacy was questioned. Reason and science* fit God into the human plan. Liberal* theological anthropology marks this period. The purpose of humanity is to use its own reason to bring about social* reforms and ultimately bring in God's "Kingdom*."

The human evils* of World Wars I and II challenged liberal theological anthropology's (often implicit) claim of human superiority over God's plan. How could human reason bring in God's "Kingdom" when human nature tends toward death and destruction? The purpose of humans became to wait on the salvation coming only from God's direction, a unidirection salvation. A strict hierarchy ensued, with every human attempt to reach God considered blasphemy*. Neo-orthodox* theological anthropology underscores this period of "Let God be God all by God's self." DWIGHT N. HOPKINS

2) A Sampling of Contextual Views and Practices

Anthropology: African American Theological Issues. North American Black theological anthropology flows out of the 1950s and 1960s Civil* Rights and Black Power movements and as a critique of the dominating white theology in divinity schools, seminaries, and churches. Because Jesus Christ is a liberator of structurally oppressed humanity and individual broken persons, the human purpose is to follow Jesus. To be human (and a Christian), one goes with Jesus. Some define humanity as a radical engagement of liberation* with the marginalized by any means necessary. Others perceive the Black Church as the hub of a black revolution in the broader society and establishing a separate black nation. Some link African American human identity to liberation, balanced by reconciliation* with white Christian supremacists. Others demand a reconnection to African spirituality*, ancestors*, and the all-powerful African God (see African Religion and Christianity Cluster).

Black theological anthropology has an international reach. Black humanity succeeds when the poor* in the USA connect with the full humanity of the poor throughout the world, particularly darker-skinned peoples. Anchored in Christianity, Black theological anthropology works with all spiritualities and religions of the global poor through the paradigm of "liberation of the oppressed." Because African American people's humanity is also shaped by their social and economic location in history's most powerful economic, political, and military country, to be human means to assume the responsibility of sharing the wealth of the USA with Third World peoples.

Black theology links the racial dimensions of the black self to ownership of wealth (see Property). How is it that the humanity of most African Americans has been defined by poverty* and working-class status? What does it mean to lack wealth or income? How is this human status amplified by the feminization of poverty (see Womanist and African American Theologies)? To be human, here, is to give substance to the eschatological thrust of Christian anthropology. The human goal is to co-labor with God to realize a healed individual self and a common wealth on earth.

Black male theological anthropology re-envisions maleness in conversation with Womanist theologians. Male anthropology is undergoing a self-examination and redefinition by learning wholeness – political and cultural, liberation and survival/quality of life, vulnerability and guarded ness, economics* and the emotional, and the academy and church together. All bodies of knowledge that foster an integrated male identity are used for individual transformation.

Being human today entails a closer working relation between the history of ideas of the academy and the wisdom of the church. Black theologians have defined their humanity as a composite of both social locations, woven together by a compassion for the wounded and for the least in all societies.

DWIGHT N. HOPKINS

Anthropology: African Theological Issues. African anthropology is an "anthropology of the whole." Africans (especially the Malagasy, inhabitants of Madagascar*) enjoy the concreteness and wholeness of things, whereas the heirs of Greek and Latin ancient cultures like abstractions. While the latter attempt to comprehend the mechanism of things, Africans try to understand their meaning. Indeed, Dubois* claimed that instead of being inclined to dominate and domesticate the world, as the heirs of the Greek and Latin cultures do, African tend to enjoy living out the mystique of the universe.

Holism, not dualism, is pertinent for traditional Africans. There is not much of a divide between the living and the dead. The "living dead," the ancestors*, are present together with the living; a person is, of course, both mind and body, both flesh and spirit, but there is no dichotomy. The terms "mind," "body," "flesh," and "spirit" are metonymic, each referring to the whole person.

Similarly, individuals cannot be envisioned apart from the community in which they flourish and which transcends them. "Alive, we live in the same house; dead, we dwell in the same tomb," says a Malagasy proverb.

While the foregoing observations have been made by sociocultural anthropologists, the Christian theological engagement with African anthropology involves wrestling with the dehumanizing forces that have shaped the modern and contemporary history of Africans. Slavery*, colonialism*, natural disasters, conflicts, and the scourge of HIV/AIDS, among others, constitute human woes of biblical proportion, which threaten the holism of life in Africa. From this standpoint, African history may well parallel biblical history as a history of rise and fall, death and resurrection. A senior anthropologist wrote, "Africa is the future . . . Africa appears to be running just slightly ahead of the history of the rest of the globe. . . . Lagos is not catching up with us. Rather we may be catching up with Lagos. Africa . . . appears to be previewing a planetary future. For good or for ill. Or both." (Weiss)

Christian "mission-doers" are those who are active in transforming African history and its future into a biblical history with its prophecy. The most indigenous Christian "mission-doers" are the agents of the so-called African* Instituted Churches. These African Christian leaders take care of the whole of human needs. They are active in prayer and celebration, but also in evangelization, in healing*, deliverance, socioeconomic production, and holistic education.

LAURENT WILLIAM RAMAMBASON

Anthropology: Asian Theological Issues. Anthropology in Christian theology concerns the origin of humanity, creation*; human ontological constitution, body and soul*; sin*; and grace* and redemption* by God in Christ and by the power of the Holy Spirit. Expressing these anthropological Christian doctrines in terms congenial to Asian cultures and religions is extremely difficult; often there are no equivalent terms and concepts.

Creation. Most Asian cultures and religions have cosmogonic myths (e.g. the Chinese *Sanwu Liji*, the Vedic *Rig Veda*, and the Tibetan* Bön religion), but none contains the belief in a creation ex nihilo, i.e. a bringing of all things into being by the transcendent deity without any preexisting material and with a divinely ordained purpose. For most Asian cosmogonic myths, both deities (gods and goddesses) and the elements of the material universe are manifestations of the Absolute, within a cyclical rather than a linear (purposeful) sense of time. Thus the Christian doctrines of divine immanence*, mystical union* with God, and cosmic order find a strong resonance in Asia.

Body and Soul. The diverse Asian views of the ontological constitution of the human person are distinct from the Christian concept of the human person as the unity of perishable matter (body) and immortal spirit (soul). In Hinduism* and Buddhism*, matter is an illusion; soul-spirit is the only real reality. In Theravada Buddhism, there is no "soul" (*anatman*), i.e. no substantial, unchanging, enduring self. In Daoism*, there is a great sense of harmony between humans and the material world. Christian anthropology can help Asians achieve a greater appreciation of the body and the individuality of the human person; Christians will learn from Asian insights into the contingency ("impermanence") of the human person and its intimate unity with the cosmos (ecology*).

Sin. While in Christianity sin is primarily a deliberate betrayal of a relationship with a loving personal God (but see Anthropology Cluster: Eastern Orthodox

Christian Theology), in Asia "sin" is the infringement of a cosmic and/or moral order (*dharma*) concretized in moral and legal codes and religious observances. In Hinduism, a set of duties is prescribed for each person according to one's place (caste*) in society and stage of life. In Buddhism, the *dharma* is embodied in the "Three Jewels" (*triratna*; Buddha, teaching, and community) and in the moral rules for monks or laity. Confucianism* emphasizes the reciprocal duties in four relationships: ruler–subject, husband–wife, parent–child, and sibling–sibling. Generally, a failure to preserve the cosmic and moral order produces shame* (more so than guilt*). Despite the absence of any notion of "original sin" or of the betrayal of a loving personal God, much in this Asian understanding of "sin" echoes Christian understandings.

Redemption and Grace. The popular understanding of *karma* and rebirth (*samsara*) often stresses the merit of one's deeds and ignores the gratuitousness of final liberation or salvation. Yet the notion of faith* and grace is central in Pure Land Buddhism; one can attain rebirth ("salvation") in the Pure Land of the Buddha Amida either through a good life or through invocation of and faith in the Buddha Amida. Christian soteriology* in Asia can insist both on personal responsibility and on faith in the gracious God who saves us in Christ and by the power of the Holy Spirit. PETER C. PHAN

Anthropology: Australian Aboriginal Theological Issues. For Australian* Aboriginal societies, humans are a part of an interrelated world, imbued with the same spiritual essence. For the Pitjantjatjara people of South Australia, our example here, in the timeless Dreaming (*tjukurpa*), spirit beings (*kurunitja*) emerged from a preexistent substance to roam the land. They metamorphosed or left imprints to form features of the environment. Spiritual essence remains within these features. These beings were the ancestors* of people, animals, and plant species. Humans share relationship, rights, and responsibilities with other species. Aborigines attribute the conception of human life to the entry of a spirit into the woman's body. The role of the male is to facilitate this entry. Death ensues when the spirit leaves the body.

Aboriginal societies emphasize social roles and obligations rather than individual rights. Reciprocity is a key principle in determining the interaction between individuals and groups, with social balance maintained as all fulfilled their responsibilities. In such an egalitarian ethos, older men and women have authority as repositories of the most sacred knowledge and control of the stories and rituals associated with the Dreaming.

The concept of a universal creator* God, which Aborigines did not have, and the story of Jesus as redeemer* were introduced by missionaries, with little understanding of or sensitivity to traditional beliefs, which were viewed as pagan*. Greater openness and translation of the Bible made it possible for Aboriginal Christians to relate aspects of their culture to Christianity, finding resonance between aspects of their hunter-gatherer lifestyle and that of biblical nomads.

Dreaming stories provide neither a model of perfection nor a concept of sin*; rather, they point toward the need for balance and provide opportunities for people to reflect on appropriate actions in specific contexts. The traditional role of a person (*ngalkilpa*) who intercedes or takes on punishment for another points toward Jesus' redeeming work.

Thus the struggle for justice* and equality became a central issue for Aborigines influenced by Christianity. Despite restrictions imposed by racial theories, government policies, and limited education, effective leaders in this struggle included David Unaipon, Douglas Nicholls, Blind Moses, Alan Mungulu, Miriam-Rose Ungunmerr-Baumann, and Djiniyini Gondarra. The influential Charismatic Arnhem Land Revival and Aboriginal Evangelical Fellowship (1970s–1980s) led to increased Aboriginal leadership. Thus theological reflection on the environment and reconciliation brought together traditional views of spiritual presence throughout the universe and their Christian Charismatic experiences. WILLIAM H. EDWARDS

Anthropology: European-American Theological Issues. European-American theological anthropology developed in response to the European Enlightenment*. Is it possible to believe in God in the Age of Reason*? It focuses on the nonbeliever and secular* culture. One wing embraces secular culture by forging a dialogue between Christian themes and philosophical theories. Another wing calls on the church to take care of its own internal demands.

The first wing sees the theologian's vocation as the application of philosophy and theory derived from broader university disciplines. Humans dare to think about and accept the latest bodies of knowledge from secular academies. No dualism exists between church or seminary and university (see Theological Education Cluster: In North America; Theological Education Cluster: In Western Europe: Germany). Correlating the nonbeliever's questions with Christian answers indicates the ongoing relevancy of Jesus Christ for a secular age. The mutual critical interaction of the Christian witness of faith and human existence is subject to the criteria of objectivity, appropriateness, credibility, pragmatic usefulness, and coherence – the same criteria faced by human and social sciences. In addition, human beings are free* subjects (independent thinkers with the power of self-transcendence), always in process (see Process Theology), impacting and being impacted by God. Taking seriously human evil, anxiety, and uncertainty, this wing still affirms humanity and its striving for justice* in human history.

The second wing of European-American theological anthropology sees Scripture* (and God and Christian witness) absorbing the world and not the opposite. The Christian "dwells *in* the Bible" rather than interpreting it for those outside the biblical world. The Christian is immersed in the uniqueness of the Christian language and culture, and confronts and changes the non-Christian world ("Christ against culture"; see Culture Cluster: Culture and Christianity). This anthropology calls on believers to learn their own native tongue, i.e. to entrench themselves thoroughly in the grammar of Christian speech rather than secular speech. Perhaps this will lead to Christianizing secular culture or helping the two cultures to better define themselves and separately pursue their respective vocations. DWIGHT N. HOPKINS

Anthropology: Feminist Theological Issues. Theological anthropology speaks of the human person in relation to God. This discourse is shaped both by an analysis of the various roles that sex and gender play in views of the human person and by a commitment to the full humanity of women. It notes the exclusion of women's voices in shaping dominant culture and, therefore, in defining what it means to be human. Throughout much of Christianity, men have been seen as normative, while women have been considered inferior. This is apparent in several doctrines, including that of creation*, as some traditional views hold that men are created in the image* of God, while women only partially or derivatively reflect the Creator; that of sin*, where women are often portrayed as inherently sinful temptresses; and that of ecclesiology* (see Church, Concepts and Life, Cluster: Feminist Perspectives), where women are sometimes barred from ordination* and leadership positions.

Feminist theological anthropology emerged as a field of study in the context of the modern Western fascination with the human subject. Feminists in Europe and the USA analyze and criticize the modern view of the human person as a rational, individual, autonomous, free subject. Such modern anthropology reinscribes dualisms* that privilege the mind over the body*, the spirit over the flesh. It supports views of humanity in which men are connected with such characteristics as reason, will, aggression, and dominance, while women are linked with the body, nature, emotion, and submission. Feminists challenge these dualistic patterns, as well as the gender essentialism that claims women and men are hardwired with distinctive traits. Many feminists discuss how the self, including gender and sexual identity, develops over time in community through social construction.

While feminists contest ways in which men universalize their own experiences as normative of humanity, the oppressive pattern of universalizing has been unwittingly repeated. As white women of privilege describe what it is to be a woman, the differences among women, including those of class, race, and sexuality, are sometimes obscured. The burgeoning of Feminist theologies around the globe, now done in conversation with Womanist* and Mujerista* theologies, has changed Feminist theology into an inherently multiple conversation. Contemporary feminist theological anthropology exists within the tension between claiming a common womanhood for ethical and political purposes, and honoring the many differences among women that destabilize the very category of "woman." Resources such as doctrines of the Trinity* and eschatology* are used in articulating such anthropologies. SHANNON CRAIGO-SNELL

Anthropology: Latin American Theological Issues. For Liberation* theology, anthropology is more than a branch of systematic theology about the human condition in relation to diverse aspects of life in history. Certainly the Bible refers to topics of theological anthropology (creation*, human in the image* of God, sin*, grace* as the gift of God), but it also includes much that does not fit into "systematic theology." Thus anthropology in Latin American theology of liberation is interdisciplinary, including history, sociology, political science, economy, social psychology, cultural studies, ethnography, and ecology.

Latin American theology is interested in speaking about the human being not as an individual, self-contained subject, but as a person who belongs to a community and is in relationship with nature. Its methodological goal is to "de-privatize" faith and theology. Therefore, it studies the historical (natural and social) process of human liberation and the struggles to build a society where, with the dignity of children of God, people can live in an environment of justice, peace, and a balanced relationship with nature.

G. Gutiérrez, in *Theology of Liberation*, proposed a helpful distinction between three levels of liberation, which are also three aspects of theological anthropology:

1. Liberation as collective: the aspiration of people in classes or sectors of society that are oppressed because of historical conflicts and their social, political, and economic ramifications.
2. Liberation as a historical process through which humans assume their own destiny, free themselves, and build an enduring new humanity.
3. Liberation as a process that leads to the biblical sources that inspire this new humanity in daily life, as it moves from the old to the new* creation, from sin* to grace*, from slavery to sin to freedom. Christ frees us from sin, from egotistical self-centeredness, the root of all separation from God, from God's life project, and from others. Thus Christ frees us to love, serve, and live in communion with God, the basis for any true human community.

Latin American theologies of liberation always underscored the original correlation of God with life, and its confrontation with a globalized system of domination with an "anti-life" logic: bringing death to the despised of the world and to the creation and its integrity (destruction of the ecosystems). The primordial will of the God of Life and God-self are broken by and for the sin of the world, a manifestation of the mystery of sin (*mysterium iniquitatis*).

The creator God is, above all, a living God who gives and defends life. Life, God's main gift, is also the most vulnerable and threatened reality. The gift of life cannot be separated from its necessary material basis: work, health, housing, rest, and food. As Irenaeus* said, "*Gloria Dei, vivens homo*," "The glory of God is the *living* human being." Monsignor Romero*, bishop-martyr of El* Salvador, added concreteness to this truth: "*Gloria Dei, vivens* *pauper*," "The glory of God is the *living* poor." VICTORIO ARAYA GUILLÉN

Anthropology: Womanist Theological Issues. Womanist* anthropology is the comprehensive study of humanity (across time, amid the intersections of biological, linguistic, and sociocultural systems) as Black women unapologetically experience communal life holistically, cognizant of how systems of sexism*, heterosexism, classism, racism*, and ageism oppress*. Such epistemology reconstructs the notion of God* and womanhood*. Womanist anthropology exposes ignorant, oppressive ideology* that subscribes to the images of Black women as mammy, whore, Sapphire, Jezebel, asexual Aunt Jemima, castrating matriarch, superwoman, and (as Zora Neale Hurston says) "the mules of the earth." These insidious stereotypes are deceptive. Black women had to be tough, self-reliant, and supportive of family, community, and strangers, loving all people; but ironically, this tenacity distorts Black women's gift of overcoming obstacles, surviving, and flourishing. By contrast, womanists reconstruct knowledge and make room for the "least of these," the excluded Black women of the world; they move to an anthropological paradigm of liberation* and survival that excavates the lives of poor Black women, by acknowledging the impact on them of everyday lived experiences contextualized by capitalistic, political economies and how this global economy shapes access, decision making, and action. Womanist anthropology affirms the God-given lives and gifts of global Black women.

CHERYL A. KIRK-DUGGAN

Anthropomorphisms, words that attribute human form, actions, or feelings to God. These three understandings of anthropomorphism are found in many religions, but also in Christianity.

God has often been envisioned in iconography and art* as an old man with white hair. This image was probably suggested by the Bible, where God is called the "Ancient of Days" (Dan 7:22) seated on a throne (Isa 6:1; Ps 11:4, 47:8; Rev 4–5, 20:11), a symbol of God's power and authority. Christ is said to sit at God's right hand, sharing God's authority (Ps 110:1, frequently cited in the NT).

Some Christians take such anthropomorphisms literally, but most take them as symbolic*. Augustine* tells how he was gradually freed from a literal understanding by envisioning God as being like the human spirit; later, he found the closest analogue to the Trinity* in the self-relatedness of the human mind. The "anthropomorphite controversy" in Egypt (c400) set the literalist monks against the enlightened Origenists*. During the controversies of the Reformation period, Lutherans retained images in their houses of worship and tolerated imagining God as an old man so long as it was not taken literally; the Reformed attacked this as idolatry and insisted that God be understood spiritually (cf. John 4:24).

God's actions are also described in human terms in the Bible: e.g. walking in the garden (Gen 3:8) or acting with a powerful "right hand" (Exod 15:12). The emphasis on actions may explain the anthropomorphisms of the first type. The modern philosophy of action insists that our notions of causality and action begin from our own experiences as embodied agents and that these are then used to imagine God as an agent.

"Anthropopathisms" are words that, following the Bible, describe God as having human feelings such as surprise, delight, disappointment, frustration, pain and suffering, wrath, and compassion. In the doctrinal tradition, the predominant view was that God is immutable and therefore "impassible*," i.e. without "passion," including emotions: the world is related to God, but God is not related to the world; God influences without being influenced. Thus passages about God's wrath or joy were taken to be metaphors, ways of evaluating events in terms of human emotions that are not appropriate to God.

In recent centuries this view has been challenged; relatedness is a perfection, not a weakness. While this has been accepted in many contexts with respect to compassion and mercy, there has been more reluctance to ascribe wrath* to God; similarly, God's pain or frustration over events in human life is much debated.

EUGENE TESELLE

Antichrist, a term (from Jewish apocalypticism*) used in the NT only in 1 John 2:18, 22; 4:3; 2 John 7 (once in the plural). These passages are often combined with images of the lawless man who claims to be God (2 Thess 2:3–4), the beast from the abyss (Rev 13), the whore of Babylon (Rev 17), and Gog and Magog (Rev 20).

"Antichrist" can refer to a false but attractive version of the Christian message (heresy*, unbelief) or to someone falsely claiming to be the Messiah – "one who assuming the guise of Christ opposes Christ" (Westcott). Medieval exegesis collated many apocalyptic passages to construct a detailed "life" of the Antichrist. Most significantly, there was a steady increase of attempts to "name the Antichrist," attaching the title to contemporaneous persons, institutions, or movements: Emperor Frederick II or Pope Boniface* VIII; the papacy*; the Enlightenment*, free thought, and Modernism*. Colonized people readily apply it to the imperial powers that held them in subjection even while preaching the gospel. In the USA, some Millennialist* beliefs have indicted as the Antichrist all movements of social reform, because these movements attempt to bring about what only the return of Christ can accomplish, namely a united, peaceful humanity. Thus these Millennialists target as Antichrist socialism, the United Nations, the World* Council of Churches, movements for international peace and justice, feminism, environmentalism, and the like.

Anticlericalism, the name given to movements, originating with Voltaire and the French Revolution, criticizing the clergy and opposing support for Roman Catholicism as the state* church and religion. The term sometimes also applied to moderate forms of separation* of church and state. **See also CHURCH AND STATE RELATIONS CLUSTER; LAICIZATION; SECULARISM AND SECULARIZATION.**

Anti-Jewish, Anti-Judaism. Often a synonym of "anti-Semitism," "anti-Judaism" refers to forms of opposition to and denigration of Jews or their religion that do not involve issues of race. **See also ANTI-SEMITISM; SUPERSESSIONISM.**

Antinomianism, a belief that the Law* (the Decalogue* and other moral commands in the Bible) is not binding on Christians because they live under grace*. Usually based on statements made by Paul (esp. Gal 3–5; Rom 2–5), it is found in various forms in Marcionism*, Gnosticism*, the medieval Brethren of the Free* Spirit, and several movements during the Reformation* and the Puritan* interregnum. The term is often extended to Christians who do not follow biblical commands in a strict or literal fashion.

Antioch, Council of (341), a council of Eastern bishops that met during the dedication of the "golden basilica." It came to be associated with two influential texts: one comprising 25 canons* concerning the deposition of bishops and one consisting of four creeds. The canons may have been adopted a few years earlier (after Constantine's* death, 337) to oppose the return of Athanasius* to Alexandria*, and some of the creeds may have been formulated in other gatherings of bishops. The creeds did not replace the Nicene* Creed but supplemented it, emphasizing God's threeness. While Arianism* was condemned, the Council said little about God's unity; in this sense it authorized both the Homoian* position of the Councils of Ariminum* and Seleucia (359) and Constantinople (360), and the alternative Homoiousian* position, which cited the second creed of Antioch.

Antioch, Its Theological Tradition. With its long tradition as a center of learning, especially of Greek philosophy and rhetoric, the See of Antioch established in the early 3rd c. a school of theology and biblical interpretation, which was flourishing by the time of Lucian* (martyred in 312). Influenced by Aristotle*, it stressed textual criticism and the literal* exegesis (in the sense of nonallegorical interpretation) of the Scriptures*. Regarding theology, Antioch focused on the idea that the humanity of Jesus must be complete if Christ* is to represent the new human who replaces the sinful human. Thus while the rival school of Alexandria* was concerned primarily with the divine Word (Logos*), which would be singly conjoined to a human nature, Antioch was concerned with the complete human assumed by the Word. Where Alexandria was concerned with guaranteeing the bond of unity between the divine and human in Christ, Antioch wished to ensure that Christ's humanity was completely intact. The 4th- and 5th-c. representatives of the school of Antioch included the exegete Diodore* of Tarsus, Theodore* of Mopsuestia, John* Chrysostom, and Theodoret* of Cyrrhus, before the school joined the school of Edessa* and finally moved to Nisibis*.

As a consequence of the ecumenical Council of Chalcedon* (451), which condemned Eutyches's* Monophysitism, the patriarchate was split into three communities. One supported the Council and was subsequently called Melkite* (the king's party), found in hellenized cities along the Mediterranean coast. The second, namely, the Syriac Orthodox* (whose members were polemically nicknamed "Jacobites," after Jacob* Baradai), rejected the Council. Ironically, the Syrians in the cities of the hinterland of the Antiochian Patriarchate, who would have been expected to welcome Chalcedon's teaching, ended up accepting Miaphysitism*, championed by the Alexandrians. The third community, the Maronite* monastery and community, which lived alongside the Syriac Church, accepted the Chalcedonian doctrine.

By the 7th c., there were three patriarchates of Antioch: the Melkite, or Greek; the Syriac; and the Maronite. By the 10th c., the Melkites had transferred to the Byzantine liturgy and influence, and subsequently followed Constantinople during the great* schism (1417). With the unions with Rome (17th and 18th c.) of some of the Greek Orthodox and of the Syrians, there were now five patriarchates of Antioch: the Melkite, Greek* Orthodox, Syriac* Catholic, Syriac* Orthodox, and Maronite*. While differences regarding doctrine and papal authority played a major part in producing this diversity, certainly political and cultural differences have also been significant factors. **See also BIBLE INTERPRETATION CLUSTER: HISTORY OF.**

CHORBISHOP SEELY BEGGIANI

Antiphon (Gk *antiphonon*, "sounding against"), a response, usually sung, to a psalm or another part of a religious service; also a sacred text sung alternately by two choirs.

Anti-Semitism refers to the projection of stereotypes on the Jewish people as a whole that portray them as essentially evil. The negative attributes projected on them are typically built on dualistic dichotomies, such as materialistic (not spiritual), deceitful (not truthful), and hypocritical (not honest). Some forms of anti-Semitism developed in ancient polytheistic culture, primarily as a reaction against the resistance of some sectors of the Jewish people to subjugation and assimilation into the Greco-Roman Empire. But the prime source of anti-Semitism in European culture has been Christianity.

Christianity developed a diatribe against the Jewish people as a religious community starting in NT times, rooted in a rivalry between the Christian affirmation that Jesus was the Messiah expected in the Jewish tradition and the rejection of this faith by the established Jewish leaders. A bitter diatribe was directed particularly against the Pharisees*, who were leading rabbinic reformers in the earliest days of Christianity. The Pharisees are stereotyped in the Gospel of Matthew*, particularly as "blind guides and hypocrites," petty legalists who were strict in superficial matters and neglected the "weightier matters of the law, justice, mercy, and faith" (Matt 23:23). They are described as "sons of those who murdered the prophets," "serpents, a brood of vipers, deserving of hell" (Matt 23:31–33) and, in the Gospel of John (8:44), as children of the devil.

This polemic directed against Jews as a religious-ethnic people hardened into fixed patterns in the patristic* writings (2nd–6th c.), expressed particularly in the *adversus Judaeos* literature (patristic writings directed against the Jews). These writings claim that the Christian Church is the true heir of God's election* of a people of God, while the Jews are the heirs of those who have always been apostate, killed the prophets, and, as the culminating perfidy, killed God's Messiah. Because of this apostasy, God is said to have cast off the Jews, condemning them to be homeless wanderers subjugated to other people (the Christians, who now identify with the Roman Empire).

When Christianity became the established religion of the Roman Empire, this polemic was translated into legal disabilities against the Jewish people. They were forbidden to proselytize, to hold slaves (eliminating them from the larger spheres of agriculture and business), and to hold political office. Rioters, often led by monks, destroyed synagogues.

This pattern of polemic as well as legal disabilities was passed on to medieval and early modern Christendom, being renewed in the 12th c. Jews were segregated in special sections of cities, forced to wear identifying garb, and forbidden the normal range of economic activities, but were allowed to function in areas forbidden to Christians, such as money lending. Stereotypes having to do with usurious practices were thus added to negative religious images. During the Crusades*, the Christian armies, on their way to fight the Muslims in the Middle East, sometimes stopped to sack Jewish communities.

Although this Christian polemic was murderous, it was not genocidal. There remained a place for Jews as a religious community in Christian society, as an object of polemic against whom Christians contrasted themselves, but also of hope for an eventual capitulation and conversion of the Jews to Christianity. This conversion was projected onto Christian eschatology*, becoming a part of the "last things" that signaled the return of Christ and final redemption*.

This ambiguity changed during the modern period as religious anti-Judaism was translated into a racial anti-Semitism. Negative characteristics thus became attributed to Jews as a race, as a matter of "blood." Jews were thus seen as people who could not truly convert or assimilate to Christian culture, but must be eliminated altogether. In 19th- and early-20th-c. Europe, Jews became the scapegoats for modernizing and secularizing* trends that challenged Christian hegemony in society. These culminated in Nazism*, which passed laws that segregated Jews, confiscated their property, expelled them, and finally physically annihilated them (see Holocaust, Jewish [or Shoah]).

Christianity bears a heavy burden of responsibility for this terrible legacy of anti-Semitism in Western society. Christians need not only to reject the negative racial and religious stereotypes of Jews and Judaism*, but also to probe their religious roots based on a rejection of Judaism as an autonomous, valid way of relating to God. Christians have to confront the question of whether it is possible to affirm that Jesus is the Messiah without, implicitly or explicitly, damning Judaism, which does not accept this claim.

Unfortunately in the late 20th and early 21st c., further confusion has arisen as a result of the political equation of anti-Semitism with criticism of the policies of the state of Israel*. This has led some people, bitter about these policies, to carry out random attacks on Jewish synagogues or social centers. It is imperative for Christians (and all people) to reject anti-Semitism, root and branch, while also separating it from legitimate criticism of particular unjust policies of the state of Israel.

ROSEMARY RADFORD RUETHER

Antony (c254–356), Egyptian hermit; inaccurately described as "the founder of Christian monasticism." His fame derives largely from the biography by Athanasius*, *Vita Antonii*, written in Greek (c358), which owes much to Athanasius's theological and political agenda. It portrays Antony as a pioneer of desert monasticism who interrupts his solitude to instruct disciples, debate pagans, work miracles, denounce heretics*, and disarm demons. The *Vita* influenced the form of all later written works on the lives of the saints. Antony's sayings and stories also appear in the *Apophthegmata* Patrum*. Recent research focuses on seven letters attributed to Antony, preserved in ancient Georgian. **See also** **EGYPT; MONASTICISM CLUSTER; RELIGIOUS ORDERS, ROMAN CATHOLIC, CLUSTER: COMMUNITIES: THEIR HISTORY AND DEVELOPMENT IN WESTERN EUROPE.**

J. WILLIAM HARMLESS, SJ

Anxious Bench, in revivalism* (since the 18th c.), a specific place for persons convinced of their sinfulness and seeking conversion* and assurance* of salvation*, utilized most notably by Charles G. Finney*.

Aphrahat (4th c.; Persian Empire), one of the oldest representatives of the Syriac spiritual tradition. His 23 homilies, *Demonstrations* (336–45; soon translated into Armenian, Arabic, Georgian, and Ethiopic), represent Syriac Christianity in its purest form, uncontaminated by Greek influence. They deal with faith*, love*, fasting*, prayer*, humility*, purity of heart, and other themes. Aphrahat expresses concerns about the temptation to adopt Jewish practices and at times addresses the contemporary pre-monastic "Sons and Daughters of the Covenant," whom he calls to a new covenant, "circumcision of the heart." Aphrahat, perhaps the earliest Christian to have written a study on prayer in general, had a large influence on Syriac spirituality in succeeding centuries.

CHORBISHOP SEELY BEGGIANI

Apocalypse (Gk *apocalypsis*, "revelation"), (1) a revelation of what will happen in the end-time; (2) the original title of the NT book commonly called "Revelation*" in English; (3) any apocryphal book with apocalyptic* teachings, such as the Syriac Apocalypse of Baruch* and the Apocalypse of Peter*. **See also** **APOCALYPTICISM CLUSTER.**

APOCALYPTICISM CLUSTER

Apocalypticism: Beginnings in Judaism and Christianity

Apocalypticism: Extension in Western History and Culture

Apocalypticism: Prolongation in the Modern Period

Apocalypticism: Beginnings in Judaism and Christianity. "Apocalypse" is derived from the Greek *apokalypsis* (revelation). "Apocalypticism" is the worldview exemplified in the Book of Revelation*. "Apocalypses" usually take the form of visions explained by an angel. There are two main types of apocalypse: (1) historical apocalypses survey the course of history, often divided into periods, and end with cosmic catastrophe and the eschatological Judgment; (2) otherworldly journey apocalypses describe tours of the heavens or nether regions. Both types include the Judgment* of the dead, and this distinguishes apocalypticism from biblical prophecy. Both types are attested in Judaism, beginning in the 2nd c. BCE, in the books of Daniel* and Enoch*. (All Jewish apocalypses are attributed pseudonymously to famous ancient figures.) The visions of Dan 7–12 stand in the tradition of symbolic visions in the Hebrew prophets (e.g. Zechariah*). Enoch, however, seems to be modeled on the legendary Babylonian king Enmeduranki, who was taken up to heaven and shown the tablets of destiny. There are Akkadian models for the extended *ex eventu* (after the fact) prophecies in the apocalypses. There was also a tradition of similar literature in Persia, but the dating is problematic.

The apocalyptic worldview, in which the world is considered the arena of supernatural forces subject to eschatological Judgment, is also reflected in many texts that are not in the form of revelations. The Dead* Sea Scrolls anticipate a final battle between the forces of light* and darkness, a motif borrowed from Persian dualism*. A major cluster of Jewish apocalypses (4 Ezra*, 2 Bar*, 3 Bar, Apocalypse of Abraham) dates from the time after the destruction of Jerusalem (70–100 CE).

The historical type of apocalypticism was a major factor in early Christianity. Whether Jesus* was an apocalyptic prophet is disputed, but he is so depicted in the Gospels. The most explicit predictions attributed to him concern the Second* Coming (Mark 13 par.) and may reflect the beliefs of the early church. Paul taught that the resurrection of Christ was the first fruit of the general resurrection (1 Cor 15) and expected that some of his contemporaries would still be alive when Christ returned (1 Thess 4). The classic expression of Christian apocalypticism is found in the Book of Revelation, written toward the end of the 1st c. CE, which predicts the downfall of Rome and the imminent return of Christ as divine warrior from heaven. **See also** **ESCHATOLOGY CLUSTER.**

JOHN J. COLLINS

Apocalypticism: Extension in Western History and Culture. From 400 to 1500 CE, apocalyptic movements identified contemporary events with biblical or other prophecies of the last days, applying new circumstances to a more or less unchanging Christian prophetic structure. Although Western apocalyptic movements sometimes advanced radical policies of social, ecclesiastical, or political reform, apocalyptic rhetoric was just as likely to be part of the dominant discourse of church and kingdom.

The Apocalypse of John (Revelation*), along with its antecedents among traditional Jewish apocalypses, provided the foundation for Christian interpretations of "last things." Western apocalypticism and its beliefs in various prophecies that offered detailed predictions of the end were kept at bay by the thought of Augustine* of Hippo (354–430), who rejected correlations between apocalyptic scripture and current historical events. Augustine's influence was significant enough to dampen overt speculation in the West about the millennium until the 11th c. After the year 1000, Western apocalypticism became linked to debates about ecclesiastical reform, playing a role in the polemics of mainstream reformers such as Gregory* VII (1073–85) and Hildegard* of Bingen (1098–1179). Among the most significant apocalypticists of the High Middle Ages was Joachim* of Fiore (c1130/35–1202), who created a new system of scriptural exegesis and apocalyptic prediction based on his theory of the three "states" (OT, NT, and end of time), although without assigning precise dates to apocalyptic events. Joachite apocalypticism became important for a number of late medieval movements, including the Franciscan* Spirituals, the Beguines*, and the Fraticelli*, whose members often espoused radical social or political ideologies. Opponents of these movements within the ecclesiastical hierarchy, however, also used eschatological rhetoric in their arguments. In the 14th c., Christians interpreted disasters such as the plague and the Hundred Years' War in light of their apocalyptic beliefs, but the century saw little in the way of prophetic innovation. Fifteenth-century reformers such as Girolamo Savonarola* and Jan Hus* stirred eschatological fears and hopes in Florence and Hussite Bohemia, while well-known Renaissance figures, including Michelangelo and Christopher Columbus, drew inspiration from traditional apocalyptic texts and images.

While modern attention has focused on the years 1000 and 2000 as crucial episodes in apocalyptic fervor, premodern Christians experienced a fairly constant state of heightened apocalyptic expectation. Such apocalypticism was both pessimistic, inasmuch as it predicted a cataclysmic end to contemporary society, and optimistic, since it envisioned a better world that would form in its wake. **See also ESCHATOLOGY CLUSTER.**

LEAH DEVUN

Apocalypticism: Prolongation in the Modern Period. Apocalypticism continues to focus on the prospect of an imminent end to the present order (eschatology*) and to draw on the Book of Revelation*. But among contemporary Christians, there have been diverse viewpoints on the interpretation and application of apocalypticism, which is highly adaptable to differing religious and social circumstances.

Some constructions of the impending end are optimistic and imply for believers a glorious conclusion to present realities. This perspective is often associated with the notion that human effort can create a better world and bring about the Kingdom* of God on earth. The positive impact of modern science* and technology* has fueled this spiritual optimism among some Christians who have experienced prosperity and the prospect of continuing good times (e.g. Social* Gospel advocates, including Walter Rauschenbusch*; the Federal* Council of Churches).

More often, apocalypticism has powerfully appealed to religious groups who presently suffer and face a dismal future, including masses of Christians in independent* churches of the Two-thirds World. Communities that experience a pessimistic outlook have repeatedly turned to scriptural texts for encouragement and for details on the prospect of divine intervention, often reading Scripture* in a literal way (e.g. the literal* interpretation of the Bible by Seventh-day* Adventists; Pentecostals*; many in the worldwide Charismatic* Movement). Many (e.g. Millerites*, Dispensationalists*, John Nelson Darby*) cling to the hope of an imminent physical return of Christ to the earth accompanied by the defeat of the forces of evil. Some (e.g. Jehovah's* Witnesses, Branch* Davidians) project a cosmic struggle on that occasion. Sometimes apocalypticism has persuaded the hopeless to follow religious leaders offering radical political or social programs, or to look for miraculous signs or wondrous phenomena (e.g. Marshall Herff Applewhite and Heaven's Gate).

These two basic alternative perspectives on apocalypticism differ on the efficacy of human efforts to solve ultimate problems. Christian movements among the dispossessed – economically, socially, or otherwise – are fertile seedbeds for this second form of apocalypticism, in which hope for better times lies in divine intervention (e.g. Nat Turner*, Latter-day* Saints, the worldwide Charismatic Movement). But the modern appropriation of apocalypticism is even more complex. Religious groups enjoying prosperity and cultural power (e.g. late-20th-c. American Evangelical Fundamentalists*) celebrate the prospect of an apocalyptic conclusion involving a literal, physical Second Coming of Christ, which, they affirm, will vindicate the righteousness* of their political and social views (e.g. variations of Dispensationalism* in Hal Lindsey's writings and the popular fictional series *Left Behind*). **See also ESCHATOLOGY CLUSTER.**

STEPHEN J. STEIN

Apocrypha Cluster

1) *Introductory Entries*

Apocrypha
Apocrypha of the New Testament

2) *A Sampling of Apocrypha*

Apocryphal Acts of Apostles
Apocryphal Gospels
Apocryphon of John

1) Introductory Entries

Apocrypha (from Gk for "hidden books"), most broadly, any books whose authorship or authority is doubtful; specifically, the books included in the Septuagint* but not part of the Jewish Scriptures. During the Reformation*, all of the non-Hebrew books were translated into the vernacular* but were printed in a separate section, between the OT and NT, usually in the following order: 1 Esdras, 2 Esdras, Tobit, Judith, Additions to Esther, Wisdom of Solomon, Wisdom* of Ben Sira (or Ecclesiasticus or Sirach), Baruch, Letter of Jeremiah, Prayer of Azariah, Song of the Three Youths, Susannah, Bel and the Dragon, Prayer of Manassas*, 1 Maccabees, 2 Maccabees. The Council of Trent* affirmed the canonical status of the Apocrypha, but placed the Prayer of Manassas, 3 Esdras*, and 4 Esdras* in an appendix. While the Apocrypha were translated in the Authorized* Version, the English Puritans* opposed any use of them that would imply doctrinal or moral authority. They have been omitted from most English translations published by Bible* societies since c1800. **See also BIBLE, CANON OF.**

Apocrypha of the New Testament. In modern usage, "apocryphal books" is used to distinguish certain early Christian texts from the "canonical" Gospels of Matthew, Mark, Luke, and John and the "canonical" Acts of the Apostles (see Present Cluster: Apocryphal Acts of Apostles and Apocryphal Gospels). The use of the concepts "apocryphal" and "canonical" for texts earlier than the 4th c. is anachronistic, because the NT canon* was not yet defined. Nevertheless, we cannot quite do without these terms. In the case of the Gospels, Irenaeus* clearly differentiated (c180) the four "canonical" Gospels of the church from all the others he knew, though he did not yet use the terms "apocryphal" and "canonical."

The literal meaning of the Greek *apokryphos* is "concealed, hidden." It seems to have been first applied to secret revelations that, in the eyes of particular groups, were more relevant than the doctrines professed in the public life of the church. The adherents of nascent orthodoxy reacted by equating "apocryphal" with "falsified, unreliable." But not all apocryphal Gospels and Acts were always and everywhere thought to be heretical. The Protevangelium of James, for example, is used in Eastern liturgies to this day.

Hans-Josef Klauck

2) A Sampling of Apocrypha

Apocryphal Acts of Apostles were written primarily in the 2nd and 3rd c. The Acts of Philip and the Martyrdom of Matthew were written later (probably 4th c.). Each of these texts honors a single apostle, e.g. Andrew, John, Peter, Paul, or Thomas. The model was not Luke's Acts* of the Apostles (which presents several witnesses and excludes the narration of Peter's or Paul's martyrdom) but the gospel story centered on one principal hero and his destiny, and ending with his martyrdom. Although all belong to the same literary genre, these Acts of the Apostles did not originate in the same milieu.

Some, like the Acts of Peter and the Acts of Paul, are products of a popular form of early Catholicism; others, like the Acts of Andrew and the Acts of John, were engendered from a more intellectual environment of dissenting Christianity. The geographical origin of the Acts varies: the Acts of Thomas* reflects Eastern Syriac Christianity; the Acts of John and the Acts of Philip*, Asia Minor; the Acts of Peter, Western Syria; the Acts of Paul,

Greece. Some of these works are composite, and their ethical or theological orientations can differ from one part of the text to another (e.g. the divergences concerning encratism* [extreme asceticism*] and Christology* in the different parts of the Acts of John).

These works do not present a unified doctrine, even if some textbooks propose such generalizations. For example, it is erroneous to say that the apocryphal Acts of Apostles as a whole are encratite or that they proclaim a docetic* Christology (the divine Christ's humanity is only apparent). Recent scholarship insists on the need to treat independently each apocryphal Acts of the Apostles.

While they differ in length, tone, and orientation, all the apocryphal Acts of the Apostles present a series of travel narratives and always include preaching and healing by the respective apostle. Each of the texts also records a developing hostility toward the apostle and finally tells, at length, a martyrdom story (or the peaceful death of the hero, as in the exceptional case of the Acts of John). Not uncommon among the Acts is a specific description of the rage of an enemy of the apostle, e.g. the jealousy of a husband, a Roman governor, a king, or an emperor.

The fate of the apocryphal Acts of the Apostles is important for understanding the history of the NT canon. While Manichaeans* read and venerated these books, possibly creating a collection of the five most ancient, Catholic leaders and theologians gradually rejected them. As early as the 4th c., certain eloquent bishops, e.g. Eusebius* of Caesarea and Augustine* of Hippo, and several councils and synods from the eastern or western parts of the Roman Empire, pronounced severe condemnations of these books. But the absence of criticism of these works in their earlier reception and a need for apostolic memories contributed to their survival. Some of the apocryphal Acts of the Apostles were rewritten according to an orthodox perspective (see the *Life of Saint Andrew* by Gregory* of Tours), or parts of them were detached and used as reading on the feast day of the apostle. New Acts of the Apostles were composed with different characteristics: the new documents had to be in harmony with the canonical Acts of the Apostles, and the apostles had to travel in pairs in order to respect Jesus' missionary speech. These more recent Acts of the Apostles were also related to local traditions and devotion (e.g. the Acts of John by Pseudo-Prochoros, closely associated with the island of Patmos), particularly at the tomb of the apostle (e.g. the *Passio Petri* by Pseudo-Linus related to Rome). FRANÇOIS BOVON

Apocryphal Gospels. The corpus of "apocryphal" Gospels in modern scholarship consists of the following: (1) narrative texts that share some affinities to the canonical Gospels and often fill gaps at their beginning (birth and childhood of Mary and Jesus) or end (Passion and Resurrection); (2) texts that carry the designation "Gospel"; (3) fragments that are derived from Gospels according to the church fathers.

The Gelasian Decree (possibly as early as 382) lists apocryphal Gospels under the names of Matthias, Barnabas, James the Younger, Peter*, Thomas*, Bartholomew, and Andrew, forgeries by Lucian* and Hesychius, and probably two infancy Gospels. Not included are the Jewish-Christian Gospels (according to the Hebrews*, of the Ebionites*, of the Nazarenes*), the Gospel of the Egyptians quoted by Clement* of Alexandria, the much later Gospel of Nicodemus, the Gospel of Judas* Iscariot, and texts barely known, e.g. the Gospels of Eve, of the Twelve, of the Seventy, and of Cerinthus.

The 1945 Nag* Hammadi discovery in Upper Egypt included another Gospel of the Egyptians, the full text of the Gospel of Thomas*, a Gospel of Philip*, a Gospel* of Truth, and a group of dialogues with the risen or earthly Jesus (Sophia Jesu Christi, Apocryphon of John*, Book of Thomas, Dialogue of the Savior, and the Gospel of Mary* Magdalene).

The importance of this corpus of "apocryphal" texts for our knowledge of the history of Christianity, for liturgical praxis and personal piety, and for art and literature can hardly be overestimated.

HANS-JOSEF KLAUCK

Apocryphon of John. See JOHN, APOCRYPHON OF.

Apollinaris, Apollinarius (c310–c390), bishop of Laodicea, born in Berytus, the son of a grammarian of the same name. When Julian* expelled Christians from the schools, the father and son paraphrased many parts of the Bible in classical forms in order to teach poetry and rhetoric. Apollinaris, a champion of the Nicene* doctrine of the Trinity*, was closely associated with Athanasius*. Like Athanasius, he taught a "Word*-flesh" Christology. When the Apollinarians spoke of "the man" (*kyriakos anthropos* or *dominicus homo*), they meant the Word in flesh, with the Word replacing a human soul.

Controversy became overt after 360, perhaps after a debate between Apollinaris and Diodore* of Tarsus. Epiphanius* reports that some of Apollinaris's followers spoke as though Christ brought his body from heaven. If Apollinaris was in fact involved, he would have meant that the flesh, being the flesh of the Word, was heavenly in its principle of animation. At the Council of Alexandria* (362), the christological problem was addressed, since those in attendance included representatives of both Apollinaris and Paulinus*, who insisted on the complete humanity of Christ. The Council's *Tome* to the Antiochenes* uses ambiguous language (Chap. 7), affirming that Christ did not have a body without soul or sense or mind; this double negative was compatible with both a Word*-flesh and a Word*-man Christology.

The dispute broke out again in Antioch, where there were already three rival bishops, when Apollinaris consecrated Vitalis, who shared his Word-flesh Christology, as a fourth bishop of Antioch (376/77). This political move prompted Epiphanius and then Basil* to gain a condemnation from Pope Damasus (377). Apollinaris and his Word-flesh Christology was further condemned by councils in Alexandria (378) and Antioch (379), probably at the Council of Constantinople* (381), and again in Rome (382). The theological answer was given during these years by Gregory* Nazianzen. EUGENE TESELLE

Apollos, a learned Jew from Alexandria who already had Christian loyalties but was more fully instructed in Ephesus (Acts 18:24–28). He was viewed as a leader by the church in Corinth (1 Cor. 1:12, 3:4). Many have supposed him to be the author of the Epistle to the Hebrews*.

Apologetics (from Gk *apologia,* "a defense"), defense of Christian beliefs with the aid of arguments thought to be convincing to the surrounding culture*.

Apologists refers in a wide Christian context to those throughout the history of the church who on the basis of reason* or other contemporary rhetorical strategies strove to defend Christian faith or practices from persecution or intellectual assault. For example, Thomas Aquinas* (1226–74) and C. S. Lewis* (1898–1963) were apologists of their respective eras.

Most commonly, scholars refer to "Apologists" as those earliest Christian thinkers who labored between the mid-2nd c. and 312 (when Constantine* ascended to power) to defend nascent Christianity from assault by both polemical criticism and violent persecution.

Early critics of Christianity, such as Celsus*, Lucian of Samasota, and Porphyry*, denounced the movement as an inferior philosophy and a "depraved and excessive superstition*," vilified Jesus as a deranged sorcerer, and characterized his followers as uneducated members of the lower class possessing, in the words of the Roman historian Tacitus, "the hatred of the human race." Beginning in mid 2nd c., however, Christian thinkers – including Quadratus, Aristides, Justin* Martyr, Tatian*, Athenagoras, Theophilus* of Antioch, Melito, Clement* of Alexandria, Tertullian*, Minucius Felix, and Origen* – began to employ the rhetorical conventions of the day to fashion thoughtful, reasoned responses to the misunderstandings, rumors, and condemnations that were leveled against early adherents of the faith. For example, in response to those who labeled Christianity an inferior philosophy, Justin Martyr described it as the most sublime of them all. Where despisers of the faith, perhaps under mistaken assumptions about sacramental practices, accused Christians of cannibalism and orgiastic behavior, Athenagoras defended Christian behavior as chaste and moral. In answer to the charge that Christians posed a threat to the Roman Empire, Tertullian insisted that the Empire prospered in direct correlation to the prayers of pious Christians.

WAYNE C. KANNADAY

Apophaticism, otherwise known as "negative theology," is a form of Christian theology that simultaneously attempts to express the transcendence* and immanence* of God. Regarding God's transcendence, apophaticism affirms the inadequacy of reason* or language* as a definitive means of knowing God; regarding God's immanence, apophaticism defines knowledge of God in terms of mystical* union. The differences notwithstanding, there are evident affinities between early Christian apophaticism and the speculative philosophies of Neoplatonism* and of the Jewish philosopher Philo* of Alexandria. Although aspects of apophatic thinking exist in Scripture and throughout early Christian literature, especially Gregory* of Nyssa's *Life of Moses,* its most sophisticated form is attributed to the 5th- to 6th-c. anonymous Christian thinker Dionysius* the Pseudo-Areopagite. The God–world relation, for Dionysius, is best understood in term of an *exitus/reditus* model. God's outpouring of Godself in creation (*exitus*) is the basis for cataphatic (positive, descriptive) statements about God; the return of all in union with God (*reditus*) requires *apophasis,* or the negation of all positive statements about God. Union with God is the result of a double negation, since God is beyond the opposition of positive and negative statements. Dionysius's apophaticism was influential in the medieval West through John* Scotus Eriugena's translation and is especially evident in the thought of Meister Eckhart*. In the 20th c, the Dionysian apophaticism is most evident in the work of the Eastern Orthodox theologian Vladimir Lossky* and the Roman Catholic theologian Jean-Luc Marion. **See also BUDDHISM AND CHRISTIANITY CLUSTER; CONVICTION; DAOISM CLUSTER; METAPHOR; MYSTICISM, MYSTICS; PARADOX; SYMBOLISM.**

ARISTOTLE PAPANIKOLAOU

Apophthegmata Patrum (Sayings of the fathers), a late-5th-c. anthology of aphorisms and anecdotes from the earliest monks of Egypt, the so-called desert fathers; considered a classic of Christian spirituality* for its wisdom on prayer*, asceticism*, and virtue. Originally in Greek, it survives in alphabetical and systematic forms. The alphabetical gathers c1,000 sayings under the names of 130 "abbas" (monks); the systematic arranges the same sayings under 21 thematic headings (e.g. humility, discernment). The systematic was translated into Latin during the 6th c. by Roman clerics and influenced medieval monasticism*. Ancient versions exist in Syriac, Coptic, Armenian, and Ethiopic.

J. WILLIAM HARMLESS, SJ

Apostasy, defection or revolt, specifically the abandonment of God, Christianity, or the true church.

Apostle (Gk "one sent forth"), an envoy or delegate; a messenger. In the NT, the term most often refers to the Twelve* and Paul* as "apostles of Jesus Christ" who have "seen" the risen Lord and have been directly commissioned by him to preach the gospel (1 Cor 15:3–11; Gal 1:15–16). Not everyone agreed with this largely Pauline definition. For example, the selection of Matthias (Acts 1:21–23) posited that one of the criteria for apostleship was having accompanied Jesus throughout his earthly ministry – possibly a source of much opposition to Paul (Gal. 1:1, 11–12 suggests that his opponents claimed that he did not have the proper credentials of an apostle, although Paul clearly saw himself as meeting all the necessary requirements, albeit in a special way). According to these NT passages about the Twelve and Paul, the "apostles of Jesus Christ" were men who, as Christ's representatives, authoritatively explained the revelation of God and exercised high authority in the church.

Yet the word "apostle" is used in other ways in the NT, e.g. when Paul refers twice to "apostles of the churches" (2 Cor. 8:23; Phil. 2:25) and when Hebrews mentions Jesus as "the apostle" whom we confess (3:1). In such cases (including Paul's dispute with the false "apostles" in 2 Cor 11–12), "apostle" is understood to entail a less specific church-leadership role. This includes the reference to both Andronicus and Junia* as "outstanding among the apostles" (Rom 16:7) that, for many contemporary scholars, points to women as apostles. (Other scholars, keeping with traditional interpretations, deny these interpretations by underscoring the possibility that the name "Junia" is an endearing diminutive for Junianus, a man's name, or that the phrase "outstanding *among* the apostles" might mean "outstanding *in the eyes of* the apostles"; see Junia.)

Throughout the history of the church, the term "apostle" has been used in a broader sense for missionaries who first brought the gospel to a region or a country, e.g. Ansgar*, the "Apostle of the North"; and Cyril* and Melodius, "Apostles of the Slavs," or for the founders of churches, such as the "African Apostles" Simon Kimbangu* in Congo* (both DRC and Congo-Brazzaville) and

John Maranke in Zimbabwe*. But most often, the title "apostle" is reserved for the Twelve and Paul. Missionaries or Christian leaders were sometimes recognized as "equal to the apostles," as Constantine* was; similarly, Nino* was recognized as "equal to the apostles and the enlightener of Georgia*." **See also TWELVE APOSTLES.** TERRY L. WILDER

Apostles' Creed, an early statement of the Christian faith, developed from the three questions that catechumens* were asked before baptism*: "Do you believe in God the Father almighty? . . . Do you believe in Jesus Christ? . . . Do you believe in the Holy Spirit?" (Apostolic* Tradition, c215, probably by Hippolytus* of Rome). The present text of the creed, based on the old Roman baptismal creed (3rd–4th c.), is the one spread during the time of Charlemagne* (8th c.) and adopted by the Western Church (c11^{th} c.). Most Protestant churches use the Apostles' Creed as the earliest confessional* statement.

Apostolic Church Order, a compilation of regulations governing church practice and discipline, ascribed to various apostles but actually originating in Egypt (c300).

Apostolic Constitution, the highest kind of decree issued by the pope of the Roman Catholic Church.

Apostolic Constitutions, a late-4th-c. eight-book compilation of canons* governing the clergy* and laity*, along with guidance for worship on various occasions. While claimed to have come from the apostles*, they are based largely on the Didache*, Papias*, and Hippolytus*, and have Arian* tendencies. **See also CHURCH ORDERS.**

Apostolicae Curae, the bull issued by Pope Leo XIII in 1896 declaring Anglican orders* to be null and void.

Apostolic Fathers, the title given to Clement* of Rome, Ignatius*, Hermas*, Polycarp*, Papias*, and the authors of the Epistle of Barnabas*, the Epistle to Diogetus*, 2 Clement*, and the Didache*.

Apostolicity and Apostolic Succession are clearly interconnected but not identical. "Apostolicity" denotes the continuity of the whole church with the apostles' witness to Christ. "Apostolic succession" refers to a specific sign or expression of such continuity.

Apostolicity is, according to the Nicene* Creed – "we believe in one holy catholic and apostolic church" – one of the fundamental marks* of the church, with a focus on continuity with the apostolic gospel lived out in the fullness of apostolic life. Apostolicity has four key dimensions: (1) "continuity" in faith* (*traditio*); (2) "succession" in ministries and structures (*successio*); (3) "incorporation" across time and space into the college of those who exercise (episcopal) oversight (*communio*); and (4) "mission" in joint service in the world (*missio*).

Apostolic succession relates primarily to succession in ministries and incorporation, although it also requires continuity in faith, apostolic life, and mission.

The NT presents the apostles (Peter*, James*, also the Twelve*) as eyewitnesses to Jesus' work, commissioned by the risen Christ, and leaders of the church. Paul's apostolic calling, while different in origin and character, had in practice the same purpose. The ministry of the apostles was unique, but their service had to be continued in the church.

Apostolicity took shape primarily during the first two centuries. Ignatius*, Tertullian*, Hegesippus*, and Irenaeus* played vital roles. Struggling largely against Gnostics* and their claims to special revelations, Irenaeus emphasized continuity with the apostles and their witness. Then apostolicity was attached mainly to the role of bishops in unbroken succession, a view generally upheld during the Middle Ages.

During the Reformation, there was in most cases a break in apostolic succession by the Protestants. Despite a commitment to doctrinal continuity and to the office of bishop, a crisis occurred when Roman Catholic bishops declined to ordain pastors for Protestant congregations. Later on a "pipeline theory" emphasizing the historic episcopate was developed within Anglicanism*.

Today, most agree that apostolicity is an essential mark of the church, yet Christian traditions diverge on the contents and role of episcopal succession. For the Roman Catholic Church, apostolicity requires not only historic continuity, but also communion with the bishop of Rome. Within Orthodoxy, historic continuity is coupled with an apostolicity of the church as a whole. Reformation and post-Reformation churches are concerned primarily with continuity in faith and doctrine. In parts of the neo-Charismatic* Movement, "pragmatism" may appear to undermine such continuity.

Ecumenical dialogue manifests possibilities of convergence on apostolicity and apostolic succession. For such dialogue, the following convictions are essential: apostolicity is, at its core, living continuity with the apostolic witness to Christ and, thus, with Christ; it is a mark of the church in its totality, which relates to its faith and life as a whole; it requires visualization through outward signs, but can also be maintained in periods when some of its signs have been lost; while avoiding juridical approaches, each church should be open to embracing as many signs of apostolic continuity as possible; and apostolicity is best expressed in and through Communion*. OLA TJØRHOM

Apostolic Tradition, an early church order with directives for appointment to the ministry, the reception of converts, community meals, and prayer. Often ascribed to Hippolytus* of Rome (c215), it is probably a composite work, developed from the 2nd to the 4th c. **See also CHURCH ORDERS.**

Aqedah See SACRIFICE OF ISAAC: THE AQEDAH.

Aquila, a Jew, born in Pontus, who with his wife, Priscilla*, lived for a time in Rome but left for Corinth when Claudius required all Jews to depart (Acts 18; cf. 1 Cor 16:19; Rom 16:3).

Aquila, Version of, Greek translation of the HB (completed c140) by a native of Pontus, first a convert to Christianity and then a proselyte* to Judaism. It was very literal so as to counteract Christian proof texts based on the Septuagint*.

Aquinas, Thomas (1226–74), theologian. Born in the kingdom of Naples into minor aristocracy, he was enrolled at the age of 5 in the school at the great Benedictine monastery of Monte Cassino. At 13 he went to the University of Naples, one of the earliest centers of Aristotelian* philosophy and an outpost of the polyglot culture at the court of the Hohenstaufen emperor Frederick II. There he met and joined the Dominican* friars, recently founded chiefly to cope with the form of Gnostic* dualism* characteristic of the Albigensians or Catharists*, who were widespread in the church, especially in France and Northern Italy. He studied first in Paris, then in Cologne, where he was taught principally by Albert* the Great (1193 [or 1206]–1280), the German Dominican friar who was among the first to introduce Aristotle's ethics, metaphysics, and philosophical anthropology into Christian thought. Aquinas lectured in Paris (1252–59; again in 1269–72), returning to Italy between these two periods to administer courses for student friars, first in Rome, then in Naples, and to act as theological consultant to Pope Urban IV and later to Pope Clement IV. Throughout his career, he composed commentaries on Scripture, Aristotle*, and Dionysius* the Pseudo-Areopagite, and wrote his *Summa contra Gentiles* and his *Summa Theologiae*. The latter he left unfinished as a result of the experience he had on December 6, 1273: "All that I have written seems to me like straw compared to what has now been revealed to me." Though fit enough to obey a summons to attend the Second Council of Lyon due to begin on May 7, 1274, he fell ill on the way and died on March 7, 1274.

While often regarded as an "Aristotelian," positively by some, negatively by others (such as Luther*), Aquinas seems to have been more concerned, especially in his second spell in Paris, to mediate between colleagues who looked to Augustine* as their master and some of the hotheads in the arts faculty (themselves, of course, clergy) who were carried away by enthusiasm for what they took to be the self-sufficient wisdom* of the ancient Greeks. The "Augustinians" were not comforted by the knowledge that Aristotle was coming to the church after centuries in which his works had been studied and commented on by Islamic scholars.

In 1277 (after Aquinas's death) a composite list of 219 theses was condemned by the bishop and theologians in Paris as prejudicial to the faith. While directed chiefly against "Averroists" in the arts faculty (those who allegedly read Aristotle* in the light of the commentaries of the Islamic* philosopher Abu'l-Walid Ibn Rushd [1126–98], Averroes* in Latin), some of Aquinas's views (perhaps as many as 16 of the theses) were included, as his contemporaries realized. These bear, one way or another, chiefly on Aquinas's proposal that (1) since matter is pure potentiality having no act of its own whatsoever and (2) since matter is the radical principle of individuation and multiplication in a species, there is only one substantial form in every composite. This arcane-sounding doctrine implies that the corporeal, vegetative, sensitive, and intellective forms predicated of the human being exist simultaneously in time in the embryo. In this way, the idea that the embryo becomes "intellectual" or "rational" and therefore "human" at a late stage is excluded. More worryingly still, Aquinas's view seemed to mean that the body of Christ in the tomb, separated from the soul*, would not be divine: there was no corporeal form antecedent to the other forms that would ensure the identity of Christ's body on the cross and in the tomb.

During his lifetime, Aquinas faced this objection many times in his works: for him the dead body of Christ remained hypostatically united to the divine person of the Word and therefore the "same body." However, adopting Aristotle's doctrine of substantial form obviously had controversial implications.

The *Summa contra Gentiles* (probably not his title), composed in 1259 64, is Aquinas's most accessible comprehensive exposition of Christian doctrine. A large part exists in his own handwriting, with his cancellations, revisions, and corrections. It was not taught in the classroom, nor did it originate there. Rather, it reads as the mature theologian's most personal attempt to expound Christian doctrine: Books I–III deal with truths about God that can be known by human reason*; Book IV with truths about divine things that can be known only by revelation*. If not entirely "against the Gentiles," Aquinas is nevertheless concerned to argue against the theological errors (as he thinks) of "the Mohammedans and the pagans," but since they accept neither the OT nor the NT "we must have recourse to natural reason, to which all are forced to give their assent" (I, 2). The first three books frequently cite Aristotle and, less explicitly, the Persian Islamic philosopher Avicenna* (Ibn Sina, c980–1037). Aquinas suspects some Muslim and pagan thinkers of denying that creatures have an active role in the production of natural effects, as if God did everything: far from glorifying God, this denial of real agency in creatures only detracts from the perfection of divine power (III. 69). Aquinas is deeply concerned to exclude the idea that the same effect may be "attributed to a natural cause and to divine power in such a way that it is partly done by God, and partly by the natural agent" – as if divine causality and human freedom were somehow in competition (III, 70).

The *Summa Theologiae* (again not his title), his most famous work, begun in 1266 when he was teaching young friars in Rome and left unfinished, was composed explicitly for "the training of beginners" (for their instructors, perhaps, more than for them personally) to put an end to the "boredom and muddle in their thinking" by which they were afflicted (Prologue). The first 43 questions of the first part deal with God, one nature and three persons; the remaining 75 with creation*, including angels*, human beings, and how the world is governed. The second part deals with the moral and spiritual life of the human being, including emotion, virtue, sin*, law*, and grace*, and, in detail, the three theological virtues* of faith*, hope*, and charity [love*], then the four cardinal virtues of prudence, justice*, courage, and temperance. The first 59 questions of the third part extend from the doctrine of the Incarnation* to the Resurrection*; the remaining 30 deal with sacrament*, baptism*, Eucharist*, and penance*.

The first part includes the famous "Five Ways" (question 2), Aquinas's "proofs of the existence of God*," followed by the much lengthier and more complicated exposition of the doctrine of God in the light of God's self-revelation as "I Am" (Exod 3:14).

Aquinas, it is now generally thought, regarded the second part as the center and most original element of the whole project: an attempt to replace the existing confessors' manuals – lists of sins based on the Ten Commandments – with a far more sophisticated portrait of the moral life. The third part, the "consummation of the whole project," deals with Christ the Savior, who "showed us in Himself the way of truth by which it is possible for us to come through by resurrection to the blessedness of immortal life" (Prologue). FERGUS KERR, OP

Aramaic, the language of the Aramaeans (late 11th c. BCE), then of the Assyrians (from the 8th c. BCE), became a lingua franca of the Middle East (7th–6th c. BCE), surviving especially in Palestine and Syria even into Greek and Roman times. Aramaic had replaced Hebrew as the language of common Jewish people (from the 6th c. BCE). Thus parts of Daniel* and Ezra* are written in Aramaic, as are the Babylonian and Jerusalem Talmuds. Jesus and his followers probably spoke Aramaic. Syriac* is an Aramaic dialect written with a different script.

Archbishop, a bishop with jurisdiction over a province*, equivalent to a "metropolitan*." At the time of Justinian*, "archbishop" was synonymous with "patriarch*," a bishop with jurisdiction over a larger region.

Archdeacon, the chief deacon, appointed by the bishop and carrying out specified tasks in the whole or part of a diocese.

Archdiocese, the diocese over which the archbishop* of a province* exercises jurisdiction.

Archimandrite, in the Greek Church, the superior over a monastery or over several monasteries (abbot* in the West).

Architecture, Church. See HIEROTOPY, THE CREATION OF CHRISTIAN SACRED SPACES.

Archpriest, chief priest* of a diocese*, often acting in the place of the bishop in his absence.

Argentina

Colonial Time. Christianity arrived in Argentina with European explorers (1516) and colonization by Spain (1580, in Buenos Aires). During this period, the challenge for Roman Catholics was the conversion* of the "Indians" and the appropriation of territory over which the Roman Catholic Church would have exclusive authority. Native people were nomadic and dispersed in lands without mineral deposits.

Without specific directions, the Jesuits* established in the northwest special kinds of "reductions*" – egalitarian settlements where numerous natives lived with Jesuit clergy following strict rules of Christian life (but no forced labor). In the Jesuit reductions, the Tupi and Guaraní people received a training unique on the continent, combining religious, social, economic, and military training. The Franciscans, with their more festive Christianity, consolidated the development of the church in the northeast. The expulsion of the Jesuits from the continent (1768) shattered an important part of colonial Christianity in Argentina. The Argentine dioceses were viewed as "marginal and miserable," as compared with those in Mexico* or Peru*. Thus the exploitation of "Indians" by Christians and the defense of Indians' rights by other Christians were in tension from the beginning and remained a fundamental contradiction through the centuries.

The 19th-c. pro-independence intellectual revolution, headed by local leaders and priests who opposed Spanish Christendom, rejected bishops and superiors of religious orders (who were often imprisoned or expelled). The revolution sought to create a Christianity without ties to Spain or the Vatican, and with very limited relations to local political authorities. In 1813 the "revolution" destroyed the instruments of torture, freed black slaves, ended the Inquisition*, and gave new meanings to Christian symbols, putting them at the service of the "revolutionary cause." The local Virgins became patronesses of the patriotic armies. With numerous priests as representatives at the Assembly, the "Southern United Provinces" proclaimed their independence (1816).

Secularization, understood to be the limitation of ecclesiastical power, continued with the 1821–22 reforms that closed convents, established norms for the designation of monastic authorities, fixed a minimum number of years for initiation into the monastic life (to avoid coercion into monastic life), and expropriated the Roman Catholic Church's economic resources, transferring them to the government. The autonomy of the Church was emphasized in worship services. Laws tolerating Protestants were passed (1825). Years later Rome sent a diplomatic mission to establish relations with the developing confederation. The end of colonial Christendom* was therefore marked by religious orders without authorized superiors, priests occupied with political responsibilities, and a growing differentiation between religious and secular spheres of life.

The Rise of the Republic of Argentina. The struggle for independence slowly gave birth to new states in the old viceroyalty of Rio de la Plata, although their borders and status were often imprecise. Christianity faced a new challenge as it contributed to building these nations, developing and affirming a national identity that gave people in each nation a sense of ownership and united them. Consequently, colonial Christianity was replaced by multiple national Christianities that in each case embodied a "credible" and "faithful" tension between strengthening its symbolic ties with the new nations and supporting a community that, beyond national borders, has a universal mission.

The immigration between 1870 and 1930 diversified Christianity. While the "Latin" majority (Spanish, Italian, and French) identified themselves with Roman Catholicism, immigrants from other nations (English, German, Russian, Ukrainian, Norwegian, Swedish, Polish, etc.) established numerous Protestant congregations, some Orthodox ones, as well as Jewish communities.

In the 1880s, the Argentine liberal state strove to "build a Christian nation," even as it weakened the Catholic institutions by relegating them to the "private domain." The civil registries (births, marriages, deaths) and cemeteries had been controlled by the Roman Catholic Church; now, the state nationalized them. The numerous religious schools became a massive public school system where education was free and religion was taught outside the regular class schedule. To "modernize" the teaching, the state created numerous teachers' colleges and brought Protestant teachers from North America to help develop and implement innovative

Christian educational practices (see Lancastrian Schools).

The vision of unlimited progress gave the state the freedom to extend to all the rights of citizenship, including universal and obligatory secret ballot in all elections (1912). In 1916, the liberal opposition (Unión Cívica Radical) won the presidential election (for the first time since 1880). But the impact of the Great War on the population of European immigrants – many thousands of male immigrants returned to their respective countries to enroll in national armies – resulted in pervasive disillusionment. A deep spiritual quest in the midst of so much death and desolation spread broadly through Christianity at the very time the Argentine state was trying to slow down the institutional growth of the Roman Catholic Church; e.g. the apostolic nuncio was expelled (1924–30, as had happened in 1884–1900).

Christianity, Nation, and Catholic Argentina. An extraordinary capitalist expansion took place between 1880 and 1930. Liberalism promised a new heaven and a new earth. In Buenos Aires, booming urbanization concentrated almost a third of all Argentines around the capital. The 1929–30 economic crisis struck at the heart of the capitalist model of the accumulation of wealth and threatened the governability and civic life of the nation. The first coup d'état (September 6, 1930) marked the beginning of the militarization of Argentina. Until almost the end of the 20th c., the Argentine Armed Forces dominated religious, cultural, social, and political life and maintained discrete links with the conservative clergy, including Father Julio Meinvielle*.

This collapse of liberalism and its promises opened the doors to its critics, including an emerging Catholic movement that sought to integrate national identity and Catholicism; to support an interventionist state; to model social justice along the lines of the church's social teachings; to reinforce social harmony; to collaborate in anti-communist and anti-liberal campaigns, because of its suspicion of democracy and of "corrupt" political leadership; and to promote the message of traditionalist Integrist* Catholicism. This vision of "Argentine Catholicism" progressively emerged and became the accepted Catholic culture for most of civil and political society.

This Integrist movement went through a long process of cultural impregnation without a direct relation to institutional Catholicism (attendance at Mass was never more than 10%). Yet it achieved a slow but steady catholicization of society and of its public spaces, at the same time that they were nationalized, or even militarized. Catholicism was an enduring but active "symbolic capital" available for use as needed from time to time, so much so that, since 1930, one could speak of Argentine society as in "natural continuity" with the "true Catholic tradition of the nation." Accordingly, Catholicism was an integral part of the "native values" and the "Argentine nationality" that was not to be contaminated by "foreign" ideologies.

This Catholic hegemony influenced other religious communities. Jews, Protestants, Muslims, and Spiritualists acknowledged the privileged legal status of the Catholic Church in the state, even as they affirmed their pluralistic views of the religious situation and advocated the separation of religion and state.

Argentine Christian groups can be understood only in their multiple relations with other social and political segments. They are not the entire focus of Argentine social history, but ignoring them would lead to major misinterpretations. Many Catholics "formed in" Integrist Catholicism occupy (and will occupy?) leadership positions and have important responsibilities in the state, the government and its departments, the universities, the unions, and sociopolitical movements, as happened in the wake of the 1930 military, religious, and business coup of General Uriburu.

Populist Christianity, promoted by the Peronist culture (1940s–1950s), with broad popular support, challenged institutionalized and clerical Integrist Catholicism. The clash between these two conceptions of Catholicism reached a critical point in 1955 when military airplanes (in rebellion against Peron) bombarded the center of the city of Buenos Aires, killing more than 300 people, with bombs inscribed "Christ Conquers"; that night, in retaliation, Peronists desecrated and set on fire the richest Catholic churches of Buenos Aires. The civil, military, and religious coup that deposed President Peron (1955) opened a new period of conflict. Both the military proclamations and those of the opposition cited papal encyclicals, church documents, and/or biblical texts. The government (1966–70) of the devout Catholic General Onganía with his project of moral reconstruction of the Christian world received radical criticism from the Roman Catholic Church, as did the Movement of Priests for the Third World, as well as the ISAL (Iglesia y Sociedad en America Latina) and its networks in slums, factories, schools, and universities. The Christian reforms of the 1960s and 1970s were shaped by memories of primitive Christianity, institutional changes, the Cuban Revolution, and the presence of acknowledged militants such as Margarita Moyano* Llerena among the "faithful and oppressed people." Even the military political radicalism of the 1960s and 1970s was partly rooted in affinities between Christianity and revolution, between Christian ethics and the spirit of guerrilla warfare.

During the 1976 dictatorship, in which 30,000 persons were arrested and disappeared, others were persecuted and exiled, and all lived in a culture of fear, there were bishops, priests, and Christian leaders who supported the terrorism of the state. The state controlled religious activities by registering worship services of all religions (less so for Catholic Masses), by offering scholarships to seminarians, and by subsidizing Catholic bishops. Meanwhile numerous Christians were murdered, tortured, or detained, "disappeared," or fled into exile, because of their religious, political, and social commitments. The murder of Catholic Bishop Angelelli* (1976), resulting from a conflict with the military and the ensuing silence of the episcopate, exemplifies the different positions. Other Christians joined the Ecumenical Movement for Human* Rights and the Permanent Assembly for Human Rights, making public the experiences and suffering of the victims.

For instance, the 1980 Nobel Peace Prize was given to Adolfo Pérez Esquivel, an Argentine Christian, for his struggle in defense of human rights and his denunciation of the crimes of military dictatorships throughout the continent. An architect, he became a pacifist in the early 1970s, founding the Ecumenical Movement for Peace and Justice (1973). He was imprisoned and tortured by the Argentine dictatorial government (1976–78) but continued his effort to develop humanitarian organizations, becoming a member of the Service for Peace and Justice and of the UN Permanent Assembly for Human Rights.

Christianity, Democracy, Deregulation, and the "Religious Market." The military defeat following the attempt to gain control of the Falklands Islands (1982) led to a removal of the military from political power and to the consolidation of democracy (1983). As part of the process to rebuild a more just society, the crimes of the dictators were denounced by many Christian leaders (including Pastor Bonino), and those responsible for the repression were judged and given prison sentences.

José Míguez Bonino (b1924), a Methodist theologian and pastor, the only Protestant Latin American observer at Vatican* II, and president of the World* Council of Churches (1975), participated in the struggle to defend human rights and contributed to the creation of the Comisión Nacional sobre la Desaparición de Personas (National Commission on the Disappearance of Persons), which was responsible for denouncing the crimes of the military dictatorship of 1976–83. He taught at the most prestigious universities around the world and received a doctorate *honoris causa* from the Free University of Amsterdam (1980).

In 1989, for the first time in its history, Argentina changed the government's ruling party by democratic means. But the shift in economic models brought about privatization, deregulation, a crisis of the middle class, indebtedness, and the transformation of the welfare state into a penal state, resulting in massive poverty and urban unemployment unprecedented in the 20th c.

Christianity was transformed along with the social and political life of the country. Because widespread poverty* was and is the primary concern both in the world of the poor and in civil society, a Christianity of action (especially in Catholicism) that looked to the state and to the upper classes to address social problems became a Christianity of action that sought to create social and spiritual popular movements that would "proclaim the Kingdom* of God." On the other hand, religion underwent a process of "emotionalization": the emotional community has taken precedence over the dogmatic community. Very diverse renewal movements emphasize healing, addressing spiritual issues (the care* of souls), speaking in tongues (glossolalia*), spontaneous dancing during worship, entering trances, seeking a direct relation with the sacred with little or no institutional mediation, together with a modern use of media*. All of these contribute to renewing the "enthusiasm" of thousands of people who participate in Charismatic* Christian groups, often several at the same time.

Other Christian groups, which emphasize the reaffirmation of Christian identity, struggle in the public sphere with (and against) the state and civil society for the symbolic control of private life (against the use of condoms, against laws concerning reproductive health, and against teaching about sexuality in the schools). They present their conception of "Christian morality" as what should be the morality of society as a whole. To their nationalism, they add preaching against corrupt political leadership. The creation of a three-way "Argentine dialogue" among the government, the UN Development Program, and the Catholic Church in early 2002 "in order to save the nation from decadence" shows the long-standing conceptual and political ties between religious and political powers.

There is a blend of complementarity and competition between Christianity and civil society and the state (see Church and State Relations Cluster: In Latin America: Argentina). In a time of Christian pluralism and religious change, accompanied by a process of Catholic deregulation, many Christians do not become members of the church they attend or hold strong personal beliefs. In this context, Christian institutions gain credibility through intense social activity, presenting themselves as "civil society," the "third sector" (*le tiers état*) engaged in social volunteerism. Recent surveys show that the Catholic Church is the most credible institution in Argentina, even as Pentecostals*, Charismatics*, and Protestants strive for space among the people. The Pentecostals do not ask for separation of church and state; they want the same privileges as the Catholics. Meanwhile, other Protestant churches advocate a clear separation of church and state in a democratic and just civil society, as well as broader human rights, including laws guaranteeing freedom of religion (which still do not exist in Argentina).

In contrast with the situation in other Latin American countries, in Argentina Christian political parties have not prospered; e.g. Christian Democracy and Pentecostal political parties have failed to become a significant political force.

Statistics: Population (2000): 37 million (M). Christians, 34.4 M, 92.9% (Roman Catholics, 33.7 M; Protestants, 2.3 M; Pentecostals/ Charismatics, 2 M); nonreligious, 1.1 M, 3.1%; Muslims, 0.7 M, 2.0%; Jews, 0.5 M, 1.3%. (Based on *World Christian Encyclopedia*, 2001.)

FORTUNATO MALLIMACI

Arianism, term applied in the 4th c. to any view denying the Nicene* doctrine that the second person of the Trinity* is of the *same* essence or substance as the Father (*homoousios*). Some scholars refer to this movement as "non-Nicene." For Arians generally (including Arius*), the One incarnate in Jesus was the Creator/Logos in person, unimpeded by a human soul (since Jesus did not have a human soul*, as Apollinaris* also taught later).

Since the Nicene doctrine seemed to make the persons identical, the alternative was to emphasize God's threeness, but in significantly different ways.

1. Arius* held that the Father alone is "God" in the proper sense. The only begotten Son is the "God" and creator of everything else, but was himself "created out of nothing" by the Father's will. This extreme Arianism emphasized that the Son is "unlike" the Father in essence, as Eunomius* further underscored.
2. A moderate "Homoian"* form of Arianism, more widespread during the 4th c., denied that the Son is "created from nothing," asserted that the Son is "like" (*homoios*) the Father, but refused to say that they are "of the same essence."
3. The "Homoiousian*" position labeled "Semi-Arian" by Epiphanius* affirmed that the Son is "*like* in essence" (but not *the same* as) the Father, in order to affirm God's threeness; this view became one component of the "orthodox" view of the Trinity.

While Arianism is usually described theologically, it had political overtones from the start. When Constantine gained power in the East (324), he found the church divided over the Trinity and thus convened the Council of Nicaea* (325). Although the Nicene* Creed became the official doctrine of the Roman Empire, its opponents, including Arius, were tolerated. At the Council of Antioch* (341), the Eastern bishops, without denying the Nicene doctrine, produced other creeds. After Constantius became sole emperor in 353, Arianism in its moderate Homoian form gained official approval at a series of councils culminating in the Council of Constantinople* in 360. Ulfila*, the bishop of the Goths*, was present at this council and adopted its moderate Arian doctrine; as a result, the Goths and other peoples (including Lombards* and Vandals*) influenced by them, who became a major influence in North African and European politics, were Arian for several centuries.

In protest against Emperor Constantius, the Homoiousians, or "Semi-Arians," kept the Eastern emphasis on threeness but were willing to say that the three were "*like* in essence." The death of Constantius and the rise of Julian* the Apostate, who removed all doctrinal sanctions, made a resolution possible. At the Council of Alexandria* in 362, the Nicene party made peace with the Semi-Arians, and the position developed by the Cappadocians* owes something to both.

The Eastern emperor Valens championed Arianism until he was killed in the battle of Adrianople (378), ironically by the Arian Goths. His successor, Theodosius*, imposed the Nicene doctrine throughout his realm, and the Council of Constantinople* (381) adopted the Niceno*-Constantinopolitan Creed, which became the standard of orthodoxy. Arian sympathies continued in the court in Milan, where Justina was regent for the young Valentinian II; yet the bishop Ambrose* was victorious in a dispute with the Arians over their use of one of the basilicas. In Constantinople, however, Gothic mercenaries were permitted to use several churches, because they were an important guarantee of stability.

After the Gothic invasions of Western Europe, Arians ruled in Italy, Gaul, Spain, and North Africa; thus Arians converted other Germanic tribes, especially the Franks, Burgundians, and Lombards. The Gothic Bible and liturgy were central to their culture; a magnificent Gothic codex containing half of the Gospels is preserved in Uppsala. In Ravenna, Arian architecture includes the baptistery and the Church of San Apollinare Nuovo.

Gothic rulers usually permitted Latin speakers to maintain their own Bible, liturgy, and doctrine. It was also assumed that they would follow Roman law while the Germanic peoples would follow their own traditions, which were soon written down in Latin. As the invaders began to speak the vernacular Latin of the time and assimilated various Roman customs, they became more susceptible to conversion from Arianism to Catholicism.

The role of queens in converting their husbands to Christianity and then to Catholicism (Nicene* Christianity) should not be overlooked. Going into new lands because of their marriages, these women took their chaplains with them and instructed their children and others, even when the kings maintained older customs. Clovis* the Frank converted to Catholicism (in this case from polytheism) under the influence of Clotilde (496); he was followed by Reccared* in Spain (587). The Vandals in North Africa remained Arian until the Byzantine Conquest (534). The Lombards, who invaded Italy (late 6th c.), gradually became Catholic over the next hundred years. After this, Arianism had no institutional continuity.

During centuries of Roman Catholic orthodoxy, the term "Arian" was used to condemn various deviations from the usual views of the Trinity and Christ. In the 17th and 18th c., it was applied to any number of views that denied the full divinity of Jesus Christ, including those of Milton*, Newton*, and Clarke. With the growth of Unitarianism* as a movement, "Arianism" became the standard designation for non-Trinitarian Christianity. **See also GOTHS; HISTORY OF CHRISTIANITY CLUSTER: IN AFRICA: NORTH AFRICA; ITALY; LOMBARDS; SPAIN; VANDALS.**

EUGENE TESELLE and RICHARD VAGGIONE

Ariminum and Seleuceia, Councils of, the Western and Eastern synods called by Constantius (359) to resolve the Arian* controversy. Under imperial pressure, both councils produced Arianizing creeds (see Arianism), which were reconciled in the Council of Constantinople* (360).

Aristides. See APOLOGISTS.

Aristotle and Christianity. The discovery of Aristotle's "lost" works by Roman Catholic scholars in Spain (12th c.) was an event of enormous significance for the development of Christian thinking from the late medieval period onward. In the centuries following the fall of the Western Roman Empire, most of Greek philosophy was forgotten by the Latin-speaking clerics and scholars of the West. Some of Plato's* ideas remained in circulation as a result of Augustine's* teachings, but for most Christians, Aristotle was little more than a legendary sage. Of all his voluminous writing, only six essays on logic (the *Organon*) remained extant (in a 7th-c. Latin translation by the Christian courtier Boethius*). The remainder of Aristotle's work – thousands of pages on metaphysics*, natural sciences*, psychology*, politics*, ethics*, and aesthetics* – passed into the hands of Greek-speaking clerics in the Byzantine* Empire and, through translations by Syriac*-speaking Christians, into the possession of Arab and Persian scholars in the burgeoning empires of the Muslim world.

The Byzantines preserved these treasures, but the Arabs and Persians did more: they commented critically on them, adapted them for practical purposes, and developed their own schools of neo-Aristotelian philosophy. As a result, when the vanished works appeared to the astonished eyes of Christian invaders in 12th-c. Spain, they were written in Arabic and accompanied by extensive commentaries by Muslim and Jewish scholars – famous thinkers like Ibn Sina (Avicenna*), Ibn Rushd (Averroes*), and Ibn Maimon (Maimonides*), all of them devoted monotheists. All that was needed to make this material available to Christian Europe was to translate it into Latin, a task accomplished by early-13th-c. teams of Christian, Muslim, and Jewish translators working in Spain, Provence, and Sicily.

The works of Aristotle and the commentators held an irresistible appeal to Western Europeans, because they were sources not only of ancient wisdom but also of modern scientific knowledge and Europe had long lagged behind the Muslim world in its general level of material and cultural development. This very fact made some Christian leaders wary of the new learning's explosive potential.

Aristotle's philosophy resonated in some ways with the worldview of the Abrahamic religions. The Greek sage viewed the universe as a single entity, harmoniously integrated, purposeful, and comprehensible. He believed in one God*, immaterial, eternal, perfect, and unchangeable, and in an immortal human soul*. Aristotle defined humans as social beings, capable of reason and of moral choice, whose highest calling was to live ethical lives. And, like Jewish, Christian, and Muslim thinkers, he viewed politics* as a branch of ethics* rather than a science of power.

But these similarities masked serious differences that worried the religious authorities in charge of Europe's new universities. Aristotle had been a pagan, after all. The natural universe, in his view, is eternal, not divinely created. His God, more a principle than a person, bears little resemblance to the biblical Father and Creator who, transcending time and space, demonstrates his concern for humanity by manifesting his will in history*. Neither the justice*-seeking YHWH of the Jews nor the messianic Savior of the Christians, Aristotle's Unmoved Mover is a passive entity, contained by the universe, and conscious only of itself. And what of Jesus Christ and his role in salvation? For Aristotle, salvation* is unnecessary, because the human will* is not imprisoned by sin* and does not require liberation* through the instrumentalities of divine grace*. Aristotle considered the soul immortal, but since he identified it with human vitality and reason, he had no conception of bodily resurrection*, divine judgment*, heaven*, or hell*.

Clearly, some of these ideas were at odds with traditional Christianity. But Jewish and Muslim thinkers had already demonstrated that Aristotle's theological "errors" could be "corrected" and his philosophical and scientific views adapted to make them palatable to biblical monotheists. The more serious problem, perhaps, was the clash between the philosopher's social attitudes and those of earlier Christian thinkers like Augustine and Jerome*. Traumatized by the fall of the Roman Empire, many Catholics had embraced a version of Christianity stressing the inevitability of sin and earthly suffering, the defects of human reason, the utter dependence of the faithful on God and the church, and the hope of a better world beyond the grave. Aristotle, by contrast, pictured humans as capable of mastering their passions, gaining true understanding of the natural world, and improving their lives by cultivating their potential for reason and moderation. The ideals of asceticism*, chastity*, saintliness*, and worldly withdrawal, so important for the development of Christian sensibilities in the monastic* age, took a back seat to the exhilarating potentialities of rational thought.

Little wonder that, following an initial burst of enthusiasm for the rediscovery of ancient wisdom, a council of bishops (1210) ruled that "neither Aristotle's books of natural philosophy nor commentaries [on them] are to be read publicly or privately in Paris, and this under penalty of excommunication." The ban, extended in 1215, permitted the study of Aristotle's logical books at the University of Paris, Europe's premier center of theological learning, but prohibited the reading of all his philosophical and scientific works. Nevertheless, almost from its issuance, the ban proved ineffectual.

Why so? One reason was that Western Europe was experiencing an unprecedented rebirth of economic, social, and cultural activity – the "medieval Renaissance" – which gave Aristotle's work new relevance. Why should rational inquiry be considered dangerous to religious faith*? It might, in fact, prove to be a way of strengthening Christianity at a time of accelerating social change. A growing confidence in human reason and interest in the natural world inspired intellectuals of the Franciscan* order, such as Oxford University's Roger Bacon*, to investigate the relationship between Aristotelian science and Catholic theology. At the same time, representatives of the Dominican* order found Aristotle's metaphysical teachings, emphasizing the unity and harmony of the universe, invaluable in combating dualistic heresies like Catharism*, which pictured a world rent by unending conflict between the principles of good and evil.

By the 1250s, Aristotle's entire body of work was *required* reading at the University of Paris, and a great debate erupted about its true meaning for Christianity. The participants in this debate – all churchmen and, by now, all Aristotelians of one sort or another – constituted a galaxy of great minds. The beloved Franciscan and future saint Bonaventure* represented the more conservative scholars; the liberals' spokesman was the greatest genius of the age, Thomas Aquinas*; and the radicals were led by a daring Belgian cleric, Siger* de Brabant. Their battle, although civil for the most part, was stormy. Alarmed by the rise of radical ideas among the liberal arts scholars, the bishop of Paris issued a series of condemnations purportedly aimed at Siger's ideas, but also inculpating some of Aquinas's teachings. The ultimate winner of the debate, from the perspective of the Catholic Church, was Aquinas, who was said to have "baptized" Aristotle, although his opponents accused him of Aristotelianizing Christianity. In 1323, the "angelic doctor" was canonized by Rome.

The Thomist* synthesis united Aristotle's ideas about the unity, coherence, and developmental principles of the universe (the universal movement of all things from potentiality to actuality) with the Christian principles of divine transcendence*, salvation*, and love*. Insisting that the natural laws of science and society reflected God's creative will, Thomism constituted the first important attempt to reconcile science* with Christian theology and ethics, and opened the doors of European universities to a great burst of scientific enterprise. But the debate was far from over. Thomism was soon attacked – again, in the name of Aristotle – by Franciscan theologians like Duns* Scotus and William of Ockham*, who insisted that the laws of nature could not circumscribe God's freedom and that human knowledge of the universe must always be provisional. Two centuries later, Martin Luther* and other leaders of the Protestant Reformation bitterly attacked both Aquinas and Aristotle, but neo-Aristotelian theology revived in the works of 20th-c. Catholic thinkers like Jacques Maritain*, Teilhard* de Chardin, and Bernard Lonergan.

RICHARD E. RUBENSTEIN

Arius (d336), theologian. Libyan by birth, Arius was a presbyter of the Alexandrian church, excommunicated by Bishop Alexander* in 318. Popular and episcopal support forced Constantine* to make his teaching a central issue at Nicaea* in 325. Arius was condemned for heresy* and exiled but was being rehabilitated when he died suddenly in 336. He was perceived by Athanasius* and others as the source of a heresy called "Arianism*." Actually Arianism was a wider stream of thought. Few "Arians" considered him personally authoritative. His few surviving writings make it difficult to discern what was personal in his theology.

RICHARD VAGGIONE

Armageddon, the place of the final battle on the day of Judgment* (Rev. 16:16); derivatively, any decisive battle of unusual size or consequence.

Armagh, the see of the archbishop of Ireland, associated by tradition with Patrick*.

Armenia. Christianity was introduced in the 2nd c. in Southern Armenia by Syriac missionaries from Mesopotamia. The Syriac tradition of Edessa* left a lasting stamp on the Armenian language, liturgy, and church discipline. The official Christianization (c314; traditional date, 301) of the kingdom by Gregory* the Illuminator, opened Northern Armenia to the influence of Cappadocia, leading to a gradual prevalence of the Greek element in the shaping of Armenian ecclesiastical culture. The Armenian alphabet, invented by Mashtots* (c405), made possible the translation of the Bible, Syriac and Greek patristic writings, and the development of original literature in numerous genres. Mashtots's endeavor also consolidated the Christian identity of Armenia even as its statehood was dismantled. Thus, in its eastern part subjugated to Persia, several generations of Armenians resisted Zoroastrian persecutions of Christianity between 428 and 575.

After the long debates provoked by Eutyches'* teaching and the ensuing Council of Chalcedon*, the Armenian Church rejected both extreme Monophysitism* and the imperial doctrine at the Council of Duin (553/55) and, in following centuries, elaborated an autonomous christological theory, strictly following Cyril* of Alexandria (see Miaphysite). Armenians expressed Christ's integral humanity in various ways but avoided designating Christ's divinity and humanity as *two* comparable entities belonging to the same abstract category of *nature*.

The Arab Conquest (699–701), although bringing new persecutions, transformed the catholicos* into the legal chief of the nation, directly responsible to the Islamic authority. Hereby, the Armenian Apostolic Church acquired a new civil role in Armenian society, maintained also under Turcoman rule (from the 15th c.). In periods of weakened Muslim power, the Armenian princes, relying on the moral weight of the Church, proved able to reunify Armenian lands and sometimes to renovate the ancient kingship. They promoted cenobitic* monasticism on their estates through protection and gifts. The monasteries became centers of economic development, learning, and art (illuminated books). Fortified, they formed a coordinated net of defense during the Seljuk, Mongol, Turcoman, and Kurdish invasions, preventing the depopulation of the country. Yet these invasions are at the origin of the vast Armenian diaspora, further stimulated by the persecutions of Christians in the Ottoman and Savafid Empires and by the Armenian* genocide (1915–16). Several autonomous ecclesiastical jurisdictions emerged because of the dispersion. In the Republic of Armenia, the See of the Catholicos is in the cathedral founded in the 5th c. on the site of Gregory the Illuminator's vision of the Son of God at Edjmiatzin, the city name meaning the "Descent of the Only Begotten."

Statistics: Population (2001): 2.97 million. Christians: Armenian Apostolic, 94.7%; other Christians, 4%. (*Source*: 2001 census.)

IGOR DORFMANN-LAZAREV

Armenian Apostolic Church. See ORTHODOX CHURCHES, ORIENTAL, CLUSTER: ARMENIAN APOSTOLIC CHURCH.

Armenian Genocide. The politics of genocide against the Armenians, accused of being a disloyal, extraneous body in the Ottoman Empire, began with Sultan Abdul-Hamid II after the 1878 Turkish military defeat. Between 1894 and 1896, from 200,000 to 300,000 Armenians were massacred, and another 30,000 were killed in April 1909 in Cilicia.

The Young Turk committee "Union and Progress," directed by Djemal, Enver, and Talaat, seized power (1913) and established the "Special Organization," the future instrument of the extermination of the Armenians. The arrest (April 24, 1915) and shooting of the Armenian intellectuals of Constantinople, among whom were deputies of the Ottoman parliament, opened the way to the elimination of Armenians from the entire Ottoman Empire under the pretext of protecting the Russian frontier from "the Christians' treason." "Confessions" extracted from Armenian notables justified the shooting of men and the deportation of the rest of the population, about 1,000,000, to the Syro-Mesopotamian desert, where, if not murdered on the way, most died of deprivation and epidemics, the survivors being killed during the summer of 1916. About 1,500,000 Armenians were victims of this genocide.

Following the Russian retreat after the 1917 revolution, the Turkish forces attempted to expand the genocide in today's Azerbaijan, which resulted in other massacres and the first exodus of Armenians from Baku (1917–18).

IGOR DORFMANN-LAZAREV

Arminianism, a movement founded by the Dutch theologian Jacobus Arminius (1560–1609, student of Theodore Beza*, Calvin's* successor), diverges from Calvinism primarily in matters of election* and "predestination* to salvation*." Arminius's Dutch followers drafted (1610) the five Articles of Remonstrance* against Calvinism: grace* is universally "prevenient" (anticipatory); election is conditional on faith*; the atonement* provided by Jesus' death was intended to be unlimited and universal; God's grace can be resisted; and perseverance in faith is not certain, making it possible for believers to fall from grace. The Articles sparked furious debate with the Calvinists led by Franciscus Gomarus, who were condemned by the Synod of Dordt* (1618). Two main branches of Arminianism can be identified: classical Arminianism adheres to Arminius's five articles, while Wesleyan Arminianism follows John Wesley*'s later modifications, which reconceived the concept of atonement to incorporate an understanding of justice*, maintained that although Christians could lose their salvation, acts of apostasy were not final, and argued that Christian perfection is possible in this life. In the contemporary world, Arminianism is most commonly found in Methodist teachings but also finds a place in some Anglican, Baptist, Church of Christ, Seventh-day Adventist, and Pentecostal churches. RENÉE JEFFERY

Arnauld, Antoine (1612–94), leading Jansenist* theologian. Born in a Parisian family linked to the Port*-Royal abbey; law and theology student at the Sorbonne; ordained priest; appointed professor of theology at the Sorbonne. In conversation with the abbot of Saint-Cyran, then imprisoned, he wrote *Frequent Communion* (1643), defending Jansenist views on the Eucharist* (their caution against frequent Communion). Contested by Jesuits* and Rome, he was expelled from the Sorbonne. A renowned mathematician, philosopher, and theologian, a disciple of Augustine*, a Cartesian, and Pascal's* friend, Arnauld participated in the important debates of his time, as his many works (42 volumes) show. **See also JANSENISM.**

JEAN LESAULNIER

Arnauld, Jacqueline Marie Angélique (1591–1661), Jansenist* abbess and reformer of Port*-Royal. Born in Paris, daughter of anti-Jesuit barrister Antoine Arnauld and sister of theologian Antoine Arnauld*. Forced to take vows, she became abbess of Port-Royal (1602). Spiritual conversion (1608) led Mère Angélique to introduce rigorous monastic Cistercian* reform and close the convent's doors; she supervised the reform of other convents. In close relationship with Francis* de Sales until his death (1622), she was subsequently heavily influenced by the cofounder of Jansenism*, Saint-Cyran. Port-Royal under Mère Angélique became synonymous with Jansenism; she maintained Jansenist tenets despite increasing persecution by Innocent IX and Louis XIV. MITA CHOUDHURY

Arndt, Johann (1555–1621), German Lutheran theologian, pastor, and author of devotional works, including his highly popular and influential *Six Books on True Christianity*, compiling materials from earlier mystical* and devotional writers (many Roman Catholic), emblems, and general directives on his favorite themes – repentance, true faith, and the holy life of the true Christian – and a prayer book, *Little Garden of Paradise*. Protestant scholastic Lutheran colleagues opposed Arndt's heretical leanings throughout his career (though John Gerhard defended him). His work had a direct influence on Pietism*, which developed later in the 17th c. and remains strong in Evangelicalism*.

PETER C. ERB

Arns, Paulo Evaristo, Brazilian churchman, Franciscan friar, priest (1945), bishop (1966), cardinal (1973), archbishop of São Paulo (1970–98). Born in Forquilhinha, Santa Catarina (1921), he was a doctor of patristic literature (Sorbonne, 1952). One of the most representative bishops of the generation after Vatican* II, pastor of the largest Catholic diocese in the world (until its 1989 division), and a supporter of Liberation* theology, he frequently confronted dictatorial security services and the wealthy, becoming a prominent defender of human* rights, struggling for social justice* and land* reform for the poor* and engaged in ecumenism. An intellectual, he wrote 49 books. **See also HUMAN RIGHTS CLUSTER: THE CHURCHES IN LATIN AMERICA: BRAZIL.**

LUIZ C. L. MARQUES

Arts and Theology. Although artists and theologians have been engaged in both supportive and contentious dialogue since the first days of the church (see Paul's Speech in Athens, Acts 18), an integrated, academic study of theology and art emerged largely after 1950. During the post–World War II arts boom in the USA, several prominent theologians and artists began a fruitful dialogue on the intersections of art, religion*, and contemporary culture. These discussions led to the inauguration of courses in many theological schools, such as Union Theological Seminary in New York City, Boston University School of Theology, and the University of Chicago Divinity School. Theologians who were engaged in research in this area included Paul Tillich*, Amos Wilder, Jacques Maritain*, Nicholas Berdyaev*, Roger Hazelton, and Walter Ong, SJ. These pioneers, followed by a second generation, mostly Tillich's students (James Luther Adams, Tom Driver, Nathan Scott, John Dillenberger, and Jane Daggett Dillenberger), examined the intersections of culture and religion and developed methods for integrating the arts into theological study. By 2000 programs for the advanced study of theology and the arts came into being in a large number of graduate theological schools in the USA and UK, while seminaries' curricula included the arts in ministerial education.

Theology and the arts is a multifaceted field taking different critical and analytic trajectories. Some programs emphasize the liturgical or performative arts (e.g. sacred music, homiletics, or dance) most often encountered in a worship context; others regard the arts more broadly, including literature, film, music, and the visual arts, whether overtly religious or not. The former programs tend to have a more practical aim (e.g. to enrich or renew a community's worship* or spiritual* life), while the latter are oriented toward a wider cultural analysis in which religion and art are two key components of research. Some programs take a more historical, analytical, or theoretical approach, emphasizing, e.g., the history of Christian art and architecture, the intellectual or theological roots of iconoclasm*, theological aesthetics*, visual culture, or art as a facet of ritual studies. Other programs direct more attention to preparing arts practitioners or training future clergy and lay leaders to appreciate and include the arts in their ministries. Church musicians constitute a large proportion of the latter group, but other arts ministries may be highlighted (e.g. chancel drama, liturgical dance*, or the design of worship environments). The theoretical side of the field now also integrates the arts into biblical studies, ethics and society, anthropology* of religion, and religion and psychology*.

All of these approaches find human artistic endeavors to be an important vehicle for expressing and examining matters of ultimate value, meaning, and the human–divine relationship. Historians view the artistic productions of a particular time and place as data that give insight into the character of a religious community and its belief system. Theologians understand the arts to be a nondiscursive and sometimes nonverbal means of conveying and reinforcing dogmatic* positions, moral* precepts, or calls for social and economic justice*. Homileticians, ethicists, and religious educators may perceive a prophetic or pedagogical role for the arts, while pastoral theologians can value the arts for their therapeutic, devotional, or inspirational function. Depending on the theologian's tradition, the arts may be understood to serve a kind of sacramental* function, mediating between the visible and invisible, or between the human and divine realms, as in the Orthodox teaching on the icon*. The role of God as creator and that of the artist as creator are then among the central points of study, along with affirming the essential goodness of the material world and its ability to serve as a vehicle for the holy* (i.e. as Incarnation*). **See also AESTHETICS AND THEOLOGY; HIEROTOPY, THE CREATION OF SACRED SPACES.**

ROBIN MARGARET JENSEN

Asbaje y Ramírez, Juana Inés de (Sister Juana Inés de la Cruz; 1651–95, Mexico), a religious of the liberal convent of San Jerónimo, theologian, philosopher, scientist, poet, music composer. Through biblical and theological arguments, she defended women's rights to study and to write. She was known as the Tenth Muse. **See also MEXICO.**

MARÍA ALICIA PUENTE LUTTEROTH and ELIZABETH JUDD

Asbury, Francis (1745–1816). First bishop of the Methodist Episcopal Church in the USA, Asbury led the movement during its dramatic growth in the new nation. Born in England, Asbury answered John Wesley's* call to serve the Methodist movement in North America (1771). After 1784, when American and British Methodists separated, he assumed the role of bishop in the USA. Although the Methodist Episcopal system and Asbury's autocratic leadership clashed with the democratic ideals of the American Revolution (see United States), Methodists thrived. Much success was due to Asbury, who believed that traveling preachers were best suited to reaching Americans who lived on farms and in small towns with no minister nearby. Though Asbury was a bishop, he rejected the prestige of a professionalized ministry. He preached constantly, traveling an estimated 300,000 miles on horseback, probably seeing more of North America than anyone of his time. Asbury embraced the controversial camp* meeting revivals* to evangelize the frontier. Through itinerant preaching and camp meetings, therefore, Asbury embraced religious practices that succeeded dramatically in the democratic ethos of the nation. Through his leadership, Methodists grew from 300 members when he arrived (1771) to more than 200,000 at his death (1816).

JAMES P. BYRD

Ascension, Christ's ascent into heaven after 40 days of resurrection appearances (Acts 1:1–9). Ascension Day, the 40th day after Easter*, always falls on a Thursday. Christ's withdrawal into heaven was used against the Gnostics'* claim to have been instructed by Christ after this period and used by Reformed theologians against the Lutherans' assertion that Christ's Body and Blood are omnipresent.

Asceticism. The Greek word *askesis* originally meant the physical discipline undertaken by an athlete, but even before the Christian Era, *askesis* came to signal a philosopher's disciplined self-restraint. Ascetic renunciation was a feature of several ancient philosophical and religious groups, including the Jewish Essenes* and some

Gnostics*. Jesus' call to prepare for the coming Kingdom* of God, and his own itinerant ministry, unencumbered by home, family, or possessions, encouraged his followers to practice similar forms of renunciation. When the Kingdom did not arrive and Jesus did not return, ascetic renunciation was nonetheless retained as a "good" in and for itself, reinforced by Paul's favoring of celibacy* over marriage* in 1 Cor 7, as well as by the apocryphal* Acts of the Apostles. Contrary to the view that asceticism arose as a protest against degraded "pagan" morals or the laxity of the post-Constantinian church, recent scholars stress that ascetic teaching and practice became a favored form of Christian living very early. Christian ascetics opted for celibacy, restricted their food, drink, and sleep, renounced properties*, and attempted to cultivate humility*. They claimed that their discipline did not signal a denigration of the body*, but improved the soul*, brought them closer to God, and was an imitation of Jesus.

Even before the advent of organized monasticism* (4th c.), beginning with Pachomius*, Christian asceticism was practiced throughout the Mediterranean world. After the inception of organized monasticism, some Christians chose to live ascetically in less regulated ways; e.g, male and female ascetics lived together as couples or in small groups (see Agapetai).

Asceticism was open to female as well as male practitioners. Several ascetic women – such as Paula*, Eustochium*, Marcella*, Melania* the Elder, Melania* the Younger, and Olympias* – came from the highest aristocracy of the Roman Empire. Their ascetic renunciation was lavishly praised by Christian writers of the day.

A large literature explained ascetic theory and practice. Christian leaders such as Athanasius*, Jerome*, Gregory* of Nyssa, Basil* of Caesarea, Ambrose*, Ephrem* the Syrian, Evagrius* Ponticus, John* Chrysostom, John Cassian*, and Caesarius of Arles laid the foundation for the theory and practice of Christian renunciation in their many writings and monastic rules.

ELIZABETH A. CLARK

Ascetic Monasticism. See MONASTICISM CLUSTER.

Ash Wednesday, first day of Lent*, six and a half weeks before Easter*. It is a time for repentance*, when ashes are rubbed onto the foreheads of the faithful.

Asian American Theologies. Asian Americans are a group of people of Asian descent who live within "the *contradictions* of Asian immigration, which at different moments in the last century and a half of Asian entry into the United States have placed Asians 'within' the U.S. nation-state, its workplaces, and its markets, yet linguistically, culturally and racially marked Asians as 'foreign' and 'outside' the national polity" (in Lowe's words). A search for an alternative religious paradigm rooted in the lived faith experiences of Asian Americans sets the context in which Asian American theology is currently being undertaken. To be sure, the impact of the dominant North Atlantic religious, theological, and cultural orientations cannot be minimized for Asian Americans' construction of theology. Asian American theology is part and parcel of a larger historical context in which theological traditions have been built and nurtured. At the same time, multivalent religious, cultural, and ethnic/racial orientations of Asian American faith communities are shaping their distinct theologies and paradigmatic frameworks that bridge "the barriers between the intellectuals at the university/divinity school and our communities so that our work takes on fresh, living meaning in the 'real' world" (Lowe).

Asian American theologies are mostly public theologies. Their interpretive scaffold can be said to be a three-legged stool of (1) the nomadic identity derived from the racialized life of Asian Americans, (2) the translocal and diasporic existence that predisposes Asian Americans to the pathos of life, and (3) the navigation among multiple religious orientations inherited from Asian and other religious traditions. These three aspects produce particular theological understandings, practices, life perspectives, and distinct Christian faith postures for Asian Americans, perspectives that offer a fresh understanding of the meaning of the "public" in the USA.

A growing number of theological themes are articulated by Asian American theologians. They include the relevance of the change and relativity expressed in the interplay of *yin* and *yang* to the coexistence of Christianity and other religions in a creative process of becoming (Jung Young Lee); postcolonial Feminist theology that examines gender, colonialism, and Christianity (Kwok Pui-lan); pilgrimage by way of marginality and liminality* that brings strangers into solidarity and community (San Hyun Lee); and the cross as a subversive effect of love, a theology that utilizes the Korean concept of *jeong* (Wonhee Anne Joh). FUMITAKA MATSUOKA

Asian Theology, Trends in. The roots of Asian theology can be traced to the appointment of Asians to the International Missionary Council (early 20th c.). In subsequent Asian ecumenical movements, the Asian theological voice began to be heard through the Indian Rethinking Christianity Movement (1930s), the *Indian Journal of Theology* (from 1952), the *South East Asia Journal of Theology* (from 1959; now *Asia Journal of Theology*), and the East Asia Christian Conference (from 1959, now Christian Conference of Asia). This Asian theological movement was empowered by decolonization, the rise of the Third World Movement, and various postcolonial struggles. Thus major themes of Asian theology include suffering* and poverty* resulting from domination and oppression, the dehumanizing of Asian women*, and interfaith conflicts and collaboration when Christians are a tiny minority. Doctrinal reformulations include the following: Jesus as one among the marginals; Christ as a cosmic principle; rejection of the doctrines of divine impassibility* and immutability in favor of a human-like God; Asian cultural and religious traditions received as sources of revelation together with the Bible; and church conceived in a praxis-oriented language regarding God's mission. Asian theologies take several forms, such as culturally oriented indigenous theologies, sociopolitically oriented contextualizing theologies, and Asian liberation theologies. Incorporating postcolonial* theories into theology is a recent trend, especially in Asian Feminist theological circles and in relatively affluent Asian countries such as Hong Kong and South Korea. SIMON SHUI-MAN KWAN

Asian Women's Resource Centre (AWRC) for Culture and Theology, established in 1987–88 as a shared dream of a community of Asian women actively engaged in a critical Feminist* theology of liberation* and transformation against a backdrop of colonialism* with a postcolonial* imagination in a pluralistic Asia, rich with natural wealth, peoples, cultures, religions, and philosophies. AWRC envisions a community of women, men, and children who are valued and value each other as equally created in God's image* with dignity, mutual respect, care, and responsibility. *In God's Image*, a quarterly journal (from 1982), focuses on women's reality, feminist struggle, vision, liberation theology, and hermeneutics. AWRC facilitates programs addressing feminist struggles and praxis in life contexts. YONG TING JIN

Assemblies of God, the largest denomination in the Pentecostal* tradition (worldwide, c50 million believers in 2000). The Assemblies of God (organized April 1914, Hot Springs, Arkansas) was an outgrowth of a felt need among the scattered local churches that featured Pentecostal theology to provide for discipline of ministers, leadership training, the promotion of a consistent theology, and support for world missions.

The Assemblies of God owes its theological identity to key personalities. In 1901 Charles F. Parham developed in his short-term Bible institute in Topeka, Kansas, the teaching that subsequent to an experience of regeneration and a second experience of sanctification*, all believers should seek a third experience of spiritual empowering, baptism* in the Holy Spirit, marked by speaking in tongues, or glossolalia*. Students in Parham's Bible institute reported experiencing this phenomenon. Associated with this empowering was the expectation of various gifts of the Spirit, most conspicuously divine healing*. Parham's protégé, William Seymour*, took this message to Los Angeles. There, at a humble church facility on Azusa* Street, Seymour led a continuous revival meeting for more than three years (1906–9). From there the Pentecostal Movement became a worldwide phenomenon. Seymour discarded Parham's insistence that the glossolalia associated with Spirit baptism need not consist of "known languages," but simply of "unknown tongues." By 1910, William Durham, a Baptist turned Pentecostal, arrived from Chicago with an additional modification, advocating "the finished work"; a crisis experience of sanctification (taught by the Wesleyans*, including Parham and Seymour) was not required for Spirit baptism. For Durham, sanctification was a process, not a crisis. When the Assemblies of God was formed, the modified Pentecostal theology of William Durham prevailed.

The theology of the Assemblies of God is strongly linked to standard Evangelical* teaching, including the authority of the Bible as Scripture* in all matters of faith and practice; the triune Godhead; the substitutionary atonement of Jesus Christ (see Atonement #2); the necessity of repentance* and faith* in Christ for salvation*; the expectation of Christ's premillennial second coming (see Millennialism Cluster). Baptism* in the Holy Spirit is understood to be an empowering for Christian witness, manifested in a vigorous world mission that encompasses North

American–sent missionaries (about 2000 at the turn of the century) and missionaries from numerous countries that once were "receiving" churches but are now "sending" churches. **See also CHARISMATIC AND PENTECOSTAL MOVEMENTS CLUSTER; PENTECOSTAL MOVEMENT, ITS HISTORY AND THEOLOGY; PENTECOSTAL WORSHIP.** WILLIAM W. MENZIES

Assumption. In Roman Catholicism, the Blessed Virgin Mary* is believed to have been assumed, body and soul, into heaven, immediately following her bodily death. The Feast of the Assumption is observed in the Roman Catholic Church on August 15, as well as in Anglicanism and Lutheranism (though without the word and doctrine of "Assumption"). The Eastern Orthodox* Churches call the Assumption the Dormition*.

Assumption of Moses, Jewish OT pseudepigraphon (early 1st c. CE; also designated the Testament of Moses), for the most part a prophecy about the downfall of Israel and its eschatological salvation. The prophecy is delivered by Moses to his successor, Joshua, shortly before the former's assumption into heaven. Christians may have been interested in its doctrines on the spirit of God. **See also PSEUDEPIGRAPHA OF THE OLD TESTAMENT.**

JOHANNES TROMP

Assurance of Salvation, an emphasis of the Reformed tradition, which affirmed both predestination* and the perseverance of saints. While the original emphasis was on the assurance that comes from faith* itself, Puritan* theologians, desiring a church of "visible saints," tried to discern the elect on the basis of their accounts of "Christian experience." **See also PRACTICAL SYLLOGISM.**

Assyrian Church of the East. See CHURCH OF THE EAST, OR ASSYRIAN CHURCH.

Athaliah, daughter of Jezebel* and wife of Jehoram, king of Judah. Seizing the throne, she reigned for six years until an insurrection led by the priest Jehoiada led to her slaying at the palace gate (2 Kgs 11).

Athanasian Creed, the *Symbolum quicunque*, named from its opening statement, "Whoever desires to be saved must above all hold the Catholic faith." Not from Athanasius, it was written between the time of Vincent* of Lerins (c440) and Caesarius of Arles (c525, who quoted it). It clarifies the doctrines of the Trinity* and the Incarnation* using formulations from Augustine* and earlier councils. The Creed has been widely used, both liturgically and doctrinally, in the Roman Catholic, Anglican, and Lutheran traditions. Its bold first line was interpreted by F. D. Maurice to mean that eternal life is knowledge of God, and eternal death* is being without God.

Athanasius (c295–373), bishop and theologian; details of his birth and education unknown. He was deacon and secretary to Bishop Alexander of Alexandria*, with whom he attended the Council of Nicaea* (325), as well as bishop of Alexandria* (328–73). He was exiled from his see five times as a result of conflicts with emperors and other bishops (335–37, 339–46, 356–62, 362–63, 365–66). Athanasius is significant for his defense of the full divinity of the Word*, or Son* of God, against opponents whom he labeled "Arians"; for his promotion of the growing monastic* movement and his work to tie it closely to the church; and for his efforts to bring unity and uniformity to the church in Egypt, as other 4th-c. patriarchs also did.

During Athanasius's career, the church was troubled by what is known as "the Arian controversy" (see Arianism). Bishops and theologians debated, in countless written works and numerous councils, the relationship between God the Father and his Son, or Word (and eventually among the Father, Son, and Spirit). Beginning with his masterpiece, *On the Incarnation of the Word* (*Inc.*, written between 325 and 337), Athanasius defended the full divinity of the Word, which he considered essential to human salvation*. In his formulation, through the Incarnation* the Word "became human, so that we may become divine" (*Inc.* 54). In the 350s he began to promote the creed adopted at the Council of Nicaea (325) as the touchstone of orthodoxy on this question: this creed declared that the Son was "of the same substance" (*homoousios*) as the Father. Athanasius argued that the language the Bible uses for the Son – e.g. "Word," "Wisdom," "Power" – makes clear that he is one with the Father and not one of the Father's creatures. Athanasius branded all who disagreed with his view, no matter how diverse their theologies, "Arians" or "Ario-maniacs," i.e. followers of the Alexandrian presbyter Arius* (c260–336), whose teachings gave rise to the controversy. As inaccurate as this labeling was, it stuck, and only recently have scholars ceased to label all the ancient theologians who questioned Nicene theology "Arians." When Athanasius was exiled from his see, it was usually because councils of bishops found him guilty of professional misconduct (especially the use of violence against his opponents), but he claimed (not without reason) that he was persecuted for his theological beliefs.

Athanasius is also a significant figure in the history of Christian monasticism*, which grew and diversified during the 4th c., especially in Egypt*. He wrote letters to desert monks and to female virgins in the cities urging them to avoid "heretical" teachings and to practice their ascetic disciplines in unity with the wider church. To female ascetics, he held up the Virgin Mary* as the model of reclusion and obedience. To ascetics throughout the world, he offered the example of the desert monk Antony* (c251–356). Athanasius's *Life of Antony* portrayed its subject as the first true desert hermit, who achieved a maximum level of virtue without the benefit of a traditional education. Antony's ascetic program constituted a form of daily martyrdom*, which gave him the power to benefit others through healing and exorcism. Written in Greek, the book was rapidly translated into Latin and other languages, and was widely read in many countries. It inspired countless Christians to take up the monastic life, became the model for all subsequent biographies of Christian saints (hagiography*), and continues to inspire Christians today. Athanasius urged nonmonastic Christians to practice a moderate asceticism of fasting, almsgiving, prayer, and temporary periods of sexual renunciation, especially during Lent*. In these ways, Athanasius promoted monasticism as the highest form of the Christian life and worked to make sure that it was firmly connected to the wider church, which consisted primarily of ordinary married Christians, their families, and the clergy.

Like many other bishops in the post-Constantinian imperial church, Athanasius sought to establish what in his view would be a single "Catholic" Church in Egypt with a unified structure and an "orthodox" theology and worship life. Each winter he issued a festal letter, which announced the dates of Lent* and Easter* to all the Christians in Egypt; in his day, Christians differed on when to celebrate Easter, and the observance of Lent was not universal. Athanasius used his letters to exhort the faithful to proper Christian living and orthodox belief. For example, in his 39th festal letter for the year 367, Athanasius defined the biblical canon* for his followers; this is the earliest Christian writing that lists precisely the 27 books that now constitute the NT (see New Testament and its Canonization). In his letters for 369 and 370, he instructed Christians on the proper way to honor the bodies of martyrs and other deceased holy persons. In these ways, Athanasius helped to establish Christian orthodoxy* not only in doctrine, but also in pious practices.

DAVID BRAKKE

Atheism, as Accusation Against Early Christians. Theoretical atheism denies the existence of God; practical atheism is the failure to honor God or the gods (cf. the modern term "Godlessness"). Since Christians refused to take part in traditional rituals, they were called atheists (see Justin Martyr); this was one reason for their persecution*. They themselves could use the term with reference to Gentiles, as those who lacked a relationship with the true God (Eph 2:12).

Atheism and Christian Theology. Atheists challenging the dominant religion, atheism rejecting and subverting theism, and biblical faith grappling with God's radical otherness are intertwined. Greek and Jew, Socrates and Jesus and his followers, were equally charged with atheism by the Roman authorities.

An atheist is one who challenges the presuppositions of the dominant religion*, as if only an atheist could subvert an established religion! This assumption belies Abraham smashing his father's idols (as both the Midrash* and the Qur'an* underscore) and history, in which today's atheism is tomorrow's religion (Feuerbach*). Then no one can really be an atheist.

Yet atheism surfaces as soon as the devil asks (see Matt 4:1–11), Will God really be there when you need him? Practical atheism confronts only a practical theism. Atheism plays the experience of God's absence against that of God's presence, driving a wedge between them. Traditional theist theology is confused when it seeks to resolve the tension between God's absence and God's presence by dissipating it under the guise of one and the same God – a metaphysical, universal explanation seeking to address a practical issue.

Metaphysical theism is as faulty as metaphysical atheism. This appears to be the case once the distinction between revealed truth and rational truth is admitted. Metaphysical theism erodes God's transcending reality when it seeks to deny metaphysical atheism without acknowledging that faith* can assert one thing and reason* another, that divine law is one thing and the laws of nature, which need no God hypothesis and make God superfluous, as atheists claim, are another. Then theists make God into a stopgap.

Whether taken for granted (by theists) or denied (by atheists), as a stopgap God is useless.

Oddly enough, metaphysical atheism stands closer to biblical faith. God's transcendence is not a matter of presence or absence but of God's radical otherness; not a matter of God being this or that, but a matter of God being closer to me than I am to myself, never able to take God for granted, although for me, a human in Christ, there is neither God nor human, as there is neither Greek nor Jew, male nor female, master nor slave. GABRIEL VAHANIAN

Athos, Mount, on the Chalkidike Peninsula (northern Greece*), is known as the "holy mountain," a center of Byzantine and Eastern Orthodox* monasticism* occupying today a preeminent position among Orthodox monastic communities. Cenobitic* monasticism was established there (10th c.), though monks sought solitude on its rocky terrain probably from the late 8th c. By the 11th c., Athos comprised a federation of numerous monasteries, populated mostly by Greek-speaking monks. Russian, Serbian, and Bulgarian monasteries emerged shortly thereafter, constituting 3 of the 20 independent monasteries at present. The "Jesus* Prayer" (since the 14th c.) and hesychasm* became the preferred methods of private prayer. An 18th-c. revival resulted in the publication of the *Philokalia*, a collection of foundational monastic spiritual writings, which influenced 19th-c. Russian spirituality. Today, Athos continues its democratic organization and its exclusion of women; it has experienced a renaissance since the 1980s. Many of its approximately 1,500 monks hold university degrees. JAMES C. SKEDROS

Atonement, or "at-one-ment" (a 16th-c. term), refers to the reestablishment of the proper relationship of sinners with God. It has come to be applied specifically to the significance of Christ's crucifixion*, understood in the context of the broader issues concerning redemption*, salvation*, reconciliation*, and the renewal of human life.

The OT sacrifices* were used to interpret the cross of Christ: the sacrifices of covenant/ Passover* (Mark 14:24; 1 Cor 5:7), sin offering (for the forgiveness of sin, Matt 26:28; 2 Cor 5:21), expiation* or propitiation* (substitution sacrifice, Rom 3:25; Heb 7–10; 1 John 2:2, 4:10), and the suffering servant (Matt 8:17; Acts 10:36; 1 Pet 2:23–24). Exactly how does the cross of Christ reestablish a proper relationship with God? Three basic answers have been given; all are grounded in the Bible, and all have strong links with their social context. The sinners' problems are seen, respectively, as bondage to the powers of evil*; guilt, or debt toward God; and a need for human transformation.

1. Ransom and Redemption from Bondage or Healing. In the patristic period, when Christianity was a minority religion within an often hostile Roman Empire, the emphasis was on bondage to death*, the law*, and the powers of evil*, from which humans were redeemed by paying a ransom*. By his death, Christ paid this ransom; "the Son of Man came . . . to give his life as a ransom for many" (Mark 10:45). For Gregory* of Nyssa and Augustine*, the devil*, who had a legitimate claim over sinners, was tricked into abusing this power in the case of Christ, who was sinless. Thus those who attach themselves to Christ through baptism* are freed from the devil's bondage. In *Christus Victor* (1931), Gustaf Aulén* emphasized the importance for 20th-c. Christians of understanding atonement as redemption from bondage; Christ's life, death, and resurrection are victorious over the forces of evil.

Similarly, Eastern Orthodox* churches view humankind primarily as a victim of the devil's deception. Death* is not God's curse on God's creation, but God's enemy and the inevitable consequence of separation from life with God. Sin* is viewed as a disease. Atonement is thus the "salvific effect of the Incarnation" that heals humans from this disease and extends to the entire cosmos.

Liberation* theology has a similar concern with structures of evil that hold people in bondage. These structures of evil are unmasked and discredited when the undeserved suffering and oppression are exposed by the Christian proclamation; the captives are not only freed from moral and psychological bondage, but also empowered for a new mode of life.

2. Honor and Juridical Satisfaction. During the Christian Middle Ages in the West, God was readily likened to a feudal overlord whose honor is offended by human sin. Sinners owe God a debt of honor; because God is infinite, this is an infinite debt that humans cannot pay. Anselm* asserted that justice requires either punishment or satisfaction. Christ, being both divine and human, offers infinite satisfaction as the representative of those who share his human nature. Luther* and Calvin* changed the focus to God's wrath, which demands punishment rather than the satisfaction of honor. Thus Christ becomes a substitute for, rather than a representative of, sinful humanity, bearing the full force of God's wrath on the cross, because the guilt of sin is transferred from sinners to Christ.

The logic of punishment, which requires the Son to bear the Father's wrath, has been criticized not only for its moral and legalistic rigidity, which engenders guilt as a condition for forgiveness and denies that God is free to forgive, but as a form of "divine child abuse," a projection of the worst human impulses. Yet contemporary theology is prepared to think about God's suffering or identifying with sufferers. Here the focus shifts from wrath to reconciliation (and potentially to the redemption view of atonement).

Christ's death is often viewed, as it was by Thomas Aquinas*, as a sufficient, indeed superabundant, satisfaction for the sins of the whole of humankind; then the satisfaction view of atonement is often combined with one of the other views of atonement to address present sin and evil. Yet in some traditions, Christ's satisfaction for sins is restricted to believers; in parts of the Calvinist* tradition, atonement is limited to the elect, predestined to attain salvation*.

3. Moral Transformation. Abelard* in the Middle Ages and modern liberal theology have emphasized the way atonement changes humans. The cross is viewed as the ultimate expression of God's love for sinful humanity, even in confrontation with human rebellion and violence; the extent of God's love evokes in believers gratitude and love for God. Because the focus is on a change in human attitude, it is called a "moral* influence" theory. This does not necessarily mean that Christ is merely a moral example; the terminology refers to a transforming appeal (often understood to be a divine intervention) to the depths of human affections.

Theologians usually display a preference for one of these ways of thinking about the cross. Yet each of them is grounded in biblical metaphors, none of which should be taken too literally or made the sole focus of reflection. The question, then, is how to think in a connected way about sin*, guilt*, suffering*, divine love*, and reconciliation*.

EUGENE TESELLE and DANIEL PATTE

Attrition, a term developed in medieval Western theology and now part of the Roman Catholic doctrine of penance*. Whereas contrition* is sorrow for sin* because of love for God, attrition is based on fear of damnation*. It is considered an "imperfect" mode of contrition, preparing the person to receive grace* through the sacrament of penance.

Auburn Affirmation, 1923 statement signed by more than 1,200 ministers and elders of the Presbyterian Church in the USA declaring that the confessions of the church cannot be regarded as infallible* and that no General Assembly has the authority to make a definitive statement of the church's beliefs, such as the five points proposed by the Fundamentalist* Movement. The 1927 General Assembly concurred.

Auburn Declaration (the), by Presbyterians of the "New School" after the 1837 General Assembly expelled four synods involved in a plan of union with the congregationalists; it refuted the accusation that this plan departed from Calvinism* and the Westminster* standards. The "Old School" General Assembly eventually approved (1868) the Declaration, stating that it contained "all fundamentals of the Calvinistic Creed," which made possible the reunion of the two groups in the northern states (1869–70).

Augsburg, Peace of, gave adherents of the Augsburg* Confession legal, though inferior, status in the Holy Roman Empire (1555). Emperor Charles* V attempted to enforce the Edict of Worms* and to eradicate the Lutheran Reformation through military action (1546–47). After an initial victory, he was defeated by Protestant princes in 1552. The Truce of Passau gave temporary legal recognition to governments that accepted the Augsburg Confession. At the 1555 imperial Reichstag (diet), final provisions were adopted for the coexistence of the papal obedience and churches of the Confession. It established the principle *cuius regio, eius religio* (the ruler determines the faith of his subjects).

ROBERT KOLB

Augsburg Confession (1530), defining document of the Wittenberg Reformation, accepted by Lutheran churches as their fundamental statement of faith. Emperor Charles* V demanded that governments introducing Luther's reforms justify this action at an imperial diet in Augsburg (1530). John Eck, a leading Roman Catholic theologian, issued his *Four Hundred Four Articles,* a wide-ranging critique of Lutheranism*, associating it with ancient and contemporary heresies*. Philip Melanchthon* led the Lutheran delegation and forged a new kind of document, a "confession*," to define the Lutherans' legitimacy as a Christian church. Twenty-one articles of faith (including the

20th on faith* and good works) asserted in a moderate language that Wittenberg Lutheran teaching conformed to Scripture and the catholic tradition. Seven additional articles argued for reforms of important aspects of ecclesiastical practice, such as Communion* in one kind, clerical celibacy*, monastic vows*, and compulsory confession*. Melanchthon rebutted the *Confutation* of an imperial Roman Catholic commission in his *Apology [Defense] of the Augsburg Confession* (1531). ROBERT KOLB

Augustine of Canterbury (d604/5), Benedictine monk, missionary to England, first archbishop of Canterbury. Sent by Pope Gregory* I with 40 monks, he evangelized Southern England (where Christianity had disappeared after the fall of the Roman Empire) and established in Canterbury a church (597) and, subsequently, a Benedictine monastery. With the arrival of more missionaries, evangelization continued, non-Christian temples were purified for Christian worship, and Augustine consecrated 12 suffragan bishops. Canterbury became the primatial see of England.

Augustine of Hippo (354–430), rhetorician, bishop, and theologian, well trained in many currents of classical life and thought. Through his voluminous writings, he transformed the classical heritage in a way that influenced medieval, Reformation, and modern thought in the West. He was born and educated in North Africa, underwent conversion in Milan (386), and served as presbyter (391), then as bishop, in Hippo, North Africa (396 until his death).

Under the influence of his mother, Monica*, he grew up thinking of himself as a Christian. After reading Cicero, he undertook a philosophical quest; in reaction against the authoritarian tone of North African Christianity, he adhered to Manichaeism* as an enlightened form of Christianity. After Theodosius* brought the full power of the Roman Empire down upon so-called Christian heresies (380) and Manichaeism (381–83), Augustine rejected Manichaeism and turned to what was held in Rome as orthodox Christianity (Milan, 386). In the *Confessions*, he cites three factors: acknowledgment that faith* based on authority* is a necessary part of reason's quest (in contrast with the Manichees' confidence that truth can be attained by reason alone); a "turn inward" evoked by his reading of Plotinus* (viewing true reality as spiritual, in contrast with the Manichees' materialism; understanding evil* as corruption or privation of the good, in contrast with the Manichees' dualism*); and a resolution of his personal struggles, which he credited to grace* speaking through Scripture*. He took up the contemplative* life, on the model of both monasticism* and philosophy. In a few years, he became a presbyter and then bishop in Hippo, where he was a prolific preacher, writer, and participant in doctrinal controversies.

Augustine continued the Neoplatonist* quest for immediate union with God, but he also limited it by insisting on the need for revelation* and grace*. His transformation of this tradition is seen most vividly in *On the Trinity*. In the first books, he probes the biblical basis of the doctrine; in Books 5–7, he develops the view that the Trinity consists of mutual relations (often called the "psychological" view of the Trinity); in Book 8, he explores several modes of ascending to God through contemplation; in Books 9–15, he develops his influential view that the human mind is the image* of God through self-relation (memory, understanding, and will, or, more specifically, immediate self-awareness, self-concept, and self-affirmation), all of them rooted in the same mind but each differentiated from the others by a distinct relation. These are fulfilled in a threefold relation to God (intuition of God, formation by the Word, and love animated by the Spirit). Augustine's understanding of the Trinity shaped later Western doctrine, including the controversial view that the Spirit proceeds from both the Father and the Son (see *Filioque*).

In conflict with the Donatists*, who saw themselves as the authentic African Church in continuity with Cyprian*, Augustine defended the validity of the sacraments* despite the human failings of those who administer them, placing greater emphasis on the bond of unity within the one Catholic Church. His interpretation of the sacraments as signs stimulated controversy during the Middle Ages, especially concerning the Eucharist*: does it signify the Body and Blood of Christ, or is it transformed into these?

As an interpreter of Paul (especially Romans*), he emphasized original* sin as affecting all descendants of Adam* and Eve; the bondage* of the will to its own disordered affections; grace* as the influence that frees the will so that it can turn toward God; and predestination* as the explanation for this priority of grace over free choice. After a brief controversy with Pelagius* over original sin and the freedom of the will (412–18), his general perspective was enforced by imperial and papal condemnations (418) and by the Council of Ephesus* (431).

The City of God, written late in his life (413–26), was occasioned by the Goths'* sack of Rome (410). In it Augustine drew together many strands of classical thought and offered a biblical perspective on the whole of human history, including political life. Books 1–10 are a defense of the city of God against critics in the "earthly city," attacking them for their political and spiritual pride; Books 11–22 interpret the biblical perspective on the origin, course, and ends of the two cities, which arise out of two conflicting loves, namely, love of self, so much so as to have contempt for God; and love of God, so much so as to have contempt for self. This work influenced medieval theories of church* and state, affirming the role of the "earthly city" even while limiting its scope.

Augustine's life began during a period of religious toleration; he became a convert, presbyter, and bishop at the time when orthodoxy was being enforced and other religions suppressed; he died with Vandal* invaders surrounding his city, a situation anticipating the early Middle Ages. His writings, soon taken to Rome, became a major source of medieval thought. The Augustinian* Rule, which was an important stage in the "monasticization of the clergy," was adopted in the Middle Ages by the canons* regular and by several mendicant orders, including the Dominicans* and the Augustinian* Hermits.

The Renaissance* looked to Augustine's intellectual and mystical interests; the Reformation* to his emphasis on sin and grace; the Catholic Church to the many ecclesial themes in his writings; Descartes* and his followers to his "turn inward" and his rational proofs. The political perspectives of *The City of God* are variously interpreted to support a Christian state, the "political realism" that relies on power, and a secular state with limited aims and space for religious freedom. EUGENE TESELLE

Augustinian Hermits or Friars, the Order of. Augustine founded three monasteries in North Africa, and his monks founded other monasteries. Augustinian monastic life somehow survived the Vandal occupation (5th c.) and the Arab invasions (7th c.); hermits following the Augustinian* Rule remained in Italy. Pope Innocent IV (1244) and especially Pope Alexander IV (1256) integrated hermitic groups to form the Augustinian Hermits, which became one of the four mendicant* orders, its members living in cities and devoting themselves to apostolic activities. The Augustinians claim Augustine as their spiritual (rather than juridical) founder; they remain inspired by his very adaptable monastic rule. T. J. VAN BAVEL, OSA

Augustinian Rule. There exist three documents entitled "Rule of Saint Augustine": one for men (*Praeceptum,* oldest ms., 6th–7th c.), another for women (*Regularis informatio* or *Obiurgatio*), and a third one (*Ordo monasterii*), which is certainly not authentic. These three documents circulated in nine different versions. After a lifelong study, L. Verheijen concluded that the *Praeceptum,* written c397 for a community of lay brothers, can reasonably be attributed to Augustine. Like other rules, the rule written by Augustine* first circulated among other monastic texts before becoming the rule for a specific community.

Its first chapter contains four basic ideas: (1) the first community of Jerusalem (Acts 4:31–35) is the model; (2) the sharing of material and spiritual goods realizes common life; (3) common life is no blind uniformity, but is built on respect for the personality of each; and (4) humility is a positive and pride a negative factor in common life. The following six short chapters apply these fundamental ideas to prayer and life in community, common life and care of the body, mutual responsibility, service of one another, love and conflict, and love in authority and obedience; the concluding chapter is an exhortation. T. J. VAN BAVEL, OSA

Aulén, Gustaf (1878–1977), Swedish theologian; professor in Lund, 1913–33; bishop in Strängnäs, 1933–52; member of the "Lundensian school of theology" (with A. Nygren* and R. Bring). In *Christus Victor* (1930), Aulén develops a typology of doctrines of redemption and reconciliation: he favors the "classical" doctrine of atonement* as redemption*, where the struggle between the God of love and the earthly powers of the devil, death, and Law results in God's victory. The Lundensian contra-positioning of *agape*/love vs. *nomos*/law intends to articulate the cosmic implications of redemption in order to overcome moralist/legalist connotations of alternative conceptualizations of atonement.

JAN-OLAV HENRIKSEN

Australia. Christianity began in Australia in unpromising circumstances, with the arrival of convicts in 1788. Initially, the Church* of England was the official religion. But the arrival of Congregationalists*, Wesleyans*, Roman Catholics, and Presbyterians* led to the Church Act of 1836, which gave financial aid to major denominations and later to Jews. Aid was also given to schools. Once the various colonies achieved responsible government, policies changed. By the end of the 19th c., state aid had ceased. All churches had equal privileges before the law, as was written into the Commonwealth Constitution in 1901, which recognized God but prohibited any establishment of religion. Church attendance was high, parliaments opened with prayer, and Christianity was seen as indispensable to national life. Most British and some North American churches were present, along with Lutheran* churches from Prussia and Scandinavia.

During the 20th c., several changes took place. Migration brought a significant Orthodox* presence (mainly Greek), along with Asian churches (mainly Chinese). Pentecostal* churches and Charismatic* networks within major churches grew rapidly beginning in the 1960s. Roman Catholics became the largest denomination. Congregationalists, Methodists, and most Presbyterians formed the Uniting Church in 1977. By the end of the century, a quarter of the population claimed no allegiance to any church, and a significant number of Jews, Muslims, Buddhists, and Hindus became Australians, weakening national Christian influences. Aboriginal and Islander Christianity, which had been scarcely visible in 19th c., became much more articulate, as all the major churches recognized the need for structures that gave Aborigines* a voice in their councils, ensuring that the racism and injustice they had experienced over two centuries would be addressed by churches and nation.

Distinctive features of Australian Christianity included meeting the challenges of traveling huge distances by agencies that brought medical help, pastoral care, and education to outback Australians, using camels, radio, airplanes, and the Internet for communication and travel where no roads existed. Initial shortages of clergy meant that lay agents were vital for the provision of ministry. A decline in ministerial and priestly vocations has made lay ministry essential again, aided by the expansion of theological education beyond the colleges that the churches established in the absence of faculties of theology in the universities until the late 19th c. Anglicans introduced synodal government (mid-19th c.), giving their male laity a voice in decision making. Women had to wait until well into the 20th c. Egalitarianism has been a feature of Australian culture. One result of that has been strong compassion for the marginalized, especially in the Salvation* Army, both within and beyond borders, and practical cooperation in philanthropy. Conversely, a regional synod in Rome in 1998 rebuked Australian Catholics for having a too democratic spirit.

Though it was not until late in the 20th c. that several world-class theological scholars emerged, such as P. Davies and C. Birch (both notable scientists), N. Habel, F. Moloney, and G. O'Collins, all the churches have had clergy and members with considerable skill in adapting European and American theologies to Australian conditions. S. Angus and P. Cameron, both Sydney Presbyterians, were tried for heresy in the 1930s and 1990s, respectively, while Fr. Collins of Missionaries of the Sacred Heart was in trouble for suggesting constitutional reform of the papacy*. Biblical authority and exegesis, Christology, miracles, ecclesiology, the role of women, and most recently homosexuality have been highly debated issues. Protestant Evangelicalism was dismissed by Liberals early in the 20th c. but has grown steadily more influential as the Liberal* theological synthesis has unraveled with the challenges posed by new theologies, ethnicity, feminism, rapid cultural change, postmodernism, and variegated spiritualities. Greek Orthodox input into these debates is slowly gathering momentum, as are contributions from ethnic churches. Sharp divisions have also occurred over the boundaries between religion and politics. Parliamentarians have sometimes been justified in their criticisms of poorly prepared submissions from churches and ecumenical bodies on controversial public issues.

A more secular* climate, the influence of multiculturalism, moral relativism, and the declining membership of the churches have meant that their public influence has shrunk over the past 50 years. Though some clergy are still guaranteed media attention, church members will not necessarily regard them as their voice, for individualism and skepticism about authority figures are cultural markers for Australians. That has been reinforced by the criminal sexual behavior of a minority of clergy and religious and by the failure of authorities to deal with such abuses, because they were concerned more for the perpetrators than for the victims. Dr. Hollingworth was forced to resign as governor-general because of his failure in this area while serving as Anglican archbishop of Brisbane.

Women have been important for the churches as volunteers, fund-raisers, educators, and caregivers. But they are no longer content to be limited to such roles and motherhood and to be excluded from the public spheres that have been monopolized by men for historical and cultural reasons. Protestant deaconesses, missionaries, and musicians had no formal roles constitutionally. Ecumenical scholarship and increasingly pointed feminist critiques of patriarchy led to the ordination of women by some denominations, though Anglicans and Pentecostals remain divided and Catholics and Orthodox are opposed to such ordination, seeing it as a surrender to culture rather than obedience to "revelation and tradition." Religious Catholic women have always included those, such as Blessed Mary MacKillop, with a vision that led them to resist episcopal authoritarians; women are now permitted a much wider constitutional pastoral and parochial role. The same is true in other churches and in the Salvation* Army, where Eva Burrows served as general from 1986 to 1993. Such changes have not prevented many younger women from opting out of church life.

Future challenges include reconnecting to the spiritual search of those under the age of 50, finding more credible ways to speak of discipleship amid a supermarket of lifestyle choices, exploring dialogue with other Australians from other world religions, meeting the challenge of environmental issues, dealing with issues of sexuality and family life, and contributing to the search for a society united in compassion, concern for peace, and commitment to changing the darker sides of Australian society.

Statistics: Population (2000): 18.8 million (M). Christians (1970): 11.6 M, 93%; (2000): 15 M, 79% (Roman Catholics, 5.4 M; Anglicans, 4 M; Protestants, 2.6 M; independents, 0.8 M; Orthodox, 0.7 M; marginal Christians, 0.2 M). The population also included in 2000: Muslims, 0.2 M, 1.2%; Buddhists, 0.2 M, 1.3%; traditional religions, 0.06 M; nonreligious, 3.1 M, 16%. (Based on *World Christian Encyclopedia*, 2001.)

IAN BREWARD

Australian Aboriginal Traditions and Christianity. Approximately 600 Aboriginal dialect groups occupied Australia at the time of colonial settlement in 1788. This entry takes the Pitjantjatjara people of northwest South Australia as an example. Their worldview is expressed in the concept of *tjukurpa*, or the Dreaming, according to which spirit-beings (*kurunitja*) that had lain dormant beneath the surface of a preexistent substance emerged as beings that shared both human and other faunal and floral species identities as, e.g., kangaroo-men, fig-men, and bower bird-women. As they traveled across the earth's surface, they metamorphosed or left their imprint to form the features of the landscape. Humans and other species are believed to be descended from these ancestral spirit beings, whose activities provided the pattern for life. Local groups descended from specific beings are responsible for maintaining the sites, stories, and rituals to ensure the continuation of these species.

Early Christian missions failed, as dispossession of land, introduced diseases, and conflict led to a rapid decline of Aboriginal populations in regions of initial contact. Although missionaries recognized the common humanity of Aborigines, mission policies reflected the dominant attitudes of the period. Aborigines were seen as a doomed race, and there was little recognition of the values of their societies. Starting in 1850, missions provided protection that enabled Aboriginal groups to survive in several regions.

During the 20th c., the Aboriginal population trend was reversed as government Aboriginal policies changed from protectionism and assimilation to self-management. Some missions similarly developed more liberal attitudes and respect for Aboriginal culture and languages. Thus in 1937 the Presbyterian Church established Ernabella Mission (in northwest South Australia) with a policy of minimal interference with the traditional culture and use of the Pitjantjatjara language. Scriptures and hymns were translated, and new Christians became involved in preaching and teaching. The Ernabella choir, singing hymns in Pitjantjatjara, toured Eastern Australia and Fiji.

In the late 1970s, the Charismatic Arnhem Land Revival Movement emerged from Methodist mission work in Northern Australia and influenced many Aboriginal communities (see Land). Aboriginal Catholics incorporated traditional symbols in church buildings and worship. In Central Australia in the 1980s, Walpiri-speaking Baptists began celebrating Christian stories through traditional ceremonial forms. In the late 1960s, the Aboriginal Evangelical Fellowship developed under strong indigenous leadership. Nungalinya College, established in Darwin in 1974, provides Aboriginal Christians with opportunities for theological education and examination of relationships between their traditions and Christianity. **See also ANCESTOR VENERATION AND CHRISTIANITY CLUSTER: IN ABORIGINAL AUSTRALIA; ANTHROPOLOGY CLUSTER: AUSTRALIAN ABORIGINAL THEOLOGICAL ISSUES; HEALTH, HEALING, AND CHRISTIANITY CLUSTER: IN AUSTRALIAN ABORIGINAL SOCIETIES.**

WILLIAM H. EDWARDS

Austria. Christianity, closely linked to the development of the Austrian nation and state and to popular religious traditions in Central Europe, spread very early (3rd–4th c.) to the region around the Danube River when it was under Roman control. The early medieval period saw successive waves of peoples – Slavs, Germans, and Huns – move into modern-day Austria and the surrounding territories that would coalesce into the Hapsburg monarchy (1526–1918). These peoples were only gradually Christianized. In the medieval period, monasteries and ecclesiastical centers (Salzburg and Passau) were crucial to the spread of Christianity.

The Protestant Reformation* made inroads in Austria. Political loyalties and religious affiliations shifted among prominent families and common people alike. The small Protestant communities of modern-day Austria trace their roots to these developments, although legal recognition by the state came only with the Edict of Toleration (1781) and in the 19th c.

The Roman Catholic* Renewal was strong in Austria, as Jesuits* and other religious orders established or reinvigorated centers of learning and reconverted people to Roman Catholicism. Throughout the Hapsburg monarchy, there was a close association of Roman Catholicism with the Hapsburgs, leading to the so-called *Pietas Austriaca*, a religious-political idea that the Hapsburgs were the defenders of Catholicism in Europe. Joseph II (1780–90) ushered in a period of controversial church reform (involving finances, ritual, and parish life) that had ongoing effects in the 19th c. Equally important were the interpenetration of religious ritual and practices with daily life (marriage, burial, child rearing, and holidays) and the role of women in maintaining day-to-day religious life. Moreover, until recent times, Austrian architecture, literature, music, and politics have been strongly conditioned by both Catholic and Protestant religious communities.

Since the mid-19th c., a reaction against the prominent place of Christianity in Austria has developed. Several constitutional and legal reforms concerning marriage, education, and other issues have been enacted to regulate the relationship between the Roman Catholic Church and the Austrian state. Gradually, new Christian denominations have been officially recognized. A troubling issue has been the relationship of Christians to Jews, who for many centuries suffered discrimination and sometimes open persecution, most dramatically during the Nazi period (the Jewish population dropping from more than 200,000 in 1938 to 4,000 in 1945) (see Anti-Semitism; Holocaust, Jewish [or Shoah]; Judaism and Christianity Cluster).

In the post-1945 period, Christianity in Austria has come into crisis. Although the cultural hold of Christianity (e.g. holidays and baptisms) has remained strong, church attendance and profession of belief have declined precipitously. Some authorities refer to an "exodus" from established churches over such issues as sexual practices and religious taxes. Only in recent years (post-2000) have there been some signs of stabilization in Christian communities. Since the 1960s, the influx of Muslims from Turkey and the former Yugoslavia has created another set of legal and cultural issues for Austria's Christians and the state.

Statistics: Population: 8 million. Roman Catholics, 74%; Evangelicals (Augsburger/Lutheran and Helvetic/Calvinist* confessions), 4.7%; Eastern Orthodox (Russian, Greek, Serbian, Romanian, and Bulgarian), 2.2%; other Christians, 0.9%; Muslims, 4.2%; Jews, 0.1%; atheists, 12%; no response, 2%. (*Source*: 2001 census.)

WILLIAM D. BOWMAN

Authority in/of the Church. "Authority" means not sheer power but legitimate power. Authority exists only insofar as those who submit to it do so by acknowledging the legitimacy of those who are in a position to use institutional or other power and/or to speak authoritatively. In Christian thought, authority belongs first to God, then to Christ, then to those who are authorized by God and Christ (prophets*, apostles*) to transmit the Christian tradition, and to the writings that were gathered together as Scripture* and, for Christians, the NT as canon within the canon. How is the divine authority transmitted from Christ to his followers? What is received as authoritative? Differing answers to these questions have occasioned many church conflicts.

In the NT, Paul's claim to authority is based on the gospel he received "through a revelation of Jesus Christ," a charismatic* authority (similar to the charismatic authority of any member of the body of Christ, 1 Cor 12:4–31) that clashed with the institutional authority of the Jerusalem church, which first received the gospel during Jesus' ministry (Gal 1–2). Yet in the Pastoral* Epistles, Paul's school refers to developing authoritative institutional structures, headed by a bishop (1 Tim 3:1–2; 1 Titus 1:7).

Ignatius* of Antioch (d107–13) underscored the authority of bishops (advocating the monepiscopate*, a single bishop in each locality guaranteeing unity in the Eucharist). Irenaeus* (c125–c200) affirmed the authority of the "apostolic proclamation," publicly handed down in the books of the NT and summarized in what we call the Apostles'* Creed. In the following centuries, authority came to be attributed to ecumenical* councils.

Meanwhile, authority became related to rival power centers. The tensions between Antioch*, Alexandria*, and Rome (and the pope*) are reflected in the doctrinal divisions (about Christology*) between Chalcedonian*, Miaphysite*, and Assyrian* (so-called Nestorian*) churches.

In the West, the "Roman" Church had a centralized structure of authority: other churches were to be "in communion with Rome;" authority resided in Rome and the authoritative dogmatic and moral teaching (*magisterium**) of the pope and papal curia.

By contrast, the Eastern Orthodox* churches, centered on Byzantium (Ecumenical* Patriarchate of Constantinople), had a somewhat diffuse authority, with autocephalous* churches "in communion with each other" (following the "principle of conciliarity"; the consensus of the whole body of believers). For these churches (until today), the seven ecumenical* councils have a dogmatic authority. But in Eastern Orthodoxy, authority is not merely (indeed, not primarily) dogmatic. Authority is experiential and doxological in character, grounded in mystical* experience. (One does not have the authority of a theologian without personal experience of God and the enlightenment it provides; consequently, authority can no longer be controlled by the institution or limited to the clergy.) Authority is tied to the experience of the "mysteries*," including the mystery of the church as a manifestation of the mysterious encounter of love between God and humankind (see Orthodox Churches, Eastern, Cluster: Introductory Entries).

As time passed, the authority of the churches became more and more entangled with that of the state (see Church and State Relations Cluster). Ultimately the Western church became an institutional authority exercising great intellectual and disciplinary authority over the whole of European society. This authority and its claim to be based on divine authority were challenged during the Renaissance* and the Reformation*, raising questions about the relative importance of biblical and institutional authority. As the Council of Trent* showed, the issue was partly a matter of the authority of Scripture* against that of tradition (see Tradition Cluster) but should also be seen as a question of who has the right to define what is the teaching of Scripture: Rome and institutional authorities (the *magisterium*) or local communities (led by preachers), and even individual believers?

The Enlightenment* and its emphasis on individualism and reason* further challenged institutional ecclesial authority, especially of the Roman Catholic Church, which in response reemphasized the authority of the *magisterium*, indeed proclaiming it to be an infallible* teaching. The Enlightenment also challenged what remained of institutional authority in Protestant churches. The right of individuals to define what is the teaching of Scripture (the more radical Protestant view) has been amplified in three ways: (1) by embracing reason* as the main authority and exercising radical criticism of the Bible (denying both institutional doctrinal authority and the authority of religious experience); (2) by locating authority in the "inspired reading" of the Bible, i.e. in the Bible as read in relationship with an individual religious experience, especially the experience of the Holy* Spirit emphasized in the Pentecostal*/Charismatic* Movement; (3) by locating authority in a threefold hermeneutical* process that includes the interpretation of Scripture (a) through an individual reading of the text in terms of (b) religious experience(s) and (c) the intellectual and ethical demands of particular contexts – the view represented by Schleiermacher*, Catholic Modernists* (especially von* Hügel), and the hermeneutic movement (from Bultmann* to Ricoeur*). In this last case, as advocacy interpreters (Feminist*, Liberation*, and postcolonial* theologians and biblical scholars) emphasize, authority resides primarily with a judgment regarding the contextual effect of a biblical teaching on others, and consequently authority is collective (not individualist) but resides with the faith community in the world (not with an aloof institution; see Scriptural Criticism).

As various churches through the centuries assumed one or another view of authority, different types of structures of church authority developed (see Church, Concepts, and Life Cluster: Church, Types of Ecclesiastical Structures, where Episcopalian, Presbyterian, Congregational, Charismatic leadership, and Charismatic/Pentecostal types of ecclesiastical structures are distinguished). DANIEL PATTE

Autocephalous Churches are Orthodox* churches that are "self-headed," with their own patriarchs* and synods of bishops, an administrative independence that does not deny spiritual unity. The Council of Ephesus* (431) established the principle of autocephaly when the Church of Cyprus became independent of Antioch; in medieval and modern times, national churches were organized in the Slavic world as autocephalous. At present there are 14 autocephalous churches: 4 ancient Eastern Patriarchates (the Ecumenical* Patriarchate of Constantinople and the Patriarchates of Alexandria, Antioch, and Jerusalem) and 10 other Orthodox churches that have emerged over the centuries in Russia*, Serbia*, Romania*, Bulgaria*, Georgia*, Cyprus*, Greece*, Poland*, Albania*, and the Czech* and Slovak Republics.

Auto da fé (Portuguese; *auto de fé*, Spanish; "act of faith"), a public ceremony of the Spanish and Portuguese Inquisition*, climaxing with a declaration of each prisoner's sins and either reconciliation through penance* or (in the case of the unrepentant) being handed over to the "secular* arm" for burning.

Autonomy has been evaluated in the Christian tradition both positively, as freedom from bondage, and negatively, as challenging God or religious institutions.

As a political term dating back to antiquity and the Stoics*, "autonomy" referred to free city-states and free men. Paul affirmed that true autonomy is a gift from God for all, including slaves and women (Gal 3:28, 5:1).

In the late Middle Ages, the Stoic and the Pauline understandings of autonomy were combined when the autonomy of the church and papacy was affirmed over against imperial power and, in the 16th c., when autonomous Protestant folk* churches in nation-states were formed, rejecting imperial and Roman ecclesiastical power.

Autonomy from church institutions was further emphasized during the Enlightenment*, but was now formulated as the freedom of human reason* from religious dogmas or institutions, and from the heteronomy* (submission to these dogmas or institutions) they involved.

In ethics, the Enlightenment understanding of the autonomy of reason led to Kant's* affirmation of the primacy of reason over revelation, by contrast with theological ethics informed by the Augustinian tradition of original* sin. Other theologians, including Tillich*, combined philosophical and theological ethics, e.g. by affirming that autonomy was deepened when related to theonomy.

Postmodern thinkers, especially feminist* theologians, have questioned the notion of the autonomous subject, in order to affirm the role of relationality*.

Autonomy has for the most part been positively evaluated in the Christian tradition. Yet according to the concepts with which one relates it, one variously affirms its excellence, its ambivalence, or its potential danger. (On the danger of individualism as an overemphasis on autonomy, see Racism and Christianity Cluster.)

CRISTINA GRENHOLM

Auxiliis. See CONGREGATIO DE AUXILIIS.

Averroes, or Ibn Rushd, 1126–98, born in Cordoba; leading Aristotelian thinker in the Islamic* world, who devoted himself to commenting on the works of Aristotle* at the request of the Almohad ruler. His writings posed serious problems for Muslim scholars such as al-Ghazali and Ibn Sina (Avicenna*), because Aristotle taught that the universe was eternal and denied the immortality of (individual) human souls*. Averroes asserted the truth of creation and the immortality of the soul, but was accused of holding that there are two truths, a religious truth and a philosophical truth. Widely cited by Thomas Aquinas* and profoundly influencing Latin Averroists such as Siger* of Brabant, Averroes was at the center of 14th-c. philosophical debates at the University of Padua. Averroes's work continued for Christian theologians who sought to adapt Aristotelian metaphysics and science as a framework for their thought, despite tensions with the Judeo-Christian view of God. Aquinas's genius lay in his analogical* approach to truth and his synthesis that drew on Augustine*, the Stoics*, Neoplatonists*, and Aristotle's theory of knowledge to bridge the gap between the Christian idea of God as creator and the belief in the immortality of individual human souls and Aristotle's architectonic science of nature. **See also BACON, ROGER.**

JAMES M. POWELL

Avicenna, or Ibn Sina (c980–1037), a brilliant polymath whose learning ranged over virtually all branches of knowledge but who was especially valued for his work in medicine, the *Qanun*, which became a standard text for Western medicine. In philosophy, his work consisted chiefly of an effort to synthesize Aristotle* and Neoplatonism* and was closely tied to Islamic* theology, which, like contemporary Christian thought, tended to find Neoplatonism much more compatible than Aristotle. He was also influenced by Gnosticism*. Yet, attracted by Aristotle's logical and scientific writings, Avicenna made important contributions to Aristotle's work on psychology. He had some influence on Scholastics such as Bonaventure* and Henry of Ghent.

JAMES M. POWELL

Avvakum Petrovich (1610–81), archpriest. A former confessor to the czar and member of church reformist circles, he was the most visible defender of old church rituals changed by Patriarch Nikon* (1654) and leader of the Old* Believer Movement. Avvakum, revered as a saint by Old Believers, wrote *Autobiography of the Archpriest Avvakum by Himself*, an important work that told of his exile to Siberia. Avvakum was burned at the stake by czarist forces in 1681.

ROY R. ROBSON

Awakening. See GREAT AWAKENING; REVIVAL, REVIVALISM.

Azusa Street Revival, a 1906–15 revival meeting in Los Angeles, California, led by William Seymour*, an African American preacher at the African Methodist Episcopal Church on that street. This revival – characterized by speaking in tongues*, ecstatic experiences, and interracial mingling – is viewed as a starting point of the spread of Pentecostalism* in the 20th c.

B

Baal (Heb for "lord" or "owner"), title given to the deities of Canaan and sometimes to the God of Israel.

Babel, the Hebrew term for Babylon*. The Tower of Babel (Gen 11:1–9) was a work of human presumption; its builders were punished by the confusion of languages, making direct communication impossible. This punishment is reversed at Pentecost* (Acts 2:1–21). According to the Christian interpretation, Babylon signifies earthly society (vs. the city of God) and Babel signifies hell*, associated with confusion.

Babylonian Captivity, the period between the deportation of many citizens of Judah to Babylonia (some leaders in 597 BCE, more in 587/86) and their return to Jerusalem after Cyrus's conquest of Babylon in 539 (Jer 25:11–12), or more exactly the reopening of the Temple in 516. For Augustine*, the city of Babylon was considered a typological* figure of the "earthly city," and Jeremiah's advice to the exiles (Jer 29:5–7) was the basis of a Christian social ethic. The removal of the papacy to Avignon (1309–77) was called its "Babylonian captivity" by Petrarch*. Luther* criticized the papacy as a "Babylonian captivity" from which the church must be freed.

Bach, Johann Sebastian (1685–1750), German Lutheran composer whose music was of fundamental importance in the development of Western music traditions and continues to receive worldwide appreciation. Beginning as a church organist in Arnstadt, Mühlhausen, and Weimar, broadening his musical horizons as court *Capellmeister* in Cöthen, he became the director of music in Leipzig, where he spent the rest of his life (1723–50). Bach composed much music, sacred and secular, instrumental and vocal, but a large proportion was written for Lutheran worship: cantatas*, oratorios*, passions*, and works for organ, in which theology and spirituality are expressed in musical form. ROBIN A. LEAVER

Bacon, Roger (c1214/20–92), a graduate of Oxford University, where he studied with Grosseteste*; one of the first to teach Aristotle at the University of Paris (c1240–50). Beyond his writing on logic in the Oxford tradition, Bacon's works on natural philosophy and metaphysics indicate a mature assimilation of Aristotle*, attuned to the implications of Averroes's* positions on the intellect, determinism, and knowledge. After 1247, Bacon developed interests in language study (wisdom languages: Hebrew, Greek, Chaldean) and the mathematical sciences. At Pope Clement V's request, he produced *The Major Work, The Minor Work,* and *The Third Work* and related works (1266). *The Major Work* presents a new educational model for the medieval university, advocating the study of the wisdom languages, the study of linguistics (semantics and semiotics*), the application of mathematics to the sciences, and the uses of the sciences in biblical and theological studies. Bacon introduced the study of *perspectiva* (optics) and used it to draw moral and religious metaphors. The last section of *The Major Work* on moral philosophy includes religious apologetics, virtue theory, and the role of rhetoric and poetics in religion. Some of Bacon's views, probably on astrology, were condemned by the Franciscan* order (1278). Back in Oxford (c1280), he wrote *Compendium studii theologiae* (c1292). JEREMIAH M. HACKETT

BAHA'I FAITH AND CHRISTIANITY CLUSTER

Baha'i Faith and Christianity: Baha'i Perspectives
Baha'i Faith and Christianity: Christian Perspectives

Baha'i Faith and Christianity: Baha'i Perspectives. The approximately 5 million adherents (in 2000) of the Baha'i Faith affirm, together with their primary texts, a number of core Christian beliefs, including the divinity and sonship of Jesus Christ, the divine inspiration of the Bible, and the significance of the Crucifixion and subsequent impact on human progress. Baha'is hold to a nonliteral interpretation of the resurrection* and future apocalyptic events predicted in the Gospels and Revelation. Although the bodily incarnation* of God's essence in Jesus Christ is not part of Baha'i teaching, Jesus is viewed as the incarnation of God's virtues and attributes and as a sinless being whose soul was preexistent. Baha'i theology describes Jesus as the "manifestation of God" (cf. "image," Col 1:15; Heb 1:3). Although they do not affirm the inerrancy* of the Bible, Baha'is reject the view of mainstream Islam* that the NT has been corrupted.

Baha'i literature on Christianity is predominantly apologetic, arguing that the founder of the Baha'i Faith, Mirza Husayn Ali Baha'u'llah, fulfilled NT prophecies on the "Second* Coming." Recent scholarly analyses of Baha'i texts on the Bible and comparative theological studies have argued that, rather than denying the uniqueness* of Jesus Christ, Baha'i texts question the exclusivity of Christianity. Christian literature on the Baha'i religion has been mostly polemical – much of it written by former Protestant missionaries in Iran* who seemingly resented the relative success of Baha'is in converting Muslims, and more recently by individuals with no knowledge of the primary languages of Baha'i texts who tried to dismiss the religion as a cult or sect. In academic works related to interreligious dialogue, Christian theologians have placed the Baha'i Faith within a theology of religious pluralism.

Baha'is and Christians share a belief in the importance of an ethical system based on personal responsibility, justice*, honesty, and compassion; of social justice*, respect for nature, interfaith dialogue, and gender and racial equality. SEENA FAZEL

Baha'i Faith and Christianity: Christian Perspectives. Many Christians remain ignorant of the Baha'i Faith, introduced to the Western world at the World Parliament of Religions (Chicago, 1893) by a Christian missionary working in Syria. He enthusiastically quoted the prediction of Baha'u'llah (Baha'Allah; 1817–92), the founder of the Baha'i religion (in Iran*), "that all nations should become one in faith and all men as brothers and that diversity of religion should cease."

Some liberal Christians greeted his son and successor, Abdu'l-Baha (1844–1921), with similar enthusiasm in London (1911). The minister of the City Temple (the historic Nonconformist Congregation where Abdu'l-Baha preached) declared, "The Baha'i movement is almost identical with the spiritual purpose of Christianity." At St. John's Church, Westminster, the archdeacon knelt with his congregation to receive Abdu'l-Baha's blessing. Pioneers of the interfaith movement welcomed the Baha'i emphasis on the unity of religions, but other Christians suspected the Baha'i Faith of "syncretism*."

Many Christians, especially Evangelicals*, have criticized Baha'is for denying the uniqueness* of Jesus and question Baha'u'llah's symbolic interpretation of the Bible in his *Tablet to the Christians* (*Lawh-I-Aqdas*). Baha'u'llah taught that God, though unknowable, is revealed through manifestations, including Jesus, along with Moses, Muhammad, and others. The essential message of these manifestations is the same, although each messenger has a distinct individuality and mission. Revelation is progressive. Baha'u'llah claimed to be the promised one of *all* religions and compared his own suffering in prison to Jesus' atoning* death. These claims are incompatible with traditional Christian belief.

Baha'u'llah's teachings anticipated many 20th-c. creative developments: the peace* movement, interfaith fellowship, equal rights for women, the International Court of Justice, and the United Nations. Christian advocates of these causes have often been happy to work with Baha'is.

MARCUS BRAYBROOKE

Baius, Michel (1513–89), Flemish theologian, teacher at the University of Louvain, participant in the Council of Trent*. Adopting an idiosyncratic interpretation of Augustine*, he held that original righteousness was natural and that redemption is a restoration of this natural state. Condemnation of his views (1567, 1579) gave impetus to post-Tridentine controversies over nature* and grace* in the Catholic Church.

Baker, Ella Josephine (1903–86). Born in Norfolk, Virginia, nurtured by a strong extended family and Baptist Church tradition, and educated at Shaw University (Raleigh, North Carolina), Baker was exposed to the social and artistic ferment of the Harlem Renaissance (1920s), which led her into the civil* rights field. From 1940 to 1986, Baker served on the staffs of the National Association for the Advancement of Colored People and Martin Luther King*, Jr.'s, Southern* Christian Leadership Conference, and was a founder of the Student Nonviolent Coordinating Committee. Her call for a group-centered leadership model conflicted with the male-dominated charismatic model represented by figures like King and Malcolm X. LEWIS V. BALDWIN

Balaam, diviner asked to curse the people of Israel but led to bless them (Num 22–24). Because he misled them into idolatry (Num 31:16), he is associated with temptation (Jude 11; Rev 2:14).

Balkans. See HISTORY OF CHRISTIANITY CLUSTER: IN EUROPE: THE BALKANS.

Balthasar, Hans Urs von. See VON BALTHASAR, HANS URS.

Baltimore, Councils of. As the administrative center of the fledgling US Roman Catholic Church, Baltimore hosted two series of important gatherings of church officials. Seven provincial councils (starting in 1829) were followed by three plenary councils (1852, 1866, and 1884) that drew leaders from recently created dioceses throughout the USA. With each meeting, the number of attending bishops and archbishops grew, reflecting the rapid growth of the Catholic community in the USA caused by immigration from Europe. Carefully worded decrees on such topics as liturgy, seminaries, parochial schools, and church property fostered a much needed sense of unity among American Catholics. The current United States Conference of Catholic Bishops traces its lineage to these Baltimore councils. THOMAS MASSARO, SJ

Bancroft, Richard (bap.1544–1610), Anglican priest, canon of Westminster Cathedral, bishop* of London (1597), archbishop of Canterbury* (1606). Dogged polemicist and able administrator, Bancroft countered the dual threats posed by Roman Catholics and Nonconformists*. Against the latter (*pace* Hooker*), he defended the church's hierarchical episcopacy as *jure divino,* apostolic*, a mark of true Christianity; bishops were both distinct from priests* or presbyters* and independent of secular control. Yet Bancroft linked religious conformity with loyalty to the English crown. In the Articles of Visitation* and the Canons* of 1604, Bancroft emphasized ceremony, the autonomy of the church, and proper preaching and catechizing*. BRETT GREGORY ARMSTRONG

Báñez, Domingo (1528–1604), Dominican theologian and professor at several Spanish universities, finally Salamanca. Confessor and spiritual adviser to Teresa* of Ávila, he led the attack on the Jesuit approach to grace* (see Congregatio de auxiliis; Middle Knowledge; Molina, Luis de).

Baptism of Christ, Jesus' baptism in the river Jordan by John* the Baptist, when he received the Holy Spirit (Mark 1:9–11, par.), associated with the festival of Epiphany*.

BAPTISM CLUSTER

Baptism as Defined by the Orthodox Church
Baptism as Defined by Protestant Churches
Baptism as Defined by the Roman Catholic Church
Baptism in the Holy Spirit

Baptism as Defined by the Orthodox Church is the first and essential sacrament*. It manifests the most radical change in the human condition by accomplishing sacramentally both a death and a new birth (Rom 6:3–11; John 3:3–8). Baptism incorporates persons into Christ and his church that they may share in his deified* humanity and, as a new* creation (2 Cor 5:17), come under Christ's rule to grow into the fullness of his nature within the church by sharing its life, faith, values, and vision. The rite of baptism consists of three parts:

1. "Catechesis," culminating in the profession of faith through the recitation of the Nicene* Creed.
2. Consecration of the font; anointing of the catechumen*, adult or infant, with the "oil of gladness"; and baptism through three immersions in the name of the Father, Son, and Holy Spirit (Matt 28:19). The newly baptized is then clothed in a white garment and anointed with the oils of chrismation*.

3. Elements of the Eucharist*, administration of Holy Communion, and tonsure.

Infants are baptized not because they are born sinful or bear guilt, but so that they may be given the gifts of sanctification*, righteousness*, and filial adoption. **See also ORTHODOX CHURCHES, EASTERN, CLUSTER: INTRODUCTORY ENTRIES.**

ALKIVIADIS CALIVAS

Baptism as Defined by Protestant Churches. Lutheran, Reformed, Anabaptist, and Baptist traditions of Protestantism have diverse interpretations of both the theology and practice of baptism. Each, however, invokes the trinitarian formula and perceives baptism in some way as an initiation into the church. Lutherans believe baptism* is sacramental*, they practice infant baptism by sprinkling, and only clergy administer baptism. Reformed Christians have a quasi-sacramental view of baptism, they practice infant baptism by sprinkling, and clergy are the sole administrators. Anabaptists advocate a symbolic view of baptism and, because of their emphasis on a believers' church, oppose infant baptism, and pastors generally perform immersion*. Baptists also affirm a believers' church, reject infant baptism, and practice immersion, and pastors are usually the administrators of baptism.

These differing views of Protestant baptism affect four theological areas. (1) Salvation*: Does one become a Christian through sacramental baptism or personal faith*? (2) The nature of the church*: Is the church composed of infants or believers only? (3) The mode of baptism: What practice symbolizes the truth of baptism – sprinkling, pouring, or immersion? (4) The nature of the ministry and the administrator of baptism: Can baptism be performed by laity or is that the right of clergy only?

WALTER B. SHURDEN

Baptism as Defined by the Roman Catholic Church is a sacrament* of initiation into the Christian community wherein, through grace*, one "puts on Christ." In modern times, the Catholic Church administers initiation for infants through baptism only (not chrismation*; cf. Baptism* for the Orthodox Church); First Communion is postponed until the "age of reason" (about 8), and confirmation until the age of 12. Vatican* II (1962–65) clarified the various parts of the ritual and enhanced the role of parents and godparents. Today infant baptisms often take place during a Sunday Eucharist*, involving the community more intimately. Although infant baptism was often associated by Catholics with the "removal of original* sin," thereby affording the possibility of entry into heaven* rather than an eternity in the "limbo* of unbaptized infants," these associations have largely faded through a more comprehensive, biblically driven understanding of baptism.

To avoid turning baptism into a social rite of passage without much religious connotation, parishes commonly require from expectant couples a period of instruction on the nature of baptism and parents' responsibilities to provide religious formation for their baptized children. While recognizing the importance of faith* for the reception of any sacrament, the church sees the parents, family, and ecclesial community as nurturing the child's faith until the time when the child will personally ratify the sacrament administered as a gesture of God's unconditional love.

The adult catechumenate*, the "Rite of Christian Initiation for Adults," was restored in the 1960s. Several months of gradual assimilation into the community culminate in baptism (frequently at the Easter vigil service, sometimes by immersion) or, if the person has already been baptized in a non-Catholic church, with a public affirmation of Catholic belief, and finally the anointing of confirmation* and reception of the Eucharist.

MICHAEL A. FAHEY, SJ

Baptism in the Holy Spirit, also called "Spirit baptism," is a term that refers to Jesus as mediator of the Spirit (Spirit baptizer), distinct from John the Baptist (baptizer in water for repentance; Matt 3:12; Acts 1:5). No established doctrine of Spirit baptism existed historically, though early evidence suggests a widespread link to water baptism and to the spiritual gifts received by Christians. Most Pentecostals* promoted the Free Church separation of Spirit baptism from water baptism to support access to the Spirit (and Jesus) apart from church rites, bringing Spirit baptism to prominence as a distinct theological concept.

Spirit baptism is associated with (1) Christian initiation by the Spirit, principally through water baptism (1 Cor 12:13) (Roman Catholic, Anglican, Orthodox*); (2) Christian conversion through the Spirit received by faith (e.g. Reformed Evangelical*); (3) a postconversion experience of "entire sanctification" (purity of heart, Acts 15:7–8) (Holiness* Movement); (4) a postconversion empowerment for Christian witness (Acts 1:8) involving extraordinary spiritual gifts (charismata), such as speaking in tongues (Acts 2:4) and divine healing (most Pentecostals*); and (5) Christian initiation or conversion by the Spirit, who is subsequently "released" in life experientially or charismatically (many Charismatics*).

Spirit baptism is perhaps an eschatological gift integrating various aspects of the Spirit's work. FRANK D. MACCHIA

BAPTIST CHURCHES CLUSTER

1) *Introductory Entries*

Baptist Churches and Their Theology
Baptist Worship

2) *A Sampling of Contextual Practices*

Baptist Churches in North America
Baptist Missionary Society

---

1) Introductory Entries

Baptist Churches and Their Theology. Historically, Baptists started out at both ends of the Protestant theological spectrum. The world's first Baptist congregation was formed in Amsterdam in 1608/9 by a group of English Separatist Puritans whose theology was Arminian*. They affirmed the role of free will* in salvation, the general atonement* of Christ (his death for all persons), and the possibility that Christians could fall from grace* along the way. Returning to England in 1612, this group became known as General Baptists. (Their heirs are often called Free* Will Baptists.) During the 1630s, another community of Baptists formed in London with a commitment to Calvinist theology centered on total depravity, election*, predestination*, and Christ's atoning death for the elect alone. Their view of limited atonement led to the name Particular* Baptists. Thus from their earliest days, different groups of Baptists held contradictory theological positions. This diversity continued in the USA and is evident in the Calvinism of the Primitive Baptists and the Arminianism of the Free* Will Baptists. Other Baptist subdenominations nuance these two theological traditions in a variety of ways that incorporate aspects of Evangelicalism*, liberalism*, fundamentalism*, and other theological positions.

What unites Baptists theologically is their belief that the church of Jesus Christ is composed of those who can attest to an experience of divine grace, followed by believers' baptism by immersion. Personal "regeneration" experienced through conversion* and new life in Christ is required of those who seek membership in a Baptist church. The concept of a believers' church* is central to Baptist theology. In general, Baptists are trinitarians who can affirm the classic dogmas of the Apostles'* Creed, although some remain suspicious of such extrabiblical documents. Many have utilized confessions of faith to summarize essential doctrines and theological ideals. Such confessions date from the 16th c. and reflect various degrees of Calvinism and Arminianism in their orientation. The confessions delineate the views of specific Baptist groups regarding God, Scripture, salvation, the nature of the church, baptism, the Lord's Supper, church discipline, and the relationship to the state. Amid differences, these confessions reflect certain distinctive beliefs affirmed by most Baptist communions.

Biblical Authority and Liberty of Conscience. Baptists affirm the authority of Scripture* as the normative guide for

Baptist Churches and Their Theology

theology, doctrine, and practice for the church and the individual. Baptists believe that their basic beliefs are taken from the Bible, and preaching from biblical texts is central to Baptist worship services. Baptists do not always agree on theories of biblical inspiration*, however; some affirm a belief in biblical inerrancy* and others hesitate to do so. They also assert that individual believers may be trusted to interpret Scripture aright, in the context of the believing community (the church) and under the guidance of the Holy* Spirit. Individual interpretation of Scripture within the context of a believers' church is a significant aspect of Baptist belief.

Sacraments, or Ordinances: Baptism and the Lord's Supper. Baptists practice two sacraments*, or ordinances*: baptism* by immersion and the Lord's* Supper. Baptism follows a profession* of faith and is administered to adults or to children who testify to an experience of God's grace*. The Lord's Supper is celebrated in churches, usually monthly or quarterly. Certain Baptist churches and groups practice "closed Communion," whereby only members of the specific congregation are allowed to partake of the sacred meal. Some Baptist groups affirm the "spiritual presence" of Christ in the bread and the wine, while others insist that the Supper is a "memorial" in which the faith of believers is nurtured by recalling Christ's death and resurrection. Some use bread and wine, while others (perhaps a majority in the USA) use bread and unfermented grape juice. A few Baptist groups also practice foot*-washing as another ordinance (John 13), a sign of servanthood among believers.

Church Order: Local Autonomy and Associational Cooperation. Baptists believe that the authority* of Christ is mediated through the community of believers; therefore, they generally adhere to a congregational* form of church government wherein decision making is based on communal dialogue and the will of the majority. Each congregation is autonomous, i.e. free to make its own decisions, develop its own ministries, and affiliate with other groups as it chooses. Yet from the early days of the movement, Baptist churches entered into "associational" relationships with other Baptist churches for fellowship, mutual encouragement, and cooperative ministries. In some cases, these regional associations led to national denominations. Churchly autonomy has led to significant divisions in Baptist life as congregations have split over differences in doctrine and practice.

Baptist Ministry: Priesthood of the Laity and the Ordaining of Clergy. Baptists readily affirm the Reformation doctrine of the priesthood* of all believers. They insist that all Christian believers are free to relate directly to God without the benefit of ecclesiastical mediators. They also suggest that all believers are ministers, called to serve God in the church and the world. Some Baptists in the UK and USA actually practiced the laying on of hands in two ways. They laid hands on all the newly baptized as a sign of their priestly calling, and laid hands a second time on those who were set aside for the "ministry of the Word," carrying out ministerial functions in the church. This kind of egalitarianism energized the laity* but also set the scene for controversies between the clergy and laity in the church.

Citizenship: Religious Liberty and Loyalty to the State. One of the most significant Baptist contributions to the modern world is the idea of radical religious liberty for all persons, believers and unbelievers alike. Baptists were the first religious group in both the UK and USA to suggest that God alone is the judge of conscience and that neither the state nor an official religious establishment can judge whether the conscience of someone is that of a heretic* or an atheist*. Each person is answerable only to God for the religious choices he or she might make. This assertion is based on Baptists' commitment to uncoerced faith* as the hallmark of the believing community. At the same time, they have also insisted on loyalty to the "earthly power" of the state as long as its actions do not violate conscience (see Church and State Relations Cluster). Baptists themselves have often disagreed on the nature of dissent in response to political and ethical issues such as civil* rights, war*, voting practices, prayer in schools, paying taxes, abortion*, and state support for religious institutions.

Theological Diversity. These shared beliefs exist in a context of significant diversity, even division, among the 40 million Baptists worldwide, some 30 million of whom live in the USA. Baptists include Arminians and Calvinists, liberals and conservatives, and a wide variety of churchly practices from congregation to congregation. Serious divisions exist over the role of women* in the church, homosexuality*, theories of biblical inspiration*, ministerial authority, the Charismatic* Movement, denominational relationships, the nature of theological* education, and other issues. Theological contrasts are evident in Baptist leaders like liberal James Forbes, former pastor of Riverside Church, New York, and conservative Jerry Falwell, former pastor of Thomas Road Church, Lynchburg, Virginia. Baptist history reflects a theological diversity that often lends itself to continuous debate and division.

BILL J. LEONARD

Baptist Worship evolved with the US Republic. Early-17th- and 18th-c. Regular (Calvinistic) Baptists utilized a Puritan* form of worship that involved praying, singing the Psalms*, Scripture reading, and lengthy sermons, all conducted in "decency and order." By the mid-1700s the revivalistic* enthusiasm of Separate Baptists led to more "enthusiastic" worship, evident in exuberant preaching, singing of "man-made" hymns, and emotional outbursts from the congregation. By the 19th c., frontier Baptists were drawn to the camp* meeting experience in which "spiritual exercises" – shouting, jerking, crying, and falling – struck the worshipping masses. Camp* meeting songs replaced the Psalms as normative worship music. Preaching*, the mainstay of the service, was presented in a more popular emotional style than the carefully reasoned homilies of the Regular Baptist ministers. A concern for immediate conversion* led to the development of the "mourners' bench" (or "anxious* bench"), a seat near the front of the church where those who fell "under conviction" might duly repent, assisted by the prayers of the faithful. The mourners' bench led to the "altar call," or "invitation to discipleship*," at the end of the service, when persons "received Christ as savior" or requested church membership. This practice continues in many Baptist churches in the USA.

Worship in African American Baptist churches developed its own forms drawn from revivalism, the slave* experience, spirituality*, and the struggle for civil* rights. It included specific types of hymnody, testimonies from the laity, prayer at the altar, and the dramatic preaching characterized by continuing discourse between the minister and the "answering congregation." Amid racial and regional differences, traditional worship in many Baptist communions consisted of a relatively simple liturgy, including an invocation, hymns, prayers, offering, solos or choral music, Scripture readings, a sermon, an "invitation," and a benediction.

By the early 21st c., many Baptist worship practices changed dramatically. Some churches gave greater attention to liturgical* renewal, evident in the use of litanies, classical music, clerical vestments, banners, and preaching from the biblical lectionary. Others moved toward more "contemporary" practices characteristic of the so-called megachurch* movement with its concern for "seeker sensitive" worship aimed at attracting people outside traditional religious communities. This "contemporary" worship included catchy "praise* choruses" (not hymns), the use of drama, drums, and guitars, folksy sermons, and few traditional Christian symbols. These changes have rejuvenated many Baptist congregations while creating "worship wars" in other churches where members differ over contemporary versus traditional styles.

BILL J. LEONARD

---

2) A Sampling of Contextual Practices

Baptist Churches in North America. Approximately 30 million Baptists in North America belong to at least 70 distinct groups. These include a theological spectrum from the Calvinism* of the Primitive

Baptists to the Arminianism* of the Free* Will Baptists. The earliest Baptists in North America were either English Particular* (Calvinist) or General (Arminian) Baptists, who helped to form the first churches in North America in Providence and Newport, Rhode Island (1630s–1640s). Seventh Day Baptists arrived soon after. By the 1700s, Calvinists divided into Regular (anti-revival) and Separate (pro-revival) Baptists. These groups made inroads into the maritime region of Canada. Baptists in the USA united in 1814 to found the General Missionary Convention of the Baptist Denomination in America. It remained intact until 1845 when Baptists north and south divided over the slavery issue and the role of the national convention.

The very conservative Southern* Baptist Convention is the largest Protestant denomination in North America, while the American Baptist Churches in the USA is one of the smaller and most racially inclusive groups. African American Baptist groups include Primitive Baptists as well as the National Baptist Convention, Incorporated; the National Baptist Convention, Unincorporated; and the Progressive National Baptist Convention. Traditionally ethnic Baptist groups include German, Norwegian, Swedish, Latino, Korean, and Japanese Baptists in the USA and Canada. The Baptist Federation of Canada unites many Baptist provincial groups. The Fundamentalist*–Modernist controversy of the early 20th c. spawned numerous Baptist bodies, including the Regular Association of Regular Baptists, the Conservative Baptist Convention, the Baptist* Missionary Association, and various Independent Baptist churches. Appalachian Baptists include Primitive Baptists, United Baptists, Old Regular Baptists, and Two-Seed-in-the-Spirit Predestinarian Baptists. Later in the 20th c., divisions in the Southern Baptist Convention led moderates and liberals to found the Alliance of Baptists and the Cooperative Baptist Fellowship. BILL J. LEONARD

Baptist Missionary Society was founded in Kettering, England (1792), by a group of Particular (Calvinistic) Baptists, including Andrew Fuller and William Carey. Carey went to Bengal (1793) and established the Serampore mission. The Society entered Jamaica (1814), where William Knibb was instrumental in securing the abolition of slavery* (1833–34). In China the mission began in 1859, with the society's most controversial missionary, the Welshman Timothy Richard. The Congo mission (1879) played an important role in the history of Leopold II's Congo Independent State. While this missionary activity had varied results, now Baptists are numerous in Mizoram (northeast India*), Jamaica*, Democratic Republic of Congo*, and Angola*. BRIAN STANLEY

Baptistery, Baptistry, a building, usually octagonal, distinct from the church but often attached to it, in which baptism is administered.

Barabbas, insurrectionist or thief whom Pilate released from prison in place of Jesus (Mark 15:6–15 par.; John 18:40).

Barbarians, those who did not speak Greek or Latin, appearing to be "babblers" (1 Cor 14:11). A term for non-Greeks in Rom 1:14 and Col 3:11; later a designation for people outside the Roman Empire.

Bardaisan of Edessa (154–222), first theologian outside the Roman Empire, who flourished at the court of Edessa* at a time of increasing Roman influence; opposed Marcionism* and astral determinism. Bardaisan came to be regarded as a heretic*. Thus his works did not survive. His thought must be reconstructed from the *Book of the Laws of Countries*, by a student, and from Ephrem*'s refutations. Bardaisan's rejection of astrology, his hymns, and his cosmology influenced later Syriac* theology and also Manichaeism*. He drew on Middle Platonism, Scripture (esp. Genesis*), and late antique science. His community later became dualist* and survived into the 10th c. UTE POSSEKEL

Bar Hebraeus (Ibn al-'Ibri) (1225/26–86), metropolitan, theologian, ecumenist, philosopher, chronicler, grammarian/lexicographer, physician. He was born in Melitene (west of the Euphrates) into a Christian (not Jewish) family and was ordained bishop (1246), then metropolitan of Aleppo (Syria, 1252). Versed in Syriac, Arabic, Persian, and Armenian, he was the greatest thinker of the Syriac* Orthodox Church during the golden age of Syriac literature. He wrote an extensive collection of *scholia* (exegetical commentaries) on the OT and NT; a doctrinal commentary on the Scriptures; and two major works of systematic theology, the *Candelabrum sanctuarii* (some call it the Syriac equivalent of Aquinas's* *Summa Theologiae*) and the *Ethicon*, an extensive guide to moral theology and mysticism*, intended for both monks and laity, concerning how to live a holy Christian life. His name is associated with a revised version of the most prestigious eucharistic* rite used in the Syriac Orthodox Church, as well as with rites of baptism* and of the blessing of water. He composed a revised, shortened version of the Anaphora* of St. James.

RIFAAT EBIED

Bar Kokhba (Aramaic, "son of a star"; see Num 24:17), designation of Simeon bar Kosiba, leader of the Jewish rebellion against Rome in 132–35 CE; his followers claimed he was the Messiah*.

Barlaam and Josaphat, venerated as Christian saints, although their vita is a Christianized version of the life of Buddha that enjoyed wide popularity throughout the medieval and early modern periods. The legend details the conversion of Prince Josaphat by the hermit Barlaam; the catechism of the prince is interspersed with frequent "examples" that foster religious belief and the ethical wisdom of a ruler. The original might have been Georgian (most likely), or Greek, or (least likely) by John* of Damascus. Their day of veneration was November 27 (early Roman martyrology) or August 26 (Greek Orthodox Church). Barlaam and Josaphat were never officially canonized.

SALVATORE CALOMINO

Barmen Declaration, written on May 16, 1934, was the authoritative statement of protest from the Confessing* Church against Nazism and, in particular, against the German* Christian Movement. Authored principally by Karl Barth*, with additional input from the Lutherans Hans Asmussen and Thomas Breit, the Declaration established the battle lines between the Confessing Church, the German Christians, and the Reich Church administration led by Reich Bishop Ludwig Müller. In particular, the Declaration rejected the legitimacy of natural* theology, instead insisting on the sole sufficiency of Jesus Christ as the one Word of God on which the church's proclamation must be based, and averring also the freedom of the church from both the state and any political ideology*.

The Declaration was adopted without alteration by the first Confessing Synod of the German Evangelical Church (Barmen, May 29–31, 1934). That the statement was called a "declaration" and not a confession was a compromise in deference to the Synod's Lutheran delegates. Nonetheless, it contained all the elements of older confessional statements, including anathemas.

Despite being a deliberate protest against the forced imposition of the anti-Semitic* Aryan Paragraph onto the church, the declaration was intended primarily to be a theological and not a political protest. However, with its repudiation of the German Christians' National Socialist ideology*, of the Reich Church government, and, therefore, of the Nazi regime's objective of bringing all aspects of German life and culture under its own auspices, the Confessing Church was inevitably also issuing a defiant political statement. In the years following Barmen, the Confessing Church became deeply divided as to the extent to which the political implications of the Barmen Declaration should be pursued. In particular, its response to the Nazis' persecution of the Jews was, and remains, hotly debated. **See also CHURCH AND STATE RELATIONS CLUSTER: INTRODUCTORY ENTRY and IN EUROPE: THE ROMAN CATHOLIC CHURCH AND POLITICS; GERMANY; JUDAISM AND CHRISTIANITY CLUSTER: WESTERN EUROPE; RACISM AND CHRISTIANITY CLUSTER: IN WESTERN EUROPE.**

MARK R. LINDSAY

Barnabas, early Jewish follower of Jesus (Acts 4:36–37), apostle to the Gentiles with Paul (Acts 9:27; 13–15; Gal 2:1, 9) until they parted ways (Acts 15:36–41), possibly because Barnabas sided with Peter in Antioch in the controversy over whether Jewish Christians could eat (non-kosher food) with Gentile Christians (Gal 2:11–13). Yet 1 Cor 9:6 positively mentions Barnabas as an apostle who, like Paul, earns his own living.

Barnabas, Epistle of, early-2nd-c. letter emphasizing the "errors" of the Jews: worship of the golden calf, erroneous cultic observances (sacrifices, fasting, circumcision, diet, Sabbath), rejection of Jesus, and misplaced trust in the Jerusalem Temple.

The notion of covenant* is central to the text. Influenced by the rhetoric of Deuteronomy*, the author stresses obedience to the Law* but excoriates Israel for misunderstanding its "true" meaning. The epistle makes extensive use of typology* and allegory*. Cultic laws are reduced to ethical ideals; other OT passages are seen as prophetic or typological references to Jesus. Ethical requirements are reinforced by means of a "Two Ways" tradition (see Didache). The author does not distinguish between "old" and "new" covenants but simply speaks of "the covenant," forfeited by Israel and inherited by Christians (see Supersessionism).

The epistle enabled Gentile Christians to lay claim to the privileges of Israel and to adopt an ethically rigorous view of the Christian life without authorizing the adoption of Jewish cultic practices. Although Israel is rejected, the author differs from Marcion* by showing reverence for the OT.

The text was probably written shortly after the Bar* Kokhba revolt. It flourished briefly among the Alexandrian fathers (Clement* of Alexandria, Origen,* Didymus* the Blind) and was falsely attributed to Barnabas*.

JAMES N. RHODES

Baroque Architecture, the complex, irregular style of late Renaissance architecture, art, and music (1600s–1750s). **See also HIEROTOPY, THE CREATION OF CHRISTIAN SACRED SPACES.**

Barot, Madeleine (1909–95), Protestant historian and archivist. As general secretary of the Cimade* (1940), she created a team to help refugees from foreign countries and Jews in internment camps during the period of the Vichy government of France (1940–44). She contributed to the creation of networks whose aim was to save Jewish children from concentration camps. In 1950 she was secretary of the YWCA*, then at the World* Council of Churches (1953–73) she was successively head of the departments of Cooperation Between Men and Women in Church and Society and of Education and Development. Throughout her involvement in Christian action, she was concerned mainly with ecumenism (see Ecumenical Movement and Its Theology), dialogue* between religions, the defense of human* rights, solidarity with victims of oppression, and the abolition of torture. JACQUES STEWART

Bar Salibi, Dionysius (Jacob). See DIONYSIUS (JACOB) BAR SALIBI.

Bar Sauma (d1294), "Nestorian*" monk in China. Probably of Turkic (Uighur) ethnicity, he learned Chinese. Intending to visit the tombs of Christian martyrs and saints, especially in Jerusalem, Bar Sauma traveled (c1280) with a companion, Mark (later Patriarch Yahballaha III), from Zhongdu (Beijing) through Khorasan and Azerbaijan to Baghdad, where they met the patriarch Denha. Eventually he was sent by the Buddhist Mongolian Il-Khan Arghun as his emissary to the West. Bar Sauma recorded his travels and encounters with popes, cardinals, kings, and the Byzantine emperor. He died in Baghdad in 1294. KATHLEEN E. MCVEY

Bar Sauma of Nisibis (5th c.), a teacher at the school of Edessa*, trained in the theology and exegesis of Theodore* of Mopsuestia. After the condemnation of Nestorius's* views (431), Bar Sauma relocated to the Sassanian Persian Empire. He became bishop of Nisibis* and was founder and patron of its school. Elected patriarch of the Church* of the East, he presided at the Council of Beth Lapat (484), which affirmed Nestorius's teaching. KATHLEEN E. MCVEY

Barth, Karl (1886–1968), pastor, theologian, opponent of National Socialism in Germany*. Following what he viewed as its decline owing to the influence of individualistic liberalism during the 19th c. (see Liberalism in Christian Theology and Ethics), he revitalized Protestant theology by producing the most comprehensive dogmatics since the Reformation. Born in Basel, Switzerland, he was educated in Bern, Berlin, and Marburg. He was professor of theology at Göttingen (1921–25), Münster (1925–30), Bonn (1930–35), and Basel (1935–62).

Born to a professor of church history, Karl was drawn early to a career in the church. His most formative influences were Harnack* and Wilhelm Herrmann, from whom he learned to critically appreciate Schleiermacher* and Kant*. He was also much influenced by the socialism of Hermann Kutter and Leonhard Ragaz and by the Pietism* of Christoph Blumhardt*.

After completing his studies, Barth was called to a pastorate in the Swiss town of Safenwil, where he formed a lifelong friendship with Eduard Thurneysen, pastor of the neighboring village of Leutwil. Initially, Barth was deeply committed to the liberalism of his teachers. However, their endorsement of Germany's war aims during World War I forced him to reconsider not only their ethics but their entire theological framework. While in Safenwil, Barth wrote his groundbreaking commentary, *Romans* (1919; rev. ed., 1922), in which he explicitly dismantled the theological presuppositions of 19th-c. neo-Protestantism. His indebtedness to the philosopher Kierkegaard* was evident during this period, particularly in his employment of Kierkegaard's "infinite qualitative distinction," by which Barth sought to emphasize the Godness of God over against human religiosity. These commentaries epitomized the postwar theological crisis in Western Europe and brought Barth instant international fame. On the strength of *Romans*, he was appointed to his first academic post (Göttingen).

During the 1930s, Barth was a vocal opponent of the Nazi regime and, along with Bonhoeffer* and Martin Niemoeller, was instrumental in founding the Confessing* Church. In 1935 Barth was dismissed from his university position in Bonn for refusing to give the Nazi salute and was expelled to Switzerland. Once in Basel, he continued to lead the fight against Nazism. He chastised the Confessing Church for not protesting more forcefully on behalf of persecuted Jews (see Judaism and Christianity Cluster: In Western Europe), was involved in underground resistance networks, and in 1944 mobilized foreign governments in an attempt to stop the Nazis' deportation of Hungarian Jews to Auschwitz (see Holocaust, Jewish [or Shoah]). Throughout it all, Barth continued to lecture and write his monumental *Church Dogmatics*.

In the postwar years, Barth championed the cause of reconciliation with the Germans, sought to ease cold war tensions by urging the West to moderate its anti-Soviet rhetoric, and was active in ecumenical circles. He was involved in the formation of the World* Council of Churches and corresponded with Rome during Vatican* II.

While reading widely across confessional boundaries, Barth was and remained a Reformed theologian. He was committed to Calvin's* legacy, although never uncritically so. Nowhere is this more evident than in Barth's restatement of the Calvinist doctrine of election*. Like his Reformed predecessors, Barth endorsed the doctrine of "double election" but argued emphatically that both election and reprobation were located primarily in Jesus Christ, and not in two separate "camps" or categories of people (see especially *Church Dogmatics* II/2). Barth similarly took issue with the Lutheran distinction between gospel* and law*; like Luther* and Augustine* before him, Barth insisted on the inseparability of the two. He contended, however, that the gospel, not the law, was both theologically and ontologically prior. Barth's legacy cannot be distilled to one main doctrinal contribution, or even to a theological system. Indeed, the sheer volume of his theological writing – 13 volumes (the last unfinished) of *Church Dogmatics* – is not simply due to his insistence that all doctrines are interrelated, but is more a product of his demand that theology make progress by constant self-correction, and thus always "begin anew at the beginning."

Nonetheless, there are certain emphases in his theology that can be regarded as characteristic of the whole. For example, throughout most of his life, Barth repudiated natural* theology, a stance that shattered his friendship with Emil Brunner. Instead, Barth was convinced that the revelation* of God can be understood only in the context of the Trinity*. This in turn involved for him a second emphasis, the so-called christological concentration. Barth was roundly criticized for this uncompromising position. However, it was precisely this commitment to Jesus as the one Word of God that enabled Barth to issue such a strong denunciation of the German* Christians' theology in the 1934 Barmen* Declaration. Moreover, in Barth's own mind, an emphasis on the divine "yes" to humanity – the unconditioned grace* of God – was the most vital aspect of a truly Christian theology. The gospel is the good news that grace saves us from any preoccupation about our own salvation*. Barth's great contribution was to restore theology to the church and restore to theology a proper concentration on the Word of God, specifically, the person of Jesus Christ as the true revelation of God to whom the Scriptures bear witness. **See also** DIALECTICAL THEOLOGY.

MARK R. LINDSAY

Bartholomew, one of the 12 disciples*/apostles*, sometimes identified with Nathanael (John 1:45–46).

Bartholomew's Day, Massacre of St., Catholic slaughter of thousands of Protestants in Paris beginning in the early hours of August 24, 1572, continuing for several days, and spreading to other French cities in the following weeks. It was a tragic reminder of the religious hatreds that attended the Reformation*. **See also** MARTYRDOM. RAYMOND A. MENTZER

Bartimaeus, a blind man healed by Jesus at Jericho (Mark 10:46).

Baruch, Book of (also called 1 Baruch), an apocryphal* book, with five chapters in the Septuagint* (the Vulgate* also includes the Epistle of Jeremiah); attributed to Baruch, Jeremiah's secretary. Following an introduction, there is a collection of three originally unrelated compositions – confession of sin (1:15–3:8), eulogy of Wisdom* (3:9–4:4), and a message to those in captivity (4:5–5:9) – held together by the theme of sin, exile, return. The different parts are of uncertain date (most likely between 2nd c. BCE and 1st c. CE).

Baruch, Syriac Apocalypse of (also called 2 Baruch), Jewish OT pseudepigraphon, an eschatological apocalypse, usually dated to c100 CE, also known as Second Baruch (as opposed to 1 Baruch, the Book of Baruch*). It is closely related to Fourth* Ezra in theme and content. According to some scholars, it may have been Christianized during its transmission. **See also PSEUDEPIGRAPHA OF THE OLD TESTAMENT.**

JOHANNES TROMP

Base Ecclesial Communities (Comunidades Eclesiales de Base, CEBs), in Latin America small groups of laypersons, normally from a neighborhood, slum, village, or rural zone, who regularly gather together to pray, sing, celebrate, commemorate, read the Bible, and discuss it from the perspective of the actual life experiences and struggles of that population. They are sometimes organized as subdivisions of Roman Catholic parishes* and are sometimes self-initiated. **See also CHURCH, CONCEPTS AND LIFE, CLUSTER: IN LATIN AMERICA: BRAZIL: BASE ECCLESIAL COMMUNITIES (CEBS) and ECUADOR: BASE ECCLESIAL COMMUNITIES (CEBS).**

Basel, Council of (1431–49), called by the Conciliarists*, who, in accordance with the decree *Frequens* of the Council of Constance*, claimed that supreme authority* in the Roman Catholic Church lies with a general council rather than with the pope*. It met north of the Alps to avoid interference by the papal party. This council (like the later Long Parliament in England) refused to adjourn, regarding itself as a "permanent council," the legislative body of the church; it took several actions that had previously been the prerogatives of the pope. The failure of the council marked the end of Conciliarism as a movement.

Basil, Liturgy of St. This anaphora*, in virtually all languages of the Eastern* churches, exists in several forms and languages (related to particular churches): the short Egyptian text (in Greek, Coptic*, Ge'ez [Ethiopian*]); the longer redactions, especially the Armenian* Versions; as well as the Syriac* and Byzantine* texts.

The prayer culminating in the *sanctus** still mirrors the Syriac preeminence of the "Liturgy of the Cherubim and Seraphim," to which other pairs of angels (not triads) were added. The prayer after the *sanctus* reflects the history of salvation. The vocabulary of the institution narrative is influenced by the verbs of the *epiclesis**; the verb pair "bless and sanctify" of the *epiclesis* is normative for the East Syriac tradition.

Especially in the Armenian Versions, but also in the other versions, the christological tenets of this anaphora reflect the formulas of the Synod of Antioch* (341) about the Son's preexistence and his relation to the Father (e.g. the Son as "Logos*," "Life," "Wisdom*," "Power," "Image"), about the Incarnation, and about the Resurrection and the Parousia. Such formulas were usually included in the prayer after the *sanctus* (sometimes also in the prayer before the *sanctus*) and in the *anamnesis**. New findings seem to preclude the involvement of Basil* of Caesarea in shaping this anaphora. Moreover, the longer versions have sometimes preserved older layers than the short Egyptian text.

GABRIELE WINKLER

Basil, Rule of, the foundation of Greek and Russian monasticism (see Monasticism Cluster). It includes the *Moralia*, 80 rules drawn from Scripture; two sets of rules in question-and-answer form, the "Small Asketikon" with 203 (or 313) short answers, probably written in 358, and the "Large Asketikon" with 55 longer answers, developed later; and several homilies depicting the ideal Christian life. These texts were extensively reworked by Basil and later editors.

The monasticism of Asia Minor probably originated in a "sectarian*" movement led by Eustathius* of Sebaste (early 4th c.) and focused not on solitary contemplation or mortification of the flesh but on the mode of life mandated in the Sermon on the Mount (Matt 5–7) and narrated in Acts (Acts 2:45, 4:32–35). It may have become further institutionalized through Macrina*, the older sister of Basil, Naucratius, and Gregory* of Nyssa. Under her influence, Basil and Gregory* Nazianzen established a neighboring monastery for men. Her brothers later underplayed her role, perhaps because of her connection with Eustathius.

In 357 (after perhaps 15 years of monastic life) Basil went on a tour throughout the East, observing the monastic life in Egypt, Palestine, Syria, and Mesopotamia; after his return, he gradually developed his Rule. Basil abandoned the punishments used by Pachomius* and emphasized mutual support and obedience to the superior, giving up self-will, and immediately following all commands not contrary to the law of God (upon overstepping his or her bounds, the superior could be rebuked by the older members of the community). The canonical* hours, based in Hippolytus* and the Apostolic* Constitutions, were regularized in this setting. The Rule of Basil became the one followed in the monasteries of the Eastern* Church. Each monastery is self-contained (there is no general administrative structure like that of the West) and follows one of the later recensions of the rule. EUGENE TESELLE

Basil of Ancyra (4th c.) was a moderate Arian* who came to disagree with the view that the Son was a creature. In 359 he and George of Laodicea championed the term *homoiousios** (of similar essence) to characterize the relation of the Son to the Father. While this position was called "Semi-Arian" by Epiphanius*, it was acknowledged by Athanasius* and others at the Council of Alexandria in 362 as a legitimate emphasis on the distinct persons of the Trinity*.

Basil of Caesarea, the Great (c330–79), a Cappadocian* who studied in Athens together with Gregory* Nazianzen (and Julian* the Apostate). Prompted by his sister Macrina*, he adopted the monastic* life (356?). After visiting monastic communities in Syria and Egypt, he became a hermit* and began composing the writings known as the Rule of Basil*. He actively opposed the Arianism* of the emperor Valens*, then became bishop (370). While participating in controversies over the extreme Arian position of Eunomius*, he worked successfully to reconcile the Nicene* party with the Homoiousians*, or "Semi-Arians." He also opposed Apollinarianism* and the Pneumatomachi*. EUGENE TESELLE

Basileia, Greek for "kingdom*," "reign," or "empire."

Basilica, a type of Roman building often used for public gatherings, with a large central hall and aisles at the sides, adapted for Christian churches after Constantine*, perhaps earlier. **See also HIEROTOPY, THE CREATION OF CHRISTIAN SACRED SPACES.**

Basilical Monastery, a monastery joined with a basilica*, built either as a memorial to a saint or as a cathedral. Paulinus* of Nola may have built the first at the shrine of St. Felix of Nola; the first in Gaul were St. Martin's in Tours and St. Denys in Paris. There were several basilical monasteries in Rome after the 5th c.; the "minsters"* in Anglo-Saxon England and Germany at the time of Boniface* were basilical monasteries. **See also HIEROTOPY, THE CREATION OF CHRISTIAN SACRED SPACES.**

Basilides, Gnostic* teacher in Alexandria (c225–50), author of a lost biblical commentary. His so-called heretical* views are very differently reported by Irenaeus*, Hippolytus*, and Clement* of Alexandria.

Basilina, early-6th-c. deacon* of the church Hagia Sophia in Constantinople*, originally from Cappadocia. Cyril of Scythopolis (*Life of John the Hesychast* 218.21–220.4) claimed to have heard from Basilina herself that she brought her nephew, a non-Chalcedonian, to the holy man John the Hesychast, who converted him to the Chalcedonian* views, as she hoped. But Basilina herself was refused entrance to John's monastery to seek John's spiritual guidance. He sent her a message that he would come to her in a dream, where she could ask what she wanted. He did; she asked and received his guidance, without compromising his monastic discipline. **See also DEACONESS.** CAROLYN OSIEK

Batak Churches. There are more than 10 Batak churches based in Batakland, Sumatra Island, Indonesia*, with an overall membership of more than 6 million, now including congregations throughout Indonesia, some with non-Batak members.

The German Rhenish mission brought the gospel to the Batak peoples from 1861 until 1942, when the Batak churches claimed themselves Lutheran* and joined the Lutheran* World Federation. Earlier several Batak churches separated from the German mission, for nationalist and self-reliance reasons. Huria Kristen Indonesia became the first self-reliant church in Indonesia (1927). After 1942, owing to religious and ethnic conflicts among Batak subgroups, other churches separated from Huria Kristen Batak Protestan church, the successor of the German mission.

As Lutheran, Batak churches regard preaching* God's Word as important for communicating God's grace* and will, and baptism and Holy Communion as sacred tradition. In daily life, Batak carefully live out their *adat* (customary law) because, they believe, there are supernatural sanctions against those who disregard the *adat* – the social and ceremonial system that regulates the rights and obligations among Batak relatives and social categories. The practice of *adat* is a potential source of tension for the churches, but it has never been totally rejected. Indeed, the German mission used elements of the *adat* to spread the gospel. Batak Christians strongly hold to *adat*, even though they follow most openly those elements of *adat* that do not conflict with the Christian faith.

Other churches (including Charismatic* churches) criticize Batak for living out the *adat* produced by Batak ancestors* in the time of darkness. Church servants (men and women elders, pastors, and bishops) sometimes criticize those who absent themselves from church services in order to attend *adat* ceremonies. But members of Batak churches keep observing *adat*. Observance of *adat* is defended as respect for ancestors or parents (Exod 20:12; Deut 5:16) and the tradition of the goodness of life that they have passed down to their descendants. Thus Batak churches live according to both the gospel and the *adat*.

Similarly, on New Year's Eve, every family conducts an evening service in which family members confess their weaknesses in the old year and ask forgiveness from one another – a moving ceremony through which Batak enter the New Year with purified hearts, forgiveness from family members, and God's blessing. **See also INDONESIA.** BATARA SIHOMBING

Bath Qol, in rabbinic theology, a voice from heaven conveying God's message (cf. Mark 1:11, 9:7; John 12:28).

Bathsheba, wife of Uriah the Hittite, whom David* is said to have seduced (taking advantage of his powerful position?); after her husband's arranged death, she became David's wife (2 Sam 11–12) and the mother of Solomon*, David's successor (1 Kgs 1–2).

Baur, Ferdinand Christian (1792–1860), professor of NT, church history, and theology, Tübingen (1826–60). He was the founder of the Protestant Tübingen school and the author of seminal studies on the doctrines of reconciliation*, Trinity*, and Incarnation* (1838–43), Paul* (1845), the canonical Gospels (1847), the history of Christian dogma (1847), church history (1853–64), and the writing of church history (1852) (see Historiography of Early Christianity as Developed in the 19th and 20th Centuries).

Baur was liberated from the scholasticism of the old Tübingen theologians with whom he studied by Friedrich Schleiermacher* and Friedrich Schelling*, but the deepest and most lasting influence on his thought was that of Georg Wilhelm Friedrich Hegel*. Baur intended to take history and the historical mediation of God with even greater seriousness than Hegel himself took them.

With Hegel, Baur affirmed that the dialectical unfolding of the Triune God is the key to historical process and that history is the clue to the divine nature. At the same time, Baur was a disciplined critical historian who attended to the details of historical evidence. Thus he sought to ground Christology in a historical-critical study of the Gospels and to apply the Hegelian dialectical principles (identity, difference, mediation) to the history of the Christian Church and dogma. He was most innovative in his theory of historical knowledge, which involves an interplay of authentic objectivity and authentic subjectivity. On the one hand, historians strive to transpose themselves into the objective course of the subject matter itself, to rethink the thoughts of the eternal Spirit, whose work history is. On the other hand, historians' own subjectivity and perspective must be acknowledged. Every biblical and theological writing reflects "tendencies," and instead of a single church historiography, there can be only "epochs" of church historiography.

Baur was the great historicizer and relativizer of theology: the flux of historical process dissolves every fixed dogmatic formulation. This is not a counsel of despair but provides insight into the nature of truth*, which is developmental. Baur established principles of historical criticism that are now taken for granted by biblical and historical theology. His most famous student was David Friedrich Strauss (of whose book on the life of Jesus he was quite critical). The historicizing of theology led at the end of the 19th c. to the work of Adolf Harnack*, Albert Schweitzer*, Wilhelm Dilthey, and Ernst Troeltsch;* and Baur's impact on NT studies is seen in the work of Ernst Käsemann*.

PETER C. HODGSON

Baxter, Richard (1615–91), English Puritan* pastor and theologian. Educated informally, he read widely in Protestant and Catholic theology. He was a Nonconformist* about various features of the liturgy, but adhered to moderate Episcopalianism, advocating bishops elected by presbyteries (see Church, Concepts and Life,

Cluster: Types of Ecclesiastical Structures). His ministry in Kidderminster (1641–60) is regarded as a model of pastoral* care. Max Weber*, in his book on the Protestant ethic, made much use of Baxter's writings. For a time during the English civil war, he joined the army to counteract the "sectaries" and Cromwell*, without success. After the Restoration (1660), he refused a bishopric but participated in the Savoy* Conference, proposing revisions of the Book of Common* Prayer; these were rejected, and under the Act of Uniformity (1662) he, like many others, was prosecuted for unlicensed preaching. A prolific author, he pursued a "Catholic" moderation and inclusiveness, anticipating both the ecumenical* movement and the Protestant Liturgical* Movement. EUGENE TESELLE

Beards, Clerical. Greek priests wore beards, a practice that continued in Eastern* churches, while priests in the West shaved; this was a point of controversy between the two sides of the church (9th and 11th c.).

Beatification, the process by which bishops, and now the pope, permit veneration* of a holy person, without full canonization*.

Beatific Vision, in Western medieval theology, after death the immediate apprehension of God's essence by the redeemed, made possible by the freely given "light of glory" and fully satisfying the human quest for happiness. In some non-Western settings today, this is the immediate experience of God's all-encompassing presence. **See also MYSTICISM, MYSTICS; UNION, MYSTICAL.**

Beatitudes (from Lat *beatus,* "blessed/happy," translating Gk *makarios*) is the term traditionally used to designate Jesus' sayings at the beginning of the Sermon* on the Mount (Matt 5:3–12; Luke 6:20–22), although this literary form is also used in the OT (especially Psalms, from 1:1) and in other parts of the NT. The beatitudes, e.g. "Blessed/Happy are the poor [in spirit], theirs is the Kingdom," have been interpreted (1) as praise for a certain behavior or attitude ("poor in spirit"), and thus as a moral exhortation ("Be poor in spirit and you will receive the Kingdom"), or (2) as a blessing (a performative word by Jesus as religious authority) that transforms the status of those designated (the "poor" or the humiliated "poor in spirit" are now and in the future "blessed" by God), or (3) as a proclamation that designates those whom the readers/hearers should recognize as blessed, as those in whom God is pleased, and as those whom they should respect as such and imitate or serve (cf. Matt 25:31–46). DANIEL PATTE

Becket, Thomas (c1120–70), archbishop of Canterbury (1162–70). A priest in Canterbury, he studied in France and Italy. As chancellor to Henry II of England (1155–62), he became the king's close companion and champion of his policies. After becoming archbishop (1162), he began defending the freedom of the church and its right to discipline clerics. He fled to France, reconciled with the king, and returned to England (1170) but insisted on the church's right to discipline. A remark by Henry inspired four knights to assassinate Becket in his cathedral (December 29, 1170). Indignation was widespread; he was canonized* (1173), and Henry made public penance* at his shrine. The veneration of Becket variously symbolized the independence of the church, preference for the French over the English royal family, and the value of penance as exemplified by Henry. It was criticized by Wyclif* and the Lollards*, with their different view of church* and state. Henry* VIII destroyed the shrine (1538).

Bede (672/73–735), "Father of English History," monk, priest, father of the church, saint. A monk in the twin monastery of Wearmouth/Jarrow from c680, he was the most scholarly author in Anglo-Saxon England. More than 30 works survive. The core of his output was biblical exegesis, but he also produced a range of educational works for his pupils, hagiographies, a martyrology, and his famous *Ecclesiastical History* (*Historia ecclesiastica gentis Anglorum,* 731), ending with a brief autobiography and a list of his works. His *History* and a second work, *Time,* in particular, exercised an enormous influence throughout the Middle Ages. NICHOLAS J. HIGHAM

Beecher, Catharine (1800–78), daughter of Lyman Beecher*, sister of Harriet Beecher Stowe*. She founded several schools for women, advocated better training of women as schoolteachers, and published *A Treatise on Domestic Economy* (1841), a much used handbook on household management (cooking, child care, health) that helped create the "cult of domesticity." Ironically, she opposed woman suffrage, arguing that the woman's sphere was the home.

Beecher, Henry Ward (1813–87), son of Lyman Beecher*, brother of Harriet Beecher Stowe*. Known for his eloquence, he was the minister of Plymouth Congregational Church in Brooklyn for many decades. As a preacher and editor, he championed woman suffrage, evolution*, and the abolition of slavery*. His reputation was compromised by a famous lawsuit alleging adultery (1875). **See also UNITED CHURCH OF CHRIST (IN THE UNITED STATES).**

Beecher, Lyman (1775–1863), Presbyterian minister in Connecticut, where he preached against intemperance (see Temperance Movement) and helped found the American* Bible Society (1816). In Boston he became sympathetic to the "new measures" revivalism* of Finney*. Moving to Cincinnati, he became president of Lane Theological Seminary, Cincinnati, following his stance against abolition during a classic debate about the abolition of slavery*; the abolitionists left to found Oberlin as a rival school, of which Finney became president. **See also UNITED CHURCH OF CHRIST (IN THE UNITED STATES).**

Beelzebub (based on the Hebrew in 2 Kgs 1), or Beelzeboul, the "prince of demons" identified with Satan* (in Mark 3:22–26, par.).

Beguine Spirituality. Beguines, female members of a lay religious movement that began in the early 13th c., were inspired by the desire to return to a more apostolic way of life and to bring the service of God into the marketplace, as the early Franciscans* and Dominicans* had done. The mendicant way of life was not open to women, so many who wished to serve God by serving the poor and needy in poverty, chastity, and obedience became Beguines. The early Beguines were mostly aristocratic and patrician women who lived together in small groups in a house provided by one of their number. The large and beautiful Beguinages of Bruges, Paris, and elsewhere are from a later period. In the early 13th c., Beguines were hailed as leading the most holy kind of Christian life because of their piety and because they did not beg, but rather worked for their living.

Their spirituality grew out of their lives of active service; spirituality required the business of everyday living to be practiced. Because of this, aspects of mystic* grace that might interfere with carrying out daily acts of service for one's fellows (such as visions, ecstasies, trances, and extreme asceticism) were generally dismissed as juvenile. For the Beguines, one is closest to union with God's divinity when living, with God's humanity, a life of suffering service, despised and rejected by others. Suffering* is not simply the means to achieve union; it is the very place of union itself. For example, Mechtild* of Magdeburg writes, "Lord what shall we now say of love? Now that we lie so close on the bed of my pain?" (*Flowing Light of the Godhead Book* 7:21). Paradox* is a defining feature of their writing. They use the Middle Dutch word *minne* (love*) to speak of God and the imagery of the Song* of Songs, and contemporary courtly love poetry to describe the intimacy and passion of their relationship. The noun *minne* is feminine and requires feminine adjectives and pronouns, which adds to the ambiguity and paradox of the texts. Beguine texts speak vividly and painfully of the awe-inspiring "otherness" of God, of a love that is beyond comprehension, fearfully great. The fear and awe evoked by the realization of the immense gulf between God and God's creatures is, for the Beguines, the other side of the intimacy they experience in sharing with God the bed of their pain. **See also HADEWIJCH; MARIE D'OIGNIES; MECHTILD OF MAGDEBURG; PORETE, MARGUERITE.**

SASKIA MURK JANSEN

Behemoth, a large animal described in Job (40:15–24), possibly based on the hippopotamus of the Nile; Leviathan* may be its counterpart.

Belarus, located in the historic and conflict-prone borderlands between Roman Catholic Central Europe and Slavic Eastern Orthodox regions. Christianity in Belarus reflects this cultural and sociopolitical marginality.

Belarus experienced only short periods of autonomy, and thus its history is integral to that of Orthodox Russia* and Catholic Poland* and Lithuania*. It can claim Christianity as its major faith for a millennium, though for many centuries the people practiced *dvoeverie* ("double faith" combining native religion and Christianity). It includes an Orthodox majority, with a large Catholic minority.

The late 16th and early 17th c. tested religious identities in the region. As Poles tried to seize the Russian throne, the Reformation* and Catholic* Renewal (Counter Reformation) washed across Belarus, each leaving a religious residue. The 1596 Brest*-Litovsk gathering (on the Polish–Belarusian border) created Uniatism* ("Greek Catholicism," as it is called in the region) to compete for Belarusian souls. The 1666 schism of the Old* Believers divided the Orthodox population. Subsequently (17th–20th c.), the Belarusians found themselves a small, marginal people, divided among Orthodox, Catholic, Old Believer, and Greek Catholic sensibilities, with some Protestant influences. The 20th c. challenged the faith of the people of Belarus through (1) the antireligious policy of the Soviet Communists and (2) the physical and spiritual devastation the region suffered as a major battlefield during both world wars. Another traumatic event was the nearby nuclear accident of Chernobyl (1986).

The Republic of Belarus, which emerged from Soviet control (1991), is a biconfessional Catholic–Orthodox state, favoring the Orthodox majority. The Belarusian Orthodox Church, an exarchate* of the Russian Orthodox Church, is headed by an ethnic Russian, Metropolitan Filaret; his struggle to master the Belarusian language exemplifies the ambivalence of Orthodoxy as both Belarusian and Russian. The general harmony between Orthodox and Catholic communities does not prevent friction from arising on official levels. The reestablishment of the Catholic diocesan structure is for Orthodox officials a violation of their "canonical territory." The coming of many Catholic clergy from Poland emphasizes the divide between Eastern Slavic- and Polish-oriented populations, and occasions government interference with visas and work permits.

The historically important Uniates (Greek Catholics), Old Believers, Lutherans, and Calvinist Protestants make up small groups today. Originating more recently (but with pre-Soviet roots) is a dynamic Protestant movement (approximately 2% of believers) made up of Pentecostals, Seventh-day Adventists, and Baptists. Among other religious traditions (less than 1% of the population), the largest groups are Jews and Muslims. There is relatively little overt inter-group conflict among these communities, though lines of tension do exist.

There has been a revival of religious identification since the end of the Soviet era, but by all indications religious life remains limited. Religious practice primarily takes the form of rites of passage associated with birth, death, and marriage. In addition, 5% of Belarusians claim to be atheists, and 25% are nonreligious.

The dominant issue in religious life in Belarus today is the role of the government. The Belarusian government has tended to support the Orthodox Church for seemingly political purposes and interferes in the affairs of all churches for political reasons. The greatest need for Christians in Belarus is freedom from meddling by the state so that they can address the serious spiritual needs of the population.

Statistics: Population (2000): 10.2 million (M). Christians, 7.1 M, 70.3% (Orthodox, 5.4 M; Roman Catholics, 1.4 M; Protestants 0.1 M; independents, 0.1 M); nonreligious, 2.4 M, 24%; atheists 0.5 M, 5%. (Based on *World Christian Encyclopedia*, 2001.)

JERRY G. PANKHURST

Belgic Confession, the confession of faith adopted in 1561 by the Reformed churches in French-speaking Belgium, modeled on the Gallican* Confession of 1559. Now one of the doctrinal standards of the Reformed Church of the Netherlands and its offspring in South Africa and the USA.

Belgium, a predominantly Roman Catholic country, has witnessed during the past two centuries an intense exchange between religion and modernity. The Christianization of present-day Belgium dates from the early Middle Ages. Protestantism was highly influential in the region in the 16th c., but after the failure of the revolt against the rule of the Spanish Hapsburgs (see Spain), the Roman Catholic religious monopoly was restored. When the Belgian provinces were annexed by revolutionary France (1795), freedom of religion was introduced. Following a brief union with the Netherlands* (1815–30), an independent Belgian state came into existence, with a liberal, parliamentary regime and a formal separation between church* and state. Since then, all religions have been granted the same opportunities for development. Yet the most important ones in Belgium – Roman Catholicism, Protestantism, and Judaism – received a form of official recognition, a protected status, and state financial support. Catholicism continued to occupy a dominant position. In 1905, out of a population of 7 million, besides a small minority of nonchurchgoers, there were about 30,000 Protestants and 3,500 Jews.

In the early years of the Belgian state, a strong liberal movement within the Catholic Church endorsed modern freedoms, since they allowed the Church to develop its own charitable and educational organizations. However, under pressure from the Holy See, more antiliberal tendencies developed (mid-19th c.), leading to a confrontation with the liberal bourgeoisie, whose influence was increasing as a result of extensive industrialization and urbanization. Ideological confrontations came to dominate political life. Between 1847 and 1884, the liberals were mostly in power and succeeded to a large extent in pushing back the Church's influence on state institutions. The Church retreated to its own structures and developed almost into a state within the state, thereby laying the basis for the segmentation of society along ideological lines ("pillarization").

After 1884, following an important shift of power, the Catholic party came to exercise a dominant influence on political life for more than a century. The subsequent Christian Democratic Party, successful thanks to the development of a powerful movement of social Catholicism, gave shape to a pillarized, neo-corporative society. (See Pillars.) The center of influence lay no longer with the state but with the intermediary structures woven into political life.

Between 1870 and 1970, the flourishing Roman Catholic Church in Belgium exercised a not negligible influence on Catholicism as a whole, mostly regarding modernization (see Modernism, Roman Catholic). It played an important part in the Catholic missionary and ecumenical movements. The Catholic University of Leuven contributed to the dialogue with modern science*. The Belgian liberal Catholic tradition, never fully lost and revived after World War II, had an important influence on Vatican* II. Its well-developed social organizations were often a model for surrounding countries. Especially after 1945, Belgian Catholic politicians played a prominent role in international Christian Democracy.

From the 1960s on, cracks became evident in the Catholic edifice; a process of "de-pillarization" emerged from the growth of individualism and secularization*. The Church gradually lost its grip on social structures and saw its influence decreasing. The number of nonchurchgoers markedly increased and religious practice declined, while the following of other religions increased. Meanwhile, Islam* (1974) and Orthodox Christianity (1985) were given official recognition and consequently received state subsidies. There is little tension among the various churches, owing in part to the ecumenical tradition within the Catholic Church. **See also LUXEMBOURG; NETHERLANDS, THE.**

Statistics: Population (2000): 10.2 million (M). Christians, 9 M, 88% (Roman Catholics, 8.2 M; Protestants, 0.13 M; marginal Christians, 72,000; Orthodox, 49,000; independents, 40,000; Christians without an expressed affiliation, 0.45 M); Muslims, 0.36 M; Jews, 30,000; Buddhists, 30,000; nonreligious, 0.77 M. (Based on *World Christian Encyclopedia*, 2001.)

EMIEL LAMBERTS

Belhar Confession, a condemnation of apartheid* and other forms of forced separation in the church "on the grounds of race and color," "descent," or "any other human or social factor," issued by the Dutch Reformed Mission Church (1986) and by the Dutch Reformed Church in Africa when they joined to form the Uniting Reformed Church (1994). In the USA, it has been adopted provisionally by the Reformed Church in America and is under consideration by the Presbyterian Church (USA).

Belial (Heb), **Beliar** (Gk transliteration). "Sons of Belial" is a term of opprobrium in the Dead Sea Scrolls; Paul uses Beliar as a name for Satan* (2 Cor 6:15).

Bells. Bells rung by hand came into Christian use by the time of Gregory* of Tours (6th c.); hanging bells were used by the 8th c. They have been rung on feast days, to summon worshippers, or to announce a death. Small bells are rung during the (Catholic) Eucharist* at the elevation* and Communion*. Popular belief holds that they can drive away demons*. Because the ringing of bells is a dramatic way of announcing the presence of a religious building, in pluralistic societies it is sometimes subdued. Where a different religious tradition is dominant, bells may be silenced, e.g. in Muslim lands (including Jerusalem until modern times); they were silenced during the French Revolution and in some Catholic countries, where Protestants could not ring bells.

Beloved Disciple, the unnamed disciple in John 13:23, 19:26, 20:2, 21:7, 21:20: "the one Jesus loved." John 21:24 suggests he was John* the Apostle.

Benedicite (Lat "Bless the Lord"), canticle of the three youths in the fiery furnace, added to the Septuagint's* Book of Daniel*; used liturgically in lauds*.

Benedict (c480–c555), born in Nurcia (or Norcia); founder of the monastery of Monte Cassino, Southern Italy; author of the Rule of Benedict*. The spiritual biography (Book II of the *Dialogues* attributed to Pope Gregory* I) credits Benedict, originally a hermit at Subiaco, with having founded several monasteries before Monte Cassino. It paints him as a charismatic preacher and teacher, only briefly mentioning his monastic Rule. The Rule provided a strong model for communal monasticism* and was later used by Cluny* and the Cistercians*.

Benedict was declared the patron saint of Europe by Pope Paul VI in 1964.

MARILYN DUNN

Benedict, Rule of, monastic* rule composed by Benedict* of Nursia, c550; in Latin, 73 chapters, about 12,000 words. Benedict envisages an audience beyond his own monastery, as he encapsulates his view of monasticism, giving comprehensive directions on communal life. Beginning in the 1930s, scholars advanced the idea that it was a derivative of the *Regula* magistri*, but the traditional view is more likely: Benedict's Rule was expanded into the *Regula magistri*.

The Rule was composed in 6th-c. Roman Italy*, where life had been disrupted by war and plague. Monasteries were now an accepted part of society, housing retired laypeople and child oblates* as well as those with more durable vocations*. Benedict suggests that they were subject to a good deal of instability and lack of discipline. Thus, while he pays tribute to the tradition that eremitism* is a higher form of monasticism than cenobitism* and recommends the works of Cassian* and Basil*, he nevertheless insists that its strongest form is communal life under a rule and an abbot*. Benedict characterizes the abbot as "taking the place of Christ," awarding him sweeping powers that place only the rule and God above him. Thus Benedict creates a charisma* of office for the head of community that is not formulated in earlier monastic writings.

The Rule defines the pillars of monastic conduct (Lat *conversatio*) as obedience, silence, and humility*. To further support the abbot, Benedict sets out a hierarchy of monastic officials – deans, cellarer (for food supplies), and porter (doorkeeper) – with specific duties and reluctantly allows the appointment of a second-in-command, or prior*. He insists on the permanence of vows made on behalf of child oblates. The Rule gives specific directions for discipline, dress, and diet, envisaging an estate-based monastic existence, separated as far as possible from the secular world, where monks may have to gather the harvest themselves or practice crafts. The community's liturgical life is based around the daily celebration of Divine Office* – in this case, matins, lauds, prime, terce, sext, nones, vespers, compline, and the night office.

The Rule's genius and durability lie in its reinterpretation of earlier traditions to create a charisma of office for the superior along with structures designed to ensure the stability and continuation of monastic life. Its views on the abbot, his officials, and monastic *conversatio* were excerpted in the "mixed" monastic rules of the 7th c. In the 8th and 9th c., it was promoted by the Carolingian* dynasty as the monastic rule of the Holy* Roman Empire and it became the basis of life at Cluny* and in the Cistercian* order.

MARILYN DUNN

Benedict XV, Pope (1914–22), born Giacomo della Chiesa (1854) into a relatively modest aristocratic family. He studied civil law (Genoa) before pursuing ecclesiastical studies (Rome). After ordination (1878), he received diplomatic training at the Academy for Noble Ecclesiastics, became secretary to Mariano Rampolla (in Madrid and Rome), was moved to Bologna as archbishop (1907), became cardinal (1914), and was elected pope (1914). During World War I, his many efforts to bring peace included a *Note* (1917) that both sides rejected as favoring the other. He organized the release of prisoners unfit for further service and established a missing persons bureau. Ecclesiastically, he tempered the campaign against Modernists*, established the Congregation for the Eastern Church, and founded the Pontifical Oriental Institute. Missiologically, he attempted to wrest evangelization from colonial ambitions by promoting indigenous clergy (see Mission Cluster: Mission and Imperialism). MICHAEL J. WALSH

Benedictine Order. There is no evidence in the Rule of Benedict* that Benedict intended to establish a federation of monasteries, though adaptation of his teaching to local circumstances was anticipated. The Rule simply circulated as a resource for other monastic legislators. Its breadth, depth, and wisdom served as its best recommendation, and its observance gradually spread to England and to the Frankish kingdom, where it became the basis of the monastic reform encouraged by Louis the Pious (778–840), successor to Charlemagne, and his monastic agent, Benedict of Aniane (c747–821). This broad adoption of the Rule established it as the norm for Western monasticism, a position consolidated and extended in later monastic reforms (e.g. at Cluny*) throughout Europe (from the late 10th c.). The 12th-c. Cistercian* reform created a stricter form of Benedictine monasticism, while the rise of other forms of religious life (from the 12th c.) reduced the number and significance of the original Benedictines. The Reformation and French Revolution were devastating for Benedictine monasticism, but there was a monastic revival (19th c.) across Europe that spread to the Americas, Africa, and Asia. Since then,

Benedictines have been leaders in liturgical* renewal, ecumenism*, and scholarship.

Despite the unity provided by a common text, Benedictine monasticism always had a variety of interpretations and applications of the Rule. Benedictines have never constituted a single "order" in the sense of the later, nonmonastic forms of religious life that appeared during the Middle Ages. Instead, there have been associations of monasteries, known as congregations, which share a particular history or interpretation of the Rule. Some congregations are highly centralized, while others are loose federations of autonomous communities. In this respect, Benedictines exemplify the ancient model of monastic life still common in the Christian East (see the following entries in the Monasticism Cluster: In the Byzantine Empire; In the Russian and Ukrainian Tradition; In the Syriac Tradition), in which monasteries themselves are the primary institutions and most authority remains with the local monastic superior (abbot*, abbess*, prior*, or prioress*), with higher levels of organization playing a supportive rather than directive role. COLUMBA STEWART, OSB

Benediction (Lat "uttering a blessing"), performatory* words conferring a blessing* on a person or group on God's behalf, traditionally by a priest, a pastor, or a bishop, but also by any believer (e.g. in everyday and family settings).

Benediction of the Sacrament, at the closing of certain Western Church services, the point at which the people are blessed with the reserved* Sacrament.

Benedictus (Lat "Blessed be God"), Zachariah's song of thanksgiving at the birth of his son John* the Baptist (Luke 1:68–79), used liturgically in lauds*.

Benefice, ecclesiastical office whose "spiritualities" are supported by certain "temporalities" (financial support); often called a "living."

Benefit of Clergy, exemption of clergy and religious* from trial by secular courts; defended by the papacy during the Middle Ages.

Bengel, Johannes Albrecht (1687–1752), was the prominent representative of the Württemberg Pietists*, whose biblical theology, with its eschatological focus, was influenced by the social disruptions that marked that region during the incursions of Louis XIV. His renowned work as a Bible scholar at Tübingen was marked by his extensive textual commentary on the Greek NT, which, in translation, had an impact on lay readers, including John Wesley*. For Bengel, an accurate reading of the Bible in its historical context would overcome an unhealthy theological dogmatism in Protestant orthodoxy. His posting a date for the Parousia* (1836) remains a controversial aspect of his work. J. STEVEN O'MALLEY

Benin (formerly Dahomey). Portuguese introduced Christianity (1640s) in this prominent West African kingdom, which became a French colony (1872), gaining independence in 1960. The proportion of Christians is still exceptionally low (28%) as compared with that of African* Religionists (52%, including practitioners of Vodoun, Vodou*) and Muslims (20%).

The Roman Catholic Church, in the south, became highly visible with the 1871 arrival in Porto-Novo of the Sisters of Our Lady of the Apostles and the Petites Servantes des Pauvres de Cotonou (1921). Following the establishment of a seminary (1913), the first African priest, Fr. Moulero, was ordained (1928), and a regional seminary was established (1930). Fr. Francis Aupiais (1877–1945) strongly affirmed Dahomey's African cultures, advocating inculturation* of Christianity and opposing colonialism. The Archdiocese of Cotonou (established in 1955) had its first African archbishop in 1960.

The first Protestant church was founded by Thomas Birch Freeman, the son of a former slave (1843), under the auspices of the Methodist Missionary Society of London. But the Protestant churches developed very slowly until 1949, owing to French suspicion of Anglo-Saxon missionaries, and despite the Goun translation of the Bible (1901–23). The Sudan Interior Mission established itself (1947) in the northeast and the Assemblies of God in the northwest.

African* Instituted Churches include the Boda Owa (Dahomey–Nigerian border, 1895), the Eledja African Methodist Church (1927), the Christian Order of the Cherubim and Seraphim (1933), and mainly L'Église du Christianisme Céleste (1952, with Prophet Samuel Otchoffa). There is a lively proliferation of sizable independent Pentecostal/Charismatic and Evangelical churches.

Despite the strong presence of African* Religion, Christianity plays a major role in all aspects of Benin society. Roman Catholics opposed the Marxist* government (1972–90); churches train the political and cultural elite in their schools and seminaries; Christian hospitals are among the best in the country; Methodist Women actively promotes AIDS prevention and educates rural girls and women; Christians played a central role during the Conference of National Reconciliation (1990); and PROCMURA (Project of Christian–Muslim Relations in Africa) promotes harmony between Muslims and the rest of the population.

Statistics: Population (2000): 6 million (M). Christians, 1.7 M, 28% (Roman Catholics, 1.26 M; Protestants, 0.2 M; members of African Instituted Churches, 0.2M); African Religionists, 3.1 M, 52%; Muslims, 1.2 M, 20%. (Based on *World Christian Encyclopedia*, 2001.)

VALENTIN DEDJI

Ben Sira. See WISDOM OF BEN SIRA.

Bequests. See WILLS AND BEQUESTS.

Berachah (Heb "blessing"), typical Jewish form of prayer, sanctifying something by praising God over it or seeking God's favor; possibly inspired the Christian Eucharist*.

Berdyaev, Nikolai Aleksandrovich (1874–1948), Russian philosopher; born in Kiev. After being arrested for revolutionary activity (1898), he was forced into internal exile (1900–3), during which he abandoned Marxism* for Christian Personalism. He became an independent writer and publisher (St. Petersburg and Moscow, 1904–22), was exiled by the Soviet government (1922), and went to Paris (1924–48), becoming the best known Russian philosopher in the West. His thought focuses on freedom*, regarded not as a social product but as a divine spark. Berdyaev combined this view with a passion for social justice*, affirming the paradoxical unity of freedom and human solidarity in Christ. Berdyaev was a Christian prophet, tirelessly contesting the powers and principalities of a fallen world. PAUL VALLIERE

Berengarius of Tours (c1010–88), theologian of the Eucharist* who affirmed the real* presence of Christ but denied any change in the elements. Attacked by Lanfranc*, he was condemned several times, definitively at a Roman council (1079), after which he confessed the conversion of the elements "in properties of nature and truth of substance."

Bergson, Henri (1859–1941). This philosopher's central concept is "duration" as inner experience. When I experience an emotion, according to Bergson, what I experience is the continuity of the experience and its heterogeneity. There is a kind of unity to the duration of the experience that cannot be separated from a multiplicity. Bergson's thought, then, is a specific form of dualism*. Yet the dualism of the duration accounts for more traditional forms of dualism, Descartes's* in particular. The heterogeneity and multiplicity of the duration can develop into the spatial separation that allows us to enumerate objects; this development is Cartesian extension. The unity and continuity of the duration, on the other hand, can develop into the indivisible and homogeneous self of the Cartesian thinking subject. Later, in *The Two Sources of Morality and Religion* (1935), Bergson extends the dualism of the duration. (1) There is closed morality and static religion, which attempt to maintain social cohesion (a closed space) by means of obedience to laws that are personified in images of God (a unified and homogeneous self). The institutional religions throughout the world are static according to Bergson. (2) However, there is open morality and dynamic religion, which attempt to open the social cohesion through the emotion of loving (continuity) all things (heterogeneity). Thus open morality and dynamic religion put themselves in touch with the duration. Such a contact with the duration is a mystical* experience. Bergson claims that Christian mystics such as Joan* of Arc are the models. While Bergson grants to Judaism* the constant demand of justice*, it is the spirit of Christianity that opens the door of love*, making it the one true dynamic religion. **See also RELIGION AS A CONCEPT AND CHRISTIANITY.** LEONARD LAWLOR

Berlin Conference (the) (November 1884–February 1885), was the occasion for the "scramble for Africa," with its resulting partition of Africa and its implications for missions and the African churches.

During the second half of the 19th c., the European powers, which had traded along the coasts of Africa, began to explore inland areas, seeking raw materials for their growing industries. Their rivalry prompted France* and Germany* to call the Berlin Conference, attended by 14 powers (including the USA, which had commercial but not territorial interests). The Berlin Act of 1885 carved up Africa into spheres of influence and gave Leopold II of Belgium personal sovereignty over the Belgian Congo. The Act guaranteed free trade, access to the Congo and Niger Rivers by all nations, free movement by "Christian missionaries, scientists, and explorers," and "freedom of conscience and religious toleration" for all persons, indigenous or foreign. The boundaries drawn up at the Berlin Conference, often dividing African nations, have continued up to the present.

Mission* organizations have often found occasion to remind colonial and postcolonial governments of the guarantees given in the Berlin Act, and have benefited from this protection. From their perspective, the guarantees regarding religious freedom have also benefited Africans. But from the African perspective, mission organizations became accomplices in the colonization and fragmentation of Africa. African churches resulting from the missionary enterprise have often recalled this fact of collusion in denominational and ecumenical discussions. African scholars often refer to the Berlin Conference as the beginning of the continent's imperial subjugation and comment critically on the role of Christian missionaries in the colonial period. **See also MISSION CLUSTER: MISSION AND IMPERIALISM.**

JESSE NDWIGA KANYUA MUGAMBI and EUGENE TESELLE

Bernard of Clairvaux (1090–1153), popularizer of the Cistercian* order, monk, preacher, theologian, diplomat; established an ecclesiology of papal plenitude of power; helped to launch a new style of preaching and a heightened devotion to the Blessed Virgin Mary*.

From a noble family near Dijon, he became a monk at Cîteaux Abbey (1112), entering the new Cistercian order with 30 friends and relatives; he then served as abbot* of Cîteaux (1115). He was highly influential in the Roman Catholic Church: he gained recognition for the Knights* Templar (1128) and traveled throughout Europe (1130) to support Innocent II as pope (after a disputed papal election); one of his former monks was elected as Pope Eugenius III (1145).

At the instigation of Peter the Venerable, abbot of Cluny, Bernard preached in support of the Second Crusade*. The Roman Catholic Church faced challenges from a new breed of academic critic, particularly in northern France. Although not trained in these schools or proto-universities and lacking skills in logic, Bernard powerfully campaigned against heretics* and their teaching, among them Peter Abelard* (condemned at Sens in 1140) and Gilbert of Poitiers (at Reims in 1148).

His book, *On Consideration*, initially written for Pope Eugenius on how to balance his duties as pope*, was developed into a treatise on the pope's jurisdiction and authority in church* and state, including his theory of papal plenitude of power. Through this book, Bernard sought to ensure the balance of power between church and state, which had been precarious since the Investiture Contest (provisionally resolved by the Concordat of Worms*, 1122) with its principle that the church was responsible for the spiritualities of the appointment of a bishop and the secular authorities for the temporalities. Thus Bernard is viewed as an authority on the powers of the pope.

Bernard's treatises on the monastic life, and on the balance between the active and contemplative* in life in general, are authoritative, as is his spiritual interpretation of Scripture, especially the Song* of Songs.

GILLIAN R. EVANS

Bethany, village to the east of the Mount of Olives, where Jesus lodged (Mark 11) and Simon the leper (Mark 14:3), Lazarus, Martha, and Mary (John 11:1) lived.

Bethlehem, town five miles south of Jerusalem; Rachel was buried nearby (Gen 35:16–19). The home of Boaz* and Ruth*, David's* forebears (Ruth 1:19; 4:9–11), it came to be called the city of David (Luke 2:11) and was the place where Jesus* was born (Luke 2:1–20). The Church of the Nativity* was built here by Constantine* and rebuilt under Justinian*.

Betrothal, originally the promise of a woman by her guardian to enter into a contract of marriage; now a mutual and freely made promise of marriage.

Beza, Theodore (1519–1605), John Calvin's* successor as leader of the variety of Reformed* Protestantism created and led from Geneva. Beza was a provincial French nobleman, educated in the humanities and law in Paris, Orleans, and Bourges, and destined for a career in the church. He became Protestant, married secretly, and took refuge in Switzerland. He was a teacher in Lausanne from 1549, then first rector of the Geneva Academy from 1559. He translated into French much of the Psalter, which became the most important service book for French Protestants. He became involved in Protestant politics during the first war of religion in France (1561–63) and remained an adviser to Protestant political leaders in France and other countries throughout his life. On Calvin's death, in 1564, Beza was elected moderator of the Geneva Company of Pastors, held that position until 1580, then continued to teach and preach until his death. He was a prolific scholar, publishing erudite biblical studies, most notably on

Greek texts of the NT, polemics directed against Catholics and Lutherans, sermons, and legal and political treatises. He remained faithful to the teachings of Calvin, although often expressing them in a more systematic manner.

ROBERT M. KINGDON

Bible, Canon of. The list of authoritative books of the Christian Bible has three forms. The shorter canon used in Protestant churches includes 66 books (in the King James Version order): Genesis, Exodus, Leviticus, Numbers, Deuteronomy, Joshua, Judges, Ruth, 1 Samuel, 2 Samuel, 1 Kings, 2 Kings, 1 Chronicles, 2 Chronicles, Ezra (also called 1 Esdras), Nehemiah (also called 2 Esdras), Esther, Job, Psalms, Proverbs, Ecclesiastes, Song of Solomon, Isaiah, Jeremiah, Lamentations, Ezekiel, Daniel, Hosea, Joel, Amos, Obadiah, Jonah, Micah, Nahum, Habakkuk, Zephaniah, Haggai, Zechariah, Malachi, Matthew, Mark, Luke, John, Acts, Romans, 1 Corinthians, 2 Corinthians, Galatians, Ephesians, Philippians, Colossians, 1 Thessalonians, 2 Thessalonians, 1 Timothy, 2 Timothy, Titus, Philemon, Hebrews, James, 1 Peter, 2 Peter, 1 John, 2 John, 3 John, Jude, and Revelation.

The Roman Catholic and Orthodox Bibles also include the OT Apocrypha*: 1 Esdras* (also called 3 Esdras), Additions to Esther*, 1 Maccabees*, 2 Maccabees, Tobit*, Judith*, Wisdom* of Solomon, Ecclesiasticus (Wisdom* of Ben Sira), Baruch*, Epistle of Jeremiah, Susanna*, Prayer of Azariah, Prayer of Manassas*, and Bel and the Dragon.

In addition, the Bible of the Eastern Orthodox churches includes 3 Maccabees, 4 Maccabees, and Psalm 151.

In addition to the books included in Orthodox Bibles, the Ethiopian Bible includes 2 Esdras* (also called 4 Esdras), Joseph Ben Gurion (or Josippon, a popular chronicle of Jewish history from Adam to Titus), Jubilees*, Enoch*, the Testament* of Our Lord, Apostolic* Church Order, Apostolic* Constitutions (or Apostolic Canons), and the Didascalia* of the Apostles. The Bible of the Church* of the East follows the Syriac translation, the Peshitta*, which includes the same books as the Orthodox Bibles but omits 2 Peter, 2 and 3 John, Jude, and Revelation and some passages of the Gospels and Acts.

Bible, Texts and Manuscripts. Since no autograph documents of the biblical canon are extant, the notion of the "text" of the Bible is a theoretical reconstruction based on a critical evaluation of the textual witnesses (inscriptions, papyri, and manuscripts). A manuscript (a handwritten document) is an individual witness to the biblical text. The oldest manuscripts, such as NT papyri or the biblical manuscripts discovered in the Judean desert (see Dead* Sea Scrolls; Qumran*), have significant authority in textual questions. The dating of later manuscripts is a more complicated question because the age of a manuscript does not reveal the date of the text it contains. Codex Bezae (a Greek manuscript containing the Gospels, Acts, and the Catholic Epistles), written in the late 4th c., may contain a 2nd-c. text. Codex Neofiti 1 (a Targum manuscript) is dated to 1504 CE but probably contains a 3rd- or 4th-c. CE text.

For the Hebrew text, most scholars consult the *Biblia Hebraica Stuttgartensia* (BHS), which is based on the Codex Leningradensis B 19 (1008 CE), a manuscript that contains the entire HB and is thought to be the best representative of the Masoretic* text (a Hebrew text transmitted by a group of scholars known as the Masoretes, c500 CE). (The *Biblia Hebraica Quinta*, when complete, will replace the BHS.) Other important witnesses to the Masoretic text include the Aleppo Codex (10th c. CE) and 6th- to 8th-c. Hebrew manuscripts from the Cairo Genizah (a synagogue repository for biblical manuscripts no longer in use). Since the manuscript evidence for the Masoretic text is relatively young, the biblical manuscripts found in the Judean desert, written between 250 BCE and 68 CE, are foremost witnesses to an earlier Hebrew text. Among the biblical manuscripts found at Qumran, the second Isaiah scroll (1QIs[b]) is quite similar to the Masoretic text and thus confirms the Masoretic text's fidelity. But others, such as 1QIs[a], diverge significantly from it. This and other divergent manuscripts suggest that the earliest witnesses to the Hebrew text were pluriform. Textual critics must discern the best reading of the Hebrew text (sometimes rejecting the later Masoretic reading) on a case by case basis. On occasion the biblical reader observes the impact of the Judean desert discoveries. In 1 Sam 10:27 the New Revised Standard Version (NRSV) adds a lengthy reading from 4QSam[a] (most English translations have not included it) that introduces Nahash and his eye-gouging practice. The NRSV editors considered this Qumran manuscript reading to be earlier and better than the Masoretic text.

These early witnesses to the Hebrew text are complemented by the Versions, especially the Septuagint* (as early as the 3rd c. BCE), the

Samaritan Pentateuch (1st c. BCE), the Peshitta* (late 2nd c. CE), the Vulgate* (late 4th c. CE), and the Targums (from the 1st c. BCE up to the 8th c. CE); these early translations offer a glimpse of the state of the Hebrew text before the Masoretic period. But the Versions contain myriad divergent readings, most of which are not superior to the Masoretic text. Textual criticism offers a method of identifying the significant readings in the Versions and for determining whether a particular reading witnesses to a Hebrew text that is earlier than and superior to that preserved in the Masoretic text.

The most widely used editions of the Greek NT are the Nestle-Aland, 27th ed., and the United Bible Societies' *The Greek New Testament*, 4th ed. These editions offer the "standard text" of the NT, which is intended to be the closest to the original NT based on a critical evaluation of the witnesses. The oldest NT documents are known as "papyri" (referring to the writing material). Some of these papyri, such as p^{52} (a fragment of John 18:31–33, 37–38, dated c125), confirm the "standard text." The Bodmer papyri XIV–XV (p^{75}), containing Luke 3:18–18:18; 22:4–24:53 and John 1:1–15:8 (dated beginning 3rd c.), is close to the later Codex Vaticanus (4th c.), thus assuring this codex a principal voice in NT textual problems regarding other texts. Similarly, p^{72} (2nd–3rd c.), containing the letters of Peter and Jude, is an important early witness to these letters. Starting in the early 3rd c., parchment replaced papyrus. Greek manuscripts up to the 9th c. are referred to as "uncials," because of their large or capital letters. After the 9th c., the manuscripts were usually written in a cursive hand and are thus referred to as minuscules.

The abundance of NT manuscripts (more than 5,000) requires scholars to identify those manuscripts that can be traced back to the same exemplar. Most textual critics appeal to early text types of the NT, such as the Alexandrine* text (Egypt), the Koine* text (linked with Antioch* and the basis for the later Byzantine text), and the text of Codex Bezae (D), to classify Greek manuscripts. The early translations of the NT also assist in establishing the NT text, since their Greek exemplar may predate the earliest uncials. The Eastern Versions include the Old Syriac Gospels (3rd c.), the Peshitta (5th c.), and the slavishly literal Harklean version (616 CE). The Western Versions include the Old Latin (2nd c.) and the Vulgate (late 4th c.). To establish the earliest form of the NT, textual critics consider readings from the best Greek manuscripts (such as from the papyri and the codices Sinaiticus, Vaticanus, Alexandrinus, and Bezae) and from the Versions (aware of each version's translation techniques). On occasion the reader will observe a textual discussion on the pages of the English NT. The Revised Standard Version removed Luke 22:43–44 to a footnote because these verses are absent in the papyri and important uncials (the Vaticanus and the corrected Sinaiticus). The editors of the NRSV decided to restore these verses to their translation, albeit in double brackets to indicate the editors' uncertainty. In the removal and restoration of these verses, one observes that textual criticism is both a science and an art.

CRAIG E. MORRISON, O.Carm.

BIBLE INTERPRETATION CLUSTER

1) *Introductory Entry*

Bible Interpretation, History of

2) *A Sampling of Contextual Views and Practices*

Bible Interpretation in Africa
Bible Interpretation in Asia
Bible Interpretation in Asia: By Asian Women
Bible Interpretation in Eastern Orthodoxy
Bible Interpretation in Latin America
Bible Interpretation in North America
Bible Interpretation in North America: African American
Bible Interpretation in North America: Latino/a
Bible Interpretation in North America and Western Europe: Queer
Bible Interpretation in Oceania
Bible Interpretation in Western Europe
Bible Interpretation Worldwide: Feminist

1) Introductory Entry

Bible Interpretation, History of. Periods in the history of biblical interpretation are defined by the church's relation to the wider society. During the 1st–4th c., the church moved from marginality to becoming the church of the Roman Empire (although Christianity was also in the Persian Empire and beyond). The Reformation in the West brought about new

Christian communities, some as state* churches, others as free* churches, both types participating in the missionary movements (peaked in the 19th c.). From the free churches came the remarkable growth of Charismatic* and Pentecostal churches in the 20th c. From the 17th c onward, the Bible was subjected to a rigorous criticism that led to the development of historical critical methods, which gradually gained acceptance in the academy.

Pre-Constantinian Interpretation. Biblical interpretation during the first three centuries laid the foundations for subsequent developments. Church Bible interpreters operated on a number of fronts: (1) interpreting the Bible in inner church struggles against heretical* groups: Marcionites*, Gnostics*, and Manichaeans*; (2) disputes with Jews, not least over the interpretation of the OT; and (3) nurturing the faith of the church. The problem lay partly in drawing out a spiritual sense from the OT narratives and the now superseded OT legislation and partly in deriving a coherent cosmology and ethics* from texts containing many views. In dealing with the OT, Christian biblical interpreters drew on the allegorical* techniques of the classical world, already taken up by Jewish interpreters like Philo* of Alexandria. Alexandrian Christian interpreters like Clement* and Origen* followed this path, seeking the higher meanings hidden in the text (see Alexandria, Alexandrian Christianity and Its Theology). In the face of the great diversity of readings of the biblical texts, the church sought unity of interpretation through the imposition of a "rule* of faith" (Irenaeus*, Tertullian*).

From Constantine* to the Reformation*. The establishment of Christianity as the religion of the Roman Empire during the 4th c. led to a flourishing of exegetical endeavor. The Antioch* school (Diodore* of Tarsus, Theodore* of Mopsuestia) preferred to establish the literal*, historical sense of the text, while still seeking its spiritual meaning, or *theoria*. Augustine* (354–430) in North Africa sought to develop a new culture based on the Bible, just as the culture of the Greco-Roman world was based on the classics; so too did Chrysostom* and Jerome*. For this they drew on the typological* and allegorical work of earlier Christian interpreters. The struggles of the 4th c. against Arianism* and Eunomianism* inaugurated a new period of conciliar orthodoxy whereby the interpretation of Scripture was controlled no longer by a simple rule* of faith but by decisions of bishops in council.

Christian exegesis of Scripture flourished again in the Middle Ages, in the monasteries and the schools – an emancipation of biblical interpretation from episcopal control. Much of the work centered on the excerpting and collection of patristic interpretation (the *glossa**). Scripture had a fourfold sense: the literal, the allegorical, the moral, and the anagogical* (indicating the progress of the soul to heaven). Thomas Aquinas's* theological work is based on his exegesis of Scripture as well as on his readings of Aristotle; he shows himself a careful reader of texts, offering a close analysis of, e.g., Paul's arguments and engaging critically with the interpretations of the glosses.

The Reformation. The Augustinian friar and professor of biblical studies Martin Luther* reasserts the importance of the literal sense of Scripture against the theological readings of the schools. His struggle to understand what Paul meant by (i.e., the literal meaning of) the "righteousness* of God" is resolved by his grammatical analysis of the genitive "of God," which he takes in context (Rom 1:17) to refer to the gift of God's righteousness. Close attention to the literal meaning of the text also characterizes Calvin's* exegesis. Lay readings flourished as the Bible was translated and distributed in printed form. Ecclesiastical control of biblical interpretation became increasingly difficult; powerful lay readings are to be found in the Radical* Reformation. Calvin laid down guidelines for Scriptural interpretation in his hugely influential *Institutes*. Luther's influence was transmitted largely through his commentary on Galatians. The groups springing from the Radical Reformation, which privileged lay interpretations of the Bible, flourished in the missionary movement and in North America; they gave rise to the Holiness* movements of the 19th c. and, from them, the Pentecostal* and Charismatic* churches of the 20th c.

The Rise of Critical Readings. The 17th c. saw the rise of critical readings prompted partly by the diversity of interpretations of Scripture with its dire consequences in the religious wars of the 16th and 17th c. in Europe and partly by the expansion of human knowledge of astronomy, geography, and history. The criticisms of Deists and Rationalists* in the 18th c were addressed by the theological faculties in Germany, notably in the biblical critical studies of Semler and Michaelis in the 18th c. and of F. C. Baur* and the Tübingen school in the 19th c. This was often linked with a liberal* theological stance, denying the veracity of miracles*, identifying Christianity with the rise of a new religious self-consciousness, and seeking to give a purely historical, non-supranaturalist account of the origins of the Christian faith. In the early 20th c., such critical readings of Scripture were linked to a more orthodox doctrine of the Word* of God by the Lutheran scholar Rudolf Bultmann*.

JOHN K. RICHES

2) A Sampling of Contextual Views and Practices

Bible Interpretation in Africa follows various approaches and methods, as interpreters seek to relate the Bible to African contexts in order to provide a biblical grounding for the burgeoning African Christianity and spirituality. Consequently, Bible interpretation in Africa is resolutely "intercultural," seeking to make intelligible the religious texts originating in particular biblical cultures for readers from other cultures and religious contexts in Africa. *Intercultural hermeneutics* describes the social and cultural factors of the world that prevailed during the composition of biblical stories. Then the culture of the biblical author and that of the target audience can be compared and contrasted. Pairing social realities of the Bible and its world, unveiled through critical analyses, with social realities of the African world promotes a liberation* hermeneutic* of the Bible for African readers and their contexts. The text can then be reread to address contemporary human experiences lived out in Africa, as it has been reread by Western people (including scholars) in their own settings. Such an approach that transcends the gaps between the settings of biblical authors and audience is plausible because a canonical text has a life and meaning of its own, beyond its original cultural context.

Intercultural hermeneutics does not neglect the specific cultural context out of which a biblical text originated in the ancient world. But it goes beyond an investigation of the history of the text. In this hermeneutics, rigorous comparative analysis of the biblical cultural contexts is paired with analysis of the African symbolic universe. The parallels between these two cultural settings confirm that the Bible can function as a transcultural book. Thus this intercultural hermeneutics is both acceptable to academically trained interpreters and valuable for ordinary readers, helping them to relate the Bible message to their cultural and life settings. Yet an intercultural hermeneutics also involves reading with and through the sociocultural eyes of many grassroots Bible groups in Africa, such as youth fellowships and women groups yearning for Christ's and God's compassion in their struggle to provide a high-quality ministry for the many caught in the HIV/AIDS tragedy. Consequently, intercultural interpretations of the Bible in Africa elucidate dimensions of biblical texts that are ignored by Western biblical scholarship. The different horizons of reading resulting from the African "symbolic universe" and social contexts yield autochthonous African theological interpretations of the Bible that provide a distinctive heritage for contemporary African Christianity.

UKACHUKWU CHRIS MANUS

Bible Interpretation in Asia. There is a lengthy history of reading, interpreting, and translating the Bible in Asia. However, "Asian biblical interpretation" more narrowly refers to the readings and interpretations of the Bible that give attention to Asian religiocultural, socioeconomic, and political contexts. How do these contexts impinge on the construction of meaning in engagement with the biblical texts? Thus rooted in the broader fields of contextualization* and contextual hermeneutics*, Asian biblical interpretation takes four forms: cultural*, liberationist*, feminist*, and postcolonial*.

Cultural hermeneutics analyze biblical texts in relation to Asian sacred texts and religiocultural realities. C. S. Song and Kosuke Koyama in the 1970s paved the way for such "cross-textual," "dialogic" approaches. Examples of such readings include the use of native religious concepts in christological thinking (the Hindu concept of *avatar* [incarnation] or the Confucian concept of Tien-tzu [Son of Heaven]) and Archie C. C. Lee's cross-textual analysis of the Chinese creation myth of Nu Kua and the biblical narratives of creation.

Liberationist approaches respond to the socioeconomic and political situations of Asia, particularly the significant poverty* level and the history of oppressive governments. In Korea, for example, the liberationist Minjung* theology was used as a lens in the analysis of the Exodus narrative in the OT and of the social classes in the NT. In India, Dalit* theology invites a dialogic comparison of the Dalits with the oppressed and ostracized segments of society in Matthew's gospel.

Feminist perspectives address the issue of gender inequality in the social fabric of Asian cultures in the critical engagement of biblical texts. Attending to the experiences of women in the intersection of sex, gender, and power, Asian feminist biblical interpretations take on such issues as the unequal treatment of women and men in Confucian* societies, the abuse suffered by Korean comfort women, the disparity of the legal system in Japan in how matters of sexuality* were and are dealt with among women and men, or the multileveled oppression of Dalit* women in India* (see the present cluster: Bible Interpretation in Asia: By Asian Women).

Postcolonial hermeneutical studies seek to address the history of colonial domination in Asia. Among the many Asian biblical scholars at the forefront of postcolonial studies, R. S. Sugirtharajah has noted various types of postcolonial readings of the Bible: dissident, resistant, heritagist, nationalist, liberationist, and dissentient. An example of this is the reading the Book of Daniel as resistance literature.

JEFFREY KAH-JIN KUAN

Bible Interpretation in Asia: By Asian Women. As a result of the Evangelical missionary heritage, most Asian Christian women belong to Evangelical traditions, which espouse a literal* interpretation of the Bible and revere Scripture* as the Word* of God and the authority in religious matters and moral life. Although these women may not challenge the patriarchal background of the Bible (see Patriarchy and Christianity), some have found elements of the Bible that affirm women's dignity, such as the teaching that women and men are created in the image* of God and that Jesus befriends women, and teaches and heals them.

Feminist consciousness emerged among Asian Christian women in the 1970s, as they began reading the Bible in the struggle for justice* and democracy* and in the fight for women's ordination* and equality in the church. Christian women reclaimed powerful and courageous biblical women, such as Miriam*, Deborah*, Mary*, and other women leaders of the early church, as role models. In Bible studies and women's gatherings, women appropriate the tradition of oral interpretation of scriptures in Asian cultures by retelling, dramatizing, and performing stories of biblical women, giving them voice and subjectivity. Through a process of dialogic imagination, they bring biblical stories and Asian stories into creative interaction with one another.

Asian feminist scholars have used insights from sociopolitical analysis and cultural anthropology to show that a patriarchal social structure defined by honor* and shame can be found in both the NT and some Asian societies today. For example, cultic purity and blood pollution condemned as social outcasts the hemorrhaging woman and the Syrophoenician woman as described in the Gospels.

By discovering the cultural dynamics that shape the biblical narratives and the similarities with Asian cultures, these scholars demonstrate the commonalities of struggles between biblical and Asian women.

Other interpreters use postcolonial* criticism in feminist biblical interpretation, paying attention to the use of the Bible in empire building and colonialism. They challenge Western scholars' complicity in supporting colonial ideology* by glossing over the imperial context and agenda. They study biblical women in the "contact zone," such as Rahab and Ruth*, the Egyptian slave girl as migrant worker, and other women suppressed or marginalized in the narrative. They investigate the deployment of gender to support class interests, concentration of power, and colonial domination. Reading the Bible as a complex ideological text, they present reconstructive readings as counternarrative and highlight liberative readings not only by experts, but also by ordinary women readers.

KWOK PUI-LAN

Bible Interpretation in Eastern Orthodoxy. The basic principles of Orthodox biblical hermeneutics include the following:

- Holy Scripture* is an incarnation* of God's Logos*. This is a fundamental christological understanding of the nature of Scripture. The divine Logos truly speaks in the words of sacred Scriptures and is active through them in the reader (see Incarnation Cluster: In the Orthodox Tradition).
- Scripture's use of human words is an expression of God's condescension toward us. This perception of sacred Scripture opens the way to an interpretation that postulates a multiplicity of meanings of the biblical texts. The same sacred text has a different sense each time it is read, the variation reflecting the differences in readers' mystical* relation to God. This posits a specific kind of objectivity: that of the concrete relation between human and God in Christ.
- Scripture and the divine knowledge it mediates are situated in the sacramental* context of the church, which means that Scripture is also sacramental. This sacramental perception of the divine truth in Scripture is synergetic: it is a gift of the Spirit, but at the same time it depends on our worthiness (holiness).
- Scripture is uniformly inspired and, indeed, "written" by the Spirit, yet expressed in the language of the human author. The Orthodox understand Scripture's inspiration* as synergetic or *theanthropic,* i.e. the fruit of the cooperation between God and human authors. Consequently, as divine, Scripture has to be treated with reverence and obedience. Since Scripture is truly the Word of God, our response to it cannot but be one of obedience, receptivity, and listening. However, the Bible is also human; thus there is room for honest and exact critical inquiry in biblical study.
- Scripture is the unique "canon* of truth" or "rule* of faith," but this does not exclude the conviction that genuine tradition* (*paradosis*) is also, in a certain sense, "inspired." The tradition, identified as the "apostolic gospel," is the "living memory of the church." Scripture and tradition are neither mutually exclusive nor complementary. Their relationship can be described neither as Scripture *or* tradition, nor as Scripture *and* tradition, but as Scripture *in* tradition. A firm Orthodox hermeneutical principle is that biblical writings can be properly interpreted only in the frame of Holy Tradition.
- The "hermeneutical bridge" that reactualizes the biblical event in the church across centuries is none other than the Holy* Spirit. It is only in collaboration with the Holy Spirit that exegetes can discern the spiritual meaning of Scripture. The interpretative vision that tries to discern the spiritual significance of God's Word is *theoria,* i.e. contemplation*. The patristic *theoria* is not really a method, but a spiritual perception inspired by the Holy Spirit (see Patristic Thought in Orthodox Christianity).

- Jesus Christ the Lord, the very object of Scripture, is also the one who gives access to its truth through the Holy Spirit. The spiritual sense of Scripture is therefore nothing else than its *christological** sense, a manifold sense that is revealed in Christ himself. Christ, who is *theanthropos* (God incarnated), is therefore the foundation and the norm of Orthodox Bible interpretation.
- The church* is the place where Scripture becomes contemporary and effective to every person and community. Outside the church's life, one can never say what Scripture really is and how it is to be understood or interpreted. One can read the Bible individually, but not as an isolated individual. One reads it as members of the church. What is true for every member of the church is also true for its theologians. The decisive test and criterion for any interpretation of the Scripture is the "mind of the church."

VASILE MIHOC

Bible Interpretation in Latin America. A complete outline of biblical interpretation types in Latin America would include imported readings oblivious to the context, readings favoring marginalization in God's name, and literalistic, academic, and liberationist* readings. Liberationist readings are distinctive of Latin America. The 1960s and 1970s were times of liberation movements, followed by dictatorships, persecution, and, lately, submission through neoliberalism. The continent suffers from poverty*, illiteracy, and several forms of slavery*. Rampant neoliberal depletion of resources is followed by a general political move toward nationalism. These contextual facts explicitly influence Latin American interpretation, even more than the Roman Catholic or Evangelical confession of the interpreters.

Latin American Bible interpretation stands on three legs: readers' life realities, the Bible, and faith communities.

Alongside their academic work, most professional exegetes are engaged in some sort of reading with marginalized people: women, the homeless, peasants, prostitutes, street children, slum dwellers, Native Americans, African Americans, etc. Since interpretation starts with readers' situations rather than with historicocritical exegesis, these groups deeply permeate professional readers' views on the texts and consequently their approaches to them.

Similarly, reading with Base* Ecclesial Communities (Roman Catholic) and with poor congregations (Evangelical) is distinctive because the participants' interests and concerns – not the text and not the professional leader – determine the agenda. God has met people in their daily lives before they meet the Bible. Text and daily struggles feed each other during question-and-answer periods, so that people leave the sessions with a deeper understanding of both. The different priorities of these readings generate tensions with official church teachings (mostly Roman Catholic) and with academic studies because of the danger of overemphasizing the subjective (experiences, needs, sufferings) over the objective (text, programs, churches' agendas) and the requirement of truly trusting the people's understanding and wisdom.

Socioeconomic readings seek to address issues of socioeconomic justice* from the prophetic words of the First and Second Testaments. The deep differences that split the world today are systemic. With input from the social sciences, socioeconomic readings take sides with the deprived. They generate tensions owing to three factors: the world sets people apart; we see each other through ideologies*; and there is an increasing awareness of the complexity of any analysis.

Another approach, liberation within liberation, focuses on the concerns of particular groups – women, Native Americans, African Americans – as well as concerns related to gender orientation and ecological issues. Tensions arise as these voices struggle to gain recognition within a hermeneutical milieu theoretically open to those without a voice.

MERCEDES L. GARCÍA BACHMANN

Bible Interpretation in North America. Until the 1970s, secular scholarly interpretation of the Bible in the USA and Canada was dominated by historical-critical methods (see Historiography of Early Christianity as Developed in the 19th and 20th Centuries). A secular "space" for critical approaches had been carved out through long, bitter battles with church interests since the 19th c.

In church-related institutions, there is still an uneven acceptance of biblical criticism, and often none at all. The immense amount of lay interpretation in faith communities was largely and is increasingly fundamentalist* with (in the USA) an unacknowledged "American inculturation*." There was (and still is) little connection between grassroots church uses of the Bible and the secular discipline of biblical criticism. The Society of Biblical Literature (SBL), the main organizing body for critical interpretation, is unrelated to any church structure.

In the 1970s, the historical-critical consensus began to be challenged from three sides: literary* criticism, including structuralism*; feminism*; and the social* sciences. Out of these impulses a dizzying variety of approaches were developed: reader-response, canonical, and rhetorical criticism; semiotic*, poststructural, and deconstructive (postmodern*) methods; political and ideological* (including Marxist*) readings; methods developed in liberation* struggles, including black interpretation; womanist*, queer*, and other gendered approaches; and psychological* methods. The SBL has become the world center for scholarly biblical interpretation of every kind, bringing together scholars from many parts of the world, using many approaches, including approaches having their origin in the Two-thirds World. New methods with intrinsic "cross-cultural" dimensions, including postcolonial* readings and cultural* studies, have been strengthened by the participation of Two-thirds World scholars.

North America provides accessible meeting places for Two-thirds World scholars, many of whom are located there as expatriates. This is both a gift and a problem. One problem is that an overwhelming proportion of global biblical scholarly discussion is in the English language. One gift is that some of the new methods, especially those emerging from liberation struggles, have surmounted the strict separation of scholarly and church engagement with Scripture*, even as it has challenged the fundamentalist view of Scripture* and its roles. Black biblical scholars in the USA, for example, are usually very active in churches. The development of the newer approaches has not meant the disappearance of historical criticism, which is still dominant in scholarly discourse. There is a division between its practitioners and exponents of the newer methods, marked, for example, by SBL's two major journals, the *Journal of Biblical Literature* (still relatively traditional) and *Semeia* (created in the 1970s as a vehicle for "experimental" methods). DAVID JOBLING

Bible Interpretation in North America: African American. African Americans' engagement of the Bible should be understood not merely as textual interpretation but as a people's "readings" of the worlds they were first forced to negotiate but then self-authorized to reshape for their affirmation. A schema of historical readings – of text and social texture – can help isolate the sentiments, practices, and orientations of a large segment of the people now called "African Americans."

First Reading: Awe and Fear. From the beginning of their contact and subsequent captivity in 16th-c. Western Africa and their transition to the Americas, where they experienced slavery* and subjugation, peoples of African descent were confronted with the colonizing, civilizing, and missionizing practices of European slavocracy. One of the most important instruments in such efforts was the Bible, common to all European slave-trading nations. Testimonies from European sailors, teachers, and missionaries, on the one hand, and from African diaspora autobiographies, on the other, register the Africans' initial lack of understanding of, and uneasy socialization into, European socioreligious orientations. The conventional literacy presupposed by these cultures at first clearly frustrated the "conversion" of the African slaves. The latter were, on the whole, incapable of meeting the literacy requirements for

Bible Interpretation in North America

conversion* and participation; even more importantly, they did not seem emotionally disposed toward the book-based religions of the slavers. The notion of divine communication effected through a book was deemed odd, awesome, fascinating, but also full of potential for world negotiation.

Second Reading: Critique and Accommodation. It was not until the late 18th c., with the phenomenal growth of Dissenting* and Evangelical* movements in England and the USA, that enslaved and formerly enslaved Africans began to engage the Bible on a large scale. Finding themselves directly appealed to by the new Evangelicals and revivalists* in vivid, emotional biblical language, and noting that nearly the entire white world explained its power and authority by appeal to the Bible, the Africans in North America engaged it. They soon came to transform the Bible from the book of the religions of the white aristocratic slavers and lower-class dissenting exhorters into their special source of psychic and spiritual power, inspiration* for learning, and language of stinging, if veiled, critique.

This reading extends well into the late 20th c. It encompasses the founding of the independent churches and denominations (late 18th c.) and of many schools and colleges (19th c.). It supplied a rhetorical framework for 19th- and early-20th-c. black nationalisms, and it was the ideological foundation for the mid-20th-c. Civil* Rights Movement and campaigns. This reading of the Bible and North American culture expressed considerable ambivalence: it was both social-critical and accommodationist-integrationist.

Third Reading: Splitting the Margins. Another reading was cultivated in the early 20th c., primarily in the urban centers of the USA. It reflected the sentiments of rural and small-town residents who migrated to the big cities in search of better job opportunities and more social freedoms. These displaced individuals formed new religious communities that gave them a sense of solidarity.

The "reading" of the Bible, and of the world, in evidence among such communities was a more critical, even radical attitude about America: there was little hope of full integration into the mainstream. America was seen as racist* and arrogant, and to be rejected as such. Among the movements associated with such an attitude were the Garvey* Movement, Father Divine and the Peace Mission Movement, the Black Jews, the Nation of Islam, the Spiritual churches, and the Pentecostal* Movement.

Fourth Reading: Leaving Race Behind. Emerging in the late 20th c., this reading was and continues to be in many respects a reaction to both the accommodationist and the separatist readings already discussed. Historically primarily Evangelical in their religious sensibilities, including the importance they attached to the Bible, African Americans have nonetheless exhibited more playfulness than doctrinalism and moralism in their interpretations. Yet in much the same way that fundamentalist* practices and beliefs among whites in the early 20th c. represented a rejection of significant aspects of modernism, so within the world of African Americans a turn toward religious fundamentalism – evidenced in the affiliation with and/or imitation of self-styled white fundamentalist churches – has come to represent a rejection or relativization of African Americans' historical experiences and sensibilities.

Fifth Reading: Women's Reading. From Phillis Wheatley to modern womanist* interpreters, women are part of each of the readings distinguished in the preceding sections. Across each of these readings, differences in historical periods, locations, classes, and other factors notwithstanding, women have added special emphases. Among such emphases, none is more perduring and radical than the challenge that African American religious communities consistently apply the moral imperative of defining the universality of the divine economy of salvation without respect to gender. VINCENT L. WIMBUSH

Bible Interpretation in North America: Latino/a. Latino/a biblical interpretation emerges from the conjunction of biblical studies and racial-ethnic studies. Biblical studies, writ broadly, involve the analysis of biblical texts in terms of production as well as consumption. This task entails not only the academic-scholarly tradition of reading, but also other major reading traditions: the dogmatic-theological, the ecclesial-liturgical, the popular-devotional, and the social-cultural. The task further involves two recent developments in the discipline: (1) an expansion of its mode of inquiry to include, beyond the traditional grand model of historical criticism, a variety of other such models – literary, sociocultural criticism, and ideological criticisms; (2) an expansion of its object of study to include not only the texts of antiquity but also the readings of such texts and the readers behind them in modernity and postmodernity.

Racial-ethnic studies involve the analysis of representations of the Other in the context of migration and the encounter of population groups. This task entails the phenomenon of migration and its processes of racialization and ethnicization that give rise to the problematic of race and ethnicity. This task also entails a set of related issues: the question of ethnoracial identity, the conditions of diaspora* and exile, the role of the state*, and the constructions and relations of dominant and minority groups.

Latino/a biblical interpretation is thus grounded in biblical ideological* criticism and racial-ethnic minority studies. Within biblical studies, ideological criticism foregrounds power relations in society and culture, with minority criticism focusing on racial-ethnic constructions and relations. Within racial-ethnic studies, minority studies highlight the mechanics and dynamics of dominant–minority formations within a state, with Latino/a studies focusing on the Latino/a population within the USA. Latino/a biblical interpretation thus constitutes an exercise in minority criticism from the perspective of the Latino/a community in the country (see Racism and Christianity Cluster).

As such, Latino/a biblical interpretation has as its base an ever-growing number of residents of Latin American origin or descent, presently constituting the largest minority group in the USA and projected to become a fourth of the population by midcentury. The group hails from all nations of Latin America and finds itself in the country as a result of conquest and migration. From this base, it examines issues of social-cultural domination and subordination in the ancient texts as well as in modern and postmodern readings and readers; it also examines uses of the Bible across the academic-scholarly and all other reading traditions of the Bible on the part of Latinos/as.

FERNANDO F. SEGOVIA

Bible Interpretation in North America and Western Europe: Queer. Queer interpretation challenges the assumption that biblical texts must be read in ways that conform to certain normative views about sex, gender, and sexuality*. Emerging in the wake of such trends as feminist* hermeneutics and increased attention to the social location of readers, queer biblical interpretation is often associated with movements for the social and religious inclusion of lesbians, gay men, and bisexuals.

"Queer" was sometimes used in the past as a pejorative term for persons known to engage, or suspected of engaging, in homosexual* practice. Instead, the word now functions as a rallying point for those who affirm such practice or contest the assumed normativity of heterosexuality.

Queer readings of the Bible may oppose the use of biblical interpretation to condemn homosexuality, or may reread biblical texts in the light of lesbian, gay, or bisexual experiences. However, as the reference to "bisexual" indicates, queer biblical interpretation also builds on queer theory's interrogation of rigid, dualistic distinctions associated with sex (e.g. "male" vs. "female"), gender (e.g. "masculine" vs. "feminine"), or sexuality (e.g. "heterosexual" vs. "homosexual," or "straight" vs. "gay"). Consequently, queer biblical interpretation can also take its point of departure from "transgender" persons and phenomena (e.g. intersexuals and transsexuals). Queer biblical interpretation is therefore defined more by its opposition to, or interrogation of, narrow views of sex, gender, and sexuality than by the sexual or gendered identities of its practitioners. In principle, at least, such interpretation can be carried out by persons of any gender or sexual preference.

Although queer biblical interpretation is in many respects distinct from traditional interpretation, it does share certain emphases with historical-critical approaches to the Bible. Like historical criticism, queer interpretation recognizes that the Bible was written in a distant historical context and is shaped by sociocultural assumptions that do not always conform to later orthodoxies. For example, whereas modern religious readers valorize monogamous heterosexual marriage, the HB tolerates polygyny, concubinage, and prostitution; and NT passages state a preference for celibacy over marriage. Both testaments make presuppositions about marriage and kinship quite distinct from those informing modern debates about, e.g., "gay marriage." Thus while some queer interpretations attempt to re-read biblical texts to make them more useful for contemporary contexts, other queer readings highlight the historical gap between biblical texts and modern contexts to suggest that biblical norms of sex, gender, and kinship cannot be imposed simplistically on the modern world.

KEN STONE

Bible Interpretation in Oceania is rippling in several places away from dominant Western hermeneutical waves. Most of these ripples are in revolt.

Attention to location (on land, in the ocean, along the edges) has stirred interested interpretations. For example, M. E. Andrew has joined the party that seeks to settle the Bible in Aotearoa/New Zealand, and the volumes of *The Earth Bible* (ed. Norman C. Habel), gathered in Australia, have raised the cries of earth and country against human neglect and abuse.

The joys of storytelling, a popular pastime in oral cultures, lurk behind the assault on the documentary hypothesis by Anthony F. Campbell and Mark A. O'Brien, who read the sources of the Pentateuch* not as end products that signal their origins but as bases for ongoing reflection and storytelling.

Several interpreters knock on the doors of critical theory (e.g. Roland Boer) and offer healing stepping-stones for the causes of women and native people (e.g. Elaine M. Wainwright, Judith E. McKinlay, and Mark G. Brett).

The Rainbow Spirit Elders (Australia) set indigenous stories and artworks alongside biblical stories. The complete range of indigenous interpretations, however, is not available in writing, partly because the public does not accommodate the languages and orality of the native people of Oceania.

JIONE HAVEA

Bible Interpretation in Western Europe is heir to more than two centuries of fierce intellectual struggle between churches and their critics. This battle was fought principally in theological faculties controlled by Protestant state* churches, notably Lutheran churches in Germany*. With the decline of state churches, free* churches and lay groups assumed greater prominence.

In academic circles, historical*-critical studies predominate, embracing since the 1980s social-historical studies and reception* history of the Bible. There has been some interest in ahistorical literary studies of the Bible (structuralist, poststructuralist, deconstructionist, and narrative readings).

Controversy surrounds the theological interpretation of the Bible. Stendahl and Räisänen argue that NT scholars should study the history of early Christianity, not exclusively the canonical texts; theological interpretation should come after this historical study. Theissen offers an evolutionary account of the emergence of early Christian religion from its Jewish matrix, an account open to theological interpretation. Others (e.g. Watson) argue that biblical interpretation, properly a matter for the church, should be conducted within the framework of trinitarian* belief. In the shadow of the Holocaust*, Stendahl attacked Lutheran interpretations of Paul linked to negative portrayals of Judaism.

Mainstream state churches have relied largely on the universities to train their ministers and provide instruction to their laity. Theological faculties were controlled by the churches, leading to a denominalization of theological departments, though greater ecumenical cooperation has developed since the 1960s (in the Protestant–Catholic ecumenical commentary series *Evangelisch-Katholischer Kommentar*). In the UK, ecclesiastical control has loosened since the 1980s.

Roman Catholic scholarship has flowered since Vatican* II (Schnackenburg, Gnilka, Pesch), as church controls were (temporarily) lifted. The Bible continues to play an important role in inner-church conflict (ordination* of women, gay men, and lesbians). Calvinist and Puritan* theologies, developed when Reformation churches were state* churches (between the 16th and 20th c.), continue to exercise great influence in such debates, particularly through the view that the OT law has continuing authority over the church.

"Nonofficial" ecclesial interpretations have flourished among Methodist and Pentecostal* churches, in a Holiness* tradition reacting to Calvinism. Evangelical* groups (both lay and clergy, e.g. InterVarsity Fellowship) have promoted a more thoroughgoing Reformed reading of Scripture. Other lay groups, such as feminist* and contextual* Bible study groups, draw on Liberationist* theologies.

JOHN K. RICHES

Bible Interpretation Worldwide: Feminist. Feminist interpretation, using a hermeneutic* of suspicion, questions the theological teachings of the Bible concerning women, which create and sustain patriarchy*. Originally Western, it is now practiced in academic circles, denominations, and churches worldwide. Early work was rightly criticized for its ethnocentrism, anti-Semitism*, disregard of class and race*, and assumption of a "universal condition" of women. Feminist interpretation nevertheless served as a point of departure for Christians globally, inspiring many to begin their own process of naming themselves, their goals, their methods, and their varied relationships to the Bible. The main methods include (1) literary studies, (2) sociohistorical studies, and (3) psychological/pastoral approaches.

1. Feminist interpretation is uniquely concerned about texts which suggest that women are the origin of all sin (Gen 2–3; 1 Tim 2:10–15), that their primary function is childbearing, and that submission to men is a reasonable part of God's creation, not to be questioned or reformed (1 Cor 14:34–35; 1 Pet 3:1–7). By retrieving positive portraits of women in the Bible, interpreters demonstrated that women's contributions to the religious and social worlds went far beyond childbearing (cf. Exod 1–2; 15; Judg 4–5; Luke 24). "De-patriarchalizing" the Bible meant the juxtaposition of texts like Gal 3:27–28 with Gal 3:26, where the goal of all Christians is to become "sons" of God. Inclusive and gender-sensitive translations* were made. The canon* was reopened to explore neglected texts or traditions (roles of female prophets*; female apostles* like Junia* and Thecla*), and questions about female authorship (Ruth*, Song* of Songs) were posed. Ultimately, the accuracy and adequacy of gendered language in theology were cast into serious doubt.
2. Interpreters focus on the social functions of patriarchy* in the history of the cultures that formed the Bible, sometimes concluding that the Bible itself resists this form of oppression. In the HB, women were shown to possess worth and dignity; studies of the Jesus Movement emphasized its egalitarian possibilities. Comparisons with polytheistic societies raised the issue of monotheism* and its historical relationship to goddess traditions.
3. The largely patriarchal biblical text is examined for women's specialized and general religious experiences, using the psychology of women. Interpreters critique and enlarge the Bible's view of women's spirituality. Woman Wisdom* was retrieved as a cosmic role model, and Jesus became a "female-identified" messiah adequate to women's needs. Gender

was exposed as a social construct (unlike "sex"), and not a divine mandate. **See also** STANTON, ELIZABETH CADY. CAROLE FONTAINE

Bible and Other "Scriptures"

See AFRICAN RELIGION AND CHRISTIANITY CLUSTER; BUDDHISM AND CHRISTIANITY CLUSTER; CONFUCIANISM AND CHRISTIANITY CLUSTER; DAOISM AND CHRISTIANITY CLUSTER; HELLENISTIC RELIGIOUS TRADITIONS AND CHRISTIANITY'S SELF-DEFINITION; HINDUISM AND CHRISTIANITY CLUSTER; QUR'AN AND CHRISTIANITY. **See also** LITERATURE AND CHRISTIANITY

Bible Translations Cluster

1) *Introductory Entry*

Bible Translations, History of

2) *A Sampling of Bible Translations*

Bible, Early Translations/Versions
Bible, English Translations
Bible, Present-Day Translations in Africa

---

1) Introductory Entry

Bible Translations, History of. The Christian faith "never exists except as *translated* into a culture*" (Bosch); Bible translation is part of this process.

Translation is an intercultural-mediated communication. Bible translation aims at sharing information and fostering communication among sender/author, messenger/translator, and receiver/reader, but not as a one-way process. Its intercultural mediation involves a give and take. Because there is never a one-to-one word correspondence between two languages, any translation process includes some degree of deletion, distortion, generalization, specification, or equivalence, and thus of interpretation. Translation of OT Hebrew and Aramaic texts and of NT Greek texts into other languages is a literary and artistic activity that creatively converts a source text into another text in another language.

The history of Bible translations begins with scribes interpreting orally the Hebrew text in Aramaic, the common language at that time (Neh 8:8; 5th c. BCE). Written Hebrew–Aramaic Bible translation (paraphrase) originated with the Targum (beginning in the early 3rd c. BCE), still within the same cultural family, Semitic culture. Bible translation became more clearly intercultural with the Septuagint* (LXX; 3rd c. BCE); the translation of the HB into Greek bridges Semitic and Hellenistic cultures, but still with a Jewish audience – possibly the Jewish Diaspora in Alexandria. The result of teamwork (traditionally, 70 or 72 translators), LXX was most influential and triggered the development of Bible translations.

For the early church, LXX served as the only sacred Scripture, was quoted by the NT writers, then was augmented by the NT books to constitute a complete Christian canon*. Many OT Versions were based on LXX, including the Old* Latin (late 2nd c.), Coptic (c2nd c.), Ethiopic (Amharic; c4th c.), Gothic (5th c.), Armenian (5th c.), Georgian (6th c.), Syriac (7th c.), and Slavic (from 9th c.) Versions. Nevertheless, the need for Christian Scriptures translated from the original language was felt by many early church communities – the Syriac Peshitta* (2nd c.), Jerome's* Latin "Vulgate*" (5th c.), Saadia ha Gaon's Arabic version (10th c.), and Rabbi Jacob Tawus's Persian version (16th c.). Vulgate gradually acquired the prestige previously reserved for LXX and Peshitta. After extensive use in the Western Church, it was recognized as authoritative by the Council of Trent* (1546).

The Eastern and Western churches were influenced primarily by LXX and Vulgate until the advent of "mixed translations" based on eclectic source texts (Hebrew manuscripts, LXX, Greek NT, Vulgate, and existing translations). The first complete mixed-translation Bibles include those in English (Oxford, 1380), German (Constance, 1450), Italian (Venice, 1471), Spanish (Valencia, 1478), French (Antwerp, 1530), Dutch (1526, Antwerp), Portuguese (Lisbon, 1784), Chinese

(Serampur, 1815–22), Malagasy (1835), Tswana (1857), Ga (Accra, 1866), Swahili (London, 1895), Tamil (1796), Hindi (Serampur, 1866–69), and Zulu (1883). This eclectic tendency is still rampant. In English, the first Bible translation fully based on original languages is attributed to William Tyndale (1526–34), superseded by the King James Version (1611), *the* Bible for English-speaking countries for about 250 years.

Bible translations and interpretations (hermeneutics*) are intertwined, presupposing each other. The translators' exegetical* choices reflect hermeneutical* and cultural choices. For instance, LXX reflects an effort to understand the text in terms of the Hellenistic* culture when it translates the Hebrew description of the earth in Gen 1:2 as "invisible and disorganized" ("empty and void" and "formless chaos" are other possibilities) and the divine name (Exod 3:14) as "I Am the Existing One." Similarly Jerome, despite his claim to have changed nothing in the message of the OT Hebrew texts, acknowledges that his renderings rely on the authority of the Holy Spirit, the Gospels, and the apostles (as understood in the Western Church).

Recent developments in hermeneutical theories have made significant contributions to Bible translation by making explicit its interdisciplinary character. Nida's functional equivalence (or common language) translation theory views translation as reproducing in the receptor language the closest "natural equivalent" of the source language message. The primary goal is to make the translation "clear and natural," while remaining faithful to the original. In the Swahili language, which has no articles, the words *mwana wa mtu* (son of man, human being) are a clear, natural Swahili rendering of the Greek NT phrase *ho huios tou anthropou* (literally, "*the* son of *the* man") and a faithful rendering of the original Hebrew/Aramaic phrase behind it. Despite inappropriate uses at times, the functional equivalence approach produced popular versions that the majority of Bible readers have used for half a century. They include the "Good News Bible," "Français Courant," "Die Gute Nachrichte," and "Swahili Habari Njema." Yet competing translation theories have emerged, including literalist, functionalist, descriptive, text-linguistic, relevance, interpretive, comparative, and literary-rhetorical approaches. Each is multidisciplinary (even the literalist approach) and requires biblical exegesis*, translation studies, linguistics, anthropology*, information technology, etc.

In sum, throughout history, Bible translations have shown a preference for common language, and a thirst for translating from original languages and for church-oriented translations, performed by competent translators/interpreters.

JEAN-CLAUDE LOBA-MKOLE

2) A Sampling of Bible Translations

Bible, Early Translations/Versions. As the HB (in Hebrew and Aramaic) migrated beyond the borders of Palestine, translations were required. In the 3rd c. BCE, the Septuagint* (LXX) version emerged as the Bible for Greek-speaking Jews in Egypt. At the same time, Aramaic-speaking Jews living in Palestine and the Babylonian Diaspora* translated the Pentateuch and most other books of the HB into Aramaic, creating a version known as the Targums* (the Babylonian Targums [Onqelos and Jonathan, 4th–5th c. CE] and the Palestinian Targums [Neofiti, 3rd–4th c. CE and Pseudo-Jonathan, 8th c. CE]). A targum to Job found at Qumran (11QtgJob) is among the earliest witnesses to this translation activity. The Jews in Edessa* translated the HB into Syriac (the Peshitta* OT, late 2nd c. CE). The NT (written in Greek) with its missionary emphasis required immediate translation. As the Gospels traveled east of Jerusalem, they were translated into Syriac – Tatian's* gospel harmony, the Diatessaron* (c170), the Vetus Syra containing the four Gospels (3rd c.), and later the Peshitta* containing 22 books of the NT (5th c.). As the Bible traveled west to Egypt and across North Africa and into Spain and Gaul, it was translated into Coptic (3rd c.) and Latin (the Old* Latin version, late 2nd c.). Jerome's* Vulgate* (late 4th c.) provided a fresh translation of the OT and a revision of the Old Latin for the NT. For biblical scholars, these Versions witness to the stages in the development of the Hebrew text. More importantly, they witness to the reception of the Bible into various cultures, as they include fascinating readings (the Palestinian Targums, e.g., are replete with explanatory readings) that render the Bible comprehensible to its target audiences.

CRAIG E. MORRISON, O.Carm.

Bible, English Translations. John Wyclif* and his followers were the first to translate the Latin Bible into English (c1382). Without the printing press and with extreme opposition to his views, Wyclif's reforms failed to flourish. Yet John Colet's success in teaching Paul's epistles in the English vernacular (early 16th c.) convinced Erasmus* of the need for the Bible in the language(s) of the people.

William Tyndale's* NT in English (1526) drew primarily on the NTs of Erasmus (1516, Greek) and Luther* (1522, German). Though it was not acceptable to print Scripture in English in England during this period, Tyndale rendered the text brilliantly and in a style of English that excited and inspired readers, illustrating with woodcuts to further engage the reader and illuminate the texts. After Tyndale's martyrdom (1536), his friend John Rogers published the "Matthew's Bible" (Matthew being a pseudonym for Tyndale).

Miles Coverdale, who was the first to publish the full Bible in English (1535), published the "Great Bible" (1539) based on the "Matthew's Bible," with improvements.

After the suppressions of Queen Mary*, Queen Elizabeth* (enthroned, 1557) tolerated the English Bible. The first domestic printing (1576) of the Geneva Bible (1560), a popular and important translation, was the first English-language Bible to have verse divisions; it included thousands of reformers' notes and references.

The first NT in English specifically for Catholics was published (1582) in Rheims (France). The OT was delayed until 1609–10, when it appeared in Douai (France).

The King James Bible (1611) dominated English Bibles for 350 years and remains the most important and influential book in the history of the English language.

The Revised Version (1885) and American Standard Version (1901) challenged the King James's supremacy, particularly among scholars. The most significant alteration was the elimination of the Apocrypha*, reducing the English Bible in most future Protestant translations from 80 to 66 books. Significant translations, owing to their attention to contemporary language issues, are the Revised Standard Version (1952); the New American Bible (1970, 2000), the official translation of the Roman Catholic Church; the New American Standard Bible (1971, 1995); the Good News Translation (1976); the New International Version (1978), which surpassed the King James Version as the best-selling English Bible by the beginning of the 21st c.; the New King James (1982); and the New Revised Standard Version (1989). Over the 25 years between 1982 and 2007, numerous translations appeared, as did revisions of existing translations. (See the Bibliography for a list of the major English translations.)

CRAIG LAMPE

Bible, Present-Day Translations in Africa. The Bible is an African book read at least in part in 665 of Africa's estimated 2,000 languages (153 entire Bibles and 293 NTs in 2003). The first translation of the Bible in Africa, the Greek Septuagint*, served primarily Jewish believers. Subsequent African translations (including Old* Latin, 2nd c.; Coptic, 2nd c.; and Ethiopian translations, c4th c.) served the needs of African churches in evangelism, teaching, and social transformation. The next wave of translations, linked to the 19th-c. missionary movement, played an essential role in the Christianization of Africa. Most African translations are now indigenous African translations (done by native speakers) and contribute to the inculturation* of Christianity. Translators developed theological lexicons proposing indigenous key terms and local equivalents for biblical features: the names and central metaphors for God and other spiritual beings, concepts, practices, festivals, rituals, and social roles. This was no easy task. For instance, to render the name of God, translators grappled with female gods such as Looa of the Iraqw of Tanzania; borrowed God's name from neighboring groups (for fear that their own was evil and unacceptable); and at times used wrong names (e.g. mistaking the Acoli traditional hunchback spirit with the creator God). Key concepts also posed serious problems; e.g. translating "holiness" in the Kenyan Luo and Luyia dialects as "white" or "clean" (hence "white or clean spirit" for "Holy Spirit") is problematic. Nevertheless, Christianity in Africa owes much to these African translations. ALOO OSOTSI MOJOLA

Biblical Commission. See PONTIFICAL BIBLICAL COMMISSION.

Biblical Theology refers to the theology found in the Bible or theology that aims to be deeply imbued with the Bible. Theology found in the Bible can be dense (e.g. Paul's* letters) or can emerge through narrative (e.g. the historical books of the OT). The difference between the OT and the NT raises the question that has existed since the 2nd c.: Are the two testaments ultimately coherent? Marcion* said no and produced his short version of the NT (Luke* and various letters of Paul). This also implied a denial of the theological coherence of the 27 NT books gathered later in the canon. Without following Marcion's massive reductionism, some have argued that the theological perspectives of NT authors differ so much as even to be irreconcilable (e.g. Paul and James* on the theological value of "works") (see New Testament Theology).

Those who, like Irenaeus* (died c200), read the two testaments as a coherent whole find unity in diversity through the Christ event. With various qualifications, they follow the NT authors by interpreting the Christ event in the light of the OT and reinterpreting the OT in the light of the Christ event. Some pursue this task by examining such themes as covenant*, creation*, faith*, promise, redemption*, sacrifice*, and salvation*, which are seen differently and more richly in the light of Christ.

One must ask: Are there only theologies (plural) of the OT and theologies of the NT? Or were many scholars correct in writing books entitled Old Testament Theology (singular) and New Testament Theology? Or should one see, with Brevard Childs, a unity, a biblical theology of the Old and New Testament?

Those drawing theology from the Bible should ask: Are they interpreting the Scriptures* as church members and in the light of Christian faith (including belief in Scripture as the inspired* Word* of God)? Do they draw theology from the whole canon, from a canon within the canon, or even from some reconstructed "original" form of the biblical text? Ten principles developed by O'Collins and Kendall indicate how theology makes the study of scriptures "the soul of theology." GERALD O'COLLINS, SJ

Biel, Gabriel (c1420–95), Scholastic theologian, follower of William* of Ockham, commentator on Peter* Lombard's *Sentences*. He studied at Heidelberg, Erfurt, and Cologne, became a member of the Brethren* of the Common Life, and was a founder of the University of Tübingen. One of the last of the Nominalists*, he influenced Luther*.

Bigamy. See POLYGAMY AND CHRISTIANITY.

Binding and Loosing, authority given to Peter (Matt 16:19) and the church (Matt 18:18) to forgive or retain sins, employed in excommunication*, penance*, and readmission to Communion.

Binitarianism, a belief in God as Father and Son, either ignoring the Holy Spirit or denying the Spirit's divinity. **See also PNEUMATOMACHI.**

Biomedical Ethics. Christian theologians helped establish the field of bioethics. Joseph Fletcher and Paul Ramsey were two of the early Protestant founders, though Roman Catholic moralists had long discussed ethical issues in medical contexts. Distinctions made within that tradition, such as "ordinary" versus "extraordinary" means of sustaining life, helped shape medical practice and law. Since the 1970s, the field of bioethics has been dominated by the application of four principles: respect for persons (also called respect for autonomy*), beneficence (doing good), nonmaleficence (avoiding harm), and justice*. The understanding of these principles has increasingly been dominated by philosophical discussion, but Christian voices continue to be important in selected issues such as cloning and stem cell research.

Christians do not speak with a unified voice on bioethical issues. Abortion*, cloning, and the use of stem cells have been particularly controversial. On the grounds that all human life is "made in God's image*" and that none should be devalued, some Christians reject any destruction of early human life, inside or outside the womb, and Catholic hospitals may refuse to perform abortions. Many Christians believe in a form of "natural* law" that prohibits interference with God's ordained order for human life; hence, they may reject sterilization or artificial modes of reproduction. Other Christians countenance abortion, sterilization, and new modes of reproduction such as in vitro fertilization and artificial insemination under limited circumstances. Stressing human freedom while mindful of human sinfulness, they argue that God gives us power to invent new means of human well-being and that new technologies can contribute to human fulfillment (such as childbearing). Increasingly, Christian commentators have emphasized the centrality of justice* issues in bioethics, with attention to the global impact of new technologies on women* and other oppressed groups. Christian feminists* have joined philosophical feminists in arguing for the priority of oppression and liberation as concerns in bioethics, while other Christian voices remain dedicated to the protection of embryonic life and of "traditional" lifestyles, including those of sexual reproduction. At stake in some debates is a basic tension between understanding humans as "stewards" of an original creation given by God and understanding them as "co-creators" who are free to shape new directions in human life.

In the USA and elsewhere, Christians have contributed to the shaping of public policy on bioethics by serving on the National Commission for the Protection of Human Subjects of Biomedical and Behavioral Research and on the President's Council on Bioethics. **See also ABORTION; BIRTH CONTROL AND CONTRACEPTION, CHRISTIAN VIEWS OF; BODY; ETHICS CLUSTER AND CHRISTIANITY CLUSTER.** KAREN LEBACQZ

Biretta, square, rounded cap worn by Roman clergy: white for priests, purple for bishops, red for cardinals.

Birgitta (1303–73), religious "feminist," Swedish medieval mystic, monastic founder; canonized (1391, Boniface IX) and named Europe's patron saint (1999, John Paul II). She corrected patriarchal* God narrative by introducing a model for female humanity at the divine level and a maternal genealogy in her "Gospel of Mary." Her vision of Christ's birth, told from Mary's perspective (Revelaciones VII:21), changed Christian iconography*. Her insistence on the mother's participation in her Son's redemptive suffering on the cross (I:10, IV:70, VII:15) is audaciously original.

Born and married into Swedish nobility, mother of eight children, and then widowed, she moved to Rome (1349–73) to promote her order. This Mariocentric double*-monastery Bridgettine order (Regula Saluatoris) is gynocentric; the abbess, as Mary's representative, rules over nuns, priests, deacons, and lay brothers. The order, accepted by Urban V (1370) as an addition to the Augustinian* Rule, spread rapidly through Europe.

Birgitta's 700 "Heavenly Visions" (Revelaciones) and eight books complete the medieval humanization of Mary and Christ. With a definition of holiness* that embraces female reproductive and sexual experiences, Birgitta inserts Mary as an active partner in salvation history mediating between God and humanity, prescribes an *imitatio Mariae*, and affirms motherhood* as a universal model of human recognition of the Other, the ethics of God's new law. EBBA WITT BRATTSTRÖM

Birkath ha-Minim, the "blessing against the heretics," added to the Eighteen* Benedictions, probably about 80 CE (but possibly before). This Jewish prayer blesses God for shattering *minim*, or heretics*, enemies of God; it targeted all traitors of the People of God – according to the times, possibly Jewish Gnostics, other Jewish sectarians, and Nazarenes, *notsrim* – the last name added (mid-2nd c.) to target specifically Jewish Christians, but now removed. The *birkath* did not involve a formal exclusion of heretics from the synagogue. But each time it was read and recited, it raised the question of heresy, forcing conversion or abstention from leadership roles or from participation in worship, because sectarians would not want to recite a malediction against themselves. Late-1st-c. Christian writings mention followers of Jesus being disciplined "in the synagogues" (Matt 10:17) or treated as "outside the synagogue" (John 9:22, 12:42, 16:2; cf. Heb 13:13, "outside the camp"). **See also EIGHTEEN BENEDICTIONS.**

Birth Control and Contraception, Christian Views of. "Birth control" refers to the active attempt to control human fertility or the timing and spacing of human births. This includes abstinence, coitus interruptus, the rhythm method, oral substances that regulate fertility (herbs, medications), barrier methods that prevent fertilization, methods that prevent implantation of a fertilized ovum, abortifacients, surgical abortion*, and infanticide. Contraception is more specifically birth control that seeks to prevent pregnancy*. Official Christian doctrine* and popular belief and practice are quite distinct.

Official Christian Doctrines. While Scripture does not specifically address the issue of birth control, the experience of the Hebrew people as a minority culture led to a pro-natalist attitude (see, e.g., Gen 1:28, 9:1, 15:5, 16:10, 22:17, 26:4; Deut 30:16; Ruth 4:11; Jer 30:19, 33:22). Early Christian attitudes toward sexuality were shaped by the teachings of Justin*, Clement* of Alexandria, Augustine*, and others that only procreative sexual intercourse within the bonds of marriage was moral. Aquinas* further argued that contraception was a sin* against nature*. Calvin* and Luther* affirmed procreation as the intended purpose of sexual intercourse. Attitudes toward sexuality began to shift in the early 20th c. when the idea of sexuality* as a good gift from God challenged previous claims. The Lambeth* Conference of the Church of England (1930) marked the first official legitimation of contraception by a church governing body, an attitude now widely accepted by mainline Protestant Christians. The Roman Catholic Church maintains an official prohibition against the use of contraception (*Casti Connubii, Humanae Vitae*).

Popular Belief and Practice. There is considerable evidence (medical textbooks, apothecary jars, pharmacy recipes, midwifery guides, newspaper advertisements) that contraceptive and abortifacient herbs and drugs have been used since the beginning of recorded history. Medieval medical manuscripts by Carolingian monks (9th c.), Hildegard* of Bingen's writings (12th c.), and 14th-c. Inquisition* court trials demonstrate that many lay Christians have regularly used these methods, provided by midwives, pharmacists, physicians, and folk healers.

Biological realities and social constraints (e.g. women are expected to care for children) mean that women's lives are more directly affected by pregnancy and birth than are men's. In addition, women in patriarchal societies who challenge sexual norms often experience social humiliation and vilification. Consequently, controlling fertility has fallen disproportionately to women.

For most Christians today, the use of contraceptive devices to control fertility is tacitly accepted if not actively supported. Overpopulation and openness to the idea of sexual intercourse within marriage as an expression of love* have encouraged wider acceptance of contraception. Abortion* remains more controversial. **See also PREGNANCY.** REBECCA TODD PETERS

Bishop (from Lat *episcopus* and Gk *episkopos*, meaning "overseer"). In the NT the term is sometimes applied to all the elders* or presbyters of a local church in their function of oversight (Acts 20:28; Phil 1:1). The term "shepherd" seems equivalent (Acts 20:28; 1 Pet 5:2; Eph 4:11). When and how there came to be a single bishop is debated (but see Monepiscopate, Monarchical Episcopate). The bishop was the pastor of the local church, elected by the people and consecrated by at least three bishops, including the metropolitan*. Today in the Catholic, Orthodox, Anglican, Methodist, and other churches, bishops normally oversee a broader area, including multiple local churches.

Bishop *in Partibus Infidelium*, Roman Catholic honorary office; appointment to a see* in a territory controlled by unbelievers and inaccessible to Catholics.

Black Canons, Augustinian* canons* regular*, who wore black habits.

Black Friars, Dominican* friars*, who wore black mantles over white habits and scapulars*.

Black Holiness Movement. See AFRICAN AMERICAN CLUSTER: HOLINESS.

Black Legend, Protestant propaganda attacking (1) Catholic Spain* for its colonial practices, using the writings of Bartolomé de las* Casas concerning atrocities against the "Indians" to discredit Spain as a colonial power and suggest that England (and eventually the USA) had more humane policies; (2) the Spanish Inquisition* and parallel activities in the Spanish Netherlands, giving rise to stereotypes of the Inquisition in European art, literature, and drama, often used symbolically to indict Roman Catholicism, religious persecution in general, tyrannical rulers, or ideological "witch hunts."

Black Madonna, a 1,000-year-old Catholic tradition of venerating nonwhite images of Mary*, the mother of Christ. There is no correlation between the color of the Madonna and the ethnicity of her devotees; numerous white European shrines honor coal black and dark

Madonnas (e.g. Einsiedeln, Switzerland; Chartres, France; Montserrat, Catalonian Spain; Loreto, Italy). "I am black and I am beautiful" (Song* of Songs) is carved above the entry to Montserrat, a possible reminder that black is associated with beauty.

Why are these Madonnas dark or black? The reasons are site specific. Study of the religious, historic, and cultural context shows that many Madonna shrines are at the sites of shrines to dark female divinities from pre-Christian traditions, usually associated with the earth, e.g. the "Mother Moist Earth" of pre-Christian Slavic traditions. The Black Madonna is also a transcultural, inculturated* devotion that grew out of earlier forms subsumed into Christianity. Known as a powerful healer and miracle worker, the Black Madonna is associated with a fierce form of Mary as the mother and protectress of the poor and excluded. She weaves national identities (Poland's Queen Black Madonna; Mexico's protective patron, the Virgin of Guadalupe; Brazil's Mother of the Excluded, Aparecida) with solidarity and nonviolent resistance. She stands for the spirit of liberation*, restorative justice*, equality, and the preservation of the earth (see Ecology and Christinianity Cluster). **See also MARY, THE VIRGIN, CLUSTER.** CHINA GALLAND

Black Monks, monks of the Benedictine* order, who wore black habits.

Black Rubric, the declaration in the Book of Common* Prayer that kneeling during Communion does not signify adoration of any corporeal presence of the Body and Blood of Christ. It was added under Edward VI (1552), removed under Elizabeth (1559), and restored under Charles II (1662). The name comes from the 19th c., when it was printed in black because it was not a "rubric"* but a doctrinal interpretation.

Black Theology is a school of constructive theology in the USA. It has historically been associated with the teaching and writings of James H. Cone and students. However, other theologians, religionists, and philosophers, such as Albert Cleage, J. Deotis Roberts, Major Jones, Shelby Rooks, Gayraud Wilmore, Charles Long, and William R. Jones, were important in the development of Black theology for their rigorous critiques throughout the 1970s. Cone's *Black Theology and Black Power* (1969) inaugurated Black theology as an insurgent discourse against white supremacy, not only in the USA but also in Latin America, Africa, and Asia. With the Black Power Movement (1964–69), blackness symbolized a radical, revolutionary race consciousness expressed in black history and black culture. Black theology is a theological interpretation of this new black consciousness. Black theology reflects on the meaning of faith in the Black God revealed in the Black Christ from the perspective of black oppression, survival, and resistance. Black culture is identified with the Christ event in which the revelation of God as liberator of the oppressed comes in and through the cultural situation of the oppressed.

A number of historians and theologians have documented the development of Black theology. Monumental is the documentary history by Wilmore and Cone, *Black Theology: A Documentary History,* in two volumes. These works show that Black theology is open to a great diversity of interests among African American theologians.

From the 1970s to the 1980s, Black theology was primarily a male-dominated discourse. By the late 1980s and throughout the 1990s, African American female constructive theologians and theological ethicists radically enlarged Black theology by their critiques of black male patriarchy* in the production of Black theology (see Womanist and African American Theologies).

In the USA, Black theology has established itself as the dominant discourse in constructive theology among African Americans. Black theology is vital and enlarges as its interests in the suffering, survival, and resistance of oppressed people expand within its global consciousness. **See also LIBERATION THEOLOGIES CLUSTER.**
VICTOR ANDERSON

Blackwell, Antoinette Louisa Brown (1825–1921), minister, lecturer, activist, author, acclaimed as first woman ordained by a regular Protestant denomination in the USA (1853) (see Women's Ordination Cluster: In North America). She participated in the Second Great* Awakening institutions and causes. Her childhood was transformed by a Charles Finney*–led revival*; she studied theology at Oberlin; and in her lectures she advocated temperance*, women's rights, and abolition. Committed to both Christianity and equality for women, she worked in uneasy partnerships with religious leaders and suffragists like Elizabeth Cady Stanton* and Susan B. Anthony*. In later years, she wrote a series of books that tried to reconcile a naturalist metaphysics with evolutionary thought and gender equality. **See also DARWINISM; UNITED CHURCH OF CHRIST (IN THE UNITED STATES).** TED A. SMITH

Blake, William (1757–1825), romantic poet, prophet, engraver. Blake was raised in London in a Dissenting* family; his works exhibit the spiritual radicalism and deep biblical knowledge characteristic of those who separated from the Church of England. The collection of his short lyric poems, *Songs of Innocence and Experience* (1794), displays a radical religious critique of slavery*, economic inequities, and religious hypocrisy. From the age of 10, Blake experienced divine visions; his mature style reflects the esoteric imagery and incantatory style of biblical prophets and visionaries. Blake's theology, honed by his reading in Paracelsus and Boehme*, is largely Gnostic*. In major poems, like *The Book of Urizen* (1794), *Milton* (1804), and *Jerusalem* (1804), Blake reflects on the entrapment of humans' divine nature in the material world and the revolutionary power that would be unleashed once humans awakened and recognized their divine origin. Blake attacked Deism*, Newtonianism*, and other Enlightenment* philosophies that denied the spiritual world. A former student at the Royal Academy, Blake illustrated his own books, as well as editions of Dante*, *The Book of Job*, and Bunyan's* *Pilgrim's Progress*. Largely unrecognized in his lifetime, Blake's idiosyncratic religious themes and imagery received a revival of interest in the 20th c. ROGER E. MOORE

Blasphemy (from Gk for "evil-speaking"), speech or action showing contempt for God. It was punished by stoning in Israel (Lev 24:16), and blasphemy against God and/or Christ was condemned by the Code of Justinian*, the Arian* Visigoths, medieval canon* law, and some of the Reformation states, although types of punishment varied.

Blessing, performatory* words that confer God's favor; hence consecration* through prayer, sanctification* with the sign* of the cross, or benediction*.

Blessing of Children. A blessing grants goodness or favor on the recipient and is indicative of a relationship. More than a good wish, the very words of a blessing do what they say. Throughout the Judeo-Christian tradition, children* are considered a sign of God's blessing and are an occasion for praising and thanking God. Thus parents and others (e.g. priests) bless children, especially shortly after their birth. Blessings of children may take place either on significant occasions or as a child dedication.

In the OT, the oldest tradition of blessing (Heb root, *brk*) of offspring is the blessing of the firstborn as a bestowal of inheritance (Gen 27, the story of Esau and Jacob) or as a sign of favor (Gen 48:20, Jacob blesses Joseph's sons Ephraim and Manasseh). The blessing of Joseph's sons is referenced in the Sabbath blessing for boys given on Friday evening (the *birkath banim*): "God make you like Ephraim and like Manasseh"; for girls matriarchs are named: "God make you like Sarah, Rebecca, Rachel, and Leah". Children are also blessed on special holy days.

In the Christian tradition, blessing children was modeled by Jesus himself when he laid hands on them (Mark 10:13–16). In contemporary society, devout parents might bless their children before sleeping at night, at the beginning of a school year, on birthdays, at graduation, and upon marriage. The US Roman Catholic Church's order of blessing of children (*Book of Blessings*, 150) remarks on the dignity of children and asks that they "may grow in Christian maturity . . . and become witnesses in the world." This blessing may be given by a priest, deacon, parent, or other person.

In traditions practicing only adult baptism (e.g. Church of the Brethren, Baptist communions), child blessing functions as a child dedication. In the religious observance of the Latter-day Saints, an infant is brought to the ward (or remains at home if the father holds the Melchizedek priesthood), where the infant is blessed and named. Blessing of children may be a formal church service or a spontaneous blessing given by anyone in the course of ordinary life. The blessing might express thanksgiving for God's gift of life and ask for peace and protection for the child. It is a concrete way parents can share their faith life and relationship with their children and can be a special, intimate moment of trust between parent and child.

JOYCE ANN ZIMMERMAN, CPPS

Blondel, Maurice (1862–1949), professor of philosophy (Aix-en-Provence). The most important 20th-c. French Catholic philosopher, he had an enormous impact on Catholic theology. In his seminal work, *L'Action* (1893), he appropriated the French positive tradition and expanded its framework to include religious practice, developing a "phenomenological"* project aimed at engaging the postmetaphysical mind of the French university. Accepting the principle of immanence*, he showed that an integral examination of the content of human action leads necessarily to an affirmation of the transcendent.

The *Letter on Apologetics* (1896) radically critiqued traditional apologetics*, showing that the subject's interior disposition is an essential ingredient in the act of faith*; Blondel thus made a significant contribution to the clarification of the relationship between nature* and grace*, as well as to the development of fundamental theology. His *History and Dogma* (1904) elucidated, at the heart of the Modernist* crisis, the role of tradition* in Catholic hermeneutics*, resolving the issue of the appropriate use of the historical method so as to avoid both historicism and relativism. Despite his loss of eyesight, in later life he dictated a monumental, five-volume philosophical trilogy. With Blondel's decisive influence on such figures as de Lubac and Von* Balthasar, Congar described him as *the* philosopher of Vatican* II. MICHAEL A. CONWAY

Blood. A symbol of life, sacrifice*, and salvation* with rich layers of meaning. In the OT, blood is understood to be the principle of life (Exod 17:14). All other blood symbolisms* derive from this basic meaning: the saving blood of the Passover lamb (Exod 12:7, 13); the prohibition of murder (Exod 20:13; Deut 5:17); blood as the seal of the covenant* (Exod 24:8); and its use in the consecration of priests (Exod 29:19–21) and during sacrifice to evoke the redeeming, atoning, life-giving union with God (Lev 1:1–14; 16; 17:3–8).

In the NT, blood is a symbol of the redemptive* sacrifice of Christ on the cross and of entrance into a new and eternal covenant with God (1 Cor 10:4,16–22, 11:23–25; Heb 9, 10). The Lord's Supper is the genesis of Christians' ritual celebration of Jesus' giving of his Body and Blood as spiritual food and drink; the cup is the Blood of the *new* covenant (Luke 22:20; 1 Cor 11:25).

The significance of Christ's shedding his blood and the understanding of the Eucharist* vary, along with the different understandings of atonement* and redemption*. Catholics and other liturgical traditions believe in the real presence of Christ's Body and Blood under the sacramental signs of bread* and wine* as they celebrate the Eucharist*, Mass*, or Orthodox Divine* Liturgy. In Protestant, Evangelical*, and Charismatic* traditions, for which the bread and wine "symbolize" Christ's presence in the celebration of the Lord's Supper, Christ's Blood is also life giving and salvific, though it is often in less liturgical settings that one is "washed... in the blood of the lamb" (Rev 7:14).

Contemporary cultures with so much violence could do well to reappropriate a respect and sense of mystery* for blood as the seat of life. All cultic and symbolic use of blood is a witness to the sacredness of all life.

JOYCE ANN ZIMMERMAN, CPPS

Blumhardt, Johann Christian, and Christoph Friedrich Blumhardt. Johann C. Blumhardt (1805–80) was educated at Tübingen and, while serving as pastor in the Lutheran parish of Mottlingen, Germany, became the center of a religious revival* that involved deliverance and healing, based on an appeal to the resurrection of Christ. An outgrowth was a spiritual retreat center he founded at nearby Bad Boll. He was succeeded in this ministry by his son, Christoph F. Blumhardt (1842–1919), who redirected its mission to advocate social reform, thus helping lay the foundations for the Social Democratic Party in Germany*. **See also PIETISM.**

J. STEVEN O'MALLEY

Boaz, a wealthy resident of Bethlehem* who, following Levirate* custom, married the widow Ruth*, becoming the ancestor of David* and of Jesus*.

Body. Surrounded by ambiguity throughout the history of Christian life and practice, the body has elicited both positive and negative responses among Christians across traditions. The human body registers profound, complex attitudes toward God, gender difference, material justice*, and nature. This ambiguity reflects deep ambivalence among Christian theologians, clergy and laity alike, in response to human finitude, suffering, and the place of change in the divine economy. This coupling of ambiguity with ambivalence requires that, to be understood, "body" always be placed in historical context.

"Body" has both figurative and literal meanings. Indeed, the line between literal and figurative is often indistinguishable. Through the Incarnation*, even God is embodied. The concept of body also marks such corporate realities as the church, understood to be the body of Christ, as well as the body of believers who partake of the Body of Christ at the sacrament of Holy Communion*. "Body" is further identified in terms of the resurrection* of the bodies of all humans at the final Judgment*.

The putative relics related to Jesus' body and the bodies of apostles and saints have historically played a central role in the worship of believers. Believers may apprehend the concept of body in either literal or figurative terms, depending on their communal affiliation or on their own interpretation. Regardless, the references are understood to be real, and the concept of body carries extremely positive connotations. These connotations reflect a Hebrew heritage that connects materiality with the goodness of God's creation* (Gen 1), distributive justice* (the prophets), and the wisdom* traditions (Proverbs).

"Body," however, also connotes negative valuations. Throughout Christian history, the human body has been associated with finitude, deterioration, material injustice, and estrangement from God. These more negative valuations and the ascetic* practices that sometimes accompany them reflect the assimilation of historical features of hellenized Judaism, Stoicism*, and Neoplatonism*. In their origin, as well as their later reappropriations, these views may reflect material conditions ranging from high mortality among women in childbirth and the infants born to them, to low life expectancies across both genders, to food shortages and high taxes, to exclusively male centered power structures that carry over into the present.

In any case, the changeability of the human body came to exemplify the corruption of the human will*, characterized as sin*, an inescapable but redeemable human condition. Though according to orthodox teaching the body's creation and its divine intention are good, as a negative marker the human body as body has been historically gendered as feminine. Based on the creation account of Gen 2–3, male theologians and clergy have traditionally portrayed the feminine-gendered body as symbolic of evil*, personified by Eve* as the author of human sin. At the same time, other male elites have interpreted this text to signify that women are merely morally inferior and therefore rightly subordinate to men, because Eve was made by God from Adam's rib. Contrary to both of these interpretations, early Gnostic* traditions often cast Eve as the author of human freedom rebelling against the Demiurge*, or evil creator God; Gnostics nevertheless just as often required that women become "as men" in order to realize the divine spark within them, because their female bodies entangled women in the material order in ways to which men were not subject. These interpretations, along with interpretations of other scriptural texts, have authorized both sexist and heterosexist practices throughout the life of the church. At the same time, across these various interpretations, the vicissitudes of the body, identified symbolically with female flesh, have required remedy through disciplines* of the flesh in preparation for a better world to come. Such disciplines include fasting*, celibacy*, voluntary poverty*, self-flagellation, and withdrawal from society, permanently or for extended periods of time.

Irrespective of negative ascriptions to the female body, practitioners have intended these practices to produce union or communion with God, or they have meant them to realize the divine within the practitioner. These disciplines, among others, have given rise to various forms of Christian mysticism* in which Christ and the believer become gendered and transgendered. In these contexts, the practitioner is represented as beloved, bride, child, and mother of Christ. Mystics of the High Middle Ages in particular write of nursing at the bosom of Mother Jesus.

The body, however regarded, has played a rich and highly variable role in the history of Christian life and practice, no more so in the past than today. For example, Christians of the 21st c. around the globe, whether Roman Catholic, Orthodox, or Protestant, discipline themselves through the regulation of their bodies, which as critics of a consumer-driven, labor-abusing, earth-destroying culture, they consider ethically requisite in a world of waste and want.

PAULA M. COOEY

Boehme, Jacob (1575–1624), a shoemaker in Görlitz, Germany. Boehme was often in conflict with local Lutheran authorities over his highly complex thought, influenced by alchemical and other hermetic*writings. God the Father, he taught, was a deep abyss or *Ungrund*, a raging fire (wrath) bequeathing as light and love the Son and the Holy Spirit in and through the revelation of creation, a revelation that the human person receives by faith in Christ. His theory influenced German philosophers, including Hegel*, and English poets, including John Milton* and William Blake*, through 17th-c. translations published by William Law.

PETER C. ERB

Boethius, Anicius Manlius Severinus (c475–c525), Roman patrician and consul (510), well acquainted with contemporary Greek Neoplatonism*. He translated into Latin, and commented on, a number of Greek works, especially on logic written by Aristotle* and Porphyry*; these became the basis of Western knowledge of logic until the 11th c. These works raised the question of universals*, debated throughout the Middle Ages.

Boethius became a member of the court of the Arian* Theoderic in Ravenna. After the reconciliation between Rome and Constantinople (519) ending the Acacian* schism, Boethius wrote his *opuscula sacra* concerning the Trinity* and Christology*.

When Theoderic discovered that some Roman leaders were secretly corresponding with the court in Constantinople, Boethius was also charged, imprisoned, and executed. While in prison he wrote his *Consolation of Philosophy*, without explicit Christian language (some have seen parallels with Bonhoeffer's* affirmation of "religionless Christianity" during his imprisonment). It became a Christian classic, translated into most Western vernaculars.

EUGENE TESELLE

Bogarín Argaña, Ramón Pastor (1911–76). Born in Ypacarai, Paraguay, he studied for the priesthood at the Gregorian University, Rome. When he returned to Paraguay (1939), the Roman Catholic Church was growing rapidly; he reorganized the Paraguayan Catholic* Action. Ordained bishop (1954–55) of the Diocese of San Juan Bautista de las Misiones, his pastoral action included a strong defense of rural and lay organizations, and efforts to promote the renewal of the Paraguayan Church in line with Vatican* II and the Latin American Episcopal Conference of Medellin*, in which he assumed a leading role. Under his leadership, the Church became one of the main opposition forces against Stroessner's dictatorship.

VERÓNICA GIMÉNEZ BELIVEAU

Bogomilism, an Eastern European Christian movement that emerged in Bulgaria* (c900), blending Orthodox monasticism* and Paulician* and Zurvanic Zoroastrian dualism. During the reign of Peter (927–69), czar of Bulgaria, its members were anathematized as heretics* who believed the devil* was the second son of God and made the world. They lived ascetic* lives like Orthodox monks, adding to their popular appeal. Cosmas the Priest first used the term "Bogomil" to describe the sect (accordingly founded by a priest of that name) and said that the Bogomils accepted only the NT, which they read in Old Slavonic and interpreted allegorically. Bogomils entered the Byzantine Empire (early 11th c.), establishing a community in Constantinople, refining their doctrine, and developing an initiation ritual (as described by Euthemius Zigabenus, who was involved in their persecution in c1100). Bogomilism was still considered a prevalent and dangerous heresy in the 1140s; yet members considered themselves the real Christians, as the Cathars* that they inspired also did in the West. Nonetheless, by 1170 (when a Bogomil leader, Papa Nicetas, came to the West), Bogomils had experienced a serious schism, some adopting the absolute dualist* belief in two co-eternal Gods. The movement thrived in unsettled political conditions, spreading to the Balkans* and surviving in Bulgaria until c1370 and in Byzantine lands until c1430.

CLAIRE TAYLOR

Bohairic, Coptic* dialect originating in the south of the Nile delta. In the 9th c, it displaced Sahidic* as the language of the Coptic scriptures.

Bohemian Brethren (Moravian Brethren, Unitas Fratrum, Unity of the Brethren), organized c1457 in Kunvald, Bohemia, by followers of John Hus* (c1373–1415). Radically sectarian until c1495, they called for biblical preaching in the common language, administration of both bread and wine to the laity in Holy Communion*, renunciation of wealth and power by the church, and reform of the corrupt clerical hierarchy. Their leading theologian was Lukaš of Prague (d1528). At their height, they numbered about 50,000. They issued confessional statements (1535, 1575) and received legal recognition from Rudolf II (1609). All but exterminated during the Thirty* Years' War, their last bishop was John Amos Comenius* (1592–1670). The Bohemian Brethren were renewed in Saxony (1722) by von Zinzendorf* (1700–60). **See also MORAVIAN CHURCH; MORAVIAN WORSHIP.** OTTO DREYDOPPEL, JR.

Bokeleale, Jean Ifoto Bokambanza (1919–2002), father of the Church of Christ in Congo, which now includes all the Protestants of the Democratic Republic of Congo*; born in Bompoma (Equator Province) into a polygamous family. After completing his primary and secondary education, he taught at the Christian Institute of Congo (Bolenge). A member of the Disciples of Christ Congo mission, he became assistant pastor at Ikongo (1936) and was later ordained a pastor (1956). He studied at, and graduated from, the Faculty of Protestant Theology of Brussels (1958–63) before studying public administration in the USA. Elected general secretary of the Protestant Council in Congo (1968), he used his talents to bring together all the Protestant churches into a unified Church of Christ in Congo, becoming its first president (1970), then its bishop (1977).

JEAN-CLAUDE LOBA-MKOLE

Bolivia. Until the 19th c., the history of Christianity in Bolivia was exclusively that of the Roman Catholic Church. It arrived with the Spanish* conquest of Alto Peru (1532), following the defeat of the Inca Empire by Francisco Pizarro; the first Catholic diocese of Sucre was established (1538). Other Christian churches arrived in Bolivia late in the 19th c., preceded by small immigrant groups of Lutherans, Anglicans, and Presbyterians. Very early on, Methodists (1906) incorporated native leaders into their church. Canadian Baptists (1898) began a mission that pioneered the development of Protestant schools, radio stations, and religious formation for rural lay leaders. Seventh-day Adventists (1898) also began schools and clinics. In 2000 there were 134 churches, 32 Christian church missions, and 9 new Christian religious movements officially registered with the Bolivian government. The National Association of Evangelicals (1968) includes 72 churches and service organizations, ranging from Baptists and Pentecostals to the Salvation Army.

The third article of the Bolivian Constitution (1967) states that the Roman Catholic Church is the national church, but grants freedom of religion to all churches. The Catholic Church was at first the baroque* Church of Spain (see Roman Catholicism Cluster: In Europe: Spain), which was imposed with very little instruction on native peoples (65% of the population, mostly Aymara, Quechua, Guarani, and Amazon basin groups). Thus there is much syncretism* of native religions and customs with Catholic worship practices, which can also be viewed as Andean inculturation* of Christian practices. For instance, the Pacha Mama of the Andean peoples (the "Earth Mother" figure of creation) and the Virgin Mary* are intertwined in popular devotion with shrines all over the country (see Mary, the Virgin, Cluster: Devotion in Latin America). This religious and cultural intermingling is visible in church art and architecture everywhere. Since Vatican II, and along with other churches, the Roman Catholic Church has begun a serious study of native cultures. Liberation* theologies have evolved into theologies of solidarity* with the poor. For almost all churches, ecumenical* dialogue now includes intercultural and gender issues.

Since the 1960s, Bolivia has seen a great influx of missionary activity by Protestant churches, the Charismatic* Movement, and other groups such as the Mormons* (with temples in several cities and their Latin American center in Cochabamba, Bolivia), all of which have a particular interest in native peoples. This increased missionary activity, with most missionaries from the USA, came in response to the internal migration of millions of Bolivians from rural communities to the cities. Pentecostal, Charismatic, and Protestant congregations, responding to the need of these uprooted people for a new sense of community, gained thousands of converts both in the cities and in the rural areas.

Yet the Roman Catholic Church remains predominant in Bolivia. Thus Sister Nacaria Ignacia, a Spanish missionary naturalized Bolivian and founder of a religious community of Bolivian women, Misioneras Cruzadas, was the first Bolivian saint (beatified by Pope John Paul II, 1992). Cardinal Julio Terrazas, archbishop of the Archdiocese of Santa Cruz, has been an outstanding figure in the Catholic Church since he was ordained a bishop in 1978. He has been a strong voice for social justice* in Bolivian society and even more so since, in 2001, he became the first native Bolivian to be named a cardinal. In 1994, Matias Preiswerk, a Methodist Swiss theologian, founded a now-growing ecumenical theological and biblical study center, Instituto Superior Ecumenico Andino Teologico.

Statistics: Population (2005): 9.1 million (M). Christians, 8.5 M, 94.1% (Roman Catholics, 7.9 M; Protestants, 0.9 M; independents, 0.3 M; Mormons, 0.1 M [including 0.7 M double affiliations]). (Based on *World Christian Encyclopedia*, 2001 and 2005.)

MICHAEL J. GILLGANNON

Bollandists, a group of Jesuits* in Belgium who have edited and published documents related to the saints* of the church since 1596, using the tools of historiography* and critical historical scholarship.

Bolsec, Hieronymus (d1584), physician, Carmelite friar, controversialist. He converted to Protestantism (c1545) and worked as a physician near Geneva, frequenting theological meetings. He disagreed with Calvin* over predestination*. He argued (citing Rom 8 and Augustine*) that instead of speaking of predestination to salvation* or to damnation* as Calvin did, one should speak of salvation because of a person's faith* in God or damnation because of lack of it. After he was tried and banished from Geneva (1551), and his doctrines officially condemned (Lyon Synod, 1563), he reconverted to Catholicism. He was influential in creating a lasting, negative image of Calvin and Geneva by publishing biographies of Calvin (1577) and Beza* (1582), presenting both as sexual degenerates and Geneva as a hotbed of sedition.

IRENA BACKUS

Bonaventure of Bagnoregio (c1221–74), influential Franciscan* theologian, teacher of the Friars Minor, Franciscan master of theology (1253), regent master and minister general (1257). As a cardinal (1273), Bonaventure played an important role in the Council of Lyon, during which he died. Critical of Aristotelian* philosophy, he favored Platonic* and Augustinian* thought. For him, the mystical* journey from the world to God passes through creation as "signs" and "footprints" of the Creator. His theology of light is based on exemplarity, emanation, and consummation. For him Scripture* is essential and the interpretive key to understanding creation* and human life.

MARY BETH INGHAM, CSJ

Bonhoeffer, Dietrich (1906–45), German Lutheran theologian and martyr of the Third Reich, with a remarkably influential legacy around the world. His early theology, in *Sanctorum Communio* (dissertation) and *Act and Being* (*Habilitationschrift*), laid the foundations for later developments by working at the interface of theology, philosophy, and the social sciences; he asserted the "sociality of humanity" (see Relationality) from a christological-ecclesiological perspective (laying the ground for contextual* theologies).

Bonhoeffer's theology was influenced by his avid interest as a youth in cultures and travel. A one-year stay (1930–31) at Union Theological Seminary (New York) helped him relate theology to social* ethics and the problem of racism*, and challenged him to become a pacifist*. Back in Berlin, where he was a *Privatdocent* at the university, his lectures, notably on Christology*, attracted a wide audience. When Hitler came to power (1933), Bonhoeffer became involved in the church struggle. Disappointed by the equivocation of the Confessing* Church, he accepted service in a congregation in London (1933–35), while seeking to isolate the Reich Church from the ecumenical* movement. During this period, Bonhoeffer's theology was developed in sermons, lectures, and essays that addressed these issues.

In 1935 Bonhoeffer became the director of a seminary of the Confessing Church in Finkenwalde. He introduced his students to the discipline* of Christian community life centered on Bible study, prayer, and rigorous study, a discipline later described in his book *Life Together.* He also wrote *Discipleship,* his classic study on faith and obedience based on the Sermon* on the Mount. After a brief exile in New York (1939), Bonhoeffer became involved in the resistance against Hitler. The Gestapo imprisoned him (April 1943) for his pro-Jewish activities. When it became clear that he was also implicated in the failed attempt to assassinate Hitler (July 20, 1944), he was sent to the Flossenburg concentration camp, where he was executed on April 9, 1945.

Bonhoeffer's considerable theological writings, now collected in *Dietrich Bonhoeffer Works* (16 volumes), include many essays and lectures in which he critically retrieved Lutheran doctrine, notably the "theology of the cross*" and the "two kingdoms*," in ways that challenged the prevailing orthodoxy and the failure of the church to counter Nazism. While working for the resistance, he drafted essays for his posthumously published *Ethics.* His *Letters and Papers from Prison* (also published posthumously by Eberhard Bethge) outlined a "nonreligious" interpretation of Christianity, awakening international interest in his legacy as a whole.

JOHN W. DE GRUCHY

Boniface (c675–754), the English monk "Winfrith," the "apostle of Germany." Under papal sponsorship and with protection by the Frankish ruler (Charles Martel), he converted leaders in Thuringia, Hesse, Franconia, and Bavaria to Catholicism (c718), establishing an orderly Christianity closely tied to the papacy. Made bishop (722), then metropolitan of Germany (731), he created new bishoprics and monasteries. As papal legate, he reformed (c745) the Frankish Church, probably playing a role in the pope's decision to replace the Merovingian with the Carolingian dynasty (751). Made archbishop of Mainz (745), he resigned to resume his mission in Frisia, where he was martyred.

Boniface VIII, Pope (1294–1303), born Benedetto Caetani (or Gaetani; c1235) in Anagni into minor nobility, studied law, entered the papal service, amassing considerable wealth in the process. He was named a cardinal priest (1291) and succeeded Celestine V as pope when the latter abdicated. Insisting that taxing clerics required his approval led him into conflict with Philip the Fair of France. In a famous bull, *Unam* sanctam* (1302), he insisted that only by subjection to the papacy could anyone be saved. He was attacked in Anagni by a few armed

Frenchmen (September 7, 1303), returned to Rome, and died a few days later.

MICHAEL J. WALSH

Book of Common Order, liturgy adopted in 1562 by the General Assembly of the Church of Scotland*, a version of the *Forme of Prayers* printed in Geneva (1556) for use by the English exile congregation there. First printed in Scotland in 1564, it was superseded by the 1645 Directory of Public Worship of the Westminster Assembly. From 1862, the name Book of Common Order was given to manuals of worship, most authorized by the General Assembly, though not as a mandatory liturgy. The 1940 edition (with 1974 and 1994 revised editions) was particularly influential within Scotland and the wider world.

JANE DAWSON

Book of Common Prayer. See COMMON PRAYER, BOOK OF.

Booth, Catherine Mumford (1829–90), mother of the Salvation* Army, advocate for women ministers. Born in Derbyshire, England, she married William Booth*, a Methodist preacher (1855). They founded the Christian Mission in London (1865) to provide help to the poor. A gifted preacher, Catherine Booth raised money for their work, while William ran the daily operation. The Christian Mission became the Salvation* Army (1878) and from the beginning accepted women as equals in leadership. The mother of eight, two of whom – Bramwell and Evangeline – became generals of the Salvation Army, Catherine Booth worked for the underprivileged and women's rights.

ROSALIE BECK

Booth, William (1829–1912), cofounder and first general of the Salvation* Army, evangelist, and advocate for the poor. Born in Nottingham, England, Booth, a Methodist preacher, married Catherine Mumford (1855). They founded the Christian Mission* in London (1865), which became the Salvation* Army (1878). William effected important social legislation to help poor working people. Under his leadership, the Salvation Army established work in 58 countries. Central to his ministry was a commitment to helping the needy physically and spiritually. In his book, *In Darkest England and the Way Out,* Booth established the Salvation Army's approach to social welfare work.

ROSALIE BECK

Bordeaux Pilgrim, first written account by a Western pilgrim to Constantinople and the Holy Land (333–34).

Boris and Gleb, Vladimirovich, Kievan princes (d1015). Princely sons of Vladimir, who Christianized Kievan Rus, Boris and Gleb refused to take up arms against their brother Sviatopolk in a struggle for succession to the Kievan throne. Though not martyred for their faith, Boris and Gleb were killed after refusing to fight. They became the models for a particularly Russian form of saint, the passion bearer, who dies in a Christ-like manner.

ROY R. ROBSON

Borromeo, Charles (1538–84; canonized 1610), played an important role in the Catholic* Renewal following the Council of Trent*. Destined to pursue an ecclesiastical career from a young age, he studied both civil law and canon* law (University of Pavia). When his uncle was elected pope (1559) as Pius IV, Borromeo was made cardinal, became cardinal-nepote (secretary of state), and was appointed archbishop of Milan. Borromeo collaborated with the pope to reconvene the Council to Trent* for its third session (1562–63), devoted to the reform of the church, especially local churches. Afterward, in his diocese, Milan, he worked at implementing these reforms – regarding discipline* of the clergy and the convents, education of the youth, and preaching – through a series of local synods. Attacked while he celebrated Mass (1569), he pardoned the would-be assassins (though they were executed). During the plague of 1576–77, he visited the sick in their houses and the hospital, serving as an example for the clergy.

GIUSEPPE ALBERIGO

Bosnia-Herzegovina. Situated between the Catholic Dalmatia and the Orthodox Serbia, the medieval kingdom of Bosnia was a meeting ground for the struggles between Eastern and Western Christianity. Breaking with Rome (mid-13th c.), the Bosnians established their own Bosnian Church, which survived until the mid-15th c. After the conquest by the Ottomans (late 15th c.), considerable portions of the population converted to Islam. From the mid-19th c., the development of the three major ethnic groups, Serbs, Croats, and Bosnian Muslims, was strongly influenced by Eastern Orthodoxy, Roman Catholicism, and Islam*, respectively. Religious and ethnic heterogeneity, and close interreligious communication and interaction, however, had a strong and lasting influence on the way in which these three communities developed throughout the centuries.

Bosnia was part of the Austro-Hungarian Empire between 1878 and 1918, then a part of the kingdom of the Serbs, Croats, and Slovenes until World War II, and a republic in Tito's Yugoslavia*. Declaring independence in 1992, Bosnia-Herzegovina suffered a three-year destructive war, which reconfigured its religious profile and prompted a significant politicization of the three major faiths, with frequent misuse of religious symbols and buildings for political aims. Ethnic cleansing during the war led to segregated ethnoreligious areas, where intolerance and discrimination against minority believers on the part of the majority group have persisted. The State Law on Religious Freedom (2004) administers the legal status of religious groups and the concessions made toward them. Interreligious dialogue* has been promoted by numerous international and local NGOs, and through the country's Interreligious Council, comprising the leaders of the four traditional religious communities: Muslim, Orthodox, Roman-Catholic, and Jewish. **See also BALKANS; ISLAM AND CHRISTIANITY CLUSTER: IN EUROPE: SOUTH-EASTERN EUROPE.**

Statistics: Population (2008): 3.94 million. Muslims, 45%; Serb Orthodox, 36%; Roman Catholics, 15%; Protestants, 1%; adherents of other faiths, 3% (with very few Jews). (Based on *International Religious Freedom Report*, 2008.)

INA MERDJANOVA

Bossey, Ecumenical Institute organized by the World* Council of Churches (1946) for conferences and study, often on emerging issues, to prepare clergy and lay leaders for service throughout the world.

Bossuet, Jacques Bénigne (1627–1704), noted preacher, Catholic bishop (Condom, then Meaux, France), polemicist. Guided by the Catholic* Renewal (Counter Reformation) and classical humanism, Bossuet preached before the court of Louis XIV (from the 1660s) and became its leading ecclesiastical intellectual. Tutor of the heir to the throne, Bossuet wrote for him *Discourse on Universal History* (1681; popular well into the 19th c.). Bossuet wished to educate the prince about the lessons from God's providence in history and to affirm the historicity of Scripture against emerging biblical criticism. Bossuet divided history into 12 epochs, from Adam* to Charlemagne*, giving primacy to the story of Israel as an example of God's universal sovereignty. In his writings and public discourses, Bossuet opposed all schism in the Catholic Church and supported Louis XIV's policies: to assert Gallican control over the church in temporal matters (against the pope; see Gallicanism), to suppress Jansenism*, and to convert Huguenots* and revoke the Edict of Nantes*. In correspondence with Leibniz* on how to restore unity to the church, he supported the divine right of kings. The agent of court opposition to Madame Guyon's* Quietism*, Bossuet engaged in a bitter polemical dispute with Fénelon* and attacked her character in writing against this "modern mysticism*."

PATRICIA A. WARD

Botswana is predominantly Christian, though Christianity is influenced by and interacts with religious ritual practices, beliefs, and ideologies of Batswana African* Religion, which historically has dominated the center stage and remains strong.

Christianity was introduced through the London Missionary Society (Robert Moffat and Mary Smith Moffat's arrival, 1820, followed by that of their son-in-law, David Livingstone*; the resulting United Congregational Church is the main Protestant church today); Methodists (1840s); Dutch Reformed Church (1870s); Lutheran Hermannsburg Mission Society (1857); Catholics (1895, with a national Roman Catholic Church established in 1959, after which it began growing); Anglicans (1902); Seventh-day Adventists (1921, the second-largest Protestant church); Pentecostals (1940, leading to the development of independent* Charismatic* churches, including women pastors, such as Rebecca Motsisi); and African* Instituted Churches (AIC's, rapidly developing since the 1960s, often with women in leadership roles, such as Queen Seingwaeng, 1883–1967, a leader in the Zion Christian Church).

Christianity made inroads into Botswana when chiefs, such as Sechele I (1833–92), Khama III (c1837–1923), and Lentswe (1876–1924), converted and in turn converted their subjects. Churches gained national identity and local leadership through, e.g., the formation of three ecumenical organizations: the Botswana Christian Council, the Evangelical Fellowship of Botswana, and the Organization of African Instituted Churches.

The emergence of Pentecostal/Charismatic churches and AICs led to theology, teaching, and practices that were much more inculturated* and contextual*, owing in part to the increased involvement of women, both as leaders and as laypersons who often preach. Worship in both Pentecostal churches and AICs, characterized by dancing, clapping, use of traditional instruments, spirit possession, and speaking in tongues*, often has a tribal association, such as going to Matsiloje (Spiritual Healing Church), Jackalas 2 (Head Mountain), or Moria (Zion Christian Church) for their festivals.

As part of their acknowledgment of the African tradition, AICs include African rites of blessing the seeds, children, and fields, sacrifices for sick people, as well as birth and death rituals. In prayers, some AICs invoke the assistance of ancestors*.

Churches have traditionally provided leadership in education and medical care. Responding to the threat of HIV/AIDS has led to closer ecumenical relations with other religions, including African Religion.

Statistics: Population (2000): 1.6 million (M). Christians, 0.97 M, 60% (members of African Instituted Churches and other independents, 0.5 M; Protestants, 0.18 M; Roman Catholics, 0.06 M); African Religionists, 0.6 M, 38.8%. (Based on *World Christian Encyclopedia*, 2001.)

FIDELIS NKOMAZANA

Branch Davidians, members of an apocalyptic* and messianic* reform movement established in 1959; it derived from Seventh-day Adventism, and more specifically from the "Davidian Seventh-day Adventists" (established in 1934). Reading Revelation* as a continuous historical prophecy, they locate the present in the climactic "Laodicean period" of Christian history. Via typology* they identify the demonic "lamb-like beast" (Rev 13) as the USA, and the mainstream Seventh-day Adventist Church as the apostate Whore of Babylon (Rev 17), while calling for repentance. On April 19, 1993, messianic* leader David Koresh (born Vernon Howell, 1959) died with 75–85 Branch Davidians at their headquarters (Waco, Texas) in a conflagration while under siege by federal law enforcement officers. Survivors continue as "Students of the Seven Seals." Branch Davidians raise issues concerning hermeneutic* assumptions in reading apocalyptic* literature, charismatic* and messianic* religious leadership, coping with the disconfirmation of religious conviction, and responsible relations between civil secular authorities and radical or insular religious communities. JOHN R. JONES

Bray, Thomas (1656–1730), founder of benevolent organizations. Assigned by the bishop of London to assist the Anglican churches in Maryland, he funded more than 80 parish libraries, founded the Society for Promoting Christian Knowledge (SPCK*, 1698) in English territories and the Society for the Propagation of the Gospel (1701) for foreign missions, and endowed the Associates of Dr. Bray (1723) to fund libraries.

Brazil

Introduction: From "Catholic Monopoly" to Contemporary Religious Diversity. In the territories that formed Brazil, five centuries of Christian presence followed various scenarios. The absolute prevalence of Roman Catholicism, a long-term phenomenon that deeply influenced the formation of the Brazilian national identity, was supplanted by a religious mobility typical of modernity, strongly felt throughout the 20th c. with the effervescence of a variety of confessional denominations. This complex dynamic makes the future of Christianity in Brazil difficult to predict, despite numerous recent academic analyses.

In colonial times (1500–1822) and during the years of the Brazilian Empire (1822–89), Roman Catholicism had the status of the official religion, with a special link to the throne in Portugal*, then in Brazil. From the early 16th to the early 19th c., the Portuguese crown mediated between Rome and the local church. From 1822 to 1889, this role fell to the Brazilian emperor. Thus for almost 400 years, it was virtually impossible to be integrated into Brazilian society without affiliating oneself with Roman Catholicism or at least respecting it. The permission granted for non-Catholic religious gatherings, introduced by the Imperial Constitution (1824), had little impact. The Republic (1889) and the enactment of the secular constitution (1891) started a slow, nonlinear, and often tense process of religious competition in Brazil. By 2000 there was a considerable religious plurality with an increased presence of Pentecostal* and Charismatic* "Protestants*" (called "Evangelicals" in Latin America).

The Catholic Church in Colonial Portuguese Brazil and the Brazilian Empire. That the motivation for colonizing the New World was in large part religious is beyond doubt, although clearly there were also economic and political motivations. Even Christopher Columbus expected to use the gold that he dreamed of finding in the newly discovered lands to finance a new crusade* against the Moors.

Decades later, in a Europe convulsed by the Protestant Reformation*, the American continent with its native populations became important missionary territories where the Catholic Church, a close collaborator in the colonial enterprise, was to recoup souls* after its losses brought about by the fragmentation of Western Christianity. Hence, the concern to bring Christian salvation* combined with metropolitan commercial interests formed the infrastructure of the European colonization of the Tropics.

The arrival in April 1500 of Portuguese explorer Pedro Álvares Cabral on the coast of what would be Brazil was hailed as a miraculous, providential event – a true epiphany* orchestrated by the Christian God. After all, the expansion of the Portuguese Empire ought to correspond to a spreading of the Roman Catholic faith (see Portuguese Explorations, Conquests, and Missions). This goal was to be achieved according to the resolutions of the Council of Trent* (1545–63), which remodeled the Roman Church through the Catholic* Renewal. Trent forged a Catholicism of reconquest based on the Eternal City, Rome (Jean Delumeau). This view emphasized the centrality of the Holy See, diluting the power of local churches.

The first organized missions among indigenous populations were led by Jesuits* (arriving from 1549), who during the following decades established their particular form of "reductions*" – mission stations where numerous natives lived together with Jesuit clergy following strict rules of Christian life (especially in the south of Brazil, as well as in Argentina*, Uruguay*, and Paraguay*). Yet as a result of the colonization process, as in many other places in Latin America, the indigenous peoples were soon reduced to a small minority of the population, with immigrants from Europe (now a majority), African slaves, and mulattoes making up the bulk of the population, which now includes Asians (Japanese immigrants, in particular) (see Mission Cluster: In Latin America: Catholic Mission in Brazil).

A paradox of extreme relevance to the Christianization of Brazil should be noted. Despite being consistent with the Catholic Renewal, the catechesis effort built into the colonial enterprise remained relatively distant from the papacy. In Portuguese Brazil, as well as during the independent imperial period, it was the Padroado* Régio (Portuguese for "Royal Patronage"; Spanish, Patronato Real) that held sway. In this regime the Roman Catholic Church, with pontifical authorization, was both financially and materially supported by the monarchy, and legally subject to its tutelage. In colonial times, owing to the Padroado and the shortage of priests in Portugal, which made it impossible to send a substantial number of missionaries to overseas colonies, the "Roman" Catholicism that arose in Brazil was a Catholicism that was Roman only in name; it was quite distant from the Tridentine thinking emanating from the Holy See in Rome. This characteristic persisted during the years of the Empire.

The social status of the Church that formed in these territories between the 16th and 19th c. was weak (it was under the political power of the state), and from the European point of view of the Catholic Renewal (following in the footsteps of the Council of Trent), it was significantly lacking in the ritual, doctrinal, moral, and intellectual/theological realms. In this Brazilian institutional and theological vacuum, late medieval Christian devotions of Portuguese origins survived untouched by the rulings emanating from Trent. Lay religious practices (see Laity Cluster) gained ground with little clerical control and gradually formed a popular Brazilian Christianity that dominated and still dominates everyday life (see Popular Christian Practices Cluster: In Latin America: Brazil). This popular Catholicism also incorporated various elements of African religiosity originally brought by slaves. This blending of Christian elements with African religiosity was officially repressed by the Catholic Church and civil authorities; yet, excluded from the Roman Catholic Church, it was free to develop independently (cf. Vodou* in Haiti).

In the midst of the lay construction of this "Brazilian-style Catholicism" (a revealing phrase commonly used in contemporary Brazil), the hierarchy sprang into action. Attempts to control sacramental and canonical practices can already be found in the early 18th c. with the First Constitution of the Archdiocese of Bahia (1707, printed 1720). Nevertheless, the Catholic Church in Brazil – weakened by the Padroado, which was supposed to support it because the state was frequently disinterested in religious affairs – did not have the strength to promote the effective Christianization prescribed by the Council of Trent. In this context, the presence of Catholic priests in the world of imperial politics was symptomatic. For instance, the priest Diogo Antonio Feijó (1784–1843, ordained 1809) was also a statesman (deputy in the General

Assembly, 1826–33), who became regent (1835–37) after the abdication of Emperor Pedro I. Feijó, whom he had opposed. Like other prelates* of the time and regardless of his clerical status, Feijó embraced Gallicanism* (independence of the local churches) and liberal views despite the Vatican's guidelines.

The Council of Trent "arrived" in Brazil only in the mid-19th c. (as Kenneth Serbin documents). Reproducing the Roman challenge to the basic precepts of Enlightenment* and to the growing secularization* and laicism* of modernity, from the 1840s the Church of Brazil sought to revitalize itself by emphasizing the doctrine formulated by the 16th-c. council. It was an attempt to "Romanize" the Brazilian Church, calling a lax clergy to appropriate religious and moral order and faithful laypeople to a daily and orthodox practice of the Catholic faith, while being mindful of the primordial role and place of the Holy See in the Church.

The seminaries acquired a central role in the enforcement of this reformed and clericalized Catholicism, to the detriment of the lay believers and their lay movements. Thus from mid-19th c., there was an effort to revitalize existing seminaries and to create new ones in which European priests imbued with the Tridentine spirit taught. Mention must be made of the Lazarist priests (Counter* Reformation order founded by Vincent* de Paul) and in particular, among the first agents of "Romanization" of the Church in Brazil, of the Portuguese Lazarist Dom Antônio Ferreira Viçoso (1787–1875), bishop of Mariana (in the state of Minas Gerais, 1844–75). In this city, Dom Viçoso reformed the old archdiocesan seminary (founded 1750, remodeled 1853), transforming it into a place of excellence. Other orders and religious congregations followed, founding not only seminaries but also various centers of studies. Examples include the Salesians (named for Francis* de Sales) during the years of the Empire and the Redemptorists (founded by Alphonsus Liguori*) and Marists in the first years of the Republic.

This program of reform and amplification of seminary education saw the number of (mostly diocesan) seminaries rise from about a dozen (mid-19th c.) to more than 600 a hundred years later. These institutions – thought of as ideal places, fortresses of God, protected from the world and its influences – were intended to produce a clerical corps that was socially superior, morally impeccable, and, in theory, apolitical, or at least distant from partisan politics and from affairs of the state, contrary to the preceding generations of priests. Paradoxically, the successful "remodeling" of Catholicism in Brazil can be measured by the most important crisis experienced in state and church relations in Brazilian history: the Questão Religiosa (Religious Question; 1872–75). This crisis arose when two already Romanized young Brazilian prelates, Antônio de Macedo Costa, bishop of Pará, and Vital Maria Gonçalves de Oliveira, bishop of Olinda, following Vatican directives, took a firm stance against Freemasonry*, although the emperor, Pedro II, and the president of the Council of Ministers, Viscount Rio Branco, were themselves Freemasons. The crisis was triggered by the imposition of canonical penalties on members of lay brotherhoods and third* orders who participated in Masonic lodges, a state of affairs previously tolerated by the Church. The two bishops were indicted, arrested (early 1874), and condemned to prison with forced labor. The sentence was commuted to prison without forced labor by Pedro II (December 1874) and, as a result of a popular uprising, revoked by the new conservative cabinet (September 1875). In the midst of the worsening decline of the imperial order, the "Religious Question" marked the distancing of the Brazilian Church from the state – the declining Empire – a distancing that, along with other factors, such as the abolition of slavery (1888), undermined support for the regime, which, in November 1889, gave way to the Republic.

The Presence and Diffusion of Other Christian Churches Before the Republic. Until 1810, Roman Catholicism was the only religion officially recognized in Brazil. In 1808, with support from England, the Portuguese Royal Court moved to Brazil because of the threat posed by the Napoleonic Wars in Europe. The so-called interiorization of the metropolis in Brazil had a great political, economic, and cultural impact, initiating in a unique way the process of national independence. There was a discrete change in the religious domain: permission was granted to hold Protestant religious services to meet the spiritual needs of English citizens, who accompanied and protected the Portuguese Royal Court, provided that their places of worship had the external appearance of houses. The Imperial Constitution of 1824 ratified this orientation, permitting private worship services for religions other than Roman Catholicism, maintaining the restrictions on the places where these could take place, and prohibiting proselytism*.

The following years saw the start of a slow Protestant penetration. In 1824 Lutheran immigrants established themselves mainly in the south of the country, founding the city of Nova Friburgo in the mountain region of Rio de Janeiro State. Missionaries of other denominations followed: Methodists (1837, 1867); Presbyterians (starting in 1859, accompanying the penetration of coffee into the interior of the province of São Paulo); and two Baptist missionary couples (1882, in Salvador, Bahia).

Proselytism, despite the law against it, and an emphasis on conversion distinguished the activities of these groups. Preaching based on daily Bible studies by believers led to literacy education in the context of traditional Evangelical/Protestant Sunday* schools. These schools had a considerable impact on members of the lower classes, including freed slaves. Schools were also created for middle-class people, among them the Presbyterian Mackenzie School (starting in the house of a pastor in São Paulo in 1870, with its own building in 1876) and the Methodist Escola do Alto (Rio de Janeiro, 1887), the embryo of the Colégio Bennett created in the same city in 1920 (see Protestantism Cluster: In Latin America: various entries on Brazil).

Orthodox Christianity, not highly visible in Brazil, first arrived in the country in 1871 (Russians were the pioneers) and has focused on immigrants from Eastern Europe and the Middle East.

The Catholic Church During the First Decades of the Republic. With the advent of the Republic (1889), its constitution (1891) defined the state as laicized (see Laicization) or secularized (see Secularism and Secularization) and cut its ties with the Roman Catholic Church. The Church was freed from the tutelage prescribed by the Padroado, but also lost financial support from the state.

The relevance of the earlier "Romanization" of the Church in Brazil (from the 1840s) increased. Beyond the earlier objective – strengthening the Roman Catholic faith in Brazil and giving to the national church unprecedented social, intellectual, and religious power – there were new urgent goals.

The first task was to guarantee the material survival of the Brazilian Roman Catholic Church by securing new financial resources, in order to ensure that the Catholic faith, formally the faith of the majority of the population, would be respected by the newly installed regime.

To this end, in this tense situation, the national episcopate adopted a moderate attitude toward the republican order, managing to mitigate more radical laicization by the new government. A significant example is the debate over private education, a sensitive issue in church* and state relations since the proclamation of the Republic. Controlling the education of new believers was, of course, of prime importance for the Church. In addition, in material terms, the Catholic schools, principally those catering to the middle and upper classes, where Catholic education prevailed, were a significant source of income for the Church. Despite the firm stance of the Brazilian Church hierarchy, it was impossible to prevent the laicization of education, a traditional claim of republicanism. Nevertheless, this was not a total defeat for the Church: it was successful in obtaining financial support from the state in compensation for its contribution to social work in various areas, including education (see Educational Practices as Christian Service Cluster).

This tense scenario, involving concessions and mutual accommodations, would set the tone for the initial decades of the Republic. In 1930, when Getúlio Vargas became president, through the work of Sebastião Leme, archbishop of Rio de Janeiro (then the national capital), the government and the Roman Catholic Church improved their relations and mutual cooperation. From 1930 to 1945, the government and clergy united around common objectives, such as maintaining order and rejecting any ideas of the ("Communist") Left. This confluence gave Catholicism a kind of semiofficial recognition.

However, the conflict between Church and modernity was not limited to church–state relations. Laicization, critical assessments of Christianity, religious indifference, materialism, and the leftist threat characterized modern times. Since the Reformation, so to speak, Rome had lived in a "state of siege," a situation aggravated by the Enlightenment*, the French Revolution, and the teachings of Marx (see Marxism and Christianity), Nietzsche*, and Freud (see Psychology and Theology). Rome reacted in a determined manner, urging the reconquest of contemporary society.

The Church of Brazil, tardily Romanized, officially closed ranks around these crusading intentions. Although the Republic was already encountering a more cohesive ecclesiastical position, it was only in 1916 that the programmatic content of the reconquest of Brazilian society would gain a formal description. Sebastião Leme*, recently named archbishop of Olinda in the northeast of the country, published a pastoral letter that united the national episcopate by inaugurating "a new consciousness-raising of Brazilian Catholicism" and proposing a "fighting program" (José Oscar Beozzo). The goal was to Christianize society on all levels, from institutions to private practices – to mark Brazil with the Latin cross. Thus, e.g., the Church created the magazine *A Ordem* (The order; 1921) and the Dom Vital Center (1922) with the intention of bringing together Catholic intellectuals; the Marian Congregation (1924) appealed to women; and the Círculos Operários (Workers Circles, 1930) appealed to workers. The Instituto Católico de Estudos Superiores (Catholic Institute for Higher Education, 1932) formed the nucleus for the first Brazilian Catholic university, in Rio. The Liga Eleitoral Católica (Catholic Electoral League, 1933) hoped to elect candidates committed to Catholic views to the Constitutional Assembly convened by Vargas.

Two symbolic initiatives are noteworthy: (1) in 1930 the proclamation as patroness of Brazil of Nossa Senhora Aparecida (Our Lady of Aparecida), originally an 18th-c. devotion based on an image of the Black* Madonna found by fishers in the Paraíba River between Rio de Janeiro and São Paulo; (2) in 1931 the inauguration of the statue of Cristo Redentor (Christ the Redeemer) in Rio de Janeiro. A part of the neo-Christianity project, the Redeemer statue, sculpted in stone, high on the Corcovado Mountain, stood out in the skies of Rio (then the national capital). Both of these symbolic initiatives had as a backdrop the heated debate among the Brazilian intelligentsia regarding the "national character" of the country. For the Roman Catholic Church, Catholicism and Brazilian identity were fully interconnected. Alceu Amoroso Lima*, a leader of the national lay intelligentsia and an active crusader for neo-Christianity in the 1930s, went straight to the point by declaring (at a national Catholic meeting, 1939), "Brazil is not Brazil without the Eucharist."

The Brazilian Catholic* Action (1935) was created in coordination with the general institution of the Catholic Action by Pope Pius XI, in order to optimize the apostolate of the laity* in ecclesiastical life. Laypeople, meeting in groups such as the Brazilian Catholic Youth (Juventude Católica Brasileira, JCB) and the Female Catholic Youth (Juventude Feminina Católica, JFC), were expected to carry out the actions decided by the hierarchy.

The neo-Christian project also aimed to compete in the religious field. It was a battle against a variety of perceived threats: popular* syncretistic* Catholicism, Spiritism and Afro-Brazilian beliefs of great appeal among the people, and the Protestant penetration reinforced by the arrival of Pentecostalism on Brazilian soil.

The First Pentecostal Wave. The national impact of the "first Pentecostal wave" is connected with the appearance of Assembléia de Deus (see Assemblies of God). Founded by the Swedish missionaries Gunmar Vingren and Daniel Berg in Belém do Pará (1911) with Baptist dissidents, the Assembléia de Deus introduced, as Clara Mafra said, a "heavyweight theological question, which would also transform the evangelical field in all Brazil": What is the role of the Holy* Spirit? Giving emphasis to divine inspiration* and to inspired improvisation, and thus viewing erudite culture negatively, Assembléia de Deus was eagerly welcomed by common people in the slums around the cities and diffused by the internal migration toward the cities. The rapid expansion of Assembléia de Deus was also assisted by its emphasis on the missionary call that each believer receives (since he or she receives gifts* of the Holy Spirit) and by less rigid theological control (as compared with mainline Protestantism). Moral practice, however, is marked by strict discipline, including modest clothing and the prohibition of smoking and drinking.

The Congregação Cristã do Brasil (Christian Congregation of Brazil), also of Pentecostal orientation, was formed in 1910 in São Paulo by Luigi Francescon, bringing together many Italian immigrants after a schism with the Presbyterian Church. As with Assembléia de Deus, Congregação Cristã do Brasil grew among low-income people struggling for better working conditions, but in this church the gifts of the Holy Spirit reinforced the authority and power of the elders (see Charismatic Authority; Charismatic and Pentecostal Movements Cluster: In Latin America: Brazil).

From 1945 to the "New Republic." The neo-Christian model of the Roman Catholic Church went into decline at the end of the pontificate of Pius XII (1939–58). Less than a hundred days after his election, the new pontiff, John* XXIII, convened Vatican* II. It was the Catholic *aggiornamento*, a process described as a Copernican turn in the history of the Catholic Church (Rufino).

In Brazil, as Vargas's dictatorship ended (1945), new questions arose for the local church, which created the National Conference of Brazilian Bishops (CNBB, 1952) to address them. In the following decades, Catholic reformism gained pastoral, social, and political strength (see Roman Catholicism Cluster: In Latin America: National Conference of Brazilian Bishops [CNBB]).

The activities of laypeople changed substantially. Brazilian Catholic Action reformed itself, adopting the specialized Belgian model, with the development between 1948 and 1950 of Catholic youth movements aimed at rural youth (JAC), high school students (JEC), freelance professionals (JIC), workers (JOC; see Young Christian Workers [Jocists]), and university students (JUC), which reinterpreted basic Christian concepts, such as that of apostolate and mission, and adopted the "see, judge, act" pedagogical method of the Belgium priest, then cardinal, Joseph Cardijn*.

Alceu Amoroso Lima, who had publicly declared his adherence to liberal Catholicism since the 1950s, became a figure of reference for reformist Catholics, together with the Jesuit Henrique de Lima Vaz, who led the JUC in the 1960s. The primary question was how to envision in the light of Christian faith the Brazilian economic underdevelopment and the massive social crisis. It was more important to be a "critical" Christian than "merely a Christian" with appropriate theological views and practices. Sacramental life is necessary, but it must lead to involvement in the social, economic, and cultural transformation of the country.

The hierarchy, divided between reformists and conservatives, followed more cautious paths. During the governments of Juscelino Kubitschek (1956–61), Jânio Quadros (1961), and João Goulart (1961–64), sectors of the Roman Catholic Church, led by the CNBB and its social pastoral letters, collaborated with state initiatives such as the Movimento de Educação de Base (Movement for Basic Education). The so-called basic reforms of the Goulart government, including the sensitive agrarian reform project, were supported by prelates and progressive intellectual laypeople. On the other hand, the more conservative clergy denounced the "Communist peril."

The military coup of 1964 prompted a significantly ambiguous and cautious document from the CNBB, which reflected the divisions in the Catholic Episcopate. While the cardinal of Rio de Janeiro, Jaime de Barros Câmara, enthusiastically applauded the armed intervention, his former assistant, now archbishop of Olinda and Recife, Hélder Pessoa Câmara*, refused to celebrate a commemorative Mass on the first anniversary of the coup d'état.

As years passed, the dictatorial character of the regime (1964–85) became evident. In a society silenced by force and subjected to brutal repression, the CNBB under the leadership of Aluísio Lorscheider and Ivo Lorscheiter called for a re-democratization and the end of censorship and political detentions. They denounced the systematic torture of dissidents and asked for the return of the exiled. They were joined in the fight against the dictatorship by Hélder Câmara and other prelates, including Paulo Evaristo Arns* (head of the largest archdiocese of the country, São Paulo), Fernando Gomes dos Santos (archbishop of Goiânia), Waldyr Calheiros (bishop of Volta Redonda, an important industrial center under the military administration), Adriano Hipólito (bishop of Nova Iguaçu in the violent and poor Baixada Fluminense), and Pedro Casaldáliga (bishop of Prelazia de São Felix do Araguaia, in the Brazilian Amazon).

The progressive clergy of the Catholic Church developed a prophetic witness in times of torment. Other bodies connected to the CNBB played an important role during the dictatorship, e.g. the Conselho Indigenista Missionário (Indigenist Missionary Council) and the Comissão Pastoral da Terra (Pastoral Land Commission), which denounced the pattern of landownership and the economic model of wealth concentration imposed by the regime (see Land, Theological Perspectives and Praxis, Cluster: In Latin America). Lay leaders, such as Alceu Amoroso Lima and Cândido Mendes de Almeida, were also part of the opposition.

During the years of the dictatorship there emerged a Catholic militancy centered on the Base* Ecclesial Communities (Comunidades Eclesiais de Base, CEBs; see Church, Concepts and Life, Cluster: In Latin America: Brazil: Base Ecclesial Communities [CEBs]), pastoral networks with a popular base in urban and rural areas where faith and demands for better living conditions were integrated. The poor communities, in the CEBs and beyond, became a privileged space for the formulation of Liberation* theology, an original Latin American contribution to contemporary theological production.

The main question is: How can one be a Christian in an impoverished world? Liberation theologies bring together theological reflection and prophetic denunciations of poverty and its causes, following the examples of biblical prophets. Leonardo and Clodovis Boff, Hugo Assmann, Carlos Mesters, João Batista Libânio, José Comblin, Frei Betto, Eduardo Hoornaert, and José Oscar Beozzo are among the most important Liberation theologians in Brazil.

Progressive Protestants also contributed to Liberation theology. Presbyterian pastor (and subsequently educator and psychoanalyst) Rubem Alves wrote *A Theology of Human Hope* (1969), a work influenced by Protestant liberal* theology and considered a precursor in the construction of the Christianity of liberation in Brazil. Subsequently, Lutheran pastor Walter Altmann interpreted the trajectory of the "Father of Reform" according to the postulates of Liberation theology in *Lutero e libertação* (Luther and liberation, 1994). Regarding the military dictatorship, despite the traditional Protestant avoidance of explicit political engagement, Evangelical/Protestant sectors cooperated with progressive Catholics in resisting the dictatorship. Two cases are exemplary.

On the occasion of the commemoration of the 25th anniversary (1973) of the Universal Declaration of Human* Rights, in the midst of the toughest period of the dictatorial government, the Roman Catholic Church and Reformed Christian churches (including Presbyterian and Methodist churches) launched a national campaign for human rights. "They had taken the first collective step in terms of denying legitimacy for the regime" (as Della Cava noted). (This campaign was not shared by Pentecostal and Charismatic denominations.)

The second example of cooperation was the project Brasil: Nunca Mais (Brazil: Never Again), a top-secret investigation (begun in 1979, published in 1985) that proved the systematic use of torture during the Brazilian military regime (1964–85). Led by Cardinal Paulo Evaristo Arns and the Presbyterian minister Jaime Wright with financial support from the World* Council of Churches, Brasil: Nunca Mais investigated the dictatorship's most violent period (1964–79), described torture methods, and named 444 torturers.

With re-democratization (the "New Republic" of 1985) and the promulgation of the Constitution of 1988, the Brazilian Catholic Church limited its action in the political arena – an attitude reflecting the changes brought about by the papacy of John* Paul II (1978–2005). During his pontificate, Karol Wojtyla limited the intellectual production and the political and social action of Liberation theologians, fearing in particular their use of Marxist analytical methodological tools (see Marxism and Christianity). The imposition of "obsequious silence" on Leonardo Boff (1985), the most popular Brazilian Liberation theologian, and on others, is extremely revealing. At the same time, Rome and many Brazilian dioceses strongly encouraged new traditionalist and conservative movements such as the Roman Catholic Charismatic* Movement (RCC), Communion and Liberation, New Song, and Neocatechumenate.

The Second and Third Pentecostal/Charismatic Waves. In the years following World War II, and especially under the Kubitschek government, the idea of "modernization" started to take shape. It had repercussions in the Evangelical/Protestant milieu, where the use of radio (see Media and Christianity), songs, and choirs of popular appeal, and of informal language during services, had a notable impact on the propagation of the Pentecostal and Charismatic* faith.

The "second Pentecostal/Charismatic wave" (see Charismatic and Pentecostal Movements Cluster: In Latin America: Brazil) started with the preaching of North American missionaries Harold Williams and Raymond Boatright of the Igreja Internacional do Evangelho Quadrangular (International Church of the Quadrilateral Gospel; see Wesleyan Quadrilateral). Emphasizing the charismatic gift of divine healing (see Health, Healing, and Christianity Cluster), the two missionaries launched an "evangelical offensive" in the city of São Paulo (1951 or 1953, depending on the source), which became a National Evangelization Crusade, spreading throughout the state of São Paulo and in other states of Brazil.

This "second Pentecostal/Charismatic wave" was helped by the characteristic fragmentation of the movement into congregations and denominations, which, for the first time, were founded and led by Brazilians. The similar Igreja Evangélica Pentecostal O Brasil para Cristo (Pentecostal Evangelical Church, Brazil for Christ) was also founded in 1951; the Igreja Pentecostal Deus é Amor (Pentecostal Church, God Is Love), founded in 1962, is aimed at the middle class; the Igreja Pentecostal de Nova Vida (Pentecostal Church of New Life) was founded in 1970.

The "third Pentecostal wave" (the independent Charismatic/Pentecostal Movement) was characterized by the appearance of the Igreja Universal do Reino de Deus (Universal Church of the Kingdom of God, 1977), founded by Edir Macedo, self-proclaimed bishop, in the impoverished suburbs of Rio de Janeiro. Macedo came from a practicing Catholic family and, before becoming Evangelist, was initiated in Candomblé, an Afro-Brazilian religion. Becoming a neo-Pentecostal/Charismatic religious leader, Macedo developed a harsh polemic against the "idolatrous Catholic Church" and "demonic Afro-Brazilian religions." The preaching of the Igreja Universal do Reino de Deus was therefore a "counterposition" (as Clara Mafra calls it) – a polemical discourse that did not prevent it from incorporating Catholic, spiritualist, and Afro-Brazilian elements in its worship services and evangelistic meetings. This church is also characterized by its massive political participation, intensive use of TV, radio, and written media*, and exploitation of the spectacular dimension of faith, such as the gathering of multitudes of worshippers in the largest football stadiums of Brazil. The institutional success of the Igreja Universal – one of the most popular and powerful Evangelical/Protestant churches in Brazil, also with international branches – is presented as providential. The same applies for the individual successes of its followers. Many of them claim in their testimonials ("witnesses") to have overcome through faith various trials – unemployment, alcoholism, illness, and emotional, family, and financial problems – associating their adherence to Igreja Universal with their successful resolution of their problems (see Prosperity Gospel Cluster).

According to Patricia Birman, the Igreja Universal do Reino de Deus is constructing a new image for the *crente* (believer), the usual and often pejorative name given to Evangelical followers. In contrast to the *crente* as humble and poorly integrated into society, the true *crente* is a cosmopolitan, rich, and successful believer.

The 2000 Census: Redrawing Borders. In the census of 2000, the Instituto Brasileiro de Geografia e Estatística (Brazilian Institute of Geography and Statistics) collected 35,000 representative answers to the question "What is your religion?" The responses provided the basis for a typological construction (with 144 classifications) of religion in Brazil, including a category entitled "without religion."

According to Marcelo Camurça, it is possible to discern from the data of the 2000 census three well-defined groupings: Roman Catholics, Evangelicals/Protestants (same word in Portuguese), and those without religion. Surprisingly, there are relatively low percentages of followers of other religions, such as Kardecism (a spiritualistic religion) and the Afro-Brazilian religions Candomblé and Umbanda, possibly because of the phenomenon of "double affiliation," a mixing of religions common in popular Brazilian Catholicism – an "invisible" syncretism not publicly admitted by those who practice it and who opted to declare themselves Catholic despite also adopting practices of other creeds (see Popular Christian Practices Cluster: In Latin America: Brazil).

Despite the inclusion of these non-orthodox, syncretistic believers in the number of Catholics, the percentage of Catholics has drastically diminished – dropping from 83.8% (1991 census) to 73.8% of the total population – although in absolute numbers Catholics increased from 121.8 million to 125 million (owing to the increase in population).

Meanwhile, during the same period, Evangelicals/Protestants jumped from 9.05% of the population (13 million) in 1991 to 15.45% (26 million) in 2000. Among these, Brazilian-led Pentecostals/Charismatics and especially Charismatics/Neo-Pentecostals predominate with 17.6 million members, the largest churches being the Assembleia de Deus, the Igreja Congregacional Cristã do Brasil, and the Igreja Universal do Reino de Deus. Slightly fewer than 7 million identify themselves as "mission Protestants," mainly Lutherans, Presbyterians, Baptists, Congregationalists, and Adventists.

This census reveals more than a change in the relations between Catholics and Evangelicals/Protestants, though in itself this represents a profound transformation of the Brazilian religious scene. Brazil is passing through a metamorphosis of Evangelicalism/Protestantism (as Maria Lucia Montes underscores). The traditional Protestant churches are losing ground to the Charismatic/Neo-Pentecostal and Brazilian independent Evangelical/Protestant churches. Thus both historical Protestantism and historical Catholicism are losing ground. Is it a Brazilianization of Christianity?

In view of the accelerated growth of Charismatic/neo-Pentecostal churches, should one project a loss of Roman Catholic hegemony in Brazil in the near future? Social scientists, such as Regina Novaes and Marcelo Camurça, believe the answer is no. Even when one takes into account the growth of those "without religion" (an important growth from 6.9 million to more than 12 million in 10 years), it is not possible to forecast a "change in cultural paradigm" in religious terms (Camurça).

An evaluation of Brazilian religious mobility must go beyond the relative numbers of religious affiliation or even beyond comparisons between the totals of followers registered in different censuses. A more detailed analysis shows that the disaffiliation of Roman Catholics occurs among those who, until recently, declared themselves Catholic only because they belonged to the Catholic Church by tradition rather than by individual choice. Thus some specialists of cultural studies (e.g. Cecilia Mariz) go as far as envisioning a Catholic "reawakening" in Brazil as a result of the Charismatic/neo-Pentecostal expansion. In the religious market, this competition could induce practicing Catholics to give more visibility to their faith. Indeed, according to 1999 studies by the Center for Religious Statistics and Social Investigations (connected to the CNBB), the percentage of Catholics attending Mass* weekly increased by more than 80% between 1991 and 1999. This increase can be attributed to two opposite influences. The progressive Liberation theology and the CEBs in which they find expression have very engaged participants. Similarly, the conservative Roman Catholic Charismatic* Movement also calls for faithful engagement, and "charismatic" priests who became media phenomena, such as Fr. Marcelo Rossi, attract multitudes to their celebrations. Internal plurality is a traditional feature of Catholicism amplified in modern times. A significant number of Catholics distance themselves from the Roman Catholic Church's teachings regarding important points such as birth* control, relationships (marriage, etc.), and sexuality*. Even in circles with a more conservative ecclesiology, such as the Roman Catholic Charismatic* Movement, where one finds a greater obedience to the Vatican directives regarding sexual matters, there are significant points of dissent; the personal religious experience of the sacred by believers, which is now more highly valued, escapes ecclesiastical control, producing tension between charisma and institution. Thus is it another form of a Brazilianization of Christianity?

Conclusion: Between Tradition and Metamorphosis, Transformation and Continuity. Although religious mobility and plurality are rapidly growing in Brazil, Roman Catholics and Evangelicals/Protestants (historical and Pentecostal/Charismatic) make up around 90% of the population. At the start of the new millennium, this situation confirmed the impact of Christianity throughout the history of Brazil – an impact open to divergent interpretations. This is a legacy that is now part of a Brazilian, dynamic, and tense process toward an indefinite future. **See also** **CHARISMATIC AND PENTECOSTAL MOVEMENTS CLUSTER: IN LATIN AMERICA: BRAZIL; CHURCH, CONCEPTS AND LIFE, CLUSTER: BRAZIL: BASE ECCLESIAL COMMUNITIES (CEBS); INQUISITION AND "NEW CHRISTIANS" IN BRAZIL; MISSION CLUSTER: IN LATIN AMERICA: CATHOLIC MISSION IN BRAZIL; POPULAR CHRISTIAN PRACTICES CLUSTER: IN LATIN AMERICA: BRAZIL; PROTESTANTISM CLUSTER: IN LATIN AMERICAN: VARIOUS ENTRIES ON BRAZIL; ROMAN CATHOLICISM CLUSTER: IN LATIN AMERICA: VARIOUS ENTRIES ON BRAZIL.**

Statistics: Population (2000): 169.4 million (M). Christians, 152.3 M, 90% (Roman Catholics, 125 M, 73.8%; Evangelicals/Protestants, 26 M, 15.45%; marginal Christians, 1.3 M, 0.75%); other religionists, 5 M, 3%; nonreligious, 12 M, 7%. (*Source*: 2000 census.)

MARCELO TIMOTHEO DA COSTA

Brazilian Literature and Christianity. The Jesuit missionaries' correspondence with their superiors in Europe (16th c.) constitutes the first literary Brazilian writing. Their evangelistic work among the Amerindians is presented in their letters in short scenes recounting the conflict between indigenous practices and beliefs and Christianity resulting from the efforts to convert the children, molding them into a new Christian generation (as José de Anchieta documents).

Throughout the baroque period (17th c.), literature, especially poetry (Gregório de Matos), gave voice to the great contrasts in the emerging Brazilian society, including indiscriminate exchanges between the native culture and Christianity, resulting in what appeared to be abuse, soon followed by guilt*, repentance*, and devotion*.

In the 18th-c. context, marked by the exploitation of precious metals and stones by colonizers, Christ's Passion* underlies all the cultural production (architecture, music, poetry, arts and crafts, painting); the Passion served as a kind of resistance language in the struggle for political independence and the liberation of slaves* (also expressed with OT images). Romanticism brings together popular culture and the myths of the Christian creed (Castro Alves).

Brazil was originally named "Land of the Holy Cross" by Portuguese explorers. The texts that most effectively express the Brazilian Christian civilization project are novels by José de Alencar (19th c.), which clearly take their ethical values from the Gospels and denounce the "Christian" aristocratic and bourgeois citizens close to the emperor, who led a life far from the Christian ideal. (Literature was addressed to the literate aristocracy and bourgeoisie; the rest of the population [90%] was illiterate.)

In the 20th c., with a greater number of readers and the introduction of higher education, local authors and editors of Brazilian literature combined Christian faith and literature in two ways.

The first is represented by poets with a Christian background, such as Jorge de Lima, Murilo Mendes, Cecília Meirelles, and Adélia Prado. Their works make explicit references to Scriptures and demonstrate their expertise in both literature and Christian theology.

The second takes the form of a quest for God in the manifestations of Christian values. These works exhibit both an impressive literary sophistication and surprisingly subtle and deep theological formulations. Such are the works of the most important 20th c. Brazilian writers: Clarice Lispector, Guimarães Rosa, Manoel Bandeira, and Carlos Drummond de Andrade.

Currently, secularism is drastically reducing the explicit impact of Christianity on mainline Brazilian literature. However, echoes of the Passion continue to sound in the social context of violence. ELIANA YUNES

Bread, in the ancient Near East, was both a dietary staple and a cultic symbol. Made of wheat or barley (for the poor), bread was the staff of life; thus the term "bread" often meant daily food. In blessing and breaking the bread at the beginning of a meal, Jewish people bless the whole meal.

Bread is a symbol of God's gift of food: the manna in the desert was "bread from heaven" (Exod 16:4). Jesus taught us to ask for our daily bread in the Lord's* Prayer (Matt 6:11, with eschatological overtones); Jesus is the "bread of life" (John 6:35); and the Eucharist* is the bread of eternal life (John 6:48–51). Bread is also a symbol of hospitality* (Gen 18:6; Ps 41:9), covenantal fidelity (Lev 24:8), and unity (1 Cor 10:16–17).

In worship, the bread of the Presence (showbread) was set before the Tabernacle (Exod 25:30), cereal offerings were of unleavened bread (Lev 2:5), unleavened bread was part of the Passover meal (Exod 12:20), and leavened (West) or unleavened (East) bread is used for the Christian Eucharist, "breaking the bread" (Acts 2:42, 46).

Although in many cultures today bread is not a staple, its symbolic meaning still evokes God's beneficence. JOYCE ANN ZIMMERMAN, CPPS

Brenz, Johann (1499–1570), Lutheran Reformer and church organizer in Southern Germany. At the University of Heidelberg (1513), Brenz studied with Johannes Oecolampadius, the future Reformer of Basel, and heard Luther* defend his theology at the Heidelberg Disputation (1518). Appointed to the Schwäbisch Hall territory (1522), he introduced Lutheran teaching, aiming to ban the Mass*, appoint qualified clergy, establish an ecclesiastical court for moral discipline, set up a poor chest, change marriage* laws, and establish free public schools for boys and girls. Brenz's primary contribution was his work with the Great Church Order (1559), a lasting system of church government and polity* adopted all over Protestant Germany.

ESTHER CHUNG-KIM

Brest-Litovsk, Union of, concluded the 1596 synod between Ukrainian* and Belorussian Orthodox bishops under Polish/Lithuanian rule and the Roman Catholic Church. A decline in the education of clergy, a lack of support from Constantinople (which had fallen to the Ottomans in 1453), and an active Catholic presence after the unification of Poland* and Lithuania* (1569) led the metropolitan of Kiev to accept the authority of Rome. The Orthodox preserved their traditional Eastern rites (Divine* Liturgy) and customs, the Julian calendar*, and married clergy, while affirming Catholic theology. Despite some resistance in Ukraine, the process of Latinization continued, leading to the formation of the Uniate (Greek Catholic) Church (see Uniate Churches). But both Russians* and many Poles, who used the Latin Mass*, opposed the Union of Brest-Litovsk, which was still a source of tension during the celebration of the 1,000th anniversary of Christianity in Russia (1988).

MARIA ROGINSKA

Brethren (the) trace their roots to the rebaptism of eight adults in the Eder River in

Schwarzenau, Germany (1708). Led by Alexander Mack, Sr., and known first as the German Baptist Brethren, their offspring in North America include several Brethren groups: the Church of the Brethren (adopting this name in 1908; headquarters in Elgin, Illinois, with about 130,000 members), the Fellowship of Grace Brethren Churches, the Brethren Church, the Dunkard Brethren, and the Old German Baptist Brethren.

The Brethren emerged from the late-17th-c. Pietist* Movement's critique of the formalism and doctrinal focus of state* churches. Echoing concerns of 16th-c. Anabaptists*, the German Baptist Brethren were influenced by both Anabaptism (beliefs about adult baptism, the separation of church* and state, pacifism*, and church discipline) and Pietism (a strong accent on love in human relationships). The celebration of a Love* Feast – a worship service that includes a modest liturgical meal, feet washing, and sharing the bread and cup of Holy Communion – became an important feature in many churches with Pietist roots. The Brethren were often nicknamed "Dunkers" or "Dunkards" because they were baptized, or "dunked," by triple immersion in lakes and rivers.

The Church of the Brethren calls its members to "another way of living: continuing the work of Jesus – simply, peacefully, together." This phrase captures distinctive Brethren values: an emphasis on discipleship*, simplicity of life, peacemaking, and the church as community. The Brethren emphasize that they are a "non-creedal church," often saying, "We have no creed except the New Testament." Two key themes include "no force in religion" (rejecting the use of coercion in religious matters) and a strong commitment to ecumenical activities, especially through the World* Council of Churches. The Church of Brethren, one of the historical peace* churches, nevertheless respects the individual conscience of members who join the military forces. The church places a strong emphasis on service programs to people in need beyond their membership.

Blending the legacies of both Anabaptism and Pietism, Brethren emphasize the importance of a loving spirit in interpersonal and church relationships. Thus the spirit of truth often takes precedence over doctrine, and the compassion of Jesus supersedes denominational dogma. Frequently citing the words of an early leader, Brethren seek to give witness to the gospel: "For the glory of God and our neighbor's good."

DONALD KRAYBILL

Brethren of the Common Life, a community that developed in the Netherlands around Gerard Groote* after c1375 to foster devotion and fight clerical abuses. Like the Beguines*, it had no formal vows; the derivative Windesheim community adopted the Augustinian* Rule. *The Imitation of Christ*, attributed to Thomas à Kempis*, came from these communities. Their schools in the Netherlands and Germany were highly honored; students included Nicholas* of Cusa, Gabriel Biel*, Erasmus*, and Charles* V.

Brethren of the Free Spirit. See FREE SPIRIT, BRETHREN OF.

Breviary, prayer book containing all readings for the Divine Office*, which priests are required to recite daily. **See also HOURS, BOOKS OF.**

Bridget of Sweden. See BIRGITTA.

British and Foreign Bible Society, lay organization founded in 1804, disclaiming any ecclesial function because its directors were members of various denominations. It initiated the publication of inexpensive Bibles without annotations and excluding the Apocrypha*.

Broadcasting, Religious. See MEDIA AND CHRISTIANITY.

Broad Church, liberal group in the Church of England during the 19th c., in the tradition of Samuel Coleridge* and Thomas Arnold.

Brown Blackwell, Antoinette Louisa. See BLACKWELL, ANTOINETTE LOUISA BROWN.

Brownson, Orestes Augustus (1803–76). Universalist* minister (1826–31), Unitarian* minister (1832), and subsequently pastor of his own religious organization (1836–42), he converted to Roman Catholicism in 1844. He was the editor of several journals (notably *Boston Quarterly Review*, 1838–42, and *Brownson's Quarterly Review*, 1844–64, 1873–75), philosopher, theologian, political theorist, and charter member of the Transcendentalist Club (1836–37). After his conversion to Catholicism, he became the foremost lay Catholic philosopher, theologian, and apologist for the Catholic community in the USA. Familiar with modern philosophy, Brownson eventually developed a doctrine of life by communion as a way of explaining the organic nature and mission of Catholic Christianity. His *American Republic* (1865) applied his theological doctrine of life to US political theory.

PATRICK W. CAREY

Bryan, William Jennings. See SCOPES TRIAL.

Buber, Martin (1878–1965), had three principal areas of concern: the philosophy of dialogue*, Hasidism, and the HB. Underlying his writings is a vision of the cultural and spiritual renewal of Judaism and Western civilization. With respect to Scripture*, he held that neither a purely literary nor a purely critical approach could adequately capture its core religious significance. Through various innovative and unconventional aesthetic* and hermeneutic* strategies, he hoped to encourage the reader to engage in an existential* encounter with the biblical text. His German translation of Scripture is guided by the premise that the Bible records God's *spoken* address. The voice of God is to be heard anew by every generation. In consonance, he propounded a "biblical humanism," which called on one to heed the address of God as refracted through other human beings in the unfolding social and historical realities of life (see I–Thou Relation). Accordingly, he was a tireless advocate of Arab–Jewish rapprochement and Jewish–Christian dialogue.

For Buber interfaith dialogue* must acknowledge genuine differences. Although he regarded Jesus as his "great brother," he did not hesitate to criticize Christianity. His critique flowed from his conception of biblical faith as positing the essential unity of life and a corresponding rejection of a distinction between the sacred and secular. All aspects of everyday existence must be permeated by the power of faith*. In contrast, he noted, by projecting salvation* as something beyond earthly life, Christianity sponsors an ontological dualism* that denigrates both divine creation* and the efficacy of human acts. Biblical faith manifests a trust in God, whereas Christianity is beholden to a Gnostic* conception of faith as saving knowledge. Christian scholars have challenged Buber's polemic for its "reckless" essentialism (ignoring the diversity of "Christianities") and for its failure to recognize the affirmation of the event of the cross as an expression of existential trust.

MARTINA URBAN

Bucer, Martin (1491–1551), Protestant Reformer, ecumenical theologian, church organizer. Born in Alsace, educated within the Dominican* order, Bucer became a leading figure in the Strasbourg Church (1523–49). The ecclesiastical structures he created for Strasbourg and Hesse were imitated by Protestant churches throughout Southern Germany; his ecclesiology* influenced Calvin*. He strove to end the eucharistic* controversy between Lutherans* (consubstantiation*) and Zwinglians* (memorial Lord's* Supper) through the Wittenberg Concord (1536). He was involved in religious colloquies with Roman Catholics in unsuccessful attempts to reunite the German Church (1540–46). Exiled by the Schmalkaldic War, Bucer taught theology in Cambridge (1549–51).

AMY NELSON BURNETT

Buchman, Frank (1878–1961), founder of the Oxford* Group and Moral* Re-armament. Born in a German-speaking community in Pennsylvania, he became a Lutheran minister. Following successful work as a YMCA* secretary (Pennsylvania State College, 1909–15), he traveled to India and China. Convinced of the need for moral revival, he organized the First Century Christian Fellowship in England (1921), nicknamed the Oxford Group (1928–29) and renamed Moral Re-armament (1938). Both praised and criticized for his attempts to bring about a moral conversion of Hitler and to prevent war, after World War II he encouraged contact between countries and religions. He was criticized for his simplistic moralism and cultivation of well-known leaders.

BUDDHISM AND CHRISTIANITY CLUSTER

Buddhism and Christianity: Buddhist Perspective
Buddhism and Christianity: Christian Perspective
Buddhist Scriptures and the Bible

Buddhism and Christianity: Buddhist Perspective. Buddhism and Christianity are often misunderstood to be contradictory to each other, because Christianity is monotheistic* and Buddhism is atheistic*. However, this is not necessarily true. Certainly if they are analyzed from a narrow perspective emphasizing the particularity of each, they may be seen to have many differences. Yet from the perspective of an all-encompassing, universal realm, the two may be seen as having a very similar position. This becomes clear when one compares a Christian's experience of God* with a Buddhist's experience of enlightenment.

For example, when Paul had his encounter with Jesus on the road to Damascus, he was described as being blind for three days (Acts 9). Whether one interprets this literally or not, it can certainly be said that Paul was changed radically, from a man of hatred and vengeance to a man of love and compassion. It is as if he had entered a furnace and been completely melted down.

The same metaphor can be applied to the Buddhist practitioner. In Zen Buddhism in particular, the term "death" is often used; it symbolizes the need to melt away all of one's linguistic and rationalistic concepts. Every belief that has up until now served as a foundation for the practitioner's existence must be obliterated by the heat of the furnace of meditation. This is called the "death" experience. It is this "death" that confers salvation*, or enlightenment, on aspirants, who are saved by the destruction of their mental prisons. From this perspective, Paul evidently experienced this "death" when meeting Jesus. All Christians, in fact, have within themselves the innate ability to have such an experience.

Another crucial similarity between Buddhism and Christianity involves the ideal of compassion*. Jesus taught that we should love* our enemies. Yet who is able to do this? Did Jesus then teach us something that cannot be put into practice? Christians say, "We can't do it alone, but with God all things are possible." A Buddhist would say, "In the narrow world of personalities and individual concerns, it is impossible, but in the world of emptiness, everything is accomplished naturally." What is this "emptiness"? The all-embracing, nonexclusive realm of interdependence, in which all beings are connected to, and thus dependent on, all other beings (see Heteronomy). Entering this realm, one will automatically feel a deep and abiding compassion, both for oneself and for others. To fully realize such a realm with one's entire being, and not just the intellect, is the goal of every sincere Buddhist. On a fundamental level, this realm can be seen as none other than what the Christians call "God" (see God, Christian Views of, Cluster).

How is the religious practitioner able to enter this realm? What does it mean to "enter the furnace"? For the Zen practitioner, it has traditionally meant abandoning not only one's sense of self, but also all reliance on words and language. Some ancient Zen masters even resorted to burning the Buddhist scriptures to make this point clear. Freedom in Zen was sought through no-language and no-words; this was the furnace through which the practitioner had to pass. Such a practice is not seen as necessary by most Christians, except perhaps by some followers of mysticism* (see Apophaticism). Yet certainly it must be agreed that a personal transformation must occur: the furnace must be entered. Only in this way can Christians meet God, and Buddhists experience emptiness. SUNG BAE PARK

Buddhism and Christianity: Christian Perspective. The Christian journey toward understanding Buddhism has been long and difficult. The 19th-c. European scholars who pioneered the study of Indian religions only gradually realized that the Buddha was not another Indian god but a historical figure who inspired a distinctive religious movement. As the traditions that stem from the Buddha's teachings were better understood, Europeans began to grasp how radical these teachings were. They seemed to suggest that Buddhism was an atheistic* religion with a nihilistic worldview, a cult of nothingness that had no place for God or for human personhood. A prejudice toward Buddhism as a life-denying religion remains influential to this day. In the early 20th c., more and more Europeans were not only attracted to Buddhism but converted to it, founding Buddhist centers and movements. A number of these converts engaged in both pro-Buddhist apologetics and anti-Christian polemics.

Despite these misunderstandings, Buddhist–Christian relations today perhaps represent the most fully developed interreligious dialogue*. Many Christians, both in Asia and in the West, practice Buddhist meditation, some after joining Buddhist communities, others while claiming to remain Christian. There is a well-established intermonastic exchange between Buddhist monks and nuns in Asian countries and their Christian counterparts in Western monastic orders. Christian participants in such exchanges insist that they have been spiritually enriched by the experience.

Those who have entered deeply into Buddhist–Christian dialogue, however, are aware of the difficulties, both intellectual and spiritual, that must be overcome if mutual understanding is to be achieved. The Buddhist teaching of "not-self" (Sanskrit, *anatman*), which states that no observable constituents of human biology or psychology allow us to verify the existence of a "person," is derived from the "mutual codependent origination" (Sanskrit, *pratitya-samutpada*) of all things. Rather than arising from a preexisting "first cause," all constituents of reality are interdependent. In the course of time, this was radicalized to mean the absolute "emptiness" (Sanskrit, *shunyata*) of all aspects of reality. Though this may seem impossible for Christians to accept, Christian "negative theology" (see Apophaticism) warns us that the transcendence of God entails our inability to know God in Godself, and human sciences have shown that the human person is not only a unique individual but a social construct. At the levels of both spiritual practice and social analysis, the encounter with Buddhism has led Christians to reexamine many things they previously took for granted in a conceptual framework derived more from Greek philosophy than from biblical revelation. The result has been a more mature Christian faith. Other Christians have been inspired by the apparent equivalent of divine grace* in Buddhist traditions, such as the Pure Land tradition, which find consolation and the promise of salvation* in devotion to bodhisattvas, who defer their own complete enlightenment and their definitive entry into *nirvana* out of compassion for suffering beings.

The more radical forms of Buddhism, such as Zen, arrive at such a thoroughgoing nondualism that they seem to eradicate not only the distinction between absolute reality and the phenomenal world, but also that between good and evil. Having transcended the illusion of a "self" and the notion of substantial existence, how does one return to the sphere of responsibility for one's actions in history? Contemporary Buddhists have developed an "engaged Buddhism," which applies the Buddhist diagnosis of human ills to the hatred, greed, and delusion underlying the injustice and violence of our world, and acknowledges the primacy of active love* of neighbor (Gk *agape*) in Christianity, while Christians have recognized the value of the wisdom (Sanskrit, *prajna*) attained in meditation. Buddhists and Christians are realizing the complementarity of their traditions, at once radically different and radically similar.

JOHN D'ARCY MAY

Buddhist Scriptures and the Bible. Like the HB, Buddhist teachings existed for several centuries as oral traditions before being written down to become scriptures at about the same time as the Christian NT. The Buddhist canon, though about 1,000 times the size of the Christian Bible, was nevertheless preserved in memory by the various schools with remarkable uniformity. The Buddhist scriptures contain vast amounts of legendary material, making it even more difficult to discover a "biography" of the Buddha than it is to reconstruct the life of the "historical* Jesus" from the Gospels. Yet in the context of a vivid portrayal of life in northeast India in the 5th c. BCE, historical scholarship can discern the words and deeds of Siddhartha Gautama, the prince who became the Enlightened One or Buddha (also known as Shakyamuni, "sage of the Shakyas").

According to tradition, immediately after the Buddha died a council was called so that there would be agreement on his authentic teachings (Sanskrit, *dhamma*) and the rules of monastic discipline (Sanskrit, *vinaya*). The individual narratives (Sanskrit, *sutras*) that make up the canon usually begin with "Thus have I heard . . . ", implying that they are authenticated by witnesses, in much the same way as the parables* of Jesus are reported by the evangelists. Much later (c100 BCE to 400 CE), new *sutras* began to appear in written form, an act of emancipation at a time when only the Brahmin caste was literate.

These scriptures, arising in the Mahayana (Great Vehicle) Buddhist movement, radicalized the Buddha's teaching on the ultimate emptiness (Sanskrit, *sunyata*) of all things by deploying a strategy known as "skillful means" (Sanskrit, *kausalya-upaya*). This allowed these scriptures to assert their legitimacy while claiming to contain definitive teachings that were too advanced to have been given to the Buddha's contemporaries but could now be revealed, much as Jesus said that he taught "in parables" until the disciples were ready to receive the full import of his message (cf. Mark 4:10–20, par.). In many Mahayana traditions, certain scriptures – e.g. the *Lotus Sutra* revered throughout East Asia – became a central focus of devotion.

At the same time, another strand of Buddhist tradition, predominant in Zen, relies on a "special transmission outside the scriptures, not founded on words and letters [but] pointing directly to one's mind." The central insight is that we already possess the transcendent "Buddha nature"; realizing this, we grasp the emptiness of all reality without dependence on written records. The paradox, of course, is that we know this only because these stories were eventually written down and themselves became scripture. Though Zen monks, too, chant the *sutras*, the practice of struggling to solve logical riddles (Japanese, *koans*) until the mind bursts through the barrier of reason and realizes nonduality, takes precedence.

Scripture in Buddhism has a somewhat different function than its Christian equivalent (see Scripture), yet there are plenty of parallels. Just as Jesus worked "signs" in order to translate his teaching into concrete practice (Gospel of John*), the Buddha performed miracles, sometimes in competition with famous magicians. Both Jesus and the Buddha taught in parables, drawing lessons from nature and everyday life. The "hard sayings" of Jesus have been compared to *koans*, and the crystal-clear imagery of the *Dhammapada* recalls the Sermon* on the Mount. Paul's saying, "I live, not I, but Christ in me" (Gal 2:20), like Jesus' words about denying oneself to follow him (Mark 8:35 par.), has seemed to some Buddhists to resemble the teaching on "not-self" (Sanskrit, *anatman*), and the hymn affirming that Jesus "emptied himself" (Phil 2) has inspired speculation about a "dynamic emptying" (*sunyata*) in the Trinity* itself. Though in different ways, both Buddhism and Christianity are "religions of the book."

JOHN D'ARCY MAY

Bulgakov, Sergei Nikolaevich (1871–1944), economist, philosopher, Orthodox priest, theologian. Born in Orel, Russia, he studied political economy in Moscow and abandoned Marxism for idealism (c1900). He was a professor of political economy (Kiev and Moscow) and a member of the Second Duma (1907) before serving as a delegate to the All-Russian Council of the Orthodox Church (1917–18) and being ordained a priest (1918). He was exiled by the Soviet government (1922). In Paris (1925–44) he was the founding dean and professor of dogmatic theology at St. Sergius Orthodox Theological Institute. The Moscow Patriarchate and an émigré synod judged Bulgakov's concept of Sophia heretical (1935), doing lasting damage to his reputation.

Bulgakov's theological achievement, aided by his friend Fr. Pavel Florensky (1882–1937), was to synthesize Vladimir Soloviev's* religious philosophy and the dogmatic and liturgical traditions of the Orthodox Church. The tensions in the synthesis are part of its creativity. At its core stands the vision of a Trinity* of divine persons embracing each other in mutual love and giving of themselves in continuing kenosis* for the life of the world. A consummate world-affirming theologian, Bulgakov believed that every worthy economic*, scientific*, and aesthetic* pursuit shares in divine Wisdom and has an offering to bring to the eucharistic feast. PAUL VALLIERE

Bulgaria. The first Christian communities in Bulgaria date back to the early ages of Christianity. King Boris I officially adopted Christianity from the Patriarchate of Constantinople (865), and he strove to promote Slavonic vernacular worship (with help from Cyril* and Methodius's translations) and Bulgarian leadership of the local Orthodox Church. The Bulgarian Church declared itself autocephalous* (927), despite Constantinople's opposition. The medieval Bulgarian Church, challenged by the Bogomils* and illuminated by hesychasm*, was subordinated to

Constantinople (1018–1235). Ottoman authorities suppressed the Patriarchate from the late 14th until the late 19th c. before restoring it through a firman (official edict) of the sultan (1870). Bulgaria gained national independence in 1878, yet it took much longer before the Bulgarian Patriarchate was officially recognized by the other Orthodox churches (1953).

After the 1989 collapse of Communism, the Orthodox Church regained its place in society. However, the Church was weakened by its Communist legacy of state-controlled pawns among its members, strict control of enrollment in the ecclesiastical academy, and a suspicion of corruption in the church leadership. Heated debates over these past compromises led to the tragic split (1992) of the Bulgarian Orthodox Church, with active interference by state authorities, which legitimated an alternative Holy Synod. This internal split had unfortunate, complex, and far-reaching consequences, despite a state-promoted (early-21st-c.) abolition of the alternative church structures. The Bulgarian Orthodox Church was also challenged by the new experience of political, cultural, and religious pluralism, for which the Church was largely unprepared and had neither an adequate theological nor an effective sociological approach.

During the post-Communist period, the heightened popularity of religion is attested to by packed churches on feast days; baptisms, funerals, and marriages in church are almost universally practiced. But other church involvement and attendance are very low, despite the fact that Orthodox Christians nominally make up about 83% of the population. For its part, the Church has not developed significant societal initiatives. Reorganized seminaries and religiously sponsored institutions of higher education seek to address a significant shortage of priests, members of religious orders, and religious specialists.

In contrast to the generally intolerant attitudes toward the new religious movements, which came to the country after the fall of Communism, sociological surveys reveal a high level of religious tolerance among and toward "traditional religions." Muslims are in a situation similar to that of Orthodox Christians. Muslims, who include a Turkish community and smaller groups of Pomaks, Roma, and Tatars, are also afflicted by internal disputes; despite efforts at revitalization, they also experience a decline in the number of regular Friday mosque-goers. Normally, Christians and Muslims live peacefully side by side, yet cooperation between them remains limited.

Statistics: Population (2001): 7.9 million. Christians, 84% (Orthodox, 82.64%; Roman and Eastern Rite Catholics, 1%; Protestants, 0.5%); Muslims, 12.2%. (*Source*: 2001 census.)

INA MERDJANOVA and
JERRY G. PANKHURST

Bull (from Lat *bulla,* "seal"), a solemn and authoritative papal pronouncement; since the 19th c., usually replaced by encyclicals*.

Bullinger, Heinrich (1504–75), Swiss theologian, architect of Reformed Covenant* theology. He embraced an Evangelical position (1522) and replaced Zwingli* as chief pastor in Zurich (1531). Along with Zwingli and Calvin*, he was one of the principal founders of Reformed Protestantism*.

Although Bullinger and Calvin differed on predestination* and church discipline*, they did come to an agreement on the Eucharist*, with the *Consensus Tigurinus* of 1549. During nearly 44 years as chief pastor in Zurich, Bullinger's sway over the Reformed* churches in Europe, England, and Scotland rivaled Calvin's own influence. Bullinger was a prolific writer. His works were widely read, and his *Second Helvetic* Confession* (1566) became a standard confession of faith in the Reformed churches.

Bullinger's doctrine of the covenant was the basis for the later development of this important Reformed concept. In his *One and Eternal Testament or Covenant of God* (1534), he argued that there was only one covenant in history, which stretched from Adam to Christ. Baptism* and Eucharist replaced the old sacraments of circumcision and Passover. Bullinger's opposition to the Anabaptists* rests in his Covenant thought, as he objected to what he viewed as their rejection of the authority of the OT.

J. WAYNE BAKER

Bultmann, Rudolf (1884–1976), German NT scholar and theologian who combined the critical-historical methods of liberal* scholarship with a biblical theology based on justification* by faith* in the salvation*-occurrence of the crucifixion of Christ. He was best known for his project of demythologizing* the NT.

Son of a Lutheran pastor, he studied theology at Tübingen, Berlin, and Marburg with Adolf Harnack* (history of dogma), Adolf Jülicher and Johannes Weiss (NT), and Wilhelm Herrmann (theology). He taught at Breslau (1916–20),

Giessen (1920–21), and Marburg (1921–51). His life spanned a tumultuous era in German history. He lost one brother in World War I, and another died in a German concentration camp in 1942. During the Third Reich, Bultmann was a member of the Confessing* Church, speaking out (1933) against the anti-Semitic policies of the Nazis and German Christians and being a principal author of a document signed by the Marburg theological faculty protesting a decree demanding absolute allegiance to the state and requiring all ecclesiastical appointees and their wives to be of the Aryan race.

Bultmann's first major work, *The History of the Synoptic Tradition* (1921), established him as a cofounder with Martin Dibelius of form criticism (*Formgeschichte*). This method of analyzing and interpreting preliterary oral traditions is based on the assumption that these traditions possess distinctive characteristics and exemplify relatively discernible patterns of development. By distinguishing among these stylistic "forms" – miracle stories, short illustrative stories, utterances (wisdom, prophetic, apocalyptic), controversial discourses, legends, etc. – and then sorting out the original and purer forms from their later embellishments, the critic is able to ascertain the earliest and most trustworthy traditions about Jesus. With this method, Bultmann concluded that many of the NT narratives about Jesus, e.g. the birth narratives, the miracle stories, Peter's confession, the triumphal entry into Jerusalem, and the Resurrection narratives, are not historically true but were written for religious or edifying purposes. Nevertheless, this analysis elucidates the historically reliable teachings of Jesus, and these are sufficient to provide a consistent picture of his ministry. These conclusions were published in his book *Jesus* (1926), which precipitated a host of responses, including "the new quest of the historical Jesus*." Equally important was Bultmann's exegesis of the NT, principally the theologies of Paul and John, presented in his *Theology of the New Testament* and his commentary on the Fourth Gospel (the Gospel of John*).

Bultmann was unique in being both a leading NT scholar and an influential theologian. His theology can, on one level, be stated simply: the crucified Christ is the revelation of God's grace* (see Cross and Crucifixion); when this revelation is understood, it asks the person to identify with Christ by surrendering the attempt to live out of one's own strength and to experience liberation from the past and freedom to take responsibility for the future.

On another level, this simply stated theology is but the tip of a highly sophisticated intellectual iceberg that includes historical exegetical inquiry, a hermeneutical* interpretive theory, and a philosophical framework for making intelligible the theological message of the NT. Bultmann's hermeneutical theory addresses the question first posed by Friedrich Schleiermacher*: "How is it possible that a present interpreter can understand an ancient text like the New Testament?" For Bultmann such an understanding is possible because both the author and the interpreter live in the same historical world and the interpreter has a "preunderstanding" of the subject matter and can have a "life-relation" to it.

The task of the interpreter of the NT is to translate the mythological language of its authors, both honoring their intentions and making their language intelligible to the present. A careful analysis discloses that the biblical authors' language is prescientific and mythological (see Myth and the Study of Christianity). The intent of this language, however, is to proclaim that human existence apart from faith is subject to transiency and the fear of death and that a new self-understanding has been made possible through the death of Christ. In this new understanding, the believer lives in the world but does not derive his or her meaning from it. The best way to make this message intellectually intelligible to modernity, Bultmann argued, was to employ the philosophy of Martin Heidegger*, which shows that we are beings who exist historically in care and anxiety and lose ourselves in preoccupation with the world.

Bultmann's exegetical studies remain authoritative reference works. Yet his main legacy is his decisive affirmation that critical biblical interpretation simultaneously involves a method of exegesis* centered on a close analysis of language, a hermeneutics* in conversation with contemporary philosophies and cultures, and a theological concern. Even as biblical scholars refine his conception of language, broaden his view of hermeneutics, and pursue other theological concerns, they show themselves to be heirs of Bultmann. **See also DEMYTHOLOGIZATION.** VAN A. HARVEY

Bunyan, John (1628–88), Puritan preacher and author of *Pilgrim's Progress*. Despite his lack of university education, Bunyan acquired a simple eloquence by reading the Bible and John Foxe's* *Acts and Monuments*. Bunyan fought in the English civil war (1644–46) as a member of the New Model Army and joined a separatist church in Bedford, England (1655), where he was recognized as a preacher (1657). With the Restoration (1660), Bunyan was imprisoned (1660–72) for nonconformity*. Bunyan's greatest contribution owes much to his inner spiritual turmoil, which he describes in *Grace Abounding to the Chief of Sinners* (1666) and, after his release from prison, *Pilgrim's Progress* (1678), an allegory of the Christian life. Continuing to preach, he published polemical tracts against Quakers* and Latitudinarians*, who, he feared, eroded the foundation of the Protestant doctrine of justification* by faith alone.

PAUL CHANG-HA LIM

Buraku Liberation in Japan, a movement aimed at liberating the Buraku people, an outcaste minority in Japan (between 1 and 3 million), from discrimination infringing on their basic human* rights, including the right to have decent living accommodations (rather than being forced to live in one of the 6,000 ghetto-like Bukaru communities), to receive an education, to enter into marriage with someone freely chosen, and to hold an occupation other than a menial job. The Buraku people, victims of oppression since the feudal system, came in contact with Christianity through the 1870s mission work of William Ball Wright of the Society for the Propagation of the Gospel in Foreign Parts. Afterward the church engaged not merely in evangelism but also in educational and medical services. Until the early 20th c., a Christianity that preached the equality of human beings was largely welcomed by the Buraku people.

While at St. Andrew Church, Tokyo, Toshimichi Imai (later the first president of the Theological Seminary of the Episcopal Church of Japan) denounced the discrimination against the Buraku people as a sin* of Japanese society and organized an evangelistic group to meet their needs (1893). Imai was joined in this mission by Kumajirou Kaiho (baptized at the oldest Protestant church in Japan) and Takeo Yasueda (active in an antiprostitution movement).

In the early 20th c., as the focus of evangelism shifted toward cities, these issues tended to be ignored. Nevertheless, Toraichirou Takeba and especially Kousuke Tomeoka worked for social welfare in Mie and Wakayama and in Hokkaido and Tokyo, respectively. In 1900 Chiki Mori founded Meiji School in Niigata for Buraku children. Yet Toyohiko Kagawa* still expressed a discriminatory view of Buraku in some of his works, despite his collaboration with the National Union of Levelers, founded in 1922 for the liberation of Buraku on the principles of human dignity, freedom, and equality. Thus the churches at large were inconsistently sympathetic to the Buraku people, but rarely critical of common, un-conscientized* discriminatory aspects of society. Some church members even refused to celebrate Holy Communion using a chalice shared with Buraku people.

After World War II, formal institutions such as the Christian Council for the Liberation of Buraku (interdenominational, since 1962) and the Buraku Liberation Center (United* Church of Christ in Japan, since 1975) were founded to challenge discrimination inside and outside the church. Since then, unjustifiably discriminatory phrases and vocabulary in the translated Bible* (see Bible Translations Cluster: History of), hymns, church documents, conferences, and Christian publications have been criticized or corrected. Pioneering research on the relation between Christianity and Buraku was undertaken by a historian, Eiichi Kudou, and theologically developed by Teruo Kuribayashi in his *Theology of the Crown of Thorns* (1986).

NOZOMU MIYAHIRA

Burial Services. There is evidence that, throughout history, human beings cared for the dead and remembered them in particular ways. The Christian history of ritual and liturgy associated with the dead is a trajectory both in universals and in elements particular to Christian theology.

The early history of Christian burial rites is a study in how common cultural practices can be imbued with new meaning. The dead were generally prepared for burial at home, accompanied (as early as the 4th c.) by the singing of psalms and hymns. The body was carried by procession to the cemetery, and in some places Eucharist was celebrated at the grave (as early as the 3rd c.). A third station at the church had been added (5th–6th c.) between home and grave. From this threefold movement developed an order of rites: the vigil* (or wake*), keeping watch and praying with the dead; the funeral liturgy in the church, in some places eucharistic liturgy focused on the story of Christ's resurrection and the "sure and certain hope" of the resurrection for all; and the final commendation and burial in the cemetery. The theological foci were on commending the dead to God, praising God for the means and promise of eternal life, and reminding the mourners that their hope was the same.

The Eastern Orthodox* churches generally solidified their funeral process around non-eucharistic liturgies, differentiating ritually between ordained and lay members, infant deaths, and deaths during Easter Week.

The Western Church liturgies began to reflect by the 8th c. a shift in theology from hope* in the resurrection* to fear of Judgment*.

Part of a complex shift in views on salvation*, dying, reconciliation, and Christian anthropology*, this eventually developed the Requiem* Mass (literally from the phrase *"rest in peace"*), which retained both ancient texts and newer rituals. The theological emphasis was on absolution* rather than commendation, and preparation for the mourners' own deaths.

The Protestant Reformation ranged from minor adaptations to the Mass to a brief burial service in the cemetery followed by a preaching service in the church. This change in practice was intended to disavow any association with praying for the dead* and instead to focus on the living and their preparation for death by proclaiming the gospel of the resurrection.

Contemporary Christian practices are increasingly diverse and divided on issues regarding inculturation* and theological differences. Theological issues are centered on the relationship between the dead and the living (see Dead, Prayers for the) and the focus of the funeral (for the dead or the living). The discomfort of many Protestants with liturgy that may affect the dead has resulted in a rise in memorial services where the dead are "remembered" as they were in life and the mourners comforted – a 20th-c. growing development in all reformed rites.

LIZETTE LARSON-MILLER

Burkina Faso (formerly Upper Volta), the home of the ancient Mossi kingdom, became a French colony (late 19th c.) and gained independence in 1960.

Islam* was introduced by Arab merchants (18th c.). The Roman Catholic White Fathers arrived among the Mossi people in 1901. Owing to the strict ban on mission schools by the French administration, Mossi Christianity started with the evangelization of adults. The progress was slow, with polygamy* as one of the major obstacles to conversion. Arriving in Ouagadougou (1930), Fr. Jean Goarnisson as a young medical doctor contributed to the expansion of missionary work by discovering a vaccine against blindness and by treating sleeping disease. He gained the government's and the elite's respect for missionaries and their work. Mass conversions occurred when the Canadian priest Fr. McCoy opened a dispensary in Dagati (northwest) and healed Poreku, a prominent traditional chief, together with many of his followers (1929); the medical center became a worship center. Starting in 1932, "rain miracles" attracted more converts in the region of Dagaa. Today the Catholic Church, strong among the elite, counts nine dioceses with numerous highly qualified personnel. Fr. Paul Zoungrana (ordained 1942) became archbishop of Ouagadougou (1960) and cardinal (1965). The theologian Anselme Sanon was made bishop of Bobo Dioulasso (1975).

Most Protestants are Evangelicals and Pentecostals*/Charismatics*; the Assemblies* of God is the largest denomination. Together these churches form the Federation of Evangelical Churches and Missions, affiliated with the World* Evangelical Alliance. The Association of Evangelical Reformed Churches of Burkina Faso (since 1986) undertakes projects among the poorest population in the Sahel.

Christianity in Burkina Faso can be described as a flowering oasis in the desert. Churches excel by their remarkable cooperation among themselves (including African* Instituted Churches) and interreligious cooperation with Muslims.

Statistics: Population (2008): 15.2 million. Christians, 19% (Roman Catholics, 11%; Protestants, 7.4%; members of African Instituted Churches, 0.6%); Muslims, 49%; African Religionists, 32%. (Based on *World Christian Encyclopedia*, 2001.)

VALENTIN DEDJI

Burning of Heretics, medieval practice first used in France (1022) and approved by Pope Lucius III (1184). A person convicted of heresy* by a church court was then "delivered to the secular* arm" for punishment (see Inquisition).

Burundi. The introduction of Christianity in this German, then Belgian, former colony is closely linked to colonialism. Earlier attempts were fruitless, mainly because of the hostility of the Arab slave* traders. Thus two pioneering Catholic White* Fathers, Deniaud and Promaux, were killed after nine months on the mission field (1881). The church was permanently planted with the coming of the German colonial masters (1896); the first Roman Catholic mission stations were built in Mugera and Muyaga (1898), and later Buhonga (1902), Kanyinya (1904), Rugari (1909), and Buhoro (1912).

The first Protestant mission stations, in Kibimba, Musema, and Muyebe, were not established until 1911 by the Neukirchner Missionsgesellschaft missionaries, but died with the departure of the Germans (1916); they were rebuilt by Danish Baptist missionaries (1928), who invited the Church Missionary Society, the Methodist Church, and the Society of Friends* missionaries to help them. The Seventh-day Adventists, who entered in 1925, confined their work to Bubanza Province in the west. From Zaire (currently Democratic Republic of Congo*) came Swedish Pentecostals (arriving in 1935).

In the early stages, Burundians, and especially the *mwami* (king), were suspicious of every foreign religion. However, the coming of the Belgians, predominantly Catholics, contributed to the growth of the Roman Catholic Church. Largely under the sponsorship of the Belgian government, the Catholic Church was involved in running social facilities, schools, and hospitals; as a result, it grew rapidly.

The Protestant Evangelical churches and the Anglicans did not grow as fast. But the growth of these churches is still considerable and is closely related to the Rwanda* revival, generally known as the East African Revival Movement (beginning in 1930). The publication of the first Kirundi Bible in 1968 for the Protestant churches also opened an opportunity for growth.

The Charismatic and Pentecostal churches (including the Swedish Pentecostal Church, the largest), with their emphasis on the Holy* Spirit, speaking in tongues*, and a strong healing ministry, appeal to many Burundians because through their traditional religion and culture they have a great awareness of the spiritual world.

The independence of Burundi (1962) ushered in an era of handing over the missionary churches to the national leadership. From then on, the most important test for both the Roman Catholic and Protestant churches was the antagonism between the Hutu and Tutsi, with major outbreaks in 1965, 1972, and 1988, and others after 1993. The attitude of the churches toward these ethnic killings can be largely characterized as laissez-faire. This attitude led to mistrust toward the churches and more killing among Burundians. A good number of churches split along ethnic lines. All this put the churches' moral authority in question.

On the contrary, Islam managed to keep both its Hutu and Tutsi members in unity. This may account for the recent growth of this small religion. The influence of the Catholics had slowed down the growth of Islam and its involvement in the top political leadership of the country. However, with Islam's capacity to unite its members above ethnic strife and its recent involvement in top political leadership positions, it can be expected to continue growing and to seriously challenge the Christian churches in Burundi.

Statistics: Population (2000): 6.7 million (M). Christians, 6.2 M, 92% (Roman Catholics, 3.8 M, Protestants, 0.8 M; Anglicans, 0.5 M); African Religionists, 0.45 M, 7%; Muslims, 0.09 M, 1.4%. (Based on *World Christian Encyclopedia*, 2001.)

THEODORE MBAZUMUTIMA

Bushnell, Horace (1802–76), pastor and theologian; born in rural Connecticut and educated at Yale College and Divinity School; an important and controversial theologian of the 19th-c. USA. He was a key figure in the shift from early-19th-c. conservative Evangelicalism* to theological liberalism*. His volume *Christian Nurture* (1848) abandoned a conversion*-oriented piety in favor of the role of family nurture. He also wrote *God in Christ* (1849), concerning Christology*, soteriology*, and the Trinity*, and tried to overcome the divisions between Unitarian* and Trinitarian Congregationalists. His theological views were controversial at the time, and Bushnell became involved in a celebrated heresy* trial. **See also UNITED CHURCH OF CHRIST (IN THE UNITED STATES).**

ROBERT BRUCE MULLIN

Business Ethics and Christianity. Christian thinkers have long been interested in ethics related to business matters. The Bible frequently discusses economic* matters and is replete with moral instructions directly applicable to business on both personal and systemic levels. For example, the OT instructs farmers to be good stewards of their land and to share their wealth in order to ensure justice* for the needy, strangers, and refugees*. Employers are instructed to pay wages on time and to use "fair weights and measures" when selling their goods. In the NT, many of Jesus' ethical teachings (e.g. love of neighbor) and parables are also directly applicable to business.

Throughout church history, theologians such as Tertullian* and Luther* saw fit to offer ethical commentary on the commercial practices of their time. Since they lived within the contexts of small-scale, zero-sum economies, their views of business and "trades people" were mostly negative.

Since the advent of modern economies, many Christians have acquired a more positive attitude toward business. Yet in today's age of large corporations and interconnected global markets, there are many new ethical concerns. Contemporary Christian business ethicists are engaged in addressing topics such as the impact of globalization*; the purpose of corporations (maximization of shareholder wealth or the well-being of other stakeholders); the treatment of workers (including those in developing countries); the implications of seeing business as a "calling" or "vocation*," honesty in accounting and finance; values-laden assumptions in management theories (i.e. views of human nature in motivating employees; see Anthropology Cluster); the impact of advertising on human values; and environmental stewardship.

Christians are far from univocal on these matters. Some generally (often tacitly) support current trends in global capitalism and many accompanying business practices. Others are more critical and see the need for reform. The roots of these differences seem to lie in factual analysis and theology, i.e. in the assessment of how far business practices are from the justice* that God wills for economic life in human communities. (See Global Ethics.)

A number of Christian corporate executives (including Max DePree, C. William Pollard, and Dennis Bakke) have worked to implement what they view as Christian-based ethics in the values and practices of their corporations. Others have been involved in the "spirituality at work" movement, aiming, in part, to reform business through the integration of spiritually based ethics. Other Christians question the neoliberal economic structure of business as they focus on globalized* solidarity and economic* ethics.

KENMAN L. WONG

Butler, Joseph (1692–1752), Anglican priest, preeminent British moralist and theologian. He wrote *Fifteen Sermons Preached at Rolls Chapel* (1726) and *Analogy of Religion* (1736), which countered 18th-c. criticisms of Christianity and were influential in Britain until the 19th c. *Sermons* appealed to the natural moral faculty of conscience* against Thomas Hobbes's doctrine of psychological determinism and self-interest. *Analogy* challenged the natural theology of the Deists*, who opposed the Christian appeal to a special revelation* in the Bible. For Butler, since nature reveals defects and ambiguities analogous to those found in the Bible, "probability must be the very guide to life." Natural religion has no privileged position over Christian revelation.

JAMES C. LIVINGSTON

Byzantine Art and Architecture, developed after Constantinople* became the capital of the Roman Empire (330 CE); characterized by the use of icons* and the construction of domes. **See also HIEROTOPY, THE CREATION OF CHRISTIAN SACRED SPACES.**

Byzantine Theology normally designates what succeeded Greek patristic* theology in the Byzantine Empire (330 [or 527/65, Justinian]–1453, although this period could technically include patristic theology). Byzantine theology continues the interests and, to some extent, the methods of Greek patristic theology, but is marked by two concerns: (1) the 5th-c. ecumenical synods* (Ephesus*, 431; Chalcedon*, 451) that divided the imperial church from those who rejected the Christology propounded by these synods; and (2) the increasing hegemony of monasticism* within the Byzantine Church (and indeed beyond it).

The long-running dispute over Christology* (especially with the Miaphysite* or Monophysite* opponents of Chalcedon) produced both a formalized appeal to patristic authority, which came to be seen as second only to the apostolic authority, especially through *florilegia,* and also a technical terminology – nature, essence, person, "hypostasis," and, later, will and activity – and a concentration on logical arguments. This is sometimes regarded as an incipient "scholasticism," but is far removed from the 13th-c. Scholastics' achievements.

The hegemony of monasticism led to a vast ascetic* literature, at the center of which is a profound reflection on human nature, fragmented by the Fall*, the restoration of which through Christ's saving work is assimilated by ascetic struggle, which leads to the restoration of communion with God, experienced in pure prayer.

These two concerns were often held together, especially in the theologians of the early Byzantine period, such as Maximus* the Confessor and John* of Damascus, and later Gregory* Palamas. Their theological synthesis combined an apophatic* approach to God (inspired both by the experience of prayer and by epistemological and ontological considerations) and a thorough development of the implications of Chalcedonian Christology, a profound interest in the created order, and a developed sense of the transfiguring* power of the sacraments* and the ascetic life, leading to deification*. These concerns were sometimes pursued separately, leading to a lay or humanist tradition of theology, concerned with learned commentary on the Scriptures and the patristic tradition, exemplified by Photios* (9th c.) and the 14th-c. lay theologians. Byzantine theology also led to a monastic tradition concerned with the transforming possibilities opened up by the pursuit of prayer, which blossomed in figures such as Simeon* the New Theologian and the 14th-c. hesychast* monks, championed by Gregory* Palamas.

Various issues occupied Byzantine theology. The iconoclast* controversy led to consideration of the nature of image/icon. For both sides, it was a matter of Christology, for the Orthodox icons* were entailed by the Incarnation*. Eucharistic* theology, too, was at issue; the iconoclast notion of the Eucharist as an icon was opposed by an Orthodox insistence on the real presence of Christ; later, attention turned to the eucharistic sacrifice. During the hesychast* controversy, Palamas defended genuine experience of the unknowable God by invoking the distinction between God's unknowable essence and his energies, in which he is truly encountered, a distinction taken up in recent Orthodox* theology. ANDREW LOUTH

Byzantium, the Greek city chosen by Constantine* when he moved the capital to the East (324), because of its strategic location and its proximity to Troy, legendary origin of the Romans. Refounded and rebuilt, it was named New Rome and, after his death, Constantinople. "Byzantine" is often used to refer to the Roman Empire after this transfer, especially after the West was conquered by Arian* Christian Germanic invaders (5th–6th c). The term can also refer to the political culture of the Empire in the East, specifically the complexity and deviousness of its diplomacy and its internal struggles for power. **See also BYZANTINE ART AND ARCHITECTURE; BYZANTINE THEOLOGY.**

C

Cabasilas, Nicholas (b c1322), Byzantine lay theologian who, though very little about his life is known (he is often confused with Nilos Cabasilas), is well known for two works: *Commentary on the Divine Liturgy* and *The Life in Christ*. A supporter of Gregory* of Palamas and the hesychasts*, he nevertheless does not mention in his works the essence–energies distinction or the Jesus* Prayer. Instead, his works expound a sacramental* piety, indebted to Dionysius* the Pseudo-Areopagite, aimed not at monks, but at laity in all ranks of society. ANDREW LOUTH

Cabrini, Francis Xavier (1850–1917), Roman Catholic nun, the first US citizen to be canonized as a saint (1946; Patron of Immigrants).

The youngest of 13 children born into a farmer's family in Italy, Maria Francisca Cabrini was twice denied entrance into a convent because of her frail health; she was finally admitted and took religious vows (1877). Though she wanted to be a missionary, following her vow of obedience she accepted an appointment as the superior of a small orphanage. Later she founded the Missionary Sisters of the Sacred Heart of Jesus (1880), modeling her actions on a treasured scriptural passage: "I can do all things in Him who strengthens me" (Phil 4:13). Devoted to works of mercy, the congregation quickly spread in Italy and Europe, establishing schools (especially for girls) and homes for the aged, the sick, and orphans.

Responding to Archbishop Corrigan's invitation to come to New York, Mother Cabrini began (1889) similar work for the sake of Italian immigrants in the USA, becoming a citizen in 1909. By the time she died (Chicago, 1917), her Missionary Sisters of the Sacred Heart had built and served more than 50 hospitals, schools, orphanages, convents, and other foundations in the USA. THOMAS MCGOWAN

Caecilian (d before 343). Bishop of Carthage during the Diocletian* persecutions (303–13), he cautioned against seeking martyrdom*. A rigorist group consecrated a rival bishop, accusing Caecilian of being associated with a *traditor* who had given the sacred Scriptures to officials (see Donatism). He was the only bishop from Latin Africa to attend the Council of Nicaea* (325).

Caiaphas, Jewish high priest who, according to Matt 26–27 and John 11:49–53, 18:28, proposed the arrest of Jesus, declared his guilt, and sent him to Pilate.

Cain, the firstborn son of Adam and Eve, who killed his brother Abel (Gen 4:1–24). The founder of the first city (Gen 4:17), he became for Augustine* the symbol of the "earthly city," whereas Abel was the first citizen of the "city of God" and a sojourner* on earth. In Jewish Midrash, Cain was sometimes called "the firstborn of Satan" (see Devil, Satan, Demons, and Demonic Powers). Conversely, for some Gnostics*, Cain became a representative of the highest deity, while Abel worshipped the Demiurge, the bungling creator. In return Polycarp* called Marcion* "the firstborn of Satan." According to later anti-Jewish Christian superstition, the Jews were often thought to have the "mark of Cain" (Gen 4:15) on their breasts (see Demonization).

Calendars. Three basic calendars have been used by Christian churches: the Julian, Gregorian, and Revised Julian.

The Julian calendar, introduced by Julius Caesar (46 BCE), was probably designed to approximate the tropical solar year. It has a year of 365.25 days divided into 12 months, with a leap day added to February every four years.

The Gregorian calendar was introduced in 1582 by Pope Gregory XIII because the Julian scheme added too many leap days; the astronomical solstices and equinoxes advanced by about 11 minutes per year (i.e. a day about every 134 years). By 1582 the year was 10 days out of alignment, which the Gregorian calendar corrected by removing 10 days. This calendar was soon adopted by most Catholic countries, then by Protestant countries (mostly in the 18th c.), and later by Eastern European countries. Thus the 1917 revolution in Russia was viewed as the "October revolution" (according to the Julian calendar), then as the "November revolution" when the Gregorian calendar was adopted by the state. But the Eastern Orthodox churches continued using the Julian calendar to establish the dates of its holidays. During this time, the Julian calendar continued to diverge from the Gregorian, the difference now being one of 13 days. Thus the Nativity/Christmas falls on December 25 according to the Gregorian calendar, but January 7 according to the Julian calendar.

The revised Julian calendar, very similar to the Gregorian calendar (they will differ by one day in 2800), was partly adopted at the Synod of Constantinople in 1923 by several Orthodox churches. The solar aspect of the revised Julian calendar was accepted by several Orthodox churches, including those of Constantinople, Greece, Romania, and Poland, but rejected by the Orthodox churches of Jerusalem, Russia, Ukraine, and Georgia. However, the lunar aspect of the revised Julian calendar, which dictates how the date of Pascha/Easter* is calculated – was rejected by most Orthodox churches, which still calculate the date of Easter according the Julian calendar. DANIEL PATTE

Calling. See VOCATION.

Calvary, "place of the skull" (Lat Calvaria; Heb/Aramaic Golgotha*; Gk Kranion), site of Jesus' crucifixion outside Jerusalem. The Church of the Holy Sepulchre* was built near the traditional location.

Calvin, Jean (1509–64), Protestant Reformer, theologian, pastor, teacher; born in the cathedral city of Noyon, Northern France. As the talented son of an episcopal official, he was able to study with the bishop's noble nephews. Benefices supplied educational support (though Calvin never advanced to the priesthood), and after receiving an arts degree in Paris, Calvin was directed by his father to study law. While so engaged, Calvin was strongly influenced by the humanist passion for original languages and sources. He became involved with the new "Evangelical" movement associated with French princess Marguerite* of Navarre, a movement in accord with but independent from German reforms (Luther*, Zwingli*, Bucer*). The question of Calvin's "conversion*," its date (c1530 or c1533) and character, continues to be debated. A very reticent man, Calvin made only one public autobiographical statement late in life, in the preface to his commentary on Psalms (published 1557), in which he spoke of his "sudden" or "unexpected" conversion. Scholars debate whether this meant his religious reorientation to the gospel (justification* by faith* and grace* alone, dependent on the sole authority of Scripture*), his break with Rome, or both. It is clear that both aspects of conversion were complete when Calvin renounced his benefices (May 1534) and left France in December for his lifelong exile.

A gifted writer, Calvin began his reform work with a small book called the *Institutes of the Christian Religion*, published in Basel (March 1536). The six chapters of this Latin text were dedicated to King Francis I of France, whose court was persecuting Evangelicals ("Protestants") as seditious heretics*. Calvin's task was to defend his fellow believers by explaining their faith: apologia and catechism in one. A Frenchman in exile and humanist-trained scholar, Calvin understood his calling to be that of a teacher-writer. Many who read his *Institutes* were impressed by his ability to organize and explain the faith; they tried to draft Calvin into active pastoral ministry. Farel* in Geneva was the first to do so, telling Calvin (simply passing through the city in July 1536) that God would trouble Calvin's peace if he did not stay to help organize the reform in Geneva.

Calvin recognized God's call through leaders of the church and stayed. With the new preaching, Geneva had already accepted Zwinglian ideas of magistrates controlling the social and moral life of the church (see Erastianism). However, Calvin insisted on ecclesiastical autonomy in discipline as well as doctrine; church and civil authority are distinct. Ideally, the two cooperate but each has its own constitutional order; the church functions independently when rulers are not members* of the faith (a conviction very important for persecuted churches and the later spread of Calvinism). Geneva's Christian civil rulers rejected this idea and exiled Farel and Calvin (April 1538). Calvin wanted to return to his writing, but Bucer, leader of Protestant Strassburg, invoked the story of Jonah to call Calvin as pastor of the French-speaking religious exiles in that German-speaking city.

The next three years of ministry were rich. Calvin's congregation in Strasbourg comprised fellow exiles; he could teach, write, and work with colleagues here and beyond. Bucer was an important influence, and Calvin became acquainted with Philip Melanchthon* and others as he participated in ecumenical colloquies (between papal and varied Protestant groups). Calvin married a widowed member of his congregation, Idelette de Bure, who shared his deep commitment to the faith and earned his heartfelt praise as "the best companion" of his life and ministry. Geneva needed Calvin, however. With personal reluctance but the conviction of following God's will articulated by church leaders, he moved back to that small city-state (1541). He spent the rest of his life preaching, teaching, and organizing the Church of Geneva, the lasting center of the international movement called Calvinism (see Reformed Churches).

Calvin is known for his writing. The *Institutes of the Christian Religion* is often called the most important book of the Protestant Reformation. Read in its final edition (1559), it was soon molding Calvin's heirs and being interpreted to fit their ecclesiastical situations. Consequently, it is often forgotten that Calvin intended this catechism-cum-textbook to be read alongside his biblical commentaries, which were the substance of his actual teaching. He lectured on Scripture*, working through one biblical book after another (*lectio continua*, "continuous reading"). The fruit was a large collection of commentaries on all the NT except Revelation and 2–3 John and on much of the OT (Genesis through Joshua, Psalms, the Prophets, although Ezekiel remained incomplete at his death). More numerous were Calvin's Sunday and daily biblical sermons (as *lectio continua*). Recorded verbatim after 1549, these include some books (1–2 Samuel, Job) for which there are no commentaries. Besides his biblical exposition, catechisms, and liturgies, Calvin wrote occasional treatises (e.g. on the Lord's Supper; Providence). However, pastoral work filled most of his time: preaching, administering sacraments and conducting marriages; promoting the metrical* Psalms, which became perhaps the most distinctive trait of Calvinist piety; working with the consistory to oversee discipline (vindicating the church's autonomy* by 1555); serving as the liaison between the pastors and the magistracy; and writing letters, receiving guests, interceding for the persecuted, and visiting the sick, despite his own increasingly severe ill health.

Calvin strongly affirmed justification by faith/grace* alone but equally emphasized sanctification* or the "third use of the Law*" (Decalogue) as the pattern for regenerate Christian life; both are the work of the Holy* Spirit. Accepted by God through faith* in Christ given by the Holy Spirit, believers are freed to worship God and called to love their neighbors. God's predestination* is the source of faith, engrafting believers into Christ and his ministry, sharing in both his cross and his resurrection. (Reprobation means that those who do not trust in Christ experience the inescapable relationship with God as hell*.) The context of this piety is corporate: the church* as the body of Christ and the world (the locus of the church's ministry). Calvin's doctrine of the church includes some of his most creative insights: the combination of "lay" (elders, deacons) and "clerical" (pastors, teachers) offices; ecclesiastical autonomy held in tension with constant prayerful engagement in civil society; and devotion to biblical teaching expounded with all the intelligence God gives to human minds and applied faithfully to living always, consciously, in God's sight and fellowship. **See also** PREDESTINATION.

ELSIE ANNE MCKEE

Calvinism. See REFORMED CHURCHES.

Camara, Helder Pessoa (1909–99), Brazilian churchman, Roman Catholic archbishop of Olinda and Recife (1964–85). A rare synthesis of mystic* and man of action, he was the founder of the National Conference of Brazilian Bishops, CNBB (1952; see Roman Catholicism Cluster: In Latin America: Brazil: National Conference of Brazilian Bishops [CNBB]). He was a cofounder of the Latin American Episcopal Conference, CELAM (1955) and a noteworthy council father during Vatican* II (1962–65). A man of prayer, brilliant orator and preacher, efficient organizer, and indefatigable advocate of justice*, peace*, and nonviolence, he became known as "bishop of the slums," "voice of the voiceless," and "advocate of the Third World," and was accused of being the "red archbishop." He received 24 major awards and published 23 books. LUIZ C. L. MARQUES

Cambridge Platform (1648). See PURITANS, PURITANISM.

Cambridge Platonists, a group of teachers at Cambridge University during the 17th c. who resisted both the Puritan* and High Anglican parties, asserting that guidance comes through direct illumination* by God.

Cameroon differs from other African countries in its geographical and human diversity; there are more than 200 ethnic groups, including Sudanese, Bantus, and Hamites (or Chamites), along with their diverse traditional beliefs. Before the arrival of Islam* from the north (1715) and Christianity from the west and south (1843), the diverse Cameroonian groups knew and worshipped God through various African* traditional religious practices.

The first contacts between Western Christians and indigenous populations on the coast occurred in the 15th c. Yet missionary work began in the 19th c with the Jamaican Baptist* Missionary Society. In their anti-slavery struggle, Baptist* former slaves* who had been kidnapped in Africa were eager to return to their native countries to preach the gospel – an Africanized Myalist revivalist gospel (see Jamaica). In response to this missionary outburst among Jamaican former slaves, the Institute of Theology was created in Calabar (Jamaica). There the first missionaries to Cameroon, black Jamaicans such as Merrick, Fuller, Pinnock, and Richardson, came to proclaim the gospel to free Africans in order to bring them the salvation* of the soul* as children of God (1843). These Jamaican Baptist missionaries were incorporated into the London Baptist Missionary Society (from 1845), leading to the establishment of English-speaking Baptist churches in West Cameroon, before being replaced by the Basel Mission and the Baptist Mission of Berlin (during the German protectorate, 1884–1916). Meanwhile in the south, the larger French-speaking Église Évangélique du Cameroon (1845) and Église Presbytérienne Camerounaise (1879) were established with the help of the Paris Mission and US Presbyterian missionaries. These and other Protestant churches became autonomous in 1957. Under Cameroonian leadership, the churches sought to serve more directly the Cameroonian diversified culture and religious contexts; they formed the Federation of Protestant Churches and Missions in Cameroon (1969).

The Roman Catholic Church came in 1890, following the baptism in Germany of a young Cameroonian, Kwa Mbange. The late arrival of the Catholic Church stimulated a quick expansion (especially in the 1930s; by 2000, 51% of Christians were Roman Catholics). For the Roman Catholic historian Jean Paul Messina, "the advent of Christianity in Cameroon is a mystery, theologically speaking. It is a real intervention of God. . . . Having a colonized layperson (Kwa Mbange) going to the Western world to reach out to his people with the gospel thereafter, is a rare story in Africa." Since the Second Vatican* Council, Cameroonian Catholics have challenged Western forms of pastoral work and undertaken an indigenization of the clergy, even as they have developed inculturated* liturgies and teachings.

Christianity has played and continues to play a primary role in the social, cultural, political, and economic development of Cameroon through turbulent times: the German protectorate (1884–1916), the French and British mandates (1916–60/61), the period of fighting for political liberation, political independence (1960), and the proclamation of the Constitution (1972) of a united secular republic, where African Religionists, Muslims, and Christians (the majority) could live together. From 1843 to the 1990s (the high point for freedom of the Cameroonian society, with a decline afterward), Christianity (all denominations) helped fashion a stable and peaceful state of Cameroon through confessional institutions such as schools, hospitals, and rural development projects, including the well-known Teachers' Training School of Foulassi (where the Cameroon National Anthem was written), the College Alfred Shaker in Douala, the College Vogt in Yaounde, the College of Mazenod, and the College Protestant in Ngaoundere, from which institutions most of the high-ranking (Muslim and Christian) administrative officers of Northern Cameroon graduated. Yet after 1990, a total lack of state control contributed to tensions among these religious institutions.

Statistics: Population (2000): 15 million (M). Christians, 8.2 M, 54% (Roman Catholics, 4 M; Protestants, 3.1 M; independents, 0.6 M); African Religionists, 3.5 M, 24%; Muslims, 3.2 M, 21%. (Based on *World Christian Encyclopedia*, 2001.)

SAMUEL FROUISOU

Camisards, French Protestants who, from 1702 to 1710, waged guerrilla warfare against Louis XIV's Catholic soldiers throughout the remote Cévennes Mountains (Southern France). They were called Camisards because of the white shirts (*camiso* in the local patois) they wore to distinguish one another during intense nighttime fighting. Following the proscription of Protestantism (1685), members of the French Reformed Church were deprived of pastors and of organized ecclesiastical structure (see Protestantism Cluster: In Europe: France). In this vacuum, movements inspired by religious enthusiasm quickly surfaced. Lay preachers, both men and women, and "prophets," mostly young women but eventually young men too, called for repentance in the face of this disaster (see Charismatic and Pentecostal Movements Cluster: Their History and Theology). Soon their message took on an apocalyptic* dimension and ultimately invited religious war. Hostilities erupted with the assassination of the Abbot du Chayla, an especially offensive royal agent who sought to convert recalcitrant Protestants forcibly (1702). Pierre Laposte, known as

Roland, quickly emerged as the most successful and charismatic Camisard leader. The crown responded with a brutal campaign of repression in which entire villages were destroyed. Roland was eventually killed and other leaders negotiated various surrenders. The struggle had effectively collapsed by 1710. Thousands died in the Camisards' unsuccessful struggle to rid themselves of royal Catholic oppression and worship freely. **See also NANTES, EDICT OF, AND ITS REVOCATION.** RAYMOND A. MENTZER

Campbell, Alexander (1788–1866), debater, editor, educator; prominent leader of the Disciples of Christ (later known as the Stone*–Campbell Restoration* Movement). Of Presbyterian* heritage, Campbell immigrated to Western Virginia from Northern Ireland* (1809), united with Baptists* (1812), and founded Bethany College (1840). Experiencing religious and social division, he committed himself to Christian unity and a restoration* of NT Christianity, including weekly Communion*. Excluded from the Baptists because of his opposition to creeds* as tests of Christian fellowship and his teaching that baptism* assures the believer of God's forgiveness, Campbell argued that slavery* is authorized by Scripture*, while opposing its continuation in the USA. **See also CHRISTIAN CHURCH (DISCIPLES OF CHRIST).** D. NEWELL WILLIAMS

Camp Meeting, a type of religious revival* characteristic of the US frontier after 1800, held out-of-doors and lasting for several days. Its background may lie in the quarterly preparatory* services held in the Presbyterian churches of Scotland and Northern Ireland. **See also METHODIST WORSHIP.**

Cana, village in Galilee, home of Nathanael* (John 21:2), place of Jesus' first miracle (John 2:1–11) and healing of a nobleman's son (John 4:46).

Canaan, "the Promised* Land," encompassing present-day Israel and Lebanon, was pledged to Abraham's offspring for an "everlasting possession" (Gen 17:8), a land "flowing with milk and honey" (Deut 6:3), given as a divine gift (Deut 9:4–5) to the Israelites. Canaan derives its name from its inhabitants, the descendants of Ham's son Canaan, cursed by Noah to serve Shem and Japheth. "Canaanite" carries a negative figurative significance throughout Scripture, associated with idolatry* (Exod 23:24) and sexual defilement (Lev 18:24–28), along with racist stereotypes (Matt 15:22–28), which Jesus resists and overcomes. Postcolonial* theology resists uses of "Canaan" as a justification for colonialism*. JEFFRY C. DAVIS

Canada. Christianity in Canada was and is characterized by a pervading sense of mission* and evangelism*, a multiplicity of denominations, a strong Social* Gospel Movement, the formation of primarily Protestant and Catholic societies in English and French Canada respectively, the challenge of a conquering secular* ethos (after 1960), and a new evangelism that challenges secularism* (early 2000s).

From 1608, the founding of Quebec* by French entrepreneurs, to 1760, the conquest of Canada by Britain, the colony of New France was Roman Catholic in law and fact. While the small French colony was centered on Quebec, Jesuit* and other Catholic missionaries evangelized scores of Amerindian nations throughout North America, called as a whole the Diocese of Quebec, led by Bishop François de Laval (1658) and his successors.

After the British conquest (1760), the Treaty of Paris (1763), which transferred most of French North America to Great Britain, made both the French language and the Catholic faith legal – at a time when Catholicism was still outlawed in Great Britain. From 1775 (the revolt against Great Britain and the formation of the USA) to the early 1900s, the vast majority of immigrants were Christian Protestants who spoke or learned English. During the 19th and 20th c., Quebec remained largely Francophone and Catholic, while Canada's other nine provinces became primarily Anglophone and Protestant.

Canada adopted constitutional frameworks and social policies that reflected its ethnic, linguistic, cultural, and religious composition. For example, from the mid-1800s, Canada created publicly funded elementary and secondary education*, usually Christian (Roman Catholic, Anglican, or nondenominational). Yet secular schools prevailed after the 1960s, following the gradual disappearance of discriminatory immigration laws (after 1945) that brought legions of religiously diverse immigrants. A growing number of Muslims (see Islam and Christianity Cluster), Sikhs*, and Hindus* now lived alongside Christians and Jews.

Christians in Canada have always emphasized mission. In New France, Jesuits* and other Catholic clergies were deeply involved in missions to Amerindian people throughout

North America. During the 1800s, Catholic missionaries, led by Oblates of Mary Immaculate assisted by Sisters of Charity of Montreal, Sisters of Providence, and Sisters of Saint Anne from Montreal, expanded their outreach to Amerindians of the Pacific slope and Northwest. They competed with Protestant missionaries, especially Methodists and Anglicans, working through missionary societies based in England, e.g. the Society for the Propagation of the Gospel and the Church Missionary Society. This renewed zeal for mission and evangelism grew rapidly among both Catholics and Protestants. Among Protestants, evangelism was rooted in Puritanism* (from Britain), Pietism* (from Germany), Methodism* and the Great* Awakening (from Britain and the USA), and romanticism*. Among Catholics, the same zealous evangelism, later known as Ultramontanism*, was based on the reformism of the Council of Trent* (1545–63) and the crusading romantic evangelism of the Church of France after Napoleon (1815). Evangelistic Protestants and Catholics focused on traditional Christian teachings about God's sovereignty, Jesus' divinity as the Son of God, the virgin* birth, the atonement* for our sins through Christ, the resurrection* of God's elect to eternal life, the divine inspiration* of Holy Scripture*, and opening one's heart to the Spirit. Evangelism, like an expanding theological and spiritual stream, ran through a variety of competing Christian denominations, including Anglican, Methodist, Presbyterian, Pentecostal, Baptist, and Roman Catholic.

The evangelistic tsunami that swept through the Christian churches in the 19th and 20th c. began to reverse the balkanization of Protestant Christianity. After 1850 Presbyterian, Methodist, Baptist, and other denominations began to federate. Various joint endeavors, societies, and interdenominational groups served multiple Protestant denominations for missions, Bible promotion, youth, the prohibition of alcoholic beverages, and social outreach. This culminated in the formation of the United Church of Canada (1925), Canada's largest Protestant Church, uniting Presbyterians, Methodists, and Congregationalists. The Church of England in Canada remained within one communion, despite the strong tensions between its traditional High Church wing and its Evangelical, or Low Church, wing. Though numerous Canadian Protestant denominations remained (including Pentecostals, Millennialists*, Baptists) by 1925 the worst of the institutional fractiousness was past.

After 1900, Canada's Evangelicals* progressively became more involved in social work, a concern that dominated the activity of Christian churches after the 1950s. The Christian gospel came to be viewed as a social* gospel; the way to personal salvation*, or liberation*, is through the salvation or liberation of one's neighbor. It is Christians' responsibility to make into their neighbor all immigrants, poor, sick, abandoned children, and oppressed and disenfranchised people of society, including Amerindians, battered and abused* women, refugees*, and minorities. This common concern led after 1960 to growing ecumenical social programs, including a wide range of joint efforts between Catholic and Protestant churches.

A fundamental effect of the Protestant and Catholic evangelistic crusade between 1850 and 1950 was the Christianization of Canadian society. By 1950, French Canada (Quebec) was a Catholic society, and English Canada was Protestant. Canada's civil society had become a Christian society. This was manifest in immigration laws (favoring Christian countries of origin for immigrants), liquor legislation, censorship laws for publications and films, marriage legislation, taxation privileges for religious institutions, laws banning commercial activity on Sunday, and education laws. In 1950 more than 90% of Canadians, including the vast majority of Canadian Amerindians, were Christians. The Dominion of Canada had become the Dominion of the Lord.

A sea change occurred during the tumultuous four decades after 1960, a time when God largely disappeared from Canada's public square. Secularism* came to prevail, leading to widespread secular schooling, as well as permissive legislation and social attitudes regarding premarital sex*, divorce*, the use of contraceptives*, homosexuality*, and abortion*. Attendance at worship services dropped dramatically. Christians and others were frequently shocked by scandals involving pedophile clergy and sexually active "celibate" clergymen. In this context, a new evangelism in Protestant and Catholic churches emerged c2000, saying, "Enough! It's time to return to basics: God*, the Ten* Commandments, the gospel, and the church." **See also GOSPEL AND CULTURE CLUSTER: IN NORTH AMERICA; QUEBEC; RYERSON, EGERTON; STRACHAN, JOHN; TACHÉ, ALEXANDRE.**

Statistics: Population (2000): 31.1 million (M). Christians, 24.8 M, 80% (Roman

Catholics, 13.1 M; Protestants, 5.4 M; independents, 1.7 M; Anglicans, 0.8 M; Orthodox, 0.6 M; marginal Christians, 0.45 M); Native Religionists, 0.8 M, 3%; Jews, 0.4 M, 1.3%; Muslims, 0.3 M, 1%; nonreligious, 4 M, 13%. (Based on *World Christian Encyclopedia*, 2001.)

ROBERT CHOQUETTE

Candlemas, feast of the purification* of Mary and the presentation* of Christ in the Temple, which became the time for blessing the candles for the year and for a procession with lighted candles.

Candles, placed on the altar, lit during services. Votive candles are set before tabernacles* or saints' representations*. The Puritans* objected to all use of candles. **See also PASCHAL CANDLE.**

Canon (Gk *kanon,* "measuring rule," thus a standard; Lat *regula,* "rule"). The term has a wide application, e.g. to the "rule of faith," canons, or decrees of councils; lists of authoritative books of the Bible*; the words essential to the Mass; and a list of saints to be venerated.

Canon, Ecclesiastical Title, for clergy of a cathedral or collegiate church. Canons "regular" live under a rule, usually the Augustinian*.

Canon within the Canon, some aspect of Scripture* that serves as the interpretive key for the rest, e.g. Paul's epistles and justification* by faith for Luther*.

Canonization of the New Testament. See NEW TESTAMENT AND ITS CANONIZATION.

Canonization of the Old Testament. See OLD TESTAMENT AND ITS CANONIZATION.

Canonization of Saints. See SAINTS.

Canon Law, the body of rules for the discipline and governance of Christian churches, especially the Roman Catholic and Orthodox* churches and the Anglican Communion. It addressed at first only internal church matters, but later other concerns, including doctrine. Its sources of authority vary widely, with increasing emphasis in the West on the legislation of the papacy*.

In antiquity and the early Middle Ages, conciliar "canons" and papal "decretals" were assembled into chronological collections, most notably by Dionysius* Exiguus (in Latin, early 6th c.) and by the patriarch John Scholasticus of Constantinople (in Greek, c570). A Frankish compiler (Pseudo-Isidore) active at Corbie added a set of forged decretals (mid-9th c.) emphasizing papal power (see Decretals, False). More easy to use were systematically organized collections appearing in Western Europe (e.g. *Vetus Gallica,* c600; the *Decretum* of Burchard of Worms, c1020).

The papal reform movement of the High Middle Ages and the attendant struggle between church and state stimulated legislation and legal analysis (see Popes, Roman Catholic, and the Papacy). New sources of authority (e.g. patristic writings and secular law) became accepted. The Western Church consolidated its claims to regulate otherwise secular matters (e.g. marriage*, commerce, war*). Gratian* summarized previous legislation in the *Decretum* (final version c1150), which includes his own commentaries. Later jurists emphasized decretals; several collections were included together with the *Decretum* in the standard compilation of canon law (*Corpus Iuris Canonici*). Juristic commentaries on this collection (strongly influenced by the Roman law of Emperor Justinian*, 533–34) are prominent examples of legal thinking, developing key concepts such as natural rights, procedural rules, and international law. The *Corpus* was supplemented by the acts of later councils and judicial decisions of the papal curia. The mass of material becoming increasingly cumbersome, the pope promulgated the *Codex* Iuris Canonici* (*The Code of Canon Law,* 1918), using European 19th-c. civil codes as models. Unlike earlier canon law, it states the law in abstract formulations without any reference to specific cases. A completely rewritten *Codex* was published in 1983.

In the Orthodox Church, ecclesiastical law collections, notably the *Nomokanon* (last version c1090), also embraced secular law. There is no modern codification. The *Pedalion* (Rudder, 1793) is the most widely used collection.

The *Corpus Iuris Canonici* continues to be valid in the Anglican Communion insofar as it has been received. The *Corpus* has been modified by the Canons of 1604 and 1969.

ANDERS WINROTH

Canon of the Mass. See EUCHARISTIC PRAYER.

Cantata, vocal composition used in worship. Developed in Germany and perfected by Bach*, it includes sections for soloists and chorus.

Canticle, hymn taken from the Bible (but not a Psalm*) and used in worship.

Canticles, Book of. See SONG OF SONGS.

Capernaum, town on the northwest shore of the Sea of Galilee, a center of Jesus' activity (Mark 2:1, par.) and site of several miracles.

Cape Verde. In this archipelago off the coast of West Africa, a former Portuguese colony (see Portuguese Explorations, Conquests, and Missions), the Roman Catholic Church had a privileged position until 1975, when political independence progressively led to democracy and religious pluralism.

Christianity arrived in Cape Verde with Portuguese navigators (1446) and Franciscans in 1465/66. A Catholic diocese* was erected on the island of Santiago in 1533 and remained until 1705, when for two centuries Cape Verde became part of a West African diocese. Today, there are two dioceses in Cape Verde, in Santiago and Sanvicente islands. Nazarenes arrived in 1901 and Seventh-day Adventists in 1935.

After the independence (1975), a Communist government secularized* the state, aggressively taking away schools and social institutions from the churches, especially the Roman Catholic Church. Religious pluralism became a reality in 1990, when democracy was instituted through the resistance against Communism led by Fr. António Fidalgo Barros and supported by Bishop D. Paulino Évora (of Santiago), and later by Bishop D. Arlindo Furtado (of Sanvicente), an outstanding Catholic theologian. With religious freedom, some independent Charismatic* churches developed with the support of Brazilian and North American churches.

A Catholic theological seminary (established in 1866, in Sannicolau) gave priests and laypeople a good secondary education. Today a master in theology can be earned at Sanjosé Catholic Seminary in Praia, the capital of Cape Verde. A bachelor in theology can be earned at the Nazarenes' theological seminary in Sanvicente. As a result, half of the clergy are natives of the islands. In all denominations, the leadership is male dominated. Since 2003 a modern Catholic hospital in Fogo has been a center for diaconal and social work led by Franciscan sisters, including Sr. Bárbara, Sr. Antonieta, Sr. Teodora, and Sr. Teodolinda.

Statistics: Population (2000): 0.43 million (M); Christians, 0.42 M (Roman Catholics, 0.4 M; Protestants, 15,000; independents, 13,000). A small number of Muslim, Native Religionists, and nonreligious people. (Based on *World Christian Encyclopedia*, 2001.)

ANTÓNIO BARBOSA DA SILVA

Capital Punishment. See DEATH PENALTY.

Cappadocians, a group of influential personages in the late 4th c., all of whom came from the province of Cappadocia in central Asia Minor, many from the same family: Basil* of Caesarea (328/29–79); his brother Gregory* of Nyssa (330–94); a younger brother, Peter of Sebaste – all of whom became bishops; their sister, Macrina* (327–80), actually the firstborn and probably the first to adopt a monastic* lifestyle; and their brother Naucratius, who adopted the solitary life around 352. After Macrina's death, Gregory of Nyssa wrote a *Life* and a discourse *On the Soul and Resurrection* that was placed in her mouth.

Macrina and Basil had been influenced by Eustathius* of Sebaste (c300–c377), who became controversial because of his moderate Arian* views (he affirmed the Homoiousian* position at the Synod of Ancyra*, 358) and because of his ascetic* mode of life.

Another Capadocian was Gregory* Nazianzen (329?–389?), who was closely associated with Basil and Gregory. Evagrius* of Pontus (345–99), born in the same region, accompanied Gregory Nazianzen to Constantinople before adopting the ascetic life, first in Jerusalem and then in the Nitrian desert (one of the centers of Egyptian monasticism in the cliff separating the Nile from the desert).

When Basil became bishop of Caesarea (370), Emperor Valens was championing Arianism* in the Eastern Empire; Basil made every effort to fill vacant sees with bishops sympathetic to the Nicene* Creed, including the two Gregories, and all of them wrote against the extreme Arianism of Eunomius*. Basil was a skilled church politician. Gregory Nazianzen was successful as a preacher and a poet but generally a failure as an administrator. Gregory of Nyssa was the most skilled as a theologian and spiritual guide.

Basil and the two Gregories were most influential in shaping the doctrine of the Trinity*. While it is often assumed that their teachings were identical, Basil held to the older Homoiousian* view of the Trinity and resisted any declaration that the Holy Spirit is of the same essence as the Father and the Son. Gregory of Nyssa used the comparison of three individuals united by a common nature – language that veers toward tritheism*. Gregory Nazianzen shaped later doctrine in two important ways. He emphasized that full divinity is in each of the persons, originally in the Father, derivatively in the Son and the Spirit; and he put forward the

concept of relation as the key to the differences among the persons, since by definition a parent has an offspring and an offspring has a parent.
EUGENE TESELLE

Capuchins. See FRANCISCANS; RELIGIOUS ORDERS, ROMAN CATHOLIC, CLUSTER: IN WESTERN EUROPE

Cardijn, Jozef (1882–1967), founder and driving force of the Young* Christian Workers Movement, Roman Catholic priest (ordained, 1906), cardinal (1965). As curate in Laeken (Brussels), he founded separate groups for working young women and men, which eventually led to the formation of the Young Christian Workers (1924). This movement quickly became the most famous of the Specialized Catholic* Action groups and spread all over the world. Cardijn's ideas and actions have at least indirectly influenced Catholic Worker* priests and Liberation* theology. At the end of his life, he became a champion of international justice and developing cooperation. EMIEL LAMBERTS

Cardinals, originally the permanent clergy of Rome, including bishops, priests, and deacons; as a college, the pope's counselors. Now bishops anywhere in the world are appointed to these positions. Since 1059 a conclave* of cardinals has elected new popes.

Care of Souls, the role of priests and other ministers of a parish*, congregation, or chapel*; traditionally regarded as the chief activity of the clergy* and the chief reason for ordination*. **See also PASTORAL CARE.**

Caribbean Islands and the Clash of Theologies. Four types of theology clashed in the Caribbean Islands, although in most instances they were not the self-conscious theologies that students do in theology classes, but the theologies by which believers live and thus the theologies reflected in their ways of life. The Christian theology brought by Europeans wiped out the theologies of the Caribs and of the Arawaks (the first inhabitants of the Caribbean) by annihilating those who held them; yet for many Africans in the islands, both Christian and African theologies survived by blending together.

The Caribs, hunters who liked to fight, believed in a superior power that guided life. They referred to this power as *maboya* (spirit); embracing one's *maboya* was a means to counteract and ward off evil forces, but it could be used for evil or good. One's own *chemmen* (god) was more powerful than one's *maboya* and could be used to counter evil *maboya* in an elaborate ceremony led by a priest (*boyez*) who divined what herbs and practices were necessary. By contrast the more peaceful and gentle Arawaks (Taino) preferred negotiation to war. They believed in a supreme creator god, Yocaju or Jucaju, who shared his powers with his mother, a goddess in her own right, as well as in other deities – e.g. the gods of fire, rain, storms – who were to be feared.

With Christopher Columbus's arrival (1492), a European theology informed by economic and political agendas clashed with that of the Arawaks and later with that of the Caribs. The Arawaks welcomed the foreigners and were decimated by them. According to a Caribbean traditional story, a practice of the Spaniards was to kill 12 Arawaks per day in honor of the 12 apostles. The Caribs fought the Spaniards and lasted well into the 18th c.

The Africans who were brought to the Caribbean Islands (starting in the 16th c.) accepted the colonizers' Christian God yet blended the beliefs of their masters with beliefs from Africa. This is illustrated in Santeria (Cuba*; see Ancestor Veneration and Christianity Cluster: In Latin America and the Caribbean), Vodou* (Haiti*), Shango (Trinidad*), and other forms of African Christian theology that have survived. **See also CARIBBEAN ISLANDS AND WEST INDIES; CONTEXTUAL THEOLOGIES.**
NOEL LEO ERSKINE

Caribbean Islands and West Indies. This region includes Cuba*, Dominican* Republic, Haiti*, Antigua and Barbuda, Bahamas, Barbados, Belize, Dominica, Grenada, Guyana*, Jamaica*, St. Lucia, St. Kitts and Nevis, St. Vincent and the Grenadines, Surinam, Trinidad* and Tobago (independent), Aruba, Netherlands Antilles (including Curaçao, Bonaire, St. Maarten, St. Eustatius, and Saba; Dutch); Anguilla, Montserrat, British Virgin Islands, Cayman Islands, Turks and Caicos Islands (British); French Guyana*, Guadeloupe, Martinique*, St. Martin (French); and Puerto* Rico and Virgin Islands (USA). The total population is 36.7 million (in 2000) in an area of 732,126 square kilometers.

This region became the frontier of various empires, each of which gave it a different name: the Spanish called it the Indies; the British, the West Indies; the French, the Antilles; and the USA, the Caribbean. The sea was baptized the Caribbean Sea, named after the Caribs, one of the most important indigenous groups, together

Caribbean Islands and West Indies

with the Arawaks, Tainos, and Ciboney. After the arrival of the Spaniards (1492), the natives of the islands, especially prey to contagious diseases, disappeared as a result of oppressive colonialism. African slaves* were then imported to meet increased labor demand on sugar plantations. Between the early 16th c. and the abolition of slavery (last decades of the 19th c.), more than 9 million slaves from Africa were forced to populate the New World. It was this institution of slavery* that had the greatest impact on the development of the Caribbean.

Religious traditions in the Caribbean are varied. In some countries, the majority is Protestant, in others Roman Catholic (see Mission Cluster: Imperialism).

During the Spanish period of colonialism, the Catholic mission was closely linked to the civil power. Bishoprics were established in 1511–12 in Concepción de la Vega, Santo Domingo, and San Juan. These first three dioceses were suffragans of the Metropolitan See of Seville. This lasted till the province of Santo Domingo was established (1546), comprising the sees of Puerto Rico, Santiago in Cuba, Coro in Venezuela*, Santa Marta in Colombia*, and Trujillo in Honduras*. In 1515 Bartolomé de las* Casas joined the Dominican Friars, who worked out a new scheme for the reorganization of Hispaniola (Haiti* and the Dominican* Republic), based on a new method of evangelization, with separate indigenous communities and respect for their cultures. The plan failed, and there is no evidence anywhere in the region of a single pastoral activity whose precondition for evangelization was respect for the indigenous cultures. Many African slaves were integrated into the Catholic Church (starting in the 16th c.), but similarly there was no respect for their African cultures.

Protestant churches were established in English and Dutch colonies (17th c.), although it was not until the 19th c. that there was a massive conversion of the black population to these churches. The Anglican and Dutch Reformed churches, the earliest non-Catholic churches in the region, did not carry out missionary work among the slaves. In 1735 German Moravian* Brethren reached Surinam and began a mission to the black population, but without much success. In the 19th c., the ruling classes in many places considered un-Christianized slaves much more dangerous than those who professed this religion. Religious instruction then became a means of preparation for emancipation. During this period, most of the Afro-Antilleans in the British and the Dutch Caribbean were integrated into the Protestant churches, especially the Methodist, Baptist, and Moravian churches.

If Christians have become the most important religious group in the region, they are not the only one. When the slaves were incorporated into the Christian churches, they did not abandon their African beliefs. As the ruling classes considered it dangerous to give religious instruction to slaves, in the 17th–18th c. the religious domain was effectively left in the slaves' own hands. And the churches, deeply involved in the slave system, had no real interest in evangelizing the blacks. There is a long list of Catholic and Protestant missionaries who owned a large number of slaves in the region. All this explains the development of Afro-Antillean religiosity. This has evolved into numerous forms, such as Vodou* in Haiti, Santeria in Cuba, Shango in Trinidad, Obeahism in Jamaica, Brua in Curacao, and Winti in Surinam. Since the churches were hostile to African religious values, the slaves had no alternative but to make use of Christian symbols, especially of public Catholic symbols, in the service of the survival of their African soul. What is viewed either negatively as syncretism* or positively as inculturation*, according to one's perspective, became the order of the day, which drew on African as well as Western Christian sources (see Inculturation Cluster: Christianity and the Gospel; Popular Christian Practices Cluster: In Latin America: Native Traditions in Mexico).

A Jewish community established itself in Curaçao (mid-17th c.) and founded the earliest synagogue still in use in the Americas. Since then, Judaism* has had a presence in the region. Hinduism* and Islam* also became major religions in some countries of the area. After the abolition of slavery, in order to safeguard the plantation economy a massive wave of Asian immigrants, especially from India and Indonesia, was brought to the region (19th c.). Today their descendants make up between a third and half of the populations of Trinidad, Surinam, and Guyana. These Hindus and Muslims have retained their original religious observance. Hinduism, Islam, and Christianity constitute the three most important religions in this region and have a considerable impact on these societies. There is a general spirit of tolerance, as shown by the recognition of religious feast days of the different religions as national public holidays.

In the last decades of the 20th c., a veritable mosaic of new religious movements took shape in the Caribbean, some imported and some native. The imported ones that have spread throughout the region include Seventh*-day Adventists, Jehovah's* Witnesses, and Pentecostal* churches, all from the USA. The Charismatic* Movement has also successfully penetrated the mainstream churches since the 1970s, practicing healing* and trances as manifestations of the Holy* Spirit. Of the native movements, the best known is the Rastafari* Movement. There is still no structure for dialogue between those new religious movements and the historic churches. Nevertheless, the ecumenical movement is strong in the region. In 1973 the Caribbean Conference of Churches was founded, an ecumenical body representing 33 Christian churches in the region (in 1996), including the Catholic, Anglican, Moravian, Lutheran, Methodist, Baptist, Reformed, Ethiopian* Orthodox, Presbyterian, and a few Pentecostal churches, as well as the Salvation* Army, the Disciples* of Christ, and the Church of God. Another notable ecumenical achievement has been the establishment, by 11 Christian churches working together, of the United Theological College of the West Indies in Jamaica, which now trains leaders for all these churches.

In the continental area, indigenous communities survived, in contrast to the situation in the islands. Belize, in Central America, was formerly known as British Honduras, until it became independent (1981). The Maya, who had been living there before the arrival of the Europeans, now constitute 11% of the population. The Mopan Maya have preserved many religious traditions. The Yucatec Maya, refugees during the "Guerra de Castas" in Yucatán, Mexico (1846–48), adopted many Spanish traditions. The Kekchi Maya are refugees from Vera Paz, victims of the military repression in Guatemala until late 20th c., and have integrated Catholic rites in their own traditions. The Garífuna are a result of the encounter between Indoamerican Caribs and African slaves and came to Belize since 1802 and constitute nowadays 7% of the population. The practices of Catholicism co-exist with their own culture and religion based on African traditions.

The Guyana coast – today the countries of Guyana, Surinam, and French Guyana – had been the object of many colonization attempts by Dutch, English, and French settlers (16th–17th c.). Many settlements failed owing to the opposition of the indigenous population, the Caribs and the Arawaks, who named the region Guiana, "Land of Waters." Today what binds the Guyana coast together is the languages of the Amerindian population, Arawak and Carib, which are still spoken in this region. In Guyana, independent of England since 1966, 5% of the population is Amerindian; in Surinam, independent of the Netherlands since 1975, 2% of the population is Amerindian; and in French Guyana, an overseas department of France since 1946, the number of Amerindians is unknown because of the constant mobility in the Amazon. Catholicism and Pentecostalism are present among the Amerindians who kept their own religious traditions. In Surinam, the Maroons (or "Bosnegers"), formerly slaves who fled plantations and who now constitute 8% of the population, preserved their own languages (Aukaans and Sarammakkan) and forms of African* Religion.

Today the idea of interreligious dialogue is more alive but remains a challenge for the Caribbean. A structure for dialogue between non-Christian religions and Christian churches remains to be created for the region, although there are some local initiatives, such as the Interreligious Council in Surinam (founded in 1989). More voices cry out for a dialogue on the theological level between Afro-Caribbean religions and Christianity. **See also MISSION CLUSTER: IN CARIBBEAN ISLANDS.**

ARMANDO LAMPE

Caribbean Literature and Christianity. In the first European text documenting the Spanish presence in Hispaniola (Haiti* and the Dominican* Republic) and Cuba*, Columbus alludes to a Christian mission to Amerindians as important for the Catholic monarchs. A Dominican friar and defender of the Amerindians, Bartolomé de las* Casas, quotes from Columbus's *Diary* (1492) in his *History of the Indies* (1561). In *A Brief Account of the Destruction of the Indies* (1552), Las Casas narrates the lives of Taino leaders like Hatuey and Enriquillo, and their reasons for rebelling against the Spaniards and Christianity. Hatuey, who fled Hispaniola, was captured in Cuba; before being burned alive, he told his confessor that if Spaniards went to heaven, he did not want to be with them.

Enriquillo, raised by Franciscan monks, accepted Christianity, profited from a Spanish-style education, then, as a rebel, negotiated a truce with the royal court while remaining a faithful Christian. Manuel de Jesús Galván wrote *Enriquillo* (1879–82), rescuing the Taino figure and investing the Dominican* Republic's national hero with noble qualities and intelligence.

In Cuban literature, Silvestre de Balboa's *Espejo de paciencia* (1608) refers to the bishop of Cuba, Don Juan de las Cabezas Altamirano, who was kidnapped by the French corsair Gilberto Girón. In the slave-poet Juan Francisco Manzano's "Ode to Religion" (1831), the speaker asks the Almighty and the Christian religion to console this humble servant. In his *Autobiography* (1835), Manzano presents himself as a sacrificial lamb*. This and other anti-slavery narratives – e.g. Anselmo Suárez y Romero's *Francisco* (1839) – hail a docile slave who "turns the other cheek"; they manipulate white Creole readers to identify with black slaves and condemn white slave masters.

Christianity became important for other Cuban writers, such as José Lezama Lima, Cintio Vitier, Fina García Marruz, Eliseo Diego, Ángel Gaztelu, and other members of the Orígenes group. Lezama founded the journals *Verbum* (1937), *Espuela de plata* (1939), *Nadie parecía* (1942), and *Orígenes* (1944–56). He and other Catholic writers preferred the aesthetic to the political, a tradition they carried into the 1959 Cuban Revolution. A priest, Gaztelu poeticized Catholic symbols. In *Paradiso* (1966), Lezama masterfully mixed classical and Catholic imageries. The Castro government ostracized these religious writers but rehabilitated them after the breakup of the Soviet Union.

In Latino Caribbean literature, written in English in the USA, some writers underscored their parents' religious and cultural values. The Puerto Rican Jesús Colón (often associated with socialism) highlights Carmencita's devout Catholic practices in *A Puerto Rican in New York and Other Sketches* (1961), which he organized as a rosary* in number and structure emphases (David García). Nuyorican (New York Puerto Rican) poets prefer to focus on the evils of US society; e.g. Tato Laviera follows this tradition while composing poems with religious symbolism. His "jesús papote" presents this Christ figure as born to a drug addict on a wintry December evening.

Dominican Loida Maritza Pérez, in *Geographies of Home* (1999), shows the cultural, political, and religious continuity from the Dominican* Republic to the USA, regardless of geographic and linguistic differences. Her Seventh*-day Adventist father demands a discipline that seems archaic in the new environment, while the grandmother's African spiritual beliefs influence the course of the narration.

Alejo Carpentier's classic *The Kingdom of This World* (1949) focused on the role Vodou* played in the slave rebellion in Santo Domingo (like Santeria, Vodou is the coming together of Catholicism and its saints* and African* Religion and its gods, *Orishas*). Lydia Cabrera's *Cuentos negros* (1940) has a comparable emphasis, and *El monte* (1954) is considered the "Bible" of African Religion in Cuba. Cristina García's *Dreaming in Cuban* (1992) has similar interests; her *Agüero Sisters* (1997) uses as a novelistic frame a religious system that relies on the coming together of Christian and African religions.

WILLIAM LUIS

Carmelite Order, a Roman Catholic contemplative religious* order that originated on Mount Carmel (near present-day Haifa) among hermits who lived there long before the Latin patriarch of Jerusalem, Albert of Vercelli, drafted (c1207) their "Primitive Rule of Our Lady of Mount Carmel," which uniquely combined contemplation* and apostolic action. When it became difficult for the hermits to remain in the Holy Land, Pope Innocent IV granted the order mendicant* status (1247) and the Rule was mitigated for use in Western Europe. The tension between contemplation and action, desert and city, Discalced* (barefoot) and Calced (wearing shoes) endured throughout the history of the Carmelites, as exemplified by the lives of the canonized Carmelites: Simon Stock (c1165–1265), Teresa* of Ávila (1515–82), John* of the Cross (1542–91), Thérèse* of Lisieux (1873–97), and Edith Stein (1891–1942). PETER TYLER

Carol, a joyous song, originally with dance, sung by people during festivals, especially Christmas. Popular in the late Middle Ages, and again since the 19th c.

Caroline Books (*Libri Karolini*), a treatise written in Charlemagne's* court, probably by Theodulph of Orleans, in response to the Eastern controversies over icons*. Claiming to pursue the golden mean, it attacked both the iconoclasts* for forbidding icons and the iconodules for excessive veneration of them. The purpose seems to have been to discredit Empress Irene*, with whom, ironically, Charlemagne would propose a dynastic marriage in 802. **See also ICONOCLASM AND THE ICONOCLASTIC CONTROVERSY.**

Carolingian Renaissance. At his capital of Aachen, Charlemagne* (c747–814) imitated many features of Byzantium*. The palace school, led by Alcuin* of York, salvaged much of ancient learning. Charlemagne acquired manuscripts from Rome, including early copies of the Rule of

Benedict*, the sacramentary*, and the authoritative collection of canon* law. From this time comes the style of writing known as "Carolingian minuscule" ("lowercase" letters, also developed for Greek during that period). The educational tradition begun in Aachen spread to Orleans, Reims, Fulda, and elsewhere in France and Germany.

In some respects, Charlemagne was the creator of Christian Europe, requiring every parish to provide basic education for its parishioners and to keep records of baptisms, marriages, and funerals (replaced by the "civil registry" by Napoleon).

Charlemagne's own time was a period of revival and reform, recovering and consolidating the classical and Christian past. The actual "renaissance" occurred under his son Louis* the Pious (educated by clerics) through reforming councils (816–17) that affirmed the freedom of the church from lay control and imposed the Benedictine* Rule on monastic life, and later through the disputes over the Eucharist* (after 830), grace* and free will* (after 850), and the theological speculations of John* Scotus Eriugena. **See also LITURGIES, HISTORY OF.**

EUGENE TESELLE

Carroll, John (1736–1815), founding father of Roman Catholicism in the USA. After being educated by Jesuits* in Europe, he joined them (1748–55). Ordained a priest (1761), he returned to the USA after a papal decree suppressed the Jesuits (1773). Supporting the movement for US independence, he took the lead in organizing Catholicism in the new nation. As (arch)bishop of Baltimore, he presided over the growth of the church from 1789 to 1815. Widely respected by Catholics and non-Catholics alike, Carroll combined loyalty to the church with acceptance of religious liberty and republican institutions, setting precedents that shaped the adjustment of Catholicism to US society and culture. PHILIP GLEASON

Carta Caritatis (Lat "Charter of Charity"), 12th-c. constitution of the Cistercian* order. The Charter stipulates that the Rule of Benedict* is to be followed in all Cistercian monasteries and establishes uniform liturgy, books, and observance together with a system of visitation for their regulation and an annual meeting, or general chapter, of all abbots at Cîteaux. It probably dates from 1165, and not, as previously thought, 1119. Rather than envisioning the spontaneous generation of a federation of new "daughter" houses from older foundations, it was designed to increase the authority of Cîteaux.

MARILYN DUNN

Carthusian Order, Catholic religious* order founded by Bruno (c1030–1101) at La Grande Chartreuse, Diocese of Grenoble, France, in 1084. Part of the 11th- and 12th-c. attempts to restore the original desert ethos of monastic* life, it combined eremitic* cells with communal elements: church, refectory, and chapter room. Thus in the distinctive Carthusian monastery plan, individual cells – actually small houses – are spaced around an extensive cloister. Monks lead a strictly enclosed life and spend much of their time in individual prayer, meditation, and study in the cell, where they also take most of their meals, meeting in church for liturgical worship at set intervals. Lay brothers* care for their material needs. The first statutes, rules for the governance of the growing order, were set down by Guigues, fifth prior of the Grande Chartreuse, in 1127.

The first Carthusian nunnery was established at Prebayon in Provence in the 12th c. The order has remained remarkably faithful to its original contemplative* ideas and is sometimes thought of as the highest and strictest form of Catholic monasticism. Today there are 19 Carthusian monasteries and 6 nunneries, mainly in Europe and the Americas. MARILYN DUNN

Cassian, John (c360–c435), monk, spiritual writer who helped introduce Egyptian monasticism* to the Latin West. Born perhaps in Scythia, Cassian became a monk in Bethlehem and moved to Egypt in 385, settling in Scetis. He went to Constantinople (c400), where John* Chrysostom ordained him deacon*. Around 415, he settled in Massilia (ancient Marseilles), where he founded two monasteries. His major work, the 900-page *Conferences,* claims to record 24 conversations with leading Egyptian masters, each focused on a core theme (e.g. discernment, prayer*, chastity*). Benedict's* Rule required the reading of Cassian in the monasteries of medieval Europe. J. WILLIAM HARMLESS, SJ

Cassock, the ankle-length garment that evolved from a late Roman robe and came to be required of the clergy, especially after the Council of Trent*.

Caste System and Christianity. In India the caste (Sanskrit *varna*) system rationalizes social stratification. Human identity is construed as hereditary and hierarchical, conflated with specific social, economic, and religious rights and duties. The caste community includes four castes: *brahmins* (priests), *ksatriyas* (rulers and warriors), *vaisyas* (business persons), and *sudras* (laborers). An economic and ritual divide separates the first three castes ("the twice-born") from the laborers' caste. "Outcastes" or "untouchables" comprise the 15–20% of Indians who are outside the Hindu caste system, being viewed as subhuman or nonhuman. They renamed themselves "Dalits*" (broken or crushed ones). In addition, Adivasis* ("original dwellers of the land") are never integrated into society (and its caste system). The Indian Christian community consists predominantly of Dalits and Adivasis.

SATHIANATHAN CLARKE

Caste System and Christianity in Latin America. See FEUDAL SYSTEM.

Casuistry, mode of ethical reasoning that resolves "cases of conscience" by applying general rules or considerations to difficult instances, especially when there are conflicting obligations or special circumstances. The term is used negatively to claim that difficult cases are being resolved in an evasive or hairsplitting way (a classic example is Pascal's* *Provincial Letters* attacking the Jesuits). Those who emphasize individual conscience* often scorn casuistic reasoning as misleading or superfluous.

Catacombs, underground burial chambers located outside the walls of Rome, since custom and law prohibited burial within the city. They were used for Christian burial starting in c200; they contain the earliest Christian art.

Cataphatic Theology speaks of God positively, in terms of who God is, according to revelation in Scripture, tradition, affective religious experience, and/or nature. It is the opposite of apophatic,* or negative*, theology.

Catechesis, Catechisms, Catechumens. In Greek, *catechesis* means "instruction." Catechumens are those being instructed. In the early church this instruction preceded baptism*, sometimes over a three-year period. The catechumens attended Sunday worship but were dismissed before the celebration of the Eucharist*. The Apostles' Creed* was taught to the catechumens only at the last stage of catechesis, during the 40 days of Lent* leading up to their baptism at the Easter* vigil* service. Several 4th-c. examples of catechetical instruction survive (from Cyril* of Jerusalem, Ambrose* of Milan, Augustine*, and Theodore* of Mopsuestia).

After the baptism of infants became the norm, catechesis was directed toward children and youth. Three traditional texts became the basis of instruction: the Apostles'* Creed, the Lord's* Prayer, and the Decalogue*; at baptism the godparents promised to teach these to the child, and they had to be memorized before confirmation*. Other kinds of instruction for the Christian life were added during the Middle Ages; the 1281 Council of Lambeth* directed priests to give instruction at least four times a year concerning the Apostles' Creed, the Decalogue, the two love commandments, the seven works of mercy, the seven deadly* sins, the seven virtues*, and the seven sacraments*. A *Lay Folks' Catechism* was prepared under John Thoresby, archbishop of York, in 1357 for the use of priests. In the 15th c., Jean Gerson's* *ABC des simples gens* was widely used.

Luther's *Larger Catechism* and *Smaller Catechism* (1529) inaugurated the use of printed question-and-answer catechism, following earlier models among the Waldenses* and Bohemians*. The genre was widely imitated in other churches of the Reformation, always using the three classic texts; the most widely used were the Geneva, Heidelberg, and Westminster catechisms. In the Catholic Church, catechisms also included instruction on the sacraments*, the virtues* and vices, and acts of popular devotion; especially influential catechisms were those of Peter Canisius* (1556, 1566) and Robert Bellarmine* (1598) and the Roman Catechism authorized by the Council of Trent* (1566).

Luther's catechisms were published with woodcuts, and the use of pictures to aid instruction became widespread in Europe and in missions throughout the world. Catechisms in Nahuatl and other languages were published in Mexico in the 16th c., and the Jesuits in Japan, China, and Vietnam prepared catechisms for these cultural settings.

Because of their origin in doctrinal statements, catechisms were sometimes criticized as being too technical; efforts were made, therefore, to base instruction on the biblical narrative rather than doctrines. The question-and-answer form has gradually been replaced by narrative or exposition.

The Second Vatican* Council decided against any universal catechism in favor of contextual* catechisms directed toward adults. The Dutch* Catechism of 1966, in preparation even before Vatican II, was criticized for being too daring, and a supplement was added to the second edition. Other catechisms were prepared in

Germany, Spain, Belgium, and France. The Catechism of the Catholic Church (1992) was prepared under Pope John Paul II, not to replace the national catechisms but to supply a "point of reference" for them. EUGENE TESELLE

Catechist (Gk "instructor"), someone who prepares candidates for baptism*; more generally, a teacher of Christian doctrine; in mission areas, an indigenous teacher.

Cathars, Catharism, a medieval dualist Christian movement that imported into Western Europe beliefs of the Balkan Bogomils*. By c1200 the Cathars had established five dioceses in Southern France (Languedoc), one in Northern France, and six in Northern Italy (with much doctrinal and organizational dispute), each diocese with its bishop, his assistants, and deacons.

Catharism asserted belief in two coeternal cosmological forces, one good (the NT loving God) and one evil (the Demiurge, the OT vengeful creator god). For the Cathars, including those with a more moderate dualism (the evil creator god simply fell from the good God's favor), all physical matter was corrupt. Consequently, Cathars did not believe in the Incarnation, although Christ had been sent by the good God to lead humankind to salvation.

The Cathars limited Scripture to the NT, often interpreted allegorically*; prayed only one prayer, the Lord's Prayer; and utterly rejected the authority of the Roman Catholic Church and the symbol of the cross.

The initiated Cathars, the "perfect" (called "good Christians" or simply "Christians"), lived a life of extreme asceticism* in order to escape at death the material realm and attain the realm of goodness. They renounced personal property* and sexual* intercourse; did not eat meat (except for fish) or dairy products, the products of coition; fasted three days a week; underwent 40-day fasts on bread and water; and were forbidden to use violence or to swear oaths. (Ordinary believers and other Christians would be reborn into an endless cycle in which their souls transmigrated into new animal or human bodies.) After training, new Cathars were initiated through a ritual, the *consolamentum,* involving the laying on of hands. But this ritual was valid only if the perfect administering it had led the pure life. Any intentional or nonintentional lapse into impure practice by the perfect rendered this ceremony invalid, and the ritual and process of self-denial had to begin again. Discovery of a lapse (even after the death of the perfect) had serious implications for the hierarchy of the Cathar Movement (e.g. the authority of Western bishops ordained by lapsed Bogomil leaders was contested).

In 1209, following the murder of the papal legate Peter of Castelnau, who preached several unsuccessful missions in the Languedoc, Pope Innocent III sanctioned the Albigensian Crusade against the Cathars. By 1229 the crusade had replaced the most important lords who had tolerated the Cathars in the region with "Catholic" northern French. Yet it was only in early 14th c. that Catharism was eliminated from the Languedoc by the medieval Inquisition*.

CLAIRE TAYLOR

Cathedra (Gk "chair"), the bishop's seat. It was customary for the Greek teacher or Jewish rabbi to sit while teaching (e.g. Jesus sat to interpret Scripture in the synagogue; Luke 4:20). In the early church, the cathedra was in the center of the apse; with the divided chancel in the Middle Ages, it was moved to the side.

Cathedral, a church with the cathedra* of the bishop, usually the most impressive edifice in a diocese. **See also HIEROTOPY, THE CREATION OF CHRISTIAN SACRED SPACES.**

Catherine of Siena (1347–80), canonized in 1461; Dominican* tertiary and visionary. Born a dyer's daughter in Siena, from an early age Catherine Benincasa practiced extreme fasting* and penance*, and entered the Sisters of Penance of St. Dominic at the age of 16. From her convent, she came to have an extraordinary influence at the time of the Great* Schism after the death of Pope Gregory XI. She had visited the last French pope at Avignon, where he was in exile, trying to persuade him to make peace with the people of Florence and return to Rome. On his death, she sided with Urban VI and drummed up support for him from dissenting cardinals and bishops in the subsequent conflict.

Chiefly remembered for her writings and political interventions, she was the author of numerous letters and a mystical text known as *Dialogues*. Here she writes in the third person, using powerful imagery to describe her sense of union with God: her soul is in God and God is in her soul as "a fish is in the sea and the sea is in a fish." She was declared a doctor of the church by Paul VI in 1970. LAVINIA BYRNE

Catholic Action, a pastoral strategy to organize the laity* for the defense of the Roman Catholic Church (early 20th c.), which developed into a movement with a strong influence in society and political life (later in the 20th c.). Popes called on Catholics, both men and women, of all social classes and age groups to participate in the apostolic task. For the first time, women were incorporated into the apostolic mission of the Church. Members received a mandate from the bishops and were organized at the parochial, diocese, national, continental, and international levels with strong ties with Rome. Leo* XIII organized the Social Catholic Action. It was developed by Pius* XI and named Catholic Action. The Specialized Catholic Action gathered youth in different social environments: as workers, students, and independent professionals. It attempted to engage the Church in a dialogue with modernity and prepared the way for Vatican* II. Pope John* Paul II did not affirm the important role of the Catholic Action, but it never disappeared. ANA MARÍA BIDEGAIN

Catholic Action and Latin America. The development of Catholic Action can be illustrated by concrete examples from Latin America.

1. From Social Catholic Action to Catholic Action: Early 20th Century. Pope Leo* XIII (1878–1903) was convinced that the Roman Catholic Church needed to organize the Catholic masses to press governments in the Church's favor, particularly to fight new social movements, such as anarchism, socialism, and Freemasonry* (*Custodi di quella fede*, 1892). He supported the creation of Catholic parties inspired by the social teaching of the Church and related to the action of Catholics in several fields (see Social Encyclicals).

Following Leo XIII (encyclical *Rerum Novarum*), Pius* X (1903–14), in the encyclical *Il Fermo Proposito* (1905), defined the object to which Catholic Action should be particularly devoted, "the practical solution of the social question according to Christian principles." He proposed the organization of Popular Christian Action (embracing the whole Catholic social movement under the strict control of the clergy), the Civic Union (to influence the political arena), and the Economic Union (including Catholic working unions and credit unions, under the clergy's control).

In agreement with these orientations, several organizations were developed in Latin American countries (especially Colombia*, Brazil*, Argentina*, Mexico*, Chile*) under the banner of Acción Social Católica. Usually these organizations were tied to right-wing political parties that confronted the liberal states and liberal political parties. In many cases, they were backed by the nuncios* rather than local bishops. They mobilized members of the elite in social assistance programs, seeking thereby to avoid a loss of church influence among the rural and urban working classes while confronting anarchist and socialist movements.

2. Catholic Action under Pius XI (1922–39). In his first encyclical, *Ubi Arcano Dei* (1922), Pius* XI defined Catholic Action as a mandate by the bishops calling laymen and laywomen to be part of the apostolic mission of the Church. Pius XII continued supporting this innovative perspective that enabled laypeople to participate in the Church's mission, for which only the hierarchy (the bishops and priests) were previously expected to be responsible. Catholic Action movements were regarded as the arms of the hierarchy in the world, with a "mandate" to engage in their mission.

In 1930 Pius XI wrote several pastoral letters to Latin American bishops strongly recommending that they organize Catholic Action in their dioceses, proposing the Italian experience as an organizational model with four branches: women, men, young women, and young men. The social work of the General Catholic Action (Acción Católica General), along with that of religious congregations, was a critical factor in the reestablishment of church and state relations in many countries in Latin America, facilitating modernization while reformist and populist governments were in power.

Meanwhile, in Latin America as elsewhere, Specialized Catholic Action movements were given the responsibility of conducting a "like toward like" apostolate, e.g. workers evangelizing workers, and students evangelizing students, all in "deep communion" with the hierarchy.

3. The papacies of Pius* XII, John* XXIII, and Paul* VI (1939–78). During this period, Specialized Catholic Action in Latin America followed the French and Belgian models, but also drew heavily on experiences in the USA and Canada*, preparing the way for Vatican* II by attempting to engage the Catholic Church in a dialogue with modernity based on the acceptance of new realities. Specialized Catholic Action was also the cradle of Liberation* theology, renewing pedagogy as liberation pedagogy (see Educational Practices as Christian Service Cluster: In Mexico). At the second Latin American Episcopal Conference in Medellín* (1968), the Base* Ecclesial Communities adopted the methodology and small-community organizational structures that Specialized Catholic Action had developed.

This inclusive approach, so important for the Roman Catholic Church and influential even in other Christian denominations, was abandoned as a more conservative church leadership arose under Pope John* Paul II (1970–2005). In Latin America, under the military dictatorships of the 1970s and 1980s, members of Catholic Action were politically persecuted. Many activists experienced exile, imprisonment, torture, and even death. Without ecclesiastic support, the movement virtually disappeared. **See also CARDIJN, JOZEF; CATHOLIC APOSTOLIC CHURCH; CATHOLIC WORKER MOVEMENT; YOUNG CHRISTIAN WORKERS (JOCISTS).** ANA MARÍA BIDEGAIN

Catholic Apostolic Church, a proto-Pentecostal* and Premillennialist Christian community in Great Britain (early 1830s), whose followers were often called "Irvingites" because of the early involvement of the Scottish Presbyterian cleric Edward Irving. The Catholic Apostolic Church was led by 12 men who regarded themselves as the restored apostolate. Organized in some 1,000 congregations around the world, the group gradually discontinued its activities after the death of the last apostle (1901).

Ecclesiologically, the Catholic Apostolic Church combined elements from Anglican and Scottish Presbyterian, Tractarian*, Eastern Orthodox, and Roman Catholic traditions. Its Premillennialist eschatology included the doctrine of the rapture*. Many of its doctrines had their origins in the prophetic utterances of women congregants, but leadership positions were strictly kept in male hands. Although theological innovators, leaders of the Church were politically active in the British Conservative Party, where they worked against what they viewed as end-time corruptions in church and society, including ecumenism*, Liberal* theology, woman suffrage, secular liberalism and communism, political Islam, and the Zionist Movement.

Although grounded in Victorian Western culture, aspects of the Catholic Apostolic Church's witness proved globally appealing. The New Apostolic Church and movement members who joined Anglican, Lutheran, and Pentecostal faith communities around the world prolonged the Church's witness after 1901. **See also MILLENNIALIM CLUSTER: MILLENNIALISM.** MARKKU RUOTSILA

Catholic Epistles, designation for seven NT documents: James*, 1 and 2 Peter*, 1, 2, and 3 John*, and Jude*. "Catholic" was used beginning in the 2nd c. to designate writings addressed to the universal church, rather than to a specific church. Eusebius* (4th c.; *Hist. Eccl.* 2.23.24–25) used this term for these seven documents to underscore that, despite questions about their authenticity, they were used "in most churches."

Catholicity of the Church. The word "catholic" (from Gk *catholicos*, "universal," and *catholou*, referring to "wholeness and integrity") has been and is understood in different ways. Ignatius* of Antioch might have been the first to use it (c100). It was commonly used in the earliest statements of the faith (2nd c.) developed from the three questions asked of catechumens* before baptism* (cf. Apostolic* Tradition, c215, probably by Hippolytus* of Rome), then affirmed in the Apostles'* Creed (first formulated in the 2nd c.) and the Nicene* Creed from the Councils of Nicaea* (325) and Constantinople* (381). The term "catholic" was also used to differentiate the "true" church from sects* and heresies*, which were excluded by the actions of councils.

At first "catholic" simply distinguished the Christian Church at large from local churches, while referring to the wholeness and integrity of the Church ("Where Jesus Christ is, there is the catholic Church," wrote Ignatius to the Smyrnaens). Cyril* of Jerusalem, in his *Catechetical Lectures* (c350), underscored the "geographical," doctrinal, and praxis meanings of "catholic": "And the Church is called 'catholic' for being in the entire world from one end of the earth to the other and for teaching wholly (*catholicos*) and lacking nothing doctrinal . . . for completely (*catholicos*) taking care of and healing every sort of sin . . . and for being of possession of . . . every spiritual gift." Cyril suggested that "catholic" should be contrasted with "heretical*." This remains the view of "catholicity" held by Eastern Orthodox Churches.

Augustine*, in his controversy with Donatism*, affirmed that what has been "universally" taught or practiced is true. Vincent* of Lerins further specified that "catholic" is "what has been believed everywhere, always, and by all" (*Commonitorium*, early 4th c.): "What all have at all times and everywhere believed must be regarded as true."

Confusion in the use of the term "catholic" was inevitable. By calling itself the Catholic

Church (and later the Roman Catholic Church), the Western Church claimed the term for itself, rejecting as heretical or schismatic Christian churches outside it. In the process, a certain ecclesiastical structure (see Church, Concepts and Life, Cluster: Types of Ecclesiastical Structures) was affirmed as a mark of "catholicity" to the exclusion of others.

But other churches, including the Arian* Church, the Eastern Orthodox Church, the Anglican Church, several national churches, and most Protestant churches, often claimed to be members of the holy catholic church, while affirming their own ecclesiastical structures and specific doctrines and practices (in the spirit of Cyril's definition). **See also MARKS OF THE CHURCH, NOTES OF THE CHURCH.**

DANIEL PATTE

Catholic Orders. See RELIGIOUS ORDERS, ROMAN CATHOLIC, CLUSTER.

Catholicos, title for patriarchs of national churches outside the Byzantine Empire (Armenian*, Georgian*, Church* of the East) denoting their independence. **See also AUTOCEPHALOUS CHURCHES.**

Catholic Renewal, the set of developments in the Roman Catholic world after the Protestant Reformation*. This concept transcends the traditional debate over the use of the term "Counter Reformation" or "Catholic Reform" to characterize the history of the Catholic Church between Luther* and Voltaire*. Catholic scholars have objected to the negative connotation of "Counter Reformation," although it is a widely used term. Many elements of reform, e.g. the 15th-c. reforms within religious* orders, predated the Protestant Reformation. The term "Catholic Reform" neglects the anti-Protestant aspects of early modern Catholicism, including the harsher censorship of books, the prohibition of the Bible in the vernacular, and the increased authority of the Holy* Office. The concept of "Catholic Renewal" incorporates both the repressive, anti-Protestant measures of the Tridentine Roman Catholic Church (see Trent, Council of) and those developments independent of the Protestant schism, including the establishment of new religious foundations, e.g. the Society of Jesus (Jesuits*), a new wave of sanctity in 16th-c. Italy, and the expansion of Catholic missions to Asia, Africa, and the Americas in the wake of the Iberian voyages of discovery and settlement (see Portuguese Explorations, Conquests, and Missions; Spanish Explorations, Conquests, and Missions). The "Catholic Renewal" also includes the process by which the Tridentine decrees were implemented, with various degrees of success in different parts of the Catholic world, through the centralization of authority and liturgy in Rome, which would profoundly mark modern Catholicism. The reaffirmation of papal supremacy (see Popes, Roman Catholic, and the Papacy), tighter central control of canonization*, the reduction of local liturgies* to Roman usages, and the doctrinal control exercised by the congregations* in the papacy came to define the nature of Catholicism until the 20th c.

RONNIE PO-CHIA HSIA

Catholic Thought. See ROMAN CATHOLICISM CLUSTER: THE ROMAN CATHOLIC CHURCH AND ITS THEOLOGY.

Catholic Worker Movement, founded in 1933 by Dorothy Day* at the urging of Peter Maurin. It is best known for its houses of hospitality*, usually located in rundown urban areas. Food, clothing, shelter, and welcome are extended by unpaid volunteers to those in need. In 2006 there were 185 Catholic Worker communities, all but 3 in the USA. "Our rule is the works of mercy," said Day. "It is the way of sacrifice, worship, a sense of reverence."

The *Catholic Worker* is also the name of a newspaper. From 1933 until her death in 1980, Dorothy Day, a journalist, was the editor.

In addition to hospitality, Catholic Worker communities are known for their activity in support of labor unions, human rights, cooperatives, and the development of a nonviolent culture. During periods of military conscription, many Catholic Workers have been conscientious* objectors. Catholic Workers have often been jailed for acts of protest against social injustice and war*. With its stress on voluntary poverty*, the Catholic Worker Movement has much in common with the early Franciscans*, while its accent on community, prayer, and hospitality has Benedictine* overtones. Each Catholic Worker community is autonomous. Since Dorothy Day's death, there has been no central leader.

JIM FOREST

CEBs, Comunidades Eclesiales de Base (Base Ecclesial Communities). See CHURCH, CONCEPTS AND LIFE, CLUSTER: IN LATIN AMERICA: BRAZIL: BASE ECCLESIAL COMMUNITIES (CEBs);CHURCH, CONCEPTS AND LIFE, CLUSTER: IN LATIN AMERICA: ECUADOR: BASE ECCLESIAL COMMUNITIES (CEBs).

CELAM (Consejo Episcopal Latinoamericano, Latin American Episcopal Conference), an organization of the Roman Catholic Latin American and Caribbean bishops that provides pastoral support and coordinates efforts to address the challenges Latin America faces. Created in 1955 during the Eucharistic* Congress in Rio de Janeiro, Brazil, CELAM (with headquarters in Bogotá, Colombia) provides training services, research, and reflection for the 22 National Episcopal Conferences to aid them in their efforts to oversee pastoral and religious development in dire socioeconomic and political situations. CELAM's General Conferences determined the direction of Catholicism on the continent. In Rio (1955), CELAM initiated episcopal coordination. In Medellín (Colombia, 1968) CELAM offered celebrated prophetic reflections on Latin American realities, including the concept of institutionalized injustice, and officially supported "Base* Ecclesial Communities." In Puebla (Mexico*, 1979), CELAM formalized the "preferential option for the poor," despite its conservative reorientation. In Santo Domingo (Dominican* Republic, 1992), CELAM celebrated 50 years of Latin American evangelization and focused on internal issues regarding control over ecclesial life. In Aparecida (Brazil, 2007), CELAM sought to revive the reception of the Second Vatican* Council in Latin America.
ANA MARÍA BIDEGAIN

Celestine V, Pope (1294), first a Benedictine, then a hermit in the Abruzzi with many followers. Elected pope at the age of 80, after a disastrous five-month pontificate he abdicated and was replaced by Boniface* VIII, who imprisoned him. The Spiritual* Franciscans had placed great hope in him, and Dante* puts him at the edges of hell as the one who made "the great refusal."

Celibacy (Lat for "single" or "unmarried"). In both philosophical and religious circles, the term also came to connote wholeness, a life uncomplicated by family concerns. The single life is preferred to the married life, as Jesus (Matt 19:12, Luke 20:35–36) Paul (1 Cor 7:7–8, 35–35, 38), and Revelation (14:4) teach. With their ascetic traditions, the Syriac* Church and the Assyrian* Church (in Mesopotamia), perhaps as late as the 4th c., considered only celibates to be true Christians worthy of baptism*.

Celibacy was a feature of the monastic* movement from its beginning and was one of its vows*. The Eastern Church permitted priests to be married but required that bishops be single. The Western Church, starting in the 4th c., required married clergy to abstain from sexual relations after ordination; there was steady pressure to require that all priests be celibate. During the Gregorian* Reform, clerical marriage was condemned as Nicolaitism*; this position, along with the condemnation of simony*, was based in large part on a desire to make the Roman Catholic Church independent of family ties and the feudal* system. A definitive prohibition of clerical marriage was enacted by the Second Lateran* Council in 1139.

The Reformation, convinced from experience that vows and requirements of celibacy were unfeasible, condemned them as merely human commands, encouraging hypocrisy, works-righteousness, and a spirit of elitism toward other Christians. Acknowledging the NT's preferential option for celibacy, they called it a *gift* (cf. Matt 19:12; 1 Cor 7:7), which may be taken away and thus is to be observed only as long as one has that gift. EUGENE TESELLE

Celsus (2nd c.) authored the earliest surviving attack on Christianity, the *True Discourse* (c180), known from Origen's refutation, *Against Celsus* (248). Celsus probably wrote in response to Justin* Martyr. He praises the Logos* doctrine and Christian morals but finds many absurdities in the Bible, objects to the exclusive claims of Christianity, criticizes the notion of incarnation*, and depicts Christianity as endangering the Roman Empire.

Celtic Christianity, Its Practices and Theology. The search for a "Celtic Christianity," with a desire to import its values and practices into Christian life and liturgy, is a notable trait of contemporary English-speaking spirituality*. The ill-defined past of "the Celtic Christians" (invariably identified simply as the victims of the "Roman party" at a mythically enlarged Synod of Whitby, 664) is perceived to offer forms of church life that, compared with traditional Western churches, are less authoritarian, are sensitive to nature and its rhythms, are less rationalist, and are more sensitive to creativity and women's insights. For others it offers a pre-Reformation unity that can legitimate and make acceptable practices, such as pilgrimage*, that otherwise would be rejected as "High Church" or "too Roman."

In stark contrast to this enthusiasm is the reaction of historians to these claims: (1) "Celtic" is a linguistic rather than a social category (referring to a language spoken in most of Western Europe in Roman time). (2) The theology of Celtic churches in Northwestern Europe is not different from that of churches bordering them, or differences are similar to those that exist (e.g. on issues relating to the calendar) across the Latin West during the Middle Ages. (3) The linguistic basis of Celtic churches was Latin, and they saw themselves, albeit in the looser manner of the time, as being linked with Rome (it was the pope who was prayed for at every Eucharist). (4) They interacted with the other Western churches in Spain, France, and Italy as within a unity. (5) Their sensitivity to nature and its rhythms is little more than what can be found in any rural, preindustrial society. However, there are three distinctive features of Celtic churches.

Sin and Forgiveness. The practice that allowed for the repeated reconciliation for sins* after baptism developed through a combination of a secular concept of using fines as reparations, rather than punishments, for crimes and the monastic notion of continual "lifestyle conversion." This "penitential" practice stands behind later auricular confession and indulgences (see Penance and Forgiveness).

Asceticism. In a nonurban society, monasteries played a more significant role in church life than elsewhere. This meant that a monastic ideal of holiness and asceticism* became dominant earlier than elsewhere in the West.

Inclusiveness. Many churches emerged within a culture of clear opposition between "Christian" and "pagan"; by contrast, Christianity arrived in Northwestern Europe as a confident culture willing to view existing practices as part of the Spirit-guided "preparation for the gospel"; upon its arrival, Christianity could purify, restore to their "true" meaning, and build on existing practices. What later writers often designated "pagan survivals" were often consciously incorporated into Christian practice (e.g. a well was rededicated to a saint) with Acts 17:16–34 as model (see Inculturation Cluster).

Often critics present "Celtic Christianity" as a fraud. Yet this view ignores the fact that Christians continually recycle parts of their past for their present needs. However, the problem of often random selection of cultural bits is at times indicative of poor theological reflection. For example, a group might wish to celebrate the Irish festival of Samhain (Halloween) on the false assumption that it can be historically isolated from a Christian cult of the dead or that it can be exclusively related to All* Saints' Day (November 1) rather than to All* Souls' Day (thus ignoring the fact that those earlier Christians prayed for the dead and believed in a purgatorial state). Yet excluding All Souls' Day fails to acknowledge both the complexity of earlier ecclesiologies and the emphasis in the festival of Samhain on graves, grave markers (many of which survive), pilgrimage, and relics.

The desires underlying the present-day quest for "Celtic Christianity" may point out certain systemic failings of churches to address felt needs. It is often through remembering what is most uncomfortable that Christians can best critique their unwitting assumptions about their religious culture. THOMAS O'LOUGHLIN

Cemetery (from Gk "sleeping place"), a term originally used only by Christians to designate a place for burial awaiting the general resurrection.

Cenobitic Monasticism, a communal form of monastic life (from the Gk *koinos*, "common") characterized by a clear set of obligations for all members, a superior who provides both spiritual and temporal guidance, and procedures for entry to the community and admission to full membership. **See also MONASTICISM CLUSTER: MONASTICISM.**

COLUMBA STEWART, OSB

Central African Republic. Named the territory of Ubangui-Shari (1894) by Savorgna de Brazza, this landlocked country became independent in 1960 (capital Bangui) with David Dacko as president.

The population includes an amalgamation of ethnic groups that immigrated in the 19th c. to escape Fulani armies and Arab slave* traders. Besides French (official language) and Sango (national language), 67 other African languages are spoken, notably Gbaya, Banda, and Bakoko.

Christianity was introduced by the Catholic Holy Ghost Fathers (1886). By 1894 a mission station was established at Bangui, and Fr. Augouard was nominated its bishop. However, owing to the ruthless exploitation of local people by French companies, Christianity was underdeveloped. This situation radically changed when in the 1920s the American Baptists* and Brethren*, together with four other Protestant missionary societies, redirected their evangelization efforts toward the "poor ones of YHWH" in the Central African Republic. As a result of this joint enterprise, the Central African Republic became the only Francophone country with 60% of Christians as Protestants. A common formula was found for the work among youth, including literature in

French and Sango. The Charismatic* renewal spread rapidly in the 1990s; African* Instituted Churches (including Kimbanguists* from the Democratic Republic of Congo*) also developed.

Beginning in 1938, the Catholic Church's presence was consolidated by the arrival of French and Italian Capuchins*. The Church's well-organized education* system attracted many Christian and Muslim students alike. Bangui was made an archiepiscopal see in 1955, but the first native archbishop, Joachim N'Dayen, was not appointed until 1970.

Sociopolitical life in the Central African Republic has been substantially influenced by churches. Barthélémy Boganda (1910–59), a gifted priest, was suspended after he founded the country's influential party, Mouvement pour l'Évolution Sociale de l'Afrique Noire, in opposition to French colonialism. He is still venerated as the "the father of the nation." In 1966 Jean Bédel Bokassa (a failed monk), then a colonel, seized power from his cousin Dacko. In late 1976, Bokassa renamed the nation Central African "Empire" and crowned himself Emperor Bokassa I in a Napoleon-style ceremony (1977). In 1979, following violent social protests during which hundreds of children were massacred, Bokassa was overthrown in a French-backed coup led by Dacko. Churches and civil society groups are striving to support the establishment of social and political stability, but unfortunately with limited success.

Statistics: Population (2003): 3.8 million (M); Christians, 50% (Protestants and independents, 1.14 M; Catholics, 0.76 M); African Religionists, 35%; Muslims, 15%. (*Source*: 2003 census.)

VALENTIN DEDJI

Centurion, a Roman officer in command of 100 soldiers. Several centurions are mentioned as believers (Matt 8:5–13 = Luke 7:1–10; Mark 15:39; Acts 10).

Cephas (from Aramaic *kepha*, "rock"; Gk *petros*), a nickname or title given by Jesus* to Simon (see Peter), apparently because of his faith and belief in Jesus as the Messiah* (Matt 16:18). Jesus' attendant promise, "On this rock I will build my church," has been interpreted to refer either to Peter's faith or to Peter himself as primary apostle and predecessor of the bishops of Rome*.

Cerdo, Gnostic teacher in Rome who differentiated between the "just" Creator* depicted in the OT and the "merciful" God revealed only through Christ. This same distinction is found in Marcion*, who may have learned it from Cerdo after coming to Rome (c140).

Cereta, Laura (1469–99), writer of epistolary essays in Latin that circulated in manuscript form among humanists in Brescia, Verona, and Venice; defender of women's education. Her first biographers claim that she lectured publicly in Brescia for seven years. While her early writings integrate religious and secular themes, her later writings reveal a tension between the two. She faced criticism as a learned woman in a society that valued women for their domesticity and religious pursuits. The Dominican friar Tommaso da Milano counseled her to abandon secular texts for religious ones. In her letters to him, she emphasizes spiritual themes and refers to God as a feminine entity (*spectatrix*, "overseer," from the Latin masculine noun *spectator*).

JENNIFER HARAGUCHI

Chaburah (from Heb "friend"), Jewish voluntary organization for religious fellowship; also its fellowship meal. The term could be applied to Jesus and his disciples, and the Last* Supper.

Chad. This former French colony, independent since 1960 (capital, N'Djamena), with 131 ethnic groups, is occupied by Muslim Arabs in the north and east, and African Religionist and Christian Black Africans in the south.

Christianity was introduced by the General Council of Cooperating Baptists of North America, which sent six missionaries to French Equatorial Africa (1920), with Paul Metzler effectively beginning work in 1925. There were hundreds of Baptist churches when in 1973 Baptists resisted a policy of tribal initiation rites enforced by President François Tombalbaye's government. Churches were closed, members were persecuted, 13 Chadian pastors were executed, and missionaries (except medical personnel) were expelled. The government formed its own Evangelical Church independent of the Baptist mission. Churches reopened in 1975 when the government was overthrown.

In the early 20th c., the Vatican placed Chad under the Italian vicariate of Khartoum (Sudan). The tensions between the French and Italian (Mussolini's) governments in the 1930s discouraged the Roman Catholic presence until after World War II. Rome signed a decree authorizing the French Roman Catholic presence in Chad (1946), reviving pioneering attempts by the Holy Ghost Fathers at Kou (1929). In 1947 the territory was divided between Capuchin* fathers and oblates in the southwest and Jesuits* in the rest of the country, including N'Djamena. Msgr. Matthias N'Gartery Mayadi was the first Chadian priest (ordained by the Capuchins, 1957) and the first Chadian bishop (1985).

Protestants (Baptists) excelled in social work, with their Koumra Medical Center, which trains doctors and nurses. Likewise, in the 1970s many Catholic nuns and brothers were trained as medical professionals to staff government hospitals and clinics. Regarding education*, Jesuit missionaries established in N'Djamena one of Africa's best seminaries. Since the 1950s, Catholic development centers have helped improve adult literacy (with some 20,000 Chadian participants in 1980).

A challenging situation evolved when Colonel Idris Deby, a warlord from the Islamic* east, headed (1990) a transition government that was supposed to lead to a pluralistic civilian regime. Starting in 1995, fundamentalist Islamic preachers propagating the Shariah Law infiltrated Chad. The possibility of a Sudanese-type development cannot be ruled out (see Sudan).

Statistics: Population (2003): 9.25 million; Muslims 53%; Christians, 29.2% (Roman Catholics, 14%; Protestants, 13.2%; members of African Instituted Churches, 2%); African Religionists, 17%. (Estimates based on 1993 census.)

VALENTIN DEDJI

Chalcedon, Council of (451). After the victory of the party of Eutyches* (who, from their opponents' point of view, affirmed Monophysitism* and its tenet that the incarnated Christ had a single nature or, from their own point of view, held the more balanced Miaphysitism*) at the Second Council of Ephesus*, which Pope Leo* I called a "robber synod," the situation dramatically changed when Eutyches' protector, the emperor Theodosius II, died. His widow, Pulcheria*, assumed power and married Marcian, who became emperor. For them reconciliation with the Church of Rome was a priority, and an ecumenical council met in Chalcedon (451).

The council recognized the authority of the second letter of Cyril* to Nestorius, the Formulary of Reunion (an agreement between Cyril and John of Antioch, a moderate of the school of Antioch*, 433), and of Leo's Tome*. The decisions of Ephesus were revoked, Eutyches was condemned as a heretic, and Ibas* of Edessa and Theodoret* of Cyrrhus were vindicated. At the emperor's insistence, the council prepared a doctrinal statement declaring Christ to be one person*, or hypostasis*, "known in two natures without division or separation, confusion or change." The language, while influenced by Leo's Tome, was drawn chiefly from Cyril. "In two natures" was added at the insistence of Rome and the Antiochenes; yet the natures were said only to "be known," not to act in distinct ways. Thus the Chalcedonian doctrine could be interpreted either in a strongly Dyophysite* way, as Rome and the Antiochenes did, or with an emphasis on the one person of the Word, as the Easterners did.

The council also declared the Church of Constantinople to be second only to Rome, creating resentment in the apostolic churches of Antioch and Alexandria. As a result, the Church of Alexandria, which considered the doctrine of Cyril* to be at odds with that of Chalcedon and held Christ to be "one nature after the union" (Miaphysites*), found additional reasons to become independent of Constantinople and of the "Melkite*" Church. EUGENE TESELLE

Chaldean Catholic Church. This uniate* church descends from the Church* of the East (East Syriac Church). As a reaction to a 1480 decree making patriarchal succession hereditary, dissident bishops and lay delegates elected John Sulaka, the abbot of the Rabban Hormizd Monastery (near Mosul, Iraq) as patriarch (1540). He sought union with Rome. Pope Julius III proclaimed him "patriarch of the Chaldean Church" (1553).

The Chaldean liturgy in classical Syriac is the Liturgy of Addai* and Mari, in which the Nicene Creed (with the *Filioque**) is chanted and communicants receive the bread species only. Baptism* is effected by immersion three times. The sacrament* of marriage* is received when the two rings are blessed. The Chaldean Church bestowed on the laity the major order of the deaconate* and the minor orders of lector and subdeacon. The austere church buildings have a rectangular nave, with a wall encompassing the sanctuary at its eastern end.

The patriarch (ecclesiastical seat in Baghdad) is elected by the bishops and confirmed by the Roman Catholic pope. There are 12 ecclesiastical sees* in Iraq* and the Middle East, and two eparchies in North America. Estimated membership in 2000 was 600,000, equally divided between Iraq and other countries.

Besides clergy (prepared in a major and a minor seminary), there are monks (the

Antonines of Rabban Hormizd), nuns (Daughters of the Immaculate Conception and the Order of the Sacred Heart), and catechists.

Pope John* Paul II and Mar Dinkha IV, patriarch of the Assyrian Church of the East, signed (1994) the "Common Christological Declaration" to promote union between Assyrian* and Chaldean churches, later (1997) approved by the hierarchies of the two churches. The Chaldean Church has been an active participant in the Council of the Catholic Patriarchate of the Orient, promoting ecumenical dialogue among Oriental churches, and in Christian–Muslim dialogue. Since Vatican* II, the many liturgical reforms have included the de-Latinization of the liturgical book and a vigorous effort to revive Syriac, both classical and vernacular, in Iraq and among immigrant communities. **See also MALABAR CHRISTIANS.** SHAWQI N. TALIA

Chalice (from Lat *calix*), cup containing the wine used in the Eucharist*.

Chancel (from Lat *cancellus*, "lattice"), the eastern* part of a church, surrounding the altar* and separated from the nave* by a wall, grillwork, a rail, or an open space.

Chant (from Lat *canere*, "to sing"), singing of a sacred text in a special liturgical way; probably of both Jewish and Greek origins.

Chantry, an endowment* to support priests saying Mass* for the soul* of the donor or persons named by the donor; originated in the Middle Ages, developed during the 12th–13th c. along with the doctrine of purgatory*. Also the name of special chapels for such Masses, built because only one Mass could be said daily at each altar.

Chapel, the structure containing the cape (*capella*) of St. Martin* of Tours; later, any shrine with relics of saints; more recently, subordinate, non-church religious structures.

Chaplain, priest or minister associated with a chapel* or with a specialized ministry serving rulers, bishops, institutions, or the military.

Chapter, an assembly of the members of a monastery* to transact business; also the room where this body gathers. A cathedral chapter is the assembly of clerics to assist a bishop in the government of a diocese.

Chardon, Louis (1595–1651), Dominican* friar, spiritual author. The first son of a prosecutor in Picardy, Chardon studied at the University of Paris, then entered the Dominican Convent of the Annunciation (Paris, 1618), a convent that belonged to the Occitanian Dominican Reform launched by Sebastian Michaëlis (1543–1618) to bring theology and spirituality together in accordance with primitive rules of the Dominican order. Very little is known about Chardon's life. We do know that he became a Dominican friar (1619), then master of novices, possibly until 1630, and that he probably went to Toulouse in 1632, then returned to Paris, where he died of the plague.

Being charged with the care* of souls, he wrote (from 1647) treatises such as the *Life of Saint-Samson* and translated the *Dialogues* of Catherine* of Siena and Tauler's *Institutions*. In his most notable book, *The Cross of Jesus* (1647), Chardon tries to understand why devout souls must suffer. By following the crucified Jesus, they are purified and can benefit from sanctifying grace*. The mystical* experience can be present in "ordinary" Christian life. Thus Chardon helps the believers whom he directs progress on the path toward holiness.

YVES KRUMENACKER

Charisma, Charism, "gift* of grace*" bestowed on the recipient to be used for the edification of others (cf. 1 Cor 12:4–11). There are a plurality of gifts (charismata, charisms), i.e. of graces and qualifications granted to Christians to perform their particular tasks or vocations* for the good of others. The Charismatic* Movement emphasizes that these gifts are from the Holy* Spirit. "Charism" is the designation of the particular tasks that specific religious* orders perform in ministering to others.

Charismatic Authority, the kind of authority that rests in a leader's unique qualities, which are viewed as gifts* (charismata) from God, contrasted by Max Weber* with traditional (e.g. inherited) and rational/legal authority. Charismatic leadership can be countercultural and stimulate cultural changes.

CHARISMATIC AND PENTECOSTAL MOVEMENTS CLUSTER

1) *Introductory Entries*

Charismatic and Pentecostal Movements: Methods for Studying

Charismatic and Pentecostal Movements: Their History and Theology

1) Introductory Entries

Charismatic and Pentecostal Movements: Methods for Studying. The Charismatic Movement encompasses Christian groups and churches that place a central emphasis on the role of the graces or gifts (Gk *charismata**) of the Holy* Spirit in the life of all their members – not merely their leaders (cf. Charismatic Authority) – as well as the sociopolitical struggles empowered by the Holy Spirit. While the statistical claim by the *World Christian Encyclopedia* (2001) that one-quarter of Christians can be viewed as Charismatic is difficult to verify, the Charismatic Movement is quite sizable. It can be divided into three Charismatic waves: that of *Pentecostal churches* (with about 65 million members) that emerged in the early 20th c.; that of *renewal Charismatic groups* inside the Anglican, Catholic, Orthodox and Protestant churches (a 20th-c. movement; may be twice or three times as large as the Pentecostal churches); and that of *independent or indigenous Charismatic churches* (also known as "neo-Charismatics"), an even larger Charismatic wave that saw the formation of independent* or post-denominational Charismatic churches that grew very rapidly during the last part of 20th c. This third wave of indigenous Charismatic churches is by definition quite inculturated*, each specific Charismatic church being shaped by the very culture that it most often rejects as the "evil world" and often characterized as empowered by the Holy* Spirit to participate in a "spiritual warfare" against demonic powers that put in bondage people who live in this evil world.

In addition to its emphasis on the gifts of the Spirit, Christian Charismatic spirituality reshapes cultures* and religious landscapes. By discerning signals of transcendence, Charismatic believers are confident that they can have a closer walk in imitation of Christ, guided by the Bible and empowered by the cross's salvific effect and the graces and gifts of the Holy Spirit that enable believers to serve Christ more than is humanly possible.

Who can be viewed as a "Charismatic"? This definition is much debated, because of the wide range of views concerning the activities of the Holy Spirit. Until recently the literature restricted the term to those who claim that the gifts of the Spirit have not ceased since the Pentecost event and who exercise the gifts within mainline churches. Yet the designation "Charismatic" also applies to Pentecostal churches as well as to many of the emerging independent churches, although Pentecostals would rather "test the spirits," since not all spirits are from God.

For a critical study of the Charismatic Movement, Africa provides a good test case, because of the importance and diversity of its various branches on this continent. An African perspective offers an alternative critical approach to account for this movement.

The Charismatic Movement has been studied from a modernist* perspective by social scientists (see Weber, Max).

Sociology* of religion, soon followed by psychology* and anthropology of religion, views religious movements as the result of social processes. Persons engaged in the Charismatic Movement attempt to make sense of (bring cognitive order to) a complex and often hostile world. Four explanations for the Charismatic Movement are given. Charismatic groups develop as:

1. an alternative and/or corrective to modernization and secularization*;
2. a response by marginalized people to a feeling of relative social and economic deprivation and of cognitive dissonance (traditional religious views are not helpful);
3. a structure in which symbolic* interaction is possible for disenfranchised persons through the recognition of their personal charismata (gifts of the Spirit);
4. an effect of globalization*, bringing about either an accommodation of indigenous religion to ideologies from North America (e.g. the focus on individualistic religious experience) or the inculturation* of Charismatics into indigenous religious contexts or a combination of both.

From an African or non-Western perspective, these critical assessments are problematic because they attribute the resurgence of religion in Charismatic revivals to an African pathology. The African indigenization of Christianity is depicted as antimodern along with fundamentalism*, as if the relationship between the African past and the modern present necessarily needed to be understood in terms of a view of history framed by social Darwinism* and its view of progress. Far from envisioning a rupture between present and past, one can envision our past as always in our present, a view of history found in several African cultures. Following Peter Berger (*Rumor of Angels*), Harvey Cox (*Fire from Heaven*), and Waldo Cesar (*Daily Life and Transcendency in Pentecostalism*), it is helpful to envision a critical approach that draws attention to the limits of the Enlightenment* critique of religion*. For this one emphasizes how religion reinvents daily life and culture by utilizing signals of transcendence in the diverse spheres of human existence. One needs to consider:

1. the inner vision and the reinvention of self and life journey;
2. the reimagining of social space and the role of visible and invisible forces in it;
3. the reshaping of the hermeneutic practice for interpreting the Bible that displaces the liberal–fundamentalist debate through a praxis-oriented hermeneutic where experience and Scripture are maintained in a dialectic relationship by the Holy Spirit. The immediacy of the Bible as Scripture* is balanced by the freedom to interpret and appropriate the multiple meanings of the biblical texts accessible to all (and not merely leaders), because of an illumination from the Spirit;
4. the reconstruction of religious life and landscape as demonstrated in missionary strategies and ethics;
5. the redeeming of the public space (the political theology of the Charismatic Movement in each specific situation).

These considerations make possible a constructive study of the Charismatic Movement in different contexts.

OGBU U. KALU

Charismatic and Pentecostal Movements: Their History and Theology. The Charismatic Movement falls into three categories (often subsumed under the single label "Pentecostal"): classical Pentecostal churches (since the early 20th c.; c65 million in 2000); renewal Charismatic groups within Catholic, Anglican, Orthodox, and Protestant churches (especially since the mid-20th c.; 175 million in 2000); and independent or indigenous Charismatic churches (also known as "independent," "postdenominational," and "neo-Charismatic," a catchall designation for a diversified movement whose membership exploded in the late 20th c. but is found throughout church history; 295 million in 2000).

Charismatic theology is as diverse as Christianity itself, taking on the hue of the groups affected and the cultures* represented, and it has influenced virtually all of the Christian Church. Christian Charismatics can be found throughout the history of the church: the early church (as Paul's* letters, especially 1 Cor 12–14, and Acts* show), the Montanist* Movement (mid-2nd–6th c.), and movements also associated with Millennialism*, including, e.g., certain French Huguenot* groups under persecution (e.g. Camisards*, 17th–18th c.) and the Shakers* (since the 18th c.). Since the early 20th c., the Charismatic Movement has become more encompassing and of great impact.

Classical Pentecostalism appeared first in North America in 1901 and spread throughout the world during the next decade. Pentecostals taught that glossolalia* (speaking in tongues) was the initial physical evidence of Spirit baptism*. All Charismatics share with Pentecostals a common emphasis on "life in the Holy Spirit," which includes exuberant worship, spiritual gifts, Pentecostal-like experiences (*not* Pentecostal terminology), signs and wonders, and power encounters. Unlike Pentecostals, renewal and independent Charismatics do not always advocate the necessity of a second work of grace* subsequent to conversion or the evidence of glossolalia* as an affirmation of Spirit baptism. Charismatics place a stronger emphasis on the full range of spiritual gifts, as opposed to Pentecostals, who treat tongues and healing* as primary (see Pentecostal Movement).

Renewal Charismatic Movement. The groundwork for the renewal Charismatic Movement in the USA had already been laid in the 1940s–1950s by the ministries of Oral Roberts, T. L. Osborne, Agnes Sanford, and Demos Shakarian and his Full Gospel Business Men's Fellowship International. Renewal Charismatics began to explore their newfound experiences in the Holy Spirit within their own traditions. During the early 1960s, individuals in virtually every major Protestant tradition (Baptist, Lutheran, Mennonite, Methodist, and Presbyterian) were experiencing a renewal in the Holy Spirit. In Britain, the leadership of Anglican Michael Harper and Pentecostal Donald Gee, together with David du Plessis, gave further impetus to the spread of the Charismatic Movement.

Aggressive opposition to the renewal Charismatic Movement subsequently developed in such groups as the Lutheran Church–Missouri Synod, the Southern* Baptist Convention, and nearly all non-Pentecostal Holiness* groups. Notwithstanding, the renewal continued to grow throughout the Protestant world, especially among those Anglicans, Lutherans, and others who assimilated its dynamic into their church life.

In 1962 Pope John* XXIII prayed that the Second Vatican* Council might bring a new Pentecost for the Roman Catholic Church. The renewal officially began in 1967, simultaneously at Duquesne University in Pittsburg and in Bogotá, Columbia. Virtually all of the early Catholic Charismatic leaders in the USA were academics who had been strongly influenced by the debates and decrees of Vatican II, which had recognized in 1964 the importance of charismatic gifts in the life of the church. The Catholic Charismatic renewal spread rapidly throughout the world, growing to almost 120 million members according to 2000 statistics (c8.7 million [M] in Africa, 16 M in Asia, 11 M in Europe, 73 M in Latin America, 9.7 M in North America, and 0.3 M in Oceania).

Independent or Indigenous Charismatic Churches are by far the largest group of Charismatics. This catchall appellation refers to almost 19,000 indigenous, independent, postdenominational churches and groups that cannot be classified as either classical Pentecostal or renewal Charismatic, but share a common emphasis on the Holy Spirit, spiritual gifts, and experiences. In virtually every other way, they are as diverse as the world's cultures they represent.

According to David Barrett, there were about 0.9 million independent Charismatics in African* Instituted Churches (AICs) by 1900 and 65 million by 2000. Indeed, since the 1970s, the Charismatic Movement has exploded in Nigeria and Ghana, and has grown steadily throughout Africa, except in the almost totally Islamic nations of the north. The new Spirit churches are different from older AICs in their Evangelical theological emphasis and more limited inculturation* (also called syncretism*). Here megachurches* (combining Prosperity* Gospel and Charismatic teachings) abound, including Canaan Land ministries (with a 50,000-seat sanctuary) and the Redeemed Christian Church of God, both with headquarters in Lagos, Nigeria.

Independent Charismatic churches in Latin America and Asia experienced similar growth (see the relevant entries in this Cluster). In China, where the Charismatic Movement and Christianity as a whole are growing rapidly, grassroots or house* churches appear in abundance because Communist repression made houses the only viable meeting places for most Christians. According to Barrett, by 1995 nearly 65% of Chinese Christians were Charismatics. Similarly, India*, the Philippines*, and South Korea* experienced strong Charismatic growth.

STANLEY M. BURGESS

2) A Sampling of Contextual Views and Practices

Charismatic and Pentecostal Movements in Africa: Eastern Africa comprise the indigenous-founded Christian groups and churches that have developed since the 1980s and are Pentecostal* in character. Their historic origins are linked (1) to renewal ferments within classical Pentecostal and other missionary churches (1920s–1930s), resulting in the emergence of Spirit-filled African* Instituted Churches and (2) to the 1930s–1940s East African Revival Movement within missionary churches. Young evangelists, fostered in the revival, witnessed through interdenominational fellowships, schools, and colleges, eventually establishing ministries and churches. Encounters with North American Pentecostalism (1980s–1990s) through print, electronic media*, and visiting exchanges embellished the revival doctrine with Prosperity* Gospel, healing*, and deliverance theologies.

The Charismatic Movement in Eastern Africa is heterogeneous, with varying doctrinal and ministerial emphasis. Beyond Prosperity teaching and Holy Spirit charismata, it is distinguished mainly by its appeal to women, its puritan morality, exuberant liturgies, evangelism*, and innovative use of media technologies.

Charismatic theology is derived from the Bible as authoritative Scripture* reinterpreted within the African world view and reflects a contextually relevant faith addressing existential and pragmatic needs. Essential to Charismatic theology is the belief in the power of the Spirit (manifested in healing* and glossolalia*) to overcome demons and other evil powers (see Exorcism), understood biblically and in traditional African ways.

The Charismatic Movement challenges patriarchal* structures and engenders new systems of egalitarian social relationships that value individuals. Women and youth have an opportunity to exercise ritual power and leadership. The ethic of transformation in Christ influences their political theology.

The movement has been assailed for antagonizing other Christian groups, for privileging loyalties to "anointed" leaders and to groups over families and attendant responsibilities; for emphasizing personal spiritual experience over theology and doctrine; for its schismatic tendency and uncritical stance toward structural evil; and for merchandising the gospel. Yet it contributed to the renewal of Christianity in Eastern Africa through the spiritual transformation of the personal and social worlds and the "charismatization" of mainline Christianity.

PHILOMENA N. MWAURA

Charismatic and Pentecostal Movements in Africa: Southern Africa are not only those whose leadership is focused on individuals with specific characteristics that attract adherents, but also neo-Charismatic groups emphasizing the charisma of each believer. Charismatic tendencies are as clearly evident in Southern Africa as elsewhere on the African continent. These tendencies are to be found in mainstream Protestant and Roman Catholic Christianity as much as in the

African* Instituted Churches (AICs) and the newer Pentecostal/Charismatic groups to which many young people flock. Southern Africa has by far the largest concentration of AICs in terms of both the number of denominations and numerical strength. Most of these churches are Charismatic in typology and in turn generate neo-Charismatic churches. Alan Anderson writes: "The new Pentecostal and Charismatic churches at the end of [the 20th] century seem to be increasing at the expense of all types of older churches. Like the older AICs before them, these churches have a sense of identity as a holy and separated community, whose primary purpose is to promote their cause to outsiders. These are the 'born again' people of God, with a strong sense of belonging to the community of God's people, chosen from out of the world to witness to the new life they experience in the power of the Spirit. This latest expression of the AIC reformation has had the effect of popularizing a new form of Christianity appealing to the urbanized and significantly westernized new generation of Africans."

The greatest strength of the Charismatic churches is their appeal to the younger generation on a continent where young people constitute the majority of the population. At the same time, one of their greatest weaknesses is the propensity for fragmentation. A charismatic leader emerges in a congregation and attracts followers. He or she leaves that congregation and establishes his or her own meeting place – a rented cinema, a warehouse, a social hall, a school, or even an open place where a tent is pitched. Before long the congregation swells and becomes too large for the available space. Other charismatic leaders emerge, and new Charismatic congregations are established. There is no necessary connection between the parent congregation and the newer ones. Sometimes the relationship is cordial, but at other times there are conflicts and tensions, especially when there are unresolved issues pertaining to leadership and property.

From the perspective of ecclesiology, it remains an open question as to what it means to be a "church" in the Charismatic Movement, whether in Southern Africa or anywhere else. If the focus of ecclesial identity is the charismatic leader, what happens when the leader's charismatic gifts decline or the leader is incapacitated by illness or death? In the more institutionalized denominations, there is a clearly established procedure for leadership transition. In the Charismatic Movement, the change of leadership seems to be chaotic and very often leads to schism as new charismatic leaders arise in the congregations, as they are actually encouraged to do. Yet for Charismatic churches, this chaotic multiplication of Charismatic communities is viewed as the work of the Holy* Spirit.

JESSE NDWIGA KANYUA MUGAMBI

Charismatic and Pentecostal Movements in Africa: Western Africa. The Christianity inherited by mainline, missionary churches in West Africa did not equip Christians to reconcile their worldview with the gospel. To address this deficit, various forms of Charismatic and Pentecostal movements developed. The major groups include the following:

1. African Instituted Churches, since the late 19th c.
2. The classical Pentecostal Movement, since the early 20th c.
3. Charismatic nondenominational evangelic Christian fellowships, attracting since the 1970s members of different Christian denominations who became Charismatics
4. Charismatic renewal groups in the mainline churches, since the 1930s
5. Independent Pentecostal and Charismatic churches and ministries, since the 1970s
6. Neo-Charismatic independent churches and ministries, since the 1990s

Arguably, the African Instituted Churches were the earliest authentically African expressions of Christianity in West Africa. Their beliefs and practices clearly epitomize the resilience of the African indigenous worldview. Thus they seek to satisfy the African's deep religious and spiritual quest and the search for authentic spirituality. Most significantly the African

Instituted Churches set the pace, blazing the path that other branches of the Charismatic Movement, first of a Pentecostal type, have followed in their quest for an expression of Christian faith in African terms. Thus between 1906 and the 1940s, the classical Pentecostal Movement adopted many features of African Instituted Churches.

Since 1970 various types of Charismatic and Pentecostal movements have recorded the fastest growth on the religious landscape in West Africa. With their message of repentance* and Holiness ethic, the gifts and power of the Holy* Spirit, spiritual warfare, healing* and deliverance, and emotional, expressive worship, they put much emphasis on mission and evangelism. The movement that began in urban West Africa has now found its way into rural areas. Furthermore, these churches are the main players in an explosion of African Christianity in the Western World. For example, the fastest-growing church in Eastern Europe is a West African–led church, in Kiev, Ukraine, founded by Sunday Adelaja. Two major African churches in the USA are the Nigerian-based Redeemed Christian Church of God and the Ghanaian-based Church of Pentecost.

Charismatic (often called Pentecostal) religiosity is becoming ever more a social phenomenon in West Africa: many people confidently use biblical phrases and names for their businesses; people who aspire to attain political positions boldly declare themselves to be born again and "Holy Spirit filled." The Charismatic churches have founded schools and universities, and offer other social services. Qualitatively, evidence of their popularity abounds with stories of people who would have been lost to secularism* had they not been influenced by the message of the movement.

Their general acceptance is related to their efforts to apply the resources of the gospel to addressing questions raised within the primal worldview of West Africans. Consequently, the ethos of the Charismatic and Pentecostal movements has been adopted by all Christian denominations in West Africa. Mainline churches in West Africa are widely "charismatized." Thus the sharp distinction between denominations and movements is becoming increasingly irrelevant. Actually, the Charismatic and Pentecostal movements are fast becoming the "mainline" Christianity in West Africa, not merely in numbers but more importantly through their spirituality*, theology, and practices, which are tailored to fit the African milieu by displaying a full awareness of the African worldview. These movements are playing a major role in shaping Christianity in Africa because they effectively respond to events and processes at work in African cultures*. Churches in West Africa are at the threshold of a new permutation of Christianity that puts emphasis on an active engagement of the Christian faith in sociocultural issues, thereby becoming relevant to people of the region.

CEPHAS N. OMENYO

Charismatic and Pentecostal Movements in Asia. In 2000 there were approximately 135 million Charismatics in Asia: 5% classical Pentecostal*, 16% renewal Charismatics in denominations, and 79% independent Charismatics (although these subcategories overlap). Pentecostal missionaries arrived in India* and China* in the 1910s; in Burma (Myanmar*), Indonesia*, and Singapore* in the 1920s; in Korea*, Thailand*, and Malaysia* in the 1930s; and in Papua* New Guinea in the 1940s. Yet there were indigenous Charismatic revivals between 1900 and 1920 in Korea, long before Pentecostal missionaries arrived. In South Korea, Charismatic Christianity has exploded since 1945. By 2000 Seoul had 11 of the 12 largest megachurches* in the world, including Yoido Full Gospel Church (c780,000 members in 2003). These and other Charismatic churches, while at the time denominationally affiliated, are increasingly involved in interdenominational relations and in networks with independent Charismatic churches and groups elsewhere. So Korean missionaries to rural China work largely with house* churches, even as independent Chinese missionaries to other parts of Asia work with Pentecostal and renewal Charismatic organizations.

As elsewhere, the independent Charismatic Movement in Asia has a literalistic* approach to the Bible, a Millennialist* worldview, and an emphasis on the person and work of the Holy* Spirit. It stresses evangelism* through revivals* and crusades (using the latest technologies), as well as through relational interactions in home cell groups (e.g. South Korea) or house churches (e.g. rural China). The spiritual gifts are especially valued, and healings, miracles, and prophecies are marks of charismatic leadership.

The Asian Charismatic Movement accentuates a holistic, this-worldly, spiritual, and communal understanding of salvation*, although as Millennialists its members also remain otherworldly. Conversion* and often an insistence on moral purity reflect the perfectionist tendencies found elsewhere in Holiness* and Pentecostal Christianity. The Pentecostal "fourfold" gospel – Jesus as savior, healer, baptizer with the Holy Spirit, and coming king – is understood to include not only bodily healing, bodily manifestations, and emotional expressions, but also material blessings and general success.

Independent Charismatics in Asia are deeply influenced by animistic beliefs. Cosmologies featuring a multiplicity of gods, ancestor* spirits, and even ghosts are adapted in the Charismatic worldview and associated with angels* and demons*. The Holy Spirit as supreme divine power enables Charismatic believers to overcome the demonic through exorcisms* and spiritual warfare. For example, among the Bible Mission churches in Andhra Pradesh, India, indigenous and Hindu cultures combine to produce *bhakti*-style liturgies and a guru mentality that elevates the anointed-of-God to the status of a charismatic leader. Charismatic gurus like Mungamuri Devadas (c1885–1960) claimed to receive revelations from the Holy Spirit through dreams and visions that were confirmed through the gift of healings. In the Spirit of Jesus Church and the Holy Ecclesia of Jesus Church in Japan, ritual chants invoke God's presence and activity in a phenomenologically* analogous way to the chanting of the Nembutsu and sutra recitation in Japanese Buddhism. These churches also Christianize and legitimatize traditional Japanese burial practices honoring the ancestors, underscoring in biblical and theological teachings that salvation extends to the spirit world. Similarly, the important Prayer Mountain Movement in Korea builds on indigenous Korean religious beliefs and practices related to sacred mountain sites, and the function of its charismatic leaders is similar to that of shamanic healers (see Shamanism and Christianity). This charismatic spirituality has been compared to popular expressions of Korean Buddhism* and Confucianism*.

Since the gift of the Holy Spirit is available to men, women, and even youth, individual lives are transformed as Charismatic Christians, especially women, are empowered to testify, pray, lead, and work for the Kingdom* of God. The Charismatic emphasis on psychosomatic healing and, in some regions, on material blessings connects with the aspirations of Asian poor and brings about upward social mobility, especially in urban contexts where interactions with Western Christians are more common than they are in the countryside. While Charismatics are mostly apolitical and socially disengaged, they have begun to realize (e.g. in South Korea) the sociopolitical impact that a large number of people can have.

Theologically, how will the ongoing growth of the independent Charismatic Movement in Asia affect the traditional doctrinal views of mainline churches? Ethically, will the Charismatic Movement in Asia produce a "clash of civilizations" with emerging Muslim, Hindu, and Buddhist groups, or will these Charismatic churches interact with their social, political, and religious environments in more positive ways? One thing is sure: these very disparate groups in Asia can no longer be ignored in the context of world Christianity in the 21st c. AMOS YONG

Charismatic and Pentecostal Movements in Australasia can be seen as originating in indigenous intra-Oceanic and extra-Oceanic cultural transactions. The engagement of European Christianities (since the 18th–19th c.) with local cultures*

in an area with some 2,000 distinct ethnic and linguistic traditions depends on preexisting cultural attitudes toward spiritual life, imported theologies, and the interactions of Christian traditions with political and social developments, such as imperialism, colonialism*, missionary* paternalism, and capitalist expansion. In 2000, Charismatic and Pentecostal members totaled an estimated 4 million (c12% of the population) in 336 denominational groupings, including 3.5 million renewal Charismatics in mainstream denominations and neo-Charismatics in indigenous independent churches.

The Charismatic Movement entered Australia, New Zealand, and the rest of Australasia in two ways. First, among mainline traditions, it was prefaced by such movements as Keswick spirituality, Camps Farthest Out, and the Healing Movement (e.g. Hickson, Sanford), as well as by international evangelists (e.g. Macpherson, Valdez, Wigglesworth, Roberts, Worley), a radical shift in ecclesial relations through Vatican* II, alternative spiritualities amid Western youth cultures (e.g. Teen Challenge, Youth with a Mission), and a widespread lay reaction against the liberalization of theology. Second, the missionary movement reflexively imported from revivals* elsewhere (Solomon* Islands, Papua* New Guinea, East Africa) alternative or intensified spiritualities* (often through business connections, e.g. the sugar industry, coffee and tea plantations, financial services, and international combines). In the islands, the Charismatic Movement was prepared for by local shamanic religiosity (see Shamanism and Christianity) and the incipient experientialism of Methodism*, particularly as articulated through classical Pentecostal and Latter Rain revival missions.

An organized Charismatic presence in Australia dates from Jim Glennon's popular healing services at St. Andrew's Cathedral (1960), bolstered by Australians (including Alex Reichel) returning from the 1969 South Bend (Indiana) /Ann Arbor (Michigan) Catholic renewal, then by the organization of the movement in the 1970s through the Temple Trust (Alan Langstaff), Charismatic communities (especially Emmanuel, Servants of Jesus), denominational service committees, and Bible colleges.

Revival was often a means of indigenization of Charismatic Christianity in the unstable political and social milieu of new or decolonizing nation-states. Australian and New Zealand Charismatic missions to the Pacific and Asia helped legitimize and sustain their Australian bases in the face of growing denominational resistance to new experiential forms and ecumenism. This opposition saw both the institutionalization of the Charismatic Movement and the formation of many independent Charismatic congregations, many of which went on to sustain significant growth in Pacific and Asian centers.

Engaging with counterculture and Latter Rain influences, the Australasian Charismatic Movement emphasized the use of popular music during worship, deliverance ministry, prophetic vision, typological* interpretations of the Bible, and apostolic leadership. Conflict has arisen over relations with indigenous cultures (e.g. brideprice, polygamy*, and pig killing in the islands; the use of totems in Aboriginal* society), the influence of US revivalism, the relatively dominant role of women, theological innovations such as "Jesus Name," shepherding, demonic oppression of Christians, the "apostolic revolution," and "Prosperity*" preaching. The contributions of Charismatic music from Scripture in Song, Hillsong, Planetshakers, and other Australasian sources to the global church has been significant.

By 2002 in Australia, the Charismatic Movement had emerged with social and political aspirations, something already evident in the heavy Christian political involvement in the rest of the Pacific (flowing from church involvement in national infrastructure building, public corruption, and ecological and economic threats). In some cases (e.g. Michael Maeliau's Deep Sea Canoe Vision Movement, 1984), charismatic dreams and visions have become significant vehicles for the articulation of local identities with global frames and for fueling mission, especially among Pacific migrant communities in the First World. In Australia, "great southland" myths have fed theologies of national renewal and a sense of global mission. Given the relatively scattered population of the region, there is no doubt that the Charismatic Movement has been a particularly energetic and global source of Christian renewal.

MARK HUTCHINSON

Charismatic and Pentecostal Movements in Europe: Eastern Europe. The Pentecostal* message of Spirit-filled experiential Christianity fell on receptive religious soil among Russians and several other peoples of Eastern Europe.

The movement reached czarist Russia and Central and East European nations in a variety of ways before the Communist takeover. The Pentecostal message was brought to Northwestern Russia and the Baltic States by some of the first Finnish Pentecostal missionaries. T. B. Barrat, the Norwegian Methodist minister who after his visit to the Azusa* Street revival in Los Angeles became the father of the Pentecostal Movement in Northern Europe, began publishing his magazine in the Russian language (1913). The expatriates who had become Pentecostal in the USA also played a strong pioneering role as missionaries when they returned to their former countries. Most successful among them was the Russian Baptist Ivan Voronaev, who laid the foundations for the Pentecostal Movement in Bulgaria* (early 1920s), then in the Soviet Union (establishing some 350 churches, mostly in Ukraine*). Many of the US missionaries were associated with the influential Russian and Eastern Europe Mission, and national leaders were trained at the influential Bible school in Danzig.

Under Communism Pentecostals were among the most fiercely persecuted Christian groups in Eastern European nations. In some countries, they were forced into unions with other neo-Protestant ecclesial communities. Governmental restrictions often led to dissident independent Pentecostal churches and unofficial associations known for their separatist and legalistic lifestyles. The collapse of the Communist regimes provided full freedom to Pentecostal and Charismatic groups. New denominations came into existence, some of them linked to global and Western Pentecostal groupings, including the Assemblies* of God and Church* of God (Cleveland, Tennessee). The largest national Pentecostal movements in post-Communist Eastern Europe are found in Romania* and Ukraine, with significant growth in Bulgaria and Belarus* as well.

The largest independent Charismatic church in all of Europe was founded in 1994 in Kiev, Ukraine, by Sunday Adelaya, a native Nigerian. God's Embassy claims more than 25,000 members (2005) who meet in 40 locations across Kiev and have planted more than 600 congregations in the former Soviet Union and around the world. The church's comprehensive mission plan includes proclamation of the gospel of spiritual freedom and empowerment for transformative sociopolitical engagement. Other independent and Word*-Faith churches have been established by strong charismatic leaders who have little or no theological education but are entrepreneurially gifted and able to communicate Christian faith as a message of hope and healing, thus attracting many urban youth. They are known for their effective use of the electronic media and their establishment of publishing houses and networks of communication. Though most of these churches resist the legalism and routinization of classical Pentecostal churches, since they plant daughter churches of their own, many of them are in the early stages of denominational structuring.

The Charismatic Movement has brought renewal to segments of Catholic churches in most nations, while it has affected national Orthodox* churches only randomly.

PETER KUZMIC

Charismatic and Pentecostal Movements in Europe: Western Europe. The Pentecostal devotion to the extraordinary power and gifts of the Holy* Spirit collided with an increasingly secularized* Enlightenment* European culture with confidence in reason and science. Inspired by European revivalism* and US

Pentecostalism, Thomas Ball Barrett came to Norway (1907) to preach Pentecostal "Spirit baptism*." He inspired international participation, except in Italy, which was evangelized by Giacomo Lombardi (1908), and Portugal, which was visited by Brazilian missionaries (1938). Pentecostalism did not achieve a large presence in secular Western Europe. Only Portuguese Pentecostalism can claim more than 2% of the population. Charismatic churches fared better.

Post–World War I isolation and a penchant for congregationalism created a heterogeneous movement, lacking widespread uniformity on issues like speaking in tongues* as evidence of Spirit baptism, eschatology*, and biblical literalism*. British West Indies Pentecostals interpreted Pentecostal power within an Afro-Caribbean cosmology that involved the defeat of evil powers. Also, though Barrett and other founders were ecumenically open, Pentecostalism and the Charismatic Movement grew in most places in tension with established state Protestant or Catholic churches (the Dutch Reformed–Pentecostal dialogue exemplifies a countertrend). Basic is the conviction that widespread conversion*, healing*, and even societal change can occur through the spiritually gifted and empowered church. The ongoing vitality of this vision, however, will require greater ecumenical understanding and cooperation across confessional and national boundaries.

FRANK D. MACCHIA

Charismatic and Pentecostal Movements in Latin America: Brazil. The development of Pentecostalism and the Charismatic Movement in Brazil is marked by three distinct phases, beginning with an isolated group of missionaries and leading to a movement fully integrated within Brazilian society.

At the beginning of the 20th c., a worldwide dissemination of Pentecostalism* was initiated by the US Holiness* Movement, which sent its missionaries to Brazil. From a timid start of a few individuals isolated in a traditionally Catholic* society, Brazilian Pentecostalism constantly increased its presence in Brazilian society.

According to the 2000 Brazil census, during 1990–2000, while the number of Catholics decreased, the number of Evangelicals* doubled to more than 26 million believers, massively increasing from 9.1% to 15.4% of the total population. Among these Evangelicals, 67.6% belong to different Pentecostal churches, most of which divided into three major denominations: "Assembléia de Deus," "Congregaçao Crista no Brasil," and "Igreja Universal do Reino de Deus."

Although different denominations and movements share characteristics with the beginning of the Pentecostal Movement in the biblical event of Pentecost*, they have distinctive emphases on the charismatic gifts* of glossolalia*, healing*, and exorcism*. Moreover, different branches of the Pentecostal Movement relate the sacred and the secular realms in various ways.

Historically, the development of the Brazilian Pentecostal Movement can be divided into three interrelated and overlapping stages.

1. Implantation. Foreign missionaries who established the Congregação Cristã (1910) and Assembléia de Deus (1911) arrived at the same time in the north in the state of Pará and in the southeast in São Paulo. These missionaries were isolated for almost 40 years and associated themselves with those who were economically less fortunate and less educated than others, and with those who could not envision any future development or migration. This first stage of the Pentecostal Movement was characterized by anti-Catholicism, glossolalia*, sectarianism, and asceticism*. Congregação Cristã remained isolated. Assembléia de Deus changed when it began to engage with the surrounding society; despite a loss of members who balked at this change, it became the major Brazilian Pentecostal Evangelical denomination.

2. Greater Openness toward Society and "Brazilization," 1950s–1960s. This development took place especially in the region of São Paulo, which was becoming industrialized. The dissemination of Pentecostalism began to take place independently of foreign influence.

This process began with a "National Evangelization Crusade" initiated by US missionaries from Igreja do Evangelho Quadrangular. This crusade had evangelization caravans, which crisscrossed different regions of the country, assembling huge numbers in tents in public places, emphasizing divine healing. This evangelization movement throughout Brazil led to a widespread and fragmented Pentecostalism, and new denominations founded by Brazilians appeared for the first time. The use of radio (see Media and Christianity) as a means of propagation had the remarkable effect of integrating the Pentecostal Movement within Brazilian society. The major denominations were Igreja Evangélica Pentecostal Brasil para Cristo, Igreja Pentecostal Deus é Amor, Casa da Benção, and Igreja de Nova Vida.

3. Rapid Growth of the Independent Charismatic/Pentecostal Movement. From the end of the 1970s through the 1980s, there was a dramatic increase in the Charismatic/Pentecostalist Movement. Initially this growth took place in the region of Rio de Janeiro, where the people were more urban and better educated than those in other areas (see Brazil). The present-day increase and visibility of the Brazilian Charismatic/Pentecostalist Movement are due to this development.

By 2000 the Charismatic/Pentecostal churches were characterized by great social integration: massive participation in politics, use of the media (television, radio, and newspapers), marketing, and an enterprising organizational structure with a strong and centralized leadership. They became sophisticated churches with new theological, liturgical, and aesthetic possibilities. They became less sectarian and more involved in social issues, rejected religious stereotypes, and freed themselves from Pentecostal rigidity – salvation* no longer meant a rejection of the world. In their greatly emotional worship services, one finds the inculturated* use of symbols and objects that have religious significance in various Brazilian religions, especially popular Catholicism, Afro-Brazilian religions, and Kardecism (a spiritualist religion) – practices that earlier would have been denounced and rejected as syncretistic*. However, they remain opposed to dialogue between religions, emphasize the devil* and exorcism*, and strongly proclaim a Prosperity* Gospel according to which God's plan for believers is that they are to be happy, healthy, and wealthy.

During this period of the Brazilian Charismatic/Pentecostal Movement, there has been a complex process of growth and internal migration, with many facets and ramifications. The primary denominations are now Igreja Internacional da Graça de Deus, Sara a Nossa Terra, and Igreja Universal do Reino de Deus, the last being a classic example of this movement.

Such indigenous Brazilian churches are best called "neo-Charismatic" or "independent Charismatic." Furthermore, these Charismatic churches that began from foreign missionaries are now themselves sending missionaries to many regions of the world. In addition, this movement has spread to mainline churches, e.g. through the Charismatic Catholic Movement. **See also BRAZIL.** PAULO BONFATTI

Charismatic and Pentecostal Movements in Latin America: Central America. In the 1940s and 1950s, the Pentecostal Movement was already established in all Central American countries. At first it spread among marginalized groups of society, but from the 1980s the Charismatic Movement became broadly accepted among middle-class and even some high-society groups. Some Pentecostal groups developed as a result of the work of foreign missionaries, primarily from the USA. But most groups have been locally developed; they are "indigenous Charismatic" (see present cluster: Studying). Pentecostals and indigenous Charismatics represent about 80% of Evangelical/Protestant Christianity in the region.

This Charismatic Movement is heterogeneous in theologies, religious practices, and political options; some are conservative and even fundamentalist*, whereas others are liberal and socially committed. Indigenous Charismatics are characterized by their great missionary fervor. Their dynamic worship includes charismatic demonstrations (like glossolalia*, prayer healing*, and "dancing in the Spirit"), communal singing of hymns, public testimonies, prayers of intercession, and tithe or offering. The renewal Charismatic Movement within the Roman Catholic Church shares many of the liturgical characteristics found in the Protestant indigenous Charismatic Movement and Pentecostalism, yet is now combined with devotion to Mary*. The Catholic Charismatic Movement is also marked by the active participation of laywomen and laymen in leadership roles and by the integration of liturgical life with diaconal action.

In all of Central America, the dominant indigenous Charismatic Movement becomes increasingly a faith focused on a quest for solutions to the crises of individuals' personal and social lives, making pacts with God to obtain prosperity*, health, and success. DANIEL CHIQUETE.

Charismatic and Pentecostal Movements in Latin America: Chile. Pentecostalism first emerged around 1909 in Valparaiso, Chile, when the US missionary W. Hoover left the Methodist Church to found the Methodist Pentecostal Church. This soon became a popular and deeply indigenous movement characterized by its beliefs in the Holy Trinity* and the Word of God, its emphasis on the active presence of the Holy* Spirit, and effusive worship services.

In its initial phase, this indigenous Pentecostalism experienced explosive growth, especially among the poor. Congregations subdivided and proliferated. Their initial relative isolation constituted an opening, spurring their missionary spirit with the goal of reaching out to the entire nation and even to neighboring countries.

Later, the evolution of Chilean Pentecostalism was marked by the political-social turmoil of the 1960s, which led Pentecostals to assume social responsibilities; and the 1973 coup d'état that led to a division of the Protestants ("Evangelicals," including Pentecostals) into two groups: those who supported Pinochet and his government and those who struggled to defend human* rights.

By 1980 Chilean Pentecostalism had consolidated itself into a religious and cultural force of about 15% of the population with a significant and active presence in Chilean society. More recently, neo-Pentecostalism and neo-Charismatic groups have developed among minority groups, influenced and linked to foreign churches, although they adapted themselves to the Chilean society.

CRISTIÁN G. PARKER

Charismatic and Pentecostal Movements in Latin America: Jamaica. Pentecostalism, the Protestant tradition with the largest membership in Jamaica, had its genesis in the religious awakening during the Great Depression (1929–33). In the midst of such socioeconomic and political crises, those most keenly affected tend to turn to God when they feel they can no longer depend on secular systems for answers to the challenges they face as individuals and societies. The New Testament Church of God and the City Mission Church founded by W. Raglan Phillips (1854–1930), with its revivalist* preaching of repentance* and healing*, enjoyed tremendous success among the poor, who feel particularly hopeless during periods of economic hardship. Another wave of Christian revival came in the aftermath of a devastating earthquake (early 1940s); many, fearing that the end of the world was at hand, turned to God "just to make sure" (that they would be saved).

The Pentecostal Movement was the religious component of the social and political revolution and riots in the late 1930s through which Jamaicans achieved universal adult suffrage (1944). Many who felt marginalized in society also felt excluded from the life of the traditional churches with their colonial* outlook and practice. In reaction to the highly Anglicized worship and leadership of the largely English-based churches, the poor and those without formal education left the mainline denominations to form their own groups, where they were free to express

Charismatic and Pentecostal Movements

themselves, linguistically and liturgically. In the new movement, much emphasis was placed on holiness, the imminent return of the Savior, freedom to choose local leaders, and freedom to discipline adherents who were not meeting the moral requirements of the children of God.

Among the features of traditional churches that came under the wrathful condemnation of Pentecostals were the requirement of formal preparation for leadership of the churches, the preparation of sermons, the wearing of vestments, the baptism of infants, and the attendance at worship of those involved in informal marital relationships. As the movement became more established and accepted, most of these rigid requirements were relaxed. Pentecostal preachers now undergo formal training for ministry, wear clerical garb, and become involved in elective politics, and women are involved in the leadership of congregations and assemblies. Aversion to mainline denominations has become nominal and vice versa. Pentecostal churches are now a part of the ecumenical movement, and as a result of the 1990s Charismatic renewal, some features of worship and discipline in mainline churches parallel those in Pentecostal churches. ASHLEY A. SMITH

Charismatic and Pentecostal Movements in Latin America: Mexico. As of the early 21st c., Pentecostals and Charismatics constituted about 70% of the sizable membership (about 8–10 million) of Protestants (called "Evangelicals" in Latin America). In Mexico one can distinguish three kinds of Pentecostal/Charismatic churches, which successively originated in traditional Pentecostalism (1910s–1960s), independent Charismatic groups ("neo-Pentecostal," 1970s–1980s), and neo-Charismatic indigenous groups (1990s).

Traditional Pentecostalism is characterized by baptism* in the Holy* Spirit, glossolalia* (the gift of speaking in tongues), and prayer healing*. It started in urban settings, then developed in rural and native communities, and now encompasses a great ethnic and social diversity. Although conversion in the Spirit represents a transformation of life, it has a very limited effect on believers' social and political values and practices as members of society.

Traditional Pentecostalism in Mexico is represented primarily by the Apostolic Church of the Faith in Christ Jesus (1914, founded by Romana Carvajal de Valenzuela, in Chihuahua) and the Assemblies of God (1921, Ann Sanders in Mexico City), as well as by the Church of God of the Complete Gospel (1931), the Pentecostal Church of Holiness of Mexico (1932), the Quadrilateral Church (1943), and the Missionary Crusade of Avivamiento (known as "Centers of Faith, Hope, and Love," 1949). Some Pentecostal churches had had Mexican leaders from the beginning, including MIEPI (Movimiento Iglesia Evangélica Pentecostés Independiente, founded by Valente Aponte) and the Interdenominational Christian Church "the Light of the World" (1926, Eusebio Joaquín), which expanded most rapidly because it addressed the common people's concerns and needs and had a significant impact in impoverished sectors of society.

Independent Charismatic Movement ("Neo-Pentecostal") often originated with renewal Charismatic groups (characterized by the experience of baptism* in the Spirit) within historic Protestant churches, and then split from these churches. The most representative communities of this movement are Castle of the King (1974, Monterrey), Christian Friendship (1972, Mexico City), New Wine (1974, Chihuahua), and Calacoaya (Mexico State, 1981). Although they retain most characteristics of traditional Pentecostalism, they can be distinguished by the fact that they do not build sanctuaries because they conduct their meetings in movie theaters; they identify themselves as "centers" or "communities" (rather than as churches) and consequently do not register with the government as official religious associations (with some exceptions). They are nondenominational, particularly focused on middle-class and upper-middle-class people.

The Neo-Charismatic Indigenous Movement is characterized by ecstatic or exotic ritual practices that emphasize liberation from demonic* powers, "spiritual war," exorcism* (liberation from evil spirits), anointing, prophecies, and visions. In their worship services, spiritual experiences are described as "labor pains," "vomiting," "holy laughter," "lion's roar," and "spiritual drunkenness." They bring this spiritual warfare to all social classes, from higher-class people to marginalized people in urban settings.

JAVIER ULLOA and REBECA MONTEMAYOR

Charismatic and Pentecostal Movements in North America. Pentecostalism in North America is estimated to have 30 million adherents. The addition starting in the 1960s of Charismatic churches that interpret "Pentecostal" experience from different church heritages has increased that number. Charles Fox Parham (c1900) first preached the Pentecostal experience of "Spirit baptism*" as empowerment for mission and as evidenced by speaking in tongues (Acts 2). Pentecostalism wished to restore to the church a "Pentecostal" or "apostolic" faith through Spirit baptism, divine healing* (and other spiritual gifts), and fervent expectation of Christ's return. Inspired by the North American Holiness* Movement and a holistic African spirituality, William J. Seymour led the racially integrated Apostolic Faith Mission on Azusa* Street in Los Angeles (1906), the global 20th-c. movement's birthplace, honing its ecumenical vision. Seymour's paper, "The Apostolic Faith," intended "to displace dead forms and creeds and wild fanaticisms with living, practical Christianity. 'Love, faith, and unity' are our watchwords." Biblical literalism* became popular in support of biblical miracles* and prophecy*, but fundamentalists* were criticized for confining the extraordinary experiences of God depicted in the Bible to the ancient past.

Despite Seymour's ecumenical vision, North American Pentecostalism soon became divided. Holiness* Pentecostals promoted an experience of "entire sanctification*" as necessary for Spirit baptism, in disagreement with "finished work" Pentecostals, who regarded the experience of Spirit baptism as following from faith in Christ's completed work. Oneness Pentecostals separated from the nascent Assemblies* of God denomination (1916) in support of water baptism* in Jesus' name and a "modalist*" understanding of the Trinity*. Doctrinal uniformity within respective camps was enforced through the formation of denominations. A racial division occurred early on, although black and white Pentecostals continued trying to structure interracial relations against the pressures of segregation. In 1994 the white Pentecostal Fellowship of North America became the Pentecostal-Charismatic Churches of North America in order to integrate racially. Pentecostalism in North America tended to wed otherworldly spirituality with a pragmatic confidence in this-worldly success (a feature of North American culture). White groups achieved this success much sooner than Latino/a and African American groups, with the latter maintaining more capacity over time to wed spiritual with critical social discernment. Though some Pentecostals seek to change existing social structures, the tendency is to exemplify the social significance of the gospel and meet human needs through alternative, spiritually gifted communities and missions.

The future challenge will consist of moving Seymour's ecumenical vision forward with a liberating social concern in a movement that is shifting from an apocalyptic* eschatology* among the urban poor to a comfortable faith among those of the middle class.

FRANK D. MACCHIA

Charisms, of Religious Orders. See CHARISMA, CHARISM.

Charity (Lat *caritas*), love*, primarily for God but also for fellow human beings, called the greatest of the "theological* virtues" (1 Cor 13); care for the poor.

Charlemagne, or Charles the Great (c747–814), king of the Franks (from 768) and "emperor of the Romans" (from 800), son of King Pippin III (714–68). In 768 the Frankish kingdom was divided between Charles and his brother, Carloman, leading to a power struggle that ended with Carloman's death (771). Now sole ruler of the Franks, Charles led extensive military campaigns on the Italian peninsula and consolidated his father's ties with the papacy. He then strove to expand the southern and eastern territories of his kingdom. On Christmas Day, 800, Pope Leo III crowned him "emperor of the Romans" at Saint Peter's Church in Rome. Although Charlemagne's involvement in planning the coronation is disputed, there is little doubt that subsequent years would see him increasingly assuming the role of head of Western Christianity, adapting his policies along this ideological line. In 813 he crowned as co-emperor his only surviving son, Louis, who succeeded him.

Charlemagne's ecclesiastical policy was initially a continuation of that of his father, Pippin III, who had assumed the leadership of the Frankish Church and actively cultivated a state ideology representing the Franks as God's chosen people and their ruler as God's representative on earth. At first Charles was content with promoting ecclesiastical reform, the homogenization of canon* law, liturgy*, and monastic* life, and a general resurgence of scholarship and learning (*Admonitio generalis*, 789; see Alcuin; Carolingian Renaissance). Later he assumed a more active role following the rise of Adoptianism (a new form of Adoptionism*, which was advocated in Spain and France in the 8th c. and which Charles viewed as heresy*) and other crises in the kingdom. Charles dictated Christian dogma and assumed the position of "king-preacher" at the head of the Frankish Church (Council of Frankfurt, 794). Lobbying by influential thinkers after his coronation as emperor strengthened his resolve to create a society based on Christian principles of justice, leadership, and individual morals.

His subsequent failure to reorganize public life according to Christian morals sobered his spirit and tempered his way of governing during the final decade of his life. Nevertheless, it soon became evident that he had succeeded in paving the way for an extensive ecclesiastical reform set in motion shortly after his death. Louis* (the Pious) benefited from his father's efforts to create a unified Frankish Church and to provide opportunities for talented individuals to take up influential roles in its institutions. Subsequent power struggles between the new emperor and the Frankish Episcopate would, however, prevent the reforms from being implemented to their intended extent. STEVEN VANDERPUTTEN

Charles V (1500–58), holy* Roman emperor (1529–58), king of Spain, ruler of the Low Countries, Naples and Sicily, and Spanish America. Educated in the tradition of the Devotio* Moderna, he was committed to the Catholic faith. Despite his hostility toward Luther*, he needed the troops of the Protestant princes to pursue his policies in Italy, suppress the Peasants' Revolt in Germany, and defend Eastern Europe against the Turks. He defeated the Schmalkaldic League (1547–48) and imposed Catholic uniformity with the Interims* (1548). But soon weakened, he gave rights to Lutheran princes in the Peace of Augsburg* (1555). After abdicating, he died in a Spanish monastery.

Charles Martel (688–741), son of Pippin* of Héristal, father of Pippin* the Short, grandfather of Charlemagne*, "mayor of the palace" of the French kings. He was known for his victory over the Moors (722) at Tours or Poitiers, though they were not expelled from France for several more generations.

Chastity, sexual purity, including both celibacy* and fidelity in marriage*.

Chasuble (from Lat *casula*, sleeveless outer garment), celebrant's liturgical vestment worn over the alb* and stole* at the Eucharist*.

Chateaubriand, René-Auguste de (1768–1848), French romantic and diplomat. A Breton noble, Chateaubriand was deeply influenced by the French Revolution, spending 1793–1800 in exile in England, where he returned to Roman Catholicism. He published *Atala* (1801), an exotic tale set in North America, about the tragic love between two "Indians," Chactas, a "pagan," and Atala, a Christian. The tale includes the description of a small agrarian Christian "Indian" utopia led by the Christ-like Fr. Aubry, who illustrates the gospel's "civilizing" force. *Le Génie du christianisme* (The genius of Christianity, 1802) is an original apology responding to the aftermath of the Enlightenment* and French Revolution. (The publication coincided with the agreement between Napoleon and Pope Pius VII reinstituting Roman Catholicism in France.) *Le Génie* is largely an aesthetic defense of the beauties of Christianity: the mysteries* of the sacraments*; Christian poetics, moral laws, scriptural truths, and Christ's teaching; the harmonies of nature; and Christian ruins. Printed in an appendix to *Le Génie*, the tale *René* recounts the protagonist's uncontrolled passion, alienation, and estrangement from European society and his attachment to Chactas (the character in *Atala*), by now a wise old "Indian."

Having become the leading voice of early French romanticism, Chateaubriand then wrote *Les Martyrs ou le triomphe de la religion chrétienne* (The martyrs, or The triumph of the Christian religion), an 1809 prose epic about the persecution* of Christians under Diocletian. Two Greeks, the Christian convert Eudorus and Cymodocea, a pagan who eventually converts because of her love for Eudorus, eventually find martyrdom in Rome in the arena where Constantine later proclaims Christianity the official religion of the Roman Empire. Chateaubriand's *Vie de Rancé* (The life of Rancé, 1844) is a biography of the abbot who reformed the Cistercian* order at La Trappe under a rule of austerity.

PATRICIA A. WARD

Chaucer, Geoffrey (1343?–1400). Living in late medieval England at a time when Christian faith and the daily, even life-structuring prominence of the Christian Church was inevitable, Chaucer's relationship to Christianity was profound and rich. One of his earliest poems, "An ABC," is an alphabetical hymn to the Blessed Virgin. His *Canterbury Tales* includes several important religious tales: the "Clerk's Tale" of patient Griselda; the "Second Nun's Tale," a saint's life of Saint Cecilia; the "Prioresse's Tale," a miracle of the Virgin; the "Man of Law's Tale" of God's protection of innocent, prayerful Custance in foreign lands among hostile "pagans." Interestingly, all of these are written in the seven-line rhyme royal stanza rather than the rhyming couplets of the majority of the tales. The "Parson's Tale," which concludes the collection, is actually a prose handbook on penance*, taxonomizing the seven deadly* sins and their "remedies."

Many of the nonreligious stories recounted in *Canterbury Tales*, even the comic, sexually charged *fabliaux* (e.g. "Merchant's Tale," "Summoner's Tale," "Reeve's Tale," "Miller's Tale") are filled with biblical allusions, some playful, some serious, and many arguably either. Chaucer's knowledge of the Bible is a matter of dispute. Many scholars argued that he had first-hand knowledge of it in an age when that would be relatively rare, while others have suggested that his biblical material came from secondhand sources like sermons. He was clearly interested in biblical commentary and patristic writings – e.g. Jerome's**Contra Jovinianum* featured prominently in the "Wife of Bath's Prologue" – and was sufficiently familiar with the exegetical tradition to allude to it, often in startling ways, e.g. in the "Merchant's Tale."

He was both keenly aware of contemporary controversies and anticlerical satire, notably in the portraits of the Pardoner, Friar, Prioresse, Summoner, and Monk of the "General Prologue," but he portrayed his village Parson as a thoroughly idealized figure. His most pointed anticlerical satire is concentrated in the "Pardoner's Prologue," in which he shamelessly reveals his frauds; the "Friar's Tale," about a corrupt archdeacon and summoner; and the astonishingly scatological "Summoner's Tale," which reveals the hypocrisy of begging friars.

A number of Chaucer's associates apparently had Lollard* sympathies. Chaucer's own position is impossible to settle, but he was intensely interested in such philosophical issues as predestination* and free will*; he translated Boethius's* *Consolation of Philosophy* and drew on it seriously in *Troilus and Criseyde* and the "Knight's Tale," and comically in the "Nun's Priest's Tale."

JOHN PLUMMER

Children. The term "children" has two general meanings in Christianity. Figuratively, Scripture and Christian tradition identify those young in faith as children adopted into the Christian family as daughters and sons of God. "Children" also refers literally to those persons who have yet to assume full responsibility and authority within and for their own life and for whom other adults remain accountable, with the age of childhood and adulthood varying in different historical periods. Christianity has held children in special, if not unique, respect in theory, although not always in practice. Children are given an honored place as heralds of God's reign and participants in the faith, but children also had to submit to the arbitrary power and punishments of adults acting on the church's behalf.

Various traditions have emphasized combinations of the following three constructions of children:

1. *Depraved.* Early theologians, e.g. Augustine*, and Reformation theologians, e.g. Martin Luther*, saw childhood as a vital moral and religious developmental phase. Children enter the world bearing the marks of "original* sin," an affliction associated with pride, self, and, above all, will. A primary parental task is to suppress and control a child's natural depravity through weekly catechism*, daily prayer and

Scripture reading, repeated admonitions, and sometimes intense reprimand.

2. *Innocent.* Under the influence of the Enlightenment* and theologians such as Schleiermacher* and Bushnell*, many Christians began to view children as inherently social and affectionate, not sinful, and as morally pure or neutral, even "sacred." A child might still be seen as having been born spiritually and morally disabled, but parental devotion offers salvific remedy. A primary parental task is to nurture a child's openness, receptivity, and intuitive proclivities toward faith.
3. *Gift.* The view of children as a gift appears dramatically in scriptural traditions in which Jesus welcomes children (e.g. Mark 9:33–37, 10:13–16); had precedent in the Jewish tradition, where the status of children was different from that of children in the surrounding Greco-Roman world; and reappeared in theologians like John Calvin*, who underscored children as God's special blessing. They are the promise, sign, and guarantee of the covenant* and also participants in it, qualifying as disciples and exemplifying God's reign. Parents are commanded to teach the love of God steadfastly and diligently (Deut 6:2, 7). Caring for children, among the least, is a sign of greatness (Mark 9:35).

Christianity in the 21st c. faces radical challenges with respect to children. Christian understandings no longer fit, yet new controlling images suggested by politics, psychology, and the market are inadequate and sometimes outright destructive. Children number disproportionately among the world's poor and are especially susceptible to exploitation and abuse. Christianity has an important role to play both in caring for children and in refashioning a better understanding of children.

BONNIE J. MILLER-MCLEMORE

Children of God. In the Bible, "children of God," like "son[s] of God," connotes a spiritual relationship to God, as well as a moral relationship: God's children have responsibilities toward others, a vocation*, as Jesus did. The people of Israel were sometimes called collectively "children of God" (Deut 14:1); the only individual called a "son of God" was the king (2 Sam 7:14; Ps 2:7, 89:26–27). In the Gospels, Jesus is called "Son* of God" (e.g. Matt 3:17; Mark 9:7; Luke 3:21–22; John 1:31–34) and calls God "Abba*," or "Father" (Mark 14:36). He also addresses his followers as children of God (Matt 5:9; Luke 20:36) and in the Lord's* Prayer invites them to address God as "Abba." Paul* regards human beings as children of God not by nature but by adoption* through Christ and the Holy* Spirit (Rom 8:14–23; Gal 3:26, 4:5). Consequently, Christians addressed each other as brothers and sisters – a status that included slaves who were Christians (Phlm 16). In subsequent history, Christians repeatedly attempted to manifest this basic equality, e.g. insisting that all receive the Eucharist* regardless of worldly status.

Chile is a Roman Catholic country with a major Protestant presence; it is one of the countries in Latin America with the largest percentage of Protestants.

16th–18th Centuries. In Chile, colonial and Roman Catholic histories are interconnected. The Spanish Conquest was the beginning of Catholic mission. Indigenous peoples saw their polytheistic practices and beliefs confronted by the religion of Jesus and of its vicar on earth, the pope. From the beginning, the Catholic Church developed through intense missionary activity among the natives, who were viewed as "pagans" and "idolaters." This Catholic Church was formally Christian, although it was an indigenous and mestizo* syncretism*, or an inculturated* Christianity, that often barely hid the survival of ancient beliefs.

South of the Bio Bio River (south of Talcahuano), the Mapuche nation ("people of the land," called Araucanos by the Spaniards) resisted both conquest (through the Araucanian War) and Christian mission until the late 19th c.

During the colonial period, Mercedarian, Franciscan*, Dominican*, Augustinian*, and Jesuit* missionaries settled in the recently founded cities, building hermitages, churches, schools, clinics, and hospitals, which were quite influential in colonial life. Processions, religious festivals, and high Masses marked the colonial life of Spaniards, natives, and mestizos.

The resulting colonial Christendom* had many mestizos and syncretistic characteristics. "Popular Catholicism" emphasized worship and various kinds of devotion to the Virgin Mary*, still celebrated today. The figure of Mary as the protector of mestizos* is at the center of large pilgrimages; she is designated by different names, ranging from the Virgin of Tirana (in the north) to the Virgin of Candelaria in the island of Chiloé (in the south).

Chile's Independence, 19th Century. The period of independence divided the Christian Church. Diocesan priests participated in the first governmental junta (1810), but a majority of the Church members remained on the side of the Spanish crown. Patriotic priests were chaplains during the diverse military campaigns against the Spaniards.

The initial constitution established Catholicism as the state religion. The Patronato* system, transferred to the president of the Republic, caused innumerable problems regarding the relations among the Chilean state, the local church, and the Holy See (Rome), e.g. each time a new bishop was named.

After 1833 growing clashes between church and state led to a reaction among ultraconservative Catholics against liberalism. In the late 19th c., laicization* and even anticlericalism became stronger in Chile, as did a more active Freemasonry*. The progressively larger gap between church and state led to the creation of a Catholic conservative party seeking to defend the interests of the Catholic Church against the state. The Catholic educational system was strengthened through the work of various congregations* and the foundation of the Catholic University (1889).

20th Century. The Constitution of 1925 finally resolved the rift between church and state. It put an end to the Patronato* system and established the Roman Catholic Church as an autonomous structure.

During this period, apostolic work was developed, in part as a reaction against the socialist and anarcho-syndicalist views that reigned among factory workers and peasants. Meanwhile this Catholic conservatism was confronted by a Christian social current. The split between conservative and social-minded Catholics still characterizes the Chilean Catholic Church.

Father Alberto Hurtado, SJ (1901–52), recently canonized as a Chilean saint, typifies this social Catholicism. In the 1940s, together with others, he led a movement that brought about the creation of workers' unions, charitable organizations, and even progressive magazines. Such initiatives in support of workers and peasants led to projects of agrarian reform in the Church's landholdings, as a forerunner of even broader changes.

The Church's social service trained many lay leaders who, in turn, founded the Christian Democratic Party (1957), which became the governing party with Eduardo Frei Montalva (1964). The Chilean Catholic Church had international influence, especially through Bishop Manuel Larraín's important role in founding CELAM* (Latin American Episcopal Conference, 1955) and at the Second Vatican* Council (1962–65).

In the 1960s, the renewal prompted by the Latin American Episcopal Conference in Medellín* (1968) advocated Base* Ecclesial Communities (CEBs*) as a church model, incarnated* spirituality, and ecclesial work in poor neighborhoods. Against conservative Catholicism, still present, groups of Christians for Socialism developed during Salvador Allende's popular government (1970–73).

Christianity, Military State, and Democratization. Set against the military coup (1973), the Catholic Church headed by Cardinal Silva Henríquez defended human* rights. An ecumenical Committee for Peace was created; a majority of Christians acted in solidarity with those in need, including those pursued by the military state. Yet a significant number of Catholics and Protestants blessed Pinochet's crusade against "atheistic Marxism*." The "Popular Church" resisted the military state (1973–1989), developing CEBs with "a preferential* option for the poor."

With the return of democracy (late 1980s–1990s), many Christian leaders played a role in the democratic governments; the influence of CEBs was weakened, while apostolic spirituality and the Catholic Charismatic Movement developed. A wind of restoration blew within the Catholic Church, and the ecclesiastic discourse became dominated by moral values (divorce, abortion, etc.), generating conflict with the democratic governments (1990s to the early 21st c.).

Protestant Churches and Religious Pluralism. While public worship other than Catholicism was legally prohibited, political pragmatism led to the authorization of Protestant worship in private precincts when British, North Americans, and Germans arrived in the 19th c. The arrival of the US missionary David Trumbull (1845) was a turning point, followed by the arrival of Methodists (1878).

The most important Pentecostal churches of the country originated under the leadership of Pastor Hoover in Valparaíso (1909), who founded the first Methodist Pentecostal Church of Chile. Internal conflicts and disputes led to the multiplication of churches, now numbering several hundred. These Pentecostal denominations rapidly expanded in impoverished lower-class and middle-class neighborhoods, became national churches, and even sent missionaries to various nearby countries. Some neo-Pentecostal/neo-Charismatic* churches developed, influenced by foreign churches (since the 1970s) (see Charismatic and Pentecostal Movements Cluster: In Latin America: Chile).

Historic Protestant churches (Lutheran, Anglican, Presbyterian, Baptist), although significant, constitute a minority; their members generally belong to families descended from immigrants. The Pentecostal/Charismatic churches, by contrast, are an integral part of the Chilean socioreligious panorama.

Formal legal equity among the churches was finally established in 1999 by a law that affirmed the religious diversity of Chilean society.

Statistics: Population (2002): 15.1 million. Christians, 87.9% (Roman Catholics, 70%; Pentecostals/Charismatic/sEvangelicals, 15%; marginal Christians, 1.9%; historic Protestants, 1%); nonreligious, 8.3%; native religionists, 2%; adherents of other religions (Jews, Muslims, etc.), 1.8%. (*Source*: 2002 census.)

CRISTIÁN G. PARKER

Chiliasm (from Gk *chilias*, "a thousand"), an alternative term for Millennialism*.

China. The history of Christianity in China is a history of encounter and dialogue with Chinese society and its age-old cultural tradition. For most Chinese, Christianity is a religion from the Western world that is still undergoing a process of accommodation to Chinese society and inculturation*.

Christianity was introduced in China in 635 when a Christian monk named Alopen arrived in Changan (modern Xian), the capital of the Chinese Tang dynasty (618–907). Alopen was welcomed as a Persian missionary from "Da Qin," a term for the Mediterranean area at that time, and his religion was understood to be "Jing Jiao" (the Luminous Religion) by the Tang Chinese. Actually, Alopen was the first Assyrian* missionary (often inappropriately called Nestorian*; see Church of the East, or Assyrian Church) in China, as told in the inscription of "Da Qin Jingjiao Liuxing Zhongguo Bei" (stele of the propagation of the Luminous Religion of Da Qin in China, discovered in the early 17th c.). With the support of the emperors Tai Zong and Gao Zong, Syriac* Christianity developed smoothly. It is said on the stele that "the religion spread throughout the ten provinces . . . monasteries abound in a hundred cities." But during the reign of the empress Wu (690–705), Christianity was attacked by Buddhists* and Daoists*. With the accession of the emperor Xuan Zong (712), Christianity was once again tolerated and continued to develop. During the Tang dynasty, Christianity established communities in Xian, Zhouzhi, Luoyang, Lingwu, Chengdu, Dunhuang, Guangzhou, and other areas. But in 845, the emperor Wu Zong issued an edict forbidding Buddhism and all other foreign religions, such as Manichaeism* and Syriac Christianity. As a result, Syriac Christianity disappeared totally from the Tang Empire, ending the first Christian mission in China.

The second introduction of Christianity into China took place during the Yuan dynasty (1271–1368). It was called *yelikewen* (transliteration of the Mongol word *erke'un*), which included in that period both the Church* of the East (commonly known as "Nestorian*") and the Roman Catholic Church. Assyrian Christians had survived in the border areas of China after the persecution of 845 and flourished among the Uighur, Naiman, and Ongut peoples. In the 11th c., the Keraits were also converted to Assyrian Christianity. Sorhahtani, mother of Khubilai (the founder of the Yuan dynasty), was a Kerait woman who believed in the teaching of the Assyrian* Church. On her death (1252), Khubilai ordered that a Mass be said for her in a Church of the East monastery in Ganzhou (Gansu Province). Assyrian Christians among these peoples moved into the northern parts of China during the Western Liao (1125–1201) and the Jin (1115–1234) dynasties. As early as 1235, there was an (Assyrian) Church of the East in Khanbaliq (the Mongol name for Beijing). Soon after, a Church of the East metropolitan bishop resided in the city. In 1289 Khubilai set up the Chongfu Si, an administrative office for Church of the East Christian affairs. During 1289–1320, there were 72 Church of the East Christian monasteries in China. Mar Sargis, a Church of the East Christian doctor from Samarkand, who was appointed governor of Zhenjiang District in South China by Khubilai in 1277, established 7 monasteries, including 6 in Zhenjiang and 1 in Hangzhou. In 1330 the archbishop of Soltania claimed that there were more than 30,000 Church of the East Christians in China.

During the Yuan dynasty (1271–1368), Catholic missionaries came to China for the first time. In 1245 the Franciscan missionary John of Plano Campini (1182–1252) was sent by Pope Innocent IV to the Mongol court of the Great Khan Kuyuk in the pre-Yuan capital of Qaraqorum (Helin). In 1253 William of Rubruck (1215–57?) also visited the court of the Great Khan Mangu at Qaraqorum. In 1260 Maffeo and Niccolo Polo made a journey to China proper and brought back a letter from Khubilai Khan asking the pope to send to China 100 missionaries well trained in science, the arts, and doctrine. In 1271 the Polos, including Nicolo's son Marco, came to China again. They were accompanied by two Dominicans with papal letters to Khubilai. But the Dominicans turned back; only the Polos arrived in China. In 1289 Pope Nicholas IV sent John of Montecorvino (1247–1328), a Franciscan, to China. When he arrived in Khanbaliq (the Yuan capital) in 1294, he was welcomed by the new emperor, Timur. John converted the Alans (a people from the shores of the Black Sea) and the Church of the East Christian Prince George (Kerguz). He built his first church in Khanbaliq (1299) and soon (1305) a second church with the help of a German brother, Arnold of Cologne. He baptized 40 boys, taught them Latin, and trained them to form a choir for Mass. In 1307 Pope Clement V appointed John of Montecorvino as archbishop of Khanbaliq and patriarch of the East, and nominated seven Franciscans as bishops in China. Three of them, Gerald, Peregrine of Castello, and Andrew of Perugia, arrived in China in 1308. They remained in the capital for five years and received *alafa* (alms) from the emperor. Starting in 1314, they went to Zaitun (Quanzhou) and became bishops there in succession (Gerald died in 1318, Peregrine died in 1322, and Andrew served as bishop from 1322 until c1330). After the death of John of Montecorvino (1328), the Alans sent a mission to Rome requesting a new bishop. John of Marignolli arrived in China (1342) as the envoy of Pope Benedict XII, bringing a "supernatural horse" as a gift from the pope to the emperor. But he left China in 1346 without assuming his role as bishop, so there had been no bishop at all in Khanbaliq since 1328. In 1362, the last bishop of Zaitun, Friar James of Florence, was killed and the Catholic Church there was also destroyed.

There were conflicts between Church of the East Christians and Roman Catholics during the Yuan dynasty. The number of Catholics during that time was approximately 30,000, but the majority of them were not Han Chinese. The Yuan Christians established their communities in Khanbaliq (Beijing), Zaitun (Quanzhou), Ganzhou (near modern Zhangye), Ningxia, Xining, Yongchang (Liangzhou), Suzhou (near modern Jiuquan), Shazhou (near modern Dunhuang), Huozhou (Gaochang), Jingzhou (in Inner Mongolia), Datong, Hejian, Daming Lu (Hebei), Dongping Lu (Shandong), Yangzhou, Zhenjiang, Hangzhou, Wenzhou, Yachi (Kunming), and other areas. In 1368 the Yuan dynasty was overthrown and all Christians in Khanbaliq were expelled. Christianity disappeared from China for the second time.

The Jesuit* approach to China was initiated by Francis Xavier* (1506–52), who came to Shangchuan Island for the first time in 1551 and returned there in 1552 until his death on December 3, 1552. Although he never set foot on the Chinese mainland, he provided important insights regarding what the forthcoming Jesuit mission in China could be. A significant breakthrough came in 1583, when Michele Ruggieri (1543–1607) and Matteo Ricci* (1552–1610) obtained permission for a permanent stay on the Chinese mainland and established their residence in Zhaoqing. They shaved off their hair and beards and dressed like "Western Buddhist monks" because they imagined the influence of Buddhism to be so strong in China. When they discovered their mistake, they allowed their hair and beards to grow again and donned silk robes like "Confucian literati" in recognition of the predominant position of Confucianism* in Chinese culture. After staying in Zhaoqing, Ricci undertook missionary activities in other places, such as Shaozhou, Guangdong, Nanchang, and Nanjing, and even made a brief visit to Beijing (1598). Together with Didaco de Pantoja (1571–1618), Ricci arrived in Beijing again in 1601, bringing many gifts to the Wanli emperor of the Ming dynasty (1368–1644). The two men were allowed to reside in Beijing. Ricci studied Chinese culture and translated into Latin the Four Books of Confucianism (*The Confucian Analects, The Book of Mencius, The Great Learning,* and *The Doctrine of the Mean*). Meanwhile, he also introduced Western knowledge to China and translated many Western books of philosophy, religion, science, and technology into Chinese. Under Ricci's influence, many renowned Chinese intellectuals converted to Christianity; among these, Xu Guangqi (1562–1633), Li Zhicao (1569–1630), and Yang Tingyun (1557–1627) became the "three pillars of the early Catholic Church." Xu

Guangqi invited Lazarus Cattaneo (1560–1640) to Shanghai to establish the Catholic Church there (1608). Later, Xu built another church on his estate at Xujiahui (Ziccawei) in Shanghai.

The success of Ricci encouraged more and more Jesuits to come to China, such as Lazarus Cattaneo (arrived in 1594), Nicolo Longobardo (1565–1655, arrived in 1597), Sabbatino de Ursis (1575–1620, arrived in 1606), Nicolas Trigault (1577–1628, arrived in 1610), and Giulio Aleni (1582–1649, arrived in 1613). Trigault returned to Europe and came back to China in 1618 together with 22 Jesuits, including Franciscus Furtado (1587–1653) and Johann Adam Schall von Bell (1592–1666). In 1597 the Jesuit province in China was established and headed by Ricci. After his death (1610), Longobardo was his successor. But Longobardo disagreed with Ricci's policy of adaptation to Chinese culture, especially the use of ancient Chinese terms for the name of God (see God, Christian Views of, Cluster: Names for God in the Bible and Church Tradition). In 1627 the Jesuits convened a conference in Jiading to discuss their differences.

Following the Jesuits, the Dominicans, Franciscans, and Augustinians began their own missionary efforts in China. Gaspar da Cruz, OP (?–1570), reached Canton in 1556 and stayed there for a short time. In 1575 Martin Rada, OSA (1533–78), visited Fujian and remained for a few months. The Spanish Dominicans entered Taiwan from the Philippines and established their first church in Jilong (1626). The first Dominican to arrive in Fujian (1631) by way of Taiwan was Angelo Cocchi (1597–1633). Juan Bautista de Morales (1597–1644) and Antonio de Santa Maria Caballero, OFM (1602–69), came to the Chinese mainland (1633), followed by Francisco Diaz (1606–46) in 1634. Luo Wenzao (Gregorio López, 1616–91), who was baptized by Spanish Franciscan Caballero in 1633, entered the Dominican order and was ordained a priest in Manila (1654). Luo was nominated as the first Chinese Catholic bishop by Pope Clement X (1673) and consecrated as bishop of Nanjing (1685). He ordained three Chinese priests in 1688. Before them, Zheng Weixin (Manoel de Sequeira, 1633–73) was ordained as the first Chinese Jesuit priest in Europe (1664).

Christian mission also met suspicion and hostility in China. Shen Que, vice president of the Nanjing Board of Rites, wrote memorials three times to the emperor denouncing the Jesuits. After a reply from Beijing (1617), he launched attacks against Christians. The persecution stopped when he was promoted to Beijing. Shen Que was one of the authors of an anti-Christian writing entitled *Poxie ji* (An anthology of writings exposing heterodoxy), edited by Xu Changzhi (1639). At the beginning of the Qing dynasty (1644–1911), Johann Adam Schall von Bell and other Jesuits were tolerated and allowed to stay in Beijing. Schall was appointed director of the Astronomical Bureau and had a good relationship with the emperor Shunzhi. But after the death of Shunzhi (1661), Schall was frequently attacked by Yang Guangxian (1597–1669) and finally imprisoned in 1664. With the assumption of supreme power by the emperor Kangxi, the Jesuit Ferdinand Verbiest (1623–88) was appointed director of the Astronomical Bureau, and Yang Guangxian was sent into exile. Kangxi had developed a friendship with Verbiest and other Jesuits and, at the very beginning, showed sympathy for their Christian beliefs. But the Chinese* rites controversy eventually destroyed this friendship and sympathy. As a result, Kangxi banned Christian mission in China.

The Dominican Juan Bautista de Morales made 17 accusations against the Jesuits and attacked the principle of accommodation with the Chinese rites (1643). Charles Maigrot (1655–1730), from the Society of Foreign Missions of Paris, promulgated an order to forbid Chinese Christians to honor Confucius and ancestors* (1693). Charles de Tournon, the apostolic visitor in East Asia sent by Pope Clement XI, issued his "Decree of Nanjing" (1707), after he had an audience with Kangxi (1705). The papal bull *Ex Illa Die* (1715) confirmed the Decree of Nanjing (later Benedict XIV prohibited these rites in the bull *Ex Quo Singulari*, 1742). Consequently Kangxi issued his edict to ban Christianity completely in China (1721). Some Jesuit missionaries were allowed to stay in Beijing, but only as advisers on science, the arts, or other cultural work. Nevertheless, the Catholic Church remained in existence in China with about 300,000 members during this period (see Mission Cluster: In Asia: Catholic Mission in China, 16th–18th Centuries).

The Russian Orthodox Church had established a mission in China in 1671. The earliest Orthodox Church in Beijing was set up shortly after 1686. From 1715 to 1956, the Russian Orthodox Church sent a mission 20 times to Beijing.

In 1627 the first group of Protestant missionaries from the Dutch Reformed Church arrived in Taiwan. In 1807 Robert Morrison

(1782–1834), the first Protestant missionary from England, arrived in Macao and then in Canton, symbolizing the beginning of Protestant mission on the Chinese mainland. In cooperation with William Milne (1785–1822), Morrison translated the Bible into Chinese (1819). As a result of their missionary activities, Cai Gao was the first mainland Chinese to be baptized into the Protestant Church in Macao (1814), and Liang Fa (1789–1855), baptized in 1816, became the first ordained Chinese evangelist (1824). Liang Fa organized the first Chinese Protestant Church and distributed the Chinese Bible and his tract *Quan Shi Liang Yan* (Good words to admonish the age), which deeply influenced Hong Xiuquan, the leader of the Taiping Rebellion (1851–64).

After the Opium Wars (beginning in 1840) and the resulting "Unequal Treaties," China was forced to open its borders, and Western Christian missionaries of various denominations swarmed into China and established their churches or missionary stations in many places. The connection of modern Christian mission in China with Western powers aroused popular hostility and resistance among many Chinese, expressed for instance in "missionary cases" and the Boxer Uprising. In this context, the missionaries paid at least some attention to social concerns in China and organized Christian social work in education, publications, relief, and medical care. Chinese Christians developed "self" consciousness and independence and founded their own indigenous churches in this process. The first independent Chinese church was the East Guangdong Zhaoqing China Evangelization Society organized by Chen Mengnan (1873). Yu Guozhen (1852–1932) established the Chinese Jesus Independent Church in Shanghai (1906). With this development, the "Three-Self" Movement following the principle of self-government, self-support, and self-propagation was put forward in the "Declaration of Churches" by the General Conference of Chinese Protestant Churches in Shanghai (May 1922).

In 1949 there were about 2.7 million Catholics, 700,000 Protestants, and 300,000 Orthodox Christians in China. In 1950 the Three*-Self Patriotic Movement" in Chinese churches formally emerged. In 1954 the Three-Self Patriotic Movement Committee of the Protestant Churches of China was founded. In 1957 the Chinese Catholic Patriotic Association was established, and since then, the Chinese Catholic Church has instituted self-election and self-consecration of its bishops and other priests. Because the number of Protestant churches and their members had declined, in 1958 they united, ushering in a period of "postdenominational development" (see Chinese Contemporary Independent and House Churches).

All church activities were forbidden during the Cultural Revolution (1966–76) in China. Since 1977, however, the Chinese churches have been restored as a result of China's reform and opening to the outside world. In 1980 the China Christian Council and the Chinese Catholic Bishops' College were established. In 2000, according to official estimates, the Chinese Catholic Church had 5 million members, about 4,000 clergy, 70 bishops, and more than 4,600 churches and meetinghouses (see Roman Catholicism Cluster: In Asia: China). Chinese Protestantism had about 15 million members, more than 18,000 clergy, more than 12,000 churches, and 25,000 meeting places (see Chinese Contemporary Independent and House Churches; Protestantism Cluster: In Asia: China; Roman Catholicism Cluster: In Asia: China).

ZHUO XINPING

Chinese Contemporary Independent and House Churches. Chinese independent and unregistered Christian communities, often called "house* churches" by both Chinese and foreign commentators, have grown rapidly and have drawn considerable attention since the early 1980s. Although Catholic house churches do exist, the great majority of these communities are Protestant. They began in the 1950s, developed further during the chaotic decade of the Cultural Revolution (1966–76), and accelerated their growth starting in the 1980s. There may be as many as a few hundred thousand such autonomous Christian communities, with the number of adherents ranging from 30 million to more than 100 million, according to the estimates. A realistic estimate is 50–55 million Protestant believers in unregistered churches in 2000, a number about three times the 16–18 million officially claimed in the registered churches. Both personal factors and issues of church–state relations account for the large size of this independent sector of the Chinese Christian Church.

Historical Development. During the first half of the 20th c., a few Protestant movements arose that were entirely independent of the established foreign missions and their churches. These included the True Jesus Church, the Jesus Family, and the Little Flock. These constituted perhaps 20–25% of the Protestant community (less than 1 million) at the founding of the People's Republic of China (1949). Thus there was some tradition of autonomy and localized independence in parts of the Protestant community.

The events of the 1950s were not easy for Chinese Christians. They were subjected to a series of stressful campaigns. The remaining foreign missionaries were expelled, and Christians were put under an elaborate system of monitoring and control centered in the newly created Chinese Christian Three*-Self Patriotic Movement. Made up of Communist Party–approved Christians, it was in turn managed by a state agency, the Religious Affairs Bureau, part of the government and party bureaucracy. In the early 1950s (perhaps as early as 1952 or 1953), some Christians began to avoid the publicly visible church and to meet in homes, but the number was not large. Later in the 1950s, pressure was put on churches to consolidate and close the remaining sparsely used church buildings. Then in 1957–58, the "anti-rightist campaign" sent many Protestants to labor camps; the intensity of the subsequent disastrous Great Leap Forward and the closing of most remaining churches resulted in a significant number of believers forming small unobtrusive home groups.

When the Cultural Revolution was launched by Mao Zedong (1966), all places of worship (of any religion) were closed, and the Religious Affairs Bureau itself was abolished. As a result, more believers attended house churches. The near paralysis of party and state structures until the late 1970s created a climate ideal for evangelization, and many new believers were added to these autonomous communities. By 1978, when churches began to be reopened for the first time in 12 years, there were almost certainly more Protestant believers than there had been in 1949, perhaps as many as 2–3 million.

Between late 1978 and 1980, the party leadership made a strategic decision to reestablish the monitoring system for Protestants that had been used in the 1950s. However, many groups of Christians had become accustomed to an essentially independent existence during the previous decade, and their leaders did not all welcome being under the scrutiny of officialdom. Moreover, when the numerous victims of the late 1950s anti-rightist campaign were released after completing their 20-year prison terms, many of the Protestants among them had little desire to have a close affiliation with the state. Finally, not only was the Three-Self Patriotic Movement reestablished, but some of the same leaders, those who in the eyes of many had collaborated with the atheistic Communist Party and had betrayed fellow Christians, were returned to leadership positions.

For all these reasons, from the start, even with the formation of a new China Christian Council (1980) designed to be more user-friendly for Protestants, large segments of the house church community were suspicious of and stayed at arm's length from the Three-Self Patriotic Movement. The key issue was registration of the congregation. As church buildings were reopened and new ones built, these obviously visible structures were the gathering places for diverse congregations, including former house churches and newly registered congregations made up largely of new converts and led by pastors who were authorized to hold office by the Religious Affairs Bureau. This registration brought with it a fairly dependable guarantee that the congregation would not be harassed by the Public Security Bureau or other arms of the government. It also facilitated access to the Protestant seminaries, which had begun being reestablished in the 1980s.

Yet many house church groups discounted the advantages of registration and affiliation with the Three-Self Patriotic Movement, seeing instead the dangers of being subjected to interference in their preaching or other activities, and especially their habits of enthusiastic evangelism, which they feared would be curtailed by the control system, which, after all, was still predicated on the assumption that religion was a retrograde social phenomenon that would become extinct someday. So although some house churches registered, many did not, and that division of the Protestants into two large sectors, registered and nonregistered, has persisted since the early 1980s, although it has grown more complex in recent years. During that time, both the Three-Self Patriotic Movement–led churches and the unregistered ones have grown rapidly, the former increasing more than 5-fold to something greater than 15 million members, and the latter well over 10-fold to the present number of probably more than 50 million members.

Distinctive Characteristics: Evangelical, Fundamentalist, and Pentecostal/Charismatic. Christian congregations in China do not have an extremely wide range of doctrinal beliefs. The vast majority of Protestants adhere to what can reasonably be called an evangelical faith* (see Evangelicals/Evangelicalism Cluster: Evangelical Theologies), including a stress on individual salvation*, the central role of Scripture*, the divinity and atonement* of Jesus, justification* by faith, and so forth. Registered and unregistered believers alike would readily subscribe to most of the major historic creeds* or confessions* of the faith. Most of the pastors and teachers at both categories of gathering are similarly like-minded in their conservative evangelical beliefs. Likewise, some in both sectors, though probably more in the unregistered sector, are "fundamentalist*" in that they see themselves in an adversarial relationship with "the world" and their own society (Christ against culture*) and have an extremely rigid code of ethical behavior and proscribed activities.

There are, however, at least two ways in which registered and unregistered churches for the most part differ. First, Pentecostalism* (the Charismatic* Movement) is prevalent in a significant part of the unregistered sector, especially in the countryside, whereas it is rarer in the urban registered churches. The Pentecostal/Charismatic concepts of the spiritual gifts (charismata*), being "filled with the Holy* Spirit," and behaviors such as speaking in tongues*, prophecy, and supernatural healing (see Health, Healing, and Christianity Cluster: In Asia) smack of superstition in the eyes of the Religious Affairs Bureau. These charismatic expressions of faith very seldom appear in large worship services in the registered churches, although they sometimes do in small groups within these congregations. Second, most of the unregistered churches have very little "quality control" in doctrinal matters. Most of the "sects*," which are deplored by both registered and unregistered Protestants and are outlawed by the state, originated in unregistered church movements. There is a lively tradition of local popular religion and of Millennialist movements in China. Most of the sects viewed as "evil cults" in China, such as Eastern Lightning, originated when the charismatic leader of a Christian group with no institutional oversight distorted Christian concepts, combining them with traditional popular religion at the local level.

Social Analysis and Trends. As the number of unregistered churches has increased during the past 25 years, the Chinese population has undergone a large shift from the countryside to the cities. The percentage of unregistered churches in the urban environment has almost certainly increased. Among those urban congregations, the number of groups made up of middle- and upper-middle-class Chinese, from the professions, business, and academe, and some from the bureaucracy and even the Communist Party (though religious belief is officially forbidden for party members), has notably increased. This means that the typical urban unregistered church is rather different from those in the 1980s; it is more confident, aggressive, and able and willing to be visible, e.g. in renting rooms in hotels or commercial buildings for their meetings. The difference is especially striking in those groups made up of young professionals, intellectuals, faculty members, and graduate students. Many of these churches apparently have no particular objection to registering with the government, but they have little interest in associating with the Three-Self Patriotic Movement, not primarily because of church–state issues, but because the intellectual level of the churches in the Three-Self Patriotic Movement is too low.

Unregistered churches in the rural areas are also changing. With the population flow to the cities, many Christians have migrated, giving rural churches and church networks a foot in urban areas. A few large nationwide networks of unregistered churches have emerged, and these became sufficiently confident in the late 1990s to issue publicly both a statement of faith and a joint open appeal to the state to grant more religious freedom.

In the 21st c., the independent and unregistered churches of China present a more complex challenge for analysis and understanding than they did at the end of the 20th c. Although there is increasing contact and interaction with the registered churches and the Three-Self Patriotic Movement, it seems likely that the phenomenon of the unregistered church will remain strong. DANIEL H. BAYS

Chinese Ethnic Minorities and Christianity. Although there are 55 officially recognized ethnic minorities in China, the number of linguistically, culturally, and religiously diversified ethnic groups might be several hundred. These groups have developed cultural and religious systems that are distinct from those of the Han Chinese people. Christianity played a role among several minorities, especially in the southwestern part of China.

In the 13th and 14th c., Christianity gained wide recognition among the Mongolian nobles, exerting a strong influence on the Yuan dynasty's court. Yet it was only in the late 19th c. that missionaries began to plant churches among the southwestern minorities. From the 1920s, Christianity played an important cultural and social role within these communities, becoming the main religion among the Lisu, Miao, Nu, Jingpo (Kachin), Lahu, Wa, Yi, and Hani. In the late 20th and early 21st c., the growth of Christianity among Chinese Mongols and Koreans in North China was also notable.

Owing to sociocultural differences, Christianity was established and grew among the ethnic minorities in China in very distinctive ways, as compared with the situation among the Han Chinese. Christianity played a stronger role in the social and cultural transformation of these minorities. Through the process of teaching from the Bible and of Bible translation, Christian missionaries brought literacy to the preliterate minorities. Schools and hospitals were founded, and health care, a different economic organization, and a new lifestyle were promoted. The Christian churches, their clergy, and their institutions strengthened the organizational structure within each ethnic community, and thus played an important role in framing these communities' ethnic identities.

Ethnic minorities have generally regarded Christianization as liberating and empowering. Even though they were asked to separate their Christian faith from their ethnic cultures, in a tacit way inculturation* took place from the beginning. Yet this process became explicit (from the late 20th c.) when Christian ethnic leaders began to encourage believers to express their Christian faith in traditional ethnic ways, and thus to develop their own form of Chinese Asian theology. In this way Christianity played an important role in helping the ethnic minorities in China to build their religious and cultural identity and to promote an interethnic dialogue in China. **See also CHINA; CHINESE CONTEMPORARY INDEPENDENT AND HOUSE CHURCHES.** YOU BIN

Chinese Literature and Christianity. The first major corpus of Christian literature in Chinese was written by early-17th-c. Jesuit missionaries who, together with Chinese Catholic scholars such as Xu Guangqi (1562–1633), Li Zhizao (1569–1630), and Yang Tingyun (1562–1627), engendered a provocative Christian–Confucian dialogue by endeavoring to identify Christian theology with certain aspects of classical Confucianism*. Prominent examples of this accommodative strategy of inculturation* include Matteo Ricci's* (1552–1610) *Tianzhu shiyi* (The true meaning of the Lord of Heaven, 1601) on the character and attributes of God and Diego de Pantoja's (1571–1618) *Qi ke* (Seven conquests, 1614) about overcoming the seven cardinal* sins.

With the aid of Chinese scholars like Wang Tao (1828–97), 19th-c. Protestant missionaries produced a large body of Chinese Christian literature. They translated Western Christian literary classics, including *The Pilgrim's Progress* (trans. William Burns, 1853), Augustine's *Confessions* (trans. William Muirhead, 1884), and *The Imitation of Christ* (trans. Henry Blodget, 1889). Their own literature includes William Milne's (1785–1822) best seller *Zhang Yuan liang you xiang lun* (Two friends, 1819), in which a Chinese believer discusses Christian tenets with his neighbor, and Griffith John's (1831–1912) *Yin jia dang dao* (Leading the family in the right way, 1882), about the Christian way of life in which a Chinese convert leads his family.

Both Ricci's and Milne's influential works were written in a dialogic form, while other works followed the pattern of a Chinese novel. The Bible was also presented as a work of Chinese literature, notably the Delegates' Version in classical Chinese (1854) and the vernacular Union Version (1919), which, it was hoped, would make an intellectual and literary impact on contemporary Chinese scholars. Owing to the patronage of the London Religious Tract Society, most 19th-c. Chinese Christian works were interdenominational and Evangelical in character.

Against the background of Western imperialism and the end of the imperial era, the May Fourth Movement (1919) aimed to reexamine China's fundamental values and purge the nation of its Confucian legacy. Some Chinese scholars saw Christianity as an alternative ideology that would be useful for national renewal. Chinese writers like Bing Xin (1900–99), Xu Dishan (1893–1941), and Ba Jin (1904–2005) were attracted by the core values of Christianity, particularly sacrifice*, forgiveness*, and universal love*, all based on Jesus' personality and teachings. Bing Xin advocated a philosophy of love in *Fan xing* (A myriad of stars, 1923) and *Chun shui* (Spring waters, 1923), collections of poems filled with images of light, expressions of hope, and praises to God. The salient Christian virtues and ethical teachings are manifest in Xu Dishan's novels, *Shangren fu* (The merchant's wife, 1921) and *Zhui wang lao zhu* (The web-mending toiling spider, 1925); their heroines, Xiguan and Shangjie, respectively, are portrayed as embodiments of mercy, faithfulness, and perseverance. Meanwhile, the institutional forms of churches and Western models of Christian theology were satirized by writers like Xiao Qian (1910–1999), whose novel *Guiyi* (Conversion, 1935) condemns the Salvation* Army and takes Christianity as a synonym for cultural imperialism. JOHN TSZ PANG LAI

Chinese Rites Controversy. In the encounter between the gospel and the Chinese people, the most explosive controversy surrounded the ancestor* veneration rites, traditionally associated with Confucius* and his teaching on filiality. Matteo Ricci* (1552–1610) and the Jesuits viewed these rites as purely honorary and ceremonial, thus gaining many converts among the Confucian literati. When Dominican missionary Juan Bautista Morales complained that these rites were superstitious*, controversy erupted and continued until Benedict XIV prohibited these rites in the bull *Ex Quo Singulari* (1742). The Roman Catholic Church reversed its prohibition through two instructions, *Pluries Instanterque* (1936) and *Plane Compertum Est* (1939). **See also CHINA.** JONATHAN Y. TAN

Chinese Women and Christianity. Early converts among Chinese women came mostly from the lower classes. The Christian Church offered them new religious perspectives on the world and themselves. Some converted because of tangible benefits and rewards, such as attending mission schools, employment, and protection. In the early 1920s, female Christians made up about 37% percent of the Protestants in China.

Church activities for women included Sunday worship, Bible studies, prayer meetings, and catechism classes. "Bible women" were hired to teach illiterate women to read the Bible and visit parishioners. Female leaders in local congregations were often active community organizers, teachers, and arbiters of disputes in their communities. In the Catholic Church, women could become members of religious orders, and some joined the group of Christian Virgins, dedicating themselves to a life of celibacy and contemplation.

In addition to evangelistic work, Christian missions provided education* for girls and women and introduced Western medicine to China. In 1844 the first mission school for Chinese girls was opened in Ningbo, and North China Union College for Women and Ginling Women's College were founded in the early 20th c. Some of the graduates of these colleges became teachers, writers, and social reformers. Christian women initiated various social reforms, such as the anti-foot-binding movement, temperance unions, and health* campaigns. Shi Meiyu and Kang Cheng were Western-trained medical doctors involved in welfare reforms for women and children. The YWCA* provided social services, organized anti-opium campaigns, and offered literary classes for female workers.

Social participation and heightened awareness of the political changes in China called for deeper religious reflection. Christian women discussed the social implications of Christianity and challenged patriarchal* practices of the Church. The churches were closed down during the Cultural Revolution (1966–76), but since they reopened in the late 1970s, women have been the most active members, and many were ordained to serve Christian congregations.

KWOK PUI-LAN

Chi-Rho. The two Greek letters that begin the title "Christ," combined in a monogram by Constantine. **See also IHS; INRI; *NOMINA SACRA*.**

Choir (Lat *chorus*), the group of singers in worship; the area in which they sing in the chancel* (though they also sing in a gallery).

Chrism, olive oil mixed with diverse substances (depending on the church), used for anointing* in the Greek and Latin churches in the sacraments of baptism*, chrismation*, confirmation*, and orders* (a different oil is used in anointing the sick).

Chrismation, the second sacrament of the Eastern Orthodox* Church, is conferred on the newly baptized (adult or infant) by the priest immediately after baptism* to impart the gift of the Holy* Spirit and signify the Spirit's indwelling presence. The chrism – a mixture of olive oil, wine, and prescribed aromatic substances symbolizing the diverse gifts of the Holy Spirit – is prepared and consecrated periodically on Holy Thursday by the ecumenical* patriarch or the heads of autocephalous* churches and distributed to the parishes. Chrismation is also used to consecrate churches and to receive baptized converts from certain other churches.

ALKIVIADIS CALIVAS

Christ (Gk *Christos,* like the Heb *Messiah**; literally translated as "the anointed one"). In the OT, one is anointed as a sign of being chosen for a task, especially kingship, but also priesthood or a prophetic role. In the NT, "Christ" is the most common title of Jesus. **See also CHRISTOLOGIES CLUSTER; JESUS, IMAGES OF, CLUSTER; JESUS, QUEST FOR THE HISTORICAL; MESSIAH.**

Christendom, a term coined in medieval England and Northern Europe to refer to the sense of a single church integrally connected with the government, and then to Christians collectively, to the territory they occupied, and most often to the ideal of a Christian nation (as opposed to evil or "pagan" society and culture*).

Christening, the act of baptizing, whereby a person is made a Christian and given a "Christian name."

Christian. The term "Christian" was first used in Antioch (Acts 11:16). Its Latin suffix suggests that it was coined by Roman officials who suspected that Jesus' followers were members of a political faction. While Paul often speaks of being "in Christ," the term "Christian" was used for many years only by outsiders (Acts 26:28). Believers were persecuted "as Christians" (1 Pet 4:16), which is probably why Ignatius*, before being martyred, appropriated the term for himself. From the 2nd c. on, it became an honorable self-designation, suggesting that Christians were both loyal to and anointed through Christ (see Hellenistic Religious Traditions and Christianity's Self-Definition). Through the centuries and in various cultures, the term "Christian" acquired many connotations, because it refers to the self-designation of anyone claiming an association with Jesus Christ, however he or she might conceive of this association.

DANIEL PATTE

Christian Church (Disciples of Christ) originated with the 1830s union on the US frontier of the followers of Barton Stone* and Alexander Campbell*. Leaders preached God's unconditional love* revealed in Jesus Christ unencumbered by teachings such as the Calvinist* doctrine of election*, believing that this simple gospel, received in faith*, overcomes the sinner's rebellion against God and unites believers with God and one another. They also called for the restoration of what they believed to be NT practices, including fellowship on the basis of confession that Jesus is the Christ (rather than doctrinal creeds*, which they labeled divisive), congregational governance, weekly observance of the Lord's Supper* as a reminder of God's love, and believers' baptism* by immersion as an assurance of God's forgiveness. They taught that unity would lead to the conversion of unbelievers and usher in Christ's millennial* reign of peace and justice. Congregations were called Christian Church or Church of Christ, and the movement was identified as Disciples of Christ. Developments related to changing social contexts have led to divisions over how to achieve unity.

The first division occurred over the use of instrumental music* during worship and the establishment of mission organizations beyond the congregation. Some congregations, located primarily in the rural South, opposed these developments as being contrary to Scripture. Identifying themselves as Churches of Christ, they were recognized by the 1906 religious census as separate from the Disciples of Christ.

The second division was recognized in 1971 with a listing in the *Yearbook of American Churches* of the Christian Churches and Churches of Christ. These congregations separated from the Christian Church (Disciples of Christ) because of its participation with other churches in the 20th-c. ecumenical* movement (viewed as condoning denominationalism*), its acceptance of historical-critical biblical interpretation* (viewed as undermining biblical authority), and its acceptance of persons as church members already baptized in some form other than believers' immersion (acceptance viewed as violating Scripture). Differences between rural and urban locations appear to have influenced this division: the 1971 census shows that the total membership of the Christian Church (Disciples of Christ) in urban counties exceeded that of the Christian Churches and Churches of Christ by 50%.

The Christian Church (Disciples of Christ) ordains women* and observes its historic practices of baptism and the Lord's Supper. Through participation in the ecumenical movement and conversations with the other streams of the Stone–Campbell movement, it calls for unity amid diversity.

D. NEWELL WILLIAMS

Christian Democratic Parties in the Low Countries, France, Italy, Austria, and Germany came to prominence after World War II. They arose from roots in previously existing Roman Catholic parties and Christian labor movements. There are similar parties in Latin America. In Germany the Christian Democratic parties are interconfessional; in Scandinavia their base is Protestant.

In the decades and countries in which Christian Democracy has been a major political force, their main opposition party has generally been socialist. This necessarily leaves Christian Democratic parties with a constituency generally right of center, though drawn somewhat to the left depending on the strength of their own non-socialist labor contingent. Their heritage, however, consists of distinctly progressive forebears who battled laissez-faire and upper-class political economies in the name of social justice*. They also had to contend with European Catholics' fear of democratic politics as dangerous and revolutionary. The experience of World War II finally discredited authoritarian regimes and showed the worth of democratic institutions in protecting human values. Christian Democracy was the most significant new development of the 20th c. in the history of Western European political parties. **See also** DEMOCRACY AND CHRISTIANITY.

PAUL MISNER

Christianity and Other Religions. See RELIGIONS AND CHRISTIANITY.

Christian Science, founded by Mary Baker Eddy* (1821–1910), popularized the metaphysical* interpretation of Christian theology that gained currency in late-19th- and early-20th-c. US culture. The term "metaphysical" denotes the primacy of Divine Mind as the controlling factor in human experience. If God is Mind and the substance of being is Spirit, then human beings, as the expression of Mind, must reflect God's eternal perfection. Original* sin is not the cause of human suffering. All negative experiences, including sin*, disease, and death*, are the result of a profound error in thinking, an error Eddy termed of "mortal mind." The fundamental perceptual error of mortal mind is the pernicious belief in the self-limiting reality of a material world. For Eddy, Spirit was the ontological and theological universal; matter was mental error.

While traditional Christian teaching commonly places the Kingdom* of Heaven in a realm beyond and hereafter, Christian Science calls for the actualization or demonstration of perfection in the here and now by *knowing* the truth of being. The Christian Scientist does not pray to a God apart for health*, security, and prosperity*. These are qualities of God's unchanging expression that human beings invariably will reflect, experientially, once they depart from erring, limited, mortal thinking. God, as Divine Principle, can be demonstrated, scientifically, by anyone who knows and affirms this principle of being. Eddy called on her followers to reflect seven synonyms for God: Principle, Mind, Spirit, Soul, Life, Truth, and Love.

The "Christian" element in Christian Science emerges in a radical reinterpretation of Jesus' role in the Gospels. Gone is the atoning*, sacrificial death on the cross. Jesus becomes the exemplar, the first and ultimate "Christian Scientist," who demonstrably overcame sin, sickness, and death through his superior perception of the allness of Spirit and the nothingness of matter. Jesus is revered by Christian Scientists, but he is not the Messiah as defined by orthodox Christology. Rather, Jesus is unique because he was the first human being to understand and fully express Divine Mind. Jesus' *at-one-ment* with God is the natural state of all human beings.

Though Eddy's many detractors scoffed at her theology, claiming it was irrational and dangerous, she stressed the practical nature of her "science." For her, it was in day-to-day challenges that Christian Scientists proved God's perfection. Thus healing became a focus of the religion, a practical manifestation of the change in thinking from the material to the spiritual.

JOHN K. SIMMONS

Christian Socialism. The intriguing relationship between Christianity and socialism has been complicated by the materialistic determinism of the dominant Marxist* version of socialism and the atheism* of most socialist political movements. However, an open-minded inspection of the topic reveals a surprising number of principles and values on which socialism and Christianity generally find ample common ground: deep concern for the well-being of workers, commitment to the equal dignity of all humans, and a justification for state interventions in the economy* to protect losers in economic competition.

Since the mid-19th c., thinkers calling themselves "Christian Socialists" have found much inspiration in scriptural* support for the communal nature of property*; e.g. Acts 2:44 and 4:32–35 portray the primitive church practicing a common holding of goods. Centering on France, Germany, England, and the USA, Christians espousing a variety of socialist ideals have, for nearly two centuries, started utopian communities, agitated in support of the labor* movement, and organized for social reform.

Among Protestants, the US "Social* Gospel Movement" led by Washington Gladden and Walter Rauschenbusch* is perhaps the best embodiment of church support for socialist principles. The early writings of Reinhold Niebuhr* and Paul Tillich's* "theology of culture" also espouse broad socialist approaches to life in society.

Much Catholic social thought overlaps with the central concerns of socialism, although Pope Pius* XI put a damper on the topic when in his 1931 encyclical *Quadragesimo* Anno* (§120) he wrote, "No one can be at the same time a sincere Catholic and a true socialist." Subsequent Catholic social teaching has refined the extent to which authentic church-based concerns regarding social responsibility and economic equity overlap with theories and practices of socialism. Socialist influences found their way into late-20th-c. Liberation* theology and even into official Catholic doctrine when Pope John* Paul II heralded (albeit in a carefully nuanced way) the notion of the preferential* option for the poor. **See also SOCIAL ENCYCLICALS; SOCIAL GOSPEL MOVEMENT.**

THOMAS MASSARO, SJ

Christina of Markyate (b.c1096–?1155), hermit and prioress of Markyate (Hertfordshire, England), renowned for the intimate portrait of her spiritual development in a contemporary biography and for her possession of the *St. Albans Psalter*, a magnificently illuminated manuscript that included scenes of direct relevance to Christina's own visionary experiences. The *Life* and the *Psalter* together provide valuable evidence regarding the religious climate of post-Conquest England, the ways someone of Anglo-Saxon birth could make a place for herself in the new Anglo-Norman monastic* world, the value placed therein on a woman's experience of God, and the rationale whereby such a woman might choose to see herself as wedded to Christ – spurning the offer of both an illicit affair with a bishop and a comfortable married life among the nobility. According to the *Life*, the abbot of St. Albans, on whom Christina relied for the material support of her priory, in turn depended on Christina for divinely inspired guidance and counsel. The *Psalter*, most likely a gift to her from the abbot, contains the oldest extant text of Old French* literature (the story of St. Alexis), an indication of the value placed on the development of a French vernacular that could vie with the Old English literature the Normans had inherited. HENRIETTA LEYSER

Christmas, festival of the birth of Christ, also called Nativity* (Lat for "birth"; Spanish, Navidad; French, Noël; Italian, Natale). The Gospels indicate no date (Matt 1:25–2:1; Luke 2:1–7). It was first observed on January 6 (see Epiphany), still the date used by the Armenian* Church. During the 4th c., in Europe it came to be observed on December 25, the date of a traditional celebration of the sun and lengthening days. It is preceded by Advent*, considered in the West to be "the beginning of the church year"; the "twelve days of Christmas" are completed by Epiphany. Since the Middle Ages, Christmas has been a time of celebration and gift giving, influenced more by popular culture than by doctrine. In the Eastern churches, the Feast of Nativity culminates on January 6 as a part of the Theophany* (Epiphany*) celebration. The Puritans* objected to Christmas as unbiblical, but it continued as a civic, cultural, and commercial holiday, and today there have been attempts to restore its religious meaning by minimizing or transforming its cultural features.

Christocentrism, any form of theology in which Jesus as Christ is the key to religious knowledge, human history, or the cosmos.

CHRISTOLOGIES CLUSTER

1) *Introductory Entries*

Christology: In Eastern Orthodox Church History
Christology: In Western Church History

2) *A Sampling of Contextual Views and Practices*

Christologies in Africa
Christologies in Africa: Images of Christ
Christologies in Asia
Christologies in Asia: The Jesus of Asian Women
Christologies in the Caribbean Islands: History
Christologies in the Caribbean Islands: Present Day
Christologies in Latin America
Christologies in North America
Christologies in North America: Feminist and Womanist

Christologies in North America: Latino/a
Christologies in South Pacific and Australia
See also INCARNATION CLUSTER; JESUS, IMAGES OF, CLUSTER

1) Introductory Entries

Christology: In Eastern Orthodoxy Church History. See TRINITY CLUSTER: IN EASTERN ORTHODOXY.

Christology: In Western Church History. Christology in the Western Church concerns the doctrine of the person of Christ, focusing on how his divinity and humanity are related (rather than on how Christ is related to the other persons of the Trinity*, as is the focus of Eastern Orthodox churches). One commonly finds an approximate distinction between "low" Christology" and "high" Christology. A "low" Christology is one that emphasizes Jesus' humanity. This was the original experience of the disciples*; it is a feature of many early Christologies, especially those that were called Adoptionist*; and it is a characteristic of many modern Christologies that are based on the so-called historical* Jesus or are concerned to avoid excessive claims. A "high" Christology emphasizes that Jesus manifests a preexisting divine being, sometimes distinct from the Father (as in Arianism*), sometimes of the same essence as the Father (as in Nicene* orthodoxy). The endemic question for Christology has been how to acknowledge Christ's full humanity while also affirming his divinity.

Within early Christianity and the NT, there were various ways of understanding Jesus: as the wonderworker (especially in Mark), virginally conceived (in Matthew and Luke), or adopted by God and filled with divine power (as in Mark 1:11 and Rom 1:3–4); as the righteous one who speaks with authority and manifests the divine Wisdom (as in Matthew); or as the incarnation of a preexistent divine being (as in John; see Preexistence).

As doctrinal debate moved into its formative stage, there were three basic approaches to answering the question "Who is Jesus Christ?" For the Adoptionists, the answer was "the man, filled with divine power"; for the "Word*-flesh" school, the answer was "the Word becoming man"; and for the "Word*-man" school, it was "the Word conjoined with the man."

Debating Adoptionism. In Rome (c250) there was a decisive rejection of Adoptionism, the view taught by Artemas (or Artemon) that Jesus was a "mere man." The alternative was to think of him as a divine person. There came to be a change in the second article of the creeds. While the Apostles'* Creed continued to speak of Jesus as "conceived by the Holy Spirit," the Eastern Creed ("the Creed," always in process as a single but ever changing living tradition) began to speak of Jesus as the divine Word*, active in creation. Thus the name "Jesus Christ" referred to the second person of the Trinity*. Along with this, there was often a denial, or perhaps only an ignoring, of Jesus' full humanity: if Jesus was a divine person, he had no need of human personhood; indeed, if he had a human mind or soul, this would seem to make him a "mere man."

Debating "Word-Flesh" Christology. According to this approach, Jesus was a divine person manifested in human flesh, without a human mind or soul. This school emphasized the divine power at work in salvation*, looking more to the divine cause and the human effect in saving others than to the mediating factors in Christ's humanity.

The Synod of Antioch (268) that condemned Paul* of Samosata gave dogmatic status, especially in the East, to the Word-flesh Christology that had already become widespread. In the early 4th c., this was the understanding shared by almost all thinkers, including Athanasius*, his Arian* opponents, and Apollinaris*, a major defender of the Nicene* faith, around whom controversy centered.

Apollinaris, by explicitly stating the widely held assumption that Christ lacked a human mind, triggered the definitive debate over the person of Christ. Damasus* of Rome held a council (377) that declared Christ to have complete humanity, yet not in the sense of "two Sons." Apollinarianism was condemned at councils in Alexandria (378), Antioch (379), and Constantinople* (381) and at another Roman council (382).

Debating "Word-Man Christology." The church now faced the question of how to affirm Jesus' complete humanity without implying "two Sons," one divine and one human. An influential answer was supplied by Gregory* Nazianzen (*Epp.* 101, 102, 202; also *Orat.* 38). He retrieved the dictum "What is not assumed is not healed," which had first been used by Irenaeus*, Tertullian*, and Origen* in an anti-Gnostic* way to defend the reality of Christ's body; on this same principle, then, a human mind must have been assumed and healed. But how? Gregory described the mind of Christ as the intermediary principle uniting Word and the animated body. This was a revival of Origen's Christology (cf. *De princ.* II,6), which spoke of Jesus' mind as so closely united with the Word, through affection and intuition, that there is a union of being. The Neoplatonist metaphor of "mixture" or interpenetration, originally developed to explain the union of soul with body, was utilized by Gregory Nazianzen, Gregory* of Nyssa, and Augustine* to explain the union of two spiritual substances, mind and Logos: Christ's human mind is the medium of union, united so completely with the Word that the two become one.

Similar, but with a fateful difference, was the position of the Antiochene* tradition (Eusebius* of Emesa, Diodore* of Tarsus, Nestorius*, Theodore* of Mopsuestia). Emphasizing God's immutability, they ascribed all change, passivity, and suffering to Christ's human subjectivity. To explain the union, they spoke of divine grace and human response. Rejecting the metaphor of mixture, they asserted a "conjunction" of *will* rather than of mind or being; this conjunction, furthermore, is dynamic, susceptible to development, as suggested by Jesus' growth in "wisdom, stature, and grace" (Luke 2:40).

The Christology of the Alexandrian* tradition (in contrast with both) thought of the Word as the subject of Jesus' human experience, being born first in eternity and then from Mary. Conflict between the Alexandrine and Antiochene traditions broke out when Nestorius became bishop of Constantinople (428) and opposed the term "Theotokos"* (Mother of God). He was immediately attacked by Cyril* of Alexandria; the conflict was exacerbated by rivalries between the sees of Alexandria and Constantinople, and by the hospitality shown toward Pelagians* in Constantinople, making Nestorius suspect in the West. Cyril issued 12 anathematisms (430) declaring that Christ is "one out of two," insisting on the "one incarnate nature of the divine Word" (hence the term "Monophysites*," or more accurately "Miaphysites*") and demanding that Christ's humanity not be called "a man" or anything other than the Word incarnate. At the Council of Ephesus* (431, held in the first basilica dedicated to Mary), Cyril's party took action before the arrival of the Antiochenes, interpreting the Nicene Creed to affirm a union in the one hypostasis* of the Word and condemning Nestorius. The Antiochene party then met separately; its creed, ironically, became the basis for the "Formulary of Reunion" agreed upon by both parties (433). The Antiochenes, however, refused to accept any condemnation of Nestorius, and many in the Cyrillian party continued their polemic against the views expressed in the Formulary.

A group of Cyrillians led by Eutyches* gained a brief victory at the Second Council of Ephesus* in 449, called a "robber synod" by Pope Leo* I. The situation was reversed at the Council of Chalcedon*, which declared Christ to be one person or hypostasis, "known in two natures without division or separation, confusion or change."

Debating Chalcedon. For the West, the Council of Chalcedon, as interpreted through the Tome* of Leo, was the end of doctrinal debate. For the East, it was the beginning of several centuries of conflict between alternative ways of understanding Christ. The Cyrillian party, emphasizing the union of the two natures in the one person of the Word, spoke of a *natural union* and asserted that Christ was "from" (Gk, *ek*) but not "in" two natures. The dynamic force of the Incarnation* made it possible to understand Redemption* as the time when all natural life would be caught up into a graced deification* (theosis*). The Antiochene party, insisting on the abiding difference between the two natures, used language that suggested two beings, and thus their opponents claimed that they taught a merely *accidental union,* a union of will rather than of being. Chalcedon had affirmed two natures or essences and one hypostasis or entity (understood as "person"), thus a *hypostatic union*. What Chalcedon did not make clear, however, was whether this meant a union through the human subjectivity of Christ, as in the Origenist and Antiochene traditions, or the taking of an impersonal human nature by the preexisting hypostasis of the divine Word, as in the line from Cyril to the later "neo-Chalcedonian" party. Even the notion of *enhypostasia** that was later set forth by Leontius* of Byzantium (c543) could be interpreted in either of these two ways.

Attempts at Compromise. Followers of Cyril either opposed Chalcedon or interpreted it as nothing more than an explication of the doctrine of the Council of Ephesus in 431. The emperors, seeking reconciliation with the Cyrillians in Egypt*, Syria*, and Armenia*, issued successive decrees intended to diminish the authority of Chalcedon (see Encyclion; Henoticon; Typos).

Rome broke communion with Constantinople over these doctrinal issues (484–519), learning in the process to take a more independent attitude toward state intervention in religious affairs. By this time, Assyrian Christians of the Church* of the East (commonly called by the misnomer "Nestorians*") began their independent life in the Persian Empire.

Inside Byzantine territory, the controversy was between the Chalcedonian and the Cyrillian parties, called respectively Dyophysites* and Miaphysites*. Although the emperors tried to modify Chalcedon's language in the direction of Cyril, the Cyrillians did not reciprocate, and they remained in control of the Coptic* Church in Egypt and the Syriac* Orthodox Church (polemically nicknamed Jacobite*; Armenia* had already developed as an independent kingdom).

The emperor Justin achieved reunion with the Western Church (519). His nephew Justinian*, trying to conciliate the Cyrillians, condemned the so-called Three Chapters* (544), and the Second Council of Constantinople* in 551 did the same. When Pope Vigilius*, under pressure, twice affirmed these condemnations (547, 553), large areas in the West broke communion with Rome as well as Constantinople.

During the 7th c., the emperors made a new attempt at conciliation on the basis of the idea of "one theandric [divine-human] energy and will" (see Monothelitism). This position was opposed in the West, aided by Maximus* the Confessor; it was condemned at the Third Council of Constantinople* in 680–81.

Separation of Three Communions. The Church* of the East was already outside the Roman Byzantine Empire and within the Persian Empire. Conquests by Persia (615–29) and more permanently by Islam (from 634) removed the Cyrillian churches of Syria and Egypt from the territories controlled by Constantinople. The emperors in Constantinople now became defenders of the faith as defined by the seven ecumenical* councils. A work by John* of Damascus, *The Orthodox Faith* (c740–50), came to be regarded as the definitive statement of Eastern Orthodox doctrine.

The meaning of "two natures in one person" was still not agreed upon even by those who acknowledged Chalcedon. The East tended to emphasize the Word as the sole person, while the West emphasized full humanity, even speaking of the Word assuming "the man." The so-called Spanish Adoptianists* were condemned because they continued to use Western language at a time when the popes were adopting Eastern language.

As the era of Scholastic theology dawned in the West, there were three predominant approaches to Christology (Peter Lombard, *III Sent.*, d. 6), influenced by a translation of the *Orthodox Faith* of John* of Damascus. The *assumptus homo* theory asserted that Christ was a man, subsisting through himself; its orthodoxy was safeguarded by the language of Augustine* and Leo that the man Jesus "was not first created and then assumed, but was created by being assumed." The *habitus* theory went to the opposite extreme, asserting that the Christ's soul and body, being assumed like a garment or habit, are not even "something" but are "nothing" without the Word. This "nihilianism" of Abelard* and Peter* Lombard was condemned at the Third Lateran Council in 1179. The *subsistence* theory speaks of the single person of the Word, subsisting first in a divine way, then after the assumption of human nature also subsisting in a human way; the humanity never subsists in and through itself, but only "in" the Word. This approach was closest to the Council of Ephesus, Cyril's 12 anathematisms, and the Second Council of Constantinople, and as these sources were rediscovered and analyzed in the 13th c., it became the predominant view, although the Franciscans* continued to hold the *assumptus homo* position.

The Reformation adhered to the doctrine of the first four ecumenical* councils, ending with Chalcedon. Debate between the Lutherans* and the Reformed* was occasioned by their differences in eucharistic doctrine. The Lutherans, in order to explain how the Body and Blood of Christ are "in, with, and under" the elements, asserted that Christ's humanity shared the attributes of the divinity, including omnipresence; consequently, they were accused of Monophysitism* by the Reformed. The Reformed asserted that the ascended body of Christ, in its human dimensions, is in heaven, that Christ is made present in the Eucharist by the power of the Holy Spirit, and that Christ's divinity is "outside" his humanity (the so-called *extra Calvinisticum*); consequently, they were accused of Nestorianism* by the Lutherans.

More intensive historical study (18th–19th c.) brought to light the differences between the four Gospels and raised questions about both their historicity and the meaning of their assertions about Jesus. As certitude about "historical truth" diminished, greater efforts were made to establish a connection between Jesus and the universal truths of reason*. This was done in an especially influential way by Kant*, who spoke of the "ideal archetype" of humanity posited by practical reason; by Schleiermacher*, for whom Jesus actualizes this archetype; and by Hegel* and his followers, for whom the ideal, first explicit in Jesus, has a life and power independent of him.

Three major trends can be identified in contemporary theology:

1. Most theologians, following Schleiermacher, revived the Origenist, Nestorian, or *assumptus homo* view that the "psychological center" in Christ is the man Jesus, not the divine Word, giving even more emphasis to Jesus' growth "in wisdom, stature, and grace" (Luke 2:52). Jesus actualized the human potentialities for relationship with God; new life on the part of Christians is the result of his historical influence through the Christian community and its sacraments.
2. Some theologians, more in line with Kant and Hegel, suggest that Jesus "represents" more than he "actualizes." Jesus primarily symbolizes a relationship that is possible without any knowledge of Jesus yet is discovered through him: the divine Word or Spirit also operates directly on other human beings. For some with a more historical perspective, Jesus becomes the initiator of a broader process that develops beyond anything that he could represent in the 1st c. Thus they speak of the "Christ principle," and feminists speak of "Christa" as a principle transcending the 1st-c. patriarchal setting and Jesus' invocation of God as "Abba."
3. The Cyrilline Christology emphasizing the Word in human flesh also has its contemporary champions. For some Liberation* theologians, the second person of the Trinity, fully divine, identified himself with the poor and oppressed (Matt 25:31–46). A fully divine power of salvation (liberation from oppression) is at work, making it possible to respond to this unconditional demand. **See also JESUS, IMAGES OF, CLUSTER; LITERATURE AND CHRISTIANITY.**

EUGENE TESELLE

2) A Sampling of Contextual Views and Practices

Christologies in Africa are cultural verbalizations of the identity and significance of Jesus, the Christ of God, as he is encountered in faith by African Christians in their historical, socioeconomic, and political situations and their religiosity, which shape the varieties of current African Christologies. New African faces of Christ arise in response to Western depictions of Jesus (based on Western historical models) that are not adequate for Africans.

In African* Religion and soteriology, there were valiant persons who fulfilled the role of savior: sages, benevolent chiefs and kings, healers – Onisegun (Yoruba), Nganga (Bakongo), and Dibia Mgborogwu (Igbo) – priests, priestesses, and great ancestors* who served as channels through which the vital force of the Supreme Being was transmitted to posterity and energized the community. Some of these mythical figures had been divinized and given different theandric attributes.

Owing to the diversity of African cultures, there has been a plethora of African responses to the question "But who do you say that I am?" (Mark 8: 29). The many images of Jesus as the Christ derived from African concepts represent African peoples' confession of the lordship of Jesus and how he meets them at the point of their needs. Culturally loaded concepts like "our Ancestor," the "African King," Odogwu n' Agha or Onwuatuegwu (Brave or Fearless Warrior [Igbo]), Omoba (Prince [Yoruba]), Nnukwu Ukochukwu (High Priest [Igbo]), and Onisegun Ode Orun (Healer from Heaven [Yoruba]), are ingeniously used to designate Jesus in African* Instituted Churches and in Charismatic* churches and given "Christ-ful" significance – especially in faith-moving hymns and praise songs, expressing the reality of Jesus in African Christians' salvation history. Such African christological constructs reflect the deep connections with Christ held in many of the vibrant Christian communities in Africa as Christ is encountered in faith and in everyday life.

African Christologies in contemporary African Christian theology indicate how African faithful discern the significance of Jesus' life cycle – birth, youth, words, work, death, and resurrection – for their culture and contexts, including the life contexts of African women, who need to retrieve human rights in overt patriarchal societies, and of people struggling with HIV/AIDS. Thus liberation and liberating ecclesiology have become essential ingredients of christological reflections in Africa.

Having crossed cultural boundaries, Christianity needs to wear different garb, namely African Christologies, the heartbeat of African Christian theology and the point around which all pastoral activities in Africa revolve.

UKACHUKWU CHRIS MANUS

Christologies in Africa: Images of Christ. Several christological images emerged as African theologians faced Jesus' challenging question: "Who do you say that I am?"

Eschatological images present Jesus as sent from God to an alienated world, where God's presence takes the shape of the Crucified One. Jesus takes on himself the conditions of the poor*, the marginalized, and the oppressed; through his resurrection, Jesus as Savior reveals God's victory over the world's alienating forces, opening a future for a new humanity (as Mercy Amba Uduyoye and Elizabeth Amoah [Ghana] and Nasimiyu-Wasike [Kenya] say).

Anthropological images of Jesus, derived from African concepts, wisdom, and knowledge, are greatly influenced by the African religiocultural heritage: Christ as the greatest ancestor* (John Pobee [Ghana]), Christ the proto-ancestor (Benezet Bujo [Democratic Republic of Congo]), Christ the brother-ancestor or elder brother (Charles Nyamiti [Tanzania]), Jesus as healer (Theresia Hinga [Kenya]), and Jesus as mother, a nurturer of life (Theresa Okure [Nigeri]; Nasimiyu-Wasike [Kenya]).

Liberational images of Jesus are articulated by several African theologians (Jean-Marc Ela [Cameroon]; Theresia Hinga and Nasimiyu-Wasike [Kenya]; Mercy Amba Oduyoye and Elizabeth Amoah [Ghana]). Jesus calls both women and men to discipleship, recognizing them as equally responsible persons (Luke 11:27–28, 8:1–2) who should work for the liberation of all people and challenge all traditional practices that are dehumanizing. Jesus especially calls African women not to accept fatalistically their hardship and suffering but to work for the elimination of those forces that limit them and reduce them to non-persons (Nasimiyu-Wasike [Kenya]).

Cosmological images present Jesus as a restorer of the cosmos who reconciles all created reality with God (Rom 8: 20–23). Natural calamities (drought, floods, famine) have claimed millions of African people. Jesus, who rebuked the winds and ordered harmony and restored tranquility, is able to restore harmony and peace to the African continent and the whole world.

ANNE NASIMIYU WASIKE

Christologies in Asia. Articulating the Christian confession that Jesus is the Word* of God made flesh and the Savior* of all humankind in Asian terms is a daunting task that Asian theologians have taken on with imagination and resourcefulness.

Assyrian* Christians (commonly known as "Nestorians," a misnomer) during the Tang dynasty made the first attempt to express christological doctrines in Asian religious terms. The famous Xi'an stele (erected 781; discovered 1623) and the "Dunhuang Documents" show that the earliest Christian missionaries to China borrowed extensively from Buddhist*, Confucianist*, and Daoist* concepts to explain the person and work of Jesus. Accordingly, Christianity is the "ever-true and unchanging Dao" itself; Jesus established a "new teaching of nonassertion" (Daoist), taught "how to rule both families and kingdoms" (Confucianist), and took an oar in "the vessel of mercy" and "ascended to the Palace of Light" (Buddhist). In India the Hindu idea of the "descent" of the gods in the form of avatars is compared with the incarnation of the Logos, and Krishna is compared with Jesus (Ovey N. Mohammed). The Hindu idea that humans can become avatars through the indwelling of the divine spirit was applied to Jesus. Christ is believed to be present and active in all authentic religions (Raimon Panikkar). Jesus was also presented as the Enlightened One, like Siddhartha Gautama (Seichi Yagi, Peter Phan), or as a poor monk who alleviates the enforced poverty of the masses by his voluntary poverty (Aloysius Pieris).

A second christological model presents Jesus through cultural categories. In India, non-Christians of the Indian Renaissance first attempted this inculturated* Christology. They saw in Jesus the embodiment of Hindu and Indian ideals, the supreme guide to happiness (Ram Mohun Roy), the incarnation of *cit* (consciousness) of the triad of *sat-cit-ananda* (Keshub Chunder Sen, Brahmobandhav Upadhyaya), *jivan mukta*, one who achieved liberation while still alive (Swami Vivekananda), the Son* of man seeking the poor of the earth (Rabindranath Tagore), and the supreme *satyagrahi*, lover of and fighter for truth (Mahatma Gandhi). Christ has also been presented as Purusha, the creator god in the form of man (P. Chenchiah); as Prajapati, lord of the created world (K. M. Banerjee); as the eternal *Om* (S. Jesudasan); as the crucified guru (M. Thomas Thangaraj); and as the elder son and ancestor* par excellence (Peter Phan).

More recently Christology accounts for the massive poverty and exploitation in Asia on the basis of ethnicity, race*, caste*, and gender. Christ is presented in India as one of the outcast and untouchable Dalits* (Arvind P. Nirmal and M. E. Prabhakar) and in Korea as a member of the Minjung*, the oppressed masses (Kim Yong Bock, Suh Nam Dong, Ahn Byung Mu). In Japan Jesus' crown of thorns is taken as a symbol of the liberation of the Buraku* people (animal slaughterers, a minority discriminated against as filthy people, in contrast to the imperial throne of chrysanthemums) (Teruo Kuribayashi). In the Philippines, Jesus is portrayed as taking part in the struggle for independence (Carlos Abesamis, Eleazar S. Fernandez). In Taiwan, homeland theology (Wang Hsien Chi) and Chhut Thau Thin theology (Huang Po Ho), respectively, emphasize the political or the cultural dimension to foster self-determination for the Taiwanese people. Asian Feminist theology highlights Christ's role in liberating women from the patriarchy* and androcentrism* that is endemic to several Asian cultures (Marianne Katoppo, Mary John Mananzan, Virginia Fabella, Elizabeth Tapia, Chung Hyun Kyung, Kwok Pui-lan, Aruna Gnanadason, Muriel Orevillo-Montenegro). PETER C. PHAN

Christologies in Asia: The Jesus of Asian Women. Jesus, fully liberated and liberator, brings fullness of life. Maleness is not essential to his Christhood. Jesus accompanies people struggling toward freedom (Virginia Fabella, Mary John Mananzan, Lydia Lascano, Sharon Rose Joy Ruiz Duremdes). Jesus is a Minjung* worker (Soon Hwa, Oh Chag-yo), the Woman Messiah in solidarity with the outcast (Chung Sook Ja), a wounded healer (Limatula Longkumer, Elizabeth Tapia), and a risk-taking servant who works for his friends' well-being (Teresa Dagdag). Jesus is crucified with women on the cross of sexual violence* (Chang Jung-nim), of patriarchy*, classism, casteism*, ethnocentrism, and imperialism*.

Jesus crossed social and cultural boundaries to become a savior and women's partner in demolishing patriarchal culture (Hisako Kinukawa). Being a *sannyasi* (ascetic*) par excellence, Jesus embodied *cit* (intelligence/awareness) of the Vedic *sat-cit-ananda* (Vandana Mataji). As a model of priesthood (Pauline Chakkalakal), Jesus the *mudang* (priest) exorcises* *han* (accumulated pain and anger against oppression and injustice), performs a life-giving dance in the *han-pu-ri* ritual, and offers an opportunity for repentance, healing, and "making things alive" at the cosmic level (Chung Hyun Kyung, Choi Man Ja). Creativity, giving new life and redemption* symbolized powerfully by Jesus' Blood, is linked to women's menstrual and birthing blood (Aruna Gnanadasun, Elizabeth Joy, Gabriele Dietrich). Like a mother* (Ahn Sang-Nim, Sun Ai Park, Rebecca Asedillo), the many-breasted Mother Christ breastfeeds her children, nourishes and redeems them from waywardness. Jesus is God-with-us, dancing with us to celebrate small victories over the multiple crosses women bear daily (Muriel Orevillo-Montenegro). Jesus is the epiphany* of God, though not the sole revelation of God (Kwok Pui Lan).

Jesus is Shakti, spiritual energy, source of living water and truth (Stella Baltazar, Gnanadasun, Monica Melanchthon). Jesus is sage, prophet, and grace of Sophia-Prajna Paramita, the beauty of Wisdom incarnate (Grace Ji-Sun Kim). Wisdom* Christology puts Jesus the Christ within a pluralist paradigm that leaves room for dialogue.

An organic Christology highlights more life-giving images of Christ in Jesus as the vine, bread, living water (Kwok), and grain (Chung). Christ is Inang Bayan, the life-sustaining motherland/mother earth. Christ is the loving and caring communities working for people's well-being (Orevillo-Montenegro). Postcolonial imagination sees Jesus as a "subject-in-process" who opens for women a new space and a new way of being-in-the-world. This "variegated Jesus" of multiple identities embodies the power of the erotic, passion for life in relationship and mutuality. The fluid space between Jesus and Christ becomes a site of resistance to all forms of oppression (Wong Wai Ching [Angela]).
MURIEL OREVILLO-MONTENEGRO

Christologies in the Caribbean Islands: History. The Moravian* Church (first in St. Thomas, 1732) spread rapidly because of its emphasis on the suffering of Christ and its vivid account of the crucifixion of Christ wearing a crown of thorns. Enslaved peoples in the Caribbean made a ready connection between Christ's suffering and their own. Moravians appealed to Zinzendorf's* *Catechism for the Heathen* to help Caribbean people understand that Christ was equal to God. The catechism instructs: "Q: Who made men and women? A: The Lord God. Q: What do you call him? A: Jesus Christ... Jesus means Redeemer and Christ means king." The cleric went on to explain the doctrines of the Fall*, Incarnation*, and Christ's cross*.

Methodists, in their preaching in the Caribbean (since 1800 in the Bahamas), focused on their parishioners' sins* and the need for punishment (see Atonemenent # 2). The answer to the problem of sin was knowing Jesus as Savior and appropriating his death on the cross; otherwise, instead of meeting Christ as Savior one would meet him as Judge.

The Baptists (in Jamaica* since 1782, with the Black Baptist Church founded by black Americans who escaped from the USA after the American Revolution, 1784) put questions to a candidate for baptism that illustrate the Church's Christology: "*Minister*: Well, Thomas, do you know who Jesus Christ is? *Candidate*: Him de Son of God, Minister. *Minister*: What did Jesus come into the world to do? *Candidate*: Him come to save poor sinners. *Minister*: Do you think he is able to save sinners? *Candidate*: Me know him able. *Minister*: How can you know that he is able? *Candidate*: Because him make de world: and if him make de world, him able to do all Tings: and minister no tell we often-time dis make him left him fader Trone, and come into dis sinful world. *Minister*: What makes you wish to be baptized? *Candidate*: Because Jesus Christ, put under water, rise up again and we wish to pattern after him. *Minister*: Perhaps you think the water will wash away your sin? *Candidate*: No, no; water no wash away me sin; nothing but precious Massa Jesus blood wash away me sin."

NOEL LEO ERSKINE

Christologies in the Caribbean Islands: Present Day. A Caribbean Jesus embodies the gospel offering salvation*, rescuing persons from the powers of sin*, the structures of death, and the forces of evil. Luke 4:18–19 exemplifies the missiological consciousness of Jesus: As Savior he saves people from all diseases and forms of human degradation and transforms their lives. As exorcist* he delivers people wrestling with the known and unknown. As liberator he is the historical ancestor*, who sacrificed his life to free enslaved blacks. This human identification solidly links Jesus with Caribbean human vulnerability. Jesus, as the Christ of faith, calls the Caribbean people to love and respect all persons, for they are "[o]ut of many, one people," despite racial, national, religious, political, linguistic, sociological, and geographic differences. As "solidarity man," Jesus stands in solidarity with oppressed women, who are bringing about revolutionary changes in society, planting seeds of justice and peace. "Christ is also the oppressed one who, by the resurrection, liberates the oppressed ones" (Williams). Jesus as Black God (Garvey* and Rastafari*) calls Caribbean "blacks" to "emancipate themselves from mental slavery" (Bob Marley) and redefine their personhood as dignified and valued.

These images of Jesus offer a new appreciation of self and Caribbean roots in Shango (Trinidad*), Pocomania (Jamaica*), Kele (St. Lucia), Vodou* (Haiti*), and Santeria (Cuba*)

LESLEY G. ANDERSON

Christologies in Latin America tend to pay particular attention to the earthly ministry of Jesus, as in the book-length Christologies of Leonardo Boff, Segundo Galilea, José Comblin, and Rubén Dri. The Central American radio adaptation of the life of Jesus by María López Vigil and José Ignacio López Vigil brings a dark-skinned, laughing Jesus close to many. José Míguez Bonino's collection of essays (1977) underlined the need to understand Jesus neither as a powerless victim nor as a celestial monarch. It is important to frame the christological question in Latin America, because, too often, the figure of Jesus functioned to justify the conquest and suffering of the many, while glorifying power and domination by the few (see Portuguese Explorations, Conquests, and Missions; Spanish Explorations, Conquests, and Missions). Such cautions are echoed by recent Feminist christological work. Jon Sobrino, the Latin American "christologian" par excellence, emphasized following Jesus as a mystagogy* that serves both as a practical confession of faith and as a way of gaining significant understanding; to follow Jesus (seguimiento) empowered by the Spirit means to proceed (proseguimiento) today along the path opened up by Jesus, to embrace Jesus' preferential* option for the poor and his way of life; the resulting opposition, persecution, and even martyrdom* are illumined by the hope* of resurrection*. See also Incarnation Cluster: In Latin America; Liberation Theologies Cluster: In Latin America; Latin American Theologies.

NANCY ELIZABETH BEDFORD

Christologies in North America. Christology is that division of Christian theology that attempts to answer the question "Who – according to faith – *is* Jesus, and what does it mean to name him 'the Christ'?" Together with the soteriological* question ("What has he done for us?"), Christology constitutes the definitive center of Christian faith and practice. It is therefore not surprising that it is also the subject of perennial controversy in the Christian Church. North American Christianity is certainly no exception.

For a numerically (and politically) significant portion of Christian groupings in the USA particularly, Jesus Christ is understood to be unqualifiedly identified with the ultimate and transcendent deity. Belief in the divinity of Christ is one of the five "fundamentals" of late-19th-c. fundamentalism*, and while it is more nuanced in "conservative" churches that would reject the nomenclature "fundamentalist," a strong feature of all Christian conservativism in the North American context is its tendency to accentuate the divine origin and nature of Christ. This has led some observers to conclude that the great danger of Christianity in North America is its propensity to embrace an undialectical monotheism* or Christomonism, "a unitarianism of the second person of the Trinity" (H. Richard Niebuhr*).

Partly in reaction to this overemphasis on Christ's divinity, liberal* Christianity in North America (see Liberalism in Christian Theology and Ethics) has consistently emphasized the genuine humanity (*vere homo*) of Jesus, seeing him not so much as an ontological extension or incarnation of God as an inspired and prophetic human being *through* whom God has revealed the divine character and purposes. Liberal and moderate forms of Christianity, as represented by most "mainstream" Protestantism and much contemporary Catholicism, locate the high significance of Jesus not primarily in his being as such but in the scriptural witness to his teaching, healing, and relationships with others.

While this liberal view may indeed represent a deviation from "classical" christological orthodoxy as expressed in the formula of Chalcedon* and other historically important decisions of evolving Christendom, it is arguably more faithful to the whole (Hebraic-Christian) *biblical* approach than are the dominant traditional Christologies, which were strongly influenced by Greek philosophical conventions *and* by the post-Constantinian political destiny of a Christianity in the service of empire. Furthermore, in the religiously pluralistic situation of the present, a Christian faith committed to triumphalistic Christologies affirming straightforwardly that "Jesus is God" virtually precludes dialogue with other faiths. **See also THEOLOGY AS HUMAN UNDERTAKING CLUSTER: NORTH ATLANTIC THEOLOGIANS DOING THEOLOGY: A DIALOGUE BETWEEN TEXT AND CONTEXT.**

DOUGLAS JOHN HALL

Christologies in North America: Feminist and Womanist. Feminist and Womanist Christologies examine the meaning of Jesus Christ in the context of women's experience, advocating for women's full human dignity. This influences women's approach to biblical accounts of Jesus and systematic theological categories related to Christology. Feminist Christologies have addressed the biblical/historical Jesus*, implications of Jesus' maleness, and Jesus' role in upending the hierarchical, patriarchal* religious and social codes of his day. Along with Feminist Christologies, Womanist Christologies have emphasized Jesus as a liberator but also accented Jesus as a co-sufferer with humanity. Asian American feminist Rita Nakashima Brock highlights Jesus' relational power, working with the community to bring salvation*. Some Womanist and Feminist theologians have underscored the importance of the Incarnation* for affirming the value of human bodies* and all of creation (Kelly Brown Douglas, Carter Heyward, Sallie McFague).

By analyzing biblical literature, some Feminist Christologies claim that Jesus clearly contradicted patriarchal codes of his day and was, in some sense, a feminist. They note that Jesus included women among his disciples, championed the most outcast women, appeared first to women on Easter morning and commanded them to preach the gospel, used female metaphors for God, and is likened in the synoptic Gospels to Sophia, or Wisdom*, a female image of divinity in the Hebrew scriptures (Elizabeth A. Johnson, Elisabeth Schüssler Fiorenza).

Jesus' maleness is a perennial christological issue for Feminist theologians. Some churches have argued that women cannot fully represent Jesus because of their gender and therefore exclude women from full church leadership (see Women's Ordination Cluster). Early Feminist theologians, in particular, questioned whether a male savior can be ultimately redemptive for women. Most argued that Jesus' maleness is incidental rather than necessary to his nature and role as redeemer and savior.

In both Feminist and Womanist theologies, the most common christological focus concerns Jesus as a liberator from oppression. In a prophetic role, Jesus consistently sides with the oppressed, calls for justice, includes women in his ministry, and reverses patriarchal hierarchies of authority (Marjorie Suchocki, Rosemary Radford Ruether). Likewise, Jesus' preaching of the reign* of God does not support gender hierarchies, because delineations between male and female are negated in the body of Christ. Jesus sets a revolutionary standard for society today.

Womanist theologians have emphasized that Black women's Christologies differ from both Feminist and Black male Christologies. Jaquelyn Grant, for example, distinguished Black women's personal and communal experiences of Jesus from white Feminist theologies of Christ. Extending Black Liberation theology, some Womanist theologists argue that Jesus' saving power offers liberation from sexism* and heterosexism* as well as racism*. A recurring theme in Womanist Christology centers on finding strength in Jesus, who is known through communities of liberation, to both bear and fight their double oppression of racism and sexism (Kelly Brown Douglas).

Since 2000, Womanist and Feminist Christologies have profoundly shaped theological discussion concerning the cross*, atonement*, and redemptive*, substitutionary suffering*. Some of these Christologies have claimed that the cross and Christian atonement theories (see Atonement #2) reinforce systems of oppression by demanding self-sacrifice and suffering from the weak while justifying and sanctifying oppression and abuse by the powerful. Since salvation* is often associated with passive suffering, theology risks supporting racial, domestic, nationalist, and imperialist violence (Kelly Brown Douglas, Delores Williams, Marit Trelstad, Rita Nakashima Brock, Rebecca Ann Parker; see Violence Cluster). These theologians may offer alternative christological emphases on baptism*, resurrection*, renewal, or the covenant*, which Jesus renews. On the other hand, some Womanist and Feminist theologians argue that Jesus' suffering on the cross is redemptive or revelatory for women since it emphasizes God's participation in suffering and promises triumph over evil and oppression (Joanne Marie Terrell, Deanna Thompson, Darby Ray).

MARIT TRELSTAD

Christologies in North America: Latino/a. Latino/a theology and its Christologies emerged at a moment when contextual and Liberation theologies exploded onto the global theological arena and sought to speak both for and from the history, spirituality, and contemporary situation of Latino/a communities. Within Latino/a religiosity, the crucified Christ plays a central role. The Jesus of Good* Friday is a central christological symbol stemming from a theological worldview that strongly emphasizes Jesus' humble origins, his prophetic message, and his active presence in the present-day lives of Christians, in particular his solidarity with the oppressed* and marginalized. The theological significance of this distinctive Latino/a understanding of Jesus is the subject of Latino/a Christologies.

Latino/a Christologies emphasize Jesus' concrete historical reality and its implications for our understanding of Jesus today. At the center, the crucified Jesus reveals God's love for humanity and God's presence with and advocacy for the poor. The Latino/a faith in the crucified Jesus cannot be found in the dogmas, official teachings, or theological treatises of academic theology, but instead is situated in the concrete faith and lives of Latino/a communities. Their popular* faith expressions are the starting point of Latino/a theological reflection, and thus play a fundamental role in Latino/a Christologies.

The image of the crucified Jesus best embodies the spirituality and theology of Latino/a communities throughout the USA. This mestizo* Jesus, one who has a preferential* option for the oppressed and accompanies them throughout their struggles, calls Christians to be concrete disciples who follow in Jesus' footsteps. The crucified Jesus of Latino/a religiosity reminds Christians of the dangerous memory of Jesus' ministry, life, and death. For Latinos/as the importance of popular religious practices demonstrates the active dimension of this faith: one not only believes, one also acts. As disciples, Christians are therefore called to follow Jesus to those marginalized spaces. On Good* Friday, as Latino/as accompany Jesus to his crucifixion, they are reminded and comforted by the fact that they do not suffer alone. The symbolic accompaniment of the *via crucis* is a reminder of the constant accompaniment of Jesus in their lives and struggles, and the accompaniment of the marginalized by believers. **See also JESUS*, IMAGES OF, CLUSTER: IN LATINO/A DEPICTIONS.**

MICHELLE A. GONZALEZ

Christologies in South Pacific and Australia. The tendency in contextual theologies in Australia, New Zealand, and the Pacific is to focus on themes that are not directly of a traditional systematic theological nature; these contextual theologies focus on themes such as identity, land*, ecology*, Spirit/spirituality*, method, and the relationship of indigenous peoples to settler societies. There is also a practice of responding to occasional, ad hoc public issues as they arise. Sometimes the language of Christ and context is used as a code to explore models of how gospel and culture*, or the local and the global, relate.

The invocation of Christology for the sake of a local theology was probably first associated with the request of Sir John Guise (governor of Papua* New Guinea, 1975–77) to the Pacific Council of Churches to "reveal to us the Pacific Christ." The purpose was strategic: (1) how might the story of Jesus be transplanted into island culture? and (2) what have been the received understandings of the person and work of Christ mediated through Western missionaries, and how might cultural symbols and practice now be employed for the sake of interpretation and relevance?

That concern for a critical engagement of a "national" story with the narrative of faith is replicated in Australia, where Christ-like images have been frequently present in literature. In both cases, the initiative for a more contextual Christology has often been located in the need to create space for the other and a concern for how difference is embraced. The tendency has been for that difference to be conceived of in terms of race and cultural diversity. The biblical and theological themes of hospitality* and the cross* are combined with the ever-present question "Who is Jesus Christ for us today?" in a range of emerging diasporic and intergenerational understandings.

The organizing principles for these Christologies in context are sometimes taken from Liberation* theology. The more common practice is to draw on cultural symbols or practices, like weaving. There is the isolated christological quest that puts to theological use popular idioms like "for Christ's sake"; the historical understanding of the antipodes has also been employed for the sake of developing a Christology on the basis of a hermeneutic of living "down under." The most recent emphasis in Australia has been on soteriology* rather than the Incarnation*. Yet these Christologies are not widely known, because publishing is difficult owing to the small domestic audience and international isolation.

CLIVE PEARSON

Chronicles, Books of, late biblical historical composition describing the history of ancient Israel from the earliest times until Cyrus's Decree (538 BCE), with many genealogical and geographical lists. Almost half of the material has parallel texts in earlier biblical writings (Pentateuch*, Joshua*, Samuel*, Kings*, Psalms*, Ruth*, Ezra* and Nehemiah). One of the largest compositions of the HB, it is placed last in the Hebrew canon*.

Writing probably in Jerusalem c400–375 BCE, the chronicler evaluates the past from his own historical context and literary theological concerns: he emphasizes the implementations of the priestly codex, the Temple and its services, and stresses the continuity of the Judean tribes as the real Israelites who survived until his times. He encourages Diaspora Jews to immigrate to Jerusalem and Judah.

Immediate personal reward and punishment is one of the core theological principles of Chronicles. Reliance on God and keeping God's commandments result in victory, peace, and prosperity*; disobeying and neglecting the Lord's word cause war, disaster, and defeat. The divine promise of the kingdom to David and his descendants is eternal; therefore, the very existence of the Northern Kingdom is intertwined with rebellion against God. The Temple (and royal city, Jerusalem) was captured by "all Israel," and since then it has been the nation's center.

Several factors combined to make Chronicles one of the least popular and least studied books of the Scriptures. It was translated relatively late into Greek and Aramaic. The 3rd-c.-CE Syriac version of the OT did not include Chronicles. Despite Jerome's* comment, "Chronicles is condensed to such an extent and so well abridged, that whoever claims to know Scriptures without having knowledge of Chronicles, would make himself a laughingstock," the book was almost completely neglected in the Christian tradition, and even excluded from scriptural studies in some communities. Hugh of Saint-Cher states that the Jewish people had a generous attitude toward Chronicles: they ranked the book among the Hagiographa*, while its appropriate place should be among the Apocrypha*.

Generally, Chronicles was better received in the Jewish tradition: verses from the book were integrated into the Jewish liturgy; they were used in the artistic works in the synagogues of Dura-Europus and En-Gedi and quoted in *Sefer haZohar* and in disputations with Christians. There are several medieval commentaries on the book. Yet Spinoza* suggested that the book be excluded from the canon. In more recent decades, there has been increasing scholarly interest in Chronicles.

ISAAC KALIMI

Chrysostom, John. See JOHN CHRYSOSTOM.

Chrysostom, Liturgy of St. John, formulary for the celebration of the Eucharist* used by Eastern Orthodox* Churches and Greek Catholic Churches. It is the second most commonly used Eucharist formulary (the Roman Catholic Mass* being the first). The primitive part constituted by the anaphora* is a recasting of a more ancient text, the Anaphora of the Twelve Apostles, composed by John* Chrysostom during his episcopate in Constantinople (398–407). This anaphora is a classical example of Antiochene* anaphora. Its ancient characteristics include the absence of the reiteration command ("Do this in memory of me") and the inclusion of the (recently) deceased in the prayer of commemoration of the saints. Before the 7th c., the Liturgy of Chrysostom (this primitive nucleus, enriched by other prayers) was used only occasionally and not as much as the Liturgy of St. Basil*. The Liturgy of Chrysostom prevailed only in the context of the post-iconoclast liturgical reform (late 9th c.), and possibly as a consequence of the spiritual movement that began at the Studios* Monastery in Constantinople in favor of everyday Communion.

STEFANO PARENTI

CHURCH, CONCEPTS AND LIFE, CLUSTER

1) *Introductory Entries*

Church, Concepts and Life: Doctrines of the Church

Church, Concepts and Life: Feminist Perspectives

---

1) Introductory Entries

Church, Concepts and Life: Doctrines of the Church. Ecclesiology, the doctrine of the church, is one of the most widely discussed topics in contemporary theology, although it was only with the Reformation* that it became a separate chapter in Christian theology, when the question of the true church came into focus.

The biblical term *ekklesia* (Gk "congregation," "assembly") denotes in the NT both the local and universal church. While the church came into existence at Pentecost as a result of the pouring out of the Holy* Spirit (Acts 2), the "founding" of the church is attributed to Jesus (Matt 16:18, a disputed verse). Among NT images for the church, the most often used are "people of God," "body of Christ," and "temple of the Holy Spirit."

Early creeds connect the church with the Holy* Spirit, forgiveness* of sins, and the coming of God's Kingdom*. The Nicene* Creed (4th c.) gave a definitive understanding of the church as one, holy, catholic, and apostolic. As the body of Christ, the church is one and holy, because its Lord is. Catholicity (Gk *cath-holou*, "according to the whole") means that the church not only is spread everywhere but also possesses the whole gospel*. All affirm these "marks* of the church" – one, holy, catholic, and apostolic. Yet their exact meaning is disputed. For example, should holiness be located in the Lord or in the members? Should apostolicity be in terms of apostolic* succession of bishops or in terms of adherence to the apostolic word of the gospel?

The Christian Church has undergone several major splits. Several Oriental Orthodox* churches* (e.g. Syriac*) disagreed with the Eastern Orthodox* and Roman* Catholic churches' adherence to the Council of Chalcedon* (451). The 1054 split between the Western Church (Roman Catholic) and Eastern Church (Eastern Orthodox) resulted from the *Filioque** dispute and other ecclesiopolitical factors. The 16th-c. division split the Western Church into Roman Catholic and Protestant* churches. Luther*, then other Reformers (Zwingli*, Calvin*, the English Reformers), began their activities with no intention of splitting the church; this schism became definitive only after the Council of Trent* (1545–63) and the founding of Protestant churches. The Radical* Reformers, out of which came Anabaptists* (e.g. Mennonites*), pushed an even more radical reform agenda with the idea of believers' baptism* and the separation between church* and state. In 17th-c. England, the Baptist* Movement arose to continue this agenda. The independent* church movements (postdenominational or free churches) that rapidly grew in the late 20th c. and early 21st c. owed their beginnings to Baptists and Anabaptists. The rise to prominence of the Pentecostal* Movement (since the early 20th c.) and later of the Charismatic* Movement were a radical challenge to all churches in that they powerfully called them to be more receptive to the power and presence of the Holy* Spirit with charismata* and spiritual manifestations.

For the Eastern Orthodox and Roman Catholic churches, the ecclesiality of the church is based on the sacraments*, especially the Eucharist*, the legitimacy of which is guaranteed by a bishop* who stands in the apostolic succession. The Eastern Orthodox Church speaks of the Church as the image (see Icon; Iconography) of the Trinity* and as a mystery* (sacrament*), emphasizing its mystical and cosmological characters. Vatican* II (1962–65) similarly anchors the church in the Trinity and, unlike in the past, regards the earthly church as less than perfect; the church is on its way to perfection. The laity is given a more prominent role, and the local churches have been endowed with greater significance.

Protestant churches regard church structures and ministry patterns as optional: the two determining indicators are the celebration of sacraments* and the preaching* of the gospel*, with distinctive doctrinal and polity* emphasis according to the denominations; in practice, however, they increasingly function as voluntary associations.

For independent* postdenominational churches, the determining factor for ecclesiality is the gathering of believers. While sacraments are celebrated and the Word preached, personal faith* is necessary. Believers' baptism* makes the church a voluntary society; the church gathers "the called-out ones" (plausible etymology of *ekklesia*, though not emphasized in NT usages). Evangelism* and mission* are highly emphasized. Independent churches also insist on the separation between church and state. The biggest independent church movement, the Pentecostal*/ Charismatic* Movement, understands itself to be restorationist, with a desire to reclaim the charismatic life and worship of the apostolic church. The empowerment of all church members by the Holy Spirit is emphasized. Even when the Word is preached and hymns are sung, "encountering" the Lord is the aim, with signs following encounters, such as healings*.

In the early 21st c the Christian Church is undergoing a transformation as its center of gravity moves rapidly from North to South, with the majority of church members residing outside Europe and North America. The Roman Catholic Church comprises one-half of all church members, Pentecostal/Charismatic and other independent churches a quarter, and Orthodox plus Reformation churches the remaining one-fourth. New challenges include, among others, the inclusion of women*, the questions of liberation* and equality, the promotion of the ministry (priesthood*) of all believers, and the acknowledgment of the missionary* nature of the church.

VELI-MATTI KÄRKKÄINEN

Church, Concepts and Life: Feminist Perspectives. What are the terms of involvement of the female members of the church, anywhere in the world? To what extent are they free to speak, contribute, teach, preach, and lead?

The fact that there are limitations for women reveals the inherent inequalities within the church structure, power, and leadership. Feminist concerns regarding the concept of "church" are tied to the understanding of the names for and nature of the Triune God*, by whom and for whom the church exists (see God, Christian Views of, Cluster: In North America: Feminist Understandings). Regarding church practice, feminists ask: Why are the voices of women considered less important or relevant than those of men? What are the implications for the church that its Scriptures* were written by – and primarily benefit – men? How can we counter the systemic neglect or dismissal of women (and other marginalized people) and their voices, perspectives, and contributions? It is not enough to pardon the past; past values and the structures and roles they created are still at work in our churches today.

While some question whether "feminist" and "church" can coexist, the reality is that people are interested in making it so. Thus feminist voices and concerns need to be attended to by the church.

JENNIFER BIRD

Church, Concepts and Life: Names for the Church. The NT word for "church" is the Greek *ekklesia*, which was the common word used for an "assembly" of citizens and of people in a group. In the NT, *ekklesia* simply refers to an "assembly" of believers. The Syriac *ɩdhta* is very close in meaning to *ekklesia*, although it is also used for the building, along with *haykla*, a common word for palace or temple (with rich symbolism). Both the Greek *ekklesia* and the Latin *ecclesia* are also reflected in the Romance languages (*chiesa, église, iglesia, igreja*). The term *gereja*, used for "church" in Bahasa Malaysia and Bahasa Indonesia, comes from the Portuguese *igreja*.

The German *Kirche*, Swedish *kyrka*, and English "church" are derived (through the Gothic) from the Greek *kyriakon*, signifying the "Lord's house" or "community." The Celtic *domnach* is similarly derived from the Latin *dominicum*, "domain" (of the Lord).

There are many other names for "church" in various languages related to particular cultures. For example, the Romanian *biserica* comes from the Latin *basilica*. The Chichewa (Malawi) *kachisi* is the word originally used for African* Religion traditional shrines. The Chinese *jiaohui*, a term foreign to Chinese culture, was coined by missionaries, combining *jiao* (teaching or religion) and *hui* (an assembly of people or a place).

Church, Concepts and Life: Types of Ecclesiastical Structures. When one considers the way in which authority* is exercised, one can distinguish five types of Christian churches.

1. Episcopalian (based on the NT references to bishops*). Authority is exercised within a hierarchy, with the bishop at the apex of the pyramid, as in the Roman Catholic, Anglican, and Orthodox churches, although they differ significantly.

The Roman Catholic Church is highly centralized, with the pope* as the supreme head of a global organization (elected in a conclave of cardinals) and with Rome as the center of administrative authority.

The Anglican Communion (including the Church of England) is much less centralized. It is organized in dioceses, each with a bishop, grouped in provinces, each with an archbishop (elected by both clergy and lay leaders), who presides over a synod deliberating on policy, ritual, and organizational matters of the Church but who does not have jurisdiction over dioceses other than his or her own. The Lambeth* Conference of Anglican Bishops (in London, every 10 years since 1888) deliberates on matters of mutual concern, but with no juridical authority over bishops and dioceses; yet the consensus affirmed by its resolutions is authoritative.

The Orthodox* churches, headed by patriarchs*, are organized in dioceses under bishops that function autonomously but in communion with each other. Autocephalous* Orthodox churches, such as the Russian Orthodox Church, are "self-headed," with their own patriarchs and synods of bishops, an administrative independence that does not deny spiritual unity.

2. Presbyterian (based on the NT references to elders*). The Council of Elders (Presbyters) exercises church authority. From the local to the national level, there are layers of representation, culminating in the General Assembly, where policy decisions are made. The moderator of the General Assembly is elected for a limited period (one to five years). National Presbyterian churches, e.g. the Church of Scotland*, are joined together in the World* Alliance of Reformed Churches. Though they have bishops, Lutheran churches (and their World* Lutheran Federation) and Methodist churches (and their World Methodist Council) nevertheless have chains of authority that are related to the Presbyterian type; the bishops' authority is derived from and is exercised along with the representative body (synod or conference).

3. Congregational (based on the NT references to local churches functioning by consensus as the body of Christ; e.g. 1 Cor 12; Rom 12). Authority is vested in each specific congregation, which periodically "constitutes itself as a business meeting" to make decisions on the governance of all aspects of the church. The pastor is hired, dismissed, remunerated, and disciplined by the congregation. Baptist churches as well as those with the label "Congregational" belong to this group.

4. Charismatic Leadership (based on NT texts such as Acts 2; 1 Cor 12). In this model, despite those texts that emphasize the charismata* of all believers, authority is vested in a charismatic leader. When the leader loses charismatic power, the leadership role is immediately withdrawn and handed over to another leader in whom the congregation recognizes significant charismatic gifts. Many African* Instituted Churches (AICs) have this charismatic leadership structure and are associated with specific charismatic leaders or founders, e.g. the Deliverance Church and the Redeemed Gospel Church (Kenya), the Kimbanguist* Church (Democratic Republic of Congo), and the Church of Prophet Harris (West Africa). Many megachurches* in the USA, tropical Africa, Central America (e.g. Tabernaculo Biblico Bautista – Baptist Tabernacle, El Salvador), and South Korea also have this charismatic leadership structure.

5. Charismatic*/Pentecostal (based on NT texts such as Acts 2; 1 Cor 12). Authority emanates from the Holy Spirit and is vested in any believer who is moved by the Spirit and receives charismatic gifts for the edification of the community. The Charismatic leadership is thus decentralized, counting on the Spirit-driven leadership of many of its members – who play important roles as leaders of cell groups – rather than that of a single leader. Such is the case of thousands of small Charismatic churches, and also of the biggest megachurches, such as Yoido Full Gospel (Seoul, South Korea) and Mision Elim Internacional (Ilabasco, El Salvador).

These five types of ecclesiastical organization are based on NT patterns, although none actually replicate the apostolic church, because their organization reflects the cultural context in which they developed. The Roman Catholic Church places great importance on central authority not only because of NT models, but also because it took over imperial authority when the Roman Empire declined. Anglicanism was established in defiance of papal authority by King Henry VIII. The Church of Scotland adopted the Presbyterian polity*, in conformity with a nonhierarchical Scottish culture. Congregationalist churches flourish in individualist cultural settings (among the rising middle class in early-17th-c. England, and spreading to North America). Charismatic leadership and Charismatic/Pentecostal churches are the most inculturated* – be they African Instituted Churches, US megachurches proclaiming a Prosperity* Gospel (see Word-Faith Movement, Its Theology and Worship), or Korean or Salvadoran mega-Charismatic churches that call people to faithfully live the full gospel by expressing it in terms of elements of their cultural and religious heritage. **See also POLITY.**

Jesse Ndwiga Kanyua Mugambi

---

2) A Sampling of Contextual Views and Practices

Church, Concepts and Life: In African Instituted Churches. AICs are Christian bodies in Africa (c60 million members) "instituted" as a result of African "initiatives" in search of "independence" from missionary domination.

Three types of AICs can be distinguished. Ethiopian churches, the earliest, originated in the 19th-c. pan-African "Ethiopian Movement" (Ethiopia representing noncolonized Africa; Ps. 68:31); they emphasized African leadership, and thus "independence" from missionary churches, while keeping most of the theological views and practices of these churches. The much larger Zionist churches, with roots in US Pentecostalism, quickly had an exclusively African leadership and are more thoroughly inculturated*, drawing on African* Religion. Apostolic churches (or Prophetic churches) were and are "initiated" by Spirit-inspired African apostles, such as Simon Kimbangu* in Congo* (both DRC and Congo-Brazzaville, from 1921) and John Maranke in Zimbabwe (from 1932).

Today most AICs are independent and indigenous Charismatic* churches. They emphasize the importance of Spirit possession, dreams, visions, and speaking in tongues*; they practice healing* and exorcism* of evil spirits and other evil powers. Because of their inculturation* (whether or not they practice polygamy* and African dietary taboos), AICs appeal to Africans through their interpretation of Scripture* (both OT and NT) and their worship using African symbols, music, and dance. TABONA SHOKO

Church, Concepts and and Life: In Asia. The concept of "church" in Asia has been shaped by both external and internal factors, such as movements for national independence, the necessity of interreligious dialogue with neighbors of other religious traditions, and the ecumenical experience in the context of mission.

The struggle for independence triggered a reconceptualization of the church as local and suffused by the cultural context. The May Fourth Movement and the socialist experience in China*, for example, led to the understanding of church as self-governing, self-propagating, and self-supporting. The indigenous church movements in other parts of the continent moved in the same direction.

The experience of Asian Christians with neighbors of other faiths has led to the realization of the church as a "community in dialogue*." The Federation of Asian Bishops' Conferences has turned dialogue into a key element for understanding the church in Asia, and according to it, the church fulfills its mission through a threefold dialogue with Asian religions*, Asian cultures*, and the Asian poor*. The minority situation in which almost all Asian churches find themselves (except in the Philippines*) has led them to a self-understanding of their life as that of a "little flock" (Luke 12:32) and their mission as that of salt and leaven (Matt 5:13, 13:33). This self-understanding of the church has served as a great force in overcoming the historically inherited division of churches and moving toward various kinds of ecumenical union. It is significant that in the context of mission the unified Church of South* India (1947) was formed from three churches that are nowhere else in union. From a theological point of view, the understanding of church in Asia has been enriched by the institution of family* – so central to the Confucian* tradition – the experience of Buddhist* *sangha* (community) of equals, and the Hindu* concept of *vasudevakudumbam* (the family of the Lord).

FELIX WILFRED

Church, Concepts and Life: House Churches. See CHINESE CONTEMPORARY INDEPENDENT AND HOUSE CHURCHES.

Church, Concepts and Life: In Latin America. The life of the Roman Catholic Church in present-day Latin America can be understood when one keeps in mind that it has gone through four political periods: predominance of liberalism, populism, predominance of dictatorships, and openings toward democracy.

Beginning in the late 19th c., the role of the Roman Catholic Church in colonial times was challenged by liberal governments and by Latin American societies influenced by modernization and laicization*; debates started in the press and in parliaments. The national states, economically liberal and politically conservative, sought to reduce the sphere of influence of the Church to private life. The life of the faithful tended to be limited to family, parish, and denominational schools. During this period, lay leaders gathered primarily to argue about the marginal role of the Church in the modern world.

In the 1920s, the existing orientation toward social issues deepened. Social organizations, unions, and Catholic political parties were established more or less successfully in different countries, achieving a massive mobilization of lay Catholics as members of Catholic organizations – first Catholic* Action, then Specialized Catholic Action movements for youth, university students, workers, and peasants; these movements provided opportunities for participation, formation, and social commitment. The radical commitment of lay Christian groups to sharing in the struggle of the poor*, the workers, and the often landless peasants led them to resist the bloody repression unleashed by the military dictatorships of Latin America starting in the 1960s, often supported by the Church hierarchy. The resulting breakup between hierarchy and laypeople of the Roman Catholic Church led to a long and difficult reorganization of the laity that began with the arrival of democracies.

The democratic context favored the pluralization of the religious sphere. Different church groups – neo-Christian or para-Christian groups; Protestant* (or "Evangelical" in Latin American terminology), Charismatic* and Pentecostal* (in Latin America, the latter term is the inclusive designation for all Charismatics and Pentecostals), Native* American, and African* American churches, as well as Orientalist and New* Age groups – gained an unprecedented visibility starting in the 1980s. This pluralization is also found inside the Roman Catholic Church, with the rise of lay movements with different liturgical, doctrinal, and theological positions, reflecting their various social milieus. All these movements within the Catholic Church are themselves quite diversified, and they include various groups of militants; yet their members remain deeply identified and committed to their movements, which occupy a growing position within the overall Roman Catholic Church and project with force their claims in the public sphere.

VERÓNICA GIMÉNEZ BELIVEAU

Church, Concepts and Life: In Latin America: Brazil: Base Ecclesial Communities (CEBs). (Portuguese, Comunidades Eclesiais de Base). During the 1960s, a "communitarian wave" swept over the Roman* Catholic Church in Brazil, in reaction to the strictly institutional conception of the Church that predominated. This new conception of "church" entered Brazil through the Movement for a Better World and its teaching aimed at renewing pastoral practice along three axes: affirming the value of the laity* and the ministry of laypeople, decentralizing parish responsibilities (previously centered on the parish priest), and gathering authentic Christian communities characterized by faith, worship, and charity (social work). This ecclesiological ideal was widely welcomed in Brazil. It was implemented in some traditional ecclesial communities but developed beyond these after becoming an explicit objective of the 1966 United Pastoral Plan of the National Conference of Brazilian Bishops (CNBB) following the Second Vatican* Council.

Base ecclesial communities became more independent in the 1970s, frequently connecting traditional communities (e.g. "rural chapels*") with the action of all kinds of "modern pastors" (bishops, priests, sisters, laity formed for Catholic* Action, theologians, and sociologists). The CEBs are small groups, normally established in a neighborhood, slum, village, or rural zone, whose members regularly gather to pray, sing, celebrate, commemorate, read the Bible, and discuss it from the perspective of the life experience and struggles of that population. As Harvey Cox says, its objective is not to reconstruct the traditional communities (with their closed and authoritarian structures), but to bring about a new type of community that embodies the most important "modern freedoms."

The members of the communities cultivate a new relationship with the Holy One, by developing a new consciousness of the struggles of the people around them and a new ethical and political commitment to participate in their struggles. A CEB can be recognized by the following: (1) Sunday celebrations without a priest, (2) communitarian leadership, (3) biblical reflection groups, and (4) action aimed at transforming life in its context in partnership with social movements. **See also** BRAZIL; ROMAN CATHOLICISM CLUSTER: IN LATIN AMERICA: VARIOUS ENTRIES ON BRAZIL.

SÉRGIO COUTINHO

Church, Concepts and Life: In Latin America: Ecuador: Base Ecclesial Communities (CEBs). Base Ecclesial Communities (Spanish, Comunidades Eclesiales de

Base) are cell groups within the parish that make room for missionary laypeople and their creativity. Formed by families from neighborhoods in communion with the parish priest and the bishop, CEBs believe that the Roman Catholic Church is not merely the hierarchy or the institution. Faith guides CEBs as instruments for the transformation of culture*, for living out a prophetic stance by denouncing organized injustice and proclaiming a new hope for and with the poor*. CEBs promote the spirit of prayer, which is understood to be the key to conversion*. Although all members are facilitators, they work with leaders who are approved and qualified by the communitarian process to serve the CEB. CEBs started in the Riobamba Diocese (1962). At present, they are active in at least 10 ecclesiastical jurisdictions in Ecuador. There are also specialized groups called "Extension Teams of CEBs" (1985). CEBs are not juridically considered movements within the Roman Catholic Church, because their dynamics vary, depending on the families and communities involved. Although some fear them, CEBs have taken a position against "diseased apostolic fervor" that leads to sectarian cults rather than to a church as a communion of members. Indeed, CEBs see as part of their mission rediscovery of the Catholic Church.

LUIS MARÍA GAVILANES DEL CASTILLO

Church, Concepts and Life: In North America. The word "church" has three meanings in North America that reflect the operative conceptions of church in contemporary society.

1. The USA and Canada* have no official state religion. The term "church" is sometimes analytically paired with "state" (as in "church* and state") to denote the relationship of all religious entities and belief groups to the state apparatus. In both societies, religious beliefs and associations are protected from governmental interference. Americans and Canadians highly value the separation of church and state, religious liberty, and the right of private judgment in moral matters.
2. "Church" also denotes a body of associated Christians who share ecclesiastical governance, on either a national or transnational basis. Thus Roman Catholics in North America refer to "the church" as the worldwide church headed by the pope; Presbyterians, Baptists, or Mennonites would typically use the same term to refer to their own denominations within a single nation. North American Christians often express concern about the church, by which they mean the chaotic organized life of Christian bodies above the level of local congregations. This phenomenon began in the 1960s; before that time, denominational expressions of Protestantism and national expressions of Catholic bodies were held in high esteem and collectively were remarkably effective in setting a religious tone for public and private morality without violating the principles of church–state separation.
3. By far the most common meaning of the word "church" in contemporary North America is that of a local congregation of believers. In contemporary North American culture, neither is one born into a church by law, nor does a territorial conception of parish* membership operate. Christians are accustomed to thinking of themselves first and foremost as members of a particular congregation, and refer to themselves as members, e.g., of St. Matthew's Church or New Life Christian Fellowship. This local identification has come at the expense of enduring association with theological and ecclesial traditions. Thus in this mobile culture, people may choose to belong to a Lutheran Church in one location and join an Episcopal Church in another without ever identifying themselves as Lutheran or Anglican. While the clergy of the respective Christian traditions continue to be more associated theologically with the tenets of those expressions of faith, "church"

for the laity has become increasingly a matter of a voluntary association with a particular gathered congregation.

JAMES HUDNUT-BEUMLER

Church, Concepts and Life: In Western European Theology. The Roman Catholic Hans Küng's *The Church* (1967) elaborated on many key insights of Vatican* II's *Lumen Gentium*, including the idea of the church as the people of God, church-in-the-making, work for the unity of the church, and the call to open up to society and world religions. The Reformed* Jürgen Moltmann's *The Church in the Power of the Spirit* (1977) similarly advocated a participatory, nonhierarchic, charismatically structured, and open view of the church. In "relational ecclesiology," the church never exists for itself but is always in relation to God and the world; therefore it is a serving, missionary church. Both Küng and Moltmann underline the charismatic* structure of the church and the charismata/charisms* of its members. For Moltmann the church is a "charismatic fellowship" of equal persons, without division between office bearers and people. Moltmann's ecclesiology searches for equality and justice among church members and also among all men and women. The Triune God as a society of equals is the model. While a hierarchical notion of the Trinity* leads to a hierarchical view of the church, an open Trinity enhances openness, mutual respect, and loyalty.

Building on the biblical and patristic tradition, the Greek Orthodox John Zizioulas's *Being as Communion* (1985) argues that all true personal existence happens in relationality, communion. Even the mode of the existence of the Triune God is relational. Thus becoming Christian means a move from "biological individualism" to an "ecclesial personhood." Communion ecclesiology soon established its place as an ecumenical conviction across denominational borders.

The Croatian Miroslav Volf entered the most foundational debate in contemporary ecclesiology: What is the ecclesiality of the church? What makes the church, church? The extreme views are represented by catholic churches (Roman and Eastern) and free or independent* churches. Unlike the former, independent churches do not require a bishop (or a priest ordained by a bishop) to ensure the presence of Christ; the presence of Christ is "ensured by faith response" apart from any officers. In the Roman Catholic tradition, Christ's presence is mediated sacramentally*, and the bishop or priest is needed to preside over the Eucharist; by contrast, independent churches speak of Christ's unmediated, "direct" presence in the entire local communion. Volf's own "ecumenical" free church view holds that while Christ's presence cannot be tied to either offices or sacraments (catholic churches), the mediation of faith is also not individualistic or absolutely unmediated. The mediation of faith happens in the community, via tradition and all church members, and not merely via ordained persons. For faith to be personal, there must be a genuine appropriation of the faith of the church.

The former missionary bishop Lesslie Newbigin has been a key voice in developing the emerging ecumenical idea of the church's missionary nature. Rather than being one of the tasks of the church, mission* is the very being of the church. When the church takes seriously its faith in the gospel as "public truth," mission flows out of its confident, yet humble and respectful sharing of the good news to all people. The flip side of the "logic of mission" is that the church that keeps the good news for itself compromises its own being as the bearer of the gospel. For Newbigin the missionary church by its very nature advocates the unity of the church. The Lutheran Wolfhart Pannenberg's *Systematic Theology*, which includes a significant ecumenical ecclesiology of contemporary times, argues that unless the church reconciles its divisions, it has little hope of convincing the world and other religions of the supremacy of the gospel.

VELI-MATTI KÄRKKÄINEN

Church Discipline is the exercise of the "power of the keys" (Matt 16:19), the power to "bind* and loose" (Matt 16:19, 18:18). Excommunication* seems originally to have resulted in permanent expulsion from the community for the sake of its purity; Hermas* claimed a special revelation permitting one repentance* for serious sins, and this became the practice of the early church (see Penance and Forgiveness).

In Celtic Christianity,* the conviction arose that no sin was beyond penance* and restoration, although the penalties listed in the so-called penitentials* were severe. The practice of secret confession, engaging in penitential acts, and being readmitted to Communion spread throughout the Western Church; uniformity was achieved at the Fourth Lateran* Council (1215). Church discipline became especially severe under the Inquisition*, whose stated purpose was to identify heretics* and seek their full repentance.

At the time of the Reformation*, Luther* reaffirmed the need for repentance but reconceived it with his doctrine of justification* by faith. In the Reformed* churches, discipline was often made a third "mark of the church," along with the proclamation of the Word and the right administration of the sacraments; here discipline was exercised by the consistory* or session*, which included lay elders* as well as the minister.

Wherever a single church is recognized and supported by government, church discipline has serious consequences in everyday life. Under conditions of religious freedom*, however, civil courts usually do not interfere with the disciplinary judgments of religious bodies. Church membership* means that one places oneself under the discipline of the religious body, but it is always possible to renounce its jurisdiction and transfer to a different denomination. Discipline remains an important feature of church life, especially for ordained ministers, whose work and livelihood depend on remaining in good standing within the denomination.

EUGENE TESELLE

Church of the East, or Assyrian Church. This branch of the Syriac Christian Church traditionally traces its roots to Addai, a 1st-c. disciple of the apostle Thomas, who was said to have come to Mesopotamia (according to the *Doctrine of Addai*, c400) and to have authored an important early liturgy, still in use in this church (see Addai and Mari, Liturgy of). In any case, Syriac-speaking Christians were well enough established to hold a synod at Seleucia-Ctesiphon (Persia) in c325, and another in 410, where they declared independence from the Church of Antioch* and organized themselves under the leadership of their own catholicos*. The 5th-c. christological controversies hardened this jurisdictional division into a theological one when the Church of the East allied itself with the School of Antioch – Diodore* of Tarsus, Theodore* of Mopsuestia, and Nestorius* – whence the erroneous designation of this church as "Nestorian." These Greek theologians' writings had been translated into Syriac by Ibas* of Edessa (early 5th c.). After the condemnation of Nestorius (Council of Ephesus*, 431) and the closing of the school of Edessa* (489), the last teachers joined the school at Nisibis*, where they refined and developed Nestorius's Christology (Jesus' humanity and divinity were joined by will, not by nature or hypostasis; yet the conjunction is so intimate that Jesus and the Word become one person, not two) and other doctrines in dialogue with the poetry of Ephrem* (praising the mystery* of the Incarnation*) and other traditional Syriac exegetical and liturgical materials. Another refugee from Edessa, Barsauma*, bishop of Nisibis, then catholicos, summoned a synod (Beth Lapat, 484), which affirmed Nestorius's teaching and advised monastics and clergy to marry. Despite efforts to stress monastic life and the teachings of Origen* (late 6th c.), the Antiochene Christology prevailed in the form articulated by Babai the Great (d628).

The Church of the East survived and prospered under Persian and Abbasid Muslim rules, producing scholars learned in medicine, philosophy, and science. Their translations from Greek to Syriac and later into Arabic provided the basis for later Muslim scholarship. A prolific missionary church, it had branches in India*, China*, and central Asia, and produced writings that constituted early evidence of attitudes toward other religions.

A 15th-c. dispute over the patriarchal succession led to overtures to the Roman Catholic Church, resulting in a uniate* branch of the Church of the East, the Chaldean* Church. Political tensions after World War I led to the relocation of the patriarchate to the West (presently in Chicago); many members of the Chaldean Church still reside in Middle Eastern countries, although less and less so in Iraq*.

KATHLEEN E. MCVEY

Church of England. See ANGLICANISM CLUSTER: ANGLICAN COMMUNION AND ITS THEOLOGY.

CHURCHES AND DENOMINATIONS

See ADVENTISM; AFRICAN AMERICAN CLUSTER; AFRICAN INSTITUTED CHURCHES CLUSTER; AMISH; ANABAPTIST MOVEMENT; ANGLICANISM CLUSTER; ASSEMBLIES OF GOD; BAPTIST CHURCHES CLUSTER; BOHEMIAN BRETHREN; BRETHREN; CHALDEAN CATHOLIC CHURCH; CHARISMATIC AND PENTECOSTAL MOVEMENTS CLUSTER; CHRISTIAN CHURCH (DISCIPLES OF CHRIST); CHRISTIAN SCIENCE; CHURCH OF THE EAST OR ASSYRIAN CHURCH; CHURCH OF GOD IN CHRIST; CONGREGATIONALISM; EVANGELICALS/EVANGELICALISM CLUSTER; FRIENDS, RELIGIOUS SOCIETY OF; GERMAN CHRISTIANS; HOLINESS MOVEMENT; HUGUENOTS; HUTTERITES; JEHOVAH'S WITNESSES; KIMBANGUISM; KIRISHITANS AND HIDDEN CHRISTIANS IN JAPAN; LATTER-DAY SAINTS, CHURCH OF JESUS CHRIST OF; LUTHERANISM CLUSTER; MALABAR CHRISTIANS; MARONITE CHURCH; MEGACHURCH MOVEMENT; MELKITES; MENNONITES; METHODISM CLUSTER; MORAVIAN CHURCH; NAZARENE, CHURCH OF THE; NORTH INDIA, CHURCH OF; OLD CATHOLIC CHURCH; ORTHODOX CHURCHES, EASTERN, CLUSTER; ORTHODOX CHURCHES, ORIENTAL, CLUSTER; PENTECOSTAL MOVEMENT; PHILIPPINE INDEPENDENT CHURCH; PRESBYTERIAN CHURCHES; PROTESTANTISM CLUSTER; REFORMED CHURCHES; ROMAN CATHOLICISM CLUSTER; SALVATION ARMY; SCOTLAND, CHURCH OF; SCOTLAND, FREE CHURCH OF; SHAKERS; SOUTHERN BAPTIST CONVENTION; SOUTH INDIA, CHURCH OF; SYRIAC CATHOLIC CHURCH; SYRIAC ORTHODOX CHURCH, UNIVERSAL; UNIATE CHURCHES; UNIFICATION CHURCH; UNITED CHURCH OF CHRIST IN THE PHILIPPINES; UNITED CHURCH OF CHRIST (IN THE UNITED STATES); WALDENSES; WORD-FAITH MOVEMENT

Church of God (Cleveland, Tennessee), formed in 1886 in eastern Tennessee; quickly became Pentecostal and a "channel for Pentecostal revival." It claims to have a worldwide membership of more than 6 million (2004) with a presence in nearly 150 countries. **See also PENTECOSTAL MOVEMENT, ITS HISTORY AND THEOLOGY; PENTECOSTAL WORSHIP.**

Church of God in Christ, a global denomination, in 58 countries (in Africa, Asia, South America, and Europe) and a major presence in the USA, has 3 million members worldwide (in 2000). Beginning in 1897 as a Holiness* fellowship among black Baptist churches in the "mid-South" USA (as the middle southern states are called in the South), it was led by Charles Price Jones, Charles Harrison Mason, and Walter S. Pleasant, who preached the doctrine of sanctification*. "Disfellowshipped" by the Baptists (1899), these leaders organized independent congregations. From 1899 to 1906, the fellowship grew throughout the mid-South and surrounding states and elected Jones (1906) to head the Church of God in Christ, a nondenominational Holiness fellowship of more than 110 congregations.

Mason, dismissed from Jones's fellowship (1907) after embracing Pentecostalism*, organized the Church of God in Christ as a Pentecostal* body, being elected its first "general overseer." Lizzie Woods Robinson, appointed (1911) by Mason, organized and led the "Women's Department," a laywomen's auxiliary and a council of women evangelists and missionaries.

Initially, Mason's Church of God in Christ (COGIC) consisted of interracial networks. Mason led the central network of predominately black congregations and permitted four white-led networks of white congregations to associate with COGIC (1909–32), although one white network left to form Assemblies* of God (1914). Education has played an important role for COGIC, which has sponsored schools and colleges in the USA and various other countries. The C. H. Mason Theological Seminary (established 1970), an affiliate of the Interdenominational Theological Center, was the first Pentecostal graduate-level seminary in the USA; in the UK, COGIC has sponsored the Calvary Theological College. Throughout the 20th c., COGIC participated both in the Civil* Rights Movement (primarily at the local level) and in various ecumenical ventures (at all levels).

Theologically, the Church of God in Christ stands within the Pentecostal Holiness tradition and holds a range of theological perspectives, ranging from Black Evangelical to Wesleyan, Liberationist*, and Womanist* theology. Scripture* as the authoritative Word of God, salvation* as conversion*, sanctification as a work of grace*, and the baptism* of the Holy Spirit are key to COGIC theology, along with the doctrine of the Trinity, which is focused on the unity of God with the Father as the Creator, Christ as the Savior and

Redeemer*, the Holy Spirit as the Deliverer and Empowerer. Doctrines concerning the Christian life as discipleship*, the church* as the family* of God, and eschatology* (second coming of Christ) are also central. DAVID D. DANIELS III

Churching of Women, attendance at church by women after childbirth for rites of thanksgiving and purification (cf. Lev 12:1–8; Luke 2:22–24).

Church Orders Early Christian writings (e.g. the Didache*, the Apostolic* Church Order, the *Didascalia* apostolorum*, and the Apostolic* Constitutions) with directions for worship, ordination, and church discipline.

Church of South India. See SOUTH INDIA, CHURCH OF.

CHURCH AND STATE RELATIONS CLUSTER

1) *Introductory Entry*

Church and State Relations

2) *A Sampling of Contextual Views and Practices*

Church and State Relations in Africa: Central Africa (Malawi)
Church and State Relations in Africa: Islamic Tropical Africa
Church and State Relations in Africa: South Africa
Church and State Relations in Africa: Western Africa
Church and State Relations in Asia: China
Church and State Relations in Asia: The Philippines
Church and State Relations in Eastern Europe: Orthodox Perspective
Church and State Relations in Europe: The Roman Catholic Church and Politics
Church and State Relations in Latin America: Argentina
Church and State Relations in Latin America: Brazil
Church and State Relations in Latin America: Chile
Church and State Relations in Latin America: Colombia
Church and State Relations in Latin America: Cuba
Church and State Relations in Latin America: Mexico
Church and State Relations in Latin America: Uruguay
Church and State Relations in the United States

1) Introductory Entry

Church and State Relations. The Persian conquest of Babylonia (538 BCE) set an influential pattern for the relations between government and religion, institutionalizing religious pluralism. Exiles from Judah were allowed to return, with the priests being responsible for governing the Jews in the Persian Empire (Ezra 1:1–5, 5:13–14, 6:3–5; Isa 44:28, 45:1–14). The so-called *millet** system applied to other religious groups as well. Greek and then Roman conquerors of the East inherited this pattern and thus grudgingly tolerated Judaism, despite its rejection of all other cults. After the Islamic* conquests, the *millet* system was adopted, tolerating the "peoples of the Book."

Christians tried at first to utilize the rights that Jews already had, but when the Romans became aware of their differences, the persecutions* began. After Constantine's* legalization of Christianity, three alternative approaches to "church and state" emerged (4th c.): *differentiation,* the state withdrawing from religious issues and offering freedom of religion; *state over church,* the state regulating religion to preserve public order (traditional Roman views of government authority, augmented by the growing ideology that rulers had been chosen by God); and *church over state,* the church asserting its freedom from the state, refusing to tolerate what it declared to be paganism* or heresy*, and exercising discipline over baptized emperors as "sons of the church."

In the West, these three basic approaches were explicitly debated from the time of Charlemagne* and Louis* the Pious. A *differentiation* of church and state was based on their different tasks and modes of governance; *royal supremacy,* reinforced by the anointing* of rulers, often achieved important reforms of church life; and *papal supremacy* grew from the time of Gregory* VII until the excesses of Boniface* VIII, resulting in a new differentiation championed by Dante*, Marsilius* of Padua, and William* of Ockham.

The Reformation* was often carried out by civil authorities. The Erastian* theory (the state should carry out the functions of Christian discipline) gave to civil magistrates many of the powers previously exercised by the church, and in the Church of England the ruler was declared "head of the church" (see United Kingdom). Where Protestant churches were persecuted, especially in France and the Netherlands, self-government by the church and differentiation from the state emerged. In the Catholic world, papal authority came to be limited by Gallicanism*, by the growing theory of "indirect power," and by Patronato* in colonial regions.

A fully secular* state emerged after the French Revolution, with parallel developments in the USA that ended the "establishment*" of religion and guaranteed religious liberty* to all. Today religious conservatives often accuse the secular state of promoting its own religion of "secular humanism" and claim that religious freedom can be preserved only if the state supports religious institutions. The liberal response is to champion religious pluralism* in a secular state. **See also POLITICAL STUDIES OF CHRISTIANITY; POLITICAL THEOLOGY.**

EUGENE TESELLE

---

2) A Sampling of Contextual Views and Practices

Church and State Relations in Africa: Central Africa (Malawi). The African* Religion usually does not perceive a radical divide between politics and religion, seeing them as two sides of the same coin. Therefore, the separation of church and state is not an African idea; it came with colonialism* and imperialism.

Under colonial administration, missionaries often represented the people in the councils of government; consequently, conflicts arose. Certain missionaries challenged and exposed the injustices perpetrated by Western colonialists against African peoples. Thus government officials began to look at missionaries with suspicion. However, African Christian leaders, like John Chilembwe and Elliot Kamwana, who worked independently of the missions in Nyasaland (now Malawi*), were viewed as most threatening. John Chilembwe eventually led an armed attack on white settlers, and Kamwana was arrested and deported.

In Malawi, under the one-party rule (1964–94), the churches were told by President Hasting Kamuzu Banda not to engage in politics, because their function was a spiritual one. The Jehovah* Witnesses refused to support the party and were exiled. When the oppression worsened, the churches spoke out, led by the Catholic bishops (1991). Negotiation with the government led to a democratic multiparty political system (1994); since then, as Malawians like to say,"the power of the church has been recognized and feared."

Democracy* has empowered the churches to take prophetic stances toward the state, and the state seeks to have the churches on its side by trying to bribe church leaders with personal gifts. Claiming to be apolitical because they are concerned with spiritual matters only, some churches are passive and thus support the status quo, while others respond to the state in reactionary ways for lack of theological grounding. But whenever the churches have acted truly prophetically, they have provided a viable alternative voice for liberation*.

AUGUSTINE MUSOPOLE

Church and State Relations in Africa: Islamic Tropical Africa. Relations between church and state in Islamic tropical Africa are as varied as the doctrinal and ideological persuasions of the various denominations and groups of both Christianity and Islam*. Significantly, these relations are dependent on local and wider political contexts.

In theory Islam is a "complete way of life"; there is no separation between private and public, sacred and secular, mosque and state. Conscious and aggressive attempts have been made to implement this teaching, an example being the Islamic

Church and State Relations in Africa

theocratic states established by the jihadists (18th–19th c.) in West Africa. The most famous was the Sokoto Caliphate in present-day Northern Nigeria. In today's Islamic tropical Africa, even though the theocratic model remains an attraction to radical Muslim groups, all countries with a Muslim majority have secular constitutions. Nevertheless, unlike the early 1960s, because of the Muslims' new political awareness it is now almost unthinkable to have a non-Muslim head of state in any of the majority-Muslim countries in tropical Africa.

On the Christian side, the Biblical dictum "Give to Caesar what belongs to Caesar and to God what belongs to God" remains theoretically operative as the basis for the separation between church and state or secularism. In practice, although all majority-Christian countries in tropical Africa have secular constitutions, there have been instances of very close relations, if not marriage, between church and state. These include countries like Ethiopia* with its long intertwined relationship between the Orthodox Patriarchate and the imperial monarchy; the relationship between the Dutch Reformed Church and the apartheid regime in South* Africa; and Frederick Chiluba's presidency in Zambia* (late 1990s). Many African heads of state and church leaders have had and continue to have "opportunistic relationships." On the whole, the church and the state function as partners in development in tropical Africa. JOHN ALEMBILLAH AZUMAH

Church and State Relations in Africa: South Africa. With the transition from apartheid to democracy (1994) led by President Nelson Mandela, in most instances the way the churches related to the government shifted from resistance (to the apartheid government) to assistance (of the democratic government). Through critical solidarity, the churches support initiatives that promote justice*, peace*, and democracy*, while continuing to protest unjust policies and protecting the vulnerable and minority groups. Critical solidarity, based on Liberation* and Reconstruction* theologies and the preferential* option for the poor*, led churches to participate through their members in the nurturing of democracy as part of their quest for a political system closer to the principles of God's household, where justice, peace, dignity, and equality are upheld. Consolidating democracy also included embracing the liberal constitution, establishing a secular state that protects South Africans from both theocracy* and antireligious atheism*.

Critical solidarity also calls churches to obey the country's laws only if they are not contrary to God's laws (Acts 4:19, 5:29). The churches also base their participation on Ps 24:1: "The earth is the Lord's and all that is in it," bringing together ecclesial and societal issues.

The churches interact with the state through the South African Council of Churches and through the National Religious Leaders Forum, which includes representatives from most religious bodies. The churches' pastoral responsibilities include accompanying the newly established democratic nation through a crucial process of confession, forgiveness, healing, reconciliation, transformation, and reconstruction. Yet there is always the danger that churches will be coopted by the state, a danger overcome when they are totally committed to championing the needs of the poor, to being sensitive to their aspirations, and to helping restore their hope and dignity by holding the state and its representatives accountable to basic principles of good governance and democracy. SIMANGA R. KUMALO

Church and State Relations in Africa: Western Africa. The advent of Christian churches in West Africa is closely related to colonialism*; Africans perceived church and colonialism as mutually reinforcing. Indeed, for both colonizers and missionaries, everything about the African peoples' culture* was satanic and worthless. At this stage, the state was run by colonial masters whose attitudes reinforced those of the missionaries. Church and state were in a mutual and cohesive relationship; the church rarely challenged colonial injustice (see Mission Cluster: Mission and Imperialism).

During the 1950s, agitation for nationalism and political independence had a profound effect on African conceptions of Christianity as a foreign imposition. While Western African nationalists were struggling for autonomy from colonial rule on the political and economic scene, African Christians sought ways to reinterpret the Christian message through their African cultural heritage. These goals were reached more rapidly on the spiritual plane; African Christianity came to the fore before political independence in most Western African nations. Significant changes took place in the 1990s with the emergence of political liberalization in many Western African nations (including Nigeria). Most mainline churches (especially the Roman Catholic, Anglican, and Methodist churches) actively campaigned against human rights abuses, corruption, and injustice perpetrated by military regimes.

Pentecostal, Charismatic, and African Instituted Churches have distanced themselves from institutional political and social involvements. With their emphasis on faith* and salvation*, they indirectly challenge political structures that are too materialistic. Some of these churches have women as founders and many have women as highly placed leaders, in contrast with the mainline churches, which are male dominated. The African Instituted Churches place great emphasis on the African cultural and religious heritage, still often despised by both the secular administration and the mainline churches. The forces of global capitalism are a great challenge to both church and state in West Africa and elsewhere.

OYERONKE OLAJUBU

Church and State Relations in Asia: China. Relations between church and state became an issue in China only after the establishment of the People's Republic of China (1949). Despite efforts at indigenization during the republican period (1911–49) – Pope Benedict XV's policy of "Sinification" (ordaining Chinese nationals as priests and bishops) and the Protestant "Independent Church Movement" stressing Sinicization and advocating the "Three-Self" principle (self-governing, self-supporting, and self-propagating) – the Roman Catholic and Protestant churches in China remained identified with Western powers.

With the establishment of the People's Republic of China (1949), the Chinese churches were cut off from their connections with foreign congregations or missions, and became self-reliant and autonomous. At first the Chinese Communist Party espoused the Marxist* view of religion as "the opium of the people" that would gradually die out as history progressed. Therefore, the Party denied that religion had any positive value and endeavored to bring about its annihilation, despite the Party's claim to guarantee the free exercise of religion. This tension was exacerbated during the Cultural Revolution (1966–76).

After 1979 the religious situation improved rapidly in an era of reform and openness. The Chinese Communist Party acknowledged ("Document No. 19," 1982) that it had erred on matters regarding religion and was willing to learn lessons from history. Churches were reopened, collective worship was resumed, and the number of believers rapidly grew.

After 1990 the Chinese Communist Party urged government at all levels to fully implement the policy on freedom of faith, to handle religious affairs in accordance with the law, and to actively guide every religion to adapt itself to the socialist society. The implementation of the separation of church and state in China means that churches are not allowed to intervene in any administrative or judicial matters (including marriages*) or in public education, and must confine their practices to religious places; conversely, the state cannot use its authority to establish or repress a religion. Religion is exclusively a personal matter left to each citizen. Religious organizations, as nongovernmental organizations, are operated entirely by the believers themselves. Thus while the Chinese churches cannot impinge on political and economical affairs, they can exert their influence in moral and cultural areas. Churches can exercise religion within a framework constructed by Chinese law. In order to be protected legally and constitutionally, their activities must be patriotic and lawful. **See also HONG KONG.**

WANG XIAOCHAO

Church and State Relations in Asia: The Philippines. Relations between church and state in the Philippines have repeatedly changed. During the colonial* period (16th–19th c.), the Roman Catholic Church and the Spanish* government were united under the Patronato*, which gave the Spanish monarchy "the responsibility of promoting, maintaining, and defending the Roman Catholic religion" (De la Costa). This gave civil power to religious authorities, leading to numerous abuses. Separation of church and state was finally introduced during the struggle for independence from Spain (1898). The Malolos Congress (1911), during the US occupation, affirmed, "The State recognizes the freedom and equality of all religions, as well as the separation of Church and State" – an affirmation reflecting a US perspective. The separation of church and state was reaffirmed with Filipino independence (1945). Nonetheless, churches continue to exercise significant political influence, specifically regarding human* rights and development projects. Religious instruction in public schools is an option that can be chosen by parents. The Roman Catholic Church continues to oppose the legalization of abortion* and divorce*, and discourages governmental endorsement of artificial birth* control in family planning and anti-HIV/AIDS campaigns. While Protestant and other non-Catholic churches publicly endorse political candidates during national elections, those elected are consistently Catholic.

VICTOR AGUILAN

Church and State Relations in Eastern Europe: Orthodox Perspective. The religious map of contemporary Europe still reflects 12 centuries of developments. In the mid-9th c., the Eastern (Byzantine) Roman Empire devised a way to maintain its universal character: the peaceful conversion of neighboring "pagan*" populations to Byzantine* Christianity (Cyril* and Methodius's mission). Slavo-Byzantine clergy translated the Byzantine ecclesiastic culture into Slavonic. Thus they transmitted the ecclesiastical understanding of the role of the state and its relation to the Eastern Orthodox* Church. The Byzantine ecclesiastical control over Slavic and Romanian* churches in the Middle Ages created the paradoxical situation in which the Church was connected to a state (Constantinople and its emperor) outside the political organization of each region – a situation resisted by local rulers. When the Balkan* States aspired to attain imperial status (13th–14th c.), they tried to replicate Byzantine church–state relations. They borrowed late Byzantine canonical sources (diverging from earlier Byzantine political theology) that described the church as an institution parallel to, or even above, the state (Matthew Blastares's *Nomocanon**).

After the Ottoman conquest of the Balkans, while Eastern patriarchates established a political agreement with the sultan, which allowed a certain degree of ecclesiastical autonomy, Moscow emerged as the political leader of Orthodoxy and gradually developed a particular theory of church–state relations, in which the czar (starting with Peter the Great) was considered head of the Church. This new policy, inspired by Western protestant models, was legitimized by reference to the (initially marginal) concept of "Third Rome," a representation of muscovite statehood as continuator of Constantinople ("New Rome"). This formula combines ecclesiastical and political organization in an undistinguishable unity (which for Western scholars was already characteristic of Byzantium in the form of "caesaropapism"). This view of the collaboration between church and state was best summarized by Dostoyevsky* (*The Brothers Karamazov*, Book II, Chap. 5): "The Church is not to be transformed into the State. That is Rome and its dream, the third temptation of the devil. On the contrary, the State is transformed into the Church, will ascend and will become a Church over the whole world [. . .] the glorious destiny ordained for the

Orthodox Church." Even in the 20th c., the newly autocephalous Orthodox churches in Balkan countries (Greece*, Serbia*, Romania*, Bulgaria*) promoted a mode of close collaboration between (Orthodox) Church and nation-state known by the legal term "symphony," Orthodoxy becoming part of national identity.

PETRE GURAN

Church and State Relations in Europe: The Roman Catholic Church and Politics. During the 19th and 20th c., i.e. since the Enlightenment* and the French Revolution, church and state relations have undergone fundamental changes. In the context of a pervasive trend from a Christendom* paradigm to the secularization* of politics, a shift occurred from a close church–state relationship, with one privileged church in each state, to a situation of religious pluralism*. Accordingly, the state, at least as a matter of principle, has come to treat all churches and religions equally.

A guiding principle throughout Christian history has been Christ's saying (Mark 12:17, par.), "Render to Caesar the things that are Caesar's and to God the things that are God's." In the Roman Catholic tradition, the various interpretations of this teaching agree on a common core: the church is not meant to replace the state (theocracy* is excluded), but the state's claim to obedience is strictly limited. The state must leave room for the "obedience of faith" toward God. In the 20th c., this aspect came to the fore in the opposition of the Roman Catholic Church to the totalitarian regimes of the Soviet bloc and Nazi Germany.

However, the road to championing modern democratic* values was a long and troubled one. The 19th-c. relations of Catholics with politics in European countries reflected anti-democratic habits and alliances with reactionary forces that hampered the process. Conversely, many governments (Protestant or "liberal" anticlerical ones) passed hostile legislation encroaching on the rights of the Roman Catholic Church. Lay Catholics then often took advantage of the possibilities of a state's liberal constitution. They formed pressure groups or even political parties to promote Catholic positions in matters such as education*, marriage* and divorce* or the activities of religious* orders.

Relations with the different governments were not uniform, though the starting position of the Roman Catholic Church in the aftermath of the French Revolution was bleak everywhere. Napoleon Bonaparte was an unlikely benefactor. However, in his design to fortify imperial France, he enlisted the authority of Pope Pius VII in the Concordat* of 1801. He pressured the pope to redraw the map of France's dioceses* and reduce their number. The long-term upshot was an unprecedented acceptance of the pope's jurisdiction by Catholics, even in local affairs ("Roman centralization," Ultramontanism*, the First Vatican* Council, 1870). It meant that, henceforth, should any nation wish to obtain concessions or agreements from its Catholics, its government would have to deal with Rome (*Kulturkampf**). In the 20th c., concordats loomed large, notably the 1929 Lateran Agreements between Pope Pius XI and Benito Mussolini (which created Vatican City as a tiny independent state within Rome) and the ambivalent Concordat of 1933 with Hitler (see Germany).

Meanwhile, changes were under way in the thinking of European Catholics. World War II stimulated the commitment to democracy* as the political system most in accord with human* dignity and rights. The cold war brought the eastern half of Europe under the domination of the Soviet Union and underscored the evils of totalitarianism. During the pontificate (1958–63) of Pope John* XXIII, contacts were made even with the Kremlin. The breakthrough, however, came with the pope from Poland (1978–2005), John* Paul II. During his pontificate, the unexpected took place: the Iron Curtain fell. By the year 2000, the European Union (EU), encompassing many Eastern and Western European states, came into being. All nation-members of the EU are committed to "freedom of thought, conscience and religion." The European bishops* had insisted on this in line with the Second

Vatican* Council and its historic Declaration on Religious Freedom (1965). **See also CHRISTIAN DEMOCRATIC PARTIES.**

PAUL MISNER

Church and State Relations in Latin America: Argentina. Ecclesiastic and political powers have been interconnected in a fluid way in Argentine life. The demands that the institution of the Roman Catholic Church placed on the state required, in reciprocity, the legitimating recognition of political authorities by the Church. This interaction continues in the present.

Although Roman Catholicism has not been established as the "state religion," this has not prevented the Catholic Church from being an active presence in the political sphere, especially since the 1853 Constitution, which protects "freedom of worship" (Articles 14 and 20). In this limited sense, the "patronage" policy (see Patronato) continued until 1966. The autonomy of the Roman Catholic Church, including freedom to appoint its own bishops, does not mean that the Church is detached from its context, and is not subject to pressures from public opinion and the state (as was the case in the 1970s). Conversely, with the end of Patronato, the Roman Catholic Church gained institutional independence, yet kept its overall goals, which it pursued, when necessary, by pressuring public authorities.

This type of relation between the Roman Catholic Church and the state continued in the 1970s following the law (No. 21,745), under General Videla's military government, that demanded the national registration of worship services (1977, still enforced) as a way of bureaucratically controlling religious groups, especially those that were not Catholic. Yet the 1994 constitutional reform (Article 76) abrogated the requirement that to be president one must "belong to the Catholic communion," although the fact that the Argentine legislation does not stipulate religious freedom suggests that the Roman Catholic Church still has a privileged place in the life of Argentina. From this perspective, the state constitutionally guaranteed "support of the Roman Catholic and apostolic worship" (Article 2). **See also ARGENTINA.**

HUMBERTO HORACIO CUCCHETTI

Church and State Relations in Latin America: Brazil. Understanding the relationship between Catholicism and politics first requires recognizing that the Roman Catholic Church is an institution. As Scott Mainwaring shows about Brazil, different "church models" lead to different conceptions of the institutional interests of the Roman Catholic Church. Internal changes in the Church bring about changes in church models that result from conflicts among groups with different conceptions of the Christian faith and of the mission of the Church. The relationship between church and state varies accordingly.

The first phase of the institutional history of the Roman Catholic Church in Brazil (1500–1822) took place under the Padroado* system. In this political regime, granted by the popes, the control of the ecclesiastical sphere – the control of the Church as an institution – was in the hands of the Portuguese sovereigns. Since the political sphere had control over church matters, in turn church leaders sought to influence political authorities. During the process of independence (1822, and the consolidation of the Brazilian Empire, under the constitutional monarchy of Pedro I), some of the clergy initially were strongly influenced by liberal and Gallican* thought and defended the special rights of the monarch with respect to the Brazilian Church and the Church's administrative independence from Rome. Yet the Brazilian Episcopate defended a greater autonomy of the Church from the state in pastoral questions and closer ties with Rome. Despite their conflicting church models, both groups defended the monarchy as the best political system to promote and maintain social order.

After the establishment of the Republic (1890–1945), the influence of the Roman Catholic Church declined; basic teachings were modified, in part, to protect the traditional interests of the Church in society. Most importantly, political struggles, including those during periods of dictatorship, and broad social movements contributed to the transformation of the "faith-vision" of sizable sections of the Church (1964–95). Deep concerns for the poor* and for social* justice* became an integral part of these groups' new vision of the mission of the Church, aimed at transforming the social order, mainly through Base* Ecclesial Communities.

However, as a result of the process of re-democratization in Brazil, the crisis of socialism, and the centralization promoted by the Roman Catholic Church, another model of church and state relations seems to have emerged in the 1990s and the beginning of the 21st c. **See also ROMAN CATHOLICISM CLUSTER: IN LATIN AMERICA: BRAZIL (VARIOUS ENTRIES).** SÉRGIO COUTINHO

Church and State Relations in Latin America: Chile. Relations between church and state in Chile reflect the historic weight of the Roman Catholic Church, its close ties with the state, and the progressive move toward the autonomy of the state and toward religious pluralism* (20th c.). During the colonial period, the Roman Catholic Church depended on the Spanish crown through the regime of the Patronato*; Christianity legitimized the colonial state, and the state supported and contributed to evangelism. The wars of independence divided the Church, but the new republic maintained the Patronato* and the union of church and state (1833). The conflicts between the Roman Catholic Church and the state (19th c.) stemmed from the Liberals' efforts to guarantee freedom of worship and of education, and civil registry of births, marriages, and deaths, all of which were monopolized at that time by the Roman Catholic Church. The 1925 Constitution separated church and state, but the national culture continued to function as if the Roman Catholic Church were the official state church. The growth of Evangelical churches led to the recognition of religious pluralism during Allende's government (1970–73). After the military state (1973–90), with the process of re-democratization of Chilean society, the government of Eduardo Frei Ruiz Tagle promulgated (1999) the new law that recognizes equal autonomous legal status for all churches.

CRISTIÁN G. PARKER

Church and State Relations in Latin America: Colombia. Colombia is one of the Latin American countries in which the conservative wing of the Roman Catholic Church resisted most powerfully the development of a secular state. The first attempts by the Liberal Party to establish a secular state through a politics of laicization* (1850s) were dismantled by the Conservative Party in 1886. This rejection of laicization was ratified by the Concordat* of 1887 (an agreement between the Roman Catholic Church and the state that is still officially in force, with some modifications). These political structures gave to the Roman Catholic Church as an ecclesial institution numerous social, economic, and political privileges, with an authority comparable to that of modern states in the exercise of their own functions. This privileged situation of the Church and its undeniable authority over citizens contributed to the creation of a state of Christendom*, in which state authorities negotiate with Roman Catholic institutional authorities on equal terms.

In 1936 Liberals tried to modify this confessionalism by instating a separation of church and state that involved suppression of the Roman Catholic Church's privileges and its statelike functions. Yet the Conservatives and the clergy reacted so vehemently against these reforms that by the end of the 1940s these measures had been dismantled. Following these years of painful conflict, the confrontation between Liberals and Conservatives shifted away from religious issues, to the point that both political parties could recognize the Roman Catholic Church as the official religion of Colombia. This agreement between the two parties was confirmed in 1957 by a plebiscite that inaugurated a period of Colombian history known as the National Front, during which Liberals and Conservatives constitutionally decreed that they would alternately govern during four presidential terms. From then on, both parties agreed to dedicate the country to the Sacred Heart of Jesus and to keep the name of God in the preamble to the Constitution.

In spite of this formal recognition of Roman Catholicism as the official religion of Colombia, Colombian society underwent a cultural process of secularization* in the late 20th and early 21st c. that led to a new laical* constitution (1991) that respects religious pluralism*. Thus Catholicism has become one of the religious options in a diversified religious world where the Pentecostal*/ Charismatic* Movement plays an increasing role. Nevertheless, the Roman Catholic Church continues to have considerable political power to defend its corporate interests and the political status quo, as well as the place of Catholic morality in Colombian life. **See also COLOMBIA.**

HELWAR FIGUEROA

Church and State Relations in Latin America: Cuba. The Roman Catholic Church has not been persecuted in Cuba, contrary to what occurred in the former Eastern European socialist countries. The Cuban Communist regime was more tolerant. Since 1968 the Roman Catholic Church's position has evolved from anti-Communist to detached critical observer. The 1968 Latin American Episcopal Conference in Medellín* and the birth of Liberation* theology made it ideologically possible to link Christian faith and social change. In 1986 the National Cuban Church Meeting took place, and for the first time the Roman Catholic Church agreed to work within the socialist context. At the Fourth Congress of the Cuban Communist Party (1991), the decision was made to abolish all forms of religious discrimination; and in 1992 the constitutional change became a reality, promoting the disassociation of the state from any form of atheism. In November 1996, Fidel Castro had an interview with John* Paul II at the Vatican, followed by the successful visit of the pope to the island (January 1998). During and since this visit, the tone of the relationship between church and state has evolved from one of confrontation toward reconciliation.

ARMANDO LAMPE

Church and State Relations in Latin America: Mexico. For three centuries, the relations between church and state in Mexico were governed by the Patronato* system, the policy of royal patronage through which the Roman Catholic Church granted sovereignty to the monarchs of Castile over Mexico, including the legal authority and jurisdiction over the Church and its mission. As Mexico began to move toward autonomy, the Constitution of Apatzingán (1814) emphasized the official role of the Roman Catholic Church. Yet since 1821, ongoing tensions have existed between the state and the Church, as modernization promoted by governmental elites has met with resistance from the Church hierarchy.

During the construction of the Mexican state (1821–67), the debate over the legal status of the Roman Catholic Church reflected the conflict between two Masonic lodges (see Freemasonry and Christianity). The Yorkino (Yorkist) Lodge viewed religion as a private matter and envisioned the Roman Catholic Church as a corporation authorized by the state, somewhat as it was under Patronato. The Escoceses (Scottish) Lodge fought for a centralist republic (or monarchy) that would protect the Church and guarantee its central place in the state through a concordat* with the Holy See. Thus in different ways both parties sought to maintain the state–church union; yet subsequently and for different reasons, both favored a separation of church and state.

The 1824 Constitution affirmed the Catholic Church as the state church, with some religious tolerance for other churches. Such tolerance was soon eliminated by the Seven Laws (1836) and the 1842 Constitution, but was restored after the US invasion (1848), but in a way that followed the French model of separation of church and state. The Conservatives, influenced by Ultramontanism*, fought for an actual separation of church and state (though with governmental support for the church) that would free the

Roman Catholic Church from the forces of Liberalism and their hegemonic pretensions. The Liberals were influenced by Gallicanism*, the North American views of freedom of religion, and antireligious European thought.

The "reform" of 1856–60 in Mexico was preceded by a period of civil war, during which the Roman Catholic Church was alone able to hold the people together; its hierarchy was respected, immensely rich, and financed by the different governments. Thus after the revolution of Ayutla (1854) that began the "reform," for economic and ideological reasons the Liberal governments sought to eliminate the dependence of the Church on the Holy See, arguing that it was impossible to be loyal to two sovereignties. They nationalized the Church's material possessions, removed its status as state church, and limited its presence in daily life. From the perspective of conservative canon* lawyers, these laws transgressed basic liberties. After the promulgation of the Republican Constitution of 1857 – discreetly secular and tolerant – some Conservatives hoped to establish a Catholic monarchy that would reestablish the role of the Catholic Church in protecting the national identity from the threats posed by diverse ideologies and other confessions. But Maximilian of Hapsburg ratified the Laws of Reform, which later (1873) were declared "constitutional" by the victorious Liberals.

Porfirio Díaz's regime (1876–1910) revived Roman Catholicism and opened the country to new Christian denominations. Catholic* Action inspired by the social doctrine of the Church participated in the political life of Mexico; in addition, the National Catholic Party was founded (1911). But this Catholic political involvement was resented by constitutional Jacobins, who succeeded in establishing a new, secular, anticlerical constitution (1917). Yet the eradication of religion from national life was prevented by the "Cristeros" uprising (1926–29; see Mexico). Thus despite the Constitution, a modus vivendi (until 1980) allowed the Roman Catholic Church to function with its buildings, hospitals, schools, and orphanages, although these were legally nonexistent. During the pontificate of Pope John* Paul II, the anticlerical laws were modified (1992, during the Salinas government) to allow for the legal recognition of religious groups and the civil rights of priests and pastors. These laws recognized that the Mexican state was incomplete if it did not recognize the necessary relationship between the state or society and the churches.

MONICA URIBE and
MARÍA ALICIA PUENTE LUTTEROTH

Church and State Relations in Latin America: Uruguay. Relations between church and state became an issue in Uruguay only with the secularization* of the country during the first capitalist modernization (1870–1930; after the Patronato* system). Secularization as the separation of church and state was a reform from the top down, until becoming a national process (early 20th c.). Yet it had deep roots in the 19th c., e.g. in the school reform led by José P. Varela (1877). As José P. Barrán notes, "The secularization of mentalities, customs, institutions, and education (a rapid process) is the primary multi-faceted cultural symptom of early Uruguayan modernity." The radical transformation of church and state relations through secularization* took two forms:

1. The marginalization of the religious, gradually relegated to the private sphere, was an expression of the modern separation between state and civil society, and between public and private spheres.
2. Official positions strongly critical of any religious hegemony (in this case by the Roman Catholic Church) combined with the transfer of the "sacred" from religious institutions to political institutions progressively brought about a civil religion, with its alternative symbols, doctrines, and rituals, and with civic liturgies aimed at reinforcing national identity and social order.

These two factors quickly transformed the relations between the Roman Catholic

Church and the state, and indeed those among religion, politics, and society for Uruguayans. During the past decades, there have been indications that the 19th-c. triumphant Jacobin secularization is losing its credibility for many Uruguayans. Yet nothing indicates that any of the alternatives is more pluralistic and libertarian; actually, the opposite seems to be true. Neither the predominance of a "neo-Christianity" invested by the media with orthodoxy and authority, nor the empire of a New* Age with its individualism prone to a lack of solidarity, nor "pseudo-multiculturalism" with its "everything goes" attitude would be better than the present secularized separation of church and state. GERADO CAETANO

Church and State Relations in the United States are based principally on language in the First Amendment to the Constitution: "Congress shall make no law respecting an establishment of religion, or prohibiting the free exercise thereof." The Constitution did not create a Christian nation: government is based on the will of "We the People of the United States" (Preamble). The "no establishment principle" means there should be no formal relationship, either positive or negative, between religion and civil authority. Government should neither aid nor hinder religion. All religions, Christian or not, and people of no religion are equal before the law.

The "free exercise principle" means government power may not inhibit or prevent the practice of religion. Not only can citizens believe what they want, but they can put those beliefs into action by attending worship, evangelizing, contributing money, or engaging in religiously motivated social action, all without government interference. Thus religious groups or individuals may try to influence government policy. People of no religious faith can abstain from religious activity. However, government may intervene if religiously motivated behavior is harmful to individuals, groups, or the society as a whole. Because separation of church and state, or religious freedom, is a constitutionally guaranteed right, disputes between religions and government units are settled by courts, the final arbiter being the US Supreme Court. In 1940 (Free Exercise Clause) and 1947 (Establishment Clause) decisions of the Supreme Court applied these federal constitutional principles to state and local laws as well.

Beginning about 1965, considerable political turmoil erupted over the scope of the Establishment Clause, a controversy that continues. The principal issues are prayer (and other religious exercises) in public schools and government aid to religious schools. The Court had declared that both violated the "no establishment" principle. The emergent "Christian Right Movement" wanted much more religious involvement in government, as a way of improving public morality, and sought ways to erode the separation of church and state and to blunt, if not overturn, decisions in the school issues. Late in the 20th c, a much more conservative Supreme Court began to accommodate that view. In reference to free exercise, the Court decided that government could be much more intrusive in religious practices than had formerly been the case. In the continuing cultural dispute, "separationists" argue that separation of church and state is compatible with Christianity; "accommodationists" claim it is not.

RONALD B. FLOWERS

Church Struggle in Germany (1930s) resulted from the Nazi policy of *Gleichschaltung* (literally "Synchronizing") that brought under Nazi control all aspects of society, including religion. German Roman Catholics, fearful of Russian Communism, capitulated to Hitler through the Concordat* of 1933. The Protestant churches battled harder to maintain their independence. Their principal antagonists were the "German* Christians," who espoused an intrinsic link between Christianity and Nazism and sought to establish a Reich Church under state control. The high point of Protestant resistance was the Barmen* Declaration (1934). In the ensuing years, however, internal divisions undermined this resistance. **See also CHURCH AND STATE RELATIONS CLUSTER: IN EUROPE: THE ROMAN CATHOLIC CHURCH AND POLITICS; GERMANY.** MARK R. LINDSAY

Church Unions, the rejoining of churches that have been separated by controversy. Some schisms* between the Eastern and Western churches were temporary (e.g. the Acacian* schism, 482–519, as well as the controversy over the Three Chapters* and Iconoclasm*, 726–87, 813–43), while the schism of 1054 became permanent despite the efforts of the Council of Florence*. A number of Eastern churches have joined with Rome (see Uniate Churches). Protestant reunions have been most numerous in Great Britain, the USA, and the Commonwealth of Nations.

Churchwarden, lay officer assisting the pastor* and representing the laity of a parish*.

Ciborium, receptacle for the reserved* host*.

Cimade, an ecumenical mutual aid service association created by the French Protestant Youth Movement (1939), inspired by Karl Barth* and the Suzanne de Dietrich Biblical Renewal Movement. Originally created by Madeleine Barot* and others to help the populations of Eastern France displaced by the war, the Cimade soon worked among foreigners and Jews in internment camps, engaging in active resistance and organizing clandestine welcome centers and underground escape networks. After World War II, the Cimade participated in social reconstruction and reconciliation services in France, Germany, and Algeria. Today it helps refugees* by providing legal assistance and supporting them morally, e.g. in illegal-immigrant centers and prisons, in cooperation with churches and numerous associations in Europe and wherever there are migrants. **See also REFUGEES AS A THEOLOGICAL CONCEPT AND AN ETHICAL ISSUE.**

JACQUES STEWART

Circle of Concerned African Women Theologians ("the Circle") gives African women from the continent and the diaspora a forum for engaging in theological dialogue with cultures, religions, sacred writings, and oral stories that shape the African context and define the women of the African continent. Members of the Circle belong to African* Religion, Christianity, Islam*, and Judaism*. In 2006 the Circle registered 616 members: 465 Anglophone, 93 Francophone, and 59 Lusophone. The criterion for membership is the commitment to research, write, and publish on issues affecting African women and women of African descent.

Mercy Amba Oduyoye is the founder of the Circle, launched in Accra, Ghana (September 1989), during a conference entitled "Daughters of Africa Arise," when the Circle also inaugurated the Biennial Institute of African Women in Religion and Culture.

The title of the second Pan African Circle conference (Nairobi, 1996) was "Transforming Power: Women in the Household of God." Musimbi R. Kanyoro was the first elected coordinator of the Circle. Mercy Oduyoye became the full-time director of the Institute of African Women in Religion and Culture.

The title of the third Pan African Circle conference (Addis Ababa, 2002) was "Sex, Stigma, and HIV/AIDS: African Women Challenging Religion, Culture and Social Practices." Isabel Phiri was the second elected coordinator of the Circle, and the list of publications by members of the Circle multiplied. **See also THEOLOGY AS HUMAN UNDERTAKING CLUSTER: AFRICAN WOMEN THEOLOGIANS DOING THEOLOGY BY MAKING CONNECTIONS** ISABEL APAWO PHIRI

Circumcellions, Latin label applied to violent supporters of Donatism* and the Donatist "Church of the Martyrs" (4th–5th c., North Africa), notorious for destroying what they viewed as pagan statues, seizing Catholic churches, attacking Catholic clergy, and seeking martyrdom. The label "Around the *Cellae*" may refer to an association with Donatist martyr shrines, the evidence comes almost entirely from hostile sources. Scholars have often identified Circumcellions as rural laborers and their rebellion as having economic or social causes; but Augustine* of Hippo and his biographer Possidius impugned their asceticism*, and their motives seem to have been fundamentally religious. It is plausible to consider them an early type of rogue monk. DANIEL F. CANER

Circumcision, Feast of the, observance of Christ's circumcision (Luke 2:21) eight days after Christmas*. Often called the Feast of the Naming of Jesus.

Cistercians, a Catholic religious* order. The Monastery of Cîteaux in Burgundy was founded (1098) by Robert of Molesme (d1111), who was inspired by the idea of a return to monastic origins characteristic of many new 11th- to 12th-c. monastic orders. Cistercians claimed to follow the Rule of Benedict* literally, cutting back the liturgical accretions of previous centuries, dressing in undyed habits, and renouncing tithes and benefices. Such claims led them into controversy with the Cluniacs*, whom by 1153 they supplanted with more than 300 Cistercian monasteries throughout Europe and in the Holy Land. This rapid expansion is partly attributable to the great Cistercian monk and preacher Bernard* of Clairvaux. The agricultural success and prosperity of the order (e.g. as sheep farmers in the British Isles) were attributable largely to the labor of lay brothers* who were a part of the order from earliest times. The organization of the order was regulated by the *Carta* Caritatis*. The first Cistercian nunnery was created in 1125. Starting in the 14th c. the order was repeatedly reformed; the Strict Observance (Trappists) emerged in the 17th c. By 2000 there were more than 200 Cistercian houses (including convents) worldwide. MARILYN DUNN

City. It is often said that the Bible begins in a garden (Gen 2:8) and ends in a city (Rev 21:1–2). Cain founds the first city (Gen 4:17); cities like Babylon, Nineveh, and Sodom and Gomorrah are punished; and the Israelites in the wilderness are warned not to return to the cities of Egypt (Num 14:1–4). Yet Jerusalem is called God's dwelling place (Ps 122, 137) and becomes a symbol of the "Jerusalem above" (Gal 4:26). The people of God are told to seek the welfare (*shalom*) of the earthly city in which they dwell (Jer 29:5–7). When Augustine* interpreted the human story in terms of the city of God and the earthly city, he was drawing on a rich symbolism* in the Bible, augmented by Greek thought, in which the *polis* was the classic form of political organization and one of the means (along with philosophical and religious contemplation) of human fulfillment.

While Jesus' ministry was mainly in the countryside and small towns of Galilee, the Christian movement quickly became urban, first in Jerusalem, then in Caesarea, Antioch, and Rome. Congregations were urban, and it is still the custom to name bishops for cities, not territories. Although monasteries were usually rural and the feudal* system was a major factor in the early Middle Ages, the life of cities became steadily more important after the 12th c. They were the locale for developments like the Lay* Piety Movement, the mendicant* orders, the Beguines*, and the universities*.

Cities as the dominant context for life raised new ethical issues. Even rural life has been affected by this commercial context, by the growing trade in commodities, and by the tendency to think of land itself as a commodity, bought and sold without regard to traditional rights. People thrown off the land have gathered in cities, offering cheap labor but living under conditions of poverty*, disorganization, and alienation from social and religious traditions. The "urban problem" became an explicit concern to the churches, which they have tried to meet through evangelism*, social ministries, house* churches, and base* ecclesial communities and advocacy for more just public policies. **See also SOCIAL GOSPEL MOVEMENT.**

EUGENE TESELLE

Civil Constitution of the Clergy, legislation of the French Constituent Assembly, July 12, 1790, essentially creating a national church. Its four sections reorganized diocesan boundaries, established direct election of bishops and clergy by laity, mandated clerical salaries paid by the state, and attempted to stop clerical absenteeism. An oath to support this act was required of all clergy by a decree of November 27. Approximately half of the clergy and two bishops took the oath, resulting in a Catholic schism. The Constitutional Church continued in modest form until the Concordat* of 1801 between Napoleon and Pius VII. **See also CHURCH AND STATE RELATIONS CLUSTER: IN EUROPE: THE ROMAN CATHOLIC CHURCH AND POLITICS.**

DALE A. JOHNSON

Civil Disobedience is an intentional, nonviolent* violation of law*, exercised as public protest on behalf of "higher" ideals that the law is thought to ignore or contravene. It is not a uniquely Christian mode of public resistance; it is also found in Judaism*, Greek culture, Jainism, Hinduism*, Buddhism*, and secular traditions. Civil disobedience campaigns launched by the distinctive figures of Mohandas Gandhi and Martin Luther King*, Jr., evidence the interreligious and intercultural provenance of civil disobedience.

As NT scholar Walter Wink has argued, however, Jesus and early Christians taught that nonviolence practiced to the point of suffering* and even death was not just political strategy, but also a "direct corollary of the nature of God" and, hence, constitutive of Christian living. Other cases of Christians' civil disobedience include: Christians' refusal of emperor worship, Mennonites'* and Quakers'* work to abolish slavery* and war*, Christians' support of the Underground Railroad against slavery, the US Civil* Rights Movement, sanctuary movements for "illegal" immigrants, and Christian soldiers' refusing deployment orders. Christian ethicists and theologians often debate civil disobedience in relation to Christian responsibility to state powers. MARK LEWIS TAYLOR

Civil Registry. Recording of births, marriages, and deaths by public officials, replacing the practice under which parish churches kept such records. The transition came during the French Revolution and was spread throughout Europe by Napoleon. In Latin America, liberal parties championed civil registry to reduce the Roman Catholic Church's influence.

Civil Religion is the religious dimension of political and civic life. In the ancient Near East, Greece, and Rome, religious ceremonies were part of public life; officials often filled priestly roles; people supported these ceremonies for the sake of social unity. The Jews* and then the Christians, because of their monotheism*, refused to take part in this older type of civil religion.

After Constantine*, however, and especially after Theodosius*, Christianity became the civil religion of the Roman Empire and of many successor states in Europe and their colonies. Each government favored a particular version of Christianity, enforcing religious uniformity and offering financial support to the state* church.

After the secularization* of Western governments, civil religion of a different sort emerged. Robert Bellah's classic essay (1967) analyzed the rhetoric of US presidents and found a civil religion based on the shared religious tradition of the West, evoking natural rather than revealed religion (cf. "nature and nature's God" in the US Declaration of Independence) and tending to promote a rather austere sense of national responsibility and readiness for sacrifice. Prayer on public occasions in the USA tends to emphasize what the religious traditions have in common.

In the non-Western world, the Chinese* rites controversy was a major test of civil religion and the degree to which Christians might participate in it. While the Jesuits' position (that participation in traditional rituals was merely a manifestation of social unity, not adherence to a different religion) was defeated in the 18th c., the Vatican adopted much the same position as the Jesuits in the 20th c. concerning Shinto* and other traditional rituals. In the USA, customs such as prayer at the opening of legislative sessions have often been defended on similar grounds, as tradition rather than a specifically religious act, or as an inculturation* of Christianity. It must be asked, however, whether such practices have any place in a secular and religiously pluralistic state. EUGENE TESELLE

Civil Rights Movement, a church-based movement that began with the leadership and involvement of Martin Luther King*, Jr., Ralph D. Abernathy, and other clergy in the Montgomery, Alabama, bus boycott (1955–56) and extended up to the planning of the Poor People's Campaign, the Memphis, Tennessee, sanitation strike, and the death of King (1968). King's Dexter Avenue Baptist Church, the First Baptist Church, the Holt Street Baptist Church, and other local black congregations in Montgomery afforded the initial context for launching the movement. In 1957 King and a hundred other clergy organized the Southern* Christian Leadership Conference, and that organization became the operational base from which they sought to mobilize the resources of black and white churches in the interest of social justice*, equality of opportunity, and peace. Although the full power of the churches was never mustered on behalf of the movement, especially in terms of material and physical resources, the Black Church became the rallying point and source of inspiration in a moral and spiritual quest to eliminate racism*, poverty* and economic injustice, war*, and human destruction. The Ebenezer Baptist Church of Atlanta, Georgia, the congregation in which King was nurtured from childhood and the one he served as co-pastor (1960–68) with his father and brother, Martin Luther King, Sr., and Alfred D. King, became a benchmark for local congregational activism and was commonly called the Mecca of church-centered civil rights protests. Other churches became equally important in terms of providing a power base, a de facto platform, or a social and political base for the movement, including the Shady Grove Baptist Church in Albany, Georgia, the First Baptist Church, Capitol Hill, in Nashville, Tennessee, the Sixteenth Street Baptist Church in Birmingham, Alabama, and the Brown Chapel African Methodist Episcopal Church in Selma, Alabama. Movement activists drew heavily on the spiritual disciplines of the church, uniting a prophetic Christian witness with the prayer circle and the picket line. From Montgomery to Memphis, the churches served as dispatch centers where bus boycotters waited for rides, became the focal point of mass meetings and prayer vigils, and provided food, funds, meeting places, staff, demonstrators, and lodging for the movement. The symbolic importance and influence of the church did not escape the Ku Klux Klan and other opponents of the Civil Rights Movement, and numerous churches were burned or bombed in Alabama, Mississippi, Georgia, and other Southern states.

LEWIS V. BALDWIN

Civil War in the United States. Fought between April 1861 and June 1865, the American Civil War was a conflict between Northern and Southern states (620,000 soldiers died; c400,000 wounded) rooted in divisions over the morality of plantation slavery*, the extent of states' rights to self-govern, and a growing divide between industrial and agricultural economies.

The war had a profound impact on Christianity in the USA, precipitating theological crises. Both Northern and Southern pulpits drew on Scripture*, tradition, and experience to validate the claim of each that God was on their side, producing numerous and theologically weak "God's-eye views" of the war. Christian theology followed politics; abolitionist theologians and preachers emerged in the North, while theology and Scripture were used to defend slavery* in the South. Massive Protestant church divisions followed; Methodists, Baptists, Presbyterians, and Anglicans in the North and the South turned against one another.

The war dealt a savage blow to the US Christian notion of being a "redeemer nation" aligned with Providence. Yet Abraham Lincoln, the wartime president (not a member of any church), offered a subtle interpretation of the war in his second inaugural address. He evoked a tragic vision of the war that acknowledged neither the triumphalism of the Northern theologians nor the self-righteous "lost cause" rhetoric of the Southern. Lincoln acknowledged the irreconcilability of the Northern and Southern positions, and insisted on the inscrutability of Providence, calling on both sides to seek peace and healing rather than divine vindication. This progressive apophaticism* was a sociopolitical benchmark that set the stage for the rise of the postbellum Social* Gospel theologies.

The war also provoked a hermeneutical crisis. Literalist* interpreters had to acknowledge (willingly or not) that some biblical cultures seemed to sanction slavery, raising the question among Northern ministers of whether mirroring biblical culture was the best way to order society. Some liberal abolitionist theologians contended that since the Bible endorsed slavery, the Bible itself should be dismissed as archaic and irrelevant, while moderates suggested that the spirit of the text, not the literal meaning, was the key interpretive principle for using the Bible in contemporary contexts.

The war shook the foundations of US Protestant theology and Bible* interpretation, deeply altering the way theology and Scripture could figure into the national discourse. Postmillennial* exuberance gave way to Premillennial Dispensational* pessimism, and literalist hermeneutics moved to the margins of national discourse, from which it later reemerged as fundamentalism*.

CALEB J. D. MASKELL

Clapham Sect (c1790–c1830), an influential abolitionist group of Evangelical Anglicans to which William Wilberforce* belonged. **See also HISTORY OF CHRISTIANITY CLUSTER: IN AFRICA.**

Clare of Assisi (1193/4–1253), first female follower of Francis* of Assisi; founded the Second Order of St. Francis (Clarissas or Poor* Clares), wrote the first monastic rule by a woman for women. Born in Assisi, Italy, to minor nobility, she fled an arranged marriage and was tonsured by Francis (1211), appointed abbess of St. Damiano (1215), founded or inspired various convents, and was canonized in 1255. Clare's devotion to Christ on the cross as a "mirror" for lay devotion led to her insistence on the "privilege of absolute poverty*" for female Franciscans. As Mueller says, "She had been inspired by Francis, who had shown her the way to live peacefully by owning nothing in a world racked with violence and litigation." Although she accepted Francis's direct request for monastic enclosure, differentiating the Clarissan lifestyle from that of the male mendicants, she struggled against the imposition of the Benedictine* Rule after the Fourth Lateran prohibition of new monastic orders. Her rejection of the ownership of property led to continued battles with Gregory IX over whether enclosure (without assurances of charitable response from the community) or poverty was key to the Clarissan vocation. Her rule, based on that of St. Francis for his community, was approved two days before her death.

JESSICA A. BOON

Clare of Montefalco, or Clare of the Cross (c1268–1308). Professed as a tertiary*, claimed by both Augustinians and Franciscans, abbess of the Augustinian Convent of the Holy Cross (1290), canonized (1881 on the fourth attempt). She was known as a devotee of the Passion, an extreme penitent, and a visionary during her lifetime. Her fellow nuns followed her directions to dissect her body after her death. Her cult in Umbria stems from the miraculous discovery through this "autopsy," confirmed by the local bishop, of the cross, crown of thorns, nails, and lance engraved on her heart, and a three pellets in her gallbladder, symbolic of the Trinity. **See also MIRACLE.** JESSICA A. BOON

Clarissan. See POOR CLARES.

Clark, Septima Poinsette (1898–1987), transformative African American teacher and selfless political organizer, who established (late 1950s) citizenship schools for teaching adults to read, a requirement for African American voters in Southern US states. These schools served as centers for the 1960s Civil* Rights Movement. Born in Charleston, South Carolina, she became a member of the African* Methodist Episcopal Church and the National Association for the Advancement of Colored People and director of education at Highlander Folk Center, where she expanded her Christianity to work with Jewish supporters. She had learned from her father to bring the spirit of Christ into her life, so she could see others as Christ saw them.

CYNTHIA STOKES BROWN

Class Meeting, the weekly meeting of a small group of Methodists*, under a class leader, to monitor conduct and spiritual progress.

Claudius, Roman emperor (41–54) who was friendly toward Herod Agrippa* and the Jews in Alexandria* but expelled Jews from Rome, c40 (cf. Acts 18:2).

Clement of Alexandria (c150–215), teacher, philosopher, elder, Apologist*, teacher of Origen*. Among the first to employ philosophy in defense of the Christian movement, he proclaimed Christianity the true philosophy, and Jesus the model of reason* and justice*, and appealed to Greeks to exchange what he viewed as corrupt pagan practices for the virtuous Christian life. Born in Athens to pagan parents, he converted to Christianity under the influence of Pantaenus (c180), succeeding him as head of the "Alexandrian* school" (190–202). Only three of his writings survived: *Exhortation to the Greeks, The Tutor,* and *Miscellanies.* Septimus Severus's persecutions forced him to go to Cappadocia, where he died. WAYNE C. KANNADAY

Clementine Literature, pseudonymous writings under Clement* I of Rome that relate his travels with Peter*, who trails and refutes Simon* Magus, especially the *Recognitions* and the *Homilies* (both early 4th c.), whose common material derives from an earlier (lost) version entitled *The Circuits of Peter* (also called the *Basic Writing*).

The Circuits of Peter was an ingenious novel written by an educated Syrian Jewish Christian around 220 CE. With broad learning and skillful rhetoric, the author argued that his or her Jewish Christian faith, originally taught by Peter, offered the true answers to the dilemmas of both polytheists and Gentile Christians. The brilliance of *The Circuits of Peter* led to the adoption of its framework by the *Recognitions* and the *Homilies* to convey their perspectives as the Roman Empire was becoming Christian. Later translations, epitomes, and rewritings kept the novel current through the ages in the East (hagiography) and in the West (here Simon eventually becomes Faust).

The early versions lift the veil on the "missing link," Jewish Christianity (e.g. its anti-Paulinism), and on the interface of educated Christians with their cultured intellectual environment. Clementine literature survived on the basis of its intriguing account of how God aids upstanding humans in coming to terms with life. F. STANLEY JONES

Clement of Rome, a leader in the Church of Rome, known chiefly for his epistle to the Corinthians (c96), urging them to resolve their conflicts and recalling that Peter and Paul were martyred in Rome because of excessive zeal. Some passages are similar to the Epistle to the Hebrews*, which may have been written at the same time and place. Clement says that the apostles appointed "bishops and deacons" from among their first converts and that others should succeed them. He does not differentiate bishops* from presbyters*; thus the former title may apply to presbyters in their collective function of oversight. If Clement had a unique role in the Roman Church, it may be that mentioned by Hermas* as "corresponding secretary" between Rome and other churches. Clement is also the alleged author of the Clementine* Literature, actually a product of the 3rd and 4th c.

Clerestory, the space above the aisles of a church, with a series of windows admitting light into the structure. **See also HIEROTOPY: THE CREATION OF CHRISTIAN SACRED SPACES.**

Clergy (Gk *kleros,* "lot," "portion," "task"), designation for those set apart for special ministries, differentiated from the laity* (Gk *laos,* "people").

Clerical Garb. In the early church, bishops and presbyters were not distinguished by their dress; if anything, they sought simplicity. Many wore the *tribonion* or *pallium* of the philosophers, a cloak of rough wool; subsequently (4th c.), clergy used the tunic that was worn by artisans and farmers, somewhat in the fashion of the worker* priests with their turtleneck sweaters. While leading worship, they merely added an early version of the stole*.

When the church was favored by the Roman Empire as the only valid religion (early 5th c.), the clergy began wearing the garb of imperial officials to indicate their social equality with them and their spiritual superiority. (This practice is analogous to that of some Protestant churches until the mid-20th c., when ministers and ushers wore morning coats during Sunday morning services.) During the early Middle Ages, when Germanic mercenaries and invaders wore trousers and grew long hair and moustaches, the clergy in Rome kept their traditional garb, which gradually changed from being old-fashioned to being priestly, or hieratic; liturgical garb became more elaborate, and each element was given symbolic meaning.

During the Middle Ages in the West, a variety of dress developed. New religious movements sought simplicity, such as the rough brown or gray garb of the Franciscans*. The cassock* (derived from the tunic and the Roman robe) became the primary garb of the clergy.

In Eastern Christianity, there are two types of cassock: a simple inner cassock and an outer cassock (or Rason). Monks always wear a black cassock. The color of the cassock of non-monastic clergy varies (black is most common; blue or gray and sometimes white during the Pascha*/Easter* season are also seen).

In the Roman Catholic Church, the cassock was prescribed for Catholic clergy after the Council of Trent*. It was only in the 17th c. that black became the standard color for Roman Catholic clergy, and gradually the clerical or "Roman" collar was required of all clergy.

The churches of the Reformation retained the custom of distinctive dress for the clergy, almost always black. While leading worship, many of them adopted the black academic gown, covered by the alb* in the case of the Lutherans*, while the Reformed* invented the white "Geneva tabs" at the neck.

Recent decades have seen two contrasting trends in all the traditional or historic Western churches: decreasing concern for distinctive garb in everyday contexts and increasing use of liturgical garb during worship. EUGENE TESELLE

Clermont, Council of (1095), pursued the agenda of the reform papacy and called for support to liberate the Eastern churches and Jerusalem from the control of the Muslims, leading to the First Crusade*. **See also URBAN II, POPE.**

Climate Change and Christianity. Contemporary Christian leaders increasingly emphasize the moral imperative to address risks of catastrophic climate change from global warming. This is a long-term rise in the earth's average surface temperature, which can alter weather dramatically. Global warming is caused by "greenhouse" gases that trap heat in the atmosphere. Burning of fossil fuels (especially petroleum and coal), deforestation, large-scale livestock production, and land use changes have increased atmospheric concentrations of greenhouse gases (carbon dioxide, methane, and nitrous oxide). Oceans absorb carbon dioxide, and trees, marine phytoplankton, and other plants transform it into oxygen. The destruction of tropical forests and changes in ocean temperatures and acidity accelerate global warming, threatening biodiversity and food chains.

Global warming is likely to bring droughts, altered rainfall patterns, melting polar ice, declining snowpack, hotter summers, heat waves and extreme temperatures, and rising sea levels and storm surges that flood coastal areas and islands. Forest fires, crop failures, water shortages, and the spread of diseases can result.

There is a strong consensus among scientists that human-induced climate change is already under way and that, if it continues, the effects will be devastating. An Evangelical* Christian, Sir John Houghton, led the most authoritative scientific assessments of the evidence for the Intergovernmental Panel on Climate Change in 1988–2002. Scientists continue to research and debate causal interactions and probabilities in climate change scenarios. Some conservative Protestant groups, especially in North America, criticize the evidence and emphasize doubts about climate science* (see Creationism; Science and Christian Theology; Scopes Trial). Dispensationalists* may interpret climate changes as signs of end-time apocalypse foretold in the Book of Revelation*. Other Evangelicals disagree with these eschatological interpretations and affirm theologies of environmental responsibility. By 2008 climate change initiatives had emerged within almost every major Christian tradition.

Ecological concerns are prominent in the OT and NT (see Ecology and Christianity Cluster). Three major biblical principles inform emerging Christian responses to climate change.

1. Stewardship of God's Creation*. The extinction of many species and loss of biodiversity are likely effects of climate change. Many theologians identify this massive degradation of the world that God created as a sin*. They emphasize that, in Genesis, "dominion" does not mean domination or destruction (see Creation; Creation, Ecology, and the Orthodox Church).

2. Social Justice*. The inseparable link between justice and ecological sustainability is fundamental to Christian environmentalism (see Justice, Christian Theological Views and Practices, Cluster). Climate change will have the greatest negative impact on the poor* in developing countries. Famines, floods, fires, and other environmental disasters destroy life and create social turmoil, suffering, and displaced "environmental refugees*."

In the 1960s and 1970s, Western environmentalists emphasized reducing population growth, which alienated Christians who saw this as advocacy for birth* control or abortion*. Contemporary environmental theory recognizes consumption patterns as more significant than simple population size. Industrialized nations, which represent only a minority of the world's population, produced about 80% of the greenhouse gases that humans have put into today's atmosphere. "Luxury emissions" differ from "survival emissions" of the poor, who use fossil fuels to meet basic needs for food and shelter. Many Christian writers emphasize the responsibility of wealthier nations (in most of which Christianity is the major religion) to promote climate change solutions and "clean" energy to help poor nations improve their quality of life without aggravating climate change (see Poverty Cluster).

3. Ethics for Healthy Societies. The climate change crisis results from economies based on burning polluting fossil fuels rather than developing locally appropriate sustainable energy sources, as well as cultures that pursue identity, status, and happiness through material consumption. Scriptural lessons of personal responsibility and simplicity affirm moral values that prioritize spiritual, not material, wealth in relations with others and with God (see Economy and Christianity Cluster).

Many theologians and environmentalists see climate change as a spiritual issue, because it forces humanity to confront basic questions about our place in the world. Its global scale, complexity, and long-term effects on unborn generations require unprecedented international cooperation, intergenerational commitments, and far-reaching solutions. As the world's largest community of ethical practice, Christianity has great influence in shaping how humanity responds. BETH A. CONKLIN

Cloister (Lat *claustra*), practice of "enclosing" monks and especially nuns; the rectangular central area of a monastery, surrounded by roofed walkways.

Clotilde (c472–545), Burgundian princess, Catholic from birth and brought up in a religious setting. After she married Clovis*, ruler of the Salian Franks (492/93), she urged him to become Christian (she would later be called "the new Esther*"). The death of their first son after baptism was one obstacle to his conversion, although her other children were said to have survived through her prayers. Perhaps in penance for violent acts by her sons, Clotilde entered a cloister in Tours and was known for her sanctity and generosity; various heroic legends were later added to her story.

Cloud of Unknowing, a book of contemplation describing how "a soul is oned with God" by an anonymous 14th-c. British author (possibly a Carthusian* monk), who also wrote the *Letter of Privy Counselling, Letter on Prayer*, and *On Discerning of Spirits* and translated *De mystica theologia* (The mystical theology) by Dionysius* the Pseudo-Aeropagite. The *Cloud of Unknowing*, a classic of mystical theology, adopts the "affective Dionysianism" of Thomas Gallus and the Victorines (13th c., Paris), who interpreted the classic texts of Dionysius from a more cataphatic* or affective stance than the previous apophatic* interpretations (e.g. by Eriugena*).

PETER TYLER

Clovis (c466–511). Chlodevech (later Ludwig and Louis), king of the Salian Franks (from 481), was the first of the "barbarian" rulers to convert to the Catholic faith, probably through the influence of his wife, Clotilde* (496, or as late as 506 or 508). France thus became the "eldest daughter of the [Roman Catholic] Church." Conversion enabled Clovis to establish stronger ties between his area of strength, in the Rhineland and the Low Countries, and the Catholic bishops in the rest of Francia. He drove the Visigoths out of Southwestern France (507). The newest son of the Church, he was the only Roman Catholic ruler of the time; in the East, the emperors were following the Henoticon*, and in the West the other rulers were Arian*. Ruthlessly eliminating rivals, he ensured the survival of the Merovingian dynasty; the Salic Law was compiled at his direction. After the fashion of Constantine, he built a Church of the Apostles Peter and Paul in Paris, in which he was to be buried with Clotilde.

Cluny, Benedictine* abbey in Eastern France, founded by William of Aquitaine (910), who renounced all authority and placed it immediately under the pope. Its abbot had direct authority over other houses, which were thus priories, not abbeys. Under a series of capable and long-lived abbots, it played a major role in the 11th-c. reform (see Religious Orders, Roman Catholic, Cluster). But the Cluniac houses became wealthy, prompting criticism, and the Cistercians* offered a dramatic alternative.

CNBB. See ROMAN CATHOLICISM CLUSTER: IN LATIN AMERICA: NATIONAL CONFERENCE OF BRAZILIAN BISHOPS (CNBB).

Cocceius, Johannes (1603–69), Reformed theologian. Born in Bremen, he studied in Holland and taught in Bremen, then in Holland. He preferred a biblical theology based on the theme of covenant* (hence the term "federal theology" from Lat *foedus*, "alliance" or "covenant"), with the "covenant of works" being succeeded by the "covenant of grace" (see New Covenant). In mid-17th-c. Holland, there was rivalry between the followers of Voetius* and of Cocceius*, both influenced by Ames and other precursors of Pietism*, but with opposing theologies. Voetius emphasized the scholastic* method, sabbatarianism*, and prayers for the dynasty of the House of Orange, while Cocceius used biblical method to develop his theology, a less legalistic practice, and prayers for the States General (the parliament of Holland).

Code of Canon Law. See CODEX IURIS CANONICI.

Codex, a book with pages bound so that they can easily be turned. In the ancient world, most books were scrolls; the codex was used chiefly for keeping financial records. Christians were the first to utilize it for copies of the Gospels and Epistles.

Codex Iuris Canonici, the Code of Canon Law, is the primary governing document of the Roman Catholic Church. Promulgated by Pope John Paul II (1983), the current Code replaces the Church's first universally binding code organized by Pietro Cardinal Gasparri and promulgated by Pope Benedict XV (the 1917 Code). The 1983 Code operates alongside the Code of Canons of the Eastern Churches (see Uniate Churches) promulgated by Pope John Paul II (1990).

The 1983 Code consists of 1,752 numbered canons (many with subdivisions) treating a wide variety of ecclesiastical governance topics, including the rights and duties of Church members, ecclesiastical structures and offices, conduct of mission and teaching activities, celebration of sacraments, Church property, ecclesiastical crimes and penalties, and administrative and judicial procedures. Notable topics not treated in the 1983 Code include most areas of liturgical law, international relations of the Holy See, and moral theology.

Most canons of the 1983 Code reflect a long history of the interplay between law* (especially ancient Roman law) and Roman Catholic theology. Ecclesiastical tribunals have very limited authority to interpret individual canons (see 1983 Code, 16). Instead, private scholarly commentaries play an important role in the development of canonical principles and interpretation. **See also** CANON LAW. EDWARD N. PETERS

Cohabitation, living together, usually without marriage.

Cold War and Eastern and Western Christianity. After the defeat of Nazi Germany, the USA and the Soviet Union entered a period of conflict, which dominated world politics until the Soviet Union and its empire collapsed (1992). Although without direct military confrontation – thus "cold war" – the two antagonists understood themselves to be in "total" conflict as the representatives of two different ways of life: liberal democracy, market economies, and individual freedom vs. socialism/communism, government-controlled economies, and equality. A bipolar political structure – NATO vs. the Warsaw Pact – was underscored by strategies of nuclear deterrence.

The cold war had an impact on Christian churches because for socialist thinkers, following Karl Marx*, religion* was "the opium of the people," a very effective weapon in the class struggle invented to manipulate the masses (see Marxism and Christianity). Accordingly, the socialist governments in Central and Eastern Europe launched an attack on Christianity ranging from replacing religious teaching in schools with courses in scientific materialism, to the introduction of secular rites and events; the dissolution of monasteries, convents, and religious orders; propaganda trials against church leaders; and censorship, threats, arrests, and the use of force.

In the Soviet Union, Stalin almost destroyed the Orthodox Church during the 1930s. Yet World War II proved to Stalin that he needed the Church (see Russia). Similarly, other socialist regimes eventually acknowledged that religion, and Christianity in particular, could not be entirely suppressed; thus they sought to neutralize its impact by keeping it inside the churches and by controlling its leaders. Consequently, Christianity was arguably the only "official" opposition within socialist states. This is why the election of the cardinal of Cracow, Karol Wojtyla, as Pope John Paul II became a crucial turning point in cold war history.

In turn, Christian leaders in Western Europe had a hostile attitude toward communism. In 1949 Pope Pius* XII confirmed a ruling of the Holy Office stating that Catholics could neither be members of Communist parties nor advocate communism. Catholic priests were not allowed to administer sacraments to such people, thereby effectively making all practicing Christians in socialist states appear to be disloyal to their governments. While Protestant and Orthodox leaders found dialogue with socialist states somewhat easier after Stalin's death (1953), the Catholic position did not change until the election of John* XXIII (1958). The Second Vatican* Council (1962–65) directly addressed pressing political problems of the cold war era and in the process introduced significant changes to Catholic dogma. Partly in response to requests from bishops and cardinals from Central and Eastern Europe, the Declaration on Religious Liberty (1965) recognized religious freedom as an inviolable right of the human person, thereby departing from the old dogma that there cannot be liberty to teach error. The encyclical *Pacem in Terris* (1963) abandoned the ancient Christian notion of a just war*, because, it argued, just wars had become impossible in a nuclear age.

The cold war politicized religion but also led to a marked influence of religion on politics (see Church and State Cluster). Ever since the Puritan* settlers had arrived in New England with the explicit purpose of building the "New Jerusalem" (Rev 21:10), US foreign policy was infused, to various degrees, with the notion that the USA was a "redeemer nation" with a universal, millennial* role. The cold war, then, positioned the "New Jerusalem" against Moscow, which according to a 16th-c. prophetic tradition was to be the "Third Rome" after the fall of Rome and Constantinople (see Russia), and thus the imperial representative of a message of salvation for the entire world. Though atheist in outlook, Soviet imperial policies were in striking accordance with this tradition.

STEFAN ROSSBACH

Colenso, John William (1814–83), Cambridge mathematician who became the first Anglican bishop of Natal, South Africa, and missionary to the Zulus (1853). A Broad* Churchman who believed in the universal knowledge of God and ethics in human cultures, and who raised the issue of the uniqueness* of Christ, Colenso published the first Zulu dictionary, grammar, and Bible translation and wrote commentaries on Romans and the Pentateuch challenging scriptural inerrancy* and engaging with Zulu culture. He fought for the rights of the Zulu people against colonial* aggression. His excommunication after a heresy trial, declared invalid by the Privy Council, led to a crisis in the Anglican Communion and the first Lambeth* Conference (1867) JONATHAN A. DRAPER

Coleridge, Samuel Taylor (1772–1834). The youngest son of a clergyman-schoolmaster, Coleridge acquired a lifelong admiration for Hebrew poetry and awareness of the prophetic intent of the Bible. Not a Pietist or irrationalist, but a post-Kantian* with a predisposition toward faith, he thought that attacks by Deists and skeptics on the authority of Scripture* and Christian doctrine should be answered by reasoned argument, including deeper investigation of reason* and the human need for religion*.

As a student at Cambridge, and as a young poet and lecturer, Coleridge shared the democratic fervor of the time, and held Unitarian* and progressivist views. This optimistic outlook had weakened by the time he wrote *The Rime of the Ancient Mariner* (1797), his best-known poem. After a winter at Göttingen (1798–99), over two decades he worked out the trinitarian position that became the basis of major works. He did not publish his most original writings on the Bible, because the public, uneducated about historical* biblical scholarship, first needed to reconsider claims for the infallibility* of Scripture*.

His prose work *Church and State* defended the national role of the Church* of England. Many in the Broad* Church party regarded Coleridge as an ally, and US Transcendentalists* admired his *Aids to Reflection* for its emphasis on the individual's self-knowledge of one's need for faith*.

ANTHONY JOHN HARDING

Collect, short prayer, derived from early Roman liturgy, comprising an address to God, a description of God's character and activity, the petition, and the goal of the petition.

Collegiality, the doctrine that bishops* are "colleagues," being a collegium of which all are a part. It was emphasized in Conciliarism* and reasserted by the Second Vatican* Council.

Colombia. In the northwestern part of South America, with coastlines on both the North Pacific Ocean and Caribbean Sea, Colombia has the third-largest population in Latin America (after Mexico and Brazil), with approximately 90% claiming to be Roman Catholic (although the percentage of those who attend Mass* is much lower) and a small but active Protestant population.

When the Spanish arrived, several indigenous nations inhabited the country, the majority belonging to the Chibcha linguistic family. The newly baptized so-called Indians were exploited without mercy by the *encomenderos** seeking slave labor for their plantations and mine exploitation. Juan del Valle, Popayan's first bishop, and the Jesuits* Pedro Claver and Alonso de Sandoval (1576–1652) denounced as contradictory to the gospel the injustice of the slavery* of indigenous and African people. Colonial* Christianity evolved in two ways: through Christendom* and through popular religiosity.

Christendom was related to the official development of the Roman Catholic Church that began with the Franciscans* in 1508 on the Caribbean Coast. By that time, women's religious orders were also present in Colombia; especially in the 18th c., women's convents played an important role in developing Christian religious tradition and social, economic, educational, and religious networks in colonial society. They also consolidated the model proposed by the Council of Trent* (1543–63) that generated a devotional form of architecture, painting, sculpture, and music, which were the base of the cultural movement known as baroque.

On the other hand, popular religiosity was based on *mestizaje* and syncretism* (see Inculturation Cluster; Popular Christian Practices Cluster). The biological and cultural "mestization" process was completed in the Andean region by the 17th c., and it set the stage for syncretism, or inculturation, in the religious field. The gods of the old cults were "baptized" as saints* and celebrated in chapels built on the very sites where the temples of these gods had been destroyed. When the destruction of the old beliefs and the process of acculturation were profound, indigenous people "went white" to form a new and inferior stratum of colonial society and therefore of Christendom. By the mid-17th c., Colombia had a vibrant religious life and had progressed both intellectually and spiritually. Clergy were educated in convents and seminaries in the metropolitan see* and in the three suffragan dioceses.

In the 19th c., the clergy were at the center of the political confrontations that marked seven civil wars between Liberal and Conservative parties. In the second half of the 19th c., Liberals, followers of French Jacobinism, violently persecuted the Roman Catholic Church and brought Presbyterians into the country to break down the Catholic monopoly. Owing to the economic and political failure of Liberal governments, politicians turned back to the Catholic Church to promote it as the official church (end of the 19th c.). They gave the Church many state responsibilities, including the oversight of education, health care, and social assistance, "civilization" of the borderlands, and control and registration of the population (birth, marriage, death) through the sacraments. The Liberal reaction to these developments resulted in new civil wars; the last one, from 1899 to 1902, the "Thousand Days' War," devastated the country. One in five persons between the ages of 18 and 30 was killed. This was the starting point of the 20th c. in Colombia.

Conservatives and Catholics reacted with intransigence, controlling the country until 1930. New Protestant missions arrived during this period. Some modernization began and, with it, new social movements and urban transformation. Owing to economic and social factors, but also to the disagreement among bishops over who should be the Conservative presidential candidate, Liberals returned to power and attempted to take total control of society; this resulted in new confrontations, particularly in the countryside. Catholics once again used an intransigent anti-Liberal and anti-Protestant discourse, as if they were calling for a new crusade.

The period from 1948 to 1953, euphemistically called *la violencia*, was the last civil war with a strong religious basis. Catholic buildings and institutions were targeted in Bogotá. In the countryside, Protestants were persecuted for their Liberal affiliation. In 1957, in accord with the "National Front" agreement, political power was divided between both traditional parties, and they agreed to recognize the Roman Catholic Church as a fundamental element of the Colombian social order; however, neither political nor religious leaders, obsessed by the division of political power, ever took into account social conflicts. The intransigent religious discourse was no longer viable, but intransigence was retrieved in lay political discourse with a cold war mentality.

The growing political conflict forced populations to move from rural to urban areas. Among many displaced people, Protestant groups developed new churches and movements centered in the cities, particularly in shantytowns. Meanwhile, new missions, particularly Pentecostal*, arrived; they would grow in the following decades, and many national Charismatic* churches would appear on the scene. The urbanization provoked by violence boosted the industrialization and modernization process, and gave rise to new cultural and social patterns that produced a loss of identification with traditional institutions, including the Roman Catholic Church and all political parties. The institutions with some social control broke down, and no alternative cohesive social mechanism arose to take their place.

After World War II, Liberals and Catholics joined forces against communism. Furthermore, Vatican* II accepted democracy and modern values; thus North American religious diversity came to be seen by Catholics as something positive. In addition, the Latin American Episcopal Conference gathered in 1968 in Medellín*; it called for the study of Latin American realities. Youth Catholic* Action movements, constituted by workers and students, began to denounce unjust institutional violence. They were aware that the only way to resolve the social conflict was through political decisions. They also appealed to the masses to increase their awareness of their own situation through literacy programs and social movements and organizations, and tried to organize a new political party. A Catholic Left began to appear among students, workers, and peasants led by the priest Camilo Torres.

Protestants also shared the concern for social issues; they made use of social sciences to find ways to transform society, establishing a trend. Among them was the group La Rosca, made up of Presbyterians such as Orlando Fals Borda, Gonzalo Castillo, and Augusto Libreros. Mennonites* began to undertake many social activities. The ecumenical dialogue helped the pacification process promoted by the National Front, but particularly opened the door for many encounters among progressive Catholics and Protestants. This context made possible the collaborative work and friendship of Camilo Torres and Orlando Fals Borda, founders of the School of Sociology at the National University of Colombia.

The Colombian Catholic hierarchy, bound to the National Front, could not find ways to assimilate the new doctrine or to emulate the transformations that took place in other episcopacies in Latin America or in other parts of the world. This situation caused a rift between the hierarchy and bishops, priests, religious men and women, and laypeople, who asked for new political leaders to take care of the poor. There was a radicalization on both sides, with slogans such as "Liberalism is a sin" and "Refraining from revolution is a sin" and the start of the "sacred socialist revolution."

The confrontation was strong within the Colombian Church in the 1960s and 1970s; many Catholics were repressed by both the Church and the state. Something similar occurred with Protestants, the movement "Evangelismo a fondo" actively sought to mobilize Protestants in an anti-Communist crusade. However, religious men and women continued to seek clearer and more determined action against social injustice and in support of human* rights activities. Consecrated religious women took very seriously the preferential* option for the poor and went to live in shantytowns and rural areas. Not merely in theory, but through action, they developed, in the 1980s and 1990s, a Liberation* theology from a women's perspective and also, through Base* Ecclesial Communities, they pushed the development of "Indian" and Black* theologies and of Bible reading from a feminist* perspective.

The National Conference of Religious developed (early 1980s) a Commission for Justice and Peace. The Jesuits founded (1970) the CINEP (Centro de Investigación y Educación Popular), a research center on social and political reality, and promoted literacy campaigns and popular awareness of social situations. As an academic center, CINEP sponsored research projects and publications (notably in 1970s and 1980s) in order to open a dialogue with the Colombian intelligentsia, mostly liberal and Marxist and strongly anticlerical. These research projects enabled some bishops to begin to understand the economic and social roots of the growing political conflict. CINEP also started its Peace Program (mid-1980s).

Social and armed conflicts (from the 1970s) pushed the governments from Turbay Ayala (1978–82) to Uribe (since 1998) to look for solutions through conflict resolution that ranged from a peace process to war intensification. The presence of the Catholic bishops in negotiations has clearly increased, as the shift in the process of negotiations has indicated. The bishops' involvement in Turbay's Commission for Justice and Peace was minimal, whereas today the bishops are strongly committed to the defense of human rights and to a political and negotiated resolution of the conflict.

The Colombian Catholic hierarchy had much difficulty moving away from its very narrow perspective on social and political matters. In the 1970s and 1980s, the hierarchy was still arguing that social and political problems were caused by the presence of foreigners – a perspective close to that of the National Front and post–National Front governments. Under the leadership of Bishop Alfonso Lopez Trujillo, the Catholic hierarchy did not support Betancour's peace negotiations, because they saw them as a movement toward surrender to subversive groups. This may have been related to the hierarchy's ties to the government and to the privileges it received, but also to the papacy's stance, which changed from a neutral position with Paul VI to a strongly anti-Communist position with John* Paul II, shaped by events in Eastern Europe.

In the meantime, bishops in rural areas began to develop another perspective on social and political issues, and looked for some kind of agreement among armed groups, as Msgr. Luis Serna did in Florencia, Caqueta. When the pope visited Colombia (1986), he talked about the need for an episcopal engagement in the search for peace in the country. Subsequently, the National Conference of Bishops created the Commission for Life, Justice, and Peace. Two conservative and controversial cardinals, Alfonso Lopez Trujillo and Dario Castrillón, were called to Rome (and therefore their direct influence was reduced). Other bishops, with better knowledge of the rural situation, assumed important positions in the National Conference of Bishops. The Conference adopted a more committed stance (end of the 1980s); it asked the bishops to thoroughly research the causes, dimensions, and characteristics of the conflict in each diocese, to formulate possible ways of correcting the situation, and to propose different ways of mediation.

The Constitution of 1991 recognized the multicultural and ethnic composition of the country, thanks largely to indigenous leaders. It recognized religious freedom, as a result of pressure from Protestant leaders organized in the Colombian Evangelical Confederation. Non-Catholic Christian churches received the same privileges as the Roman Catholic Church through the signing of new agreements between the state and the different churches and congregations. But these *concordatitos* (small concordats) excluded all non-Christian religious institutions and reinforced the Roman Catholic Concordat*. Under the Gaviria government (1990–94), the bishops and Roman Catholic Church institutions played an active role in the search for a peaceful resolution to the political conflict and openly defended human rights. During the presidential campaign, while the Samper government (1994–98) was concerned with defending itself against charges of money laundering, the Roman Catholic Church, bishops, priests, and men and women religious took a stand to try to resolve the social crisis of displaced people from rural areas, where the civil war continued to intensify. They investigated this matter and denounced the situation. Meanwhile, Cardinal Rubiano, archbishop of Bogotá, criticized Samper's attitude and denounced drug trafficking as socially destructive, financing war, and promoting an extralegal culture with easy money that caused corruption. At the same time, through organizations to which church institutions were committed, such as the Permanent Assembly for Peace, and with the help of the German Bishops' Conference, the church leaders initiated a peace process with the National Liberation Army.

This change of perspective of the Catholic hierarchy reinforced the action of many laypeople, men and women religious, and priests, usually with a Liberation theology perspective who were working for the defense of human rights and organizing communities and social movements. The organizations that contributed to this process included the dioceses of Barracabermeja, Socorro y San Gil, Uraba, Mogotes, and Quibdo, and the Feminine Popular Organization, which started the national social movement of women, a pacifist and feminist movement. However, the political and social awareness of religious leaders and the Roman Catholic Church still needs to find a path for promoting the organization of civil society, as well as democratic values and tolerance.

Protestant and Pentecostal/Charismatic churches offer different ways to face the social and political conflict. The more active minority of "historic" Protestants is committed to a negotiated peace and the defense of human rights. In the 1990s, the Conference of Evangelical Churches organized a commission on human rights and the peace process. This commission has done much research into the complexity of the conflict. Also in ecumenical endeavors, they have worked with the Roman Catholic Church in several projects on development and peace that included the civil society in the process of peace building. Some fundamentalist Pentecostal churches used to believe that secular authority comes from God and that therefore there is no room for criticism of the state. However in the past decades, the political participation of Pentecostal/Charismatic churches (more and more of them locally led Charismatic churches) has changed; they formed at least five different political parties during the 1990s, and some of their leaders have been elected members of the Senate and Council. Recently, they have also been involved in a paramilitary political scandal; several of their leaders were jailed for having associated with right-wing extremist and illegal paramilitary groups.

Pentecostals/Charismatics have played an active role in the resocialization of internally displaced persons in the slums of the big Colombian cities, although their work (always resulting from grassroots initiatives) has not been very systematic or organized. Forced displacement is also a main concern of the Roman Catholic Church; according to the National Conference of Bishops, the number of displaced people in Colombia between 1985 and 2005 is 3.8 million, reflecting a new wave of displacement that began in the 1980s partly because of the expanded drug market, which led to the multiplication of common criminals, guerrillas, and paramilitary groups.

By 2000, the commitment of all Christian churches to the peace process was growing. Both Catholics and Protestants criticized Plan Colombia and its implementation, but owing to the history of disagreements and violence among these churches, it is still difficult for Catholics and Protestants to join in a united ecumenical front. The human cost of the churches' involvement in the peace process has been extremely high, although this has not discouraged them. Among Catholics, 1 archbishop, 3 bishops, more than 50 priests, 9 men religious, 2 missionaries, 3 women religious, and many lay members of the church were killed in the first years of the 21st c. Many have been kidnapped, and even more have been threatened. Among Protestants the situation is no better; in the same period, more than 50 pastors were killed, and many were kidnapped. The Vatican news agency says that Colombia has the highest rate of religious murder in the world. **See also** **CHURCH AND STATE RELATIONS CLUSTER: IN LATIN AMERICA: COLOMBIA; PROTESTANTISM CLUSTER: IN LATIN AMERICA: COLOMBIA; ROMAN CATHOLICISM CLUSTER: IN LATIN AMERICA: COLOMBIA.**

Statistics: Population (2008): 45 million (est.). Christians, 96% (Roman Catholics, 90%; Protestants, 6%; other Christians, 1%; as many as 20% of Christians can be viewed as Charismatics); adherents of indigenous and African-related religions, 1.5%; small Jewish and Muslim communities; nonreligious, 1.4%. (Estimate based on the 2003 census and Bidegain, *Historia del cristianismo en Colombia*.)

ANA MARÍA BIDEGAIN

Colonialism and Imperialism and Christian Theology. If Christian theology* is "thinking about God," oriented by a symbol*, Jesus Christ, and carried by its mythologies* and rituals, then Christian theology has played key roles in both colonialism and imperialism. Theology has functioned in diverse, contradictory ways within what Edward Said has called the "imaginative culture" of colonialism and imperialism.

Colonialism and imperialism are closely related phenomena. Both are complex forms of organized power, and both predate Christianity and its theologies. Colonialism involves three interactive processes: (1) a society's will to dominate people of another society, setting up structures for controlling those people; (2) rationalizing this domination by marking dominated peoples as dissimilar and inferior, usually in terms of race; and (3) masking both the domination and the racism by claiming a necessary or virtuous vocation to "Christianize," "civilize," or "develop" the dissimilar and inferior others.

Imperialism is a society's ability to project transnational power to achieve political rule over other societies. This rule is achieved by a combination of economic and military power to make war and enforce subordination. Imperial power has usually been necessary for colonial domination.

Christian theology has played reinforcing and resisting roles in relation to both colonialism and imperialism.

Christian Theology and Colonialism. Christian theology as thinking about God, the creator and sustainer of the whole of life, bequeathed to colonizing cultures a myth* and ethos* of universal visioning. Colonizers drew on this universalizing discourse to support their global designs for domination.

One of the most influential examples of Christian theology's global design for colonialism is found in the T and O maps of medieval periods. These maps place Asia at the top of a circle (maps faced east, the direction of rising sun, before the invention of the compass), above a T (the horizontal line of the T representing the Nile River as an extended line dividing both Europe and Africa from Asia; the shorter vertical line representing the Mediterranean Sea, separating Europe from Africa). The entire landmass organized by the T was positioned at the center of a circle (surrounding oceans). Three worlds were thereby divided and named after the three sons of the biblical figure Noah: the fair and favored Japheth (Europe, on the lower left), Shem (Asia, extending across the top), and the cursed Ham (Africa, on the lower right). In the 16th c., a "fourth continent" (the West Indies or Americas) was interpreted as the enlargement of Japheth (Gen 22:9). Japheth (Europe) thus had religious sanction for laying colonizing claim to the Americas. Here theology provides, as Walter Mignolo says, an "overarching geopolitical imaginary for the modern/colonial world system."

The same sacred text, Genesis, however, could be used to resist European colonizers' global designs. Especially those segments teaching that persons *qua* persons were made in the image of God (Gen 1:27) cut against colonizers' aims to treat and exploit some societies as inferior. Thus even though Christian missionaries often supported colonizers, philosopher Albert Memmi noted that colonizers were also often fearful of Christians' conversionist strategies because they could suggest full and equal assimilation of the colonized. Theological notions of "the image of God" or of God being "no respecter of persons" (Acts 10:34), not showing favoritism, could help fuel resistance to colonialism.

Christian Theology and Imperialism. Christian theology's discourse about God, however, not only provided to colonizers a mythos and ethos for a global design, a *universum* for colonial power. It also proffered a hierarchical ordering, a *dominium*, for imperial power.

Especially with the rise of Constantinian theology, political rulers could be seen as representative of God, the transcendent ruler over all creation. In the modern/colonial world system, spawned from the 16th c. on, God has routinely been associated with political rule, anchoring what Michael Hardt and Antonio Negri refer to as the "transcendental apparatus" of colonial and imperial domination. The all-ruling and transcendent Ruler conveys to earthly rulers a transcendence of command, bestowing on them a divine right to imperial rule.

Again, however, Christian theology generates a discourse of resistance to imperial power. Numerous studies confirm that Jesus' life and teachings in 1st-c. Israel have to be viewed against the backdrop of Jewish people's suffering and resistance. Familiar NT terms used by Paul and Jesus (e.g. kingdom*, faith*), which theologians have used in traditionally depoliticized forms, actually take on fuller and more adequate meaning when seen within the early Jesus movement's resistance to Rome's imperial power. This explains why Christian theology still generates theologies of resistance to empire.

In the late 20th and early 21st c., Christian theologians had just begun to acknowledge and study the diverse functions of their beliefs in the Western history of colonialism and imperialism. The theological initiative for turning to colonialism and imperialism has come largely from Christian thinkers in colonized regions of the world, and especially Liberation and postcolonial theologians. **See also DECOLONIZING THEOLOGY; LIBERATION THEOLOGIES CLUSTER; POSTCOLONIALISM AND CHRISTIAN THEOLOGY.** MARK LEWIS TAYLOR

Colors, Liturgical. The use of specific colors for vestments* and paraments* developed during the 12th c. and was standardized much later: violet for repentance* (Lent*, Advent*, although blue for hope is also used during Advent); white for purity and joy (Christmas*, Easter*, Trinity* Sunday, All* Saints' Day, Nuptial* Masses); black for mourning (All Souls'* Day, Requiem* Masses); red for blood and fire (Pentecost*, feasts of martyrs, more recently Palm* Sunday and Good* Friday); and green for life (after Epiphany*, after Pentecost).

Colossians, Epistle to the, written in the name of Paul*, c70–80, in Asia Minor to a general audience. Colossae is most likely a pseudo-addressee. The letter represents Pauline tradition, which releases Christians from Jewish laws of ritual purity, for a new generation.

Most scholars contest the authenticity of Paul's authorship, because of differences with the language, theological concepts, and ways of thinking found in Paul's undisputed letters (Romans, 1 and 2 Corinthians, Galatians, Philippians, 1 Thessalonians, Philemon), although the text has the typical form of Paul's letters. Colossians exhorts its readers to hold fast to their faith* in Christ and warns of deviant teachings (2:16–23). Its opponents practice a sort of "angelic worship," "dwell on visions," and demand that believers observe Jewish purity rules (Moses' Law*), but their identity is obscure. Scholars often regard their teaching as a kind of heresy* and Colossians as part of the "pure" teaching of the NT. The author and his opponents may, however, merely represent competing early Christian traditions. The opponents may have been among those Jewish Christians who wrote Revelation* and Jude*. Alternatively, the author may simply have sought to protect the Pauline heritage. The letter's exhortations include a household* code (3:18–4:1) reinterpreting this aspect of the patriarchal Hellenistic culture (see Hellenistic Religious Traditions and Christianity's Self-Definition).

The writer is acquainted with Paul's letters, and imitates his style in order to refer to the apostle's authority, but now describes Christ as the head of all earthly and heavenly rulers. Therefore, believers in Christ are free from "angelic worship" and strict regulations. The author thus releases Christians from the purity laws more categorically than Paul did (cf. 2:20–21; Rom 14:3).

Colossians was included in the Pauline letter collections early on and was thus accepted into the NT canon* and respected by many church fathers (e.g. John Chrysostom*). Its descriptions of Christ influenced the development of Christology*. OUTI LEPPÄ

Colporteurs (French), peddlers of devotional literature; specifically, men and women who sell the Bible at a nominal price (often giving it away for free) and promoting its use. During the 19th c., they traveled great distances, often under difficult conditions, to bring the Bible to people who had no access to it.

Columba (521–97; Lat for Gaelic Colum Cille, "dove of the church"), Irish monastic leader, member of the Ui Neill clan, founder of monasteries at Derry and Durrow. He was exiled from Ireland* after the Battle of Cul Dremnhe (561) and settled at Iona* (c563). From there, Columba traveled throughout Scotland, where he is credited with having attempted to Christianize the Picts. The main source for his activities is the *Life* composed by Adamnán, ninth abbot of Iona (d704). Columba's relics were shared by Scotland and Ireland in the early Middle Ages, reflecting his influence and veneration in both countries. MARILYN DUNN

Columbanus (543–615), Irish monastic leader (590s). He arrived in France, an "exile for the sake of Christ," where he founded the triple monastery* (including monks, nuns, and tertiaries*) of Luxeuil-Annnegray-Fontaines. He was expelled from France (c613) and died in Italy (615).

His pastoral success in France aroused episcopal hostility; initially welcomed by Merovingian rulers, he was later driven out by Queen Brunichildis. The subsequent creation of family monasteries under the influence of his successors at Luxeuil formed a cornerstone of 7th-c. aristocratic power in Northeastern France. In Italy he founded Bobbio and campaigned against Arianism* and the Three* Chapters controversy. Columbanus's letters and sermons reveal his spiritual background and struggles; his brief Rule for Monks reflects his charismatic style and the influence of Basil* and Cassian* on Irish monasticism; his Communal Rule and Penitential demonstrate Irish penitential practice. Elements of Columbanus's rules were combined with parts of the Rule of Benedict* and others in the 7th-c. "mixed" monastic* rules.

MARILYN DUNN

Columbarium, an assemblage of niches in a church or churchyard, designed to house the cremated* remains of deceased members.

Comenius, Johannes Amos (1592–1670), theologian, philosopher of education, linguist, diplomat, bishop of the Bohemian* Brethren (Unitas Fratrum). Born in Moravia, educated in the schools of the Brethren and at Heidelberg, he was ordained (1614) and was active as teacher in Prerov and as a priest in Fulnek. In 1628 he led a group of Brethren into exile in Lissa, Poland, and traveled extensively seeking an end to the Thirty* Years' War. His educational innovations included the use of pictures in textbooks and a graded curriculum. His lifelong project was a "pansophia" to collect and classify all human knowledge. He revised the Brethren's *Ratio Disciplinæ* (1660), which later inspired Zinzendorf*. He died in Amsterdam, never having returned to his homeland.

OTTO DREYDOPPEL, JR.

Comity Principle (the), often adopted by Protestant mission organizations, is a principle of interchurch relations emphasizing reciprocity: extending courtesies to other missions, especially recognizing their validity, with the expectation that those missions will reciprocate. In accord with this principle, areas are apportioned to various missions that agree not to compete in a region in which another mission organization is already working.

Committee on Cooperation in Latin America, partnership of Protestant churches in the USA, growing out of a conference in 1913, for the coordination of mission efforts. Because Latin America was predominantly Catholic, US Protestants saw the continent as a mission field. They became active there during World War I, especially after the Panama* Conference in 1916.

Common Good (also commonweal or commonwealth), the purpose of life in society and the chief task of the state (Aristotle*, Thomas Aquinas*, Leo* XIII's 1879 encyclical *Rerum* Novarum*). John* XXIII defined it as "the sum of those conditions of social life by which individuals, families, and groups can achieve their own fulfillment."

Common Prayer, Book of (the "Prayer Book"), the only legal liturgy* in the Church of England from 1549 to 1554, 1559 to 1645, and 1662 until the 20th c., it shaped subsequent Anglican liturgical books. It was the most elaborate and directive liturgy used by any Protestant Church during the Reformation*. After experiments with vernacular* worship (1540s), Thomas Cranmer* presided over the Prayer Book's compilation, which had been authorized by Parliament (1549), adding an ordination service (ordinal*) in 1550. Influential Protestants criticized its compromises with traditional rites; thus a Reformed* Prayer Book was authorized in 1552. Elizabeth I's religious settlement (1559) brought back the 1552 book, slightly modified to accommodate Lutheran views. A Catholicizing version for Scotland prepared by High Church Scottish bishops (1637) caused an uproar among the Scots, culminating in open war with England (1638). Subsequent wars throughout Britain saw the English Prayer Book abolished by the Westminster* Parliament (1645). Charles II's Restoration brought a 1662 modified Reformed version that kept the general shape and Cranmer's* prose style (with Miles Coverdale's version of the Psalms). It has been unaltered since, although alternative books have been used in the 20th and 21st c. Despite its Reformed origins, its ceremonial style and stability over time have contributed to the theological bridge-building ethos central to Anglicanism*. **See also ANGLICANISM CLUSTER: ANGLICAN WORSHIP AND LITURGIES.**

DIARMAID N. J. MACCULLOCH

Communion (Gk *koinonia*), referred to in 1 Cor 10:16–17 as fellowship or participation in the Body and Blood of Christ by sharing the bread and cup of blessing.

Communion is historically restricted to the baptized. Some churches delay the Communion of baptized children. Penitents* under discipline may be excommunicated* or prohibited from receiving Communion. Some churches restrict Communion to their own members or to the churches with which they are in fellowship.

By late antiquity, the frequency of receiving Communion declined because of the requirements of abstinence and fasting*. The Fourth Lateran* Council (1215) required Christians to receive Communion once a year at Easter, after making a confession*. Both Protestant and Catholic reformers urged more frequent reception. In the Reformed* tradition, the whole congregation received Communion together four times a year. In all Christian traditions, the frequency of receiving Communion has increased in modern times.

Communion practices vary among churches. In some, Communion is received at the altar* individually or in groups, standing or kneeling; in others, it is received by individuals in their seats. Some celebrations use a broken loaf and a common cup or chalice; others use small wafers and individual cups. Some use unleavened bread and wine; others use leavened bread and grape juice. Communicants with wheat allergies may receive rice bread. Alcoholics may receive only bread. **See also EUCHARIST CLUSTER.**

FRANK C. SENN

Communion in Both Kinds, reception of both bread and wine (both species*) at Communion*. The cup, withdrawn from the laity in the 13th c., was restored by the Hussites*, the Reformation* churches, and the Second Vatican* Council.

Communion of Saints, one of the affirmations of the Apostles'* Creed ("I believe in the

Holy Spirit, the holy catholic church, the communion of saints . . ."). How does the communion of saints differ from the church*, which is also affirmed? It is variously understood to be the union of all the faithful (on earth, in purgatory*, and in heaven), the union of the elect, or the sharing of holy things (especially the sacraments; see Communion), in which case it can include unbelievers (who share the visible signs but not the grace signified by them). **See also SAINTS; SAINTS, DEVOTION TO, IN THE ORTHODOX TRADITION; SAINTS, DEVOTION TO, IN THE ROMAN CATHOLIC TRADITION.**

Communion Table, eucharistic* table, made of wood in Protestant and Low Church Anglican churches, versus the stone altar* in High Church and Catholic churches.

Communion Tokens, metal tokens given to those who attended the preparatory* service in Puritan* or Presbyterian churches, indicating their fitness to receive Communion.

Communism and Christianity. See COLD WAR AND EASTERN AND WESTERN CHRISTIANITY; MARXISM AND CHRISTIANITY.

Compassion, suffering* with another; deep sympathy or empathy for another; sorrow or concern for the plight of a needy person, leading to words or deeds that are meant to help the person. For Christians, Jesus is the epitome of compassion. He did not just feel with those who suffered; he gave his life for them. He was not just concerned about individuals' earthly existence; he also sought to heal humanity's broken relation to God. His compassion was not limited to friends; it also embraced those who persecuted him and sought to kill him. **See also *AGAPE*; LOVE; MERCY.** LEROY H. ADEN

Compatibilism, theological view that freedom* is compatible with the totality of factors that influence one's decisions: God's will, external circumstances, and one's own inclinations. The Jesuit theory of "middle* knowledge" is one way of showing how freedom of choice is compatible with grace* and predestination*.

Complementarity, a term applied to the relation between men and women as "made for each other" for mutual support (cf. Gen 2:18, 24 and Mark 10:8; Eph 5:28–33). It is contrasted with both patriarchy* and equality*.

Compline, the night prayer of the Roman Catholic Church, may be recited by supplicants privately or communally before going to sleep, asking for a "perfect night and peaceful death." Anglican evensong* has incorporated some elements of this office. KEITH F. PECKLERS, SJ

Complutensian Polyglot Bible, the first multilingual edition of the Bible, in six volumes (1514–17), prepared at Alcalá (Lat Complutum) under Cardinal Ximénes* de Cisneros. The OT contains, in parallel columns, the Hebrew text, the Latin Vulgate*, and the Greek Septuagint; the NT contains the Greek text and the Vulgate.

Concelebration, joint celebration of the Eucharist by two or more priests, restored by the Second Vatican* Council.

Conciliarism, the movement in the Roman Catholic Church that holds that a council has jurisdictional authority in the Church and can act independently of the pope* in an emergency. In the midst of the Great* Schism of 1378–1417, when two rival popes claimed authority, two German scholars residing in Paris, Conrad of Gelnhausen and Henry of Langenstein, put forward (1380) the notion of rescuing the Church by convoking a council independent of both rival popes, which was supported by Paris scholars, including Pierre d'Ailly and Jean Gerson* (1383), and ultimately by the cardinals who had elected the rival popes. These cardinals jointly called the unsuccessful Council of Pisa* (1409). The high point of Conciliarism came with the Councils of Constance* (1414–18) and Basel* (1431–49). Gallicanism* made similar claims about the authority of councils. When Angelo Roncalli was elected pope in 1958, he said, "My name shall be John." This was not only an allusion to the statement of Zechariah (Luke 1:63); it was a revival of Conciliarism, in at least a moderate form, for there had been no pope named John since the antipope John XXIII, deposed in 1415. One of his first acts as John* XXIII was to call the Second Vatican* Council. EUGENE TESELLE

Conclave, the place of assembly where the cardinals* meet to elect a pope*; hence the name of the assembly itself.

Concord, Formula of, and *Book of Concord*. Disagreements among Lutherans over the interpretation of the Augsburg* Confession led the "authentic Lutherans" to state their position more explicitly. The Solid Declaration and the Epitome (adopted 1577) constitute the Formula of Concord, which denies that human merit and free will have any role in justification* yet rejects antinomianism*, as it deals with various topics, including the relationship between law* and gospel*, Christology*, and adiaphora*. These, along with the classic creeds*, the Augsburg Confession (1530), the Schmalkaldic Articles (1537), and Luther's two catechisms (1529), were published together as the *Book of Concord* (1580). It was adopted by most of the German and Scandinavian rulers, but not in Nassau, Hesse, or Branschweig, which retained the Augsburg Confession alone. When Lutheran institutions bear the names "Concordia" and "Augustana," they may indicate loyalty to one or the other tradition.

Concordat, an agreement between church and state, specifically the Roman Holy See* and a government. (For the importance of concordats, see especially Church and State Relations Cluster: In Europe: The Roman Catholic Church and Politics.)

Concubinage, the cohabiting* of a man and a woman without marriage, often for social reasons.

Concupiscence, inordinate desire for temporal things (Rom 7:7; Gal 5:6; Jas 1:13–15), often understood to be the result and chief manifestation of original* sin.

Confessing Church (the) was founded during the German Church* Struggle as German Protestantism's answer to the Nazis' attempt to bring Christianity in line with National Socialist ideology. Protestant resistance was galvanized around two main issues: the attempt by the German* Christian Movement to create a united Reich Church under state control and the imposition in November 1933 of anti-Semitic legislation – the Aryan Paragraph – onto the German Church. The Pastors' Emergency League, under Martin Niemöller*, was the first major resistance movement organized by German Protestants. However, key leaders such as Karl Barth* and Dietrich Bonhoeffer* argued that the German Church was *in statu* confessionis* and that the only remaining option was the publication of a common confession of Christ against the Nazi heresy. This occurred in January 1934 when delegates of 167 Lutheran, Reformed, and United communities gathered in Barmen. In the process, they established themselves as the Confessing Church. The Barmen* Declaration (May 1934) was the high point of the Confessing Church's resistance. The presence of the Confessors enabled German Protestants to successfully resist coordination by the Nazi state. Yet members of the Confessing Church never agreed on the extent to which the Church should engage in political, as well as theological, resistance.

MARK R. LINDSAY

Confession, acknowledgment of sin* by the congregation in a general way (see *Confiteor*) or by an individual by him- or herself before God (as in Protestants churches) or to a priest as an act of penance* (as in the Roman Catholic Church). **See also SEAL OF CONFESSION.**

Confessions. See CREEDS, SYMBOLS, AND CONFESSIONS OF FAITH.

Confessor, in the early church, a person who suffered for the Christian faith without dying, thus not a martyr*.

Confirmand, a candidate for confirmation*.

Confirmation, a ritual prayer for the coming of the Holy* Spirit through which a believer is empowered to witness for Christ. The word has its origins in Gaul (5th c.), where bishops juridically confirmed the baptisms* administered by presbyters, deacons, and others, using some ritual elements of initiation: hand laying, anointing, and/or prayer. Theologians then linked the practice to two passages from Acts (8:14–17; 19:5–7), in which Peter, John, and Paul imposed hands on previously baptized disciples.

By the Middle Ages, the Western Church had made confirmation a ceremony distinct from baptism, administered by a bishop, during which he anointed a previously baptized Christian with chrism*. Chrismation became the equivalent of confirmation. When a bishop baptized, on rare occasions he administered confirmation in the same ceremony. When heterodox Christians were received back into the fold, the ceremony also included confirmation.

Throughout this time, the Eastern Church maintained a different pattern. The presbyter who baptized also chrismated in the same ceremony (see Chrismation).

In time the word "confirmation" took on the meaning of "strengthening," and it came to be seen as an expression of one's Christian maturity.

The 13th-c. Western Church included confirmation among its seven sacraments*, but Martin Luther* excluded it from the list, preserving only baptism and the Lord's Supper. The Reformed churches regarded confirmation as a personal expression of faith made by those baptized as infants. It usually concluded a period of comprehensive catechesis.

The Roman Catholic Church calls confirmation one of its sacraments of initiation. When a priest baptizes an adult, he administers confirmation immediately. Usually this ceremony takes place at the Easter vigil. Most Catholics are baptized as infants, however, and a bishop confirms them after they have completed a period of catechesis. The recommended age for confirmation varies considerably throughout the Catholic world; in the USA alone, the age ranges from about 7 to about 16. Some are confirmed much later; others never. When other Christians become Catholic, a priest confirms them immediately upon receiving them into the full communion of the church.

In the Orthodox churches, chrismation*, a sacrament, is conferred on the newly baptized (adult or infant) by the priest immediately after baptism* to impart the gift of the Holy* Spirit.

The meaning of confirmation, sometimes with other titles, varies among other Christian groups. Many see it as a person's reaffirmation of baptism in the presence of a church leader or community. PAUL TURNER

Confiteor (Lat "I confess"), mutual confession and forgiveness of sins by the priest and congregation at the beginning of the Roman Mass, a practice that originated in monastic communities.

CONFUCIANISM AND CHRISTIANITY CLUSTER

Confucianism and Christianity: Confucian and Christian Perspectives
Confucianism and Christianity in Hong Kong
Confucian Classics and the Bible

Confucianism and Christianity: Confucian and Christian Perspectives. The term "Confucianism" was introduced by Jesuit missionaries in China as a neologism for a scholastic tradition rooted in Chinese culture and philosophy that is various referred to as *rujia* (school of the literati), *rujiao* (traditions of the literati), *ruxue* (teachings of the literati), or simply *ru* (literati). While the *ru* tradition itself predates Confucius, the ethical vision of Confucius (c551–c479 BCE) and his followers has come to define and enrich this tradition.

The point of convergence of various schools within Confucianism is the existential questions regarding the ultimate values that shape human living. Confucius and his successors answered these questions by presenting an ideal person who is adept at relating to others and able to trust in the validity of these relations for familial and social harmony. In the *Analects,* Confucius called this ideal person a *junzi* (exemplary person), and the highest existential virtue that this exemplary person embodies he called *ren* (humanness).

The classical Confucian paradigm for virtuous living is the proper self-cultivation of the "Five Constants" (*wu chang*), i.e. *ren* (humanness), *yi* (appropriateness), *li* (ritualized propriety), *zhi* (wisdom in thought and action), and *xin* (keeping to one's word). Confucians insist that one must go beyond merely knowing these virtues in an intellectual sense; one must engage in the actual personal self-cultivation of the Five Constants. Complementing the Five Constants are the "Five Relations" (*wu lun*), which define the five foundational relations of a Confucian society on which the complex, interlocking human relations in Chinese society are constructed: parent–child, ruler–subject, husband–wife, elder–younger siblings, and friend–friend. The first four relations are hierarchical, whereas the fifth is a relation of equals. The Confucian conception of society presupposes that there are no strangers in society, defining the basic social relation as at least friend-to-friend (compare with friendship* in Christianity).

For Confucians the proper relational ordering of society as a human macrocosm takes the family as its inspiration and starting point. Society is ordered and harmony is promoted at all levels based on *filiality,* the source of order and harmony within a family. Ritually, filiality is expressed through ancestor* veneration offered by son to father, by scholar-gentry to Confucius as ancestor par excellence, and by emperor to his ancestors and to *tian* (heaven) for the well-being of the nation. Because filiality together with its public ritual expression of ancestor veneration became the glue that held religion, culture, and society together in imperial

China, the attempts by some 17th- and 18th-c. missionaries to prohibit Chinese Roman Catholic converts from participating in ancestor veneration were viewed as attacks on filiality and on the very cohesion of Chinese culture and society, triggering the Chinese rites controversy*.

The Jesuit missionary to China, Matteo Ricci* (1552–1610), was convinced that the core teachings of Confucianism did not conflict with the Christian gospel. In an early work, *Jiaoyou lun* (On friendship), he sought to reassure the Confucian literati with his appreciation of the social significance of friendship and other foundational human relations within the Confucian Five Relations framework. His magnum opus, *Tianzhu shiyi* (True meaning of the Lord of Heaven), is grounded on the premise that the "original" Confucianism of Confucius, rather than the neo-Confucianism of Zhu Xi (Chu Hsi), enshrined an incipient monotheism and moral and ethical truth that were compatible with Christianity. History remembers two of Ricci's Chinese students, Xu Guangqi (1562–1633) and Li Zhizao (1565–1630), together with Yang Tingyun (1557–1627) as the "three pillars of the early Chinese Church." All three remained staunch Confucians, seeing no profound conflict between the Christian gospel and their Confucian way of life and asserting that Christianity replaced their earlier Buddhist practice (*buru yifo*). A student of Ricci, Xu Guangzi (Paul Hsu Kuang-ch'i) is best remembered for his summary of the fundamentals of Christianity in a letter he wrote in a powerful defense of Christianity, revealing a brilliant synthesis of Confucian and Christian ideas: "The service of Shangdi [the Sovereign Above] is the fundamental principle; the protection of the body and the salvation of the soul are of utmost importance; loyalty, filial piety, compassion, and love are accomplishments; the reformation of errors and the practice of virtue are initial steps; repentance and the purification [of sin] are the prerequisites for personal improvement; the true felicity of celestial life is the glorious reward of doing good; and the eternal misery of hell is the recompense of doing evil."

Contemporary scholars and theologians have continued the dialogue between Confucianism and Christianity. For example, Yao Xinzhong and Kim Heup Young have explored the intersection of *ren* and *agape* and considered their theological ramifications, while Yeo Khiok-Khng is interested in rereading biblical texts through a Confucian–Christian hermeneutical lens. Other theologians have proposed constructive Confucian–Christian Christologies of "Jesus as the Eldest Son and Ancestor" (Peter Phan) and "Jesus as the Crucified and Risen Sage" (Jonathan Tan). John Berthrong and Robert Neville are proponents of "Boston Confucianism," asserting that Confucianism transcends its Chinese sociocultural roots to speak to a Western audience.

JONATHAN Y. TAN

Confucianism and Christianity in Hong Kong. These two traditions encountered each other almost immediately after the colonization of Hong Kong. Two events particularly shaped their subsequent encounters. The first was James Legge's arrival (1843). Both a missionary and a Sinologist, he completed the first translation of the Confucian classics into English and thus introduced Confucianism to the West in a sympathetic way that also, however, aroused serious debates. The second event ties in with the neo-Confucian manifesto on the crisis in Chinese culture published in 1958, which elicited serious local Christian responses. This later event evidenced a change in the basic motive of the encounter between the two traditions from a sociopolitical one (e.g. for national salvation through theological indigenization or inculturation*), which was prominent on the mainland, to the cultural motive of the diasporic Chinese Christian communities striving to define their identity.

SIMON SHUI-MAN KWAN

Confucian Classics and the Bible. The Confucian classics and the Bible are "classical" or "canonical" (regulative) in that they embody the normative and communal wisdom of two great civilizations. Yet the ideals and precepts of these "scriptures*" (*shengjing*) or "sacred books" (*shengshu*) transcend the historical circumstances of their origins and shape the modern world.

Beyond historical differences in linguistics, thought patterns, and content, the Confucian classics and the Bible have much in common, which is elucidated by the study of their genre, their moral and spiritual teachings, the process of their redaction, and the commentaries written on them throughout history. The varied contents of the texts allow for multiple points of dialogue and resonance.

The Confucian classics are called the Four Books (*Sishu*) – the *Great Learning* (*Daxue*), the *Doctrine of the Mean* (*Zhongyong*), the *Analects* (*Lunyu*), and *Mencius* (*Mengzi*). They contain a comprehensive understanding of the moral, philosophical, and political worlds of human endeavor in China*. In addition to proverbial sayings, the Four Books also contain history, oracles, poetic texts, dialogues, and debates. The complementarity of Confucian classics and the Bible (see Bible, Canon of; Bible Interpretation Cluster; Bible, Texts and Manuscripts) becomes apparent when one holds their radical differences in tension (cf. *Doctrine of the Mean*) – a challenging, interpretive move that highlights the incompleteness of both Confucian and biblical texts, while holding them sacred (cf. Ricoeur's* textuality) (see Scripture).

The Judeo-Christian Bible holds to the cosmogonic belief that the universe is theocentric; the cosmos is initially created and sustained by a divine power of goodness. The Confucian "heaven" (*tian*) as a naturalistic cosmos lacks personal narrative, yet the transcendent nature of heaven is thought to be *ren* (benevolence) of the moral order. The immanent nature of heaven is expressed in human nature as virtues. Thus human virtues are anthropocosmic. A balanced worldview that is both theocentric and anthropocosmic is most beneficial; otherwise, religion becomes divorced from ethics, alienating divine grace from human endeavor.

Although Confucian classics assume neither Adam's fall* (sin*) nor one's existential estrangement from *tian*, both scriptures seek to overcome social conflicts, moral collapse, and spiritual chaos. The difference between the two scriptures lies in the Confucian virtue of self-cultivation and the biblical faith in God's grace*. However, the Confucian self-cultivation ethic grounded on *ren* (benevolence) and *li* (ritual propriety) can be subsumed under a biblical ethic that is based on the Holy* Spirit; together, these two traditions encourage a complete obedience of faith*.

The cyclical history of the Confucian classics and the linear eschatological view of the Bible can mutually critique each other's interpretive assumptions about space and time, held in each case as "either space or time." Such mutual critique can move toward a more holistic and dynamic understanding of a multidimensional universe envisioned as a spiral movement.

The biblical understanding of love* as cruciform (i.e. exemplified by Jesus' cross) fulfills the Confucian ideal of *ren*; in addition, Confucian ethics on propriety (*li*) and music (*yue*) supplements the biblical theology that lacks detailed ethical explication.

The relationship between human nature or goodness and divine grace in the Bible is antithetical to that in Confucian classics, yet both scriptures agree that only the love of neighbors expresses concretely how to be fully human (*Analects* 15:9) or holy (Lev 11:44; Matt 5:48; 1 Pet 1:16).

The scholarly tradition of *rujia* (Confucianism) and God's Messiah as the suffering servant in the Judeo-Christian Scripture emphasize that living the Way (Dao) or living God's love is to love others as one self, who is loved by God.

An intertextual reading between these two scriptures fulfills the intertextuality inherent in the Confucian classics and in the Bible – an intertextuality resulting from the plurality of texts each canon includes and puts in dialogue (Fishbane).

YEO KHIOK-KHNG

Congo, Democratic Republic of (DRC). Since 1482 (when Roman Catholics arrived), Christianity has become greatly diversified owing to different levels of inculturation* in the complex cultural, political, and religious context in what is now the Democratic Republic of

Congo. Political independence was achieved in 1960, and since that time, the political and socioeconomic climate has been one of turbulence, to which some Christians have contributed even as others have been victims. The dominant Roman Catholic Church in the Congo (51% of the population) took prophetic positions against colonialist* practices and in favor of independence (since 1956), experienced a renewal movement, developed a pastoral option for "Small Christian Communities," and now has its own inculturated* rite, the Zairian or Congolese Rite, for the Mass (approved by the Vatican in 1988; see Malula, John). In the meantime, all the churches arising from Protestant missions (since 1878) have been united into a single Protestant Church, L'Église du Christ au Congo (Church of Christ in Congo, since 1970, 21% of the population), while 23% of the population are members of the Kimbanguist* Church (originating in 1921; as of the early 21st c., there were about 8 million members in the DRC) and other independent churches that developed remarkable Congolese forms of Christianity.

The Congolese Horizon. The DRC, successively named Independent State of Congo (1885–1908), Belgian Congo (1908–60), Republic of Congo-Kinshasa (1960–64), Democratic Republic of Congo (1964–71), and Republic of Zaire (1971–97), now named the Democratic Republic of Congo (since 1997), is a large tropical African country that has more or less retained the political boundaries of the 1885 Berlin* Conference, and has about 60 million inhabitants, belonging to more than 365 ethnic groups, with more than 200 distinctive languages, including a majority of Bantus (who arrived from Nigeria and Chad more than 1,000 years ago), as well as Sudaneses and Nilotics from Ethiopia (who arrived more recently) and the Batwa ethnic groups (Pygmies; the first occupants of the DRC).

Congolese people were socially and politically organized in families, villages, clans, ethnic groups, kingdoms, and empires (at least since the 8th–9th c. CE). Religion* was an integral part of these sociopolitical systems and the most conspicuous feature of life. Religion was life, and life was religion. Solidarity was the most ethical virtue sustaining individual and community life. People believed in one God, creator of everything, and they could interact with God through ancestors*. Beginning in the 15th c., contacts with Europe progressively undermined the traditional sociopolitical and religious harmony. Sociopolitical organizations based on ethnic affinities were replaced by new structures, which led to turbulence that was caused by poor management and that culminated in repeated wars, including one that claimed more than 3,500,000 lives between 1996 and 2006.

Christian Origins and Developments in the DRC. Christianity arrived with the Roman Catholic Church in 1482, followed by the Protestant churches (since 1878), the Kimbanguist* Church (1921), and other independent churches.

Roman Catholic Church. In 1482 the Portuguese explorer Diogo Cão landed at the estuary of the river Congo. Franciscan missionaries arrived sometime later and baptized the first Congolese Christian, Chief Manuel Mani of Soyo, on Easter Sunday, 1491, followed in the ensuing months by the baptism of Prince Mvemba a Nzinga, who took the name Dom Afonso, and the baptism of his father, the king of Mbanza Kongo (the kingdom at the mouth of the river Congo, now partly in Angola), Nzinga Nkuwu, and his wife (1491), who took the names João and Eleonora, respectively (the names of Portugal's King João and Queen Dona Eleonora). Subsequently, many people flocked to get baptized. Because of this early Catholic presence, Congo has been called the "elder son of the Church in black Africa" (Beeckmans). This first phase of Catholic evangelization was interrupted in 1835 with the departure of the last priest.

The second phase of the Catholic evangelization (1880–1980) started with the arrival of the Scheut missionaries (Congregatio Immaculati Cordis Mariae, a congregation from Belgium) at Boma (in Bas-Congo, original capital of the Belgian Congo) and ended with the celebration of its centenary. During this colonial* period, the Catholic Church enjoyed a privileged status, but it faced a series of challenges: juridical conditions for missionary establishments; competition with Protestants; integration of local cultures; church–state relations, especially at the time of independence (1960); anticlericalism during the disintegration of Congolese society; the murder of 200 sisters, brothers, and priests (1960–65); and (during the presidency of Mobutu) the nationalization of all foreign-owned institutions, and thus Catholic schools and institutions (1971). Amazingly, this period witnessed a significant growth of the

Catholic Church in terms of basic structures and number of Congolese lay leaders, priests, and sisters – a growth that endured beyond the colonial period, in part owing to the 1956 declaration by the Catholic Bishops of the Congo (and Rwanda and Burundi) denouncing colonialist practices and expressing support for independence. This growth of the Catholic Church was also manifest in the lives of Congolese Catholics, including Isidore Bakanja (1885–1909, beatified in 1994), a young mason killed for refusing to stop functioning as a catechist, and Anuarite Nengapeta (1941–64, beatified in 1985), a sister murdered during the 1960–65 upheavals as she resisted rape; the erection of the first Catholic university (1957); the birth of African theology (1960); and the launching of the pastoral option for Small Christian Communities (1961) that developed inculturation* theology, the focus of the "Kinshasa school of thought." Proponents of this school argue for a church whose theological thinking, liturgical celebrations, and community life should be "incarnated" in Congolese culture. Inculturation is found in numerous theological books and articles, in dialogued and sung Masses, and in the life of self-supportive Small Christian Communities, including the Jamaa (Swahili, "family") Movement (from 1953), which started in the mining region of Katanga, was initiated by the Belgian Franciscan missionary Placide Tempels, and includes as many as 200,000 members. This renewal movement within the Congolese Catholic Church – a most impressive attempt to Africanize Christianity – consists of communities of married people (except for a few priests, nuns, and widowers or widows) who practice their Christian faith following an African lifestyle and conception of community life, and who commit themselves to growing in this faith-practice through ongoing instruction led by members of the Jamaa. By 1980 approximately half of the population of the DRC was Catholic; there were about 50 dioceses with many schools, medical centers, and philanthropic centers, run by mostly Congolese personnel.

The third phase of the Roman Catholic evangelization began in 1980. The first decades consisted of harvesting the fruits of previous efforts. The Congolese Catholic Church was affirmed by the successive beatifications of two Congolese Christians (Anuarite and Bakanja) by Pope John Paul II and the 1988 Vatican's approval of the "Roman Missal for the Dioceses of Zaire," commonly known as "Zairian or Congolese Rite." In addition to cultural elements like songs, dances, and traditional symbols for kingship, the Mass in Zairian Rite includes, in the invocation of saints, the invocation of good ancestors*. The ritual of reconciliation, symbolized by the shaking of hands, takes place immediately after the sermon instead of being performed before the Eucharist, as it is in the usual Roman missal. Though culturally and theologically significant, these particularities do not make the Zairian Rite a different rite in the technical sense of canon law.

In spite of criticism from Liberation* and Reconstruction* theologians, inculturation has moved beyond the DRC and become a key aspect of the mission of the Catholic Church in Africa, alongside evangelization, dialogue*, justice and peace, and media. All these aspects might overlap at some points, but they can be summarized as the main concerns of an incarnated church. For the sake of the Roman Catholic Church, some bishops have sacrificed their life to defend human* rights, though others were accused of complicity with the warlords. However, the Episcopal Conference of the Congo issued many declarations, appealing for a stop to the war and promoting human dignity. This testimony of the Episcopal Conference displays the diaconal and prophetic roles so highly valued by ordinary Christians.

Protestant Church. There is a single Protestant Church, L'Église du Christ au Congo (Church of Christ in Congo), recognized in the DRC since 1970. The history of Protestantism in Congo can be divided into two phases: before and after 1970.

In 1878 the Baptist missionaries H. Craven and Strom arrived in Palabala (Bas Congo) and founded the first Protestant stations along the river Congo (Braekman). They were members of the Livingstone Inland Mission (named for David Livingstone*, who had reached the Congo in 1869), later replaced by missionaries from the American Baptist Missionary Union and Svenska Missions Förbundet and eventually joined by other Scandinavian Baptists. American Southern Presbyterians concentrated more inland in Kasai Province (in Luebo, where they built a hospital), and the Disciples of Christ went farther north (to Bolenge, where they replaced the American Baptists in 1899). The African Inland Mission established itself in the northeastern part of the DCR (1912); Methodists established themselves especially in the southeast (Katanga Province, since 1918, where they have a seminary) and were followed by

Pentecostals (in different parts of the country). Educational and social joint organisms, and particularly the Protestant Council of Congo (since 1924), coordinated all these diverse missionary activities, until all these developing churches were replaced by the Church of Christ in Congo in 1970.

The second and ongoing phase of Congolese Protestantism began in 1970 with the creation of Church of Christ in Congo under the influence of Rev. Bokeleale* and Revs. Makanzu, Masamba, and Bossekota, among others. Despite the opposition of the Evangelicals, the government supported this unification in order to control Christians in three churches: the Roman Catholic Church, Church of Christ in Congo (Protestant), and Kimbanguist Church. Since 1970, the Church of Christ in Congo has taken many initiatives for socioeconomic growth, increasing its participation in education, health, social development, microfinance, and business enterprises (like industrial fishing and printing presses).

On the theological front, Congolese Protestant theologians produced a great deal of contextual theology and addressed the role of the Church of Christ in Congolese society, e.g. by emphasizing the importance of women not only in social work but also in the ordained ministry. An example of Congolese contextual theology is the "psycho-pastoral approach to witchcraft*, a main concern for Joseph Kufulu Mandunu, a Congolese Protestant theologian. Unlike many pastors and theologians who prefer to ignore witchcraft, proponents of the psycho-pastoral approach admit the reality of this phenomenon and suggest a pastoral care based on the biblical practice of healing* and exorcism*. While articulating Reconstruction* theology to respond to the appeal of the All Africa Church Conference, other Congolese seek a new theological paradigm that claims to go beyond inculturation and liberation. Yet exactly what such a unifying paradigm, capable of mobilizing contributions from different individuals and perspectives, would be is still not clear.

The Kimbanguist Church. The Kimbanguist Church (see Kimbanguism) started in 1921 as a popular and messianic movement led by the prophet Kimbangu*. After his death in 1951, his followers spread out and formed different sects inspired by his teaching. In 1956–57, Joseph Diangenda, the prophet's youngest son, succeeded in unifying these diverse Kimbanguist sects and created the church officially known as the "Church of Jesus Christ on Earth by the Prophet Simon Kimbangu." MacGaffey (1992) described the Kimbanguist Church as "the largest African-founded Protestant Church." It became a member of the World* Council of Churches (in 1969), 10 years after its official recognition by the colonial government (1959). However, the Church of Christ in Congo (since 2002) and then the Roman Catholic Church (since 2004) suspended ecumenical relationships with the Kimbanguists. The Kimbanguist Church nevertheless continues to preach the gospel and maintain its ecclesial structures.

From an outsider's perspective (for an insider's perspective, see Kimbanguism), the Bible seems to be the most important heritage that Kimbangu left to his followers. He is reported to have said, "I do not leave you orphans, I leave you with the Bible." In addition to the Ten Commandments, the Kimbanguist Church has an ethical code, which includes the following rules: (1) Respect the government (Rom 13:1–3). (2) Love everybody, even your enemy (Matt 5:43–45). (3) Do not smoke either tobacco or hemp. (4) Do not imbibe alcohol. (5) Do not dance or attend dances. (6) Do not bathe naked or sleep naked. (7) Do not quarrel. (8) Do not use charms or magic. (9) Pay taxes. (10) Do not harbor resentment. (11) Admit your wrongdoing before witnesses. (12) Do not eat monkey or pig. The basic theology of the Kimbanguist Church confesses Kimbangu as the prophet of Jesus and someone who was with God since the creation (John 1:1–18). Baptism is practiced without water, but in the name of the Father, the Son, and the Holy Spirit, who descended upon Kimbangu. In a later theological development, Kimbangu's three sons have been confessed as (being like) the three persons of the Trinity. Nkamba, Kimbangu's native village, is a symbolic New Jerusalem. The social engagement of the Kimbanguist Church includes loyalty to the government and self-support campaigns. Kikongo is the official language of the Kimbanguist Church.

Other Independent Churches. The history of independent churches in the DRC can be dated from 1704, when Dona Beatriz Kimpa Vita (c1682–1706) founded her own church, known as the Antonian Church. She used Christian symbols but revitalized traditional Congolese cultural roots, questioned the traditional view of the cross, and preached a black Messiah and a kind of Prosperity* Gospel. She was captured and burned at the stake for heresy at the instigation of Catholic missionaries. Since the 1970s, the phenomenon of African* Instituted Churches has significantly increased in the DRC. More than 2,600 independent churches are found in Kinshasa City alone. They are inspired by the Charismatic Movement, reformism, Pietism, Gnosticism, Millennialism*, thaumaturgy, and utopia. They build their communities on the basis of practices selected from Catholicism, Protestantism, Kimbanguism, African traditional beliefs, and oriental religions. For example, "liberal Catholics" relate to some Catholic traditions, "Evangelical sects" are associated with Protestantism, while the "Ngunzists" claim to be part of the Kimbanguist heritage. Generally, independent churches preach the gospel of prosperity or of purity, and their theologies are popularized through audio- and videocassettes. These theological principles easily reach the majority of Congolese Christians, while those of the denominational churches are limited to elites who study or teach at theological institutions. The "new churches" literally dominate the world of Christian music.

Statistics: Population (2000): between 52 and 60 million. Christians: 96% (Roman Catholics, 51%; members of African Instituted Churches (including Kimbanguist*) and independent Charismatic churches, 23%; Protestants, 21%; marginal Christians, 1%); African Religionists, 2.4%; Muslims, 1.6%. (Based on *World Christian Encyclopedia*, 2001.)

JEAN-CLAUDE LOBA-MKOLE

Congo, Republic of (Congo-Brazzaville), is situated in the western part of the Kongo kingdom, where Christianity flourished in the 15th and 16th c. Yet when Holy Ghost missionaries arrived (late 19th c.), they found no Christians. The present Congolese statistics on Christianity depend on the 1978 definition of sect* as any association or church not recognized by the Marxist state. Three denominational churches and two African* Instituted Churches (AICs) were recognized: Roman Catholics, Evangelical Churches of the Congo, Salvation* Army, the Kimbanguist* Church, and the Lassy Zepherin Church. Other AICs were viewed as sects. When these are included, there are 2.7 million Christians in a population of 2.9 million (1.5 million Catholic, 0.5 million Protestant, and 0.37 million members of AICs). Many Christians (0.59 million) are Charismatics.

The lower Congo culture is the cradle of messianic-prophetic movements (*ngunza*) inspired by charismatic leaders who suffered imprisonment and/or death in colonial hands. Kimpa Vita led the Antonian Movement in the 17th and 18th c. to reunite the Kongo. Simon Kimbangu*, Baptist catechist in Congo-Leopoldville, led a politicoreligious revival in 1921 that became the Kimbanguist* Church; and André Matsoua, who died in Brazzaville prison (1942), provoked a nativistic liberation movement, Matsouanism. These movements espouse political liberation*, health*, and deliverance from occult forces. "Witchcraft*" (*kindoki*), the ambivalent power or knowledge to heal or destroy, dominates narratives of clan and national disorder, economic and political success or failure. In this context, the Catholic Charismatic Movement, Protestant revivals, AICs, and nativistic sects combat Evil (as a transcendent power). Through trance, prayer, confession, the imposition of hands, and the administration of "revealed herbs" or holy water, prophets, shepherds, and pastors divine, heal*, exorcise*, and impose change in personal moral and social behavior. They displace and denounce the traditional *nganga* (healer), whose therapeutic field they justify and occupy. The practice of African* Religion is rare. But the importance attached to healing and exorcism, and to ancestral and messianic founders' tombs, authenticates ancestral cosmology (see Ancestor Veneration and Christianity Cluster: in Africa).

Since the civil war of 1993–94, Congo-Brazzaville has been scarred by ethnic conflict despite the sovereign national government. References to diverse religious phenomena escalated as distress and anxiety increased; conversely, the religious movements and churches reinforced the political power of various groups and the national goverment.

Ecumenism is highly developed; however, the 1998 massacre of church representatives who were killed as they attempted to reconcile the warring factions weakened the sociopolitical impact of the movement. The Catholic majority (six dioceses and one prefecture) is retraining its laity to assume civic responsibilities through "Basic Christian communities," especially in the south. The Charismatic Movement, fraternities (*mabundu*), youth associations, and other groups fill the vacuum created by social fragmentation and provide mutual aid and witness to the faith. **See also EXORCISM.**

Statistics: Population (2000): 2.9 million (M). Christians, 2.7 M, 91% (Roman Catholics, 1.5 M; Protestants, 0.5 M; members of African Instituted Churches, 0.37 M); African Religionists, 0.14 M, 5%; Muslims, 1%; nonreligious, 2%. (Based on *World Christian Encyclopedia*, 2001.)

ELOCHUKWU EUGENE UZUKWU, CSSP

Congregatio de Auxiliis (Lat "Commission on Divine Aid" [given by grace]), appointed (1597) by Pope Clement VIII because of intense intra-Catholic debate over grace* and freedom*. Because the Jesuits*, following Miguel de Molina*, affirmed free will* despite the role of grace, they were accused of Pelagianism*. Because the Dominicans, following Domingo Báñez*, defended predetermination (thus predestination*), they were accused of Calvinism*. Pope Paul V exonerated both, leaving the debate unresolved (1607).

Congregation. In the Jewish and Christian traditions, a religious gathering (Heb *qahal*; Gk *synagoge* and *ekklesia*; Lat *congregatio*). In Roman Catholic usage, a community or order not required to take solemn vows; a group of monasteries; one of the permanent committees of the College of Cardinals in Rome. In Protestant churches of the Congregational* type, the local body responsible for calling and ordaining to all ministries.

Congregationalism. Congregationalism, an ecclesiological reform movement, grew out of the Reformation*. Its radically independent and proto-democratic church polity sought to enable a faithful approximation of the style and structure of the NT church in the social context of European Protestant society. The Congregational model took root among Dissenters* in England, France, and the Netherlands; it was most thoroughly incorporated into the social fabric of Puritan* New England, where it remained the official ecclesiology* for more than 200 years.

While Congregationalism does not have a specific creedal formulation, given its emphasis on the autonomy of each congregation, a few characteristics of the movement can be discerned.

Congregationalism is against ecclesiastical hierarchy, denying that there is an "official" church through which salvation* is administrated. Rather, each congregation possesses within itself all that is required to be a fully realized Christian Church, namely the preaching of the gospel and the administration of the sacraments (baptism* and Communion*) by a settled minister, called to a church by a vote among the members.

Congregational theology is covenantal* and, historically, Calvinist*. The covenantal relationship within the Trinity and the covenantal relationship between God and God's people (as understood in the Westminster* Confession of Faith) are the exemplars by which Congregational churches classically seek to relate. Each church has its own covenant by which incoming members testify to God's saving work in their lives and commit to one another in fellowship, discipline, and mission.

Congregational churches are also voluntarist*; fellowship is not determined by geographical parish* but by the decision of the individual member to join the covenant community. Voluntarism was a strike against ecclesiastical hierarchy and also an attempt to form a community of "visible saints," in which all members are mature Christian believers. In Congregational New England, such communities became quasi-theocratic*; only members of the church voted on town issues, which lent credence to the notion that the vote of the church represented God's will. The aspiration to maintain God-centered civil societies as an example for the world was crystallized in John Winthrop's famous sermon, "A Model of Christian Charity," regularly invoked by US politicians to this day.

While Congregationalist contemporary theology tends to have little to do with theocracy and leans away from the Reformed beliefs of its early adherents, the ecclesiology of sacramental, autonomous covenant community remains the same. **See also CHURCH, CONCEPTS AND LIFE, CLUSTER.**

CALEB J. D. MASKELL

Congregatio de Propaganda Fide. See PROPAGANDA FIDE, CONGREGATIO DE.

Congress of Asian Theologians, a movement that organizes regular congresses (1997, Korea; 1999, India; 2001, Indonesia; 2003, Thailand; 2006, Hong Kong; 2009, Philippines) of Asian theologians related to the Programme* for Theology and Cultures in Asia and its founding bodies. Each of these congresses, attended by about 100 theologians and ecumenical leaders, promotes the formation of networks of Christian theologians throughout Asia, so that they may "come together to share life and work, project together concerns for the future, and help in the renewal and reinvigoration of the life and mission of the Church and of the ecumenical movement in Asia." SIMON SHUI-MAN KWAN

Consanguinity, a specified relation by descent from a common ancestor. Specified degree of consanguinity is an obstacle to marriage* in Scripture*, canon* law, and civil law.

Conscientious Objection, refusal on moral grounds to obey certain laws or to participate in carrying them out. It has its roots in the Stoic* position that natural law takes precedence over the laws enacted by the state. Early Christians were "conscientious objectors" to the Romans' demand that they offer incense to the traditional deities or the image of the emperor. At the time of the Reformation, conscientious objection took new forms among the Anabaptists* and later in the Society of Friends*. In the USA, those who disagreed with slavery* and the Fugitive Slave Law openly engaged in conscientious objection; Henry David Thoreau (see Transcendentalism) articulated many of its principles in his essay on civil disobedience*, which was then studied and effectively adapted by Mohandas Gandhi in India's struggle for independence and by Martin Luther King* during the civil rights struggle.

Members of the traditional "peace* churches" have been given the right, throughout US history, to abstain from active participation in war, often being given "alternative service." New legal controversies have been occasioned by conscientious objectors who are not members of the peace churches but act on their individual convictions, religious or nonreligious, and by "selective conscientious objection" to particular wars but not to war as such. **See also NONVIOLENCE; PACIFISM AND CHRISTIANITY; PEACE MOVEMENTS; PEACE AND PEACEMAKING.** EUGENE TESELLE

Conscientization (Portuguese, *conscientização*), consciousness raising, a term coined by Paulo Freire (*Pedagogy of the Oppressed*, 1970) to refer to the process of learning to recognize social, political, economic, cultural, and ideological structural powers and the action that can lead to liberation from their oppressive elements. **See also LIBERATION THEOLOGIES CLUSTER: LIBERATION AND THEOLOGY.**

Consecration (from Lat *consecrare*, "to render a person, place, or thing holy" [*sacer/sacra*]). In the OT, there are references to consecrations or dedications of altars (cf. Exod 40), the firstborn (Exod 13:2), the Temple (cf. 2 Chr 5–6), kings (1 Sam 10; 2 Sam 2), and prophets (Isa 6:5–13; Jer 1:5; cf. Rom 1:1; Gal 1:15, Paul "being set apart" as an apostle).

In Christian history, consecrations developed for churches, altars, altar stones, chalices, and patens, these being dedicated for sacred use unless subsequently "reduced" to profane status.

The ordination* of priests* as bishops* is traditionally called a "consecration." The profession of vows by men and women religious is likewise a "consecration," though not an "ordination" (the sacrament of holy orders is not involved).

Roman Catholics sometimes make personal "consecrations" to various devotions, such as the Sacred Heart of Jesus or the Immaculate Heart of Mary. Roman Catholics also speak of the "words of consecration," pronounced by the priest to change the bread and wine into the Body and Blood of Christ. The Eastern Orthodox, however, usually regard the invocation (*epiclesis*) of the Holy Spirit or the entire eucharistic prayer (anaphora) as effecting the change of the bread and wine rather than the words of consecration alone. ROBERT FASTIGGI

Consensus Tigurinus (Lat "Zurich Agreement"), the declaration of faith, in 26 articles, agreed upon in 1549 by Calvin* and Bullinger*, representing the Reformed churches of French and German Switzerland, respectively. Its chief purpose was to reconcile the conflicting eucharistic* doctrines of Zwingli* and Calvin, rejecting both the Roman Catholic and the Lutheran positions.

Consequentialist Ethics emphasizes the effects (consequences) of choices and actions, especially their effects on others, and the intentionality of actions. In contrast to deontological ethics, which emphasizes conformity to moral norms, consequentialist ethics (the most common ethical approach in business) is goal oriented and thus also called "teleological" or, with John Stuart Mill, "utilitarian." Theological consequentialist ethics can be most directly concerned with the question: For the sake of whom are we acting? (our neighbors), and therefore with the question: What is desirable for others? (By contrast, deontological ethics is concerned with the negative imperative: "harm not.") It is an ethical approach particularly helpful in an eschatological perspective (a "Kingdom* ethics"). **See also DEONTIC, DEONTOLOGICAL ETHICS; PERFECTIONIST ETHICS.**

Conservatism in Christianity: A Sociological Perspective. Sociologists study the relations between religion and society. A sociological approach to the study of contemporary religion divides adherents of world religions into traditionalists (or conservatives), who reject significant aspects of modernity, and modernists (or liberals), who accept modernity.

The "Christian Right" (taking various forms in different religious and cultural contexts) embodies religious conservatism. The Right seeks to create a Christian society where the state enforces the morality propounded by the Right; other religions are not respected; and the Right's "Christian" worldview dominates all of culture. The Right espouses "ordered liberty": people should be free only to do what is "right."

There are various explanations for the appeal of conservative Christianity. One is that people are attracted to strict rules: strictness conveys a desirable seriousness (Kelley, 1977) and eliminates "free-riders," allowing congregations to more effectively reward participants (Iannaccone, 1994). Another possible explanation is that conservative Christianity survives because it is more helpful than conventional Christianity to the poor and powerless; e.g. it allows them to feel good about themselves as members of a spiritual elite (Tamney).

Conservative Christianity may grow in the future because of this appeal and because conservatives tend to have large families and to be more successful than liberals at retaining the loyalty of their youth (Greeley and Hout). Moreover, many throughout the world are attracted by the Pentecostal* and Charismatic* forms of conservative religion, which combine indigenous, Shamanistic*-like elements and Christianity, and are thus able to offer premodern people continuities with their past and a bridge to modernity (Gifford).

As conservatives in the North Atlantic world become middle class, some develop a modified form of conservatism, more adapted to modernity. This "modernized conservatism" is appealing because people value traditional gender roles or rituals that evoke religious experiences, or because they fear being on a slippery slope to "moral relativism." **See also POSTMODERNISM AND THEOLOGY.** JOSEPH B. TAMNEY

Consistory, a place of meeting; now the meeting of church officers: in Catholicism*, the pope* and cardinals*; in Protestantism, the bishop and clergy, or congregational officers.

Constance, Council of (1414–18), the major achievement of the Conciliar* Movement, occasioned by the Western Schism (or Great* Schism, 1378–1417), when there were rival popes in Avignon and Rome, and the election of a third pope by the Council of Pisa* (1409–15). The call to the Council was issued at the demand of Emperor Sigismund. The Council functioned as a kind of Congress of Europe, with representatives of rulers, bishops, and universities; the voting was by nations. As a "general council," it was able to deal with questions about the schism, the reform of the church, and heresy*.

About heresy, there was little disagreement. Although Sigismund gave a safe-conduct to Jan Hus*, the Council imprisoned him and urged him to recant; however, Hus refused and was burned at the stake (1415).

The schism was resolved when the Pisan pope, generally termed "antipope," John XXIII, tried to dissolve the Council and then fled. The Council took a Conciliarist* view and adopted the decree *Haec sancta* (1415), declaring that it had direct authority from Christ and that persons of every rank, including the papal, were obliged to obey it in matters of faith, the extirpation of the schism, and the reformation of the church in head and members. From 1415 to 1417, no pope was recognized; the Council held supreme authority in the church, and a series of reforming decrees was passed, including *Frequens* (1417), requiring the pope to convene general councils at regular intervals.

The Council, losing its momentum, decided to elect a pope and chose Martin V. He immediately contravened some of its measures. Not prepared to depose the pope it had just elected, the Council adjourned (1418); Pope Martin was in control. *Haec sancta* remained authoritative, since the legitimacy of the popes depended on it. Further councils were held in accordance with *Frequens*, especially the Council of Basel*.

EUGENE TESELLE

Constantine (272/73–337), first Christian sovereign of the Roman Empire. Born in Naissus (modern Serbia), Constantine served as a military tribune, then lived in Nicomedia (303–5). His father, Constantius, had become Western emperor (305). Constantine was in Britain when his father died (at York, 306). The army saluted Constantine as emperor of the West. Constantine marched against Maxentius, who also claimed to be emperor (312). On the eve of battle, Constantine had a vision in which he was promised victory under the sign of the cross. He adopted this insignium (the *Chi-Rho** monogram), defeated Maxentius, and entered

Rome a monotheist, if not yet a Christian. He gave the Lateran basilica to the pope and ordered a new structure built over the tomb of St. Peter*.

Constantine and Licinius, one of two competitors for the Eastern throne, met in Milan (313), and the two sent letters to provincial governors repealing the persecution of Christians, which was being prolonged by Licinius's rival Maximinus Daia. After the defeat and death of Maximinus, Licinius ruled the East as Constantine's ally. Yet Constantine invaded his dominions under the pretext of resisting a barbarian invasion (316). Alleging heavy taxation and persecution of Christians, Constantine deposed Licinius, then (324) moved the capital from Rome to Constantinople, the "Second Rome."

Because of the unrest caused by the Arian* controversy, Constantine called and dominated the Council of Nicaea* (325; see Trinity in Eastern Orthodoxy; Trinity in the Western Tradition). In his religious policy, especially toward the Donatists* and the Arians*, he punished intransigence. Having already governed the church as a Christian in the West for some years, he now passed laws that favored Christians, though probably suppressing only what he viewed as the most immoral "pagan" cults and religious intolerance. He ruled as sole emperor for 13 years, waging successive wars for the protection of Christians outside the empire – a threat that engendered persecutions of Christians as "pro Roman," e.g. in Persia (see Church of the East, or Assyrian Church) – and died on the eve of a campaign against Persia, receiving baptism on his deathbed.

In Constantinople he had prepared a shrine to the Twelve Apostles, with his tomb in the center, both to share their honor and to receive their merit (thus Eastern Christians called him "the equal of the apostles"). After his death, he was deified in the traditional Roman manner, which Christians were able to interpret in their own way. Thus in death as in life, Constantine was at the boundary where classical Greco-Roman and Christian traditions met, both Christianizing the former and adapting the latter to the growing spirit of imperial absolutism.

MARK J. EDWARDS and EUGENE TESELLE

Constantinople, Councils of, four general councils that met in present-day Istanbul during the church's first millennium. They were preceded by the Homoian Council of Constantinople (360), which should not be ignored.

The Homoian Council of Constantinople (360), called by Constantius II, the Roman emperor of the East, reaffirmed, against Nicaea* I (325), the moderate Arian* view that the Son is "like" (*homoios*) the Father while avoiding saying that he is "of the same essence" (*homoousios*). Like the following council, it was attended almost exclusively by bishops from the East and is often ignored because of its theological position (deemed heretical* by its opponents), although it is an important reminder of the fact that Arianism remained a very strong movement in the Christian Church until the 6th or 7th c.

Constantinople (381), one of the ecumenical* councils*, called "Constantinople I" by those who reject the Homoian Council, completed the work of Nicaea I, once again rejecting Arianism*. It formulated the Niceno*-Constantinopolitan Creed (what is commonly known today as the Nicene* Creed), which reaffirmed Jesus' full divinity and extended Nicaea's minimal language on the Spirit to say that Christians believe "in the Spirit, the holy, the lordly and life-giving one, proceeding forth from the Father, co-worshipped and co-glorified with Father and Son." Although no Western bishops attended, Pope Damasus I (366–84), who did not send delegates, accepted the Niceno Constantinopolitan Creed. It said only, "The Spirit proceeding forth from the Father." *Filioque** ("and the Son") was added later and became standard in the West. Eastern bishops objected to this addition because Eastern theology on the whole held that the Spirit proceeds from the Father alone, adding to the East–West split.

Constantinople II (553) addressed the continuing confusion concerning Jesus and Mary, specifically the Nestorian* position that Mary was the mother of Jesus the human being (*Christokos*), but not the mother of God's Son (*Theotokos**). The Council condemned the "Three* Chapters," referring to the essays of three men – Theodore* of Mopsuestia, Theodoret* of Cyrrhus, and Ibas* of Edessa – who seemed to sympathize with Nestorianism*. The weak pope Vigilius* (537–55) hesitated. While he had been supported by the Byzantine empress Theodora*, he had leaned toward Miaphysitism. But after her death, the Byzantine emperor Justinian* overshadowed Pope Vigilius. Vigilius ultimately endorsed the decrees of the Council, but only after issuing inconsistent public and private statements. The Council's creed provides a useful summary of a half-millennium of Christology*, Mariology*, and Trinitarian* theology.

Constantinople III (680–81) resolved the remaining question of how many wills Jesus had. Monothelitism* argued for one, saying the human and divine wills had merged in Jesus' unique person. The Council condemned this position, holding that Jesus is one person with two natures and two wills (one human and one divine). This position meant that the Council had also to condemn a prior pope, Honorius I (625–38), who had followed the monothelites. Later arguments would be made that Honorius had held this position as an individual Christian but not as a pope, that he was well-meaning but misguided, or that he did not hold the position but had failed to oppose it.

Constantinople IV (869–70), the least prestigious of the West's 21 general councils, is typically not accepted as a general council in the East. It was more a local political event than a theological summit, despite its repetition of the theology and creeds of the prior seven general councils. The Council concerned itself with the competing claims of two bishops, Photius* and Ignatius, to be patriarch of Constantinople, who alternately held the see, a situation complicated by the assassination of one Byzantine co-emperor by the other – a possible reason for the repeated assertion of the ultimate authority and honor to be accorded bishops over secular rulers. Several Roman popes were involved before, during, and after this meeting, inappropriately, according to some in the East. In subsequent years and centuries, popes and Eastern bishops rejected or accepted this Council.

CHRISTOPHER M. BELLITTO

Constantinople, Patriarchate of. See ECUMENICAL PATRIARCHATE.

Consubstantiation (Lat for "with another substance"), Lutheran doctrine of the Eucharist*, according to which after consecration the Body and Blood of Christ are "in, with, and under" the elements.

Consultation on Church Union (COCU) grew out of a joint proposal by Episcopal Bishop James Pike and Presbyterian Eugene Carson Blake in 1960. In response, nine US mainline denominations committed to agreeing on and manifesting a form of unity faithful to the NT and effective in carrying out common mission* today. From 1962 to 2002, scholars and laypersons from these churches – African* Methodist Episcopal Church, African Methodist Episcopal Zion Church, Christian* Church (Disciples of Christ), Christian Methodist Episcopal Church, Episcopal* Church, International Council of Community Churches, United Presbyterian Church in the USA (Presbyterian Church USA, after 1983), and Methodist Church (United Methodist after 1968) – worked out a theological consensus on ministry and forms of church order, united worship, and ways to combat racism* and discrimination against disabled people (see Disability and Christianity) and women (see Feminist Theology Cluster: In North America: various entries). Fellowships involving shared eucharistic worship and common mission including thousands of people emerged. Plans to achieve full communion were accepted by eight of these churches; the Episcopal Church did not vote on this proposal. After each church accepted all the others, the work of COCU passed to an association, "Churches Uniting in Christ," for completion and implementation.

GERALD MOEDE

Contemplation, Contemplative Prayer and Life. Disciplined dedication to prayer is a feature of all religions. The roots of Christian contemplative life are both biblical and Hellenistic. Contemplation was not a distinct path in the life of the early church, but it was inseparable from its missionary and communal life.

In the 4th-c. Roman Empire under Constantine*, Christendom emerged both as a religious and as a secular force. This shift led radical Christians (especially those practicing asceticism*) to seek holier lifestyles on the margins of the Empire. The traditions of contemplative life as a distinct form of Christian commitment therein emerged. The deserts in Egypt*, Palestine, and Syria* were the first cradles of the contemplative monastic* movement (see Eremitic Monasticism; Monasticism Cluster). The focus of the monks and nuns in this movement was an inner journey, a personal search for God.

In many sources, the term "contemplation" means "intellectual vision" or speculation. This sense of the term fails to grasp the full meaning of religious contemplation and mysticism*. Contemplation is not merely a matter of analogical* knowledge of the infinite (e.g. in a personal search for the reality of God), but one of immediate intuition (see Apophaticism; Heteronomy [as kenosis*]). Realizing the love of God is a central aim of Christian contemplation; therefore, emotions, as well as intuition, are central to it. Contemplatives' search aims not at the extraordinary, but at the ultimate reality that gives meaning to our lives.

Contemplatives sought (and still seek) solitude and silence, and forsook mundane preoccupations in order to hear the Word of God. Thus the deserts gave way to different paths of institutionalization, to spaces and structures such as monasteries and hermitages, and to monastic orders and rules of life (see Monasticism Cluster: Monastic Rules). Multiple traditions emerged in Byzantine and Latin Christendoms, which in turn produced different schools of spirituality (e.g. Byzantine and Eastern Orthodox* monasticism*, Cistercian*, Carmelite*). The monastic movements usually began as an initiative of the laity*, not of clerics. Many mystics have been women, laity, and nonordained religious. The early emphasis on withdrawal was later balanced with models combining the active life and the contemplative life. Modern spirituality also promotes the flourishing of contemplation in the midst of the secular city.

From the *Sayings of the (Desert) Fathers* (*Apophthegmata* Patrum*) down to writings by Thomas Merton*, the tradition has amassed a vast corpus of literature that aids in the contemplative enterprise, combining asceticism, theology, spiritual psychology, and mystical phenomenology. Great masters, such as Teresa* of Ávila, John* of the Cross, Ignatius* Loyola, and, among Protestants, Sebastian Franck, Valentin Weigel, and Jacob Boehme*, have played important roles as spiritual directors. Even though contemplation is a personal journey, it is recommended that one receive guidance in view of the psychological effort demanded.

Today, many lay Christians are seriously interested and involved in contemplation. Persons outside the church also seek spiritual insight by examining the wisdom of the great Christian mystics. Finally, the fruitful dialogue between contemplatives of different religions has demonstrated the interreligious ecumenical potential of contemplation (see Dialogue, Ecumenical; Interfaith Dialogue). **See also PRAYER OF THE HEART.**

ANA MARÍA BIDEGAIN and JUAN SANCHEZ

Contextualization, a term introduced into the theological vocabulary by the Theological Education Fund (World* Council of Churches) in 1972, as an outgrowth of the work of its leader, Skoki Choe of Taiwan. Contextualization is built on the assumption that, consciously or not, all theologies are born out of a social condition and the needs of a particular context.

Contextualization reverses the direction from which theology is approached. Rather than assuming theological truths and then finding cultural language with which to formulate these truths, contextual theology starts by studying the context and its historical, socioeconomic, political, cultural, ethnic, racial, and religious dimensions. It then uses these dimensions to articulate a theology at once appropriate to that situation and pointing to a universal reality.

Contextualization is important for three reasons (Robert Schreiter). (1) Methodologically, while Christian hope is rooted in the Bible, it is shaped by language and the cultural specificity of both the Bible and the interpreter's culture. There is a dialectic relationship between text and context, each helping the other to elucidate the hope that seeks expression. (2) Sociologically, the environments in which we find ourselves play a critical role in the way our theologies develop. (3) Perhaps most importantly, Christian theology is based on an incarnational God, who became manifest in a particular time and place. A docetic* theology is as unhelpful as a docetic Christology*. A theological response to God's initiative must be as particular as the initiative itself was.

Contextual theology came to the fore with the global perspective common today. As we become aware of the universal dimensions of humanity, how local context shapes that humanity becomes apparent to us. Well-crafted contextual theology addresses local situations and in so doing contributes to global conversations without suppressing other voices from other contexts.

However, while context is the medium through which theology must be articulated if it is to have substance, context is not without flaw. Christianity assumes that sin* is pervasive; we are both too broken and too finite to speak definitively of God. The Christian message has a critical prophetic edge that speaks of an alternative vision of a world as God intends it. Doing contextual theology requires the use of a hermeneutic* of suspicion. Just because something is contextual does not mean that it is inherently good. Each theology must be tested by the gospel message and alternative voices. **See also INCULTURATION CLUSTER.**

DAMAYANTHI M. A. NILES

Contextual Theologies

See AFRICAN AMERICAN CLUSTER: THEOLOGIES; ASIAN THEOLOGY, TRENDS IN; ASIAN AMERICAN THEOLOGIES; BLACK THEOLOGY; COLONIALISM AND IMPERIALISM AND CHRISTIAN THEOLOGY; CREATION THEOLOGY IN SCANDINAVIA; CRISIS THEOLOGY; DALIT THEOLOGY; DECOLONIZING THEOLOGY; DIALECTICAL THEOLOGY; FEMINIST THEOLOGY CLUSTER; GAY AND LESBIAN THEOLOGIES; INDIAN CHRISTIAN THEOLOGIES; LATIN AMERICAN THEOLOGIES; LATINO/A THEOLOGIES; MINJUNG THEOLOGY; PALESTINIAN LIBERATION THEOLOGY; RECONSTRUCTION, AFRICAN THEOLOGIES OF. **See also CHURCHES AND DENOMINATIONS AND THEIR THEOLOGIES CLUSTER.**

Contraception. See BIRTH CONTROL AND CONTRACEPTION, CHRISTIAN VIEWS OF.

Contrition, sincere sorrow for one's sins, based on love for God (contrasted with attrition*).

Convent, a building in which nuns (members of a Roman Catholic women's* religious order) live. The community is ruled by the mother superior, considered God's representative, who reports to her major superior in the mother house, which in turn reports to the Vatican.

Conventicle, in British law, a private, clandestine, or illegal religious gathering, e.g. of Nonconformists* or Dissenters* in England or Covenanters* in Scotland.

Conversion (from Lat *conversio*, "turning around" or often "turning toward") is not designated by a particular term in the Bible, although the Hebrew *shuv* and the Greek *epistrephein* sometimes convey the "turning toward" God that characterizes conversion, in contrast to repentance*, which emphasizes the "turning away from" evil. As the process of radically rejecting evil and embracing a relationship with God through faith*, conversion is commonly viewed as involving radical alterations in people's beliefs, behaviors, and affiliations, as A. D. Nock emphasized, contrasting conversion in Christianity and Judaism with conversion in other religions. Although conversion is often experienced as a sudden radical change, and although some scholars and Christian traditions limit it to such a sudden experience, other scholars and Christian traditions affirm conversion as a *process*; the sudden experience is the experience of a paradigm shift. As a process of religious change, conversion is cumulative and contextual, taking place "in a dynamic force field of people, events, ideologies*, institutions, expectations, and orientations" (Rambo). Thus the study of conversion benefits from social scientific approaches (psychology, sociology, anthropology), as well as from theological and missiological inquiries.

The scholarly study of Paul's* conversion as presented in Gal 1:11–17 (and Phil 3:3–14) exemplifies this diversity of views. For traditional Western scholarship that emphasizes "Paul the theologian proclaiming justification through faith," conversion established for Paul a totally new relationship with God through faith, a complete rejection of his Pharisaic Judaism and of his evil behavior as persecutor of the church. Following this model, most Western missionaries in Africa, Asia, and Latin America preached a gospel demanding from converts a total rejection of their former religious and cultural traditions by turning "from darkness to light" (see, e.g., Mission Cluster; Portuguese Explorations, Conquests, and Missions; Spanish Explorations, Conquests, and Missions).

By contrast, following Stendahl, scholars of the "New Perspective" underscored that Paul's experience was not a "conversion" in this traditional sense. Paul remained a Jew, e.g. holding to fundamental beliefs in the God of Abraham and to the Jewish Scripture, and proclaiming a Jewish message about Jesus as Messiah. His radical experience was rather a call to a prophetic role as missionary to the Gentiles* or Nations, as Jeremiah (1:5) and Isaiah (49:1) were before him. According to this perspective, conversion is a process through which the gospel finds expression in continuity with the very religious and cultural views and practices that it transforms for converts. And conversion is a call to contribute to a transformative mission in a particular context and is always inculturated*, as the church already recognized in the Hellenistic* period or during its early expansion in Africa (see Orthodox Churches, Oriental, Cluster: Ethiopian Orthodox Tewahedo Church), China*, and later in Latin America (see, e.g., Mexico; also Culture Cluster: Culture and Christianity; Inculturation Cluster).

Still other scholars underscore that in all cases conversion is the experience of being freed from bondage. They take note of the apocalyptic character of Paul's message (a messianic message) and its emphasis on the power of sin (in its many forms) to keep humans in bondage. While affirming the specificity of his own experience (Gal 1:11–17), Paul describes his readers' conversions as a liberating experience similar to his own. This transformative experience makes believers in Christ "a new creation" (6:15). Conversion as a foundational liberating experience has been underscored through the centuries in the Eastern Orthodox* tradition, with its view of sin as a disease and the conversion process leading to a theosis* (the making of a new creation), Christians becoming agents of this ongoing transformation in the world. Similarly, Liberation theologies emphasize that liberation from all forms of sin, including structural sin through which people are oppressed, is a fundamental conversion experience that call those who are free to contribute to the liberation of others. **See also** LIBERATION THEOLOGIES CLUSTER. DANIEL PATTE

Conversos (Spanish, "converted"), Spanish Jews who converted to Roman Catholic Christianity after undergoing severe persecution (late 14th–15th c.). Suspicions against these "New Christians," still viewed as Jews by the populace (also referred to by the derogatory term *marranos*, "pigs"), led in part to the establishment of the Spanish Inquisition* (1478). The Inquisition accused *conversos* of secretly observing their Jewish faith and ordered the execution of many. The civil and ecclesial rights of *conversos* and their descendants (Christians with Jewish ancestry) were severely curtailed by 15th- to 16th-c. laws, although many or most *conversos*, including Roman Catholic saints such as Teresa* of Ávila and John* of the Cross, practiced an orthodox Catholic faith. **See also** SPAIN.

Conviction. While this term designates a juridical process (someone being convicted of a crime) that can refer to true and false beliefs (convincing a person of error, compelling a person to admit the truth), in theological perspectives that question the limits of rationalism*, conviction has become a helpful concept in referring to the state of being convinced, free of doubt – a primordial experience (Gadamer*) housed in language (Heidegger*). Conviction as the state of being convinced is at the center of Quaker* worship. A conviction as a truth perceived by believers to be self-evident, "proprioceptive" (arising within the organism), or "intuitive, vocational, mystical" (von* Hügel) imposes itself on believers and drives their lives. Directly related to faith as trust (see Faith #2) and as primordial religious experience (see Faith #4), conviction precedes understanding but can be brought to understanding through theological reflection (*fides quaerens intellectum* [Anselm*]) and then questioned. **See also** APOPHATISM; GADAMER, HANS-GEORG; HERMENEUTICS; METAPHOR; MODERNISM, ROMAN CATHOLIC; MYSTICISM, MYSTICS; SYMBOLISM. DANIEL PATTE

Cooperative, a voluntary association engaged in economic activities, committed to democratic control and equitable sharing of assets and profits, and championed by socialists, liberals, Catholics, and liberal Protestants. A cooperative enables small operators to increase their bargaining power and efficiency through joint action, whether in marketing or buying products (agriculture, fishing, manufacturing), providing services (transportation, utilities), or gaining mutual security (health care, insurance, savings, housing). The Rochdale Pioneers (1844) formulated classic cooperative principles; a major modern example is the Mondragon network (France), founded by a Basque priest (1956).

Cope, long cloak of semicircular cloth worn by clergy in processions or at vespers*, when the chasuble* is not used.

Copernicus, Nicolas (Niclas Koppernijk; 1473–1543), astronomer, mathematician, medical practitioner, clerical administrator. Born in Torun (Thorn), Poland; studied in Kracow, Bologna, Padua, and Ferrara. He formulated the first successful mathematical version of heliocentric astronomy. However, he delayed publication of his theory, in part because it challenged the literalist* scriptural interpretation (several biblical passages mention the sun's motion or the earth's immobility). He was presented with a copy of his *De revolutionibus orbium caelestium* on his deathbed. At first regarded simply as a useful mathematical device, the book soon incited growing opposition among theologians, culminating in the condemnation in Rome of the Copernican worldview as "contrary to Scripture*" (1616). ERNAN MCMULLIN

Coptic Orthodox Church. See ORTHODOX CHURCHES, ORIENTAL, CLUSTER: COPTIC ORTHODOX CHURCH.

Corinthians, 1 and 2 Epistles, collections of letter fragments (perhaps eight) written by Paul to the church at Corinth over several years (c42–56) that record Paul's turbulent relationship with a diverse congregation and defend his apostolic ministry.

Initially Paul and his colleagues stayed in Corinth for more than 18 months (Acts 18:11), converting both Gentiles (1 Cor 12:2) and a significant minority of Jews (1 Cor 16:19), including the former "ruler of the synagogue" Crispus (Acts 18:8). For the first time, the Pauline mission succeeded in crossing social class boundaries. Most converts were from the lower classes (1 Cor 1:26–28). But converts from the upper strata functioned as patrons of the Christian community and included Gaius, "the host of the whole church," and Erastus, "the treasurer of the city" of Corinth (Rom 16:23; 1 Cor 1:14). For these few upper-class Christians, "learned eloquence" held an attraction (1 Cor 1:17; 2:1, 4); they admired the learned and eloquent Apollos (Acts 18:24–28; 1 Cor 1:12, 3:4) and instigated factions. To such elite Christians, Paul was an embarrassment owing to his weakness, the defects of his oratory, his vulgar occupation, and his gospel focused on the "crucified Christ." Thus they welcomed rival Jewish Christian apostles who questioned the legitimacy of Paul's apostleship. Seeking to reestablish his authority, Paul made a second visit to Corinth, with disastrous results: one of the leaders of the church "did Paul wrong" (2 Cor 2:1–11, 7:12). In response, Paul composed the "painful epistle" (now 2 Cor 10:1–13:10), then pursued reconciliation through a conciliatory apology (now 2 Cor 2:14–6:13, 7:2–4) and through Titus's* mediation. Paul eventually celebrated the Corinthians' repentance (2 Cor 1:1–2:13, 7:5–16, 13:11–13) and their contribution to the collection for the poor in Jerusalem (2 Cor 8, 9).

Paul draws on the primitive Christian *kerygma** of Jesus' sacrificial death (1 Cor 1:18–31, 11:23–26; 2 Cor 5:14–15) and resurrection (1 Cor 6:14, 15:1–11) to deepen the Corinthians' understanding of their experience. For Christians of Jewish origin, Paul cites the Scriptures of Israel: presenting typological*/midrashic* interpretations of Israel's wilderness wandering (1 Cor 10) and of the veil of Moses (2 Cor 3). For Paul the Jewish Scriptures are authoritative, yet he reverses the direction of hermeneutical inference; the meaning of events in Israelite history is determined by the Christians' contemporary experiences (1 Cor 10:11). His portrayal of Moses as a deceiver (2 Cor 3:13–16) anticipates Marcion*.

Paul's appropriations of traditions from Greco-Roman culture are most significant. Beyond citing comic writers (e.g. Menander in 1 Cor 15:33), he adapts religious, political, and theatrical discourse, e.g. the "proof" of the resurrection of the dead (1 Cor 15), modeled on the "proof" of the immortality of the soul (Plato's *Phaedrus* and Cicero's *Tusculan Disputations*), or the "fool's speech" (2 Cor. 11:1–12:10), based on the speeches of fools in farce and mime.

The gospel of the "crucified Christ" nullifies the cultured elite's values, but empowers the weak and lowborn (1 Cor 1:18–31). This divinely ordained reversal of values requires a self-limiting regard for others, especially the poor and the weak, for whom Christ died (1 Cor 8:11), a discernment of the needs of others, and the sharing of possessions (1 Cor 11:17–34; 2 Cor. 8, 9). Christian existence is a paradox of "power made perfect in weakness" (2 Cor 12:8–10), of "life manifested in death" (2 Cor 4:7–12). Christians are given the "ministry of reconciliation," to "live no longer for themselves" (2 Cor 5:11–21). LAURENCE L. WELBORN

Cornelius, a centurion of the Italian cohort living in Caesarea, who was associated with a synagogue* as a God fearer*. After a vision he sought out Peter*, who had also received a vision declaring the acceptability of Gentiles* who had not been circumcised* as followers of Christ (Acts 10). For Peter and for Christians today, this was evidence of God's inclusiveness of all people.

Cornelius, Bishop of Rome. See POPES, ROMAN CATHOLIC, AND THE PAPACY.

Corporatism, the political theory that the state should balance the organized interests of all sectors of society (agriculture, labor, industry, the professions, the arts) for the common good. The encyclicals *Rerum Novarum* (1891) and *Quadragesimo Anno* (1931) envisaged justice being achieved through neither capitalism nor socialism, but through negotiation among representatives of these "corporations." While these social* encyclicals assumed that corporations would be autonomous, in fascism* they were controlled by the state.

Corpus Christi, Feast of, a commemoration of the Eucharist* on the Thursday after Trinity* Sunday. **See also JULIANA OF LIÈGE.**

Corruption (from Lat "disintegration" or "destruction"), the physical disintegration of the body; moral deterioration through sin*.

Cosmology, the study of the universe as a whole, using the methods of philosophy, theology, and/or the natural sciences. **See also WORLD.**

Cosmos. See WORLD.

Costa Rica. Christopher Columbus arrived in Costa Rica during his fourth voyage (1502) in the territories inhabited by Huetares, Bruncas, and Chorotegas. The first Catholic parishes were established in San Blas of Nicoya (1544) and Cartago (1562). But the Bribries and Cabécares of the Talamanca region resisted until the 19th c., after repeated efforts by the Spanish governors and the Franciscans to conquer and evangelize them.

Near Cartago, Juana Pereira, a mulatto woman, discovered on August 2, 1635, a dark stone bearing an image of the Virgin. Since then the "Negrita," or "Virgin of los Angeles," has been much venerated.

With independence from Spain (1821), a concordat* with Rome stipulated that Roman Catholicism would be the exclusive religion of the country (signed by Pius IX in 1852). The Constitution of 1871 tolerated other religions but reaffirmed the position of the Catholic Church as the state church. Following the expulsion of the Jesuits and of Bishop Bernardo Thiel, however, laws passed by Liberals limited the legal jurisdiction (e.g. regarding civil registration, matrimony, cemeteries, education) of the Catholic Church (1884).

Protestantism first arrived following trade agreements with Great Britain; an Episcopal Church was established in San José (1864) for members of the embassy and merchants. Then Jamaican workers arrived on the Atlantic Coast (at Limon) to construct a railroad; new Protestant churches were founded by the Jamaica* Baptist Missionary Society (1887) and the Methodist Church of Jamaica (1894). Until 1940 Protestants sought to develop, in addition to religious services, medical, educational, and agricultural programs with the support of North American organizations such as the Central American Mission, the Latin American Mission, and Methodist Churches.

The archbishop of Costa Rica, Victor Manuel Sanabria, supported both Calderón Guardia, president (1940–44) and leader of the Republican Party, and Manuel Mora, leader of the Communist Party, in order to ensure passage of social legislation establishing, among other things, social security and medical insurance for workers.

Struggling for religious freedom, the Protestant churches founded a federation of churches, Alianza Evangélica Costarricense (1950). From 1940 to 1960, Protestantism spread throughout the nation, with a steady increase in Pentecostal* missions. The Charismatic* Movement of the 1970s, among both Catholics and Protestants in Costa Rica, was animated by the Cuban Pentecostal Pastor Gerardo of Avila, the Argentine pastor Juan Carlos Ortiz, the North American priest Francis McNutt, and Sr. Cecilia Arias. The Charismatic Movement deeply influenced many Catholic communities and was one of the reasons for the interruption of the broadcasting of "Radio María" (early 2000s) and for the crisis during the last years of the tenure of Msgr. Arrieta (Román Arrieta Villalobos) as archbishop (1979–2002). Protestants constituted 4.3% of the population in 1960, but 18% by 2000, with more than half of the Protestants in Charismatic* (Pentecostal) churches.

Another movement, Liberation* theology, was initiated (early 1970s) by the group "Exodo"; its journal, *Exodo*, is read in schools and seminaries, including the Ecumenical School of Religious Studies (Escuela Ecuménica Ciencias de la Religión), the Latin American Biblical Seminary, and the Department of Ecumenical Studies (Departamento Ecuménico de Investigaciones).

Statistics: Population (2000): 3.8 million. Christians, 89% (Catholics, 70.1%; Protestants, 18% [the larger Protestant churches: Assemblies of God, Seventh-day Adventists, Church of God]); other religionists, 1.8%; nonreligious, 9.4%. (*Source*: 2000 census.)

JAIME ADRIÁN PRIETO VALLADARES

Côte d'Ivoire. The geographical and historical portals to Côte d'Ivoire were the northern Sahel, gateway to Islam* (since the 18th c.), and the southern Atlantic Coast, gateway for Christianity.

Trading posts for ivory and slaves, established by the Portuguese in the 15th c., initiated the first contacts with Christianity, but no attempts to evangelize were undertaken until 1637, when French Catholic missionaries settled there. The inhospitable climate, however, soon took its toll.

Active evangelization resumed more than two centuries later, when Côte d'Ivoire became a French colony in 1893.

In conjunction with colonization, Catholic missionaries settled along the coast, forming the first and major Christian denomination. The largest Christian worship center on the African continent is the basilica Notre Dame de la Paix in Yamoussoukro. The Roman Catholic Church celebrated the centenary of evangelization there in 1995.

In 1960 Côte d'Ivoire gained its independence. Before that, from 1913 to 1936, other Christian denominations from Europe and North America sent missionaries. Methodists* attained prominence among the mainline Protestant churches. In 1927 Evangelical* churches began to take root. Among the most recent groups to achieve missionary success have been the Assemblies* of God and Jehovah's Witnesses*.

Until the late 1970s, Côte d'Ivoire experienced remarkable economic growth. The influx of immigrants from many West African nations brought with it African Instituted Churches. Two major examples are the Harrist Church, founded by William Wadé Harris from Liberia, who personally traveled to Côte d'Ivoire in 1912 to establish the denomination there, and the Celestial Church of Christ, which was founded in 1947 in Benin by Samuel Biléou Oshoffa and has spread throughout Côte d'Ivoire since 1975.

Among the major Christian churches (Catholic, Methodist, Harrist), there has been a long tradition of cooperation, understanding, and hospitality, particularly within leadership circles. Côte d'Ivoire is noted for having established a Ministry of Cults to maintain harmony among all religions.

The number of Roman Catholics and members of African Instituted Churches has nearly tripled since 1970. There has also been a significant increase in the number of Christians who identify themselves as Charismatics*. According to 2005 estimates, Christians comprise 20–30% of the population, Muslims 30–40%, and indigenous religionists 25–40%. Migrants (one-third of the population) are estimated to be 70% Muslim and 20% Christian. Such statistics, however, are as fluid as the boundaries between African* Religion and Christianity or Islam. Syncretism* and inculturation* are challenges or opportunities for Christian churches. Moreover, since the beginning of the North–South civil war in 2002, religious positions have become entwined with political struggle.

Statistics: Population (2000): 14.8 million (M). Christians: 4.7 M, 32% (Roman Catholics, 2.2 M; members of African Instituted Churches, 1.34 M; Protestants, 0.8 M); African Religionists, 5.5 M, 38%; Muslims, 4.4 M, 30%. (Based on *World Christian Encyclopedia*, 2001.)

FRANÇOIS ROSSIER

Council, Synod, an assembly of bishops convened to regulate doctrine or discipline. "Council" (derived from Latin) and "synod" (derived from Greek) have the same meaning, but the former term is often applied to ecumenical* councils and, in the West, to gatherings of bishops representing the entire Roman Catholic Church (listed by their location, e.g. Vatican* II). The early councils, especially in the West, followed the procedures of the Roman Senate and city councils. The term "synod" is usually used for regional or less solemn gatherings of bishops in the Roman Catholic Church and in autocephalous* Orthodox* churches, and of representatives or delegates in Protestant churches – for which, in several cases, "synod" is also the designation of a regional level of administration.

Counsels of Perfection, not binding on all Christians, but rather advice to those who have the gifts of grace* necessary for complete dedication to God (especially poverty*, chastity*, obedience*). **See also MONASTICISM CLUSTER: MONASTIC VOWS; VOWS.**

Counter Reformation, the repressive, anti-Protestant measures of the Roman Catholic Church (e.g. in Spain*) following the Council of Trent* (meeting in three periods between 1545 and 1563). It is best understood as part of the broader Catholic* Renewal.

Courtly Love. The tradition of romantic love that developed in the 12th c., expressed in the poetry of the Provençal *troubadours*, the French *trouvères*, the German *Minnesänger*, and Dante*. It exalted the "lady," expressed emotions of longing and self-denial, and encouraged genteel manners and "chivalrous" behavior toward women. While it had some connections with the Albigensian* Movement, it was also promoted among Roman Catholic clergy (especially Andreas Capellanus, Andrew the Chaplain); it stimulated scholastic debate over the nature of love*, especially whether it is self-seeking or self-denying; and it influenced the language of Christian devotion and spirituality, especially among the Beguines*.

Covenant (Heb *berit*), biblical covenants that originated as political treaties. Their ratification by a slaughtered ass among Hittites gave rise to the language of "cutting a *berit*," preserved in the Bible. The two main types of Hittite treaties, suzerainty–vassal and parity, consisted of (1) historical prologue, (2) stipulations (what each party commits itself to doing), (3) provision for deposit and reading, (4) witnesses. (5) blessings and curses, and (6) ratification.

The P source in the Pentateuch* mentions covenants between God and Noah*, Abraham*, and Moses*, each sealed with a visible sign (rainbow, circumcision, Sinaitic legislation). Another tradition refers to a covenant with David*, its sign being a scepter. Among ordinary people, covenants were often broken. The divine promise to Abraham was distorted into a concept of privilege, leading Amos* to insist that election* was a call to assume responsibility toward others and leading Jeremiah* to prophesy a new* covenant of flesh and blood, a responsive heart-mind to replace one of stone, the Decalogue. The checkered history of Israel gave rise to various groups who considered themselves the true people of the covenant. Outside mainstream Judaism, Covenanters withdrew to the vicinity of the Dead* Sea, while Christians saw themselves as recipients of Jeremiah's promised new heart and called their sacred writing *kaine diatheke*, the new covenant (later Latinized as "testament"). **See also** ELECTION; NEW COVENANT.

JAMES L. CRENSHAW

Covenanters, Covenanting. Scottish Protestants often bound themselves by oaths to defend their religion, first against the papacy, then against bishops and royal supremacy, finally against patronage*. The first covenants were drawn up during the reign of Mary (1556, 1557, 1559). The King's Confession of 1581, designed to prevent a revival of Catholicism by excluding all doctrines not in accord with the Scots* Confession (1560), was signed by James VI and by the clergy and many of the people (reaffirmed, 1590, 1595; incorporated into the National* Covenant, 1638). The Solemn* League and Covenant (1643) sought to establish Presbyterianism in Scotland, England, and Ireland (accepted by the Westminster* Assembly and Parliament). Later Covenanters resisted attempts to impose episcopacy on Scotland. With the removal of the Stuart regime (1688), the "Cameronians" dissented from the Revolution Settlement (1689–92) because it did not require the Church of Scotland to adhere to the National Covenant and the Solemn League and Covenant. Their Reformed Presbyterian Church refused to participate in any government that failed to acknowledge, by covenant, the "crown rights" of Jesus Christ as head of both church and state. In the USA, the Reformed Presbyterian Church similarly objected to a constitution that did not acknowledge God and Christ.

Cranmer, Thomas (1489–1556), England's most prominent early reformer. Born in Nottinghamshire, he studied and taught at Cambridge University. Archbishop of Canterbury from 1533, he facilitated Henry VIII's marriage to Anne Boleyn. Though closely allied with Thomas Cromwell* in religious reform, he continued to enjoy Henry's esteem despite Cromwell's execution (1540) and conservative hostility. He spearheaded Edward VI's Protestant reforms, including two English Books* of Common Prayer (1549, 1552), his lasting memorial being their sonorous prose. Judged a traitor by Mary's* government (1553) for supporting Jane Grey's royal succession, he was convicted of heresy* (1554). Just before his burning in Oxford, he dramatically recanted his earlier abject return to Catholicism.

DIARMAID N. J. MACCULLOCH

Creatianism, the theory that each soul* is newly created by God, either at conception or at some stage in the development of the body. Alternatives are preexistence* and traducianism*.

Creation. Christians commonly affirm, following Gen 1, that God created the heavens and the earth. God's creation of the world is first among the acts of God recounted in the ecumenical creeds*, and Christians often express such a belief in the routine course of worship, e.g. in the thanksgiving portions of eucharistic* prayers or when renewing baptismal vows. Beliefs about creation are clearly important, then, to Christians, but that does not mean their sense is equally clear. Among the questions in dispute are the following:

1. Does God's creation of the world refer specifically to the world's origins, in ways that might bring Christian belief into conflict with scientific descriptions of how the universe began? Many Christian theologians believe, to the contrary, that the world is God's creation whether the world had a beginning and whatever its manner of origination. To say the world is created is

to say that the world exists in dependence on God, and this relation of dependence holds, however the world began, and even if the world has no beginning and always existed.

2. Did God create from something or nothing? Creation ex nihilo has been the dominant Christian view, but many theologians now argue that this view distorts the biblical record and is impossible to square with contemporary understandings of natural processes. If God works on or with something that God does not create, does that mean, however, that there are limits to God's power and therefore to Christian hopes for the world's future?
3. Does God create everything? If so, how can one account for evil in the world? Most theologians distinguish sharply between the way God is responsible for the good as its creator and the way God is involved in evil (e.g. by merely permitting it or maintaining in existence those solely responsible for their own sinful acts). But how can one make such a distinction without compromising the common claim of the universal extent of God's creative work?
4. Finally, if God creates ex nihilo the world alone and by fiat, is not this an unhealthy model for human imitation, a charter for absolute human power? Theologians hoping to deflect this charge must provide some alternative account of what is at stake in the creation ex nihilo, e.g. not power so much as a concern for the universal beneficence of a God intimately related to absolutely everything. KATHRYN TANNER

Creation, in the Bible. There are several distinct creation stories in the Bible, including Gen 1:1–2:3; Gen 2:4–25; Isa 40–55 (especially 40–48); various Psalms (e.g. 8, 19, 104); Prov 8:27–29; creation by God as a potter (Isa 29:15–16, 45:9–13; Jer 18; Rom 9:20–21); and creation by the Word (Gen 1; Ps 33:9, 148:5; John 1:1–3; Heb 11:3; 2 Peter 3:5–6). With this diversity of biblical views, one should not be surprised to find through the centuries a diversity of Christian understandings of the Apostle Creed's statement about God as "creator of heaven and earth." **See also** METAPHYSICS AND CHRISTIAN THEOLOGY.

Creation, Ecology, and the Orthodox Church. Creation, the Orthodox believe, is a manifestation of God's love for humankind and all creatures; creation should be in harmonious relation with the Creator. Thus rather than being either servants or rulers of creation, humans should approach creation as priests and ministers. Created in the image and likeness of God, they offer back to God with love what is given to them with love. With this ministerial attitude, creation will survive. Indeed, through the risen Lord, creation can enter into eternal life. The liturgical life and ascetic* practices of the church teach us to respect rather than exploit the material world. Consequently, for the past generation, the Orthodox Church has consistently emphasized the urgent need to address the ecological crisis and has taken concrete steps to do so, e.g. by calling for the use of environmentally conscious agricultural methods in monasteries and by establishing September 1 as the Day of Creation. The Ecumenical Patriarchate initiated church services, conferences, encyclicals, and books for the preservation of creation. The ecological crisis is to be viewed in terms of the Fall and sin*; it calls all humans to repentance (*metanoia*), to a change of mind, abandoning purely utilitarian attitudes to adopt a ministerial attitude toward creation. **See also** CLIMATE CHANGE; ECOLOGY AND CHRISTIANITY CLUSTER. TAMARA GRDZELIDZE

Creationism. Historically, creationists have been distinguished by their belief that God created each and every thing, rather than by any contingent statement as to how this was achieved. Since Darwin's* day, however, an increasing number of so-called creationists, rejecting evolution as a creation method, have campaigned to equate creationism with their belief in the miraculous origin and fixity of living "kinds" according to Genesis. This narrow creationism – based mainly in the USA, where populist values have long shaped biblical* interpretation and many Evangelical* Christians readily call themselves fundamentalists* – at first accepted modern geological evidence of an ancient earth. But "old-earth creationism" (from the 1920s) was challenged by a minority of Evangelical exegetes and scientists who believed a yearlong catastrophic global flood, according to Genesis, had reshaped the earth's crust and lent it the appearance of great age. "Young-earth creationism," positing that the earth is only some tens of thousands of years old, took root among believers, some of whom acquired formal technical and scientific credentials. An early-19th-c. doctrine almost unknown among professional geologists and biblical scholars became the basis of creationists' efforts (1970s and 1980s) to mandate the teaching of "creation science" in US state schools. After judicial defeats, supporters restored some of creationism's historic scope by seeking to rally creationists and Evangelical evolutionists behind the teaching of "intelligent design*."

JAMES E. MOORE

Creation Theology in Scandinavia emphasizes how God's redemptive* work rests on God's prior work in and for the creation. Grundtvig* (19th c.) adopted the phrase "first a human, then a Christian" as expressing this point. G. Wingren and K. E. Løgstrup independently developed (mid-20th c.) an understanding of creation based on concrete phenomena in human life that are positive preconditions for a full theology. The concept of "creation" refers a) to God's works for which redemption takes place and b) to the basis for self-expression of all human life (eventually made explicit by philosophical analysis). This integrative approach is viewed as an alternative to a revivalist* Pietistic theology that fails to affirm the inherent qualities of God's creation after the Fall*. It is important for the Scandinavian national churches, as it partly serves to recognize and affirm the religious stance of their members, despite low regular church activity.

JAN-OLAV HENRIKSEN

Crèche (French, "crib"), representation of the infant Jesus' crib, as well as various figures from the birth narratives; initiated by Francis* of Assisi (1223).

Creeds, Symbols, and Confessions of Faith. A creed is a statement beginning "I believe" (Lat *credo*). The name "symbol" was given to the Apostles' Creed, shared by believers in different localities, by analogy with the tokens ("symbols") shared by contracting parties.

A "confession of faith" is similar in character to a creed. But "creed" has come to connote a fixed statement of doctrine; confession, a statement that consciously speaks from and to its time. The Reformed* churches proclaim themselves to be confessional but not credal. Congregational* and Baptist churches leave it to each congregation to write its own confession of faith; statements of any bodies broader than the congregation are understood to be expressions of consensus, not requirements.

Creeds and confessions fill a variety of functions, and thus take different forms. The oldest, in rough historical sequence, are (1) liturgical and catechetical, (2) controversial, and (3) irenic, or church-uniting. The Reformation brought forth new genres of confessional statements: (4) reforming, (5) apologetic, and (6) church-founding.

Liturgical and Catechetical Function. The first of the creeds was the Apostles' Creed or Old Roman Symbol (mid-2nd c.), developed in Rome as a baptismal confession. Used by Irenaeus* (c180) as a convenient summary of the apostolic proclamation, when both the NT canon* and the doctrines of the church were still in formation, it stated the current consensus of the Western Church. The wording varied among local churches. The Apostles' Creed continued to be used in the West for purposes of catechesis* or instruction, first for adult converts, then for all baptized persons as they matured. It has remained the most widespread summary of Christian doctrine for the laity in the West.

Controversial Function. The Apostles' Creed was expanded in the Eastern churches to declare the preexistence* of the second person of the Trinity before the Incarnation*. Adapting the Eastern creeds, the first two ecumenical* councils added language that gave greater definiteness to the doctrine of the Trinity*: the Nicene* Creed (325) and the Niceno*-Constantinopolitan Creed (381). While the latter came to be used in worship (after 489 in the East, after 589 in the West), these creeds originally functioned as doctrinal standards to which bishops and the universal church must conform – hence the rise of "dogma*" (here meaning a "decree" by church authority). The so-called Athanasian* Creed is widely used, for both liturgical and doctrinal purposes, in the Catholic, Anglican, and Lutheran traditions.

Since councils* were usually called to resolve doctrinal disputes, they often made more condemnatory than positive statements. In interpreting creeds emerging from such councils, it is necessary to understand what doctrines were being opposed, and on what grounds. During the Middle Ages, decrees of popes and councils responded to various issues of doctrine and practice, especially the sacraments, and various so-called heresies* were condemned, especially those of the Cathars*, the Waldenses*, Wyclif*, and Hus*.

Irenic Function. Official statements of doctrine became longer and more complex as the Catholic Church engaged in dialogue with the Eastern Orthodox churches. This was an irenic setting in which it was appropriate to emphasize

Creeds, Symbols, and Confessions of Faith

what the two traditions shared. The first comprehensive statements of Catholic doctrine were those adopted by the Councils of Lyons (1274) and Florence* (1439) for reunion with the Greek Orthodox Church. The latter council adopted similar statements intended to achieve reunion with the Armenians* (1439) and the Syriacs*, Copts*, and Ethiopians* (1442).

Reforming Function. The Reformation* occasioned even more extensive doctrinal statements, since the Reformers agreed with the classic doctrines expressed in the creeds but challenged many practices and beliefs that had gained currency in the Middle Ages. Since they looked beyond church doctrine to the authority of Scripture*, against which all ecclesial statements must be tested, they called their statements "confessions of faith," intended to express their best understanding of what was revealed, while acknowledging its provisional character.

The first statements with a reforming function were written in German principalities and Swiss cities (1520s). But the classic reforming confessions were drawn up in England: the Forty*-two Articles (1553), the Thirty*-nine Articles (1562), and the Westminster* Confession (1643–47), all intended for the reform of the Church of England.

Apologetic Function. When reform movements came under attack, it was necessary to take an apologetic or defensive stance. The Augsburg* Confession (1530) was presented to Charles* V and the Reichstag. The Second Helvetic* Confession was presented to this same body (1566) when the Reformed churches in Germany were under attack from Catholics and Lutherans. Calvin's* *Institutes* also had this function, being addressed to the king of France during a period when the Reformed church was on the defensive.

The Reformation had begun as an attempt to reform the Catholic Church (a theme of Conciliarism* from 1380 to 1417). For several decades, there was hope that an ecumenical council would be convoked by the emperor; instead, the pope called the Council of Trent* (1545–63), which rejected most Protestant doctrines, clarified Catholic doctrine, and reformed a number of practices. The Roman Catechism of 1566 summarized Catholic doctrine in a comprehensive way.

Church-Founding Function. When reform of the Catholic Church was no longer thinkable, Protestants wrote confessions of faith with a church-founding role. Reformed confessions were adopted in France (1559), Scotland (1560), and Belgium (1561), along with Presbyterian forms of government. The separate existence of the Lutheran Church in Germany is dated from the Peace of Augsburg (1555) and even more decisively from the Reichstag of 1566. The Lutheran Book of Concord*, which excluded Reformed and Melanchthonian* perspectives, took final form in 1580. There were proposals to prepare a common confession for the Reformed churches as well, but instead a *Harmony of the Confessions* was published (1581). Lutheran controversialists depicted it as a weak substitute, while the Reformed responded that it is of the nature of confessions to speak from their time and place and that harmony is preferable to uniformity.

Controversial Function. As the Protestant churches developed internal disputes, controversial confessions arose. The most dramatic of these came with the Synod of Dort*, when the Dutch Reformed Church condemned the doctrines of the Arminians* and insisted on predestination* and limited atonement*.

Which Statements Are Definitive? The Oriental Orthodox* churches have regarded the statements of the first three ecumenical* councils – those of Nicaea* (325), Constantinople* (381) and Ephesus* (431) – as the only authoritative statements of faith. The Eastern Orthodox churches have regarded the statements of the seven ecumenical* councils – adding Chalcedon* (451), Constantinople* II (553), Constantinople* III (680–81), and Nicaea* II (787) to the first three – as authoritative. The *Orthodox Faith* of John* of Damascus was regarded as a convenient summary. Contacts with both Catholics and Protestants made it necessary, however, to differentiate the Orthodox perspective from that of these two Western traditions, because Orthodox theology is experiential and doxological rather than doctrinal (see Orthodox Churches, Eastern, Cluster: Introductory Entries). The confession of Cyril Lucaris* (1629) was widely condemned for its Calvinism*. To replace it, confessions were written by Peter Mogila* (1638) and Dositheus* of Jerusalem (1672).

During the Enlightenment* and up to the 21st c., doctrinal orthodoxy fell on hard times. There were strong sentiments against "strict subscription" to the confessions of the churches, justified by the Reformation principles that "God alone is the Lord of the conscience"; and all persons have the responsibility to interpret Scripture for themselves. Romanticism* and idealism* (19th c.) put doctrine on a different footing as an expression of religious intuitions. Historical study also gave a better understanding of the formation of existing doctrines. And as old disputes receded in importance and the gospel came to be understood in new ways, reformulations were often proposed. New confessions of faith were adopted, usually with the purpose of summarizing Christian doctrine in a brief but comprehensive way, using language that would be relevant to 19th- and 20th-c. contemporaries.

In the Roman Catholic tradition, this kind of updating has been done through catechisms*. The Second Vatican* Council decided against any universal catechism in favor of contextual catechisms directed toward adults. Yet the Catechism of the Catholic Church (1992) was prepared under Pope John Paul II to supply a "point of reference" for the national catechisms.

Church-Uniting Statements. The irenic function of doctrinal statements is once again seen in the union of Protestant churches, especially those growing out of the British traditions, resulting in the United Church of Canada* (1925), the Church* of South India (1941), and similar "united" or "uniting" churches in Ceylon, Ghana, Zambia, New Zealand, and Australia. Their "basis of union" typically acknowledges the faith and ministries of all the uniting churches and seeks participation from all of them in future ordinations.

Another approach to the diversity of creeds and confessions was taken by the World* Council of Churches in 1948, when it offered membership to all churches that confess Jesus Christ as "God and Savior," leaving all other matters to mutual discussion, which has led to further doctrinal agreements, especially the Lima* Declaration.

Othodoxy and Orthopraxy. Finally, concerns for doctrinal "orthodoxy" have been joined by concerns for "orthopraxy"* in the Christian life and its relation to social, economic*, and political* structures. This is seen in the Social* Gospel and Christian Socialism* (19th c.) and in Liberation* theologies (20th c.). The Confession of 1967 of the United Presbyterian Church in the USA applied the biblical theme of reconciliation to the racial and economic issues of the time; the Presbyterian-Reformed Church of Cuba (1977) related the Christian tradition to a revolutionary situation. EUGENE TESELLE

Cremation, burning the body of one who has died; the ashes are sometimes stored in a church's columbarium*. Now permitted in Western churches, it was initially prohibited because it seemed to contradict hope in the resurrection*.

Crisis Theology, or theology of crisis, was a school of theological methodology that emerged in Germany* in the aftermath of World War I, particularly during the 1920s. Key figures included Friedrich Gogarten, Rudolf Bultmann*, and Paul Tillich*, for whom the prevailing cultural and political crises were deemed to have determinative theological significance. Karl Barth* has often been included within this movement, largely because his 1922 commentary on Romans is replete with the word "crisis." However, the crisis of which Barth spoke was not the political calamity facing Germany, but the dialectic of judgment* and grace* revealed always anew in the Word of God.

MARK R. LINDSAY

Croatia. Historically the Croats and the Serbs have been at the crossroads of Eastern and Western, Byzantine and Roman, Christianity since the 4th-c. division of the Roman Empire, reinforced by the Great* Schism (1054).

The beginnings of Christianity in the region of Western Illyricum, the Roman provinces of Dalmatia and Panonia, are still obscure, although Rom 15:19 and 2 Tim 4:10 claim that this area was evangelized in the apostolic era. The Croats, Slavs who migrated and settled the present area (7th c.), were gradually Christianized (7th–9th c.) by Frankish, Roman, and Byzantine missionaries (respectively, from the north, west, and south) – a diversity that contributed to subsequent political, cultural, and religious tensions.

Croatia, united under King Tomislav (925), became for the first time an independent country, reaching its zenith (11th c.) just before submitting to Catholic Hungary. Croats came under the Hapsburgs in 1527 as part of the larger European defense against the Ottoman Turks, being named "bulwark of Christianity" (*antemurale christianitatis*) by Pope Leo X. They were reinforced by many Eastern Orthodox Serbs who had been invited to settle in its southwestern region. Thus predominantly Catholic and shielded from the Reformation, Croatia gained a considerable Serb Orthodox minority, a source of ethnoreligious tension leading to atrocities during World War II and the recent Croatian war for independence.

At the end of World War I (1918), Croatia became part of the Kingdom of Serbs, Croats, and Slovenes (renamed Yugoslavia* in 1929). Following the German invasion (1941), the pro-Nazi "Independent State of Croatia" was created, and after World War II, Croatia was incorporated into Tito's Yugoslavia. During the Communist rule, religion was seriously repressed and many clergy, including the archbishop of Zagreb, Alojzije Stepinac, made cardinal by Pius XII and beatified by John Paul II during the second of his three extraordinary visits to Croatia, were convicted of treason.

Croatia is the only Slavic country in the Western Christian tradition that preserved the Old Slavonic liturgical language (originating with the 9th-c. "apostles of the Slavs," Cyril* and Methodius). Protestants from Germany, where the Croatian Matthias Flacius* Illyricus became famous for his theological writings, produced the first translation of Scripture and other Christian books in the Croatian language. Today, owing to Croatia's joint history with Bosnia*, Muslims are the third-largest religious grouping in the country. Although religious freedom in present-day Croatia is legally ensured, strong identification of ethnicity, culture, and public life with the Catholic Church makes the lives of ethnic and religious minorities tenuous. **See also HISTORY OF CHRISTIANITY CLUSTER: IN EUROPE: THE BALKANS.**

Statistics: Population (2000): 4.5 million (M). Christians, 4.3 M, 95% (Roman Catholics, 4 M; Orthodox, 0.2 M); Muslims, 0.06 M; nonreligious, 0.2 M. (*Source*: 2001 census.)

PETER KUZMIC

Cromwell, Oliver (1599–1658), of minor Huntingdonshire gentry, led Parliament to victory against King Charles I during the English civil war. He crushed rebellion in Ireland (1649) and Scotland (1651). As commander-in-chief of the army, he dominated the government after Charles's execution and ruled England as lord protector (1653–58). Deeply pious, Cromwell saw himself as an instrument of Providence. He supported liberty for all Protestant consciences, vigorously promoted the gospel, and negotiated for the return of Jews to England. A biographer called him "God's Englishman"; no English ruler was more firmly convinced of his and his country's divine mission.

ROBERT MICHAEL ZALLER

Cross, Sign of, Christians have traced the cross on their foreheads at least since the 4th c. as a private act of sanctification and to ward off the devil* (see Ransom), as well as during the liturgy. After the 4th c., the cross was traced on the breast, from right to left (Eastern churches) or from left to right (Western churches).

Cross and Crucifix. Both symbols denote Christ's crucifixion. The plain or empty "cross" refers to the Crucifixion, while pointing to the Resurrection; the crucifix, a cross with Christ's body affixed to it, focuses on the Crucifixion in and of itself.

Cross and Crucifixion. Jesus' crucifixion under Pilate is a historical fact, supported by Christian, Jewish, and Roman sources. A quintessentially Roman form of execution, crucifixion was noted for its heinous social and psychological consequences. Executed publicly, naked, denied burial, and left as carrion, the crucified attracted vicious ridicule. Roman procedures varied, but typically included a flogging, with victims carrying their own crossbeams to the site of execution, where they were bound or nailed to the cross with arms extended or raised up. Variations in the way victims were crucified served as sadistic entertainment and prolonged life for maximum deterrent effect.

From the outset, interpretations of Jesus' crucifixion differed. Generally, for Rome, it demonstrated Rome's intolerance of attempts to incite rebellion; for the Jerusalem leadership, according to the Gospels, the cross marked Jesus' demise as a religious deceiver and false prophet; and for Jesus, the cross was to be interpreted in relation to his mission, a process that, according to the Gospels, Jesus began while he anticipated his violent death. In the NT, the cross is the means by which God achieved salvation* – understood in various ways, e.g. as sacrifice*, as a demonstration of God's love, and/or as a way of conquering evil. As a pattern of discipleship, Jesus' Passion exemplified service and ennobled undeserved suffering for those who embody the ways of God in a world hostile to God. In addition, the cross is inescapably political: Jesus was crucified because he was a threat to Rome, and his acceptance of his death was a rejection of the politics of coercion and violence.

Attempting to explain how the cross saves, theologians subsequently developed numerous theories of atonement*. The cross also became the focus of Christian piety, evidenced in iconography*, including jewelry; anointing persons and objects by tracing the cross with oil; crossing oneself as an act of dedication or to avert evil; reports of stigmata* (marks resembling the wounds of the crucified Christ); during the medieval era, increasingly morbid dramatizations of Christ's Passion; and the practice of praying the stations of the cross. Identification with the crucified Christ has taken other forms, e.g. as a political weapon sanctioning submissive passivity on the part of others (e.g. the European colonization of Latin America) or as self-mortification (e.g. Opus* Dei). Identification with the cross is sanctioned not when it provides religious legitimation of oppression*, but when it serves as an instrument in the struggle against the politics of violence in the name of the politics of the crucified Christ. JOEL B. GREEN

Crowther, Ajai Samuel (1807–91), the first African Anglican bishop. A Yoruba (Nigeria) captured by slave traders (1820) and rescued by British naval forces from Portuguese traders during a transatlantic crossing (1822), he was relocated with other liberated slaves in Sierra* Leone. "Convinced of another worse state of slavery, namely that of sin and Satan," he converted to Christianity (c1825). After being educated at the first higher-education school in tropical Africa (the Christian Institution in Freetown), he taught in villages of liberated slaves while helping develop books to teach missionaries the Yoruba language. Following his ordination, he returned to Nigeria as part of a Church Missionary Society team of the Anglican Church (1842), promoting an indigenous African mission among the Yoruba. In 1864 he became bishop. **See also ANGLICANISM CLUSTER: IN AFRICA: EASTERN AND WESTERN AFRICA.**

Crozier, Crosier, bishop's staff, shaped like a shepherd's crook.

Crummell, Alexander (1819–98), African American theologian, born in New York, brought up as an Episcopalian. As a youth, he was introduced to biblical languages at the Oneida Institute and was ordained in the Episcopal Church, despite having been denied admission to the Episcopal Seminary. He received his bachelor's degree and mastered biblical Greek at Cambridge University (graduated 1853), then took up missionary work in Liberia. His sermons and addresses attempted to reconcile his fervent black nationalism with a Victorian, Anglocentric civilizing mission*. After returning to the USA (1872), he established St. Luke's Church in Washington, D.C. Crummell's theology was a typically American "Arminianized* Calvinism." A solid advocate of African American political rights, he gravitated toward High Church ritual because he was hostile to plantation religion, which he viewed as a slaveholder's conspiracy to undermine the moral and intellectual development of African Americans.

WILSON J. MOSES

Crusades, a series of military campaigns fought by "Latin" (Roman Catholic) Christians against peoples believed to be threatening Christian territory, Christian people, or Christianity itself. Crusades were waged against Muslims, other Christians, and "pagans" in medieval Western Europe (11th–16th c.).

Crusades were generally initiated by the pope. The participants took the religious vow to join a crusading expedition, wore a distinctive badge (a cross), and believed that their participation replaced all penance* due for their confessed sins. Thus the Crusades were very much like pilgrimages* in their spiritual purpose. Both men and women could take the Crusade vow, but starting in the early 13th c., noncombatants were encouraged to make a monetary donation, purchasing an "indulgence*" instead of fulfilling their vow in person.

The Crusades developed from a Western Christian discourse of holy war* rooted in the OT. They derived from the European Christians' defensive wars against Muslim invasions of Southern Europe (8th–9th c.) and the successful expeditions to free the Iberian Peninsula and North Africa (second half of the 11th c.). The Byzantine emperor Alexius Comnenus appealed to the West (1095) to help him recapture Anatolian territories lost to the Muslim Seljuk Turks. At the Council of Clermont (1095), Pope Urban II initiated a military expedition, which recovered former Byzantine territories and also captured Jerusalem*, an important focus of Christian pilgrimage. By the 1130s, the Muslim ruler Zenghi of Mosul used the Islamic concept of *jihad* (holy war) to unite his subjects against the Latin Christian invaders, though it was not until 1291 that they were finally driven from Palestine.

Giles Constable identifies four scholarly definitions of "crusade": (1) any Christian religious war fought for God (*generalist view*); (2) a religious undertaking for the masses and/or for warriors (*popularist view*); (3) military-religious expeditions to recover or defend Jerusalem (excluding other expeditions) (*traditionalist view*); and (4) any military campaign recruited and organized by the pope (*pluralist view*).

The Crusades did not succeed in holding Jerusalem, although the crusaders did conquer the Iberian Peninsula, retard the Ottoman advance into the Balkans, ensure that the Baltic States' interests would be oriented toward the West, and provide an ideological basis for Latin Christian expansion into the New World.

In the medieval period, Muslims regarded the Crusades as less threatening to Islam* than the conflict between Sunnis and Shi'ites or Mongol invasions. It was not until Western imperialism impinged on the Islamic world (19th and 20th c.) that Muslim historiographers took interest in the Crusades, depicting them as the cause of modern-day Christian–Muslim conflict in the Middle East. **See also HOSPITALLERS; MILITARY ORDERS; TEUTONIC KNIGHTS.**

HELEN J. NICHOLSON

Crypto-Calvinism, a term used by opponents of Melanchthon* to condemn his teachings concerning the Eucharist*. For the sake of unity with the Reformed* churches, he merely asserted that Christ's Body and Blood are "truly exhibited" by the elements, and did not affirm that the unworthy actually receive Christ's Body and Blood.

Cuba. The sharp tension between the Christian churches (except for Presbyterians and Pentecostals) and the state in Cuba that arose because of the nationalization of education* in 1961 remains, although it has eased up.

The missions of the Franciscans* (1511), Dominicans* (1515), Jesuits (1566), and other orders introduced Catholicism on the island. The Diocese of Santiago de Cuba was established in 1522 (archdiocese, 1803), and that of La Havana in 1787 (archdiocese, 1925). In Santiago there is a national sanctuary where the faithful venerate the image (found in 1604) of the Virgin of Charity, also called Virgin of El Cobre, declared the patroness of the Republic of Cuba in 1916. The Catholic Church has devoted much attention to educational institutions, serving the middle and upper classes.

A few Anglicans arrived in Cuba in 1741. From 1880 onward, Methodist, Episcopal, and Baptist communities were established; in 1884 a Presbyterian Church was founded. The Spanish-American War of 1898 challenged the Catholic dominion and led to the Americanization of Cuban Protestantism. Many North American Protestant missions, including Seventh-day* Adventists, and then Pentecostal* churches were established. Many Protestant educational facilities, serving primarily the middle and upper classes, were established.

After the defeat of Batista's dictatorship (1952–59), the churches were sympathetic to the revolution led by Castro. But the Law of June 6, 1961, which stated that education was to be public and free, and decreed the nationalization of all private centers of learning, brought all the churches into conflict with the state and many missionaries left the island. Only the Pentecostal and Presbyterian churches, though few in number, generally welcomed the revolution. Since 1968 the Catholic Church's position has evolved from anti-Communist to that of "detached critical observer," to openness, and to rapprochement with the government (visit of Pope John* Paul II, 1998). By contrast, the Ecumenical Council of Churches, uniting 14 Protestant churches, maintained throughout this period a positive dialogue with the revolutionary state and society. After 1959, Santeria, an Afro-Cuban religion, developed with the support of the Cuban Revolution. **See also CHURCH AND STATE RELATIONS: IN LATIN AMERICA: CUBA; RASTAFARI MOVEMENT.**

Statistics: Population (2000): 11.2 million (M). Christians, 5 M, 44.5% (Roman Catholics, 4.3 M; Protestants, 0.2 M; independents, 0.1 M; marginal Christians, 0.1 M); nonreligious, 4.1 M, 37%; Spiritists, 2 M, 17.9%. (Based on *World Christian Encyclopedia*, 2001.)

ARMANDO LAMPE

Cult (from Lat "veneration" or "worship"). The term refers to many forms of Christian worship of God or veneration of saints*. Often used as a sociological term for a small, dedicated movement with definite beliefs and practices, usually in response to a charismatic leader, and rejecting other forms of belief and practice. "Cult" in this sense most often has negative connotations, to suggest an unusual degree of syncretism, implying manipulation, fanaticism, and heterodoxy*. Yet syncretism* is a complex phenomenon that is actually an aspect of any religion, including Christianity, in the form of inculturation* or contextual* theologies. **See also SYNCRETISM.**

Culture Christianity, in Scandinavia and other secularized* settings, consists of a Christian-influenced worldview, a concept of the human person, and some basic ethical and existential values deriving from Christianity, together with a preference for using Christian-inspired language in important situations. For Culture Christians, most parts of their cultures are Christian, but others most certainly are not, nor are certain of their religious beliefs, if they have any. Culture Christianity does not arise by itself, nor is it sustained by itself. It presupposes the teaching and rituals of the churches (especially folk* and state churches) throughout the centuries and today. Culture Christians have no ways or rituals of their own for transmitting Culture Christianity to their children. Culture Christianity is the historical result of compulsory confirmation classes (e.g. in Denmark*, from 1736) or religious education. Also what is heard by those attending the rituals of the churches (baptisms, funerals, marriages, and feast days, especially Christmas and Easter) contributes to the upholding of Culture Christianity in the broader population. This prevalent situation in Scandinavia (Denmark*, Norway*, Sweden*) is also found in other secularized contexts (e.g. Bulgaria*) where Christianity is privatized: "I am religious in my own way."

HANS RAUN IVERSEN

CULTURE CLUSTER

1) *Introductory Entry*

Cultural Studies

2) *A Sampling of Contextual Views and Practices*

Culture and Biblical Studies
Culture and Christianity
Culture and Christianity in Eastern Orthodoxy
Culture and Christian Theology
Culture and Worship

1) Introductory Entry

Cultural Studies is a broadly defined scholarly field that draws from new forms of literary* criticism (emphasizing multiple readings over authorship), revisionist Marxist* critiques (with a fundamental suspicion of capitalist economies and deep engagement in the politics of culture and the social), and semiotics* and Lacanian psychoanalysis (underlining signs and representations that proliferate in all forms of media). Consequently, cultural studies is less a methodological discipline than a constellation of critical theories investigating all kinds of cultural practices and their multiple processes of circulation, contestation, negotiation, and accommodation at any one location or across the globe.

Cultural studies had a significant impact on the understanding of Christianity, through, e.g., its theoretical turns toward the material*, the ordinary, and the mass of ordinary believers (see Popular Christian Practices Cluster). Far from H. Richard Niebuhr's* definition of culture as human civilization characterized by essences and values and his interest in Christianity's distinctive place in culture, Kathryn Tanner appropriated the modern anthropological* conception of cultures as everyday life and thereby proposed a new theological agenda. An understanding of Christianity depends not only on abstract concepts and theories about the divine, but also on its material constitution in specific historical and social location and through processes of community formation and concrete religious practices, including the use and reception of symbols, rituals, and beliefs in everyday life. From this perspective, Christianity is as much a product of culture as it is a contributor to historical cultural formation; change and development in Christianity involve as much negotiation and consensus as contestation and disputes. Such an approach challenges the study of Christianity to distance itself from transcendental ideation of the divine good and to focus on a detailed examination of its diversified contextualized practices. Hence the primary sites for understanding Christianity cannot be traditional theology and biblical scholarship, but rather the spontaneity, contradiction, and conflicted daily practices of the Christian masses.

The turn to the material and the popular has put into question not only the subject matter but also the methodological assumption of studies of Christianity. Recent forms of biblical and theological scholarship begin to pay attention to the politics, discursive formation, and power negotiation within and beyond the biblical and theological texts, by following newly emerged themes, such as gender, race, and postcolonial politics. Their aim is to expose Christianity's production and dissemination of hegemony in contemporary culture and to capitalize on the power of difference and resistance in the practices of the diverse Christian communities.

WONG WAI CHING (ANGELA)

2) A Sampling of Contextual Views and Practices

Culture and Biblical Studies. The word "culture" refers to the ways of life (material substance, norms of behaviors, values, and beliefs) that offer systems of meaning and explanation in the life-world of human society. Those who emphasize the social sciences view culture as a "complex whole" that makes up a society or its ways of life. Those who take the humanities approach understand culture as that which "cultivates" virtues and aims at fostering ways of life that lead to human flourishing.

Biblical studies, in its task of interpretation, involves both a methodology and a process of understanding the meaning of the biblical texts, of the authors, and of the readers. The relation between Scripture* and culture is a complex dialectic of values in which interpreters are both recipients, socially constructed persons (as heirs of culture and tradition), and hermeneutic agents – choosers of meaning, negotiators of values. The writer (who is the first reader) and the readers (i.e. interpreters) are co-producers of the meanings of the biblical text.

Cultural biblical studies include Scripture interpretations (reading Scripture through the lens of culture) and culture interpretations (reading culture through the lens of Scripture). "Multicultural" biblical study involves studying of the Bible from various cultural perspectives and resources. "Intercultural" biblical study involves comparative study of the Bible through the engagement of multiple cultural lenses. "Cross-cultural" biblical study has two meanings. Descriptively, the term refers to either (1) the use of cultural resources (e.g. the myths, philosophy, or concepts of the Sumerian, Egyptian, Jewish, or Greco-Roman world) by biblical authors to express their understanding of God or (2) the use of contemporary cultural resources (e.g. indigenous texts or cultural frameworks) by biblical interpreters as interpretive tools for reading Scripture. Prescriptively, cross-cultural study refers to either (1) the relevance of the text to *new* readers or (2) the ethical obligation of doing biblical interpretation across cultures and with a diverse community of interpreters sustained by the gifts of courage, authenticity, and humility.

Cultural biblical studies advocate contextual and indigenous interpretations of Scripture, noting that the Bible can speak to all cultures. While every interpretation may be legitimate and valid in its context, every interpretation is partial, yet its limitation is overcome by an ever-enlarging spiral process of cross-cultural (global) interpretation. The ambiguities of an interpretation and the contextuality of the interpreter, though culturally conditioned, are partially clarified and expanded through the process of global biblical interpretation.

YEO KHIOK-KHNG

Culture and Christianity. The relationship between Christianity and culture is a perennial problem. In his book *Christ and Culture*, H. Richard Niebuhr* analyzes the different ways in which this relationship has been conceived. His typology of five conceptions of this relationship is helpful for discerning how Christianity has been appropriated in various cultural contexts, taking Africa as the main example.

Christ against Culture. When Christianity is presented as an alternative to the existing culture, the prospective convert must choose either to follow Christ or to remain in the "evil world" or "paganism." This is a common conception when Christianity is viewed as an apocalyptic* or sectarian* movement, and also as Christendom*. Most missionaries from the North Atlantic to Africa presupposed this view, without acknowledging that for them Christianity was their own cultural and religious heritage. Since Christianity cannot exist in a cultural vacuum, any claim to preach the "pure gospel" is pretense. Christians are necessarily products of their cultures. When they go out to win converts, they do so from their own cultural backgrounds, using the languages and cultural tools they have accumulated through the process of socialization and education. In practice, portraying Christ as against culture puts in conflict the missionaries' culture with the prospective converts' culture and engenders serious social crisis. The proliferation of African* Instituted Churches is a manifestation of that crisis. Ngugi wa Thiong'o's novel *The River Between* portrays this crisis in the conflict between Joshua, a staunch Christian, and Muthoni, his daughter, who seeks wholeness in the traditional African way of life. Okot p'Bitek's long poems, *Song of Lawino* and *Song of Ocol* portray the same crisis. Kosuke Koyama's *Waterbuffalo Theology* describes a similar crisis in Thailand, where local people could identify with Christ, while the missionaries portrayed Christianity as a movement against their Buddhist tradition.

The Christ of Culture. On the opposite end of the spectrum, some Christians consider Christ to be the "Son of God" and "Son of man" who comes to affirm the cultural and religious heritage of peoples. The gospel is the fulfillment of culture, not a threat to it, as the Sermon on the Mount (Matt 5–7) exemplifies. Christ, the "man for all cultures," helps people discern and live according to God's will in the context of their respective cultural and religious traditions. Thus Christianity cannot be culturally uniform. The churches of the apostolic period presupposed this relationship between Christ and culture. Though Jewish-Christian and Hellenistic-Christian churches were in communion with each other, each retained its unique cultural particularity. One should then expect significant differences among, e.g., African, European, and North American churches.

Christ above Culture. Seeing Christ as above culture is a way of avoiding the conflict between the two preceding perspectives. Making a distinction between the heavenly and earthly cities (Augustine*), Christianity becomes transcendentalist, concentrating on "salvation*" in heaven and the future. In practice, such religiosity becomes irrelevant to the needs and demands of the present.

Christ and Culture in Paradox. Seeing Christ and culture as paradoxical is another way of avoiding the conflict: Christ is both identified with and contrasted with culture. The church is in the world, though it is not of the world – the view of the Protestant Reformation, especially Luther*. The problem is the lack of clarity regarding the circumstances under which Christ is portrayed in support of or against culture. Who has the authority to decide? In the modern Christian missionary enterprise, this authority has been vested in missionaries, who in general are biased in favor of their own cultures and against the cultures where they are guests.

Christ the Transformer of Culture. According to this perspective, Christ makes all things new (Rev. 21:5). Conversion is viewed as a challenge for converts to change their ways and become new beings. Paul's conversion is often cited as an example. He was transformed from a "persecutor" of Christians to a "perfector" of Christianity. Yet "transformation" presupposes that the earlier way of life is not abandoned; it is transformed through the adoption of new insights and commitments. In practice, the ingredients of transformation are most often taken from the culture of the missionaries; the resulting change is then comparable to any other process of acculturation*. In Africa most cultural changes under colonial rule and missionary tutelage have been of this kind. Thus many of the African elite blamed the modern Christian missionary enterprise for the cultural alienation that Africans have suffered under the pretext of modernization.

These five perspectives on the relationship between Christianity and culture are often simultaneously present in a given cultural context and/or a given denomination, causing tension and confusion and giving rise to factions. This is the case in Africa. Part of the cultural crisis in Africa arises from the lack of consensus among Christians and churches on the most relevant and constructive approach to reconciling Christianity and culture.

JESSE NDWIGA KANYUA MUGAMBI

Culture and Christianity in Eastern Orthodoxy. The Eastern Orthodox* proclamation and presentation of the eternal Christian gospel has penetrated and transfigured many cultures throughout the world during its 2000-year history. Eastern Orthodox have been very aware of the dangers of imposing a particular culture along with the gospel; thus, they have consciously sought to understand and respect different cultures from their first encounter. Pentecost clearly revealed how the Holy* Spirit infuses every language and culture, and can not only transform culture into a carrier of the Divine, but in fact even lift it up in creative and dynamic ways to discover new expressions and realities.

The Eastern Church's respect for other cultures can be seen during the first centuries in the ways the gospel penetrated and flourished outside the Greco-Roman world, as it helped develop cultures and peoples in Ethiopia*, Armenia*, and Egypt*. How this contrasts with the approach to culture of the Latin Church can be seen in the Latin clergy's attack of the Byzantine missionaries Cyril* and Methodius (9th c.) for their creation of a Slavonic alphabet and translation of liturgical services into the local language, which demonstrated their respect for the Slavic culture. A representative response of these Byzantine missionaries to the Latin belief in limited "sacred cultures" was (quoting Methodius addressing German representatives of the Latin Church): "Aren't you ashamed to accept only three languages [Latin, Greek, and Hebrew] and to say that the other languages are deaf and dumb?...We know that there are many people who read books and praise God in their own languages: the Armenians, the Persians, the Abasgi, the Iberians, the Sogdians, the Goths, the Avars, the Turks, the Khazars, the Arabs, the Egyptians, and others." Western Christianity came to have a similar respect for other cultures and languages in part through the Protestant Reformation seven centuries later, as well as through, e.g., the Jesuit* missionaries and the Second Vatican* Council (1960s).

The Orthodox theological approach when other cultures are encountered is first to try to understand and affirm the good that already exists within this culture and that coincides with the essence of the gospel message. Second, if any elements of the culture fundamentally stand against the spirit of the gospel, the Church rejects these. Finally, those rudiments of culture that are not seen as totally irreconcilable but in need of new meaning and understanding would then be "baptized" with the creative spirit of the gospel and transfigured into something new, while still holding onto the old structures of the culture. **See also MISSION CLUSTER: MISSION AND EASTERN ORTHODOXY.**

LUKE A. VERONIS

Culture and Christian Theology. Culture in a "high-culture" sense refers to intellectual or spiritual achievement in great works of art, literature, or philosophy. Culture in an anthropological sense refers to the meaning dimension of social action generally, to the beliefs, values, and symbols pervading a whole way of life. Whenever one talks about any human activity, with a recognition of its self-fashioning capacities and its socially and historically conditioned character, one is talking about culture in the latter sense.

Culture in this second sense is central to contemporary ways of doing theology. Culture figures in post-liberal theology's worry that the distinctiveness of Christian witness is diluted by modern culture, in liberal or revisionist theology's effort to show the meaning and relevance of Christianity for new cultural situations, and in Liberation theology's support for contemporary cultural trends toward greater equality and inclusion. Culture in all these theologies identifies the non-Christian "world" that theologians must either oppose or applaud. In the influential terminology of H. Richard Niebuhr*, opposition suggests "Christ against culture"; a more collaborative stance is that of a "Christ of culture."

Moreover, Christian theology is itself a cultural formation in this broad sense of culture, with a number of implications for how theology is done. First, the way theology is influenced by context can be talked about in cultural terms. Christian theology might arise, e.g., in and through the process by which elements of the wider culture are assimilated and revised from a Christian point of view. Second, theological disagreements can be understood in cultural terms, e.g. in terms of the degree to which a Christian way of life requires cultural uniformity, a shared body of basic beliefs and values. Third, thinking of theology in cultural terms allows one to identify theology primarily with beliefs and values that are ingredients in day-to-day Christian life. Rather than being a religious form of literature or philosophy, as the idea of high culture suggests, theology becomes the meaning dimension of socially significant Christian action. All Christian action has a theological dimension by virtue of the way it is permeated by a sense of what Christians believe and value. Theology as a specialized intellectual activity would simply bring this meaning dimension of everyday Christian life to more explicit critical reflection. Finally, thinking of theology in cultural terms foregrounds the practical consequences of Christian beliefs and values, the way those beliefs and actions are bound up with Christian social action. **See also** INCULTURATION CLUSTER. KATHRYN TANNER

Culture and Worship. The relationship between culture and worship has been popularly called "liturgical inculturation*" since the 1960s (from the anthropological term "enculturation"). Inculturation involves the dialogue between worship and the values, rites, symbols, and customs of the particular local culture. Some of those cultural elements are judged to be worthy of inclusion in the church's rites and are subsequently incorporated into worship for its enrichment. Although the term is relatively recent, the concept itself is as ancient as Christianity itself. The mere fact that there are four Gospels rather than one suggests something of a cultural need to adapt the Christian message accordingly to particular cultural contexts. From the earliest centuries, the history of Christian liturgy* has revealed an exchange between local culture and worship, especially evident in the Greco-Roman world, where there was much borrowing between Christian ritual and mystery* religions (e.g. Mithraism*). Consequently, there were similarities in liturgical language and initiation rites, post-baptismal catechetical formation, use of liturgical vesture*, and bodily posture. Yet those shared cultural symbols were interpreted differently according to each religious tradition and belief system.

The evolution of the Ambrosian*, Gallican*, Mozarabic*, and Roman rites offer further examples of inculturated worship; each contained strong cultural components of the context and region in which the rite emerged. The church's missionary* history reveals similar concerns of cultural adaptation. When missionaries arrived in any region, one of the first things they did was to translate* the Bible into the language of that region and advocate the use of local languages for worship. Thus the brothers Cyril* (d869) and Methodius (d885) promoted vernacular worship among the Slavic people, just as Jesuit* missionaries would do among the Chinese (17th c.). Vatican* II (1962–65) called for a recovery of the Catholic Church's missionary role in the world; its Constitution on the Liturgy, *Sacrosanctum Concilium* (Nos. 37–40), advocated the importance of culturally adapted worship, especially in mission lands. The 1988 "Roman Missal for the Dioceses of Zäire" (or Zairian/Congolese* Rite) offers a significant example within the post-conciliar church. The Lutheran World Federation's Nairobi Statement (1996) helps contemporary reflection on inculturation by highlighting four relationships of worship and culture: worship as transcultural or universal; contextual; countercultural; and cross-cultural.

KEITH F. PECKLERS, SJ

Cure of Souls. See CARE OF SOULS; PASTORAL CARE.

Cursillos de Cristiandad (Spanish), "short courses" conducted during a three-day weekend, preparing participants for "fourth-day"

activities in their everyday life. They began in Mallorca, Spain, in 1943–44 in preparation for pilgrimages to Compostela* and received ecclesial approval in 1949. Similar programs include Tres Dias, Via de Cristo, Walk to Emmaus, and Kairos, a program for prisoners.

Cyprian of Carthage, Thascius Caecilianus Cyprianus, bishop of Cathage and martyr; born into a noble family of Carthage in Roman Africa, raised in traditional religious practice, and apparently educated in rhetoric. He never married and no mention is made of siblings. He converted to Christianity (c246) and was elected bishop by the Christian community in Carthage (248). He became the leader of the bishops of Africa and guided the church through a series of crises. In January 250, Emperor Decius enjoined everyone to participate in a sacrifice to honor the deities guiding the Roman Empire. When the bishops stipulated that those who did not resist and "lapsed" must submit to lifelong penance*, some of the confessors* (who resisted the emperor's order) – anticipating martyrdom and immediate entrance into heaven – offered to win forgiveness for others directly from Christ. Rebellious clergy readmitted the sinners under the martyrs' patronage, thereby dividing the church against the bishops. The majority of the people remained loyal to the bishops, who then accepted back into communion all those who had lapsed but had subsequently submitted to public penance under their authority. This accommodation provoked a second schism of rigorists, who refused to readmit any apostates to communion.

Cyprian led the African bishops in developing three theological positions during this controversy: (1) that Peter and the apostles, as the original college of bishops, had received from Christ the power to forgive major sins committed after baptism; (2) that the unity of the church derives from God, so that the sin of attempting to divide it was equivalent to apostasy*; and (3) that only bishops legitimately established within the unity of the church could sanctify through baptism and the Eucharist. Thus no one could be saved outside the unity of the bishops' church (which they viewed as the one Catholic Church). This theology was the foundation for the Donatist* schism in the African Church after the Diocletian persecution, in the early 4th c. Cyprian was expelled from Carthage in the initial stages of the Valerian persecution, in the autumn of 257. He was tried by the Roman proconsul and executed on September 14, 258, the first martyr-bishop of the African church.

J. PATOUT BURNS

Cyprus. A large island in the Eastern Mediterranean. Its importance as well as its misfortunes derive from its proximity to Asia Minor, Palestine, and Egypt. Influenced by both Phoenician and Greek cultures, it also acquired a large Jewish population; it was the birthplace of Barnabas*, and some of the Christians persecuted with Stephen* fled to Cyprus (Acts 11:19–20). It was visited (c 45) by Paul, Barnabas, and Mark (Acts 13:4, 15:39). Barnabas was traditionally considered its first bishop, and his tomb and relics were later found (478). Epiphanius*, the 4th-c. "hammer of heretics," was archbishop of Salamis (later Konstantia). Cyprus became the first autocephalous* church by action of the Council of Ephesus* (431), making it independent of the patriarch* of Antioch*. The island came under moderate Islamic influence (653–965), then Byzantine (965–1191); during the Crusades*, it was under European control, Frankish (1191–1489) and subsequently Venetian (1489–1571), with Greek Orthodox bishops subordinated to the Roman Catholic hierarchy. After Turkish reconquest, the Orthodox Church alone was recognized, and the Christian community was considered a millet*, with the hierarchy responsible for its obedience. The island was administered by Great Britain after 1878 and gained independence in 1960. Archbishop Makarios, already considered the ethnarch in the tradition of the millet, became the first president. He created controversy by advocating union with Greece*, a policy opposed by the Turkish population. Turkey invaded (1974), and there was a transfer of populations. Today Turks occupy the northern third of the island and Greeks the southern two-thirds, although there is technically one Republic of Cyprus recognized by the United Nations (while a Republic of Northern Cyprus is recognized by Turkey alone).

Statistics: Population (2007): 790,000. Christians 82% (Orthodox, 78%; Maronites and other Christians, 4%); Muslims, 18%. (*Source*: Cyprus Demographic Report, 2007.)

EUGENE TESELLE

Cyril and Methodius, brothers born in Thessaloniki. Cyril (826–69; also Constantine-Cyril) was a teacher, and Methodius (c815–885) an official in Constantinople. On diplomatic missions to the Khazars (860) and Moravia* (862), they translated the Bible and the liturgy into a Slavic dialect ("Old Church Slavonic") and invented an alphabet (an earlier version of Cyrillic). When they were in Rome, the pope permitted them to celebrate the liturgy in Slavic. Cyril died in Rome; Methodius was appointed bishop of Moravia, but his work was blocked by German bishops. The brothers' influence in the Slavic world continued in Serbia*, Bulgaria*, Poland*, and Russia*.

Cyril of Alexandria (c378–444), a powerful Greek bishop and an eminent patristic theologian. His insightful christological writings emphasizing the dynamic force of the Incarnation* (deification* process, theosis*) had broad effects, influencing the Councils of Ephesus I (431) and II (449), of Chalcedon (451), and of Constantinople II (553).

A native of Egypt, Cyril attended his uncle, Archbishop Theophilus, at the Synod of the Oak (403), which deposed John* Chrysostom. After a violently contested election, Cyril became archbishop of Alexandria (412); his early administration was tumultuous. After 428 Cyril clashed with the archbishop of Constantinople, Nestorius*, who conceived of two centers of operation simultaneously present in the life of Christ: one human and one divine, with one sometimes predominating over the other. Cyril abruptly denounced this as heretical*, insisting that Jesus was wholly and completely divine, thus one single person (the "Miaphysite" view), and that person was God. Scholars wonder whether Cyril overinterpreted Nestorius's language about "two persons" when he understood it as a doctrine of two subjects. Cyril's reputation suffered after the 18th c. (he was depicted as "too much the politician"); very little of his work was translated into English. Yet recent studies have underscored how significant a theologian and exegete he is.

JOHN A. MCGUCKIN

Cyril of Jerusalem (c315–386), bishop of Jerusalem, best known for his "Catechetical Lectures," which provide insights into 4th-c. Christian instruction and initiation. For Cyril's early life and his career, which was punctuated by several exiles, we have only disparate sources, e.g. Epiphanius*, Jerome*, and the 5th-c. historian Sozomen.

After becoming bishop of Jerusalem (c349), Cyril, who defended Nicene Christology (see Nicaea, First Council of), was exiled a first time (357) for his opposition to Arianism* by Acacius, a strong "non-Nicene" Arian and bishop/metropolitan of Caesarea. Despite reservations about the term *homoousios* for its nonbiblical provenance, Cyril held a high, de facto Nicene, Christology; Gregory* of Nyssa witnessed to Cyril's correct christological confession before the Council of Antioch (379). Cyril attended the Council of Constantinople (381), where the Niceno*-Constantinopolitan Creed was once and for all ascertained to be the badge of Christian orthodoxy.

Cyril's "Catechetical Lectures" (c350), 18 Lenten sermons to the catechumens preparing for baptism*, deal with sin* and God's pardon; how the water* of baptism cleanses the body, and the Holy* Spirit cleanses the soul; true faith; and the Apostles'* Creed. The later five post-baptismal mystagogical* lectures provide fascinating details about the 4th-c. Palestinian liturgy. Cyril was probably the originator of "Holy Week," reliving the events day by day in their historic setting. PAUL CHANG-HA LIM

Czech Republic. The beginnings of church organization in the Czech Republic are associated with the Byzantine mission of Cyril* and Methodius (diocese established and the Old Slavonic liturgy approved by the pope, 869). But very little survived the fall of the Moravian Empire (906) and Christianity ultimately spread (in its Latin form) from the West (Bishopric of Prague, 973).

The successful development culminating during the reign of Charles IV (Archbishopric of Prague, 1344; Charles University, 1348) was interrupted by religious wars following the execution of popular preacher Jan Hus* in Constance (1415). The independent Hussite Church was formally recognized in 1436, with distinctive features of vernacular Mass and Communion "under both kinds" (both the loaf and the cup – hence the name Utraquists†). Several other churches emerged, of which the Bohemian* Brethren (also called Unitas Fratrum, Unity of the Brethren, 1457) became most prominent. Its contribution to learning and cultural life is most significant; its translation of the Bible (the Kralice Bible, 1579) was accepted as the standard in the Czech language.

The 16th-c. Reformation further contributed to religious pluralism (Lutheranism* in German-speaking areas, Anabaptists* and other radicals elsewhere), but the Hapsburg victory (1620) ultimately led to a ban on non-Catholic confessions. After several waves of exile – in the 1620s (including the exile of Comenius*, bishop of the Brethren, and his followers) and 1730s (exile of the Moravians*) – the country became predominantly Catholic. After passage of the Act of Toleration (1781), only 2% of population left the Roman Catholic Church.

While in the 19th c. most of the population remained Catholic, national leaders and intellectuals glorified the Hussite Movement and stressed the resistance against Germans and Rome as its legacy to the nation. This contradiction is understood by some to have been the starting point of the secularization of Czech society. The foundation of the independent Czechoslovak Republic (1918) strengthened this trend, when several Protestant churches based on the Hussite tradition were established.

The Communist regime in Czechoslovakia (1948–89) launched a severe antireligious campaign, marked first by open attacks on churches (show trials of church leaders, closures of monasteries, etc.), later by focusing on education and propaganda (religion as something irrational and old-fashioned compared with a rational and modern worldview).

A substantial part of Czech society today sees itself as secular* and antireligious. In 2001 only approximately one-third of the population declared a religious affiliation, but there are persisting doubts about these figures (reflecting the participants' common distrust of the census and the notion that religion is exclusively private). Other surveys suggest that many people seek the supernatural outside of traditional church structures ("believing with no belonging"), a reason for the stagnation of membership in traditional churches, in contrast to the relative growth of Charismatics and Jehovah's Witnesses. **See also** **JEROME OF PRAGUE; SLOVAK REPUBLIC.**

Statistics: Population (2001): 10.2 million (M). Religious affiliation, 1921: Roman Catholics, 82%; other Christians, 9.4%; Jews, 1.3%; atheists, 7.1%. 1950: Roman Catholics, 76%; other Christians, 16.3%; Jews, 0.1%; atheists, 7.2%. 1991: Roman Catholics, 39%; other Christians, 4.7%; others, 0.2%; without religious affiliation, 39.9%; unknown, 16.2%. 2001: Roman Catholics, 26.8%; other Christians, 2.9%; others, 2.5%; without religious affiliation, 59%; unknown, 8.8%. (*Source*: 2001 census.)

MARTIN ELBEL

D

Dalit Theology, an influential strand of Indian contextual* thinking, collectively reflects on the ongoing Christian activity of resisting oppression and advancing liberation among outcaste communities (Dalits) dehumanized under the comprehensive, contemporaneous, cumulative, and apartheid-like caste* system. The Indian Christian community consists predominantly of Dalits (and Adivasis*). Yet it was only beginning in 1981 that these oppressed communities became self-reflective participants in the development of Christian theology. Dalit theology derives from the effects of caste* oppression; it is a protest against the dehumanizing consequences of the long, weighty, and widespread subjugation of the Dalits by the caste communities. As a counter-theology (in contrast to other Indian Christian theologies developed since the early 1800s), it unveils the legitimizing role of traditional Hinduism* and resists the coopting predilection for inculturation* by Hindu-Christian theologies.

Dalit theology is remarkably original in its constructive contribution. It strives to collect and circulate Dalits' special knowledge about God, the world, and human beings. It reclaims for Indian Christian theology the Dalit outlooks, themes, motifs, and revelations from and about the Divine, received and preserved in media other than the written text. Because Dalits were forbidden access to the Hindu Vedas and their recitation in temples for fear that the Dalits would pollute the holy scriptures and pure Hindus, Dalits imaginatively used drums, dances, oral narratives, paintings, and sculptures to register and recall their sustaining and healing experiences with the Divine.

Deeply affected by the person of Jesus and passionately aligned with the liberating work of Christ, Christian Dalit theology is a specialized discipline that arises from reflection, by Liberation-identified Dalits and Dalit-identified Liberationists, on the interlocking of divine and human things that are relevant now and will affect the future of Dalit communities. Thus Dalit theology is based on the "pathetic" experience of specific Dalit communities, filtered through the inspirational person and work of Jesus Christ and integrated into the lives of all oppressed peoples in its goal of funding and finding life in all its fullness. As a contextual Liberation theology in India, it is collective and comprehensive in scope, humanizing in objective, profusely (even if naively) dependent on God for help and support, deeply rooted in Jesus' liberative teaching and practice, connected with the natural world of earth, wind, and water, and hopeful that life before death is both a gift from God and a right of all peoples.

SATHIANATHAN CLARKE

Dalmatic, knee-length vestment with wide sleeves and two stripes, used by deacons* during High Mass* and by bishops* on certain occasions.

Damian of Alexandria (d605), patriarch, theologian, 35th pope of Alexandria (578–605). Of Syrian origin (Edessa), he was contemporary with four Byzantine emperors, Justin II (565–78), Tiberius II (578–82), Maurice (582–602), and Phocas (602–10). A vigorous and reforming pope of the Coptic* Church, he revived the authority of his office, especially by disentangling the various strands that troubled his argumentative and factious church. He first had to deal with burning problems of an ecclesiastical and doctrinal nature with Antioch, becoming involved (c586) in a stormy controversy with Peter* of Callinicus, patriarch of Antioch (581–91), over a problem that arose during the tritheist controversy. Peter accused him of Sabellianism* because in refuting tritheism* he had declared that the characteristic properties of the divine persons, i.e. fatherhood, sonship, and procession, were the hypostases* themselves. Thereupon Damian accused his critic of tritheist sympathies. Damian claimed that the tradition stemming from the Cappadocian* Fathers legitimized the notion of the persons of the Trinity as "subsistent relations" and believed that tritheism must be refuted by a restatement, a "repristination," of the divinely inspired traditional teaching. He claimed that he was contributing to the clarification of patristic teaching.

RIFAAT EBIED

Damnation, the consciousness of bearing divine condemnation for eternity*. In one sense, damnation is simply existence in hell*. As compared with hell, however, "damnation" (from Lat *damnum*, "loss") emphasizes the pain of loss (absence from God) more than the pain of sense (endured physically). Augustine* speaks of a double damnation: in the present life and after death*. As all life is punitive, those who reject God suffer now. Then there is the interim period, when the disembodied soul* suffers alone. After the resurrection*, as Augustine says, the souls of the damned receive their flesh back "not to alleviate, but to aggravate" the suffering (*non ad beneficium, sed ad supplicium*). Damnation can also be the condition of those living but predestined for hell in theological systems like Calvin's* with double predestination*. Augustine regards the most severe punishment as exile from God (*Enchiridion* 112). Calvin concurs: it is "being estranged from all fellowship with God"; "those to whom the Lord will thus publicly manifest his anger will feel that heaven, and earth, and sea, all beings, animate and inanimate, are, as it were, inflamed with dire indignation against them, and armed for their destruction" (*Institutes* 3.25.12).

Damnation, like hell, is not only a threat, a deterrent, but also the worst conceivable fate. Death camps, gulags, and natural disasters evoke these theological terrors. Sickness, depression, and injustice can elicit a despair, a forsakenness, akin to damnation, a self-contraction so profound that one doubts God's presence and one's ability to escape hell. Cassian* called this "sadness" (*tristitia*), Luther* *Anfechtung*. This is the call *de profundis* (Ps 129 [130]), the "abyss" for Hadewijch* of Brabant, the pit of Dante's* *Inferno*, and the dark night of the soul in John* of the Cross. The return from the depths, a spiritual rebound, reverses the threat of despair. **See also** JUDGMENT; PURGATORY.

ALAN E. BERNSTEIN

Dance, already a part of religious ceremony at the time of the Paleolithic cave paintings, is mentioned in the OT in connection with Miriam* (Exod 15:20), David* (2 Sam 6:14, 22), and praise in the Temple (Ps 149:3). In Judaism dancing on the Sabbath, the Feast of Tabernacles, and the Day of Atonement continued, and in Hasidism dancing was encouraged.

In Greek theater, the chorus (*choros*, which originally meant "dance") was generally circular, with the leader in the center. Philo* says that the Therapeutae* engaged in song and dance; circular dance is mentioned in two Gnostic* texts, symbolizing the harmony of the original and restored creation*. Platonist philosophers likened the turning of the chorus toward the center to the circling of the heavens around the One or to the turning of distracted and fallen souls toward the One; among Neoplatonists and in Augustine*, conversion* (*epistrophe*) meant this positive "turning toward."

Dance came to acquire negative connotations because of its association with banqueting and lascivious stage plays. Usually excluded from worship and the sanctuary, dance was nevertheless associated with marriage* ceremonies, feasts held at the tombs of Christian martyrs, and with popular celebrations (e.g. in the West at Christmas*, Mardi Gras, and Carnival). Most 19th- to early-20th-c. Protestant missionaries forced indigenous people to give up their dance traditions as pagan*, idolatrous, or lascivious.

Nevertheless, religious dancing was encouraged in the USA by the Shakers* and at times by Pentecostal* and Holiness* groups. Since the late 20th c., it has commonly occurred in many Charismatic* and other churches in Africa, Asia, and Latin America (e.g. members of the congregation dance as they bring their offerings to the altar).

In North Atlantic mainline denominations, liturgical dance came to be performed after a more positive attitude toward the human body* developed (19th–20th c.) through the influence of Ruth St. Denis (1877–1968). Dance may be narrative (e.g. dancing the parable of the prodigal son), interpretive (interpreting Ps 23, the Lord's Prayer), thematic (portraying the creature before the Creator), or expressive of various religious feelings. The song "Lord of the Dance" (words by Sydney Carter, 1963, set to a Shaker hymn tune) brought the metaphor of dance into many hymnals.

The Second Vatican* Council, in its Constitution on the Liturgy, encouraged popular participation in worship with "acclamations, gestures, and bodily attitudes" as well as the adaptation of indigenous rites of passage.

EUGENE TESELLE

Dance of Death, originally a late medieval morality play featuring a dialogue between Death and all classes of human beings; subsequently, a visual representation of Death as a corpse or skeleton, leading all humans in a dance to the grave.

Daniel, Book of, belongs to the third division of the HB, the Writings, coming apparently too late to be ranged among the Prophets. Numerous allusions (especially Dan 11) to Antiochus

IV's persecutions (2nd c. BCE; a historical "premiere") may indicate Daniel's date. Conservative interpreters, however, antedate Daniel (6th c.), with God inspiring the seer with the events of 168–67 BCE (see also 1 Macc 1:41–67; 2 Macc 6:1–7:43).

Chapters 1–6 are stories about Daniel and his companions exiled in Babylon; Chaps. 7–12 are an apocalypse on the end-times. The book is bilingual: Chaps. 2–7 in Aramaic; 1 and 8–12 in Hebrew. There are also Greek words in Dan 3. The structure follows a dual 1:5 pattern: one Hebrew chapter followed by five Aramaic ones; one Aramaic chapter followed by five Hebrew ones. The Greek versions include five additions (apocrypha).

In Dan 2 and 4, Daniel interprets dreams and accedes to the highest position at the royal court. The central apocalyptic* part, a genre present in Isa 24–27 and Ezek 38–39, deals with "the manifestation of secrets unknowable by natural means" (Theodotion* on Dan 2:19), especially about the end times. In the midst of the persecutions of the faithful, the apocalyptist sees the coming of the "son* of man" (Dan 7) and forecasts the resurrection* of the just (Dan 12), two major breakthroughs in biblical revelation. The perspective is marked by historical pessimism, dualism*, and determinism, but also by a total faith* in the divine ultimate intervention. Then human history ends and the Kingdom* of God (e.g. 2:44, 4:3, 6:26) comes. Thus the final historical cataclysm entails coincidently the ultimate theophanic redemption*. From being historical, as among the prophets, eschatology* has become suprahistorical.

André LaCocque

Dante Alighieri (1265–1321) rapidly rose to a position of political power in Florence, becoming a member of its governing council, the *signoria*. Internecine strife resulted in his expulsion in 1301. During his peregrinations in exile until his death, he composed fundamental works, including *The Divine Comedy*. This work, written in the vernacular, is responsible more than any other for establishing the Florentine dialect as the literary and eventually the national language of Italy.

The Divine Comedy is an incomparable summing up of the medieval Roman Catholic vision of the universe. The poem recounts the journey of its author through the three realms of the afterlife – hell*, purgatory*, and paradise* – where all truth, human and divine, is revealed in an eschatological* perspective. Dante's dialogues with the dead reveal the depths of the human soul, for good and for ill, along with the unfathomable dispensations of Providence for bringing the drama of history to a just end. Adapting epic tradition, especially Virgil's epic of imperial Rome (the *Aeneid*), Dante personalizes the form, incorporating romance and lyric modes. This poetic summa constitutes a veritable encyclopedia of culture drawn from all the arts and sciences, as well as from world history and contemporary chronicle. All these elements are melded into a quest for total knowledge and ultimately the vision of God.

Dante thereby founds a tradition of Christian epic that continues in such authors as Tasso, Spenser, Milton*, Blake*, and even Joyce. This sub-biblical genre constitutes a literary extension of Christian revelation* based on the claim that poetry can be a vehicle of divine vision, a disclosure of truth of a prophetic order that may be in tension with priestly, ecclesiastical authority*. Dante's theological poetics and his exemplary figure as poet-prophet thus open the path for literature to become an original discovery of divinity, as well as of human life and the universe, as seen through the optics of God that a poet may gain access to through exceptional grace and by virtue of his or her special art and discipline.

In exile (1301–21), Dante composed fundamental works of political philosophy (*On Monarchy*) and literary theory (*On the Vulgar Tongue*) and, above all, *The Divine Comedy*. Other vernacular works include the story in poetry and prose of his love for Beatrice (*The New Life*) and his digest of philosophical knowledge (*The Banquet*).

See also AESTHETICS AND THEOLOGY; ITALIAN LITERATURE AND CHRISTIANITY.

William Franke

Daoism and Christianity Cluster

Daoism and Christianity: Daoism and Christian Perspectives

Daoism and Christianity: Daoist Canon and the Christian Bible

Daoism and Christianity in Neo-Confucian Korea

Daoism and Christianity: Daoism and Christian Perspectives. Daoism, one of the two major native religious traditions of China* (along with Confucianism*), traces its original insights from *Laozi* (the name of both a person and a book). According to tradition, Li Er, subsequently known as Laozi (an honorific name, "Old Master"), was a native of Southern China during the 6th c. BCE During the Tang dynasty (618–907 CE), Daoism was highly valued because Laozi was regarded as the ancestor of Li Yuan, the founder of the Tang dynasty. According to the tradition, the book *Laozi*, or *Book of the Way (Dao) and Its Virtue* (*Dao De Jing*), was edited in the 3rd–4th c. BCE. Laozi's thought was further developed by Zhuangzi (4th c. BCE), who contributed a concrete teaching on apophatic* contemplation: "sitting in forgetfulness" and "fasting of the heart." While the literary style of *Laozi* is sober and poetic, the sentences written by *Zhuangzi* are long and prosaic, and the book contains many allegorical, witty, and humorous stories.

Laozi and Zhuangzi initiated the concept of *wu* (nothingness, nonbeing), emphasizing the limitation of human reason*. Since the Dao has no shape, no smell, and no color, we have to go beyond our ordinary perception and stay in the quiet state of emptied mind. While "being" (*you*) signifies nameable individual objects, the source and foundation of all of these is "nonbeing" (*wu*). Against Confucianism, Laozi and Zhuangzi pointed out the limitation of social norms and propriety. Laozi and Zhuangzi's philosophical tradition was later incorporated, along with other traditions, by leaders of Daoist religious orders and schools.

Historical Encounters of Daoism and Christianity. The first encounter occurred in 635 when Alopen, an Assyrian* Christian (often inappropriately called "Nestorian*"), came to the capital city of Tang, translated the essence of Christian teaching, and dedicated it to the emperor. The emperor Taizhong permitted missionary activity, and Syriac monks placed portraits of succeeding emperors on the wall of the monastery and prayed for them. This 150-year-long Syriac mission to China and the names of priests (in both Chinese and Syriac) became known through the "stele of the propagation of the Luminous Religion" (built in 781, buried in 845 during the Huichang persecution, unearthed in 1625), which expresses how Daoism was employed as a bridge to Christianity.

Syriac and Assyrian missionaries did not hesitate to use Daoist terms. They translated YHWH Elohim as the "Heavenly Lord" (*Tianzun*), adopting the Daoist name for the highest divinity, and explained that God is *empty* and calm, but transforms myriad things in mysterious ways. They portrayed the Christian Trinity as "our triune and mysterious God" (*Sanimaoshen*) who is the "lord of *silence* and truth" (*Wuyanzhenzhu*). "Emptiness" and "silence" are characteristics of the Daoist Heaven rather than of the Christian God. Similarly, they introduced Jesus as a "heavenly immortal" (*tianxian*) – the highest level of immortals in Daoism – who ascended to heaven before his disciples after he opened the gates of faith, hope, and love and composed 27 sacred books. Jesus' death on the cross is not mentioned.

The second encounter between Daoism and Christianity was very different from the first. Daoism had lost its influence during the Ming dynasty. When Jesuit missionaries came to China (16th c.), the dominant ideology was neo-Confucianism. Thus Matteo Ricci* criticized Daoism as superstitious and nihilistic (as he did Buddhism) and claimed that Confucianism was closest to the truth.

Contemporary Encounters between Daoism and Christianity. Daoist classics and Daoist masters can be rich resources and good dialogue partners for contemporary Christians because of both parallelisms and differences between the two traditions.

1. Both traditions conceive of ultimate reality as the source of life and value. The *Laozi* (Chap. 42) states that all things originated from, and are nurtured by, the Dao, the mother of myriad things. The Dao is compassionate and forgiving (*Laozi* Chaps. 63, 67), as God is (Luke 17:20). Yet for Daoism, ultimate reality is primarily immanent in each being as its nurturing principle, while for Christianity, God forms a personal relationship

(a covenant*) with humans. When dealing with ecological* issues, Christians would benefit from learning from Daoism about the immanence of ultimate reality. In turn Daoists can be stimulated by the Christian understanding of God as relational.

2. Both Daoism and Christianity recognize the importance of revelation*. For example, both oral and written revelations played a significant role in the establishment of new Daoist schools. Christian scriptures are full of revelations from God through Abraham, Moses, the prophets, and finally Jesus Christ. Differences concern the way of transmission: words are valued in Christian revelation, wordless signs of heaven and earth in Daoist revelation.
3. Both traditions developed rich contemplative* methods as a way to attain eternal life or immortality. Daoist immortals are said to have completely transformed their life energy through the exercise of "inner alchemy," and so returned to the purity of the Dao (in some schools, with invisible bodies). Christians also hope for eternal life when the death of the body is overcome; revelation (of Christ as sacrament, a channel of salvation who makes what is invisible visible) and contemplation lead to purification that is necessary for union with God. But while Daoism classifies immortals according to the level of their "contemplation," the Christian notion of eternal life relies heavily on God's grace and depicts the "communion* of saints" as egalitarian.
4. Both Daoism and Christianity try to stay near the people, fulfilling their needs for healing, blessings, and peace. The possibility of becoming an immortal or a saint is open to everyone. Both traditions aspire to establish a society of equals and have concern for the poor.

SUNG-HAE KIM, SR.

Daoism and Christianity: Daoist Canon and the Christian Bible. The Daoist Canon, or *Daozang,* is a comprehensive collection of numerous, diverse scriptures that is several hundred times the size of the Christian Bible. It came about through successive compilations of Daoist texts that date from the beginning of the Tang dynasty (618–907 CE). The Ming Canon of 1445, *Zhengtong daozang* (Daoist Canon of the Zhengtong Reign Period), which includes almost 1,500 texts (among them, texts produced under the Tang, Song, Jin, and Yuan regimes), lies at the heart of all modern editions of the Daoist Canon.

Following the example of the Buddhist Tripitaka, the Daoist Canon had originally been divided into "Three Grottoes" (*Sandong*), "Four Supplements" (*Sifu*), and "Twelve Divisions" (*Shi'er bu*). The present-day Canon preserves these core divisions, yet considerable variations occurred owing to later additions of commentaries, revelations, and texts elaborating on the core divisions.

Daoism does not have a single, standard view of scripture* or of its origin and roles (as is also the case for Christianity). Daoism is characterized by complexity and flexibility, qualities that are reflected in its view of scripture, which encompasses the diverse views of other religious traditions.

Generally speaking, in Judaism*, Christianity, and Islam*, scripture is considered to be a record of revelation from and about the Absolute, i.e. from and about God or Allah; consequently, these traditions attach the highest value to their own scriptures (although each has several, very different views of the roles of scripture). In other religious traditions, including Buddhism* and Confucianism*, scriptures are construed as human texts produced by human deliberation. Thus Buddhism and Confucianism emphasize an individual's (a sage's) authentic religious experience and wisdom more than they do revelation from a divine being, and strive to implement the sage's valuable teachings in deeds of their religious and daily life.

Daoist views include these diverse understandings of scripture and its roles. Roughly speaking, a group of traditions, such as the Great Purity Tradition, Numinous Treasure Tradition, and Celestial Masters Tradition consider their scriptures to have a divine origin and divine power. For such traditions, scriptures are literal expressions of the Dao, i.e. the primordial chaos of nondifferentiation. They believe that scriptures are sacred in that they manifest the Sacred itself and possess sacred power themselves. These traditions grant absolute authority to their scriptures.

In contrast, a group of Inner Alchemy (Neidan) traditions, such as the Complete Reality Tradition, lend more weight to the practical value of scripture than to its absolute authority as literal revelation. For these traditions, their scriptures present a gateway to the Dao, but are distinguished from the Dao itself because of their inherent limitations owing to the fact that they employ human language. In this context, scriptures are an auxiliary means to accomplish the religious goal.

Different attitudes toward scriptures are linked with different understandings of religious language and of salvation, i.e. whether salvation is attained via divine power or through human effort. Daoism has permitted the free interpretation of scriptures. As a result of such flexibility, an ongoing process of editing has led to broad variations and the continuous re-creation of the Daoist Canon. The tolerance and flexibility of Daoism occasionally threaten its identity. SOOBIN CHOI

Daoism and Christianity in Neo-Confucian Korea. Korea is greatly influenced by both Confucianism and Christianity. Although Confucianism originated in China, Korean society was thoroughly structured by neo-Confucianism – a Confucianism in which Daoist thoughts are deeply embedded. Yet in this neo-Confucian country, Christianity is a major religion (at least 30% of the population is Christian), in contrast with other traditionally neo-Confucian countries – China, Hong Kong, Japan, Taiwan, and Vietnam – in which less than 3% of the population is Christian.

The success of the several branches of the Presbyterian Church in Korea – becoming during the 20th c. the largest Reformed Church in the world – is due in part to the strong similarities in the thought of John Calvin* and Korean neo-Confucianists, culminating in the work of Yi T'oegye (1501–70). Despite their distinctive premises (God vs. Heaven), both traditions claim a transcendental anthropology (the human being as the image of God [*imago Dei*] or the mandate of Heaven [*T'ien-ming*]), an ontology of co-humanity (*agape* or *jen*), a rigorous discipline of humanization (sanctification vs. self-cultivation), and the priority of piety (*pietas* or *ching*) and order.

The Confucian–Christian relationship in Korea does not fit any Western Christian categorization pertaining to the relationship between Christianity and other religions, such as exclusivism, inclusivism, pluralism*, or syncretism*. Korean Christians cannot adopt a hermeneutical distance from the indigenous tradition that governed Korean life for more than a millennium. In the family, most self-identified, churchgoing Christians still practice neo-Confucian moral norms and social customs. This distinctively Confucian–Christian context conjures up an intriguing issue concerning dual religious identity.

Although Daoism as a religion takes popular forms such as Shamanism* and folk religions, Daoist thought is influential and deeply embedded in neo-Confucianism. The Dao, the normative-generative way of life and of the cosmos, has been the all-embracing root metaphor of East Asian thought. The first Korean Christians conceived of Christ as the intersection of the heavenly Dao and the human Dao (cf. John 14:6). The Dao was taken to be a more biblical notion than the Logos because the first name of Christianity in Greek is *hodos*, "the way" (Acts 16:17, 18:25–6). Some argue for the adoption of the Dao as an alternative theological metaphor (theo-Dao) to both the problematic Logos (theo-Logos) and the reductionistic praxis (theo-praxis). HEUP YOUNG KIM

Darby, John Nelson (1800–82). Ordained in the Church of Ireland (1825) and instrumental in the development of the dissident Plymouth* Brethren Movement, he advocated the dissolution of existing churches (1842). Convinced that a clear separation of Israel and the Christian

Church should be maintained and that a clergy separated from the people was unbiblical, he energetically espoused a Dispensationalist* reading of Scripture* and church history that led to his conviction that a "secret rapture*" would signal the end of the present age. His teachings mark the beginning of the contemporary Dispensationalist Movement in Evangelical Christianity and are the basis for the popular belief in a Premillennial "rapture." **See also MILLENNIALISM CLUSTER.** STEPHEN E. LAHEY

Darwin, Charles Robert (1809–82), naturalist, originator of the theory of evolution* by natural selection. He rejected the Bible as a scientific authority and explained the origin of living species by natural laws given by God. For his devotion to science and his upright life, he received England's highest religious honor when scientists joined churchmen and politicians to inter him in Westminster Abbey.

Born to wealth and christened an Anglican, Darwin attended Unitarian* services with his mother. His father, a freethinker, sent him (1825) to study medicine at Edinburgh University, where Robert Grant, an evolutionist and unbeliever, stimulated his interest in natural history. Abandoning medicine, Darwin entered Cambridge University (1828) to prepare for ordination in the Church of England. He accepted his professors' beliefs about an ancient earth formed according to God's laws, the fixity and divine design of living species, and the authority of the Bible. But a botanist, Rev. John Stevens Henslow, got him a place on the survey ship HMS *Beagle* during a five year voyage around the world. In South America, impressed by nature's power and diversity, he began to see how the appearance of new species in time and in space could be explained by laws, just as Christian geologists explained the formation of the earth's crust.

Darwin saw that humans, too, were subject to God's laws – as Unitarians believed, laws of material perfecting. Just as the races descended from one another and belonged to one family, so all species were "netted together." It was "more humble . . . and true" to believe that humans were "created from animals." He devised a theory of creative evolution that he called "natural selection" (1837–39), working on it privately for 20 years, giving up faith* in the Bible and then in Christianity after his father's and eldest daughter's deaths.

His *Origin of Species* (1859) showed that he remained a strong theist, though in later years he sometimes considered himself "agnostic." In *The Descent of Man* (1871), Darwin stated that "our minds refuse to accept" evolution "as the result of blind chance" and that "the highest form of religion" was "the grand idea of God hating sin and loving righteousness." In accepting his body for burial, the church reclaimed its own. **See also EVOLUTION AND CHRISTIANITY.** JAMES MOORE

Darwinism, a loose label for the various interpretations of Darwin's* theories about evolution* and natural selection in *Origin of Species* (1859). His work posed many challenges to Christians and is still a subject of intense controversy (with Process* Christian theologians integrating evolution into their theology; Cobb).

For fundamentalists* and other literalist* interpreters of Scripture*, Darwinism conflicts with the creation story in Genesis*. For liberal Christians, geologists and biblical historians had already undermined the Genesis cosmology. For biologists, Darwin seemed to complete a program already victorious in the physical sciences: a rejection of final causation, or of any purposeful agency, in the explanation of physical processes. Physicists had continued to believe in a creator God who ordered the universe, but they did not include God in their descriptions of transformations in nature. Yet there was a great deal more dynamite in Darwin's theory.

One reason is that Darwin developed a historical, not a mechanical, explanation. Thus Darwin seemed to be explaining the origin of new life forms in much the same language as the Bible. What God had seemed to do, "natural selection" did just as well, though the process depended on random variations. The theory was most disturbing for those people, including many theologians, who had always found the best "proof" for the existence of a God in the complex biosphere or in the wondrous adaptations noted by Darwin. One could still assert that a God was behind the evolutionary process, but such an assertion was gratuitous, with no explanatory role. For such people, theism itself was at stake.

Darwin's theory was also threatening because it encompassed humans. For Christians, *The Descent of Man* was the most challenging of Darwin's books. By narrowing the perceived differences between humans and other primates – the gradual evolution of language and self-consciousness explained human distinctiveness – Darwin seemed to leave no place for a human spirit or soul*. For Darwin and his very high estimate of higher mammals, this was not depreciating humans; but it was so to many critics. It seemed more so when some of Darwin's disciples, not always against his wishes, used his theory to support undisciplined forms of capitalism or heinous types of eugenics. In time the term "social Darwinism" often became identified with these purported social or economic implications of his evolutionary theory. **See also BERLIN CONFERENCE; RACISM AND CHRISTIANITY CLUSTER: IN WESTERN EUROPE.** PAUL K. CONKIN

David, king of Judah and Israel (10th c. BCE). In 1 Sam 16–31, David is presented as having been chosen by God to replace Saul* as the anointed king of the people of Israel*. After triumphing over the Philistine Goliath and escaping from Saul's wrath, he ruled as king of Judah, then of all Israel. After his conquest of Jerusalem*, which became his capital, David established a vast kingdom of Israel. Though condemned for his adulterous relationship with Bathsheba*, blamed for the death of her husband, Uriah, and politically weakened by the revolt of his son Absalom*, David was the recipient of a divine promise that his dynasty would never disappear.

Although there are no contemporary, extra-biblical sources on David's life, the general historical background of the early Iron Age in Israel (12th–10th c. BCE) has been described archaeologically. The rise of the Philistine city-states is well documented, although the biblical descriptions of David's wars with Israel's other neighbors may be shaped by later conditions. Yet the Tel Dan Inscription seems to indicate that, by the late 9th c. BCE, the name "David" was firmly associated with the ruling dynasty of Judah.

Throughout the books of Samuel and Kings, David's heirs are regarded as the sole legitimate, divinely appointed rulers of Israel, whose faithfulness or not to the covenant* profoundly influences Israel's fortunes. The expectation of a Davidic messiah* features prominently in prophetic literature (e.g. Isaiah, Jeremiah, Ezekiel); in Psalms, Chronicles, and later Jewish literature, the image of David becomes more a religious archetype than a political model.

In the NT, Jesus is repeatedly presented as a direct descendant of the Davidic line and as a messiah of the Davidic type. Church fathers and particularly Augustine* regarded the life of David as an allegorical* or typological* precursor of the earthly ministry of Christ. NEIL SILBERMAN

Day, Dorothy (1897–1980), born in Brooklyn, New York, founder of the Catholic* Worker Movement. Though active as a young adult in radical secular movements, she was drawn to Christianity. To express her gratitude for the birth of her daughter Tamar, she arranged for the infant's baptism in the Roman Catholic Church. Soon after, she herself became a Catholic (1927).

In 1932 Day met Peter Maurin, whose vision of a social order "in which it would be easier for men to be good" inspired her. In response to his proposal, she started a newspaper to publicize Catholic social teaching. On May 1, 1933, the first copies of the *Catholic Worker* were handed out on Union Square, Manhattan.

The paper soon led to the creation of the first Catholic Worker "house of hospitality" (185 such houses in 2006), where food was served to the homeless and unemployed, clothing made available, and a welcome given.

On her 75th birthday, the Jesuit magazine *America* devoted a special issue to Day as the individual who best exemplified "the aspiration and action of the American Catholic community during the past forty years." The Archdiocese of New York proposed her canonization. The Vatican has given her the title "Servant of God."

JIM FOREST

Deacon, Diaconate (from Gk *diakonia*, "service"; *diakonein*, "to serve"). Words based on *diakonia* appear 102 times in the NT, a frequency that indicates that the early followers of Jesus were deeply impressed by Jesus' person and ministry as ones of service. *Diakonia* is, in the NT, the major characteristic of all ministries; it does not refer simply to the ministry of a deacon.

By the middle of the 1st c. CE, particular individuals serving in a local church were called "deacons." In early Christian texts, the role of such deacons was neither uniform nor evident in every community. Early data indicate that the service of the deacon was in part liturgical. Deacons were officially ministers during the Eucharist*: reading the gospel, preparing the gifts, and assisting at Communion. Deacons were liturgical ministers in baptism*. Often, deacons went into the water with the one to be baptized and asked the person, "Do you believe in the Father? the Son? the Holy Spirit?" The deacon with his hand on the person's head submerged the person in the water. In a few recorded instances, a deacon also served as the minister of reconciliation and even celebrated the Eucharist and preached. Beyond these liturgical duties, the deacon was often the major pastoral minister (see Pastoral Care) for a

Christian community, providing for the poor*, the sick, orphans, and others in need; he was frequently the financial administrator for a community. Christians generally had limited contact with the bishop or priest; on a daily basis, it was the Apostolic* Tradition (c215), which cites an actual ordination ritual. Thus "ordination" as a ministerial entry rite began only in the late 2nd c. (theological descriptions of earlier such ordinations are conjectural), and this in a specific geographical area (around Rome; not necessarily in other areas). It is only from the 4th c. that one can speak more generally about ordination rituals. In the Western Church, the pastoral ministry of deacon began to disappear starting in the 6th c., leaving the diaconate as an order through which one passed on the way to priesthood*. Only a few permanent deacons are mentioned in church literature from the 8th to the 12th c. In the Eastern* Church, the role of the deacon remained strong down to the present age – a role primarily liturgical but not exclusively so.

The renewal of the permanent diaconate after Vatican* II is not a renewal of the diaconate as it existed in the ancient church. The contemporary permanent diaconate has been established to meet the pastoral needs of the third millennial church – pastoral needs that reflect the liturgical, pastoral, and social needs of the Catholic Church today.

Two issues remain the same. First, all ministries in the Christian Church center on Jesus the deacon, the one who came to serve and not be served (Mark 10:45) and the one who washed the feet of the disciples (John 13). These words and actions of Jesus are the benchmark for all Christian ministries: episcopal, presbyteral, diaconal, and lay.

Second, pastoral needs rather than a theological position have been the seedbed from which all church ministries have developed. The structures and forms of church ministries have changed in the course of history in response to specific pastoral needs. Ordained ministries, in their historical development, show adaptation. The current permanent diaconate needs to measure itself by the actual and serious pastoral needs of present contexts.

KENAN B. OSBORNE, OFM

Deaconess, title for female deacons. In the earliest church period, women were called deacons*, the same title given to men (Rom 16:1–2; probably 1 Tim 3:11); they were most likely delegates or representatives of local churches and later assistants to church leaders. Pliny the Younger (*Letter* 10.96 to Trajan) refers to two slave *ministrae* in Bithynia-Pontus, who probably have a similar role. From the 3rd c. in Syria, there was a distinctive office for women, as described in the *Didascalia** (3rd c.) and Apostolic* Constitutions (4th c.). The office flourished in the East in the 4th, 5th, and 6th c., witnessed by numerous texts and funerary inscriptions, and survived beyond that. The titles *diakonos* and *diakonissa,* with occasional variants such as *diakone,* seem to have been fairly interchangeable, sometimes varying even within the same text. The office appeared in the West only rarely beginning in the 6th c. in monastic contexts.

The liturgical role of deaconesses consisted primarily of assistance at the baptism* of women, since baptism entailed immersion of the naked candidate and anointing of various parts of the body. It was deemed improper for a male bishop or presbyter to perform this ritual. Women without the title most likely assisted in places where there were no female deacons.

The pastoral role of female deacons was much broader. They prepared women and children for baptism and did the catechetical follow-up afterward. They undertook pastoral visitation of sick women and provided protection and support to female penitents and pilgrims. They served in monasteries as liturgical leaders in the singing of the Divine* Office and sometimes as superior, though the two offices were always kept distinct.

The sacramental ordination* of deaconesses has sometimes been questioned. They do not seem to have been ordained *for* sacramental ministry, but the language of ordination is generally used in reference to them, e.g. Canon 15 of the Council of Chalcedon*, which legislates that they are not to be ordained until the age of 40. The usually recognized term for ordination, *cheirotonia,* is used in this text. While most legislation either presupposes or states plainly the expectation that deaconesses will be celibate (virgins or widows*), some surviving funerary inscriptions place them in family relationships. **See also BASILINA; JUSTINA; LAMPADION; MARTHANA; OLYMPIAS; PHOEBE; SABINIANA; SOPHIA ("SECOND PHOEBE"); VIRGINITY, THEOLOGY OF.**

CAROLYN OSIEK

Dead, Prayers for the. Praying for the dead is controversial among Christians, both historically and today. At the heart of the disagreement is defining the relationship between the living and the dead, whether the living can have any effect on the dead, and whether the dead can change.

Evidence of praying for the dead in the early church is ambiguous; the extant materials can be interpreted in different ways. The evidence is as varied as early graffiti at martyr* shrines that asks for the martyrs to keep the living in mind (*in habite mente*), the early-3rd-c. martyr account of Perpetua* containing a story of efficacious prayer for her dead brother, and Augustine's* differentiating between the dead who remember us before God and the dead for whom we pray.

The practices of praying to the saints* and for other dead multiplied in many ways in the second millennium, including the articulation of the doctrine of purgatory*, the saying of (Requiem*) Masses for the dead, and an increasing emphasis of the dependence of the dead on the living.

In the 16th c., a primary protest of Luther* was the misuse of these practices, especially indulgences*. Many Protestants claimed the dead were beyond change and engagement with the world, thus making prayers for the dead irrelevant. They forbade prayers to the saints* because they were a denial of the sole mediatorship* of Christ; thus a chasm developed between the living and the dead, which was challenged by the Catholic* Renewal.

In the 20th and early 21st c., the harsh dualism of Protestant and Catholic stances has been diversified by ecumenical agreements and inculturation*, especially as Christianity is shaped by cultures where ancestor* veneration has expanded categories of thinking. At the same time, the veneration of saints has found new adherents beyond Catholicism and has been influenced by interfaith conversations.

LIZETTE LARSON-MILLER

Deadly Sins. Gregory* I's list of deadly sins – pride, covetousness, lust, envy, gluttony, anger, and sloth – draws on Evagrius* of Pontus's eight "evil thoughts" quoted by John Cassian*.

Dead Sea Scrolls. In 1947 Arab Bedouins found an ancient Jewish library in a cave on the northwestern shores of the Dead Sea. Subsequently, 10 other caves were found to contain scrolls belonging to a group of Jews living nearby and identified by many scholars as Essenes*, who were "prepar[ing] in the wilderness the way of the Lord" (Isa 40:3), i.e. God's coming as the final act in the process of fulfilling the promises in the Scriptures*.

No fewer than 930 scrolls (dating from c250 BCE to 68 CE) belonged to the library of this Jewish community, which was led by a prophetic figure, an anonymous "Righteous Teacher" revered for his genius and revelatory power. Following his lead, the community emphasized that God was trustworthy and just and had established "a new* covenant" in Israel: the community living at Qumran*.

The scrolls, hidden from the conquering Roman armies led by Vespasian (c68 CE), represent not only the beliefs, ideas, and aspirations of the Qumran community, but also those of other Jews of Galilee* and Samaria*, and were held by Jews contemporaneous with Jesus of Nazareth.

The Dead Sea Scrolls include the following:

1. All the books of the HB except Esther. The large Isaiah Scroll proves that biblical books had been carefully copied over a period of more than a thousand years. Some scrolls appear to be expansions of the Bible or "Rewritten Bible." The canon* was not yet closed (c70 ce); scribes continued to alter, expand, or abbreviate the biblical texts.
2. Apocrypha* and Pseudepigrapha* in Hebrew and Aramaic previously known only in late medieval copies, notably the Damascus Document, Books of Enoch* or 1 Enoch, and Jubilees*.
3. Previously unknown works indicative of the life of the Qumran community, most importantly the Rule of the Community; the Thanksgiving Hymns; a scroll about the final battle between "the Sons of Light" and "the Sons of Darkness," the War Scroll; an explanation of how to interpret Torah, entitled "Some Works of the Torah"; and commentaries of the prophets, the Pesharim.

The authors of the Pesharim* (1st c. BCE) stressed the fulfillment of the prophecies of the HB in events surrounding the community and within it. These interpretations, inspired by the Holy Spirit*, focused on how the history of the group reflected and fulfilled prophecies, demonstrating God's trustworthiness. God did not disclose to the prophets the "secret mysteries"; now God revealed to the Righteous Teacher all the mysteries of the words of the prophets (Habakkuk Pesher).

The Jewish group at Qumran emphasized the Holy* Spirit, anticipated the coming of the Messiah* (sometimes two messiahs, a priestly and a kingly messiah), and emphasized that their time was "the latter days," or the end of time. They stressed that all humanity was divided into the Sons of Light and the Sons of Darkness. The Sons of Light, the Qumran group and other Essenes, were the elect* of God and drank salvific water that provided full or eternal life. This prophetic group first conceptualized the Holy Spirit as separate from God, the notion of two messiahs, the doctrine of double predestination*, and the Spirit-inspired interpretation of Scripture*.

This group of Essenes was similar to the group of Jewish followers of Jesus. Both Jewish groups lived in the Holy Land about the same time (although the Essenes had already existed for 150 years). Both emphasized the Holy Spirit, the Messiah, and the prophecies fulfilled in their own time and group. Both groups imagined a future, not far off, when the wicked would be punished and the righteous rewarded. The Jewish followers of Jesus, however, believed that the Messiah had come and was Jesus of Nazareth.

John the Baptizer clearly had some relation with the Qumran Essenes, but he was not one of them. Jesus was neither an Essene nor anti-Essene. His teaching indicates that he was intermittently positively and negatively influenced by the Essenes. The Gospel of John* was influenced, indirectly or directly, by the Essenes. In sum, the Dead Sea Scrolls have revolutionized our perceptions of the origins of Christianity. The Essenes, while not the precursors of the Christians, did influence Jesus and his followers in significant and symbolic ways.

JAMES H. CHARLESWORTH

Dean, originally, title of an official supervising 10 persons in a monastery; now applied to various kinds of subordinate officials.

---

1) Introductory Entry

Death in the Bible and Early Patristic Literature. Early in the OT, Israel's understanding of death was shaped by its covenantal* relationship with God, seen as the giver of life. Since death seemed to be a part of God's creation*, it could be accepted as a natural culmination of life. Persons who lived a long life and had children to perpetuate their names died a "good death."

But death meant separation from God. The dead went to Sheol*, a shadowy underworld beyond God's immediate care. This fate seemed contrary to God's graciousness. The tension became worse when a personal rather than a communal relationship with God gained ascendancy (Jer 31; Ezek 18). Should not the righteous be rewarded and the wicked punished? This belief collapsed experientially (Job* and Ecclesiastes*), leading to a belief in life after death where the righteous would get their reward. Yet this idea remained nebulous, even in the direct references to something like a resurrection (Dan 12:2–3; Isa 26:19).

In the NT, death is connected causally with sin*. "The wages of sin is death" (Rom 6:23). Paul postulates that through Adam sin came into the world and with sin came death (Rom 5:12). Death cuts a wide swath. It refers to physical cessation but, before this, to anything that diminishes life. It also refers to a cosmic power that subjects all creation to futility and decay (Rom 8:20). Paul suggests different views of the link between sin and death: To sin is to live by the flesh, which is mortal. To sin is to be separated from God, the source of life; this separation yields death. To sin is to incur God's wrath; death is the punishment. Death is the last enemy of humankind and of God to be destroyed (1 Cor 15:26).

According to the NT, Christ takes away the power of sin and of death. Believers still die a physical death, but in all other ways they are alive to new life in everlasting communion with God.

Paul's complex understanding of death and sin led to different views. Within the main trend of the Western Church, Irenaeus*, Augustine*, and Luther* believed that turning away from God (sin as guilt) eventuates in death (as punishment), from which humankind can be rescued only by Christ. The Eastern Orthodox* Church, following Basil* the Great, John* Chrysostom, Athanasius*, and Cyril* of Alexandria, views death as God's enemy, resulting from separation from life with God due to sin as a disease. **See also ESCHATOLOGY CLUSTER; REDEMPTION.**

LEROY H. ADEN

---

2) A Sampling of Contextual Views and Practices

Death, Christian Views of, in Africa. In African* Religion, "life" and "death" are not mutually exclusive. Death does not end an individual's personality; life goes beyond the grave as the dead become ancestors*, "living dead," who remain alive for the living.

In African cultures, funeral rites are community affairs; visits are paid to the bereaved family by the community. The day before the funeral, the corpse is brought home. A night vigil takes place, often until morning. The dead must be mourned in order to create an environment of tranquility and harmony for both the living and the dead. After the funeral, all wash their hands in cold water, washing away death's "coldness" before the funeral meal, which is a celebration of life and a return to "normal life."

Christians observe these traditional African rites, with their related view of death, introducing Christian perspectives that vary from one denomination to another and from one African culture to another. The night vigil is a time to convey Christian messages, sing vibrant hymns, and share pastoral care that brings healing to the community. The funeral meal is celebrated in the spirit of the Eucharist. Death is sad, but it is not shameful*, when through such rites those who grieve are assured of God's mercy and God's endless glory.

PAUL JOHN ISAAK

Death, Christian Views of, in Asia. Three dimensions converge in Christian views of death in Asia. First and most basic is the biblical view that acknowledges the reality of death as part of the human condition, which is affected by sin*. God created the life of all beings, and Jesus Christ, through his Resurrection, saves them from the power of death. The Spirit empowers the life of all beings in the universe, individually and collectively.

Second, this biblical view enters into conversation with views of death in Asian cultures and religions, including the Hindu* view of death as a natural process in the cycle of birth, life, death, and rebirth (*samsara*) and of liberation (*moksha*) from this cycle; the Buddhist* view of death as a point of awakening from the continuous cycle of death and rebirth in order to renounce and overcome the futile life of desire (and thus attain *nirvana*); the Confucian* view that "life and death are determined by Heaven" and that a life of compassion, justice, propriety, and wisdom is essential, thereby emphasizing life rather than death (*T'ai Ping*, "Great Peace"); and the view of Daoism*, which seeks deliverance, immortality, and the state of "living in eternity" in oneness with the Dao.

Third, the scientific and biomedical view of death as the permanent end of the life of a biological organism has evolved with advances in science and technology. Transhumanists, who believe that life (health and longevity) and death (end of the biological mechanism) can be managed by technology, are now seeking to justify their aims in religious terms. A convergence between Asian religious views on death and the modern biomedical understanding of death is desirable on religious grounds in order to deal with biomedical* ethical issues.

Asian Christian theologians view life and death holistically and integrally, and are struggling to understand them in light of war*, political oppression*, poverty* and hunger, disease, violent social conflict, religious cultural conflict, and biological and ecological destruction.

KIM YONG-BOCK

Death, Christian Views of, in Latin America. As in the Caribbean, in the popular psyche in Latin America life and death are inextricably intertwined. The living already experience death. Preoccupation with death is prevalent, and the downturns and sufferings of life are seen as its intimations.

The Spanish colonizers brought with them the austere Roman Catholicism of the Inquisition* and the penitential devotion (see Penance and Forgiveness) characterized by *escarmientos*, punishments of the flesh. Thus there is much comfort in the sight of a profusely bleeding Christ, fully identified with the human reality of a living death. In death one's destiny is concretized.

Death is also present among the living. In death relatives become saints* in the family circle, and their last wishes have power over the living. They are frequently referred to in quotidian conversations and are considered efficient agents in prayers to God. Their remains are, at times, venerated. In this way they seem not to be dead at all. When life and death are thus intimately conjoined, however, life is devalued.

HEROLD D. WEISS

Death, Christian Views of, in Latin America: The Caribbean Cult of the Dead. The earliest narratives about slavery* in the Americas frequently note blacks' determination to celebrate the funerals of deceased companions. Father Dutertre (17th c.) reported that slaves walked great distances at night to participate in songs and dances at wakes. This devotion did not make any sense to their masters. But if slavery is a social death, the cult of the dead is for the slave a symbolic negation of this social death. Masters sought to reduce funerals to a minimum, signifying that slaves remained merchandise even in death. From this perspective, the cult of the dead is a radical opposition to slavery. Thus one finds this practice throughout the Americas.

The funerary rituals last several days and even years, because of the belief that the dead (their spirits) remain in water* and protect the living members of their family. The rituals link dead individuals to the ancestors*, thus to African divinities and to lost Africa. In the French West Indies, November 2 serves as a day when the community is reconstituted through a dialogue between the living and the dead, and all the cemeteries are illuminated. In Haiti, the November 2 celebration is a national holiday involving the worship of *Gede* (death divinities), including people possessed in the streets and in the cemeteries. **See also THE PRESENT CLUSTER: IN LATIN AMERICA.**

LAËNNEC HURBON

Death, Christian Views of, in North America. Like the biblical understanding, the contemporary North American view of death ranges from seeing it as a natural event to seeing it as a catastrophe of human existence. The common thread is that death is not just physical cessation but a wholistic shutting down of life.

Contemporary theologians give more attention to collective death than to individual death by focusing on the end of this world. Some believe that this transformation will come within human history; others that the end means the destruction of the present world in favor of a kingdom beyond human history. Most North American theologians favor the Hebraic understanding of person as an animated body. Thus if they believe in life after death, they believe in the resurrection* of the body*. Yet popular Christian beliefs often favor the Greek idea that a person has a mortal body and an immortal soul*.

Some contemporary North American theologians put the emphasis on what

God will do at the end of time to overcome death, while others see Christ's suffering and death as an identification with, and God's salutary answer to, our suffering and death.

LEROY H. ADEN

Death, Christian Views of, in Western Europe. Christ's* redemption of humans from sin* and from death is the distinctive doctrine emphasized by Christianity according to Western European Christians. They note that, in the HB, death confines all, regardless of character, to a neutral land of the dead, Sheol (Hades), and that during Christ's "descent into hell*," he experienced physical death, invading this land, defeating death, and rescuing the righteous. Furthermore, according to the apocryphal* Gospel of Nicodemus (4th–6th c.), during his descent, Christ cast the wicked dead into Tartarus, abolished Sheol, and separated salvation* from damnation*. Until the second* coming, after a person's physical death there is an interim existence, purgatory*, when the soul* exists separately until, at the general resurrection* of the flesh, the person is reconstituted and judged. While Eastern Christians, citing 1 Pet 3:19 and 4:6, long maintained the possibility of postmortem expiation and even conversion, Protestants deny the existence of purgatory*. Calvin* interpreted this experience as accepting the divine wrath* owed by all humans and a momentary near isolation from life and God*. At the Last Judgment*, there is a possibility of new life, life after death, but also the second death, death after death (Rev. 20:14, 21:8). Damnation* is the only real death. **See also ETERNITY; JUDGMENT.**

ALAN E. BERNSTEIN

Death, Christian Views of, among Western Feminists. In her work, culminating in *Foundations of Violence*, Grace Jantzen outlines the fascination with death, destruction, and violence* that has characterized Western culture from classical antiquity through Christianity and into contemporary postmodern thought. This emphasis results in a repudiation of all that is corporeal and in the present – the body*, the senses, sexuality*, and sensuality – and perpetuates a mystical fascination with worlds beyond the here and now.

In her elaborate genealogy of this Western preoccupation, Jantzen demonstrates that this "necrophilia" is *gendered*. Our death obsession is largely a male symbolic construct and preoccupation that seeks to repress and veil a masculinist fear and anxiety of the maternal body specifically and of female sexuality generally.

Feminist philosophers of religion like Jantzen refuse this obsession with death and destruction and instead focus on forces of "natality" that celebrate beauty, desire, and the creative impulse over Western "necrophilia." Life and new creation trump violence, death, and sacrifice*; newness, rebirth, transformation, and even redemption are essential to human flourishing. They further argue that unless the West learns to cherish natality, and the feminine symbolic, our obsession with death and destruction will continue to have real consequences in the world and eventually bring about our demise. **See also ORTHODOX CHURCHES, EASTERN, CLUSTER: INTRODUCTORY ENTRIES; THEOSIS, DEIFICATION.**

KATHLEEN O'GRADY

Death of God Theology, from the Greek myth of the dying and rising God ("We don't kill gods, they die") to Nietzsche's* "God is dead" ("We have killed God") through Luther* and Hegel*. The rhetoric of the theme triggered liturgical or historical rather than theological treatment. Conceptualizing the claim that, in God, the Father suffered the death of the Son (3rd c.), patripassianism* was declared heretical; it downgraded the Son's salvific work ("He dies for us"). This condemnation marked the end of an era. The Greco-Roman pantheon and Jewish Temple had collapsed, pointing to a metaphysic* Trinity* and its essentialist soteriological-ontological theism (God as Highest Being; see Heidegger, Martin; Metaphysics and Christian Theology). Given Jesus' option for the primacy of the Kingdom* of God over salvation*, ontological theism was initially challenged in the 1960s by Death of God theology: end-time (eschatic) existence consists not in changing worlds, but in changing the world in which the Word has become flesh.

Highest Being or Clockmaker, a stopgap God is useless and superfluous, an idol*. As with Luther and Calvin's* predestination*, the believer is freed from God *as well as* by God. There is no temple in the New Jerusalem. The useless and superfluous God is dead. Still, the Death of God theologies maintained by others, for whom we are saved from God rather than by God, appear to be a secular reappraisal of faith wrapped in apocalyptic or humanistic garments.

GABRIEL VAHANIAN

Death Penalty (the), one form of the state's claimed "right to kill," is a *punitive* form of killing for violation of a rule or law. It has never been completely separable from other uses of state-sanctioned violence, militarily (for war*) or politically (for removing rivals to state power).

New Testament teachings of Jesus on love* and forgiveness* and against revenge, and early followers' vulnerability to lethal force amid the Roman Empire, instilled in them a resistance to Christian support for or exercise of the death penalty. When Christians assumed imperial power (4th c.), however, they codified, sanctified, and wielded lethal and brutal force for centuries, authorizing state killing for both punitive and military purposes. It was also used politically against "heretics*" who threatened religiopolitical orders.

Christian resistance to the death penalty never died out, persisting among members of repressed, nonviolent heritages: Waldenses*, English radicals, Anabaptists*, Quakers*, and African slaves. Jesus' teachings, and his own death by imperial execution, were used to criticize Christian support of the death penalty and state violence. Christian resistance was strengthened by later, secular currents pressing for abolition of the death penalty. Most formal Christian Church organizations today oppose the death penalty, even if a large number of Christians still support it. **See also** IMAGE OF GOD.

MARK LEWIS TAYLOR

Deborah. Alluding to "word," "deed" (Heb *dabar*), and the useful, busy "bee," Deborah clearly evokes positive connotations. She is a leader in Judg 4, which tells of Barak's and her victory over Sisera and his army, and in Judg 5, where Deborah is portrayed as singing and celebrating victory, a rare instance of lyrical poetry in the Bible. One of the few well-known women among biblical characters, she is unique in embodying everything a major or minor judge is supposed to do: achieve military victory, rule, and perform justice, respectively. In Deborah, epic and lyrical poetry come together.

MIEKE BAL

Decalogue. See TEN COMMANDMENTS, DECALOGUE.

Decius, Roman emperor (249–51). After defeating Philip the Arabian, reputed to be a Christian sympathizer, Decius upheld old Roman traditions and civic religion. He required all citizens and noncitizens, males and females to make sacrifices to the traditional deities and obtain certificates. Christians were not required to abandon Christianity, but when they refused to perform the required rituals they were persecuted. The Decian persecutions*, the first to be empire-wide, created a major dispute within the church, centered around Cyprian's* requirement of strict penance* for the lapsed* and those who secured false certificates of sacrifice.

Decolonizing Theology. Theology and colonialism* have been closely related throughout history, although their connection has been investigated only recently. Many of the most significant Christian theological developments took place simultaneously with significant shifts and developments in the political structures of empire and colonialism.

One of the earliest christological confessions, "Jesus is Lord," developed in the context of the Roman Empire (mid-1st c. CE), when all its subjects were to assert that the Roman emperor was Lord. The Councils of Nicaea* (325) and Chalcedon* (451), which shaped the doctrines of the Trinity* and of Christ*, were convened and supported by Roman emperors. Anselm* of Canterbury wrote his well-known *Cur Deus homo* as the second archbishop of Canterbury, a position instituted by the Normans after the 1066 Norman Conquest. Martin Luther's* 16th-c. Reformation in Germany, and perhaps even his doctrine of justification*, cannot be imagined without the changing politics of empire in Europe. While the opposition by Bartolomé de las* Casas (d1566) to the Spanish Conquest is well known, his theology nevertheless proposes colonialist models that, though milder, were realized in the 18th- to 19th-c. colonialisms of other European nations. The father of liberal theology, Friedrich Schleiermacher* (d1834), was deeply interested in and influenced by European colonialism, as was recently recognized. The relation between the works of 20th-c. theologians and various postcolonial and neocolonial forms of empire remains to be clarified.

The major insight that requires fresh study of these phenomena is that the power of empire and colonialism is not limited to politics and economics. If empire and colonialism have an impact on all areas of life, including the realm of ideas, the exploration of relations between theology and colonialism becomes imperative. This insight does not imply, however, that empire and colonialism are able to control all aspects of life and of theology all the time. Decolonizing theology therefore faces at least two tasks: (1) to explore how theological thought is shaped by empire and to offer a critique; and (2) to identify which aspects of theology resist assimilation by colonial powers and to highlight tensions with these powers and instances of resistance. Such tensions and resistance potentially exist even in the above-mentioned theologies developed in close proximity to empire. As a result of these investigations, theological moves that push beyond empire and colonialism can be identified, and fresh understandings of the contributions of theology to the history of the world emerge. **See also COLONIALISM AND IMPERIALISM AND CHRISTIAN THEOLOGY; POSTCOLONIALISM AND CHRISTIAN THEOLOGY.**

JOERG RIEGER

Decretal, Papal, a pope's letter containing a decision regarding a matter of discipline written in response to a specific question or appeal.

Decretals, False (Pseudo-Isidorean), a collection of documents ascribed to Isidore Mercator, including genuine and forged canons* of councils and papal decretals*. Written in France around 850 in order to enhance the bishops' independence from both secular rulers and metropolitans*, the decretals authorized them to appeal directly to the pope. First quoted in 852, they were welcomed in Rome (864) because they enhanced the pope's authority both in the church and in relation to secular rulers. **See also POPES, ROMAN CATHOLIC, AND THE PAPACY.**

Dedication of Churches, setting aside of buildings used exclusively for worship; in high-liturgical traditions, marked by celebration of the Eucharist* and blessings outside and inside the building.

de Foucauld, Charles Eugène (1858–1916), desert hermit. Born in Strasbourg to an aristocratic family, he served in the French army, joined the Cistercian* Trappists, and went on pilgrimage to the Holy Land. There he conceived of a new model of religious life based on the "hidden life" of Jesus in Nazareth. In Algeria he pursued this life, bearing witness to the gospel among his poor Muslim neighbors until his assassination by Islamic insurgents. His spirituality later inspired the Little Brothers of Jesus and other "fraternities." He was beatified as a martyr by Pope Benedict XVI (2005). **See also HISTORY OF CHRISTIANITY CLUSTER: IN AFRICA: NORTH AFRICA.**

ROBERT ELLSBERG

Deification. See THEOSIS, DEIFICATION.

Deism, Enlightenment* emphasis on God as known through nature. It usually regards revelation* as a reiteration of what can be gained by reason*; it views clergy as unnecessary and parasitic, and God as acting through nature as a whole, without special providence.

de Marillac, Louise (1591–1660), wife, mother, religious founder of the Daughters of Charity (with Vincent* de Paul), 1633; canonized, 1934. In her widowhood, she turned to spiritual pursuits. Vincent de Paul was her spiritual director (c1624), and he increasingly relied on her to visit and maintain the spirit of his Confraternities of Charity. She also guided the formation of young rural women in their service of the poor* (assistance, education, hospital nursing, work with orphans and prisoners), at first in Paris, but eventually most of France. Her spirituality centered on a meditation on the centrality of union with Jesus crucified.

JOHN E. RYBOLT

Demiurge, Greek word for "artisan" used by Plato* and then by early Christians for God as forming the world. Today, commonly used negatively (as among the Gnostics) to refer to the inferior deity they associated with the material world. **See also GNOSTICISM.**

Democracy and Christianity. The roots of Western democracy can be traced to ancient Athens and Renaissance Italy, but it developed as the polity of modernity only after the European Enlightenment. The relationship between democracy and Christianity is historically ambiguous, dependent on the forms of Christianity that are present. Although democracy is secular in character, four trajectories within Christian tradition have made significant contributions to the development of its theory and praxis, as follows:

1. Notions such as subsidiarity* and the common good*, which emerged when medieval Roman Catholicism brought Christianity into creative interaction with Aristotelian* political philosophy
2. The Calvinist* tradition, which emphasized the need for mutual responsibility before God within a covenantal* relationship of the people of a society.
3. Heirs of the Radical* Reformation, English Nonconformity*, and liberal* Protestantism who affirmed the dignity of the individual, human* rights, freedom of conscience*, separation of church* and state, and religious toleration
4. The Christian Socialist* tradition, which stressed human solidarity, egalitarian participation in the democratic process, and economic* justice* as the basis for the sustainability of democracy

Each of these trajectories rejects tyrannical government in its own way. All acknowledge that human sinfulness* leads to political corruption, even in democracy, although some are more optimistic about human nature than others; and all eschew selfish individualism and seek to develop forms of community as the place within which human beings find fulfillment.

Although Christianity has provided many of the building blocks for democratic theory and contributed to its practical development around the world, Christianity as such does not unequivocally support one particular political system, whether a democracy or not. The Anglo-Saxon world more readily views democracy as related to Christian values (e.g. human rights). Yet democracy has inherent problems. As continental Europe suspected until well after World War II, it can be the harbinger of anarchy and revolution, and it is open to corruption of all kinds. But this does not mean that all systems of government are equally acceptable. Especially after the 20th-c. experience of Nazi and Stalinist totalitarianism, ecumenical Christianity now appears to be irrevocably committed to the retrieval of democracy as essential to its vision of a just world order. **See also CHURCH AND STATE RELATIONS CLUSTER; POLITICAL STUDIES OF CHRISTIANITY; POLITICAL THEOLOGY.** JOHN W. DE GRUCHY

Demonic Powers. See DEVIL, SATAN, DEMONS, AND DEMONIC POWERS.

Demonization. In the original sense, demonization means the reinterpretation of pagan* deities as demons by Christian theologians, foremost regarding polytheistic* religious systems in ancient Egypt, Greece, and Rome, as well as among early medieval Germanic, Celtic, and Slavic peoples. In the early modern period, deities of Native* American and Asian peoples were still demonized by Christian conquerors and missionaries.

Other monotheistic* religions were not demonized. However, as Islamic and Jewish believers were not members of the Christian community, they were associated with crime or conjurations in periods of crisis (see Islam and Christianity Cluster; Judaism and Christianity Cluster). The suspicion of support from demons in their supposed evildoing applied to Christian minorities as well. The gatherings of Cathars* and of Waldenses* were interpreted as devil worship. According to the persecution handbook (*Practica Inquisitionis heretice pravitatis*, c1320) of the French Dominican inquisitor Bernardo Gui, heretics were generally to be seen as allies of demons (see Inquisition).

The most striking example of demonization is the labeling as demonic in origin of popular beliefs in divination, fortune-telling, amulets, and magic. According to Augustine*, these things or acts require at least an implicit pact with the devil*, since believers or practitioners expect an effect they could not produce naturally, and hence implicitly expect demonic support. Augustine's theory of the implicit pact was approved by Thomas Aquinas* and put into practice by late medieval inquisitors, as noted by Henry Kramer (aka Heinrich Institoris), author of *The Witches' Hammer* (*Malleus Maleficarum*, 1486), a book that served as the theological foundation of witch-hunting in Europe.

Even contemporaries noticed that marginal people were the main targets of these prosecutions and that they were held responsible for all kinds of misfortune, particularly when moral entrepreneurs or "crusading reformers" (as sociologist Howard Becker has called them) took the initiative.

Demonization is not unique to Christianity or monotheistic religious systems; it also occurs among polytheistic civilizations even if they are open to accepting and absorbing foreign deities.

As an analytical term, "demonization" means the stigmatization of outsiders or minority groups. It prepares the ground for legal prosecution, mob violence, or war. **See also DEVIL, SATAN, DEMONS, AND DEMONIC POWERS; WITCHCRAFT, WITCHES.**

WOLFGANG BEHRINGER

Demons, in the Greek world, intermediate beings between earth and heaven; in Christian theology, fallen angels* who tempt humans to rebel against God, and evil spirits with the power to possess humans. **See also DEVIL, SATAN, DEMONS, AND DEMONIC POWERS.**

Demythologization. Bultmann's* project of using existentialist categories to interpret critically the mythological thinking that frames the NT. As defined by the history* of religion school, mythological thinking is prescientific; the natural world is the theater for supernatural agencies: demons*, evil spirits, angels*, and gods. Bultmann further argued that the NT proclamation about Jesus is framed in Jewish apocalyptic* and Gnostic* mythologies. Because these past mythologies are not Christian and are mutually contradictory, theologians should elucidate their inner meaning: the intuition that our familiar world does not have its ground in itself and that we desire redemption* from guilt and the anxiety that precedes death*. Bultmann argued that Heidegger's* conceptuality is most adequate for demythologizing because of its philosophical description of human beings as unique in being called by conscience to come out of their "inauthentic" preoccupation with worldly concerns and take responsibility for themselves and their freedom. **See also BULTMANN, RUDOLF.**

VAN A. HARVEY

Denmark. Arian* and Celtic* Christianity had some influence in Denmark before the 9th c. through Viking warriors who sailed as far as Canada and the Caspian Sea (late 8th--mid-10th c.). The Catholic mission began in 826 with the German monk Ansgar*. Christianization and development of the Danish nation were closely connected (10th–11th c.). Local landlords and monks built 1,800 stone churches in the 13th c. Competition between Roman Catholic bishops and kings came to an end in 1536, when King Christian III expropriated the church and turned it into an Evangelical Lutheran* state church. Since then the church has been governed by the state, although it was renamed a Folk* Church in the 1849 democratic constitution and local congregational boards were instituted (1903). Denmark was unique in Nordic countries in never experiencing the triangular split between state, church, and people. During the cultural and Pietist* religious revivals (19th c.), with Grundtvig* as its leading figure, one-quarter of Danes became "professing" Christians.

Today, 70–75% of Danes are "Culture* Christians," who use the church for baptism, confirmation, and funerals and sometimes for weddings, though without personal relation to congregational life, creed, or Bible. "Churched Christians" (10–15%) attend church services and activities more or less regularly, and a few "individual Christians" personally relate to Christianity without attending church. Twelve bishops (including one in Greenland and one in the Faeroe Islands) formally supervise more than 2,000 parishes with pastors who are state civil servants and are required to have a master of theology from one of the state universities.

With only 2% of church members attending church on a normal Sunday, Denmark has the world's lowest religious participation in weekly services. With little competition from the small "free churches," the Evangelical Lutheran Church in Denmark is thus the weakest "monopoly church" in the world. In the 20th c., old folk religiosity in modern dressing and, through immigration, Islam have become visible alternatives to Christianity. Thus church leaders have become aware that the church can remain Christian only as a church in mission – a difficult proposition when the church is governed by the secular state and most of its members are Culture Christians. **See also LUTHERANISM CLUSTER: IN NORDIC COUNTRIES.**

Statistics: Population (2003): 5.3 million (M). Christians, 4.6 M, 86.7% (Evangelical Lutherans, 4.5 M; other Protestants, 0.03 M; Roman Catholics, 0.03 M); Muslims, 0.2 M, 3.7%; nonreligious, 0.45 M; 8.8%. (*Source*: Danish Governmental Statistics, 2003.)

HANS RAUN IVERSEN

Denomination, a self-designation first used by English Dissenters* (Presbyterian*, Congregationalist*, and Baptist*) in the early 18th c. to suggest both their differences and their acknowledgment of each other; now often used, in an ecumenical spirit, to designate any church tradition.

Denominationalism, form of religious organization that is preeminent in the USA. Denominations differ from the classic models of church* and sect* in three ways. (1) They presuppose no established religion and put all religious bodies on the same footing. (2) They are both voluntaristic* (like sects) and inclusive in membership (like churches), and do not normally posit an absolute or exclusive claim to possess the truth. (3) Although they are often competitive with respect to membership, they can cooperate with other denominations for broader purposes. Denominationalism emerged in 18th-c. colonial America and became dominant with the collapse of the colonial established churches (19th c. in the USA; later elsewhere in the world). ROBERT BRUCE MULLIN

Dentière, Marie (1495–c1561), Reformer. Daughter of a noble family (d'Ennetières), she left her Augustinian convent and joined French Reformers in Strasbourg. She married Simon Robert, and the couple followed William Farel* to the Swiss Valais (1528), where she participated in her husband's ministry. Widowed (1533), she married Antoine Froment. The couple moved to Geneva (1535) and worked to establish the Reformed* religion. In August 1535, she exhorted nuns in the Poor* Clares' Convent to leave their order and renounce celibacy. When the Council of 200 exiled Farel and John Calvin* (1538), Dentière wrote a letter to Marguerite* de Navarre, which was published in Geneva (1539) as a *Very Useful Epistle*. The *Epistle*'s dedication defends women's rights to interpret and teach the Bible. Its "Defense of Women" presents exemplary women from the OT and NT and refutes the notion that women are the source of evil. The final section affirms salvation* through faith* alone, attacks the Mass*, and excoriates Roman Catholic clergy and the papacy. In a 1546 letter to Farel, Calvin reported a confrontation with Dentière, who had been publicly preaching in Geneva. A 1561 copy of Calvin's sermon on 1 Tim 2:8–12 carries a preface in which Dentière criticizes extravagant clothing and cosmetics.

MARY B. MCKINLEY

Deontic, Deontological Ethics (from Gk *to deon*), the approach to ethics* that emphasizes obligation and duty; a choice is right when it conforms to a moral norm. Deontological ethics calls for a quest for basic moral principles, which many Christians envision as a law* – God's will as revealed in Scriptures* (and/or church tradition*). Yet for Kant* and many theologians, conformity to a moral norm should not be confused with legalism. Through regard for others ("harm not"), pure practical reason both establishes *what* morality unconditionally demands and determines the will to do it. **See also CONSEQUENTIALIST ETHICS; PERFECTIONIST ETHICS.**

de Paul, Vincent. See VINCENT DE PAUL.

Descartes, René (1596–1650), mathematician, scientist, philosopher. A key figure in the scientific revolution, Descartes sought to reconcile scientific inquiry with Roman Catholic doctrine. He invented the Cartesian coordinate system and founded analytic geometry. His rationalist epistemology shaped the great debates of modern Western philosophy. The son of a councilor at the Parliament of Brittany, he studied at the prestigious Jesuit* college of La Flèche (1606–14), earned a law degree (Poitiers, 1615–16), joined the army of Prince Maurice of Nassau, then of Maximilian of Bavaria (1618–19), took up residence in Paris (1625), settled in the Netherlands (1628–49), and died in Stockholm in the service of Queen Christina of Sweden (1649–50).

With Mersenne, he rejected final causes and vitalist elements of Aristotelian* natural philosophy, seeking to explain physical phenomena in mechanical terms. However, intimidated by Rome's censure of Galileo* (1633), he chose not to publish his mechanist account of the world and human physiology. Instead, he summarized his conclusions in the *Discourse on Method* (1637), in which he abandoned his schooling and laid out a vast program of research in physics, metaphysics*, medicine, and ethics*. He intended the *Discourse*, written in French, to appeal to a broad audience – "even women" – but returned to Latin in the *Meditations on First Philosophy* (1641) to establish the metaphysical credentials for his mechanist natural philosophy. From one indubitable intuition (*cogito, sum* – "I think, I am"), he identifies a criterion of truth (clarity and distinction) by means of which he goes on to prove both God's existence and the reality of our perceptions, claiming in this way to overcome the skeptical critique of knowledge popularized by Montaigne and Charron. His correspondence with Princess Elizabeth of Bohemia led him to broach ethics. He tempered Stoic* impassibility in the *Passions of the Soul* (1649); to live happily, one must channel rather than suppress the passions.

Descartes courted the powerful Jesuits his whole life but never won the approval of the Roman Catholic Church. His assertion of the radical distinction between mind and body (dualism*) contradicted the Catholic doctrine of transubstantiation*; his works were placed on the List of Prohibited Books (*Index* Librorum Prohibitorum*) in 1663. The Jansenist* Pascal* noted the originality of Descartes's *cogito* with respect to a similar formulation in Augustine's* *City of God*, yet he dismissed Descartes's confidence in reason as "uncertain and useless." The epistemological questions raised by Descartes proved more enduring than his natural philosophy, which waned in the shadow of Newton's* *Principia* (1687). REBECCA WILKIN

Descent into Hell, a clause concerning Christ, based on 1 Pet 3:18–20 and Ps 16:10 (Act 2:27), in the received version of the Apostles'* Creed, recorded by Rufinus* of Aquileia (c400). It has been variously interpreted to mean that Christ (1) conquered death* and hell*, freeing captive souls, or (2) fully experienced the wrath of God against sinful humanity, or (3) continued in the state of the dead until resurrected.

Desert, any deserted place, not necessarily arid; "wilderness" is often a better term. Deserted places, not being subject to human control, symbolize that which is wild, chaotic, and thus fearsome and demonic*. Egyptian monks of 4th-c. eremetic* monasticism* sought deserted areas in order to live apart from others in contemplation and self-discipline, and perhaps to pursue demons into their last places of refuge. Metaphorically, a time of spiritual uncertainty and testing is often called a "wandering in the wilderness," like that of the Israelites before their crossing of the Jordan and their entry into the Promised Land. **See also WILDERNESS.**

Design, Argument from, an 18th-c. argument that the adaptations of life forms to their environments must be the result of intelligent design. A theory of "external teleology*" rather than Aristotle's "internal teleology" of finite beings, it was dealt a blow by Darwin's* theory of natural selection: that characteristics are shaped *by* their interactions.

Desire. Early theologians appropriated the Song* of Songs to develop the idea that desire is the link between the human and the divine. They identified the problem of humanity as estrangement from its essential nature and interpreted redemption* as theosis* (divinization) through which desire is purged of attachment to created goods. Desire as longing for and joy in the divine restores fallen human nature. Desire emphasizes the fundamental goodness of human nature and the nonduality of the human and the divine; it underlines the creative and redemptive quality of the divine kenosis* that eternally empties itself as love* and for love. These themes remain prominent in the Eastern Orthodox* Church.

During the Middle Ages in the West, desire was a common trope used by contemplatives* and mystics* to express the relationship between God* and the soul*. Bridal imagery and erotic metaphors gave expression to the joy and intimacy that arises as "self-will" is displaced by the divine will.

In line with a Middle Age trend in Roman Catholic theology (Anselm*, Aquinas*) Protestant theology privileged legal metaphors and interpreted the problem of humanity to be guilt before a cosmic judge. Christ was no longer the divine bridegroom but an atoning sacrifice* (see Atonement #2). *Eros** was interpreted to be a selfish and indulgent love in contrast to the gracious power of *agape**.

The importance of desire as an important theological theme reemerged in the 20th c., especially in Feminist* and Queer* theology. A juridical model of atonement* and redemption* appeared woefully inadequate in light of the atrocities and oppressions of the 20th c. Desire reemphasizes the love of God for humanity and corrects the negative assessment of the body* and sexuality* characteristic of much Christian moral thought. It unifies God and humanity, body and soul, *eros* and *agape*.

WENDY FARLEY

Deus Absconditus (Lat "hidden God"), Luther's expression for God apart from revelation* and grace*, often depicted as arbitrary and wrathful.

Deus Revelatus (Lat "revealed God"), Luther's expression for God as revealed through Christ, gracious and justifying* sinners.

Deuterocanonical Biblical Books are viewed as "also belonging to the canon" (the approximate meaning of "deuterocanonical"), although there was hesitation about including them, as their exclusion from the Jewish canon (the HB) and from the canon of certain churches – especially Protestant churches – exemplifies. Thus what Protestants (and biblical scholars) call "OT Apocrypha*" are viewed as "deuterocanonical books" by Catholics and Orthodox. **See also BIBLE, CANON OF THE.**

Deuteronomistic History. Martin Noth proposed (1943) that Joshua*, Judges*, 1–2 Samuel*, and 1–2 Kings* were written as a unified history of Israel from conquest to the Exile*, with Deuteronomy* as a preface. He called this work the "Deuteronomistic History." It explains Israel's changing fortunes and eventual destruction as a consequence of its disobedience of the laws of Deuteronomy. Noth's proposal became the standard model for understanding these books. Yet scholars now tend to find a greater level of optimism in the book than Noth did. Rather than a single exilic edition, some now hold that it was twice redacted to express prophetic and legal concerns. Most scholars now date the "Deuteronomistic History" to King Josiah's reign (late 7th c. BCE) and view it as King Josiah's charter for his religious reforms. An exilic-era redaction brought the history up to date by blaming the Exile on King Manasseh, whose sins were depicted as so heinous that Josiah's actions were insufficient to convince God to revoke his judgment. Recently, the very idea of these books forming a "Deuteronomistic History" and the nature of a "deuteronomistic school" has come under closer scrutiny and critique. JAMES R. LINVILLE

Deuteronomy, the fifth book of the Jewish and the Christian canon. Its title in Hebrew is *devarim*, or "words," a term from the opening phrase of the book (1:1); titling books in this way was a common practice in ancient Judaism. By contrast the title "Deuteronomy" is a transliteration of the Greek title in the Septuagint* based on a controversial interpretation of Deut 17:18. The Hebrew *mishne hatora hazot* (lit. "a copy [a double, a second copy] of this law") is translated in Greek *to deuteronomion touto*, "this second law," implying that Deuteronomy is a second, perhaps distinct body of legal tradition rather than a form of the same law (of Moses).

Deuteronomy recounts the journey of the biblical community from Horeb to Moab. In its retelling of the story, Deuteronomy casts itself as Moses' farewell speech to the biblical community, and it places the people of Israel on the brink of entering the land of Canaan. Deuteronomy has a distinctive method of telling the story about how the people of Israel escaped bondage in Egypt, wandered in and through the wilderness, engaged and defeated their opponents in combat, and were now poised to enter the land that YHWH promised to Abraham*, Isaac*, and Jacob* – figures to whom the literary and cultural traditions of ancient Israel ascribe prominent roles in the history of the biblical community.

Deuteronomy opens with a narrative that places the biblical community just east of the Jordan River (Deut 1:1–5), then begins to cite sermons Moses delivered to Israel (Deut 1:6–4:40, 5:1–11:32). These speeches introduce a large block of legal injunctions that give the people guidelines regarding how they should live once they enter the land of Canaan (Deut 12:1–26:19). Deuteronomy then includes another speech of Moses that delineates incentives for obeying and curses for disobeying deuteronomic legislation (Deut 27–28). Deuteronomy suggests that Moses delivered still another address in which he discusses the journey from Egypt to the land of Canaan and reiterates the covenant* into which YHWH entered with Israel in Moab (Deut 29–30). Miscellaneous items appear in the final chapters, including the "Song of Moses" (Deut 32), the narrative detailing Moses' blessings of the tribes of Israel (Deut 33), and an account of the death of Moses and the investiture of Joshua (Deut 31 and 34).

Deuteronomy 12–26 contains a compilation of diverse legal regulations, many of which appear in Exod 20:22–23:19. Yet layers of law in Deut 12–26 are absent in Exodus. These legal injunctions deal with the monarch and civil magistrates. They prohibit the presence of images in the Israelite cultic system, centralize the Israelite cultus, and regulate behavior toward social subgroups that existed on the fringes of the socioeconomic structure. Ideology embedded in Deut 12–26 includes the belief that peace, fecundity, abundance of food, well-being, and the keeping of the Law are closely intertwined, a "YHWH alone" theology, and the claim that individuals in the biblical community should love YHWH with all of their heart.

The ideology* in Deut 12–26 is far-reaching. It shapes the reconstruction of history in Joshua*, Judges*, 1–2 Samuel*, and 1–2 Kings*. In fact, it is probable that this ideology played a role in the Josianic* reformation. Moreover, Deut 12–26 and the Book of Jeremiah* share ideas about YHWH, religiosity, and the Israelite cultus. Scholars account for this phenomenon by postulating the existence of a deuteronomic movement at work in the biblical community. While subgroups of tradition in Deuteronomy may come from the Kingdom, during the 8th c. BCE, it is probable that the book of Deuteronomy received its final form during the late 6th c. BCE.

HAROLD V. BENNETT

Devil, Satan, Demons, and Demonic Powers. In the Bible there is mention of evil spirits, sometimes called "demons" (usually using the diminutive, Gk *daimonion*), resembling the concept of demons (Gk *daimon*, "spirit") in Greek philosophy, causing disease or madness; but there is also the dualistic* concept of an evil force in opposition to God, sometimes imagined as an army and in few instances personalized as Satan. The concept of an evil anti-God, which was to become influential in the Christian tradition, can be traced back to the Iranian culture of Zoroastrianism, where God was opposed by "Ahriman," an evil counterpart. This cosmological opposition was echoed by "Satan" in the Jewish tradition. "Satan" (transl. "the accuser") originally served as a kind of prosecuting attorney at God's court and only later developed into a director of evil, without ever becoming too prominent.

Satan started a new career in the early Christian Era. In the period of their persecution, desperate Christians perceived Satan as the "ruler of the world" (2 Cor 4:4). The "leader of the demons" was called "*diabolos*" (Gk; Lat *diabolus*), a term that entered the European languages (e.g. French, *diable*; English, "devil"; German, *Teufel*). In the central narrative of Christ's temptation (Matt 4:1–11), the devil is portrayed as acting in person. In the Book of Revelation, he is even "king of hell" (Rev 9:11) and acts explicitly as the Antichrist (Rev 20). But the message of the Bible remains ambivalent, since in some parts of the OT and NT the role of demons is marginal (Genesis, Deuteronomy) or explicitly denied (Acts 23:8).

Although Augustine* (354–430), earlier a follower of Manichaeism*, sometimes described the material world as the realm of the devil – the *Civitas diaboli* as opposed to the *Civitas Dei* – the widespread attitude was to downplay the power of demons during the period of Christianization. Since the Christian God had to be powerful in order to attract new believers, and since Germanic and Slavic rulers – in the footsteps of Emperor Constantine* – would convert only to a powerful God, demons were portrayed as less important (from the Carolingian* period to the High Middle Ages). During the period of the European expansion (10th–12th c.), a period of favorable climate and economic and demographic growth, urbanization and the inculturation of Scandinavia, Eastern Europe, Southern Italy, the Iberian Peninsula, and the Holy Land, the image of the triumphant God continued to prevail.

It was only when expansion came to an end, when the climate turned less favorable, and when endemic as well as epidemic diseases led to a shrinking economy and even to decreasing populations, that the pessimistic ideologies of Augustine and Thomas Aquinas* took root. Starting in the 13th c., "demonology" – the science of demons – rose to prominence and began to shape European minds. An increasing number of theologians saw human society on the brink of the Apocalypse*, and the devil with his supposed human allies (minorities like the Muslims in Spain* or the Jews*, Christian heretics* like the Cathars* and Waldenses*, or imaginary terrorists like witches*) seemed to endanger the future of humankind. Pogroms* and the persecution of witches were being interpreted as part of the final struggle between good and evil, as a prelude to the final Judgment*.

However, even at the climax of European witch-hunting (c1600), skepticism concerning the power of demons was widespread. In the worldview of many groups, such as Anabaptists* and Spiritualists*, there was no space for the devil. For leading intellectuals, e.g. Michel de Montaigne, stories of the devil were but fairy tales. In the Reformation* and Catholic* Renewal periods, institutional pressure was too enormous to articulate openly such rejections of demons. It was only the generation of Thomas Hobbes (17th c.) that started to object to the theologians and their views, and this more impolitely owing to the fact that their monopoly of interpretation was over. Subsequently, unbelief in the existence of the devil was equated with atheism*. Nevertheless, it was up to Christian theologians like the Dutch minister Balthasar Bekker (1634–98) to deconstruct the idea of any impact of spirits or demons, let alone Satan, on the material world, thus contributing to the end of the witch-hunt.

From the early 18th c., the figure of the devil was historicized by enlightened authors like Christian Thomasius and Daniel Defoe. Belief in demons was ridiculed by an increasingly strong current of secular* unbelief. Under the impact of the scientific revolution, economic success, political stability, and other aspects of modernity in Europe and the Americas, Christian theologies started to deconstruct traditional demonology accordingly (e.g. from psychological perspectives). In the present, theologians seem to avoid the subject, but Pope John* Paul II repeatedly confirmed the existence of the devil. **See also** DEMONIZATION; WITCHCRAFT, WITCHES. WOLFGANG BEHRINGER

Devotio Moderna. This spiritual movement spread in the Netherlands* and the Rhine valley (14th–15th c.). It originated with Geert Groote* (1340–84), was propagated by the Brothers* and Sisters of the Common Life and the canons regular of the religious houses and schools of Windesheim (Netherlands), and had a major influence on Gabriel Biel*, Erasmus*, and Charles* V. The most famous text of the Devotio Moderna is *The Imitation of Jesus Christ*, attributed to Thomas* à Kempis (d1471). It delineates a form of spirituality for laypeople, underscoring devotion to Christ and to his Passion, devotion to the Eucharist, systematic meditation, and reform of moral life for laymen.

GUY-THOMAS BEDOUELLE, OP

Devotion (from Lat "vowing," "giving"), solemnly giving oneself to God or Christ (see, e.g., Devotio Moderna), through formal action (monastic vows*, worship*, prayer*), intense informal worship (meditation of Scripture*, private spiritual life), or inward zeal. In popular Roman Catholicism (and Anglicanism), the term "devotion" also designates acts of veneration* associated with shrines, icons*, or places of pilgrimage* dedicated to a saint* or to the Virgin Mary*, as well as special veneration of Jesus (e.g. devotion to the Sacred Heart of Jesus) or of the sacrament (e.g. adoration of the Holy Sacrament).

Devotional, a written or customary guide to private acts of devotion, aimed at deepening the spiritual* life.

Dewey, John (1859–1952), one of North America's preeminent philosophers identified with US pragmatism. One of Dewey's earliest writings, *Principles of Psychology*, was based on the evolutionary science of his day, especially the philosophy of T. H. Huxley. Dewey's reconstructive philosophy was a reaction to speculative idealism, rationalism, and classical British empiricism. His was a "radical empiricism." Thought, reason, intelligence, and categories of knowledge are instrumental and experimental, as is religion. Knowledge is instrumental for seeing the consequences* of existing events and is used as a plan and method for conducting human actions. As with knowledge, religion (ritualized and organized) historically grows from the religious need of traditional societies to manage precarious events in experience. When societies advance scientifically and technologically, the traditional functions that religion once offered will be transcended by creative intelligence, and the religious function of experience will be assimilated into a common, social faith. The works that best describe Dewey's understanding of religion are *The Quest for Certainty* and *A Common Faith*.

VICTOR ANDERSON

Diaconate, the office of deacon* or the period of time a deacon serves.

Diakonia (Gk "service"), a frequently used term in the NT designating the major characteristic of all ministries, including liturgical ministries – that of preaching and serving others (including the poor and the needy) as Christ did. Today the term *diakonia* most commonly refers to the shared ministry whose purpose is to serve God among suffering people, among the poorest, among those who suffer, among those most in need. Thus *diakonia* is not simply the ministry of deacons* and deaconesses*, although through their services they often epitomize *diakonia*. **See also DEACON, DIACONATE; DEACONESS.**

Dialectic, originally a form of logical argumentation associated with Socrates and dramatized by Plato*, involving refuting an argument by evaluating definitions of concepts and their relationships. Kant* used a "transcendental dialectic" to expose the illusion of knowledge beyond phenomena and possible experience. For Hegel* dialectic is the passing over of a notion into its own negation because of conflict between its inherent aspects. Thus Hegel viewed reason as developing through historical interactions, a notion applied by Karl Marx* to social and economic processes.

Dialectical Theology emerged as a school of theological thought after 1918, primarily as a reaction against liberal Protestantism. It was developed (early 20th c.) chiefly by Karl Barth*, Emil Brunner, Friedrich Gogarten, and Rudolf Bultmann*, who were united by similar assumptions about theological methodology. Inspired by the Kierkegaardian* and, to a lesser extent Dostoyevskian*, use of dialectical method, the dialectical theologians proceeded on the assumption that humanity's essential condition is one of crisis before God. Humanity and God are separated by a "barrier of death*," the solution to which is found, not in religion, but in the encounter with Jesus, in whom is revealed both God's *no* to human self-sufficiency and God's *yes* of grace*.

Barth, whose influence was of pioneering significance to dialectical theology, argued in his

1919 commentary on Romans and again in his famous Tambach lecture, "The Christian's Place in Society," that there exists a "dialectic between time and eternity." For Barth this was essentially a code for his insistence that God and humanity are fundamentally discontinuous, that neither God nor God's revelation can be equated or synthesized with human philosophical or cultural presuppositions. Barth thus sought to emphasize the necessity and yet, from the human side, the impossibility of encounter with divine revelation.

In contrast, Brunner, Bultmann, and Gogarten gradually developed their respective theologies in more anthropocentric directions. For them, following Heidegger, the dialectical character of theology came to be based less on the negation of humanity by revelation than on the dialogic nature of human existence itself. Brunner therefore thought it possible to locate the "point of contact" between humanity and the Word of God, while Gogarten argued that it was both possible and necessary to develop a secular ethics.

The content and objectives of dialectical theology were articulated principally through the journal *Zwischen den Zeiten* (Between the times), founded by Barth, Gogarten, and Eduard Thurneysen in 1922, when the unity of the dialectical school was still intact. It soon became clear that the major proponents of dialectical theology were heading in divergent directions, leading them to differing political reactions to Hitlerism. Thus by 1933 both the journal and dialectical theology as a school had ceased to exist.

MARK R. LINDSAY

Dialogue, Ecumenical, is the conversation among Christians of different churches or communions; it is "intrafaith" (in contrast to interfaith) dialogue*. Ecumenical dialogue is a conversation of discovery. "In speaking the truth in love" (Eph 4:15), one discovers not only one's ecumenical partner but also oneself. Bilateral or multilateral, dialogue is contextual* and takes place on various levels. Each dialogue is shaped by the identity, culture*, language, and symbolic* order of the interlocutors and of the churches they represent. At the local, regional, national, or international level, one finds either formal official dialogues sponsored by ecclesial authorities or informal dialogues conducted by ecumenical centers and groups. Because of the disparity of ecclesial structures of authority* (see Church, Concepts and Life Cluster: Types of Ecclesiastical Structures), a given dialogue is not always viewed in the same way by different churches.

Dialogue among Christians draws on Scripture* that presents unity as both a gift and a call. Jesus prayed for his disciples' unity: "May all be one . . . so that the world may believe that you have sent me" (John 17:21). Paul grounds the Christian vocation in "one Lord, one faith, one baptism" (Eph 4:5). From its scriptural base, dialogue searches tradition* to find the foundation on which to build ecumenical consensus. The consensus that is sought concerns full visible unity* in apostolic faith*, life rooted in Word* and sacrament*, and missional* witness* to church and world. This unity has come to be understood in terms of *koinonia* (communion*). The dialogue's task is to identify shared elements of faith, life, and witness and to discern differences, and among these to distinguish between differences compatible with the consensus and church-dividing differences.

Ecumenical dialogue is theological, historical, and pastoral. As theological, it is an encounter among equals, this equality being discerned from the perspective of each tradition's ecclesiological self-understanding. As historical, ecumenical dialogue studies the Christian past so as to explore the variety of understandings of the church's faith, life, and witness, and examines how these findings might assist the churches in drawing closer together. As pastoral, ecumenical dialogue opens the institutional encounter of churches through the personal encounter of individuals. Doing theology* together, interlocutors engage in faith formation by sharing their Christian experience and by praying together.

Dialogue does not exist for its own sake. Nor is its goal merely the writing of interchurch reports. Rather, dialogue serves the people behind the documents and promotes the reception of ecumenical findings in the churches.

LORELEI F. FUCHS, SA

Dialogue, Interfaith. Dialogue between Christians and the followers of other faiths is not a luxury reserved for Christian intellectuals but a daily necessity as globalization* and the mass media bring believers of different religions into frequent contact with each other. Furthermore, political events and acts of violence by fanatics of all faiths (not only Muslims) have made interfaith dialogue a matter of extreme urgency.

Interfaith dialogue as a genuine opening of persons of different faiths to one another with a readiness to share and be enriched by other faiths serves a multiplicity of functions. It helps overcome fear of the "other," removes misunderstanding of and prejudices against other religions, promotes collaboration with others in areas of life beyond religion, and enhances the understanding and practice of one's own faith.

The Pontifical Council for Inter-religious Dialogue of the Roman Catholic Church has suggested four modes of interfaith dialogue: (1) the dialogue of life consists in sharing daily life, which fosters mutual understanding, neighborly assistance, and cordial friendship among adherents of different religions; (2) the dialogue of collaborative action brings believers of different faiths together to promote justice, human rights, peace, human development, and ecological well-being; (3) the dialogue of reflection makes possible a deeper understanding of and enrichment by the beliefs and practices of religions other than one's own; and (4) the dialogue of spiritual experience, the deepest and most transformative, brings people together to pray, each in the way of his or her tradition and later, possibly, to pray together, in a common way. The dialogue between Christianity and Judaism* is unique, governed by a different dynamics and theology, given the special relationship between these two religious traditions.

Interreligious dialogue is often looked on with suspicion by non-Christians. It is feared to be a covert attempt by Christians to convert them, especially when it is presented as part of Christian mission* (as official documents of the Roman Catholic Church often do). Even the widespread view that believers of non-Christian faiths are "anonymous* Christians" (Karl Rahner*), though legitimate from a Christian point of view, may be misunderstood as a theological cooptation of non-Christian religions and as a refusal to encounter the other as other. Interfaith dialogue should not be allowed to eclipse the dialogue that the church must carry out with atheists and nonbelievers who still present a formidable challenge to the Christian faith. **See also** RELIGIONS AND CHRISTIANITY. PETER C. PHAN

Diaspora (Gk *diaspeirein*, "to scatter") generally connotes the displacement and dispersal of a people from their homeland. The term is used primarily in reference to the Jews, whose separation from Palestine began in the biblical era, becoming a paradigm of much of their existence. Diaspora was often conflated with *galut* (exile*) and interpreted as punishment for Israelite sins* (Lev 26:33; Deut 4:26–28, 28:63–65; Jer 5:19, 9:15). Long before the destruction of the Second Temple (70 CE), Jews had settled outside Palestine, a principal migration having taken place in the Hellenistic period (after 323 BCE), and most of it voluntarily. Jews lived all over the Mediterranean, usually in Greek-speaking cities, in communities where they could engage freely in a wide variety of occupations, enjoy civic privileges, and maintain their distinctiveness through adherence to the Torah and communal participation in synagogues (1 Macc 15:22–23; Philo*, *Leg.* 281–83). Paul's missionary activity regularly brought him first to the synagogues of diaspora Jewry (e.g. Acts 13:14, 14:1, 17:2–3, 18:4, 18:19, 18:26, 19:8–9), the most logical sites for the initial spread of Christianity. Ancient Jews outside Palestine never developed a theory of diaspora and rarely categorized it negatively. Though Jerusalem was their "mother city," their own communities were their native lands (Philo, *Flacc.* 46). ERICH S. GRUEN

Diatessaron (Gk "through four"), created by Tatian* (c170), is a harmony integrating the four Gospels into a single text. Its original language was most likely Syriac, though it survives in translations only.

A onetime student of Justin* Martyr, Tatian, born in Syria, left Rome after being accused of heresy and returned to obscurity in the East. In his Diatessaron, he gave the Oriental Church its first version of the four Gospels. The Diatessaron remained the main form in which, until the late 4th c., Syriac Christianity read the gospel. Yet it was banned (early 5th c.), and the four Gospels were read instead.

In addition to the Gospels, the Diatessaron integrated material from a fifth source, probably an ancient gospel tradition known to the Syriac* Church. Tatian conformed the OT quotations in the Gospels to the Peshitta* (the Syriac version of the OT). This receptivity toward local textual traditions helps to explain the early popularity of the Diatessaron in the East.

The Diatessaron was translated into Latin at an early date, then from Latin into many European languages. Yet these Western harmonies, though used in popular religion, never competed with the canonical Gospels.

Scholars painstakingly recovered part of the original Syriac text of the Diatessaron, giving them access to a version of the gospel text that was older than most other manuscripts and that in some ways throws new light on beliefs and practices of the early church. JAN JOOSTEN

Didache, a compilation of earlier sources (rather than an original composition), has four thematic sections: a Jewish "Two Ways" instruction (Chaps. 1–6), a liturgical treatise (Chaps. 7–10), a treatise on church organization (Chaps. 11–15), and an eschatological section (Chap. 16). The manual was composed around 100 CE for a Christian congregation in (Western) Syria. What was the purpose of the Didache? The Jewish roots apparent in each section show a community within the larger fabric of Judaism*. Yet certain features in 8:1–3, 9:4, 10:5, and 14:1 typify the manual as non-Jewish. The present text probably reflects a process of transition. By the time the document was created, so many Gentiles had already been adopted into the community that it became sociologically a Gentile Christian group.

The Didache attempts to overcome the tension between non-Jewish and Jewish Christians by establishing an identity separate from contemporary Judaism.

Claiming apostolic authority, the manual was widely known and highly esteemed in the churches during the first five centuries. The influence of the original Two Ways instruction (without 1:3a–2:1 and 6:2–3) lasted even longer: it served as a model for the basic instruction of neophytes and Christian believers through the early Middle Ages. HUUB VAN DE SANDT

Didascalia Apostolorum, a church order written in Syria (first half of the 3rd c.). Modeled on the Didache*, it became in turn the basis of the first six books of the Apostolic* Constitutions. While this work and the Constitutions made use of Jewish sources, it attacked Jewish Christians, drawing a contrast between the original Law (the Decalogue*, identical with natural* law) and the ceremonial "second Law" given as a punishment after the rebellion in the wilderness (cf. the negative views of the Law in Stephen's speech, Acts 7:42–50, and the Epistle of Barnabas*).

Didymus the Blind of Alexandria (309–94 or 313–98), biblical commentator, theologian, spiritual writer. Blind by the age of four or five, Didymus had texts read to him, memorizing their philosophical and theological arguments. Didymus's commentaries employ allegorical* exegesis and show his opposition to Manichaeism* and to Arian* and neo-Arian (Eunomian*) theology. His commentaries are important contributions to the Greek exegetical tradition, and his teaching on ascetic* life was highly regarded by Evagrius* Ponticus and other educated ascetics of the 4th–7th c. Didymus's works were anathematized (553) because he sympathized with Origen's* teaching on the preexistence of souls. BYARD BENNETT

Dies Irae (Lat "day of wrath"), opening words of a rhymed hymn depicting the soul facing Judgment. Originating in Benedictine* circles and rewritten by a Franciscan* (probably Thomas of Celano), it was used in the Mass* for the Dead at funerals and in the liturgy for All* Saints' Day. Composers, notably Hector Berlioz and Sergei Rachmaninoff, adopted the initial chanted tones as a musical theme.

Dietary Laws, scriptural or traditional regulations concerning what to eat or not to eat, when to eat, and sometimes how to prepare food.

Diocese, the territory under the pastoral* jurisdiction of a bishop*. Several dioceses form a province*.

Diocletian (245–313), Roman emperor (284–305) who reorganized the Empire by distributing power among four regional rulers and creating a new degree of autocracy. At first he continued the tacit toleration of Christianity, but his loyalty to Roman traditions, encouraged by Porphyry's* belief that Christians were too exclusive, eventually led him to issue four edicts of persecution* with increasing severity, starting in 303. In 305 he abdicated and retired to Salona. Some persecutions continued; soon edicts of toleration were issued in the West and East (306, 311) and in the Edict of Milan* (313).

Diodore of Tarsus (d c390), bishop, theologian, exegete. Educated in Athens, Diodore was ordained a priest by Meletius of Antioch, founded an ascetic school near Antioch*, and became bishop of Tarsus (378). He was a leading figure at the Council of Constantinople* (381). Diodore attacked polytheism and was a firm opponent of Arianism* and Apollinaris*. He is best known as the dominant figure of the Antiochene* school of exegesis*, insisting on literal* and historical interpretation of Scripture as opposed to the allegorical* method favored in Alexandria. Diodore's students included John* Chrysostom and Theodore* of Mopsuestia. His Antiochene Christology*, emphasizing the humanity of Christ, is believed to have anticipated Nestorianism*. ANDREA STERK

Diognetus, Letter to, a 2nd-c. anonymous letter by a Christian to an inquirer, explaining Christians' dissent from the doctrines of both Jews* and Gentiles*. It is notable for its depiction of Christians as sojourners* living in but not of the world, for whom "every foreign place is their homeland, every homeland foreign." Despite this they are "the soul of the world" (Chaps. 5–6).

Dionysius Exiguus (Lat "small," "poor," "skinny") (c470–c545). Born in Scythia (now Romania*), he was a monk in Rome and translated an influential collection of canon* laws from Greek into Latin. While calculating the dates of Easter* for coming years (525), he also developed a chronology of past events and for the first time dated them "before Christ" (BC, now BCE [before the common era], out of respect for other religions) and "after Christ" (*anno Domini*, AD, or the common era, CE). This system of dating became the standard method throughout Europe after being used by Bede* in England.

Dionysius (Jacob) bar Salibi (early 12th c.–1171), rhetor, polemist, deacon, bishop, metropolitan. Born in Melitene (west of the Euphrates); known as Dionysius, his name as bishop of Mar'ash (Germanicia, 1154), then as metropolitan of Amida (Northern Syria, 1167). He played a major role in the Syriac theological renaissance (12th–13th c.), writing many homilies, liturgical works (on the Syriac Orthodox liturgy, especially baptism), canon law, commentaries on classical and patristic texts (on Dionysius* the Pseudo-Aeropagite and Evagrius* Ponticus), polemical treatises (against Muslims, Jews, Nestorians*, Chalcedonians, Melkites*, Armenians*, and idolaters), theological works, and biblical commentaries. These writings distill the Syriac intellectual tradition of the first millennium, and offer rare and illuminating insight into relations between Christians, Jews, and Muslims, not from the perspective of Western crusaders*, but from within the frequently neglected viewpoint of the Oriental Orthodox* tradition. His *Against the Muslims* is unique among Christian works on Islam from the medieval period (Griffith). His commentaries on portions of Aristotle's *Organon* and on Porphyry's *Isagoge* were prominent in the Syriac theological curriculum; it was said in the East that without them "it is not possible to obtain an understanding of the scriptures." **See also** ISLAM AND CHRISTIANITY CLUSTER.

RIFAAT EBIED

Dionysius the Pseudo-Areopagite (5th–6th c.) is the name given to the author of the *Corpus Dionyiacum*, comprising *De divinis nominibus*, *De mystica theologia*, *De coelesti hierarchia*, *De ecclesiastia hierarcha*, and some remarkable theological epistles. Throughout the Middle Ages, this author was thought to be the disciple converted by Paul on the Acropolis in Athens (Acts 17:34). The author's quotations and paraphrasing of the Neoplatonist* Proclus (412–80) are among the important clues enabling scholars to establish that he flourished in the 5th–6th c., perhaps in Syria as a Greek-speaking monk. His theological tractates and letters articulate a mystical* theology revolving in good part around the Nameless God of Many Names (see Apophaticism) and the notion of hierarchy in the manifestation of the Supreme Divinity through all the orders of creation. This world picture is a synthesis of Neoplatonic teaching and Christian revelation. Dionysius's writings are fundamental, particularly to later Greek theology. He continued to be recognized as a first-rank authority on angelology, ecclesiology, and negative theology, even after it was disclosed that he had not been the convert of Paul on the Acropolis. He still guides speculation on the limits of theological knowledge, and so reminds us of the "Unknown God" evoked by Paul in his preaching to the Greeks. **See also** NEOPLATONISM AND CHRISTIANITY.

WILLIAM FRANKE

Diphysites. See DYOPHYSITES.

Diptychs, folded tablets with two leaves listing persons, living and dead, to be commemorated at the Eucharist*. Entry or removal of the names of bishops* in the diptychs was a sign of communion* or excommunication*, respectively. A diptych is also a pair of Byzantine icons* that depict two themes side by side.

Disability and Christianity. Disability can be found everywhere once you know how to look for it. The challenge for Christian theologians has been to develop conceptual frameworks, intellectual practices, and pedagogical awareness that investigate the presence of disabilities rather than perpetuate the "absent presence" of disabilities in texts, teaching, and institutions. Disability is no longer seen as the biological condition of an individual body*, but rather as a complex product of social, political, environmental, and biological realities. Disability studies as a field of interdisciplinary inquiry – including religious studies, biblical studies, and Christian theology – have emerged from three primary sources.

1. *The theological imaginings of caretakers of people with disabilities.* Religious bodies established many caretaking facilities for people with various forms of disabilities. Chaplains who spent much time with people with disabilities, especially developmental disabilities, began to write about their patients' lives. Brett Webb-Mitchell's theological work relates the struggles and triumphs, frustrations and joys of children and adults with disabilities. Jean Vanier, who began ministering to the disabled in 1964, helped to found an international organization, L'Arche, which creates communities where people with developmental disabilities and those who assist them share their lives. Vanier's writings have been widely influential in their depictions of disability and of theological responses to people with disabilities.
2. *Theologians who have a family member with a disability and express their care through formal theological accounts.* Thomas Reynolds's disabled son embodied for him the Christian story in which strength always comes from weakness. Amos Yong engages his experience as the sibling of a person with Down syndrome to raise fundamental issues about theological anthropology*.
3. *New theological views from people with disabilities themselves.* Through his writings, Harold Wilke, who helped with the passage of the Americans with Disabilities Act (1990), advocated full inclusion of people with disabilities in congregations (e.g. by accommodating their needs and acknowledging their dignity as persons and the authority of their voices). His presence as a clergy member often surprised members of the congregations who wondered how he could do pastoral ministry without arms. Nancy Eiesland, both a sociologist and theologian, employed Liberation* theology to frame her lifelong experience with disability and the hidden history of Christianity's "disabled God" (the crucified Son of God). Kathy Black, a theologian and preacher, disputed the common notion that disability is a punishment for sin* (see Atonement #2). Ethicist and theologian Sharon Betcher argued that people with disabilities are a reproach to cultural images of body* and health, to consumerist values, and to global economic* patterns that embody these values. Biblical scholars Sarah Melcher, Hector Avalos, and Jeremy Schipper engage biblical studies in groundbreaking conversation with the wider field of disability studies. Scholars with disabilities are becoming the primary authors of theologies of disabilities.

Recent developments in disability theology and religious advocacy [*Editor's note*: especially the late Nancy Eiesland's] led to the formulation of the UN Convention on the Rights and Dignity of Persons with Disabilities (came into force in 2008), which includes the right to practice spirituality (a first for rights treaties). The Convention is prompting further exploration of the link between civil society and religion in support of full inclusion of people with disabilities in all areas of life. This can only continue to stimulate research on disability in Christian texts, congregations, and global work. **See also PASTORAL CARE; PASTORAL THEOLOGY.**

NANCY L. EIESLAND

Discalced (Lat "unshod"), term applied to religious* congregations whose members wear only sandals, a practice introduced in the West by Francis* of Assisi. **See also CARMELITE ORDER; TERESA OF ÁVILA.**

Disciples of Christ. See CHRISTIAN CHURCH (DISCIPLES OF CHRIST).

Discipleship. Being a disciple of Jesus Christ seems a simple enough concept. Is it not being like the Twelve*, who, according to the Gospels, followed Jesus during his ministry? Yet they are less than reliable models (e.g. Judas's betrayal; Peter's denials; the disciples' misunderstandings). Furthermore, the canonical Gospels (and other NT books) offer different views of discipleship, reflecting particular practices of the Christian life in various 1st-c. church contexts.

Discipleship, as the life practice of followers of Christ, has been and is understood differently according to (1) the aspects of biblical text(s) deemed most significant, (2) the theological views one holds (especially regarding anthropology*, sin*, atonement*, faith*, God's role in life, and ethics*), and (3) the practical life context issues that Christians have to address (see Scriptural Criticism). From this perspective, one can distinguish two broad understandings of discipleship, whose central feature is either

(1) doing God's will, as taught by Jesus, or (2) imitating Christ.

1. Discipleship as Doing God's Will Revealed by Jesus is a matter of obeying the authoritative teaching of Jesus, who calls disciples for a particular ministry – with two variations. First, discipleship involves learning from Christ the basic moral principles (God's will) that should govern disciples' lives and that they should model for others in society. The presupposed basic human predicament (the root of sin) is that humans *do not know* God's will regarding the "moral life" (here in Kant's* deontological* understanding of it). Then, e.g., the beatitudes (Matt 5:3–10) are read for their teaching of basic moral principles: being poor in spirit, humility, meekness, and righteousness.

Second, discipleship is being called by Christ to play a role in society and being willing to play it. The presupposed basic human predicament is that humans *do not want* to do God's will (which they already know), because they do not recognize the "consequences" of their actions (cf. John Stuart Mill's consequentialist* understanding of the moral life). Jesus' call (with its promises, e.g. "I will make you fishers of people," Matt 4:19) reveals the positive consequences of choosing a life of discipleship and the negative consequences of not doing so. The beatitudes are then read as a call to discipleship, enticing the hearers to become disciples through their promises (e.g. "theirs is the Kingdom").

2. Discipleship as Imitating Christ (*imitatio Christi*; see Imitation of Christ as Disciple) posits that discipleship requires a close, intimate relationship with Jesus, through which disciples are progressively trained and equipped to become disciples; when Jesus called Peter and Andrew, he promised to "make you fishers of people" (Matt 4:19), a training completed only when they finally went in mission (Matt. 28:19–20). The presupposed basic human predicament is that humans are *neither equipped nor trained* to do God's will (even if they already know it and want to do it), as in the Aristotelian perfectionist* view of the moral life that requires apprenticeship (imitating an expert) to acquire character (*ethos*), virtues, and practical wisdom. Disciples need to be transformed into Christ's likeness. Three variations emphasize different primary transformations.

First, by imitating Christ, disciples are resocialized, acquiring a new identity (character) as they share Christ's "symbolic world" – including his vision of the Kingdom – and thus learn to be children of the Kingdom and children of God (e.g. praying with Christ, "Our father in heaven"); thus disciples are enabled to be like Christ and can accept being "poor in spirit," "meek," and "persecuted for righteousness' sake," as Christ was.

Second, by imitating Christ, disciples share Jesus' discerning faith and receive the ability to discern in society both those who are actually "blessed" by God (not the rich or joyful ones, but the poor and repressed, those who mourn) and other manifestations of the Kingdom that should orient their ministry as disciples.

Third, by imitating Christ, disciples share in his power. Although the forces of evil and oppression seem overwhelming, as they imitate Christ disciples discover that God empowers them to overcome these obstacles, even if they have to go "the way of the cross" following Christ (undergoing various kinds of hardships and eventually martyrdom).

Theologians, churches, denominations, and individual Christians usually display a preference for one of these ways of understanding and practicing discipleship. Yet each choice is grounded in biblical texts and traditions, intertwined with choices regarding other theological concepts, and needs to be weighted in terms of its contextual implications. **See also APOSTLE; IMITATION OF CHRIST.** DANIEL PATTE

Disciplina Arcani (Lat "teaching of what is secret"), a 17th-c. term that refers to the early church practice of teaching the Lord's* Prayer, the mystery of the Trinity*, and the Apostles'* Creed to catechumens just before baptism (to avoid profanation by pagans; Matt 7:6; 1 Cor 3:1–2) and to the recitation of some eucharistic prayers silently.

Discipline. Both the Roman Catholic* Renewal and the Protestant Reformation* emphasized the importance of communal and personal discipline in forming Christian life and community. Discipline was viewed as preserving the integrity of the church, being a sign of the true faith, nurturing holiness of life, and being necessary for social order (see Ethics and Christianity Cluster).

Discipline in the Roman Catholic Church is associated with the last session of the Council of Trent* (1561–63). It introduced tools to strengthen Catholic public discipline, especially by stressing the sacrament of penance* and enhancing bishops' oversight of confessors so that a moral agenda might be highlighted in the confessional. Archbishop Charles Borromeo* of Milan (1538–84) was exemplary in such efforts. Reform of existing monastic* orders and clerical life (chiefly through seminary training) and support for new reformed religious communities emphasizing moral and ascetic* discipline was also undertaken. Examples were the reform of the Carmelite* order as the Discalced Carmelites (1562) at the initiative of Teresa* of Ávila and John* of the Cross and the founding of the Society of Jesus (Jesuits*, 1540), the Theatines (1524), Barnabites (1533), and Ursulines (1535). Vigorous spiritual practice was encouraged for both religious and lay Catholics. Young people were encouraged in the Catholic life through the establishment of the catechetical Confraternities of Christian Doctrine. The ministry of spiritual direction flourished. Key to spiritual reform were the Jesuits, who in their schools and varied ministries promoted spiritual* exercises (daily examination of conscience, meditation on the life and Passion of Christ) to discipline individuals for service to Christ's church and people. Francis* de Sales's (1567–1622) popular *Introduction to the Devout Life* promoted a spiritually and morally disciplined life for laypersons that stressed interior prayer, the acquisition of virtue, acts of charity, chaste and spiritually oriented relationships, devotion to the examples of the saints, and active participation in the sacramental life of the church.

Protestant discipline centers on Bible study and prayer and is often individual; Protestant discipline for community life follows a similar pattern, as Bonhoeffer's* book *Life Together* exemplifies. WENDY M. WRIGHT

Dismas, the name given later to the penitent thief crucified with Jesus (Luke 23:40–43). Dismas Houses, founded (1974) by Jack Hickey, OP, offer transitional housing and support services to men and women recently released from prison or jail in the USA and Ireland.

Dispensationalism, the belief that history is divided into divinely ordained periods, or "dispensations." Joachim* of Fiore (c1135–1202) argued that the history of the world comprised three ages: an Age of the Law*, governed by God the Father; an Age of Grace*, brought on by the Incarnation*; and an Age of the Spirit*, during which the Antichrist* will be defeated and the world renewed. Darby* initiated a renewed Dispensationalist theology (early 19th c.), still influential in Evangelical Protestantism. The Scofield Reference Bible (1909) describes seven dispensations. Progressive Dispensationalists (20th c.) argued for fewer ages. "Ultradispensationalists" argued for different dividing points. With the popularity of the *Left Behind* novels, the movement edged into the mainstream. **See also MILLENNIALISM CLUSTER: INTRODUCTORY ENTRY and IN NORTH AMERICA.** STEPHEN E. LAHEY

Dispersion. See DIASPORA.

Disruption of 1843. Led by Thomas Chalmers, almost 40% of the ministers left the Church of Scotland (forfeiting salaries, manses, and pulpits) and established the Free* Church of Scotland. The cause of the secession was chiefly the issue of patronage*. The split ended in 1929.

Dissenters, official designation for Nonconformists* (Presbyterians*, Congregationalists*, and Baptists*) who separated themselves from the Church of England, especially after the Restoration* and the Act of Uniformity* (1662).

Dissolution of the Monasteries. Henry VIII, in his role as supreme head of the Church of England (see Supremacy, Acts of) and on the basis of several acts of Parliament, confiscated monastic* properties in England, Wales, and Ireland (1538–40). Luther* and others had questioned the legitimacy of monastic vows*, and monks and nuns were widely regarded as unproductive parasites. The monastic communities owned more than one-fourth of the land in England, and confiscation of their properties was presented as a way of reducing taxation. The lands were sold to the nobility for country estates, and buildings were dismantled for their materials. The role of the monasteries in local economies, social services, and learning was lost and not easily replaced. **See also ANTICLERICALISM; COLD WAR AND EASTERN AND WESTERN CHRISTIANITY; LAICIZATION; ROMAN CATHOLICISM CLUSTER: IN EUROPE: FRANCE; SECULARISM AND SECULARIZATION; SPAIN.**

Divination, foretelling future events or disclosing by magical methods what is hidden. Condemned throughout the Bible as superstitious* or the work of demons*.

Divine Command Ethics is an ethical theory that grounds judgments of good and evil in God's commands in natural* law and/or Scripture*.

Divine Liturgy of the Orthodox Churches is their primary act of worship. It is a eucharistic* service conducted with great solemnity and joy* and composed of prayers, litanies, Scripture readings, hymns, solemn processions, and participation in Holy Communion.

The Divine Liturgy is regarded as a presentation of and participation in the sacred meal Christ imparted to his disciples, called in Orthodox theology "the Mystical Supper." It is concomitantly viewed as a symbolic* rendering of the life of Christ, an eschatological revelation of the Banquet of the Kingdom*, an imitation of the angelic worship in heaven, and a bloodless sacrifice* (though not a repetition of the sacrifice of Calvary).

The Divine Liturgy has two parts: the Liturgy of the Catechumens*, in which Scripture is read and preached, and the Liturgy of the Faithful, in which Holy Communion is consecrated and offered. The chief versions of the Divine Liturgy are those of St. John* Chrysostom, St. Basil* the Great, and St. James*. These differ primarily in the composition of the anaphora*, the long prayer rehearsing God's wondrous works leading up to the words of institution and the *epiclesis** (invocation of the Holy Spirit). Because the joyous* character of the Divine Liturgy was considered incongruous with a sense of penitential compunction, a separate service called the Presanctified* Liturgy was developed for distributing Communion on weekdays in Lent*.

The Divine Liturgy presupposes involvement by all worshippers in various ways. The Orthodox ecclesial ethos prohibits a clergyman from celebrating the Eucharist in the absence of others. In continuity with the ancient Christian practice of celebrating the Eucharist on the tombs of martyrs*, Orthodoxy requires the Divine Liturgy to be celebrated around the holy table (consecrated with the relics of martyrs*), or at least on an *antimension*, a decorated cloth into which relics are sewn.

Prosphora (loaves of leavened bread marked with a seal) and sweet fermented wine are prepared for consecration with prayers and ritual actions, along with specific commemorations of the saints of the day and prayers for the living and the departed.

The Orthodox Church regards Communion* as a real reception of the Body and Blood of Christ but does not accept the philosophical commitments inherent in the Latin doctrine of transubstantiation*. Clergy and laity receive both elements; since the 9th c., the laity has been communed by means of a spoon.

ARCHBISHOP DEMETRIOS TRAKATELLIS

Divine Office of the Liturgy of the Hours consists of the liturgical offices that mark the different times of the day (morning, midday, evening, nighttime) and is shaped by the liturgical seasons of the church year. In the East, it was established as a popular office of the laity* with their clergy, whereas in the West it came to be adopted by monastics* and other religious*. Today it has been rediscovered in the West as the prayer of the whole Church. **See also LITURGICAL MOVEMENT; LITURGIES, HISTORY OF; LITURGY OF THE HOURS.**

KEITH F. PECKLERS, SJ

Divine Right (*ius divinum*), doctrine that both state and church authority originate from God (Rom 13:1–2) and are specified by God. The 17th c. was the high point of claims for the "divine right of kings" as well as for claims that episcopal or presbyterian forms of church governance are of divine right (*iure divino*). The modern concept of sovereignty is somewhat comparable: it can be ascribed to the people, the ruling or executive power, or a diversity of governing agencies.

Divorce, dissolution of marriage, permitted in ancient Israel (Deut 24:1–4) but condemned by Jesus as contrary to God's intention in creation (Mark 10:6–9; Gen 1:27, 2:24). In Mark 10:10–11, remarriage is considered to be adultery as long as the former spouse is living; in Matt 19:9, divorce is permitted in the case of adultery. Paul permits a Christian to separate from an unbelieving partner (1 Cor 7:15). **See also SACRAMENTS IN WESTERN CHURCHES.**

Docetism (from Gk *dokein*, "seeming," "apparent"). When Jesus was understood to be the manifestation of a preexistent* divine being, some Christians assumed that his humanity was merely "apparent." This notion, especially among Gnostics*, is opposed in 1 John 4:2–3 and 2 John 7, Ignatius*, and several anti-Gnostic writers. An analogous notion (which later influenced Islam*) was that Jesus was not crucified, having changed places with Simon* of Cyrene. Metaphorically, any way of thinking that relies solely on intellectual or spiritual factors, ignoring social and material factors, can be called "docetic."

Doctors of the Church, "teachers" officially recognized in the Roman Catholic Church because of their contributions to doctrine* owing to their knowledge and insight.

Dogma (Gk "opinion" or "decree)". In the LXX and NT, dogma was usually an "edict" (e.g. Dan 2:13; Luke 2:1). In patristic and medieval Latin theology, "dogma" referred to a "tenet," whether true of false. Thus the "true" dogmas of the Catholic Church were opposed to the "false" dogmas of heretics*, or the "true" dogmas of the Waldenses* were opposed to the corrupt "dogmas" of the Roman Catholics. Dogmas were summary formulations of the beliefs of a church or movement, such as creeds* and, later, confessions and symbols (see Creeds, Symbols, and Confessions of Faith). Since the 18th c., "dogma" has been a technical term for an authoritative propositional truth taught by the churches as revealed by God and as binding on all members of these churches.

This relatively new use of the term "dogma" posits that certain beliefs may not be contested by believers and thus presupposes a particular view of faith: faith as "believing that" (Augustine's *fides quae creditur*) (see Faith #3). This view of dogma can be based on both OT and NT texts (e.g. the Shema*, Deut 6:4–25; the apostolic tradition, 1 Cor 15:1–11) and the early councils that gave authoritative expressions of the "faith" about the Trinity* and Christology*. Yet the relative role of dogma varies among church traditions, according to the emphasis they put on faith as "believing that."

For Eastern Orthodox* churches, the doctrinal formulations of the seven ecumenical* councils are alone received as dogmatically authoritative. This is so, despite what other see as a lack of specificity of these formulations, in part because Orthodox theology is experiential and doxological in character. With this experiential emphasis on faith, dogmas are not at the center and thus need not be specified further (see Orthodox Churches, Eastern, Cluster: Introductory Entries).

For the Roman Catholic Church and its emphasis on "orthodoxy*" (as correct belief), it was essential to develop always more precise doctrinal formulations in medieval and modern Western councils (including Trent*, Vatican* I, and Vatican* II), against what was viewed as "nonorthodox" or even "heretical" views. Thus Vatican I (reaffirmed by Vatican II on these points) distinguished between two kinds of dogma: "solemn judgments" of popes (thus papal infallibility*, itself a "divinely revealed dogma") and those taught by the "ordinary and universal *magisterium**" i.e. by the bishops in communion with Rome. Heresy is then defined as obstinate doubt or denial of a dogma of the Roman Catholic Church (as Avery Dulles underscores).

For Protestants* the concept of dogma has generally been less central, expressed in confessions* or symbols, if not bracketed out (as for "noncreedal" churches, e.g. Baptist churches). Yet two trends can be distinguished. First, many Protestants who emphasize faith as "believing that" seek to formulate dogmas (doctrines) corresponding to the Reformation*. This means that dogmas must be constantly tested against Scripture* or against the Reformers' interpretations of Scripture. Thus for Karl Barth* dogmas are doctrinal propositions acknowledged and confessed by the church as contained in the Word of God. In a less sophisticated way than Barth, Protestant fundamentalists* seek to formulate "biblical dogmas."

Second, with more relational and experiential views of faith (see Faith #1, 2, 5, 6), other Protestants negatively or positively underscored the inculturated* character of dogma. For example, for liberal Protestants, such as Harnack*, (Catholic) dogmas were hellenized deformations of the gospel, and thus were authoritarian and legalistic. Yet 20th-c. ecumenists (e.g. Wolfhart Pannenberg, George Lindbeck, David Tracy, Elizabeth A. Johnson) affirmed the inculturated character of dogma in a positive light; for Lindbeck traditional dogmas were authoritative in their original contexts, but as the cultural setting shifted, dogmas lost their force and had to be replaced by new dogmas or new formulations of these dogmas.

Similarly, because they commonly emphasize orthopraxy*, contextual theologies and the Christian communities out of which they emerge tend to reformulate dogmas so that they might support the effort to address contextual issues (see Contextual Theologies; Feminist Theology Cluster; Liberation Theologies Cluster).

In the contemporary Charismatic* Movement (in its many forms), as in the mystic* and apophatic* movements through the centuries, the amplified emphases on the experiential character of faith pushes dogma (and "orthodoxy" as affirmation of dogma) to the side; it is not central. Even though members of such movements might commonly provide "orthodox" answers when asked what they believe about particular doctrines (answers that seem, therefore, very conservative and completely divorced from their particular life contexts), these beliefs are not what authoritatively shape their faith and their lives as Christians in life contexts marked by specific religious experiences. **See also CHARISMATIC AND PENTECOSTAL MOVEMENTS CLUSTER: STUDYING.** DANIEL PATTE

Dome of the Rock, Muslim* shrine in Jerusalem*, built (691–92) on the site of the Jewish Temple*, believed to be where Muhammad* ascended to heaven.

Dominic (1170–1221). Born in Caleruega, Spain, he became canon of the Cathedral of Osma. During a journey to Scandinavia, he and his bishop, Diego, were confronted by Cathars* and their heresy* in Languedoc and by non-evangelized people in Prussia. These encounters were for them an apostolic vocation*. Pope Innocent III sent them to preach to the Cathars.

Since, following their doctrine, the Cathars lived in poverty*, the two men adopted evangelical poverty. Their preaching produced some fruit. Before returning to Spain, Bishop Diego founded a monastery at Prouille to shelter converted women (1207). Continuing to preach, Dominic was joined by some companions, the nucleus of a community that was supported by Bishop Fulk of Toulouse. Dominic obtained from the pope the establishment of a new order and immediately dispersed the first brothers to the nascent universities of Paris, Oxford, and Bologna.

Then Dominic divided his time between preaching in Italy (he died in Bologna) and the organization of the order, characterized by the superiors' election, begging, and intellectual formation. Contrary to traditional views, Dominic initiated neither the Inquisition* nor the rosary*. Since he left almost no writing, his spirit must be found in his work, namely the Dominican* Order of the Preachers.

GUY-THOMAS BEDOUELLE, OP

Dominican Order. Friars, nuns and now apostolic sisters, and laypeople (Dominican Laity) form the Order of Preachers. It was founded by Dominic* (early 13th c.) and quickly grew both in number and in quality. Albert* the Great and Thomas Aquinas* gave to the Dominican order a doctrine that became normative in the (Western) Church. Dominican mystics (Eckhart*, Suso*, Tauler*) had a far-reaching influence. During this period, the Dominicans were (among others) put in charge of the Inquisition*.

The 16th c. was a crisis period; the Protestant Reformation* was a harsh challenge for Dominicans, e.g. in England. But long after her death, Catherine* of Siena, OP (d1380), helped the order to overcome this crisis through the enduring influence of her call to reform through "the total love for God" achieved through repentance and renewal. Yet the order had a powerful voice in Spain*, with Vitoria, Las* Casas, and Luis of Granada, and (in the 17th c.) in Latin America, with Martin of Porrès and Rose* of Lima. The Dominican pope Pius V (d1572) enthusiastically led the Catholic reformation movement (see Catholic* Renewal) following the Council of Trent*. A long debate about the doctrine of grace* opposed Dominicans and Jesuits in that period.

The 17th and 18th c. were an age of mysticism* (among French Dominicans) and of prospering missions all the way to China* and the Philippines*, as well as the West Indies (presented in John Baptist Labat's remarkable narratives). The French Revolution was a blow for the Dominican order in France and beyond; while the Spanish provinces partially and temporarily disassociated themselves from the authorities of the order.

The 19th c. was a time of reconstruction, led by Edward Dominic Fenwick in the USA (from 1804) and Lacordaire* in France (c1840). One of Lacordaire's first companions, Vincent Jandel, became master general of the order. Congregations of sisters proliferated everywhere, with specialized apostolates in schools and hospitals. Cloistered monasteries were restored and new lay organizations organized.

The Dominican order participated in the Thomist* revival and founded the École Biblique de Jérusalem with Marie-Joseph Lagrange. In the early 20th c., the brothers were exiled from France* because of anticlerical* laws, while the English province developed under the direction of Bede Jarrett. Between 1920 and 1970, there was a remarkable growth; Dominican theologians (including Chenu and Congar) played an important role at Vatican* II. Yet the order did not escape the crisis that followed. By the end of the 20th c., some Dominican provinces were near extinction, but others are very much alive.

GUY-THOMAS BEDOUELLE, OP

Dominican Republic. Evangelization of the Caribbean began in Santo Domingo through the work of Bernardo Boil (1505), a Franciscan*

friar*, previously named vicar apostolic of the new regions discovered by Columbus and conceded to the kings of Spain by Pope Alexander VI Borgia's bull *Eximiae Devotionis Sinceritas* (1493). Spiritual and temporal powers were so intertwined that the agents of the Inquisition* were commissioned (1516) to pursue Jews and heretics that might have settled in the island. Meanwhile, as early as 1501 and 1510, the first black slaves were brought to work, together with the Tainos (whom the conquistadores called "Indians"), in the gold mines. But after the mid-16th c., the Spaniards regularly brought boatloads of Africans as slaves to work in the sugar plantations and workshops. Church authorities demanded that the masters build chapels to facilitate the slaves' religious practice. In 1622 the bishops of Venezuela* and of Puerto* Rico met in council at Santo Domingo to discuss the baptism of slaves and their religious instruction, which the masters did not favor; this became a frequent source of conflict between masters and clergy.

The slaves' resistance took the form of "chestnut camps" (*marronnages*) – after the slaves escaped to remote areas in the mountains – as well as numerous, more ambivalent religious associations (e.g. of St. John Baptist, of the Virgin, of St. Cosme and Damiens) through which the slaves reappropriated their beliefs in African divinities by expressing them in the cult of saints, promoted by the Catholic* Renewal.

The slave insurrection that took place in Saint Domingue (now Haiti*) in the wake of the French Revolution (1789) had a great impact on the political and religious evolution of the Spanish colony (which became the Dominican Republic); it was invaded and occupied by Toussaint-Louverture (1801), who proclaimed the liberty of all the slaves, in the city of Santo Domingo.

When the Dominican Republic gained independence from the Haitians (1844), Roman Catholicism was proclaimed the state religion. Thus Freemasonry* and Protestant worship were prohibited (1862). A concordat* (1954) between President Trujillo and the Vatican further established Roman Catholicism as the religion of the Dominican state, which "recognizes the Church as a perfect society." Other denominations were tolerated, but not in public; there were several periods of persecution, especially of Jehovah's* Witnesses. Similarly, Vodou*, which had developed among African slaves since the 16th and 17th c., was rejected as essentially Haitian and foreign, and thus for both racial and nationalist reasons. The Dominican nation conceives of itself as composed of whites and mestizos* (from Spanish and Amerindian [Tainos] origins), and not of blacks – a racist ideology* omnipresent in Dominican society, which nevertheless includes a sizable minority of blacks (11%), in addition to mestizos* (73%) and whites (16%). In 1937 about 20,000 (black) Haitians who came to work in the country were slaughtered at the border, essentially for racist reasons, as were (in 1962) 200 members of a messianic religious movement that integrated Vodou* and the cult of saints. The Dominican national identity was defined during Trujillo's long dictatorship (1930–61) as simultaneously Hispanic, Roman Catholic, and Dominican. This conflated national identity was sometimes contested by the Catholic hierarchy and bishops who called for an alleviation of the regime's repressive practices against opponents. Nevertheless, the Roman Catholic Church remained closely associated with political authorities and tended to be intolerant of Protestants, including Evangelicals and Baptists, and the more numerous Pentecostal*/Charismatic* churches developed in the country after the US occupation (1916–24). **See also HAITI.**

Statistics: Population (2000): 8.5 million. Christians, 94.5% (Roman Catholics, 88.3%; Protestants [including independent Pentecostals/ Charismatics], 5.6%; marginal Christians [Jehovah's Witnesses], 0.6%). (Based on *World Christian Encyclopedia*, 2001.)

LAËNNEC HURBON

Dominus Vobiscum (Lat "The Lord be with you"), liturgical salutation to the congregation, answered by "And with your spirit"; based, respectively, on Ruth 2:4 and 2 Tim 4:22.

Domitian, Titus Flavius (51–96), Roman emperor (81–96), under whom Christians were probably persecuted (cf. Revelation*, Heb 12:4, 1 Clem 7), most likely because they were denied the Jews' exemption from taking part in civil religious ceremonies or the imperial cult. In the imperial cult, Domitian was treated as a "present deity"; temples were dedicated to him during his lifetime. **See also PERSECUTIONS.**

Domitilla, Flavia (d c100), wife of Titus Flavius Clemens, a possible successor as emperor. Clemens and Domitilla were accused of "atheism" and leading a "Jewish way of life," which could mean that they were Christians or sympathizers; Clemens was executed (95) and Domitilla was exiled. Christians may have begun to use her catacombs before her death.

Donation of Constantine, a forgery in which Constantine* granted to Pope Sylvester supreme authority in the church and temporal rule over Rome (understood, after the 11th c., to mean the Roman Empire in the West). It is usually thought to have been produced in Rome (750–80), but others have suggested it was written in France, perhaps as early as the disputes surrounding Louis* the Pious (830–33). Even when it was assumed that the Donation was historical, some (including Dante* and Marsilius* of Padua) asserted that Constantine never had the right to give the Empire in the West to the pope, or the pope to receive it. Various doubts were expressed about its authenticity, and Lorenzo Valla demonstrated that it was a forgery in 1439.

Donatism, historically, a movement that separated itself from the Western Church in North Africa; doctrinally, any tendency that emphasizes the personal holiness* of ministers and church members, making such holiness the definitive mark* of the true church or the source of the validity of the sacraments*.

The Donatist Movement grew out of the great persecution* (303–5) under Diocletian*. Rigorists denounced as *traditores* those clergy who had handed over copies of the Scriptures and viewed them unfit to administer sacraments and ordinations. They rejected the bishop of Carthage, Caecilian*, because he had been consecrated by an alleged *traditor*, and elected a rival bishop, Majorinus, soon succeeded by Donatus.

The Donatists considered themselves the only authentic church. Their zeal for holiness was found in an earlier African, Tertullian*, and they could claim Cyprian* in their support, specifically his demand for the rebaptism of persons baptized by the impure. Ethnic and regional factors played a role: the Donatists were especially strong in Berber areas; they gave voice to economic misery and class inequities, most clearly through the violent Circumcellions*.

Against the Donatists' regionalism, Augustine* insisted on the universality of the church. Against their claim that the sacraments depend on the purity of the minister, he argued that Christ is the principal agent, acting through the sacramental signs and thus bypassing personal failings (see *Ex opere operato*). Against their self-identification as a pure church, he argued that the church is inevitably a mixture of wheat and tares, with a clear separation being made only at the Last Judgment (Matt 13:24–30).

Reunion was proposed by the Catholic bishops (401), and a decisive conference was held under the auspices of the Empire in Carthage (411). Gradually the Donatists were reconciled with the Catholic Church through a combination of pressure and leniency.

Throughout the history of Christianity, purist tendencies have been called "Donatist." During the Gregorian* reform, Cardinal Humbert* was accused of Donatism because he attacked ordinations tainted by simony* and urged the laity to boycott priests guilty of simony and Nicolaitism*. Other reform movements (e.g. Waldensian*, Anabaptist*, Pietist*, Evangelical*) have been called Donatist insofar as they make personal holiness a test of membership or ordination, or claim to be the only true church. Conciliarists*, Protestants*, and Gallicans* attacked the "Roman Church" for claiming to be the only true church; one task of the Second Vatican* Council was to show that the church is more Catholic than Roman.

EUGENE TESELLE

Donne, John (1572–1631), was born to a prosperous Roman Catholic family. His mother was a descendant of Sir Thomas More*, and her brother was head of the Jesuit* mission in England. Donne was educated at home by Catholic tutors and attended Hart Hall, Oxford, preferred by Catholics. Prevented by his religion from obtaining a university degree, Donne sought patronage and a place at court. In 1593 his younger brother was arrested for harboring a Catholic priest and died in prison. Donne apparently abandoned Catholicism at about this time and later wrote a number of withering satirical attacks on Catholics (*Pseudo-Martyr,* 1610), especially Jesuits (*Ignatius, His Conclave,* 1611). Eventually persuaded by friends and King James himself to take holy orders, he did so (1615), ultimately becoming dean of Saint Paul's Cathedral. Renowned during his ecclesiastical career for his exciting sermons (more than 150) and his meditations, *Devotions upon Emergent Occasions* (1624), he wrote "metaphysical" love poems and religious lyrics equally bold in language and metrical effects, marked by wit, conceits, argument, and intellectualism. His erotic poetry often uses religious imagery, and his religious verse is sometimes sexual (e.g. Holy Sonnets 10 and 18).

JOHN PLUMMER

Dormition (Lat "falling asleep"), festival in the Eastern Church that corresponds to the

Assumption* of the Blessed Virgin Mary in the Western Church (August 15).

Dort, Dordt, or Dordrecht, Synod of (1618–19). In 1610 the followers of Arminius*, known as the Remonstrants*, including Jan Uytenbogaert and Johan van Oldenbarneveldt, suggested revisions to the Belgic* Confession, softening the Reformed doctrine of predestination*. While the Amsterdam merchants and the States General favored tolerance in doctrinal matters, the ministers and people in less urban areas tended to be zealous Calvinists*; thus religious passions were brought into political life.

The military leader, Maurice or Maurits, harnessed the populist spirit of the Counter-Remonstrants. After his troops occupied towns and expelled Remonstrant magistrates, Maurits forced the States General to call a national synod at Dort in 1618–19, with the Remonstrants attending not as participants but as the accused. It was the most representative of all Reformed gatherings, with representatives from Switzerland, the Palatinate, England, and Scotland, yet its decrees have been adopted only by the Dutch churches of the Netherlands, South Africa, and the USA.

The synod's "five points" asserted unconditional election*, limited atonement*, total depravity, irresistible grace*, and perseverance of saints. Remonstrant ministers were removed; in a parallel trial, Oldenbarneveldt was executed in what historians usually call a "judicial murder", and Grotius* escaped life imprisonment by being smuggled to safety.

Dositheos (Lat Dositheus) (1641–1707), patriarch of Jerusalem. Born in the Peloponnesus, as an orphaned youth he entered the Holy Apostles Monastery in Corinth. Appointed archbishop of Caesarea (1666), then exarch of Jassy, Romania (1667), he was named patriarch of Jerusalem at the age of 28 (1669), serving in that capacity until his death.

Through his extensive travels and prolific publishing efforts (stemming mainly from the print shop he founded in Jassy), Dositheos defended the Orthodox faith against both Protestant and Roman Catholic theologies, notably in the "Twelve Chapters," published posthumously (1715) as a history of the patriarchs of Jerusalem with a strong attack against the pope of Rome.

The crowning glory of Dositheos's career was his convocation (1672) of the Synod of Jerusalem, or Council of Bethlehem, its actual locus; its purpose was to condemn the Calvinistic "Eastern Confession of the Christian Faith" (1631), attributed by many to the ecumenical patriarch Cyril Lucaris*. In the Synod's acts, the lengthy condemnation (rejecting unconditional predestination* and justification* by faith* alone) was followed by Dositheos's own "Confession of Faith," composed of 18 decrees, four questions, and an epilogue. This Confession teaches the true faith of the Eastern Church and is regarded by many as a symbolic or canonical book of the Eastern Church.

RONALD POPIVCHAK

Dostoyevsky, Fyodor Mikhaylovich (1821–81), a Russian writer, created a new genre of psychological religious novels, including the masterpieces *Crime and Punishment, The Idiot, Demons,* and *The Brothers Karamazov*. He saw writing as a religious mission to restore the divine image of fallen humans.

Born to an Orthodox family, he joined the Petrashevsky group of atheists and revolutionaries, was arrested, and sentenced to death. He saw as a kind of resurrection and the beginning of a new life the last-minute commutation of his sentence to four years in Siberia, where the only book he had was a copy of the NT, which he retained until his death.

Dostoyevsky, like a Russian Dante*, offers a journey through a psychological hell, purgatory, and paradise. His "hell" also has a social embodiment – gloomy Saint Petersburg crowded with poor people. Fiery passions, despair, spitefulness, fixed ideas, false theories that justify murder, or the building of an "ideal" society by violence bring hell to one's soul. He believed in natural sin and showed how destructive ideas infect the mind and, consequently, freeze the heart, a psychological punishment. He presented characters in extremes of sinfulness and holiness. We are redeemed and saved through suffering, repentance, and love. Dostoyevsky's Christ-like characters mostly refer to the Russian Orthodox traditions of kenotic* monasticism* and "folly" for Christ's sake (see Holy Fool). Dostoyevsky sees the divine image* in all people, despite their sins. Many of his writings are apocalyptic* and express his belief in the all-forgiving Christ.

ELENA VOLKOVA

Douai-Reims Bible, English translation made for Catholics by the English College, located first in Douai and then in Reims (NT published 1582, OT 1609–10). Based on the Vulgate* rather than the original languages, its vocabulary is highly Latinate; it was utilized but also criticized by the translators of the Authorized* Version.

Double Monastery, religious house with men and women living separately but with a common superior, usually a noble woman (e.g. Macrina*, Melania* the Elder, Hilda*, Etheldreda*).

Doubt, strictly speaking, "hesitation" (Gk *distazo*, "to be of two minds," "to hesitate"; in Plato and Matt 14:31, 28:17). It is the opposite of having a firm conviction* or faith*. Thus different views of doubt correspond to different views of faith. (1) Doubt can involve a withholding of assent, a hesitation to commit oneself to faith in the sense of trust. (2) It can reflect a lack of trust, and thus irresolution, which might lead to moral failure. (3) It can be a matter of doubting a belief, i.e. the content of faith (*fides quae creditur*), because of deliberation or inquiry (as emphasized in the Greco-Roman world) or because of new information or new perspectives in the light of which firmly held beliefs crumble; Victorian Britain gave full expression to this kind of doubt, and the results varied: atheism*, agnosticism*, or revisions of traditional belief. (4) Doubt can entail calling into question the view that faith is the way toward understanding, emphasizing the difference between faith and knowledge. (5) Finally, doubt can refer to a lack of experience of God or to the experience of the silence or distance of God, a kind of doubt that is frequently associated with apophatic* experiences of the mystery of God. In this case, doubt is a part of faith, rather than opposed to faith; thus the disciples worshipped the risen Christ even as they doubted (Matt 28:17, literal translation). Then, with Augustine*, one can find consolation in "I doubt, therefore I am," or, with Kierkegaard*, one can relish the continued uncertainty and instability. **See also FAITH.** DANIEL PATTE

Douglass, Frederick (1817–95), best known as an anti-slavery lecturer, editor of abolitionist newspapers, and author of three autobiographies, was licensed as a local preacher of the African* American Methodist Episcopal Zion Church (1839). Douglass denounced Christian slaveholders and the clerics who defended them. He ridiculed a program to distribute Bibles to the slaves as a travesty, arguing that slaves had no legal right to own anything. His religion focused less on vicarious atonement* than on the imitation* of Christ and a belief in a moral government of the universe. His public friendship with the atheist Robert G. Ingersoll, who took public stands against racial injustice, led to accusations of heresy*. Douglass responded by observing that "the loving Jesus" had given proof of "his Messiahship" when he "especially identified himself with the lowest classes of suffering [people]." Douglass's assertion that geological evidence contradicted the biblical account of creation led to another accusation of heresy; he defended himself in an oration on Galileo, "It Moves, or the Philosophy of Reform" (1884). WILSON J. MOSES

Doxology, glorification of the three persons of the Trinity*, originally added after the recitation of a psalm.

Dowry, payment given with the wife at the time of marriage*.

Dualism, a philosophical or theological doctrine that posits an irreducible "twoness" or duality between God and matter (as in Plato*), or between good and evil (as in Manichaeism*), or between "spiritual" humanity and nonspiritual persons (as in Gnosticism*), or between mind and body (as in Descartes*). Dualism seems to be supported by certain aspects of experience: the differences between male and female, inner and outer, thought and matter, good intentions and bitter defeat, oppressors and victims, or simply "ours" and "theirs."

Dualism may be resolved by making one factor the source of the other (e.g. God creating* matter), or by interpreting one factor as a transformation of the other (e.g. seeing evil* as a corruption of what is good), or by seeing both as manifestations of an underlying unity (e.g. pantheism or interpretations of mind and body as diverse modalities of the same reality).

The Christian doctrine of the Trinity* seemed to some in the early church to involve dualism: if the Father and the Son are fully divine, this seems to imply two eternal principles, and even three when the Spirit is considered. This potential dualism was resolved by emphasizing that the Father eternally begets the Son, as light comes from the sun, naturally but freely.

Moral dualism may involve contrasts not only between good and evil behavior, but between honor* and shame, purity and pollution. Moral dualism is resolved through the appropriate moral attitude and behavior marked by goodness, honor, or purity.

Modern anthropology* reinscribes forms of dualism that privilege the mind over the body, the spirit over the flesh, by viewing the ideal human person as a rational, individual, autonomous, free subject. Then, as feminist* theological anthropologists* show, this dualism supports views of humanity in which men are connected with such characteristics as reason, will, aggression, and dominance, while women are linked with the body, nature, emotion, and submission. "Binary" thinking privileges one factor over another, since it operates in terms of *a* and *not-a*. It is preferable to think in terms of "difference," e.g. *a* and *b*. EUGENE TESELLE

DuBois, W. E. B. (1868–1963), is one of the great figures in African American intellectual history. He was a philosopher, sociologist, educator, civil rights activist, and pan-Africanist. DuBois attended Fisk College (1885–88), and was profoundly confronted there by overt racial* discrimination, which he had not experienced during his youth in Great Barrington, Massachusetts. DuBois's experience in the South deepened and solidified his commitment to racial uplift though education, entrepreneurship, and organization. After leaving Fisk, DuBois studied at Harvard, earning B.A., M.A., and Ph.D. degrees. His dissertation was entitled *The Suppression of the African Slave Trade in America* (1896). His training in philosophy, history, economics, and sociology provided DuBois with critical insight into the US dilemma, the race problem. Among his earliest works in social research is *The Philadelphia Negro* (1896), based on his research for the University of Pennsylvania. After completing this research, DuBois returned to the South, where he taught at Atlanta University. There he vested himself in the social history of the race as reflected in black expressive and institutional cultures such as in the Negro Spirituals* and the Black* Church. No text is more frequently read in African American cultural studies than DuBois's *The Souls of Black Folk* (1905). Social reform through civil rights activism dominated most of DuBois's mature life. No controversy catapulted him into radical, racial reform as much as his exchange with Booker T. Washington's conservative reform platform expressed in Washington's Atlanta Exposition speech in 1895. DuBois called it "the Atlanta compromise." DuBois's position on race reform was radical and made him one of the great voices for the NAACP (National Association for the Advancement of Colored People). Most of his writings during the years before his expatriation from the USA to Ghana (1957–1963) survive in *The Crisis Writings* (1972). The Washington debate demarcated DuBois as advocating a subversive Christianity that promoted political equality, prophetic social witness, and absolute social justice embodied in concrete human relations. From 1957 until his death in 1963, DuBois devoted himself to supporting postcolonial Africa. He died in Accra, Ghana. VICTOR ANDERSON

Dulia (from Gk *douleia*, "service"), veneration* of the saints, contrasted with *hyperdulia** toward Mary and *latria*, worship*, of God alone.

Duns Scotus, John (1265–1308), Franciscan* logician, metaphysician, theologian. He was born in Scotland, studied and taught at Oxford University, and taught in Paris (1300–7) and Cologne (1307–8). Major works include his commentaries on Aristotle's* *Logic, Metaphysics*, and *De Anima*, Peter* Lombard's *Book of Sentences, Quodlibetal* questions, and *De Primo Principio*, a philosophical demonstration of the existence and attributes of God. He was famous for his position on the Incarnation*, univocity of being, rational will*, primacy of freedom*, and contingency of the created* order.

Scotus belongs to the second generation of scholars who were critical of Aristotle*, following the Parisian Condemnation of 1277. As a Franciscan, he reacted against the neo-Augustinian positions of Henry of Ghent on the analogy* of being and the will's freedom. He reacted as well to the intellectualist positions of Godfrey of Fontaines. His teaching on the rational will was inspired by Aristotle's theory of causality and Anselm's* teaching on the two affections in the will. His demonstration of God's existence (*De Primo Principio*) brings together Platonic* and Aristotelian arguments for a first being.

Scotus's Franciscan identity is evident in his writings. He affirms the primacy of love* for God (*Deus diligendus est*) as the foundation for natural law. He rejects the intellectualist and naturalist project of post-1260 Aristotelian ethics in order to highlight the rationality of ordered loving. His attention to the particular individual (*haecceitas*) corrects Aristotelian hylomorphism and defends a unique unrepeatable principle of identity belonging to each created being. His affirmation of the univocal concept *being* defends the possibility of language* about God without reducing the transcendent to the sphere of immanence. His clarification that theology is a practical science rather than a speculative endeavor continues the Franciscan attention to praxis* as the full perfection of human nature. His defense of the contingency of the created order, the centrality of divine love and freedom, and the Incarnation as independent of original sin offer a Christocentric vision of human history that places divine abundant love at the center of Christianity.

Often mistakenly contrasted with Thomas Aquinas*, Scotus is properly understood as an early-14th-c. theologian who rejected the post-1277 return to Augustinianism* and who sought to refine the arguments in the debates surrounding human and divine freedom, the nature of individuation, and the rationality of faith. His thought was extremely influential in the 14th–17th c., and his legacy can be identified in thinkers like Suárez*, Christian Wolff, Kant*, Charles Sanders Peirce, and Heidegger*.

MARY BETH INGHAM, CSJ

Duplessis-Mornay, Philippe (1549–1623), French Huguenot* statesman, military leader, writer, theologian. An early proponent of toleration for Reformed* worship in France, he pressed for a national council of Protestants and Catholics, whose purpose would be to reform the church in accord with an ancient Gallic model. Duplessis-Mornay also appealed for a European Protestant union to include general synods of Protestant theologians and a military league of princes. He was a lifelong adviser and diplomat in the service of Henry of Navarre, later King Henry* IV of France, and participated in the negotiations that culminated in the Edict of Nantes* (1598) and the end of religious warfare. Duplessis-Mornay wrote several important religious and political treatises. His *Traité de l'Église* (1578) severely criticized the Roman Church, while *De la vérité de la religion chrétienne* (1581) explored truths of the Christian faith through a study of classical authors. *De l'institution, usage et doctrine du saint sacrement de l'Eucharistie en l'Église* (1598) attacked the pope as Antichrist and led to a fiery public exchange with the Bishop of Evreux. He was most likely among the principal contributors to the anonymous *Vindiciae contra Tyrannos* (1579), an influential political tract that allowed for resistance to a monarch who violated Christian faith.

RAYMOND A. MENTZER

Durand, Marie (1715–76), emblematic figure of French Protestant courage and resistance in the face of religious intolerance and persecution following the revocation of the Edict of Nantes* and the proscription of the Reformed Church of France (1685). Imprisoned in 1730 while a teenager, with many other Huguenot* women who refused to deny their faith, she remained in the Tour de Constance (Aigues-Mortes, Southern France) for 38 years, until 1768, when everyone was released. The word "register" ("resist" in the local patois), which she and other prisoners carved into the prison wall, summarized the meaning of their lives and their faith.

RAYMOND A. MENTZER

Durham, William. See ASSEMBLIES OF GOD.

Durkheim, Emile David (1858–1917), along with his followers, referred to as the Année Sociologique group (Paris), established sociology* as a university discipline. Along with Weber* and Marx*, Durkheim is generally viewed as a founding father of sociology. For him sociology covered a wide range of subjects – theory, method, social division of labor, suicide, law, art, morals, among others. Religion*, however, was of supreme importance, for him it was crucial for understanding any society. Although the son of a rabbi, as a critical rationalist he rejected the truth value of all religions. However, there were no "false religions": all were true insofar as they were at the heart, and vital to the well-being, of the society in which they were located. They provided society with cohesion, morality, and social energy (dynamism, collective effervescence).

In *The Elementary Forms of the Religious Life* (1912), he defined religion not in terms of a god, gods, or spirits, but rather as a system of beliefs and practices relative to sacred things that unite people in a single community. His notion of the sacred* was that which is determined by society and is inviolable. He contrasted it with the profane*, but both terms were subdivided into beneficent and malevolent forces. His emphasis on the sacred proved particularly fruitful in the analysis of religion and societies. He also emphasized the great importance of ritual*, correcting the overly rational approach to examining religion, which concerned itself mainly with belief. He classified rites as positive, negative, and piacular (atoning). Ritual is contrasted with belief, but it is open to debate which, for Durkheim, was sociologically prior, or whether they had equal significance.

A too simple reading of Durkheim suggests that he equates religion with society. The relation between the two is complex. Nonetheless, stressing the social component of religion has been a most fruitful source approach to the study of religion. Durkheim's disregard of the role of the individual in religion brought criticism, especially from Western Christian theologians.

In the face of the decline of Christianity in the West, Durkheim supported the notion that the emerging religion would be the cult of the individual*, which he held was based on fundamental moral ideas found in Christianity. He wrote little about Judaism and was an admirer of medieval Catholicism. On his deathbed, he declared that he had received no personal consolation from his study of religion. **See also SECULARIZATION AND DESECULARIZATION IN EUROPE AND NORTH AMERICA.**

WILLIAM S. F. PICKERING

Dwane, James Matta (1848–1916), left the Methodist Church to join Mokone's Ethiopian Church in 1896. He later assumed the leadership of the Church and negotiated links with the American African Methodist Episcopal Church. The latter's failure to recognize African leadership forced his withdrawal, leading him and his church to join the Anglican Church as the Order of Ethiopia. **See also SOUTH AFRICA.**

MOKGETHI MOTLHABI

Dwight, Timothy (1752–1817), Congregationalist minister, poet, theologian, educator. Grandson of Jonathan Edwards*, Dwight was educated at Yale College, served as a chaplain during the American Revolution, and was one of the founders of the first school of literary criticism in the USA, the "Connecticut Wits." His literary work, marked by millennial* themes, was strongly patriotic in tone, making him a vocal proponent of US exceptionalism. Dwight's most famous poem, *The Triumph of Infidelity*, was a shrill denunciation of European religious skepticism. In 1795 he returned to Yale as president. Under his leadership, Yale became the premier training ground for pastors and theologians, among them Lyman Beecher* and Nathaniel William Taylor (see New Haven Theology), who would shape 19th-c. Evangelical religion. Though he was not a systematic or highly skilled theologian, Dwight exerted a powerful influence on New England Christianity. Suspicious of the New Divinity theology of Samuel Hopkins* and Nathaniel Emmons, Dwight translated the religious practices of the Puritans and the Calvinist theology of Edwards* into popular language that resonated with westward-moving frontier folk. Dwight's popularity extended well into the 19th c., notably in his five-volume *Theology, Explained and Defended*, a series of 173 sermons he preached in the Yale Chapel.

JOHN R. FITZMIER

Dying, Care of the, an Eastern Orthodox Perspective. The dying process compels most people to take stock of their lives and confronts them with numerous challenges. With the diagnosis of a terminal illness, spiritual issues, often set aside or ignored for most of life, arise both for the dying person and for many of the caregivers – family, friends, or health care workers. The broad spiritual questions as to life's meaning and/or one's relationship with the Divine often find expression in more specific concerns regarding pain and suffering*, patience and endurance, loneliness and isolation, the dignity and value of every human being, honesty and openness, as well as in questions regarding prayer and its comfort, the meaning of dreams, visions, and other end-of-life phenomena, the actual death, the soul's* departure from the body*, and the afterlife.

The clergy and lay Christians who visit the sick seek to offer insight into the specific spiritual question(s) raised by the dying person, often addressed to family members, friends, or health care professionals. The dying person and those around the person can find hope* and peace when clergy and lay visitors help them to deal with these difficult questions.

The Orthodox Church defines the sacrament* of holy unction as healing and forgiveness. Since physical recovery may not be God's will, the prayer of Christ that God's will be done is at the heart of the sacrament. By the anointing of the sick body, the person's suffering is sanctified and united to the suffering of Christ; the wounds of the flesh are consecrated: strength is given that the suffering may lead not to the death of the soul* of the sick, but to eternal salvation in the resurrection and life of the Kingdom* of God. Healing is not a final goal; it is merely a sign of God's mercy and further opportunity to live for God and for others.

As death approaches, the Orthodox priest recites special prayers for the "separation of the soul and body." The sacrament of holy unction is not reserved for the moment of death; it does not constitute the "last rites" or "extreme unction" (as is sometimes thought). Holy unction is the sacrament for the complete restoration of a sick person, whatever the illness may be.

In contrast, the Roman Catholic Church previously viewed holy unction as extreme unction with emphasis on resolving guilt. However, the newest edition of the Catechism of the Catholic Church (1499–1532, 1997) shows that Rome's understanding of holy unction falls more in line with Eastern Orthodox Christianity.

MATTHEW P. BINKEWICZ

Dyophysites, advocates of two natures, divine and human, in Christ, opposed by the Miaphysites* (and Monophysites*). For dyophysites in the Western and Antiochene churches, the Council of Chalcedon* (451) supported dyophysitism; Eastern Orthodox Churches did not espouse this interpretation of Chalcedon.

E

Easter, the annual celebration of the resurrection* of Christ, called the Pasch (Gk and Lat *Pascha*; similar terms in the Romance languages) or Passover. The English term "Easter" and the similar German term are of Anglo-Saxon origin (related to a spring goddess of fertility, Eostre).

Celebrations of Easter. The early church continued the observance of the Jewish Passover, giving it additional meaning (1 Cor 5:7). For several centuries, the Pasch was a single event, celebrating Christ's death and resurrection, often with an evening vigil followed after midnight by baptisms, since baptism was viewed as a union with Christ in his death and resurrection, renouncing the devil and evil, and making a transition from the society of sin to the society of the redeemed.

The observance of "Holy Week" – from Palm Sunday to the Last Supper, Good* Friday, and the Pasch – emerged in the 4th c. in connection with the holy places identified under Constantine* and Helen*. This became a "historicizing" of the liturgy, an opportunity to relive the events at the place of their occurrence in order to share their power, including Christ's resurrection as a victory over the power of darkness – hence the joyful proclamation "Christ is risen!"

Easter as the paschal mystery* of human redemption* from evil powers including death* has been celebrated in the Northern Hemisphere with metaphors and symbols of new life related to spring folk festivals, including the old custom of hunting for "Easter eggs."

Controversy over the Date of Easter. The Quartodecimans* of Syria and Asia Minor continued to observe the 14th day of the lunar month (Jewish Passover). In Rome it was the 16th day; subsequently, it was celebrated only on a Sunday, on or after the 16th day. The Council of Nicaea* (325) decreed that the Pasch was to be observed on the Sunday after the full moon following the spring equinox (between March 21 and April 25).

Controversies over the date continued up to the 7th c.; because of the use of different calendar* systems, observances were sometimes up to four weeks apart. Dionysius* Exiguus (5th–6th c.) calculated much used paschal tables and in the process dated the years before and after the supposed birth of Christ.

The Gregorian calendar (1582), which made a 10-day adjustment in accordance with the actual length of days, led to a new kind of dissension. Catholic Europe adopted the calendar, while the Anglican Church kept the old system until 1752, and the Eastern and Uniate* churches remain divided. **See also** CALENDARS; LITURGICAL YEAR.

DANIEL PATTE and EUGENE TESELLE

Eastern Catholic Churches, autonomous (Lat *sui iuris*) churches, in full communion with the bishop of Rome, the pope. These ecclesiastic branches of various Eastern or Oriental Orthodox* churches maintain the language, liturgy, and canon law of the various Eastern or Oriental Orthodox churches from which they separated in order to unite with the Roman Catholic Church. **See also** UNIATE CHURCHES.

Eastern Churches, a shorthand designation for all Orthodox churches, including both Eastern Orthodox* churches and Oriental Orthodox* (non-Chalcedonian) churches.

Eastern Orthodox Churches. See ORTHODOX CHURCHES, EASTERN, CLUSTER.

East Timor. See TIMOR-LESTE.

Eastward Position, position of the celebrant during the Eucharist* in the Roman Catholic Church, standing with his back to the people (the altars of churches usually face east), a tradition that has been observed since the early Middle Ages in France, then elsewhere in Catholicism, until Vatican* II changed the position (the celebrant now faces the people). This was a controversial issue in the Church of England in the 16th and 17th c.

Ebenezer (Heb "stone of hope"), monument erected by Samuel* after the routing of the Philistines (1 Sam 7:10–12) at the same place where Israel had earlier been defeated and lost the Ark of the Covenant (1 Sam 4:1–11).

Ebionites (Heb *ebionim,* "the poor"), possibly the name of members of the early Christian community in Jerusalem (cf. Gal 2:10). The term came to be applied later to Jewish Christians who continued to observe many features of the Jewish law, rejected Paul and his doctrines, and understood Jesus to be a man on whom the Holy Spirit descended at his baptism. Their relation to the Clementine* Literature and to the Nazarenes*, another Jewish Christian group mentioned in the 4th c., is a matter of continuing controversy and inquiry.

Ebionites, Gospel of the, a Jewish–Christian gospel known through seven fragments quoted by Epiphanius* and possibly through other Jewish Christian writings (e.g. the sayings of Jesus in the [pseudo] Clementine* Literature).

The name does not derive from a legendary founder called "Ebion" (as Epiphanius thought) but from the Hebrew *ebionim,* "the poor," an honorific title among pious Jews. These Ebionites* probably lived in Transjordania or Syria.

In the late 2nd c., the Ebionites created a gospel for their own use, which they ascribed to Matthew but which was based on all three synoptic* Gospels (excluding John). The infancy stories were omitted, indicating Jewish–Christian reservations about the virginal conception of Jesus.

The fact that the Ebionites were vegetarians led to other revisions in their gospel: John the Baptist eats "honey cakes" instead of "locusts"; Jesus denies ever wanting to eat meat at the Passover meal (in the new version of Luke 22:15); and Jesus is critical of all sacrifices.

At the baptism of Jesus, the heavenly voice further quotes the second part of Ps 2:7: "Today I have begotten you" (see Luke 3:22). This makes possible an Adoptionist* or even a docetic* interpretation (according to Epiphanius, the Ebionites favored an "angelic Christology*"). **See also APOCRYPHA CLUSTER: APOCRYPHAL GOSPELS; HEBREWS, GOSPEL ACCORDING TO THE; NAZARENES, GOSPEL OF THE.** HANS-JOSEF KLAUCK

Ecclesiastes, one of the Megilloth*, responds to a collapsed moral order by denying that human existence has any meaning. A thematic statement about life's futility begins and ends the unknown Qoheleth's reflections, and poems that follow and precede create a chiastic structure. An opening inscription and two epilogues comment on Qoheleth's profession as a teacher of wisdom reaching out to ordinary laity.

The book's language and Aramaic influence, apparent in its vocabulary, grammar, and syntax, indicate a late Ptolemaic or, more probably, a Hellenistic period (c250 BCE) characterized by multitiered government, economic entrepreneurial ventures, and rapidly changing fortune. The fiction of Solomonic authorship seems intended to legitimize unorthodox views: death cancels everything; wisdom cannot achieve its goal; the deity is unknowable; the world is amoral; and pleasure commends itself. Indeed, Qoheleth advances the view that humans and animals share a single fate, but he also urges those who can to enjoy life. Affinities between Ecclesiastes and Greek philosophy suggest that Qoheleth was forging philosophical discourse in a linguistic system poorly equipped for abstract thinking. His apparent Epicureanism and coolness toward a distant deity vexed some readers – hence the epilogue's orthodox advice: fear God* and keep the Ten* Commandments. Modern nonreligious people are familiar with the refrain "Vanity of vanities, says Qoheleth, all is vanity," and the poem stating that there is a time for everything.

Early church fathers valued the book for its depiction of existence without Christ, and to offset its pessimism Jewish leaders eventually associated it with the joyful days of Sukkot.

JAMES L. CRENSHAW

Ecclesiasticus, Book of. See WISDOM OF BEN SIRA (or Sirach [Gk] or Ecclesiasticus [Lat]).

Ecclesiology, doctrine and discussion about the church* in relation to God, human history, and salvation. **See also CHURCH, CONCEPTS AND LIFE CLUSTER: INTRODUCTORY ENTRIES.**

Eckhart, Meister (c1260–1327), philosopher, theologian, preacher, administrator. John Eckhart studied in Cologne, where he met Albert* the Great. A lecturer in the *Sentences* at the University of Paris (1294), he was recalled to Erfurt to be prior of the Dominican Studium. He returned to Paris (1302) as a master in theology and wrote *Questiones parisiensis.* Provincial of Saxony in Northern Germany (1303–11), he produced a collection of sermons, *Paradise of the Intelligent Soul,* an excellent example of Latin meeting the German vernacular. In Paris for a second mastership (1311), he wrote the incomplete *Opus tripartitum* ("Work of Propositions," "Work of Questions," and "Work of Expositions," surviving in the form of commentaries on the Scriptures). Interpreting Scripture with the help of natural science and philosophy and influenced by Maimonides'* *Guide of the Perplexed,* he came to understand the spiritual or "parabolic" meaning of Scripture. This is shown by his six surviving Scripture commentaries from his time at Strasbourg and Cologne (1313–27), when he gained a reputation as a preacher in the vernacular.

For Eckhart, God is the ultimate "Ground" (*Grunt*) from which all things flow in trinitarian pattern. His "God-talk," carefully crafted with hermeneutical depth and precision, is based on the idea of Albert* the Great about the flowing of all things from God. For human beings, the return to God culminates in a breakthrough to simple divinity. In referring to God as one, Eckhart introduces a dialectical way of speaking in which God negates all that is knowable, leading to God as absolute wholeness (following Neoplatonic* views). His collection of sermons provides central metaphors of *Grunt*/Ground/God and uses the patristic doctrine of the birth of God in the human soul*.

Eckhart's careful distinctions were not always understood by his audience. Charged with heresy* related to the "Free* Spirit Movement" (1326), Eckhart defended himself in public; his case was moved to the papal court in Avignon. The papal bull *In agro dominico* (1329) officially condemned him on 28 propositions (17 held to be heretical and 11 "evil sounding," although they could be given a Catholic meaning). Eckhart denied making them. Yet they are found in his works. In the 19th and 20th c., Eckhart was "rediscovered" as a master of the spiritual* life.

JEREMIAH M. HACKETT

1) Introductory Entry

Ecology and Christianity. How do Christians view nature and their relation to the natural world? Christian theology*, like all theologies in any religious tradition, elucidates and posits the foundational theological frame in which believers and interpreters conceive of God, humans, nature, and their interrelations. These foundational frames make room for a variety of interpretations, but limit their range. Thus mainstream Western Christian traditions frame their conception of God*, humans (see Anthropology Cluster), and nature in ways that ascribe very little, if any, theological or spiritual relevance to nature.

As critiques often note, the devaluation of nature is related to anthropocentric presuppositions that frame most interpretations of Scripture and tradition. This anthropocentrism is rooted mainly in the influence of Greek classic philosophy on early and medieval Christianity.

Creation* stories (Gen 1, 2) are often interpreted as a divine command for humans to reign over the earth; in effect, humans are viewed as co-creators with God of the rest of creation (Gen 2:8–20). This perspective might eventually be ecologically sustainable, as foundational for a stewardship* theology; a number of ecologically aware theologians have suggested it. Humans have a unique responsibility to take care of the earth. But this interpretation of the creation stories also easily becomes a justification for a more or less unlimited right to utilize and exploit natural resources and animals to satisfy human needs and interests.

The redemption* theological key concepts – sin*, atonement*, salvation*, and Christology* – are also traditionally framed in an anthropocentric perspective. Sin is primarily a human activity or stance opposed to God or other humans, while human acts against nature and animals are less relevant, if at all. Consequently, salvation concerns humans exclusively. Furthermore, for certain traditions, salvation is envisioned as the rescuing of individuals from the sinfulness of the earth (the evil material "world") so that they can attain a state of grace in a heavenly or divine realm.

Christology and the Christ event are traditionally viewed by Western theology from an anthropocentric perspective, similarly problematical for ecologically aware theologians. Since God was incarnated in a human being, is it not obvious that humans are especially close to God and that salvation is exclusively for humans? The Gospels' themes of Jesus defeating the forces of nature – further demonstrated by the bodily resurrection – affirm that it is possible (and good) to subordinate nature to humanity.

Some forms of eschatology in the Western Christian tradition are also anthropocentric. They find in the Book of Revelation* and other apocalyptic* biblical texts affirmations that, according to God's plan, earth and material reality should be abandoned for another, nonearthly dimension. Then working for environmental protection and prohibiting the exploitation of nature and animals are irrelevant, indeed against God's will or plan.

It is possible to interpret ecological issues from a Christian perspective in more constructive ways by questioning and reconsidering the theological frames through which Christian tradition is interpreted. Instead of an anthropocentric view, one can readily adopt a creation*-centric interpretation of the creation stories or an interpretation centered on the covenantal* tradition of the HB. Similarly, theology can readily underscore that the Incarnation is an affirmation of the centrality of the created, natural world. Such views are present, e.g., in Francis* of Assisi, diverse mystical* and ascetic* traditions, and theologies beyond the North Atlantic world.

Christian theologians often connect ecology and social justice issues, because the people of the Two-thirds World, among them women, are more directly exposed to water and air pollution (including chemical pollution), the devastation of forestland, water scarcity, floods, and other consequences of climate change. **See also CLIMATE CHANGE AND CHRISTIANITY; LAND, THEOLOGICAL PERSPECTIVES AND PRAXIS, CLUSTER; WATER.**

MARIA JANSDOTTER-SAMUELSSON

2) A Sampling of Contextual Views and Practices

Ecology and Christianity: Eastern Orthodox Perspective. Each year, on September 1, the commencement of the ecclesiastical calendar, Orthodox Churches worldwide pray for the protection of the natural environment. The practice was established by Ecumenical Patriarch Demetrios in 1989 and was continued by his successor, Ecumenical Patriarch Bartholomew, whose ministry has focused on environmental issues with annual encyclicals, regular seminars, and international, interdisciplinary, and interfaith symposia focusing on the Mediterranean Sea (1995), the Black Sea (1997), the Danube River (1999), the Adriatic Sea (2002), the Baltic Sea (2003), and the Amazon River (2006).

This concern for nature is deeply rooted in theological principles. Orthodox Christianity underlines the intimate connection between human beings and the natural environment, emphasizing equally Adam's creation "in the image and likeness of God" (Gen 1:26) and "from the dust of the earth" (Gen 2:7). Humanity shared the sixth day of creation with "all the living creatures and creeping things of the earth" (Gen 1:24–26). The environmental crisis is a painful reminder of this reality. In response to this crisis, Orthodox Christianity draws on three characteristic values:

1. Icons* are central to Orthodox spirituality, revealing the eternal dimension of everything. Icons offer a corrective to a secular culture, which values only the here and now. In icons the heavenly God assumes a human face. Thus all humanity is rendered an image of God, while the entire world assumes iconic significance. Everything in this world is a sign of God's presence.
2. The Divine* Liturgy performs in time what the icon achieves in space. Our age is guilty of relentless waste because it has lost the spirit of worship. Maximus* the Confessor (7th c.) describes creation* as a "cosmic liturgy." The Orthodox Church

regards this world as a gift from God, which we have polluted by ceasing to relate to the world with a sense of awe and thanksgiving. Isaac the Syrian (7th c.) speaks of acquiring "a merciful heart, burning with love for the whole of creation – for humans, for birds, for the beasts . . . and all of God's creatures."

3. In this life, altering the way we perceive the world requires repentance of our practices and redirection of our perspectives. Orthodox spirituality underlines *ascesis* (self-restraint; See Asceticism), which enables us to live more frugally, remembering the poverty* of others and rendering human beings more compassionate and the world more inhabitable. Through asceticism*, we move away from what we want to what the world needs, valuing everything as created by God and as intended for God.

See also CREATION, ECOLOGY, AND THE ORTHODOX CHURCH; LAND, THEOLOGICAL PERSPECTIVES AND PRAXIS, CLUSTER; WATER.

JOHN CHRYSSAVGIS

Ecology and Christianity: Ecofeminist Theology. Françoise d'Eaubonne coined the term "ecofeminism" in 1974 to describe a mass movement modeled on contemporary ecological and feminist understandings of human society. Ecofeminist theology takes this as a context for its interpretation of Christian tradition.

While either ecology or feminism* may function as an entry point into this conceptual field, it is their critical interaction and projected integration that defines its theological character. This is marked by a reimagining of the concept of God* from one of patriarchal* domination over others, specifically over women* and nature*, to one envisioned in terms of an evolving relationship between God and the whole community of life on earth. The ecological framework for this relationship presupposes that the planet's ecosystems and the lives of the organisms they support are constitutively interconnected and interdependent. Therefore, the relationships between us are ideally characterized by cooperation, compassion* and justice*.

Ecofeminist theologians highlight positive religious and philosophical insights offered by Process* theology, Feminist* theologies, and the worldviews of indigenous communities with a strong matriarchal tradition that stress the importance of ecological interdependence and the value of biodiversity in all its forms. This transformative dialectic creates and at the same time exposes the need for models of God that foster a sense of our belonging within the whole community of life on earth rather than within a supposedly closed system of exclusively human salvation*. "The sacred" is seen as a totality that cannot be separated from whatever we perceive as the whole of existence. It is understood as the internal transcendence* of every living being and its environment.

An ecofeminist worldview consistently challenges theological traditions that systematically favor an ontotheology privileging the infinite, immaterial, objective, and rational* over the evolving, material, and emotional aspects of human existence. It demonstrates that granting primacy to spirit* and will* over the body* has led to unquestioned and apparently indissoluble connections being made between sexuality*, sin*, and female fertility. These Christian postulates have in turn served as a religious legitimation of Western hierarchical concepts of mastery over both women and nature.

This legitimized domination reduces the biophysical environment to instrumental or commodity value alone, seeing nature as something external to ourselves that is to be controlled and exploited for our sole benefit. Therefore, ecofeminists unite with social and environmental justice* and peace* movements to counter the destructive effects of global military–industrial complexes on the whole community of life. **See also LAND, THEOLOGICAL PERSPECTIVES AND PRAXIS, CLUSTER; WATER.** ANNE PRIMAVESI

Ecology and Christianity: Ecotheology. With its roots in the 1960s and the growing awareness of environmental problems parallel with the growing critique of the Christian heritage as anthropocentric, ecotheology has developed as a distinctive perspective within the theology and praxis of Christian denominations all over the world. Its general aim is to challenge Christian worldviews and ethics that make a strong division between God and nature, and to interpret the Bible and Christian tradition in a way that includes and safeguards the dignity of nature and animals. There is also a post-Christian* field of ecotheology, founded on the presupposition that the Christian heritage is too corrupted by anthropocentrism to be reinterpreted in a constructive way. Among the post-Christian ecotheologies are ecofeminist goddess perspectives. (see the present cluster: Ecofeminist Theology).

Ecotheology can be done by taking biblical texts, e.g. the creation stories, as proof of the divine origin of not just humans, but also of nature and animals. The creation* stories can be read as the foundation of both a covenantal* theology and a theology of spiritual immanence. The covenantal ecotheology takes into account the ancient Hebrew tradition about the covenant relation between God and humanity (including the Noah tradition). Presupposing that God's covenant is with all of creation and not merely with humans, the covenant makes humans responsible for establishing right relations with the earth. In an ecotheology of spiritual immanence, the earth is thought of as a holy interdependent community where God is encountered in humans and nature, although not reduced to immanent features. This view has been articulated primarily within the Roman Catholic and Orthodox traditions (see the present cluster: Eastern Orthodox Perspective). Modern Western Process* theology is one of the strong voices of ecotheology that rearticulates this perspective within Protestant theology. Ecotheology has also found inspiration in Christian medieval mystical traditions and the spiritual heritage from, e.g., Francis* of Assisi and Julian* of Norwich.

Other options include Ecofeminist theology and ecotheology in the liturgical* and ritual movement, often combined with feminist perspectives (see Women's Christian Practices and Theologies Cluster). The rhythms of nature and the human body are included in the language and activities of liturgy and rituals. Significantly, strong voices in ecotheology also come from the Two-thirds World and often combine ecotheology and a social justice perspective. **See also LAND, THEOLOGICAL PERSPECTIVES AND PRAXIS, CLUSTER; WATER.**

MARIA JANSDOTTER-SAMUELSSON

ECONOMY AND CHRISTIANITY CLUSTER

1) *Introductory Entry*

Economy and Christianity

2) *A Sampling of Contextual Views and Practices*

Economy and Christianity: Economic Ethics and Christian Theology

Economy and Christianity: Economic Studies of Christianity

Economy and Christianity: Economic Studies of the History of Christianity in the United States

---

1) Introductory Entry

Economy and Christianity. Economy (from Gk *oikonomia*, "administration of the household"; Lat *dispensatio*) is the social system of production, exchange, distribution, and consumption of goods and services in a community, a region, a nation, or the world. This is the economy that is the concern of the entries in the present cluster. Yet "economy" is also a theological concept. In the doctrine of the Trinity*, the "economy" is God's action toward the world (Eph 1:10, 2:9): creation*, redemption*, and sanctification*. In Eastern Orthodoxy, "economy" means the pastoral administration of canonical* or moral principles, relaxing them for the sake of a greater good as long as essentials are not violated. Casuistically* and humorously, "economizing the truth" means that not everything must be disclosed in every possible situation.

---

2) A Sampling of Contextual Views and Practices

Economy and Christianity: Economic Ethics and Christian Theology. The thought of Plato*, Aristotle*, and Stoicism* conjoined with the Torah*, the Prophets*, and the teachings of Jesus (see Kingdom of God, The Concept of, Cluster) was the substance of patristic and medieval theology's understanding of economy*. In Christendom* God was considered implicit in economy, and questions of economy were at the heart of theology. The church fathers generally followed Aristotle in extolling the virtues of *oikonomia* (Gk *oikos* + *nomos* = "the law or management of the household") and derogating the shaping of life according to commerce ("chrematistics"). Human beings are constituted by their associations and the goods their associations serve. The tradition through Aquinas* generally held that human community and the polis/state must regulate economy; the tradition regularly argued, as part and parcel of its doctrine, for fair price, just wage, complex space in which there was a place free of commodity exchange, and the wisdom of sumptuary laws (concerning personal expenditures). This economic perspective also led to the condemnation of usury as the unnatural assumption that an inanimate thing, money, is able to produce anything (as work does).

In the 17th c., Grotius* and Locke* laid the groundwork for a new ethical take on economics that featured a new form of natural* law and individualism, which had been on the rise since the Reformation. From that point, economic theology and ethics* have taken their bearings from the perceived centrality of the market. Although *economy* is an element of all antique and modern societies, *economics* is a modern science. Accompanying the rise of economics, there has been a decreasing sense of the involvement of God and faith in the economy. Deism*, as in the case of Adam Smith, highlighted the importance of religion in producing the virtues necessary for the practice of economy but sought to interdict those aspects of Christian doctrine, ritual, and ecclesial structure that squandered wealth or hindered the free play of economic practices

Since the 19th c., the market has loomed ever larger in economic theology and ethics. The old concerns of Christian political economy (the allocation of resources for production, the distribution of what it takes to live and thrive, the relations of those in the household, and the harm done to communities and nature by production, inequitable distribution, and unjust relationships) have been reduced to the modern concern of the science of economics: the allocation of scarce resources to meet "unlimited" human wants through the expression of preferences in the market. Economic theologies and ethics are divided in their views of God and Christian values in relation to the market.

One approach accepts the neoclassical definitions of the market (now perceived by many as an all-encompassing system replacing religion*; see also Idol, Idolatry) and construes the market as the key to understanding and practicing Christianity. The teachings of Jesus exemplify market rules and the human inclination toward competition and accumulation. Faith* is closely identified with individuals' economic acts of pricing, valuing, and expressing preference. Religion will succeed only if the internal, "natural" laws of the market are heeded. In the "marketplace of Christianity" approach, economic analysis provides the standard of ethics. Neoclassical market theory and Christian faith are not antagonistic but actually collude.

A second approach, the mainstream approach, however, focuses on the limits, failures, and deformations of the market and points to the necessity of community in the interstices left open by the market and its institutions. Once land, labor, and money completely become commodities, there is little space in which communities can resist the market and thrive. The sociological insights of Weber*, Durkheim*, and Troeltsch* are fundamental here. The point is not necessarily to criticize the logic of the market but to find political and communal means for limiting the market. This ethical approach generally assumes the possibility of a civil society and churches not controlled by the market. It seeks sources other than the market for value creation and prizes the thought forms of democracy* and communitarianism. Theologians and ethicists as different as Rauschenbusch* and other Social* Gospel thinkers, Reinhold Niebuhr*, and William Temple, and two generations of their disciples, ply this way.

A third approach emerged in the late 20th c., when two themes predominated: poverty* and ecology*. The failure of the globalized market following US neoclassical designs to ameliorate poverty and stanch the degradation of nature led to a deeper criticism of market economy. This third trend depends more heavily than the others on a critical retrieval of the Christian Scriptures and tradition and an alternative narrative of economy and Christian faith. Refusing to accept the modern definitions of the market as the criterion of what may be true in the Christian faith, this perspective criticizes the presuppositions of the market and seeks critically to retrieve ancient forms of economy: house holding, redistribution, and reciprocity. It also assumes that faith must have its own economy. This trend pays close attention to the fundamental practices of giving, forgiving, and hospitality*, arguing that the market, if unregulated, obviates these practices in its global reach. Yet these practices are necessary for any economy that humanely issues in just production, distribution, human relations, and the survival of nature. **See also** **ETHICS AND CHRISTIANITY CLUSTER.**

M. DOUGLAS MEEKS

Economy and Christianity: Economic Studies of Christianity. For the 18th-c. Scottish moral philosopher and economist Adam Smith (*Wealth of Nations*), the discoverable laws of the market are the uncontested standard of what is to be publicly retrieved and supported in Christianity. Following in Smith's and Hume's* footsteps, Christian theology employs economic studies of Christianity of various types and to often divergent ends.

1. *Christianity as supporting capitalist principles.* The contemporary study of Christianity can be seen in the publications of Acton Institute, which promotes a free society informed by Christian faith and moral absolutes. From this perspective, Christianity is primarily a source of individual virtue and offers little with regard to the actual operation of the market. Forms of this approach are favored by conservative Evangelicals who see capitalist principles as the guarantor of the liberties of free speech, religion, and an unregulated market. Christianity offers justification and support of capitalist principles.
2. *Using economic theories to explain Christianity.* By and large, neoclassical economic theory considers religion to be outside its bounds. However, a thoroughgoing neoclassical economic reading of Christianity is found in the work of Rodney Stark and Robert B. Ekelund, in which the tools of economic theory illuminate the emergence, development, and crises of Christianity and make normative judgments about the plight of the church and contemporary religion-influenced issues. Market logic (pricing, supply and demand, preferences) can explain all aspects of Christianity. The teachings of Jesus exemplify market rules and the human inclination to accumulate.

   The econometric economist Robert William Fogel measures the interaction between religious revival* and political reform and the material conditions in which they take place. According to Fogel, the post-1960s Evangelical revival is primarily about spreading spiritual meaning, now that material needs in the USA have been basically met.
3. *Economic studies critical of the foregoing.* Karl Marx criticized Christianity as an opiate that numbed the suffering of the oppressed. But he also saw it as a cry of the oppressed. Liberation*

theologies, epitomized by Gustavo Gutiérrez and Leonardo Boff, take up the Marxist economic analysis. Postcolonial* theologies follow the economic and cultural analysis of Edward Said and of new forms of empire adopted by Michael Hardt and Antonio Negri.

Another strand of economic study of Christianity (Max Stackhouse and others) has developed from Weber's* hermeneutical approach, which concentrates on the effect of Christian ideas on the development of economies. Weber conjectured that the capitalist pursuit of economic gain was in part engendered by Calvinist* and Puritan* self-denial and planning. Joseph Schumpeter, however, argued that capitalism began not with Reformation influences on the industrial revolution but rather in the 14th-c. small Italian city-states.

Richard Henry Tawney's Christian Socialist criticism of 18th-c. economic and social thought forms a milieu in which contemporary theologians, e.g., John Milbank, rework a Christian Socialist perspective. The steady-state economist Herman Daly and the Process* theologian John Cobb analyze the destructiveness of the global market economy and propose a new autarchy for local economy. Karl Polanyi's critical and prophetic history of the destructiveness of the modern unregulated market is the backdrop for the retrieval of biblical and traditional forms of economy for the practice of the church today. M. DOUGLAS MEEKS

Economy and Christianity: Economic Studies of the History of Christianity in the United States. Christianity in the US colonial period (16th–18th c.) replicated the economic patterns of European and English churches. Religion was a public good, and all members of a particular society were expected to adhere to the established church, whose ministry and ministers were supported by the public treasury. As the colonial period developed, however, early Americans brought an increasing variety of expressions of Christianity to the English colonies; by 1775–83 (the American Revolution) nearly every expression of British or continental European Christianity – established or Dissenter* – existed on the US mainland. National unification of formerly disparate colonies leveled the question of whether there would be a single national church.

The First Amendment to the Constitution (1791), soon followed by similar state constitutions, provided that there would be no national establishment of a particular denomination. This elimination of state establishment forced the privatization of religion as a public good. Without resort to even town-level funding, and without long-established churches supported by an aristocracy or lands, churches quickly turned to their own members for support. The new principle of voluntarily supported churches has profoundly affected the understanding of Christianity in the USA and created the conditions for Christian institutions to both proliferate and compete with one another.

This voluntary model of financial support of Christianity caused a series of innovations in financing technique and a new self-understanding by religious groups and their leaders. In the 19th c., Christian groups became the collective basis for founding most US colleges, hospitals, orphanages, missionary and tract societies, and programs of poor relief. Protestants faced competition from other churches in the same geographic region; they progressively redefined the scale and purpose of religious activity by the sorts of capital investments needed. Without geographical parishes*, US churches became characterized by relatively high expenditures by congregations for church building to attract and retain members in competition from other churches.

After the Civil War (1861–65), church leaders enunciated a divine-command basis for supporting churches as a form of religious obligation. They argued that a biblical tithe* (or 10%) of all one's weekly proceeds had never been repealed, only forgotten. This development paralleled the rise of an income-dependent new middle class that formed the basis of organized Protestantism and increasingly of

Roman Catholicism. Middle-class Protestants embraced the institutional* church (which supports social works in the community), and this greatly expanded the scope and expense of the typical congregation's activities. Middle-class Catholics, meanwhile, built a vast system of parochial and diocesan schools supported by voluntary gifts.

The emphasis of the Progressive Era (1890–1920) on responsibility for talent and wealth found an analogue in Protestantism's new emphasis on a person's "stewardship* under God's ownership of all things." This view of stewardship led both to a deemphasis of rule-based obligation and to broadened religious giving and spending. Religious causes well beyond the congregation – colleges, the YMCA* and YWCA*, camps, and missionary boards – with lay control and initiative began to receive greater funding. With support going to philanthropic institution building instead of local congregations, Protestant clergy families sometimes lived in "genteel poverty." Ministers' wives spoke to one another eloquently of the sacrifices and surprises a spiritual domestic life entailed. In Catholicism the labor supply that made the institutional life of schools and parishes possible was based on willing self-sacrifice by hundreds of thousands of women* religious. Priests, nuns, and ministers alike were not especially well paid until the mid-20th c., but their vocations were at the peak of respect conferred by general society.

During the post–World War II years (1950s–1960s), there was tremendous growth in the number of "new church starts" and denominational budgets for new programs. Raising money for Protestant churches, old and new, was relatively easy, but was accompanied by a crisis in understanding of the nature of the professional ministry. Clerical pay reached its high point in US history, but the socially ascribed value of clerical labor began to decline, leading to a later crisis in vocations, particularly acute in Catholicism and rural Protestant church leadership.

Late-20th- and early-21st-c. organized religion in the USA faces pressures wrought by its own successes in the postwar years. Like firms that overexpanded in flush economic times, Protestant churches and Catholic parishes now operated in more than 300,000 locations, maintaining facilities, programs, and staffs, while facing intense competition from one another and with other ways of being religious – North Americans affiliated less with formal religious groups and consumed more spiritual* literature, ranging from the Dispensationalist* *Left Behind* series to books fusing Eastern religions with the quest for self-fulfillment (see New Age Spirituality and Christianity). In a crowded marketplace, more than half of those who continue to affiliate with a Christian congregation belong to churches with large memberships (500 and more), while congregations of fewer than 100 members form the majority of all religious institutions. JAMES HUDNUT-BEUMLER

Ecthesis, the decree issued by the emperor Heraclius (638) forbidding discussion of "energies" (activities) in Christ and asserting that Christ's two natures are united in a single will. **See also** MONOTHELITISM.

Ecuador, straddles the equator (hence its name) on the west coast of South America. The Andes Mountains divide the country into three isolated regions with different cultures (Costa, Sierra, and East) and the Galápagos Islands (site of Darwin's* investigations). The country is multiethnic (self-identified native, 7%; black, 3%; mestizo* [racially mixed], 77%; mulatto, 3%; white, 10%) and multilinguistic (Spanish, Quichua, and a dozen languages of the Amazon region). This cultural diversity finds expression in different religious practices, symbolisms, and customs. Roman Catholicism, embraced by most of the population, shapes the common cultural identity.

The 16th Century. The aboriginal populations had religions related to nature and agricultural cycles. Yet the Incas superimposed on these religions the worship of the sun, Inti, and the moon, Quilla, during the time of the Inca Empire (1438–1533). The development of Christianity marched in step with the colonial* conquest (Quito was conquered in 1534). The Spaniards did not dismantle the existing social, cultural, and religious organizations, but incorporated them into the complex system of colonial Christendom. In 1535

Franciscans*, Dominicans*, and Mercedarians (a Spanish order), and later Augustinians* and Jesuits*, began missionary activities. They wrote grammars for indigenous languages, strove to improve social conditions (introducing new ways of farming and creating trade centers for native arts and crafts), and established various institutions, including monasteries. The first synod (1570), called by Bishop De la Peña, resolutely sided with the natives, defending their rights, but the viceroy of Lima rejected this "excessively pro-native" position. Although the Roman Catholic Church took measures to protect indigenous people from the *encomenderos* (colonists to whom the Spanish crown "entrusted" the indoctrination of the natives in exchange for services and taxes), the Church most often was the colonists' docile instrument and condoned the injustices they perpetrated.

The 17th Century witnessed an architectural explosion (the Jesuit and Franciscan churches in colonial Quito, the work of natives and mestizos), the establishment of impressive universities (San Fulgencio, 1586; San Gregorio Magno, 1620; Santo Tomás, 1688), and the Amazon missionary expansion – all as a result of the harsh colonialist exploitation of the natives. The Roman Catholic Church had become a colonial institution; resources derived from colonial exploitation were used to promote the education of the clergy and the development of religious art (to be used for catechesis*) at the famous School of Quito by mestizos and native artists (Pampite and Caspicara, sculptors; Miguel de Santiago and Goríbar, painters), and the construction of sumptuous church buildings. In contrast to many religious, who were considered lax, the first Ecuadorian saint, Mariana de Jesus (1618–45) led a life characterized by mysticism* and asceticism*, although she did not belong to a religious order.

During the 18th Century, cathedrals and religious communities increased their wealth and their ideological-political control over the population. Yet sociocultural turmoil erupted in the late 17th c. and continued with the expulsion of the Jesuits (1767), including Father Juan de Velasco, whose *History of the Kingdom of Quito* helped to galvanize Ecuadorian nationalism, and with the first declaration of independence (1809) led by men, such as Eugenio Espejo (who died in prison), women, such as Manuela Espejo (his sister) and Manuela Cañizares, and ordinary priests, such as Juan Pablo Espejo (the brother of Eugenio and Manuela), Correa, and Loyola.

In the 19th Century, during the short-lived period (1819–30) of the Republic of Greater Colombia (encompassing present-day Colombia, Venezuela, Ecuador, and Panama), the Roman Catholic Church inherited colonial power and promoted an economic ideology. Subsequently, in independent Ecuador (from 1830), following a concordat* with the Vatican (1862), García Moreno (president 1869–75) used the Church as an instrument to consolidate his theocratic program: leaving education in the hands of European religious and establishing Roman Catholicism as the official and exclusive religion. Three Ecuadorians were remarkable for their social ministry during this period: Mercedes de Jesús, Narcisa de Jesús, and Brother Miguel.

Following the suspension of the concordat (1877), the Liberal Revolution (1895), headed by Eloy Alfaro and supported both by rich exporters and by the poor, brought about a radical transformation of the ideological-political structures. The separation of church* and state left the Roman Catholic Church without its large land estates. The government decreed freedom of conscience and of worship. Protestantism, which since 1820 had had great difficulty establishing itself, could now develop beside Roman Catholicism. Public education took education* out of clerical hands. The conflict between laic anti-clerics and pro-clerics would last until the signing of the *Modus Vivendi* (1937) with the Vatican. As a result, the Pontificia Universidad Catolica del Ecuador was founded (1946).

The 1960s witnessed profound transformations. Vatican* II (1965) and the Medellín* Latin American Episcopal Conference (1968) urged the Roman Catholic Church to abandon its overly defensive anti-liberal stance. Committed Christians led by Monsignor Proaño experimented with Liberation* theology. But with Pope John* Paul II, the process of liberation was reversed. Movements like Opus* Dei – with two archbishops, schools, and centers for higher education – and other integrist* groups began to grow, although they were far removed from ordinary people. With the Law of Religious Liberty (1999), the state guaranteed the right to give religious instructions in all educational establishments, including public schools.

Protestantism in Ecuador. Anglicanism arrived in 1820, and the first pastors, many of them martyrs (professing another religion was a state crime), came mostly from the USA; Diego Thompson (Lancastrian* education), Lucas Mathews, Francisco Penzotty, Andrés Milne, and Zoilo Irigoyen. After the Liberal Revolution, Eloy Alfaro allowed the Methodists to found the first schools for teachers (Juan Montalvo and Manuela Cañizares). Rosina Kinsman created the first kindergarten. Evangelical churches have greatly expanded since 1960. The Ecuadorian Evangelical Confraternity (1968) comprises more than 50 denominations, which are active in health*, broadcasting, and education (HCJB Christian radio station and hospital; the Latin American Christian University). The Latin American Church Council vigorously works for ecumenical dialogue.

Ecuadorian Inculturated Religious Life. Native Andean elements have survived in religious festivities. For instance, the Inti Raymi (Celebration of the Sun) underlies the Corpus* Christi festivities; the singing of the "Salve Regina" is associated with the singing of *Yupaichishca*, a traditional hymn addressed to the divinity or to the emperor. The *prioste* is the outstanding figure who sponsors religious feasts. If formal religious ceremonies are brief (Mass* or transitional rites, e.g. funerals, nuptials), attendant celebrations, with a carnival-like flavor (including costumed dancers), may last for days or even weeks. Throughout the country during Christmas, the Pase del Niño (a procession for the Baby Jesus), the feast of Corpus Christi (especially at Cuenca), and the Holy Week processions (Jesus del Gran Poder, Quito; Cristo del Consuelo, Guayaquil), the logic of two cultures is combined: the Spanish and the mestizo*. In Quito the *cucuruchos* (penitents), dressed in purple, accompany others who compete in self-flagellation, a kind of pageantry of suffering. Besides each locality's patron saint, the most profoundly venerated figure is the Virgin Mary*. The pilgrimages to different sanctuaries (which entail long walks for the sake of expiation or to fulfill promises and are paid for with *ex-voto** offerings) culminate in crowded processions in which a special statue of Our Lady is carried with great respect, a cultural climax. Thousands of pilgrims are attracted to sanctuaries such as El Cisne (Loja), Huayco (Guaranda), El Quinche (Quito), and Agua Santa (Baños-Tungurahua).

The Roman Catholic Church, an institution with credibility and influence, has the largest number of believers, with groups promoting ecumenical dialogue. But the Roman Catholic Church faces complex challenges, including the decreasing number of believers, most of whom were baptized but never evangelized. Only some accept Christian values as components of their cultural identity; young people are becoming secularized*, although they reject, not the Church, but its deformed image. The people of God long for a church that discerns without feeling superior, that evangelizes and allows itself to be evangelized, that is sensitive to the cry of the poor and values deeds more than words. There exists a hidden, underground missionary minority with intense evangelical courage that continues working, hoping for the right time for and new signs of a revival. **See also MERCEDES DE JESÚS; MIGUEL, BROTHER; NARCISA DE JESÚS; PROAÑO, LEONIDAS.**

Statistics: Population (2000): 12.65 million (M). Christians, 12.3 M, 97.6%; (Roman Catholics, 8.7 M, 69.0%; Protestants/Evangelicals, 0.4 M, 4.1%; Pentecostals/Charismatics, 1.6 M, 12.5%; independents: 0.2 M, 1.8%); nonreligious, 0.2 M, 1.5%; other, 1.5 M, 11.8%. (*Source*: CEHILA [Comisión para el Estudio de la Historia de la Iglesia en América Latina y el Caribe] Studies, 2000.)

LUIS MARÍA GAVILANES DEL CASTILLO

Ecumenical Association of Third World Theologians (EATWOT) was initiated by Fr. Sergio Torres, who, while in Nairobi (1974) to prepare for the Fifth World* Council (WCC) of Churches Assembly, held exploratory discussions with several theologians and church leaders, including Kofi Appiah-Kubi (then working for the All Africa Conference of Churches) and Jesse Mugambi (then theology secretary for the World Student Christian Federation, Africa Region). During the Fifth WCC Assembly (1975), Fr. Torres made plans to hold the first meeting of EATWOT at Dar es Salaam (1976), with Appia-Kubi and Mugambi facilitating the local logistical arrangements and Fr. Torres providing the international mobilization.

Theologians from Africa, Asia, and Latin America needed a forum to discuss Christian theology from their own contextual perspectives, without restriction or inhibition by the dominant perspectives from Europe and North America. Thus the self-presentation was as follows: "The Ecumenical Association of Third World Theologians – EATWOT – is an association of men and women committed [to] the struggle for the liberation* of Third World peoples, by promoting new models of theology for a religious pluralism, social justice* and peace. As Third World theologians, EATWOT members take the Third World context seriously, doing theology from the vantage point of the poor* seeking liberation, integrity of creation, gender co-responsibility, racial and ethnic equality and interfaith dialogue. Thus Third World theologies are those which offer an alternative voice to the marginalized and exploited people of the planet."

EATWOT was born in Dar-es Salaam, Tanzania (1976), with 22 representatives from Africa, Asia, and Latin America, and one Black theologian from the USA to share with one another theological efforts in their denominations – Roman Catholic, Protestant, and Orthodox. At that time, Third World Christians had become aware that the "universal" theology they had inherited from the West was not pertinent to their context of poverty and marginalization; traditional theology had to be reformulated to become meaningful to peoples struggling for a more just and egalitarian world.

Thus EATWOT endeavors to (1) interpret the gospel using the hermeneutical* circle to link God's word to the life of marginalized people; (2) encourage the interchange of theological views through the publication of books and journals with themes of interest in the Third World, including Liberation theologies; (3) foster the mutual interaction between theological formulation, science*, art*, spirituality*, and ecology*; (4) motivate the interaction of theologies within the diverse cultures and religions of peoples of the Third World; (5) give support to social movements for spiritual, social, and interreligious liberation; and (6) organize regional, continental, and intercontinental meetings of Third World theologians.

A general assembly of EATWOT was convened in Johannesburg in 2006 (the organization's 30th anniversary) and adopted a five-year program, involving (1) the development of and engagement with gender theologies and new methods for such theologizing that challenge patriarchal privileges and require the reconstruction of ideologies* of all genders; (2) an exploration of the authority of the biblical text (Scripture*) in the theological endeavors of Third World Christians along with naming additional oral and written sources to be engaged and explored in the formation of these new theological endeavors; (3) the reaffirmation of praxis* methods that constructively engage the tensions between action on the ground and theological formulations and constructions; (4) the affirmation of EATWOT members' commitment as theologians to working with gender, racial, ethnic, indigenous, and sexual groups in mutuality, learning from one another to enhance the building of viable liberatory communities; and (5) the development of dialogical styles and approaches to interaction among EATWOT members and with members of other religious groups that are nonhegemonic and affirm the humanity and worthiness of all parties in the dialogue. **See also CONTEXTUAL THEOLOGIES.**

JESSE NDWIGA KANYUA MUGAMBI

Ecumenical Councils, assemblies of bishops from the "whole inhabited world" (implicitly defined as the Roman Empire), whose decisions on doctrine, ethics, discipline, and worship are held to be binding on all Christians. The list of authoritative councils is disputed.

For the Eastern Orthodox* churches, the seven ecumenical councils are Nicaea* I (325), Constantinople* I (381), Ephesus* I (431), Chalcedon* (451), Constantinople* II (553), Constantinople* III (680), and Nicaea* II (787). All of these were called by Roman Byzantine emperors. Several other councils, while later rejected on various grounds, were similarly called and approved by emperors; these include Sardica (342/3), Ariminum* and Seleuceia (359), Constantinople* (360), Ephesus* II (449), and Constantinople* IV (754).

The Oriental Orthodox* non-Chalcedonian churches recognize only the first three ecumenical councils. Most of the churches of the Reformation* recognize only the first four. The Roman Catholic Church, which holds that the pope must call, preside over, and promulgate the decrees of a council, recognizes 14 more, from the Middle Ages through Vatican* II.

Ecumenical Movement. "Ecumenical," a word derived from the Greek *oikumene,* was used as early as the 5th c. BCE to denote "the inhabited earth." In the rare NT usages, it frequently refers to the whole world (Matt 24:14) or the Roman Empire (Luke 2:1). Over time, "ecumenical" came to refer to the whole church, specifying its universality, and to describe the seven ecumenical* councils convened from the 4th to the 8th c. and held by many as authoritative for the whole church.

Since the World Missionary Conference in Edinburgh* (1910), the start of the modern ecumenical movement, the word "ecumenical" has come to refer to the whole church and to be associated with the movement for the unity of the church, a unity called for by the church's sense of mission. In 1951 the Central Committee of the World Council of Churches (WCC) defined "ecumenical" as pertaining to everything that relates to "the whole world. It therefore covers equally the missionary movement and the movement toward unity." Most often, then, the word is defined as "the whole inhabited earth."

There is not a single expression of the modern ecumenical movement. This can be illustrated by the perspectives of the Orthodox churches, the WCC, and the Roman Catholic Church. In 1920 the Holy Synod of the Church of Constantinople issued an encyclical, *Unto the Churches of Christ Everywhere*, calling for a global league or fellowship (*koinonia*) of churches to meet the needs of the world. This was later described by the Dutch general secretary of the WCC, W. A. Visser 't Hooft (1900–85) as "an initiative which was without precedent in church history."

The WCC was formed in 1948 in Amsterdam and has obviously come to be a major instrument of ecumenism. Streams from the Faith* and Order Movement, the Life* and Work Movement, and the missionary movement came together in this formation. The WCC now has more than 350 member churches, largely Protestant (although not all these church bodies wish to be called by that name) and Orthodox.

The Roman Catholic Church has never become a member of the WCC, although increasingly it participates fully in certain WCC activities, notably its Commission on Faith and Order. Since Vatican* II and its decree on ecumenism, *Unitatis Redintegratio* (1964), the Church's involvement in the movement for the unity of the church has been undisputed. Pope John* Paul II went so far as to affirm, in his encyclical *Ut Unum Sint* (1995), the "irrevocable commitment" of the Roman Catholic Church to the ecumenical movement as "an organic part of her life and work."

To these instances must be added such activities as the formation of national and regional councils of churches; the organic union of church bodies in countries such as India, Pakistan, Canada, and the USA; the ecumenical activities of the Christian World Communions (Anglican, Lutheran, Reformed, Roman Catholic, and others) expressed frequently in bilateral dialogues on theological issues that historically have divided church bodies from one another; and, surely, the joint witness and activities of church bodies on issues of social justice, e.g. racial and gender discrimination, refugee relief, the struggle to overcome world poverty*, the prevalence of violence in a world at war, and the quest for ecological* sanity.

There is no single "ecumenical theology," although no theology relevant to both the nature of Christian faith and the needs of the world can be without strong ecumenical dimensions. The Faith and Order Movement has fostered a willingness on the part of many ecclesial bodies to face historic theological and ecclesiological issues that have divided the churches. Since the latter part of the 20th c., new streams of theology with clear ecumenical implications have arisen, including such movements, among many, as Third World Liberation* theology, Feminist* and African* American theologies, and new ways of approaching and understanding the classic biblical texts. All of these are frequently concerned to emphasize the corporate, communal nature of the church. And all now deal with new questions of mission in a world that is diverse, pluralist, and increasingly marked by religious fundamentalism* and fanaticism. The ecumenical movement in its many forms has always seen its work as designed such "that the world might believe" (John 17), and that task is increasingly crucial and difficult.

In the long run, the ecumenical movement is not concerned merely with cooperation between church bodies. The quest for the unity of the church – in community and in mission* – is a quest for *koinonia*, unity as communion* at the deepest levels of life, made possible by the gracious quest of God for communion with God's own creation. NORMAN A. HJELM

Ecumenical Patriarchate of Constantinople (present-day Istanbul) is the ranking church within the communion of the 14 autocephalous* churches that constitute Eastern Orthodox* Christianity. The Patriarchate includes metropolitanates, archdioceses, and dioceses in Turkey* and Greece*, as well as in the Americas, Western Europe, Australia, and the Far East. The archbishop of "Constantinople and New Rome" (present-day Istanbul), known as the ecumenical patriarch, is recognized as the presiding bishop within the worldwide Orthodox Church of about 250 million believers.

Early Christian tradition identifies Andrew* the Apostle as an evangelizer in the region of the ancient Greek trading city of Byzantium*. Emperor Constantine* selected this strategic city for the new capital of the Roman Empire (324) and dedicated it as New Rome (330). From then onward, the role of the bishop of New

Rome gradually increased. The Council of Constantinople (381) stated (Canon 3) that the bishop of the new capital had "prerogatives of honor" after the bishop of Rome. The Council of Chalcedon* (451) identified the bishop of Constantinople as a recipient of appeal (Canons 9 and 17) and stated that this church had "equal privileges" with that of old Rome (Canon 28). The same council broadened the jurisdiction of Constantinople beyond the boundaries of the Roman–Byzantine Empire and the other ancient patriarchates. Then (from the late 6th c.) the archbishop of Constantinople was also called the "ecumenical patriarch" to indicate his importance not only within the Church but also within the Roman–Byzantine Empire.

From the 4th c., many prominent patriarchs played a leading role in the theological discussions at the ecumenical councils, in missionary work, charitable activity, iconography, architecture, and liturgical developments. With the church divisions following the Council of Chalcedon* (5th c.) and the Muslim conquests of Palestine, Syria, and Egypt (7th–8th c.), the Patriarchate's influence only increased.

Between the 9th and 15th c., tensions between the Church of Rome and the Ecumenical Patriarchate (chiefly over papal authority and the *Filioque**) led to a gradual estrangement. Limited excommunications were exchanged (1054). However, a formal schism did not immediately follow, although Constantinople consistently rejected the growing claims of papal jurisdiction throughout the Church. The sack of Constantinople (1204) by Western crusaders* and the temporary appointment by Rome of Western bishops in Constantinople and other Eastern cities profoundly compounded differences in theology, church polity*, and liturgical practices. Constantinople sent representatives to the Councils of Lyon (1274) and Florence* (1438–45) to discuss differences. However, the decisions of both were subsequently rejected in the East, and this deepened the alienation between Catholicism centered in Rome and Orthodoxy centered in Constantinople. For the Orthodox, the schism was formalized in 1484.

The city of Constantinople fell to the Muslim Turks in 1453. While the Roman–Byzantine Empire came to a tragic end, the Patriarchate continued under new political conditions that frequently impeded its witness. During the 16th c., the Patriarchate was engaged in limited theological discussions with Lutherans and Anglicans. It also granted autocephalous status to the Church of Russia* (1589). With the subsequent breakup of the Ottoman Empire and the creation of new Balkan nations (19th c.), the Ecumenical Patriarchate granted autocephalous status to the churches of Greece* (1850), Serbia* (1879), Romania* (1885), Albania* (1937), and Bulgaria* (1945). More recently, autocephaly was granted to the Church of Georgia* (1989) and the Church of the Czech* Lands and Slovakia* (1998).

The Ecumenical Patriarchate has expressed its primatial ministry by encouraging greater unity among the autocephalous Orthodox churches and has identified common issues needing attention by the entire Church. It continued to be a center of appeal arbitrating in disputes involving other regional Orthodox churches. The Patriarchate led Orthodox participation in the global expressions of the ecumenical movement and especially the dialogue with both the Oriental Orthodox churches and the Roman Catholic Church. It also was a champion of interreligious understanding and peaceful cooperation, notably in the charitable and environmental areas (see Ecology and Christianity Cluster: Eastern Orthodox Perspective). Finally, the Ecumenical Patriarchate exercised a particular responsibility for overseeing the development of new regional churches beyond the boundaries of other autocephalous churches. Resulting from both missions and immigration, the growth of the Orthodox Church in the so-called diaspora of the Americas, Western Europe, Australia, and the Far East is both significant and complex. In these areas, the Ecumenical Patriarchate has exercised its primacy by guiding a united mission and witness of the Orthodox in these diverse societies. **See also AUTOCEPHALOUS CHURCHES; MISSION CLUSTER: AND EASTERN ORTHODOXY.**

THOMAS FITZGERALD

Eddy, Mary Baker (1821–1907), US writer, theologian, founder of the Church of Christ, Scientist (1879). Born in New Hampshire, she spent the first 40 years of her life coping with chronic illness. She met "science of health" itinerant Phineas Quimby (1862) and began preaching a version of Quimby's message after her sudden recovery from a nearly fatal illness (1866). Christian* Science emerged in a period (late 19th c.) marked by intense interest in the relationship between spirituality and health* as well as an increasing respect for science*. In *Science and Health with Key to the Scriptures* (1875), Eddy combined eschatology*, spirituality, health, and science by offering an authoritative interpretation of Scripture* that focused on healing. She claimed that matter was illusory and Spirit real. A proper, scientific reading of Scripture deemphasized the supernatural aspects of Jesus Christ and focused on his message that disease, sin*, and death* would vanish if a person understood the monistic nature of reality. Although Eddy's teachings, especially her admonition not to seek medical treatment for illness, disturbed people outside the movement, her message proved particularly congenial to middle- and upper-class urban women. At a time when many such women felt powerless, Christian Science provided empowerment and individual well-being. **See also** **CHRISTIAN SCIENCE.** SARAH JOHNSON

Eden (translated "paradise*," a Persian term, in LXX) is the "garden of delight" where Adam and Eve lived (Gen 2:8) before being driven out after sinning (Gen 3:23–24). Many Christians supposed that Eden was still somewhere on earth, empty, guarded by the angel with a flaming sword (Gen 3:24), probably in Mesopotamia or Ethiopia. Some saw natives of the Amazon, north Mexico, or the South Seas as living in "Edenic simplicity." Luther* and others with a more radical view of human sin* suggested that Eden had been erased by the Flood*, increasing the sense of transience and deprivation.

Edessa, present-day Urfa, in Southeastern Turkey, center of Syriac* Christianity. Under Roman control from 213 CE, it fell to Persia (609) and was then under Arab rule (from 639) until the Crusades (1098). King Abgar's* conversion in apostolic times is legendary. Marcionites*, Bardaisanites*, and Manichaeans* flourished in early centuries. A church building existed in 201. The Syriac Church had three martyrs during the Diocletian* persecution (Shmona, Guria, and Habbib) and used Tatian's* Diatessaron* until the 5th c. Succeeding the school of Antioch*, the school of Edessa, a center of theological education (4th–5th c.; moved to Nisibis*, 489), included the theologians and church leaders Ephrem*, Rabbula, Jacob* of Serug, Bar* Sauma, and Narsai. Its famous icon of Christ (*mandylion*) was transferred to Constantinople in the 10th c.

UTE POSSEKEL

Edict of Milan. See MILAN, EDICT OF.

Edinburgh Conference (1910), World Missionary Conference, leading to the founding of the International Missionary Council (1921). The Eastern Orthodox* and Roman Catholic churches were not invited, but neither were mission societies seeking converts from these churches; participants were confined to those working among non-Christians (contrast the Panama* Conference of 1916). Non-Europeans were present only as members of delegations from mission societies, not as representatives of "younger churches"; active participation was thus limited to churches based in colonial nations, ironically at the time of nationalist revolutions in Mexico (1910) and China (1911). John R. Mott* chaired most meetings; J. H. Oldham was secretary. The later Faith* and Order Movement grew directly out of Bishop Charles Brent's protest at the Conference's avoidance of issues of doctrine and ministry; the parallel Life* and Work Movement was nurtured by Oldham.

Edinburgh Conference (1937), the second World Conference on Faith* and Order, gathering 414 delegates from 122 churches and 42 countries. The Conference was centered on five themes: (1) the grace of our Lord Jesus Christ, (2) the church of Christ and the Word of God, (3) the communion of saints, (4) the ministry and sacraments of the church of Christ, and (5) the church's unity in life and worship. It adopted a theological statement, *Affirmation of Union in Allegiance to Our Lord Jesus Christ,* and committed the Faith and Order Movement to integration, together with the Life* and Work Movement, into the World Council of Churches officially formed in Amsterdam (1948) after World War II. NORMAN A. HJELM

EDUCATIONAL PRACTICES AS CHRISTIAN SERVICE CLUSTER

1) *Introductory Entry*

Educational Practices and Institutions as Christian Service

2) *A Sampling of Contextual Views and Practices*

Educational Practices as Christian Service in Africa
Educational Practices as Christian Service in Asia

Educational Practices as Christian Service in Mexico
Educational Practices as Christian Service in the United States

1) Introductory Entry

Educational Practices and Institutions as Christian Service. From the earliest development of the Christian faith, education has been a central mission of the churches. Jesus is called "teacher," and much of what he did in his public life was to transform through teaching. The introduction to the Sermon on the Mount (Matt 5:2), a collection of the teachings of Jesus, begins "Then he began to speak, and *taught* them, saying" (emphasis added).

Early church leaders were engaged in education as teachers and writers. For example, Clement* of Alexandria (c150–215) wrote extensively, served as head of the catechetical school, and influenced the formation of an orthodox tradition. Augustine* of Hippo (354–430), in *On Christian Doctrine*, wrote profoundly about Christianity's educational responsibilities; his thought and that of Thomas Aquinas* (1125–1274) have shaped the Roman Catholic understanding of education. The Protestant Reformers, Martin Luther* (1483–1546) and John Calvin* (1509–1564), further developed Christianity's understanding of education. Luther's views are contained in the *Large* and *Small Catechisms*; Calvin founded educational institutions and was a humanist scholar whose vast publications reflect a strong commitment to the educational dimensions of faith*. Both saw education as a means of conversion* and transformation.

The aims of education within Christianity have been and continue to be (1) to inform, (2) to discover and disseminate knowledge, and (3) to use that knowledge for good. Christians understand the world to be the creative work of God, and this creation* can be understood through education as a means of "loving God with one's whole mind" (Mark 12:30 par.)

In addition, Christianity has been committed to advancing knowledge as a means of human development, enrichment, and preparation for a life of service. Christians are called (see Vocation) to prepare themselves through education to love God and all people, and to serve the causes of peace and justice.

Christian educational institutions can be found in nearly every corner of the world. They exist within local congregations in Bible study and catechetical teaching for all ages. Schools, colleges, universities, and theological institutions also represent Christianity's enduring commitment to education. Today, these institutions face all the challenges of the global context and information age – crossing language and culture, confronting resistance from established ways and seats of power, finding the necessary financial resources to sustain the effort, and discerning ways to accommodate the varieties of government policies in different countries.

Many of these institutions provided education well before the rise of public education and have been incorporated into public systems. Some of the distinctive Christian features of these institutions are less visible as a more secular educational model becomes the dominant mode. This is particularly true in Europe and the USA. But the trajectory of the founding values of these institutions, such as dedication to the welfare and development of every student, the teaching of life as a gift to be used for service, and the concern to make a contribution to a more just world, continues into the present.

At every level of education, regional and international associations and institutions exist to advance Christian education, and individual institutions do their work in complex environments. For example, within higher education, there is the United Board of Christian Higher Education in Asia and more than 200 institutions participate in the All India Association of Christian Higher Education. Forman Christian College in Lahore, Pakistan*, recently returned to the Presbyterian Church by the government after several years of nationalization, is thriving, although it is faced with the complexities of being a minority institution in an Islamic republic. The Mar Elias Institutions in the Galilee serve students from many backgrounds and at all levels and include on their faculty Christians, Jews, Muslims, and Druze. DUNCAN S. FERGUSON

2) A Sampling of Contextual Views and Practices

Educational Practices as Christian Service in Africa. Formal Western education came to Africa with missionaries (see Mission Cluster: In Africa). Most mission stations established schools, hospitals, and sometimes printing presses and agricultural projects. Thus mission stations were centers of faith and educational development.

The primary aim of the schools was to convert* African people to Christianity. All the students of a particular school were to be members of the denomination that established the school. The teaching of the Bible was a priority. The teaching of religion at school had the same goals as Sunday school teaching at church. School teachers were also trained to be evangelists.

Missionaries also introduced professional training of Africans in teacher training colleges, medical and nursing colleges, and training centers for artisans and administrators. Special mission work for women and girls was introduced in order to establish Christian families, following the belief that women shape the next generation and have a great influence on their husbands. Missionaries wanted the mission-trained teachers, evangelists, preachers, and church members to marry Christian women who would encourage their husbands in their faith.

Mission education produced most of the first generation of political leaders in Africa, including Kwame Nkruma of Ghana*, Jomo Kenyatta of Kenya*, Julius Nyerere of Tanzania*, Kenneth Kaunda of Zambia*, and Kamuzu H. Banda of Malawi*. Religion in Africa has continued to contribute significantly to the democratization of politics.

Although independent African governments have taken over as the major provider of Western education, churches continued to manage boarding schools; teacher training colleges and hospitals are still popular among Africans in many countries as providers of the best Western education and medical facilities. In many church schools, the aim of religious education is now educational. Church schools enroll children from different denominations and religions. Girls and boys have the same school curriculum. Some African countries, like Zambia, Malawi, and South* Africa, have encouraged the teaching of multi-faith religious education to promote tolerance among adherents of different religions. This trend has been supported and promoted by International Consultations on Religious Education in East, Central, and Southern Africa.

ISABEL APAWO PHIRI

Educational Practices as Christian Service in Asia. Christian schools were first founded in Asia by missionaries (see Mission Cluster: In Asia) amid the colonial* expansion of the Western powers. Catholic missionaries came along with the Portuguese and Spanish, who were seeking trading opportunities in the early 16th c. (see Portuguese Explorations, Conquests, and Missions; Spanish Explorations, Conquests, and Missions). Since their early years of missionary work in places like India*, Siam (Thailand*), Japan*, and especially the Philippines*, the Catholic missionaries have established schools for teaching Christian children and training priests. At the turn of the 17th c., some of these schools in the Philippines were turned into tertiary educational institutions – the oldest universities in Asia.

Later, the Dutch colonial power and its Protestant missionaries arrived (mid-17th c.). Christian schools were set up in Indonesia*, Formosa (Taiwan*), and Ceylon (Sri* Lanka). The greatest influence on the development of modern education in Asia, however, was exerted by the British and US Protestant missionaries. Since the opening of schools by the English Baptists in Calcutta in the first few years of the 19th c., Protestant missionaries had established educational institutions throughout Asia, ranging from preschools to colleges. Catholic missions also continued

Educational Practices as Christian Service

their educational endeavors, often in competition with their Protestant counterparts.

Aims of Education. Besides serving as an important means of evangelism*, the missionary educational practices also aimed (1) to provide Christian education to converts* and their children; (2) to provide preparatory education for training local preachers, catechists, or priests; (3) to reform oppressive local customs like the exclusion of women from education; and (4) to abolish local superstitions* by transmitting Western knowledge.

As the missionary educational enterprise grew larger (late 19th c.), educational missionaries began to highlight the significance of Christian schools and colleges in transforming Asian religions and cultures* and making the local people more receptive to the gospel. Some missionaries and local Christians also supported the idea of reforming a given nation by building up the character of the people through Christian education.

Education, Culture, and Nationalism. Before Western missionaries arrived, many Asian peoples already had strong religious cultures, including Hinduism*, Islam*, Buddhism*, and Confucianism*. The beneficiaries of the local dominant cultures often found the mission schools threatening or detestable. Thus in the beginning, mission schools faced resistance from the local dominant cultures and attracted children from underprivileged families or ethnic minorities.

However, with the rise of nationalism (19th c.), the attitude of leaders of the Asian nations toward missionary education became more ambivalent. While they valued the mission schools as an indispensable provider of Western learning for modernizing Asian nations, they also feared that the propagation of Western religion would harm the building of national identity. The general rule was that when resources were sufficient and the nationalistic spirit was high, nation-states would by all means reclaim the control of education. In some extreme cases, like that of Communist China*, all mission schools were closed. More often, Christian schools were allowed to continue but were required to observe some restrictions; e.g. compulsory Bible lessons and religious activities were prohibited.

In general, Christian schools and colleges, if allowed to exist, have become recognized players in national educational systems. Many of them, because of their own long histories, have continued to enjoy a good reputation. They are in direct competition with the public schools, but may also receive subsidies from Asian governments. The balance between the pursuit of academic results and the nurture of Christian values is an important issue that has to be addressed constantly. At the level of higher education, the United Board for Christian Higher Education in Asia has established the Asian Christian Higher Education Institute (Asian Institute), so as to strengthen the Christian presence in colleges and universities.

GUSTAV K. K. YEUNG

Educational Practices as Christian Service in Mexico

Education and Original Evangelization. In Mexico, education was intimately connected to the evangelization process. Primary education, which took place in courtyards, open chapels, or schools attached to convents, made use of bilingual texts to teach grammar, vocabulary, and catechism, and of theater or painting to represent dogma (and in the process some training in arts and crafts). Priests, sisters, and other religious were assisted by native teachers. The Jesuits'* arrival greatly promoted higher education. The Real y Pontificia Universidad (Royal and Pontifical University) of Mexico (1550s) functioned independently. The Conciliar Seminary (17th c.) offered theological education for the secular clergy, while the education of women, also the Church's responsibility, was provided in convents and in informal women's schools "of friends."

18th and 19th Centuries. The need to instruct the growing population led to the creation of religious schools (18th c.) that offered free education to poor children. Yet the Roman Catholic Church's educational work was reduced during the Bourbon reforms (1750–1808), when the viceroy created primary schools that functioned under the supervision of the government and were publicly financed. The expulsion of the Jesuits (1767) further reduced the role of the Church in education. During the empire of Agustin de Iturbide (1822–23), Lancastrian* schools – schools emphasizing peer tutoring as advocated by the British Quaker educator Joseph Lancaster – were developed, expanding a secular program of popular education. In 1833 the independent state took over the responsibility of education, supervising the schools, without nevertheless relieving the Church of its educational role and its opportunity to provide free education by opening schools attached to convents and in parishes. Likewise, the *Catechism* of Father Ripalda remained the center of moral education during the 19th c.

From the Revolution to the Present Day. Porfirio Díaz (president, 1876–80; 1884–1911) gave religious groups permission to come to Mexico and establish private schools. But with the Mexican Revolution (1929), the project of secular education prohibited religious associations from having religious education programs in public schools. This struggle for ideological control between church and state lessened toward the middle of the century, owing to more lenient state policies and a less aggressive attitude of the National Union of Parents of Family and other movements related to the Roman Catholic Church. Today several religious orders – including female congregations – have educational institutions ranging from those offering primary education to those providing university-level education (especially Jesuit, Lasallian, Marist, and Salesian colleges or universities). JAVIER OTAOLA MONTAGNE

Educational Practices as Christian Service in the United States. Christianity emphasized education from its beginnings, following the example of early Christians who met to study the teachings (*didache*) of the apostles (Acts 2:42) and the "great commission" "to teach them everything I have commanded you" (Matt 28:19–20).

From these injunctions and the growing awareness that Christianity must be taught in order to be understood and practiced, the Christian churches devoted themselves to education. Christian teaching, from its entrance into the USA (16th–17th c.) to the present, falls into three categories: (1) informational, (2) transformational, and (3) vocational. In the family, in the church, and in the institutions of the church, there was a need for people to learn about the basics of Christianity: the stories and content of the Bible, the theology and practices of the church, morality and the expectation of service. These teachings were intended to nurture learners in their spiritual lives and transform them into Christian people. The information that led to transformation in turn pointed to an understanding of vocation*, one's calling in life.

Numerous institutions devoted to education became a part of the US Christian landscape and have continued to evolve. In the family*, young people were and continue to be expected to learn about faith*. Sunday* school and catechetical classes were and are integral to parish life. Christian schools at all levels and retreat centers were developed by a vast spectrum of denominations and theological perspectives. Theological seminaries for the training of clergy became foundational for providing priests and ministers for the Christian Church. Publishing supported and continues to support this vast educational endeavor.

The educational mission of Christianity in the USA varies among denominations and historical traditions. The Roman Catholic Church has a network of educational institutions that makes it possible for Catholics to receive the majority of their education within Catholic institutions. Generally, mainline Protestants have less complex networks and in many cases have been supportive of public education. There is a growing trend among the Evangelical community to provide schools at all levels in order to cultivate the formation of a Christian mind and spirit.

DUNCAN S. FERGUSON

Edwards, Jonathan (1703–58), born in Connecticut, Yale graduate, Congregational and Presbyterian minister. Because of a major revival*, and his sermons and writing, he became widely known during the 24 years he spent as pastor of a congregation in Northampton, Massachusetts Bay Colony. After losing this pulpit as a result of controversy over the halfway* covenant (1750), he became a missionary to Native Americans in western Massachusetts. Here he had time to write and to teach a few young ministers. They and their successors would dominate theological training in the USA for the next century. Just after assuming the presidency of the College of New Jersey in Princeton, Edwards died from a smallpox inoculation (1758).

Edwards distinguished himself in four areas: in probing the nuances of religious experience, in his brilliant defense of divine sovereignty and moral determinism against Arminians*, in utilizing an idealistic ontology in his understanding of God and of the Trinity*, and in an aesthetic understanding of conversion and human virtue.

Edwards first gained fame for his sensitive, even awestruck description of a remarkable revival that began in his own congregation in 1734. His *Faithful Narrative* became a literary classic, was widely read in Britain, had a direct impact on John Wesley*, and launched a literary genre in the USA (detailed, moving accounts of great revivals that often converted readers). He believed the revival, or Great* Awakening, was the work of the Holy* Spirit, despite some unwanted excesses. He condemned a cold, unmoving, lifeless form of religion in his *Treatise on Religious Affections*, a defense of affectional religion and a manual of self-examination that even today remains a widely read devotional guide.

Edwards defended complete piety, or an unqualified love of, or trust in, a sovereign deity. His more soaring conceptions of God as an eternal ground, as a divine mind fully immanent in all its expressions, informed his defense of divine omnipotence. His *Freedom of the Will*, a powerful philosophical polemic, drew a series of careful distinctions, most importantly between physical and moral determinism. Human choices are not a part of the physical processes of nature. Yet Edwards argued that they have their own order. Humans are able to consider options and to choose among them. This means that they are free. But even human choices have a cause: the developed likes and dislikes of the one choosing. Thus one's identity, one's developed personality, determines choice, but one's identity is not an object of choice. Edwards wrote a devastating critique of the intellectually absurd and morally dangerous beliefs defended by some English Arminians. In their defense of a free will, they argued that human choices reflected no physical or moral determinants. They disassociated choice from developed character, from preferences, from all reasons for choosing one option over another. Such a freedom entailed an absurdity: accidental or uncaused choices. One was free only when nothing determined choice or when one not only wanted an object but wanted to want it (this leads to an infinite regress; see Free Will, Freedom).

Even as a youth, Edwards came to the belief that ultimate reality was "mind-like." Later, influenced by English Neoplatonists at Cambridge and possibly by John Locke's* *Essay on Human Understanding*, Edwards used idealistic and Neoplatonic motifs in his more philosophical theology. This meant that, to him, the best image of God was that of an all-inclusive mind, whose ideas were emanations outward, or modes of self-expression, or a form of self-edifying communication. The divine ideas of such a mind provided him, like many earlier theologians, with a rationalization of the Logos*, or Son* of God, while the love and spirit of mutuality that obtained between a mind and its thought, or between a figurative father and son, provided an image of the Holy* Spirit. All creation is continuous, not an act in past time. And the physical universe reflects, not rational intent at some point of creation, but the rationality (the harmony, symmetry, and rhythm) of God's own sustaining thought.

Such an idealistic and immanent* conception of God was suffused with aesthetic* content. The whole of being is harmonious, mutually supportive, and beautiful. The divine mind, when perceived in all its beauty, when grasped in an immediate and moving way, is so winsome that no person can do other, morally, than respond to such a sensibly present God with consent, trust, and love. True virtue is the beauty present in such consent to the unity, delightfulness, and sweetness found only in God. God does not coerce humans, but seduces them.

But ordinary humans, without special illumination from the Holy Spirit, without the gift of grace*, never really perceive or grasp the loveliness of God and thus do not, morally cannot, respond to him in faith*. PAUL K. CONKIN

Egeria or Aetheria, a woman, probably a Spanish nun or laywoman, who made a pilgrimage to the Holy Land and holy places in Egypt and Syria (c381–84) and wrote to her circle of women ("sisters" or "ladies") an account of her travels. Known through a 11th-c. Latin partial manuscript, her account includes a detailed description of the Liturgy of Jerusalem, both daily liturgies (matins, sext and none, and vespers) as well as Sunday services at different times of the liturgical year.

Egypt. Christianity in Egypt is associated with the NT and very early Christian traditions. The Gospel of Matthew* (2:15) mentions that the holy family came to Egypt (the only country outside Palestine where Christ lived) and came out of Egypt as Israel did in the time of the Exodus*. Acts* (2:10) mentions persons from "Egypt and the parts of Libya belonging to Cyrene" among the Jews listening to Peter's Pentecost sermon in Jerusalem. Similarly, those who debated with Stephen* included Jews from Cyrene and Alexandria (Acts 6:9). Acts 18:24 may allude to a mid-1st-c. Christian community in Egypt. According to a tradition mentioned by Eusebius* of Caesarea, the Egyptian Church was founded by Mark the Evangelist.

In the 2nd c., Alexandria was an important economic and commercial center of the Roman Empire, because of its location at the junction of the great maritime and land route connecting Europe to Africa and Asia. It also had an important cultural role as a major center of Greek learning and as a Christian center where Gnostic* groups and anti-Gnostic groups confronted each other.

Clement* of Alexandria, Origen*, and Didymus* the Blind were influential throughout the church, even as Gnosticism and Manichaeism* were in Egypt (3rd and 4th c.) (see Alexandria, Alexandrian Christianity and its Theology; Nag Hammadi Codices).

The vitality and rapid spread of Christianity in Egypt in the 3rd and 4th c. can be measured by the violent persecutions that the church suffered under the emperors Septimus Severus (193–211; when Leonides, Origen's father, suffered martyrdom), Decius (249–51), Valerian (253–59), and especially Diocletian (284–305) and Maximus Daia (308–13).

In the 4th and 5th c., after the Edict of Milan was issued by Constantine* (313), the life of the Coptic Church was characterized by theological debates and monasticism*. Preeminent in the theological debates that followed the rise of Arianism* was Athanasius*, viewed as the 20th patriarch of the Coptic* Church (326–73). Born in Alexandria (c295), Athanasius became the secretary and companion of Patriarch Alexander I, accompanying him to the Council of Nicaea*, strongly emphasizing the full divinity of the Word* or Son* of God against opponents whom he labeled "Arians." Athanasius was exiled five times by Arian emperors. Preeminent in the theological debates against Nestorianism* was Cyril, the 24th patriarch (412–44; see Cyril of Alexandria). An eloquent preacher and great theologian, he confronted Nestorius, who conceived of two centers of operation simultaneously present in the life of Christ, one human and one divine, and thus denied the title Theotokos for the Virgin Mary (see Mary, the Virgin, Cluster: Theotokos). Cyril emphasized the dynamic force of the Incarnation* and affirmed that Jesus was wholly and completely divine, thus a single person.

Egyptian monasticism* is commonly associated with Antony* (c254–356), who, according to Athanasius's biography, was the founder of Christian monasticism. Antony was a pioneer of desert monasticism who interrupted his solitude to instruct disciples and to perform other pastoral duties. Pachomius* (c292–346) was another early Egyptian monastic leader, commonly described as "the founder of cenobitic* monasticism." Born of pagan parents, he enlisted in the army, served for several years, and converted; on his release from the army, Pachomius was baptized and later founded a monastic community in Tabennesi (c323). In the Pachomian system, the monastery consisted of a group of buildings surrounded by an enclosure wall.

The late 5th–7th c. was marked by the schisms that followed the Council of Chalcedon* between the non-Chalcedonian churches (see Orthodox Churches, Oriental, Cluster: Coptic Orthodox Church) and the different Chalcedonian churches. Among the significant figures of this period were Timothy Aelurus* (d477), Dioscorus of Alexandria (d530), and Severus* of Antioch (who had fled to Egypt, 518).

During the Arab conquest (635–40), the weakened Byzantine provinces of the Near East were overthrown. After the reign of the Umayyad dynasty (661–750), during which the Coptic Church had eight patriarchs, the church became the target of Arab governors. A tax was levied on monks, and many churches and monasteries were destroyed, including the monastery at Bawit.

With the 10th-c. establishment of the caliphate of Shia Fatimid (909–1171), in independent Egypt Copts enjoyed a fair amount of religious freedom. Yet for nine years, al-Hakim (996–1021) persecuted Christians, including women, destroyed many churches and monasteries, and humiliated, tortured, and exiled Patriarch Zacharias (1004–32) to a monastery. But after 1005, al-Hakim restored all their confiscated property to Christians and allowed the patriarch to return to his see.

After the peak of the golden age of Coptic Arabic literature (13th c.), the Mamluk dynasty started a persecution (late 13th c.); by the 14th c., once again, many churches were destroyed, property was confiscated, and heavy taxes were levied against the Coptic community. The number of Christians drastically decreased, notably as a result of the plague (the Black Death). After experiencing a loss of influence in the 14th and 15th c., during the Ottoman period (especially the 17th–18th c.), Copts occupied important administrative positions in the government, a situation that facilitated the restoration of the churches and the translation of new books from Greek and Syriac.

The relations between the Coptic Church and Western churches began to change in the 15th c. For the first time after the schism following Chalcedon, the Roman Catholic pope entered into contact with the Coptic Church. The Roman pope Eugene IV (1431–47) sent to Cairo his delegate, the Franciscan Albert de Sarteano (d1450). The pope informed his Alexandrian counterpart of the discussion of union between the Western and Eastern churches. A Coptic delegation was sent to the Council of Florence* (1438–45) but arrived late. From the 16th to 19th c., many letters were exchanged between the two prelates. Then, beginning in the 19th c., Protestant missions arrived in Egypt.

What is the status of Christianity in Egypt today? There are no accurate statistics. One can estimate that there are between 7 and 10 million Christians (approximately 10% of the population) in Egypt, mostly Copts. **See also ORTHODOX CHURCHES, ORIENTAL, CLUSTER: COPTIC ORTHODOX CHURCH.**

Statistics: Population (2007): 80 million (M). Christians, 8 M, 10% (Copts, 7 M; Protestants, 0.5 M; Roman Catholics, 0.3 M; independents, 0.2 M); Muslims, 72 M, 90%. (*Source*: 2001 studies on Coptic Christianity.)

YOUHANNA NESSIM YOUSSEF

Eighteen Benedictions (Heb *Shemoneh 'Esreh*), Jewish daily prayer practiced before and after the fall of Jerusalem (70 CE), known only in a much later Babylonian (longer) and Palestinian (shorter) version. Both versions are a prayer for the gathering of the dispersed (Diaspora*), the reinstatement of proper judges, God's mercy on Jerusalem, proper worship in the Temple, and significantly, in the 14th benediction, the coming of a Davidic Messiah* to rebuild Jerusalem – one of the infrequent references in early Jewish literature to a Jewish expectation of the Messiah, although it was certainly formulated in this form after 70 CE. The "blessing against the heretics" (Birkath ha-Minim) was added probably about 80 CE. **See also BIRKATH HA-MINIM.**

DANIEL PATTE

Ekandem, Cardinal Dominic (1917–95), born into a non-Christian royal family in Obio Ibiono, Nigeria, converted to Christianity, baptized (1925), ordained a priest (1947); the first Anglophone West African bishop (auxiliary bishop of Calabar, 1954). Appointed bishop of Ikot Ekpene (1963) and, after the Nigerian civil war, administrator of the Port Harcourt Diocese (1970–73), he was named cardinal (1976), then metropolitan archbishop of Abuja (1989–92). He presided over the Catholic Bishops Conference of Nigeria (1973, 1976) and the Association of Episcopal Conferences of Anglophone West Africa (1977), promoting inculturation* in the African Church, encouraging evangelization of Africa by Africans, and founding the National Missionary Society of St. Paul.

CAMILLUS UMOH.

ELCA. See LUTHERANISM CLUSTER: IN THE UNITED STATES: EVANGELICAL LUTHERAN CHURCH IN AMERICA (ELCA).

Elder, one who is older (Gk *presbyteros**), term used in Presbyterian, Congregational, and Baptist churches to designate both "teaching" and "ruling elders," ministers of Word and sacrament, and laity elected for church administration, respectively.

Election, God's "choice" of some peoples (i.e. Israel, the Christian Church*) or individuals ("the elect") for some purpose. As there are both "general" predestination* and "salvific" predestination (see Predestination), there is "election for a specific function" and "election for salvation*."

In both cases, election is an act of divine freedom through which God favors the "elect." One can then ask whether God still acts with both justice* and mercy*. Paul addresses this question by affirming that God's choice cannot be understood by human beings (Rom 11:33). He also raises a major issue for Christian theology when he speaks of God's foreknowledge* and mentions it in connection with predestination (Rom 8:29–30). Does Paul imply that predestination is based on foreknowledge? If so, is it foreknowledge of works or of faith? Or did God choose Jacob rather than Esau before they were born and before they had made any choices (Rom 9:11), so that election is based not on works but on God's call (Rom 9:12), as Augustine* emphasized? In the latter case, election is God's free "predilection" for some rather than others, and predestination is God's preparation of the means by which God's purpose will be fulfilled.

Election is often presented as election for salvation – often in apocalyptic texts of the NT (Mark 13; Matt 24) – and, throughout Christian history, is often expressed in views of predestination*. Yet in the OT (especially in Deuteronomy*), this election – as YHWH's free choice – results in a covenantal* relationship in which the two parties (YHWH and the chosen/elect people) have responsibilities; thus the election of Israel is for a particular task: being the people of God among the nations. For the elect, the election is always the blessing of a particular relationship with God and can therefore be equated with "salvation" (in the sense of overcoming the separation between God and the chosen individuals or groups). But in both the Jewish tradition and Paul (in all the aforementioned passages), "election" is associated with "calling" or "vocation" for a particular task. **See also VOCATION.**

EUGENE TESELLE and DANIEL PATTE

Eli, priest and judge (1 Sam 1–4), who trained Samuel* as a priest and prophet*. Because he failed to discipline his sons, they were killed in battle. When Eli died, he was replaced by Samuel.

Eli, Eli, Lema Sabachthani, Aramaic, "My God, my God, why have you forsaken me?" (Ps 22:1; Matt 27:46), among Jesus' last words on the cross.

Elijah, considered by the early church to be the greatest prophet, revived the son of a widow at Zarephath, challenged the prophets of Baal at Carmel, and ascended in a whirlwind to heaven (1 Kgs 17–19, 21:17–29; 2 Ks 1–2). Malachi 4:5–6 prophesied that Elijah would return before the day of the Lord, and the NT declares that the prophecy was fulfilled by John* the Baptist (Matt 11:14, 17:1–13; cf. Luke 1:17). Luther* compared the prophet to the Reformers, and the prophets of Baal to the Roman Catholic Church. Elijah's story exemplifies devotion, providence, and divine empowerment. JEFFRY C. DAVIS

Eliot, George (1819–80), pseudonym of Mary Ann or Marian Evans, a translator of scholarly works and author. Following her youthful orientation to Evangelical Christianity, George Eliot was exposed to German critical theology through her translations of Strauss and Feuerbach, and to the "religion of humanity" by followers of Auguste Comte. With the publication of *Middlemarch* (1872) and *Daniel Deronda* (1876), she was recognized as the greatest English writer of her time.

George Eliot remained a deeply religious thinker, and religious themes and figures appear in all her novels. She explored how redemptive transformation occurs through ordinary historical and psychological processes. For her the objective of religion is to reorient human beings from self-centeredness to reality-centeredness, with "reality" understood to include other persons, the larger human and natural community, and the ultimate mystery of things. She imagined thinking of God not as a transcendent supreme being but in terms of divine sympathy, suffering, and immediate presence. In her last novel, *Daniel Deronda*, in which she explores the spirituality of Judaism, the divine presence becomes an omnipresence, a whole that contains and preserves every part as a part. She did not abandon the figure of Jesus. She saw in his story the mythos and pathos of the human story, and his story hovers in the background of the stories of her heroines and heroes, many of whom exemplify an *imitatio Christi*.

Interest in George Eliot's fiction has revived with feminist literary scholarship, which has found in her work powerful depictions of women. Theologians and ethicists have discovered in her a valuable resource for thinking about questions of meaning, truth, and purpose in the context of postmodernity*. Several of her novels have been successfully adapted to television. PETER C. HODGSON

Eliot, T. S. (Thomas Stearns) (1888–1965), poet, critic, editor, dramatist. Main poet in the 20th-c. revolution in the arts that included Picasso, Stravinsky, and Joyce; educated in literature and philosophy at Harvard and Oxford Universities.

While a student, he wrote "The Love Song of J. Alfred Prufrock," an existentialist* monologue of the divided self; after World War I, *The Waste Land*, a snapshot of personal and cultural trauma; after his baptism, the penitential lyric *Ash-Wednesday*; and during World War II, *Four Quartets*, a theodicy*. The last three suggest the stages in Dante's* spiritual journey: hell, purgatory, and paradise. As a literary and social critic, Eliot defended tradition* as a self-renewing community of the living and the dead; he founded and edited an influential journal (*Criterion*, 1922–39) and wrote five verse plays.

Eliot was born in St. Louis, Missouri, into a family distinguished for its contributions to US culture. His forebears, who lived in New England starting in the 17th c., included preachers, judges, historians, two presidents of the American Unitarian Association, two of Harvard University, and two of the United States (John Adams, John Quincy Adams). His ancestors helped establish Unitarianism* at Harvard Divinity School; his grandfather, transplanted to Missouri, founded the Unitarian Church of the Messiah and Washington University. The "guardians of the faith" in Eliot's circle were the American Transcendentalist Ralph Waldo Emerson* and the English poet and critic Matthew Arnold.

Eliot began his religious quest during the reevaluation of Christianity forced by the science of Darwin* and the philosophy of Nietzsche*. Dissatisfied with Emerson's Unitarianism and Arnold's Culture, he proceeded down a crooked road leading roughly from aestheticism* (art as religion) to agnosticism* (F. H. Bradley's neoidealism) to relativism (J. G. Frazer's *Golden Bough*, primitive mythology) to the Church of England. He was baptized in 1927 and soon thereafter became a British citizen and active churchman. Eliot moved forward by looping back to his pre-American English roots and to pre-Enlightenment* Christian orthodoxy, a complex return to origins marked by modern education and experience. His new commitment was evident in his poetry ("Journey of the Magi," *Ash-Wednesday*, *Four Quartets*), plays (*Murder in the Cathedral*), and criticism (*Idea of a Christian Society*). His journey, religious in the radical sense (*religare*, "to rebind fragments," "to reconnect"; see Religion as a Concept and Christianity), illustrates a quest for wholeness by a poet of immense intelligence and erudition who found in common life moments that opened windows on transcendence and supported faith in the Incarnation*.

JEWEL SPEARS BROOKER

Elizabeth, wife of the priest Zechariah*, mother of John* the Baptist, and cousin of Mary*, who visited her before the birth of Christ (Luke 1; commemorated in the Feast of the Visitation*).

Elizabeth I (1533–1603), queen of England and Ireland (1558–1603). As Henry VIII's younger daughter, by his second wife, Anne Boleyn, she was illegitimate under Roman canon law (which did not recognize the marriage) and under English law (because her mother was executed, 1536). Yet she was named third in the Succession Act of 1544, should her half-siblings, Edward and Mary, die without heirs, as happened. She succeeded to the throne without challenge.

She was given an excellent education by tutors who were identified as "Christian humanists," or "Evangelicals," and subsequently emerged as Protestants. She was a remarkable scholar, fluent in Latin, French, and Italian, with some Greek and Spanish. Although Elizabeth had held to the Reformed religion since at least 1547, when Mary* (Tudor) succeeded to the throne (1553) she was forced to conform to the established Roman Catholic faith, although Mary (rightly) did not trust her sincerity. Elizabeth spent 18 months in prison and under house arrest. After Mary's pregnancy failed (1555), Elizabeth was generally looked to as the heir.

An orthodox Edwardian Protestant (shaped by Thomas Cranmer* and Nicholas Ridley), Elizabeth took her responsibilities as both monarch and church leader with extreme seriousness. Knowing that most of her subjects preferred the old ways and believed that a woman was disqualified from leading the church, she called herself supreme governor rather than supreme head of the church settlement, keeping it ecclesiastically conservative while theologically Protestant. God had given her the job of shaping and running the English Church, and she would brook no interference with that prerogative and her authority. Her responsibility to God was personal and immediate. Conformity was to her always more important than unity. Thus it was in response to her excommunication by the pope (1570) that she made the Church of England a Protestant establishment.

DAVID LOADES

Elizabeth of Hungary (1207–31). Daughter of the king of Hungary, at 14 she married Duke Louis IV of Thuringia; the pious couple had three children. Following his death during the

Crusades*, she took refuge in Marburg, where she founded a hospital and humbly took care of the poor. Exhausted by this work and by acts of penance*, she died at the age of 24. Canonized only four years after her death, she is revered for embodying the spirit of St. Francis* of Assisi. There are many poetic stories and legends about her, illustrated by a rich iconography, in particular that of the miracle of the bread transformed into roses when she carried bread to the poor, despite the interdiction to do so. These hagiographies praise her as a figure who is both emblematic and full of contrasts: of royal standing yet profoundly humble; wealthy and generous; afflicted and patient; with a deep piety and a genuine love for the poor; with an abiding affection for her husband, who was fighting to liberate the tomb of the Christ and after whose death she took a vow of chastity. As such, Elizabeth of Hungary was a figure with great appeal to romantic piety both in and beyond Catholic Germany and Hungary.

GUY-THOMAS BEDOUELLE, OP

Elkesaites, members of a 2nd-c. Jewish sect in Mesopotamia, named from the "Book of Elkesai." The book was adopted by a Jewish Christian group similar to the Ebionites*.

El Salvador. Spanish Catholic priests first arrived in El Salvador in 1525, but mission got under way slowly in a country that had no resources that were of interest to the Spaniards. Secular priests under the jurisdiction of the Diocese of Guatemala* initiated mission work in El Salvador. This foreign control of the Church was long resisted, until in the early 19th c., when through the national independence movement (1821) a local bishop was named by the civil government and finally recognized by the pope in 1842. This troubled relation between church and state continued. In 1886 the Liberal government secularized* cemeteries and education*, religious orders were abolished, and religious liberty was affirmed.

In the 20th c., some priests chose to side with the poor against elite dictatorships, rejecting the traditional union of the Roman Catholic Church with the aristocratic landowners. Church leaders, inspired by Liberation* theology's emphasis of the preferential* option for the poor, became subject to military persecution. The military dictatorship, armed by the USA as part of its anti-Communism crusade, tortured and killed tens of thousands of peasants. Numerous priests and catechists were assassinated, including Archbishop Romero*, four US nuns, and six Jesuit priests (early 1980s). Dissension within the Church lessened institutional loyalty.

As in Honduras* and Nicaragua*, the people are predominantly mestizos* (91%); 5% are Pipil and Lenca ("Indian"), 3–4% white, and a small number black. The great scarcity of priests has made ministry to local churches extremely difficult. About 40% of rural parishes are without priests. Barrett gives a typology of Roman Catholicism in the land: bourgeois Catholicism (traditional, European Catholicism; 4% of Catholics); popular Catholicism (30% of Catholics; see Popular Christian Practices Cluster: In Latin America); Mayanized Catholicism (60% of Catholics; practiced by mestizos who hold onto certain ancient Mayan religious traditions and mix them with Catholicism and popular Catholicism); a kind of Christo-Mayanism (4% of Catholics; practiced by pure Mayans who keep most Mayan traditions in which they introduce Christian practices).

As in much of Latin America, Bible societies were instrumental in initiating "Evangelical missions" (as all Protestant and Pentecostal missions are called in Latin America). Francisco Penzotti began the work (1892) of the Central American Mission. Other groups followed: American Baptists* (1911), Assemblies* of God (1929), and Church* of God, Cleveland (1930). Several independent Pentecostal*/Charismatic churches grew rapidly, becoming about 80% of Protestants in El Salvador by 2000 (Protestants constitute between 16 and 20% of the population).

The religious situation is complex. Base* ecclesial communities (Comunidades Ecclesiales de Base, CEBs) were strong during the civil war (late 20th c.), and some continue. But Catholics are divided on issues of church and society, structural oppression, and attitudes toward the poor. A significant number are Charismatics. Conservative Protestant churches remained largely apolitical during the civil war, except for the Lutherans* and the American Baptists, who supported the peasant movement alongside the CEBs. The rapid growth of Pentecostals/Charismatics* was a response to population displacement, broken community and family bonds, and a sense of hopelessness in troubling times. The message of God's acceptance, direct access to the divine through Jesus, a concrete ethical code, self-expression through the speaking of tongues, and an assured hope of personal future fulfillment converted many to the new faith. **See also MEGACHURCHES IN EL SALVADOR.**

Statistics: Population (2000): 6.3 million (M). Christians, 6.1 M, 97.6% (Roman Catholics, 5.7 M; independents, 0.7 M; Protestants, 0.5 M; marginal Christians, 0.1 M, with 15% doubly affiliated – baptized Catholics [still counted by the Catholic Church] who converted and became members of independent Charismatic and Protestant churches); nonreligious, 0.1 M, 1.6%. (Based on *World Christian Encyclopedia,* 2001. The move toward Charismatic churches continued; according to 2008 estimates, nearly one-third of the population claimed to be "Evangelical.")

SIDNEY ROOY

Elvira, Council of, a Spanish council (either 300–6 or 312–14) presided over by Hosius*. Its 81 canons are the first to have survived intact; they reflect Christian attitudes just before Constantine's* victory, when city officials were becoming Christian and there was apprehension that they might take part in idolatrous rituals. The Council stipulated that clergy were to maintain self-control. Lifelong excommunication was specified for a number of sins without reconciliation, even at death.

Emerson, Ralph Waldo (1803–82), leader of the Transcendentalist* Movement, essayist, spiritual philosopher. After resigning from his Unitarian* pulpit (1832), Emerson delivered lectures in Boston that culminated in his 1838 address at Harvard Divinity School, a call for the dramatic reform of conventional theology and lifeless preaching. These lectures, as well as his volumes *Nature* (1836) and *Essays* (1841), were the basis of Transcendentalism, a movement of spiritual enlargement, literary innovation, and political reform that deeply influenced US culture. Emerson formulated an intuitive and experiential religion, and emphasized the revelatory powers of nature. He conceptualized God as the "Over-Soul," a spiritual force both within and beyond the self. His later work stressed the evolution of religion into pure ethics. He was an important figure in US romantic thought, and his work had a profound impact on contemporaries such as Henry David Thoreau, Margaret Fuller, and Walt Whitman, and on later thinkers such as William James* and Friedrich Nietzsche*. **See also SPIRITUALITY CLUSTER: CHRISTIAN FORMS OF, IN NORTH AMERICA.**

DAVID M. ROBINSON

Emmanuel, Immanuel (Heb "God with us"), a name in Isa 7:14 and 8:8 (probably referring to a child born in Isaiah's time without connection to the Messiah, as Jewish interpretation posits) and in Matt 1:23, which opens up the possibility of identifying Jesus as the Messiah* or Christ*. The identification of Jesus with "Emmanuel" mentioned by Isaiah encouraged the development of the doctrine of the Incarnation*. **See also INCARNATION CLUSTER.**

Emmaus, a village 60 stadia (seven miles) from Jerusalem (Luke 24:13), where two disciples recognized Jesus during the breaking of bread.

Encomenderos, Encomienda, in Latin America, colonists to whom the Spanish crown "entrusted" the Christian indoctrination of the natives in exchange for services (slave labor) and tribute (e.g. gold, corn, chickens). **See also LAS CASAS, BARTOLOMÉ DE; REDUCTIONS; SUBLIMUS DEI.**

Encratism (from Gk *encrateia,* "self-control"). The term was applied by the Greeks to the control of both desire and anger. Among Christians it was applied primarily to the former. So-called Encratites, or extreme ascetics*, are attacked by several 2nd- and 3rd-c. writers. Some of the apocryphal* Gospels and Acts may have been written in these circles. It has also been suggested that their views form the background of the emerging doctrine of original* sin.

Enculturation, an anthropological term that designates the process by which people adapt to and assimilate the culture in which they live, integrating themselves into that culture. Since the 1960s, this term has been replaced in the study of Christianity by "inculturation" to indicate that the encounter of a culture and Christianity is a two-way process in which the gospel and the culture of a particular people are integrated and mutually enriched. **See also INCULTURATION CLUSTER.**

Encyclical, a "circular" letter sent to all churches under the jurisdiction of a bishop or the pope. **See also SOCIAL ENCYCLICALS.**

Encyclion, decree issued by the emperor Basiliscus (486), condemning Chalcedon* and adopting Miaphysitism* as the religion of the Empire. After Zeno's restoration as emperor, he issued the Henoticon*, attempting unsuccessfully to reconcile the Dyophysites and the Miaphysites.

England, Church of. See ANGLICANISM CLUSTER: ANGLICAN COMMUNION AND ITS THEOLOGY; UNITED KINGDOM.

English Literature and Christianity. Christianity and the Bible have been important to English literature from its beginnings. The earliest surviving poem in English, "Caedmon's Hymn," is a prayer praising God for the creation of the world and humankind, and the most important Old English poem, *Beowulf*, describes – disapprovingly – "pagan" religious practices, contrasting them with Christian beliefs.

The work of the late medieval poets Geoffrey Chaucer* and William Langland is steeped in biblical allusion and quotations, and is often concerned with ecclesiastic controversies. During this period, Christian drama, both morality plays and biblical mystery plays, lyrics, biblical paraphrases, and devotional prose, were popular.

The language of the various 16th- to early-17th-c. English translations of the Bible*, along with the Book* of Common Prayer, profoundly influenced the language of English literature. Renaissance literature expanded its scope to include more secular subjects, but (Protestant) Christian beliefs and assumptions continued to dominate literary production. In his 1579 *Defense of Poesy*, Sir Philip Sidney defended literature against Puritan* attacks of frivolousness by arguing that poets create imaginary worlds under God's inspiration, moved by "the force of a divine breath." Edmund Spenser's *Faerie Queene* (1590) is a highly complex allegorical epic celebrating Protestant faith in a magical, perilous land of giants, monsters, and heroic knights.

Shakespeare's* plays, though secular in subject matter, resonate profoundly with religious thought and biblical allusions. His position, if any, on contemporary doctrinal issues continues to be a matter of dispute, in part because his use of philosophical and theological material always appears to be generated by the plays rather than vice versa.

Among the poets of the 17th c. who took up explicitly Christian subjects was John Donne*, dean of Saint Paul's Cathedral. George Herbert's *The Temple* is a metaphoric collection of devotional verse that examines the conflicts within his own faith. Robert Herrick, Richard Lovelace, Richard Crashaw, and Andrew Marvell produced important poetry on Christian subjects. John Milton's* *Paradise Lost* (1667, 1674) is perhaps the most ambitious English Christian poem, seeking nothing less than to "justify the ways of God to men." His contemporary John Bunyan*, a Baptist preacher with much less formal education, wrote the enormously popular *Pilgrim's Progress* (1678).

During the Enlightenment, Christian themes and subjects gave way to social and political ones, while the romantic period saw these combined in the biblical imagery of William Blake*. John Keats seems not to have been much interested in religious ideas, and Percy Bysshe Shelley was a devout atheist. William Wordsworth's poetry was produced over a very long career, and both its religious and political ideas shifted from an early radicalism to a later orthodoxy. Samuel Taylor Coleridge* (*The Lyrical Ballads*, 1798) likewise moved through Unitarianism* and conservative Anglicanism*. Byron's upbringing in Calvinistic Presbyterianism perhaps lies behind his creation of the "Byronic hero," rebellious, brooding, guilt-wracked, and exemplified by the defiant hero of the closet drama *Cain*.

The Victorian period was marked by religious tensions brought on in part by scientific investigations, including the writings of Charles Darwin* on evolution. With the exception of the poems of Gerard Manley Hopkins, Victorian poetry is marked more by expressions of doubt – notably Alfred Lord Tennyson's *In Memoriam* – than those of faith. Novelists varied in their doctrinal positions but shared an easy and frequent use of biblical allusion, and Anthony Trollope explored the mundane politics of church life itself.

Twentieth century English writers only infrequently voice Christian themes, important exceptions being T. S. Eliot* and C. S. Lewis*, but Christian imagery and biblical allusions continue to be important, if operating in heterodox fashion, as in W. B. Yeats's "The Second Coming."

JOHN PLUMMER

Enhypostasia, doctrine that Christ's humanity has its hypostasis*, or existence, "in" (and not separate from) that of the Word.

Enlightenment, an intellectual and cultural movement in the 17th and 18th c. (For a very different kind of enlightenment, see Buddhism and Christianity Cluster: Buddhist Perspective.) The European Enlightenment joined the humanistic spirit of the Renaissance* and the scientific* revolution of the 17th c. and ushered in the modern* world. This diverse, complex, often inconsistent era deeply influenced subsequent Christian thought. It sought to bring about a new order based on the model of natural science, i.e. testing what before had been taken for granted. No longer a received heritage of knowledge, reason was now an ongoing process of autonomous critical analysis. "Enlightenment," the philosopher Immanuel Kant* (1724–1804) declared, "is the release from... the inability to make use of one's understanding without direction from another... *Sapere aude* [Dare to know]! Have courage to use your own reason*." It was this insistent revolt against settled assumptions, traditions, and authority that challenged Christianity on many fronts.

Reacting to the bloody religious wars of the 17th c., Enlightenment writers viewed religious dogmatism, intolerance, prejudice, and coercion as the enemies of liberty of conscience and of communal peace. John Locke's* (1632–1704) *A Letter Concerning Toleration* (1689) became, for writers such as Voltaire (1694–1778), Gotthold Lessing (1729–81), and Thomas Jefferson* (1743–1826), the cornerstone of true religion. Since no religion can indubitably be proved true, forced uniformity denies personal freedom*. Teaching, persuasion, and prayer are the only legitimate means of spreading religious belief. Enlightenment writers further argued that there should be no conflict between religious faith and reason. Beliefs may appear to be above reason but never can be contrary to reason once known. In *Christianity Not Mysterious* (1696), the Deist John Toland (1670–1722) argued that revelation* never can be inherently mysterious or incomprehensible. Others went further, insisting that biblical revelation can add nothing to a natural religion that is eternal, perfect, and universal. Christianity may be of more recent origin, yet its essentials must have come from an all-loving and wise God, i.e. at creation itself – the theme of Matthew Tindal's (1655–1733) *Christianity as Old as the Creation* (1730).

The inerrancy* and unquestioned truth and authority of the Bible as Scripture* also were challenged. Voltaire believed that the historical errors, outmoded science, and primitive morals found in the Bible only breed superstition and fanaticism. Biblical scholars, notably H. S. Reimarus (1694–1768) and J. S. Semler (1725–91), were discovering that the Bible consists of various strata and genres of literature, passed on orally, edited, and arranged for certain purposes, thus challenging the Bible's historical veracity and divine inspiration. The result was a series of naturalistic accounts and explanations of the development of the biblical canon and the origins of Christianity itself. Such studies raised an issue current today: the genuine historical reality and message of Jesus vis-à-vis the earliest Christian community's memory and portrayals of him in the NT.

Furthermore, the so-called truths of history, based as they are on testimony, are open to question, and thus can never become the proof of the necessary truths of reason. As the philosopher David Hume (1711–76) put it, "A [historical] miracle can never be *proved* so as to be the *foundation* of religion" (emphasis added). Hume and Kant also argued that we cannot *know* the nature of God, e.g. his infinity, oneness, perfection, or goodness, through our empirical examination of the contingencies and uncertainties of either nature or human history. Religion is, rather, a natural belief, a want of reason, or a deep moral demand. The Enlightenment ran its course, and a Counter Enlightenment followed. Yet the seedbed of the latter is present in the writings of the Enlightenment thinkers themselves. Hence it remains true that Christianity is deeply indebted to the heritage of the Enlightenment. JAMES C. LIVINGSTON

Enlightenment in the United States. The European Enlightenment had an important influence on religion in the USA in the late 17th and 18th c., especially during the revolutionary era and the founding of the nation. The effects of this relationship were not entirely anticipated. The American Enlightenment was significantly moderated by evangelical Protestantism, by earlier Calvinistic* Puritanism*, the First Great* Awakening (1730–60), and the Second Great Awakening (1800–30). Most Americans were alarmed by the skepticism and cynicism of the radical French *lumières*, e.g. Voltaire. They also disavowed the likes of the Protestant Dissenter and pamphleteer Thomas Paine's (1737–1809) fiery attacks on the Bible as "a book of lies, wickedness, and blasphemy" (*Age of Reason*, 1794–96). Yet, surprisingly, Calvinists, liberal Christians, and dissenting Millennialists* allied with Paine's *The Rights of Man* (1791) and with the radical republicanism of, e.g., Thomas Jefferson, in their revolutionary political aims.

Many Christian moderates, e.g. John Adams* (1735–1826), rejected Calvinism and creedalism, while Christian Deists, e.g. Thomas Jefferson* (1743–1826), censured Protestant orthodoxy as introducing "new absurdities" into Christianity. At the same time, these and more skeptical thinkers, e.g. Benjamin Franklin* (1706–90), spoke openly and warmly of "God's kind providence." Contradictions abounded. What enlightened moderates and radicals together attacked was church establishment, priestcraft, creedal dogmatism, and "enthusiasm." The Christian religion was to be reasonable, free, and, in its essential part, moral.

The American Enlightenment's greatest contributions to Christian thought are its principles of religious liberty* and relations between church* and state. James Madison's (1751–1836) *Memorial and Remonstrance against Assessments* (1785) insisted on "a perfect separation between ecclesiastical and civil matters," as did Jefferson's principle that "the legislature should make no law respecting an establishment of religion, or prohibiting the free exercise thereof" (1802), words enshrined in the First Amendment of the US Constitution (1791).

JAMES C. LIVINGSTON

Enoch, Books of

1 Enoch, a collection of Jewish writings claiming to transmit revelations about the cosmos and the end-time received by Enoch (Gen 5:21–24), but actually written between 350 BCE and 50 CE. The various parts of 1 Enoch reflect the political upheavals created by the Hellenistic and Roman overlords of Palestine; internal Jewish disputes, especially about the nature of the calendar and right practice in the Jerusalem Temple; and social tensions between the rich and powerful and the oppressed "righteous and pious," who were the authors' clients. Foundational to the Enochic revelations is an interpretation of Gen 6:1–4 that depicts "the sons of God" as angels ("holy watchers") who rebel against God by revealing forbidden secrets, mating with mortal women, and breeding a race of giants who devastate the earth. Central to the "parables of Enoch" (Chaps. 37–71) is an interpretation of biblical texts about the Davidic king, the "Son* of man" (Dan 7), and 2 Isaiah's "Servant* of the Lord," which posits a heavenly figure who will enact God's imminent judgment against "the kings and the mighty." Essential to much of the collection is the belief that the audience comprises the righteous and pious of the end-time, constituted by revelation and awaiting vindication in the Judgment.

The myth of the watchers was widely used in early Christianity as an explanation for the demonic* presence in the world. The parables' expectations about the "Son of man" were a source of early Christian speculation about the exalted Christ and his imminent return as judge. 1 Enoch, however, is considered canonical only by the Ethiopian Church and has been preserved only in manuscripts of its Bible.

2 Enoch, a Jewish apocalyptic writing (c1st–2nd c. CE) that reinterprets a collection of Enochic traditions very similar to 1 Enoch. Its speculation focuses on the content of the seven heavens, it emphasizes ethical obligations, and its eschatology is concerned primarily with the fate of the individual immediately after death. A legend about the miraculous birth of Melchizedek (Chaps. 71–72) is of comparative value for the study of the NT infancy narratives and the Melchizedek–Jesus speculation in the Epistle to the Hebrews. Composed probably in Greek, it is preserved only in Old Church Slavonic manuscripts from the 14th c. and later, which contain various Christian interpolations and revisions.

3 Enoch, a collection of Jewish mystical traditions, the earliest from the 4th to the 9th c. CE, that describe Rabbi Ishmael's ascent to heaven, where he sees Enoch enthroned as the angel Metatron at the right hand of God and many heavenly mysteries. It is an important testimony to the mystical speculation that continued to flourish in the Middle Ages alongside the Torah instruction embodied in the Talmuds.

GEORGE W. E. NICKELSBURG

Enthusiasm (from the Gk "being possessed by a deity"), term for those who claim to be inspired, usually connoting intensity, excess, lack of control, zeal, and fanaticism. It is roughly equivalent to the German *Schwärmerei*, used by Luther* in opposing the Spiritual* party. It is also used by scholars to describe the intensely charismatic* group that Paul confronts in his letter to the Corinthians*.

Environment, all that surrounds and supports human life, including society and culture, but especially the natural* world. **See also ECOLOGY AND CHRISTIANITY CLUSTER.**

Ephesians, Epistle to the, a general Pauline letter* probably composed by an associate after Paul's martyrdom. Unlike Paul's letters, Ephesians does not refer to particular situations. Its Gentile Christian audience is to celebrate the divine plan that has incorporated them into God's holy people. It paints a heroic image of Paul's suffering for the gospel.

Ephesians incorporates traditional material using an ornate Greek style, unlike Paul's own: liturgical language of hymns and baptism; elements of Paul's letters, especially Colossians; and an apocalyptic* emphasis on demonic* powers.

Paul's descriptions of the local church as the body of Christ (4:1–16) have been combined with hymnic celebration of Christ exalted over all powers in the cosmos (Phil 2:6–11) to produce a vision of the church as a cosmic body with Christ as its head (unlike 1 Cor 11). In adapting the conventional household* code for dominant and subordinate members, Ephesians transforms marriage into a relationship between Christ (husband) and his body, the church (wife; Eph 5:22–33, cf. Col 3:18–19). Paul's argument that both Jewish and Gentile believers are righteous through faith has been reformulated as God's eternal plan or predestination* of the elect*.

Ephesians develops a theology that is both universalist and sectarian. Images of believers as "children of light" who must live in a world of constant combat with powers of darkness are sectarian. Images of the divine Christ as head of a cosmic body in which groups that had been hostile (Jew and Gentile) are united in a new humanity are universalist. Ethical values like the household code match those of the larger society.

Gnostics* in the 2nd c. saw Ephesians as evidence of the true God (light), as opposed to the demonic ruler of the material world. The images of a universal church, of marriage as a sacrament, and of believers as predestined for salvation were key to later Christianity.

PHEME PERKINS

Ephesus, First Council of (431). Summoned by Emperor Theodosius II to settle an emerging dispute between Alexandrine* and Antiochene* views on Christology*, two rival groups met in Ephesus (431). The larger group, under Cyril* of Alexandria and Memnon of Ephesus, affirmed Cyril's Christology, deposed and condemned Nestorius*, "the new Judas," linking him with Pelagius*, and, gathered in the Basilica of Mary, affirmed her as Theotokos (see Mary*, the Virgin, Theotokos); the influence of earlier devotion to Artemis on the cult of Mary has been disputed. The smaller group, under John of Antioch, criticized Cyril's views as Apollinarian* but refrained from passing judgment on Nestorius or the title Theotokos. Although present in the city, Nestorius attended neither gathering, refusing to appear before the first, but not invited to the second. Consistent with an earlier Roman decision against Nestorius and swayed by his purported association with Pelagius, Pope Celestine supported Cyril. The emperor, initially strongly critical of both sides, first ordered Cyril and Memnon as well as Nestorius to be deposed and imprisoned, but eventually endorsed Cyril's group and its decisions, thus giving them the status of ecumenical conciliar decrees. Nestorius's deposition and retirement to his former monastery in Antioch was followed by a compromise Formulary of Union in 433, but the disputes continued. Exiled in 436 to the Great Oasis in Upper Egypt, Nestorius continued to defend his position. KATHLEEN E. MCVEY

Ephesus, Second Council of (449). In the controversy between the Alexandrian and the Antiochene views of Christ (see Christologies Cluster: Introductory Entries; Ephesus, First Council of), an extreme Cyrillian position was voiced by the archimandrite Eutyches* in Constantinople. Eusebius* of Dorylaeum, who in 429 had raised the alarm over Nestorius*, now attacked Eutyches as heretical in the opposite direction. Eutyches acknowledged that Christ was "*from* two natures" but insisted on "*in* one nature after the union," seeming to deny the reality of Christ's humanity. But this allowed him to emphasize Christ's divinity as the power at work in transforming other human beings, overcoming the power of evil (rather than emphasizing that the cause of this transformation must be human as well as divine, as Antiochenes did). Flavian*, patriarch of Constantinople, brought Eutyches before a local synod (448), where he was condemned. Eutyches was championed, however, by the emperor Theodosius II and the eunuch Chrysaphius, who set aside the synod's judgment and called for a new council in Ephesus (449). Eutyches was exonerated; his bishop, Flavian, and his accuser, Eusebius of Dorylaeum, were deposed; and the doctrine of the Antiochene leaders, Ibas* of Edessa and Theodoret* of Cyrrhus, was condemned. Because of the manner in which the council was conducted and the extreme doctrine that it adopted, Pope Leo* called it a "robber synod." Its decisions were reversed by the Council of Chalcedon* (451). Yet this council remained significant for Miaphysites* and the Oriental Orthodox* Churches.

EUGENE TESELLE

Ephrata Cloister, founded near Lancaster, Pennsylvania, by a German Pietist, Conrad Beissel (1691–1768), in 1732. At its height, the cloister numbered some 80 members of a celibate sisterhood and brotherhood and, nearby, 200 or more married "householders." Emphasizing Saturday worship, celibacy, and a religious rhetoric strongly influenced by Jacob Boehme* (1575–1624), the monastic* community practiced a highly ritualized liturgical life (its distinctive a cappella music was memorialized in Thomas Mann's *Doctor Faustus*), composed numerous

hymnals and theological treatises, and supported a thriving German-language press. With Beissel's death, the community declined rapidly, despite its energetic and scholarly leader, Peter Miller (1710–96). The last celibate died in 1813.
PETER C. ERB

Ephrem the Syrian (c306–73), theologian, poet, exegete, deacon, saint. Raised by Christian parents, Ephrem spent most of his life in Nisibis* on the Roman–Persian frontier. After the city's cession to Persia (363), he resettled in Edessa*, a city of great religious diversity. He lived the single, ascetic life of the Sons and Daughters of the Covenant, a proto-monastic movement, valued learning, and was a teacher. In Edessa, he organized famine relief.

Ephrem is best known for his numerous hymns (*madrashe*), sung by female choirs and focused on liturgical, biblical, and theological themes (e.g. the Nativity, Epiphany, the Crucifixion, the Resurrection, the Trinity, the Christian Church). He frequently employed symbols* and types*, parallels and paradoxes* to express theological insights. Drawing on symbols from Scripture and nature, he praised the mystery* of the Incarnation* and God's care for humankind. Other hymns address contemporary events, such as the Persian sieges of Nisibis, the Eastern campaign of Emperor Julian, and Nicomedia's destruction by earthquake (358).

Ephrem commented on many biblical books; extant are commentaries on Genesis, Exodus, and the Diatessaron*. His interpretation of Genesis shows affinities with Jewish exegesis, despite his anti-Jewish polemics in other contexts. Rejecting the diverse theological views flourishing in Northern Mesopotamia, Ephrem allied his community with the normative Christianity of the Roman Empire. In the controversy over Arianism*, he vigorously defended Nicene* theology against neo-Arian positions, especially in his *Hymns on Faith* and *Sermons on Faith*. In his *Prose Refutations*, Ephrem uses arguments from Greek philosophy to refute the followers of Marcion*, Bardaisan*, and Mani.

One of the most eloquent and influential of the Syriac church fathers, Ephrem with his symbolic theology shaped the later tradition. Pseudo-Ephremic treatises exist in many languages, most numerously in Greek. The modern revival of scholarship on Ephrem in the West was initiated by E. Beck's critical editions and studies.
UTE POSSEKEL

Epiclesis (Gk "invocation"), the petition in the eucharistic* prayer that the Holy* Spirit come upon the elements to make them the Body and Blood of Christ. The Eastern Church regards this as the moment of consecration; the Western Church, the words of institution*.

Epiphanius of Salamis (c315–403). Born in Palestine, he lived as a monk in Egypt, led a monastery in his hometown, and was known for his learning. He became bishop of Salamis, or Constantia, on the island of Cyprus (367) and devoted much energy to fighting heresies, especially Arianism*, Apollinarianism*, and Origenism*. His *Ancoratus* (374) and *Panarion* (374–77) are important sources of information on early creeds and doctrines.

Epiphany (Gk "manifestation," "showing'), the "shining forth" or revelation of God to humans. More specifically a feast day (January 6) celebrating the revelation of God in human form in the person of Jesus Christ. On this day, Western churches commemorate the visitation of the Magi* to the Baby Jesus and thus his manifestation to the Gentiles. Eastern churches also, and primarily, call this feast Theophany ("manifestation of God") – if they use the Julian calendar, January 6 is the equivalent of January 19 in the Gregorian calendar used in the West – commemorating the baptism of Jesus, his manifestation as the Son of God to the world. **See also** CALENDARS; LITURGICAL YEAR.

Episcopal Church See ANGLICANISM CLUSTER.

Epistle Reading, the portion of the NT Epistles read during worship, as directed in the lectionary*.

Erasmus, Desiderius (c1466–1536), educator, scholar of the Christian tradition, theologian; mastered classical literature in both Greek and Latin. He was born in Holland and educated there by the Brethren* of the Common Life; he subsequently studied theology in Paris. His earliest prose works included a collection and commentary on adages from classical literature (1500) as aids to education (and in nine long essays added in the 1508 and 1515 editions, to advocate adherence to the "philosophy of Christ" in both church and state); an attack on the "barbarians" who despised letters and learning; and a treatise on his "philosophy of Christ" (*Enchiridion*, 1503). The caricatural repackaging of the *Enchiridion* in his *Praise of Folly* (1511, augmented 1514), his most brilliant and lasting work, is an ironical and satirical treatise that by its end identifies the fool in a paradoxical* way with the Christian believer as depicted in Paul's letter to the Romans.

By the time Luther* posted his theses in 1517, Erasmus was the most famous humanist in Europe. In 1516 he published the first edition of the Greek NT, together with his own Latin translation and annotations. Augmented editions appeared in 1519, 1522, 1527, and 1535. The publication of Erasmus' first edition gave great impetus to the translation of the NT into various vernaculars and to biblical exegesis*. Luther was lecturing on Romans when the edition appeared, and from Rom 9:16 forward, Luther used it in his teaching. When Luther was in trouble in 1519 and his ruler, Elector Frederick of Saxony, asked Erasmus his opinion of Luther, he replied that opposition to Luther came from the "barbarians." Erasmus's support at this time was important for Luther's survival. But in the 1520s, Erasmus entered into debate with Luther over the question of free will*, publishing a tract against Luther's notion of the bondage of the will (1524), which Luther answered (1525) with his *Bondage of the Will*. They were never reconciled.

Erasmus published editions of the church fathers, Jerome*, Cyprian*, Arnobius and Athanasius*, Hilary*, Irenaeus*, Ambrose*, Augustine*, John* Chrysostom, Basil*, and Origen*, between 1516 and 1536 – a period when he also wrote much on the sacraments*. With respect to marriage*, he suggested the possibility of granting divorce*, raising questions regarding whether marriage was a sacrament. He always sought reform from within the church and maintained his allegiance to the Roman Catholic Church.

Erasmus was not fully appreciated until the 20th c., when serious scholarship on him began; it continues into the 21st c. ALBERT RABIL, JR.

Erastianism, doctrine that the state should carry out the functions of Christian discipline*. Thomas Erastus (1524–83), a physician from Zurich, championed this approach to church* and state, so as to avoid giving too much power to the Reformed Church and the risk of a new Inquisition*. Erastianism, looking to Josiah* and Hezekiah, Constantine*, Theodosius*, and Justinian* as its models, assumed that government may not only reform the church but supervise its discipline. The exercise of discipline by bishops and elders for many centuries (in the NT as well as the early church) was explained as an "abnormal" situation, resulting from the lack of Christian magistrates. The pope* was called Antichrist* because he had usurped the role of the Christian emperors. The Church* of England has many of the features of an Erastian approach.

Eremitic Monasticism, a solitary form of monastic life, from the Greek *eremos*, "desert," the classic setting for it; also known as "anchoritic" monasticism (Gk *anachoresis*, "withdrawal"). Hermits have often lived in relation to a monastic community that provided material and spiritual support.

COLUMBA STEWART, OSB

Eritrea. The history of Eritrea is closely tied to that of Ethiopia*, which throughout history included large parts of what is now Eritrea. In recent times, Eritrea was a colony of Italy (1890–1941), then a British protectorate (1941–52) – although it was in federation with Ethiopia (1952–61) – and a northern province of Ethiopia (1961–93). The history of Christianity in Eritrea is therefore part of the history of Ethiopian Christianity. The Diocese of Eritrea (where, along the Red Sea, Christianity predated Frumentius's* arrival in Aksum) was a strong part of the Ethiopian* Orthodox Tewahedo Church. A vital part of the kingdom of Aksum (Christian from the 4th c.), it was the region in which Islam* encroached on the kingdom (from the 7th c.). While northern and western parts of Eritrea were largely under Muslim rule, efforts to conquer the southern part of Eritrea (10th–15th c.) were stopped by Ethiopian Christians. For instance, Emperor Zar'a Ya'eqob (reign, 1434–68) contributed to the spread of Christianity in Eritrea by granting land to the followers of Ewostatewos. These Ethiopian Christians strictly followed Jewish ritual life (dietary laws, Sabbath, circumcision) and established monasteries in present-day Eritrea.

The Eritrean Orthodox Tewahedo Church played a significant role in the struggle for independence, achieved in 1993 after a long and bloody war with Ethiopia. Now the country is almost equally divided between the Eritrean Orthodox Church, an autocephalous* Oriental Orthodox* Church since 1993 (an autocephaly recognized, though reluctantly, by the Ethiopian patriarch) and Sunni Mulims. **See also ORTHODOX CHURCHES, ORIENTAL CLUSTER: ETHIOPIAN ORTHODOX TEWAHEDO CHURCH**

Statistics: Population (2000): 3.9 million (M). Christians, 1.9 M, 49% (Orthodox, 1.8 M; Roman Catholics, 0.1 M; Protestants, 0.02 M); Muslims, 1.9 M, 49%; nonreligious, 0.07 M,

2%. (Based on *World Christian Encyclopedia*, 2001.)

Eriugena, John the Scot. See JOHN SCOTUS ERIUGENA.

Esau, son of Isaac* and Rebecca*, older twin brother of Jacob*. The two struggled with each other in the womb (Gen 25:22–23), foreshadowing the deception through which Jacob secured Esau's birthright and incurred his anger. They are viewed as the ancestors of rival nations, Edom* and Israel*.

ESCHATOLOGY CLUSTER

1) *Introductory Entry*

Eschatology

2) *A Sampling of Contextual Views and Practices*

Eschatology and Apocalypticism in Africa
Eschatology and Apocalypticism in Eastern Orthodox Europe
Eschatology and Apocalypticism in Mexico
Eschatology and Apocalypticism in North America
Eschatology and Apocalypticism in North America: Feminist Perspectives

1) Introductory Entry

Eschatology (Gk *eschaton*, "the final reality"; *eschata*, "the last things") typically includes such topics as death*, particular and universal judgment*, purgatory*, hell*, heaven*, the resurrection* of the body, the fulfillment of history, and the destiny of the universe itself. Eschatology offers no guided tour of the afterlife, but seeks to give a critical account of what is to come, in its individual and collective aspects, by extrapolating from what has already occurred in the incarnation*, death, and resurrection of Christ (Rahner*). Through the gift of the Holy* Spirit, the future of God is already present in its active and attractive power, drawing history to its completion (Pannenberg).

The expansive, indefinable reality of the *eschaton* occurs as a judgment on the present world; it summons to action even though the end is never fully possessed or realized in any age (Moltmann). Thus theology*, as "faith* seeking understanding," finds a necessary complement in eschatology as "hope* seeking understanding." There is an eschatological dimension present in every theological theme, even if eschatology is a particular branch of theology dealing with a range of special questions such as the destiny of the individual, history as a whole, and, indeed, the universe in its entirety.

Since medieval times, eschatological reflection has oscillated between a "warm," often overheated style with dramatic declarations of the imminence of the end and the final age of the Holy Spirit (Abbot Joachim* of Fiore, the Spiritual Franciscans*) and a "cooler", more objective systematic account of our "last end" (Aquinas*). In the contemporary context of interreligious dialogue*, such polarities continue in new forms. For example, the hopes of Abrahamic religions (Judaism*, Christianity, and Islam*) find God's promise of fulfillment revealed in history, whereas many Eastern religions and spiritualities (e.g. Buddhism*, Hinduism*, Daoism*) are suprahistorical in their views of enlightenment or self-realization.

Contemporary forms of eschatology attempt to relate hope for the ultimate to practical responsibilities in the penultimate areas of political*, social*, and economic* structures of the present. A hope-filled vision of the end disturbs any acceptance of deficiencies, distortions, and sinfulness as "the way things are." Insofar as eschatology recognizes that the crucified Jesus has been raised in his compassionate solidarity with the poor and the marginalized, it assumes a socially critical function (see Preferential Option for the Poor). With this "apocalyptic sting" (Metz), eschatology both inspires and learns from the praxis of liberation, which refuses to disconnect the "world to come" from the suffering peoples of the present. If the Eucharist* is the liturgical proclamation of "the Lord's death until he comes" (1 Cor

11:26), it demands, even now, an energetic anticipation of what God is bringing about in communities based on the values of justice*, peace*, and human dignity (see Human Rights Cluster). Such "sacramental" conduct is both a sign and a present realization of what God has in store.

In dialogue with evolutionary*-oriented sciences*, new questions arise regarding eschatology. For example, how is the ultimate God-given future ("eternal life") to be related to the genesis of the cosmos and the evolutionary dynamics of life on earth, with its unimaginable dimensions of space and time? How is the resurrection of the body, in Christ and eventually for all, related to the transformation of the material universe? How would the eventual ending of the solar system or the universe itself figure in a scientifically attuned eschatology?

However such questions are addressed, "what God has prepared for those who love him" (1 Cor 2:9) is not simply a homogeneous extension of the present. The form of the eschatological consummation of history lies hidden in the mystery* of God. But because of what is already revealed in Christ, the end is an object of hope and a longing for that fulfillment when God will be "all in all" (1 Cor 15:28). **See also APOCALYPTICISM CLUSTER; HOPE.** ANTHONY J. KELLY, CSSR

2) A Sampling of Contextual Views and Practices

Eschatology and Apocalypticism in Africa. Diviners have been part of African religious traditions and have revealed past, present, and future events for either individuals or communities. In the face of formidable problems that tend to darken one's future, people need hope*, and they turn to diviners at such critical times. It is not surprising that the Book of Revelation* is popular in many branches of the Charismatic* Movement because of the vision it paints about the end of human history, catastrophic world events, and anticipation of a new heaven and a new earth.

John Mbiti has sought to explain the African fascination with the future. He asserts that the African concept of time* has a long past, a short present, but no future dimension. He goes on to say that African time moves backward into the past and not into the future. Therefore, he suggested that it was Christianity that brought the future dimension to Africa, thus reversing the concept of time among African peoples. For Mbiti, this explains why the Christian faith in Africa is centered now on a future brought about by God and not made by human beings through material development. The eschatological future is the new element in Africans' philosophy of time.

This theory has been greatly criticized, opposed, and modified by other African scholars. For Jesse Mugambi, the concept of time can be adequately discussed only by taking into account matter, duration, and space. Benjamin Ray and Kwesi Dickson are of the opinion that Mbiti did not take the idea of destiny into account, while Lugano Sankey thinks that to deny people a sense of future is to deny them hope. Others have seen the processes of initiations common in Africa as confirming a future dimension of time. Thus Mbiti did not fully analyze the concept of time.

Furthermore, one of the major reasons that many African Christians adhere to the Christian faith is their aspiration to go to heaven upon death or when Jesus returns. Therefore, one can wait for the end time, since historical time is like being on a watch tower (hence the Watch Tower Movement) or in a waiting room. However, the ideas of heaven*, hell*, and their attendant rewards are all new to the African worldview, which is, according to Mugambi, a monosectoral reality.

AUGUSTINE MUSOPOLE

Eschatology and Apocalypticism in Eastern Orthodox Europe. Although Chiliasm* (Millennialism*) has been repudiated by the Eastern Orthodox* Church Councils, eschatological sentiments were recurrent among mainstream Orthodox churches and dissident groups. Among the theological sources that informed their eschatological outlook were the Book of Revelation* (popular in Slavonic

Orthodoxy in the 11th–13th c. despite its rejection by some church fathers) and numerous apocryphal* and pseudepigraphal* apocalyptic books. Some of the early Christian eschatological texts survived only in Slavonic translation (e.g. 2 Enoch* and the earlier version of the Book of Daniel*). In Russia some of these texts were adopted by popular culture and influenced paraliturgical spiritual verses (*dukhovnye stikhi*).

In 11th- and 12th-c. Bulgaria*, probably because of the Bogomil* Movement, apocalyptical sentiment was expressed through apocryphal prophesies ascribed to the prophet Isaiah that gave a special place to Macedonia* in the topography of the "last things." The Ottoman conquest of Bulgaria had also given rise to eschatological prophesies (14th–15th c.).

Eschatological motifs were present in the religiopolitical notion of Moscow as "the Third Rome" (14th c.) and in the symbolism of the reign of Ivan the Terrible.

The Brest*-Litovsk Union between the Roman Catholic and Orthodox churches (1596) gave rise to a vigorous Orthodox polemic in Ukraine* in which eschatological prophesies were used to discredit the Union, as in the early-17th-c. anti-Union polemical writings of Zakhariia Kopystenskii, Stefan Zizaniia, and Ivan Vishenskii.

The religious schism in the Russian Orthodox Church (late 17th c.) developed in an atmosphere of intense Millennialist expectations and produced a prolific body of eschatological texts. Apocalyptic sentiments were widespread during the reign of Peter I (1682–1725) and his 18th-c. successors; popular rumor portrayed Peter I as the Antichrist*. Eschatological fears accompanied many state-sponsored campaigns in modern Russia, such as vaccination against smallpox and population censuses. Several religious sectarians practiced various forms of "escape" from the Antichrist: some refused to accept passports or money, some burned themselves alive, while others barricaded themselves in caves.

Millennialism nevertheless was also shared by elites: Alexander I (1801–25) presented himself as the leader of a new mystical union of Europe based on spirituality and devotion rather than on the ideas of the Enlightenment*. Dostoyevsky* ("The Legend of the Grand Inquisitor" in *Brothers Karamazov*) and Vladimir Soloviev* (*Three Conversations*, 1900) were inspired by the Book of Revelation. **See also MILLENNIALISM CLUSTER.** IRINA PAERT

Eschatology and Apocalypticism in Mexico. The processes of conquest and evangelization had different impacts on the various native peoples of Mesoamerica. In some cases, the reality of a hostile presence was projected into a utopian future through further elaboration of native prophetic or apocalyptic myths. The opposition to the colonial* order was thus at first nourished by the people's own history and myths. But owing to prolonged contact with the colonizers, these native myths ended up amalgamated with the Judeo-Christian messianism and apocalypticism in socioreligious movements that can be included in the history of resistance to colonialism. Yet in the 19th and 20th c., these movements confronted more directly the plunder and exploitation resulting from the insertion of the country into the modern capitalist system.

Contradicting the image of peace* erected around the colonial history of New Spain, some 30 messianic native movements (with several including blacks and mestizos*) struggled against the abuses of religious and/or political-administrative authorities. These were found primarily in the Mayan region, which includes the Yucatán Peninsula and the current states of Chiapas and Tabasco, as well as among the native people of the states of Guerrero and Oaxaca in the south, and the nomadic and semi-nomadic people who inhabited the area from Jalisco to New Mexico in the north. It is noteworthy that such movements are absent from the center of the country.

The best-known cases include the Mixtón rebellion (1541), those of Tepehuanes (1616), Tarahumaras (1646–1690), Tzeltales in Cancun (1712), and Tepic (1801), and the "caste war" (the revolt of the Maya people of Yucatán, 1847–1901). In each case, the prophetic dreams and apocalyptic hopes of liberation of an oppressed community led the community to seek to free itself from subjugation through anti-Spanish revolts or, as in the case of Cancún, through the creation of indigenous churches. The rise of such indigenous churches was ferociously repressed during the colonial period, but in the 19th c. the Cruzob (People of the Cross) Mayan Church was established (1850), as was the Tzotzil Mayan Church of Chamula (1868). The most recent, nonnative, Millennialist movement is the New Jerusalem colony, in Michoacán, founded in the wake of a series of apocalyptic Marian messages that announced the imminent destruction of the world because of the "Modernist corruption" that had pervaded the Catholic Church since Vatican* II.

JAVIER OTAOLA MONTAGNE

Eschatology and Apocalypticism in North America. The future has always been prominent in North American life. From the outset, this so-called New World has seen itself as the cutting edge of civilization, humankind's "last, best hope." Its true (if unacknowledged) religion has been "the religion of Progress" (George P. Grant). Christianity, North America's culturally established religion, has on the whole accommodated itself to this optimistic predisposition, providing the rhetoric and symbolism requisite to its articulation and celebration.

While such a predisposition in fact constitutes a decisive eschatology, no theological term or emphasis has been less familiar to Christians in North America than has "eschatology." Conventional introductions cryptically labeled it "the doctrine of last things." But the "last things" have not been an existential concern for the North American general public and church, since "the end" (in both its teleological and chronological senses) could appear to be positive and reassuring.

With the breakdown of the modern vision, however, and the impact of globally ubiquitous threats and instabilities on public consciousness, a new and vital interest in this neglected dimension of Christian tradition has emerged in North American Christian circles. Perhaps this interest could be dated from the 1954 General Assembly of the World* Council of Churches in Evanston, Illinois, with its theme, "Jesus Christ – the Hope* of the World." With the postmodern assault on all one-sidedly optimistic assumptions about the future of civilization (especially Western civilization), theologians began to reflect more earnestly on the explicitly Christian sources of hope – a hope that did not require the repression of the data of despair, but could be more realistic about the negations that were appearing on the horizon and more capable of the moral and practical courage required to counter them. It would be hard to underestimate, e.g., the impact of Juergen Moltmann's *Theology of Hope* on theological dialogue in this context.

At the same time, the "future shock" felt by North Americans since 1960 evoked in much popular Christianity a resurgence of the apocalypticism that had perhaps always been an undercurrent in North America's officially optimistic society, for an exaggerated utopianism easily and regularly begets in some the suspicion that it cloaks devastating possibilities. Moreover, the "otherworldliness" and antiworldliness of much Christian Pietism* in North America naturally favors end views in which salvation* entails the destruction of the fallen creation (see Hal Lindsey's Popular *The Late Great Planet Earth*).

Clearly, a biblically based faith that affirms the "goodness" of God's creation* cannot endorse such an apocalyptic scenario. It is a questionable redemption* theology that requires the damnation of creation! At the same time, the Christian "liberalism" that locates redemption in historical evolution has difficulty today taking seriously the real threats to planetary existence that are the subject of every honest news broadcast. Eschatology is no longer an addendum to Christian theology, but a necessary ingredient of all serious Christian reflection. DOUGLAS JOHN HALL

Eschatology and Apocalypticism in North America: Feminist Perspectives. There is no more potent source of judgment* of the status quo, encouragement of the high-risk prophetic* witness, and hope* for an ultimate vindication and new* creation than the biblical tradition of eschatology – especially when apocalyptically* intensified. Bitter or promising, violent or peaceable, patriarchal* or egalitarian, religious* or secular*, revolutionary or reactionary – every radical movement in the West betrays the traces of the Apocalypse. The Women's Movement comes spiked with images of a positive Millennialism*.

The Shakers* (18th c.) declared that "Woman's Rights are fully recognized, by first giving her a Mother in Deity, to explain and protect them" (DeBerg). Claire Demar (early 19th c.) wrote, "The word of the WOMAN REDEEMER WILL BE A SUPREMELY REVOLTING WORD" (capitals in the original). Increasingly secular, the eschatology of feminism* only mounted: "Pealing! The clock of Time has struck the woman's hour" (a toast at an 1891 Women's Press Club). Yet Feminist theology – as in Rosemary Ruether's *New Woman, New Earth* – reconnects gender justice* to eschatology.

Still, the deployment of apocalyptic binaries of messianic* vs. demonic* forces requires complex symbolic* maneuvers. A symbolic figure of feminine sexuality* embodies historical evil: the Great Whore, all-consuming and finally consumed, "for all the nations have drunk of the wine of the wrath of her fornication" (Rev 18:2). John of Patmos's fury against a female competitor as "Jezebel" (Rev 2:20–23) provided a template for fans such as Bockelson, who practiced polygamous and gynocidal terror in his 16th-c. "New Jerusalem," or for fundamentalism's* inscription of the 19th-c. New Woman as "silly women of the last days." Apocalypse has promoted an ascetic*, heroic, and dominative masculinity, suffering a perceived (and often real) oppression. Its adherents declared the pope or the Ottoman Turk, suffragists or feminists, the Whore of Babylon, with an absolutism unavailable to "lukewarm" mainstream Christians. Mary Daly answered with a "Holy War waged by Wholly Haggard Whores casting off the bonds of whoredom" – an apocalyptic denunciation of the Apocalypse.

Feminist readings of Christian eschatology may pursue a radical cultural "anti-apocalypse" (Lee Quinby); a theological neo-apocalypse, as in Elisabeth Schüssler Fiorenza's retrieval of John of Patmos as a hero of social justice; or a "counter-apocalypse," which proposes to detoxify and recycle eschatological radicalism for a just and sustainable "new heaven and earth."

A hallucinatory proliferation of gender-charged imagery has always inflected the great drama of good and evil, denunciation and promise, now and then. How would we cease negotiating with its strange angels, messianic warriors, and virgin brides? CATHERINE KELLER

Escrivá de Balaguer, Josemaria. See OPUS DEI.

Esdras, First Book of (sometimes designated 3 Esdras; See Bible, Canon of the), one of the Apocrypha*. It is a free Greek version of biblical history from the time of Josiah's reform (621 BCE) to that of Ezra's reform (444 BCE) as found in 2 Chr 35:1–36:21 (1 Esd 1:1–55) and Ezra and Nehemiah (1 Esd 2:1–30, 5:7–9:55). The independent text, 1 Esd 3:1–5:3, presents the story of three youths in a riddle contest at the Persian king Darius's court. What is strongest in the world? Zerubbabel won by claiming it was women and truth. As a reward, he obtained permission for the exiled Jews to go home. Josephus* used 1 Esdras as the basis for the postexilic history of the Jews. It was possibly written shortly after 165 BCE. DANIEL PATTE

Esdras, Second Book of (also designated 4 Esdras), is better known as Fourth* Ezra.

Esoteric Theology (from Gk "hidden within"), theology communicated to an inner group of disciples and understood only by the initiated. The Greek mystery* religions and Plato's* Academy differentiated between esoteric and exoteric teachings; the distinction entered Christianity with the Gnostics*. In mainstream Christianity, there is an analogous principle that faith* is the only path to true understanding*. Since the Renaissance*, esoteric theology has been linked with the recovery of the Hermetic* corpus and the thesis that a "perennial philosophy," reconciling many different religious traditions, has been available to those who seek it. **See also THEOSOPHY.**

Esquivel, Adolfo Pérez. See ARGENTINA.

Essenes, a group of Palestinian Jews (2nd c. BCE to 1st c. CE) devoted to a life governed by a strict interpretation of Torah. Descriptions of the organization, practices, and discipline of the group in Philo*, and especially Josephus* and Hippolytus*, concur sufficiently with some of the Dead Sea Scrolls to indicate that the Qumran* community was an Essene group. Taken together, these texts depict a group that claimed to have a revealed interpretation of Torah* constituting them as exclusively the chosen people of God, and a revealed interpretation of the Prophets (see Pesher) that assured them that they were living in the end-time, when God would vindicate their righteousness. At Qumran, the leaders of the group were Zadokite priests, and strict ritual purity was enforced by stringent sanctions. Celibacy* seems to have been the rule at the male community in Qumran, but not in other Essene settlements in the land. Although the Essenes are not mentioned by name in the NT, aspects of their organization, practice, and eschatological* expectations suggest that some members of some early Christian communities may have come from communities of Essenes or like-minded Jews. **See also DEAD SEA SCROLLS.**

GEORGE W. E. NICKELSBURG

Essentialism, the assumption that all the members of every species or "kind" of thing have the same characteristics, because these are "essential" to all members of the species. Today Feminist* and Liberation* theologians attack the assumption that all women or all cultures have the same inclinations and needs, regardless of social and cultural factors. **See also NOMINALISM; REALISM; UNIVERSALS.**

Establishment, in ecclesiastical usage, a relation between church and state established by law, usually favoring one church over others.

Esther, Book of, a 2nd-c. BCE biblical book, recounts how, at the court of the king of Persia, Ahasuerus (Xerxes I?), Esther became the royal consort and with her kinsman, Mordecai, saved the Jews from extermination by the grand-vizier, Haman. It also tells of how the festival of Purim was established to celebrate the destruction of the enemies of the Jews. In the Hebrew Masoretic* text, this story is strikingly devoid of any allusion to God; two Greek versions (the Septuagint* and the "Alpha Text") give Esther a religious dimension by repeatedly mentioning God and by adding chapters (parts of the Apocrypha*).

Because of its secular character, the Hebrew Book of Esther has been historically received with much reluctance in Christian churches (especially in Eastern Christianity). Martin Luther believed that Esther should not figure in the Bible. But rabbinic Judaism, despite dissenting voices, considered Esther to be divinely inspired; Maimonides* ranked it right after the Torah. Such discrepancy is the result mainly of diverging perceptions of the literary genre of the book. To see Esther as a historical report (slanted or not) leads to a legitimate dis-ease with its secularism and its violence. But when it is read as a "carnivalesque" novella in the image of the festival it establishes, Purim, one can appreciate it as the only biblical book that is Diaspora*-oriented with an observance that is not rooted in the land of Israel and is not pentateuchal. In that case, this "ethnocentric" Esther belongs to the Bible as an affirmation of the people of God in the secular world of the Diaspora*.

ANDRÉ LACOCQUE

Estonia had contacts with Christianity from the 11th c. on. With the conquest of Estonia in the 1220s by the troops of the Order of the Brethren of the Sword (see Military Orders; Teutonic Knights), the Christianization of the population took place. Many impressive church buildings and monasteries were built.

The Reformation reached Estonia early, in the 1520s. Swedish rule in Estonia in the 17th c. led to the publication of religious literature in the Estonian language (NT, 1686; complete Bible, 1739) and to theological education (Tartu University, founded 1632). After the annexing of Estonia by Russia (1721), the Russian Orthodox* Church developed. Since the second half of the 19th c., other Christian movements have gained some following in Estonia.

After Estonia became independent in 1918, the Evangelical Lutheran Church was recognized as the main church in Estonia. Under the Soviet occupation, Christians suffered from repressive measures: the property of the churches was confiscated and some denominations were pronounced illegal. However, the majority of the churches were allowed to use the state-owned church buildings.

When Estonia regained its independence (1991), churches had an unprecedented revival. Publishing of religious literature was resumed, and theological education is offered now in at least five institutions, among them Tartu University. Most high school programs include religion. Recently, however, because of secularization*, a decline in membership has been observed in many churches. Many people attend only special services, such as annual festivals, weddings, and confirmations.

Statistics: Population (2000): 1.4 million (M). Christians, 0.89 M; 63.5% (unaffiliated Christians, 0.36 M; Protestants, 0.24 M; Orthodox, 0.23 M; independents, 0.05 M); atheists and nonreligious, 0.50 M, 36%. (Based on *World Christian Encyclopedia,* 2001.)

HEIKKI SILVET

Eternity, the temporal dimension of infinity. Holding God* to be eternal, Christians consider "eternity" a synonym for salvation* or the Kingdom* of God. Unlike eternity, time* has a beginning and an end, and a course or path, called history*. Like the other monotheistic religions, Christianity gives the "Eternal One" a power and a love that is paternal and royal or – more neutrally – supervisory and loving – through providence*, grace, sacraments, and miracles. Unique to Christianity is the interaction between time and eternity implicit in the doctrines of the Incarnation* and salvation* through the efficacy of divine sacrifice*. From a "pneumatic" perspective, the Holy* Spirit removes "the sacrifice on the Cross from its historical coordinates and propels the redemptive act throughout time" (Vondey). The potential of eternity and infinity to articulate Christian ideas was clear as early as Paul, who expressed fundamental unities by speaking of how "all" may be present "in all" (1 Cor 12:6, 15:28; see also Eph 4:6; Col 3:11) when the world comes to union with its Creator and vice versa.

Especially in the Western* churches, Christian thought orders time by defining the key points as if on a line: creation*, the Fall*, the Nativity*, the Crucifixion*, the Resurrection*, Pentecost*, and the expected Parousia* (the Second* Coming), resurrection*, and the Last Judgment*. Consequent to that reckoning, Christ sentences persons (souls* and their bodies, now reunited) to an eternity in either heaven* or hell*. From these premises, the question arises: Does divine foreknowledge, being eternal, determine human choice? The solution Boethius* proposed radically divides eternity from time (and therefore divine knowledge from sequence). There can be no foreknowledge, because there is no "before" in the Divine Mind.

The Greek terms that imply "eternity" have provoked debate over the duration of hell. *Aidion* (Rom 1:20, referring to God's eternity) combines the Greek root *aei,* meaning "always," with the adjectival suffix *-dion* to become an adjective meaning "always-like." *Aionion* (Matt 25:41, 46, balancing eternal life and punishment) derives from *aion,* for "eon" or "an age," and could mean "merely" extensive duration. Augustine* defended the eternity of hell (opposing Origen*), arguing that the same eternity applied to hell as to heaven; otherwise the saints would be cheated of unending bliss.

Nicholas* of Cusa (1401–64) and Georg Cantor (1845–1918) have enriched the concept of eternity through their mathematical explorations. **See also DAMNATION; JUDGMENT.**

ALAN E. BERNSTEIN

ETHICS AND CHRISTIANITY CLUSTER

1) *Introductory Entry*

Ethics

2) *A Sampling of Other Views and Practices*

Ethics and Christianity in Africa
Ethics and Christianity in Eastern Orthodoxy
Ethics and Christianity as Ethic of Risk and Womanist Ethics

1) Introductory Entry

Ethics. "Christian ethics" refers to the theological or theoretical study of morality (which takes several forms) and often to the subject matter of this study, "morality" (or one of its specific implementations, e.g. business ethics).

Morality is a matter of relationships: right and wrong, good and bad, virtuous and vicious, just and unjust interactions with others. While Christianity is a religion of salvation* and redemption*, it is also a religion of morality, since it is rooted in relationships: with God; with other Christians (in communities of various kinds; see Church, Concepts and Life, Cluster: Doctrines of the Church; Church, Concepts and Life, Cluster: Types of Ecclesiastical Structures); with other people, including followers of other religions (see Religions and Christianity); and with the world, God's creation (see Ecology and Christianity Cluster). The foundation of Christian morality is therefore often summarized in the twofold commandment to love God and to love one's neighbor" (Mark 12:30–31, par.; see Love). Christians are called to assume responsibility for their behavior, their acts and their failure to act, in all dimensions of their lives.

Consequently, churches and their theologians have developed social* ethics, economic* ethics, business* ethics, global* ethics, and medical* and biomedical* ethics. They have formulated ethical stances concerning the place in society and the church of women (see Feminist Theology Cluster; Women's Christian Practices and Theologies Cluster; Women's Ordination Cluster) and of other marginalized groups (see African American Cluster; Australian Aboriginal Traditions and Christianity; Black Theology; Dalit Theology; Native American Traditions and Christianity; Palestinian Liberation Theology; Womanist and African American Theologies) and concerning family*, sexuality*, abortion*, ecology*, politics*, refugees*, war*, and justice*, as well as behavior within the church (see Canon Law; Church Discipline; Discipline; Polity).

This concern for ethics and morality does not mean that Christians have not been responsible for much evil throughout church history, be it through sins* of commission or omission (see Colonialism and Imperialism and Christian Theology, as well as entries on countries colonized by Christian nations, i.e. most of the countries in Africa, Asia, Australasia, and Latin America; Crusades; Heresy; Holocaust, Jewish [or Shoah]; Inquisition; Poverty Cluster; Racism and Christianity Cluster). Christians strive to alleviate these evils, even as they unwillingly condone them by participating in societies or cultures that contribute to them.

Many Christians aspire to, or claim to have, an objective and absolutist ethics, such as the "divine* command ethics" that grounds judgments of good and evil in God's commands in natural law and/or Scripture, in contrast to "subjectivist" or "situationist" ethics, viewed as relativist. Yet from an ethical perspective, one cannot ignore the fact that throughout history much evil has been committed by Christians with an objective and absolutist ethics (see Postmodernism and Liberation Theologies; Postmodernism and Theology). Furthermore, history shows that the formulations of "natural* law" – the moral norms shared by Christians and others – vary with cultural and social contexts, as do the formulations of ethical teachings resulting from reading of the Bible as Scripture* (a "Word-to-live-by" that Christians relate to their changing life contexts). The fact remains that Christians envision themselves as moral agents and act on the basis of what they perceive to be self-evidently (and thus objectively and absolutely) good or wrong (see Conviction). They act on the basis of preunderstandings about the moral life. Following philosophers, Christian theologians view these preunderstandings as falling into three broad types, named here following Ogletree.

Perfectionist Ethics emphasizes the formation of the self as moral agent, through the use of moral discernment or "practical wisdom" to reach human happiness (Aristotle*) or everlasting life with God (Augustine*, Aquinas*). When applying moral principles, a moral agent needs "virtues*": a "know-how" to address moral issues in concrete situations, the cardinal virtues of self-control, endurance, wisdom, and justice (Plato and Aristotle), and the theological virtues of faith*, hope*, and charity* (Augustine, Aquinas), which one acquires as "practical wisdom" through imitation of a teacher. In this view (of much traditional moral Roman Catholic teaching), a disciple* is formed through imitation of God and Christ (*imitatio* Christi*) as well as of dedicated, saintly persons, who might or might not be church leaders. Loving God leads to loving neighbors.

Deontological Ethics emphasizes obligation and duty; a choice is right when it conforms to moral norms, basic moral principles that derive from the intersubjective character of action. For Christians, these basic moral principles, often envisioned as a law*, are God's will as revealed in Scripture*, both in the OT and in its reinterpretations by Christ (e.g. the Sermon* on the Mount) and in church tradition*. Deontological* ethics easily becomes legalistic. Yet for Kant* and, following him, many (Protestant) theologians, conformity to moral norms should not be confused with legalism. Through regard for others, pure practical reason both establishes what morality unconditionally demands ("harm not"; "respect other persons' dignity") and determines the will to do it.

Consequentialist Ethics emphasizes the effects (consequences) of choices and actions, especially their effects on others; it examines the intentionality of actions, since it is goal oriented (as John Stuart Mill's utilitarianism is, e.g., in business). Theological consequentialist ethics is most directly concerned with the for-the-sake-of-whom (unconditional responsibility to and for the other) and therefore with what is desirable for others (rather than the negative "harm not" of deontological ethics). The neighbor is always the middle term between God and me; it is through the face and voice of the neighbor that I am in relation to God (see Levinas, Emmanuel), as Liberation and contextual theologies (preferential* option for the poor) also emphasize.

These classical views of ethics are constantly challenged by situations that call for other types of practices. **See also SERMON ON THE MOUNT.** DANIEL PATTE

2) A Sampling of Other Views and Practices

Ethics and Christianity in Africa. Classical philosopher-theologian Thomas Aquinas* described ethics in terms of the good* to be done and the evil* to be avoided. But good and evil can be understood only within a certain context. African theologians (e.g. Bujo) and ethicists (e.g. Nyerere) situate ethics in Africa by making community its defining principle.

Approaches to ethics depend on perceptions of sources of ethical criteria: God, individual person, "natural law," state, or community. These lead to distinctive ethical systems or schools: "natural law" ethics, idealism, individualism, situation ethics, rationalism, and communitarian ethics, among others. How do some of these relate to Africa?

Divine will as source of ethics, the common view in mainline African Christianity, bases itself on "revealed" sources, the Bible in particular. Deductive in approach, it preserves the uniqueness of God but often clashes with Africa's aspirations for human freedom. It fails to address Africa's questions about the slave* trade, colonialism*, effects of globalization*, poverty*, or underdevelopment*.

Individual as source of ethics preserves the Christian perception of the person's integrity, yet leads to an un-African overemphasis on the individual at the expense of community. Buttressed by and buttressing laissez-faire capitalism, it promotes competition, contradicting Africa's ethic of sharing and cooperation.

"Natural law" as source of ethics claims that every person has the ability through reason* to know good and bad; the choice for either is open to human freedom*. Preserving the idea of God's image* in every person, this theory is blind to human perversity, exemplified in Africa by tyrants such as Idi Amin Dada (Uganda*) and Mobutu Sese Soko (Democratic Republic of Congo*).

State as source of ethics is expressed radically in communism* and mildly in forms of (African) socialism*. The state is invested with absolute power, much as God is in the divine will approach. This clashes with the African ideal of the individual's rights in community.

Community as source of ethics is the African approach in which moral traditions, found in customs and taboos, safeguard and enhance the life of the community and the individuals within it. God, the foundation of moral order, channels power for ethical conduct through the community in its fourfold dimensions: the ancestors*, the living, the yet-to-be-born, and the community of goods*.

The human potential to choose right or wrong conduct regarding oneself and others is recognized by African moral traditions. Thus theories that deny human beings the capacity for moral freedom, leading to ethics of determinism (in philosophy) or predestination (in theology) are largely foreign to Africa.

LAURENTI MAGESA

Ethics and Christianity in Eastern Orthodoxy. Ethics is the normative aspect of theology, focusing on the "ought" aspect of living the Christian life. The ultimate source of ethics is the "Good," understood to be the one God in the triune divine reality of Father, Son, and Holy Spirit (see Trinity in Eastern Orthodoxy).

Humanity as a whole and human beings as persons in community find in God the norm of their personal and corporate human existence as created beings in the "image and likeness of God" (Gen 1:6). In this they follow the injunction of Jesus Christ, "Be perfect as your heavenly Father is perfect" (Matt 5:48), Jesus Christ being the model for this perfection through his incarnation*, example, and character.

For Eastern Orthodox Christianity, there are several sources for implementing this ethic. The "natural moral law" (*physikos ethikos nomos*) is an elemental ethical guideline allowing for ordered social and personal life, as embodied in codes such as the Decalogue* in the Judeo-Christian tradition, but also expressed by the authorities of other world religions (see Culture Cluster: And Christianity in Eastern Orthodoxy). Yet the corpus for ethical reflection on both theoretical and practical ethical guidelines for living the Christian faith includes the NT, the writings of the recognized church fathers of the first millennium, conciliar canon law, ascetical writings, as well as liturgical texts and, to a lesser extent, the writings of contemporary Orthodox Christian ethicists.

In many practical applications, the Orthodox Church is socially conservative, but the evangelical supreme value of love* (Christian *agape*) can turn any given situation into an opportunity for radical moral action. In every moral situation, two dynamics are at work: (1) the struggle (*agon*) against evil and sin*, sin being the absence or denial of the God-like life (*theosis**), and (2) the struggle to realize (*ascesis*, "exercise") in practice and in each situation God-like behavior and values.

STANLEY S. HARAKAS

Ethics and Christianity as Ethic of Risk and Womanist Ethics. Katie Cannon's groundbreaking exploration of "the moral wisdom found in the black women's literary tradition" (1988) challenged ethicists to rethink our understanding of the nature and sources of ethical action. She found in the work of African* American women a tradition of strength and persistence, which is one of the richest heritages facing humankind. Cannon analyzed the ethical impact of "unshouted courage, . . . the incentive to facilitate change, to chip away the oppressive structures bit by bit, to celebrate and rename their experiences in empowering ways. . . . 'Unshouted courage' is the quality of steadfastness, akin to fortitude, in the face of formidable oppression" (Cannon, *Black Womanist Ethics*).

In the writing of many African American women, we find an ethic of risk, a definition of responsible action within the limits of bounded power. These writers describe the nature of responsible action when control is impossible and name the resources that evoke persistent defiance and resistance in the face of repeated defeats. Within an ethic of risk, actions begin with the recognition that far too much has been lost and there are no clear means of restitution. The fundamental risk constitutive of this ethic is the decision to care and to act even though there are no guarantees of success. Such action requires immense daring and enables deep joy.

The ethic of risk, as expressed in the lives and writings of African American women and men, poses a foundational challenge to Euro-American ethics. Our moral and political imagination is often shaped by an ethic of control, a construction of agency, responsibility, and goodness which assumes that it is possible to guarantee the efficacy of one's action. We often assume that being responsible means ensuring that the aim of one's action will be carried out. This understanding of responsible action leads to a striking paralysis of will* when one is faced with complex problems. Euro-Americans are challenged by African American women and men to criticize such understanding of responsible action insofar as it distorts the implementation of communally accepted norms.

The ethic of risk is characterized by three elements, each essential in maintaining resistance in the face of overwhelming odds: a redefinition of responsible action, grounding in community, and strategic risk taking. Responsible action does not mean the certain achievement of desired ends, but the creation of the conditions of possibility for desired social ends, the creation of a matrix in which further actions, further resistance, are possible, sustained, and enabled by participation in an extensive community, a community that offers support in struggle and constitutes the context for work that spans generations. **See also** LIBERATION THEOLOGIES CLUSTER: IN NORTH AMERICA: WOMANIST; WOMANIST AND AFRICAN AMERICAN THEOLOGIES. SHARON D. WELCH

Ethiopia. The history of Ethiopia since the 4th c. is also the history of Christianity in Ethiopia, specifically the history of the Ethiopian* Orthodox Tewahedo Church. Until 1974 Ethiopia was a kingdom or empire of variable size, including for a long time large parts of what is now Eritrea*. Ethiopia claims to have been the second Christian state (after Armenia*).

Early Period. The earliest plausible account of the origins of Christianity in the Aksumite/Ethiopian kingdom comes from Rufinus* Tyrannius (4th c.), according to whom Frumentius* was brought to the royal palace (c340) as a servant of the king of Aksum (or Axum). Freed upon the king's death, at the queen's request he stayed to function as regent. Frumentius founded a Christian church in Aksum; he also gathered together Christians already in the kingdom, most of them merchants from the Roman Empire, primarily from Syria and the Byzantine world, along the Red Sea coast, including Adulis. After his regency, Frumentius went to Alexandria (c347) to plead with Patriarch Athanasius* to send a bishop to the new Christian community in Ethiopia. Instead, Athanasius ordained Frumentius himself as the "first" bishop and apostle of Ethiopia (although there might already have been a bishop in Adulis).

Rufinus's account is corroborated by other evidence regarding this period in Ethiopia, including a letter of the Byzantine Arian Roman emperor Constantius (preserved in Athanasius's *Apologia ad Constantium*) demanding that the Aksumite princes send Frumentius back to Alexandria to be instructed in Arianism*, although this never took place.

There are no reliable sources from which to draw a complete picture of subsequent developments in the Ethiopian Church in Aksum. However, we can assume that, for the next two centuries, basic liturgical books, including the Psalter, and then the entire Bible were translated into Ge'ez, the local language. Yet 6th-c. accounts testify to the strength of the Ethiopian Church and its contact with the Byzantine Christian world. For instance, the monk Abba Matta, who came to Ethiopia and established a monastery, was said to have been supported by the bishop of Aksum and to have collaborated with another monk. Similarly the Egyptian monk Cosmas Indicopleustes's travelogue enthusiastically records his visit to Ethiopia (c525) and its many churches and their bishops.

The arrival (6th c.) from the Byzantine Empire of the "Nine Saints," the fathers of Ethiopian monasticism*, could also have energized the Ethiopian Church. Each of them founded a monastery around Aksum. Dabra Damo, the monastery of their leader, Abuna Aregawi (Ze-Mikael), is still an important religious center. The translation of the Rule of Pachomius* during the same period is probably not coincidental.

Aksum's significant role as an administrative center of the kingdom ended around the 10th c. or earlier. The cause of its fall was probably the revolt of a non-Christian ethnic group against the Ethiopian Church. The uprising put members of the ruling house to flight and inflicted incalculable damage on church property, including the destruction of the church in Aksum. The rebel group did not, however, hold power for long.

The Zagwe Era (1137–1270). Another Christian dynasty, known as Zagwe, took power in c1137, establishing its capital at Adafa (or Roha) in Lasta, the Zagwe's home province (south of Aksum). This new Christian dynasty was more concerned with spiritual matters than with state affairs. Its kings constructed the several rock-hewn churches in Lasta, their lasting monumental legacy. Some of these kings were also priests (now honored as saints by the Ethiopian

Church). Still, the dynasty did not seem to have enriched the Church educationally; no literary work of any significance, original or in translation, remains from this time. Actually, some manuscripts copied during the Aksumite era disappeared.

The Solomonic Dynasty (from 1270). The Zagwe were overthrown in 1270 by Yekuno Amlak, an energetic young man who claimed to be a descendant of the Aksumite royal family. Tradition maintains that the Ethiopian Church played a significant role in putting Yekuno Amlak on the throne. In subsequent years both the dynasty founded by Yekuno Amlak and the Church denounced the Zagwe reign as illegitimate.

Yekuno Amlak was a good friend of Abuna Iyyasus Mo'a, the abbot of the Dabra Hayq Estifanos monastery (from the 9th c.) – a monastery that Yekuno Amlak helped strengthen – and apparently a close relative of the abbot of another monastery, Abuna Takla Haymanot. In subsequent years, the Dabra Hayq Estifanos monastery used its political power to contribute to the literary life of the Church. Similarly, according to tradition, Yekuno Amlak rewarded Abuna Takla Haymanot by granting a third of the state's revenue to the Church (actually the Church collected only a tithe [10%] on certain lands – a revenue that ended in the 20th c.).

The Golden Age of the Church. For better or worse, the period during which Yekuno Amlak's dynasty controlled the throne is the most memorable in the Ethiopian Church's history. The king's heirs managed to propagate the idea that Ethiopian Christians replaced the Israelites as God's chosen people, because Ethiopians had accepted Christ as the expected Messiah whereas the Jews rejected him (see Election; Supersessionism). What set Ethiopians apart from other nations that had accepted Christ was reflected in two foundational stories recorded in the *Kebra Nagast* (the Glory of kings), a book about the origins of the Solomonic line of emperors. The first story claimed that the royal family descended from Menelik, son of King Solomon and Queen Makeda of Ethiopia (or the Queen of Sheba, of the South). The second claimed that the Christian faithful were the descendants of firstborn Israelites who accompanied Menelik from Jerusalem, stealthily taking the Ark (*tabot*) with them, and settled in Ethiopia. Empowered by this legend, the Solomonic dynasty ruled without challenge, except from several Muslim communities that felt excluded from the national government.

The installation ("restoration" says the tradition) of the Solomonic dynasty coincided with the development of Arabic Coptic literature in Egypt*. The Coptic* metropolitans and their entourages brought to Ethiopia Arabic religious books hitherto not known in the local Church, and so did Ethiopians who visited monasteries in Egypt and the Holy Land. The Dabra Hayq Estifanos monastery and the clergy at the royal palace translated such works into Ge'ez. They also produced important theological works, including the 14th- to 15th-c. works by Metropolitan Salama, Emperor Zar'a Ya'eqob, and Giyorgis of Gasecca as well as the anonymous homilies *Retu'a Haimanot* (True Orthodoxy). These works were in part prompted by the late-13th-c. controversies regarding the place of icons* (especially of the Virgin Mary*) in worship; should one bow (a form of worship) before an icon? Monks rekindled these controversies (15th c.); they viewed bowing before the emperor and icons as incompatible with their monastic rules, views that were suppressed by the emperor.

Another controversy arose when a group of theologians (Zamika'el and his followers) disapproved of the king's "obsession" with Mary and the king's teaching that observing holy days in honor of Mary exonerates sinners from their sins.

The question of how to reconcile God's unity and God's trinity* also created division. Some of the anaphoras* seem to have been composed to emphasize the Miaphysite* Church's position: "three with one nature" (Anaphora of Mary). Consequently, manuscripts and murals often have three identical pictures, each representing one of the three persons in the Trinity, or have three suns with one light coming from them. Similarly, how does one reconcile the fact that God often has an anthropomorphic image in the Bible and that he is unlimited and invisible? Other sources of controversy were the nature of Christ's second* coming (alone or, according to the Ethiopian Church, with the Father and the Holy Spirit?) and the observance of Saturday as the Lord's Sabbath.

As always, the emperor's words became the position of the Church, including that regarding the scope of Scripture*; Jubilees*, Enoch*, and the Maccabees* provided a basis for the angelology and Millennialism* of Emperor Zar'a Ya'eqob, who also waged a fierce campaign against witchcraft*, magical practices, and fortune-telling, though with little success.

Although his legacy is debated, Emperor Zar'a Ya'eqob voluntarily and involuntarily contributed to the further spread of Christianity. He granted land to the followers of Ewostatewos, Christians who strictly followed Jewish ritual life (dietary laws, Sabbath, circumcision) and systematically destroyed pagan shrines as they established monasteries in present-day Eritrea. Yet he also involuntarily spread Christianity by banishing to non-Christian regions the Estifanosites (monks rejecting much of the emperor's teaching by commitment to their monastic rules), who successfully preached Christianity and built churches in these regions.

The Civil Wars and Their Consequences. Ethiopia's monarchs have always been Christian, whereas the country's peoples were always diverse in language and religion. Every revolt against the government – by non-Christians, leading to the fall of Aksum (c10th c.), by the Jewish Falasha (or Felasha; 14th c.), and by Muslims (15th c.) – inevitably affected the Ethiopian Church. The most devastating revolt (1527–43) was that against Christian dominance when Imam Ahmad ibn Ibrahim al-Ghazi took control of the autonomous Muslim principality of Adal with help from the Ottoman Turks. The Ethiopian peasant army was no match for the trained Arab mercenaries with guns and cannons. The Imam's army overran the entire country, putting to death Christians who refused to embrace Islam. Monasteries and church buildings were looted. The monks of Dabra Hayq Estifanos were among the fortunate few to save their manuscripts and church building. The rebellion was finally put down in 1543 with military help from Portugal.

The Catholic Challenge. As Emperor Galawdewos (1540–59) was again taking control of his kingdom and the Ethiopian Orthodox Church, the Portuguese claimed that they had provided assistance on the condition that the Church submit to the pope of Rome. The Portuguese claimed that the Ethiopian Church harbored Eutyches'* heresy* and taught Judaic practices rejected by the Roman Catholic Church. The Ethiopian Church had to defend its teachings in a written statement of faith by Emperor Galawdewos.

Although the emperor might have been sympathetic to the Roman Catholic demands, local opposition forced him merely to settle the Catholics in some regions where they could practice and teach their faith. In time most Portuguese settlers left Ethiopia. The kingdom and the Ethiopian Orthodox Church were then faced with the problem of migrating Oromo, who invaded the country from the south. Many of the churches that escaped the imam's sword were wiped out by the Oromo people (with long-lasting consequences).

Under continuing pressure from the Oromo in the south and Islamic raids from the east, as well as internal struggles for control of the throne (the capital moving westward to Gondar), despite the successful reign of the politically astute Emperor Sarza Dengel (1563–97), his successors were once again forced to seek help from the Roman Catholic West. Emperor Zadengel (1604–1605) began doing away with religious practices to which the Catholics objected, and his successor, Emperor Susenyos (1607–32), officially embraced Roman Catholicism and installed (in 1625) Cardinal Afonso Mendez, a Spaniard, as head of the Ethiopian Church.

The attempt to introduce Roman Catholicism failed. The clergy were asked "to reason" in discussing theological issues, but as Merid Wolde Aregay notes, those "who argued with conviction and zeal were beaten" and countless Ethiopian Christians, including Metropolitan Sam'on, were martyred. The king's demand that all Christians be rebaptized, that the clergy be reordained, and that the Church follow Latin rites brought about a popular uprising. The king was forced to abdicate. His son Fasiladas (1632–67) immediately restored the Ethiopian Orthodox Church, expelling or executing foreigners and their converts.

But the restoration of traditional ways did not bring peace to the Church. A new theological controversy regarding the sense in which Christ was "anointed" rehearsed in a different way the disagreements between Miaphysite Orthodox churches (including the Ethiopian Orthodox Tewahedo Church) and churches that followed the Council of Chalcedon* (including the Roman Catholic Church). The Ethiopian Church's integrity was preserved by the king's power to resolve theological and christological controversies and by the suppression of dissident views. Ultimately, any deviation from the Ethiopian Orthodox Tewahedo Church's christological views was rejected by the last royal council (Boru Meda, 1878), which also condemned the worship of Mary, changing the liturgical statement "worshipping [Mary] with her Son" to read "worshipping [Mary's] Son and bowing before her."

The Era of the Princes. From 1769, the emperors were little more than symbols of the unity of the country. Real political power was divided among feuding governors or princes of the provinces. Lawlessness was the order of the day. The Church was again deeply affected.

The era of the princes came to a close with the rise of Emperor Tewodros (1855), who reaffirmed Tewahedo doctrines and practices (proscribing other views). Although nominally under the Coptic* Church of Alexandria (until 1953), the Ethiopian Church has been as much a national institution as the monarchy, and the two have been closely connected. The kingdom was called a "Christian kingdom." As head of the Church, the king appointed all important Church officers, including the abbots of the important monasteries. He presided over national councils dealing with religious matters. In the event of disagreement among the clergy, the king's words became the official position of the Church. Yet individual parish churches remained largely independent of the central administration, although greater supervision appeared when the Church became autocephalous*. The newly arrived Protestant missionaries (late 19th c.–early 20th c.) approached vulnerable peasants and ridiculed Church traditions – most of the time without any awareness of their contents.

Emperor Haile Selassie, born Tafari Makonnen, ruled as regent from 1916 (as Ras Tafari; see Rastafari Movement), was crowned (1930), and reigned until 1974 (except for the Italian occupation, 1936–41). He promoted the formal independence of the Ethiopian Church, which, since the 4th c., had been under the authority of the Coptic pope of Alexandria. In 1948 an agreement between the Coptic and the Ethiopian churches led to autocephaly for the Ethiopian Church, a process formalized by the 1959 crowning of Abuna Baslios as the first patriarch of Ethiopia.

With the fall of Emperor Haile Selassie (1974), the Ethiopian Orthodox Tewahedo Church lost its status as the state church. The Derg Marxist government (1974–91) nationalized church property and land, and hundreds of thousands, including thousands of priests and monks, were killed during a "Red terror." In addition hundreds of thousands died from famines during the droughts of the 1970s and 1980s. Ethiopia is one of Africa's poorest countries. Since 1991 the renewal of the Orthodox Church (located primarily among Amhara and Tigre rural populations) has been linked mainly to the education and training of priests and laypeople in newly established seminaries and nearly 2,000 schools (not enough in a country where more than half of the 76 million inhabitants are illiterate). Protestant churches have similarly created some 500 schools. Indigenous Charismatic* churches, long underground despite their progression in rural areas, are developing.

Christian Spirituality and Theology. Spirituality is an important matter of daily life for the faithful of the Ethiopian* Orthodox Tewahedo Church. They communicate in prayer not only with God but also with angels and with the "righteous who died in body": the Virgin Mary, the prophets, apostles, saints, and martyrs. The Church teaches that these celestial beings pray for the living and intercede on their behalf. Construing such beings as deities, believers commonly observe their holy days. According to the "Homiliary in Honor of the Archangel Michael," all ailments are caused by demons* from the army of Satan*. Special prayers based on Scripture (some bordering on magic, using God's names to cast a spell) ward off ailments.

Churches are dedicated to a saint, such as Mary, Gabriel, or George, or to one of the names of God, such as Trinity, Savior, Emmanuel, or Jesus. Dedication makes the building a holy place, the dwelling place of God and the saint(s) when the church building is blessed and a *tabot* is placed in it. A *tabot* is a replica of the Ark of the Covenant, feared and revered, becoming a personification of the saint or God (as named) to whom it and the church are dedicated. When a church is dedicated to, e.g., Saint Mary, she is in her own *tabot*, her own "house."

The faithful believe that *tabot*s or the saints they represent have the power to hear and answer prayers. The clergy read about miracles performed by the saints to people (including the sick) who pray to them, observe their holy days, and name their children after them. They vow to bring offerings (carpets, ornamental umbrellas, a cow, or a ram) if their prayers are answered. Churches with especially powerful *tabot*s are centers of pilgrimages.

Eschatology* is framed by the clergy's teaching about rewards and punishments meted out after death, as encapsulated in "Journey (of the Soul) to Heaven" (a recently discovered document). According to it, while the soul* is still in the agony of death, the Angels of Light and the Angels of Darkness ask the soul about its faith, especially about the mystery of the Trinity and Incarnation, and about its good deeds. According to the response, the soul has an easy or difficult journey to heaven to appear before the

Lord for judgment, and then is taken either to paradise* or to hell* until the final Judgment*, after the second* coming of the Lord and his reign of 1,000 years with the righteous (see Millennialism Cluster). At that time, the righteous move to the Kingdom* of Heaven and the sinners to Sheol (hell). But punishment in Sheol is not eternal. The church father Retu'a Haymanot writes, "No Christians are abandoned . . . even if [they] died in sin, without penance, [they are] given penance in hell commensurate to [their] sin, after which [they are] saved for the sake of Christ."

Judaism in Christianity. Ethiopian Christians observe Judaic practices: circumcision, dietary traditions, and Saturday as Sabbath. Why? This has not been satisfactorily answered. Traditional scholars (pointing to Acts 8:26–38) maintain that Ethiopia accepted Judaism before it accepted Christianity. Most historians propose, instead, that the practices were taken from the OT, when Ethiopians embraced Christianity, because these Judaic practices could be associated with local pre-Christian traditions (e.g. circumcision), and combined OT traditions (e.g. dietary traditions) with teachings of the Apostolic* Church Order and Apostolic* Constitutions (parts of the Ethiopian Bible). **See also** **ORTHODOX CHURCHES, ORIENTAL, CLUSTER: ETHIOPIAN ORTHODOX TEWAHEDO CHURCH; RASTAFARI MOVEMENT.**

Statistics: Population (2008): 80 million (estimate). Christians, 60.8% (Orthodox, 50%; Protestants, 10%; independents, 0.6%.; Roman Catholics, 0.2%); Muslims, 32.8%; African Religionists, 4%; other religionists and nonreligious, 2.4%. (*Sources*: 2008 United Nation Population Fund estimate; 1994 Ethiopian census [for religion percentages].)

HAILE GETACHEW

Ethiopian Orthodox Tewahedo Church. See ORTHODOX CHURCHES, ORIENTAL, CLUSTER: ETHIOPIAN ORTHODOX TEWAHEDO CHURCH.

Ethos. Christian thinkers have used the term "ethos" for a cultural style, tone, or orientation permeating collective life. The Greek, *eithos*, denoted a person's or group's character as embodying distinctive ideals. "Ethos" is used in contemporary anthropology and rhetoric. In theology, Paul Tillich*, among others, described religious ideals as uniquely carried in the ethos of group and personal life.

MARK LEWIS TAYLOR

EUCHARIST CLUSTER

Eucharist in Eastern Orthodox Churches
Eucharist in Oriental Orthodox (Non-Chalcedonian) Churches
Eucharist in Western Churches

Eucharist in Eastern Orthodox Churches. See DIVINE LITURGY OF THE ORTHODOX CHURCHES.

Eucharist in Oriental Orthodox (Non-Chalcedonian) Churches follows different liturgical texts. Nevertheless, the theology it involves is not so different, striving to remain faithful to the tradition of the ancient church.

Eucharist is one of the seven sacraments* of Oriental Orthodox churches. Along with baptism*, the Eucharist is deemed essential for salvation*. It symbolizes the final unity of the faithful with Christ through the communion in the Blood and Body of our Lord Jesus Christ.

The Eucharist in Oriental Orthodox churches symbolizes the bloodless sacrifice of our Lord Jesus Christ on the holy altar, the symbol* of the crucifixion* of our Lord. Through the Eucharist, every believer communes with Jesus Christ and participates in the Lord's Supper, at which only Christ's apostles were present. Through the receiving of the holy sacrament, the believers' relationship with God is transformed; now God dwells in each of them; each of the faithful dies for sin and obtains new life, in union with Christ and in hope of resurrection for eternal life.

The Oriental Orthodox churches strongly strive to preserve that union with Christ: the priest delivers both the Body and the Blood of Christ to the faithful, who, having repented and confessed their sins, are strengthened with faith and approach Christ. According to the apostolic order and as a confirmation of this union with Christ, the priest can celebrate the Divine Liturgy only once, and with one bread and one chalice, so that everyone can be one in Christ: "For we being many are one bread, and one body: for we are all partakers of that one bread" (1 Cor. 10:17).

BISHOP YEZNIK PETROSSIAN

Eucharist in Western Churches. From the 3rd c. onward, the beginnings of a distinctively Western approach to eucharistic theology can be noted. Earlier a diversity of eucharistic meanings and definitions coexisted with little apparent difficulty. But there was also a substantial unity that undergirded the various approaches: the Eucharist was seen as a sacrificial* act of the whole Christian community made in union with Christ, and it provided the nourishment for the community's own self-recognition as Christ's body* within the world. When the debates did eventually come – and there were some very serious ones during the Middle Ages and the Reformation – they often focused on the subject of sacrifice and presence*: the relationship between the sacrifice of Christ on Calvary and the Eucharist, and exactly how Christ was present in the Eucharist elements. What is abundantly clear in the Western patristic eucharistic tradition is the emphasis given to the communal dimension: the grace* that was given in the Eucharist bound members of the liturgical assembly one to another and corporately into the body of Christ, the church*. This is evident in the North African writings of Cyprian* of Carthage (d258) and especially Augustine* of Hippo (d430). Gradually, attention shifted to Christ as both the one who offers the sacrifice and who is himself offered. Ambrose* of Milan (d397) gave emphasis to the personal encounter between the communicant and Christ in the Eucharist and paved the way for a medieval shift toward concerns about the individual in relationship to the eucharistic sacrifice.

The 9th c. witnessed the first controversies over the nature of the eucharistic presence in contrasting the approaches of two monks from the same monastery of Corbie: Paschasius* (d860) defended a more realistic approach that would become normative within medieval eucharistic theology, while Ratramnus* (d868) argued for a more symbolic approach. In the 11th c., a new controversy was introduced by Berengarius* of Tours (d1088), who opposed the real presence of Christ. The Fourth Lateran* Council (1215) definitively established the doctrine of transubstantiation*, affirming that during the Mass* the bread and wine are substantially changed into the Body and Blood of Christ with only the accidents (i.e. outward appearances) remaining. Thomas Aquinas* (d1274) added significantly to the discussion in applying the categories of Aristotelian metaphysics to the Eucharist. Such theological developments led to greater eucharistic devotion outside of Mass (benediction, processions, etc.) and the establishment of the Feast of Corpus Christi (the Body and Blood of Christ) in 1264. Mass came to be viewed as a personal devotion for clergy as well as laity. Private Masses abounded and the "fruit" of the sacrifice of the Mass came to be applied to living and deceased, with monetary offerings given to clergy who officiated. Indeed, 12th-c. England witnessed the emergence of "chantry priests," who did nothing more than say Mass throughout the day for the list of intentions they had received. Numerous liturgical abuses grew in this period, especially around Mass stipends and the giving of indulgences*.

The 16th-c. Reformation was strong in its condemnation of such abuses and criticized a eucharistic piety that was a far cry from what the patristics had promoted. Faithful to his Augustinian roots, Luther* (d1546) accepted the language of the Mass as a sacrifice of praise and thanksgiving, but found the medieval language of propitiatory* sacrifice linked to Christ's death on the cross to be more problematic. He also challenged the doctrine of transubstantiation, arguing that during the Eucharist Christ is present "in, with, and under" the elements (consubstantiation*) even as the bread and wine coexisted with the Lord's Body and Blood. The Swiss Reformer Zwingli* (d1531) advocated the Eucharist as a memorial in which the bread and wine remained completely unchanged. Calvin* (d1564) attempted a *via media* between the two, arguing that through the power of the Holy* Spirit, Christians are raised up to eat and drink with Christ at the Eucharist, whom they receive spiritually by faith in eating the bread and drinking the wine.

The Council of Trent* reaffirmed the doctrine of transubstantiation in its 13th session (1551) in much greater detail than what had been established at the Fourth Lateran Council. Ten years after Trent's decree on the Eucharist, the doctrine of the sacrifice of the Mass was discussed and affirmed at the same council in its 22nd session (1562), stating that the Mass was the true and propitiatory sacrifice instituted by Christ and could be offered for the living and dead, but did not detract from the sacrifice of the cross. Special attention was given to the efficacy of the sacrifice.

Vatican* II (1962–65) reaffirmed the sacrificial nature of the Eucharist as defined by Trent. But it was posited within the wider context of the liturgical community, recognizing the manifold presence of Christ within the Eucharist and the church. Post–Vatican II theology has given much attention to the threefold presence of Christ in the Eucharist: in the gathered assembly, in the Word proclaimed, and in the Eucharist. Moreover, Western churches are recovering the important role of the Holy Spirit in transforming not only the bread and wine but also the community as it lives the Eucharist within the world. The later 20th c. also saw the Christian churches reaching significant convergence not only on liturgical structures but also on how Christians can speak together about eucharistic sacrifice and presence. This was especially evident in the 1982 Lima text of the World* Council of Churches, *Baptism, Eucharist and Ministry*. Globalization* and postmodernism* offer fresh challenges for the continuing evolution of eucharistic theology in the 21st c. **See also ATONEMENT; COMMUNION; SACRIFICE.**

KEITH F. PECKLERS, SJ

Eucharistic Congresses. The First Eucharistic Congress, held in Lille (1881), was initiated by a Roman Catholic laywoman, Emilie Tamisier (d1910), herself inspired by the "apostle of the Eucharist," Peter Julian Eymard (d1868). The theme was that "the Eucharist saves the world," offering the remedy of faith in the real presence of Christ in the Eucharist as a corrective to religious indifference (see Secularism and Secularization). During the 20th c., the congresses continued to grow and became internationalized during the pontificate of Pius* XI, being celebrated on all continents and taking on a missionary as well as ecumenical and interreligious dimensions. Their fundamental intention is to increase understanding of and participation in the eucharistic mystery*. In 1986 Pope John* Paul II promoted the Vatican office for International Eucharistic Congresses to the level of a pontifical committee. **See also EUCHARIST CLUSTER.** KEITH F. PECKLERS, SJ

Eucharistic Fast. Less an ascetic* practice than a means of proper disposition for receiving Holy Communion, the eucharistic fast consists of complete abstinence from food and drink until the sacrament has been received. It originated in the 4th c. In the Roman Catholic Church, until the 1950s fasting began at midnight on the night before Eucharist. Changes in the law on eucharistic fasting were brought about by Pope Pius* XII (1953, 1957), Pope Paul* VI (1964), and the Congregation for Divine Worship and the Discipline of the Sacraments (1973). The 1983 Code of Canon Law states that one normally abstains from food and drink for one hour before communicating and that the drinking of water does not constitute a break in the fast. **See also EUCHARIST CLUSTER.**

KEITH F. PECKLERS, SJ

Eucharistic Prayer (Canon of the Mass), central prayer of praise and thanksgiving within the Eucharist*. Trinitarian in structure and recited by the president (bishop, priest, pastor), it recalls God's salvific deeds in the paschal mystery of Christ. The Eucharistic Prayer begins with the preface dialogue "Lift up Your Hearts!" and concludes with the "Great Amen." In the Roman Catholic Church, it was formerly called the "Canon," meaning something fixed or unchanging, normally referring to the Roman Canon (Eucharistic Prayer I in the current Roman Missal); dating from the late 4th c., it is the oldest extant eucharistic prayer in the West. In the Middle Ages, it came to be prayed silently by the priest both to increase its sacral nature and sense of mystery and because it was no longer necessary for the Mass* to take account of the assembly in a direct way.

Since Vatican* II (1962–65), the consecratory nature of the entire prayer has been recovered, so that consecration is not limited to the words of institution, "Take and eat," "Take and drink." Today the Eucharistic Prayer's communal dimension has also been recovered along with the Holy* Spirit's role in transforming not only the bread and wine but also those present who partake of the sacrament. The assembly participates actively in the prayer, singing the various acclamations interspersed throughout. As in the liturgical books of other Christian churches, the current Roman Missal offers a number of new eucharistic prayers to be used in certain contexts and circumstances.

KEITH F. PECKLERS, SJ

Euchological Prayers (of praise to God) include the Eucharistic* Prayers (a major type) as well as, e.g., prayers of dedication of a new or renovated church, the prayer of dedication of a new altar, and the prayer of blessing over the water to be used for baptism.

Euchologion, in Orthodox* churches, a liturgical book that contains the services and prayers used for the sacraments. One of the earliest one (4th c.) is that of Serapion of Thmuis.

Eudocia (c460), Roman empress. Originally named Athenaïs, probably from Antioch, the daughter of an Athenian intellectual, she was Theodosius* II's wife. Before being married she was baptized, taking the Christian name Eudocia (421). As empress she used her influence to promote tolerance of non-Christian intellectuals and teachers in the nascent "university" of Constantinople. She traveled to Jerusalem (438), visited the monastery of Melania* the Younger on the Mount of Olives*, was at the dedication of the Church of St. Stephen*, and brought back relics of Stephen. Because of rivalry with Pulcheria*, she left permanently for Jerusalem (443) and favored the doctrine of Eutyches* concerning the "one nature" of Christ.

Eudoxius (c300–70), Anomoian* leader. Born in Armenia, he became successively bishop of Germanicia, of Antioch*, and of Constantinople* under the sponsorship of Arian* bishops and emperors.

Eugenicus, Mark (1394–1445), scholar and monk declared a saint by the Eastern Orthodox Church (1734). Born in Constantinople, son of a deacon, he served as metropolitan of Ephesus and as a delegate to the Council of Florence*, where he was an outspoken opponent of the *Filioque** and of reunion with the West. Despite being threatened in Florence, he returned safely to the East and continued to write against Western doctrine and against union. On his deathbed, he persuaded George Scholarius (later Patriarch Gennadios* II) to assume leadership of the opponents of the union.

Eunomius (c325–96), theologian. Like his master, Aetius, who was considered a radical Arian*, Eunomius rejected *homoousios**. For him Father and Son could be distinct only if their essences were *anomoios*, "dissimilar," to one another. His followers were therefore called "Anomoians" by their opponents. Appointed bishop of Cyzicus, Eunomius was soon exiled for heresy*. According to his unique theory of language, God's name (expressed verbally as "Unbegotten") revealed his essence perfectly but not discursively. Nicenes and Arians alike rejected him but were required to clarify their own positions. Condemned by the Council of Constantinople*, his church survived into the 6th c.

RICHARD VAGGIONE

Eunuch, castrated male. Commonly used in harems, eunuchs often became important court officials. The Bible refers to their presence in Egypt (Gen 37:36, 40:2, 7), Israel (1 Kgs 22:9; 2 Kgs 8:6, 9:32, 24:15, 25:19), Babylon (Esth 1:10, 2:21), and Ethiopia (Acts 8:27–39). Because of their physical mutilation, eunuchs were initially excluded from worship (Deut. 23:1), but later were welcomed (Isa 56:3–5: Acts 8:36–38).

Europe, History of Christianity in. See HISTORY OF CHRISTIANITY CLUSTER: IN EUROPE: EASTERN EUROPE; HISTORY OF CHRISTIANITY CLUSTER: IN EUROPE: WESTERN EUROPE.

Eusebian Canons, the tables prepared by Eusebius* of Caesarea to enable readers to find parallel sections in the four Gospels*, often copied in manuscripts of the Gospels. Their function has been succeeded by Gospel parallels and the division of the text into chapters and verses.

Eusebius of Caesarea (c260–c339), Christian Apologist, theologian, scholar. Eusebius studied in Caesarea under Origen's pupil Pamphilus; after Pamphilus's martyrdom, he completed Pamphilus's *Apology*. Like Origen, he became a prolific theologian and exegete, compiling *Onomasticon* (a glossary of Hebrew names in scripture), although Eusebius did not adopt Origen's allegorical methods in his commentaries on Luke, Isaiah, and the stories of God's appearances in the OT. His most notable apologetic work is the *Preparation for the Gospel*, a 15-book compilation of texts designed to reveal convergences of Greek thought and Christianity. Among his early theological works, the 10-book *Demonstration of the Gospel* corroborates the main tenets of Christianity from the OT.

Eusebius's *Ecclesiastical History*, the chief source of the history of the church before Constantine*, is particularly important because it incorporates unedited documents. The last of its 10 books was heavily revised around 317, after the dissolution of Constantine's alliance with Licinius, the non-Christian emperor of the East; some scholars maintained (though this is doubted) that the original version terminated before the persecution of 303.

Elected bishop of Caesarea (c313), Eusebius welcomed the return of synodical government after Constantine's seizure of the Eastern throne (324). He signed the creed promulgated at the Council of Nicaea* (325), which affirmed the consubstantiality of God the Father and God the Son (see Trinity in Eastern Orthodoxy; Trinity in the Western Tradition). But he never admitted that the Son was equal to or coeternal with the Father, and resented the later attempts of Athanasius* to force these views on the church.

There is evidence that Eusebius's enemies secured a condemnation of his views (because of Arian* tendencies) in Antioch before the Council of Nicaea, yet it was not he but his bugbear, Bishop Marcellus of Ancyra (the interlocutor of his *Against Marcellus* and *Ecclesiastical Theology*), who was finally deposed. Constantine offered the See of Antioch to Eusebius, who declined it. Admiring the emperor to the point of adulation, he wrote a four-book hagiography of him, again transcribing many original documents, and extolled him as the vicar of Christ on earth in his *Tricennial Oration* (336).

MARK J. EDWARDS

Eusebius of Dorylaeum (mid-5th c.). A lawyer in Constantinople, he sounded the alarm over Nestorius's* teachings; he accused him (wrongly) of Adoptionism* (429). Once again in reference to the humanity and divinity of Christ, as bishop of Dorylaeum, Eusebius attacked Eutyches'* teaching, claiming it was heretical for committing the opposite error, Monophysitism* (according to which Christ had a single, divine nature) (448). Deposed by the Second Council of Ephesus*, he took a leading role in the Council of Chalcedon* (451) after the new emperor reinstated him.

Eusebius of Emesa (c300–c354/59), bishop, theologian, exegete; born in Edessa*, where he was educated in Scripture and Greek literature. Eusebius was a student of both Patrophilus of Scythopolis and Eusebius* of Caesarea; then he studied in Antioch* and Alexandria*. He declined the Episcopal See of Alexandria during Athanasius's* exile and became bishop of Emesa. His surviving works include Greek fragments, sermons in Latin translation, and *Commentary on the Octateuch and Reigns* in Armenian translation. As an exegete of the Antiochene school, Eusebius discussed translation problems and drew on Jewish traditions. He opposed Arianism* and emphasized the limits of human knowledge.

UTE POSSEKEL

Eusebius of Nicomedia (early 4th c.). Bishop of Nicomedia and a disciple of Lucian* of Antioch, he championed the Arian* party. He obtained the deposition of Athanasius* (335), baptized Constantine* before his death (337), and was a leader at the Council of Antioch* (341), which attempted to supplement or replace the Nicene* Creed with four others.

Eusebius of Vercelli (d371), a supporter of the Nicene* Creed; exiled in the East (355–62). He was one of the first bishops to live with his clergy under a rule*, a pattern adopted in the Augustinian* Rule and by the canons* regular.

Eustathius of Antioch (early 4th c.). As bishop of Antioch, he played a major role in the Council of Nicaea* (325). Because of his insistence on divine unity and the reality of Christ's human soul, he was accused, respectively, of Sabellianism* and Adoptionism*. He was deposed within a few years at the instigation of Eusebius* of Caesarea and died in exile.

Eustathius of Sebaste (c300–c380), bishop in Pontus, a moderate Arian* who affirmed the Homoiousian* position at the Synod of Ancyra* (358). Later he supported the position of the Pneumatomachi*, denying the full divinity of the Holy* Spirit. He exerted his greatest influence in organizing a new mode of monastic life, with an asceticism* based on the Sermon on the Mount (Matt 5–7) and the earliest church (Acts 2:44–45, 4:32–35); he emphasized manual labor and works of charity, and minimized differences of class and gender. He probably influenced Macrina* and Basil* of Caesarea more than they or their admirers acknowledged.

Eustochium, Julia (c368–419/20). Born in Rome, daughter of the Roman senator Toxotius and Paula*, she directed a monastery for women in Bethlehem (404), where she died.

Eustochium was one of five children born to Paula and Toxotius, descending from the Scipios and the Gracchi on her mother's side and the Julians on her father's side (after whom Eustochium was called "Julia"). Around age 16, Eustochium vowed to remain a virgin* (384) and adopted a life of ascetic* discipline, directed by her mother, Paula, and the Roman noblewoman Marcella*. Along with these women, she studied under Jerome* and was praised for her learning, especially her proficiency in Hebrew. After her father's death, she accompanied Paula on a pilgrimage to the Holy Land and a visit to the monks of Egypt. She settled in Bethlehem, helping to establish two monasteries – one for men and another for women – and a hospice for pilgrims (see Hospitality). Upon her mother's death in 404, she assumed supervision of the women's monastery until her own death.

Jerome dedicated to Eustochium several biblical translations and commentaries, and addressed numerous letters to Eustochium, among which is *Epistle* 22, his best-known outline of (female) ascetic discipline.

KRISTI UPSON-SAIA

Euthanasia (Gk "gentle death"), termination of life for humanitarian reasons: unbearable suffering, incurable physical degeneration, cessation of brain function, loss of quality of life, and even (most controversially) "defective" mental or physical capacity (of infants or adults). Christian views of euthanasia balance in different ways the "sanctity" and "quality" of human life. At the minimum ("passive euthanasia"), euthanasia involves not pursuing extraordinary, difficult, or burdensome means to prolong life, or not resuscitating a patient after heart failure with his or her consent. Intermediate measures ("active euthanasia") include withdrawal of artificial medical support (e.g. feeding tubes, electrical stimulation). The Roman Catholic Church has explicitly condemned active euthanasia as incompatible with the sanctity of human life, but despite recent ambivalence it has had a long tradition of supporting passive euthanasia. The Eastern Orthodox* Church seeks to maintain a balance between quality of life and sanctity of life. Other churches express even greater concern about the "quality" of human life. Protestant and independent churches hold diverse views all along this continuum. But euthanasia that involves physician-assisted actions to stop vital functions – physician-assisted suicide – is most often rejected. **See also DEATH, CHRISTIAN VIEWS OF, CLUSTER; DYING, CARE OF THE, AN EASTERN ORTHODOX PERSPECTIVE; HOSPICE; MEDICAL ETHICS.**

Eutyches (c378–454), archimandrite* in Constantinople. He opposed Nestorianism* (according to which Jesus' humanity and divinity were joined by will, not by nature) but was accused by Eusebius* of Dorylaeum of taking the opposite view: that of Monophysitism* (according to which Christ had a single nature) (448). He acknowledged that Christ was *"from* two natures" but insisted on *"in* one nature after the union," which seemed to deny the reality of Christ's humanity. This allowed him to emphasize Christ's divinity as the power at work in transforming human beings, overcoming the power of evil (rather than emphasizing that the cause of this transformation must be human as well as divine, as Antiochenes did). Eutyches, championed by Theodosius* II, was exonerated at the Second Council of Ephesus (449), but deposed and exiled by the Council of Chalcedon* (451) and rejected by Miaphysites*.

Evagrius of Pontus (345–99), monk, early theorist of Christian mysticism*. Evagrius grew up in Pontus, near the Black Sea. Ordained deacon* by Gregory* of Nazianzus, he earned fame in Constantinople defending (c380) the emerging trinitarian* doctrine. After an affair with an aristocratic woman, he fled to Jerusalem, where Melania* the Elder convinced him to become a monk. In 383 he moved to Egypt, settling first in Nitria (one of the centers of Egyptian monasticism on the cliff separating the Nile from the desert), then in Kellia. He apprenticed under Macarius the Egyptian and emerged as the leader of a circle of intellectual monks.

Evagrius's writings, terse, technical, and sometimes cryptic, appear mostly in collections of numbered paragraphs (chapters, *kephalaia*). In *The Monk* (*Praktikos*), he classifies temptations according to "eight thoughts," a scheme that shaped later medieval teaching on the seven deadly* sins. In *Chapters on Prayer*, he advocates unceasing wordless and imageless prayer* and plots stages in the soul's* journey to God.

The Second Council of Constantinople (553) posthumously condemned Evagrius for Origenism*; his friends and disciples, branded Origenist heretics*, were hounded out of Egypt. His works survived, preserved mainly under others' names or in Syriac translations. Twentieth-century scholars rediscovered his works and recognized how profoundly he had influenced classic mystical traditions, in both the East and the West. **See also MONASTICISM CLUSTER: SYRIAC TRADITION.**

J. WILLIAM HARMLESS, SJ

Evangelical, having to do with the gospel (Gk *euangelion*). (1) The adjective often refers to the teachings and way of life found in the Gospels*. (2) The verb "to evangelize" has been used, starting with the NT, to refer to the proclamation of the gospel as good tidings (see Evangelism or Evangelization). (3) During the Reformation*, "Evangelical" was the name given to Protestant* churches in Germany and Switzerland because of their emphasis on the gospel of justification* by faith*. Likewise in Latin America it is the common designation for Protestants. The Evangelical* Alliance of the 19th c. was an international partnership of Protestant churches, emphasizing the gospel as that which unified them. (4) Since Wesley* and the Great* Awakening, the term has been applied to movements emphasizing proclamation and personal transformation, usually in reaction against liberalism* or conventional religiosity (see Evangelicals/Evangelicalism Cluster). (5) Negatively, "evangelical" can denote excessive zealousness in proclaiming or defending a cause.

Evangelical Alliance, voluntary organization founded in London (1846), building on the heritage of John and Charles Wesley* and the London Missionary Society. Its initial emphasis was on Christian unity, but it has diverged from the ecumenical* movement because of its stricter Evangelical* doctrinal standards. The organization in the USA is called the World Evangelical Fellowship; globally, the World Evangelical Alliance is based in Vancouver. Parallel organizations are the Lausanne* Group and the National* Association of Evangelicals.

Evangelical Lutheran Church in America (ELCA). See LUTHERANISM CLUSTER: IN THE UNITED STATES: EVANGELICAL LUTHERAN CHURCH IN AMERICA (ELCA).

EVANGELICALS/EVANGELICALISM CLUSTER

1) *Introductory Entry*

Evangelicals/Evangelicalism and Evangelical Theologies

2) *A Sampling of Evangelicals/Evangelicalism*

Evangelicals/Evangelicalism in Asia
Evangelicals/Evangelicalism in Asia: The Philippines
Evangelicals/Evangelicalism in Australia and the South Pacific
Evangelicals/Evangelicalism in Latin America
Evangelicals/Evangelicalism in Latin America: Mexico
Evangelicals/Evangelicalism in North America
Evangelicals/Evangelicalism in the United Kingdom

1) Introductory Entry

Evangelicals/Evangelicalism and Evangelical Theologies. Evangelicalism is a largely modern, interdenominational movement with roots in both early Christianity and the Protestant Reformation*. Evangelicals and their theologies are diverse, but virtually all of them adhere to the authority and sufficiency of Scripture*, the centrality of the cross*, the imperative of transdenominational gospel promotion (see Evangelism or Evangelization), and the necessity of spiritual rebirth. The story of modern Evangelical theology began in Europe, gained momentum in the larger Western world, and now flourishes throughout the Southern Hemisphere.

Evangelicalism in Continental Europe. The 16th-c. Protestant Reformation* in Europe called for a return to what its leaders (Luther*, Zwingli*, most Anabaptists*, Calvin*, and others) deemed the central teachings of the NT: *sola fide, sola gratia, sola scriptura,* and *solus Christus.* Most of them taught that Scripture should function as the ultimate doctrinal norm (*sola scriptura*) and that salvation* from sin* and death* (see Atonement #2) is granted by grace* alone (*sola gratia*) through faith* (*sola fide*) in Christ* alone (*solus Christus*). They differed among themselves over other doctrinal matters (Christology*, the Eucharist*, and the relation of church* and state). But they agreed that the medieval churches needed major reforms and that the reforms they favored had apostolic warrant. This understanding of "Evangelicals" remained nearly unchanged in continental Europe until today.

Evangelicalism in the United Kingdom and North America from the 18th Century. A different understanding of "Evangelicals" appeared in the 18th c. with the renewal movements that spanned the Atlantic Ocean during the so-called Great* Awakenings of Great Britain, Ireland, and the Americas. These renewal movements reaffirmed the faith of the Reformation, infusing it with Pietist* and revivalist* practices inspired by British Puritanism* and Continental Pietism. The need for conversion*, personal piety, and ecumenical witness became essential to Evangelicalism after the Awakenings.

Jonathan Edwards* and John Wesley* were key leaders of the Awakenings. Edwards was a Calvinist* minister who clarified the tenets of Reformed Protestantism in the midst of the revivals. His theological treatise *Religious Affections* distinguished true religion as a matter of love for God, and his *Freedom of the Will* gave Calvinists theological ground from which to evangelize cross-culturally. Wesley was an Arminian* minister who helped to inaugurate the Methodist Movement within the Church of England. His doctrine of entire sanctification* fueled the development of the Holiness* Movement in subsequent centuries. He believed that Christians should seek and receive a second work of divine grace* (after the first work of justification*). He taught that this "second blessing" rendered them entirely sanctified and no longer prone to sin voluntarily.

During the 19th c., Evangelicals institutionalized revival and used it to foster further renewal through the Holiness* Movement. Holiness people are deeply committed to personal sanctification, set apart from worldliness, and empowered by the Holy* Spirit. Charles G. Finney* and Phoebe Palmer* were their important early leaders. They preached in both Britain and North America. Finney rooted his gradualist notion of Christian perfection ("Oberlin Perfectionism") on Edwards's doctrine of "natural ability" (rather than Wesley's second blessing). Palmer popularized a Wesleyan form of perfectionism by means of her so-called altar theology.

By the late 19th c., Pentecostalism* emerged out of the Holiness revivals. Pentecostals are the most intense Holiness adherents, fervent about the special gifts of the Spirit (charismata*). They practice speaking in tongues*, a *third* blessing, which they believe attends the baptism* in the Spirit. Charles Fox Parham and William Seymour were key founders of Pentecostalism. The Charismatic* Movement introduced Holiness/Pentecostal concerns in the mainline churches, gaining prominence near the mid-20th c.

Evangelicalism in the Two-thirds World. Holiness/Pentecostalism proliferated in the Southern Hemisphere during late 20th c., although it had penetrated Africa, Latin America, and Asia in the early 20th c., often from Europe. Thus in Latin America, and often in Africa and Asia, the term "Evangelical" refers to all Protestants, as it does in continental Europe.

Most 21st-c. Christians live in the Southern Hemisphere, and Charismatics* (also known as Pentecostals) there constitute the fastest-growing segment of Evangelicalism today. Africa contains a wide constituency of Evangelicals in African* Instituted Churches and in traditional congregations (e.g. Anglican, Catholic, Methodist, Presbyterian), most of which include charismatic groups. Charismatics account for the vast majority of Protestant growth in recent Latin American history. They also thrive in East Asian contexts, such as China and Korea.

North American and British Evangelicals continue to fight for orthodoxy in cultures inclined to question their convictions regarding traditional Christian worldviews. Fundamentalists* and neo-Evangelicals, e.g., defend the literal truth of Scripture in the face of Modernism*. Non-Western Evangelicals also maintain a vibrant orthodoxy, but do so with less concern for defending the traditions of the West. They stress supernatural intervention in daily living and nurture a Restorationist* desire to repristinate the faith of the apostles. They are spiritually exuberant and exceptionally prolific. Many of them now look to the West with missionary intent. Indeed, Evangelical theology continues to thrive today, shaped by the members of an increasingly global community.

ELIZABETH MASON CURRIER and DOUGLAS SWEENEY

2) A Sampling of Evangelicals/Evangelicalism

Evangelicals/Evangelicalism in Asia. The word "Evangelical" is rather loosely used in the Asian context. Most Protestant churches in Asia were established in connection with the Evangelical revival* within the mainline Protestant churches in Europe and share with them a common "Evangelical tradition" in theology and spirituality. Furthermore, the conflict in the USA between Christians rooted in a conservative approach to Scripture* and theology and those considered "liberals" would gradually have an impact on countries worldwide, including Asia. Building on the formation of the World Evangelical Alliance (1846), the National Association of Evangelicals in the USA (1942) developed a specific theological and missionary profile that deeply influenced Asian Evangelicalism. In addition, the International Conference on World Evangelization (Lausanne, 1974) popularized and reinforced Evangelicalism in Asia.

The Evangelical Fellowship of Asia (founded in 1983) is a fellowship of national Evangelical alliances in Asian countries, where in various configurations one usually finds two kinds of Evangelical expression. (1) In most mainline Protestant churches, there are groups that identify themselves as "Evangelicals," including youth groups and movements such as the Evangelical Union, Campus Crusade, and Youth for Christ. (2) The National Alliance brings together Evangelical churches, as well as mission agencies and movements with an Evangelical orientation. Evangelicalism in Asia, following the conservative–liberal controversies in the USA, is primarily a theological movement aimed at safeguarding what it views as the "orthodox" Protestant faith, namely the belief that the Bible/Scripture* is divinely inspired and is the final authority in matters of faith and practice; the atoning death of Christ on the cross for human salvation* (see Atonement #2); personal faith*; spiritual renewal through the power of the Holy* Spirit; and the conviction* that Christians are called to engage in the evangelizing mission* to bring others to personal faith in Jesus Christ. Even though these convictions are the kernel of Evangelicalism everywhere, they are developed in various ways in Asia.

Beside safeguarding the "orthodox" Protestant faith, the Evangelical Fellowship of Asia has a seven-point emphasis as it develops networks and strengthens Evangelicalism in Asia: two traditional emphases, mission and church planting, and theology and church renewal; and five forward-looking emphases, regarding religious liberty, social concerns, women's ministry, youth ministry, and leadership development. The Asia Theological Association (since 1970) brings together the theological educational institutions in Asia committed to Evangelical faith and scholarship. S. WESLEY ARIARAJAH

Evangelicals/Evangelicalism in Asia: The Philippines. In the Philippines, the term "Evangelical" designates the members of the many Charismatic*, Pentecostal*, and fundamentalist* churches and parachurches* that have been organized primarily since the 1950s. The missionaries who established most of these churches came from fundamentalist and Pentecostal groups in North America.

In the 1960s, the leaders of these denominations and parachurches* felt the need to organize but did not want to join the National* Council of Churches in the Philippines because they believed that it had become too "modernist" or "liberal" in its theological orientation. These Charismatic, Pentecostal, and fundamentalist Evangelical groups define an Evangelical as one who affirms the traditional fundamentals of the faith, particularly the divinity, humanity, and substitutionary atonement* (see Atonement #2) of Jesus Christ; the total depravity of humans (see Sin*) and salvation* by grace* through faith in Christ alone (see Faith #3); and the inerrancy* and final authority of the Scriptures* in faith and practice.

In 1964 a core of Christian leaders met at the First Baptist Church Manila and discussed the founding of an organization that would express the Evangelicals' oneness in Christ. After several meetings, they formed the Philippine Council of Evangelical Churches, Inc., composed of more than 54 denominations (in 2000), with Bishop Efraim Tendero as general secretary (from 1993). The two largest denominational members are the Association of Bible Christian Communities of the Philippines and the Christian and Missionary Alliance Churches of the Philippines. **See also PHILIPPINES.** VICTOR AGUILAN

Evangelicals/Evangelicalism in Australia and the South Pacific. Evangelicals were the pioneers of Christianity in Australia* and the Pacific Islands. The convict chaplains were mostly Evangelical Anglicans* and Methodists*. As the number of settlers grew, other denominations were established – Presbyterian*, Baptist*, and Congregationalist* – all strongly committed to Evangelicalism. Another Evangelical strand came with Lutherans* from Prussia. Pacific Islanders were actively involved in regional evangelism as far away as Melanesia. In Australia successive visiting evangelists reinforced the Evangelical message, also regularly proclaimed by ministers, lay preachers, Sunday school teachers, and youth leaders. Agencies such as the YMCA* and YWCA*, Christian Endeavour, and temperance* movements also underlined conversion*, education*, and social service, which fostered Evangelical identity, as did burgeoning overseas missions, and new denominations.

Evangelical theology was challenged by new emphases in biblical scholarship (see Bible Interpretation Cluster: History of), science*, and philosophy*. By the mid-20th c., these dominated the major denominations, but Evangelicals' Bible colleges upheld traditional convictions. The Anglican Diocese of Sydney was an Evangelical stronghold. Melbourne Anglicans founded Ridley College, vital to Evangelical identity. Annual conventions nourished lively piety, missionary enthusiasm, and support by many generous business and professional families. Crusaders in high schools and Evangelical groups in universities linked Evangelical theological positions with modern knowledge. Periodicals, books, and papers kept Evangelicals in touch with worldwide developments. North American influences grew during the late 20th c.; Billy Graham's visits gave Evangelicals fresh inspiration. Sydney Anglicans such as Archbishops Mowll, Loane, Robinson, and Jensen and theologians such as T. C. Hammond and D. B. Knox were influential far beyond Australia. The Evangelical Fellowship in the Anglican Communion owed much to the Sydney leadership, as did the Lausanne* movement. World Vision Australia symbolizes the social conscience of Evangelicalism and its ability to tap into compassion for social justice, making it the largest aid and development agency in Australia (as exemplified by Alan Walker, a Sydney Methodist). Many Pacific Islanders contributed to evangelism in the Papua New Guinea Highlands starting in 1945.

The emergence of strong Pentecostal*/Charismatic* churches and groups in major churches contributed to the renaissance of Evangelicalism. Important networks of Aboriginal* Christians grew out of the revival that started on Elcho Island. Migrant churches from Asia and the Pacific brought additional strands into Evangelicalism. Innovative media work and the development of Christian music and hymnody and of a younger generation of scholars, along with ministerial and lay leaders, have given Evangelicalism the ability to deal with changes. IAN BREWARD

Evangelicals/Evangelicalism in Latin America. See PROTESTANTISM CLUSTER: IN LATIN AMERICA.

Evangelicals/Evangelicalism in Latin America: Mexico. "Evangelical" commonly designates in Mexico all Protestant churches (as in continental Europe). North American Protestant missionaries started arriving in Mexico in 1840. By 1916 Protestantism still followed the model of the American Evangelicalism of the Second Awakening* and of revivalism* characterized by individualism, salvation* through Christ's vicarious atonement (see Atonement #2), and sanctification*.

After World War II, a new wave of missionaries belonging to the Holiness*

Movement arrived in Mexico, often emphasizing Millennialist* and fundamentalist* interpretations of the Bible. This early Charismatic* Evangelical Movement represented a "reactionary faith" – a faith reacting to what believers perceived as the threat of secularism*, science*, and communism (see Marxism and Christianity). By contrast, the Methodist, Presbyterian, and Baptist churches were hardly influenced by these reactionary attitudes, although many of the members of this early Charismatic Evangelical Movement came from these churches. This movement was marked by dualism* and Holy* Spirit experience, by an ethics of separation from the "world," and by a legalistic inflexibility. As in the rest of the Protestant tradition, for this movement the Bible remained the only basis for faith* and ethics*, yet now with a literalistic* reading of the Bible, an emphasis on individual conversion* (being "born again"), and missionary zeal.

With this radicalization of the Evangelical ethos*, and in the context of the cold war, Evangelical communities, particularly in institutions of theological education, developed alternative positions that emphasized, together with a more ecumenical attitude, Christians' social and political responsibilities. The Congress of Oaxtepec (1979) and the journal *Cristianismo y sociedad* (Christianity and society) represented a shift in the conceptualization of the mission of Evangelicals in Latin America: an integral component of mission now includes the transformation of society. Similarly, the Latin American Theological Fraternity (1970) reestablished the connection of Evangelicalism with the Evangelical tradition of the 16th- to 17th-c. Anabaptist Movement, and reread the Bible in light of the integral commitment of the mission of the church.

JAVIER ULLOA

Evangelicals/Evangelicalism in North America. Evangelicals in North America are characterized by diversity, voluntarism, and allegiance to their mission of gospel witness around the world. Most members of this movement are Protestant, but others identify with Evangelicalism without affirming all of its tenets. The Evangelical Movement is rooted in a view of classical Christian orthodoxy defined largely by a Protestant understanding of the gospel (see the present cluster: Introductory Entry) and distinguished by its origins in 18th-c. European and North American colonial revivals*.

These practices sprang up during the Great* Awakenings (c1720s–1750s) of Europe and the colonial USA, which called for adherence to biblical teaching from the pulpit, as well as from small-group and individual Bible study. The goal of revivalism* was personal and corporate repentance* from sin* and personal and corporate devotion to Jesus as Lord*, a transformation empowered by Scripture* and the Holy* Spirit. On the social level, the Great Awakening saw unprecedented interethnic, interregional, and interdenominational efforts to promote the gospel in North America, which emerged as the center of the Evangelical Movement.

America's Second Great Awakening (late 18th c. to the 1830s) was diverse. It was led by Calvinist* Edwardsian* ministers in New England, Charles Finney* and his "inconsistent Calvinism" in upstate New York, and Methodists*, along with Baptists* and Presbyterians* with Arminian* tendencies, in the Cumberland River valley. The disestablishment and democratization of US religion accompanied these revivals. Previously marginal groups gained a greater opportunity to minister; grassroots gospel promotion led to a populist orientation and contextual expression of Evangelicalism.

Evangelical institutions propelled by a new voluntarism moved to the center of US culture, spearheading social reform in the early 19th c. Evangelicals, women prominent among them, led the Temperance* Movement, worked for the abolition of slavery*, and ministered to the poor*. The rise of naturalism and Modernism* provoked the 20th-c. fundamentalist* controversy and the retreat of Evangelicals from social involvement. Many Evangelicals gathered around the fundamentals of their faith, defined in the *Five Point Deliverance* (1910) as the inerrancy* of Scripture, the virgin* birth, penal substitutionary atonement*, Jesus' bodily resurrection*, and the historicity of biblical miracles*, yet many ignored the social implications of these fundamentals.

Neo-Evangelicals emerged from the doldrums of a defeated fundamentalism in the 1930s and 1940s to reengage North American culture. Their goal was "cooperation without compromise": to uphold fundamentalist doctrinal convictions *and* sociocultural involvement. Billy Graham was their unmistakable leader.

With the shift of the center of the Evangelical Movement from North America to the Southern Hemisphere, the prevailing tenor has also changed, dominated now by Holiness*, Pentecostal*, and Charismatic* congregations. Since Evangelicals are "people of the book" committed to constant renewal and contextual expressions of historic Christianity, the future of Evangelicalism in North America depends on engagement and collaboration, not only with its historic roots, but also with these newer Christian traditions.

ELIZABETH MASON CURRIER and DOUGLAS SWEENEY

Evangelicals/Evangelicalism in the United Kingdom. Evangelicals claim to represent the most authentic tradition of biblical Christianity and Reformation Protestantism*, even though their existence as a recognized movement dates only from the late 1730s. In that decade, the preaching of John Wesley*, George Whitefield*, and others not only launched Methodism* but established the broader Evangelical tradition as a seminal influence in British Protestant churches. Evangelicals strongly emphasize the authority of the Bible as Scripture* (although not necessarily insisting on its verbal inerrancy*), the necessity of personal conversion* and acceptance of Christ, the belief in the pivotal theological and devotional significance of substitutionary atonement (see Atonement #2), and zealous activism in spreading the gospel in order to transform society.

By the mid-19th c., Evangelicals had become a substantial party in the Church of England (see Anglicanism Cluster: Anglican Communion and its Theology; United Kingdom), and their influence was a key factor in the Disruption* of the Church of Scotland* (1843). They also had a major impact on the Baptists* and Congregationalists*, as they shaped the ethos of the Methodist* churches. Evangelicals founded numerous societies to promote their evangelistic agendas, notably the London Missionary Society (1795), the Church Missionary Society (1799), the British and Foreign Bible Society (1804), the London City Mission (1835), and the Evangelical Alliance (1846). Wider social and political agendas were promoted by leaders such as William Wilberforce* (1759–1833) in his campaign against the Atlantic slave* trade and Anthony Ashley-Cooper, earl of Shaftesbury (1801–85), in his efforts to ameliorate the working and living conditions of the poor.

There was a loss of momentum in the late 19th and early 20th c. Internal tensions between liberals and conservatives increased, although Britain, unlike the USA, never developed a powerful fundamentalist* movement.

After World War II, however, Evangelicals again became a major force, strengthened by international influences, such as the Billy Graham crusades (1950s), but remained a distinctive indigenous movement. Their renewed strength in the Church of England was apparent at a congress in Keele (1967); the formation of the Evangelical Alliance Relief (TEAR) Fund (1968) was symbolic of their recovery as a strong social conscience and commitment to Third World aid. Since the 1960s, many British Evangelicals have been influenced by the Charismatic* Movement. In the 1980s and 1990s, the Evangelical Alliance, led successively by Clive Calver and Joel Edwards, developed into an influential umbrella organization and pressure group. As liberal and Catholic traditions have declined, Evangelicals have increasingly set the tone of British Christianity.

JOHN WOLFFE

Evangelism or Evangelization (both from Gk *euangelion*, "good news") is, for many Christians, a term equivalent to "mission*," including any number of local and foreign-soil ministries. From a more Evangelical* perspective, however, evangelism is more the global proclamation of the best news of all – "in Christ God was reconciling the world to himself" (2 Cor 5:19, NIV). Evangelism is a ministry of reconciliation given to us by "God, who reconciled us to himself through Christ" (2 Cor 5:18, NIV). Although the creation and all creatures are totally disconnected from God, God has not only reconciled believers to God, but has chosen to use believers as instruments of reconciliation. "How then, can they call on the one they have not believed in? And how can they believe in the one of whom they have not heard? And how can they hear without someone preaching to them? And how can they preach unless they are sent?" (Rom 10:14).

For Evangelicals, evangelism begins in the OT with a people chosen and blessed by God to be a blessing to others. In Abraham*, the children of Israel* were called to bear witness to a God who was faithful to the covenant* promises, who would deliver and sustain all who would call faithfully on the name of the One who loved them. Israel soon forgot. The sacrifices instituted for covenant renewal became a mindless ritual. God became weary. Centuries of unfaithfulness betrayed the inability of the covenant with Abraham to sustain a lasting relationship with God. Jeremiah* 31:31–34 revealed the ultimate plan. God would institute a new* covenant whereby sin was not only "covered over" (propitiated*), but "rooted out" (expiated*), whereby God would "forgive their wickedness and remember their sins no more" (v. 34) (see Atonement #2). The ultimate good news on which evangelism is grounded is the new covenant sacrifice* of God's own son that fulfilled this prophecy in "the greater and more perfect tabernacle*" that is not made with human hands, eternal in the heavens" (Heb 9:11) (see Supersessionism).

The church has received the commission from the resurrected Christ to "go and make disciples of all nations, baptizing them in the name of the Father and of the Son and of the Holy Spirit" (Matt 28:19). Acts* describes many examples in the lives of the apostles, who spread Christianity throughout the Roman Empire. The apostle Paul* perhaps best epitomizes the nature of evangelism. Church history reveals countless Christians who have felt that same call, as Christianity would eventually become a worldwide movement that included men and women of all backgrounds and races.

Styles of evangelism vary greatly. For some, evangelism is more "propositional," seeking to "get the word out." It attempts to create a need (the unfortunate caricature being, "You are a sinner, and if you don't do better you will go straight to hell"). For others evangelism is more relational, seeking to establish a relationship and then allowing the need to surface within the relationship so that the gospel* can be applied to a felt need.

Types of evangelism vary as well. Most associate evangelism with mass crusades in which the evangelist proclaims the good news with an invitation to respond as a crisis event. Others see evangelism more as a process whereby individuals are gradually won to faith in Christ. The media* are used for mass appeal through talk shows and televised worship services.

Many Evangelicals believe that local church evangelism is the most effective. Here church members realize that, although there is a "gift of evangelism" (see Eph 4:11), which is available to the few for specific tasks, the overall work of evangelism is the responsibility of the church as a whole. Every member has a sphere of influence in which only he or she can minister most effectively. Women have traditionally played and continue to play an essential role as evangelists in their own important spheres, often praying for wayward sons and daughters and interceding for others, their role in evangelizing should not be overlooked. There are also various parachurch* groups whose focus is evangelism (e.g. Teen Challenge, Youth with a Mission, Campus Crusade). Evangelism can be an appeal to individuals, one on one (a more Western approach) or to groups of peoples in parts of the world where decisions are made in community – in a family, an ethnic group, or even a nation.

Evangelicals insist that in evangelism God takes the initiative in the drama of rescue. The Holy* Spirit is at work the world over preparing the hearts of people to receive the gospel message. When Ananias (Acts 9) got to Saul, the Spirit of God had already done the work. When Peter (Acts 10) got to Cornelius, the Spirit had prepared the way. When Philip (Acts 8) got to the eunuch, the Spirit had gone before him. For many Christians, the heart of evangelism is simply showing up and paying attention. **See also MISSION CLUSTER.** ROBERT G. TUTTLE, JR.

Evangelist, NT term for one who communicates the gospel through proclamation or otherwise (Acts 21:8); also applied to the writers of the four Gospels; modern Evangelical* Movement term for preachers urging conversion or revival.

Evangelization. See EVANGELISM OR EVANGELIZATION.

Eve, the first and most infamous of biblical women (Gen 2–3), has been judged by Christian tradition as responsible for human depravity and emblematic of the sinfulness lurking in all women; Irenaeus* contrasts Eve as the source of sin* with Mary* as the source of salvation*. Misleading translations and interpretations with their own patriarchal structures made a problematic text for women much worse. Eve's offer to Adam*, and his speedy blame of her (Gen 3:12), led Christian readers to see Eve as primarily a seductress, bringing to humanity the dual problems of sexuality*/fertility and death*. The story also seems to blame women for their own oppression, since not only the pain of childbirth but also women's subordination to men is presented as punishment for disobedience (Gen 3:16). NICOLE WILKINSON DURAN

Evil, the Problem of. Religions* intend, among other things, to identify that which is problematic in the human situation and to propose a resolution (see Anthropology Cluster). Within Christianity this process is itself problematic because of tensions within Christianity's fundamental presuppositions: God* is all-powerful and benevolent, and God creates* the world good. Why, then, is there evil in the world? A perennial task of Christian theology, then, is to resolve these tensions, first in the very definition of evil and second in rendering that definition compatible with a good world created by a good God.

With regard to the definition, there were traditionally three categories of evil: (1) natural evil, such as earthquakes and floods; (2) physical evil, such as illness and death; and (3) moral evil, such as sin*. Of these, the primacy was given to moral evil. Augustine* considered all evil to be the result of sin and its punishment; were it not for the human sin of pride and disobedience, there would be neither illness nor death, and natural events would not be experienced as evil. Given that there is evil, however, balance is restored to the world through punishments that reestablish the harmony of a good world.

There were two routes for explaining the existence of evil, again in Augustine: (1) the plenitude of being and finitude, wherein God creates all possible forms of existence; and (2) human freedom*: the first humans were given the option of conforming themselves to God's commands. Refusing to do so, humans lost their original purity, turning away from love of God to love defined by lust.

A variation on the plenitude of being approach was developed by Leibniz* in his publication *Theodicy* (1710). "Theodicy*" refers to the justification of God in the face of evil. For Leibniz God created the very best possible world, but it was not possible to create that world without the presence of evil. Evil must be balanced by harmony, as Augustine also argued; but unlike Augustine, Leibniz maintained that this harmony was accomplished not through an everlasting hell*, but through a city of God composed of all rational spirits, living together in an ultimate preestablished harmony fully determined by God.

The optimism of Leibniz's *Theodicy* was radically challenged by Voltaire and other Enlightenment* philosophers following the physical and emotional shock waves left by a major earthquake in Lisbon (1755). Voltaire satirized Leibniz in his novel, *Candide*, which denied that this world is the best of all possible worlds, and suggested instead that finitude is the issue. Other Enlightenment thinkers brought the notion of an "Adam*" into question, and Deistic* notions undercut the need to "justify" God. Moral evil occurs because of environmental influences such as climate and geography, social influences, and the natural frailty of the body.

Twentieth-century theologians continued to follow either freedom or finitude as the fundamental root of evil, in both cases devising intricate arguments that maintained the goodness of God. However, the radical movement toward historicity*, and with it the movement from theoretical accounts of evil to descriptive accounts of evil, changed the dynamics of the topic. Liberation* theologians bespoke the evils of oppression*, systemic evil, and a God of the oppressed, and all theologians had to account for the radical forms of evils in the 20th c. (see Holocaust, Jewish [or Shoah]).

Process* theologies introduced a new dynamic by redefining not the goodness of God, but the power of God, arguing that God's power is persuasive rather than coercive and that God creates with the world, not on the world. In Process views, freedom and finitude together account for the problem of evil and together argue for a shift in the conception of God's power.

MARJORIE HEWITT SUCHOCKI

Evil Spirit. See DEVIL, SATAN, DEMONS, AND DEMONIC POWERS.

Evolution and Christianity. The origination of living species in the ordinary course of events and their modification into a diversity of forms were long found compatible with Christian doctrines of creation* and Providence*. Even the soul* could be thought of as generated during human reproduction (see Creatianism; Traducianism). But no one offered a widely convincing explanation of how species originated until Darwin* (1809–82).

In Europe, theories of "transmutation" were linked with political efforts to undermine established Christianity by ascribing life's progress and diversity to nature's powers rather than God's. Evolution was used to undermine the Bible by making humans the soul-less offspring of apes.

Darwin's theory of evolution by "natural selection" differed. Its premise was the adaptation of organisms to survive in their environments. Natural* theology saw this as proof of God's existence and inexplicable. But Darwin asked how adaptation came about. He argued that in the constant struggle for life, according to a law stated by Rev. Thomas Malthus, organisms with some survival advantage tend to leave more offspring than those without it. The offspring inheriting this advantage are better adapted to their environments and thus are naturally "selected," like the prize livestock selected by breeders. Humans were no exception. Darwin believed that an animal ancestry, far from degrading humans, raised the status of beasts, "our brethren in pain, disease, death and suffering." For him, when or whether humans acquired an immortal soul* during evolution was no more a problem than the soul's advent in fetal development.

Before Darwin's *Origin of Species* (1859), only a few liberal Christian scholars professed a belief in organic evolution – usually exempting humans from the theory by insisting on the separate creation of the soul. Darwin's influence made evolution increasingly acceptable to believers, with Unitarians* in the lead, closely followed by liberal clergy and theologians in many denominations. Yet until the mid-20th c., Christian believers seldom accepted human evolution, and almost never the primacy of natural selection. Rather, evolution was commonly seen as a series of divine edicts, or as an organic growth inspired by divine power, or even as a process in which the Divine Being participates and to which that Being is subject. To an extent, this diversity reflected disagreement among biologists about the causes of evolution. Since the late 20th c., theologians have evaluated post-neo-Darwinian theories. Even so, many believers still hold with those in Darwin's day who argued that evolution calls less for changes in received doctrines than for a recovery and reemphasis of the fullness of the Christian tradition. JAMES MOORE

Exarchate, a semiautonomous province of the Eastern Orthodox Church under the pastoral jurisdiction of a metropolitan ranking immediately below a patriarch.

Excommunication, the most severe sanction the Roman Catholic Church can impose on a member of the faithful. Its long and sometimes sensationalistic history can obscure the sober canonical realities of the penalty. The chief effects of excommunication are exclusion from the sacraments* (notably the Eucharist*, or Communion, hence the term "excommunication"), restrictions against ministerial participation in public worship, and possible loss of ecclesiastical office or functions (1983 *Codex Iuris Canonici* [CIC] 1331).

Classified as a "censure," excommunication is fundamentally oriented to bringing about the reform of the individual; it is not an "expiatory*" penalty intended to uphold legal justice* or defend social values (1983 CIC 1312). This is why excommunication, which assumes the presence of objective grave sin*, cannot be imposed or declared without prior warning (1983 CIC 1347); likewise, once an excommunicated person withdraws from contumacy, he or she has a right to the prompt lifting of the penalty (1983 CIC 1358). Dying excommunicated does not of itself consign one to everlasting punishment*. The Catholic Church claims no jurisdiction over the departed.

Excommunications can be incurred automatically (*latae sententiae*) for a few very specific ecclesiastical offenses listed in the 1983 Code. In the past 150 years, the number of offenses punishable by automatic excommunication in the Roman Catholic Church has dropped steadily, and Eastern Catholic (Uniate*) canon law has no automatic excommunications. A larger number of offenses are punishable by excommunication if the penalty is imposed or declared as a result of a judicial or administrative penal process. EDWARD N. PETERS

Exegesis (Gk "leading out of" [the complexity of a text]), detailed exposition, explanation, and interpretation of the Scriptures*, guided by hermeneutics*.

Exemption, a monastic community's freedom from the bishop's jurisdiction, making it directly responsible to the pope or to its religious order, first granted to Bobbio (628, 643).

Exiit, the bull* issued by Pope Nicholas III (1279) during the controversy among the Franciscans* over the meaning of poverty. **See also POVERTY CLUSTER: POVERTY MOVEMENT; PROPERTY.**

Exile, an involuntary departure from one's homeland. Biblically, it refers to the deportation of Judah from Jerusalem by the Babylonians (597–39 BCE) and the earlier exile of the Northern Kingdom by the Assyrians following the fall of Samaria (722 BCE). The first exiles were actually Adam and Eve (Gen 3), demonstrating that exile is the result of sin* (cf. 2 Kgs 17:7–8; Jer 25:8–11; Ezek 1). Exile prompts the hope of restoration by God on the basis either of repentance* (e.g. Deut 30:1–10) or of gracious redemption* (1 Peter, where Christians are viewed as "exiled," now with a positive connotation). JEFFRY C. DAVIS

Existentialism and Christian Thought. Existentialism, partly a reaction against German idealism* (Hegel*), is expressed in Kierkegaard's* emphasis on how Christianity implies a certain mode of personal "existence" and life that must be appropriated, in contrast to Christian belief as a mere custom or as believing a given doctrinal point of view. After World War I, influenced by dialectical* theology and the rise of phenomenology*, existentialism developed in several directions, building mainly on the insights of Kierkegaard. It concurred with the emphasis in modern Western Christianity on the individual and on choice, and participated in the criticism of bourgeois modes of faith. Along with other anti-metaphysical trends, existentialism offered Christian thought a way out of the dilemma posed by historical* criticism and positivism* by emphasizing that personal commitment, choice, and engagement are what matters, not objectively secured facts of history.

Existentialism was able to establish links with Christianity partly because revivalist* movements also emphasized choice and individuality, and partly because existentialism criticized the depersonalization of humanity often brought about by the modern scientific approach. By emphasizing authenticity, existentialism offered significance to personal existence in the depressed cultural climate on the Continent after World War I. Yet atheistic currents in modern existentialism have sometimes been hostile toward Christianity.

Existentialism is critical of forms of Christianity too closely based on scientific reason (historicism*, neo-Kantianism*, liberal* theology). When choice, anxiety, dread, and death are given a phenomenological interpretation along with the rest of human existence, this interpretation can be articulated within the framework of Christian faith. Hence, faith* is more than belief ("believing that"); it (or the lack of it) also involves psychological conditions that account for the different possibilities for being and becoming a human being. The most consistent existentialist approach to theology is that of Bultmann*. Although mainly a Continental movement, existentialism influenced North American theology, especially through Tillich* and his students.

Existentialism has helped Christian theologians to voice a critique of a modern culture marked by the alienation of individuals and to emphasize that Christian faith is anchored primarily in personal existence rather than in ecclesial life and popular customs. Conversely, it has contributed to the development of a somewhat problematic individualistic mode of Christianity and has sometimes stressed the significance of the present in ways that neglect the importance of Christianity's historical roots.

JAN-OLAV HENRIKSEN

Exodus, the second book of the HB, contains a master narrative of freedom from bondage and community formation in three parts. Exodus 1:1–15:21 describes the oppression of the Israelites in Egypt and their miraculous release into the Sinai wilderness. Then, in 15:22–24:18, their journey toward the Promised* Land takes them to the mountain of God, where God reveals (through Moses*) community guidelines: the Ten* Commandments and the Covenant* Code. Finally, in Chaps. 25–40 (often called the "tabernacle texts"), God reveals instructions for a national shrine (the Tabernacle*), which is then constructed.

Exodus was most likely given final form during the Exile* (6th c. BCE) or shortly thereafter, when it was important to establish national identity after the trauma of the Babylonian destruction of Jerusalem and Judah, but it contains earlier material. The compelling story of escape to freedom in the first part of Exodus is a highly constructed narrative; consequently, the historicity of all its dramatic details (e.g. the 10 signs and wonders; splitting of the Reed Sea) is unlikely. However, the basic storyline – descent into Egypt, servitude in the eastern Nile delta, and escape against great odds into the wilderness – reflects the actual movements of small groups in the 13th c. BCE. The intense experiences of relatively few people were retained, embellished, and expanded by their descendants over many centuries. Early versions of this narrative may date to the first part of the divided monarchy (9th–8th c. BCE).

The second part of the narrative (15:22–24:18) contains the social norms of the Israelites. Its guidelines for community life are presented as constituting a covenant* between Israel and its deity. Although most likely dating to the monarchic period, some of its precepts may be earlier; yet all are presented as having been revealed to Israel in the wilderness.

The same pattern can be discerned in Exod 25–40. The national shrine (the Jerusalem Temple) as it existed at the end of the monarchy or the beginning of the postexilic period, is retrojected into the wilderness period as a portable shrine or tabernacle. Its elaborate and costly details are a product of the exilic imagination remembering the Jerusalem Temple, but the basic concept of a tent of meeting as a community shrine at which divine oracles could be received may be an authentic remnant of the premonarchic and early monarchic era (12th–10th c. BCE).

Although Moses is not called a prophet in Exodus, his prophetic identity is indicated by his call narrative (3:1–10) as well as by the fact that all the community regulations and the instructions for the national shrine are presented as having been conveyed from God to the people by Moses. As ancient Israel's prophet *par excellence,* he models the importance of prophecy* as the medium for communicating the divine will. Similarly, the important role of Aaron* in effecting the Exodus and especially in serving God through the holiness of the priestly office at the national shrine sanctions the office and functions of Israelite priesthood*.

The narrative of the Exodus provides the paramount HB example of God's salvific involvement with humankind. The covenant section indicates that people can enter into a binding relationship with their deity; in so doing, they take on the obligation to obey God's will and carry out a vocation*. The tabernacle section provides a way for people to experience the abiding presence of God in their midst.

Central aspects of Israelite and then Jewish beliefs and practices – Passover*, circumcision, redemption of the firstborn, covenant, Ten Commandments, Sabbath*, Holy Ark, menorah – are validated by appearing in Exodus as part of the collective memory of the foundational experiences of early Israel.

CAROL MEYERS

Ex Opere Operato, a term that suggests that the sacraments convey grace by being administered, independently of the worthiness or intentions of people involved.

Exorcism, the art of dislodging Evil (as a power that possesses people and things) from persons, places, or objects, exists in most religions. The practice, recorded throughout history, presupposes enabling cosmologies and anthropologies*. Demonic* possession is framed by social, economic, political, and cultural narratives. Exorcism is effective where the Evil is named, identified, expelled, or contained through the deployment of a ritual symbolic apparatus related to these narratives. Since Evil destabilizes the normal/local, it is often identified as *an-other,* as foreign – Beelzebub* or even "legion."

The Christian Gospels present Jesus at home with the cosmological assumptions of his time in a context marked by sociopolitical crisis and anxiety that encouraged religious fervor, occult practices, and exorcisms. The Targum on Num 6:24 illustrates such assumptions: Aaron's blessing of the people is expanded to include protection from "demons" of the night, midday, morning, and evening, and "evil spirits." The line between moral and physical evil is blurred. Through exorcism Jesus identified with and brought relief or liberation to the sufferer, inaugurating the Kingdom* or reign* of God. Consequently, he directed attention away from himself, focused on the Kingdom, and totally opposed the search for scapegoats ("who sinned?"). Jesus' style provides a specific Christian horizon for practicing exorcism. "In the name of Jesus," the disciples performed miracles and exorcisms. These cosmological perspectives continued to influence the early and later Christian understanding of Evil and practice of exorcism. Baptismal exorcism was a battle launched against the demonic occupant of the candidates. Jesus' command *ephphatha* (Aramaic for "be opened," as explained in Mark 7:34) became a baptismal incantation. In the Catholic

Church, canonically appointed exorcists engage demons possessing persons, places, and objects.

Modernity and rationalism encouraged the receding of the cosmology and anthropology of evil. Scientific accounts and psychological* theories led people to associate spirits (good and evil), witchcraft*, witch* hunts, and exorcisms with superstition and an unscientific view of the universe.

The postmodern world, wounded by traumatic occurrences like Auschwitz (see Holocaust, Jewish [or Shoah]) and the Rwandan* genocide, is a theater of anxiety, crisis, and a resurgence of Evil inhabiting persons, objects, and places. Mainline missionary churches, Pentecostalism*, African* Instituted Churches, and the Charismatic* Movement have reinvented rituals of exorcism. In places like Africa, spirits inhabiting the ancestral universe that are ambivalent in nature are reduced, in Manichaean terms, to evil spirits or demons. Through exorcisms and deliverance ministries, Evil/Satan is summoned to depart from the possessed or sufferers, who confess they are witches or "containers of the devil." Exorcism occupies the ritual energy and imagination of these Christian churches.

ELOCHUKWU EUGENE UZUKWU, CSSP

Expiation, making up for an offense against God or neighbor by performing a favorable act. The Crucifixion* as expiation emphasizes the positive merits of Christ; propitiation*, by contrast, emphasizes placating God's anger* (see Atonement #2).

Exposition of the Sacrament, in Roman Catholicism, displaying the eucharistic host (elevating it during Mass* or placing it in a monstrance*) for veneration.

Ex-voto (Lat "from the vow"), a votive offering to a saint, Christ, or God given in fulfillment of a vow or in gratitude or devotion; often a part of popular* Christian practices and of pilgrimages*. Shrines are often decorated with ex-votos.

Ezekiel, Book of, an OT prophetic book, containing stories about and speeches attributed to the prophet named Ezekiel. The prophet was born in Judah but was taken into Babylonian* captivity in 597 BCE. The content of the book reflects the Babylonian Exile* as well as references to the continuing Judean community.

Ezekiel's prophecies began in 592 BCE and continued over a span of about 20 years. They included letters to those still in Jerusalem (before the exile of 587/86) as well as those already relocated to Babylonia. Most of the book (Chaps. 1–39) was probably written during the Exile. Ezekiel combines typical features of a prophetic book (such as oracles against the nations, Chaps. 25–32) with priestly interests, including a focus on the purity of the Jerusalem Temple.

Ezekiel 4–24 concentrates on the fall of Judah, arguing for the rightness and inevitability of Babylon's conquest of Jerusalem in 587. The prophet performed several sign-acts and pronounced oracles indicating that Jerusalem's fall was the will of God, justified because of Judah's sin*.

Despite the exile of the Jews to Babylonia, the Book of Ezekiel does offer hope*. In future times, God will spare those who choose righteousness* over sin (33:10–20). God will place a new heart and a new spirit among these survivors (36:26–28). God will also revive the people who have been reduced to dry bones (37). God will lead the people back to their former homes and pour God's spirit upon them (39:25–29).

Ezekiel 40–48 details the reconstruction of the Jerusalem Temple. This does not follow the construction plans of the First Temple, nor was the Second Temple (522 BCE to 70 CE) built according to Ezekiel's plans. Ezekiel's vision of the Temple was symbolic rather than architecturally practical, for it meant to emphasize God's presence (48:35).

Ancient Jewish tradition questioned whether Ezekiel should be considered canonical, because it disagreed with the Pentateuch about whether sins affected only the sinner or the sinner's family (Ezek 18:4, 20, cf. Exod 34:6–7) and provided different dimensions for the Temple (Ezek 40–48, cf. Exod 26–27 and 1 Kgs 6–7). Among Christians, African American tradition has especially treasured Ezekiel, and images such as the dry bones (37) and God's chariot (1:16) have inspired gospel songs as well as many sermons.

JON L. BERQUIST

Ezra, 4. See FOURTH EZRA.

Ezra and Nehemiah, the Books of, originally a single literary work (written after 332 BCE), tell an idealized story of a reconstituted but small Jerusalem community threatened with obliteration by imperial rule (Ezra 9:7–10), interethnic strife (Ezra 9–10; Neh 13), and abusive excesses of an elite class (Neh 5).

Presented as cultural heroes, Ezra and Nehemiah responded to the Jerusalem community's suffering by enacting similar internal reforms to strengthen the community's cultural identity and restore order and hope* to a people in disarray.

The positions that Ezra and Nehemiah occupy complicate the story; they are imperial authorities, trusted by the Persian crown (Ezra 7:11–26; Neh. 1:11–2:8), but with loyalties to the Jerusalem collective (Ezra 7:1–6; Neh. 1:1–6). Thus they deploy strategies of both accommodation and resistance. The reforms reflect this ambiguity. The horror of mass divorces that separate Israel from the peoples of the land (Ezra 9:1–4; 10; Neh. 13) and destroy families simultaneously creates a space of cultural flourishing for the Jerusalem community. The reaffirmation of the Law of Moses (Neh. 8) calls the people toward a cultural unity that resists imperial domination and also gives the province the political stability that the Persian officials desire. The reforms allow both the Persian crown and the Jerusalem community to affirm the same rhetoric, although at cross-purposes. The two officials succeed in appeasing the Persians while saving their people.

The two books culminate in separatist rhetoric (Ezra 9–10; Neh. 10, 13), poignant and provocative in its stark language but morally disturbing in its content. Were Ezra and Nehemiah too intent on pleasing the Persians at the expense of the people? Were they unwittingly complicit in Persian repression by pitting one marginalized group against another, constructing an interethnic conflict that disempowered both and bolstered imperial dominion? Or were their problematic reforms the only reasonable means to ensure the survival of the devoted to YHWH? These are important questions for marginalized communities in struggles against repression.

HERBERT ROBINSON MARBURY

F

Fabiola (d399), Roman matron of the *gens Fabia* who, as a widow, adopted a life of austerity (asceticism*) and traveled to Bethlehem* to join the monastic* community of Paula*, Eustochium*, and Jerome*. After the outbreak of the Origenist* controversy, she returned to Rome. She was canonized as a Roman Catholic saint*.

Faculty (Canon Law), permission from an ecclesiastical superior to hold an office and/or perform an action.

Facundus of Hermiane (6th c.), a bishop in North Africa who, in his "Defense of the Three* Chapters" (547–48), argued that the three accused theologians were in accord with the decrees of the Council of Chalcedon*. After the Second Council of Constantinople* (553), large portions of the Western Church broke communion with Constantinople and Rome. Facundus's writings are a valuable record of the dispute and its background.

Faith, a term that suggests, in both its everyday and religious meanings, an intense relationship, generally understood in interpersonal terms.

1. Faith as Faithfulness. In most languages, "faith" applied originally to human relationships, namely to the "good faith" with which one makes a promise and to the "faithfulness" with which the promise is kept. In the HB, the primary terms for faith are based on the root *'mn* ("amen"* is derived from this root), which connotes trustworthiness or faithfulness. God has good faith and is faithful to God's promises. Human faithfulness to God is a response to God's faithfulness. Paul's language about "the faith of Jesus Christ" (Rom 3:22) may refer to such a faithfulness of Jesus to God.

2. Faith as Trust. Faith as trusting God the promiser (*credere Deo*) involves submitting to God and living according to God's promises (a possible meaning of "the obedience of faith," Rom 1:5, 16:26). In the Bible, faith often suggests a confident trust in God or in Christ as worthy of trust.

3. Faith as Believing a Speaker's Words ("Believing That"). When focused on what the trustworthy speaker says, faith means "believing that certain affirmations are true." Faith is a trustful assent to divine truth or revelation expressed in the words of the prophets, Jesus, the Bible, or other authoritative voices. Faith is then defined by its content.

Augustine distinguished between the faith ("trust") *by which* we believe (*fides qua creditur*) and the faith *which* is believed (*fides quae creditur*), or the content of faith, e.g. the 2nd-c."apostolic proclamation," summarized in the Apostles'* Creed, elaborated and defined in subsequent doctrinal decisions.

4. Faith, Knowledge, Understanding, and Reason. Paul contrasted people who have "faith" (and might be weak) with those who have "knowledge" (Gk *gnosis;* 1 Cor 8). The Gnostic Valentinians* also emphasized this contrast. Clement* and Origen* more cautiously affirmed that faith is perfected through knowledge, i.e. personal appropriation and understanding of the content of faith. Augustine often said (following the Old* Latin version of Isa 7:9), "Believe in order to understand." Then faith is the way toward understanding. Similarly, Anselm* defined theology as *fides quaerens intellectum* (faith seeking understanding). Through theological understanding, what is already believed gains in consistency and clarity (e.g. Anselm's *Cur Deus homo*). Theology has also utilized the more pedestrian activity of reasoning* to seek coherence in what is believed and perhaps to confirm it through argumentation; reasoned knowledge discerns the validity of beliefs.

5. Faith as Movement toward, and Experience of, God. To speak of "believing *in*" God or Christ is a distinct usage that began in the Septuagint* and was further developed in the NT. "Believing *in*" (or "faith" without qualifier, as in the synoptic Gospels and Paul) is more than "believing *that*," for "even the demons believe and tremble" (Jas 2:19), and more than believing/trusting a promiser; it is a personal adherence to, and movement toward, God (or Christ). In Augustine and Catholic theology, faith as movement toward God is often linked with love*; faith is completed by love (Gal 5:6). Faith, hope*, and love are aspects of the same personal orientation, all working together until love alone persists (1 Cor 13:8–13). Faith as movement toward God can be the beginning of spiritual union with God, as suggested by Gregory* of Nyssa, Dionysius* the Pseudo-Aeropagite, and Maximus* the Confessor. It is an initiation into mysteries*, i.e. being enabled to perceive and understand what is otherwise beyond human perception and understanding. In similar ways, in apocalyptic* and Charismatic* perspectives, faith involves discerning the mysteries of God's interventions in one's present context (see Typology).

6. Faith as Gift. The Protestant doctrine of justification* by faith alone led to an emphasis on faith as trust in the good news (gospel*) of God's purpose of salvation through Christ, linking the believer to Christ through the influence of the Holy* Spirit; faith is not a human achievement but God's gift, receiving God's gift (charisma; 1 Cor 12:9). Protestantism also speaks of faith as "believing that," i.e. assent as well as trust, based on revelation. For 20th-c. Roman Catholic theologians (including Rahner*) the primary constituent of faith is an interior acceptance of God's grace*. Vatican* II affirms the element of assent ("believing that") but subordinates it to the "obedience of faith" (Rom 1:5, 16:26), faith as trust.

The philosophers Hume* and Kant*, by limiting the range of reason, seemed to ascribe a new role to faith. But they also raised the question as to what faith could be based on. Schleiermacher* defined faith as a "feeling of absolute dependence," while Ritschl* emphasized "value judgments" of practical reason. In the 20th c., Barth* tended to follow Ritschl, as he called attention to the Word of God as direct address and faith as total response. Dewey* underlined the religious function of experience as a common, social faith. Tillich* tended to follow Schleiermacher; for him faith was "absolute concern" shaped by specific cultural questions and religious symbols. **See also RATIONALISM AND CHRISTIAN THEOLOGY; REASON; REVELATION.**

EUGENE TESELLE and DANIEL PATTE

Faith and Order Movement, a key contributor to the modern ecumenical* movement, was born early in the 20th c. Inspired by the American Episcopal bishop Charles H. Brent (1862–1929), the movement came into being to provide a platform for theological dialogue on fundamental questions of Christian faith and ecclesial structure with the intention of moving churches toward visible unity – "to proclaim the oneness of the Church of Jesus Christ and to call the churches to the goal of visible unity in one faith and one eucharistic fellowship, expressed in worship and in common life in Christ, in order that the world may believe."

This movement was from the beginning parallel both to the Life* and Work Movement, associated largely with the Universal Christian Conference on Life and Work, Stockholm (1925), and to the modern missionary movement that issued from the historic World Missionary Conference, Edinburgh* (1910). Decisions of the Faith and Order and Life and Work movements in 1937 led to their inclusion in the World* Council of Churches (WCC), formed in 1948. Faith and Order retained its existence as a commission within the WCC. Since Vatican* II, the Roman Catholic Church has been a member of the commission, and increasingly persons from the Pentecostal*, Evangelical*, and Charismatic* traditions participate in its work.

Faith and Order has held five important world conferences, from Lausanne (1927) to Santiago de Compostela (1993), including those in Edinburgh (1937), Lund (1952), and Montreal (1963). Its most widely known and significant accomplishment for churches has been the convergence document "Baptism, Eucharist, and Ministry," shaped in Lima (1982).

NORMAN A. HJELM

Fall is the answer to the question, What is the beginning of human sin* (Lat *lapsus*)? Because the answer was found in interpretations of Gen 2–3, the beginning of sin was called the "Fall." The Genesis story suggests that the human situation is not what it might have been: there is pain in childbearing (3:16), laboring by the sweat of one's brow (3:19), and death (3:3, 19; emphasized by Paul in 1 Cor 15; Rom 5). What sin causes these predicaments? A range of answers can be identified throughout church history.

Two emphases are found in traditional interpretations: (1) Adam* bears the primary responsibility, since the prohibition against eating from the tree of knowledge is addressed only to Adam, prior to Eve's creation. (2) Eve* alone had contact with the serpent, and thus appears to be the mediator of temptation – a common interpretation based on the threefold presentation of the serpent, the woman, and the man in that order (Gen 3:1–7, 12–13, 14–19).

Gnostics* followed another line of interpretation. They saw in the eating from the tree of knowledge the victory of more spiritual forces over the bungling or evil creator, the Demiurge*, whose activity is defined by the world of material and animate beings.

Irenaeus* responded by suggesting the gradual development of sin. Adam and Eve were created neither mortal nor immortal, but with the capacity for both mortality and immortality: disobedience would lead to death and obedience to life.

This interpretation was elaborated in two ways: (1) the doctrine of original* sin, according to which Adam and Eve's sin affects all their descendants, and (2) the Pelagian* doctrine, according to which their sin affected only themselves and is perpetuated by imitation.

Origen*, by contrast, posited that finite spirits were created in union with God. How could free and intelligent beings lapse into sin? Origen's answer was that they drifted away through *koros* (carelessness, weariness, satiation).

Augustine* suggested that, before committing any outward act, they sinned inwardly through pride, self-concern, and self-exaltation.

Modern Western approaches to the Fall stem largely from Kant*, who transformed "original sin" into "radical evil" (see Evil, the Problem of): by the time we come to full moral awareness, we find that we have given in to bad rather than good impulses. Since humans are capable of acting on rational incentives, evil, while perhaps inevitable, is still a human responsibility.

Likewise, Schleiermacher* said that humans sin from the first, but added that this occurs through God's wisdom; God wills that all humans experience guilt so that they will be all the more grateful when they are offered salvation.

In Liberation* theology, original sin or radical evil is understood chiefly as "systemic evil" or "structural evil" of social institutions that perpetuate dominance and slavery, self-indulgence and deprivation.

DANIEL PATTE and EUGENE TESELLE

FAMILY, CHRISTIAN VIEWS OF, CLUSTER

1) *Introductory Entries*

2) *A Sampling of Contextual Views and Practices*

---

1) Introductory Entries

Family, Christian Views of, in Eastern Orthodox Churches. For Orthodox, the family is the context in which we work out our salvation* as children of God. In and by meeting the physical and psychological needs of its members, the family nurtures the souls of its members. The daily life of the family in the world serves to purify, sanctify*, and deify (see Theosis, Deification) its members in Christ as the church of the home.

The family, while within and connected to the world and broader culture, is oriented toward the Kingdom* of God. Orthodox understand family life as sacramental*. The Kingdom of God becomes a lived experience in the daily struggles of life. The family is necessarily linked to the eucharistic* faith community and finds its fulfillment within the body of Christ. In and through the family, as the church of the home, we live in the world as citizens of heaven. The family lives out the sacramental reality of church in daily life by living out the gospel mandate to love* God and neighbor; it participates in missions*, outreach, evangelism*, education*, hospitality*, service to the poor*, prayer*, repentance*, and ascetic* practices. The vocation of the family is to nurture the souls of all members in order that they seek first the Kingdom of God and pursue righteousness in all interactions. The family finds it fulfillment as its members live as brothers and sisters in Christ within the body of Christ. In this sense, family is not necessarily limited to a particular structure or arrangement but can comprise a variety of relationships. Nevertheless, Orthodox maintain the marital dyad as the center of the family and child rearing as a central purpose of family life. Within a hierarchy of love (see Trinity in Eastern Orthodoxy), all members share an equality of persons while having distinct roles.

The family is called to live in the world as the church of the home – a Christian community of love within a Christian community of love. **See also MARRIAGE, THEOLOGY AND PRACTICE OF, CLUSTER: IN EASTERN ORTHODOXY.**

PHILIP MAMALAKIS

Family, Christian Views of, in Western Churches. "Family" refers to the social unit that includes those related by blood, adoption, or marriage* and, by extension, to the Christian community of those related to one another through faith* in Christ. Tension between these two meanings creates ambivalence within the tradition about the family within Christianity. Scripture* and theology have been used to bolster several different forms of living.

The New Family in Christ. Distinct from Hellenistic Jewish and Greco-Roman religions, which sanctioned the home as one of the sites of prayer, education, and celebration of festivals, the Christian movement gradually shifted religious loyalty from the hearth to extrafamilial relationships. In the synoptic Gospels, Jesus subordinates kinship to discipleship* (Luke 14:26; Matt 10:37) and declares those who do God's will to be "my brother and sister and mother" (Mark 3:33–35; Luke 8:19–21; Matt 12:46–50). Over the next several centuries, martyrdom* and monasticism* led followers to reject family responsibilities for a more radical testimony. Early Syriac* Christianity identified celibacy* as a higher religious calling than marriage and procreation.

Hierarchical Male-Ruled Families. Other Scriptures endorse marriage, children*, and the patriarchal* family. Gospel texts reveal Jesus blessing wedding wine, welcoming children, and opposing divorce* and adultery. Biblical authors of the "household* codes" (Eph 5:22–6:9; Col 3:18–4:1; 1 Pet 2:18–3:7; 1 Tim 2:8–15; Titus 2:1–10) exhort subordinate family members (wives, slaves, children) to submit to their superiors (husbands, masters, fathers). Reformation theologians reclaimed marriage as a religious calling and interpreted the codes as a definitive statement on the proper relationship between church and family. The family became a "little church" with the father at the helm.

Egalitarian Families. Some scholars argue that early Christianity established communities of greater gender equality. Men and women gathered in "house* churches" that sometimes placed women in important leadership roles (e.g. Rom 16:3). Baptismal creeds leveled human relationships (Gal 3:28). The household codes in fact responded to disruptions caused by the new family ethos of the early movement. Liberation* theology and progressive denominations confirm the importance of mutuality in marriage, shared responsibility for parenting, and support for a diversity of families as representative of basic Christian convictions.

Contemporary debate over *the* Christian family results from ambiguity in the tradition from the start. Emphasis on freedom in Christ, the priesthood* of all believers, and God as ultimate authority strain family loyalty. At the same time, Christianity has long sanctioned committed marriage, procreation and care of children, and strong families. **See also MARRIAGE, THEOLOGY AND PRACTICE OF, CLUSTER: IN WESTERN CHURCHES.**

BONNIE J. MILLER-MCLEMORE

2) A Sampling of Contextual Views and Practices

Family, Christian Views of, in Africa: African Instituted Churches. The view of the family in African Instituted Churches (AICs) is conceptualized in both indigenous and Christian terms. In Africa, family as a lineage–ancestry system is the foundation of social, economic, and religious life, provides identity, and affirms the worth and integrity of every individual. An AIC congregation becomes a surrogate kinship group, with the spiritual leader as its head. Each AIC views itself as a family, "God's household"; faith in Jesus Christ, our Ancestor*, provides access to the Father in one Spirit (Eph 2:18–19; Gal 3:26, 6:10) and transcends ethnic, gender, and class limitations (Gal 3:28).

Tensions are evident. AICs struggle to balance cultural values, Christian ideals, and modernity. Ethnic composition hinders efforts to be a unified "household of God." While the lineage structure offers a sense of belonging, it may promote dependency. Monogamy, the Christian ideal, is challenged by polygamy* associated with traditional values and social and economic structures. Women have central roles in AICs' leadership on a scriptural basis, but their functions are circumscribed by cultural prescriptions about gender roles.

The fact remains that AICs provide an intense experience of community. Despite some limitations, Christian values embodied in the church as "household of God" are experienced and mediated within this new lineage framework.

PHILOMENA N. MWAURA

Family, Christian Views of, in Africa: Eastern Africa. Views of the family in Eastern Africa are multilocal, multigenerational, multiethnic, and multireligious, owing to migration, marriage, and conversion*, and are marked by tensions between African cultural values and Christian teachings.

While rapidly changing, Eastern African families are primarily socioeconomic units sustaining the life of their members through socialization and multiplication. Christian communities embody the same family values, multiplying their members and socializing them; like any African ancestor*, Christ longs for many descendants. Yet tensions exist regarding reproduction; polygamy* is anti-Christian and celibacy* is anti-African. Consequently, many profess Christian values but practice traditional African values.

Eastern African values reinforce those scriptural teachings advocating a hierarchically patriarchal* family, heterosexual* marriage, and children*, opposing divorce*, and envisioning Christian communities as male-ruled families. Yet households and churches headed by women have emerged with the popularization of women empowerment programs and Feminist* theology (Gen 1:26–28; Matt 13:33–34; Luke 15:8–10; Gal 3:28).

Socioeconomic strains and the breakdown of African cultural values rejected by Christianity have engendered a tragic neglect of familial responsibilities. This crisis is to be attributed to the missionary introduction of Christianity as a profession of faith in Christian values, including celibacy and monogamy, rather than as a way of life that upholds the economic welfare of all members of the extended family according to East African values.

EUNICE KAMAARA

Family, Christian Views of, in Africa: Southern Africa. Southern African societies can be divided into two groups: matrilineal societies trace their descent from a common ancestress and patrilineal ones from a common ancestor*. Examples of matrilineal societies include the Yao, Chewa, and Bemba of Malawi*, Zambia*, and Mozambique*. The husband settles in his wife's village and does not pay "bride-wealth." The offspring of her marriage belongs to the wife and her kinsfolk. However, this arrangement does not amount to matriarchy. In patrilineal societies, the husband pays bride-wealth to the family of the wife. The children and property of the family belong to the husband and his kinsfolk. Examples of patrilineal societies include the Tumbuka, Tonga, Zulu, Xhosa, Shona, Tswana, and Sotho of Malawi, Zambia, Mozambique, Zimbabwe*, Lesotho*, Botswana*, and South* Africa. Christian families simply continued these practices. The Christian missionaries were opposed to the (British) colonial governments' introduction of the "hut tax," which forced men to labor in the colonial economy and to migrate to the cities and neighboring countries to look for jobs and raise money for the tax. In turn this caused the breakup of many Christian families. Similar labor migration is also mentioned by the UN as a contributor to the spread of HIV infection in Southern Africa. ISABEL APAWO PHIRI

Family, Christian Views of, in Asia. The family in Asia is a social unit based on blood or marital ties. Except in a few predominantly Christian communities (e.g. in Northeastern India), the Asian Christian family is usually part of a big clan whose members embrace different religions; thus it is often caught up in the cultural and religious practices of the prevalent religion, culture, or philosophy (e.g. indigenous religion, Confucianism*, Daoism*, Hinduism*, Buddhism*, Islam*). Such practices include filial piety, respect for (veneration* or worship of) ancestors*, general preference for boys, and privileging of boys. In the very few matrilineal communities found in some indigenous communities of Indonesia*, India* and Bangladesh*, some Christian families may accord certain privileges to girls and women, including ownership of property. Literal* use of Scriptures*, such as the biblical household* codes (e.g. Eph 5:22–6:9; Col 3:18–4:1), reinforces the patriarchal and hierarchical relations of Asian cultures, religions, and philosophies. Asian Feminist* theologians critique oppressive practices and interpretation of Scriptures, and call for the family to model a more egalitarian community with Christ (rather than the husband/father) as head of the whole Christian family. Owing to migration for economic or political reasons, more frequent occurrences of interracial and interreligious marriage and divorce or legal separation, and a decline in traditional marriages, the Christian family in Asia is changing rapidly. **See also MARRIAGE, THEOLOGY AND PRACTICE OF, CLUSTER: IN ASIA.** HOPE S. ANTONE

Family, Christian Views of, in Australia. In contrast to the nuclear family structures of nonindigenous people in Australia*, in Aboriginal* societies each person identities every person in the group by a relationship term (classificatory system of kinship); e.g. a father's brothers are known as fathers and a mother's sisters are known as mothers. Although Aboriginal societies tend to be egalitarian, as an individual identifies all others in the society by a relationship term, a wide range of obligations and rights are established. Older men and women have authority in their kin group. In the past, women had a degree of autonomy in their sphere of food gathering and preparation and in rituals relating to fertility and nurturing. In traditional education, parents, older siblings, and other relatives passed on their knowledge through training in social relationships, which included defining eligible marriage partners. Polygamy* was common, with men often having two or three wives.

Early missionaries assumed that their mandate of "Christianizing and civilizing" involved imposing the model of monogamous nuclear families. Men were refused baptism until they restricted themselves to one wife. Some missions relaxed this rule when it was realized that women sent away by their husbands lacked support and protection. Yet the statement in the early 1900s of a Roman Catholic priest, later Bishop Gsell, was typical: "The nomadic family group is the antithesis of the Christian family." Many Aboriginal orphans and children of mixed descent were removed from their extended families and found nurture and support in mission homes (e.g. Colebrook, South Australia; Mount Margaret, Western Australia) as the home residents became their new family.

Some missions supported traditional family structures, as Aboriginal Christians found resonance with biblical family structures and marriage arrangements. As relationship (*walytja*) is a central concept in Aboriginal societies, references to God as "father" and Jesus as "elder brother" were soon absorbed into prayer and preaching. The Pitjantjatjara term for Christians is *Jesuku walytja* (relatives of Jesus). The church is God's extended family in which previous barriers between different Aboriginal groups and between Aborigines and other Australians are broken down.

In contemporary society, many Aboriginal families experience problems as individuals face tensions between traditional kinship obligations and the demands of modern political and social roles. Some churches, having apologized for removing Aboriginal children from their families, seek to help Aboriginal families as they adjust to these changes and to contribute to the church's understanding of family from their own tradition and experience. **See also ANCESTOR VENERATION AND CHRISTIANITY CLUSTER: IN ABORIGINAL AUSTRALIA; ANTHROPOLOGY CLUSTER: AUSTRALIAN ABORIGINAL THEOLOGICAL ISSUES.** WILLIAM H. EDWARDS

Family, Christian Views of, in Latin America. The family is still viewed as an important institution in Latin American society, despite the multiplicity of contexts (from Argentina* and Chile* to Mexico* and from Brazil* to Ecuador*) and the repeated claims that it is in crisis. According to 2000 and 2008 surveys, "traditional families" as conceived of in the modern period – headed by married couples (a man and a woman) for whom having children and achieving financial stability are highly important – are still a majority. However, these surveys also show fundamental changes in the way family relations are envisioned.

For most Latin Americans, the family founded on a married couple should be the cornerstone of society. The state should adopt policies that promote family life as a solution to problems such as youth delinquency, addictions, and violence, and as a factor of social cohesion. Yet many acknowledge that the quality of family life has deteriorated in the late 20th and early 21st c. and expect further deterioration in the future.

Recent surveys show that marriage* has lost some of its attraction. The number of married people is decreasing. Contributing factors include fear of divorce* (which has increased), workplace demands, economic problems, changes in cultural values, women's independence, and, above all, the sense that living together before getting married is acceptable. Cohabitation as the beginning of a first union has increased sharply since the beginning of the 21st c. For some this shows that the taboo associated with sex has given way to a fear of commitment and of love*. Work and personal aspirations, rather than love, are vital concerns in relationships.

Highly educated young people with good jobs tend to postpone marriage. Once men and women have reached a greater level of psychological and social development, building a stable and healthy relationship is nonetheless not without difficulties, because each partner has a complex life and must learn to adapt to that of the other.

The single-parent family (generally a mother and children, but also a father and children) has always existed; yet according to 2000 and 2008 surveys, this type of family has multiplied (especially among relatively well off people), mainly because of the number of breakups and divorces. One-person homes have also increased (about 8% of the inhabitants of big cities). Family units tend to fragment. There are also a growing number of unions of divorced men and women who include their children from previous marriage(s) in the new family. Simultaneously, the importance of the extended family (which upholds traditional values of solidarity for the protection and help of relatives) is declining, though it is still important in lower-class and low-middle-class segments of society.

The high level of poverty* in Latin America affects families; many poor people cannot afford to marry, and many couples cannot afford to have children and support a family. Relationships within Latin American families change. Compared with their parents' generation, men have assumed more responsibilities for child care and household chores, but most domestic work remains women's responsibility. Yet economic and work-related conditions often make it difficult for parents to assume their traditional responsibilities toward children, who have been described as "horizontal children" (because their parents see them only at bedtime) or "orphan children" (because the parents' working hours are so long). In addition, surveys show a decrease in the number of children and the postponement of the birth of the first child, especially in the middle and upper classes.

The churches respond in three ways to these cultural changes in the concept and sense of family, and especially to the discovery that there are "nontraditional" families and couples in the churches themselves.

1. *Perplexity*. The churches recognize the new realities, but without adopting a critical stance. Often this attitude simply leads to conformity to the new cultural realities, without providing church members any orientation in light of the Christian faith.
2. *An Integrist* or fundamentalist* attitude* that uses Christian values in a reactionary way, without taking social problems into account and without showing mercy, compassion, or empathy to those who are struggling in these situations. Some of the Christians who adopt this stance are associated with conservative political groups or movements that advocate discrimination or authoritarian rules.
3. *Biblical and theological reflections* taking on the challenges posed by these new social, family, and personal realities. These reflections lead to an enriched understanding of the family in terms of its cultural essence rather than of unchangeable principles and laws. The church discovers that its responsibility includes pastoral* care for the family, viewed as a space for the protection, growth, nurturing, and enrichment of life. The church as the family of a variety of families through its pastoral ministry provides family counseling for its members, both in good times and in periods of crisis. The church can then use its prophetic voice to challenge society to strengthen and enrich those intimate spaces where life takes place and is nurtured – the family in its many forms. HUGO N. SANTOS

Family, Christian Views of, in North America: African American Traditions. The family in African American Christian traditions is an elastic and highly diversified entity that includes nuclear two-parent families, extended families, single-parent families, and "fictive" families that often incorporate close friends from church or the community who do not have living or close relatives. The scholar W. E. B. DuBois* observed that the origins of the Black Church (see African American Cluster: African American Churches and Their Theologies) preceded the origin of the black family. This refers to the fact that during slavery*, when marriage between black men and women was illegal, the earliest Black churches were permitted. Churches became "extended families" to include and affirm every community member, especially those members who had been sold or otherwise separated from their biological kin.

With freedom, black families achieved high rates of marriage and family stability. This strength was manifest during the Civil* Rights Movement, when Dr. Martin Luther King*, Jr., led Black Church members, both adults and children, in desegregating US society.

Since then, there has been urgent concern about the future of black families as rates of marriage* decline, divorce* rates increase, rates of father absence are high, and the percentage of nonmarital births is above 65%. Although the vast majority of African American Christians are Protestant, there are a large number of black Catholics. Both Protestants and Catholics have focused on strengthening black families. Among the most contentious issues being actively debated are women's* ordination and the status of homosexuals* within churches and within the larger matrix of family life. Increasingly, with parental absence, black families are relying on grandmothers as surrogate parents. Black churches support family life through a variety of creative practices, such as the celebration of "Men's Day" and "Women's Day," as well as the cultural acknowledgment of Mother's* Day and Father's Day. **See also** **MARRIAGE, THEOLOGY AND PRACTICE OF, CLUSTER: IN WESTERN CHURCHES**

ROBERT M. FRANKLIN

Family, Christian Views of, in the United States. Different religious views and practices of family formation are reflected in the demographic patterns in the USA. Family relationships that developed among Protestants, Roman Catholics, and Native American and African practitioners of indigenous religions contributed to tensions among different forms of family structure and patterns of hierarchy and equality.

In settling Massachusetts, e.g., many families were Puritan* and Calvinist, sought freedom to practice their religion, and expected a patriarchal* form of family life that exemplified "subordination and equivalence" – a Christian convention established as early as Augustine*. As a practical, social matter, women were understood to be subordinate to men, though from a theological standpoint women were equal to men. "Subordination" reinforced a father's and husband's control over property and inheritance and offered women little recourse in situations of domestic violence*. "Equivalence" met practical concerns during the Revolutionary War when women ran farms, repelled enemies, and were rewarded for their defense of the colonies with control over families and property.

In California, Roman Catholic Spanish military explorers sought gold. Armies consisted of single men who intermarried with Native Americans. When, e.g., the Spanish intermarried with Pueblos, they encountered matrilineal kinship systems that placed economic power among women and immediate responsibility for offspring with a mother's male relatives, even though children lived with fathers. The power of women in Pueblo families intersected with the reverence for Mary* in Roman Catholic tradition, changing the balance of power between men and women in some Southwestern families.

In the southern states, family formation was influenced by slaveholding. Some slaveholders perceived their households as "my family, white and black." As in the Greek household, a slaveholder had life-and-death control over slaves. The stability of slave families depended on the benevolence, wealth, and age of the slaveholder; slave families were disrupted by punishment, sale, or death of owners. Biblical arguments both supported and denied such family formation, and slaveholding by prominent religious families contributed to denominational schism in the 19th c. (see Slavery and the Christian Churches in North America).

In Minnesota, Lutheran family formation was linked to that of community, as entire communities of Scandinavian families relocated together in the Upper Midwest.

Scholars continue to debate the effects of such historical patterns on the poverty* of Native American and African American families, the "liberal" and "conservative" mentality of regions of the North American continent, and the support or lack thereof for family public policy in contemporary times. **See also** **MARRIAGE, THEOLOGY AND PRACTICE OF, CLUSTER.**

PAMELA COUTURE

Family, Christian Views of, in Western Europe. The "ethical landslide" of the 1960s (which culminated in the May 1968 youth revolt against all traditional values and literally paralyzed Europe for several weeks) shook up the status quo. Many people at the bottom of the hierarchical ladder in society and churches became conscious of their personhood and responsibility for their lives. A sense of freedom from traditional norms pervaded all of life, and especially views of family. Tradition as a source of true values lost its self-evidence for more and more people, especially the young, both in society at large and in the churches. There are still traditional Christian families in Western Europe, especially in traditional churches, where the father is the head of the family and the mother the general provider of care. But they are no longer a clear majority. Christian political parties, especially in Roman Catholic countries, as well as leaders of more traditional Protestant churches, have attempted to fight this trend, but without much success.

With increased mobility, children generally leave home in their late teens to be independent. Their point of reference becomes youth culture. The sense of belonging to a family dissolves and is replaced by a sense of belonging to a group of friends. When one thinks of "a family," one thinks of parents (often, one parent) with *young* children.

In this context, many young Christian people live together and do not marry; they have lost their trust in the institution of marriage. In Western Europe, about one-third of marriages end in divorce (Council of Europe statistics). These young people believe that it is better to live in love and responsibility for each other without a wedding than to have a sordid divorce. Commonly they marry, often in their 30s, when children are planned. Fertility manipulation, in order to either have or not have children, is generally practiced, even when a church prohibits it. Christians generally understand this as part of God's instruction to be responsible human beings.

Many women do not see themselves as first defined by family roles; their identity is framed by their work outside the home. Slowly, men are assuming half of the responsibility for child care and housekeeping. Many young children spend at least part of the week with other children in child care centers.

Christians on the whole no longer start to think about their lives and their identity in terms of the family, but in terms of their individual responsibility and accountability as persons, endowed by God with special gifts. In this individualistic culture, the churches give the opportunity to experience community. This community is not imaged as a family, but rather as a God-given group of friends. **See also FRIENDSHIP; MARRIAGE, THEOLOGY AND PRACTICE OF, CLUSTER.**

RIET EN PIM BONS-STORM

Family, Christian Views of, and Worldwide Issues: Feminist Theological Perspectives. Second-wave 20th-c. European-American feminists, as distinct from feminist adherents of earlier movements, identified the family, not just society in general, as the source of women's oppression. Books such as Betty Friedan's *The Feminist Mystique* and Simone de Beauvoir's *The Second Sex* contested homemaking as exploitative, fought against domestic violence, and pushed for equality in jobs and salaries. Christian and Jewish feminists contributed to this development by challenging religious justification for male domination, edicts such as "Wives, be subject to your husbands" (Eph 5:22; Col 3:18), and views of the order of creation* that placed women and children under men and God.

Divergent understandings of the family, however, marked both secular and religious feminists from the beginning. Liberal, humanist, and individualist forms of feminism of the 1960s and 1970s criticized the family as an obstacle to women's fulfillment. In the 1980s, social, radical, gynocentric, and relational* feminism shifted the critique to the wider cultural constructions and suggested that denigration of the female body*, procreativity, and maternal thinking (see Motherhood*) was a more fundamental problem. For women of color, the feminist critique of family failed to take account of their desires for safe homes, viable jobs for men and women, and protection of children* in a racist* society.

Approaches to the family among religious feminists fall roughly into three groups, which correspond to developments in feminist secular theory. Early white Feminist* theologians joined the humanist critique of religious norms of male rule and female service. In the 1980s and 1990s, Womanist* theologians saw the dismissal of motherhood and family as problematic and promoted broader norms of community mothering. Evangelical* Protestant and Roman Catholic feminists accepted some secular feminist tenets, such as affirmation of women's worth or protest about abuse, while reclaiming more explicitly religious mandates about marriage*, responsibility for children*, and social justice*.

Despite these differences, feminist scholars in religion and theology have made several significant contributions on the family that secular feminists and the general public often overlook. They have critiqued and reconstructed Scriptures* and traditions and offered important arguments for radical mutuality and egalitarian relationships in the family, the creation of women and children in God's image*, and the integral connection between reconstructing the family and reforming society.

BONNIE J. MILLER-MCLEMORE

Family, Christian Views of, and Worldwide Issues: Genocide and Modern Wars. The modern phenomenon of genocide and the proliferation of wars that specifically or collaterally target noncombatant families challenge traditional conceptions of God's power and justice* as well as the notion of suffering as redemptive. Racial and ethnoreligious forms of genocide aim to destroy the family as the future of a community: mass rape and mutilation, abduction and enslavement of children as soldiers, and systematic killing and maiming characterize ideologically motivated wars. Such genocidal wars degrade and dehumanize the entire community through extravagantly cruel treatment of women as childbearers and -rearers. Traditional theodicy* explains such suffering as (1) a chastening for past transgressions, (2) a test that will ultimately strengthen faith, and (3) redemptive suffering in the larger scheme of sacred history while asserting God's omnipotence*, benevolence, and omniscience*. However, the logic of theodicy ascribes a higher meaning to senseless suffering and thereby justifies the perpetrators and encourages the submission of victims to degradation and atrocity. Instead, the biblical traditions of Lamentations* and of protest against God can serve as starting points to develop faithful responses that foster resistance to oppressive ideologies and state-sanctioned cruelty inflicted on entire communities.

KATHARINA VON KELLENBACH

Family, Christian Views of, and Worldwide Issues: Nonheterosexual Two-Parent Families. Christian conservatives are alarmed by the heightened visibility and cultural acceptance of families headed by same-sex couples, the legalization of civil marriage* for same-sex couples in several countries (Canada, Belgium, the Netherlands, Spain, parts of the USA), and the movement within various religious traditions to bless same-sex unions. Traditionalists insist that the practice of nonmarital sex, including homoerotic intimacy, is not biblically authorized and threatens personal and social well-being. Progressives welcome nonheterosexuals fully into the life and leadership of the church, support their civil and human rights, including the freedom to marry, and call for a reformation of Christian sexual ethics in light of the biblical mandate to seek justice for the marginalized.

Christian conflict about sexuality*, marriage, and family is nothing new. The Reformers* challenged the Catholic ban on married clergy and allowed divorce* with the possibility of remarriage, but without reversing the tradition's sex negativity and patriarchal bias. They elevated a male-dominant model of marriage, restricted sexual activity to procreative activity between married spouses, and expected all eligible adults to marry and form families.

Within contemporary Christianity, sharp divisions have surfaced about women's power and roles, the acceptability of diverse sexualities, including homosexuality, bisexuality, and transgenderism, and the authority and sources for revising Christian sexual and family ethics.

Opponents of same-sex marriage idealize a 19th-c. Western middle-class nuclear family as the Christian norm, arguing that marriage as an immutable God-given institution is heterosexual for the purpose of rearing children, moral and complete because it brings together two sexually differentiated persons into a complementary union of "opposites." In contrast, progressives view marriage and family as changing institutions. Seeking to transform the anti-sex and patriarchal biases of Christian traditions, they argue for a relational* ethic focused not on identity, but on moral conduct and the character of relationships. Emphasizing the unitive rather than procreative purpose of marriage, they conclude that same-sex couples can fulfill the requirements of committed love and mutual care that marriage promises, and they invoke Jesus' nonconventional attitude toward family and community as a warrant for their stance.

This debate poses questions about the respective role of church* and state in family life and whether the marital family should be privileged over other kinds of intimate associations. It challenges Christians to consider whether faithfulness requires standing in continuity or discontinuity with their tradition when it comes to sexuality and relational justice.

MARVIN M. ELLISON

Families, Christian Views of, and Worldwide Issues: Substitute Families in Squatter Camps. Substitute families comprise persons not necessarily related by blood who form a family system, by choice, for mutual protection and sustenance. Roles and structures within these families usually attempt to mirror local social and religious ideals. Unaccompanied children, the elderly, and women displaced by economic, natural, or political disaster and/or by violence especially benefit from these relationships.

Massive squatter camps, unsanctioned by local government or international agencies, are often located in Two-thirds World countries (Latin America, Africa) where notions of family are influenced by Roman Catholicism and/or Evangelical Protestantism, and are also found in Western Europe, the Pacific, and Asia. While reflecting the gospel imperative to protect the vulnerable (Jas 1:27; Matt 25:40), substitute families usually portray the Pauline tradition of male hierarchy (Eph 5:23). The autonomy of women as heads of households, though, is common and accepted in regions prone to war and political instability (Ruth 1).

Traditional Christian views of procreation as the central purpose of family (Gen 1:28) conflict with the need for economic sustainability and the control of health and disease through the limitation of offspring within substitute families. For unaccompanied children, adoption threatens links to blood kin, potentially violating the Christian ethic* of care for one's family (I Tim 5:8).

M. JAN HOLTON

Farel, Guillaume (1489–1565), founder of the Reformed* Church in French-speaking Europe. The son of a notary in Gap (Southern France), he pursued advanced education in Paris. First under the spell of moderate Reformers like Jacques Lefèvre d'Etaples and Bishop Briçonnet of Meaux, he soon felt called to go all the way in becoming Protestant. He wrote several devotional works but was best known as an inflammatory preacher, capable of provoking riots with his sermons, with particularly strong attacks on Roman Catholic eucharistic* theology, using arguments parallel to Zwingli's*. He spent most of his career preaching in French-speaking areas along the border with Switzerland, sometimes with material support from Zwinglian Bern, as part of a campaign to spread its faith. His greatest success was in Geneva, where he persuaded local authorities to throw out their prince-bishop, to adopt laws outlawing the Mass and mandating Protestant worship (1535, 1536), and to hire Calvin* to assist him. Calvin, Farel, and others were thrown out of Geneva in 1538. Calvin alone returned in 1541 to consolidate the Reformation there. Farel spent most of the rest of his life directing the Reformation in and from Neuchâtel.

ROBERT M. KINGDON

Fascism and Christianity. See GERMAN CHRISTIANS AND THEIR THEOLOGY; RACISM AND CHRISTIANITY CLUSTER: IN WESTERN EUROPE.

Fast, Fasting. Abstention from food was practiced in Judaism and in early Christianity. Wednesdays and Fridays became the Christian fast days. Fasting became part of Lent* and, in the Eastern Church, several other seasons of the church year. In Protestantism, fast days have been called at times of crisis. Fasting is also an element of civil* disobedience.

Father, an honorific title for bishops, then confessors, and finally most priests, based on Paul's claim of spiritual fatherhood (1 Cor 4:14); a designation for one of the persons of the Trinity*.

Fátima. The apparitions at Fátima (1917), which gave rise to Portugal's premier pilgrimage center, are the subject of continuing controversy. Most non-Catholics have considered the veneration to be based on fraudulent claims. Although successive popes have affirmed the authenticity of the visions, many Catholics inside and outside Portugal remain unconvinced. Some skeptics interpret what happened as an example of popular religiosity imposing itself on the official church, as in medieval times (see Popular Christian Practices Cluster).

The Virgin appeared at the Cova da Iria, in the parish of Fátima, on the 13th day of each of the months of May to October 1917 to three young shepherds (although in August the date was actually the 19th because the children were held for questioning by a local republican official on the 13th). On October 13, thousands of witnesses at the Cova da Iria claimed to have seen the sun miraculously dance in the sky. Two of the children, Francisco and Jacinta Marto, died in an influenza epidemic (1919–20) and were beatified in 2000. Their older cousin, Lúcia de Jesus Santos (1907–2005), the principal visionary, became a Dorothean and later a Carmelite* nun living in seclusion in Coimbra. The local bishop declared the apparitions "worthy of credence" after canonical inquiry (1930). The visionary messages of 1917 were further elaborated by Lúcia in three "secrets." The first two were the reality of hell* and the need to consecrate Russia to the Immaculate Heart of Mary. The third secret, written down in 1944 and conveyed to the pope, was not revealed until 2000. The vision included the shooting, in an apocalyptic setting, of a "bishop dressed in white," which Cardinal Ratzinger (now Benedict XVI) interpreted as referring to the attempted assassination of John Paul II on May 13, 1981 (64th anniversary of the first vision).

RICHARD A. H. ROBINSON

Faustus of Riez (5th c.). Probably of British origin, he became a monk and abbot at Lérins, then bishop of Riez in Provence. Opposing predestination*, he wrote a treatise on grace* (472), insisting on the role of free choice as well as of grace (a semi-Pelagian* view). His views were condemned at the Second Council of Orange* (529).

Fear of God, in a negative sense, a feeling of impending danger from God's justice* and anger* ("servile" fear); in a positive sense, awe and reverence for God, as a child reveres a parent ("filial" fear), or in a mystical* experience.

Federal Council of Churches (FCC), an interdenominational North American organization founded in 1908. It had no authority over member churches and no creed*-making powers; its purpose was to express Christian unity and promote shared public action in evangelism*, education*, and social* justice. The founding assembly adopted the so-called Social Creed of the Churches (see Social Gospel Movement). The FCC became an indispensable means of interchurch cooperation during World War I, pioneered radio* broadcasts by leading preachers, and developed television* programs. The successor organization is the National* Council of Churches.

Felix of Urgel (d818), one leader of so-called Spanish Adoptianism*. Probably influenced by the language of an older approach to Christology* in the West, its proponents were attacked during the reign of Charlemagne* from the perspective of earlier doctrinal decisions, especially the Second Council of Constantinople* (553).

Fell, Margaret (1614–1702), English "mother of Quakerism*" (Religious Society of Friends*), leader, publisher, petitioner, prisoner of conscience. Daughter of a "gentleman" of Dalton (Furness, Lancashire), widow (1658) of judge Thomas Fell, she married (1669) George Fox*, founder of the Quaker Movement, whose preaching had convinced her to become a Quaker in 1652.

For 50 years, Fell promoted Quakerism's post–civil war radical Christian agenda: for Spirit*-led renewal*; a clergy-less church; social* justice*; refusal of oaths*, tithes*, militarism, and status-defining dress and politeness; and the spiritual equality and public ministry of women.

Despite hostility from the state and the Anglican Church, her home, Swarthmoor Hall (Ulverston), was Quakerism's hub, an illegal meeting place for worshippers, as well as a respite center for traveling ministers. She corresponded with Fox, who was frequently absent; published epistles to Quaker groups; remonstrated with individuals, from magistrates to Quaker dissenters; wrote tracts to European Jews (translated into Hebrew); and supported controversial women's meetings for Quaker governance. Some doctrinal publications (e.g. on Quakers' marriage rites and peaceability) predated Fox's on those subjects. Imprisoned for being a Quaker (1666–67), she wrote *Women's Speaking Justified*, a spirited Bible-based defense of women's* ministry.

Variously loved or loathed by factions in Quakerism, Margaret Fell was committed to the life of the Spirit, freedom of worship, and justice, as her writings make clear.

CHRISTINE TREVETT

FEMINIST THEOLOGICAL PERSPECTIVES

See BIBLE INTERPRETATION CLUSTER: WORLDWIDE: FEMINIST; CHRISTOLOGIES CLUSTER: IN NORTH AMERICA: FEMINIST AND WOMANIST; CHURCH, CONCEPTS AND LIFE, CLUSTER: FEMINIST PERSPECTIVES; DEATH, CHRISTIAN VIEWS OF, CLUSTER: AMONG WESTERN FEMINISTS; ECOLOGY AND CHRISTIANITY CLUSTER: ECOFEMINIST THEOLOGY; ESCHATOLOGY CLUSTER: ESCHATOLOGY AND APOCALYPTICISM IN NORTH AMERICA: FEMINIST PERSPECTIVES; FAMILY, CHRISTIAN VIEWS OF, CLUSTER: WORLDWIDE ISSUES: FEMINIST THEOLOGICAL PERSPECTIVES; GOD, CHRISTIAN VIEWS OF, CLUSTER: IN NORTH AMERICA: FEMINIST UNDERSTANDINGS OF; GRACE OF GOD CLUSTER: NORTH AMERICAN FEMINIST PERSPECTIVE; INCARNATION CLUSTER: IN NORTH AMERICA: FEMINIST UNDERSTANDINGS; JUSTIFICATION, THEOLOGICAL VIEWS AND PRACTICES, CLUSTER: IN WESTERN EUROPE: FEMINIST VIEWS; LIBERATION THEOLOGIES CLUSTER: FEMINIST; POVERTY CLUSTER: POVERTY, THEOLOGY, AND ETHICS: NORTH AMERICAN FEMINIST VIEWS; RACISM AND CHRISTIANITY CLUSTER: IN NORTH AMERICA: FEMINIST THEOLOGY AND SYSTEMIC RACISM

FEMINIST THEOLOGY CLUSTER

Feminist Theology in Africa. "The way forward is a 'new community of men and women,' not reversal; participation, not takeover or handover. Feminism in theology springs from a conviction that a theology of relationships might contribute to bring us closer to human life as God desires it." These words, written by the "mother of African theology," Mercy Amba Oduyoye, remain relevant to African Feminist theology today.

African women theologies and biblical hermeneutics are important not only because sub-Saharan Africa has become more Christian than Europe, but also because African women theologians have published much. An attempt to capture all African women's theologies (theories and/or praxes) under the rubric "Feminist theologies" is problematic, because these women have not yet adopted a uniform designation for their work. The label "African women's theologies" better captures what these women do and say in women-identified God-talk and in their theological efforts (theories and/or praxes) at the heart of their constant struggle to seek affirmation as human beings of equal worth despite patriarchal structures, be they social, religious, cultural, economic, or political. African women theologians, some of whom founded the Circle* of Concerned African Women Theologians (or the Circle), participated in the women's Commission of the Ecumenical* Association of Third World Theologians (EATWOT) in the late 1970s. The Circle was formed (1989, Accra, Ghana) because of these women's painful observation that EATWOT theologies did not take African women's experiences seriously. Since its inception, the Circle has provided space to African women theologians for networking, mentoring, attending academic meetings, and writing. Established in the Anglophone, Lusophone, and Francophone African contexts, Circle members hold continental meetings every five years. Circle chapters in different regions cater to local needs. Since the publication of their first book, *The Will to Arise: Women, Tradition and the Church in Africa* (1992), Circle members have published more than 100 books. The various strands of African women's Feminist theology, i.e. Circle and non-Circle ones, written or oral, focus on the critique of patriarchy as manifested in the African culture and religion, in the church, and in the neocolonial imperial structures that continue to have a negative impact on women's lives. In addition, in aural African contexts, including many nonliterate women and female children, although not authored, African Feminist theology is either orally articulated in various churches and women's organizations or lived in women's daily lives in private and public spaces.

Although relatively recent compared with its Western counterpart, Feminist theology in Africa has matured, in relative terms, more quickly. However, as can be expected owing to the smaller number of African women theologians and biblical scholars available, in many parts of the continent Feminist theology is still taking root and sprouting. **See also THEOLOGY AS HUMAN UNDERTAKING CLUSTER: AFRICAN WOMEN THEOLOGIANS DOING THEOLOGY BY MAKING CONNECTIONS.**

MADIPOANE MASENYA (NGWAN'A MPHAHLELE)

Feminist Theology in Asia. Asian Feminist theology emerged in the late 1970s, as Christian women related the Bible and faith to Asian sociopolitical and religious-cultural realities after political independence. Associations of theologically trained women were formed in different parts of Asia, while ecumenical networks such as the Ecumenical* Association of Third World Theologians and the Asian Women's Resource Center for Theology and Culture facilitated exchange and dialogue.

The Bible occupies a pivotal place in church life, and Asian Feminist theologians emphasize the liberating heritage of the Bible by lifting up biblical women such as Ruth and Naomi, Hannah, Miriam, Deborah, and Mary, the mother of Jesus, as role models. Some have used Asian myths, stories, and legends to reinterpret biblical stories and the faith traditions. They have insisted that Western culture does not have a monopoly over Christianity, which must interact with different cultures of the world. Because Christians make up less than 3% of the Asian population, an important concern is interreligious dialogue and solidarity with other women working for justice*.

Asian Feminist theologians have presented different images of Jesus*. Filipino Feminist theologians stress Jesus as a fully liberated human being, whose prophetic ministry challenged the status quo and transgressed the religious and ethnic boundaries of his time. Korean feminists appropriated their Shamanistic* tradition and reinterpret Jesus as a priest of *han*, a feeling of hopelessness and indignation against unjustifiable suffering. Indian feminists speak of Jesus as the embodiment of Shakti, the creative Hindu feminine principle. Others have presented organic metaphors for Christ and postcolonial interpretations of Jesus.

Instead of a docile and obedient mother, Mary is seen as a co-redeemer for human salvation, a model of true discipleship, and a fully liberated human being. Mary challenges the cultural norms and partakes in God's mission with a profound historical sense of the destiny of her people. Asian Feminist theologians challenge the churches to recognize women as full members of the body of Christ and equal partners in ministry. They seek to develop an ecofeminist* spirituality that is life affirming, respects the sacredness of the earth, and empowers women to struggle against the exploitation of the global economic order, sex tourism, militarism, and gender oppression. In an age of globalization,

Asian Feminist theologians condemn the structural sin* of oppression* brought by the market economy and search for alternative orderings of the world that value women's sexuality* and dignity and justice for the marginalized*. KWOK PUI-LAN

Feminist Theology in Latin America takes into account the historical context in which women live in this region and, above all, their poverty* and marginalization*, not only as women, but also as members of a society that has been historically marginalized by the imposition of colonialism* under the capitalist system. Therefore, Latin American Feminist theology focused, and still focuses, on the triad characterizing the domination inflicted on Latin American women (class, gender, and ethnicity) and on an ecumenical approach seeking to retrieve noncanonical and/or forgotten traditions of feminine wisdom*. Latin American Feminist theological reflections are also rooted in and nourished by pastoral work.

Feminist theologians Elsa Tamez, Ibone Gebara, María Pilar Aquino, and Mary Judith Ress identify three phases of Latin American Feminist theology. (1) the 1970s, during which there was little differentiation from the issues and perspectives of Liberation* theology, (2) the 1980s, during which there was an increased focus on gender issues and problems affecting women as women (vs. those affecting them as, e.g., poor or as Latin American); and (c) the 1990s to the present, a period that has seen a full-fledged antipatriarchal stance and radical gender perspectives in language, theology, and biblical hermeneutics. This last phase includes holistic ecofeminism* (Ivone Gebara and Con-Spirando), queer* theory (Marcella Althaus-Reid), positions legitimizing heterodox views challenging traditional Christian anthropology* and cosmology, appreciation of insights coming from African and Amerindian spiritual and mythical traditions, and even some forms of post*-Christian spirituality.

Feminist theologians have created communal spaces of reflection and fellowship. Some of the prominent groups are Con-Spirando in Chile* (with a journal on Latin American ecofeminism), Talitha Cumi in Peru*, and Gaia in Venezuela*. One trend in Latin American Feminist theology reconceptualizes the fundamental themes of traditional theology from an ecofeminist* perspective; another trend is concerned with developing a feminist biblical hermeneutics (Carmiña Navia Velasco, Alicia Winters, Tania Sampaio, Elsa Tamez, Irene Foulkes, and the biblical journal *RIBLA* of Costa Rica). *Ecofeminism in Latin America* by Mary Judith Ress includes reflections by several of the women working on these issues: Agamdilza Sales de Oliveira, Marcia Moya, Coca Trillini, Sandra Duarte, Fanny Geymonat-Pantelís, Sandra Raquew, Graciela Pujol, Alcira Agreda, Clara Luz Ajo, Doris Muñoz, Gladys Perentelli, and Silvia Regina de Lima Silva. Teolgandas, a group of women theologians based in Buenos Aires, follows a more orthodox perspective. Each group has a surprisingly unique, beautiful theological voice, denoting the richness, strength, and depth of insight of the movement.

ANA MARÍA BIDEGAIN and JUAN SANCHEZ

Feminist Theology in North America, as a formal academic field, emerged in 1968 with the publication of Mary Daly's *The Church and the Second Sex*, a powerful critique of the second-class status of women in Roman Catholicism. Reflecting the broader movement of "second-wave" feminism of which they were a part, early Feminist theologians claimed women's experience as a primary authoritative source. From that ground, Daly and others unmasked the damage done to women by traditional theological ideas. As Daly put it in her second book, *Beyond God the Father*, "If God is male, then the male is God." Feminist theologians not only critiqued male dominance in church and society, but argued that masculinist bias also shaped gender roles and underwrote environmental exploitation. Understanding sin* as pride and salvation* as self-giving love* encouraged women to sacrifice their own ambitions and desires for others, as Valerie Saiving and Judith Plaskow argued. As a corrective, they claimed self-abnegation as a distinctively feminine form of sin. Meanwhile, other Feminist theologians drew on neglected sources in Western religious traditions (including neopaganism) to cultivate alternative images of God, a project carried forward by Sallie McFague and Elizabeth Johnson. Catherine Keller and Laurel Schneider have moved beyond *reimaging* God to *reimagining* the divine. Other loci taken up for critique and reconstruction over the years include Christology* and atonement* theory (Brock, Joh, and Ray).

Feminist theology continues to reflect larger trends in women's studies. In the 1980s and 1990s, Feminist theology, like other fields, came under fire for its own exclusive tendencies, grounded in the content given to "women's experience." Womanist* (African* American Feminist) and Mujerista* (Latina Feminist) theologians argued persuasively that Feminist theologians framed their understanding of women's oppression – and thus their agenda for liberation – in terms of white middle-class women's needs and ambitions (Williams and Isasi-Diaz). Living at the intersection of racism*, sexism*, and classism* means women of color face distinctive forms of oppression that white Feminist theologians failed to take into account. Another important trend in Feminist theology prompted largely by attempts to address more adequately women's diversity has been the turn to theory. In addition to theories of race, gender, and sexuality, Feminist theologians have found postcolonial* and poststructuralist* theories useful analytical and constructive tools (Armour, Fulkerson, Joh, Keller, Kwok, and Welch). Feminist theologians are also increasingly engaged in work that crosses the lines that separate religious traditions (Farley, Joh, and Kwok). ELLEN T. ARMOUR

Feminist Theology in North America: African American. See LIBERATION THEOLOGIES CLUSTER: WOMANIST; WOMANIST AND AFRICAN AMERICAN THEOLOGIES.

Feminist Theology in North America: Latina. Focusing on women who are poor, Feminist theology is a critical reflection of the religious experiences and thought of peoples and communities living in the USA whose shared values and understandings express Latin American cultural and religious traits. It seeks to contribute in feminist religious terms both to sustaining the struggles to change kyriarchal* silencing, marginalization, and domination, and to actualizing the Christian vision of justice* for a renewed creation (see New Creation). Comprising diverse approaches from particular theological fields, the conceptual framework of Latina Feminist theology articulates the following shared methodological features.

Critical Analysis. Meeting the aspirations of subordinated women for human dignity, self-worth, and freedom from poverty entails recovering the historical legacy of Latina women's initiatives against colonization* and dehumanization. It also entails empowering the voices and agency of women today through conscientization*, which identifies oppressive* situations caused by multidimensional, multiplicative, and interrelated systems of domination and discloses viable paths for transformative theological interpretation.

"Border Crosser" Hermeneutics. While fostering a consciousness of being historical subjects of change, Latinas move across symbolic and physical boundaries, becoming themselves "border bodies." As such, whether found in biblical narratives, in religious traditions, or in daily life, theological interpretation brings together plural forms of wisdom to affirm new ways of *convivencia* (living together).

Commitment to Transformation. Recognizing diversity and difference as characteristics of human beings, this theology values dialogue*, relationality*, and interdependence as crucial to overcoming social and religious hostilities. In shaping alternatives of justice* for humanity and the world, this theology affirms shared intellectual practices to provide helpful interpretations of the Christian faith and supports common religious, ethical, and political spaces to renew spirituality and hope. The critical adoption of interdisciplinary, interreligious, and intercultural approaches into theological elaboration is an asset of this theology, but other pressing issues remain insufficiently addressed, such as women's sexual health, sexuality* and power, and radically changing power structures of institutional churches and religions. **See also** LATINO/A THEOLOGIES. MARÍA PILAR AQUINO

Feminist Theology in North America: Mujerista. Mujerista theology is a liberative praxis* – a reflective action that contributes to the liberation of Latinas and their communities in the USA. Mujerista theology enables Latinas by helping them to develop strong moral agency, clarifying the importance of who they are and the value of what they think and do. It helps Latinas affirm God's presence and revelation in their communities and daily lives. It exposes the many oppressive societal structures that are offensive to God because they hide God's presence in the world. Mujerista theology emphasizes Latinas' preferred future, providing glimpses of the "kin-dom"* of God, the family of God, in the midst of present social, economic, and political realities. The source of Mujerista theology is Latinas' lived experience, viewing Christian theology as "faith seeking understanding," its age-old definition. Mujerista theology does not exclude church teachings, biblical traditions, or popular religions with their mixture of Christian, African, and Amerindian religions. It is a communal theology based on Latinas' reflection on their religious understandings and practices and the role these play in their daily struggle for fullness of life and liberation. Because of its recent development and the small number of Latina theologians, Mujerista theology is but a small daughter born of the hope* of Latina women for their liberation* and the liberation of all peoples. Yet as a small daughter, Mujerista theology participates in the family of liberation and women-centered theologies that have emerged around the world since 1960. By its serious critique of Latino culture* as well as of the U.S. dominant culture from the perspective of gender, race and ethnicity, and class, Mujerista theology seeks to have an impact on mainline theologies that implicitly or explicitly support what is normative in church and society without taking into consideration Latinas' faith traditions and practices.
ADA MARÍA ISASI-DÍAZ

Feminist Theology in Pacific Islands and Australia. The Pacific region covers a broad area, stretching from Papua New Guinea in the north, to Hawaii in the east, to Australia* and New* Zealand in the south, and to New Caledonia in the west. European colonization began in the 1700s, and Christianity was a major force in introducing indigenous peoples to European culture, mainly through the establishment of church missions. There is widespread evidence that before European colonization, busy trade routes within the Pacific tied together strong, and highly varied, indigenous cultures.

Predictably, church mission* most often involved the degradation of local religions – often very violently – in the establishment of a European style Christianity. Nevertheless, Christianity in the Pacific today reflects more often than not a blending of traditional rites and beliefs with various Christian theologies and church practices, and a high percentage of Pacific Islanders are Christian.

Feminist theology is relatively new in this region and is certainly characterized by a wide diversity of theologies, reflecting engagement with various Christian traditions and cultures. However, women across the Pacific have been involved in reevaluating their religious and theological traditions from a variety of cultural and feminist perspectives. There have been numerous forums and publications in which such feminist theologizing has been communicated. Two examples are the EATWOT (Ecumenical* Association of Third World Theologians) consultation "Pacific Women and Theology" and "Weaving Women and Theology," a second consultation of "Weavers," the women's subcommittee of the South Pacific Association of Theological Schools. A special issue on Pacific women was published in Vol. 15 of the *Pacific Journal of*

Theology (1996), edited by Lisa Meo. The Weavers writer's workshop in April 2001 resulted in the 2003 publication of *Weavings: Women Doing Theology in Oceania.*

Feminist theology has been a dynamic discourse in Australia and New Zealand among nonindigenous women; there have been many publications, conferences, and organizations, which have resulted in changes to patriarchal church practices, such as the ordination* of women in Anglican and Uniting churches, changes in sexist liturgical language, and the participation of women in liturgies and church institutions. More recently, Women Scholars in Religion and Theology (WSRT) has been networking between nonindigenous and indigenous women in the Pacific to set up forums and publications around issues in Feminist theology. The WSRT publishes an online journal, *Seachanges* (wsrt.com.au/seachanges), and holds conferences every four years.

ELAINE M. WAINWRIGHT

Feminist Theology in Western Europe. The *Yearbook of the European Society of Women in Theological Research* (from 1993) and its annual bibliographies provide a route into the spectrum of Feminist theology across linguistic, cultural, and ecclesiastical differences. Differences between countries, however, can be profound, depending on access to education in theology/religious studies. In, e.g., Ireland*, Feminist theology is in its infancy, whereas in Italy* researchers on women in the history of the church (e.g. Ricci) and theologians such as Cettina Militello (who have organized international colloquiums since 1985) have undertaken pioneering work. A European "new feminism," in constructive dialogue with Pope John* Paul II's insights in particular, discusses the positions that may advance a Christian case for the full human dignity of women (Schumacher). Writing as a Norwegian Roman Catholic, Kari-Elisabeth Børresen has since 1968 challenged some of the foundations of inherited Christian anthropology* and, in France*, Elisabeth Behr-Sigel voiced the profound concerns of Orthodox women about their ministry in the church, with inevitable implications for theology (Behr-Sigel) (see Women's Ordination Cluster: The Orthodox Church). Feminist theology in the Netherlands* has made inroads since the 1970s, and the Dutch research program on religion and gender (e.g. de Haardt) relates closely to a wider "women and faith" network across the denominations. In the Federal Republic of Germany*, Feminist theology has also developed since the 1970s, especially in connection with biblical studies in the Evangelical churches and faculties (Moltmann-Wendel), and major work has been achieved on the study of Christian origins (Schottroff, Schroer, and Wacker). Some of the best-known biblical interpreters now working in North America were originally from the Federal Republic. In the UK, some provocative new writers have emerged (Althaus Reid and Beattie) with no inhibitions about the re-evaluation of Christianity's core symbolism and doctrines.

ANN LOADES

Fencing the Table, in the Reformed* churches, protection against desecrating the Eucharist* by excluding all who have not repented*, specifically at a preparatory* service.

Fénelon, François de Salignac de la Mothe (1651–1715), Catholic cleric, writer, proponent of Quietism*. Fénelon earned a reputation as tutor to Louis XIV's grandson (1689) and as author of *Treatise on the Education of Girls* (1687) and *Telemachus* (1699), a novel about how to rule wisely and create a productive society. The novel's classicism suggested a biblical frame of reference and an indictment of Louis's absolutism.

At the court, Fénelon met Jeanne Guyon*, a lay spiritual adviser and mystic*. As bishop of Cambray (1695), he defended Madame Guyon*, the subject of an official ecclesiastical inquiry into Quietism*. She advocated contemplative* prayer, abnegation of the self, union with the divine will, inner repose, acceptance of suffering and persecution*, and disinterested or pure love*. Fénelon engaged his former mentor Bossuet* in a public debate over this "new" mysticism*. Fénelon's treatise *Explication of the Maxims of the Saints* (1697) maintained that the doctrine of pure love belonged to a continuous tradition of church teaching. Madame Guyon was imprisoned in the Bastille, and Fénelon was exiled to his bishopric. The pope (following Louis XIV) condemned the *Explication* (1699); Fénelon submitted to papal authority. In exile, he achieved mythic status for his acts of charity. Posthumously, his letters of spiritual direction were influential. PATRICIA A. WARD

Feudal System, a form of social, political, and economic order based on mutual oaths between a lord and a vassal. The lord granted land and the people who labored on it (a fief) to a member of the warrior class (the vassal) in exchange for a promise of military service. The vassal then had a similar relation to his people. The system was regularized in the empire of Charlemagne* and continued for many centuries in Europe and its colonies (*encomienda* and *hacienda* in the Spanish colonies [see Reductions]). Feudalism did not prevail everywhere in Europe; there were always some areas in which there were farmers or city dwellers who developed institutions of self-government. To some extent, the feudal pattern of relationship (lord-vassal) became reflected in the Christian conception of the God-human relationship (e.g. Atonement #2).

Feuerbach, Ludwig (1804–72), atheistic critic of Christianity and father of projection theories of religion*. After studying theology in Heidelberg, he transferred to Berlin to study philosophy with Hegel*. He was fired from his first academic position at Erlangen for his book *Thoughts on Death and Immortality* (1830), which espoused a form of pantheism* and rejected a personal deity and personal immortality. He left academia to become an independent scholar. In the 1830s, he sided with the Young Hegelians for whom Hegel's idealism was incompatible with Christian doctrine. He became famous in the 1840s for *The Essence of Christianity* and writings calling for a "philosophy of the future" that repudiated idealism and embraced a naturalistic humanism founded on I–Thou relationships (see I–Thou Relation) and social solidarity. After 1859, bankruptcy forced him to live out his life with the financial aid of friends.

In *The Essence of Christianity,* Feuerbach argued that in religion the human being projects or objectifies his or her own image of the self and then turns this objectified image into a subject for whom human beings are objects. Deities are objectifications of human nature, the Christian deity being the objectification of the essential human attributes of reason*, will*, and love*. The imagination clings to this projection because it expresses the deepest human desire for recognition and immortality. But the idea of God* as a separate being is contradictory, and if one follows the inner logic of the Christian doctrine of the Incarnation*, one will be led to an atheistic* humanism because this doctrine states that God sacrificed God's own nature out of love for humankind.

Feuerbach continued to refine his theory of religion, increasingly stressing that the origins of religion lay in the feeling of dependency on nature and our desire to transcend its necessities (especially death) by humanizing it. **See also ATHEISM AND CHRISTIAN THEOLOGY.**

VAN A. HARVEY

Fiat (Lat "Let it be"), Mary's* response to the Annunciation* (Luke 1:38); a primary instance of human acceptance of divine grace*.

Fideism, emphasis on faith* at the expense of reasoning; the term usually has a negative connotation.

Fiji. The Christian experience in Fiji can be divided into two major phases. The first entailed the proselytization of the native Fijians by 19th-c. missionaries who came from the United* Kingdom, Australia*, and New* Zealand beginning in 1835. Under one of these missionaries, John Hunt, a Methodist theologian, Fijians converted from a polytheism that may have recognized the concept of a supreme being among many nature gods. Hunt's influence was instrumental in the "submission to Jehovah" of the Fijian chief Ratu Seru Epenisa Cakobau and subsequently, with the assistance of Tongan and Fijian teachers and other sympathetic chiefs, the conversion of all Fijians by 1900. Over these years, the Methodists* (65%) were joined in Fiji by Roman Catholics, Anglicans*, and Seventh*-day Adventists.

The second phase of Christianity in Fiji (20th–21st c.) was influenced by the arrival of the Indo-Fijian population (1879–1920), indentured through colonialism* to work in the sugar industry; their numbers eventually grew to 45% of the total population. Christian churches worked diligently among the Indians, yet have gained relatively few converts. Preserving community identity in a foreign and sometimes unwelcoming environment (without secure access to land resources) has been a rallying point for Hinduism* and Islam* in Fiji. Yet Indo-Fijians generally accept the education and welfare facilities, such as orphanages, that Christians provide.

Social and political change arising from urbanization also influenced modern Christianity in Fiji. Although today's Fijians still celebrate their faith with devotion and passion, they retain a predominantly exclusivist, Sabbatarian* heritage, averse to liberalizing influences and ecumenicism*, which is a weak and divided movement within Fiji. This conservative Christian expression applies equally to the newer Pentecostal*/Charismatic* religious groups that have proliferated especially among urban dwellers struggling to cope with Western modes of life. Meanwhile, the established churches – notably the influential Methodists – are slow to address social issues central to effective urban mission, such as the amelioration of poverty*. Fiji's four "coups" since 1987, provoked mainly by grievances expressed through a Fijian-dominated army, have intensified the image of Christianity as inimical to the interests of the Indo-Fijian minority and their religious beliefs. For this reason alone, interfaith dialogue* is critical to the future social stability of Fiji.

Statistics: Population (2000): 817,000. Christians, 463,600, 57% (Methodists, 34.5%; Roman Catholics, 7.2%; members of Assembly of God, 3.8%; Seventh-day Adventists, 2.6%; independents/Charismatics, 8.9%); Hindus, 34%; Muslims, 7%; nonreligious, 2%. (Based on *World Christian Encyclopedia*, 2001, and 1996 census.)

ANDREW THORNLEY

***Filioque*.** The doctrine that the Spirit* proceeds from the Father *and the Son* (Lat *Filioque*) rather than from the Father alone (John 15:26 and the Niceno*-Constantinopolitan Creed).

The West, following Augustine*, held this doctrine and, at the Council of Braga (675), officially augmented the Nicene Creed with these words. This form of the Creed was widely disseminated in Charlemagne's* Frankish empire, but was condemned by the Eastern Orthodox* Church and by the pope. The *Filioque* was finally inserted into the Roman creed in 1014, at a time marked by tensions with the East.

The *Filioque* remains a major point of dissension. The Western churches insist that the giving of the Spirit through Christ is a manifestation of intradivine relations. The Eastern Church acknowledges that the Spirit is given through Christ (John 20:22), but only in connection with the Father's creation*, redemption*, and sanctification*. But saying that Christ gives the Spirit blurs the distinction between persons of the Trinity* and implicitly denies that in the Incarnation* the person of the Son was fully united to human nature. The Anglican bishops have permitted the removal of the *Filioque* from the Nicene Creed.

The *Filioque* implies that the Spirit comes with or through the Word* (Scripture, proclamation, sacraments) and thus through the church and its ministries. Is this the case? Or is the Spirit "free," poured out independently of an institutional church? EUGENE TESELLE

Finland. In predominantly Lutheran Finland, Western and Eastern Christianity have met through history. Christianity in Finland has long been associated with two "folk* churches," the Lutheran Church and the Orthodox Church.

Christianity arrived in Finland from both the West (Roman Catholic) and the East (Orthodox) in the 11th c. In the 16th c., the primarily Catholic Finland became Lutheran with Finnish Michael Agricola* (1510–57) as its reformer. The arrival of small religious minorities (Jews, Muslim Tatars), new Christian influences (Methodism, Evangelical Free Church, Pentecostalism), and an increasing number of nonreligious persons changed the religious scene (late 19th–early 20th c.). National independence (1917) made it possible to pass the Freedom of Religion Act (1922), renewed in 2003 to take into account the increasingly multireligious scene. The official ties between the state and the Lutheran Church have been gradually severed. The state is neutral on religious questions.

Finnish spirituality has been marked by five revivals* within the established Lutheran Church. The four 19th-c. revivals had Pietist* roots – with one of them, Laestadianism, also spreading in Sweden and Norway. The Neo-Pietist Movement (which originated after World War II) has close links with the Anglo-Saxon Evangelical* revival. Since the 1970s, the Charismatic* Movement has gained a foothold in the Lutheran and other Protestant churches.

Although Lutherans are not frequent churchgoers, church-officiated life cycle rites (baptism, confirmation, wedding, burial) are highly regarded. New types of church services (Thomas* Mass) have become popular, along with the summer festivals of the revivalist movements, which tens of thousands attend.

The Evangelical Lutheran Church has nine dioceses (c500 parishes). Women have long played a central role in church social services. In 1986 women's ordination was accepted. The autonomous Orthodox Archbishopric of Finland (three dioceses) has belonged since 1923 to the

Patriarchate of Constantinople. The clergy of both folk churches are trained at theological faculties of state universities (Helsinki, Åbo, Joensuu). Free churches have their own theological schools. Religious education in one's confession is provided in primary and secondary schools. The Finnish church religiosity serves as civil religion: church services are a part of the opening of Parliament and of Independence Day celebrations.

The Lutheran Church, an active defender of a "welfare society" and an advocate of solidarity with the poor of the world, has promoted cooperation between Lutheran and Anglican churches (Porvoo* Declaration).

Statistics: Population (2000): 5.2 million (M); Christians, 4.8 M, 86% (Lutherans, 4.35 M, 84.2%; Orthodox, 0.05 M, 1%; other Protestants and Roman Catholics, 0.04 M, 0.08%); nonreligious, 0.68 M, 13%; Muslims and Jews, 0.2%. (*Source*: 2000 census.)

EILA HELANDER

Finney, Charles Grandison (1792–1875), revival leader; president (1851–66), professor of systematic theology (1835–58), and professor of pastoral theology (1835–75) at Oberlin College. The most famous 19th-c. revival* preacher, Finney developed beliefs and practices that still exert a powerful influence across multiple strands of Christianity.

Finney grew up with transformations in the wake of the American Revolution (see United States): westward migrations, the disestablishment of churches, democratic sentiments, an expanding industrial and consumer economy, and new anxieties concerning gender and race. Finney developed "new measures" for revival that complemented and deepened these shifts. He led mass revivals throughout the northeastern and mid-Atlantic states (notably in Rochester, New York, 1830–31) and in Great Britain (1849–50, 1859–60).

A descendant of old New England families, Finney radicalized the New* Haven theology's emphasis on free will (see Freedom, Free Will) and later blended it with Wesleyan* notions of perfection*. Converted in a revival, Finney adapted practices developed by itinerant and camp* meeting preachers – preachers who were lay and ordained, male and female, African American and European American. Trained as a lawyer, Finney cultivated an orderly but expressive style that appealed to an emerging white middle class. Finney made the ecstatic repeatable and the sensational respectable.

Finney's sense of holiness* required both personal conversion* and social transformation. He led movements for temperance*, educational* reform, new opportunities for women, and the abolition of slavery*. Finney's synthesis became the dominant form of Protestant Christianity in the USA. This synthesis began to break down (late 19th c.) into several movements. Finney's stress on second baptism and perfection informed the Pentecostal* Movement. His call for social reform flowed through the Social* Gospel Movement into mainline Protestantism. His demand for personal conversion and mass revival influenced Dwight Moody*, Billy Graham, and Evangelicalism* more broadly.

TED A. SMITH

Firmilian (d268), bishop of Caesarea in Cappadocia. An admirer of Origen* (perhaps through Gregory* Thaumaturgus), he went to Caesarea in Palestine to hear him. He corresponded with Cyprian* during the controversy over the lapsed*, supporting him against Rome. He presided over the first council that condemned Paul* of Samosata (264) and died on the way to the second (268).

Flacius, Matthias Illyricus (1520–75), a student of Luther* and Melanchthon*, first leader of the "Gnesio*-Lutheran Movement." Italo-Croatian by birth, Flacius came to Wittenberg (1541) in a spiritual crisis, from which Luther freed him. Instructor of Hebrew at Wittenberg (1544), he resigned in protest against what he perceived as Melanchthon's compromise with the papacy. Flacius's ongoing rancorous exchanges with Melanchthon and his radical interpretation of Luther's thought helped organize opponents of Melanchthon's policy into the "Gnesio-Lutheran group. He taught theology at Jena (1557–61) but otherwise remained a private scholar, pioneering Protestant hermeneutics (*Clavis Scripturae Sacrae*, 1567) and biblical studies (*Glossa Novi Testamenti*, 1570 texts) and experimenting with new forms of church history that critiqued papal claims (he composed *Catalogus Testium Veritatis* [1556] and planned though did not write the first Protestant church history, the *Magdeburg Centuries* [1559–74]). In Magdeburg he led the opposition to the "Interim*" of Charles V (1548). This led to Flacius's doctrine of *status* confessionis*: when indifferent matters are made essential, they are no longer indifferent and must be opposed. Flacius's assertion that original* sin was the

"substance" of sinners and reshaped them in the "image of Satan" alienated most of his followers during the last 15 years of his life.
ROBERT KOLB

Flagellants, those who scourged themselves, often in public procession, in penance* for the sins of the world; first noticed in 1260, they were possibly influenced by the ideas of Joachim* of Flora.

Flavian (d449), patriarch of Constantinople, who aroused controversy in 448 when he secured the excommunication* of Eutyches* for his Monophysite* views about Christ. The Second Council of Ephesus* (449) was called under imperial pressure; Flavian died after a severe beating (apparently by three deacons from Alexandria) and was declared a heretic. He was vindicated by the Council of Chalcedon* (451).

Flavia Vitalia, a freeborn, married (*matrona*) presbyter*, was the agent of the church for the sale of a burial plot, according to the 425 CE inscription found in Salona, Dalmatia (present-day Solin, Croatia): "Under our Lord Theodosius, consul for the eleventh time, and Valentinian, most noble man of Caesar, I, Theodosius, bought [a tomb] from the matron Flavia Vitalia, the holy presbytera, for three golden solids." Though "presbytera" can designate a presbyter's wife, that is not likely here: "holy" is a common title for clergy, and she, not her husband, represents the church for the sale of property. It is impossible to say what other presbyteral functions, e.g. sacramental, she exercised. **See also** LETA.
CAROLYN OSIEK

Flesh, in the NT, a characterization of the person driven by human, earthly concerns of any kind or, in both the NT and theological tradition, the human body influenced by carnal lust, along with all disordered impulses, including "spiritual" sins of curiosity and pride.

Flood (the) is presented in Genesis as a divine act of punishment, destroying life on earth. Noah* and his family, along with animals, survive in the ark built according to God's directions (Gen 6:11–8:19). Augustine* followed Philo* in allegorically linking the ark to one's body, Noah to the righteous mind, and the waters to the cleansing of one's soul. Medieval commentators noted the flood's connection to baptism* (cf. 1 Pet 3:20–21). Contemporary scholars often parallel more than 200 ancient extrabiblical flood stories. The flood portrays the saving, judging, and patient character of God in redemptive history.
JEFFRY C. DAVIS

Florence, Council of (1438–45), also named Ferrara–Florence (it met one year in Ferrara). It was called by the pope as a continuation of, and substitute for, the Conciliarist* Council of Basel* (1431–49), held north of the Alps and controlled by the emperor Sigismund. The chief purpose was to consider reunion with the Greek Orthodox* Church at the request of the emperor John VIII Palaeologos, who attended the Council along with the patriarch of Constantinople and other bishops and scholars.

The chief doctrinal issues for the Greeks were the *Filioque**, unleavened bread*, purgatory*, and papal supremacy. Eventually these issues were resolved, at least verbally. Differences of ritual and canon* law were more easily agreed upon, and the Decree of Union was signed July 5, 1539, under Brunelleschi's dome in the Florence *duomo*. Mark Eugenicus* of Ephesus refused to sign and organized opposition to the reunion in the East, where the union was repudiated.

The Council adopted similar statements intended to achieve reunion with the Armenians* (1439) and the Syriac* Orthodox (polemically nicknamed "Jacobites*"), Copts*, and Ethiopians* (1442), leading to reunions with portions of the Armenian, Syriac, and Chaldaean churches. **See also** UNIATE CHURCHES.
EUGENE TESELLE

Florovsky, Georges (1893–1979), theologian, historian, Orthodox priest; pioneering ecumenist with the World* Council of Churches. Born in Kirovograd, raised in Odessa, Russia*, he studied philosophy (Odessa and Prague, 1911–23), fled to Bulgaria* (1920), and then taught in Europe (1923–48) and North America (1948–79). Reacting to Sergei Bulgakov's* "sophiology," Florovsky developed an Orthodox theology called "Christian Hellenism" or "neopatristic synthesis."

Florovsky taught that the Orthodox Church providentially "baptized" Hellenism*, and this Byzantine* Greek heritage was expressed in the fathers* who witnessed to, and taught concerning, the Church's experience of Christ. They are authoritative because they bear the "catholic mind" or identity of the Orthodox Church – Christ himself "in head and body." This patristic mindset is the Church's "living tradition" – scriptural*, eucharistic*, and charismatic* in character – embracing both continuity and growth (see Patristic Thought in

Orthodox Christianity). The Orthodox Church is identified with the creedal *Una sancta*, but beyond its canonical limits exist separated Christians who are called to return to it.

Orthodox Theology, for Florovsky, is called to be patristic* because it follows the patristic spirit and vision; neo-patristic because the fathers help us face our current problems and queries; and a contemporary synthesis because we respond patristically to our age.

Florovsky's theological vision became normative in Eastern Orthodoxy* through such students as Alexander Schmemann, John Meyendorff, John Romanides, and John Zizioulas. **See also ORTHODOX CHURCHES, EASTERN, CLUSTER: INTRODUCTORY ENTRIES.**

BRANDON GALLAHER

Florus of Lyon (d c860), deacon who served several archbishops of Lyon as a scholar. His excerpts from earlier commentaries on the epistles of Paul, especially from Augustine, were influential throughout the Middle Ages. During the controversy on predestination*, he defended Gottschalk* against John* Scotus Erigena.

Focolare (Italian, "hearth"), lay movement, primarily Roman Catholic, whose watchword is Christ's prayer "that they all be one" (John 17:21); thus it encourages a "spirituality of unity" and dialogue across religious and cultural lines. **See also ITALY.**

Folk Christian Practices. See POPULAR CHRISTIAN PRACTICES CLUSTER.

Folk Churches in the Nordic Countries are the former "Lutheran state* churches" that progressively adopted democratic church rules when democracy and freedom of religion were introduced (19th–20th c.). Despite their new freedom of choice, the majority of people in these countries have remained members of these churches, which have made considerable contributions to the cultural and political coherence of the Nordic countries.

The theology of the Folk Church in Denmark, Finland, Iceland, Norway, and Sweden was developed primarily for the people as an interpretation of this historical development rather than as a religious critique of institutionalized forms of Christian practice. Yet since affiliation, church buildings, and ceremonies are no longer connected with the specific theological belief of an institution, in each case there are tensions between the authority of the Folk Church and the people's experience. For example, social coherence demanded the Church's commitment to building and sustaining a welfare state, but implied the repression of different, more local religious expressions, especially among the Sami people (the Lapland people), an issue that is being addressed. Overall, women have supported the Church; but the Church has not supported women. Consequently, women had to "cross gender borders" in a variety of ways, among them by seeking international and ecumenical cooperation. As a result, more and more women are ordained as priests and bishops (see Women's Ordination Cluster: In Western Europe). Women have also created their own rituals.

The Folk Church in each of the Nordic countries came into conflict with religious freedom (implemented last in Sweden*, 1951) because it continues to have a privileged status. Both Finland* and Norway* substantially invest in the Christian upbringing of the youth. Sweden has chosen another path; the teaching for confirmation is officially regarded as a resource for young people in interpreting their lives and in their existential choices.

Folk Church practices are closely linked to life rituals: baptism, confirmation, weddings, and funerals. In each case, ritual and ordinary life merge, shaping most of the population's conception of what should take place at different stages of life. However, Folk Church rites are often interpreted quite freely by the individual. Yet the link between context and church is constantly reshaped. For example, women's full participation in the life of the Folk Church has highlighted issues such as violence against women, the global economical crisis from a gender perspective, and the consequences of racism for women.

A clear distinction between church practices and folk practices cannot be drawn in the Nordic countries. In each case, the Folk Church is increasingly looked upon as a supplier of services in response to people's needs and less as a hierarchical and doctrinal authority. However, issues concerning underprivileged groups tend to be neglected.

JAN-OLAV HENRIKSEN, ELINA VUOLA, and CRISTINA GRENHOLM

Fontevrault, Order of, a "double order" of monks and nuns founded by Robert of Arbrissel (d1116), with rigorous observance of the Benedictine* Rule. Its houses were principally in France*; the order was suppressed during the

French* Revolution, but an order for women was revived in 1806.

Foot-Washing. Washing a guest's feet was a gesture of hospitality* (Luke 7:44). Jesus humbly washed the disciples'* feet at the Last* Supper (John 13:5). It became a practice for bishops* and the pope* to wash the feet of 12 persons under their care on Maundy* Thursday, reflecting the new commandment that the disciples love one another (John 13:34).

Foreigners. See REFUGEES AS A THEOLOGICAL CONCEPT AND AN ETHICAL ISSUE.

Foreknowledge, God's knowledge of things still to occur, considered to be "present knowledge" because God's knowledge is timeless.

Forgiveness. See PENANCE AND FORGIVENESS.

Forgiveness, Christian Discourses of. Christian discourses proclaiming the promise of God's unconditional forgiveness*, commonly viewed as the "good news" of the gospel, have several possible emphases. The message that every human being remains within God's loving care and concern is profoundly important for communities torn apart by interethnic strife, terrorist regimes, and atrocities. However God's forgiveness might be understood, it is for everyone, no matter how wicked or depraved (see Justification, Theological Views and Practices, Cluster: A Central Doctrine for Western Christianity; Lutheranism Cluster: Martin Luther).

But this promise of God's unconditional forgiveness turns to "cheap grace"* (Dietrich Bonhoeffer*) when practiced in political contexts that discount personal accountability and promote a culture of forgetfulness and premature closure. The Christian emphasis on forgiveness may have dubious side effects when designed to prevent confrontation with painful political and personal truths and to maintain stability during tumultuous regime changes (e.g. Germany*, South* Africa, Chile*, Rwanda*, Guatemala*, Argentina*). Furthermore, forgiveness as a supreme Christian virtue can lead to moral paralysis when used to silence victims' cries for justice* and restitution. Similarly, the gospel's numerous admonitions against judgment, intended to induce spiritual humility*, can be deployed to derail criminal prosecutions and to prevent historical truthfulness. Such a lopsided emphasis on forgiveness is rooted in theological anti-Judaism by (implicitly) contrasting the Christian belief in God's love* and mercy* with the Jewish belief in God's wrath and commandment to do justice, although the dialectic between God's love and wrath is fundamental to biblical God-language (see Anger or Wrath of God). Because of Christian calls for reconciliation* without restitution, most perpetrators of state-sanctioned crimes feel politically, legally, morally, and often religiously justified, and see no need for remorse or repentance* despite the frequently gruesome nature of their deeds. Such Christian discourses of forgiveness "demoralize" both victims and perpetrators.

Another kind of Christian discourse of forgiveness takes into account that the condemnation of evil* is a biblical commandment and not (always) attributable to hasty, haughty, or hypocritical attitudes. The biblical practice of justice* requires empathy, love, and sustained support for the perpetrators by insisting on treating them as moral* agents endowed with freedom* and the ability to choose between good and evil and to undergo change. Far from dehumanizing perpetrators, insistence on repentance and restitution as necessary parts of the reconciliation process encourages transformation and distancing from harmful ideologies such as racism*, anti*-Semitism, sexism*, and heterosexism*. In this discourse, the establishment of justice and Jesus' call to repentance are central to the "good news" of forgiveness. KATHARINA VON KELLENBACH

Fornication, voluntary sexual intercourse between two unmarried persons. It is differentiated from adultery*, which involves at least one married person.

Forty-two Articles of Religion. Throughout the Reformation* period, statements of doctrine* were an important feature of the changes in religion (see Creeds, Symbols, and Confessions of Faith). In continental Europe, the Augsburg* Confession (1530) provided both an outstanding witness and compelling driving force of the Lutheran Reformation. In England, King Henry* VIII used articles of religion as instruments of policy – in 1536 opening the door to some Reformation possibilities and in 1539 slamming the door again.

King Edward VI imposed the Reformation on his kingdom by requiring Reformed Books of Common* Prayer (1549, 1552), along with homilies, orders in council, and new episcopal appointments. However, Archbishop Cranmer* preferred to reinforce the teaching of the Prayer Book by means of doctrinal articles to which the clergy would have to subscribe, resulting in the Forty-two Articles, signed by the king and published in May 1553. Their wording enforces a Reformed understanding of the faith*, especially with respect to the supremacy of Scripture*, justification* through faith, and a receptionist* doctrine of the sacraments* (e.g. in the Eucharist*, the Body and Blood of Christ are received not physically but through faith*, and thus are not received by unbelievers).

King Edward VI died within weeks of the completion of the Articles, and so they never achieved authority or even currency. In Queen Elizabeth's* reign, however, they provided most of the corpus of the Thirty-nine* Articles of 1571. BISHOP COLIN O. BUCHANAN

Fosdick, Harry Emerson (1878–1969), Baptist author, preacher, educator; one of the chief spokespersons for liberal* Protestantism in the fundamentalist controversies (1920s) in the USA. Although not an outstanding scholar, Fosdick was a respected member of the faculty of the prestigious Union Theological Seminary in New York (1908–46). A great preacher, Fosdick was pastor of the interdenominational Riverside Church in New York (1926–46), a congregation that he created with the help of John D. Rockefeller, Jr. A gifted and prolific writer, Fosdick had a knack for producing accessible and compelling books such as *The Secret of Victorious Living* (1934), *On Being a Real Person* (1943), *A Faith for Tough Times* (1952), and *Dear Mr. Brown: Letters to a Person Perplexed about Religion* (1961). He was a courageous champion of unpopular causes; e.g. he advocated Christian pacifism* during World War II. Through his sermons and books, he made a strong case for the desirability of thinking men and women simultaneously embracing modernity and Evangelical* Christianity.
DAVID HARRINGTON WATT

Fourth Ezra, Jewish apocalypse. Chapters 3–14, usually dated to c100 CE, were superficially Christianized during their transmission. Chapters 1–2 and 15–16 are later Christian additions. The theme of Fourth Ezra is theodicy* in the light of Jerusalem's destruction. The book is a major source of information concerning Jewish eschatology*, including descriptions of the awaited Messiah*. **See also PSEUDEPIGRAPHA.**
JOHANNES TROMP

Fox, George (1624–91), founder of the Religious Society of Friends*. Born in England, he experienced Christ (1647), began itinerant preaching, authored numerous pamphlets and books, and married the widow Margaret Fell* (1669). Paralyzed by periods of depression and withdrawal, he died after defeating challenges and consolidating the movement.

Fox flourished during the chaotic English Revolution and hoped to draw the English people to his movement. He met Oliver Cromwell*, but their views diverged and he was frequently jailed. Convinced of the failures of other churches, whose services he occasionally interrupted, he believed Quakers* might recapture the primitive Christianity lost to apostasy, by stressing, without rituals or hierarchy, the inward leadings of God's Spirit, and he appealed to the democratic sentiments of the "lower and middling orders."

After the Stuart Restoration, Fox and 12 others issued the famous 1661 "Peace Testimony" eschewing warfare and political goals. The Quakers stressed the mystical* side of Christianity, with little emphasis on outward forms or reliance on Scriptures* without the guidance of God's Holy* Spirit. The group's government was a modified Presbyterian system with final authority culminating in the Yearly Meeting. The 1666 "Testimony from the Brethren" effectively gave authority to the central leadership. Over time, the Quakers were actively involved in women's rights, as well as opposition to slavery* and to war*. H. LARRY INGLE

Foxe, John (1517–87), martyrologist, minister, author of *Acts and Monuments of the English Martyrs* (the *Book of Martyrs*). After completing his studies as a fellow of (Roman Catholic) Magdalen College (1539–43), he should have been ordained a priest, but he became a Protestant and married.

In London (1547), while a tutor in a Protestant household, he was encouraged to write a church history in defense of the Reformation*. In danger after Mary's* accession, he escaped to Basel and converted his Reformation history into an English martyrology. After Elizabeth's* accession (1559), he returned to England as a tutor and published the *Acts and Monuments* (1563). Although much of it was patched together from the works of John Bale and the Magdeburg *Centuries*, this work was immediately recognized as important, burning with a passionate hatred of persecution and of the Roman Catholic clergy. Sensitive to criticism (of which there was plenty), Foxe revised his magnum opus three times (1570, 1576, 1583), changing the content and emphasis. He also published many sermons and other tracts, in both Latin and English. There were five posthumous editions and several abridgements of the *Acts and Monuments* before 1684, and several in the 18th and 19th c. DAVID LOADES

France. The history of Christianity in France cannot easily be distinguished from that of Christianity in Western Europe as a whole (see History of Christianity Cluster: In Europe: Western Europe). To understand the place of Christianity in early-21st-c. France, it is necessary to review the 19th- and 20th-c. history.

Before the 19th c., the history of Christianity in France was predominantly a history of the Roman Catholic Church, which traces its origins to Irenaeus* (2nd-c. bishop of Lyon) and the baptism of the Merovingian barbarian Clovis* in Rheims (early 6th c.), and continues through the empire of Charlemagne* and the Carolingian* Renaissance, which reached its height during the reign of Louis* the Pious (9th c.) and his sons. The Benedictine* Rule was imposed on monastic* life, and there were important reforms exemplified by the establishment of Cluny* (10th c.) and by the creation of the Cistercian* (12th c.; see Bernard* of Clairvaux) and the Carthusian* (11th–12th c.) orders. Catharism* in Southern and Northern France (early 13th c), was suppressed by the Inquisition*, led by Dominicans* who also played an important role in the university in Paris where Thomas Aquinas* taught.

Before the French Revolution, the link between the Roman Catholic Church and the state remained close, enshrined in the 1516 Concordat* (between King Francis I and Pope Leo X), although conflict between the spiritual and the temporal power – and between the Gallican* Church and Rome – was a constant feature of the relationship. During the Reformation* period, France was divided between Roman Catholics and Protestants (Huguenots*), who included Calvin*, Farel*, Beza*, as well as the sister of King Francis I, Marguerite* de Navarre, and the future Henry* IV. Henry converted to Catholicism in order to become king but proclaimed the Edict of Nantes* (1598) to end the wars between Catholics and Huguenots* (exemplified by the massacre of St. Bartholomew's* Day, 1572). The Jansenist* controversy (including Pascal*) with the Jesuits* and Bossuet* (17th c.) reflects the theological ferment of the period. Yet even as the Catholic* Renewal promoted the development of new religious orders during the 17th c. (e.g. by Francis* de Sales and Jane* Frances de Chantal), the revocation of the Edict of Nantes (1685) made Protestantism illegal and opened a period of persecution of the Huguenots, until the 1789 revolution.

The 1789 revolution produced a seismic rupture, and thereafter its legacy shaped the relationship between church, state, and nation. Whereas the *clergé patriote* of 1789 had looked to religion to bind the nation together, the Jacobins proclaimed the Republic one and indivisible, and their onslaught on Roman Catholic Christianity in effect turned France not into one nation, but into two. The 1801 Concordat (signed by Napoleon in 1802 and thus known in France as the 1802 Concordat) restored some order to the religious field and provided the legal basis for relations between church and state until 1905, but it did not of itself end all religious conflict. By the late 19th c., the French Protestant community, which was divided into the Reformed Church and the Augsburg Confession, numbered only around 600,000 (less than 2% of the population), although it had an influence on national life that was entirely disproportionate to its size.

The Religious Revival. The 1815–80 period witnessed a spectacular religious revival in France, as elsewhere in Europe. This reinvigorated and crusading Catholicism was not a French manifestation of a new, militant, and, above all, Roman Catholicism that developed especially under the papacy of Pius* IX (1846–78). Rather, out of the ruins of the Revolution, the Roman Catholic Church rebuilt itself: vocations to the priesthood rose, as did recruitment to religious orders and, in particular, to female religious orders. Between 1800 and 1880, almost 400 new female orders were founded and some 200,000 women took religious vows.

The Catholic revival owed much to the change in the intellectual climate produced by romanticism*. Yet it was by no means confined to an intellectual elite; it was evident also in the real, if uneven, re-Christianization of the French countryside. Mass attendance rose, as did the number of Easter communicants, although under the impact of the anticlerical policies of the Third Republic after 1879, there was some falling away again. In the 19th c., the Roman Catholic Church succeeded as never before in narrowing the gap between the religion of the people and the religion of the clergy, largely by embracing beliefs and practices that resonated powerfully with the religious impulses of the rural masses: the devotion to saints, the veneration of shrines, the organization of local pilgrimages, and enthusiasm for miracles.

Marianism (see Mary, the Virgin, Cluster) was a notable feature of the new Ultramontanist* Catholicism and was fostered by frequent apparitions of the Virgin – in 1830 (Paris), 1846 (La Salette), 1858 (Lourdes*), and 1871 (Pontmain) – as well as by official pronunciations of the Church such as the doctrine of the immaculate* conception (1854). Marian visionaries came from humble backgrounds and were usually women or children – a reminder to arrogant, rationalist, male intellectuals that they had no monopoly on truth or wisdom. Another thing that was dear to Ultramontanists was devotion to the Sacred Heart. Centered on the visions of a 17th-c. nun, Marguerite-Marie Alacoque, the devotion was adopted in the 19th c. as the symbol of a Catholic vision of the nation and led to the building of the great Sacré Coeur basilica in Paris (late 19th c.) and the eventual canonization of Marguerite-Marie Alacoque (1920).

The French Culture War, 1879–1905. Fearful of the consequences of revolution, which recurred at frequent intervals (1830, 1848, 1871), the ruling classes generally subscribed to the view that religion was "good for the people," if not necessarily for the educated bourgeoisie. Eventually, however, after 1879, under the Third Republic, a new generation of anticlerical republicans (see Anticlericalism) was ready to challenge the rise of aggressive Ultramontanist Catholicism, personified in France by the crusading journalist Louis Veuillot (1813–83) and his team at the newspaper *L'Univers*. In the ensuing culture war (1880s), republicans enacted legislation that took forward their agenda of realizing the *idée laïque*, laicization*, the creation of a completely secular polity and society. The key battle was in education*. Legislation in 1881 and 1882 made primary education free, compulsory, and nondenominational for both sexes. A further law (1886) provided for the progressive laicization of the teaching profession: around half of the nuns and brothers who taught in the nation's primary schools were removed by the early 1890s. The education of girls was a particular target of the republicans, who were convinced that women's greater allegiance to organized religion was both a source of division in families and a barrier to the spread of the republican ideal. Accordingly, legislation of 1879–80 established teacher training colleges for women teachers and a network of state secondary schools for girls. Other anticlerical measures included the reintroduction of divorce (1884) and a conscription law (1889) that obliged seminary students to do their military service like everyone else.

The 1880s legislative culture, however, stopped well short of a full-scale assault on religion. Only the extreme Left wanted to abolish the 1801 Concordat altogether. For a brief moment there were even signs of détente. In 1892 the new pope, Leo* XIII (1878–1903), initiated the movement known as the Ralliement, through which French Catholics were exhorted to rally to the Republic. At the same time, Leo issued his celebrated encyclical on social justice, *Rerum Novarum* (1891; see Social Encyclicals), which greatly boosted the burgeoning Catholic social movement and notably encouraged the emergence of a second generation of Christian Democrats (the first having been associated with the era of 1848). Some were priests, others laypersons like Marc Sangnier, founder of *Le Sillon* (the Furrow, 1899). All were concerned, above all, with the plight of the industrial working class.

The Ralliement failed to make much headway at the grassroots level, however, and and it came to an end in the wake of the Dreyfus Affair, where once again Catholics were seen to be on the wrong side of the political divide, largely because of the high-profile role played by the Assumptionist order and its widely read, rabidly anti-Semitic* newspaper *La Croix* in the campaign against the Jewish army captain Alfred Dreyfus, falsely convicted of treason. Thus by 1900 the culture war moved into a new and decisive phase that led directly to the severing of the ties between church and state, which had endured for more than a century. Following the persecution of religious orders (especially those involved in teaching) and the rupture in 1904 of diplomatic relations with the Vatican – now under the new and more intransigent leadership of Pius* X (1903–14) – the French government, pushed by anticlerical parliamentarians, passed the Separation Law of December 9, 1905, aimed primarily at breaking the power of the Roman Catholic Church as a political force.

From the Separation of Church and State to the 21st Century. The influence of Rome continued to shape the French Church up to 1914 and beyond. Unrestrained by the French state, Pius X and his secretary of state, Merry del Val, took full advantage of their freedom to appoint bishops who shared their reactionary outlook, many of them sympathetic to the extreme right-wing nationalist organization Action Française. The Vatican also cracked down on intellectual tendencies within the French Church that it regarded with suspicion, condemning as heretical so-called Modernism*, a term of abuse applied to clerics such as Alfred Loisy* who were deemed to have maligned traditional church doctrine in a search to accommodate their scholarship to the findings of modern science.

World War I did something to heal the breach between French Catholics and the Republic. Catholics were loyal to the concept of the *union sacrée*, the political truce (1914) initiated by President Poincaré, and Catholic propagandists were not slow to point out how the exemplary war service of the 25,000 priests and seminarians mobilized at the front gave the lie to the Church's alleged lack of patriotism. French Catholics, committed to a fight to the finish, also spurned the peace initiatives of Pope Benedict* XV (1914–22). Reconciliation with Rome took place when full diplomatic relations were restored (1921). On the other hand, anticlericalism was far from dead and resurfaced after the election of a government of the Left (1924), though it was met with stubborn and successful resistance from the National Catholic Federation (from 1925). Rome's condemnation of Action Française (1926) also appeared to bode well for future relations between Catholics and the Republic.

The 1920s and 1930s were a period of renewal in the French Catholic Christianity. In the wake of the condemnation of Action Française, the episcopate underwent renewal, while the number of priests began to rise again. New lay Catholic elites – both men and women – emerged through the program of specialized Catholic* Action sponsored by Pope Pius* XI (1922–39) with the ambitious aim of re-Christianizing society. The prototype of the JOC (Young* Catholic Workers, Jocists) was emulated by the JAC (farmers) and the JEC (students), all of them complemented by separate female groups. Youth movements with a focus on sports and the outdoors likewise flourished, notably the Catholic Boy Scouts and Girl Guides. The Christian trade union (the Confédération Française des Travailleurs Chrétiens, known as the CFTC) recruited approximately a fifth of wage earners. The interwar period was also a golden age of Catholic thought, epitomized by the likes of Maritain* and Emmanuel Mounier, as well as a distinguished period in the history of Catholic literary culture (Paul Claudel, François Mauriac, Georges Bernanos) (see French Literature and Christianity). A small but vibrant group of Christian Democrats supported the Spanish Republicans. These, however, were denounced as traitors by the majority of Catholics, who retained many of their traditional anti-Republican sentiments, as the experience of war and defeat soon revealed.

Most Catholics, headed by the bishops, had no difficulty in rallying to the Vichy regime (1940–44) set up under Marshal Pétain as an antidote to the defeated and discredited Third Republic. It was the established power, recognized by the Vatican and Vichy's "National Revolution" in favor of "family, fatherland, and labor." It appealed to conservative Catholics, not least the parish clergy. Disenchantment set in only gradually, when the realities of occupation and Vichy's subservience to Nazism became apparent, although only a heroic minority engaged in active resistance. From the ranks of the Resistance, however, would come a new, more open, and, above all, more democratic and pluralist Catholic vision of politics in the postwar years. Despite its checkered record under Vichy, under the Liberation government of General de Gaulle, himself a practicing Catholic, the Church entered the postwar era with more political clout than it had enjoyed since the 1870s. Catholics, notably those of the new Christian Democratic Party, the MRP, would feature prominently in French governments throughout the life of the Fourth Republic (1946–58).

Yet by the 1940s, Catholics were aware that they lived in a country that in many respects was only nominally Christian. A book produced by two priests in 1943 called France a "missionary country" (H. Godin and Y. Daniel, *La France pays de mission?*). To meet the new challenge, some priests abandoned their parishes and became workers ("worker* priests"), but in 1953–54 the worker priest experiment was suppressed by the Vatican under Pius* XII (1939–58). In the climate of the cold war, "progressive" Christians were viewed with suspicion in Rome (and Washington) and Catholic peace activists were likewise condemned. Nevertheless, the reforming impetus of the 1930s was far from spent, and the French Catholic contribution to the *aggiornamento* of the Church launched by Vatican* II (1962–65) under Pope John* XXIII (1958–63) and Pope Paul* VI (1963–78) was considerable, not least in the area of theological expertise provided to the Council.

The Council profoundly transformed the entire Catholic world, but reactions to the new liturgy* in the vernacular and to the Council's other decrees were mixed. Traditionalists hated the innovations, while many enthusiasts of the Council thought that the reforms did not go far enough, particularly with regard to clerical celibacy* and artificial contraception (birth* control), the latter of which was condemned once more by Paul* VI's encyclical *Humanae Vitae* (1968). The price of upholding traditional teaching in the age of the sexual revolution was a steep decline in the Church's authority. By the early 1990s, polls revealed that even among women who still attended Mass, more than 80% ignored the papal teaching on contraception.

"À la carte" Catholicism had arrived, and the decline of traditional religious practice went on apace. From more than 20% of the adult population in 1972, weekly attendance at Mass had fallen to just 8% by the mid-1990s and to 4.5% in 2008. At the dawn of the new millennium, the secularizing trend was bucked only by Protestant Pentecostals/Charismatics*, who had made surprising gains in some of the toughest suburbs of Paris, and by a growing Muslim minority numbering at least 4 million, which made Islam* the second largest religion in France. Ironically, some French Catholics now regard the secularization* laws enacted against them in the culture war of 1879–1905 as the best defense against Islamic militancy. The long-cherished aim of a Christian reconquest of society has been definitively shelved, and Catholics now hope at best to foster respect for Christian values in a pluralist society. **See also FRENCH LITERATURE AND CHRISTIANITY; PROTESTANTISM CLUSTER: IN EUROPE: FRANCE; ROMAN CATHOLICISM CLUSTER: IN EUROPE: FRANCE; SECULARISM AND SECULARIZATION.**

Statistics: Population (2000): 60 million (M). Christians, 41.8 M, 71% (most "secularized") (Roman Catholics, 39 M [decreasing]; independents [including Pentecostals/ Charismatics], 1.3 M [rapidly increasing]; Protestants, 0.8 M [decreasing]; Orthodox, 0.6 M [increasing]; marginal Christians [e.g. Jehovah's Witnesses, Mormons], 0.3 M [increasing]); atheists and nonreligious, 11.6 M, 19.6%; Muslims, 4.2 M, 7.1%; Jews, 0.6 M. (Based on *World Christian Encyclopedia*, 2001.)

JAMES F. MCMILLAN

Francis of Assisi (c1182–1226), penitent, charismatic preacher, founder of orders, deacon, mystic*, saint (canonized by Gregory IX, 1228); born and died in Assisi (Umbria, Italy). Francis abandoned a worldly lifestyle (1205) and embraced an apostolic life of poverty* and preaching* (1207). With his first followers (eventually named "Friars Minor" or "Lesser Brothers"), Francis obtained from Pope Innocent* III (1209) a global commission to preach penance* and verbal confirmation of a gospel-based rule – later expanded (1221), codified, and confirmed in a papal bull by Pope Honorius III (1223) – which was called Francis's First Order. With Clare* of Assisi, he founded the Second Order (1212), for contemplative nuns, later known as "Poor* Clares." He attracted secular penitents into his Third* Order and, with Cardinal Hugolino (future Pope Gregory IX), gave them a rule (1221). Francis attempted to end the Fifth Crusade* by preaching to Al-Malik al-Kamil, sultan of Egypt (1219), who remained sympathetic but unconverted. He supported the Fourth Lateran* Council program (1215) with encyclical letters encouraging eucharistic devotion. After resigning from the office of minister general (c1221), Francis received stigmata* in a mystical experience of Christ's Passion at Monte della Verna in Tuscany (1224).

Francis decried the avarice of the Italian mercantile revolution (see Economy and Christianity Cluster: Economy and Christianity; Economy and Christianity Cluster: Economic Ethics and Christian Theology), violence* in society, and contemporary dissatisfaction with clergy perceived as worldly and silent. Francis's Rule challenged the friars to a life based on Jesus' "words and footprints," i.e. teaching and lifestyle. Embracing gospel terms (brother, minister), Francis minimized distinctions among friars except for ordination*. Poverty was radical, based on Matt 19:21 and Luke 9:3; it was characterized by giving everything to the poor and rejecting money and property*, both individual and corporate; friars were to support themselves by working and begging. They were to preach first by example; those who had been approved by the Roman Catholic Church would preach by word; those "inspired by God" would preach by example and by word to Saracens and other nonbelievers. Modifications of Francis's Rule in 1223 allowed preachers access to books, and in 1224 Francis authorized Anthony of Padua to lecture to the friars on theology.

In contrast to the Cathars*, Francis emphasized the humanity as well as the divinity of Christ. In contrast to the Waldenses*, he taught the real presence of Christ in the Eucharist and the authority of an ordained clergy – hence the early description of him as "a totally Catholic and apostolic man": *vir catholicus et totus apostolicus*. Friars were to be brothers to all. Indeed, in his *Canticle of Creatures*, Francis taught a brotherhood of all creation, inasmuch as all creatures come from God and reflect God. Pope John* Paul II named Francis "patron saint of ecology*" (1983). CONRAD L. HARKINS, OFM

Franciscans, Christians inspired by the religious experience and values of Francis* of Assisi (c1182–1226), including members of the Catholic religious* orders he founded and other communities within and outside the Roman Catholic Church. Common to all these groups is conversion to Jesus Christ and a gospel-centered life.

Francis founded two religious orders, giving both a rule of life: Friars Minor or Lesser Brothers (1209) and Poor Ladies of San Damiano (later known as Poor* Clares), founded with Clare* of Assisi for contemplative* sisters (1212). He also founded an order for secular people, clergy and laity, male and female, Brothers and Sisters of Penance (1221). Each of these Franciscan communities, the First, Second, and Third* Orders, lives gospel values according to the status of its members (men under vows, women under vows, or laypersons). Religious communities soon developed in the Third Order, with gradual separation into Third Order Regular (for those under vows) and Third Order Secular (for those not under vows). Among Friars Minor, zeal for gospel poverty worked against unity: the Franciscan Spirituals* broke with the community (1294), only to be suppressed; the leaders of the order were condemned by papal authority and replaced (1328). For the next two centuries, the dispute over poverty resulted in the formation of subordinate reform groups, until the 1517 division of the order into Friars Minor Conventual and Friars Minor of the Observance. Further fragmentation continued, one group, the Friars Minor Capuchin, obtaining separate status through papal approbation (1528). Fragmentation continued within the Friars of the Observance, Friars of the Strictest Observance, Reformed Friars, and Recollect Friars, until the suppression of these distinctions and the imposition of the simple term Friars Minor by Pope Leo XIII (1897).

Members of the First Order live according to the Rule of Francis finalized in 1223; divergent groups of Poor Clares live each according to one of several medieval rules. Modern members of the Third Order Secular live according to the Rule of Paul* VI (1978), and members of the Third Order Regular according to the Rule of John* Paul II (1982). Protestant Franciscan communities appeared in the 20th c., particularly in the Anglican and Lutheran churches, e.g. the Society of St. Francis and the Order of Ecumenical Franciscans. Since Vatican* II (1962–65), new Catholic Franciscan communities have been formed, among them Friars of the Renewal. Catholic Franciscan communities today exemplify, according to their specific norms, the gospel values lived by Francis: conversion to Christ, loyalty to the Roman Catholic Church, penance, prayer, evangelization, missionary activity, peace, justice for the poor and marginalized, and ecology*.

CONRAD L. HARKINS, OFM

Francis de Sales (1567–1622), French-speaking Savoyard bishop (of Geneva, in exile in Annecy), Catholic saint, doctor of the church. De Sales devoted his clerical career and episcopacy (1602–22) to the renewal (especially spiritual) of the early modern Roman Catholic Church. An early mission took him to the Chablais region to reclaim it for the Catholic faith. A persuasive preacher, spiritual director, and influential devotional writer, he was most remembered as a promoter, especially through his *Introduction to the Devout Life* (1609), of a deep spirituality* adapted to the lives of lay Catholics. De Sales's *Treatise on the Love of God* (1616) presented his theological, spiritual, and pastoral vision of a world of interconnected divine and human hearts linked by the gentle, humble heart of the crucified Jesus (Matt 11:28–30). It emphasized the primacy of love* in the Christian life (see Anthropology Cluster: In Western Christian Theology). His "optimistic" vision, rooted in the Christian humanism of the era, conceived of human nature (most distilled in the heart) as essentially good and God directed – thus the importance of gentle, loving personal and pastoral practices, such as spiritual friendship, spousal love, individualized spiritual direction (see Discipline), and affective writing, preaching, and teaching, which can win the hearts of others. He was cofounder (1610, with Jane* de Chantal) of the religious* order known as the Visitation of Holy Mary. **See also CATHOLIC RENEWAL.** WENDY M. WRIGHT

Francis of Xavier. See XAVIER, FRANCIS OF.

Francke, August Hermann (1663–1727), educated in centers of Lutheran orthodoxy, developed a concern for "useful" rather than merely "pure" doctrine, under the influence of Spener*.

Personal living for God, in response to personal visitations of grace*, was the intended lifelong outcome of repentance* and conversion*. As pastor in Glaucha and professor at the adjacent University of Halle, he instituted a program of Pietist* renewal that touched many facets of society, including the religious education of children and youth of all social classes, care for orphans, Bible distribution, and pioneering efforts in world mission that were ecumenical in nature. J. STEVE O'MALLEY

Françoise-Marguerite de Joncoux. See JONCOUX, FRANÇOISE-MARGUERITE DE.

Franklin, Benjamin (1706–90), printer, pragmatist, US founding father. Franklin's relationship to Christianity is paradoxical. A friend of George Whitefield*, he advanced the Evangelicalism of the Great* Awakening by printing works by Whitefield*, Gilbert Tennent, and other revivalists. Yet he himself was not an adherent of either the Calvinism* of his New England heritage or the dominant Quakerism* of his Philadelphia home. A Freemason*, he adopted a noncreedal Enlightenment* Deism* and looked to Christianity as a utilitarian means of cultivating virtuous living in society. His Deistic virtue-driven ethics informs much of the language about God in the first documents of the American Republic. CALEB J. D. MASKELL

Fraternity, a group of men organized for a common purpose (especially spiritual discipline* and mutual support) who thereby become "brothers." Fraternities became a significant part of lay* piety during the Middle Ages and in subsequent centuries, in Western Europe as well as in the "colonies."

Fraticelli, a breakaway group of Spiritual* Franciscans, followers of either Angelo Clareno or Michael of Cesena.

Free Churches. See INDEPENDENT OR FREE CHURCHES.

Freedom, Free Will. Experience suggests that many of our actions are freely chosen; by this we usually mean that we could have carried out at least one alternative action and that the decision to act is our own. The adjective "free" is set in contrast to captivity, bondage, or necessity, a situation in which one is not free to choose or to do what one chooses. In the West, several issues related to the concept of free will arose:

1. Terms like "choosing" or "willing" may be more accurate than "having free will," since we do not know whether there is an entity called the "will" behind our acts. The Scholastics* came to differentiate three kinds of willing: liberty of exercise (whether to act or not act), liberty of specification (the choice of this or that good), and liberty of indifference (freedom for both good and evil).
2. Freedom may be defined by spontaneity (willing out of motives that seem good to oneself) rather than choice among alternatives. From this perspective, true "freedom," in contrast to "free choice," consists of love* for God without any consideration of alternatives; love for God is the fulfillment of free choice (a tendency in the Augustinian* tradition and in certain kinds of mysticism*; see HETERONOMY).
3. One may be free within a horizon narrower than what free choice in the abstract might suggest. Paul suggests (Rom 5:16–23) that those who are "free from sin*" are "slaves of righteousness," and those who are "free from righteousness" are "slaves of sin." Thus for Augustine*, Luther*, and Calvin*, the language of external slavery is internalized as a moral or subjective slavery: one becomes the slave of the one who is obeyed (Rom 6:16).
4. How do free agents become "slaves of sin"? Christian answers sometimes emphasize temptation by the devil* and sometimes by original* sin, or its contemporary version, structural* evil. These influence the process of willing by narrowing the range of viable possibilities, offering only limited suggestions, or rewarding some inclinations rather than others. Bondage in willing is usually explained as the outcome of free choice, either one's own or Adam's. For example, both Augustine and Calvin argued that even under the influence of original sin, sin occurs "willingly" or "not without willing."
5. How is the will liberated from bondage to sin? This is the classic problem of "free will and grace*." Some (e.g. Jansenists*) think of grace* as overpowering the will. Others (e.g. Augustine*, Jesuit* theologians, Edwards*) think of grace in terms of persuasion, offering motives that arouse new depths of willing.

See also COMPATIBILISM; MORAL INFLUENCE. EUGENE TESELLE

Freemasonry and Christianity. In 1717 four old London lodges consolidated and formed a remarkable social organization, the Grand Lodge of London, an umbrella organization to which other lodges would give their affiliation. Within two decades, Benjamin Franklin* joined a Masonic lodge in Philadelphia; by 1750 the organization was steeped in controversy yet growing in popularity in both Europe and the USA.

Since the Middle Ages, masons, carpenters, bakers, bell makers, and barber-surgeons in many European countries had been protected and supervised by guilds, which safeguarded their wages and benefits and monitored the quality of their work; members identified themselves with secret words and handshakes. Only the masons' guilds survived the transition into modern market conditions by becoming "Freemasonry." Besides conviviality and fellowship, the Masonic lodges held other cultural attractions. Master masons were literate and known for their mathematical and architectural skills, particularly in the construction of military and urban fortifications. Myth and lore associated the masters' geometrical skills with ancient learning supposedly inherited from the legendary Egyptian priest Hermes Trismegistus, who allegedly taught Moses and transmitted to him a mystical understanding of the heavens related to mathematics. The mystical combined with the utilitarian to bond brothers who became increasingly interested in the first, while abandoning the second.

Freemasonry's development in the 18th c. has been difficult to investigate. Many grand lodges were secretive, ritualistic, and devoted to hierarchy. But the lodges also consistently spoke about civic virtue and merit, about men meeting as equals, about the need for brothers to become philosophers, about their being "enlightened." By the late 18th c., the egalitarian logic had spread, particularly in France, where women flocked to the new "lodges of adoption."

The Masonic ideology of rising by merit, which justified egalitarian fraternizing among men of property who were free to choose their governors, belonged first and foremost to the English republican tradition. The lodges had a tendency to become schools for government – more, rather than less, democratic government.

Freemasonry's relationship with Christianity is controversial; Freemasonry is rejected by most churches because of its ambivalence toward religion, although different lodges and individual Freemasons have various attitudes toward Christianity, since Freemasonry "excludes none on account of belief." Benjamin Franklin, who was a Freemason, serves as an example. A friend of George Whitefield*, he advanced Evangelicalism by printing works by Whitefield and other revivalists*. Yet he held to a noncreedal Enlightenment* Deism*, viewing Christianity as a means to cultivate virtuous living in society. **See also CHURCH AND STATE RELATIONS CLUSTER: IN LATIN AMERICA: MEXICO.**

MARGARET C. JACOB

Free Spirit, Brethren of, an antinomian* movement that flourished c1270–1350. Accusations about its beliefs tended to be stereotyped ("union with God frees a person from the moral law"; "fornication is not a mortal sin"), probably through misconstrual or malice. The Beguines'* vernacular piety aroused suspicions of association with this movement. One Beguine, Marguerite Porete*, was burned at the stake in 1310, and theses drawn from her book were condemned (Council of Vienne, 1311–12). Yet her *Mirror of Simple Souls* became an anonymous classic of spirituality*, and similar language can be found in Eckhart* and other late medieval mystics*.

Free Will Baptists, the name given to the heirs of the Baptist congregation formed in Amsterdam in 1608/9 by a group of English Separatist Puritans who were Arminian* in theology and were known in England as General Baptists. They affirmed the role of free will* in salvation, the general atonement* of Christ (his death for all persons), and the possibility that Christians could fall from grace* (contrast with Particular Baptists). **See also BAPTIST CHURCHES CLUSTER.**

French Literature and Christianity. The first vernacular literary texts in France illustrate the cultural dominance of Catholic belief until the Renaissance. The *Sequence of Saint Eulalia* is a 9th-c. hagiography*. The *Song of Roland*, the earliest extant epic (c1100), depicts Charlemagne* as the ideal Christian ruler, his nephew Roland as a Christian tragic hero, and their conflict as a battle of Christian forces against "pagan" (Muslim) Saracens.

Religious drama in Latin began as an embellishment of the Mass*, evolving into dialogues about the Nativity and Resurrection; some vernacular refrains became part of this material. The earliest vernacular plays were the 12th-c. *Holy Resurrection* and *Play of Adam*. The latter dramatizes elements of the Mass, emphasizing the psychology of Adam* and Eve* in the story of creation, their temptation and fall*. Miracle plays, centering on the lives of saints and performed by the laity, dominated the 14th c. Mystery plays, often depicting the Passion of Christ, emerged in the 15th c., became huge communal productions, and were banned in the mid-16th c.

With the Renaissance, the first Catholic reformers, called Evangelicals*, were followed by Protestants, called Calvinists* or Huguenots*. Lefèvre* d'Etaples (c1450–1536) published French commentaries on Paul and the Gospels, as well as a translation of the Bible (1523–30). Opposed by the Sorbonne, he was protected by Marguerite* de Navarre. Calvin* himself is viewed as a major contributor to the development of French prose through his sermons and, especially, the *Institutes*.

François Rabelais, a contemporary of these figures, engaged in a comic indictment and satire of Catholic scholasticism and asceticism. Clément Marot, a Protestant poet and satirist, translated 49 psalms (1533–43), later completed by Théodore de Bèze (or Beza*, 1551–62); this poetry was sung in Huguenot worship services. Beza's revision of earlier Bible* translations became the official Geneva translation (1588) used by Huguenots. (The 1550 Louvain translation was the approved Catholic text.)

The Wars of Religion between Catholics and Protestants were formally ended by the Edict of Nantes* (1598), but conflict continued in the 17th and early 18th c. *Les Tragiques* by Agrippa d'Aubigné (1579) is a poetic account of the wars and a justification of the Protestant cause.

In the aftermath of the Counter* Reformation (in France often a more appropriate term than "Catholic* Renewal"), the 17th c. was marked by religious controversy and fervor. After the revocation of the Edict of Nantes (1685), Protestant influence on French literature was greatly diminished. With the rise of classicism, literature followed Greek and Latin models rather than those of the Bible. A notable exception was two plays based on the OT by Jean Racine, *Esther* (1689) and *Athalie* (1691). Yet the devotional* literature of figures such as François (Francis*) de Sales and Surin assumed great importance, as did the genre of spiritual biographies and autobiographies (influenced by translations of Teresa* of Ávila) and of sermons (already important in the 16th c.).

The Jansenist* and Quietist* controversies influenced French literature. Pascal's* *Provincial Letters* (1656–57) was a devastating series of 18 polemical letters condemning the Jesuits* and their attack against the Jansenists*. Devotional work such as Madame Guyon's* and great spiritual prose such as Fénelon's* and Bossuet's* reflected the Quietist debates.

The Enlightenment and the French Revolution (1789) brought skepticism and sweeping criticism of special revelation* and of the biblical text by figures like Voltaire. Anticlericalism* became a dominant theme in French culture after the nationalization of the holdings of the Roman Catholic Church and the institution of the worship of the Supreme Being during the Revolution.

Romantics tended to displace onto the poet and poetry the power once vested in the priest, the mystic, and the Bible. The most notable Catholic among early-19th-c. writers was Chateaubriand*, whose apology for Christianity, *The Genius of Christianity* (1802), emphasized its civilizing role and its beauties. Lamartine exemplified the romantics' faith crises and their unorthodox form of faith. The figure of Christ was an example of their religious anguish, as in Alfred Vigny's *The Mount of Olives* (1844).

Secularism* increasingly characterized French literature after the separation of church and state (1905). Nevertheless, an important renaissance of Catholic philosophical thinking occurred before World War II, (see Marcel, Gabriel; Maritain, Jacques). The most important writers were Charles Péguy, Paul Claudel, Georges Bernanos, and François Mauriac. The theoretical impulses of French intellectual life during the later 20th c. reduced the impact of Christianity on literature, although one finds rich echoes of Christian images and allusions, used in an ironic, secular context, in writers such as Samuel Beckett. **See also** FRANCE.

PATRICIA A. WARD

Friar (from Lat *frater*, "brother"), member of a mendicant* order. Friars are principally Franciscan*, Dominican*, Carmelite*, and Augustinian.

Friends, Religious Society of. The Religious Society of Friends, or "Quakers," began in the 1640s during the English Revolution. Its leader, George Fox*, wanted to "revive primitive Christianity," in contrast to the apostasy of contemporary groups. Hence Quakers dispensed with clergy, met in simple settings, and convened in silence, to await the leadings of the Holy* Spirit (see Quaker Worship). The group remained united and free of formal divisions until the 19th c.

Within the Society, the system of control was a modified Presbyterian* system, with the top decision-making body being the Yearly Meeting. (Quakers eschewed the word "church," designating bodies as simply meetings.) After 1666, and the issuance of the *Testimony from the Brethren* in London, power gradually devolved to the Meeting for Sufferings, an executive committee, within each Yearly Meeting. Since women enjoyed equal rights to speak during worship, they organized bodies parallel to the men's.

In 1661 a small group of Quaker men in London announced that Christ had commanded the Friends not to participate in war* or outward conflict, a hallmark of the movement that was more important than theological speculation. In 1675 Robert Barclay penned *An Apology for the True Christian Divinity,* which became the authoritative rendering of Quaker thought. For Quakers, Christian faith was based on two sources: Scriptures* and Quakers' encounters with the Holy* Spirit. Differences could be resolved by recognizing that revelations* from the Spirit, whether biblical or experiential, did not contradict each other. Such recognition, however, did not forestall conflict.

By the 19th c., influenced by Methodism*, English Quakers had become more "Evangelical," emphasizing the Bible and the atoning* blood of Christ, a development that also affected American Friends. In the USA, a formal division in 1827–28 spread to five Yearly Meetings, with the separatists known as "Hicksites," after Elias Hicks*, and the Evangelicals dubbed "Orthodox." Further splits ensued: by the 1840s, Wilburites were reacting to Evangelical inroads among the Orthodox, now called "Gurneyites." By the late 1860s, Orthodox in the US Midwest had evangelists and, by the 1890s, pastors; soon their Yearly Meetings, including a holiness* emphasis with a quest for perfection, differed little from Methodist churches. In 1887, in Richmond, Indiana, a declaration defined Orthodox Quakerism in Evangelical terms.

Such developments had an impact beyond North America, as Orthodox missionaries took their faith to Africa, Latin America, and Asia. **See also QUAKER WORSHIP.** H. LARRY INGLE

Friendship, defined by Cicero as "a relationship of mutual affection, based on agreement about all human and divine matters, together with goodwill and affection." Christians adopted ideas from classical antiquity to define spiritual friendship; they were also influenced by biblical references to the friendship of David and Jonathan, and Christ and the "beloved disciple" (possibly John*), to Christ's commandment to love* one another, and to early community in Jerusalem, despite the difficulty of reconciling the ideal of mutual, exclusive friendship with love of neighbor. Augustine* and Basil* the Great transposed these classical ideals in the context of doctrines, such as the body of Christ; monastic* writers (e.g. Cassian*) described friendship as a key element in spiritual progress. Later writers also discussed questions of friendship with God and with the self.

CAROLINNE WHITE

Fruits of the Spirit. Paul lists these fruits (Gal 5: 22–23) as love*, joy, peace*, patience, kindness, goodness, faithfulness, meekness, and self-control. The Vulgate* adds modesty, continence, and chastity, making a total of 12.

Frumentius (c300–c380), the first bishop and apostle of Ethiopia*. According to Rufinus* Tyrannius's reliable account (4th c.), a philosophy teacher from Tyre, Meropius, and his students, Frumentius* and Aedesius, went to "India" (as Rufinus called Ethiopia). Their boat was attacked. Frumentius and Aedesius survived and were taken to the royal palace (c340), where the king held them as servants. Before his death, the king granted them freedom for years of faithful service as teachers and advisers. At the queen's request, they stayed to help run the government until the crown prince could assume power. Frumentius used his good offices to found a Christian church in Aksum and gathered together Christians already in the kingdom, namely Roman merchants from Syria and the Byzantine world. After this regency, Aedesius returned to Tyre, becoming a parish priest. Frumentius went to Alexandria (c347) to plead with Archbishop Athanasius* to send a bishop to the new Christian community in Ethiopia. Instead Athanasius ordained Frumentius himself as the "first bishop" and apostle of Ethiopia. **See also ETHIOPIA.** GETACHEW HAILE

Fundamentalism is the label applied to aggressively conservative movements in many of the world's religious faiths.

North American Fundamentalism. Fundamentalism (term first used in 1920) was originally a movement in US Protestant Christianity, both inside and outside the denominations, that defended traditional beliefs, biblical authority, and the uniqueness of human beings against the challenges of modernism, e.g.

historical criticism and evolutionary biology. This Protestant fundamentalism grew out of 19th-c. revivalist* and Premillennialist* movements, entrenched patriarchalism*, and the Bible Conference Movement. Yet fundamentalism is not simply another name for popular* religion, religious conservatism, traditionalism, or orthodoxy. It is a movement that seeks to resist, oppose, and defeat selected aspects of modernity both by self-isolation (in independent congregations, subcultures, or families) and by appropriating the power of the media or politics.

Interpretations and assessments of fundamentalism vary and tend to be matters of emphasis, yet certain themes in Protestant Christianity persist. These themes include the absolute and literal* authority of biblical verses and passages on whatever subject they proclaim; certain fundamentals of belief, such as miracles*, the virgin* birth, and the bodily resurrection* of Jesus; the scenario of the end of the world taken from the books of Daniel and Revelation; the patriarchal*, nuclear family* and the importance of male authority in both the family and the congregation; and the replacement of a secular and religiously pluralistic society with a Christian society modeled on colonial times. In the last decade of the 20th c., the Fundamentalist Movement took on a moral-political dimension with the rise of the New Christian Right, which focused on selected moral issues having to do with public schools, the family*, sexuality*, and the media*, e.g. school prayer, Christian symbols in government places, homosexuality*, abortion*, pornography, and creationism*.

The distinctive religious dimension of fundamentalism is the sense of threat from a secular and religious pluralistic culture to the life of faith. At the same time, the use of communication technologies, modern genres of music, and multiple types of ministry give fundamentalist congregations an ethos of enthusiasm, energy, and even fun. Fundamentalists find a way to exist in a secular culture by reclaiming aspects of traditional religion and creating a certain distance from culture by way of independent congregations, homeschooling, Bible colleges, independent television networks, and religious publishing. Sociologically speaking, the Fundamentalist Movement is centered on relatively affluent, middle-class young adults rather than on a disenfranchised social class. From the beginning, fundamentalism has tended to be a grassroots movement, a populism suspicious of official religion and hierarchical institutions and maintaining a supernatural worldview. As a movement, it has tended to embody a certain pessimism about the state of the world, a pessimism directed both toward other religious groups as either "pagan" or apostate and toward society as corrupt and under the rule of Satan. This is why Christian, Jewish, and Islamic forms of fundamentalism engender a rhetoric and strategy of opposition that identify specific enemies such as psychoanalysts, evolutionary biologists, liberals, feminists, gays and lesbians, and secular humanists. A social-political conservatism associated with fundamentalism has included opposition to the Social* Gospel and to movements for civil rights (including the rights of women and gays and lesbians), virulent anticommunism, and a militaristic stance in international relations.

Global Fundamentalism. Because fundamentalism pervades many world religions, we can speak of "fundamentalisms." Roman Catholic fundamentalism (Integrism*) and Episcopalian fundamentalism center less on the inerrant Scriptures* than on an unchangeable tradition* monitored by an authoritative institution. The reforms of Vatican II were the primary event that evoked a Roman Catholic integrism that opposes the vernacular Mass*, any diminishment of papal and episcopal authority, and any moderation of canon* law on issues of priestly celibacy*, the ordination* of women, or altered family* and sex ethics. Muslim fundamentalism was evoked by the long history of Western domination of the Middle East after the division of the Ottoman Empire. Because its primary conviction is that the practice of Islam* is not possible in a Western (secular, religiously pluralistic) nation-state political setting, it has been from the beginning a religiopolitical movement whose aim is to restore a Muslim state as the context for the practice of *shari'a* (religious law). Hindu fundamentalism likewise arose as an anticolonialist, anti-Western movement that hoped to create a Hindu nation-state based on the Dharma (piety, spirituality). Jewish fundamentalism in the form of Haredi and Hasidic Judaism is centered in the texts of the Torah and Talmud, as well as various handbooks and commentaries, as a way of ensuring Jewish survival in the modern age.

The one feature that all of these fundamentalisms share is the determined, even militant rejection of aspects of modernity on behalf of traditional forms of faith. Hindu, Muslim, and

Jewish fundamentalisms all battle for a national or cultural setting sufficiently distant from Western influence to permit their practices of faith.

EDWARD FARLEY

Fundamentals, The. The title of two series of books, one in 4 volumes (1909), another in 12 (1910–15), which saw many dangers in "higher criticism" (historiography*) and liberal* theology. The Presbyterian General Assembly listed five fundamentals (1910; reaffirmed 1916, 1923): inerrancy* of Scripture, virgin birth, substitutionary atonement*, bodily resurrection*, and historicity of miracles*. Among Premillennialists*, the last was replaced by the second* coming of Christ.

Fundamental Theology. In scholastic* thought, an examination of the presuppositions of Christian faith (God's* existence, the possibility of revelation*, the human capacity to know God, and the basis of the "act of faith*"). Reshaped by transcendental* Thomism and Karl Rahner* into a broader description and analysis of the human situation, it includes the universal call of grace*. **See also ANONYMOUS CHRISTIANS; EXISTENTIALISM AND CHRISTIAN THOUGHT; SUPERNATURAL.**

G

Gabon, named "Gabão" by Portuguese explorers (15th c.) who were the first Christian contacts for several Bantu groups that had immigrated there around the 13th c. A former French colony (1850, first as part of the French Congo, now Republic of Congo*, Congo-Brazzaville), independent since 1960, Gabon is the richest country in the Central West African region (owing to dense rainforests logged for precious tropical woods and to offshore oil), although most people do not benefit from this wealth. The capital, Libreville, was a settlement for former slaves who had been freed from slave ships (1849).

Christianity was introduced to Gabon (1841) by the Congregation of the Sacred Heart of Mary (a French nun order; see Jane Frances de Chantal). Father Jean Bessieux established St. Mary of Gabon (1844), the oldest Catholic church building in modern Africa. The first Protestant missionaries were sent by the Congregationalist American Board of Commissioners for Foreign Missions (1842); they were followed by Presbyterians (1870). When French became a requirement in mission schools (1889), these earlier Protestants were progressively replaced by French Protestant missionaries (including Albert Schweitzer*). After a slow beginning, the Protestant Church grew rapidly, resulting in the (autonomous) Evangelical Church of Gabon (Église Évangélique du Gabon, 1961). The traditional religion of the Banzie (Initiates), or Bwiti, originating with the Fang people, became increasingly Christian (from 1945), with an emphasis on Jesus as Savior, and emerged after independence (1960) as a vigorous African* Instituted Church, l'Église des Banzie.

The Roman Catholic Church in Gabon grew rapidly through mass conversions in the 1930s (from 16,000 in 1910 to 120,000 in 1940) and "second evangelization" efforts in the 1960s (c300,000 in 1972). The latter were significantly aided by the teaching and social activities of the Daughters of Mary (Ekwa Maria) and the Soeurs de Sainte-Marie de Gabon. Some studies have indicated that there was further growth of the Roman Catholic Church, although other studies have reported a slower growth – indeed a stagnation – owing to the lack of Gabonese priests, despite the effort of Gabonese Msgr. André Raponda-Walker (1871–1968), a linguist and scholar, who composed African hymns. The hierarchy of the Church (now four bishops) was under the authority of the archbishop of Brazzaville until 1961, when Msgr. François Ndong was appointed the first auxiliary bishop of Libreville.

The Evangelical Church of Gabon (weakened between 1970 and 1997 by a succession of internal divisions, mostly resolved in 1997) oversees almost 25% of all primary schools in Gabon, and runs seven secondary schools and a teacher training college. It has a theological school for the training of its pastors and lay leaders.

Statistics: Population (2000): 1.2 million (M). Christians, 1.1 M, 90.6% (Roman Catholics, 0.5–0.75 M; Protestants, 0.2–0.3M; independents [including members of African Instituted Churches], 0.2–0.3.5 M), Muslims, 0.06 M, 4.6%; African Religionists, 0.04 M, 3.1%, nonreligious, 0.01, 1.2%. (Based on *World Christian Encyclopedia*, 2001.)

VALENTIN DEDJI

Gabriel, the angel who was sent to the prophet Daniel* (Dan 8:16–27, 9:21–27) and who announced to Zachariah* the birth of John* the Baptist (Luke 1:11–12) and to Mary* the coming of the Messiah* (Luke 1:26–38). He described himself as "standing in the presence of God" (Luke 1:19) and was later listed among the seven archangels*.

Gadamer, Hans-Georg (1900–2003), born in Marburg, a student of Heidegger*, who supervised Gadamer's *Habilitationsschrift* on Plato's* ethics. Later professor of philosophy at the University of Heidelberg, he was one of the most important figures in the discussion of hermeneutics*, particularly after the publication of his major work, *Wahrheit und Methode* (1960; *Truth and Method*, 1975). Building on Heidegger's work in ontology*, Gadamer's book is broadly interdisciplinary, drawing on art criticism, literary criticism, theology, and jurisprudence. Hermeneutics move beyond all theoretical categories, and even beyond such historically defined ideas as "reason*" as understood by Enlightenment* thinkers, to an experience of the whole of life, practical wisdom being preferred to abstract theory. In his discussion of aesthetics* and art, Gadamer lays great emphasis on the concept of play, as an event with its own life within which disclosure may take place. Play, properly, is deeply serious, "absorbing the player into itself" and its world. By extension, any act of interpretation is not a mechanical process, but a creative event. Gadamer's hermeneutics are an extension of the earlier work of Schleiermacher* and Dilthey. Like them he emphasizes the universality of the hermeneutical problem, but more than them he seeks a return to primordial experience, rejecting all claims to historical* objectivity on the grounds that modern hermeneutical scholars inevitably fail to take their own specific historical standpoint seriously. Gadamer's insistence on the importance of language* in the final part of *Truth and Method* betrays the influence of Heidegger: as the medium of hermeneutical experience and all understanding, language allows "being" to reveal itself. Language is no "prisonhouse" but allows an experience of the world that opens the self to the other and entertains the universal possibility of attaining the truth. **See also APOPHATISM; CONVICTION; HERMENEUTICS; METAPHOR; SYMBOLISM.** DAVID JASPER

Gaius (early 3rd c.), Roman presbyter who reported that Rome had the "trophies" (memorial monuments) of the apostles Peter* (on the Vatican hill) and Paul* (on the road to Ostia). He rejected the Apocalypse* (Revelation*) because of its materialism, ascribing it to Cerinthus. Eusebius* summarized his writings.

Galatians, Epistle to the, one of the oldest extant epistles of Paul* (c51–52) written from Corinth* to churches he recently founded in the Roman province of Galatia (Asia Minor). It reflects conflicting views on the full incorporation of Gentiles* into the new religious community. Should Gentiles be circumcised and follow dietary laws? This issue threatened church unity first in Jerusalem* and then in Antioch* (2:1–14). Paul had heard that other missionaries later sought to convince the Galatian churches to uphold Jewish rites to ensure their righteous status (1:6–7, 3:2–3).

To counter this teaching, Paul stresses the divine origin of his autonomous Gentile mission, authenticated by Christ's revelation* and by charismatic* experiences (1:15–16, 3:1–5). Paul reinterprets salvation* history about Abraham*, Isaac*, and Moses* to emphasize the temporary nature of the Law/Torah* and the primacy of faith* (3:6–4:31). The Christ-believing churches, free of Torah obligations, are marked by "the law of Christ," i.e. sacrificial love*, as demonstrated by the cross* (5:13–14, 6:2).

Paul soon modified his polemical way of defending the community identity as he faced the intricate reality of Jew–Gentile cohabitation (see 1 Corinthians* and Romans*). Ironically, Galatians, which intended to defend the marginalized Gentiles, was used in marginalizing rhetoric against Judaism* by the later church (e.g. John* Chrysostom and Luther*). The Reformers* used Galatians as a primary text for the doctrine of justification* by faith alone. Its polemical treatment of the Law/Torah also attracted Marcion* and other Gnostics*. The concern in Galatians for both universalism* and particularism provides a framework for various Liberation* theologies. ATSUHIRO ASANO

Galileo Galilei (1564–1642), mathematician, natural philosopher, astronomer. Born in Pisa, taught in Pisa and Padua; as a mathematician-philosopher adorned the Medici court in Florence.

In 1609–12 Galileo made a series of telescopic discoveries, published in *The Starry Messenger*, that challenged the long-held earth-centered worldviews of Aristotle* and Ptolemy. They also seemed to conflict with the Bible, e.g. when one interprets literally the few texts that describe the sun as in motion or the earth as at rest. The ensuing controversy ended (1616) in Galileo's being formally admonished to abandon the Copernican* view as "contrary to Scripture*." The accession (1623) of a new pope, Urban VIII, encouraged Galileo to resume his work, leading to the publication of his *Dialogue on Two Chief World Systems* (1632). An angry pope ordered Galileo to be tried on suspicion of heresy*. Condemned for defending a view contrary to Scripture and for ignoring the personal admonition he had received in 1616, he was forced to abjure the Copernican worldview and sentenced to permanent house arrest. He returned to his early work on falling bodies, publishing the foundational work of modern mechanics, *Two New Sciences* (1638).

His (uncirculated) *Letter to the Grand-Duchess Christina* (1615) drew on Augustine's *De genesi ad litteram* to enunciate, in classical form, the principles that should govern apparent conflict between Scripture and natural knowledge. Had the Roman judges been guided by these principles, the Copernican view would never have been condemned, as finally conceded by the Vatican (1992). Later critics of the Roman Catholic Church would construe the condemnation of Copernicanism as an attack on science*. But in 1616, most natural philosophers and astronomers were entirely unpersuaded by the Copernican view. The scientific issue thus played little, if any, part in the theologians' discussions. The issue was the apparent challenge to Scripture; the bitter Reformation* debates of the day allowed that consideration to swamp all others. ERNAN MCMULLIN

Galla Placidia (c390–450), Roman empress. Daughter of Theodosius* I, she was taken from Rome by Alaric the Goth (410) and married his brother, Ataulf. On his death, she was returned to the Roman court as part of a treaty between the Goths and Romans. Forced to marry the Roman general Constantius, she was named Augusta (empress) when he became co-emperor in the West. She served as regent for the first 12 years of her son Valentinian III's rule. She supported Augustine* during the Pelagian* controversy and Leo* during the Monophysite* controversy.

Gallicanism, a movement among French Catholics that defended the rights of the French Church to govern itself without papal control, a view also adopted by Catholics in other parts of the world (see, e.g., Brazil; Mexico). Ultramontanism* represented the opposite position. The decrees of the Council of Constance* (1418) and Basel* (1431–37) gave councils an authority independent of the pope and were cited by the French kings in defense of their special rights in the French Church. During Louis XIV's reign, the French bishops adopted the four "Gallican articles" (1682) affirming that kings are not subjects of the pope; general councils have an authority independent of the pope; the pope must respect the national churches' traditions and decrees; and papal statements in matters of faith are not binding without the whole church's consent. Louis XIV, in return for abandoning Gallican views, gained from Rome the right to appoint bishops and approve the publication of papal decrees and visits by papal legates. Gallicanism, promoted by the Jansenists*, was revived by the Civil Constitution of the Clergy (1790) and Napoleon's concordat with the pope (1801). The declaration of papal infallibility* at the First Vatican* Council excluded Gallicanism, but the Second Vatican* Council reaffirmed the role of national conferences of bishops. **See also POPES, ROMAN CATHOLIC, AND THE PAPACY.**
EUGENE TESELLE

Gallican Rite, a liturgy widespread in the West after the 4th c. (Gaul, Spain*, Milan, and probably the Celtic* churches), more elaborate than the Roman Rite, with many features derived from Eastern liturgies, especially that of Antioch. Under Charlemagne*, the Roman Rite was adopted, but with Gallican features, which influenced the Roman liturgy in coming centuries. **See also LITURGIES, HISTORY OF.**

Gamaliel (d c50), a Pharisee*, member of the Sanhedrin*, and teacher of Paul* (Acts 22:3), who advised against persecuting the apostles (Acts 5:34–39).

Gangra, Synod of (c341), a regional synod in Asia Minor whose canons* were directed chiefly against the extreme asceticism* of Eustathius* of Sebaste for its negative view of marriage* and for its confusion of gender and class roles.

Garcés, Julián (c1452–1542), Dominican priest, first bishop in the Diocese of Tlaxcala, New Spain. His letter to Paul III describing the appalling treatment of the indigenous peoples helped to inspire the bull *Sublimus* Dei* (1537) on the dignity of these peoples. **See also MEXICO.** MARÍA ALICIA PUENTE LUTTEROTH and ELIZABETH JUDD

Garvey, Marcus (1887–1940), emigrated to the USA from Jamaica* (1915) and founded a black nationalist movement that thrived until his deportation (1940). Much of Garvey's activity centered on plans to establish political and commercial ties between Africa and the Americas. He also spoke of uniting, "civilizing," and Christianizing Africa in order to make it a modern military and industrial power. Garvey found support among numerous African American religious groups, including the Moorish Science Temple, a group of Black Hebrews who eventually migrated to Ethiopia*, and numerous Protestant ministers. The African Orthodox Church (with bishops legitimately claiming apostolic succession) adopted the Garveyite doctrine that Christ was the black man of sorrows. **See also RASTAFARI MOVEMENT.**
WILSON J. MOSES

Gay and Lesbian Theologies. During the era of "gay liberation" (1970s in North America and Western Europe), gay and lesbian people claimed the right to define themselves, wrestling that power from the legal and medical professions. Gay people began to construct themselves as a stable minority group and to make claims to equality under the law. Debates raged among gay and lesbian people as to whether sexual orientation was an objective, transcultural fact or a social construction. Lesbian feminists* challenged gay men to interrogate their investment in and collusion with the complex systems of patriarchy*. This social movement forced the churches to face the whole issue of homosexuality*. A body of gay liberal theology began to emerge. In these works, the authority of the gay or lesbian self was audaciously positioned as a challenge to the authority of Christian tradition and contemporary systems of Christian authority.

The concepts of a universal self and universal experiences were eventually challenged by Liberation* theologies, and the inherent goodness of gay culture came under scrutiny from feminist, black*, and lesbian sources. The specter of AIDS cast a terrifying cloud over gay liberation. Thus a much more self-critical body of gay and lesbian Liberation theology emerged (1980s). Influenced by Process* theology and the idea of God who suffers-with, the emergence of the Divine as erotic power is a persistent theme in sexual theology of this period. God was conceived as the power of right relationship, radically immanent, and experienced most intensely not in the patriarchal system of marriage* but in the fluid bonds of friendship*. But so radically immanent is this God that God often disappears into human experience, providing no critical horizon and no sense of mystery* or hope*.

In the 1990s, the work of queer* theorists began to have an impact on Christian reflection on sexuality* (see Bible Interpretation Cluster: In North America and Western Europe: Queer). Queer theory challenged the very concepts of sexuality, arguing that these are matters of performance, not hard, eternal reality. A new body of theology developed out of queer theory, characterized not by the perspective of a particular sexual orientation but rather by a belief that sexual orientation and gender are not stable enough concepts on which to build theologies. Queer theology claims that neither heterosexual nor homosexual experience can claim any kind of divine authority. Sexual ethics then has to be built on foundations other than gender. **See also SEXUALITY, ISSUES OF, CLUSTER.**

ELIZABETH STUART

Gehenna (from Heb *ge hinnom*, "place of woe," where children were sacrificed to Moloch). It became a term for the place of everlasting punishment (Mark 9:43, 48 par.). **See also HELL.**

Gelasian Sacramentary, the oldest Roman sacramentary* (Vat. Reg. Lat. 316), with liturgies for the feasts in the church year and containing the canon* of the Mass* in traditional form.

Gender Studies. See FEMINIST THEOLOGY CLUSTER.

Genesis, Book of, the first book of the Bible, reports traditions about the origins of the world and of Israel (primeval beginnings and ancestral sagas). The historical*-critical approach to Genesis distinguishes literary sources – J (Yahwist), E (Elohist; an expansion of J?), and P (Priestly) – and attributes to P the final edition. Some critics think of one original source, preceded by oral narratives and subsequently expanded to include other traditions reflecting Israel's later experiences.

A "prologue" (Gen 1–11) shows a progressive corruption of the world that was originally created good. By contrast, Abraham* (12–25) inaugurates the history of salvation (of "all the families of the earth"; 12:3). The book ends with Joseph's bones being carried from Egypt to the land of Israel. In between, Isaac* (26), Jacob* (27–35), and Joseph* (37–50) are presented without complacency as complex personalities on whom divine promises (of posterity, land, and bliss) are repeatedly bestowed. Structurally, Genesis's framework is built around genealogical lists ("These are the generations of" occurs 10 times, starting with "heaven and earth" in 2:4a). They are attributed to P. They fill enormous chronological gaps and define Israel's historical relationship with its neighbors (see 9, 10, 16, 19, 25) and within its own families and tribes (see 4, 12, 20, 26, 34, 38).

Parallels with ancient Near East myths* are abundant: sibling rivalries, universal degradation, a deluge (flood*) divinely sent, personal deities, various designations of the gods, impure divine–human commerce, and punished human hubris. Documents from Canaan, Mesopotamia, Egypt, Turkey, and Greece shed much light on a treasure trove of myths shared by Israel but often fundamentally reworked through "demythologization*."

Genesis's drafted picture is realistic, especially in terms of the problematic kinships that expand on the basic one between man and wife in

Gen 2–3. While a conservative viewpoint would read Genesis as history, critics consider it mostly legendary, i.e. meant to bear a faith* testimony rather than to belong to historiography. Actually, Genesis displays a "theological history" in which God is Lord in spite of the persistence of evil*, as the primeval narratives (3, 4, 6, 11) show in a paradigmatic way. These narratives are not paleographic; they state that God is creator* of all that is living, a message with its eschatological* apotheosis entrusted by God to Israel. Thus for believers through the centuries, Genesis as Scripture* binds past, present, and future in a historical complex marked by trust and meaningfulness. **See also CREATION; IMAGE OF GOD; MYTH AND THE STUDY OF CHRISTIANITY.** ANDRÉ LACOCQUE

Geneva Bible, English translation of the Bible (and Apocrypha*), published in Geneva in 1560, prepared by exiles from the England of "Bloody Mary." Its notes promoted Calvinist theology and resistance to tyrannical heretical rulers. It was the Bible most widely used in England for a century and was purposefully replaced by the King James* Version.

Bible de Genève, a revision of Olivétan's French translation by Beza* with pastors and professors of Geneva, published in 1588, was the official Bible of Geneva and French Huguenots.

Geneva (Calvin's) and Its Theological Traditions. The Reformation* in Geneva had its roots from c1531 in political rebellion against the prince-bishop (the last one, Pierre de la Baume, left in 1533). Guillaume Farel's*, Pierre Viret's, and Antoine Froment's preaching of Zwinglian* doctrine from 1534 led to the abolition of the Mass* (August 10, 1535) and the adoption of the Reformation (edict of May 21, 1536). The city was politically under the protection of Zwinglian Bern after separating from the Roman Catholic Diocese of Geneva. Calvin* arrived in July 1536 and was persuaded to stay and consolidate the religious changes. He and Farel were banished from Geneva (1538–41) for attempting to introduce church discipline (Communion* four times per year, moral censorship, excommunication*) that was judged too strict by the Zwinglian Church in Bern and the population of Geneva. Called back (1541), Calvin introduced a presbyterian* system of church government. The Church of Geneva was ruled by the Company of Pastors, headed by Calvin. The consistory, a mixed body of clergy and laypeople, shared with civil magistrates the task of policing morals and church discipline. Unlike civil courts, it could excommunicate but could not impose prison sentences. The powers conferred on the consistory curtailed civil authorities' prerogatives in religious matters. Church discipline and its partial enforcement by the Church distinguished Geneva from the Zwinglian churches. To implement his system, Calvin relied on refugees from France and other countries. But the Calvinist Movement was not consolidated until 1555, because the original citizens remained favorable to the Zwinglian system. The movement also included a number of theological specificities, especially its emphasis on divine providence* and predestination* with the corresponding devaluation of human powers in the realm of salvation*. There were controversies, e.g. the Bolsec* affair, in which other Swiss churches showed a more reserved attitude. The movement gradually reinforced its image as anti-Catholic, rigorist, and biblicist. The execution of Michael Servetus (1553) for his heterodox views on the Trinity* prompted an outcry in favor of religious toleration and earned Calvin a reputation for cruelty, although not he but the Geneva Council imposed the death sentence. The Geneva Academy (founded 1559, with Beza* as its first rector) became the training ground for Protestant pastors from all over Europe. Most of Geneva's theological traditions of the period were embodied in Calvin's *Institutes of Christian Religion* and numerous sermons and biblical commentaries. Eventually the movement was to have an influence in many parts of the world, ranging from Northern Europe to North America and Asia. **See also CALVIN, JEAN.** IRENA BACKUS

Gennadios II (George Scholarios) (c1405–c1473), the first patriarch of Ottoman Constantinople, a Byzantine theologian. As a layperson, George Scholarios served as a secretary, judge, and lay preacher at Emperor John VIII Palaiologos's court in the final years of the Byzantine Empire. Scholarios participated, along with many other Byzantines, in the Council of Florence* (1447), supporting an agreement on church unity. But Scholarios soon opposed this agreement, as did many other participants. Following John VIII's death (1449), Scholarios retired to the monastery of Pantocrator, Constantinople (1450), taking the name Gennadios. After the fall of Constantinople (1453), he was a prisoner of the Ottomans. The sultan Mehmed II turned to him to become patriarch, responsible politically for the Greek Orthodox population within the Ottoman Empire; the Greek Orthodox Church became a civil authority, according to the *millet** system. On two occasions, Gennadios was temporarily forced from this very difficult position. When he abdicated (c1463), he retired to the Prodromos monastery in Thessalonica, devoting himself to writing commentaries on Thomas* Aquinas, apologies in support of Aristotle, and many other works on theology, ethics, and liturgy. Interestingly, he is the only Byzantine theologian known to use the term "transubstantiation*" to refer to the changing of bread and wine into the Body and Blood of Christ. **See also *MILLET*.** JAMES M. POWELL

Gentiles (Gk *ethne*; Lat *gentiles*), all the nations of the world (*oikoumene*), often in contrast to Israel (Rom 2–3, 9–11); according to the context, this distinction could be religious (Jews vs. non-Jews), ethnic (Israelites vs. non-Israelites), or political (an Israelite world vs. a Roman world). Because of Israel's election*, the Gentiles/nations were often viewed as sinners and idolaters*; the Torah* placed restrictions on contacts with them. But Israel's election was as "a light to the nations" (Isa 49:1–6). Paul is called as the apostle to the Gentiles/nations (Gal 1:16); the mission to the Gentiles/nations is approved by Peter and James (Gal 2; Acts 10, 15). In Christian usage, "Gentile" can also refer to a recalcitrant member of the church (Matt 18:17; cf. 21:31–32) or to a "pagan"* or idolater.

Genuflection, bending of the right knee to express reverence for the reserved sacrament or the name of Jesus (cf. Phil 2:10).

George of Cappadocia, Arian* bishop who replaced Athanasius* in 357; he was killed by a mob in 361 for an iconoclastic action, plundering a shrine.

George of Laodicea (4th c.), moderate Arian* bishop who opposed the Anomoian* views of Eudoxius* (for whom the Son is *anomoios*, or "unlike," the Father in essence). With Basil* of Ancyra, he championed the Homoiousian* conception of the Trinity* (the Son is *homoi-ousios*, "like in essence," with the Father, but not *homoousios*, "identical in essence").

Georgia. National identity has always been closely associated with the Orthodox Church of Georgia: "Georgia is the country where church services are held in the Georgian language," says *The Life of St. Gregory of Khandzta* (written 10th c.). Whether Christians, nonbelievers, or non-Christians, culturally all Georgians belong to the tradition preserved by the Orthodox Church of Georgia, although since 1991 this attitude has had ambivalent effects on the process of democratization and on church life.

According to tradition, the apostle Andrew was the first to preach Christianity in Georgia, and a Cappadocian woman, Nino*, converted the royal couple (King Mirian and Queen Nana); Christianity became the state religion of Iberia, the eastern part of present-day Georgia (c330). The kingdom of Colchis (Western Georgia) was Christianized shortly afterward (the two kingdoms unified in the early 11th c). Under Muslim rule, few Georgians ever converted to Islam*, even though after the fall of Constantinople (1453) the Church of Georgia was considerably weakened. Under Russian rule (from 1801), the Orthodox Church of Georgia was subordinated to the Russian* Orthodox Church (1811–1917). When the Soviet rule began (1921), the Orthodox Church of Georgia had 2,455 parishes, before being systematically silenced and suppressed.

Christian practice has dramatically increased since Ilya II became catholicos*-patriarch of Georgia (1977), encouraged a revival of daily devotion by writing a prayer book, and instituted reforms to enable the Georgian Orthodox Church to regain its role in social life and prestige in society. These reforms, which began with a confrontation with Soviet ideology, led to a revival of monastic life (in 1977, 4 monasteries with 20 monks and nuns; in 1988, 7 monasteries with 55 monks and nuns; in 2003, 65 monasteries with 250 monks and nuns). A great number of churches were reopened (in 1977, 25 parishes with 50 clergy; in 1988, 200 parishes with 180 clergy; in 2003, 550 parishes with 1,100 clergy).

The Constitution of 1995 affirms freedom of religion (for Roman Catholics, Baptists, Muslims, Jews, among others), yet mentions "the special role of the Orthodox Church of Georgia in the history of Georgia"; in a 2002 agreement between the Church and the state, the Orthodox Church of Georgia was granted the status of *primus inter pares*.

Statistics: Population (2007): 4.6 million. Christians, 89% (Orthodox, 83%; Armenian Non-Chalcedonian Orthodox, 5%; Roman Catholics, 1%; Baptists, 0.2%; Pentecostals, 0.1%); Muslims, 10%; Jews, 0.25%; nonreligious, 0.7%. (*Source*: 2002 census.)

TAMARA GRDZELIDZE

Georgian Apostolic Autocephalous Orthodox Church. See ORTHODOX CHURCHES, EASTERN, CLUSTER: IN GEORGIA.

German Christians. The German Christian Movement, founded in 1927, was one of many similar religious movements that, emerging from the spiritual crisis following Germany's defeat in World War I, sought to harmonize Lutheranism* with extreme German nationalism. "German Christians" became the most representative group and enthusiastically greeted the rise of Nazism (1932). They regarded Hitler as God's new revelation*, believed in the ideological* inseparability of Christianity and Nazism, and sought to unite German Protestants in one church under the control of the Nazi government. The Church* Struggle in Germany was based primarily on this issue. **See also CHURCH AND STATE RELATIONS CLUSTER: INTRODUCTORY ENTRY.**

MARK R. LINDSAY

German Literature and Christianity. Soon after the arrival of Christianity in Germany* (6th c.), early medieval vernacular literature provided Christian instruction and edification through texts such as paraphrases of the NT (Otfried's *Evangelienbuch*, c870), depictions of Christ as liege lord in an old Saxon epic style (*Heliand**, c830), poems on Christ's life by Ava (c1125), dramatic performances of Christ's Passion (*Osterspiel von Muri*, c1250), and mystical writings by Mechthild' von Magdeburg (1207–82) and Meister Eckhart* (1260–1329).

When clergy ceased to be the sole carriers of culture (12th c.), a courtly literature harmonized chivalric and Christian virtues. In his *Parzifal*, Wolfram von Eschenbach (1170–1220) presents an ideal Christian knight transcending his duties in the world by becoming the king of the Holy Grail*.

The most influential book for German language and literature was Luther's* Bible translation (1522–34). Its bold language has inspired writers and poets to the present day.

Throughout the Renaissance* and Reformation*, most prose literature was satirical and polemical, used in the controversies between the Reformers and their opponents. In the subsequent Catholic* Renewal (Counter Reformation), Jesuits* wrote plays with biblical subjects to be performed in schools. Meanwhile, the Protestant devotional book *Six Books on True Christianity* (1605–21) by Johann Arndt* edified Christians until the early 19th c. and inspired both sacred baroque poetry and early Pietism*.

Seventeenth-century German literature remained deeply religious. Protestant Boehme* and Catholic Angelus Silesius (1624–77) continued the mystical* literary tradition. During the devastating Thirty* Years' War in Germany, great Christian poetry was created, such as the still-popular church hymns by Paul Gerhardt (1607–76) and Protestant religious sonnets and heroic martyr tragedies by Gryphius (1616–64) that celebrated Christian stoicism. The Catholic convert Johannes Jacob Christoffel von Grimmelshausen (1621–76) in his picaresque novel *Simplicissimus* (1668–69) about the brutality of war portrayed a hero who withdraws from the world as a hermit.

German Pietism*, reacting to rigid Lutheran orthodoxy, had considerable influence on 18th-c. literature. With its introspective concerns, it shaped confessional and autobiographical writings. With its stress on the experience of God through feeling, Pietism inspired Friedrich Gottlieb Klopstock's *Messias* (1748–73), a series of cantos that form a biblical heroic epic in hexameter representing Christ's Passion and the Resurrection in an emotional, visionary manner.

Through the secularization* of the Enlightenment*, Christianity slowly lost its hold on German culture. Secular humanist authors such as Goethe (1749–1832) and Schiller (1759–1805) became the new prophets and spiritual leaders of the nation. In early romanticism, literature and art usurped the role of religion and became vehicles of spiritual revelation, as Novalis (Georg Philipp Friedrich Freiherr von Hardenberg, 1772–1801) emphasized. However, many later romantics, such as Joseph Karl Benedikt Freiherr von Eichendorff (1788–1822), Clemens Brentano (1778–1842), and Annette von Droste-Hulshoff (1797–1848), rediscovered the pre-Reformation Middle Ages and wrote with traditional Catholic sensitivities.

By the mid-19th c., as a result of the firmly established historical-critical method of biblical hermeneutics, the Bible understood as a historical document was nevertheless used as a storehouse of literary allusions, images, or story lines, often in an ironic vein, as in Thomas Mann's (1875–1955) tetralogy *Joseph and His Brothers* (1933–42), or for satire, as in Stefan Heym's (1913–2001) *King David Report* (1972). German expressionist writers around World War I voiced deep spiritual needs and experienced God as the inaccessible Other, somewhat akin to Barth's* early theology; the dramas of

Ernst Barlach (1870–1938) are good examples. In the Third Reich, the Catholic writers Reinhold Schneider (1903–58) and Werner Bergengruen (1892–1964) were forbidden to publish, but their poems, clandestinely distributed, sustained many Germans. During the postwar 1950s and 1960s, the Christian novelist Heinrich Böll (1917–85) became the "conscience of the nation" through his attacks on the hypocrisy of the church and the new German affluence during German reconstruction. The use of biblical images in contemporary German poetry continues to be an intrinsic part of intertextual communication, as in the works of Paul Celan (1920–70), Peter Huchel (1903–81), Hans Magnus Enzenberger (b1929), and Ernst Jandl (1925–2000). BARBARA CARVILL

Germany. Present-day German culture is Christian through and through. Half of the official monuments are churches and monasteries. After the Reformation*, the relationships among Roman Catholic, Lutheran, and Reformed churches were strained, yet the ecumenical movement finally dissolved these tensions. The state and the three large confessions are still interconnected. Religious socialization has declined, especially in Eastern Germany, but the need for spiritual support and transcendence is increasingly recognized. Loss of membership and shrinking financial resources in mainline churches have led to the closure and sale of church buildings (mostly built in the 1950s). Yet revivalist*, Evangelical*, and Charismatic* independent churches are growing.

History. Christianity spread within the boundaries of the present-day Federal Republic of Germany from the 6th to the 13th c. primarily through monastic missions, the sword, and monastic colonization (see Hospitallers; Military Orders; Teutonic Knights). The new religion was firmly rooted in all areas when the initial proclamation was followed by the building of churches and the establishment of dioceses and archdioceses. Parishes were often organized and supported by laypersons, the so-called proprietary churches (*Eigenkirchenwesen*), which still exist in the form of the patronage rights of influential people who determine parish appointments. In addition, when kings awarded land and legal sovereignty to bishops and archbishops (10th c.), they created independent ecclesiastical principalities. Although these divisions were officially erased by the secularization* of church properties (1803), they still influence confessional relationships. The religious authority of the imperial sovereign was acknowledged by the crowning in Rome of all the rulers of the Holy* Roman Empire of the German nation, from 800 (Charlemagne*) to 1530. Despite the limitation of power mutually agreed upon following the investiture* controversy (1122), medieval church history was a continual power struggle between pope (*sacerdotium*) and emperor (*imperium*). During the Crusades* (12th and 13th c.), both powers worked together to liberate Palestine from the "infidels."

Indulgences* granted in connection with the Crusades introduced an indulgence-based piety (reinforcing the juridical view of sin* and atonement*), whose abuse provoked the protest of the monk Martin Luther*. Excommunication* drove Luther and his followers into final opposition. The Protestant Reformation* grew in many territories and cities under princely protection. Luther was concerned to guide the church, theology, and piety back to the gospel of a freely given personal justification* by faith* and to declare all pious practices to be ineffective for salvation*. In order to lend a solid basis to the changed understanding of faith, Luther translated the Bible into German, wrote hymns, developed liturgies (see Lutheranism Cluster: Lutheran Worship), and wrote catechisms*. He replaced church hierarchy and the pope with a pastoral ministry concentrated on the proclamation of the Word and the administration of the sacraments.

Zwingli* and Calvin* had similar concerns but could not achieve agreement with Luther regarding the Eucharist* and other issues, and the Reformed* churches took a separate course. Luther's supporters gathered around the Augsburg* Confession of Faith (1530) and were acknowledged as a religious party at the Augsburg Reichstag (1555). The Reformed cited the Heidelberg* Catechism (1563) but remained unprotected until the Peace of Westphalia (1648). Anabaptists* and Spiritual* Reformers were granted tolerance only at specific locations and generally only much later. With the exception of the imperial cities, the Catholic and the Protestant state churches and territorial churches once again were monoconfessional.

In the Protestant sphere, city magistrates and princes, supported by consistories, took over the administrative functions of the bishops. This territorial church government existed until 1918 and continues to have an effect today, e.g. in the state's levy of church taxes for the three major churches.

In the Catholic sphere, a phase of consolidation and definition followed the Reformation upheaval. Catholicism undertook a fundamental reorientation at the Council of Trent* (1545–1563), supported by the Jesuit* order and other monastic foundations. The *Index* Librorum Prohibitorum* (List of prohibited books) had an isolating effect (1559–1966).

After the development of the territorial churches, Protestantism concentrated on securing the legacy of the Reformation through dogmatic theology. In addition, during the Thirty* Years' War (1618–48) and afterward, pre-Reformation mysticism* took on new life in Pietism*.

The repeated efforts to achieve peaceful coexistence despite bitter polemics remained ineffective. Paul Gerhardt's hymns, however, overcame confessional barriers. With the foundation of the institutions at Halle, Francke* provided social-ethical and reformist-pedagogical influences. Von Zinzendorf* gave basic social relevance to the piety of individual conversion; the Moravian* Church that he founded, centered in Herrnhut, still serves a worldwide Bible-reading community through its publication of "Daily Watchwords [verses]" (*Losungen*).

The unease of all these churches regarding the constraints of dogma* and of the authoritarian state–church system favored the development of the Enlightenment*, which took a specifically German form under the influence of Gottfried Leibniz, Christian Wolff, Lessing*, and Kant[1]. Consequently, a biblically critical, moral, and tolerant Christianity within the limits of reason emerged. In reformist Catholic circles, even the idea of a national church independent of Rome began to germinate.

The most lasting effect on German Christianity until the late 20th c. was that of the French Revolution (1789), the Napoleonic expansionist wars of liberation (1792–1813), and the end of the old Holy* Roman Empire (1806). The integration of the lands of the abolished ecclesiastical territories into secular territories strengthened regional church structures even in Catholicism and made religious tolerance more urgent than ever. Despite the continued existence of territorial church governments, the democratic awakening in the German Federation and in the Bismarckian Empire (late 19th c.) led to a cautious "democratization" of Protestant Church administrations taking the form of church councils and synods. Of course, only men were eligible to vote and to be elected. Women obtained the ecclesiastical (and political) right to vote only in 1919. When unions between Lutherans and Reformed – administrative, liturgical (Prussia), and (occasionally) confessional unions – were ordered by political authorities, numerous union opponents (later tolerated as Free Church Old Lutherans) emigrated to North America (see Lutheranism Cluster: In the United States: Lutheran Church–Missouri Synod) and Australia. The fossilized religion of the Enlightenment (early 19th c.) was enlivened by romanticism*, idealism, and a German revivalism* – a movement prolonging Pietism embraced by individual Protestants enthusiastically preaching the Kingdom* of God and its justice.

Representatives of all three confessions – the Catholics Johann Michael Sailer and Johann Adam Möhler, the Lutherans August Tholuck and Matthias Claudius, and the Reformed Friedrich Schleiermacher* – strove to overcome the undue influence of the Enlightenment in theology and piety. Regenerative forces arose in Catholicism through the highly motivated monastic orders, the new scholasticism*, and orders devoted to social work. Catholic Sisters of Mercy and Protestant deaconesses as well as diverse Catholic and Protestant associations worked with great commitment to improve social conditions (early 19th c.). Until Vatican* I (1869–70), there was very little tension between Catholics (liberal and often critical of the pope) and Protestants. The promulgation of the dogmas of the immaculate* conception of Mary (1854) and of the doctrinal infallibility* of the pope (1870) was resisted even among Catholics; in protest the Old* Catholic Church separated from the Roman Catholic Church (1870/71). Yet Catholics who opposed such movements against Rome were strengthened by resisting Bismarck's legislation against the Catholic Church (the *Kulturkampf** directed against Ultramontanist*) and by the development of a political Catholicism (Center Party). Despite the peace laws (from 1886), civil marriage and state supervision of the schools remained in effect.

Long-term challenges for Christianity in the modern world arose from the social problems caused by industrialization; the socialism* promoted by Karl Marx* and Friedrich Engels; the atheistic movement initiated by Feuerbach* and Nietzsche*; various social movements of emancipation; World War I and the collapse of the monarchy; the Protestant churches' sudden independence from the state; the unloved Weimar Democracy; the National Socialist (Nazi) tyranny; the "Church* Struggle"; World War II; de-Nazification; the processing of the past and ecclesiastical reconstruction with ecumenical aid; the reshaping of the relationship between Christians and Jews after the Holocaust*; German political division; the churches of the German Democratic Republic (GDR) under socialist rule until 1989; the peace* movement at a time of rearmament and nuclear threat; the questions posed by ecumenical* Christianity, the Two-thirds World and colonialism*, ecology*, and ongoing technological* development; and the search for meaning and orientation in a global world becoming ever more secular (see Secularization and Desecularization in Europe and North America). These complex circumstances deeply shaped contemporary Christianity.

Churches in Contemporary Germany. Within the 16 federal states of the Federal Republic of Germany, there are 7 Roman Catholic archdioceses (and 27 dioceses), 23 Lutheran, Reformed, and United regional churches, and numerous free and independent churches.

The presiding bishop of the German Bishops' Conference represents the Roman Catholic Church in its relationship with the German state and with Rome. The Central Committee of German Catholics, a lay Catholic organization, has the responsibility of preparing the Katholikentag (Catholic Day, since 1848), a cultural gathering of Catholic Germans held every two years and also, more recently, the co-responsibility for organizing the ecumenical Kirchentag (Church Day).

The Protestant regional churches (*Landeskirchen*), each with its own administrative office (with three women as bishops, 2007), still reflect the earlier territorial organization. Yet since 1948, they have been united in a church federation, the Evangelische Kirche Deutschlands (EKD, led by the chair of its council), to deal with matters of common concern, including revising Bible translations, worship lectionaries, and hymnals, supervising theological education, issuing statements on current questions in church and public life, and especially representing more effectively the whole church in its relations with the state.

In 1969, the (East) German Democratic Republic demanded the dissolution of the Alliance of Protestant Churches (Bund der Evangelischen Kirchen) in the GDR. Yet Protestant churches strove to develop Christian life in a socialist context, promulgating courageous resolutions criticizing social conditions that contributed to the political "turning point" of 1989.

Since 1991 the Protestant church federations from Western and Eastern Germany have been united, and there is an ongoing movement toward church union among Protestant churches. Protestantism has also developed a Deutscher Evangelischer Kirchentag (German Protestant Day), held every two years and led by laypeople (like the *Katholikentag*). The Protestant Day promotes discussion forums on current issues, musical performances, liturgical and worship innovations.

The Evangelische Kirche Deutschlands also encompasses three confessional alliances (reflecting the movement toward church unions): The United Protestant churches (Union Evangelischer Kirchen, 2003; earlier under other names); the Vereinigte Evangelisch-Lutherische Kirche Deutschlands, which unites eight Lutheran churches (since 1948); and the Reformed Alliance (Reformierter Bund), which unites two Reformed regional churches and numerous Reformed congregations (progressively since 1884). Most Protestant free or independent churches (with the exception of the Mennonites*) are gathered in a union (the Vereinigung Evangelischer Freikirchen, since 1926) that includes those churches that originated from German revivalism* and the rejection of liberalism, as well as the Baptists.

Certain churches are not included in any of these alliances, namely conservative Lutheran churches (the Selbständige Evangelisch-lutherische Kirche), which separated themselves in 1972, rejecting both the ordination* of women and the Leuenberg* Agreement (1973, a theological consensus establishing full communion among the majority of Lutheran, Reformed, and United churches in Germany). Nevertheless, these conservative Lutheran churches remain in contact with other churches and are members of the broader and more informal association of churches, the Arbeitsgemeinschaft christlicher Kirchen (since 1974), which includes the Catholic German Bishops' Conference and three Orthodox churches, and sponsors the yearly "Week of Prayer for Christian Unity."

Although the three major churches (Catholic, Lutheran, Reformed) continue to experience a declining membership (owing to loss of members and low birthrate), they still have relatively stable "folk* church" structures remaining from their former roles as state* churches, providing for rites of passage (baptism, confirmation, marriage, funeral services) with a growing emphasis on the pastoral counseling associated with these rites. Celebrating the Sabbath and devoting long weekends to the main Christian feasts are affirmed as rights. There are, of course, differences between city and countryside, and between East and West Germany. In the former GDR, 40 years of socialist government and the opening of the state security files have left deep wounds in the churches.

Catholic Masses, celebrated in the German language since Vatican* II, are generally better attended than the liturgically simpler Protestant services. But even those dissociated from the church still fill the pews for concerts of sacred music (by, e.g., Bach* and Handel*). Thematic worship services with modern music and special presentations find increased favor. Despite what some view as obstacles – priestly celibacy and gender inclusiveness for pastors in the Protestant churches (see Women's Christian Practices and Theologies Cluster: In Western Europe: Germany), the priestly or pastoral ministry is highly esteemed and centered on mission, preaching, and counseling. Church work with children, youth, and women's and men's groups, as well as social work, are performed by lay co-workers and volunteers. Protestant and Catholic schools and institutions, with challenging educational and social programs, also reach people on the periphery of the church.

Piety in Germany. Piety, religious life devoted to the gospel, has taken many forms through the centuries in Germany. The medieval church made a clear distinction between the piety of laypeople (focused on doing God's will in secular life; see Laity Cluster) and those of religious* orders observing the evangelical counsels* of perfection (through asceticism*, prayer, and praise of God behind cloister walls). When Luther emphasized salvation* through faith* active in love and the priesthood* of all believers, and when, consequently, Protestantism abandoned cloisters, Protestantism also lost havens of intensive discipleship* that nurtured specific charisms* as well as art. Except for a few surviving Protestant religious foundations for women (*Damenstifte*), it was only after 1945 that men and women, deeply moved by traumatic war experiences, but also by Pietistic, High Church, or Charismatic religious experiences, gathered together in Protestant *Kommunitäten*. The members of these Protestant religious monastic communities renounce marriage and private property in order to lead a common spiritual life in communities financially supported by their own work and by donations. In 2004 more than 1,300 persons followed this way of life in 40 Protestant *Kommunitäten* and approximately 5,000 men and 25,000 women in Catholic religious* orders lived in cloisters with ordered prayer and binding vows.

The common form of Christian piety today is expressed in active church participation (including volunteer church work). Exaggerated forms of Christian piety (cult of the saints*, abuse of indulgences*) belong to the past. But the common quest for a modern form of spirituality* (as in Taizé*) connects all Christians with one another. Family devotions and private Bible reading are exceptional. Only a few still have a personal (theistic*) conception of God*. Yet pious Evangelicals are found everywhere, e.g. in the Gnadau Communal Movement, which sees itself as a provider of religious revivals* for the Protestant regional churches. Extreme conservatives are more prominent in Catholicism (Opus* Dei) than in Protestantism.

Theology. The relationship between theology, piety, and the church was and is not always harmonious. Pietism and revivalism were considered for a time to be theologically heterodox. The papal Syllabus* of Errors (1864) condemned 80 religious, ethical, and political "modern errors"; from 1910 to 1965–67, Catholic clergy were required to pledge themselves to the condemnation of Modernism*. Vatican* II brought an opening not only in liturgy and administrative structures, but also in theology. In 1966 the prohibition of Protestant books was lifted. Romano Guardini (1885–1968, who taught in Berlin, Tübingen, and Munich and had a major influence on the Liturgical* Movement in Germany) and Rahner* took up ideas from Aquinas* while in dialogue with modern philosophy (Heidegger*) and the natural sciences. Rahner's prognosis that the pious person of the future would be a mystic* applies to all denominations. Toward the end of World War I, Protestant liberal theology (Ritschl*) collapsed together with the optimism expressed in Culture* Protestantism with its quest for a present-day Kingdom* of God (Harnack*). The Religious Socialists sought to combine the concerns of communism and the workers' movement with the gospel. Through his proclamation of the infinite distinction between God and the world, Barth* rejected every form of hyphenated Christianity.

Encouraged by the Reformation jubilees (1883 and 1917), neo-Lutheranism took up concerns (expressed in the reinterpreted Lutheran doctrine of the two* kingdoms and in the theology of the orders of creation*) that accommodated the German* Christians and National Socialists (Nazis). The national sense of having been deeply hurt by the Treaty of Versailles at the end of World War I was mitigated by the religiously charged concept of *Volkstum* (nationalism). The Confessing* Church, influenced by Barth's* theology, was just as unsuccessful after 1933 as was faithful Lutheranism in resisting the cult of the *Führer*, the dictatorship of *Gleichschaltung* (coordination), and the inhumane racial ideology* of Nazism (as Bonhoeffer* noted). Nevertheless, the Barmen* Theological Declaration (1934) and the Confessing* Church's ideologically critical memorandum addressed to Hitler (1936) motivated individuals to resist in words and deeds. German Roman Catholics, fearful of Russian Communism, accepted an ambivalent concordat* with Hitler (1933). Bishop Clemens August Graf von Galen and the encyclical *Mit brennender Sorge* (With deep anxiety, 1937) strengthened the Catholic opposition, which was more pronounced than that of the Protestant camp. Yet clergy and laity in all the churches fell victim to the regime, opposing Nazism in only a limited way.

After 1945 German theology was dominated by Barth and other Church* Struggle theologians (including Niemöller* and Helmut Gollwitzer), as well as Erlangen Lutherans (who did not participate in the Church Struggle because of their views of the relationship of faith* to history*; Paul Althaus, Werner Elert) and Tillich*, who exerted an influence from exile in the USA. Bultmann's* demythologization program progressively reached church members. In the 1960s, the death* of God debate questioned theology after the Holocaust*. Bonhoeffer's views, developed in prison, about "the nonreligious interpretation of biblical concepts," the "this-worldliness of Christianity," and the danger of a "cheap grace*" influenced a generation of young theologians. Gerhard Ebeling fruitfully reinterpreted Reformation theology for the present. Jürgen Moltmann's "theology of hope*" (1964) not only invigorated eschatology*, but also showed the church the way into an ecumenical future. The youth and students' movement of 1968 with its systematic critique of society did not leave church and theology untouched.

Diaconal and Social Engagement. In pre-Reformation times, cloisters and monastic foundations (Hospitallers*) took care of the poor and sick. In addition, the giving of alms, which was considered meritorious, mitigated acute distress. The Reformers organized public welfare in the congregations with the aid of church assets and freewill donations. But since these "good works" were no longer of use in achieving salvation*, the churches' contributions to welfare shrank so much that communal care of the poor had to be increasingly supplemented by the city or principality.

To combat more effectively the social misery caused by 19th-c. population growth, loss of farmworkers' jobs, and industrialization, Wichern* called the Protestant churches to address the "social question" in a historic speech at the Wittenberg Kirchentag (1848). In 1849 he founded the Central Committee for Inner* Mission, which would coordinate private and church initiatives. For Wichern lack of faith and moral decline were the major causes of the social crisis; he thus combined social assistance and mission. A complete network of social relief institutions was established all over Germany.

During the Third Reich, the Inner Mission was forced to compete with the Nazi people's welfare organization; the employment of the Nazis' euthanasia policies (outside the facilities of the Inner Mission) could be prevented in only a few cases. In 1975 the Inner Mission (within the diaconal work of the Evangelische Kirche Deutschlands) and other professional associations regained their economic independence as "public corporations," shifting from care for the sick, handicapped, and old people to counseling as well as integration of refugees*, foreigners, the poor, and the oppressed* in Germany and abroad (including the Two-thirds World).

Since 1897 the Caritasverband, the association of Catholic relief and social service agencies, has worked side by side with the Protestant welfare agencies in Germany and abroad. Together they make a vital contribution to welfare in Germany and the humanization of society. The fund-raising drives conducted by the relief organizations benefit projects in the Two-thirds World for the most part. The declaration "For a Future in Solidarity and Justice" (1997), jointly issued by the Council of the EKD and the German Bishops' Conference, reminds those who are becoming ever richer of their responsibility for the growing number of poor people (see Poverty Custer). Not to be forgotten here is the Christian-motivated peace movement led by the historic "peace* churches" (Mennonites*, Quakers*, Brethren*), who speak out for nonviolence*, justice*, the preservation of creation*, and an effective education* for peace.

Religious Education. According to the constitution of the Federal Republic, there is no state church. Nevertheless, Protestant and Catholic religious instruction is a required subject in public schools, taught under state supervision "in agreement with the principles of the religious denominations." Yet the parents or legal guardians of students can elect to replace it by courses on, e.g., ethics or comparative religion.

At state universities, there are Catholic and Protestant theological faculties (see Theological Education Cluster: In Western Europe: Germany) in accordance with the still-valid 1933 Reich Concordat and regional concordats with Rome, and similar conventions between Protestant churches and states – a situation that sometimes gives rise to conflict between academic freedom and church commitment. Chaplaincy in hospitals and the military follows a similar pattern of church and state relations.

Christians and Jews in Germany. For centuries, Jews were required to pay for the limited protection granted to them by the emperor and regional princes. In times of crisis (Crusades*, plagues, epidemics, crop failure), they fell victim to scapegoating, being persecuted as "Christ murderers" and deniers of the Messiah. Initially, Luther* had hoped for the conversion of many Jews to Christianity. Later, he recommended and approved severe measures against them.

The Enlightenment* mitigated Christian anti*-Judaism. Astonishing rapprochements took place between Christianity and Reform Judaism, from which many baptisms resulted. In 1871 Jews gained equal rights in the Second German Empire. Yet this success engendered new resentments that grew into a racist* anti*-Semitism after World War I. The German* Christians made anti-Semitism a part of their basic policy and therewith played into the hands of Nazi policy (Nuremberg racial laws, 1935). Although individual Christians interceded on behalf of Jews and Jewish Christians and, in return, were imprisoned or killed, as a result of the Nazi policy of *Gleichschaltung* (bringing under Nazi control all aspects of society, including religion), the Christian churches could not prevent the genocide of 6 million European Jews beginning in 1941 (see Church Struggle).

The Stuttgart Declaration of Guilt, issued by Protestant theologians in October 1945, laments the "infinite suffering" that was brought "upon many peoples and countries," but does not mention the Holocaust*. Only in 1950 did the Synod of the EKD confess a partial Christian responsibility, a confession that opened the process of Jewish–Christian dialogue. Official declarations by Protestant churches on the church and Israel followed. Similarly, Vatican II paved the way for a transformed relationship with the Jews. Now a broad consensus affirms the inseparable connection of the Christian faith with Judaism*, the enduring election of Israel, the need to stop the mission to the Jews, and the need to recognize the state of Israel. The canonization (1998) of the Carmelite nun of Jewish origin, Edith Stein, murdered at Auschwitz in 1942, was viewed in different ways by Jews and Christians. Since 1973 the academic year of study at the Benedictine abbey Dormitio in Jerusalem for Catholic and Protestant German-speaking students of theology also contributes to the understanding among Christians, Jews, and Muslims (see Judaism and Christianity Cluster).

Ecumenism and Interreligious Relations. The streams of refugees from the East during and after World War II caused the largest confessional shifts since 1803. In this situation, the willingness to live in tolerant, peaceful coexistence was more than ever put to the test. All previous attempts to overcome divisions among Christians, including among the churches of the Reformation, had been unsuccessful. But after years of doctrinal discussion, reconciliation between Lutherans and Reformed was achieved in the Leuenberg Concord (1973). The 105 Protestant churches (including small groups like the Bohemian Brethren*, Waldenses*, and Methodists*) gathered together in the Community of Protestant Churches in Europe (2003), allowing pulpit exchange and intercommunion (joint participation in the Eucharist). The churches of the EKD have agreed on intercommunion with the Mennonites, and conversations with the Anglican Church progress.

The Catholic Church is not a member of the World* Council of Churches but is represented in its Faith* and Order Commission. In 1985 the Ecumenical Working Group of Protestant and Catholic Theologians produced a study on the repeal of the central doctrinal condemnations of the 16th century (so far accepted only by the Protestants). In 1999 representatives of the Lutheran* World Federation and the Roman Catholic Council on Unity signed the "Official Finding on the Joint Declaration on the Doctrine of Justification*." On the Catholic side, the acceptance of the Protestants as a church, the recognition of Protestant pastoral offices, and the permission to hold joint celebrations of the Eucharist (especially in mixed marriages) are still open questions. Nevertheless, all of these are often simply practiced by Christians at the grassroots level. The recent removal of the wall that for more than 450 years separated the Protestant nave in St. Michael's Church at Hildesheim from the Catholic crypt is a sign of reconciliation. As the claims to possess absolute truth are abandoned, the negative images of other Christians fade; the dialogue between Christianity and other religions not only is possible, but is in full swing.

Conclusion. Although the role of Christianity in society and the financial powers of the churches will continue to decline, the Christian origins of German art, architecture, music, and literature endure. Although the state* church structures have faded away, the gospel continues to be experienced as a force that preserves values and provides meaning, orientation, and hope in the peaceful contest among religions. **See also MISSION CLUSTER: IN WESTERN EUROPE: GERMANY; THEOLOGICAL EDUCATION CLUSTER: IN WESTERN EUROPE: GERMANY; WOMEN'S CHRISTIAN PRACTICES AND THEOLOGIES CLUSTER: IN WESTERN EUROPE: GERMANY.**

Statistics: Population (2004): 82.5 million (M). Christians, 66.3% (Roman Catholics, 25.9 M; Protestants, 25.6 M; members of free churches, 0.5 M; Orthodox, 1.4 M; independents, 0.6 M); Muslims, 3.2 M; Buddhists, 0.2 M; Jews, 0.1 M; Hindus, 0.1 M; nonreligious, 20 M (or more). (Based on *Statistisches Jahrbuch*, 2005; *Kirchliches Jahrbuch*, 2001; *Gütersloher Verlagshaus*, 2004; *Kirchenamt der EKD in Hannover*; and *Materialdienst der Ev. Zentralstelle für Weltanschauungsfragen* 68, 7/05.)

INGE MAGER

Gerson, Jean Charlier de (1363–1429), a highly influential French theologian, who was and remains an extremely controversial figure. Born into a peasant family, he became the chancellor of Paris University, royal adviser, ecclesiastical leader, humanist poet, pedagogue, and outstanding preacher. Holding a perplexing combination of traditional and innovative attitudes, simultaneously referred to as Ockhamist* (see Ockham [Occam], William) and Scotist (see Duns Scotus), Gerson was also called "the most Christian and consoling doctor" for his genuine piety and ability to lead others from desperation to hope. A mystic*, but also rational* and practical, he longed for a compromise between love and reason*, advocating a Christ-centered faith* over theoretical learning. Gerson played a crucial role in the revival of affective Pastoral* theology expressed in his famous motto, "Do penance and believe the gospel." Influenced by Dionysius* the Pseudo-Aeropagite, the school of Richard* of Saint Victor, Bernard* of Clairvaux, and Bonaventure*, he reveals remarkable knowledge of human psychology and strong democratic tendencies. Seeking to open contemplative life to laity* and particularly to women, Gerson laid down the conditions and methods preparatory to contemplation*. His dialectic "theology of seeking" or "covenantal causality" (M. S. Borrows) represents a compromise between active and passive approaches, Quietism* and theology of merits*, safeguarding both divine sovereignty and human freedom. This mystical quest of God, which aimed at solving the dilemma of grace* by finding a via media between fideism and voluntarism, influenced such 15th- and 16th–c. theologians as Nicolas* of Cusa and Lefèvre* d'Etaples. Without being anti-sacramental, Gerson developed his Christology with Christ as the medium of grace. One of the most eminent orators of his time, strongly influenced by Petrarch*, whom he imitated, Gerson encouraged the study of the classics. A linguistic innovator, he preached and wrote in Latin or French, according to his audience. A conservative Catholic, he promoted devotion* to the Blessed Virgin Mary* and St. Joseph but severely criticized the Roman Catholic Church for corruption and abuses. He admitted, for the sake of emerging from the Great* Schism (1378–1417) and returning to unity, the superiority of the ecumenical council over the pope in extreme cases. Because of his French patriotism and Conciliar* views, he has been traditionally associated with Gallicanism*. Gerson's lifelong concern being that of preserving the unity of Christendom, he was a leader in condemning John Hus* during the Council of Constance*. His influence can be traced up to Francis* de Sales and Cardinal Bossuet*.

YELENA MAZOUR-MATUSEVICH

Gertrude the Great (1256–1302), mystic*, nun, writer, proponent of devotion to the Sacred Heart; background, parentage unknown; member of the Saxon monastery of Helfta from the age of four until her death; often confused with Gertrude of Hackeborn, Abbess* of Helfta (1251–91).

The monastery of Helfta employed Benedictine* and Cistercian* traditions and was under the spiritual direction of Dominican* friars. Helfta provided Gertrude with a solid education and companions such as the mystics* Mechthilde* of Magdeberg and Mechthilde of Hackeborn, whose mystical experiences she helped record in Latin. Gertrude, influenced by Augustine*, Gregory* the Great, the Victorines*, and Bernard* of Clairvaux, produced works in German and Latin. The former (letters, commentaries, prayers, etc.) are lost. She is remembered for the Latin pieces, *Spiritual Exercises* and *The Herald of Divine Love* (*Legatus memorialis abundantiae divinae pietatis*). *Herald* was completed by fellow nuns shortly after her death, incorporating autobiographical material, including her experiences since her first vision at the age of 25.

Her Dominican advisers approved her works and later recommended them to Teresa* of Ávila. Gertrude was designated "the Great" by Cardinal Lambertini (Pope Benedict XIV). Recent studies concern her focus on female monastic communities and their spirituality*.

SABINA FLANAGAN

Gertrude of Nivelles (626–59), abbess of a monastery in Nivelles (Belgium), known for her hospitality* to pilgrims and her generous benefactions to Irish monks.

Ghana (former British colony, "Gold Coast," 1874–1957). Vibrant Christianity in Ghana is culturally marked, contextualized, and inculturated* both in ritual practices and in community and social practices, reflecting the roles of women and of the popular majority. These inculturated features are apparent in the interactions of Christianity with African* Traditional Religion and Islam*.

Historical Survey. Christianity in Ghana can be traced back to the arrival of Augustinian*, Capuchin*, and Dominican* friars, Roman Catholic missionaries from Portugal*, first in Shama, a coastal village (1482). They were displaced by the Dutch (1637) but reentered the Gold Coast in 1880 (at Elmina) through the Society of African Missions. By 1906 Roman Catholicism had been introduced to Northern Ghana, where it greatly expanded between 1914 and 1917.

Protestantism was introduced in Ghana (primarily in the coastal region) by missionaries of the Moravian United Brethren (c1618), the Netherlands Reformed Dutch (c1742), and the Church of England Society for Propagation of the Gospel (1751). But the Presbyterian and Methodist churches (including the African Methodist Episcopal Zionist and Christian Methodist) were established primarily on the foundation laid by missionaries from the Basel mission (Christiansborg, 1828), Bremen mission (1847) (both replaced by missionaries from the United Free Church of Scotland, 1917), and Wesleyan Methodist Mission (1835). Other Protestant denominations were also established in Ghana, including the Anglican, Mennonite, Evangelical Lutheran, Baptist, and Society of Friends*. These major Protestant churches are now members of the Christian Council of Ghana and are affiliated with the World* Council of Churches and other ecumenical bodies. All these "mission churches" resulted from efforts by missionaries not only to evangelize, convert people, and build churches, but also to establish schools for training members of the African elite to assume important positions in the church and political government.

Apart from the mission churches, Pentecostalism* (from the early 20th c.), led by William Wadé Harris (1860–1929), John Swatson (1855–1925), and Kwame Sarpong Oppong (1884–1965), played an important role in Ghanaian Christianity. Pentecostalism and, following it, the Charismatic* Movement gave birth to African* Instituted Churches (AICs), which broke away from the mission churches by emphasizing revivalism* that, through the "African worldview," seeks to address Africans' authentic need for deep spirituality and religiosity. Pentecostalism and the Charismatic Movement made room for women's active participation in Christianity. For example, the first and largest AIC in Ghana (the Twelve Apostle Church, a 1914 offshoot of Harris's work) was jointly founded and led by John Nackabah and the prophetess Grace Tani.

The most recent development in Ghanaian Christianity is the New Religious (or neo-Charismatic*) Movement within the mission churches; it purposefully remains within the mission churches but brings about revivalism* by incorporating "Spirit-filled" charismatic tendencies into worship, focusing on the vibrancy of the work of the Holy* Spirit (speaking in tongues*, loud praying, healing*/deliverance, animated Bible study, use of incense and candles), as do Pentecostal and Charismatic churches.

Throughout the country, these various Christian denominations are often characterized by cultural and linguistic affinities. Thus there are two Presbyterian churches: the Evangelical Presbyterian Church, found mainly in the southeast (Volta region), with mainly Ewe-speaking members; and the Presbyterian Church of Ghana, found mainly in Accra among Akwapim-speaking peoples. The Ashanti and central region Christians are mainly Roman Catholic. The Fante-speaking peoples are mainly Methodists.

Christianity is pervasive but is found mainly in Southern Ghana, while the north is largely Muslim (since the 15th c., before the arrival of Christianity). Islam's great appeal is that it fosters continuity with African Religion (especially polygamy*) rather than propagating Western ideals. Although Christianity, Islam, and African Religion tend to coexist amicably, they nevertheless compete.

Distinctive Features of Christianity in Ghana. Several important features mark the diversity in religion in Ghana. In the mission churches (e.g. Roman Catholic, Presbyterian, Methodist, Anglican, Baptist), traditional worship is serene and calm, whereas in the AICs and Charismatic churches, the atmosphere is robust, lively, and body and soul moving. In addition, the mission churches tend to follow Western/Eurocentric literary liturgical practices, while the AICs and Charismatic churches tend to blend "received" Western traditions with practical African sociocultural and contextual elements that cater to believers' everyday needs. The outcome of this "hermeneutic* of grafting" (Akoto) is neither one nor the other but a unique flavor of both. For example, whereas the mission churches see salvation* as repentance* from sin* (personal and "original" sin), the AICs and other "Spirit-filled" or Charismatic churches see salvation as directed toward well-being and success in earthly life now (see Prosperity Gospel Cluster: In Africa). Although the idea of God* seems similar to that of mission churches and Western mainline churches, for the AICs and Charismatic churches God, "the Supreme Being," is construed not only as transcendent, but also as in control of the universe, including daily life. This conception of the Supreme Being (see God, Christian Views of, Cluster: In Africa) is manifested in the names and attributes accorded to the Supreme Being and to individuals at birth. As in the mission churches, where God is accessible through Jesus (and saints), in the AICs the Supreme Being is ultimate and cannot be directly approached; hence in addition to Jesus, intermediary-like divinities ("lesser" gods), consulted through local priests/priestesses or prophets/prophetesses, are employed to reach the Supreme Being for material and spiritual success. Furthermore, whereas Western mission churches are infused with the Cartesian philosophy and theology of rationalism and empiricism (*cogito, sum*; "I think, I am"; see Descartes, René) of the 17th- and 18th-c. Enlightenment*, which is skeptical of the impingement of the supernatural on the material realm, Ghanaian Christianity of the 21st-c. AICs and Charismatic churches sees life as populated by both benevolent and malevolent spirits, which influence the course of human life for good or for evil. Equilibrium is, therefore, maintained by "propitiation*, expiation* and reconciliation*" (Bediako).

Statistics: Population (2000): 20.2 million (M). Christians, 11.2 M, 55% (Protestants, 3.4 M, members of African Instituted Churches, 3 M; Roman Catholics, 2 M; Anglicans, 0.25 M; marginal Christians, 0.21 M); African Religionists, 4.9 M, 24%; Muslims, 4 M, 20%. (Based on *World Christian Encyclopedia*, 2001. The Ghana Statistical Service 2000 Population Census has different figures: Christians, 69.0%; Muslims, 15.6%; African Religionists, 8.5%.)

DOROTHY B E A AKOTO

Ghetto (Italian, contraction of *borghetto*, "little borough"), section of a city to which Jews were restricted; often walled, with gates closed at a definite hour. Legally required segregation began in Portugal* and Spain* (late 14th c.); the practice spread to Italy and involved the greatest number of Jews in Germany. **See also ANTI-SEMITISM; HOLOCAUST, JEWISH (OR SHOAH).**

Gibbon, Edward (1737–94), historian of the later Roman Empire. He read widely in classical literature, and on a visit to Rome in 1764, he conceived his *Decline and Fall of the Roman Empire*, published in three volumes (1776–81). Building on several centuries of work by Catholic and Protestant scholars, it set a new standard for comprehensiveness, detailed analysis, and stylistic subtlety. Gibbon's discussion of Christianity tends to be vitriolic ("triumph of barbarism and religion," "monks, eunuchs, and women"), but he accurately highlighted many issues and is still profitably read.

Gideon, one of the "judges*," whose call was confirmed by the miracle of the fleece (Judg 6:36–40). With a force intentionally reduced to 300, he routed the Midianites (Judg 7).

Gideon Bibles, Bibles placed in hotel rooms and other places of accommodation by an organization of Christian business people. The Gideons were founded by a small group of traveling salesmen in Janesville, Wisconsin (1899), taking their name from Gideon*. The organization now operates widely in the English-speaking world.

Gifts of the Spirit. This phrase is not found in the NT, which merely refers to the Holy* Spirit as a "gift" (of God) (Acts 2:38, 8:20, 10:45, 11:17; possibly John 4:10). In Roman Catholicism, "gifts of the Spirit" are those listed in Isa 11:2 (the spirit of wisdom, understanding, counsel, strength, knowledge, and fear of the Lord). In Protestantism and the Charismatic* Movement, this phrase designates the plurality of "graces" (charismata*; often translated "gifts") given by the Spirit* to perform particular tasks or vocations* for the good of others (cf. 1 Cor 12:4–11). Paul includes the utterance of messages of wisdom* and of knowledge, faith*, healing*, the working of miracles*, prophecy, discernment of the spirits, and tongues, or glossolalia*.

Gilbert de la Porrée, or Gilbertus Porretanus (1070–1154), an early scholastic theologian who taught in Chartres and Paris, then became bishop of his native city of Poitiers. He is known chiefly for his "realist"*view of the Trinity*, holding that the essence* of God is distinct from and prior to the three persons*. He was condemned (1148) for teaching, in effect, a "quaternity."

Gilbert of Sempringham (c1083–1189), monastic reformer and founder of the Gilbertines. Born in Lincolnshire, he studied in France before becoming a priest at Sempringham. About 1131 he became spiritual director of a small group of anchoresses*, from which developed the nunnery of Sempringham. Failing to persuade the Cistercians* to assume their oversight (1147), with the aid of Bernard* of Clairvaux he subsequently drew up a rule derived from both Benedictine* and Augustinian* models for his communities, which typically comprised nuns, canons*, lay brothers, and lay sisters. Toward the end of his life, he relinquished their direct control. He was canonized in 1202.

BRIAN GOLDING

Gilead, territory east of the Jordan (inhabited by the tribes Gad and Manasseh), where a famous balm grew (Gen 37:25) – hence Jeremiah's yearning cry, "Is there no balm in Gilead?" (Jer 8:22).

Giles of Rome, or Aegidius Romanus (c1245–1316). Philosopher and theologian, possibly born in Rome, he became an Augustinian* hermit, studied in Paris with Thomas Aquinas*, was elected general of the Augustinians (1292), and founded many convents. Perhaps the greatest impact of his many treatises was in the political sphere. His treatise on papal authority was the basis of Boniface* VIII's notorious bull *Unam sanctam* (there is no salvation outside the Roman Catholic Church; to reject the pope's authority is to exclude oneself from the Church); his work on the duties of princes was written for the future King Philip the Fair, Boniface's opponent.

Gladden, Washington. See SOCIAL GOSPEL MOVEMENT.

Gladstone, William Ewart (1809–98). Raised an Evangelical Anglican, Gladstone moved to Old High Church principles by his 1832 election as a Conservative member of the English Commons. He served in both Conservative and Whig cabinets, most influentially as minister of the exchequer, and was the Liberal prime minister four times (until 1894). An active lay theologian, he defended the Anglican Church establishment in *The State in Its Relations to the Church* (1838, 1841): "The state is a person, having a conscience, cognizant of matter of religion, and bound . . . to advance it." In 1845 he resigned from the cabinet to remain consistent with the position. He supported the Oxford* Movement's concerns, but not its "Romewards" aspects. Gladstone's political shift to Liberalism marked his opposition to the Ecclesiastical Titles Act against Roman Catholicism (1851) and his support of Jewish emancipation and a number of Nonconformist* concerns, including an atheist's right to sit in Parliament, as well as Irish* political and religious rights. He nevertheless remained a theological traditionalist: defending Anglo-Catholic interests, arguing against anti-ritualist legislation (1874), writing against papal infallibility* in a 1874 pamphlet, *The Vatican Decrees,* and publicly debating with Darwin's* defender, Huxley*, on the origins of religion and biblical interpretation (1885–90).

PETER C. ERB

Global Ethics, the range of ethical or theological positions about the necessity of, possibility of, and practical strategies to address the need for minimal standards of ethical conduct between and within nations in an increasingly interdependent world. (1) Given pluralism and conflicting ideals, is it possible to envision a common morality based on universal values? (2) Could the values of the United Nations Declaration of Human Rights serve as a common morality? Or is it, itself, controversially "Western" ? (3) Should we seek universal ethical consensus based on the minimal ethical consensus shared by all the world's religions? Or should we mainly expand our own tradition-dependent theory of global ethics?

Kantians* point to a common morality. The natural law tradition, appealing to common human needs, aspirations, and potentialities, suggests universally binding moral codes. But the commonalities of human nature can be consistent with substantially different moral codes and thus underdetermine morality.

The theologian Hans Küng envisions a common global ethic based on the minimal ethical consensus shared by all the world's religions. Küng argues that there can be "no new global order without a new global ethics." He parses his major premise, "every human being must be treated humanely," into four major commitments: (1) to nonviolence* and respect for life; (2) to solidarity* and a just economic* order; (3) to tolerance and truthfulness; and (4) to equal rights and partnership between men and women." Critics argue that such universal principles, if they are to cohere and receive a general assent, are so vague as to be virtually empty.

Other authors espouse human* rights theory as the foundation of a global ethic. Yet for many, any transcultural or foundational bases for a global ethic of rights should be avoided. Thus, reflecting on the UN Declaration, Jacques Maritain* says, "We can agree about rights on condition that no one asks why." The why is rooted primarily in practical reason*, with global principles as guides to action. Universal global ethics must, perforce, return to tradition-bound theories to find resonating resources.

Perhaps the wisest approach admits the tradition dependence of all ethical schemes (philosophical or theological) but works toward establishing transcultural claims through a process of reflection on the commonalities and overlap of different traditions and invites a richer probe by the various religious traditions into their account of global oughts. A global ethic is less some given bestowed by a preexisting universal morality than a project for an urgent, hoped-for, real possibility.

JOHN A. COLEMAN, SJ

Globalization: Christian Responses. Protestant denominations associated with the World* Council of Churches, Roman Catholicism, and Orthodoxy tend toward a partially critical, yet positive view of globalization. In a series of addresses, Pope John* Paul II asserted that "globalization, in itself, is neither good nor bad. It will be what people make of it." His encyclical *Centessimus Annus* set out some guidelines for a humane globalization: a new world order must not be reductively economic but must also pay attention to politics*, culture*, the state (see Church and State Relations Cluster), and the environment (see Ecology and Christianity Cluster). While he endorsed market economies*, the pope noted that markets remain blind to collective and spiritual needs and, without regulation, may not serve the common good: "It is necessary to globalize solidarity*, too." Although expressing fear that globalization might increase poverty* and inequality or erode local cultures, on balance, he asserted, "For all its risks it offers exceptional and promising opportunities, precisely with a view to enabling humanity to become a single family, build on the values of justice*, equity and solidarity." "Globalization without marginalization*" was another papal slogan.

The World Council of Churches has registered some of its fears of a globalization based on neoliberal economic models: a loss of cultural identity; greater concentration of power in corporations and in states; unequal distribution of power and wealth; and the erosion of the state and of safety nets. Drawing on a suggestion of Orthodox Patriarch Bartholomew, the World Council of Churches proposes that the older Christian notion of "ecumenicity" (i.e. the whole world as interconnected, in God's care, rooted in cooperation) replace the term "globalization." Theologians from the Reformed tradition tend to emphasize the covenant* and God's orders for creation* to address a new world order.

Evangelicals vary greatly in their response to globalization (a phenomenon that greatly facilitates the growth of their movement). Some groups, such as those who sponsor the magazine

Sojourners, endorse globalization for its positive possibilities (one world in consciousness) while remaining critical of its failure to address global poverty and aware of its incomplete human governance structures. Others stress the unique Evangelical opportunities that result from globalization and are likely to assert that a free market, in the long run, benefits everyone. They remain wary of criticism of presently constituted capitalism. Christian voices are found at the global forums at Davos and the World Social Forum. Most would agree with the former that there is a need for reform of current globalization and with the latter that "another world – another kind of globalization – is possible." **See also ECONOMY AND CHRISTIANITY CLUSTER.**

JOHN A. COLEMAN, SJ

Global Warming. See CLIMATE CHANGE AND CHRISTIANITY.

Gloria in Excelsis (Lat "glory in the highest"), the first words of the angels' song narrated in Luke 2:14, often used as a canticle* in worship. An expanded Greek version has been incorporated into the worship of various traditions since the 4th c.

Gloria Patri, a song of praise to the Trinity* that follows the singing of any psalm; added to the worship service in Western churches in the 4th c.).

Glossa Ordinaria, the marginal glosses on the Bible that originated in patristic times as comments on difficult or confusing passages and later included quotes from patristic commentaries (added by Eugippius, Bede*, and Florus* of Lyon). In the 11th c. a more formalized, Talmud-like version developed, with the text in the center of the page and the commentary in the margins or between the lines. Major contributions were made by Anselm of Laon, Gilbert* de la Porrée, and Peter* Lombard.

Glossolalia, "speaking in tongues" under the inspiration of the Holy* Spirit (1 Cor 14), emphasized in the Pentecostal* and Charismatic* movements. One of the gifts* of the Spirit.

Gnesio-Lutherans, modern label for a group of Luther's students (1549–77) whose interpretation of Luther's* break with the medieval church was a radical departure from medieval soteriology*. Against Melanchthon* and his followers (the "Philippists"), their bold, explicit confession included their views of the Law* and good works in Christian life, original* sin, the role of the will* in conversion, and definitions of "repentance*" and "gospel*." They argued for a strict limitation of the power of secular government within ecclesiastical affairs and favored more drastic departures from medieval ceremonies and ecclesiastical polity*. The Formula of Concord* offered a solution to these disputed issues.

ROBERT KOLB

Gnosticism. The term "Gnosticism" seems to have been coined in the 17th c. to denote certain religious movements dating from the first few centuries CE. The Greek adjective *gnostikos* ("leading/pertaining to knowledge") was used by Plato to designate the intellectual dimension of learning as opposed to the practical. By the 2nd c. CE, the word appears as a self-designation by certain Christians, who were attacked as presumptuous by their critics (see Irenaeus). However, the modern category "Gnosticism" is most commonly applied to a much wider assortment of teachers and groups than the tiny number for whom the self-designation *gnostikos* is actually attested. Therefore, "Gnostics" are best understood not as members of a single sect or movement, but rather as believers who introduced diverse religious innovations that were linked to various degrees by notable overlapping doctrines or themes.

One usual feature is that the transcendent God or order of being is distinguished from one or more inferior creators of the material world. Another frequently shared view is some variation on the theme of humanity's preincarnational origin in a transcendent realm, subsequent descent to the material cosmos, and eventual salvation and return, effected by revelation that reawakens the knowledge (Gk *gnosis*) of one's kinship with the Divine.

Relatively few of the original writings of such circles survive, but several important examples are included among the tractates in the Nag* Hammadi Codices and a few other Coptic manuscripts. Important evidence is also found in polemics attacking these groups, such as the heresiology by Irenaeus* (c180), "Exposure and Refutation of Knowledge (*gnosis*) Falsely So-Called" (conventionally known by the title *Adversus haereses,* "Against the Sects") – a catalog that also includes teachers or groups who are virtually never classified as "Gnostic" in modern research (e.g. the Ebionites*) or for whom the appropriateness of this label has been disputed (e.g. Marcion*, Tatian*). Irenaeus's work was expanded upon by numerous later writers, e.g. Clement* of Alexandria (c160–215), Tertullian* (c160–225), Hippolytus* (c170–235),

Origen* (c185–251), and Epiphanius* (c315–403).

Several Nag Hammadi texts contain myths of origin, as in the important Apocryphon of John*. Often in the form of "rewritten scripture," they refashion the Genesis creation stories so that the creator God is an entity inferior to the transcendent Divinity. Such speculations are interesting instances of theodicy*: explanations that protect the true God from responsibility for imperfection or evil* in the cosmos. Earlier cosmologies giving some role to intermediate agents can be found in Platonic, neo-Pythagorean, Jewish, and other ancient sources. "Gnostic" myths of origin emerged within this wider tradition of theodicean speculations, although they are often considered the most radical examples, and "Gnosticism" is frequently defined in terms of an alleged negative attitude toward the material cosmos and its creator(s). However, in fact there is remarkable variety in how negatively the creator and cosmos are portrayed in "Gnostic" sources, ranging from demonization* of the creator as a willful, animal-like figure, ignorant of the Divinity that transcends him and malevolently intent on the domination of his realm, including humanity, to the creator as merely intermediate and imperfect rather than a hateful adversary.

The distinction between "spiritual" humanity and nonspiritual persons typical in "Gnostic" soteriologies* has often been labeled deterministic, although in very many cases this is an incorrect characterization. For example, according to some texts, the reception of spiritual identity is available ritually, e.g. by baptism* or chrism*. Spirituality can be depicted as a potential for all humans, though realized only in individuals who respond to revelation.

Social behavior, communal organization, or ritual practices in such groups were apparently quite diverse, but the details are not extensively or reliably documented. Although "Gnostics" are commonly portrayed as rejecters of the world, the activities of some of them suggest less social deviance and greater social conformity than that in more "orthodox" circles (e.g. fewer dietary scruples, social interaction at civic religious celebrations or public entertainment, aversion to radical social resistance such as martyrdom*). The spectrum of sexual mores was probably not so unlike that in the rest of the Christian population. Ascetic* renunciation of sexuality* was certainly the ideal in several groups, although marriage* and procreation were condoned in others. The heresiologists accused some groups of sexual excess or uses of sex in ritual, but these polemical charges are highly suspect.

In the early centuries of Christianity, before the standardization brought about by creeds, canons, and organizations, these often elaborate myths of origin and eschatology* constituted some of the earliest attempts at a systematic articulation of Christian doctrine in relation to Jewish tradition and Greco-Roman philosophy. Controversy over such experiments played a role in shaping fundamental features of what became Christian "orthodoxy." **See also VALENTINIANS; VALENTINUS.**

MICHAEL ALLEN WILLIAMS

GOD, CHRISTIAN VIEWS OF, CLUSTER

1) *Introductory Entries*

God, Christian Views of: In Eastern Orthodoxy
God, Christian Views of: A Historical Overview
God, Christian Views of: Names for God in the Bible and Church Traditions

2) *A Sampling of Contextual Views*

God, Christian Views of, in Africa
God, Christian Views of, in Asia
God, Christian Views of, in Australia
God, Christian Views of, in the Caribbean Islands
God, Christian Views of, in Latin America
God, Christian Views of, Latino/a
God, Christian Views of, in North America
God, Christian Views of, in North America: Feminist Understandings
God, Christian Views of, in Western Europe

1) Introductory Entries

God, Christian Views of: In Eastern Orthodoxy. God is Trinity. As Trinity, God is the coexistence of the full divinity of the Father, Son, and Holy Spirit. An affirmation about Jesus that involves less than full divinity cannot lead to an understanding of God as Trinity. Trinity is thus more than a way of understanding God's relation to the world. It is a way of understanding God. **See also TRINITY IN EASTERN ORTHODOXY.**

God, Christian Views of: A Historical Overview. In Christian belief, "God" is the name (but not a proper name; see the present cluster: Names for God in the Bible and Church Traditions) for the sole reality deserving of human worship*. This idea that there is only one real deity reflects Christianity's historic derivation from monotheistic* Judaism* and accounts for the ancient church's polemic against polytheistic* modes of worship as an idolatrous* offense against the one true God. According to biblical tradition, God is the ultimate power that created* the world and continues to sustain and rule over it by ordering the relationships among all creatures. Of special concern to God is humankind, which, created in God's own image*, has the possibility of serving God with the distinctive human capacities of heart, mind, and will*. Since the failure of humanity to conform to the divine ordering (sin*) is the central problem to which the gospel* is addressed, God is also the judge* of human failings as well as the redeemer* realigning persons to the divine purposes for them. Hence God is creator, sustainer, providential governor, judge, and redeemer or savior*. While God intends what is good for human beings, all of God's creatures exist ultimately for the sake of glorifying their maker.

Through their appropriation of Greek philosophy (see Inculturation Cluster: Of Christianity in the Greco-Roman World), Christians availed themselves of sophisticated conceptual tools to clarify their theological convictions both to themselves and to non-Christians. Against Christian dualists* (Gnostics* and Marcionites*) who called into question the identification of the redeemer known through Christ with the creator-judge of Israel, it was necessary to reaffirm the monotheistic premise of the teachings of Jesus and of his earliest Jewish followers. Against "pagans*" it was important to stress the basic difference between monotheism and Greco-Roman polytheism, as well as to argue for the rational superiority of the former. By building a bridge between gospel and philosophy (see Gospel and Culture Cluster: Introductory Entry), Christians integrated the Greek quest for a rational understanding of the world with their biblical heritage. Nevertheless, this adaptation of philosophy also occasioned difficulties for classical Christian theology, since the anthropomorphic*, or person-like, depictions of God in the biblical narratives were now seen to be in tension with the metaphysical* attributes assumed to be self-evident as descriptions of the divine nature, such as impassibility*, timelessness, and absolute simplicity. An enduring question is: Can the personal deity of the Bible truly be accounted for in Greek philosophical thought? (see Philosophy and Christian Theology).

Christianity departs from Judaism by affirming that Jesus is not only Israel's long-awaited Messiah* (Christ) but also the incarnate Son* (Word*, Logos*) of God through whom all things have been created. The full explication of this confession culminated in the trinitarian and christological doctrines of the 4th and 5th c.; accordingly, God is "one divine essence in three persons" (Father, Son, and Spirit) and Jesus Christ (the second person of the Trinity*) is both "fully divine" and "fully human." Whether this trinitarian Christology* results in a doctrine of God that is no longer legitimately a species of monotheism is a question raised by both Jews (see Judaism and Christianity Cluster: Jewish Views of Christianity) and Muslims (see Islam and Christianity Cluster: Muslim Views of Christianity) as well as by Christian Unitarians*. Nonetheless, Christian orthodoxy* has insisted that its doctrine is not tritheistic*; how God is both one and three remains a mystery* of faith that cannot be rationally grasped by the finite mind.

Before the Enlightenment*, it was assumed that knowledge of God comes primarily through the Bible's supernatural revelation* as authoritatively taught by the church's tradition*. This did not preclude a limited knowledge of God based on natural reason or general illumination (natural* theology), although it was insufficient to guarantee the revealed truths of Christian faith (e.g. the Trinity). In the modern period, when the maturation of natural science* suggested the possibility of explaining the world's operation on immanent grounds alone, apart from recourse to God as a causal factor, the philosophical basis of natural theology was severely called into question. The loss of the inherited philosophical assumption that all rational persons naturally believe in the existence of one God opened the door to the increasing influence of agnosticism* and even atheism* in the post-Christian West and required theologians to explore alternative ways of making Christian religious convictions intelligible to the wider culture. One prominent route has been to argue that belief in God is important for sustaining moral* agency and existential* meaning even if it bears little relation to scientific explanations of the non-human world. Furthermore, historical-critical study of biblical and other religious traditions has impressed on contemporary theologians the essential role of human creativity in generating ideas about God throughout history. As a result there has arisen a new awareness that traditional beliefs about God are subject to critique and revision in the light of new questions arising in different cultural and religious contexts. Still, the crucial issues remain the nature of God and the bases for believing in God. **See also THE PRESENT CLUSTER: NAMES FOR GOD IN THE BIBLE AND CHURCH TRADITIONS; TRINITY IN EASTERN ORTHODOXY; TRINITY IN THE WESTERN TRADITION.** PAUL E. CAPETZ

God, Christian Views of: Names for God in the Bible and Church Traditions. The noun "God" is not a proper name; thus it is not transliterated, but translated from one language to another.

The Hebrew *El* and Greek *Theos* are translated in Syriac as *Alaha* (closely related to the Arabic *Allah,* a name commonly used by Christians in Arabic-speaking countries) and, by Ephrem* the Syrian (4th c.), as *Alahutha,* an abstract name meaning "Deity" or "Divinity," grammatically feminine, when he wants to stress the maternal characteristics of God. *El* and *Theos* are translated by the English "God," Swedish *Gud* (on Runic stones from c1000), German *Gott* (originally neuter, became masculine when adopted by Christianity) – terms that might be derived from the Indo-European root *ghut-* (the one invoked or the one sacrificed to). The Latin *Deus* is reflected in the Romance languages (*Dieu, Dios, Dio, Deus*). The Romanian *Dumnezeu* is derived from the Latin *Dominus Deus* (Lord God). In Chichewa (Malawi), the terms *Mlengi, Mulungu,* and *Mphambe* refer to God as the creator of all things, while *Chauta* and *Leza* refer to the presence of God as creator: *Chauta,* like rainfall; *Leza,* like a mother nurturing her children. Other examples are the many traditional names of God used by Christians of different ethnolinguistic groups in Angola* (as well as parts of the Republic of Congo* [Congo-Brazzaville] and the Democratic Republic of Congo*), e.g. *Nzambi* (in the Kikongo, Kimbundu, and Chokwe languages), *Suku* (in Umbundu), *Kalunga* (in Ambo), *Nzambi-Kalunga* (in Herero), and *Huku* (in Nyaneka-Humbe). Through such inculturated* naming, the conception of God is linked with each religious worldview.

A generic, indefinite term, "God" can be used in the plural. The Hebrew term *Elohim,* designating the one God of Israel, is grammatically plural. Most biblical books assume that there are other gods (Exod 20:3, Deut 5:7; 1 Cor 8:5; 2 Cor 4:4). The angels are addressed as "gods" (Ps 82:6; John 10:33–34). "God" is sometimes used as a qualifier (e.g. of the Logos* in John 1:1, meaning that the Logos is "a god," or "divine," or "God"). Yet "God" is primarily an indefinite term, an "*x*" requiring further specification and a name.

God can be named by description, e.g. "the God who appeared at the burning bush," "the God who raised Jesus from the dead." People speak of "my God" (see Jer 7:23, 31:33) or of "the God of Abraham and Sarah." When people reject "the God of Calvin" or "the God of Islam," they imply that the other party worships a different, erroneous or fictitious, God.

"God" is also named by reference to God's function or activity in relation to the world. For Gregory* of Nyssa, "God" refers to God's activity rather than God's essence; for John* of Damascus, it describes God's providential care. Tillich* and Schleiermacher* speak of a generic function – respectively, the "dimension of ultimacy" or "ultimate dependence" – that gains specificity in each religion.

For Paul, these descriptive ways of naming God can become idolatrous: although God's "eternal power and deity" are understood through the things God made, God's truth can be changed into a lie when the powers that impinge on human life are addressed as deities (Rom 1:20–25). Conversely, designating God through function titles, such as "Creator" and "Lord," might raise questions regarding the view of God as everlasting. Could God be Creator and Lord before there was a world? Or must creation be everlasting (as Origen* thought), since God could never not be Creator? The traditional answer has been that these function-titles refer to the everlasting God, who decides whether and when to create (thus these titles are always appropriate), rather than to the created temporal world.

The Question of God's Proper Name. For both Jews and Christians, God's "proper name" is expressed by the so-called tetragrammaton*, *YHWH*. Knowing the name of the supreme deity might enable one to compel lesser deities or demons to obey. During the postexilic period, the divine name ceased to be pronounced (as is still the case for most Jews); its consonants continued to be written, but the term *Adonai* (my Lord) was substituted in reading. The Massoretes* added the vowels for this reading. Then, Calvin* and others in the Reformed* tradition combined these consonants and vowels and pronounced the divine name "Jehovah."

While *YHWH* functions as a name, it may have originated as some kind of description. When Moses asks God's name, the answer is "*Ehyeh asher ehyeh*" (Exod 3:14). Because the Hebrew verb can mean "to be" or "to become," this name can be translated in two ways:

1. "I am who I am" – a tautology, or a refusal to give a name, or, according to many ancient commentators, "I am the one who is," "being itself," the source of all other beings.
2. "I will be who I will be," emphasizing either the sense of "becoming" and God's freedom rather than God's permanence or the sense "I cause what I cause."

God is often called *YHWH Sebaoth*, "Lord of hosts," as though to give definiteness to the name. Yet the "hosts" are rather indefinite. Are they the armies of Israel, heavenly bodies, powers of nature, or angels?

Christian "Proper" Designations for God. Names (those that apply directly to God and not merely in relation to the world) include trinitarian terms and absolute perfections.

1. *The Trinity**. For some the trinitarian names are "function terms" based on three different modes of divine action: God is called Father because of creation*, Son because of redemption*, and Spirit because of sanctification*. Against this modalism*, others declared the Trinity to be eternal and affirmed that Father, Son, and Spirit intrinsically apply to God's essence (see Trinity in Eastern Orthodoxy; Trinity in Western Traditions). Since the Syriac designation for God, *Ruha* (Spirit), is grammatically feminine, it acquired female symbolism in the earliest (pre-4th-c.) form of Syriac Christianity. Recent theology, aware that the use of masculine terms "makes God male," tends to use gender-free or feminine terms as a corrective.
2. *The perfections*, such as "being," "truth," "wisdom," "good," and "benevolence" in their absolute sense, might refer properly to God's divine essence, shared by the three persons. Yet the theory of analogy* acknowledges that we do not understand the "mode of signification" of these terms when they are applied to God and thus are outside their usual contexts.

EUGENE TESELLE

2) A Sampling of Contextual Views

God, Christian Views of, in Africa. African Christian concepts of God have developed from both African* Religion and the Bible. The worldview of the HB is strikingly similar to African worldviews; Africans feel at home within the Bible. Thus instead of inventing names to describe God, African Christians simply use existing local names.

For Africans, as for the Bible, a name denotes the character or personality of the person designated by this name. Thus to get a sense of African concepts of God, we must consider a few appellations and "praise names" that African Christians use for God. When, like their ancestors, the Akan Christians of Ghana* call God *Onyame,* they affirm that God is "the Provider of All Things" and that those who know and worship God-*Onyame* have everything they could ever need. To describe the omniscience of God, the Barundi of Burundi* call God *Indaavyi,* "the Watcher of Everything." Traditionalist and Christian Yoruba of Nigeria* call God *Olodumare,* "the Almighty." To ascribe creation to God, the Ngonis of Malawi* call God *Uluhlanga,* "the Original Source." For the Akans, God's reliability is expressed in the name *Twereduampong,* "The tree that does not bend when leaned upon." God is seen not only as Father but also as Mother. The Krobos from Ghana call God *Mau Kpetekplenye,* "Mother of All Big or Wonderful Things." The Gas from Ghana balance the parenthood of God by calling God *Ataa Naa Nyonmo,* "Father-Mother God" (also see Angola).

These traditional concepts were incorporated into Christian views of God because traditional understandings of who God is and of God's role in daily life are remarkably similar to those of the biblical God. The African cultural context is such that even though Christianity cannot be said to be an "African religion," it is very clearly an "African's religion."

For African Christians, God is not a distant or absentee landlord but a very present help in times of joy and sorrow, and in the day-to-day drudgery of living. God is in charge of all and over all. Life begins and ends with God; God is the One, to be feared and obeyed above all. Thus the Akans say, "*Gye Nyame,*" meaning that without the blessing of God, human efforts are bound to fail in any endeavor. For African Christians, God is the creator of all, above all, and in all. ROSE TETEKI ABBEY

God, Christian Views of, in Asia. The Christian views of God in Asia are in a process of transformation that can be characterized by four parallel, yet independent trends.

The initial and most predominant is the biblical/classical view of God that Protestant and Roman Catholic missions brought with them to Asia. Most missionaries, looking on the Hindu* tradition as polytheistic and the Buddhist* as devoid of God, challenged Asian peoples to abandon their religions and cultures and adopt the Western Christian trinitarian understanding of God. At the center of this teaching was Christology, which proclaimed Jesus as the Son of God who by his death and resurrection brought about salvation*. To this day, this theology informs the preaching and teaching ministry of the mainline churches, their worship, and their missionary endeavor.

A second trend was present from the beginning. Some missionaries and native theologians were dissatisfied with the total rejection of the Asian religious heritage. They attempted to interpret or to augment the classical Christian understanding of God with Hindu, Confucian*, and other Asian cultural symbols, myths, and images. Asian religious terminologies and concepts like *Dharma, Tien, Chu,* and *Dao* have been employed to speak about God. But much of this remains at the level of theological and philosophical exploration, including attempts to relate the Christian notions of the Ultimate with the Hindu Advaitic teaching of Brahman and Buddhist notions of, e.g., *nirvana* and *shunyata.* Interfaith dialogue* and discussions of the theology of religions have also challenged traditional views of God, although without significant impact on the Asian Church's understanding of God.

The third trend, which has had a much greater impact, is found in the theological reflections related to the subaltern cultures of Asia, e.g. the Minjung* theology in Korea and the Dalit* theology in India. These begin with the Bible, but interpret the biblical understanding of God and Jesus Christ from the experience of the suppressed, excluded, and marginalized* peoples of Asia.

The fourth trend, which is gathering increasing momentum, is the Asian feminist* critique and reflections on God, especially in the Philippines, India, Korea, and Hong Kong. These not only offer a critique of the patriarchal character of God in Christian traditions and in dominant Asian religious traditions, but also seek to revive the liberative elements of some Asian forms of spirituality* that have been suppressed or undermined in Christian teaching. S. WESLEY ARIARAJAH

God, Christian Views of, in Australia. Christian views of God have been shaped by changing contexts in Australia. Although until the 1970s almost all Australians identified with Christianity, practical help for the needy has been and still is seen as more significant than religious belief, ritual*, or experience – much as in the biblical prophetic tradition. Amid a strongly secular culture, traditional Christian views of God prevail within the churches.

Christianity arrived in Australia in 1788 with the "First Fleet" of convicts, soldiers, and one Church* of England chaplain, the Evangelical Richard Johnston. He preached and lived a Christ centered faith, but his ministry was tolerated rather than welcomed. Enlightenment* views of God as "moral governor" predominated to maintain order in "the most godless place under heaven" (as the saying went). "Killjoy" remains a common view of the Christian God.

Penal colonies evolved into women-scarce agricultural settlements where fire, flood, and drought decimated crops, sheep, and cattle. Within Christian religious forms, men placed their faith in fate* (often feminized) and one another ("mateship," with God as the "mate upstairs"). Sayings like "She'll be right, mate", "Just cop it sweet," and "When your number's up" reflect this fatalistic streak, evidenced in the prevalence of gambling. God's sovereignty* and rationality* were correspondingly emphasized in the churches, and much of Christian piety* was feminized.

The gold rushes of the 1850s saw the population treble, and life became less capricious. Christianity spread and prospered, displacing and evangelizing Australian* Aboriginal peoples but bringing coherence to Torres Strait Islanders. Sectarian* rivalries among Protestants (British), Catholics (Irish), members of the Church of England, and members of "free" churches strengthened the belief that "deeds, not creeds," are what matters. "Mateship" was reinforced by hardship during the two world wars; sacrificial dying, "in remembrance," and "greater love hath no man" became the focus, softening fatalism but offering "Christ substitutes."

Since 1960, Australia has been a multicultural, multi-faith country: the Buddhist* and Islamic* presence, and a growing appreciation of indigenous perspectives, are blunting secularism*. Spirituality* and God as "spirituality sponsor" are accepted, but "consumer religion" is common. Protestant and Catholic tribalism may have ended, but Pentecostalism* and new forms of conservatisms" have sharpened the contrasts between church and society, notably in Sydney. Conversely, Christendom's* demise, the leavening presence of the Orthodox* Church, Charismatic* revivals, and feminist* insights, as well as the ongoing orthodox teachings have seen trinitarian* faith permeate the churches' life in a more evident way.

Diverse views of God are tolerated in Australia today, as religion and spirituality are viewed as private matters. Christ-centered, Spirit-enlivened faith generally predominates in the churches: how this translates into public life is an issue for the future. CHARLES SHERLOCK

God, Christian views of, in the Caribbean Islands. Caribbean peoples have always expressed belief in God. For Amerindians in the Caribbean, the

Supreme Being "was immortal, invisible, omnipotent but not uncreated, because he had a mother who presided either in the Sun or Moon. He was called by several names, chiefly that of *Jocahuna*, and lived in the skies" (W. J. Gardner). While animists at heart, Amerindians blended their views about God with Roman Catholic beliefs. "Many Indians resented having been practically forced to become Christians.... Most of them were able to accommodate the beliefs and practices of the new religion by understanding them in terms of their native beliefs. God the father, of Catholic belief, they identified with the creator-god, *Wamurreti-Kwonci*, whom they otherwise knew as the benign *Jocahuna*. Sometimes they identified Jesus Christ with *Jocahuna*; at other times they believed him to be the son of *Jocahuna* or *Wamurreti-kwonci* and the Virgin Mary, whom they confused with *Atabei*, a goddess of Arawak belief" (Dale Bisnauth).

The African presence in the Caribbean islands led to a fusing of African beliefs in God with Christian language and beliefs. These fused beliefs have been variously expressed as Vodou* in Haiti*, Shango in Trinidad*, Santeria in Cuba*, and the Rastafari* Movement in Jamaica*. In each case, certain African beliefs are preserved and blended with Christian categories. For instance, the Rastafaris assert the existence of a creator God who is responsible for the governance of the world and who rules over the affairs of humankind. But while using the Christian Scriptures* to make their case, they change the language and adapt Christian categories to fit their existential situation. The creator God is black and called *Jah*.

Caribbean conceptions of God are often formulated in reaction to the colonial* theology articulated by the Christian Church. The genius of the indigenous expressions of God is that, in such a context, Caribbean people began to make a connection between God and freedom*. God is the source of healing*, the one who will overthrow the unjust order and help them hold body and soul together in the midst of oppression*. In colonial theology, while the soul belonged to God, the body belonged to the master. In Santeria, Vodou*, Shango, and Rastafari, the body is the site of freedom, as these religions assert that their participants are witnesses of God's freedom in the midst of an unjust world. NOEL LEO ERSKINE

God, Christian views of, in Latin America. God – the experience of God and reflection about God – is at the very heart of theology (Gk *theos*, "God"). The key question is not about God the "transcendent mystery," but about the God of the "underside of history." How are God's grace* and God's love* to be proclaimed to the millions of human beings who are marginalized*, excluded, condemned to being nobodies, and denied identities as persons?

God, the eternally unchangeable mystery, is set against injustice and oppression*, and thus escapes transcendence and takes sides. God is the mystery paradoxically revealed where life is destroyed, on all the Golgothas* of the world. For Latin American theology, it is not enough to say that God is revealed in history*. On the basis of this central truth of the Christian faith, Latin American theology also affirms God's suffering for life and justice* and God's loving solidarity* with those deprived of their rights. Thus Latin American theology proclaims the God of life, the God of the poor, the liberating* God, who is present in the midst of history on the side of the excluded, listening and freeing people through the divine victorious power that conquers death and recreates life.

The words of the old story of the Exodus are still valid in the present context: "I have seen the affliction of my people.... I have heard their cry because of their oppressors; I know their sufferings; I have come down to deliver them [my people].... So come, I will send you to Pharaoh to free my people" (Exod 3:1–10). In the NT, God's option for love* takes the form of the incarnation* of Jesus and of his proclamation of the Reign* of God and of God's justice, good news for all, including all who are oppressed.

For the Latin American theology of liberation, faith* in the liberating God requires discernment and struggle against the idols* of oppression and death. The opposite of faith* in God is not atheism*; it is idolatry* – the adoration of the false god: power, capital, consumerism, and the market taken as absolute, as a god in whose name the life of millions of human beings and nature are destroyed. Such idolatry is the most serious betrayal of the will of the God of life.

From this perspective, the life of faith in the mystery of God is ultimately a matter not of understanding the idea of God, but of experiencing God's reality. It is a matter of entering into and sharing God's very life, in a "praxis according to God" (G. Gutiérrez), a praxis of justice and of love that corresponds to God's practice of justice and love through Jesus and the manifestation of the Reign of God. Love and the practice of justice are the primary means of gaining access to God.

VICTORIO ARAYA GUILLÉN

God, Christian Views of, Latino/a. Latino/a theology and thus its view of God is at the intersection of academic concerns and the faith* and struggles of Latino/a communities, because Latino/a theologians address at once the theological academy, the ecclesial realm, and broader Latino/a communities. The concept of God found in this theology is intimately shaped by the faith life of Latinos/as. The starting point of theological reflection is the popular expressions by Latinos/as of God's presence in their lives.

Within Latino/a popular religiosity, God is understood as the one who accompanies* Latino/a peoples in their everyday struggles. The crucified Christ of Good* Friday points toward a God who suffers for and with marginalized* peoples. For Roman Catholic Latinos/as, the importance of the saints* and Mary* is a further expression of God's presence in everyday life. This God of everyday life who encounters us in the mundane is at the center of Latino/a views of God. This is expressed in all aspects of Latino/a culture*, from idiomatic phrases of Latin American Spanish to the rituals celebrated in the streets and homes of Latino/a communities. This cultural expression of the significance of everyday life reveals a God who is present in all moments and aspects of one's life.

The prominence of Marian devotions (see Mary, the Virgin, Cluster: Devotion in Latin America), a fundamental aspect of Latino/a religiosity, offers a window into Latino/a understandings of the divine. Whether it is a Mexican American devotion to Our Lady of Guadalupe (see Mary, the Virgin, Cluster: Of Guadalupe) or a Cuban American devotion to Our Lady of Charity, the different Marian apparition stories depict the Mother of God as being in solidarity* with the oppressed*. This Mariology informs an understanding of God who has a preferential* option for those who are marginalized*.

Latino/a peoples are at the curious intersection of Spanish, Indigenous, African, and US cultures. The hybridity of Latino/as, expressed most often in the categories of *mestizaje* and *mulatez*, contributes yet another feature to Latino/a views of God. The divine is often depicted as non white, and these representations have sociological, political, and theological value. This is a manner of expressing the image* of God (*imago Dei*) present in Latino/a peoples. For Latinos/as, the Christian God is present in their everyday lives, accompanies them in their suffering, and is revealed within and through their culture and religiosity.

MICHELLE A. GONZALEZ

God, Christian Views of, in North America. Despite rampant secularity and materialism, US society is vociferous in its claim to believe in God (see United States). A 2006 survey affirms that "the U.S. is overwhelmingly a nation of believers," 85% of whom follow the Christian faith; only 5% admit to believing in "nothing beyond the physical world." By contrast, in Canada*, 16% of the population indicated no religious affiliation in the national census of 2001, and there is an intentional-verging-on-legal rejection of "God-talk" in the Canadian political and professional landscape.

While people in the USA are extraordinarily united in their (largely "Christian"-

inspired) claim to believe in God, they are divided with respect to God's nature and purposes. According to the 2006 poll, 31% believe in an "authoritarian" God, "deeply involved in daily life" and "angry at sin"; for 23% God is "benevolent" and involved as a "positive force"; 16% believe in a "critical" God who does not interact with the world but is "unhappy with its current state"; and 24% think of God as "distant" and not interactive – a "cosmic force."

Despite its lack of theological sophistication, this sociological breakdown indicates a great deal about the function of theistic belief. The kind of conviction*, i.e. religious "certitude," especially represented in the first ("authoritarian") and also somewhat in the second ("benevolent") categories, explains the political and moral self-confidence of recent US administrations. The theism of "the Christian Right" leaves no room for doubt*, whether religious, ethical, or political; and the "benevolent" God of the middle classes prefers harmony over probing thought that may disturb. The third ("critical") and fourth ("distant") categories, which assume a continuing struggle with a God whose nature and intentions are still a mystery*, are views that would fit those of deeply engaged classical theological reflection and contemporary Liberation*, Feminist*, African* American, and Process* theologies*.

The social and religious climate in North America, and particularly the USA., presents a profound challenge to theologians, both Protestant and Catholic, whose primary assumption is God's "otherness" or transcendence. The God of the Judeo-Christian traditions remains both sovereign and, even in self-revelation, hidden – *Deus absconditus*. Such a God cannot be equated with any nation, race, gender, political ideology, or way of life. Thus while North American culture is permeated by God-talk at the popular level, serious Christian theology in this context manifests a continuing need to distinguish God from the most prevalent popular assumptions about the deity at work in our midst. Hence the most important scholarly attempts to comprehend and honor God are likely to seem strange or even a-theistic or agnostic. **See also DEATH OF GOD THEOLOGY; THEOLOGY AS HUMAN UNDERTAKING CLUSTER: NORTH ATLANTIC THEOLOGIANS DOING THEOLOGY: A DIALOGUE BETWEEN TEXT AND CONTEXT.** DOUGLAS JOHN HALL

God, Christian Views of, in North America: Feminist Understandings. Theology teaches that God is Spirit beyond gender identification and that speech about God is analogical*, not literal. However, traditional images of God, such as Father, Lord, and King, communicate that God is male or at least more fittingly addressed in male than in female terms. In response to this exclusively male imagery, feminist critics contend that exclusive speech for God is idolatrous*, making a graven image of divine mystery*. Moreover, they point out how the symbol* of God functions. Exclusively patriarchal naming of God degrades women and privileges men in church and society. In so doing, it distorts relationships within the community and sanctions structures of dominance and subordination.

Feminist theology proposes that using female symbols of God effectively challenges idolatrous patriarchal understandings of God. This language for God in female images emerges from women's encounter with God present in the depths of themselves. These encounters inspire varieties of metaphors* and models drawn from women's experiences of bodiliness (see Body), passion, cognition, and relationality*. The Scriptures enrich this variety with dynamic images of God such as midwife and mother*, nursing and protecting her offspring. These metaphors point to God's maternal relation to the world, often eclipsed by paternal metaphors. Reclaiming the female symbol of Divine Wisdom* (Prov 3:19–20, 8:22–31; Wis 6:22), creating, ordering, and redeeming the cosmos, provides a viable interpretative framework for God's presence and action in Christ* and in the Spirit*. In the Gospels, Jesus images God as a baker-woman (Matt 13:13 par.) and as a woman searching for a lost coin

(Luke 15:8–10). Female images of the Divine enable women to claim the fullness of their identity as created in God's image, redeemed by Christ, and graced by the Spirit. Such imagery effects an experience of God as beneficent toward the female and as an ally of women's flourishing. Moreover, it gives rise to a community characterized not by domination and submission, but by mutuality and reciprocity, one that values and calls forth the gifts of a discipleship* of equals for the sake of mission. Recognizing women's humanity and ways of being in the world as *imago Dei* (God's image) offers diverse options for naming God, who is nonetheless beyond all names (see the present cluster: Names for God in the Bible and Church Traditions). Diverse symbolism recovers the richness of God's self-revelation throughout salvation history and restores right relationships in church and society.

ELIZABETH A. JOHNSON and GLORIA L. SCHAAB

God, Christian Views of, in Western Europe. Since Augustine, no century has been as challenged as the 20th by a radical reappraisal of the doctrine of God or has failed so dramatically. The pinnacle of Christendom*, this "Christian century" presided over the inculturation* of faith but was bound to collapse when the secular* was severed from its religious twin.

Disqualified by scientific* imperialism, God soon becomes useless, a superfluous hypothesis. Nature*, no longer God's handiwork, goes by laws that point to no extraneous power, as does history* in the aftermath of genocidal apocalypses. Nevertheless, Nietzsche*'s diagnosis (we have killed God) is downplayed, if heard. Under the Christian aegis, faith* no longer prods reason*. Nor is the religious enchanting the secular. The world is disenchanted, not with religion, but with Christianity. Theology tries to rescue a doctrine that has collapsed instead of coming to grips with God by first asking not whether God is this or that, but whether there is a Christian doctrine of God and at what cost, especially if Jesus can be no surrogate God.

Inklings abound of apophatic* theology, of speculations about the names or namelessness of God (see the present cluster: Names for God in the Bible and Church Traditions), the unknown or hidden God. "No object besides objects," writes Buber*, who adds, "God is not to be found by subtraction and not to be loved by reduction." Nor (with Bultmann*) is God "the cause (*aitia*) to which thought refers the world, or the source (*arche*) in terms of which the happenings in the world can be grasped in their unity and lawfulness." Otherwise, God is reduced to an idol*, a god that is not quite God (Maritain*).

What matters is not *what,* but *that,* God is, a question nowhere raised except through language where "the inevitable elusiveness of the divine name is the logical safeguard against universal idolatry" (Ramsey).

Neither Barth*'s Wholly Other God (christological concentration notwithstanding) nor Tillich*'s God as being-itself (unconditioned and yet, as ground of being, somehow contingent on that which is) and as the power of being go quite beyond the traditional dualism* of natural vs. supernatural, literal* vs. symbolic*, Word* of God vs. word of man, real vs. virtual language. The field of faith* lies neither in nature nor in history, but in covenant* and in Incarnation* – "worlding the Word."

By retrieving Marcion*, who drastically pitted law* against gospel*, history against theology, Harnack switched faith to a language so native to the believer that God never can be hostage to any idea of being (Macquarrie) nor faith to dogma (Kittel). Indeed, "that Jesus spoke of God not in dogmas but in poems should be the starting point of all our efforts to speak of God" (Theissen). **See also ATHEISM AND CHRISTIAN THEOLOGY; DEATH OF GOD THEOLOGY.** GABRIEL VAHANIAN

Goddianism. A form of African Religion reconstituted by 20th-c. African elites in Nigeria. **See also AFRICAN RELIGION AND CHRISTIANITY CLUSTER: CULTURAL INTERACTIONS.**

Godparents, witnesses to a Christian baptism* who assume responsibility for Christian nurture of the newly baptized person, especially when a child.

Golden Legend, also known as *Lives of the Saints,* a collection of stories about saints and explanations of feast days, written about 1275 by Jacob* of Voragine; very popular in the late Middle Ages.

Golden Rule, precept in the Sermon on the Mount: "Whatever you wish others to do to you, do so to them" (Matt 6:12; cf. Luke 6:31). A "negative" form of the rule is ascribed to Rabbi Hillel, and parallels are found in a number of the world's religions.

Golgotha (Heb/Aramaic, "place of the skull"; Lat Calvaria, "Calvary*"), site of Jesus' crucifixion outside Jerusalem.

Gómez Morín, Manuel (1897–1972), Roman Catholic ideologist; rector of the National Autonomous University of Mexico in Mexico City (1933–34), who defended its autonomy as a liberal alternative to the Pontifical University of Mexico. He was founder and president (1939–49) of the Partido Acción Nacional (PAN, National Action Party), a Mexican Roman Catholic party, a conservative "Christian Democracy" party that views itself as pursuing "national action" that is neither Left nor Right.

MARÍA ALICIA PUENTE LUTTEROTH and ELIZABETH JUDD

Good Friday, the Friday before Easter, on which the anniversary of the crucifixion of Christ is observed. Originally the church had a single celebration on the Pasch, the Christian Passover (see Easter); separate observance on each of the days of "Holy Week" began during the 4th c. in Jerusalem, then was progressively adopted elsewhere. For the Roman Catholic Church, Good Friday is a day of fasting, abstinence, and penance*; the Mass* is not celebrated. In the Eastern Orthodox Church, after extended celebrations of the Divine* Office, the day ends with a symbolic burial of Christ. A three-hour devotion on Good Friday, from noon to 3 PM, was developed in Lima, Peru, by Fr. Alphonsia Messia, SJ (1687) and quickly spread through Latin America and then Europe. It often used the seven* last words of Christ on the cross, set to music by Haydn, Dubois, and others. Protestant churches have adopted this custom, with readings, sermons, and prayers commemorating the events of the Crucifixion and celebration of the Lord's* Supper.

Goods, Community of. In Acts 2:44–45, 4:32–35, members of the early church in Jerusalem sold their possessions, held all things in common, and distributed food and other material things to those in need. After the community of goods was adopted as a monastic ideal, debates persisted regarding possessions because of the understanding of poverty* (Matt 10:9–10) espoused by Franciscans* and Nil* Sorsky, in Russia.

GOSPEL AND CULTURE CLUSTER

1) *Introductory Entry*

Gospel and Culture

2) *A Sampling of Contextual Views and Practices*

Gospel and Culture in Africa
Gospel and Culture in Asia
Gospel and Culture in Australia
Gospel and Culture in the Caribbean Islands
Gospel and Culture in Eastern Europe
Gospel and Culture in Mexico
Gospel and Culture in North America

1) Introductory Entry

Gospel and Culture. Gospel (Gk *euangelion;* Old English, *godspell,* "good news") is the good news about Jesus Christ, the central message of Christian proclamation. The cognate verb is used in the LXX* (Isa 52:7, quoted in Rom 10:15; Matt 11:5 = Luke 7:22). An inscription in Priene (9 BCE) speaks of the "good news" of Augustus Caesar; the proclamation of Jesus as Lord thus competed with the imperial cult, especially in the East.

The title of Mark*, "The Gospel of Jesus Christ" (Mark 1:1), was used as a model to designate other written narratives about Jesus (or collections of his sayings) that began to be called "Gospels," or rather the one gospel "according to" Matthew*, Mark*, Luke*, and John*.

In addition, there were many other "apocryphal*" Gospels (1st–2nd c.), including those "according to" or "of" the Ebionites*, Hebrews*, Judas*, Mary* (Magdalene), the Nazarenes*, Peter*, Philip*, and Thomas*. Each gospel (including the canonical ones) presents the central message of the Christian proclamation ("the gospel") in its own way, related to a specific cultural and religious context. This message was summed up (2nd c.) as the "apostolic proclamation," summarized by the Apostles'* Creed. Yet the gospel (as message) continued to be expressed in new ways in different cultural contexts, as illustrated in the entries in this cluster. **See also** CULTURE CLUSTER: CULTURE AND CHRISTIANITY.

2) A Sampling of Contextual Views and Practices

Gospel and Culture in Africa are interrelated in three ways. At first, the gospel was viewed as a revelation coming from outside of Africa and was proposed to be the new path of truth that should replace the "pagan*," "savage," "barbaric" African culture in its entirety. This view, which dominated colonial* Christianity from the 16th to the 19th c., but is still present, demanded that African populations abandon their ways of thinking, feeling, and acting, their sense of humanity, and the norms, values, and customs governing their life in society, and enter the new life promised by the Christian God. The primary theologies called for Africans to become a *tabula rasa,* to forget completely their own culture; the missionaries spoke of "planting the church." Conversion was in the image of colonialism; "savage," "barbaric" Africans were "born again" by accepting Western dogmas and social norms that were viewed as the only possible and true understanding of the gospel.

Gospel and African culture are related in a second way when the gospel as the Word* of God is viewed as revealing, and allowing to flourish, deep spiritual, ethical, and theological insights already present, though hidden, in the African culture. The gospel does not come "to abolish" the African culture, but rather "to fulfill" it by incorporating it into God's sublime project for humanity (as Jesus did not come "to abolish" the law or the prophets but "to fulfill" them; Matt 5:17). The African culture, like any culture, is a womb to be impregnated by the gospel, a field where wheat must be separated from weeds (cf. Matt 13:24–30), or a battleground in which the forces of good and evil must be distinguished (cf. Matt 13:37–43). Two theological trends developed this vision in Africa: the theologies of the "hidden treasure" (Matt 13:44) and of "indigenization"; they inaugurated a positive attitude toward African culture, although keeping a distance between gospel and a culture that prevents resistance to neocolonialism.

Gospel and African culture are related in a third way, namely through the contemporary theologies of inculturation*, reconstruction*, and invention. These theologies do not locate the gospel outside the dynamics of cultural creativity. Inculturation theologies recognize that African Christians interpret the gospel as Scripture* and as the Word* of God from the perspective of their direct encounter with God in their own cultural experience, without mediation by Western culture and its hermeneutical blinders. Africans encounter God at the African "initiatory bush" (a bush that is not consumed by fire, according to Bimwenyi-Kweshi) to engage in a dialogue where the gospel offers a vantage point for seeing the African culture in a meaningful way. For Reconstruction* theology, the gospel empowers the African culture as an agent of rebirth and resurrection through which the whole of society can be transformed on the basis of spiritual values. For Invention theology, the gospel inspires and nourishes human creativity for building the future and winning future battles against cultural oppression*. KÄ MANA

Gospel and Culture in Asia. The good news of God's self-gift in the Word* made flesh resonates with various Asian cultures and is the foundation for the Christian affirmation of cultural pluralism. In spite of negative attitudes toward Asian cultures (e.g. condemnation of Chinese ancestor* rites and of Malabar rites in India), there have been efforts to translate and adapt the gospel to Asian ways of thinking, customs, and traditions (e.g. the May Fourth Movement in China and the "Rethinking Christianity" group in India; see Church, Concepts and Life, Cluster: In Asia; Indian Christian Theologies). This positive trend has found spokespersons in missionaries such as de Nobili* and Ziegenbalg in India and Ricci* in China. The traditions of Thomas Christians (Malankara* Orthodox Syrian Church) in India and the Sian-fu stele inscription in China bear witness to Christian communities living harmoniously with their respective cultural worlds from quite early times.

Besides this "incarnational" approach to the relationship between gospel and culture, there has also been a "prophetic" engagement in which the gospel is an effective prophetic critique of cultures. Yet history and experience demonstrate the importance of being rooted incarnationally in cultures in order to offer an effective prophetic critique. The absence of such prophetic engagement easily leads to an uncritical conformity to cultures.

A challenge that Asia faces is to blend the incarnational and prophetic approaches in the relationship between gospel and culture. Another major challenge (yet to be undertaken) is to relate the gospel to a "reconstructed understanding of culture," not as an essentialized and closed system divorced from history and social realities, but as a reality continuously constructed by a given community that takes into account the differences within a culture. **See also CULTURE CLUSTER: CULTURAL STUDIES** and **CULTURE and CHRISTIANITY**. FELIX WILFRED

Gospel and Culture in Australia. The gospel has been preached in Australia* since the "First Fleet," but popular understanding has varied. Protestant chaplains were government employees, and some, as magistrates, sentenced men to flogging; consequently, the gospel's demands were heard as punitive moralism. Roman Catholic clergy shared their flocks' trials, but their ministry was restricted. English Anglicans, Scottish Presbyterians, and Irish Catholics each assumed that theirs was "the" church. Sectarianism* strengthened secularism*, with doctrine minimized in favor of "deed, not creed" religion. Thus the gospel was commonly identified with self-serving establishment religion, life-denying Protestant moralism, guilt-inducing "pie-in-the-sky" Catholicism, or sheer irrationalism.

In outback communities, the gospel was commended by ministers willing to serve sacrificially; in the cities, churches in which laity and clergy worked together, especially in public evangelism, grew. The Depression and world wars saw more holistic gospel ministries emerge; the years since have seen cooperation in evangelism* and growing ecumenical openness (contested by some conservative Protestants) but a decline in church attendance.

In today's multicultural Australia, reconciliation* in Christ, the grace-giving work of the Spirit, and the importance of living out the gospel are viewed as crucial for believable proclamation in a society open to the spiritual but suspicious of religious institutions. **See also GOD, CHRISTIAN VIEWS OF, CLUSTER: IN AUSTRALIA; JUSTIFICATION, THEOLOGICAL VIEWS AND PRACTICES, CLUSTER: IN AUSTRALIA.** CHARLES SHERLOCK

Gospel and Culture in the Caribbean Islands. Caribbean peoples, despite centuries of colonialism and mismanagement, are most inventive, creative, and committed to struggle to make a better world. Despite differences in language, religion, and ethnicities, they share a history; a vocabulary (e.g., colonialism, underdevelopment, production of sugarcane and bananas, racism, and tourism), and a central problem, poverty*. Thus the gospel is the gospel of Christ only insofar as it proclaims justice* for the poor.

Poverty – entailing a lack of health care, homelessness, and the AIDS epidemic – cuts across the Caribbean cultures. The Christian Church also cuts across cultures.

Thus it is in the best position to speak the word of justice, especially when the gap between rich and poor widens, and to adopt a Liberation* theology that will make a material difference in people's living conditions. In the past, the church was content to walk beside those condemned to a harsh life of poverty, offering spiritual encouragement and a home in heaven after their death, and thus reinforcing a culture that makes people powerless. Becoming a "justice church" involves leading Caribbean people to abandon cultural traditions that render them voiceless and economically and socially dependent. For this the gospel of Christ must be translated into social praxis.

NOEL LEO ERSKINE

Gospel and Culture in Eastern Europe. See CULTURE CLUSTER: CULTURE AND CHRISTIANITY IN EASTERN ORTHODOXY.

Gospel and Culture in Mexico. Theology* interrelates gospel and culture* as it seeks to conceive of the relationship between believers' faith* in spiritual, transcendent realities and the individual and collective religious experience in the cultural reality of daily life. Theology has existed in Mexico since the time of the Mesoamericans, who expressed their religious wisdom in myths*, rites, religious practices, and beliefs in the Anáhuac region and throughout Mesoamerica.

Two kinds of Western theology arrived with Christian evangelization (see Mexico). One was mystical* and was lived out in convents with their own European cultures. The second kind of theology was missionary, which aimed at communicating the gospel in two ways: either by demanding a *tabula rasa* (a total abandonment of previous beliefs and practices) or by recognizing the voice of the Spirit* in Mesoamerican peoples and their cultures. At first Christian and Mesoamerican theologies collided; eventually, however, they began to interact: Christians allowed native theologies to contribute to the life of the church, and Mesoamericans endorsed popular expressions of Christian faith (see Popular Christian Practices Cluster: In Latin America: Mexico).

After the colonial period, the institutional church in Mexico framed its life around diverse European theologies, thus defining itself as against Mesoamerican cultures. But following the Liberals' political triumph (1856), the Mexican government abolished the state church status of the Roman Catholic Church; thus Protestant churches arrived in Mexico with their own theological perspectives. In addition, since 1940, North American religious organizations have contributed to a broader theological and religious diversity.

After the Second Vatican* Council (1962–65) and especially after the Latin American Episcopal Conference in Medellín* (1968), the Liberation* Theology Movement paid attention (from a Marxist perspective) to the structure of production of authoritative teaching. Who was empowered to produce theology? Liberation theologians removed "theological production" from the hands of clergy in the sanctuaries and entrusted it to laypersons in public places; theological production became associated with the struggle of the poor for a more human and just world. Then new producers of Christian theology emerged: Mesoamericans, African Americans, rural people, youth, women, and others, each group having specific theological proposals, distinguished by their contents and methodologies, but with similar ways of relating gospel and particular cultures and life conditions.

Latin American and Feminist theologies, developed elsewhere in Latin America, have found a unique Mexican voice, shaped by their reflection on life experiences in Mexico. Professional theologians, social activists, and pastors of churches seek to correlate fidelity to the received faith and commitment to addressing the new challenges of life in the world.

ELEAZAR LÓPEZ

Gospel and Culture in North America. There are two basic North American views of "gospel." With the definite article ("*the* gospel") and without the definite article, as "good news."

"Gospel" (Gk *euangelion*) means "good news." The source of this good news, for

Christians, is the life, death, and resurrection of Jesus, the Christ – the normative biblical and theological bases of the Christian message. But the articulation of the Christian message *as gospel* depends on the context in which it is proclaimed. This "news" can be thought "good" only insofar as it engages, illumines, and "answers" the problems (the "bad news") of a given culture. Gospel for one time and place is thus not necessarily gospel for another. Hence for many in North America, ranging from members of mainline churches to members of Charismatic churches, the quest for "gospel" is an ongoing task of the disciple* community, involving it in a continuous attempt to "discern the signs of the times" in which it finds itself and in ever new proclamation (*kerygma**) responsive to the cultural reality for which it is intended.

By contrast, with the definite article, "the gospel" is associated with supracontextual doctrinal claims as though it were fixed and unaffected by historical actuality – a fundamentalist*, biblicist view. Ironically, "*the* gospel" that is upheld by the most determined users of the term in the USA is in fact highly determined by the presuppositions, anxieties, and conflicts of the contemporary religious situation in which it was fashioned and is perpetuated. DOUGLAS JOHN HALL

Gospel Music. The term has informally come to mean all modern, composed religious music and is thus differentiated from hymns*, classical sacred music. It has also been loosely applied to US Southern religious music (close-harmony, country-influenced quartets) and contemporary Christian music (pop melodies with religious lyrics).

However, the term "gospel music" is most commonly applied to a genre that emerged from the early African American sacred music tradition (see Spirituals). Also called black gospel music, it is a composed sacred music form created from the melding of spirituals, jubilee, and blues (and, later, rhythm and blues) with the emotionalism and instrumentation of Pentecostal* worship services. It is characterized by overtly religious lyrics, a love of improvisation, call-and-response choruses and performances, and a pronounced beat.

Gospel music is particularly identified with African Americans, and the term was first popularized by composer Thomas Dorsey (1899–1993) in Chicago (in the 1930s, although the term had been in use since the early 1900s). Gospels were originally performed either a cappella or with a piano or organ, but gospel artists eventually added other instruments, including guitars and drums. Singer Mahalia Jackson (1911–72) was the most influential gospel artist, the first to "cross over" into mainstream white North America.

Gospel music has traditionally been performed by large choirs, usually fronted by a soloist (as in the Mississippi Mass Choir), mostly male quartets (e.g. the Dixie Hummingbirds), or soloists (Shirley Caesar). Although first popularized in black churches, not all black denominations welcome gospel music performances in their services.

During the "golden age" of gospel music in the USA (1945–late 1960s), gospel artists played an important role in the Civil* Rights Movement. A more "urban" version of the music (incorporating elements of funk, rock, and/or rap music) became more popular in the early 21st c. Still, traditional gospel music remains a potent force in contemporary black culture. Gospel songs like "Precious Lord, Take My Hand," "O Happy Day," and "Peace in the Valley" remain staples in black and white church services, revivals*, and funeral services alike. **See also MEDIA AND CHRISTIANITY; MEDIA AND CHRISTIAN WORSHIP; MEGACHURCHES REMAKING RELIGIOUS TRADITION IN NORTH AMERICA; PRAISE AND WORSHIP.** ROBERT DARDEN

Gospel Reading, during worship the reading of a selection from one of the Gospels after all other biblical readings, traditionally with the congregation standing to show reverence in "high liturgy" churches.

Gospel of Truth. The untitled third treatise in the first codex of Nag* Hammadi begins with the words "The gospel of truth," which became the modern title of this writing, although it seems more like a homily or meditation on the topic of "truth." Irenaeus* knew of a "Gospel of Truth" used by the Gnostic* Valentinian* school. That gospel, about which Iraneus says that it "agrees in nothing with the Gospels of the apostles," might be identical with the surviving (middle to late 2nd c.) text of the codex of Nag Hammadi. Some scholars' assumption that it was composed by Valentinus* himself cannot be substantiated.

The Gospel of Truth consists of a nearly unbroken stream of associations and displays considerable poetic vigor, though its underlying structure is not easily discerned. Some biblical concepts (truth* and error, knowledge and ignorance, the anointing, the cross), metaphors (the living book, the good shepherd, sleep, and blindness), and literary forms (parables* and beatitudes*) can nevertheless be identified. The beautiful passage on Jesus' activity as a teacher is probably a reminiscence of Luke 2:46–49. The underlying theme of this enigmatic text progresses from "searching" and "finding" to "rest." "Rest" is a shorthand for ultimate salvation*, which the preacher of this discourse has at least partially already found. HANS-JOSEF KLAUCK

Gothic Architecture, church building style, developed from the 12th-c. Romanesque* basilica, featuring pointed arches, continuous shafts from floor to apex, stained glass windows, and a large apse* with several chapels. **See also HIEROTOPY, THE CREATION OF CHRISTIAN SACRED SPACES.**

Goths, a Germanic people whose two branches, the Ostrogoths and the Visigoths, embraced Arian* Christianity (c364–78), the moderate "homoian" Arianism (asserting that the Son is "like," *homoios*, the Father, but refusing to say that they are of the same essence). Under the influence of Ulfila*, the "apostle to the Goths," and other Arian missionaries, the Goths converted to Christianity while they and other Germanic people were fleeing from the Huns and first settled in the Danube region (including Romania* and Hungary*), before migrating to and occupying the entire western Mediterranean region.

Arian Christian Visigoths ruled Spain* and (Southern) Gaul (415–587); the Arian Church saw itself as the "Catholic" Church (denying this title to the Roman Church). The Spanish Church became Catholic in the Nicene sense once again when King Reccared* converted from Arian Christianity to Latin Christianity (587). The Visigothic monarchy lasted until it was swept away by the Muslim invasion (711–19).

Similarly, Arian Christian Ostrogoths ruled Italy* (493–552); Arian and Roman churches coexisted, although there was much tension between them. Because the Ostrogoths preserved much of the Roman mode of governing – Christian dioceses continued to correspond to the *municipia* (cities with their own local governments according to Roman law) – Arian rulers maintained close control of the local churches; the bishops were in most instances Arians (a situation that changed with the Arian Lombards*, who succeeded the Ostrogoths in Northern Italy). **See also ARIANISM; ITALY; SPAIN.**

Gottschalk, or Godescalc (c804–69), German monk and theologian; was dedicated to monastic life, was tonsured, and took vows while still a child at the Abbey of Fulda. He sought release on the grounds that he had been made a monk against his will. A council gave him his liberty (829), but he continued to reside in several monasteries. He developed an extreme doctrine of predestination* ("double predestination," with respect to both salvation* and damnation*), based on Augustine's* last writings, which he preached in Italy and the Balkans. (His own fate as a child, having been "drawn into salvation" against his will, may have reinforced this theology.) He returned to Germany (848), where he engaged in a new and sophisticated discussion of predestination, one of the high points of the Carolingian* Renaissance, which included all the notable theologians and church politicians of the time. Several regional councils formulated complex statements denying double predestination and ascribing salvation to grace* and damnation to human guilt. Gottschalk died in confinement (869), holding to his theory of predestination until death. Many of his writings have been retrieved and studied only in recent decades.

---

1) Introductory Entries

Grace of God in the Eastern Orthodox Tradition is understood as the experience of God's presence as a step toward the realization of the ultimate goal of Christian life: divine–human communion (theosis*, divinization). Absent in Eastern Orthodox theology are distinctions between different kinds of grace, such as prevenient grace and sanctifying grace. According to most contemporary Orthodox theologians, the Greek patristic tradition developed an understanding of grace as a communication of the divine energies, in which one participates to a greater or lesser degree.

This notion of grace as a self-communication of God is rooted in the Incarnation*, in which humanity is saved from death and corruption through union with the Divine (see Atonement #1). Grace is communicated sacramentally and iconically. Sacrament* within the Orthodox tradition is an event of the divine presence made possible through the iconic* structure of a particular medium. In addition to the formal sacraments in the Orthodox Church, such as Eucharist* and baptism*, the Orthodox theologian Alexander Schmemann affirms that all of creation is potentially sacramental. Grace is a gift received through synergy, i.e. the performance of ascetic* practices, such as liturgical worship, prayer, fasting, and almsgiving. Such practices do not make demands on God's grace, but make one available to receive the presence of God that permeates all of creation. **See also ORTHODOX CHURCHES, EASTERN, CLUSTER: INTRODUCTORY ENTRIES.**

ARISTOTLE PAPANIKOLAOU

Grace of God in the Western Tradition. Grace is God's favor to human beings. In the OT, grace encompasses creation*, Israel's redemption* from Egypt and its election*, the covenant*, the gift of the Law*, sending prophets*, and other acts of divine favor. According to the divine self-revelation of Exod 33:19–34:9, God's grace is threefold: God acts with "faithful love" (Heb root *hesed*), is "merciful" (Heb root *rhm*), and is "gracious" (Heb root *hnn*). First, God's "faithful love" presupposes an existing relationship (specifically the covenant) to which God is faithful and underscores that grace is an action by God (rather than simply an attitude) that fulfills an essential need that humans cannot meet by themselves, e.g. an action of deliverance, healing, and overcoming barrenness (such as that of Sarah). Second, God's "mercy" expresses the benevolence of a superior toward a weak or needy inferior. Third, "graciousness" as applied to God refers to a type of relationship that God has with humans and that humans can also have with others; grace is the action of freely and unilaterally offering an undeserved gift or favor; although it can be requested or withheld, it cannot be coerced.

In the NT, the Greek *charis* is the central term for God's grace; according to the NT passages, this term refers to God's acts of faithful love, God's mercifulness, or God's graciousness (expressed by different terms in the OT). *Charis* is found especially in the Pauline letters and Luke and Acts, but also in 1 and 2 Peter, as well as in John 1:14–17, Hebrews, and James.

Charis thus has three connotations, comparable to the OT connotations:

1. Grace may refer to lovingly giving aid to someone who needs help (2 Cor 8:6, 7, 19, about Titus's gracious work) and especially to God's loving help and empowerment of people in need – a sense of "grace" found in the Pauline letters, as well as in Jas 4:6 and 1 and 2 Peter. This view of grace as intervention on behalf of someone in need is closely related to salvation* as the redemption* of humans who are powerless to free themselves from bondage – physical bondage or any other bondage that separates them from God – or are powerless to achieve sanctification*. Here, grace designates a divine intervention through Christ and empowerment through Christ and the Spirit that effects salvation and/or sanctification*.
2. Grace may refer to God's saving benevolence in Christ; what is emphasized is not so much God's action but God's inclination. Here *charis* evokes the image of a loving father or a forgiving judge. "God's grace" is

 Grace of God in the Western Tradition

especially manifested through Christ's death, which saves sinners from the condemnation they justly deserve – according to (especially Protestant) interpretations of Paul's letters, e.g. Rom 3:24–25a: "They are now justified by his grace as a gift, through the redemption that is in Christ Jesus whom God put forward as a sacrifice of atonement by his blood."

3. As God's "graciousness," grace is the action of freely and unilaterally endowing persons with specific tasks or ministries by offering them an undeserved gift, "charisma," or favor. Luke often uses *charis* in this sense (e.g. about Mary, Luke 1:10; about Jesus, 2:20, 52, 4:22; about the apostles, Acts 4:33, 6:8), whereas Paul often uses "charisma" in this sense (e.g. 1 Cor 11).

These multivalent understandings of God's grace in Scriptures have given rise to different interpretations through the centuries. While all three connotations (which parallel in some ways the three understandings of atonement*, of salvation*, and of sin*) are found in all traditions, in each instance one or another is given primary emphasis.

Following the Greek fathers, Eastern Orthodoxy* primarily emphasizes grace as God's "faithful love" (connotation 1), the experience of God's presence as a step toward the realization of the ultimate goal of Christian life, divine–human communion. From a Western perspective, this Orthodox view of grace is envisioned as the divine helping humans by healing them of sin as a disease of the soul and freeing them for cooperation and union with God. Thus the Virgin* Mary, the Theotokos*, is the paragon of fallen humanity renewed by divine grace (but see The Present Cluter: In the Eastern Orthodox Tradition).

In a similar vein, Augustine begins his *Confessions,* "You have made us for yourself, and our hearts are restless until they rest in you." On this basis, he raises questions concerning the relation between reason and revelation (as grace), the earthly city and the city of God (as God's gracious gift), as well as liberation* and salvation*.

As they have confronted these issues, Western Christian theologians have adopted the biblical term "good pleasure" (*eudokia, beneplacitum*) to describe God's willing (see Revelation) (connotation 2). While this might mean that God acts arbitrarily, it usually carries the connotation of generosity and favor. Medieval thinkers often quoted the Neoplatonist* dictum that goodness extends or spreads itself (*bonum est diffusivum sui*); to avoid the implication that this happens by necessity, they added that God acts freely, but always in accordance with the goodness of God's nature. God's good pleasure confers benefits that go beyond anything that created things deserve or are able to accomplish. It is usual to emphasize three successive ways in which God acts graciously: creating things that did not exist, inviting human beings into a communion with God that is beyond their intrinsic capabilities, and offering salvation after they fall into sin.

Grace in a narrower sense applies not to creation but to the invitation to communion with God. In Scholastic* discussions, the term was seen to have at least three applications. In its origins, grace is an attitude and decision on God's part to turn toward human beings. Grace does not merely remain within God but is communicated through action (the "actual grace" of the Scholastics), mediated through Word and sacraments or immediately through divine influence. And when grace takes full effect, there is a change in human beings (the "sanctifying grace" of the Scholastics). The latter is understood to be a "new being" and a new mode of acting, animated by faith*, hope*, and love* (1 Cor 13:13).

Roman Catholic theologians focus on the relationship between divine grace and nature. Nature is associated with human capabilities, and grace is associated with divine influence beyond those capabilities. Thomas Aquinas* asserts that grace presupposes and perfects human nature and acknowledges human achievements in work, culture, science and technology, and politics; yet humanity is satisfied only through God's self-communication in grace.

By contrast Protestants tend to discuss grace* as a resolution of sin*, considering how God's grace in Jesus Christ overcomes human sin, which separates human from God.

The Charismatic* Movement, while emphasizing grace as God's "faithful loving" interventions (e.g. in healings*) (see connotation 1) give greater weight to God's "gracious" gifts, charismata, that empower believers for specific ministries.

DANIEL PATTE and EUGENE TESELLE

---

2) A Sampling of Contextual Views

Grace of God: Asian Perspective. Grace as anchored in the person of Jesus Christ, the Word of God, "full of grace and truth," is in tension with the universality of grace so important in the pluralistic context of Asia. This is the recurring problem of the relation between the saving event in Jesus Christ and God's unbounded and effective love for all peoples and God's universal saving action. In the Asian context, grace is therefore understood as that divine wisdom* which enables human beings to recognize and acknowledge God and to transcend difference. Grace enables us to attain the fullness of our humanity and to build a community of equals. Grace empowers us to challenge and change dominant systems and structures and to promote social relations most beneficial to people. For this, God's grace bestows on us the gifts* of the Spirit, as well as justice*, love*, joy, and peace*. Hence grace is a community-building force that frees human beings from all ghetto attitudes.

MONICA JYOTSNA MELANCHTHON

Grace of God: Latin American Perspective. Reflecting on grace from a Latin American perspective involves taking as a starting point the economic, social, and cultural hardships experienced by poor* people, the majority of the population. Social inequality, lack of dignity, and other signs of structural* sin* challenge the traditional ahistorical conception of grace. According to Liberation* theology, grace empowers people by reminding them that as children of God, created in God's image, they have a place in the world. In a mercantile society in which everything is bought and sold, the excluded, the marginalized*, the invisible non-persons experience grace as that through which they are included and made visible in society. This gift from God that they receive is an invitation to radiate grace in their daily life, carrying within their soul, mind, and body the message of God's love* in a world that knows no mercy. Conversely, grace reminds the powerful, the wealthy, and those with authority of their complicity in structural sins that create inequality, even as grace affirms that they are themselves children* of God. The affirmation that here and now by grace all humans are God's kin can lead to mutual respect and to the suppression of inequalities and discriminations in society and the church.

ELSA TAMEZ

Grace of God: North American Feminist Perspective. Traditionally, grace is the unmerited acceptance and ever-present love of God that forgives and restores sinners through Jesus Christ. Christian feminists readily affirm grace as the antithesis of sin*, suffering*, and death* that are met by God's mysterious, redemptive* power. Feminists also have different understandings of grace. A critical assessment of power in divine–human–cosmic relations is key to naming and explicating grace. Amid systemically disordered and violent relations of domination and subordination, grace is the power of the Holy Spirit – the unexpected gift of sustenance, empowerment, and redemption for freedom* and dignity – that transforms people into persons respectful of self and others. Divine grace is thus the transformative, surprising, and uncontrollable wellspring in which one can seek healing*, justice*, and love*, and find strength to resist evil*, to build dynamic communities of peace and compassion, and to support the flourishing of all creation. Images of graced experiences include the exodus of liberation*, the rainbow of covenant*, the jubilee of new beginnings, the power of people to bring one another into well-being, the Christic identification with the discarded and downtrodden, and the breaking of bread – "the welcome table" – where hospitality* to strangers* and outcasts and the promise of life abundant are shared.

MARILYN J. LEGGE

Grace at Meals, custom of giving thanks before meals, inherited from Judaism and ascribed to Christ (John 6:11) and Paul (Acts 27:35).

Grail Legend. In medieval romances, starting in the 12th c., the Holy Grail is a vessel with unique powers, sometimes identified as the cup used by Christ at the Last Supper, transmitted to Joseph* of Arimathea, and producing effects like those often attributed to the Eucharist*.

Gratian (12th c.), teacher of canon* law in Bologna, Italy, author of the *Concordia discordantium canonum* (known as *Decretum*), a comprehensive collection of laws relating to most aspects of church governance and discipline. Gratian created the foundation for medieval and modern canon law and possibly served as an adviser to a papal judge (Venice, 1143). There is very little evidence that he was a monk or a bishop, as has been suggested.

Gratian collected legal statements deriving from general and provincial councils, papal decretals*, patristic writings, the Pseudo-Isidorian forgeries (False Decretals*), penitentials*, and secular law. As sources, he used recent legal collections and contemporary theology. Gratian's innovation was to include his own brief comments (*dicta*), which apply the methods of early Scholasticism* to reconcile the seemingly contradictory statements passed down by tradition.

The *Decretum* is preserved in two recensions, perhaps from different authors. The first, finished shortly after 1139, contains most of the *dicta* and 1,860 chapters. The second is more juristic. It was already in use by 1150 and contains 3,945 chapters. Some 200 excerpts were taken directly from the sources of Roman law. The *Decretum* remained foundational for Catholic Church courts and the teaching of canon law until 1918.

ANDERS WINROTH

Great Awakening, a name applied to Evangelical* revivals* that took place in Great Britain, Ireland, and the American colonies from the mid-1730s to the mid-1740s. It involved hundreds of ministers and churches, with Whitefield*, then Edwards* and the Wesleys* as iconic figures.

The thousands of conversions that took place during the revivals were unified by the religious experience of the "new birth," an intensely personal, often emotional form of Christian conversion that places primary importance on the direct operation of the Holy* Spirit on a person.

People turned out by the thousands to participate in or evaluate the revival gatherings. Many, referred to as the "New Lights," embraced the Great Awakening as God's work, and many others, the "Old Lights," rejected it as overenthusiastic and irrational.

The revivals had a socially democratizing effect. The spiritual experience of the common person was often prioritized over the minister's hierarchical authority; women and ethnic minorities had a personalized voice in the once-restricted public square. Subjective understanding began to challenge doctrine* in the pursuit of truth.

This dramatic turn toward "heart religion" among 18th-c. Enlightenment Protestants led some to consider the Great Awakening as the archetypal mass media* event in the dawning age of Evangelicalism*.

CALEB J. D. MASKELL

Great Bible, the edition of the English Bible, based on the translation of Miles Coverdale, that was ordered to be used in every parish church in England (1539). **See also BIBLE TRANSLATIONS CLUSTER: ENGLISH TRANSLATIONS.**

Great Commandment, the twofold commandment of love for God (Deut 6:4) and love for neighbor (Lev 19:18) declared greater than all others by Jesus (Mark 12:28–34) and by the Jewish lawyer (Luke 10:27).

Great Commission, Jesus' command (Matt 28:19) to "go and make disciples of all nations, baptizing them in the name of the Father, the Son, and the Holy Spirit."

Great Entrance, in the eucharistic* liturgy of the Eastern* churches, the solemn procession in which the bread and wine are carried to the altar*.

Great Schism, a term that refers to two different schisms: the schism of 1054 and the schism of 1378–1417.

"The Great Schism of 1054" refers to the break between the Eastern* and Western* churches, usually said to have occurred when

Pope Leo IX and Patriarch Michael Cerularius excommunicated each other. Many factors contributed to the growing alienation between the two groups: divergent theological understandings and liturgical practices, but also cultural gaps and political rivalries. The heated disputes in 1054 over the ecclesiastical calendar, the use of leavened or unleavened bread, or additions of the *Filioque** clause to the Nicene Creed, although liturgical and theological, reflect a fundamental split in the conception of the church* and of the ecclesiastical structure (see Filioque; cf. Orthodox Churches, Eastern, Cluster: Introductory Entries; Roman Catholicism Cluster: The Roman Catholic Church and Its Theology). The schism of 1054 was not regarded as final; in fact, the Crusades* were mounted at the request of, and for the benefit of, Christians in the East. But the sack of Constantinople (1204) increased Greek resentment toward the Latins, and this was a major factor in the failure of the reunion negotiated at the Council of Florence* (1439).

"The Great Schism of 1378–1417" refers to the period in the Western Church following the Babylonian* Captivity, when rival popes sat in Avignon and Rome and a third pope was elected at the Council of Pisa* (1409). The impasse was resolved at the Council of Constance* with the removal or resignation of the rival popes (1415) and the election of a new pope (1417). **See also CONCILIARISM.** EUGENE TESELLE

Greece. For most of its history, Christianity in Greece has been comparatively homogeneous and united despite historical vagaries.

Paul* brought Christianity to Greece (mid-1st c.), establishing communities in Philippi, Thessaloniki, and Corinth. Little is known of pre-Constantinian Christianity in Greece. Eusebius* preserves 2nd- to 3rd-c. correspondence between Corinthian church leaders and Rome and attests to the existence of communities in Athens and Crete. The 4th c. and following centuries provide evidence for the vibrancy and spread of Christianity. At the Council of Chalcedon* (451), 42 bishops from the provinces of Macedonia, Epirus Nova, Epirus Veta, Thessaly, Achaia, Crete, and the Greek islands were in attendance or represented. Important pilgrimage sites at Philippi, Corinth, and Thessaloniki attracted faithful from around the Mediterranean. The closing of the academy of Athens by Justinian (529) marks the final demise of the polytheistic Greek lifestyle. Non-Christian Slavs overran much of Greece (end of the 6th c.), although their cultural impact was limited to the north. Eighth-century Iconoclasm* resulted in the realignment of the Roman vicariate of Thessaloniki from its historical jurisdiction under Rome to the ecclesiastical authority of Constantinople. Thessaloniki produced the two missionary brothers Cyril* (Constantine) and Methodios (9th c.).

During the medieval period, Greece remained part of the Byzantine Empire. Important ecclesiastical and monastic buildings survive from this period: the church of Hagia Sophia (Thessaloniki), Hosios Loukas (Stiris), and the monastery of Daphne (outside Athens). The period from the 9th to the 11th c. witnessed a marked increase in monastic foundations, Mount Athos* being the most significant and lasting. The Great* Schism of 1054 between Rome and Constantinople along with the Crusades* provided Western rulers an opportunity for eastward expansion. The Fourth Crusade (1204) brought further western expansion and Roman Catholicism. The late medieval Byzantine city of Mistra (near the site of ancient Sparta) was a hub of political and ecclesiastical activity; Mistra's artistic and religious vibrancy is attested to by several churches along with their frescos.

By 1460, with the exception of a few islands, Greece was under Ottoman control, resulting in four centuries of stagnation and decline. Local Ottoman authorities extracted fees for many of the activities of the Christian community, especially for appointment to high ecclesiastical offices. The training and education of clergy were limited. A new category of martyrs* emerged, the "new martyrs," referring usually to Christians who had converted willingly or forcibly to Islam* but were martyred for returning to Christianity. The Orthodox hierarchy of Greece continued to be under the jurisdiction of the Ecumenical* Patriarchate of Constantinople, and absenteeism among local Greek bishops, who sought advancement in Constantinople, was common. The Orthodox Church remained the only viable institution among Greeks; through its daily, weekly, and yearly liturgical and festal cycle, it preserved religious, ethnic, and later national identity.

Greece's independence from the Ottomans (1821), opened a new chapter for Christianity. Calls for a church independent of the Ecumenical Patriarchate of Constantinople, the latter still under Ottoman authority, were realized, though not universally welcomed.

The Orthodox Church of Greece became closely tied to the nascent state. Early constitutions identified all Greek citizens as Orthodox Christian; today the constitution guarantees religious freedom but acknowledges the Orthodox Church as the "prevailing religion." During much of the 19th c., Roman Catholic communities flourished on many Greek islands. A sizable Muslim minority of Turkish ancestry resides in Thrace. The 1923 adoption of the Gregorian calendar* by the Church of Greece proved controversial. Resistance was strong and brutally repressed by the state. Initially, the Old Calendarists in Greece numbered perhaps 1 million. Today they constitute about 5% of those who identify themselves as Greek Orthodox.

Greek identity and Orthodox Christianity continued to be closely linked throughout Greece's modern history. In the last quarter of the 20th c., secular reforms (e.g. civil marriage and divorce by consent) reflected a shift away from this monolithic identification. Nonetheless, the Orthodox Church remains a strong force in the cultural, religious, and political life of Greece. **See also ORTHODOX CHURCHES, EASTERN, CLUSTER: IN GREECE.**

Statistics: Population (2000): 10.6 million (M). Christians, 10 M, 95% (Orthodox, 9.9 M; independents, 0.23 M; Roman Catholics, 0.06 M); Muslims, 0.35 M, 3.3%; nonreligious, 0.2 M, 2%. (Based on *World Christian Encyclopedia*, 2001.)

JAMES C. SKEDROS

Greek Koine. See KOINE.

Greek Orthodox Church. See ORTHODOX CHURCHES, EASTERN, CLUSTER: IN GREECE; ORTHODOX CHURCHES, EASTERN, CLUSTER: GREEK ORTHODOX CHURCH AND ITS THEOLOGY.

Greene, (Henry) Graham (1904–91), British novelist, essayist, playwright, and scriptwriter, who converted to Roman Catholicism (1925) and became one of the great 20th-c. Roman Catholic literary authors. A brilliant writer of political thrillers throughout his long career, he is most celebrated for his series of "Catholic" novels, *Brighton Rock* (1938), *The Power and the Glory* (1940), *The Heart of the Matter* (1948), and *The End of the Affair* (1951). These novels portray characters in extreme situations in which faith* and belief, doubt* and betrayal are set in the political and social upheavals of his time.

Major theological themes in his novels include the idea of "the sinner at the heart of Christianity" and God as the "Hound of Heaven" pursuing the errant soul. Greene focuses on the spiritual life of failed and sinful characters who eventually gain the privileged status of experiencing the "appalling strangeness of the mercy* of God."

Greene was deeply influenced by Newman*, and he was an astute reader of Catholic theology before, during, and after the Second Vatican* Council (1962–65). Critics often assume that Greene's late novels eschew Christian themes for political ones, but there is much evidence to suggest otherwise, especially in two novels, *The Honorary Consul* (1973) and *Monsignor Quixote* (1982), which reveal his full engagement with issues vital to Vatican II Catholicism and liberation theology. MARK BOSCO, SJ

Gregorian Calendar. See CALENDARS.

Gregorian Chant. See PLAINSONG.

Gregorian Sacramentary, the name given to several sacramentaries* (liturgical books) attributed to Pope Gregory* I (590–604). The oldest was sent by Pope Hadrian I to Charlemagne* (c790); only a copy (811/12) survives. Because it did not have services for parts of the church* year, it was augmented from French copies of the Gelasian* Sacramentary, possibly by Alcuin*. This compilation became the basis for the later Roman Missal.

Gregory I, Pope (c540–604), "Gregory the Great," theologian. Born into a wealthy senatorial family, he became prefect of Rome (573). He sold his estates, spent his wealth helping the poor, and founded six monasteries in Sicily and one in Rome, where he became a monk (c574). The pope made him one of the seven deacons of Rome, then apocrisarius at the emperor's court in Constantinople (c578); he returned to Rome (c585) as abbot of his monastery. He reluctantly became pope (590) when the Roman Church was largely responsible for public order during the fall of the Roman Empire. He made peace with the Lombard* invaders (592–93) and sent Augustine* of Canterbury as a missionary to England (597). By refusing to recognize the claim of the patriarch of Constantinople to the title of ecumenical* patriarch, he asserted papal primacy.

Gregory was the first to establish the norm of exegesis* according to the four senses: literal (or historical), allegorical, moral (or tropological), prophetic (or anagogical) – probably derived from John Cassian* (c360–435).

Gregory wrote *On Pastoral Care* to guide popes and bishops in keeping a balance between practical duties and spiritual lives. He preached several series of exegetical sermons in the Western patristic tradition. His *Moralia in Job*, a moral interpretation of Job, emerged from conversations with his fellow monks. In his *Dialogues* (authorship disputed), Gregory provided a biography of Benedict* of Nursia and a series of exemplary stories and apothegms from the tradition of monastic asceticism*, which he eagerly promoted. GILLIAN R. EVANS

Gregory the Illuminator (c260–c326/8). King Tiridates IV of Armenia* (298–330), like his benefactor, Emperor Diocletian*, persecuted the Christians. According to his "life" (by Agathangelos, c455), Gregory, a preacher of Parthian origin, was tortured and thrown into a deep pit for his refusal to worship the goddess Anahit. After a long confinement, to the amazement of all he was discovered alive; the king, hoping to be healed by the saintly man, released him. Gregory converted the king, urging him to destroy the idols*. Gregory, "the Illuminator of Armenia," was ordained a bishop in Caesarea (Cappadocia), baptized the king and his court, and evangelized the country, which became the first official Christian state (c314).
IGOR DORFMANN-LAZAREV

Gregory Nazianzen (c330–c390), one of the Cappadocians*. Son of the bishop of Nazianzus, he studied in Athens together with Basil* of Caesarea (and Julian* the Apostate). He and Basil compiled the *Philocalia*, excerpts from Origen's* writings.

His father ordained him against his will as a priest; Basil, as part of his anti-Arian* campaign, appointed him bishop of the small town of Sasima, but he refused to live there. He went to Constantinople (379) as a champion of the Nicene* doctrine, preaching in the church building of the Anastasis (a converted house), since the court of Valens had given all the basilicas to the Arians. He participated in the Council of Constantinople* but soon resigned and spent his time writing poetry and orations in an ornate Greek style. He is called "the Theologian" because of his five "theological orations" on the doctrine of the Trinity*; they are important for their emphasis on the crucial role of *relation* in the Trinity and their insistence on the full divinity of each person. Gregory's letters against Apollinarianism* were decisive in changing the course of thinking about Christology*; like Origen, he saw the humanity of Christ as linked to the Word through acts of mind, i.e. knowledge and love. EUGENE TESELLE

Gregory of Nyssa (c335–c395), one of the Cappadocians*. The younger brother of Macrina* and Basil* of Caesarea, Gregory was attracted by the revival of classical culture in Athens under Libanius; he married and became a teacher of rhetoric. As bishop of Caesara, Basil appointed Gregory to the See of Nyssa to counter Valens's Arian* policies.

When Basil died (379), Gregory inherited his brother's role. *On the Making of Man* demonstrates his interest in setting forth the consistency (*akolouthia*) of the biblical message, and develops his four-stage theory of the creation of human beings and their restoration through the Incarnation*, Redemption*, and Resurrection*. After Macrina's* death (380), he wrote her *Life*; he also placed in Macrina's mouth his work *On the Soul and Resurrection*. A leading figure at the Council of Constantinople* (381), Gregory issued his massive *Against Eunomius* to refute Arianism. His *Catechetical Oration* seeks to help catechists answer philosophical objections to the Incarnation.

After retreating from ecclesiastical politics (387–94), he produced spiritual writings, including 15 homilies on the Song* of Songs and the *Life of Moses*, which allegorizes the Exodus narrative (as Philo* and Origen* had done) as the ascent of the soul*, growing in virtue and rising to the "perfection" that consists in unending progress toward God, "straining ahead" (*epektasis*; Phil 3:13). EUGENE TESELLE

Gregory Palamas (c1296–1359), Greek monk, archbishop, theologian, defender of hesychasm*. Born in Constantinople, Palamas became a monk, went to Mount Athos* (c1318), fled to Thessaloniki to escape the Turks, but soon returned to Athos. He was consecrated archbishop of Thessaloniki (1347, during a civil war), was a captive of the Turks for one year (1354), and engaged in a dispute with a mullah. More than 60 sermons survive from this period.

Living in the Byzantine Empire, caught between the Turks' advance and increasing interest in the brilliant theological edifice of Western Scholasticism, Palamas was involved in a controversy with Barlaam*, a Greek monk from Calabria, initially over the *Filioque** (1337), then over the hesychasts' claim to behold the uncreated light of the Godhead through their practice of the Jesus* Prayer. The controversy divided Byzantine intellectual society. Palamas, opposed by Gregory Akindynos and others, was vindicated by the 1341, 1347, and 1351 synods in Constantinople. Palamas's defense of the hesychasts (*Apodeictic Treatises on the Procession of the Spirit; Triads in Defense of the*

Hesychasts) was based on the distinction between God's unknowable essence and God's energies, through which God is known. Such Palamism characterized the liveliest traditions of Orthodox theology in the 20th c. ANDREW LOUTH

Gregory VII, Pope (1073–85). Hildebrand, possibly an offspring of Jewish converts in the Pierleone family, a monk in Rome, became chaplain to Pope Gregory VI and went to Germany (1046), becoming acquainted with the "northern" or "imperial" reform movement. Upon returning to Rome (1049) he was a key adviser to reformer Leo IX and several other popes, who changed the reform from a lay to a clerical movement.

After Hildebrand became Pope Gregory, decrees were issued against simony* and Nicolaitism*, and against lay appointment and the investiture* of clerics. In Germany, Henry IV persuaded two synods of compliant bishops to declare Gregory not the pope; Gregory deposed Henry and freed his subjects from their oath of allegiance. Gregory called for a council in Augsburg in February 1077, and in January Henry stood dressed as a penitent before the gate of Matilda of Canossa's fortress, where Gregory was staying. Gregory, in releasing Henry from excommunication*, acted too quickly and mercifully. A counter-emperor was elected, and a three-year civil war devastated Germany. Henry besieged Rome; Gregory called on the Normans for aid, but they sacked the city and he died a few months later.

While some see Gregory as a power-mad despot, others appreciate his efforts to differentiate between church and state. His example taught people to criticize both clergy and monarchs, paving the way for revolutionary movements. The independence of the church was greatly enhanced by the universal requirement of clerical celibacy*, which loosened the ties between the church and the feudal* system and encouraged the clergy to devote their energies to the church rather than to offspring.

EUGENE TESELLE

Gregory Thaumaturgus (c213–c270). Born in Neocaesarea in Pontus, he studied with Origen*. He returned to his native city, was made bishop, and is said to have converted the entire city and region. The many legends about his miracles are the reason for his title "Wonderworker." He perhaps exerted his most notable influence on Macrina*, Basil* of Caesarea, and Gregory* of Nyssa through their grandmother, also named Macrina.

Gregory of Tours (538–94), bishop of Tours, author of *History of the Franks*, a compilation of earlier traditions and a detailed account of Gregory's own times. He also wrote a number of accounts of the miracles wrought by martyrs* and saints* (e.g. *Life of Saint Andrew*), enhancing the authority of the church and warning about the consequences of heresy* and immorality. The content of his writings vividly exhibits the differences between his day and that of classical Rome; his "late Latin" style is perhaps the manifestation of this dramatically changed setting.

Grimké, Sarah Moore, and Angelina Emily Grimké (later Weld), noted Quaker abolitionists and women's rights advocates, born into a prominent Charleston, South Carolina, slaveholding family. After moving to Philadelphia in 1821, Sarah (1792–1873) joined the Religious Society of Friends*; her more assertive sister, Angelina (1805–79), followed in 1828.

Having reacted against slavery* and the overly formal Presbyterian religion, the Grimké sisters were attracted to Quakerism, with its emphasis on equality. Sarah found especially appealing Quaker John Woolman's testimonies against slavery and his travels devoted to this cause. She lectured against slavery and wrote some of the first feminist* articles to appear in North America (1837). Angelina also addressed Southern women, speaking out against the evils of slavery. In 1838, Angelina testified before a legislative committee (in Massachusetts), becoming the first woman to do so; she won renown and much notoriety as an orator. Both sisters allied themselves with the most radical abolitionists.

Disowned by their meeting when Angelina married Theodore Dwight Weld (1838) in a non-Quaker wedding, they became itinerant speakers (addressing mixed race and gendered audiences) and writers. Retiring into private life, they played behind-the-scenes roles in the movement for women's rights. Their influence gave Quakerism further impetus to push social reform. H. LARRY INGLE

Groote, Geert (1340–84), Dutch reformer, founder of the Brethren* of the Common Life, or Devotio* Moderna. Born in Deventer, he studied in Paris and became a professor in Cologne. Turning away from worldliness (1374), he retired to a Carthusian* monastery and was influenced by Jan van Ruusbroeck*. Ordained a deacon but never a priest, he preached in the Diocese of Utrecht, gathering groups committed to the "common life," but also arousing discontent. Thomas* à Kempis wrote about Groote's life and compiled *The Imitation* of Christ*, possibly using materials from Groote.

Grosseteste, Robert (c1170–1253), bishop of Lincoln; a prominent figure in 13th-c. English intellectual life. Probably educated at Oxford and Paris, he wrote on astronomy and Aristotelian logic, and lectured on theology at Oxford (c1225–30). In 1230 he resigned in order to teach the new community of Franciscans* outside Oxford; this began a long association with leaders of both the Dominicans* and the Franciscans. In 1235 he became bishop of Lincoln, where he worked vigorously in the spheres of administration, reform, and preaching. With his knowledge of Greek, he translated a number of works in philosophy and theology (including the epistles of Ignatius*); he also continued his reflections on natural science. In the church*-and-state disputes of his time, Grosseteste opposed the efforts of Henry III to control ecclesiastical appointments, but he also rebuked the abuses of the curia in a direct address to Pope Innocent IV (1250). His influence was multifaceted: his pupils Adam Marsh and Bacon* continued in his spirit at Oxford; his translations from Greek stimulated scholastic* theology more broadly; and his writings, preserved at Oxford, encouraged Wyclif* in his later efforts to reform the church.

Grotius, Hugo (1583–1645), Dutch lawyer, historian, theologian, politician, diplomat; studied at Leiden (1594–97) and received an honorary doctorate of law from the University of Orléans (1598). He was imprisoned for participating in the Remonstrance* (1618), but escaped to Paris (c1621), where he remained in exile throughout his life and served as Queen Christina of Sweden's ambassador. Often called the "father of international law," Grotius is most famous for the legal work *De Jure Belli ac Pacis* (1625) and the theological work *De Veritate Religionis Christianae* (1627). An adherent of Arminianism*, Grotius argued against the Calvinist view that the church ought not to be subject to the authority of the state and the Calvinist doctrine of predestination* to salvation*, arguing instead that salvation, while predestined, was conditional on faith*. A tireless advocate of religious toleration and doctrinal unity in a time of religious conflict, Grotius argued that Scripture* should not be used as a divisive instrument in sectarian polemics, petitioned King James I of England to reunify the Christian churches under his headship, and called for the reconciliation of the Roman Catholic and Reformed Christian churches. Grotius's *Annotations* (to the OT and NT, 1641–50) were believed by many, including Spinoza*, to constitute a new form of Biblical criticism. RENÉE JEFFERY

Grundtvig, Nicolai Frederik Severin (1783–1872), a pastor, historian, poet, and politician, who became a modern father of church and nation when Denmark* was transformed from a feudal* society to a democracy. Five hundred of his songs and hymns are still used. Strongly trinitarian* he emphasized a creation* theology influential in Scandinavia. Partly influenced by romanticism*, he emphasized the importance for Christians of politics*, culture*, myths*, and local history. He initiated the Folk High School, a boarding school for adults; although it did not grant degrees, it promoted cultural consciousness, contextual* theology, and peoples' participation in local society building, and was emulated around the world. HANS RAUN IVERSEN

Guadeloupe. In his account of religious life in the 17th-c. Caribbean, Father Jean-Baptiste Labat (1663–1738) noted that blacks enthusiastically received Christianity, baptism, confessions, and Communion, while remaining attached "to the sorcery of their African countries." Morning and evening prayers, led by elders or taskmasters, were integral parts of the slaves' lives on sugar plantations or in factories. Evangelization was a fundamental part of the slavery* system, which was further regulated by the 1685 Black Code (see Haiti).

In the 18th c., Roman Catholic missionaries often complained that colonial masters did not see to the slaves' religious instruction. Indeed, the masters' primary concern was to hold onto their absolute power over slaves. Thus they resisted missionaries, especially Jesuits, whom they deemed too close to the slaves, possibly inciting them to revolt. Official regulations (sent by Louis XVI, 1777) emphasized that missionaries should be exclusively concerned with "public order, the masters' interest, and the salvation of souls*" (and thus not with the slaves' physical, social, and economic needs). In fact, the slaves themselves organized revolts, especially in Grande Terre (Eastern Guadeloupe) and sometimes attacked plantations. In 1794 they gained liberty for all, as proclaimed by the French Convention. But Napoleon reestablished slavery (1802) and the racial hierarchy prescribed by the Black Code.

Before the official abolition of slavery (1848), slaves often deserted plantations and factories. Fr. Dugoujon, despite the traditionally prudent position of the Roman Catholic Church, supported slaves' revolts and followed the abolitionist Victor Schoelcher (1804–1893) and his republican call for the equality of all citizens, including blacks in the Caribbean. By the end of the 19th c., defying the Church, blacks and mulattos embraced the republican ideals and secularization* (strict separation of state and religion), including the secularization of public education; religious orders were barred from public schools. Yet in the 1970s, some priests (including Fr. Céleste) associated with farmworkers called for a greater involvement of the Church in social problems.

Many Guadeloupians feel uneasy in a church culturally tied to the metropolis. Thus some participate in Hindu* worship (transplanted in Guadeloupe by laborers brought from India in the mid-19th c.); others are turning to new religious movements – Jehovah's* Witnesses, Mahikari (from Japan), Mormons*, Seventh*-day Adventists, and Charismatic* groups. Roman Catholic Guadeloupians reappropriate or critically reread their African religious inheritance in their devotions to the saints* in religious Catholic associations (see Ancestor Veneration and Christianity Cluster: In Latin America and the Caribbean), e.g. receiving "gifts" from the saints through the intermediary of a *gadèdzafè* (a holy person in the African tradition).

Statistics: Population (2000): 456,000 (90% black or mulatto). Christians, 95.3% (Roman Catholics, 95%; Protestants, 4.9%; marginal Christians, 4.3%; independents, 0.3% [doubly affiliated, 9.2%]); nonreligious, 3.1%; Hindus, 0.5%; other religionists, 1.1%. (Based on *World Christian Encyclopedia*, 2001.)

LAËNNEC HURBON

Guadalupe, Virgin of. See MARY, THE VIRGIN, CLUSTER: OF GUADALUPE.

Guatemala is the most populous and ethnically diverse of the Central America republics. The Maya, comprising more than 20 linguistic groups, make up more than half of the population. Almost all Guatemalans consider themselves Christians. The ways they live their faith have resulted from complex processes of translation and adaptation during more than 500 years.

After the Spanish* conquistadors arrived (1524), Franciscans* and Dominicans* settled the Maya in "Indian towns." Confraternities (*cofradías*) of Maya organized day-to-day religious life, incorporating what they understood of Roman Catholicism into their worldview. The *cofradías* venerated the saints*, sacred figures that took on complicated identities as histories and legends brought from Europe were blended with local ideas. Visiting priests offered access to the sacraments of the Roman Catholic Church. Traditional Mayan ritual leaders, both men and women, also continued their own practices, often in secret. Catholic elements were incorporated into these rituals. This process produced the Mayan Catholic beliefs and practices known in Guatemala as *costumbre* and still observed in many highland villages.

Guatemala's independence from Spain (1821) weakened the institutional structure of the Roman Catholic Church. Freedom of worship was first sanctioned in anticlerical legislation (1824). The Liberal government seized power (1871) and implemented measures to greatly restrict the influence of the Church. This government permitted the presence of organized Protestantism*. Presbyterians* from the USA arrived first (1882), immediately opening a school at the government's request and initiating efforts to attract converts.

The Central American Mission (CAM), a conservative Evangelical faith mission (claiming inerrancy* of Scripture, Dispensationalism*, and fundamentalism*) founded by Cyrus Scofield, arrived in 1899, soon followed by Nazarenes* (1901), Quakers* (1902), and the Primitive Methodists* (1914). Almost immediately Guatemalan preachers broke away from missionary tutelage and established independent churches. Yet in the early 20th c., it was the Dispensationalist theology of the CAM that set the tone for Guatemalan Protestantism.

Pentecostalism* appeared in Guatemala in the 1910s. The largest classical Pentecostal denominations are the Church* of God (Cleveland, Tennessee) and the Assemblies* of God (1930s). Guatemalans soon started their own Pentecostal churches; the Church of God of Prophecy (1941) and the Prince of Peace Church (1955) are the most prominent.

In the 1940s, Catholic* Action was promoted by the bishops as a way of purifying and modernizing the Roman Catholicism of the Maya. Catholic Action relied on the training of lay catechists, who often clashed with the traditional leadership of the *cofradías*. With the influx of foreign priests and women religious (from the 1950s), Catholic Action also became a vehicle for community organizing among the Maya.

Guatemala's brief experiment with democracy, beginning in 1944, was brought to an abrupt end by a CIA-sponsored coup (1954). The ensuing military governments became more and more repressive. By the late 1970s, Mayan communities and Catholic Action activists were especially targeted by the army. The Roman Catholic bishops began to speak out in defense of human* rights. During this time, the Protestant groups grew (peaking c1980). A new form of Protestantism emerged; several Guatemalan preachers founded independent Charismatic* (neo-Pentecostal) churches, calling on adherents to embrace a gospel of prosperity*. Four of the largest independent Charismatic megachurches in Guatemala City are the Fraternidad de Dios (1978), El Shaddai (1983), Familia de Dios (1990), and Casa de Dios (1994). With their control of Evangelical telebroadcasting and media*, these groups set the tone for Protestant practice and understanding in the cities and beyond.

The peace accords that brought an end to the internal conflict were signed in 1996 in the context of increasing self-assertion by many Maya of their cultural rights. Mayan religious practice emerged in the public sphere, and many began asking openly how ancient Mayan spirituality and Christianity can be related to one another.

Christian belief and practice in Guatemala continue to diversify. Approximately 25% of Guatemalans identify themselves as Protestants or Evangelicals, a percentage that has remained stable since the early 1980s. Most participate in charismatic forms of worship. Some groups, particularly the independent Charismatic churches, reject Mayan spirituality as demonic*. Other groups provide space for believers to affirm their Mayan cultural identity as they worship Jesus Christ. While 70% of Guatemalans identify themselves as Roman Catholic, a much smaller number participate actively in one of the several options now available to Roman Catholic believers. Catholic Action remains a force in some Mayan communities. The Charismatic* renewal (from 1970s) allows those with charismatic experiences to remain within the Roman Catholic Church. In the early 21st c., many pastoral agents have embraced models of inculturation*, incorporating elements of Mayan culture into the liturgy and encouraging Mayan men and women to enter religious vocations.

Statistics: Population (2000): 11.4 million (M). Christians, 11.1 M, 97.7% (Roman Catholics, 9.6 M; mainline and independent Protestants, 2.5 M). Practitioners of Mayan traditional religions might also be members of a church. (Based on *World Christian Encyclopedia*, 2001.)

KARLA ANN KOLL

Gunpowder Plot (1605), failed attempt to blow up the houses of Parliament and to kill King James* I of England, in the hope that Roman Catholics could seize power. It resulted in increased anti-Catholic feelings.

Gutenberg, Johann (c1396–1468), first European to print with movable type (separate letters cast in molds). The first book he printed was the Bible, although the dates are uncertain and he never listed himself as the publisher. He lived in Strasbourg for some years, but his famous work was done in Mainz, beginning with a Psalter (1457) and then the entire Bible (before 1461).

Guyana. Berbice and the United Colony of Demerara and Essequibo were unified as British Guiana (1831), which later became the independent Republic of Guyana (1966). The population became very mixed as a result of the turbulent early history of the Guiana colonization. Native Americans are only 7% of the population. Early settlers included Dutch, English, French, Germans, and Sephardic Jews; later, slaves from different African regions were imported for the plantation economy. During the 19th c., following the abolition of slavery (1834), a large number of East Indians (from India; today 50% of the population) were brought to replace slaves (today, 36% are of African origin).

The mission of the Moravian* Church (1738) was followed by Congregationalist* (1808), Anglican (1826), Presbyterian (1818), and Roman Catholic (Apostolic Vicariate, 1837) missions. The churches regularly denounced human rights violations. Thus a slave uprising in 1823 led to the imprisonment of Rev. J. Smith, the Congregationalist minister of Demerara, who died in jail (and became known as the Demerara martyr). Father Dark, a Jesuit priest, was murdered by the Guyanese dictator F. Burnham (ruled 1964–87). In the 1970s–1980s, the ecumenical Guyanese Council of Churches played an active role in denouncing the violation of human* rights by this repressive government.

Hinduism* took firm roots in Guyana through the Indian immigrants, of whom a small percentage were Muslims and established Islamic communities. Presbyterians were successful in converting East Indians to Christianity, their mission becoming like an Indian church. The White-Robed Army (Jordanite) Movement originated in 1895 in Guyana; predominantly Afro-Guyanese, it is a Millennialist* movement characterized by its anticipation of the Last Day, "possession" by the Holy* Spirit, and "African" ideas and practices.

Statistics: Population (2000): 861,000. Christians, 440,000, 51.0% (Protestants, 170,000; Roman Catholics, 87,000; Anglicans, 77,000; independents, 27,000); Hindus, 280,000, 32.5%; Muslims, 70,000, 8.1%; native religionists, 39,000, 4.5%. (Based on *World Christian Encyclopedia*, 2001.)

ARMANDO LAMPE

Guyard, Marie (1599–1672), a founder of New France, was a mystic known as Marie de l'Incarnation. She joined the order of the Ursulines after being widowed in France and went to Canada* in 1639. Her spiritual works included her lectures given to nurses under her authority and her correspondence, particularly with her son, a Cistercian* monk. Combining contemplation* with action, her spirituality is filled with confidence and trust in the love of the Lord, contributing to her personal liberty, since as a lover, "He seeks to do the will of the one he loves."

RAYMOND LEMIEUX

Guyon, Jeanne Bouvier de la Mothe (1648–1717), French mystic and lay teacher. She experienced apophatic* mysticism* (contemplative* prayer to the highest form of divine union). Influenced by Francis* de Sales and Jane* de Chantal, John* of the Cross and Teresa* of Ávila, Madame Guyon emphasized both interior prayer and absorption of the individual will into the divine will, with ensuing peace, plenitude, and pure love. In *Short and Easy Method of Prayer* (*Moyen Court*) (1685), she taught that interior prayer is available to all, that reliance on the intellect inhibits spirituality, and that clergy should preach the way of simplicity of the Gospels. With a sense of apostolic mission, she was in Savoy, Piedmont, and Grenoble, and then in Paris as a spiritual guide to a devout court aristocrat. She influenced Fénelon* and the school at Saint Cyr, founded by Madame de Maintenon, wife of Louis XIV, who, together with Bossuet*, eventually opposed her. When the pope condemned Molinos* for Quietism*, Madame Guyon was examined by clergy (1694) and signed an act of submission. Meanwhile, Fénelon and Bossuet engaged in their famous public debate about pure love and "passive" mysticism (Quietism). Madame Guyon was interned (1696), imprisoned in the Bastille (1698), and eventually released (1703, after Bossuet's death). She lived under house arrest, teaching devotees, including Protestants. Her 40-volume collected works include a spiritual commentary on the Bible.

PATRICIA A. WARD

Gypsies, Charismatic Movement among. The history of Gypsy populations has been a history of discrimination and rejection. The worldwide Charismatic Movement among Gypsies is most unusual. With more than 600,000 members, it traces its roots to the ministry of the French Pentecostal *gadjo* (non-Gypsy) pastor Clément Le Cossec (1921–2001), founder of the Evangelical Gypsy Mission of France (or "Life and Light Mission"). Started in the early 1950s in Brittany, this mission was part of the French Assemblies* of God until 1968. Many of its doctrines and practices remain classical Pentecostal*. In 1975, for sociological and ecumenical reasons, it became a member of the French Protestant Federation. Rapid growth brought Pentecostal/Charismatic spirituality among Gypsies throughout Europe, North America, and Asia. An International Gypsy Committee (formed in 1965) convened a first world congress with delegates from 14 countries in 1971. With a strong emphasis on conversion* and healing*, evangelism, church planting, leadership training, musical discourse, and social justice (more than 30 children's homes in India), the Charismatic Movement among Gypsies gives a new sense of personal belonging and acceptance to people who have been and continue to be treated as second-class citizens because of a lifestyle that conflicts with the *habitus* of sedentary life.

RAYMOND PFISTER

Habakkuk, Book of, one of the Minor Prophets, opens with a dialogue between God and the prophet about God's apparent indifference to the evil* inflicted on righteous people, a charge that God denies (1:2–2:5). The book continues with a series of woes pronounced on those who do evil (2:6–20) and concludes with a lament, invoking God to save God's people again, as God had in the past (3:1–19).

Habakkuk was a prophet in Judah, perhaps even Jerusalem, who flourished during the early days of the neo-Babylonian period, from c608 (before the fall of Assyria to Babylon in 605) to 598 (when Babylon first attacked Jerusalem).

The book employs three main traditions: (1) justice*, which requires fair and even generous treatment of the poor; (2) the Day of the Lord (YHWH), the day God (YHWH) will punish God's enemies, in particular those who did not treat the poor* mercifully; and (3) the hymnic tradition, which in this case praises God for the past deliverance of faithful believers and implores another deliverance.

Habakkuk uses the tradition concerning the Day of the Lord to predict God's judgment* and punishment of sinners, especially the Babylonians. At the same time, Habakkuk promises salvation* to the righteous among the Judeans.

Habakkuk extols God as holy, in this case not simply as the One who is majestically above sin and condemns it, but as the One who promises to deliver and vindicate innocent sufferers and those steadfast in their trust of God. The justice of God demands God's protection of the innocent. PAUL L. REDDITT

Habit, a garment, specifically the distinguishing dress of persons in the religious* life.

Hades (Gk for the place of the departed; used in LXX* as a translation of the Heb *Sheol**), in the NT and the Apostles'* Creed, the abode or state of the dead before the Last Judgment*, sometimes a hell*-like place of punishment.

Hadewijch is a woman's name associated with a mid-13th-c. collection of mystic* texts probably written near Brussels or Antwerp. Both the Flemish mystics Jan van Ruusbroec* and Jan van Leeuwen knew these texts and thought highly of a woman they referred to as Hadewijch. Nothing is known for certain about her life, but it is thought that she may have been a Beguine*. Hadewijch's writing focuses on the relationship between the soul* and God. Her chosen name for God is Minne, "Love," a feminine noun in Dutch, so she refers to God using feminine pronouns and adjectives. Using the conventions of courtly love poetry, she speaks of herself as the humble lover-knight and God as the demanding, fickle lady. Her writing appears to be intensely personal, but it has didactic rather than cathartic intent. The five Hadewijch manuscripts are closely related and contain some or all of the following texts: 45 poems in stanzas, 32 letters, 14 visions, 16 poems in mixed forms (or epistolary poems), 8 other poems, and a short prose text. The authorship of some of these texts has been debated, but as a collection they provide us with a vivid picture of a particular form of mystic* spirituality. **See also BEGUINE SPIRITUALITY.**

SASKIA MURK JANSEN

Hagar, the Egyptian maid of Sarah, herself the barren wife of Abraham. Sarah gave Hagar to Abraham to bear a child. When rivalry developed between the women, Hagar fled to the wilderness, only to return at God's command. Later Sarah, having become a mother, expelled Hagar and her child (Gen 16, 21). Judaism* vacillates between denouncing Hagar and claiming her as a prototype of the Hebrew slaves. The Christian Paul allegorizes her as Mount Sinai "bearing children for slavery" (Gal 4:21–26). The Islamic* tradition exalts her as the mother of the Arabs and the matriarch of monotheism.

PHYLLIS TRIBLE

Haggadah (Heb "narrative"), in rabbinic Judaism, sermon-like interpretations of biblical texts and story-like illustrations and expansions in a moralizing or edifying (at times mystical or apocalyptic) mode, found especially in midrash* (as contrasted with halakhah*, especially in Mishnah and Talmud). Much use of Scripture in the NT is haggadah-like. The Passover haggadah are the readings that accompany the Passover* meal.

Haggai, Book of, one of the Minor Prophets, blames drought and deprivation on the people's failure to rebuild the Temple after their return from exile, urges the reconstruction of God's house, the seat of YHWH's life-giving presence (1:4–11), and anticipates both renewed prosperity (2:6–9) and the restoration of Davidic (messianic*) kingship (2:23).

Haggai's prophecy is divided into five precisely dated sections (1:1–11; 1:12–15a; 1:15b–2:9; 2:10–19; 2:20–23). He was active for four months during the reign of the Persian king Darius I in 520 BCE, when Zerubbabel was governor and Joshua was high priest (Ezra 5:1–2).

Like other prophets*, Haggai addresses the connection between sin* and judgment*, and emphasizes that a responsive turning to God elicits God's turning to the community with blessing (2:16–19) rather than curse. For Haggai, the repercussions of the restoration of the Temple echo beyond Israel (2:19) to affect world events, as seen in God's "shaking" heaven and earth and overturning "the throne of kingdoms" (2:21–22). The prophet's vision suggests that Judah will be independent once again, ruled by Zerubbabel, not just the current governor, but YHWH's chosen one, a descendant of King David (2:23). Indeed, he is the "signet," the medium through which God's authority will be exercised.

Early church fathers emphasized typological* connections with Zerubbabel, e.g. pointing to Christ and his signet, reflecting Christ's authority and power as king. More generally, however, Haggai reminds both Jews and Christians of the transformative power of God's presence, not just in the eschatological future, but in the contemporary life of both communities.

BETH GLAZIER-MCDONALD

Hagiographa. See WRITINGS.

Hagiography. The writing of lives of the saints*. The form and content of the lives were originally influenced by Hellenistic novels, the NT Apocrypha*, and panegyrics of the philosophers.

Hail Mary (Lat *Ave Maria*), a prayer to Mary* based on the salutations of Gabriel and Elizabeth (Luke 1:28, 42): "Hail Mary, full of grace, the Lord is with thee. Blessed art thou amongst women and blessed is the fruit of thy womb, Jesus. Holy Mary, Mother of God, pray for us sinners, now and at the hour of our death. Amen."

Haiti. On December 5, 1492, Columbus believed he had discovered India. In fact, he was in the presence of Tainos, Amerindians who had divided the island into five regions called *caciquats*, following their own well-developed political system and their own customs and religion. Their entire way of life was destroyed by the conquistadores, who carried out their own project: finding gold, enslaving the Tainos, and forcing them to convert to Christianity. Of about 1.5 million inhabitants in 1492, only 10,000 remained on the island in 1530; the Tainos had died not only from their inhumane treatment as slaves, but also because of epidemics brought from Europe.

A voice cried out in the wilderness, that of the Dominican* Antonio de Montesinos, followed by Bartolomé de las* Casas, who espoused the cause of the inhabitants of Hispaniola, becoming their defender. From the early 17th c., Jews and Protestants fleeing persecution in Europe brought a new wave of colonization to the island. As early as 1635, Cardinal Richelieu (King Louis XIII's prime minister) created the Compagnie des Cent-Associés (which became in 1664 Compagnie des Indes Occidentales), a colonizing trading company that brought slaves* from Africa to the island under the pretext that they would be baptized. In 1697, the island was divided into two countries; a French colony, Saint Domingue (which would become Haiti in 1804), and a Spanish colony (now the Dominican* Republic). Christianity presents itself, then, as an ideology that justifies the slavery of blacks. There were no official protests against slavery by the popes. In 1685, as a prolongation of the revocation of the Edict of Nantes*, the "Black Code" was enacted; for two centuries, it regulated slavery as an institution on a racist basis, proclaiming Roman Catholicism the only authorized religion in the island; Protestants and Jews had to either leave the island or hide. As for the slaves, they were not allowed to have a religion of their own; their "assemblies" were declared "illicit and rebellious" (Black Code, 3).

A general insurrection of the slaves on the night of August 22, 1791, in the northern part of the country was probably preceded by clandestine Vodou* meetings. A majority of the missionary clergy supported the rebels. Toussaint-Louverture became the leader, who organized and consolidated the final liberation of the slaves. He sent for a dozen priests authorized under the Civil Constitution of the Clergy, but Napoleon sent 30,000 troops to reestablish colonial status and slavery. Following a two-year revolutionary war, in which the slaves battled slavery and racism*, Haiti became the first independent state in the Americas after the United States. Nevertheless, the political leaders retained Roman Catholicism as the official religion; a concordat* was signed in 1860 between the Vatican and the Haitian state to promote the official recognition of Haiti's independence and its place among civilized nations.

With this goal in mind, the Catholic clergy who came from Brittany (France) worked intensely to eliminate Vodou, which they considered barbaric. The Catholic Church provided for all the education* and social services in the country. Yet there were conflicts between the Church and the state (1860–1900), as political leaders sought to use the Church for administrative (official record keeping, e.g. registry of baptisms, marriages, and deaths) and political purposes. In 1915 the clergy supported the US occupation because it helped them in their fight against Vodou*. Under the dictatorship of Duvalier (1957–1986), many priests and bishops and two entire congregations (those of the Spiritains of France and Jesuits* of Canada) were expelled. But in 1966, Duvalier signed an agreement with the Vatican aimed at establishing an "indigenous" episcopate; several Haitians were consecrated as bishops. The dictator hoped that, as a result, the clergy would be totally dedicated to his service. But inspired by Vatican* II, the Roman Catholic Church led the fight for human* rights. Furthermore, liturgical texts and hymns were translated into the Creole language; the language spoken by the entire population, which had so far been treated as inferior to the French language, was now recognized as a sacred language.

Following a free election (1991), Jean-Bertrand Aristide, a priest (formerly a Salesian) was elected president. However, the Roman Catholic Church was weakened by this direct involvement of one of its priests in a political role in a government, which was viewed by most as extremely disappointing. Since then there has been a sizable expansion of Protestantism in Haiti; the Charismatic* and Pentecostal* movements seem particularly apt at addressing the needs of numerous believers among the Haitian poor. Religious pluralism is now a fact of life. Thus the 1860 Concordat will have to be revised, and the separation of church and state normalized so as to guarantee tolerance and religious freedom.

Statistics: Population (2000): 8.2 million (M). Christians, 7.8 M, 95.8% (Roman Catholics, 6.5 M; Protestants, 1.4 M; independents, 430,000; Anglicans, 105,000); practitioners of Vodou and other traditional religions, 0.3 M, 2.5%; nonreligious, 0.1 M, 1.4%. (Based on *World Christian Encyclopedia*, 2001.) LAËNNEC HURBON

Halakhah (Heb "way to walk"), in rabbinic Judaism, the body of law regulating all aspects of life, including religious ritual; the Oral Torah as codified in Mishnah, then Talmud*. Halakic interpretations of Scripture and traditions have the purpose of guiding the Jewish community in all aspects of life (contrast with Haggadah).

Halfway Covenant, a form of partial church membership created by Puritans* in New England (late 17th c.) for people (usually offspring of members) who agreed to follow the creed and the rules of the church (the covenant) without claiming a spiritual experience of conversion. They could participate in the Lord's Supper, on the grounds that it was a "converting ordinance."

Hallel, psalms* of praise (Ps 113–18) recited as a unit at major Jewish festivals and at the Passover* meal.

Halloween (shortened form of "All Hallows Eve"), evening vigil (October 31) before All* Saints' Day. Often associated with tales of the dead and masquerading, it has assimilated local customs: lighting bonfires and preparing for the Celtic New Year, November 1.

Halo, circle of light around a person's head, used first in depictions of Greco-Roman deities, then of emperors, and adopted by Christians in depictions of Christ and the lamb, then of saints and angels.

Ham, youngest son of Noah*. Because he saw his father's nakedness, he incurred a curse on his own son Canaan* (to be "a slave of slaves," Gen 9:22–27) and, by implication, on all of his descendants, including Cush, Egypt, and Put (Gen 10:6). The so-called curse of Ham was used to justify the enslavement of Africans, first in the Islamic world, then among Europeans (from the 17th c.). In fact, the text (Gen 9:25–27) speaks of Canaan rather than Ham, and the original function of the curse was to justify the conquest of the land of Canaan.

Handel, George Frideric (1685–1759), German-English composer, organist. Although he never held a permanent appointment as a church musician, he wrote much sacred music for Reformed* worship (in Halle, c1702–4, though the music is now lost), Roman Catholic worship (in Rome, 1707–8), and Anglican worship (from c1711). During the 1730s, he developed the English oratorio*, the genre of *Messiah** and *Judas Maccabaeus*, which gained him lasting fame. His choral writing continued to inspire English church music until well into the 19th c. His sacred works include about 20 oratorios*, 1 passion*, 25 anthems*, 5 *Te** *Deum*s, 2 jubilates, cantatas*, motets*, and vesper* psalms. **See also MESSIAH, HANDEL'S.** TASSILO ERHARDT

Harnack, Adolf von (1851–1930), one of the most important German theologians between the time of Schleiermacher* and that of Barth*. Born in Dorpat, appointed professor of church history at the University of Berlin (1888), he was also significant in his role as the first president of the Kaiser Wilhelm Society for the Advancement of the Sciences, today's Max Planck Society.

Raised in a strict confessional Lutheran environment, Harnack specialized in the history of early Christianity, where he saw prefigured the main problems in the entire history of Christianity. Convinced early on that the Christian faith stood in need of systematic theological reformulation in the modern age, he strove to render Christianity historically plausible. His *History of Dogma* (1886–90) served this program by tracing the hellenization of Christianity since the 2nd c. and thus making the historically conditioned character of emerging Christian doctrine transparent (see Hellenistic Religious Traditions and Christianity's Self-Definition; Inculturation Cluster: Of Christianity in the Greco-Roman World). As a result, Harnack became one of the most controversial theologians of his time, as well as one of the most important international figures promoting a liberal and enlightened Protestantism (see Liberal Theology).

His popular *Essence of Christianity* (1900) offers a concise summary of his theology. Part 1 identifies three main characteristics of Jesus' proclamation against which Harnack gauges the subsequent development of Christianity: Jesus' preaching of the immanent Kingdom* of God; his message concerning the fatherhood of God* and the infinite value of the human soul*; and his demand for a higher righteousness* epitomized by the love command. He then relates this threefold gospel to the social, political, cultural, and legal orders as well as to the soon to emerge christological question. Part 2 pursues the development of the gospel through history, condensing the essential developments into three types: Greek Catholicism, Roman Catholicism, and Protestantism. Because it is based on Jesus' message of the unconditional worth of each person as a child of God, Protestantism is the religion of individual freedom*.

Harnack's multifaceted engagement with university, educational, social, and political questions served the aim of introducing these Protestant ideas and values into modern culture. After 1918 he supported the Weimar Republic politically and theologically because he believed it best capable of guaranteeing individual as well as Christian freedom.

CHRISTIAN NOTTMEIER
(trans. by BRENT SOCKNESS)

Hartshorne, Charles (1897–2000), inspired much Process* theology. He worked with Alfred North Whitehead at Harvard University, finding clarification of his own intuitions. Whereas Whitehead's major interests were mathematics and physics, Hartshorne focused on philosophy of religion and metaphysics. Much of Whitehead's influence on theology was mediated by its systematization and development in Hartshorne's teaching at the University of Chicago.

Hartshorne thought that traditional arguments for the existence of God could regain their cogency if the idea of God was reformulated in a process way. The traditional ontological argument fails because its idea of perfection is incoherent. Process theology clarifies how God is absolute and immutable, but also how God is affected by events in the world. It presents divine power as persuasive rather than coercive in a way that avoids divine responsibility for unnecessary evil*. It satisfies the human need to believe that our efforts are ultimately meaningful whatever their outcome in the course of time.

Hartshorne developed a Buddhist–Christian doctrine of the nonsubstantial self, which exists only in successive moments. Pure selfishness is impossible, because each occasion cares at least for its successor. Since each momentary self feels the feelings of previous selves, compassion (feeling with) is fundamental to the nature of things.

JOHN B. COBB, JR.

Haynes, Lemuel (1753–1833), African American minister (ordained 1785), Puritan*

controversialist, resident of Connecticut, Massachusetts, Vermont, and New York. Abandoned at birth, reared by white Presbyterians, Haynes became a staunch defender, against free-will Evangelicalism, of New Divinity theology, the "consistent Calvinism*" of Jonathan Edwards's* students. Haynes's important contribution was his argument that Calvin's* and Edwards's theological tradition was most fully, even most biblically, understood as anti-slavery and pro-black (in advance of the abolitionist era inspired by free*-will Evangelicalism). For Haynes, Edwards's benevolentist ethics, predestinarian and providentialist theology, and emphases on biblical covenants* and the beauty of God's design revealed their incommensurability with the slave trade and slavery*. JOHN SAILLANT

Healing. See HEALTH, HEALING, AND CHRISTIANITY CLUSTER.

HEALTH, HEALING, AND CHRISTIANITY CLUSTER

---

1) Theologies and Practices of Health and Healing

Health, Healing, and Christianity in Contemporary Western Theologies.

Philosophers and theologians have been debating the meaning of "health" ever since 1946, when the World Health Organization promulgated its definition of health as a state of "complete physical, mental, and social well-being." This definition was immediately criticized for being too broad, almost equivalent to notions of human happiness. As such, there could be no comparing the value of health with other values, no weighing of policy options if health includes everything from lack of illness to justice* and peace*, and no taking responsibility for ill health (since health had become an impossible ideal).

The core insight of the World Health Organization definition, however, is that health is not just the absence of injury, disease, or disability. It has something to do with the whole of ourselves. We do not just have bodies; we are embodied. Yet we are more than embodied. A Christian theological anthropology* understands human persons to be embodied spirits, inspirited bodies. Hence health of mind* (or soul*) and health of body* are not separate matters; each influences the other. Each has to do with the health of our "selves."

The Christian understanding of what it means to be a person includes a capacity for free* choice and a capacity for relationship. Because of these capacities, persons are transcendent – capable of self-determination, of introducing the "new" into the meaning of their lives and destinies, and of coming into relation with all that can be known and loved, reaching for relationships ultimately of communion with God and all persons in God (see Person, the Trinity, and the Self). Moreover, Christians understand a call to all persons to become what they are called to be (see Vocation), to live in solidarity with one another, and to heal and be healed by one another. Our histories, cultures, institutions, and education are all of concern.

An example of the relationship between bodily health and other dimensions of health can be found in the 20th- to 21st-c. AIDS pandemic, concentrated in the global South. The problem is not only one of clinical infection and disease. It is intertwined with issues of worldwide justice*: intractable poverty*, colonial* and postcolonial* confusion of cultures*, stigmatization of persons based on gender inequality, and coerced sexual* behavior. The development of contextual Christian theologies of health and healing has therefore required not only theological anthropologies* and theories of Christian love*, but also careful and comprehensive social analysis. **See also HOSPITALS AND HEALING PROGRAMS AS CHRISTIAN MINISTRY.** MARGARET A. FARLEY

Health, Healing, and Christianity in Eastern Orthodoxy. Orthodox Christian anthropology* teaches that the human being is a psychosomatic whole and emphasizes the importance of synergy and interdependence in the healing disciplines. Derived from the Hebraic tradition, the custom of holistic healing, or attending to emotional, spiritual, and physical needs, began with early Christians. In the 4th c., Byzantine institutions began to focus on curing the sick, integrating religious rituals with medical treatment. Byzantine hospitals were often built near churches: they were founded on the Byzantine belief that patients would regain full health when connected to God and the church community.

The ancient Greeks described medicine as "the most philanthropic of the sciences" (*philanthropotate ton epistemon*); faith expressed the instinctive quest of humans for wholeness through the divine. The importance of scientific engagement in Byzantine culture reflected the belief that reason* is a God-given faculty that empowers humans to develop innovative methods for holistic healing.

The practice of Byzantine healing stems from the understanding of Christ's mission as a healing ministry, delivering people from physical, mental, and spiritual suffering. Inextricably connected to experiences of the mystical*, Eastern Orthodox* theology requires openness to God's participation, or the God vision (*theoptia*), in one's life. **See also HOSPITALS AND HEALING PROGRAMS AS CHRISTIAN MINISTRY.**

JOHN T. CHIRBAN

Health, Healing, and Christianity in North American and European Pentecostal/Charismatic Movements. Healing in Pentecostalism implies that salvation* is not just a juridical solution to the guilt of sin* (see Atonement #2), but also deliverance from physical oppression (see Atonement #1). The spiritual gift of healing through prayer is thus regarded as having been won by Christ in his death and resurrection, and thus as part of the "apostolic faith*," along with conversion*, Spirit baptism*, and Christ's return to establish the Kingdom* of God on earth.

The relevance today of healing stories in the Bible is accepted without question. Pentecostal healing was anticipated in North American Holiness* and European Holiness/Pietist movements (e.g. Johann Blumhardt*, Dorothea Trudel, Charles Cullis, A. B. Simpson). Healing began to wane in both Europe and North America near the dawn of Pentecostalism (c1900), implying that Pentecostalism* grew initially as a haven for those who valued healing. The Pentecostal founder, William J. Seymour*, with his background in African* holistic spirituality and the Holiness* Movement, was predisposed to advocate healing as part of the gospel, calling it the "sanctification of the body." Healing became popular among all Pentecostal groups, although African Americans tended to set it within a broader vision of God's authoritative claim on the entire creation. After World War II, popular healers (e.g. Oral Roberts and T. L. Osborne) emerged in the USA, conducting mass healing campaigns internationally and building organizations comparable to US Pentecostal denominations in terms of resources, a legacy continued after 2000 by Benny Hinn (born in Israel) and the German evangelist Reinhard Bonnke. These ministries represented one of the major inspirations for the spread of Pentecostalism and the Charismatic Movement globally.

Tensions did arise over healing. German Protestants were condemned in the "Berlin Declaration" (1909) by the Evangelical Church for "many manifestations in common with spiritism*." Pentecostals in Italy and Spain considered Catholic healing stories involving saints or relics as superstitious*. German Lutheran Charismatic Arnold Bittlinger interpreted healing as an enhancement of natural healing processes rather than the typically Pentecostal supernatural intervention. Many Pentecostals in the USA reject the popular "health and wealth gospel" and the idea among "deliverance" ministries that genuine Christians can be demonically possessed.

The future challenge for North American and European Pentecostals will be to speak of extraordinary healing while also including God's healing hand within natural processes and human efforts to alleviate suffering. FRANK D. MACCHIA

2) A Sampling of Contextual Views and Practices

Health, Healing, and Christianity in Africa: African Traditional Practices. Health, wholeness, and holiness are fundamental values in traditional and Christian Africa. Influenced by the world-affirming and therapeutic African* Religion, and rooted in Jesus' practice during his ministry, African* Instituted Churches (AICS), the Charismatic* Movement, and priest-healers of mainline churches pay close attention to everyday human needs. In contemporary Africa, health and healing practices demonstrate the resilience of the African Religion's view of the universe.

A person in community, a composite of visible and invisible elements, lives in dynamic relationship with the visible and invisible worlds. Health implies the happy maintenance of a web of relationships with humans, spirits, and God, while sickness, particularly psychosomatic and serious illnesses, could result from a flaw in those relationships.

Sickness threatens life, the highest good. Healing reestablishes harmony through a process that discerns the cause(s) and prescribes holistic cures. Experts (*dibia, nganga, babalawo*, African traditional medical practitioners), empowered by tutelary spirits to penetrate the forces of the night, wrestle from nature hidden curative potential and mystically assail all enemies of life. They integrate cosmic, social, psychological, religious, and pharmaceutical aspects of African life and world (the *Lebenswelt* of phenomenology) into integral health care.

With the declining number of practitioners of African Religion, Christian prophets, visionaries, and pastors or priest-healers of AICs, and of African Charismatic, Pentecostal, and mainline churches, have a commanding influence. As Jesus' disciples, they heal by prayer, discern causes of illnesses, impose the confession of sins and fasting, and recommend rituals or prayers. Empowered by the Holy Spirit, they struggle against all human and spiritual enemies of life; thus they exorcise* evil spirits and assail witchcraft* and sorcery. Holy water*, holy oil*, and candles replace medicinal herbs. Although medication is not totally excluded, ultimately God is the healer. Healing is never limited to the physical; in both African Religion and Christian practices, the ailment is cured, the evil cause is contained, and harmonious relationships in the community are reestablished.

ELOCHUKWU EUGENE UZUKWU, CSSP.

Health, Healing, and Christianity in Africa: Dealing with AIDS. In the African worldview, health is understood to entail harmonious relationships between the physical and spiritual worlds, among the living, and between the living and the environment. God*, ancestors*, and evil people are believed to be the source of harm and misfortunes that befall people and animals and the environment. Diviners are consulted to identify the cause of sickness or misfortunes and prescribe the best way of restoring harmony. Healing rituals are performed to restore the damaged relationships.

When mission* Christianity came to Africa, the majority of the missionaries prohibited their members from seeking out African healing methods and promoted the use of hospitals and clinics. Unfortunately, these institutions concentrate on physical healing without connecting sickness to spiritual causes, as in African and biblical healing. The rapid growth of most African* Instituted Churches and Charismatic* ministries can be attributed to the fact that they have sought to address the absence of spiritual healing in the mission churches. Fortunately, some mission churches now include healing in their services.

The high rate of HIV/AIDS in sub-Saharan Africa has been a challenge to all churches. The churches have come a long way in changing their attitude toward people living with HIV/AIDS. The Ecumenical HIV/AIDS Initiative in the Africa 2001 Action Plan is a positive example of an attempt to help the churches develop the competence they need to care for people with HIV/AIDS. The 2003 All* Africa Conference of Churches General Assembly HIV/AIDS Covenant is another example of churches pledging to deal with HIV/AIDS.

ISABEL APAWO PHIRI

Health, Healing, and Christianity in Africa: Spiritual Healing. Spiritual healing, the practice of casting out evil spirits (through "dry fasting," prayers, and the therapeutic reading of psalms) is practiced by African* traditional medicine men and women with spiritual powers that can deliver the afflicted from demonic* attacks.

In traditional West African society, people seek deliverance and wholeness by going to the homes of reputed medicine men or women and participating in pilgrimages to oracles. Diagnosis and the procurement of remedies were the central preoccupation of traditional health care deliverers. In African anthropology*, a person is considered to be both a visible and an invisible entity, experienced in physical, psychic, and mystical ways; illnesses can enter the person through the actions of sorcerers, witches*, and evil spirits*. Psychosomatic problems are usually given mystical, supernatural interpretations. Even today people are usually dissatisfied with Western medical explanations and patronize healing centers and redemption camps.

Spiritual healing as attested to by the earliest NT witnesses (e.g. Mark 1:27, 34; Acts 2:22) was inseparable from the proclamation of the gospel. Christ remains the model for all African Christian faith healers. They engage negative supernatural powers with potent words, psalms, holy water or oil, and the burning of colored candles. Ebullient Pentecostal*, Charismatic*, and Evangelical preachers, as well as lay "brothers" and "sisters" of the Roman Catholic Renewal Movement, are leading prophet-healers, performing their healing ministry when there is a demonstration of faith* in Jesus as Lord. Women leaders, prophetesses, and evangelists affirm Christ as "the only husband who conquers all principalities and powers."

Mainline Christian missions built hospitals and clinics for converts and healed the sick with ritual prayers and unction. But spiritual healings, especially as "deliverance," "Holy Ghost fire," and "spiritual warfare" against "territorial demons," came in the wake of the African* Instituted Churches (AICs) and the Pentecostal, Charismatic and Evangelical movements. Hundreds of prophet-healers, priest-healers, and exorcists* active in prayer houses, redemption camps, and crusade grounds see themselves as heirs of the gift of spiritual healing given by the Holy* Spirit. UKACHUKWU CHRIS MANUS

Health, Healing, and Christianity in Asia. Christians constitute c8% of Asia's 3.6 billion people. Amid poverty* and religious diversity, Christians understand health as multidimensional, addressing physical, mental, social, spiritual, and ecological needs.

For Asians the source of illness may be the body, the mind, the psyche, or the spirit; illness may be caused by persons, the environment, or an evil spirit*. Sickness could come from malnutrition as well as from social, economic, political systemic injustice. Capitalist globalization brings untold suffering to many.

Healing is diversely attributed to divine grace*, the patient's receptivity, a healer's spiritual development, and justice-based relations. Western colonization* reintroduced Christianity (15th–16th c.; see History of Christianity Cluster: In Asia) and condemned indigenous spirituality and its healing practices as "pagan*."

For Asian Christians, Jesus is the Christ*, God incarnate*, who saves and heals. He is a divine healer, as the great prophets proclaimed (Isa 65:17–23; Mic 6:8), ministering to all, especially the poor. He came so that all will have abundant life (John 10:10). Christian churches today provide healing ministries, such as prayer healing, counseling, visiting of the sick, anointing*, as well as hospitals and health clinics, and relief aid to tsunami survivors and to refugees*. Through interfaith dialogue*, religious violence is addressed.

Christians adopt healing practices like tai chi, aromatherapy, acupuncture, yoga, herbal cleansing, ayurvedic medicine (India), and healing by means of *prana*, or subtle energy. Pranic healing, popularized by Filipino-Chinese Master Choa Kok Sui and his books, makes use of the principle that "energy follows thought." This practice is based on both Asian traditions and biblical healing.

Filipino churchwomen combine tai chi with praying in order to relieve stress. They honor *babaylan*s (indigenous priestesses or healers). Nuns practice pranic healing with the poor. Some Korean Christian feminists combine prayers with Shamanism*. Chinese house* churches offer prayers for healing and herbal remedies. Pentecostal*/Charismatic* churches offer healing through divine invocation and healing touch.

The National Council of Churches in the Philippines established community-based health programs, as well as shelters for abused women and migrant workers. In the 1990s, faith-based groups, such as those in Hong* Kong, Thailand*, and India*, undertook HIV/AIDS ministries. Indigenous peoples of Asia had an impact on Christian consciousness of "earth care" and ecojustice (see Ecology and Christianity Cluster).

Because health care is unavailable to millions, health becomes a justice* issue. Erlinda Senturias, a Christian medical doctor from the Philippines*, writes, "Health can be achieved by changing structural injustice, promoting community involvement in health, and personal knowledge and practices that will contribute to health and healing." Healing ministry is participating in God's mission in a fragile world. Asian Christianity today promotes health and healing for all creation.

ELIZABETH S. TAPIA

Health, Healing, and Christianity in Australian Aboriginal Societies. To many Australian Aborigines, the biblical healing stories are still relevant; Aborigines consider prayer* to be an important component of the healing process, even if they call on the powers of traditional healers (*ngangkari, mabarn,* or *galka*). Traditionally, they attribute illness to a variety of causes: extreme heat or cold, spirit beings (*mamu*), humans (who cast spells or insert objects into the body), and the breaking of taboos. The healers' methods include massage, binding, rubbing with red ochre or other minerals, administering plant medicines, sucking, cauterizing, and enveloping with smoke.

Colonial settlement introduced new diseases, such as smallpox, measles, and tuberculosis, with devastating consequences. Recently, changes in diet and lifestyle (including substance abuse) have contributed to an increased incidence of diabetes, hypertension, cancers, and physical and mental disorders. Primary health care, once provided mostly by missions, is now accessed through community or general health services. While Aboriginal people utilize these services, they still seek assurance that the basic spiritual causes of their illnesses will be dealt with, seeing prayer as an important component of the healing process. As their traditional worldview (see Australian Aboriginal Traditions and Christianity) provided no precedents for dealing with the effects of introduced diseases and substances, they look to modern medical services and prayer to mediate healing in these situations.

WILLIAM H. EDWARDS

Health, Healing, and Christianity in Latin America. The impoverishment and marginalization of Latin American countries are major factors in the proliferation of sick people. Pentecostal* and Charismatic* churches, whose members are primarily from the poorest social classes, conceive of illness as a direct assault on people as children of God. Consequently, Pentecostals/Charismatics often seek explanations and solutions from the spiritual realm rather than from medical services – to which, at any rate, they have very limited access. In their quest, the Bible plays a central role. Generally, they interpret Jesus' healings as victories of life over death, of faith* over disbelief, of the Kingdom* of God over the kingdom of Satan*. They are signs of the coming Kingdom. Thus Pentecostals/Charismatics live their faith in an eschatological dimension.

Pentecostals/Charismatics closely associate health and salvation*. Health is a concrete manifestation of the coming final salvation, a proof that God accepts and loves them, and thus forgives their sins, blesses them by the presence of the Holy Spirit, and empower them for a renewed life.

A large part of the social and religious force of the Charismatic Movement resides in its therapeutic dimension, in its ability to provide a religious answer to health problems in social and economic situations that produce illness, and thus to offer a concrete and tangible salvation. The conviction that drives the Charismatics' quest for health is the certainty of God's faithfulness* and God's promise of health for all nations.

DANIEL CHIQUETE

Health, Healing, and Christianity in North America: African American Perspectives. Health pertains to the multiple, dynamic ways that African Americans relate to their bodies, minds, and emotions, and to God, as well as to their fitness and balance, for the sake of survival. For Emilie Townes, health, as a cultural production, relies on sociocultural constructs, biology, and environment. Healing involves curative, restorative, transformative processes that move one from illness to wholeness. In the African American Christian context, health is a gift, and people are the stewards. People are to care for themselves with proper diet and exercise, be conscious of systemic (political, social, and economic) oppression*, and live so that their awareness of evil* does not make them sick. The systemic oppression of African Americans has worn down their bodies, minds, and spirits with words and deeds that thwart health and deny wholeness. Personal and communal health and healing concern the social justice* ministry of Jesus Christ. Thus believers, under covenant* obedience, are to model and support the health and healing of others: to feed the hungry, give drink to the thirsty, and clothe the naked; help the blind see, the lame walk, and the deaf hear; raise the dead; and preach the good news to the poor (Matt 9:35, 11:5).

CHERYL A. KIRK-DUGGAN

Health, Healing, and Christianity in North America: Feminist Perspectives. Feminist* theorists have for a long time been concerned about approaches to ethics, particularly medical* ethics, that are dominated by a concern only for principles. Especially if principles are wielded primarily as a part of deductive patterns of reasoning, they can obscure the actual persons and their situations whose needs and possibilities must be respected. Hence among many feminists, including Christian feminist theorists, a strong interest has arisen in what has come to be called an "ethic of care" as contrasted with an "ethic of justice*." While an ethic of justice is judged to be concerned primarily with the logic of ethical principles, an ethic of care is concerned with people and relationships.

Nevertheless, many feminists are reluctant to eliminate principled analysis and argument altogether. Moreover, they see that "care," like love*, can be mistakenly focused and susceptible to distortion. Hence some Christian feminists advocate an ethical method that makes justice a normative measure of good and right caring. This approach ("principled care") is especially consonant with a Christian articulation of the command of love for one's neighbor. It offers the possibility of aiding responses to human needs across cultures and time, for it requires that the concrete reality of persons be the primary focus of ethical concern and active caring.

MARGARET A. FARLEY

Health, Healing, and Christianity in the Western World. Jesus' ministry uniquely combined the proclamation of the gospel with healing, as a sign of the Kingdom* of God; Jesus mandated his disciples to do likewise so that all might have "life, and have it abundantly" (John 10:10). Until the 19th c., however, the Christian ministry (except for charismatic* individuals) was shaped less by actual "healing" than by *caritas*, "caring" in Christ's name, supporting an unprecedented range of institutions for people in need, the sick in body and mind among others. While these institutions laid the foundation for the modern welfare state in the Western world, their various health care programs and social activities, it was only after medicine began to cure fatal diseases that Christians came to appreciate the healing mandate anew, this time generally stressing not so much the miraculous aspect of divine intervention as the divine provision for adequate medical care, proper nursing, and sensible counseling. Nonetheless, the church does not endorse the "wellness craze" so typical of affluent societies, but the quest for genuine life.

Spiritual healing – either healing by nonmaterial means or healing of things not physical (the spirit) – became of special interest only in the context of post-Enlightenment* rationalism* (late 16th c.) and has received increasing attention ever since. While distinct from "faith healing" in that it does not explicitly focus on faith, spiritual healing developed into something unique in Western Europe either by complementing established ways of healing with prayerful counseling or by competing with these established ways of healing for the sake of manifesting spiritual power, the power of the Holy* Spirit in particular. The advent of scientific medicine (19th c.) and of psychology and psychotherapy (20th c.), along with the growing realization of the limits of medicine's capacity to heal, made the church reconsider its healing ministry. The Church* of England took the lead in 1953 by appointing a commission to study the subject; other churches followed. However, there is still no unanimity regarding what spiritual healing is all about. Some hold it to be exclusivistic and not reconcilable with any other way of healing, while others maintain that it consists in consoling a troubled mind by bringing about inner peace, even if the physical ailment cannot be cured.

CHRISTOFFER H. GRUNDMANN

Heathen (from Old English), "not Christian or Jewish," equivalent to NT Greek *ethne* (nations, Gentiles*), a term used by Christians (as well as Jews and Muslims) for adherents of nonmonotheistic religions. **See also PAGAN, PAGANISM.**

Heaven, in the OT, the visible sky and the realms beyond it; the dwelling place of God*, the "most high" (Gen 14:20; Isa 57:15), who, however, cannot be contained even by the "heaven of heavens," to say nothing of any temple built by human beings (1 Kgs 8:27). In the NT, Jesus speaks of heaven as the throne of God (Matt 5:34) and lifts his eyes to heaven in prayer (Mark 6:41); he ascends into heaven (Acts 1:9–11), and from there he is to return (Matt 24:30). Consequently, the capitalized term "Heaven" is used as a metonymy for God – a way of referring to God without using God's name according to Jewish practices, e.g. Matthew's "Kingdom of Heaven" as equivalent to "Kingdom of God." Yet God is not spatial; worship is to be "in spirit and truth" (John 4:24; cf. Rom 12:1; John 4:24; Col 3:1–3). Thus, for many Christian traditions, God's dwelling is in the faithful (John 6:56, 14:17; Rom 8:9; 2 Cor 6:16; 1 John 4:14–16); Origen* and Augustine* interpreted heaven metaphorically as all those created spirits in whom God dwells.

In Christian eschatology*, heaven is understood to be the place (or the state) of the souls* of the faithful after death and of their bodies after their resurrection*. The emphasis is not on physical characteristics but on the beatitude* or happiness that comes from communion with God as "all in all" (1 Cor 15:28).

Hebrew Bible, an inclusive designation (although it also contains Aramaic) for what Jews call the Tanakh* and Christians call the Old* Testament.

Hebrews, Gospel According to the, a Jewish-Christian gospel, mentioned by Papias* and Hegesippus* and quoted by the Alexandrian theologians Clement*, Origen*, and Didymus*, then more liberally by Jerome* (although at times he confuses it with the Gospel of the Nazarenes*). The text may have been written in Greek in Alexandria (early 2nd c.). It was respected because of the legend (cf. Eusebius*) that the Alexandrian teacher Pantaenus brought it from India* as the original Hebrew version of the Gospel of Matthew*. Among the fragments, we find mention of the Holy* Spirit as the mother of Jesus (reflecting Semitic thinking, where the word for "spirit" is feminine) and an independent version of the story of the woman caught in adultery (John 8:3–11). Jesus' saying on "seeking and finding" has been expanded by recourse to wisdom traditions (Sir 6: 27–31) and by allusions to Platonic philosophy. Jesus' baptism still contains some traces of a prophetic Christology when the voice of the Spirit declares, "My Son, in all the prophets I was waiting for you. . . ." James, the Lord's brother, plays a key role alongside Jesus. The first appearance of the risen Lord is to James (modifying 1 Cor 15:7), thus legitimating him as head of the post-Easter (Jewish) community. **See also APOCRYPHA CLUSTER: APOCRYPHAL GOSPELS; EBIONITES, GOSPEL OF THE.** HANS-JOSEF KLAUCK

Hebrews, Letter to the, the longest argument in the NT*; self-identified as a "word of exhortation" (13:22). As a "letter," Hebrews presents a riddle. The author, destination, and background are unknown. The riddle vanishes if Hebrews' essential literary character – as a persuasive text (more sermon than letter), written by a gifted individual (60–100 CE) and directed to a general Christian audience – is taken seriously.

The author affirms the old covenant* as a valid revelation* of God, but one pointing forward to its fulfillment, now emerging in the new covenant (see Typology). Four scriptural arguments are constructed. Psalm 8 (2:5–18) asserts that humanity, though humbled for a season, is destined by God for glory, honor, and universal authority in its attachment to Jesus. Psalm 95 (4:1–13) reminds readers to seize now the opportunity to enter God's rest. Psalm 110 (7:11–25) shows that the Messiah* is of a prior priesthood (Melchizedek*, not Aaron*) and thus the legitimate prototype of the new order. Jeremiah 31 (8:1–13, 10:11–18) promises that a new covenant will deal more effectively with sin's* power, opening access to God for all through Jesus' sacrifice*. Hebrews also rehearses exemplary models of faith* and exhorts pilgrims to persevere in the journey of faith. Its central aim is pastoral*. While there may be reasons for spiritual sluggishness or drooping morale, God's people are summoned to a life of constant engagement, striving toward maturity as demanded and made possible by Jesus, "the pioneer and perfector" of faith (12:2). JON ISAAK

Hecker, Isaac (1819–88), a member of the Brook Farm Community (Massachusetts) and a participant in the Transcendental* Movement (1843), Hecker converted to Roman Catholicism (1844), became a Redemptorist priest (1849–57), then founded and became the religious superior (1858–88) of the Congregation of Missionary Priests of St. Paul the Apostle (the Paulists). As a Paulist, Hecker became a theological consultant and adviser to the Second Plenary Council of Baltimore (1866) and Vatican* I (1869–70). He tried to deepen Catholic spiritual life and win Protestants to Catholicism by publishing the *Catholic World* (starting in 1865) and establishing the Catholic Publication Society (1866). PATRICK W. CAREY

Hegel, Georg Wilhelm Friedrich (1770–1831), completed theological studies in Tübingen (1793); served as a lecturer in Jena (1801), a professor of philosophy in Heidelberg (1816), and a professor of philosophy in Berlin (1818), where he lectured on all the major topics of philosophy, including the philosophy of religion, until his death.

A product of two movements of the Enlightenment*, romanticism* and rationalism*, Hegel sought to reestablish a comprehensive knowledge of God, world, and humanity in light of the Kantian critique of the limits of theoretical reason. He did so by arguing that the structure and process of thinking itself connect the thinker with objective and ultimate reality. He described his position as one of *absolute idealism*, in contrast to Kant's* subjective idealism. Ideality is not something that is given outside of and apart from reality; rather ideality is the *truth** of the finite, of reality. "Absolute" connotes that which encompasses all relations within itself, including relations with the finite and empirical. God as the absolute idea releases or "absolves" the other to be other. Nature and finite spirit constitute the otherness of God, and they are necessary for the actualization of God as absolute spirit. Hegel's system is holistic, not monistic or dualistic.

Hegel's *Lectures on the Philosophy of Religion* (critical English ed., 1984–87) offers a speculative redescription of the Christian metanarrative, which is that of the Triune God unfolding. Narrative applies to the immanent as well as the economic or worldly Trinity;* thus process* and movement are introduced into divinity. The inward dialectic of the divine life (identity, difference, mediation; or Father, Son, Spirit) is outwardly reenacted in the creation, fall, redemption, and consummation of the world. God creates the world by a primordial judgment or "release" of otherness. Conflict and estrangement are a tragic by-product of a world of finite forces. But God redeems the world by making manifest the implicit unity of divinity and humanity; reconciliation appears in and as a concrete human being, Jesus Christ, through whose life and teaching the divine idea courses. The death of Christ is also the death* of God, and thereby death itself is overcome, absorbed into the divine life as a negated moment. Spirit* is the power to overcome evil* and death, and God's Spirit manifests itself in the formation of the community of faith, whose destiny is to serve not only itself but the world as the latter moves toward its consummation in freedom. Christianity is regarded as the "consummate religion," in contrast to the "determinate religions" that form the history of religion – a topic to which Hegel gave unprecedented attention in his lectures. This reconstruction of the main themes of Christian theology owes much to a heterodox trajectory that can be traced to Gnosticism*, Neoplatonism*, and German mysticism*, but it is set forth in a distinctly modern framework.

Controversy over Hegel's philosophy, and his philosophy of religion in particular, erupted after his death and continues to this day. His immediate followers split into left, right, and center parties. The left wing (David Friedrich Strauss*, Ludwig Feuerbach*, Bruno Bauer, and Karl Marx*) read his thought as implicitly pantheistic or atheistic, and Marx in particular converted it into a dialectical materialism that became the basis for an economic interpretation of history. The right wing (I. H. Fichte, C. H. Weisse, and Friedrich Schelling* in his late writings) sought to establish a pan-logistic theism or a "positive" philosophy of mythology. The middle Hegelians (Karl Daub, Philipp Marheineke, Karl Rosenkranz, and Ferdinand Christian Baur*) carried forward the agenda of a demythologizing* theology that affirms the Hegelian mediation of God, nature, and humanity in such a way that each retains its integrity.

Hegel has had an enormous impact in the realms of logic, ethics, politics, aesthetics, and philosophy of history* as well as the philosophy of religion*. Many recent philosophers (Emmanuel Levinas*, Jacques Derrida, Michel Foucault, Jürgen Habermas, and Paul Ricoeur*) imbibe deeply of Hegel even as they criticize his totalizing tendencies. Whether Hegel's social ontology, which is rooted in his unique conception of "spirit" (*Geist*), and his dialectical method, which is based on the principle of negation, deserve the epithet of "totalizing" is one of the contested issues in the ongoing controversy over his thought. Hegel's philosophy of religion provides resources for a critically liberal revisioning of Christian theology*, in contrast to the philosophical skepticism and religious fundamentalism* that often prevail today.

PETER C. HODGSON

Hegesippus (2nd c.), church historian, who drew up the "apostolic* succession lists" of the early bishops of Rome and other apostolic churches.

Hegesippus (Pseudo-), the spurious name of the author of a five-volume Latin history of Jerusalem's fall (70 CE), erroneously attributed to Hegesippus*, but composed c370 (possibly by Ambrose* of Milan or Evagrius* of Antioch). Perhaps inspired by Emperor Julian's failure to rebuild the Temple (363), "Hegesippus" sought the Christian truth in Jerusalem's fall: as divine punishment for the rejection and death of Jesus. Though acknowledging and borrowing much from Josephus's* *Judean War*, he dismissed that "partner in the treachery of the Jews" and removed much military and political detail, major speeches, and tragic and prophetic ethos. Competing with Josephus's *War* (in Latin translation), "Hegesippus's" influence appears in Christian theology and art. STEVE MASON

Heidegger, Martin (1889–1976), was raised a Roman Catholic, studied briefly for the Catholic priesthood (1909–11), and unsuccessfully sought a Catholic chair of philosophy (1915). He abandoned scholastic-dogmatic Catholicism in 1917.

As a young scholar, he read Schleiermacher*, Luther*, Kierkegaard*, and Barth*, but rejected dialectical* theology (*Gesamtausgabe*, 9, 162n). In the early 1920s at the University of Marburg, he taught courses on Paul* and Augustine*, and he delivered a lecture "Luther and Sin" at Bultmann's* Pauline seminar. His lecture "Phenomenology and Theology" (1927) mandated a strict separation between faith* and philosophy and between God* and being – a Lutheran position that he maintained throughout his career. In 1929 he declared that his book *Being and Time* (1927) made no argument for or against God's existence (*Gesamtausgabe*, 9, 159n), although privately he wrote that human existence "must remain open to divine grace" (*Briefwechsel Blochmann*, 32).

In the 1930s, Heidegger attacked Christian theology for being based on an untenable metaphysics*/ontotheology. Insofar as metaphysical Christianity relegated God to the status of highest entity, Heidegger saw it as a major source of contemporary nihilism (*Gesamtausgabe*, 65, 139–40). Before the God of the philosophers, he wrote, "one cannot fall to one's knees in awe." He claimed that his "god-less thinking, which abandons the philosophical God . . . is perhaps closer to the divine God. That means it is more open to Him than onto-theo-logy would like to admit" (*Gesamtausgabe*, 11, 77; see also Death of God Theology).

In a 1966 *Spiegel* interview, Heidegger declared, "At this point only a god can save us" (*Gesamtausgabe*, 15, 671). He made it clear, however, that this "god" was not the Jewish-Christian divinity but only the god of the poet: being as "the holy" in Hölderlin's nonmetaphysical sense (*Anstöße*, I [1954] 33). Heidegger's work has nothing to do with preparing for Christian revelation* and grace*. The "god" that Heidegger's philosophy awaits is simply "the possible arrival of world" (*Gesamtausgabe*, 79, 73–77), wherein world as the source of all meaning is at last recognized in its utter groundlessness. The arrival of such a world within the lives of human beings would constitute "the turn from the forgottenness of being to the protection of its presence." That event would also be the arrival of the "last god" (*Gesamtausgabe*, 65, 288–93), i.e. world as such, and with it the possibility of secular-philosophical salvation.

THOMAS SHEEHAN

Heidelberg Catechism, the Reformed* catechism* prepared at the command of the elector Frederick III by Zacharias Ursinus and Caspar Olevianus (1562). It is notable for its personal tone. The three parts deal with (1) human violation of the "law of God," i.e. the great* commandment of love*; (2) redemption* through Christ*, justification*, and sanctification*, and the sacraments*; and (3) gratitude, expressed by obeying the Ten* Commandments, understood as guidance (the "third use" of the Law*), as well as by prayer modeled on the Lord's* Prayer. Question 80 ("What difference is there between the Lord's supper and the popish mass?") was added by command of the elector in response to the final decrees of the Council of Trent* (1564). Long used by the Reformed churches in Germany* and the Netherlands*, it has also been added to the Book of Confessions of the Presbyterian Church in the USA (1967).

EUGENE TESELLE

Helena, (248–328), mother of Emperor Constantine*. Born in Drepanium, in Bithinium, Asia Minor, she married Constantius Chlorus in 270. He became Roman emperor of the West in 270 and abandoned her for dynastic reasons. When her son, Constantine (born 272), became emperor in 306 and was converted to Christianity (312), he restored her fortunes. She zealously supported Christians, and in old age she traveled extensively, visiting Jerusalem and eastern provinces of the Empire. She discovered the so-called true cross on what she claimed was the site of Golgotha and built the Church of the Holy Sepulchre in Jerusalem. LAVINIA BYRNE

Heliand, Old Saxon epic, commissioned by Louis* the Pious (c830); an example of inculturation*, depicting Christ as hero and liege lord, and the apostles as his courageous vassals. Despite its imperial commission, its point of view is Saxon, implicitly linking the Frankish Empire with Rome. **See also** FEUDAL SYSTEM.

Hell, place of eternal punishment for opponents of God*. Hell presupposes the judgment* of the dead, which preexisted Christianity in the Egyptian *Book of the Dead*, Plato's dialogues, the Eleusynian mysteries, Zoroastrianism, and, according to Josephus, among the Pharisees* and Essenes*. Infernal torments mentioned in the Bible include fire (Matt 25:41), fire and brimstone (Rev 20:10), worm and fire (Mark 9:43–49), and darkness (Matt 8:12; 2 Pet 2:4). The Apocalypse of Peter* (2nd c.) introduced punishments far more vivid than the biblical ones.

Opposition to an eternal, unchanging hell began early. Origen* claimed that divine punishment must be curative, and so could be neither physical nor eternal. The Vision of Paul retains the tortures in the Apocalypse of Peter*, but includes a descent of the heavenly* court into the pit of hell, where Christ* suspends torments on Sundays. Some medieval visions also mitigated hell's tortures so that, for centuries, purgatory* and hell overlapped. Scholastics* like William of Auxerre (1220s) debated whether one should pray for the damned. Caesarius of Heisterbach (c1225) claimed that angels* punish in purgatory* and demons* in hell. Dante* combined the physical and emotional reality of hell by saying, "Each one swathes himself in that which makes him burn" (*Inferno*, 26:48).

Though rejected in the West and condemned twice by Justinian*, Origen's* allegorical interpretation, "The fire by which each person is punished is proper to oneself" (*First Principles* 2. 10.4, cf. Isa 50:11), remained influential in the East. While skirting Origen's* belief in *apokatastasis* (restoration) and its corollary, reincarnation, the Greek* fathers also allegorized hell's torments. The Greek and Latin Bibles refer to both Tartarus (2 Pet 2:4) and Gehenna*, whereas the translation in the Old* Latin version and the Vulgate* of Hades as *infernus* (or "hell," rather than as the *inferi*, or "underworld") colored the afterlife differently in the West than the East. For example, Byzantine* iconography presents not the "descent into hell," but the *anastasis*, or "resurrection." Luther* compared the inner torment of a confused soul* (*Anfechtung*) to hell. In the *Psychopannychia of the Soul* (1534), Calvin* considered hell and its exile not a place, but a condition (p. 224b). This interpretation dramatizes the distinction between hell and damnation*. In 1999 Pope John* Paul II pronounced hell "the ultimate consequence of sin*," not a place, but a source of suffering* for the sinner. **See also DEATH, CHRISTIAN VIEWS OF, CLUSTER; ETERNITY; JUDGMENT.**

ALAN E. BERNSTEIN

Hellenistic Religious Traditions and Christianity's Self-Definition. "Christianity" (to use the word anachronistically) began as another 1st-c. Judaism, embroiled in many of the same controversies that preoccupied other forms of Judaism of the period (including those of the Pharisees*, Sadducees*, and Essenes*), e.g. the reimagination of Torah and Temple, kingship and sacrifice, the importance of circumcision, diet, calendar, and ethnicity. Christianity's self-definition over against Judaism and the wider Hellenistic world emerged as a question in different periods, locations, and circumstances, for individuals and groups far removed from the time, place, and issues that preoccupied Jesus or Paul. Those who struggled with self-definition were confronted with an astonishing variety of texts and traditions (see Apocrypha Cluster: Of the New Testament), a diversity that was a problem, not an answer, for defining "Christianity." They had to look elsewhere for arguments to forge a new sense of identity. Christian self-definition was and is an ongoing process of improvised differentiation and innovative negotiation. The categories "Christian," "Jewish," and "pagan" (as non-Christian and non-Jew) are neither stable nor essentially known entities, but social formations continuously engaged in self-re-creation.

In some of his letters (c50–60), Paul* warns new Gentile* recruits against the persistent dangers of their former religions. Drawing on existing Jewish polemics against "idolatry*" (e.g. Wis 13–15), Paul criticizes all religions other than his own as a "lie" (Rom 1:25), the debased worship of "images" resembling human beings and animals (Rom 1:23). Like other Hellenistic Jews, Paul linked the spiraling descent into immorality directly to idolatry (Rom 1:29–31). The line of demarcation still seems to be the simplistic "Israel vs. the nations" (read: "us vs. them"). Elsewhere Paul exhorts his recruits to "shun the worship of idols," because this is in fact the worship of demons*, not of God (1 Cor 10:14, 20–21). The belief that the gods of Greek religion and myth were demons likewise derives from Jewish polemic (1 Enoch 15:8–12, 19:1, 99:7; Jubilees 1:11, 22:17), but is also found in the contemporary philosophical critiques of popular religion (e.g. by Plutarch).

Paul* as envisioned by Luke in Acts* (c100–20) takes a more conciliatory approach in his speech on the Areopagus in Athens. Claiming to have seen an altar dedicated "to an unknown god," Paul declares, "What you worship as unknown, this I proclaim . . . , the God who made the world and everything in it does not live in shrines made by human hands" (Acts 17:23–24). All people have an obligation to seek this God, "for he is not far from each one of us" (17:27). Then Paul quotes the well-known line from the Stoic Aratus's poem *Phainomena*: "For we are indeed his [according to Aratus, Zeus's] offspring" (17:28). Rather than condemning people for willfully believing a lie (Rom 1:25), Paul in Acts declares that "God has overlooked past times of human ignorance, [and] now commands all people everywhere to repent" (17:30). A definition of "Christianity" emerges, constructed not in terms of inner-group polemics, but with a wider view of the 2nd-c. political, social, and religious world.

These few passages by their paucity underscore how little the NT is really interested in the question of Christian self-definition vis-à-vis Greek and Roman religion. But Justin* Martyr (mid-2nd c.) offered a more developed "history of religion." Drawing on the Greek philosophical critique of popular religion, Justin declares all religions apart from Christianity to be the invention of evil demons (*daimones*) who have masked themselves as "gods" in order to mislead and enslave humans. In their effort to counterfeit the "true religion," these demons are responsible for the apparent similarities that exist between Christianity and certain aspects of Greek cult and myth. But in the very anxious attempt to mark out boundaries and to envision a Christian virtual identity, Justin began laying the groundwork for the very categories of "Christianity" and "paganism" and for defining the divide that separates them. His immediate point is as much political as it is religious: Christians are indeed "atheists*," as they are accused of being, but only insofar as they refuse to participate in the cultic worship of demons. In this sense, they are like Socrates, who was similarly accused of "atheism" for trying to deliver humankind from the power of the demons by means of "true reason."

A more sophisticated attempt at Christian self-definition is found in the *Exhortation to the Greeks* of Clement* of Alexandria (c150–215), who presents a concise account of the origin and history of religion in seven stages, from primitive simplicity to present-day corruption. Clement's distinctive achievement is his attempt to explain religion* as a *human* phenomenon. The trope is one of decline and fall ("error"), set in sharp relief against the "true religion," Christianity; yet Clement acknowledges that the original natural affinity between humans and the divine has never been completely lost. Like Justin, Clement recognizes that a handful of Greeks (most notably Plato*) laid hold of the truth*, but they derived their knowledge from the Hebrews. Some of Clement's arguments appear in writers both before and after him, but none present as comprehensive and philosophically informed an account of the history of religion, until Eusebius.

Eusebius* of Caesarea's monumental *Preparation for the Gospel* (c314–18) is much more than a refutation of Porphyry's* *Against the Christians*; it attempts to provide a fully developed history of religion and a definitive statement about the place of Christianity in it (indeed, apart from it). The first five books lay out the history of religion under three main headings: the natural, the mythical, and the political. Again, it is a story of decline and fall, aided and abetted in its final phase by the increasing power of the demons. Eusebius even fixes a precise date for the "death of paganism": "in the time of [the emperor] Tiberius, when our savior [was] making his sojourn among men." Eusebius constructs both a different origin and a separate history for Christianity, tracing it back in an unbroken lineage to the "original" and "true" religion of the Hebrew patriarchs.

With the conversion of Constantine*, Eusebius's constructed history came to enjoy the status of imperial history and exercised its influence down to the modern period. Yet the artifice and artificiality of these projects of self-definition and social formation should be kept in mind. For grassroots Christianity, there was much more convergence of religious and cultural identities than would otherwise seem the case. For example, the Christian historian Sozomen reports that late-4th-c. Jews, Christians, and pagans were participating in a common religious festival at Mamre, the Palestinian site of the Abrahamic theophany*, until Constantine instructed the bishops to shut it down. **See also** INCULTURATION CLUSTER: OF CHRISTIANITY IN THE GRECO-ROMAN WORLD; POVERTY CLUSTER: AND THE EASTERN ORTHODOX CHURCH. A. J. DROGE

Hellenists, in Acts 6, Jews from the Diaspora*, a minority (among the "Hebrews," Aramaic-speaking Jews) in Jerusalem and probably in the early Christian community. One of them, Stephen, became the first martyr of the Christian movement, not because he followed Jesus but because of his radically "Hellenist" teachings, against the Temple, the Law, and the customs (the Oral Torah*) given by Moses. The Hellenists possibly were the pre-Pauline source of central motifs in Paul's teaching.

Helvetic Confession, First, adopted (1536) by the Reformed* churches in Switzerland*, but not by Constance or Strasbourg.

Helvetic Confession, Second, adopted (1566) at the request of Elector Frederick III of the Palatinate when called to defend himself before the *Reichstag* of the German Empire. To meet this emergency, Bullinger's* personal statement of faith (1561) was quickly revised and adopted by many Reformed churches. Moderate in tone, it emphasizes the authority of Scripture* in the church's government and reformation; predestination,* emphasizing trust in God's free and gracious election*; and the practical life of the church, worship*, church order, ministry, the sacraments, and marriage.

Helvidius (late 4th c.), Italian theologian known as a result of Jerome's* attack on him for denying the perpetual virginity of Mary* and saying that the "brothers" of Jesus were the natural sons of Joseph and Mary. This incident reflects the 4th-c. conflict between those who exalted virginity* and those who defended marriage*.

Hemmingsen, Niels (1513–1600), the leading Danish theologian of the late Reformation and early Lutheran orthodoxy. He was influenced by the Aristotelian and humanistic ideas of Melanchthon* during his studies in Wittenberg. He lost his official positions in 1579 because of the crypto-Calvinist* element in his teaching about the Eucharist*. He gained international renown from more than 100 books in Latin, dealing with issues concerning dogmatics, ethics* and nature, pastoral* theology, preaching*, and good morals of citizens. Outstanding among his works are *Enchiridion theologicum* (1557), *Syntagma institutionum* (1574), and *De lege naturae* (1562). **See also DENMARK.**

HANS RAUN IVERSEN

Henoticon (Act of Union; 482), the doctrinal declaration, written by Patriarch Acacius of Constantinople, issued by the emperor Zeno in an attempt to reunite the Miaphysites*/Monophysites* with the Church of Constantinople. While it condemned Eutyches* as well as Nestorius*, it interpreted the Council of Chalcedon* as purely disciplinary, making no reference to the question of the "natures" of Christ, anathematizing anyone who set forth a creed other than the Nicene* Creed (in fact, the Niceno*-Constantinopolitan Creed), "whether at Chalcedon or at any other synod." The *Henoticon* led to the Acacian* schism (482–519) between the Eastern and Western churches.

Henry IV (1050–1106), German king (1056–1105) and emperor of the Holy* Roman Empire (1084–1105), central figure in the investiture* controversy. Caught between the reforming zeal of Pope Gregory* VII aimed at separating church* and state and the desire of German bishops and nobles to continue traditional patterns according to which the bishops were appointed by the king, King Henry declared Gregory deposed (1076). The latter excommunicated Henry and released Henry's subjects from their oath of fealty. When Henry made a private peace with the pope at Canossa (1077), a counter-emperor was elected. Ultimately Henry was elected emperor (1084). Yet Henry's last years were plagued by rebellion, even by two of his sons, and he was forced to resign the year before his death. **See also INVESTITURE CONTROVERSY.**

Henry IV (1553–1610), king of France (1589–1610) and of Navarre (1572–1610). As a Huguenot*, he was involved in the wars of religion before becoming king of France (changing his faith to Roman Catholicism "to better serve the country"). He enacted the Edict of Nantes (1598) to end the civil war, guaranteeing religious liberties to the Protestants. A very popular king, showing great care for the welfare of his subjects and an unusual religious tolerance for the time, he was murdered by a fanatical Catholic, François Ravaillac. **See also NANTES, EDICT OF.**

Henry VIII (1491–1547), king of England and Ireland (1509–47). Heir to Henry VII when his elder brother, Arthur, died (1502), he married Arthur's widow, Catherine of Aragon. He allowed Cardinal Thomas Wolsey to dominate day-to-day government for nearly two decades. He claimed that the first of several wars with France (1512–13) were "in defense of the papacy." Horrified by Luther*, he commissioned *Assertio Septem Sacramentorum* (Defense of the seven sacraments), for which he was rewarded (1521) with a papal title still used by English monarchs: "Defender of the Faith."

Henry's marriage to Catherine was soured by his obsession with fathering a male heir; the couple had only one surviving daughter, Mary* (Tudor). From 1527, the king's love for Anne Boleyn spurred his quest to have his marriage* declared null, made especially difficult by his insistence that the pope acknowledge that the papacy had erred in granting a dispensation for this marriage. The resulting deadlock destroyed Wolsey's power (1529); Henry abandoned papal loyalty for his long-standing conviction of his God-given headship of the English Church. Academics, including Cranmer*, formalized this conviction into a claim of royal supremacy, and Cromwell* rose to political power by steering legislation through Parliament to recognize it and repudiate papal obedience. Henry delegated his new power to Cromwell as "vicegerent in spirituals." Cromwell dissolved all monasteries, nunneries, and friaries (1536–1540), and worked to authorize the publication of an official English Bible (the Great* Bible, 1539).

Anne Boleyn's enemies convinced Henry of her (almost certainly imaginary) adultery; after her execution (1536), his marriage to Jane Seymour at last provided him with a son, Edward, but she died as a result (1537). Heartbroken, Henry nevertheless pursued matrimonial adventures: an embarrassing mismatch with Anne of Cleves (1540) was disentangled so that Henry could marry Catherine Howard, the marriage ending in her undoubted adultery and execution (1542). Only with the Evangelical Catherine Parr (1543) did Henry find contented partnership.

Many across the religious spectrum died for not conforming to his idiosyncratic religious agenda. He lost any strong sense of purgatory*, remained proud of the English Bible and suspicious of clerical power, curbed cults of images, and destroyed shrines; he entrusted the education of his son Edward and his daughter Elizabeth* to Evangelical scholars. Nevertheless, he never accepted the Protestant emphasis on justification* by faith alone and maintained the Latin Mass*, compulsory clerical celibacy, and other doctrinal provisions of the self-consciously traditionalist Act of Six Articles (1539).

DIARMAID N. J. MACCULLOCH

Heresy. While the term has come to mean erroneous, deviant, or misleading versions of Christian teaching, originally the Greek word *hairesis* had no negative connotations; neutral and descriptive, it referred to a school of thought "chosen" by members of a group (etymologically, "a choice"). The corresponding Latin term, *secta*, was similarly neutral (deriving not from *seco*, a "cutting off," but from *sequor*, voluntarily "following" opinions or a way of life).

In Acts (5:17, 15:5, 26:5) *hairesis* refers to the Pharisees and Sadducees as Jewish parties. For later interpreters, Acts 24:5, 24:14, 28:22 (describing Jews as rejecting the Christian *hairesis*) and 1 Cor 11:18–19 (in which Paul regrets that there are *haireseis*, "factions" among the Corinthians) reflect a more negative use of the term. Accordingly, Paul would have assumed that difference or plurality of belief was a danger sign, since unanimity (*homonoia*) was the "normal" expectation in "Hellenistic culture" (just as Ignatius*, a generation later, rejoiced over the lack of division in the churches to which he wrote; Eph 6:2, cf. *Trall* 6:1). Yet the neutrality of the term remained intact, because Luke and Paul needed to add negative terms to condemn the problematic interactions among factions. It is possible that Paul and Ignatius simply condemned factions for opposing and excluding each other, and not for holding different views (a plausible interpretation of 1 Cor 11:18-19). In fact, Christianity began with a diversity of doctrine, practice, and authority.

Nonetheless, *hairesis* was clearly used negatively by Justin* and Irenaeus*, who condemned Gnostics* and Marcionites* for denying that the Creator is the Father of Jesus Christ and for rejecting the authority of the OT.

In the history of Christian doctrine, various themes have been the focus of intense controversy, and some views held by one's opponents have been pronounced heretical (conflicting groups have often declared each other heretical). After the Gnostic controversy (2nd c.), noteworthy conflicts concerned the Trinity*, Christology*, original* sin and the need for grace*, the *Filioque**, the Eucharist*, the unity of the church, the Protestant doctrine of justification*, and Modernism*. Manuals listing and refuting various heresies, written during the 3rd and 4th c., were expanded during the Middle Ages and with the division between the Western and Eastern churches and between Catholics and Protestants.

The political enforcement of doctrine began with Constantine* and especially with Theodosius*, whose decree of uniform belief in the Trinity* (*Cunctos populos*, 380) became part of Roman law until the Reformation* and the Enlightenment*. Medieval rulers punished heresy as a counterfeit version of Christianity, since religious uniformity was politically valuable. The Inquisition* developed out of concern for the Albigensian* and other heresies. The role of inquisitors was to seek out information and gain confessions of heresy, then to hold hearings under the procedures for the sacrament of penance*. Persons who refused to recant were handed over to the "secular* arm" for burning.

Theories about the development of dogma* recognize that doctrines come to be formulated only gradually, usually in opposition to emergent formulations. Even when doctrines are clarified in this oppositional way, they are susceptible to further interpretation. Beyond the tragedies of persecution, exclusion, or religious war, there is always the danger that "heresy-hunting" will stifle open discussion of doctrinal issues and lead to an "external orthodoxy" that fosters "internal sterility of faith," as Karl Rahner* warned.

At the height of a controversy over a doctrine or a practice, feelings are intense and lines are drawn very closely, because *both sides of the controversy* perceive the central relevance of the issue to their own lives or proclamations. This is what later generations often recognize in retrospect, eventually moving toward improved relations, or even reunion.

DANIEL PATTE and EUGENE TESELLE

Hermas, Shepherd of, sometimes considered canonical (e.g. by Clement* of Alexandria, Origen*, Irenaeus*, and Codex* Sinaiticus); the most popular noncanonical text in the first five centuries of the church. The Muratorian* canon (late 2nd c.) relegates the work to secondary helpfulness because it lacks apostolic authorship.

The author, Hermas, a *threptos* (an abandoned baby raised in slavery) and eventually a freedman, had a family and household in (or near) Rome in the late 1st or early 2nd c. Clement* of Rome, a church leader of the time, might be the Clement mentioned in *Vis.* 2.4.3. Hermas writes of visions received, in three sections probably written over a period of time and intended as notes for oral proclamation: the "Visions," "Mandates" (or "Commandments"), and "Similitudes" (or "Parables"). The revelatory figure of the "Visions" is a woman (the church) who grows progressively younger. The revelatory agent in the "Mandates" and "Similitudes" is an angel dressed as a "shepherd," from whom the text takes its name.

The visionary message is communicated by both apocalyptic* images and allegory*: the female church, the building of a tower with stones brought from various places, trees, mountains, etc., form the basis for moral instruction until the tower is completed at the end of the age.

The conversion of church members who were instructed to share their wealth suggests a relatively wealthy community. The text contains the earliest Christian treatment of the discernment of spirits*, based on Hellenistic Jewish teaching.

The Shepherd had great popular appeal because its ethical teaching was the right combination of intriguing imagery and practical instruction.

CAROLYN OSIEK

Hermeneutics is the theory or science of interpretation, relating especially to the Bible and to be distinguished from exegesis* and from practical exposition. The word comes from Hermes in Greek mythology, whose task as messenger of the gods was to explain divine decisions to humans.

Christian hermeneutics has its origins in the Bible itself; the NT is, in large part, an interpretation of the HB, e.g., through typological* readings whereby figures or typical events in the OT are seen as prefigurements of figures and typical events in the NT. The early church quickly established two major hermeneutical "schools" in Antioch* and Alexandria*. The school in Antioch emphasized literal* readings of Scripture. The school in Alexandria emphasized allegorical* interpretations, following Clement* (c150–215) and Origen* (c185–c254), both deeply influenced by Greek philosophy. The greatest hermeneutical scholar of the West, Augustine* of Hippo (354–430), was trained in classical thought and developed, in *On Christian Doctrine,* a semiotics*, or theory of signs, distinguishing between "natural" signs and "given" signs, i.e. divinely revealed signs in the words of Scripture* and requiring careful interpretation. Looking back to earlier Christian interpreters like Irenaeus* and Tertullian*, Augustine finally depends on the judgment of the rule* of faith within the church; this later ensured that the medieval church maintained an iron grip on the interpretation of Scripture, which remained essentially unchanged in principle until the Reformation of Luther* and Calvin*. As in the early Christian interpreters, medieval hermeneutics pursued multiple levels of meaning, such as the literal, allegorical, moral, and anagogical meanings of Nicholas* of Lyra (c1270–1349).

Luther's (1483–1536) hermeneutical revolution was made possible in part by the new technology of the printing press; for the first time, a standard text free from the vagaries of hand copying was available to a relatively large readership. Furthermore, the availability of vernacular Bibles in a growing number of languages encouraged both the spread of literacy and the freedom of the individual reader to interpret Scripture apart from the authoritative and dogmatic demands of the church. But above all, it was Luther's principle of *sola scriptura* (Scripture alone) that firmly shifted attention to the text of the Bible (and no other book), free from the interpretative strategies of the church. The *sola scriptura* principle (Scripture* principle) together with an emphasis on the *literal* meaning alone turned hermeneutics toward its modern forms. In many ways, the Reformers anticipated the hermeneutics of the Enlightenment*, the "Age of Reason*." Descartes's* (1596–1650) *cogito, sum* (I think, I am) heralded the Enlightenment by distinguishing clearly between the realms of the sacred and the secular, and confirming reason as the interpreter's primary tool. The interpretation of Scripture no longer begins with prayer, but is based on an exercise of cool reason and even doubt* with the aspiration to achieve a complete understanding.

Schleiermacher* (1768–1834), the "father of modern hermeneutics," set down principles that have guided biblical interpretation to this day. For him, hermeneutics is an art, an endlessly renewed task born of a wish to understand (the reader) and to be understood (author and text) in a never completed circular movement. Interpretation has two parts: the *psychological*, concerned with the interplay between the reader and the text, and the *grammatical*, requiring precise knowledge of the text's grammar and syntax. With Schleiermacher, hermeneutics is subject to universal principles; the Bible must be read with the same critical attention as any other texts. Wilhelm Dilthey (1833–1911) extended Schleiermacher's approach by placing hermeneutics within the broad context of the human sciences. In reaction the first major hermeneutical figure of the 20th c., Barth* (1886–1968), like Luther, regarded the reading of Scripture as essentially a "listening" to the Word* of God, an opening to God's revelation to prompt the words of the preacher. In distinction to Barth, Bultmann* (1884–1976) was deeply influenced by contemporary existential* thinking, and for him the task was to demythologize* the ancient cultural assumptions of the Bible and renew its message in the idiom of modern thought. Perhaps the greatest evaluation of hermeneutics in the second half of the 20th c. is Gadamer's* *Truth and Method* (1960), which explores the dialogue between the claims of truth and the processes of method – a hermeneutics of faith* (see Conviction) against a hermeneutics* of suspicion (Ricoeur's* term).

In the wake of postmodernity*, it is not easy to anticipate the future of the hermeneutical task of scriptural interpretation. Varieties of "liberation*" hermeneutics (feminist*, postcolonial*), the shift from the verbal to the visual, and the advent of texts in "cyberspace" are having an effect on interpretation, just as the technology of the printing press affected the hermeneutics of Luther's time. **See also APOPHATISM; BIBLE INTERPRETATION CLUSTER; CONVICTION; METAPHOR; SCRIPTURAL CRITICISM; SYMBOLISM.** DAVID JASPER

Hermeneutics of Suspicion, term coined by Paul Ricoeur* (referring to Marx*, Nietzche*, and Freud*, in *Freud and Philosophy*, French original, 1965; English, 1970) for a method of interpretation which assumes that the surface-level meaning of a text (including the Bible) conceals the political interests it serves (see Ideological Studies of Christianity; Ideology). Hermeneutics of suspicion became an important methodological tool in feminist* studies to unmask the patriarchal* and androcentric* perspectives of (biblical) texts.

Hermetic Writings, texts attributed to the Hellenized Egyptian god of wisdom, Thoth-Hermes (1st–3rd c. CE), divided into "technical" works (astrology, alchemy, and magic) and "philosophical" treatises (the Byzantine collection *Corpus Hermeticum*, the Latin *Asclepius*, the Armenian *Hermetic Definitions*, and three Coptic texts from the Nag Hammadi "library").

Hermetic writings originated in the sophisticated multicultural milieu of Alexandria, notorious for the blending of Greek philosophical ideas with "Oriental" traditions, especially Egyptian wisdom literature and the biblical creation story (Genesis). Affinities with Christian–Gnostic systems stem from this shared intertextual network.

Hermetic texts combine cosmological speculation with a desire to attain salvation* through a noetic experience (*gnosis*) of God. They resolve the theological problem of God's transcendence vs. immanence by the intercession of intermediary divine powers. Contrary to Gnostic* attitudes, they praise the physical world as God's beautiful creation. Their anthropology* derives from a modified Platonic soul–body dualism*: the goal of Hermetic experience is the soul's deliverance from the body, but bodily sensation remains an essential preliminary to spiritual enlightenment.

Ancient Christian attitudes toward Hermetism range from polemical rejection to the appropriation of "Hermes" as a herald of Christianity. Hermetic writings have influenced various esoteric currents, including the New Age Movement.

ZLATKO PLEŠE

Hermit, or Eremite, person who lives alone in a deserted place in order to concentrate on prayer, self-discipline, and contemplation. **See also ANCHORITE LIFE; EREMITIC MONASTICISM.**

Herod Family. The tangled family tree of the Herods begins with Herod I, also known as

Herod the Great (73–4 BCE), who ruled (from 37 BCE) over much of Palestine in collusion with the Roman Empire. King Herod slaughters males under the age of two in Matthew's infancy narrative (Matt 2:1–18), an indication that some saw him as an enemy of the Jewish people. Upon Herod I's death, his kingdom was divided among his three sons, Archaeleus (the south, including Judea), Philip (the north-east), and Herod Antipas (the north, including Galilee). Antipas, whom Jesus calls "that fox" (Luke 13:32), ruled until 39 CE, presiding, according to Josephus* and the Synoptic Gospels, over the execution of John* the Baptist. Antipas lost public support when he divorced his first wife and married Herodias*, the wife of his half-brother, Philip. According to Luke, since Jesus was from Galilee, Pilate initially sent him to Antipas for trial. The fact that Mark's Gospel calls Antipas a king (6:14–30) does not reflect history (Matt 14:1) as much as it does Mark's presentation of Antipas as a type of foolish foreign king, familiar from Hebrew narrative. Acts also mentions Herod Agrippa I, a favorite of Josephus for his skillful cooperation with the Romans (*Antiquities* XVIII, v–viii; Acts 12:3–11), and records that Herod Agrippa II tried the apostle Paul (25:13–26:32).

NICOLE WILKINSON DURAN

Herodians, twice mentioned in the NT; in each instance, the group conspires with the Pharisees* against Jesus (Mark 3:6, 12:13; Matt 22:16). Historically, the pairing is unlikely, because the Pharisees were members of a reform movement with no investment in Rome, whereas the Herodians presumably supported the secondhand Roman rule of the Herods*.

NICOLE WILKINSON DURAN

Herodias, initially married to her uncle, Philip, until another uncle, Herod Antipas, divorced his first wife and married her (Josephus, *Antiquities* XVIII, v). In Mark, Herodias is conniving and murderous, using her daughter's appeal and her husband's weakness to kill John* the Baptist, who criticized her marriage to Herod (6:14–30).

NICOLE WILKINSON DURAN

Hesychasm (from the Gk for "silence" or "stillness"), a method and theory of prayer and contemplation* in the monastic* tradition of the Eastern Church; closely identified with the 13th- to 14th-c. spiritual* revival in the Byzantine Empire as defended by Gregory* Palamas and centering on Mount Athos*. As a spiritual practice, its roots are much earlier. A noted feature of hesychasm is the use of the Jesus* Prayer, often in conjunction with psychosomatic techniques and under the experienced guidance of an elder. The hesychastic tradition is reflected in the *Philokalia*, a collection of ascetic* and spiritual writings (between the 4th and 15th c.; first published, 1793).

JAMES C. SKEDROS

Heteronomy, as an ethical or theological concept or as a mode of existence, is often viewed negatively by Christian theologians. However, it also carries positive connotations, which can be cautiously appropriated, with full awareness of its oppressive potential.

1. As an ethical concept, heteronomy (Gk *hetero,* "another"; *nomos,* "law") literally refers to ethical norms and values that are externally imposed on the subject. These norms and values can be regarded either as a threat to the autonomy* of the individual, who should instead make her or his own moral choices (Kant*), or as a necessary guide for the individual, who would otherwise go astray (Barth*). Thus in Christian dogmatics, heteronomy is to autonomy as law* is to gospel*, as creation* is to salvation*, or as government is to the church (the Lutheran doctrine of the two realms [or kingdoms*]).
2. As a mode of existence, heteronomy is closely related to the two other modes of existence: autonomy* (its opposite) and relationality*. According to Tillich*, heteronomy is autonomy gone astray; the individual has given up the search for true faith* (ultimate concern) and has passively accepted traditional norms and values. He proposes "theonomy," a harmonious synthesis of autonomy and heteronomy. In that heteronomy implies a lack of control, it has negative connotations. Nevertheless, it also has the connotation of "vulnerability," which, when regarded as a life condition, is related not only to exposure and oppression*, but also to love* and empowerment.
3. The heteronomous character of Christian faith, submitting to divine revelation, has been a target of the Enlightenment* critique of religious institutions and also of post-Christian feminist critique (Hampson), because it may contribute to resistance to the emancipation from oppression of women or of any humans. However, heteronomy can also be seen as a fundamental dimension of Christian faith,

kenosis*, exemplified by the empowering experience of contemplative* prayer (Coakley) and corresponding to breaking through in psychodynamic therapy (Heyward).

4. Beyond Christianity and its institutions, there are heteronomous risks in contemporary society arising from institutions beyond the control of the individual, such as mass media, multinational companies, and large bureaucracies, none of which promote mutual relations.

Heteronomy is necessarily interrelated and in tension with autonomy and relationality. Each of these three modes of existence is ambivalent, becoming oppressive when it denies the other two modes. Heteronomy is oppressive when it smothers mutual relations and fails to respect the individual. However, heteronomy is also the positive empowering that occurs when one ultimately abandons control of oneself, trusting God (rather than relying on oneself or human [relational] institutions) or receiving the gift of love*.

CRISTINA GRENHOLM

Heterosexuality denotes a person's sexual* feelings and fantasies about and sometimes sexual activities with (a) person(s) of the other sex. Until the late 20th c. (at least in Western cultures), all humans were assumed to be heterosexual unless sick, abnormal, or immoral. For the majority of Western Christians, heterosexuality is morally superior to homosexuality*, although some have modified their views in the light of scientific research and Western gay and lesbian Christian movements.

Heterosexuality as an Embodiment of Patriarchal Power. This most distinctly religious understanding is steeped in a patriarchal* worldview in which a male God creates the human male above the female, sexually and otherwise. This view is frequently shared by Judaism* and Islam*. Since Scripture portrays Adam* and Eve* as suitable partners, figuratively joined by God and commanded to procreate, Roman Catholic, Eastern Orthodox, and Protestant Christians have commended heterosexual marriage* as the only moral context for sexual activity, childbearing (pregnancy*), and family*. The traditional image of Christ and the church as bridegroom and bride, the basis for much Christian prayer, liturgy, and hymnody, makes heterosexuality sacred; the bridegroom–bride image is a "hetero-fetish," as the feminist ethicist Beverly W. Harrison pointed out. Contemporary Christians tend either to accept the church's basic teachings about heterosexuality as morally normative or to challenge these teachings as oppressive, discriminatory, and generating violence* against women and persons perceived as non-heterosexual.

Heterosexuality as Morally Neutral. In the late 20th and early 21st c., Feminist*, Womanist*, Queer*, and various other Liberation* theologians have argued for more inclusive Christian understandings of scriptural* authority, tradition, sexual morality, marriage, and family. They hold that heterosexuality is one of several morally neutral ways of experiencing and expressing one's sexuality*.

Like homosexual behavior, heterosexual activity can be destructive or creative, coercive or cooperative, abusive or healthy; thus heterosexuality can be moral or immoral. **See also** ABUSE AS PASTORAL CARE ISSUE.

CARTER HEYWARD

Hexaemeron (Gk "six days' work" of creation*; Gen 1) was the subject of many early Christian commentaries.

Hexapla, edition of the OT produced by Origen*, with six columns (Hebrew, Hebrew transliterated into Greek, and four translations by Aquila*, Symmachus, the Septuagint*, and Theodotion*). Further columns were added when other versions became available. It was begun in Alexandria and completed in Caesarea, where the original remained. The "Hexaplaric" text of the LXX was widely copied; other selective copies were also made, especially of the four Greek translations.

Hicks, Elias (1748–1830), Quaker* farmer, minister, reformer. Born on Long Island, New York, he traveled widely among Quakers, voicing his opposition to slavery. His preaching and support for continuing revelation* led to a major split among Quakers. Hicks reacted to the amassing of wealth* and integration of Quakers within the larger society. He bluntly attacked Friends* who differed with him, many who embraced Evangelical theological views. He emphasized inward seeking and less reliance on the Scriptures. His mostly rural followers challenged Quakers' urban leaders in Yearly Meetings, especially in Philadelphia, New York, and Baltimore, bringing about long-lasting splits.

H. LARRY INGLE

Hidalgo y Costilla, Miguel (1753–1811), Roman Catholic priest, a national hero of Mexico for initiating the movement of independence in 1810 in response to the colonialist* exploitation of indigenous people, his parishioners. His call to arms was heralded by the banner of the Virgin of Guadalupe. He was defrocked, excommunicated, captured, killed, and beheaded. But the revolutionary movement continued. **See also MARY, THE VIRGIN, CLUSTER: OF GUADALUPE; MEXICO; SPANISH EXPLORATIONS, CONQUESTS, AND MISSIONS.**

MARÍA ALICIA PUENTE LUTTEROTH and ELIZABETH JUDD

Hierotopy, the Creation of Christian Sacred Spaces. The term "hierotopy" consists of two Greek roots: *hieros* (sacred) and *topos* (place, space, notion); it refers to the creation of sacred spaces as a special form of human creativity, as well as to a field of study analyzing particular instances of the creation of sacred spaces as "hierotopical projects." Hierotopy, as a recently established theoretical concept, relates to a specific and neglected research field that spans art history, anthropology, and religious studies and how they are interrelated so as to form a space that reflects believers' previous experiences of the sacred and invites new encounters with the mystery of the holy.

Hierotopy as a Field of Study accounts for artistic images and the symbolic* world they form (see Aesthetics and Theology; Arts and Theology), but also investigates the combination of material objects that occupy and organize a sacred space, the rituals and social mechanisms that take place in them, and the theological and liturgical aspects through which a sacred space is created in a "hierotopical project." A created sacred space cannot be interpreted as the synthesis of arts, as the age of baroque, and later *art nouveau,* seem to suggest. Hierotopy deals with a different subject matter, created sacred space, which cannot be described simply as a combination of artifacts and of various ephemeral effects. On the contrary, a created sacred space embodies specific images (visions) of sacred space that subordinates a realm of stable architectural forms (e.g. basilica*, cathedral*, monastery*) and various pictures (e.g. icons*, stained glass windows) to changeable liturgical clothes and vessels, lighting effects and ritual gestures, invisible fragrance, and prayers. In fact, almost all objects of Christian art were originally conceived of as elements of a hierotopical project that sought to construct an immaterial but real space as the center of the universe around which the world of objects, sounds, perfumes, lights, and other effects revolved.

Such research fields as lighting and fragrance find their proper context within an overall hierotopical framework. Several written sources (including Byzantine monastic ceremonials) provide a detailed description of the practice of changing lighting during worship services according to a sophisticated scenario. At times light accentuates certain images or holy objects, organizing a perception of the entire space of the church and providing a logic for "reading" its most significant elements. Similarly, the realm of fragrance presents ever new combinations of incense, wax candles, and aromatic oils in lamps (see Incense and Olfactory Experience in Worship) that mark and organize the sacred space of worship in the church; this had deep roots in the OT Temple, and also in ancient Near East and Roman imperial cults.

Hierotopy as the Making of Sacred Space in the Bible. In earlier studies, sacred space, associated with God's actual presence and the holy, was the subject of a phenomenological* interpretation reflected in Mircea Eliade's notion of hierophany as "an irruption of the sacred that detaches a territory from the surrounding cosmic milieu." Eliade used the well-known biblical story of Jacob's dream (Gen 28:12–22) as a characteristic illustration of hierophany. However, in this phenomenon, one can isolate a hierotopical part. In the biblical story, the hierotopy starts with Jacob's awakening. Inspired by his dream-vision (hierophany), he creates a sacred space (making a pillar with the stone, pouring oil on it, calling the place Bethel, house of God), presenting a model to all of his successors – creators of innumerable churches and shrines. The permanent relation and intensive interaction between hierophany (mystical* appearance) and hierotopy (the creation of an environment conceived of by minds and made by hands) determines the specificity of the making of sacred spaces as a form of human creativity.

The making of the Tabernacle provides another biblical model. According to Exod 25–40, the Lord himself conveyed to Moses on Mount Horeb the entire project of the Tabernacle, from the general structure of the space to details of the sacred vestment production. God chose the master Bezalel (Exod 31:2) to implement the plan, positing a model relationship between creators of sacred space and creators of objects.

Creators of Sacred Spaces. The most powerful paradigm for creators of sacred spaces has been inherited from King Solomon, who was inspired by God to build the Temple in Jerusalem. He established for centuries an iconic* behavior of earthly rulers in relation to the Ruler of the Universe. In the Byzantine tradition, emperors were often creators of sacred space, following the model of the holy emperor Justinian* as the builder of the Hagia Sophia. According to a popular Byzantine story, Justinian did his best to surpass Solomon in his project of building the great church of the Empire.

A representative figure of such creators of sacred space in the West is Abbot Suger, who conceived of the first Gothic space in the abbey church of St. Denis (1140–44). His roles included endowing the project and casting masters, but it also entailed the development of a theological vision (possibly influenced by the theology of Dionysius* the Pseudo-Areopagite), as well as the elaboration of new rituals and artistic modeling (as he explains in his extensive writings). This multifunctional activity, comparable to the role of future film directors, integrated various arts into the creation of a single sacred space.

The Creation of "Holy Land Sacred Spaces." A key element of the medieval hierotopy was the re-creation of the Holy Land or some of its parts. For instance, the Pharos chapel in Constantinople functioned not merely as an imperial storage place for the main Passion relics, but also as the Byzantine "Holy Sepulchre" – the sacred center of the Empire. In the West, the most striking examples are Santa Croce in Gerusalemme in Rome and Campo Santo in Pisa, for which the "holy earth" from Golgotha was brought by ships in the 4th and 13th c., respectively. The 17th-c. New Jerusalem complex near Moscow, representing the largest re-creation of the Holy Land in world history (about 50 square kilometers), combined an iconic image and a narrative illustration, presenting both Byzantine and Western hierotopical traditions. The creation of such spatial images as sacred spaces did not mean that the locus "Holy Land" disappeared. Actually, the topographical, material concreteness of the Holy Land conveyed power and religious efficacy to the sacred spaces re-creating the Holy Land.

Similarly, one large sacred space can imbue smaller sacred spaces with religious power and efficacy. This is the case in many Romanesque and Gothic cathedrals, yet the most striking example is the overall environment of Hagia Sophia in Constantinople, which provided the framework in which several hierotopical projects belonging to different periods could coexist. Thus Hagia Sophia was filled with installations that created particular sacred spaces: around the altar table; at the Samaritan's well in the southeast section; around the icon reliquary with the chains of St. Peter in the northern aisle; and near the northwest pillar, which included relics of St. Gregory the Wonderworker. The latter was covered by gilded brass plates and adorned by a venerated icon of this saint. On particular days, a movable altar table was installed in front of the pillar and special services took place. Deliberately modeled micro–sacred spaces were activated in particular moments of the daily or annual liturgical services.

The creation of sacred spaces is a dynamic matter. Hierotopical projects were usually presented in permanent movement. Performativity, dramatic changes, and flexibility were connected with the Byzantine notions of *chora* (metaphysical, divine space) and *choros* (circular movement in space), which were sometimes reflected in iconography, e.g. in the early-14th-c. mosaics of the Kariye Camii (in the Chora Monastery, Constantinople) conceived by Theodore Metochites. This donor and creator of the sacred space clearly pointed out the origins of his imagery, symbolically presenting different images of the Virgin with the Child inscribed with the same words – *Chora tou achoretou* (space of the uncontainable) – and two images of Christ above the entrances to the narthex and to the naos (where the liturgy is performed) inscribed as *Chora ton zonton* (space of the living). The entire church building and all its images were intended to represent this "divine space."

In Byzantine minds, the icon* (of Jesus* Christ or of Mary* the Theotokos) was not merely an object and a flat picture on a panel or wall, but a spatial vision emanating from the image into the environment in front of it, creating a sacred space between the picture and its beholder in which various other media (lighting, smells, sounds) were interacting. This can be illustrated by the medieval Holy Tuesday performance with the icon of the Hodegetria of Constantinople, which happened each week in the Byzantine capital from the 12th c. The image on the panel icon of the Hodegetria was perceived as animated and as an inseparable part of the iconic spatial milieu. The holy icon was actively participating and interacting with the beholders, who became an integral part of the sacred space created by the image, together with the other images, lights, smells, gestures, and sounds. In a way, the beholders, with their collective and individual memory, spiritual experience, and knowledge, participated in the creation of the sacred space.

The Palm Sunday ceremony, or the "procession on a donkey," in 16th- to 17th-c. Moscow provides another striking example. The czar led the patriarch, seated on a donkey in remembrance of Christ's entrance into Jerusalem, from the Kremlin to St. Basil's Cathedral on Red Square. The space of evangelical Jerusalem was reproduced in the center of Moscow and became a "living picture," a dynamic and spatial reenactment of what was also a popular iconographic theme.

A comparative approach reveals different religious and national models of Christian hierotopy. In Byzantium a dominant iconic vision of sacred space breaks down the barrier between the material body of the church and the external milieu. The inner space of the church could be displayed and re-created in squares and streets, in fields and mountains, which were, at least temporarily, transformed into an icon of the sacred universe, created by God. Furthermore, the church building itself is considered a transparent structure and a moving spiritual substance: indeed, relics* were sometimes inlaid in walls, pillars, and cupolas of Byzantine churches. In post-Byzantine churches in Romania*, the altar iconography is reproduced on the facades of the church building; in this way, the hidden space of the "holy of holiest" is open to the external world, in turn conceived of as a cosmic sacred space, a church-cosmos.

Byzantine models were adopted and transformed in different countries according to their national characteristics and even climatic conditions. The architecture of ice that framed Russian hierotopical projects for the Epiphany* and other winter festivals simply could not exist in the Balkans. The sublime Constantinopolitan patterns were being reworked in the folk milieu: the well-established "academic" hierotopy was combined with spontaneous sacralization of the human environment.

As a living entity, a hierotopical project could change over time: the original framing vision was subject to developments and additions. Cathedrals of the Moscow Kremlin provide a good example: their sacred space considerably changed over the centuries. Liturgical textiles covered icons and great parts of walls until the late 17th c., when most were removed from the cathedrals. This created a very different image of sacred space.

Sacred Space in Minor Arts and Written Texts. The hierotopical approach relates not merely to the sacred spaces of churches, cities, or landscapes, but to spatial imagery in minor art forms and in written texts.

Byzantine manuscripts provide characteristic examples. Their first pages sometimes looked like a solemn gate to the sacred space of the book, e.g. representing the heavenly city made up of churches (as in the manuscripts of the 12th-c. homilies of James of Kokkinobaphos and the sermons of St. Gregory* Nazianzen from Sinai).

Liturgical vestments provide another example of hierotopical imagery. The 14th- to 15th-c. embroidered Byzantine episcopal liturgical robes, *sakkoi,* of the Moscow Metropolitan Photios, e.g., with their sophisticated system of images, created a microcosm of the church space, which was incorporated into the sacred milieu of the actual cathedral; they revealed their true meaning in the liturgical movements and gestures.

The same is true of liturgical vessels and numerous reliquaries. The 10th-c. Constantinopolitan stone chalice from San Marco in Venice (the Chalice of the Patriarchs), adorned by a gold medallion with an enamel image of Christ Pantocrator on the bottom, reflected the sacred space imagery of Byzantine cupolas, also bearing the Pantocrator image. In the Communion rite, both images had to be perceived as interrelated parts of the same sacred space (see Jesus, Images of, Cluster).

The so-called Limburg *Staurothek* (968–85), consisting of a piece of the true cross framed by 10 other relics, mostly kept in the church of the Virgin of the Pharos, created a sacred space out of this reliquary chapel, which had belonged to the Byzantine emperors. Some Byzantine reliquaries of St. Demetrios reproduced not merely the iconography of the saint, but the arrangement of his shrine in Thessaloniki, which is represented by a sequence of flat and volume images, gradually appearing in the process of the opening of a reliquary. Thus the reliquary created an image of venerated sacred space – or re-created this sacred space – widely known for the miracles that were said to have regularly happened there.

Finally, the descriptions of a sacred milieu (e.g. the dwelling place of a saint) are a regular topic of medieval writings. Characteristically, the realistic features of landscapes (such as distances) are obliterated in these texts, which present a recognizable but iconic image of the sacred place. The modeling of sacred space by word images entails not merely direct descriptions of paradise, a monastery, or a church, but also some attempts to present an image of a specific milieu, becoming "sacred" beyond commonly recognized characteristics, as in some of the novels of Tolstoy and Dostoevsky.

In large spaces (church and city), in minor arts, and in literary texts, there is one and the same type of creativity, shaped by the idea of sacred space imagery and by an iconic perception of the world. **See also ICONOGRAPHY.**

ALEXEI LIDOV

High Christologies emphasize that Jesus manifests a preexisting divine being, sometimes different from the Father (as in Arianism*), sometimes of the same essence as the Father (as in Nicene* orthodoxy). The endemic question for Christology has been how to acknowledge Christ's full humanity (emphasized in low* Christologies) while also affirming his divinity, as high Christologies emphasize. **See also CHRISTOLOGIES CLUSTER: INTRODUCTORY ENTRIES.**

High Church Party (the) comprises members of the Church of England (see Anglicanism Cluster) who emphasize its continuity with the Roman Catholic Church and the centrality of the sacraments*. During the 19th c., they were often associated with the Oxford* Movement, but condemned its divisiveness.

High Mass. See MASS, ROMAN CATHOLIC.

Higumen or Hegumen (from Gk), title for the head of a monastery of the Eastern Orthodox Church, comparable to abbot* in the Western Church. **See also MONASTICISM CLUSTER: IN THE BYZANTINE EMPIRE.**

Hilary of Poitiers (c315–c367), convert to Western Christianity from paganism (and not from Arianism), bishop of Poitiers (from c350), chief supporter of Nicaea* and Athanasius* in the West. In 356 he was exiled to the East and defended the Nicene doctrine at the Council of Seleucia* (359). Like Athanasius he encouraged an alliance between the Homoiousians* and the Homoousians*, since both were opposed to the Arians*; this was achieved at the Council of Alexandria* (362). His work *On the Trinity* (359) influenced Augustine* and others; *On the Synods* (359) informs the West about the Eastern councils and their creeds; after the Council of Constantinople* (360), which made Arianism the official doctrine, he wrote several polemical works. Because of his eagerness for debate, he was sent back to the West (360), where he continued to attack Arianism. He introduced into the West the practice of writing hymns, a practice already used in the East by both the Arians and their opponents to promote their doctrines.

Hildegard of Bingen (1098–1179), abbess*, visionary, writer on natural history and medicine, hagiography*, cosmology, and theology*; composed a song cycle and musical drama; maintained a voluminous correspondence with religious and secular figures, exalted and humble; made several journeys within Germany preaching before clergy and laity. Understanding herself as a prophet*, privy to the secrets of God, she gained acceptance for her writings, initially from the monks* of Disibodenberg and later at the Synod of Trier (1147–48) from Pope Eugenius III, who encouraged her to record and circulate whatever she learned from the Holy* Spirit through her visions.

Born the 10th and last child of a noble family from Bermersheim in Rheinhesse, early on she showed signs of her unusual gifts. Dedicated to God by her parents at the age of eight, she joined the anchoress* Jutta of Spanheim in a cell at the Benedictine* monastery of Disibodenberg, either at that time or somewhat later. When Jutta died (1136), Hildegard was elected head of the small convent, which had grown from the original anchorage. In 1141 Hildegard experienced a vision that changed the course of her life. In it she not only was granted the ability to understand the inner meaning of the texts of her religion (which she describes as "the Psalter*, the evangelists* and other catholic books of the Old and New Testament*") but also was commanded to say and write what she had understood for the edification of others, despite the fact that she was a woman and lacking all but a rudimentary education. After some hesitation, compelled by an illness that she took to be a divine chastisement, she started to write *Know the Ways [of God]* (*Scivias*), which took 10 years to complete. This was followed by the *Book of Life's Merits* (*Liber vitae meritorum*) (1158–63). The *Book of Divine Works* (*Liber divinorum operum*) (1163–73/74) completed her visionary trilogy.

While writing *Scivias* and amid opposition from the abbot* and monks, Hildegard moved her convent from Disibodenberg to Rupertsberg, a divinely indicated location, near Bingen on the Rhine (1150). After some initial difficulties, the convent flourished and she established a second (1165) at Eibingen on the opposite side of the Rhine. However, as a Benedictine*, she remained technically subject to the abbot of Disibodenberg and, beyond him, to the archbishop of Mainz. Her other works (some lacking the explicit claim of a divine source), including her musical, medico-scientific (*Physica* and *Causes and Cures*), and hagiographical writings (*Life of St. Disibod* and *Life of St. Rupert*) can all be related to her activities as abbess and founder of convents.

Hildegard corresponded with a range of important people of her day, including Frederick Barbarossa, who also consulted her in person, Henry II of England and Eleanor of Aquitaine, several popes, and spiritual luminaries such as Bernard* of Clairvaux. Various bishops, priests, monks, and nuns were the recipients of her letters, which often chided them for laxity in their role as teachers and defenders of the faith. This was in the context of the high expectations for renewal of the faith* that had been raised by the reforms of Gregory* VII, the alarm over the spread of non-Catholic movements such as that of the Cathars*, and the fact that the church in Germany was riven by a papal schism* (1159–77).

Hildegard saw herself principally as a teacher, interpreting by her writings, counsel, and preaching "the ways of God" to humanity. Given this broad task, her writings are truly encyclopedic, encompassing biblical and salvation* history from its beginnings to the end of the world. She expected the end to occur sooner rather than later, although she was careful never to predict a date (unlike her younger contemporary and fellow visionary, Elisabeth of Schoenau). Because of her early papal recognition as a conduit for God's words, the usual strictures against teaching by women were waived for her. Her writings were also acceptable because what she said, although strikingly original in form and expression, remained well within the bounds of 12th-c. Catholic orthodoxy; nor did they challenge the role of the male hierarchy in the Roman Catholic Church.

Although Hildegard's works were never completely lost sight of, in the last decades of the 20th c. her life and works were extensively studied, making her, if not a household name, recognizable to a wide range of people. She is claimed to be a female role model and inspiration not only by Christians of various confessions (there have been efforts to have her declared a "doctor* of the church"), but also by New* Age practitioners, followers of alternative medicine and "creation spirituality," ecologists* and feminists*, and musicians, both traditional and contemporary. SABINA FLANAGAN

Hincmar (806–82), Frankish churchman, educated at the abbey of St. Denis, he joined the court of Louis* the Pious, then supported his son, Charles the Bald. Appointed archbishop of Reims (845), he became the focus of several controversies over his rights as a metropolitan*. The False Decretals* (which he ironically quoted) were forged around 850 to strengthen the bishops' hand against their metropolitans, enabling them to appeal directly to the pope. He played a major role in the rejection of Gottschalk's* view of "double predestination*" (for both salvation* and eternal reprobation); his own position (God wills the salvation of all, but the human will remains free; God predestined a few to be saved out of mercy, yet Christ died for all) was confirmed at the Synod of Quiercy (853) but was opposed at Valence (855).

HINDUISM AND CHRISTIANITY CLUSTER

Hinduism and Christianity. Conversion* has been the bone of contention between the two religions. The built-in missionary* stance of Christianity (Matt 28:16–10; see Mission Cluster) and the intractable loyalty to the hierarchical caste* order of Hinduism (Manu's Code of Law, *Manava-Dharmasastra*, c2nd c. CE) have led to an uneasy relationship.

Christians take human activity in history* as central; Hindus presuppose the interdependence of all happenings. Christian beliefs stress uniqueness ("outside the Church there is no salvation*"; the uniqueness* of Christ), while Hindu beliefs include interconnectedness and harmony (*dharma*). There are differences in their perception of the goal of life (death* and resurrection* for Christians;

rebirth and liberation for Hindus) and of truth and reality (historical approaches for Christians; ontological approaches for Hindus).

Missionaries like Francis Xavier* perceived Brahmins and their teaching negatively. Roberto de Nobili* (15th c.) refuted beliefs like rebirth. However, Thomas Stephens (1549–1619), a Jesuit missionary and poet, proficient in Marathi, Konkani, Sanskrit, English, and Portuguese, wrote a salvation-history "inculturation*" epic, *Kristapurana*, on the life of Jesus Christ, employing Vaishnava terminology (from one of the main Hindu traditions) but eschewing apologetics and exclusive Hindu language as Veda and Shruti texts do.

Bartolomaeus Ziegenbalg's papers (1719) contain both Christian views on polytheism* and the "immorality" of the Hindu deities and the rejoinder by the "Malabarian Brahmins" concerning the illogicality of eternal punishment*, the impossibility of Jesus being savior* of the world owing to his mean parentage, and the impossibility of belief in a God who suffered and died.

In the Bombay controversy, John Carey (1810–82) ridiculed inconsistencies in the Puranas. Conversely, Narayana Rao (1832), interpreting the Bible literally, pointed out its inconsistencies. Wilhelm H. Mill (1792–1853) and John Muir (from 1837) refuted Hindu doctrines in order to present the truth of Christianity. Subaji Bapu disdained the idea of a 6,000-year-old creation* but conceded that salvation in non-Hindu religions was possible because it is the universal Atman that is honored as Buddha, Jina, Christ, Allah, and all other deities. Haracandra Tarkapañcanana heaped contempt on those who converted to Christianity out of a desire for liquor and meat. He argued that the Veda, unlike the Bible, is eternally pre-existent and coeval with creation. Nilakantha Goreh refuted doctrines like Christ's salvific suffering and death.

K. C. Sen (1838–84) criticized the Christian churches but believed in the Trinity* and the omnipresent and universal Christ*. Swami Vivekananda* and M. K. Gandhi* revered Jesus but were critical of missionaries who belittled and undermined Hinduism.

Since Vatican* II (*Nostra Aetate*, also known as *The Declaration on the Relation of the Church and Non-Christian Religions*, by Pope Paul VI, 1965), Catholics view other religions sympathetically. Raimon Panikkar (b1918) speaks of the universe of faith* and the "pluriverse" of beliefs wherein the complementarity of religions and the polarity and distinctiveness of religions are maintained (see the present cluster: Interreligious Dialogue).

Christians (Wilkinson, 1839) have drawn attention to the inhumanities of caste* structures. Today the Christian churches are becoming acutely aware of problem of the oppression of Dalits*, many of whom have become Christians. The Viswa Hindu Parishad accuses Christians of enticing the poor* to convert to Christianity. Others question the value of service that aims at conversion but not all agree with this (e.g. Mani Shankar Aiyar, as Shourie notes).

Mutual interaction has led some Christians (Brahmabandhav Upadhyaya) to inculturate* their beliefs employing Hindu symbols and metaphors* and Hindus to become missionaries (Ramakrishna Mission) and more conscious of the relevance of Hinduism to all (Vivekananda), but some lament its overall lack of social spirituality. FRANCIS X. D'SA, SJ

Hinduism and Christianity: Interreligious Dialogue. Raimon Panikkar's work illustrates one of the possible relationships between Christianity and Hinduism: interreligious dialogue*. His contributions center on the theme of interculturality. His translation of the Vedic hymns made these Hindu texts intelligible to readers of other traditions. His interpretation of Indian myths* invites readers to discover the mystery* of reality that is cross-cultural. From *Unknown Christ of Hinduism* (1964) to *The Fullness of Man, A Christophany* (2006), Panikkar attempts to discover the Christic mystery hidden in Hinduism and elsewhere.

For Panikkar this is possible because reality is trinitarian. This awareness shapes the primordial form of human consciousness; every culture has envisioned reality in terms of three primordial worlds: the world of gods, that of humans, and the material world; heaven, earth, and the underworld; sky, earth, and in between; a transcendent aspect, a noetic factor, and an empirical element. Reality is characterized by interrelations and in this interrelationship one observes a trinitarian principle. "Every real existence is a unique knot in this threefold net." The root cause of present-day malaise is the fragmentation of reality into the dichotomy between spirit and matter, science* and religion*, reason* and revelation*, and, above all, God, world, and human beings. This truncated outlook manifests itself in such problems as colonization, consumerism, ecological imbalance, religious persecution, and economic and social injustices. Healing comes through the cosmotheandric vision – the vision of the interrelatedness of cosmos, human, and the divine.

For Panikkar, interreligious dialogue begins with a clear distinction between faith* and belief. Faith is not the monopoly of believers; it is the constitutive dimension of every human being. Beliefs are shaped by cultures, and yet they have a constitutive claim to transcend those very cultures. The ideal aspired to by interreligious dialogue* is to foster *communication* between diverse religious traditions – and first, for him, between Hinduism and Christianity – in order to bridge the gulf of mutual ignorance, in order for each tradition to speak the other's mythical language while sharing the other's faith experience. This ideal may be reached at certain moments, but it does not imply a reduction of rich religious experience into a single system. ANAND AMALADASS

Hindu Scriptures and the Bible. "Bible*" refers to the written narrative of the Judeo-Christian revelation* (Vatican* II). It begins with the creation of the world and culminates in Jesus* and his movement and leads to a new heaven* and a new earth (new* creation). The expression "Hindu scriptures" (a misnomer employed mostly by Christians) refers generally to authoritative (*pramanam*) oral traditions like the Vedas, and the Agamas of the Shaivas, the Samhitas of the Vaishnavas, and the Tantras of the Shaktas. Their common concern is liberation from *samsara*, the world of rebirth.

"Bible as God's written word" (Scripture*) and Shruti (listening to the eternally revealing Veda) of the Hindus are specific designations that refer to their historical and transhistorical belief worlds. The personal character of biblical religion has often been argued by Christians to be the one true understanding of the Divine (Martin Kähler) and is sometimes used indirectly as an argument against religions like Hinduism (de Nobili*).

In contrast the eternal Veda excludes human and divine authorship (*apaurusheya*) and consequently is free of error (Mimamsa, Vedanta). But the "theistic" non-Vedic Pancaratra tradition (Yamuna) attributes the exclusion of error to Vishnu's omniscience*. Others believe that Vishnu is only the revealer, not the source of the revelation (Nyaya). The authority of the Veda with respect to the non-Vedic traditions has not remained unchallenged.

At home in a culture of reading, writing, analyzing, objectifying, and interpreting (biblical hermeneutics*), the Bible (the OT and NT) is believed to be God's Word* in human language. To understand the Bible, one has to be aware of the literary genres it employs to tell the story of salvation*. Its purpose is to make us familiar with the way God works in history and particularly in Jesus of Nazareth. Jesus' story, the centerpiece of the Christian Bible, highlights the presence of God in the neighbor and illustrates and actualizes love of God in and through love* of the neighbor (as Soares-Prabhu repeatedly emphasized). Jesus' total self-emptying (kenosis*) enabled him to be filled with the Spirit. It is this Spirit that renews the face of the earth (Ps 104:30) and will ultimately lead to a new heaven and a new earth (Rev 21:1–27).

Revelation in the Hindu world has generally to do with a culture of hearing and listening (*shruti*), and meditating on and discerning the forces that have introduced a state of blindness (*moha*)

into the world (as explained in the Upanishads). These make us see that the world is a projection of our desires and dislikes, which renders us incapable of perceiving the world as it is. The dynamic of desire holds us captive to the inexorable world of *karma* and rebirth (as explained in the *Bhagavadgita*). Awareness of the active effects of desire* leads to *moksha*, liberation from the process of rebirth. To come to such awareness, the Hindu traditions have proposed different paths (*margas*), like meditation (*shankara*), loving devotion for Vishnu, and detached engagement in the world (Bal Gangadhar Tilak, Gandhi). Still others (including the Hindu teacher and Vaishnava monk A. C. Bhaktivedanta, founder of the International Society of Krishna Consciousness) advocate the recitation of names of the Divine (*mantra*) to obtain release from *samsara*.

As Soares-Prabhu stresses while interpreting Scripture* with the poor, the Bible places stress on love and service of the neighbor; this brings one in touch with the Christ who is present in all persons, especially the needy (Matt 25:31–46). Human persons constitute the center of biblical concern because they are the primary locus of God's presence in the world.

The different Hindu revelatory traditions concentrate on liberation from the inexorability of rebirth. This is their common goal. Thus the only content of Hindu revelation refers to escape from *samsara*, the cycle of rebirth. Interestingly, however, Hindus at the grassroots level are speaking today of the whole world as God's family, which perhaps goes back to the all-embracing theophany in the 12th chapter of the *Bhagavadgita*.

FRANCIS X. D'SA, SJ

Hippolytus (c170–c236), a major theologian of the early-3rd-c. Roman Church, heard by Origen* when he visited Rome (c212), and the probable author of a major work against heresies*. He opposed the view of the Trinity* presented by Sabellius*, as well as the popes Zephyrinus and Callistus, as too monarchian*. After 217 he became the "anti-pope" against Callistus and his successors. During the persecution under Maximinus, he and the pope Pontianus were exiled to Sardinia; apparently they reconciled before being martyred. A statue of Hippolytus was discovered in Rome in 1551; on its base is a list of many of his works, including the Apostolic* Tradition, an early church* order.

Hispanic Theology. See LATINO/A* THEOLOGIES.

Historiography of Early Christianity as Developed in the 19th and 20th Centuries. Historiography is "the study of the study of history," i.e. the study of approaches and methods used in the historical discipline, and of the assumptions and theories of historians across time. "History" here does not mean "what happened in the past," but refers to a discipline of the modern academy.

Whether history became an academic subject before the development of the 19th-c. Western research university has been debated. Before that, history was usually considered a branch of "letters." Nineteenth-century German scholars such as Leopold von Ranke altered this approach: the historian was to locate primary source documents pertinent to the period and subject being studied and offer a factual and unbiased presentation based on these sources. History was to be an objective "science*"; historians' accounts were to correspond to "what actually happened."

The historiography of early Christianity did not strictly follow this pattern of development. Patristics, the study of the early "church fathers" (2nd–6th c.), was considered a branch of theology. Although 19th-c. historians of Christianity learned to "go to the sources," many approached their subject with an apologetic and polemical aim, often related to their denominational affiliations. In countries where Protestantism dominated, patristics focused especially on Greek and Latin Christian writings of the first three (rather than later) centuries, which were deemed close to the source of Christian truth, the NT. Considerable confidence was placed in the accuracy and credibility of the fathers' accounts of early Christian history and theology.

Augustus Neander, professor of church history at Berlin (mid-19th c.), is often considered the "father" of the modern study of church history. Neander, who saw the providential hand of God directing the course of Christian history, praised the benefits that Roman Catholicism brought to late antiquity and the Middle Ages – an emphasis considered too "Romanizing" for many North American Protestants. Ferdinand Christian Baur* and the Tübingen school developed a historiography marked both by critical historical studies and by Hegel's perspective.

Some decades later, Harnack's* studies of early Christian history and literature were instrumental in the development of patristics as a scholarly discipline.

An issue of paramount importance in the creation of the field was the editing and publication of primary source patristic texts, and in this enterprise, scholars from across Europe took part. France led the way with editions by Benedictine monks (from the 17th c.) and by J.-P. Migne*, the editor of *Patrologia Latina* and *Patrologia Graeca*. Italian scholar Giovanni Battista de Rossi's research on Roman catacombs and inscriptions greatly advanced knowledge of early Christian material culture and practice. In England the Oxford* Movement and the reactions to it spurred scholarship on the church fathers. English translations of patristic texts were offered in the Ante-Nicene Christian Library, a series begun by two Scotsmen (1864). Later in the 19th c., a Swiss-born professor in the USA, Philip Schaff, organized the Nicene and Post-Nicene Series. The late 19th to 20th c. saw the founding of *Corpus Christianorum Series Latina* and *Series Graeca*, then of *Texte und Untersuchungen zur Geschichte der altchristlichen Literatur, Corpus Scriptorum Ecclesiasticorum Latinorum,* and *Sources Chrétiennes.* Writings by fathers in Coptic*, Syriac*, Armenian*, and other "Oriental" languages of their churches – increasingly deemed important – were published in the *Corpus Scriptorum Christianorum Orientalium* and the *Patrologia Orientalis.*

The study of early Christianity moved beyond its primary home in seminaries into humanities departments in secular colleges and universities (middle to late 20th c.). In tandem with the development of the field of "late antiquity" within history departments, patristics acquired a new name, "late ancient (or "antique") Christianity." Now, social history approaches abounded, as evidenced in research on women*, asceticism*, law*, slavery*, writing, the family*, children*, and so-called heresy* (the latter of which was much stimulated by the finding of the Nag* Hammadi documents). Social-science* disciplines (especially anthropology) provided "mental tools" quite different from the theological approaches that had dominated traditional patristics. In the English-speaking world, Peter Brown pioneered the introduction of anthropology to studies of late ancient Christianity.

In the early 21st c., social history and social science methods were joined by new approaches stimulated by literary studies and critical theory. History was now understood to be an analysis of the processes of representation. Sharp criticism was leveled at earlier assumptions regarding the "transparent" nature of texts and "authorial intention." The interest in discourse, power, texts, and language fostered by semiotic* theory seemed well suited to the rhetorical and ideological* nature of much patristic writing. How these newer emphases will meld with more established approaches, theological as well as social historical and social scientific, remains an issue for scholarly debate in the 21st c.

ELIZABETH A. CLARK

History, Concepts of. In *The City of God,* Augustine* warned Christians against the cyclical concept of history among the Greeks, insisting that the straight line was the path to salvation*. The cyclical view was characteristic of Greek philosophy after Plato, who located perfection outside time and portrayed the visible world as "a moving image of eternity" (*Timaeus* 37). Stoics believed in periodic conflagrations of the world, after which everything takes place again. Yet Greco-Roman historical writing was generally informed by a "linear" conception; the past furnished *exempla,* because human nature was held to be consistent (Thucydides 1.22.4; Tacitus, *Hist.* 4.74). Yet the point of Augustine's warning was not merely to contrast cyclical and linear time, but to present the past as a series of supernatural transactions manifesting God's anger* or wrath and forgiveness* (see Penance and Forgiveness), culminating in the end of history – history as a process of redemption* inherited from Judaism, rooted in the covenant* and in apocalypticism*.

Luke's* history of his people written for non-Christian Gentile readers (Luke and Acts) was a novel amalgam of Greek and Jewish concepts. As Luke 1:1–4 reveals, the author adopted the double criterion on which Greek historical writing was founded: a choice determined by the intrinsic value of events and the best information available. An elaborate sixfold synchronism (Luke 3:1–2) bridges the stories of different nations. The lives of Jesus and his apostles furnish *exempla* (Acts 10:38). The aim of Luke and Acts – to ensure that nothing about Jesus and his followers escaped the notice of Roman readers (Acts 26:26) – is consistent with the compendious perspective made possible by Roman hegemony. Yet as the continuation of a narrative from Adam (Luke 3:38), Luke and Acts perpetuate the Jewish notion of history as a series of interventions by God in the created world.

Ecclesiastical history, the invention of Eusebius*, is founded on a dichotomous concept: history divided in two by the Incarnation*. The Christian nation was born in heaven, "with the first dispensation concerning the Christ himself," yet appeared on earth in the time of Augustus (*Eccl. Hist.* 1.1.8). Although Eusebius took models from the histories of the philosophic schools and Josephus's* apology for Judaism, his account of the struggle of the church against "heresy*" and persecution was a departure from classical canons. The chronographers of late antiquity and the Middle Ages incorporated mundane events into the Eusebian framework of providential history.

The modern Western concept of history as an immanent and autonomous process in chronological time is part of the non-Christian heritage, even if philosophers of history, such as Hegel*, posit an absolute spirit realizing itself in the dialectic of world history. Against the outlook of historicism (Ranke), Walter Benjamin revives an apocalyptic* concept of history as "a configuration pregnant with tension" in the revolutionary fight for the oppressed. **See also** TIME.

LAURENCE L. WELBORN

History, Theological Concepts of. History is a theological concept because Christians believe in the incarnate* presence of God in history. The emergence of Western historical consciousness and critical methods for the study of history (historiography*) raised a twofold question for theologians in Western Europe and North America: How does God act in history? Can evidence of God's presence be acquired from historical knowledge? H. Richard Niebuhr's* typology of relations between Christ and culture* works well for the relations between God and history.

1. *God against history* is the type of mutual and total opposition that is evident in apocalyptic* and sectarian views which anticipate the imminent end of history and regard history itself as fallen, corrupt, and passing away. God acts only to end history, and knowledge of God is strictly supernatural, based on miraculous disclosures.
2. *God above history* is the view of mainstream Catholic theology. Augustine* posited two cities, heavenly and earthly, in which Christians live. World history transpires in the earthly city, while the city of God is the realm of eternal salvation*. The cities are not disconnected, and a hierarchical synthesis forms between them. God acts in the historical realm, but principally to judge and confute worldly designs.
3. *God of history* is a view that espouses an organic relationship between God and history. God is the immanent power or spirit of history, moving the historical process and manifesting God-self in it. Here the concept of God* is itself historicized, and God can be known from an understanding of the depth and purposes of history. Hegel* is the preeminent exemplar of this type with his image of the divine idea as a weft that drives across the warp of human passions, weaving the fabric of world history.
4. *God and history in paradox** represents a form of dualism, in contrast to the separatism of God "against history", the synthetic view of God "above history," and the holism of the "God of history." This is the view of the Protestant Reformation, especially of Luther*. Christians are subject to the tension of obedience to two authorities or kingdoms, which do not agree and cannot be synthesized but must be accepted. The relationship between God and history is paradoxical and cannot be fully understood.
5. *God the transformer of history* is a modification of the third and fourth types. Against the third type, it expresses a stronger differentiation between God and history. Against the fourth type, it emphasizes the transformative activity of God in history; it recognizes history to be a realm of tragic conflict in which good can be brought out of evil; and it asserts that historical knowledge can serve as corroboration but not as source of faith. This type is associated with some forms of Protestant liberalism*.

PETER C. HODGSON

HISTORY OF CHRISTIANITY CLUSTER

1) *Introductory Entry*

History of World Christianity: A Survey

2) *A Sampling of Regional History*

History of Christianity in Africa
History of Christianity in Africa: North Africa

---

1) Introductory Entry

History of World Christianity: A Survey. Christian history began with a small group of Jewish followers of Jesus* of Nazareth. He was a Galilean who had been crucified under Roman rule. His followers, however, claimed he was the Messiah* whom God had raised from the dead. From Jerusalem they spread the message to surrounding cities. Soon Gentiles were admitted to the group without being required to keep Jewish Law. Drawn from various urban classes, these early Christians gathered in house* churches. They shared the teachings of the apostles*, practiced baptism* and the Eucharist* (Lord's* Supper, Communion*), and experienced charismatic* gifts. As the movement began to accommodate itself to its surrounding social world, it modified its earlier egalitarian tendencies. The social inversion implied by the message of the crucified Christ nevertheless provided a permanent source of internal prophetic* critique.

By the 3rd c., Christian communities were scattered from India* to Iberia (Spain*), with their greatest concentration in the Mediterranean world. Opposition from the Roman government was local at first, and always sporadic; and when it did occur, martyrdom* helped spread the faith*. Within the movement, a variety of interpretations and teachings emerged. One of the most important parties, that of the Gnostics*, taught that Christ had brought secret teachings for an elite body of believers. Responding to them, another group of writers whom later generations deemed to be orthodox gave lasting shape to the contours of Christian doctrine.

The 4th c. brought political establishment. The first kingdom to do so was Armenia*. More important for the history of Christianity worldwide was the conversion of the Roman emperor Constantine*. His new capital, Constantinople, became the center of a grand Christian political experiment. Establishment within the Empire took another half-century to complete. With it came the persecution of Jews in the Roman world (see Judaism and Christianity Cluster). Christians in the Persian Empire, on the other hand, suffered the consequences of Roman establishment as their Sassanid rulers began to persecute them.

Organized monasticism* arose in the deserts of Egypt* in the 4th c. and quickly spread to every region of the Christian world. Monasticism's ascetic* practices continued the spiritual tradition of martyrdom. Its structures provided a vehicle for the leadership of women and an effective missionary force for the spread of Christian faith, especially through the practice of hospitality*.

New disputes, such as the one between Donatists* and Catholics in North Africa, challenged the unity of the church. The most important of these was the Arian* controversy, which led Constantine to call the Council of Nicaea* (325). Nicaea's creed eventually became the trinitarian standard for Christian faith. Arian missionaries meanwhile took their form of Christianity across Rome's northern borders, where it found a reception among Germanic tribes (see Goths; Lombards; Vandals). At about the same time, the kingdom of Ethiopia* formally embraced Christian faith.

The 5th c. was one of christological controversies as competing schools argued over the precise relationship between Christ's human and divine natures (see Christologies Cluster). The Council of Chalcedon* (451) provided a definition that became the standard of orthodoxy in Constantinople and Rome. A dissenting party, called Nestorian* by its detractors, eventually found a home in the Persian Empire in the Assyrian* Church. In Egypt*, Ethiopia, Nubia, Armenia*, and Western Syria* another group of non-Chalcedonian Miaphysite* churches, labeled Monophysite* by their detractors, emerged.

Pressure from immigrating Arian Christian Germanic tribes (5th c.) resulted in the breakdown of imperial control over the western regions of the Roman Empire (including Spain, Italy*, and North Africa). The conversion of the Arian Franks to the Catholic faith (late 5th c.) opened a new chapter in Christian history there. In the eastern Mediterranean, Roman civilization continued in its Greek form. Growing cultural and theological differences between Latin and Greek traditions began to strain relations between the pope* in Rome and the ecumenical* patriarch in Constantinople.

In the 7th c., from Arabia came the Prophet Muhammad, whose teachings became the basis for Islam*. Followers of Islam rapidly conquered Syria, Palestine, Egypt*, Persia, North Africa, and Spain*. Within a century, approximately half of the Christians of the world were under Muslim rule as religious minorities. Farther east, Assyrian* Christian missionaries along the Silk Road found a reception in imperial China* (mid-7th c.). Christian *sutras* and a variety of liturgical texts were produced in Chinese. A small community lasted several centuries before withering away.

Several thousand miles away, the Franks were the dominant political force in the region now known as Europe. Their greatest ruler was Charlemagne*, whom the pope crowned as a new Roman emperor in 800. The Franks sought to impose the Christian faith on their neighbors, but the true task of conversion fell to wandering monastics who brought spirituality to the people.

Charlemagne's coronation was not well received in Constantinople, where Roman imperial rule continued unabated. The Iconoclast* controversy dominated the church there (resolved at Nicaea* II, the seventh ecumenical* council, 787). As in the West, monastic communities were the most important centers of spiritual life. From Constantinople, Christianity spread to the Bulgars*, Slavs, and Russians*. Meanwhile, in the West, the faith made its way north to Scandinavia* by the year 1000.

A series of reforms in the 11th c. significantly strengthened the office of the pope as relations with Constantinople further deteriorated. In Iberia Christian kings began a "reconquest" of Muslim lands. When Muslim rulers closed Jerusalem to Christian pilgrims*, the pope called for the Crusades* – holy wars – against Islam. For the next four centuries, Western Christendom* was on crusade. Muslims in Palestine and Iberia, Jews and other "heretics*" in the West, and Constantinople itself were all its targets. The Crusades failed in their primary goal to establish Latin rule in Palestine. They succeeded in taking Iberia (Spain and Portugal), severely weakened the Byzantine Empire, and opened up a new chapter on terror in the West through the office of the Inquisition*.

A host of new religious movements sprouted in the West during the 12th–14th c. Some were deemed by Rome to be heretical, but others, notably the Franciscans* and Dominicans*, gained official recognition as spiritual orders. Aided by a recovery of classical learning, in part through contact with Arabic learning from Spain, a new intellectual movement, Scholasticism*, took shape. Anselm*, Abelard*, Thomas Aquinas*, and Bonaventure* are just a few of the names associated with their endeavors.

In 1204 a crusading army from the West sacked Constantinople and installed a Latin king for several decades. The office of the ecumenical* patriarch was disrupted, leading indirectly to the formation of autocephalous* Orthodox* churches in the eastern Mediterranean world. Greek rule was eventually restored, but political and theological pressure from the Latin West continued to weaken the Eastern Christian city.

In the 13th c., the most decisive event in world political affairs was the rise of a Mongol ruler named Genghis Khan. His descendants established an empire that extended from the Pacific Ocean to Europe and included China, Central Asia, Persia, Russia, and Armenia. The first Mongol rulers were shamanists* who practiced a moderate degree of religious toleration. By the end of the 13th c., most had converted to Islam or Buddhism*, putting renewed pressure on Christians who lived within their territories.

In Egypt a new dynasty arose and brought about the end of the Christian kingdom of Nubia in the 13th c. Ethiopia* remained the lone Christian kingdom in Africa, and its churches found themselves facing new pressures from Islam. A revival of the Semitic roots of Ethiopian culture helped revitalize Ethiopian Christianity during this period.

Disruptions in the papal office and a time of competing claimants coincided with the growth of power of national kingdoms in the West. The kingdom of Muscovy emerged from under Mongol rule to carry Russian national aspirations forward. The Ottoman dynasty, in the meantime, had come to power in Asia Minor and in 1453 conquered Constantinople, bringing the Byzantine Empire to an end.

The 15th c. opened the history of the modern world. Portuguese and Spanish seafarers led the way in the violent conquest of the Americas, rapid expansion of the African slave* trade, and European colonial incursions into Asia (see Portuguese Explorations, Conquests, and Missions; Spanish Explorations, Conquests, and Missions). At the same time, the internal disintegration of Western Christendom* began. Humanists* led the way, undertaking a renaissance* in arts and letters. They were soon joined by church reformers*. While some remained under Rome, others, called Evangelicals* or Protestants*, separated. In England the crown took direct control of the church. New confessional state* churches emerged, e.g. in Germany*, Switzerland*, Holland (Netherlands*), and Scotland*. Throughout Europe radical communities of Anabaptists* separated from any civil government. The result was a century of warfare and religious strife.

In the Americas, the Spanish Conquest, coupled with the introduction of new diseases, was brutal. Christianity was forced on the native population, but indigenous expressions soon began to appear. African slaves also began embracing Christianity, often identifying traditional deities with Christian saints. In the Congo*, an independent African Christian kingdom arose, prefiguring forms of African Christianity that would later flourish. Farther east the Portuguese brought Catholic missionaries to India*, Japan*, China*, and Vietnam*. In China converts were initially allowed to maintain rites of ancestor* veneration, a practice Rome later forbade.

France*, Sweden*, Holland, and England (United* Kingdom of Great Britain) soon joined the colonial venture in North America. The English were the most successful, allowing religious dissenters such as Puritans* and Quakers* to undertake new settlements.

Protestant and Catholics alike sought to exert pressure on the office of the ecumenical patriarch in Istanbul, who was now appointed by the Ottoman rulers. Roman Catholic missions were active farther east in Syria, Ethiopia, and India, exerting pressure there on the indigenous Christian communities. Russia, too, felt the pressures from the West as churches left the Orthodox faith to enter communion with Rome. The 17th-c. schism between Old* Believers and the Russian Orthodox* Church resulted when reformers sought to introduce changes from within.

Western Europe was home to a 17th- to 18th-c. intellectual revolution that became known as the Enlightenment*. Supported by the gains of science* and the growth of rationalism* in philosophy, the Enlightenment attacked the authority of tradition* in all its forms. Against the power of church and state alike, it posed the rights of the individual "man of reason." The response from within the churches was varied, but in some places new enlightened forms of Christian belief began to emerge.

For Roman Catholics, spiritual life continued to be associated primarily with the various religious* orders. Within the state-sanctioned Protestant churches of the Continent, Pietists* began to organize *collegia*, or small groups, for prayer and spiritual renewal. Pietists were prominent among the first Protestant missionaries from the

West to join Roman Catholics in Asia. Prominent preachers, most notably the Methodists*, stirred revival* in England, while in North America the Great* Awakening took place. The Awakening brought African slaves* into Protestant Christianity for the first time in the 18th c. Invisible institutions of slave religion emerged on plantations in the Southern USA, and independent African churches were formed in the North (see African American Cluster).

The War of Independence (1775–83), which resulted in the formation of the USA, and the French Revolution (from 1789) marked the birth of the modern nation-state. Political disestablishment was at the heart of the new political enterprise. Meanwhile, the industrial revolution was under way in Europe, fueling the growing economy* of global capitalism. In Europe, liberal democratic political ideals took hold among the middle classes (from the early 19th c.). Socialism and more radical communistic ideas spread (later 19th c.; see Marxism and Christianity). Historical* criticism was embraced in the universities and brought to bear on biblical studies (see Bible Interpretation Cluster, Introductory Entry), while the advances of science* forced a fundamental rethinking of basic cosmology.

Criticism of a different sort brought an end to the African slave trade that had provided forced labor for agricultural production in the Americas. Abolitionism involved Europeans and Africans alike in its efforts. The revolutionary spirit of the age bought about political independence and the abolition of slavery in Latin America as well (see Mission Cluster: And Antislavery; Slavery and the Church in Brazil; Slavery and the Church in North America; Slavery and the Church through the Centuries). The Catholic Church, which had been closely connected with the colonial regimes there, initially suffered a considerable loss of influence. It was soon able to reforge its alliances with the new leadership, however, and continued its dominant religious role on the Latin American continent.

Revivalism*, romanticism*, transcendentalism*, and social* reform all characterized the 19th-c. US religious context. The new nation was Protestant in character. As it expanded westward, it annexed half of the territory of Mexico and continued warfare against Native Americans. A bloody civil war tore apart the nation (mid-19th c.) and led to the emancipation of people of African descent. Within a decade, a new system of racial terror emerged in the South. Immigration reshaped the ethnic and religious character of northern urban areas as they underwent rapid industrialization (late 19th c.).

The 18th- to 19th-c. European colonial enterprise grew, opening the door to Western missionaries throughout Asia and Africa (see Colonialism and Imperialism and Christian Theology). A number of new Protestant missionary societies were organized (early 19th c.) as part of what soon became the largest missionary movement in history (see Mission Cluster). European warships forced imperial China to open its doors to foreigners (mid-19th c.). European powers formally divided all of Africa into colonial territories (Berlin* Conference, 1884–85). These were viewed by many in the West as providential acts, paving the way for further missions. From Russia, Orthodox missionaries traveled east into Siberia and Alaska. Many of these missionaries did succeed in planting Christian churches in new territories. As they did, however, the importance of older confessional identities, marked as they were by national and historical factors of their land of origin, declined.

The 20th c. saw the rapid growth of anticolonial and postcolonial* forms of Christianity under successive generations of indigenous leadership in Asia, Africa, and Latin America. European civilization meanwhile tore itself apart through two world wars, then fell into a cold war that placed the entire planet under the shadow of nuclear annihilation. By the end of the century, a new global network of Islamic militants, employing the methods of terrorism and fueled by anti-Western sentiments, dominated the global political scene. This was a century of great death and destruction. Human beings died in the gas chambers of Auschwitz and in the killing fields of Cambodia. It was also a century of great scientific and technological advance. Human beings walked on the moon and were tied together through a global system called the Internet.

The Christian vocabulary expanded significantly in the 20th c. to include the ecumenical* movement, Pentecostalism*, African* Instituted Churches, fundamentalism*, Vatican* II, the Charismatic* Movement, and Liberation* theology. Interfaith dialogue* joined conversion* and church planting as forms of mission*, while many churches opened the ranks of leadership to women*. Perhaps the most important historical event of the 20th c., however, was the shift in the center of world Christianity. After more than a millennium of Christian culture and 500 years of dominating world Christianity, Europe underwent rapid secularization* to become a post-Christian* continent. Meanwhile, Christianity registered enormous growth in Asia and Africa, joining Latin America to create a new global Christian majority. Two thousand years after that small band of Jewish disciples first appeared to spread the news of Jesus, Christians now number between 1.5 and 2.1 billion persons with churches found in every continent.

DALE T. IRVIN

---

2) A Sampling of Regional History

History of Christianity in Africa

Christianity in Egypt and the Maghreb. When the Pan-African Liberian Edward Wilmot Blyden visited Egypt in 1866, the experience transformed his life's journey. He was deeply impressed by the creativity and achievements of his ancestors and determined to encourage Africans to recover the glory of their heritage. Skeptics, unwilling to accept that the early church fathers were Africans, questioned whether Egypt was actually an African country and utilized the alleged curse of Ham* to ignore the Kushites, Nubians, Abyssinians, and Africans south of the Sahara desert. Admittedly, Africa is a medley of ancient cultures: Nilotic, Berber, Numidian, Nubian, East African Negroid, and remnants of marauding groups – Punics, Romans, diasporic Jews, and others. But from the earliest stories in the Bible, through the Prophets, the childhood of Jesus, and the ministry of the early apostles, Africans featured prominently; Jacob, Jesus, and apostles took refuge during various periods in Africa. The internal history of the Coptic* Orthodox Church reclaims this past: when the center of gravity of Christianity shifted from Palestine to the Greco-Roman world, Africa was central to the development of early Christianity; according to tradition, the apostle Mark, whose parents were from Cyrene, was the first *abuna* (bishop) of the Coptic Church and was martyred in the cosmopolitan city of Alexandria. Indeed, Africa produced much of the patristic literature that shaped the dogma. The school in Alexandria* set forth the methods of text examination, exegesis, and philosophical language under Pantaneus (2nd c.; the first head of the catechetical school in Alexandria, according to Eusebius*) and Clement* that became normative. Christianity has a longer history in Africa than in the northern globe.

Early African Christianity at first benefited from association with Judaism, the only *licita religio*, and the Septuagint*, the Greek translation of the OT by Jews in Alexandria. Christianity followed the inculturating* pathway of the indigenous religious worldview that already affirmed resurrection*, life after death*, salvation*, miracles*, and divine kinship. Its strength, however, lay in its intellectual vitality; the Alexandrian school provided both the apologetics for this persecuted minority and a consolidation of the doctrine, polity*, liturgy, and ethics of Christianity in its formative period, when very diverse texts competed for authority before the canon* of Scriptures* was established.

From Egypt, Christianity spread to Libya and "North Africa," Tunisia, and Algeria (known at that time as Africa, Carthage, and Numidia) along the Mediterranean breadbasket of the Roman Empire (see the present cluster: In Africa: North Africa).

African intellectuals dominated the effort to establish the new Christianity. Origen* was invited by the teachers of Caesarea; Diocletian invited Lactantius* to teach literature in his palace at Bithynia, just as Augustine* was invited to teach in Milan. Africans pioneered Conciliarist* and ecumenical traditions and won the ears of the Syriac*, Cappadocian*, and Greco-Roman teachers during the synodal debates that raged throughout the Roman Empire. The avid debater Tertullian* represents another tendency in African Christianity, namely charismatic* spirituality. Martyrdom strengthened the appeal of the spiritual route and linked it to the search for identity and national resistance. The eremitic* tradition flowered. Pachomius* and his tradition of sacrificial, radical discipleship* and daily ordering of life constitute the root of many Western traditions, especially the Benedictine*. Similarly, Optatus* shaped Western penitential practice.

Translation of the Scriptures into indigenous languages followed apace as the movement expanded; growth was often illustrated by the number of bishops at synods, the intellectual achievements of Augustine* of Hippo, and the endurance of persecutions reflected in vigorous diatribes against *traditores* who betrayed their faith. Stories of faithfulness during persecution, like that of Perpetua* and Felicitas, represented a new development, noble women opening their homes to protect poorer sisters (the origin of nunneries). Tertullian's *Ad uxorem* exemplifies the internal dynamics of Christians' care for one another, evangelistic ardor, construction of community, and spiritual devotion. This was a vibrant age of Christianity in North Africa until the end of Constantine's* rule and was prolonged by a more subdued Christianity under the rule of the Arian Christian Vandals* (429–534).

By 500, there were c8 million (M) Christians in Northern Africa, but only 5 M by 1000, 2.5 M by 1200, and 1.5 M by 1500 – a decline that was caused by multiple factors (see the present cluster: In Africa: North Africa).

Origins of Nubian and Ethiopian Christianity. The relationship between Egypt and Nubia (farther south) was cultural, commercial, and religious. The ancient Nubian kingdom of Meroe was linked to Christianity through the Ethiopian eunuch (Acts 8:26–40), traditionally known as Judich, the treasurer of the *candace* (queen) of Meroe. Formal Christianity was established in the 5th c. in the three Nubian kingdoms: from north to south along the Nile river, Nobatia (Nobatae), Makuria (Maqurrah), and Alwa (Alodia). The Byzantine emperor Justinian* sent a pro-Chalcedonian* mission led by Longinus (543), but his queen, Theodora*, outwitted him with a Miaphysite* mission led by Julian that arrived first in Nobatia. Longinus arrived in Alwa. When the three kingdoms united for security and political reasons, Nubia witnessed a Christian revival evident in the conversion of pagan temples into Christian worship places, royal patronage, and the erection of cathedrals and monastic* houses.

Earlier, two young Syrians, Frumentius* (c300–c380) and his friend Aedesius, were brought as slaves to the Aksum court (Ethiopian highlands), where Frumentius became the tutor of the young king Ezana and persuaded him to convert to Christianity (see Ethiopia). Frumentius, later trained in Alexandria, was ordained as the first *abuna* in Ethiopia. He brought some of the ancient documents from Alexandria before the Arabs burned the city's large library. Ethiopian Christianity revolved around the king, the *abuna*, and the heads of the oldest monastic houses. It had strong Hebraic roots, a tradition of icons*, and crosses, a lively liturgical tradition that increasingly absorbed elements of indigenous culture, numerous monasteries, and a wealth of legends, including one concerning the Ark of the Covenant that the son of the queen of Sheba had duplicitously brought from Jerusalem.

The Christian presence up the Nile continued to be important until the 14th c. in Nubia and much later in Ethiopia.

Early African Christianity and Islam, 7th–15th Centuries. The decline of Christianity in Northern Africa points to the insurgence of Islam* in the 7th-c. Maghreb. It is surmised that Christianity had shallow roots or was emasculated by philosophical, doctrinal debates and the tax burdens of the dysfunctional Byzantine emperors. Muslims with their military strategy, horsemanship, and ascetic discipline appeared to be liberators. Yet a closer look indicates that there was a measure of resistance, possibly because the Arabs avoided mixing with the local infidel population, squabbled among themselves, and delegated the mundane task of governance to the bishops and local authorities. The process of Islamization came later amid the hybridization of Islamic identity; Muslims outlawed proselytization and used marriage as an instrument of increasing their numbers. Thus the Christian population was reduced through emigration, incorporation, forced conversion, and cultural exchanges. Still, Christianity consolidated itself in rural Coptic* villages, becoming a marker of national identity, and started a slow decline from the 13th c. in Nubia. Ethiopia was saved from the Islamic pressure by its reconnection with European Christianity in the 15th c. By that time, Ahmad Gran (the left-handed Arab) had seized the region that is now Eritrea.

Iberian Catholicism and Africa, 15th–17th Centuries. Islam also presented challenges to Europe. Islam controlled the breadbasket of Southern Europe and the Levant route to the sources of spices in the Far East. The Muslims established a lucrative trade in salt from the Saharan oasis Taghaza and the trans-Saharan gold trade in the Futa-Jallon basin. They developed an intellectual center in Timbuktu (also known as Tombouktu), the first university in Africa; its huge library collections are currently being edited and indexed.

Challenges elicit responses. Europeans first responded with futile crusades. By the 15th c., Spain* and Portugal* united in the *reconquista* project. The Portuguese prince Henry the Navigator (1394–1460) experimented with new sails, astrolabe, compass, keel, and many naval projects and finally recaptured Ceuta (North Africa, 1415). By 1460 Prince Henry's captains had reached Sierra* Leone in search of an alternative sea route to the trans-Saharan gold and spices of the Far East. The Portuguese crown secured the monopoly of each new territory with papal bulls and the Padroado* agreements that left evangelization and Christian activities under the control of the Portuguese crown. Christianization was articulated as a motive in this predominantly commercial enterprise, along with the hope of reconnecting with the mythical empire of Prester* John. But the Portuguese cautiously stayed on the islands and forayed only a few miles from the coast into a few places, such as the Gold Coast. The Cape* Verde Islands became a little Portugal, while São Thomé served as a major refueling depot. Only in the Kongo-Soyo kingdoms (Angola*) did they establish a significant Christian community. A court alliance bound the monarchy and the elite into a ceremonial Roman Catholic spirituality and immersed the Catholic Church in political intrigues and the slave* trade. In the 17th c., an African girl who belonged to a *ngunza* prophetic cult claimed to be possessed by the spirit of St. Antony* and to have received a message to mobilize the Christians to stop the violent civil warfare. The Roman Catholics hanged this patron of popular Catholicism as a heretic*.

When the Portuguese made incursions into Zimbabwe*, the conversion of the king and queen of the Mutapa kingdom was short-lived. They later encountered the Oman Arabs on the islands of the Indian Ocean and the coast of Eastern Africa, and established themselves in Zanzibar, Malindi, and Sofola, where they crossed to India, Sumatra, and Java (mid-1600s). The shoestring empire yielded spices, gold, slaves, and few Christians. Various approved religious orders made evangelistic efforts. Records indicate the ordination of a number of indigenous priests, mostly mulatto sons of traders, domestic servants, and assistants.

Evangelization also occurred in Dahomey (now Benin*) and Nigeria* (17th c.) when the Portuguese made incursions into the Benin and Warri kingdoms from Cape* Verde. The kings were hosts to the church and school, and the Portuguese exchanged guns for pepper. In Warri the *olu* (king) sent his son to study in Portugal. He ascended to the throne but was quickly dethroned, because the Portuguese abandoned the treaties and purchased pepper from India. The *oba* (king) of Benin deported the priests. Commercial enterprise was more important than Christian evangelization. The Portuguese celebrated by striking a gold coin named the *cruzado*.

Chaplaincy and Christian Presence in the 17th and 18th Centuries. Other European countries joined the lucrative venture: Spain disengaged from the united monarchy and competed with Portugal. Spaniards, the seafaring Danes and Dutch, who provided the transport haulage, then the French and English seized portions of the Portuguese African shoestring empire. The slave trade dominated and stifled evangelization as prospective converts were enslaved. By the late 17th c., there were 21 slave-trade forts on the West African coast alone. Some appointed chaplains. Many did not. The chaplains were ridiculed and paid in trade goods. The Danes and Dutch trained some Africans in Europe and brought them back as chaplains, among them Philip Quaque, Jacob Capitein, Christian Protten, Frederick Svane, and Anton Amo. Each failed out of frustration. Amo became a prominent philosopher and professor in Europe.

Abolitionism and Evangelical Revival. As the slave trade stifled evangelization, abolitionism* was the engine of the Evangelical revival. Whether as a result of conscience, economic calculation, or humanistic philanthropy (the influential abolitionist Clapham* sect of Evangelical Anglicans exemplified this ambivalence), the evangelization of Africa became a solution. There were many stakeholders: African Americans adopted a number of strategies that included the option to redeem mother Africa through Christianity; diasporic Africans such as Equiano wrote moving reminiscences of enslavement that stirred consciences; and liberated slaves like Paul Cuffee invested resources in establishing a commercial relationship with Africa and in mobilizing abolitionist groups on both sides of the Atlantic. Quakers* invested in abolitionist organizations. The American Revolution yielded enough liberated slaves to create a climate that resulted in the 1807 abolition of slave trade in the British Empire. The British philanthropist and politician Fowell Buxton suggested in his *Africa Slave Trade and Its Remedy* (1839) a combination of treaties with chiefs, legitimate trade in raw materials that could feed British industries, and Christianization as a civilizing agent.

These political, economic, and religious projects catalyzed geographical explorations and the experimental colony of freed slaves in Freetown, Sierra* Leone. When the experiment almost collapsed in 1792, the British shipped African Americans from Nova Scotia to the rescue. Some were Baptist and Methodist, and many had imbibed the New Light Charismatic* Movement. They forged a new Christian spirit and nurtured those who were freed by British squadrons from slave ships on the West African coast. The Holy Ghost Fathers played the same role on the East African coast. Many of these freed slaves returned later to evangelize their native countries.

The enlarged missionary enterprise in the 19th c. changed the face of Christianity in Africa with respect to the number of men and women missionaries and associations, their strategies and foci, resources, and the areas covered (see Berlin Conference). The voluntarist principle sidestepped denominational obstructions, ensured mass support and funding, and enhanced evangelical zeal. Translation* of the Bible into the vernacular, education* programs, charitable institutions, and the recruitment of indigenous personnel combined to engage African responses. By 1914 Christianity had invaded the hinterlands of many African countries. The expansion was uneven, depending on the colonizing nation, accessibility to water and rail transport, and rivalry among missionaries. Education* was the most successful instrument of evangelization.

African responses to missionary and colonial structures took three forms: loyalty, voice, and exit. The educated elite created a movement, Ethiopianism, that sought to rebuild African identity through religion and championed the idea that Africans should evangelize Africa. They gave voice to African discontent and contested the Western monopoly on church doctrine and cultural expression. Some made an exit to found native African churches (based on indigenous forms of African* Religion). Prophets emerged all over the continent, emphasizing the resonance between indigenous worldviews and the charismatic* dimensions of the gospel. Some emerged from within indigenous African Religion; others had had previous contact with Christianity.

From World Wars to Decolonization. What characterized African Christianity during that period included the disruption of missionary structures, increased space for indigenous agency, the consolidation of Christianity during the interwar years, an increase in the number of Christians through indigenous adjustment to the colonial situation, the multiplication of African* Instituted Churches, known as "Zions" in Southern Africa, *aladura* (prayer people) in Western Africa, and *abaroho* in Eastern Africa. Emphasis on prayer and the inculturation* of indigenous ingredients into doctrine, polity, liturgy, and ethics created a new Christianity that would merge with nationalist struggles for decolonization after 1945 when war-weary Europeans reassessed the cost of colonization. Churches fought against colonization by developing state theology, indigenization projects that included native leadership (theological education and the ordination of Africans), liturgical renewal following Vatican* II, engagement with freedom fighters, and ecumenical* ventures such as church union projects. But these initiatives were attacked from three directions. (1) From the inside, the educated elite rejected limited indigenization, called for a moratorium, and started the African theology project. (2) Revivals* broke out in secondary schools and universities among students who later founded Pentecostal* or charismatic* ministries. (3) From the outside, the cultural nationalists in the new states attacked Christianity. The pace of decolonization of African churches intensified. By 1975, when the World* Council of Churches met in Nairobi, it was obvious that the church in Africa had come of age. Since then, the growth of Christianity with charismatic Pentecostalism at the cutting edge has remained unstoppable. The denominational churches are now charismatized*. **See also** **CHARISMATIC AND PENTECOSTAL MOVEMENTS CLUSTER: IN AFRICA; CHURCH AND STATE RELATIONS CLUSTER: IN AFRICA; PROTESTANTISM CLUSTER: IN AFRICA** (various entries); **ROMAN CATHOLICISM CLUSTER: IN AFRICA.**

OGBU U. KALU

History of Christianity in Africa: North Africa. Christianity first entered Africa in Egypt and spread to Libya (see the present cluster: In Africa). The Gospel of Mark* and Acts* mention, in particular, the presence of disciples coming from the town of Cyrene (Mark 15:21; Acts 2:10, 11:20). The history of Christianity in Western North Africa (modern Tunisia, Algeria, and Morocco) can be divided into three chapters: (1) the expansion and disappearance of a Latin church (2nd–12th c.); (2) a period dominated by captives, slaves, and merchants (12th–19th c.); and (3) colonial times and their aftermath.

The Expansion and Disappearance of a Latin Church (2nd–12th Centuries). Christianity arrived in North Africa first on the coast and later inland with traders and settlers from all regions of the Mediterranean world. Historical documents show that Christian communities had been formed by the end of the 1st c. Soon, every small city shaped its organization around a bishop and his clergy. By 250 CE, regional councils drew 100 bishops. Around 350 there were twice that number. In 411 a council drew 470 bishops, and 50 years later, c700.

This expansion took place despite the many periods of persecution* in the 2nd and 3rd c., during which many Africans gave their lives for their faith. Numerous accounts of their martyrdom* are extant, and some of these martyrs are still venerated by the Roman Catholic Church, e.g. Felicitas and Perpetua* (d203) and Cyprian* (d258).

Among all the figures of the North African Church, special mention should be made of Tertullian* (155–240). Born in Carthage, he was one of the key witnesses of that period and the author of many works written in defense of the faith. He is known as well for his radicalism in matters of morals and his negative views of women. Cyprian*, bishop of Carthage, was viewed by the other bishops as their leader. He regularly called regional councils, which gave a sense of unity to this growing church. Between two bouts of persecution, he encountered a problem that was later to divide the church: the reconciliation of apostates.

The greatest figure of the North African Church remains Augustine* (354–430), who lived during the period after the Roman persecutions had ended with Constantine's* Edict of Milan (313). This return of peace brought about a new period of expansion for the church, but also triggered a split. The quarrel occurred over the reintegration of those Christians who had denied their faith at the time of persecution. Some wanted the church to be rather lenient, while others rejected the lapsed and even doubted the validity of sacraments* conferred by clerics who had fallen and been reconciled. The latter were led by Donatus, their bishop in Carthage, who gave his name to the rigorist group: the Donatists*.

As time went on, the church split into two groups, with two bishops and two clergies in most cities, and violence erupted again and again. In some cases, religious difference was reinforced by social troubles between rich and poor. Elected bishop of Hippo in 397, Augustine led the opposition to the Donatists through teaching, preaching, debates, and councils.

Another danger was already threatening this divided Roman Catholic Church: the Vandals*, a Christian Arian* people from Germany who invaded North Africa. Their kingdom with Carthage as its capital (in modern Tunisia) lasted from 428 to 534. In the name of their Arian beliefs (asserting with the moderate Arians that the Son is "like" [*homoios*] the Father, but denying that the Son has the same essence as the Father, as the Nicene* doctrine of the Trinity* does), they persecuted Catholic Christians: most of the bishops were deposed or expelled and replaced by Arian bishops. Many Catholic faithful were killed or tortured; their church leaders took refuge in Europe; others were deported and sold into slavery to the Moors (as they would come to be known).

It fell to the Byzantine emperor Justinian* to put an end to the Vandal occupation in 534, at least in a large part of North Africa. Under the rule of Justinian, who cultivated the Chalcedonians of the Eastern churches and the rapprochement with the West, the Roman Catholic Church enjoyed another period of peace, which could not conceal, however, that its strength was no longer what it had been.

This decline became evident when the Arabs arrived and, in spite of strenuous Roman or Berber resistance, launched successive expeditions to conquer North Africa from 647 to 705. The military victory of the Muslim armies did not mean the end of the Christian presence in North Africa. As in the East, Islamic* rule meant that non-Muslims – Jews and Christians – were relegated to *dhimmi* status (lit. "protected" people, because they are "people of the Book," *Ahl al-Kitab*), which entailed the payment of a head tax and the acceptance of an inferior position in social and political life.

Suddenly, the links between Europe, Rome in particular, and North African Christians were severed. From 630 onward, written sources, formerly abundant, become scarce, almost nonexistent. People and land were now integrated into a new world, that of the nascent Islamic Empire in the East. Yet one finds signs of a Christian presence far into the 11th c. Repeatedly, Arab geographers spoke of whole regions and villages peopled by Christians. Apparently these communities were left to fend for themselves. Many, clergy included, fled to Europe. The new rulers recruited many Berbers for their armies, requiring them to convert to Islam before enlistment. In cities and villages, Christians went on as before, speaking Latin, tilling the land, or trading, taking care of those churches that they were able to maintain. Rome noted that the number of bishops had dramatically fallen (there were fewer than five in 1053) and some priests were sent to the pope to be ordained as bishops in the 1070s.

New developments hastened the disappearance of Christianity. Around 1050 the arrival of nomadic peoples from Arabia destroyed the old farming system, bringing insecurity to the countryside and ruin to the cities. Muslim religious leaders had often expressed anti-Christian feelings, while rulers and common people seemed to favor peaceful coexistence. The final blow came c1150 when the Almohads, a group of Islamic zealots, took power in Morocco, conquered North Africa and Spain, and in present-day Tunisia, forced Jews and Christians to embrace Islam or be killed.

Christianity did not disappear, purely and simply, on account of persecution. The Christian Church, in fact, was weaker than Eastern Christianity in Egypt for various reasons. Local culture had never been given the chance to give birth to a "native liturgy." Internal strife had weakened its energy. It was a church present in cities, but without surviving monasteries (monks in Eastern North Africa preserved Christian identity in their monasteries, which provided needed theologians and bishops). Moreover, under the Vandals and the Byzantines, and finally at the time of the Arab conquest, clergy and laity fled to Europe in great numbers.

Christians as Captives, Slaves, and Merchants (12th–19th Centuries). The native Christian presence that had faded away was replaced by the Christianity of foreigners in North Africa: trade went on between the northern and southern shores of the Mediterranean Sea. In most harbors, Christian traders from Italy, Spain, France, and Portugal took advantage of commercial treaties between European powers and North African rulers and lived in the cities. At times a priest came with them, officially accepted as their chaplain.

Muslim rulers sometimes felt the need to enlist Christian European troops to ensure their personal security. They came as a body, led by noblemen from Europe and an occasional priest.

Most of the Christian presence, however, consisted of slaves* and captives. Privateers attacked merchant ships of European countries or raided European shores, bringing back with them thousands of captives. They were usually treated harshly. Many were harassed until they turned Muslim. Christian religious, especially Franciscans*, came to ransom them, if they could, or give them spiritual or physical comfort in their trials. Christianity and Islam were not religions in dialogue, but warring empires. Religious conversion meant an act of treason against one's own people.

Colonial Times and Their Aftermath. With the conquest of Algeria by France (from 1830) and the establishment of protectorates over Tunisia (1881) and Morocco (1912), thousands of people of the Christian tradition came to live in these countries, where the bulk of the population was Muslim. The Christian presence was a simple extension of European Christianity. The Muslim and Christian communities met not on religious grounds, but on the political and social levels, where suspicion, then opposition and downright hostility, led to riots, war, and finally independence (Morocco and Tunisia, 1956; Algeria, 1962). Most of the Christians left with their clergy.

Roman Catholic leaders (Cardinal Duval, other bishops, as well as a number of priests and men and women religious*) stayed on. A new spirit developed between members of that tiny community. They did not conceive of their presence as a means to gain converts and establish a large native church. They felt called to bear witness to God's unconditional love toward all peoples. This love could be expressed by selfless service toward these new nations and their people. As time went on, that attitude brought about a change of atmosphere: friendship began to displace enmity.

When Algeria entered a near civil war in 1992, moderate people suffered at the hands of radical groups. Tens of thousands of persons were killed. Christians remained to offer what help they could, unwilling to desert their friends in time of danger. Nineteen of them – bishop, monks, religious, and nuns – were killed. Even though some Muslims embraced Christianity, most Christians in North Africa are still of foreign origin. Their aim is to be recognized as a "church of non-Christians."

FR. JEAN-MARIE GAUDEUL

History of Christianity in Asia. There are at least two approaches to understanding the history of Christianity in Asia: an expansionist and a postcolonial* approach. The expansionist approach reflects a West-centered understanding of Christianity. It was written in the West from the perspective of churches in Europe and North America whose missionaries sought to expand the churches' influence to the southern continents with royal or state blessings (see Mission Cluster: In Asia). By contrast, the postcolonial approach reflects a historical consciousness that arose primarily in the 20th c. among peoples of colonized regions who determined to rewrite history from the perspective of the "young churches" and who wanted to elucidate how Christianity is grounded in the history of the new Asian nations. While both approaches are political and, to a large degree, mutually exclusive in principle, when read critically together, they contribute to a rich understanding of Christianity as a whole in Asia.

A major expansion of Christianity took place in the colonial era (16th–early 20th c.). It started as a competition for resources and overseas influence between Spain and Portugal (see Portuguese Explorations, Conquests, and Missions; Spanish Explorations, Conquests, and Missions). Other European countries, Britain, France, and Germany, filled the gap as soon as Spain and Portugal retreated. The US historian Kenneth Scott Latourette describes the 1800–1914 period as the "Great Century" when Christianity expanded extensively into Asia (and Africa), with missionaries from Europe and North America setting up numerous missionary stations and later "young churches." Stories of "success" have been recorded in massive missionary journals and correspondence, which speak of the steady increase in the number of churches and converts in the Philippines*, India*, China*, Southeast Asia, Indochina, and the South Pacific Islands and Australia*, where colonial conquest took hold. In the cases of some "tribal*" and rural areas of North India, the borderland between Southern China and Indochina, including Northern Thailand*, Laos*, Cambodia*, Myanmar*, and the mountain ranges in Taiwan*, entire villages were converted to Christianity and remained Christian thereafter. In the cities, education, medicine, and charity services became the chief means by which Christian missions won over the hearts and souls of "heathen" people.

Many missionaries of the time carried out their work with a heavy imperialistic impulse (see Mission Cluster: And Imperialism). Their task was to save the wrecked souls* of the evil-driven colonies through the conversion* of "uncivilized pagans" to the one true religion, Christianity, and to the superior science and values of the culture* and civilization of the West. Missionary boards presupposed that their role was to preach "the Truth" and to assume political control and governance. It was therefore not a coincidence that the relations between the missionary churches of the West and the young churches in Asia were structured exactly like the relations between the home colonial bureaucracy in Western nations and the government in Asian colonies. Many missionaries enjoyed the privilege of extraterritorial protection and special access to colonialist facilities similar to that of colonial officers. The organic relationship between Christianity and Western colonial powers placed the churches of Asia in the position of being firmly identified with foreign domination and added a subtle weight to the colonial constitution of Christianity in Asia.

Nevertheless, many missionaries played a dual role in the various colonies. In some remote areas in the mountains or poor inlands, missionaries were reported to have often suffered from tremendous health problems and endured much cultural isolation as they dedicated themselves to education* and medical work with the "natives." In the cities, some missionaries frequently sent critical comments to their countries, denouncing the cruel exploitation of the "natives" by settlers and colonial offices. In some cases, utilizing the authority of their respective missionary boards, they actually influenced local colonial legislation, e.g. against women and child abuse in such cases as *sati* and the prostitution of girls in India and foot-binding and the slavery of girls in China. Missionaries were also pioneers in the education of girls and the training of women as teachers and nurses in colonized territories. Confronted by the tragedies they saw on the front line, some missionaries were among the few voices of conscience opposing, e.g., the opium trade in China. Thus even from the perspective of Western expansion, it appears that Christianity advanced in Asia from the 16th c. because it was driven both by imperialistic and economic forces and by the humanistic instincts of concerned missionaries.

The 1910 World* Missionary Conference in Edinburgh* was one of the first occasions when Asian Christians consciously articulated their regional identities and resisted continuous control by their founding churches in the West. National consciousness in Asian countries grew tremendously between the two world wars and was heightened with the successive independence of Asian nations after World War II until the 1970s. Since the 1950s, Asian historians such as K. M. Panikkar have raised serious questions regarding the political, economic, and cultural domination of the West, and Asian theologians such as D. T. Niles*, M. M. Thomas*, Masao Takenaka, and K. H. Ting have called for indigenous churches and the development of Asian theology in order to rid Christianity of any remaining imperialistic tinge. The subsequent establishment of regional ecumenical structures such as the Asian Office of the World* Student Christian Federation, the Christian* Conference of Asia (originally the East Asian Christian Conference), and the Asian Alliance of YMCAs* set the stage for a new Asian Christian self-understanding.

It is not uncommon today to read the history of Christianity not only as an eastward movement but also as a westward one. Christianity did not originate from the West, as came to be assumed in the 20th c. Its origin was actually in Asia, given that some of the first church centers, in Bethlehem, Jerusalem, Antioch*, and Armenia*, were geographically located in Western Asia. Early Christian communities were established outside the Roman Empire starting in the 1st c. long before the Western imperialist era. Assyrian* Christians (commonly but inappropriately called Nestorians*, to refer to the early Asian Christian communities) expanded extensively in the East between the 1st and 10th c. Probably the oldest and one of the strongest traditions in the history of Christianity in Asia is the alleged mission of Thomas* the Apostle, who not long after Jesus Christ's resurrection, brought the gospel to India*. A Christian in Edessa*, on the bank of Euphrates River (see Iraq) between Roman Asia and Persia (see Iran*), wrote a lively account called the Acts* of Thomas, a 3rd-c. popular apocryphal text that has survived as the oldest account of a church in Asia beyond the Roman Empire. Despite its partially legendary status, the tradition of the "apostle to the East" provides clear testimony to the spread of Christianity in Asia outside the Roman Empire and east of the Euphrates long before the regional name of Asia came to be used. In sum, from the 1st c., Christianity stretched from West Asia (the ancient Near East) along the Old Silk Road through Persia to China* and along the water routes from Mesopotamia and Arabia to India* and Sri* Lanka; it was adapted in a variety of ways by these cultures over the centuries.

This recent "recovery" of the Asian origin and Asian tradition of Christianity represents a postcolonial politics of resistance to the continued imperial legacy of the West. A strong sense of Asian identity emerged as an outcome of the extensive Western conquest of land and peoples starting in the 16th c.; a strong quest for an Asian Christianity followed. A rewriting of history attempts to incorporate the rise and fall of Christianity into the history of the vast continent that came to be known as Asia. Over against the Imperial West, this recovered history aims to minimize the influence of Western churches in the development of churches, beliefs, and faith practices in the formerly colonized territories. Internally at the high time of nationalistic movement around Asia after WWII, this recovered history corresponds to the quest of Asian Christians for autonomous and independent identities and their will to contribute to the national reconstruction of the newly independent nations. Thus, reclaiming Christianity as a cultural and religious tradition deeply rooted in Asian history and soil serves both external and internal purposes.

Since the 1950s, Christianity in Asia has proceeded in three main directions: (1) the development of structural and financial independence; (2) a theological movement toward indigenization and contextualization; (3) continued expansion through mission and evangelism of developing countries and interior areas.

Development of Structural and Financial Independence. The formerly "young churches" gradually sought independence from their European and North American mother churches along with the political independence of their respective countries. Some of the most notable examples were the united church movement in India* and China*, which involved, in particular, the Church of South* India, the Church of North* India, the Church of Christ in China (Hong Kong District after 1953), and the United Church of Christ in Japan*. Despite political controversies, the postdenominational Three*-Self Patriotic Movement of Chinese Protestants and Catholics has continued to uphold the three principles of self-governance, self-support, and self-propagation. All these churches represent efforts to seek structural and financial independence, and autonomy from outside clergy; they shun overseas influence. Nevertheless, despite local leadership and functioning with local resources, few of these churches have cut themselves off from the tutelage of their mother churches in the West. In many cases, doctrinal and theological positions of the early church fathers and the medieval churches of Europe are still considered the ultimate reference for Christian orthodoxy.

A Theological Movement toward Indigenization and Contextualization was called for in Asia and quietly took place in various parts of the continent, such as India and China, as early as the 1920s. This theological movement started as a response by early Asian Christian intellectuals to the national movements. They took part in the drastic 20th-c. social transformation in Asia and contributed to the theological articulation of a liberating social role of Christianity in decolonization. By setting up national and regional ecumenical councils, these Asian Christian intellectuals drew theological reflection from the processes of nationalism, social revolution, Marxist revolution, and democratic governance. In turn, various attempts were made by local indigenous movements to accommodate Christianity and vernacular cultures. Because of the early theologians' dedication (from the 1920s), much creative Asian theological thought emerged, which laid the ground for the ongoing development of a movement of Asian Christianity.

Although primarily a theological movement, the movement of Asian Christianity defined much of what we understand by Christianity in Asia today. Through various ecumenical vehicles, such as the World* Student Christian Federation (Asia-Pacific), the Christian Conference of Asia, the Association of Theological Education in Southeast Asia, the North Asia Association of Theological Schools, the Board of Theological Education of the Senate of Serampore College, the Programme for Theology and Cultures in Asia, and the Asian* Women's Resource Centre for Theology and Culture (see Theological Education Cluster: In Asia), clergy and laypeople joined together in a contextual theological movement and contributed enormously to the identity of an Asian church and its sociopolitical relevance to the postcolonial reconstruction of Christianity in the midst of multiple and sometimes conflicting Asian cultural and religious traditions.

Continued Expansion through Mission and Evangelism. Both Protestant and Catholic churches are actively pursuing mission and evangelism. Nineteenth-century US revivalism* was translated into strong and persistent evangelical movements throughout Asia, taking hold of many free, independent* churches, such as the evangelistic Baptist Alliance and the Christian and Missionary Alliance in Asia. Facilitated by networks such as the World Evangelical Alliance, members of these churches seek to evangelize all Asian natives despite a hostile political atmosphere and an economically deprived environment. Following in the footsteps of European and American missionaries of earlier centuries, some of these evangelical preachers worked on "the frontiers," in poor villages and remote inland areas, for the conversion of estranged souls. Most recently, newly industrialized countries, including South Korea* and Taiwan*, as well as Hong* Kong, have begun to send missionaries to inner China, "tribal*" areas of Thailand* and Myanmar*, and newly reopened developing countries such as Cambodia* and Vietnam* for long- and short-term Evangelical missions. **See also CHARISMATIC AND PENTECOSTAL MOVEMENTS: IN ASIA; CHURCH AND STATE RELATIONS CLUSTER: IN ASIA; PROTESTANTISM CLUSTER: IN ASIA; ROMAN CATHOLICISM CLUSTER: IN ASIA.** WONG WAI CHING (ANGELA)

History of Christianity in Europe: The Balkans. On the Balkan Peninsula, Eastern* and Western* Christianity interacted intensely in the aftermath of the 4th c., when the Eastern Roman Empire, or the Byzantine* Empire, was established in that part of the world. The arrival of Muslims (14th–15th c.) and Jews (16th c.) added to the region's religious and cultural heterogeneity (see Islam and Christianity Cluster: In Europe: Southeast Europe).

South Slavs who settled in the Balkans (6th and 7th c.) were eventually Christianized by the Byzantines (9th c.). Particularly important in this process was the missionary work of Cyril* and Methodius (later declared the "apostles of the Slavs") and their disciples. Cyril created a Slavonic alphabet and translated the Gospels and church service books from Greek into church Slavonic. This allowed for both the development of a Slavonic–Byzantine culture and the formation of autonomous churches by the South Slavs. Bulgarians* succeeded in establishing an independent, autocephalous* patriarchate (10th c.), and Serbs followed suit (14th c.).

The gradual cultural and political estrangement between the Byzantine world and the Latin world, coupled with ecclesiastical and theological disputes (specifically on the issues of the *Filioque**, papal claims, and the use in the Eucharist* of leavened bread by the Greeks and unleavened by the Latins) culminated in the Great* Schism (1054). The rift between the two great churches was deepened by the Crusades*, and particularly by the conquest and pillage of Constantinople (1204) during the Fourth Crusade. Attempts at securing reunion between the Christian East and West in the 13th and 15th c. were short-lived. The Ottomans conquered the Balkan Peninsula (late 14th to early 15th c.).

Under the Ottoman Empire, the region was administratively organized in the "*millet** system," whereby membership in a "nation" was determined by religious affiliation. At the top was the Muslim *millet,* whose members enjoyed religious, political, and administrative privileges. Christians and Jews under Islam were second-class citizens, yet they enjoyed protections and special rights; they were *dhimmi* (protected) as "people of the Book" (*Ahl al-Kitab*). The Orthodox *millet,* headed by the patriarch of Constantinople, was higher in the hierarchy than the "Armenian*" *millet,* which included all Christian churches (including non-Chalcedonian* Oriental* Orthodox churches) that did not recognize the authority of the ecumenical* patriarch of Constantinople. "Jews" formed a *millet* of their own. The Ottomans treated the patriarch of Constantinople as the head of all Orthodox Christians in their dominions. By the mid-18th c., the churches of Serbia* and Bulgaria* had lost their independence and were directly under the Ecumenical Patriarchate.

The close link between church and nation in the Balkans became a key component of the nation-building projects that appeared with the rise of nationalism (from the late 18th c.). The struggle for national liberation was thus intertwined with a struggle for ecclesiastical independence. Throughout the 19th c., a number of national churches emerged – the Church of Greece*, the Church of Serbia, the Church of Bulgaria*, and the Church of Romania* – in a process parallel to the emergence of these independent nation-states.

Churches and various religious communities suffered oppression under the atheistic* Communist regimes established throughout the Balkans after World War II. The end of the cold* war was marked by the return of religion to the public square. Because of the multiple transitions undergone by post-Communist societies, and particularly with regard to the violent dissolution of the Yugoslav Federation into new nation-states, the Balkans experienced a new instrumentalization of religious identities for various nationalist projects as well as inter- and intrareligious tensions related to the newly emerging religious identity politics. **See also ALBANIA; BOSNIA-HERZEGOVINA; BULGARIA; CROATIA; GREECE; MACEDONIA; ROMANIA; SLOVENIA; YUGOSLAVIA.**

INA MERDJANOVA

History of Christianity in Europe: Eastern Europe. The area south of the Danube lay within the Roman Empire and was Christianized from the 2nd c. Incursions of Goths* and Slavs interrupted the process, but missionaries, including Ulfila*, the "apostle of the Goths," who introduced Arian* Christianity to them before they moved to North Africa and Western Europe (c364–378), as well as Cyril* and Methodius, the "apostles of the Slavs," from Byzantium (Constantinople), brought Eastern Orthodox Christianity beyond the Danube basin to the Czech*, Slovak* and Polish* lands (end of the 9th c.), where Catholic Frankish and German missionaries were also active. Russia* was Christianized by missionaries from Byzantium (10th c.); the Baltic States by missionaries from Poland and Germany (from the 12th c.).

The emerging states in Central Europe and the Balkans eventually had to choose between Rome and Constantinople, and the divisions became permanent in 1054 (the Great* Schism). To this day, a "fault line" in Eastern Europe separates the Catholic/Protestant and Orthodox worlds. Several territories bordering or straddling the fault line are of mixed faith (Albania*, Bosnia*, Hungary*/Transylvania); farther north, particularly where the Catholic* Renewal (Counter Reformation) was active (from the mid-16th c.), Eastern-Rite Catholicism was common (Ukraine*, Romania*/Transylvania). The Orthodox world had no experience of the Renaissance* and Reformation*, with the important exception of Ukraine.

When the Orthodox Balkans were under Ottoman (Muslim Turkish) rule (15th–19th c.), Christians were treated as second-class citizens. They were generally allowed to exist in peace, but their activities were limited: church building, monasticism, charity, and education were restricted; many parish clergy were illiterate; theology lost originality and vigor; and missionary activities ceased altogether. One of the main problems for the Balkan Slavs was Greek ecclesiastical control and "hellenization" of their churches. (see the present cluster: In Europe: The Balkans).

Meanwhile, Russia emerged from two centuries of Mongol rule and, after the fall of Byzantium to the Ottomans (1453), began to assert leadership in the Orthodox world. In the 17th c., Russia came back into contact with the rest of Europe. Then the partitions of Poland (late 18th c.) brought Orthodox Ukrainians and Belarusians*, as well as Roman Catholic Poles and Lithuanians*, under Russian rule. The Russian Orthodox Church remained under close state control but maintained a tradition of spirituality*, monasticism*, and missionary activity (to the north and east).

Centuries of confrontation with the Ottoman Empire had some important repercussions in the religious history of Western Europe. It enabled the Protestant princes of Germany to consolidate their political power after the Reformation while their potential Roman Catholic opponents were preoccupied with developments in the east. It also explains the tenacity of Reformed Protestantism in Hungary and Transylvania, in contrast to its eclipse farther north after the Catholic Renewal (from the Polish–Ukrainian ethnic boundary in the east to the German–Polish boundary in the west). In the south, the Catholic Renewal was delayed (until the late 17th c.) by the Ottoman occupation, which made political use of Protestantism as an anti-papal and anti-imperial force, thus allowing Protestantism to establish tenacious roots.

In Poland, Slovakia*, Slovenia*, Croatia*, and Lithuania, the historically close identification between the nation and the Catholic Church was consolidated. Thus Catholicism kept Polish national identity alive during the long periods when the country as a political entity disappeared from the map. In the Czech lands, Catholicism was challenged by Hussitism* (early 15th c.), one of the earliest European Protestant movements. Eastern Germany later became the heart of the Reformation.

Levels of religiosity came to vary widely in Eastern Europe. Poland and Slovakia were highly religious; the Czech Republic and East Germany were heavily secularized (the former partly as a result of the harsh Catholic reaction to the Hussite tradition during the Catholic Renewal).

The first Balkan peoples to gain their independence from the Ottomans were the Greeks (1821). The Serbs followed (1830). The Romanian lands, always semi-autonomous, remained so until 1877. Meanwhile, in 1860 the Bulgarian* Orthodox Church declared its autonomy before the Bulgarian state achieved independence, and the identification of Orthodox churches with particular nations (autocephaly*, phyletism*) became typical of Eastern Europe.

World War I brought about the collapse of four empires, the Russian, German, Austro-Hungarian, and Ottoman, and independence for nation-states that had been taking shape in Central and Eastern Europe.

Meanwhile, Communist control was consolidated in the Soviet Union. Efforts to eradicate religion in the 1930s gave way to uneasy coexistence after World War II and an ambiguous position for the Russian Orthodox* Church. Between 1945 and 1948, the Soviet authorities encouraged the Russian Orthodox Church to extend its authority over the Orthodox churches in the countries of Eastern Europe now under Soviet political control. Thus the Eastern-Rite Catholic Church of Western Ukraine was suppressed (1946) and declared aggregated to the Russian Orthodox Church. After 1948 church representatives regularly promoted the Soviet concept of "peace" in international gatherings. In 1961 the Russian Orthodox Church became a member of the World* Council of Churches; it could not have done so without the Soviet authorities' consent.

In the new nation-states of Central and Eastern Europe under the Soviet Union's control after World War II, Communist governments first attempted to severely restrict religious practice, closing places of worship, arresting and even murdering clergy and believers; later they attempted to co-opt the churches for political ends, even as they neutralized their capacity for independent witness. Constitutional guarantees of religious freedom were interpreted to extend only to the individual's right to believe and to worship.

In Eastern Europe, Communist policies and the churches' responses varied widely, in part owing to the relative strength of the churches within each country. Frequently, the churches found that a combination of "discretion" and "valor" enabled them to retain a visible presence in society. Besides Albania, where all religions were declared illegal (1967), Czechoslovakia saw the most sustained application of repressive policies. Yugoslavia was at the other extreme; from the mid-1960s, there was mutual tolerance and recognition between the Catholic Church and the state.

The national Orthodox churches proved least able to offer resistance to Communist policies, because their identification with a particular nation meant weaker ties with fellow believers abroad and because of the traditional Orthodox relationship with those holding political power. In Bulgaria the Communists brought church–state relationships to a logical conclusion. During the 1940s, the Orthodox Church was reduced by persecution and threats of withdrawal of state subsidy to a position of submission; then the state named it the "traditional church of the Bulgarian people" (1949). In Yugoslavia the Communist authorities viewed nationalism as the most dangerous dividing force in the country; thus they aimed at reducing the social influence of the Orthodox Church in Serbia and of the Catholic Church in Croatia.

The Catholic Church presented special problems because its administrative center was in the Vatican. Communist policies had the least success in countries with a Roman Catholic majority, as in Poland, where the Catholic Church retained far more authority and legitimacy than the government throughout the Communist period.

Communist policies also had limited success when applied to certain Protestant churches: the Protestant Church in East Germany succeeded in making its authentic voice heard on important social and political issues; in the Soviet Union, a significant section of the Baptist Church went underground and assumed the freedom of the outlaw.

Religion was just one of the factors involved in the end of Communism in Eastern Europe. It played its part in several interrelated ways. At the individual level, religious ideas in their broad sense helped to form an ethical alternative to the Communist system. At the social level, the churches were the only public institutions not initiated and organized by the Communist Party and thus proved a haven for alternatives to official activities. At the national level, the churches in several Eastern European countries helped preserve the identity of particular nations in the face of sovietization or its local equivalent, at a time (1970s–1980s) when nationalism was viewed as a vehicle for personal and communal freedom.

After the Communist system collapsed in the Soviet Union and Eastern Europe (1989–91), the churches faced a range of opportunities, challenges, and problems. Great expectations were placed on the churches as vehicles for social and even political change, but they were hampered by shortages of resources, property, personnel, and experience. Moreover, they were often divided internally by disputes over their performance under Communist persecution. Authoritarianism had usually become a feature of church leadership under Communism: the leadership had tended toward doctrinal and liturgical conservatism in the face of the atheist challenge, reinforced by a lack of exposure to developments in the wider 20th-c. Christian world. Consequently, the challenges of the new pluralism* were particularly acute. The place of the churches in political debate was an open question (cf. Political Theology), although they were all by and large in favor of integration into the European Union; despite misgivings about Western secularism*, they saw no real political alternative. Meanwhile, the national churches raised their voices against proselytism* by the influx of missionaries from a range of Protestant and new religious movements; the international ecumenical movement faltered. Another problem was the identification of religion with interethnic conflict, particularly in the former Yugoslavia.

The general tendency in Eastern Europe after the end of Communism was a decline in religious practice. In 1999 surveys throughout the region showed an average 15% decline since 1991 (Poland remained an exception). During the Communist era, the phenomenon of "practicing nonbelievers" (persons attending church to demonstrate their disapproval of the official ideology*) had been common. When Communism came to an end, sociologists of religion increasingly wondered whether patterns of religious observance in Eastern and Western Europe would begin to resemble each other, with an increase in the East of "believing without belonging": having religious faith without showing allegiance to any specific denomination.

PHILIP WALTERS

History of Christianity in Europe: Western Europe. Western Europe includes some 17 countries and a small number of microstates (e.g. Vatican City and Monaco). The historic and contemporary Christian identities could be represented as follows: strongly Lutheran (Iceland, Norway*, Sweden*, Denmark*, Finland*), strongly Roman Catholic (Ireland*, Belgium*, Luxembourg*, Austria*, Portugal*,

Spain*, Italy*), mixed Catholic and Protestant (Switzerland*, Germany*, Netherlands*), mixed Protestant with a Catholic minority (United* Kingdom), and historically Catholic but largely secular (France*).

Early European Christianity was basically Mediterranean, framed within the Roman Empire. The influence of the church in Rome grew not only because of the increasing number of Christians, but also because of the gradual acknowledgment of a single leader, the bishop of Rome, later also called pope*. Church organization was muted by religious persecutions* (especially in the late 3rd c.). The conversion of Emperor Constantine* (313) and the later acceptance of Christianity as a legal religion within the Roman Empire established a new foundation for advancement and also for the involvement of secular rulers in the affairs of the church.

In the 5th and 6th c., Germanic tribes (e.g. Arian* Christian Goths* and Lombards*, Catholic Franks) took over the western half of the Empire. The establishment of monastic* communities, most notably Benedictine*, sustained the worship, devotional, and intellectual life of the Latin Church and provided numerous missionaries to carry the Christian message to such distant lands as Britain, Ireland, and Germany. Meanwhile, successive bishops of Rome, especially Gregory* I (590–604), claimed authority over the Western Church and contested the positions and actions of the Eastern emperors. During the Middle Ages, this assertion of papal power, together with the parallel claim of authority over secular rulers, was supported by the "Donation* of Constantine," a document that the 4th-c. emperor had presumably issued, giving all of this authority to the pope (although 15th-c. scholars showed the document to be an 8th-c. forgery).

In 800 the Frankish king Charles the Great (later conflated into "Charlemagne*"), who had significantly expanded his kingdom, met Pope Leo III in Rome. After Mass on Christmas Day, Leo placed a crown on Charles's head and declared him to be emperor. However regarded at the time, this event was later seen as marking the beginning of the Holy* Roman Empire, separating itself from the East and bringing together political and religious authority over much of Western Europe. Never a unified territory, it gave special status to the person of the emperor, especially in encounters with the papacy. Eventually the position was determined by a vote of seven German "electors," among whom were the archbishops of Mainz, Cologne, and Trier.

From the 10th through the 15th c., Christianity in Western Europe was shaped by several significant developments: the establishment of new religious orders (e.g. Carthusians*, Franciscans*); the increased presence of itinerant preachers, focusing especially on lay* devotion and local renewal; the emergence of popular movements that protested church doctrine or practice (led by, e.g., Valdès* in Italy, Wyclif* in England); theological debate over such issues as the Eucharist* and the work of Christ; ecclesiastical councils (e.g. Lateran* IV, 1215, and Constance*, 1414–18) that codified dogma and settled governance issues; the systematic consolidation of doctrine by Thomas Aquinas* and others; the encouragement of an interior piety through the writings of Eckhart* and Tauler* and the work of communities of the Devotio* Moderna; and the biblical and historical scholarship of Northern humanists, chiefly Erasmus* of Rotterdam, and the ensuing critiques of immoral clergy, lax bishops, overly scholastic theologians, and worldly religious orders.

The 16th-c. Protestant Reformation* resulted in the formal end of Christendom* in Western Europe, i.e. the sense of a single church integrally connected with the secular government. By the late 16th c. there were Lutheran churches (primarily in Northern Germany and the Scandinavian countries), Reformed churches (in Switzerland, France, Netherlands, Scotland, and the Rhineland area of Germany), Anabaptist churches (small pockets of resistance, chiefly in Southern Germany and the Netherlands, to these ecclesiastical options), and the Church of England (Anglican* Communion). Protestants (so named from the "protestation" of princes and cities at the Diet of Speyer, 1529, who objected to the imperial ban against Martin

Luther*) differed from Catholics in appealing to the sole authority of Scripture*, declaring the central doctrine of the faith* to be justification* by grace through faith, and affirming two sacraments* (baptism* and the Lord's* Supper) instead of seven. The Reformed churches, originating out of Zwingli's* and Calvin's* reforming movements in Zurich and Geneva, respectively, came to be organized mainly by country. Each of the Protestant branches appealed to confessions written at crucial moments in the century: for Lutherans, the Augsburg* Confession (1530) and the collection called the Book of Concord* (1580); for the Reformed, several national documents (e.g. Scots, 1560; Heidelberg, 1563; Westminster, 1646); Anabaptists, the Schleitheim Confession (1527); and for the Anglicans, the Thirty-nine* Articles (1571) (see Creeds, Symbols, and Confessions of Faith). Reformed churches differed from the Lutheran Church on several key questions, such as the understanding of the Lord's Supper and the presence of Christ; the interpretation of the Bible's direction regarding worship, the ministry, and church government; and resistance to idolatry (the list of the Ten* Commandments, in which Reformed include condemnation of graven images and Lutherans do not, is a small but significant sign of this difference). Anabaptists, despite considerable variety, differed from the other groups over the nature of baptism (believers, not infants, were to be baptized), over the relation of the church to the secular government (including the church as a voluntary community), and over the relation of grace to the sacraments. The Church of England, while basically a Reformed church in the 16th c., affirmed the monarch as "supreme governor," established the Book of Common* Prayer as the core of its worship, and acknowledged the historic episcopate as key to its connection to the early church. These particularities created their own internal conflict, leading to the emergence of more self-consciously Reformed communities later known as Presbyterian* and Congregationalist*.

Catholic activities in the 16th c., traditionally labeled "Counter Reformation," are now commonly termed Catholic* Renewal (or reformation). The Council of Trent* condemned Protestant positions, but also proposed significant reforms, such as forbidding absentee bishops and priests, expanding bishops' control over activities within their dioceses, and encouraging better training for priests. A number of new religious orders were founded for women (Ursulines, Discalced Carmelites*) and men (Theatines, Barnabites, Capuchins*); several combined a traditional contemplative* life with activities in the world. The Society of Jesus, or Jesuits*, approved by the pope in 1540, became the most successful of these new forms of religious life, both in the number of Jesuits and in the kind of work undertaken (as missionaries, teachers, advisers to royal courts).

The classic Christian conviction that there is one God and one truth led to the further convictions that there is only one true form of the Christian religion and that government should have an interest in supporting that religion, in order to avoid popular confusion, reduce occasions for conflict, and promote the good of society. This view, called "Constantinian," continued in Western Europe; virtually every country before the 19th c. had some form of religious establishment (see State Churches). That might take the form of government appointment of bishops, mandatory religious education in schools, public financial support through taxes or payment of clergy salaries, required church attendance, and the involvement of religious leaders in the government (one of the "estates" in France and Sweden; bishops of the Church of England were members of the House of Lords). In several countries, a sectarian or dissenting opposition to state churches also existed, e.g. Reformed communities in France, Pietist* movements in Norway and Sweden, and Nonconformists* and Catholics in Britain. The acceptance, not without struggle, of the principle of religious freedom, the removal of various political disabilities, and the disengagement of some governments from the church (sharply in France, gradually in Sweden) eventually changed dissenting communities into "free* churches." Several of the continuing state churches have come to prefer the terms "national" or "folk*" churches, to illustrate cultural rather than political connections.

Despite the world wars, the Depression, the rise of totalitarian regimes, and the Holocaust*, several developments in the 20th c. have been notable for Christianity in Western Europe. The beginnings and growth of the ecumenical* movement have extended to the entire world, but European Protestants have played significant roles, from holding international conferences in Edinburgh* (World* Missionary Conference, 1910), Stockholm and Oxford (Life* and Work, 1925 and 1937), and Lausanne and Edinburgh (Faith* and Order, 1927 and 1937), to hosting the first meeting of the World* Council of Churches in Amsterdam (1948). European churches have continued to engage each other toward the end of overcoming historic conflicts and divisions, as demonstrated by the Leuenberg* Agreement (1973) between Lutheran, Reformed, and United churches; the Porvoo* Common Statement (1992) between British and Irish Anglican churches and Nordic and Baltic Lutheran churches; the Joint Declaration on the Doctrine of Justification* by the Lutheran World Federation and the Catholic Church (1999); and the dramatic way in which the Catholic Church encouraged religious dialogue through the documents of Vatican* II and the welcome offered to a number of ecumenical observers there.

Church leadership changed visibly in the second half of the 20th c. with the ordination of women to the ministry. Such change did not happen easily, and some opposition continues even in those churches that have permitted it. Some free churches (e.g. English Congregationalists*, 1917) were able to ordain women earlier than state churches because they faced fewer constitutional restraints. Wartime conditions created opportunities for the ordination of women because pastors were enlisted, but such opportunities tended to vanish after 1945. In state churches, the ordination of women usually followed official decisions by a year or two. Among the earliest churches to allow such ordination were the Evangelical Lutheran Church of Denmark (1947) and the Church of Sweden (1958); more recently, the Church of Finland (1986) and the Church of England (1992) have joined them. Pastorates for women in larger churches gradually became possible only after some years, and women were elected to episcopal office or its equivalent even later. Numbers alone reflect the most significant change; by 2000, one-quarter of the ministers of the Evangelical Church in Germany and more than 40% of those in the Church of Sweden were women. The Catholic Church has consistently opposed such ordinations, but some Catholic organizations have continued to advocate them, even though women ordained by retired bishops are immediately excommunicated (see Women's Ordination Cluster).

Beginning around 1980, the topics receiving the most attention from commentators and the churches themselves were the dramatic decline in church attendance and the extent of religious belief, leading Grace Davie, e.g., to characterize the decline as "believing without belonging" and European Christianity as "the exceptional case" when compared with other regions of the world. "Secularization" (see Secularization and Desecularization in Europe and North America) is the umbrella term, having largely replaced the earlier and more aggressive "de-Christianization" (see Post-Christian Thought). While contested as a theory or as *the* master narrative, its causes, consequences, and implications have been widely explored. Factors as diverse as the Enlightenment*, revolutions that included the churches among its targets, urbanization and industrialization, the emergence of a vigorous anticlericalism*, the 19th-c. liberal spirit that was rejected for so long by the dominant churches, the challenge of socialism to working conditions and the class system, the gradual assumption by government of social functions such as education and public welfare that the church had performed for hundreds of years (see Laicization), the student protests of the 1960s, dramatic shifts in gender roles since then, and the persistence of privilege on the part of established churches themselves have all been cited as reasons for this decline. It has sharply changed the religious situation, not least by focusing on religion at the popular level (see Popular Christian Practices Cluster: Introductory Entry; Popular Christian Practices Cluster: In Western Europe). What does it mean for religious participation to occur at key points in life (birth, marriage, and death) but seldom at other times? If attendance is down, why are pilgrimages* to some 6,000 sacred sites and shrines in Western Europe more popular than ever? If belief, too, has declined, why are church taxes and other ways in which governments support religious expression financially not seriously protested? If regular worship life is broadly disdained, why has the Liturgical* Movement begun in the 1930s by European Catholic scholars been so influential among Protestant churches worldwide? Why is the Taizé* community attracting thousands of young people for retreats, with a worship style imitated around the world? Why did 2005 World Youth Day in Cologne, Germany, attract some 800,000 youth for Mass with Pope Benedict XVI? Why has a development like the Thomas* Mass (Helsinki, 1988), intended for doubters and seekers, been so successful, spreading throughout Northern Europe? And why has the Community of Sant' Egidio, begun in 1968 in Rome for disaffected youth and emphasizing solidarity with the poor, attracted followers around the world? In their collective ways, the realities and the conundrums of Christianity in Western Europe will ensure continued interest and attention for many years to come. **See also CHARISMATIC AND PENTECOSTAL MOVEMENTS: IN EUROPE; CHURCH AND STATE RELATIONS CLUSTER: IN EUROPE; PROTESTANTISM CLUSTER: IN EUROPE; ROMAN CATHOLICISM CLUSTER: IN EUROPE.**

DALE A. JOHNSON

History of Christianity in Latin America and the Caribbean Islands. Following Columbus's expedition (1492), the "New World" became a disputed space and a missionary territory. European Christendom assumed a self-conscious position of global centrality (an ideological stance still active for many) that initiated "world Christianity" as a missionary enterprise of the "Latin Church" (Roman Catholic Church); hierarchical, clerical, and evangelical interests were interconnected in this missionary enterprise. Christianity in Latin America bridged the civilizations of both peoples indigenous to the Americas and Iberian (Spanish and Portuguese) peoples, who were in the process of transitioning from medieval feudalism* to the early modern consolidation of sovereignty in nation-states. This diversity was further complicated by the cultural contributions of African enslaved populations brought en masse to Latin America from the 16th to the mid-19th c. when other Europeans and Asians arrived with their own cultures and religious traditions. The militant Iberian Catholics encountered a mosaic of religious traditions rather than a single homogeneous "pagan" front, even though European ideologies subsumed all these cultural-religious identities under one homogeneous representation. The Spanish Conquest resulted in an ideological and cultural destruction of the Amerindians' past, which too often was also genocide (see Portuguese Explorations, Conquests, and Missions; Spanish Explorations, Conquests, and Missions).

Two primary contrasting ideological trends informed the pastoral actions of the (Roman Catholic) Church in Latin America: conversion* by force and the foundation of an "Iglesia Indiana." The traumatic confrontation between the conquistadors and Amerindian peoples marked the religious history of the region. Evangelization took place in a context of violence; conversion by force was self-legitimated. Yet some missionary enterprises differentiated genuine evangelization from conquest, in two distinct ways: (1) the setting aside of territorial havens (the reductions*) from which civil and military Iberian authorities would be excluded and (2) direct ideological confrontation with traditional beliefs and practices and advocacy. Yet most Iberians failed to distinguish between their national identity and their Christian identity, between the interests of the monarchy and of the gospel, as they had on the Iberian Peninsula, despite the incisive appeals of priests (e.g. Bartolomé* de las Casas). Out of pastoral concern, such priests declared a prophetic partiality for the poor and against injustice, and advocated for the welfare of Amerindians by means of legal, anthropological, and theological arguments.

The 17th-Century Institutionalization of the Church. The Christian presence was the result of both the friars'* evangelization of "Indians" and the growing population of Iberian settlers. A stable ecclesial system with parishes and dioceses was necessary, along with religious* orders, including women's* religious orders, since women religious had multiple functions beyond the spiritual domain in the financial, social, and cultural spheres. The different ethnic and social strata – European and indigenous populations, as well as a large mestizo* population – developed distinctive ecclesial styles. In addition, alongside official Christendom, multiple popular* forms of Christianity ranged from European-like Marian devotions (see Mary, the Virgin, Cluster: Devotion in Latin America) to indigenous kinds of Christianity that preserved full-fledged ancestor* veneration rituals and, in between these extremes, different levels of "syncretism"* or "inculturation*", an ever-present phenomenon. In some areas, such as Cuba* and the coast of Brazil*, the richest forms of syncretism or inculturation incorporate African rather than Amerindian components.

The 18th-Century Establishment of the Bourbon Dynasty in Spain brought profound changes in colonial policy, moving toward a greater centralization of power, denoting a shift from the corporate mentality to a modern perspective of individualism and rationalism. The Spanish crown attempted to abolish ecclesial practices not aligned with "regalism" (the king's perspectives and political goals). The starting point of these "enlightened reforms" was the expulsion of the Jesuits* by Charles III (1767), the weakening of religious orders, and the systematic subjection of the Roman Catholic Church to the authority of the state (see Church and State Relations Cluster: In Latin America). Social movements nourished by ideals spread by sectors of the Church resisted such reforms, which retrospectively can be seen as the prelude to the end of the Spanish Empire. Creoles and poor Europeans often joined revolts against the colonial system by indigenous and mestizos church members; members of wealthier classes and Church leaders, as well as most priests and members of religious orders, adopted ambivalent stances. But opposition to religious and political movements became progressively more visible. The viceroyalties of Peru*, New Granada, and River Plate (Argentina*) were shaken by the 1780s popular movements against the Bourbon reforms, progressively leading to the independence process (1810–30).

The 19th-Century Independence and Rule by Liberal States resulted from the disintegration of the Spanish Empire. Christ and Mary, along with Christian ethical notions, were invoked as liberating symbols. Still, some insurgents and their supporters were integrists*, conservative members of the Church and even of the clergy. Christians belonged to the different political factions; Creoles and lower clergy were usually more supportive of independence, whereas Spanish-born people and the Episcopate tended to be "regalist."

In the wake of the postcolonial period, the church endured a profound institutional crisis. The void left by the Patronato* Real called for the establishment of direct relations with Rome, but for decades, the papacy hesitated to recognize the sovereignty of the new republics. In the interim, many episcopal sees were vacant, seminaries empty, and men's religious orders depleted. The Divine Office* of the liturgy of the hours celebrated by women religious in their convents and family prayers kept religiosity alive.

The emancipation process transformed, but did not dissolve, the ties between the former colonies and Europe. British merchants replaced Spain's colonials, as a result of international events and the colonial societies' response to them. The social stratification remained unchanged; some "revolutionary" leaders, seeking a nationally controlled church under the banner of the new states, welcomed new colonial masters.

The Liberal reforms (1850–80) reopened the debates concerning church* and state relations and the role of clergy in education and in the welfare system. Religious reforms involved not only church and state separation, but also confiscation of the wealth of the Roman Catholic Church; the Church's wealth, particularly land and urban properties, passed into lay hands. Convents, seminaries, and Catholic schools and universities were confiscated by the state. Priests, religious, and monastic orders practically disappeared and lost much of the wealth that gave them the capacity to carry out their social work and exert a social influence among the poor. Furthermore, the state often gained control over the Church, not only regarding political and economical issues, but also regarding liturgical and religious matters (as in Colombia*, 1853; Mexico*, 1857). Some leaders of these reforms were secular* modernists more or less opposed to Catholicism. Others were anticlerical, but profoundly attached to Christian religious signifiers. The institutional church struggled against liberalism and modernization. By 1900 the Catholic Church did not have legal status in nine countries in Latin America, and the states did not have diplomatic relations with the Vatican (only two had concordats*).

Because liberals favored the insertion of Protestantism*, it became viable in the region. Protestants founded schools, Bible societies, and missions. European migration, particularly to the Southern Cone (including Brazil), became another source of Protestant institutionalization, albeit along the lines of national churches with ethnic identities and enclaves. Proselytizing groups came from the USA to Central America, the Caribbean, Mexico, and the Andean region.

Church and State Reintegration and Rupture. The 1930s economic crisis made it clear that some traditional welfare functions of the Roman Catholic Church had not been successfully replaced by the state. Following the failure of liberal states, new political leaders sought a reconciliation with the Church in order to secure the masses' support and delegated to the Church some welfare functions, including education, health care, the management of social organizations, and even civil registry in rural areas. As the Church regained relevance in the life of the nations, religious orders and the lay Catholic* Action, both with an overwhelming majority of women, attended to social needs and thus became protagonists in the process of church and state reintegration.

In the 1940s and 1950s, some Latin American bishops saw the importance of the Specialized Catholic* Action model and backed its development in Latin America. Following this model, many Catholics shifted their commitment from defending the Roman Catholic Church and the Christian faith from the dangers of modern secularism and secularization* to embracing a Christian vocation requiring concrete dedication to social justice* and liberation* of the poor*. This shift led to the pastoral renewal of the Church (second half of the 20th c.) and the formulation of Liberation* theologies. Following Catholic Action's national and international experience of pastoral coordination, Dom Helder Camara* (Brazil*) and Dom Manuel Larraín (Chile*) proposed and led the foundation (Rio, 1955) of the Latin American Episcopal Conference (CELAM*) to coordinate Latin American pastoral action. In 1959 religious orders of men and women and their congregations formed in the same spirit the Latin American Religious' Conference (CLAR). CELAM and CLAR prepared the continent to receive the Second Vatican* Council, publicizing its proposals and adapting them to Latin American realities. The second general conference of CELAM at Medellín* (1968) effectively responded to the renewal spirit of Vatican II and provided fresh insights into the mission of Christians in the concrete reality of Latin America. Pastoral priorities were redefined, with an emphasis on service and evangelization of the poor and marginalized groups, such as indigenous and black populations. Many religious, particularly women, relinquished their traditional settings in large convents and as administrators of large educational and health institutions at the service of the middle classes and established smaller communities in lower-class neighborhoods in order to work and live among the poor.

Following the Specialized Catholic Action organization and adopting its methodology, the pastoral initiative known as Base* Ecclesial Communities favored the role of laypeople and women religious as pastoral agents and sought to apply the gospel to people's struggles in their lives. Base Ecclesial Communities provided a new context for ecumenical* dialogue* and collaboration and, from a committed Christian perspective, further criticized the ills of Latin American societies' dependence on capitalism.

Women's religious orders, Catholic Action youth movements, and priests developed social activities, e.g. literacy campaigns, unions, cooperatives, social movements, and new political forces among blacks, indigenous peoples, women, and other people traditionally marginalized from social, political, and economic activities. A biblical movement with possibilities for a popular hermeneutics* also emerged (see Bible Interpretation Cluster: In Latin America). These lived experiences informed the critical discourse that came to be known as Liberation* theology.

In 1972 conservative bishops started to rule CELAM, led by Alfonso Lopez Trujillo. An ideological confrontation arose in the Roman Catholic Church during the cold war and the implementation of national security regimes.

The dispute within the Church included the internal persecution of the progressive Catholic wing. Christian leaders were also persecuted by the dictatorships in the name of national security in Brazil*, the Southern Cone (1960s–1970s), and Central America (1980s) and in the drug war in Colombia* and Mexico* (since the 1990s). Thousands of people were threatened, jailed, tortured, "disappeared," or murdered. A large number of the victims were Catholic and Protestant Christians who, out of their faith commitments, struggled along with the poor and defended human* rights. The list of these thousands of martyrs is yet to be compiled systematically.

By the mid-20th c., many historical Protestant denominations had become largely autonomous, with Latin American leaders and vernacular identities and ecclesial styles. The Council of Latin American Churches was created in 1982. Ecumenical relations among Catholics and Protestants became significant after Vatican II, taking the form of diverse interdenominational collaboration and dialogue, particularly after the Medellín conference. Ecumenical dialogue has been almost nonexistent, however, with the fast-growing Pentecostal* and Charismatic* churches.

Under the papacy of John* Paul II (1978–2005), more conservative prelates replaced the bishops who led the implementation of Vatican II's reforms. Conservative movements such as Opus* Dei gained key positions of leadership. The laity favored the more spiritual Charismatic renewal movement within the Roman Catholic Church over the more socially laden Christian movements of the 1970s. In the meantime, a newer generation of Liberation theologians articulated fresh Christian reflections on gender, ethnicity, ecumenism*, and ecology*.

Some peoples of African and Amerindian descent have renounced the Christian components of their syncretistic* or inculturated traditions, seeking to rediscover their ancestral traditions afresh. A significant segment of Latin Americans, especially from the lower classes, have turned to Pentecostalism and the Charismatic Movement, especially as they are shaped by Latin American leaders and struggle to address social issues. Nevertheless, the 2000 census data indicate that, in several Latin American countries, an increasing number of people do not belong to any church. **See also CHARISMATIC AND PENTECOSTAL MOVEMENTS CLUSTER: IN LATIN AMERICA; CHURCH AND STATE RELATIONS CLUSTER: IN LATIN AMERICA; POVERTY CLUSTER: POVERTY, THEOLOGY, AND ETHICS: LATIN AMERICAN VIEWS; PROTESTANTISM CLUSTER:**

IN LATIN AMERICA; RELIGIOUS ORDERS, ROMAN CATHOLIC, CLUSTER: IN LATIN AMERICA; ROMAN CATHOLICISM CLUSTER: IN LATIN AMERICA (various entries). ANA MARÍA BIDEGAIN and JUAN SANCHEZ

History of Christianity in the Middle East: Syriac Christianity. Syriac Christianity is at the center of the history of Christianity in the Middle East. With its distinctive theological and liturgical views, Syriac Christianity was responsible for the initial spread of Christianity in the East (India*, China*) and the South (Ethiopia*). It endured in the Middle East through the centuries despite repeated political and religious turmoil.

The Aramaic language, spoken by the people of Syro-Mesopotamia for centuries before the Christian Era, was also the language of Jesus and his first followers. In its eastern dialect, called Syriac, it became the cultural vehicle of Christianity in that area. While several empires rose and fell, Christians continued to live, thrive, and develop theologically and culturally despite their minority status. Their descendants continue to practice their religion in traditional churches in their ancient homelands, which are identified on current political maps as Israel*/Palestine, Lebanon*, Jordan*, Syria*, Iraq*, Eastern Turkey*, and Iran*. Although Arabic gradually replaced Syriac as the vernacular in most places, Syriac has survived not only as a liturgical language but also as the spoken language in several villages in Turkey, Syria, Iraq, and Iran, and the classical language was revived in the 19th and 20th c.

An early tradition links a local king, Abgar*, with Jesus himself, the apostle Thomas*, and his disciple Addai* (Thaddeus). More certain evidence comes from the 2nd c., when Tatian* "the Assyrian" compiled his Diatessaron*, the first gospel harmony, and Bar Daisan* the "Aramean philosopher" taught in Edessa*. Mani* also taught in this region east of the Roman Empire in the Sasanian Persian Empire. The themes of these early sources include doctrinal diversity, hymnody*, and asceticism*.

Two major writers emerge in the 4th c.: Aphrahat* and Ephrem*. Both attest to an early form of asceticism unique to this branch of early Christianity: the "sons and daughters of the covenant." Each also shows a close relationship with the substantial Jewish communities of Mesopotamia (Babylonia). Ephrem, a Nicene-Orthodox poet and theologian, had a lasting impact on all later branches of this tradition.

The 5th-c. christological* controversies resulted in permanent divisions, since most Greek and Latin Christians endorsed the Council of Chalcedon* and Syriac Christians followed either the Council of Chalcedon (Melkites*, Maronites*) or the Antiochene* Christology of Nestorius* (the Assyrian Church, or Church* of the East) or the Miaphysite* Alexandrian Christology of Cyril* as interpreted according to the perspective represented later on by Severus* (of the Syriac* Orthodox Church).

Syriac versions of the Bible* (e.g. the Peshitta*, Harclean, and Philoxenian versions), of great interest to modern scholars of Scripture, also nurtured indigenous intellectual and spiritual traditions. Theodore bar Konai, Michael the Syrian, and Gregory Abu'l Farag (or Bar Hebraeus*), among others, produced scriptural commentaries, theological treatises, histories, and grammatical and philosophical writings in Syriac well into the Islamic* period. Mystical* traditions also flourished, most notably in Isaac of Nineveh.

Baptism and eucharistic worship are central to this tradition, whose members still celebrate these rites in forms established in the earliest centuries. The Anaphora* of Addai* and Mari, still used in the Assyrian Church, is both the oldest known eucharistic rite and the only one lacking words of institution. Syriac baptismal liturgies include anointings* both before and after baptism. Emphasis on the Holy* Spirit, Mary as Mother of God (in most Syriac churches), poetry, and hymnody – eventually accompanied by musical instruments – are central to the communal worship.

Having shared the Thomas tradition with Indian Christians from an early date,

Syriac Christians have cultivated ties with Asia and Africa over the centuries. In 345 Thomas of Cana led a group of Assyrian Christians from Syro-Mesopotamia to India*, where their Knanaya Christian descendants still survive along with other Syriac-tradition Christians in Kerala*. The Sian-fu stele inscription (781) attests to the presence of the Assyrian Christian missionary Alopen in China* in 635. The Syrians Frumentius* and Aedesius converted the Ethiopian* emperor Ezana of Aksum in the 4th c. Their common Miaphysite Christology and the rise of Islam contributed to the strengthening of ties among Syriac Orthodox, Coptic*, and Ethiopian Christians that continues today.

Syriac Christians have interacted with Islam* from its formative period to the present. Scholars debate questions of Christian influence on the Qur'an* and *hadith* (traditions of the Prophet). Jacob* of Edessa* and other Miaphysite Christians translated Aristotle*, studied Greek scientific texts, and mediated the transmission of other aspects of Greek culture to the Romano-Byzantine Umayyad Empire (661–750, centered in Damascus). Their East Syriac counterparts played a similar role in the Abbasid Empire (750–c1300, centered in Baghdad) and its Persian culture. Classified as *dhimmi* (literally "protected" people, loosely "people of the Book"), Christians under Islamic rule engaged in dialogue and debate. Whereas John* of Damascus considered Islam to be a Christian heresy*, Timothy I started from points of agreement between Christians and Muslims in arguing for his Dyophysite (two natures) view of Christ. Dionysius bar Salibi and others expanded the religious debates to include Judaism as well as Islam and the various christological factions.

Under Seljuk and especially Ottoman Turkish rule with its *millet** system, Christians were governed by the religious leaders of their own ethnic and confessional communities, subject in turn to the Turkish rulers. This system provided a significant degree of autonomy but also reinforced the subordinate status of religious minorities. At the same time, Western Christians, first as crusaders*, then as missionaries*, later as traders and diplomats, and finally as rulers by mandate, interfered in "Middle Eastern" affairs. Their well-intentioned efforts often jeopardized delicately balanced political arrangements. Since the conversion of Muslims was difficult or impossible to achieve, both Roman Catholic and Protestant missionaries eventually directed most of their evangelistic efforts toward the Syriac Christians (and other "Oriental Orthodox" Christians, such as Copts and Armenians). Ecumenical and interreligious dialogues* are healing many of the divisions.

Emigration, especially to Western Europe, the USA, Canada, and Australia, increased in the later 20th c. for economic as well as political and religious reasons. Despite all of these factors leading to division and a diminution of their numbers, Syriac Christians continue to maintain a presence in their traditional lands. The US wars in the Persian Gulf and Islamist* fundamentalism* may prove to be the greatest challenges to this tenacity. **See also CHALDEAN CATHOLIC CHURCH MALANKARA ORTHODOX SYRIAN CHURCH; MONASTICISM CLUSTER: IN THE SYRIAC TRADITION; ORTHODOX CHURCHES, ORIENTAL, CLUSTER: SYRIAC ORTHODOX CHURCH, UNIVERSAL; SYRIAC CATHOLIC CHURCH.**

KATHLEEN E. MCVEY

History of Christianity in North America. See CANADA; UNITED STATES.

History of Christianity in the South Pacific and Australia. Australian and South Pacific Christians are connected economically and culturally by their shared experience of colonialism*. Australian Christians were deeply convinced that God had placed them on the continent to further the civilization and evangelization of the islanders to the north. Aboriginal* peoples did not see colonization so positively. The churches' members rarely protested about dispossession, exile, or the cruelties of frontier warfare. Few Aborigines responded to attempts to convert them, and colonists who learned any of their many languages were a rarity. Lutherans* in South Australia and Benedictines* in Western Australia were exceptions.

History of Christianity in the South Pacific

In Australia*, from the arrival of convicts in 1788 to the 19th c., Christians were predominantly Protestant. Yet a quarter of the population was Roman Catholic. Initially, they were severely discriminated against, even denied priests, because the authorities feared rebellion. The appointment of some clergy and then Bishop Polding (1794–1877) enabled them to take their part in the construction of colonial society. Carolyn Chisholm (known as "Mrs. Chisholm") (1808–77) worked tirelessly for female Irish migrants. In South Australia, persecuted Prussian Lutherans were helped by a compassionate Baptist to settle, bringing another strand of Protestant Christianity to the colonies, although their connections with the Pacific did not emerge until later in the century.

Anglicans, Congregationalists, Presbyterians, and Wesleyans shared the planting of Christianity on Polynesian islands, in Fiji*, and in parts of the New Hebrides, while Scots and Nova Scotians pioneered in Melanesia; Anglicans established Christianity in New* Zealand through the initiatives of Samuel Marsden (1765–1838). Parent British churches saw the planting of churches in Australia and the South Pacific as part of the same missionary imperative. Sydney became a center for provisioning missionaries and trading with the newly Christianized islands, sometimes providing refuge for those who had fled tribal wars. French Roman Catholic missionaries also saw the advantage of Sydney contacts, even though Australian Protestants were distrustful of French colonial expansion into the Society Islands and New Caledonia and lobbied a reluctant British government to annex, or at least protect, the New Hebrides, Papua New* Guinea, and Polynesia against further French incursions into what was believed to be a divinely ordained sphere of British influence.

Until the pace of free settlement increased (1830s–1840s), Polynesian Christians outnumbered settlers in Australia, who nevertheless were entrusted with increasing oversight of their Pacific brothers and sisters. Although there were far more Pacific Islander missionaries than British ones, colonialist ideas about white superiority made British missionaries reluctant to share authority with the Islanders, lest the young churches be corrupted by local customs. That changed more quickly in London Missionary Society (LMS) areas, although Tongans and Samoan Wesleyans refused to honor a vague British comity* agreement that had awarded Samoa to the LMS. Islanders found European Christian divisions politically useful. Chiefs enhanced their status by linking with a different church than their rivals or defended their newfound faith by war with their denominationally different neighbors. No dissent was permitted in villages, or even on entire islands.

Islanders saw the advantages of literacy and European technologies, but did not adapt to missionary teachings about the time-bound life of the British worker. Large churches showed how quickly Islanders adopted British and French building methods and steel tools. The Bible was accepted as a sacred book, and some of its precepts were speedily integrated into communal life, for the advantages of peace were obvious. Australian colonists could be selective in their hearing of Scripture*, especially in the way they related it to business and politics, and its authority could be interpreted differently in such matters as keeping the Sabbath, the place of music in worship, and the sacraments*. Disputes over divorce* and marriage* with a deceased wife's sister were settled by legislation rather than theological agreement. Evangelical Protestants campaigned against gambling, sexual impurity, and alcohol abuse, while Roman Catholics and Anglo-Catholics adopted a more relaxed attitude toward the first and the last. Many Protestants felt so strongly about alcohol abuse that they opted for total abstinence. With the help of female temperance* advocates, many replaced wine with grape juice at the Lord's* Supper. On the Pacific Islands, where there were neither wheat nor grapes, some missionaries chose to use coconuts rather than bread and wine.

Education for ministers was essential in the Islander churches. Theological colleges were established from the 1840s, some of which, like Malua in Samoa, continue to flourish, with a highly qualified faculty.

The refusal of Australian universities in the 19th c. to award degrees in theology forced the churches to explore alternatives. The Australian College of Theology (1891) and the Melbourne College of Divinity (1910) provided long-distance education and external examinations, until Sydney and Queensland provided limited access to degrees. It was not until the 1970s that amendments to the Melbourne College of Divinity Act and the participation of Catholic seminaries made undergraduate degrees in theology possible. Other centers copied the model. Catholic universities have further widened the options, as has recognition of a whole range of other degree-granting institutions.

Two independent churches were developed in Melbourne by evangelists. Alexander Dowie, later founder of Zion City in Illinois, founded an independent church in Melbourne (1880s). Similarly, Dr. Charles Strong established the Australian Church in 1885, which lasted till the 1960s, with a strongly liberal and democratic ethos. Small independent churches of Pentecostal* origins emerged in the early 20th c., but were not independent churches in the sense that they initiated dramatic changes in doctrine and worship that were uniquely Australian. They were inspired by churches in the USA.

Theological disputes were not important in the Islands, but were of great public interest in Australia. The emergence of liberal* theology, the development of the sciences*, and the criticism of dogma challenged the churches to allow for more freedom of conscience and to offer defenses of the faith. Although no world-class thinker emerged from Australian churches, there were many able exponents of the faith and numerous publications on the relation between religion and science, Christology, ethics, eschatology, and the questions debated by Protestants and Roman Catholics. By the end of the 20th c., the form of the disputes had changed, but the limits of adaptation and change were discussed as vigorously as ever. In both Polynesia and Melanesia, there were lively debates about the possibilities of Pacific versions of Christianity across the denominational spectrum, as more and more had received a postgraduate education.

Few South Pacific churches ordain women* for the ministry, but a steady widening of leadership opportunities for educated women has occurred. Some Aboriginal churches have ordained women, but there are still strong regional cultural constraints against women having sacred authority over men. A number of Pacific Islanders have shared in the leadership of the World Council of Churches. Similarly, Roman Catholics have been consulted in Rome, although the number of cardinals in the region is small.

Political independence has posed great challenges to the Pacific churches. They have not always been able to rise above the challenges of tribalism, so that financial impartiality is rare. Ecumenism is fragile. Law and order have broken down in many parts of Papua* New Guinea, with a resumption of tribal fighting. Civil wars in Bougainville and the Solomon* Islands have been very destructive, as have the military coups in Fiji*. Australian churches have contributed modestly to peacemaking and reconciliation. They also have the demanding task of bridging Christian–Muslim differences after jihadist attacks on Australians in Bali and Jakarta.

Independent* churches with indigenous leaders who rejected the tutelage of missionaries emerged early in Polynesia. The Siovili and Mamaia movements were attacked by missionaries as perversions of Christianity. That could not be said of the Free Wesleyan Church in Tonga, founded in 1885. King George Tupou II rejected the authority of the Australasian Conference but did not change local polity* or doctrine, apart from enhancing his authority over the church, ensuring the primacy of Tongan priorities. In l924 reunion with thc Wcslcyan rcmnant was achieved, but a small group stayed outside as an independent church. In Fiji, Apolisi Nai led a group out of the Methodist Church seeking to develop Fiji for the Fijians during the 1930s.

Nothing similar occurred among Aborigines in Australia. The number of converts was too small, and the group was linguistically divided. Although Aboriginal churches had emerged by the mid-20th c., they were closely controlled by their founding bodies and were interdenominational rather than independent, like the Ratana Church in New Zealand. In contrast, "adjustment cults" (also called "cargo cults"), which often had some features of independent churches, were not uncommon in Papua New Guinea; they sought to gain access to European wealth and power by quasi-religious means, especially after 1945. They provided a total culture for their followers, accompanied by strong eschatological* hopes, which sometimes spilled over into politics. The Christian Fellowship Church on the Solomon Islands broke with Methodism and became an independent church, as did Maamafo'ou in Tonga during the 1970s.

In Australia the emergence of mega-congregations, such as Hillsong in Sydney and City Life in Melbourne, may lead to their becoming independent churches with a different relation to Australian culture than the historic denominations.

Urbanization in the South Pacific has undermined customs of social control and weakened religious authority, although as yet individualism, secular views, and a free market in religious and moral choices have not undermined religious commitment as significantly as they have in Australia. The rapidly changing context challenges all the churches to find new ways to transform their societies. IAN BREWARD

History of Religion School (from the German *Religionsgeschichtliche Schule*, sometimes inaccurately translated "history of religions school") was a group primarily of biblical scholars who were drawn to study under Albrecht Ritschl* in Göttingen (late 1880s). The senior figure in the formation of the school was Albert Eichhorn (1856–1926). One of the most influential younger scholars was Hermann Gunkel (1862–1932), who abandoned his studies of the NT to become one of the great pioneers of critical OT study, particularly in his groundbreaking *Schöpfung und Chaos* (Creation and chaos, 1895). Other members were the NT scholars William Wrede (1859–1906), Wilhelm Bousset (1865–1920), and Ritschl's son-in-law, Johannes Weiss (1863–1914), the OT critic, Alfred Rahlfs (1865–1935), and a student of comparative religion, Heinrich Hackmann (1864–1935). Others who were later associated with the school were Wilhelm Heitmüller (1869–1926), Hugo Greßmann (1877–1927), Paul Wernle (1872–1939), Heinrich Weinel (1874–1936), and Richard Reitzenstein (1861–1931). Ernst Troeltsch* (1865–1923) was known as the school's "systematic theologian." While never sharing a common manifesto, all were concerned to investigate religion using a thoroughgoing historical method. This led to a number of publications, including the influential popular series *Religionsgeschichtliche Volksbücher* and the massive encyclopaedia *Die Religion in Geschichte und Gegenwart*. J. C. B. Mohr, the publishing house controlled by the Siebeck family, was particularly influential in ensuring that the writings of the school were widely disseminated.

At Göttingen they soon began to distance themselves from Ritschl, who sought to isolate Christianity from the broader history of religion through the imposition of what was called a "dogmatic" method. Unlike other scholars influenced by Ritschl, the members of the school tended to avoid the isolation of religion through a "value judgment of faith." Instead, they understood religion* to be a universal human phenomenon enmeshed in the nexus of history. Some members, including Bousset and Troeltsch, were attracted to Ritschl's Göttingen sparring partner, Paul de Lagarde (1827–1891), professor of Oriental languages, who sought to study Christianity in its historical context. Another important influence was the OT professor Bernhard Duhm (1847–1928), who understood religion to be a matter more of spiritual experience than of dogma. From the outset, many members of the school studied spiritual experience in the individual. Gunkel, e.g., wrote his dissertation on the effects of the Holy* Spirit on Paul. Where Ritschl derided religious experience as "Pietism*" the history of religion school emphasized the study of what William Wrede called "appearances and moods." Bousset, in his influential work *Kyrios Christos*, studied the life of early Christian communities, focusing on the sacraments* and mysticism* rather than the more common Lutheran themes of law* and gospel*: it was religion rather than dogma that formed the subject matter of theology. Similarly, Gunkel wrote that the aim of the school was "to look in the hearts of the people of religion, to experience their thoughts inwardly and adequately to describe them." The study of ancient texts revealed the spiritual life of the individual and of the early Christian communities. Many such experiences were shared with other non-Christian religions. Some members of the school, including Bousset, were deeply influenced by Hegelian* philosophy, which understood history to be the march of the spirit through time. Others were less willing to apply such a constricting teleological framework. Troeltsch, e.g., wrote in 1913 of the impossibility of constructing "a theory of Christianity as the absolute religion on the basis of a historical way of thinking or by the use of historical means."

Some members of the school espoused the post-Kantian* philosophy of J. F. Fries (1773–1843), who had earlier influenced the OT scholar W. M. L. de Wette (1780–1849). Bousset, e.g., felt that in religion there was an immediate grasp of the underlying essence of things, the thing-in-itself, which allowed for an utter security despite the vagaries of history. Such a philosophy was also adopted by Rudolf Otto in his influential work, *The Idea of the Holy*. For others, especially Troeltsch, this emphasis on an underlying essence of religion beyond history was a form of mysticism, which meant that Christianity could easily lose its impact in the social world. Members of the school could thus adopt very divergent social and political positions, as is evidenced by the different stances taken by Bousset and Troeltsch after World War I.

The influence of the school on subsequent scholarship, both in biblical studies and more broadly in religious studies, has been immense: its ideas spread quickly beyond the German-speaking world into the USA and Britain. If there was a weakness in the school's understanding of religion, which often owed more to philosophy than to historical study, it nevertheless attempted to approach Christianity as a religion among religions. In some quarters, its work can still provoke controversy. **See also RELIGION AS A CONCEPT AND CHRISTIANITY.**

MARK D. CHAPMAN

Hodge, Charles (1797–1878). As a professor for 56 years at Princeton Theological Seminary, a Presbyterian minister, and the editor of *Princeton Review*, Hodge was a major representative of Calvinist* orthodoxy. He defended biblical infallibility* against historical-critical Bible* interpretation, opposed revivalists* like Finney* for reducing true piety to superficial emotionalism, rejected theological liberalism* because it downplayed original sin* and Christ's atonement*, and called Darwinism* "atheism." A leading intellectual, Hodge argued that theology, like all sciences*, derived from facts; theology's facts were induced from Scripture* as scientific facts were induced from nature (and the terminology of his commonsense realism). Hodge taught more than 3,000 students, and his *Systematic Theology* (1873) was a standard textbook into the 20th c.

JAMES P. BYRD

Holiness. In the biblical tradition, holiness is posited to be a characteristic unique to God. Thus Leviticus* has God say, "For I am the Lord your God; sanctify yourselves [= make yourselves holy] therefore, and be holy for I am holy" (11:44; see 19:2). Holiness (Heb *qodesh*) is what "separates" God from all that is limited. Every other person, place, act, or thing falls under the rubric of holiness by having some connection to God (emphasized in the NT by the Gk root *hagios*) or being dedicated to God (emphasized by the Gk root *hosiotes*). From this perspective, Christ reflects in visible form the holiness of God, and for those who follow Christ he is the model and source of holiness: to the degree that one is "in Christ" one is holy. Consequently, Paul could address his congregations as "saints" or holy ones (e.g. Rom 1:7). Thus holiness (or "sanctity," a term derived from Lat *sanctus*) for the person of faith is relative to the absolute holiness of God revealed in Christ. To the degree that one is close to God, one can be called "holy."

Every generation had to find different ways of living out the holiness to which it was called by grace*, i.e. to have a "sanctified" life. Was one to follow Christ as a missionary, preacher, servant of the poor, or teacher, or less explicitly as a faithful Christian spouse, parent, or person otherwise engaged in the world? The criterion for personal holiness, then, is the degree to which persons' lives conform to the model of Jesus Christ, who is the way, truth, and life. To the degree that such persons strive to be followers of Christ, they become more holy (sanctified) in that their lives belong to and conform more exactly to God, the source of holiness.

The term "holiness" as applied to persons is also analogously applied to space (holy places; see Hierotopy, the Creation of Christian Sacred Spaces), times (festal seasons), ritual acts (the holy liturgy), and objects (holy water, the Bible [Scripture*] as "the holy Bible"). The applications of the term vary depending on the emphasis given to external manifestations of observances. For example, the Eastern Orthodox* tradition, with its core emphasis on the Divine* Liturgy, uses the term for more things (e.g. vestment.) or persons (monks) than Evangelicals, who tend to use the term for persons who are "converted* to Christ" and "sanctified," which is an etymological equivalent of holiness (see Holiness Movement). Indeed, some Charismatic* traditions call their congregations "Holiness churches."

Holiness also has an eschatological* dimension; holiness for humans is fully attained at the end of this life (the *eschaton*), when they return to God, who is holy and the final source of all holiness. This completes the circle: humans come out from God, who is holy, and return to God, the source of all holiness. In the Christian tradition, this eschatological dimension of holiness has both an individual and a corporate character. Individually, persons reach their capacity for holiness when they are with the Lord in heaven*. Similarly, according to the biblical tradition, the world will be saved at the end of history when the New Jerusalem is achieved, as described by the language of holiness in Rev 21:1–2: "I saw a new heaven and a new earth, for the first heaven and the first earth have passed away and the sea was no more. And I saw the holy city, the New Jerusalem coming down out of heaven from God."

LAWRENCE S. CUNNINGHAM

Holiness Movement. The Holiness Movement represented a 19th-c. US renewal of the Wesleyan doctrine of Christian perfection, blended with the themes of revivalism* and perfectionism* that were inherent in antebellum US religion. Emphasis was placed on the immediacy of the experience of sanctification* (subsequent to conversion*/justification*), typically characterized as "baptism* in the Holy* Spirit." The latter theme derived from the Pietists* via John Fletcher and John Wesley*. Emphasis was placed on the social as well as the personal dimension of holiness, particularly the abolition of slavery*.

Leaders included the evangelist Charles Finney* (1792–1875), the Oberlin school, and the American Antislavery Society. Phoebe Palmer* (1807–74) nurtured a generation of Holiness leaders in her Tuesday meetings in New York, and her work in England inspired the Booths* to launch the Salvation* Army. The Holiness Movement grew to several million adherents, thanks to the international mission work of the Methodist bishop William Taylor (1821–1902), the European Holiness crusades of Hannah and Robert Pearsall Smith (1874–75), and the National Camp Meeting Association for the Promotion of Holiness (1867), among others. Holiness denominations included the Wesleyan Methodist Connection (1843), the Free Methodists (1860s) (see Methodism Cluster), and later the Nazarenes*. These Holiness bodies were among the first to ordain women* ministers.

J. STEVEN O'MALLEY

Holocaust, Jewish (or Shoah), was the systematic, state-organized persecution and murder of approximately 6 million Jews (including 1.5 million children) by Nazi Germany* and its collaborators. Under Adolf Hitler (1889–1945), the Nazi state, a radically anti-Semitic, racist*, and genocidal regime (1933–45), slaughtered two-thirds of Europe's Jews and one-third of the world's Jewish population.

While "Holocaust" designates the Nazi destruction of European Jews, that name does not always or necessarily refer exclusively to them alone. Hitler's murderous regime destroyed millions of other defenseless people, including Roma and Sinti (Gypsies*), Polish* citizens, as well as homosexuals*, the handicapped, Jehovah's* Witnesses, and other religious and political dissidents within Germany. For racial, cultural, or political reasons, members of these groups were attacked in ways that were related to but not identical with the Jews' fate under Hitler. Jews were consistently the foremost targets of Nazi Germany's racism and the mass murder that followed from it.

Historical Context. From 1933 until the beginning of World War II (September 1, 1939), the strategy of Nazi Germany's racist anti-Semitism was to deprive Germany's Jews of their citizenship, employment, and property, thus forcing them to emigrate. Even with Germany's relatively small prewar Jewish population (c550,000), that approach was less than completely successful from the Nazi point of view. Once the war began, Germany's military gains brought millions of Jews under the swastika. Such overwhelming numbers made plans for the forced relocation of European Jews unworkable. By late 1941, the mass killing of Jews was under way in Eastern Europe. It eventually reached continental proportions when Jews throughout Europe were deported to killing centers that the Germans constructed on Polish soil. At Auschwitz, the most notorious site, more than a million Jews were gassed to death.

Religious Character of the Holocaust. As one considers the religious contexts and implications of the unprecedented tragedy that is now called the Holocaust, it is important to note that at least three terms name this event. All of them raise questions concerning why and how it happened. Masters of euphemistic language, the Nazis spoke of *die Endlösung*, the "Final Solution" of their so-called Jewish question. If Hitler had fully gotten his way, the "Final Solution" would have resulted not only in the annihilation of every Jewish man, woman, and child but also in the eradication of Judaism and every aspect of Jewish tradition. The intention of the Nazis' assault on the Jews was to rid the earth of everything Jewish.

In the early 1940s, Polish Jews used the Hebrew term *shoah* to designate their plight under Hitler. The roots of that word go back to biblical sources: Psalms*, Isaiah's* prophecies, and Job's* lamentations. Its meanings are multiple. Sometimes *shoah* denotes dangers that threaten Israel from surrounding nations; at other times, it refers to individual distress and desolation. If catastrophic destruction is signified in each case, the biblical meanings of *shoah* imply divine judgment. Those ancient meanings, however, are called into question by the "Final Solution," for in what credible sense could God's judgment be embedded in the Nazis' intended destruction of Jewish life and tradition? In contemporary usage, *shoah* conveys the old sense of destruction but sounds disturbing notes of fragmentation and questioning where religious traditions are concerned.

Although "Shoah" is widely used in Israel and in some European countries, and Yom Hashoah is Israel's official remembrance day for the catastrophe, "Holocaust," a term that began to achieve prominence in the 1950s, remains this event's most common name. It derives from the Septuagint*, a Greek translation of the HB (3rd c. BCE), which employs *holokauston* for the Hebrew *olah*. Those biblical words refer to a completely consumed burnt offering. As a name for Nazi Germany's genocide against the Jews, the term "Holocaust" is also surrounded by problematic religious connotations. In no credible sense could the destruction of the European Jews be called a sacrifice to God.

For both Jews and Christians, the Holocaust raises anguished problems about God's relationship to history*. For Christians those problems are especially difficult because the Christian tradition is deeply implicated in and indicted by the Holocaust. Specifically, Nazi Germany's targeting of the Jews in the Holocaust cannot be explained apart from anti-Jewish images – Christ killers, willful blasphemers*, unrepentant sons and daughters of the devil*, to name only a few – that were deeply rooted for centuries in Christian thought and practice. What can rightly be called Christian anti-Semitism provided the essential background, preparation, and motivation for the Germans' "Final Solution." That same long-standing Christian hostility toward Judaism and Jews goes a long way toward explaining why overtly Christian resistance to the Holocaust was as scarce and sporadic as it turned out to be. In the dominant Christian worldview before and during the Holocaust, Jews were considered "outsiders" to such a degree that help in their times of acute need was unlikely to be much of a Christian priority. After the Holocaust, Christian attitudes toward Jews have changed significantly for the better, but the price paid for that reformation is beyond calculation. **See also ANTI-SEMITISM; SUPERSESSIONISM.** JOHN K. ROTH

Holy. See HOLINESS; HOLINESS MOVEMENT.

Holy Days of Obligation, Roman Catholic feast days during which laity and clergy are obliged to attend Mass*, abstaining from work that might prevent this observance.

Holy Fool (fool for Christ's sake) is a type of Christian saint* who pretends to be insane and imitates Christ, willingly subjecting him- or herself to homelessness, poverty, disdain, and persecution. The biblical model is provided by prophets and by Paul's juxtaposition of heavenly and earthly wisdom ("We are fools for Christ's sake," 1 Cor 4:10). Holy fools sacrificed their private lives, names, and identities to God, spoke in parables, and enacted scenes in public to accuse people of their sins and to preach. They first appeared in Egypt* in the 4th c., then in Byzantium* and, in great number, in Russia* (14th–16th c.). **See also MONASTICISM CLUSTER: IN THE RUSSIAN AND UKRAINIAN TRADITION.** ELENA VOLKOVA

Holy Innocents, children massacred by Herod's order in an attempt to destroy the infant Jesus (Matt 2:16–18); commemorated on December 27 in Oriental Orthodox* churches, December 28 in Western* churches, and December 29 in Eastern Orthodox* churches.

Holy Name, Veneration of, refers to the practice of bending the knee (Phil 2:10) upon hearing or seeing the name of Jesus. Bernardino of Siena promoted this veneration; at his trial for heresy* (1426), he argued that adoration is not that of the letters (IHS*) but of the person to whom the name refers (cf. icons*).

Holy Office. The Congregation of the Holy Office (Congregatio sancti officii), originally established as the Congregation of the Holy Roman and Universal Inquisition* by Pope Paul III (1542), received the former name from Pius X (1908).

Distinct from national inquisitions, the Holy Office set up by Paul III was a central tribunal directed by a cardinal secretary for judging questions of heresy* and schism*. The focus initially was on Protestants* but soon shifted to Catholics themselves. From the early 17th to the mid-20th c., the Holy Office issued numerous decrees on sacramental, doctrinal, and moral matters.

In 1965 Pope Paul VI changed the name of the Holy Office to the Congregation for the Doctrine of the Faith (Congregatio pro doctrina fidei [CDF]). The List of Prohibited Books (*Index* Librorum Prohibitorum*), which had been under the Holy Office since 1917, was discontinued (1966). The CDF, however, retained the right to examine books for doctrinal and moral problems. Pope John Paul II reorganized the Roman Curia by his 1988 apostolic constitution, *Pastor bonus*, and reinforced the CDF's duty "to promote and safeguard the doctrine on faith and morals in the whole Catholic world" (Article 48).

ROBERT FASTIGGI

Holy Oils. See CHRISM.

Holy Places, places in Palestine associated (sometimes only by legend) with biblical events, especially those in Christ's life. **See also HIEROTOPY, THE CREATION OF CHRISTIAN SACRED SPACES; HOLY SEPULCHRE, CHURCH OF THE.**

Holy Roman Empire. After Roman rule ended in the West (c476), the Roman Empire continued in Constantinople. Relations between Constantinople and the West were strained by schisms over the Henoticon* (482–519), the Three* Chapters (from 547), monothelitism* (649–81), and iconoclasm* (726–87). The last of the Greek-born popes sponsored the Carolingian* dynasty (751) and relied on its military support in Italy*; the "Donation* of Constantine" seemed to give the pope control over the Empire in the West. Thus the way was paved for Pope Leo III to crown Charlemagne* emperor (though only of the West) in St. Peter's on Christmas Day, 800. The title was retained by his heirs and was always conferred by the pope; after an interruption in the line of succession, it was resumed when Otto received the title (962). Despite the power of some imperial dynasties, the position of the emperor of the "Holy Roman Empire of the German Nation" steadily weakened and the role of the electors among the German nobility became increasingly important. The last emperor to be crowned personally by the pope was Charles* V (1530). The Empire (which, as Voltaire said, had become "neither holy nor Roman nor an empire") was ended in 1806 by another French ruler, Napoleon, who, in the presence of the pope, crowned himself emperor of the French (1804).

EUGENE TESELLE

Holy Sepulchre, Church of the, rock-hewn tomb of Jesus in Jerusalem, allegedly discovered by Constantine* or his mother, Helena*. Over the "cave" were built a memorial (*aedicule*) and later, enclosing it, the rotunda called the "Anastasis" (place of resurrection). These structures were demolished under Sultan Hakim (1009); the rotunda was replaced by the Greeks (11th c.), and the church by the crusaders (12th c.). The Templars'* churches in London and Paris were built in imitation of this composite structure.

HOLY SPIRIT CLUSTER

1) *Introductory Entries*

Holy Spirit
Holy Spirit in Eastern Orthodoxy

2) *A Sampling of Contextual Views and Practices*

Holy Spirit in African Christianity
Holy Spirit in Asian Christianity
Holy Spirit in Caribbean Christianity
Holy Spirit in Latin American Christianity
Holy Spirit in North American Christianity
Holy Spirit in South Pacific Christianity
Holy Spirit in Western European Christianity

1) Introductory Entries

Holy Spirit, in Christian theology, denotes both the third person* of the Trinity* (alongside the Father and Son) and the idea of God as Spirit (John 4:24), spiritual presence, or spiritual creative force. Recently, the Holy Spirit has received greater recognition in theology. The reasons are many, including a better knowledge of Eastern Orthodoxy* with its rich pneumatological tradition, the rise of the Pentecostal*/Charismatic* movements, and a general postmodern* interest in spirituality and new religiosity.

The Bible uses a number of metaphors for the Spirit: wind (Gr *pneuma*, thus "pneumatology," the doctrine of the Spirit), dove, and Paraclete (comforter, advocate). The foundational biblical insight, especially in the OT, is the Spirit as the life principle that makes all life possible and sustains it (Gen 1:2; Ps 104:29–30). The Spirit is also presented in the Bible as mighty charismatic power, subtle wisdom, and cosmic presence of God. In the NT, the integral connection between Jesus and the Spirit becomes the leading theme.

It took several centuries for Christian theology to come to any kind of doctrinal understanding of the Spirit in the emerging trinitarian doctrine. While early Christian creeds connect the Holy Spirit with the church* and forgiveness* of sins, later Christian tradition, especially Protestant, came to emphasize the Spirit's role in the individual Christian's life as the agent of sanctification*. The Eastern tradition (especially that of the Cappadocians* and Athanasius*) helped establish the deity of the Spirit alongside the Father and Son. In the Christian West, Augustine* consolidated the idea of the Spirit as the bond of love between Father and Son. The Western tradition also established the *Filioque** (and from the Son) according to which the Spirit proceeds not only from the Father but also from the Son. The charge that the West had subordinated the Spirit to the Son led to the split between the East and West (1054).

Along with these doctrinal developments, the history of lived theology acknowledges a number of pneumatological traditions that places greater emphasis on the experience of the Spirit than on theological definitions. These include the 2nd-c. enthusiastic Montanist* Movement, the highly mystical* medieval movements, various Spirit movements of the Radical* Reformation, and more recently the rapidly growing Pentecostal/Charismatic movements. Pentecostals believe in a universal empowerment of all Christians by the Spirit (Spirit baptism*). All of these Spirit movements emphasize unmediated access to the Spirit, rather than tying the Spirit mainly to sacraments and church offices (especially that of bishop) as the established traditions do, and thus challenge church structures and doctrinal formulations.

Contemporary theology is experiencing a resurgence of pneumatology alongside a reconsideration of the role and nature of the Spirit. The Holy Spirit was connected mainly with salvation*, inspiration*, individual piety, as well as some aspects of church life. Without denying these emphases, contemporary theology also connects the Holy Spirit with other theological topics, such as creation*, God*, Christology*, and eschatology*. Political, social, environmental, liberationist, and other "public" issues are discussed from pneumatological perspectives. Contemporary theology also acknowledges the relation of the Spirit to particular contexts by taking note of the distinctive experience of the Spirit in Africa, Asia, and Latin America, as compared with the North Atlantic world and acknowledging the role of the Spirit as empowering and giving voice, for instance, to women*, the poor*, and the oppressed*. Contemporary theology also investigates the relation of the Holy Spirit to other religions and their respective understandings of "spirits," as well as the correlations between science and pneumatology now that a dynamic worldview, more sensitive to everything "spiritual," has replaced the mechanistic one.

VELI-MATTI KÄRKKÄINEN

Holy Spirit in Eastern Orthodoxy. See TRINITY CLUSTER: IN EASTERN ORTHODOXY.

2) A Sampling of Contextual Views and Practices

Holy Spirit in African Christianity. Holy Spirit, *Mzimu Woyera* in Malawian Chichewa, is the feminine divine power behind Christian living and transformation, the breath (life giver) of the church, the internal witness of God's revelation, and the Ancestor* facilitating daily communion between the Supreme Being and creation.

In African* Religion, ancestors facilitate communion by bringing revelation from the Divine to humans, who respond through ritual worship. Means of revelation include dreams, visions, and spirit possession. In African Christian theology of conversion*, healing*, and interconnectedness, when this role is conceived of as mediation, it is that of Christ, but when it is conceived of as living communion, it is that of the Spirit as breath of the church. The Spirit-filled Christian remains in daily communion with Jesus Christ, the model *par excellence* of a transformed and transforming life guided by compassion*, grace*, justice*, and mercy*. The Spirit, as the Ancestor, convicts and empowers in order to transform the heart and community, inaugurating repentance (*metanoia*) in response to the call to mission. For inspiration, the Spirit reveals the compassionate work of Jesus, who journeyed with the marginalized, reflecting with them and leading them to praxis as a way of ushering in the Reign* of God.

The Spirit also reveals God's will and empowers the intercessor (bishop, prophet-preacher, messianic figure) in sustaining health and in healing. Health is the harmonious functioning of every part of the body in relationship with a particular environment (Weatherhead). Healing restores such harmonious relationships. Faith healing involves prayer and ritual, heavily relying on the disposition of faith of those seeking healing (Moyo). The Spirit reveals the cause of ill-health, effects the healing, and enables human agency for healing.

Women's embodied spirituality interconnects their sexuality with the rest of creation as mother earth. Spirit-possessed women therapeutically sing and dance barefoot in rhythm with the sacred earth, to whom creation owes its survival. Women's barefoot theology presents three levels of interconnectedness rooted in a vulnerable kinship relationship and based on compassion, grace, justice, and mercy. They associate the Spirit first with the Triune God: father and mother creator God, Jesus (the victorious model), and Spirit (Jesus' sister, who facilitates divine interconnectedness with creation, partly embodied in mother earth); second, with divine creation relatedness; and third, with intercreation interconnectedness.

In African Christianity, the Spirit also has an important role in the Charismatic* renewal and the conception of the Bible as revelation (rather than as word) related to the Spirit's internal witness.

FULATA MOYO

Holy Spirit in Asian Christianity. Even though the idea of Spirit or spirits is not foreign to the peoples of Asia, articulating the doctrine of the Holy Spirit involves many challenges, given the multireligious and multilingual Asian context. Asian Christian theologians have carried out this task in five ways.

1. The process of translating the Bible into Asian languages has engendered a theological activity that looks for dynamic equivalents in the local language. While the Tamil Bible uses the word *aavi* (vapor, ghost, or steam) for Spirit, the Sanskritic tradition considers *atman* (soul) appropriate. The very choice of a dynamic equivalent brings in new meanings.
2. Theologians draw from the religiocultural traditions of Asia to construct an Asian doctrine of the Holy Spirit. Jung Young Lee proposes the concept of *chi* (or *ki* in Korean) in presenting the Holy Spirit as a feminine and vital energy embedded in the life of the Trinity*. A. J. Appasamy presents the Holy Spirit using the Hindu idea of *antaryamin* (indweller). P. Chenchiah uses *shakti* (the energy of God, represented in the feminine iconic form) to name the Holy Spirit "Mahashakti." Vengal Chakkarai, employing the concept of *avatar* (decent or incarnation), explains the Holy Spirit as the incarnation of Christ in the hearts of the believers.

3. Korean theologians have linked the Holy Spirit to the Shamanistic* traditions of Korea and the spirits of ancestors*. Such a linking may raise questions about the symbolism of evil* in some of the Shamanistic categories. Minjung* theologians of Korea have grappled with this in varied ways. The Charismatic*/Pentecostal traditions within Asia have found indigenous ways of expounding the Holy Spirit, taking into account some of the traditional spiritual practices in Asia.
4. Liberation theologians expound the idea that the Holy Spirit is a companion who empowers the poor* in their struggle for freedom and dignity. The Dalit* theologians of India, such as Arvind Nirmal, utilize the concept of the Holy Spirit as the empowerer.
5. K. C. Sen, a 19th-c. Hindu theologian, saw the Holy Spirit as the initiator of the Church of Third Dispensation.

These five ways of construing the doctrine of the Holy Spirit clearly indicate that Asian theologians are no longer bound by the categories and conceptual frameworks inherited from the Western missionary enterprise; they are engaging in creative theological exposition of the Holy Spirit. M. THOMAS THANGARAJ

Holy Spirit in Caribbean Christianity. In the Caribbean, the person and work of the Holy Spirit are conceived of in perhaps as many ways as there are groups that claim to embrace the Christian faith. In the main, these notions are informed by historical and cultural influences related to Africa, where the ancestral roots of the vast majority of Caribbean people are (though some are also from Asia); to Europe, owing to colonial influences; and to North America, as a result of regional proximity and the current global influence of the USA.

From Eurocentric dogmatic theology has come the notion of the Holy Spirit as the divine power who imbues us with the capacity (see Grace of God Cluster) to become the best we can be, despite the odds confronting us. In the context of the Caribbean colonial heritage, the Holy Spirit is the divine resource made available to humans, enabling them to overcome the challenges of this life in order to make the transition to the next life, where such challenges will be no more. Much emphasis is placed not only on the experience of genuine perfection in the hereafter, but also on the capacity to endure hardship faced in the present.

The Afrocentric influence is found in the quest for a here-and-now experience. In this perspective, the Holy Spirit's work is considered liberative, endowing humans with the capacity to confront and conquer hardship. It is this confidence in the Spirit's liberating* power that undoubtedly inspired the expression of the spiritual "And before I be a slave, I'd be buried in my grave and go home to my Lord and be free."

More recently, the influence exerted by an aggressive materialism rooted in the US Prosperity* Gospel emphasizes the realization of our God-endowed capacities. Then the Holy Spirit is deemed to be the one who heals, who provides all the material and nonmaterial resources required to live an abundant life, and who equips the believer for faithful Christian witness.

For the most part, Caribbean understandings of the Holy Spirit are rooted in the biblical presentation of the Spirit, especially in the Acts of the Apostles and 1 Cor 12, 14. They portray the Holy Spirit as God's means of transforming and renewing fallen humanity to fulfill their divinely ordained role as God's partners in redeeming the world. HENLEY BERNARD

Holy Spirit in Latin American Christianity. Diverse experiences of the Spirit during the 20th c. in Latin America led churches and theologians to pay closer attention to the Holy Spirit. Pentecostalism*, the Catholic Charismatic* renewal, popular* religions originating with indigenous peoples (in independent Latin American Charismatic churches), and Base* Ecclesial Communities, among others, have brought about a renewed understanding of the active presence of the Spirit.

For nearly 500 years, the religious experiences of American indigenous peoples were disqualified as diabolic by both Catholic and Protestant Christianity. In institutional Catholicism, the Spirit was understood to be present only in the sacraments and through the clergy's mediating liturgical acts. In Protestantism the Spirit was associated chiefly with the liturgical celebration and, above all, with the reception of the Word. Pneumatology reflected the dogmatic positions of each ecclesiastical tradition and was viewed as secondary to other theological themes.

The eruption of Pentecostalism (from the early 20th c.) and of the Charismatic renewal (since the 1960s) revealed dimensions of the Spirit's role, such as healing (of both individual bodies and communities), inciting believers to a liberating mission, ecstatic experiences, liturgical renewal, glossolalia*, and concrete ecumenical efforts. Also since the 1960s, the Liberation movement has attributed a large part of its motivation to the power of the Spirit; thus Liberation theology has devoted more of its reflection to the liberating Spirit, underscoring the Spirit as the power of liberation, of community solidarity, and of the defense of life.

In Protestant communities, especially Pentecostal and Charismatic communities, the communal character of the manifestations of the Spirit is also emphasized, although these communities give more importance to the concrete manifestations of the Spirit for individuals. The Spirit is understood to be a power that renews life, health in all its dimension, and eschatological* hope* – with a tendency toward reductionist, magical, and exhibitionist views of the actions of the Spirit (see Charismatic and Pentecostal Movements Cluster: Studying).

Recent social, cultural, ecclesiastical, and theological changes in Latin America have brought about significant changes in the perception of the Spirit. A more holistic view of the Spirit, determined less by dogmatic considerations than by the communities' concrete experiences, is emerging. This holistic view theologically retrieves and affirms the Spirit's "community management," the Spirit's ability to renew and preserve life, the Spirit's configuration of liberating and just communities, the Spirit's role in inspiring the quest for dialogue and understanding among diverse groups, and the Spirit's support in promoting the values of the Kingdom*.

DANIEL CHIQUETE

Holy Spirit in North American Christianity. Much of the theology of the Holy Spirit in North America is a continuation of European traditions as well as an attempt to revise and expand pneumatology in order to speak to multiculturalism, the diversity of Christian churches, the postmodern* mindset, as well as Evangelical* and Pentecostal*/Charismatic* movements.

The Lutheran Robert W. Jenson's discussion of the Spirit in his *Systematic Theology* is representative of traditional mainline approaches. The trinitarian pneumatology of the Roman Catholic Elizabeth Johnson similarly builds on tradition but does so with a view to developing a feminist* interpretation of the Spirit in search of a holistic, egalitarian perspective. Johnson has also attempted to find connections between femininity and the environment. The Protestant Mark I. Wallace's *Fragments of the Spirit: Nature, Violence, and the Renewal of Creation* similarly makes a passionate case for a theology of the Holy Spirit sensitive to the "biocentric" dimension and preservation of nature as it faces "ecocide." Process* theology's first attempts to offer pneumatological reflections likewise echo many of these concerns.

The Evangelical theologian from Canada, Clark Pinnock, has endeavored to construct a full-scale systematic theology from a pneumatological perspective, thus challenging theology that in general has given the Spirit a secondary role. The American Malaysian-born Pentecostal theologian Amos Yong produced a major Pentecostal theology of the Holy Spirit with a global aim and in dialogue with ecumenical voices. Unlike most Evangelicals and Pentecostals, Yong has also written substantively on the theology of religions from a pneumatological perspective, arguing that the work of the Holy Spirit extends beyond the church and encompasses the whole created cosmos. The discussion of Spirit baptism* by another US Pentecostal theologian, Frank Macchia, is the first attempt not only to clarify theologically this central Pentecostal concept and experience, but also to put it in dialogue with Roman Catholic and Protestant theologies.

VELI-MATTI KÄRKKÄINEN

Holy Spirit in South Pacific Christianity. The traditional life of the peoples of the South Pacific is immersed in and derives from the various spirits. Nothing happens without being caused by spirits, and much of the way of life is shaped by a determination to serve the spirits in order to be blessed by them.

The Christian message was introduced (19th c.) into this context of a complex "spiritual" existence. Until recently, most of the theological attention of the missionary churches has been "christological" rather than "pneumatological." The clear assumption was that acceptance of Jesus Christ meant the rejection of the spirits of traditional culture.

However, despite the heritage of Christian missionary teaching and its widespread success in planting Christian churches in the South Pacific, there remains a strong sense among Pacific Islanders that their lives are influenced, if not controlled, by the various spirits in their culture. For some, the Christian faith is a variation of their own traditional system of belief and offers yet another spirit (the Holy Spirit) that has the power to bestow good or evil and is to be manipulated in order to seek blessings.

In recent years, with an increase in the number of Evangelical movements with a Pentecostal* or Charismatic* focus throughout the South Pacific, there is a heightened focus on pneumatology in the churches. "Holy Spirit movements" have evolved, both within and beyond the established churches. Elements of these movements include a profound personal experience of conversion*, a renewal of personal life, healing* from affliction, speaking in tongues*, and, in some cases, more unusual events. How are these experiences of the Holy Spirit related to the manifold spirits of traditional cultures? This remains an open question.

These recent developments provoked a mixed response among established churches. An awareness of the genuineness of the movements as a work of the Holy Spirit often existed side by side with accusations or suspicions about the non-Christian nature of the movements. Nevertheless, the impact of these developments in the past generation has been such that the established churches have had to work out ways of accommodating it within their structures. In some cases, this has not been possible and new religious groups have emerged. However, serious engagement with the important theological issue of the relationship between Holy Spirit and the spirits of traditional cultures is still needed.

RANDALL PRIOR

Holy Spirit in Western European Christianity. One of the architects of contemporary Roman Catholic theology, Karl Rahner*, argued that it is the Holy Spirit who makes possible the human reception of divine grace* and the self's experience of existential transcendence. During Vatican* II, Rahner also encouraged his church to appreciate "the dynamic element in the church." Eastern Orthodoxy's rich pneumatological tradition is represented by the Russian-born Vladimir Lossky's* mystical* theology. In a different vein, the Orthodox John Zizioulas's take on the Holy Spirit is guided by his "communion theology": as the Triune God exists as a community of personhood, so the Holy Spirit is the principle of communion.

The most widely debated Protestant pneumatology is delineated in German Reformed Jürgen Moltmann's *Spirit of Life: A Universal Affirmation* (1992). Although it discusses traditional topics (e.g. justification* and sanctification*), it also relates the discussion to pressing contemporary themes, such as the environment, justice, and equality, in search of a "holistic," "all-encompassing," or "comprehensive" approach to the Spirit. Moltmann wishes to perceive God's presence in the Spirit in all things and all things in God ("immanent transcendence.") The pneumatology of another Reformed German, Michael Welker, presents a unique approach in *God the Spirit* (1994). On the basis of biblical materials, he critiques "metaphysical," "speculative," and "abstract" forms of pneumatology in search of "concrete" and "realistic" voices. His main concern is to pursue the question "Where can we discern the Spirit in life?"

The most distinctive feature of the Lutheran Wolfhart Pannenberg's pneumatology is that he interweaves the Spirit with all major loci of his rigorous systematic argumentation, such as creation* and eschatology*. In search of a theology as public discipline, Pannenberg opposes the idea of the Spirit as the principle of individual piety. Eager to relate the Spirit to science*, Pannenberg takes his cue from the biblical statement of the Spirit as life-giving principle, which he calls the "field-concept" (from modern physics). He believes there are surprising possibilities for agreement between new scientific theories and theological conceptions.

VELI-MATTI KÄRKKÄINEN

Holy Synod, the Russian Orthodox Church's supreme governing body, created by Peter the Great (1721) to displace the patriarch's authority. It was abolished after the Russian Revolution of 1917, and the patriarch's authority was restored.

Holy Water, water set apart and blessed for religious purposes, including dedication, exorcism*, burial, and ritual cleansing on entering a church.

Holy Week, week preceding Easter*, beginning with Palm* Sunday, reenacting in succession all the events of Jesus' last week; probably instituted in Jerusalem; Egeria's* narrative (380–83) is the first account of it.

Homiletics, the theory of preaching. **See also** PREACHING; RECEPTION STUDIES OF PREACHING.

Homily (Gk *homilia,* "familiar discourse"), a type of preaching*, usually in a spirit of edification rather than proclamation or argumentation.

Homoousians, Homoiousians, Homoians, Anomoians, the parties in the 4th-c. debate over the Trinity*. The Homoousians asserted with the Nicene* Creed that the Son is *homoousios,* or "identical in essence," with the Father. The Homoiousians asserted that the Son is *homoiousios,* or "like in essence," with the Father. Their concern was to affirm the threeness of the divine persons. Although they were called "Semi-Arians," they were reconciled with the Homoousians at the Council of Alexandria in 362 and contributed to the completion of the doctrine that the Trinity is "one essence" in three persons. The Homoians supported the Arians*, arguing that the Son is *homoios,* or "similar," to the Father. The Anomoians were extreme Arians who insisted that the Father alone is "God" in the proper sense; the only begotten Son is the "God" and Creator of everything else, but was himself "created out of nothing" by the Father's will, and thus is *anomoios,* or "unlike," the Father in essence.

Homosexuality denotes a person's sexual* feelings, fantasies, and sometimes sexual activities with (a) person(s) of the same sex. Throughout much of Christian history, homosexuality has been considered sinful and later was viewed as a disease. Although these traditional attitudes remain strong, a growing number of Western Christians in the early 21st c. view homosexuality as medically and morally neutral.

1. *Homosexuality as sin**. The oldest and most tenacious view of homosexuality as contrary to both God's supernatural law and the laws of nature is held by the Roman Catholic, Eastern Orthodox, and conservative Protestant churches. According to this view, with roots in Scripture* (Gen 19; Lev 18:22; Rom 1: 26–27), homosexuality is morally wrong and represents a turning away from our human nature in God's image. Those who espouse this view think that granting social justice* to gay, lesbian, or bisexual persons amounts to condoning sin against God.
2. *Homosexuality as sickness.* To members of movements in the late 19th and 20th c. that advocated pathologizing and "treating" human beings in medical and psychological terms, homosexuals were diseased individuals who needed help. Although Sigmund Freud is often cited as a source of this view, his studies suggested that most people are naturally bisexual. Because the "sickness" theory frees homosexuals

from moral responsibility, many Christians stressed the difference between homosexual "orientation" (the disease) and homosexual "behavior" (the sinfulness).

3. *Homosexuality as medically and morally neutral.* In the late 1960s, psychologist Evelyn Hooker showed that the "sickness theory" was based solely on research involving homosexuals in psychiatric treatment. In 1973 the American Psychiatric Association officially removed homosexuality from its list of mental disorders. Subsequently, in the USA and other Western cultures, through the ongoing work of feminists, and gay, lesbian, bisexual, transgender, and queer* activists and theologians, many Christians began to understand homosexuality, and sexuality* as a whole, to be morally neutral. Like heterosexual* behavior, homosexual activity can be destructive or creative, coercive or cooperative, abusive or healthy, and thus immoral or moral.

Reverend Troy Perry's founding of the Metropolitan Community Church (1968) and its growth around the world signaled a new visibility and activism on the part of gay, lesbian, and other queer Christians. The Presbyterian Church (USA), despite overwhelmingly defeating a more inclusive report on sexuality, forcefully articulated a Christian vision of sexual justice, inclusivity, and acceptance of homosexuality as a morally neutral orientation and behavior (1991). Of concern are the churches' oppression of their own homosexual, bisexual, and transgender members and issues of social justice (e.g. housing and employment equality; the some 1,000 legal and economic benefits associated with marriage).

Throughout Protestant, Roman Catholic, and Eastern Orthodox communities, a Queer theological movement is struggling to transform Christian understandings of homosexuality and sexuality and their root in Scripture*. The 2003 election of an openly gay man, Gene Robinson, as a bishop in the Episcopal Church (USA) and thereby in the worldwide Anglican Communion, as well as the acceptance of openly gay and lesbian priests and bishops in Lutheran churches (e.g. the Church of Sweden and the Evangelical Lutheran* Church in America), signaled a global struggle among Christians to come to terms, or not, with new understandings of homosexuality. CARTER HEYWARD

Honduras, Republic of. The Christian faith got off to a slow start in Honduras. The Mayan people and culture disappeared for unknown reasons c300 years before the Spanish Conquest. Several Amerindian groups, especially the Lenca, became amalgamated with the Spanish. Consequently, 91% of the population is mestizo*, 6% indigenous, 2% Garifuna (black), and only 1% white.

Early mission efforts by Franciscans* had moderate success. The slow establishment of settlements (because of the lack of exploitable resources) hindered the progress of colonization and of evangelization. Since the colonial period, Honduras has had the lowest proportion of priests (most from foreign lands) to people in Latin America. This has militated against meaningful commitment to the Roman Catholic Church. After national independence was achieved (1838), the Church fought to retain its traditional role in politics and society. However, some of those privileges were taken away in the 1880s. Civil registers of births and marriages, public education, and freedom of religion were adopted. Yet because of its overwhelming presence, the Church continued to exercise significant power in national decisions.

In the 1950s, a serious evangelistic effort was launched by the Catholic Church to resolve the nominal membership of most Catholics. Many lay "delegates of the Word" led worship, received the Communion elements from an urban priest, and distributed the previously consecrated bread to those who came to the services. This grassroots movement, under distant priestly supervision, brought many into a meaningful relationship with the Church. A significant social activism on behalf of the poor* was initiated in Honduras, the second-poorest country in Latin America.

Adventists began mission work in 1891, followed by the Dispensationalist Central American Mission (1896), Quakers* (1902), Evangelical and Reformed (1920), Moravians* (1930), and members of Assemblies* of God (1937). Yet the growth of the Protestant Church was slow until the late 20th c., when the tremendous expansion of Pentecostal*/Charismatic* groups made deep inroads into nominal and folk Catholicism. Complex factors created a milieu conducive to change: the spontaneous rise of lay leaders, the growing disenfranchisement of the poor, the search for transcendental security, faith in biblical teaching, dependence on the supernatural for the solution of concrete personal problems, a future resolution of the crises of this life, and the unconditional recognition of personal worth by the spiritual community.

Pentecostals/Charismatics (now 80% of Protestants/Evangelicals) include classical Pentecostals (members of Assemblies* of God, Church* of God), the Charismatics who are renovating existing denominations, neo-Charismatics, including members of "spiritual warfare" groups, adherents of the Prosperity* Gospel, and others. Most Evangelical groups have little political influence in national affairs.

Statistics: Population (2000): 6.5 million (M). Christians, 6.3 M, 97% (Roman Catholics, 84%; Protestants/Evangelicals and Charismatics, 14%; 1% with dual membership). (Based on *World Christian Encyclopedia*, 2001.)

SIDNEY ROOY

Hong Kong. The first Catholic missionary, a Swiss named Theodore Joset, landed in Hong Kong in 1841, one year before the beginning of its colonization. The first Protestant missionary, Jehu Lewis Shuck from the American Baptist Missionary Union, came in 1842. During the following decades, as a British colony Hong Kong became a gateway to mission in mainland China*.

In 1874 the Roman Catholic Church established an apostolic vicariate. In 1880 the first All-China Catholic Synod was held. It became a diocese* in 1946. However, it was not for another 23 years, in 1969, that the Church had its first Chinese bishop (Francis Chen-peng Hsu). In 2000 there were 55 parishes and 98 places for religious services.

The Protestant community now includes about 1,300 congregations in more than 50 denominations, with many independent churches. The Baptists form the largest denomination. Others include Anglican, Lutheran, Christian and Missionary Alliance, Methodist, Church of Christ in China, Adventist, Pentecostal, and the Salvation* Army. The Hong Kong Chinese Christian Churches Union* and the Hong Kong Christian Council* facilitate ecumenical and joint endeavors among Protestant churches.

The Hong Kong Chinese Christian Churches Union, a congregation-based organization, was established in 1915 as a joint effort between the London Missionary Society, the China Congregational Church, the Anglican, the Methodist, the Chung Tsin missions, the Baptists, and the Chinese Rhenish Church to deal with matters pertaining to the Christian cemetery. Its membership now covers almost one-third of the local congregations, which implies that more than half of the total Protestant population is connected to the Union through their churches. Its ministry now extends to the provision of medical services, education, elderly services, and other social services. The Hong Kong Christian Council was established in 1954. It is a member of the World* Council of Churches, and its core membership contains mainline denominations, ecumenical agencies, and the Orthodox Metropolitanate of Hong Kong and Southeast Asia. It is committed to ecumenism, interfaith dialogue, and the promotion of unity of witness, serving as a bridge between local and worldwide churches.

Between 1980 and 1997, many significant developments occurred. Facing the return of Hong Kong to Communist China in 1997, the churches became highly vocal in negotiating their independent identities, serious about fostering church growth, and cautious about developing a relationship with the churches in mainland China. Many declarations and position papers formulated how the church should theologically and politically face the "1997 issue*," and the number of Chinese-speaking congregations grew dramatically, from 634 in 1980 to 1129 in 1999.

The local Christian community is characterized by its heavy commitment to providing social services and education. Its relationships with other religions or ideologies have been harmonious. Nevertheless, tensions have resulted from the condemnation of Chinese ancestral* veneration as sinful by many Evangelicals and most Charismatics*.

There are now more than 20 seminaries in Hong Kong. However, indigenization of the leadership did not take place until the 1970s. Because Hong Kong is highly Westernized, theological contextualization* and inculturation* are not receiving much attention. Yet since the 1950s, there has been a substantial dialogue between Christianity and Confucianism*.

The most distinctive contribution of Christianity in Hong Kong had to do with the return of Hong Kong to Communist mainland China in 1997 (the "handover"). With the signature of the Sino-British Joint Declaration on the question of Hong Kong in 1984, Hong Kong entered into an era of decolonization. People were, however, in the somewhat ambivalent position of both celebrating the decolonization and finding themselves neither culturally nor politically ready to be integrated into Communist China. Contextual theologization conditioned by this ambivalence became active to an unprecedented extent. In 1984 several statements were formulated by Christian leaders: "Statement on the Catholic Church and the Future of Hong Kong," signed by Cardinal John Baptist Wu Cheng-Chung and the Diocese of Hong Kong; "A Manifesto of the Protestant Church in Hong Kong on Religious Freedom," by the Hong Kong Christian Council; "The Convictions Held by Christians in Hong Kong in the Midst of Contemporary Social and Political Change," by a group of Evangelical Christian leaders in Hong Kong; "A Position Paper on the Future of Hong Kong" by the delegation of Hong Kong Protestant Church leaders. In 1987 Arnold Young published his *Theology of Reconciliation*, which discussed the 1997 handover. Reconciliation* as a contextualized theological theme, however, lost its impact after the Tiananmen June Fourth event of 1989. Kwok Nai-wang wrote a great deal about pro-democracy and pro–human rights theologies; Archie Lee contributed an Asian perspective on the "1997 issue" with his cross-textual hermeneutics. These theologizations, among others, however, seemed to lose their local audience after the peaceful handover. SIMON SHUI-MAN KWAN

Statistics: Population (2000): 6.86 million (M). Christians, 0.59 M, 8.6% (Catholics, 0.24 M; Protestant, 0.35 M) in a city where popular religions that blend Buddhism*, Daoism* and Confucianism* make up the vast majority; Muslims, 80,000, 1.2%. (Based on Information Services Department, *Hong Kong Annual Report*; David Wu and M. H. Liu, eds., *Ministry and Challenge in the 21st Century* [in Chinese]. HK: HKCRM, 2002; Hong Kong Catholic Truth Society, *Hong Kong Catholic Directory and Year Book*.)

Honorius, Pope (d638), during his papacy (625–38), took great interest in the Anglo-Saxon mission and granted the first exemption* to the monastery of Bobbio* (628). He is best known for approving monothelitism*, the doctrine of Emperor Heraclius and Sergius, patriarch of Constantinople. He stressed Christ's unity of person (638), using the expression "one will" without clarifying whether there are one or two "activities"; later he declared that Christ is one "agent," with the divine nature acting through the human. The Third Council of Constantinople* (680–81) condemned monothelitism and anathematized Honorius, fueling later arguments against papal infallibility from Conciliarists*, Gallicans*, and Protestants, since this episode indicated that a council may correct a pope.

Honorius of Autun, or Augustodunensis (early 12th c.), monk and scholar who worked in both England and Germany. His writings, widely read, offered an edifying synthesis and popularization of doctrine; some works were translated into the vernacular.

Honor and Shame. Anthropological and sociological studies have introduced the concepts of honor and shame to describe key elements in the cultures* of the Mediterranean at the time of the origins of Christianity. They are paired values used to structure status and all social interactions. "Honor" refers first and foremost to public reputation. The honorable man (honor is conceived of particularly as a male trait) exhibits personal readiness to maintain or extend the honor of his family. Similarly, "shame" refers primarily to public disgrace but also to the personal sensitivity that seeks to avoid it. Such shame (or modesty) is particularly a female virtue.

Honor and shame helped to shape the culture's morality, i.e. the generally accepted rules of correct behavior. A freeman was expected to function in public roles, competing to maintain his household's status. Women, as less public figures, could not normally add to the honor of the household but were expected to avoid any behavior that might detract from it.

Honor could be inherited or bestowed in response to competition. In general, a reputation for gravity, effective authority, liberality toward friends and clients, and respect for the property of others defined an honorable man. The author of the Pastoral Epistles wanted just such men in the leadership of the Christian churches (1 Tim 3:1–13; Titus 1:5–9). Women showed that they had a good sense of shame by dressing modestly and remaining in the background, although some Christian women were apparently testing these assumptions (Titus 2:3–5) (see Household Codes).

Honor and shame shaped sexual behavior by defining approved sexual couplings. Among Greeks and Romans, a freeman might honorably penetrate others, including not only his wife and concubines, but also slaves and prostitutes, male and female. It was shameful, however, for a free man to be penetrated by another man. Jews differed in that they also prohibited the penetration of another male (see Homosexuality).

Similarly, it was shameful for a married woman to be penetrated by anyone other than her husband or for a freewoman to be penetrated by a slave. In female–female sexual relationships, the assumption was that one woman would play a male role, and this reversal of genders was considered shameful.

While not one of the primary ethical principles of either Scripture or ancient philosophy, honor and shame were powerful forces in the structuring of society. Accordingly, they influenced efforts to set ethical guidelines.

L. WILLIAM COUNTRYMAN

Hooker, Richard (1554–1600), studied, then became a fellow, at Corpus Christi, Oxford, tutored by the "godly" (Puritan) divine John Rainolds and apparently numbered among the "godly"; however, Hooker and Rainolds were expelled c1580. After a ministry in Drayton-Beauchamp, Buckinghamshire (1584), Hooker was appointed master (senior priest) of the Temple Church (London, 1585 until 1591, when he resigned) and now held theological views diametrically opposed to those of his "godly" assistant, Walter Travers. In 1595 he became rector of Bishopsbourne near Canterbury, where he lived until his death. Sponsored by George Cranmer and Edwin Sandys, he wrote (late 1580s) the eight-volume *Of the Lawes of ecclesiasticall politie*, defending the status quo of the Church of England (see Anglicanism Cluster: In Europe: The United Kingdom). The *Lawes*, never a best seller, were criticized by many "godly" writers for being obfuscatory. Since the Restoration, Hooker has been regarded as an icon typifying Anglican theology. This "urban myth," which began with Isaak Walton's *Life of Hooker*, has increasingly come under scrutiny in more modern historiography. Contemporary treatments of Hooker's theology identify him as Reformed* rather than as specifically Anglican. The question, then, is: What was it that made Hooker's Reformed theology sound so unreformed to his Reformed (Puritan*) contemporaries?

BRYAN SPINKS

Hooker, Thomas. See PURITANS, PURITANISM.

Hooper, John (c1495–1555), bishop, martyr, divine. He is remembered for his stand against ecclesiastical vestments* during the reign of Edward VI and martyrdom* in the persecution during Mary's reign. A graduate of Oxford and a Cistercian*, Hooper was converted to Protestantism after reading Zwingli* and Bullinger*. After 1539 Hooper became a religious exile and studied in Zurich with Bullinger. Returning to England (1549), he was offered the See of Gloucester, which he declined because he objected to the vestments required at consecration. This caused a serious crisis, resolved only by the intervention of Bullinger and Hooper's reluctant recantation. A model bishop, he was involved in preparing the 1552 Book of Common* Prayer and in revising the canon law. Despite his support for Mary after the death of Edward VI, Hooper was arrested (September 1553) and imprisoned until he was burned at the stake in Gloucester as a heretic* (February 9, 1555). Considered a "proto-Puritan*" because of his strong positions and severe manner, Hooper was nothing of the sort. He governed his diocese with common sense and a generous wisdom that was anything but doctrinaire. But his radical views (attested to by his many writings) and uncompromising personality made him as much an enigma to his contemporaries as he remains today.

DAVID G. NEWCOMBE

Hope. Throughout biblical history, hope is portrayed as an especially forward-looking virtue. Hope presupposes that humans need to be "saved" from something (that there is something wrong, beyond human control). Hope expresses trust in God to bring about the fullness of salvation* in the time and the manner determined by God alone. It implies a resolute attitude: hope arises at the core of Christian existence by the grace* of God, acting within the present experience of suffering, endurance, and love* (Rom 5:1–5; cf. 8:22–25). The love that "bears all things, believes all things, hopes all things, endures all things" (1 Cor 13:7) underpins the tough, patient, and enduring character of hope. Through it, Christian life is strengthened for the long haul: its future fulfillment in "God all in all" (1 Cor 15:28). The goal of hope is anticipated in Christ's rising from the dead. But this "already" is ever looking to a fulfillment that is "not yet." Confronted by inevitable suffering and struggle, and by those who have "no hope and are without God in the world" (Eph 2:12), Christian witness demands a courageous "accounting of the hope that is within you" (1 Pet 3:16) (see Eschatology Cluster).

With its God-given and God-ward character, hope is traditionally classified, along with faith*, charity, and love*, as a "theological virtue*." Directed to the future, it relies on God to make clear what faith holds to and what love (or charity) most desires; love for God arouses desire for God. Hope without faith would be blind. Without love, it would be narrowly individualistic, thereby failing to embrace the God who "desires everyone to be saved and to come to the knowledge of the truth" (1 Tim 2:4). Three perspectives on hope can be considered.

1. The virtue of hope has four features. First, it is intent on the supreme good, God, and the Kingdom* (understood as the reign of God over all). Second, it seeks a future good: although we already share in the life of God, "it has not yet appeared what we shall be" (1 John 3:2). Third, it seeks a possible good, in a future guaranteed by God's promise. Finally, it nonetheless pursues a difficult good, for hope demands the surrender and self-giving love involved in following Christ's way. Thus it differs from natural optimism or human planning because it moves toward a future that only God can give.
2. In *Homo Viator: Introduction to a Metaphysic of Hope,* Gabriel Marcel* has noted the existential* relevance of hope to a world ravaged by two world wars; being human is to be "on a journey" through time, a *viator*. As hope moves forward, it is not wishful optimism; it comes into its own when one is most tempted to fall into despair. Because it contests all closed visions of human existence, it takes a prophetic* stance, breathing the atmosphere of an ultimate gracious mystery* that can never be fully named or imagined.
3. In *The Principle of Hope,* Ernst Bloch locates hope at the very heart of historical progress. It animates all quests for freedom*, striving to bring a new society into being. Hope is therefore "utopian," not as a vague aspiration, but as the active, realistic anticipation of new forms of a just society. For the Marxist Bloch, "God" is a symbol for the as yet unrealized possibilities of human freedom. Jürgen Moltmann's *Theology of Hope* has proved seminal for a critical assimilation of Bloch's work into Christian theology.

Along with the thanksgiving, longing, and intercession of prayer*, the task of hope is to reclaim the heights already occupied by the martyrs*, reformers, saints*, and mystics*. It extends to solidarity with all hopeful people who, however implicitly, insist that there is something worth living and dying for. Christian hope, anchored in Christ, supports and enlarges the hopes of the world for fulfillment, unity, and lasting life (Teilhard* de Chardin).

ANTHONY J. KELLY, CSsR

Horologion, in the Eastern Orthodox* Church, a book containing the offices for the canonical* hours. **See also DIVINE LITURGY.**

Hosanna (Gk form of the Heb petition "Save, we pray"; Ps 118:25), uttered by the multitude during Jesus' entry into Jerusalem and adopted into Christian worship.

Hosea, the Book of, collection of oracles from the 8th-c. prophet Hosea; best known for its use of metaphors of marriage* and adultery to describe the relationship between God and Israel.

Hosea prophesied during the tumultuous years before the Assyrian conquest of the Northern Kingdom (721 BCE). In Chaps. 4–14, the prophet's political concerns are evident as he castigates priests, princes, and other power brokers for their bloody political intrigues, ill-advised foreign alliances, corruption, and idolatry* at national shrines. Hosea evokes many ancient traditions, including the Jacob* story, the escape from Egypt, and the wilderness experience to underscore the nation's dependence on YHWH and the dire consequences of rejecting his Law.

Chapters 1–3 dramatize the nation's transgressions and its possible fate through prophetic acts and metaphors involving Hosea's marriage to a promiscuous woman (or prostitute), the ominous names given to their children, the wife's pursuit of her "lovers," divine threats of divorce, and the promise of a new betrothal in the wilderness. This extended metaphor, most likely original to the prophet, draws on societal expectations of wifely fidelity to underscore the covenantal demand for exclusive worship of YHWH.

The metaphor of covenant* as a divine–human marriage has been influential in both Jewish and Christian thought. The metaphor appears again in the oracles of later prophets (e.g. Jer* 3; Ezek* 16, 23), shaped Jewish interpretation of the love* imagery in the Song* of Songs, and provided the model for Christian self-understanding of the church* as the bride of Christ. Many modern readers, however, are troubled by the marriage metaphor's patriarchal* determinants and question its theological utility today.

ALICE A. KEEFE

Hosius or Ossius (c255–c358), bishop of Córdoba. He participated in the Synod of Elvira*. After Constantine's* victory in the West (312), he functioned as his chief theological adviser and was sent to Alexandria to deal with the Arian* controversy. He presided over the Council of Antioch (325), was a leading figure at the Council of Nicaea* (325), and presided over the Council of Sardica (343). Because of his defense of Athanasius* and the Nicene* Creed, he was banished (355). Under pressure at the Council of Sirmium (357), at the age of 100 he subscribed to its Arianizing* creed and was allowed to return home. There is a possibility that he is the addressee of Calcidius's Latin commentary on Plato's *Timaeus*.

Hospice, a movement dedicated to improving end-of-life care with a team approach, so that dying persons will have medical, emotional, and spiritual support tailored to their own wishes, in the home or a homelike setting. Care is also extended to family members and loved ones.

Hospitality, the practice of sharing one's home and resources with guests, travelers, and other Christians (including the opening of one's home as a house* church), but also with needy persons: strangers, foreigners, and refugees* as well as the poor (see Poverty Cluster; Preferential Option for the Poor), the sick*, homeless, orphans, and widows. Repeatedly emphasized in the Bible (OT and NT), this practice remained a central element of the Christian life for centuries, although it became less prominent with the advent of Christendom*. Hospitality is presupposed by ascetic* movements, the many forms of renunciation of property* and of ownership*, and monastic* movements; it has been institutionalized in hospitals* and social programs of many kinds. **See also CHRISTIAN SOCIALISM; ECONOMY AND CHRISTIANITY CLUSTER: ECONOMIC ETHICS AND CHRISTIAN THEOLOGY; SOCIAL ENCYCLICALS; SOCIAL ETHICS; SOCIAL GOSPEL MOVEMENT.**

Hospitallers. Founded as the Hospital of St. John in Jerusalem (late 11th c.) before the beginning of the Crusades*, for more than 900 years the religious* order of Hospitallers has served Christ by caring for the sick and poor. For nearly seven centuries, this military*-religious order also carried out military activities in defense of Christians against Saracens, Mamluks, and Ottoman Turks from its base in the Holy Land, then on Rhodes and Malta. Today, the order's headquarters are in Rome and it continues charitable work through its national associations throughout the world.

As a hospice in which brothers under religious vows gave spiritual care to the sick poor, with limited medical care, the Hospital of Jerusalem was typical of the hospitals established in Western Europe at this time. By the 1130s, the military needs of the crusaders in Syria and Palestine led the Hospitallers to take up active military functions, and the Hospital was gradually transformed into a military* religious order.

The Hospitallers regarded military activity against the enemies of Christendom* as a labor of love toward other Christians: warrior-brothers who fought and died in that service won spiritual merit. Other members of the order included servants, priests, and sisters who followed a largely contemplative* lifestyle, as well as male and female associates. In their devotional practices, members placed special emphasis on martyr-saints, such as their patron St. John the Baptist, St. Sebastian, and St. Catharine of Alexandria, as well as warrior-saints such as St. George.

After the Mamluk conquest of Palestine and Syria (1291), the Hospitallers moved their headquarters to Cyprus, then to Rhodes, where they set up a new infirmary to care for sick, poor pilgrims to the East and warred against Ottoman shipping vessels. After Rhodes was captured (1522) by the Ottomans, the Hospitallers set up a new base on Malta (1530), from which they continued naval operations against the Barbary pirates. Their military activity ended with Napoleon Bonaparte's conquest of Malta (1798).

During the medieval period, the Hospitallers' infirmary cared for all comers, Jews and Muslims as well as Christians, while its diplomatic contacts with Muslim leaders were beneficial for the defense of Christendom (e.g. their alliance with the Ottoman prince Jem, 1481–95). The modern order continues to undertake essential medical work in some of the most needy areas of the world. HELEN J. NICHOLSON

Hospitals and Healing Programs as Christian Ministry. Caring for *all* in need and not just for one's own kin has been an essential element of Christian life and the life of the church from the beginning. Jesus charged those who wanted to serve him to serve the needy (Matt 25:31–46), and the apostles appointed congregational attendants to look after those in need of help (Acts 6:1–6). Soon after Christianity was elevated to the rank of an official religion in the Roman Empire, Bishop Basil* of Caesarea (the Great) established in 369/70 the "Basilias," an institution for the care of the poor and the sick, setting an example for many similar initiatives. It heralded the unprecedented history of institutionalized charity* motivated by the desire to witness to God's unconditional love to humankind in Christ.

"Hospital," meaning a place for the reception and welcoming of guests ("hotel" and "hostel" are derivatives), was the general term by which these institutions became euphemistically known. Staffed by members of religious or lay orders, often founded just for that purpose, hospitals usually were comparatively small charitable institutions serving not only the sick, but orphans, widows, and the destitute alike. Accordingly, until the 19th c., by which time medicine had evolved from an art to a science, with the laboratory and microscope, hygiene and antisepsis at its core, hospitals hardly resembled contemporary hospitals.

Once medicine proved capable of healing fatal diseases, turning hospitals from places of care into places of curing, pious physicians, in their desire to imitate Christ, felt compelled to bring healing to all people in need, the "all" now having a truly global ring. Supported by philanthropists and later joined by the still very young profession of nursing, they established hospital-based medical missions at home and abroad where, motivated by disinterested benevolence, they rendered medical help gratuitously irrespective of gender, race, or creed.

But when hospitals turned into highly sophisticated, expensive institutions and once national health care services and the World Health Organization (1948) were in place, it was realized that, in order to remain truthful to its mandate, the Christian ministry of healing should focus on programs of disease prevention and comprehensive healing accessible to all rather than remain a competitor in the health care business. Consequently, most of the hospitals were transferred to other hands; healing programs of various kinds were developed and continue to receive support from the churches. **See also HEALTH, HEALING, AND CHRISTIANITY CLUSTER.**

CHRISTOFFER H. GRUNDMANN

Host, sacramental bread used in the ritual of the Eucharist*.

Hostel (Gk *xenodocheion*), a place providing accommodations for Christian travelers, especially those on pilgrimage* to Jerusalem's holy* places (from the 4th c.); often found in monasteries.

Hours, Books of, books for daily devotion by the laity*, based on the Breviary*, often richly illustrated in the late Middle Ages.

Hours, Canonical, regular times of daily prayer, with several different patterns: the third, sixth, and ninth hours, plus midnight; sunrise and sunset; and cockcrow. **See also DIVINE OFFICE.**

House Churches. Jesus often stayed in private houses on his travels. Paul mentions the "church in the house" of Aquila and Prisca (1 Cor 16:19; Rom 16:5), and other names he mentioned are probably those of hosts and hostesses ("heads of household" could be wives or widows) in house churches (Rom 16:2 and 23; 1 Cor 16:15–16; cf. Col 4:15). But the church gathering is sometimes differentiated from the home gathering (1 Cor 11:22 and 34), and for several centuries, Christianity was criticized for undermining the family and the household.

Thus English Nonconformists* and Friends* used appropriate language when they called their places of worship "meeting* *houses.*" Early Christians usually met in private homes, although Justin* rented a hall "above Martinus" in Rome. In the Greco-Roman world, homes were often the locale of various *collegia*, or associations, philosophical schools, mystery cults, and synagogues. While leadership might be exercised by a guest (priest, philosopher, apostle, or prophet), the etiquette remained that of the household; the householder, a person of some means, inevitably acquired informal or formal authority. Hospitality* toward strangers, praised in the NT (1 Pet 4:9), is one of the requirements for becoming a bishop (1 Tim 3:2; Titus 1:8). The Eucharist* and the *agape** began as meals in household settings, and Paul was aware of the tension between customary dinner practices and the needs of gathering "as the church"; he said that if the former are predominant, "it is not the Lord's supper that you eat" (1 Cor 11:18–22).

Early Christian vocabulary seems to move from the "house church" to "the whole church" (Rom 16:23), i.e. all the house churches, which can be called collectively the "household of God" (1 Tim 3:15), then to the church "in the city" (cf. the salutations of Paul's letters). Even when there were multiple meeting places, there was unity through the presbyters* and eventually the monepiscopate*. By the early 3rd c., as the excavation at Dura-Europos shows, a portion of a private home might be rebuilt for exclusively religious use, with a baptistery* and a platform for the eucharistic table. In the late 3rd c., buildings called "the house of the church" were constructed, apparently according to the basilica* plan.

With the subsequent institutionalization of the (Eastern and Western) churches, the center of church life and of communal worship shifted to basilica and church buildings (see Hierotopy, the Creation of Christian Sacred Spaces), with accompanying shifts in ecclesiology. Yet throughout Christian history, house churches can be found as a sole place of worship and church life, especially during persecutions – e.g. in North* Africa (7th–11th c.), where Christianity survived under Islamic rule before disappearing – as well as in branches of Christianity excluded (or excluding themselves) from mainline churches (e.g. in the West, Hussites*, Valdese*, Anabaptists*, Dissenters*, members of the Independent* and Free Church and of the Restoration* Movement). The factor that determines whether a location is a church* is neither sacred space (church buildings) nor sacred institution, but the gathering of believers and a sense of mission* (the church exists not for itself, but for others).

In the early 21st c., in addition to house churches developed in situations of actual or potential persecution (see, e.g., Chinese Contemporary Independent and House Churches), house churches have been established by the Charismatic* Movement, particularly in its indigenous, postdenominational form. These independent groups of laypersons meet together for biblical studies and prayer in homes, apartments, compounds, or other informal places, participating in charismatic worship, often using "praise* and worship" music adapted to their religious and cultural contexts around the world. Another growing use of the house church model is related to megachurches*, composed of many "cells" that meet in homes.

EUGENE TESELLE and DANIEL PATTE

Household Codes are instructions regarding how groups in the "extended family" or "household" should interact with each other. As first discussed, though not labeled "household codes," by Aristotle (*Politics*), such sociopolitical norms addressed the *paterfamilias* in his three household roles of husband, father, and master (with authority over wife, children*, and slaves*). Within the Christian canon, household codes start to show up in the pseudonymous Pauline literature (Eph 5:22–6:9; Col 3:18–4:1), in 1 Pet 2:18–3:7, and throughout the Pastoral Epistles (and are possibly found in other NT passages, if one also includes instructions that are addressed to any member of a household or that encourage obedience to elders and other ecclesial authorities). This adoption of household codes is an indication that with the organizational development of the Jesus movement, certain Roman or imperial standards had to be embraced (see Inculturation Cluster: Of Christianity in the Greco-Roman World). Rather than addressing the *paterfamilias*, the NT adaptations of the household codes address the wives, slaves, and children directly. Are their presence and importance acknowledged, as some say? The household codes also become a vehicle for inscribing a patriarchal* (kyriarchal) structure in ecclesial gatherings and valorize the suffering of slaves and wives as Christ-like. The adaptation of a sociopolitical norm in Christian texts affirms its prevalence as social expectation – indeed, as a political norm – since proper maintenance of the household was the most important support of Empire.

The texts requiring that slaves be submissive to their masters (Eph 6:5–8; Col 3:22–4; Titus 2: 9–10; 1 Pet 2:18–25) became primary texts for sermons addressed to African slaves in the North American colonies, and the texts that wives be submissive to their husbands (Eph 5:22–33, Col 3:18; 2 Tim 2:8–15; Titus 2:3–5; 1 Pet 3:1–7) are understood to imply that no woman should be a teacher or leader of men. **See also COLOSSIANS, EPISTLE TO THE; EPHESIANS, EPISTLE TO THE; PASTORAL EPISTLES, 1 AND 2 TIMOTHY AND TITUS; PETER, 1 AND 2 EPISTLES OF.**

JENNIFER BIRD

Howe, Julia Ward (1819–1910), author of the US "Battle Hymn of the Republic," inventor of Mother's Day, women's rights reformer. Born to a wealthy New York family, she married (1843) Dr. Samuel Gridley Howe, a pioneer in education for the blind, then lived in Boston.

Stifled by Samuel's insistence that as a wife and mother she remain in the domestic realm, Howe wrote poems, plays, philosophy, and theology (1860s). A tour of Union army campsites (November 1861) inspired her to pen the words to "The Battle Hymn of the Republic." After the Civil War, Howe joined the woman suffrage and club movements, helping found the New England Woman's Club and the *Woman's Journal*.

Her opposition to the Franco-Prussian War (1870–71) prompted her to call on women around the world to celebrate a "Mother's Day of Peace" annually, arguing that humanity would never fully appreciate its creation in God's image* until it allowed the nurturing love embodied by mothers to moderate male aggression. In Howe's theology, God* was just as much a mother as a father.

After her husband's death (1876), Howe campaigned for woman suffrage, the cause of peace, and the ordination* of women. Both Mother's Day and the "Battle Hymn" remain American icons. VALARIE H. ZIEGLER

Hubmaier, Balthasar (c1485–1528), Anabaptist* leader in Southern Germany and Austria. Following studies at the University of Freiburg im Breisgau and, in scholastic theology, at the University of Ingolstadt (with Johann Eck, future adversary of Luther), Hubmaier became cathedral preacher in Regensburg, pilgrimage preacher at the Chapel of the Blessed Mary, and pastor in Waldshut (Austria), remaining dedicated to Catholic observances. In 1523 he became an open proponent of the Reformation and challenged the Catholic clerics to a religious disputation (1524) with 18 theses affirming justification* by faith alone and the Mass* as a memorial of Christ's death (not a sacrifice), and denouncing all the major scholastic theologians, belief in purgatory*, and most traditional Catholic practices, including pilgrimages. Hubmaier's first theological treatise, *On the Christian Baptism of Believers* (1525), was a defense of believers' baptism*, which he promoted as a part of the general Reformation program. Hubmaier and his wife joined Anabaptists seeking refuge in Moravia, where various religious confessions were legally tolerated, settling in Nikolsburg (Mikulov, 1526). But he was extradited to Vienna (July 1527) when Ferdinand of Austria assumed the crown of Bohemia and Moravia. Charged with rebellion while in Waldshut, he was interrogated and burned at the stake (March 1528). ESTHER CHUNG-KIM

Huddleston, Trevor (1913–98), Anglican priest, best known for his book *Naught for Your Comfort* (1956). He was involved in the campaign against Bantu education and the removal of blacks from Sophiatown (1955–56). Recalled to England (1956) by his religious order, the Community of the Resurrection, he revisited South Africa briefly after its independence, and his ashes were buried there. **See also SOUTH AFRICA.** MOKGETHI MOTLHABI

Hügel, Baron Friedrich von. See VON HÜGEL, BARON FRIEDRICH.

Hugh of St. Victor (also Hugo or Hugues; c1096–1141), medieval theologian, who studied at the monastery of St. Victor (Paris), became head of the school of St. Victor (or Victorine school), and wrote numerous spiritual and mystical* works, as well as commentaries combining literal* and allegorical* interpretation. His *De sacramentis* (*On the Mysteries of the Christian Faith*, c1134) was an influential systematic theology. This work affected the development of Scholasticism*, because it was the first to synthesize patristic teachings and to systematize them so as to organize them into a coherent and complete body of doctrine – a systematic theology.

Huguenots. "Huguenots" (along with "Calvinists") was the appellation frequently given to members of the French Reformed* Church. The movement, inspired largely by the French John Calvin's* reform of the Francophone city of Geneva, took root in France (1550s).

The etymology of the word "Huguenot" remains controversial. Does the label suggest association with the early king Hugh Capet? Or, more likely, was it a corruption of *Eidgenossen* (confederates), referring to the Genevan protective alliance with Protestant Bern (1536) and then applied to French Reformed Protestants? Catholics initially employed "Huguenot" in a pejorative sense. Still, French Reformed Protestants appropriated the word, applying it particularly to their military and political activities: the Huguenot army and the Huguenot cause. The designation took on new life among the Protestants who fled France after the proscription of the Reformed Church (1685; see Nantes, Edict of, and Its Revocation). Refugees clung to their Huguenot identity as they sought asylum in Switzerland*, the Netherlands*, Germany*, the British Isles, North America, and elsewhere.

While subscribing to the theological tenets espoused by Calvin, Huguenots contributed their own distinctive sense of order. The national Confession of Faith (1559, revised in 1571 and thereafter known as the "Confession de foi de la Rochelle") established the fundamentals of belief, while the Discipline (1559) instituted polity*. Taken together, the two statements elaborated a theology founded on the directives of Scripture* and a liturgy focused on its explanation through the pastor's sermons. The administration of the sacraments, notably baptism and quarterly celebration of the Lord's* Supper, completed the life of worship. The Huguenots exhibited a strong sense of order in their polity; they were the first Reformed Church to have a structured series of representative bodies. Each local church possessed a consistory* staffed by pastor*, elders*, and deacons*. They met weekly to confer on details of church administration, oversee the distribution of poor* relief, and discuss breaches of Christian conduct.

Above the consistory, a synod* regularly gathered representatives from the various local churches in a region then at the national level. At each level, the delegates clarified belief, developed polity, and settled disputes among the faithful. A strong need for the correction of sin* added to the sense of order and discipline. Consistories regulated marriage and sexuality, rooted out superstition, and settled people's quarrels in the expectation of constructing a godly society. **See also PROTESTANTISM CLUSTER: IN EUROPE: FRANCE.**

RAYMOND A. MENTZER

Humanae Vitae (Of human life), a 1968 encyclical by Pope Paul VI on the regulation of birth that reaffirms the traditional teaching of the Roman Catholic Church regarding abortion*, contraception (see Birth Control and Contraception, Christian Views of), and other issues pertaining to human life.

Humani Generis, encyclical of Pius* XII "concerning some false opinions threatening to undermine the foundations of Catholic doctrine," issued (1950) to correct the questioning attitude and research priorities of the new French theology and other forms of postwar theological revival. It emphasizes two basic convictions: the indivisibility and timeless nature of truth*; and a corporate view of theology (theologians are assistants who communicate the official teachings of the Roman Catholic Church and not their private thoughts). Pius XII also acknowledged that biological evolution* was compatible with the Christian faith, yet argued that God's intervention was necessary for the creation of the human soul*.

Humanism and Renaissance. In Italy a *umanista* (14th c.) was a practitioner of the *studia humanitatis* – the disciplines of grammar, poetry, rhetoric, history, moral philosophy, and politics. Humanism was distinguished from professional studies in law, medicine, and theology. The earliest statement of the humanist program of education is Pier Paolo Vergerio's *The Character and Studies Befitting a Free-Born Youth* (c1402). (Renaissance humanism has no relation to humanism as a nontheistic philosophy of life that originated in the 19th c.) The Renaissance humanist curriculum had many associations with and implications for Christianity.

Grammar included proficiency in languages. Coluccio Salutati (1336–1406) argued that grammar is not Christian but that no Christian can understand Holy Scripture* without it. Humanists used their knowledge to translate and annotate classical texts: Lorenzo Valla (1407–57) wrote *Notes on the New Testament* (1449–50), later (1504) published by Erasmus*; Giannozzo Manetti (1396–1459) translated the NT into Latin. From the early 1500s, humanists were instrumental in the translation and exegesis of the Bible in French, German, English, and other languages.

Rhetoric. Vergerio, in a series of sermons at the papal court (c1405), introduced Jerome* as the model of a Christian scholar. Erasmus, who viewed Jerome as his patron saint, penned the most enduring example of humanist oratory in *Praise of Folly* (1511 and 1514, anticipating Luther's* criticisms of the Roman Catholic Church), the book that justifies the assertion that "Erasmus laid the egg Luther hatched."

History. In his *Donation* of Constantine*, Valla used grammatical and historical arguments to refute the belief that Constantine had willed the western half of his empire to Pope Sylvester. Luther cited this text in his critiques of the papacy. Many Protestant historians followed Valla's example in rewriting the history of the Church.

Politics. Niccolò Machiavelli (1469–1527) transformed political thought with his contention in *The Prince* that politics is about power, not morality, a notion that in the centuries since has proved profoundly disturbing to Christians. More* (1478–1535) argued in *Utopia* (a new genre based on Plato's *Republic*) that the problem with contemporary civilization is greed and the solution is to curb it.

Moral Philosophy. Humanists addressed a host of moral philosophical questions: Is the human condition vile or dignified? Does nobility lie in birth or personal virtue? Does authority rest in Scripture* and tradition* or only in Scripture? Is the human will* bound or free? Humanists remained open on most questions before the Reformation*. Thereafter, they became embroiled in the struggles it engendered.

ALBERT RABIL, JR.

Human Rights Cluster

1) *Introductory Entry*

Human Rights

2) *A Sampling of Contextual Views and Practices*

Human Rights and the Churches in Africa
Human Rights and the Churches in Asia: The Philippines
Human Rights and the Churches in Latin America
Human Rights and the Churches in Latin America: Brazil
Human rights and the Churches in Latin America: Mexico

1) Introductory Entry

Human Rights. The concept of human rights entered the political realm with the English Magna Carta (1215), the British Bill of Rights (1689), the Virginia Declaration of Rights (1776), the French Declaration of the Rights of Man (1789), and the US Bill of Rights (1791). These guarantee "negative rights," limiting the range of government action; they were animated by opposition to absolutism or the divine right of kings. They have since been supplemented by the more controversial notion of "positive rights," claims on society or government (e.g. clean air and water*, land*, opportunities for housing, employment, and retirement income). Both kinds of rights are enshrined in the Universal Declaration of Human Rights (1948), which was motivated by an awareness of the "barbarous acts" committed during World War II and by protests against many aspects of colonialism*.

The Christian tradition has adopted various attitudes toward human rights. The affirmation of human dignity is often justified by appeal to the creation of humans in the image* of God, to God's grace*, and to the Incarnation*.

The early church asserted that faith* must be voluntary and not coerced, and the Edict of Milan* (313) made this an official policy. Dissenting movements throughout Christian history have often reasserted this position in the face of coercion by church and state; theoretical justifications were developed by Anabaptists* and especially Spirituals* during the Reformation, by Independents* during the English Revolution, and by Roger Williams* in Rhode Island. Religious pluralism was championed in some countries, most notably Poland*. Bartolomé de las* Casas and others, building on the tradition of natural* law, asserted the rights of indigenous peoples in the Spanish colonies in the Americas.

Other perspectives often dominated. Beginning with Theodosius*, imperial laws were directed against "pagans*," Jews (see Judaism and Christianity Cluster), and Christian "heretics*." The growing partnership between church* and state fostered not only the punishment of dissenters but forced conversion of conquered peoples (especially under Charlemagne* against the Saxons). When inquisitors* declared persons to be heretics, they could be delivered to the "secular* arm" for execution. Rulers not only enforced the church's judgments, but often tried to control the church for the sake of political unity. The Edict of Nantes* (1598), which permitted a degree of religious diversity in France, was later revoked (1685) by Louis XIV.

The modern affirmation of human rights emerged from criticism of the actions of both church and state, and from actual experience of religious pluralism, showing that it was a permanent fact, was not destructive, and even enhanced civic life. Holders of these views continued to struggle against the older notion that "error does not have the same rights as truth" and that religious conformity is needed for public order. Gradually, human rights were affirmed during the 19th c., after World War II, and at the Second Vatican* Council; but authoritarian governments (at times with the complicity of churches) continue to deny human rights in various ways. Missionary activity in the non-Western world has been met with hostility among the populace and governmental action against those who change their religion, especially in Islamic but also in Hindu regions.

Yet the churches have defended human rights in the face of dictatorships, especially in Latin America and in Africa, documenting abuses and encouraging the creation of truth* and reconciliation commissions (see Reconciliation as Christian Praxis).

Christians continue to disagree over how far human rights should be extended, especially in Western Europe and the USA. Some insist on gender equality, while others adhere to traditional views of gender roles. Some see legal safeguards for reproductive freedom, including abortion* and birth* control, as human rights, whereas others insist that they are contrary to natural* law and demand the right to abstain from participation (as physicians, nurses, or pharmacists). Some believe that the civil institution of marriage* includes rights for same-sex couples, whereas others see it as a violation of both natural law and the traditions of church and society. **See also CHURCH AND STATE RELATIONS CLUSTER; JUSTICE, CHRISTIAN THEOLOGICAL VIEWS AND PRACTICES, CLUSTER.** EUGENE TESELLE

2) A Sampling of Contextual Views and Practices

Human Rights and the Churches in Africa. In Africa, deeply affected by past and ongoing colonialism*, slavery*, forced labor, and exploitation of all kinds, churches see human rights in terms of a theology of creation* and of redemption* based on God's will (the Ten* Commandments, Exod 20:1–17), the creation of humans in God's image*, God's everlasting love* for humans reflected through their love for one another (John 13:34–35), and the redemption of God's people through Moses and Jesus (emphasized by Liberation* theology). African Christians understand creation and redemption as people of faith* who love God and depend on God with a living confidence and trust in God's love, grace* (in Christ Jesus), guidance, and care.

From this perspective, human rights and the gospel are understood in terms of each other. The right to freedom is God given; it is part of people's humanity as creatures in the image of God (whether they believe in God or not), and is not granted by the state or other institutions, including the church. Christian churches have simply the duty to stand for the God-given rights of human beings as they live in communities.

The church exists to serve the world and thus should not withdraw into spiritualistic isolation from worldly matters, as it often did by denying or ignoring the violations of human rights. For instance, in Angola*, the church long ignored flagrant violations of human rights by the two main factions involved in a bloody civil war. Finally assuming their duty, the Roman Catholic Church and the Protestant churches issued statements (pastoral letters) denouncing the violation of basic human rights and the resulting degradation of Angolan society through loss of its core values of humanness and the ensuing violence and dehumanization. For instance, looking at Angolan women, one can see on most of them deep scars of violation, of having been forced to serve as human shields in war, as food gatherers for their families and for armies, as combatants' wives, and as carriers of munitions, and today these women are reduced to foraging in garbage dumps for survival and are themselves treated as garbage of society. A sound society is not possible if the wounds of past ill treatment are not cared for. As they become aware of these violations of human rights, churches are working together across denominations and with secular nongovernmental organizations. Yet Africa and African churches have a long way to go in the struggle for human rights and in dealing with the long-term consequences of their violations.

LUCIANO CHIANEQUE

Human Rights and the Churches in Asia: The Philippines. A peaceful "people's power revolution" brought down a mighty dictatorship on the strength of prayer, public statements, and courageous actions (1986). Jaime Cardinal Sin led Roman Catholics, other Christians, Muslims, and political groups, ending 14 years of brutal violations of human rights.

Church–state relations had soured when President Ferdinand Marcos declared martial law (1972), ostensibly to reform society, arresting without warrants thousands of opponents, ranging from feudal oligarchs to idealist youth. Hundreds disappeared. Many were routinely tortured.

The churches awoke. For Catholics, Vatican* II reforms had prepared the ground for church social action. Protestant churches were even more ready. The 1974 national assembly of United Church of Christ in the Philippines called for "freedom of speech" so that "voters could speak out their minds in a national referendum"; it cried out that "many of those detained have not been charged in court," that "citizens were maltreated." It called for justice*, asserting that "every individual, however lowly, is a child of the Heavenly Father." Protestant pastors and church members were among those detained and tortured. In 1978 the United Church called for the dismantling of martial law. The Protestant Church was promptly labeled a "subversive front." The battle was joined by Roman Catholics, and culminated in the defeat of the dictatorship in 1986, one step in the ongoing struggle for human rights. NOEL VILLALBA

Human Rights and the Churches in Latin America. The struggle of the Dominican Bartolomé de las* Casas and other clergy in the 16th c. to defend the "Indians" signaled a major landmark in the history of human rights. As a result of that struggle, the Spanish crown formally recognized "Indians" as persons with the same rights as Europeans. In practice, however, Christian natives were exploited, and non-Christian natives were not accorded the same rights. Furthermore, the Roman Catholic Church tolerated black slavery*, although it did protect slaves against abuses and upheld their right to marry and maintain stable relationships. During the wars of independence, Creole clergy (whites born in Latin America) fought for democracy* and equal rights for natives and blacks in the new societies. During the 19th c., the Church became very conservative politically and socially. Nevertheless, in many instances, bishops and priests intervened in favor of natives during antigovernment rebellions.

After Vatican* II, and especially after the episcopal conference of the Latin American bishops in Medellín* (1968), the Catholic Church emerged as one of the principal defenders of human rights, especially during the repressive right-wing dictatorships in Brazil*, Bolivia*, Paraguay*, and Central America. Many churchmen and churchwomen were imprisoned, tortured, and murdered because they defended workers, peasants, and others victims of human rights violence. Archbishop Oscar Romero*, murdered in El* Salvador in 1980, and Luis Espinal, a Jesuit murdered the same year in Bolivia* by a paramilitary group, have become symbols of that era. In Chile* the Vicariate of Solidarity, founded by Cardinal Silva-Henríquez, protected Chileans during the Pinochet dictatorship. In São Paulo, the Peace and Justice Commission founded by Cardinal Paulo Arns* protected prisoners during the military dictatorship in Brazil*. In El Salvador, Tutela Legal, founded by Archbishop Romero, had the same function.

But Catholic bishops were deeply divided over the issue of personal and social rights. For progressive bishops, the rights to own land* and enjoy job security were perceived as a necessary complement to individual rights. Conservative bishops recognized only the rights to life and to physical integrity. In Argentina* the episcopate maintained an overly discrete silence during the "dirty war" (1976–83), when the military kidnapped and executed thousands of Argentinians. In Peru* during the period of terrorism unleashed by the Shining Path (1980–92), Liberation* theology Christians defended the rights of the poor* who were victims of both the terrorists and the military. But the Opus* Dei archbishop of Ayacucho – the home of the Shining Path – refused to deal even with human rights organizations of the Roman Catholic Church. In Castro's Cuba*, the churches are not allowed to speak out on political issues, including human rights.

 Human Rights and Churches, Latin America

The historical Protestant churches also took a strong stand in defense of human rights and frequently collaborated in ecumenical peace efforts with the Catholic Church. In Peru the Department of Peace and Hope, founded by Protestants, worked closely with the Catholic bishops' Social Action Commission during the war against the Shining Path. However, Protestants of a fundamentalist persuasion, frequently encouraged by politically conservative Evangelicals from the USA, openly supported right-wing dictatorships.

In every country, individual Christians, with or without official church support, also contributed to the human rights movements. In Argentina Adolfo Pérez Esquivel*, a layman and Nobel Peace Prize winner (1980), helped organize the Mothers of Plaza de Mayo, mothers whose children had been kidnapped because they were considered "subversives" by groups acting on behalf of government officials. In Uruguay* the Jesuit José Luis Pérez Aguirre founded the Justice and Peace Service for Uruguay. Certain Jesuit-founded centers, like Tutela Legal (El Salvador) and the Miguel Agustín Pro Human Rights Center in Mexico*, have gained both national respect and official harassment for their work. JEFFREY KLAIBER, SJ

Human Rights and the Churches in Latin America: Brazil. Although the expression "human rights" is not explicitly mentioned in Scripture, many biblical passages stress human dignity. For instance, since human beings were made "in the image* of God" (Gen 1:27), any human rights' violation disfigures the Creator. Similarly, the gospel accounts of Christ's unjust and violent death reveal, for the faithful, an incarnated God totally identified with human suffering.

In Latin America, contemporary Christian analyses, especially those inspired by Liberation* theology, have reinterpreted the Bible to discern its teaching regarding how to fight for the rights of the oppressed*: the poor*, the weak, and other marginalized* people. Brazil is the largest and richest Latin American country, but it is also the country with the greatest inequality in wealth distribution. Theologians, clergy, and religious groups denounced state agencies, especially security forces, for constantly abusing human rights. These religious groups strove to link gospel practice and social justice by creating movements for land* and urban reform and for the defense of slum dwellers, the homeless, Amerindians, immigrants, prisoners, and other oppressed people. These movements inspired the creation of nongovernmental organizations to denounce racial, social, and gender prejudices and injustices.

This connection between Christian faith and the needs of the oppressed was forged in Brazil in the late 1950s by Roman Catholics and, subsequently, by Protestants, especially Lutherans, Presbyterians, and Methodists (and, to some extent, neo-Charismatics*/Pentecostalists). Specialists argue that ecumenical projects on human rights and other social problems must cast a broader net in Brazilian society, following the successful model of the CPT (Comissão Pastoral da Terra, the "Pastoral Commission for Land") and of the project known as "Brasil: Nunca Mais" (Brazil: Never Again). The CPT, a commission of the Brazilian Roman Catholic Ecclesial Conference with Protestant (mainly Lutheran) cooperation, struggles for land policy reform and denounces violence against rural workers. "Brasil: Nunca Mais" was the name of a top-secret investigation (begun in 1979, published in 1985), which furnished proof of the systematic use of torture during the Brazilian military regime (1964–85). Led by Cardinal Paulo Evaristo Arns*, former archbishop of São Paulo, with financial support from the World Council of Churches, "Brasil: Nunca Mais" investigated the dictatorship's most violent period (1964–79), described torture methods, and named more than 400 torturers. See also Land, Theological Perspectives and Praxis, Cluster.

MARCELO TIMOTHEO DA COSTA

Human Rights and the Churches in Latin America: Mexico. The Pontifical Council for the Laity in Rome is the place where one can find information about the repression exercised by South American dictatorships; about the exile of Christians who struggle for human rights in Central America; about Guatemalan* refugees; as well as about the selective political repression practiced by the Mexican* government against bishops, religious, and laity, primarily because of their denunciation of violations of human rights of other people and only secondarily because they protest violations of human rights of which they are victims. They were inspired in this present-day defense of human rights by those missionaries who defended the dignity of the natives as Friar Bartolomé de las* Casas did. Following in his footsteps were the bishops Sergio Méndez* Arceo, Samuel Ruíz, and Arturo Lona; the novelist and poet José Álvarez Icaza; Miguel Concha, OP; Jesús Maldonado, SJ; and Digna Ochoa (a human rights lawyer, who was killed in her Mexico City office, 2001). There are several human rights centers in Mexico struggling against human rights violations. RAQUEL PASTOR

Hume, David (1711–76), Scottish philosopher, economist, historian. He propounded the principle of "empiricism," whereby all other concepts must be definable in terms of basic empirical (sensory or introspective) and formal (logical) concepts. The test is whether the words expressing an alleged concept are definable without remainder in words expressing only empirical and logical concepts. "God*" and "soul*" cannot be so defined; thus these words do not express (actual) concepts. The same principle applies to sentences. An apparent declarative statement is meaningful only if it can be stated in sentences made up of words that express only empirical and logical concepts. "God and souls exist" fails this test. This seems to provide a powerful criticism of theology and traditional philosophy, neither of which survives the test. Each is self-defeating.

Having used his theories against his opponents, Hume quietly ignores them in writing his own works. He criticizes natural* theology, especially the argument from design, in *Dialogues Concerning Natural Religion*. He offered a theory of the origins of religion in *The Natural History of Religion*. According to this theory, belief in God arises from human propensities to form beliefs that had been awakened by widespread if not universal experiences, especially the awareness of order in nature. Since these propensities do not operate in everyone, and do not produce the same beliefs in everyone in whom they operate, the propensities that give rise to religious beliefs are not part of human nature. Hence they do not result in natural beliefs – beliefs that it is our nature to have. We thus cannot justify having such religious beliefs in the same way that we can justify our belief in empirical and logical concepts. Justifying our religious beliefs is not a matter of having any reason or evidence for thinking these beliefs to be true, but only of rendering us blameless in having them.

KEITH E. YANDELL

Humility (from Lat for "lowly"), the quality or state of being lowly, of having a lowly opinion of oneself; it stands in contrast to pride. Understood by Christians as submission to God, especially when linked with contrition* (Isa 58:57:15), it was considered a religious virtue*. Christ is praised for humbling himself (kenosis*), to the extent of having died on the cross (Phil 2:8). In Christian practice, submission to God has been understood as not having too high an opinion of oneself (Rom 12:3), and receiving correction, especially from superiors but also from others. Feminist*, Liberation*, and postcolonialist* theologians have criticized this self-abasement, especially when it involves acceptance of inequalities originating in human society.

Hungary. The history of Christianity in the territory of the present Republic of Hungary is as complex as its political history. Christianity first arrived in the 3rd c. in the Pannonian Roman province (west of the Danube). Then Arian*, Roman Catholic, and Orthodox missionaries worked among the Huns, Goths*, Lombards*, Avars, and Franks (ruled by Charlemagne*), who successively occupied the region, before the Magyars (Hungarians) with ties to the Orthodox Church invaded it from the east (896). The Magyars' princes opted for the Latin Church; Stephen I (later canonized) was given the title of apostolic king by the pope (1000) and made Hungary a Catholic kingdom. He converted to Catholicism a population that had been partly Orthodox and partly non-Christian with the help of Italian, German, and Bohemian missionaries, but also through the establishment of a feudal* system that involved adopting the religion of one's lord. Following an initial defeat by the Mongols (1241), the Hungarian kingdom was fortified and reached its peak, repelling Mongol (13th c.) and Ottoman (15th c.)

invasions, becoming a shield for Western Christianity and occupying a vast territory in Central Europe.

In 1526 the kingdom was defeated by the Ottomans and divided into three parts. The west, under the control of the Austrian* Hapsburgs, remained Roman Catholic. In the central part, occupied by Turks indifferent to Christian divisions, Lutheran and Reformed churches were established (late 16th c.). The eastern part, Transylvania, was independent and granted freedom of worship to Roman Catholics, Lutherans, Reformed, and Unitarians*. By 1600 a majority of Hungarians were Protestants, primarily Reformed. But when the Austrian Hapsburgs expelled the Ottomans (1686–99), they introduced the Counter* Reformation, led by Jesuits*; a series of anti-Hapsburg and anti-Catholic uprisings by Protestants and Unitarians seeking freedom of religion (1704–11) were crushed. When the Edict of Toleration was finally granted (1780), Protestants had been reduced to less than a third of the population. In the late 19th c., the Roman Catholic Church experienced an "awakening" that resulted in many religious vocations to the priesthood and the monastic life; the Roman Catholic Church grew in influence, all the more so when Hungary lost many of its Lutheran territories as it achieved independence from Austria after World War I.

Judaism* became *religio licita* (late 19th c.) in this Christian nation. The Jewish community numbered more than 800,000 before World War II; the anarchy and economic crisis of the interwar period were blamed on "the Jews," and it was this anti-Semitism that fueled the Hungarian Holocaust in 1944 (when 600,000 Hungarian Jews were deported and died, most in Auschwitz).

During the Communist period (1947–89), the churches faced both the official atheistic propaganda and the secularization* of church schools and institutions. Religion was banned from public life. The totalitarian Communist mobilization of society created a schizophrenic division between the private and public lives of people. In Hungary, satirically called "the happiest barrack" among the Communist societies, the religious segment of society was officially under state control, although it remained active in rural areas and behind closed doors in the cities. Since the establishment of a new democratic regime in 1989, there has been freedom to practice one's religion in both private and public life. As a consequence, many different forms of religion have emerged, with widespread participation in birth, marriage, and death ceremonies, in Christmas and Easter celebrations, and in popular Catholic devotions. More than 200 churches, denominations, sects, and cults are registered. Yet the effects of secularization* are strongly felt.

Statistics: Population (2001): 10.2 million. Roman Catholics, 51.9%; Reformed, 15.9%; Evangelicals (Lutherans), 3.0%; Greek Catholics, 2.6%; Orthodox, 0.1%; other Christians, 0.8%; Jews, 0.1%; other religionists (including Muslims), 0.1%; nonreligious, 14.5%; no response, 10.8%. (Based on 2001 census.)

ANDRÁS MÁTÉ-TÓTH

Hurley, Dennis (1915–2004), Catholic archbishop of Durban and, for a long time, the lone voice in the Roman Catholic Church in South Africa in the struggle against apartheid* and in the advocacy of human* rights. As president of the Southern African Catholic Bishops Conference, he also worked for reconciliation among the churches and promoted joint communal celebrations. **See also SOUTH AFRICA.**

MOKGETHI MOTLHABI

Hus, Jan (c1373–1415), theological reformer, priest; catalyzed the Hussite revolution in Bohemia and Moravia, which led to the development of the Moravian* Church. Condemned at the Council of Constance for heresy* and burned at the stake, he remained an important symbol for Czech* nationalism.

Educated at the University of Prague (1390–1409) and a preacher at Bethlehem Chapel in Prague (1402–1415), he welcomed Wyclif's* thought, which was promoted by Czechs who studied at Oxford. Wyclif's reforming ecclesiology resonated with Czech discontent but was condemned by Archbishop Zbyněk Zajíc and university officials (1403). Yet Hus and Jerome* of Prague continued to preach against clerical ownership of property. For them claiming ecclesiastical office without embracing apostolic poverty* evinced a lack of the grace that was necessary to hold that office. Their anti-papalism was agreeable to Wenceslas IV, the Bohemian king. But when Hus began to condemn the papacy as Antichrist*, Wenceslas turned against him (1412), forcing Hus to go into hiding.

While in exile, Hus wrote *De Ecclesia*, arguing that the church* is the universal body of the predestined*, who alone are members of the body of Christ. The division between Roman and

Eastern Christianity, he said, suggests the impossibility of the Roman Church's claim to be universal; the church, furthermore, has no need of a pope or cardinals. While borrowing many of Wyclif's arguments, Hus forgoes the philosophical and theological depth of Wyclif's treatises for the sake of brevity and clarity of exposition. Hus did not deny transubstantiation*, but favored utraquism*, in which the communicant takes both bread and wine, over the usual custom of taking the bread alone.

In 1414 Emperor Sigismund and John XXII called the Council of Constance*; Hus was tricked into going. After being tried by the council (under Jean Gerson's* influence), he died at the stake on July 6, 1415. STEPHEN E. LAHEY

Hutchinson, Anne Marbury (1591–1643), lay leader in England, then New England, central figure in the "free grace" controversy, considered a progenitor of feminism*, Quakerism*, and American individualism. Though excluded from the ministry as other women were, she exemplified Puritanism* in her daily life, teaching Scripture at home, "preparing souls for me to convert," Rev. Cotton said. After the Church of England silenced Puritans, she followed Cotton to Boston (1634), taught Scripture to large groups, questioned ministers' "covenant of works" as against the Calvinist* "covenant of grace*," and opposed the 1636 war against the Pequot Amerindians. Banished as a heretic (1637–38), she cofounded Rhode Island with Roger Williams*. She was killed in New Amsterdam by Amerindians fighting the Dutch.
EVE LAPLANTE

Hutterites. Early in the Anabaptist* Movement (1528), the Hutterites formed a group in Moravia, sharing material goods in the spirit of the apostolic church (Acts 2:44–45, 4:32–35). Their leader, Jacob Hutter, was burned alive (1535); more than 2,000 Hutterites died for their faith.

From 1870 Hutterites enjoyed remarkable growth in the USA and Canada (c50,000 in 2008). Hutterites live in large agricultural colonies clustered like small villages, following three core values: sharing material goods, surrendering self-will for communal harmony, and separating themselves from an evil world. For Hutterites, private property symbolizes selfishness, greed, and vanity. They constitute the oldest surviving Christian communal movement (outside monastic orders). DONALD KRAYBILL

Huxley, Thomas Henry (1825–95), biologist, essayist, defender of Charles Darwin*. Huxley's aggressive repudiation of the authority of theology and Scripture* in scientific matters forced a rethinking of the relationship between science* and religion. Born in England to a lower-middle-class family, he studied medicine, held professorships at the Royal School of Mines, the Royal Institution, and the Royal College of Surgeons, and was dean of the Normal School of Science (South Kensington). Huxley, often seen as an implacable enemy of Christianity, publicly debated proponents of conservative Christianity (e.g. Bishop Wilberforce* and Gladstone*), defended Darwin's right to put forward a purely naturalistic theory of evolution, and coined the term "agnosticism*" (1869). Nevertheless, Huxley saw himself as purifying the Christian Church, just as Luther* had. Pledging allegiance to what he called the "New Reformation," he aligned himself with liberal Anglicans and Nonconformists who called for Christianity to modernize itself. Huxley was deeply indebted to Unitarianism* for the evolutionary theodicy* that grounded his entire view of the world. He used agnosticism as a way of distancing himself from lower-class atheists* and materialists, but also to underline his links to the ancient church. As an agnostic ("against Gnosticism*"), he stood with the early church, which rejected Gnosticism. BERNARD LIGHTMAN

Hymn, Hymnody. Augustine* (354–430) defined "hymn" as a song in praise of God, sometimes a vehicle of spontaneous praise, uttered under the influence of the Holy* Spirit. Augustine reflected and refined (for Christian purposes) what he had absorbed from earlier Greek and Roman sources, which expressed elemental human needs articulated through inward and outward "speaking" addressed to mysterious forces beyond ourselves with the expectation that these needs would be heard and met.

The expression of these fundamental desires through hymns has taken many forms throughout Christian history. Attentive to resources (the kinds of musical sounds available), appropriateness (sounds deemed sacred), theological development (various understandings of God), and liturgical expectations (formal, traditional, cultural, informal, emerging), communities have developed repertoires of communal singing, most often referred to as hymnody.

Tracing the history of hymnody reveals that the questions that regularly confronted Christian communities in their decisions about hymns in the past continue to challenge us today: What makes a hymn sacred? What sounds and words connect human beings to a divine presence? How do words and sounds convey the human qualities of God as we know them in Jesus the Christ? Whose experience is primary in deciding what sounds transmit notions of transcendence and immanence? How do our hymns convey the availability and intermingling of the Spirit?

Because hymns are intended primarily to be sung, their power is amplified. Sung music reverberates in the muscles of our bodies. This physical connection with our memories and imaginations influences powerfully what we feel, believe, and do about others and ourselves in relation to God. Hymns can reinforce evil as well as good, they can limit rather than include, shun rather than welcome, as well as evoke shared strength and express collective sorrow and joy.

Choosing hymns requires respectful attentiveness and imagination. Whereas familiar words and sounds provide comfort and certainty, varied rhythms, harmonies, and melodies that reflect the particularities of an array of cultures, ethnicities, and human experiences can help us expand our grasp of divine and human possibilities. Hymns, as Augustine suggested, reflect a mingling of spirits, human and divine. We sing ourselves into what we are coming to know and believe. As such we receive hymns and write them, we change them and treasure them. Hymns remind us of, urge us toward, support and prick us in pursuing an evolving faith* in God and in one another. **See also WORSHIP CLUSTER.**

JANET WALTON

Hypatia (c375–415), mathematician and philosopher of the Neoplatonist* school in Alexandria. Although a non-Christian, she taught many Christians, including Bishop Synesius of Cyrene. Because she espoused an alternative tradition, defending science* against religion, she was attacked by a mob of Christian health care workers, who scraped off her flesh. Bishop Cyril* of Alexandria (c378–444) may have been involved. While he evaded any penalties, an imperial decree placed restrictions on the activities of the bishop's health care workers.

Hypostasis (Gk for the reality underlying appearances), a key word in the trinitarian* controversy, first used as a synonym of the term *ousia* (nature) to mean a self-subsisting reality. The Cappadocians* made a distinction between the two terms: "one ousia in three hypostases" – one "nature" in three "realities" or three "persons" – became the accepted view of the Trinity for many churches. Hypostasis became a focal issue in the christological* controversies, when the Council of Chalcedon* declared that Christ was "one person (hypostasis) *in* two natures," while the Miaphysites* spoke about Christ as "one incarnate nature of the divine Word."

I

Ibas (5th c.), bishop of Edessa (435–57), a leader of the school of Edessa*, translator of Greek works into Syriac. He succeeded Rabbûla*, a partisan of Cyril* and an opponent of the Antiochene* position on Christology* (see Nestorius). Ibas, along with Theodoret*, defended the Formulary of Reunion (433), which mediated between the rival positions. His letter to the Persian bishop Maris (433) denounced Cyril's behavior. Condemned at the Second Council of Ephesus* (449), he was rehabilitated by the Council of Chalcedon* (451). Yet his letter to Maris was included in the Three* Chapters condemned by Justinian* and the Second Council of Constantinople* (553).

Ibn Rushd. See AVERROES, OR IBN RUSHD

Ibn Sina. See AVICENNA, OR IBN SINA.

Ichthus (Gk "fish"), acrostic using the initial Greek letters for "Jesus Christ, Son of God, Savior"; often suggested by a schematic fish design.

Icon (Gk *eikon*, equivalent to Lat *imago*, "image"), a two-dimensional visual image, either painted or done in mosaic, of Christ, the Virgin Mary*, and/or one of the saints. **See also ICONOGRAPHY.**

Iconoclasm and the Iconoclastic Controversy. While early Christians objected to and sometimes destroyed the idols (sacred images) of "pagans*," an internal controversy broke out in the Eastern Orthodox Church. The "iconoclasts" ("image breakers") sought to destroy, or at least marginalize, icons*; the "iconodules*" defended both the production and the veneration* of icons.

During the 7th c., opposition to icons arose within the Eastern Church (and, to a lesser extent, the Western Church) on four grounds: a reassertion of the older view that only the Eucharist* and the cross* can represent Christ; the Monophysite* tendency to minimize the human side of the Incarnation*; Jewish and especially Muslim criticism; and a sense of emergency fueled by the expansion of Islam. In 726 the emperor Leo III (717–41) sided with the iconoclasts, declaring all images idols, ordering their destruction, removing the main icon protecting Constantinople, and persecuting monks and other Christians who venerated icons. In 730 he deposed Germanos, the patriarch of Constantinople, who opposed his measures. John* of Damascus defended icons in three writings (726–30), ironically from within Islamic territory (Damascus), attacking the emperor's interference in matters of doctrine. In 754 a council in Constantinople condemned both the making and the veneration of icons. A "decade of blood" followed, with many "new martyrs," most of them monks.

The situation changed when Leo IV died (780) and authority passed to his wife, Irene*. A devotee of icons and a supporter of the monks, she prepared the way for the Second Council of Nicaea* (787), which approved the veneration of images of Christ, Mary, and the saints (veneration as contrasted with worship* offered only to God, a distinction lost at first in the translation used in the West). It quoted a statement made by Basil* of Caesarea (comparing images of the emperor to the Son as an image of the Father): "the honor rendered to the image rises to the prototype."

After Irene's death (802), persecution revived. This less extreme "second Iconoclasm" was ended in 842 by another empress, Theodora*. In 843 a new patriarch was installed, and on the first Sunday in Lent, the icons were restored. This day continues to be observed in the Eastern Church as the "Triumph of Orthodoxy." From this time on, the Eastern Church looked to the authority of the seven ecumenical* councils, and the emperors settled into a different role, not one of determining, but of defending, orthodoxy. **See also *CAROLINE BOOKS*.**

EUGENE TESELLE

Iconoclasm as a Theological Concept refers to breaking idols*. It has nothing to do with Iconoclasm* or the Iconoclastic controversy of the 8th and 9th c. Despite connotations of fanaticism, iconoclasm harks back not merely to the biblical prohibition of graven images but to its roots, the radical otherness of God, to God's namelessness, whose worship must be guarded against every idolatrous corruption of faith*. Most adamant in denouncing such inborn proclivity is Calvin*, who compares the imagination to an idol-making factory that obfuscates one's capacity for criticism by negating its capacity for self-criticism.

Iconoclasm deals not so much with the cleavage of image and word, icon* and idol, flesh and spirit, as with the dialectic of literal* and symbolic* according to which the literal is a parable* of the symbolic and nothing is more symbolic than the literal that is not taken literally (the sun "rises"; "he is risen") and objectified as though it were a mere world event. Biblical iconoclasm consists in the mutual debunking of divine and human, of religion* through religion, so long as the language through which this occurs – pictographic or alphabetic, visual, or phonetic – does not become a cliché but "speaks" to us.

Creation debunks nature as a matrix of religion, as creation also debunks history insofar as it proleptically "caps" Israel's exodus from Egypt. A similar role is played by the virgin birth (the Incarnation*) with respect to Abraham's descendants according to the flesh (the Jews) and the historical covenant of God with Israel. In keeping with biblical iconoclasm, Christianity, like Judaism, is not a religion of a book but of the living Word. The God that speaks can be silent. The idol is mute. GABRIEL VAHANIAN

Iconodule, Greek for "one who serves icons*." **See also ICONOCLASM AND THE ICONOCLASTIC CONTROVERSY.**

Iconography, the Greek term for the painting of sacred images (*eikones*). John* of Damascus and others insisted that the translation be simply "writing of icons," but this is a wooden application of the verb *grapho*, which connotes painted figurative art as well as normal "writing."

The proper subjects of a true icon are Christ*, the Virgin Mary*, or the saints*. Other topics and themes are not regarded as the subjects of mainstream icons, since the purpose of this religious art, as understood in Eastern Christianity, is not so much a didactic presentation (an attitude that predominates in the Christian West) as a personal (hypostatic) invocation*. The "writing" or painting of icons is a form of praying, and icons are meant to be prayer forms, to be used in the practice of worship. To this day, the distinction between didactic art and icon can be observed between, e.g., a wall fresco depicting an NT or other biblical scene, and a panel depicting Christ or one of the saints. The latter is regarded as a classical example of an icon and used in public worship (typically being incensed* by the clergy or kissed by the faithful), while the fresco is more "illustrative."

There is a sense, deeply rooted in Eastern Christian attitudes, that the icon opens a door to the spiritual presence* of the holy* one represented. This is probably related to the fact that the early use of the iconography of saints in the churches was related to their tomb relics, which were an important part of Byzantine Church services. While the Orthodox faithful are clear that they are not idolaters* who worship the icon as such (the niceties of this theology were set out at the seventh ecumenical council, the Council of Nicaea in 787), they understand the veneration they give to the icon as passing immediately, and directly, to the person represented there. Icons, therefore, have a generally more substantive "sacramental*" aspect than does any religious art in Catholic or Protestant experience.

The roots of the Christian use of icons have been much disputed over the years. Some see their appearance (as wall paintings in the 2nd c. and as portable panels in the 7th) as a decadent "hellenization" of the early "pure" practice of having no religious images at all in a church building (a position especially favored by Protestant commentators). Others trace the rise of the icon to the emperor cult of the late antique period or to lesser-known traditions of domestic worship of the old gods being displaced by the increasingly important "new god" Jesus, especially in early Christian Egypt* (where most of the ancient surviving portable panels were found). The discovery of new exemplars of ancient art is continually changing perspectives on the debate about origins.

One thing is clear enough, however: when icons do make their regular appearance in Eastern Christian churches, after the 7th c., they already come with a sophisticated technique and a reasoned *apologia*, one that is added to with remarkable profundity until the 9th c. Some of the most important Orthodox theologians of the icon are John* of Damascus, the patriarchs Nikephoros and Germanos, and Theodore* of Studium. **See also ICONOCLASM AND THE ICONOCLASTIC CONTROVERSY.**

JOHN A. MCGUCKIN

Iconostasis, a wall with three doors that is covered with icons and separates the nave from the sanctuary in Byzantine Orthodox* churches. Originally it was a relatively low wall but now extends from floor to ceiling, as it is covered with icons in certain traditional arrangements.

Identity, Christian. See HELLENISTIC RELIGIOUS TRADITIONS AND CHRISTIANITY'S SELF-DEFINITION.

Ideological Studies of Christianity. Ideological studies scrutinize the expressions of ideologies* in religious metaphors*, psychological* archetypes, master stories, confessional myths* that distinguish between "sick" and "healthy" religion, violence*, and mutuality. Religious metaphors and psychological archetypes interact in the human unconscious, shaping constructive and/or destructive spirituality*. Religious master stories and myths provide believers with a framework of ideas for interpreting existence, both mundane and transcendent. That ideological framework both shapes and reflects human spirituality: personal piety, worship ritual, and social action. Christianity is rooted in OT and NT historical narratives. A mythic interpretation of those idealized biblical narratives as Scripture* forms Christianity's ideological framework of meaning, its master story.

All religious master stories and ideologies should be constantly critiqued to discern whether they cultivate growth and health, and can be affirmed to be true, or foster pathology and destruction, and should be rejected as false. Thus scholars continually analyze Christianity's biblical sources, traditions, master stories, and confessional ideologies with methodologies that function as lenses through which to discern the constructive or destructive qualities of the Christian tradition.

Psychological and sociological analyses are useful for assessing the psychosocially constructive and destructive effects of the master story behind the biblical texts, within the texts, and in front of the texts (Kille, Ricoeur*). Master stories and confessional ideologies convey their messages by metaphors, which can be studied through literary analysis. Religious metaphors insinuate themselves through learning processes into believers' unconscious minds (see Metaphor). They provide the content of their psychospiritual archetypes (Freud, Jung).

If religious metaphors are destructive, they fill believers' unconscious minds and their psychological archetypes with pathological content, producing destructive value systems, self-defeating emotions and behavior, and unhealthy responses to life situations. If religious metaphors are constructive, they fill believers' unconscious minds and shape their archetypes with wholesome and growth-inducing content. This creates healthy value systems, growth-inducing emotions and behavior, and constructive responses to life situations (see Psychology and Theology).

Christianity's confessional myth contains an ambiguous representation of God's nature and behavior that derives from the ambiguous narratives of the Bible. In one set of biblical narratives, God is a violent paranoid warrior in cosmic conflict with evil deities (other gods, idols*, Satan*), the battleground being history and the human heart. In this biblical metaphor, God solves ultimate problems with ultimate violence*. Moreover, "he" is so disturbed with humans that to retain psychospiritual equilibrium he must kill somebody: humans or his own beloved son (see Atonement #2). In this master story, God is a (borderline) paranoid schizophrenic, with psychotic episodes. Such a sick God makes for sick people; sick people project such a sick God. This is an ideological construct (a representation of an imaginary relationship of individuals to the real conditions of existence), not an empirical, phenomenological, or heuristic presentation of the existence of an ontological evil or of a cosmic conflict between good and evil, God and the devil.

An alternative biblical narrative presents a Christian master story leading to a quite different confessional ideology, the biblical narrative about God's unconditional, universal, and radical grace* – the good news of much OT teaching and of the Christian gospel. According to this alternative Christian ideology, God embraces all humans unconditionally in spite of themselves. In this master story, God's radical acceptance frees believers from each other and themselves, affording them true mutuality, a truly healthy community and personal life. Christians historically have tended to cling to the sick confessional ideology, eclipsing the healthy confessional ideology of the gospel of grace.

J. HAROLD ELLENS

Ideology. Neutrally defined, "ideology is a representation of the imaginary relationship of individuals to their real conditions of existence" (Althusser). In this strict sense, an ideology usually takes the form of a master story about human experience and the external world, expressed in multiple historical narratives, myths*, and/or personal narratives recording memories of origin and development. In this way, an ideology provides the contours and content of people's confessional interpretation of life, their worldview, the ideas they claim to be true, and the values they idealize. Thus an ideology also sets forth a program of social* and political* organization that entails a struggle and the task of recruiting adherents; an ideology creates a deep bond among all those who share it or, conversely, sets them apart from other communities that do not embrace this ideology. An ideology that promotes congeniality facilitates peaceful communication and close association between communities or persons. An ideology that sets people apart can lead to a sense of superiority (our ideology is better, purer, truer) and an "us and them" mentality. The ideology of religious communities that perceive themselves under threat tends to become defensive and aggressive, whereas the ideology of a secure community tends to be open and harmonious.

"Ideology" as used by Marx* is a disparaging term referring to "false consciousness," which is necessarily destructive and pathological. In the neutral sense, ideologies can be either false and destructive, or true and constructive, promoting growth and health. J. HAROLD ELLENS

Idol, Idolatry. Idolatry is the worship of idols, condemned in ancient Israel because they represented false deities or were claimed to represent God, who cannot be depicted, or were made of impotent wood or stone, silver or gold. The early church followed a similar policy as it confronted, not without ambivalence, the problem of eating idol* meat. It broadened the meaning of "idolatry" by defining it as the absolutization of a true but partial revelation, manifestation, or gift from God (e.g. the creation, Rom 1:19–23; or money/Mammon, Matt 6:24). During the period of Christian persecution*, apostates denied their Christianity by making an offering to idols. As modern theologians (including Liberation* and Death* of God theologians) emphasize, idolatry is a present-day issue. The opposite of faith* in God is not atheism*; it is idolatry – the adoration of a false god, such as power, capital, consumerism, and the market taken as absolute, as a god in whose name the life of millions of human beings and nature are destroyed. For these theologians, such idolatry is the most serious betrayal of the will of the God of life. **See also GOD, CHRISTIAN VIEWS OF, CLUSTER: IN LATIN AMERICA; ICONOCLASM AS A THEOLOGICAL CONCEPT.**

Idol Meat (the usual translation of Gk *eidolothyta*, "meat offered to idols"). The question of eating meat offered to idols – eating in a temple (e.g. during the meeting of a guild), eating meat that had been sacrificed before being sold in the market, or eating meat served to guests in a home – was addressed in an ambivalent way by Paul. In 1 Cor 8 and 10 and Rom 14:20, Paul permits the eating of idol meat, but discourages such practice for the sake of those with a "weak conscience." In so doing, he applies to a specific circumstance Jesus' teaching that all foods are clean (Mark 7:29). Paul's followers express a similar ambivalent attitude in Col 2:16; 1 Tim 4:3; and Heb 9:10, 13:9. However, eating idol meat was specifically condemned in Rev 2:14, 20 and throughout the 2nd c. in the nascent Eastern and Western churches. It remains an issue today, especially for Christian converts in homes where food is traditionally offered to ancestors*.

Iglesia Filipina Independiente. See PHILIPPINE INDEPENDENT CHURCH.

Ignatius of Antioch (d c107/13), bishop of Antioch, known only through seven letters that he wrote while traveling through Asia Minor, guarded by 10 soldiers, on his way to being martyred in Rome. (A longer recension of these letters, along with four others, came to be widely circulated, but Ussher and other scholars have shown that this was a 4th-c. expansion.)

One letter was sent to the church in Rome, asking that it not intervene to save him from martyrdom*. Five letters were written to churches that had sent delegates during Ignatius's journey to encourage him, and one to Polycarp*, bishop of Smyrna. Ignatius staged his journey as a triumphal march, dramatized by the delegations and his own letters. He warned against the errors of "Judaizers*" and "Docetists*" (some scholars think that these two names may designate two tendencies in a single group). His insistence on the reality of Christ's flesh is like that of the Johannine* epistles, although he did not quote them directly. He referred to several Pauline Epistles (1 Corinthians, and probably Romans and Ephesians), and either the Gospel of Matthew or an oral tradition related to it.

Ignatius offers the first evidence for the monepiscopate*, according to which a single bishop* in each locality, assisted by presbyters* and deacons*, was the guarantor of the church's unity with Christ in the Eucharist. Consequently, for some scholars, his journey and death may have occurred in the middle or late 2nd c. During his time, however, the monepiscopate may have been one organizational form competing with others; while it seems to have been common in some of the churches in Asia Minor to which he wrote, Ignatius may have been pressing it on others as a plausible way to ensure the unity of the church, and his status as a martyr may have helped to promote it.

EUGENE TESELLE

Ignatius of Loyola (1491–1556), founder of the Society of Jesus (see Jesuits). At the dawn of modern times, when humans became aware of their autonomy, Ignatius opened a spiritual path for loving God and devoting one's life to serving God in the world by using spiritual discernment in decision making.

Born in Aspeitia, Guipúzcoa (in the Basque country), Inigo, the 13th child of the lords of Loyola, was a page at Arevalo, then a *gentilhombre*-soldier in the service of the viceroy of Navarre. Following an injury in battle and his conversion* in Loyola, he became a hermit* at Monserrat and later at Manresa (1523). After a pilgrimage* to Jerusalem (1524), he studied in Barcelona, Alcalá, Salamanca, and especially Paris (1530–37), where he adopted the name of Ignatius and, with 6 companions, took the "vow of Montmartre" to lead a Christ-like life in the Holy Land (1535). Ordained a priest in Venice (1538), with 10 companions (including Francis Xavier and Peter Favre), he founded the Society of Jesus in Rome (approved by Pope Paul III, 1540). Elected superior of the order, he wrote its "Constitutions" and led its development, sending Jesuits to Germany*, Brazil*, India*, and Japan* (including Francis Xavier* to Japan, 1544). When he died (Rome, 1556), there were 1,000 Jesuits*. The *Spiritual* Exercises,* the "Constitutions," his letters (more than 6,000), an autobiography, and *Spiritual Journal* are the founding documents of Ignatian spirituality.

The autobiography shows the relationship between Ignatius's own spiritual experience and what he sets forth in the *Spiritual Exercises*. Ignatius seeks to discern God's will for him. His year as a hermit at Manresa, "his primitive church," was a time of profound illumination regarding the mysteries* of the Trinity*, the creation*, the Incarnation*, and the presence* of Christ in the Eucharist*. This was also a period during which he developed his two central meditations on the Kingdom of God and the "two standards" (of Christ and Satan), which provided the framework for his vision of the Society of Jesus. Ignatius often said that even if there was no Scripture to teach these matters, he would readily die for them simply on the basis of his visions – a stance that made him a suspect in the eyes of the Inquisition*.

For Ignatius one must seek, and indeed find, God in all things. According to Nadal, his vicar*, Ignatius "had received from God the unique grace to contemplate freely the Holy Trinity, especially in his last years. Furthermore, in all things, actions, and conversations, he contemplated the presence of God; he was a contemplative in action." This unique grace drove him to search for God not only in prayer, but also in action, in order to conform his will to God's through righteous intent and spiritual discernment of God in the world, where the Incarnation takes place and where humans make decisions about their lives. It is in the world that he wanted "to help souls" and "feel with the Church," whose head is "the vicar* of Christ on earth." "In between the Christ our Lord, the Bridegroom, and the Church, his Bride, the same Spirit guides us for the good of our souls."

Ignatius's spirituality is thus marked by constantly seeking to discern God's will, following Christ in his mission, having confidence in humans, nourishing their freedom, and respecting their spiritual meditations. Ignatius wrote, "God wants to be glorified as much through what God gives as Creator, that is, through (human) nature, as through what God gives us as Redeemer, that is, through supernatural gifts." Thus for Ignatius, theology and spirituality are intimately related. The graces* he received at Manresa gave him an architectonic vision of creation and redemption. Christ is "our Creator and Lord"; his mission is to gather together all of humanity in the Kingdom* of the Father, by freeing humans from the traps set by the "enemy of human nature." And Christ's task is not finished. Raised from the dead, Christ continues his mission in the (Roman Catholic) Church by calling each and all to become his companions and friends and to work with him under harsh conditions in order to share the joy of his victory.

The expected response to Christ's call is not mere goodwill, but love* reflecting one's conformity with Christ and gratitude for all the gifts one has received, a love that frees one from random devotions and allows one to discern the Spirit's role in all life events and the ways God's will is at work in all things. The Jesuit Hevenesi summarized Ignatius's rule for acting: "Put your self confidently in God's hands, as if the whole success of the action depended on you and not on him; then expect everything from God who will do everything, and you nothing." In early modern times, marked both by a human desire to assume responsibility for life in society and to transform it and by the lack of helpful guideposts and the limited usefulness of traditions, Ignatius opened a way to Christian decision making.

CLAUDE FLIPO, SJ

IHS, monogram based on the first three Greek letters of the name of Jesus (IHSOYS). Veneration of the holy* name in this form was promoted especially by Bernardino* of Siena (15th c.). **See also CHI-RHO; INRI; NOMINA SACRA.**

Image of God (Lat *imago Dei*), an expression used in connection with the creation* of humanity, male and female (Gen 1:26–27). Later, however, only males, Adam and Seth, are said to be in God's image (Gen 5:1–3); 1 Cor 11:7 also suggests that males alone are the image and glory of God; here, however, Paul might be quoting the Corinthians, expressing his own view in 1 Cor 11:11–12. In Gal 3:28, Paul affirms that there is "no male and female" (among those baptized into Christ; Gal 3:26–29; cf. Col 3:10; Eph 4:22–24). Similarly, Philo* and the Gnostics believed that in the true sense of humanity created in the image of God, males and females were identical.

Wisdom of Solomon (2:23) states that God created humanity for incorruption, in the image of God's own eternity*, but that death entered the world through the devil*. This view influenced the patristic interpretation of Rom 5:12–14 and 1 Cor 15:21, 56, despite Gen 3:5, 22, 32, in which Adam and Eve, by gaining knowledge of good and evil, become like gods or like God and, according to the narrative, would live forever if they were to eat from the tree of life. This complex biblical tradition gave rise to several distinct interpretations.

If the image is something visible, it might be the human form itself, or it might be "dominion" over all created things (mentioned in Gen 1:27). If linked with the prohibition on making and worshipping images, then humanity, as the image of God, has no need for images. Perhaps being created in God's image implies a co-humanity (Barth*). Perhaps God's image is the mental and/or spiritual aspect of humanity, shared by males and females; or immortality or incorruption, as belonging properly only to God (as developed in complex ways by Irenaeus*, Clement*, and Origen*, who at times quoted Plato's comment about becoming "like God" [*Theaetetus* 176B]).

In a very different vein, Philo and later thinkers interpreted the image of God to be God's Word or Wisdom, the only true, undistorted, permanent expression of God (cf. 2 Cor 4:4; Col 1:15; Heb 1:3). Then humanity bears God's image only as long as it is oriented toward and formed by the true Image/Word, and the image is lost if one turns away from God (as is occasionally suggested by Irenaeus and Clement, and made most explicit by Origen, Athanasius*, and the early Augustine*). Thus for some (including certain Protestant thinkers), the image of God is totally lost through sin*.

However, the later Augustine saw human beings as intrinsically the image of God, since their self-relationship is an image of the Trinity*: memory, understanding, and will; self-remembrance, self-understanding, and self-love fulfilled in remembrance, understanding, and love of God. Following him, others underscore that the image abides at least in a minimal way despite sin, although the right relationship with God is lost and must be restored through the grace of Christ.

During the Iconoclastic* controversy, Theodore* of Studios argued that human nature is "God's own iconography"; the Incarnation*, furthermore, appropriates humanity to the Word's own person. Not only does humanity bear a likeness to its archetype, that likeness has been affirmed explicitly by God.

Contemporary theologians in marginalized communities or in solidarity with them affirm that any human being is intrinsically the image of God, and remains so, and thus has a dignity worthy of the respect owed to God – a view that challenges slavery*, oppression of all kinds, and the death* penalty.

EUGENE TESELLE

Image of God: Contemporary Feminist and Liberation Theological Views. The biblical assertion that men and women are made in the image of God (Gen 1:27) is fundamentally egalitarian, affirming that all people are intimately related to God. Yet many Christian communities have interpreted the claim that humanity is made in the image of God in hierarchical ways. Thus women often have been viewed as being in the image of God in a deficient way, e.g., derivatively, through men. Similarly, humanity in the image of God has been seen as wielding unbridled dominion over the earth and all creatures. Such hierarchical interpretations support the oppression of women and the careless destruction of the environment (see Ecology and Christianity Cluster).

Contemporary Feminist and Liberation theologies reclaim the egalitarian meaning of the *imago Dei*, celebrating the God-given dignity of all persons. Many theologians seek to embrace the universal affirmation that all humans are made in the image of God, while avoiding essentialist statements regarding traits such as gender, sex, and experience. Christians from various traditions challenge views of the image of God that focus on individuality and imply a dualistic* view of the body and mind. Drawing on doctrines such as Trinity* and Christology*, theologians honor plurality and diversity through interpretations of the image of God that highlight embodiment, community, and relations characterized by justice*.

SHANNON CRAIGO-SNELL

Images of Jesus Christ. See JESUS, IMAGES OF, CLUSTER: IN LITERATURE.

Imitation of Christ (*Imitatio Christi*), a spiritual classic comprising four books, written for a monastic setting; published in Latin (early 15th c.) and soon translated into many languages. While no author's name was given, it is ascribed to Thomas* à Kempis. He most likely compiled and translated into Latin some writings of Geert Groote*. **See also DEVOTIO MODERNA.**

Imitation of Christ (Lat *imitatio Christi*) is one of the ways discipleship is defined (see Discipleship #2) as early as Paul (1 Thess 1:6, 2:14; 1 Cor 4:16, 11:1). According to this definition, discipleship requires a close, intimate relationship with Jesus, through which Jesus' followers are progressively trained and equipped to become disciples. The presupposed view of faith* is that it is a process of moving toward God and Christ (see Faith #5). The presupposed basic predicament is that believers are neither equipped nor trained to do God's will (even if they already know it and want to do it), as in the Aristotelian perfectionist* view of the moral life, according to which one is required to undergo apprenticeship (imitating an expert) in order to acquire character (*ethos*), virtues, and practical wisdom. Disciples need to be transformed into Christ's likeness. Three variant emphases can be found independently or in combination.

1. By imitating Christ, disciples are resocialized, acquiring a new identity (character) as they share Christ's "symbolic* world" – including his vision of the Kingdom* – and thus learn to be children of the Kingdom and children of God (e.g. praying with Christ, "Our father in heaven"); thus disciples become like Christ, willing to be "poor in Spirit," "meek," "persecuted for righteousness' sake."
2. By imitating Christ, disciples share Jesus' discerning faith and are given the ability to discern in society those who are actually "blessed" by God (not the rich or joyful, but the poor and repressed, those who mourn, as in Matt 5:3–10; Luke 6:20–26) and other manifestations of the Kingdom that should orient their ministry as disciples.
3. By imitating Christ, disciples share in Jesus' power. Although the forces of evil and oppression seem overwhelming, as they imitate Christ disciples discover that God empowers them to overcome these obstacles, even if the disciples have to go "the way of the cross" following Christ.

See also DISCIPLESHIP; PERFECTIONIST ETHICS.

DANIEL PATTE

Immaculate Conception, the Roman Catholic dogma according to which the conception of Mary*, the mother of Jesus, was without any "stain" (Lat *macula*) of original* sin, as defined in the constitution *Ineffabilis Deus* by Pope Pius IX (1854), which affirms that Mary* (as the Blessed Virgin) "in the first instance of her conception, by a singular privilege and grace* granted by God, in view of the merits* of Jesus Christ, the Savior of the human race, was preserved exempt from all stain of original sin." The Feast of Immaculate Conception has been celebrated on December 8 since the 15th c. (long before it became a matter of dogma). (The immaculate conception of Mary should not be confused with the dogma of the virginal conception of Jesus; see Incarnation Cluster). **See also MARY, THE VIRGIN, CLUSTER.**

Immanence, the state of being "within" something else. The term is used most commonly with reference to the immanence of God* in the world*, which is often related to the Incarnation* (see Phenomenology and Christianity). In the doctrine of the Trinity*, the "immanent Trinity" is eternally "within God," while the "economic Trinity" is in God's external activities of creation*, incarnation*, and sanctification*. The "method of immanence" is associated with both Blondel* and Husserl*, starting "within" human experience but remaining open to the disclosure of that which transcends experience.

Immanuel. See EMMANUEL, IMMANUEL.

Immersion, baptism by submerging the body in water (rather than pouring or sprinkling water over the body). This was the usual practice of the early church, at first using "living water" in streams, then water in baptismal fonts. Trinitarian triple immersion is practiced in the Eastern Orthodox Church. **See also BAPTISM CLUSTER.**

Immortality (from Lat for "undying") is ascribed primarily to God*, who is without beginning or end. It is considered superior to mere survival as a "shade" after death, implied by the Hebrew Sheol* and the Greek Hades*. The view that the soul* is immortal and that its destiny is determined by its own decisions is found first among the Pythagoreans and the Platonists*.

The biblical tradition tends to speak in terms of resurrection* of the dead. When the idea of immortality entered the biblical tradition, it was viewed as a gift of the immortal God as the Creator*: the soul is not immortal as God is, and is thus not preexistent; it is given immortality by God. Thus Wis 2:23–24 says, "For God created us for incorruption, and made us in the image of his own eternity, but through the devil's envy death entered the world, and those who belong to his company experience it." The gift of immortality (incorruption), lost through sin*, is retained by "blameless souls*." The Christian tradition continues to understand immortality in relation to God as the Creator. Without God's act of creation, creatures would cease to exist; thus immortality and resurrection* of the body are at times understood to be a "new" creation."

The NT authors, along with the Pharisees* and Jewish apocalyptic* writers (but not the Sadducees*) anticipate the resurrection of the body. If that is to happen, the body must be "further clothed" and its mortality "swallowed up" by true life from God (1 Cor 15:53–57; 2 Cor 5:4). More than the survival of an immortal soul, the hope is for an abiding union with the risen Christ (see Resurrection of Christ), because Christ defeated the "power of death." Thus the church fathers (e.g. Irenaeus*, Athanasius*, Gregory* of Nyssa*) based the hope* for immortality on the redemptive work of Christ (see Redemption). Yet under Platonist and Neoplatonist* influences, the church fathers and early Scholastics* tended to oscillate between affirmation of the immortality of the soul* (as separable from the body; thus Origen* could envision the soul as preexistent) and affirmation of the resurrection, which involves the reunion of body and soul (e.g. Augustine* at times stressed the immortality of the soul and at times the resurrection). But this uncertainty was largely laid to rest by Aquinas's* emphasis, with Aristotle*, that the soul is the form of the body; resurrection of the body is necessary for full human immortality.

This doctrinal tradition is challenged by atheist* views, in that the Christian hope of immortality depends on God's immortality (although this is not the case for Spiritism* and other religious movements). Yet the Christian tradition continues to emphasize the themes of corruption and death, the need for divine grace*, the role of freedom* in determining one's destiny, God as the giver of true life, and final resurrection.

EUGENE TESELLE and DANIEL PATTE

Impanation, eucharistic* theory that the body of Christ becomes present in the bread after consecration, but without transubstantiation*.

Impassibility, God's lack of "passion" ("passivity," lack of emotional disturbance) and even of "compassion*" ("suffering with") for other beings, challenged in modern times on biblical, theological, and philosophical grounds. **See also ANTHROPOMORPHISMS.**

Imperialism and Christianity. See COLONIALISM AND IMPERIALISM AND CHRISTIAN THEOLOGY.

Imposition of Hands. See LAYING ON OF HANDS.

Imprimatur (Lat "let it be printed"), in the Roman Catholic Church, certification by a bishop or other authority that a book is free of doctrinal error.

Imputation (Lat "reckoning," "ascribing"), God's crediting believers with righteousness because of their faith (Gen 15:6; Rom 4:3, 9, 22; "Faith was reckoned [by God] to Abraham as righteousness"); thus not counting sin because of Christ (2 Cor 5:19; "In Christ God was reconciling the world to himself, not counting their trespasses against them"). **See also JUSTIFICATION, THEOLOGICAL VIEWS AND PRACTICES, CLUSTER.**

INCARNATION CLUSTER

1) *Introductory Entries*

Incarnation in the Orthodox Tradition
Incarnation in the Western Tradition

2) *A Sampling of Contextual Views and Practices*

Incarnation in Africa
Incarnation in Asia
Incarnation in Latin America
Incarnation in North America
Incarnation in North America: Feminist Understandings
Incarnation in South Pacific and Australia
Incarnation in Western Europe

---

1) Introductory Entries

Incarnation in the Orthodox Tradition is understood to be the union of the divine and human natures in the person of Jesus Christ. The definitive texts on the Incarnation in Orthodox theology are Athanasius* of Alexandria's *On the Incarnation* and *Orations*. Athanasius argues that Jesus' divinity must be identified with that of the true God; otherwise, there is no hope for salvation*. In what is now a classic phrase, Athanasius declares that "God became a human being (*anthropos*) so that a human being can become god." This logic of divine–human communion functioned as a first principle throughout the history of Orthodox theology, both patristic and contemporary. This understanding of the Incarnation in terms of the divine–human union in the person of Jesus Christ is the foundation of the well-known Orthodox notion of theosis* (divinization). It is also the basis for the Christian doctrine of the Trinity*, which is the conceptualization of God's communion with creation through the person of Jesus Christ, by the power of the Holy Spirit. Orthodox theologies of the church, liturgy, sacrament*, and icon* were also shaped by this understanding of the Incarnation.

From the 5th to the 9th c., Orthodox theology contended with objections to the doctrine of the union of the divine and human natures in the person of Jesus Christ, primarily raised from the point of view of Monophysitism* (although the adherents call their movement Miaphysitism*) and Monothelitism*. Although it is often assumed that patristic theology offers a "high Christology," the main concern of the fourth, fifth, and sixth ecumenical* councils was asserting the full humanity of Jesus Christ against tendencies in Monophysitism and Monothelitism to prioritize the divine nature over human nature (a view that Miaphysites vehemently reject). The culmination of Orthodox theology of the Incarnation is the affirmation of the use of icons* in the seventh ecumenical council. Debates, however, over Orthodox theology of the Incarnation reemerged in the 14th-c. controversy over hesychasm*. In response to theologians who argued against the possibility of an experience of the divine light, Gregory* Palamas defended hesychastic practices, such as the Jesus* Prayer, as means to experience the divine light on the basis that it is the same light that Jesus Christ revealed in his transfiguration*. **See also ORTHODOX CHURCHES, EASTERN, CLUSTER: INTRODUCTORY ENTRIES; SOLOVIEV, VLADIMIR SERGEEVICH; TRINITY IN EASTERN ORTHODOXY.**

ARISTOTLE PAPANIKOLAOU

Incarnation in the Western Tradition denotes the belief that God has entered into human history in an act of solidarity and redemption*, and that this entrance and embodiment are focused on the specific historical individual Jesus* of Nazareth. Though rooted in the NT, the doctrine was formalized and given systematic expression during the patristic* period. The first four centuries of Christian reflection on the identity and significance of Jesus of Nazareth involved the exploration and assessment of a number of possible christological* models, including Ebionism* (leaning toward Adoptionism*, according to which the human Jesus is the adopted Son of God) and Docetism* (according to which the humanity of Jesus is merely apparent). Both were eventually judged to be inadequate.

During the Arian* controversy (4th–7th c.; Arianism, in its prevalent form, asserted that the Son is "like" [*homoios*] the Father, but refused to say that Father and Son are "of the same essence"), the idea of "incarnation" was subjected to rigorous scrutiny.

Debate centered on a number of questions. First and foremost, was this a legitimate way of interpreting the identity of Jesus* of Nazareth? It seemed to raise several philosophical difficulties; e.g. classical Greek philosophy was unable to accommodate the idea of a God* who became incarnate. Furthermore, the concept of the "two natures" of Christ was seen as creating logical tensions that undermined confidence in the belief. Second, writers such as Athanasius* of Alexandria argued that some such belief in the Incarnation was necessary to do justice to the NT witness to the significance of Jesus of Nazareth, especially as the bearer of salvation* and the object of Christian worship. Other issues concerning the relation of the human and the divine in Christ arose during the Nestorian* controversy (particularly the early 5th c.; Nestorianism affirmed that Jesus' humanity and divinity were joined by will, not by nature).

The issues were discussed at a series of ecumenical* councils, culminating in the Council of Chalcedon* (451), which gave formal expression to the doctrine using categories drawn from contemporary Greek metaphysics. The "Chalcedonian definition" spoke of Christ as "being of one substance with the Father as regards his Godhead, and at the same time of one substance with us as regards his humanity; like us in all respects, apart from sin; as regards his Godhead, begotten of the Father before the ages, but yet as regards his humanity, begotten, for us and for our salvation, of Mary* the Virgin, the God-bearer (Theotokos*)."

This basic notion has subsequently played an important role in Christian thought. Two ongoing debates can be identified in subsequent Christian theology, each continuing the discussions of the patristic period. First, the question of whether the concept of the Incarnation is the best way of expressing the NT's witness to Christ remains open and subject to debate, particularly during the modern period. Second, the specific role of classical Greek metaphysics in the Chalcedonian formulation of the doctrine of the Incarnation has been argued to be an unnecessary imposition on the ideas of the NT. Some Christian writers have sought to distance themselves from these ontological* concepts, replacing them with relational or existential notions more acceptable to contemporary cultures. More recently, however, a new debate has developed, resulting from growing awareness of the religious diversity of the world. Some have argued that the doctrine of the Incarnation represents an inappropriate affirmation of the uniqueness* or superiority of Christ, insensitive to other religious sensibilities. Others, however, argue that the doctrine must be retained on account of its credentials, while conceding that thought must be given to its mode of presentation in this new cultural climate. **See also CHRISTOLOGIES CLUSTER.**

ALISTER E. MCGRATH

---

2) A Sampling of Contextual Views and Practices

Incarnation in Africa is most important not only because it has a central place in the Christianity brought to Africa by missionaries, but also because the Christian faith must be "incarnated" into the African context, just as God entered into the human context by taking a human form in the man Jesus of Nazareth. Thus beyond the Chalcedonian dogma, African interpretations of the Incarnation are necessary, such as the following ones related to the Haya tradition (Northwestern Tanzania).

Incarnation of the Father Ancestor. Who is incarnated and can be identified with the first person of the Trinity? African ancestral anthropology answers: Ruhanga, the Creator, the Source of All, the Proto-ancestor, the Greatest Father of Humans, Father Ancestor, the Ancestor par Excellence.

Incarnation of Brother Ancestor / Son of God. Who is Jesus Christ for Africans, from the perspective of African anthropology and culture? What is the significance of God's incarnation through Jesus Christ to Africans? "A Christ who is not present is not relevant, as he does not address people's needs and problems encountered in existential life" (as a 2006 Lutheran

World Federation Document states). For many Africans, Jesus Christ is Kazoba, the Illuminator and Eternal Light who guides humans and all creatures, and the Elder Brother, "the First Born," and thus the Brother Ancestor, the archetypal model for both humans and spiritual beings. Ancestral incarnation integrates well the two natures of Jesus Christ, humanity and divinity, into one nature without confusion, contradiction, or change – a view that complies with classical formulations, while being fully African.

Incarnation of Sister Ancestor / Spirit of God. The first two African views of incarnation are incomplete unless they are related to the Spirit of God and its sanctifying role. A Haya tradition provides an anthropological pneumatological model of Ntangaire (or Amagara, "Vital Force") that offers a way to conceive of Christian pneumatology as an integral part of incarnation. The Holy Spirit is "Sister Ancestor," who gives life and distributes talents, who as Ntangaire participates in the creation as the breath breathed in the nostrils of the clay figure created by the creator God, Ruhanga, in collaboration with his Son, Kazoba the Illuminator. Thus the Christian experience of the Holy Spirit can be envisioned from a Haya perspective.

In Africa, incarnation is and should be understood in terms of African trinitarian models rather than Greek and Neoplatonist ones, as they invite Africans in general and African believers in particular to participate in the mystery of God incarnated and to become true brother or sister descendants of Jesus.

SYLVESTER KAHAKWA

Incarnation in Asia. Alexandre de Rhodes (1593–1659), a French Jesuit missionary in Vietnam*, remarked that the doctrine of the Incarnation is the hardest Christian mystery* for Asians to accept. It offends the imagination and sensibilities of Asians, even those well disposed to the Christian message. Thus Ram Mohan Roy, the founder of the Brahmo Samaj, an Indian society dedicated to the promotion of monotheism and the eradication of social abuses in India, denounced the Incarnation as polytheistic. Yet the notion of a god "descending" to the human and even animal world is not absent from Asian religions. Thus in Hinduism, Krishna tells of his 10 embodiments in both animal and human forms (avatars), not by necessity but out of the deity's gracious choice.

Some Christian theologians have attempted to express the Incarnation in terms of the concept of avatar. A. J. Appasamy calls Jesus the supreme avatar. V. Chakkarai affirms that Jesus as mediator of God to the world is the incarnation of *cit* of the triad *sat, cit, ananda* (being, consciousness, bliss). For P. Chenchiah, Jesus is God taking a body permanently in God's historical process of ever-new creation. These praiseworthy attempts nevertheless risk the danger of eclipsing what is unique in the Christian doctrine.

PETER C. PHAN

Incarnation in Latin America. The Incarnation ("the Word became flesh and lived among us," John 1:14) emphasizes the historicity of Jesus' life. Paul describes the Incarnation as happening at "the fullness of time" (Gal 4:4) and thus at the culminating point of history. Through the fullness of love and grace (John 1:14, 1:16–17), God became human – indeed, God became a poor person (2 Cor 8:9). Jesus assumes human life in all its beauty and its vulnerability, in its wealth* and its poverty*. Through his incarnation, the Son of God, "born of a woman," gives himself to the poor of the world, assuming the full humanity of the poor, as the Gospels show. Jesus was born, lived, and died as a poor person. As contemporary Latin American theologians underscore, through his radical preferential* option for the poor, Jesus proclaimed the Kingdom* of God and God's justice*, as good news for the poor.

Through Jesus' birth, the God of the poor burst into the history of the poor in a special way and yet in continuity with the history of salvation*. Salvation history is fulfilled through Jesus' life, death, and resurrection.

The Incarnation is presented in Paul's text as a liberation giving to the poor as well as to everyone else the possibility of being children of God. Jesus' coming is liberation from the yoke of a law that is powerless to save (whatever that "law" might be) and the adoption of all as children of God (Gal 3:23–25; 4:4–5). Through the Incarnation, the poor and everyone else receive the gift of being daughters and sons of God, rather than slaves. "In Christ Jesus you are all children of God through faith" (Gal 3:26–28).

The Incarnation is the foundation of discipleship* and of the life and mission* of the church. As a community of Jesus' brothers and sisters, the church prolongs Jesus' incarnation by serving those who are excluded and vulnerable ("the little ones," in the language of the Gospels) .

The Incarnation is also the central point of the liturgical celebration of the mystery of faith for Latin American Christians. We celebrate, in Leornado Boff's words, "the humanity and the joyfulness of our God," who was born and became poor among us to save and give life through the community of Jesus' brothers and sisters who follow an incarnational praxis as Jesus did.

VICTORIO ARAYA GUILLÉN

Incarnation in North America. There are two basic trends in North American views of the Incarnation. Most North American Christians hold to classical ("orthodox", Chalcedonian*) Christology, a substantialist (ontological*) view of the Incarnation, which popular religious rhetoric reduced to mere slogan and formula ("Jesus is God"). North American theologians tend toward relational* theologies of incarnation.

Profoundly affected by ontologies emanating from the Hellenistic world, the doctrinal language of the 4th-c. church transformed the "enfleshment" of the divine Logos (John 1:1–18) into a straightforward identification of Jesus with God at the level of substance or being itself, the view most often held in North America. Many of the more reflective Christologies that have emerged in North America (and elsewhere) during recent years, including some Feminist* theologies, have been attempts to move away from substantialist and toward relational theologies of incarnation. They emphasize that the fundamental interest of biblical faith is not in being as such (whether that means God's being or ours) but in being-in-relation (see Relationality; Heteronomy). Thus Jesus is the incarnation of God's Word, not because he is "of the same substance" (*homoousios**) or even "of a similar substance" (*homoiousios**) to God, but because believers experience him through faith* as the supreme manifestation of God's being *with* us – Emmanuel*.

DOUGLAS JOHN HALL

Incarnation in North America: Feminist Understandings. The doctrine of the Incarnation* affirms that the Word* of God became human in Jesus Christ to liberate* and redeem* creation. Rather than focusing on Jesus' human nature, however, certain interpretations of incarnation, patriarchal* interpretations, emphasize that Jesus' maleness is essential to his divine identity and redemptive work. This distorts the liberating significance of incarnation for women by subordinating female humanity and excluding women from full identity as *imago Christi* (image* of Christ). It reinforces male images of God and legitimizes male superiority, since God "chose" to become flesh as a male. Theoretically, it jeopardizes women's salvation*, because as the ancient maxim holds, what is not assumed is not redeemed.

Redeeming incarnation as liberating for women requires inclusive interpretations of this mystery*. Feminist theology asserts that incarnation actually subverts patriarchal dualisms* by connecting the divine with bodiliness. This theology retrieves the biblical Wisdom* tradition, identifying Jesus' redemptive ministry as God's enduring creativity in the world. As prophetic Wisdom, Jesus incarnates the divine inclusive love that effects and delights in the flourishing of all, especially the poor and marginalized. Recast in these terms, the mystery of incarnation unleashes hope* and vision for relationships of mutuality that create a discipleship* of equals in Christ.

ELIZABETH A. JOHNSON and GLORIA L. SCHAAB

Incarnation in South Pacific and Australia. Incarnational approaches to theology were rare in early Pacific contact histories; exceptions were those of William Ridley and Daniel and Janet Matthews, who engaged early-19th-c. indigenous cultures on equal terms. The irrefutable cost of colonial* regimes to indigenous peoples, crises and advances in anthropology, theology, and ministry training, and the obvious failure of traditional models of the church (thus, e.g., the crisis of Roman Catholic vocations*) have moved Christian thinkers toward more dispersed and laicized ecclesial models. The papal exhortation *Ecclesia in Oceania* (2001) is typical of traditional church responses, proposing "communion, inculturation*, and a renewed proclamation of the gospel in ways appropriate for the peoples of Oceania." The recognition that early missions had sought to impose elements that were culturally alien to the people unleashed diverse attempts to find Christian patterns in Pacific and Australasian indigenous cultures. Rainbow Spirit theology, "women's business" theologies, the use of Maori *karakia* (incantations), and Deep Sea Canoe missions are the result, with both European and indigenous thinkers (e.g. at Wontulp-Bi-Buya and Nungalinya Colleges) working on symbolic transferences that enable indigenous practices to enrich Christian praxis. This form of intellectual incarnation has proved easier to find among declining mainstream churches. How Christianity should incarnate itself in indigenous societies is viewed very differently in expansionary neo-Pentecostal/Charismatic* traditions, which look to revivalist* experience to radically change cultures. Revival movements (e.g. Elcho Island, 1979) have produced adherents of both approaches; the creation of national churches and autonomous indigenous commissions has not solved the tension over quite different understandings of incarnation.

MARK HUTCHINSON

Incarnation in Western Europe. See THE PRESENT CLUSTER: IN THE WESTERN TRADITION.

Incense and Olfactory Experience in Worship. Often mentioned in the OT and NT, gradually introduced since 312 in Orthodox, Catholic, and high Anglican worship, and almost universally used in ancient Mediterranean religions, incense accompanies individual, collective, domestic, monastic, and civic worship or symbolizes sacrifice and conveys prayers; its scent, together with that of perfumed holy oil, marks spaces (see Hierotopy, the Creation of Christian Sacred Spaces), actions, implements, and persons as holy (Exod 30:22–38).

In biblical and theological traditions, incense signals human initiatives toward the divine, such as sacrifice or prayer (e.g. Ps 141:2). Holy oil (perfume) signals the divine presence and divine favor or blessing toward humans. Thus olfactory encounters signal human–divine relations, interactions, and exchange as 2 Cor 2:14–16 invites believers to join Paul in spreading the fragrance of the knowledge of Christ as a sign of salvation and of Christ's power.

As a category of religious experience, smell was tied to ancient, pan-Mediterranean symbolism. Good smells signaled health*, blessing*, divine presence, immortality*, and paradise*. Bad smells were associated with decay, mortality, death*, sin*, and hell*. These associations were rooted in ancient medical and hygienic practices: herbs and spices healed, cleansed, disinfected, decontaminated, and purified. Patristic writers shifted attention away from the functional use of incense toward its epistemological meaning. Smell provides an effective physical signal of human–divine encounter: experienced in concretely affective terms, yet invisible, intangible, and silent. Smells move incomprehensibly: they are uncontainable, transgressive, contagious, and dangerous. Scent wafts ahead of encounter and lingers afterward; it provokes memory and emotion. Patristic writers cited all these characteristics to attune Christians to the way olfactory experiences in daily life provided constant reminders of God's presence and action in the world.

SUSAN ASHBROOK HARVEY

Inclusive Language is a system of vocabulary and syntax that does not exclude, diminish, or render invisible any person or group on the basis of gender, race, class, disability, legal status, or other criteria. The strategies by which inclusive language is developed are in the realm of grammar and thus are specific to each language, yet the ethical and theological significance of inclusive language cuts across such differences.

Gender is the most obvious arena in which one encounters changes in language in order to make it inclusive. Today women as well as men hold jobs such as "firefighter," so older forms like "fireman" no longer reflect reality. Women's visible presence in society is not honored by generic words like "mankind." Supposedly generic terms that privilege one gender over the other have been used to justify the exclusion of women from occupations and places. Simply put, such generic use of gender-specific terms or of masculine pronouns to encompass both genders or a person of unspecified gender is untrustworthy and consequently disempowers women.

Gender is not the only issue addressed by those who advocate inclusive language. People with disabilities are people first, and their disabilities are merely descriptors. "People who are blind" are not "the blind." Crayon manufacturers recognized that the beige crayon is not the only one that is "flesh-colored." "Black" and "dark" as metaphors for evil or impurity perpetuate racist prejudice against persons with black or brown skin in many cultures.

Inclusive language is a theological issue. It is related to language and images for God*. To speak about God, the Ultimate, the Transcendent, the Ground of Being, the Infinite, using finite human speech is at heart an impossible task. At best, such words and images can point to God, without naming God directly. To use only male terms to refer to God obscures the theological affirmation that God transcends all human categories of race, gender, culture, and time, and that all humankind has been created in that inclusive divine image (Gen 1:27).

Far from being a matter merely of political correctness, inclusive language goes to the heart of religious language and ethical practice. Although its specific forms and strategies are still being developed, inclusive language identifies a profoundly theological agenda. **See also DISABILITY AND CHRISTIANITY; FEMINIST THEOLOGY CLUSTER; IMAGE OF GOD; RACISM AND CHRISTIANITY CLUSTER.**

SHARON H. RINGE

Incubation, practice of sleeping at the tombs of martyrs, later in churches and other holy places, to seek healing or visions.

INCULTURATION CLUSTER

1) *Introductory Entries*

Inculturation of Christianity and the Gospel
Inculturation of Christianity in the Greco-Roman World

2) *A Sampling of Contextual Views and Practices*

Inculturation of Christianity in Africa: Central and Southern Africa
Inculturation of Christianity in Africa: Eastern Africa
Inculturation of Christianity in Africa: Western Africa
Inculturation of Christianity in Asia
Inculturation of Christianity in Latin America and Elsewhere

---

1) Introductory Entries

Inculturation of Christianity and the Gospel. A coinage introduced in the 1960s, "inculturation" refers to the process whereby the gospel and the culture of a particular people are integrated and are thereby mutually enriched. Yet inculturation is as old as Christianity itself (see the present cluster: In the Greco-Roman World); the gospel has never been acultural. First clothed in Jewish culture and religion, in the Western* churches the good news took on Hellenistic, Latin, Teutonic, Anglo-Saxon, Iberian, and other elements. It is this Western-inculturated Christianity embodied in layers of theology, canon* law, liturgy*, and spirituality* that was exported primarily by missionaries to the so-called Two-thirds World.

In the late 20th and early 21st c., inculturation became for many Western missionaries a self-conscious effort to prolong the Western process of inculturation of Christianity by promoting inculturation of Christianity in other cultures around the world. This practice goes far beyond what it was for the early missionaries and takes different forms according to each cultural context (described in the following entries). Yet from a Christian theological perspective, the inculturation process can be viewed as having the following characteristics, the emphasis varying from one culture to another.

1. Inculturation is a two-way process of inserting the already inculturated gospel into a particular culture and this culture into the gospel, so that the resulting inculturated Christianity will be something different and new (as a dialogue between two cultures, it could be called "interculturation").
2. Inculturation is an integral and constitutive dimension of mission*.
3. Inculturation is guided by the mysteries* of Jesus' incarnation*, death, and resurrection* and the descent and active presence of the Holy* Spirit, the guiding force of inculturation.
4. The principal agents of inculturation are the local church and the native people, not the missionaries, the experts, or the central authorities.
5. Inculturation embraces all aspects of church life, from theology to ethics, law, liturgy, catechesis, and spirituality.
6. Inculturation must criticize and reject aspects of culture that dehumanize human beings and thus goes hand in hand with Liberation* theologies.
7. Since culture is often bound up with religion, inculturation is often carried out as part of interreligious dialogue and pays special attention to popular religion.

Ideally, a self-conscious practice of inculturation seeks to keep in tension the promotion of diversity and pluralism and the preservation of the unity of faith by assessing its compatibility with the gospel and communion with the universal church. **See also CULTURE CLUSTER: CULTURAL STUDIES** and **CULTURE AND CHRISTIANITY; GOSPEL AND CULTURE CLUSTER.**

PETER C. PHAN

Inculturation of Christianity in the Greco-Roman World. The Christian message, originally based on Jewish apocalyptic* premises, was soon reexpressed in Hellenistic terms in both form and content, becoming accessible to the Greco-Roman world even as it challenged some of its aspects, as a few examples show.

Christianity initially spread in Mediterranean cities where the dominant Greco-Roman culture was omnipresent. The earliest formulations of the Jesus tradition already reflect this Hellenistic context. The saying "The eye is the lamp of the body" (Matt. 6:22–23; Luke 11:34–36) is related to the philosophical debate about sense perception and cognition; the closest analogy to the genre of Q* (as a collection of sayings) may be the "Principal Doctrines" of Epicurus, a philosophical catechism. The collections of Jesus' miracle stories have an epiphanic* function, like those of Hellenistic "divine men." The canonical Gospels may follow the genre of Greco-Roman biography. The complex role of inculturation as both accommodation and challenge to a culture becomes apparent when one asks, How did Hellenistic audiences subjected to Roman rule receive the message about Jesus as "Son* of God" and "Savior*" when the same terms were used for Augustus and when Caesar's birthday was celebrated as "glad tidings" (*euangelion*, gospel) for the world?

Paul's* apostleship to the Gentiles is a thoroughgoing inculturation. 1 Thessalonians draws on Cynic traditions in differentiating Paul's behavior from that of other missionaries (2:5–12) and alludes to Greek epitaphs in consoling the bereaved (4:13–18). The creed "Jesus died and rose" (4:14; cf. Rom. 10:9) uses familiar vocabulary for readers accustomed to savior gods who die and rise. Paul's extended debate with elite converts at Corinth adapts the Greco-Roman discourse form to pastoral purposes: 1 Cor 1–4 is an "appeal for concord," a subgenre of deliberative rhetoric; to glorify love*, 1 Cor 13 follows the model of Plato's speeches in *Symposium*; 2 Cor 11:1–12:10 is a mime-inspired "fool's speech." Paul's inculturation was not an accommodation to the values of Greco-Roman society, but a transformation of the concepts appropriated, in accordance with the paradoxical revelation of the "crucified Messiah." Thus Paul reinterpreted the political idea of "reconciliation*" (2 Cor 5:18–21).

Late-1st- to early-2nd-c. Christian literature shows an infiltration of Greek philosophical concepts that made Christianity more meaningful to Hellenistic elite: Middle Platonism* in Hebrews* and the Stoic vision of cosmic harmony in 1 Clement* 20. The Christian–Platonic synthesis of Clement* of Alexandria completed the transformation of the Jewish apocalyptic Jesus movement into a Hellenistic religion of the salvation* of the soul*. Fourth-century Christian art reflects the depth of inculturation: the Good Shepherd is represented as Hermes. **See also HELLENISTIC RELIGIOUS TRADITIONS AND CHRISTIANITY'S SELF-DEFINITION; POVERTY CLUSTER: AND THE EASTERN ORTHODOX CHURCH.** LAURENCE L. WELBORN

2) A Sampling of Contextual Views and Practices

Inculturation of Christianity in Africa: Central and Southern Africa. The general tendency among Western missionaries to Central and Southern Africa was to assume that European culture was Christian and that African culture and religion were demonic* and therefore should be dismissed. However, many African Christians wanted Christianity to take root in African culture and religion so that the gospel might be truly African. While the inculturation of music* and liturgy* has been relatively easy, rites of passage were the battleground where mission churches and indigenous churches confronted each other most strongly. For instance, all the mission churches of Malawi* struggled over the practice of initiation ceremonies for men and women – ceremonies highly valued in most cultures in Southern Africa. Thus in 1903 the Dutch Reformed Church Mission banned its members from taking part in traditional initiation ceremonies. By 1920 the missionaries realized that the local Christians, especially women, preferred to be suspended from church membership for a period in order to initiate their daughters and sons and be reconciled to the church afterward. Thus by the 1930s, most mission churches in Malawi decided to develop Christian versions of the initiation ceremonies, which are still practiced today. Similarly, among the Shona of Zimbabwe*, the major struggle has been over burial rituals (see Death, Christian Views of, Cluster: In Africa). Firstborn sons are bound by culture to bury their parents in a traditional way, something that African Christians did, even if they were temporarily excommunicated from the church. The result has been the Christianization of traditional funeral rites in the Roman Catholic Church. In South Africa, most mission churches have Christianized the traditional unveiling of tombstones because of its value in local traditions. ISABEL APAWO PHIRI

Inculturation of Christianity in Africa: Eastern Africa. Starting in the mid-19th c., European missionaries introduced and consolidated Christianity in the Eastern African region, according to the form in which it had been molded in their own countries. Since they largely ignored or sidelined the religious perceptions and sensibilities of the indigenous people, "missionary Christianity" has remained a sort of "second-layer" faith imposed on and parallel to indigenous beliefs and practices.

The question of inculturation* has become urgent since the 1960s. It concerns how to express Christianity in African cultural terms so that it speaks through local mythical*, symbolic*, and conceptual religious "language." This language for Christianity entails the importance of the spiritual universe, ritual, and human relationships through community, cooperation, and sharing.

Since ancestors* and spirits* play a significant role in Eastern African spirituality*, it is not surprising that they do so in Eastern African Christianity. Ever present and involved in the life of society, ancestors are the custodians of the people's moral traditions, entrusted to them by the Creator. They are responsible for the strength and life of the community.

All elements of creation are powers, "vital forces" (forces of life), mutually interdependent and supportive. The greatest vital force is the life of humanity, sustained by proper relationships. Ritual* activity is geared toward enhancing human life with the help of the ancestors. Rites of passage – birth, puberty, marriage*, old age, and death* – are extremely significant. Concepts drawn from ritual activities and applied to Jesus as healer, elder brother, and diviner form a new theological language of inculturation.

Situating Christianity in the socioreligious context of Eastern Africa began with evangelism* and its reception. In Eastern African Christianity, perceptions of religious mediation through ancestors and spirits refuse to die. Similarly, notions of evil* as powers (related to witchcraft*) are still very common. Thus whether secretly or openly, Christianity in Eastern African can be viewed as syncretistic*. It needs to recognize this syncretism and its ambivalence, although some want to view it as a form of inculturation*. **See also TANZANIA.** LAURENTI MAGESA

Inculturation of Christianity in Africa: Western Africa. "Inculturation," the incarnation* of the gospel in the context of living Christian communities, is fraught with tension. The gospel transforms every culture*, but its reception also empowers West Africans to live the good news in dialogue with their culture. Inculturation (not decorative *adaptation* of cultural patterns) challenges West African churches to undertake a vital reception of the gospel through new liturgies, catecheses, ethical practices, ministries, church structures, and theological formulations, which have nevertheless to be recognized as *"catholic,"* as expressions of the universal church. Fear of syncretism* results in superficial adaptations of deep African traditional psychoreligious practices, instead of enriching the religious treasury of humanity.

The Bible in West African languages is foundational for inculturation. Translations display the compatibility of the biblical and African worlds penetrated by and embodying revelation by the *same* God. Sermons and interpretations highlight the continuing relevance of the text present in peoples' lives.

Vernacular liturgies accompanied by gestures, songs, instrumentation, and new ritual texts exemplify the West African reception of Christianity. Experiences vary according to regions and Christian churches. Christian initiation* integrates the stages and rhetoric of traditional African initiation in Burkina* Faso; African* Religion's child-naming and marriage* ceremonies are integrated into Nigerian Catholicism; healing* rituals reflecting traditional rituals abound in all churches.

African* Instituted Churches (AICs) expand ministries and church structures. They create new rites tying together the Bible and West Africa, e.g. the ordaining of prophets and visionaries for the healing* ministry. AICs and the Charismatic* Movement integrate traditional West African mysticism* into Christianity. The experience of the descent of the Holy* Spirit into the elect, women and men, is displayed in ways similar to "possession" by West African spirits.

Systematic theological reflection focuses on methodology, family* and community ethics*, ecclesiology, and Christology*. The titles of Christ – Chief or King, Ancestor*, Master of Initiation, Liberator. and Healer – integrate West African traditions into Christianity.

ELOCHUKWU EUGENE UZUKWU, CSSP

Inculturation of Christianity in Asia. Christianity that was brought to Asia in the 16th c. was primarily Iberian in form, since mission in all of Asia was undertaken under the patronage* of Portugal* (and Spain* in the Philippines). For good and for ill, Christian mission was associated with Western imperialism and often perceived as its handmaiden. Later, other Western powers joined in the military conquest, commerce, and Christian mission in Asia: the Netherlands*, the UK, France*, and the USA (see United Kingdom; United States).

Even if the Christian faith was often identified with its Western form, many missionaries were aware of the difference between the gospel they were to preach and the Western civilization they carried with them. Early examples of those who promoted inculturation were the Syrian* (non-Chalcedonian) Orthodox missionaries to China* who in the 7th–8th c. attempted to express the Christian faith in Buddhist*, Confucianist*, and Daoist* terms. Thus they taught that Christianity is the "ever-true and unchanging Dao" itself; that Jesus established a "new teaching of nonassertion" (Daoist), taught "how to rule both families and kingdoms" (Confucianist), and took an oar in "the vessel of mercy" and "ascended to the Palace of Light" (Buddhist). Similarly, many 16th- to 17th-c. missionaries (mainly Jesuit) – such as Alessandro Valignano in Japan*, Matteo Ricci* in China, Roberto de Nobili* in India*, and Alexandre de Rhodes in Vietnam* – self-consciously sought to explain Christian beliefs and practices in terms understandable to the native peoples.

For its practitioners in the early 21st c., inculturation goes far beyond what it was for the early missionaries in Asia. **See also THE PRESENT CLUSTER: AND THE GOSPEL.**

PETER C. PHAN

Inculturation in Latin America and Elsewhere. See POPULAR CHRISTIANITY CLUSTER.

Indebtedness, the sense of monetary, social, or personal obligation that a person or group owes to another person or group for something received. Seneca, in "On Benefits," describes the concept of indebtedness as essential to the patronage system – a system of social reciprocity that characterized human relating during the Pax Romana. Yet with the Roman Empire and its patronage system, indebtedness was often a concept reflecting basic inequality, a relation between unequals. More generally, the concept of indebtedness is also central to the honor*/shame system. In the NT, this concept (expressed by the verb *opheilo* and the nouns derived from it) is frequently found, referring positively or negatively to a sense of indebtedness to God or to other people (as in the Lord's Prayer in Luke 11:4 and John 13:14, reciprocal foot-washing). Paul (especially in Romans) refers to it in order to encourage people in Christian communities to imagine themselves in relationships that emphasize a sense of mutuality and interdependence – what Filipinos might call "indebtedness of the heart" and Paul the "indebtedness of love" (Rom 13:8). More specifically, Paul uses this concept to express a mindset that acknowledges other people's talents, gifts, and contributions and thus one's indebtedness to this other person or group.

MONYA A. STUBBS

Independent Churches Worship. See CHARISMATIC AND PENTECOSTAL MOVEMENTS CLUSTER; EVANGELICALS/EVANGELICALISM CLUSTER; GOSPEL MUSIC; MEDIA AND CHRISTIANITY; MEDIA AND CHRISTIAN WORSHIP; PENTECOSTAL MOVEMENT; PENTECOSTAL WORSHIP; PRAISE AND WORSHIP.

Independent or Free Churches, churches that (1) were founded without government sponsorship (e.g. the Anabaptist churches); (2) were forced out of a relationship with a government (e.g. the denominations* of the Dissenters* after the English Restoration); (3) left one of the established churches (e.g. in the Netherlands*, Sweden*, and Norway*); (4) were indigenously instituted, independent of foreign missionary churches (see African Instituted Churches Cluster); (5) developed apart from the purview of any denomination (post-denominational churches, a widespread phenomenon at the beginning of the 21st c., sometimes arising from political situations. **See also CHARISMATIC AND PENTECOSTAL MOVEMENTS CLUSTER; CHINESE CONTEMPORARY INDEPENDENT AND HOUSE CHURCHES; HOUSE CHURCHES; WORD-FAITH MOVEMENT.**

Index Librorum Prohibitorum (List of prohibited books), issued by the Inquisition* in 1557, it prohibited Protestant books, among others. It was originally enforced by the Congregation of the Index and then by the Holy* Office. Since 1966 it no longer has the force of canon* law but retains moral force.

India, a country whose civilization has spanned several millennia, with the rare distinction of having welcomed the gospel during the time of the apostles. According to tradition, Thomas preached the gospel in Northwest India, landed (52) in Cranganore, Kerala (on the western coast of South India), and suffered martyrdom in Mylapore (the eastern coast, today part of Chennai, formerly Madras). His memory is alive, particularly in Kerala, where a group of Christians call themselves "Thomas Christians" and follow the Syriac tradition and liturgy; they are members of the Malankara* Orthodox Syrian Church, which has maintained a relationship with Syrian* Orthodox churches; their bishops were sent from Chaldea (Iran* and Iraq*). In addition, in 345 Thomas of Cana (Kanai) led a group of Assyrian* Christians from Syro-Mesopotamia to Kerala (India), where their Knanaya Christian descendants still survive (see History of Christianity Cluster: In the Middle East: Syriac Christianity).

Although the Christian tradition in India is ancient, Christians there have remained numerically a "little flock." According to the Indian census of 2001, Christians constitute just 2.3% of the population, in contrast to Hindus, who make up the overwhelming majority (80.5%), and Muslims (13.4%.). In absolute terms, however, the number of Indian Christians is significant: a total of about 28 million people (more than twice as many according to nongovernmental sources), a larger number of Christians than in many traditionally Christian countries of the West.

Christians are not uniformly spread throughout the country; they are concentrated in certain pockets, with a sprinkling of Christians elsewhere. There is a strong concentration of Christians in the southern states of India (Tamil Nadu, Kerala, Karnataka, Andhra Pradesh, and Goa), in the eastern parts, among the Adivasis* ("original dwellers of the land," also called "tribals"; see Tribalism and Christianity), and in the northeastern parts, among the Adivasis of Mongoloid origin. In the sparsely populated states of Nagaland, Mizoram, and Meghalaya, the majority of people are Christians. A sizable majority of Indian Christians are Adivasis and Dalits* (formerly known as "untouchables"), who embraced Christianity through mass conversion (especially in the 19th and early 20th c.).

Practically every Christian denomination is represented in India. Roman Catholics, Orthodox, Lutherans, Baptists, and Anglicans have a longer history than do those of other denominations. However, it would be incorrect to identify Indian Christianity with the history of the various denominations. Indian Christianity is a river with its own route into which the streams of the histories of the various denominations flow. Their active involvement in mission led the various churches to set aside the inherited Western denominational divisions and collaborate in the work of the gospel. For example, historical divisions among Christian churches are much less visible in India than elsewhere, as was demonstrated by a highly significant event with global ecumenical implications. The Church of South* India (CSI) was formed in 1947 as a single communion comprising Episcopal and non-Episcopal churches. It was the culmination of persistent efforts on the part of outstanding church leaders and long negotiations. The Church of North* India (CNI) was formed (1970) on the same basis. This unique union of churches is a challenge to a divided Christianity and has served as an inspiration for church union in other parts of the world.

The Spread of Christianity. We have scant information about the period between apostolic times and the modern missionary era (from the 16th c.), e.g. the arrival of Franciscan* friars, including John of Montecorvino, who spent some months (1291–92) in Mylapore before setting sail to Khan Balik (Beijing), China*.

The expansion of Christianity in India really started with Portuguese traders, who brought missionaries with them to India and eventually came to hold political power (see Portuguese Explorations, Conquests, and Missions). These missionaries established themselves in Goa, which would become the hub of Christianity for the whole of India and East Asia. Francis Xavier*, SJ, came to India in 1542 and worked tirelessly in the southern coastland to convert and baptize its fishing peoples. The Jesuit* order established its mission center in Madurai (Madurai Mission), and the well-known Italian missionary Roberto de Nobili*, a nephew of Cardinal Bellarmine, did his missionary work in and around that city. The caste* system was already a crucial issue in Indian Christianity. Fearing that any interference with the system might jeopardize their missions, the missionaries followed a strategy of division of labor: some became missionaries exclusively for members of the low castes and outcastes, and others, like Roberto de Nobili, worked among the Brahmins and members of the upper castes. The outcome of this strategy is apparent to this day in the caste conflicts among Christians in the southern states.

With the suppression of the Society of Jesus (1773), missionaries from other religious orders came in large numbers. The Carmelites* began their missionary involvement in Kerala, whereas the Paris Foreign Missionaries, with Pondicherry as their headquarters, expanded their work in Tamilnadu, Andhra Pradesh, and neighboring regions. One of the issues that plagued the Indian Church was the patronage rights (Padroado*) retained by the Portuguese crown by which they exercised ecclesiastical jurisdiction over the churches in India. Noting that the missionary work was attuned to Portuguese national interests, Rome attempted to control the affairs of the Catholic Church through its newly established Congregatio de Propaganda* Fide (Congregation for the Propagation of Faith, 1622). The missionaries of Padroado and those from the Propaganda Fide were locked in conflicts and feuds, resulting in many scandalous clashes. Some villages today have two adjacent churches: one that had been under Padroado jurisdiction and the other that had been under Propaganda Fide. The Roman Catholic mission could not make much headway during the 17th and 18th c. owing to a lack of missionary personnel and, above all, to the internal conflict of jurisdiction between the Portuguese Padroado missionaries and the Rome-appointed apostolic vicars and priests working in these territories.

In the northern parts of the country, the earliest Christian mission was associated with the Mogul emperor Akbar. He was deeply interested in understanding religions and concerned about religious harmony. Such was his openness that he had the Virgin Mary* and angels* painted on his palace walls. His eagerness to learn more about Christianity led him to invite Jesuit missionaries from Goa to his court, though the missionaries were disappointed because they had entertained false hopes of converting the emperor.

While the Catholic mission was in a state of confusion, following Portuguese domination, the Protestants began their mission. The German missionary Bartholomäus Ziegenbalg brought Protestant Christianity into the Danish colony of Tranquebar, Tamilnadu (1706). By then the British East India Company was politically entrenched and did not allow missionaries, lest its commercial and political interests be adversely affected. So Ziegenbalg's and his companion Plütschau's missionary work took the form of translating the Bible for the first time into an Indian language, Tamil. This great missionary learned Tamil, to a considerable degree, through dialogue with Hindus. More than a century later, another Danish colony, Serampore in West Bengal, became the center of mission work for Baptist missionaries. Best known among them was William Carey, whose contributions covered many areas; chief among these was his involvement in higher education and translation of the Bible into several Eastern Indian languages.

When the charter of the East India Company was up for renewal (1813), the Evangelicals of England spearheaded by Charles Grant and Wilberforce* wanted a "missionary clause" to be included that would permit the entry of missionaries into India. After heated debate in the British Parliament, the clause was approved; missionaries of different denominations set sail to India and established mission centers, especially in Southern India. Missionaries from the London Mission Society, the SPCK* (Society for Propagating Christian Knowledge), and other organizations worked side by side. As a result of the Protestant and Roman Catholic efforts, there was mass conversion of outcastes (Dalits) and people from the lower castes. During the same period, Baptist and other Protestant groups established mission centers in Northeast India, working with Adivasi groups there and in the East. The mission work also challenged traditional practices such as the live cremation of a widow on her husband's funeral pyre (*sati*), child marriage, and denial of remarriage to widows, and aided in enacting new legislation by the colonial government to reform these traditions.

During this conversion work, there was a fresh realization of the "civilizing mission" of Christianity. This eventually led to the institution-building phase in Indian Christianity. Beginning in the mid-19th c., numerous educational institutions from the primary level to colleges, medical services offered by village dispensaries and modern urban hospitals, and social and economic development activities were established. These institutions constitute the visible face of Indian Christianity throughout the country. An evolution of the self-understanding of Christian educational institutions has taken place. At first, they were viewed as a means of converting members of the upper castes and classes; during the post-independence period, they were viewed as contributing to nation building; and today educational involvement is a means of empowering the most powerless groups, such as the Adivasis and the Dalits. It is noteworthy that literacy among Christians, especially among Christian women, is strikingly higher than the national average. Christian educational institutions are known for their excellence and high quality of education.

This tradition was set by great missionaries like W. Miller of Madras Christian College and C. F. Andrews of Stephen's College, Delhi. The challenge facing Christian higher education is how to reconcile the twofold commitment to the education of the poor and the maintenance of high standards.

Hindu–Christian Relationship. During the early centuries of Christianity in India, the Thomas Christians accommodated themselves to the Hindu environment and have continued to maintain many Hindu customs and traditions. In other parts of the country, a deep spiritual affinity between Hindus and Christians is manifest, especially during mutual visits to pilgrimage centers or local religious festivals. Popular* Christianity in India has adopted many elements of Hindu symbolism and modes of religious worship.

The relationship with Hindus was strained during the time of the Portuguese mission, which condemned the Hindu practices and instituted the infamous Goan inquisition. Another period of conflict with Hindus occurred in the 19th c., at the beginning of the Indian war of independence (1857). Hindu and Muslim soldiers revolted against British authorities for attempting to convert them and for stealthily introducing Bibles into the barracks. At the time of the revolt, Christians were found on the side of the British, which provided a motive for inflicting violence on Christian communities. Christians were killed in large numbers in North India. These events are to be viewed against the backdrop of growing animosity of Hindus toward Christians; Hindus suspected that the colonial government and its officials were undermining Hinduism by joining forces with the missionaries in swelling the Christian ranks and that the converts or "apostates" (in the Hindu perception) were collaborating with the missionaries. The missionary support of state policy such as banning *sati* and the introduction of the Bible in English classes in government schools seemed to confirm the Hindus' suspicion. Added to this was the passing of the Caste Disabilities Removal Act of 1850, which gave the converts the right of succession as in the Hindu tradition. Furthermore, there was, rightly or wrongly, a general perception that the colonial government and its officers were supportive of Christians and missionaries. It is an irony of history that anti-Christian sentiments contributed to the forging of unity among Hindus across caste, religion, and language (see Colonialism and Imperialism and Christian Theology).

Ambiguity has characterized Hindu–Christian relations since the mid-19th c. There was vehement opposition to the Christian mission (including bitter criticism by Gandhi), especially to conversion efforts. Yet movements like the Brahmo Samaj in Bengal saw Christianity as a great resource for the renewal of Indian society and culture, and the stalwarts of this influential association, Rammohun Roy, Keshub Chunder Sen, and others, were attracted by the Christian message. Several missionaries, influenced by Orientalists who brought the riches of Indian culture and tradition to the West, began to cultivate a positive attitude toward Hinduism and sought to incorporate some of its traditions and customs into Christianity.

By the early 21st c., opposition to Christianity had grown, and the Brahmo Samaj legacy of an intellectual rapprochement between Hindus and Christians had waned. This is not to deny the peaceful coexistence of Hindus and Christians in daily life. The opposition to Christianity and Christian mission might be explained by the steady rise of Hindu militancy, starting in the 1920s with the founding of Hindu Mahasabha, and the emergence of Hindu right-wing politics represented by the Bharatiya Janata Party. Since the late 20th c., sporadic attacks against Christian ministers and institutions in the northern parts of the country have increased.

Underlying the general Hindu attitude toward Christians, at every level and at all times, is the fact that Christianity is alien to the Indian nation and culture, and it expanded in the country with the support of the colonizers. Another issue is conversion*. Although the Constitution of India ensures religious freedom, there is suspicion that Christians use numerous methods to entice the uneducated and rank and file of the poor classes to Christianity. Many Hindus make an argument similar to Gandhi's: conversion infringes on the freedom of the masses. This argument fails to note that the poor have their own agency, and it is they who decide to convert to one religious group or the other (see Hinduism and Christianity Cluster).

Development of Indigenous Christianity. Obviously India has been influenced by the West, and Christianity has been an important channel of influence, as the numerous educational institutions of Western education run by the churches indicate. But Indian Christianity itself did not remain Western. During the period of Roman Catholic and Protestant missions, the missionaries dominated the affairs of the churches. Many missionaries were convinced that indigenous people were not capable of and not yet ready for ordination as ministers. Yet local catechists, teachers, "Bible women", and others were crucial for the expansion of Christianity in India, and without these men and women, missionaries could not have reached out to the people. The story of these indigenous ministers of the gospel is yet to be written. In spite of this general climate, the ordination, amid stiff resistance, of Aaron, a Lutheran of India, in 1733 foreshadowed things to come. In the Roman Catholic Church, the emergence of an indigenous movement took much longer. The trend toward ordaining indigenous priests and bishops became more pronounced only in the late 19th and early 20th c., particularly under the impetus of Pope Leo* XIII.

The dependence of churches on foreign missionaries continued throughout the 19th c. and until the mid-20th c. However, even in the early 20th c., indigenous people began questioning the control missionaries exercised on Indian Christianity by occupying leadership positions and controlling finances. A very powerful voice for autonomy was that of Bishop V. S. Azariah, who forcefully raised this point at the World Missionary Conference in Edinburgh* (1910). The movement toward autonomy led Indians to take over leadership of the churches and to shape the future of Christianity there. It is important to note that this movement toward autonomy was triggered by the Indian national struggle for independence. The political struggle had repercussions for the transformation of churches into indigenous ones.

With national independence (1947), the number of Western missionaries declined rapidly. Any missionaries that remain today are exceptions. A new development has taken place: Indians from regions with a strong Christian presence, especially in the south, go to other parts of India to serve as missionaries. Indian missionaries today even serve in Africa, Latin America, and other parts of the world. While there were only two indigenous Roman Catholic religious orders in the 19th c. (Carmelites of Immaculate Mary and the Society of St. Francis Xavier, or "Pillar Fathers"), the 20th c. witnessed the emergence of numerous indigenous congregations in response to local needs.

Christianity and Indian Culture. In spite of opposition from many missionaries and conservative local Christians, indigenization sought to adapt Christianity to the Indian religious ethos and its way of thinking and worshipping. This kind of adaptation was even stronger in the Roman Catholic Church, especially after Vatican* II. More recently, cultural adaptation efforts have raised some critical issues (see Inculturation Cluster). First, it is impossible to define Indian culture as a homogenous reality. Although there is an increasing realization that Indian culture is composite, made up of many elements from different regional, linguistic, and ethnic groups (e.g. Aryans, Dravidians, people of Mongolian ancestry), adaptation or cultural contextualization* was typically thought of in terms of *the* dominant Brahminical culture. A similar adaptation took place theologically, by employing Brahminical religious concepts to interpret various aspects of Christianity. Dalits and the Adivasis, who constitute the majority of Indian Christians, strongly oppose this type of indigenization of the dominant culture. Dalit Christians, struggling against oppression by the upper castes (including in the churches), are betrayed by the adoption of symbols from dominant Brahminical Hindu culture. Indian Adivasis seem to be less inclined to accept any such adaptation, and they retain to large extent the Western form of Christianity. This is particularly true of the Adivasis of Northeast India, including the Nagas and Mizos.

Indian Nation and Christianity. Whereas in most parts of Asia there are official or state-sponsored religions, in India the constitution ensures religious freedom and equality for all religions, regardless of their numbers. Christians also enjoy protection under the law as minorities, and they are given the right to run educational and other charitable institutions. Nevertheless, in spite of a history of tolerance within India, the ideology and praxis of the religiously inspired right-wing Bharatya Janata Party and Hindu militant movements like Rashtriya Swayasevak Sangh have created a sense of alienation and insecurity among Christians.

Along with most other Indians, Christians viewed the British government as beneficial to the country. However, many Christians joined the struggle for full independence, including some prominent members of Congress (Kalicharan Banerjee, J. C. Kumarappa, S. K. George, and the Joseph brothers).

At the time of independence, there was serious apprehension about the future of Christianity. Christian leaders were unsure of the kind of treatment Christians would receive from the majority community of Hindus once the British were no longer ruling. One suggestion for ensuring the safety of Christians as a minority was to create a separate electorate for Christians. By choosing their own representatives, they could be sure their voice would be represented politically, but the British had already rejected this idea of separate electorates for minorities like Christians and Muslims. The idea was vehemently opposed by Gandhi and other national leaders, not to mention by many Christians themselves. In the constituent assembly that framed the present-day constitution, Christians, trusting in the fairness of the majority community, gave up any such claim to a separate electorate, a move that was highly admired for its spirit of openness.

The contribution of Christianity to the nation and its development spans many and diverse areas. Because missionaries sought to translate the Christian Scriptures into native languages, they were able to make significant contributions to the grammar and literature of Sanskrit, Tamil, and other Indian languages, beginning as early as the 17th c. (see Indian Literature, the Bible, and Christianity). Some Christian missionaries served as mediators by transmitting to the West some of the riches of Indian culture and civilization, but many projected a distorted picture of India and its culture – something resented by many Hindus even today.

Christianity did contribute to the creation of new social and egalitarian thought in India. In an atmosphere that excluded the poor and those of the lower castes from knowledge, because members of the upper castes and classes thought that education was their privilege, Christians introduced the idea that education was everyone's right, irrespective of a person's social and economic conditions; thus schools for those in the lower castes and for women were started by Indian social reformers like Jyotirao Phule. Christians contributed to the emergence of the idea of equality of all before the law. In particular, Christian missionaries defended the cause of the Adivasis, protected them from rapacious exploiters, were involved in the struggle for liberation of the oppressed castes – e.g. in the princely state of Travancore in South India – and defended workers from exploitation by colonial and local landowners.

Dalit and Adivasi Christians. Christians of Dalit origin and Adivasis make up the overwhelming majority of Indian Christians. Dalit Christians suffer discrimination both in the church and in society. Within the church, discrimination extends from segregated seating for Dalits to refusal to accept them as equal partners in the management of it affairs. One of the most serious problems encountered by Dalit Christians is that they are not eligible, according to current legislation, to receive those benefits protecting non-Christian Dalits from discrimination, even though Christian Dalits suffer the same kind of discrimination, political powerlessness, and economic deprivation as others. The reason cited is that Christianity does not recognize caste, which is something characteristic of Hinduism. Once Dalits are converted to Christianity, so goes the argument, they lose their caste status and cannot claim the constitutional provisions that favor Dalits.

Dalits have an ambiguous relationship with Christianity. Christianity contributed to their social uplift through education, medical care, and other developmental and social activities. But Dalit Christians are treated as second-class citizens in most churches and are prevented by upper-caste Christians from exercising their agency in almost all of the churches in India. In many instances, Christian mission has created a new sense of dignity and self-confidence for the Dalits. But there is also the widespread view that Christianity dampened their political involvement, in comparison with Hindu Dalits. Dalits are developing their own theology (see Dalit Theology).

Christianity has also empowered Adivasis in several ways, especially through education and many social and developmental initiatives, resulting in greater self-confidence. Christianity is so deeply rooted among some Adivasis, like the Nagas, that it has become part of their self-identity. But from the perspective of some sections of the Indian population, Christianity has alienated the Adivasis from their culture and has imposed Western culture on them. Moreover, the insurgency among the Adivasis* of Northeast India and the emergence of secessionist tendencies are attributed to the influence of Christianity. The relationship of other Christian churches to Christian Adivasis is also ambiguous. **See also NORTH INDIA, CHURCH OF; SOUTH INDIA, CHURCH OF.**

Statistics: Population (2001): 1.2 billion. Hindu, 80.5%; Muslim, 13.4%; Christian, 2.3% (c28 million); Sikh, 1.9%; other, 1.8%. (Based on the 2001 census. The percentage of Christians given in the *World Christian Encyclopedia*, 2001, is 6.2% (62 million); apparently the discrepancy exists because the Dalits and Adivasis were underrepresented in the census.)

FELIX WILFRED

Indian Christian Theologies. Although the origins of Christianity in India, according to tradition, date back to the apostle Thomas*, there is little to say about Indian Christian theologies of apostolic times. This is because the ancient Indian Church of Thomas Christians (Malankara* Orthodox Syrian Church), in the state of Kerala on the west coast of South India, was dependent on Middle Eastern churches for theology, worship practices, and even their bishops. The theology from that time can only be glimpsed today in the liturgical tradition of Thomas Christians. Undoubtedly, their theology had a Nestorian* influence, i.e. the belief that the human Jesus was taken hold of by the Logos* to become lord and creator of the universe: Jesus' humanity and divinity were joined by will, not by nature, although Jesus and the Logos become one person, not two. Their liturgical books were in East Syrian and contained not only the names of Nestorius*, Theodore*, and others, but Nestorian formulas as well. This theological orientation did not change until the 20th c.

The missionary era in India began with the arrival of Vasco da Gama on the western coast of India (1492). The missionaries taught the scholastic* theology that they had learned in their native country. There were laudable exceptions, such as Stephen Thomas, Ernest Hanxleden (popularly known as Arnos Padri), the Carmelite* priest Paulinus of St. Bartholomew (1748–1806), and most exceptionally, the Italian missionary Roberto de Nobili* (1577–1656). Nobili followed an apologetic method of trying to prove the truth of the Christian message to Hindu Brahmins, while allowing his Hindu interlocutors to expound their doctrines; but Nobili also pioneered a method of adaptation to Hindu customs and traditions, which caused a confrontation with Rome. His greatest contribution to Indian theology was his praxis of inculturation*, or contextualization*, which continues to be a source of inspiration for many forms of Indian theologies.

De Nobili's way of life as a Christian *sannyasi* (ascetic*) – closely resembling that of a Hindu *sannyasi* – fully embodied his theology of inculturation. His belief was that if Greco-Roman modes of thought were initially incorporated into Christian thought and praxis, the same must be true of Indian tradition. Thus he tried to give a Christian theological interpretation of Hindu customs and traditions. His praxis of dialogue* led to the development of some Indian Christian theological vocabulary. On the Protestant side, Bartholomäus Ziegenbalg (1683–1719), in his life and missionary work at the Danish colony of Tranquebar, Tamilnadu, showed great sympathy toward Hinduism, as is evidenced in his works, *Description of Malabar Books* and *The Genealogy of Malabar Gods*.

These seeds of a new Hindu–Christian theological orientation began to bear fruit (late 19th c.) when a Brahmin convert to Christianity, Brahmobahdhav Upadyaya (1861–1907), carried forward this task. He was a pioneer in relating Christian faith with the culture, philosophy, and genius of India. Although Upadyaya did not create any theological system, his developments of Hindu–Christian concepts influenced subsequent theologians, who interpreted Christianity through *advaita*, or nondualism, in which God* and soul* are viewed neither as one nor as two distinct entities. The same is true of the relationship between God and nature or the world. The Christian *ashram* movement has further developed the *advaitic* interpretation of Christianity. Bede Griffiths, an English Benedictine monk associated with the Saccidananda Ashram in Thaneerpalli, in the center of Tamilnadu, developed many theological insights through the *advaitic* experience and interpretation of the gospel. The encounter with Hinduism, in this way, led also to a development of an Indian theology of religions. This theology passed through various stages, starting from a theory that Christianity is the "crown of Hinduism," to the recognition of revelation in other religious traditions ("the unknown Christ of Hinduism") and the working of God's Spirit and plan of salvation through the symbolism and sacramentality in these religions.

Such Christian efforts parallel the Hindu attempt to interpret Christianity. This is something quite unique, and it enlarges the horizon of Christian theology as well as its methodology. Hindu social reformers like Rammohun Roy (1772–1833) focused on the significance of Jesus Christ and his "ethical precepts"; Keshub Chandra Sen, another towering intellectual figure of 19th-c. Bengal, saw in Jesus a true Asian and affirmed the importance of recovering the original Asian Jesus from the accretions and distortions that have taken place over two millennia. Sen viewed Jesus Christ from an "evolutionary*" perspective and saw the destiny of every human being and the whole universe to become the Christ, something the Western theologian Teilhard* de Chardin would later call "Christification." Sen interpreted the mystery of the Holy Trinity* through the Hindu concept of *sat-cit-ananda*.

A creative movement of Indian Christian theologies is represented by the "Rethinking Christianity in India" group, including P. Chenchiah, V. Chakkarai, and A. J. Appasamy. Chenchiah (1886–1959), a convert from Hinduism, attributed to the Indian scriptures a role similar to the OT with respect to the NT. He saw in Jesus the birth of a new creation, and those who are joined with him are on the move toward the Kingdom* of God, being fashioned by the creative energy of the Spirit*, or *shakti*. In this interpretation, he was greatly influenced by the modern evolutionary Hindu thinker Sri Aurobindo. Chakkarai (1880–1958) developed an understanding of Jesus through the key Hindu concept of *avatar* (descent of God) and showed how, unlike Hindu avatars, the avatar Jesus is not a momentary intervention of the Divine, but a permanent feature in the relationship of the Divine to human beings. For his part, A. J. Appasamy interprets Christianity as a way of *bhakti*, or personal devotion of love and surrender. He draws inspiration from the great medieval Hindu theologian Ramanuja, who systematically developed the concept of *bhakti*.

Involvement with the sociopolitical realities of the country has also been important for developing Indian theologies. In the post-independence period, under the influence of general social ferment, theologies of nation building emerged, followed by a theology of development. These theologies explored the relationship between humanization, salvation*, and liberation*. An Indian theology of liberation emerged from the unique experience of oppression in the nation, was stimulated by secular movements for liberation and peoples' struggles throughout the country, and drew on many sources: the liberative thoughts, narratives, and symbols in Indian religious traditions, peoples' movements, and secular ideologies. M. M. Thomas* among Protestants, and Sebastian Kappen, Samuel Rayan, and Soares-Prabhu among Catholics, were outstanding representatives of Indian Liberation theology. In short, there have emerged two broad streams of Indian theology: one with the religiocultural heritage of India as the interpretative key; the other with the sociopolitical condition of the country as the perspective from which the gospel message is to be read. The more recent trend of Indian contextual theology has attempted to merge these two streams.

The most significant development in recent decades is the emergence of Dalit* theology, based on the experience of negativity, brokenness, and oppression suffered by the Dalits (so-called untouchables) owing to the ideology* of the pollution of purity, a caste-based social hierarchy, the traditional Indian semifeudal system, and exploitation through the neoliberal economy. (Dalits constitute the majority of Indian Christians, although the churches are still controlled by middle- and upper-caste Christians.) Immediacy, concreteness, and radicalism characterize the Dalit theology, which is critical of futile theoretical discussion and theological narcissism, and is suspicious of Indian theology based on the classical Hindu worldview and concepts. In the Hindu religious justification of caste, Dalits see the root of their oppression and therefore reject any Indian Christian theology that accommodates Brahminical tradition (as those just mentioned do). The Dalits' theological critique of caste draws inspiration from Jesus' attitude toward purity and pollution, his suffering, humiliation, and death outside the gates of the city.

Another major group of Indian Christians are the Adivasis*, or "tribals," concentrated in the east and northeastern parts of the country. An "Indian Tribal theology" is developing, with deep roots in their slighted and neglected traditional cultures. The Adivasis, the "original dwellers of the land," are alienated from their lands and are therefore undergoing an identity crisis. They are caught up in a situation of armed struggles in the midst of political convulsions and cultural crises caused by modernity and globalization that may completely destabilize them. Their engagement with the Christian message has resulted in fresh "tribal theologies" that can inspire other forms of theology developing in India.

An Indian Feminist theology is struggling to emerge, countering patriarchy colored by the reality of caste and traditional cultural factors, and dealing in particular with the issues of dowry, *sati*, rape, domestic violence, and female feticide, as well as with the social and cultural constructs of the feminine in India. Pandita Ramabhai (1858–1922) converted to Christianity and fought against patriarchy* in both Hinduism and Christianity. Her legacy as a pioneer in the liberation of Indian women is alive in Indian Feminist theology. Feminist theologians are also critical of the Indian churches, in which discrimination against women persists. The distinct strident voice of criticism from Dalit feminists, victims of gender discrimination compounded by caste and economic deprivation, has posed many challenges to developing Indian theologies. FELIX WILFRED

Indian Literature, the Bible, and Christianity. A highly romanticized legend portrays Jesus receiving wisdom in India. Yet, although this Hindu chronicle, *Bhavishya Purana,* contains a reference to Christianity in 8th-c. India, it is viewed as a 19th-c. interpolation. The first authentic Christian record can be found in Tarisapalli copper plates (849, Malayalam language) in Kerala. Pope Gregory XV's 1623 permission granted to Roberto de Nobili* to dress in Brahmin's robes anticipated a synergetic relationship between Christianity and non-Judaic religions and cultures.

The Bible mediated between Christianity and Indian literatures. The missionary aim to make the Bible available in Indian languages led to revolutionary growth of literature in all Indian languages, through the preparation of grammar books and dictionaries. De Nobili learned Sanskrit and Tamil; so did Constanzo Beschi (1680–1747), whose Christian poems became Tamil classics. Beschi Indianized Christian figures, giving them the dress and weapons of Hindu gods and combining concepts like *karma* with divine decree and original sin*, rebirth of an avatar with Christ's second* coming. Jerome Xavier translated or wrote Christian texts in Persian, Urdu, and Arabic; J. S. Thomas Stephens in Kokkani and Marathi; William Carey in Bengali, Sanskrit, Oriya, Marathi, and Hindi; and John Hanxleden in Malalayam. Pandita Ramabai (1858–1922, a woman advocating the education of women) translated the Bible from Hebrew and Greek into Marathi. The Bible is now available in 50 Indian languages (it was first translated into Tamil, 1726).

Thomas Ramban and a disciple, who described St. Thomas's coming to Malabar (c52) in *The Ramban Song* (*Thooma Parvam* in Tamil, 1601), were the first Indologists; their two-way translations initiated comparative literary and religious studies. Eighteen-century *bhakti* (devotional) literature presented Christ as a figure of divine manifestation, just like the avatars of the larger Hindu traditions, and compared the Christian Trinity and the Hindu *trimurti*.

In the 18th and 19th c., Christianity became a catalyst for social reform, in part through its development of literature in different languages, e.g. by writing in Roman script the (primarily oral) languages, thus Christianizing local literary traditions. Ramkrishna Paramahamsa's experiments with multireligious mysticism* integrated religions found in the writings of Brahmo Samaj (and the Bengal Renaissance), Raja Rammohun Roy, Keshub Chander Sen, Brahmabandhab Upandhyay, Sri Aurobindo, and Gandhi. Sadhu Sunder Singh's *With and Without Christ* is well known for combining Christian and Indian religious practices. In the 20th c., Indian English, Hindi, and Marathi fiction presents a more realistic picture of Christian life. Christianity has been most influential in the revolutionary development of Dalit* literature in all Indian languages. SUNANDA MONGIA

Indigenization. See INCULTURATION CLUSTER.

Indonesia, the fourth most populous country in the world (after China, India, and the USA). Of its 225 million citizens (2007), 88% are Muslims, but it has a strong Christian minority, 9% (six-tenths Protestants, four-tenths Roman Catholics). Christians are found mostly in the "outer islands," with only 3% in the central island of Java. A protected and somewhat privileged group during the colonial period, Christians were able to establish a strong community in the independent Republic of Indonesia starting in 1945 owing to better educational facilities. Since the 1990s, various administrations have allowed a stronger Muslim influence in public life, a source of some increased tension between Muslims and Christians.

Some have speculated about early Persian Assyrian* Christians (commonly called "Nestorians*") in the archipelago. But the only firm facts about Christianity date from the arrival of the Portuguese in Malacca (1511) and the Moluccas (Ternate, 1522). The Portuguese came for the spice trade, and they found that the local dynasties had converted to Islam only some 50 years earlier. They started the conversion of some local communities, leading to a mosaic of Christian and Muslim villages in the Moluccas (see Portuguese Explorations, Conquests, and Missions). When the Dutch took over the Portuguese trading factories (after 1605), the small Christian communities of the Moluccas became Protestant. Under the Dutch East India Company (1598–1800), most efforts to spread Christianity were stopped. Only after 1830, Protestant missionary societies started organized work in the outer islands with remarkable success in restricted regions. In the 1830s, the conversion of most people of the Minahasa (North Sulawesi) took place in combination with a very strong colonial presence that drastically changed the local economy through the forced cultivation of coffee. A 1859 agreement with Portugal brought East Flores and parts of West Timor under Dutch colonial rule, and subsequently Catholic priests started missionary work in Flores and West Timor. In the 1860s, a successful campaign of the German Rhenish Mission (Ludwig Nommensen) was begun in Batakland, North Sumatra, resulting in the largest Lutheran Church of the country.

During Dutch colonial rule, many inland regions of the outer islands were occupied in 1900–10 through campaigns labeled "wars of pacification." The Dutch preferred Christianization of the inland and mountainous regions, as well as on islands where the coastal areas had accepted Islam for centuries. This resulted in a strong Christian presence after 1910 in inland South and Central Sulawesi (various Toraja tribes), where the coastal region had accepted Islam since 1605. Inland regions of Flores, Timor, and Sumba accepted Christianity as a majority religion during this period. The Christian presence also became strong in the easternmost island of West New Guinea or West Papua.

To bring an end to headhunting and rituals in which large groups had sexual intercourse with women and spread venereal diseases, men and women were ordered to leave the traditional longhouses and live in new villages organized around a school with a teacher from other islands, a church, and small family houses. The colonial government prevented "double mission," and therefore West Papua was divided into a northern Protestant region and a southern Catholic one. Four Indonesian provinces (out of 31) have a Christian majority with a strong political influence: East Nusa Tenggara, 3.8 million (M) (88% Christians); Papua, 2.2 M (76% Christians); North Sulawesi, 2 M (67% Christians); and Maluku, 1.2 M (50% Christians).

In the last year of the "Pacific War" (the Japanese occupation of the archipelago during World War II), a committee for the preparation of Indonesian independence debated the status of the new independent Republic. Several Muslims proposed an Islamic state, but the threat of Christian secession in the eastern islands necessitated the *pancasila* (five pillar) compromise: a state ideology based on five pillars of belief in one God, democracy, nationalism, humanism, and social justice. During the war of independence against the Dutch colonial army (1945–49), the strong Christian presence in the guerrilla struggle (with a large number of Christians earlier trained in the colonial army) was a good start toward Christian participation in nation building in the following decades.

Protestant missionaries started to establish independent regional churches in the early 1930s, while the Indonesian Catholic hierarchy was formally instituted in 1960. In reality, however, expatriate missionaries still dominated much of the Christian churches until mid-1960s when a double movement of independence and new relations took place. There was then an infusion of money in the form of developmental aid, in which the churches played a major role until the mid-1980s. But for religious activities outside theological education, most churches were self-reliant owing to the improvement of the economy in the 1970s under the harsh and increasingly corrupt regime of General Suharto (1966–98) that took place after the economic decline under the first president, the strongly nationalist but chaotic and corrupt Sukarno (1945–67).

Although Christians lost many of the privileges they enjoyed during the colonial period, after 1945 they nonetheless continued to oversee many educational institutions, hospitals, and activities for social welfare and thus exercised a strong influence in society. They were and are strongly present in the media*, from newspapers to radio and television. The strongly anti-Communist policy of General Suharto after the 1965 coup (a first step toward the removal of President Sukarno) required everyone to be a member of one of five global religions (Islam*, Hinduism*, Buddhism*, Protestantism, or Roman Catholicism), and this brought many Muslims to Christianity, especially on the major island of Java, where Christians are now about 3% of the population. Christian–Muslim relations became more tense, however, as a result of this success of Christianity, especially since 1990.

Both sides feel threatened. Christians fear that the growing application of *shari'a* Islamic law (as in the westernmost province of Aceh and several other districts) will restrict their religious freedom and make it very difficult to build new churches, schools, and hospitals. However, hard-line Muslims spread the fear of *Kristenisasi,* the ongoing efforts of Christians to seek adherents among Muslims. From a global perspective, Indonesia seems to be the single example of a dominant Muslim society in which a considerable number of people have embraced Christianity.

Regional ethnic and cultural differences are very important in Indonesia, and most classical Protestant churches have an ethnic identity. The great Lutheran Batak* Church is found in all major towns of the country. It serves Batak people who migrated from Sumatra to other parts of the archipelago. Many other churches, however, encourage their members to join the "local" Protestant churches that are members of the Union of Protestant Churches.

Chinese Christians are a case apart in Indonesia: they have established Protestant churches of their own, although the language used in most of them is not Chinese but modern standard Indonesian. In the Catholic Church, Chinese were not given the privilege of ethnic cultural expression as other ethnic groups, such as the Flores, Dayak or Batak Catholics, were. Starting in the late 19th c., Batak Christians, wishing to take matters in their own hands, became more independent of foreign missionaries. In the towns of Java, they make up c20–30% of the Christians.

Unlike the Indian, Japanese, and Chinese Christian communities, Indonesia has not produced internationally known theologians. This may be the result of the Indonesians' modest character. Similarly it has been said that Indonesian Muslims, whose numbers are larger than in any other country in the world, have never taken the lead. Nationally the best known Christian thinker was the gifted architect, novelist, political activist, and Catholic priest Yusuf Bilyarta Mangunwijaya (1929–99).

Women have prominent positions in Indonesian churches. They were admitted as ordained ministers decades before the missionary churches of the Netherlands admitted female ministers (see Women's Ordination Cluster). Nearly all Protestant churches have female ministers. Theologian Marianne Katoppo, who wrote the English-language *Compassionate and Free* (1979), is the best known internationally.

Until the 1950s, Protestant churches were mostly classical or mainstream: Lutheran in Batakland and Kalimantan (from German and Swiss missions), Reformed in the rest of the country (from Dutch missions). Since the 1960s, many new churches of the Evangelical* and Pentecostal*/Charismatic* traditions have been established with strong ties to US missionary societies. The Christian and Missionary Alliance started (1929) in Sulawesi and Kalimantan, but many other churches started missionary work in the 1960s, especially among the Chinese population. Although these new churches claim to address non-Christians, in fact they often attract members from established ethnic churches. Prayer meetings of Pentecostal/Charismatic groups or churches are often spirited, with modern music played on a guitar rather than an organ, held in convention halls or hotels rather than in traditional churches, and attended by well-to-do and urban people. Pentecostals/Charismatics are much more active on the island of Java than in the more rural areas of the outer islands. In the major towns of Java, this has resulted in the creation of many, sometimes hundreds of, scattered small Christian churches among a Muslim majority. All religions in Indonesia, but mostly Islam and Christianity, have shown an increasing vitality in the late 20th and early 21st. **See also BATAK CHURCHES.**

Statistics: Population (2007): 225 million (M). Christians, 20 M, 9% (Protestants, 13.3 M; Roman Catholics, 6.3 M); Muslims, 198 M, 88%. (*Source*: *A History of Christianity in Indonesia*, 2007.)

KAREL STEENBRINK

Indulgence, relaxation of the "temporal" penalties for sins* that have been confessed and forgiven. Indulgence began in the 3rd c. with the promise of martyrs* to intercede for sinners and the practice whereby confessors* (those who had been imprisoned but not martyred) readmitted the "lapsed*" ("sinners" who had denied the faith during persecution) to the church. With the growth of the juridical view of sin and atonement* (the necessity of satisfaction and/or punishment for atonement), purgatory* came to be seen as the place where, in the interim between an individual's death* and the general resurrection*, the soul* of a person to be saved temporally expiates venial* sins* or mortal* sins* after contrition* and confession*. Penance* under the supervision of the church came to be understood as a substitute for "temporal" punishment in purgatory (in contrast to "eternal" punishment in hell*). With the presupposition that the Roman Catholic Church has the right to administer the "merits" of Christ and the saints (the "treasury of merits") in order to alleviate temporal punishments, plenary indulgences for all temporal punishments were first issued by the popes for those participating in the

Crusades*, then on Jubilee* years (e.g. the turn of a century) and on other special occasions.

Abuse of indulgences increased in the late Middle Ages, when mendicant* orders were often accused of the indiscriminate sale of indulgences. This was the occasion for Luther's* call for reform, which led to a number of reforms by the Catholic Church. After the sale of indulgences was prohibited (by Pope Pius V, 1567), plenary indulgences were still used to encourage piety and good works. After the Second Vatican* Council, Paul VI substantially restricted the use of indulgences (in *Indulgentiarum Doctrina*, 1967), while retaining the concept.

EUGENE TESELLE

Inerrant, incapable of or exempt from error, particularly as ascribed to Scripture. **See also INFALLIBLE; SCRIPTURE.**

Infallible, incapable of or exempt from failing or error (inerrant). Infallibility has been ascribed to Scripture*, the church and its councils, and the pope*.

Infallibility or Inerrancy of Scripture has been affirmed by most Christian groups, but the Protestant Reformation affirmed it to the exclusion of any infallibility on the part of the church or the papacy. This claim has been based on (1) God's calling of the prophets* and apostles* to proclaim God's Word to their contemporaries and (2) the inspiration* of the writings they later set down. There has been disagreement since the Reformation over several questions: whether the Bible *is* the Word* of God or contains it or conveys it; whether the Bible is infallible in all aspects (including scientific or historical statements) or only in matters affecting the human relationship with God. Usually it is said that the Word of God is heard and understood only under the guidance of the Holy* Spirit, and that certitude about the authority or infallibility of Scripture comes not from human reasoning or from the authority of the church, but from self-authentication by the Word of God (see Scripture).

Infallibility of the Church. Infallibility is also ascribed (on the basis of John 16:13 and Acts 15:28) to various aspects of the church: its unanimous tradition (see Tradition Cluster; Vincentian Canon), the sense of the faithful (which Pope Pius* IX sought before declaring the dogma of the Immaculate* Conception), councils of the church (see Conciliarism), and the pope.

Papal Infallibility may first have been suggested by Peter John Olivi*, a Franciscan* Spiritual, in order to guarantee the permanence of the bull of Pope Nicholas III (1279) that affirmed the Spirituals' practice of poverty*. Papal infallibility was championed by many in the Catholic Church. It was defined as a dogma by the First Vatican* Council (1869–70), which stated that the pope, when he speaks *ex cathedra* on issues of faith and morals, has "that infallibility which Christ willed his church to have." Thus it does not take away anything from the church but affirms that the church's infallibility may be concentrated in the one person of the pope.

In all these cases, infallibility is not considered an inherent quality of the human beings or documents involved, since it is a function of divine infallibility, to be received gratefully and humbly by human beings – and sometimes in opposition to what they regard as their best insights and inclinations.

EUGENE TESELLE

Infant Baptism, while not practiced by "believers' churches" (Anabaptists*, Baptists*), is practiced by other churches with different ecclesiologies and theologies. Among Roman Catholics, it was often associated with the "removal of original* sin," thereby affording the possibility of entry into heaven* rather than an eternity in the "limbo* of unbaptized infants." There is evidence that, by 200, baptism was regarded as essential for salvation* when the infant was in danger of death (hence the permission for women to baptize infants in an emergency). Since Vatican* II, these associations have largely faded through a more comprehensive, biblically driven understanding of baptism as a sacrament of initiation into the Christian community wherein, through grace*, one "puts on Christ." This is close to the Lutheran view of baptism* as sacramental, and even of the quasi-sacramental Reformed* view of baptism (the covenant* applies to children of believers; cf. the "households" that were baptized, Acts 16:15, 33; 1 Cor 1:16). In the Orthodox* Church, through baptism, infants are incorporated into Christ and his church that they may share in his deified* humanity, being given the gifts of sanctification*, righteousness*, and filial adoption. **See also BAPTISM CLUSTER; SACRAMENTS IN WESTERN CHURCHES.**

Infralapsarianism, the view of predestination* according to which God's election* of some for redemption* is "subsequent" to God's foreknowledge of the Fall*. Most 17th- to 18th-c.

Reformed* theologians affirmed infralapsarianism, rather than supralapsarianism*, which placed God's election "prior" to foreknowledge of the Fall.

Inner Mission, a term coined by Wichern* for his work in Hamburg (from 1833); used after the first Kirchentag* (1848) to refer to all activities undertaken to reclaim, through preaching, tracts, and charitable works, persons who had fallen away from the faith in the midst of social upheaval related to industrialization. It became a vast network of social relief institutions all over Germany*.

DAVID CROWNER and GERALD CHRISTIANSON

Innocent III, Pope (c1161–1216), born Lotario di Segni. After being elected pope (1198), he sought to work with reform groups such as the Humiliati and the Trinitarians, and supported Francis* of Assisi. He strengthened papal rule of the Papal States and took a leading role in the disputed election of a successor to Emperor Henry VI and the election of an arch bishop of Canterbury (1207). He was greatly conflicted when the Fourth Crusade* conquered Constantinople (1204), becoming a major obstacle to East–West relations, especially when he imposed the use of the Latin Rite. Against the Albigensians*, he initiated both the mission of Dominic* (1205) and the crusade (1208–29) that led to French domination of Languedoc; he also sponsored the Teutonic* Knights' conquest in the Baltic region. Later Innocent focused chiefly on the summons of the Fourth Lateran* Council (1215), the most important of the medieval reform councils that defined the doctrine of transubstantiation*, approved new procedures for confession and penance*, and prohibited the writing of new rules for religious* communities.

JAMES M. POWELL

Inquisition (from Lat *inquisitio*, "inquiry"). Special tribunals to detect and eradicate heresy* developed in several stages:

1. Investigations of heresies predated the actual Inquisition. In 1184 Pope Lucius III directed bishops to investigate heresy in their dioceses and hand those who would not recant over to the secular authorities for punishment. Pope Innocent* III approved the mission of Dominic* (1205) in the hope that there would be conversions* among the Albigensian heretics (see Cathars, Catharism), but this by itself proved ineffective. Pope Gregory IX (c1233) commissioned certain members of the Dominicans and Franciscans, with direct responsibility to the pope, to investigate this and other heresies and take corrective measures.
2. An actual "inquisition" arose when these investigations were coordinated in the dioceses. When an inquisitor came into a district, people had one month to come forward to abjure* heresy and receive penance*; then information from other persons could be used to call them to a hearing. Inquisitors functioned as pastors or theologians, not as canon lawyers. Trial was voluntary, and the inquisitors sought repentance; if the accused recanted, the sentences were those of the sacrament of penance, accepted voluntarily (on the theory that satisfaction* means voluntary suffering). The bishop had to be involved in any sentencing. Despite many abuses and major flaws in the system, features of due process also existed.
3. Voluntary confinement gradually became a part of penitential procedures and required the construction of facilities. Refusal to appear or to be confined for purposes of inquiry and refusal to recant were taken as admissions of guilt. Torture was eventually permitted by the pope (1252) in the case of stubborn suspects, but it was not to cause mutilation, bleeding, or death.

   To ensure that penances were carried out, the sentences were stated publicly; confinement (understood to be voluntary) might be included, but penances usually involved wearing a yellow cross and performing public acts of penance. The property of imprisoned penitents could be confiscated by temporal rulers to pay for the inquisitors, their staffs, and the prisons that had to be maintained. Unrepentant heretics were handed over to the "secular* arm," which usually burned them at the stake.
4. Inquisitors utilized the classic manuals about heresies; thus they often tried to fit the beliefs of the accused to the older heresies. The possibility of arbitrary judgment increased when translation between the vernacular and Latin was involved. Thus it has been suggested that the inquisitors imagined "phantom heresies" (e.g. the Free* Spirit) or helped to make real heresies more definite among their adherents. Witchcraft* was not originally within their scope, but on the theory that it involved a pact with the devil* it was eventually

added (1398), and in Germany the *Malleus Maleficarum* (Hammer of heretics, 1487) was written by two inquisitors. Inquisitors played a minor role in the prosecution of the Templars*; they were more active against the Franciscan Spirituals* and Joan* of Arc. In the Papal States, they were involved in the burning of Giordano Bruno in 1600.

5. The Spanish Inquisition was a new institution, established by Ferdinand and Isabella* (1478) with the reluctant permission of the pope. It operated as an instrument of the rulers, and its *autos* de fe* were staged as public spectacles to intimidate the populace. Its first role was to examine converted Jews (*conversos**) and Muslims (*moriscos**), then the *alumbrados* (those perceived to be false mystics) and followers of Luther*, but it even investigated Ignatius* Loyola and Teresa* of Ávila.

See also BLACK LEGEND; DEMONIZATION.

EUGENE TESELLE

Inquisition and "New Christians" in Brazil. "New Christians" was a name given at first to Jews and Moors who were forced by law to convert to Catholicism as a result of the Inquisition*, a procedure supported by the state in Spain* (end of the 13th c.). The name "New Christians" segregated the newly converted Christians from the "old Christians," in order to preserve the prerogatives of the latter. Consequently, new Christians were also called *conversos** (converted) or *marranos* (a derogatory term, "pigs," from the Arabic *mahran*), used in a pejorative sense seemingly to designate those who did not eat pork, like the Moors and Jews. Such terms were used starting in the early 12th c., when the "recently reborn" (Lat *nuper renati*) started to be excluded from public offices and official dignities.

With the mass coercive conversions ordered after 1497 by the Inquisition on the Iberian Peninsula, most of the recently converted, mainly from Judaism, fled to the New World. Thus "New Christians" participated in the "discovery" of Brazil*, among them Gaspar da Gama and Fernando de Noronha. Different groups of New Christians spread across Brazil in the northeast (Maranhão, Pernambuco, Bahia) and southeast (Espírito Santo, Rio de Janeiro, São Paulo). The New Christians did not form a homogeneous group; they slowly became assimilated into the colonial society in Brazil without a particular ideology. Following the Iberian union (1580–1640), the Inquisition became active once again in the New World. Inquisitors frequently arrested some New Christian apostates and took them back to Portugal*, where they were judged and occasionally sentenced to death. During the Dutch invasion of Northeast Brazil (1624–54), some New Christian groups, actually crypto-Jews, reconverted to Judaism. When Brazilian explorers found gold in the Southeast (late 17th c.), an enormous number of people moved there, many of them New Christians who became rich, influential bourgeois. Inquisitional persecutions started again, showing that the Inquisition had economic as well as religious motivations. Finally, the laws that distinguished old Christians from new were gradually phased out after the 1750s and abolished by the Act of 1773.

MARCOS CALDAS

INRI, initial letters of the Latin words over the cross (John 19:19–22), "Iesus Nazarenus Rex Iudaeorum," "Jesus of Nazareth, King of the Jews." **See also** *CHI-RHO*; IHS; *NOMINA SACRA*.

Inspiration (Lat *inspiratio*, "in-breathing"; Gk *theopneustos*, "God-breathed," 2 Tim. 3:16). Common to all Christian notions of the inspiration of Scripture* is the idea that the Holy* Spirit influenced the coming into existence of the Christian canon as authoritative Scripture* (see Bible, Canon of). The basis of this doctrine is the self-witness of Scripture to its divine origin and inspiration. The nature and extent of inspiration can be determined by focusing on the biblical writers' own statements (found throughout the canon) as well as by considering the phenomenon of Scripture; the latter approach, however, raises all sorts of issues, especially when it is held that inspiration also means infallibility* or inerrancy*.

Similarly, the locus of the Holy Spirit's action in inspiration is commonly held to be either the authors (as in 2 Pet 1:21) or the writings themselves (as in 2 Tim 3:16). These two notions are not necessarily opposed.

The view of the intensity and power of inspiration varies in different theological schools. A classical, traditionalist view makes inspiration almost an act of "dictation," as found in many historical statements, both Protestant and Catholic. The contemporary Fundamentalist* Movement emphasizes a somewhat similar idea of inspiration as verbal or plenary inspiration, thus making every word authoritative. At the other extreme, for 19th-c. liberalism and later liberal movements that arose as a result of the Enlightenment (see Liberalism in Christian Theology and Ethics), inspiration is an enhancement of the human capacity to grasp essential insight into divinity, as in an artistic act of inspiration; in that case, inspiration is mostly a function of the human spirit, and its "authority" is the authority of an authentic experience of the divine. The neo-orthodox school (e.g. Karl Barth*), while holding to the divine source of inspiration (as the traditionalists do), made inspiration a matter of an authentic, though not necessarily infallible testimony (as the liberals do). Most theologies locate themselves between the traditionalist and liberal extremes, trying to negotiate the complex relationship between the divine and human agency in inspiration, as illustrated in *Dei Verbum* (No. 11) of Vatican* II, which states, "God chose men and while employed by Him they made use of their powers and abilities." The Protestant Reformation*, while insisting on divine inspiration and authority, also spoke strongly for the human element in the process, thus opening the way to a critical study of Scripture.

VELI-MATTI KÄRKKÄINEN

Institution, Words of, words of Christ during the Last Supper (1 Cor 11:23–24; Mark 13:22–24, par.), used in the central prayer of the Eucharist*. **See also ANAPHORA; *EPICLESIS*.**

Institutional Church. (1) Since the late 19th c., an urban church providing specialized ministries and social services to a vulnerable population, e.g. women, children and youth, laborers, and ethnic groups. (2) In contemporary parlance, an often derogatory characterization of the church* as a human "institution" rather than as a "faith community," "mission," or "true church."

Insufflation, breathing or blowing on a person or thing to symbolize the influence of the Holy* Spirit (cf. John 20:22).

Integrism, Integralism, Integrist Movement, in the Roman Catholic Church, a trend opposing liberalism* (specifically, ecumenism and modern Bible studies) and Modernism*. It is associated especially with Pope Pius* X's "Oath against Modernism" (1910). It is often linked with socially and politically conservative movements in Roman Catholicism, which supported dictatorships in Spain*, Italy*, and Latin America (including Argentina*).

Intercession (Lat "a coming between"), prayer* on behalf of others, usually for very specific issues or events in their lives.

Intercommunion, sharing of the Eucharist* by two churches or denominations, usually considered a key manifestation of agreement on matters of both faith (doctrine) and order (system of government).

Interdict, exclusion of persons or regions from participation in the rituals of the church, especially the sacraments*.

Interfaith Dialogue. See DIALOGUE, INTERFAITH.

Interims, decrees attempting to secure temporary religious unity between Catholics and Protestants after the defeat of the Protestant princes in the Schmalkaldic War (1546–47). The Augsburg Interim decreed by Charles* V (1548) made concessions to the Protestant doctrine of justification*, but imposed outward conformity with bishops and the Mass. The milder Leipzig Interim (1548) gained the assent of some Lutheran leaders. Others (in Magdeburg) objected that the doctrine of justification was contradicted by the emphasis on works, decreed by rulers rather than the church. This led to Flacius's* doctrine of *status* confessionis*, according to which there is a need for "confession" when a given situation sends a wrong message about the gospel; when indifferent matters are made essential, they are no longer indifferent and must be opposed.

Internet Technology has changed society and dramatically altered congregational life and the practice of communal religion. As members of congregations increasingly adopted e-mail, the Web, and other Internet technologies, so too did churches, mosques, and synagogues and their leaders. In North America from 1997 to 2007, the percentage of congregations with Web sites increased from 11 to more than 50%. Those using electronic newsletters, digital projection equipment, blogs, text messaging, and member databases increased almost as dramatically. In 2005 nearly 90% of US clergy reported having Internet access and using e-mail. National surveys in the USA have found a strong correlation between the adoption of these technologies and membership growth. This trend will increase as Internet technologies continue to facilitate the work of congregations by enhancing communication among members and clergy, improving the delivery of goods and services, revolutionizing the worship experience, and developing new congregational configurations, including cyber-linked church sites and online campuses. **See also TECHNOLOGY AND CHRISTIANITY.**

SCOTT THUMMA

Intinction, practice of dipping the bread into the cup during Communion. It is often recommended for hygienic purposes.

Introit, a psalm or hymn sung when the celebrant enters the church or approaches the sanctuary.

Investiture Controversy, the dispute between popes* and emperors (of the Holy* Roman Empire) over the right of secular rulers to confer the symbols of spiritual office (crozier* and ring*) on bishops and abbots. "Lay investiture" was prohibited by the Easter Synod in Rome (1059), the decrees of Gregory* VII (1074), and another Roman synod (1075). Henry* IV in Germany denounced Gregory's position (1076), and the controversy continued (involving Anselm* of Canterbury, among others). Under the Concordat of Worms* (1122), it was agreed that bishops would be canonically elected, but rulers could be present at the election, confer "temporalities" (temporal powers), and receive feudal* homage.

Investment Funds are funds that seek investments from religious congregations or individuals at a lower interest rate than the market rate. For example, the Grameen Bank in Bangladesh* was a pioneer in making small loans (enough to plant a crop or buy basic tools) at a low rate of interest through peer lending groups whose members continue to offer support and advice. The Ecumenical Development Cooperation Society, nicknamed Oikocredit, is related to the World* Council of Churches and is based in Holland. Loans are offered to church-related cooperatives or other grassroots organizations, which lend money for sustainable, income-generating projects. The Nicaraguan Community Development Loan Fund was started in 1991 in cooperation with CEPAD, the Nicaraguan Council of Protestant Churches; loans are made to cooperatives, home-based businesses, and women's organizations.

EUGENE TESELLE

Invisible and Visible Church, a differentiation made by Augustine* and revived by the Protestant Reformation*, according to which, since its inception, the true but invisible church consists of the elect*, all those who will believe* in the grace* of God, will be justified*, and will receive salvation*, whereas the visible church also includes those who remain captives of sin* (cf. the parable of the wheat and the weeds, Matt 13:24–30).

Invocation, calling upon God*, or angels* or saints* in their role as God's servants, in praise*, thanksgiving*, or supplication*.

Iona, a small island off the west coast of Scotland, where Columba* founded (563) a monastery. From there, Columba set out to preach and evangelize in Scotland. (The surviving medieval buildings and crosses all date from after his time.) The influence of Iona as a center of learning and monasticism* continued after Columba's death, and monasteries founded by monks from Iona, such as Melrose and Lindisfarne, continued its Irish monastic and artistic traditions into the 7th c. The Book of Kells (an illuminated manuscript of the Gospels) may have been begun in Iona. Although sacked by Vikings (806), Iona became a place of pilgrimage; it was the burial place of a number of medieval Scottish, Irish, and Norwegian kings and, in 1994, of the British political leader John Smith. In the Middle Ages, it was home to a Benedictine* nunnery and monastery. In 1938 Iona Abbey became home to the Iona Community, a dispersed Christian ecumenical community working for peace and social justice, the rebuilding of community, and the renewal of worship.

MARILYN DUNN

Iran. Non-Persian minorities – Assyrians*, Chaldeans* (both descendants of Syriac-speaking Christians from Mesopotamia), and Armenians* (brought to Persia as deportees, 604) – constitute 97% of Christians.

In the early 2nd c., Syriac* Christianity entered ancient Persia, first among Jewish-Christian communities of Parthia, via Edessa* and Adiabene. There were Christian communities in Parthia and Media c200–230. Shapur II (309–79) severely persecuted the church, which was distinguished by the contribution of Aphrahat* (d339) to Syriac spirituality. After the Council of Chalcedon* (451), Dyophysite ("two natures") Christology became church doctrine. With the expansion of Islam* (7th c.), the church faced persecutions but remained true to its faith and vigorous in evangelization.

Western missionary activities (gaining converts primarily from Oriental Orthodox* churches rather than the Muslim community) began with the Roman Catholics (15th c.); Protestants arrived much later (18th c.).

Since the implementation of the Islamic *shari'a* (law) (1979), Christians have experienced new restrictions. Many churches and affiliated institutions have been closed. Protestant missionaries were forced to leave.

The church "families" in Iran include the Catholic (including Chaldean*, Armenian*, and Latin), the Eastern and Oriental Orthodox* (Assyrian* Church of the East, Armenian* Apostolic, and Russian Orthodox*), and small Protestant churches.

The Oriental Orthodox churches are sustained by ancient liturgy and rituals, with high attendance and participation. Despite their variety, two factors have united Iranian Christians: a common faith and a shared experience as ethnic minorities. Since apostasy is proscribed in Islam, evangelization has produced few converts, who remain, by necessity, crypto-Christians. Because of the rise of Islamic fundamentalism and political instability in the region, many Christians are emigrating to the West. The prospects for the survival of Christianity in Iran are dim. **See also** IRAQ.

Statistics: Population (2000): 67.7 million (M). Christians, 363,000, 0.5% (Orthodox, 202,000; independents, 80,000; Roman Catholics, 16,400; Protestants, 14,000); Muslims, 64.7 M, 96%; nonreligious, 205,000, 0.3%. (Based on *World Christian Encyclopedia*, 2001.)

SHAWQI N. TALIA

Iraq, a new nation whose multiethnic and multireligious population is proud to lay claim to its ancient roots in the Mesopotamian "cradle of civilization." Iraqi Christians (especially Assyrians* and Chaldeans*) have ancient ethnic and religious roots. Those Christians of the Syriac* (East Aramaic) tradition can trace their roots with certainty to the 2nd c., although some claim the 1st c. (see Abgar; Addai and Mari). Despite their long history as a minority that is usually tolerated and respected, they have sometimes suffered persecution (see History of Christianity Cluster: In the Middle East: Syriac Christianity).

Though subject to the ecclesiastical See of Antioch*, the Church* of the East declared its autonomy at the Synod of Markabta (424); the final schism took place after the Council of Chalcedon* (451). At the Synod of Seleucia (486), the Syrian Church of the East affirmed a Dyophysite ("two natures") Christology* and adopted the appellation "the Assyrian* Church of the East." In 1553 the Chaldean* Church was established as a uniate* church; today it is the largest church in Iraq.

The East Syrian Church had illustrious scholars, including Tatian* (2nd c.; author of the Diatessaron*); Rabbula*, bishop of Edessa (c350–c435 who revised the Peshitta*; and Ephrem* (c306–373), the great Bible exegete and a doctor of the church. From 400 to 1100, the Assyrian Church was engaged in vigorous evangelization in India*, China*, and Central Asia.

During the Abbasid caliphate (750–1258 CE), many Christians reached high positions in the state Muslim administration and, as scholars, translated Greek philosophical and medical texts (see Islam and Christianity Cluster: In the Middle East). Since the invasion of Baghdad by Tamerlane (1373 CE), the church has faced many persecutions, the last one during World War I.

Established under British mandate with arbitrarily drawn boundaries after World War I, Iraq achieved independence in 1932, first under a king, then as a republic (1958), which initially came under Ba'ath Party control (1961–2003), then under US occupation, and eventually under the government elected during the US occupation.

The Christian community is divided into Catholics (including Chaldean* and Syriac* Catholics), Orthodox (Assyrian*, Syrian* Orthodox, and Armenian* Apostolics), and Protestants (converts from the various communities through evangelization by Western missionaries since the 19th c.).

Despite the current violence, Iraqi Christians are determined to maintain their presence in the place they feel is their homeland, just as it is for the larger populations of Sunni and Shi'ite Muslim Arabs and Kurds. Yet the number of Christians is dwindling.

Statistics: Population (2000): 23.1 million (M). Christians, 740,000, 3.2% (Roman Catholics, 268,000; Orthodox, 139,000; Protestants and independents, 315,000); Muslims, 22.2 M, 96%; nonreligious, 157,000, 1%. (Based on *World Christian Encyclopedia*, 2001.) 2009 (after massive emigration): fewer than 400,000 Christians.

SHAWQI N. TALIA

Ireland. Christianity in Ireland has been marked by a close association of religious and political allegiances, giving organized religion an unusual resilience, but also making it a source of deep and sometimes violent divisions.

Ireland was Christianized (5th–6th c.) by missionaries, including Palladius* and especially Patrick*, who became the island's patron saint. English monarchs established control over part of the island from 1169, but their grip in the early 16th c. remained too weak to extend the Protestant Reformation to a peripheral and religiously conservative population. The Church of Ireland (episcopal in governance and Protestant in doctrine) found its adherents almost exclusively among English immigrants drawn to Ireland by the opportunities created as the Tudor state extended its political and military control. An influx of Scots (17th c.) created the basis for a substantial Presbyterian presence in the northern province of Ulster.

This identification of Protestantism with a process of conquest and expropriation ensured that religious and political allegiances became closely linked. Civil wars (1642–53, 1689–91), both resulting from crises in England (see United Kingdom), gave the victorious Protestant minority a monopoly of political power and a near monopoly of landed property, while Roman Catholics were subjected to strict penal laws. Even after the last of these had been repealed (1829), resentment of continuing social and economic inequalities contributed significantly to the rise of Irish nationalism among Catholics. Yet Protestants saw a continued political union with Great Britain as essential to their survival as a threatened minority.

The 19th c. was a period of religious revival. Historians of Catholicism speak of a midcentury "devotional revolution," characterized by a sharp rise in church attendance, the spread of lay pious associations (sodalities and confraternities), and the replacement of popular rituals, many of them linked to the rhythms of the agricultural year, by the orthodox devotions of Ultramontane* Catholicism. Meanwhile Protestants of all denominations were powerfully affected by Evangelicalism*, in particular by the great transatlantic revival* movement (1859).

During 1920–22, conflicting political aspirations were resolved by the creation of an independent Irish state in the predominantly Catholic south, while six counties of Ulster, where Protestants had a two-thirds majority, remained within the United* Kingdom as a self-governing region, Northern Ireland. Independent Ireland, though never formally adopting a state church, became a strongly Catholic society, in which the Roman Catholic Church controlled schools, hospitals, and other institutions, and exercised a strong if informal influence over legislation. In Northern Ireland, Catholics were subjected to widespread discrimination in employment and other areas, leading eventually to an outbreak of sustained political violence in 1969.

Religion in early-21st-c. Ireland is in a state of transition. In the Irish Republic, two decades of unprecedented prosperity have undermined both nationalism and Catholicism. The proportion of adults attending church at least weekly, which was as high as 90% in the 1970s, has fallen sharply, although whether this decline will continue or attendance will stabilize at its current level (about 50%) remains to be seen. In Northern Ireland, church attendance has also declined, but more slowly: the 14% decline in the number stating a religious affiliation is an index less of secularization* than of the pressures of a divided society. Survey evidence suggests that the proportion of genuinely nonreligious is around 5% and shows a strong correlation with disassociation from the dominant political ideologies of nationalism and unionism.

Statistics: Population (2002): 3.9 million (M). Christians, 3.7 M (Roman Catholics, 3.5 M; Anglicans, 0.1 M; Presbyterians, 0.02 M; Methodists, 10,000); nonreligious, 0.1 M.

Northern Ireland: Population (2001): 1.7 M. Christians, 1.6 M (Roman Catholics, 0.67 M; Presbyterians, 0.35 M; Anglicans, 0.26 M; Methodists, 0.06 M); no religion/not stated, 0.23 M. (Based on Louise Fuller, *Irish Catholicism since 1950*, 2002.)

SEAN CONNOLLY

Irenaeus (c125–c200), bishop of Lyon. Born in Asia Minor, he heard Polycarp* in his youth. He became a presbyter in the Greek-speaking church in Lyon, which commissioned him to go to Rome to request toleration for the Montanists*. While he was absent, persecutions broke out in Lyon (c177), and when the bishop Pothinus was martyred, Irenaeus was chosen as his successor. He also sought toleration for the Quartodecimans* during their controversy with Rome (c190).

Two works by Irenaeus survive, largely in Latin, Syriac, and Armenian translations: *Against Heresies* (or *Exposure and Overturning of the Falsely Called Knowledge*) and *Exposition of the Apostolic Proclamation*. For him the "apostolic proclamation" is the teaching handed on publicly (not in secret traditions) in the apostolic churches, orally but chiefly in writing, i.e. the books of the NT; he thinks of the Apostles'* Creed as a summary of this teaching.

Confident about this common heritage, he offers a comprehensive synthesis of Christian doctrine, attacking Gnosticism* in detail, then presenting his own position, a developmental view of human history that has been attractive to modern thinkers: Adam and Eve were to be educated gradually in God's ways, but their sin* brought serious malfunctioning into human life; Christ has "recapitulated" human life, correcting what Adam and Eve did and leading it back to God. EUGENE TESELLE

Irene (750/55–803), Byzantine regent (780–90) and emperor (797–802). Upon the death of her husband, Leo IV (780), she became regent for her son, Constantine VI, and devoted her efforts to overthrowing Iconoclasm*.

She carefully prepared the way for an ecumenical council; after the army broke up the first session in Constantinople (786), it was reconvened in Nicaea (787). This Second Council of Nicaea* approved the making and veneration of icons*. After Constantine asserted power as sole emperor (790), she engineered his removal (797), had him blinded in the purple chamber where he had been born, and assumed the title of "emperor" (*basileus* in official documents, *basilissa* on coins). The fact that a woman sat on the throne in Byzantium was one of the reasons offered by Charlemagne* for assuming the title of emperor of the Holy* Roman Empire in 800 (the *Caroline* Books* had been written a few years earlier, likewise to discredit the Eastern Empire, saying that the West neither worshiped icons nor venerated them). After Charlemagne became emperor, he and Irene entered into friendly negotiations so that the Empire could once again be united, and marriage may have been contemplated. Instead, she was removed from power and exiled (802).

EUGENE TESELLE

Irish Articles, the 104 articles of faith adopted by the Irish Episcopal Church (1615), probably compiled by James Ussher*, a Calvinist* in doctrine, like a majority of bishops in the Church of England at the time. They affirm predestination* and perseverance*, call the pope Antichrist*, teach Sabbatarianism*, and make no mention of the threefold* ministry or the need for episcopal ordination. These articles were the chief model for the drafting of the Westminster* Confession (similar order and headings of chapters, and even similar language).

Isaac. The Bible presents Isaac as the long-awaited son of the covenant* whom God promised to Abraham* and Sarah* (Gen 21:1–3). Yet by God's command and Abraham's obedience, Isaac nearly became the victim of child sacrifice (Gen 22). Shortly thereafter, his mother died. Through a servant, his father arranged for him to marry the formidable and attractive Rebekah*. Upon Abraham's death, Isaac received his inheritance. Soon he and Rebekah had twins, Esau* and Jacob*. But in an encounter with the Philistine king Abimelech, Isaac protected himself from potential death by lying about Rebekah, calling her his sister. In his old age, Rebekah and Jacob deceived the blind Isaac so that he mistakenly blessed Jacob rather than Esau (Gen 25:19–28:5).

Judaism* praises the young Isaac as a willing victim of sacrifice*. Although spared death, Isaac becomes a paradigm for martyrs (4 Macc 13:12). Christianity sees his story as foreshadowing Jesus' crucifixion (Rom 8:31–32). Isaac also foreshadows the church, the heir of God's promise (Gal 4:21–28). In Islam* the Qur'an* reports the near sacrifice of Abraham's son without naming the son. The subsequent section, however, announces "the good news of Isaac as a Prophet, one of the righteous" (Surah 37:100–112). **See also SACRIFICE OF ISAAC: THE AQEDAH.** PHYLLIS TRIBLE

Isabella I of Castile (1451–1504), born to John II of Castile and Isabella of Portugal; married Ferdinand of Aragon (1469), uniting two powerful kingdoms over which they held equal authority. She was given the title "Catholic" by Pope Alexander VI, signaling both her devotion to the Catholic faith and her determination to promote cultural hegemony through religious practice. She used the Spanish Inquisition* (established 1478) to guarantee Catholic orthodoxy, with its forced conversion and expulsion of Jews and Muslims. She sponsored Christopher Columbus (1492) and articulated the first Spanish responses to the "Indies," and achieved the "reconquest" (of the Iberian Peninsula from Muslims; 1492) by retaking Granada. She was the patron of a significant spiritual reform led by her confessor, Cardinal Francisco Ximénez* de Cisneros, including the foundation of the University of Alcala, the production of the Complutensian* Polyglot Bible, and Castilian translations of important medieval mystical* treatises. **See also SPAIN; SPANISH EXPLORATIONS, CONQUESTS, AND MISSIONS.**

GILLIAN T. W. AHLGREN

Isaiah, Ascension of, a Christian document, possibly incorporating some earlier Jewish traditions, that tells how, because of unfavorable predictions, the prophet Isaiah is sawed in half by

Manasseh at the behest of the devil*. The main emphasis is on the prophet's visions concerning Christ and Antichrist*, the church, and the end of time. **See also PSEUDEPIGRAPHA.**

JOHANNES TROMP

Isaiah, Book of. Modern translations of the Bible locate Isaiah first among the Latter Prophets followed by Jeremiah, Ezekiel, and the Book of the Twelve, but the Babylonian Talmud (14b–15a) locates it immediately before, and the Septuagint immediately after, the Twelve, with which it has much in common. The standard division of the book into First Isaiah (1–39), Second or Deutero-Isaiah (40–55), and Third or Trito-Isaiah (56–66), widely accepted in critical scholarship, represents no more than a very rough chronological sequence; First Isaiah is itself a compilation that includes very late material. The book attained its final form not haphazardly but as the end product of an incremental process of rereading, reinterpreting, and reapplying earlier prophecies – a process that was complete before the publication of the Septuagint version and the Isaiah Scroll from Qumran* (1QIsa[a]), by which time interpretations could not be incorporated into the book itself as they had been, but took the form of a commentary apart from the book.

The earliest of these commentaries are the six fragmentary Qumran Pesharim* (4QpIsa[a-e] and 3QpIsa), comparable in some respects to the fulfillment sayings in the Gospel of Matthew*, most of which cite Isaiah. Together with Deuteronomy and Psalms, Isaiah was the most cited book at Qumran, and its interpretation was, in general, of major significance for the Jewish sects of the late Second Temple period (see Dead Sea Scrolls). It was no less important for early Christians in their attempt to grasp and articulate the meaning of the identity and mission of Jesus – especially as the Servant* of the Lord – together with their own identity. However, there are no Christian commentaries before Origen's (early 3rd c.), which is now lost but mentioned by Jerome.

The title (added later) attributes the book to Isaiah ben Amoz, who was active under successive Judean rulers from c742 to c701 BCE. There is no reason to doubt Isaian authorship of a nucleus of sayings found in Chaps. 1–12 and 28–32, which expand on Amos's powerful critique of his Israelite contemporaries, especially the political and religious leadership. In addition to numerous (mostly prose) expansions of oracular sayings, First Isaiah contains a compilation of poems directed against foreign nations, principally Babylon (13–23), as well as a section somewhat misleadingly known as "the Isaian Apocalypse" (24–27). The long narrative in 36–39 about Hezekiah's revolt against Assyria followed by the Assyrian punitive campaign of 701 was taken, with slight modification, from 2 Kgs 18–20. It features a prophet who plays a supportive role, heals, and works miracles, in contrast to the Isaiah who elsewhere in the book fearlessly condemns corruption in high places.

The Deutero-Isaiah (40–55) focuses on the expectation of a new beginning aroused by Cyrus's victories and the anticipated fall of Babylon, the return from exile*, Jerusalem's restoration, and the servant mission of Israel to the world, which, by default, will pass to an unnamed prophet, the Suffering Servant (53). In Trito-Isaiah (56–66), from the late Persian and early Hellenistic period, the disappointment of these high expectations led to conflict and schism within the Judean community and the emergence of an apocalyptic* worldview, fully developed in the Book of Daniel*.

We therefore find represented in the book three distinct profiles of its putative author: the prophet as man of God, a kinder and gentler version of Elijah or Elisha; as apocalyptic seer; and as social critic. The first is dominant in the early history of interpretation (Chronicles, Sirach, *The Lives of the Prophets, The Martyrdom* of Isaiah*); the second carries over into Daniel, Qumran, and early Christianity; and the third reemerged only in the early modern period with the beginnings of critical study of the prophetic literature.

JOSEPH BLENKINSOPP

Ishmael was the firstborn son of Abraham and his second wife, Hagar*. After the birth of Ishmael's half-brother, Isaac, Abraham expelled him and his mother to the wilderness. In time, Ishmael fathered 12 tribes (Gen 16, 21, 25:12–17). Judaism* deems him the rejected son of the covenant* who became the ancestor of the Arabs. Christianity makes him a symbol of the Jews, born "according to the flesh" (Gal 4:21–31). The Qur'an describes him as a messenger and a prophet, faithful to his promises (Surah 19:54). Islamic* tradition holds that Ishmael assisted Abraham in building the Kaaba (the "House of God" at Makkah [Mecca]).

PHYLLIS TRIBLE

Isidore of Kiev (c1385–1464), scholar and monk, delegate from the Greek Orthodox* Church to the Council of Basel* (1434), appointed metropolitan* of Kiev and all Russia (1436). He attended the Council of Florence* to negotiate reunion between the Eastern and Western churches (1438–39). As the papal legate for all of Eastern Europe, he tried to persuade Poland* and Lithuania*, which favored the Council of Basel*, to accept a council called by the pope. He entered Moscow, went to the Church of the Ascension (with a Latin cross, it was said), and had the decree of union read out. Four days later, Vasili, grand prince of Moscow, confined him to a monastery on charges of heresy*. He escaped and had a long career in Rome as a cardinal, archbishop for Russia, and legate to the East, with jurisdiction over the Venetian Empire. As the Turkish siege of Constantinople tightened, Isidore went to the city with 200 archers (1452). He persuaded the people to accept union, and a synod of the clergy proclaimed the union in Hagia Sophia. When the city fell in May 1453, Isidore was captured, although he escaped to Cyprus and Rome, where he raised money to ransom those captured in the city and promoted a crusade to retake Greece* from the Turks.

Isidore of Seville (c560–636), born to a noble family in Cartagena, educated in Seville, probably under his brother Leander, who was a monk before he became bishop of Seville (c580). Leander was vigorous in the conversion to Roman Catholicism of the Arian* Christian Visigothic rulers (see Goths*), and Isidore, who succeeded him (c600), built even closer relations with the royal house. His *History of the Goths, Vandals, and Suevi* is a useful source for the history of his times. Presiding over several councils and associated with a major collection of canons, he defended the *Filioque** against criticism from Rome and Constantinople. His *Etymologies*, a classification of all learning in 20 books, was based on his own fragmentary knowledge and mistranslations from the Greek; but it was much cited throughout the Middle Ages.

1) Introductory Entries

Islam and Christianity: Christian Views of Islam. Islam arose in the 7th c. amid Christianity, Judaism, and Zoroastrianism (the main religion of Persia). From the beginning, it was ambiguously formulated both as a continuation of these religious traditions and as a pure and Arab revelation, correcting the deviations of its predecessors. This ambiguity marked the Christian perception of Muslims throughout history. Christians either perceived a deep connection with the basic doctrines and practices of Islam or exaggerated the differences by characterizing Islam as a negation of Christianity because it rejects the divinity of Jesus and his death on the cross*. Like Manichaeans* and some Christian sects (see Docetism), Muslims believe that someone else was placed on the cross to die, while Jesus was rescued by God.

Assyrian* Christians (also called Persian Nestorians*), Syriac*, Egyptian* and Ethiopian* Miaphysites*, and Chalcedonian* Greeks were the Christian neighbors of Islam during its quick expansion after Muhammad's death (632 CE). Some of the first reactions were apocalyptic* in style, like the vision ascribed to Shenute*: "After that shall arise the sons of Ishmael and the sons of Esau who hound the Christians and the rest of them will be concerned to prevail over and rule all the world and to rebuild the Temple that is in Jerusalem." John* of Damascus, son of the finance minister of a Muslim caliph, had a more theological and balanced view. Islam was included in his book about "Christian" heresies because Muslims recognize Christ as the Word of God and as God's Spirit, although they differ from Christian orthodoxy in many details. Themes central to both religious traditions were later debated by Eastern* Christians and Muslims, who were viewed as respected heretics. Yet in Western* Christianity, not much was said about Islam until the Crusades* (1096–1291).

During the European Middle Ages, Islam was the stronger party. In his theological writings, Thomas* Aquinas (d1274) paid great honor to Muslim thinkers, especially Averroes* (Ibn Rushd), for their efforts to bring Greek philosophy into harmony with monotheistic belief. At that time, Muslim civilization was economically and politically far superior to Christian societies. But Muslims turned from respected heretics into "members of a backward religion" when the power relation changed after the fall of the Caliphate of Baghdad (1258). European power expanded, starting with the Portuguese travels to India and the Far East from 1498 on. In the heyday of colonial* imperialism (1880–1940), most Muslim lands (except Turkey and Arabia) came under the rule of Christian countries, and Islam became a distinct "backward" religion.

Vatican* II (1962–65) reevaluated this conception of Islam, stating in its document *Nostra Aetate*, "The Muslims adore the one God, living and subsisting in Himself; merciful and all-powerful, the Creator of heaven and earth, who has spoken to men; they take pains to submit wholeheartedly to even His inscrutable decrees, just as Abraham, with whom the faith of Islam takes pleasure in linking itself, submitted to God. Though they do not acknowledge Jesus as God, they revere Him as a prophet." Other churches formulated similar statements. However, the religious and political uprising of Islam since the late 1970s, and numerous violent acts linked to Islamic doctrines, have caused much anxiety, fear, and animosity among Christians. The ambiguity remains.

KAREL STEENBRINK

Islam and Christianity: Muslim Views of Christianity. From its inception, Islam was touched by the spirituality of desert monks (see Eremitic Monasticism; Monasticism Cluster: In the Syriac Tradition) and other Christians who lived in and around Makkah. The Qur'an* and the Prophetic tradition (Hadith) praise the piety of Christians, but decry their belief in the Trinity and the divinity of Jesus. Although the Qur'an and subsequent tradition assert that Christ is the Word of God and a "spirit from Him" (God), they nonetheless insist that he is a human creature of God and one of God's messengers. This mixed assessment of Christian faith and piety rendered Muslim views of Christianity at best ambivalent.

In spite of the rapid expansion of Muslim rule into both Latin and Byzantine areas of Christendom* from the 7th to the 16th c., Muslims treated Christians with deference. This attitude changed with the development of the legal and theological sciences under Abbasid rule [750–1258], which led many Muslim scholars to adopt a critical attitude toward Christianity.

Among the first to write about Christianity were early historians like 'Ali b. Rabban al-Tabari (d870) and al-Ya'qubi (d897) and heresiographers like Ibn Hazm (d1064) and Shahrastani (d1153). Apart from Ibn Hazm, who lived in turbulent times in Islamic Spain and thus condemned Christianity as utter madness, the rest were generally sober historians.

With deepening Muslim–Christian political and economic conflicts starting at the end of the 11th c., Christian polemics against Islam, its Prophet, and its scripture increased. Muslims retaliated by attacking Christians and what they considered to be their creedal errors. Soon a literary genre known as "answering" or "refuting Christian errors" appeared. It has persisted in one form or another to the present. Muslims, however, have from the beginning been constrained by the Qur'an's veneration of Jesus and his mother and its repeated injunction to "debate with the people of the Book in the fairest manner."

Muslim attitudes toward Christians and Christianity were profoundly affected by the Crusades*. Modern Muslim thinkers coined the phrase "international crusadism," which they connected with ideas of Western neocolonialism. Three additional elements contributed to the growth of this critical attitude: Christian missionary work in Muslim lands, Orientalism, and colonialism*.

Beginning in the second half of the 19th c., the Muslim world witnessed the rise of numerous intellectual and social reform movements. Increasingly, Christianity came to be regarded as a tool of Western colonialism*. Until World War II, many educated Muslims both hated and admired the West; they sought to emulate it in the fields of science and technology but rejected what they considered to be its corrupt morality and irrational religion. Postcolonial Muslim discourse has since tended to view Western civilization negatively and to see Islam as a self-sufficient faith and worldview, capable of restoring the Muslim Ummah to its rightful place on the stage of world history.

Muslim immigration to the West, and the good efforts of the World* Council of Churches and the Vatican (Vatican* II), have contributed to constructive Muslim–Christian dialogue. Such dialogue remains the only hope for international cooperation and world peace, particularly after the 9/11 tragedy. MAHMOUD AYOUB

---

2) A Sampling of Contextual Interactions

Islam and Christianity in Africa. Present-day Sudan*, Egypt*, and Ethiopia* were Christian strongholds by the early 7th c. During the colonial period (19th–20th c.), European missionaries penetrated the rest of the continent. Christian missionary efforts brought about the Christianization of the equatorial zone of West Africa, as well as Central, Southern, and Eastern Africa. The exponential growth of Christianity took place during the post-independent era (from the late 1950s), when church leadership was transferred to indigenous African hands. The ecclesiastical traditions now include the Coptic* Church in Egypt and North Africa and the Ethiopian* Orthodox* Church (the oldest Christian traditions in Africa), as well as the Roman Catholic, mainline Protestant, Pentecostal*, African* Instituted, and Charismatic* churches.

With the emergence of Islam (7th c.), Arab Muslim armies invaded Egypt (641), subduing the rest of North Africa in the subsequent centuries. The Islamic Conquest was followed by the dispersion of Muslim traders (of slaves, ivory, gold, and salt) and clerics into tropical Africa. Along the East Coast, Arab and Persian Muslims formed trading communities on the shores and the coastal islands (e.g. Zanzibar, Pemba, the Comoros). In West Africa, itinerant Muslim traders and clerics settled among indigenous communities. Although they were not formally "missionaries," their presence and activities became the main means of converting indigenous Africans into Islam. As Islam passed to indigenous African leadership, it was blended with African* Religion practices and customs. Sufism (mystical Islam) offered to African Muslims what the African* Instituted Churches have more recently offered to African Christians, namely the opportunity to take responsibility for the faith and give it a specific African imprint. The legal and political tenets of Islam were deliberately ignored in most places, haphazardly appropriated in some, and fiercely resisted in others. By the 18th c., Islam was firmly established in North Africa and along the East Coast of Africa, but it remained a class religion of the mercantile bourgeois and an additional royal cult in most of Africa.

Some African Muslims viewed as a "corruption of Islam" its apparent "stagnation" in tropical Africa, the blending with African traditional elements, and the non-application of Islamic law (*shari'a*) in public life. Such Muslims launched a series of military campaigns (jihads), especially in the Western Sudan* (late 18th and early 19th c.), ostensibly to purge Islam of African traditional elements, to extend the influence of Islam territorially, and to enforce the legal and political content of Islam. The celebrated "jihad" of Uthman Dan Fodio (d1817) affected present-day Northern Nigeria*, Southern Niger, and parts of Cameroon*. The political and legal dictates of Islam have remained major sources of controversy and conflict in places like Nigeria* and the Sudan*. Yet Sufism in its varied orders (or branches), with its capacity for incorporating African elements, remained the main attraction to Africans and the main vehicle for the propagation of Islam in Africa.

Just when Islam appeared to be on the ascendancy in Africa (early 19th c.), the modern European Christian missionary enterprise entered the continent with its three-pronged agenda: Christianity, commerce, and colonialism* (see Mission Cluster: In Africa; Mission Cluster: Introductory Entries). Despite suspicion, and occasional direct confrontation between the colonialists and Muslims, on the whole Islam enjoyed a favorable patronage under colonial rule and achieved more success in converting Africans during the century of colonization than during the previous 12 centuries.

Nevertheless, the 19th-c. European scramble for Africa and the Christian missionary attacks against the slave* trade caused tensions and open confrontation between Muslims and Christians. Western/Christian civilization was regarded by most Africans as more advanced than that of Arab/Islamic civilization. Those communities that regarded Islam as the religion of their oppressors (e.g. natives of Southern Sudan and middle Nigeria) regarded Christianity and Western civilization as attractive alternatives to Arab/Islamic domination. Conversely, Muslim rulers responded to Western/Christian civilization during the colonial period with self-protective withdrawal, especially from Western education. British colonial policies of indirect rule and the ban on missionary work in Muslim areas contributed significantly to keeping African Muslims and Christians asunder.

The African sense of community and extended family ties helped to overcome the theological and ideological divide between Islam and Christianity. There are numerous examples of "interfaith households" across the continent in which members of the same families are of different religious persuasions. Some ethnic communities, such as the Yoruba of Nigeria, are almost half Muslim and half Christian. Religious festivals like Christmas, Easter, and Ramadan are jointly celebrated by all. Muslim and Christian relatives and neighbors attend religious services during such occasions as marriage and funeral ceremonies. Occasionally Christian family members are called on to contribute to Muslim relatives' pilgrimage to Mecca (the Hajj), and Muslims to contribute to the theological training of their Christian relatives and friends. Senegal, a majority-Muslim country, had a democratically elected Christian president, Leopold Senghor, while a Muslim, Bakili Muluzi, was elected president of Malawi*, a predominantly Christian country. In Tanzania* the elected presidency rotates between Christian and Muslim leaders through the ballot.

Both Islam and Christianity remain missionary in Africa. Several Islamic missionary groups have sprung up, drawing their funding and training from North Africa and the Middle East. Similarly, Christian missionary groups, funded mainly from Europe and North America, have also stepped up their activities in evangelizing Muslims. The theological and ideological postures of these groups have been a source of tension and occasional open conflicts in various parts of Africa. However, the nondogmatic, nonideological, and therefore less confrontational African ethos neutralizes the competitive sting of Islam and Christianity. **See also HISTORY OF CHRISTIANITY CLUSTER: IN AFRICA.**

JOHN ALEMBHILLAH AZUMAH

Islam and Christianity in Africa: North Africa. See HISTORY OF CHRISTIANITY CLUSTER: IN AFRICA: NORTH AFRICA.

Islam and Christianity in Asia: Indonesia. With 178 million Muslims (88% of the population) in 2000, the Indonesian Muslim community was by far the most numerous worldwide (with 8.9% of Christians in Indonesia). Since independence in 1945, the "five-pillar-ideology," or *pancasila*, the basis of the Indonesian Constitution, protects the great religions. The five pillars – belief in one supreme deity, humanism, democracy, social justice, and national unity – were chosen as a middle road between an Islamic and a secular state. The island of Java, the most populous, is almost exclusively Muslim (less than 2% Christian); Christians live in a number of ethnic and Christian pockets in the so-called outer islands. Thus the relations between Christians and Muslims are also interethnic. In 1945 Christians of the outer islands warned that they would leave the young nation if it became an Islamic state.

Observers have defined Muslim–Christian relations in Indonesia as those between two minorities. Muslims, by far the largest group, lack economic power (because ethnic Chinese dominate much of the economy); until the 1990s, they lagged behind in education and cultural manifestations (newspapers, books, prestigious schools) and in participation in the army (because the Dutch rulers preferred Christians to be members of the colonial army) and could not gain political power (because moderate Indonesian Muslims were opposed to Arab-style fundamentalism). Religious harmony has been a great concern for all governments since 1945. Sukarno (1945–65) promoted unifying secular and nationalist ideas. Muhammad Suharto (1965–1998) initially sought the support of all religions against Communism, yet he soon excluded all religions from politics and ordered the acceptance of *pancasila* as the "foundation of all social organizations." Some fundamentalist Muslims and committed Christians rejected this creation of a "civil religion" as a catalyst for interreligious harmony. In the 1990s, Suharto and other politicians increasingly played the "Islam card," creating unrest that was fueled by economic problems (after 1997) and growing ethnic tensions. Radical Muslims expressed fear of aggressive Christian missionaries, while Christians blamed the political opportunism that introduced Islamic elements into the national laws (a ban on mixed marriages; the establishment of *shari'a* in the rebellious province of Aceh; the prohibition of religious propaganda). Indonesia is the only country in the world where a large number of Muslims converted to Christianity (about 2% of the inhabitants of Java, or 2.4 million) without many problems until the 1970s. Since then, however, tensions have sharply increased.

KAREL STEENBRINK

Islam and Christianity in Asia: The Philippines. Islam arrived in the Philippines c1380 (about 200 years before Christianity) through Arab traders and missionaries in the Sulu islands (south of the Philippine Archipelago). The first Muslim sultanate was established in Sulu (1450); subsequently other sultanates were established on the larger Mindanao island (c1475) with Islamic institutions (mosques; *madrasas*, or schools; and *shari'a*, or law). Local traditions (*adat*) were blended with orthodox Islamic practices and teachings; this local Islam, called *Luwaran* (especially among the Cotabato Muslims), governed Philippine Muslims until 1900, when the more orthodox Sunni Islamic *shari'a* gained ground.

Roman Catholic Christianity had been firmly established in the Philippines* by 1565. North American Protestantism was introduced by US missionaries after the defeat of the Spanish colonial forces (1898).

Spanish wars against the Moros (Philippine Muslims), from 1578, when Spanish forces invaded Sulu, until 1898, limited the spread of Islam in the Philippines. The succeeding US regime and the independent Philippine government (with Christian ties) tried to improve Christian–Muslim relations.

The progressive immigration (from the early 17th c.) of Christianized Filipinos from Luzon and the Visayas into the island of Mindanao, along with the evangelization of the indigenous Filipinos (most people practiced native religions in Northern and Eastern Mindanao), made the Moros a minority in Mindanao, even though they claimed Mindanao to be historically theirs. This minoritization of the Moros caused endless troubles and bloodshed – most recently the rebellion against the Philippine authorities, first (1971) by the Moro National Liberation Front (MNLF) and later the Moro Islamic Liberation Front (MILF). A peace agreement was reached with the MNLF (1996), but not with the MILF.

Both Islam and Christianity interacted with animistic Philippine religions, leading to the development of "folk Christianity" (with popular* Christian practices) and "folk Islam" alongside the more orthodox Christianity and Islam. Three forms of Christianity had a lasting impact on Philippine Islam, with differing modes of interaction: Spanish Roman Catholicism (through wars, now dialogue*); North American mainline Protestantism (through dialogue); and the triumphalist indigenous non-Catholic groups (Iglesia ni Kristo and Filipino Millennialist* sects, such as the Tadtad and Ilaga) along with the more recent Charismatic* and Pentecostal groups (through the total rejection of Islam).

With the end of the long period of Moro wars, which hardened negative attitudes and suspicions, Muslim–Christian encounters are now more peaceful. In Mindanao and large urban centers in Luzon (Manila, Baguio) and the Visayas (Cebu), dialogue in various forms makes this peaceful situation possible.

These encounters have produced a deepening of Islamic and Christian self-consciousness, along with some degree of acculturation*. Christians influenced by these encounters have considered more seriously their Christian faith: the biblical tradition of creation* (Gen 1, 2); Abraham's* role in both Islam and Christianity; the role of the Virgin Mary* and Jesus Christ (as savior* and prophet); the biblical canon (e.g. the recognition that besides the four canonical Gospels there are other gospels, including the Gospel of Thomas*); Christian beliefs about "salvation* only in Jesus Christ"; the possibility of God's manifestation in Islam and other religions; and challenges to the celebrations surrounding Christmas* and Holy* Week. A growing number of Filipino Christians have converted to Islam (the Balik–Islam Movement).

The impact of Christianity on Filipino Muslims includes a deepening respect for and veneration of the Qur'an* as the Word of God; following the *shari'a* in Mindanao (for the more orthodox); the importance of the *madrasas* (Islamic/Arabic schools), the *ulama* as interpreter of the *shari'a*, and of the *dawah* (call or mission); and the Balik–Islam (Return to Islam) Movement. Practices surrounding marriage (with a trend toward monogamy), the wearing of the veil among women and the growing of the beard among men (as markers of Islamic identity), and the improved status of Muslim women are visible signs of Christian influence on Filipino Muslims. **See also PHILIPPINES.**

BISHOP HILARIO M. GOMEZ, JR.

Islam and Christianity in Europe: Southeast Europe. While the Muslim presence in Southeast Europe dates to the 10th c., when members of various Asiatic tribes settled in different parts of the Balkan Peninsula, it was the Ottoman Conquest (14th–15th c.) that led to the massive expansion of Islam in Southeast Europe and added to the long-term coexistence and interplay of multiple religions and cultures in that part of the world, notably Eastern Orthodox Christianity, Roman Catholicism, Islam, and Judaism*. The Muslim expansion was achieved both by the influx of Turkic-speaking populations and by the gradual conversion of parts of the local Slavic population.

The coexistence of Islam and Christianity has created modes of living together with tolerance and respect for others in everyday life. Muslims and Christians sometimes share shrines and pilgrimage places, and a number of saints have both a Christian and a Muslim identity. Various forms of religious syncretism*, crypto-Christianity, and biconfessionalism were not uncommon (particularly between the 17th and 19th c.). Generally, however, established Muslim–Christian relations fit into the practice of *komshiluk* (from the Turkish word *komshiya*, "neighbor"), according to which people of different ethnic and religious groups live peacefully side by side and often interact positively, while preserving their structural and cultural differences and sustaining generally unbridgeable boundaries.

Theological interaction between Christianity and Islam in Southeast Europe went through various stages. Islam was initially seen as a variation of Arianism*. Among the major points of the Christian critique of Islam were Muhammad's status as Prophet, and the Muslim belief that the Qu'ran* is the uncreated Word of God. Muslims, in turn, criticized the doctrines of the divinity of Jesus Christ* and the Trinity*. Theologians on both sides interpreted the other religion as incoherent.

With the decline of the Byzantine Empire and the Ottoman conquest of Constantinople, and under the pressure of new historical developments, the initially derisive and hostile attitudes toward the spreading Ottoman Islam were replaced by attempts at better understanding, more objective interpretations, and greater interest in dialogue*. While this dialogue between Christianity and Islam in Southeast Europe subsided between the 16th and 19th c., it reappeared in the 20th c., specifically under the influence of the interreligious activities undertaken by the World* Council of Churches and the Second Vatican* Council. Interreligious dialogue was massively fostered by various international agencies as a means for peace building after the secessionist Yugoslav wars (1990s). **See also HISTORY OF CHRISTIANITY CLUSTER: IN EUROPE: THE BALKANS.** INA MERDJANOVA

Islam and Christianity in Europe: Western Europe. In the 1950s, many came from the rest of the world to find work when Europe faced the task of reconstruction after World War II. Colonial history often determined where people immigrated. For example, the UK received people from Pakistan and India, France received those from North Africa, and Germany those from Turkey. At first, the religious affiliation of these immigrants mattered little: they planned to leave after a few years and usually suspended their religious practice for the duration of their stay.

European Christians initially saw them as foreigners who needed help in settling down and feeling at home. As time went on, social problems came to the fore. Christian groups, e.g. in France the (Protestant) Cimade* and Catholic* Action groups, were accustomed to providing social assistance. In the 1970s, the economic crisis led these countries to curb their immigration policies drastically. Foreign workers realized that reentry to Europe would be impossible if they returned to their homelands. Hence they stayed in Europe for good, and their families joined them. Religious practices could no longer be set aside: new generations needed education in the faith of their ascendants.

Several facts have emerged: (1) Many of Muslim descent are no longer keen to be identified as "Muslim" (in France, this is the case of 40% of such Muslims). This is especially true of the younger generation born and educated in secular Europe. (2) Nevertheless religious practice, estimated to involve 5–10% of the community, requires buildings and religious personnel, which are still lacking in many places. (3) Muslims in Europe are as divided over religious issues as are those in the rest of the Islamic world, which is torn by warring factions. (4) Muslim communities organized themselves along widely different lines, e.g. ethnic groups in Britain and dispersion in France.

Christians face the Muslim presence in Europe with a whole range of attitudes. Many have an image of Muslims that is totally negative. Others have become friends with them, helping them as immigrants or refugees*. Some churches have set up structures of dialogue*: interfaith activities in the UK, a Service for Relations with Islam in France, and centers for documentation and dialogue in Germany (CIBEDO in Frankfurt) and Belgium (el-Kalima in Brussels).

Muslims and Christians are gradually discovering that their encounter is only a small part of the wider interreligious encounter in a very pluralistic world.

FR. JEAN-MARIE GAUDEUL

Islam and Christianity in the Middle East. Islam originated and developed in a world deeply influenced by Christianity.

 Islam and Christianity in the Middle East

By the time of the Prophet Muhammad (c570–632), Christianity was firmly established among the Arabs of Northern Arabia, and there were also strong communities in parts of the Arabian Peninsula. When Arab armies conquered parts of the former Byzantine Empire in the Middle East and North Africa (7th and 8th c.), they became rulers of substantial Christian populations, which maintained their own beliefs and practices. As Muslims reflected on the doctrinal and ethical implications of their own scripture, they did so in an interreligious context in which they both influenced their Christian subjects and were influenced by them (see History of Christianity Cluster: In Africa: North Africa).

The Qur'an* contains many references to Christianity. It portrays those in the Christian community as recipients of revelation (e.g. Q 3:3–4, 5:82), although it pointedly asserts that Christ was human and not divine (e.g. Q 3:51, 5:116–17), and it makes allusions that were later formulated into acerbic criticisms, primarily that Christians believed in three gods (Q 4:171, 5:73) and that their scriptures, originally revealed to Jesus (Q 5:110), had been corrupted over time (e.g. Q 3:78, 5:41; in the Qur'an, the criticism is usually leveled against Jews, but it was later generalized).

Such teachings decisively shaped Muslim attitudes toward Christians. These gradually developed into the view that, as recipients of a scripture from God, Christians were part of the line of faith that culminated in Islam and therefore merited respect as *Ahl al-Kitab*, "people of the Book," but that they had divinized the messenger sent to them and distorted their scripture; they had strayed from monotheism into illogical beliefs in a triple Godhead and in a being both divine and human. The denial of the crucifixion in Q 4:147 ruled out any consideration of the atonement*.

For their part, Christians usually looked down on Muslims. At first they saw them as a manifestation of God's punishment for the christological* divisions that divided Christians or as heralds of the Apocalypse*; later, they simply found little time for their beliefs. The most charitable Christian assessment of Muhammad was that he had delivered to the "pagan" Arabs an elementary form of Abrahamic faith that prepared them for the fullness of Christianity. More frequently they dismissed him as a self-seeking fraud who had borrowed his teachings from Christian heretics (John* of Damascus's condemnation of him in these terms exerted a lasting influence) or, relatively rarely, as possessed by the devil* (see Demonization).

In the formative 8th and 9th c. of Islam, Muslims and Christians interacted closely in the burgeoning cities of the Islamic Empire, where Christians were often esteemed by their Muslim rulers for their learning and skills. The caliph's own doctor was usually a Christian, while Christian secretaries maintained the bureaucratic and fiscal structures of the Empire. Above all, Christian translators, the most important of whom were the group led by Hunayn ibn Ishaq, opened the doors to Greek learning that stimulated intellectual exploration in the late 8th and 9th c. by a monolingual Arabic-speaking Muslim readership and led to a surge in Muslim theological reflection about the being of God and God's involvement with the world. Whether Christian theology provided actual models for Muslim thinking is uncertain, but it is clear that at this time theologians from both faiths debated their respective doctrines according to the same logical methods and in Arabic, which by 800 CE had largely replaced Greek and Syriac. For a period at least, Arabic-speaking Christians, among them the Melkite* Theodore Abu Qurra, the Syriac* Orthodox (polemically nicknamed Jacobite*) Habib ibn Khidma Abu Ra'ita, and the Assyrian* Christian (commonly named Nestorian*) 'Ammar al-Basri, articulated their traditional doctrines in forms shared by Muslims. This helps explain why debates were focused on the common issue of the being of God: Muslims insisted that Christians violated reason* by portraying the Godhead as triple and confining God to a human form, while Christians contended that Muslims demeaned God by depicting him as a bare singularity.

Such theological exchanges led to significant points of cross-fertilization. But any respect that accrued was strictly limited by the uneven social relationships that prevailed. Christians, like other non-Muslims, were cast as *dhimmi* (more specifically *Ahl al-dhimma*, "people of protection," based on a pact supposedly agreed on under the 7th-c. caliph 'Umar), a status that theoretically accorded them legal redress against wrong but effectively divided them from Muslims by requiring them to dress distinctively, yield to Muslims in public, and pay a poll tax. These regulations accentuated the differences produced by religious disagreements; Christians increasingly felt reduced in social status, conversion to Islam gathered impetus, and communities dwindled in confidence and numbers. **See also CRUSADES; DIONYSIUS (JACOB) BAR SALIBI.** DAVID R. THOMAS

Islam and Christianity in the Middle East: Lebanon. Although interreligious relationships in Lebanon* have been strongly influenced by the politicization of the different religious communities, which tended to obscure common interests, recent developments have shown that many kinds of interreligious relationships can exist and, perhaps less visibly, have existed over the years. Not only do Christians, Muslims, and Druze share common political goals, such as the secularization* of politics and liberation from foreign political interference, in daily life the boundaries between Christians, Druze, and Muslims are far less rigid than the political structures suggest. Intermarriage is not uncommon, and in public schools children of all communities are educated together. As in the past, class is often more important than religion, and Muslim–Christian relationships within a certain social layer are often more important than those across class boundaries within the same religious group. Over the years, many organizations for interreligious cooperation and study have been established and play a role in easing the tensions between Christians and Muslims not only in Lebanese society but also in the wider Middle East. Cooperation in relief activities (e.g. during and after the 2006 war between Israel and Lebanon) is coupled with dialogue on political, social, and religious issues, as well as religious experience shared by Christians and Muslims in prayer and pilgrimage, among which a renewed Marian devotion (see Mary, the Virgin, Cluster) plays an important role. Among the active institutions are the Islamic–Christian National Dialogue Committee (initiated in 1993, working with the official leadership of the communities), the Lebanese Gathering for Dialogue (since 2002, focusing on political dialogue; one of the founders, Tareq Mitri, was active in religious dialogue and became a cabinet minister), the Arab Group for Christian–Muslim Dialogue (since 1995, with members in various Arabic countries; Riad Jarjour was one of its general secretaries), and the educational Institut d'études islamo-chrétiennes at the University of Saint Joseph.

HELEEN L. MURRE-VAN DEN BERG

Israel. While Christians disagree as to the place of Israel in Christian theology and feel particular concern for Arab Christians in Israel and Palestine, for Jews the centrality of the land of the Bible (see Promised Land), and the survival of a third of world Jewry, are at stake.

When dispossession arose following the destruction of the Temple (70 CE), Christians argued that the Exile* occurred as a result of divine punishment. Traditional Christian interpretation emphasized punishment for failing to believe in Christ, a supersessionist* view – the belief that Christians replaced Jews as the people* of God – that contributed greatly to anti-Semitism*. The possibility of a rebuilt Temple caused great concern in the 4th c. As long as Jerusalem and the Temple lay in ruins, and Jews remained in exile, Christians appeared to be correct in claiming that Judaism had lost its legitimacy.

These views have changed in more recent times, particularly since the creation of the state of Israel (1948). The Palestinian Church, whose members are a small minority in Israel, faces a major crisis, both practical and theological, partly as a result of the belief that the Bible has been used as a political Zionist text. For Palestinian* Liberation theologians, Arab Christians have paid the price of Western Christian anti-Semitism. Furthermore, churches are generally controlled by those who are foreigners to the indigenous Arab Christians, who trace their Christianity back to the 1st c.

Initially, there was a noticeable lack of Christian comment on the establishment of the state of Israel, possibly because of Israel's challenge to the traditional stereotype of Jews as a suffering and persecuted minority (according to Alice Eckardt). The first modern Christian document to discuss the place of Israel, by the Synod of the Reformed Church of Holland (1970), stressed that Christians must appreciate the significance of the land of Israel for Jews. The Synod of the Evangelical Church of the Rhineland (1980) stated that "the continuing existence of the Jewish people, its return to the Land of Promise, and also the creation of the State of Israel, are signs of the faithfulness of God towards His people" – a view endorsed by other Protestant denominations. Some Evangelical Christians – including US evangelists such as Jerry Falwell (1933–2007) and Pat Robertson (b1930) – view the Jewish return to Zion as a fulfillment of biblical prophecy and to some extent see Jews as pawns used to fulfill God's final predetermined game plan in history. Today many manifestations of this position, sometimes called Christian Zionism, disagree on many points, including the conversion of Jews.

Roman Catholics, before Vatican* II, traditionally saw Jews only as victims rather than as people capable of power and sovereignty. However, the 1965 document *Nostra Aetate*, while not explicitly mentioning Israel, began the process that eventually led to the Vatican's recognition of the state of Israel (1994) and the pope's pilgrimage to Israel (2000).

Only a very small proportion of Israelis are Christians. Of the 7 million inhabitants, about 20% are non-Jewish. Of this group, about 85% are Muslim and 15% Christian. Most Arab Christians date their origins to the time of the Crusades*, and even to the 1st c., and many of the holy places are in the possession of Greek Orthodox, Roman Catholics, and Armenians*. "Solidarity groups," another type of Christian presence, seek "solidarity with Israel" – e.g. the Christian village of Nes Ammim in Galilee – following their conviction that there is a special relationship between the Christian churches and the Jewish people and that Christians bear historical responsibility for centuries of anti-Judaism and anti-Semitism.

EDWARD KESSLER

Israel, People of. Israel, the name given to Jacob during his struggle with the angel (Gen 32:29, 35:10), has an unknown etymology, deriving perhaps from the phrase "God [El] is fighting" (see Hos 12:4–5). The earliest attestation to an Israelite entity is the Egyptian "Merneptah stele" (13th c. BCE). Originally a league of 12 tribes – traditionally all founded by sons of Jacob – the people of Israel were united by their monotheistic faith in YHWH as creator of the universe and lord of history.

Moved by the conviction* of God's election* (Deut 4:37; Amos 3:2; Acts 13:17), Israel saw itself as a priestly nation (Exod 19:6; 1 Pet 2:9; Rev 1:6; 5:10). Its relations with other peoples knew heights and lows, owing mainly to the frequent hostility and incomprehension of neighboring powers. Israel's "otherness" and difference of values set it apart, reinforcing the conviction of a divinely appointed destiny (on the condition of heeding God's Word, Deut 6:4). Jesus is proclaimed "king of Israel" (John 12:13).

Israel's perennial character (Rom 11:28–29) is seen by some as proof of God's existence. Others insist on the supersession* of Israel by the church, veritable heir of the promises (according to certain readings of Rom 9:6; 1 Cor 10:18; Gal 5:16). The role of the OT in Christianity depends on the (anti)supersessionist stance one adopts.

ANDRÉ LACOCQUE

Italian Literature and Christianity. Italian literature was from the beginning influenced by Christianity in spirit, form, genre, theme, and gender roles, owing to the predominance in Italy of the Roman Catholic Church in all its variety and complexity.

The Latin origins of Italian literature can be traced back to Jerome's* Vulgate* (385–404), which made the Scriptures* available in medieval Latin. All texts in the vernacular (Italian, *volgare*) reflect some contact with Latin texts. Francis* of Assisi wrote the first vernacular poetic text of value, the *Canticle to Brother Sun* (*Il cantico di Frate Sole*, c1225); Jacopone da Todi popularized the *laudi* (songs in praise of the Lord) and, through them, religious theater.

Dante's* *Commedia* universalizes Christianity. Unlike Dante's, Petrarch's* Christianity is influenced by Augustine's* philosophy. He expresses the (male) individual's anxieties before God's unknowable power. However, the work that best represents the profound 14th-c. Christian faith is Catherine* of Siena's *Letters* (*Le lettere*).

During the Renaissance, Pope Nicholas V created the Vatican Library, while Pope Pius II worked to unite humanism and Christian culture. Pietro Bembo, author of the seminal

Prose in the Vernacular (Le prose della volgar lingua, 1525), was in charge of the official pontifical documents and later became a cardinal. In response to the Reformation and the challenges to the religious basis of the temporal power of the Roman Catholic Church, the Church created the (in)famous *Index* Librorum Prohibitum,* a brutal form of censorship. Nonetheless, the Church remained a powerful cultural center. Torquato Tasso's *Jerusalem Delivered* (*Gerusalemme liberata,* 1598) brought Italian literature outside its geographical borders.

After the Enlightenment, in Milan, Carlo Porta and Alessandro Manzoni (author of the novel *The Betrothed* (*I promessi sposi,* 1827) put Catholicism back at the center of Italian literature. Anti-Jansenism* flourished. Romanticism combined the Catholic attachment to Rome with the idea of an Italian nation.

During the Italian unification (*risorgimento*) and the modern era, Catholicism maintained a central place in Italian literature, especially in the many works of Vincenzo Gioberti, in Antonio Fogazzaro's *The Patriot* (*Piccolo mondo antico,* 1881), Giovanni Papini's *Life of Christ* (*Storia di Cristo,* 1921), Federico Tozzi's *Three Crosses* (*Tre croci,* 1920), philosopher Benedetto Croce's *Why We Cannot Not Define Ourselves As Christians* (*Perche' non possiamo non dirci cristiani,* 1942), political theorist and Communist leader Antonio Gramsci's "The Catholic Question" in his posthumous *Prison Notebooks* (*Quaderni del carcere,* 1948–51, 1975), Clemente Rebora's *Curriculum vitae* (1955) and *Songs of Infirmity* (*Canti dell'infermita',* 1955–56), and Mario Luzi's *Complete Poems* (*L'opera poetica,* 1988).

SAMUELE F. S. PARDINI

Italy. Although the political unity of Italy is relatively recent, the homogeneity of the area (the peninsula south of the Alps, and the islands of Sicily and Sardinia) was accentuated after the 14th c. by the shared use of the Italian language.

Evangelization and Birth of the Christian Community. The origins of the Christian communities in Italy are poorly documented. The marginal and often precarious condition of Christian groups in the Roman Empire explains the scarcity of historical documentation, yet archeological findings can complement it.

As the capital of the Empire, Rome attracted the apostles*, all the more so since a flourishing Jewish community was already there. Some NT writings testify to the spread of Christianity in Italy, centered on the two major apostles, Peter* and Paul*. Paul addressed a significant letter to the Romans* (c54–58). A few years later (c61), he arrived in Rome as a prisoner. The apostle Peter was martyred there (perhaps in 64, as his martyrdom is traditionally related to the burning of the city under Nero). Similarly Paul was thought to have been martyred (possibly c67) in Rome, where the Christian faith was already considered suspect for cultural and political reasons (see Persecutions). Regarding liturgy and church order in the Christian community in Rome at that time, much information is provided by the Apostolic* Tradition, an early church* order, probably written by Hippolytus* (c170–c236). The Christian faith was also preached in other cities – Naples, Ravenna, Milan, and Aquileia – and in Sicily and Puglia.

The Edict of Toleration (313) by the emperors Constantine* and Licinius opened a new period. Christian churches were erected in Rome, and pagan temples were transformed into churches. The custom of burying Christians in underground necropolises (catacombs*) ceased. Until the 3rd c., the liturgy in Italy was conducted in Greek; the transition to Latin* came during the 4th c.

Following Constantine's decision to transfer the capital of the Empire to Constantinople (324), Rome saw an increase in its ecclesiastical importance because of its association with the apostles Peter and Paul. In Northern Italy, the people's choice of the popular provincial governor Ambrose* (c338–97) as bishop of Milan (to replace an Arian* bishop) testifies to the integration of political life and Christianity, and the increased social prestige of ecclesiastical officials. Milan under Ambrose gained importance as an ecclesiastical center beside Rome. The Council of Aquileia (381), presided over by Ambrose, had a decisive role in this process.

By the end of the 4th c., the Christian communities were grouped in approximately 100 dioceses. The distinction between clerics and laypeople was still tenuous and fluid. A variety of liturgical traditions emerged; the Ambrosian* Rite in Milan and the Aquileian Rite (in the northeast of Italy) differed from that of Rome.

Italian Christianity under "Barbarian Rule" (5th–10th Centuries). The sack of Rome by the Visigoths of Alaric (410) – followed by the rise of the Ostrogothic kingdom of Italy (493–552) established by Theodoric – constitutes a turning point, because it signaled the sunset of a culture that had been hegemonic for nearly two centuries. For peoples within the area of Latin culture, Rome had become the center of the Latin Christian faith, assuming a role analogous to that of Jerusalem in the 1st c. The "barbarians" (Germanic tribes; the Goths*, often identified with the Vandals*) were Christians themselves, but as Arian* Christians they challenged the catholicity of the Roman Church.

With the slow evangelization of the countryside, distinct centers of Christian life, often monasteries of the Roman Church, were formed there. Nevertheless, the cathedrals in the cities, each presided over by a bishop with a college of presbyters, remained the central points of reference for Christian life. Christian dioceses corresponded to the *municipia* (cities with their own local governments according to Roman law, continued under the Goths). The bishop (often Arian) had social and political standing; he often assumed the titles and roles associated with other imperial functionaries.

During this period, Benedict* of Nursia (c480–c555) was a hermit at Subiaco and then founded several monasteries, most notably that in Monte Cassino (Southern Italy). With the monasteries, an authoritative Roman Christian presence outside of the cities was established. Yet popular forms of Christianity – "syncretistic" or "inculturated" Christian practices and doctrines, according to one's perspective – also developed. The piety of common, lay Christians – often Arians – was centered in the family, with traditional prayers and simple celebrations transmitted orally from generation to generation. The Lombard* conquest (568–605) added new pressures from Arian rulers. Yet as Lombard rulers minimized in their governmental administration the role of Christian dioceses as *municipia*, the churches were more independent; Latin-speaking Christians could assert their distance from the Arianism of the rulers.

In the meantime, the violent doctrinal controversies about Christ, his person and nature, though centered in Constantinople, reached Italy, and the West was often the center of opposition to developments later judged to be heretical* (see Arianism; Christologies Cluster; Miaphysite; Monophysite; Three Chapters).

The Centrality of the Roman Church. The growth of the territorial domain of the Church of Rome, the nucleus of the future temporal power of the popes, was given a legal foundation by the "Donation* of Constantine*," a forgery produced in Rome (c750–80) granting to the pope supreme authority in the church and temporal rule in Italy. The bishop of Rome, like all bishops, had been elected by the "clergy and people" of the city, but a Lateran Synod (769) sanctioned their exclusion from active participation in such a selection. Thus began the relationship between church* and state (and the broader society), which led to envisioning Christendom* as a society in which the ecclesiastical and the political and civic were so closely associated that they often became indistinguishable, in terms of both mutual support and contamination.

The Christian life of laypeople was very simple: they were to take Communion at least at Easter (later also at Christmas and Pentecost), know the "Our Father" (see Lord's Prayer) and the Apostles'* Creed, and frequent the Sunday Mass. Regarding morality, there was an effort (not always successful) to purify popular customs. With the conquest of Sicily by the Muslims (831), a radically different religion with its own cultural and social structure was present side by side with Christianity.

With the second millennium, important changes took place on the peninsula. In the north (under the rule of the German emperors of the Holy* Roman Empire, successors of Charlemagne*), there was economic growth and the beginning of a reform movement. In the south, the Norman settlements (since the early 11th c.) ended Arab/Muslim domination and stabilized the situation. A Christian faith more disposed to take up its own armed defense and to undertake military expeditions and crusades* grew in Italy as well as north of the Alps. New social classes surged to prominence and called for an urgent reform of the Roman Catholic Church that would free it from both ecclesiastical and imperial control; e.g. the movement of the Patarini in Milan and Florence led by laypeople and the lower clergy protested the simony* and the wealth of the higher clergy.

During that period, a major Western institution was born: the *universitas studiorum* (Bologna), the "university," where the inheritance of the past was studied and conflicting perspectives analyzed. Gratian* compiled at Bologna the *Concordantia discordantium canonum,* which would constitute the nucleus of the *Corpus Iuris Canonici* (see Canon Law) destined to regulate the life of Roman Catholics until 1918.

From Francis* of Assisi to the Council of Trent* (13th–16th Centuries). The reformist ferment became concrete in the Lay* Piety Movement, as seen most dramatically in the religious revivals of 1233 (the "Alleluia" Movement) and 1260 (the flagellants of Northern Italy, who whipped each other to atone for their sins and calling on the populace to repent). The figure of Francis* of Assisi (c1182–1226) synthesizes the complex spiritual pressures of the moment. Unlike the clergy, Francis rendered tangible and explosive the imitation of Jesus in late medieval society. His followers gave rise to the Franciscans*. The need to preach the gospel motivated another layperson, Peter Valdes*, to engage ordinary Christians, including women, in the task of preaching; but the radicalism of Valdes's followers* resulted in their condemnation by the official church at the Council of Verona (1184). This confrontation led to the creation of a "heretical" church, the Waldensian* Church in the Piedmont valleys, whose members, like the "Poor Lombards," were subjected to relentless persecution.

Between the mid-15th and early 16th c., denunciations of the institutional, theological, moral, and pastoral decadence of the Roman Catholic Church multiplied. Girolamo Savonarola (1452–98), a Dominican, sought ecclesiastical, social, and political reform in Florence, and was eventually executed; Catherine of Genoa (1447–1510), a canonized mystic, offers another example of the spiritual commitment of this period. While Martin Luther's* movement was maturing in Germany, the spiritual climate in Italy was very different. From 1542 the relentless work of the Roman Inquisition* limited the Protestant expansion in Italy, creating a climate of frustration and spiritual collapse in many places. Flight to Protestant lands was the solution for many: Bernardo Ochino (1487–1564), a Franciscan reformer in Venice, escaped the Inquisition by going to Geneva (1542); Peter Paul Vergerio (1498–1565), formerly bishop and papal nuncio* to Germany, became Protestant while attempting to refute Lutheran writings and introduced the Reformation in parts of Northern Italy, but soon had to escape to Germany (1549). The Waldensian communities felt affirmed by the Protestant reform; at their synod of Cianforan (1532), in which Farel* participated, they adhered to Calvinism*. Rather than flee, others preferred to keep their beliefs to themselves (Calvin called them "Nicodemites*"): they shared the Catholic liturgy and outward behavior, but professed in the privacy of their own consciences the "true religion." But most Italian Catholics simply accepted the demonization* of Luther and Protestants relentlessly presented by Roman propaganda. For common Italian Roman Catholics, the Council of Trent* (1545–63) was a remote assembly of grand ecclesiastical dignitaries far removed from their daily life.

The Modern Period (16th–20th Centuries). The political division of the peninsula into three zones influenced Christian perspectives: the north was sensitive to contact with Catholicism on the other side of the Alps; in the central region, primarily the States of the Church, the "government of priests" progressively fed anticlericalism and a greater disposition toward secularization*; in the southern region (including Sicily and Sardinia), subject to Spanish and then French influence, a relaxed ecclesiastical regime coexisted with an awareness of the dignity and independence of the clergy in the care* of souls. During the 17th–18th c., the civil and religious became interwoven. The baroque developed as a cultural attitude that also involved the religious. Jansenism* had a moderately significant impact, with adherents in certain circles, whereas the anti-Jansenist reaction was much more vigorous and produced a literature of contestation (see Italian Literature and Christianity). The age of worldwide exploration expanded the missionary sensibility toward the "pagan" continents.

The suppression of the Jesuits* (1750–73) provoked in Italy the constitution of the "Christian Friendships" (Amicizie cristiane), a secret society fighting the rise of modern culture. In this context, Scipione de' Ricci (1741–1810), bishop of Pistoia-Prato, sought at the Synod of Pistoia (1786) to reform the Tuscan Church along the lines advocated by the Jansenists by promoting a rediscovery of the Bible, a greater liturgical devotion, the use of the vernacular* in the Mass, and the Church's renunciation of social privileges. But all this was rejected in Italy (de' Ricci recanted in 1794); it was realized in France with the French Revolution, which was viewed as a frontal attack on Catholicism.

In the early 19th c., the first germs of secularization* became manifest in Italy. The later 19th c. was dominated by the "Roman Question." The process of unification of the peninsula put an end to the States of the Church. Rome became annexed to the kingdom of Italy (1870). In protest, one of the high apostolic tribunals, the apostolic penitentiary (1871, confirmed by Pius IX, 1874), forbade Catholics to participate in political elections. Yet national unification was accepted by certain lay Catholics – especially Giovanni Acquaderni and Mario Fani, who founded the Italian Catholic Youth Society (1867, later called Catholic* Action) – and resisted by others, the "intransigents" of the Opera dei Congressi (1874–75). The predominantly rural population, very poor and still profoundly religious, called for Christians to confront social issues. Thus Catholic social movements developed especially in Northern Italy, forming the embryo of a postclerical Catholic ruling class. Toward the end of the century, a young priest, Romolo Murri (1870–1944), attempted to bridge the separation of Catholics from democratic political life in a movement that led to the creation of "Christian Democracy."

A harsh reaction and repression was the response of the Roman Catholic Church to the need for the cultural renewal of Catholicism. This climate of suspicion and denunciation marginalized many young intellectuals and spiritually gifted individuals (the "Modernists*"). As a result, both clergy and laity were impoverished, pushed as they were to avoid theological issues and cultural research (illustrated by the 1871 abolition of the theological faculties in state universities).

After World War I (1918), fascism appeared to be a providential answer to the threat of "Red" socialism and anticlericalism. The fascist movement promised to reestablish social order and to respect religion. The papacy and a great part of the clergy regarded fascism with sympathy; Cardinal Gasparri for the Holy See and Mussolini, as head of the Italian government, signed the Lateran Pacts (1929) that resolved the Roman Question and created the Vatican City as a sovereign state. The Christian antifascist minorities were marginalized. Catholicism was established as the "state religion." On the cultural level, the Catholic University of the Sacred Heart (Milan, 1923) was established through the initiative of the Franciscan Agostino Gemelli. The laity became more active, developing Catholic Action; yet the movements that animated Christians elsewhere in Europe at that time barely touched Italy.

Christianity in Contemporary Italy (20th–21st Centuries). At the end of World War II (1945), Catholicism lived with the conviction that it was definitively shaped and established; no improvement was necessary. After the reconstitution of the democratic regime, the Catholic presence in Italian society had two forms: Catholic Action, now directly controlled by the Church hierarchy; and the Christian Democratic Party, indirectly controlled and supported by Catholic Action. Preventing the expansion of the Communist* Party's ideology was the dominant concern. Many Catholics were convinced that with the proper social and political commitments (Catholic Action and the Christian Democratic Party), the democratic system could bring about a "Christian state" that would concede to them the management of power and ensure that faith would have the influence that is due to the gospel. But the Holy See's excommunication of Communists and their supporters (1949) had the opposite effect; it marginalized Catholics. The ferment of renewal was nevertheless present, especially among the youth. Many groups embodied a spirit of freedom, an intense spiritual commitment to a Christian presence in society, and the quest for a mature life of faith. The majority lived an activist spiritual and political life under the leadership of Luigi Gedda, the general president of Catholic Action, and the Jesuit father Riccardo Lombardi, promoter of the "Crusade for a Better World." The government and magistrates, however, interpreted the Lateran Pacts (Article 7) in a way that was often oppressive and discriminatory with regard to religious minorities (Waldenses, Methodists, Jews). Freedom of religion, though sanctioned by Article 8 of the constitution, had a difficult time.

The Second Vatican* Council (1962–65) rapidly aroused profound interest in Italian public opinion. The events of the Council taking place in Rome brought Italian Catholicism out of its peripheral condition. Even ordinary people became involved in the great themes of Christian renovation. In the last years of the pontificate of Paul VI (1963–78), a spiritual flowering became manifest, especially with the birth of spontaneous monastic communities (Monte Sole, Bose, Spello), characterized by an intense commitment of faith that attracted the participation of a broad range of Christians. Such communities coordinated and enriched myriad prayer and Bible study groups.

With the election, after four and a half centuries, of two non-Italian popes (Karol Wojtila, 1978; Joseph Ratzinger, 2005), the Catholicism of the Italian Peninsula entered a new phase of its history. The pope's diminished involvement in Italian affairs was accompanied by deep sympathy for "movements," ranging from the Focolare* (emphasizing ecumenical and interfaith dialogue) to "Communion and Liberation" (emphasizing collaboration in the mission of the Church in all spheres of life) and Sant' Egidio (emphasizing solidarity with the poor). These movements find it difficult to maintain a balanced relationship with ordinary believers. Their efforts to root Christian identity in certainties that are historical and temporal betray a kind of fundamentalist* tendency. The conciliar impulse nevertheless triggered processes of renovation: the spread of direct contact with the Bible, participation in the liturgy, and a slow but ongoing diffusion of historical and theological studies on Christianity in the university. All these are helping to overcome centuries of passivity and marginalization of lay believers. In the 1980s, while Catholic Action was losing vitality, other commitments developed. The volunteer sector involves many Christians in services on the "frontier," such as assistance and rehabilitation of drug addicts, assistance of the elderly, and service in Two-thirds World countries.

Church and state relations in Italy have extended to the Reformed churches, which became beneficiaries of public funds; a similar agreement was made with the Jewish communities. The rapid decomposition of the Christian Democratic Party after the fall of the Berlin Wall necessitated a strenuous search for a new mode of presence in Italian society. The climate of greater freedom, resulting from Vatican II and the ecumenical initiatives of contact and dialogue, has calmed the tensions between Christian confessions, while the rapid evolution toward a multireligious tradition has profoundly changed the spiritual climate and the increasingly secularized culture of Italy.

Statistics: Population (2000): 57.3 million (M). Christians, 47 M, 82% (baptized Roman Catholics, 55.6 M [10 M are "disaffiliated" and only 6% attend Mass regularly]; Protestants, 0.4 M; marginal Christians, 0.4 M; independents, 0.4 M; Orthodox, 0.1 M); Muslims, 0.7 M, 1%; nonreligious, 9.5M, 17%. (Based on *World Christian Encyclopedia*, 2001.)

GIUSEPPE ALBERIGO

I–Thou Relation, an intimate, loving union, usually between persons, human or divine, who view each other as free, self-directed individuals possessing intrinsic value and dignity. (The English "thou" is a translation of the familiar form of "you" in French [*tu*], German [*du*], and other languages). It is contrasted with an I–him/her relation between persons who view each other as separate things or objects whose value lies in their particular features and functions. The loving bond between I and thou enhances each party, for it entails a sharing of lives and experiences while respecting the mysterious uniqueness of each. **See also BUBER, MARTIN; MARCEL, GABRIEL; LEVINAS, EMMANUEL; HETERONOMY; RELATIONALITY.** THOMAS C. ANDERSON

J

Jackson, Rebecca Cox (1795–1871), Shaker* preacher and founder of an African American Shaker community in Philadelphia (1859). Born in Pennsylvania, she was converted to Christianity in 1830 and became an itinerant preacher (1833–40) before joining the Shakers (1843). Jackson's life draws together the Holiness* Movement, perfectionism*, and race. Her spiritual visions, recorded in *Gifts of Power*, indicated a desire for both spiritual perfection and physical protection. As an itinerant preacher and an African American woman, Jackson faced persecution*. Her visions taught her that hardship was inevitable but that God would protect her if she became an obedient and pure spiritual vessel. As direct communications from the Holy* Spirit, Jackson's visions also provided her with a source of spiritual authority; she left her marriage, embraced celibacy*, and began preaching. She abandoned the African* Methodist Episcopal Church, in which she had experienced conversion* and sanctification*, for the Shakers, whose theology cohered with her beliefs regarding purity. But the overwhelmingly white Shaker community did not make sufficient inroads among African Americans. Creating her own religious community gave her spiritual authority uncommon among 19th-c. women, black or white, and the opportunity to work among African Americans.

SARAH JOHNSON

Jacob, son of Isaac* and Rebecca*, younger twin brother of Esau*. Isaac favored Esau*, but through deception Jacob received the Abrahamic blessing (Gen 27). Fleeing Esau's wrath, Jacob was employed by Laban and married his daughters, Leah* and Rachel* (Gen 29–30). His 12 sons, by four mothers, were considered the ancestors of the 12 tribes of Israel*, so called because of Jacob's name change after wrestling with God at Peniel (Gen 32). Late in his life, he and his sons went to Egypt, where Joseph* was a high official and gave them assistance (Gen 46). The Israelites were later enslaved in Egypt, leading to God's deliverance, the Exodus*.

Jacob Baradai, or Baradaeus (c500–578), the name deriving either from "Bar Addai" or from "Bardaya" (saddle blankets), referring to his humble garb. Born in Tella and educated at a monastery near Nisibis, Jacob spent 15 years in Constantinople as a member of the circle of Theodora*, a sympathizer of the Miaphysites*, at a time when her husband, Justinian*, was enforcing the doctrine of Chalcedon*. Through her influence, he was secretly consecrated metropolitan of Edessa* and traveled through the East, consecrating an underground hierarchy of bishops and priests, without ever being betrayed. Because of their invisibility, they were called the *akephaloi*, the "headless ones." This was the beginning of the non-Chalcedonian Syriac* Orthodox Church, called "Jacobite," a polemical name.

EUGENE TESELLE

Jacob of Edessa (c640–708), scholar, exegete, bishop. Born near Antioch, Jacob studied in the monastery of Qenneshre, then in Alexandria, before becoming bishop of Edessa* (684–688, 708). He resigned over a conflict with clergy about ecclesiastical discipline; he spent 11 years in the monastery of Eusebona and 9 in the monastery of Teleda, where he revised the Syriac translation of the OT. He died shortly after resuming his episcopate of Edessa. Jacob wrote biblical commentaries, letters, a chronicle, canons, and treatises on liturgical, philosophical, and philological subjects. His encyclopedic learning and uncompromising attitude contributed to the redefinition of Miaphysite* Christian identity after the Arab Conquest.

UTE POSSEKEL

Jacobite, a polemical (and offensive) nickname given to the Syriac* Orthodox Church, after the name of its Miaphysite* bishop, Jacob* Baradai (c500–78), who revived the spiritual life of the Church in Syria*, Armenia*, Egypt*, Persia, and Cyprus*.

Jacob of Serug, or Sarug (c451–521), Syriac poet-theologian and author, important writer about non-Christian religion in Syro-Mesopotamia, bishop in Serug (Sarug) (519). Together with the Syriac* Church, Jacob distanced himself from Chalcedonian* doctrines, although he was never directly involved in christological* controversies. Known chiefly for his metrical homilies (*memre*) – including those on the Mother of God (see Mary, the Virgin, Cluster: Theotokos) – Jacob also wrote letters and festal homilies in prose. His significant anti-Jewish* polemic and positive attitude toward women are associated with Ephrem* the Syrian. Three early biographies, one by Jacob* of Edessa, survive. He is credited with having written a liturgy and an order of baptism. He was influential in the Malankara* Orthodox Church of India.

KATHLEEN E. MCVEY

Jacob of Voragine (c1230–98), member of the Dominican* order (1244), provincial of Lombardy (1267–86), archbishop of Genoa (1292–98), author of the *Golden* Legend.*

Jamaica. Christianity on this island situated in the Caribbean Sea includes African-rooted movements and churches, as well as other denominations.

Originally populated by the Arawak Indians, who disappeared during Spanish rule (from 1509), Jamaica became Catholic when the pope created an abbacy (1516). When Jamaica became a British colony (1655), Anglicanism* became the official religion, until 1869, when the separation of the Anglican Church and the colonial state occurred. Jamaica has been an independent nation since 1962.

In 1837 the Roman Catholic mission became an apostolic vicariate*, and Jesuits* have been active since then in the educational* field. The vicariate became the Diocese of Kingston (1956), then the archdiocese (1967).

Arriving in 1754, the Moravians* were the first Protestant missionaries among slaves* in Jamaica, followed by the Wesleyan-Methodist* Church (1789). The Jamaican Baptists became independent in 1842. The Scottish Missionary Society and Secession missionaries formed the United Presbyterian Mission in 1848. In 1965 the Congregationalists and Presbyterians came together as the United Reformed Church of Jamaica. The Jamaican Council of Churches has existed since 1941.

Starting in the late 18th c., conformist missionary churches attracted an increasing number of slaves and free blacks. The arrival of freed slaves from the US colonies during the War of Independence stimulated a Native, or Black Baptist, tradition in Jamaica. Many slaves practiced different forms of African* Religion. There were increasing "outbreaks" of Myalism, a Jamaican syncretism* of African spirit belief and apocalyptic Christianity (also called "revivalism," as an inculturation* of apocalyptic Christianity into African slaves' religious culture). Jamaican Myalism evolved over time to combat the effects of *obeah*, the word for witchcraft* practice, that was disseminated in West Africa and Jamaica (see History of Christianity Cluster: In Latin America).

The Jamaican Christian tradition developed a peculiar interpretation of the faith*, according to which Jesus is the Savior who will liberate God's people from "Babylon" (the evil and oppressive world). It was found among earlier groups, including the "revivalists," and it continues among the Pentecostals and Charismatics* today (250,000 members in 1970; 385,000 in 2000). This theme of "Babylon" is also present in the Rastafari* Movement.

Statistics: Population (2000): 2.5 million (M), more than 90% of African origin. Christians, 2.1 M, 84.0% (Protestants and independents, 60%; Roman Catholics, 8%); Spiritists, 10.1% (including Rastafari); Hindus, 5%; nonreligious, 3.9%) (some double affiliations). (Based on *World Christian Encyclopedia*, 2001.)

ARMANDO LAMPE

James. In the NT, the name "James" (Gk *Iakobos*) refers to at least three different persons:

1. James, the son of Zebedee, brother of John. The brothers were the second pair of disciples to be called by Jesus (Mark 1:19; Matt 4:21) and part of the Twelve* (Mark 3:17; Matt 10:2; Luke 6:14; Acts 1:13), as well as the inner circle of Jesus' disciples (Peter, James, and John; Mark 5:37, 9:2, 14:33, and par.; Luke 9:28). He was killed by Herod Agrippa (Acts 12:1–2), the only one of the Twelve whose martyrdom the NT records.
2. James, the son of Alpheus, is another of the Twelve, identified as such only in the four lists of apostles (Mark 3:18; Matt 10:3; Luke 6:15; Acts 1:13).
3. James, the brother of Jesus or "the Lord's brother" (Gal 1:19), a "pillar" of the Jerusalem Church (Gal 2:9) and participant in the Jerusalem conference (Gal 2:1–20; Acts 15:1–20), who saw the risen Lord (1 Cor 15:7). This is the person referred to as James in Acts 12:17, 15:13, and 21:18, i.e. after the death of James, the brother of John (12:1–2); he is also the brother of Jesus mentioned in Mark 6:3 and Matt 13:55 (see also Jas 1:1; Jude 1). "James, the brother of Jesus" is interpreted to mean (a) James, a younger son of Joseph and

Mary; or (b) James, a son of Joseph by a previous marriage, a foster brother of Jesus (on the basis of apocryphal sources), a view favored by many Orthodox and Protestants; or (c) James, a cousin of Jesus (based on the Semitic idiomatic use of "brothers" to designate "cousins"), who was identified with James, the son of Alpheus, the son of Mary ("mother of James and Joses," Mark 15:40, Matt 15:40), the preferred Roman Catholic interpretation, following Jerome* and Augustine*. DANIEL PATTE

James, Letter of, a pseudonymous* letter (c90s, Rome?) written to poor Jewish-Christian communities, is the most radical NT document speaking out against the rich (5:1–6, 4:13). It seeks to give hope* (1:2–4, 12) to oppressed* people and to exhort them to undertake a coherent practice in which actions are consistent with faith (1:22–27, 2:4–17, 3:13) (see Faith #1). There was discrimination against the poor within the community (2:1–6, 2:14–16) and exploitation of the farmworkers by landowners (5:1–6). Apparently, the majority of the poor were women, since the Letter of James uses the feminine *adelphe*, "sister" (2:15) (in those days, inclusive language was not a concern).

The Letter of James is known for affirming "justification* by works" (2:24) and for eliciting Luther's* scorn ("epistle of straw"). Nevertheless, when read from the perspective of the historical Jesus* (since it includes Jesus' sayings), James advocates a Christology of the Way centered on the practice of justice* and what has been called more recently the preferential* option for the poor (1:27, 2:5–6, 14–17). Paul's phrase "justification by faith" was misinterpreted to imply that faith does not demand a commitment to neighbors*. In the presence of the poor, James corrects this view by emphasizing that works of justice are an important element in justification and the unity of faith and works (in agreement with Paul himself; see Gal. 5:6). James constantly challenges the churches to demonstrate their faith through commitment to the oppressed and discriminated, especially women.

ELSA TAMEZ (translated by Gloria Kinsler)

James, Liturgy of St., eucharistic formulary in the Greek language, probably elaborated in Jerusalem on the basis of the anaphora* of the *Mystagogical Catecheseis* (post-380) and the two stages of the Liturgy of St. Basil*. Until the 12th–13th c., the Liturgy of St. James was used in the Orthodox Patriarchate of Jerusalem and the Catholicate of Georgia. It was subsequently replaced by the Byzantine liturgies of St. John Chrysostom* and of St. Basil. The Liturgy of St. James (in Syriac translation) is also used by the Syriac* Orthodox Church and the Malankara* Orthodox Church of India, both Oriental Orthodox* (non-Chalcedonian) churches, and by Oriental churches in communion with Rome, including the Syro-Malankara Catholic Church. Some Eastern Orthodox churches celebrate the Liturgy of St. James on October 23 and the Sunday after Christmas, both feasts of St. James.

STEFANO PARENTI

James, Protoevangelion, or Gospel of, one of the Greek apocryphal Gospels (2nd c.). The purported author, James*, the brother of the Lord, describes the birth and childhood of Mary, her coming of age and betrothal to Joseph* (who was a widower with several children, as Origen* discussed), and Jesus' birth and early childhood. It emphasizes God's work in Mary's life, her purity and perpetual virginity*, i.e. before, during, and after the birth of Jesus. Widely read and translated (in Syriac, Ethiopic, Coptic, Georgian, Old Slavonic, Armenian, Arabic, Irish, and later in Latin), the Protoevangelion was one of the bases of the Orthodox doctrine of Mary as Theotokos. **See also MARY, THE VIRGIN, CLUSTER: THEOTOKOS.**

James I of England (1566–1625), king of Scotland and England, political theorist, ecumenist, peacemaker. Born in Scotland, he became James VI on the abdication of his mother, Mary*, queen of Scots (1567). He became James I of England on the death of Elizabeth I* (1603), then proclaimed himself king of Great Britain (1604).

As king of Scotland, James successfully balanced rival political and religious factions and played a significant if controversial role in governing the Church of Scotland*. He defended the monarchy against Calvinist* resistance theories. On his accession in England, he proposed an ecumenical council to resolve disputes among churches. James convened the Hampton Court Conference (1604) to consider Puritan* proposals for reform. One result was a new English translation of the Bible*, the Authorized or King James Version (1611). Under his direction, the Church of England was administered by capable bishops and was largely Calvinist* in theology, but included some Arminians*. James sent British representatives to the Synod of Dort* to resolve theological disputes in the Netherlands; he patronized in England French Huguenots* and exiled Roman Catholics; he initiated relations with the Greek Orthodox Church through Patriarch Cyril Lucaris*. After ending the war between England and Spain (1604), James assisted in the peaceful resolution of disputes elsewhere in Europe, attempting without success to negotiate settlements at the beginning of the Thirty* Years' War and to forge an alliance with Catholic Spain.

Long derided for his undignified appearance, his fondness for male favorites, his extravagance, the corruption at his court, and his frequently contentious relations with the English Parliament, James is now also admired for his virtues and achievements. A shrewd politician, he brought stability to his kingdoms; he was an able theologian, an ecumenist and peacemaker, and the pungent writer of *The Trew Law of Free Monarchies* (1598), *Basilicon Doron* (1599), *Triplici Nodo, Triplex Cuneus* (1607), and *A Premonition to All Christian Monarches* (1609). **See also BIBLE TRANSLATIONS CLUSTER: ENGLISH TRANSLATIONS.** W. BROWN PATTERSON

Jane Frances de Chantal (1572–1641), widow, Roman Catholic saint, cofounder (with Francis* de Sales) of the Visitation of Holy Mary, a diocesan congregation (Annecy, Savoy, 1610), which became a formal monastic order (1618). The Visitation was an innovative early modern Catholic women's religious community that emphasized interior rather than austere exterior discipline*. Entrants included widows and handicapped women who were not eligible to enter other reformed orders. The Visitation's motto, "Live Jesus," captured the idea that one's heart should be inhabited by the gentle, humble heart of Jesus (Matt 11:28–30) through the practice of the "little virtues" such as gentleness and humility*. Spiritual guidance was undertaken in this same spirit of gentleness in order to "win hearts." The characteristic prayer of Mother de Chantal and the Visitandines was a simple, nondiscursive entrustment of self to God. This spirituality reflected the changing spiritual ethos of early modern Catholicism, which emphasized an individualized and inward faith focused on the acquisition of virtue, a spirituality that gradually replaced the more exteriorized, concrete spirituality of the late medieval world. After de Sales's death, Mother de Chantal oversaw the phenomenal growth of the order, especially in France. **See also CATHOLIC RENEWAL.**

WENDY M. WRIGHT

Jansen, or Jansenius, Cornelius (1585–1638), author of *Augustinus* (1640), taught Scripture* in Flanders (now Belgium) and wrote biblical commentaries. Together with the abbot of Saint-Cyran, who was theologian and spiritual counselor of Port-Royal, he studied the church fathers, especially Augustine*, compiling from them a *summa theologica,* in which he emphasized Augustine's main doctrinal points: original* sin, predestination*, and grace*. Humans are powerless under sin* and need to be empowered by divine grace* to do God's will; he affirmed predestination* and irresistible grace*. Named bishop of Ypres, he prematurely died of the plague. His name will remain attached to "Jansenism*." JEAN LESAULNIER

Jansenism, a movement that emerged following the posthumous publication of Jansen's* *Augustinus* (1640). The term "Jansenism" or "Jansenist" was first used polemically to designate the "new" doctrine of this volume, rejected as such by Roman authorities. In reality, it was an effort to return to Augustine's* thought, in reaction to the Renaissance's anthropology*, which minimized the effects of original* sin. Jansen used Augustine to affirm the depth of human sin, against the Renaissance view as well as against the view of the Jesuits* (especially the disciples of Molina*); Jansen rejected the notion that humans have received free will, a free agency giving them the potential to choose what is good (see Freedom, Free Will), and the Jesuits' toleration of lax morality.

Augustinian theology as presented by Jansen was attacked, even though it was closely related to the views of Pierre de Bérulle, cardinal and mystic* (1575–1629), and Francis* de Sales. But the Roman condemnation of statements from Jansen's *Augustinus* and comments by Jansen and Saint-Cyran, and the suspicions of political authorities such as Richelieu, had a negative impact on the monastic renewal of the Port*-Royal Abbey, its remarkable nuns (including Angelique Arnauld*), and intellectuals (including Antoine Arnauld* and Blaise Pascal*) who gravitated around Port-Royal.

A center of spirituality and theology, Port-Royal became, for many, an object of condemnation, even though its spirit won over many dioceses and much of French society. Outside of France, there was a parallel development of Jansenism and anti-Jansenism, which resulted in renewed Roman condemnation in the 18th c. (for, among other things, Janenism's association with Gallicanism*) and in the transformation of the movement. Without severing its roots, it moved away from its original inspiration, emphasizing the propagation of the Christian message through study of the Bible and of patristic literature, and demanding freedom of conscience, as well as a rigorous moral life and ecclesiastical discipline. By becoming synonymous with rigorism, Jansenism obscured the true spirit of Port-Royal. JEAN LESAULNIER

Japan. In 1549 the Jesuit Francis Xavier* introduced Christianity in Japan, which was impoverished spiritually and physically as a result of recurring bloody civil wars. Christianity was spread among local rulers and the people by the Catholic missionaries; in 1582 Kyushu Christian rulers sent a delegation of four Japanese boys with the Jesuit Alessandro Valignano to Gregory XIII in Rome. Despite this initial success, the process of national unification and a policy of isolation after the late 16th c. led to the official proscription of Christianity, partly out of fear of Western colonization* and ideological* subversion. Christians were oppressed and almost eradicated (see Kirishitans and Hidden Christians in Japan). Most notably, 26 Christians were crucified at Nagasaki (1597), when the number of Christians was about 300,000.

When Japan opened itself to the world (1850s), Catholics and Protestants came to the country. In 1865 B. T. Petitjean, a Catholic missionary, discovered the "hidden" Christians and invited them to Ooura Cathedral at Nagasaki; later more than 3,000 Christians were persecuted by the authorities. When this event became an international diplomatic issue, the authorities officially lifted the proscription on Christianity (1873). The first Protestant church was founded in Yokohama (1872).

Christianity contributed to the modernization of Japan by creating educational* institutions, supporting civil* rights, forming labor, farmer, and consumer unions, teaching personal and social ethics, enriching Japanese* literature, and enhancing social* welfare. The 1889 Japanese Imperial Constitution established freedom of religion, but only insofar as it did not infringe on the national order and subjects' duties. Consequently, from 1889 Christian pacifists*, pastors, and educators who opposed nationalism* were persecuted. In 1891 Kanzou Uchimura, who later created the Non-church Movement, had to resign his teaching position in Tokyo because he refused to comply with the Imperial Precept on Education signed by the emperor (see Chinese Rites Controversy). Yet Japanese Christendom was ultimately incorporated into Japanese nationalism, as was the case with the United Church of Christ in Japan and with a union of Protestant churches.

After the Allied defeat of the Japanese in 1945, full freedom of religion, provided by the new constitution written during the US occupation, contributed to a renewal of Christianity. Since the 1960s, issues such as the inculturation* of Christianity in Japan, Christians' collaboration with the wartime government, and the stagnation of Christianity have been reexamined. Christians still constitute a small percentage of the population, but Christianity has contributed immensely to the improvement of various aspects of the Japanese society. **See also BURAKU LIBERATION IN JAPAN; KAGAWA, TOYOHIKO; SHINTO AND CHRISTIANITY.**

Statistics: Population (2000): 127 million. Christians, 3% (independents [including isolated "radio-believers" and "hidden Christians"], 1.3%; marginal Christians [e.g. members of Church of Christ Scientist, Jehovah's Witnesses, Mormons], 0.7%; Protestants, 0.5%; Roman Catholics, 0.4%; Anglicans, 0.1%); Buddhists, 55%; new religionists, 25.9; Shintoists, 2.1%; atheists and nonreligious, 13.1%. (Based on *World Christian Encyclopedia*, 2001.)

NOZOMU MIYAHIRA

Japanese Literature and Christianity. Christianity intersects with Japanese literature mainly in the modern era and introduces a new rhetoric of individual moral and spiritual quests.

After the ban on Christianity was lifted (1873), Christianity provided a context and a language to define spiritual freedom, individualism, love, and aesthetic and poetic ideals crucial to the development of Japanese romanticism and naturalism in the Meiji period (1868–1912). Kitamura Tokoku (1868–94), Shimazaki Toson (1872–1943), Kunikida Doppo (1871–1908), and Tayama Katai (1871–1930), all Christian converts, incorporated Christian themes (the divine, sin*, guilt, sacrifice*, commandments) into works that are essentially secular yet soul searching. In the Taisho period (1912–26), Arishima Takeo (1878–1923) questioned the hypocrisy of conventional Christians in *A Certain Woman* (1919) but condemned the moral degeneration that followed the rejection of Christianity. Miyazawa Kenji's (1896–1933) indebtedness to Christianity is evident in his description of a transcendental world in *The Night of the Milky Way Express* (posthumous) and the figure of humility* and self-denial in his poem "Undaunted by Rain" (1931).

Biblical motifs are found in Natsume Soseki's (1867–1916) works, such as the image of the lost sheep in *Sanshiro* (1908) and the herd of pigs hurtling themselves over the cliff in the *Ten Nights of Dream* (1908). In *The Confessions of a Mask* (1949), Mishima Yukio (1925–70) constructs his ultimate vision of beauty and tragedy using the tension in the biblical iconography of the Madonna* (purity), Sodom* (corruption) and St. Sebastian* (martyrdom). Abe Kobo (1924–93) borrows from the image of the Apocalypse (the Book of Revelation*) and a surviving ark of humanity (*The Ark Sakura*, 1984) to describe a haunting post–nuclear world of doom.

The works of Christian writers range from church history in Japan to the use of a religious rhetoric for moral investigations. Endo Shusaku (1923–96) depicts the difficult and at times tortuous encounter between a pantheistic Japan and a monotheistic West. His fictional depictions range from the persecution of Christian converts in Japan (*Silence*, 1966) to a Jesus to whom a "yellow man" can relate (*A Life of Jesus*, 1973). Sono Ayako's (1931–) *Watcher from the Shore* (1979–80) raises questions about faith* and moral judgment through the daily confrontation of life and death in a gynecologist's work (see Medical Ethics). Other Christian writers include Ariyoshi Sawako (1931–84), Inoue Hisashi (1934–), Miura Ayako (1922–99), Shimao Toshio (1917–86), Shiina Rinzo (1911–73), and Kaga Otohiko (1929–). ANGELA YIU

Jaspers, Karl (1883–1969), philosopher, psychopathologist, cultural critic, professor in Heidelberg (dismissed in 1937 by the Nazis because his wife was Jewish; reinstated in 1945) and later in Basel (1948). He wrote the standard work on psychopathology and numerous works in philosophy influenced by the Bible (mainly the OT), Kant*, Kierkegaard*, Weber*, and Nietzsche*.

As a result of his Protestant and politically liberal upbringing and his career as a psychopathologist, Jaspers realized the limits of scientific knowledge about humans, who spiritually "live out of" sources transcending nature. He developed a phenomenology* of faith* as a basis for any vision of ultimate truth by time-confined humans. Jaspers affirms the value of Christianity for teaching a sense of individual freedom and dignity arising from a personal relatedness to God ("transcendence") and transmitting the unconditional morality of the OT. For Jaspers God* transcends time and human grasp. The biblical stories of God's acts and commanding presence are myths* and symbols* ("ciphers of transcendence") that inform our faith and guide our practice. Hence Jaspers critiques the emphasis of Christianity on confessing to creeds (*fides quae creditur*) instead of undertaking the risk of living by one's belief (*fides qua creditur*) (see Faith #3).

Jaspers takes issue with the modern neglect of the Bible, its theological dogmatization, and attempts to demythologize* it. Against Bultmann*, Jaspers insists that truths conveyed by myths or symbols are translatable only into other myths or symbols. Any myth, including that of the Christian act of salvation*, "is to be tested from the standpoint of the earnestness of existential actuality, for the power emanating from its language and the truth issuing from it in the actuality of life."

Jaspers sharply criticizes the Christian doctrine of revelation* and its claim that Christian truth supersedes or excludes the validity of other religions (thus in *The Great Philosophers* Jaspers puts Confucius, the Buddha, and Socrates on a par with Jesus). Claims to the exclusiveness of truth lead to intolerance, religious wars*, and persecution*. God transcends all historic revelational religions. The validity of my faith does not require that others believe as I do. Encountering different religions calls for solidarity among believers and mutual tolerance, rather than the intolerance that arises when believers are "militant defenders of a creed."

LEONARD H. EHRLICH

Jeanne de Jussie (1503–61). Born into a family of lesser nobility, she professed at the Convent of St. Clare* in Geneva* (1521), where she was a scribe (*écrivaine*) and eventually the abbess (1548). Sometime before 1555, she wrote the *Petite chronique* (Short chronicle), which concerned the threat to, and subsequent translocation of, her Catholic convent as a result of the Reformation in Geneva (1530–35). She describes soldiers and Protestant civilians constantly threatening the inviolability of the convent (and of its nuns). Local preachers and newly married former nuns (including Marie Dentière*) repeatedly entered the convent to preach the value of marriage*. In 1535 the Clarissan nuns undertook a difficult trek to Annecy in order to take refuge in the convent of Sainte-Croix. Jussie freely disputed the doctrines and practices of the Reformers, including Luther*, and caricatured the former nuns and priests who attempted to persuade the nuns to give up enclosure. Her narrative is rich with details about daily life during the Reformation, the hardships of travel, and the strength of women (the nuns, as well as the wives of Protestant civilians) during the crisis. A Catholic press published Jussie's chronicle as *The Leaven of Calvinism* (1611; nine editions; Italian and German translations between the 17th and 19th c.).

JESSICA A. BOON

Jefferson, Thomas (1743–1826), third US president, founder of the University of Virginia, author of the Declaration of Independence. Baptized Anglican, he became a Deist*, distanced himself from traditional Christianity, and yet left perhaps the most important religious legacy of any president. An advocate of religious liberty, he wrote the "Statute for Establishing Religious Freedom," which became Virginia law (1786). Later he supported a "wall of separation between church* and state" in a letter to the Danbury Baptist Association. For Jefferson, Baptists* were colleagues in the struggle for the disestablishment of state churches. Despite his Deist beliefs, Baptist preacher John Leland called Jefferson a "patriarch of liberty" for his defense of church–state separation. Jefferson considered himself an authentic Christian because he followed Jesus' moral teachings, although he rejected traditional doctrines about Jesus' divinity, which he considered superstitions and divisive. These convictions led him to produce *The Life and Morals of Jesus*, later called the "Jefferson Bible," which contained Jesus' teachings from the Gospels, with miraculous and theological stories removed. For Jefferson traditional Christianity would eventually lose credibility in an enlightened* age, and he expected Unitarianism* to become dominant in the USA. JAMES P. BYRD

Jehovah's Witnesses, with its origins in the late-19th-c. teachings of the US evangelist Charles Taze Russell*, has at present some 7 million active members around the world. The Watch Tower Bible and Tract Society of Pennsylvania, with its headquarters in New York, is the main corporate vehicle of the organization. The name "Jehovah's Witnesses" was adopted in 1931.

Russell was convinced that the world was in its last days, and this view remains a core part of the group's doctrine. Witnesses are expected to devote a number of hours each month to spreading the Millennialist message (see Millennialism Cluster). They conduct much of this activity by talking to people while distributing publications door to door.

Jehovah's Witnesses regard the Bible as the source of all theological knowledge. It is held to be factually true and the only basis for sound belief. Other Christian groups are thought to be in error because they rely on nonbiblical traditions or on misinterpretations of the Scriptures*; they are thus part of the (evil) world that is coming to an end.

Witnesses believe that the idea of the Trinity* is nonbiblical and false. God* has a proper name, Jehovah. Jesus Christ is his son, but he is neither part of Jehovah nor equal to him. Likewise, the cross* is seen as a "pagan" symbol; Witnesses believe that Jesus died on a vertical stake.

The group teaches that death* brings life to a complete end; there is no immortal* soul* and hence no hell* in which existence would continue. When God's Kingdom* is established on earth, those who are worthy of renewed life will be resurrected (see Resurrection of the Body in Western Christianity). Most will live forever in this world, which will have been transformed into a paradise; only 144,000 people have been anointed to join Jehovah and Jesus Christ in heaven.

There has often been tension between Jehovah's Witnesses and public authorities because members refuse to swear oaths* of allegiance, serve in the military (see Pacifism and Christianity), or vote. Their refusal to accept blood transfusions has also been controversial. Witnesses do not celebrate birthdays or holidays (including Christmas* and Easter*), although an annual memorial service commemorates Christ's death.

All Witnesses are responsible for evangelizing, and congregations are led by male "elders" rather than professional ministers. Local groups meet in buildings called "kingdom halls" (not churches). The organization is highly centralized, with directives coming from the governing body via national offices to every individual congregation and member. DAVID VOAS

Jeremiah, Book of. Jeremiah reflects theologically on the military threat facing Judah* (late 7th c. BCE), the Babylonians' siege of Jerusalem*, and subsequent efforts of Judean political groups to develop strategies for life under occupation and in diaspora*.

Jeremiah prophesied from 627 through the fall of Jerusalem (587), then briefly in Egypt* (43:8–13, 44:1–30). Judah was caught in the geopolitical tensions between weakening Egypt and ascendant Babylon. Jeremiah's role as royal adviser during those unstable times brought him into conflict with the kings Jehoiakim and Zedekiah (Chaps. 36–38).

Jeremiah's theology of history underlines the persistent spiritual stubbornness of the people of Israel*, the culpability of Israel's political and clerical leaders, and God's power to punish (e.g. 15:1–9) and to restore (30:18–31:14). Intense lamentations ("jeremiads") are employed to dramatic effect as a form of prophetic biography (11:18–12:6, 15:10–21, 17:14–18, 18:18–23, 20:7–18). Jeremiah's turbulent poetry also makes visible the suffering of personified Zion* and the pathos of God. Emphasis on Israel's accountability for apostasy is balanced by the promise that God will renew the covenant* with Israel.

Jeremiah preserves divergent voices struggling to make sense of the disaster that had befallen Judah. Most clearly articulated is the position that Nebuchadnezzar of Babylon was God's instrument deployed to punish Judah for its disobedience to God. "Submit to Babylon and live!" was the rallying cry of those who, to preserve belief in a sovereign God, interpreted the devastation of Judah as God's will. But the book records subtle opposition to the accommodationist position, as well. Thus a key ethical question is left unresolved: should the faithful inhabit a threatening world as pragmatic assimilationists (29:5–7) or as idealistic resistance fighters (35:1–19)?

Fierce debates about false prophecy* (23:9–17, 28:1–17) reveal that much was at stake for Judean leaders vying for authority. Internecine accusations (24:1–10, 42:7–22) show a community bitterly divided against itself. These traditions, ostensibly exilic, may reflect an ongoing tension within postexilic Israel regarding the benefits of cultural assimilation versus the importance of guarding communal boundaries.

The commissioning of Jeremiah (1:4–10) is read in services of Christian ordination*. Jeremiah's laments offer an iconic model of spiritual wrestling with the costs of vocation*. Jeremiah's "new covenant*" (31:31–34) has been extraordinarily influential in Christian liturgical theology since the 1st c. (Luke 22:20; 1 Cor 11:25; Heb 8:8–13, 9:15), appropriated as a central idiom for Christ's redeeming work and its memorialization in the practice of the Eucharist*.

CAROLYN J. SHARP

Jerome (Lat Hieronymus) (c331/347–419), biblical scholar and commentator, translator, polemicist, ascetic*, transmitter of classical learning and Greek biblical, theological, and monastic scholarship into the Christian Middle Ages. Born in present-day Croatia*; studied in Rome. Having chosen an ascetic* life, he lived as a hermit* in the Syrian desert for about three years, studying Greek and Hebrew. After returning to Rome (382), he served as papal secretary until 385. Subsequently, Jerome moved to Bethlehem and founded a monastery* with Paula*, one of the aristocratic Roman women with whom he had a lifelong friendship. There he translated the Bible from Hebrew and Greek into Latin, wrote commentaries, engaged in polemic consisting of much satire and abuse, and writing letters (of the c120 extant letters, c40 are addressed to women), and corresponding with Augustine* on theological and biblical questions. These works are of historical, literary, as well as theological and biblical interest.

Immersed in classical culture and literature, and a brilliant literary stylist, Jerome used his wide learning in the service of the developing Christian culture. An exponent of the ascetic life, he was criticized by some for overemphasizing the value of sexual chastity*, as in his Letter 22 to the young girl Eustochium, his works against Jovinian and Helvidius, and his *Life of Malchus*. Suspected of Origenism*, he became a critic of Origen's doctrines and later wrote against Pelagius*.

He was hugely influential in the Middle Ages as a model of an ascetic, as a biblical commentator, and as a compiler of reference works such as the list of famous people (*De viris illustribus*) and the translation and expansion of Eusebius's* Chronicle and dictionary of biblical places names. Later writers gave many of his sayings the status of proverbs. His Latin translation of the Bible, later known as the Vulgate*, became the standard text in Western Europe.

CAROLINNE WHITE

Jerome of Prague (c1373–1416), theological reformer who, with Hus*, led the early stages of the Bohemian* reform movement that would develop into the Moravian* Church and inspire Luther*. With Hus, Jerome was tried and burned at the Council of Constance in 1416.

Educated at the University of Prague (1398), Oxford (1399–1402), and Paris (1406), and expelled from Heidelberg for his Wycliffite* leanings (1408), he may have gone to Jerusalem on pilgrimage (1403). He actively promoted Wycliffism in Prague in 1409 and in the presence of Emperor Sigismund in Hungary (1410). He was tried in Vienna (1410) and excommunicated; he escaped to Moravia, where he preached against the papal crusade against Naples (1412). He followed Hus to Constance in 1415, where after Hus's murder he recanted on September 23. Despite this, he was imprisoned, reaffirmed his Wycliffite beliefs, and was burned on May 31, 1416.

Jerome was, along with Oxford scholar Peter Payne (d1455), instrumental in bringing Wyclif's texts to Prague. Influenced by Wyclif's *Trialogus*, he promoted Wyclif's philosophical and theological ideas throughout Europe. Like Hus, he rejected Wyclif's denial of transubstantiation*, but argued for the church as the universal body of the predestined* and vigorously attacked the clerical hierarchy.

STEPHEN E. LAHEY

Jerusalem. Old Assyrian *Ursalimmu*, "City of Peace," also called "Jebus" (Judg 19:10–11; 1 Chr 11:4–5); political and religious capital of Israel after David moved the Ark of the Covenant there (2 Sam 5–7). Isaiah 52:1 refers to Jerusalem as the "Holy City," while Ezekiel interprets Jerusalem as "YHWH is here" (48:35) and "center of the world" (5:5, 38:12; cf. Judg 9:37); Jerusalem is also viewed as the repository of God's Name (Ps 122; Isa 54). Because it is the locus of messianic expectation (Isa 2:3), all nations are to come to Jerusalem on pilgrimage (Zech 8:20–23). Jesus' death and resurrection occurred there, and from Jerusalem, Christianity sprang (Acts 1:8). Revelation 21–22 offers a vision of the New Jerusalem, along with a new heaven and a new earth. **See also ZION.**

ANDRÉ LACOCQUE

Jerusalem Council (51 or 49), an apostolic council attended by Paul*, Peter*, and James*. As Paul described it (Gal 2:1–10), this conference addressed the tensions between James's and Peter's mission to the Jews – proclaiming a gospel *with* the Law – and Paul's mission to the Gentiles – proclaiming a gospel *without* the Law. Both forms of the gospel were recognized as authentic; the gospel is necessarily inculturated*, even as it maintains its continuity with Judaism*, and a fundamental unity exists among Christians who follow different forms of the gospel. This ideal was difficult to implement, as the incident in Antioch (Gal 2:11–21) already showed. Acts 15:1–30, and other passages in Acts 11 and 18, seem to reflect a similar reluctance; Acts' secondhand reports seem to have been reshaped by conflating several meetings and softening the agreement (15:29 requires Gentiles to follow part of the Law).

Jesuits (Society of Jesus), Roman Catholic religious* order of priests with a distinctive vow of obedience to the pope in order to serve the gospel and the universal church.

Founded by Ignatius* of Loyola and his companions (Rome, 1540), the Society of Jesus counted at the time of his death (1556) 1,000 members in Europe, Brazil*, and Japan*. Its Constitutions, approved by Pope Paul III, inspired other religious orders. According to the 1975 General Congregation, "To be a Jesuit is to know that, although a sinner, one has been called to be a companion of Jesus as was Ignatius, who implored the Virgin Mary to 'put him in relationship with her Son,' and who then saw the Father himself asking Jesus, carrying his cross, to take this pilgrim in his company. What is, today, to be a companion of Jesus? It is to be under the cross as a standard and to be committed to the decisive struggle of our time, namely the struggle for faith* and for the justice* that faith implies."

The years 1550–1645 constituted the golden age of the Society of Jesus. The 15,000 Jesuits included famous theologians, scientists (who welcomed Galileo* to their Roman "college" [high school], 1611), pedagogues who established many "colleges" and universities throughout Europe and beyond, and missionaries who traveled to India* (de Nobili*, 1606), China* (Ricci*, 1583), Tibet* (Andrade, 1624), Canada* (Brébeuf and Jogues, 1640), Paraguay* and its "reductions*" (separate mission colonies where converted natives resided), Brazil*, and Japan. The lay Marian congregations, inspired by Ignatius's *Spiritual* Exercises* (especially among students), multiplied all over Europe. After 1645 the Jesuits were deeply involved in major controversies, notably over Jansenism*, Gallicanism*, and Chinese* rites (condemned by the pope, 1704, when the mission in China counted 300,000 Christians).

The Jesuits' successes and power prompted jealousy and international intrigues, related especially to the reductions in Paraguay, the rise of nationalism*, and the Enlightenment*. The Jesuits were banished from Portugal* (1754), France* (1763), Spain* and Naples (1767), and were abolished by Pope Clement XIV (1773) (except in Russia and Prussia). Restored in France in 1815 (where Clorivière had prepared novices), Jesuit missions and educational work resumed (especially in the USA, where the Jesuits opened "colleges" and universities, and conducted missions among Native Americans). By 1950 the Society had 36,000 members.

In 2000 there were 19,800 Jesuits (Latin America, 3,000; North America, 3,200; Asia, 5,600; Europe, 6,600). Since Vatican* II, and the "updating" (Italian, *aggiornamento*) led by Pedro Arrupe, the Society has devoted itself primarily to promoting justice*, inculturation*, and the service of the marginalized*, especially refugees*.

CLAUDE FLIPO, SJ,

Jesus. See CHRISTOLOGIES CLUSTER; JESUS, QUEST FOR THE HISTORICAL.

Jesús, Felipe de, OFM (1572–97). Born in Mexico*, he went as a missionary to Japan and was crucified in Nagasaki along with 26 other Franciscans* and Jesuits*. He died first and thus is known as the first martyr of Japan. Canonized by Pope Pius IX (1872), he is the patron saint of Mexico City.

MARÍA ALICIA PUENTE LUTTEROTH and ELIZABETH JUDD

JESUS, IMAGES OF, CLUSTER

1) *Introductory Entry*

Jesus, Images of

2) *A Sampling of Contextual Views*

Jesus, Images of, in Byzantine Iconography
Jesus, Images of, in Latino/a Depictions
Jesus, Images of, in Literature
Jesus, Images of, in Movies
Jesus, Images of, in Western European Art

1) Introductory Entry

Jesus, Images of. Historical Christianity is rich in visual imagery, conveyed in poetry, song, and pictorial arts, most often centered on the figure of Jesus. Much of the iconographic evidence can be subsumed under three overlapping rubrics: typology, portraiture, and narration.

Typology. Christian typology seeks to demonstrate that all of reality (nature and history) prefigures and culminates in Jesus Christ (or in the time of the believers, or in the future; see Typology). Typology was used by early Christians to assert themselves against Jews and pagans. Typology consists of "types," or prefigurations, and "antitypes," their fulfillments. Types are inferred, allusive, or associative; they depend on the interpreters' creative imagination. In visual art, Christian interpreters and viewers found iconographic types of Jesus virtually everywhere.

The most familiar OT iconographic types of Jesus include Adam*, Daniel*, David*, Isaac*, Job*, Jonah*, and Moses*. There also were Greco-Roman mythopoetic typological figures of Jesus, including Asklepios, Helios, Herakles, and Orpheus. Generic figures functioning as iconographic types include images of Jesus as king, philosopher, shepherd, soldier, and teacher. There are animal types (dove, fish, eagle, lamb, peacock, phoenix, unicorn) along with cosmic images (air, earth, fire, light, sun, water). Cultivated plants (grape, olive, palm, wheat) have also been pictorial shorthand types of Christ, along with letters (e.g. alpha and omega, iota and chi), geometric figures (circle, octagon, triangle) and inanimate objects (e.g. the cross).

Portraiture. The earliest surviving portraits of Jesus date to the 6th c. The most famous is the painted bust of Christ at St. Catherine's Monastery, Mount Sinai (most likely executed in 6th-c. Constantinople). Christ as "Pantocrator" (the Almighty One) is shown facing front, looking out at the viewer, dressed in a purple tunic, his right hand raised in a gesture of blessing, his left arm holding a large codex (presumably the Bible). Surrounding Christ's head is a gold halo*. Such icons*, executed on a thin wooden board, were originally portable pictures patronized by private persons, often set up in private chapels and houses. As devotional images, such icons of Jesus have been popular in Eastern Christendom from the 6th c. to the present.

Since there are no eye-witness accounts of Jesus' physical appearance, by definition icon portraits of Jesus are products of the creative imagination of Jesus' followers. But to devout viewers, the veracity and reality of the Jesus portrait icon remain. Devotees bow down before the Jesus icon, and touch, kiss, and speak to the image, engaging it as if it were a beloved living person. The Christ icon is what it represents, the presence of God in a palpable form, accessible to human sight and touch.

In Orthodox churches, icon piety lives on. To Western Christians, piety directed to icons of Jesus (or Mary* and the saints*) is foreign and difficult to comprehend; such difficulties led to the Iconoclastic* controversy (7th–9th c.) and the condemnation of icon piety as idolatrous by many Protestants. Nevertheless, echoes of Jesus icon portraiture can be found in Western medieval and modern art history (see the present cluster: In Western European Art).

Narration. Pictures illustrating Jesus' story play a major role in Christian iconography. The clearest figural renderings of Jesus engaged in actions described in the NT are found in 6th- and 7th-c. illustrated Gospels (e.g. Rabbula codex, Rossano codex, Latin codex of Bishop Augustine of Canterbury); still earlier visual narratives are those of catacomb* paintings and early Christian sarcophagi. The basic story line depicting Jesus' life in visual form includes his birth, infancy, and childhood, adult ministry, and especially the last days (entry into Jerusalem, the supper, the garden scene, betrayal and arrest, trial and crucifixion, post-resurrection appearances). Since the late 5th c., Jesus' crucifixion* has dominated Jesus visual narratives. Typology often overlaps: OT types are exhibited alongside or in juxtaposition to Jesus as fulfillment of these types.

PAUL CORBY FINNEY

---

2) A Sampling of Contextual Views

Jesus, Images of, in Byzantine Iconography. Since there is no NT description of Christ's physical appearance, the 4th-c. Eastern church fathers described Christ either as an ordinary and even ugly man who "had no form or majesty" (following Isa 53:2) or, on the contrary, as more beautiful than any other human (following Ps 44:3).

1. Christ Pantocrator. By the 9th c., literary descriptions of Christ as a handsome middle-aged man with hair down to his shoulders, an oblong face, and full beard had taken shape. This iconographic type was readily accepted because it resembled the extremely popular statue of Zeus at Olympia made by Phidias. Since the 11th c., these iconographic representations were inscribed "Jesus Christ Pantocrator" (the Almighty or All-Ruler), pointing both to Christ's power in heaven and on earth, and to his eternal existence as the second person of the Trinity. After "the triumph of Orthodoxy" ended the Iconoclast* controversy (843), this representation took the dominant position in the cupolas of churches and became the most widespread representation of Christ in Byzantine iconography.

2. Christ as Handsome Young Man was preferred by some Christian authors (e.g. Theodorus Anagnostus, 6th c.), who rejected the "Zeus-like" image. The image of Christ as a beardless youth with wavy hair symbolizing the eternal beauty of the embodied God (as in the mosaic image of the altar in the Church of San Vitale, Ravenna, 6th c.) remained popular until the Trullo Council (692) demanded "realistic" representations, as it rejected allegoric images of Christ, such as Christ as the Lamb.

By the mid-11th c., other types of Christ iconography were established and ascribed specific names (the miniatures of the *Paris Gospel* Gr. 74).

3. Jesus Christ the Ancient of Days named the image of a gray-bearded old man (Dan 7:9; Rev 1:14) – representing Christ as he appeared in the visions of prophets, before the Incarnation*, as an eternal being in heaven, the second person of the Trinity*.

4. Christ Emmanuel presents "God with us" as an innocent and unprotected child; for Byzantine theologians, it is a reminder of the Incarnation* and of the redemptive* sacrifice.

5. Christ as Priest reflects this liturgical quest of Byzantine iconography. Following an early Byzantine apocryphon, it represents Christ as a youth with an outlined beard, crownlike hair style, and priestly tonsure (a mosaic image at St. Sophia, Kiev, mid-11th c.; a fresco of Nerezi, Macedonia, 1164). In manuscripts and church decorations, various images of Christ were deliberately juxtaposed to reflect Christ's priestly role at different stages of salvation history and of the mystery* of the Eucharist*, in which the same Christ offers, is offered, and accepts the offering in heaven together with the Trinity. After the 13th c., the Byzantine "Christ as High Priest" represents the Lord in the robe of an officiating bishop or patriarch (sometimes with a royal crown, a sign that Christ is supreme ruler and high priest).

6. Anapeson (the Vigilant Eye) represents Christ as a child sleeping with open eyes. It can be traced back to biblical images (Judah as a lion, Gen 49:9) combined with ancient legends of lions born dead and becoming alive on the third day. With its stress on the Resurrection*, this image was set on the western wall of a church, above the entrance (e.g. frescoes of Protaton at Mount Athos, late 13th c.).

7. Christ the Angel, representing Christ as a winged youth with crossed nimbus, was inspired by the second Easter homily of Gregory* Nazianzen. The earliest depictions are illustrations of this homily in 11th- to 12th-c. manuscripts, and since the late 13th c., it appears on church murals (Church of St. Clement, Ochrid).

8. Byzantine Images of Christ connected with renowned miracle-working icons of Constantinople. The most venerated and widespread was the *Mandylion* – a representation of the holy face on a cloth. Tradition claimed that this image was "not made by human hands" and presented the "self-portrait" of Christ, first brought to Edessa*, then to Constantinople (944), and extensively reproduced, taking a prominent place in the Orthodox Church. Other Byzantine images of Christ were inscribed as "Chalkitis" or "Antiphonitis," indicating their connection with miracle-working icons of Constantinople.

In the mid-16th c., a major controversy related to the iconography of Christ erupted in Moscow (the "Viscovaty affair"). Kremlin icon painters, influenced by Western art, inserted new allegoric images of Christ, e.g. Christ as crucified angel or as warrior. Despite protests and discrepancies with the Byzantine tradition, these iconographic experiments were approved.

Since the 17th c., there has been no significant development in iconography except some discussions with Old* Believers concerning the gesture of blessing and the abbreviation of Jesus' name in Russian icons. Most images replicated renowned miracle-working icons, frequently connected with the Russian royal family (e.g. the "Savior of Smolensk" icon). **See also HIEROTOPY, THE CREATION OF CHRISTIAN SACRED SPACES.**

ALEXEI LIDOV

Jesus, Images of, in Latino/a Depictions. Latino/a theologians, writers, and artists evoke images of the *barrio* Christ, the *mestizo** Christ, and the intimate Christ. Latino/a theology often emphasizes the earthly Jesus, the one exposed to abject circumstances, human suffering, and death. Jesus suffers as we do, and identifies with the poverty* and social marginalization* that many Latinos/as experience. However, the earthly Jesus also challenges entrenched power to respond justly to the needs of the oppressed*. He is the "hard-hitting" Jesus, the "*barrio* Christ," who comes from and for the neediest (Recinos). He is the "*mestizo* Christ," who hails from Galilee, on the margins of power, but confronts Jerusalem, the center of entrenched power (Elizondo). Jesus also stands with women, outcasts in society because of gender discrimination and health challenges. Jesus heals them, and many join his gathering of disciples. In the end, only women stand with Jesus in death and bear first witness to new life (Aquino). Finally, many Latinos/as identify with this suffering but confrontational Jesus in intimate ways, even naming their children after him, as depicted in the book *Jesus Is My Uncle* (Pedraja). **See also CHRISTOLOGIES CLUSTER.** EFRAIN AGOSTO

Jesus, Images of, in Literature. The plethora of noncanonical and later fictionalized appearances of Jesus in world literature makes the hyperbole in John 21:25 something of a reality: everything written about him, let alone a useful description of each, would require many volumes.

Aside from his portrayal in noncanonical Gospels, the earliest Western literary appearances of Jesus occurred in the period of Mediterranean and European translation of the Bible; they were often highly imaginative paraphrases (e.g. Juvencus's *Historiae Evangelicae libri quattor*, Spain, early 4th c.; *Christ and Satan*, Anglo-Saxon, late 8th c.). Paraphrasing, gap filling, and fictional departures from biblical narrative have created distinctive views of Jesus. Beyond such paraphrases, H. Richard Niebuhr's* *Christ and Culture* (1951), with its fivefold classification system, offers a helpful nexus (see Culture Cluster: And Christianity).

1. The "Christ against Culture" Images. When traditional Germanic* epics met Christianity, a heroic "Christ against culture" figure emerged, as seen in the Old Saxon alliterative epic *Heliand** (c830) and in the 8th- to 9th-c. Anglo-Saxon Jesus poems. The triumphalist Jesus reappears with Roman overtones in works as varied as the 1602 Portuguese* *Life of Jesus* (later in Persian and Latin translations) by the Indian* Jesuit Hieronymus Xavier; Giles Fletcher the Younger's *Christ's Victorie, and Triumph in Heaven, over, and after Death* (1610); and John Milton's* *Paradise Regained* (1671). He is the ethical model countering revived Stoic classical virtues in Sir Richard Steele's *The Christian Hero* (1701). Such characterizations of Jesus faded in the 18th–19th c. and reemerged in Liberation* theology and literature in the 20th c. Thus in Ernesto Cardenal's *Cosmic Canticle* (1993, Nicaragua*), Jesus is a Communist hero, or in James K. Baxter's "The Maori Jesus" (1966), he is a postcolonial countercultural prophet.

2. The "Christ above Culture" Images are most dominant in mystical* literature, such as the devotionals of the European Middle Ages. Among these images are the rapturous, ethereal Jesus of Teresa* of Ávila, Madame Guyon*, and the Pre-Raphaelites, as well as the evanescent, almost hallucinatory Jesus as the muse of the Syrian poet Tawfiq Sayigh ("The Sermon on the Mount," 1970).

3. The "Christ of Culture" Images followed German romantics such as Annette Droste-Hulshoff ("Gethsemane" in *Das Geistliche Jahr*, 1839) and might be better labeled "Jesus of Culture." One important variant makes Jesus a kind of romantic hero, at one with nature, as in English poet Felicia Heman's "Mountain Sanctuaries" (1825), echoed in Ernst Renan's best-selling *La Vie de Jésus* (1863). Another, more predominant in modernity, is exemplified in William Blake's* *Jerusalem* (1820), as well as Walt Whitman's "To Him that was Crucified" (1860) and *Leaves of Grass* (1855), and is apparent in the opening lines of Heinrich Heine's "Deutschland: A Winter Tale" (1844). This approach permits a radically personalized reading of the Gospels; a portrait of Jesus becomes self-portraiture. In the 20th c., this trend accelerates. With the loss of belief in the divinity of Jesus, he appears as a locker-room buddy approving of self-indulgence and adultery, as in Canadian Rudy Wiebe's *My Lovely Enemy* (1982); as disillusioned and desultory as Casy in John Steinbeck's *Grapes of Wrath* (1939); as the cynical and defiant antihero Jesus in New Zealander R. A. K. Mason's "Nails and a Cross"; or as depressive as Reiner Maria Rilke's Jesus in "The Olive Garden" (1906). Occasionally the irony of postmodernism's loss of the sense of loss produces an infernal reading of Jesus, as in Gore Vidal's *Messiah* (1954); or a failed Messiah and lost religious hope, as in Russian Vladimir Lvov's untitled postwar poem about the Crucifixion, exemplified by "We can only pity Christ today, / So, of course, he's no longer great. / Our earth loves the victorious."

4. The "Christ Transforming Culture" Images are a counterdevelopment, clearly present in Marxist* and neo-Marxist literature. Initially European, this strain is first visible in Christian Socialism, as in Elizabeth Linton's *The True History of Joshua Davidson* (1872), Elizabeth Phelps's *A Singular Life* (1895), and perhaps Upton Sinclair's *They Call Me Carpenter* (1922). This political theme is developed in Africa by Senegalese Leopold Senghor, Congolese Tchicaya U Tam'si , and Nigerian Chinua Achebe, in all of whose work Jesus is a poignant but exemplary figure to whom a proper response would produce reconciling rather than violently revolutionary social change.

5. The "Christ in Paradoxical Relation to Culture" Images – never quite at home in culture, never quite able not to be in culture – is found in postmodern writers' portrayal of Jesus as a complex, problematic teacher, but also in many modernist works that drew heavily on postcanonical or Gnostic* Gospels to create an ambivalent Jesus, such as Robert Graves's *King Jesus* (1946), Nikos Kazantzakis's *The Last Temptation of Christ* (1953), and the quasi-biographical account *A Life of Jesus* by Japanese Shusiako Endo (1973), and still more sensationally in Dan Brown's *The Da Vinci Code* (2003). By their opposition to a paradoxical representation of Jesus, Dorothy Sayers's *The Man Born to be King* (1943) and Francois Mauriac's *Vie de Jésus* (1936) highlighted the trend toward problematizing the Jesus of the Gospels, reflecting this sense of ambivalent struggle with the claims of faith, even though, as Miguel de Unamuno (*The Christ of Velasquez*), has written, "Jesus, you are as a living fount / which, in the thick of the forest, / sings ever new songs of eternal love."

DAVID LYLE JEFFREY

Jesus, Images of, in Movies. In the history of cinema, from the late 19th c. to the present, there have been literally dozens of biographical films about Jesus. These films follow the overall conventions of the "biopic" (biographical film) genre: they are explicitly based on textual sources – the four Gospels – and they make a claim to be historically authentic, and perhaps even historically accurate, at the same time as they clearly invent numerous elements of the story. The number, variety, appearance, and content of the Jesus movies demonstrate that these films do not tell us about the past so much as they reveal tensions, concerns, assumptions, and anxieties about the present. For example, North America's understanding of itself as the champion of the individual against an oppressive regime, or of a democracy* against tyranny, can easily be detected in the films' portrayals of Roman rule in Galilee and the people's longing for salvation*.

The Jesus movies span all eras and all genres. In the early silent era, they tended to be static and episodic, little more than slightly animated tableaux of famous biblical paintings. An exception was Cecil B. DeMille's 1927 film, *King of Kings*, which presented a highly developed and often entertaining narrative, including a raunchy "backstory" that explains how Mary* Magdalene came to follow Jesus. After DeMille's film, there was no full biopic of Jesus until the era of the biblical epics (1960s). This long break was due in part to the enormous influence of DeMille's movie, but perhaps even more to the Production Code (1930–1960), which greatly limited the types of stories and images that could be shown on the screen. The major biblical epics, such as *The Greatest Story Ever Told* (Stevens, 1965), were, and continue to be, enormously popular. Some films drew explicit connections to the modern era. For example, Pasolini's moving black-and-white film, *The Gospel According to Saint Matthew* (1964), used Jesus' life as an allegory for the class conflicts in Southern Italy after World War II. These films were soon followed by the Jesus rock musicals *Jesus Christ Superstar* (1973) and *Godspell* (1973), in which Jesus is treated with both humor and irony as he sings his way through his mission and parables*. Palpable in these films are such current issues as the Civil* Rights Movement and the conflict in the Middle East, as well as the countercultural ethos of the hippie movement. The 1980s saw two major iconoclastic* films, Scorsese's *Last Temptation of Christ* (1988) and the Canadian film *Jesus of Montreal* (Arcand, 1989), which, like Pasolini's film, used the story as an allegory* of their own time and place. These two films made no claims to historicity and hence can be placed at the boundaries of the biopic genre. Another, shorter hiatus ensued, causing some critics to suggest that the era of Jesus movies has finally ended. The appearance of *The Gospel of John* (Saville, 2003), *The Passion of the Christ* (Gibson, 2004), and *The Nativity Story* (Hardwicke, 2006) dispelled this notion and showed that the Jesus story continues to be amenable to interpretation in many different ways.

The great variety in these cinematic depictions demonstrates that Jesus' story remains useful as a vehicle for exploring issues that resonate far more with the films' audiences than do the concerns of 1st-c. Galilean Jews. Furthermore, underlying these films, as well as their popularity among viewers, is the idea that Jesus himself, whether as Messiah, prophet, champion of the poor and oppressed, flower child, wise teacher, or superhero, continues to intrigue us and to be a vehicle through which we can view and attempt to understand ourselves and our problems and issues as they change over time.

ADELE REINHARTZ

Jesus, Images of, in Western European Art. Western iconographic traditions – with a narrative and/or didactic character, in contrast to Eastern Orthodox icons* – mirror the hopes, fears, and convictions of Christians during nearly two millennia.

Early Christianity. The earliest images of Jesus (catacomb* frescoes and sarcophagus reliefs) show Jesus in three iconographic types: those of generic figures (e.g. healer, king, philosopher, shepherd, teacher); OT types (e.g. Jonah, Moses); and pagan gods and heroes (e.g. Asklepios, Herakles). In the 5th and 6th c., the first fixed pictorial conventions for the rendering of Jesus emerged, especially in basilicas*: Jesus was shown seated, facing front, his right hand raised (gesturing speech or blessing), his left hand holding a codex. This enthroned Pantocrator Christ, a figure of authority and power, was often flanked by images of apostles, disciples, evangelist symbols, martyrs, and saints.

Medieval Christianity. From the 7th to the 14th c., Jesus images in illustrated Gospels and Bibles that presented narrative, pictorial versions of Jesus' life largely followed early Christian precedents. Yet the enthroned Christ appeared especially in larger public formats (e.g. tympana of Romanesque and Gothic cathedrals), together with images of Jesus crucified. Throughout the medieval period in Western Europe, crucifixion iconography was ubiquitous as book illustration, fresco painting, relief sculpture, engraved glass and gemstones, enamels, mosaic, bone and wood carving, metalwork, and textiles.

Modern Christianity. From the late 13th c. to the present, pictorial arts have been rich and variegated. Giotto's frescoes in the 1305/6 Arena Chapel (Padua) include Jesus crucified, the *pietà* (Mary holding the dead body of her son), and Christ enthroned (the Last Judgment). The style of Giotto's traditional iconography points to the 15th- and 16th-c. Italian Renaissance, when well-known artists elaborated the narrative sequence of Jesus iconography, from his birth to his public ministry, from the Last Supper, the agony in the garden, the betrayal, to the Messiah's ignominious death, his descent from the cross, his resurrection, and his ascension. The Italian Renaissance tradition was adopted and then continued into the 17th and 18th c. throughout Western Europe; yet in Protestant territories, the traditional iconographic repertory was either diminished or altogether eliminated. In the 19th c., Jesus iconography declined in artistic importance.

In the 20th c., Jesus iconography all but disappeared in large sectors of traditionally Christian Western Europe. At the mid-20th c., the so-called *art sacré* movement (led by the Dominican Marie-Alain Couturier) attempted to revive traditional Christian religious iconography, but soon died a quiet death in the 1960s. Thereafter, there has been little of artistic note.

PAUL CORBY FINNEY

Jesus, Quest for the Historical. The quest for the historical Jesus began during the Enlightenment*. Thomas Emlyn and Thomas Woolston, both Unitarians* (early 18th c.), challenged the veracity of the Gospels' accounts. But the four stages of "the quest" began with the book of H. S. Reimarus that is variously entitled in English translation *On the Aim* (or *Purpose* or *Intention*) *of Jesus and His Disciples* (German original, 1778).

The First Quest. Reimarus's book posed what became the central question of the quest: How much continuity and discontinuity is there between the historical Jesus and the canonical portraits of him? Was Jesus somewhat different from what the NT says about him? Sharply different? Or even, as a few have occasionally argued, was he a fiction?

Reimarus argued that Jesus' aim and that of his followers were very different: Jesus proclaimed the Kingdom* of God; his followers proclaimed Jesus. The details of his portrait of Jesus as an anti-Roman political Messiah whose life ended in bitter disappointment and his claim that Jesus' followers stole his body and invented a religion about Jesus have been discounted. But Reimarus's distinction between Jesus as a figure of history* and the way the Gospels tell his story, as well as doubts about the veracity of Jesus' miracles* (D. F. Strauss, 1835), led to a study of the sources. Scholars assigned historical priority to the Synoptic* Gospels rather than to John* and concluded that Q* and Mark* are the oldest layers of the synoptic tradition, as is still broadly accepted today. "Lives of Jesus" proliferated in the 19th c., although what effect the first quest had on churches, clergy, and laity is unclear.

Within the academic world, Schweitzer* brought the first quest to an end with his enormously influential *Quest of the Historical Jesus* (1906; a sequel to his *Mystery of the Kingdom of God,* 1901). Schweitzer narrates brilliantly the quest up to his time, presents his argument that Jesus' message and mission were dominated by apocalyptic* eschatology*, and concludes with the theological claim that it is not the historical Jesus who matters for theology, but the living Christ who "comes to us as One unknown." His argument that the historical Jesus does not matter was anticipated by Martin Kähler, a theologian, in *The So-Called Historical Jesus and the Historic Biblical Christ* (1892). Yet Schweitzer admired the historical Jesus and thought we could know quite a bit about him. Far from discrediting him, Schweitzer's portrait of Jesus as a heroic but deeply mistaken eschatological figure was and remains persuasive to many.

The Second Stage of the Quest (a time of "no quest") resulted from Schweitzer's book and lasted until the mid-20th c. Although C. H. Dodd, Rudolf Bultmann*, and others wrote important books, there was a relative lack of interest in the historical Jesus and considerable skepticism about what we can know, as well as theological uncertainty about whether the quest mattered for Christian theology.

The Third Stage: The Second Quest (from the 1950s) was motivated by the conviction that the historical Jesus does matter for theology. It focused on the understanding of existence mediated by the *kerygma** (preaching) of early Christianity and by the message of the historical Jesus. Notable authors include James Robinson, Günther Bornkamm, and Norman Perrin.

The Fourth Stage: The Third Quest (a renaissance of Jesus scholarship, from the 1980s) is differentiated from the second by a multidisciplinary approach that incorporates models drawn from the social sciences and history of religion (see History of Religion School); a greater and more appreciative understanding of the Jewish context of Jesus and his Jewishness; collaborative studies of the sources (the Jesus* Seminar and the International Q Project; see Q, a Collection of Sayings Ascribed to Jesus).

Regarding sources, a strong majority continue to affirm the priority of Mark and Q. Recently, some scholars have emphasized the importance of the study of orality, which can be combined with the study of written sources.

The Expanded Context for Jesus Research. The first and second quests focused on "Jesus within Christianity" (the NT and Christian theology), and often entailed a negative or negligible treatment of Judaism*. In the third quest, a larger context emerged: Jesus within Christianity within Judaism. Shaped by a post-Holocaust* awareness of the ways that Christian perceptions of Judaism have fed anti-Semitism* and by detailed research into the varieties of Judaism in Jesus' time, the third quest produced a thoroughly Jewish Jesus who was in conflict with some forms of Judaism (assessments of the conflict vary). An even larger context has been emphasized by some: Jesus within Christianity within Judaism within the Roman Empire. This emphasis includes an understanding of christological terms like Son* of God, Lord*, and Savior in the context of Roman imperial theology.

To what extent do the Gospels report "what happened"? And how much is based on subsequent beliefs (from a post-Easter perspective)? Third quest scholars range from minimalists to maximalists. At the minimalist extreme, a few argue that Jesus never existed, and others affirm his existence but assert that only a very small portion of the gospel tradition is based on what he actually said or did (mostly wisdom sayings). Maximalists defend the historical reliability of most of what is in the Synoptic Gospels.

In the center, the majority of Jesus and scholars of the Gospels agree that Jesus existed; the Gospels are a developing tradition that combines memory, testimony, and metaphorical narrative; and it is possible to know some things about the historical Jesus with various degrees of probability. They emphasize in various combinations that Jesus was a Jewish charismatic/mystic; a wisdom teacher; a healer and exorcist; a prophet of the Kingdom of God; and the initiator of a movement. Other issues include eschatology, the political Jesus, and the relevance of the quest to Christian theology.

Eschatology. Scholars in North America seem about evenly divided. Many agree that Jesus proclaimed an imminent interventionist eschatology ("apocalyptic* eschatology"): the Kingdom would come by divine intervention in the near future. But some argue that Jesus espoused no eschatology; the eschatological sayings in the Gospels are the product of early Christian beliefs. Still others argue for a fulfilled eschatology; Jesus himself was the eschatological fulfillment of God's promises to Israel. Others argue that Jesus held a participatory eschatology: the Kingdom would come through human participation. The notion of imminent intervention is gone, yet eschatology as God's purpose for the earth remains central to the message and activity of Jesus.

How Political Was Jesus? Those who affirm imminent interventionist eschatology commonly see Jesus as apolitical. Because Jesus believed God would soon transform the world through divine intervention, what did political institutions and systems matter? They would soon be irrelevant. Those who say that Jesus was primarily a wisdom teacher also commonly see him as apolitical. But many argue that Jesus was concerned about politics in the way that much of the Bible is: God's purpose, God's passion, for the earth is that it be a world of justice* and peace*. Jesus' passion for the Kingdom of God led him to criticize the system of domination of his time and to advocate an alternative vision; all this led to his arrest and execution.

The Relevance of the Quest to Christian Theology and Practice Remains Disputed. Some third quest scholars set the question aside and concern themselves only with the historical task. Others argue, as Kähler did, that only the canonical Jesus matters for theology. By contrast, others argue or imply that only the historical Jesus matters. Still others believe that both the historical Jesus and the canonical Jesus are relevant to Christian theology and practice.

The quest will continue, although its shape is impossible to predict. As long as Jesus matters, historical and theological interest in the quest and its significance will abide. **See also PARABLE.**

MARCUS J. BORG

Jesus Prayer (not to be confused with the Lord's* Prayer), originated in Greek hesychasm*: "Lord Jesus Christ, Son of God, have mercy on me (a sinner)." Following the injunction to pray unceasingly (1 Thess 5:1), in the Orthodox* tradition the faithful repeat the Jesus Prayer again and again as a means of concentration. At first they engage in a simple recitation of the prayer, but as they enter more deeply into the process of prayer, they make their own the words of the prayer; ultimately the prayer becomes a "prayer of the heart," the prayer of adoption, "when we cry, 'Abba! Father!'" (Rom 8:15).

Jesus Seminar, a group of mostly North American scholars who began meeting in 1985 to analyze and discuss the historical authenticity of sayings and deeds attributed to Jesus in the Gospels and other early Christian documents and then to vote on their authenticity, reporting the vote in *The Five Gospels: What Did Jesus Really Say* using four colors (red, pink, gray, and black) to indicate the probability that a particular saying or deed was authentic (red) or not (black).

MARCUS J. BORG

Jewish Christian Relation. See JUDAISM AND CHRISTIANITY CLUSTER.

Jewish Christians. See EBIONITES; JUDAIZERS; NAZARENES, GOSPEL OF THE.

Jewish Traditions. See JUDAISM AND CHRISTIANITY CLUSTER.

Jiménez de Cisneros, Francisco. See XIMÉNEZ DE CISNEROS, FRANCISCO.

Joachim of Fiore (c1135–1202), biblical interpreter. After having experienced several visions on a pilgrimage to the Holy Land, he entered a Benedictine* monastery (later a Cistercian* one) and eventually founded his own monastery. Claiming to have received the gift of understanding, he developed an original interpretation of the Bible providing an alternative to the traditional view that history will end with the return of Christ in judgment*.

He wrote concurrently *Concord of the New with the Old Testament, Exposition of the Apocalypse,* and *Ten-Stringed Psaltery.* According to his doctrine, which is one of remarkable simplicity, there is a correspondence between the events and persons of the OT and NT, and those (foretold by Revelation*) of a third age – the age of the Holy* Spirit that began with Benedict* (6th c.), continued with Bernard* of Clairvaux (1090–1153), and was to be fulfilled in 1260 ("a thousand, two hundred, and threescore days," Rev 11:3, 12:6) when the reign of the Son would be superseded by the reign of the Spirit, new religious orders would be founded, and a truly "spiritual church" would arise. In this third earthly period, humankind would leave its condition of tutelage and be guided inwardly by the Holy Spirit.

The Franciscans* saw their own order foretold in Joachim's writings. A Franciscan, Gerard of Borgo San Donnino, wrote *Introduction to the Eternal Gospel* (Paris, 1254). In addition to reproducing excerpts from Joachim's writings, it introduced the notions of a "third testament" superseding the other two and the coming of the "eternal gospel" (Rev 14:6) – views quickly condemned by the pope (1255). Yet Joachimist beliefs persisted among Franciscans, especially the Fraticelli*.

Movements of innovation or renewal (e.g. the Lay* Piety Movement, the Free* Spirit, the Radical Reformation, hopes about the New World and about progress, the American and French Revolutions, the new spirit of liberty) were not directly influenced by Joachism, although, in hindsight, Joachimism seemed to be the earliest formulation of a new, more hopeful approach to human history.

Lessing* gave intellectual legitimacy to this way of thinking, which was widely followed in the 19th c., as a distillation of the loving and emancipatory aspects of Christianity; as a religiosity outside the church, even in post*-Christian perspectives. At the dawn of the 21st c., Joachimism was either viewed with favor by progressive and liberationist Christians or blamed by conservatives as a major source of disruptive hopes for an infeasible earthly future.

EUGENE TESELLE

Joan of Arc (1412–31), virgin* martyr, military leader, French national hero. Born into a farming family, Joan claimed she had been divinely inspired to lead the French army in victories against the English that turned the tide of the Hundred Years' War. She facilitated Charles VII's coronation; later captured by the English and deserted by her French king, she was burned at the stake for heresy* (a conviction overturned 24 years later). Joan's rejection of clerical authority and insistence on personal religious experience somewhat anticipate the Reformation*. Beatified (1909) and canonized (1920), Joan remains an inspirational figure as a woman who defied the standards of her time.

MAUD BURNETT MCINERNEY

Job, Book of. One of the wisdom writings of the HB, Job is a literary rendering of a traditional story concerning a pious and wealthy man who inexplicably experiences devastating loss and suffering. Although the character Job is not an Israelite, the book is the product of a Judean author, writing probably in the 5th c. BCE.

The book is written in two contrasting styles, including a frame tale, composed in simple but elegant prose (1:1–2:13, 42:7–17), and a series of poetic speeches, consisting of a dialogue between Job and his three friends (Chaps. 3–27), a poem on the elusiveness of wisdom (28), a final speech by Job (29–31), a speech by a fourth friend, Elihu (32–37), and God's speeches from the whirlwind with Job's brief replies (38:1–42:6).

The frame tale focuses on the motives for human piety. Is it, as the adversary suggests (1:9–11, 2:4–5), an implicit bargain in which piety is exchanged for wealth and security? Or can piety be disinterested? The sufferings inflicted on Job provide the conditions for determining the answer. In the frame tale, Job retains his piety, his wealth is restored, and new children are born to him.

By contrast, in the poetic section, Job bitterly criticizes the lack of moral order in the world and the abusive behavior of God toward humans, even as he yearns to meet God in a trial at law. His friends defend God's governance of the world and treatment of Job, whom they see as justly punished. The most radical perspective in the book, however, is that of God, whose enigmatic speeches from the whirlwind implicitly reject the belief, widespread in antiquity, that God acts according to the principle of retributive justice*. Traditional Christian interpretation, however, has tended to focus on the suffering of Job rather than on the book's radical theological claims. **See also THEODICY.**

CAROL NEWSOM

Jocists (members of Jeunesse Ouvrière Chrétienne). See CATHOLIC ACTION; YOUNG CHRISTIAN WORKERS (JOCISTS).

Joel, Book of. In the Book of the Twelve Prophets, Joel appears second, after Hosea*. The prophecy was evoked by calamitous economic events, described poetically as an attack by locusts, an invading army, and severe drought. A balanced structure depicts the disaster in the first half of the book (1:1–2:17) and promises complete restoration in the second half (2:18–4:21, Hebrew text). Divine judgment of sinners from all nations follows the restoration of God's elect. There are sociological indications of a postexilic date: a reference to trade in slaves by the Ionians (Greeks) and Sabeans, and language about the day of YHWH, especially frightening cosmic symbolism similar to later apocalyptic* symbolism. Affinities with the Book of Jonah* exist, but it cannot be determined which author, if either has borrowed from the other. The question asked by both, "Who knows whether he [God] will turn and repent?" comes from the divine proclamation in Exod 34:6–7 about God's nature as merciful and just. Joel's message, addressed to the inhabitants of Jerusalem, is best known for two things: the reversal of the utopian vision concerning transforming swords into plowshares and spears into pruning hooks (Isa 2:4; Mic 4:3) and the extraordinary prediction about the outpouring of the divine vital force (spirit) that erases distinctions of gender, age, and social class. Early Christians interpreted the events associated with Pentecost recounted in Acts 2 as the reversal of the confusion of language recorded in the story about the Tower of Babel in Gen 11 and the fulfillment of Joel's prophecy. JAMES L. CRENSHAW

Johannine Comma, an interpolation in the text of 1 John 5:7–8, "the Father, the Word, and the Holy Spirit," a trinitarian formula added c800 to the Vulgate* after "There are three that testify." The interpolation became part of the official Latin text but is missing from Greek and other manuscripts.

John. In the NT, "John" (Gk *Ioannes*), a common Jewish name, refers to at least four different persons.

1. John, the son of Zebedee, called by Jesus with his brother James* (as the second pair of disciples; Mark 1:19; Matt 4:21), one of the Twelve* (Mark 3:17; Matt 10:2; Luke 6:14; Acts 1:13), and one of the inner circle of Jesus' disciples (Peter, James, and John; Mark 5:37, 9:2, 14:33 and par.; Luke 9:28). Luke associates John with Peter, the two being leaders of the disciples both in the Gospel of Luke (e.g. 22:8) and in Acts (Chaps. 3, 4, 8); yet after James's death (12:2), John does not play any major role in Acts. By contrast, in Gal 2:9–10, the earliest record, Paul identifies John, alongside Peter*/Cephas and James* ("the brother of the Lord"), as one of pillars of the church in Jerusalem. In the Gospel of John*, John is never mentioned by name, although the "sons of Zebedee" (John and James) are said to have seen the risen Christ (John 21:2). Church tradition associates John with the "beloved disciple" (John 13; 19; 20; 21), the presumed author of the Gospel of John (21:24), an authorship doubted by most scholars (see John, Gospel of).
2. John of Patmos, the seer and presumed author of the Book of Revelation* (1:1, 1:4, 1:9, 22:8).
3. John Mark, an early Jewish Christian who participated in Paul's, Peter's, and Barnabas's missionary activities (Acts 12:12, 12:25, 13:5, 15:37–39). Church traditions identify him as the presumed author of the Gospel of Mark* and as Mark, the companion of Paul (Phlm 24; 2 Tim 4:1).
4. The Elder (*presbyteros*) (2 John 1; 3 John 1) was sometimes identified with John the Apostle (as Papias* seems to do). Eusebius* clearly distinguished John the Presbyter from John the Apostle.

See also JOHN THE BAPTIST. DANIEL PATTE

John, Acts of. See APOCRYPHA CLUSTER: APOCRYPHAL ACTS OF APOSTLES.

John, Apocryphon of ("Secret Book of John"), often considered a classic example of Gnosticism*, purports to be a revelation by Christ to the apostle John about the divine realm and its relationship to the visible cosmos and humanity. A 2nd-c. original Greek version may have been the source of the mythology that Irenaeus* ascribed to certain *"gnostikoi."* Three copies in Coptic translation (c4th c.) survive among the Nag* Hammadi Codices, and a fourth in Berlin Codex 8502 (c5th c.).

The myth portrays an ineffable transcendent Spirit, from whose self-contemplation emerges a perfect realm or family of personified attributes ("aeons"). The material cosmos is an imperfect copy fashioned by a lesser being named Ialdabaoth, an offspring of the lowest entity (Wisdom*) in the transcendent realm. True humanity is the spiritual family in the realm of perfection, including the spiritual Adam*, his son Seth*, and the race or offspring of Seth. Earthly humanity possesses the physical form created by Ialdabaoth, but also the spiritual element, or seed, of Seth, which bears the image of God and is capable of salvation* if one is receptive to this revelation.

MICHAEL ALLEN WILLIAMS

John, Epistles of, a collection of three letters directed to an open public (1 John), an individual church (2 John), and an individual Christian (3 John), exhorting them to remain faithful to their vocation*. The main topics are faith*, truth*, and love*. The language echoes the Gospel of John* and OT covenant* traditions.

The addressees seem to be Christians in Asia Minor, organized in house churches, subject to the influence of Judaism*, Hellenism*, mystery* religions, and the Roman imperial cult, at the beginning of the 2nd c. CE.

The readers stand in the Johannine tradition, but the meaning of this tradition is debated. In the Gospel of John, there is a tendency toward a spiritualization of the Christian message, of Christ, and of Christian existence. The adversaries of 1–3 John seem to be "Ultra-Johanneans" who are proud of their spiritual "unction," lack social responsibility, and are influenced by contemporary enthusiastic* movements leading to Gnosticism*.

In 1 John, the central issues are the conditions of the new* covenant relationship with God: faith* in Christ incarnate and love* of one's brothers and sisters in readiness to share the daily bread (1 John 3). Only in this way can one be proud of knowing God, loving God, and being God's child. 2 John takes up the same criteria, and 3 John applies them to a concrete situation.

The twofold emphasis of 1–3 John on Christology* (faith and truth) and ethics (love) can be explained by a particular anthropology*: instead of boasting about one's communion with God through the Spirit and disregarding Christian solidarity, one should continue to confess Jesus Christ, who has "come in the flesh" (1 John 4:2; 2 John 7) for the redemption* of sinners, and acknowledge one's communion not only with God, but with fellow Christians.

JOHANNES BEUTLER, SJ

John, Gospel of, or "Fourth Gospel," authorship unknown but attributed pseudonymously* to "John," often identified as John, son of Zebedee; written c90 CE, probably in Asia Minor, independently of the Synoptic* Gospels but drawing on some similar traditions. Unlike Matthew* and Luke*, the Gospel of John begins not with an infancy narrative but with a cosmological introduction proclaiming Jesus to be the preexistent Word* of God. In John 1–12, Jesus' ministry is built around a series of "signs" narratives; John 13–20 has a lengthy set of "farewell discourses" at its heart, followed by the Passion narrative and Resurrection* appearances. Chapter 21 is an epilogue.

The Fourth Gospel was probably written within and for the use of a Jewish-Christian group, the "Johannine community," which had a distinctive theology and history. The Gospel of John suggests considerable tension between Johannine believers and Jews who did not share their view that Jesus was the Christ* and Son* of God. While some passages imply that the Jews had expelled Johannine Christians from the synagogue* (9:22, 12:42, 16:2; cf. Martyn), this cannot be proved.

In keeping with its heavily christological focus, John draws from the broad range of Jewish speculation on the nature, title, role, and origins of the Messiah*, in order to emphasize that Jesus is the Savior* – the Messiah, the prophet, the king of Israel – anticipated by Jews and Samaritans alike. Most important, Jesus is the Son of God, who through his life, death, and resurrection will remove the sins of the world and provide the way to eternal life for those who believe (1:19–22, 4:26, 20:30–31).

John calls upon witnesses (God, John* the Baptist, Scripture*; 5:31–47). It also uses a strident rhetoric of binary opposition, in which believers are associated with positive terms such as life, light, and spirit, and nonbelievers with their opposites: death, darkness, and flesh (e.g. 3:17–21, 5:22–24). The negative characterization of "the Jews" symbolizes those who are condemned to God's wrath* on account of their unbelief (8:31–58).

The Gospel of John was the subject of homilies and commentaries by the church fathers (e.g. Origen*, John* Chrysostom, Augustine*) and became a part of the Christian canon*. In the modern era, it has furnished the "born again" label and other slogans adopted by some Christians (3:3, 3:16). Negatively, John 8:44, in which Jesus tells some Jews that "[y]ou are from your father the devil*," has contributed to anti-Semitic* discourse throughout the centuries. ADELE REINHARTZ

John of Ávila (1499–1569). A preacher and Catholic reformer (see Catholic Renewal), he is best known for his influence on the reform of the Council of Trent* and his spiritual treatise *Audi, Filia* (1556; definitive, complete version published posthumously, 1574). Born into a wealthy *converso** (New Christian) family, he studied at the University of Alcalá (1524?), was ordained (1526), and then was posted to Seville. But he was imprisoned under suspicion of being a lapsed *converso* and an *alumbrado* heretic (false mystic) by the Inquisition* (1531). After being declared innocent (1533), he spent two decades focusing on Christian education* and reform of the church. An unauthorized version of the complete *Audi* was put on the 1559 Index* of Prohibited Books.

John of Ávila was a renowned preacher of Passion spirituality at the beginning of his career. His treatises on pastoral, clerical, and papal reform influenced several Spanish delegates to the Council of Trent. The *Audi, Filia,* an exegesis of Ps 45:11–12, was written as a guide for a female follower, then expanded for a larger audience. It focuses on Bible study, obedience to God, and contemplation of the Passion. In the final expanded edition, John also describes the city of God, warns against the devil's* temptations*, and advocates the glory of Christ. JESSICA A. BOON

John the Baptist, a 1st-c. apocalyptic* prophet* and ascetic* ("neither eating nor drinking," Matt 11:18 cf. Mark 1:6 and par.). From Josephus* (*Jewish Antiquities*) and the NT Gospels, one can conclude that John was from a lower, rural, priestly family (Luke 1, 2) and possibly associated temporarily with the Essenes* of Qumran* (in the "wilderness of Judea"), and that in defiance of the aristocratic religious and political authorities (Pharisees and Sadducees, Matt 3:7; Herod Antipas, who killed him, Mark 6:14–29), he preached the imminent coming of God's wrath* upon faithless Israelites. He called them to do works fit for repentance* (Matt 3:7), namely works of social justice* (Luke 3:10–14) and ritual purification (John 3:25) through baptism* (Mark 1:2–11 and par.), and proclaimed the coming of a further purification by the "Holy* Spirit and fire" (Matt 3:10–12).

Building on this tradition, the four Gospels present John as the precursor of Jesus. The early church absorbed most of John's movement (although some claimed John's superiority to Jesus). Mark presents John as Elijah* incognito (1:6, 911–13), preparing the way of Jesus, who is mightier than John (1:1–8, 6:14–29). Matthew explicitly presents John as (the new) Elijah (17:12–13) and puts Jesus' words on John's lips (3:2, 4:17); yet Jesus' baptism scene involves a rebuke of John for misunderstanding Jesus' ministry (3:14–15). For Luke John's ministry is completely separate from that of Jesus: he still belongs to the period of the "Law and prophets" (16:6). In the Fourth Gospel, John the Baptist is simply "the voice" witnessing to Jesus as the light (1:6–8), as the Christ who increases while John decreases (3:23–30); here John is the first confessing Christian, a model missionary*. Thus despite original ambivalences in the history of the church, John was viewed as a saint, a model of discipleship. DANIEL PATTE

John Chrysostom (c349–407), theologian, ascetic*, archbishop of Constantinople; viewed as one of the greatest preachers of the early church, hence the epithet "Chrysostom" (golden-mouthed). Born in Antioch, Syria, he studied rhetoric under the renowned Hellenistic orator Libanius. He was ordained a deacon* (381) and priest* (386) in Antioch and became archbishop of Constantinople (398–404). Twice deposed and banished for involvement in political and ecclesiastical intrigues, he died in exile.

John's life spanned a pivotal period of transition in the Roman Empire and the ancient world. Christianity was gaining political and social ascendancy, but it continued to compete with older religions, the imperial cult, and Judaism, and struggled with internal tensions. Politically the Empire was officially divided between East and West, and ecclesiastically the rise in power of Constantinople provoked the jealousy of the more prominent Eastern sees* of Antioch* and Alexandria*. Chrysostom's career reflects these rivalries and tensions.

Born into an educated upper-class family, after his father's early death John was raised by his mother, Anthusa. A gifted student, he received a traditional classical education and was possibly headed for a career in law or the civil service. But John soon turned away from a secular career and began to prepare for ministry in the church, where his rhetorical training would serve him well. For three years, he was an aide to Meletius*, the bishop of Antioch, studying the Scriptures* under him; he also frequented a form of ascetic school led by the priest Diodore*, later bishop of Tarsus. John was ordained as a lector, a minor clerical position, but soon retreated to the nearby mountains to pursue an ascetic life, first under the tutelage of an elderly monk and later in greater isolation. His rigorous austerities are said to have damaged his health; after approximately six years in the Syrian desert, he returned to Antioch to resume his duties as a lector, was ordained a deacon (381), and was largely responsible for administration of the church's charity.

Ordained a priest in Antioch (386), John pursued for the next 12 years an active pastoral and theological career. He preached regularly in the churches of Antioch and was involved in civic affairs. His sermons are an excellent source of information about the city and the diverse Christian and non-Christian factions that competed for popular attention. John became embroiled in high-level ecclesiastical and imperial politics when leaders in Constantinople appointed him as their bishop (398). He already had enemies, chief among them Bishop Theophilus* of Alexandria, a rival episcopal see. John's efforts to reform church administration and finances, outspoken criticism of the higher clergy, scorn for the affluent lifestyle of the imperial court, and persistent reclusiveness provoked further opposition. His imprudent remarks about Empress Eudoxia and his reception of the Tall* Brothers, Egyptian monks accused of Origenism*, served to mobilize his enemies. Deposed by the Synod of Oak* (403), he was quickly reinstated. Despite popular support, John was again deposed and banished, and he died in exile in Armenia*.

Well trained in the classical tradition, John Chrysostom was one of the most eloquent Christian orators in late antiquity and is admired among classical scholars for his elegant prose. Most of John's writings are sermons on books of the Bible or in honor of saints and treatises on practical Christian living. In exegesis* he leaned toward the literal and historical interpretation of the Bible favored in Antioch* rather than the allegorical* interpretation emphasized by the Alexandrian* school. Yet John was deeply concerned with the application of the biblical text to Christians' spiritual and moral lives. He condemned luxury and abuses of wealth and emphasized charitable giving and the needs of the poor.

John's sermons also reflect the political issues and theological controversies that marked the late 4th c. Soon after his ordination, he faced a great civic upheaval as the citizens of Antioch destroyed imperial statues in protest against the imposition of new taxes. In a series of sermons, John both rebuked the people for their acts of violence and consoled them in the face of probable imperial repercussions. He preached a series of sermons against radical Arian* Christians in the city and another series, *Against Judaizing Christians*, warning against participation in Jewish festivals and observances. The inflammatory rhetoric of these sermons helped promote anti*-Jewish attitudes during the Middle Ages and beyond.

The most prolific of the Greek fathers, John is best known as a preacher* and exegete. Besides his many letters and treatises, more than 900 of his homilies are extant. His sermons began to be translated into Latin soon after his death; he was the most popular Eastern Christian writer in the medieval West. John also wrote an influential treatise, *On the Priesthood*, the first full-fledged treatment of Christian ministry. In Byzantium his name was attached to the Constantinopolitan liturgy* in honor of his liturgical reforms. With Basil* the Great and Gregory* of Nazianzus, he is counted among the three holy hierarchs for his leadership of the church. ANDREA STERK

John Climacus (c525–606), or John of the Ladder, revered as a saint* by Roman Catholic, Oriental Orthodox, and Eastern Orthodox churches. A monk, he lived for 20 years as an ascetic* hermit* at the foot of Mount Sinai, studying the lives of saints. After becoming abbot*, John wrote the *Climax* (or *Ladder*) *of Divine Ascent* describing the 30 steps of spiritual progression in monastic life, reaching dispassionateness (*apatheia*) as the ultimate contemplative and mystical good, which became a classic for Eastern Orthodox monastic life.

John of the Cross (1542–91), mystical* theologian and founder, with Teresa* of Ávila, of the Discalced Carmelites*. Born into a poor family in Old Castile, he entered the Carmelite house of Medina (1563) and studied theology. Ordained a priest (1567), he met Teresa, a prioress of a Carmelite convent in Ávila, who sought his assistance in spreading a new form of contemplative monastic lifestyle. Juan de Santo Matía adopted a new name, Juan de la Cruz, John of the Cross (1568).

He served as master of the Discalced (barefoot) Carmelite College in Alcalá and as confessor of Teresa's convent (1571–77). The reformist spirit sparked by Teresa and John's collaboration was resented by the Calced Carmelites, who incarcerated John for nine months (1577–78) in their monastery – a harbinger of the separation between Calced and Discalced Carmelites (1579–80). When, after Teresa's death, the provincial Nicolás Doria imposed additional ascetic strictures on the Discalced Nuns, John opposed him and was banished (1591) and died.

John's writings, treasures of Renaissance Spanish literature and of Western Christianity, ironically juxtapose a mystical imagination and apophatic* wonder with medieval Scholastic philosophy and thus represent a unique contribution to Western theology. Active submission to the Supreme Lover, the source of life and love's energy and longing, lies at the center of John's mystical contemplation. *The Spiritual Canticle*, *The Dark Night of the Soul*, and *The Living Flame of Love*, perhaps his best-known works, show the influence of Teresa of Ávila; both see the process of purgation, illumination, and union as the trajectory of the human soul seeking union with God. *The Spiritual Canticle* also displays an indebtedness to Bernard* of Clairvaux; both writers see in Song* of Songs a canonical blueprint for the journey of the soul seeking union with the Divine. John's dedication to describing "God's mysterious ways upon the human soul" has left an indelible mark on subsequent Catholic theology. Beatified (1675) and canonized (1726), he was made a doctor of the church (1926). PAUL CHANG-HA LIM

John of Damascus (c675–c750), monk, theologian, prolific writer of liturgical poetry, epitomizer of the Greek patristic* tradition. His family played a prominent role in the fiscal administration of Syria during the 7th c., a period of political change, and he himself served under the caliph in Damascus. He became a monk (early 8th c.) in or near Jerusalem.

John was the first Christian to write about Islam* with direct knowledge of it (see Islam and Christianity Cluster: Introductory Entries and In the Middle East), but he primarily defended the Greek patristic tradition of the ecumenical* councils against those who, having found relative freedom under the Muslim yoke, rejected it. He served as a defender of conciliar orthodoxy while among the monks of the Holy Land and gained great renown as a preacher. He is still regarded as one of the greatest Byzantine hymnographers.

Apart from his polemical works, his works epitomized the Greek patristic tradition and became a vehicle for monastic meditation. These included a handbook (*Dialectica*) that focused on logic and the technical language of Greek theology; a "century" on heresies* – 80 chapters of an epitome of Epiphanios's* *Panarion*, supplemented by 20 chapters of John's own composition, the last of which was on Islam; and a "century" summarizing the essential points of the Christian faith (*On the Orthodox Faith*, or *Expositio fidei*) on the doctrines of God* and the Trinity*, creation* (including a great deal of astronomical, geographical, physiological, and psychological learning), Christology*, and various points concerned with Christian worship, the sacraments*, icons*, and the last things (see Eschatology Cluster). This concluding treatise was translated into many languages, including Latin, in which form it provided valuable access to Greek patristic theology for the Scholastics and later Western theologians up to Schleiermacher*.

John also wrote three treatises (including *On the Divine Images*) against Byzantine Iconoclasm* (under Leo* V), which contained a classical defense of the place of icons* in Christian worship, based principally on the doctrine of the Incarnation*. This was translated into Slavonic in the early modern period and provided an Orthodox defense of religious painting against Calvinist Protestantism. ANDREW LOUTH

John of Ephesus (c507–89), also known as John of Asia. An energetic ascetic* leader of the Miaphysites*; founder and archimandrite* of the monastery at Sycae near Constantinople. Of Northern Mesopotamian origin, ordained as a deacon, and titular bishop of Ephesus (though he never resided there), he was an important historian and a major leader of the persecuted "underground" church organized by Jacob* Baradaeus. KATHLEEN E. MCVEY

John Paul II, Pope (1978–2005), born Karol Wojtyla (1920) in Wadowice, Poland, educated at Jagellonian University, at the secret seminary housed in the archbishop's palace during World War II, and in Rome after World War II. He wrote poetry, a number of plays, and some theatrical criticism. His philosophical doctoral dissertation was later published as *The Acting Person*. He taught for a time at the University of Lublin and was made assistant bishop, then archbishop of Cracow (1963). The first non-Italian pope* since 1522, he had the second longest pontificate in history, marked by a somewhat conservative theology combined with a vigorous defense of human* rights. He produced a large number of encyclicals*, including three on Catholic social doctrine (see Social Encyclicals), and gave support to the Polish trade union Solidarity as it successfully confronted the Communist regime. He traveled more than any pope before him, and was the first pope to enter a synagogue* and visit a Muslim country. His final years were marred by ill health, perhaps exacerbated by a wound from an assassination attempt (1981). More than 4 million people attended his lying-in-state; a large number of world leaders attended his funeral. Moves were made to declare him a saint shortly after his death. MICHAEL J. WALSH

John Scholasticos (c503–77), patriarch of Constantinople (from 565). Theologian and jurist, he compiled (c545) the earliest preserved version of the *nomocanon** that combined both canons* of the church and imperial laws, reflecting the close relationship between the Eastern Orthodox* Church and the state.

John Scotus Eriugena, or Erigena (c810–c877). "Scotus" indicates that he was Irish, "Erigena" that he was born in Ireland. In Ireland he learned Greek and became acquainted with philosophy and theology; he went to France, probably because Ireland was vulnerable during the Viking raids, and became a resident scholar in the court of Charles the Bald at Laon. He seems never to have become either a monk or a cleric; thus he was free from certain kinds of ecclesiastical discipline and could be bolder in his philosophical speculation than others who were subject to such discipline. At the request of Charles, he translated the writings of Dionysius* the Pseudo-Areopagite, two works by Maximus* the Confessor, and *On the Making of Man* by Gregory* of Nyssa. His *Periphyseon*, or *On the Division of Nature*, is a daring speculative work. During the controversy over predestination* aroused by Gottschalk*, he defended freedom* in a highly speculative way.

John XXIII, Pope (1958–63), born Angelo Giuseppe Roncalli (1881) into a large peasant family in Sotto il Monte; studied in Bergamo and Rome; after ordination became secretary to the bishop of Bergamo. During World War I, he was a hospital orderly, then a chaplain, and entered the papal diplomatic service, going to Bulgaria*, Turkey*, and Greece* before being sent to Paris (1944). He was named cardinal (1955) and shortly afterward patriarch of Venice. After his election as pope* (1958), he summoned a general council (Second Vatican* Council) to update the Roman Catholic Church's theology and mission. He greatly supported the movement for human* rights (see his encyclical* *Pacem* in Terris*, 1963) and Christian unity. His stances had a great impact, even on the Soviet Union, leading to his receiving in audience the son-in-law of the Soviet Communist Party's general secretary. He was beatified* in 2000.
MICHAEL J. WALSH

Jonah, Book of, a popular biblical narrative, is complex and problematic. Who was the prophet? Is the story historical? When was it written? For what purpose? Is the present ending genuine? Why did Jonah start by running away? Why was he angry at the end? What are we to make of his being swallowed by a "whale"? Of his speaking Assyrian? Of a five-word (in Hebrew) discourse producing a massive conversion of a wicked empire? Of a tree growing in one night?

Jonah ben Amittai was an obscure prophet in the 8th c. BCE (2 Kgs 14:25; but is this verse decisive for dating the Book of Jonah?). The extraordinary events reported in Jonah are seen as divine interventions (cf. 3 Macc 6:8; Josephus*, *Judean Antiquities*, Book 9, 10:2). But modern scholars emphasize the fantastic elements of the document, its late linguistic features, and its anthological composition, and suggest the 4th–3rd c. BCE as a date. Indeed, the Book of Jonah interprets earlier traditions and is itself interpreted. The Gospels (Matt 12:38–41, 16:1–4; Luke 11:29–32) speak of "the sign of Jonah," in which one recognizes Jesus' message, death, and resurrection (cf. Christian sarcophagi and catacombs*).

Read symbolically – for the church fathers, Jonah is a type of the Messiah* (see Typology) – would the book denounce Israel's "narrowness" regarding the nations (see Gentiles)? Jonah refuses to "evangelize" Israel's notorious oppressors and is incensed by their conversion, which shames Israel's obduracy. Spared by God, Nineveh will destroy Israel in 721. Does God's universalistic justice* amount to a historic injustice? The book balks at giving a definitive answer and ends on a question mark (4:9–11).

ANDRÉ LACOCQUE

Joncoux, Françoise-Marguerite de (1668–1715), Jansenist* activist, spiritual writer. Born in Paris, Joncoux defended the Jansenist cause persecuted by Louis XIV. In the publication process, she was a link between theologians, such as Pasquier Quesnel, exiled in the Netherlands, and the Parisian Jansenist world, where she hosted gatherings that included theologians like Jacques-Joseph Duguet. She collaborated on the *Histoire abrégée du jansénisme* (1697) and, with Quesnel, on the *Histoire du cas de conscience* (1703). Speaking out for Port-Royal, she coordinated attempts to save the convent before its destruction (1709). She spent her last years fighting the anti-Jansenist bull *Unigenitus* (1713).

MITA CHOUDHURY

Jordan. The Hashemite kingdom of Jordan, whose royal family successfully steers a balanced political course in the Middle East, guarantees its minority of Christians (about 4% of the population) freedom of worship and freedom of conversion – a socially difficult issue in most countries with a Muslim majority.

The majority of Christians in Jordan belong to the Greek Orthodox* and Greek-Catholic (Melkite*) churches; smaller groups belong to the Syriac* Orthodox Church or the Armenian* Apostolic Church, or are Roman Catholics and Protestants. Christianity seems to be growing, partly because of the increasing number of Evangelical* (especially Seventh day Adventist*), Pentecostal*, and Charismatic* converts, but also because of the immigration of a considerable number of Christians from Iraq*, mainly from the Chaldean* Church.

Christianity has been present in the region at least since the 4th c. (when the area around Mount Nebo, near Madaba, became an important site of pilgrimage). Western Protestant and Catholic missions put their mark on the Christian landscape in the 19th c., mainly winning over Orthodox Christians to Uniatism* (Melkites) or Protestantism, but also converting smaller groups of Muslim Bedouins. From 1948 the Jordanian royal family acted as protectors of the holy places in Jerusalem and Bethlehem. Israel's occupation of the "West Bank" and East Jerusalem made this more difficult and caused many Palestinians – including many Orthodox, and Lutheran Christians – to migrate to Jordan.

More than in other Middle Eastern countries, there is an official dialogue between Muslims and Christians (see Dialogue, Interfaith), supported by the royal family (cf. the Royal Institute for Inter-Faith Studies, Amman). This is part of a general atmosphere of mutual tolerance and acceptance, often attributed to the shared tribal background of Christians and Muslims. See Islam and Christianity Cluster: In the Middle East.

Statistics: Population (2000): 6.7 million (M). Christians, 0.27 M, 4.1% (Orthodox, 2.0%; Roman Catholics, 0.7%; independents, 1.2%; Protestants, 0.2%; Anglicans, 0.1%); Muslims, 93.5%; atheists, nonreligious, 2.5%. (Based on *World Christian Encyclopedia*, 2001.)

HELEEN L. MURRE-VAN DEN BERG

Joseph, Husband of Mary, the mother of Jesus, was praised as a just and righteous man, a son of David (Matt 1:19–20; cf. Luke 1:27, 2:4). An angel of the Lord visited him three times, guiding him to take Mary as his wife, to travel to Egypt for safety, and to take his family to Israel (Matt 1:20, 2:13, 2:19). A carpenter (Matt 13:55), Joseph remains obscure, although he is discussed in apocryphal* writings: the Gospel of James, the Gospel of the Nativity of the Virgin Mary, the Story of Joseph the Carpenter, and the Life of the Virgin and Death of Joseph. The Gospel of Mark does not mention him.

JEFFRY C. DAVIS

Joseph, Son of Jacob and Rachel, sold into slavery by his brothers, eventually rising to power in Egypt as a result of his ability to interpret dreams (Gen 37, 39–50). The Dead* Sea Scrolls view Joseph as the ideal person. Justin* Martyr, Tertullian*, and Irenaeus* identify Joseph as a type of Christ; Ambrose* devoted an entire book to this concept (see Typology). Athanasius* considers Joseph to be a model of godly faithfulness*. Joseph's story significantly exemplifies the providence of God* (e.g. Gen 45:5, 45:7–8, 50:20) and presents an example of one who resists temptation (Gen 39). The

NT recognizes Joseph as a person of faith* (Heb 11:22). JEFFRY C. DAVIS

Josephus, Flavius (37–c100), Judean priest, statesman, soldier, historian, immersed in Greek culture. His writings were exploited by Christian writers for background to the NT and theological proof of divine wrath* against Israel. He served as a general in the war against Rome, was captured (67), and was eventually freed because he predicted that Vespasian and Titus would become emperors (69). After Jerusalem's fall (70), he traveled to Rome with Titus (71) and there wrote *Judean War* (70s), *Judean Antiquities* with *Life* (93/94), and *Against Apion*.

Writing against the backdrop of celebration by the Flavian dynasty (69–96) of victory in Judea, Josephus challenged the image of his nation as rebellious by showing its admirable character. His presentation of the causes and course of the war and the nation's origins and age-old constitution dismisses hostile accounts of these. The old picture of Josephus as Flavian mouthpiece is not defensible.

Josephus's works were preserved in Christian circles, as a companion to the Gospels. Origen* and Eusebius* quoted his portrait of Jerusalem's* sufferings, allegedly fulfilling gospel predictions of woe in retribution for the city's rejection of Jesus; his references to Jesus*, James*, and John* the Baptist; and his information about conditions in Judea* and Galilee*. Known not to be a Christian, Josephus was valued as a reliable, independent witness of Jerusalem's fall and as the unquestioned authority on NT background. **See also HEGESIPPUS (PSEUDO-).** STEVE MASON

Joshua, Book of, presents Israel's conquest and occupation of the land of Canaan as having taken place in obedience to divine commands and in fulfillment of divine promises.

Joshua underwent a complex process of composition, during which diverse materials and traditions were assembled, edited, and expanded over time for inclusion within the Deuteronomistic* History (7th–6th c. BCE).

The book constructs a sense of Israelite identity by rendering its story in the distinctive idiom of Deuteronomy*. It accentuates God's initiative in choosing Israel, fighting its battles, and giving it the land. It also demonstrates that the unity of Israel, obedience to the commandments of Moses, and separation from other peoples are essential to the achievement of God's promises. This depiction is undercut, however, by a counternarrative that recounts internal squabbles, transgressions of the commandments, agreements with the indigenous peoples, and failure to occupy their lands.

The intricate interplay between divine grace* and human obedience configures the book's plot, which portrays God's faithfulness and power while exemplifying the vigorous faith* called for in response. Its account of divinely ordained conquest, however, confronts the reader with disturbing questions of war*, ethnic violence*, oppression*, and dispossession – and God's* implication in them.

Early Christian interpreters saw Joshua as a foreshadowing of the work of Christ (Heb 4:8–9; Barnabas* 12:8–9) or read the book as an allegory* of the war against sin* or evil*. During the era of Western colonialism*, Joshua influenced the construction of national mythologies of election and destiny, and the legitimization of programs of militarism, dispossession, and ethnic cleansing. DANIEL HAWK

Josiah, king of Judah (640–609 BCE). While renovating the Temple in Jerusalem, workers found a "book of the Torah*" (2 Kgs 22:8), probably Deuteronomy*. Following its commands, Josiah destroyed all places of Canaanite (and syncretistic*?) worship and centralized the sacrifices in Jerusalem. Christian interpreters through the centuries have seen Josiah as a significant example of a ruler concerned with the purification of religion (see Erastianism).

Jovinian (d c405), a monk who argued that virginity* is not a higher state than marriage*, attacked the belief that some modes of life gain a higher heavenly reward, and shared Helvidius's* denial of the perpetual virginity of Mary. He was condemned as a heretic* by synods in Rome (392) and Milan (393).

Juana Inés de la Cruz, Sister. See ASBAJE Y RAMÍREZ, JUANA INÉS DE.

Jubilee, Year of, presented in Lev 25, comes at the end of a cycle of seven sabbatical years (the 50th year, 25:11), when all Israelites enslaved for debt are set free and returned to their families, and the lands that had been taken over by others are returned to the original families. The Jubilee reflects a theologically significant socioeconomic perspective. "The land shall not be sold in perpetuity, for the land is mine [God]; with me you are but aliens and tenants" (25:23). As resident aliens before God (see Refugees as a Theological Concept and an Ethical Issue) and as God's freed slaves (freed from Egypt; 25:42, 55), Israelites are not to make slaves* of each other (25:39, 42); those enslaved for debt should be freed. Although there is no evidence that the Jubilee system was ever implemented, its themes of liberation* and restoration were emphasized by the prophets (e.g. Isa 35, 42, 58, 61) and shaped the hope* for the messianic redemption* and restoration* and the challenge for justice* to the oppressed* – including, in the NT, Jesus' proclamation of the Kingdom*, most explicitly in Luke 4:16–30. Contemporary Christians struggling for justice* for the economically oppressed underscore the importance of the Jubilee view of the land*, just as Liberation* theologians call for the liberation and restoration of the oppressed.

DANIEL PATTE

Jubilees, Book of, Jewish OT pseudepigraphon (early 2nd c. BCE.; Qumran fragments confirm its antiquity). Ascribed to Moses and recounting biblical history from creation until the giving of the Law, this history is divided into periods of 50 years ("Jubilees") and enriched with many apocryphal traditions. Once an important source of Byzantine chronology, the Book of Jubilees is now fully preserved only in the Ethiopian* Church and provides examples of retold sacred history and typology*. **See also PSEUDEPIGRAPHA.** JOHANNES TROMP

Judah, fourth son of Jacob* and Leah*; also, the tribe descended from Judah and the territory occupied by this tribe in Southern Palestine, from the Dead Sea to the Mediterranean, where it encountered the Philistines*. After the division of the kingdom, the southern portion (including the territory of Benjamin) was called Judah. This usage continued after the Exile*; hence the inhabitants were called Jews, and their religion Judaism*.

JUDAISM AND CHRISTIANITY CLUSTER

1) *Introductory Entries*

Ancient Judaism, the New Testament, and Early Christianity
Judaism and Christianity: Christian Views
Judaism and Christianity: Jewish Views

2) *A Sampling of Contextual Interactions*

Judaism and Christianity in North America
Judaism and Christianity in Western Europe

---

1) Introductory Entries

Ancient Judaism, the New Testament, and Early Christianity. Christianity arose as a messianic movement within Palestinian Judaism. Jesus and his disciples were Jews, at home in the teachings, practices, experiences, and hopes of their people. Understanding the rise of Christianity requires taking into account the writings and archeological remains of contemporary Jewish religion and culture, and scrutinizing how the NT writers adopted, transformed, or discarded their Jewish heritage.

First-century Judaism was diverse, indeed a plurality of "Judaisms," including those of the Sadducees*, Pharisees*, Essenes*, and other apocalyptic* groups. Yet these diverse groups had common elements. Central to the Jews' self-identity was their belief in their election*: the one true God had chosen them and accepted them into a unique relationship of reciprocal fidelity (faithfulness; see Faith #1). Their vocation* – their responsibilities within this covenant* – was laid out in the divinely revealed Torah* ("instruction" and "Law" – much more than simply a legal code; see Law), and they believed that their God would reward and punish their obedience and disobedience. By the turn of the era, most Jews accepted as the authoritative repository of sacred tradition most of what was becoming the HB, also available in Greek translation, the Septuagint* (LXX). The Jerusalem Temple was a major religious institution, a place where priests offered daily sacrifices* for the nation, people brought sacrifices of thanksgiving for blessings received, and other sacrifices atoned for sin.

These points of commonality, however, were expressed in a cultural, intellectual, social, and religious pluralism; and there were outright sectarian* dissenters, among whom the Jesus movement can be placed. Although most biblical texts applied the notion of election to the nation as a whole, some Jews such as the Qumran* Essenes* and other Apocalyptic Jews limited the terms "Israel" and "the chosen" to their own group. For them Torah was their particular revealed interpretation of the Mosaic laws, and since they alone could properly obey divine law, only they would receive divine blessing and salvation* from sin* and evil* (viewed as a power, in a dualistic perspective; see Apocalypticism Cluster: Beginnings in Judaism and Christianity).

In these apocalyptic sectarian groups, the view of the nature of blessing and salvation varied widely and stood in sharp contrast to that of other strands of Judaism, for which blessing might be experienced as a prosperous and happy life and salvation was not really an appropriate concept. In the midst of suffering and unjust death, Apocalyptic Jews anticipated blessing and salvation in a resurrection* or a blessed existence in heaven*. The agent of salvation might be God, an angel, a heavenly figure called the "Son* of man," or the anointed king (Messiah*) in a restored Davidic dynasty. The Qumran Essenes and parts of 1 Enoch* rejected the viability of the Temple cult and criticized its priesthood. A true high priest, the anointed one of Aaron, had yet to appear. One could atone for sin through almsgiving and other righteous deeds and through rituals of self-abasement and purification.

Such beliefs were expressed in a wide variety of sectarian writings. Noteworthy are the apocalyptic* books, which claimed to transmit revelations that a notable figure of the past (Enoch*, Daniel*, Moses*, or Ezra*) received from a heavenly revealer. Beliefs constituted communities of like-minded people, often persecuted minorities, who gathered to reinforce their beliefs and pursue a God-pleasing lifestyle. Some groups (e.g. the Essenes, and the authors and readers of 1 Enoch), claiming revelation through visions or inspired interpretation of Scripture*, believed that the end-time and the moment of their deliverance was near.

Early Christianity is best viewed as such a sectarian movement. Inspired by the revelatory appearances of the risen Jesus, and informed by their own interpretation of Scripture, the earliest disciples announced that the end of the age was at hand and that Jesus would return from heaven as God's judge. Alongside their belief in resurrection (of Jesus and later of Christians), they drew many of their symbols, institutions, and practices from their Jewish context, not least the identity, titles, and functions applied to Jesus. Even their belief that non-Jews (Gentiles*) could become members of God's people has a Jewish parallel (1 Enoch, based on prophetic texts of the HB). But whether non-Jews were bound to obey the Torah was vigorously debated. Some Christians continued to observe the Torah's prescriptions into the 2nd c. (see Ebionites; Judaizers; Nazarenes, Gospel of the). Others, like Paul*, strongly opposed the necessity of Torah obedience for Gentile Christians (although he left open the possibility of Torah obedience for Jewish Christians). Still others, like Matthew*, sought a middle ground. Essential to the 1st-c. church was the conviction that Jesus of Nazareth, crucified and raised from the dead, variously identified as Christ (Messiah), Son of man, Son* of God, or Lord*, was the end-time agent of God's beneficent activity. Strands of early Christianity espoused a supersessionist* perspective, understanding themselves to be the new Israel that replaced the old Israel as God's chosen; these Christians excluded from their community Jews who continued to find their religious center in the Torah rather than in Jesus; they interpreted the Roman destruction of Jerusalem and the Temple (70 CE) as God's judgment on the nation that largely had not accepted Jesus as Christ. Yet, the only witness to the history of earliest Christianity, the NT, is striking for its Jewish character, even as the Gospels express antipathy toward Jews who did not believe in Jesus as Christ. **See also DEAD SEA SCROLLS.**

GEORGE W. E. NICKELSBURG

Judaism and Christianity: Christian Views. Christianity grew out of Jewish monotheism* and the traditions of Judaism as they existed 2,000 years ago.

Judaism and Christianity: Christian Views

Although Jesus* of Nazareth came to be understood as the founder of Christianity, he did not intend to start a new religion. Jesus was a practicing Jew, and he died as one. His original followers were practicing Jews. Following Jewish traditions, Jesus' teachings emphasized love* of one's neighbor, the need for repentance*, and liberation* for the oppressed*. Although he rejected violence, Jesus suffered a violent death when Pontius Pilate*, the Roman governor of Palestine, executed him as an expedient way to stop the political upheaval that Jesus and his followers might cause. Roman, not Jewish, power put Jesus to death by crucifixion*.

Jesus' death left his followers dismayed and scattered. Jesus probably would have been a mere footnote to history if his Jewish disciples had not come to believe that Jesus had been resurrected from death, that he was the Messiah* promised in Jewish tradition, and that he was the Son* of God.

Most Jews did not share these beliefs. Nevertheless, Paul*, with his Jewish prophetic view of mission to Gentiles (non-Jews), and others had greater success in sharing the Christian faith with the Gentiles of the Mediterranean world. When the Romans destroyed Jerusalem (70 CE), the small, struggling sect within Judaism was on its way to becoming the Christian religion that would gain cultural dominance in Western civilization.

The divorce between Christianity and Judaism was not a happy one. Although Christianity's power grew in the West, especially from the 4th c., Jewish belief and practice persisted as counter-testimony to Christianity's most basic claims. Christians could not accept the Jewish interpretation of events surrounding Jesus of Nazareth. Christians embraced what Jews rejected: that Jesus is Lord*, the Messiah, and that the revelation given to the Jewish patriarchs, Abraham*, Isaac*, and Jacob*, to Moses*, and to the prophets prefigured and was fulfilled in Jesus. Thus Christianity historically understood itself to be the religion God intended Judaism to be, but, allegedly owing to a failure of understanding or will, the Jews were incapable of receiving God's most precious gift, Jesus as Lord.

A structured, official Christian position toward Jews and Judaism eventually emerged, which scholars identified as a "teaching of contempt." This *adversus Judaeos* literature (patristic writings directed against the Jews and Judaism; 2nd to 6th c.) began with Apologists*, such as Justin* Martyr (*Dialogue with Trypho*) and Tertullian* (*Adversus Judaeos*) and continued with other church fathers such as John* Chrysostom (*Orations against the Jews*) and Augustine* (although later in his life he adopted a more positive view of Judaism). This anti-Judaism teaching of contempt achieved ever greater influence as Christian authority and Roman power joined hands, leading to an essentially Christian civilization in the West.

The anti-Judaic teaching of contempt, vestiges of which remain, pivots around supersessionism (Lat *supersedere*, "to sit above," "to replace"). Supersessionism's defining convictions include the following: God's revelation in Jesus Christ surpasses the revelation to Israel; the NT fulfills the OT; Judaism is an overly legalistic religion; Christians replace the Jews as God's people; Jews neither heeded the prophets' warnings nor understood the prophecies about Jesus; and the Jews were Christ killers, guilty of the crime of deicide.

Contemporary Christianity strives to repudiate any "teaching of contempt" toward Jews and Judaism, but this change in attitude took place only after European Jewry was nearly destroyed in the Holocaust* unleashed by Nazi Germany and its allies. As Christians came to realize that their tradition's anti-Jewish hostility implicated Christianity in the Holocaust, much-needed reform of Christian understanding about the Jewish tradition got under way. That reformation remains a work in progress. Supersessionism is in question, but it has not been eradicated. Yet Christian–Jewish relations in the 21st c. are arguably the best they have been for two millennia. **See also ANTI-JEWISH, ANTI-JUDAISM; ANTI-SEMITISM; HOLOCAUST, JEWISH (OR SHOAH); SUPERSESSIONISM.** JOHN K. ROTH

Judaism and Christianity: Jewish Views. Christianity and Judaism have a unique relationship, not least because Jesus was born, lived, and died a Jew. The first Christians were Jews, and it was centuries later that Christianity and Judaism parted ways. By the completion of the Talmud (c500), Judaism and Christianity had diverged (see Birkath ha-Minim) and Jewish* Christianity ceased to exist. Nevertheless, Christians and Jews remained (and remain) intricately connected through their claim to follow the same Scriptures*. What Christians call "Old* Testament" and Jews "Tanakh" is mostly the same, although they interpret Scripture quite differently – thus the aphorism "Jews and Christians are divided by a common Bible."

The main theological divide concerns Christian claims about the divinity of Jesus*. Gradually the church came to view Judaism as the outdated people of Israel, which had been replaced by the new and true people of Israel, the church. Yet many Christians in the early centuries attended synagogue services. Church leaders (e.g. John* Chrysostom, c350–407) complained bitterly about their attendance and delivered vitriolic sermons against Judaism (creating a literary genre, *adversus Judaeos*), insisting that Jews did not understand the OT. Augustine* (354–430) portrayed Jews as children of Cain*, whose dispersion was God's punishment; yet Jews served as witnesses to Christian truth and were not to be harmed.

Once Christianity was established as the official religion of the Roman Empire (late 4th c.), the Jews' situation became more difficult. However, this was a gradual process, because the energy of Christian Europe was directed toward defeating pagans and Christian heretics. Nevertheless, the Justinian* Code (535–53) removed many Jewish rights and legitimized the closure of synagogues* as well as forced baptisms (despite some church opposition).

Judaism was a minority in both the Islamic world and Christendom*; Jews thus asked themselves why God allowed these faiths to flourish. One view was that Christianity was a form of idolatry*, perhaps not in the full biblical sense but because of inherited patterns of idolatrous worship. Another approach categorized Christianity in terms of the Noachide laws (see Noah), which formulated moral standards without a demand for conversion to Judaism. Judah ha-Levi (1075–1141) and Maimonides* (1135–1204) viewed Christianity as preparing the way for nations to worship the God of Israel and thus redemption*. Menahem ha'-Meiri (1249–1316) even argued that Christianity should be understood as a form of monotheism* and coined the phrase "nations bound by the ways of religion" to relax certain rabbinic laws and allow for a more fruitful interaction between Jews and Christians.

From c1100, as Christendom became more homogeneous, Jews were seen as one of the last "different" groups. Jews were accused of the ritual murder of Christian children, host* desecration, and causing the Black Death, all such accusations usually leading to group executions. Dominicans* and Franciscans* were fiercely anti-Jewish and implemented the Inquisition*, burned thousands of Jewish books (Paris, 1240), preached conversionist sermons at which Jewish attendance was compelled, held enforced public disputations (Paris, 1240; Barcelona, 1263), accused Jews of "blood libel" (using human blood in rituals, 1246, 1475), and promoted the wearing of a distinctive badge by Jews (authorized by the Fourth Lateran Council, 1215). By the 16th c., Jews had been expelled from most of Western Europe.

Jews therefore viewed the Reformation* as a positive development, partly because it diverted Christian attention away from Judaism and partly because the Protestant return to the HB contributed to a rise in messianic fervor among Jews. Despite its early promise, however, the Reformation continued the Christian "teaching of contempt."

A shift in Jewish attitudes toward Christianity can be noted following the Enlightenment* and Jewish emancipation. Reform Judaism figures such as Abraham Geiger (1810–74) embraced the Jewishness of Jesus, and even some Orthodox Jews argued that Jesus embodied the essence of Judaism. It was not a huge step for Martin Buber* (1878–1965) to call Jesus his "elder brother."

At the same time, Jews continued to hold negative views of Christianity as a result of continuing anti-Jewish prejudice and the rise of anti-Semitism*. The Enlightenment doctrine that, while society could be remade, certain persons were beyond redemption provided the basis for modern racism* and reached a crescendo during the Nazi* period and the Holocaust*. The rise of Nazism, the Holocaust*, and especially the failure of the churches from 1933 to 1945 resulted in anger toward and distrust of Christianity.

The reassessment of Christian attitudes toward Judaism in modern times – e.g. in the writings of James Parkes (1896–1981) and Robert Travers Herford (1860–1950) – and after the Holocaust slowly brought about deep-seated theological changes. Consideration of the Roman Catholic Church's "teaching of contempt" for the Jewish people was placed on the Second Vatican Council's agenda by Pope John* XXIII (1881–1963) at the urging of Jules Isaac (1877–1963) and resulted in *Nostra Aetate* (1965). Its insistence that "Jews should not be presented as rejected . . . by God" was a significant turning point for the Roman Catholic Church. When Pope John* Paul II (1920–2005) led the Vatican to recognize the state of Israel* (1994) and made a pilgrimage to the Holy Land (2000), he overturned centuries of teaching that tied Jewish eviction from their land* to their sinful rejection of Christ. Yet the Church was still not seen as guilty of any error or wrongdoing.

Since 1970 mainline Protestant churches have adopted positive views of Judaism and rejected supersessionism*. The Evangelical Church of the Rhineland's 1980 document asserted that Jews were permanently elected as God's people and that the church was taken into this covenant* with God through Jesus Christ the Jew.

The change in modern Jewish attitudes toward Christianity took place more slowly, partly owing to suspicion about Christian motives and the legacy of the "teaching of contempt." Nevertheless, the publication of *Dabru Emet* (2000), a cross-denominational statement exploring the place of Christianity in Jewish terms, represents the most positive portrait of Christianity in many centuries. However, for many Jews, Christianity is unimportant to their Jewish identity, except in their opposition to anti-Semitism and support for the state of Israel. EDWARD KESSLER

---

2) A Sampling of Contextual Interactions

Judaism and Christianity in North America. In the predominantly Christian North American countries (in 2007, Christians constituted c80% of 300 million residents in the USA, 95% of 107 million in Mexico*, 70% of 33 million in Canada*), there are about 6.4 million Jews (slightly more than 2% of the population) in the USA (a total that rivals the Jewish population of Israel*), between 40,000 and 50,000 Jews in Mexico, and about 330,000 Jews (1% of the population) in Canada. Most North American Jews have ancestors who fled European anti-Semitism and persecution.

Christianity's dominance in North America originated from 15th- to 16th-c. European colonization*. Roman Catholicism was especially strong in Spanish territories that became modern-day Mexico and the southwestern United States; in Maryland, one of England's Atlantic colonies; and in northern regions controlled by France until the 18th-c. British conquest that eventually brought Canada into existence. Protestant Christianity achieved hegemony in most of the 13 British colonies that declared their independence from England (1776) and created the USA by framing and ratifying a federal constitution (1787 and 1789, respectively).

The earliest North American Jews included so-called *conversos**. Forcibly converted to Christianity during the Inquisition*, they went to Nueva España (present-day Mexico) in the 16th c., where, despite persecution, many secretly maintained their Jewish traditions. Other early Jewish arrivals in North America were Spanish-Portuguese Jews who fled from Brazil to Dutch New Amsterdam (1654). Governor Peter Stuyvesant sought to bar them from the colony, but his superiors at the Dutch West India Company overruled him. In 1658 a Jewish group from Barbados established a community in Newport, Rhode Island, where Roger Williams's* leadership fostered an unusual degree of religious toleration. George Washington, the first US president, was welcomed at Newport's Touro Synagogue (1790). His response underscored the notion that the US government "gives to bigotry no sanction, to persecution no assistance."

Washington's words are engraved in the United States Holocaust* Memorial Museum in Washington, D.C., but anti-Semitism* akin to Stuyvesant's 17th-c. hostility has not disappeared. In 2006, for example, more than 900 anti-Semitic incidents were reported in Canada, the highest level in 25 years. In another 2006 report, the American Jewish Committee found that 26% of American Jews took anti-Semitism to be a "very serious problem" in the USA. Another 65% identified it as "somewhat of a problem," while less than 10% stated that anti-Semitism was "not a problem at all." JOHN K. ROTH

Judaism and Christianity in Western Europe. While Christianity has long been the dominant religion in Europe, Jews have also lived in one European country or another for much of the past 2,000 years. The Christianization of the Roman Empire put Jews in the precarious situation of a minority, although at first their economic activity was not restricted and they could be found in all professions. However, hostile and popular prejudice against Jews grew, later fed by the "blood libel," which originated in England with the case of William of Norwich (1144) when Jews were falsely accused of reenacting the Crucifixion by murdering a Christian child on Easter. During the Crusades*, mob violence inspired by Christian preaching prevailed and Jews suffered; they were expelled from the guilds, and their professional opportunities were greatly diminished. With the Roman Catholic Church prohibition of usury* by Christians, making loans with interest and pawnbroking became the main occupation of Jews.

There were exceptions, such as the *convivencia* (living together), i.e. the relatively harmonious coexistence of Jews, Christians, and Muslims in medieval Spain* and Portugal*. However, the later medieval period (13th–15th c.) was characterized primarily by the widespread expulsion of Jews, signaling the social decline of the Jewish communities in Western Europe. The center of Jewish life gravitated to Eastern Europe and Turkey. In Paris in 1242, a "Talmud trial" took place and 24 cartloads of the Talmud were burned, marking the decline of Talmudic study, which had been stimulated by scholars such as Rashi; this culminated in the expulsion of French Jews in 1394, although the Jews of Avignon, known as "the pope's Jews," were spared a similar fate by papal intervention and flourished.

The Reformation* led to more positive attitudes toward Jews among Christians. The humanist tradition emphasized the enduring qualities of Jewish religious teaching, although the ensuing religious wars also gave rise to anti-Jewish violence, partly inspired by Luther's* tractate *On the Jews and Their Lies* (1543), but there were smaller philo-Semitic Christian reform movements, such as that of the Anabaptists*.

Modernity* and the Enlightenment* brought the equalization of the civil status of Jews with that of Christians, but many Jews sought equality with Christians through baptism. The poet Heinrich Heine, for example, saw his baptismal certificate as an "entry ticket to society."

During the 19th c., some Jews took their place in European high society, but there was also an increase in anti-Semitism, demonstrated by the Dreyfus affair, the trial and court-martial for treason of French Jewish captain Alfred Dreyfus (1859–1935), found guilty by anti-Semitic army officers on the basis of forged documents and banished to life imprisonment. The affair motivated Theodor Herzl to write *The Jewish State* in 1896 and eventually led to the 1905 law separating church* and state in France*.

An influx in Western Europe of impoverished Jewish refugees* fleeing from persecution in Russia increased the Jewish population, e.g. in the UK, from about 25,000 in 1881 to 350,000 in 1914. Even before the rise of the Nazis, some British Christians, such as James Parkes, recognized Christian responsibility for anti-Semitism* and organized dialogue began. Many British Jewish leaders and some Christians were strong supporters of Zionism.

The destruction of European Jewry from 1933 to 1945 resulted in an awareness among Christians of the immensity of the burden of guilt that the Christian Church carried not only for its general silence, with some noble exceptions, but also because of its many centuries of "teaching of contempt" toward Jews and Judaism.

Through soul searching, many Christians in Europe began the painful process of reexamining Christian sources and institutions. Notably the Vatican, the World* Council of Churches, and most Protestant denominations have issued declarations against the perpetuation of anti-Jewish teaching. The Holocaust* not only caused Christianity to reassess its relationship with Judaism but also stirred greater Jewish interest in Christianity and Jewish participation in dialogue*, exemplified perhaps by Chief Rabbi Sir Jonathan Sacks' contribution through numerous influential books and lectures.

Dangers of division and violence remain, including a potential spillover from Middle East conflicts involving Israel and divisions resulting from the efforts of some Christians to convert Jews. Yet there are friendly relations between many leaders of Jewish and Christian communities and between local churches and synagogues. **See also HOLOCAUST, JEWISH (OR SHOAH); ISRAEL.**

EDWARD KESSLER

Judaizers (from Gk *Ioudaizo*, Gal 2:14, "to live like Jews"), Jewish Christians (more precisely, followers of Christ of Jewish origin) for whom the observance of the Law of Moses (circumcision, dietary laws, etc.) was a necessary part of being a follower of Christ Jesus, whether one was Jewish or Gentile in origin. They were welcomed by at least some of the (Gentile) Galatians. Some Jewish Christians – among whom were Peter*, James*, and primarily James's followers in Jerusalem (whom Paul, another Jewish Christian, opposed, Gal 2; in contrast to Acts 10–11) – refused to eat with Gentiles who did not observe the Law. Addressed at the "Council of Jerusalem" (Gal 2:1–10; Acts 18:22 [or Acts 15, or 11:30]), this issue was not truly resolved, as ongoing conflicts suggest. With the disappearance of the Christian community in Jerusalem during the Jewish–Roman war (67–70), the issue lost significance rather than being addressed, even though Jewish Christians are still mentioned by Ignatius* of Antioch and Justin* Martyr (early 2nd c.) and formed two major movements: the Nazarenes* and the Ebionites*. Yet addressing this issue might have helped with the question of the relationship between Judaism* and Christianity.

DANIEL PATTE

Judas, Gospel of, a 2nd-c. Gnostic* "revelation dialogue" between Jesus and his disciples, known by Irenaeus* but discovered only recently in a damaged Coptic manuscript and published (2006). Its major themes concern the transcendental realm, various false spiritual leaders, the origin of the cosmos, the creation and destiny of humanity, and the threat of the stars. Jesus, the revealer of right knowledge, frequently criticizes his disciples for misunderstanding. The only disciple who understands Jesus' teaching is Judas Iscariot, who also hands him over to the authorities. Some scholars assume that this is because of his demonic character; others maintain that Judas is Jesus' favorite disciple, who helps him escape his earthly body and conquer the powers of Hades.

ANTTI MARJANEN

Judas Iscariot, one of Jesus' disciples. In the canonical Gospels, Judas is last in the lists of disciples (Mark 3:19; Matt 10:4; Luke 6:16) – the treasurer of the group (in John 12:6). Iscariot may indicate Judas's hometown ("man from Karioth"). Judas handed Jesus over to Jewish authorities, identifying him with a kiss. Although his motivation remains ambiguous in Mark (14:10), in Matthew Judas acts out of love for money (26:15). In Luke (6:16, 22:3) and John (6:71, 13:2, 13:27), Judas is an agent of the devil*, consciously betraying his master. In Matthew (27:5), Judas repents and hangs himself. According to Luke, Judas bought land with the money of betrayal, fell, and died (Acts 1:18). According to Papias* (2nd c.), Judas swelled so much that he became wider than a carriage and finally burst.

The noncanonical Gospel of Judas* presents Judas as the disciple who best understands

Jesus' teaching but who also turns him in to Jewish authorities. Scholars debate whether the text pictures him as Jesus' favorite disciple or as a demonic agent of the archons.

ANTTI MARJANEN

Jude, an apostolic letter of exhortation to Christians from the fictive author, Jude, a brother of Jesus (Mark 6:3) and James*, leader of Jewish Christians in Jerusalem (Acts 21:18). Christians must reject teachers who undermine traditional Christian beliefs. Its rhetorical style and polemic against heresy*, a development predicted by prophets and apostles, suggest a Greek-speaking author writing to second- and third-generation Christians. Examples of God punishing the unfaithful are taken from both Jewish Scriptures and traditions associated with Enoch*. If God "delivered his people out of Egypt, but later destroyed those who did not believe and the angels who did not keep their positions" (Jude 5–6), disloyal Christians can expect the same. 2 Peter* adopted Jude's warnings to bolster expectations of divine judgment*.

PHEME PERKINS

Judge, God as, God as the source of all human obligations, whether natural or revealed (see Law); the arbiter who judges human responsibility and guilt; the one who can justify* sinners* by declaring or making them righteous* (see Atonement); the one who denounces human, social, and ecological injustices that distort creation* (see Justice, Christian Theological Views and Practice, Cluster).

Judges, Book of, is a collection of stories about Israel's tribal period, when military leaders called "judges" ruled after Joshua's conquest of Canaan and before Israel became a monarchy (c1250–1020 BCE).

Judges is part of the Deuteronomistic* History (Joshua* to 2 Kings*), which was compiled from oral and written sources during the Babylonian Exile (6th c. BCE). This history tries to give a theological rationale for this traumatic event.

The rationale given in Judges is a disintegrating cycle of apostasy*, oppression*, repentance*, and liberation*. The Israelites demonstrate their lack of faithfulness* to God by worshipping the Canaanite god Baal and goddess Astarte. God dispatches a foreign oppressor. Israel cries out, and God sends a judge as deliverer. Peace rules the land until the judge dies and the cycle begins again. Religious and social chaos marks the end of the book: "There was no king in Israel; all the people did what was right in their own eyes" (Judg 21:25).

Although the book seems to be about male heroes, their decline is often expressed through their fractured relationships with women. Intermarriage with foreign women seduces Israel into worshipping their gods, setting the theme for the book. Barak refuses to fight unless Deborah* accompanies him (Judg 4–5). The tyrant Abimelech is dishonored when a woman kills him (9). Jephthah gains military victory at the price of his daughter's life (11). Samson's* romantic entanglements with foreign women lead to his downfall (14–16). At the book's end, a Levite's wife is betrayed, gang-raped, and dismembered, and 400 more women are seized and raped to replenish a tribe, which atrocity sparks a civil war (19–21).

Judges is almost absent in the Christian lectionaries. However, the narrative power of its stories over the Christian imagination is evident in Western art (Rembrandt, Rubens, Doré), literature (Milton*), and music (Handel*, Saint-Saëns).

GALE A. YEE

Judgment, the act of distinguishing good from evil*. Whether it is the weighing of the heart in the Egyptian Book of the Dead, scrutiny of the naked soul* in Plato's *Gorgias* (525), or the meditations of an anxious psalmist, it is clear that the idea antedates Christianity. Belief in future judgment colors one's life. For John (3:18), those who do not believe are "judged already" or "condemned already," and Augustine* (*City of God* 20, 1) insists that God has been judging since the beginning of the world: by banishing the first parents from paradise* and casting the rebellious angels* from heaven*. Moreover, God judges the acts of individuals during their lives sometimes visibly, sometimes not, with punishment imposed either now or after death*. This judgment is a corollary to Providence: supervision includes chastisement (see Habakkuk, Book of). The visible punishment in this life harkens back to Deuteronomy's* threats against those who are disobedient. The Nicene*, Athanasian*, and Apostles'* Creeds agree on Christ's* coming to judge the living and the dead.

The very fact that a judgment is needed presupposes that, from God's perspective, something is wrong. The Bible presents various criteria for passing judgment. "For all of us must appear before the judgment seat of Christ [the eschatological* Judgment], so that each may receive compensation for what has been done in the body, whether good or evil" (2 Cor 5:10;

also Rev 20:12–13). This Judgment concerns the way people treated "the least of these who are members of [Christ's] family" (Matt 25:40, 45, NRSV), as well as the good or evil words they uttered (Matt 12:37). In Romans* the Law is inscribed in the heart, thoughts accuse and defend, and the conscience testifies. Thus "God will judge the secret thoughts of all" (Rom 2:15–16). Through the conscience, divine judgment supervises individual human judgment of moral options.

Some metaphors represent the idea of judgment: the separation of wheat from chaff, goats from sheep; cutting the vine from the root; inscription (or not) in the book of life. *The Shepherd of Hermas** (early 2nd c.) relates a vision in which a designer trims stones to fit a church under construction and casts away those that do not fit. Using an image from Zoroastrian eschatology, Pope Gregory* I (d604) referred to a bridge over which souls pass insofar as their virtues* permit them to do so. If successful, they attain green meadows; if not, they fall into a stinking stream. Byzantine illuminators adapted the story of Jacob's* ladder. The Judgment scenes on the tympana or inside the west walls of medieval churches portray Christ the Judge on his throne, right hand upraised to welcome the blessed, left hand turned down to repel the damned. Often (e.g. at Autun), the archangel Michael holds a scale, in whose pans he weighs the good and wicked deeds of each at the final reckoning. A competing idea locates judgment at a person's death, during which one is assigned to heaven*, hell*, or purgatory*. In a popular image of individual judgment, angels* and demons* compete for the soul as it leaves the body at death.

Metaphors signifying judgment sometimes acquired literal application through penitential practices such as almsgiving*, charity* work, pilgrimages*, and crusades*. Eventually these penances could be commuted by the endowment of land or revenues, the subsidization of Masses in chantries*, or the purchase of indulgences*. Although Scholastic theologians insisted there could be no direct exchange of donations for credit in God's eyes, the practices were widespread.

The Reformers' insistence that works counted for nothing beside faith* and the free bestowal of grace* received some impetus from objections to these practices. For them predestination* makes divine judgment not a historical or lifelong process, but an aspect of eternal knowledge and will that is divine and, from a human, time-bound perspective, "prior" to creation. God's freedom to save or damn, to make vessels for glory or for destruction (cf. Rom 9:21–23), is independent of any human effort. Human life, however, is still under the inscrutable judgment of God. **See also DAMNATION; ETERNITY; HELL; PURGATORY; SALVATION; SON OF MAN.**

ALAN E. BERNSTEIN

Judith, Deuterocanonical Book. With a name that means "Jewish woman" or "female Judean," the character Judith has been read as an idealized embodiment of the Jewish nation. Like the "*Judea Capta*" images on Roman coins, the widowed Judith seems to represent the nation in the form of a bereft woman. Yet Judith is a childless widow* who does not weep for her husband or his unborn offspring. Ascetic* and pious, Judith fasts* more or less all the time, refuses all suitors, and successfully keeps the lascivious Holofernes at bay until she can decapitate him. Her bodily boundaries are represented as imperiled, as are the nation's, but by vigilantly defending her own body, Judith singlehandedly defends the boundaries of the nation as well. Taken up by European art of recent centuries as a story of the nation imperiled, the book has an ambiguous message about gender roles and women who break them. Judith accomplishes what none of the male council can do, but she does so by the powers emanating from her great beauty as much as by her wits and courage. **See also BODY.**

NICOLE WILKINSON DURAN

Julian the Apostate (332–63), Roman emperor (361–63), nephew of Constantine* (emperor, 306–37), cousin of Constantius II (emperor, 337–61). Following the massacre of his family, he was educated under the forced tutelage of clergy in Constantinople and Cappadocia. Although he was baptized and served as a reader in the church, he also studied the classical tradition and became more sympathetic to it than to Christianity. Since he was technically a Christian, he was an "apostate" in Christian eyes. To cleanse himself of baptism*, he was initiated into the Eleusinian and Mithraic mysteries*. He was named Caesar in 355 and scored military successes in Gaul. Proclaimed emperor by the army in 360, he became sole ruler upon Constantius's death in 361. He excluded Christians from teaching positions, encouraged traditional sacrifices, promised to rebuild the Temple in Jerusalem, and wrote diatribes against the "Galilaeans." By letting all exiled bishops return, he increased Christian dissension, but he also made possible the reconciliation of conflicting parties in the disputes over the Trinity* at the Council of Alexandria* (362). He was killed in 363 during a campaign against the Persians.

EUGENE TESELLE

Julian Calendar. See CALENDARS.

Julian of Eclanum (c381–c454), Pelagian theologian, often depicted as a champion of independent inquiry in the face of dogmatism. When Pope Zosimus condemned Pelagianism* (418), Julian led the resistance. Zosimus excommunicated* him and 17 other bishops in Italy and Illyria (419). Emphasizing the permanent goodness of human nature, Julian accused Augustine* of Manichaeism* in asserting original* sin and called for a council to resolve the issues. But the excommunication was not lifted, despite his appeal in 439 to Pope Sixtus III (probably a repentant Pelagian).

Julian of Norwich (1343–c1416), theologian, visionary, anchorite* (by 1394), who lived in a cell in the Church of St. Julian in Norwich, England. Near death in 1373, Julian experienced a series of visions of Christ's Passion that she recorded in the first book written by an Englishwoman. She produced a short text, the *Showings*, a few years after the event; sometime after 1393, following two decades of intense meditation on the theological significance of her visions, she dictated a much longer version, *Revelations of Divine Love*.

Although it is unknown whether Julian was a recluse at the time of her visionary experience, she already had a reputation for sanctity (mentioned in the *Book of Margery Kempe**) and led an intensely devotional life. As she wrote in *Revelations of Divine Love* (Chap. 2), she had previously "asked for three gifts from God: (i) to understand his passion; (ii) to suffer physically while still a young woman of thirty; and (iii) to have as God's gift three wounds... namely, the wound of true contrition*, the wound of genuine compassion*, and the wound of sincere longing for God" (see Faith #5). A year later, after paralysis resulting from a sudden illness and reception of the last rites, Julian experienced over the course of one day 15 visions about Christ's Passion, the doctrine of sin*, and the Trinity*. A 16th vision of the devil* attempting to frighten her took place in her sleep that night. Scholars have noted Julian's distinction between "ghostly sights" and "bodily sights" as a means to distinguish her visions from the suspect "corporeal" visions that could, according to medieval understanding, as easily be given by the devil as by God.

Julian's work is remarkable because it records the development of her theology from an intense visionary experience of the Passion to a Trinitarian theology in which she explores Jesus' role as the mother of humanity (see Motherhood). This development is apparent when one compares the two versions of the text. In the short text, *Showings*, Julian draws her authority from personal details about herself and her family that stamp her work as a record of an individual's visionary experience; but in *Revelations of Divine Love*, she omits personal references in favor of greater graphic detail about the Passion as well as extensive theological reflection on the Trinity (as Johnson shows). Julian notes the difference between the content of the vision and the revelation* of its meaning over her lifetime: "I... began to understand that every revelation was full of deep secrets.... The first quality is the literal meaning of the words as I then received them; the second is the inner significance that I have discovered since; the third is the whole revelation itself, which from beginning to end – cover[s] the contents of this book" (*Revelations of Divine Love*, Chap. 51). Julian offers a model of a visionary turned theologian (the transition between experience and doctrine) and is an important source of information about the religious options open to women in late medieval England.

Julian's most notable theological contribution stems from her consideration of the role of Jesus in the Trinity as a result of his role on earth in his Passion. For example, in *Revelations of Divine Love* (Chaps. 16, 17), Julian dwells on the state of Christ's flesh as it slowly desiccated. "I saw his dear face, dry, bloodless, and pallid... then, dead, it turned a blue color, gradually changing to a browny blue, as the flesh continued to die.... At first, when the flesh was still fresh and bleeding... I could see that the dear skin and tender flesh... seemed about to drop off, heavy and loose... sagging like a cloth." Meditation on the events of Jesus' life and death was a late medieval phenomenon. But Julian was distinctive in moving from physical details to theological explorations, rather than focusing on the narrative of Christ's life alone. She attributes "fatherhood, motherhood, and lordship" to the Trinity, then posits that an understanding of the Trinity comes through a threefold process: an attention to anthropology* and human predicaments; and the revelation that "the great power of the Trinity is our Father, the deep wisdom

our Mother, and the great love our Lord" (*Revelations of Divine Love,* Chap. 58). Julian unites the themes of the humanity of Christ and his role as mother in the Trinity by representing the compassion that led to Jesus' sacrifice as his mothering, nurturing quality: "But we make our humble complaint to our beloved Mother, and he sprinkles us with his precious blood.... And this sweet and lovely work he will never cease from doing until all his beloved children are born and delivered" (*Revelations of Divine Love,* Chap. 63).
JESSICA A. BOON

Juliana of Liège (c1192–1258). As an advocate of inaugurating a feast of Corpus* Christi, she experienced much opposition. A member and then superior of an Augustinian* convent near Liège, she was forced to leave because of her beliefs, becoming a recluse in the city. She gained the support of the archdeacon of Liège, the future pope Urban IV. The feast was observed once in Liège (1246), but she experienced much opposition and was exiled. Urban IV instituted the feast of Corpus Christi in 1246, after her death.

Junia (mid-1st c.), designated an apostle* and, with Andronicus, "outstanding among the apostles" by Paul (Rom 16:7). She was Paul's compatriot (a Jewess), imprisoned like Paul, and a Christian prior to Paul. Confirmed to be a woman by Origen (c185–254) and into the 12th c., and a wise woman with the "title of apostle" by John* Chrysostom (c349–407), she was canonized in Constantinople (608; feast day, May 17 in Eastern Orthodoxy*; her feast day has been officially observed in various Episcopal* dioceses since 1984).

Junia became a foil for gender issues. Giles* of Rome (c1245–1316) called Andronicus and Junia "men," and "Junia" became "Junias" (male) in critical editions of the Greek NT from 1927 to 1998, after which the name "Junia" was restored. She was a man in Luther's Bible; English translations normally read "Junia" until the late 19th c., then "Junias" until the late 1980s, after which "Junia" became dominant. The editorial change to "Junias" was supposedly justified grammatically by its designation as a contraction of the common name Junianus; but "Junias" has not been found to exist anywhere, nor could "Junianus" be contracted to "Junias." Grammatically, "outstanding among the apostles" signifies "prominent apostles," and not "well known to the apostles," as is often suggested when Junia is acknowledged to be a woman. Most often it was because of the bias that an apostle could not be a woman that Junia was turned into a male. **See also BIBLE TRANSLATIONS CLUSTER.**
ELDON JAY EPP

JUSTICE, CHRISTIAN THEOLOGICAL VIEWS AND PRACTICES, CLUSTER

1) *Introductory Entries*

1) Introductory Entries

Justice, Theological Views and Practices, in Eastern Orthodox Christianity. Beyond varied understandings of justice, the Eastern Orthodox* Church tradition fundamentally holds that true justice has its source in God. God's justice is inherent in the Divine Nature, and is therefore complete and perfect. In the created world, only approximations of this justice can be comprehended or achieved.

In human terms, justice is not one of many virtues, but "the good" in itself, the harmony by which all elements of virtue are integrated in an appropriate way.

According to Scripture, a portion of Christ's mission is "to proclaim justice" (Matt 12:18); it is a sacred duty to "proclaim justice" (Heb 11:32), and it is evil to "neglect justice" (Luke 11:42). For Basil*

(4th c.) human justice seeks to emulate divine justice, both as a means of rectifying the injustice in human relations (*epanorthotike*) and as a means of retribution (*antapodotike*), even though justice is difficult to comprehend and achieve (*dystheoriton*). Because of "passions" (human imperfection expressed in sinful conditions and actions), it is a constant struggle to achieve justice, to give to all their due, and to reduce injustice, especially by challenging the powerful or attending to the needy (*Homily* 12.8).

In the past, challenging powerful political authorities took the form of written counsel on governance, which was directed primarily to the Byzantine emperors. Thus for the deacon Agapetos, "equity" was a key element of justice; rulers should keep their "mind fixed on equity... exemplifying humanity as a quality that is God-like" (*Advice and Counsel*, Chap. 40). Rulers should exercise justice on behalf of the weak, fatherless, poor*, widows*, and strangers*. Rulers are not above the law*; they are morally obligated to follow it themselves, thus conveying to the governed the importance of just behavior by all. Considerations of the parallel obligations of the rulers and the ruled are a condition for governing justly. The amount of power that rulers exercise ought to be in proportion to what is needed for the good of the governed. The goal of the rulers' exercise of justice is to help the governed "advance in things good and not evil" (Chap. 46).

Eastern Orthodox Christians recognize all the aspects of justice that various philosophies identify: harmony, divine* command, natural* law, mutual agreement, and civil and economic treatment, coupled with the exercise of mercy* and compassion* (humanity). In Eastern Orthodoxy, all these aspects of justice are integrated into a holistic perception of the human sphere that reflects its origin and its roots in divine justice, i.e. in the Triune God. STANLEY S. HARAKAS

Justice, Theological Views and Practices, in Western Christianity. In Western Christian discussions of the question of justice, we can discern a trajectory, starting from Greek and Hebrew terms and concepts, which successively emphasized interhuman justice as divine command; the just individual; justice as a divine attribute over against sinful humanity; forensic justice in the nominalist* tradition; and a recovery of the sense of interhuman justice as the claim of the divine.

Interhuman Justice. The literature of ancient Israel, especially the Prophets* and the Psalms*, insisted on *tsedeq* and *mishpat* (Hebrew terms for "justice") as the claim and command of the Divine. These terms function in parallel to indicate the imperative of interhuman, distributive justice (*tsedeq*) and the divine intervention to establish that justice through the vindication of the wrongly accused or the violated and vulnerable (*mishpat*). The denunciations of the absence of justice take the form of condemnations of the unbridled avarice and arrogance of the powerful.

From Interhuman Justice to the Just Individual. While the social and public character of the OT concern with justice is relatively noncontroversial, the NT reference to *dikaiosyne* (translated as both "justice" and "righteousness") has less often been associated with social relationships than with the individual's relation to God.

Plato and Aristotle presented justice as the ideal characteristic of the good society or constitution, as well as the designation of the ideal character of the human being. Thus *dike* is the theme of Plato's *Republic*, in which the ideal society and the appropriate character of the (aristocratic) human person are correlated. While social (interhuman) and individual justice were similar during the period of the city-state (a good city consists of good individuals), the emergence of the empire relegated the hope* for a just social order to the messianism characteristic of emergent forms of Judaism and Christianity, while the just person (apart from the social order) was the theme of Stoicism* and related movements.

Distributive Justice and the Just Individual. Patristic theologians like Basil* and Chrysostom*, relying on the Gospels*, insisted on a redistribution of wealth* as a condition of divinely mandated distributive justice (focusing on social justice). But Alexandrian* Christianity inherited the emphasis on justice as the attribute of a good person. This ran afoul of the growing sense of human incapacity for justice, especially in Augustine* and his heirs. Thus while God was just, humans could not be. The theme of retributive justice (God's just punishment* of sinful* humanity) became the background for an attempt to reconcile divine justice with mercy*.

Forensic or Nominal Justice. The idea of forensic or nominal justice responds to the problem of the apparent contradiction between justice and mercy through the notion that the judge may pronounce the verdict that a guilty person is innocent or at least will be regarded as if innocent (see Atonement #2). This appears to be a counterfactual claim that rests on the judge's sovereign power to declare the guilty innocent. This is accompanied by the claim that the innocent one (the Son or Christ) suffers and dies in the place of the guilty so that the guilty can be pronounced innocent or just (righteous*) and in that sense "justified." This apparent double violation of simple justice has not gone unnoticed in the theological traditions (Abelard* or recent feminist* criticism of substitutionary atonement). The declaration that those who are guilty (unrighteous) are nevertheless innocent may also cut the nerve of the claims of interhuman justice and indeed promote injustice, as seemed to happen in Lutheran Germany* during the Holocaust* or Catholic Latin* America during the reign of the death squads.

The Recovery of Interhuman Justice. The recovery of the understanding of justice as interhuman (rather than as forensic or nominal justification*) is found in the Social* Gospel and in modern social* papal encyclicals and is most vigorously recovered in Latin American Liberation* theology. The work of Miranda in rereading the Bible from the standpoint of the divine claim of justice that can be actualized only as the commitment to the welfare of the other, especially the most vulnerable, draws on the Prophets and Psalms and also on Paul* and even John*. Justification is the call to become an agent of justice and love (see Justification, Theological Views and Practices, Cluster).

In more recent European thought, especially in the work of Derrida but also in that of Agamben and Badiou, justice is understood in Pauline fashion to be "outside the law," which nonetheless impels the law* toward an approximation to justice, even if this always fails to correspond to the claim and call of justice. Justice is understood to be social justice that takes the form of welcoming and making an individual commitment to the other. This European recovery of justice outside the law occurs through a reading of Paul outside the confines of Christianity proper and is correlative to the awareness of the new global situation as one of empire that has certain features in common with the imperial context of Pauline counter-imperial thought and practice.

THEODORE W. JENNINGS, JR.

---

2) A Sampling of Contextual Views and Practices

Justice, Theological Views and Practices, in Africa. The African worldview, generally speaking, is infused with religion. The earth is a creation of God, known in Africa by many names, the one God in control of the universe and all that it contains (see God, Christian Views of, Cluster: In Africa), while human beings are children of God and deities are agents of God. In African myths, folktales, and proverbs, commonly God is actively involved with human beings, urging justice, respect, and compassion* among them. When a person is cruel, selfish, unkind, oppressive, exploitative, or callous toward others, the Akan of Ghana* say, "That one is no human being"; the Zulu of South* Africa say that such a person does not have *ubuntu* i.e. has no humanity. The Luyia of Kenya* prefer to forget such a person and prohibit naming children of the next generation after this person.

People of Africa, a huge continent, have developed a spirituality shaped by Africa's primal religious imagination (African*

Religion, also called African Traditional Religion), Christianity, and Islam*; each of these traditions grounds social justice in the nature of God. The Islamic *zakat* (almsgiving) has its roots in the righteousness of God, which God also enjoins on human beings who are God's stewards on earth. To be an African Muslim, one must adhere to this God-centered view of social justice. Similarly, in the Bible, a holy book for many Africans, several prophets, especially Isaiah*, Amos*, and Micah*, speak of social justice. Isaiah 58 is one of the most pungent denunciations of social injustice, as are Chaps. 1–5 of Amos (God commands in Amos 5:24, "Let justice run down like water and righteousness as a mighty stream"). The biblical teaching protects the weak: widows*, children*, the sick, and all who are vulnerable. In the narration of Jesus' life, in which he is portrayed as one devoted to the vulnerable and to overcoming opponents, Mark says, "The common people heard him gladly" (Mark 12:37, King James Version). Social justice, from the Christian perspective, is anchored in the affirmation that God is righteous and requires right dealings among human beings.

In Africa, one finds that African Religion, Islam, and Christianity all teach that the religious basis of life is the nature of God as one who requires just dealings among human beings as a way of life. Social justice is not benevolence; it is a demonstration of our humanity. It is with these shared views that African believers can confront the manifestations of injustice and violence ever present in Africa as elsewhere. **See also RECONCILIATION AS A CHRISTIAN PRAXIS.**

MUSIMBI KANYORO

Justice, Theological Views and Practices, in Asia: The Philippines. Legal or forensic justice is formally enshrined in the nation's laws, but substantive justice in the sense of having real and meaningful access to the requisites of a decent human existence is the justice for which Filipino peoples long. This longing has driven Philippine history since the awakening of Philippine nationhood.

Centuries of struggle against colonial* and domestic oppression* provide the matrix for the specific understanding and practice of justice in the Philippines. Christian evangelization of the Philippines took place under the auspices of Spanish* colonialism (three and a half centuries) and US imperialism (half a century). The struggle for land* and democracy* forms the core of the struggle against the colonial and church authorities. More recently, it has come to include the aspirations of other marginalized* segments of society. Justice is served to the extent that the goals of the struggle are achieved; there goals are, for peasants and fishers, procuring land and fishing grounds; for workers and employees, decent wages and working conditions; for indigenous peoples, ownership of ancestral land; for marginalized women and children, social services; and for all the people, freedom from foreign domination.

Justice and human* rights are closely related in the context of a struggle against foreign domination and domestic oppression. Most victims of human* rights violations by agents of the state are perceived to be involved in one way or another with antigovernment forces, both legal and underground. A very significant number of these victims come from the ranks of religious, priests, pastors, nuns, and lay workers.

The biblical view of justice was introduced in the midst of the anti-Spanish struggle. Soon after, biblical images began to surface in the rhetoric of peasant uprisings. Quasi-religious political organizations formed the core of movements seeking justice from the Spanish colonial authorities. Religious views of justice pervaded the ideology* of the late-19th-c. national revolution. It was in the name of justice biblically understood that priests, religious, and other church workers formed the Christians for National Liberation, which joined a Communist-led insurgency in 1972 that continues to the present.

EVERETT MENDOZA

Justice, Theological Views and Practices, in the Caribbean Islands. It is sobering to acknowledge that domination, oppression*, and colonization* came to the Caribbean with the arrival of the Christian Church. Missionaries came with the colonizers, were often paid by them, and sought to fulfill their wishes. The presence of "the colonizer and the colonized" brought to the fore issues of justice, freedom, and identity, from two perspectives.

From the perspective of the planter class and the majority of the missionaries, issues of justice, freedom, and identity were conceived of in terms of a plantation ethic that included slavery*. From the master class's point of view, justice meant peace* without conflict. Peace as an expression of a just society is not a far-fetched or unrealistic goal, yet it requires changing perspective.

Slave narratives suggest that the master class really wanted peace without justice. For the enslaved peoples, justice meant freedom* (and liberation*); the master class overlooked the fact that peace was predicated on an admission that a change was needed because something had gone amiss. A peaceful community is a community that addresses a wrong that needs to be made right.

The problem was that peace as envisioned by the planter class did not lead to the creation of a just society. The missionaries did not understand this problem either, as they often proclaimed peace without justice, as they declared the master class to be at peace with God, without understanding that such "peace with God" includes being in conflict with oppressive* orders (see Justification, Theological Views and Practices, Cluster).

The enslaved community understood justice in terms of freedom. In many instances, freedom meant a change of geographical place; it meant returning home to Africa; being reunited with the ancestors as well as going back to the forests in Africa. The slaves' understanding of hell* was separation from place and community: "Way down yonder by myself I couldn't hear no'body pray." Freedom meant the ability to make decisions about running away and to take responsibility for one's destiny.

The Caribbean adage "out of many people one people" expresses a vision of a just community; an identity beyond masters and slaves; a new humanity beyond race and class, in which human worth lies in relationship to God; a just society in which peace and freedom are a reality.

NOEL LEO ERSKINE

Justice, Theological Views and Practices, in Latin America. Latin American theologians note that justice has a clear ethical and theological dimension, as it seeks to construct equitable and family-like interhuman relations and to struggle against oppression*. Justice is directly tied to God, who "works vindication and justice for all who are oppressed" (Ps 103:6) and who acts as "the *go`el* of Israel," the next of kin, protector, and redeemer of the widow*, the orphan, the foreigner* (Ps 146:7, 9, 68:5; Zech 7:10). Injustice is sin*, the negation of God's will of justice, as the prophets repeat again and again, because knowing God, authentic worship*, and the practice of justice are interconnected (Jer 22; Mic 6:6–8; Isa 58:6–7) and because the practice of justice prolongs God's liberating* act; it is being faithful to the covenant* between God and the people. Thus in the Bible, justice is synonymous with salvation* and redemption*.

Latin American theologians also emphasize that Jesus' mission is in continuity with this prophetic tradition. In Jesus' teaching, the Kingdom* of God and its justice are inseparable (see Sermon on the Mount), although this is often obscured by English translations, which render all the terms for "justice" (e.g. *dikaiosyne*) and "injustice" (e.g. *adikia*) by terms referring to individual morality (e.g. "righteousness" and "wickedness"). Similarly, despite many English translations, Paul speaks of those who practice injustice (often translated "wickedness") as hindering the truth and justice of God (Rom 1:18) and of salvation as "justification," which is a manifestation of the justice of God that results in "graced lives." "For the kingdom of God is . . . justice [*dikaiosyne*] and peace and joy from the Holy Spirit" (Rom 14:17).

Latin American theology prolongs the prophetic tradition of the Bible; the practice of justice is a dimension of the life and the mission of the community of faith (see Latin American Theologies). Following Jesus, the faith community is gathered for the sake of the Kingdom of God, both in its ecclesial life and in social services, in order to practice justice and peace and to preserve the integrity of the creation. To practice justice is to struggle for the ongoing satisfaction of people's fundamental needs: food, housing, work, and education; to struggle for human* rights for those who are excluded and impoverished; to struggle for gender equity; to struggle to take care of the creation, our home; and to struggle against every form of systemic violence*, while remembering those, e.g. Bishop Romero*, who gave their lives in the struggle for justice.

VICTORIO ARAYA GUILLÉN

Justice, Theological Views and Practices, in North America. The issue of justice includes questions of distribution, reparation, retribution, and restoration. In the North American context, economic distributive justice has been a primary theoretical focus, although contemporary Christian discussions also include reparation, making amends for past wrongs, reconciling opposing parties, and restoring community.

Christian ethicists draw on Liberation* theologies to emphasize the gap between rich and poor* and the need for redistribution of goods and services. Roman Catholic ethicists link justice to questions of common good and human* rights; the bishops' statement on the US economy* ("Economic Justice for All," 1985) has been highly influential. Protestants stress the biblical bases of justice: justice encompasses both specific commandments and fundamental claims to "right relation." Justice requires redistribution of power, analyses of oppression*, and action for liberation. Christian approaches to justice incorporate global concerns: balance of trade, remission of debts, women's rights, and North–South relations.

Christians also utilize philosophical theories: John Rawls's "difference principle," Martha Nussbaum's "capabilities theory," and Iris Marion Young's "five faces of oppression" are influential theoretical constructs, as is the "communitarian" approach of Michael Walzer.

The legacy of slavery* and racism* in the USA makes racial justice a particular concern. Womanist* and Mujerista* (Latino/a) approaches to justice attempt to take seriously the tangled web of race, class, and sex, although all agree that formulating an adequate theoretical perspective is difficult. Christians have also debated justice for gay, lesbian, transgender, and bisexual people. In addition to theoretical concerns, justice praxis has included advocating for the liberation of prisoners, for an end to selected wars*, and for equal rights and empowerment of women, those with disabilities, and other oppressed groups.

KAREN LEBACQZ

Justice, Theological Views and Practices, in North America: Latino/a. Justice, the main concern of social* ethics*, involves claims about how available social goods and services are to be distributed along with responsibilities and social burdens. For Latinos/as, at the heart of talk about justice is the question of the legitimate criteria used to determine how distribution ought to take place. From a theological point of view, justice concerns are dealt with in relation to God as the source and ground of the good and of the meaning of human life; just relationships in society express our view of the fitting relationship with God and God's creation.

From a Latino/a point of view, justice has to do with the creation of relationships that enable people to fulfill their humanity and to generate and sustain caring communities of mutual support involving a fair exchange of the available social goods and services. Beyond procedural notions of justice, Latinos/as claim that the well-being of the poor* and marginal* provides the standard by which to judge the objectivity, impartiality, and fairness of all social institutions and procedures of justice. The theological concern for the poor and marginal is given precedence over philosophical and scientific notions of justice. Religiously grounded notions of justice take precedence over rationally grounded notions of justice, and indeed are alone to provide the core motivation of love, care, and compassion that initiates and sustains a radical commitment to justice.

The church, called to be faithful to the memory of Jesus and his mission, is given the vocation to move forward the cause of justice among the poor. Nevertheless, the church has opted to ally itself with the powerful and wealthy and has contributed to the unjust state of affairs that has led to massive human poverty. To reestablish its true mission*, the church must become a church of and for the poor. This preferential* option for the poor takes the concrete forms of social and political advocacy and of solidarity with the struggles by which the poor, the marginal, and the voiceless seek their liberation. The church must contribute to the struggle to socialize wealth and democratize power so that "the least of these" and, through them, all of us might be able to fulfill our humanity. This entails a radical transformation of society and of our way of being. In this new society, service to the Other gives our individual and collective power, wealth, and freedom their reason for being.

ISMAEL GARCÍA

Justice, Theological Views and Practices, in North America: Womanist. Womanists*, compelled to expose evils* perpetrated against all humans, define justice-making as a communal, religious engagement. Justice, a moral virtue, concerns fairness, equal distribution, retribution amid wrongdoing, and an impartial treatment of all persons in all settings. Thus justice is philosophy and praxis, thought and action. Justice arises from biblical traditions requiring social activism and life-empowering witness, a praxis opposing evil and suffering (Clarice Martin). Justice-making necessitates human participation with God*, to interpret Law* and Scripture* with the aim of securing equality.

Thus justice calls for opposing social and ecclesial systems that place yokes of injustice on women: pathological degradation, silencing, dismissing, or ignoring them (Frances E. Wood). Antithetical to Jesus' teachings, injustice ignores the dehumanization of slaves*, the plantation's misogyny, and the present-day patriarchy* in church and society. Womanist justice involves seeking and loving righteousness, kindness, and walking humbly with God.

Black women, committed to scrutinizing multifaceted, systemic oppression*, have long had a race–gender–class consciousness; they have formed social clubs that valued connections between critical self-understanding of, and socioeconomic response to, oppressive realities, which they internally addressed with self-help and economic self-determination (Marcia Riggs). Against injustice, they embodied a Black* Liberationist* ethic that required action toward collective advancement, because God's justice required them to respond to institutionalized moral evil* with social responsibility.

Womanist justice ethics rejects suffering* as God's will (Emilie Townes). Suffering is unscrutinized, cyclical, static, unmetabolized pain; by contrast, pain is a recognized, named experience used for transformation (Audre Lorde). Thus for Townes, by moving from a reactive posture about suffering to a transformative posture of pain, one engages in liberative messages of love* and resurrection*.

Womanist justice engages with alternative sources of empowerment: resisting sin and evil, by using power from the periphery (Rosita Mathews). Womanist justice denounces naive biblicism, idealism without critical knowledge of actual experience, and dogmatic moralism; by remembering and retelling the stories of those who have suffered and overcome, Womanist justice pursues a recentering, redemptive resistance that redefines Black women's realities toward transformation (M. Shawn Copeland).

Womanist justice seeks wisdom* through cultural artifacts: music, art, and literature that examine ideas of the Divine and the benevolence of beauty amid evil within an African holistic, religiocultural worldview that provides renewal and healing* power. These cultural artifacts afford collective exorcism*: they name and expose oppression through stories of coded communication allowing a platform for "speaking truth to power" (as Quakers* say): birthing just engagement. **See also WOMANIST AND AFRICAN AMERICAN THEOLOGIES.** CHERYL A. KIRK-DUGGAN

JUSTIFICATION, THEOLOGICAL VIEWS AND PRACTICES, CLUSTER

1) *Introductory Entries*

2) *A Sampling of Contextual Views and Practices*

---

1) Introductory Entries

Justification, a Central Doctrine for Western Christianity. Paul* is the most important source of the Christian doctrine of justification, which adopts the OT understanding of reality as both forensic and at the same time efficacious, as both a demanding challenge and the appropriate response. It represents the center of his theology, especially in Galatians and Romans, although this is contested by the "new perspective on Paul" (see Paul, the Apostle). An intensive revival of Paul was initiated by Augustine*, who asserted against Pelagius* the sovereignty of divine grace* and contested the freedom* of the human will* to accept or reject grace. Thomas Aquinas* adopted his position in that he excluded any necessary and active human cooperation in preparation for grace. By contrast, late medieval theologians such as Gabriel Biel* enunciated the thesis that God does not deny grace to those who do what they can.

Luther* passionately opposed this thesis, citing Paul above all; he saw the turning point in his own life and theology in his discovery of the "correct" understanding of Rom 1:16–17, according to which God's righteousness makes the ungodly righteous (Rom 4:5). This happens only through the Word (*solo verbo*), only through grace (*sola gratia*), only through Christ (*solo Christo*), only through faith* (*sola fide*); the forensic declaration of righteousness (or justification) through the promise of grace makes one who is effectively embraced by this promise into a new* creature (2 Cor 5:17). This means that the Creator validates God's own justice toward the creature, taking it into the realm of God's righteousness* and away from the realm of sin*; thereby God restores righteousness. In faith, which is not a human work (see Faith #6), not even a human deed, but solely the work of God by which God comes to the creature (*fides adventitia*, Gal 3:23, 25), the creature justifies God and accepts God's care. In this sense, the righteousness of faith is *iustitia passiva*: the righteousness given and imparted by God in Christ (*iustitia aliena*), which I lose if I try to bring it reflexively into what I possess by myself. The passivity of the righteousness of faith does not mean denial of good works; actually it releases one for higher activity, indeed freeing one for the highest activity of all, the love* through which faith manifests its energy ("faith working through love," Gal 5:6). Faith by its own nature brings forth good works; but faith is not grounded in these good works and the believer is not justified through them. Thus Luther's radical understanding of justification leads to a new understanding of ethics*: *ethos* is relieved of soteriological* burdens and is freed to care genuinely for the world and its actual needs. The person who is justified solely through faith is reconstituted as a responsible, ek-centric, eschatological agent (Joest): addressed by the accusing and convicting law and by the liberating gospel, and challenged to answer, one lives in faith outside oneself (*extra se*), only in God and in love directed toward one's neighbors and their sorrows and joys (conclusion of the *Treatise on Christian Freedom*, 1520). This ek-centric being consists in a vertical relation to the Creator and a horizontal relation to fellow creatures; one becomes what one already is, the image* of God. Looking only on oneself, one sees oneself only as a sinner; looking on Christ, one sees oneself as fully righteous (*simul iustus et peccator*, "both righteous and sinner").

The epoch-making significance of Luther for theology, church history, and indeed world history consists in his understanding of all of theology as a doctrine of justification; the correlation between sinful humans and the justifying God is the criterion for structuring all theological motifs. The Council of Trent* opposed Luther's doctrine of justification at decisive points. In Protestantism the dominant position of justification as the criterion and center of theology became less clear, as it already was for Calvin, and even for Lutherans during the debates with Reformed* and Arminians* about the "process of salvation" (*ordo* salutis*). In Pietism* (then Arminianism and Methodism*) self-examination became important for gaining certitude about justification; faith was no longer, as in Luther, a looking away from self and toward Christ. Schleiermacher* moved regeneration, inclusion into living communion with Christ, to the center of piety. Later in the 19th c. various attempts were made to renew the Lutheran doctrine of justification – energetically by Ritschl*, who, however, eliminated the doctrine of God's wrath that was so decisive for Luther. Martin Kähler made the most persuasive attempt, presenting all of systematic theology (apologetics, dogmatics, and ethics) as a doctrine of justification. In the 20th c., his student Tillich* tried to vindicate the doctrine of justification within the modern horizon, as the answer to the question about the meaning of life in the face of meaninglessness. The Luther renaissance rediscovered the significance of the doctrine of justification as a basic criterion of the distinction between Rome and Wittenberg and sought to bring its centrality to recognition. Whether the "Common Declaration on Justification" (1999) can overcome the division between Roman Catholics and Lutherans is debated.

OSWALD BAYER

Justification for Eastern Orthodox Churches. See ORTHODOX CHURCHES, EASTERN, CLUSTER: INTRODUCTORY ENTRIES.

2) A Sampling of Contextual Views and Practices

Justification, Theological Views and Practices, in Africa. Africans view human misbehavior against God's order as the disruption of proper interaction and communion not only with God, but also with fellow humans and with departed relatives (ancestors*). According to African philosophy, one's life and religion are inseparable from the community, from which one receives maturity, identity, justice, and survival.

Upon conversion, African Christians spontaneously applied this traditional perspective to their understanding of justification by asking: How does justification affect human relationship? How does it help me be a gracious neighbor to my fellow humans regardless of gender, nationality, color, religious, and ideological affiliation (Kahakwa)? They found that justification addresses structural sins related to social, economic, cultural, and religious factors. Thus instead of limiting justification to the vertical relationship between individuals and God – following the "spiritualized" understanding of sins*, faith*, grace*, and justification of both mission Christianity and post-mission Christianity – Africans conceive of justification as encompassing all horizontal relationships. It entails being God's gracious instrument of powerful liberation for the oppressed* and victimized.

Justification involves liberation* and freedom*, along with the gospel of Jesus, who identified himself with the poor*, the deprived, and the marginalized* (Luke 4:18).

For different denominations in Africa, justification with both its vertical and horizontal dimensions is demanded by a faith in the Trinity* that calls Christians to interact with the Triune God. Justification necessarily encompasses all interactions with fellow humans and departed relatives who join hands in addressing people's problems and needs, in liberating them from oppressive and unjust systems and powers that threaten their lives. Sinners are *justified with and for others* (Greive).

SYLVESTER KAHAKWA

Justification, Theological Views and Practices, in Asia. Theologians in Asia emphasize the social implications of "justification," because doctrine or faith (see Faith #3) has ethical implications. In the Asian context of religious, cultural, and ethnic pluralism*, of widespread poverty*, oppressive* social* systems, globalization*, and violence*, justification involves the affirmation of God's acceptance of all people, of the equality of all; justification calls people to accept one another irrespective of differences of caste*, color, gender, and/or creed. God's inclusive and embracing love* and grace* endow all people with inherent dignity given that they are created in God's image. God's inclusive love, also revealed in Jesus Christ, works among all people, calling them to repent* and return to God. All those who respond in faith are accepted by God and "justified," and thereby associated with the human quest and struggle for justice and liberation, both grounded in God's divine nature (see *Ordo Salutis*). The works of a righteous or justified person stem from obedience to covenant* regulations and result in justice*, a good and upright life, the preservation of peace*, and a guarantee of the prosperity* of the community as a whole. Asian Christian teaching on justification emphasizes a call to solidarity or communion with the poor, oppressed, and stigmatized in their struggles for dignity and humanity. Through this solidarity, the good news of the gospel is being shared.

MONICA JYOTSNA MELANCHTHON

Justification, Theological Views and Practices, in Australia. Justification (however understood) is widely believed to be the reward for self-effort in Australia*, because self-reliance is a dominant ethos. Many experienced Christianity as oppressive and life denying in the early colonies: a man believed that only he and his mates could be relied on. This attitude has remained as Australia has prospered.

Justification as a reward for self-effort was attacked by many Protestant clergy (while accusing Catholics of such teaching). Yet "deeds, not creeds" has remained pervasive in the churches. Thus, paradoxically, rationalist* and separatist* trends in the (traditionally Evangelical) Anglican Diocese of Sydney have fostered a climate of spiritual "effort" in its circle of influence.

Making room for justification "by grace*," the end of the 20th c. saw the "Protestant work ethic" and workaholism questioned, and indigenous and orthodox Protestant perspectives heard. "Being" became as significant as "doing," and spiritual disciplines* were defined more in relational" than in "rule-of-life" terms. A renewed appreciation of grace* in Roman Catholic, mainline Protestant, and Pentecostal churches was a source of ecumenical* convergence that fostered spiritual life in which faith*, grace, and works are integrated and related to corporate as well as personal life – as in the Australian Lutheran–Roman Catholic agreement on justification.

CHARLES SHERLOCK

Justification, Theological Views and Practices, in Latin America. In Latin America, it is impossible to understand justification without considering the reality of exclusion, injustice, and structural* evil and sin*. In that case, justification cannot be a synonym of "forgiveness of sin by grace," i.e. without accountability or, from the victims' perspective, with impunity (see Forgiveness, Christian Discourses of). Rather, justification is through grace in the sense that it comes from God and occurs as a response to structural sin (see Grace of God Cluster: Latin American Perspective). Sin is generated by human beings through unjust practices that imprison the truth in injustice (Rom 1:18) and turn them into victims as well as into victimizers, accomplices of this sin. Through justification, God's justice* actually becomes present to liberate us from the logic of sin that dehumanizes both victims and victimizers. While grace rehabilitates us, with the goal of making us a new* creation despite our sins, justification calls us to practice justice* with freedom, dignity, and honesty, following Jesus. If sin leaves visible deadly marks, justification should also leave a visible mark: the radiance of a life as a new creation, displayed by those who, here and now in our historical context, have been resurrected, as Jesus was.

ELSA TAMEZ

Justification, Theological Views and Practices, in North America. The radical teaching of Luther* and the Reformers about "justification by grace*, through faith*" – salvation as a sheer gift of God's grace, appropriated by faith and not earned by our "works" – was perennially misunderstood by their contemporaries and in subsequent (including North American Protestant) history by two recurrent deviations.

1. Thinking that human justification before God is a "given" that frees believers from any personal obligations. Bonhoeffer*, most influential for mainline North American Christians, criticized this assumption, calling it "cheap grace."
2. In response to this "cheapening," reintroducing "works righteousness" through the back door, in the declaration of unwarranted grace, by adding "faithfulness" (see Faith #1) and moral and legal requirements for the "faithful." This, although not the intention of Calvin's "third use of the law," typified much of the Calvinism* so formative in North American Christian history.

The more taxing contemporary hurdle for this central Protestant teaching is linguistic: the language of "justification," fraught with legalistic overtones and almost inextricably bound up with the guilt consciousness of earlier epochs, is barely understood in a society whose typical anxiety is related not to guilt but to the loss of meaning. In his sermon "You Are Accepted," Tillich* suggested a provocative way of translating justification theology into this contemporary idiom.

DOUGLAS JOHN HALL

Justification, Theological Views and Practices, in North America: Latino/a. Since Hispanic Americans belong to different theological traditions, they profess diverse interpretations of justification. Protestants, emphasizing the radical nature of human sinfulness* and of God's transcendence, understand justification as a gift beyond human possibilities and completely undeserved. Roman Catholics see God as immanent within history and see justification as God's restoring or revitalizing those powers that are part of our nature; justification is part of the process by which, with the assistance of the Holy* Spirit, we continue to grow spiritually and morally toward the righteousness that prepares us to live in God's Kingdom*.

Latino(a) theologians, pressed to announce the good news to their communities of the marginal* and poor*, sought new forms of ecumenism that brought different churches closer to each other in a common understanding in which justification is closely associated with justice*. For the poor, justification is no longer merely being comforted. By being justified, they are empowered to lead lives of disciplined commitment and sacrifice for a new order and a new humanity. For the powerful, justification is a call to become accountable to the poor. In both cases, the justified are empowered to engage in the political task of living life for the sake of others, whether by God's grace alone or by God's restoration of our powers, to live more authentic lives, seeking right relationships with God, creation, and others. ISMAEL GARCÍA

Justification, Theological Views and Practices, in Western Europe: Feminist. Justification constituted a special challenge to Feminist theologians, since it presupposes specific understandings of creation*, sin*, and freedom* that are often gender biased.

Feminist theologians have diversely emphasized justification as a liberating power through its connotation of human equality (since this doctrine affirms that God accepts everybody regardless of differences) or as a source of hope* in a sinful world. Like other Liberation* theologians, they also linked justification to a concern for justice*. Thus they are wary of spiritual interpretations of justification that make a sharp distinction between the individual before God and interhuman relationships. In such cases, the doctrine of justification no longer provides means to resist women's subordination and other forms of oppression*; it risks condoning these conditions and disregarding concerns for non-human life forms (see Ecology and Christianity Cluster: Ecofeminist Theology). Instead, a feminist view of justification emphasizes the connections between the spiritual and the social dimensions of life. It offers a critique of interpretations that neglect the value of all creation and structural* evil and sin, sometimes by exploring the relation of justification to grace* and new* creation. It also balances a positive view of individual freedom (autonomy*) with a sense of relationality[F].

CRISTINA GRENHOLM

Justina, legendary 4th-c. character in the *Acts of Saints Cyprian and Justina*. She converts the magician Cyprian, who has been hired to cast a spell on her. He becomes a bishop and ordains her a deacon*. According to various versions, during a period of persecution* of Christians in Damascus or Nicomedia under either Decius* or Diocletian*, they are tried and executed together, she first because he fears that she will weaken in the face of death and lapse*. Cyprian is sometimes confused with Cyprian* of Carthage. Gregory* Nazianzen (*Orat.* 18 [24]) mentions the fact that the two Cyprians are confused, but does not refer to Justina. Cyprian has become the center of the legend, although in the original story Justina converts him. **See also DEACONESS.**

CAROLYN OSIEK

Justinian (c483–565). As Roman emperor (527–65) and before, during the reign of his uncle, Justin, he pursued a *Westpolitik*, reconquering areas in Africa, Italy*, and Spain* that had been governed by the Arian* Christian Goths*, seeking better relations with the popes in Rome, and ending the Acacian* schism. To Christianize the Roman Empire, he closed the philosophical schools in Athens (529), forced many to be baptized, and built many churches, including the impressive Hagia Sophia (Constantinople, 538). He sponsored the Justinian* Code and its classic differentiation between church and state (and their harmony).

Conflict persisted in the East between Chalcedonians* and Miaphysites* (or Monophysites*). Perhaps by mutual agreement, Justinian cultivated the Chalcedonians, who were allied with the West, while his wife, Theodora*, supported a clandestine non-Chalcedonian church in Egypt* and Syria* (see Jacob Baradai, or Baradaeus; Orthodox Churches, Oriental, Cluster: Coptic Orthodox Church). In a futile attempt to placate the Miaphysites*, Justinian condemned the "Three* Chapters," intimidating Pope Vigilius and causing a schism with large segments of the Western Church.

EUGENE TESELLE

Justinian, Code of, a collection of Roman laws compiled by the order of Justinian*, containing all imperial laws from the reign of Hadrian; published between 529 and 534. It incorporated the Theodosian Code (438) and two 4th-c. collections on which the latter had been based (*Codex Gregorianus* and *Codex Hermogenianus*). In addition to the Code itself, the *Corpus Iuris Civilis* included the Digest (selections from classical jurists), the Institutes (a training manual), and the Novellae (laws issued after 534). This formed the law of the Byzantine* Empire. Much attention is given to religion. While Justinian differentiated between church and state, he desired a "harmony" (*symphonia*) between them; he governed the "externals" of the church's life and penalized all (including Jews and heretics*) who did not follow orthodoxy* as he saw it. The *Corpus* was studied in the West after 1170, especially in Bologna. The legal profession found it more useful than the older Germanic and feudal law in a commercial society, and increasingly it became the law of the Holy* Roman Empire in Germany. Its methods and principles also influenced canon* law after Gratian*. Most European law codes, except in England, were built on its tradition. EUGENE TESELLE

Justin Martyr (c100–c165), philosopher and martyr (in Rome), Christian Apologist*. Born of pagan parents in Neapolis, Samaria, he describes exploring various philosophies and converting to Christianity. He wrote his two apologies, one to the emperor and one to the Senate, during stays in Rome (c40–50; c155–65). In his *Dialogue with Trypho,* a Jewish scholar, Justin argues that the new* covenant with Gentiles has superseded* the old covenant with Israel, that Jesus is both the Messiah* and the preexisting Logos* of God's self-revelation in Scriptures (in Judaism and Christianity Cluster, see Christian Views; Jewish Views). His (lost) writing against Marcion* and Gnosticism* probably influenced Irenaeus*, Tertullian*, and Hippolytus*. Thus he responded to the three major stimuli to the development of theology: apologetics, controversy with Jews, and opposition to heresies*.

He established the framework for the Christian doctrine of the Logos. The Word, uttered by God for the sake of creation, is the Platonists'* "intelligible world," giving form to matter by becoming the World Soul*. This Word illuminates all people, including Greek philosophers, but only in a partial and fragmentary way; the Word becomes fully present in Jesus Christ, who enables people to know God, lead virtuous lives, and defy demons* worshipped in pagan religions. The pagan philosopher Celsus* (c180) attacked Christianity, perhaps in response to Justin's arguments.

EUGENE TESELLE

K

Kagawa, Toyohiko (1888–1960), Christian social reformer in Japan; born in Kobe, brought up and baptized in Tokushima by a US Presbyterian missionary, H. W. Myers (1904). He studied in Presbyterian institutions: Meiji Gakuin (1905–7) and Kobe Theological Seminary (1907–11). Pulmonary tuberculosis (eventually fatal) led him to devote himself to serving and evangelizing the underprivileged in Kobe (1909), where he kept his residence (despite further study at Princeton Theological Seminary, 1914–17, and a trip to Tokyo to help the victims of the Kanto great earthquake in 1923). Throughout his life, he made significant contributions to the improvement of social conditions by helping to create labor, farmer, and consumer unions. In the 1930s, he developed the "Kingdom* of God Movement," a nationwide evangelistic movement partly influenced by the US Social* Gospel, based on his conviction that Jesus' love consists in redeeming underprivileged people. After the war, he contributed to the founding of the Socialist Party of Japan (1945) and social movements, while undertaking extensive evangelistic tours in Japan, Europe, and the USA. His collaboration with the wartime Japanese army and the discriminatory descriptions of "the poor" in his book, *Study on the Psychology of the Poor* (1915), have been severely criticized. His autobiographical novel, *Crossing the Death Line* (1920), was a best seller. NOZOMU MIYAHIRA

Kairos (Gk "right time"), a divinely assigned time or period; an opportune or special time (of fulfillment of prophecies, of the Kingdom*; Mark 1:15, par.); or a time of crisis. "Kairos theologies" are contextual* Liberation* theologies developed in a time of crisis by spiritual communities themselves rather than by theologians; an example is *The Kairos Document* written in Soweto (South* Africa, 1985).

Kant, Immanuel (1724–1804), last major Enlightenment* philosopher; taught at the University of Königsberg, Germany. There is some debate whether Königsberg Pietism* influenced his philosophy. Kant's *Critique of Pure Reason* (A, 1781; B, 1787) changed the course of modern thought through its "Copernican revolution" in philosophy.

Just as Copernicus* explained the heavens' apparent movement by postulating the movement of the spectator, so Kant explained the possibility of our knowledge of objects by postulating that objects must conform to the mind (B, xvi). Because our capacity for receiving impressions is constituted in a certain way, the way objects are received must conform to this constitution. The forms in which the "matter of sensibility" (sensible intuition) is received can thereby be known a priori, since they are given through the mode in which we are affected by objects. The two pure forms of sensible intuition are space and time; through them appearances are ordered in certain relations. Furthermore, experience must itself conform to the concepts (categories) of understanding, which provide rules necessary for unifying the manifold of intuition if experience is to be possible. Through these concepts, the mind actively synthesizes the data of intuition and gives it unity. The two fundamental sources of human knowledge are sensibility and understanding; both are necessary for cognition. Objects are *given* through sensibility (receptivity); they are *thought* through understanding (spontaneity). Kant notes, "Thoughts without content are empty; intuitions without concepts are blind" (A, 51; B, 75). Consequently, (1) we can never transcend the limits of possible experience, because the *content* of all thought is given through sensibility. (2) We have knowledge only of *phenomena* (objects as experienced), not of things-in-themselves. (3) We have no "theoretical knowledge" of God* or the soul*. Kant found it "necessary to deny knowledge to make room for faith*" (B, xxx). Theoretical reason cannot provide definite answers regarding the questions concerning God, freedom*, or immortality*.

Kant's ethics reflect the moral outlook of an enlightened citizen of the world. In the *Critique of Practical Reason* (1788); he argued that, even though we cannot affirm the existence of God, freedom, and immortality from a "theoretical" point of view, their existence must be posited from a "practical" one. Contra Hume* (1711–76), who believed that reason could determine only the means to ends already desired, Kant argued that if morality is to be possible, pure "practical reason" must be able to determine the "necessary ends" of the rational will. Not only can pure practical reason establish "what morality unconditionally demands" (action in accordance with the categorical imperative), pure practical reason is also sufficient to determine the will. And if we can be moved to act purely out of respect for the moral law, we must be transcendentally free (see Deontic, Deontological Ethics). Morality cannot be derived from religion. Action in accordance with morality because God commands it is heteronomy* and contradicts all genuine morality. Rather, God and immortality are objects of a practical faith. The individual committed to morality must hope* that God exists and that God's duration is endless. Kant's *Religion within the Bounds of Reason Alone* (1793, 1794) explains Christianity in terms of practical reason. Kant tackles the problem of radical evil* (the corruption of the fundamental principle or disposition guiding all a person's actions) and how to understand the redemptive* work of Christ. The historical Jesus* is understood to be an exemplar of an ideal archetype already lying within our reason; only through such an archetype can any historical person be known as good. It is the individual who must effect the change from an evil disposition to a good one; faith in expiation* effected by another cannot be the ground of an individual's conversion*. Only the individual already committed to a good course of life can have genuine faith in God and God's forgiveness*.

JACQUELINE MARIÑA

Käsemann, Ernst (1906–98), NT scholar, influenced by both Bultmann* and Barth*, but critical of both. His 1956 "Old Marburgers Lecture" stressed (against Bultmann) that faith* is possible only when one takes history* seriously, especially the history of Jesus, since the earthly and the exalted Lord are identical (see Jesus, Quest for the Historical).

After completing studies in Bonn, Tübingen, and Marburg (he wrote his dissertation under Bultmann, 1931), a pastorate in the Ruhr, and war service, he became a professor of NT in Mainz (1946–51), Göttingen (1951–59), and Tübingen (1959–71). His life context* profoundly influenced his scholarship and approach. Käsemann was committed to the theological significance of the NT and to its opposition to all totalitarian regimes (including Nazi Germany*). For Käsemann, apocalyptic* was the mother of all Christian theology; eschatology* and the theology of the cross* are decisive for the NT and theology. Human existence is not autonomous* but conditioned by which "lord" one serves. The lordship of Christ is primary and leads to corporate rather than individualistic existence.

Following Adolf Schlatter, Käsemann interprets Paul and Romans under the unifying theme of righteousness/justice. The righteousness/justice of God is both gift and salvation-creating power, because in and with the gift comes the lordship of Christ from which it is inseparable. Abraham was the prototype of faith* (as opposed to a model of faithfulness, when one presupposes an understanding of faith as a piety characterized by works). Justification* by faith as a theology of the cross is a polemical doctrine calling for a faithfulness to the covenant* (in relation to Judaism*) and to the creation*.

Käsemann's wide-ranging research also included the quest for the historical Jesus, hymnic and creedal elements in early traditions, the Lord's* Supper, "early catholicism" in the NT, diversity in NT theologies, and the history* of religions. As a radical critic of both church and society, Käsemann fought to demonstrate faithfulness to the gospel as the final arbiter of life and truth.

WILLIAM S. CAMPBELL

Kazakhstan, Kazakstan. Christianity in Kazakhstan has had a checkered history, with alternating periods of flourishing and decline. From the 6th c., the Church* of the East maintained several metropolitan sees in the Central Asian region, with Christians living in the south and southeast part of present-day Kazakhstan. The closest metropolitan sees were those of Samarkand (Uzbekistan) and Nawakat (Kyrgyzstan), and there was a local center in Taraz (Dzambul). The decline of central Mongol power (late 14th c.), accompanied by military raids, plague, famine, and the conversion of many local rulers to Islam*, caused a steep decline in the number of Christians. When the region became part of Czarist Russia (18th c.), emigrants introduced Russian* Orthodox* and Ukrainian* Orthodox Christianity; proselytization among the local population was discouraged by the government. A variety of Protestant (Lutheran, Baptist, Mennonite) and Catholic communities were introduced in the 19th c., mainly via German settlers. Further Christian growth was hampered by the Soviet regime (most of the 20th c.), which placed numerous restrictions on religious activities, although they were less severe than in other parts of the Soviet Union.

After independence (1991), many Russians left the country, causing a significant drop in the number of orthodox Christians, which constituted the large majority of Kazakhstan Christians. This decline was not compensated by the growth of Baptist and Pentecostal*/Charismatic* churches, although accurate assessments of their missionary activities and successes are hard to come by, partly because these churches are wary of attracting unwanted attention from the government. Traditional Protestantism has experienced a decline, whereas Roman Catholicism continues to grow. A majority of the population adheres to Islam; the Muslim community has grown in the wake of recent reawakening processes following the demise of the Soviet atheist ideology. Conversion* activities among this part of the population are looked upon with suspicion. Several laws impose strict state control of all religious communities (including Muslim and Christian communities), but their effects on Jehovah's* Witnesses have been especially severe. Nevertheless, freedom of religion is generally granted to religious organizations that register with the government; failure to register, however, is punished by fines and short jail sentences. Socially, it is often difficult for those from Muslim backgrounds to convert to Christianity, but less so than in other Central Asian states.

Statistics: Population (2000): 16 million. Muslims, 42.7%; atheists and nonreligious, 40.2%; Christians, 16.7% (Orthodox, 8.6%; independents, 4.0%; Roman Catholics, 3.1%; Protestants, 0.2%). (Based on *World Christian Encyclopedia*, 2001.)

HELEEN L. MURRE-VAN DEN BERG

Keble, John (1792–1866), educated at Corpus Christi College, Oxford, elected a fellow at Oriel College, Oxford (1811, at the age of 19), a tutor there from 1817 to 1823. Widely recognized as a poet because of his book *The Christian Year: Thoughts in Verse for the Sundays and Holydays* (1827), he was elected professor of poetry at Oxford (1831). His "Assize Sermon" of July 14, 1833 (published as *National Apostasy*, 1833), warned against the increasing control of the church by secular authorities (see Church and State Cluster: Introductory Entry) and was credited with having initiated the Oxford* Movement, in which he played a leading role. He served as vicar of Hursley (1836–66).

PETER C. ERB

Kempe, Margery (c1373–c1438), visionary, cataphatic* mystic*, considered a model of medieval lay sanctity. In her *Book*, a dictated autobiography that was lost until 1934, she describes a life of constant compunction, devotion to the humanity of Christ, and "sanctification of the ordinary" (Pellegrin).

Born in Bishop's Lynn, England, she received permission from her husband, John, to live chastely (1413) and went on pilgrimages* in England, the Holy Land, Assisi, and Rome (1413–15). She was tried on suspicion of Lollardy* (1417). A priest revised the illegible manuscript of *Book I* (1436) and transcribed *Book II* (1438).

Kempe lived a publicly devout life, gaining both supporters (including Julian* of Norwich) and detractors owing to her vociferous weeping during Mass, frequent fasting, return to virginal white clothes after choosing continence, claims to have received revelation, and uncontrollable "roaring" at every thought of Jesus. Watson interprets her "imitation* of Christ" as a form of public ministry (Watson). Frequently dismissed by modern scholars of mysticism as hysterical, Kempe is championed by scholars studying the thesis that "bodiliness provides access to the sacred" (Lochrie; Bynum; see Body). Given her era's restrictions on female preaching and its concerns with heresy*, Kempe's insistence on her extreme spirituality as a married, nonreligious woman is unique.

JESSICA A. BOON

Kenosis, Kenotic Christology. "Kenosis," emptying, is a Greek word in the "Christ hymn" (Phil 2:7–11) that Paul may have taken from an earlier source: Christ, "who was in the form of God, emptied himself, taking the form of a slave," embracing human vulnerability; therefore, God exalted him and bestowed on him the title of Lord. The sequence of emptying and exaltation has been emphasized in later theology as the "two states" of the incarnate* Christ and a model to be followed by Christians. In Russian Christianity, there is a "kenotic" tradition of monasticism, humbly serving others (see Monasticism Cluster: In the Russian and Ukrainian Tradition; Sketic Monasticism). During the 19th c., a "kenotic" movement in theology asserted that the second person of the Trinity* emptied himself to the extent of giving up divine knowledge and power, living in a vulnerable human mode until his exaltation. For Bulgakov* the relations between the persons of the Trinity are best understood in terms of kenosis as a movement of self-giving and self-receiving that has the capacity to overflow and reflect itself in the creation of the world. More broadly, Hegel's* suggestion that the historical process involves a divine self-emptying has been suggestive to many theologians. A more moderate version of this kenotic theology is that God, rather than being impassible*, sympathizes with the human condition and suffers with it.

Kenotic Christology has implications for Christian life, suggesting that it not be limited to autonomous* and relational* modes of life, but also be heteronomous* and thus kenotic, when, like the persons of the Trinity, believers are involved in a movement of self-giving and self-receiving – a mode of life that is problematical for some Feminist* theologians, because it reinforces customary views about the role of women, but that is affirmed by others (Coakley; Grenholm).

EUGENE TESELLE and DANIEL PATTE

Kenotic Monasticism, Russian style of monastic life based on the Gospels and emphasizing humility and charity. It originated in Kiev with the "cave monasteries" founded by Antonii in imitation of Mount Athos* and the "aboveground" monastery of Feodosii in imitation of the Studios* in Constantinople. It was further developed among the "non-possessors" (including Nil Sorsky) in the trans-Volga region. Monks engaged in works of charity and spiritual guidance of laypeople. Father Zossima in Dostoyevsky's* *The Brothers Karamazov* belongs to this tradition. **See also NIL SORSKY.**

Kenya. The Republic of Kenya has a secular constitution, which recognizes and appreciates the constructive role of religion in society. This constitutional position has provided space for religious communities to contribute to basic social services such as medical care (see Health, Healing, and Christianity Cluster: In Africa: African Traditional Practices and Christianity), schooling (see Educational Practices as Christian Service Cluster: In Africa), relief, and rehabilitation (see Poverty Cluster: Poverty, Theology, and Ethics: African Views). Christianity is the most influential religion in Kenya, although it is manifested in a wide spectrum of denominations: Orthodox, Roman Catholic, Episcopal/Anglican, Presbyterian, Congregational, Evangelical, Charismatic, Baptist, and Pentecostal. This diverse expression of ecclesial identities is rooted in the history of Christian missions in Kenya. As early as 1914, more than 35 missionary societies were competing for African converts in the Kenya colony, which was at that time under the British Empire. Similar diversity characterizes the expressions of Islam* and Vedic religions (see Hinduism and Christianity Cluster) in Kenya.

Roman Catholicism has the largest number of adherents. The Portuguese arrived in 1498 (Vasco da Gama visited Mombasa en route to India*) and settled at Mombasa and Malindi during the 16th and 17th c. (see Portuguese Explorations, Conquests, and Missions). But the small Christian community established by Augustinian* friars disappeared when the Portuguese were driven out of East Africa by the Arabs (1693), who established a sultanate until the colonization of East Africa by Britain (late 19th c.). The Catholic mission started again with the arrival of Holy Ghost priests (1889), and Catholicism grew rapidly throughout the country. By 1948, 8% of the population claimed to be Roman Catholic. Growth was even more rapid immediately after World War II: the percentage of Roman Catholics reached 20% in 1962, then continued to increase at a slower pace (23% in 2000). The struggle for the Roman Catholic Church is the slow progress in indigenous vocations (in 2000 less than half of priests were African). In an effort to overcome this limitation, missionary agencies from all over the world have established novitiates and seminaries in and around Nairobi. The Catholic University of Eastern Africa (based in Nairobi) is one of the largest private tertiary institutions in this region. It has constituent colleges owned and managed by various religious orders, including those of the Jesuits*, Marists, Dominicans*, Franciscans*, and Capuchins*, as well as that of the Maryknoll* missionaries.

Numerically, Anglicanism* is the next most influential denomination, with 30 dioceses and 3 archbishoprics. The Anglican Church of Kenya was introduced through the Church Missionary Society (CMS), closely associated with the 19th-c. Evangelical* revivals* in Britain. Since the late 1920s, the East African Revival Movement has played a significant role in Kenya. The Anglican Church of Kenya (with about 3 million members in 2000) has hundreds of sponsored primary and secondary schools, all under the patronage of the respective bishops in whose jurisdiction the schools are located (see Anglicanism Cluster: In Africa: Eastern and Western Africa). The Presbyterian Church (with c0.6 million members) also has a strong influence, especially in Central Kenya among the Kikuyu. The influence of the Methodist Church is significant in Eastern Kenya and on the coast (notably among the Meru). The Africa Inland Church (which originated from the interdenominational Africa Inland Mission in 1875 and became autonomous in 1971) is the largest "independent" church (c1.5 million members), with most of its members in the Rift Valley. A wide range of African* Instituted Churches attract adherents in most parts of Kenya, both in rural areas and in urban centers. New Pentecostal, Evangelical, and Charismatic churches have been introduced in urban centers, attracting adherents among the schooled elite, especially the youth.

Demographic Features. More than 70% of Kenya's population is under 25 years of age. Anyone on a casual visit to any church on a Sunday morning will notice the dynamism and youthfulness of Kenyan Christianity irrespective of denomination. Young people are greatly influenced by the mass media* – newspapers, magazines, radio, television, the Internet*, and advertising – the content of which is increasingly shaped by the vested interests of transnational corporations. Most pastors have great difficulty responding to the needs of young people, having been trained in formal ecclesiastical structures, with which youth are uncomfortable. One of the consequences of this challenge is that young people are increasingly joining Charismatic* and neo-Pentecostal initiatives that are transient and highly mobile. To retain the youth, formal Christian denominations seek to recruit younger pastors.

Ecclesiastical Features. Kenyan Christianity is both dynamic and diverse, ranging from conservative to highly innovative. Liturgically, the prayer books and hymnals inherited from the colonial period are still used in some congregations, while some congregations in the same denomination have undertaken innovative initiatives in worship and social service. Open-door immigration policies tend to encourage the introduction of ideas and experiments from various parts of the world, with the consequence that Kenyan Christianity reflects liturgical influences from all the continents.

Social Impact. Through denominationally sponsored schools, colleges, and hospitals, Kenyan Christianity has had a very strong social impact. Most members of the Kenyan elite have been schooled and have served in a denominationally sponsored institution. This impact is often taken for granted, particularly because of the secular emphasis of the Kenyan civil service. Many civil servants have prominent leadership roles in the congregations where they worship on Sundays, but their church leadership roles do not necessarily influence their conduct at work as civil servants during the week. This inconsistency has persisted since the colonial era and is indicative of a form of Christianity that has yet to permeate the cultural identity of African Christians. John V. Taylor described this form of Christianity as "classroom religion," which is practiced as long as the adherents are in the classroom or in the cathedral, but is suspended when they are back home.

Kenyan Christianity has had a strong political influence throughout Kenya's history. During the colonial period, some African converts to Christianity supported the nationalist struggles against colonialism* and imperialism, while others identified themselves as loyalists together with the missionaries. Others identified themselves with Christ and refused to participate in partisan politics. More recently, some church leaders have become outspoken advocates of political liberalization, while others support the status quo. During the 1990s, the Inter-Religious Forum led by the National Council of Churches of Kenya became the most visible expression of alternative political stances at a time when political dissent was frowned on. Thus Kenyan Christianity has been identified with both transformative and conservative political tendencies.

Ecumenical Relations. Kenyan Christianity embraced the modern ecumenical movement as early as 1908, two years before the Edinburgh* World Missionary Conference (1910). Progressive missionaries met at Kikuyu to form the Alliance of Missionary Societies. Through that alliance, many ecumenical initiatives were facilitated, including the Alliance Boys High School, the Alliance Girls High School, and St. Paul's United Theological College. Despite this long history, however, there has been no real support for the attempt to develop a united church (1960s); this initiative did not go beyond the drafting of a united liturgy between the Anglicans, Lutherans, Presbyterians, and Methodists. Christian denominations seem to be content to continue worshipping within their denominational cocoons.

Missionary Outreach. The older denominations have not been involved in missionary outreach outside their diocesan localities. However, "Christian initiatives" led by young people include a strong concern to travel outside of Kenya to proclaim the gospel. Many young Kenyans have been sent for short periods to Ethiopia*, Sudan*, Tanzania*, Uganda*, Rwanda*,

Burundi*, Democratic Republic of Congo*, Europe, and North America. This concern for missionary outreach among young people coincides with their international exposure through schooling and their interactions through the mass media and the Internet. The success of these initiatives can also be explained in terms of the availability of surplus capital, which comes from their salaries as well as from planned fundraising.

Kenyan Christianity is generally self-centered with regard to interfaith relations. Whenever there is a serious national crisis, church leaders convene and invite leaders from other faiths for consultation. They may issue a communiqué addressed to the political elite. However, such occasional meetings and consultations have not yet coalesced into an initiative to form a permanent interfaith forum.

Future Prospects. Kenyan Christianity is outwardly dynamic and vibrant. At the same time, the forces of secularization* and urbanization are strong. It is difficult to predict the impact of these processes on Kenyan churches and Christian communities. Whereas secularization in Europe and North America was facilitated by industrialization, the process of secularization in Kenya (as elsewhere in tropical Africa) is advancing without industrialization. Most young people moving into urban centers from the rural areas live in informal settlements without formal employment and without basic social amenities. With Christians living under such conditions, the development of predictable ecclesial structures is difficult. Thus Christianity in Kenyan informal urban settlements is a great challenge to ecclesiology as it has been formally taught in theological institutions, although transient and highly mobile Charismatic and neo-Pentecostal initiatives and African* Instituted Churches seek to address these situations.

The African Church will come of age when it becomes self-critical and moves beyond self-congratulation. This process has begun. Many excellent research monographs on Kenyan Christianity have been written by Kenyan students in universities, theological colleges, and pastoral institutes in Kenya. Yet these monographs are neither published nor codified, remaining in archives and known only in the small circle where they originated. Bringing them into the public domain will be an important step in helping the African Church to become self-critical. African theologians can then interact among themselves, learning from one another and critically evaluating the North Atlantic intellectual heritage and methodology in which they have received their academic formation. In this way, African theology can find an important role in an African Church in the process of coming of age, at a time when the demographic center of gravity of global Christianity has shifted from the North Atlantic to the rest of the world, including tropical Africa. **See also RECONSTRUCTION, AFRICAN THEOLOGIES OF; THEOLOGICAL EDUCATION CLUSTER: IN AFRICA: ISSUES IT FACES; THEOLOGY AS HUMAN UNDERTAKING CLUSTER: AFRICAN WOMEN THEOLOGIANS DOING THEOLOGY: MAKING CONNECTIONS.**

Statistics: Population (2000): 30 million (M). Christians, 23.8 M, 79.3% (Roman Catholics, 7 M, 23%; independents, including members of African Instituted Churches, 6.6 M, 22%; Protestants, 6.4 M, 21%; Anglicans; 3 M, 10%; Orthodox, 0.7 M, 2.5%); African Religionists, 3.5 M, 11.5%; Muslims, 2.2 M, 7.3%. (Based on *World Christian Encyclopedia*, 2001.)

JESSE NDWIGA KANYUA MUGAMBI

Kerygma (Gk "preaching"), the activity and content of Christian preaching, often contrasted with *didache*, or instruction.

Kerygma Petrou. See PETER, PREACHING OF.

Keswick Movement, Calvinistic holiness movement, from c1870 in England (with roots among the Plymouth* Brethren and Moody's evangelistic campaigns and the Holiness* Movement in North America). It diverged from Wesleyan Methodism* regarding what happens in believers' hearts at the moment of sanctification*. In contrast to the Wesleyans' Arminianism*, the Calvinistic Keswick Movement held that the sanctified are not made holy but are victorious over sin*, which remains in their hearts, and thus are in constant need of grace*.

Keys, Power of the, given to Peter* (Matt 16:19) and the community (Matt 18:18) "to bind and loose" – usually understood in Roman Catholicism as "to excommunicate* and restore" and thus regulate access to salvation*.

Kiddush (Heb "blessing"), blessing recited over a cup of wine in order to sanctify an occasion; a feature of the Last* Supper.

Kierkegaard, Søren Aabye (1813–55), Danish writer, theologian, philosopher. Born in Copenhagen, he graduated in theology (1840) and defended his thesis, *On the Concept of Irony* (1841). In 1840 he became engaged to Regine Olsen (1822–1904). The engagement, dissolved after only 11 months, had a lasting influence on his life and authorship.

Kierkegaard wrote approximately 40 books and pamphlets and a similar number of newspaper articles. Approximately half of his publications were written under various pseudonyms. The other half, edifying discourses, were published in his own name.

Kierkegaard's impact on Christian theology is multifarious. In *The Concept of Anxiety* (1844), his pseudonym, Vigilius Haufniensis, revises the traditional doctrine of original* sin* going back to Augustine*. Kierkegaard emphasizes that sin always enters the world through the concrete sin of each individual; thus sin must not be understood as a hereditary deformity of human nature.

In *Philosophical Fragments* (1844), under the pseudonym Johannes Climacus, Kierkegaard sharpens his understanding of faith* and Christianity. He takes as his point of departure Socrates*, who presupposes that truth is posited within the human being and can be reached in an immanent way. As an alternative, Climacus claims that Christianity presupposes that one is in a state of sin because of one's own guilt, and therefore it is not possible to relate to the truth by oneself, but only through transcendence. From this thought stems Kierkegaard's understanding of God as the absolute paradox*, which he fully developed in *Concluding Unscientific Postscript* (1846), also by Climacus.

Paradox is a key concept in Kierkegaard's attempt to interpret Christianity as a contradictory unity of time* and eternity*, which defies discursive understanding. The Christian paradox is that the infinite God has become a finite human being at a certain point in history and as such has suffered death on the cross. Kierkegaard's view of paradox is also found in his doctrine of "the stages," a theory about the relation between the three spheres of existence: the aesthetic*, the ethical*, and the religious. In the religious stage, the ethical commitment is combined with faith in a personal God who not only demands obedience (religiousness A), but also forgives in Christ the person's disobedience or sin (religiousness B, or the paradoxical religiousness). The transition from religiousness A to religiousness B happens by a leap.

After 1846 Kierkegaard radicalizes his understanding of Christianity and stresses that suffering*, martyrdom*, and imitation* are essential signs of true Christianity. *Works of Love* (1847) analyzes the relation between human love* and love of one's neighbor, and represents Kierkegaard's contribution to Christian ethics. But already in *Works of Love*, the radicalization of his view of Christianity and his critique of "Christendom*," the notion of Christianity as a cultural artifact, are visible. In *The Sickness unto Death* (1849) by Anti-Climacus, Kierkegaard continues his reflections on sin beyond *The Concept of Anxiety* by analyzing key concepts like despair and offense as constitutive of true Christianity. In *Practice in Christianity* (1850), by Anti-Climacus, Kierkegaard sharpens his view and draws a dividing line between the false triumphant church and the true struggling church.

In February 1854, Professor H. L. Martensen's declaration at the funeral service of Bishop J. P. Mynster that Mynster was a martyr gave rise to Kierkegaard's attack on the Danish Church. In a newspaper article in December 1854, Kierkegaard severely criticized Mynster as the representative of the official church; during the following months, he extended his attack to include every pastor in the Danish Church. Inwardness is an essential part of Kierkegaard's description of existence; it is often put on the same footing as appropriation and redoubling. "Redoubling" means that one should exist according to what one believes, even if this results in a collision with the world, a collision that could end in martyrdom rather than in a comfortable position as a vicar. Kierkegaard accuses Mynster and all the pastors of the Danish Church of lacking inwardness, whereby they "make a fool out of God" by only "pretending" to be Christians. In 1855 Kierkegaard published his own series of pamphlets, *The Moment*. After the publication of the ninth volume, he suddenly collapsed in the street and died on November 11.

Kierkegaard's emphasis on the responsibility of the individual for his or her own life has had an enormous impact on French existentialism*, whereas his religious thought has been taken up primarily in German, Danish, and later North American contexts, with the early Barth*, Bultmann*, and Tillich* being the most famous of those influenced by him. PIA SØLTOFT

Kimbangu, Simon (c1887–1951), whose teaching led to the creation of "the Church of Jesus Christ on Earth by the Prophet Simon Kimbangu," or Kimbanguism*. Born in Nkamba (Bas-Congo, Republic of Congo* [Congo-Brazzaville]) to non-Christian parents, who named him "Kimbangu" (one who reveals hidden things), he was raised by his Christian aunt near a Baptist Missionary Society station, where he was educated. Baptized (1915), married to Marie Mwilu (with whom he had three children, Charles Kisolokele, Salomon Dialungana-Kiangani, and Joseph Diangienda [or Diangenda]), he became a catechist in his native village while continuing to care for his fields. According to Kimbanguist sources, in repeated visions (from 1918) Kimbangu heard himself being called and sent by Jesus as an "apostle" to his brothers and sisters, because of the unfaithfulness of the church. After he finally accepted his calling, Kimbangu's mission started on April 6' 1921, when through prayer and the laying on of hands, he healed a woman. This and other instances of healing (see Health, Healing, and Christianity Cluster: In Africa: African Traditional Practices and Christianity), together with his preaching (in the Kikongo language), soon brought crowds to Nkamba; a revival* had begun. From then on, people called Simon Kimbangu *ngunza* (prophet) and *mvuluzi* (messiah, savior). With seven collaborators ("disciples"), Kimbangu preached repentance*, conversion to Jesus, love* for God and neighbors, God's judgment*, forgiveness*, and liberation* from all evil* through Jesus Christ. He called his followers to receive the Kingdom* of God, which had been taken away from unfaithful servants (the European missionaries; cf. Matt 21:33–43). Emphasizing the authority of the Bible, he asked his followers to reject alcohol, tobacco, dancing, fetishism, sorcery, and polygamy*. Since Kimbangu was leading a revival movement within the Baptist Church, he sent those who wished to be baptized* to that church rather than baptizing himself. He did not want to found a church. Yet Catholic and Protestant catechism schools were deserted by his followers.

Kimbangu's preaching, strongly Africanized, emphasized that some biblical texts, including the parables and Exodus, directly addressed Africans and the fundamental issues of their lives, and called for their liberation. At first, he emphasized spiritual liberation, but he soon concerned himself with political liberation as well, prophesying about independence, a time when "blacks will become whites, and whites blacks." On October 1921, Kimbangu was arrested, brought before a military court, and publicly condemned to death for threatening national security and for preaching about a "new God" who would be worshipped in a national Black church. However, King Albert commuted his sentence to life in prison, where he died on October 12, 1951.

LÉON NGUAPITSHI KAYONGO and
JEAN-CLAUDE LOBA-MKOLE

Kimbanguism began as a 1921 revival movement that arose out of the preaching and ministry in Bas-Congo of Simon Kimbangu (see Kimbangu, Simon), a Congolese Baptist catechist, and that gave rise to the Church of Jesus Christ on Earth by the Prophet Simon Kimbangu (Église de Jésus Christ sur la terre par son envoyé spécial Simon Kimbangu; EJCSK), a member of the World* Council of Churches.

Several years after Kimbangu's death in prison (1951), his disciples met in Matadi-Mayo (1958). Joseph Diangienda (1918–92), Kimbangu's youngest son, became the spiritual leader of the Church (assisted by his elder brothers, Charles Kisolokele and Salomon Dialungana-Kiangani) and began organizing it (1959). (The spiritual leader of the hierarchical and centralized EJCSK must be a descendant of Simon Kimbangu.) The EJCSK is trinitarian*, although it symbolizes the Trinity in an African way (symbolized as African persons; God is black). Its spirituality is charismatic*. Its pastors include both men and women. Women are ordained pastors because of the example set by Mama Mwilu, Kimbangu's wife, who led the revival movement while her husband was in jail, and because the Holy* Spirit inspires women as well as men.

With its 15 million members, the EJCSK is an important Christian presence, besides Catholicism and Protestantism, in the Democratic Republic of Congo*, Republic of the Congo* (Congo-Brazzaville), and Angola*; it is a missionary church in other parts of Africa and Madagascar, as well as in Europe and North America. Following Kimbangu's teaching, the EJCSK is financially independent, so as to avoid any dependence on Western churches. Its members support the church through *nsinsani*, an African socioeconomic communal practice of mutual aid (whereby different groups compete to meet the needs of the Church and its mission).

Kimbanguism has generated two kinds of theology: an oral theology and a more systematic written theology. The oral theology is expressed in inspired hymns, African melodies, spontaneous prayers, and sermons that make use of African illustrations, proverbs, and wisdom teachings. This theology is totally inculturated*. All the key themes of the gospel of Jesus

Christ emphasized in Baptist churches (e.g. repentance, faith, grace, love) are expressed in hymns, prayers, and sermons, alongside Kimbanguist history and theology. Following Kimbangu, preachers do not hesitate to underscore the liberation* message of all the parts of the Bible and to identify (typologically*) the people of Israel under slavery with the persecuted Kimbanguists (under Belgium colonialist power); to interpret the Exodus as both revivalist spiritual liberation and political independence; and to identify the Pharisees, who opposed Jesus, with the white missionaries of the colonial period. The "black race" (like the "lost sheep" [Luke 15:4–6] and those brought to the king's banquet from the streets [Matt 22:1–14]) is an important Kimbanguist theological theme. Kimbangu had proposed such biblical interpretations. Joseph Diangienda further pondered the origin of black humanity, its ongoing pauperization and suffering, and its place in the history of salvation. From this perspective, hymns and sermons evoke the problem of evil and envision not only Adam and Eve, but also God as black: "For we too are his offspring" (Acts 17:28), created in God's image. Thus the black race is divine and blessed, but this blessing became a curse because of "original* sin*," which for Kimbanguists is sorcery and "black magic"; the church must be freed from these through rituals of repentance (such as the repentance ritual in which people covered themselves with sackcloth and ashes [following Jonah 3:6], a ritual led in December 1992 by Salomon Dialungana-Kiangani, the brother and successor of Joseph Diangienda).

The written Kimbanguist theology was developed especially in 1965–1971 in preparation for admission to the World* Council of Churches and the Conference of the Churches of All Africa. The resulting 1977 document spelled out the Kimbanguist views on all the main theological topics, from creation to the Trinity, salvation, the sacraments, liturgy, ethical issues, and ecclesiology, clarifying the African inculturation of many aspects of the Kimbanguist oral theology that might seem alarming. For instance, during the celebration of the Lord's* Supper, the Body of Christ is an African cake (made with corn, potato, and banana) and the Blood of Christ is honey mixed with holy water. Salvation* is conditional, in that grace and faith must be complemented by the "fruits of faith," namely good deeds. The Kingdom, from an African Millennialist* perspective, is still completely in the future. The "communion of saints," those who overcame Satan, include Kimbangu. The EJCSK believes in the Trinity, yet the Trinity is symbolized by Simon Kimbangu's three sons, paths to the trinitarian God. Regarding gospel and culture*, the EJCSK respects the culture and identity of each ethnic group.

LÉON NGUAPITSHI KAYONGO

King, Martin Luther, Jr. (1929–68), African American Baptist clergyman, theologian, civil* rights leader. Born in Atlanta, Georgia, King, a descendant of generations of clergymen, was steeped in the traditions of the Ebenezer Baptist Church and Southern Black Baptist Protestantism. He graduated from Morehouse College (1948), Crozer Theological Seminary (1951), and Boston University (1955, Ph.D., philosophical theology). Doubts surfaced as King moved through his studies, compelling him to reject much of the Christian fundamentalism* of his church heritage in favor of biblical and theological liberalism (see Liberal Theology). The shift in King's thinking became glaringly evident when he was introduced to historical-critical biblical studies and embraced insights from Boston Personalism* and the Social* Gospel of Walter Rauschenbusch* and others. While serving as pastor of the Dexter Avenue Baptist Church in Montgomery, Alabama (1954), he was catapulted to leadership of the Montgomery bus boycott (1955–56). King was involved in the founding of the Southern* Christian Leadership Conference (SCLC, 1957), a civil rights organization led by ministers and rooted in the Black church. Returning to Atlanta (1960), he used the Ebenezer Baptist Church as a platform for his civil rights activities. Drawing on the teachings of Jesus and the nonviolent* philosophy of Mohandas K. Gandhi, King led church-centered civil rights campaigns in many US cities, including Albany, Georgia (1961–62), Birmingham, Alabama (1963), Washington, D.C. (1963), St. Augustine, Florida (1964), Selma, Alabama (1965), Chicago (1966–67), and Memphis, Tennessee (1968). In these and other campaigns, he elevated the politics of civil disobedience and nonviolent confrontation to unprecedented levels, without compromising what he saw as the essential core of traditional Christian truths and values. He applied the biblical principles of love* and justice* in a determined effort to eliminate racial oppression*, economic exploitation, war*, and human destruction. Although best known as a pastor and civil rights leader, King was a polished academic who combined theological liberalism, biblical piety, and sociopolitical analysis in a manner that suited the changing political, intellectual, and cultural climate of the 1950s and 1960s. His six books and numerous essays advance the major themes in his thought, namely the personal God of love and reason, the redemptive power of love and nonviolence, the sacredness of the human personality, the moral obligation to resist evil, the beloved community as the highest human ideal, and the social mission of the church. **See also CIVIL RIGHTS MOVEMENT.** LEWIS V. BALDWIN

KINGDOM OF GOD, THE CONCEPT OF, CLUSTER

1) Introductory Entry

Kingdom of God, the Concept of, in the New Testament (Gk *basileia tou theou; basileia ton ouranon* [Kingdom of Heaven; Matthew]), at the core of Jesus' teaching, is a symbolic figure that, by definition (see Symbolism), "represents connections between individual, community, and ultimate reality." Its significance varies in the NT and throughout history according to the ways the figure is constructed and represented, namely in parables*.

The Kingdom as the Reign of God is envisioned as the ideal people of God over whom God reigns, especially when the Kingdom figure is constructed as a prolongation of the covenant* and the wisdom* tradition. This ideal community submits to God's authority as king, walks humbly with God, loves the neighbor, and exemplifies God's justice in a new family-like egalitarian community, a "kin-dom." "Your kingdom come" points to the establishment of the kin-dom/kingdom by believers who do God's will; thus while its full realization will take place in the future, pockets of the kin-dom are already found. Most directly expressed by Luke's presentation of the parables*, this view of the Kingdom is found throughout history in all movements striving to establish a new social order, e.g. the Social* Gospel.

The Kingdom as the Eschatological Empire of God is envisioned as the age to come, which will bring to an end the evil*, demonic* empires of the present age, when the figure is constructed in an apocalyptic* perspective, as a future reality on earth although it is seemingly conceived as a present reality in heaven ("Your kingdom come. Your will be done, on earth as it is in heaven"; Matt 6:10). As an eschatological* promise (e.g. Matt. 5:3–12) of a new order to be established by God in an imminent future, the proclamation of the coming of God's Kingdom (*basileia*) is a potent source for judgment of the status quo, which in NT times was the empire or kingdom (*basileia*) of Rome and of satanic or demonic powers that keep people in bondage. This is most directly expressed by Matthew's presentation of the parables* read in light of the coming Judgment*.

The Kingdom as God's Series of Powerful Kingly Interventions is envisioned when the figure of the Kingdom is constructed as an ongoing and decisive prolongation of God's powerful activity in history, following the type* of God acting as king (Heb *malek*) when freeing Israel from Egypt in Exod 15:11–18, or of God's kingly activity (Heb *malkuth*) or mighty deeds in Ps 145:11–12. In the end-time (Jesus' ministry and beyond), one can see God's ongoing kingly interventions, which are a mystery that is by definition beyond understanding (Mark 4:11). One experiences and encounters these kingly activities of God when one reads the parables as pointing toward this mystery, as the Gospels of Mark and Thomas do in different ways. **See also PARABLE.**

DANIEL PATTE

2) A Sampling of Contextual Views and Practices

Kingdom of God, the Concept of, in Africa. The Lord's* Prayer, well known and often recited in African Christianity, requests that "Your kingdom come." "Kingdom" is understood by many ordinary African Christians in spatial terms, similar to earthly kingdoms, the only difference being that God's Kingdom is in heaven. It is accessible only at death when one is a baptized member of a church here on earth. The Kingdom of God is conceived of as a spiritual realm. This is the popular understanding usually found in missionary churches in Africa.

A political version of the Kingdom was presented by Ghana's first president, Kwame Nkrumah, when he said, "Seek ye first the political kingdom and the rest shall be added unto you." He put "political kingdom" where Jesus had " Kingdom of God or Heaven" (cf. Matt 6:33). This "materialist" reading of the gospel texts about the Kingdom contrasted sharply with the missionary churches' teaching.

In between these two views, a third view has emerged: a so-called liberation view of the Kingdom. Here the focus is on the Reign of God as the abundant life that African people need today as they begin the third millennium. Therefore, the Kingdom or Reign of God is understood as liberation* from sin*, i.e. from any form of oppression* – cultural, economic, political, or social; as the promotion and establishment of socioeconomic justice*, democratic governance, and human* rights; and as the realization of full *uMunthu* or *Ubuntu* (humanness) as seen in the face of Christ.

Harvey Sindima comments, "To pray for God's kingdom to come is to ask God to intervene in human history and establish divine rule, that is, to liberate people bound by socio-economic ad political powers – this advent of God into history is liberation." Sindima continues by arguing that this petition asks God to set in motion a resistance movement against the current social, political, and economic order, which by its very nature is oppressive* because it is permeated by sin; and encourages Christians not to surrender to the current powers or become immobilized by fear, but to become instruments of God in bringing about a new order of justice.

AUGUSTINE MUSOPOLE

Kingdom of God, the Concept of, in Asia. The concept of "Kingdom of God" occupies a central place in Asian theologies of liberation*, such as those of Choan-Seng Song, Aloysius Pieris, Michael Amaladoss, Peter Phan, Minjung* theology (Korea), Homeland theology (Taiwan), theology of struggle (the Philippines), Dalit* theology (India), and Asian Feminist* theology. These theologies argue that the primary mission of the church is to proclaim and bear witness to the Reign of God, and not simply to save souls and plant the church. The symbol of the Reign of God allows Asians to overcome the pronounced individualism of their religions and ethics and to view salvation* as necessarily comprising the sociopolitical, economic, and cultural dimensions of human existence. It requires Asian Christians to commit themselves to the "preferential* option for the poor," to join with those who are oppressed* in their struggle for human* rights and freedom*, and to identify and fight against the forces that enslave their fellow Asians (e.g. communism, neocapitalism, sex tourism, human labor trafficking, ecological destruction). Furthermore, it enables Asian to recognize the gratuitousness of God's gift of salvation* over against the common emphasis on earning merit. Finally, the symbol of Kingdom of God directs Asian attention away from the golden age of a mythic past and turns it toward the eschatological* end-time (*eschaton*), when the risen Christ himself will "come again" to judge the living and the dead and to bring the Reign of God to ultimate fulfillment. PETER C. PHAN

Kingdom of God, the Concept of, in North America: Latino/a. Latino/a Christians emphasize the political relevance of the Kingdom but disagree as to the locus of the political.

For some the political for which the Kingdom is relevant is the all-encompassing public dimension of life. In the OT, God's rule is manifest in Israel's history and awaits full establishment through the coming of the Messiah. The NT claims that the fullness of the Kingdom will ultimately be established by God in the future, yet also claims that God's power and sovereignty were present in history through Christ's acts of healing and liberating the poor, the sick, and the needy. The community of faith gets a glimpse of life in the Kingdom when it acts in ways fitting the Kingdom that "is and is not yet." The establishment of the Kingdom is a gift from God, and not a human achievement. Thus Latino/a Christians use the image of the Kingdom to motivate the faith community and people of goodwill to commit themselves to the tasks of reforming the present distribution of power, wealth, social positions, and social services and of empowering the poor* and marginalized* to achieve fullness of life. The Kingdom is a standard of love* and justice* that calls for more inclusive and harmonious social and political communities.

Other Latino/a Christians, with a narrower definition of the political, limit the Kingdom to the quality of life that ought to be maintained within the church as a loving, caring, and egalitarian community. The church's task is not so much to transform the world as to witness to the world a better way of living. This view of the Kingdom had an ambiguous political history. Whenever the church claimed to be the only true representative of the Kingdom, it tended to curtail all other legitimate claims of justice* and social reform.

Still other Latino/a Christians have argued that the normative vision of the Kingdom transcends history. It enables the church to denounce the evils and shortcomings of our present social and communal life, but it is not continuous with this life; we cannot bring our world in harmony with the Kingdom.

In all cases, Latino/a Christians see the Kingdom as transforming life through denunciatory judgments and acts of mercy; and as the vantage point from which the meaning and purpose of history can be perceived. ISMAEL GARCÍA

Kingdom of God, the Concept of, in the Western World. A question commonly raised in the West has been: How is the Kingdom of God related to the kingdoms of this world, which are always in some tension with it? Augustine* differentiated the earthly city from the city of God. Luther* spoke of two* kingdoms or two realms in which human life takes place. Are the Kingdom of God and the kingdoms of this world opposed? Or in tension with each other? Or parallel? Or can earthly life be transformed by the Reign of God? Answers vary with the degree of optimism about the current situation and about possibilities for transformation through human or divine action.

These questions show that the Western tradition has privileged, among the views just listed, the view of the Kingdom as the ideal community over which God rules and which submits to God's authority, loves the neighbor, and exemplifies God's justice in a new family-like egalitarian community. Thus it is appropriate to speak of it as the "Reign of God" or as the "kin-dom" – to avoid patriarchal* or kyriarchal* connotations.

The Reign of God as the central theme of Jesus' preaching was also revived in 19th- to 20th-c. liberal* theology as an eschatological* notion, oriented toward the future. While God was regarded as always sovereign, God's rule has not taken full effect. But there is hope* for God's effective rule. Just what this future might be is not clear from the texts, and conflicts of interpretation have multiplied.

EUGENE TESELLE

Kingdom of God in the Eastern Orthodox Tradition: Kingdom and Wilderness. In the Eastern Orthodox tradition, the Kingdom of God and the eschatological fulfillment of creation* to become a new* creation have been associated with wilderness. Wilderness is the site of the integration of the material and spiritual realms, whereupon both realms are fulfilled in an embodiment of the new creation and Kingdom of God, fulfilling all cultural histories. Wilderness is a place of repentance*, illumination, and theosis*. St. Catherine's monastery in the Sinai Desert was established close to where Moses* spoke with God and is where John* Climacus wrote his *Ladder of Divine Ascent*. From the wilderness, Isaac the Syrian stated that theosis is burning compassion for all creatures, even demons*. In contemporary Orthodox theology, wilderness also provides insights into how the evolution of the material realm is brought into union with the spiritual realm. The ecological* dynamics of the nested natural systems of wilderness can be outlined by noting that within it each human being is potentially a microcosm reflexively aware of nature as a whole and of the Holy* Spirit, which makes possible this awareness (see Ecology and Christianity Cluster: Eastern Orthodoxy Perspective). The indwelling of the Holy Spirit in individual human creatures enables responsible and compassionate communion with all of nature to fulfill our creative capability and thus become a new* creation, God's Kingdom.

Furthermore, from this perspective, the sin* of Adam* is understood to be the denial of death* that arose as human individuals emerged as the first creatures conscious of death as an existential reality. As evolutionary* biology indicates, the purpose of individuation is to allow death, and the purpose of both individuation and death is to allow evolution of new life. Accordingly, from the Orthodox perspective of the Kingdom, the evolutionary dynamics of wilderness over the 4 billion years of the evolution of life can be seen to be a cosmic Eucharist* in which created beings come to the door of the new* creation – a door opened by Jesus Christ to fulfill all cultural histories, enabling all to discover the meaning of life in communion with, and in self-sacrificial compassion for, all of creation. The contemporary struggle for sustainable development and global social justice*, inspired by the Holy* Spirit, is the cosmic Eucharist, a liturgy in which we ourselves participate. **See also** **TEILHARD DE CHARDIN, PIERRE.**

KEITH MORRISON

Kingdom or Reign of Christ. In the NT, Jesus is called Lord because of his resurrection and exaltation (Rom 1:4; Phil 2:11; Acts 2:36). In the infancy narratives, he is said to be the inheritor of David's kingship (Matt 2:2; Luke 1:32–33). Yet Jesus' rule is not always equated with God's. The OT verse most commonly quoted in the NT is Ps 110:1: "Sit here at my right hand until I make your enemies your footstool." Paul anticipates that Christ will "deliver the kingdom to God the Father" (1 Cor 15:24), after which Christ will also be subject to God (1 Cor 15:28). In the 4th c., Photinus* emphasized this as part of his allegedly modalist* view of the Trinity* and was condemned by several councils; this is the reason for the words "of his reign there will be no end" in the Niceno*-Constantinopolitan Creed.

Augustine*, who adhered to the doctrine expressed in this creed, still asserted that the Reign of Christ has different characteristics than the Reign of God. He equated the millennium* with Christ's reigning in the hearts of the faithful as they struggle against inward and outward temptations (*De civ. Dei* XX.8–9). It is similar, then, to the Reign of the Holy* Spirit, described by Paul as "groaning in travail" (Rom 8:12–25). This perspective is adopted by many contemporary theologians who see the present as a time of struggle and hope* rather than one of triumph.

EUGENE TESELLE

King James Authorized Version. See BIBLE TRANSLATION CLUSTER.

Kings, 1–2, Books of (3–4 Kingdoms in the Septuagint*), are the last components of the Former Prophets (in the Jewish Bible), which also include Joshua*, Judges*, and 1–2 Samuel*. Traditionally ascribed to Jeremiah*, most scholars now consider 1–2 Kings to be part of the Deuteronomistic* History, which spans the Former Prophets, with an initial edition during King Josiah's reign (late 7th c. BCE), updated during or just after the Exile (for other scholars, the time of the books' entire composition). 1–2 Kings narrates the succession of David* by Solomon*, the building of the Temple*, Solomon's apostasy, the division of the kingdom into Israel (Northern) and Judah (Southern). Continuing apostasy leads to the destruction of Israel by Assyria and then of Judah by Babylon, despite Josiah's reforms.

1–2 Kings addresses a dispersed Judean population, justifying the Exile. The theme of royal obedience to divine law is central. Significant, too, are the exclusivity of worship in Jerusalem, the fulfillment of the covenant* curses for apostasy, and the role of prophecy as warnings and predictions of divine judgment. Thus dynastic promises to David are portrayed as conditional. The ending of the book, narrating the release of the imprisoned king Jehoiachin, is highly enigmatic. It intimates that the dynasty is not entirely defunct, although the degree to which a monarchic restoration is envisioned is probably minimal at best.

Often considered a direct historical source, 1–2 Kings is a literary and ideological document demonstrating the continuing relevance of Israelite religion and identity as a defense against assimilation. It ensures the sacrality of Jerusalem* as a holy site despite the loss of the Temple. The Northern Kingdom's fall is depicted in such a way that Judah becomes the continuing focal point of "Israelite" identity. This plays not only into the later distinction between Samaritans and Jews, but also into the legends of the "lost tribes of Israel." Jewish tradition looks to 1–2 Kings in recollection of former national glory and independence, whereas the fall of the Temple is commemorated on the solemn occasion of Tisha B'ab, "Ninth of Ab" (usually in August). Along with the rest of the Former Prophets, Kings provides perspectives on the nature of political power and the relationship between national fortunes and the divine will. Its theme of exile helped solidify later Jewish identity as a people in diaspora*.

JAMES R. LINVILLE

Kirchentag, annual gathering of all Protestant churches in Germany, with significant lay participation. It is marked by three historical phases: from 1848 to 1872, inspired by Wichern*'s speech at the founding of the Inner* Mission (1848), the Kirchentag functioned as an alternative to the spirit of the 1848 revolutions in Germany; from 1919 to 1930, it was an official gathering of the German Evangelical Church, with nationalistic emphasis; and from 1949 to the present, continuing the heritage of the Confessing* Church, it was ecumenical and concerned with the renewal of church and society, uniting Protestants in East and West Germany until the Berlin Wall was built (1961) and supporting the peace movement of the 1980s.

Kirishitans and Hidden Christians in Japan. "Kirishitan" is the Japanese pronunciation of the Portuguese *Christão*. The history of Christians in Japan* has three stages: (1) from 1549 (Francis* Xavier's introduction of Roman Catholic Christianity) to 1644 (the martyrdom of Manshiyo Konishi, the last missionary in Japan); (2) from 1644 to 1873, the proscription of Christianity (lifted in 1873); and (3) from 1873 until today.

1. 1549–1644. When the Catholic missionaries pursued evangelism, Japanese language and customs often impeded conversion. Some local rulers, like Sumitada Oomura, showed an interest in Christianity partly because of the potential benefits of trade relations with the missionaries' countries; others, like Ukon Takayama, adopted the Christian faith themselves and were baptized, and mass conversion in their territory often followed.

2. 1644–1873. The shogunate isolation policy led to the persistent persecution, martyrdom, and banishment of Kirishitans and missionaries. Thus some Kirishitans formed underground groups, called *confraria* or *companhia*, to pass their teachings and rituals on to future generations. Kirishitans, now called Senpuku (underground) Kirishitans, covertly maintained their faith at the risk of their life without any teaching priests.

3. 1873–Today. When Christianity was once again tolerated, some Kirishitans returned to the Roman Catholic Church and were called Fukkatsu, or "resurrected," Kirishitans by Francisque Marnas (1896). Others, called Kakure, or "hidden," Kirishitans (although they did not need to hide as before), maintained their form of Christian faith, which had been syncretistically fused (some would say, inculturated) with local conventional religions and customs, including Buddhism* and Shintoism*. The Catholic Church tended to call them Harare, or "separate," Kirishitans, because they separated themselves from the Church. Today a few hundred Kakure Kirishitan households remain, mainly in Nagasaki Prefecture, with their particular *oratio*, relics, tombstones, rituals, and literature.

NOZOMU MIYAHIRA

Kiss of Peace, mutual greeting of the faithful during the Eucharist*, originally with a kiss on the lips, more recently by placing one's hands on another's shoulders or with a handshake.

Kitagana, Yohana (1868–1938), important Bugandan chief with five wives. Baptized Roman Catholic, he abandoned his wives, declaring, "God must suffice for me." An outstanding Roman Catholic catechist, he left his native area, becoming a pioneer missionary in Southwest Uganda*.

ROBERT KAGGWA

Knights of Malta. See HOSPITALLERS.

Knights Templar. See MILITARY ORDERS.

Knox, John (c1514–72). Leading Scottish and British Reformer and icon of Protestant Scotland, he had a British and European perspective. His most significant contributions were the Protestant triumph during Scotland's Reformation crisis of 1559–60 and his tenure as Edinburgh's minister, 1560–72, which placed him at the heart of the kingdom's affairs. On her return, he vigorously opposed Mary, queen of Scots, regarding private Mass (1561) and supported her deposition in 1567. While his outspoken preaching made him the leading voice in the first years of the Church of Scotland* (the Kirk), its organization was largely the work of others. Knox's *History of the Reformation* (1587) became the model for Scottish Presbyterian historiography, and his 1558 resistance tracts, including *The First Blast,* influenced European political thought. He had previously served as minister (1549–53) within the Edwardian Church of England* and Marian exile congregations* (1554–59), and remained in close contact with Elizabethan Puritans*. His ecclesiological and theological views, especially on predestination*, were influenced by his friends John Calvin* and Theodore Beza*.

Knox regarded himself as a preacher and prophet offering a black-and-white, apocalyptic* view of the world, where Protestants battled against Antichrist*, which they identified with the papacy. In God's cause, it was legitimate to resist "ungodly" rulers. One of the main attributes of Christian commonwealth was to maintain purity in worship and avoid idolatry*, with a strict adherence to the principle that nothing lacking scriptural warrant was acceptable. Knox was a forerunner of Scottish covenant* thought, teaching that by openly accepting Protestantism, a kingdom entered into covenant with God, parallel to the experience of OT Israel.

Knox's part authorship and his authority shaped the fundamental texts of the Scottish Reformation – the Geneva* Bible, the Book* of Common Order, the Scottish Confession of Faith, and the First Book of Discipline – which together helped mold the character of the nation's Kirk and people. *The* Scottish Reformer, he was also regarded as a founding father of the Reformed* tradition and of English Nonconformity*. In Scottish contemporary thinking, he personifies the country's Reformation and the adoption of an uncompromising Protestant stance, and is sometimes unfairly caricatured as a killjoy and woman hater.

Knox's surviving writings are found in Laing's *Works* (1846–64); they comprise his *History,* his resistance tracts, *First Blast of the Trumpet, Letter to the Regent, Appellation to the Nobility, Letter to Commonalty* (1558), and other polemical, devotional, and theological tracts, as well as his liturgical and ecclesiastical papers and letters (1548–72).

JANE DAWSON

Koine (Gk "common"), Gk dialect of NT; language of the Greco-Roman Empire, which developed as its common ground after the conquests of Alexander the Great.

Koran. See QUR'AN AND CHRISTIANITY.

Korea, North. Liberation from the Japanese colonial occupation (1905–45), the subsequent division of the Korean Peninsula, and the occupation of the North by the Soviet Union brought about drastic changes for Christian communities in North Korea. Until 1948 Christianity was vibrant and dynamic; the churches were centers of the anti-Japanese independence movement. But the establishment of the pro-Soviet Communist government of the Democratic People's Republic of Korea (1948) had a disastrous impact on the Christian communities that opposed the atheist ideology of Communism and the government's antireligious policies and land reforms. Tens of thousands of North Korean Christians, including church leaders, fled to the South.

When the Korean War broke out (1950), hundreds of dissident Christian leaders were imprisoned and executed without trial, and most church buildings were either destroyed or confiscated. Even though the Federation of Korean Christians was organized in 1946 (a pro-Communist government organization), no Christian activities were known until 1972, when the North and South governments began a process of peace and reconciliation. The Pyongyang Theological Seminary, the only institution for pastoral training, opened in 1972. By 1992 two state-sponsored Protestant congregations (the Pongsu Church and the Chilgol Church, built respectively in 1988 and 1992) and one Roman Catholic parish (Changchun Catholic Church) were under the supervision of the Federation of Korean Christians and held regular worship services. Although their members number less than 1,000, they serve as a conduit between the tightly closed Korean society and the Western world. Leaders of the

Federation of Korean Christians attended various meetings that addressed the peaceful reunification of Korea. These were organized by international ecumenical bodies such as the World* Council of Churches, which in turn sent delegates to North Korea in the 1980s and 1990s, along with thousands of Christian leaders (from, e.g., US and Canadian churches) and members of humanitarian relief organizations (including some from South Korea).

The majority of Christians (only about 10,000 in the early 1990s) worship in house* churches, where 10–15 persons regularly meet for Sunday services. They use Bibles (OT and NT) published in North Korea since 1984 (reprinting the South Korean Catholic–Protestant common translation) and a hymnal (a slightly revised 1939 hymnal). Yet young people under the age of 18 are prohibited by law from participating in worship services. The three-year theological school admits fewer than 10 students a year, selected among college graduates. As of 2009, nearly 90 seminary graduates were active in the churches.

As a state-sponsored religious organization, the Federation of Korean Christians must have a theology that accommodates the state ideology* of *juche* (self-reliance) framed by an atheistic humanism of a Feuerbach* type. Yet it is possible that indigenous contextual theologies will emerge in North Korea.

DAVID KWANG-SUN SUH

Korea, South. Christianity in Korea is marked by a twofold tension. Since 1950 it has grown from a tiny minority proclaiming a gospel of justice* and empowerment for the weak to a powerful movement emphasizing personal salvation* and a gospel of prosperity*. Second, it has gained distinctive features through its interactions with Shamanism*, Buddhism* and Confucianism*, even as it contributed to the modernization and westernization of Korea.

Late 18th and 19th Century: Implantation of Catholicism. Christianity was first introduced in Korea in the 17th century by young Confucian *Silhak* scholars who studied Christian literature brought from China. It was in Beijing that the first Korean, Yi Sung Hun, was baptized; returning to Korea in 1784 he founded a Catholic church. Catholicism quickly spread, despite harsh persecutions due primarily to the Christians' refusal to observe ancestral* rites. For Confucians, this was a clear evidence that western culture and religion desecrated Korean culture; ultimately Taewongun (regent, 1864–73) outlawed foreign cultures and religions. Persecution ceased after the Japanese invasion in 1876 and the treaty with the United States in 1882. During the bicentennial commemoration of Korean Catholicism (in 1984), Pope John Paul II canonized 103 Korean martyrs – starting with Kim DaeGon (1822–46). Korean Catholics played an important role in the struggle against political and economic oppression through the 1970s and 1980s.

Late 19th Century: Early US Protestant Missions. These missions began with Horace Allen, a US doctor and Presbyterian missionary, who had been transferred from China to Korea in 1884 and provided health* services for the imperial court. In 1885 another Presbyterian, Horace G. Underwood, and a Methodist, Henry G. Appenzeller, came to Korea. Protestant missions maintained a balance between evangelism*, social welfare, and educational* programs, building medical clinics and Christian schools. Besides the establishment of churches, the fruits of this missionary work included social reforms led by Koreans trained in Protestant mission schools, the empowerment of disenfranchised people, and the opening of Korean society to Western culture.

Starting in 1890, Samuel Moffett established a different form of Protestantism in Pyongyang, now the capital city of North Korea. His teaching was focused on repentance* and personal salvation*, appealing to Koreans' spiritual hunger for freedom but not explicitly confronting the social issues resulting from Japan's brutal rule over Korea. In fact, the American Board for Foreign Missions and the US government instructed missionaries in Korea not to engage in politics. Korean churches were nevertheless viewed as anti-Japanese through their association with the West and the USA; many Christians actively participated in the independence movement in 1919 and resisted, with Moffett and other missionaries, the Japanese imposition of Shinto* shrine worship in the 1930s.

1945–1960: After the Liberation of Korea. Following much political upheaval, a US-backed government headed by Syngman Rhee, a US-educated Methodist, was established in South Korea in 1948. The Korean War in 1950 brought a large number of North Korean Christians to the South. Since then South Korean Protestantism has tended to side with anti-Communist ideologies, reinforcing the governments' policies against the Communism of North Korea.

After 1960: The Rapid Growth of Christianity. Christians increased from 18.3% of the population in 1970 to 40.8% in 2000. This growth took place while the country was undergoing rapid industrialization; several military coups supported the economic exploitation of the masses by government-supported conglomerates. Most of the Protestant churches remained silent about this political and economic situation. Implicitly supporting the dictatorial governments by leading prayer breakfasts for the presidents, pastors of megachurches* taught and preached the blessings of economic and spiritual success and upward social mobility. The charismatic* services with their exuberant expressions of faith and their appeal to the Prosperity Gospel were viewed as a return to the enthusiasm of the early church. Yet this success-oriented faith and charismatic practice are also an inculturation* of Christianity reflecting traditional Korean Shamanistic* religious practices.

This period witnessed a rash of divisions and subdivisions of Protestant churches. Fully one-third of Protestants are members of churches that have seceded from the main denominations or of the hundreds of independent denominations in Korea. These divisions, caused mostly by leadership conflicts, reflect a conception of the church* strongly influenced by the Confucian hierarchical culture. Church communities separate themselves from very similar ones in order to maintain their own family-like authority structures. In most Korean Protestant congregations, the pastor is the "big father" (the patriarch); the elders are the "second fathers" (sharing and extending the authority of the patriarch); the anointed deacons are "big hands" (overseers to whom authority has been delegated in a specific domain); non-anointed deacons are "workers" (bearing authority through their work for the family); all other members, including women and children, are ordinary family members. Each congregation remains in a denomination only insofar as its authority structure is respected. Each denomination has founded its own theological school where pastors are trained to assume authority over congregations. Graduating pastors are in competition with each other to prove their authority by founding new congregations of the denomination.

Women's leadership in the church is either denied or very limited in this hierarchical culture: women are ordained in only a few denominations. Nevertheless, women's role in Korean churches cannot be underestimated. More than 50% of members are women; their sacrificial faith is often viewed as an example of Christian discipleship*, and women have developed safe spaces within the churches for the free exercise of their faith and upward social mobility. Feminists and advocacy groups for women's rights actively assume more leadership roles in both church and society.

Christian social witness, comparable to that of the early Protestant missionaries, did not disappear altogether despite the prevalence of the Prosperity Gospel and personal salvation. Minjung* theology is a response to the political and economic oppression of the "people" (*minjung*). In the Gospel of Justice Movement, Christian students, professors, and pastors repeatedly protest against oppressive social and economic policies of the government.

Charismatic early-morning prayer services that begin at 4 o'clock everyday are a typical Korean ritual practice influenced by Buddhism and Shamanism. Buddhist temples have early-morning services. Shamanism has highly emotional rituals before sunrise. In their own charismatic early-morning prayer services, Christians pray for the success and prosperity of their family, their particular church, and the nation, often in prayer houses in beautiful mountain settings.

The most important theological issues for the 19 million Christians in South Korea include bearing witness to the gospel as the good news of justice* and peace* in the midst of division between North and South Korea and huge economic disparities between the haves and the have-nots. How does preaching the Prosperity Gospel address the needs of the poor and the marginalized*? Do churches contribute to the cycle of poverty* through their implicit support of the present economic system? A second issue concerns the lack of interfaith dialogue, for exclusive claims of salvation ignore the many ties between Christianity and other religions in Korea. Finally, the numerous divisions in Korean Protestantism raise important issues concerning the relationship between Christian and cultural structures of authority.

Statistics: Population (2000): 46.8 million (M). Christians, 19 M, 40.8% (Protestants, 12.3 M; Roman Catholics, 3.7 M; independents, 2 M; marginal Christians, 0.8); Shamanists, 7.2 M, 15.6%; Buddhists, 7.2 M, 15.3%; new religionists, 7.1 M, 15.2%; Confucianists, 5.1 M, 11.1%. (Based on *World Christian Encyclopedia*, 2001.)

YUNG SUK KIM

Krapf, Johann Ludwig (1810–81), a German from Leipzig, the pioneer missionary to the east coast of Africa (1844) sponsored by the Church Missionary Society (CMS; see Anglicanism Cluster: In Africa: Eastern and Western Africa). After unsuccessful missionary work in Ethiopia*, he spread the Anglican faith to the interior from a base at the coastal town of Mombasa. Despite a great commitment to evangelization, Kraft and his colleague, Johannes Rebmann, were much more preoccupied with anthropological, language, and geographical documentation. Krapf's greatest achievement was laying the foundation for the development of Kiswahili. He wrote the *Kiswahili Grammar* and *Kiswahili Dictionary*, the first of their kind. Kiswahili has become the lingua franca of Eastern, Central, and Southern Africa and one of the official languages of the African Union; it is now spoken by at least 200 million people. It is taught in Western Africa at the University of Ghana, and a version of Microsoft Word exists in Kiswahili.

Krapf learned the designation of Mount "Kenya" (which he spelled "Kenia") from his Kamba guides and made it a European designation for the mountain and the region.

JESSE NDWIGA KANYUA MUGAMBI

Ku Klux Klan. See RACISM AND CHRISTIANITY CLUSTER.

Kulturkampf (German, "culture war"), Bismarck's legislation against the Roman Catholic Church in Germany (1871–87), which included governmental control of education*, withholding of financial assistance from the Church, and the expulsion of religious* orders. Bismarck soon found it prudent to make peace with the new pope, Leo* XIII; most of the laws were repealed by 1887.

Kuyper, Abraham (1837–1920), Dutch religious and political leader. After studying literature, philosophy, and theology at Leiden University (doctorate in theology, 1863), Kuyper was sent to his first parish at Beesd, where, in response to his parishioners' Calvinistic piety, he began to reassess the rationalistic modernism of his theological training, After assuming the pulpit in Amsterdam (1870), Kuyper protested anemic theological liberalism and sought to provide a genuine orthodox Calvinist alternative. Consequently, he was increasingly uncomfortable with the monarchy's role vis-à-vis the church and became a vociferous proponent of the separation of church* and state in the Netherlands. His influence further grew when he began writing for the *Herald* (1871) and then founded his own paper, the *Standard* (1872). He began a long political career (1874) as a member of the Second Chamber of Parliament (founding the Anti-Revolutionary Party, 1879) and prime minister (1901–5).

Ecclesially and theologically, Kuyer was responsible for the secession of the more historically Reformed faction from the Dutch Reformed Church (1886). He founded the Free University of Amsterdam (1880) to further combat the zeitgeist of philosophical and theological liberalism*. His perspectives on the comprehensive lordship of Christ, with a distinct emphasis on "common grace," deeply influenced Dutch Calvinism. **See also REFORMED CHURCHES.**

PAUL CHANG-HA LIM

Kyrgyzstan, Kirghizia. In Kyrgyzstan, Christianity has had a long but largely unwritten history. Under Mongol rule (13th–14th c.), probably building on an earlier Christian presence (6th c.), a metropolitan see of the Church* of the East existed in Nawakat, and the existence of Christian settlements west and southwest of Issy Köl Lake is attested to. Although Christianity took root among local populations, many nomadic peoples remained faithful to Shamanistic* traditions, which today still complement official (Sunni) Islam*, the dominant religion.

After the decline of central Mongol power and the conversion of local rulers to Islam, Christianity disappeared from the region, only to return with the advent of Russian power. Russian* and Ukrainian* Orthodoxy* remain important, although independence from Russia (1991) led to Russian out-migration. The descendants of German settlers make up the majority of the small Protestant (Lutheran, Baptist, Mennonite) and Roman Catholic communities in Kyrgyzstan. Religious freedom accompanying the fall of the Soviet Union encouraged Evangelical and Pentecostal missionaries from various national backgrounds to enter Kyrgyzstan and evangelize the local population. Their activities met with modest success, both among nominal Christians of Russian or German backgrounds and among those of Sunni Kyrgyz or Uzbek descent. This evangelization effort caused unrest, especially in the orthodox Muslim regions of the south, where official adherence to Islam grew considerably after the atheist policies of the Soviet government were abandoned. The government of Kyrgyzstan upholds freedom of religion, including freedom of conversion, although new communities focusing on converting Muslims are often wary of official registration and prefer to gather clandestinely in private homes.

Statistics: Population (2000): 4.7 million. Muslim: 60.8%; atheists and nonreligious, 27.9%; Christians, 10.4% (Orthodox, 7.7%, independents, 1.5%; Roman Catholics and Protestants, less than 1%). (Based on *World Christian Encyclopedia*, 2001.)

HELEEN MURRE-VAN DEN BERG

Kyriarchy. A term introduced by Feminist* theologians, "kyriarchy" designates a sociopolitical reality as hierarchically structured; it includes relations of class, race, and religion in addition to gender, indicating the multiple layers of oppression* and domination. **See also ANDROCENTRISM; PATRIARCHY AND CHRISTIANITY; SEXISM.**

Kyrie Eleison (Gk for "Lord, have mercy"), a brief prayer used in the liturgy in the East by the 4th c, It was soon adopted, without being translated, in the West.

Kyrios (Gk equivalent of Heb *Adonai*, "Lord"). In the Septuagint* (reflecting the usage in the HB), the term refers to God; in the Gospels, to Jesus, both as a counter to the *kyrios* (emperor = lord) in Rome and as a title of respect, "master."

L

Labadists trace their lineage to Jean de Labadie (1610–74), who proceeded from ministry as a Jesuit, to secular priest, to Reformed pastor/teacher in Geneva and Middleburg, where his separatist tendencies led to expulsion from the Dutch Synod. His disciples, organized into a separatist community of the regenerate, modeled a cloistered life that was authoritarian and pneumatic (charismatic*) in nature and included a community of goods. The principal community settled in Wiewert (Netherland), where it survived into the 18th c. Labadist communities briefly existed in Surinam and Maryland. Labadism provided a stimulus for Pietism* in the German territorial churches.

J. STEVEN O'MALLEY

Labarum, the standard designed by Constantine*, carried by a select group of soldiers. It was probably an adaptation of the cavalry standard, modified with the *Chi*-Rho* monogram surrounded by a wreath of gold and precious stones.

Labor, Theologies of. Theologies of labor describe the meaning of human work in light of God's* work as creator, redeemer, and sustainer of the world. Although the term came into prominent use in the 19th and 20th c., theologies of labor are as old as the varied Christian traditions themselves.

The Bible. Biblical understandings of labor vary, although each assumes the necessity and value of work. In Genesis work is portrayed as one of God's own activities (Gen 2:1–3; Exod 20:11) and one of God's intentions for human beings, as Adam is instructed to till the garden and maintain it (Gen 2:15). With its slavery* in a foreign land (Exod 5), however, Israel experiences the dehumanization of backbreaking work. A vision of humane work emerges in Israel's journey to the Promised Land: Sabbath* rest and the Jubilee* year, where debts are forgiven (Lev 25). In the NT, God's blessing of manual labor is exemplified by Jesus' identity as a carpenter (Mark 6:3) and reflected in Jesus' parables* and preaching about laborers. In John's vision of the New Jerusalem at the conclusion of the Scriptures, work does not disappear, but is redeemed in a city renewed by God (Rev 21).

Monasticism*. Monastic traditions within the church have long upheld the centrality of work in Christian life. Manual labor glorifies God and prevents sloth and laziness. The Rule of St. Benedict* (6th c.) exhorts monks to work at specified hours of the day, a tradition that continues in contemporary monasteries and is integral to modern understandings of the workday.

Vocation. Protestant Reformers Luther* and Calvin* argued for an expanded understanding of work as vocation*. In their eyes, *all* human labor necessary for survival and flourishing is the result of a divine calling. Labor is an expression of thanks to God. Some, such as Weber*, have argued that this vision of vocation assumes that industriousness is a sign of God's election* (see Protestant Ethic).

Labor as Co-creative. Several recent theologies of labor argue that human work adds worth to God's creation. In *Laborem Exercens*, John* Paul II extols work for its capacity to transform the world. When our work honors persons in constructing something new, we participate in the redemption* of the world. Echoes of this perspective can be found in the Charismatic*-inspired theology of Miroslav Volf, although each is also aware of the dehumanizing aspects of work in both capitalism and communism (see Economy and Christianity Cluster).

The Modern Labor Movement. In the midst of industrialization and urban poverty*, Leo* XIII's encyclical *Rerum Novarum* (1891; see Social Encyclicals) promoted the unionization of workers and the practice of collective bargaining. Pope John Paul's 1983 meeting with Lech Walesa, leader of the banned Polish labor union, signaled renewed engagement of Catholic social teaching with the labor movement. Latin American Liberation* theologians, however, have been the most forceful exponents of workers' rights. The "preferential* option for the poor" implies that the advancement of God's Kingdom* is evident in the struggles for justice* among the working classes. In Protestant thought, Rauschenbusch*

(1861–1916) represents a watershed. His expression of the "Social* Gospel" includes criticism of child labor and unrestrained corporate profit at the expense of workers. Contemporary Womanist* theologian Joan Martin incorporates remembrances of slavery* in her theological ethics and articulation of workers' rights.

The Legacy of Christian Reflection on Labor. In an age of globalization*, in which lower-class workers on one continent are subject to upper-class management decisions on another, it is essential for theologies of labor to address the ambiguity surrounding work. Even though labor is one way in which people can praise God, it frequently becomes a curse because of greed and injustice. One possibility for a vision of humane labor includes reflection on the doctrine of the Trinity*. In this doctrine, Christians address God's work for the world: labors that are *shared* among the triune persons, not "owned" by one at the expense of another; labors that celebrate the distinctiveness of each person's work and stress the interdependence of persons. In this divine economy*, we witness abundance, where gifts and work are given to all, rather than scarcity, where work is hoarded so that others go without. Another resource for reflection is Christian liturgy*. Etymologically, "liturgy" means "work of the people." In the Eucharist*, Christians encounter the risen Christ in bread baked with human hands and wine pressed by human labor. Remembering that the Communion* elements stem from the labor of agricultural workers (often migrant workers), the celebration of Communion links human labor to the work of Christ that sustains the world. DAVID H. JENSEN

Labyrinth (Gk), or maze (Old English), built in churches at least since the 4th c., is an intricate winding path moving toward a center; sometimes it splits into two or more paths, thereby causing confusion – an appropriation of the classical Greek tradition linked with Theseus's slaying of the Minotaur. In churches in North Africa (4th–5th c.), labyrinths had a Roman rectangular design oriented from west to east, symbolically moving from sin* to salvation*. In the medieval West, labyrinths were first drawn in manuscripts but were later built of stone in the floors of cathedrals and churches, opposite the altar*. In Chartres and its region, they were circular, whereas in Reims, they were octagonal; in both cases, they were partitioned into four quarters by the cross*.

As Craig Wright documented, each path advanced and then regressed, suggesting salvation's* ordered complexity, gradually overcoming sin and dissonance. At the center was a representation of the Minotaur (Satan); Christ enters the labyrinth, conquers Satan, and frees the imprisoned souls*. Worshippers, retracing with Christ the path that goes through sin and death, are freed from hell*, given new life, and empowered to move through purgatory* to heaven*. From the perspective of God's wisdom* and providence*, a seemingly complex and confusing path has order. Contemporary labyrinths, which emphasize the latter aspect, are aids to individual meditation and "centering."

Lacordaire, Henri-Dominique (1802–61). A French lawyer and skeptic, he converted (1824), entered a seminary, and was ordained (1827). Always sympathetic to liberal politics, he became a contributor to Lamennais's* *L'Avenir* (1830) and made with him a dramatic pilgrimage to Rome (1831) to ask the pope to support liberal politics; instead, they were condemned. In 1835 he began his *conférences* in Notre Dame. Seeing the religious* orders as the key to the revival of Catholicism in France, he joined the Dominican* order (1840), reintroduced it in France (1843), and organized the Dominican Third* Order of teachers (1852). He enthusiastically greeted the French Revolution (1848) and was elected a deputy to the National Assembly. After the coups of Louis Napoleon (1851, 1852), he concentrated on church life, but was frustrated by internal divisions in the Dominican order.

Lactantius (c250–c325), Christian educator and Apologist*. Born in Africa, where he studied rhetoric and literature and taught Latin rhetoric at Diocletian's* court in Nicomedia, he was converted to Christianity. When persecution broke out (303), he lost his post, left Nicomedia, and wrote his *Divine Institutes* (305–10), a defense of the Christian faith using non-Christian resources and arguing for tolerance. At the court of Constantine* in Trier (310), he formally presented the *Institutes*, one source of Constantine's policy of religious toleration (involving a new definition of "religion"). *On the Deaths of the Persecutors* (313–15) describes the gruesome deaths of several emperors, including Nero*, Domitian*, Decius*, and Diocletian*. **See also RELIGION AS A CONCEPT AND CHRISTIANITY.**

Lady, Our Lady. See MARY, THE VIRGIN, CLUSTER.

Lady Chapel, a chapel dedicated to Mary, usually at the east end of the apse.

Laicism, Laicity, Laical, pertaining to laity* rather than clergy* in the context of laicization*.

Laicization. Beyond its application to the laity, "laicity" acquired additional connotations in France*, its (former) colonies, and Latin America, where the term means strict separation of state and religion. Under such circumstances, "laicization" means legal secularization or disestablishment of religious institutions – especially schools, so as to free public education from religious interference. **See also ANTICLERICALISM; SECULARISM AND SECULARIZATION.**

1) Introductory Entries

Laity, Theology of. The term "laity" refers to the "people of God," specifically those who are neither clergy* nor religious*. A theology of laity is concerned with recovering the active role and responsibilities of laypersons in both the church and the world. Although there have been differentiated roles in the church since NT times, for its first 150 years Christianity did not always make a clear distinction between clergy* and laity. However, a distinction between Christian people as a whole and church leadership had emerged by the late 2nd c. This distinction became hard and fast by the fifth century, as the laity were gradually reduced to passive recipients of clerical ministrations. During the Middle Ages, the Lay Piety Movement was a protest or at least an alternative to this state of affairs (see the present cluster: Laity and the Lay Piety Movement During The Middle Ages).

Theologies of the Laity Emerging out of the Reformation. The Reformers further challenged the separation of clergy and laity. Luther* underscored the biblical teaching on the priesthood* of all believers (1 Pet 2: 9–10). He insisted that all Christians are priests by virtue of their baptism* and held that no other priesthood ought to be granted a separate ontological status. The Catholic* Renewal's reaction to the Reformers led to an even more restrictive view of the laity, eventually culminating in Pope Pius* X's declaration in *Vehementer Nos* (1906) that the church was an "unequal society" composed of two ranks, clergy and laity, the primary obligation of the latter being to docilely follow their pastors.

An Orthodox Theology of the Laity. Eastern Christianity's theology of the laity is grounded in the Divine* Liturgy. Since baptism* initiates the believer into the distinctive *ordo* of the Christian assembly, the laity are defined, not passively, but by their active participation in Christian worship (see the present cluster: Laity and Their Ministries in Eastern Orthodoxy).

Mid-20th-Century Theologies of the Laity. In the mid-20th c., a number of Catholic theologians sought an alternative to the largely passive and reductive theology of the laity dominant at the time. Karl Rahner* defined the laity by the full integration of the life of the world into their Christian existence. Marie-Dominique Chenu described the task of the laity as that of consecrating the world to Christ. Yves Congar was the first theologian to apply the threefold office of Christ – priest, prophet, and king – to the laity by virtue of their baptism. As priests the laity are called to make their ordinary lives a living sacrifice to God. As prophets the laity receive God's Word, penetrate its depths, apply it to their life in the world, and participate in handing it on in the life of the church. Their kingly office is fulfilled through their exercise of Christian service in the world. Congar's thought had a major influence on the Second Vatican* Council's more positive teaching on the laity. The Council saw the distinctive participation of the laity in the Roman Catholic Church's mission grounded in the "secular character" of the laity. This secular character recognized the typical (but not exclusive) orientation of the layperson to the world.

Post-Conciliar Theologies of the Laity. John* Paul II endorsed Vatican II's positive teaching on the laity, combining the Council's typological view (that the laity are secular given their ordinary involvement in the world) with its theological interpretation of the laity's secularity (that they embody in a particular way the Church's mission to the world). He also affirmed the possibility of lay ministry, even as certain official documents during his pontificate expressed concern that lay ministry might undermine priestly ministry.

After the Council, Congar questioned the helpfulness of the lay–clergy distinction, wondering whether it ought to be replaced by a focus on the relationship between community and ministries in service of the community. Finally, a number of contemporary theologians, particularly from the Two-thirds World, have questioned whether the laity–clergy language remains helpful. The entire church ought to be considered in terms of its secularity, i.e. its mission to be a sacrament* of the Reign of God in its mission to the world.

RICHARD R. GAILLARDETZ

Laity and the Lay Piety Movement during the Middle Ages, an outgrowth of the Gregorian Reform (11th c.; see Gregory VII, Pope). By attacking abuses by the clergy, and especially by urging the laity to boycott unworthy priests, the popes encouraged lay participation. A new wave of wandering preachers, of whom Norbert* of Xanten is the best known, encouraged poverty* in imitation of Jesus' earliest followers (Matt 10:9–10). Many viewed the Gospels as the true "rule*," and baptism* as authorizing poverty and simplicity, a welcome alternative to the wealthy church of the bishops and abbots. The movement took three forms: encouraging a worthy clergy; bypassing clergy and sacraments in mysticism*; and founding alternative organizations.

The most extensive new movement was that of the Waldenses*, who conflicted with the church because their laity preached. The Humiliati, centered in Milan, were acknowledged by the Roman Catholic Church on condition that they form three orders: clergy leading the canonical life, laity leading the religious* life in communities, and married persons with families. This pattern of three orders was adapted in the mendicant* orders, which were also part of the background of the "Radical Reformation," especially the Anabaptists*. The Beguines* and Beghards, in Northern Europe (13th c.), were similarly required to become third* orders of Franciscans* or Dominicans*.

EUGENE TESELLE

2) A Sampling of Contextual Views and Practices

Laity and Lay Catholic Organizations in Mexico. Since the colonial period, the laity in Mexico* have been organized in brotherhoods and sisterhoods according to their social class and status. Inspired by the social* encyclical *Rerum Novarum* (1891), these lay organizations were involved in social action through Catholic congresses, agricultural weeks, and social weeks, and initiated the National Confederation of Catholic Circles of Workers and other movements.

During the Mexican Revolution (1910), lay organizations – including the National Catholic Party, the Catholic Association of Mexican Youth, the Union of Catholic Women, the National Union of Parents, the National Confederation of Catholic Students, the National Confederation of Catholic Workers, the Congregations of Mary, the Nocturnal Adoration Movement, and the Knights of Columbus – became active defenders of Roman Catholicism against the anticlericalism of the government. They formed the National

League for the Defense of Religious Liberty. Together they defended their faith and their church against the "evil government" (1926–29) through the Popular Union, the Women's Brigades of Joan of Arc, and armed peasant groups called the Cristeros (who led armed resistance against the government).

To end the armed uprising of the Cristeros, in 1929 certain bishops went along with the government's policy of politically neutralizing lay organizations by coopting them into Mexican Catholic* Action (ACM). Some laypersons continued the armed fight, while others founded other movements (e.g. the Legion, the Base) that later became political parties. In 1939 even members of the ACM and of student movements participated in the formation of the antigovernment party, Political National Action.

In the 1940s, the bishops' pastoral action aimed at the Mexican elites led to the formation of new lay organizations, including the Social Union of Mexican Businessmen and subsequently Opus* Dei and Regnum Christi. Anti-Communist groups were also formed at that time. In the larger population, a notable movement was the Mexican Social Secretariat led by Fr. Pedro Velásquez, who later (1960s) headed the campaign "Christianity yes, Communism no" with the Conference of National Organizations; yet the focus of this campaign changed from anti-Communism to social initiatives. The bishops created the National Council of Laypersons, while civic groups such as the National Association of Women, Integral Human Development, and Pro-Life defended Catholic morality.

The Second Vatican* Council, the theology of liberation*, the Latin American Episcopal Conference (CELAM*, Consejo Episcopal Latinoamericano) in Medellín* (1968), and the massacre of students during the 1968 movement together drove a wedge between religious and civil authorities and between the organizations belonging to the Mexican Social Secretariat and those related to the Mexican Bishops' Conference. These events inspired the formation of Base* Ecclesial Communities (CEBs), the movement "Christians for Socialism," and the Movement of Christians Committed to the Popular Struggle (1980s) and its various centers supporting the poor. At the end of the 20th c., there were efforts to promote a dialogue between conservative and progressive lay movements. **See also CATHOLIC ACTION; MEXICO.**

RAQUEL PASTOR

Laity and Their Ministries in Eastern Orthodoxy. "One Christian is no Christian." Eastern Orthodoxy asserts that the entire body of the faithful, both clergy and laypersons, comprises the laity, or "people of God" (*Laos tou Theou*) (1 Cor 12: 27; Eph 2:22, 1 Pet 2:9). Every baptized member of the Orthodox Church is a complete member and "co-worker" with God in the process of the salvation* of the world (1 Cor 3:9), thus enjoying a full share in the royal (leadership), prophetic (teaching), and priestly (offering) ministry of Christ. There is a proper differentiation between the general priesthood of believers established through baptism* and the particular priesthood of the pastoral office. Unfortunately, tension exists in some places between the legitimate responsibilities of clergy and laypersons. Orthodox theologians identify the essential responsibilities of each while promoting the avoidance of the dangers of "clericalism" on the one side and of "congregationalism" on the other.

Every gift* is meant ultimately to be shared. Vocations* to intercessory prayer*, good works and charitable* acts, marriage*, family* life, monasticism*, formulating theology, education*, ministries of healing*, spiritual* direction, care for the earth (ecology*), mission* and witness, hymnography and music*, philanthropy and stewardship, advocacy for the vulnerable, administration, writing and publishing, iconography* and the arts, pastoral* care and leadership are but some of the many areas in which laypersons may serve today. At the heart of every vocation, lay and ordained, is the call to holiness*. Gregory* of Nyssa urges responding to this call by emulating "peacemakers*", "who reveal in their own lives the characteristics of God's activity. This work he also directs for you. Namely, to cast out hatred and abolish war, to exterminate envy and banish strife, to get rid of hypocrisy, and to extinguish from within resentment of injuries which linger in the heart" (*On the Beatitudes*, Homily 7).

KYRIAKI KARIDOYANES FITZGERALD

Laity and Their Ministries in Scandinavia: Parish Boards. Such boards were introduced in Scandinavia during the transformation of the Lutheran state churches into Folk* churches (from 1850). During the 17th and 18th c., a lay ministry as "assistant of the pastor" was introduced, but was never popular because the main task was limited to church discipline*. Parish boards (since 1862) have been very popular. Because the Swedish Church kept most of the property owned by the medieval Roman Catholic Church, the parish boards and the boards at the diocesan and national levels have been dominated by members of political parties. In Norway (from 1920) and especially in Denmark (from 1903), parish board members have been recruited from among church members of all kinds, including a great number of Culture* Christians. Should the boards be primarily administrative bodies, acting on behalf of the state and/or local society, or should their function be the ministry of all believers? This has been a long-standing debate. The legitimacy of the boards has also been questioned, since only 10–20% of church members participate in the elections. Nevertheless, the boards have catalyzed good relationships between local people and parish churches in Scandinavia.

HANS RAUN IVERSEN

Laity and Their Participation in Worship. In the NT, the church is called the people (*laos*) of God (1 Pet 2:9; cf. Exod 19:6). While the earliest church was highly participatory (cf. 1 Cor 12, 14, esp. 14:26), leadership came to be concentrated in the clergy*; the role of the laity was to say "Amen" or make brief responses. The Lay* Piety Movement in the Middle Ages emphasized that baptism* itself is a qualification for Christian leadership; Protestantism* emphasized the priesthood* of all believers and gave the clergy a functional rather than a hieratic status; and the Second Vatican* Council directed that the laity have a role in worship.

Lambeth Articles, an appendix (1595) to the Thirty*-nine Articles (1571). Calvinistic in theology, written by William Whitaker (Cambridge) to settle a controversy over predestination*, approved by John Whitgift, archbishop of Canterbury, and prelates gathered at Lambeth Palace, the articles were not sanctioned by Queen Elizabeth; thus their status was that of an "explanation" of points already established.

Lambeth Conferences are meetings of bishops* from throughout the Anglican Communion, convened by the archbishop of Canterbury of the time, usually at 10-year intervals. They originated with a request to Archbishop Longley from Canadian bishops in 1865 that the diocesan bishops be brought together from around the world to redress a South African situation that was seen as a scandal in the Communion. The bishop of Natal, William Colenso*, had been convicted of Modernist* "heresy" by an ecclesiastical court in South Africa, but had been confirmed in his episcopate by the Privy Council in London. Longley convened a conference of the Anglican bishops worldwide, though without Colenso, at Lambeth in 1867. Once gathered, the bishops discussed Natal and deplored Colenso's confirmation.

Thereafter, the conferences were convened on a regular basis, and the approximately 10-year cycle continued, except during the two world wars. The conferences are convened by the archbishop of Canterbury, at his own discretion. Until the formation of the Anglican Consultative Council (ACC) in 1971, it was arguable that the archbishop's invitation list for the Lambeth Conference alone constituted the Anglican Communion and decided its limits. Since 1968 the conferences have been widened to include first theological consultants, then the members of the ACC, and, in 1998, all serving bishops. Recent conferences have been serviced by the ACC office in London. In 1978 a conference of bishops' wives was held alongside the Lambeth Conference – and by 1998 this included a sprinkling of women bishops' husbands.

From the start, the concept of a "conference" was that it would not have conciliar powers, but would carry only the moral or spiritual weight of any findings the members reached. Thus the constitutional autonomy of the Anglican provinces was respected. Nevertheless, the conferences have at intervals set down important markers, such as the "Lambeth* Quadrilateral" (1888), the "Appeal to All Christian People" (1920), the launch of the Decade of Evangelism (1988), and a strong resolution on homosexual relationships (1998). This resolution anticipated a decade of widening splits in the Anglican Communion over the issue of homosexual relationships, precipitated most notably by the consecration in 2003 of an actively homosexual presbyter as bishop of New Hampshire in the Episcopal Church (USA). The archbishop of Canterbury, Rowan Williams, did not invite this bishop to the 2008 Lambeth Conference, but in several African and other provinces, the invitations to the other US bishops who had supported the New Hampshire appointment were viewed as provocatively divisive. Overall about 25% of those invited from around the world declined to attend; an informal alternative "Gathering for the Anglican Future Conference" was held in Jerusalem. At the Lambeth Conference itself, for the first time there was no plenary resolution; the focus was on fellowship, mutual support, and engagement.

BISHOP COLIN O. BUCHANAN

Lambeth Quadrilateral. Following an initiative by the American House of Bishops at the general convention in Chicago (1886), the 1888 Lambeth Conference set forth the "Lambeth Quadrilateral," which defined the minimum standard for Anglicans to adopt when uniting with other ecclesiastical bodies. The four "sides" of the Quadrilateral were as follows:

1. The Holy Scriptures* as the rule and ultimate standard of faith;
2. The Nicene* and Apostles'* Creeds as sufficient statements of the Christian faith;
3. The two sacraments – baptism* and the Lord's* Supper – ministered with unfailing use of Christ's words of institution and of the elements ordained by him;
4. The historic episcopate locally adapted.

Further Lambeth Conferences (1920, 1948, 1958, 1998) reaffirmed the Quadrilateral, exhibiting subtle variations without change of substance.

BISHOP COLIN O. BUCHANAN

Lamb of God (*Agnus Dei*), NT metaphor for Christ (John 1:29, Rev 5:12), linking him with the Passover* lamb (1 Cor 5:7; 1 Pet 1:19), suggesting that the cross* is a Passover sacrifice, Christ suffering without complaint (Isa 53:7). In Revelation* the Lamb who had been slain becomes powerful (5:6–14), unleashing vengeance (Chap. 6), conquering all enemies, becoming king of kings (17:14).

Lamennais, Félicité Robert de (1782–1854), priest (1816), leader of French Catholic conservatism, advocate of the separation of church* and state, but later advocate of liberalism and social reform. In his *Essay on Indifference in Matters of Religion* (1818–23), he developed an argument espousing the authority of the community as the source of truth – a position later condemned as "traditionalism*." He became an ally of the Ultramontanists*, advocating papal authority against the compromises of the Gallican* bishops and emphasizing the church's freedom from the state, which led him to champion freedom of religion and the press and other "liberal" causes. This sentiment was fomenting in other Catholic countries, especially Belgium* and Poland*, both of which were seeking political independence, and "Mennaisians" could also be found in Britain and the USA.

In 1831 Lamennais made a disappointing pilgrimage to Rome to ask the pope to heed the signs of the times, to which the pope responded by condemning civil liberties and the separation of church* and state. His *Words of a Believer* (1834), also condemned by the pope, looked beyond the church with an apocalyptic vision of transformation by God. Lamennais, asserting his individuality, drifted away from the church, although his liberal vision of a church freed from political ties was perhaps realized in the 1905 secularization* laws in France.

EUGENE TESELLE

Lamentabili, decree of the Holy Office (July 3, 1907), under Pope Pius* X, condemning 65 propositions drawn from the writings of the Modernists*. It was followed by the encyclical *Pascendi* (September 8, 1907), which also condemned the Modernists.

Lamentations, Book of, one of the Megilloth*, portrays a community enduring the devastating collapse of its life-defining worlds: the nation's defeat, the Temple's destruction, the monarchy's downfall, and the people's exile. Lamentations' five poems, with their rich diversity, are held together by the acrostic device in Chaps. 1–4 and the use of 22 verses (the number of letters in the Hebrew alphabet) in Chap. 5.

The Septuagint* ascribes authorship to Jeremiah*, but modern scholarship commonly rejects this tradition. The historical context of Lamentations was probably a time shortly after the Exile (587 BCE).

The theological traditions of David's divine chosenness and of Zion's inviolability are shattered by Israel's historical experience. The cause of the disaster remains in question. Is it the people's sin? God's punishment? The enemies' cruelty? All are parts of the theological explanation.

Personified as a bereaved mother, Jerusalem laments the loss of her children. This literary genre parallels Sumerian city laments. God is both a violent and destructive enemy (Chaps. 1–2) and a merciful God to whom suffering people address petitions (Chap. 3). Lamentations resists a simple resolution of this tension between the two views of God and defies any closing. The final prayer is open-ended, anticipating God's new initiative in the midst of human enigmatic suffering*.

Lamentations helps Judeo-Christian communities to give lament a place in their religious life. It has been used in Jewish worship at annual commemorations of the Temple's destruction (Tisha be Av), in Christian Lent and Holy Week liturgies, and in services following disasters.

ARCHIE CHI CHUNG LEE

Lampadion, female deacon* in the monastery of Macrina* in Annesi, Pontus, mid-4th c. She exercised leadership as "*protetagmene* of the choir of virgins," which may refer to liturgical leadership in the Divine* Office, but not to the position of the monastic superior (*hegoumene*), a position held by Macrina. When Macrina died, her brother, Gregory* of Nyssa, was uncertain about her burial wishes. An intimate of Macrina, Lampadion knew her wishes and Gregory followed them. She provided a good example of the probable roles of a female deacon in a women's monastery who was not superior. **See also DEACONESS.**

CAROLYN OSIEK

Lamps. The burning of lamps, later frequently replaced by candles, has been a widespread practice, symbolizing the light of revelation* and the human act of devotion.

Lancastrian Schools. Joseph Lancaster (1778–1838), a Quaker*, used more advanced students to teach beginning students from a nonsectarian perspective. The first Lancaster Schools were established in Chichester, 1810 for boys and 1812 for girls. Interest in this style of teaching spread, as indicated by the opening of a school by Czar Alexander in Kishinev (1824). Imprisoned for debt in England, Lancaster moved to Baltimore and published a book on his method (1821). He was invited to Caracas by Simón Bolívar, and the method spread in Latin America. After Bolívar's death, Lancaster went to New York, where he died in poverty. **See also EDUCATIONAL PRACTICES AS CHRISTIAN SERVICE CLUSTER: IN MEXICO.**

LAND, THEOLOGICAL PERSPECTIVES AND PRAXIS, CLUSTER

1) Introductory Entries

Land, Theological Perspectives and Praxis, in Eastern Orthodoxy See ECOLOGY AND CHRISTIANITY CLUSTER: EASTERN ORTHODOX PERSPECTIVE.

Land, Theological Perspectives and Praxis of Indigenous Peoples in India, Other Asian Countries, and North America. In the biblical tradition, the term "land" combines economics, politics, history, sociology, ethnicity, tradition, identity, and spirituality. "Land" refers to a special relationship between God, humans, and land. It is more than just a habitat or a political boundary; it is the basis of social organization, economic systems, and cultural identification. The creation stories maintain that land is not only sacred but also co-creator with the Creator: "Let the earth bring forth. . . ." (Gen 1:24). Together with land as a partner, God nurtures, sustains, and gives life to all beings. The land owns people and gives them an identity. The land is also a temple in and through which people become one with the sacred power. In the Jubilee* tradition, political, economic, and social justice* and liberation* also apply to the land.

Like the Israelites, many communities, particularly indigenous people around the world, affirm that it is the land that owns people and gives them an identity. Their religious systems, ceremonies, rituals, festivals, and dances are all centered on and deeply rooted in the land itself. Like the HB, indigenous people's myths* and rhetoric speak of the land as belonging to the Creator. Villages, clans, and individuals may own the land, but within the wider understanding that the land belongs to the Creator, the ultimate owner of land. Thus the land belongs to all equally, and all have equal rights and freedom to live on it, and no one can claim it exclusively for him- or herself, nor can one sell it as though it were one's exclusive property*. Land means survival and life. Land is people's identity and spirituality.

Christian theology has not given adequate attention to this important component of life. First, from a scientific perspective, the physical world was merely viewed as the sum total of many material components and energies. Humans believe they can understand, predict, and control everything in it. We are separate from, and think we are masters of, all created things, including the land (see Science and Christian Theology). Second, for several Christian theologians, the natural world is understood within a hierarchical structure, created by God. In this hierarchy of creatures, humans are the highest, having ultimate right over the land and its resources. Intellectual or rational nature is superior to the rest of creation. Theology is thus primarily about God and humans. The land is merely a "theater" for the actualization of God's plan of salvation. The land has no history and is not redeemed; it is merely used. Humanity alone is redeemed in Jesus Christ.

In the history of Christianity, different voices have communicated a theology of land. But these voices have remained muffled. In recent years, indigenous theologians, along with other theologians (including ecofeminists*, Process* theologians, and the "Justice, Peace and Integrity of Creation" Program of the World* Council of Churches) have sought to correct this dualistic*, anthropocentric, androcentric*, and hierarchical view of reality by developing a theological methodology from the perspective of land. Drawing on resources from their own traditions, some indigenous theologians (e.g. George Tinker, Yangkahao Vashum) have articulated a central and crucial theological perspective in a quest for justice and liberation from the perspective of "land." Since culture, religion, history, spirituality, and even the Supreme Being cannot be envisioned without "land" or "space," "land" is not merely a justice issue alongside other justice concerns. It is foundational to a theological self-understanding out of which liberation, justice, and peace will naturally and necessarily flow (see Liberation Theologies Cluster: In North America: Native American.) Poverty*, oppression*, ethnic conflicts, and identity issues cannot be understood so long as they are not related to the integrity of the land. Justice toward the land is the key to liberation, human dignity, and fullness of life.

When justice is present in the land, the fields and forests and all living things will dance and sing for joy (Ps 96: 11–13). Authentic liberation can be experienced only in harmony with the land. This is the context for considering and taking part in struggles for economic* justice against the exploitation of humans, for human dignity and human* rights against the political oppression* of humans, and for peace and justice in relations between humans and nature against the industrial destruction of the environment. Issues concerning identity, hunger, disease, illiteracy, culture, and religion are intrinsically related to the land. This methodological and theological priority of justice toward the land is essential not only because of the "earth-centered" worldview and tradition of indigenous people, but because of the present-day ecological crisis and misuse of resources that threaten the survival of many people around the world. **See also ECOLOGY AND CHRISTIANITY CLUSTER.** WATI LONGCHAR

Land, Theological Perspectives and Praxis

2) A Sampling of Contextual Views and Practices

Land, Theological Perspectives and Praxis, in Africa. Land politics is a sensitive issue in Africa owing to its political, economic, and sociocultural connotations. Colonial and postcolonial wars were fought primarily over land and boundaries. An infrequently discussed issue is the relation of land to economic* justice* pertaining to mineral wealth. Other issues related to land politics are gender imbalance and racial and class discrimination regarding landownership. Instead of treating land as a gift from God, all land has been converted into a commodity for a few in Africa. The history of land dispossession is simple. Before the arrival of the European colonialists in the 16th c. (indigenous black Africans had land. They had socioeconomic systems and rules in place that governed their land administration and conservation. Now many indigenous black Africans are dispossessed and landless, while the descendants of Europeans own vast pieces of land and mineral wealth therein, such as gold and diamonds.

Role of Labor and Survival. In many biblical traditions, Christians who participate in the liberation* struggle in Africa often refer to the story of Naboth's vineyard (I Kgs 22:1–19). The land that used to be a resource for the livelihood and sustenance of families who occupied the African land from time immemorial was taken away and converted to produce commodities and is accessible to only a few elite landowners. Indigenous Africans who used to own land collectively (a common practice) were turned into landless farmworkers. In view of this continuing land dispossession, the African Churches are faced with the challenge of standing in solidarity with landless poor while wrestling with its own dual identity crisis. Indeed, most often the churches are both "landed" (the churches of landowners) and "landless" (without land themselves and churches of landless people). The churches seek to amplify the voice of the voiceless and strengthen the resilience of local landless communities against dispossessing and oppressive forces.

Communal Dimension. The African concept of landownership can be likened to a circle of seated people (Zulu, *indilinga*) in which no one is above another and all are treated and viewed as equal custodians of this gift of land from God or ancestors* and as having an equal duty to preserve the land for the next generation(s). Thus land is designated not as a possession but as an "inheritance"; the connection between the social unit and the land is inalienable and endures to perpetuity.

Although most land dispossessions occurred through the barrels of guns, most dispossessed communities in Africa now hope to have their land restored to them, although through the market that prioritizes individual ownership and profit making (e.g. South Africa's "willing seller/willing buyer" approach to land reform).

As most societies or communities in Africa are patriarchal and landownership is governed through customary laws, gender imbalances are prominent. While customary laws can provide poor households with greater access to land and security, they too are in need of reform. In many African countries, women are prevented from owning and inheriting land, because their property rights are often tied to their social relations with men. For example, some customary land registrations require women to receive authorization from their husbands to independently acquire a land title. This is especially problematical for women who are unmarried, widowed, or divorced, and can limit women's ability to grow food for their families. Strengthening women's rights will require working with both state and customary laws.

Ecological Issues. According to the indigenous African concept of relationship between humankind and land, people do not own land but rather belong to the land. Those who use the land are expected to respect it and the One who has given it as a gift. The use of harmful agricultural chemicals such as pesticides and genetically modified seeds is generally unacceptable in African traditional agricultural practices. A recent spate of exclusive housing development projects on arable land is becoming an issue of concern among many land activists, as projects of this type result in a scarcity of arable land.

Land is a gift from God that can be used to reconcile divided communities, restore dignity, and bring about sustainable development and livelihood to the millions of marginalized, landless, and poor indigenous Africans. **See also ECOLOGY AND CHRISTIANITY CLUSTER.**

THULANI NDLAZI

Land, Theological Perspectives and Praxis, in Latin America. In the theologies of the global peripheries, especially in Brazil* and other Latin American countries, land is one of the central themes of a spirituality* closely tied to the struggle for life and to the defense of human* rights and of territories threatened by the globalizing economical model.

Land as a Site of Exploitation, Banishment, and Suffering in Latin America. In Latin America, colonization* under the cross and sword made the land a site of exploitation. Colonization followed the "civilizing logic" that exploits social classes, creates poor and oppressed people, and exploits and marginalizes territory and nature, exhausting the land's resources. The way of life and the cultures of the original peoples were disrupted and corrupted by the wholesale slaughter of people and animals. Land as a site of banishment and suffering was reinforced by the massive kidnapping of African peoples to be used as slaves in the Americas.

Land as Mother Earth, the Site of life, in Latin American Traditions. By contrast, according to the religions of the original peoples, the land is "Mother Earth" (Pachamama in the Aymara and Quechua languages, Olokuadule in the Kuna language, or Papa Egoró in the Embera language), a sacred and alive territory, the source of life, which cannot be bought or sold and which is inherited from the ancestors*. The land is the site of life. It unites the visible with the invisible world, the community with its ancestors, and is the root and support of culture*. In the Guarani tradition (see Paraguay), this experience is translated into the search for the Land without Evil (Terra Sem Males), a search that embodies both resistance and utopia. Through the "*tore* ritual," the Kiriri indigenous people of northeastern Brazil celebrate the struggle to defend the territory (Mother Earth) against large economic projects, affirming the land as holy ground where the "enchantments" and all knowledge live.

In the Afro-American religions in Brazil, *axé,* the sacred power, is contained and transmitted in the elements and substances of the natural world, animal, vegetal, or mineral, related to each other either through water – sweet or salty – or through land and forest. Nana, the *orixa* (intermediary between the Creator and creatures) of land and water, is the humid womb that contains all forms of life.

The Afro-Brazilian communities that have survived from the time of the *quilombolas* (descendants of slaves that escaped from plantations) find in their religion a vital source of resistance and struggle for the land they have occupied since their struggle against slavery*.

The Land and Latin American Theology. Throughout the history of Latin America, many Christians (e.g. Bartolomé de las* Casas, Antonio Valdivieso, Toribio de Mogrovejo) struggled for the rights of the peoples of the land; today many Christians, both men and women, are dying once again as they defend "terra," a term that in the Romance languages means both "land" and "earth" (as well as "soil"). For Latin* American theology, the conflict between possession of the land (terra) and life on earth (terra) is highly significant.

In Latin America, the deepest motivation of those who struggled for independence and took part in social revolutions was always the defense of the liberated land; there was strong participation by farmers and landless farmworkers. Such resistance and liberation movements shaped a Liberation theology that goes beyond national and property* issues. This theology affirms that the land is a collective household: the land of God, the land of brothers and sisters. The Christian farmers' popular theology redefines ways of living on earth (terra) and with the land (terra); it is a religiosity associated both with the land and with the farmers'

Land, Theological Perspectives and Praxis

struggle, their rituals of resistance, and their celebrations of the land. Celebrating terra is both an expression of Latin American spirituality* and a form of revolutionary struggle. God is revealed both in the created world (terra as the earth) and in the struggle for the land (terra as the land that people farm as a means of survival). In its perspective on the land/earth (terra), Latin American Liberation* theology combines the theologies of creation*, of nature, and of social struggle.

Rereading the Teaching of the Bible about the Land in Latin America. From the perspective of Latin America, one can readily appreciate the way the biblical story of Genesis plays on the different connotations of the terms for "earth," "land," and "soil" (Heb *eretz, adam*), since "terra" has all these connotations. Land or earth is created by God and creates in relation to God's work. From the land (terra as soil, as part of creation), we are created; through the land, we re-create ourselves in the multiple forms of sustenance and pleasure, occupation and territory, as the traditions of the original peoples of Latin America also affirm.

"Land" is always more than the land that a farmer cultivates. Land places a diversity of beings in relation to each other: water and sky, trees and minerals, animals and vegetation (Gen 1). As a condition of human existence, the ordering of land is a part of the organization of the human family through the vital materiality of productive and reproductive work (Gen 2). Yet as it is appropriated by humans, the land becomes and is the site of conflicts and projects (Gen 3), of disputes among human groups and among models of economic occupation (Gen 4), including that which distinguishes between city and country. This conflict over land occupation motivates and explains the human drama of death, revenge, and disaster. As the site of human activities, the land is the place in which human groups search for living and working space.

Deserts, valleys, and mountains are subjects of mythical and historical narratives in the biblical tradition, just as other traditions associate deities with ecogeographical features. Shaped by competing economic projects, the land appropriated by empires becomes a site of oppression and exploitation of human labor (Exod 1), while enslaved groups organize themselves and go in search of the Promised* Land (Exod 3). These migratory waves, stimulated by hunger, war, and military and economic control of the land, are also processes of organization and resistance of social groups against hegemonic powers and processes of struggle to achieve other models of occupation of the land, and of labor and power.

As a promise and as a project, the land binds together different ethnic groups, forges societies (Josh 9), and shapes social structures and forms of labor, distribution, and consumption. Territorial control, privileged economic relations, agricultural production, and access to water, wood, and minerals (1 Sam 8) reflect the role of land in tribal, national, and imperial conflict. Absent from metaphysical, essentialist, and idealistic theological systems, because it is "merely material," a redeemed land is nevertheless prophesied in eschatological and futurist visions.

Consequently, in Latin American popular Christianity, the land is a reason for and a promise of life; it organizes the faithful around the defense of a territory and a model of communal occupation, a life to be fully accomplished in eschatological time. The land articulates the conflict of classes and the ecological struggle through the organization of peasant movements in the defense of territories, in the occupation of lands controlled by the great landed estates of the latifundium and agribusiness, depriving traditional populations of land and reducing them to the status of landless farmworkers or slave laborers.

Associated with the feminine "mother earth," the struggle for the liberation of land and water*, the defense of the environment, and agro-ecology are also a struggle against patriarchal* and sexist* violence and against the domination of women that is extended to the land through a model of development that subordinates the reproduction of life to progress and profit. In sum the popular reading of the Bible in Latin America reinstates the land as God's promise, by interpreting it from the perspective of the experience of the Exodus and from that of the Jesus* movement and its concern for the oppressed. **See also ECOLOGY AND CHRISTIANITY CLUSTER.**

NANCY CARDOSO PEREIRA

Landázuri Ricketts, Juan (1913–97). Archbishop of Lima, Peru (1955–90), and president of the Peruvian National Episcopal Conference (1955–88), he played a decisive role in transforming a conservative church into a progressive and pluralistic one. Born in Arequipa, he entered the Franciscan* order. As archbishop he followed a policy of diversity within unity. He reinforced the social orientation of the Roman Catholic Church and worked in harmony with the reformist military government of General Velasco (1968–75). Named a cardinal in 1962, he played important roles at Vatican II and the episcopal conferences of Medellín* (1968) and Puebla (1979). **See also PERU.**

JEFFREY KLAIBER, SJ

Landmarkism, a movement originating in the Southern* Baptist Convention in the mid-19th c., but eventually breaking away from it. Its distinctive ecclesiology (sometime called "Baptist successionism"; cf. Apostolicity and Apostolic Succession) claims that the Baptist churches, with their believer* baptism and local congregational* church government, are the NT church, and that its continuity (though usually concealed) has been maintained through the centuries.

Langton, Stephen (c1155–1228), archbishop of Canterbury; born in Lincolnshire, studied and taught in Paris. Langton was influential as a preacher, theologian, moralist, and biblical commentator. He delineated the chapter divisions of the Bible (still in use with some modifications), prepared a standard text of the Vulgate*, and wrote the hymn *Veni Sancte Spiritus*. He was created a cardinal, then appointed archbishop of Canterbury by Innocent* III (1206–7). When King John kept Langton from occupying his see, the pope excommunicated the king and placed England and Wales under an interdict* (1208–14); this was ended by John's submission, after which the kingdom was made a papal fief, an act Langton opposed. He supported the barons who sought to reaffirm English traditions concerning the government and the church, but he also functioned as a mediator when John was forced to sign the Magna Carta (1215). The pope criticized this document as a threat to kingship and to the Fourth Crusade*, and suspended Langton for declining to excommunicate the barons (1215–18). Restored by a new pope and with a new king, Langton initiated improvements in education, discipline, and pastoral care, implementing the decrees of the Fourth Lateran* Council of 1215. In a dramatic confirmation of the freedom of the church, he presided over the transfer of the relics of his predecessor, the martyred Becket*, on the 50th anniversary of his death (1220).

EUGENE TESELLE

Laodicea, city in the Phrygian Lycus Valley, Asia Minor. (1) Mentioned in Colossians*, indicating that a church had been established there during Paul's missions; (2) one of the "seven churches" in Rev 3:14.

Lapsed (Lat *lapsi*, "the fallen"), Christians who denied the faith during persecution*; readmitting them to the church became a serious issue during the Decian* persecution (see Cyprian).

Las Casas, Bartolomé de (1484–1566), a Spanish missionary, nicknamed "the Apostle of the Indies" for his indefatigable defense of the human* rights and dignity of indigenous peoples. He was the first European to denounce the economic, political, and cultural injustice of colonialism* in Latin America.

Born in Seville and trained as a lawyer, Las Casas traveled to Hispaniola (1502), where he witnessed much Spanish brutality against the native people. After studying for ordination in Rome (1507), he returned to the Caribbean in order to resist exploitation by the conquistadors. He celebrated his first Mass in the Americas (rather than in Spain) in 1510, symbolizing his commitment to combating injustice. Las Casas forsook his own ownership of "Indians" and his business holdings (1514), decrying the systemic evil of colonization and oppression of the indigenous peoples – including the *encomienda** system (forced labor in return for protection and instruction in the Christian faith). Although he tried to help the indigenous peoples, he failed to oppose the importation of slaves from Africa. He carried out an unsuccessful experiment, a "benign colony" (Venezuela, 1519–22, a precursor of the egalitarian "Jesuit reductions*," where numerous natives lived together with Jesuit* clergy) designed to protect native peoples from the Spanish settlers. Following this failure, Las Casas joined the Dominicans* (1522), continuing his role as defender of indigenous people and making several trips to the Spanish royal court for this purpose.

His articulate defense of "Indian" human rights in debates – especially, against Juan Ginés de Sepúlveda's claim that indigenous people were inferior beings (1550, Valladolid, Spain) – complemented his written work chronicling both the native peoples' civility and humanity and the Spaniards' cruelty and depravity: *The Devastation of the Indies: A Brief Account*; *The Only Way of Drawing All Peoples to the True Religion*; *In Defense of the Indians*; and the *History of the Indies*.

PAUL CHANG-HA LIM

Last Supper, Jesus' last meal with his disciples on Thursday evening, at which the Eucharist* was instituted. **See also LORD'S SUPPER.**

Lateran Councils, four general councils of the Western, Latin Church held in Rome in 1123, 1139, 1179, and 1215. As a part of the medieval papal revolution, they were different from the collaborative eight general councils of the first millennium under imperial leadership.

Lateran I (1123) ratified the Concordat of Worms*, allowing secular lords to invest bishops with signs of civil authority, making the selection of bishops relatively independent, and reserving for church officials the investing of symbols of spiritual authority. Lateran II (1139) focused on heresy*, which would be of even greater concern at later medieval councils. Lateran III (1179) legislated that cardinals* play the leading role in papal elections and permitted a two-thirds majority, not unanimity, for election. The council singled out the Cathars*, or Albigensians*, as heretics.

Lateran IV (1215) was the largest and most prestigious of the medieval councils, touching nearly every issue impacting medieval society and religion. The council upheld Lateran III's grant of the crusader's* indulgence* and privileges to those who fought heretics and stipulated penalties for recalcitrant heretics – including unlicensed, wandering preachers – and for secular authorities and laypeople who failed to root them out. A bishop who failed to investigate and excommunicate heretics was subject to deposition. The council required Jews* and Muslims* to dress distinctively (without providing specifics), prohibited Jews from serving in public office, and mandated that Jews remain indoors on Palm* Sunday. Lateran IV was the first general council to use the scholastic word "transubstantiation"* to describe the ancient Catholic belief that bread and wine were fully and substantially changed into Christ's Body and Blood. It mandated what came to be called "Easter duty": the confession of sins and reception of the Eucharist* at least once a year. Unknowingly anticipating Luther's* criticisms, Lateran IV cautioned against the sale of indulgences* and false relics*.

CHRISTOPHER M. BELLITTO

Lateran Treaty (1929), concordat* in which the Kingdom of Italy* recognized the Vatican City as a sovereign state (the Holy See* similarly recognized Italy, giving up all claims to Rome and the former Papal* States). Its provisions favoring the Roman Catholic Church were significantly modified in 1984.

Latin, Ecclesiastical, began to appear in early Christian societies between the 2nd and 4th c. Some regard ecclesiastical Latin as a decadent form of classical Latin; however, recent scholarship has acknowledged its linguistic sophistication. Differences between classical and ecclesiastical Latin arose from several factors, including the ecclesiastical need for a larger and more precise theological vocabulary and a desire to make the translation of Greek Christian sources, particularly inspired texts, more literal than was possible with classical Latin. The pronunciation system of ecclesiastical Latin, as primarily preserved within the Roman Catholic Church, is somewhat different from that of classical Latin.

EDWARD N. PETERS

Latin America, History of Christianity in. See HISTORY OF CHRISTIANITY CLUSTER: IN LATIN AMERICA.

Latin American Literature (Spanish) and Christianity. Christianity has always been present in Latin American literature, beginning with the accounts of those who chronicled their adventures in the Indies, through the songs and poems of Juana Inés de Asbaje* y Ramírez (1651–95, Mexico), to the most recent hymns by Ernesto Cardinal. But the literary presence of Christianity is more a cultural environment than a biblical/theological reflection or testimony.

In the 19th c., historic novels were written, especially for the Catholic and ecclesiastic culture of the colonial capitals: Mexico*, Lima (Peru*), and Cartagena de Indias (Colombia*). Some featured priests' sermons or the excesses of the Inquisition*, e.g. *Monja y casada, virgen y mártir* (1868, Nun and married woman, virgin and martyr) by the Mexican Vicente Riva Palacio (1832–96) and *El Pecado Del Siglo* (1869; The sin of the century) by the Mexican José Tomás de Cuellar (1830–94). Others portray traditional customs; e.g. *Peruvian Traditions* by

Ricardo Palm (1833–1919) recounts the founding of convents and the adventures of members of religious orders (nuns, monks, brothers) in their missionary work, and tells the stories of infamous excommunications. Other novels, e.g. *Cumandá, o, un drama entre salvajes* (Cumandá, or a drama among savages) by the Ecuadorian Juan León Mera (1832–94), sought to portray Christianity, and specifically Roman Catholicism, as a religion that was superior to others.

In the 20th c., Christian themes are more visible in poetry, e.g. in the poems of the Chilean Gabriela Mistral (1889–1957) and the Peruvian Cesar Vallejo (1892–1938), who express their religious experience at times in mystical* ways and at times in deeply rebellious ways. Novels are infused with the traditions and beliefs of Christendom*, especially its dark sides, support indigenous traditions, and denounce the many methods of evangelism or mission* that fail to respect indigenous people, their religious customs, and their gods. More recent novelists denounce the ecclesiastical institution, its rigor, fanaticism, and intolerance; they are often centered on the figure of the priest, who navigates among diverse political factions, seeking among them his evangelical vocation. The works of the Guatemalan Miguel Angel Asturias (1899–1974), from the *Leyendas de Guatemala* (1930; Legends of Guatemala), which describes Mayan civilization before the Spanish Conquest, to his largely autobiographical last novel, *Viernes de dolores* (1972, Friday of Our Lady of Sorrows) are good examples. Among the works of the Mexican Agustín Yañez (1904–80), *Al filo del agua* (1947; *The Edge of the Storm*, 1963) is particularly notable for its allusions to biblical texts. Another such book is *El Cristo de espaldas* (1952, The backward Christ) by the Colombian Eduardo Caballero Calderón (1910–93).

In Latin American literature in Spanish, there are works that reflect Liberation* theology as well as distinctive works, such as the brilliant novel *El Signo del Pez* (1987, The sign of the fish) by the Colombian Germán Espinosa (1938–2007), which re-creates the world of Jesus of Nazareth. **See also BRAZILIAN LITERATURE (PORTUGUESE), CHRISTIANITY IN.**

CARMIÑA NAVIA VELASCO

Latin American Theologies. In thinking about Latin American theologies, it is fundamental to keep in mind the cultural complexity and dynamism of this subcontinent, in which religiosity is both hidden and manifest, both within and outside the prevailing Roman Catholicism. Many scholars in Mexico, the Caribbean, and Central and South America question the very concept of "Latin America," for it often obscures the diversity of indigenous languages and faith expressions, the African spiritualities, and the non-Iberian European and Asian influences.

The contours of early Latin American theologies can be glimpsed paradigmatically in the work of Felipe Waman Puma de Ayala (born c1550 in Peru*) and Sister Juana Inés de Asbaje* y Ramírez (b1651 in Mexico*). They were not officially theologians of the church, but both made implicit and explicit use of theological categories. Their works exhibit three features that repeatedly appeared in later theologies: (1) a fundamental awareness of the tragedy that faith in a God of justice* can be utilized to sanction injustice; (2) the ability to carry out theological reflection on the margins of hegemonic discourses; and (3) an aesthetic creativity not limited to deductive reasoning. Inasmuch as their writings allowed them to transcend a given place and time, they came to occupy a paradoxical place of relative symbolic privilege, as is the case with those contemporary Latin American theologians whose works are published and distributed beyond their immediate circles. Most Latin American theologians, however, are virtually unknown, although they produce theology in many forms: as academic articles and monographs, but also as pamphlets, Bible studies, sermons, radio programs, Weblogs, plays, and artwork. In Clodovis Boff's words, these theologies are at once professional, pastoral, and popular. Ideological and financial obstacles affect the circulation of theological knowledge, although valiant attempts are being made to socialize theological production, as in the work of the *Teologanda* collective led by Virginia R. Azcuy, which has been mapping out and making known "theologies made by women" in all areas of the subcontinent.

Early Latin American Liberation theologians, both Protestant and Roman Catholic, such as Rubem Alves, Hugo Assmann, Gustavo Gutiérrez, José Míguez Bonino, Leonardo Boff, and Jon Sobrino continue to exert an influence. Their most significant contributions include the insistence on the centrality of the poor* for God; the use of the social sciences as a tool for interpreting reality; the epistemological weight of the theologian's social location; the development of a liberating biblical hermeneutic accessible to all; the centrality for Christology of Jesus' earthly ministry (see Christologies Cluster: In Latin America); and an insistence that the church needs to withdraw from the pursuit of privilege and engage in the prophetic denunciation of injustice. Two strands have coexisted in these theologies from the beginning: the frank celebration of the symbols and practices of popular* religiosity (Juan Carlos Scannone) and the need for a "liberation of theology" that exercises ideological* suspicion, especially of its own idolatrous* tendencies (Juan Luis Segundo). Protestant theologies have tended to be more in tune with the latter; however, Pentecostalists* and Charismatics* continue to incorporate and transform aspects of popular religiosity, in particular those that have to do with bodily healing*.

The "new way of doing theology" proposed by the first Protestant and Roman Catholic Liberation theologians required its practitioners to pay close attention to liberating praxis and to the "signs of the times;" this necessarily led to the diversification of the movement. In a memorable 1977 conference in Mexico City, James Cone demanded where the people of color were among Latin American theologians, whereupon Dora Valentín stood up and added, "And where are the women of all ethnicities among the theologians?" In response, one might mention the feminist liberationist method of Elsa Támez, the indigenous theologies of Eleazar Hernández and Aiban Wagua, the Afro-Latin American feminist hermeneutics of Silvia Regina de Lima Silva and Maricel Mena López, and the ecofeminist moral theology of Ivone Gebara.

Not all theological strands in Latin America belong to the genealogy of Liberation theology: in many Roman Catholic seminaries, neo-Thomism* continues to be the most influential voice; Evangelicals and Pentecostals often give priority to individual piety, while others (e.g. Fraternidad Teológica Latinoamericana) draw on Anabaptist* and Pietistic* traditions to arrive at a theology focused on holistic mission*. Still, the questions placed at the heart of the theological discussion by Liberation theologians cannot easily be ignored: all forms of Latin American theology face the challenge of the earth itself crying out for justice*. What Jon Sobrino calls "honesty with reality" is demanded by the complexities of a subcontinent where hope* and despair, natural resources and an unequal distribution of wealth, land* and landlessness, fertility and desertification, life and death continually pressure theologians to come to grips with the palpable implications of their faith commitments. **See also** **LIBERATION THEOLOGIES CLUSTER: LIBERATION AND THEOLOGY; PREFERENTIAL OPTION FOR THE POOR.**

NANCY ELIZABETH BEDFORD

Latino/a Theologies, an articulation of Hispanic theologies that emerged during the 1960s. Hispanics, owing to their location in the United States, are heirs of indigenous, African, Asian, and various European cultures, including that of medieval Catholic Spain. They are white, black, and everything in between. They are Catholics, Protestants, worshippers of Orisha (African quasi-deities), Jews, Muslims, atheists, spiritualists, and followers of Amerindian religious traditions. There is no typical Hispanic, no normative, unifying, or monolithic Latino/a theology; there is a plurality of Latino/a theologies related by a common theological methodology.

Hispanic religious identity has been described in terms of *mestizaje* (mixture; see Mestizos). For US Latinos/as, the borderlands are not solely a geographic location; they are also a social location of *mestizaje* in which Latinos/as attempt to construct their theological perspectives. Because of the US cultural views of the "nature of race," both Hispanic/Latino/a Catholics and Protestants find abuse and neglect within their own denominations. The *comunidad* (community) serves as a resource to counter this abuse, becoming an important unifying factor in the new *mestizaje* in the USA. Operating from the perspective of exiles, aliens, and outsiders, Latino/a theologies develop into a study of God from the margins of Euro-American power and privilege. Their theological methodology seeks "truth" as an ongoing process called *teología de conjunto* (collaborative theology), the coming together of the community of believers to work collectively in seeking theological precepts.

The spirituality* of Latinos/as is a dynamic grassroots religion practiced in *lo cotidiano* (the everyday); it stresses home devotional practices, such as worshipping at home altars, praying to saints, or taking *promesas* (vows). This popular* religion (devotional piety), a part of the shared cultural roots emerging from different traditions, is where individual and communal feelings find religious symbols and actions that make sense of the world and provide a concrete point of contact with the Divine in the midst of daily life.

Latina Feminist and Mujerista theologies follow a similar theological methodology with, in addition, concerns for the sexism* prevalent in Hispanic culture and the lack of race and class analysis by North American feminists.

The ethos of the cultural and social contexts of the Latino/a community affects what is theologically important to Hispanics. Their cultural context shapes popular religious manifestations. In their social location, the concepts of family* (an important social institution) and justice* (with praxis, action, as the central tenet) powerfully inform what the *comunidad* deems to be important. **See also FEMINIST THEOLOGY CLUSTER: IN NORTH AMERICA: LATINA** and **IN NORTH AMERICA: MUJERISTA.**

MIGUEL A. DE LA TORRE

Latitudinarianism, the name applied in 17th-c. England to Anglican clergy who conformed with episcopacy and the Book of Common* Prayer but regarded them as matters of human ordering rather than divine command. Calling these "things indifferent" (see Adiaphora, Adiaphorists), they affirmed much "latitude" in applying the church doctrines. Among the Cambridge* Platonists, to whom this label was originally given, this stance was linked with scientific* thought and rationality, easily lending itself to indifferentism or skepticism and to individualism.

Latria, the Latin term for "worship," based on the Greek; the worship of God alone (contrast with *Dulia*).

Latter-day Saints, Church of Jesus Christ of. The Church of Jesus Christ of Latter-day Saints emerged in the 19th c. out of a Restoration* rather than a Reformation* ideology. Joseph Smith* organized the Latter-day Saints in Fayette, New York, in 1830, shortly after he produced the Book of Mormon*, which, he claimed, he received from the angel Moroni and translated from an ancient record.

Latter-day Saints under Smith's Leadership. Smith reported that God the Father and Jesus Christ appeared to him, telling him that all Christian churches had departed from the truth and that he should join none of them. The Book of Mormon* offers evidence of Smith's stature as God's designated prophet, empowered to effect a complete restoration of gospel truths, priesthood authority, and church organization.

Smith gathered converts in Kirtland, Ohio (1831–38), and other locations in Missouri (1831–38), and later (1839) transformed the village of Commerce, Illinois, into the thriving church center of Nauvoo, a virtually independent theocratic city-state. Assisted by a "Quorum of Twelve Apostles," Smith led a people and a city teeming with refugees expelled from Missouri and converts from the East and from England. Mormons administered local courts, municipal offices, and a powerful militia.

Latter-day Saints under Young's Leadership. Smith was murdered in 1844, and most Saints rallied around Brigham Young*, who led thousands of exiles to the Salt Lake Valley. They colonized the West, practiced polygamy* from 1852 to the turn of the century, and swelled with converts; they continued to immigrate to Utah until the "gathering" stopped around 1900.

Latter-day Saints Today and Their Theological Views. Envisioned as the final incarnation of Christ's church, the Latter-day Saints preach the centrality of Christ and his atoning* sacrifice in the soul's* progression from pre-mortal existence through earthly incarnation and toward celestial glory. Through faith in Christ's atonement and by obedience to his laws and ordinances, such exalted men and women, married or "sealed" together for eternity, become like God, enjoying eternal life and a continuing posterity. In addition to the Book of Mormon*, the Doctrine and Covenants and the Pearl of Great Price contain revelations and ancient writings revealed to Smith and his successors and, along with the Bible, constitute the Latter-day Saints' canon of scripture.

Mormons support a vigorous missionary effort (some 60,000 self-supporting missionaries serve for 18–24 months), subscribe to a stringent health code (no coffee, tea, alcohol, or tobacco), commit themselves to a life of chastity (no pre- or extramarital sex), and are expected to contribute 10% of their gross income to the Church. These demands, coupled with a history of "gathering" (that frequently overwhelmed and threatened old settlers) and recurrent oppression, combine to produce a Mormon culture that is intensely cohesive. At the same time, hundreds of thousands of annual converts make the group's constitution dynamic and fluid.

Organizationally, the church is hierarchical and centralized. From headquarters in Salt Lake City, a prophet and two counselors receive "continuing revelation" to lead the Church. Next in authority are the Quorum of Twelve Apostles and several Quorums of Seventy, all of whom, as worldwide or "general" authorities, preside over a membership that has been growing at a prodigious rate (from 3.1 million in 1970 to 8 million in 1995, according to *World Christian Encyclopedia,* 2001). More than half of their members live outside the USA, and that proportion will continue to increase because Mormon conversion rates are the highest in Latin America and Africa.

Smaller bodies of Mormons include the "Reorganized Church of Jesus Christ of Latter Day Saints" (claiming direct continuity with Joseph Smith; centered in Independence, Missouri), "Temple Lot," "Bickertonites," and "Strangites." **See also MORMON, BOOK OF; MORMON WORSHIP; SMITH, JOSEPH; YOUNG, BRIGHAM.** TERRYL GIVENS

Latvia. Lutheranism is the traditional official faith in Latvia, but in Southeast Latvia Roman Catholicism prevails as a more "popular" faith, and Russian Orthodoxy is important because of the high percentage of Russians in Latvia. There have been attempts to revive the national indigenous religion.

Latvians and Estonians were conquered by crusading orders of Teutonic* Knights (12th c.). In the aftermath of the Reformation*, the ruling German landowning class adopted Lutheranism and controlled the clergy and peasantry. After Latvia was gradually absorbed into the Russian Empire (18th c.), Latvians experienced a "dual" (Lutheran/Orthodox) occupation (19th c.).

Following a period of independence (1920–40), Latvia became part of the Soviet Union; anyone who practiced religion was persecuted. In contrast to the situation in Lithuania*, in Latvia Soviet rule was more overtly dominated by the Russians, and there was little national or religious dissent. There was some involvement of the churches in the process leading to Latvian independence (1991), but as in most post-Communist countries, since independence both internal and external problems have prevented the churches from playing an active public or political role; these include a lack of resources, expertise, and experience; internal debate; and a new environment of pluralism and secularization*.

During the Communist period, the established denominations tended toward authoritarianism and doctrinal and ritual conservatism as a result of enforced isolation from developments in Europe and the wider world and a "fortress mentality" in the face of persecution and aggressive atheism*. In the post-Communist period, this conservatism has been both reinforced and challenged by the influx of Western Protestant missionaries and "new religious movements." The Latvian Lutheran Church has reacted against the perceived liberalism of Lutheranism in the wider world, e.g. by rejecting the ordination of women*.

There is an unofficial distinction between traditional and nontraditional religions, with the former enjoying privileges such as the right to teach religion in schools, a right that other social groups have challenged. There are also some potential problems of discrimination connected to the registration of religious communities. However, under the Religion Law of 1995, there are no serious restrictions on religious freedom, and Latvia complies with the standards of the European Union, which it joined in 2004.

Statistics: Population (2000): 2.3 million (M). Christians, 1970: 1.2 M, 51%; 2000: 1.6 M, 67% (Protestants, 0.56; Orthodox, 0.55; Roman Catholics, 0.49; independents, 0.12); nonreligious, 0.76 M, 32%. (Based on *World Christian Encyclopedia*, 2001.)

PHILIP WALTERS

Laud, William (1573–1645), archbishop of Canterbury. Matriculated (1589) and was then a fellow (1593) at St. John's College, Oxford; its substantial Catholic leanings had a formative influence on Laud's liturgical sensibilities and theological trajectory. Laud argued (1602) for the perpetual continuity of the church, posited the indispensable nature of diocesan bishops (1604), and remained an avowed opponent of Calvinist* theology. Throughout Laud's career, both at Oxford and at Canterbury, rumblings were heard that he was too close to being Roman Catholic and bent on disfiguring the Protestant identity of the Church of England.

Appointed bishop of St. David's (1621), Bath and Wells (1626), and London (1628), before becoming the chancellor at Oxford University, Laud was poised to become the archbishop of Canterbury (1633) under Charles I. With the authority to reconfigure the shape and identity of the Church of England, and convinced that the Puritan* factions were inimical to the unity of the Church, Laud began to implement draconian policies, which further alienated the Puritans. He emphasized the beauty of holiness, a sacramentarian piety focused on the Eucharist*, deliberately turning away from the sermon-focused piety of the Calvinist puritans.

During the personal rule of Charles I (1629–40), Laud's power was both bolstered and hotly challenged. He was impeached by the Commons during the Long Parliament and brought to the Tower of London (1641). He was tried (1644) and executed (January 1645) on the charge of popery. PAUL CHANG-HA LIM

Lauds (literally "praise"), ancient morning prayer of the church; originated in Judaism. After Vatican* II, it became increasingly popular in Roman Catholic parishes as it was in Anglican churches after the Reformation.

KEITH F. PECKLERS, SJ

Lausanne Movement. With a focus on evangelization (evangelism*) and a nondenominational rather than ecumenical* emphasis, the Lausanne Movement is in many respects the counterpart of the World* Council of Churches, which is based in Geneva. Both independent mission organizations and Evangelical churches participate in the Lausanne Movement. It grew out of a World Congress on Evangelism held in Berlin (1966) at the initiative of Billy Graham. A subsequent International Congress on World Evangelization in Lausanne (1974) drafted the Lausanne Covenant with six emphases: "the authority of Scripture*; the nature of evangelism; Christian social responsibility; the urgency of world missions*; the problems of culture*; and spiritual warfare." Numerous conferences (global, regional, topical) have been held since then.

Lavra (Gk for "alley"), or laura, among 4th-c. Palestinian monks, a row or cluster of monastic cells around a common center, including a church for gathering for worship. Later, any Greek and Russian monastic community without a formal cenobite* organization. **See also MARTHANA.**

Law. In the OT, the term *torah** (instruction) refers to narrative instruction, social regulation, and directives concerning, e.g., temples, vestments, and liturgies. In Judaism "Torah" refers to the Pentateuch*, which contains relatively little material that would be termed "legal" in the later Roman sense. Reducing the "OT Law" to the legal codes found in the Torah is a later Christian innovation. On this assumption, the paradigm for this legal material is the giving of the Decalogue* at Sinai, into which much of the remaining legal material is assimilated.

In the NT, the term *nomos* often has the wider Torah in view. However, for many interpreters, Paul* often restricts *nomos* to mosaic legal codes that do not apply to Gentiles*. In Paul's terms, the love of neighbor "fulfills" or completes the Law. The Gospels* tend to contrast the way of Jesus with the "Law of Moses" or to emphasize compassion* instead of compliance with legal codes.

As Western Christianity took over both the judicial functions and the legal assumptions of the Roman Empire, it tended to emphasize the "positive law" of legislation or decree. This resulted in the codes of Justinian* and Theodosius* as the basis of church-sanctioned law; subsequently, OT Law was most often understood according to the same pattern. When linked with the Greek view of law as the order that governs the cosmos, this produced a view of "natural* law" that grounds moral* law.

The Reformation* regarded law as that which the human cannot fulfill (because of sin*). Thus law first indicates the need for salvation* "apart from the Law" (through the gospel of grace*) and for punishing criminal behavior (murder, theft) in a fallen world. The Reformed tradition also found in the legal and covenantal traditions of the Torah the basis for a "third use of the Law" that would govern Christian communities and commonwealths. Radical* Reformation movements maintained that the Law is fulfilled by love of the neighbor (Paul) or through interhuman justice* and mercy* (Gospels).

More recent European discussion has emphasized the justice* that is heterogeneous to law yet indissociable from it, a justice to be understood in terms of radical welcome of the other (Derrida). Agamben noted that messianic movements (in Judaism*, Christianity, and Islam*) maintain that law is both consummated and abrogated with the coming of the Messiah and emphasize the violence of the law in contrast to a justice, which, like love*, cannot be coerced.

THEODORE W. JENNINGS, JR

Lay Brother or Sister, (1) member of a religious order engaged in manual labor, who is not obliged to recite the Divine* Office; (2) nonordained member of a Christian community. **See also LAITY.**

Lay Movements, Lay Participation in Worship, Lay Theology. See LAITY CLUSTER.

Laying on of Hands is a gesture used in many religions. For Christians, it has biblical roots in both the OT and NT. Spanning centuries and cultures, it continues to carry different meanings depending on context and tradition.

In the OT, the laying on of hands was a gesture concerned with setting things, animals, and people apart, sanctifying them for sacrifice or consecrating them; it was also a gesture of blessing*. To these practices, the NT added the laying on of hands for healing* and initiation.

In Christian liturgical history (as attested from the early 3rd c.), the laying on of hands continued to be used for healing and initiation (with or without anointing) and, in addition, was practiced during ordinations* of all ranks and for reconciling penitents. It was also used for marriage* in Eastern Orthodox Christian rites (from the 4th c.) and later in the Latin-speaking church (from the 10th c.).

There are a variety of theological interpretations of the laying on of hands, even when joined to a verbal prayer. However, it is often seen as a way of imparting or transferring something, as in the act of blessing*, especially as conferring the Holy Spirit, highlighting the role of the third person of the Trinity* in liturgical rites.

LIZETTE LARSON-MILLER

Lazarus, (1) the beggar in Jesus' parable (Luke 16:19–31); the name was later used for any beggar. (2) Mary and Martha's brother, who was resurrected (John 11:1–44).

Leah, older daughter of Laban. By deception she became Jacob's* first wife and bore him six sons: Reuben, Simeon, Levi*, Judah*, Issachar, and Zebulun.

Leaven, sourdough or yeast that ferments dough, causing it to rise and making it lighter. As a metaphor for an inconspicuous potency that brings impressive results, it is used positively in Jesus' parable of the leaven (Matt 13:33 = Luke 13:21), comparing leaven to the Kingdom* of God working quietly but inevitably. Elsewhere it is used negatively to suggest a sinful influence (e.g. Jesus warns against "the leaven of the Pharisees," Mark 8:15, par.) or an impurity contrasted with Passover, the feast of "unleavened bread" (1 Cor 5:6–8). Passover was called the feast of unleavened bread because eating leavened bread, and even the presence of leaven in one's house, was and still is prohibited for practicing Jews during Passover as a reenactment of Exod 12:15–20 (before leaving Egypt, the Israelites did not have time to leaven their bread).

Lebanon. Although no recent statistics on Lebanon's religious communities are available, the almost 40% that is usually attributed to the Christian population is the highest percentage of Christians in any Middle Eastern country. Politically, their influence is even more pronounced, because since the conclusion of the civil war (1975–89), exactly half of the 128 seats of Parliament are reserved for Christians. Of these, half are taken by politicians belonging to the Maronite* Church, the largest Christian community in the country. The president also comes from this group. Maronite and Christian dominance in the political and economic structures of Lebanon contributed to the outbreak of the civil war, as did the disrupting influences of regional power politics involving Israel*, Syria*, and the Palestinians*. A Christian majority had been purposely created by the French during the League of Nations mandate period, was confirmed by the 1932 census, which showed 51% Christians vs. 49% Muslims, and was institutionalized during independence in 1942. However, the politicization of religious communities, the accompanying negotiations over representation, and the increase of Muslims vis-à-vis Christians created a rather unstable political entity.

The focus on the political aspects of the religious communities has obscured many other aspects of Christianity in Lebanon, among which are its rich liturgy and its denominational variety alongside numerous formal and informal interconnections in social institutions, education, and daily life. In addition to the Maronite Church, which has long-standing relationships with the Roman Catholic Church, the Greek Orthodox* and Greek Catholic churches are important elements of Lebanese Christianity; the Gregorian Armenian* and Armenian Catholic churches have also long been present. In the 20th c., Syriac Orthodox* and Syriac Catholic as well as Assyrian* and Chaldean* churches were established by refugees from Turkey*, Iraq*, and Iran*. Starting in the 16th c., missionaries strengthened and modernized Catholicism, whereas in the 19th c., North Americans helped create Protestant churches. Together with more recent Pentecostal* denominations, these constitute a small minority, but the Maronite Church has been especially influenced by the Charismatic* Movement. Western missionaries were instrumental in the establishment of a number of famous educational institutions, such as the (Protestant) American University of Beirut and (Roman Catholic) Université de St. Joseph. Whereas many of their Christian and Muslim graduates have contributed to Lebanon's lively Arabic literary and scholarly scene, the use of English and French as languages of education have also contributed to a strong Western focus of many of Lebanon's educated elites. **See also ISLAM AND CHRISTIANITY CLUSTER: IN THE MIDDLE EAST: LEBANON.**

Statistics: Population (2000): 3.9 million. Christians, 39% (Maronite, 37%; Orthodox, 2%; independents, 02%); Muslims, 59%; nonreligious, 2%. (Estimates based on diverse governmental reports; no recent statistics are available.)

HELEEN L. MURRE-VAN DEN BERG

Lectionary, "lessons" (portions of Scripture*) to be read on specific days in the church year (from the 4th c.). A three-year "common lectionary" is now used by Roman Catholic, Orthodox, Anglican, and mainline Protestant churches.

Lecturer, a preacher appointed by a parish to provide regular sermons. The Puritans* used such appointments to install preachers with their own views, and the Long Parliament encouraged this practice, but it was halted by the Act of Uniformity (1662).

Lee, Ann (1736–84), evangelist and founder of the United Society of Believers in Christ's Second Appearance (Shakers*). Born in England, she had a difficult marriage marked by the deaths of infant children. She emigrated to the British colonies in North America (1774) and was the leader of the Shakers until her death. In the Millennialist* milieu of late-18th-c. England, Lee joined the Shaking Quakers, who predicted the imminent return of Christ. When she emigrated to North America, she proclaimed a message that combined Millennialism and Perfectionism*. She claimed that the millennium had come in her church. The millennium was marked by the direct experience of the Holy* Spirit – a source of authority more important to Lee than Scripture or traditional creeds – and by moral perfection, particularly exhibited through compulsory celibacy*. Celibacy, however, did not signal the erasure of gender differences. To bolster her spiritual authority, "Mother Ann" (as her followers called her) used feminine imagery, speaking of the labor she undertook for her followers. Later Shakers claimed that Lee herself was the second coming of Jesus. The Shaker Movement survived Lee's death and reached its heyday in the mid-19th c. SARAH JOHNSON

Lee, Jarena (1783–?), born in Cape May, New Jersey; the first authorized (1819) female preacher in the African* Methodist Episcopal (AME) Church. After she informed Bishop Richard Allen* that the Lord had revealed to her that she must preach the gospel, he replied that the AME Church's *Discipline* did not allow for women preachers. Lee responded, "O how careful ought we to be, lest through our bylaws of church government and discipline, we bring into disrepute even the word of life. And why should it be thought impossible, heterodox, or improper for a woman to preach seeing the Savior died for the woman as well as for the man?" Lee's apologetic appeals for women's equality did not succeed, but her spiritual gifts and skills did. Years later, Bishop Allen was so moved by Lee's spontaneous "exhortation" during a worship service that he "rose up in the assembly, and related that [she] had called upon him eight years before, asking to be permitted to preach, and that he had put [her] off; but that he now as much believed that [she] was called to that work, as any of the preachers present." Although Lee still experienced hostility in her ministry, she enjoyed a fruitful career (at least until the late 1840s) as an itinerant preacher, activist, and author. **See also AFRICAN AMERICAN CLUSTER: HOLINESS; AFRICAN METHODIST EPISCOPAL (AME) CHURCH.** MONYA A. STUBBS

Lefèvre d'Etaples, Jacques (c1470–1536). Viewed as the first French humanist, he wrote commentaries on Aristotle, then on early Christian writings, medieval mystic literature, and Nicholas* of Cusa. As vicar general in the Diocese of Meaux with responsibility for evangelism*, he insisted on a return to the Bible, teaching himself the Psalms, Paul's letters, and the Gospels. Suspected of heresy* by the Faculty of Theology of Paris, he took refuge in Strasbourg (1525), apparently adhering to Protestant ideas. Back in France under the protection of Marguerite* of Navarre, sister of King Francis I of France, he did not express his personal religious views and devoted himself to the first translation of the entire Bible in French.

GUY-THOMAS BEDOUELLE, OP

Leme Cintra, Sebastião (1882–1942), archbishop of Olinda and Recife (1916–21), coadjutor archbishop (1921–30), and cardinal archbishop of Rio de Janeiro (1930–42), is considered a crusader for Brazilian neo-Christendom. As director of the conservative Romanization process, he claimed a central role for the Roman Catholic Church in such important areas as politics (creation of the Catholic Electoral League) and education (foundation of Rio de Janeiro's Catholic University). He also fought to improve church and state relations, which was difficult after 1889, when a secular republican regime was proclaimed (see Laicization). During Vargas's presidency (1930–45), when both the Roman Catholic Church and the state had similar objectives, including fighting Communism and maintaining social order, Dom Leme established an efficient collaboration with the federal government, which led to the semiofficial recognition of Roman Catholicism. **See also CHURCH AND STATE RELATIONS**

CLUSTER: IN LATIN AMERICA: BRAZIL.

MARCELO TIMOTHEO DA COSTA

Lent, the 40-day period (Quadragesima) during which believers prepare themselves for Holy Week through fasting, prayer, penitence, almsgiving, and self-denial. In the Western churches, Lent begins on Ash Wednesday and ends on Holy Saturday (the six Sundays of the period, each of which commemorates the Resurrection, are not fasting days, and thus are not counted). In the Eastern Orthodox* churches, the "Great Lent" (or "Great Fast") begins on Clean Monday (Sundays are included in the 40 days) and ends on the Friday before Palm Sunday (Holy Week being a distinct period of fasting). The Great Fast is contrasted to the Nativity Fast, the 40-day fast before Christmas. **See also LITURGICAL YEAR.**

Leo I, Pope (440–61), possibly born in Rome, a saint and doctor of the church, one of two popes to be called "the Great." Leo was a particularly influential deacon. His election occurred while he was on a diplomatic mission to Gaul. He rapidly asserted his authority over the Church in Rome and Christians in the West. When Eutyches* appealed to him during a dispute with the patriarch of Constantinople over the nature of Christ, Leo addressed a document, now known as "The Tome," to the patriarch, a document that played a crucial role in the decision-making process at the Council of Chalcedon* (451). Leo persuaded Attila the Hun not to attack Rome (452), and although he failed similarly to dissuade the Vandal* Genseric, he did convince him not to set fire to it or to massacre its inhabitants. **See also POPES, ROMAN CATHOLIC, AND THE PAPACY.**

MICHAEL J. WALSH

Leo XIII, Pope (1878–1903), born Gioacchino Vincenzo Pecci (1810) in Carpineto. After his ordination (1837), he served as nuncio* in Belgium, became bishop* of Perugia (1846) and a cardinal* (1853). He was appointed *camerlengo* (chamberlain) of the Roman Catholic Church (1877), which impressed the cardinal electors. Because Leo was ill, it was thought that his pontificate would not be a long one; in fact, however, his was the third longest pontificate in papal history. Determined to win back the Papal States, he tried unsuccessfully to win allies against the Kingdom of Italy. He encouraged the study of Thomas Aquinas*, opened the Vatican archives to scholars, and issued a number of encyclicals*, especially on church*–state relations, most significantly *Rerum* Novarum* (1891), known as "the workers' charter." He condemned "Americanism" and declared Anglican orders invalid (the bull* *Apostolicae Curae*, 1896), though he desired the reconversion of England to Roman Catholicism. **See also POPES, ROMAN CATHOLIC, AND THE PAPACY.**

MICHAEL J. WALSH

Leonine Sacramentary, the earliest surviving volume containing prayers for the Mass* in the Roman Rite. The early-7th-c. manuscript is attributed to Leo* I, but it also draws on later materials.

Leontius of Byzantium (6th c.), defender of the Christology* of the Council of Chalcedon*. He argued that this council found the golden mean between the Monophysites*, who thought that one hypostasis* implies one nature (a misunderstanding of Miaphysitism*), and the Nestorians*, who thought that two natures imply two hypostases. To show how Christ can have two natures in one hypostasis, he used the notion of *enhypostasia**: a nature can be real by "subsisting in" a hypostasis shared with another nature. This can be interpreted in several ways, as D. B. Evans and B. E. Daley have shown. Leontius may have had Origenist* leanings; if so, Jesus' creaturely life would be absorbed into the person of the Word through knowledge and will. After the Second Council of Constantinople* in 553, it was understood to mean that the divine Word assumed an individual "humanity" but not a "man."

Leontius of Jerusalem (6th c.), author of two writings, one against the Monophysites* (the polemical name given to Miaphysites*) and one against the Nestorians*, that were formerly ascribed to Leontius* of Byzantium. He was the more clearly "neo-Chalcedonian*" of the two, interpreting the Christology of the Council of Chalcedon* in the light of the writings of Cyril* of Alexandria; thus Christ is the divine Word* acting through a complete humanity.

Lesotho. The history of Christianity in Lesotho goes back to 1833 when King Moshoeshoe I (1786–1870), the founder of the Basotho nation, invited three Paris Evangelical Missionary Society missionaries in the hope that they would help him establish his sovereignty in the Mohokare (Caledon) Valley. Moshoeshoe also wanted a footing in the "new world" being established around his frontiers by the Afrikaners (Boers) and the British (as noted by Moshoeshoe's biographer, Thompson).

When Roman Catholic missionaries made a request to found a mission in Lesotho, Moshoeshoe gladly assented (1862). The first Catholic mission began in Tloutle (Roma). The Roman Catholic missionaries were followed by the Anglicans* (1867).

As of the early 21st c., most Basothos were Christian. The Roman Catholic Church is the largest church; all of its leaders and priests are Basotho. The Lesotho Evangelical Church is the largest Protestant church and the first major church to ordain women as ministers and evangelists. The Anglican Church is much smaller.

A large number of smaller churches and spiritual movements are active in Lesotho. They include the Methodist Church of Southern Africa, the African Methodist Episcopal Church, the Apostolic Faith Mission, Assemblies of God, Seventh-day Adventists, and numerous Pentecostal*, Charismatic* and Evangelical churches – all of whose leadership is local, contributing to the lives of Basotho. Other religious groups have gradually gained a small but significant membership of committed followers: Baha'i*, Jehovah's* Witnesses, the Church of Jesus Christ of Latter*-day Saints (Mormons), and Islam*.

The Christian Council of Lesotho, an ecumenical body (since the mid-1960s), began the process of ecumenical dialogue with some success, breaking down the barriers among churches and cooperating in the fight against the HIV/AIDS pandemic.

Christians from most if not all these churches follow a number of African* religious customs and rituals, often contrary to official church teachings.

Statistics: Population (2000): 2.1 million (M). Christians, 1.95 M, 91.0% (Roman Catholics, 0.80 M; Protestants, 0.28 M; members of African Instituted Churches and other independents, 0.25 M; Anglicans, 0.1 M); African Religionists, 0.17 M, 7.7%. (Based on *World Christian Encyclopedia*, 2001.)

TEFETSO HENRY MOTHIBE

Lessing, Gotthold Ephraim (1729–81), major figure in the German Enlightenment*, proponent of religious tolerance. His plays were performed in Berlin and Hamburg; as a critic, he dealt with issues of dramatic theory. While serving as the librarian at Wolfenbüttel, he published fragments from H. S. Reimarus, one of the first historical critics of the Bible, and engaged in his own biblical criticism. His view of religion emphasized universal morality apart from historical revelation; this was dramatized in *Nathan the Wise* (1779) and advocated programmatically in *The Education of the Human Race* (1780), where he wrote the well-known dictum that "accidental truths of history cannot prove necessary truths of reason." In this work, he also gave currency to the theory of three ages and the eternal gospel, linked with Joachim* of Fiore.

Leta, a *presbytera* according to an inscription from 4th- to 5th-c. Tropea, Calabria: "Sacred to her good memory. Leta the *presbytera* lived forty years, eight months and nine days. Her husband made [this monument]. She preceded him in peace on the day before the Ides of May." What she did is unclear, but she certainly was not simply the wife of a presbyter*, since her husband gives no indication of holding that office. The inscription coincides well with the letter of Gelasius*, bishop of Rome (494), complaining of the admission of women to sacred ministry at the altar in South Italy. **See also FLAVIA VITALIA.**

CAROLYN OSIEK

Leuenberg Agreement, a statement adopted by the major Lutheran and Reformed* churches in Europe (1973), formulating a common position on points that had divided them at the time of the Reformation* (Christology*, the Lord's* Supper, and predestination*) and declaring that the doctrinal condemnations of the past no longer apply. They formed the Leuenberg Church Fellowship, renamed the Community of Protestant Churches in Europe (2003).

Levinas, Emmanuel (1906–95), a Lithuanian Jew who lived and worked in France; a hermeneutical* phenomenologist* and moral philosopher. As the latter, he sought to identify the ground of unconditional responsibility to and for the other. As a phenomenologist, he located this not in some transcendent reality such as Plato's Good or the biblical God but in intentionality, the immediate experience the self has of itself and its world as meaningful. But for him intentionality is reversed. Meaning does not arise as I confer it by my gaze or speech. It arises rather from the gaze and the voice of the other, by which I find myself identified as the one called to categorical obligation and infinite responsibility.

As a hermeneutical phenomenologist, Levinas does not pretend to occupy the view from nowhere but rather inhabits a specific site within the history of traditions. His reflection arises within the horizon of his understanding of Jewish traditions, and for this reason "the other to whom and for whom I am responsible is most specifically the widow, the orphan, and the stranger."

Levinas offers his critique of Christianity largely through his critique of Kierkegaard*. For Kierkegaard, God is the middle term between me and my neighbor. It is because God commands me to love my neighbor as I love myself and, through the acts of creation* and redemption*, gives me good reason to do so that I am a responsible self. By contrast Levinas insists that the neighbor is always the middle term between me and God. My only relations to God come through the face and voice of the neighbor.

Levinas fears that unless the ethical* relation is given priority over the God relation, the self will become self-centered, so concerned with its own salvation* (eternal happiness) that an all too possibly violent amoralism will supplant ethical responsibility. By focusing on texts in which Kierkegaard develops the God relation and completely ignoring his major ethical treatise, *Works of Love*, Levinas fails to notice that love of God and love of neighbor are as inseparable for Kierkegaard (and Christianity) as they are for Levinas (and Judaism*). Nevertheless, Levinas provides a prophetic warning against a danger to which every theistic religion is vulnerable: allowing religious interest in personal or collective happiness to lead to the neglect of the neighbor's needs or to violent oppression* of the weak. MEROLD WESTPHAL

Levites, one of the 12 tribes of Israel*, given the role of maintaining the Temple, leading worship, and performing sacrifices.

Leviticus is the third of the five books of the Torah*, the Pentateuch* (also called the Five Books of Moses). The Hebrew name is *wayyiqra'*, "He called," according to the first Hebrew word of the book. *Leviticus* is the Latin form of the Greek *levitikon*, which connotes "priestly."

Leviticus is the central book of the Pentateuch. The narratives in the first two books, Genesis* and Exodus*, are concerned with Israel until it arrives at Sinai; in the last two books, Numbers* and Deuteronomy*, Israel continues on its way to the Promised* Land. Leviticus stands in between, and the events it portrays are located in Sinai. It is written in the language of the "priestly" (P) level (or source) of the Pentateuch.

From inside the Tent of Meeting (1:1), God gives Moses all "the commandments for the people of Israel" (26:46, 27:34). The first part of Leviticus (1–16) concentrates on sacrifices*. Chapters 1–7 contain the rules about performing the following sacrifices: burnt offering (1), grain offering (2), peace or well-being offering (3), sin offering, or purification offering (4:1–5:13), and guilt offering (5:14–26[6:7]) (there are minor changes in 6:1[8] –7:38). In Chaps. 8 and 9, Moses installs Aaron and his sons as the first priests, who then perform their first sacrifices. The cultic rules culminate in the Day of Atonement (Chap. 16): once a year Aaron (i.e. the high priest) shall make atonement* for the sanctuary, the Tent of Meeting, the priests, and the whole people of Israel (16:33, 34).

The second part of Leviticus (17–26), often called the "Holiness Code," is less structured; it is dominated by the theme of holiness* (e.g. 19:2, 20:26), as earlier, in Chaps. 11–15 (cf. 11:44, 45). There are commandments on keeping away from unclean animals (11), the cleansing of bodily impurity (12–15), sexual and family matters (18, 20), cultic rules (17, 22, 23), and special commandments for priests (21).

Chapter 26 summarizes both the Book of Leviticus and the divine lawgiving from Sinai. The central term is "covenant*." God will keep the covenant as long as Israel keeps God's commandments (vv. 1–13), and God will retract it when Israel breaks God's laws (vv. 14–39), but ultimately God will remember it (vv. 40–45).

The cultic laws in Leviticus are given for the Temple, which no longer exists. But the ethical laws are still observed by the Jewish people today. Of particular relevance is the Day of Atonement (Lev 16). ROLF RENDTORFF

Lewis, C. S. (Clive Staples) (1898–1963), literary scholar, novelist, spiritual writer, Christian apologist. Born in Northern Ireland, studied philosophy and English literature at Oxford, was a fellow of Magdalen College, Oxford (1925–54) and then chair of medieval and Renaissance literature at Cambridge (1954). He converted from atheism* to theism* (1929) and then to Christianity (1931) under the influence of friends like J. R. R. Tolkien and Hugo Dyson. He became the founding president of the Oxford Socratic Club (1942), where issues related to Christianity were debated.

His main apologetic works were written between 1941 and 1947, a period dominated both by World War II and, intellectually, by starkly naturalistic* philosophical movements, such as logical positivism*. His most famous apologetic book, *Mere Christianity* (1952), originated as series of radio talks on the BBC during the war. His vigorous and creative arguments for the supernatural along with his accessible style made him one of the most widely read 20th-c. authors and arguably the most influential apologist of his era, especially among Protestant Evangelicals*. He also authored several novels with spiritual and moral themes, including the famous children's series *The Chronicles of Narnia,* which was made into several motion pictures.

JERRY WALLS

Liberalism in Christian Theology and Ethics describes a movement that began in the early 19th c. in response to the challenges of modern culture and continues to the present day. It seeks a mediation between faith* and reason*, God and world, tradition and culture*, to avoid the undesirable alternatives of authoritarian dogmatism and aggressive secularism*. This mediation is never settled and must be rethought by each new generation.

The word "liberal" (Lat *liberalis*) designates something that is free (*liber*), open-minded, and generous. Theologically, to be liberal means to be free from the constraints of dogmatic orthodoxy and to employ critical methods (historical, literary, philosophical, psychological, sociological) that belong to a broader intellectual life. It also indicates that the subject matter of theology is freedom* itself, understood to be a reference to God (as the radically free One), to human beings (created in the image of the divine freedom), and to God's activity in the world (a gracious liberality).

Liberalism is oriented toward experience, both individual and collective, as a source of religious faith* and practice. It works in tandem with the resources of Scripture* and tradition* and the criteria of rationality* to form relative judgments about truth, being, and goodness. Experience in all its forms, including emotion and feeling, connects persons with what is real, objective, and abiding. Some liberal thinkers supplement the experiential element with a visionary or spiritual dimension, which entails an awareness of the mystery* beneath the real. The mystery can be articulated in negative or positive form; the emphasis may fall on mystical fragments or a theological system.

Most liberal thinkers are committed to a prophetic, culturally transformative theology. This is the ethical mandate of late-19th-c. liberalism, radicalized by postmodern critiques of culture, society, and politics. Whereas "culture* Protestantism" was once considered a temptation of liberals – an accommodation to the values and interests of a culture oriented toward material progress – liberal thinkers have learned from the culture critiques of neo-orthodoxy* and from liberation* struggles related to race, class, gender, and sexual orientation. Liberalism is committed to the realization of God's Kingdom* or "freedom project" in history*, knowing that such a realization is always unfinished and subject to tragic distortions.

PETER C. HODGSON

Liberal Theology refers to several movements in modern theology. Although few theologians labeled themselves "liberal," the term can be appropriately applied to those who have accepted Enlightenment* thought, particularly the principle of criticism of tradition, authority, and dogma. In some countries, holding such a critical attitude was considered a subversive political act. W. M. L. de Wette, for instance, lost his post in Berlin (1819) for espousing liberal causes. Protestants widely accepted liberal methods from the 19th c., but with a few notable exceptions, it was not until the Second Vatican* Council that Roman Catholic theology began to adopt a moderate critical approach to Scripture and tradition (see Bible Interpretation Cluster: History of).

Liberal theology has strong national characteristics. In Germany it emerged from the critical questioning of tradition* (late 18th c.). While most German theology remained antiliberal, a number of figures accepted the principles of the Enlightenment, including Friedrich Schleiermacher*. Later theologians, including Otto Pfleiderer, who drew on the system of Hegel* and sought a reconciliation of all thought, were also labeled liberals. Others, notably Adolf von Harnack*, sought to reduce Christianity to its purest essence, removing the accretions of the past. In the eyes of their opponents, who derided them as "culture* Protestants," some liberals, including Harnack and Ernst Troeltsch*, were regarded as overoptimistic about technological progress*. This charge became particularly common after World War I, when liberal theology quickly lost its preeminence.

In England, with its liberal political tradition, many theologians accepted forms of liberalism. A number adopted a belief in progress through education*, producing the notorious *Essays and Reviews* (1860), which called for critical study of the Bible. Later English liberals tended toward apologetics, seeking reconciliation between modern thought and religion.

Others, like John Robinson, preferred the term "radical" and were closer to German dialectical theology than to either liberal tradition. In the USA, a number of seminaries (most important, Union Theological Seminary in New York) adopted liberal methods. In Chicago, under the influence of Shailer Mathews, the Divinity School adopted a close interplay of sociology*, history*, and theology. Such liberalism was criticized by theologians like Reinhold Niebuhr*, who sought to revitalize Christian orthodoxy.

In more recent years, many theological movements, including Radical* Orthodoxy, have been deeply critical of the Enlightenment and liberal theology, regarding both as a compromise between secular thought forms and the truths of Christianity. Others see little alternative to liberalism for the survival of a culturally relevant Christianity. MARK D. CHAPMAN

1) Introductory Entry

Liberation Theologies: Liberation and Theology. The great theological treatises have not given attention to the theme of liberation. However, in the past decades, theologians have begun to reflect on liberation from a theological perspective, seeing liberation as the essence of faith* itself. Theologies of liberation have contributed most to this Christian truth; but the church also sees liberation as central to the evangelical message (as the Congregation for the Doctrine of the Faith affirmed in *Libertatis Conscientia*). Proclaiming the gospel is proclaiming liberation.

In the HB, the aspirations for liberation of the people of Israel in Egypt, and subsequently in Babylonia, as well as for liberation from oppression* during the time of the judges, show the importance of liberation in the biblical tradition. Liberation comes as a faith experience in which one knows that God* is merciful and attentive to the cries of the oppressed. In the OT, the verbs "liberate," "save," "rescue," and "have well-being" are translations of the same Hebrew root (*yasha*); the choice of the English equivalent varies with the passage. Similarly in the NT, the Greek verb *sozo* means "liberate," "save," or "heal," according to the context. Other roots, whose literal meaning is "release" or "liberate," connote "redeem," "save," or "rescue." This signals that salvation* cannot be reduced to an abstraction, a thought, or a feeling. Salvation also relates to concrete sociocultural realities. When there is liberation, the saving presence of God is experienced. Liberation amplifies the traditional concept of salvation by opening it up to a profound and integral experience for humans, especially for those who suffer economic*, gender*, racial*, or sexual*-orientation oppression*. God is revealed as liberator and savior. Two questions must be raised: Liberation from what? Liberation for what?

Liberation from What? Paul emphasizes liberation from sin*, the law*, and death*. Closer examination of this teaching shows that liberation from sin includes liberation from structural sin – manifested in unjust economic systems and sinful sociocultural relations, which affect people, the environment, and even individuals' intimate relationships. Therefore, liberation involves both personal and collective transformations. Liberation from sin is also liberation from death* and the law, because death is the product of sin, which is legitimated by the law when the law is followed blindly and placed above the human being. One is liberated from all that oppresses, harms, marginalizes, or kills humans and their habitat and from all that contributes to this destructive oppression, including, eventually, the law. Life is God's supreme gift; therefore, life as liberation from death is central.

Liberation for What? Liberation is a process in which God and human beings participate. Sin prompts divine salvation in the form of liberation, and humans are challenged by historic reality to carry out the task of liberation as God's sons and daughters obedient to the message of the Kingdom*. Liberation makes us free to liberate others who suffer from injustices of any kind. Before being freed, one cannot free others. The practice of liberation demands a process of personal conversion* that simultaneously unites one with the others in a collective process of historic transformation toward justice.

This theological reading does not allow freedom to be spiritualized, as often happens in an unjustly structured society. Liberation and liberty must remain tied together to prevent the concept of liberty from becoming abstract. Indeed, there is no justice* without liberty, but there cannot be full freedom unless there is liberation with justice. Full liberation will happen when there is a perfect communion between humans among themselves, with nature, and with God. Meanwhile, it will always be a process.

ELSA TAMEZ
(translated by Gloria Kinsler)

---

2) A Sampling of Contextual Views and Practices

Liberation Theologies: Feminist. See FEMINIST THEOLOGY CLUSTER.

Liberation Theologies in Africa. See RECONSTRUCTION, AFRICAN THEOLOGIES OF.

Liberation Theologies in Asia. In South Asia, a liberation paradigm is consciously adopted by theologians from marginal groups, such as the Dalits*, Adivasis* ("tribals," indigenous people), fish workers, and women. For these South Asian Christians, theology is not a systematic explication of timeless truths, nor is it a matter of applying a prefabricated system of ideas to a situation. It is a reflection on the articulation of faith* experience of people as they try to overcome unjust and oppressive forces that dehumanize them, be they caste* structure or economic* exploitation and patriarchy*. The primary objective of theological reflection is to help people in their struggle for justice* and freedom*.

Liberative praxis* is the method of doing theology. Emphasizing praxis does not mean rejecting theory. On the contrary, South Asian Christians assert that rigorous theoretical reflection should emerge from practice that is oriented toward transformation. Unlike Latin American and other liberation theologians who found Marxist analysis to be a useful tool for understanding poverty and marginalization, South Asian liberation theologians have recourse to cultural and religious analysis. These types of analysis allow them not only to grasp their situation as oppressed people deprived of freedom, but also to construct a theology that sustains them in their struggle. They appropriate for themselves liberative and humanistic visions and values in their Adivasi or Dalit culture* that have been suppressed by the dominant culture and its symbol system. Therefore, in their struggle against historical as well as contemporary processes of domination, the Dalits and indigenous groups have become conscious of their identity as people. Cultural realities like pathos and symbols like drums, which evoke a feeling of community, are frequently employed by theologians. Adivasi theologians are involved in an effort to reclaim the ecocentric "tribal" worldview for developing a contextual theology. A. P. Nirmal, a Dalit, describes Dalit theology as a "countertheology" in relation to dominant theologies. Understandably, protest is a characteristic of this theology, but at the same time, it is integral to people's ongoing search for identity and their struggle for justice*.

Scripture*, the Bible as the testimony of men and women who have experienced God's freedom, is now read and interpreted in relation to the experiences of marginal groups. Christ, the liberator, has a special appeal. Jesus is in solidarity with the crucified of this world. This has provided a bridge, and not a barrier, to oppressed people of other faiths.

K. C. ABRAHAM

Liberation Theologies in Asia: Dalit Theology. See DALIT THEOLOGY.

Liberation Theologies in Asia: Japan. See BURAKU LIBERATION IN JAPAN.

Liberation Theologies in the Caribbean Islands. Caribbean churches have been slow to warm up to Liberation theology. One of the reasons is the view that over generations the "church fathers" have handed down church teaching, thereby making the churches' theology a received theology. Therefore, the task of the church is not to create a new theology but to preserve the received theology. With their long colonial history, many islanders have been reared to look to the metropolis for an answer to their problems. Similarly, Christian islanders look to Europe and North America for doctrinal standards and teaching, whether they are members of the mainline churches (established by colonial powers or with their blessing) or of the relatively new churches, including the many Pentecostal* or Charismatic* churches. The fact that Karl Marx's name is often associated with Liberation theology further convinced many church leaders that this theology does not come from God.

However, a noticeable shift is starting to take place among some church leaders, in part as a result of the work of theological schools in the region. Early pathfinders, including Idris Hamid and Robert Cuthbert of Trinidad, Dale Bisnauth of Guyana, Lewin Williams of Jamaica, and Ophelia Ortega of Cuba, have begun to make a substantial difference in the church's relationship to Liberation theology. For instance, Robert Cuthbert, a leader of the Moravian Church in Jamaica (1980s), changed the Church's relationship to the land* by insisting that the Church, one of the country's largest landowners, cultivate its land to provide food for the masses of people.

The church has made progress in taking sides with the poor* and actively changing ecclesial practice to accommodate the poor, but it has not made the same kind of progress in issues raised by Womanist* and Feminist* theologies. Women are still not widely accepted into positions of church leadership and are subordinate to men in their roles in the church, which in this respect lags behind secular institutions. Similarly, the churches have not had much open discussion of gay rights (see Gay and Lesbian Theologies).

Even more important, Caribbean theologians have not been in conversation with indigenous expressions of religion. What would it mean for the church in Trinidad to engage the Shango religion, or for the church in Cuba* to engage Santeria, and the church in Jamaica* Rastafari*? A Caribbean Liberation theology must not only seek to relate the Bible to church doctrine and practice but actively address issues that affect "the least of these."

NOEL LEO ERSKINE

Liberation Theologies in Asia: Minjung Theology. See MINJUNG THEOLOGY.

Liberation Theologies in Latin America. See LATIN AMERICA THEOLOGIES.

Liberation Theologies in North America: African American. See BLACK THEOLOGY.

Liberation Theologies in North America: Native American. Speaking of Latin American Liberation theology, Vine Deloria, Jr., argued that Liberation theology is as oppressive to Indian peoples as are the old dogmatic theologies of the colonial missionary movement. Both are equally rooted in the Euro-Western conceptual framework that privileges individualism and holds indigenous peoples in bondage to these ways of thinking – even about liberation. All Christian theology, says Cherokee scholar Andrea Smith, even Liberation theology, is "complicit in the missionization and genocide of Native peoples." Even Liberation theology's "option for the poor" is ultimately based on a worldview of radical individualism and of material production and consumption that divides people according to class structures that are alien to the value system of Native nations. Rather than be lumped by Liberation theology with a class of other people (the poor), Indian people simply want their peoplehood recognized as discrete nations with valid cultures.

Because the modern state needs to homogenize culture in either its capitalist or socialist version, Deloria argues, the invention of Liberation theology was an absolute necessity for controlling the minds of minorities. Thus genuine liberation will require Indian people to take seriously their own communitarian value systems and epistemology rather than to adopt Euro-Western individualist paradigms of thinking.

The classic liberationist radical interpretation of Jesus fails to work for Indian people, simply because historically the proclamation of Jesus was an integral part of the colonial conquest, which entailed totally displacing centuries-old religious and cultural traditions and replacing them with a one-size-fits-all Euro-Western Jesus. Historically for Indian peoples, Jesus has always meant bondage, not liberation.

Besides recalling the history of violence against Indians perpetrated by Euro-Christians, Robert Warrior underscores the longer Judeo-Christian history of glorified conquest. The Exodus story was already a narrative about the conquest of indigenous peoples (the Canaanites) by Israel, and for the Puritans* this story was replayed in North America with Indians in the role of the Canaanites and the Puritans as the grateful recipients of the new promised land. This has made it very difficult or even impossible for Indians to redeem this story as liberatory.

Thus, consistent with Deloria, Liberation theology for Indian people who are serious about freedom and independence may require saying a firm "no" to Jesus and Christianity and adopting a different starting point – namely, reclaiming the ceremonial structures that promoted peace, harmony, and balance for millennia and the values that accompanied them. **See also LAND, THEOLOGICAL PERSPECTIVES AND PRAXIS, CLUSTER: OF INDIGENOUS PEOPLES IN INDIA, OTHER ASIAN COUNTRIES, AND NORTH AMERICA.**

GEORGE E. "TINK" TINKER

Liberation Theologies in North America: Womanist. Womanist* theology, organic to Black women's experiences, their activities in societies, and their faith communities, is global, ecumenical, interfaith, and at root Liberation theology.

Delores S. Williams notes that "faith seeking understanding" is liturgical, dialogical, and pedagogical. "Womanist," the term derived by Alice Walker from "womanish," denotes women of African descent who are audacious, outrageous, in charge, and responsible. Womanist emancipatory theology engages God-talk and human relationships with God amid hope, engenders mutuality and community, honors the image* of God (*imago Dei*) in everyone, champions basic human goodness, and focuses on liberation amid lived fragmentation. This epistemology questions the quality of life, stewardship, and decision making within sociopolitical, cultural contexts.

Womanist thought includes traditional theology, Bible and/or other sacred texts, ethics, and context. Yet it also transcends the limits of these fields and engages creative imagination to achieve personal becoming, communal solidarity, health, and justice. In analysis and lived experience, Womanist theology understands salvation* to be ultimate freedom. Enslavement is antithetical to salvation* (see Slavery and the Church through the Centuries). This liberative view engages hope* that acknowledges abuse, pain, violence, and separation and engenders courage to move from endurance to total well-being. This hope liberates as it challenges oppressive paradigms, institutions, and symbols that deny love and health. Womanist Liberation theology sees global social structures that shape Black women's lives while asking about God; sees how Black women engage God; and sees how they must reject a God mired in abusive, establishment ideologies that care nothing for Black women.

Womanist Liberation theology is a field of study and a way of incarnated life. People from various contexts do womanist analysis when they ask how oppression affects one's view of self, the world, and God. To live womanism is to be Black, female, and poor. Womanist Liberation theology tests the limits of freedom – from the use of symbols, storytelling, listening to and analyzing the stories of others, to personal relationships. It is dynamic and relational, requiring that one question cultural systems of classism, sexism, heterosexism, racism, ageism, and ableism: beliefs, belief practices, and those disconnects indicating hypocrisy. Liberation theology seeks to liberate the total person. Such theology requires rigorous self-assessment in which, like Katie Cannon, one develops critical, methodological tools and frameworks to challenge various inherited religious traditions in collusion with androcentric patriarchy. Amid this critique, these tools serve as catalysts for rebellious, revolutionary acts to overcome oppressive realities. Rebellion emerges from our ethical analysis; from this analysis emerges a reflective, Womanist liberation theology. **See also ETHICS AND CHRISTIANITY CLUSTER: AS ETHIC OF RISK AND WOMANIST ETHICS; WOMANIST AND AFRICAN AMERICAN THEOLOGIES.** CHERYL A. KIRK-DUGGAN

Liberation Theologies in Palestine. See PALESTINIAN LIBERATION THEOLOGY.

Liberation Theologies in the South Pacific. In this relatively unknown region of the world, Liberation theology has made its mark in a unique way. When Liberation theologies were evolving during the 1970s, many of the South Pacific nations were agitating for political independence from colonial powers. Because the traditional cultures of the South Pacific make no separation between religion and politics, it was commonly church leaders who were the pioneers in political independence and who subsequently became their nation's first political leaders. Liberation theology and its categories provided a powerful theological framework for understanding the movement toward political independence as the work of a God who is on the side of the colonized, is committed to their struggles, and promises liberation in the form of independence.

Since independence was achieved in many of the South Pacific island nations, indigenous theologies emphasizing decolonization have developed. This has been most clearly represented in the articulation of "coconut theology," in the mushrooming interest in the relationship between the gospel and local cultures*, and in theological reflection on personal experience among the young generation of South Pacific theologians.

However, Liberation theology remains a powerful theme in those situations where a struggle against oppressive* powers remains a reality. This takes two general forms: a political struggle against colonizing powers (e.g. the struggles of Kanaks in New Caledonia, indigenous people in West Papua, and Aboriginals in Australia) and a struggle for emancipation against oppressive cultural powers. In the latter category, women in the South Pacific are becoming an increasingly vocal group, developing a distinctive form of Liberation theology, evoking images of the womb and birthing as they deal with the heritage of their own cultural oppression. On a wider regional level, issues of justice* and peace* continue to be a major theme of leaders across the South Pacific.

RANDALL PRIOR

Liber de Causis, treatise made up of extracts from Proclus's* *Elements of Theology*, compiled by an Arab scholar and translated into Latin (12th c.). It was ascribed to Aristotle, but when Proclus's work was translated into Latin (1268), Thomas* Aquinas recognized that this was its source.

Liberia, one of only two countries (with Sierra* Leone) specifically founded by an imperial power to repatriate and resettle its slaves*, was established by the USA (Sierra* Leone by Great Britain).

The American Colonization Society was launched in 1816 by both wealthy slave owners who wanted to remove freed slaves from the USA and committed abolitionists, who thought that a settlement for freed slaves in Africa would enhance their campaign. These white upper-class men, including James Monroe (after whom the Liberian capital, Monrovia, is named), Bushrod Washington, Andrew Jackson, Francis Scott Key, and Henry Clay (presiding), met in Washington, D.C., raised money, and lobbied Congress, which finally (1819) awarded them $100,000 for the resettlement of former slaves in Liberia.

The first ship, the *Elizabeth*, arrived in Liberia from New York in early 1820, with 88 former slaves and 3 white male agents of the American Colonization Society; the agents soon died of yellow fever, as did 22 former slaves. Thereafter, more former slaves settled in Liberia. Joseph Jenkin Roberts became the first non-white governor of Liberia (1842), and when the legislature declared Liberia a republic, he became its first president (1847). However, it took more than five generations for Liberia to elect a president of indigenous African descent. Indigenous Liberians were excluded from national leadership, despite their demographic majority, a factor that contributed to social, cultural, religious, political, and economic conflict.

Cultural and religious plurality was already prevalent. Since the 12th c., Islam had blended with the African cultural and religious heritage. Multiethnic diversity was taken for granted. The former slaves were Christians, primarily members of the African* Methodist Episcopal Church, African Methodist Episcopal Zion Church, Christian Methodist Episcopal Church, and the Liberia Baptist Missionary and Educational Convention. Later Roman Catholic and mainline US Protestant denominations (Episcopal, Lutheran, Presbyterian, United Methodist) established local branches in Liberia. During the 20th c., Pentecostal and Charismatic churches were introduced; among them were the Little White Chapel, New Apostolic Church, Redeemed Fellowship International Church, Three Brothers Ministries of Faith Church, United Church of God in Christ, United Pentecostal Churches of Christ, and Don Stewart Christ Pentecostal Church. African Instituted Churches, including Church of the Lord (Aladura) and the Church of Prophet William Wade Harris, also have adherents in Liberia.

The political conflicts and civil war of the late 20th to early 21st c. resulted from unresolved tensions and grievances of the indigenous people of Liberia, which were based primarily on the resettlement of former US slaves without consultation with the local population. Such conflicts cannot be resolved militarily. The Inter-Faith Mediation Committee of Liberia (later called Inter-Religious Council of Liberia), which includes both Christians and Muslims, played a significant role in mediation and reconciliation* by seeking to diffuse the tragic civil war through the religious frames of reference of both communities and individuals. In 2003 the All* Africa Conference of Churches awarded the Archbishop Desmond Tutu Peace Prize to the Inter-Faith Mediation Committee of Liberia. Under Ellen Johnson Sirleaf, the first woman elected president in Africa, Liberia is struggling to establish new social norms, despite its tension-loaded history.

Statistics: Population (2000): 3.1 million (M). Christians, 1.2 M, 39.3% (independents [Charismatics and members of African Instituted Churches], 0.5 M; Protestants, 0.4 M; Roman Catholics, 0.15 M); African Religionists, 1.3 M, 43%; Muslims, 0.5 M, 16%; nonreligious, 0.05 M, 1.5%. (Based on *World Christian Encyclopedia*, 2001.)

JESSE NDWIGA KANYUA MUGAMBI

***Liber Pontificalis*,** a collection of biographies of early popes, striving for chronological accuracy. Probably begun in the 6th c., it was supplemented in stages until as late as the 15th c.

Liberty. Often used synonymously with "freedom*," "liberty" has distinctive connotations: (1) a morally neutral freedom of choice (while freedom is the willing of what is good); (2) a natural* or civil* right to be respected by the state; (3) a goal to be sought, through liberation* from captivity or oppression*.

Liberty, Religious. See CHURCH AND STATE RELATIONS CLUSTER; TOLERATION.

Life of Adam and Eve, an OT pseudepigraphon ascribed to Moses, which relates the story of the first sin* (cf. Gen 3–4), embellished with much apocryphal material. Its main themes are the inevitability of death*, as well as the justified hope for continued existence after death and for eschatological resurrection. Scholarly opinion differs on whether it is of Jewish or Christian provenance; it dates from somewhere between the 1st and 4th c. CE. **See also PSEUDEPIGRAPHA.** JOHANNES TROMP

Life and Work Movement, ecumenical* movement organized by Nathan Söderblom, archbishop of the Lutheran Church of Sweden*, to formulate a unified Christian response to the economic, social, and moral crisis resulting from World War I. A first conference (Stockholm, 1925), in which Protestant and Orthodox* churches participated, used the phrase "life and work" to indicate that "the Christian way of life" is "the world's greatest need." These hopes were frustrated by the rise of totalitarian regimes (1929–33). A second conference (Oxford, 1937) sought to relate the Christian hope* for the Kingdom* of God to the church's responsibility in the world and (with the Faith* and Order Movement) led to the formation of the World* Council of Churches. **See also** UNITED CHURCH OF CHRIST IN THE UNITED STATES.

Liguori, Alphonsus (1696–1787), canonized (1839), declared a doctor* of the church (1871), and the patron of confessors and moralists (1950). After a brief career in law, he was ordained (1726) and led an extraordinary pastoral, literary, and theological life. His strongly affective emphasis on the Incarnation* set the tone for Catholic spirituality* that prevails to this day. His hymns are still sung in Italy (e.g. *Tu scende dalle Stelle*). His *Theologia Moralis* (1753–79), a guide to the pastoral* direction of conscience, is central in the history of moral* theology. He founded a religious community (1732), whose members are now called Redemptorists (CSsR), to evangelize the most abandoned.
ANTHONY J. KELLY, CSSR

Lima, Alceu Amoroso (1893–1983, pseudonym Tristão de Athayde), essayist, literary critic, and university professor, was the most influential intellectual layperson in Brazilian Roman Catholicism. Converted in 1928, he occupied a leading position among Brazilian laity until his death. During this long trajectory, Amoroso Lima underwent a substantial change in his religious identity. This shift, inspired by French thinkers like Maritain*, Congar, and Mounier, began in the 1940s and drove him from a conservative model of faith to a liberal catholic ecclesiology. Because of that change, Amoroso Lima gave enthusiastic support to the Second Vatican* Council (1962–65) and was a tough critic of the Brazilian dictatorship (1964–85). MARCELO TIMOTHEO DA COSTA

Lima Text, a statement entitled "Baptism*, Eucharist*, and Ministry" (BEM) that was coordinated by the World* Council of Churches (1982). It formulates points of agreement among churches and notes remaining doctrinal differences. It has furnished a basis for mutual recognition of ministries, and for church unions, throughout the world.

Limbo (Lat *limbus*, "edge"), "borderline" state of souls* whose only punishment is an inability to enjoy the beatific vision of God. In popular Roman Catholic theology since the Middle Ages, this is the state of unbaptized infants. This is not, however, an official doctrine of the Roman Catholic Church.

Liminality (from Lat *limen*, "threshold"), a ritual process in which the "structure" of society is negated by the "anti-structure" of *communitas*, the ritual space. **See also** HETERONOMY.

Lindisfarne, an island near the northeast coast of England where a monastery was founded (635) by monks from Iona* under the sponsorship of King Oswald of Bernicia. Here the Celtic* tradition was combined with new currents from Rome, and as such exerted a major influence on Christianity in both England and Scotland.

Litany, a series of petitions with a repeated response by the congregation, e.g. "Have mercy" or "Deliver us."

Litany of the Saints, prayer to the Trinity*, Mary*, and a list of angels and patriarchs, prophets and apostles, martyrs, and saints.

Literal Interpretation of the Bible, usually contrasted with allegorical* interpretation, which finds a "spiritual" meaning different from the literal meaning of the words. Literal interpretation acknowledges that some words are used metaphorically, that a parable* does not refer to an actual event, and that narrated events may also have typological* meaning (anticipating future events that are the fulfillment of Scripture as promise or prophecy). Today, Evangelicals* and fundamentalists* claim that literal interpretation uncovers "the only true meaning" of the text. This assertion presupposes a choice of certain aspects of the text as most significant and a specific view of Scripture* and its role (usually its moral teaching, when Scripture is read as a "lamp to my feet" or "rule of the community").

LITERATURE AND CHRISTIANITY

See AFRICAN AMERICAN CLUSTER: LITERATURE AND CHRISTIANITY; AFRICAN LITERATURE (ANGLOPHONE) AND CHRISTIANITY; AFRICAN LITERATURE (FRANCOPHONE) AND

CHRISTIANITY; AFRICAN LITERATURE (LUSOPHONE) AND CHRISTIANITY; BRAZILIAN LITERATURE AND CHRISTIANITY; CARIBBEAN LITERATURE AND CHRISTIANITY; CHINESE LITERATURE AND CHRISTIANITY; ENGLISH LITERATURE AND CHRISTIANITY; FRENCH LITERATURE AND CHRISTIANITY; GERMAN LITERATURE AND CHRISTIANITY; INDIAN LITERATURE, BIBLE, AND CHRISTIANITY; ITALIAN LITERATURE AND CHRISTIANITY; JAPANESE LITERATURE AND CHRISTIANITY; JESUS, IMAGES OF, CLUSTER: IN LITERATURE; LATIN AMERICAN LITERATURE (SPANISH) AND CHRISTIANITY; PORTUGUESE LITERATURE AND CHRISTIANITY; RUSSIAN LITERATURE AND CHRISTIANITY; SCANDINAVIAN LITERATURE AND CHRISTIANITY; SPANISH LITERATURE AND CHRISTIANITY

Lithuania. As in Poland*, Roman Catholicism has been a major element in shaping and preserving Lithuanian national identity over the centuries. In 1387 Lithuania, the last non-Christian state in Europe, concluded an alliance with Poland that led to the acceptance of Christianity. From the Reformation until the late 18th c., the Polish-Lithuanian Commonwealth rivaled Russia* politically in the area from the Baltic to the Black Sea; thus the Catholic faith rivaled Russian Orthodoxy. Successive partitions of Poland (late 18th c.) led to the country's becoming a part of the Russian Empire, but Catholicism remained strong among the Lithuanian peasantry and became linked with the growth of Lithuanian nationalism (19th c.). After Lithuania gained independence in 1920, the Roman Catholic Church became the state church, claiming 85% of the population.

During World War II, Lithuania became a part of the Soviet Union; it was unique among Soviet republics in that it was predominantly Roman Catholic. From the beginning, the Church was harshly persecuted: clergy were executed or deported, Church property confiscated, religious education prohibited (and later severely limited), religious orders abolished, and priests closely monitored. Nevertheless, the Church played a major role in defending religious, national, and civil rights; 81 volumes of the clandestine *Chronicle of the Lithuanian Catholic Church* (1972–89) have been printed.

Lithuania was the first Soviet republic to declare its independence (1990). Church attendance reached a high point over the next three years, but then began to decline again. As in most post-Communist countries since independence, an active public role for the churches has been hampered by both internal and external problems: lack of resources, expertise, and experience; internal debate; and a new and unfamiliar environment of pluralism and secularization*. Social and welfare work and religious education in schools have been areas of expansion. The Roman Catholic Church remained the most trusted social institution in the late 1990s.

During the Communist period, the established denominations tended toward authoritarianism and doctrinal and ritual conservatism as a result of enforced isolation from developments in Europe and the wider world and a "fortress mentality" in the face of persecution and aggressive atheism*. In the post-Communist period, this conservatism has been both reinforced and challenged by an influx of Western Protestant missionaries and new religious movements.

Although more than 70% of Lithuanians still considered themselves Catholics in 2005, only 10–15% regularly attended church. The 1992 Constitution explicitly rules out the creation of a state religion, but the Religion Law of 1995 deemed certain long-established faiths "traditional" and granted them some privileges, including state aid for the restoration of their buildings and the right to teach religion in state schools. As a result of agreements between the state and the Vatican (2000), the Roman Catholic Church enjoys some informal recognition. However, there are no serious restrictions on religious freedom, and Lithuania complies with the standards of the European Union, which it joined in 2004.

Statistics: Population (2000): 3.7 million (M). Christians, 3.2 M, 88% (Roman Catholics, 3.1 M; Orthodox, 0.11 M; Protestants, 0.04 M; independents, 0.03); nonreligious, 0.44 M, 12%. (Based on *World Christian Encyclopedia*, 2001.)

PHILIP WALTERS

Liturgical Colors, colors used for paraments, vestments, and hangings at specific times of the church year. The practice of using specific colors originated among the Augustinian* canons in Jerusalem (12th c.) and gradually became standardized; it is now widespread among all Western churches. Although there are some variations, the standard colors are as follows: purple during the penitential seasons of Advent* and Lent*; white during the festivals of Christ (e.g. Christmas* and Easter*) and on Trinity* Sunday; red on Pentecost* and the feasts of apostles and martyrs; and green during the "ordinary times" of spiritual growth between Epiphany and Lent, and between Trinity Sunday and Advent.

Liturgical Movement (the) promoted the 20th-c. renewal of worship within the Roman Catholic Church, paving the way for the Second Vatican* Council (1962–65) and influencing liturgical renewal within other churches.

Until recently, many thought that the movement began in 1833 with the refounding of the Benedictine* monastery of Solesmes by Prosper Guéranger (d1875). But Guéranger opposed liturgical creativity and advocated a strict adherence to the Roman celebration of Mass* and the Divine* Office. More recent scholarship claims that the movement was founded by the Belgian Benedictine Lambert Beauduin (d1960) of Mont César during a national Catholic labor conference in Malines (1909). Beauduin was convinced that liturgy was foundational for Christian social activism, and thus the Liturgical Movement in Belgium was marked by a strong pastoral concern that emphasized the social dimension of Christian worship.

In Germany the movement centered around the monastery of Maria Laach. It was led by Benedictine abbot Ildefons Herwegen, Odo Casel, OSB (d1948), and diocesan priest Romano Guardini (d1968); important contributions were made by Aemeliana Löhr (d1972) and other German women. The German Liturgical Movement was more intellectual and academic than the movement in Belgium. Very soon the movement took hold in Austria under the leadership of Augustinian Pius Parsch (d1954) and in France with the 1943 founding of the Centre de Pastorale Liturgique and the important periodical *La Maison-Dieu* (from 1945). The US Liturgical Movement was founded in Collegeville, Minnesota, by a monk of St. John's Abbey, Virgil Michel (d1938), a student of Beauduin's at Sant'Anselmo in Rome. Like its Belgian forebear, the US movement registered a strong social consciousness and substantial lay involvement.

Before Vatican II, the Liturgical Movement did not seem to have taken root in Africa, Asia, or Latin America. The possible exception was Brazil where, from their monastery in Rio, German Benedictine monks published the *Folheto liturgico* (a pamphlet given out at Sunday services that helped people better appreciate the Mass) and devoted themselves to other pastoral concerns (in the 1930s). Beyond the Liturgical Movement itself, Vatican II opened a wave of liturgical innovations, e.g. in Latin America (in Base* Ecclesial Communities and popular* expressions of Christianity) and in Africa (especially in the Congo* [now Democratic Republic of the Congo]), with the development of the Zairian or Congolese Rite – officially approved in 1988 – possibly under the influence of the Belgian Liturgical Movement.

KEITH F. PECKLERS, SJ

Liturgical Vestments. See VESTMENTS OR VESTURE.

Liturgical Year, or Christian year, refers to the cycle of annual Christian feasts in celebration of God's acts of salvation* as manifested in the mystery* of Jesus Christ, from the creation* up to Pentecost* and the expected second* coming of Christ. The foundation of the liturgical year is the weekly Sunday celebration, commemorating Jesus' suffering, death, and resurrection (especially in the Eucharist*); the highlight of the year is the celebration of Easter*. The liturgical year is structurally defined by two categories of feasts: the temporal cycle (marked primarily by Advent*, Christmas*, Lent*, Easter, and Pentecost) and the sanctoral cycle (feasts of saints*).

The Temporal Cycle is centered on Easter and Christmas. The celebration of Easter, originally lasting one day, has been extended to three days, the *Triduum sacrum* (from Good* Friday to Easter Sunday). It is preceded by a time of preparation, either Quadragesima (Lent), a 40-day period of fasting and prayer in preparation for Holy Week (the dates of which are calculated differently in the Western and Eastern churches), or Septuagesima, a 70-day period including Lent and a 30-day pre-Lent season (no longer observed except in the Lutheran Church). Easter is followed by Eastertide, culminating in Pentecost*. In the Byzantine tradition, the celebration of Easter, including Lent and Eastertide, dominates.

A cycle of feasts is also centered around Christmas*, starting with a period of preparation (Advent* or Nativity fast in Eastern churches) and leading to Christmastide, which ends on the Sunday after Epiphany*. In the Western tradition, the celebration of Advent and Christmas is considered the beginning of the liturgical year.

These two principal cycles are followed by a series of Sundays ("ordinary time") that are connected neither to each other nor to any particular theme.

Sometimes the feast cycles overlap one another because the Easter cycle based on the lunar year cannot be synchronized with the other feasts that are based on the solar year. Moreover, Sunday corresponds to neither the lunar nor the solar calendar because the seven-day week does not have an astronomic reference.

The Sanctoral Cycle includes the calendar of saints. On the anniversary of the death of a saint, his or her birth into heaven is celebrated; thus the date of death is referred to as *dies natalis* (birthday), a sharing in the mystery of Easter, as the saint is united with the resurrected Christ. In addition, during the Middle Ages, "devotional feasts," such as Trinity Sunday and Corpus* Christi, were celebrated.

Despite the cyclic concept of time and the cyclic order of feasts, the liturgical year is not a cycle that repeatedly returns to its starting point. By connecting the course of time with events from the history of salvation and through anamnesis* (remembrance), feasts are put in historical perspective: the remembrance of God's acts of salvation in the past is celebrated in the present from the perspective of the future: the second coming of Christ. The historical and eschatological* perspectives provide the cyclic perception of time with a linear dimension. The image of a spiral makes it easier to understand this connection between the cyclic and linear.

The liturgical year made sense for centuries because, in the Northern Hemisphere, it is linked with the seasons (Easter–Spring, Pentecost–Summer, Advent–Fall, Christmas–Winter); moreover, many feasts originated in an agricultural setting. But the liturgical year loses this connection with the seasons in the Southern Hemisphere (where a large percentage of Christians now live). In the Northern Hemisphere, secularization* and industrial, technological, and social developments have also resulted in a decline in the plausibility of the liturgical year. The feasts have become separated from their agricultural origin. For centuries the social calendar had been influenced by the liturgical year. Now the socioeconomic agenda and the leisure culture have become increasingly determinant, and the liturgical feasts have become secular "leisure days" rather than holy days or "holydays." **See also CALENDARS.**

LOUIS VAN TONGEREN

Liturgies, History of. Christian worship has always comprised different traditions, developing and influencing each other in various social, cultural, linguistic, and ecclesial contexts. The fluid and diverse practices of the early church gradually coalesced into common patterns, with more fixed elements (see Worship Cluster: In Early Christianity). Eventually this led to the formation of several liturgical "families," or rites. As Paul Bradshaw has shown, this formation was not a divergence from a single "Urtext," which never existed; rather, commonality developed out of more varied early practices. The major centers of Antioch, Alexandria, and Rome – as well as Jerusalem and Constantinople in the 4th c. – were most prominent in influencing practice elsewhere.

By the end of the patristic period, liturgical traditions in the East included the Byzantine, Alexandrian (Coptic* and Ethiopian*), Greek-speaking West Syriac, Syriac-speaking East Syriac*, and Armenian*, all of which are maintained in various Eastern churches today.

In the West, besides the Roman Rite, there existed the Milanese (Ambrosian*), Gallican*, Celtic*, and Hispanic (eventually "Mozarabic") rites. The differences among them were not only based on language and culture; each also underwent its own liturgical evolution, with its own liturgical forms. In Eucharistic* prayers, e.g., Antiochene and Alexandrian forms have distinct structures. Common elements, like the *sanctus**, one or two *epiclese*s*, institution* narrative, *anamnesis**, and offering, were inserted at different points. The Roman prayer, the Roman canon of the Mass, was even more fundamentally distinctive in its structure and content – it had a variable first section (the "preface") – and in other Western rites there were a number of variable elements throughout the prayer.

In late antiquity and into the Middle Ages, both East and West experienced a significant synthesis of practices from different regions. The Byzantine Rite as we know it (see Divine Liturgy of the Orthodox Churches) emerged from two great syntheses of "cathedral," urban monastic*, and Palestinian monastic practices in Constantinople, which Robert F. Taft has called the "Studite" and "neo-Sabaitic" syntheses, after the Studios* Monastery and the Sabas Monastery. In the West, the Roman Rite underwent major transformation in the wake of Carolingian* liturgical reforms. Seeking liturgical unity in his empire, Charlemagne* suppressed the more prolix and ornate Gallican and Celtic liturgies, attempting to impose the more austere Roman liturgy. The effect, however, was a synthesis of Gallican and Roman liturgical material, which was later imported back into Rome. It is this complex Roman–Gallican hybrid, and not simply the Roman Rite of antiquity, that eventually supplanted most of the non-Roman Western rites and became the late medieval "Roman Rite."

The Reformation* increased the diversity in Western Christian worship, as Reformers and the traditions following them developed different liturgical forms over time. James White has identified nine traditions in the wide range of Protestant worship practices (from the 16th to the 20th c.): Lutheran, Anglican, Reformed, Anabaptist, Separatist or Puritan, Methodist, Quaker, "Frontier," and Pentecostal. These traditions vary widely in their departure from late medieval Catholic practice, the allowance made for liturgical practices without explicit biblical warrant, the use of ceremonial, and the adherence to fixed forms or insistence on spontaneity. Both the traditions that emerged in the 16th c. and those that emerged later were affected by successive developments in church and society. Movements in spirituality and church life, such as Methodism*, Pietism*, the Great* Awakening, Anglo-Catholicism, global missionary activity, ecumenism*, and the modern Liturgical* Movement, had an impact on worship, as did cultural currents like the Enlightenment* and romanticism*.

Roman Catholic worship in the same period was theoretically much more fixed. The Council of Trent* and the Catholic* Renewal introduced a thorough liturgical reform, with a very strong emphasis on standardization, unification, and centralization of official liturgical books. Nonetheless, Tridentine uniformity should not be exaggerated. Roman Catholic worship was strongly affected by baroque European culture and tensions over inculturation* in "mission lands," such as the Chinese* rites controversy. Medieval forms of popular devotional piety, like Eucharistic* adoration* and benediction, were supplemented by newer, highly emotional forms (such as devotion to the Sacred Heart or newer Marian devotions; see Mary, the Virgin, Cluster) in reaction to the rationalism* of the Enlightenment. Concern for catechesis* led to developments in preaching*, which was often more moral or doctrinal than biblical or liturgical, but affected liturgical practice. Starting with the 19th-c. establishment of the Benedictine* monastery of Solesmes (France), historically informed revival and reform of liturgical practice led to the growth of the Liturgical* Movement. In Roman Catholic practice, this culminated in the liturgical reforms of the Second Vatican* Council, with an emphasis on Scripture, grounding liturgical forms in early sources, and *aggiornamento* (updating), paying attention to the social and cultural context of the modern world and to its pastoral needs. The shared efforts of the Liturgical Movement in Western churches, which relied on the same historical sources, led to an "ecumenical convergence," with increasingly similar forms in modern worship books, although greater diversity is arising once again, from a more complex and varied appropriation of history in a postmodern and global context. **See also INCULTURATION CLUSTER; MISSION CLUSTER: IN AFRICA.**

MAXWELL E. JOHNSON and CHRIS MCCONNELL

Liturgy (Gk, leitourgia), originally meaning a public duty, a service to the state undertaken by a citizen, has come to designate a public "service to God" – a "work of the people" for God's sake (e.g. praising God or sanctifying* parts of human existence, such as the hours of the day and night) and thus a worship service*, as well as the whole complex of worship services, all the rites, ceremonies, prayers, and sacraments of the church, in contrast to private devotions. **See also LABOR, THEOLOGIES OF.**

Liturgy of the Hours. Whether celebrated communally or in private, its purpose is to sanctify the hours of the day and night with fixed times of prayer. Like their Jewish forebears, early Christians gathered in the morning to give thanks to God for the light of a new day and in the evening to ask forgiveness and protection for the coming night. Early church sources (e.g. Clement* of Alexandria, Origen*, Tertullian*, Cyprian*) refer to praying at other times as well, such as at midday, before meals, before retiring, and briefly during the night. This tradition of praying at fixed times began as a practice among the laity* and was only gradually taken over by monastics*. Lay participation in the liturgy of the hours was especially evident in the popular "Cathedral Office," which grew in the 4th c. mostly in the East, although Ambrose* attests to the presence of this liturgy in Milan. The Cathedral Office was celebrated in the presence of the bishop and included processions, the use of candles and incense, and the singing of psalms by the assembly. With the 6th-c. advent of Benedictine* monasticism in the West, the liturgy of the hours became the property of monasteries and other religious communities, thanks especially to the use of Latin, which few laypeople were able to grasp. And with the clerical obligation to pray the Divine* Office, it became privatized and clericalized. Over the centuries, there were various revisions of the Roman Office, especially in 1568 with the Roman Breviary (office book of the clergy) of Pius V. Vatican* II's attention to the liturgy of the hours focused largely on reforming the Breviary rather than attempting to revive the traditional Cathedral Office for popular usage. Nonetheless, both Trent* and Vatican II encouraged Sunday vespers in parishes, but with rather unimpressive results. Anglican churches and chapels have been far more successful at sustaining the tradition of morning and evening prayer, especially in the tradition of evensong, which contains elements of both Roman vespers* (evening prayer) and compline* (night prayer).

KEITH F. PECKLERS, SJ

Livingstone, David (1812–73), missionary, explorer, publicist. Born in Scotland, died in Chief Chitambo's village in Zambia*; trained in science and medicine before being ordained by the London Missionary Society. He arrived in South Africa* in 1841 and left in 1852, seeking, as a pioneer traveler, to open up Africa north of the Limpopo to the gospel and to "development." He gained fame for his missions, yet was deeply misunderstood, and his memory was misused in the era of the "scramble for Africa" (see Berlin Conference). Although he alerted the Christian world to the horrors of the Swahili and Portuguese slave* trade, his passionate belief in racial equality was ignored in the enormous body of literature about him that was produced shortly after his death. ANDREW C. ROSS

Llaguno Farías, José (1925–92), Jesuit*, parish priest, administrator, apostolic vicar, bishop of the Diocese of Tarahumara in Mexico, known especially for his communitarian openness with indigenous people, struggling with them to claim their human* rights. His publications include *La personalidad jurídica del indio* (The legal personality of Indians) and a study of the Third Mexican Provincial Council (1585). **See also MEXICO.**

MARÍA ALICIA PUENTE LUTTEROTH and ELIZABETH JUDD

Llull, Ramon (1232–1316), lay philosopher and theologian, largely self-educated. Scion of a wealthy Majorcan family, he underwent a "conversion* to penitence" around 1263, then devoted his life to constant travel, promoting the evangelization of non-Christians (especially Jews and Muslims), undertaking private missionary campaigns, and perfecting a "great universal art," elaborated in more than 300 Arabic, Catalan, and Latin writings, through which he sought to demonstrate the truth of Catholic doctrine. Llull taught his "great art" (published as the multiple-volume *Ars magna,* 1305–8) in Paris and convinced the Council of Vienne (1311) to support the study of Oriental languages at major European universities. He died returning from a missionary journey to Tunis.

Devoted to the ideals of both the Dominican* and Franciscan* orders, Llull was the preeminent lay evangelist of his era. His major mystical* writing (*Book of the Lover and the Beloved*) remains widely admired, as does his promotion of interfaith dialogue. Adaptations of his "great art" enjoyed tremendous popularity during the Renaissance. Despite occasional official opposition to his teachings, Llull's example of devotion and sacrifice – along with his reputation as a polymath and his alleged martyrdom – has ensured his veneration in Spain to this day.

MARK D. JOHNSTON

Locke, John (1632–1704), censor in moral philosophy, Christ Church, Oxford (1663–64); secretary to Sir Walter Vane in Cleves (1665–66), then to Anthony Ashley Cooper; official posts on either side of exile in Holland (1683–89).

Locke lived through turbulent times: the English civil war (1642–46, 1648), the execution of Charles I (1649), the restoration of the monarchy (1660), the laws against Dissenters, the Glorious Revolution (1688), and the Toleration Act (1689).

In his *Essay* (1689), Locke discusses the origin and extent of human knowledge, ("grounds and degrees of belief, opinion, and assent"). He holds that our ideas are derived from experience (they are not innate); knowledge results from the operation of reason* upon ideas. God-given reason is supplemented by revelation* – God's illuminating of the mind with otherwise inaccessible information. By faith we assent to revealed propositions that are above, but not against, reason. In *Paraphrases* (posthumous), Locke discusses faith* in terms of trust. The Bible contains "infallible truths" as well as mysteries* beyond comprehension. It checks the enthusiasts'* claims to direct illumination by the Holy* Spirit.

Locke's opinion that intuited ethical principles have the demonstrative certainty of mathematics gradually weakened. Fortunately, those who accept Jesus as king and savior receive authoritative moral principles from him. Children should learn morality from the Bible. As to our capacity for moral action, a willed act is free only if we have the power to perform it.

Initially opposed to religious toleration, he later advocated the toleration of orthodox Protestant Dissenters*, but not of Roman Catholics (deemed subservient to a foreign power) or atheists (perceived as repudiating the fount of morality, God).

For Locke adherence to the doctrine "Jesus is the Messiah" was sufficient to designate the subscriber a Christian, although Christians need additional beliefs. His reticence with respect to the Trinity* led some to brand him a Socinian (follower of Socinus*). ALAN P. F. SELL

Logos (Gk for "word," applied to the second person of the Trinity*; cf. John 1:1 and 14). Philo* of Alexandria had already spoken of the Word of God as a distinct entity and interpreted God's speaking in Gen 1 as the uttering of this Word for the purpose of giving form to the created world. The 2nd-c. Apologists* adopted this understanding of the Word as a mediating principle between an unchangeable God and the changeable world. The Logos was also understood to be the source of both human intelligence and the "natural law*" of conscience. **See also REVELATION; WORD OF GOD.**

Loisy, Alfred (1857–1940), French Modernist* biblical scholar. Educated at the Institut Catholique in Paris, he became a protégé of the historian Louis Duchesne and specialized in the study of the Bible. He taught at the Institut Catholique (1881–93) but was dismissed and directed to confine himself to study of "Oriental languages." He continued his critical studies of early Christianity from the perspective of history* of religion (e.g. comparing the development of Christian rituals as "Christian mysteries" with pagan mystery* religions) and advocated what he saw as a new apologetic for Catholicism, based on the ongoing formulation of doctrine. The publication of *The Essence of Christianity* by Adolf van Harnack* (1900) gave him the opportunity to publish his views, in the form of a reply to Harnack, in *The Gospel and the Church* (1902). Pope Leo* XIII did not respond, but his successor Pius* X placed his works on the *Index* Librorum Prohibitorum* (List of prohibited books, 1903). Loisy became part of the Modernist* movement, organized chiefly by Friedrich von* Hügel. Pius X condemned Modernism in its various aspects in the decree *Lamentabili** and the encyclical *Pascendi** (both 1907). By this time, Loisy had left the Roman Catholic Church. He became a professor of the history of religions at the Collège de France (1909) and continued to publish works of scholarship as well as several retrospective analyses of the disputes that had surrounded him.

EUGENE TESELLE

Lollardy (also Wycliffism) remains England's only native "heresy*." It originated in Oxford c1380 among the followers of John Wyclif* (d1384). Influenced by Wyclif's increasingly realist* (vs. nominalist*) later theology, Lollard texts are characterized by polemical arguments against clerical endowments, fraternal orders, priestly confession*, indulgences*, pilgrimages*, a professional priesthood, and transubstantiation*. Early Lollard writings in English, including a translation of the Bible (see Bible Translations Cluster: English Translations), a gospel commentary, and a sermon cycle, are distinguished by their academic erudition. Lollard texts often skirt Donatism*, and worship and education were practiced in informal conventicles. Trial records show that women often advanced in these secret groups as teachers or preachers. In 1382 several Oxford Lollards, John Aston, Philip Repingdon, and Nicholas Hereford, were disciplined and Lollard conclusions condemned. (Hereford later recanted, becoming a bishop and Lollard inquisitor.) Virtually all Lollard texts remain anonymous; an exception is William Thorpe's biographical narrative (dated 1407). Members of the gentry often protected Lollards through the early 15th c. Persecution increased under Archbishop Thomas Arundel of Canterbury after 1400. The death penalty was authorized for heresy* in 1401, and in 1409 biblical translation in English was prohibited. Persecutions continued until the 1520s.

DERRICK G. PITARD

Lombards, a Germanic people that, together with other Germanic people (Goths*, Vandals*), embraced Arian Christianity, the moderate "homoian" Arianism* of Ulfila* and other Arian missionaries. When they invaded Northern Italy* (568–605), unlike the Goths* who preceded them, Lombard rulers minimized in their governmental administration the role of the churches. As a result, Latin-speaking Christians could begin to reassert their church identity as distinct from the Arianism of the rulers. **See also ARIANISM and ITALY**

LORD. In translations of the OT, the capitalized term "LORD" is used for the tetragrammaton* in the original Hebrew text; it is used out of respect for the Jewish tradition of not speaking or writing the name of God. In the NT, "Lord," a translation of *Kyrios**, is used for Jesus.

Lord's Day, Christian name for Sunday (Rev 1:10). For Sabbatarians*, the term underscores their advocacy of making Sunday a day of rest like the Sabbath*.

Lord's Prayer, the prayer taught by Jesus to his disciples (Matt 6:9–13; Luke 11:2–4). The longer, Matthaean version is the one used by Christians of all traditions. In early catechesis*, it was taught (along with the Apostles'* Creed) to catechumens shortly before their baptism. It is still used as a model when instructions about prayer are being given. As a communal prayer (its origin, as its opening words, "Our Father," indicate), it is commonly recited in worship services of most Christian traditions.

Lord's Supper, a title for the Eucharist*, especially among Lutherans* and other Protestants who, following Zwingli*, understand it to be primarily a memorial, based on Paul (1 Cor 11:20, 25). **See also COMMUNION.**

Lossky, Vladimir (1903–58), son of the renowned Russian philosopher Nicholas Lossky; exiled from Russia (1923), eventually settled in Paris, studied at the Sorbonne with the medievalist Étienne Gilson. Lossky's earliest published work on the apophaticism* of Dionysius* the Pseudo-Areopagite, related to his posthumously published dissertation on Meister Eckhart*, was formative for his understanding of Eastern Orthodox* theology. Theology for Lossky begins with the event of divine–human communion in the Incarnation*, which reveals that knowledge of God is an experience of mystical* communion with God, or theosis*. Theology is thus inherently apophatic; it cannot be reduced to logical propositions established by reason*. Apophaticism is not simply naming what God is not. An apophatic mode of doing theology is necessary to lead one to true knowledge of God as a mystical union beyond reason. Because it is apophatic, theology is antinomic: it necessarily affirms the nonopposition of opposites (rather than attempting to resolve the opposition; see Paradox). Lossky was particularly instrumental in establishing the centrality of the neo-Palamite distinction (see Gregory Palamas) between the essence and energies of God in contemporary Orthodox theology. His Trinitarian theology of personhood in terms of uniqueness and freedom also had an influence on contemporary theologies of the Trinity in Eastern Orthodoxy, especially on the thought of the Greek theologians Christos Yannaras, and John Zizioulas.

ARISTOTLE PAPANIKOLAOU

Louis I, "the Pious" (778–840), Charlemagne's third son, who succeeded his father upon Charlemagne's death (814). He sponsored the monastic* reforms of Benedict of Aniane; his decrees (816–17) brought greater uniformity to both Benedictine* monasticism and the life of canons* regular. During his reign, the "Carolingian* renaissance" gained new force. He sponsored the mission of Ansgar* to Denmark* and Sweden*, and the composition of the *Heliand** as a way of inculturating* Christianity into German culture.

Family rivalries led to his doing public penance* twice (voluntarily, 822; imposed, 833). His reign is a prime example of "political Augustinianism," a political (mis)application of Augustine's view of the superiority of spiritual to temporal authority; papal actions in these years prepared the way for the investiture* controversy (11th c.).

Louis IX (1214–70), king of France, son of Louis VIII and Blanche of Castile, declared a saint (1297). He succeeded his father (1226) under his mother's regency. Following his marriage to Margaret of Provence (1234), he gradually asserted his personal rule, most clearly by deciding, against his mother's advice, to go on a crusade* (1248) – a disastrous expedition ending with his capture, which confirmed his sense of unworthiness. He reformed the kingdom in order to strengthen it; preferring negotiations to war, he strongly defended royal interests, while remaining deeply religious. With the intention of leading another crusade, he moved first to Tunis in the hope of converting its ruler but died of illness soon after his arrival.

JAMES M. POWELL

Lourdes, small town in the French Pyrenees where Bernadette Soubirous, a 14-year-old shepherdess, experienced a series of apparitions of the Virgin Mary in 1858. The Lady (*Aquéro*) told Bernadette (in patois), "I am the Immaculate* Conception." Marian visions, not uncommon in 19th-c. Europe, occurred almost invariably among poor and uneducated people like Bernadette. The Lourdes site rapidly established itself as the most famous Marian shrine and became an international pilgrimage* center. The Virgin appeared to Bernadette (canonized, 1933) by a fountain in a grotto, and the alleged healing properties of the water were the main attraction for pilgrims, many of whom claimed to have been miraculously cured. **See also FÁTIMA; MARY, THE VIRGIN, CLUSTER.**

JAMES F. MCMILLAN

Love has always been considered central in Christian faith. It refers both to the nature of God and to the orientation and quality of Christian discipleship*. The Bible confronts Jews and Christians with the divine command to love God, other humans, and their own selves. Thus in both traditions, love is more than feeling, emotion, and passing sensation. It involves the acceptance of God's gift of loving relationship and covenant*; a willingness to develop faithful relations with God, other people, God's creation, and one's own emerging self; and a desire* for transcendence and transformation of both self and other. Like apophatic* Western mysticism*, Quietism*, and the Holiness* Movement, Eastern Orthodoxy* emphasizes love as the link between the human and the divine, leading to is distinctive doctrine of theosis* (divinization, human transformation). Love is the quality of eternal relations.

The Christian praxis of love developed in response both to particular interpretations of biblical notions and traditions and to changing views of human nature and its potential in spiritual, cultural, and intellectual contexts.

The Hebrew Scriptures use a number of expressions for God's love and care for people and their relations to God, friends, and strangers in Israel. By contrast the Septuagint* and the NT express God's love mostly through the Greek term *agape**, and sometimes through *philia* (friendship*), but never through *eros*. This term would have invited confusion with the Greek god of love, Eros, and related notions of cosmic power, fertility, lust, and temptation. The terminological distinction between *agape* and *eros* gained additional significance when Christian love was further developed in contrast to other traditions and notions of love.

The Synoptic Gospels quote Jesus' confirmation of Israel's dual love command (Deut 6.5–6; Lev 19.18) and thus emphasize that Jesus' proclamation of the command to love God, neighbor, and enemy was firmly in line with Jewish praxis. However, the Gospels differ in terms of their exploration of love's horizon. While Luke's good Samaritan story identifies every person as neighbor, the Gospel of John and his letters limit the horizon of love to the Johannine community itself, even as they offer the deepest reflections on God as love (1 John 4). The Pauline letters praise love as God's gift to the church for dealing with conflict and otherness and for promoting an intimate spiritual relationship between Christ and his disciples.

Under the influence of Neoplatonist* anthropology, Christian thinkers have understood love ultimately as God-given eternal fulfillment beyond bodily constraints, worldly limitations, and human sinfulness. Hence Augustine* (354–430) identified one form of true love that alone deserves our full praise and desire, namely God's love. God alone can love. When we love one another, it is in reality God who loves in us. Mystics* in and beyond Christianity have approached the mystical nature of love in terms of union between God and the human soul*.

The reassessment of human agency in medieval Europe promoted new attitudes toward the human potential for love in Scholastic philosophy and theology. Thomas Aquinas* (1225–74) considered friendship* to be granted to us by God as the highest manifestation of divine love. Love (Lat *caritas*) is one of the three theological virtues* (with faith* and hope*). In the God-given light of love, human beings are able to love God and the human other.

Luther* (1483–1546) and the Protestant Reformation affirmed love as God's free gift and rejected any claim that humanity transcends sinful nature on its own. Human love is never free of self-interest, even when directed to God. True love comes only from God. However, as a result of divine grace*, human beings can and ought to love their neighbors by attending to their genuine and concrete needs.

Both the dichotomy between divine and human love and the praxis character of love were further explored in modern Christianity (e.g. by Kierkegaard*). *Agape*-love coming from above was sharply distinguished from worldly love and desire* (cf. Nygren*). Accordingly, romantic love was rejected as misguided desire and human projection.

More recently, Christian thinkers, attentive to the need to reassess human emotions, the erotic quality of desire, and the human body* as divinely created for love, have begun to explore the unity and complexity of love in new ways. Now personal and social neglect of love and violations of love are considered sinful, but sexuality, the body, and other natural foundations of human love, partnership, and community are no longer considered sinful.

Recent Western trends of idealizing the human body, however, complicate efforts to relate love and body and love and sexuality more adequately. Feminist* insights into the interdependence of love and self have brought into question the indispensability of self-sacrifice in Christian love. It is not the self that must be overcome, but the ego. Moreover, reconsidering the social and political dimensions of love has increased attention toward the eschatological* nature of love: Christian love is neither a mere object of faith, nor an occasion for isolated acts of charity*; rather, guided by the Holy* Spirit, it initiates a praxis of personal, ecclesial, and universal transformation.

WERNER G. JEANROND

Love Feast, the Eucharist* or Lord's* Supper, often called the *agape** in the early church.

Low Christologies emphasize Jesus' humanity, which was the original experience of the disciples*. It is a feature of many early Christologies, especially those called Adoptionist*, and a characteristic of many modern Christologies that are based on the so-called historical Jesus* or are concerned to avoid excessive claims about Jesus. **See also CHRISTOLOGIES CLUSTER; HIGH CHRISTOLOGIES.**

Low Church Party, the group in the Church of England that gives a "low" place to the episcopate, priesthood, and sacraments, in a manner similar to that of the Puritan* party of the 16th and 17th c. The term is now applied to the Evangelical Movement in the Church. **See also ANGLICANISM CLUSTER.**

Loyola, Ignatius. See IGNATIUS OF LOYOLA.

Lucaris, Cyril (1572–1637), patriarch of Alexandria (1601–20), then of Constantinople (1620–37). Born in Crete (under Venetian control), he studied in Venice and Padua. While attending the Synod of Brest*-Litovsk (1596), he became suspicious of Rome and the Jesuits* and turned toward Calvinist* theology, which he tried to synthesize with Orthodoxy*. He sent priests to study in the West, corresponded with leading Anglicans and Lutherans, and gave the *Codex Alexandrinus* (the most valuable early-5th-c. Greek manuscript of the OT and NT) to Charles I of England. His Western sympathies led to his being deposed several times, but he was restored through the efforts of the Dutch and British ambassadors. The sultan had him put to death on suspicion of being involved in an anti-Turkish plot. His *Confession of Faith* (1629) was condemned after his death for its Western and Calvinistic bias; in its place, the confessions of Peter Mogila* (1638) and Dositheus* of Jerusalem (1672) became the most widely approved summaries of Orthodox doctrine.

Lucian of Antioch (d312), presbyter in Antioch, martyr. He revised the text of the Greek Bible, and the "Lucianic text" became the accepted one in most of the Eastern Church. Arius* and his allies, who held a subordinationist* view of the second person of the Trinity*, regarded themselves as followers of Lucian; his status as a martyr enhanced the Arians' position. The second of the four creeds adopted by the Council of Antioch* (341) was said to be his.

Lucifer (from Lat *lux,* "light," and *ferre,* "to bring"; "bringer of light"), a name given to the Devil*, the prince of demons, viewed as a fallen angel (like a fallen star; Isa 14:12). The use of this name was popularized in works such as Dante's* *Inferno* and Milton's* *Paradise Lost.*

Luis de Granada (c1504–88), Dominican* preacher, writer, mystic*; born in Granada, Spain, to poor parents. After his father's death, his mother had to work as a laundress at a Dominican convent, probably the Convento de Santa Cruz recently founded by Ferdinand and Isabella*. Luis entered this priory (1524) and was later given a fellowship at the Colegio de San Gregorio at Valladolid (1529), where he was an outstanding student until 1534. Sometime afterward he was elected prior of the Convento of Escala Coeli near Cordoba and set about the task of reforming it. He gained the reputation of being a fluent and confident preacher, even as he spent several hours a day in solitary prayer away from the community. Based for a time in Badajoz, he composed his most famous work, *The Guide for Sinners* (*Guia de Peccadores,* 1555), then moved to Portugal (1557 until his death) as the provincial of the Portuguese Dominicans and the confessor of Queen Catherine. During this period, he wrote several additional books expressing a fiery enthusiasm for the Christian life in a gentle and charming style, particularly describing the revelation of Christ in the natural world. His writings continue to be read today in Roman Catholic spiritual circles.

PETER TYLER

Luke, Gospel of, one of the four Gospels of the NT. Literary comparison indicates that the author, named Luke, most likely knew the Gospel of Mark and another source (Q*) shared with Matthew. The Gospel of Luke includes much material otherwise unknown, such as the narratives of Jesus' birth and childhood and parables like those of the good Samaritan and the prodigal son. It was written in the late 1st c., some time before the writing of the Acts of the Apostles.

Luke mastered the literary conventions of his time; his work represents a Christianity both deeply embedded in Jewish tradition and defending itself on Greco-Roman grounds. Luke sees the person and mission of Jesus as a fulfillment of prophecies; the infancy narratives are permeated with references to the sacred texts of the Jews. God's history with his people is marked by a recurrent pattern of promise and fulfillment. Jesus' mission is to restore the people of God as it continues toward its universal purpose as promised to Abraham. Luke does not hold a supersessionist* view. While reaching out to the Gentiles and including them without requiring them to comply with Jewish tradition, he supports the special role of the Jewish people. The Jews, however, become divided over Jesus when he calls for a reversal of social distinctions and status, as predicted by Mary in the *Magnificat* (1:46–55).

Women are portrayed as acting and speaking in their own right, and Luke's composition features gender complementarity as part of more comprehensive patterns of parallelisms.

Good news is proclaimed to the poor, but the primary targets of the Gospel of Luke are the rich and prominent. They are called to meet the needs of others without expecting anything in return. The many meals depicted in this gospel refer not only to nourishment but to social interaction and community with those held in contempt by elite society. Conventional practices of reciprocity are redesigned to promote a provocative inclusive practice. In the end, only God's justice* will balance the accounts but the end-time is not imminent. Eschatological excitement is tempered by a moral and philosophical discourse aimed at conversion and perseverance. Luke also intensifies an ethos of voluntary abandonment to support an ascetic* lifestyle marked by sexual renunciation, even reinterpreting the virgin motherhood of Mary as a motherhood constituted by the fruitful reception of the Word of God, which in the Gospel of Luke is characteristic of a disciple*.

TURID KARLSEN SEIM

LUTHERANISM CLUSTER

1) *Introductory Entries*

Luther, Martin
Lutheran Churches and Their Theologies
Lutheran World Federation (LWF)
Lutheran Worship

2) *A Sampling of Lutheranism in Context*

Lutheranism in Germany
Lutheranism in the Nordic Countries
Lutheranism in the United States
Lutheranism in the United States: Evangelical Lutheran Church in America (ELCA)
Lutheranism in the United States: Lutheran Church–Missouri Synod

1) Introductory Entries

Luther, Martin (1483–1546), German Protestant Reformer, theologian, translator of Scripture. He initiated the Reformation* and influenced other Reformers, even when they disagreed with him. Luther was born and died in Eisleben, Germany, but spent most of his life as a professor of biblical interpretation at the University of Wittenberg. In 1505 he became an Augustinian* monk but left the order after he was excommunicated in 1521. Four years later, he married Katharina von Bora, a former nun, and they had six children. Although he was the acknowledged leader of the Lutheran Movement, his only official position was the academic chair he received in 1512 and held until his death.

Luther did not intend to leave the Roman Church or to start a reformation. As an earnest monk and teacher of Scripture, however, he began to question three features of medieval religion that led to irresolvable conflict with the papacy*: the Scholastic* theology in which he was trained; practices like indulgences* and praying to saints*, for which he could find no warrant in Scripture*; and papal claims to supreme authority in the church.

During his early lectures, Luther stumbled over Rom 1:16–17. He could not understand how the righteousness* of God could be revealed as good news (gospel), since the Nominalist* theology he had studied defined God's righteousness as the standard by which God judged sinners. In a moment of inspiration, which Luther described as "entering paradise through open gates," he decided with the help of Augustine* that Paul* intended that the righteousness of God be understood as a gift received through faith*. In academic debates (1516, 1517), Luther criticized the medieval notion that one could merit* grace* and salvation*, and the authority of Scholastic theology gave way to the Bible and Augustine.

Luther's discovery also led him to question the medieval piety in which he was raised. Indulgences were based on a theology that presupposed that contrite sinners* had to earn forgiveness by acts of penance* that made up for (satisfied) their sin. Since the purpose of indulgences was to release people from having to perform this satisfaction, for Luther they were superfluous once he was convinced that forgiveness was received in faith. Furthermore people no longer needed to pray to Mary and the saints since Christ was the only savior and object of faith. In a provocative set of 95 theses prepared for academic debate in 1517, Luther questioned not only the need for indulgences but also the power of the papacy to grant a full (plenary) indulgence that claimed to forgive sin in exchange for a contribution to the building of St. Peter's basilica in Rome.

This criticism of papal power initiated the conflict with Rome. During a crucial debate with John Eck at Leipzig in 1519, Luther rejected the traditional biblical basis for the divine origin of papal authority in Matt 16 and John 21. After persisting with his critical views and insisting that the authority of Scripture* remained "lord even over the pope," he was threatened with excommunication* (1520); in 1521 he was both excommunicated and declared an outlaw in Germany.

Owing to the protection of his immediate overlord, Elector Frederick of Saxony, Luther escaped capture and execution and returned in 1522 to his teaching duties in Wittenberg. By that time, Luther found himself the leader of a popular movement that was called evangelical* because it was based on the good news that salvation* was mediated by faith in Christ alone and not by any merit to be gained through religious activity. This principle, often called justification by faith, meant that the work of Christ was the sufficient basis of salvation and did not need to be supplemented by other works like satisfaction, invocation of saints, private masses, monastic vows, or fasting (see Justification, Theological Views and Practices, Cluster: A Central Doctrine for Western Christianity.) Accordingly, Luther and his colleagues had to construct a new Protestant piety that required an expansion and refinement of his theology. Redefining the sacramental life of the church proved to be especially controversial. In *The Babylonian Captivity of the Church* (1520), Luther had argued that only baptism* and the Lord's* Supper met the biblical standard for a sacrament*: commanded by Christ, joined with a promise, and requiring a material element. The medieval Mass*, understood to be a sacrifice offered to God, was replaced by the Lord's Supper as a means through which Christ bestowed the promised gift of forgiveness*. This promise was first applied to believers during baptism and remained valid for the forgiveness of all their sins* (not only original* sin) for as long as they recalled that promise in faith. Most Reformers, however, rejected Luther's sacramental views. Neither Ulrich Zwingli* nor the Anabaptists* believed that forgiveness of sin and regeneration occurred during baptism; the Anabaptists, moreover, rejected the baptism of infants and small children. Zwingli also rejected Luther's literal interpretation of the words of institution at the Lord's Supper, arguing that the Body and Blood of Christ were not really present in the sacrament. That disagreement, sealed in Marburg in 1529, led to the rise of separate Lutheran and Reformed churches.

Luther's main goal as a Reformer was to put in place a Christian way of living that was more biblical and Christ-centered than medieval piety. His template for that life was explained in *Freedom of a Christian* (1520): through faith Christians were the freest of all people and subject to none, but through love* they were servants of everyone and subject to all. After 1521 his work was dedicated to the nurture of that faith and love: he translated the Bible into German; wrote hymns and services of worship in German; composed the catechisms*; taught a new generation of pastors and found them parishes; wrote pamphlets on marriage, education, war and peace, and business ethics; and defended his movement politically and theologically. When he died in 1546, he still did not know whether the German Reformation would survive.

Luther's theology shaped the confessions of Lutheran churches around the world and became a prominent current of modern religious thought, but his authority has been mostly indirect and unofficial. Three of his writings acquired the status of Lutheran confessions in the *Book of Concord** (1580). Most influential is the *Small Catechism* (1529), but the *Augsburg* Confession* (1530), authored mainly by his closest colleague, Philip Melanchthon*, is acknowledged as the founding document of Lutheranism.

Luther's works include the following: lectures on Psalms, Romans, Galatians, and Hebrews (1513–21), Galatians (1531), and Genesis (1535–45); programmatic treatises of 1520: *The Papacy at Rome, To the Christian Nobility, The Babylonian Captivity of the Church,* and *Freedom of a Christian*; controversial and theological works: *Against Latomus* (examination of sin, grace, and faith, 1521), *Bondage of the Will* (1525) against Erasmus*, *Confession concerning Christ's Supper* (1528), *Schmalkaldic Articles* (1537), and *Councils and the Churches* (ecclesiology 1539); works on reform and education: *Estate of Marriage* (1522), *Temporal Authority* (1523), *To the City Councils of Germany* (schools, 1524), *German Mass* (1526), *The Large Catechism* and *The Small Catechism* (1529); a German translation of the NT (1522) and prefaces to books in the German Bible; hymns, sermons, and letters; and prefaces to his collected German (1539) and Latin (1545) works. SCOTT H. HENDRIX

Lutheran Churches and Their Theologies. Lutheran churches throughout the world claim continuity with the apostolic church. As "Lutheran," however, they trace their beginnings to the Reformation* initiated by Martin Luther*. It was not Luther's purpose to break from the Roman Catholic Church, and surely not to establish a denomination named after himself. Yet his proposals regarding the substance of the basic Christian message and church renewal set off a movement that in time was institutionalized.

In complicated ways that involved the Emperor Charles* V (1500 58), royalty and politicians in the German and Nordic states, popes*, and countless theologians of various points of view, the Lutheran Movement grew up alongside both the Roman Catholic Church and a number of other Reformation bodies. It soon lost its provisional character and a denomination was born.

Lutheran church bodies throughout the world have taken various paths. A state* church system characterized parts of Europe, and vestiges of that system remain in several countries. Lutheran churches in North and South America started as churches of immigrants. Lutheran churches in Asia and Africa are children of missions from Europe and North America. At the end of 2006, there were more than 200 Lutheran church bodies throughout the world, with a total membership of more than 70 million persons. Of these churches, 140 form the Lutheran* World Federation, which has a total membership of more than 66 million. The Lutheran churches outside the Federation, with more than 3 million members, led by the American Lutheran Church–Missouri Synod (see the present cluster: Lutheranism in the United States: Lutheran Church–Missouri Synod) are generally biblicist and nonecumenical.

Luther's original proposals were first fleshed out in the Augsburg* Confession, a document of 28 articles written by his colleague Philipp Melanchthon*

(1497–1560), signed by nine German territorial rulers, and presented to Charles V (1530). This confession found no agreement among the theologians of the Roman Catholic Church, and thus the complex process by which Lutheran churches came into being was begun. Consistently, these churches have retained the Augsburg Confession as their standard of faith and theology. In 1580 *The Book of Concord**, a formidable 700-page collection of seven "Lutheran" documents following the three "ecumenical creeds" (Apostles'*, Nicene*, and Athanasian*) was agreed to and Lutherans attained something like unity. Many Lutheran churches today continue to hold *The Book of Concord** as binding in its totality.

Thus Lutheran theology is always to be described as *confessional*. That theology has, to be sure, developed historically and contextually* as new circumstances and cultures have been encountered. Holding that a nonconfessional Christianity is a contradiction in terms, Lutherans find in the 16th-c. confessions an authoritative theological exposition of what is and what is not "Lutheran."

The original proposal of the Lutheran Reformation as developed in these confessions was that the Christian gospel should be seen in accordance with the Bible as God's gracious offer of unmerited salvation* in Jesus Christ, the message of "justification* by grace* through faith*" (see Justification, Theological Views and Practices, Cluster: A Central Doctrine for Western Christianity). This, Lutherans hold, is "the article by which the church stands or falls." The famous hallmarks of Luther's cause were *sola gratia* (by grace alone), *sola fide* (by faith alone), and *sola scriptura* (by Scripture* alone). This basic understanding was accompanied by other calls for reform: to give both the bread and wine in the Mass*, to conduct the Mass and to provide the Bible in local languages, to allow priests to marry, and to provide for great freedom in church government. Each of these calls has been theologically refined and developed over the years in ways, subtle and not so subtle, that have at times widened the gap between Lutherans and other Christians.

Certain dominating principles are found in Lutheran theology. That theology, in one current presentation, is trinitarian*, Christocentric*, highly sacramental*, church* centered, and thoroughly ecumenical*. Lutherans have participated in virtually all of the great theological debates of the past five centuries: orthodoxy and Pietism* in the post–Reformation Era, the role of human experience in relation to the operations of grace, the use of historical* criticism in biblical studies, and often divisive eucharistic* controversies. Lutheran social* ethics – based largely on views of law* and gospel* and the "two* kingdoms" – have at times, most notably in Germany before and during World War II, been seen as dualistic* and quietistic, separating the gospel from life in the world. Many ethicists since that war have worked to make classic Lutheran ethics more relevant to contemporary struggles for liberation* and social justice*.

It has largely been the modern ecumenical* movement that has caused Lutheran theology and ethics to be increasingly clarified and broadened. Several bilateral dialogues* – e.g. with the Roman Catholic Church, the Anglican Communion, and the Orthodox and Reformed churches – have required Lutherans to reexamine centuries-old positions. A notable result of these conversations has been the 1999 Joint Declaration on the Doctrine of Justification, signed by the Roman Catholic Church and the churches of the Lutheran World Federation. Whether the Lutheran tradition now has the generosity and will to move with other traditions toward unity is perhaps the chief question concerning its future.

NORMAN A. HJELM

Lutheran World Federation (LWF), a global "communion of churches," includes 140 church bodies in 78 countries, with a membership of more than 66 million. It was preceded by the Lutheran World Convention (1927, Eisenach, Germany), which could not reconvene because of World War II. The LWF was founded in 1947 in Lund, Sweden, with 47 churches from 26 countries; it was remarkable for bringing together German, Nordic, and North American Lutherans, whose nations had only recently been at war with each other.

The LWF faced four challenges at its inception: rescue of the needy, common initiatives in mission*, joint efforts in theology, and a common response to the ecumenical* movement. These challenges have continued to exist in various forms and contexts. The influx of refugees after the devastation of World War II led to a worldwide program of relief and development. The urgent support of mission churches that had been "orphaned" during World War II soon expanded to include the support of indigenous churches of the Two-thirds World. The Lutheran theological traditions were enriched by the ecumenical influence of Liberation*, Third World, and other theologies*. Ecumenically, the LWF has engaged in numerous bilateral dialogues. A significant result was the signing in 1999 by the Roman Catholic Church and the churches of the LWF of the Joint Declaration on the Doctrine of Justification* (1999); that central doctrine of Christian faith, so prominent in Reformation controversies and condemnations, is no longer a point of division between the two traditions.

At the intersection of doctrine and social concern, the LWF took an unprecedented stance in 1984 by suspending the membership of three churches in Southern Africa over the issue of apartheid. In keeping with Lutheran tradition, in 1977 the LWF had declared apartheid a *status* confessionis*, meaning that the very nature of Christianity is denied by the separation of races within the churches. After a lengthy pastoral process, this suspension was lifted in 1994.

The LWF, at first "a free association of Lutheran churches," declared itself "a communion of churches" (1990). In this deeper ecclesiological understanding, small, struggling church bodies from the Two-thirds World are on equal footing with large, wealthy churches from the Reformation heartlands. Women and laity have assumed positions of leadership alongside male clergy. Global social concerns of poverty*, violence*, and discrimination preoccupy the LWF and its Departments for World Service, Mission and Development, and Theology and Studies. Its headquarters are in Geneva, Switzerland.

NORMAN A. HJELM

Lutheran Worship. The distinct forms and styles of Lutheran worship can be traced back to the models provided by Martin Luther* (1484–1546). Lutheran worship remained in continuity with the Mass* of the Roman Catholic Church even though it has been regulated by various church orders in many countries and inculturated* into the folk cultures of many peoples.

Luther did not abolish the forms of worship practiced in the medieval church. His concern was to reform worship so that it might better serve the proclamation of the gospel. Luther revised the canon of the Mass so that Christ's words of institution of the Lord's Supper would stand in clear relief. His *Form of the Mass* (1523) was in Latin. His *German Mass* (1526) was for congregations that lacked choral resources; the German texts of the Mass were versified and set to tunes that the people could sing. Luther also encouraged the composition of hymns* for the congregation and set an example by providing 36 of his own.

Lutheran worship was regulated by official ordinances in countries that adopted the Reformation. Luther's models were influential but were not slavishly followed. Some church orders were more conservative than others in retaining traditional practices. The liturgical* year calendar* and lectionary*, altars* with their appointments, and vestments* for ministers remained customary in Lutheran practice. Lutheran worship gave a new emphasis to expository preaching* and frequent reception of Holy Communion* in both kinds. Communicants were expected to announce their intention to receive the sacrament to the pastor and to be examined and absolved (confession* and forgiveness*).

Lutheran worship gives prominence to church music* and congregational singing. The cantatas of Johann Sebastian Bach*

(1685–1750) are the high points of church music with multiple voices and/or instruments. The proliferation of hymns and spiritual songs helped to inculturate Lutheran worship into the folk cultures of many countries and regions, from Germany*, Scandinavia*, and Eastern Europe, to North America and to Eastern and Southern Africa, Southeast Asia, and the Far East. The multicultural character of Lutheran worship is reflected in recent worship books, such as *Evangelical Lutheran Worship* of the Evangelical Lutheran Church in America (2007) and *Lutheran Service Book* of the Lutheran Church–Missouri Synod (2007).

Lutheran worship is most distinctive when it remains Catholic in form, Evangelical* (i.e. gospel-centered) in content, participatory in practice, and multicultural in experience.

FRANK C. SENN

2) A Sampling of Lutheranism in Context

Lutheranism in Germany. Institutionally and organizationally, by far the largest number of Lutheran Christians in Germany* are members of the traditional territorial churches (see State Churches) that go back to the 16th c.; the main exceptions are the Independent Evangelical Lutheran Church and Lutheran communities in Baden. Free and independent of political rule since the end of World War I, all of these territorial churches belong to the Lutheran* World Federation, which was founded in 1947. In 1948 the United Evangelical Lutheran Church in Germany (VELKD) was organized as a federal church, now encompassing eight independent member churches (Bavaria, Brunswick, Hannover, Mecklenburg, North Elbe, Saxony, Schaumburg-Lippe, Thuringia; together, 10 million members). Outside the VELKD, the Lutheran churches in Oldenburg, Württemberg, and Pomerania (together, 3 million members) are nevertheless members of the Lutheran World Federation. In addition many communities within the United* Churches have a Lutheran character; their confirmands* are instructed according to Luther's *Small Catechism**. Altogether more Lutherans live in Germany than in any other country. The relation of the VELKD to the Evangelical Church in Germany (EKD), to which it is institutionally linked, and to the Union of Evangelical Churches has been debated since 2002. The conclusion was that the VELKD will continue with its own general synod, administration, bishops' conference, presiding bishop, and church offices. The work of the VELKD has put its stamp on Lutheranism through the service book (liturgy) and lectionary, the Doctrinal Ordinances and the Guidelines for Church Life, Service Regulations, and the Seminary for Theological Studies in Pullach, the Pastoral Seminary, and the Institute of Liturgical Studies in Leipzig.

Lutheranism in Germany (and worldwide) is distinguished by the Lutheran confessional documents *Book of Concord** (1580) and, especially, the Augsburg* Confession of 1530 and Luther's *Small Catechism*. A proper Lutheran Church is defined in the Augsburg Confession VII: "the congregation of saints, in which the gospel is purely preached and the sacraments rightly administered." The charisma of Lutheranism (the gift historically entrusted to it) is clarity of doctrine and worship with a focus on sinful humanity and the justifying God (see Justification, Theological Views and Practices, Cluster). Like every charisma, this charisma is not for self-display but for service. The Lutheran confession is not an end in itself but is to be a service to the *oikoumene*. Similarly, German Lutheranism is engaged in many ecumenical activities, chiefly through membership in the World* Council of Churches but first in the broader Protestant context.

Following the Arnoldshain Theses on the Lord's Supper (1957), the "Concord of the Reformed Churches in Europe" (Leuenberg Concord), which was concluded in 1973, brought Lutherans and Reformed closer together into a communion of churches, not a union. Lutheran theology and piety remain characteristically distinct from Reformed theology and piety (see Reformed Churches); there are distinct understandings of the Lord's* Supper, the relation between law* and gospel*; God's two* kingdoms or realms, and thereby social ethics, views of the church, ordination, and office. The Roman Catholic Church more readily seeks dialogue with the Lutherans than with the Reformed. The Joint Declaration on the Doctrine of Justification, accepted by the Roman Catholic Church and the churches of the Lutheran World Federation (Augsburg, October 31, 1999), provoked lively controversy among German Lutherans. The decisive points of Lutheranism, such as "by faith* alone" and "*simul iustus et peccator*" (both righteous* and sinner) and, above all, the significance of the doctrine of justification as a basic criterion of theology and ecclesiology, continue to be contested between Rome and Wittenberg and need further theological attention and development (see Justification, Theological Views and Practices, Cluster: A Central Doctrine for Western Christianity). Discussions are also taking place between Lutheran and Anglican theologians, as documented in *Worship and Ethics: Lutherans and Anglicans in Dialogue* (1994). Doctrinal discussions with the Methodist Church led, within the framework of the Leuenberg* Agreement (or Concord), to a mutual declaration of church communion. Dialogues with Mennonites* and Old* Catholics have resulted in a mutual declaration of eucharistic hospitality.

Not tied organizationally to the constituted churches, a number of Luther societies carry out their work, advancing knowledge of the person and work of Luther and clarifying his significance for the present. To this end, the Luther Society (*Luthergesellschaft*) was founded (1918) in Wittenberg. It disseminates the research of the "Luther renaissance," publishes the periodicals *Luther* and *Luther-Jahrbuch*, and sponsors lectures and conferences. Since 1932 the *Luther-Akademie Sondershausen-Ratzeburg* (as it is called today) has brought together German Lutheran theologians, along with others from the Nordic countries, for regular conferences to revive the theological heritage of Luther and introduce students to Luther studies, which also occurs in the universities.

Less visible institutionally but not to be undervalued is the cultural significance of Lutheranism in Germany. The language of Luther's Bible and many insights of Luther's theology, variously transmitted, remain more or less explicit in the present. Lutheranism is influential in Germany, not least through the hymns of Paul Gerhardt and the music of the arch-Lutheran Johann Sebastian Bach*.

OSWALD BAYER

Lutheranism in the Nordic Countries

(Denmark*, Finland*, Iceland, Norway*, Sweden*) has been and remains tied to the governments in a state–church system, although changes are taking place; thus the Church of Sweden* has become more autonomous since 2000. This is so because Lutheranism was introduced (in the 1530s) in Nordic countries partly for political reasons and partly because kings, princes, and/or leading clergy embraced Reformation theology, but not because of a broad public movement. The population abandoned Roman Catholic customs and theology slowly.

The governments used Lutheranism to maintain national identity and common values. Conversely, Lutheranism as the dominating confession had a religious quasi-monopoly that gave it a strong confessional character. Thus despite variations among countries, Nordic churches presently have a distinctive attitude toward ecumenism*; they are both more restrictive (maintaining their confessional stance) and more open to it than Lutheran churches in other countries.

Lutheranism is the core of the Nordic civil* religion; more than 80% of the population are baptized members of the national churches who limit their participation in the Lutheran churches to attending worship services for important national events, disasters, and tragedies that affect the population as a whole and for rites of passages (especially baptisms and funerals (see Secularization and Desecularization in Europe and North America). But Lutheranism has also been shaped (since the early 19th c.) by various revivalist* movements, which were theologically conservative but at times socially and politically radical. Thus these movements gave Lutheranism a clear direction with regard to mission* and *diakonia**, providing an opportunity for many women* to assume leadership roles in church work. There is often tension between Lutheran civil religion and Lutheran revivalism, resulting in the constituting of small, independent Lutheran churches that criticize the alleged conformity of the state church. Conversely, the state church provides a religious alternative for those who find that revivalist religious movements demand too much from their members.

The state–church system with its open form of Lutheranism makes possible the coexistence of groups with significantly different opinions about theological and moral issues, within one common framework. Although not without controversy, Lutheranism has taken moderately liberal stances by accepting recent social developments in church life, e.g. concerning the role of women (the ordination of women* in Sweden from 1958, including several bishops) and issues of global justice (e.g. the World* Council of Churches in Uppsala, 1968). **See also FOLK CHURCHES IN NORDIC COUNTRIES; PIETISM IN SCANDANAVIA.**

JAN-OLAV HENRIKSEN

Lutheranism in the United States. American Lutherans trace their roots to the 16th-c. Reformation*. Colonial Lutheranism depended for at least a century on European-trained and temporarily posted clergy, until German and Swedish ministers ordained Justus Falckner (1703).

Henry Melchior Muhlenberg* organized the Pennsylvania *ministerium* (1748), creating the first US based structure for recognizing ministers, training teachers, resolving disputes, and starting new churches. After the American Revolution, the needs of the missions on the frontier forced the colonial churches to adapt, and they formed "synods" that brought laity and clergy together to plan for expansion. Throughout the 19th c., the number of Lutherans in the USA, Canada, and the Caribbean increased as new immigrant groups arrived.

Theological disputes among 19th-c. Lutherans dominated the history of Lutheranism. In addition, Lutherans split along sectional lines during the Civil War. Widespread efforts to achieve reconciliation began in the 1930s when English replaced various immigrant languages as the common language in place of the various immigrant languages; these efforts resulted in the formation of the American Lutheran Church (ALC, 1960) and the Lutheran Church in America (LCA, 1962). Together with the Lutheran Church–Missouri Synod (LCMS), more than 90% of US Lutherans now belonged to three distinctly US churches. Two of these – the more congregational and Pietist ALC and the ecumenically oriented LCA – merged with a "moderate" offshoot (Evangelical Lutherans in Mission) of the staunchly confessional LCMS, forming in 1988 the Evangelical Lutheran Church in America (ELCA). Smaller groups, like the Wisconsin Synod and the Evangelical Lutheran Synod, remain independent and conservative, while the ELCA maintains the ecumenical and social ministry commitments of the American Lutheran tradition and represents American Lutheranism in the Lutheran World Federation.

Lutheran colleges, hospitals, social services, and missions carry on the social ministry and educational traditions of the several ethnic Lutheran streams and have expanded the reach of Lutheranism to make it an increasingly multicultural US tradition. MARIA ERLING

Lutheranism in the United States: Evangelical Lutheran Church in America (ELCA). Founded by a merger (1988), the ELCA is the largest American Lutheran denomination (5 million members; 10,700 congregations) in the USA and Caribbean. Its purpose is "to participate in God's mission and proclaim God's saving gospel of justification* by grace* for Christ's sake through faith* alone."

Broadly ecumenical, the ELCA has entered formal "full communion" with five other churches. Social* justice* and service are carried out through multiple partnerships, including Lutheran Services in America (the largest US nongovernmental social service network), the Lutheran* World Federation, and Lutheran World Relief. While congregations exhibit broad diversity, adherence to the Lutheran confessions and the widespread use of common liturgies and hymnody (*Evangelical Lutheran Worship*, 2006) bind them together as one church with 65 geographical synods (each led by an elected bishop). Churchwide offices in Chicago provide resources to congregations and coordinate partnerships with 74 international companion churches. Clergy (more than 17,500 active and retired women and men) are educated at eight seminaries. Persons from all backgrounds are served by 28 affiliated colleges and universities, as well as a vast array of schools and youth camps. MICHAEL L. COOPER-WHITE

Lutheranism in the United States: Lutheran Church–Missouri Synod, originally Die Deutsche Evangelisch-Lutherische Synode von Missouri, Ohio, und Andern Staaten, formed (in Chicago, 1847) by 12 pastors and 16 congregations (c3,000 members). German speaking, the Missouri Synod emphasized biblical doctrine and the Book of Concord* as a faithful exposition of God's inspired word. Centered in the Midwest, the Lutheran Church–Missouri Synod numbered more than 600,000 baptized members (early 20th c.). German immigration to the USA subsided, and two world wars forced it to anglicize. Questions about polity*, fellowship with other Lutherans, the nature and character of Scripture*, election* and conversion*, justification*, and inculturation* led to serious controversies (some ongoing). The Lutheran Church–Missouri Synod had nearly 3 million members in 1971, but only 2.5 million members and c6,000 congregations and c8,000 pastors in the early 21st c. With seminaries in Fort Wayne, Indiana, and St. Louis, Missouri, and colleges and universities in Ann Arbor, Michigan, Austin, Texas, Bronxville, New York, Irvine, California, Mequon, Wisconsin, Portland, Oregon, River Forest, Illinois, St. Paul, Minnesota, Selma, Alabama, and Seward, Nebraska, the Lutheran Church–Missouri Synod has the nation's largest Protestant school system, with more than 1,700 preschools, elementary schools, and high schools and 10,000 teachers. The Lutheran Church–Missouri Synod also has deaconesses*, directors of Christian education and of Christian outreach, a department of archives and history at Concordia Historical Institute, and headquarters in St. Louis, Missouri.
LAWRENCE R. RAST, JR.

Luwum, Janan (1924–77), saint, martyr, parish priest; Anglican bishop in Northern Uganda*, Anglican archbishop of Uganda, Rwanda*, Burundi*, and Boga (now in the Democratic Republic of the Congo*, 1974–77). Hero of the resistance, he publicly denounced Amin's brutal regime and abuse of human* rights, was arrested, and executed. ROBERT KAGGWA

Luxembourg. The Grand Duchy of Luxembourg encountered Christianity through traders and soldiers during the Roman occupation (3rd and 4th c., although historical evidence is lacking). Systematic attempts to Christianize the territory began in the 6th c. with Irish itinerant missionaries who wandered among the Germanic peoples of Northwest Europe. The first institutional Christian presence came with the foundation of Benedictine* monasteries (7th c.). The monastery of Echternach, founded by Willibrord (697), served as a missionary and spiritual center for the whole of Northwest Europe throughout the Middle Ages. During the Austrian Hapsburg occupation, Roman Catholicism became the state* church. In 1815 Luxembourg became a grand duchy ruled by the first Dutch king, William I, who recognized Protestantism.

Although the influence of the official church has been decreasing over the past decades, Roman Catholicism remains the dominant religion. Popular devotions to the Blessed Virgin Mary* and other saints are flourishing. The Christian presence in public media and politics remains strong. Thirty percent of the Luxembourg people are Roman Catholic immigrants (especially Portuguese, French, and Italian). Religious groups other than Christian are very small. Islam is not recognized as an official religion by the Luxembourg state, although freedom of religion is guaranteed.

Statistics: Population, 0.5 million (including 42% immigrants). Christians, 66.9% (Roman Catholics, 50.5%; Protestants, 0.8%; Eastern Orthodox, 0.4%; members of other Christian denominations, 15.2%); Jews, 0.2%; members of Eastern religions, 1.5%; members of other non-Christian religions, 0.6%; formerly religious, 13.3%; never religious, 16.5%. Attend religious services apart from special occasions: never, 32.5%; only on special holidays, 22.8%; once a week, 11.5%. Pray every day, 14.0%; never pray, 40.9%. (*Source*: 2004–5 *European Social Survey*.) Importance of religion: very important, 15.5%; quite important, 29.6%; not important, 30.6%; not at all important, 24.4%. Unpaid volunteers for a church or religious organization, 6.1%. (*Source*: 1999–2000 *European Values Study*.)

FRANS WIJSEN

LXX, shorthand for Septuagint*, the earliest and most influential Greek translation of the HB.

Maccabees, Books of

1 and 2 Maccabees are deuterocanonical* books found in the Septuagint* (in Greek) and the Catholic and Orthodox Bibles, but not in the HB and Protestant Bibles (see Bible, Canon of).

1 Maccabees (written in the late 2nd c. BCE), a unified composition in the style of the biblical historical books (e.g. Judges, Samuel, 1–2 Kings), has a conservative theological outlook similar to that of 1–2 Chronicles (possibly written by a Sadducee*). It presents Judea's struggle under the leadership of Mattathias and his sons, especially Judas Maccabeus, for liberation from the Hellenistic Seleucid kings, and especially from Antiochus Epiphanes, who sought to suppress Jewish worship and institutions.

2 Maccabees, a composite work, apparently redacted at different times, has a more Hellenistic theology; its final redaction, apparently addressed to a different audience (perhaps the Jewish Diaspora* in Egypt), seems to have intended to introduce Hanukkah, the Jewish holiday commemorating the rededication of the Temple during the Maccabean revolt. In 1 and 2 Maccabees, Judas Maccabaeus, portrayed as a heroic figure doing "God's will," became a well-known symbol through his re-presentation by Dante* (in *Paradiso*) and Handel* (in the oratorio *Judas Maccabaeus*).

3 and 4 Maccabees are deuterocanonical books (part of the Bible) only for Eastern Orthodox churches.

3 Maccabees (written in the 2nd or 1st c. BCE) refers not to the Maccabees' revolt, but to similar situations in which God's miraculous deliverance of the Jews from threatened destruction by foreign oppressors occurred.

4 Maccabees (possibly written in the 1st c. CE) emphasizes martyrdom* (of Eleazar and the mother and her seven sons) and is most significant for its presentation of martyrdom as a vicarious sacrifice* redeeming God's people Israel – a notion that made this book important for Christians (although there is no evidence of direct influence on the NT), especially for the development of martyrology. Thus this book was significant for, e.g., Gregory* Nazianzus, John* Chrysostom, Ambrose*, and Augustine*.

DANIEL PATTE

Macedonia is a region in the Balkans covering Northern Greece* and the southwest corner of Bulgaria*, where Paul* established Christian communities in Philippi and Thessaloniki, with the latter dominating Southern Macedonia to the present. The bishop of Thessaloniki held the title of vicar of the Church of Rome (from 412), and the city housed the relics of the 4th-c. martyr Demetrios, whose basilica attracted pilgrims from the 5th c. to the present. The Balkan Wars of 1912–13 carved out the current Greek and Bulgarian boundaries of Macedonia. At the end of World War II, Yugoslavia created the autonomous Republic of Macedonia.

JAMES C. SKEDROS

Macedonia, the Republic of, a small Balkan country bordered by Serbia*, Bulgaria*, Greece*, and Albania*.

Christianity was established in Roman cities (e.g. Stobi, Ohrid) as early as the 4th c. under the jurisdiction of the bishop of Thessaloniki, who held the title of the vicar of the Church of Rome (from 412). Non-Christian Slavs moved into Macedonia (from the mid-6th c.). The missionaries Clement and Nahum (disciples of Cyril* and Methodios) established themselves in Ohrid (late 9th c.) and trained numerous native Slavic-speaking clergy. Successive Bulgarian and Serbian expansion dominated the medieval period; Ohrid became the seat of the autocephalous* Bulgarian Patriarchate (11th c.). Ottoman advances (second half of the 14th and 15th c.) resulted in several centuries of Muslim rule, which contributed to the multifariousness of an already diverse population. At the end of World War II, Yugoslavia created the autonomous Republic of Macedonia. In 1991 the Republic gained its independence.

Eastern Orthodoxy* in its Slavic expression has remained the dominant form of Christianity within Macedonia. The Macedonian Orthodox Church plays an important role in national and ethnic identity, and declared its independence from the Serbian Orthodox Church (1967). Yet no other Orthodox church has recognized its autocephaly. Several important monasteries and churches (St. George near Kumanovo; the Monastery of the Archangel Michael near Kratovo) survive from the medieval Serbian kingdom. Nearly one-quarter of Macedonians are Muslim, the vast majority of ethnic Albanian descent.

Statistics: Population (2000): 2 million. Christians, 64% (Orthodox, 59.5%; Roman Catholics, 3.5%; independents, 0.05%; Protestants, 0.04%); Muslims, 28%; nonreligious, 8%. (Based on *World Christian Encyclopedia*, 2001.)

JAMES C. SKEDROS

Machen, J. Gresham (1881–1937), Presbyterian scholar who played an important role in the liberal–fundamentalist controversies (1920s) in the USA as a spokesperson for fundamentalists*. Many fundamentalists (and other conservatives) found Machen's polemical writings deeply compelling, including his claim in *Christianity and Liberalism* (1923) that Protestant modernism is not a modern version of the Christian faith, but rather a set of beliefs and practices that are clearly un-biblical and un-Christian. Machen taught at Princeton Theological Seminary (1906–29) and played an important role in the creation of Westminster Theological Seminary (Philadelphia) and the Orthodox Presbyterian Church. DAVID HARRINGTON WATT

Mackay, John A. (1889–1983). The first Protestant missionary to gain acceptance in intellectual circles in Peru, Mackay exercised great influence over Protestant missionary activity in all Latin America. As president of Princeton Theological Seminary (1936–59), he fostered ecumenical studies and called for tolerance in the face of Senator McCarthy's anti-Communist campaign. He arrived in Peru in 1916 and transformed the Anglo-Peruvian (today San Andrés) school into one of the most prestigious preparatory schools. Among his close friends were Luis Alberto Sánchez, a leading man of letters, and Víctor Raúl Haya de la Torre, founder of the Aprista Party. **See also PERU.**

JEFFREY KLAIBER, SJ

Macrina (c327–c380), one of the Cappadocians*. The first child of Basil and Emmelia, Macrina was named for her grandmother, Macrina the Elder, a martyr. Her secret name, revealed to her mother three times, was Thecla*, after the 2nd-c. saint widely honored as an example of a celibate. After the death of the spouse chosen by her parents, Macrina claimed for herself, at the age of 12, the rights of a widow* and adopted the monastic* life (c339 or 340). After the death of her father (probably sometime between 341 and 345), Macrina and her mother gradually transformed their home in Annisa into a monastic* community, where they engaged in activities reserved for slaves* (baking bread and weaving garments); this suggests the influence of Eustathius* of Sebaste, who was rebuked by the Synod of Gangra* for minimizing the differences between slaves and free persons. Macrina persuaded her brother Basil* to return from his studies in Athens and adopt the ascetic* life (probably 355/56); their younger brother Naucratius had already adopted the solitary life (probably 352). It was most likely Basil (357/58) who organized a double* monastery with areas for men and women, sharing a church. After Macrina's death, her brother Gregory of Nyssa wrote the *Life* of Macrina and a discourse *On the Soul and Resurrection* that was placed in her mouth. EUGENE TESELLE

Madagascar, "the Big Island," off Africa in the Indian Ocean. The population is composed of descendants of immigrants from the South Pacific (who arrived mainly between the 3rd and 5th c. CE). These people, the Merina (comprising many ethnic groups, who speak Malagasy), are the dominant people of the island and live in the central highlands. Christians among them are mostly Protestants. There are also "coastal people" from Africa (Bantu), who settled shortly after the Merina in the coastal areas, where Muslim Arabs established trading posts (from the 7th c.). Christians among them are mostly Catholics. About half of the population is Christian, almost equally divided between Protestantism and Roman Catholicism.

Christianity arrived on the island with the Portuguese (1500), who brought the first missionary, the Dominican João de San Tomas (1585). They were followed by Jesuits, including Luis Mariano (1613); Fr. Nacquat produced a catechism in Malagasy (1657). These sporadic missionary efforts were unsuccessful until the 19th c., when David Jones, a missionary of the London Missionary Society (LMS), was welcomed by King Radama I (1810–28), who sought to open the island to European culture. LMS missionaries (not associated with a colonialist occupation; the British never occupied the island) started a network of schools and brought artisans to found industries, developing a Christian presence in the fabric of society. At the same time, they preached the gospel, using

Fr. Nacquat's catechism, and translated the Bible (completed 1836).

Queen Ranavalona I (1828–61) expelled all the missionaries and persecuted Christians (with hundreds of martyrs). But when missionaries returned (1861), the number of Christians had increased to about 5,000. When Queen Ranavalona II became a Christian (1869) and made Christianity the religion of the island, the number of Christians quickly grew (to 39% of the population by 1900); thereafter, growth was very slow.

Political struggle between the Merina rulers and the French colonists resulted in two wars (1883–86, 1895–96), during which all the Catholic missionaries were expelled. When Madagascar became a French colony (1896), there was a new wave of persecution against Christians (during which many were killed, and churches were burned), and the anticlericalism* of the French administration severely limited church activities.

While Protestantism is firmly rooted in the Merina intellectual, upper social class (on the plateau), the Roman Catholic Church oriented its work toward coastal people, the peasant masses.

The Roman Catholic Church, which in 2000 had about 3.7 million members in more than 300 parishes, progressively gained a Malagasy identity, with the first nine Malagasy priests ordained in 1925, the first Malagasy bishop in 1939, and the first Malagasy archbishop in 1960. The Second Vatican* Council bought about a greater Catholic Malagasy identity (with the National Synod called by the bishops in 1975). Although a great number of priests and religious are of foreign origin, the creation of the Catholic Theological Institute (1980s) seeks to reverse this trend. The network of youth centers compensates for the limits placed on Catholic schools by the laicization* imposed by the French (until 1960), although the teaching of (Catholic or Protestant) catechism in public schools and subsidies for private schools (including Catholic) since 1972 opens new possibilities for the Roman Catholic Church.

Protestantism, based on the work of the LMS, was strongly reinforced by the conversion (to Protestantism) of Queen Ranavalona II (1869), which led to a mass movement (*rebik'ondry*) into Protestant churches, especially among Merinas. Missionaries from the British Friends* (1869) and from the Paris (Protestant) Mission (1897) cooperated with LMS missionaries, developing local churches (according to comity* agreements), until 1968, when all these churches were united in the Church of Jesus Christ in Madagascar (a Reformed church, l'Église de Jésus Christ à Madagascar, two-thirds of Malagasy Protestants). Following the emphasis of the LMS missionaries, the Church of Jesus Christ has a vast network of primary and secondary schools and is actively integrated into Malagasy daily life through social work institutions. Similarly, the missionaries of the Norwegian Missionary Society (since 1866), joined by other Lutherans, led to the formation of the Malagasy Lutheran Church (south of the island), the second-largest Protestant church (one-quarter of Malagasy Protestants). Most Protestant pastors are Malagasy, now trained in two seminaries: the Faculty of Theology of the Church of Jesus Christ (since 1979) and the Lutheran Faculty of Theology (since 1985).

Christianity in Madagascar faces the issue of the relationship between church* and state, including laicization*, a legacy of the French colonial period. Laicization is resisted by Catholics. Protestants, theoretically in favor of a strict separation of church* and state (e.g. they banned national flags from Protestant sanctuaries), have among their members many Merina political figures and heads of government.

Christianity is also confronted by the fact that about half of the population practices the traditional religion that combines Merina and African* Religion. This religion involves faith in a supreme deity, Zanahary, and primarily the veneration of ancestors*, who are believed to reward or punish the living. For instance, the Merina and Betsileo engage in the reburial practice of "turning over the dead" in order to celebrate spiritual communion with ancestors, the "living dead," and receive blessings; during the ritual, the relatives' remains are removed from the family tomb, rewrapped in new shrouds, and returned to the tomb following festive ceremonies in their honor. Many Christians practice such veneration of ancestors, even though they regularly attend Mass or worship services; Catholic and Protestant attendance is very high.

In addition, spirit possession and medium activity are central to the Malagasy culture. Mediums ("shepherds"), traditionally women, have significant spiritual authority. Early Protestant missionaries brought to Madagascar concepts of a male deity whose worship was led exclusively by males; they strove to repress "emotional" worship, which they claimed was a reflection of "pagan" ritual, and did not associate worship with healing. Thus Christianity was incoherent to many islanders. Hence, Madagascar's Healing Shepherds, a Christian Charismatic* movement affirming the leadership and healing power and authority of women, and offering an effective model for healing the mentally ill, attracted many.

Statistics: Population (2008): 20 million (M). Christians, 50% (Protestants, 25%; Roman Catholics, 23%; Anglicans, 2%); African Religionists, 47%; Muslims, 3%. (Based on *World Christian Encyclopedia*, 2001, and United Nations: World Population Prospects, 2008.)

VOLOLONA RANDRIAMANANTENA ANDRIAMITANDRINA

Madonna (Italian, "my lady"), a title of address for Mary*; also a designation for pictures or statues of Mary. **See also BLACK MADONNA; MARY, THE VIRGIN, CLUSTER.**

Magdala, town on the Sea of Galilee*, probable birthplace and home of Mary* Magdalene; important fishing and fish-exporting center of the Roman Empire.

Magdalene. See MARY MAGDALENE.

Magi, originally a priestly caste among Medes and Persians; among Greeks the term "magus" acquired various connotations: sage, astrologer, magician, or charlatan. Magi are represented as the first Gentiles* to have honored Christ (Matt 2:1–12). Through the centuries, they were interpreted in ways that reflected evolving cultures. The fact that they offered three gifts led to the conviction that the Magi were three in number. Gradually they came to be considered kings (Ps 72:10–11; Isa 60:3); they were named (Gaspar, Balthasar, and Melchior in the West); and they were viewed as representing three age groups (youth, middle age, old age) and three races (yellow, white, black). Today at least one of them is sometimes represented as a woman.

Magisterium (Lat *magister*, "teacher"), in Roman Catholicism, the authoritative* teaching function of the Church, whose formal pronouncements on faith and morals are infallible*; even "ordinary *magisterium*" (teaching by bishops) is to be obeyed in a general way.

Magnificat, Mary's* song of praise (Luke 1:46–55), is named from its opening word in the Vulgate*; part of vespers* in the West, morning office in the East.

Mahabane, Zacheus R. (1881–1970), Methodist minister and president general of the African National Congress in 1924 and 1937; vice president of the All African Convention and first president of the Non-European Unity Movement (1943). In 1956 he became president of the Interdenominational African Ministers Federation. He worked for change through both politics and the church. **See also SOUTH AFRICA.** MOKGETHI MOTLHABI

Maimonides, Moses ben Maimon (1138–1204), born in Cordova, the capital of Andalusia (Muslim Spain). A Jewish scholar, he lived amid the intercultural splendor of this largest and most affluent city of Europe until 1148, when an invasion of North African Berbers, ostensibly to assist local Muslims against the Spanish *reconquista**, forced his family into exile. They fled first to Fez (Morocco) and then, via the Holy Land (in the throes of the Crusades*), to Cairo, where he remained until his death. His prodigious intellectual output included scientific treatises on the calendar, the art of logic, a commentary on the Mishnah, and a codification of Jewish religious law from its sources. At 33 he became the supreme religious authority of Jews in Egypt and the medical consultant at the court of the sultan, Saladin. There he composed a set of reflections on faith* and reason*, Torah and philosophy for his pupil, Joseph, which were compiled in the *Guide of the Perplexed*. This work inspired Thomas Aquinas* (1226–74) to undertake a similar project. Like Thomas's work, Maimonides' *Guide of the Perplexed* did not always meet with appreciation by his own community, yet it reflects the ability of Jewish scholars to address religious issues in the larger Islamic world. DAVID B. BURRELL, CSC

Malabar Christians. A Christian community known as Thomas Christians, or Malabar Christians, has existed on the southwest coast of India since ancient times, as attested to by 4th-c. sources. The community claims that it was founded by the apostle Thomas*, who evangelized India in the late 1st c. Located in the state of Kerala, these Christians form a distinct religious community fully integrated into Indian society. During the early centuries, they were in full communion with the Assyrian* Church in Persia, which sent bishops to India. Since these bishops did not speak the local language, real jurisdiction was placed in the hands of an Indian priest who was given the title of archdeacon of all India and who served as the civil and religious superior of the community of the Malabar Christians until the arrival of the Portuguese (late 15th c.).

The Persian connection was beneficial to the Malabar Christians in that it opened the small Christian community to the larger Christian world. But for many, this relationship compromised the independence of the community. The core elements of Christian life remained foreign in a country with a rich culture, philosophy, and body of religious thought. However, the Malabar Christians early on developed a lifestyle of their own. In the social and cultural realms, they followed the customs and practices of their Hindu brothers and sisters (see Hinduism and Christianity Cluster). Socially, they became the peers of those in the higher classes. The social and ecclesiastical life of Malabar Christians before the arrival of the Portuguese reflects a unique Christian vision of this community. The oneness with their social and cultural milieu implied an inculturated* approach, an awareness that Christ in becoming human assumed everything human and redeemed all social and cultural values. However, the Portuguese* colonization* was the beginning of a sad history of forced Latinization and Westernization that caused unrest and schisms among Malabar Christians. Thus in the early 21st c., the 8 million Malabar Christians in India are divided among five Oriental churches, including the Syro-Malabar Catholic Church, and their adherents are spread throughout the world. **See also ORTHODOX CHURCHES, ORIENTAL, CLUSTER: MALANKARA ORTHODOX SYRIAN CHURCH.** JOSEPH PATHRAPANKAL

Malachi, Book of, concludes the collection of the Twelve Prophets, reflects the weaknesses of a disheartened postexilic community (1; 2, 3:6–12), and announces God's certain coming to fulfill all the people's hopes (3:1–5, 3:16–4:6). Although Malachi (Hebrew for "my YHWH's messenger") may be a personal name, modern scholarship suggests it is a title, an editor's attempt to identify the author with the promised messenger of 3:1.

The book is dated to the Persian period (470–50 BCE), primarily because the author confronts the same sorts of abuses (lax priesthood, prevalent intermarriage, lack of social justice) that Nehemiah and Ezra* set out to reform.

Composed of six sections in question-and-answer dialogic style (1:2–5, 1:6–2:9, 2:10–16, 2:17–3:5, 3:6–12, 3:13–4:3), Malachi stresses covenant* obedience: the levitical covenant that the priests have corrupted and that YHWH is determined to uphold (2:4); the marriage covenant (2:10, 14) desecrated by individuals desirous of upgrading their status; and the Sinai covenant, the Law of Moses (4:4), which still functions as the unchanging authority for the community.

Malachi addresses issues of religious indifference (3:6–12), social justice* (3:5), and doubts caused by the prosperity of the wicked (2:17–3:16). He anticipates a judgment* when the wicked will be destroyed and the righteous rewarded, when a renewal that begins with the nations (1:11) will culminate in the transformation of God's own people (3:13–4:3).

Malachi's identification of Elijah* as foreshadowing "the great and terrible Day of the Lord" (4:5) has influenced both Jewish and Christian eschatology*. In the NT, John* the Baptist is identified as Elijah (Matt 11:14, 17:10–13), and in Judaism at the Passover meal, a place is set for Elijah, the long-awaited guest.

BETH GLAZIER-MCDONALD

Malankara Orthodox Syrian Church. See ORTHODOX* CHURCHES, ORIENTAL CLUSTER: MALANKARA ORTHODOX SYRIAN CHURCH.

Malawi (Nyasaland when a British protectorate, 1891–1964) had five overlapping phases of Christian development.

1. *The arrival of the historical churches.* Christianity was brought to Malawi (1861–85) by the Universities' Mission to Central Africa, which established the Anglican Church. The Livingstonia Mission (1875, the Free Church of Scotland), Blantyre Mission (1876, the Church of Scotland), and Dutch Reformed Church Mission (1889) joined together to form the Church of Central Africa Presbyterian (1924–26). The Roman Catholic Church arrived with the Montfort Fathers (1889–1901) and the White Fathers (1902).
2. *Independent African leadership* was fostered by the English missionary Joseph Booth in churches as diverse as the Zambezi Evangelical Church (1892), African Evangelical Church (1893), Churches of Christ (1906), Seventh Day Baptists (1898–1910), and Seventh-day Adventists (1902). Subsequently, the Malawians also founded churches, e.g. Providence Industrial Mission (John Chilebwe, 1900) and the Watch Tower Church (Elliot Kamwana, 1908). Thereafter, African* Instituted Churches of various types proliferated.
3. *The handing over of leadership to Africans.* This occurred in most mission churches

(c1964, when political independence was achieved). New missions also arrived, including the Southern Baptist Mission (1960), Wisconsin Evangelical Lutheran (1962), Christian Brethren (1964), Free Methodist Church (1973), Church of God of Prophecy (1977), and Pentecostal Assembly of Canada (1978), founding churches of their traditions.

4. *The interdenominational revival movement (from the 1970s).* Through parachurch* organizations, e.g. New Life for All and the Scripture Union, young people brought the gospel to the streets, schools, and churches; these youth became educated Christian leaders in church and society.
5. *The Charismatic* revival.* Although the Charismatic Movement started with fellowships and ministries mostly for the educated class, it soon came to include self-funded, mostly urban Charismatic churches, such as Agape (Pastor Mgala, 1982), Faith of God (Pastor Matoga, 1984), Living Waters (Pastor Ndovi, 1985), All for Jesus (Pastor Zalimba, 1993), Frames of Victory (Pastor Katchire, 1993), Calvary Family Church (Pastor Mbewe, 1994), and Vineyard (Pastor Gama, 1994).

Women's ordination is controversial. The Assemblies of God and the Church of Central Africa Presbyterian are the only mission churches that ordain women. However, the interdenominational and Charismatic revivals opened a door to churches founded by women, including the Chilobwe Healing Centre (Mayi Nyajere, 1986), Revival Ministries (Mayi Gonthi, 1986), Blessed Hope Church and Ministries (Bishop Yami Mchika, 1992), Namatapa Miracle Centre (Mayi Chipondeni, 1992), and Chisomo Worship Centre (Mayi Chapomba, 1998).

Statistics: Population (2008): 14 million. Christians, 77% (Roman Catholics, 25%; Protestants, 20%; members of African Instituted Churches, 18%; Anglicans, 3%; marginal Christians, 1%; other Christians, 10%); Muslims, 15%; African Religionists, 5%. (Based on *World Christian Encyclopedia*, 2001, and United Nations: World Population Prospects, 2008.)

ISABEL APAWO PHIRI

Malaysia is a tropical nation, multicultural, multiracial (Bumiputera [mostly Malays], 60.3%; Chinese, 26%; Indians, 7.7%) and multireligious (Islam, Buddhism, Christianity, Hinduism). Malaysia's official religion is Sunni Islam, popularized by Indian and Arab merchants (15th c.). The Malay-predominant government is joined by Chinese, Indians, and major indigenous peoples in East Malaysia (e.g. Sabah and Sarawak). Its constitution specifies that Malays must be Muslims. Evangelism among Muslims is banned by state law. Apostasy from Islam is rarely allowed or publicized. Despite recent and increasing Muslim antagonism toward other religions, non-Muslims are entitled to practice their religious beliefs and rituals. Chinese and Indians can also run their own school systems, using their languages, although students must learn Malay, the official language, especially if they want to attend local universities.

Roman Catholicism was introduced in Malaysia when the Portuguese conquered Melaka (1511, for the spice trade; see Portuguese Explorations, Conquests, and Missions). Evangelism by missionaries (e.g. Francis* Xavier) bore little fruit, partly because of tensions between the Vatican and Portugal* over the control of Catholic missions. With the Dutch becoming the new colonists (1641), Protestantism arrived and Catholicism was repressed until 1703. The first Malay (1733) and Chinese (1823) Bibles were published. The British, when they occupied Penang (1786), brought with them Anglicanism and Methodism; Christianity started to progress, and freedom for all religions was implemented. In 1813 William Milne, the first Protestant missionary (London Missionary Society), settled in Melaka. With the help of Munshi Abdullah, a local English-speaking Muslim, missionary work and publication developed. Meanwhile, the Anglican Church advanced under Robert Hutchings but remained a white, English-speaking ministry until the early 20th c. By 1874 the British ruled most of Malaysia. Throughout their colonial rule, they remained neutral toward Islam as they courted collaboration from Muslim elites. When West Malaysia became independent (1957), the privileged status of Malays and Islam was guaranteed by the constitution. British colonial policy, however, has led to racial and economic tensions. To secure social stability, laws such as the 1960 Internal Security Act and the 1969 Emergency Act can be invoked to detain suspects without formal charges.

Beginning in the late 19th c., American Methodists and Overseas Missionary Fellowship contributed to the evangelism of many Chinese and Indian communities. Both William F. Oldham (1854–1935) and Sophia Blackmore (1857–1945) greatly promoted education* for men and women. By the 20th c., the Chinese were the largest Christian group; the work of Chinese missionaries (e.g. Sung* Shang-Jie, 1901–44) was not insignificant. Reformed theology propounded by Stephen Tong (b1940), a Chinese Indonesian theologian, has also received a wide audience since the 1990s. In 1984 the Christian Federation of Malaysia began providing a unified front for Catholics and Protestants. Some noted Christian leaders and scholars actively participate in politics. Social service ministries focus on orphanages and rehabilitation for gambling, drug, and alcohol abuse. Many of the 10 major Pentecostal/Charismatic, Catholic, and Protestant seminaries are underfunded.

Statistics: Population (2007): 27.17 million. Christians, 9.1% (Roman Catholics, 3.3%; Protestants, 3%; Anglicans, 0.9%; independents, 0.8%); Muslims, 60.4%; Buddhists, 19.2%; Hindus, 6.3%; Confucians, Daoists, and Chinese folk religionists, 2.6%. (Based on *World Christian Encyclopedia*, 2001, and United Nations: World Population Prospects, 2008.)

MENGHUN GOH

Malcolm X, born Malcolm Little (1925), often viewed as the father of black power, emerged soon after his release from prison (1952) as the most important minister in Elijah Muhammad's Nation of Islam (Black Muslim Movement). From 1957 until his assassination (1965), he tried unsuccessfully to develop a dialogue between the Nation of Islam and Martin Luther King's* Southern* Christian Leadership Conference. Differences over the love ethic, retaliatory violence, integration, and the relevance of the Christian faith to the African American freedom struggle prevented the two leaders from cooperating, although they seemed to be moving along converging paths at the time of their deaths.

LEWIS V. BALDWIN

Malines Conversations (1921–25), a series of meetings, following the 1920 Lambeth* Conference, between Anglican and Roman Catholic theologians, held in Malines, Belgium, under the sponsorship of Cardinal Mercier. The participants reached agreement about episcopacy, the pope's primacy, and the Eucharist, making significant inroads into unity or re-union within the church. The conversations were viewed with suspicion by Protestant-leaning factions in the Church of England and by conservative Roman Catholics. The conversations ended with Cardinal Mercier's death, and Pope Pius XI's encyclical* *Mortalium Animos* (1928) warned Catholics to stay out of ecumenical dialogues.

Malula, John (1917–89), born in Kinshasa (1917), ordained a priest (1946), consecrated a bishop (1959), made a cardinal (1969). Received the degree of *Doctor honoris causa* from both the Catholic University of Leuven (1978) and Boston College (1980). Upon his episcopal consecration, in the Congo* under Belgian rule, he expressed his pastoral stance in terms of "a Congolese Church in a Congolese state" and of social and political justice. As a result, he was expelled from Kinshasa and, for a time, sought refuge in Rome (1972).

Malula's pastoral legacy includes the composition of liturgical songs; the founding of the Sisters of Saint Theresa of the Child Jesus; the elaboration of the "Zairian/Congolese Rite" of Mass; the erection of four seminaries, an institution for lay leaders of the Small Christian Communities, and centers for disabled people, as well as for the pastoral and intellectual training of Catholic women; and the convocation of the Diocesan Synod (1986–88). His *Oeuvres complètes* (edited by De Saint Moulin) show that Malula sought to found a Congolese Church and be a prophet of justice*, often repeating that he preferred to be crucified than to crucify the truth.

JEAN-CLAUDE LOBA-MKOLE

Mammon (Heb "wealth," "property," "money"), a term used in Matt 6:24 and Luke 16:13 to designate wealth as an idol* that people serve instead of serving God. "No one can serve two masters.... You cannot serve God and Mammon" (see also Luke 16:9).

Manassas (or Manasseh), Prayer of, a deuterocanonical book (although the Council of Trent* put it in an appendix of the Roman Catholic Bible; see Apocrypha Cluster; Bible, Canon of), is a prayer attributed to Manasseh (687–42 BCE; 2 Chr 33). An individual lament of personal sin*, it emphasizes God's infinite mercy and grace*. Throughout history, because of anti*-Jewish prejudice ("hypocrite Jews" could not pray such an introspective penitential prayer), it was viewed as a Christian prayer. But scholars agree that it was composed by a Jew, perhaps near Jerusalem sometime before the destruction of the Temple (70 CE).

Mani, Manichaeism. Mani (216–76) was born near Ctesiphon, Mesopotamia. His father, Pattek, a native of Ecbatana, joined a Mughtasilite community of Elkesaites*, which Mani left at the age of 24 after receiving a second revelation from his divine "twin" about his role as the successor of Buddha, Zoroaster, and Jesus. After traveling extensively in the newly founded Sasanian Empire and in India, he wrote in Aramaic the seven books that formed the canon of his church. He enjoyed the patronage of the Sassanid Shâh, Shapur I (220–73). Under Vahram I, who favored Zoroastrianism, Mani was imprisoned and died.

Manichaeism spread rapidly (3rd and 4th c.) but became one of the most persecuted heresies* under Christian Roman emperors. It reached China (7th c.) and became the state religion of the Uighurs in Central Asia (8th c.). Its prophetology, universal evangelism, and key doctrine of the suffering of the divine in matter motivated extensive accommodation to the various mission fields of the church. This was supported by a firm ecclesiastical organization and an interdependent relationship between clergy and laity, elect and hearers.

The key Manichaean doctrine of radical dualism* of spirit and matter, light and darkness, is based on an elaborate cosmogony that explains the past, present, and future situations of the world. Among the deities, emanations of the Father of Greatness, who fight the forces of Darkness besieging human minds, are Jesus the Light (one of several Jesus figures) and the Light-Nous. Equipped with divine properties, the Manichaean elect worked for the liberation of the divine light in two significant ways: they preached and disseminated the words of truth in order to instill enlightenment in the human mind, and they daily consumed light-containing vegetarian food by which light was released through digestion. This required regular purification through fasting, prayer, hymn singing, and confession.

GUNNER BJERG MIKKELSEN

Manning, Henry Edward (1808–92), Anglican priest, closely associated with the Oxford* Movement. Manning was received into the Roman Catholic Church (1851) and appointed archbishop of Westminster (1865); he rigorously supported poor relief and promoted Catholic education. His commitment to social justice* led to close working relations with other Christians; he had a significant role in negotiating the end of the 1889 London dockers' strike. He was influential at the Vatican, supporting the centrality of the pope* and Ultramontane* causes generally and pressed for the 1870 Vatican I declaration of papal infallibility. PETER C. ERB

Manuscripts of the Bible. See BIBLE, TEXTS AND MANUSCRIPTS.

Maphrian, title of the bishop of the Syriac* Orthodox Church, next in rank after the patriarch*.

Marburg Colloquy, meeting held in October 1529 between Martin Luther* and Ulrich Zwingli* and their supporters to resolve differences concerning the Lord's* Supper, which would in turn make possible a defensive political alliance among Protestant cities and territories against the Catholic emperor Charles* V. The participants adopted a statement of faith in which they agreed on 14 articles but acknowledged in the 15th article their differences on the sacrament. Nevertheless, the colloquy effectively ended polemical exchanges between Lutherans and Zwinglians and ultimately led to the Wittenberg Concord (1536), establishing a consensus on the Lord's Supper between Luther and the cities of South Germany. AMY NELSON BURNETT

Marcel, Gabriel (1889–1973), existential philosopher, playwright, composer, literary critic, book editor; friend of Bergson*, Maritain*, and Ricoeur* and a critic of Jean-Paul Sartre's atheistic existentialism*. A convert to Roman Catholicism (1929), he criticized the modern obsession with technology* that ignored the God-given dignity of each person*, the value of intimate interpersonal relations, and the deep human need for being (God). Using phenomenological* analysis of lived experience, he was among the first to explain the distinction between I–thou* and I–him/her relations, between being and having: the phenomenon of lived body; the situated dependent character of the self; the characteristics of fidelity, hope*, love*, and humility*; and the experiences involving obscure participation in an Absolute Thou, ensuring eternal* fulfillment. THOMAS C. ANDERSON

Marcella, an aristocratic widow and close friend of Jerome*, was the head of a religious community of Christian virgins* and widows* in her home in Rome. According to Jerome (*Epistle* 127), after her husband's death, she shunned remarriage and became the first nun in Rome, dedicating her life to asceticism* and the rigorous study of Scripture under Jerome's tutelage. After Jerome's exile to Bethlehem (385), in his name she mediated theological disputes in Rome and played a critical role in bringing about the condemnation of Origenism*. Marcella died from injuries sustained during the Gothic invasion of the city (410). ARIEL BYBEE LAUGHTON

Marcion (d c160), originator of Marcionism, a Christian movement that emphasizes Paul's contrast between law* and gospel as antithetical ways of salvation*. Born in Sinope (Black Sea), after some time in Asia Minor he went to Rome (c135), probably learning from Cerdo* the doctrine of the two Gods. Expelled from the church in Rome (144), he founded his own church, keeping the threefold office (bishop, presbyter, and deacon) and the two sacraments (baptism and Eucharist, substituting water for wine). Marcionism was eventually absorbed by the Manichaean* Movement of the 3rd–4th c.

Taking the OT literally, Marcion rejected the "OT God," the Creator, a God of rigid justice, as inferior to Jesus' merciful God, having nothing to do with creation but acting through sheer pity to rescue humanity held captive to the Creator. Jesus suffers the Creator's wrath* on the cross and thereby ransoms those who believe in him. In his major work, *Antitheses*, Marcion, like some Gnostics*, devalued the heroes of the OT who obeyed the OT God and sympathized with those who had been passed by or hardened in their sins by the vengeful Creator. Marcion called Jesus "Chrestos" (worthy, holy) rather than "Christos"; Jesus is not the Jewish Messiah*.

Marcion accepted only the letters of Paul, the true apostle, plus an edited version of the Gospel of Luke, which he considered "Paul's gospel" (Rom 2:16). The most avid Paulinist in the 2nd c., he brought many of Paul's themes to the fore. Marcion may have gathered together the corpus of Paul's letters (without the Pastorals*); in any case, he made use of it. This helps explain the caution about Paul in the mid-2nd c.: there are warnings against misinterpreting him (2 Pet 3:15 16); Paul is "corrected" by pseudonymous writings (2 Thess, the Pastorals, 3 Cor); Justin* ignores him; and Marcion's *Antitheses* are attacked along with the Gnostics' "genealogies" (1 Tim 5:20). Nonetheless, Paul was accepted by the church as one of the apostles (see New Testament and Its Canonization; Paul the Apostle).

Irenaeus*, Tertullian*, and Origen* answered Marcion by affirming the connection between the OT and the NT and arguing that the same God can be both just and merciful. The label "Marcionite" continues to be used today for various forms of Christianity that diminish its relation to Israel and the OT (e.g. Schleiermacher* and Harnack*) or deny that God can be known through the created world (e.g. Barth*).

EUGENE TESELLE

Margaret of Scotland (1045–93; canonized 1250), wife, queen, mother. A Saxon princess, she was exiled to Hungary as a child, while Canute*, the Danish invader, took over England. After the Norman Conquest (1066), she was married to Malcolm III, king of Scotland. She brought sophistication to the Scottish court, reformed the church by introducing Roman practices, such as the use of Latin, keeping the Sabbath, and Communion at Easter. Her daughter Mathilda married Henry I of England, thereby reconciling Saxon, Danish, and Norman claims to the English crown. She was renowned for her charity and love of the poor.

LAVINIA BYRNE

Marginalized, term referring to people who are relegated to the margins of a society. In their own countries, they have the status of refugees, those designated in the OT by the term *ger* (stranger, alien). Thus what applies to refugees applies to marginalized people. **See also REFUGEES AS A THEOLOGICAL CONCEPT AND AN ETHICAL ISSUE.**

Marguerite of Navarre (and of Angoulême) (1492–1549), French Renaissance humanist, sympathizer with early church reformers ("evangelicals"). Sister of King Francis I of France, Marguerite was spiritually sensitive, with mystical* and Neoplatonist* tendencies. She was influenced (1520s) by Guillaume Briçonnet, bishop of Meaux, and his circle of "evangelicals," including Lefèvre* d'Etaples (who translated the NT into French), and by Luther* and Calvin*. Because of her political importance, her protection of evangelicals placed her in a difficult position when official French persecution began (1534); on occasion she withdrew prudently to her own court. A patron of writers such as Clément Marot, a Protestant, and François Rabelais, a Protestant sympathizer, she is best known for the *Heptaméron*, her collection of 72 tales. Yet Marguerite's correspondence, plays, and religious poetry are also important. *Le Miroir de l'âme pécheresse* (1531), censored by the Sorbonne but translated by the future Elizabeth I of England as *The Glass of the Sinful Soul* (1544), is a poem, printed with marginal scriptural references, emphasizing the redemption* of the sinful* soul in Christ, Pauline theology, and the traits of the soul of the true disciple as mother, bride, and sister of Christ. A collection of Marguerite's spiritual poetry (*Marguerites de la Marguerite des Princesses*, 1547, a title playing on her own name, "Marguerite," meaning "daisy") ranged from spiritual songs to a dialogue on perfect love* (see Apophaticism). Her theatrical works include a four-part play, *Comedy of the Nativity of Jesus Christ.*

PATRICIA A. WARD

Marian Devotions. See MARY, THE VIRGIN, CLUSTER.

Marie d'Oignies (1167–1213), born in Nivelles (near Liege, Belgium) to wealthy parents. Married at 14, she convinced her husband to join her in a life of chastity and service to the poor*. They gave away their wealth and devoted themselves to the care of lepers. Marie retired to a hermitage of the Augustinian priory of St. Nicholas d'Oignies and attracted a number of disciples, including Jacques of Vitry, renowned for his preaching, who attributed both his decision to become a canon regular and his preaching ability to her intervention. Marie is commonly held to have been one of the first Beguines*; in 1215 Jacques of Vitry used her example to obtain papal sanction for the Beguine way of life.

SASKIA MURK JANSEN

Mariology, the doctrine and discussion of the Virgin Mary* in relation to God, human history, and salvation. **See also MARY, THE VIRGIN, CLUSTER.**

Maritain, Jacques (1882–1973), French Catholic philosopher. Raised as a liberal Protestant, Maritain, with his Russian Jewish wife, Raissa Oumansoff (a poet and intellectual), converted to Catholicism (1906), becoming the leading philosopher of the 20th-c. Catholic intellectual renewal. At the Sorbonne (1901–6), he rejected positivism and initially embraced Bergson's* vitalist philosophy, then abandoned it to articulate a neo-Thomist* position that he brought to bear on epistemology, metaphysics*, politics*, and aesthetics*. Modern thought could be in harmony with Thomistic realism. Logical reason* could engage with spatiotemporal, quantitative, metaphysical reality, but intuitive reason, a nonconceptual way of knowing, characterizes art. Aesthetic* creativity extends divine creativity. Maritain criticized the legacies of Luther*, Descartes*, and Rousseau* as fragmenting reason* from faith*, mind from body, feeling from knowing. From the 1930s, Maritain was identified with Christian social philosophy, criticizing secular culture and defending the rich potential of the individual and the need for a just society. Much of Maritain's thinking was in evidence at Vatican* II, although late in his career, he warned against the extent of Vatican II reforms. The author of more than 50 books, Maritain taught modern philosophy at the Catholic Institute of Paris (1914–33), the University of Toronto (1933–45), and Princeton University (1948–52). He was the ambassador of France to the Vatican (1945–48). After his wife's death, Maritain lived in a Dominican* community in Toulouse, becoming a monk (1969).

PATRICIA A. WARD

Mark, Gospel of, the earliest and shortest of the canonical Gospels, in which suffering* and conflict are prominent. Its hope is mysterious and dark.

Like the other Gospels, Mark was originally anonymous and given its name by later tradition. The only clues we have about the historical context of the Gospel of Mark come from within the Gospel itself. From Mark's presentation of the Temple as doomed and his sense of a coming cosmic conflict, scholars usually set Mark's date as during or just after the Jewish–Roman war (66–70) that ended in Rome's sacking Jerusalem and destroying the Temple. Eusebius* cites Papias* to the effect that Mark was Peter's interpreter, but this could be a nice way of taming Mark's urgency and explaining its unwieldy narrative style. Others relate Mark with Paul* (cf. shared apocalyptic outlooks, and Acts 12, 15; Col 4). Despite some well-accepted guesses, the place of the Gospel's writing is unknown.

The tone of the Gospel's story is grim, tense, and urgent; violent conflict seems ready to erupt at any moment. In the light of Jesus' crucifixion and the Temple's destruction, this Gospel seems in search of some continuity between the present political and social oppressive chaos and the biblical tradition's sense that God cares for and will save the people.

Mark is most well known for what it lacks: it has no birth story, no stories of Jesus appearing after the Resurrection (manuscript evidence shows that it ends at 16:8), and no extended ethical teachings. These absences (it is not known whether Mark's author does not know them or deliberately shuns this part of the early Christian tradition), together with the Gospel's overall brevity and its choppy literary style, have led scholars to the conclusion that this is the earliest of the Gospels. Matthew and Luke, in particular, seem to add to Mark's basic plot framework and, most likely in those authors' own minds, to clarify Mark's murky message (see Synoptic Gospels).

Unconcerned with Jesus' birth or ancestry, the Gospel of Mark presents as central the question of Jesus' suffering, death, and resurrection.

Mark weaves the story of betrayal, humiliation, and pain that we know as the Passion*, maybe for the first time. The Gospel's brief account of the empty tomb* forms a frightening, yet hopeful epilogue to the concluded story of Jesus' death. Mark's exposition of Roman oppression and Jewish brokenness offers, as its best hope*, the mysterious sense that, despite it all, something survives. There is that which even the combination of human frailty (the disciples' betrayal and abandonment) and human depravity (Roman oppression and cooptation of the high priest) cannot kill.

NICOLE WILKINSON DURAN

Mark, Liturgy of St., eucharistic formulary in Greek, proper to the Patriarchate of Alexandria*. Its most ancient witnesses are the Strasbourg (4th–5th c.) and the John Rylands (6th c.) Papyri. The Liturgy of St. Mark remained in use by the Orthodox* churches until the 13th c., when the Byzantine liturgies of St. Basil* and of St. John* Chrysostom replaced it, strongly influencing the Alexandrian liturgy. In this non-Chalcedonian Patriarchate, the Liturgy of St. Mark was restored in the 20th c. by Patriarch Cyril VI (1959–71) and is now also known as the Anaphora of St. Cyril. As usual in the Coptic* Church, it is recited in a loud voice. As with the Liturgy of St. James*, there is a movement in the Eastern Orthodox churches to celebrate the Liturgy of St. Mark. The formulary is characterized by a double *epiclesis** (which petitions the Holy Spirit to come upon the elements to make them the Body and Blood of Christ), before and after the eucharistic narrative, and by long intercessions interpolated between the pre-*sanctus* and the post-*sanctus*. It contains traces of ancient forms of concelebration*, in which several priests participated with gestures (extending of the hands), but without reciting the texts simultaneously.

STEFANO PARENTI

Mark Eugenicus (c1392–1445), scholar, teacher, monk with a reputation for learning and sanctity, who became metropolitan* of Ephesus (1436). A member of the Greek Orthodox delegation to the Council of Florence* (1438–39), he was an outspoken critic of Rome and its doctrines and practices; he refused to sign the decree of union. The emperor gave him safe passage home, and he spent the rest of his life attacking the union, intensifying opposition to it among the monks and the people. On his deathbed, he persuaded Gennadius* II to assume leadership of the opposition. He was declared a saint in 1734.

Marks of the Church, Notes of the Church (Lat *notae ecclesiae*), the characteristics of the "true church." Initially, the marks of the church were those designated by the adjectives applied to the church* in the Nicene* Creed: one, holy, catholic, and apostolic. These four marks were claimed by Catholic controversialists to confer authenticity on the Roman Catholic rather than the Protestant churches and by Tractarians* to emphasize Catholic aspects of the Church of England. At the time of the Reformation*, the Augsburg* Confession affirmed two marks: the church is where the gospel is purely preached and where the sacraments* are rightly administered. The Reformed* tradition added a third: discipline, the "binding* and loosing" authorized by Christ (Matt 18:18). In the Anglican* Communion, the Lambeth* Quadrilateral identifies the essentials of the true church and the basis for reunion. Since the 1960s, a more functional view of the church, "the church is mission*," sometimes emphasizes evangelism* and sometimes liberation*.

Maronite Church. The Maronite Church traces its origins to a hermit and a monastery. According to the historian Theodoret* of Cyrrhus, the hermit Maron (4th-c. Syria) gained renown for his ascetic* life and for his gift of healing* both bodies and souls. After his death, his disciples established a monastery that became known as the "House of Maron." The monks and the laity to whom they ministered became identified as the followers of Maron, or Maronites.

Because of geography and culture, the Maronite community found itself involved in the christological* debates of the 4th–5th c. It championed the teachings of the Councils of Ephesus* and Chalcedon*, which distinguished it from the followers of Nestorius* in the Church of the East and the Miaphysites* (or Monophysites) of the Syriac* Orthodox Church. The trinitarian* and christological* controversies are reflected in the Maronite liturgy in the prominence given the Holy* Spirit and the emphasis given the divine prerogatives of Christ. Owing to persecutions and the arrival of Islam*, the Maronite community established itself in the mountain recesses of Lebanon*, where it formed itself as a church with its own hierarchy. By the beginning of the 8th c., it had its own patriarch and considered itself an authentic representative of the Church of Antioch*.

With the coming of the Crusades* (from the 12th c.), the Maronites solidified their ties with the Church of Rome and opened themselves to

Western culture. From the 15th c., various religious orders of the West established themselves in Lebanon and opened schools throughout the country. This raised the literacy of the Lebanese of all religious backgrounds and further introduced Western culture.

Through the centuries, the Maronite Church has helped to form the nation of Lebanon. It has contributed to making Lebanon a refuge for those suffering religious and ethnic persecution, and thus has carried out a significant ecumenical role with the various Eastern churches in the area. It has sought to achieve coexistence and dialogue with its Muslim neighbors.

From the late 19th c., Maronites and other Lebanese began emigrating for economic reasons. At first they went to countries in the Middle East, but subsequently emigrated to all parts of the world. The largest Maronite communities are in North and South America and Australia. At present, the Maronite Church is the third-largest Eastern* Catholic Church (see also Uniate Churches). More Maronites live in the Western world than in Lebanon and the Middle East.

Having originated and developed in the region straddling Antioch and Edessa*, the Maronite Church was the heir of both of these rich liturgical traditions. The Maronite Anaphora of Third Peter and the Edessan Anaphora of Addai* and Mari are derived from a common source, which is the oldest eucharistic prayer in the Christian Church. Its Divine Liturgy, mystery of baptism, and Divine Office contain many hymns and prayers of Ephrem* the Syrian and his successors. This Edessan heritage preserves some elements of early Judeo-Christianity and witnesses to an expression of faith grounded in the Scriptures and Syriac poetry, with little Greek philosophical and cultural influence. The Maronite liturgy also incorporates the liturgical patrimony of the ancient Church of Antioch, especially in the more than 40 anaphoras* (eucharistic prayers) that it has preserved, particularly the ancient Anaphora of the Twelve Apostles, which was the basis for the Anaphora of St. John Chrysostom of the Byzantine Church (see Chrysostom, Liturgy of St. John).

The principal source of Maronite theology is the liturgy itself. Maronite theology is a witness to the Syriac theology of Ephrem, Aphrahat*, and Jacob* of Serug, or Sarug. It is grounded in the mysteriousness* of God, who out of love creates the world and is revealed in the very act of creating. The Incarnation* is both the ultimate revelatory event and the climax of God's creation. It is part of the divine plan that nature and Scripture prefigure and prepare the way for the coming of creation's fulfillment. The personages, events, and practices of the old covenant are types* foreshadowing the divine realities that will be finally disclosed in Christ. Christ's work as Savior and Redeemer is the expression of divine compassion and benevolence. The cross* represents the new "tree of life," restoring the Edenic tree of life lost through the sin* of Adam and Eve. Just as Eve was born from the side of Adam, so the church, the new Eve, is born from the side of Christ. Baptism and the Eucharist, which are foreshadowed by the blood and water that flowed from the side of Christ, are the elements that constitute the universal church and are the vehicles of divinization* of its members.

CHORBISHOP SEELY BEGGIANI

Marprelate Tracts, satirical diatribes attacking episcopacy* that were authored by the fictional Martin Marprelate and clandestinely published in 1588–89 by radical Puritans* intent on replacing bishops in the Church of England with a Presbyterian government that emphasized preaching. Several bishops responded to them. The Elizabethan regime perceived them as treasonous; in 1593 John Penry was executed for involvement in the circle from which they emanated. Most likely the parliamentarian Job Throckmorton was their chief author. By their outrageous ridicule, the tracts demystified the authority of lordly prelates, but ultimately discredited the Presbyterian cause by their extremism, as moderate Puritans had feared.

DEWEY D. WALLACE, JR.

Marranos. See *Conversos.*

MARRIAGE, THEOLOGY AND PRACTICE OF, CLUSTER

Marriage, Theology and Practice of, in Asia

Marriage, Theology and Practice of, in Eastern Orthodoxy

Marriage, Theology and Practice of, in Western Churches

Marriage, Theology and Practice of, in Western Churches: Ceremony

Marriage, Theology and Practice of, in Western Churches: John Calvin's Geneva

Marriage, Theology and Practice of, in Western Churches: The Roman Catholic Church and Annulment of Marriage

See also FAMILY, CHRISTIAN VIEWS OF, CLUSTER

Marriage, Theology and Practice of, in Asia. Marriage in Asia is generally considered a socially and religiously sanctioned union between a man and a woman, as well as their respective families or clans. Christian marriage practices and rituals often follow the Western tradition inherited from mission churches. Marriage as a permanent and monogamous contract ("till death do us part"; Gen 1:27, 2:7–25; Matt 19:4–6; Mark 10:6–9) is, for Asian Catholics, a sacrament* ordained by God for procreation and, for Asians of other church traditions, a public vow and sacred contract. Remarriage is allowed for widows and widowers and for divorcees in countries where divorce is legal (1 Cor 7:8–9); in predominantly Catholic societies like the Philippines*, divorce is not allowed, although legal separation is possible. As elsewhere, gay and lesbian, bisexual, and transgendered groups claim their right to a love-based union. Some people oppose institutionalized marriage, opting to live together and have a family without official marriage.

More and more Asians contextualize their marriage rituals, incorporating Asian cultural motifs and symbols. Many Christian couples hold two marriage ceremonies: a Western one and an ethnic/cultural traditional one. Many Asians enter marriage because of mutual love, but in certain communities marriages are arranged by parents or elders. As a result of interactions with the wider world, Asian marriage is becoming more interracial and interreligious.

Asian Feminist* theologians criticize the inequality between women and men implied by certain symbols in the rituals and the oppressive dowry tradition required of the bride's families (a tradition that was incorporated into Christian marriages in India, despite its link to female feticide and infanticide). Asian Feminist theologians also challenge the justification of hierarchical relations between husband and wife through the uncritical use of Scriptures*. For instance, Feminist theologians reread the household* codes (e.g. Eph 5:22–33) to emphasize the mutual loving submission of husband and wife to each other for the full flowering of each family member. HOPE S. ANTONE

Marriage, Theology and Practice of, in Eastern Orthodoxy. Orthodox believe that marriage is instituted by God with the hope that it will reflect Christ's union of love with his church (Eph 5:20–33, the epistle reading for the marriage service). Thus marriage is a call to witness to Christ (see Martyrdom in Eastern Orthodoxy).

Marriage is one of the great sacraments*, or mysteries*, of the Orthodox Church. It is God who unites a man and woman in a wedding service; as the priest prays, "O holy God, who didst create man out of the dust, and didst fashion his wife and join her unto him as a helper, . . . Do Thou, the same Lord, . . . unite this Thy servant *N.*, and this Thy handmaid *N.*; for by Thee is the husband united unto the wife." No vows are said, as the marriage is understood to be accomplished by God, in cooperation with the good intentions and efforts of the couple, rather than by their expressed promises to each other.

A major purpose of marriage is to provide a means for spouses to help each other as they walk together on the path of salvation* toward eternal* life. The procreation and nurturance of children is also important and expected. Marriage provides the only God-sanctioned realm for the full expression of human sexuality. Marital relations are understood to be inherently good and have no taint of sin* when engaged in with dignity and mutual respect (in contrast, see Original Sin), Marriage is also considered to be essential for the stability and well-being of society.

Marriage can be only between one man and one woman, and ideally it is to last forever. Yet in pastoral recognition of human weakness and sinfulness, divorce* and remarriage have always been allowed.

The Orthodox Church's lofty view of marriage is reflected in the practice of allowing clergy to be married. It is also reflected in John Chrysostom's* exhortation to every married couple to make their home "a little church."

DAVID FORD and MARY FORD

Marriage, Theology and Practice of, in Western Churches. Since the time of Jesus, Christian marriage has been distinguished by its strong emphasis on mutual consent, permanence, and sanctity. In medieval Western Europe, the sacramental* status of marriage resulted in an assumption of legal jurisdiction by church courts, triggering many conflicts between canonical formulations based on these values and traditional notions of familial and communal control. In the 16th c., Protestants attempted to resolve such problems by redefining the validity of marriage as well as rejecting the married estate's long-established spiritual inferiority to virginity. By the modern era, legal jurisdiction over marriage passed to secular authorities in all countries with large Christian populations. Nevertheless, the ancient values of free consent, sexual fidelity, and indissolubility are still proclaimed by all modern Christian denominations.

Since the early church, Christian marriage has shared many characteristics with its Jewish, Roman, and Germanic counterparts, most notably the goals of establishing an exclusive sexual relationship and of producing legitimate heirs. Only Roman law, however, put equal emphasis on the free consent of both parties, although Romans did not recognize the indissolubility of the union in the same way or consider the covenant a spiritual estate as Christians did. Following Jesus' reported pronouncements (Matt 5: 31–32, 19:3–6, 18; Mark 10: 2–12; Luke 16:18), Christians rejected divorce* – with the possible exceptions of adultery (Matt 19:3–9) and the so-called Pauline privilege for spouses of hostile unbelievers (1 Cor 7:15) – and they permitted any two adults to marry, regardless of differences in social status. At the same time, Christians since the time of Paul have displayed a pronounced preference for celibacy* and virginity* over marriage, allowing the latter only for the legitimate outlet of sinful sexual urges (1 Cor 7) – a text later interpreted in terms of the doctrine of original* sin. Church fathers consistently rejected the Gnostics' equating of marriage with fornication itself, but with the growth of asceticism* in the 3rd and 4th c., the negative characterization of marriage as a *remedium* became even more pronounced. Even Augustine* (354–430), who wrote extensively about the "triple goods" of marriage – offspring (*proles*), fidelity (*fides*), and permanency (*sacramentum*) – acknowledged that the estate belonged to the postlapsarian "city of man" rather than the "city of God" and remained decidedly inferior to virginity and chastity. Virtually all Christian writers until the High Middle Ages placed the greatest emphasis on the procreative function of marriage (cf. Gen 1:28).

During the Middle Ages, both the Eastern and Western churches continued to teach the consensual, "sacramental," and indissoluble nature of marriage, with various degrees of social impact. Both churches expected to approve marriage, but in the Byzantine Church this entailed a formal rite, while in the West the requirement was interpreted as a priest's subsequent blessing and was rarely enforced. The turning point in Western Europe came during the 12th c., with the writings of canonists Gratian* (d1159?) and Peter* Lombard (c1100–60). Although both agreed on the importance of uncoerced vows of consent between the couple, they differed on the point at which a marriage became valid. As a compromise, the lawyer-pope Alexander III (1159–81) decreed that "words of present consent" ("I take you") were sufficient to establish a valid marriage but that "words of future consent" or engagement ("I will take you") required consummation for validity. Later Canon 51 of Lateran* IV (1215) reaffirmed the sacramental nature of matrimony (based especially on the Vulgate's translation of Eph 5:32) and added a stricter requirement of publicity in the form of three successive weekly banns, and the presence of at least two people and a priest at the wedding as witnesses (the ministers were the couple themselves). About the same time, new diocesan courts, known as officialities, assumed jurisdiction over questions of marriage vows, deciding questions of validity based on canon* law.

Martin Luther* and other Protestant Reformers of the early 16th c. objected to the Roman Catholic Church's marriage theology and law on several grounds. Most fundamentally, following the scholarship of Valla (1407–57) and Erasmus* (1469–1536), they rejected the scriptural basis for declaring marriage a sacrament*, arguing that a better translation of the term in Eph. 5:32 would be "mystery." Accordingly, the Roman Catholic Church's claims to jurisdiction were considered contrived means of raising money (e.g. manufacturing legal impediments to marriage and charging for dispensations). All of these "abominations," Luther argued in his *Babylonian Captivity of the Church*, defiled rather than elevated marriage, as did the "false and impossible" teaching of the celibate ideal. Instead, Luther, Calvin*, and others proposed that marriage was the highest earthly estate, both a symbol and an embodiment of God's covenant* with his people. While holding true to the traditional consensual and indissoluble ideal of marriage, Protestants redefined each attribute in significant ways, also requiring parental approval for the validity of all unions and allowing divorce and remarriage in some instances. During the last session of the Council of Trent*, Catholic leaders responded by making parental consent and church solemnization essential for validity but resisted any major changes in the Church's teachings on impediments and divorce. Virginity and celibacy were likewise reaffirmed as spiritually superior to marriage.

Beginning in the 18th c., marriage jurisdiction became an increasingly secular affair in predominantly Christian countries, and by the beginning of the 20th c., only Eastern Orthodox churches resisted the trend of dual civil and religious ceremonies, though not for long. Today, although commitment to the oldest theological elements of fidelity, sacredness, and permanence remains strong, all Christian denominations have experienced internal tensions and in some cases schisms over changes in their teachings on the importance of procreation (and thus contraception* and sexual* pleasure), divorce*, and annulment*, as well as gay* and lesbian unions. Even the Roman Catholic Church, which is among the most doctrinally conservative body on such issues, at Vatican* II modified the traditional preeminence accorded to procreation in doctrines concerning marriage and the vocation of women. Meanwhile, the World* Council of Churches and other ecumenical assemblies continue to struggle for consensus on the contemporary significance of the theological tradition in urgent discussions regarding human sexuality, biotechnology, and violence* against women. **See also** **FAMILY, CHRISTIAN VIEWS OF, CLUSTER.**

JOEL F. HARRINGTON

Marriage, Theology and Practice of, in Western Churches: Ceremony. Marriage is a rite of passage from the single state to the conjoined state of marriage as a social institution. Christian tradition admits both secular ceremonies (marriage as a consensual contract) and religious ceremonies (marriage as a covenant rooted in faith).

In antiquity the marriage ceremony was primarily a family event in which the bride's father gave his daughter in marriage, the groom carried the bride over the threshold of his house, and cake was eaten or a wedding feast was celebrated. Before c1000 in Western Europe, no Christian wedding ceremony existed; marriage was not an ecclesial matter. However, starting in the 4th c., a clerical blessing might take place (often at the wedding feast); thereafter, clergy progressively had a more active role in marriage ceremonies, until all marriages were effectively under the jurisdiction of the church. By 1100 there was an established Christian wedding ceremony consisting of consent, handing over of the bride and the giving of a dowry, blessing of the bride's ring, and blessing of the marriage (all at the church entrance); the nuptial Mass* was then celebrated, with the bride being veiled and blessed and the priest giving the groom the ritual kiss of peace, who then gave it to the bride;

sometimes the priest blessed the wedding chamber.

In Western Europe, two main issues surround the ceremony of marriage. The first is whether marriage is constituted by consent (Roman tradition) or by intercourse (Frankish and Germanic traditions, in which consent was exchanged at the betrothal); the Western Church decreed that consent alone was essential (12th c.). The second issue is whether marriage is a sacrament*. Augustine claimed that marriage is a visible sign of the invisible relation of the union of Christ and his church and is a sacred pledge of fidelity between husband and wife. For Luther and Calvin, since marriage existed from the beginning, it could not be a sacrament instituted by Christ; thus the church has no right to regulate marriage.

Since 1789 in France, civil weddings have become mandatory (as they subsequently have in all of Europe); a religious ceremony follows (mandatory for Catholics, optional for Protestants). When marriage is celebrated with only a religious ceremony (as in the USA), the minister must also have the credentials to file a civil wedding certificate.

Many cultural customs surround the celebration of marriage around the world, but the deliberate consent of the couple is essential. Contemporary societies tend to regard marriage merely as a contract, and thus take a much more liberal stance on divorce. JOYCE ANN ZIMMERMAN, CPPS

Marriage, Theology and Practice of, in Western Churches: John Calvin's Geneva. Before the Reformation, Geneva was an episcopal city run by a prince-bishop, assisted by nearly 1,000 clergymen, all committed by vows to a celibate life. It also permitted prostitution, under government supervision. With the Reformation, both of these lifestyles were abolished, and all sexual impulse had to be channeled into marriage.

Before the Reformation, marriage was a sacrament* and was under the control of a bishop's court. After the Reformation, marriage technically became a civil matter. It was placed under the control of a new semi-judicial body called the Consistory, which John Calvin* created through ecclesiastical ordinances (1541). This committee of the city government included 12 lay elders elected once a year, and all (about 12) of the ordained pastors of Geneva, including Calvin. Calvin, as a professional lawyer, had thus created the body that controlled marriage, created a set of marriage laws it applied (although these laws were not formally endorsed by the city government for several years), and sat upon it as a judge.

Marriage in Geneva was technically a contract created by a formal agreement between a man and a woman to live together for the rest of their lives, witnessed by at least two honorable people, normally approved by the couple's two sets of parents. It was registered with the city government, announced from the pulpit of the parish in which the couple lived on three successive weeks, and then celebrated at a wedding a short time later. It was often accompanied by a notarized contract outlining the property each family involved brought to the new household, but this was not theologically necessary. The wedding at which the marriage was celebrated had to be held in a parish church and presided over by one of the city's ministers, as part of any regular church service, except for the four Sundays during the year in which Geneva celebrated Communion. Marriage could be dissolved with a divorce*, granted by the city government on recommendation of the Consistory, on grounds of either adultery* or desertion. This provision for divorce was new in Christian Europe, but remained rare. Toward the end of his life, Calvin argued that the marriage contract was a form of covenant*, since it also involved an agreement with God. This led to a doctrine of covenantal marriage, as distinct from both sacramental marriage and secular marriage.

ROBERT M. KINGDON

Marriage, Theology and Practice of, in Western Churches: The Roman Catholic Church and Annulment of Marriage. Annulment is a "declaration of matrimonial nullity" in Roman Catholic canon* law, i.e. an official determination that what appeared to be a valid marriage was not one. Given the presumption of validity that canon law accords to marriage (1983 *Codex* Iuris Canonici* [CIC] 1060), the nullity of an impugned marriage must be carefully proved (1983 CIC 1608). Annulments are not granted upon request or as favors to "deserving" persons. Civil annulments are not recognized by the Roman Catholic Church.

A declaration of nullity is usually sought in order to facilitate one's desire to enter a subsequent marriage in the Roman Catholic Church. If granted, it declares both former spouses free to enter marriage in the Church without risk of bigamy. All annulment cases are reducible to questions of matrimonial capacity, consent, and form (1983 CIC 1057). On these matters, the jurisprudence of the Roman Rota (which functions as a court of appeal) is considered illuminative but not binding on local tribunals (1983 CIC 16).

Annulment petitions are usually filed by one of the parties to the impugned marriage before an arch-/diocesan tribunal (1983 CIC 1673). Major tribunal officers must have requisite academic degrees and are appointed by the bishop (1983 CIC 1419, 1432). The Defender of the Bond (an independent office, since Pope Benedict XIV, 1740–58) is specifically charged with proposing the reasonable arguments that can be offered against finding nullity. Declarations of nullity require ratification by an appellate tribunal (1983 CIC 1682). At times the tribunal declaring nullity might impose a *monitum* (suggestion) or a *vetitum* (prohibition) on either or both parties, rendering a future attempt to marry by same illicit or invalid, respectively, until the matter occasioning the restriction (say, active alcoholism) is addressed to the tribunal's satisfaction.

The recent dramatic increase in the number of annulments worldwide, especially in the USA, has occasioned sharp criticism from those who fear that the Roman Catholic Church's commitment to lifelong marriage is being undermined by the annulment process. Others observe that, besides changes in the 1983 Code that facilitated such an increase, annulment figures might reliably indicate a deterioration in the ability or willingness of many to enter marriage as proclaimed by the Church. EDWARD N. PETERS

Marsilius (or Marsiglio) of Padua (c1275–1342), theologian, political theorist. After studying in Padua, he went to Paris, served as rector of the university (1313), and spent time in Avignon and Italy as well as Paris. He became a partisan of the German emperor Ludwig IV ("the Bavarian") after his excommunication by John XXII. His major work, *The Defender of the Peace* (published 1324), depicted the medieval popes, especially Boniface* VIII, as sources of "scandal and strife" because of their claims to supreme authority in both church and state, based on a misinterpretation of the Donation* of Constantine. Peace could be restored if the church limited its authority to spiritual matters, and if bishops (all of whom were equal except by mutual agreement) were chosen by the faithful (as in the early church), not by the pope (who was himself elected), in accordance with regulations established by general councils*. Marsilius pointed out that the ecumenical* councils of the undivided church had all been called and enforced by emperors, the only ones who had "coercive" authority. After his authorship of *The Defender of the Peace* was discovered, Marsilius fled to the court of Louis, or Ludwig, the Bavarian (later Holy Roman emperor). Propositions from the work were condemned (1327), and the author was excommunicated. Marsilius accompanied the emperor to Rome (1327–29) for his coronation and was made imperial vicar. After Louis's efforts to gain the pope's support failed, Marsilius spent the rest of his life at the court in Munich, along with William* of Ockham. His theory of church* and state was utilized by the Conciliar* Movement, by Henry* VIII to assert his claim of supremacy over the church, and by the Long Parliament to call the Westminster* Assembly. His view that political sovereignty comes from the people anticipated modern democracy; his position that it is undivided anticipated both absolutism and totalitarianism. EUGENE TESELLE

Marthana, deaconess* renowned for her virtue and as a monastic* superior of women at the sanctuary of Saint Thecla* in Seleucia (modern Silifke on the south-central Turkish coast), where Thecla is thought to have died. The only named local character in Egeria's* account of her travels in biblical lands, probably in the late 4th c., Marthana was encountered by Egeria on a pilgrimage in Jerusalem, then at the Shrine of Thecla, where Marthana governed a group of *apotactitae*, or ascetic* virgins*, in monastic cells, i.e. probably in a laura, or *lavra**, a monastery with solitary cells for the nuns around a church building for communal prayer and discipline. Such a walled-in compound made eremitical* life possible for women in an environment that was not as dangerous as the wilderness. The Shrine of Thecla was a large monastic and pilgrimage compound centered on a cave and church with a pilgrim hospice; thus Marthana's influence and authority must have been considerable. CAROLYN OSIEK

Martha and Mary. In most comparisons of Martha and Mary (Luke 10:38–42), Martha is said to typify the active life, whereas Mary is an exemplar of the superior contemplative life, which is totally directed toward God. Meister Eckhart*, however, suggested that the higher mode of life is represented not by Mary's contemplation, but by Martha's care for many things, which was acceptable so long as she remembered the "one thing necessary" (Luke 10:42), namely God and constant unity with God, which can be accomplished even in the midst of activity. Similarly, feminist scholars have pointed out that the traditional denigration of Martha's "service" (10:40) reflects a marginalization of women's "service" (*diakonia*, the major characteristic of all ministries) in the church. **See also DEACON, DIACONATE; DEACONESS.**

Martínez, Luis María (1881–1956), Mexican-educated archbishop of Mexico* (1937–56); chargé d'affaires of the Holy See who negotiated with the government of the Republic of Mexico during the period of religious conflict (1930s). Despite the fact that the law severely restricted public worship and prohibited other activities of the Roman Catholic Church, a *modus vivendi* – a legal fiction according to which the law would be neither modified nor applied – remained in force as Martínez supported the government of Cárdenas (e.g. during the expropriation of oil cartels, 1938). **See also MEXICO.**

MARÍA ALICIA PUENTE LUTTEROTH and ELIZABETH JUDD

Martinique. The history of Christianity in this "colony," an integral part of France (an overseas "department" and thus part of the European Union), is tied to its colonial history.

Christianity arrived with French Protestants (late 16th c.) who succeeded in settling in France's American colonies. But when Louis XIII (1601–43) intervened in Martinique by giving charters to trading companies, he established Roman Catholicism as the official religion. Carmelites*, Capuchins*, Jesuits*, and Dominicans* were sent to make Protestants and Jews renounce their respective faiths and to evangelize the native Caribs.

In 1635 Cardinal Richelieu established a trading company charged with providing slaves from Africa to work on the sugar plantations. In 1685 the "Black Code" was enacted to regulate slavery* as an institution, proclaiming Roman Catholicism as the only authorized religion, explicitly banning the slaves' African Religion (see Haiti). Nevertheless, numerous slaves escaped to the mountains and organized revolts. Since the clergy and religious owned slaves, they were not inclined to take a stand in favor of the rebelling slaves. The proclamation of general freedom decreed by the French Convention (1794) could not be applied in Martinique because at that time the island was briefly occupied by the British.

In the 1840s, clergy and religious, especially the Brethren for Christian Education of Ploërmel, were devoted to bringing religious instruction to the slaves. They were deeply concerned about the African beliefs ("delusions") that survived among slaves, as well as by the numerous religious devotions to which the slaves participated and which combined Christian and African beliefs. Although determined to bring religious instruction to the slaves, clergy and religious did not bring them freedom. An exception was Fr. Castelli, who propagated abolitionist republican ideas. He did not convince many members of the clergy of the merit of these ideas because of the planters' constant hostility and because, in becoming abolitionists and followers of Victor Schoelcher, the mulattos assumed a republican anticlerical stance. The abolition of slavery (1848) in all French colonies was achieved by the French abolitionist movement led by Schoelcher, who, often in Martinique, also advocated the republican anticlerical ideal of public education, which the clergy strongly resisted. Later the Law of Separation of Church and State (promulgated in 1905 in France) was denounced by the Roman Catholic Church as a threat to the identity of Martinique. Thus Bishop Cormont argued against the administrative authorities in the Catholic newspaper *Les Antilles*, so much so that the law could not be applied in Martinique before 1911.

Today, many religious movements, including those of Seventh-day Adventists*, Jehovah's* Witnesses, and Pentecostals*/Charismatics*, are attracting numerous Catholics, possibly indicating a shift in cultural identity.

Statistics: Population (2000): 395,000. Christians, 97.0% (Roman Catholics, 92.7%; Protestants and other Christians, 4.3%); nonreligious, 1.9%. (Based on *World Christian Encyclopedia*, 2001.)

LAËNNEC HURBON

Martin of Tours (c316–97), ascetic* and bishop, subject of an influential biography by Sulpicius Severus. Born in present-day Hungary, he devoted himself to Christ as a child but served in the Roman army (when, reportedly, he cut his cloak in half to share it with a beggar), until he left to lead a solitary ascetic life near Poitiers, France. His followers built cells nearby, forming the first known monastic* community north of the Alps. Elected bishop of Tours (371), he continued to lead an ascetic life while working to eradicate pagan worship, building churches, performing miracles, and providing a model of spiritual focus and rejection of worldly values. A cult spread after his death: Gregory of Tours mentions the occurrence of miracles at Martin's shrine.

CAROLINNE WHITE

Martyrdom (Gk *martus*, "witness"). Originally applied to the apostles as witnesses of the resurrection (Acts 1:8, 22, 10:21), the term was soon applied to those who made their witness through death (Acts 22:20; Rev 2:13, 17:6), which became the primary meaning of the word. The term "confessor," while it originally had the same meaning, came to be applied to those who confessed the faith without suffering death.

The "acts" of the martyrs' trials were sometimes based on eyewitness accounts, perhaps even transcripts of court records, although they came to be a literary genre with a standardized form. While martyrs were those who died confessing Christ, the Maccabean* martyrs, specifically the seven brothers (2 Macc 7), were also appropriated by Christians during the first few centuries of the common era as martyrs in their own tradition. The limits of what counted as dying for one's faith were tested in specific cases. Dionysius of Alexandria wrote to Novatian* that martyrdom to avoid schism was not less noble than that to avoid idolatry, for in the latter case one died for one's own soul, while in the former one did so for the entire church. The Council of Elvira* (early 4th c.) decreed that a person killed for destroying an idol was not a martyr. Thomas Becket* was killed by the king's knights because he had defended the freedom of the church, not because he defended the faith and not for his own salvation; the question was raised, therefore, whether he was a martyr. Dietrich Bonhoeffer* is often called a martyr, but the appropriateness of the designation has been questioned because he was executed as a traitor and conspirator. The designation "martyr" will always be contested. In recent centuries there have been many "new martyrs" – in mission areas, under governments strongly favoring another religion, and under oppressive or Communist governments. While all are remembered in their immediate communities, some have been more broadly acknowledged and honored as martyrs – e.g. canonized* by the Roman Catholic Church. **See also SAINTS.**

EUGENE TESELLE

Martyrdom in Eastern Orthodoxy. In the Orthodox tradition, martyrdom (Gk *martyria*, "witness") is central to the Christian life. While some are called to be put to death in witness to Christ, all are called to witness to Christ through a life of self-sacrificial love. Thus monasticism*, marriage*, and the Christian life in general are paths of bloodless martyrdom.

Many Christians have been killed for their faith in Christ throughout the history of the church, beginning with Stephen's stoning (Acts 7:54–60); thousands died during the persecutions* of the first three centuries, and many unbelievers came to believe in Christ after beholding the courage of the martyrs as they endured the torture leading up to their death. The *Account of the Martyrdom of St. Polycarp* (c157) declares, "Blessed, then, and noble are all the martyrdoms. . . . For who would not admire their nobility and patience and love of their Master?" While only a few hundred Orthodox Christians were killed for their faith under the Islamic Ottoman Turks (beginning in the 15th c.; see Islam and Christianity Cluster: In Europe: Southeast Europe), millions of Orthodox died under the Soviets in Russia and Eastern Europe (in the 20th c.).

Another form of dramatic witness to Christ, prominent in Orthodox Christianity, is monasticism* – the surrender of one's life to Christ through a life of poverty* and celibacy*, in solitude or community (eremitic* and cenobitic* monasticism, respectively).

Marriage* is seen in the Orthodox tradition as a call to witness to Christ through living in self-sacrificial love for the other. Hence, marriage is also considered to be a form of martyrdom. Accordingly, two of the three hymns sung in the Orthodox marriage service speak of the Church's holy martyrs. Indeed, the Orthodox tradition underscores that every Christian is called to "crucify the flesh" (Gal 5:24) through ascetic* effort in order to witness to the new life in Christ (cf. Mark 8:34; Rom 6:3–13; Gal 2:20). Such a life transcends egotism and death and radiates divine love for all (see Spirituality Cluster: Denominational View: Eastern Orthodox).

Hence martyrdom, either literally the shedding of one's blood or figuratively an ongoing "bloodless" self-sacrifice, is central to the Orthodox understanding of the Christian life.

DAVID FORD and MARY FORD

Martyrium, a church built over the tomb or relics of a martyr; sometimes a memorial structure.

Marxism and Christianity. According to Marxist theory, Christianity is a form of ideology* that masks the injustices of class-structured societies by legitimating the power of the ruling classes and preventing oppressed peoples from changing the social order by offering them a reward in the afterlife. For much popular Christianity, and for some Christian theology, Marxism is an atheist* ideology, denying the spiritual dimension of human existence and antithetical to all things Christian.

Between these two extremes lie far more interesting and theologically fruitful interpretations, based on the awareness that Marx's interpretation of history* and his expectation of a society without domination and injustice were themselves dependent on certain Christian and Jewish understandings of history and the hope* for a messianic transformation establishing the Kingdom* of God. The mediating figure was Hegel*, who attempted to give a philosophical account of the truth of the Christian religion, an interpretation of history that he understood explicitly as a theodicy*, a justification of historical conflict and human suffering*. For Hegel the whole of human history was the dialectical unfolding of Spirit or Mind (*Geist,* Hegel's term for God*) through successive stages of human self-understanding. All these stages involved conflict and suffering, but would culminate in the achievement of full self-consciousness: as Infinite Spirit became fully embodied in Finite Spirit (Hegel's philosophical rendering of the doctrine of the Incarnation*), humans would become aware that they were and are makers of their own history. Hegel thought that this full realization of *Geist* in history was being realized in his time: ideationally in the critical-historical understanding of his own writings; historically and institutionally in the French Revolution, the development of the idea of individual rights (see Human Rights Cluster), including the right to property*, and the development of the modern nation-state based on constitutions chosen by the people.

Marx argued that Hegel's philosophy remained too ideational and overlooked the extent to which the modern nation-state expressed the power and property of one class, the bourgeoisie. The Communist Revolution, led by the proletarians who were without property rights, would usher in a classless society in which bourgeois rights were universalized and no single class could use the right to property to subjugate others. Although Marx intended the self-conscious transformation of existing human economic and political institutions ("The philosophers have only *interpreted* the world, in various ways; the point, however, is to change it" – his famous 11th "Thesis on Feuerbach"), his conviction that a society without domination and suffering was possible was fully dependent on Hegel's philosophy of history, especially the theodicy. All the suffering of history was justified because it had led to this new historical possibility, dialectically present but unrealized in capitalism; and the new society he envisioned bore a striking resemblance to the Reign (or Kingdom*) of God in which sin* and suffering* are overcome.

Marx is, according to this interpretation, a member of the Christian (and Jewish) family, perhaps a rebellious child but one from whom the parents can learn. Marx's interpretation of the crises of history in which new forms of human social cooperation emerge from the injustices of the old can be understood as a restatement of the biblical prophetic* tradition. His hope for the liberation* of the poor* and oppressed* in a classless society revives the messianic and eschatological hopes of Christian teaching, too often obscured by the institutional and cultural accommodation of the churches. His astute critical analysis of the power relations and injustices of industrial capitalism offer a social interpretation of the doctrine of sin*, with critical potential. These three points are taken up by three of the most important approaches to Marxism by 20th-c. theologians.

1. Neo-orthodox Protestant theologians responding to the crises of the two world wars, general economic collapse, and Fascism and Nazism* took seriously the Marxist critique of religion* as ideology, proposing a prophetic Christian faith that stood over against all forms of political *and* ecclesial idolatry*, and against social and economic* injustice. While differing in important ways, Barth* (1886–1968), Tillich* (1886–1965), and Reinhold Niebuhr* (1892–1971) put the prophetic tradition at the center of their theology, supporting various forms of social democracy and promoting social justice*.
2. Liberation* theologies (middle to late 20th c.), originating in Latin America with the work of Gustavo Gutiérrez, adopted a more explicit Marxist framework for interpreting the possibility of the emancipation of oppressed peoples from national and international structures of capitalist political and economic forms. Having studied with Rahner* (a German Catholic deeply influenced by Barth), Gutiérrez combined Barth's "crisis theology" with Marxist social analysis for a this-worldly interpretation of Christian eschatology* and the possibility of genuine social transformation.
3. Some recent theology has looked to "critical theory," associated with thinkers of the School of Social Research in Frankfurt, Germany, during the 1930s. These thinkers tried to account for the historical failures of Marxist theory by combining Marx with Weber*, Freud, and other social thinkers. The early generation (including Walter Benjamin, Theodor Adorno, Max Horkheimer, and Herbert Marcuse) tried to find a basis for social criticism without Marx's grand theory and theodicy, influencing theological contemporaries such as Tillich*. The most important thinker of the next generation, Jürgen Habermas, has articulated a critical theory for understanding how human interaction is distorted by the power relations of advanced capitalism. Habermas offers a theory of communicative ethics* which combines, in part, Marx, Kant*, and Christian moral commitments. Although his theory implies the increasing secularization* of society, Habermas's work has been used by both Protestant and Catholic theologians as a resource for social critique.

See also **HISTORY, THEOLOGICAL CONCEPTS OF; HOPE; KINGDOM OF GOD, THE CONCEPT OF, CLUSTER; LIBERATION THEOLOGIES CLUSTER.**
JON P. GUNNEMANN

Mary, Gospel of. The Gospel of Mary, a 2nd-c. Christian text, is preserved in one fragmentary Coptic manuscript, Codex Berolinensis (of the original 19 pages of the Gospel, pages 1–6 and 11–14 are missing), and in two short Greek papyri. The work consists of two parts. The first contains a revelation dialogue between the risen Jesus and his disciples; the second comprises a conversation between Mary* Magdalene and the male disciples after the departure of Jesus. During that conversation, Mary Magdalene discloses a special instruction imparted to her by Jesus in the form of a vision, which troubles her male colleagues, especially Peter and his brother, Andrew. Both the content of the vision and the fact that it was given to a woman provoke anger and jealousy. The controversy ends with a comment by Levi, who sides with Mary Magdalene since "the Savior made her worthy . . . [and] loved her more than [the male disciples]" (18:10–15). Thus Levi implies that Mary was Jesus' favorite disciple and therefore also capable of receiving his special message.

The Gospel of Mary shows very few ties to Judaism. Its theological perspective originates in an early Christian interpretation of Jesus' teachings within a pluralistic context combining popular Platonic and Stoic motifs. The Gospel of Mary belongs to those writings that regard not Jesus' death and resurrection but his teaching as a means of gaining salvation*. Likewise, the work represents a form of early Christianity that presented a strong defense of women who wanted to take part in spiritual leadership and in interpreting Jesus' teachings. This form of Christianity should not be called Gnostic* because the Gospel of Mary does not contain the idea of a creator distinct from the highest God.

ANTTI MARJANEN

MARY, THE VIRGIN, CLUSTER

1) *Introductory Entries*

2) *A Sampling of Contextual Devotions*

Mary, the Virgin: The Black Madonna
Mary, the Virgin: Devotion in Latin America
Mary, the Virgin, of Fátima
Mary, the Virgin, of Guadalupe
Mary, the Virgin, of Lourdes

See also IMMACULATE CONCEPTION

1) Introductory Entries

Mary, the Virgin. Mary of Nazareth, mother of Jesus in history and proclaimed mother of God in faith, is the most celebrated female religious personality in the Christian tradition. Her figure is extraordinarily complex, portrayed and interpreted in diverse ways throughout history. This diversity begins in the Gospels, which present Mary in relation to Jesus and her husband, Joseph, in a range of theological perspectives. The different Christian traditions amplify this diversity. Following the depiction of her in the Gospel of Mark, Protestants tends to treat statements concerning Mary as meditations that reflect biblical themes and clarify beliefs about Jesus Christ. Drawing on John's portrayal, Orthodox opt for an iconic* and symbolic approach to the mother of Jesus. Catholics are drawn to Luke's presentation of Mary as a woman of faith*, highly favored by God and responsive to God's invitation to bear the Redeemer through the power of the Holy Spirit. Catholicism generally regards theological statements about Mary as historically factual or as affirming Jesus' divine origins. Ecumenical dialogue among these traditions seeks common ground in the Scriptures and in creeds to harmonize their different understandings of Mary. Beyond Christianity, Islam* reveres Mary as the mother of Jesus the prophet and as one of God's chosen in the line of prophets herself.

These interpretations of Mary are expanded by her influence on cultural, social, and political spheres. Centuries of artwork, architecture, literature, music, prayers, and titles from all cultures extol her virtues and highlight the events of her life. The Byzantine Empire credited the Virgin Theotokos* with protecting it during invasions; many North American Catholics drew strength from Our Lady of Fátima* during the time of the cold war; migrant workers enlist aid from Our Lady of Guadalupe* in their struggle for just wages and living conditions; New York's Italian immigrants find solace in the Madonna* of 125th Street. Moreover, the message of God's mercy and reversal of the social order in Mary's biblical song, the *Magnificat**, proclaims the subversive promise of hope* and liberation* for those who are poor* and oppressed* throughout the world.

Theologians offer a range of interpretations of the virgin-mother Mary as well. Some envision Mary as the "maternal face of God." This helps to compensate for overly patriarchal* images of God and affirms that women have the capacity to represent God. However, it hinders the direct use of maternal imagery for the mystery* of God*. Other theologians suggest that Mary represents the "ideal feminine." This casts Mary as a model for all other women and elevates certain virtues as characteristically feminine. However, this model trades on a patriarchal understanding of male and female nature that is dualistic*. It emphasizes Mary's private life of obedience, childbearing, nurturance, and self-sacrifice and suggests that these are ideal feminine virtues women ought to embody. Feminist* critics argue that this hinders women's personal and intellectual flourishing, encourages dependence and submissiveness, and restricts women's public participation and leadership in church and society. A viable alternative approach follows the lead of Vatican* II and places Mary within the people of God and the communion of saints*, that vast company of witnesses, living and deceased, who seek God and who join with one another in hope. It returns to the Gospels to discover the historical woman of faith and situates her within her Jewish traditions, her rural village life, her oppressive political situation, and her faith-filled partnership with God in the work of liberation*. Such a theology of Mary inspires fidelity to the living God, prophetic action toward justice*, and uncompromising discipleship*. Moreover, it reveals women's full and indispensable participation in God's redemptive activity.

ELIZABETH A. JOHNSON and GLORIA L. SCHAAB

Mary, the Virgin, Theotokos, mother of Jesus of Nazareth, proclaimed "Theotokos" (God-bearer) by early Greek-speaking Christian faithful. For the Christian East, the established traditions surrounding the historical mother of Jesus draw, in part, from the meager details of her life presented in the four canonical Gospels, but primarily from the rich apocryphal* texts that circulated widely and in many languages during late antiquity. These texts often emphasize her life before the birth of Jesus; an example is the early-2nd-c. Protoevangelion of James*, which details her conception, birth, youth, and the selection of Joseph as her protector. Alternatively, they describe her actions after the resurrection* of Christ, e.g. her supposed missionary journeys with John the Evangelist and her "dormition" (literally, "falling asleep"). Following these apocryphal traditions, the Byzantine Church assigned dates of commemoration for her birth (September 8) and her dormition (August 15) and included them in the 12 major feasts of the liturgical calendar.

The affirmation that Mary was Theotokos most likely originated in a 3rd-c. liturgical petition calling on her to intercede with her son on behalf of the Christian community. The title was not universally accepted and became one of the key points of dispute in the protracted christological* debate between Cyril*, archbishop of Alexandria, and Nestorius*, archbishop of Constantinople (420s). Nestorius refused to accept the title, arguing that it both undermined God's sovereignty and implied that Mary gave birth to the entire Godhead. Cyril and Proclus* of Constantinople countered that the title was necessary to affirm the hypostatic unity (see Hypostasis) of the God-man Jesus Christ beginning at the moment of his conception: if Mary was not Theotokos, then Christ was not divine. The title was affirmed at the First Council of Ephesus* (431) and was reaffirmed at the reunion council (433). It has remained an essential dogma of the Eastern Orthodox* (Chalcedonian) and Oriental Orthodox* (non-Chalcedonian) since that time.

Because of her role as Theotokos, Byzantine commentaries, sermons, and hymns devoted to the Virgin (e.g. the Akathistos Hymn) ascribed to her a role in salvation* history. The same texts also affirmed her preeminence among the saints*, both in terms of prayer for her intercession and in terms of a diversity of models for pious emulation (as both mother and virgin, servant and queen, Mary provided panegyrists and hymnographers with an endless number of models to inspire faithful imitation).

GEORGE E. DEMACOPOULOS

Mary, the Virgin, Theotokos, in Byzantine Iconography. The earliest preserved images of the Virgin Mary date back to the 3rd c. (catacombs of Priscilla, Rome). Such images are mentioned in 4th-c. written sources (e.g. a letter of Gregory* of Nazianzus). The iconography of the Virgin proliferated after the Council of Ephesus (431), which rejected Nestorius*'s doctrine and established the veneration of the Virgin Mary as Theotokos*, the Mother of God. Since the 5th c., the images of Our Lady accentuated important theological concepts: the Incarnation*; Our Lady's intercession for sinful* humankind before her Son and the Supreme Judge*; the Holy Virgin's glorification as the Queen of Heaven; the identification of Our Lady with the church (*ecclesia*); and the veneration of the Virgin as the Temple of Wisdom*.

In Byzantine iconography, the Virgin was represented as a young woman with ideal features (9th-c. descriptions), hair covered with a headdress and a long, dark blue or purple veil often decorated with stars symbolizing her divine nature. The Virgin's image is regularly inscribed with "MP ΘY," the Greek abbreviation for *Meter Theou*, "Mother of God" (or *Hagia Maria*, "Holy Mary," before the 9th c.).

There were images of the Virgin Mary by herself or with Christ the Child (early examples can be seen in 6th- to 7th-c. mosaics of the altar apses on Cyprus;

icons of the Sinai Monastery; five 6th- to 8th-c. icons from churches in Rome). In the single images, the Virgin's hands are raised in the gesture of prayer; these images are either frontal ("Virgin Orant") or are turned sideways. Both iconographic types embodied the idea of intercession* and supplication before Christ. The Virgin Orant was often represented in conches of altar apses as the major image of a church (e.g. a mosaic of St. Sophia in Kiev, mid-11th c.). In several cases, these images were inscribed *Theotokos Blachernitissa,* referring to the venerable image in the Blachernae, the major church of the Virgin in Constantinople. The Virgin in prayer (sideways image) was often inscribed *Hagiosoritissa* (of the holy shrine), indicating its connection with another miraculous icon in the Chalkopratea Church, Constantinople. Some variants of this image, called *Paraklesis* (Supplication), represent the Virgin with an open scroll in her hand; these images are paired with the image of Christ, to whom the Virgin appeals. The text on the scroll consists of a dialogue between the Virgin and Christ (frescoes of Lagoudera, Cyprus, 1192; icon from the cathedral of Spoleto, 11–12th c.).

Icons of the Virgin Mary with the Child emphasized the paradox* of the fundamental Christian miracle: an earthly woman holds the eternal and heavenly ruler of the universe as an unprotected child. The most symbolic and abstract icons present the Virgin Orant with Christ the Child on her chest in a roundel, sometimes inscribed *Nikopoios* (victorious) (since the 7th c. in Byzantium) or "Our Lady of the Sign" (since the 12th c. in Old Russia, associated with the miraculous icon of Novgorod).

Images of the enthroned Virgin with the Child (well known from early Christianity) symbolized universal power and Divine Wisdom creating her temple in the body of the Virgin (the 9th-c. sanctuary mosaic of St. Sophia, Constantinople). Among 11th- to 15th-c. icons, the image of the Virgin pointing to the Child with her right hand was most popular and was often inscribed *Hodegetria* (Gr "pointing the way"), connecting all replicas with the miraculous icon of the Hodegon Monastery, which was perceived as the main defender of Constantinople.

From the 11th c., new "animated" images, often called *Eleousa* (merciful) or *Glykophilousa* (sweetly embracing), accentuated intimate relations between Mother and Child (tenderly holding the Virgin's cheek). An early-12th-c. replica of such an image of the Church of Blachernae in Constantinople was brought to Russia and became the major miraculous icon of the country, known as "Our Lady of Vladimir." In Russia during the 15th–17th c., there were about 100 types of the Virgin with Child (usually icons "specialized" in certain kinds of miraculous help). In the 18th and 19th c., the number grew to more than 500. During this period, large icons, combining in a single panel hundreds of small-scale miracle-working icons, created a sort of iconographical dictionary. **See also** **HIEROTOPY, THE CREATION OF CHRISTIAN SACRED SPACES; JESUS, IMAGES OF, CLUSTER: IN BYZANTINE ICONOGRAPHY; SYMBOLISM.** ALEXEI LIDOV

---

2) A Sampling of Contextual Devotions

Mary, the Virgin: The Black Madonna. See BLACK MADONNA.

Mary, the Virgin: Devotion in Latin America. Devotion to Mary is a common feature of Roman Catholicism in Latin America. It is expressed through different national devotions, such as the Copper Virgin of Charity for Cubans*, the Virgen Purisima for Nicaraguans*, Aparecida for Brazilians*, Chiquinquira for Colombians*, Lujan for Argentines*, and Guadalupe for Mexicans* (see the present cluster: Of Guadalupe). Even for those who profess no religious belief, the different Virgins are a symbol of what it means to be Cuban, Nicaraguan, Brazilian, Colombian, Argentinean, or Mexican. They are strong symbols of national and religious identity that has roots in the colonial period in each country. Devotion to the Virgin Mary is built on the cultures and ethnic interstices that have shaped Latin American history. For instance, the Copper Virgin of Charity started as a local devotion in a slave* community in the 17th c. and, in the 19th c., came to represent the Cuban process of building identity as the Copper Virgin of Charity was venerated as the national patron of Cuba during the war of independence from Spain. This devotion has also been associated with Ochun by the Afro-Cuban community. And it has come to play a central role for the Cuban community, particularly exile community in the USA.

At a different level, the Virgin Mary is a syncretistic* (or inculturated*) figure through whom indigenous peoples relate aspects of their Christian worship to features of the pre-Columbian worship of feminine deities. The Christian female figure of the Virgin Mary also represents the mother earth as the axis of creation. In Latin America, this inculturated devotion to the Virgin Mary acquires stronger meaning, since the absence of the father, who is often unknown, is a recurrent phenomenon that gives a higher place and value to the mother; the Virgin Mary represents the mother* figure *par excellence.* The female figure dominates the Latin American ethos, and the Virgin Mary plays the symbolic role of female power. On the other hand, devotion to the Virgin Mary is also related to the *marianismo,* a practice that provided a cultural source for an idealized femininity. Such idealization was based on the spiritual and moral superiority of women over men that legitimated the suffering of women in subordinated domestic roles. The consolidation of all the national devotions in the Virgin of Guadalupe as patron of the Latin American continent was proposed several times in the 20th c. and more recently by John Paul II. This proposal may be rooted in an attempt to strengthen pro-life discourse through the icon of the pregnant virgin (see Pregnancy). Devotion to the Virgin Mary is also seen as a mark of identity for Roman Catholics, particularly in the face of the growing Pentecostal* and Charismatic* movements and the increase in Charismatic practices within the Roman Catholic Church.

Ana María Bidegain

Mary, the Virgin of Fátima. See FÁTIMA.

Mary, the Virgin of Guadalupe. The first evangelization in Mexico emphasized primarily the gospel of Christ and the church. It is therefore surprising that devotion to the Virgin of Guadalupe became the most significant religious characteristic of Christianity in Mexico. John Paul II declared, in Santo Domingo, that "[i]n the Virgin of Guadalupe we have a perfect example of inculturated* evangelization." This appropriately reflects the historical development of this devotion, and particularly the "Guadalupe event," as presented in *Nican Mopohua,* written in Náhuatl, a highly symbolic-mythological language.

The event occurred at the sacred place where Mesoamericans worshipped Tonántzin, Our Mother the Land, a place they perceived to be the active, maternal presence of God. The apparitions restored the dignity of Mesoamericans. They demonstrated that it was possible for their world to change, even though it had been invaded and was in chaos. The Virgin was considered the mother of four of the main Mesoamerican deities. In this apparition, she proposed an evangelization whose purpose would be to show and give love, compassion, aid, and protection, and thus to listen to and remedy all the distress, misery, sorrow, and pain of the inhabitants of the land, and of those who invoked her (in inculturation and mission, see Mission Cluster). This intention of the Virgin was to be symbolized by the construction of a temple in Mesoamerican territory; it demanded that Mesoamericans value and have confidence in themselves and that the (European) bishop trust their ability to evangelize Mesoamericans.

Juan Diego, a poor Indian, was the authorized representative chosen by the Virgin. She required the collaboration of the bishop, the highest ecclesiastic authority. The bishop turned down her request on three occasions. Although Juan Diego pointed out that the Virgin's message was a valid Christian teaching about evangelization, the bishop still objected to it.

Meanwhile, Juan Bernardino, the uncle of Juan Diego, was sick and dying. Juan Diego cared for him, rather than doing what the Virgin had requested of him, namely to return to the bishop and meet her at the sacred place where she normally appeared to him. So instead, she came to him. The Virgin said that she had taken upon herself the tragedy of Mesoamericans; she promised that she would heal Juan Bernadino and asked Juan Diego to continue his mission to convince the bishop to build the temple. She asked him to cut some flowers, which were miraculously blooming in a place that was intensely cold, and to bring them to the bishop, as a sign that he should agree to build the temple. When Juan Diego gave the flowers to the bishop, the image of the Virgin suddenly appeared on Juan Diego's clothes. The bishop was converted; he invited the people to build the temple, and he saw that Juan Bernardino had indeed been healed. Thus devotion to the Virgin of Guadalupe began.

As time passed, the Virgin of Guadalupe became a well-established devotion; she was officially recognized as the Virgin Mary, named patroness of New Spain (1746); she was crowned as the queen of Mexico (1895) and named patroness of Latin America (1910). The veneration of the Virgin as protector has grown, although some ecclesiastic sectors do not demand that respect for her be expressed as social action.

It is necessary to distinguish among apparitions, devotions, political uses of these, and lost experience and integrity.

MARÍA ALICIA PUENTE LUTTEROTH

Mary, the Virgin of Lourdes. See LOURDES.

Maryknoll Missionaries, the popular name for the Catholic Foreign Mission Society of America (Maryknoll Fathers and Brothers) and for independent allied groups: Maryknoll Sisters, founded by Mary Josephine Rogers; Maryknoll Lay Missioners; and Maryknoll Affiliates. The Maryknoll Society was founded (1911) by two diocesan priests, Thomas F. Price and James A. Walsh, with headquarters outside Ossining, New York.

The Society's first assignment (1918) was in the Canton vicariate, China*; later it served in Northern Korea*, Japan*, and Manchuria (1920s) and eventually in more than 30 countries. The Maryknoll priests, brothers, and sisters often work together.

The Maryknoll Society trains people to be lifelong missioners, educates North Americans about missions*, and solicits prayer for missions. Its magazine, *The Field Afar* (*Maryknoll /Revista Maryknoll*), along with printed and audiovisual material, interpreted other cultures and religions for North American Catholics. Maryknoll men and women fostered indigenous leadership through seminary teaching and founding women's religious communities in several countries. Their mission engagement is focused on small Christian community formation, social justice*, direct evangelization, medical and youth work, communications, and parish development. Since 1970 the Society has sponsored Orbis Books, which publishes Catholic and Protestant authors from around the world who write about mission, theology, spirituality, and interreligious dialogue*, thus contributing to an understanding of Christianity globally. ANGELYN DRIES

Mary Magdalene, the most important woman "disciple of Jesus," accompanied him from Galilee to Jerusalem (Mark 15:40–41). A native of Magdala*, according to Luke (8:2) she became one of Jesus' followers after he had driven out seven demons from her. It is historically less likely that she was a financial sponsor of Jesus and his male disciples as Luke suggests (8:3). Luke's claim reflects his literary tendency to present Jesus and his followers as a movement surrounded by influential and wealthy supporters (a tendency also apparent in Acts). The view that Mary Magdalene was a prostitute is untenable. It is based on a questionable identification of Mary Magdalene with Mary in John 12:3 and with the anonymous anointer in Luke 7:36–50. Luke mentions Mary Magdalene for the first time in 8:2, immediately after the anointing story, without any indication that 7:36–50 spoke of her.

Both Matthew (28:9–10) and John (20:14–18, apparently reflecting an independent tradition) refer to Mary Magdalene as a person who saw the risen Jesus (see also Mark 16:9–10). The fact that Mary Magdalene was viewed as an eyewitness to Jesus' resurrection suggests her influential position in the early Jesus movement.

Mary Magdalene is a prominent figure in several 2nd- and 3rd-c. Christian texts. For example, the Gospel of Mary* and the Gnostic Gospel of Philip* and Pistis* Sophia depict her as the favorite disciple* of Jesus who best understands his teachings. Mary's spiritual superiority arouses jealousy among her male colleagues, especially Peter, but Jesus defends her (Gospel of Philip, Pistis Sophia, Gospel of Thomas*), as does Levi (Gospel of Mary). Some texts refer to Mary because they regarded her as an important heroine of the past (Gospel of Philip, Pistis Sophia); others appeal to her authority in discussing women's ecclesiastical position at the time (Gospel of Mary). ANTTI MARJANEN

Mary Tudor (Mary I) (1516–58), queen of England. After her father Henry* VIII's estrangement from Catherine of Aragon, Mary was bastardized (1533). During her half-brother Edward VI's reign (1547–53), she faced troubles anew for stubbornly maintaining the traditional Catholic liturgy. The government made Jane Grey the queen (1553), but Mary exploited widespread outrage to stage a coup d'état. As queen (1553–58), she moved swiftly to restore both traditional worship and papal obedience; she also brushed aside objections to marriage with Philip II of Spain. Equally single-minded was her commitment to burning Protestants. She longed for a child and thought she was pregnant, but she had fatal stomach cancer. Her death led to Elizabeth* I's reversal of her religious program. DIARMAID N. J. MACCULLOCH

Mashtots, Mesrop (c361–439/40), served as a translator at the Armenian court and participated in expeditions to convert remote parts of Armenia*. Apparently troubled by the use of military force to impose Christianity, he embraced the monastic* life, searching for other ways to make the Christian Scripture and liturgy "native" for his compatriots. Supported by the catholicos* Isaac and the king Vram-Shapuh, Mashtots visited Syriac and Greek literary centers of Mesopotamia in unsuccessful attempts to adapt an extant script to Armenian. Instead Mashtots invented a phonetic alphabet (c405) and translated the Book of Proverbs from Syriac. Mashtots and his disciples translated into Armenian the entire Bible within two years; they later translated the works of the Syriac* fathers. Mashtots thus allowed the two parts of Armenia, divided since 387 between the Sassanian and Roman Empires, to maintain their Armenian identity and to associate it with Christianity. The peace of 422 enabled him and his disciples to travel to Western Armenia, teaching the alphabet beyond the border and translating the Greek fathers and the Jerusalem Lectionary. Literary activity in Armenian has never ceased henceforth. According to his disciple Koriun and Moses* of Khoren, Mashtots also invented alphabets for Georgia and Ałuania and trained local translators. IGOR DORFMANN-LAZAREV

Masoretes, scholars (scribes*) who through the centuries maintained the strict rules for hand-copying Hebrew biblical texts for liturgical and scholarly use, in scroll and codex forms, respectively. They first added vowels (c6th c. CE), accents, and later some marginal notes (from the *Masorah,* "tradition") to the biblical text, establishing the Masoretic Text.

Masoretic Text (MT), a Hebrew biblical text with vowels and other markings transmitted by the Masoretes (6th–8th c.). **See also BIBLE, TEXTS AND MANUSCRIPTS.**

Mass, Roman Catholic. "Mass," from the Latin *missio,* a medieval term for the eucharistic celebration, refers to the dismissal rite *"Ite missa est"* ("Go, you are sent)," which establishes a relationship between Christian worship and mission within the world. The Mass includes the Liturgy of the Word* (biblical lessons, proclaimed and preached) followed by the Liturgy of the Eucharist* (including the Eucharistic* Prayer and sharing of Communion*). In Rome, the language of the entire liturgy was originally largely koine* Greek. By the middle of the 3rd c., when the spoken language shifted to Latin, so too did the biblical readings for the purpose of intelligibility, but the prayers remained in Greek. Only with the papacy of Damasus I (d384) did the Roman Church completely adopt Latin for the entire eucharistic celebration.

In the late 4th c., the Roman Eucharist took on strong cultural traits that reflected the Roman cultural genius of sobriety and simplicity. The 5th–8th c. marked the classical period of the evolution of the Roman Mass, especially evident in the "Stational Liturgy" (including processions to designated churches, presided over by the pope). Although the entrance rite reflected Roman imperial court ceremonial customs, the rest of that Mass exhibited classical Roman sobriety: there was little use of incense*, there were no genuflections* and no elevation of the bread and cup. Vested clergy remained in their places throughout the Mass and did not approach the altar during the Roman Canon, whose language appealed more to the intellect than to the heart.

In the Franco-Germanic regions, the Mass was much more elaborate, consistent with that cultural genius and appealing more to the heart than to the head. There was greater use of drama and poetry, candles and incense; prayers were lengthier and more evocative. With Franco-Germanic pilgrims*, who began visiting Rome after the baptism of Clovis* (496), Roman liturgical traditions found their way into the "Gallican* Mass." In the 8th c., Charlemagne* (d814) followed the lead of his father, Pepin the Short (d768), in attempting to Romanize and unify the Franco-Germanic people using the Roman Rite as the primary instrument. A reverse influence occurred in the 10th c. when Gallican liturgical elements made their way into the Roman Rite and its classical form was lost. The Mass increasingly became the clergy's property with the laity as passive spectators. By the year 1200, the offertory* procession ceased, as did offering the chalice to the laity. Communion was now received on the tongue, and Mass was uniformly celebrated with the priest turned toward the altar (and thus "toward the east," *ad orientem*) with his back to the people. Private Mass without a congregation became standard fare and was often celebrated simultaneously at different altars in the same church. The Mass had become a private devotion, and liturgical abuses abounded.

The Council of Trent* (1545–63) attempted to correct some of those abuses, especially regarding the inappropriate proliferation of Masses and Mass stipends, superstition around the number of fixed Masses, and the problem of indulgences*. The Mass was reformed with special attention to liturgical unification for the entire Roman Church, aided both by the promulgation of the Roman Missal of Pius V (1570) and by the establishment of the Congregation of Rites (1588). Such liturgical centralization was accomplished through strict adherence to the new Roman Missal and priests were forbidden to deviate under pain of sin. The Roman Rite would remain untouched for 400 years, until Vatican* II (1962–65).

Vatican II promoted a reform of the Mass that balanced tradition with progress, building on the Tridentine liturgical reforms but open to the pastoral needs of the 20th-c. church. Returning to biblical and patristic sources, the Council's Liturgy Constitution, *Sacrosanctum Concilium* (massively approved by 2,147 to 4), spoke of the Eucharist as the "source and summit of the Christian life" and recovered the principle of full and active participation by the liturgical assembly, with baptism* as the common denominator. Like the early church and the 16th-c. Reformation, a renewed emphasis was placed on intelligibility; thus vernacular languages were introduced. Cultural adaptation was encouraged, especially in mission lands, so that the Mass could more aptly reflect the cultural genius of each local church. One of the greatest gifts of Vatican II was increased ecumenical liturgical cooperation. Today the Eucharist celebrated in mainline churches is often quite similar to the Roman Catholic Mass and vice versa; people pray the same liturgical texts and read the same biblical lessons. In large cities, liturgical assemblies are increasingly multicultural and multiracial, making the call to liturgical inculturation* and authentic liturgical renewal more urgent than ever. KEITH F. PECKLERS, SJ

Mater et Magistra. See SOCIAL ENCYCLICALS.

Matins, morning service of prayer, ideally between dawn and sunrise, eventually differentiated from lauds*.

Matriarchy refers to a legal, social, economic, cultural, and political system that validates and enforces the sovereignty of female heads of families; it is rare in Christianity, although it is sometimes found in matrilineal societies (in parts of Africa and in the Philippines). **See also PATRIARCHY AND CHRISTIANITY.**

Matrimony. See MARRIAGE, THEOLOGY AND PRACTICE OF, CLUSTER.

Matthew, the Gospel of, a carefully crafted story of Jesus, moves skillfully between narrative and discourse (see markers: 7:28; 11:1; 13:53; 19:1; 26:1). It depicts Jesus as a preacher, teacher, and healer (4:23; 9:35) in the context of 1st-c. Palestinian Judaism.

Generally, scholars locate the origins of the Gospel in the last decades of the 1st c., in Syria, most likely Antioch, a cosmopolitan city of the Roman Empire with a long-standing Jewish enclave. Within such a Jewish context, the Matthean community struggles with its parent body concerning issues of authority and authoritative interpretation of their sacred tradition/s (5:21–48; 16:13–20; 18:18–20). Others from a variety of ethnic origins ("Gentiles") challenge the boundaries of the Matthean community and some of the Gospel's stories reflect a rethinking of the way Gentiles might be included (2:1–11; 8:5–13; 15:21–28).

The program that shapes this story of Jesus is found in 4:17: the *basileia**, or empire of the heavens (see Kingdom of God, the Concept of, Cluster), is near at hand. A group of disciples* (men and women; 4:18–22; 8:14–15; 9:9)

experience this *basileia* through Jesus' preaching (5–7; 10; 13:1–52; 18; 21:23–25:46) and healing (8–9; 12:9–14; 15:21–28; 17:14–23; 20:29–34; 21:14). They, in turn, are commissioned to go forth and tell people that Jesus has been raised (28:7), reconcile failed disciples (28:10), and teach and make disciples (28:19–20).

Jesus is characterized in continuity with Israel's traditions of holy ones and prophets*. He is named the one born of God or Son* of God (2:15; 3:17; 4:3, 6; 14:33; 16:16; 26:63; 27:40, 43, 54). He gives a new law from the mountaintop as Moses* did (5–7), and he heals as Elijah* and Elisha* did (8–9). He is also, however, a sign of divine discontinuity. He is in the line of Tamar*, Rahab*, Ruth*, and Bathsheba* (1:3, 5, 6) and is child of an endangered woman (1:16, 18–25). His deeds of prophetic healing* draw forth the title "Sophia" (Wisdom*), justified by her deeds (11:19), and he learns to extend his understanding of the *basileia* vision of God from a Canaanite woman (15:21–28).

Containing tensions within, the Gospel has created tensions without: it has been used, e.g, as a foundation for the structure of the Roman Catholic Church (16:13–20) and as an anti*-Jewish weapon (27:25). In addition, tensions in the text concerning authority, membership, women's leadership, and other issues continue to engage contemporary women in their practices and theologies. ELAINE M. WAINWRIGHT

Maundy Thursday. The term "Maundy" derives from the "new commandment" (*mandatum novum*) of foot-washing (John 13:34); "Thursday" refers to the Thursday before Easter*, the time of the Last* Supper and the institution of the Eucharist*.

Maurists, Benedictine monks of the Congregation of Saint-Maur, who edited and published texts of many Christian writers of the early and medieval periods. Most of these editions were republished in the *Patrologia* of J.-P. Migne*.

Maximos (Maximus) the Confessor (c580–662), Greek theologian, spiritual writer. Born into the aristocracy, he was secretary to the Byzantine emperor Heraclius before becoming a monk in Chrysopolis (614) and then Cyzicus (c625). During the Persian invasion (626), he fled to the Mediterranean islands and then to Carthage (628), while dealing with questions raised by the spiritual writings of Gregory* Nazianzen and Dionysius* the Pseudo-Areopagite. He gave a mystical* interpretation of the liturgy; several of his works were later translated into Latin by John* Scotus Erigena.

Maximos wrote against Monothelitism* (encouraged in Emperor Heraclius's *Ecthesis** [638] and Constans II's Typos* [647–48]) and took part in the condemnations of this doctrine by councils in Africa and Rome (646) and by the Lateran Synod (649). Arrested, tried in Constantinople, exiled (655–56), and brought once again to Constantinople, he was condemned by a synod (662); his tongue and right hand were cut off to keep him from propagating his views. Exiled to the Caucasus, he died later in the same year.

Against the Monothelites, he insisted that each nature of Christ has its own mode of willing and acting; indeed, the human nature is freely self-actuating. This affirmation of a human will* and activity is testimony to the reality of God's creation; freedom of will and difference from God persist even in the Incarnation*, as they also persist in mystical* union. With the neo-Chalcedonians*, however, he denied a human person or agent in Christ, for the only agent is the divine Word*. In the case of Gethsemane (Mark 14:36 par.), the Word in human mode both expresses human temptation and consents to the divine will. There remain two wills and activities, which are united but never "one." EUGENE TESELLE

McPherson, Aimee Semple (1890–1944), Pentecostal* evangelist and founder (1923) of the International Church of the Foursquare Gospel (c2 million members in 83 countries in 2000). Born in Canada, she converted to Pentecostalism (1908) and went as a missionary to China with Robert Semple, her husband, who died there (1910). She married Harold McPherson (1912; divorced 1921) and was an itinerant evangelist from 1914 until 1923, when she founded Angelus Temple in Los Angeles.

McPherson combined Pentecostal and Evangelical* theology to become one of the most popular evangelists of the 20th c. Her "foursquare" message (from the "foursquare" holy city of Rev 21:16) included traditional Evangelical, Holiness*, and Pentecostal emphases – Jesus Christ as savior, baptizer with the Holy Spirit, healer, and soon-coming king – and social commitment to help the poor. Worship at the Angelus Temple downplayed Pentecostal particularities (e.g. glossalia*) and focused on a Protestant salvation* message. McPherson demonstrated the affinity between conservative Evangelicals and popular media. Her sermons blurred the line between worship and entertainment (with costumes and lavish sets). In 1924 she became the first woman granted a radio license by the US Federal Communications Commission. Her station, KFSG (Kall Four-Square Gospel), her periodical, the *Bridal Call*, and books such as *In the Service of the King* (1927) further disseminated her message.

SARAH JOHNSON

Means of Grace, sensible signs (especially sacraments*, the words of Scripture*, preaching*) through which divine revelation* and grace* are communicated to human beings.

Mechtild of Magdeburg (1207–82), born of wealthy and possibly aristocratic parents, moved (1230) to Magdeburg to become a Beguine*, lived there for 40 years before retiring (1270) to the convent at Helfta. Her book, *Flowing Light of the Godhead* (*Fliessende Licht der Gottheit*), written mostly while she was a Beguine (with the encouragement of her Dominican confessor, Heinrich of Halle), consists of accounts of visions and descriptions of conversations between Mechtild and God. The ordering of the books is not her own, although it follows the description of Mechtild's life given by God in Book 7:3: "Your childhood was the playmate of my Holy Spirit, your youth the bride of my Humanity, and now your old age is the mistress of the house of my Divinity" (not "housewife" as some translations have it). Mechtild uses Minne, "Love," as her name for the Divinity, and her most profound understanding of God is the paradox* that his withdrawal is the highest manifestation of his awful presence. It is in the depths of despair, when the soul feels the farthest from God, that Mechtild, like other Beguines, experiences the comfort and presence of Minne. **See also** APOPHATICISM.

SASKIA MURK JANSEN

Medellín (Colombia), location of a meeting of CELAM (Consejo Episcopal Latinoamericano, Latin American Episcopal Conference) in 1968. **See also** CELAM.

Media and Christianity. The church views media (film, television, radio, the Internet) with both hope and despair. Conservative traditions see media as powerful instruments for evangelism*, whereas liberals look optimistically to them as means for powerless people to gain a public voice. Traditionalists decry secular media's immorality, while liberal groups criticize the commercialization and conservative politicization of media. Both groups agree that media can help build religious community.

The worldwide growth of Christian broadcast and film media has been fueled primarily by Evangelicals'* belief that these technologies have the power to convert persons and even whole societies to faith. Some historians identify the origins of this perspective in Europe's Protestant Reformation, which entailed the first religious use of mass printing and distribution. For modern North American Evangelicals, the invention of the radio (late 19th c.) elicited a similar hope in mass-mediated evangelism. North American Premillennialists, who believe that Jesus Christ's second coming and eternal judgment are immanent, turned to electronic media to proclaim the gospel around the globe.

Mainline Protestant and Roman Catholic groups focus on freedom of speech and the need for decentralized, localized media decision making throughout the developed and developing world. They hope to prevent modern nation-states and corporations from selfishly controlling media to the exclusion of indigenous cultures and minority faiths.

The global church agrees that excessive media secularization* ought to be resisted because it would weaken religious communities. But conservatives focus on secular media's immorality – especially the sex, violence, and profanity it disseminates – whereas mainline and other more liberal Christians emphasize the commercialization and politicization of media and their role in creating consumer-oriented, materialistic culture, as do conservative or "right-wing" Christian movements. North American–produced religious media had this effect particularly in Latin America.

Christians of all traditions see mass media as powerful means of organizing and strengthening religious communities. They generally believe that so long as the media are free of antireligious legislation and regulation, religious groups can use television, radio, film, and the Internet to maintain their distinct local cultures and international identities. To the worldwide church, the media are both symbols and technologies, with much promise and yet fraught with danger. **See also** TELEVANGELISM AND WESTERN CULTURE.

QUENTIN J. SCHULTZE

Media and Christian Worship. The church has always defined itself primarily in and through the medium of worship*, as believers have "gathered together" for praise, prayer, teaching, and especially sacrament. The intrinsically localized, sacred, and exclusive aspects of worship gatherings led to tensions over the appropriateness of transmitting worship to heterogeneous, unregulated audiences.

For many traditions, worship is a local practice meant to be undertaken in person, just as Jesus Christ was God's incarnate Son and is present (see Presence of Christ) in the worship service. This presence of Christ is understood in different ways by different traditions. Thus the Roman Catholic Church and (in a slightly different way) the Eastern Orthodox Church, which affirm a "real presence" of Christ in the Eucharist*, have resisted mediating the Mass* or the Divine* Liturgy through broadcast technologies. Catholics made exceptions based on the fact that even within the local parish some shut-ins are unable to participate in Mass. Except on high holidays, Catholics tend to broadcast the Mass only locally.

With the Reformation, many Protestant traditions deemphasized the sacredness of a particular space (see Hierotopy, the Creation of Sacred Christian Spaces) or time, including those set aside for worship. As a result, Protestants began mediating worship through radio, television, and eventually online internet technologies. A few even claim to have established "virtual" churches online. Roman Catholic, Orthodox, and mainline Protestant groups have criticized Evangelicals (and others) for creating semi-religious versions of worship services that imitate "secular" broadcast programs, such as musical variety shows.

Worshipping via mass media has also been controversial because of differing perspectives on whether worship should be open to the public or restricted to members of the believing community. Mainline Protestants and Roman Catholics wanted to make sure that worship did not become a public spectacle for audiences unfamiliar with Christian practices. Since broadcast media attract comparatively wide audiences, such critics tend to advocate "narrowcasting" services, via closed-circuit, subscription-only, or even online media that are not likely to be accessed by unaffiliated people.

Worship through mass media elicits within the church the same kinds of discussions and practices that Christians have had from the early days, when believers met secretly in homes and at times in underground caves. Concerns about the appropriateness of mediated worship help the various church communities to articulate who they are as local communities of faith, how they should worship a holy God, and how they can define their distinct identities in contrast to the wider culture. **See also GOSPEL MUSIC; LITURGIES, HISTORY OF; MEGACHURCHES REMAKING RELIGIOUS TRADITION IN NORTH AMERICA; MEGACHURCH MOVEMENT; PRAISE AND WORSHIP; WORSHIP CLUSTER.** QUENTIN J. SCHULTZE

Mediating Theology, the movement in German theology, inaugurated by followers of Schleiermacher*, to achieve a "true mediation" between Christianity and contemporary thought, thus between supernaturalism and rationalism*. Its vehicle was the periodical *Theologische Studien und Kritiken,* founded in 1828. Most of the participants, including Schleiermacher, supported the Prussian Union of Lutheran and Reformed churches (see Germany). Some of them built on Hegel's* revival of the themes of Trinity* and Incarnation*; others followed Schleiermacher in starting with religious experience and developing a new conceptuality. The movement (especially as articulated by Isaak August Dorner and Richard Rothe) offered an alternative to biblicism and confessionalism by seeking connections among theology, philosophy, and critical study of the Bible.

Mediator, one who intervenes between two parties for the purpose of communication or reconciliation*. Paul applies the term to angels* (Gal 3.19–20) to suggest their inferiority as communicators of God's will. Yet Christ is called "the mediator of a new covenant" (Heb 8:6, 9:15, 12.24) or "the one mediator between God and humans" (1 Tim 2.5). In christological* doctrine, the term becomes more frequent, and more precise. Christ's role as mediator implies no distance or inferiority, for there is immediate union of the divine and the human.

Mediatrix (Lat feminine form of "mediator"), term applied to Mary* in her capacity of mediating the grace* that comes from her son Jesus Christ.

Medical Ethics. Although the term "medical ethics" became prominent only after the 1803 publication in England of Thomas Percival's influential book, *Medical Ethics,* it had been around for a long time as a concept, field of learning, and practice. There are, in fact, multiple traditions worldwide in which concerns for ethics and medicine appear: ancient and modern traditions, religious and secular, from both the East and the West, as well as the global South. Central to human experience in every culture and society are experiences of birth and death, and of disease, injury, and disability*. Peoples everywhere have therefore sought meaning in these experiences, as well as remedies and support. Since major values and vulnerabilities are at stake, ethical frameworks have governed ways of thinking about the practice of "medicine."

Christian medical ethical frameworks are distinctive but not wholly unique; they overlap with other traditions, both secular and religious. For example, all traditions have had to address the moral character of healers or physicians, and medical choices such as whether to treat or not to treat. Many traditions, including Jewish, Christian, Muslim, and contemporary secular traditions, have been commonly influenced by, e.g., the Greek Hippocratic collection of writings from the 5th c. BCE (particularly the Oath of Hippocrates).

Religious traditions of medical ethics have always been shaped by beliefs about the causes of disease, the meaning of suffering*, the worth of the human individual and the common good, the value of life, and the place of death* in life. Christianity, Judaism*, and Islam* share beliefs in a God* who cares about all creation* and who makes human beings in God's own image*, calling them to have compassion* for one another. These traditions, therefore, also share a belief in the intrinsic worth of persons and a concern for human flourishing in community.

A Christian medical ethical framework is further shaped by belief in Jesus Christ as the incarnation* and revelation* of God, and as the model of healing* as well as companioning in suffering and death. In this framework, human physical life in this world is a fundamental good, a gift from God to be stewarded and lived with reverence and respect. Yet physical life is not an absolute good; it need not be preserved at the price of other goods such as faith* or freedom*. Moreover, Jesus' twofold love commandment emphasizes an ethic whose center is love* of God and neighbor*.

Shaped by fundamental beliefs, Christian medical ethical discernment relies on four primary sources and employs a variety of methods of analysis and argument. Scripture*, tradition* (theological and ecclesiastical), secular disciplines, and contemporary experience are the standard sources (in the past, Protestants emphasized Scripture, and Roman Catholics emphasized tradition, ecclesiastical authority, natural* law, and case studies). Patterns of reasoning in Christian medical ethics are "teleological*" (taking account of consequences and/or more ultimate ends; see Consequentialist Ethics) or "deontological*" (considering what is right, regardless of consequences). Narratives are also important in gaining insight into ethical issues, as in the overall Christian "story" or the story of a patient's own life. Moreover, Christian medical ethics encompasses "virtue*" or "character" ethics, discerning what ought to characterize givers and receivers of care as well as the relationship between them.

The long history of Christian medical ethics was marked by clarity and continuity (for Protestants, in terms of general attitudes and guidelines; for Roman Catholics, in terms of explicit principles formulated in the 16th c. and specified in new contexts thereafter). In the mid-20th c., however, massive developments in science and technology called for the critical retrieval and reconstruction of past work in medical ethics. Urgent choices loomed regarding the limitation of treatment, assisted suicide, technologically assisted reproduction (see Pregnancy), research on human subjects at all stages of development, cloning, organ transplantation, and genetic manipulation. New insights arose regarding patient rights, physician–patient relationships, and justice* in the delivery of health care.

Christian thinkers (Protestants such as Joseph Fletcher and Paul Ramsey; Roman Catholics such as Richard McCormick and Charles Curran) worked with others to formulate principles that would be intelligible in religious and secular discourse – principles demanding informed patients' choice, prohibiting unjust harm and requiring positive consequences for individual and communal well-being, and obligating distributive justice in the allocation of scarce medical resources. New debates (within and between forms of Christianity) emerged regarding contraception and birth* control, euthanasia*, abortion*, and embryonic stem cell research. Traditions are no longer monolithic with respect to most contested issues, and there is strong agreement on central principles of respect for persons and responses of care. Even Roman Catholicism, which continues to hold some clear official positions, has sustained conversations and debates on diverse views among its moral theologians. **See also HEALTH, HEALING, AND CHRISTIANITY CLUSTER.**

MARGARET A. FARLEY

Meditation, reflecting, pondering, or exercising the mind through sustained consideration of a religious text, doctrine, or mystery, for the sake of devotion* to God and spiritual growth.

Megachurches. A megachurch is a Protestant congregation with 2,000 or more in attendance (adults and children) at services on an average weekend. However, these congregations and the larger global Megachurch Movement are far more complex and nuanced than an arbitrary size marker. The Megachurch Movement can be characterized as a unique collective response to cultural* shifts and changes in societal patterns throughout the industrialized, urban, and suburban areas of the world.

Very large churches have existed throughout the history of Christendom. But in recent decades, the number of megachurches has dramatically increased, growing in the USA from a handful in 1900 to 50 in 1970 to nearly 1,300 in 2008; similar increases, though somewhat smaller, have occurred worldwide. Individual megachurches are diverse in style and visionary approach; there is no single megachurch model. Overall, however, these churches are quite uniform in structure, owing in part to their size and organizational complexity.

The average megachurch has c4,000 weekly participants and an annual budget of 6.5 million US dollars, although the international megachurches are generally much larger. Globally, they are found predominantly in densely populated urban centers of Korea*, Brazil*, Australia*, South* Africa, and Nigeria*. In the USA, the majority are located in the southern Sunbelt, clustered around suburbs and exurbs of the largest sprawling metropolitan areas, such as Houston, Phoenix, Orlando, Los Angeles, and Atlanta. This pattern shifted as the phenomenon developed, beginning in urban areas (with "tall-steeple" megachurches), then dramatically expanding in the suburban Sunbelt, and now increasingly being established in Northwest, Northeast and Midwest suburban areas.

Half of these congregations were founded after 1971, and in 2008 fully 80% were still led by the senior pastor under whose tenure the dramatic growth took place. These senior pastors are predominantly male, well educated, and on average 50 years of age, and are strong visionary, entrepreneurial leaders. They are primarily responsible for the distinctive vision, clear mission, and well-defined sense of purpose common to nearly all megachurches. These central leaders are assisted by a large number of additional clergy, staff, and volunteers. Almost all megachurches hold conservative theological beliefs and describe themselves as Evangelical*.

Worship at these congregations often takes place in a theater-style auditorium, adorned with few traditional religious symbols. The professional, elaborately produced service is characterized by expressive contemporary music and singing accompanied by electric guitars, keyboard, and drums, with music and words projected onto huge screens and enhanced with sophisticated technology. The fast-paced worship culminates in a polished, entertaining sermon that is practical and culturally relevant as well as biblical and inspirational (see Gospel Music; Media and Christianity; Media and Christian Worship; Praise and Worship).

These churches provide countless services, ministries, and activities throughout the week. Their programs meet both the spiritual and physical needs of participants and local community members. These programs also offer a place for participants to live out their religious commitments in service to others. Nearly every megachurch employs small groups and provides intimate fellowship opportunities that structure intentional community building and enhance commitment on a large scale.

When compared with national profiles of church members, participants in megachurches are found to be similar in gender makeup (60% female, 40% male) but on average younger and less likely to be married; there are twice as many single persons among megachurch participants. Megachurch attendees are both more highly educated and have higher incomes than either participants in smaller churches or the US adult population in general. Overall, megachurches have much greater ethnic and racial diversity than any other grouping of congregations. Many participants in these churches (70%) have come from other congregations locally or joined after having moved from other geographic locations, but 25% were previously not affiliated with a church or had not attended church for years. Most attend megachurches because they are attracted by the church's size, its vision and mission, the pastor's charisma, the contemporary worship forms, and the many activities and programs. The participant turnover rate in these churches is considerable, with two-thirds having attended for five or fewer years. Yet the level of commitment and the spiritual activities of megachurch participants on average are at least equal to those of participants in smaller churches.

Megachurches offer participants new ways of being religious in community. These churches allow attendees to participate by choice, at levels and in ways that suit their individual desires. The many programs and options allow them to choose and customize their experience of the church so that it meets the needs of each family member. For participants who have moved from other localities, megachurches offer ready-made social networks and intimate groups that allow them to integrate into a new community quickly, with others of similar values and demographics.

Megachurches have vast resources of money and people. They are also surprisingly daring and inventive in terms of programs and organizational structures. In addition, their senior clergy are popular speakers, authors, and religious leaders. This combination has resulted in megachurches generating many innovative shifts in religious expression, music, and organizational forms. While these largest churches represent less than half of 1% of all US churches, they garner considerable attention and influence within the religious world and secular society.

The growth of the megachurch phenomenon is, in part, the result of an economy of scale and efficiency that smaller churches seldom match. However, the growth of megachurches also parallels the movement of other institutions toward larger structures, technological innovation, and pop cultural expressiveness. This church form fits the contemporary suburban social milieu. It offers choice, flexibility, and even customization of spiritual expression to its participants and declares to an increasingly secular society that religion is alive and flourishing. **See also WORD-FAITH MOVEMENT AND ITS WORSHIP.**

SCOTT THUMMA

Megachurches in El Salvador. Almost one-third of El* Salvador's Christians now profess to be Evangelicals/Protestants, 75% of whom are Charismatic* or Pentecostal. Most of them attend the thousands of very small churches that proliferate in poor barrios and rural villages; yet at least 10 urban churches have attendance figures above 5,000. Two notable examples illustrate fundamental differences among these megachurches.

The Tabernaculo Biblico Bautista "Amigos de Israel Central" was founded by US-educated Edgar Lopez Bertrand. The Baptist Tabernacle boasts a membership of more than 80,000 and has spawned at least 40 smaller churches, some of them in North American Salvadorian communities. The mother church in a middle-class sector of San Salvador occupies a square block, with two schools, a theological training center, and a plush 8,000-seat sanctuary hosting six consecutive, highly choreographed Sunday services. Bertrand's politically passive and theologically conservative message is spread throughout Latin America by means of radio and television broadcasts.

The Mision Elim Internacional is located in the slums of Ilabasco. Elim is a church of the very poor with an active membership of more than 150,000 (usually considered the second-largest church in the world). Along with continuous Sunday celebrations held in its massive open-air auditorium, the church broadcasts over radio and television and offers numerous midweek services, as well as a weekly all-night prayer vigil attended by more than 3,000. Unlike the Baptist Tabernacle, which is under Bertrand's autocratic leadership, Elim is not pastor driven. Modeled after the world's largest church – Yoido Full Gospel (Seoul, South Korea) – the Elim community is organized according to districts, sectors, zones, and small neighborhood cells. Each cell and sector has an appointed leader, and each district has a pastor. Also unlike the Tabernacle, Elim is Charismatic*/Pentecostal. Its worship is animated by fiery preaching, open weeping, speaking in tongues*, and healing*. Women are active as cell group leaders, yet in worship they wear veils, sit separately from men, and do not serve as pastors or teachers.

These two churches represent a widening theological gulf that separates Central American Evangelicals. While the Baptist Tabernacle emphasizes the Prosperity* Gospel common in many North American megachurches, Elim is becoming socially and politically prophetic, increasingly speaking out against political injustice and the economic structures that foster poverty*, violence*, and emigration to the USA. Despite these differences, however, both churches function as alternative societies for their members. They are constructed islands of common faith and support that shelter Salvadorian believers from the turbulent seas of political unrest, violence, and crushing poverty.

TIMOTHY WADKINS

Megachurches Remaking Religious Tradition in North America. The emergence and rapid growth of megachurches represented one of the most significant changes in North American Christianity at the end of the 20th and the early 21st c. The majority of megachurches, customarily defined as Protestant churches with

2,000 or more weekly attendees, identify themselves as conservative, often combining orthodox Evangelical* theology with practical, therapeutic (see Health, Healing, and Christianity Cluster: In North American and European Pentecostal/Charismatic Movements) religious messages. Many employ the latest in audiovisual technology in their worship services (see Media and Christianity; Media and Christian Worship) and offer attendees a wide range of services and religious events (from fitness classes to Bible studies). While small in number (there are only c1,300 megachurches among the 335,000 congregations in the USA), megachurches wield extraordinary influence over denominations through their ministry activities and worship styles and over millions of Christians around the world through the Internet (Thumma and Travis). Many megachurches draw heavily on the marketing strategies and entrepreneurialism of the contemporary marketplace to effectively sell their brand of Christianity and their products to other churches, often through new, quasi-denominational bodies like the Willow Creek Association (Twitchell, Sargeant, Thumma and Travis). Scholars have begun to identify three ways in which megachurches are affecting the traditions and practices of congregations.

The primary and most profound way megachurches influence historical Protestant denominations is through the process of "mimetic isomorphism." Many congregations of Lutheran*, Methodist*, Presbyterian*, and other historical denominations see megachurches as offering a model for worship*, Christian education, and decision making that works stunningly well in a religious market where interest in preserving or following historic traditions is very low. Thus some congregations abandon the hymns, rituals, and theological orientations grounded in older, often Reformation-based traditions and adopt the pop rock–inspired praise music (see Praise and Worship), Evangelical or conversion*-oriented liturgy, and conservative theology of megachurches in a bid to survive and compete (Sargeant).

A second way that megachurches influence historical Protestant traditions is through "selective isomorphism," in which congregations borrow elements from megachurches that they can easily incorporate into the life of the congregation and that dovetail with their own understanding of what is essential and what is nonessential within their historic tradition. Thus in early 21st c., several Lutheran churches blended the worship approach from Willow Creek or Saddleback Community Church with Lutheran liturgical elements. For example, two Lutheran congregations made rock-and-roll music a central part of their worship services, justifying it on the basis of Luther's own use of the music of his day, but they kept the sacrament of Holy Communion as a regular part of worship (Ellingson). Under pressure from the religious market to conform, they adopted the rituals, forms of worship, or theology of the successful newcomers but did so in incremental ways that did not so radically change the tradition held by longtime or "cradle" members (Chaves).

A third way that megachurches influence religious traditions is by pressuring congregations in local religious markets to return to their historic roots and to define themselves as "niche" congregations that specialize in offering an authentic denominational church experience. Rather than directly competing with megachurches, some congregations intentionally remake themselves as exemplars of Lutheranism, Methodism, or Presbyterianism, e.g. in order to offer local churchgoers a clear alternative to the relatively standardized experience offered by megachurches (Eiseland, Ammerman). Thus megachurches lead some congregations of historical denominations to rediscover their tradition.

While it is clear that megachurches are here to stay and that they will continue to wield an enormous influence in both local and national religious ecologies, mainline Protestant congregations will also continue to respond creatively, sometimes rediscovering their tradition and sometimes blending old and new traditions into what may become new forms of Protestantism. **See also** **MEDIA AND CHRISTIANITY; MEDIA AND CHRISTIAN WORSHIP; PRAISE AND WORSHIP; TELEVANGELISM AND WESTERN CULTURE; WORD-FAITH MOVEMENT AND ITS WORSHIP.**

STEPHEN ELLINGSON

Megilloth (Heb "scrolls"), the five scrolls recited on Jewish festivals and in Jewish liturgies: Ruth* (Shavuot, celebration of the giving of Torah), Song* of Songs (Passover), Ecclesiastes* (Sukkot, Tabernacles), Lamentations* (ninth of Av, commemoration of the destruction of the Temple in Jerusalem), and Esther* (Purim).

Meinvielle, Julio (1905–73), Roman Catholic priest who for several decades was the spokesperson for important sectors of Argentine Catholicism. A prolific intellectual who contributed to such magazines as *Criterio* and *Sol y* *luna,* he is viewed as the mentor of the fundamentalist (integrist*) and authoritarian Catholic Argentine nationalists, and later of anti-Semitic youth movements such as the Tacuara (in the 1950s–1960s). These youth movements and Meinvielle promoted in diverse publications and conferences their conception of the social order as a corporate society organized and framed by the spiritual (the Roman Catholic Church); Meinvielle strongly condemned Jacques Maritain*, accusing him of selling out the Church to Rousseau-type liberalism* and Marxist* communism. **See also ARGENTINA.**

LUIS MIGUEL DONATELLO

Melanchthon, Philipp (1497–1560), Reformer and humanist, Luther's* colleague at the University of Wittenberg (1518–60), where he taught theology and humanities. Besides writing popular books on Greek and Latin grammar, rhetoric, logic, and world history, he published commentaries on Psalms, Proverbs, Matthew, John, Romans (five on Romans), 1 and 2 Corinthians, Colossians, and 1 Timothy, the first Protestant systematic theology (*Loci Communes Theologici* [Theological topics]), and several Lutheran confessional documents (the Augsburg* Confession, the Apology [in defense of the Confession], and the *Treatise on the Power and Primacy of the Pope*).

Melanchthon was the first Pauline interpreter to apply systematically the rules of rhetoric for analyzing the letters' structure and figures of speech and to employ the rules of dialectic for identifying their topics and logic. The first edition of his *Loci Communes* (1521/22) follows the basic topics of Romans (sin*, law* and gospel*, grace*, faith*). Like Luther, he understood that God justifies* (declares righteous) Christians by grace through faith because of Christ alone. His definition of the capacity of law and gospel to terrify and comfort Christians remains fundamental to Lutheran hermeneutics. Controversies after Luther's death called into question his teachings on free will* and the Lord's* Supper. With Bucer* he drafted the 1535 Wittenberg Concord, which held that Christ is present with the bread and wine. TIMOTHY WENGERT

Melanesia. See HISTORY OF CHRISTIANITY CLUSTER: IN THE SOUTH PACIFIC AND AUSTRALIA.

Melania the Elder (342–410). Born in Spain, she founded and directed monasteries in Jerusalem (377–400). The granddaughter of a wealthy consul in Rome, Melania devoted her life to asceticism* after losing a husband and two children. After visiting desert fathers in Egypt (372/4), she settled in Jerusalem and founded a monastery on the Mount of Olives, which became a double* monastery when the monk, historian, and translator Rufinus* soon joined her. Jerome* referred to Melania as a "second Thecla*" because of her commitment to asceticism. Jerome later expunged her name from his *Chronicle* owing to her friendships with Rufinus, Evagrius* Ponticus, and Palladius* and her implication in the Origenist* controversy.

SUSANNA DRAKE

Melania the Younger (c385–439). Born in Rome, married to Pinian (399), she founded a monastery on the Mount of Olives (431/2). The granddaughter of Melania* the Elder, the wealthy Melania the Younger took a vow of celibacy* with her husband, Pinian, after their two children died. With her mother, Albina, and Pinian, she lived in Thagaste, North Africa, and later in Jerusalem, where she founded a double monastery after her husband died. She practiced a rigorous asceticism* and renounced much wealth. By selling many of her properties, she funded monasteries in Egypt, North Africa, Antioch, and Palestine. SUSANNA DRAKE

Melchizedek (Heb "king of righteousness"), king of Salem (= Jerusalem*) and priest of the highest God (Gen 14:18) who blesses Abraham*. An enthronement psalm* calls the king "a priest forever after the order of Melchizedek" (Ps 110:4). This description is also applied to Christ* in Heb 5–7.

Melkites, Arabic- and Greek-speaking Christians who accept the Christology of Chalcedon*, all of the first seven ecumenical councils (those recognized by the Eastern Orthodox* churches, although the Miaphysite* Oriental Orthodox* churches in Syria* recognize only three; see Ecumenical Councils), *and* the primacy of the pope of Rome. Their name, from the Syriac *malkâ,* "king," originated among Miaphysites* as a pejorative designation of "the king's people," who sided with the Byzantine emperor in endorsing the Chalcedonian christological formula. Overtures from Rome (14th–18th c.) led to formal recognition of papal claims by some, who kept the name Melkites (1724). Others, who rejected the Roman claims, are now known simply as Greek Orthodox of the Diocese of Antioch, or Antiochian Orthodox. The Melkite patriarchs of Antioch, Jerusalem, and Alexandria have counterparts in the Greek Orthodox*, Syriac* Orthodox, and Coptic* Orthodox churches.

KATHLEEN E. MCVEY

Memory, the "presence" of the past. **See also TIME.**

Men, Alexander (1935–90), priest, apologist, and thorn in the side of Soviet authorities, Fr. Alexander Men was one of the best-known voices of Russian Orthodox Christianity during the late Soviet period. A Jew who converted to Christianity, Men held an ecumenical view of faith at odds with Russian Orthodox officialdom. He was murdered, probably by anti-Semitic nationalists, with an ax on his way to serve the liturgy. ROY R. ROBSON

Méndez Arceo, Sergio (1907–92), historian, bishop of Cuernavaca, Mexico (1952–83). Before Vatican* II, he initiated pastoral and liturgical renewal. He denounced the repression of students (1968), showed solidarity with political prisoners, actively participated in "Christians for Socialism" in Chile* (1972), supported psychoanalysis in Benedictine* monasteries with the abbot Gregorio Lemercier and the intercultural experiments promoted by Iván Illich, and supported Base* Ecclesial Communities. Because of his international solidarity with the oppressed*, he was called the bishop of the "cathedral without borders" by Latin American intellectuals. He was the author of *La Real y Pontificia Universidad de México*.

MARÍA ALICIA PUENTE LUTTEROTH and ELIZABETH JUDD

Méndez Medina, Alfredo (1877–1968), Jesuit priest, founder and director of the Mexican Social Secretariat and of the journal *Social Peace* (*La paz social*, 1923–35). He made important proposals addressing the agrarian problem in Mexico. **See also LAND, THEOLOGICAL PERSPECTIVES AND PRAXIS, CLUSTER: IN LATIN AMERICA.** MARÍA ALICIA PUENTE LUTTEROTH

Mendicant Orders, the "begging" orders, with no personal ownership of property; principally the Franciscans*, Dominicans*, Augustinian* hermits or friars, and Carmelites*.

Mennonites. Mennonites trace their origins to Anabaptism*, a renewal movement in Europe (first half of the 16th c.). The Anabaptists, the so-called "radical wing" of the Reformation, shared with the Protestant Reformers a high regard for Scripture and a rejection of papal authority; early Anabaptist leaders frequently referred to the Apostles' Creed as the foundation of their theology. But Anabaptists and their descendants – Mennonites, Amish*, and Hutterites* – differed with both Roman Catholics and Protestants* in their practice of believer's baptism*. This conviction, combined with a strong affirmation of Christ's teachings against violence*, resulted in a view of the church as a voluntary gathering of believers whose way of life would inevitably be in tension with the unredeemed world.

Mennonite theology has been, as a rule, oriented more toward ethical practice (orthopraxis*) than systematic doctrinal formulations (orthodoxy*). This is in part a consequence of the 16th-c. persecution, which deprived the movement of its university-trained leaders. More fundamentally, however, the Anabaptist/ Mennonite understanding of faith is inherently "incarnational*." Thus Hans Denck, an early Anabaptist leader, underscored, "No one can truly know Christ unless one follows him in life."

This incarnational and Christocentric approach to faith has several important consequences for Mennonite theology. Because Christ* is the fullest revelation of God to humanity, all Scripture must be read through the lens of his precepts and practices. Mennonite theology generally regards the exemplary character of Christ's life and teachings as inseparable from the salvation offered by his death and resurrection: Christians today, like the disciples of the 1st c., are called to follow Christ in their daily life. Likewise, the voluntary church is understood to be a visible embodiment of the resurrected Christ. Its distinctive practices – including the sharing of economic possessions, the practice of mutual accountability or discipline, egalitarian forms of leadership, and believer's baptism – offer a corporate witness to the world of a redeemed, transformed life in Christ.

Perhaps the most distinctive aspect of Mennonite theology today is its commitment to an ethic* of love* in all human relationships. Mennonites have understood biblical pacifism* (sometimes called nonresistance) to be a natural concomitant to God's free gift of grace*: just as God has graciously offered forgiveness to unworthy sinners, so too are Christians – as recipients of that love – called to extend God's grace to others, including enemies. Mennonites do not always agree about the political consequences of biblical nonresistance. But they are united in their conviction that the body of Christ transcends national boundaries and that Christians are called to be peacemakers by exemplifying Christ's love in word and deed.

The Mennonite emphasis on believer's baptism and ethical accountability was sometimes accused of Pelagianism*; Mennonites, however, clearly regard salvation* as a free gift of God's grace, a gift that human beings have the freedom to accept or reject.

Despite their skepticism about systematic approaches to theology, Mennonites have produced numerous confessions of faith. These have tended to be somewhat fluid documents, periodically revised to reflect shifting emphases and concerns.

The influences of Pietism* (especially in the 19th c.) and fundamentalism* (first half of the 20th c.) on Mennonites in North America have attenuated some of the distinctive features of Mennonite theology; more recently, the strong emphasis on peacemaking and social concerns have led some toward theological liberalism. Thus Mennonites debate the question: Should Mennonite theology be rooted in Christian orthodoxy? Or be grounded in distinctive premises, such as a nonviolent understanding of atonement*? JOHN D. ROTH

Mennonite Worship. The 16th-c. Anabaptist groups, forerunners of the Mennonites, met secretly for worship in homes, forest clearings, or caves to avoid persecution. This practice of worshipping in homes – or, later, in simple meetinghouses – continued in North America well into the 19th c. Today, Mennonite churches vary widely in design, but tend to be simple, strongly emphasizing function over form.

Mennonite worship has no fixed regiment. Generally, it is nonliturgical, with an emphasis on exegetical and practical sermons. Its communal dimension is reflected in four-part congregational singing and in a structured time set aside for congregational sharing or public responses to the sermon. Announcements of upcoming activities during the week are a reminder that the life of the body extends beyond Sunday morning worship. Mennonite worship often includes a "children's time" (during which a story related to the sermon topic is told) and is often followed by a period of informal fellowship and a Sunday school hour.

Mennonite worship styles have become more fluid. Some congregations have more contemporary worship styles – with amplified instruments, choruses, and clapping – while others reflect "high church" liturgical influences that include responsive readings, the use of the lectionary, and a more intentional focus on the seasons of the church year.

Mennonites generally celebrate Communion* (the Lord's Supper) two to four times a year. The elements, bread and grape juice, are understood to be a commemoration of Christ's sacrifice, a celebration of the unity of the gathered community, and a reminder of the suffering* that a Christian might be called to endure. Although the age at which people are baptized varies, baptism follows a confession* of faith and a period of instruction, and is associated with congregational membership. The mode of baptism can be that of sprinkling, pouring, or immersion.

JOHN D. ROTH

Menologion (Gk "monthly account"), in the Greek church, a liturgical book containing the lives of the saints*, arranged by months.

Mercedes de Jesús (1828–83), "the Rose of Guayas." Born in Baba, Ecuador*, she renounced her family inheritance to serve the poor*. She was the first missionary laywoman among the Shuar people (1869). In Cuenca (1871) she directed an orphanage for girls. She founded in Riobamba the "Santa Mariana de Jesús" Institute (1873). She died of pneumonia as a modest doorkeeper and was beatified in 1985. LUIS MARÍA GAVILANES DEL CASTILLO

Mercersburg Theology developed from the collaboration of John W. Nevin (1803–86) and Philip Schaff (1819–93) at the seminary of the German Reformed Church (Mercersburg, Pennsylvania). From the Presbyterian "Old School" tradition, Nevin opposed the "new measures" revivalism* associated with Finney*, and was influenced by Coleridge* and German theology. In *The Mystical Presence* (1846), Nevin interpreted Christ's presence in the Eucharist* as a "spiritual [rather than corporeal] real presence" of the whole person of Christ through the Holy Spirit, received by faith. Schaff, a Swiss who had studied in Germany and became a major historian of doctrine, emphasized Protestantism's "Catholic substance"; Protestantism maintained the classic doctrines of the early centuries but purged non-Scriptural accretions. In *The Principle of Protestantism* (1845), Schaff envisaged a future reunion of "subjective" Protestantism and "objective" Catholicism. Resisting the informality that pervaded US Protestantism, Nevin and then Schaff developed a new liturgy for the Reformed Church, retrieving the perspectives of Calvin* and Knox*, the Reformed* churches in Germany, and the Puritans* at the Savoy* Conference (1661). Although accused of being too sympathetic to Roman Catholicism, like members of the Oxford* Movement they were influenced primarily by German idealism and the

Romantic* movement, as well as the Prussian* Union grounded in the Reformed* churches in Germany. They are among the founders of both the ecumenical* movement and the Liturgical* Movement in Protestantism.

EUGENE TESELLE

Mercy, compassionate behavior by those in power toward those who are powerless, do not deserve to be treated with compassion, and are not expected to offer compensation. In the Christian tradition, it is first an attribute of God, then a human action in response to God's mercy.

Mercy as an Attribute of God (e.g. 2 Cor 1:3; Rom 9:15–18, 15:9; Heb 4:16) overlaps with God's compassion* and grace*, and with the expressions of these in atonement*, redemption*, and salvation*. The understanding of God's mercy varies along with the understanding of these key theological concepts. "Lord have mercy!" (the gospel phrase used in the liturgy of both Eastern and Western churches) has, therefore, at least three diverging meanings: (1) God's mercy may refer to the healing of a disease (whether this disease is sin* or an illness) or to the deliverance of persons who are in bondage to some evil power (whether this is a demonic power or an enslaving and oppressive power, as in Egypt; see Atonement #1), an interpretation found in the earliest church, Orthodox* churches, Liberation* theologies, and the Charismatic* Movement. (2) God's mercy may refer to the mercy of the divine judge bestowed on persons who should be condemned but are forgiven (see Atonement #2), an interpretation found in Western* church traditions. (3) God's mercy may refer to God calling people out of their rebellion against God or to God's transforming appeal to lead a life of love, compassion, and mercy, comparable to God's love, compassion, and mercy (see Atonement #3; Sanctification).

Mercy as Human Action in Response to God's Mercy and Made Possible by It. "Be merciful, just as your Father is merciful" (Luke 6: 36; see also, e.g., Hos 6:6; Matt 5:7). The liturgical prayer "Lord have mercy!" implies the willingness to "be conformed" to God's mercy and to act not out of moral independence but with the awareness of one's dependence on others (and God as Other), as in Rom 12:1: "I appeal to you . . . by the mercies of God, to present your bodies as a living sacrifice" (see Almsgiving). The understanding of what this merciful self-sacrifice entails varies according to one's view of God's mercy.

Hermeneutics* of suspicion since Nietzsche* emphasize the pathological effect of such merciful attitudes, especially when this call to be merciful is understood as forgiving and is addressed to people who are oppressed*; the call to forgive one's oppressors is commonly used to justify oppression, as Liberation and Feminist* theologians have underscored (see Forgiveness, Christian Discourses of). But referring to different views of the mercy of God, other theologians point out that a merciful attitude and a moral life are demands grounded not in an ethical, juridical principle (resulting in forgiving the guilty), but in the true encounter with others and the perception of their needs that one mercifully strives to address.

DANIEL PATTE

Merici, Angela (c1474–1540), founder of a religious order, the Ursulines; canonized (1807). Born in Venice (where she remained until 1516) and orphaned at a young age, Angela Merici had a vision (1506) in which she was told that she would found a society of pious and charitable virgins in Brescia. She led a prayerful and charitable life and eventually moved to Brescia (1516), where she organized (starting in 1531) a small group of 12 young women to help her with the catechetical work. She founded (1535) the first religious order devoted to the teaching of young girls, with Ursula as patron saint. The goal was to re-Christianize family life and society through the Christian education of future wives and mothers. Each member of the Company of St. Ursula was to continue living in her own home, exercising her apostolate among the members of her family, her social acquaintances, and the children of her neighborhood. The order was approved by Pope Paul III (1544). However, Archbishop Charles Borromeo, a leader of the Catholic* Renewal, changed the administrative organization of the Company to bring it into harmony with the Council of Trent*. Since then, the nuns have been cloistered.

YVES KRUMENACKER

Merit, the quality of deserving reward from God for a work done for God. The scholastics* distinguished "condign" merit (*meritum de condigno*), based on a strict accounting, from "congruous" merit (*meritum de congruo*), based on a relationship established by grace*, such that Christ and the Holy Spirit make up for the limitations of finite and sinful human beings. This doctrine was repudiated by Luther*, who underscored the sinfulness of all human works and acknowledged merit only in Christ.

Merton, Thomas (1915–68), US monk, spiritual writer, contemplative*, poet, essayist, social critic, agent of interfaith dialogue. His 1948 autobiography, *The Seven Storey Mountain*, became a post–World War II religious classic. He died by accidental electrocution in Bangkok.

On December 10, 1941, three days after the bombing of Pearl Harbor, he entered the Cistercian* Abbey of Gethsemani, Kentucky. His early writings focused on solitude and silence as prerequisites for the contemplative* life. The Second Vatican* Council (1962–65) engaged him in redefining the roles of contemplation and action in the modern world.

Merton cultivated the apophatic* mystical* tradition, simultaneously articulating God's mediations (cataphatic tradition) in poetry and prose. His theology was Augustinian, emphasizing the action of grace* on the (unaided) will* and the primacy of love* of God and neighbor.

Merton was an ardent advocate of peacemaking* in a world of violence and war. He appropriated Gandhi's nonviolent* theory and practice to address contemporary social problems. He forthrightly opposed the US war in Vietnam as unjust, condemned white liberals' superficial role in addressing US racism*, and challenged society's ephemeral ethics evidenced in "mass man," "post-Christian" identity, and consumerism. Important correspondents included Boris Pasternak, Jean Leclercq, Dorothy Day*, Daniel Berrigan, Czeslaw Milosz, and Ernesto Cardenal. GEORGE KILCOURSE

Mesrop. See MASHTOTS, MESROP.

Messalians. Derived from the Syriac word *msallyane*, "people who pray," the term "Messalian" was used from the late 4th c. to designate Christian ascetics* who devoted themselves to constant prayer, refused to practice physical labor, and claimed to attain spiritual perfection thereby. First identified as a heretical "movement" by Epiphanius* of Salamis (in *Panarion*, c377), such "people who pray" became associated with specific doctrines after some were questioned in the 380s and 390s: at issue were beliefs that a demon* dwelled in the soul* from birth and could be expelled only through constant prayer (not simply by baptism*) and that a soul thus purified would receive the Holy* Spirit and be liberated from passions. Messalianism and its practitioners (also identified as Euchites, i.e. "Prayers," and Enthusiasts*) were universally condemned at the Council of Ephesus*, but the Messalian profile continued to evolve and to be condemned throughout the Byzantine period.

The problematic evidence for the "Messalian controversy" has prompted different reconstructions of its origin, nature, extent, and significance. Most historians agree that the term "Messalianism" quickly became used (mainly in the East) to conceptualize an array of early monastic views, practices, and tendencies that originally had no definite connection.

DANIEL F. CANER

Messiah (Heb *Mashiah*, "anointed one"; transliterated in Gk as *Messias*; translated in Gk as *Christos*). Despite traditional Christian readings of the OT, in the HB the term *Mashiah* is never used for an individual who would be a future savior* or redeemer*. Kings (see 1–2 Samuel), but also priests (beginning with Moses anointing Aaron, Exod 29:7; Lev 8:12) and even prophets (Elijah is told to anoint Elisha, 1 Kgs 19:16) are anointed as a sign of being chosen for a task. The term is found in Isa 45:1 (Cyrus, the Persian king, is "anointed") and Hab 3:13 (which refers to the anointed who need to be saved by God). But beyond these two instances, the term "anointed" is not found in Isaiah*, Jeremiah*, Ezekiel*, or the Twelve Prophets, despite the repeated mention that future Davidic rulers ("branch of David") are expected to inaugurate a new era of peace and justice that will not end, a view also expressed in the Royal Psalms* (Psalms 2, 18, 20, 21, 45, 72, 89, 101, 110, 132, 144). In sum, in the Prophets and the Psalms "the emphasis is not on the person of the future king but on the fact that, at last, the Davidic ideal... will be realized" (Jonge).

That Jesus was "the Messiah expected by Israel" is a basic Christian conviction expressed in the proclamation of Jesus as the Christ*. Yet one should not conclude from this claim that Jews in the time of Jesus eagerly expected the coming of the Messiah. This generalization, long presupposed in biblical studies, is contradicted by critical analyses of the Palestinian Jewish literature of this period: Wisdom* of Ben Sira; 1–2 Maccabees*, Jubilees*; Testaments* of the Twelve Patriarchs; Dead* Sea Scrolls (which refer to three messianic figures: a Davidic one, a priestly one, and a prophet-like figure); Psalms of Solomon*; Josephus*; 1 Enoch*; and 4 Ezra*. This literature shows that the expectation of the Messiah was relatively unimportant; expectations of future salvation are extremely diverse. The salvific action is often performed directly by God. When other agents of salvation are mentioned, they might be angels, suffering righteous ones, prophetic figures, a figure called the "Son* of man," or, relatively infrequently, a messiah (an anointed one). While expectation of a messiah is found in Pharisaism* (to the extent that its views are reflected in later sources, such as the Eighteen* Benedictions) and among apocalyptically* minded Jews, by explicitly claiming that Jesus was the Messiah expected by Israel, the followers of Jesus located themselves on the margins of mainline Judaism of the time.

Messianism, as a waiting for the Messiah, remains an important feature of Christianity, with the expectation of the Second* Coming and of the Parousia*. **See also APOCALYPTICISM CLUSTER; CHRISTOLOGIES CLUSTER; ESCHATOLOGY CLUSTER; JESUS, QUEST FOR THE HISTORICAL.** DANIEL PATTE

***Messiah,* Handel's Sacred Oratorio;** libretto by Charles Jennens, music by George Frideric Handel*; first performance, Dublin, April 13, 1742. The libretto is a compilation of biblical passages, including Isa 40:53; Luke 2; Ps 2; and 1 Cor 15. Presumably inspired by Richard Kidder's *A Demonstration of the Messias* (London, 2nd ed., 1726) and similar apologetic* works, it defends fundamental Christian claims against the challenges of Deism* and Judaism*. Handel's setting became (after some controversy concerning the 1743 London performances) his most celebrated work and has enjoyed a tradition of uninterrupted, worldwide performance to this day. **See also HANDEL, GEORGE FRIDERIC.**

TASSILO ERHARDT

Mestizos, Spanish term designating (in Latin America and the Philippines*) racially mixed persons, usually persons of Spanish and indigenous origins. The classification of mestizos as a "race*" – neither indigenous nor white – is a colonialist* social, cultural, and economic construct that was (and still is) used to maintain a caste*-like hierarchical structure in these societies. **See also LATINO/A THEOLOGIES; TRIBALISM AND CHRISTIANITY.**

Metaphor. Metaphoric language refers to an extraordinary affirmation that two unlike "things" – two known concepts firmly established in different fields of meanings – are actually the same despite their strong incongruity (see Paradox).

Metaphoric language has religious significance when, e.g., it arises as a response to both negative limit-experiences (fear of one's own death* or that of a loved one, suffering*, catastrophic loss, guilt) and positive limit-experiences (birth of a child, gratitude, unexpected joy, or forgiveness). Because denotative language is typically inadequate in limit-situations, people are constrained to invoke figurative expressions (metaphoric, symbolic*, analogical*, paradoxical*). Metaphoric statements twist the ordinary meaning of words, concepts, and actions to refer to a way of being in the world beyond that of the everyday. A "live-metaphor" preserves the tension in the claim that something "is" and "is not" at the same time.

Metaphoric language abounds in the Christian Scriptures*. Metaphoric process is evident in the central image of Jesus* Christ*, both human and divine: "I am the vine," and the "first" is "slave of all" (Mark 10:44, par.). At its best, theology elaborates on and illuminates the meaning and adequacy of particular metaphoric language. Some theorists see theology itself as metaphorical. MARY GERHART

Metaphysics and Christian Theology. The general definition of metaphysics in the *Cambridge Dictionary of Philosophy,* "the philosophical investigation of the nature, construction, and structure of reality," reflects the general confusion over the concept. Andronicus of Rhodes penned the tantalizing label *ta meta ta physika* (located "after *The Physics*") for Aristotle's (384–22 BCE) shorter works about "first philosophy," guided by the question "What is the being of beings?" – the ontological question that became central to Christian theology for centuries, before it was questioned from several directions.

"What is real," "What is a thing," or "What is the difference between what is real and what appears" are metaphysical questions. Metaphysical options include realism*, dualism*, idealism, materialism, naturalism, and epiphenomenology, and subtle variations of each. Christian theology has long assumed some form of metaphysical realism, at least since Thomas Aquinas*, even if such realism is not empirically verifiable; this lack of verifiability was problematized by many philosophers in recent centuries.

Stoic* philosophical theology assumed that the universal status of a reasoned theo*logical* (or cosmo*logical*) explanation (grounded in Logos*) was superior to common religious convictions* – "so-called" knowledge about God, assertions without proof. About the knowledge of God, Paul (1 Cor 8:1, 5) discussed and questioned the "real/so-called" distinction used to differentiate God and the gods of the cosmos (1 Cor 8:1, 5).

Augustine's* metaphysical proposal that God created the universe out of nothing (*creatio ex nihilo*) posited that God alone was responsible for the creation* of both form and matter. Thereby Augustine rejected the long-standing assumption held by Plato*, Aristotle, and Stoics that the material of the world was uncreated and that divine creation imposed order upon matter. Aquinas (c1226–74) employed Aristotle's query regarding being *qua* being in an interpretative flourish on the name of God* (Exod 3:14, read as "I Am Being"), concluding that "Being" is the name of God. Thereby Aquinas united Aristotle's impersonal deity with the personal deity of Jewish scripture in a Christian "ontotheism" (God as Supreme *Being*). Duns* Scotus, Henry of Ghent, and William* of Ockham among others offered critiques of Aquinas's metaphysical theology.

Descartes* (1596–1650) sought to counter the skeptical critics of classical Christian theology by establishing, in *Meditations on First Philosophy*, the self-certainty of "I am thinking" (*cogito, sum*) as the unquestionable foundation of knowledge, including knowledge of the existence of God and the external world. The influence of Cartesian thought persists in the privilege given to private or personal experience in modern Christian thought and practice and in individualistic piety (e.g. praying with closed eyes). Rationalist philosophers and theologians concerned with such metaphysical issues include Spinoza* (1632–77), Leibniz (1646–1716), and Hegel* (1770–1831). The privileging of epistemological concerns (how do we know?) became widespread in Anglo-Saxon philosophy, where empiricism flourished in the thinking of Hobbes (1588–1679), Locke* (1632–1704), and Hume* (1711–76). Hume distinguished "natural religion" (metaphysical theology) from "revealed religion," criticizing the former as philosophically indefensible. Other philosophical critics of metaphysics include Feuerbach* (1804–72), Comte (1798–1857), Nietzsche* (1844–1900), Carnap (1892–1970), and Russell (1872–1970).

Kant* (1724–1804), seeking to determine the limits of reason in knowing, questioned the possibilities of knowing the principles of cosmology or metaphysics (*Critique of Pure Reason*). Protestant theologians influenced by Kant – Ritschl* (1822–99), Barth (1886–1968), Reinhold Niebuhr* (1892–1971), and Richard Niebuhr* (1894–1962) – shifted the emphasis of their theology from metaphysics to ethics.

Heidegger* (1889–1976) argued against Thomism* that an inquiry into the being of beings is not a query into a supreme or first being, but rather a query into the meaning of "to be," the verb (in the infinitive) that makes possible thinking about "what is." But because thinking is dominated by "what is," by "beings" (metaphysics), and thus is unable to construe properly *what it means* "to be" (ontologically), we often render the (verb) "to be" of beings as another "being" (a noun). Tillich* (1886–1965), following Heidegger, argued that God is not a being, not even the highest being – a blasphemous confusion of category. For Tillich, God is "being-itself" or the ground-of-being or power-of-being. Process* philosophers and theologians – Hartshorne (1897–2000), Wieman (1884–1975), Williams (1910–73), and Cobb (1925–) – influenced by Whitehead* (1861–1947), questioned the appropriateness of what they call the "substance" ontological assumptions of classical metaphysics (Plato, Aristotle, Aquinas) and propose as an alternative "process," "relational" metaphysics for Christian theology.

The plurality of metaphysical (ontological and cosmological) assumptions posited by Judeo-Christian traditions, authors, texts, rituals, and institutions undermines the conflation of a specific ontology or cosmology (metaphysics) and faith. For instance, the presence of several distinct creation* stories in the Bible should dissuade Christians from inferring that any one canonized story defines a particular "Christian cosmology." Bultmann's* demythologization* project (following Heidegger) interpreted biblical texts existentially rather than cosmologically. Similarly, the controversies and conflicts over issues such as the origin of the universe or the human species between science*, philosophy, and Christian theology result in part from a lack of agreement as to what counts as reason and/or evidence. **See also PHILOSOPHY AND CHRISTIAN THEOLOGY.** DAVID W. ODELL-SCOTT

METHODISM CLUSTER

Methodism: Methodist Churches and Their Theology
Methodism: Methodist Episcopal Church
Methodism: Methodist Worship
Methodism in the United Kingdom

Methodism: Methodist Churches and Their Theology. The Methodist Movement (now c75 million members worldwide) that John Wesley* (1703–91) initiated within the Church of England (see Anglican Cluster: Anglican Communion and Its Theology) developed from several theological strands: (1) the "holy living" tradition of Thomas* à Kempis, Jeremy Taylor, William Law, and the Puritans*; (2) the Anglican "religious societies" epitomized by the Society* for the Propagation of Christian Knowledge (SPCK); (3) Lutheran piety mediated by the Moravians*; (4) late medieval and English mysticism*; (5) the early church fathers (see Patristic Thought); (6) Calvinism*; and (7) Arminianism*. Wesleyan theology was shaped by the way John Wesley appropriated and rejected aspects of each of these traditions under the exigencies of the Wesleyan revival*. The extraordinarily wide range of Christian thought inherited by Wesley partly explains the many different theological expressions of Methodism/Wesleyanism today, from liberal* and Evangelical* churches to Pentecostal* revivalism. Both North American and British Methodism drifted away from Wesley in the 19th c., but there has been a significant renaissance of Wesleyan theology since the mid 20th c.

John and his brother Charles Wesley* (1707–88), the poet and hymn writer of Methodism, were raised in a large family of strict Puritan/Anglican piety, disciplined learning, and high-church devotion. Diminutive in stature, abundant in spiritual energy, John Wesley traveled about a quarter million miles and preached more than 40,000 times. He outlived the prejudice against him for his religious enthusiasm and died in great esteem.

"The First Rise of Methodism" (as Wesley's *Journal* refers to it) occurred during the years 1725–34. With his 1725 decision to become ordained, Wesley began a highly regimented life of self-examination and diary keeping. As students at Christ Church, Oxford, John and Charles were instrumental in forming small groups of university students, including George Whitfield*, for praying, studying Scripture and the church fathers, visiting prisoners, and educating poor children. They appeared to be so methodical in these endeavors that they were derisively called "Methodists." From this period came three convictions of Methodist belief and practice: (1) that the Christian life is to be disciplined in the pursuit of perfection* (maturity) in obedience to God's law, (2) that this discipline should manifest itself in ministry to the poor*, and (3) that Christian life should develop in small covenanted groups.

The "Second Rise of Methodism" (1735–38) began when Wesley accepted an invitation of the Society for the Propagation of the Gospel (see SPCK, Society for Promoting Christian Knowledge) to be a missionary in the new US colony of Georgia founded by James Oglethorpe. Although Wesley was industrious, publishing a hymnbook and equipping himself to convert Native Americans, this period was largely one of failure. He proved too overbearing in pressing the church's rubrics and moral standards on roughhewn colonists. This failure, together with his disappointment in not sensing assurance* of salvation through holy living (see Holiness), led to a severe crisis that was the background for his conversion* experience. On the way to Georgia, he had met Moravians* who pressed on him salvation* by faith and the necessity of assurance that one is saved. Upon his return to London, he became active in religious societies, in particular the Fetter Lane Society. Having failed to be perfect in obedience, Wesley was ready to accept the Lutheran emphasis on salvation* by grace* as interpreted by the Moravians and was "converted" at Aldersgate on May 24, 1738. After holy living, grace* in its multifarious senses became the second theme of Methodist theology. Although he experienced doubts shortly after his Aldersgate experience, Wesley preached grace and the possibility of the assurance of salvation in such a forceful way that he was banned from some Anglican parishes.

Following Aldersgate three factors contributed to the development of Wesley's theology: (1) his visit to the Moravian community in Herrnhut and his observation of Francke's* pietistic social work in Halle, a highly organized form of diaconic spirituality that had a positive impact on social conditions; (2) his reading of Jonathan Edward's* account of the revival* in New England; and (3) his reading of the Church of England *Book of Homilies* (see Cranmer, Thomas), in which he found the key to his open theological questions and the form of his own theology.

The "Third Rise of Methodism": Revivals and Methodist Societies. In response to Whitfield's plea, Wesley made himself more "vile" by preaching to thousands of the working poor in the open spaces around Bristol (1738–39). It is arguable that the Wesleyan revival materialized as Wesley saw the surprising response to his preaching of grace from the miners and other persons suffering from a loss of place and community in the move from the land to the cities and into the first stages of a brutal labor-intensive economy.

Wesley's theology developed on the ground, as it were, out of the exigencies and new experiences of the revival. The hallmarks of Wesley's theology emerged in constant tension with the Moravian emphasis on faith* alone and the Calvinist* emphasis on election* leading to the doctrine of predestination*. The simple assumption that faith* was the only prerequisite for salvation led, in Wesley's view, to Quietism*. And predestination cut off the lifeblood of Christian discipleship*. Thus took shape the distinctive Wesleyan claim that both faith and good works are constitutive of salvation*.

In the revival, Wesley saw God raising up the Methodists "to reform the nation, especially the church, and to spread scriptural holiness throughout the land." Wesley served as the theologian, teacher, and organizer of the revival, which in the beginning was led primarily by laypersons: mostly uneducated, unordained preachers, class leaders, stewards, and trustees. In addition to visiting sites of new Methodist societies and preaching houses, Wesley furnished an educational and devotional literature for lay leaders (at least 400 books and tracts for the movement; *Collected Works* [1772–74, first ed.] numbered 32 volumes). Organization of the revival and the maintenance of the Methodist "Connexion" required commonly held doctrine and disciplined living. The preachers were to preach no doctrine other than what was contained in the collection of Wesley's published sermons and his *Notes upon the New Testament*. Wesley's published sermons (eight volumes, 1787–88 ed.) were basically short treatises on Christian doctrine and practice rather than the more engaging sermons he actually preached. The *Journal* is not so much an autobiography as a propagandistic defense of Methodism against its detractors. It shows how Wesley's theology developed in relation to the organization and mission of the movement and relates vivid portrayals of persons who shaped the movement, their piety, their temptations, and their deaths. His 50-volume *Christian Library* includes what Wesley judged to be the crucial works of the Christian tradition.

The Methodist societies, classes, bands, and quarterly and annual conferences were considered means of grace by which the objectives of the revival were to be realized. Published minutes of conference meetings became the record of the theology and practice of Methodists. Rules and methods were developed for lay leaders and members of groups. The "General Rules" stood at the center of the common life: "Do no harm, by avoiding evil in every kind. Do good of every possible sort and, as far as possible to all men. Attend upon the ordinances of God." Quarterly examination of members gave force to these rules. Wesley's revival turned out to be more resilient in the end than Whitfield's because he spent as much time organizing his societies, classes, bands, and the "Connexion," as he did preaching and writing theology.

Methodism in North America. Wesley began sending preachers to the small number of Methodists in North America in 1769. Having become convinced that a presbyter can also serve as a bishop, Wesley ordained several persons to provide sacraments and episcopal leadership to the fledgling church in the USA, thus sealing

Methodism: Methodist Churches

the split with the Church of England. With the American Revolution, all persons Wesley had sent to the USA returned to England, save Francis Asbury*, who became the "new Wesley" in the rise of the North American church. After the Peace of Paris, Wesley provided a plan for a separate structure of the North American church, which officially began as the Methodist Episcopal Church at the "Christmas Conference" of 1784. North American Methodism assumed an ambiguous relation to Wesley and took on a shape of its own in the context of US republicanism and expansiveness. During the Second Great* Awakening, with its camp* meetings and close identification with people affected by the vast economic and social changes of the period, Methodism proved to be a major democratizing influence in the nation. The Methodist Protestant Church (1830) assumed a more republican form of polity*. In 1939 the Methodist Episcopal Church and the Methodist Episcopal Church, South, merged to form the Methodist Church, which in 1968 united with the Evangelical United Brethren Church and the Methodist Protestant Church to form the United Methodist Church.

The Methodist Episcopal Church gradually became an "established" church, taking on the organization of the US federal government, with executive, legislative, and judicial branches, and becoming the largest Protestant denomination in the nation by the mid-19th c. In agreement with Wesley, who in a letter to Wilberforce* called US slavery* "that execrable villainy," the "vilest" known to history, the earliest Methodist legislation provided that slave owners could not be Methodists. Within a short time, this was overturned in practice. Succumbing to the economy of slavery and regionalism, the Methodist Episcopal Church split in 1844 into Northern and Southern churches, a harbinger of the bitter division of the country and the horrendous Civil War. African American churches – the African* Methodist Episcopal Church (1816), African Methodist Episcopal Church Zion (1821), and Christian (initially called "Colored") Methodist Episcopal Church (1870) – separated from the Methodist Episcopal Church on racial grounds (see African American Cluster: African American Churches).

Methodist Theology. The three basic doctrines of the Methodist tradition, original* sin*, justification* by faith, and holiness*, were styled by Wesley thus: repentance* ("the porch of religion"), justification by grace through faith ("the door of religion"), and sanctification* ("religion itself"). The main tenets of Methodism today – the centrality of grace (prevenient, justifying, and sanctifying), holy living, salvation as open to all, and social holiness – generally follow suit.

Although his theology was Evangelical in flavor, Wesley always maintained that Methodists were in harmony with the doctrinal standards of the Church of England (the Thirty*-nine Articles, the *Book of Homilies*, and the Book of Common Prayer) and only a "hair's breadth" different from the Calvinists. Wesley's Evangelical theology is quite different from many forms of 21st-c. Evangelicalism*. He was critical of preachers who reduced the gospel to the grace that led to an oversimplified view of conversion without emphasizing fulfilling the "law of grace." Wesley's Evangelical theology is also opposed to the individualism of much current Evangelical theology. The fullness of salvation can take place only in the beloved community of disciples; the only true holiness is "social holiness." Methodist theology can be summed up by the phrase "faith that works through love." Justification that does not lead to sanctification withers in the struggles of discipleship. Love* of God must be expressed in love of neighbor* and finds its realistic, practicable forms in the directives and judgments of Matt 25.

The most distinctive and contentious of Wesley's doctrines was the possibility of experiencing entire sanctification* or Christian perfection*. It prevented Lutheran, Calvinist, and Church of England clergy from joining his movement and led to endless clarifications (1760s–1770s) that did not persuade his critics. Sanctification is a gift of God's grace. He did not mean thereby works-righteousness or perfectionism and never claimed perfection for himself. The Wesleyan doctrine of assurance of salvation also led to much controversy; Wesley was faced with exaggerated perversions of these doctrines among his own preachers. The second most prominent theologian of the Methodist revival, John Fletcher, sought to clarify the doctrine of sanctification in his *Checks Against Antinomianism.* Several denominations have split off from mainstream Methodism as a way of maintaining a true doctrine and practice of perfection/holiness, e.g. the Wesleyan Methodist Connection (Church) (1843–1947, 1947–68), Free Methodist Church (1860), and Primitive Methodist Connection (Church) (1811; 1889, USA; 1902, UK).

Methodist Social Principles. Mainstream Methodism has sought to hold together works of piety (prayer*) and works of mercy*, personal holiness and social holiness. Methodists have often followed Wesley's example in collecting clothes, food, and money to distribute to those in need; organizing medical clinics for the poor; microlending for small business undertakings; and subsidizing houses for widows and children. At various times, such as before and after the Civil War in the US South, Methodists have tended to stress "personal holiness" in order to make the church apolitical. But other strands of Methodism, e.g. those heavily involved in the Social* Gospel Movement and those who sympathized with the New Deal, have been engaged not only in personal acts of compassion, but also in "social holiness" that seeks to serve justice in society. Following Wesley's impulse, Methodists have embodied their theology in prison reform, education* for the masses (numerous colleges, universities, and seminaries have been founded by Methodists), the labor movement, women's rights movements, antiwar engagement, temperance actions, child labor elimination, economic* equity, and environmental witness. These commitments were codified in the Methodist "Social Principles," which are still effective in the United Methodist Church (1968). The United Methodist Church, however, continues to be subject to Wesleyan tensions as it seeks to deal with bitter differences over homosexuality*, racism*, economic* justice*, and war* and peace*.

M. DOUGLAS MEEKS

Methodism: Methodist Episcopal Church. See ASBURY, FRANCIS; THE PRESENT CLUSTER: METHODIST CHURCHES AND THEIR THEOLOGY.

Methodism: Methodist Worship.

Originally a reform movement within the Church of England (see Anglicanism Cluster), Methodism is an amalgam of Roman Catholic and Evangelical* elements. The distinctive tension in Methodist worship reflects John Wesley's* insistence in the 1740s that Methodists attend Anglican parish worship as well as utilize the new forms of worship and devotion in the Methodist societies and preaching houses emerging from the revivals*. Wesley revered the Anglican liturgy and Cranmer's* 1549 Book of Common* Prayer, but under the influence of the Pietists*, Latitudinarians*, and Nonjurors, he understood the authority of Scripture* to be interrelated with that of the tradition* (especially during the Patristic* period), reason*, and experience as the standards of true worship. Methodist worship has subsequently been known for combining freedom and flexibility with established form.

Scripturally based preaching forms the core of Methodist worship. Wesley's emphasis on the social character of faith is usually reflected in participative worship – especially hymn singing and extempore prayer – but also in revival forms of worship, e.g. Love* Feasts, personal testimonies, watch night services, covenant renewal, weekly prayer meetings, and occasional congregational fasts.

North American Methodist worship was originally shaped by Wesley's "Sunday Service of the Methodists in North America," which was adopted as the "prayer book" of the new Methodist Episcopal Church (1784 Christmas Conference). Post–Revolutionary War developments took North American Methodist worship away from its roots. The Second Great* Awakening phenomenon of camp* meetings (c1800) developed out of quarterly meetings and shaped Methodist worship sensibilities. People camped for several days in tents and wagons, hearing revival preaching and participating in highly emotional worship. Some fainted, "got the shakes*," or "melted." Many experienced conversion. Camp meetings both reflected and counteracted the explosive character of life on an expanding frontier and around urban centers.

Though Wesley encouraged Communion* every Lord's Day, Methodists generally practiced Communion quarterly because of the scarcity of clergy. The use of wine gave way to the use of grape juice, because of the Temperance* Movement. When camp meetings declined, Sunday* school, revivals in churches, and camping experiences emerged as centers of Methodist worship.

Post–Civil War worship grew more formal, especially in the 20th-c. ecumenical movement and Liturgical* Movement, to which the Methodist churches contributed significantly. Preaching remained at the center but was now set in the solemnity and beauty of structured liturgy, reflective of Anglican and Lutheran roots (see Anglicanism Cluster: Anglican Worship and Liturgies; Lutheranism Cluster: Worship). The Wesleyan simplicity of functional worship edifices gave way to more elaborate symbolic buildings in the Federal and later the Romanesque or Gothic revival architectural style. The Akron*-style semicircular sanctuary brought corporate worship and Sunday school into symbiosis as education* rivaled worship in importance. Sophisticated organs, robed choirs, cushioned pews, stained-glass windows, processions, and ornate clergy vestments increasingly became the norm. Successive 20th-c. Methodist hymnals recovered the Christian liturgical* year, the lectionary*, the Psalter in the form of responsive readings, and more traditional rituals for baptism and Communion. Newer hymnals emphasize songs from the global church and a broader spectrum of North American ethnic and social groups.

M. DOUGLAS MEEKS

Methodism in the United Kingdom arose out of an international awakening of Evangelical religion (see Great Awakening) and a sense of dissatisfaction with the prevailing condition of the Church of England (see Anglicanism Cluster). Its origins can be traced to the meetings of a small religious society at Oxford University beginning in 1729. Among the participants were John Wesley* (1703–91) and his brother Charles Wesley* (1707–88), who emerged from the turbulent decade of the 1730s as the leaders of the Methodist Movement, with John supplying much of Methodism's theological and organizational content and Charles its poetic hymnody. The early stages of the movement were characterized by rancorous theological conflicts as the Wesley brothers began to distance themselves from Moravians*, Calvinists*, and mystics. The Methodism that emerged from these conflicts embraced a connectional system of church government in which societies and classes were serviced by itinerant and local preachers. The annual conference, at which John Wesley met with his itinerant preachers, emerged as the ruling body of the church. In its theology, Methodism reflected mainly the orthodox creedal statements of historic Christianity, but it had distinctive emphases on Arminianism* (the universal offer of salvation*; see Universalism), Christian perfection* or entire sanctification* (the idea that perfect love* is achievable on earth as in heaven), and assurance* of faith based on an experiential sense of sins* forgiven (see Atonement #2).

Methodism remained a self-governing society within the Church of England, at least until 1795, when the Plan of Pacification effectively resulted in sacramental independence. In 1797 Methodism experienced the first of many splits that characterized the movement throughout the 19th c. These divisions, often based on social class, religious style, and competing ideas about church government, were largely repaired in the 20th c., but by then the percentage of Methodists in the English population had begun a decline that shows no sign of reversal.

Methodism recruited many members among women, artisans, miners, and small farmers. Its greatest gains in both town and country were in those areas least susceptible to Anglican paternal control. Its growth was particularly strong in some of the new industrial areas of the north of England, Wales, and parts of Ireland, and less so in Scotland. Methodism also spread to the USA, where it became the largest Protestant denomination in the country. By the late 19th c., its mobile laity and dynamic missionary movement exported Methodism to most countries in the world.

Throughout their history, Methodists' self-declared mission to "spread scriptural holiness throughout the land" has been reflected in their various commitments to education*, temperance*, and trade unionism, and in their opposition to slavery* and blood sports. Although no longer the potent force it was in the 18th and 19th c., Methodism continues to have a voice in ecumenism*, international justice*, and world mission*. Some of its "daughter" churches in the Holiness* and Pentecostal* traditions continue to thrive.

DAVID HEMPTON

Methodius. See CYRIL AND METHODIUS.

Methodius of Olympus in Lycia, Asia Minor (?–c311), philosopher, bishop, martyr. Acquainted with the Stoic and Platonist traditions, he opposed dualism* – both the notion that matter, coeternal with God, is the source of evil and the notion that soul* must be freed from body*. He followed Irenaeus* in seeing human life as indeterminate and in considering evil* the result of human freedom*. The image* of God, compromised through disobedience, is restored by the Incarnation*, conveyed to others through baptism* and the Holy* Spirit, and fulfilled in the resurrection* of the body and eternal* life. While Methodius learned much from Origen*, he later opposed Origen's highly spiritualized view of resurrection. Methodius's *Symposium*, modeled on Plato's, praises virginity*. While it is often seen as an early expression of monasticism* (leading some scholars to think he was a charismatic teacher rather than a bishop), virginity is treated as a metaphor for striving after perfection*, applicable to all (L. G. Patterson). This work, like the parable of the ten virgins (Matt 25:1–13) on which it is based, remains partly parable.

EUGENE TESELLE

METHODOLOGIES FOR THE STUDY OF CHRISTIANITY

See AESTHETICS AND THEOLOGY; ANTHROPOLOGY CLUSTER; BIBLE INTERPRETATION CLUSTER: HISTORY OF; CHARISMATIC AND PENTECOSTAL MOVEMENTS CLUSTER: STUDYING; CHURCH AND STATE RELATIONS CLUSTER; CULTURE CLUSTER; ECONOMY AND CHRISTIANITY CLUSTER; ETHICS AND CHRISTIANITY CLUSTER; HERMENEUTICS; HIEROTOPY, THE CREATION OF CHRISTIAN SACRED SPACES; HISTORIOGRAPHY OF EARLY CHRISTIANITY AS DEVELOPED IN THE 19TH AND 20TH CENTURIES; HISTORY, CONCEPTS OF; HISTORY, THEOLOGICAL CONCEPTS OF; HISTORY OF RELIGION SCHOOL; HOMILETICS; ICONOGRAPHY; IDEOLOGICAL STUDIES OF CHRISTIANITY; IDEOLOGY; METAPHYSICS AND CHRISTIAN THEOLOGY; MYTH AND THE STUDY OF CHRISTIANITY; PHENOMENOLOGY AND CHRISTIANITY; PHILOSOPHY AND CHRISTIAN THEOLOGY; PHILOSOPHY OF RELIGION; POLITICAL STUDIES OF CHRISTIANITY; POLITICAL THEOLOGY; POSTCOLONIALISM AND CHRISTIAN THEOLOGY; POSTMODERNISM AND LIBERATION THEOLOGIES; POSTMODERNISM AND THEOLOGY; RECEPTION STUDIES OF PREACHING; RECEPTION STUDIES OF SCRIPTURE; RELIGION AS A CONCEPT AND CHRISTIANITY; SCRIPTURAL CRITICISM; SEMIOTICS AND THE STUDY OF CHRISTIANITY; SOCIOLOGICAL STUDIES OF CHRISTIANITY; SYMBOLISM; THEOLOGY AS HUMAN UNDERTAKING CLUSTER

Metrical Psalms, translations of the Psalms* with meter and usually rhyme, from the Reformed* tradition, which initially used only the Psalms and canticles* from Scripture in worship. Numerous versions were published in France (by Marot and Beza*), England, Scotland, and New England into the 19th c.; thereafter, most Reformed churches adopted "hymns of human composure."

Metropolitan, title of the bishop of the capital city of a province that includes several dioceses; equivalent to archbishop*. The metropolitan convenes provincial synods, supervises other bishops, and attends the consecration of new bishops in the province.

Mexico. Christianity in Mexico is complex, because it incorporates two major cultures – Western and Mesoamerican – and many subcultures, interwoven in some places with Afro-American elements.

15th-Century Incorporation of Christianity into Mesoamerican Cultures

Spanish Christianity and its mix of cultures. Christianity in Mexico originated from Spain*, arriving during the Conquest. Iberian Christianity had distinctive characteristics reflecting the diverse beliefs and practices of a population with Iberian, Roman, Celtic*, and Visigoth* cultural roots. Furthermore, Spanish Christianity was forged by seven centuries of interaction with and resistance to Islam*.

Inculturation* in Mesoamerican cultures. In Mesoamerica, Spanish Christianity was further shaped by political transformations linked with colonization and by inculturation* in a territory with a variety of cultures and religions. Four types of Christianity emerged:

1. A Roman Catholicism interwoven with indigenous cultures resulted from the Spanish military conquest of more than 60 sedentary peoples (including the Maya, Mexicas, Purépechas, Mixtecos, and Zapotecos), which had previously been a part of the Mexica, or Mexica-Aztec, Empire. These cultures left pictorial representations of their knowledge and skills, codices conveying their sense of history, religious and civil calendars, pyramids, and ceremonial centers. The reactions of local populations to the Spanish Conquest ranged from armed defense to legal fights and cultural resistance; similarly, their reactions to the arrival of Christianity and European culture ranged from adaptation, to acceptance or to rejection. Thus the Spanish Conquest was more than a military event that came to an end in 1521; it became a long-term process.
2. A Roman Catholicism of mission was developed in regions inhabited by nomadic and seminomadic peoples, whose sense of the universe followed another rhythm. In such cases, mission work initially took the form of itinerant, intermittent evangelization. The missions were associated with the expansion of the Spanish Empire in America (the viceroyalty of New Spain) and reinforced the politics of "reductions*" and "congregations." The aim of these settlements of Mesoamerican people was to inculcate within them a "better" (Western) religious life and civilization.
3. A Roman Catholicism of transfer was found in regions with few inhabitants, where the Spanish settled, worshipped, and established religious organizations similar to those on the Iberian Peninsula.
4. A Christianity of immigration was practiced by the populations originating in Africa, who, as in other aspects of their lives, sought to hold onto their traditions; they expressed their devotions and religious feasts with iconography, songs, and dances with both African and Christian characteristics.

The 16th-Century Implantation of Roman Catholicism was initiated by Cortés and the priests who accompanied him (1519). Christianity took new forms according to the specific populations that received it and responded in quite different ways to the religious orders' strategies of evangelization. Different peoples processed the Christian message in accordance with their particular regional, cultural, political, and ethnic perspectives and configurations.

The God of the sedentary groups mentioned earlier, Ometéotl, was dual, both male and female (Ometecuhtli–Omecihuatl), and there were many other deities, including Quetzalcóatl Kukulcan, Tláloc, Huitzilopochtli, Xilonen, Tlalzolteotl, and Ipalnemohuani (the one who gives us life). There were three interconnected levels of reality – terrestrial, heavenly, and underworld – which provided a sense of interrelation with the environment and allowed for pain and death in life. Their social organization around the *altepetl* (city-state) and the smaller *calpullis* (collective living units providing space for work, interactions with others, worship, and the shaping of a sense of identity) reflected their vision of the organization of the universe along four axes, each related to a deity, a color, a symbol, and a tree.

Friars used diverse pedagogical approaches to evangelize these different populations. Some sought to impose Christian doctrines by making their acceptance and the formal rejection of traditional religions a requirement for having a function in the new society. By contrast, some friars used a more inculturated* approach; for them, evangelism involved affirming the presence of the Holy* Spirit in the experience of the indigenous populations.

Religious orders. The mendicant* religious orders (principally the Franciscans*, Dominicans*, and Augustinians*), who arrived in 1524–26 and 1539, developed their missions as autonomous provinces* of their orders; by virtue of papal exemption, the missions were independent, i.e. free of episcopal control. Subsequently the Jesuits* arrived, as did the Conceptionists (a branch of the order of St. Clare*, related to the Franciscans) and other female congregations; thus the diversity of religious orders progressively increased. The orders built convents, schools (with specific educational systems), and social institutions (retreat centers, orphanages, asylums, hospitals) that addressed social and medical needs. Friar Pedro de Gante (c1480–1572) created the School of San José de los Naturales in Tenochtitlán (the first Franciscan school in Mexico). Other Franciscans created the School of Santa Cruz Tlaltelolco (1536–76), which was directed for two decades by its own Nahuatl students, who were instrumental in writing the important *Historia general de las cosas de la Nueva España* (History of the New Spain) coordinated by Bernardino de Sahagún* (written in the 16th c.; published in the 19th c.). Antonio Valeriano (a student of this school) is said to have written *Nican Mopohua,* the controversial document about the apparitions of the Virgin of Guadalupe (see Mary, the Virgin, Cluster: Of Guadalupe); even if one contests the historicity that Valeriano attributes to this religious experience, the *Nican Mopohua* is a valuable example of inculturation. Purépecha students actively participated in the San Nicolas School, founded by Vasco de Quiroga* in Pátzcuaro, Michoacán, electing the school's authorities and teaching their instructors the Purépecha language. One of the objectives of these schools was the education of Nahuatl and Purépecha priests. This unique and effective intercultural experience acknowledged the value of true interchange between the two worldviews that had been brought into contact. Yet these intercultural experiments were quickly replaced by a project of Hispanization, which involved the destruction of non-Hispanic cultures. The education of Mesoamerican priests was prohibited by the first Mexican Provincial Council (1555).

Ecclesiastical organization. Following the old Mesoamerican organization, which was based on the *altepetl* (city-state) and *calpullis* (collective living space), the Roman Catholic Church was organized into dioceses, and divided into parishes and smaller "chapels." This promoted stability in the central region of Mexico. The first Mexican apostolic assemblies (1527–38) made decisions regarding ecclesiastical organization and the sacraments. After the Council of Trent* limited the autonomy of religious orders, the entire ecclesiastical organization was placed under the authority of the bishops. Three Mexican provincial councils (1555, especially 1565, and 1585) defined the approved forms of evangelization that still frame ecclesiastic and liturgical life. Tlaxcala was the see of the first bishop, the Dominican Julián Garcés, who in a letter to Pope Paul III described the Tlaxcala population and their values, influencing Paul III's bull, *Sublimus Deus* (1537), which recognized the dignity of the "Indians" as rational beings who had souls and were thus entitled to enjoy liberty and receive the sacraments.

The resolutions of the 1585 Mexican Provincial Council included a law aimed at protecting indigenous populations but prohibiting the use of zoomorphic symbols that perpetuated the worship of Mesoamerican deities. Yet the Council also sought to carry forward aspects of the first friars' utopian projects by promoting the popular Mesoamerican devotions to Mary* (under various names) and the saints*.

The Court of the Holy Office (Inquisition*), created in Mexico in 1571, punished deviations in matters of faith, blasphemy, bigamy, and witchcraft*. Nevertheless, after the condemnation and death (at the stake) of Carlos Ometochtzin, the *cacique* (chief) of Texcoco, the Inquisition was forbidden to intervene among indigenous peoples, because they were new to Roman Catholicism.

Reception and rejection. For the conquerors and missionaries, the destruction of idolatry* was essential. They put an end to ceremonial centers, their priests, and all public ceremonies of the old religion, especially human sacrifice. As a result, popular religion retreated to the sphere of private life.

The substitution of church worship services for traditional religious ceremonies, and of Catholic saints for old gods, allowed traditional beliefs, rituals, and mythic expressions to survive by being rooted in Christian soil, even as they remained framed by Mesoamerican traditions. Especially in the baroque* period (from the late 16th c.), diverse elements of Christian medieval traditions were appropriated and adapted by indigenous peoples.

Yet conflicts were also common. In reaction to a caste system that condemned indigenous populations to the lower caste, there were many forms of resistance: armed, legal, and cultural.

In the late 16th c., the Spanish expansion to the north, motivated by a search for silver, brought a great number of missions, Spanish villages, and military prisons into territories inhabited by battle-hardened nomadic and seminomadic (*chichimecas*) peoples, causing constant rebellion, which continued into the 17th c.

17th-Century Strengthening and Expansion of Christendom. After the collapse of the Mesoamerican populations (16th c.) owing to wars and epidemics, New Spain in the 17th c. saw a continual growth in population, with a proliferation of mixed cultures, beliefs, and traditions. Meanwhile, in the parishes, another source of conflict was the replacement of the friars of various religious orders by secular clergy. One of the architects of this "secularization" of the parishes, Archbishop Juan de Palafox* y Mendoza, opened the way for a baroque church that sought to replace the worship of "pagan idols*" by popular but appropriate devotions to Mary and the saints, which found expression in the arts and letters. This was a time of Creole pride expressed in the writings of scholars such as Sr. Juana* Inés de la Cruz and Carlos de Sigüenza y Góngora, who claimed the Mesoamerican past as their own and celebrated the natural and cultural wealth of the land, as well as its wonders and miracles (e.g. among many others, the apparitions of the Virgin of Guadalupe).

Formal religious organization was buttressed by the "brotherhoods," which grouped the faithful by caste and position and performed important religious and social functions. Brotherhoods organized the feasts of patron saints and attended to the moral, spiritual, and economic needs of their members, e.g. during times of bereavement. Brotherhoods also facilitated the control, maintenance, and production of common goods, e.g. providing financially for parishes and convents.

18th-Century Liberal–Monarchical Tensions. At that time, the clergy of New Spain were primarily Creole priests, who strove to differentiate themselves from the Spanish Church and who, because of their strong social presence and the institutional autonomy they enjoyed under Bourbon–Austrian rule, managed to accumulate enormous political and economic power. When the Bourbon monarchs ascended to the Spanish throne (1700), the state strengthened its position, promoting secularization (distancing church from state) and limiting the influence of the religious civil corporations (which performed the civil functions commonly held by city hall in modern states), the brotherhoods, and the Church. The inspector José of Gálvez (sent by Charles III, king of Spain) promoted these changes.

The Bourbon reforms promoted economic development through the exploitation of silver, commerce, and intervention in "Indian" communities. The culmination of the Bourbon measures was the expulsion of the Jesuits (1767), which clearly demonstrated that the objective was to put an end to the autonomy of groups that criticized and thus hindered the governmental practices that benefited the Spanish crown. The populations associated with the Jesuits reacted violently, but were repressed. In cultural terms, the departure of the Jesuits meant a decline of educational opportunities and an increased dependence on a rigid monarchical state, severely weakening communal structures. In Italy several of the expelled Jesuits, including Francisco Javier Clavijero, Francisco Javier Alegre, and Juan Benito Díez de Gamarra, wrote important works on Mexico.

The Fourth Mexican Provincial Council (1771) reflected the tensions resulting from the Bourbon reforms and the pressure that the crown exercised on the clergy. Prelates and parish priests, king and pope were divided. These tensions contributed to the Mexican independence movement. Similarly the blunt preaching of the Dominican friar Servando Teresa de Mier prefigured modernity, the environment in which leaders of the independence matured.

By the end of the 18th c., an increase in Mesoamerican consciousness was apparent in the large number of people involved in projects that would primarily help Mesoamericans (rather than the Spaniards). This indigenous resistance clearly shows the appropriation of Christianity by Mesoamerican groups, also exemplified by the iconography and literary works about the veneration of Guadalupe that clearly incorporated Mesoamerican views. Benedict XIV expressed this in 1754 when he approved the patronage of the Virgin of Guadalupe over New Spain – "She did not do anything similar in any other nation" – making her one of the most important components of Mexican nationalism.

19th Century: Rome's Renewed Control of Catholicism before the Republican–Liberal Triumph

Struggle for control. The period from the expulsion of the Jesuits (1767) to the beginning of the Mexican Revolution (1910) is perceived as a long "Mexican 19th century" – a period marked by a protracted conflict among religious authorities, civil authorities, and society.

Political emancipation from Spain (1821) – a movement that was initiated in 1810 by the priests Hidalgo* and Morelos* but that evolved in ways they had not expected – and the beginning of the Republic gave rise to the conflict over the Patronato* system. The relevant questions were: Who would inherit the rights of the crown? What should be under the control of the state? What should be under the control of the Roman Catholic Church?

Because the pope did not acknowledge Mexican independence (until 1836), no bishops were appointed; the 10 Mexican dioceses remained vacant. Consequently, state representatives were the main protagonists at the important meetings of 1822, where decisions were made regarding ecclesiastical organization. It was not until 1831 that Gregory XVI, taking into account the changes in Mexico, appointed some bishops. The opposing groups – "the realists" associated with the Virgin of los Remedios and "the supporters of independence" associated with the Virgin of Guadalupe – were all Catholics but separated by their views regarding the form, type, and significance of the relation between civil authorities and religious authorities, and their views about the best type of government.

Throughout most of the century, sociopolitical leaders had to contend with two Masonic rites – the Scottish (Escoceses) and York (Yorkino) lodges (see Freemasonry and Christianity) – which conceived in a different way the respective functions and missions of the state and the Roman Catholic Church. There was an ongoing struggle, with frequent shifts of power, between "centralists" (seeking greater political centralization and supporting Roman Catholicism as the state religion) and "federalists" (liberals and anticlericals favoring a political federation with greater autonomy for the states). Thus centralists supported a Patronato concordat* in the 1824 Federal Constitution, which included laws recognizing Roman Catholicism as the exclusive religion. But federalists promoted a liberal type of secularization*, through the reforms proposed by Gómez Farías (1833), the Constitution of 1857, and especially the "organic laws" of "the reform" (1855–60). Wherever these laws were implemented, they involved the suspension of special ecclesiastical status, the nationalization of the properties of the clergy, religious liberty, the separation of church and state, and the institution of civil marriage and secularization of cemeteries. These laws were further reinforced by the 1874 Constitution. Federalists and centralists alternatively promoted other changes, including the successive closing and reopening of the Pontifical University and the other Catholic universities and colleges; formal welcoming of other Christian denominations or official support of Roman Catholicism; nationalization of the properties of the clergy or their restitution; the expulsion of bishops and religious (e.g. the expulsion in 1861 of Luigi Clementi, the apostolic nuncio, and other bishops) or the return of bishops (e.g. in 1864 under Maximilian); and the establishment of new religious congregations and the reinstatement of previously established ones.

Defending the dignity of indigenous peoples. The restitution of properties to the community by centralists made people aware that the lands that belonged to indigenous peoples had been plundered; this issue and other matters regarding the dignity of indigenous people fueled tensions between the centralists in power and the liberal federalists and their respective political agendas. Unexpectedly, the government most in favor of indigenous peoples was that of Maximilian, who, with the support of the bishops, pursued bilingual politics (issuing documents in Nahuatl) and used his political power to help indigenous peoples with land problems. The Maya retained an extensive autonomous zone, and their military force provided them with important political leverage throughout the century. The Yaquis in the north had been harshly oppressed and deported to Oaxaca and Yucatan; they demonstrated great endurance and dignity in their struggle for liberty, however, confronting the injustice and repression they suffered by walking more than 13,000 kilometers to return to their lands.

The arrival of new denominations. With religious liberty and political support for foreign economic investment, the 19th c. saw the official recognition of other Christian denominations in Mexico. Chaplains and missionaries belonging to other churches arrived to minister to diplomats and business people. In addition, invasion by the US resulted in the appropriation of half of the country (1847; Treaty of Guadalupe Hidalgo,

1848, formally ending the Mexican–US War, with the USA appropriating the territory that became Utah, Nevada, California, most of New Mexico and Arizona, and parts of Oklahoma, Colorado, and Wyoming), and the French intervention (1863) resulted in the installation of Maximilian as emperor (1864–67). Diverse missionaries societies were given authorization to enter Mexico (1871); according to the liberal ideal, along with political participation that was less corporate and more individual, anyone was free to cultivate new forms of religious experience and of education.

Strengthening the diocesan structure. The establishment of new dioceses began again during Maximilian's rule, although he did not actively support the reform laws. A total of 24 new dioceses were established during the 19th c., including the period of Porfirio Díaz's regime (the "Porfiriato," 1876–1910). Eight of these dioceses soon became ecclesiastical provinces.

The provincial councils were reinstated, including those of Oaxaca (1892), Durango, Guadalajara, and Michoacán (1895) and that of the archdiocese of Mexico (1896). In addition the First Plenary Council of the Latin American Bishops was convened in Rome (1899), with the purpose of implementing the decrees of the First Vatican* Council (1869–70). Vatican I, which directly contributed to the centralization of the Roman Catholic Church, was attended by seven bishops and three archbishops from Mexico – the largest delegation from Latin America.

With respect to popular devotions, ecclesiastical authorities continued to support the growing veneration of the Virgin Mary. Pope Leo XIII authorized the coronation of the Virgin of Guadalupe (1895), and Pius X proclaimed her patroness of Latin America (1910) (see Mary, the Virgin, Cluster: Of Guadalupe).

This period culminated in the first decade of the 20th c. with the Social Catholic Congresses, the "social weeks," and other initiatives that followed the social* encyclical of Leo XIII, *Rerum Novarum* (1891). These social Christian activities in the midst of difficult economic conditions and the impoverishment of the majority of the population laid the groundwork for the participation of Christians in the Mexican Revolution, despite its anticlericalism.

20th Century. In 1910 the Mexican Revolution was initiated by the convergence of various political and cultural trends around a single issue: anticlericalism*. In reaction, the National Catholic Party (1911) supported the Roman Catholics in the exercise of their political rights.

Legal restrictions and modernization. The triumph of the Constitutionalist Party during the Revolution led to the establishment of a new constitution (1917). The Jacobin members of the constituent congress built into the constitution a series of anticlerical restrictions: Article 3 prohibited the Roman Catholic Church's involvement in primary and secondary education (education was nationalized and made available to the Mexican masses) and prohibited the Church's organization of workers' and peasants' movements (see Catholic Action); Article 5 prohibited monastic orders as an irrevocable sacrifice of liberty; Article 24 restricted public worship and other religious activities to places of worship; Article 27 strictly limited the possession of real estate by religious groups; and Article 130 denied the legal status of religious groups and the political rights of priests and other religious leaders. In reaction to these measures, there were public demonstrations and a pastoral letter from the bishops protesting the constitution with support from Pope Benedict* XV. But the legislators refused to amend the constitution.

During the government of Plutarco E. Calles (1924–28), "regulation laws" (including anticlerical measures, such as the Law on Worship, 1926) required the implementation of the articles of the constitution by municipal authorities. Political, social, and cultural reactions followed. The Catholic associations, unified in the League for the Defense of Religious Liberty, promoted economic boycotts, legal interventions, and political debates. Their resistance culminated in 1926 in an armed uprising (by the Cristeros, "followers of Christ"). Other movements also resisted the "regulations laws" from the perspective of their diverse religious, political, and economic concerns. In 1929 the Church hierarchy negotiated with the government, reaching agreements that were perceived as treasonous by grassroots Christians (Cristeros, who were excluded from these negotiations). These agreements initiated a *modus vivendi* – a legal fiction according to which the law would be neither modified nor applied – which was still in force in 1938 when the bishops supported the government of Cárdenas during the expropriation of the oil cartels. The *modus vivendi* allowed the Church to function with its own buildings, hospitals, schools, and orphanages, although these were legally nonexistent. In 1970 Sergio Méndez* Arceo, bishop of Cuernavaca, in his letter of Anenecuilco to the presidential candidate (later the president), Luis Echeverría, expressed the need for constitutional changes in ecclesiastical matters.

During the two following decades, the Church's involvement in political and social issues increased, so much so that in 1987, once again, the government tried to limit the clergy's political involvement by promulgating an electoral federal code that restricted their participation. The promulgation of this code triggered renewed efforts to make official the *modus vivendi* by procuring the recognition of the legal status of religious groups, of priests and pastors (with civil rights comparable to those of other citizens), as well as of the churches' educational activities, properties, and public worship, including those outside of church buildings. The weakness of President Carlos Salinas de Gortari (1988–94; whose legitimacy was marred by suspicion of electoral fraud) led him to modernize church*–state relations and to modify the inviolable anticlerical laws (1992). As a result, diplomatic relations between Mexico and the Vatican were strengthened. Pope John* Paul II played a significant role in the development of these constitutional amendments, which facilitated the pope's five visits to Mexico.

Changes in lay organizations. During the first decades of the 20th c., lay organizations were initiated primarily by the pope or by the bishops and priests; they were conceptualized and shaped by "the long arm of the hierarchy." At the initiative of Pope Pius* XI (1922–39), the bishops called lay Catholics to found Catholic Action in Mexico by directing their social involvement exclusively toward Catholic social programs; conversely lay Catholics were to limit their involvement in the social and military actions of the anticlerical society.

From 1952, and more clearly after Vatican* II, the social actions of lay Catholics were further justified by the formal recognition that it was their own baptism* (and not the bishops) that called laypersons to assume Christian responsibilities (see Vocation). José and Luz María Alvarez Icaza, a Mexican couple, were invited to the Second Vatican* Council as lay participants. New lay associations were created with objectives directly related to the laity's spiritual life and needs, e.g. the Christian Family Movement, the Courses on Christian Doctrine, and Family Education in the Faith. Vatican II and the Latin American Episcopal Conference (CELAM*) in Medellín* (1968) called Catholics to seek gospel-congruent solutions for the social consequences of impoverishment and structural violence. New lay movements (and the priests, religious, and some bishops who supported them) tried to address these issues as a response to what they viewed as the historical Jesus'* call to his disciples*.

These developments polarized lay Catholic movements and secular, anticlerical movements involved in social actions. As a result, the Catholic movements were banned by the government. Before the student movement of 1968 (which occurred in Mexico as well as in North America and Western Europe), the official position of the hierarchy toward these post–Vatican II lay Catholic movements, their action, and their repression by the state was silence. Nevertheless, a bishop, Méndez Arceo, and several groups of priests and religious publicly denounced the repression of the lay movements and stood with the victims.

It was in this period that Base* Ecclesial Communities (CEBs, Comunidades Eclesiales de Base) were established. Their relatively horizontal spirituality resulted from a collective community-building process by men and women – lay, religious, and clergy – who brought to the gatherings their poverty and their life struggles so that they might be seen in the light of the Word of God of the Bible; from this new perspective, the community envisioned concrete actions as expression of its social commitments. Emanating from the CEBs, a series of civil associations of men and women became involved in education efforts and social awareness raising (*concientización*); they functioned as nongovernmental organizations for human* rights viewed from a Christian perspective. Since the ecumenical meeting at Oaxtepec (1979), other Christian denominations have actively participated in the ecumenical construction of an alternative world, with greater justice* for all.

Christian involvement beyond church borders. Some dioceses and episcopal regions adopted a radical pastoral orientation in their interaction with the rest of society. Bishop Sergio Méndez Arceo struggled to bring about structural changes that would open the diocese in Cuernavaca to experiments such as the Centro Intercultural de Documentación (CIDOC; 1961–76) of Ivan Ilich. Following the intercultural orientation of the CIDOC, missionary activity was envisioned as an "Alliance for Progress" (as initiated by J. F. Kennedy) requiring that the missionaries identify themselves as guests of the host countries (see Ilich's book,

Deschooling Society, a critique of education as practiced in "modern" economies). The involvement with the CIDOC, as well as the "Christians for Socialism" orientation of Bishop Sergio Méndez Arceo, and the use of psychoanalysis by the monk Gregorio Lemercier in the Monastery of the Resurrection in Cuernavaca, led to a break with the Mexican Bishops' Conference and the Vatican. Nevertheless, Bishop Sergio Méndez Arceo received many expressions of clear support: Christians and nonbelievers throughout the world, convinced of the necessity of change, named him their bishop "of a cathedral without walls and without borders."

Toward an autochthonous church. After the Indigenous Congress (1974), D. Samuel Ruiz García, bishop of San Cristóbal, Chiapas, promoted an "autochthonous church," an initiative welcomed by many bishops in Latin America and elsewhere. Despite suspicion on the part of the Mexican Roman Catholic hierarchy and the Vatican, the autochthonous church initiative gained the support of other bishops of the region, including D. José Llaguno, bishop of the Tarahumara. The commemoration of the fifth centennial of Columbus' arrival on the continent (1992) became the occasion for promoting a more inclusive sense of collective identity that truly accounts for the presence of Mesoamerican peoples and for making people increasingly aware of the injustices suffered, of the ongoing resistance against the European cultural, political, and economic hegemony, and of the indigenous cultural wealth that can contribute to bringing about urgently needed changes. Thus it was in Chiapas that the Mexican government began to recognize the demands of the Zapatistas and the Zapista Army of National Liberation (1994). For his role as a peacemaker in these negotiations, Bishop Samuel Ruiz García received the 1996 Pacem in Terris award and was nominated for the Nobel Peace Prize.

In the early 21st c., Christianity in Mexico had become less monolithic. While the number of active lay Roman Catholics had significantly decreased, members of other Christian denominations had increased, especially in the southern part of the country. In addition, other religions had progressively settled in Mexico. This religious plurality affects the Christian churches and groups in different ways. For many churches, it has occasioned greater ecumenical openness, dialogue, and cooperation. But for numerous other churches and groups, this plurality is perceived as a threat demanding intra-institutional consolidation and closed Christian communities.

Statistics: Population (2000): 97 million. Roman Catholics, 88%; Evangelicals, 2.87%; Pentecostals and neo-Charismatics, 1.62%; Jehovah's Witnesses, 1.25%; mainline Protestants, 0.71%; Seventh-day Adventists, 0.58%; members of Iglesia de Jesucristo de los Últimos Días, 0.25%; Jews, 0.01%; nonreligious, 3.53%; no response, 0.83%. (*Source*: 2000 census.)

MARÍA ALICIA PUENTE LUTTEROTH

Miaphysite (Gk "one nature"), the christological tradition that grew from Cyril* of Alexandria's emphasis on the Johannine tradition encapsulated in the phrase "the Word became flesh and dwelled among us." To represent fully the unity of divine and human in Christ, Cyril (c375–444) originated the term "hypostatic union" from the Greek *hypostasis*, meaning "underlying reality," but taken at the Council of Chalcedon* (451) to be the equivalent of "person" (Gk *prosopon*) and contrasted with "nature" (Gk *physis*). For Cyril, the Incarnation* brought a real and permanent union between human and divine, i.e. "one incarnate nature of the divine Word" (the Greek phrase begins with *Mia physis*). Although this union is *"out of* two natures," the two natures can be perceived only by an act of pure intellection (mystical contemplation), not by any sensory evidence; neither in his consciousness nor in his activities did Jesus alternate between human and divine; his mother may be called Theotokos* (God-bearer or Mother of God) without hesitation. The dynamic force of the Incarnation* made it possible to understand redemption* as the time when all natural life would be caught up into a graced deification* (theosis*). The formulas of the Council of Chalcedon – "one person (hypostasis) *in* two natures," Mary as "Theotokos" – adopted and adapted Cyril's language, invoking his authority. But would Cyril have accepted the council's decrees? This is an open question, since he died seven years before. Following Severus* of Antioch, most Christians in Egypt*, Armenia*, Ethiopia*, and much of Syro-Mesopotamia rejected the Chalcedonian definition and affirmed Cyril's heritage as their own – hence their self-identification as "Orthodox"; they are properly known as "non-Chalcedonian" or "Miaphysite" to distinguish them from those who accept Chalcedon. Yet they vehemently reject Eutyches*, deeming him worthy of the epithet "Monophysite*" (emphasizing "only one nature"). KATHLEEN E. MCVEY

Micah, Book of, attributed to a rural Judean prophet, a younger contemporary of Isaiah* of Jerusalem, represents a stinging social critique of the conditions of Israel and Judah in the 8th c. BCE. The book deftly juxtaposes prophecies of judgment (1:2–2:11, 3:1–12, 6:1–7:6) with prophecies of restoration (2:12–13, 4:1–5:15, 7:7–20).

Micah reflects the decades following the height of power and prosperity of Israel and Judah and the context of the fall of the Northern Kingdom. The ancient traditions of the march of the divine warrior, Zion, and messianic hope are all invoked but with a twist. YHWH comes to destroy (1:2–7). Zion shall be plowed because of its iniquities (3:9–12). In its place, the new Zion will signal peace*, justice*, and security (4:1–4). The new shepherd-king will reunite the people and bring peace (2:12–13). The classic exhortation in 6:8 (to do justice, love kindness, and walk humbly with God) brings together some key emphases of 8th-c. prophetic preaching: justice (Amos), steadfast loyalty (Hosea), and humility as contrasted with pride (Isaiah). Each of these issues is seen not only in relation to God–human relationship but also in terms of human–human interaction in all aspects of life.

By placing the call to demilitarize back to back with the agrarian dream of secure, self-sufficient living, Micah makes a critical point of timeless import that there can be no peace without justice. DEVADASAN PREMNATH

Middle East, History of Christianity in. See HISTORY OF CHRISTIANITY CLUSTER: IN THE MIDDLE EAST: SYRIAC CHRISTIANITY.

Middle Knowledge (*scientia media*) is a kind of knowledge that God has which is "between" the knowledge of pure possibles and the knowledge of actual events, according to Molina*, Bellarmine*, and Suarez*. For these Jesuit theologians, God knows what persons "would do," quite freely, if offered grace* under certain circumstances and plans accordingly. God offers grace to the elect, yet leaves the decision in their hands: God offers the inducements to which God knows the elect would respond, *infallibly* but without directly *determining* the human response. The notion of "middle knowledge" develops Augustine's* observation (similar to Origen's* earlier comment) that Luke 10:13–15 (= Matt 11:20–24) speaks of what the people of Tyre and Sidon "would have done." For Augustine the call and the inclinations toward a positive response come from God, but consent is the person's own; grace operates through moral* influence rather than through physical determination (see Predestination).

Midrash (Heb), rabbinic form of interpretation of the Bible or commentary, in the mode of halakhah* (legal aspects) or haggadah* (narrative).

Migne, Jacques-Paul (1800–75), editor and publisher of historic texts. Originally a parish priest, he founded a publishing house in Paris that produced the *Patrologia Latina* (1844–64, 221 volumes) and the *Patrologia Graeca* (1857–66, 162 volumes), using many previous editions of early and medieval texts. "Migne" has come to stand for the *PL* and *PG* canons.

Miguel, Brother (1854–1910), "the Azuayan Lily" of Ecuador*; member of the Roman Catholic Institute of the Brothers of the Christian Schools, catechist*, educator, academic, member of the Ecuadorian Academy of Language (1892). Born in Cuenca, Ecuador, he was known for his long and dedicated labor in the school "El Cebollar." He was sent to Europe to translate into Spanish texts to be used by Christian Brothers and to teach in a novitiate in Spain, where he died. Beatified in 1977, he was canonized a saint (1984), patron of catechists for First Communion children.

LUIS MARÍA GAVILANES DEL CASTILLO

Milan, Edict of (313), a letter from Licinius to the governors in the East, reporting that he and Constantine* had agreed in Milan to tolerate Christianity and all other religions, and to restore the properties that had been confiscated. It was the third edict of toleration (Maxentius in 306, Galerius in 311). It did not "establish" Christianity but gave it official toleration.

Militarism is a pejorative term referring to undue trust in military might, not only as a means of defense against a direct attack, but as means of solving problems. Militarism is especially problematic for Christian theologians because it uses religion* to identify God with a nationalistic and military cause, demonizes* opponents as aggressors, and marginalizes Jesus. For example, the pamphlet of the Fifth Monarchy Men in 17th-c. England called people to a hopeless revolution, citing the OT 18 times, Revelation 14 times, two other NT texts, and never Jesus. Other examples are the many German pastors who, at the beginning of World War I, preached from Rom 8:31: "If God is for us, who can be against us?"

Jeremiah 2:13, 2:37; Isa 30:1–5, 31:1–3; and Hos 5:5 7:10–12 say that placing trust in horses, chariots, and military alliances is like placing idolatrous* trust in broken cisterns that hold no water. Militarism exaggerates what military strength can do, creates false pride and foolhardiness, and leads to the destruction and exile that result from war.

Military spending builds interest groups that push for the appropriation of money that could be used for other causes. In 2007 a full 42% of US income taxes went to past and current military expenses; 22% to health care; 9% to antipoverty programs; 4% to education, training, and social science; and 1% to international relations. **See also PACIFISM AND CHRISTIANITY; WAR, CHRISTIAN ATTITUDES TOWARD.**

GLEN H. STASSEN

Military Orders are religious orders initially established during the 12th c. to defend Christian pilgrims* and to assist in the defense and expansion of Christian-held territory in Palestine and later in the Iberian Peninsula and elsewhere. Several developed from older Hospitaller orders. In the medieval period, the leading military orders were the Templars, the Hospitallers*, and the Teutonic* Knights. Members of such orders followed a papally approved religious rule and, when not involved in military activity, followed a religious lifestyle similar to that of other orders; several survive to the present day as charitable and Hospitaller organizations.

The military orders' emphasis on the active religious life was typical of 11th- and 12th-c. reform movements in the Latin Church. Their belief in serving God by fighting derived from the OT concept of holy war*, the cults of the warrior-saints of the early church, and the newly developing concept of crusading*. Against the objection that those who live an active life and shed blood cannot be the spiritual equals of traditional cloistered contemplatives, Abbot Bernard* of Clairvaux (1090–1153) argued that they were an example of Christian charity since they defended their fellow Christians. Members of the military orders included knights, other warriors and servants, priests and sisters, and male and female associates. Only the warriors fought; the rest served God through prayer. Typically the early orders attracted the lower nobility and non-nobles, but in time the orders became more aristocratic.

The military orders played an important military role in the Crusades: as standing armies they brought discipline to medieval military forces. In the medieval period, they also made the religious life available to many from the military and lower social classes who were excluded from traditional monastic* orders. Their military involvement ceased (19th c.), but the surviving orders are still involved in charitable work worldwide. **See also RELIGIOUS ORDERS, ROMAN CATHOLIC, CLUSTER.**

HELEN J. NICHOLSON

Millenarianism, the belief in a coming major transformation of corrupt, unjust, or otherwise errant society under the sway of evil spiritual powers found in various religious traditions; in Christianity it takes the more specific form of Millennialism. **See also APOCALYPTICISM CLUSTER; ESCHATOLOGY CLUSTER; MILLENNIALISM CLUSTER.**

MILLENNIALISM CLUSTER

1) Introductory Entry

Millennialism (from Lat *mille anni,* "a thousand years"; also called Chiliasm, from Gk *chilias,* "a thousand"), the belief that Christ will reign on earth for a thousand years at the end of time, has played an important role in Christian history. The belief derives from Rev 20:2–7, which prophesies that after a series of apocalyptic events, Satan will be bound for a thousand years, during which time Christ and the holy martyrs will reign on earth. Since Revelation next describes the New Jerusalem, Millennialist tradition has assumed that Christ will reign in a rebuilt Temple in Jerusalem. Christian Millennialism, in turn, drew on Jewish apocalyptic writings and even older Mesopotamian religions, notably Zoroastrianism.

Millennialism pervaded early Christianity. About 172 or earlier, Montanus, a convert in Phrygia (in modern-day Turkey), proclaimed that the millennium would soon begin in Phrygia. Montanists'* teachings influenced many, including the patristic writers Irenaeus* and Tertullian*.

Pope Zephyrinus condemned Montanism (early 3rd c.), and Millennialism gradually faded as Christianity gained a secure position in the Roman world. The theologian Origen* (c185–c254) vigorously rejected belief in a literal millennium. The thousand-year reign, he argued, allegorically represented Christ's sovereignty in believers' lives. Augustine's* masterpiece, *The City of God* (413–26), saw a divine plan unfolding in history, but made no reference to a literal thousand-year reign of Christ.

By the 4th c., Catholic dogma, as summarized in the Nicene* Creed (325 and later revisions), foresaw Christ's return and a final Judgment* but otherwise ignored Revelation's more elaborate end-time scenario. Millennialism survived, however, among reformers and wandering prophets and in cathedral sculpture, stained glass, and the visionary music of Hildegard* of Bingen. A central goal of the Crusades* (1097–1270) was to expel Jerusalem's Muslim rulers so the city could fulfill its millennial destiny. The visionary monk and prophecy interpreter Joachim* of Fiore (c1135–1202) saw history unfolding in three great ages, culminating in the Age of the Spirit, when Christ will indeed reign on earth, along with a church radically reformed along monastic lines (see Dispensationalism). The Franciscan* order, founded by Francis* of Assisi soon after Joachim's death, proved receptive to his version of Millennialism. The Hussites, followers of the proto-Protestant Reformer Jan Hus* of Prague, burned at the stake in 1415, were influenced by millennial anticipations.

In the East, meanwhile, the Council of Constantinople* (381) declared Millennialism a heresy*, and the various Eastern Orthodox churches have historically discouraged millennial speculation. As in Catholic Europe, however, it survived at the popular level.

As the Protestant Reformation* unfolded (early 16th c.), its leaders generally rejected Millennialism, and most Lutheran and Reformed churches remain amillennial today. But the Reformation's impact stimulated popular millennial zeal. German peasants who revolted against their rulers (1524–25) and suffered terrible retribution were influenced by Thomas Müntzer*, a Protestant preacher who interpreted their uprising as a harbinger of the millennium. Among the Anabaptists*, who rejected all state authority in religious matters, Melchior Hoffmann and other firebrands espoused Millennialism. When Anabaptists took over the Westphalian city of Münster (1534), a young Dutch tailor, Jan Bockelson, proclaimed the millennium's arrival, with himself as Christ's regent on earth, entitled to take multiple wives. While Bockelson and his entourage lived in luxury, the populace starved. The authorities besieged Münster (1535), and as the desperate residents fled, they were slaughtered. In more benign forms, Millennialism influenced the Pietist* Movement in 17th-c. Germany and the Moravian* Brethren in the 18th c.

Millennial anticipations also inspired the 17th-c. English Puritans* and other Dissenters* who viewed not only the pope but also the Anglican bishopric as agents of the Antichrist* whose overthrow would usher in the millennium. The Puritan poet John Milton* saw the English civil war (1642–48) and its aftermath as the prelude to Christ's earthly reign. Puritan settlers brought Millennialism to North America (from the 1630s), where it would enjoy a long and vigorous afterlife (see the present cluster: In North America).

As interest in prophecy revived in 19th-c. England, such figures as Edward Irving, Henry Drummond, and John Darby* of the Plymouth* Brethren delved into Revelation, Daniel, and other apocalyptic texts to determine the precise sequence of end-time events that will culminate in Christ's millennial reign.

With its apocalyptic* scenario of good and evil in mortal combat, and its seductive vision of a coming age of justice* and peace*, Millennialism has attracted Christians in every era. While the poor* and oppressed* have been especially drawn to it, Millennialism's appeal is by no means limited to the downtrodden. Thomas More's* *Utopia* (1516), the radicalism of the French Revolution, the world-historical philosophy of Georg Friedrich Hegel*, Karl Marx's* vision of a communist utopia, and even Adolf Hitler's "thousand-year Reich" have all been interpreted as secularized but still recognizable forms of Millennialism. **See also** DISPENSATIONALISM. PAUL S. BOYER

2) A Sampling of Contextual Views and Practices

Millennialism in Africa. "Millennialism" refers to the Christian orientation toward the future – the expectation of the return of Jesus Christ, the Parousia*, or the rapture* of the faithful for a thousand-year reign, an escape from the suffering* that the rest will undergo. The churches in Africa believe in such a vision, but they differ in their emphasis.

Most mainline missionary churches in Africa adopt a cautious attitude of wait and see. Other missionary churches, like the Seventh*-day Adventist Church and Jehovah's* Witnesses, make Millennialism one of their distinctive beliefs, and live and work in the light of it. The Watch Tower Movement of Jehovah's Witnesses has spread like wild fire riding on this expectation.

Independent African churches (both Charismatic* and African* Instituted Churches) with their "African view of the future as potentially present" (Mugambi) see their acts of healing (within their prophetic movements) as millennial signs that they will indeed be part of the millennial realization. The Mwana Lesa Movement in 1925 Zambia (described by Ranger) is a good example. At times these millennial expectations have taken on political overtones in situations of oppression, suffering, and discrimination or have been driven by the ideology of some leader, e.g. the head of the Lord's Resistance Army in Uganda. AUGUSTINE MUSOPOLE

Millennialism in China. Before China encountered the Western millennial tradition, the most powerful millennial idea in China was found in Buddhism*, in the Pure Land traditions and the expectation of the coming of Maitreya Buddha, a kind of messianic incarnation of the Buddha. Millennial strains of Buddhism have given birth to secret societies (White Lotus) and some powerful popular movements; one toppled the Mongol dynasty (14th c.). After Christianity was introduced in China, Christian Millennialism, along with native Buddhist tradition, played an important part in mass movements. The Taiping rebellion under Hong Xiuquan, a messianic leader influenced by Christian Millennialism, almost overthrew the Qing dynasty (mid-19th c.). The Boxer Rebellion (late 19th c.) again demonstrated the power of millennial beliefs, including the magical belief, shared with North American Ghost Dancers and African Kartelite cults, that certain incantations could render believers invulnerable to bullets. Premillennialism, the mainstream theological thinking of the revivalist* movement in Britain and North America (late 19th c.), which was introduced into China by missionaries, widely influenced the conservative wing of the Chinese churches; it was perceived as the only correct interpretation of Scripture*. Premillennialism dominated the churches in China until c1980, but gradually lost its singular importance with the development of popular* Christian practices. TAO FEIYA

Millennialism in North America. The belief in Christ's thousand-year reign on earth, foretold in Revelation (see the present cluster: Millennialism), looms large in North American Christianity. In the early 17th c., leading New England Puritans* concluded that Christ's millennial kingdom would arise in North America once the French Catholics and the Indians, whom they identified with the Antichrist*, had been vanquished. In the mid-18th c., Jonathan Edwards* speculated that revivalism* and prayer could bring on the millennium. Charles Finney* and other antebellum revivalists similarly viewed their efforts as hastening the millennium.

In the early 1840s, William Miller, after studying the prophecies, foretold Christ's imminent return. In an age of utopian hopes, Miller attracted many followers. Widespread disillusionment resulted when his calculations failed to come to fruition, but from the ashes arose the Seventh*-day Adventist* Church.

In its hopeful guise, known as Postmillennialism*, this belief inspired reform-minded North American Christians to work for justice* and peace* in order to prepare for Christ's millennial reign. In the 20th c., Social* Gospel ministers and Martin Luther King* all invoked millennial themes.

In its pessimistic and apocalyptic* form, Premillennialism, this belief encouraged the view that wickedness and war will increase as the end approaches and that only a remnant of believers will survive the end-time cataclysms to share in Christ's thousand-year reign. In the late 19th c., many North American Evangelicals embraced premillennial Dispensationalism*, formulated by John Darby* of the Plymouth* Brethren. Citing Bible passages, Darby taught that the millennium will be preceded by the rapture*, when true believers join Christ "in the air" (1 Thess 4:17); the seven-year tribulation dominated by the Antichrist; and the Battle of Armageddon, when Christ vanquishes the Antichrist.

Popularized by paperback writers (*Left Behind* series), televangelists, and fundamentalist* churches, Dispensationalist Millennialism won millions of adherents. According to some surveys, by the early 21st c., some 40% of Christians in the USA embraced some aspects of Darby's system. Dispensationalism had real-world implications, as believers found the United Nations, the global economy, and Israel's divinely ordained boundaries all foretold in Scripture*. **See also** JEHOVAH'S WITNESSES.

PAUL S. BOYER

Millennium. See MILLENNIALISM CLUSTER.

Miller, William. See ADVENTISM; SEVENTH*-DAY ADVENTIST WORSHIP.

Millet (Persian, "nation"; Arabic, *millah*, "people"), the Qur'an's* term for religions of the peoples of the Book (Jews and Christians). In the Ottoman Empire, religious groups, including Christians, were governed by their own religious authorities and laws under the supervision of the Empire, which defined a people purely by their religion. **See also** GENNADIOS II (GEORGE SCHOLARIOS).

Milton, John (1608–74), poet, religious controversialist, shaper of English religious and political history in the turbulent years of the English civil war and protectorate, author of *Paradise Lost* and other influential Christian poetry; born in London, educated at St. Paul's School and Christ's College, Cambridge. But for his Puritan* sympathies, he would most likely have entered the priesthood in the established Church of England. Instead, he turned to poetry. Milton's struggle over his vocation colors his early poem *Lycidas* (1638), a pastoral elegy that also satirizes contemporary clerical abuses.

Milton came into his own as a writer in the 1630s and 1640s, when conflicts among divergent church factions roiled England and eventually led to the overthrow of the monarchy. He wrote many treatises urging ecclesiastical reform, including *Of Reformation* (1641) and *The Reason of Church Government* (1641). Milton's skill as a polemicist led Cromwell* to commission him to write *Eikonoklastes* (1649), a defense of the republican government and the execution of King Charles I. In this period, Milton also published *Areopagitica* (1644), a spirited attack on press censorship that articulates his Protestant commitment to the individual search for truth.

During the protectorate, Milton served as the "secretary for foreign tongues." After the restoration of the monarchy in 1660, he was briefly imprisoned but later lived quietly in London and turned his energies to biblical poetry. Blind from 1651, he relied on his daughters as readers. *Paradise Lost* (1667, 1674), an epic poem in 12 books, tells the story of Adam* and Eve's fall* and explores the nature of evil* and its place in God's providential plan. Milton consciously evokes Virgil, Dante*, Ariosto, Tasso, and Spenser, even as his subject leads him to "Things unattempted yet in Prose or Rhyme." *Paradise Regained* (1671) treats Christ's temptation in the desert. *Samson Agonistes* (1671), a verse drama, retells Samson's fall into blindness and weakness.

Milton's theology is difficult to categorize. Although a staunch opponent of the Roman

Catholic Church, he also eschewed rigid Protestant orthodoxies and flirted with "heretical" positions. Unlike the Puritans, he believed in free will* and, in *Of Christian Doctrine*, he even questioned the Trinity*. William Blake* thought Milton was a Gnostic* ("of the Devil's party without knowing it") and praised him as a theological maverick. Milton's works pulse with the energy of an age when Bible reading led the citizenry to overthrow the monarchy and attempt, if only briefly, a new Christian commonwealth. **See also** ENGLISH LITERATURE AND CHRISTIANITY. ROGER E. MOORE

Mind, the human intellect, has been understood quite differently throughout Western intellectual history. "Mind" has been used to refer to the human mind and to the divine mind (cf. the Word*). Within this framework, one can distinguish (1) mind as the thinking aspect of the human person, (b) mind as a share of the Divine, and (c) mind as a pragmatic tool (rather than animal instinct) for self-preservation.

For Plato*, mind and intelligibility were the measure of all being. To be *is* to be intelligible. Mind is one of two fundamental options of the human soul*: either the "senses" (focused on the changeable, sensible realm; turning away from the light of the Good) or the mind (the intelligible), through which one *is* known by, and knows, the Good itself, an ethical perspective (following Socrates) that equates knowledge with virtue*.

For Augustine*, adapting the Platonic teaching, the Christian God* is the Good itself, the source of being, and also the guarantor of our ability to know with certitude. Jesus Christ, the Logos*, the Truth, illuminates the human mind, rescuing it from the deceptive world distorted by sin*. Furthermore, the human mind (now part of the soul) mirrors through its three aspects – memory, understanding, and will*– the divine Trinity*.

With the rediscovery of Aristotle* (12th c.), a more naturalistic notion of mind (or intellect) emerged. Thus for Aquinas* special divine illumination was not needed for the mind to know truths with certitude and to possess science*.

Nominalists* (e.g. Ockham*, 14th c.) raised concerns about the extent to which the mind yields an accurate picture of the external world, and whether the universals* of the human mind correspond to real natures in things or are creatures of human reason*. Perspectivism and the provisional nature of mind's ideas were emphasized by, e.g., Nicholas* of Cusa (15th c.), Montaigne (16th c.), and Pascal* (17th c.). Mind is no longer merely the locus of truth where being is reflected; mind is a zone of constructive creativity where the world can be modeled and *re-presented*, provided that one observes critical norms, owing to the limitations of the human mind (see Hume, David; Kant, Immanuel). Theological truths like God's existence and the immortality of the soul become mere postulates of the practical mind or reason.

The romantic movement (including Hegel*) resisted this critical trend through a more vigorous notion of Spirit or Mind (*der Geist*), seeing in history the workings of divine Providence or Spirit itself (i.e. Mind).

In opposition, existentialists or humanists such as Kierkegaard*, Nietzsche*, Heidegger*, and Sartre shared the intuition of the absence or "death*" of God. The mind needs to account for the human condition without recourse to traditional Christian or Neoplatonic notions of a God who is Truth or a supreme Creator Mind structuring the world. Mind becomes more personalistic, dialogical, a pragmatic tool integrated into the whole person.

Thus for Levinas*, Buber*, von* Balthasar, and Wojtyla (John* Paul II), the mind integrated theoretical and practical concerns, privileging pragmatic concerns in the service of the human person. Mind is thus (re)united with ethical considerations. DANIEL O'CONNELL

Ministry, Ministries. The NT Greek word *diaconia* (service or ministry) had mundane origins (e.g. serving table; Luke 10:40), but gained theological meaning in relation to the church's mission, not without controversy. Against the disciples' concern to be the greatest among his followers, Jesus taught them, "Whoever wants to be first must be last of all and servant of all" (Mark 9:35, 10:43).

This tension between humble service and pride of position and power (cf. Paul's self-presentation as both "slave/servant" and "apostle"; Rom 1:1) is found throughout history as a matrix of the church and its mission, whether it led to the rejection or adoption of cultural patterns. Paul emphasized the diversity and unity of ministries through the one Spirit and the one body of Christ (1 Cor 12), as he confronted competition among ministers of the gospel (1 Cor 3). The various ministries (as apostles, prophets, evangelists, pastors, teachers) are gifts of Christ "to equip the saints for the work of ministry, for building up the body of Christ"

(Eph 4: 12). Yet by the late 1st c., the churches (mostly house* churches) developed various hierarchical forms of leadership to ensure the integrity of their ministries, often patterned on the patron–client relationship and hierarchical household* codes of the Greco-Roman world. Furthermore, the Western Church progressively assumed the cultural patterns and structures of the Roman Empire (4th c.). Eventually this led to a tripartite, hierarchical structure: bishops*, presbyters* (priests*), and deacons*, with a radical distinction between ordained* ministries and the laity's* largely passive ministry. Parallel to the "secular*" clergy emerged the religious* or "regular*" priestly orders and various lay movements. The 16th-c. Protestant Reformation affirmed "the priesthood* of all believers" but did not completely overcome elitism in its ecclesiastical structures and among its highly trained clergy.

The 18th- to 20th-c. missionary movement spread Christianity throughout Africa, Asia, and other regions, with considerable complications. There the model of highly trained, ordained, and paid clergy was not feasible, but it was possible to find indigenous leaders for all the ministries (as R. Allen pointed out). Furthermore, emerging indigenous churches, especially African* Instituted Churches and Pentecostal*/Charismatic* churches in Latin American and elsewhere, have not required professional pastors with formal training. Decentralized theological* education programs begin to offer widespread training for indigenous leaders, whatever their geographical, cultural, economic, gender, or educational location, preparing for both social and ecclesial ministries.

Similarly, the emergence of Base* Ecclesial Communities brought renewed spiritual life, prophetic relevance, and a new model of ministry to the Roman Catholic Church in Latin America and elsewhere, to some degree in direct confrontation with the hierarchy (as exemplified by the silencing of Liberation* theologians by the Vatican). ROSS KINSLER

Minjung Theology. The Korean term *Minjung* means "oppressed* people." In the 1970s, the Minjung suffered under a military dictatorship, a "development dictatorship" that assumed the role of "political messiah" ostensibly to save the people from the evils of poverty and communism. One response to this situation was the publication of the "Theological Declaration of Korean Christians (1973)" and its clandestine circulation within the ecumenical movement in Korea and overseas, which acted as a spark for the new theological movement.

An oppressed worker discovered the biblical message, noting that "Jesus was a worker, too," which invited the Minjung theological statement "Jesus is Minjung." This led to reading the Bible through Minjung eyes, a development in biblical hermeneutics started by Ahn Byung-Mu.

Minjung theologians also began to reread Korean history as a history of the Minjung. One clear historical reference is the Tonghak Peasant Movement (1894), similar to the T'aiping Movement for the Heavenly Kingdom (1850–60) in China*. A second is the historic March First Independence Movement (1919) against the Japanese colonial empire.

Minjung theology uncovers the religious dynamics in the life of the Minjung. Tonghak, a Minjung religion, is a convergent religious movement incorporating Minjung expressions of Confucianism*, Buddhism*, Daoism*, and Shamanism*. Minjung theology also catalyzes a Minjung religious hermeneutics to integrate the respective religious texts and histories in its understanding of religion. Thus Minjung theology has opened a new religious horizon in Korea.

Minjung culture, such as Korean mask dance (*talchum*), is a key resource for Minjung theology. Hyun Young-Hak, one of the original Minjung theologians, discovered a religious dynamic of critical transcendence in *talchum*. Additional such resources are Minjung painting (represented by artists Hong Sung-Dam and Lee Chul-Soo) and Minjung music and literary writings that express the *han* (deep feeling of resistance against injustice done) of the Minjung – their suffering under oppressive power. The late Suh Nam-Dong developed a theology of *han*, taking the theme from various Korean poems and novels.

The social biography of the Minjung posits that the political sovereignty of the Minjung is derived from the sovereignty of God. Jesus is affirmed as the Messiah of the Minjung, and the Minjung are the people of Jesus. "Minjung as sovereign subject" is the theological foundation for Minjung struggle. KIM YONG-BOCK

Minster (from Lat *monasterium*), cathedral or large church in Anglo-Saxon England where the clergy lived under a rule*. *Münster* is a German adaptation of the term introduced by English missionaries.

Miracle, event that evokes wonder or astonishment and thereby promotes reverence or fear. Miracles are generally viewed as exceptions to the usual workings of nature and thus as evidence of supernatural power that validates the authority of a miracle worker when one is involved. Miracles entail a certain amount of ambiguity. They may be divine or angelic, demonic, or the result of human deception, or simply unusual events.

The biblical expression "signs and wonders" suggests that the emphasis may be not simply on unusual power but on the "sign" character of the miraculous events. In the OT, certain impressive events are produced "so that you may know that I am the Lord" (e.g. Exod 11:7, 14:18, 16:6, 16:12 31:13). Specific signs may validate God's promises (Judg 6:36–40), but seeking or expecting signs or miracles may be "tempting God" or "putting God to the test" (Isa 7:12; Exod 17:7; Deut 6:16; Luke 4:12, par. 1 Cor 1:22). Furthermore, miracles could also be produced by magicians calling on false gods or demons; thus all miracles must be "tested" (Deut 13:1–3; 1 Thess 5:21; 2 Thess 2:9; Rev 16:14).

Most OT miracles are associated with the Exodus (specifically with Moses* and Aaron*) and with Elijah* and Elisha*. Jesus' miracles, including exorcisms*, healings*, the raising of the dead, and "nature miracles," are presented as the fulfillment of prophecy (e.g. Luke 7.22), a sign of the "last times" (e.g. Luke 11:20), and the overcoming of evil powers that keep people in bondage (see Redemption). Some are linked with the forgiveness of sins (Mark 2:1–12). Some are based on the faith of those healed (Mark 10:52) and may *not* happen because of a lack of faith (Mark 6:5–6). The beneficiary sometimes spreads the news about Jesus (e.g. Mark 5:20), but there may be a lack of response (Luke 10:13).

Similar miracles are attributed to the disciples and apostles in the Gospels, Acts, and the apocryphal* Acts of various apostles, being interpreted as evidence of Jesus' continuing activity through the Holy Spirit. Visions, prophecies, and speaking in tongues were also considered manifestations of divine power.

Throughout the history of Christianity, miracles, especially healings, are often associated with successful missionaries, with saints and their relics, and later with the reserved host* or with especially powerful images or icons* of Christ or the saints. Miracles were often used to validate the authority of one party or another. In the canonization* of saints, miracles (produced by God through the intercession of the saint) came to be expected as a confirmation of the person's sainthood. Miracles of healing are associated with special sites, such as Lourdes* and Fátima*.

During the Enlightenment*, miracles came under criticism as either the delusions of credulous people or fraudulent. The documents that recorded miracles were examined with the conviction* that miracles cannot be viewed as historical (because, being beyond natural laws, they cannot be verified). This notion had been promulgated earlier by Spinoza*, who emphasized that God acts only through natural laws, and by Hume*, for whom miracles were out of keeping with the general expectations developed in the course of one's experience. Protestants often viewed the continuing miracles claimed by Catholics as either fraudulent or diabolical.

Thus following Lessing* and others, a new emphasis was placed on "moral miracles" through the "demonstration of Spirit and power" (1 Cor 2:4), such as Jesus' sinlessness, conversions such as Paul's, life transformations ("fruits of the spirit"; Gal. 5:22–23), the preaching of the gospel by uneducated people, and the rise of an egalitarian community of men and women. While not contravening the laws of nature, "moral miracles" go beyond normal expectations, given human weakness. The view of moral miracles played an important role in revival* and Holiness* movements, but was expanded in subsequent Pentecostal*/Charismatic* movements to include once again healings and other powerful manifestations of the Holy* Spirit against evil powers.

A broader view of miracles, adopted by many theologians and found throughout Christian history, underscores that God's creation of the world is the greatest miracle. The entire cosmos is a miracle; "miracles" in a narrower sense are only the most astonishing manifestations of God's power. In this connection, Schleiermacher* said that "miracle is merely the religious name for 'event.'" EUGENE TESELLE

Miranda y Gómez, Miguel Darío (1895–1986), bishop of Tulancingo, Mexico*; archbishop primate of Mexico (1956–77); cardinal (1969); director of the Mexican Social Secretariat. A staunch advocate of social justice, he attended the Second Vatican* Council and served as first president of the Latin American Episcopal Conference (CELAM, Rio de Janeiro, 1955).

MARÍA ALICIA PUENTE LUTTEROTH and ELIZABETH JUDD

Mirari Vos (1832), the encyclical of Gregory XVI condemning the liberal doctrines of Lamennais*, Lacordaire*, and Montalembert (who advocated civil liberties and separation of church* and state) following their dramatic pilgrimage to Rome.

Miriam, Moses'* and Aaron's* lesser known sister, Miriam is named as one of the sibling triumvirate (Num 12:4) and leads a victory song after the crossing of the Red Sea (Exod 15). The sister who watches over baby Moses is not named, but readers have assumed that this clever girl is the same Miriam later referred to as Aaron's sister. Miriam's many namesakes include the mother of Jesus in the Christian Scriptures. NICOLE WILKINSON DURAN

Miskito Coast, Caribbean shore of Nicaragua and other Central American countries, not settled by the Spanish because of the tropical climate. The English established themselves in Belize (1638) and had an impact on the entire Caribbean coast; they established a protectorate (1678) over the "Miskito king," helping him rule over the Sumo and Rama peoples. When it came under Nicaraguan sovereignty (1860), the Mesoamericans retained autonomy, and continued to use English and their indigenous tongues. **See also** NICARAGUA.

Missal. In the Roman Catholic Church, book containing the service of the Mass* for the entire year, including all readings and chants for each day.

MISSION CLUSTER

1) *Introductory Entries*

Mission, Theologies of, and Western and Asian Churches
Mission and Eastern Orthodoxy

2) *A Sampling of Contextual Views and Practices*

Mission: Thematic Issues: Anti-slavery
Mission: Thematic Issues: Emigration or Colonization
Mission: Thematic Issues: Imperialism
Mission: Thematic Issues: Race
Mission in Africa
Mission in Asia
Mission in Asia: Catholic Mission in China, 16th–18th Centuries
Mission in the Caribbean Islands
Mission in Europe: Germany
Mission in Europe: Post-Communist Eastern Europe
Mission in Latin America: Catholic Mission in Brazil
Mission in Latin America: Catholic Mission in Mexico
Mission in North America: Mission as Conquest
Mission in the South Pacific

---

1) Introductory Entries

Mission, Theologies of, and Western and Asian Churches. It is customary today to distinguish between "mission" and "missions." By *mission* is meant God the Father's own "mission" or activities in history through Jesus and in the power of the Holy Spirit. This mission actualizes in time and space the eternal relations among the divine persons of the Trinity*. It is the mission of the church only insofar as the church is empowered to participate in it. By *missions* is meant the various forms and activities by which the church carries out God's mission at a particular place and time. Today there is a keen awareness that missions are not restricted to certain individuals, i.e. missionaries, but are incumbent on all Christians. The church is missionary by its very nature.

Like other church activities, Christian missions are undergirded by theologies that both shape the understanding of the church's mission and dictate the strategies and methods for missions themselves. Different theologies of mission dominated during certain periods of church history, and these paradigms (though they never disappeared) waxed and waned, depending on changes not only in religious but also in sociopolitical, economic, and cultural conditions.

Mission as Proclamation and Witness to Save Souls. This model of mission is inspired primarily by Matt 28:19–20. Jesus' command to go and make disciples of all nations, baptize them in the name of the Father, Son, and Holy Spirit, and teach them to observe all that he has commanded is taken to mean proclaiming, through words and deeds, the good news of God's salvation to all people and converting them to the Christian religion. Salvation* is exclusively that of the soul*, for which conversion* and baptism* are absolute requirements. Missions are made urgent by the doctrine of original* sin according to which all humans are born as enemies of God and by the belief that very few indeed will be saved. All non-Christian religions are condemned as idolatry* and superstition* or at least as powerless human attempts at self-salvation. A modern version of this theology of mission is found in D. A. McGavran's "church growth movement" and in many Evangelical* and Pentecostal* missionary circles.

Mission as Planting the Church. This model is inspired by Luke 14:23. In this parable, the master orders his servants to go to the roads and country lanes and bring everybody to the banquet so that his house may be full. Conversion and baptism are the first steps toward the final goal of mission, i.e. establishing the church, with all its institutional and sacramental structures. This model is operative in most mainline churches, especially the Roman Catholic Church.

Mission as Serving God's Kingdom of Truth, Love, and Justice. This model is rooted in Luke 4:18–19, which speaks of Jesus' mission of preaching the good news to the poor*, releasing captives, giving sight to the blind, setting the oppressed* free, and proclaiming the favorable year of the Lord. Salvation is understood not in spiritualistic and individualistic terms (as the salvation of souls) or in ecclesiastical terms (as the planting of the church), but as comprising the social, political, economic, and cosmic dimensions of human existence. Paradoxically, this model of mission was facilitated by the Enlightenment* with its ideals of autonomous reason*, individual freedom*, and technological* progress. Today, it is favored by Liberation* theologies of all types, which see the church as servant of the Kingdom* of God, committed to the preferential* option for the poor.

Mission as Dialogue. While not denying the necessity of witness, proclamation, baptism, church planting, and serving, this model of mission focuses on finding the most effective way to carry out God's mission amid cultural diversity, religious pluralism, and massive poverty*. This modality is dialogue*, based on the mystery* of God's incarnation*. The dialogue is fourfold: dialogue of life, which entails living with people of non-Christian faiths; of action, which entails collaborating with them in projects of peace* and justice*; of theological exchange, which entails learning from their different beliefs and practices; and of religious experience, which entails praying with them. The three areas of this fourfold dialogue are liberation, inculturation*, and interreligious dialogue. This model of mission as dialogue has been strongly espoused by the Federation of Asian Bishops' Conferences.

PETER C. PHAN

Mission and Eastern Orthodoxy. The Eastern Orthodox* Church's distinctive missionary goal is and has always been to create indigenous eucharistic communities while respecting the indigenous culture, using the local language, offering translations of Holy Scripture and the Divine* Liturgy, creating an alphabet and writing system when necessary, and training indigenous leaders to serve as soon as possible.

The missionary legacy of the apostolic church continued in the 4th c. through missionaries such as Gregory* the Illuminator of Armenia*, Nino* (or Nina) of Georgia*, and Frumentius* of Ethiopia*. During the 4th–6th centuries, the Byzantine Church evangelized the vast regions of the Byzantine Empire, while simultaneously sending missionaries to Syria*, Mesopotamia, Persia, Armenia, Phoenicia, Arabia, Nubia, Ethiopia, and India*. The most famous Byzantine missionaries were the brothers Cyril* and Methodius, who evangelized the Slavic peoples of Moravia (9th c.), creating a Slavic alphabet for their translation work; their 20-year labor resulted in more than 200 indigenous clergy, who in turn evangelized the Slavic lands of Serbia*, Bulgaria*, Moldavia*, and eventually Russia*.

With the fall of Constantinople (1453) to the Ottoman Empire, the Orthodox Church in Russia carried the mantle of missions through such pillars as Stephen of Perm, the evangelizer of the Zyrian people (Northwestern Siberia); the 18th-c. philologist Makarius Glukarev, who spent 14 years in the rugged northern Siberian Altai mountains; Innocent Veniaminov, who ministered for 45 years in Alaska and Eastern Siberia and established the Russian Orthodox Mission Society, along with Nicholas Kasatkin, who entered Japan* in 1862 when the country was one of the most xenophobic in the world, and concluded a 50-year mission with more than 33,000 Christians in 266 communities. The Russian Orthodox Mission Society helped send hundreds of missionaries throughout the vast lands of the eastern end of the Russian Empire, as well as to Alaska, Japan, China*, and Korea*, and published more than 2 million copies of hundreds of translations of the Bible and spiritual writings into 20 languages for various missions.

The best example of a leader of the contemporary Orthodox missionary movement is Anastasios Yannoulatos, archbishop of Albania*, who has led a missionary renewal in Greece* (from 1950s) and influenced many of the Orthodox churches worldwide in their missionary outreach. His academic work in missiology and world religions as a professor at the University of Athens for 25 years, combined with his missionary efforts in East Africa and Albania (from 1981), have set the model for modern Orthodox missions. **See also** CULTURE AND CHRISTIANITY IN EASTERN ORTHODOXY.

LUKE A. VERONIS

---

2) A Sampling of Contextual Views and Practices

Mission: Thematic Issues: Anti-slavery. Christian missions had an ambiguous relationship with slavery*. Before the Enlightenment*, few Christians questioned its legitimacy, although some Spanish priests in the Americas urged that slaves be treated with humanity. The first Anglican missionary society, the Society for the Propagation of the Gospel (1701), inherited a slave plantation in Barbados, and its first missionary to Africa, Thomas Thompson, published a book in defense of the slave trade (1756). Even some pioneers of the 18th-c. Evangelical missionary awakening (e.g. Thomas Haweis of the London Missionary Society, 1795) were implicated in slave owning.

The Evangelical missionary movement, influenced by Enlightenment thought, nevertheless presumed the equality of all humans and their potential to be raised by grace to the heights of civilization. This ideology of Christian improvement was not a "political theology." The missionary societies instructed their Caribbean* missionaries to avoid politics and teach slaves to be obedient to their masters. But dissenting chapels created an alternative society in which Bible reading, lay preaching, and open prayer dissolved distinctions between slaves and free persons. Alarmed slave owners placed restrictions on missionary operations, but such repression (which was intensified after the slave rebellions in Demerara, 1823, and Jamaica*, 1831) turned cautious Evangelicals into champions of emancipation. The abolition of slavery was now regarded as essential to ensure freedom for the gospel and elevate degraded and enslaved Africans to full human dignity. Missions contributed directly to slave emancipation in the British Empire (1833–34).

From the 1840s, Christian hopes for the regeneration of Africans shifted from the Caribbean to West Africa, where the colonies of Sierra* Leone (1807) and Liberia* (1820) had been founded as bases from which Christian freed slaves (both African and African American) could evangelize other Africans. T. F. Buxton's African Civilization Society (1839) and the resulting Niger expedition (1841) aimed to counter the African slave trade by "legitimate commerce" and the gospel. Although the expedition ended in disaster, its goals lived on in the principles of Henry Venn (Church Missionary Society) and David Livingstone*. Venn encouraged cotton cultivation in West Africa to stifle the slave trade and nurture a middle class that would support an indigenous church. Livingstone expected Zambezi cotton to drive out the slave trade from East Africa and remove from Lancashire consciences the burden of dependence on cotton grown by US slaves. In the later 19th c., anti-slavery was a preoccupation of the Catholic missionary strategist Cardinal Lavigerie, founder of the White* Fathers. BRIAN STANLEY

Mission: Thematic Issues: Emigration or Colonization. When mass emigration from Europe to North America began (18th c.), its volume and direction expanded as technology and communications improved; in the 19th c., 50 million emigrants left Europe. Some followed a specific missionary vocation, and the writings of these pioneers may have stimulated secondary, secular emigration to countries where mission stations were becoming centers of a spreading Western culture* and commerce. Others, conversely, sought the mission field in response to the "heathenism" encountered and publicized by explorers and colonial administrators; other emigrants had socioeconomic betterment as a primary motivation. Few churches, except that of the Mormons*, promulgated a theology of emigration or colonization, and the link between missions and overseas settlement was generally pragmatic and indirect.

Minority emigrants, such as Scandinavian and German Pietists, and Russian Mennonites or Doukhobors, fled religious persecution. Clergy – like the rusticated Scottish Presbyterian Norman McLeod in Nova Scotia in 1817 and the Anglican Isaac Barr in Saskatchewan in 1903 – occasionally orchestrated colonization schemes, while in the 1840s Christian colonies were promoted in New Zealand's South Island, at Christchurch by English Anglicans and in Otago by Scottish Presbyterians. More commonly, home churches offered financial and practical assistance to emigrants, raising money from congregations to build and staff colonial churches and schools with ministers, catechists, and teachers. Religious and ethnic issues were sometimes indistinguishable, as colonial mission committees responded to pleas from clergy and laity to reinforce transplanted identities, as well as meet spiritual needs. For example, across Canada, Gaelic-speaking priests and Presbyterian ministers alike complained that inadequate clerical provision was damaging the linguistic as well as the spiritual health of adherents.

From the late 19th c., Christian charities, particularly in Britain, advocated and aided the emigration of unemployed and surplus citizens. The Salvation* Army, advertising itself as the world's largest emigration agency, used its international network to supervise recruitment and relocation. While attempts to establish Salvationist colonies foundered, thousands of emigrants were transported and found work through the Salvation* Army well into the 20th c. After 1922 unprecedented state funding bolstered collaborative colonization schemes operated by the Salvation Army, the YMCA*, and other Christian charities throughout the British Empire.

The evangelistic dimension of emigration waned during the 20th c, but this does not detract from the lasting religious and cultural impact made by missionaries and emigrants alike in a complex, worldwide network of overlapping relationships whose full implications are not yet fully understood. MARJORY HARPER

Mission: Thematic Issues: Imperialism. Christian missions have been associated throughout history with both a divine command and the assumption that they bring a religion "superior" to preexisting local or indigenous religious beliefs and practices. Thus missions were commonly linked with imperialism, the control or subordination of peoples by more powerful and superior ones. Secular authorities since Constantine* and the Roman Empire saw the advantages to imperial rulers of linking Christian expansion to their preoccupations with power, wealth, and security. Conversely, missions – e.g. Spanish and Portuguese (16th c.), and British (19th c.) – often valued the protection and political and material support provided by an imperial power for secure evangelism and the prospect of successful conversions (see Portuguese Explorations, Conquests, and Missions; Spanish Explorations, Conquests, and Missions).

Such relationships were often purely functional or opportunistic, rather than based on principle, whether in missions' relationships with European powers or with indigenous non-European state and empire building – e.g. through dependence on strong local rulers like the *kabaka* of Buganda, Tswana rulers, or the "king" of Fiji.

Missions generally become enthusiastic agents of imperialism in those regions where indigenous peoples were overtly hostile or deeply resistant to the promulgation of Christianity, as they maintained their own ancient religion and culture. For example, in Muslim regions, China*, and Japan*, and, among the Ndebele in Central Africa, vigorous rejection of Christianity was the norm, with missions increasingly approving of the use of imperial force to break down local resistance. In India*, British missions deplored the government of India's reluctance to support Christian proselytism*. Elsewhere the bitter competition of Catholics and Protestants prompted demands for government backing and expulsion of religious rivals. By contrast missions were the most critical of imperialism in white settler societies, whose treatment of indigenous peoples was usually harsh.

Missions had only limited success either as supporters or as critics of imperialism. Both at home and abroad, mission relations with peoples, governments, and elites remained ambiguous and shifting. Missions' attempts to undermine local cultures were resented, although missions' offerings – literacy, education, medicine, diplomatic mediation, and economic opportunity – were warmly received. Local peoples often selectively plundered missions and the imperialism they frequently peddled, appropriating what seemed useful and discarding the irrelevant. This process gradually broke apart the 19th-c. Enlightenment's* linkage of Christianity, commerce, and civilization. Since then missions' imperialism has become an increasingly local phenomenon at odds with the claims of empires. African and Asian indigenous Christians assisted the process of decolonization as they acquired the means to challenge imperial hierarchies and controls. Simultaneously, the implications of local beliefs for Christianity taking root became better understood.

ANDREW PORTER

Mission: Thematic Issues: Race. Race* became a problem for missions with the expansion of missionary work from Western Europe after 1492. This expansion was closely associated with the creation of the Spanish* and Portuguese* empires and a massive movement of Europeans into the New World, where they occupied the lands of the indigenous people whom they enslaved. This was justified by the assertion that the humanity of the "Indians" and later that of imported Africans was inferior to that of the invaders. The missionary orders, particularly the Franciscans* and Dominicans*, and later the Jesuits*, converted a large number of the indigenous peoples, while asserting their full humanity and attempting to protect them by creating autonomous Christian "Indian" enclaves or reductions*.

The Roman Catholic Church clearly taught that "Indians" and Africans were fully human, but the power of the settlers in the Americas was such that racial discrimination became so entrenched that the episcopate gave in to it and denied "Indians" ordination as priests. In contrast, in Japan* and China*, free from settlers in the 17th c., indigenous men were ordained and even raised to the episcopate.

With the expansion of Protestant Europeans, overwhelmingly British, to North America, the local people were dispossessed of their lands and a large number of Africans were brought to the continent as slave* laborers. This occurred with little or no discussion of the treatment of either "race" in the various Protestant churches.

The Evangelical revival* changed the situation. Slavery was challenged on the basis of the oneness of humanity, and the new Protestant missionary movement became inextricably involved with abolitionism. In the US South in the early 19th c., most Protestant denominations divided (schisms healed only in the mid-20th c.), with the Southern churches developing a biblical defense of slavery and of white racial supremacy. A similar theological development took place in South Africa in the Dutch Reformed churches. These churches produced missions, but they were missions that planted racially defined churches.

The racial egalitarianism of the Catholic and Protestant missions was subtly distorted from c1860 to c1950 by the pervasive impact in the West of "scientific racism" and Anglo-Saxonism, which produced in the missions not crude racism but a pernicious paternalism. For example, until the 1950s, despite the existence of local synodical or episcopal structures, real power in Protestant churches was held by all-white mission councils.

ANDREW C. ROSS

Mission in Africa. Throughout the history* of Christianity in Africa, the understanding of mission and its practice has evolved. Africans were initially on the receiving end of Christian mission before becoming missionaries themselves.

Mission as Conversion and Church Planting. For the early (since the 15th c.) Catholic and Protestant missionary enterprises in Africa, "conversion*" was the primary goal. The missionaries' commitment to education, health and social care, and agricultural projects was a means to achieve this goal.

The Roman Catholic Congregation for the Propagation of the Faith underscored that "mission is that element of ecclesiastical ministry which accomplishes the establishment of the Catholic faith among non-Catholics." Consequently, "conversion" meant the profession of Christian teaching and baptism* in the name of the Trinity*. Conversion implied "the expansion of the Reign of God" and "the founding of new churches" (as Thomas Ohm, OSB, wrote); missionary adaptation was viewed as a threefold process: that of accommodation, assimilation, and transformation.

For Protestants in general, and Evangelicals in particular, mission required a special vocation* through the Holy* Spirit and sending by a church. It aimed at the baptism of non-Christians and at church planting and church growth. As for present-day Charismatic* and Pentecostal* churches, the first evangelistic goal is to bring people to an explicit commitment to Jesus Christ, because the core of the Christian message is the person of Jesus Christ, who must be proclaimed in his fullness in believers' lifestyle and in their words.

Mission as a Quest for Authenticity. In the 1940s, "voices from the margins" (like the Senegalese politicians Léopold Sédar Senghor and Alioune Diop) warned the church in Africa that its survival would depend on its ability to become more authentic in its mission. This was reminiscent of Blyden and Ajayi Johnson's 1870s pioneering works calling missionaries to interpret the gospel as a meeting place with African culture – an approach that Bediako calls a quest for the "hermeneutic of Christian identity." The issue was how the old and the new in African religious consciousness could become integrated into a unified vision of what it meant to be authentically African and Christian. Across most denominations, this view gave impetus to the use of vernacular prayers and songs, in both public and private, formal and informal settings; the spirituality* that grew from such experience became the vehicle for an authentic African Christianity.

Mission Adaptation, Inculturation, and Liberation (Late 1950s to Late 1960s). The formulation of genuinely African theological concepts and practice of mission amounts to the conviction that conversion to Christianity must be coupled with cultural continuity and political freedom. Inculturation* and adaptation were the concerns of church leaders in tropical Africa, while Black Liberation* theology, together with "confessing" and "kairos*" theologies, were the main options chosen in South* Africa. A crisis emerged: the concept of "adaptation" used by North

Atlantic missionaries in response to the quest for an African approach to mission was branded inadequate, because the adaptation model aimed at translating a Christianity developed elsewhere into the so-called mission lands. Meanwhile Liberation theology emerged as a "mission call" to the church to liberate the entire personhood of the African threatened by a severe "anthropological poverty*" – not just a poverty of not having, but one of not being. Jean-Marc Ela directed the attention of African churches to their prophetic role as defenders of the oppressed*. These same issues were raised in South Africa by Gabriel Setiloane, Itumeleng Mosala, Desmond Tutu, Allan Boesak, and others in their struggle against the apartheid system.

Mission as Incarnation and as Fostering African Ecclesial Structures. The Fourth Episcopal Synod of the Catholic Bishops of Africa and Malagasy (1974) urged the church to embrace the concept of mission as "incarnation*." The emphasis was now on the Africanization of the church's structures and personnel. The same year (1974), Protestant churches gathered at the All* Africa Conference of Churches in Lusaka and adopted the "moratorium issue," a call for the self-assertion, self-reliance, and self-government of the church in Africa. The Pan-African Conference of the Ecumenical* Association of Third World Theologians (EATWOT II; Accra, 1977) radically stimulated a new momentum in African theological thinking. For the first time, African theologians, including Roman Catholics and Protestants, Francophones and Anglophones, convened.

Mission as Liturgy prolongs the "logic of incarnation" by letting Christian faith "become flesh and blood in African cultures"; the rhythmic melodies that identify the African personality enlivened church services throughout tropical Africa. This movement was observed in Protestant congregations, and especially in the Charismatic* Movement and African* Instituted Churches.

In the Roman Catholic Church, the prescribed Latin language was a handicap. Consequently, the first African renderings of the Holy Mass* (late 1950s) tried to combine African melodies with the Latin text, as in the *Missa Luba* from Zaire and the *Messe des Piroguiers* (Canoeists) from Cameroon. In East Africa, Stephen Mbunga excelled by composing the *Misa Baba Yetu* as the first original text and melody in Swahili, followed by the *Misa Kwango* in Lingala (Western Congo's lingua franca). In 1967 the Cameroonian priest Fr. Pie-Claude Ngumu initiated an African celebration of the Mass in Ndzon-Melen (near Yaoundé), which was highly praised at the Eucharistic Congress in Lourdes (1982). Similarly, Cardinal Malula, archbishop of Kinshasa, inspired and supervised the three-year elaboration of the Zairean Rite at the local faculty of theology, which was finally approved under the title "Roman Missal for the Dioceses of Zaire" (see Congo, Democratic Republic of; Inculturation Cluster; Liturgies, History of).

Mission as Healing. The practice of healing* is one of the strongest elements of African churches, both mainstream and independent. As the Ghanaian theologian Appiah-Kubi said, "Priest-healers and prophet-healers in AICs [African Instituted Churches], blending elements of African culture into their services and beliefs, have achieved some remarkable successes in the areas of chronic psychiatric problems." Andrew Walls has commented, "Healing is addressed to the person as the centre of a complex of influences." For Archbishop Milingo, what is at stake is to bring "the liberating power of Jesus Christ as the source of healing to people."

Mission as the Empowerment of Women. "Today it is impossible for African theology . . . to emerge and to bloom unless both African churches and African theology start out from and develop around the situation of women in Africa," as Louise Tappa and Mercy Oduyoye, founding members of the Circle* of Concerned African Women Theologians, say. In general, African women theologians reject the doctrinal approach to Christology that prevails in the male-dominated church. Instead, they accept the "Christ of history," who "defines his mission as a mission of liberation" (see Theology as Human Undertaking Cluster: African Women Theologians Doing Theology: Making Connections). What is at stake here is the wholehearted acceptance of Jesus as the one who brings total liberation, embracing every aspect of life. **See also** **RECONSTRUCTION, AFRICAN THEOLOGIES OF.** VALENTIN DEDJI

Mission in Asia. Asia, where Jesus was born and where Christianity began, was never without a significant Christian presence. According to the Malankara Orthodox* Syrian Church (Mar Thoma), in 52 CE the apostle Thomas converted some upper-class Hindu families in Cranagore, went to China, returned to India, organized Christian communities in Malabar, then moved to Coromandel on the east coast, where he suffered martyrdom, and was buried in Mylapore (south of Madras).

In the 3rd and 4th c., the monastic communities of the Syriac Orthodox* Church moved farther east, into Armenia*, Persia, and India*. In China* the mission of a group of monks (led by Aluoben or Alopen) prospered from 635 to 936 under the Tang dynasty (618–907) but disappeared with the Mongol Conquest. Later during the Yuan (Mongol) dynasty (1271–1368), Syriac Orthodox and (for the first time) Catholic missionaries entered China. But Christianity again disappeared when the Yuan fell to the Ming in 1368. In the 17th c., waves of Catholic missionaries, at first Jesuits*, then Dominicans*, Franciscans*, Augustinians*, and members of the Missions Étrangères de Paris, came to China and other Asian countries under the patronage (Padroado*) of Portugal* – except the Philippines*, which was under Spanish jurisdiction. Thus in tandem with Western military conquest and commerce, Christian missions were carried out in India*, Japan*, the Philippines*, Taiwan*, Vietnam*, Cambodia, Laos, Malaysia*, and Indonesia*. An exception was Korea*, in which missions were initiated by the Koreans themselves in 1784. Later Iberian imperialism was joined by Dutch, English, French, and US imperialism.

Roman Catholics were followed by Protestant denominations, especially starting in the 19th c., with their mission "societies" (e.g. the Baptist Missionary, the London Missionary Society, the Netherlands Missionary Society, the Deutsche Christentumsgesellschaft, the Danish-Halle Mission, the Moravian Mission, the American Board of Commissioners for Foreign Mission, the American Baptist Missionary Board, the Basel* Mission, and the Berlin Society). Today, the presence of Pentecostals* and Charismatics* is significant in many Asian countries.

A recent important development in Asian missions is the emergence of a number of Asian-born missionary societies of apostolic life aimed at mission to non-Christians (*ad gentes*), in foreign countries (*ad exteros*), and for life (*ad vitam*). Notable among these are the Mission Society of the Philippines, the Missionary Society of St Thomas the Apostle (India), the Catholic Foreign Mission Society of Korea, the Missionary Society of Heralds of Good News (India), the Missionary Society of Thailand, and the Lorenzo Ruiz Mission Society (the Philippines).

In Asia there are many kinds of mission* theologies and practices: proclamation and witness to save souls (especially among Evangelicals, Pentecostals, and Charismatics); planting the church (among mainline churches); serving God's Kingdom* of truth, love, and justice (related to Liberation theologies); and mission as dialogue*, strongly espoused by the Federation of Asian Bishops' Conferences.

PETER C. PHAN

Mission in Asia: Catholic Mission in China, 16th–18th Centuries. Modern Roman Catholic Missions were opened in China* by Jesuits* (1583–1630s; for earlier periods, see History of Christianity Cluster: In Asia). The pioneer, Matteo Ricci* (1552–1610), adapted the gospel to Chinese culture. According to Ricci, Christianity, the "teachings of heaven," was the only true universal religion; its monotheism, moral rigor, and intellectual foundations agreed with the pristine teachings of the ancient Chinese sages, which were subsequently "corrupted" by

Buddhism* and Song scholars. By mastering Confucian* culture, Ricci and his companions attracted Chinese elites by the novelty and brilliance of their intellectual and social actions, including the presentation of Western scientific knowledge. When Ricci died (1610), there were 2,500 converts, and in 1636 there were 40,000 (served by 20 Jesuits), despite rebellion, warfare, and dynastic change (1630s–1660s). The arrival of Dominicans* and Franciscans* (1630s) initiated a long dispute over the methods of conversion. Opposed to Ricci's accommodation of Confucianism, his successor, Niccolo Longobardi (1565–1655), and other Spanish friars accused the Jesuits of preaching an adulterated Christianity. The first major persecution (1664–71) was unleashed by a Beijing mandarin: most European missionaries were deported to Guangzhou, although a Jesuit astronomer, Ferdinand Verbiest, won imperial favor. Between 1664 and 1692, with the promulgation of an imperial edict favoring Christianity, the number of converts doubled, from 100,000 to 200,000. But the number of Christians dwindled in the 18th c. to about 120,000, for two reasons. (1) Opposition to Ricci's accommodation resulted in the "Chinese rites* controversy" over the "term question" that led to the condemnation of Chinese "superstitions*" – rites in honor of Confucius and ancestors* – and the condemnation of Christianity by the Qing emperors. The papal decree of 1742 banned the Chinese rites and the use of Shangdi and other terms, except that of Tianzhu, for naming* God. During major persecutions between 1745–48 and 1784–85, European missionaries, Chinese priests, and Christians were martyred. (2) Intense rivalries among religious orders from different European countries developed among Spanish Jesuits, Dominicans, and Franciscans, and newly arrived missionary orders and secular priests from France and Italy. To facilitate missionary work under persecution, more Chinese were recruited and trained for the priesthood, both in China proper and in Italy, France, and Siam. While there were only 4 Chinese priests vs. 86 Europeans in 1724, their number rose to 26 out of a total of 109 in 1739 and 44 out of 101 in 1765. By the end of the 18th c., native clergy constituted the core of the Chinese Catholic Church. RONNIE PO-CHIA HSIA

Mission in the Caribbean Islands. Iberian Roman Catholicism came to the Caribbean islands through explorers, conquistadors, and friars (late 15th to early 16th c.). Pope Alexander VI's bulls giving the territories "discovered" by Columbus to Spain made Christian mission a synonym of conquest and domination. The *encomienda** system organizing both Christian evangelization and exploitation of native groups resulted in the almost total annihilation of Amerindians. Under the banner of Christian evangelization, converted Caribbean Amerindians were enslaved, exploited, and killed.

Nevertheless, some Roman Catholic friars lifted their prophetic voices against the exploitation of the natives. Antonio de Montesinos's sermons powerfully raised the issue of justice*, inspired Bartolomé de las* Casas, "defender of the Indians," and anticipated the Valladolid* debate concerning whether Amerindians had souls* (if not, they could be enslaved).

With the genocide of natives, Africans were violently brought as slaves* to sugar and cotton plantations. The dominant mission theology and practice continued: "saving souls while keeping bodies in shackles." Nevertheless, the Jesuit Alonso de Sandoval resisted the treatment of slaves, promoted the use of African languages by Christianized African slaves, and developed a new missiology toward them, *De Instauranda Aethiopum Salute.*

Until Vatican* II, the Roman Catholic mission theologies and practices generally remained the same: serving the interest of the powerful and rich, with tenuous critical voices reminding the Church of its sinful interests. With Vatican II and the development of ecumenical emancipation theologies, mission theologies became more concerned with social justice and the Afro-Caribbean character of Christianity in the region. Since the late 20th c., the Caribbean Roman Catholic Church has actively participated in the ecumenical Caribbean Conference of Churches, which developed theologies of religion, cultures*, and emancipation.

In the early 17th c., Protestantism arrived in the Southern Caribbean, where the British and the Dutch, first through pirates and later through missionaries, brought a similar gospel of "saving souls and keeping bodies in shackles." In the late 19th and early 20th c. in the Latin Caribbean, missionaries from the USA preached a gospel emphasizing education*, social services, and the promotion of US-style democracy* and capitalism.

By contrast the African* Methodist Episcopal Church's missionary work in the Dominican* Republic and Haiti* and Puerto* Rican missionaries in the Dominican* Republic encouraged, respectively, a Protestant Afro-Caribbean identity and the development of a national Protestant church, La Iglesia Evangélica Dominicana.

Starting in the early 20th c., Pentecostal* and Charismatic* mission theologies and practices varied as Caribbean Pentecostals/Charismatics created a collage of conservative, "saving souls" mission practices and social justice concerns that breaks down traditional theological structures.

In tension with the inherited Iberian Catholic and European/North American Protestant and Pentecostal/Charismatic theologies and practices, current Christian mission in the Caribbean is discovering its own agency and vitality based on its Amerindian–African–European/North American cultural and religious heritage. Mission focuses on both preaching the gospel for the unsaved and engaging in social justice and the emancipation, liberation, and reconciliation of the Caribbean people. It struggles with Afro-Caribbean religions, once identified as demonic*, while developing strong ecumenical* and interfaith programs and searching for an Afro-Caribbean Christian identity.

This "reversal" of mission theology, which involves cross-cultural, cross-religious perspectives, also brings about a "reversal" of mission practice as Caribbean missionaries go to other parts of the world.

CARLOS F. CARDOZA-ORLANDI

Mission in Europe: Germany. From the time of the Crusades*, the task of spreading the gospel was viewed in Germany* as primarily incumbent on the mendicant* orders, later the Jesuits*, and frequently in cooperation with colonial expansion. Important missionary instructions emanated from the Congregatio de Propaganda* Fide in Rome (from the 17th c.).

For the Protestant Reformers, mission was not initially an urgent concern, because Christ's return was expected in the near future. But in the 18th c., Francke* and Zinzendorf* took up the idea of mission. Protestant missions fully developed in the 19th c. under the influence of the German Awakening through missionary associations and societies. For example, Louis Harms trained at the Hermannsburg Missionary Institute the first "messengers of faith" sent to Africa (1853). They planted Lutheran theology, piety, and church organization in the native African cultures following the program of accommodation and indigenization typical of colonial times (organized at the Berlin* Conference, 1884–85).

Meanwhile, to combat more effectively the social misery caused by 19th-c. industrialization, Wichern* in a historic speech at the Wittenberg Kirchentag* (1848) called the Protestant churches to address the "social question" through the Inner* Mission," which would complement "foreign mission" and coordinate private and church initiatives. For Wichern lack of faith and moral decline were the major causes of the social crisis; he thus combined mission and social assistance, and a network of social relief institutions was established all over Germany.

With the end of colonialism and the formation of autochthonous churches (1960s) throughout the world, the methods and goals of mission fundamentally changed. Contextualization* and inculturation* are now the guiding concepts for the German churches' support of Two-thirds World churches, a support offered in the spirit of partnership that ought to characterize the propagation of Christianity in other religious, sociocultural, and political contexts. In this process, preaching and instruction are just as important as medical, diaconal, and social involvement advocated by missionaries such as Albert Schweitzer*. Since World War II, Protestant mission has focused primarily on supporting the development of existing churches (rather than opening new missionary fields). Following Vatican II, German Catholic missionary practice similarly emphasizes dialogue and partnership. German missions participated in the ecumenical movement, which arose from national and international unions and conferences that sought to unify mission efforts and, in the process, led to the founding of the World* Council of Churches in 1948. **See also GERMANY.**

INGE MAGER

Mission in Europe: Post-Communist Eastern Europe. The most crucial and controversial issue of missions in post-Communist Eastern Europe concerns the level and nature of the involvement of Western churches in the lands traditionally dominated by Orthodox or Roman Catholic state* churches. Although the degree of religious practice differs from country to country across the region, except in the mostly secularized Czech* Republic and former East Germany*, most people in other nations claim allegiance to the dominant religious confession, considering it constitutive of their national and cultural identity. The demise of totalitarian states and discrediting of the imposed Communist ideologies and their atheistic worldviews has thus in most nations been accompanied by a resurgence of the old national but suppressed legacy of religious pride, now emphasized in the new nation-building processes. Ethnoreligious homogenization has been encouraged by the new rulers, who have deliberately empowered the old national churches at the expense of religious minorities and placed restrictions on foreign missionary work.

Many of the Western Evangelical* and Charismatic* mission agencies saw the demise of Communism as a providential opening of long-closed mission fields and took advantage of the immediate post-Communist era of anarchy and spiritual confusion. Lacking proper cultural and ecumenical sensitivities and disregarding the long presence of the Christian faith in these nations, they aggressively promoted Western individualistic concepts of conversion* and church planting. Their claims of doing Evangelism in areas long dominated by godless Communism have been perceived in most cases, however, as threats to national and cultural identity and as needless proselytizing in territories Christianized for centuries. Rare cooperative partnerships between Western mission agencies and national Orthodox and/or Roman Catholic churches, initially conceived as ecumenical support aimed at their internal renewal, did not bear much lasting fruit and were in most cases dissolved under the suspicion that the underlying intention of all Western missionary efforts in Eastern Europe was to win converts away from their ethnoreligious roots (see Proselytism). Some of the Western, mostly North American missionaries and a surprising number of Korean* missionaries continue to operate from the conviction that traditional confessions are moribund, compromised, and spiritually deficient because they do not take personal faith* and Christian morality seriously.

The growth of mutual distrust, confusion, and antagonism is due mostly to differences in ecclesiology and divergences between Orthodox, Roman Catholic, and Evangelical concepts and models of ministry* and missionary activity. On the Protestant Evangelical side, the problems are compounded by disturbed relationships, missionary competitiveness, and a plethora of new denominations and independent churches.

PETER KUZMIC

Mission in Latin America: Catholic Mission in Brazil

Indigenous Peoples and Missionaries during the Colonial Period in Brazil. Beginning in 1549, Jesuit* priests Nobrega and Anchieta worked together with the Portuguese* authorities to colonize their territory in Latin America. They first settled in the central Bahia province of Brazil among the Tupi-Guarani, then (18th c.) moved farther north (Belém) and south (São Paulo). Mastering the different native languages served both the efforts to keep the indigenous peoples under control as laborers and to convert them, laying the foundations for mission stations and "reductions*." The Jesuits' defense of the "Indians' freedom" and their position against slavery* resulted in their expulsion from São Paulo, Belém, and other regions and in attacks against the mission stations and reductions in the south. In 1654 Fr. Viera succeeded in obtaining laws protecting the mission stations and reductions, which granted autonomy to the missionaries and controlled the enslavement of indigenous peoples. When the Jesuits lost their influence before Portuguese courts, their opponents, the Bandeirantes (members of an armed militia of early settlers) and proslavery partisans increased. Having reached an agreement with the colonial authorities, the Jesuits shared the missionary work with Carmelite*, Franciscan*, Mercedarian, and other religious orders. Nonetheless, the Jesuits lost favor in Lisbon (1759) and were expelled from Brazil.

Mission and Indigenous Peoples' Cultures, 19th and 20th Centuries. During this period, indigenous peoples of the northern and western regions of Brazil had an experience similar to that of the populations of the coastal areas during the preceding centuries: they encountered colonization* and its enormous potential for destruction. Colonization was justified as a means of facilitating progress and of exploiting natural resources that were deemed necessary for development. For many indigenous peoples, contact with whites meant extinction or marginal survival. As in earlier centuries and until the 1960s, the Catholic missions of the Salesians*, Capuchins*, and Dominicans* continued to impose a Christianity that demanded acculturation and disregard for the religious practices of indigenous people. Influenced by Vatican* II, the 1968 Latin American Episcopal Conference (CELAM*) fought to protect indigenous populations with the support of defenders of indigenous peoples and many missionaries who denounced massacres. Ultimately CELAM founded the Indigenous Missionary Council (1972). Catechetical instruction was revised to protect the life and culture of the indigenous populations, thus setting a new standard for evangelization.

FERNANDO TORRES-LONDOÑO

Mission in Latin America: Catholic Mission in Mexico. When Tenochtítlan, the Nahuatl city-state, was defeated and colonized, three Franciscans asked permission from Pope Leo X to evangelize the populations. The pope promulgated the bull *Alias Felicis Recordationis* (1521), which granted to the missionaries full ecclesiastical authority over their mission territories, and even over priests. For the Franciscans, this opened the door to the pursuit of their "Franciscan utopia" (see Mexico). With the next pope, Adrian VI (1521–23), the missionary friars were organized under the authority of Franciscan provincials, and the first 12 missionaries came to Mexico (1524) charged with "catechizing" and "indoctrinating" indigenous peoples.

The 12 missionaries constructed church buildings, learned the languages, and translated catechisms and creeds, pursuing their Franciscan inculturation* projects. Other religious orders – Dominicans (1526), Augustinians (1533), and Jesuits (1572) – soon arrived to help with this complex task, settling in different parts of the territory. After these missionary inroads were made, parishes and convents were established from Central America to California in order to deepen the evangelization and education of indigenous, Spanish, and mestizo* people. The growth of the missions was due in part to their economic importance, resulting from the prosperity of their landholdings, which provided surpluses to support new missions.

In the 17th c., Rome again took control of missionary activities by creating the Congregation for the Propagation of the Faith. The Franciscans founded colleges for the Propagation of the Faith – first that of Santa Cruz de Querétaro (1682), then those of the Sierra Gorda led by Friar Antonio Margil de Jesús – to prepare new missionaries and to revitalize evangelism, especially in the northern part of Mexico. This missionary effort coincided with the Jesuits' missions of Sonora, Sinaloa, and California, led by Eusebio Kino, SJ. After the Mexican independence, missions were run in vastly different ways; some were abandoned or destroyed, while other became church buildings.

At present several dioceses have developed a special pastoral activity toward indigenous people following the directives of Vatican* II. In Mexico religious orders and congregations now promote the *missio ad intra* (internal mission) in many regions with an indigenous population. This is a pastoral activity that presupposes a faith already preached and accepted, and that aims at bringing to maturation the faith of believers, including their sanctification (through the sacraments). Yet these religious groups also pursue the *missio ad gentes* or *ad extra,* bringing the gospel to diverse parts of the world, even to regions (and indigenous churches) that have already been evangelized. CLODOMIRO SILLER

Mission in North America: Mission as Conquest. The conversion of "Indian" peoples to Christianity began almost from the beginning of the European invasion of the Americas. Such conversions were invariably coerced, always involving the intense political, economic, and social pressure of colonial governments and most often persistently supported by or under the constant threat of colonial military intervention. The first missionary to enter any native community immediately divided that community against itself, to the advantage of the colonial political establishment, forcing an individualist choice between self and the ceremonial and spiritual unity of the community.

Roman Catholic missions in North America followed the paradigm of mission work already developed in Latin America. While Dominicans (eventually including Bartolomé de las* Casas) arrived early in the Caribbean* and worked to bring some sense of justice* to native peoples there, the strategy of Hernán Cortés defined centuries of European colonialism*. Upon dislodging the Aztec government in a murderous war, Cortés imported Franciscan* missionaries explicitly to assist in the pacification of Mexico. This model – rather than the Dominican and las Casian model – became the rule.

In North America, Catholic missionaries worked consistently as agents of the conquering colonial administration in French and British Canada. In territories claimed by the USA, Jesuit missionary Pierre-Jean DeSmet pursued missionary expansion under a non-Catholic colonial government, and yet made himself very useful to the US military in convincing Indian peoples to sign treaties that greatly favored the colonial invaders. Catholic schools became persuasive in implanting a Euro-value system in young Indian children in the 19th and 20th c. (according to the European calendar) and equally so in their attempts to destroy Indian cultural systems – from Indian family* systems to structures of self-governance that had functioned in Indian communities for multiple generations.

The early Protestant paradigm followed the Catholic model; e.g. the "praying towns" in New England were very similar to the mission compounds and "reductions*" (*reducciones*) in Latin America. In the 1640s, John Eliot worked in the direct hire of the Massachusetts General Council. The model shifted when colonial governments began to move toward disestablishment and a separation of church* and state (18th–19th c.). Missionary endeavors became more directly related to their colonial governments in the USA, as elsewhere. It was more than a coincidence that Episcopal missionary Bishop Henry Benjamin Whipple became a key US government functionary on an important commission dedicated to negotiating the total submission of Lakota Sioux peoples to US hegemony (1870s). The commitment of these missionaries to a cultural*conversion of Indian peoples to a Euro-Western worldview and value system (and not merely a religious conversion to Jesus) can be clearly traced even in the more heroic story of missionary resistance to the US federal government removal plan (1830s) when Samuel Worcester and Elizur Butler spent time in a Georgia state prison to voice their objections to the removal of the Cherokees.

GEORGE E. "TINK" TINKER

Mission in the South Pacific. Missions began in 1797 in the Society Islands, through the London Missionary Society, which believed that its goal was to rescue the heathen from damnation and civilize them through conversion* and repudiation of their religious and cultural heritage. Wesleyans* held similar views, as did the French Picpus and Marist* Fathers, who were also anxious to establish the true church.

London Missionary workers believed that their converts should develop their own churches and skillfully used local Christians as missionaries. The resulting converts incorporated Christianity into Polynesian political patterns, built large churches, and enthusiastically adopted literacy and European technology. Protestant–Catholic rivalries led to some religious wars. Leading chiefs were fascinated by Hebrew models of kingship. Missionaries advised chiefs on Christian laws and communities as alternatives to historical religious bases and ethical boundaries.

Progressively Catholic missionaries took a more gradualist approach. Bishops Pompallier and Navarre issued important guidelines dealing with cultural differences. Protestants' theology of the Word led them to emphasize translation into local languages, the education of indigenous pastors, and strict discipline.

Work in Melanesia was much more difficult. Apart from some success in New Caledonia, the Solomons, and New Hebrides, it was not until the 1880s that sustained attempts were made to evangelize newly colonized Papua* New Guinea. Experience in Polynesia enabled missionaries to avoid earlier mistakes. French Sacred Heart and German Divine Word fathers sought contact points with tribal cultures as a basis for Christian proclamation. The periodical *Anthropos* (1906–) published articles about this, based on the fledging discipline of anthropology. In New Caledonia, the notable French Protestant missiologist M. Leenhardt explored Kanak culture at great depth from 1902 to 1926. German Lutherans like C. Keysser rejected individual conversions*, arguing for baptism* only when the tribe as a whole was ready. These theological and practical changes were important for planting churches in the New Guinea highlands. All missions agreed on the need for indigenous churches, apart from sectarian Protestant groups that were still operating with early 19th-c. evangelistic paradigms and rejecting traditional cultures. The emergence of movements combining Melanesian and Christian motifs made vital the wise assessment of remaining tribal culture. The ecumenical Melanesian Institute (established in 1968), played a vital missiological role, although it did not reach many pastors, whose traditional theology of mission was shaped by tribal rivalries. Liberation from wars and from fear of witchcraft* or demon* possession has been important for Pacific Christians, but conservative interpretations of village unity have often been authoritarian, restrictive, and unhelpful in urban contexts despite the value of communal mission. IAN BREWARD

Mit Brennender Sorge (German, "with burning concern"), encyclical of Pius* XI, smuggled across the Alps and read from all Roman Catholic pulpits in Germany on Palm* Sunday (March 21, 1937), denouncing violations of the 1933 Concordat* between Germany and the Vatican, the abolition of the OT from the schools, and other features of the Nazi regime and the German* Christian Movement.

Miter, headdress worn by a bishop on solemn occasions, removed during prayers; used since the 11th c. in the West and since the fall of Constantinople (1453) in the East.

Mithraism and Christianity. Mithraism was one of the Greco-Roman mystery* religions that existed during the Roman Empire. One of the several stages of initiation into the mysteries of Mithras apparently involved a sacred meal of bread and water (or water and wine). According to Tertullian*, initiates may also have joined in lustrations. Justin* Martyr, conceding that the Mithraic sacred meal resembled the Christian Eucharist*, viewed the former as a diabolical imitation of the Christian meal. The Mithraic view of salvation* (shedding eternal blood, being piously reborn and created) recalls Christian formulations; the central image of the Mithraic sanctuary, Mithras slaying the bull, is reminiscent of the central place of the crucifixion* and sacrifice* of Christ within Christianity. Avoiding simplistic notions of dependence of one tradition on the other, scholars usually view the development of religions in late antiquity as interdependent. MARVIN MEYER

Mixed Cup, water mixed with eucharistic wine; an ancient practice, disapproved of by the Armenian* Church, Puritans*, and Evangelicals of the Church of England; championed by Anglo-Catholics.

Mixed Marriage, marriage between a Christian and an unbaptized person or between Christians of different churches or denominations.

Modalism, belief that the Trinity* merely represents three modes of operation by a single being (see Monarchians; Patripassianism*; Sabellianism*). The language of baptism formulas that attempt to avoid gendered terms (Father, Son) by using "Creator," "Redeemer," "Sustainer" is deemed modalist.

Modernism, Roman Catholic (1890–1907) was a late-19th- and early-20th-c. movement of English and Continental Roman Catholic scholars who wrestled with questions posed by modernity. Modernism, an originally pejorative name, designated an intellectual orientation of Christians who attempted to incorporate the results of historical criticism and the sciences into contemporary theology. Exchange among Catholic and Protestant biblical scholars, theologians, and philosophers was facilitated by Friedrich von* Hügel, who played a role in bringing together work by scholars in England, France, Italy, and Germany. The movement was condemned in 1907 by Pope Pius X as "a synthesis of errors" and a serious threat to the unity, orthodoxy, and stability of the church. Two documents, a list of errors (*Lamentabili*) and an encyclical (*Pascendi*) culled ideas from the writings of Loisy*, Tyrrell*, von* Hügel, Petre*, Ernesto Buonaiuti, and others to systemize the movement under the name "Modernism." The remedies prescribed to overcome Modernism were severely restrictive of biblical interpretation and theology. Viewed in its historical context, Modernism can be interpreted as a movement for renewal within Catholicism that offered an alternative to the liberal Protestant outlook and in some ways anticipated the Second Vatican* Council.

ELLEN M. LEONARD, CSJ

Mogila, Peter. See MOHILA, PETER.

Mohila, Peter (1596–1647) ("Mogila" in Russian; "Movila" in Moldavian-Romanian; "Mohila" in Ukrainian), Moldavian Orthodox monk, theologian, metropolitan of Kiev, author of the *Orthodox Confession of Faith*; son of the Moldavian prince Simeon and the Hungarian princess Marguerita. Peter was educated in what was then the Polish Ukraine, probably at, among other places, the Brotherhood School in Lviv, Ukraine; the site of his more advanced education is disputed (perhaps the University of Paris or the Jesuit school in Kraków, Poland).

The young Peter Mogila had a military career (from 1616) under the patronage of the Polish crown (battling the Russians with the Hetman [military commander] and Chancellor Stanislav Zholkiwski, then battling the Turks with the Hetman Jan Carl Chodkiewych). Turning to spiritual warfare, Peter entered the Monastery of the Caves (Pechersky Lavra) in Kiev, Ukraine (August 1627), becoming its archimandrite* (superior; Christmas 1627). In 1631 he founded the Monastery Academy, the first such institution of higher learning in Eastern Europe.

Elected, appointed, and consecrated as the metropolitan of Kiev (1632), he ruled with a fierce independence until his death. He led the struggle to reclaim for the Monastery Academy former monastic properties around Kiev that landowners had appropriated during prior regimes. Yet his 15-year tenure was devoted primarily to a threefold mission: education of both clergy and laity, uniformity of liturgical books and services, and the unification of all Christians. This noble undertaking can be vividly seen in his masterwork, "The Orthodox Confession of Faith" (1640), intended to present the main tenets of Orthodox theology over against Roman Catholic and Protestant claims.

Composed in Kiev, most likely in Polish, the "Confession" was translated into Latin and presented in 1642 to a church council in Jassy, Moldavia, for approval by the Greek Church. Theologian Meletios Syrigos translated the text into Greek with some minor emendations and sent the "Confession" to Constantinople for the patriarchal seal of approval. It was sealed and signed (1643) as a canonical work of the Eastern Church by Patriarch Parthenios of Constantinople, Patriarch Joannikios of Alexandria, Patriarch Paisios of Jerusalem, and Patriarch Makarios of Antioch.

The tripartite "Confession" has a question-and-answer format. Part One concerns the faith and is based on the Niceno-Constantinopolitan Creed. Part Two concerns hope and is based on the Lord's Prayer, the beatitudes, and works of mercy. Part Three focuses on charity and is based on the Christian virtues and the Ten Commandments. RONALD POPIVCHAK

Möhler, Johann Adam (1796–1838), Roman Catholic priest, historian, theologian, preeminent figure of the Catholic Tübingen school of theology in Germany. He was influenced by German romanticism and its sense of history's evolving organic wholeness, as reflected in Hegel's* and Schelling's* idealism. In *The Unity of the Church or the Principles of Catholicism* (1825), Möhler begins not with defined doctrine but historically with the inner, living, evolving church, guided by the presence of the Holy Spirit*. The church "forms itself from inward out" through the spiritual convictions and needs of the Christian community. The church's consciousness is collective and communal, the test of faith being its identity with this consciousness. In *Symbolics or Presentation of the Dogmatic Differences of Catholics and Protestants* (1832), Möhler speaks of the Catholic bishops and hierarchy as emerging "from below" out of the life of the faithful and of the pope's primacy as symbolizing this unity of the Roman Catholic Church. Möhler contrasts a genuine Catholic theology with both Protestant individualism and its *sola* scriptura* doctrine and the Council of Trent's* (1545–63) dependence on external tradition and authority. Möhler's theology, revived after World War II, influenced the theology of the Second Vatican* Council (1962–65). JAMES C. LIVINGSTON

Mokone, Mangena (1851–1936), father of the African* Instituted Church movement known as Ethiopianism (1892). He was a Methodist minister, as well as the founder and a staff member of the Kilnerton Training Institution in Pretoria. As a lecturer, he experienced racial discrimination and differential treatment, which led to his leaving the Institution and founding his own church. **See also HISTORY OF CHRISTIANITY IN AFRICA; SOUTH AFRICA.** MOKGETHI MOTLHABI

Moldova Republic (or Basarabia), largely Orthodox*, is closely related to Romania*, with which it shares parts of its history.

Christianity has been in the region since the 3rd c. and developed as a part of the Romanian Church. When Moldova was under the Kievan Rus (10th–12th c.), the Orthodox Church was further implanted. The Hungarians, victorious in a battle against the Tatars, brought Roman Catholicism into Moldova (14th c.). But after 1382, with the Musat House reigning over the principality, Eastern Orthodoxy became once again the main church, although the independent-minded Moldavians were soon in tension with the Constantinople Patriarchate. Stephen III the Great (c1457–1504) long resisted the Ottomans and was hailed as "true champion of Christian faith," although he finally submitted to them; he is honored as a saint and supported monasticism* (including Mount Athos*). Other religions were tolerated (with sizable German and Hungarian Roman Catholic communities, as well as Armenians* and, after 1460, Hussite* refugees).

In 1812 Moldova was incorporated into the Russian political sphere, while the Eastern Orthodox Church remained under the jurisdiction of the Patriarchate of Romania until 1940, when it was placed under the jurisdiction of the Patriarchate of Moscow; since the 1990s, there have been attempts to bring the Church back under Romanian jurisdiction. The Eastern Orthodox Church among the Gagauz (people in Southern Moldova, whose Turkic language was adopted during the Ottoman rule) has closer links with the Greek Orthodox Church.

The Moldavian Orthodox Church follows the revised Julian calendar* (since 1923, also adopted by the Romanian Church but rejected by the Russian Church). Accordingly, all the holidays, including Christmas, coincide with Western holidays. Yet the major holiday, the Orthodox Pascha, or Easter*, is celebrated according to the Julian calendar.

Moldavian Orthodox Christians are tolerant of other Christians and other religions, including Islam*. They follow the tradition inherited from Romanian and Russian Orthodoxy. Thus as a sign of appreciation and respect, the young kiss the hands of older men and women. They read the OT following the Septuagint* version and are deeply immersed in patristic and mystic literature (emphasizing Russian mystic literature since 1940). These are emphasized in the theological education offered at the Theological Academy from Chisinau, where men can prepare for the priesthood, and women for the license in theology leading to teaching positions. Laypeople are active in church choral music, usually polyphony in local dialect and Russian.

Statistics: Population (2007): 4.4 million (M). Christians, 69% (Orthodox, 2.6 M [including Gagauz Orthodox]; independents, 0.3 M; Protestants, 0.1 M; Roman Catholics, 0.07 M),

Muslims (primarily Gagauz people), 5%; Jews, 1%; nonreligious, 25%. (Based on *World Christian Encyclopedia*, 2001, and United Nations: World Population Prospects, 2008.)

ILIE MELNICIUC-PUICA

Molina, Luis de (1535–1600), Spanish Jesuit* theologian. His *Concordia Liberi Arbitrii cum Gratiae Donis* (1588) argued that grace* is efficacious not "intrinsically" but through God's middle* knowledge, i.e. God's foreknowledge of what human beings "would do" and the preparation of appropriate inducements to which they freely but infallibly respond. **See also COMPATIBILISM; JANSENISM; MORAL INFLUENCE.**

Molinos, Miguel de (c1628–c1696). Born in Teruel (Valencia), he entered the priesthood and went to Rome (1663), where he counted among his friends Cardinal Odescalchi, who became (1676) Pope Innocent XI. Molinos is remembered chiefly for his popular book on prayer, *La guía espiritual* (*The Spiritual Guide*, English ed.), a guide to the interior life of prayer and the "progress to perfection." Enormously popular, the book was condemned (1687) for a number of errors later collected in the papal bull *Coelestis Pastor* (1688) under the general term "Quietism*." Condemned to life imprisonment, Molinos died in the prison of the Holy Office. The book, prohibited and placed on the List of Prohibited Books (*Index* Librorum Prohibitorum*), is a readable enough guide to the spiritual life. But its emphasis on the division between "inner" and "outer" and its deemphasis on the role of Jesus in the spiritual life explains why it would not find favor in the Roman Catholic Church. A chapter entitled "Excessive Love and Fervor for Others Can Destroy Inner Peace" (2.3) and advice on how we need detachment from "God himself" (3.18) are reminiscent of the problems faced by the interpreters of Meister Eckhart* three centuries earlier.

PETER TYLER

Monarchians, those who deny that God is a trinity*. In the 2nd and 3rd c., this position grew out of fear that the Logos* doctrine was polytheistic. Modalistic* Monarchianism, or Sabellianism*, claimed that the Trinity is simply three different modes of God's acting toward the world (creation*, redemption*, sanctification*). Adoptionism* was another form, asserting that Jesus was merely the recipient of divine energies. A third position, anticipating Arianism*, stated that only the Father is truly God, the Son* and Spirit* being creatures.

MONASTICISM CLUSTER

1) *Introductory Entries*

2) *A Sampling of Monastic Traditions*

1) Introductory Entries

Monasticism a form of Christian life characterized by ascetic practices, including frequent prayer, renunciation of material goods, celibacy, and some degree of separation from society. As a recognizable movement, monasticism emerged from the various traditions of Christian asceticism* (early 4th c.), most notably in Egypt*, where the terrain lent itself to sharp distinctions between settled areas and the desert regions that came to be associated with the new form of asceticism. Egypt produced two models of monastic life, communal (cenobitic*) and solitary (eremitic*), although the practices were similar, and solitaries formed loose communities around a spiritual guide. The exemplar of eremitic monasticism was Antony the Great (c254–356), whose biography (written in Greek, soon translated into Latin) circulated throughout the Mediterranean world. The key early figure in cenobitic monasticism was Pachomius* (c292–346), whose biography and writings were translated from Coptic into Greek and partially into Latin.

Similar patterns of life were soon evident in Palestine and elsewhere, often overlying more ancient forms of Christian asceticism such as consecrated virginity*. The Egyptian model, disseminated through hagiography, spiritual writings, and traveling monks, found favor among bishops for its emphasis on discipline and loyalty to the episcopate. In regions with strong native ascetic* traditions (e.g. Syria/Mesopotamia), the Egyptian model had a less immediate impact, although it influenced later development and eventually entirely replaced the native ascetic model. Monastically inclined bishops, e.g. the Cappadocian* Basil* of Caesara (c330–79), fostered the development and regulation of monasticism in their regions, creating their own syntheses of the ascetic and monastic traditions.

In the West, translations of Egyptian and other monastic texts into Latin and the creation of Western monastic rules (with content strongly influenced by the Egyptian tradition) led to the replacement of less organized forms of ascetic/monastic life (e.g. that of Martin* of Tours, 317–97, in Gaul) by the more structured models favored by John Cassian* (c365–c435) and his episcopal patrons. In Latin Africa, with a strong native tradition of ascetic practice, Augustine* (354–430) embraced communal monastic life (influenced by, but not directly patterned on, the Egyptian model) and provided an ordered, recognizably monastic form of asceticism.

In the 5th c., monasticism in its various forms, communal and individual, became the dominant ascetic paradigm for both men and women throughout the Christian world. This dominance was encouraged by bishops who had been monks or who saw monasticism as a means of easing tensions between ascetic movements with their nonhierarchical structure and the institutional church. As a clearly defined way of life subject to episcopal regulation, monasticism provided an approved outlet for ascetic inclinations and came to play a vital ecclesiastical and social function in both eastern and western Mediterranean regions. With the requirement (from the 4th–5th c.) that bishops be unmarried, monasteries provided the leadership for the church, further strengthening monastic and episcopal ties.

The communal (cenobitic) form of life, by far the most prevalent form of monasticism, drew inspiration from the lives of renowned hermits while providing a more stable and secure environment. In the West, monasticism has been traditionally associated with Benedict* of Nursia (c480–c540), whose "Rule for Monks" drew from several previous rules and other spiritual texts. Benedict's interpretation of the monastic tradition slowly became predominant over 300 years, greatly aided by its adoption (early 9th c.) as a tool for monastic reform in the Frankish kingdom (see Louis I, "the Pious"). Benedictine monasticism experienced several waves of renewal and reform, most notably with the 12th-c. rise of the Cistercian Movement with its appeal to a more primitive observance of the Rule. The Islamic conquest of the Middle East and, eventually, of the rest of the Byzantine Empire was a great blow to Eastern monasticism. Even so, great centers of Greek monastic life, such as Mar Saba (Palestine), Mount Athos* (Macedonia), and the Studion (Constantinople), codified monastic practices and established liturgical customs that became universal throughout the Orthodox* churches (both Greek and Slavic).

Among Eastern Christians, monasticism has remained the dominant paradigm for nonmarried vowed life. In the Western Church, new forms of vowed life appeared with the Franciscans* and Dominicans* (12th c.), and later (16th c.) the Jesuits*. But these should not be confused with actual monasticism. In the modern era, Western monasticism was severely affected by the French Revolution and its aftereffects in Germany and Austria, although it revived (mid 19th c.) and spread to North America, Africa, and Asia. After a great flowering (19th c.), monasticism in the Slavic world was devastated by the 1917 Russian Revolution and the spread of Communism after World War II, but revived after the collapse of the Soviet Union. There was a monastic revival in Egypt and on Mount Athos* (late 20th c.). Among Armenians* the genocide* in Turkish Armenia (early 20th c.), combined with Soviet rule in Eastern Armenia, effectively destroyed monastic life for men, while it continues in a greatly diminished form for women. Syriac monasticism in the Middle East suffered similarly, with early indications of a revival, especially in India and among

Syriac Christian emigrant communities in Europe.

The basic pattern of monastic life has been universal throughout Christian history and across geographic and cultural divides. Daily communal prayer at regular intervals, normally including a nocturnal vigil, is the fundamental obligation and marker of the monastic life. Traditionally, monastic prayer has consisted largely of sung or recited psalms, accompanied by readings from other parts of the Bible, and hymns. Dietary restrictions such as fasting and abstinence from meat or other animal products are typical, especially on certain days and during liturgical seasons of penance*. Monks and nuns have been distinguished from nonmonastic Christians by their dress – a difference evident even in the early period of monastic life when the form of monastic dress more closely resembled conventional clothing. In the West, monks tended to have shorn hair, normally with a distinctive cut (tonsure), while in the East hair and beard were typically left untrimmed. In both East and West, following prevailing cultural norms, monastic women were veiled, although some now dispense with the veil.

Monasticism exists as an expression of baptismal* commitment, with an additional formal commitment to the monastic life through vows. The form and understanding of monastic* vows have varied greatly, but the fundamental obligations to monastic practices, including celibacy*, renunciation of private property*, and obedience to a spiritual father or mother, are universal, as is the concept of permanent commitment. In the medieval West, monasticism came to be divided into different groups according to the foundational figure or rule followed by certain communities. The concept of "order" remains ambiguous among Benedictines with their decentralized structure and has never been characteristic of the Christian East, where monasticism is understood to be a way of life that follows various patterns but is not subdivided into canonically distinct groups.

Monks and nuns have been regarded as intermediaries and intercessors, providing counsel and spiritual assistance. Monasteries became providers of social services, receiving abandoned infants and orphans, caring for the sick, offering material provisions to those in need, and providing hospitality to pilgrims and travelers. Monks and nuns are typically literate and have served as educators both within and outside of their monasteries. With their traditional orientation, monasteries have normally been conservative forces in the church and have sometimes viewed themselves as defenders of doctrines or customs in times threatened by change. The emphasis on education characteristic of monastic life meant that monks and nuns have often played vital roles in spiritual and liturgical renewal. The biblical and liturgical basis of monastic life has provided inspiration to many who are not formally monastic and served as a bridge across ecclesiastical divides: monasticism predates the division between the Latin West and most of the Eastern churches and the 16th-c. breakup of Western Christianity into Protestant and Catholic forms. **See also RELIGIOUS ORDERS, ROMAN CATHOLIC, CLUSTER.**

COLUMBA STEWART, OSB

Monasticism: Monastery. Place of residence of a community of monks* or nuns*, who are secluded from the world and live under monastic vows. Double* monasteries include both men and women, living separately but with a common superior. In addition, triple monasteries include a house for tertiaries* associated with the mendicant* orders. **See also HIEROTOPY, THE CREATION OF CHRISTIAN SACRED SPACES.**

Monasticism: Monastic Rules (Lat *regula*, "rule"; hence "regular* life" and "regular clergy"), documents setting out the regulations for leading a monastic life.

The earliest Christian monks did not live by specific written codifications: the fathers of the Egyptian desert passed on their wisdom to their disciples by example and their teaching, which was eventually set down in the *Apophthegmata* Patrum*.

With the rise of communal monasticism, more detailed and specific regulations were produced by the communities of Pachomius* and in Cappadocia by Basil* of Caesarea, who was always influential in the East and seems to have been widely followed in the 5th-c. West. Augustine* produced a short rule capable of being used by both monks and nuns (390s). Bishop Caesarius composed a lengthy rule for the women of his nunnery in Arles (c512–534). The most sophisticated and integrated Western monastic rule was created by Benedict* of Nursia c550; half a century later, Columbanus's* Monastic Rule attempted a brief encapsulation of Irish tradition, apparently influenced primarily by Cassian* and Basil; the surviving monastic rules from Ireland are later creations. The period of the "mixed rules" in the West (7th c.) saw the combination of sections from the rules of Benedict, Columbanus, Caesarius, and others to meet the needs of aristocratic family monasteries. The Iberian Peninsula produced distinctive texts to meet its own sociopolitical circumstances.

By the early 9th c., the Carolingian Empire had decreed that monasteries were to follow the Rule of Benedict*; however, the increasing complexity of liturgy and the multiplication of monasteries led to its being accompanied by the "customs" and "uses" of individual monasteries and sets of accompanying regulations. This was paralleled by the formation of the Studite Constitutions in the Byzantine Empire, where, however, rules and orders did not conform to the Western pattern. The 11th and 12th c. saw an attempt in Western Europe to return to the ideas and rules of the desert fathers and early monasticism.

Monastic rules represent a move toward structure and organization and underpin the formation of Western monastic orders. The tension between spontaneity and organization is demonstrated by the difficulties experienced by the charismatic monastic leader Francis* of Assisi when asked by the Roman Catholic Church to set down a monastic rule for his growing order (1220s). MARILYN DUNN

Monasticism: Monastic Vows, promises typically made in a liturgical setting to undertake the obligations particular to the monastic life: obedience to a rule of life and a superior, celibacy*, and the renunciation of property*. To these are added in some traditions a commitment to a particular monastic community.

COLUMBA STEWART, OSB

---

2) A Sampling of Monastic Traditions

Monasticism in the Byzantine Empire. Monasticism may have begun in the Byzantine* Empire (330–1453) as a movement of withdrawal among the laity*, a secession from the cities of late antiquity in order to live a simplified life in the hinterland; but almost simultaneously many of these ostensible solitaries occupied the highest positions in the church, claiming the roles of bishops and priests that, by their very nature, were urban and political offices (Sterk). Within a few hundred years, this movement of withdrawal had been so successful that it transformed the nature of Christian leadership into a predominantly ascetic* endeavor. Although the rhetoric of monastic sources stresses the role of monasticism apart from society, monasticism played important political functions within the Byzantine experience, not least after the 10th c., when monasteries were significant landowners. In the middle Byzantine Era perhaps half the literate class of the Empire consisted of monks. This accounts for the wholesale glorification of the ascetic imperative in Eastern Christianity. The Byzantines (who were so adept at, and who delighted in, paradoxes) soon perfected the idea of the "city monk," the "cosmopolitan hermit." The image of emperors seeking advice on intimate matters of state policy from the leading ascetics of the day is not merely a rhetorical trope.

Monasteries made their appearance relatively early in Constantinople. The first was the community of Dalmatou built by the senator Saturninos for the Syrian monk Isaac (382). At first the ascetic houses were a ring of suburban "retreats," but as the capital expanded, these came to be embedded in almost every part of town; thus Constantinople became a veritable "city of monasteries" (Janin, Dagron, Charanis, Talbot). In 430, when Archbishop Nestorius* tried to restrict the social interactions of Constantinopolitan monks, the furious resistance played no small part in his downfall (McGuckin). When Eutyches* was condemned (448), his deposition was signed by no fewer than 23 resident higumens* (abbots*). The official notice ending the Acacian* schism listed 53 major city higumens, and the Synod of 536 listed 63. Special monasteries existed in the capital for different ethnic groups, especially the Syrians, Latins, and Egyptians (Janin). Very little is known about the number of female convents, although there were several in Constantinople. Almost a third of all known monasteries existed within the capital's walls (Bryer). With regular imperial and aristocratic endowments, monasticism flourished throughout the lifetime of the Empire. Even times of apparent setback (e.g. under Iconoclastic* emperors or when Nikephoros Phokas limited the landholdings of monasteries) were merely temporary or reformatory measures. The Byzantine palace always supported (and regulated) monasticism. When destruction came, it was inevitably from outside, at the hands of Latin or Islamic enemies.

Monasticism was socially active in Byzantium. By the mid-5th c., many hospitals (*nosokomeia*), poor houses (*ptocheia*), hostels for strangers (*xenones*), orphanages (*orphanotroheion*), and old-age homes (*gerokomeia*) had been pioneered in Constantinople (Constantelos). Most monastic complexes, whether they had a social ministry or not (and several existed primarily to celebrate the life of prayer among hesychasts*), were governed by a triumvirate: the higumen, the oikonomos (steward), and the ekklesiarches (sacristan). The higumen had the obligation of teaching and ordering the entire household, and frequently was expected to hear the "confession of thoughts" of each monastic, although it was common for a higumen, at least in larger houses, to appoint an especially revered elder to be the "soul-friend" and confessor of the monks (*pneumatikos*). The relation between the monk and the spiritual elder was an important one, and the theme of spiritual fatherhood (especially in later Byzantine monastic writing) is considerable (Turner).

Throughout the Byzantine world, the *typikon* (rule) of Basil* of Caesarea (see Basil, Rule of) and the administrative order of the Studium Monastery (drawn up by Theodore* the Studite) dictated the standard pattern of monastic life. Byzantine monks were fluid and mobile, unlike their Western counterparts with their vows of stability. Each house, in theory, was founded with its own local *typikon*, a charter determined by the aristocratic founder who endowed the house originally.

The progressive loss of the Byzantine hinterland in the last imperial ages proved no less disastrous for monastic life than it did for the Empire as a whole. After the Latin occupation of Constantinople (13th c.), most monasteries were desperately impoverished; yet after the fall of Constantinople (1453), no fewer than 18 monasteries were still functioning. The outlying monastic centers, such as those on Crete, Cyprus*, and the Slavic lands, clung on tenaciously through a succession of oppressive overlords, and their painted churches remain an eloquent testimony to the dissemination of Byzantine culture through monastic foundations. Some of the fortress monasteries, e.g. St. Catherine's at Sinai or St. Sabas' Great Lavra* in Palestine, also survived, as did (most spectacularly) the great monastic colonies on Mount Athos*. **See also SKETIC MONASTICISM.** JOHN A. MCGUCKIN

Monasticism in the Russian and Ukrainian Tradition. The earliest Russian and Ukrainian monasteries were urban foundations on the Byzantine model and may date to the 10th c. Literary tradition traces its roots to the Pechersky (from *pechera*, "cave") complex of monasteries near Kiev, founded in the 11th c. by Antonii, a native of the region, who had spent several years at Mount Athos*. His younger associate and successor, Theodosii, introduced the Rule of Studios* (or Studite Rule). This suggests a *lavra** monastic type with cenobitic* elements.

During the Mongol invasions and subsequent domination (13–14th c.), monasteries farther from population centers and farther to the north and west were eventually linked to the rising power of Muscovy. Emblematic of this development was Sergius* of Radonezh (d1392), founder of the Trinity Monastery, 70 kilometers northeast of Moscow. A towering figure, Sergius renewed the anchoritic* and cenobite* models of monastic life. The vita tradition depicted him and later his followers as seekers of solitude, joined by admirers seeking guidance. The gradual expansion of the settlement to a large cenobitic complex ensued, and the pattern then repeated itself. The result was the diffusion of monastic life (especially to remote lands of the north) (Stella Rock). Monasteries became large fortified cultural centers where chronicles, illuminated manuscripts, icons, and frescoes were produced. For instance, Andrei Rublev (d1430) painted unsurpassed icons* at Andronikov Monastery (southeast of Moscow). Miraculous icons located in monasteries served as palladia (divine guarantees of protection). For example, the famous Vladimir Mother of God, a gift of the Constantinopolitan patriarch to one of the Kievan princes (c1131), was placed in a monastery, but then moved as a palladium first to Vladimir and later to Sretenskii Monastery, which had been founded as a place of meeting (*sretenie*) for the people of Moscow.

Women embraced monastic life, although they were fewer in number and less well known than men. Women of imperial households (like some of their male counterparts) were sometimes forced into monastic life; some wealthy women were founders or patrons of convents (Thyret).

The anchoritic and cenobite strands of Russian monasticism came into conflict over the question of monastic property* in the 15th c. with Nil* Sorsky (1433–1508), who represented the hesychast*, mystical* emphasis of the "Non-Possessors," and Joseph of Volokolamsk (1439–1515), who represented the cenobitic, socially activist type, the "Possessors." Loss of the prophetic charism of monastic life has typically been traced to the victory of the cenobites, but recent studies suggest the contrast has been overdrawn (Rock, Dykstra).

A more radically prophetic type of monk, the "holy* fool" (Russian, *yurodivyi*) had already appeared in the 11th c. in the form of Isaac of the Pechersky Monastery of Kiev. The "holy fool" tradition was reinforced by the translation into Slavonic of Byzantine "lives" of those who made themselves "fools for the sake of Christ." As Muscovite autocracy grew under Ivan IV ("the Terrible," 1530–84), the distinctive Russian type of "holy fool" reached its apogee; stories circulated of "fools" who taunted the czar with impunity, while the czar himself imitated their behavior. Eventually the famous cathedral of Moscow was named for one named Vasilii. Others continued in this role into the early 20th c. (Ivanov).

Peter the Great's hostility toward the spiritual ethos of monasticism and the seizure of monastic lands and revenues by Catherine II ("the Great") resulted in a radical reduction in the number of both monasteries and their inhabitants. Catherine also granted women's monasteries autonomy from male direction, with the result that their numbers increased dramatically; some female monastic leaders managed their economic affairs well, while others did not.

At the end of the 18th c., Paissii Velichkovskii's publication of an abridged Slavonic version of the *Philokalia** sparked a monastic renewal centered on the "prayer* of the heart" and spiritual guidance for all – monks and laity alike – from elders (*startsi*) whose holiness was marked by compassion and insight. Optina Pustin, the preeminent center of this piety, attracted many pilgrims*, among them Turgenev, Gogol, Dostoevsky*, and (the more skeptical) Tolstoy*.

Suppressed and persecuted under Communist rule, monastics found new strategies of resistance. Under the New Economic Plan and its collectivization of farms, some monasteries redefined themselves as collective farms. Faced with mass arrests, confiscation of properties, imprisonment, and execution, beginning on February 18, 1932, some persevered by becoming "secret monks," covertly embracing a life of prayer and Christian asceticism (Wynot). Some large monastic complexes were transformed into prison camps. Perestroika and the fall of Communism resulted in a revival of monastic life and restoration of monasteries. **See also** SKETIC MONASTICISM.

KATHLEEN E. MCVEY

Monasticism in the Syriac Tradition. The earliest Syriac Christianity was characterized by asceticism* rooted in biblical notions of covenant*, holiness, and eschatology. Sons and daughters of the covenant (*bnai* and *bnat qeiama*), sworn to celibacy*, lived in towns and cities alongside married Christians, who might also choose abstinence from sexual intercourse, thus embracing *qaddishuta* (chastity, holiness). The term *ihidaya* (solitary one) simultaneously implied resemblance to Christ the Only Begotten, singleness (celibacy), and single-minded devotion to the Kingdom* of God.

An influx of Egyptian and Greek monastic literature (Antony*, Shenoute*, Basil* of Caesarea, Palladius*, Evagrius*) introduced new cenobitic* and eremitic* ideals and Origenist* currents for both men and women. Unusual forms of ascetic behavior marked by radical rejection of human culture* in the name of the "angelic life" – that of itinerants (wandering ascetics), stylites* (e.g. Simeon*), and "holy* fools" – are attested to by Theodoret* and John* of Ephesus. The tale of the "man of God," a wealthy young man who embraced poverty and anonymity, spread from Edessa* to the West, where its ideal was echoed by medieval mendicants*. Cenobitic monasteries became the norm in both Miaphysite* and Assyrian* traditions and served variously as centers of scholarship, translation, and scientific and philosophical study, and as patriarchal residences, hospices, and strongholds under persecution. KATHLEEN E. MCVEY

Monepiscopate, Monarchical Episcopate, single bishop. In the NT, bishops are often mentioned in the plural, suggesting either that each house church had its own bishop or that presbyters exercised authority in a collegial way. The monepiscopate is first mentioned in the letters of Ignatius* (106–13), as an emerging pattern of governance. Some see the negative side of the monepiscopate in Diotrephes's "love of preeminence" (3 John 9–10). In Rome, however, there may not have been a single bishop until Pius (c140). In Alexandria a body of presbyters, with a rotating chair, was replaced (c190) by the monepiscopate of Demetrius.

Monica (331–87), mother of Augustine*. Because of her, Augustine always thought of himself as a Christian (he even viewed Manichaeism* as a more enlightened form of Christianity). She is a major figure in his *Confessions*, manifesting constant concern for him and urging him toward Catholic (rather than heretical*) belief and commitment; while he was trying to assert his independence, she followed him from Carthage to Rome and then to Milan. The narrative portion of the *Confessions* ends with her death, shortly after their conversation in Ostia, which is described in mystical terms. In the dialogues from the time immediately after his conversion, Monica is represented as the simple believer who repeatedly comes to insights that are later confirmed by rational investigation.

Monk, a man living under a vow of singleness and simplicity, in isolation from the world; a term not properly used for canons* regular or mendicant* friars*.

Monogenes, Greek term used to describe Jesus Christ in the NT (John 3:16, 18; 1 John 4:9) and in most early creeds. While usually translated "only begotten," it is rendered "unique" (*unicus*) in some Latin creeds. It was interpreted to mean that only Christ is God's offspring by nature, while others are adopted (Gal 4:5).

Monophysite ("only one nature"), term given by its opponents to the christological tradition that developed from Cyril* of Alexandria and his emphasis on the "one incarnate nature of the Word." **See also** MIAPHYSITE.

Monotheism (Gk for "one God"), belief that there is one sole God*; worship and service of one God. Monotheism is contrasted with polytheism*, belief in a number of deities; with henotheism, service of one god while assuming the existence of other deities; and with pantheism*, belief that God and the cosmos are basically identical. In actuality monotheism often uses a more flexible vocabulary (at times close to that of henotheism), e.g. "you are gods"

(Ps 82:6, John 10:34) and "the god of this world" (2 Cor 4:4). Because the word "god" can take a plural form, a differentiation is made between the "one true God" and the "false gods" (see God, Christian Views of, Cluster).

Judaism* and Christianity have regarded the most basic threats to monotheism to be (1) the supposition that another independent and conflicting principle exists alongside God (cf. Zoroastrianism and Manichaeism*) and (2) the introduction of literal plurality into God. The doctrine of the Trinity* has often been thought to be polytheistic (a view that led to Monarchianism*); in Nicene churches, this problem was resolved by speaking of God as one essence* in three persons*. In actual life, believers may be polytheistic in their loyalties while professing monotheism – hence the emphasis of H. Richard Niebuhr* on "radical monotheism," setting all values in relation to the one God.

Monothelitism, the doctrine that Christ, being "divine-human" ("theandric"), has only "one will" and activity. Dionysius* the Pseudo-Areopagite had spoken of "one divine-human energy/activity" of Christ (*Ep.* 4). Severus* of Antioch and Miaphysites* used this designation, which seemed congruent with Cyril's* view of "one incarnate nature of the divine Word." With this dynamic force of the Incarnation*, redemption* can be understood as theosis*, the graced deification of all natural life.

Emperor Heraclius (624) thought that the Chalcedonians and Cyrillians could be reconciled by avoiding the Miaphysite language while emphasizing "one divine-human energy/activity" ("monenergism"), and thus "one divine-human will" ("monothelitism"). Patriarch Sergius supported this twofold doctrine. But Pope Honorius* merely affirmed monothelitism (encouraged in Heraclius's *Ecthesis**, 638, and approved by Constantinople councils, 638, 639).

From a neo-Chalcedonian* perspective, Maximus* the Confessor objected that will and activity belong to the natures, not to the hypostasis*; each nature acts in its own way and even has its own will, though without conflict or separation. This affirmation of a human will* and activity is testimony to the reality of God's creation; freedom of will and difference from God persist even in the Incarnation, as they also persist in mystical* union. Yet any action by Christ involves the joint and coordinated activity of both natures, without confusion, since his human will is always responsive to the divine will of the Word.

Maximus persuaded several councils in Africa and Rome (646) and the Lateran synod (649) to condemn monothelitism as heretical and to reaffirm "two natural wills." Emperor Constans, forbidding talk about either one or two wills in his Typos, deposed Pope Martin I, exiling him along with Maximus for refusing this compromise (653).

After Syria and Egypt came under Islamic control, with less political need to seek conciliation with the Miaphysites, councils in Rome (680) and Constantinople II (680–81) affirmed Christ's two natural wills and operations. The Maronites* (Lebanon) rejected this doctrine until 1182, when they entered into communion with Rome (1182). EUGENE TESELLE

Montanism, prophetic movement named after a founder, Montanus, who with two women Prisc[ill]a and Maximilla, was a prophet-leader in Phrygia, Asia Minor, from the late 150s (for Epiphanius*; Eusebius* improbably suggests the late 170s). In its early phases, it was called "the New Prophecy"; its members were also known as Cataphrygians or Pepouzians (from Pepouza, their geographic headquarters); later subgroups included Quintillianists, Priscillianists, Artotyrites, and Taskodrougites. It was a movement of prophecy and spiritual (charismatic*) renewal within Christianity, spreading very rapidly until its followers seceded from, or were driven from, emerging Catholic congregations that viewed them as "heretics*". By 200 they were established in Rome and North Africa, where the martyrology of Perpetua* and Felicity showed contact with Montanism. Tertullian* of Carthage embraced Montanism, but was perhaps not typical of it.

Initially orthodox in doctrine, Montanism was rigorous in discipline (e.g. fasting*) and stressed spiritual gifts*. The prophets sought to interpret "suffering, covenant and promise" (Epiphanius, *Panarion* 48.13.1). Montanism showed affinities with Jewish*-Christian thought and some sources suggest a much-heightened eschatological* expectation. Commentators (exaggeratedly) assume its particular zeal for martyrdom*. Fragmentation into subgroups over centuries brought doctrinal and liturgical deviations. Critics debate as to whether and to what extent it was indebted to the religion and concerns of rural pagan Phrygia and mantic prophecy (see Inculturation Cluster). It showed clear links to existing Asian

Christian theology, including Revelation's* interest in the New Jerusalem (Rev 21) and the Johannine Paraclete* (John 14:16, 16:7). Its lively early gatherings were characterized by enthusiasm* and possibly some unintelligible speech (glossolalia*). Prophecy remained characteristic of it. The prophets' shrine in Pepouza, the site where Montanism's "Jerusalem" headquarters may have been located, was destroyed in the 6th c.

The surviving oracles of the prophets Montanus, Prisc[ill]a, and Maximilla are intelligible snippets of longer utterances, chosen by critics to present Montanism in the most negative light. Women's prominence in prophesying and teaching sharpened opposition to it. Other sources (almost all from its opponents) vary in quantity and quality of information: from Origen* to the Code of Justinian*; from Epiphanius of Salamis to Hippolytus* of Rome; from Eusebius's 2nd- to 3rd-c. informants to Praedestinatus*. Epigraphy, from Asia Minor, Africa, and Rome, mentions (Montanist) officials, supporting *some* of their opponents' claims about aberrant doctrine.

Montanism's popular success prompted the emergent Christian tradition to develop greater self-definition and to make more decisions about what was to be authoritative for Christians. Gnosticism* had the same effect on the church. CHRISTINE TREVETT

Montenegro. See YUGOSLAVIA.

Moral Agency, accountability for one's actions, which one has undertaken freely, with awareness of norms and consequences. **See also ORIGINAL SIN; WILL.**

Moral Influence, a type of causality, suggested by many theologians to be an explanation of conversion* by the grace* of God and subsequent moral acts. During the 16th-c. debates over grace and free will*, some argued that grace acts "physically," as one thing acts on another. Others argued that grace acts "morally" by appealing to the affections, without overpowering free will. Ambrose* and Augustine* evoke the depths of divine love manifested in the Incarnation*, Christ's words, deeds, and willing crucifixion*, as motivating a believer's responding love for God. Abelard* spoke of such a response as the chief meaning of atonement* ("moral influence" theory of atonement). A "moral suasion" (or influence) of grace is associated with the Wesleyan* Movement, Edwards* and his followers, and the "new measures" revivalism* of Charles Finney*. This perspective entails a strong theory of the bondage of the will: although we are "physically" capable of willing the good, we are "morally" unable to do so until freed from our disordered inclinations (affections). **See also PREDESTINATION.**

Morality. See ETHICS AND CHRISTIANITY CLUSTER.

Moral Re-armament, the name by which the Oxford* Movement became known after founder Frank Buchman's* call (1938) for "moral and spiritual rearmament."

Moravian Church. Under the official name of Unitas Fratrum, the Moravian Church originated as the Bohemian* Brethren (1457) organized by followers of Jan Hus*. Severely persecuted and almost exterminated during the 17th-c. religious wars, they were renewed in 1722 by Nicholas Ludwig von Zinzendorf*, who articulated the Church's threefold mission: communal pietism, promotion of experiential religion in the European state churches, and cross-cultural evangelization.

With headquarters in Herrnhut, Germany, it was first organized as a transconfessional mission society (until the mid-19th c.), then emerged as a Protestant denomination. Moravians began work in England in 1728 and were recognized as an "ancient Protestant Episcopal church" by the British Parliament (1749). Missions were begun in the Caribbean* (1732), Surinam (1735), Georgia (1735), Pennsylvania (1740), South Africa (1748), and Labrador (1771). In the 19th c., missions included work in Central and South America, North India and Tibet, Palestine, and German and British colonies in East Africa. The immigration of Scandinavians and Germans to North America led to significant growth of the Moravian Church in the USA and Canada. World Wars I and II disrupted Moravian missions and led to a decentralization of the Moravian Church in 19 provinces; this involved, worldwide, about 1 million members, with the largest single concentration in Tanzania*.

Moravian theology begins with a strong Christocentrism. The Bohemian Brethren distinguished among things essential to salvation* (relationship to God in Jesus Christ), ministrative to salvation (church, Scriptures, sacraments), and incidental to salvation (doctrines, rituals, ecclesiastical structures). Moravian theology in the Zinzendorfian period was shaped by the contending themes of Pietism*, Lutheran* orthodoxy, and Enlightenment* thought. Although the Moravian Church adopted a statement of theological principles entitled "The Ground of the Unity" (1957), Moravian theology remains more devotional and relational than dogmatic or confessional. The best expressions of the Moravian Church's theology can be found in its hymnody and liturgy. OTTO DREYDOPPEL, JR.

Moravian Worship. Inspired by the reforming principles of Jan Hus*, worship among the earliest Bohemian* Brethren was starkly simple. The reading and expounding of Scripture* were the focus of their gatherings. Their liturgy was based on free prayer and the singing of spiritual songs in the common language. Communion* in both kinds, in which both the bread and cup were offered to the laity, was their central concern. In later generations, Moravian worship took on a more churchly character. Luke of Prague (d1528) published an agenda for worship (1501), and the Brethren's priests began to wear vestments. The Church Litany of 1571 has been carried over into the liturgical practice of the Renewed Moravian Church. Under Nicholas Ludwig von Zinzendorf*, Moravian worship was highly influenced by the Lutheran* liturgy. At the same time, Moravians developed the *Singstunde*, which became paradigmatic for their later worship practices. In it, verses from different hymns followed one after another in such a way as to develop a spiritual theme. The Love* Feast, based on the *agape** meal of the early church, the Christmas Eve candle service, and the Moravian celebration of Holy Communion all follow the form of the *Singstunde*. Zinzendorf was the author of many hymns, and he began the Moravian practice of writing "liturgies" for various seasons and occasions. These are prayers and responsive readings, most often using the language of Scripture, interspersed with hymns. Elements of the Zinzendorfian liturgies survive in the 1995 Moravian Book of Worship.

Moravian worship in North America has been highly influenced by frontier revivalism*, with its preaching for conversion, and by the free church worship that emerged from it. Contemporary Moravian worship most often begins with hymn singing and the praying of one of the liturgies, continues with the reading of Scripture and the presentation of tithes and offering, and ends with a sermon, hymn, and benediction. Holy Communion is celebrated seven times a year in most Moravian congregations, on the major festival days of the Church, although many Moravians, influenced by the World Council of Churches' document, "Baptism, Eucharist, and Ministry" (1982), advocate a more frequent observance. Recent growth of the Moravian Church in Great Britain and in North America has come as the result of immigration of Moravians from the Caribbean and Central and South America who have brought with them their own hymns and worship practices. These have made Moravian worship as a whole increasingly multicultural.

OTTO DREYDOPPEL, JR.

More, Hannah (1745–1833), writer, educator, associate of the Evangelical Anglican Clapham sect. Born in Western England, she had a brief career as a playwright in London. After an Evangelical conversion*, she joined the campaign for the abolition of the slave* trade and began a lifelong friendship with William Wilberforce*. At his suggestion, she founded (1789) her first Sunday* school in Cheddar. The author of *Village Politics* (1793), the *Cheap Repository Tracts* (1795–98), and *Coelebs in Search of a Wife* (1808), she exerted the greatest influence of all the Evangelical woman of her generation through her literary and philanthropic activities.

ANNE STOTT

More, Thomas (1478–1535), English humanist, statesman, Roman Catholic. More was a contemporary of Erasmus, and his humanistic endeavors extended beyond his classic *Utopia* (1516; a perfect version of Plato's *Republic* that includes tolerance of all religions) and other Latin works to encourage fresh engagement with ancient sources. Alongside his political roles – including speaker of the House of Commons (1523) and lord chancellor (1529–32) – he was committed to the Roman Catholic Church during some of its most turbulent decades. In the interest of religious reform, More shared with his contemporaries a desire to return to the texts and piety of the early church as norms for spiritual renewal. Meditative treatises on suffering* (*The Last Things*, c1522; *A Dialogue of Comfort*, 1534; *De Tristitia Christi*, unfinished, 1535) offer Christian commentaries on the vicissitudes of worldly affairs in which More was fully embroiled. A defender, alongside Henry* VIII, of the sacramental system when Luther* first attacked it, More later was Henry's opponent in supporting papal sovereignty over the entire church – a confrontation with the king that ultimately cost him his life. An indefatigable and erudite polemicist in both Latin and English, More defended traditional doctrines such as those of purgatory* and the Eucharist* against critiques originating on the Continent. As a religious writer and a humanist, More took the risk of addressing European issues in an English context. RALPH KEEN

Morelos y Pavón, José María (1765–1815), priest whom Hidalgo* named as his deputy during the Mexican war of independence. After Hidalgo's death, he called the National Constituent Congress (1813) to endorse the *Sentiments of the Nation*, which he wrote, declaring Mexican independence from Spain*, making the Roman Catholic Church the state religion, abolishing slavery*, racial social distinctions, and torture, and establishing a system of government. Called "servant of the nation," after brilliant political-military campaigns, he was declared a heretic and defrocked; he was captured and executed as a traitor. But the revolutionary movement continued. **See also MEXICO.**
MARÍA ALICIA PUENTE LUTTEROTH and ELIZABETH JUDD

Moriscos (Spanish, Moorish), Muslims who remained in Spain* after the Christian reconquest (11th–15th c.) and who were forced to convert to Christianity, especially after the fall of Granada (1492). The newly converted tenaciously held to Islam through the 16th c. Between 1609 and 1611, the entire *morisco* population was expelled from Spain. **See also SPAIN.**

Mormon, Book of. In 1830 Joseph Smith* published a book he claimed to have translated "by the gift and power of God" from ancient gold plates buried in a hillside in upstate New York. The book records the details of three ancient peoples who had inhabited the North American continent. The bulk of the record was purportedly made by "Nephite" prophets of Jewish extraction, who presided over their people from 600 BC until their extinction in the 5th c. AD. Throughout this period, Nephite prophets maintained records of wars, missionary labors, prophetic writings by Isaiah and other Old World figures, predictions of a coming Christ, and teachings about atonement*, faith* and baptism*, charity*, and other doctrines consistent with modern Christianity. Abridged by a Nephite warrior-prophet named Mormon, then buried in the ground by his son Moroni, the record was delivered to 21-year-old Smith in 1827 by that same Moroni (in the form of a resurrected being, or angel).

The Book of Mormon contains little in the way of innovative doctrines, but it does recount a visit of Christ to the New World after his Jerusalem resurrection. Its major theological contribution and readerly appeal have been its modeling of a kind of "dialogic revelation" as literal as OT versions, but more individualized and egalitarian. Although Mormons believe it is an authentic historical record of ancient peoples, its language and topics are in some cases germane to 19th-c. theological concerns, including those of the Restoration* Movement. It is esteemed by Mormons as "the Word of God," a companion to the Bible, and the principal evidence of Joseph Smith's status as a prophet of God and restorer of the true church of Jesus Christ. **See also LATTER-DAY SAINTS, CHURCH OF JESUS CHRIST OF; MORMON WORSHIP; SMITH, JOSEPH; YOUNG, BRIGHAM.** TERRYL GIVENS

Mormon Worship. Mormons, members of the Church of Jesus Christ of Latter*-day Saints (LDS), worship God, the eternal Father, and Jesus Christ.

Sacred Spaces. LDS doctrine designates temples as the most sacred sites of worship, the believers' homes as the second most privileged spaces for devotional acts, and the chapels, or meetinghouses, as the third most important. A temple (more than 100 worldwide in 2000) is a holy place, a "house of the Lord."

Sacraments. Only members in good standing may enter the temple to perform sacraments or "saving ordinances" for themselves and vicariously for the dead, such as the following: proxy baptism*, priesthood* ordination, washing and anointing, clothing in sacred garments worn throughout life, "endowment" (the making of a covenant, including obedience and sexual purity), marriage, and sealing (a ceremony that promises that family bonds will endure eternally). Mormons are reluctant to discuss the particulars of temple worship publicly, for it is the most sacred aspect of their faith.

The home is the most sacred locale outside the temple. LDS families are encouraged to practice personal and family prayer, daily Scripture readings, and Monday night "family home evenings," which include song, prayer, a lesson based on a theme from the Gospels, and/or a family activity.

The majority of a Mormon's public devotional life unfolds in a congregational meetinghouse known as the ward house or chapel.

The principal weekly worship service is the "sacrament meeting," attended by all members. LDS prophet Joseph Smith taught that everything in the gospel is an appendage to the doctrine of Christ's atonement*. Accordingly, the purpose of the Sunday meeting is to partake of the Eucharist, "the sacrament," in commemoration of the Lord's suffering in Gethsemane and death on Calvary. Broken bread and cups of water are passed to members of the congregation with solemnity; two rote prayers are spoken by priests (usually young men of 16–18 years), who consecrate the emblems. Congregational singing opens and closes the meeting and precedes the passing of the sacrament, and devotional talks given by lay members follow it (there is no professional clergy). No formal liturgy exists. The only variation in format occurs on the first Sunday of the month, when members spontaneously approach the pulpit and "bear testimony," or publicly profess their faith in Christ and cardinal LDS tenets. Services are always conducted in the local language, but are otherwise essentially identical in all countries and cultures.

Like many Christians, Mormons believe that true religion and worship require a life of service. With no paid ministers, the largest missionary force in the world, and a comprehensive welfare program, committed Mormons attempt to enact the LDS Scripture passage that "when ye are in the service of your fellow beings, ye are only in the service of your God." **See also** **LATTER-DAY SAINTS, CHURCH OF JESUS CHRIST OF; MORMON, BOOK OF; SMITH, JOSEPH; YOUNG, BRIGHAM.**

TERRYL GIVENS

Mortal Sin, a sin "unto death" (1 John 5:16), i.e. death of the soul*, loss of grace*, and damnation*, unless there is repentance*; a deliberate decision that goes against God's will, in contrast to venial* sin.

Mortification, metaphorically "killing" the flesh and its desires (cf. Rom 8:13; Col 3:5) through self-denial and the willing of higher values.

Mortmain (French, "dead hand"), legal status of properties held inalienably by a monastery or other ecclesiastical body, which led governments to limit or prohibit further transfers of property.

Mosaic (from the Gk for "muse"), pictures or patterns produced by cementing together small pieces of colored stone or glass (*tesserae*); used in early church buildings.

Moses, a Hebrew with an Egyptian name, called by YHWH to lead his people out of bondage in Egypt, to preside over the giving of the covenant* and Law* to the Hebrews on Mount Sinai, which established them as the people* of God, and to lead them to the Promised* Land, is portrayed in different ways by historians, various HB traditions, early Judaism, and the NT.

Historians debate the historicity of many aspects of Moses' story (is it the conflation of an exodus*-settlement story and a Sinai tradition?) but conclude that the broad outline of Moses' story could be historical.

In the Pentateuch*, three portrayals of Moses can be distinguished:

1. In the Yahwist-Elohist traditions, the oldest strata (especially Exod 1:15–2:22; 3:1–12, 5:1–15:21; 19–24; 32–34; Num 10–36), Moses is portrayed as YHWH's commissioned agent, to whom God's name, YHWH, is revealed; who confronts Pharaoh in YHWH's name; through whom YHWH acts; and who appeals for Israel's covenant obedience on the basis of God's gracious act of freeing the people from Egypt (Exod 19:4, 20:2). As a mediator of the Law, or lawgiver, Moses receives from God the Ten* Commandments and other laws (20:1–20) for the people. It is with Moses as a mediator of the covenant that YHWH makes a covenant on the people's behalf (Exod 34:27). Yet Moses remains humble (Num 12:3), functioning as a nursing mother for the people (Num 11:12) and interceding for them.
2. In Deuteronomy, Moses continues to be the mediator between God and the people (5:5, 27), but now as the Law's interpreter; thus in a series of homilies, Moses explains the commandments to a rebellious people for whom he intercedes with God (Deut 9:25–29); Moses is also portrayed as vicariously bearing YHWH's wrath against his people; he is punished for their sake by being forbidden to enter the Promised Land, dying in Moab (Deut 1:37; 3:25–26; 34).
3. The Priestly Tradition claims that YHWH revealed to Moses all the laws of Exodus and Numbers, and in particular the instructions for making the tabernacle where YHWH will reside (instead of on Mount Sinai), written and rewritten on tablets

"with the finger of God" (Exod 24:16–18, 31:18, 35:1–40:33). In the Priestly tradition, Moses is a sinner (not trusting in God; Num 20:12); not entering the Promised Land is his punishment.

In Hellenistic Judaism, as propounded by Philo* of Alexandria, Moses is a superhuman "divine man" (familiar in Greek culture), a perfect ruler and legislator, a high priest, and a prophet who reveals what cannot be understood by reason (*Vita Mosis* presents Philo's allegorical* interpretation of Moses). Josephus* adds that Moses is both a Greek "divine man" and an Israelite "man of God," the founder of a theocracy.

In Palestinian Judaism, all of the Pentateuch (Torah) has been revealed to Moses (including the narrative of his own death and burial). The whole Torah is interpreted by a growing tradition of midrash*.

In the NT, Moses and the Law (Torah) are generally portrayed positively, but are presented as having been superseded (see Supersessionism) or fulfilled by Christ (see Typology). Paul associates Moses with the period of the Law (Rom 5:14; 9:15; 10:5, 19) when revelation (including the Law) is veiled (2 Cor 3:7–18), contrasting him with the period ushered in by Christ, when the glory of God revealed to Moses is now unveiled. In the Synoptic Gospels* and Acts*, despite disputes with the Pharisees and their Judaism* based on Moses' authority (e.g. Acts 6:11–14, 21:21), Moses appears during the Transfiguration as one of the precursors (with Elijah) of Christ, and Jesus is figuratively presented in Matthew* as a "new Moses" (a typological fulfillment of Moses). In John, Jesus is said to surpass Moses (Jesus fulfills the Law given through Moses, John 1:17; cf. 3:14, 6:32), but those who truly believe Moses would believe in Jesus (5:46; 9:28 is ambivalent). In Hebrews, Moses is portrayed as being similar to Jesus but inferior to him. DANIEL PATTE

Moses of Khoren (c8th c.), author of the *History of the Armenians**. Combining his vast antiquarian and geographical erudition with the imagination of a brilliant novelist, Moses integrates legends and traditions, narrating the past of his people, as well as the writings of the 5th-c. Armenian historians Koriun, Agathangelos, Faustus, and Lazarus into the world history known to him from the Bible, Josephus*, Eusebius*, and Socrates of Constantinople, and from Anania of Shirak's *Geography* (7th c.). Some of what he records has been confirmed by archaeological findings. He presents himself as a mid-5th-c. author and contemporary of the first Armenian writers and the last Armenian kings, but he is not mentioned by Mashtots* or his disciples before the 9th c.

Moses seeks to provide the Armenians with a summary of their history that describes their genealogical, ecclesiastical, and cultural characteristics, in order to help them overcome the disruptions of their political history. He apparently writes at the request of a Bagratid patron, giving to this princely family a prominent role in the consolidation of national identity after the fall of the Arsacid kings – probably in the period when the Bagratids were gaining the upper hand over their Mamikonean rivals, between the establishment of the Abbasid Caliphate (750) and the Armenian uprising of 771–2.

IGOR DORFMANN-LAZAREV

Motet, musical composition for several voices, with words generally taken from Scripture. Motets are most often sung during the offertory* and the elevation* of the Mass*.

Mother of God. See MARY*, THE VIRGIN, CLUSTER: THEOTOKOS.

Motherhood is ambivalent in Christian thought. It is associated positively with creativity and life and negatively with salvation and eternal life. Together Eve, the first mother and the first sinner, and Mary, a virgin and the mother of Jesus, represent this ambivalence. Actual motherhood and its symbolic interpretations are related in complex ways, often obscuring the fact that motherhood differs throughout history and in various cultural contexts.

Motherhood as the Fulfillment of Womanhood. Because the vast majority of women give birth, motherhood is connected with what it means to be a woman. Thus Adam and Eve were originally given specific tasks, respectively cultivating the soil and giving birth (with pain). The most common images of women in the Bible are those of daughter, mother, and wife. Motherhood is even seen as a means to salvation* (1 Tim 2:11–15). Still, this ideal has been relativized by, and often subordinated to, celibacy* in spiritual life.

Feminists have pointed out the important distinction between the biologically necessary, and thus gender-specific, aspects of motherhood and care for children, which is not gender specific. Women's movements are concerned with the negative consequences of motherhood; they affirm the importance of reproductive health and social care and underscore the tension between motherhood and women's full participation and authorization in society. Control of women's reproductive capacity has been crucial for maintaining male power. One aspect of patriarchy* is the control of women's sexuality*, defining motherhood as its proper expression while imagining motherhood to be an essentially asexual position, opposed to that of "virgin" or "whore."

Motherhood as an Aspect of Personhood. Motherhood is related to the ideal of self-sacrificing love*, giving life even to the extent of self-extinction. The Madonna* is the primary image of this ideal. Mary*, the "servant of the Lord," unconditionally accepts giving birth to the Son of God. Women throughout history and in many cultures have assumed the task of giving birth as God given, while never being able to live up to the ideal of Mary's purity. The ethos of the biblical household* codes has put mothers in the service of their husbands, as well as public and ecclesial authorities. Male consent to fatherhood* has been a prerequisite for a child to be considered legitimate.

Feminist philosophers have shown that moth erhood is in conflict with personhood, whereas fatherhood is not. Mothers are not expected to be agents who are in a position to deal with moral and emotional complexity. The self-sacrificing ideal hinders mothers from expressing their autonomy* and thus from developing relationships (relationality*). However, motherhood has positive aspects: children and others have to be cared for and love must be given. The crucial issue is that caring and love giving should neither be restricted to motherhood nor subordinated to patriarchal power, as is too often the case in theology and church practice.

Motherhood as a Metaphor. Motherhood is used metaphorically as an ideal that is projected in various ways on women in different situations and in theological analogies. Ideal self-sacrificing and subordinate motherhood has set the standards for the proper conduct of mothers. Motherliness has been expected of women in situations where they are not literally acting as mothers, e.g. in congregations, monastic life, schools, and hospitals. In theology motherhood has been marginalized in relation to the dominating metaphor of the heavenly Father.

The motherhood metaphor raises theological and ethical concerns, because it emphasizes the traditional subordinate aspects of motherhood. Instead, women and men should use this metaphor to make sense of their experience of the challenges of and resources of motherhood. Different forms of motherhood should be analyzed (single mothers, collective mothering, adoptive mothers), and the idea of compulsory motherhood should be questioned. A critical reinterpretation of the motherhood metaphor can be a means of confronting patriarchal* theology and bringing more progressive images of God into play in the service of life in congregations and society.

Becoming a mother means becoming connected to another person without being able to control that person (see Heteronomy). As she gives birth, the mother has to face not only the possible death of her child, but also her own human finitude. Thus reflection on motherhood leads to the insight that we are not in control of life, neither our own nor that of others. Motherhood embodies the ambiguity of vulnerability and exposure. Instead of being affirmed as human, this ambiguity has been unduly gendered and constructed as female. While oppression* is a problem to be solved, vulnerability is a life condition with which we need to cope and with which we can cope through love*. The traditional monolithic view of motherhood exposes mothers to different kinds of sexual oppression in family life and in society. A critical reinterpretation should emphasize that in motherhood we can envision a clear distinction between exposure and vulnerability, between oppressive relationships and love in personal, social, and spiritual life.

CRISTINA GRENHOLM

Mother's Day, initiated by Julia Ward Howe* after the 1870–71 Prussian War as an annual "Mother's Day of Peace," which eventually became commercialized.

Mott, John Raleigh (1865–1955), North American Methodist layperson, evangelist, promoter of ecumenism; often called "Protestants' leading statesman" of his era and "father of the ecumenical movement"; Nobel Peace Prize laureate (1946), honorary chair of the first World* Council of Churches conference (1948).

After making a commitment to Christian service (1886), he became the college secretary of the YMCA*, organizing its Student* Volunteer Movement for Foreign Missions (1888). He then founded the World* Student Christian Federation (1895), which he chaired from 1920 to 1928 (see Rouse, C. [Clara] Ruth). He chaired the Edinburgh* Missionary Conference (1910), which launched the modern ecumenical* movement.

Mott came of age in an era of Protestant optimism about the Social* Gospel, world evangelization, and ecumenism and during the industrial revolution, when global transportation was facilitated. He traveled some 2 million miles for the World Student Christian Federation to evangelize university students especially, to "unite in spirit as never before the students of the world," and to hasten Jesus' prayer "that all may be one."

During the fundamentalist*–Modernist* controversy, when liberals and conservatives debated mission* priorities, Mott taught, "Evangelism without social work is deficient; social work without evangelism is impotent." His *Evangelization of the World in This Generation* (1900) became a missionary slogan in the early 20th c. MARK GALLI

Mourning Rites. See DEATH, CHRISTIAN VIEWS OF, CLUSTER.

Movable Feast, festival that is always on the same day of the week (e.g. Maundy* Thursday), but the calendar date of which varies according to calculation of Easter*.

Movement in Worship comprises various types of individual and corporate expressive movements, reflecting devotion and worship because bodies* are "a living sacrifice" to God (Rom 12:1). Such movements, which differ from one culture to another, range from liturgical gestures (processions, genuflection*, making the sign* of the cross, standing in praise*, prostration*) to liturgical dance and dancing in the Spirit (in Charismatic* worship).

Moyano Llerena, Margarita (1928–2003), leader of Catholic* Action in Argentina*. In the 1960s, she was the president of Youth of Catholic Action in Argentina and then worldwide. She was one of the 12 laypersons who were observers at the Second Vatican* Council and a participant at the Latin American Episcopal Conference in Medellín* (1968). Subsequently she worked with the brothers of Taizé*, both in France and Argentina, in Base* Ecclesial Communities such as the Institute of Popular Culture and the Seminars of Theological Formation. LUIS MIGUEL DONATELLO

Mozambique. In this war-devastated country, Christianity is multidenominational and coexists with African* Religion and Islam*; there is a notable degree of religious tolerance among Mozambicans.

Long before the Portuguese Vasco da Gama reached the Mozambican coast (1498), Arab settlers had trading posts there. In fact, the name "Moçambique" is derived from "Musa bin Ba'ik," the name of the Arab sheikh who was ruling the area when da Gama landed. The arrival of da Gama signaled the arrival of both Portuguese rule and Christianity; the navigator's purpose was both the development of commerce and the propagation of the Christian faith. Implanted through missionary work – Dominican* (since 1506), Jesuit* (since 1560), and Augustinian* (since the 17th c.) – the Roman Catholic Church was closely tied to the colonialist regime; it was a tool for Europeanizing the natives (*assimilados*), or civilizing and transforming them into "Portuguese-like" people. This was carried out for the purpose of commerce, including slave* trafficking. Missionary work was consequently seriously compromised (Butselaar). Only the Roman Catholic Church was allowed to operate throughout the country.

Mozambican Christianity is unique in that many of the Protestant and African* Instituted Churches (together with a membership similar in size to that of the Roman Catholic churches), which during the Portuguese regime were under strict scrutiny and restricted to certain zones, were not founded by foreign missionaries but by Mozambicans themselves who had emigrated to South Africa, converted, and brought the gospel back home. Thus there "grew in Mozambique, a Church with an African Spirituality, independent or almost independent from a European Mission" (Butselaar).

For a long time, Protestant and African Instituted Churches were confined primarily to the southern region, so that the colonialist regime could exercise control over them; the government suspected that the activities of these churches were related to revolutionary and liberation movements. Muslims lived in the central and northern regions.

Protestant missionary efforts began in the 1880s, with the arrival of (North American, then Swiss) Presbyterian missionaries and North American Methodists (leading to the creation of Congregationalist and United Methodist churches among the Matswas in Inhambane Province), then of Wesleyan Methodists from South* Africa (leading to the creation of Wesleyan Methodist Churches among the va-Ronga and the Changanas, in Maputo and Gaza Provinces). The Anglican Church flourished among the Txopis, the Changanas (Gaza and Southern Inhambane provinces), and the Nyanjas. Since Mozambique gained its independence (1975), Protestant churches have spread throughout the country and there is freedom of religion, although during the first five or six years of the civil war (1975–1992), there was much tension between FRELIMO (Frente de Libertação de Moçambique, the Liberation Front of Mozambique) and all organized religions (including Islam), because they were viewed as having collaborated with the Portuguese and as being ruled from outside (by Roman Catholics from Rome, Presbyterians from Geneva, and Methodists from the USA).

Since 1982 Christianity in Mozambique has grown rapidly. In contrast to their European counterparts, most churches – Roman Catholic, missionary Protestant, and independent churches, as well as African Instituted Churches – are full to capacity every day, and a good number of Christians worship outdoors rather than in a building. Besides reflecting a lack of financial resources, the "under tree" or "open space" worship practice is an interesting inculturation* phenomenon; it parallels practices of African* Religion in its Mozambican form (more specifically, ancestor* veneration), while manifesting the fact that the church provides an open space for everybody.

The Christian community played an important role in bringing about peace in Mozambique. Through the initiative of the Christian Council of Mozambique, the Mozambican churches came together to work for peace with other stakeholders, a process that led to the signing of the Rome General Peace Accords (1992, brokered by the Sant'Egídio community in Italy*). The process of preserving and developing a "culture of peace," which requires the involvement of all Mozambicans, is ongoing, and the church still plays a role. Initiatives like the "Swords into Plowshares" project (of the Christian Council of Mozambique) were still active in the early 21st c.

The growing understanding that global issues require global intervention led to an increasing interdenominational and interfaith collaboration that stimulated mutual understanding and acceptance, opening space for dialogue and cooperation. Today Christians in Mozambique have joined hands with other religions in peacebuilding efforts and conflict transformation initiatives such as monitoring elections, governance, and development, and contributing to HIV/AIDS programs.

Statistics: Population (2000): 19.7 million (M). Christians, 7.5 M, 39% (Roman Catholics, 3.1 M; Protestants, 1.8 M; members of African Instituted Churches and other independents, 1.4 M; Anglicans, 0.1 M); African Religionists, 10 M, 50%; Muslims, 2 M, 11%. (Based on *World Christian Encyclopedia*, 2001.)

DINIS MATSOLO

Mozart, Wolfgang Amadeus (Joannes Chrysostomus Wolfgangus Theophilus [Latinized to Amadeus] Mozart, 1756–91), Austrian composer, pianist, knight of the papal Order of the Golden Spur. Served at the court of the prince-archbishop of Salzburg (1769–81); freelance composer in Vienna (1781–91). A Freemason* from 1784, he composed numerous cantatas, songs, and occasional works for lodge meetings (e.g. *Maurerische Trauermusik*). In his operas, he expresses ideas of the Enlightenment* (*Le nozze di Figaro*) and Freemasonry (*Die Zauberflöte*). His sacred works include 17 Masses*, Mass movements, *Requiem** (incomplete), 2 vespers*, 4 litanies*, 3 cantatas*, 2 sacred dramas, 21 minor sacred vocal works, and 17 church sonatas.

TASSILO ERHARDT

Muhlenberg, Henry Melchior (1711–87), Lutheran pastor, organizer of churches, recorder of Pennsylvania colonial life. Muhlenberg trained at Göttingen University, then tutored at the Franke Institute in Halle with its missionary, spiritual, and educational program. Muhlenberg accepted the Institute's appointment as minister to colonists in the USA (1743). During his travels across the religiously and politically charged territory of the mid-Atlantic and during revolutionary upheavals, Muhlenberg dispensed medicines and Halle publications, sent reports to his superiors, organized churches, regularized ministerial practice, and kept a rich record of colonial life. He is known as the patriarch of North American Lutheranism*. MARIA ERLING

Mujerista Theology. See FEMINIST THEOLOGY CLUSTER: IN NORTH AMERICA: MUJERISTA.

Mukasa, Spartas Reuben (c1880–1982), Ugandan, baptized Anglican but fascinated by the aim of the African Orthodox Church (AOC) in North America (inspired by Marcus Garvey*) to become a universal Black church rooted in ancient Christianity, which did not espouse racism* or colonialism*. He became affiliated with the AOC in South Africa, left the Anglican Church (1929), and established an AOC in Uganda*, which was later affiliated with the Greek Patriarchate. He was ordained a Greek Orthodox* priest. ROBERT KAGGWA

Munguía, Clemente of Jesus (1810–68), first archbishop of Michoacán (1863–68), he was frequently named visitor and apostolic delegate in Mexico. He was expelled for his opposition to the Laws of Reform and to Maximilian's liberal decisions. **See also MEXICO.**

MARÍA ALICIA PUENTE LUTTEROTH and ELIZABETH JUDD

Müntzer (Münzer), Thomas (c1488–1525), Radical Reformer, mystical theologian, and leader in the Peasants' War of 1524–25. Native of the Harz region (East Germany), after completing biblical studies (Leipzig) and earning a bachelor's degree (Frankfurt/Oder), he was ordained a priest (c1514). A chantry priest in Braunschweig and a confessor for nuns in a convent nearby, he repeatedly visited Luther at Wittenberg (1517–19), became a pastor in Zwickau (1520) and Allstedt (1523–24), married, and had a son. He journeyed to Prague (1521) to support followers of John Hus*. Influenced by the Millennialist* Joachim* of Flora (c1132–1202) and the mystic* John Tauler* (1300–61), he advocated a restitution of 1st-c. spirited apostolic faith; the reformation he espoused, unlike that of Luther*, rejected the exclusive authority of the Bible and temporal power and called for an egalitarian society as a spearhead of the imminent eternal rule of Christ. In 1524 Müntzer organized several hundred followers in a "covenant of the elect" and joined the peasants in their rebellion against their landlords. The rebellion failed. Caught, tortured, and beheaded, Müntzer was branded by Luther as an incarnation of the devil. He was considered by 19th- and 20th-c. revolutionaries, linked to Karl Marx (1818–83) and Friedrich Engels 1820–1895), to be a forerunner of socialist and communist thinkers.

ERIC W. GRITSCH

Muratorian Canon, a list of NT writings discovered in 1740 by Lodovico Antonio Muratori (1672–1750) in an 8th-c. manuscript. It is usually dated to the late 2nd c., but others claim that it was a 4th-c work; its poor Latin suggests that the original was in Greek. It mentions all the NT books, except Hebrews*, James*, and 1 and 2 Peter*, and includes the Apocalypse* of Peter and the Wisdom* of Solomon as canonical; it rejects the Shepherd of Hermas*, the Marcionite* epistles of Paul to the Laodicaeans and Alexandrians, and several Gnostic* and Montanist* writings.

Music in/as Worship. Although music is not an essential part of worship, it is a vital element of it. Worship, during which people honor and serve one another and God, depends on engagement. To relate to God*, a reality, mysterious* and human, that can never be fully grasped, yet tangibly present in many varied experiences, is challenging. Sounds, body movements, space, objects, and words are principal means by which communities make the connection with God real for themselves. Since the 4th-c., when Christian communities adopted patterns of public court rituals as their structures for worship, music has accompanied processions, called attention to important ritual moments, and communicated formality, seriousness, and power. Most of all, music makes it possible to know from within ourselves what it feels like to believe in God through a wide spectrum of emotions, unbounded love*, paralyzing fear*, anger*, or doubt*.

By way of melodies, rhythms, harmonies, and texts, music reaches beyond rational knowing to open our hearts, stretch our vision, and give us personal and collective energy to make commitments in light of what we grasp through sounds. The purpose of music is not to express proof or argument. Music works within each person through whispers and hunches. Music carries the heart of our different stories, cultures, and traditions. Through music we understand what life and death require. When we make music, we add personal and collective layers to these resonating elements of faith*.

Because music anchors the present moment at the same time that it expresses what is beyond it through a complex weaving of remembering and imagining, choices of music pose both possibilities and difficulties. Whereas for many years, worshipping communities depended on European precedents as the primary resources of sacred sounds, we know now the limits of that dependence. Whereas most worshipping communities were made up of people from the same tradition, now they comprise people of multiple denominations, multiple ethnicities and cultures, and varied needs in the same church community. These situations require meticulous and respectful attention to questions about music. What words and sounds awaken and energize faith in emerging contexts?

With Bach* and rock, complex rhythms and timeless chants, worshipping communities experience their faith as both familiar and unfamiliar. Music makes it possible to discover again and again what it is to be Christian in a world that changes quickly and is instantly interconnected. JANET WALTON

Myanmar (Burma). Despite government-imposed restrictions on missionary activities (since 1962), Christianity in Myanmar is a vibrant, rapidly growing faith, as Christians witness to their faith and Burmese church leadership is developed through theological education and the increasing role of women.

The earliest Christian work in Myanmar was that of the Franciscan Pierre Bonfer (1554), but the Catholic mission was actually established by the Italian Barnabite Fathers (1721), followed by the Congregation of Propaganda (1829) and the Oblates of Turin (1840). The Catholic missionaries established schools, seminaries, and other social institutions. They are noted for their work in publishing primers, catechisms, and histories of Myanmar and the Catholic mission.

Protestant mission work began in 1807 with English Baptists and was carried on by North American Baptist missionaries, Adoniram and Ann Judson, who arrived in 1813. They were joined by other Baptist missionaries and missionaries from the Paris Foreign Mission Society (1856).

At the time of the three Anglo-Burmese wars (between 1826 and 1885), Anglican chaplains accompanied the British troops. The first diocese was established by Jonathan Holt Titcomb (1877). Dr. Jonathan Ebenezer Marks, a missionary educator, founded schools and was invited by King Mindon to establish one in Mandalay. The US Methodists began their mission in 1878 and the British Methodists in 1880. All denominations reported substantial growth among the Karens, Kachins, Chins, and other ethnic minorities under British colonial rule and after Myanmar achieved independence (1948); but there has been little growth among Burmans, the majority ethnic group.

A coup by General Ne Win in 1962 (who ruled until 1988) led to a socialist rule. All missionaries were expelled (1966). Mission and private schools, as well as social work institutions (e.g. orphanages, hospitals), were nationalized. Despite pro-democracy demonstrations (1988) and the victory of the National League for Democracy (led by Aung San Suu Kyi, who received the Nobel Prize) in the 1990 national elections, the army continues to control the country. Christians face difficulties in building churches and doing mission work. However, the churches continue to grow. Seminaries report record enrollment, churches are full, and Christians continue to witness to their faith.

As a result of the expulsion of missionaries (1966), the churches urgently needed to develop local leadership. Theological schools from mainline denominations were instituted; the Association for Theological Education in Myanmar included 30 theological schools (2006) representing nine major Protestant denominations (among them, the Myanmar Institute of Theology for higher theological education) and made connections with the Roman Catholic major seminaries and the Evangelical/Pentecostal schools. The reason for the large enrollment in seminaries could be that theological education provides an alternative to the state secular education or that revival* and mission programs prepare believers for the ministry. The forms of theological education vary, but they all aim to be contextual (see Contextualization).

Burmese culture does not encourage leadership by women, even though women bear half the economic and social burden of the home. Traditional views of women's roles continue to dominate even the churches, so that women are rarely found in decision-making bodies and few women are ordained. Yet a large number of women now teach in the theological schools, and some are heads of these schools.

Christianity, despite its deliberate contextual character, is still regarded as a "potted plant" in Buddhist Myanmar, and Christians are regarded as pro-Western and non-nationalist. Christian missionaries' triumphalist approach has not helped matters. What is needed is genuine dialogue* with the large Buddhist* majority.

Christians were instrumental in initiating development work in health*, education*, community welfare, agriculture, and work with marginalized people like orphans, the blind, the elderly, migrants, refugees, exploited women, and the poor. New ideas about development are needed to meet the growing food crises, especially among the rural and urban poor.

Statistics: Population (2000): 45.6 million. Christians, 8% (Protestants, especially Baptists, 6%; Roman Catholics, 1%; independents, 1%); Buddhists, 85%; native religionists, 1%; Muslims, 4% (in the south); others, 2%. (Based on *World Christian Encyclopedia*, 2001.)

ANNA MAY SAY PA

Mystagogy, a Greek term referring to initiation into a particular mystery*. The Hellenistic mystery* religions used this term to refer to their secret rites of initiation. In Eastern churches, mystagogy is initiation into the sacraments* (mysteries), into fundamental doctrines (especially the mysteries of the Trinity*, Christ*, the Incarnation*, the Holy* Spirit), as well as into the mystical relationship with God, Jesus Christ, and the Holy Spirit, whether in individual religious experience, in communal worship, or in secular life. In the Roman Catholic Church, mystagogy is the post-baptismal initiation and instruction of believers. More generally, mystagogy refers to the principles and practice of the interpretation of mysteries.

Mystery (Gk *mysterion*), that about which one should not speak (a secret) or cannot speak (since it is beyond words). The Hellenistic mystery* religions illustrate the first perspective; their emphasis is on "secret": initiates had "experiences of mystery" (e.g. rebirth or mystical experiences in ceremonies), about which they were not to speak. The Dead* Sea Scrolls illustrate the second perspective; in them "mystery" (Heb *raz*) refers to the mysterious ways in which God acts in history and to the divine plan to bring about the end of time. This active presence of God was "revealed" to the prophets – they recognized it, pointed to it – but it remained a mystery, i.e. something that cannot be known directly and spoken about because it is beyond human understanding. This mystery was in turn revealed to those who diligently studied the prophets' oracles (i.e. to the apocalyptically minded members of the Qumran community).

Given these two perspectives, Paul's references to his proclamation of Jesus Christ as based on "the revelation of the mystery kept secret [silent] for long ages" (Rom 16:25) and to other "mysteries" (Rom 11:25, referring to the "mystery" of the hardening of Israel; various mysteries in 1 Cor) are understood in two ways. They are understood in the Greek sense as referring to "secrets" that have been explained and/or can now be told openly (in which case, no mystery remains) – a line of interpretation that is prolonged in dogmatic theologies that emphasize the role of reason*. Or they are understood in the prophetic and apocalyptic sense as referring to experiences of mystery, to divine interventions that have been revealed but are and remain beyond human understanding and beyond words (the proclamation points to the presence of a mystery, which remains a mystery). In the latter case, Orthodox* churches perceive the sacraments* to be mysteries. A theological approach to mystery, prized in Alexandria by Clement* and Origen*, emphasizes that a mystery can be known and revealed, but it is and remains paradoxical*; such an apophatic* theology (or "negative theology") is associated with mysticism*. To encounter a mystery is to encounter the holy or sacred, which overwhelms the believer – an experience of heteronomy* (in the positive sense of this term, although it remains fraught with danger).

DANIEL PATTE

Mystery Play, medieval dramatization of a biblical narrative, often performed in the vernacular. **See FRENCH LITERATURE AND CHRISTIANITY; PORTUGUESE LITERATURE AND CHRISTIANITY.**

Mystery Religions and Christianity. The mysteries, or mystery religions, were secret religious organizations that flourished during the Greco-Roman period, frequently alongside early Christianity. Typically rooted in ancient tribal and fertility worship, the mysteries proclaimed the salvation* of individuals who chose to be initiated into the inner secrets of life in this world and beyond.

Among the most prominent of the mystery religions were the Eleusinian mysteries of Demeter and Kore and the mysteries of Dionysos, of the Great Mother and Attis, of Isis and Osiris, and of Mithras*. Initiation apparently involved secret ceremonies, but little is known about the actual rituals. The ceremonies of a number of the mystery religions probably included a sacred meal shared by those initiated. The experience of initiates may be described as a passage through death to new life, so that some texts on the mysteries refer to one who is *renatus* (reborn or born again), and divine figures may be depicted, in one way or another, as dying and rising.

Like the mystery religions, early Christianity was a religion of salvation and personal decision, and Christian worship was also expressed in ceremonial rituals, forms of initiation (see Baptism Cluster), and sacred meals (see Communion; Eucharist Cluster). Christianity often understood salvation in the context of death* and resurrection*, and of rebirth (the Gospel of John*), and in relation to Jesus as a dying and rising figure (e.g., in Paul's letters and the Gospels). Clement* of Alexandria (in *Exhortation to the Greeks*) concludes that Christianity may be considered a mystery religion, although it is the only true manifestation of the mysteries. Today most scholars avoid simplistic conclusions about the connection between the mystery religions and early Christianity; instead, they recognize the parallel development of religions deeply concerned with salvation in a Mediterranean environment that employed syncretistic* (inculturated*) means of announcing ways of salvation. **See also MITHRAISM AND CHRISTIANITY.** MARVIN MEYER

Mysticism, Mystics. No fewer than 26 definitions or descriptions of "mysticism" and "mystical theology" are listed by the 20th-c. English prelate and theologian William Ralph Inge in his book *Christian Mysticism*. There is no simple, universally accepted definition of this element of the Christian tradition. Prominent authors have advocated radically incompatible understandings of mysticism.

The interrelated terms "mysticism," "mystery*," and "mystical" are etymologically related to the Greek adjective *mystikos*, which means "hidden" or "secret." In a preliminary way, we can say that mysticism is the whole set of beliefs and practices arising from a conviction about, and a more or less intense awareness of, realities that are otherwise hidden. Above all, this hidden reality is God's presence, experienced by Christians either in and through Scripture*, the sacraments*, and the world of nature, or in a more immediate and direct way without the apparent need for such intermediaries.

Scripture. The best place to begin the study of Christian mysticism is the Bible. Although the adjective "mystical" does not appear in the NT, the cognate noun "mystery" (*mysterion*) is found in a number of important passages. The NT concept of mystery should be interpreted not in light of the ancient Greek mystery religions, as some earlier scholars believed, but in light of the OT, especially the prophets, as most contemporary scholars recognize. Whereas most of the ancient Israelites did not consider themselves privy to God's plans and decisions, which God was believed to make in consultation with those heavenly advisers called either "the council of the holy ones" (Ps 89:8, NAB) or "the divine assembly" (Ps 82:1), the prophets did have access to this otherwise hidden (i.e. "mystical") realm. According to Jeremiah, the distinction between a true and false prophet depended on whether or not one "has stood in the council of the Lord, to see him and to hear his word" (Jer 23:18). For this reason, and contrary to the position of an older author like Friedrich Heiler (d1967), who made a sharp distinction between prophetic and mystical prayer, one could say that the earliest mystics in the Judeo-Christian tradition were the Hebrew prophets*.

In the NT, Jesus himself is portrayed as very much in the line of these prophets. He too has knowledge of his Father's plan of salvation* and is able to reveal it to his disciples*, as when he tells them, "To you is granted the mystery of the kingdom of heaven" (Mark 4:11; cf. Matt 13:11; Luke 8:10), or when he breaks forth in the exultant cry, "I give praise to you, Father, Lord of heaven and earth, for although you have hidden these things from the wise and the learned, you have revealed them to the childlike" (Matt 11:25). Paul is also to be numbered among the early Christian mystics by virtue of his claim that he and his fellow apostles are to be regarded as "servants of Christ and stewards of the mysteries of God" (1 Cor 4:1), for they "speak God's wisdom, mysterious, hidden [*en mysterio*], which God predetermined before the ages for our glory" (1 Cor 2:7). Joseph Fitzmyer has in fact concluded that *mysterion* is so central to Paul's thought that "it conveys for him the content of his gospel."

Patristic Era. *Mysterion* was an equally fundamental term for Origen* (c185–c254), who has been called the church's first great theologian. In his voluminous commentaries on individual books of the Bible, Origen regularly sought the "mystical" or "spiritual" sense of the text, i.e. its deeper meaning, hidden from those who remained only at the narrative level but open to anyone who, gifted by God, could grasp "the inner meaning, the Lord's meaning." Origen was convinced that this was possible precisely because the Bible was not just another book but was one pervaded by God's presence, even though that presence was hidden to those who did not read the text with the eyes of faith*. Other patristic writers, convinced of a similarly real but hidden presence of the Lord in the sacraments, likewise called them mystical, as when Nilus of Ancyra (d c430) spoke of the Eucharist "not as simple bread but as mystical bread" or when Eusebius* of Caesarea wrote of baptism as "mystical regeneration in the name of the Father, Son, and Holy Spirit."

This awareness of God's presence in the Bible and sacraments* was, understandably, sometimes characterized by what we today would call profound religious experience. Although these early writers did not often speak of their experiences in an autobiographical way, from time to time they did break through. In Origen's first homily on the Song of Songs, which he interpreted "mystically" as referring to the loving union between Christ as bridegroom and the individual soul as bride, he wrote, "Often, God is my witness, I have felt that the Bridegroom was approaching, and that he was as near as possible to me; then he has suddenly gone away, and I have not been able to find what I was seeking.... He does that often, until I hold him truly and rise leaning on my well-beloved."

A patristic writer of a somewhat later generation, Gregory* of Nyssa (c335–c395), sometimes called the father of Christian mysticism, emphasized much more insistently than Origen the ultimate incomprehensibility of God, but this insistence was accompanied by an equally strong assertion that one can still have "some sense of [God's] presence," as Gregory writes in his commentary on the Song of Songs. In the West, and at approximately the same time, the most influential of the Latin fathers, Augustine* of Hippo, wrote about an experience of the Divine Presence that he and his mother, Monica*, underwent simultaneously. Using the language of ascent, he writes in his *Confessions* (Book 9) that the two of them "rose beyond ourselves and in a flash of thought touched the Eternal Wisdom which remains over all. If this could be sustained and other quite different visions disappear, leaving only this one to ravish and absorb and envelop its beholder in inward joys so that life might forever be such as that one moment of understanding for which we had been sighing, would not this be: 'Enter into the joy of your Lord' [Matt 25:21]?"

Medieval and Early Modern Era. Augustine's depiction of that mystical experience as a vision, together with his attempt in *The Literal Meaning of Genesis* (Book 12) to distinguish among different kinds of visions, provided a theoretical basis for the "visionary literature" that came to form a large part of the corpus of medieval mystical texts, as in the works of Hildegard* of Bingen (1098–1179), Henry Suso (1300–66), and Julian* of Norwich (1343–c1416). The ongoing popularity of their works, distinguished not only by detailed descriptions of visions but also by acute theological reflections on them, has contributed to the widespread assumption that mystics regularly experience visions or other extraordinary phenomena, such as locutions (divine words heard inwardly) or ecstasy (a sense of "standing outside" oneself in a trance-like state of felt timelessness). Near the dawn of the modern era, Teresa* of Ávila (1515–82) analyzed such phenomena in great detail, especially in her masterpiece, *The Interior Castle* (Part 6). Teresa's analyses are penetrating, but the very brilliance of her work has almost inevitably reinforced for many the impression that Christian mysticism is something extraordinary, reserved for a chosen few, while most followers of Christ are consigned to a more ordinary way of discipleship. This was certainly the understanding of mysticism in what was, according to the *Oxford English Dictionary*, the first recorded use of the word in English, when Henry Coventry wrote in *Philemon to Hydaspes* (1736), "How much nobler a Field of Exercise... are the seraphic Entertainments of Mysticism and Extasy than the mean and ordinary Practice of a mere earthly and common Virtue!"

Some More Recent Understandings. Coventry's once widely accepted depiction of mysticism as something extraordinary has more recently been subjected to criticism by various scholars. The two opposing viewpoints can be illustrated by the work of two theologians of the 20th c., both of them referring to the life of Thérèse* of Lisieux (1873–97), revered by millions as a great saint. In his study of Thérèse, Hans Urs von* Balthasar stated categorically that she never "crossed the threshold into what is known as mysticism." He justified his position by noting that her life was free of the presence of or even the longing for extraordinary "mystical phenomena" such as visions, ecstasies, and locutions. Yet Louis Bouyer, also fully aware that such phenomena were absent from Thérèse's life, drew a very different conclusion, namely that she offers us "the most convincing testimony of the fact that genuine mysticism does not consist so much in the experience of ecstasies or 'visions',... but quite simply in total self-abandonment in naked faith, through an efficacious love of the Cross that is one with the very love of the crucified God." The main thing, according to Bouyer, is to be fully convinced of the Divine Presence within oneself and others, "and especially to act accordingly, not to experience more or less directly the feeling that this is indeed so."

It would be pointless to argue that one of those understandings of mysticism is correct and the other simply wrong, for in fact the term has long been used in both these senses. However, it is worth noting that Bouyer's understanding is more in accord with the way the mystical was understood in the early Christian centuries, when a conviction of God's presence in the Bible, the sacraments, other human beings, or the world of nature was not necessarily associated with the kinds of unusual phenomena that von Balthasar had in mind. In this earlier understanding, the mystical is viewed as something that, to one degree or another, is part of any devout Christian's life journey. The Trappist monk Thomas Merton* (1915–1968) expressed this continuity of the mystical with other stages of spiritual growth in a particularly felicitous way in one of his essays: "To reach a true awareness of [God] as well as ourselves, we have to renounce our selfish and limited self and enter into a whole new kind of existence, discovering an inner center of motivation and love which makes us see ourselves and everything else in an entirely new light. Call it faith*, call it (at a more advanced stage) contemplative* illumination, call it the sense of God or even mystical union: all these are different aspects and levels of the same kind of realization: the awakening to a new awareness of ourselves in Christ, created in Him, redeemed by Him, to be transformed and glorified in and with Him." One of Merton's contemporaries, the monk David Steindl-Rast, has expressed this understanding even more succinctly by writing that "a mystic is not a special kind of human being; rather, every human being is a special kind of mystic" (see Heteronomy).

Mysticism and Interreligious Dialogue. Christians in all parts of the world would do well to reflect on the fact that the theologian Friedrich von* Hügel (1852–1925) convincingly argued that the mystical element of religion is just as indispensable as what he called the other two basic elements: the institutional and the speculative. It is only when one of the three becomes top-heavy or undervalued that problems arise. It is equally important to realize that the same three elements are to be found, to some degree, in all the great world religions. Just as Christians sense God's presence in the Bible, so too do Jewish mystics find that presence above all in the Torah, Muslims in the Qur'an, and Hindus in the Vedas, Upanishads, and *Bhagavad Gita*, while Buddhists experience the ongoing presence of the Buddha in their sutras and other scriptures. In our time, when encounters with members of other religious traditions are becoming more and more common, this element of the mystical may well offer a more common ground for dialogue* than the institutional and speculative elements, if only because religious institutions are often associated with memories of hostile actions in the past and theological speculations have frequently been characterized by charges and countercharges of heresy.

JAMES A. WISEMAN, OSB

Myth and the Study of Christianity. In its early Greek usage, the term *mythos* was largely synonymous with *logos**. Thinkers such as Plato made a distinction between the two, qualifying myth as something implausible or fabulous, viewing *logos* as a more positive term. From this early period up to the present, the various presentations and interpretations of myths, and the debates over their function in culture, society, and religion, have constituted the field of mythology.

Despite its secondary status as "implausible," myth is found in every culture and during every epoch; it is as widespread as it is diverse. A primary characteristic of myth is the language it uses. It tends to speak of the very nature of creation* in a declarative and constative way, in a tone beyond simple proposition or description. Thus mythical language speaks directly to the order and meaning of human existence, typically through an account of the beginnings of things. Often in archaic language, these narratives provide us with cosmogonies, creation stories at a point in time somehow removed from our own. Mythical language also typically supplies the meaning behind various ritual acts or sacred objects. Thus the significance and connotations of the rite of Communion*, or Eucharist*, may be approached through the lens of mythology.

Beyond its contribution to the development of literature, myth is central to our attempts to understand religion*. Since all religions appear to rely on it, myth may be seen as an expression of something essential to both human religiosity and culture*. Yet how are we to translate those insights from mythical language into scholarly discourse? Some of the most significant answers to this problem are the following.

One approach, which originated with the Greeks, is to read myths as allegories* that speak to the human condition or as questions of ultimate significance. For example, stories of the battling gods are to be understood simply as providing insight into the conflicting impulses found within all human beings. This type of allegorical reduction remains a common practice even today.

When 18th-c. North Atlantic empires arose and expanded across much of the known world, the comparative models of modern science came to be applied to myth. In their encounters with a bewildering variety of societies, religions, and languages, North Atlantic travelers and later ethnographers sought to compare myths gathered from all cultures. In the face of such variety, a notable project was the search for the origins of religion*; comparative mythology was seen as a uniquely useful method for such a vast scientific exercise.

For mainstream Christian theology, the question of myth came to center stage only in the 19th c. As a part of his contribution to modern theology, and most likely inspired by 18th-c. ethnographers, Schleiermacher* embraced certain elements of myth in order to explain the variation of forms God* had taken over time. God is to be known mythically; the hidden truth is eternal and unchanging, but divinity moves across the ages assuming various forms. Schleiermacher also contributed to the debates arising over the principles of hermeneutics*, or scriptural* interpretation. The concept of myth was important in these discussions, but Bultmann* and his followers objected and in fact attempted to free their biblical readings of myth, seeking to "demythologize*" Scripture.

With the advent of modern psychology, efforts began anew to translate the language of myth. In an effort to access the shared unconscious of the human mind, Carl Jung turned to the common patterns and symbols* recurring in myth. Another modern figure to systematically research commonalities among the myths of various cultures was the historian and comparative religionist Mircea Eliade.

RICHARD J. MCGREGOR

N

Nag Hammadi Codices, collection of 12 papyrus codices (probably 4th c. CE) and pages from a 13th, found in 1945 by villagers near the town of Nag Hammadi, Upper Egypt, and containing Coptic translations of more than four dozen tractates. Several of these bear some relation to Valentinian*, Sethian, or similar traditions described by earlier Christian heresiologists and often labeled "Gnostic*." Before 1945 knowledge about such groups came primarily from these polemical accounts, since the original works were not yet known (except for a few, found primarily in three early Coptic manuscripts discovered in the 18th–19th c.).

Most of the tractates were originally composed in Greek, probably between the 2nd and 4th c. CE, and some possibly earlier (a fragment of Plato's *Republic*). They vary in genre: collections of sayings (e.g. the well-known Gospel of Thomas*, the Gospel of Philip*, the Gospel* of Truth), apocalypses (e.g. Apocalypse of Peter*), treatises in epistolary form, homilies, and others. Several (e.g. Apocryphon of John*) contain myths* of origin, describing the emergence of the divine realm and the creation of the cosmos and human beings, with the creation of the material world typically ascribed to lower creators rather than the highest God.

MICHAEL A. WILLIAMS

Nahum, Book of, one of the Twelve Prophets and containing some of the HB's most vivid poetry, offers no criticism of its own people (unlike other prophetic books), but describes the "devastation, desolation, and destruction" (2:10) of Nineveh, the capital city of the Assyrian Empire. Thus the prophet's name, which means "comfort" or "comforter" (or is a shortened form of "YHWH comforts"), is quite appropriate for a Judahite audience that suffered deeply at Nineveh's hands (1:15, 2:2) but is ironic from the perspective of the Ninevites, whose "name shall be perpetuated no longer" (1:14).

Scholars agree that Nahum's prophecy is to be dated to around 612 BCE, the year Nineveh fell to a coalition of Mede and Babylonian forces. That event was either imminent or had recently occurred.

The execution of justice* against Nineveh, clearly warranted because of its endless cruelties (3:19), is a demonstration of the belief that YHWH, the universal sovereign, "takes vengeance on his adversaries and rages against his enemies" (1:2) with punishments that are appropriate to the crimes committed. Indeed, given the prophet's description of Nineveh as a prostitute (other cities like Jerusalem [Ezek 16:1–43] and Rome [Rev 17:1–6] were similarly portrayed in other prophetic literature) and its treachery as sexual seduction (3:4), YHWH's punishment of sexual violence and humiliation (3:4–7) is metaphorically apt. Nevertheless, the idea that God's anger* may express itself in sexual violence* against women is disconcerting (see Abuse as Pastoral Care Issue) and suggests why these verses rarely find an audience in Christian and Jewish teaching and preaching.

BETH GLAZIER-MCDONALD

Nakedness, Nudity, had a number of meanings in the Christian tradition. Adam* and Eve's* discovery that they were naked (Gen 3:10) is interpreted in two ways: (1) Earlier they were not ashamed of nakedness; thus for some (Adamites, Doukhobors), nakedness without shame* or guilt is regarded as a fruit of salvation*. (2) Earlier they were clothed in wisdom and glory but became naked and vulnerable through sin* (Wis 2:23–24; Rom 8:19–22; 2 Cor 5:4), whose power is overcome through Christ's death (Rom 6:6–11). Literal nakedness connotes poverty and vulnerability (Job 1:21; Matt 25:36). For Jerome* the ascetic* life consisted of "nakedly following the naked Christ"; Francis* of Assisi left his previous life by literally becoming naked. In the early church, a person being baptized* was naked, signifying transition, rejection of the old, and putting on of the new.

Name of Jesus, Feast of the, medieval celebration held in January; on the Roman calendar until 1969; for Anglicans, an alternative to the Feast of the Circumcision (January 1).

Namibia, a large, sparsely populated country, has large diamond, copper, zinc, uranium, and salt deposits, vast tracts of cattle grazing land, and a sea laden with fish. It was colonized by Germany (1884–1919) and was then under South African rule until it achieved independence (1990). A policy of "divide and rule" (apartheid*) left the settlers rich and the Namibians poor.

Christianity arrived in Namibia shortly after 1652, when the Nama (Hottentot) people and "Coloureds" from present-day South Africa crossed the Orange River, bringing what they had learned from Dutch settlers. The first European missionaries arrived in 1812 from the London Missionary Society. An indigenous Christian woman, Zara Schmelen (c1793–1831), translated the Bible into Khoekhoegowab (the Nama language). German Lutherans from the Rhenish mission (1842) followed by Finnish Lutherans (1870) established Lutheran churches that formed the United Evangelical Church of South West Africa, the largest church in Namibia.

For their worship services, Namibians have adapted Christian rituals and icons to include indigenous music, songs, artwork, drumming, singing, and dance. Christians regard the cross of Jesus Christ and the Bible as the most sacred Christian symbols and have them in their homes. The churches promote programs dealing with HIV/AIDS by maintaining that AIDS is a disease, not a sin.

Since the peace accords (1988) and independence (1990), the constitution guarantees freedom of religion. Through interreligious and joint social activities, African* Religion is accepted as being on a par with Christianity (and the small Muslim and Jewish communities). Some Christians retain indigenous beliefs and practices; e.g. African Religion speaks more intimately to their spiritual needs during the difficult moments of death* and mourning.

Statistics: Population (2000): 1.7 million (M). Christians, 1.6 M, 92.3% (Protestants, 0.8 M; Roman Catholics, 0.3 M; members of African Instituted Churches and other independents, 0.2 M); African Religionists, 0.1 M, 6%. (Based on *World Christian Encyclopedia*, 2001.)

PAUL JOHN ISAAK

Nantes, Edict of, and Its Revocation. The Edict of Nantes was a decree issued in 1598 by Henry* IV of France to end the wars between Catholics and Huguenots*; it embodied many features of earlier peace agreements (1564, 1570, 1576).

The Edict gave Protestants liberty of conscience and private worship and of public worship in many localities and on the estates of Protestant nobles (though not in Paris); royal funds for Protestant schools, including several universities; special courts, with both Catholic and Protestant judges, for cases involving Protestants; and control of about 200 cities and 5 garrisoned cities.

This last provision conflicted with the absolutist policies of Richelieu (in power 1624–42), and later Mazarin and Louis XIV. The fall of La Rochelle (1628) led to the disarming of other military forces. It became increasingly difficult for the Reformed Church to hold national gatherings. After 1665 Protestant children were required to be educated as Roman Catholics; the special courts were abolished in 1679; and the Edict was revoked in 1685 at the request of the Assembly of the Clergy, on the pretense that the majority of Protestants had been converted to Catholicism.

Though forbidden to emigrate, at least 400,000 fled to other countries, enriching their economies at France's expense. The revocation was one of the justifications for England's removal of the Roman Catholic king James II and the installation of William in 1688, with the provision that no Catholic was to occupy the British throne. The demand for external conformity fostered duplicity and guarded attitudes as ongoing marks of French culture; the contrast with England's religious tolerance gave weight to criticism by Voltaire and other Enlightenment figures. EUGENE TESELLE

Narcisa de Jesús (1832–69), "the Violet of Nobol." Born in Nobol, Ecuador, she consecrated her life to the service of God as a humble dressmaker. She moved to Lima (1868), where she lived a life dedicated to spirituality and service to others. She was beatified in 1992.

LUIS MARÍA GAVILANES DEL CASTILLO

Narthex, vestibule to the nave, separated from it by a railing, columns, or a wall.

Nathanael, disciple* from Cana (John 1:45–51), not listed as an apostle* in the Gospels other than John but possibly identical with Bartholomew*.

National Association of Evangelicals, a coordinating agency facilitating Christian unity, public witness, and cooperative ministry among some 60 Evangelical denominations, congregations, educational institutions, and service agencies (e.g. the Salvation* Army) in the USA; it started in St. Louis, Missouri (1942), and expanded in the 1950s (as Billy Graham, associated with the agency, gained visibility). It sponsored the New International Version of the Bible (1978). It is usually contrasted with the liberal National* Council of Churches and the conservative American* Council of Christian Churches.

National Baptist Convention, USA, founded in 1895 with headquarters in Nashville, Tennessee. Claiming more than 8 million members, it is the largest body of African American Baptists. A dispute over the National Baptist Publishing Board led to the organization of the rival National Baptist Convention of America (1915). Differences over the tenure of the presidency and the Convention's role in civil* rights resulted in a second split in 1961, as Gardner C. Taylor, Martin Luther King*, Jr., and other Evangelical liberals rejected the "gradualism" and "progressive accommodationism" of its president, Joseph H. Jackson, in favor of the politics of confrontation and organized campaigns of nonviolent direct action. King and others on the "Taylor team" supported the decision to organize the Progressive National Baptist Convention, USA, a second rival body. The programs and priorities of the National Baptist Convention, USA, have over time included foreign missions, cooperation with white Baptists, and racial uplift and empowerment. The election of Theodore J. Jemison, an adviser to King, to the presidency of the Convention in 1982 inaugurated a gradual shift away from the sociopolitical conservatism of Jackson toward a more liberal philosophy, a trend that continues in the early 21st c. LEWIS V. BALDWIN

National Council of Churches (NCC), leading ecumenical* organization in the USA, founded (1950) by the merger of the Federal* Council of Churches and seven other interchurch agencies. It includes 36 Protestant, Anglican, Orthodox*, African*American, and peace* churches. Affiliated with the World* Council of Churches, it seeks interchurch and interfaith cooperation and advocates social justice. It sponsored two new translations* of the Bible*: the Revised Standard (1946, 1952) and the New Revised Standard (1989). Churches that disagree with the NCC are affiliated with the National* Association of Evangelicals and the American* Council of Christian Churches.

National Covenant (1638), covenant* of Scottish Presbyterians protesting the imposition of the Book* of Common Prayer on the Church* of Scotland.

Nationalism and Christianity. Nationalism is an ideological* formulation of a society's culture*. It can be based on language, kinship, history, or religion, or a combination of these elements. To be useful as one of these foundational elements, religion (whether Christianity or another religion) has to be nationalized. In societies where religions are pitted against each other, they have to be cleansed of their divisive potential by being encapsulated in nationalism – being made part and parcel of national identity, and having histories of religious conflict tailored to fit a tale of national unity. Religious worship comes to be connected with moments of national glory and national remembrance. This process of homogenization is never entirely successful, because nationalism not only unifies but also diversifies by giving rise to alternative forms of nationalism or regional identities. Since in modern nation-states a politics of numbers, producing majorities and minorities, is important, religion can be used as the foundation of majority nationalism as well as of minority identities.

Nationalism can be secular or religious. In the modern period, the relation of secular nationalism to religion is particularly significant. Secular nationalism as an ideology helps create the space in which religions are allowed to operate. This does not mean that the role of religion is necessarily limited. Religious traditions as interpreted in a nationalist way are crucial to the formation of state–society and society–individual relations in the modern nation. Religious traditions become fields of disciplinary practice in which modern civil subjects are formed and contribute to the creation of the modern public. Religious institutions make possible notions of individual conscience and civilized conduct; religious movements produce notions of what is "public" and shape public opinion.

At a theoretical level, secular nationalism can be seen as replacing religion (becoming the religion of the nation-state), and modern statecraft as a secularized political theology. However, religious communities are never entirely absorbed by nationalism and continue to be the object of secular regulation, such as in the separation of state and church (see Church and State Relations Cluster).

Nationalism can also be religious in nature. Religious nationalism may amount to not more than a civil* religion in the sense that national leaders express their belief that the nation is "a nation under God." Themes of death, sacrifice, rebirth, and a mission in the world are celebrated in religious fashion during national holidays and in the form of national monuments. In certain cases, when war and death are involved, the nation has to acquire a metaphysical existence beyond individual life.

Important theological concepts have been adopted by modern nationalism, such as that of the chosen people* of God, formulated from the OT – a notion that can justify an almost racial sense of superiority and fuel nationalist projects abroad and at home; that of rebirth or revival* of the nation, connected to the Protestant metaphor of awakening*; that of the coming of a messiah*, a leader who will take his people to a promised land. A religious symbolic repertoire of divine election*, of ordeals to test one's convictions*, conversion* to higher truth, and martyrdom* is routinely applied to the biographies of great nationalist leaders and their nations.

World religions like Christianity can never be entirely captured by particular forms of nationalism, because they have a global mission*. From the 19th c., this global mission has been transformed by the emergence of a world system of nation-states in which a Christian is at the same time a member of a worldwide community and a citizen of a nation-state. Members of Christian minorities all over the world are constantly questioned about their national loyalty. This is clearest in the case of Roman Catholics, especially those with an Ultramontanist* position, who affirm their allegiance to the pope and are consequently accused of national disloyalty. The nationalist question of loyalty concerned Roman Catholics in 19th-c. Britain as much as it concerns Coptic* Christians in Egypt today. Particularly, conversion to Christianity in nations that consider themselves to be non-Christian is often considered to be antinational. One strategy for coping with this is to show the deep, historical roots of Christianity in periods of national history that are important to the nationalist imagination.

The global character of Christianity makes it transnational, despite its being aligned with nationalism in many places. While Protestant state* churches are directly connected to nation-states, the religious cause is always seen as expanding beyond the boundaries of the nation-state, especially in missionary activities and theologies of dialogue. While the Christian mission* is as old as Christianity itself, missionary activities receive new salience and new challenges owing to the emergence of nationalism. In the contemporary phase of globalization, transnational Christian movements, such as Evangelicalism* and Charismatic* Catholicism, align themselves with nationalism in different parts of the world, while simultaneously remaining outside the control of national states.

PETER VAN DER VEER

Native American Traditions and Christianity. A lingering question in the minds of many Euro-Christians and even in the minds of some Indian people has to do with the possible connections between Christianity and the cultures* and religious traditions of Native peoples in North America. Are not the spirits that Native peoples call on similar to the angels of the Christian holy text? Do not all Indian people have a name for that Sacred Other identified by Euro-Christians as "God"?

Before these concerns are addressed, the radical cultural differences between American Indians and all those cultures associated with European modernity – a complex issue – must be noted. We limit ourselves here to two principal differences between these two cultural sets and try to demonstrate their ultimate incommensurability.

Two cultural values won the day in Europe with the emergence of European modernity: individualism and temporality. With the concurrent emergence of European colonialism*, these values were then imposed on all the lands and peoples dominated by the European military, economic, and political machinery. These values were internalized by European peoples to such an extent that they are presumed to be universal values, when they are recognized at all (so dominant is the cultural conditioning). Yet most of the world's indigenous peoples, and particularly American Indians, live according to a very different and contrasting set of deeply rooted cultural values, marked by spatiality and communitarianism.

Because the basic notion of salvation* in the Euro-Western schema is heavily individualized (individual or personal salvation in Jesus Christ), the colonial missionary imposition of this model of salvation immediately worked for the destruction of Indian communitarian values. A well-known story involves a missionary who finally achieved the conversion of the chief of a tribe. When the chief capitulated, received catechetical instruction, and agreed to baptism, he discovered that the missionary refused to baptize the whole tribe because the members had not been likewise instructed. The chief therefore deferred his own baptism until the missionary was able to instruct the whole tribe. To this day, Indian cultures are strongly characterized by communitarianism, in spite of the concurrent greed of individualism that is taught by the missionaries, schools (stressing personal achievement over community good), and US government officials and the dysfunctionality that such individualism creates. One of the characteristic behaviors in Indian communities that continues today is called the "give-away," whereby an Indian family would honor the community by generously giving gifts that they had been collecting for a long time. The missionaries condemned these give-aways as demonic. Their reasoning seems to have been that it hindered the development of the newly imposed regime of individualism, not merely that it detracted from the Sunday morning offering.

The difference between spatiality and European temporality is perhaps even more foundational for both cultures, yet is much less readily acknowledged by Euro-Americans. While the sacred is measured in terms of time in the West (e.g. seventh day, Sunday mass, the Julian and Gregorian calendars*, liturgical time, the time clock, production schedules, the value of labor, annual reports to stockholders), space and place are much more significant to Indian peoples. Where we live, the territories where we are sovereign, the orientation of our homes (with doors facing east in most tribes), the direction of our heads when we sleep, how we bury our dead: these are key issues in our cultures. Ceremonies always have a spatial orientation: Sun dances and green corn dances are oriented toward the rising of the sun. A sweat lodge may face east or west, depending on the tribe and/or the particularity of the ceremony. The lingering sense of spatiality in Euro-Christianity is reduced to speaking of the altar in a church as "liturgical east," even when the orientation is north by northwest, an architectural decision predicated largely on economic and temporal concerns.

These two fundamental cultural differences mean that any Indian convert to Christianity must deeply sacrifice cultural values and habits of behavior that affect the well-being of the whole of a community.

Finally, Indian peoples universally lack a word for "god*," just as most tribes lack a word for "war." These have been provided by missionaries and US government officials over the years of colonial intervention in Indian affairs. Our understanding of the world, as Apache scholar Viola Cordova has argued, is radically different from European understandings of God and is complex to the point of having evaded successful interpretation by Eurocolonial scholars to this day. At this point, comparisons should be made not with Christianity but between Native understandings and the explanations of modern theoretical astrophysicists.

GEORGE E. "TINK" TINKER

Nativity (from Lat for "birth"), festival of Jesus'* birth, observed in Western churches on Christmas*, December 25, and in Eastern churches culminating on January 6 as a part of the Theophany* (Epiphany*) celebration. The term is also used for the birthdays of John* the Baptist (June 24) and Mary* (September 8).

Natural Law, moral norms shared by Christians and others. Paul assumes that all people have an awareness of God's Law* through conscience, so that it is possible for them to do "by nature" what God also commands in the Law (Rom 2:14–16).

How is this to be understood? Emphasis may be placed on an intuitive sense of good and evil, or on rational deduction from the first principles of practical reason*, or on natural human tendencies. Thomas Aquinas* combined these: natural law consists in precepts of practical reason formulated after careful inquiry into natural inclinations and needs; thus life, reproduction, care of the young, life in society, and religion ought to be respected in private actions and in the laws of states.

A rival theory, building on the feudal* notion that rights are based on a mutual oath*, was that rights are not "natural" but are based on social customs, oaths and contracts, or divine revelation. In the history of colonization*, conquering powers often made the claim that people may enslave themselves freely. This perspective was opposed by Bartolomé de las* Casas, who argued that rights have a status independent of personal choice. Eventually this was to develop into the theory of "inalienable rights." The US Declaration of Independence and the Declaration of the Rights of Man brought theories of inalienable natural rights into public law. The Universal Declaration of Human* Rights, formulated by the United Nations (1948, 1949), has become part of international law.

EUGENE TESELLE

Natural Theology, without appeal to revelation*, endeavors to show that the propositions that God exists, God more probably exists than not, God is more reasonably believed to exist than not, or the like, are true. This contrasts with natural atheology, which tries to prove the contradictory, or some logical contrary, of these propositions, and with a defense, which replies to a natural atheology argument. Coming with various strictures – among them deductive, probabilistic, abductive (to the best explanation), and cumulative – it may use perceptual, introspective, metaphysical, moral, historical, aesthetic, or epistemological premises. Pascal's wager that belief in God is more rational than unbelief, since a believer may gain infinite benefit and risks minor loss, whereas the unbeliever may gain minor benefit and risks infinite loss, is not an argument that God exists, but for its being a better gamble to believe that God exists than not to believe. It is not an instance of natural theology.

The "moral argument" refers to a variety of arguments to the effect that there being true moral propositions entails the existence of God, or that our obligation to obey such laws arises only from God commanding us to do so, or that the existence of things possessing value can be explained, or is best explained, only by reference to God.

The "ontological argument" endeavors to show that "God does not exist" is not possibly true, since a proper understanding of the concept of God includes necessary existence or existence in all possible worlds.

The "cosmological argument" infers from there being things that might not have existed, whose existence possibly has an explanation, to there being something that cannot not exist that has caused them. Stronger versions make no claims regarding infinite regress and stress the necessity of there being an explanation for there being things that might not have existed.

The "teleological argument" rests on the idea that the best explanation of the natural order that makes science and everyday life possible is the world being created and sustained by a mind with sufficient power. A specific form begins with the enormous improbability of life having arisen from what the initial physical conditions are believed to be, concluding that it happened only because God brought it about. This idea is challenged by the notion of an infinity of "parallel universes." Religious experience (someone at least seeming to experience God) is appealed to as evidence that God exists, or as best explained by theism*. KEITH E. YANDELL

Nature (Gk *physis;* Lat *natura*), that which makes things, and the world as a whole, act as they do. The earliest Greek philosophers suggested that this factor is matter in one or another mode (water, fire); Plato, that it is transcendent forms in the ideal realm; Aristotle, that it is the form in each individual thing. Theology, while acknowledging that natural things are self-forming and self-sustaining (in contrast to miracles*), sees matter and form as created and sustained by God*. Ancient, medieval, and modern sciences have increasingly traced the lawlike regularity of natural processes. Process* theology sees God as both source and sustainer of these regularities.

Nature and Grace. In Christian life, nature is associated with human capabilities, and grace* with divine influence beyond those capabilities. While Protestants tend to discuss "sin* and grace," Catholic theologians focus on "nature and grace," considering the prior question of the role of grace apart from sin. Hence Thomas Aquinas* asserts that grace presupposes and perfects human nature, and acknowledges human achievements in work, culture, science and technology, and politics; yet the human spirit is satisfied only through God's self-communication in grace, echoing Augustine's opening statement in his *Confessions*: "You have made us for yourself, and our hearts are restless until they rest in you."

Naude, Beyers, minister of the Dutch Reformed Church and member of the Broederbond. After the Cottesloe Consultation (1960), he was forced to leave his church and founded the Christian Institute of Southern Africa (1963). The Christian Institute promulgated a gospel of justice and equality of races, suffered persecution from the government as a result, and was banned (1977). Naude was placed under a five-year house arrest. **See also SOUTH AFRICA.** MOKGETHI MOTLHABI

Nave, main portion of many churches (excluding the chancel*) where the laity worship.

Nazarene. Jesus is called "the Nazarene" in the Gospels and Acts; early Christians are called "Nazarenes" by Jewish leaders (Acts 24:5). "Nazarene" continued to be a Jewish designation (*Notzerim*); it was used by other Christians for Jewish-Christian groups in Syria. Today it is a self-designation for Christians, especially members of the Church of the Nazarene.

Nazarene, Church of the, arose out of the 19th-c. Holiness* Movement in North America. Urban mission on the East and West Coasts (late 19th c.) led to the organizing of two small regional church bodies: the Church of the Nazarene (in the West) and the Association of Pentecostal Churches of America (in the East). The two groups merged (1907) as the Pentecostal Church of the Nazarene. The Holiness Church of Christ, located in the south central USA and committed to evangelism among the mostly rural poor, joined with the other two (1908), followed in 1915 by the Pentecostal Mission in Nashville, Tennessee, and the Pentecostal Church of Scotland in Glasgow. All were committed to evangelism in the USA; to the education of young people for Christian faith, life, and service; and to mission around the world. In 1919 the denomination dropped the term "Pentecostal" from its name.

Having arisen out of the Holiness Movement, the Church of the Nazarene traces its theological heritage to John Wesley*. Theologically, that entails the following commitments:

1. To the primary role and authority of Scripture* in all things pertaining to Christian belief and practice – locating the denomination within Protestantism*. The authority of Scripture lies most fundamentally in its disclosures concerning how humankind may come to know and experience God's redeeming work.
2. To Arminianism*, the theological understanding of the 17th-c. Dutch Reformed* theologian Jacobus (James) Arminius*
3. Most important, to the theological view that humans may experience sanctification* in the present world, to the extent that they know their inner lives to be nothing but undivided love* for God and for others. After conversion, this is a second work of grace called "entire sanctification*."

With more than 1.5 million members in 150 countries (in 2005), the Church of the Nazarene is governed by the quadrennial General Assembly, consisting of delegates from each district that organizes the congregations in a given area. In between sessions of the General Assembly, the affairs of the denomination are supervised by six general superintendents and by a general board, which consists of elected ministerial and lay members.

The Church's relatively successful missionary outreach raises two challenging questions: (1) How can a view of Christian belief and life that arose in a North Atlantic cultural setting be translated into the varied cultural contexts of the world? (2) How can the Church of the Nazarene remain a single, international denomination by minimizing or avoiding domination by its North American "mother church"?

HAL CAUTHRON

Nazarenes, Gospel of the, medieval name for excerpts from a Jewish-Christian gospel, most of them found in Jerome*, some in the Latin version of Origen's* commentary on Matthew and in Eusebius* (although the attributions are often disputed).

The name alludes to Nazareth, Jesus' hometown. Based mainly on Matthew and perhaps on free-floating traditions, the Gospel of the Nazarenes could have been composed in the Jordan area or Syria* (late 2nd c. or, according to Lührmann, the 4th c.).

The narrative of the rich man (Matt 19:16–24) in the Gospel of the Nazarenes contains the comprehensive formula uttered by Jesus: "Man, fulfill the law and the prophets." Appended is the injunction to love "your brothers, Abraham's sons," alluding to the Gospel's background in a Jewish-Christian community. The "daily bread" in the "Our Father" is understood to be "our bread of tomorrow," perhaps rightly so.

The baptism* of Jesus creates some problems, as usual: Is it conceivable that Jesus may have sinned, even in ignorance? In a moralizing version of the parable of the talents, the Lord punishes not the servant who had hidden the money but another who had "spent it on harlots and flute-girls."

HANS-JOSEF KLAUCK

Nazism and Christianity. See GERMAN CHRISTIANS; RACISM AND CHRISTIANITY CLUSTER: IN WESTERN EUROPE.

Negative Theology. See APOPHATICISM.

Nehemiah. See EZRA AND NEHEMIAH, THE BOOKS OF.

Neighbor, "one who is near" (from Old English for "near dweller," a translation of Greek and Hebrew terms with similar connotations). Leviticus 19:18, "You shall love your neighbor as yourself," summarizes the Law in the NT (Matt 19:19, 22:39; Mark 12:31, 33; Luke 10:27; Rom 13:9; Gal 5:14; Jas 2:8). Inevitably the question arises, "Who is my neighbor?" In the OT, "neighbor" generally refers to a member of Israel, but also to people of neighboring countries (especially in Job and in exilic texts). Similarly, in the NT, "neighbor" usually designates a member of the church or of one's social community. But in Luke 10:29–37, Jesus reverses the question. In response to the lawyer's query "Who is my neighbor?" Jesus asks, Who "became a neighbor" to the wounded man (in the parable of the good Samaritan)? In this way, Jesus expanded the neighbor relation to involve universal love*. DANIEL PATTE

Nemesius of Emesa (late 4th c.), bishop of Emesa, author of *On Human Nature,* which makes much use of the Platonist* tradition in discussing the soul*. This work was used by John* of Damascus and, in Latin translation, by the Scholastics*.

Neo-orthodoxy, catchall term for the new approach to theology that emerged after World War I in Germany with "Crisis* theology" (Karl Barth*, Rudolf Bultmann*, Emil Brunner, Friedrich Gogarten, Paul Tillich*) and later in the USA (H. Richard and Reinhold Niebuhr*, Paul Lehmann, Edwin Lewis, Elmer Homrighausen), all liberals who challenged the optimism of liberal* theology and reemphasized the Reformation themes of sin* and justification*. In criticizing modern confidence in progress and emphasizing revelation* rather than natural* theology, they tended to overvalue the European Christian tradition as it had evolved since Constantine* and had benefited from colonialism*. But Barth and Reinhold Niebuhr associated themselves with secular rather than religious socialism, and Tillich paid increasing attention to non-Western religions.

Neoplatonism and Christianity. With Plotinus (204–69 CE), Platonism* took on a new level of both transcendence and complexity, and this had various consequences for its interaction with a soon-to-be triumphant Christianity. Plotinus himself had little direct influence on Christian thinking; the influence came primarily through his pupil Porphyry* (232–c305). The irony is that Porphyry was a noted opponent of Christianity, such that his work *Against the Christians* was condemned to be burned by imperial decree (448). However, his distinctive metaphysical position, identifying the first principle with the "Father" of the intellectual triad (Being, Life, and Intellect), provided a welcome stimulus to the Cappadocians* Gregory* of Nazianzus and Gregory* of Nyssa (late 4th c.) in developing the doctrine of the Trinity*.

With Porphyry's pupil Iamblichus of Chalcis (c245–325), Platonism took a turn toward Sacramental* theology, with the adoption of the rituals of theurgy into a philosophical system (cf. *Myst.* II.11), and this was continued in the Athenian school of Syrianus (c370–435), Proclus (412–80), and Damascius (c465–535). While this paralleled the development of Christian sacramental theology, it is not clear that there was any direct influence from Platonism before the time of Dionysius* the Pseudo-Areopagite (early 6th c.), who was clearly influenced by the Athenian school, particularly in his love of triads and in his adoption of the process of procession and return as a cosmic principle.

However, Platonism constituted primarily a pole of opposition for Christian thinkers of this period; much polemic was directed at it. Particular bones of contention were the Platonist doctrines of the eternity* of the world, the preexistence of the human soul*, and the absolute unity, suprarationality, and impersonality of the first principle. The Alexandrian Christian philosopher John Philoponus (c490–570) inveighed against the former two doctrines, Augustine* (354–430) particularly against the latter. Plotinus had argued that his first principle, the One, must be superior to intellect and being, and thus absolutely impervious to passions, and this position, maintained by all subsequent Platonists, undermined the Christian concept of a personal God*.

Interesting figures on the interface between Platonism and Christianity include Synesius of Cyrene (370–413), a Hellenic philosopher sympathetic to Christianity, who was prevailed upon to become bishop of his native city; Marius Victorinus (mid-4th c.), a Roman lawyer and Platonist philosopher (influenced by Porphyry) who converted to Christianity late in life; and Boethius* (c480–524), who wrote *The Consolation of Philosophy.* **See also PLATONISM AND CHRISTIANITY.** JOHN M. DILLON

Nepal. Although Christianity arrived in Nepal much earlier, present-day Christianity cannot trace its roots before 1950. Since then Nepalese Christianity has experienced phenomenal growth.

When Nepal was still divided into small kingdoms and principalities (18th c.), Capuchins* did missionary work among the Newar people in the Kathmandu Valley, establishing a Christian community with several thousand members. But when Nepal became unified, all Nepalese Christians were deported to Betiya, India (1769), and Christian mission was prohibited.

With the end of the royal Rana regime (1951) and the introduction of democracy, Christian professionals were allowed to come to Nepal for the promotion of health* and education*, although the constitution banned any conversion to Christianity. The punishment for converting to Christianity was a one-year imprisonment; that for preaching or trying to convert someone was a three-year imprisonment; and that for baptizing a convert was a six-year imprisonment. This law, active until 1990, was officially removed in 2008 with the declaration of Nepal as a democratic federal republic, a secular state.

In the midst of these persecutions, Christianity has grown, gaining converts among Hindus, Buddhists, and indigenous people (including Kirants). Denominational differences have been minimal among churches, although some denominational differentiation arose after 1990. The indigenous and autonomous church movement with an Evangelical*, Pentecostal*, and Charismatic* character is predominant. Signs, miracles*, and prayers for healing* are common during church services and during witness among non-Christians.

Church worship takes place on Saturday; baptism* and the Lord's* Supper are the main sacraments*. Most churches are congregational, and the relationship between laity and clergy is nonhierarchical. Women ministers are accepted in most churches. All ministers receive theological education at several Bible training centers.

Nepalese Christians believe that the Bible is the inspired Word of God (see Scripture) and that being born again is absolutely necessary to experience salvation* and entrance in God's kingdom*. Yet Christians also strive for the inner transformation of society and for a better quality of life through education and health care. Christians show patience and respect when dealing with people of other faiths and ideologies.

The main challenges for Nepalese Christian leadership in this period of rapid growth include how to maintain faithful discipleship in their society and work toward the unity of the body of Christ.

Statistics: Population (2008): 29 million. Christians, c4% (almost all independents, with a few Protestants, Roman Catholics, and Orthodox; most are Charismatics); Hindus, 80%; Buddhists, 9%; Muslims, 4%; Kirants, 3%. (Based on 2001 census and *World Christian Encyclopedia*, 2001.)

BAL KRISHNA SHARMA

Nepotism, conferral of office or other benefits on family relations. It became an issue with the 16th-c. popes and was formally condemned in the next century.

Nero (37–68), Roman emperor (54–68). The last emperor descended from Julius Caesar, he was adopted by Claudius and proclaimed emperor at the age of 16. The philosopher Seneca was his adviser early in his reign, and government was orderly. But his murder of family members, his erratic activities, and his tyrannical measures turned the senatorial class against him. After the fire in Rome (64), which was blamed on the Christians, the city was rebuilt with regular streets and impressive buildings. The discovery of a plot against Nero (65) led to the execution of Seneca, Lucan, and Nero's wife, Poppaea. He was killed after a revolt by several generals, joined by the Praetorian Guard. Since he was hated by the Romans, Christian apologists found it useful to associate the persecutions* with his name. The "number* of the Beast" (Rev 13:11–18) is the total of the numerical values of the letters in *Neron Kaisar*.

Nerses IV Shnorhali (1102–1173), Armenian* catholicos*, author of historical, exegetical, doctrinal, pastoral, and liturgical works. He was called Shnorhali, "the Gracious," in homage to his meekness and charity, and to his religious poetry. He was educated in the Karmir Vank Monastery, ordained a priest, then a bishop. As the assistant of the catholicos Gregory III Pahlawuni (his brother), he contributed to the discussions over the doctrinal and ritual disagreements with the Roman Catholic Church (1139–41).

In 1166 Nerses became a catholicos, advocating persuasion over coercive methods of conversion* in the struggle against the "Children of the Sun" (a syncretistic* sect). In negotiations with the Byzantine Church (1165–72), he demonstrated an irenic spirit and affirmed the primacy of common faith over ritual and disciplinary divergences. Although Nerses remained faithful to the mitigated Julianist positions of the Armeno-Syrian Council of Mantzikert (726; affirming, following Julian of Halicarnassus [d528?], that Christ's body was incorruptible, though capable of all human experiences, including suffering), for Christian reconciliation he was ready to abstain from the Miaphysite* formula.

IGOR DORFMANN-LAZAREV

Nestorian Church, common but erroneous name for the Church* of the East, also called the Assyrian*, Chaldean, or East Syriac Church. While it adheres to the view of Christ held by Nestorius*, Diodore* of Tarsus, and Theodore* of Mopsuestia, it refined and developed Nestorius's Christology by emphasizing the mystery* of the incarnation*.

Nestorianism, the position defended by Nestorius*.

Nestorius (c351–c451), patriarch of Constantinople (428–31). A native of Syria*, he entered a monastery in Antioch, where he assimilated the Antiochene* tradition in biblical interpretation and Christology, probably studying under Theodore* of Mopsuestia. His reputation as a preacher led to his being appointed patriarch of Constantinople (428). He supported a member of his clergy who preached against calling Mary "Theotokos*," or "Mother of God," because for him Jesus' humanity and divinity were joined by will, not by nature or hypostasis, although the conjunction is so intimate that Jesus and the Word become one person, not two. Eusebius* of Dorylaeum accused him (wrongly) of Adoptionism*. His position was attacked by Cyril* of Alexandria, who issued 12 anathemas, and by a council in Rome (430). At the Council of Ephesus* (431), Nestorius was removed from office and his doctrines condemned. Upon returning to his monastery, he was banished (436), supposedly to Petra but actually to Upper Egypt and the Great Oasis, where he wrote his *Book of Heraclides,* responding to the two Councils of Ephesus* (431, 449) and arguing that his views agreed with those who were now condemning Eutyches*. EUGENE TESELLE

Netherlands, The. According to a legend, Christianity was brought to what is now the Netherlands by Servatius, who moved his episcopal see* from Tongern (present-day Belgium) to Maastricht (383), where the episcopal see remained until 722, when it was moved to Liège (Belgium). Nevertheless, we can say that the southern parts of the Netherlands were Christianized during the last century of Roman rule (late 4th to early 5th c.). The northern parts (on the other side of the rivers Maas and Waal) were Christianized from 689 onward by Willibrord, who was ordained archbishop of the Frisians, with his see in Utrecht.

The ecclesiastical division of the territory, the south under the Diocese of Liège and the north under the Diocese of Utrecht, remained more or less the same (except for some parts along the borders, which belonged to the dioceses of Münster and Cologne in present-day Germany) until the Dutch revolt (with a decentralized state and freedom of religion as its main targets), when the Republic of Seven United Provinces declared itself independent from the Spanish kings (1581). The Dutch Reformed* Church obtained a monopoly position in the north, while Roman Catholicism continued to be strong in the south, which remained under Spanish rule. After the Vienna Conference (1815), the United Kingdom of the Netherlands (Kingdom of the Netherlands since the separation of Belgium, 1830) was established, and its new constitution (1848) recognized freedom of religion.

Despite social mobility, the north–south divide is strongly felt in Dutch Christianity and contributed to a strong differentiation among regions in which almost total church affiliation from birth until death was the norm: the Protestant "pillar*" in the north, the Roman Catholic "pillar" in the south, and liberal and socialist "pillars" in between. During the 1960s, church membership decreased rapidly. In 2004 the Dutch Reformed Church, the Reformed Churches in the Netherlands (separated from the former in 1886), and the Lutheran Church united to form the Protestant Church in the Netherlands, the second largest Christian denomination in the Netherlands after the Roman Catholic Church.

For years now, the Central Office for Statistics, the Social and Cultural Planning Office, and the Scientific Council for Government Policy have been producing different, and partly contradicting, statistics on church membership owing to different definitions of Christian and religious affiliations and various instruments for measuring them. Whereas some scholars speak about an ongoing secularization* in the Netherlands, others speak about a slowing of this process, or even a resurgence of religion in the public domain.

According to the study "God in Nederland" (God in the Netherlands), conducted every 10 years from 1966 to 2006, 55% of the Dutch people associate themselves with Christianity in a general way. In 2006, 30% said that they belonged to a church (61% said they did not); 40% of church members attended church services regularly (vs. 77% in 1966).

While 66% of Dutch people say that the churches should not express themselves on (personal or social) ethical or political issues, they value religion highly when it comes to matters of life and death* (73%) and hold that religion has a social function in maintaining norms and values (74%), in creating social cohesion (63%), in drawing the public's attention to wars and other disasters (63%), and in celebrating national holidays (56%). For 66%, religion and politics are connected, but only 15% favor politics based on religion.

Despite declining church membership, a majority show an interest in religious or spiritual matters. More than 50% indicate that they seek deeper meaning in life and that there is something beyond the visible world, something that connects human beings, the world, and the universe; 33% say that they have had a mystical experience, and 66% say that they pray regularly.

The Netherlands is commonly referred to as one of the most secularized countries of the world, although Dutch scholars have become more cautious in explaining what this signifies exactly. Most would speak about a deinstitutionalization, which applies not only to churches and mosques but also to other social organizations, whereas a substantial part of the Dutch population practices religious rituals or prayers in a noninstitutional context, which many call spirituality*.

The situation of Dutch Christianity is ambiguous: a majority of Christians practice a postmodern* spirituality outside the institutional churches, and the faithful who remain within the churches are becoming more orthodox or conservative. The Netherlands has not become areligious, but it is too early to speak about a "resurgence of religion" as some have suggested.

Statistics: Population (2006): 16.5 million. 55% are affiliated with Christian values in a general way, but only 30% belong to a church (Roman Catholics [primarily in the south], 60%; Protestants [primarily in the north], 40%); Muslims (mainly of Turkish and Moroccan descent), 5%; members of Eastern religions, 1.1%; Jews, 0.2%. (*Source*: "God in the Netherlands," 2006.)

FRANS WIJSEN

Nevin, John R. See MERCERSBURG THEOLOGY.

New Age Spirituality and Christianity. New Age spirituality became a clearly identified movement in the 1970s, but its several dimensions were not necessarily new. It grew out of ancient thought, of trends already present in North American culture, and of developments in other parts of the world. As a quest for a spiritual pathway that would offer an alternative to traditional Christian ways associated with mainline churches, sincere seekers sought a spirituality* that felt congruent with their experience, and more responsive to dramatic global changes and to the new realities of contemporary life.

The Christian community responded in diverse ways, in some cases with interest and a desire to learn, often with caution, and frequently with clear rejection. These different responses reflect the diversity of the New Age Movement, as well as the complexity and many-sidedness of Christianity. Should New Age be viewed as an arena for tarot or integral spirituality, crystals or ecology, witchcraft* or holistic health, astrology or planetary transformation? Three patterns have characterized New Age spirituality:

1. New Age as a journey toward the divine, which is generally viewed as within oneself or as one's higher self, in contrast with the transcendent personal God often emphasized in Christianity. Through developmental processes, meditation drawn from Eastern traditions, and channeling that puts one in touch with one's past lives, one nurtures the divine within.
2. New Age as a journey toward self-discovery (implied by the preceding) is the effort to know oneself and to realize one's full potential as a human being, an endeavor undertaken through reflection, inquiry, and discussion in small groups, and meditation focused on "right mindfulness." On occasion, this inward journey employs the grammar of science, speaking about vibrations, energy, and evolution, but more frequently links spiritual maturation with the ancient Hindu/Buddhist understanding of karma and samsara that connects human growth to past lives.
3. New Age as a journey toward the world embraces all peoples and cultures and has affirmed the goodness of the original creation*. Those engaged in New Age thought often commit themselves to issues of ecology* and justice*.

Christian churches have been positive about New Age sensitivity to ecology and holistic health, but are more critical of the absence of a clear statement about a personal God* and about Jesus, and the emphasis on reincarnation rather than eternal* life. Christians ask whether New Age communities are truly committed to a more just and humane world or are preoccupied with personal fulfillment and trivial practices. **See also SPIRITUALITY CLUSTER, CHRISTIAN FORMS OF: IN NORTH AMERICA.**

DUNCAN S. FERGUSON

New Caledonia. See HISTORY OF CHRISTIANITY CLUSTER: IN THE SOUTH PACIFIC AND AUSTRALIA.

New Covenant (Heb *berit hadasa*; Gk *kaine diatheke*; also translated "new testament") is a designation that, since NT times, the Christian Church has claimed for itself as "the people of the new covenant." From patristic times, this designation was used both in a supersessionist* sense, emphasizing discontinuity between "old" and "new" covenants, and in a qualitative sense, emphasizing continuity.

In polemic writings against Jews, Justin* Martyr (c100–c165), and later, e.g., Irenaeus*, Tertullian*, and Origen*, emphasized that the church has supplanted the people of Israel, which has been rejected – a supersessionist view reiterated throughout the history of the church and grounded in multiple NT texts.

Yet the same church fathers affirmed the continuity between the old and new covenants as they rejected Marcion's* teaching and Gnostic* views that emphasized complete discontinuity. Continuity is recognizable when one notes that the concept of "new covenant" originated in Jeremiah and was an early Apocalyptic* Jewish doctrine (though rarely found in midrash*). As distinct from the several renewals of the covenant (e.g. in the time of the Josianic reform; 2 Kgs 23), Jer 31:31–34 (cf. Ezek 36:25–28) speaks of an eschatological* "new covenant." It is new, not because of a discontinuity with the "old" covenant, but because it is written on the human heart cleansed from sin* (or "forgiven"; cf. Atonement #1); not because God changed the covenant, but because, in this cleansed/forgiven condition (through the role of the Holy* Spirit, adds Ezek 36), humans will at last be faithful to it – whether they are Israelites or Apocalyptic Jews (Jubilees*), Essenes* of Qumran, or the people of God in the broader sense that includes the Gentiles*/nations* envisioned by Paul in 2 Cor 3:2–6. The Last* Supper tradition presents Jesus as saying, "This cup is the new covenant in my blood" (1 Cor 11:25), integrated into (the longer version of) Luke 22:20; while Mark 14:24 merely has "blood of the covenant," Matt 26:28 adds "for the forgiveness of sins" (a new covenant language).

The ambivalence between the supersessionist view of "new covenant" (originating in the polemical separation of Christianity from Judaism) and the qualitative view (emerging in the HB and early Jewish origins of this concept) persists. The choice of one or the other option has significant theological and ethical implications, especially since "covenant" includes a call (an election*) to a particular task for the glory of God. **See also ANTI-JEWISH, ANTI-JUDAISM; COVENANT; UNIQUENESS OF CHRIST.**

DANIEL PATTE

New Creation refers to God's work of re-creation, understood as renewal, replacement, or making new things. The idea of God's re-creation, already implied in God's covenant with all living things (Gen 9:1–17) after the Flood*, becomes explicit in Isa 43:19 and 65:17: God creates new things, specifically new heavens and a new earth. Paul* employs the expression "new creation" (2 Cor 5:17; Gal 6:15), which the authors of Jewish apocalyptic writings such as 1 Enoch* (72:1) and Jubilees* (1:29, 4:26) previously used.

As Pelagius* notes, "new creation" has been diversely interpreted to refer to (1) the inner transformation of individual believers by the Holy* Spirit (Augustine*, Basil*, John* Chrysostom); (2) the personal experience of rebirth through baptism* that often provides a new identity (Theodoret* of Cyrrhus; see Grace of God Cluster); (3) the new community of faith formed through the ministry of Christ and the apostles (John* Chrysostom); (4) God's establishment of a new world through divine interventions in history in order to replace the present age with an eschatological new kingdom*, a process beginning with Christ's death and resurrection (Cyril*); (5) God's preservation and restoration of the natural world, according to theologians' and ethicists' recent interpretation of Rom 8:18–25. SEJONG CHUN

New Haven Theology, a revision of Edwardsian* Calvinism that Nathaniel W. Taylor (1786–1858) developed with Chauncey A. Goodrich and Eleazar T. Fitch at Yale College. Taylor redefined the doctrines of original* sin* and freedom of the will* in order to urge the unrepentant to convert. He also employed God's moral government as a theological superstructure, rejected the sinfulness of "unregenerate doings," and insisted that God did not condemn anyone to hell* before creating the world (see Infralapsarianism). These teachings sparked the "Taylorite" controversy, which divided Connecticut

Congregationalists* (early 1830s) and eventually dissolved New England's Edwardsian tradition. ELIZABETH MASON CURRIER and DOUG SWEENEY

New Israel. See JUDAISM AND CHRISTIANITY CLUSTER; NEW COVENANT; SUPERSESSIONISM.

Newman, John Henry (1801–90). Anglican priest and fellow of Oriel College, Oxford, Newman served as vicar at the university church (1828–43). Received into the Roman Catholic Church (1845), he was made a cardinal (1879). He opposed liberal* theology, which he described as "the doctrine that there is no positive truth in religion, but that one creed is as good as another."

Closely allied to the Oxford* Movement, he played a central role in producing the *Tracts for the Times* (1833–41) and the journal *British Critic* (1836–42), preaching and writing extensively on the early church, the independence of the church* from state infringements, the apostolic priesthood*, and the sacraments* as means of grace*. In "Tract 90" (1841), he argued that the Anglican Thirty*-nine Articles could be read in a fully Roman Catholic sense. He published *Essay on the Development of Christian Doctrine* shortly before his reception into the Roman Catholic Church.

Appointed rector of the Catholic University of Ireland*, he published his inaugural lectures, *The Idea of a University* (1852), his most influential work. As editor of the liberal Catholic journal the *Rambler* (1859–60), he wrote "On Consulting the Faithful in Matters of Doctrine" (1859). In 1864, following an attack on Catholic honesty, Newman published his *Apologia pro Vita Sua*, establishing his reputation as a stylist, apologist, and theologian. He replied (1865) to Edward Boverie Pusey's* *Eirenicon*. His *Letter Addressed to the Duke of Norfolk* (1875) defended individual conscience in Catholic life and Catholic national loyalty against Gladstone's* argument. Among his poems, only his "Lead, Kindly Light" and "The Dream of Gerontius" (1865, in Edward Elgar's musical setting) are remembered. Newman's most important theological/philosophical work, *An Essay in Aid of a Grammar of Assent* (1870), summarized his life's thought on faith* and reason*, the place of probability in human decision making, and the nature of certitude. PETER C. ERB

New Measures. See FINNEY, CHARLES GRANDISON.

New Testament and Its Canonization. The use of the NT writings as authoritative scriptural* documents developed slowly during the 2nd c. Early in the 2nd c., local churches used the Gospels (most often Matthew*) and a few other writings. Three of the Pauline Epistles – 1 Corinthians*, Romans*, and Ephesians* – were often cited. 1 Peter* and 1 John* are mentioned by Papias*. Hebrews* and Revelation*/Apocalypse were in circulation. But explicit interest in gathering together the apostolic writings did not begin until after 150.

The transition can be seen in Asia Minor. The generation of Papias* and Polycarp* (first half of the 2nd c.) was satisfied to claim continuity with the apostles*, looking first to living traditions* (e.g. sayings of Jesus independent of the Gospels) and only then to writings. Paul was often ignored, except by Marcionites*, as was the Fourth Gospel, except by the Valentinians*. But after 150, the canon principle was at work: disputes over the content of the apostolic proclamation, arising from the confusing diversity of apostolic traditions, could be resolved only by consulting the apostles' writings. The canon principle, possibly invented by Marcion* when he recognized only Paul and Luke as authoritative, was used against him and the Gnostics* by Irenaeus*, whose career began in Asia Minor, followed by Tertullian*, Clement*, and Origen*. Thus Asia Minor was the center of the formation of the NT canon, followed by Rome and then Alexandria. Paul and the Fourth Gospel were no longer ignored, but the aspects that seemed to aid Gnostics* were neutralized through their juxtaposition with writings ascribed to other apostles, including James and Peter. James 1:14–26 affirms but also corrects Paul's emphasis on faith, and 2 Pet 3:15–17 cautiously accepts Paul's letters. Regarding the Gospels, Irenaeus noted that each had distinctive features that could be used by one of the groups he viewed as heretical. Yet together, as the "fourfold gospel" (one gospel, "according to" four different writers), these distinctive scriptural texts supplemented, corrected, and interpreted each other. Simultaneously, the OT, specifically the Septuagint*, including the Apocrypha*, the Bible of the Greek synagogue, was asserted against Marcionites and Gnostics. By 200, something very much like the present NT was taking shape, but this was not yet the "canon."

The canonization process continued, with debate over the authorship and standing of a number of books, including Hebrews (questioned in the West), James, 2 Peter, and

Revelation/Apocalypse (questioned in the East). In Alexandria, several other writings (including Hermas* and Barnabas*) were included, while in Syria only the Gospels (with Tatian's* Diatessaron*), Acts, and Paul were included; James, 1 Peter, and 1 John were added only after 400.

Only in the 4th c. was there agreement about the canon, a specific list of books. The first list of writings that corresponds exactly to the later NT is in Athanasius's* festal epistle (367); his inclusion of Revelation/Apocalypse is probably due to his alliance with the West, just as Damasus of Rome agreed with the East and affirmed Paul's authorship of Hebrews. The canon was thus finalized as part of a diplomatic agreement among Nicene leaders in the decades following the condemnation of Arianism in Nicaea* and in the first decades of Arian* power in the Western Roman Empire. North Africa followed the lead of Rome (councils in Hippo, 393, and Carthage, 397), still expressing some doubts about the authorship of Hebrews.

At about this time, Jerome* rediscovered and translated the HB, suggesting that it had greater validity than the Septuagint, the earlier Greek translation. Luther retained the traditional NT canon, but raised questions about several of its writings because they lacked a strong doctrine of justification by faith. He also raised questions about the Apocrypha*, which the Reformation churches usually include only as an appendix to the Bible. **See also BIBLE, CANON OF; BIBLE, TEXTS AND MANUSCRIPTS.**

EUGENE TESELLE

New Testament Theology arose out of a perceived need for inquiry into the meaning of the NT independent of contemporary theological bias (19th c.). In approaching the task, scholars confront questions about (1) the sense in which NT theology is historical*, (2) what is meant by "theology*," (3) whether NT theology should be limited to canonical writings, and (4) how the diversity of viewpoints reflected in the NT writings should be assessed. The following are representative answers.

William Wrede (1859–1906). (1) The task of NT theology is strictly historical. One goal of the history* of religion school was to present a history of the thought-world of early Christianity. (2) Theology involves the personal viewpoint of the scholar and thus obscures the historical investigation of the NT. The NT does not provide answers to the questions of dogmatic theology. (3) Inquiry should not be limited to canonical texts, because the goal is to understand the wider thought-world of early Christianity. (4) The diversity of the NT results from the historical development of early Christianity.

Adolf Schlatter (1852–1938). (1) NT Theology is historical because its subject matter is that of the past. However, theology and history are interrelated. The NT is designed to evoke faith* and is best understood from that perspective. (2) Theology expresses the convictions* of early Christians as found in NT writings, especially in the self-understanding of Jesus. (3) The NT is the primary source of NT theology. Other ancient texts (and their choice) introduce the historian's bias. The OT is also important for understanding NT faith. (4) Diversity in the NT does not imply opposition, for it arises from diverse reactions to the powerful message of Jesus.

Rudolf Bultmann* (1884–1976). (1) Historical reconstruction is necessary to interpret the NT in a way that has meaning for the present. The theology of Paul and John developed out of the message of Jesus and the proclamation of the early church. (2) Theology is found in the religious self-understanding of Paul* and John*. These two writers convey an understanding of human existence – an existential* understanding – that can be apprehended by modern people. (3) Noncanonical texts are important sources. Within the canon, Paul and John are privileged as sources of theology. (4) NT writings are diverse, but not all express "theology."

Some biblical scholars question this formulation of the task, but, explicitly or not, all engage these questions on some level. **See also BIBLICAL THEOLOGY.** SUSAN E. HYLEN

Newton, Isaac (1642–1727), born in Lincolnshire, England, in the year Galileo* died; studied at Cambridge University; became a revolutionary philosopher and mathematician. His first love throughout his life was theology and a millennial* interpretation of the Bible, a seemingly ironic perspective for one who made the world seem like an ordered, rational place, bounded by mathematically knowable laws. Yet he made explicit that he wrote *Mathematical Principles of Natural Philosophy* (1687) in order to make humankind believe more deeply in the deity, although this might not be obvious to modern readers.

Newton's science* rested on the bedrock assumption that "nature is exceedingly simple and conformable to herself" and that whatever "holds for greater motions, should hold for lesser ones as well." Rules are universal; the laws that hold for the physics of local motion, or mechanics, also hold for planetary motion. Thus to tackle the problem of why bodies on the surface of our planet are not thrown into space by its rotation and orbital revolution, Newton rigged up "a conical pendulum" that would be analogous to the earth, so as to measure its swing and the hold that earthly gravity exacted on it. This illustrates Newton's style of reasoning and his demand for experimental proof, which complemented his demonstration that mathematics applies to mechanics. MARGARET C. JACOB

New Zealand. Anglican missionaries from New South Wales, Australia*, arrived in 1814, followed by Wesleyan and French Marist missionaries. Before colonization (1850s), the large majority of Christians on the islands were Maori, who became missionaries themselves. Maori movements combining Maori culture* and Christianity developed rapidly, until the colonial wars over land and sovereignty in the 1860s disillusioned many Maori.

The main settler churches were the Church of England, as well as Presbyterian, Roman Catholic, and Wesleyan (Methodist) churches. Abolition of state aid to church schools in 1877 was supported by many Protestants, who were content with the education provided by Sunday schools. Roman Catholics disagreed. Religious orders provided low-fee education until state aid resumed (1970s). Because of secularist and Catholic opposition, there was no teaching of divinity in the University of New Zealand until 1945.

By 1900 all churches had established newspapers, theological colleges, national governing bodies, and networks of pastoral care and advocacy, as well as missionary work in the Pacific and Asia. Sectarian bigotry was strong, but it largely disappeared after Vatican* II and the introduction of Roman Catholic ecumenical initiatives. Formal ecumenical initiatives were only partially successful: Protestants formed the National Council of Churches (1942); Catholics joined a freshly structured Conference of Churches (1988), which disbanded in 2004. Attempts to unite Anglicans, members of Churches of Christ, Methodists, and Presbyterians fell apart in the 1980s. Yet much informal local cooperation endured. The rapid growth of Pentecostal churches and Charismatic* networks in the major churches left liberals and Evangelicals alike mystified by changes in worship and by Spirit-centered theology and piety. Pacific Islander migration also brought new configurations and the emergence of churches linked to parent bodies, rather than with New Zealand denominations.

Although all the churches grew after 1945, dissension about adaptation to cultural change emerged. Thus in 1967 Presbyterians attempted to try for heresy Principal Geering, the mentor of those who see no future in theistic Christianity. Feminists mounted a broader critique, to which women's* ordination, inclusive* language, and action against male sexual misbehavior were not sufficient answers. Increasingly articulate Maori Christians from the 1970s mounted a critique of the overt and covert racism* that had long belittled them. Their appeal to the much-neglected Treaty of Waitangi (1840) required all the churches to develop new forms of partnership with the Maori. Anglicans have gone the farthest along the bicultural path. Churches have also been divided in their response to homosexuality*. Evangelicals have increasingly challenged liberal solutions to such issues, but as yet Christian political parties have failed to gain representation in Parliament. New Zealand Christianity has produced a number of theological scholars, and informed ministers and laity, who have brought Christian perspectives to bear on national issues.

In the early 21st c., the majority (69%) of New Zealanders were Anglo settlers; Maori, the Polynesian inhabitants of the islands, were a minority (10%). Despite the dramatic fall in church attendance and involvement among major denominations, the Christian heritage remains important, although many no longer identify themselves as Christians in the census. New* Age spirituality has some popularity. The great world religions are poorly represented in New Zealand. The churches face a huge challenge to reconnect effectively with the major concerns of many New Zealanders. Nonetheless, Christian missionary and humanitarian concerns are still strong, though not wholly expressed through Christian organizations.

Statistics: Population (2000): 3.9 million (M). Christians, 3.2 M, 84% (Protestants, 0.9 M; Anglicans, 0.8 M; Roman Catholics, 0.5 M; independents, 0.2 M); Buddhists, 0.04 M, 1%; nonreligious, 0.5 M, 14%. (Based on *World Christian Encyclopedia*, 2001.)

IAN BREWARD

Nicaea, First Council of (325). The first of the ecumenical* councils, it was called by the emperor Constantine* because of the controversy aroused by Arius's* assertion that the Son was a creature, brought forth by the free choice of the Father. Arianism had already been condemned at a regional synod in Antioch (325), presided over by Hosius*, but a council of all the world's bishops seemed desirable.

A creed offered by the Arians was rejected by the angry majority. Subsequently, Eusebius* of Caesarea, whose views had been condemned at the synod in Antioch, offered the creed of his church; the emperor approved it but suggested the addition of *homoousios* (i.e. an affirmation that the Son is "of the same nature" as the Father). The wording of the creed finally adopted by the council seems in fact to be based on the creed of Jerusalem rather than Caesarea. Four anti-Arian anathemas concluded the creed.

The key assertion of the Council of Nicaea was that the Son is *homoousios* with ("of the same nature" as) the Father. Since the Arians had attacked the term, the Council may have felt that this was an appropriate way to draw a line, especially since Constantine supported it. The Council failed, however, to explain how the Father and the Son are distinct; in fact, it anathematized those who said that the Son is of a different "ousia or hypostasis" than the Father. This lack of clarity resulted in 50 more years of controversy, which ended only with the rapprochement of the Homoousian* party (arguing that the Son is "of the same nature" as the Father) and the Homoiousian* party (arguing that the Son is "like in essence" with the Father) at the Council of Alexandria* (362) and the distinction made by the Cappadocians* between one ousia and three hypostases. **See also** **CHRISTOLOGIES CLUSTER: INTRODUCTORY ENTRIES; TRINITY IN EASTERN ORTHODOXY; TRINITY IN THE WESTERN TRADITION.**

EUGENE TESELLE

Nicaea, Second Council of (787). Called by the empress Irene* to end Iconoclasm*, this broadly representative council first met in Constantinople (786), was interrupted by the army, which had Iconoclastic sympathies, and moved to Nicaea (787). It approved images of Christ, Mary, and the saints, painted or mosaic or depicted by other suitable media. A differentiation was made between worship* of God and veneration* of saints, quoting Basil* of Caesarea (comparing images of the emperor to the Son as an image of the Father): "The honor rendered to the image rises to the prototype." **See also** **ICON; ICONOCLASM AND THE ICONOCLASTIC CONTROVERSY; JESUS, IMAGES OF, CLUSTER: IN BYZANTINE ICONOGRAPHY; MARY, THE VIRGIN, CLUSTER: THEOTOKOS: IN BYZANTINE ICONOGRAPHY.**

Nicaragua. The population of Nicaragua today includes mestizos* (69%), whites (17%), blacks, including mulattos (9%), and only a small percentage (5%) of indigenous peoples, whom Dominican* monks, including Bartholomé de las* Casas, and later Franciscans*, initially evangelized. The Roman Catholic Diocese of Nicaragua (which included Costa* Rica until the independence period) was first based in Leon. Granada had the first established church in Central America.

During the Central American Federation of the Central American Republics (1821–38), the constitution named Roman Catholicism the only religion, "with the exclusion of the public exercise of any other." From 1838 to 1858, the Liberal Party prevailed with anti-Catholic measures, but from 1858 to 1893 the Conservative Party was in control. A strong liberal reaction after 1893 guaranteed religious liberty, to the detriment of the Roman Catholic Church. Civil registration, matrimony, cemeteries, judicial rights, and public education, which were administered by the Roman Catholic Church, were placed under state control. However, under the Somoza family dictatorship (1934–79), certain favors were granted, such as financial support, return of expelled monastic orders, and religious education in the schools, in exchange for ecclesiastical support for the regime.

Many external hindrances (common in Central America) worked to the detriment of the Roman Catholic cause: lack of clergy, abolition of tithes, expropriation of church lands, lack of cultural integration, economic dependence, and popular resistance to political and ecclesiastical domination. Tensions existed among the clergy over questions of political loyalties, actions on behalf of the poor*, and foreign interference in domestic affairs. Foreign powers seeking rights to construct a canal across the isthmus through Nicaragua vied for control during the 19th c.

Early British relations with the Miskito people, the lumber trade, and the establishment of settlements presaged the first pre-independence Anglican (Episcopal) groups in the coastal area. The arrival of Jamaican* Baptists* signaled the beginning of limited Protestant activity. In 1849 the German Moravians* began fruitful work with the Miskitos and the Sumos until World War I, when the work was taken over by the US group from Bethlehem, Pennsylvania. Under the Conservative government, the foreign Bible societies experienced mixed success, and the arrival of Protestants was largely hindered; but under the Liberals (after 1893), more arrived, including the Central American Mission (1900). As a result of division, however, work progressed slowly.

At the Panama* Missions Conference (1916), Nicaragua and El* Salvador were assigned to the Northern Baptist Church (now American Baptist Church). Together with the Moravians, the Baptist Church made important contributions to efforts to resolve national issues, especially in defense of the poor, despite the population's significant resentment against the USA owing to the nearly continuous occupation of Nicaragua by US Marines from 1912 to 1933, US support of the Somosa dictatorships, and the US role in the destructive Contra War (1980s).

Especially strong has been the growth of the Assemblies* of God congregations, alongside that of numerous other Pentecostal/Charismatic* groups, the Seventh-day Adventists*, Nazarenes*, and Jehovah* Witnesses. Slowly at first, Protestantism has in recent times grown rapidly, constituting around 15% of the population. The ecumenical CEPAD (Evangelical Council for Aid to Victims) united more than 40 churches and agencies in response to the 1972 earthquake. Under the leadership of Gustavo Parajón, this movement helped to meet the urgent social, medical, and educational needs of the marginalized*.

Statistics: Population (2000): 5 million (M). Christians, 4.9 M, 96.3% (Roman Catholics, 4.3 M; Protestants, 0.6 M; independents, 0.2 M); native religionists, 0.1 M; nonreligious, 0.1 M. (Based on *World Christian Encyclopedia*, 2001.)

SIDNEY ROOY

Nicene Creed. Properly speaking, the creed adopted by the Council of Nicaea* (325), based on the baptismal creed of Jerusalem. The "Nicene Creed" used today in both Eastern and Western churches is a slightly longer creed adopted by the First Council of Constantinople* (381), more accurately called the Niceno-Constantinopolitan Creed.

Niceno-Constantinopolitan Creed (the) differs from the Nicene Creed in its omission of the anathemas*, its presentation of several formulations about Christ (emphasizing Jesus' full divinity), and its extension of Nicaea's minimal references to the Holy* Spirit. Christians believe "in the Spirit, the holy, the lordly and life-giving one, proceeding forth from the Father, co-worshipped and co-glorified with Father and Son" (but not "proceeding forth from the Father *and the Son*" [*Filioque**], later added in the Western Church).

Nicholas of Cusa (1401–64), German philosopher/theologian, canon* lawyer, administrator, cardinal; engaged in a lifelong effort to reform and unify the universal and Roman Catholic church. Chancellor to the archbishop of Trier and expert at the Council of Basel* (1432–38), he wrote the Conciliarist* *Catholic Concordance* (1433), then moved to the papal side (1437), was a papal delegate to Constantinople* (1438), then cardinal and bishop of Brixen (1450), and finally part of the papal curia in Rome (1458–64).

He wrote 20 philosophical/theological treatises and dialogues, as well as 10 works on mathematics. (His pastoral efforts are reflected in more than 200 sermons.) His *On Learned Ignorance* (1440) extended Christian Neoplatonic* thought and was the basis for his subsequent writings. It expounds central ideas on God*, the universe, and Christ, acknowledging the limits of human knowing about what God is. Reason* is appropriate for the finite realm but cannot measure the infinite God, because there is no proportion between God and creatures. The created universe is at once "enfolded" in God's oneness and "unfolded" as a limited or "contracted" image of that oneness. Since God is its center and circumference, learned ignorance proposes that the universe is neither centered on the earth nor limited in extent. Only Christ provides a measure that unites the finite and infinite. Nicholas's later *On Conjectures* (1442), *About Mind* (1450), and *Vision of God* (1453) propose conjectural metaphors* for exploring the limits of our knowledge and for seeing the transcendent God. **See also APOPHATICISM; ETERNITY; MIND; MYSTICISM, MYSTICS.** CLYDE LEE MILLER

Nicholas (Nicolas) I, Pope (858–67), champion of papal power, used the False* Decretals against metropolitans*; criticized Photius*; sought the Bulgars'* loyalty; invited Cyril* and Methodius to Rome (867).

Nicholas of Lyra (c1270–1349), biblical exegete, professor at the Sorbonne (from c1309), provincial (head of the Franciscans*) of France (from 1319).

He learned Hebrew (possibly at the center of Jewish learning in Évreux), became acquainted with the Talmud, midrash, and the work of Rashi (Rabbi Solomon ben Isaac, 1045–1105), became a Franciscan (c1300), and moved to Paris, where he flourished in the university setting, despite conflicts over evangelical poverty* between the papacy and the Franciscan order (see Olivi, John Peter). He participated in the trials of the Knights Templar* (1307) and of the Beguine* mystic* Marguerite Porete* (1310, burned at the stake). His *Literal Postill on the Whole Bible* (c1322, 1331), which became a manual of exegesis, was a running commentary on the OT and NT, known for its double literal* sense (rather than mystical or allegorical sense), its affirmation of history and literary context, and Jewish interpretations of the OT. The double literal sense served as his key to the interpretation of OT prophetic passages, allowing him to draw one sense for the prophet's own time and another (usually christological and typological*) for the future. Among many other works, *Moral Postill on the Whole Bible* (1333–39) is a typological* and allegorical* series of notes on passages of Scripture that could be given both a moral and a spiritual interpretation. **See also HERMENEUTICS.**

PHILIP D. W. KREY

Nicholas of Myra (4th c.), bishop legendary for his generous acts in Myra, Asia Minor; widely revered in Byzantium, patron saint of Russia and other countries. His feast day (December 6) became the occasion for gift giving in the Low Countries. Under the influence of Germanic traditions, he became known as St. Nicholas, a figure that was secularized in the Protestant Netherlands and New York, gradually becoming the contemporary Santa Claus.

Nicodemites, term coined by Calvin* (1543), based on Nicodemus's* behavior, to characterize Protestants in Roman Catholic areas who kept their beliefs quiet or attended Mass without communing, contrary to Calvin's view that testimony to the true faith must be bodily and spiritual; the true church must be visibly set in contrast to the false.

Nicodemus, Pharisee* and learned member of the Sanhedrin*, who came secretly to Jesus (John 3:1–15), cautiously defended Jesus' activities, and helped bury him (John 19:39–42).

Nicolaites, group condemned in Rev 2:6, 14, 15; followers of Nicolaos (Acts 6:5) according to Irenaeus* (c180). Clement* of Alexandria relates Nicolaos's offer to share his beautiful wife in order to counter the charge that he was excessively proud to be her husband and as a sign of Christian self-sacrifice (and male superiority). Nicolaitism referred to the practice of concubinage among clergy and the marriage of clergy after celibacy* was imposed on all priests (1059).

Niebuhr, H. Richard (1894–1962), US theological ethicist who, like his brother Reinhold, found his voice during the 1930s against a background of economic depression, totalitarianism, and World War II. Niebuhr understood human agents as responders in the midst of interactions with others; the interactive stances of persons and communities are always ordered and oriented by faiths* in valued realities. Different faiths in different objects support different patterns of practical life. Accordingly, Niebuhr decried the idolatries* of the age, e.g. nationalism*, racism*, capitalism, and communism, which took a human community, activity, or desire as a limiting and distorting center of value and brought with them a train of bad consequences. For Niebuhr the radical faith in God that comes to us in Israel and in Jesus Christ demands a revolution in our more usual devotions. His influential book, *Christ and Culture**, addressed what he considered the primary problem of Christianity: the relation between devotion to God-in-Christ and the many ends, achievements, and values to which culture invites our allegiance. In response he outlined five types of moral theology: Christ against culture, Christ of culture, Christ above culture, Christ and culture in paradox, and Christ the transformer of culture. **See also CULTURE CLUSTER: CULTURAL STUDIES; CULTURE CLUSTER: CULTURE AND CHRISTIANITY; HISTORY AS A THEOLOGICAL CONCEPT; JESUS, IMAGES OF, CLUSTER: IN LITERATURE.**

DOUGLAS F. OTTATI

Niebuhr, Reinhold (1892–1971), US theologian and political thinker, influential interpreter of Christian social ethics*. Son of a German immigrant pastor, pastor in Detroit (1915), professor at Union Theological Seminary in New York (1928), leading figure in the theological movement known as Christian Realism.

Niebuhr developed his own theological position during a time of general disillusionment following World War I. In contrast to earlier Social* Gospel theologians, who expected to transform modern industrial society by moral ideals drawn from the teachings of Jesus, Niebuhr insisted that change can be brought about only by power* and that those with power are inevitably influenced by their own interests. The teachings of Jesus therefore provide little direct guidance for Christian social ethics, which must be concerned with a rough justice* among competing interests rather than a community of mutual love*. Niebuhr's early works, *Moral Man and Immoral Society* (1932) and *An Interpretation of Christian Ethics* (1935), developed this approach to social problems, which became known as Christian Realism.

Niebuhr's most important work, *The Nature and Destiny of Man* (1943), offers a more positive view of the social and political relevance of Christian tradition. While we must avoid sentimental efforts to turn the sacrificial love that Jesus reveals into a simple historical possibility, we need the biblical view of humanity, balanced between the image* of God and the sinful creature, to face the realities of history without thinking that we can end evil in the world and without giving in to despair. During World War II and the cold war that followed, Niebuhr became increasingly convinced that democracy needed to be guided by the substance of this Christian interpretation. In the words of an aphorism that he coined for *The Children of Light and the Children of Darkness* (1944), "Man's capacity for justice* makes democracy possible; but man's inclination to injustice makes democracy necessary."

Later authors and religious leaders had mixed views of Niebuhr's legacy. Martin Luther King, Jr., found Niebuhr's realistic emphasis on power important in shaping his own view of nonviolence* and social change. Others have suggested that Niebuhr's Christian Realism made him slow to support movements for justice among the powerless and insufficiently critical of the realities of US power. Nevertheless, no figure has emerged since Niebuhr's time with a comparable ability to make persuasive connections between Christian tradition and contemporary political choices. **See also DEMOCRACY AND CHRISTIANITY; SOCIAL ETHICS; UNITED CHURCH OF CHRIST (IN THE UNITED STATES).** ROBIN W. LOVIN

Niemöller, Martin (1892–1984), U-boat commander during World War I, captain of a Freikorps troop during the unsuccessful Kapp putsch against the Weimar Republic. After he completed theological studies in Münster (from 1919) and was ordained as a Lutheran pastor (1924), his first post was with the Lutheran Home Mission in Westphalia; he later (1931) became a pastor in the wealthy Berlin suburb of Dahlem, where he was assisted by Dietrich Bonhoeffer's* close friend, Franz Hildebrand. Conservative and nationalistic in his politics, Niemöller was initially enthusiastic about Nazism*; even its anti-Semitism* did not overly concern him. However, he became increasingly troubled by the regime's intrusion into church affairs, founded the Pastors' Emergency League, and joined the Confessing* Church. His preaching became openly critical of the government. He was imprisoned in Sachsenhausen (1938), then in Dachau, until he was liberated by US troops (1945). Even in prison, though, his attitude toward Nazism was ambivalent. Critical of the government's neopaganism, he nonetheless lobbied former naval colleagues to secure his release so that he could fight for Germany*. In the years following the war, Niemöller remained a controversial figure. Unpopular in Germany because of his insistence that Germany acknowledge its wartime guilt, he courted controversy in the wider West because of his opposition to the arms race and the Vietnam War. He was the principal author of the 1945 Stuttgart Declaration of Guilt and served as president of the Hesse-Nassau Lutheran Church (1947–62) and president of the World* Council of Churches (1961). MARK R. LINDSAY

Nietzsche, Friedrich (1844–1900), German philosopher whose impact on 20th-c. Continental philosophy and critical theory is perhaps unmatched. Son and grandson of Lutheran pastors, trained as a philologist and scholar of classics (University of Leipzig), appointed professor of philology (University of Basel, 1868). Early in his career, he was influenced by the thought of Schopenhauer and the operas of Wagner; he left the academy in 1879. His most well known work is *Thus Spake Zarathustra* (1883–85), but the works most important for understanding his vehement and incisive criticism of Christianity and religion are *The Gay Science*, in which Nietzsche's madman announces the death* of God, and *On the Genealogy of Morals*. This criticism focused on the psychological and social needs served by beliefs, rituals, and religious practices and culminated in a "genealogical" method that explains moral and religious beliefs in terms of social interests and power struggles. In the *Genealogy*, Nietzsche argued that Christianity's "ascetic* ideal" promises an afterlife that can be achieved only by denying life in this world. This, he claims, is a strategy of the "will to power of the weakest" that both consoles the weak and infects and renders powerless the strong. Despite Nietzsche's attack on religion*, there are clear signs in his writings of prophetic, ascetic, and mystical* sensibilities, whether expressed in the "redemptive" mission of Zarathustra, in his reflections on body, spirit, and discipline, or in his ecstatic invocations of Dionysus.

Nietzsche's impact on Christian thought has been significant. Barth* countered Nietzsche's attack on Christianity but also applauded his insightful analyses of the drive to human self-aggrandizement that marks "religion." This Christian appropriation of Nietzschean suspicion is found more recently in Ricoeur* (hermeneutics* of suspicion) and Merold Westphal. Tillich* embraces Nietzsche's existentialist* analysis of human "existence as estrangement" and interprets Nietzsche's "will to power" as an affirmation of human life in spite of this estrangement. In this, Tillich claims, Nietzsche provides a genuine alternative to the Christian affirmation of life "in spite of" estrangement. Finally, Nietzsche has had an enormous impact on Death* of God theologians such as Thomas Altizer and Gabriel Vahanian and on postmodern religious thinkers and "secular theologians" such as Mark C. Taylor and Charles Winquist. In general, these thinkers accept some version of Nietzsche's proclamation of the "death of God" and embrace Nietzsche's critique of metaphysics*, his perspectival and bodily epistemology, and his Dionysian celebration of life and love for reality.

TYLER ROBERTS

Nigeria. Christianity in Nigeria, with its large youth membership, is dynamic and vibrant. It plays a more important social role than African* Religion or Islam*, the two other major religions in the country. It is highly diversified, comprising traditional mainline churches (Anglican*, Protestant – including Methodist*, Presbyterian*, and Baptist* – and Roman Catholic), Pentecostal/Charismatic* Evangelical, Prosperity* Gospel, and African* Instituted churches, as well as new religious movements founded by Nigerians. In a situation of rampant poverty*, the traditional African understanding of religion as the source of both spiritual and material well-being and the contemporary materialistic culture have combined to make the Prosperity Gospel, according to which wealth is a sign of divine favor, the most popular among the common people.

Late 16th–18th Centuries. The introduction of Roman Catholicism marked the first wave of evangelization in Nigeria. In 1515 Oba Osuola, the king of the Binis, and in 1571, the *olu* (king) of the Itshekiris, with the help of Portuguese traders in their territories, had asked that Roman Catholic Portuguese missionaries be sent to Benin City and Warri in Southern Nigeria (see Portuguese Explorations, Conquests, and Missions). At that time, Nigeria was not yet a political entity but comprised different kingdoms. The approach of the missionaries was to convert the king first and thus win the kingdom. Hence the focus of attention was the courts of the kings. The kings allowed their children and some prominent men in their kingdoms to become Christians. In 1600 Domingos, the son of Sebastião, a prominent Warri Christian, was sent to Portugal to study for the priesthood. He was not successful and returned home in 1608 with a Portuguese wife and some missionaries to work in Warri. Spanish and Italian missionaries, and possibly Brazilian Catholic missionaries of African descent, later joined the Portuguese missionaries in Warri.

Because there were not enough missionaries in Europe, and because of the death or illness of many missionaries, this first wave of contact could not continue beyond 1770, when the last group of missionaries went to these two kingdoms. During the intervening period, many people had been baptized and churches built, but only in the courts of the kings. Christianity did not penetrate the interior of the kingdoms and died out in the 19th c., when missionaries could no longer go there. Today one reminder of this first encounter is an Africanized church in Benin City, called Arousa Church, whose liturgy contains Latin terms, such as *sanctus* and *introit*, reminiscent of Roman Catholic Latin Mass, while elements of African Religion are used also in worship. In Warri, a huge cross in the center of old Warri town serves as another reminder.

Mid-19th–Mid-20th Centuries. The second wave of evangelization that resulted in the implantation of Christianity in Nigeria was initiated in the 19th c. by Protestant missionaries. The impetus was an Evangelical revival* in England and France that led to the formation of missionary societies in these countries to bring the gospel to non-Christians. This coincided with the period of the "European scramble for Africa" (see Berlin Conference), British colonization, and the amalgamation of Nigeria into a single political unit under British control. It was also the period of the abolition of Atlantic slave* trade and the resettling of liberated slaves in Sierra* Leone and Liberia*.

Among the liberated slaves in Sierra Leone were Nigerians of the Yoruba ethnic group, who became Christians and later emigrated to Badagry and Abeokuta in Western Nigeria. From Nigeria they invited the missionaries they had known in Sierra Leone to bring Christianity to Nigeria. Initial responses came from Methodists (1842) and Anglicans (Church Missionary Society, 1845). In the Church Missionary Society team was Rev. Ajai Crowther*, a Yoruba, who later became the first African Anglican bishop. The liberated slaves who had returned to Nigeria greatly facilitated the work of the missionaries. The success of these missions inspired the United Presbyterian Church and the Southern* Baptist Convention (USA) missions to the Efiks in Calabar in the Southeast (1846), and the Yoruba in Badagry (1850), respectively, as well as the Roman Catholic mission to Lagos (1867). However, by 1859 a Roman Catholic community, probably the fruit of an earlier Portuguese missionary effort, was discovered in Lagos under the leadership of a catechist known as "Padre Antonio," a native of Sao Tomé. From the 1860s, Presbyterian, Roman Catholic, Qua Iboe (Church of Scotland Mission), and Methodist missionaries entered Nigeria from Calabar in the Southeast, and expansion of missionary work in Nigeria began in earnest. In 1884 a Roman Catholic mission to the Igbo in Onitsha entered Nigeria from the East. Meanwhile, the Protestant mission in Western Nigeria had spread to Idah and other places in the north.

The 19th-c. missionaries adopted a different approach than did those of the earlier period. Rather than seek the conversion of the king first, they sought to convert individuals. They called for complete severance of Christians from their traditional culture, which they saw as evil, and expected African Christians to imbibe European culture and practice Christianity as it was practiced in Europe. They established "Christian villages" (Roman Catholics) and "mission villages" (Protestants) where Christians lived together apart from others (a practice later discontinued). Protestant missionaries studied the people's (oral) languages, reduced them to writing, and analyzed and formalized their grammar, translated the Bible into the local languages, and introduced literacy education for adults so that they could read the Bible (see Bible Translations Cluster). Both Protestant and Roman Catholic missionaries introduced Western education* and Western health care. These gave people a new lease on life and made Christianity attractive not only because of its religious value but also because of the social benefits that came with it.

The late 19th c. involved many challenges within the Christian fold. There were two schisms born of personal conflicts between pastors: one in the Presbyterian Church (Calabar, 1882), and another in the Baptist Church (Lagos, 1888). The most significant challenge was the breakaway in 1890 of about 600 Nigerian members from St. Paul's Breadfruit Anglican Church in Lagos to establish the "African Church," the first African* Instituted Church (AIC) in Nigeria. This was attributed to racism* in the church, the high-handedness of Bishop Herbert Tugwell in dealing with African members, and the disdainful attitude of the European missionaries toward African culture*. Many other breaks followed. While these early AICs held on to traditional Christian theology, there emerged others that, under the weight of colonial oppression, preached apocalyptic*, political theology. These new AICs include the Aladura Movement, which encompasses a group of AICs of a common type but of diverse origins that arose among the Yoruba (early 20th c.) – equivalent to the AICs called "Zionist" in Southern* Africa – which see the church as God's city of refuge for Africans. Other AICs preach ultimate victory for suppressed Africans (equivalent to Ethiopianists); others look for the coming of a messiah to deliver Africans from their bondage and are called "Messianic." For all of them, the Bible is the basis of their beliefs and practices.

Mid-20th–Early 21st Centuries. The flowering of the Christian missionary efforts started about the middle of the 20th c. This the period has been the coming of age of Christianity in Nigeria. It is marked by the rapid spread of Christianity to all parts of the country, a large increase in the number of Christians, and a large body of Christian elite and well-educated native clergy. It corresponds to Nigeria's post-independence (1960) period, a failed attempt by the Protestants to form a National Church of Nigeria, the Roman Catholic Church's post–Vatican* II (1962–65) period, and Nigeria's post–civil war (1967–70) period. During the war, the Christian churches were seriously engaged in caring for the hungry, the wounded, the sick, and the dying. After the war, they were engaged in reconstruction and rehabilitation work. The Catholic Church distinguished itself in all this by the support it offered through international Catholic agencies.

The civil war (1967–70) slowed the growth of Christianity, and afterward the government made matters worse by taking over Christian schools and hospitals. In spite of this, Christianity continued to spread rapidly, and the government started handing back the schools and hospitals, and allowed churches to establish universities.

Since the mid-20th c., the Christian churches have shown great commitment in grappling with social issues. During the 1983–99 military regimes, often called the "dark years" of Nigerian political history, the nation experienced the most severe government repression it ever knew. The Christian churches resisted this strongly. From year to year and with dogged determination, the Christian Association of Nigeria, the umbrella body of all the churches in Nigeria, denounced the military government and its repressive policies. When in 1993 the incumbent military president, Ibrahim Babangida, a Muslim, annulled the presidential election that was believed to have been won by Chief M. K. O. Abiola, also a Muslim, the Christian community in the country reacted in strong protest, because the election was attested to have been free and fair by international observers; at stake was the issue of justice*.

Since Nigeria returned to democratic rule in 1999, political elections have been a thorny issue, as every aspirant wants to win by fair means or foul. This has resulted in the use of violence, cheating, and manipulation of election results. The Roman Catholic Church in particular has played a major role in monitoring these elections through its Justice, Development, and Peace Commission.

This period has witnessed great dynamism in Nigerian Christianity. Since the 1970s, Christians have been going on organized pilgrimages* to the Holy Land in large numbers yearly. A proliferation of new religious movements has led to the establishment of new kinds of independent churches of Pentecostal and Charismatic* orientation that do not fit into traditional patterns. A notable one is the Deeper Life Bible Church, which started as a movement that helped Christians of all denominations toward a life of holiness* and whose members first met in people's homes. Today the Deeper Life Bible Church has branches all over the country. The Synagogue Church of Pastor Joshua in Lagos, which focuses on healing*, is tied to the personality of the pastor. Since its founding in the 1990s, it has not established any branches. The Spiritan ministry of Rev. Fr. Edeh, a Catholic priest, also focuses on healing and is tied to the personality of the priest. Others are more open and have branches. They include the Winners Chapel, the Charismatic Movement, the Solid Rock Church, the Foursquare Gospel Church, and the Open Bible Church. It is impossible to count or keep track of these churches, as they spring up very fast. Most of them engage in televangelism, with healing and prosperity as their main topics.

Distinctive Features of Christianity in Nigeria. An impressionistic picture emerges from a listing of the features of various churches. While some of these features are common to all the churches, some are particular to certain churches.

Common to all the churches is the highly structured nature of the leadership. In the African Instituted Churches, some of which were either founded or are led by women, women* play significant leadership roles. In the other churches, even though women constitute about 70% of the membership and workforce, they occupy very few leadership positions. Probably because of the influence of the male-oriented traditional culture, there is no massive movement to change the situation. Only recently have women Liberation theologians appeared on the scene (see Circle of Concerned African Women Theologians).

All churches take theological* education seriously. The Roman Catholic Church has 10 theological seminaries with an average of 350 students in each, 1 graduate school of theology jointly operated with other West African Bishops Conferences, and 5 universities, one of which is operated by the Nigerian Bishop's Conference and the others by different Catholic organizations and individuals. The other churches have several theological colleges and seminaries, and more than 20 universities between them. In the Catholic Church, seminary training lasts five to seven years beyond secondary school, while some churches require two or three years of training beyond secondary school.

Ecumenism is a vital rallying point for a Nigerian Christianity that faces a constant threat from Islamic* insurgence. It is concretized in the formation of the Christian Association of Nigeria at the national and state levels, and the establishment of a Christian Social Center in Abuja, the nation's capital. However, there is still much to be done at the level of theological and pastoral unity of the churches.

All the churches express a concern for the poor* through community development projects and material relief programs. They also take the worldview of the people seriously. In a situation where nearly every disease is attributed to evil spirits and many people cannot afford to pay hospital bills, midnight rituals and healing* services, hitherto practiced only in the African Instituted Churches, have become important features of Nigerian Christianity, cutting across all denominations. Inculturation*, including the introduction of elements from contemporary "pop culture," such as the playing of guitars and trumpets during worship, is practiced by all the churches, including the Roman Catholic Church. This has led to a reduction of the traditional European elements in Christian worship such that, e.g., a Roman Catholic from Europe would find it difficult to feel at home at some Nigerian eucharistic celebrations.

Nigerian churches are very missionary minded. Many of the locally founded churches, such as the Brotherhood of the Cross and Star, take their evangelistic crusades to the USA and Britain, and have outposts in these countries. The Roman Catholic Church sends missionaries to the USA and Europe. In the 1990s, the Missionary Society of St. Paul was established by the Nigerian Catholic hierarchy to train and send priests to various parts of the world. The priests of this missionary society work in many parts of Africa, the Caribbean, and the USA.

In 1994 an apparition of the Blessed Virgin Mary* experienced by a teenage Catholic girl in Aope, Benue State, was in the news all over the country. The apparition was accompanied by messages calling for repentance and conversion. Large crowds of people visited the apparition grounds to witness the event, which was reported to take place weekly. Since then, the place has become a center of pilgrimage*, although the Nigerian Catholic hierarchy has neither officially condemned nor commended the incident.

In the early 21st c., the conservative Convocation of Anglicans in North America (CANA) placed itself under the spiritual jurisdiction of Archbishop Peter Akinola, Anglican* primate of Nigeria.

Some of the African Instituted Churches use the Bible and particularly the Psalms as a means of protection against evil spirits. They counsel members to sleep with the Bible under their pillow (see Bible Interpretation Cluster: In Africa). Only two sacraments* are emphasized in these churches: baptism* and the Eucharist*. In the Brotherhood of the Cross and Star and the Cherubim and Seraphim churches, baptism is administered in rivers by immersion and the Eucharist is celebrated with peanuts and cookies. Marriage* is not emphasized and is rarely celebrated.

Christianity faces constant confrontation by Islamic fundamentalists. Nearly every year, serious clashes occur between Christians and Muslims, resulting in the burning of churches and mosques, and the killing and maiming of people, particularly in the Muslim-dominated northern part of the country. One such clash occurred because a Christian unknowingly drove his car over a Qur'an that a Muslim had accidentally dropped on the road.

Christianity has helped to bring Western civilization to Nigeria and to form an educated generation of Nigerians that led the fight for Nigeria's independence. The missionaries helped to reduce mortality and morbidity by introducing Western medical services in the country. By studying some Nigerian languages and committing them to writing, Christian missionaries have contributed immensely to the development of these languages. However, because the current wave of Christianity came to Nigeria alongside the colonization* of the country, some Africans see it as heavily implicated in the colonization of Nigeria and as a form of imperialism*, particularly as it has displaced the African Religion of the people. In a country with a strong Christian presence, corruption, embezzlement of public funds, tribalism*, and the big divide between the rich and the poor in the midst of enormous natural wealth constitute an embarrassment to Christian witness. **See also AFRICAN RELIGION AND CHRISTIANITY CLUSTER; CHARISMATIC AND PENTECOSTAL MOVEMENTS CLUSTER: IN AFRICA: WESTERN AFRICA; PROTESTANTISM CLUSTER: IN AFRICA: WESTERN AFRICA; ROMAN CATHOLICISM CLUSTER: IN AFRICA: WESTERN AFRICA.**

Statistics: Population (2000): 111.5 million (M) (main ethnic groups: Yoruba, 17.5%; Hausa, 17.2%, Igbo, 13.3%, Toroobe Fulani, 4.9%, Yerwa Kanuri, 3.0%). Christians, 51 M, 45.9% (independents, 21 M; Anglicans, 20 M; Protestants, 14 M; Roman Catholics, 13.4 M; 17 M of these Christians are doubly affiliated, identifying themselves with more than one denomination); Muslims, 49 M, 43.9%; African Religionists, 11 M, 9.8%. (Based on *World Christian Encyclopedia*, 2001.)

JUSTIN UKPONG

Nikon, Patriarch (1605–81), sixth patriarch of the Russian Orthodox* Church and architect of church reforms. Shortly after ascending to the patriarchal throne (1652), Nikon brought Russian liturgical and textual traditions into line with contemporary Greek norms in an effort to reform the church and to centralize the power of the patriarchy. His changes (especially the new hellenized spelling of "Jesus" and the revised sign of the cross) encountered fierce resistance across Russia and engendered the Old* Believer Movement. Nikon's reforms were accepted at a Russian church council (1666–67), but the patriarch was removed from the throne for extending his power into secular domains.

ROY R. ROBSON

Niles, Daniel Thambyrajah (1908–70), along with Paul Devanandan and M. M. Thomas*, was seminal in shaping the ecumenical movement and the theological conversation in South Asia. A deeply committed Methodist, like Wesley* D. T. Niles shaped his books through his sermons and ministry rather than through a theological system. Although influenced by the neo*-orthodox thought prevalent in the ecumenical movement, he was also a contextual* theologian searching to understand the theological message for particular places and times. Deeply Christocentric (see Uniqueness of Christ), Niles nevertheless clearly believed he could live out his faith only in the midst of discussion and interaction with people of other faiths with equal passion and commitment. His ability to hold together seemingly opposite ideas as complementary ones helped him provide vision for the church in the early 1900s. **See also INDIA.**

DAMAYANTHI M. A. NILES

Nil Sorsky (c1433–1508), monk and spiritual leader of the Russian trans-Volgan fathers. Nil traveled throughout the Christian East, including Jerusalem and Mount Athos*, and learned hesychasm*. In Russia*, Nil founded a cloister on the Sora River. He taught a form of monasticism* that questioned the need for worldly goods, making him known as a "Non-Possessor." He also taught the importance of simplicity, tolerance, and mystical* Christianity. Although most large monastic communities did not follow his example, his influence spread through small hermitages. Nil's Rule was revived at the famed Optina Monastery in 19th-c. Russia.

ROY R. ROBSON

Ninety-five Theses, questions for academic debate posted by Luther*, October 31, 1517, and sent to church authorities. They challenged current teaching and practice concerning indulgences*, which were clearly subject to abuse and later reformed at the Council of Trent*. The theses open with a statement that the whole Christian life should be one of penance*, and end with an exhortation to follow Christ through tribulation as the way to genuine peace.

Ninian (c360–c432), first Christian missionary to Scotland and Northern England. Although many traditions are not historically verifiable, there is no doubt that Ninian was the first bishop of Galloway after planting a church (c397) and later a monastery in Whithorn, and that his mission was particularly successful among the Celts*.

Nino or Nina (early 4th c.), venerated as a saint, "equal to the apostles and the enlightener of Georgia"; a Cappadocian woman, who converted the royal family (King Mirian and Queen Nana) of Iberia (Eastern Georgia*). According to the Georgian tradition, she preached the gospel and performed healings first in Rome, then in Georgia; according to the Western tradition, she was brought to Georgia as a slave of the royal family.

Nisibis, School of. Founded under Bishop Barsauma, with Narsai (d502) as first head, and joined by scholars from Edessa* after 489, the school flourished (until the 7th c.) as an East Syrian center of exegesis and liturgical studies. Statutes from 496 and 590 reveal the school's community life. From Nisibis emerged the genre of "cause" literature on the origins of liturgical feasts. During Henana's directorate, a controversy over the normative role of Theodore* of Mopsuestia led to the exodus of many teachers and students. The school was also famous in the West and served as a model for Cassiodorus's plan of study for monks.

UTE POSSEKEL

Njangali, Florence Spetume (1908–84), canon in the Anglican Church and member of the revival movement in Uganda*; first woman deacon in East Africa (1973); campaigner for women's ministry in the Anglican Church. Njangali actively influenced the decision to allow women's* ordination as priests (1980).

ROBERT KAGGWA

Noah, son of Lamech, was the father of Shem, Ham, and Japheth. He found favor with God, built an ark, survived the Flood*, and ultimately preserved humanity (Gen 6–9). After the Flood,

God made a covenant* with Noah never to destroy life on earth again. In later biblical texts (Isa 54:9; Matt 24:37–38), Noah is recognized as righteous (Ezek 14:14, 20; 1 Pet 2:5) and a person of great faith (Heb 11:7). Early church commentators noted Noah's obedience, seeing him as a new Adam*. Conversely, early rabbinical commentators questioned his righteousness because of his drunkenness (Gen 9:21).

JEFFRY C. DAVIS

Nobili, Roberto de (1577–1656), a controversial Jesuit missionary in Indian Church history, began his work in Madurai (South India, 1606), questioning the Portuguese approach to mission and initiating a "new Madurai mission" that defined what it is to be a Christian within the Indian cultural context.

His option to work among the Hindu* society elite had consequences in the mission field. But Nobili was very creative. Having mastered Tamil and Sanskrit, he cited Sanskrit sources in his three Latin treatises, in which he spoke highly of Indian culture and civilization, for an European audience. Conversely, his Tamil writings sought to communicate traditional Roman Catholic Christian doctrines and to prove the superiority of Christianity over Hinduism through arguments based on the scholastic theology of his time. But the God of reason did not win over his audience.

Nobili attempted to differentiate sociocultural aspects, such as the caste* system, the wearing of saffron, the "sacred thread," and tuft of hair by Brahmins, and vegetarianism, from Hindu religion. This was an insightful way of carrying out his mission but, in the context of the Indian worldview, where it is not clear where culture* ends and religion begins, his efforts were misguided and failed.

The most important aspect of his missionary approach was his search for a sense of a pristine and monotheistic God in India, and he found it in the concept of Brahman, the one, true, immaterial God dimly apprehended through the natural light of reason – as Paul referred to the "unknown God" before the Athenians (Acts 17). But his zeal to prove that his religion was the fulfillment of all others prevented him from appreciating the nuances of the Hindu concept of God. Nevertheless, the questions he raised remain relevant and still need to be adequately answered. What is it to be a Christian in the Indian cultural context? Could the Christian message be made intelligible to people of India by using symbols of Indian religions? In intercultural and interreligious dialogue*, Nobili's approach calls for a revisioning of the mission* in India today. **See also INDIA.**

ANAND AMALADASS

Nominalism views universals not as "real" but only as names or concepts in the mind. Most likely developed by Johannes Roscellinus (Abelard's* teacher), it became an issue in 1092 when Roscellinus was accused of tritheism*, affirming three persons but denying the "reality" of unity in the divine essence. Nominalists of the later Middle Ages (beginning with William* of Ockham) argued that many theological concepts have no grounding in reality and can be resolved only by revelation*. Deconstruction (see Postmodernism and Liberation Theologies) advances a nominalist view that order is imposed by human discourse. Feminists* also do so when critiquing the "essentialism" in facile assumptions regarding women. Many postmodern, postcolonial, and Liberation theologies (see Liberation Theologies Cluster; Postmodernism and Liberation Theologies; Postmodernism and Theology; Postcolonialism and Christian Theology) as well as contemporary cultural studies of Christianity (see Culture Cluster: Culture and Christianity Cluster) adopt similar nominalist positions. **See also UNIVERSALS.**

Nomina Sacra (Lat "sacred names"), In (handwritten) Christian manuscripts, abbreviations of "Jesus," "Christ," "Lord," "God," and other holy names formed by the first and last letters (omitting the intervening letters), with a line over both letters. This is the practice of most early Christian manuscripts. **See also *CHI-RHO*; IHS; INRI.**

Nomocanon in the Eastern Orthodox* Church, a collection of laws including both canons* of the church and imperial laws; it reflected a close alliance between church* and state in the Orthodox world. It was compiled in different versions from the 6th c. (John Scholasticus) and the 8th c. (Photios*) to the 13th c.

Nonconformists, a term first applied to those Protestants (soon called "Puritans*") who declined to conform to certain prescriptions of the Church of England's 1559 Book of Common* Prayer. With the Act of Uniformity (1662) requiring assent to "all and everything" in the revised Book of Common Prayer, more than 2,000 clergy (of some 9,000) refused to comply, and "Nonconformist" then meant separation from the Church of England. Until the 19th c., "Dissenters*" was the more common term for groups such as Presbyterians, Congregationalists, and Baptists. By the late 19th c., "free churches" became the favored label, implying a positive rather than negative difference from the established church.

DALE A. JOHNSON

Nonconformity and Theological Education. Protestant Nonconformity in Britain emerged after 1660 from the restoration of the Church of England as the nation's established church (see United Kingdom). Its 17th-c. groups included Presbyterians*, Congregationalists*, and Baptists*; later Evangelical movements such as Methodism* were subsumed under the label "Nonconformist."

Since their members were excluded from the Universities of Oxford and Cambridge, Nonconformist places of theological* education first took shape as "Dissenting academies," often conducted in the homes of local ministers. Several of these provided the basis for the more substantial "theological colleges" formed by the mid-19th c., with more than one tutor and 25–40 students. By 1850 Congregationalists had more than a dozen colleges (three in Wales, one in Scotland), Baptists six (two in Wales), and Presbyterians one. With greater central government, English Methodists established branches of the Theological Institution in Manchester (1842) and London (1843), followed later by additional branches in Leeds and Birmingham.

General programs of study involved a literary course (languages, philosophy, mathematics, and science) of two to three years and a theological course of three to four years. With no capacity to offer degrees, colleges could only hope that students would stay the full course. Many feared the loss of faith* that would come when piety was married to education, while the colleges argued that the education of ministers had to keep up with the general educational pattern within the churches. The absence of denominational support for Congregational and Baptist colleges often placed the institutions in financial straits.

Opening the older universities to Nonconformists after 1870 produced a new pattern: separation of the arts and theology courses and the relocation of several colleges to Oxford, Cambridge, Manchester, and Bristol. First to move was the Congregationalist Spring Hill College to Oxford in 1886, taking the name Mansfield College. Others followed over the next 40 years, enabling the denominations to think of themselves as integral parts of the larger society. This development provided the foundation for yet another pattern that emerged in the later part of the 20th c., the establishment of theological federations of colleges in ecumenical partnerships, usually connected with a university and often including Anglican institutions. In addition to greater resources provided by such relationships and the ability to offer various degrees and certificates, these programs frequently included emphases on mission* and on education for laity* in a variety of ministry situations.

DALE A. JOHNSON

Nonjurors, English and Scottish clergy who, when William III came to the throne (1688), refused to swear allegiance on grounds that they would violate their previous oath to James II; hence they were also called Jacobites. Disobeying the law of the realm, they kept their own hierarchy and worshipped separately. Most adhered to the doctrine of the divine* right of kings, which also meant passive obedience to established authority.

Nonviolence, refusal, especially for religious or moral reasons, to use violent means to defend oneself (e.g. Matt 5:37–48) or achieve one's goals. **See also KING, MARTIN LUTHER, JR.; MENNONITES; PACIFISM AND CHRISTIANITY; PEACE CHURCHES.**

Norbert of Xanten (c1080–1134), Reformer, founder of the Premonstratensians. Following his conversion* (1115), he tried to reform the house of canons* in his hometown of Xanten. At his request, Pope Gelasius II permitted him to be a wandering preacher in Northern France. The order of Premontré was founded (1120) with the aid of the bishop of Laon; an order of canons* living under the Augustinian* Rule, it was recognized by the pope (1126). Norbert became archbishop of Magdeburg (1196) and helped prevent a renewal of the investiture* controversy.

Nordic Countries. See DENMARK; FINLAND; LUTHERANISM CLUSTER: IN NORDIC COUNTRIES; NORWAY; SWEDEN.

North Africa. See HISTORY OF CHRISTIANITY CLUSTER: IN AFRICA: NORTH AFRICA.

North America. See CANADA; QUEBEC; UNITED STATES.

North India, Church of (CNI), is a united and uniting church formed in 1970 that brought together six denominations after 41 years of dialogue. The denominations that united were the Council of Baptist Churches in Northern India, the Church of the Brethren* in India, the Disciples* of Christ, the Church of India (formerly the [Anglican] Church of India, Pakistan, Burma, and Ceylon), the Methodist Church (British and Australasian Conferences), and the United Church of North India (Congregationalists and Presbyterians). In the early 21st c., the CNI had a membership of 1.25 million in 3,000 pastorates covering, despite its name, all of India, with the exception of Kerala, Tamil Nadu, Andhra Pradesh, Karnataka, and Lakshwadeep Islands.

Espousing a firm belief in the Apostles'* and Nicene* Creeds, the CNI makes an attempt to draw on the theological insights of all its constituent churches. Its union and life as a united church have made possible the evolution of theological positions that are both ecumenical and contextual*. Likewise its liturgy represents the diversity of its constituent member churches and seeks to articulate the love of God in the midst of present reality.

The polity* of the CNI brings together the Episcopal*, Presbyterian*, and Congregational* elements of its constituent members. In its episcopacy, the CNI is both constitutional – bishops are appointed and perform their duties according to the constitution – and in historic continuity with the early church. Furthermore, the CNI is not committed to any one interpretation of episcopacy.

The CNI is divided into 26 dioceses, each with a bishop. The highest body, the synod, meets once every three years to elect an executive committee and a moderator, who acts as the presiding bishop and the head of the church.

The CNI is made up largely of members of subaltern communities: Dalits* ("outcastes," about 150–200 million persons) and Adivasis* (about 60–70 million "original dwellers of the land," indigenous persons). Therefore, the CNI has always been actively involved in social action and solidarity with subaltern communities through its social and health service boards. This solidarity is also expressed in a theological and pastoral praxis and mission agenda (see Dalit Theology). The CNI is committed to becoming radically transformed and to transforming communities. **See also INDIA; SOUTH INDIA, CHURCH OF.** ENOS DAS PRADHAN

Norway. Most Norwegians presently combine a public ritual Christianity limited to important life transitions and a strong private Christian religiosity, although there is tension between a large state church with modest demands on its members and groups (including Charismatic groups), inside and outside the state church, whose doctrinal and ethical demands on their members are much stricter.

The transition from Norse to Christian religion lasted about two centuries, through trade contacts with Europe, Viking raids, and missions from England, Germany, and Denmark. Having died (1030) fighting for Christianity, King Olaf* Haraldsson gained a reputation as a saint, which strongly contributed to the spread of Christianity among Norwegians. In 1539, when Norway was a weak province of Denmark, the Reformation was decreed by the Danish–Norwegian king. In the 17th c. an absolute monarchy was combined with a strict, law-protected Lutheran orthodoxy.

A process of religious pluralization of the monolithic Lutheran culture began in the 19th c. Norway was separated from Denmark* and entered a union with Sweden* (1814). The new constitution consolidated the state* church. In 1845 religious freedom was established; Methodists, Baptists, Lutheran free churches, and others progressively organized, but their membership never became large. Ascetic* revivalist* movements remained within the state church, because the lay preacher Hans Nielsen Hauge*, who inspired these movements, was loyal to the state church, despite his criticism of its religion.

By 2000 about 86% of Norwegians were members of the state church, while the number of Roman Catholics, Muslims, and Buddhists grew with the arrival of immigrants and refugees after 1970. Many Lapps (the Sami people, an old ethnic minority) joined a conservative Christian movement within the state church, that of the Laestadians.

While a large majority of the population takes part in life cycle rites (baptism, confirmation, weddings, funeral services) and Christmas Eve worship services, only 2 to 3% attend services on Sunday. The Church of Norway performs some "civil* religion" functions on solemn national occasions or in times of crisis. By contrast, the relatively few members of free* churches (and members of conservative religious organizations within the state church) frequently attend meetings; yet the free churches are stagnating. Charismatic groups (mostly within the state church) have grown rapidly since 1970.

The Church of Norway has a complicated system of state and ecclesiastical government, with an increasing role given to democratically elected councils. The first female pastor was ordained in 1961. In 2000, out of 11 bishops 2 were women.

In public schools, all pupils receive religious education. Christianity dominates in the curriculum, but religious tolerance and dialogue are emphasized. Theological education with liberal tendencies was established with the first university (1816). In reaction, the more conservative Norwegian Lutheran School of Theology (Menighetsfakultetet; 1907) was established. The recently founded Missionary College provides theological education for the many missionaries (sent since 1850 around the world).

Christians involved in 19th-c. revivalist* movements combined modernizing concerns for individuals and social issues and antimodernizing ethical impulses. During the 20th c., these groups strove to maintain a Christian stamp on social institutions (e.g. public schools) while fighting liberal laws (e.g. on abortion). Despite these conservative trends, the Church of Norway broadened its Christian ethical commitments in a liberal direction to include social (global exploitation; discrimination against immigrants), ecological*, peace*, and sexuality* issues. Although less importance is now given to doctrinal issues and more to spirituality*, Norwegian churches remain relatively conservative, dogmatically speaking.

A charter member of the World* Council of Churches, the Church of Norway participates in the Christian Council in Norway, which provides a forum for dialogue among all denominations and facilitates some dialogue with Muslims and Buddhists.

Statistics: Population (2000): 4.46 million (M). Christians, 4.2 M, 94.7% (Protestants, 4.14 M; independents, 0.13 M; Roman Catholics, 0.04 M); Muslims, 0.06 M; nonreligious, 0.11 M. (Based on *World Christian Encyclopedia*, 2001.)

PÅL REPSTAD

Notes of the Church. See MARKS OF THE CHURCH, NOTES OF THE CHURCH.

Novatianism, rigorist movement in the Western Church that grew out of the Decian* persecution (249–50). Novatian was a Roman presbyter who opposed the election of Cornelius and became a rival bishop of Rome. He and his followers revived the position of the Montanists* that those who committed serious sins* must be excluded permanently from the church.

Novena, Roman Catholic devotion with special prayers on nine successive days, in imitation of the apostles' nine-day preparation between the Ascension* and Pentecost*.

Novice, Novitiate, new member of a religious community who is under probation, and may be dismissed or may voluntarily leave.

Number of the Beast, 666 (Rev 13:28; in some manuscripts, 616). Hebrew and Greek letters had numerical values, suggesting a connection between names and numbers. It has often been argued that the letters for "Neron Kaisar" (Greek for "Nero the Emperor"), when written in Hebrew, add up to the number of the beast.

Numbers, fourth book of the Pentateuch*, recounts Israel's wilderness* journey from Mount Sinai to Canaan*. Its title derives from the census lists in Num 1 and 26.

The book moves from preparations for Israel's march through the wilderness* (Num 1–10), the old generation's slide into rebellion and death (11–20), to signs of hope* in the midst of the death of the old generation (21–25), and the rise of a new generation on the edge of the Promised* Land (26–36).

Numbers was compiled by priestly groups in the 5th c. BCE to provide renewed identity, devotion, and hope to Jews who returned from the Babylonian Exile* (587 BCE) to Judah* under the aegis of the Persian Empire.

Earlier wilderness journey traditions associated with Northern Israel (Ephraim) (e.g. Ps 78) were reshaped in Numbers as a paradigm for all Israel, offering both warning and hope for the reconstruction of the Jewish community after the Exile. The unique prophetic authority of Moses* (Num 12) was supplemented by affirmations of Aaron's* authority as high priest (Num 16–17, 25), reflecting shifting leadership patterns in the postexilic Jewish community.

Numbers encouraged diligent obedience to the Torah*, offered hope to returnees from the Exile as a new generation in the Promised Land, reinvigorated devotion to a rebuilt Jerusalem* Temple* (symbolized by the wilderness Tabernacle* in Num 1–10), and supplemented earlier biblical law codes with new legal traditions and interpretations (e.g. Zelophehad's daughters in Num 27, 36).

Numbers includes the Aaronic priestly blessing* (Num 6:22–27), the manna story (11; see John 6), the miraculous water from the rock (20; see 1 Cor 10), the bronze serpent (21; see

John 3), and Balaam's* promise about a future king and a star (24:17; see Matt 2).

DENNIS T. OLSON

Nun, strictly speaking, a woman leading an enclosed* life; in popular usage, any woman under religious* vows. **See also WOMEN'S RELIGIOUS ORDERS CLUSTER.**

Nunc Dimittis, Simeon's song (Luke 2:29–32), named from its opening words in Latin; used in daily prayer since the 4th c.

Nuncio, permanent diplomatic representative of the Roman See* to a government (the representative to the USA is called an "apostolic delegate" because of the differentiation of church* and state).

Nuptial Mass includes the ritual celebration of Christian marriage*, which takes place within the liturgy of the Word and after the homily. On a day other than a Sunday or feast day, the liturgical texts (prayers and biblical readings) may be chosen by the couple from options within the Roman Missal and Lectionary. The nuptial blessing is normally imparted by the assisting minister within the Communion rite after the Lord's Prayer and before the peace.

KEITH F. PECKLERS, SJ

O

Oak, Synod of the (403), synod held by order of Emperor Arcadius in a suburb of Chalcedon, attended by enemies of John* Chrysostom, most of them from Egypt. Condemned on 29 charges, Chrysostom was removed from the See of Constantinople and exiled by the emperor. Soon recalled because of popular protest, he was nevertheless permanently exiled the next year.

Oath, solemn appeal to God, or another sacred person or thing, as witness that a statement is true or a promise is binding. Christian groups that forbid oaths (following Matt 5:33–37) are often permitted to make an "affirmation" rather than take an oath.

Obadiah, one of the Twelve Prophets; shortest book of the OT, comprising only 21 verses, mostly in poetic form characterized by vivid language and imagery. Obadiah (Heb "servant" or "worshipper of YHWH") was identified by later Jewish tradition (*Sanh.* 39b) with King Ahab's administrator (1 Kgs 18:3–16), yet this is a relatively common biblical name, possibly that of a Judean prophet of the 6th c. BCE.

The book, identified as a "vision" of Obadiah (v. 1; cf. Isa 1:1; Nah 1:1), begins with a prophetic judgment against Edom, Judah's hostile neighbor, possibly alluding to its having seized part of the Judean territory during the Babylonian rule. The book consists of two sections: (1) an oracle against Edom (vv. 1–14), announcing the coming defeat of Edom (vv. 1–9) and describing Edom's crime against Judah (vv. 10–14); and (2) the day of YHWH (vv. 15–21), proclaiming both the coming judgment* to all nations and the deliverance of Israel (vv. 15–18), when the Promised Land previously occupied by other nations will be repossessed by Jerusalem and the kingdom shall be YHWH's (vv. 19–21).

The oracle against Edom is well connected with the "oracles against nations" of other prophetic books, especially Jer 49:7–22; Ezek 25:12–14; Amos 1:11–12, 9:12; and Joel 3:19. The pronouncement of the coming judgment upon Edom (vv. 1–14) broadens to include all nations on the "day of the Lord" (vv. 15–21). Thus through the centuries, "Edom" has been interpreted as symbolic of the alien outside world that will be condemned.

PHILIP CHIA PHIN YIN

Oblate, in the early Middle Ages, a child dedicated to a monastery*; more recently, any person devoted to specific work in a monastery.

Oblation, bread and wine offered at the time of the offertory* for consecration in the Eucharist*; by extension other gifts presented during the service for charitable purposes.

Ockham (Occam), William of (c1285–c1347), Scholastic philosopher, controversial theologian, political writer; was born in England, entered the Franciscan* order, was educated at Oxford and Paris, studied with Duns Scotus*. While teaching at the University of Paris (1320–23), he composed works on Aristotelian physics and logic. His work on the rule of parsimony (already apparent in Aristotle*), known as "Ockham's [or more usually Occam's] razor," asserting that theories should not be multiplied without necessity, has been used ever since to assess competing theories in a broad range of disciplines (sciences, philosophy, theology, law). Ockham's major contribution to Scholastic metaphysics* was his distrust of claims of human certitude with respect to the reality of universals*; universals are "names," mental "abstractions," rather than existing things in reality. The contention that Ockham was simply a nominalist* is now widely contested. Ockham argued that everything real is individual and particular. Thus he came to reject the assumption that matters of faith* were also matters of reality, thereby criticizing the ontology argued for by Aquinas*. Therefore, the immortality* of the soul* and the existence, unity, and infinity of God* are not matters of reality discernible by human reason*; they are matters of faith through revelation* alone. Later in his career (after 1328), Ockham devoted himself to ecclesiastical politics, joining the Franciscan dispute with Pope John XXII over apostolic poverty* and church possessions, and arguing for a strict separation of church* and state on religious grounds.

DAVID W. ODELL-SCOTT

Offertory, originally an anthem* sung during the Mass* while the people's offerings were collected and the elements were placed on the altar; currently, that part of the worship* service during which offerings are made.

Office, Divine, daily public worship services of the Western Church. In the early church, the practice of the Divine Office was simply a series of stated times for prayer during the day. The monastic movement appropriated it and made it more formal (see Benedict, Rule of). The usage spread to the nonmonastic clergy during the Middle Ages. The Breviary* is a compilation of prayers and readings for the Divine Office for private as well as public use. (The Divine Office should not be confused with the Divine* Liturgy of the Eastern Orthodox* Church.) **See also DIVINE OFFICE OF THE LITURGY OF THE HOURS.**

Olaf Haraldsson (995–1030), patron saint of Norway*. A Viking king baptized in Rouen (1012), he established Christian laws in Norway and brought English clergy to the country (1016). Forced into exile (1028), slain in Stiklestad while trying to return (1030), like Christ, he attained victory through death. His cult* quickly spread, and his reliquary* in Nidaros Cathedral became a site of pilgrimage*. He was canonized* in 1164, and presented as a martyr*, model Christian, and "eternal king of Norway" in the Divine* Office for St. Olaf (feast, July 29). Hundreds of European and North American churches are dedicated to him. The number of people who go on pilgrimage to Nidaros (now Trondheim) continues to grow.

VIDAR L. HAANES

Old Believers (Russian, *starovery*), also known as *staroobiradtsy* (Old Ritualists), is a generic term for a diverse group of religious dissidents who separated from the Russian Orthodox* Church in the late 17th c. because of changes in the Russian Orthodox liturgy (1660s). The violent methods used by the reformers, social and economic disasters, and eschatological* sentiment led to religious unrest. In the 18th–19th c., the important centers of Old Believers were in the north (on the White Sea), the trans-Volga region, the border between Russia* and the Polish Commonwealth, the Baltic provinces, Bessarabia, Moscow, the Urals, and Siberia, but their geographic distribution was uneven.

According to official data, 190,944 persons registered as Old Believers in 1716–26 and as a consequence payed a double poll tax. To avoid this tax, many Old Believers remained nominal members of the Orthodox Church. Thus the actual number of Old Believers could not be precisely determined until 1905, when they were granted full legal rights. In 1912 there were 1.8 million Old Believers (less than 2.5% of the population in the Russian Empire). However, the Old Believers' strength lay not in their numbers but in their literacy, economic power, and strong communal identity.

Except during a period of enlightened toleration (1763–1814), the imperial government did not grant legal rights to Old Believers and tried to assimilate them into the Orthodox population. They finally received the same legal rights as the Orthodox Church in 1905. In the Soviet Union, the number of Old Believers declined owing to religious repression, and some migrated to Australia, the USA, South America, China, and European countries. After the breakdown of the Soviet Union (1991), there was a revival of Old Believer religious life, but its impact remained limited in post-Soviet Russia.

There are two main types of Old Believers: priestly (*popovtsy*) Old Believers, who differ from the mainstream Orthodox Church only on the issue of ritual; and priestless (*bespopovtsy*) Old Believers, who accept lay ministry and have fewer sacraments than the Orthodox Church. Among priestly Old Believers, some (*beglopopovtsy*) recruit priests from the Orthodox Church, while others (*belokrinitskie*) have had their own church hierarchy since 1846, when the Bosnian bishop Amvrosii (Popovich) ordained bishops for the "Old Orthodox Christian Church." The priestless Old Believers have many divisions (ranging from moderate to radical), which are divided over the understanding of the Antichrist* and other eschatological views (see Eschatology and Apocalypticism in Orthodox Eastern Europe) and over the role of sacraments. Marriage* became a subject of fierce debate among priestless Old Believers: some advocated celibacy* as the only way to salvation* (in the absence of priests who could perform the sacrament of matrimony); others concluded that marriage was a sacrament performed by God that a priest merely witnessed (see Marriage, Theology and Practice of, Cluster: In Eastern Orthodoxy). Moderate Old Believers who kept their own rites were recognized by the Orthodox Church and formed the United Faith (Edinoverie, officially approved in 1801).

Old Believers preserved the medieval Orthodox rite and liturgy, including the monophonic (*znamennyi*) chant of Byzantine origin, traditional iconography, and book culture.

Generally, Old Believers' culture and way of life are regarded as reflecting the way of life typical of Russia before Westernization under Peter the Great.

Like many other religious dissenters, Old Believers were and are active in trade and business, differing from average Russian peasants by their well-organized and sustainable agricultural economy. For both priestly and priestless Old Believers, the role of the laity is conspicuous. Laypeople interpret the Scripture and participate in interconfessional debates. Women as a rule have a higher status among Old Believers, both in everyday life and in religious life than do women in the Russian Orthodox Church; among priestless Old Believers, it is not unusual for women to carry out the roles of ministers (cf. Women's Ordination Cluster: In the Orthodox Church). IRINA PAERT

Old Catholic Church, separated from the Roman Catholic Church in 1870–71 in protest against the promulgation of the dogma of the doctrinal infallibility* of the pope (First Vatican* Council, 1869–70) "as an innovation contrary to the traditional faith of the Church." After the signing of a letter of protest (by 1,400 German laypeople and clergy, September 1870) and the excommunication* by the pope of leaders of the protest (including Johann Joseph Ignaz von Döllinger), a first Old Catholic congress met in Munich (1871) with representatives from Germany*, Austria*, and Switzerland*. The main tenets were adherence to the ancient "catholic faith" and its origin in the early church, the rejection of "new dogmas," and the reformation of the Roman Catholic Church. The affirmation that the (Old) Catholic Church (as independent from Rome) was the true Catholic Church – an affirmation accepted by several governments in Germany and Switzerland – led to the Old Catholics' claim on church buildings and other properties owned until then by the Roman Catholic Church in these countries. Other congresses (Cologne, 1872; Breisgau, 1874; Breslau, 1876; Baden-Baden, 1880; Krefeld, 1884) and synods established the Old Catholic Church, following models of earlier groups in the Netherlands*, resulting in the election of a first bishop, Professor Joseph H. Reinkens (1873, ordained by the non-Roman archbishop of Utrecht). In 1874 they abolished the requirement of clerical celibacy* and declared the "Catholic Diocese of the Old Catholics in Germany" to be autonomous, episcopal, synodal in organization, and catholic in liturgy. Beyond the German-speaking countries in Europe, the Old Catholic Church spread to Poland* and North America, and in 1995 had a worldwide membership of approximately 800,000.

Old Latin Version (*Vetus Latina*), Latin translation of the Bible from the Septuagint* and the Greek NT, probably completed in North Africa and Southern Gaul (late 2nd c.). There are three "text types," K, I, and D, formerly known as the African, Italian, and European manuscript traditions, respectively. **See also BIBLE TRANSLATIONS CLUSTER: EARLY TRANSLATIONS/VERSIONS.**

Old Testament and Its Canonization. Speculating about the growth and development of the OT canon – the books of Tanakh* for Jews and of the OT for Christians – is complex and challenging because there are no surviving ancient records that describe the processes of its formation and recognition either by Jews or subsequently by Christians. Several references in books later included in the canon suggest that there was a recognition of their sacredness, but the reasons for including them in Tanakh/OT are nowhere explicitly stated. Essentially the literature that was included in the canon of Tanakh was that which clarified the identity and mission of the Jewish people as the people* of God and that subsequently had a similar function in the Christian community as its OT canon.

Initially this literature included the Law of Moses*, then the whole Pentateuch*, and later the additional books of the Prophets* and the Writings*. Torah, the Law or Pentateuch, was recognized as authoritative c500 BCE, the Prophets (*Nebiim*) c200 BCE, and the final collection of Writings (*Ketubim*) between the late 1st c. CE and the mid-2nd c. CE. The OT writings that gained sacred status among the Christians *before* their separation from the Jews (between 70 and 135 CE) included many books now classified as noncanonical books, the Apocrypha* and Pseudepigrapha* (see Septuagint).

The scope of Tanakh and the OT canon was not settled for either the Jews or the Christians before their separation, but those books that were considered sacred by the Jews of the 1st c. CE are the same books that were initially accepted as Scripture* by the early Christians. Both Jews and Christians ceased recognizing most of the pseudepigraphal writings by the 3rd c. CE , but most Christians continued to include in their OT much of the apocryphal literature. The Protestant churches later accepted the same OT sacred books that were recognized by rabbinic Judaism and included only 39 OT books. No official decisions settled the matter for either the Jews or the Christians. The primary criteria for inclusion in the Tanakh or OT were widespread use in the respective communities and adaptability to the needs of both religious communities.

The churches have never reached complete agreement on the scope of their OT. Also, the Christians, unlike the Jews, organized their OT canon with the Prophets at the end, pointing to the continuing revelation* of God in their NT. **See also BIBLE, CANON OF.**

LEE MARTIN MCDONALD

Olga (Old Norse Helga, 890–969, christened Helena), Varangian princess, wife of Igor and mother of Svjatoslav (Sviatoslav), rulers of Kiev, regent during the early years of her son, grandmother of Vladimir*. In 957 she paid a visit to the Byzantine emperor Constantine VII in Constantinople* and was baptized by him. Her conversion and practice of Christianity in Kiev attest to the gradual process of Christianization of Kievan Rus' in connection with Byzantinium*, rather than with Latin Christianity. **See also UKRAINE.** PETRE GURAN

Olives, Mount of, a hill east of Jerusalem*. It is represented as a place of worship and revelation (2 Sam 15:32; Ezek 11:23; Zech 14:4). According to the Gospels, Jesus* met the crowd there on Palm* Sunday (Mark 11:1), taught there (Luke 21:37, 22:39), and prayed there after the Last* Supper (Mark 14:26); his ascension* took place nearby (Luke 24:50–51; Acts 1:12).

Olivi, Peter John (c1247–98), charismatic Franciscan* teacher in Narbonne, France. As the order gained prestige and influence, he became critical of Aristotle* and pagan philosophy; he defended a return to authentic Franciscan life in *Questions on Evangelical Perfection*. Controversy centered on his teachings on the vow of poverty* (*usus pauper*); these teachings were censured (1283), and his writings were banned by the order (1285). After being rehabilitated (1287), he taught at the convent of Santa Croce (Florence). Olivi's writings were in the tradition of Joachim* de Fiore and influenced Ubertino de Casale, the Spiritual Franciscans, and other 14th-c. members of apocalyptic* movements.

MARY BETH INGHAM, CSJ

Olympias (late 4th–early 5th c.), illustrious, wealthy noblewoman. She was born in Constantinople, the granddaughter of the Praetorian prefect and consul Ablabius. Around 385 she married the much older Nebridius, who became prefect of Constantinople (386). Soon widowed at the age of about 20, she refused to remarry, even when, to exert pressure, Theodosius* I forbade her to administer her own property. She adopted an ascetic* life and founded a monastery* next to the great church of Constantinople, where she became patron of bishops, monastics, and the poor, and presided over a center of spiritual life and influence in church and imperial politics. Gregory* Nazianzen wrote a poem for her wedding. Gregory* of Nyssa dedicated his commentary on the Song of Songs to her. She was ordained a deaconess* in her 30s by Nectarius, bishop of Constantinople (381–97). Two sisters, a niece, another relative, and 50 of her servants, among others, belonged to her monastery of 250 ascetic* women, which was later burned in the Nika riots of 532 under Justinian, but apparently rebuilt. Olympias is a saint of the Eastern Church.

Olympias was a friend, confidante, and loyal supporter of John* Chrysostom as bishop of Constantinople. After his exile (404), she too was tried and exiled because of her support of him. From exile John Chrysostom wrote 17 surviving letters to her; hers to him have not survived. Olympias died in exile before 419.

Several sources mention Olympias and her life, including the anonymous 5th-c. *Life of Olympias*; the 7th c. *Narration Concerning St. Olympias* attributed to Sergia, a successor in her monastery; Palladius's* *Lausiac History*; and Sozomen's *Ecclesiastical History*. Sergia's account relates miraculous events surrounding the transfer of her bones from a grave outside the city to a place in her monastery. **See also DEACONESS.**

CAROLYN OSIEK

Omnipotence of God. God is omnipotent in that he is all-powerful, ruling over or administering all things and in all aspects. The Hebrew *Shaddai* is translated in Greek as *Pantocrator* (All-Ruling; LXX*), which became *omnipotens* (able to do everything) in Latin. In Christian usage, the term is found chiefly in the Book of Revelation* and the Apostles* Creed.

This language is rooted in the doctrine of creation*; finite things would not exist or have any power of action without the creating and sustaining activity of God. God's power is not merely physical "might"; it is power or authority exercised on and through the world and compatible with God's wisdom and goodness. Without God the world *might* not exist at all, or it *might* be a different kind of world; God is understood to be the cause of what is *actual*. (Note the differentiation between what *might* happen and what *actually* happens.)

The Scholastics* distinguished between God's "absolute power," all that God "can do," and God's "ordered power," what God actually wills to do; God acts consistently with God's own purposes (in creation*, covenant*, salvation*) and remains faithful to those purposes. Because God acts in a consistent way, it can happen that something that is "logically possible" will be "circumstantially impossible."

The reality of evil*, both in nature and in human life, raises issues of theodicy*: How could a good God create a world with so much suffering*, and a humanity that freely commits so many evil acts? Since the time of Plato*, some have posed a dilemma: given these facts, God must either be all-powerful but not good, or be good but not all-powerful. The Book of Job* seems at times to suggest the former, just as Paul must finish a discussion of election* with an exclamation about the unsearchable depths of God's ways (Rom 11:33–35).

Omnipotence is sometimes understood to be "omnicausality," whereby God not only causes but determines all events, including sin*; this was the position of the Stoics* and Spinoza* among philosophers, and Calvin* and Schleiermacher* among theologians.

Theologians have usually affirmed, however, that the omnipotent God "permits" sin. Thus for Barth*, because God wills to be "God for human beings" and calls them to respond, God made it possible to reject this call, i.e. to sin, although it is morally illegitimate, impossible, fruitless, and tragic to do it. Sin is the "impossible possibility," a contradiction of what both God and humanity properly are.

An influential response to the problem of evil* is found in the narrative of Joseph, whose brothers intended evil while God intended good (Gen 45:5–8). For Augustine*, God permitted only those kinds of evil that could be used to accomplish some good. While this may seem to be small consolation to those who suffer great evil, the emphasis is on God's activity to overcome it (thus for Tillich*, God is "the power of being to overcome nonbeing"). For Bonhoeffer*, God shares human suffering and rejection; God identifies with the oppressed* and has a "preferential* option for the poor" (Liberation* theology).

From these diverse perspectives, God's omnipotence is incompletely manifested in the present world. The eschatological* hope* is that Christ will subject all things to God (1 Cor 15:24–28; Phil 3:21; 1 Pet 3:22; Heb 2:5–8; Rev 19–21), not through an exercise of absolute power but through the establishment of a community in which God is "all in all" (1 Cor 15:28) or of the New Jerusalem in which God dwells with God's own people (Rev 21:1–4). **See also GOD, CHRISTIAN VIEWS OF, CLUSTER.**

EUGENE TESELLE

Omnipresence of God, God's presence "everywhere" or "to all." It is not that God is diffused throughout space and divided – hence the traditional dictum "All of God is everywhere," like a sphere whose center is at every point.

The objection that ancient Israel assumed that God is not present in Sheol* (Ps 88:4–5, 10–12) is contradicted in Ps 139:8. Is God too pure to behold evil* (Hab 1:13)? Conversely, does God dwell or abide in particular places? In the Tabernacle? In the Temple? In the faithful (John 6:56, 15:5; cf. 1 John 2:6)? Is God "more present" in Christ than elsewhere? In the debates over Christology*, it was agreed that the Incarnation* cannot mean that God is localized in Jesus. To avoid this view, the followers of Cyril* spoke of the Word's dwelling in Jesus' humanity, while the Antiochenes*, stressing God's transcendence of space and time, explained Jesus' unique relationship to God. EUGENE TESELLE

Omniscience of God, God's all-knowing. The "all" is usually understood to include not only what is actual but also what is possible but never actualized. Traditionally, it was assumed that God's knowing is eternal*, without temporal sequence, so that all events are known "now" by God; God's "foreknowledge" of future events is really a "present knowledge" to God, without detriment to the human exercise of finite freedom. Modern theologians have generally favored a more "living" understanding of God, as knowing actual events as they occur, but against the background of God's awareness of all possibilities and God's purposes for what should be actualized. **See also MIDDLE KNOWLEDGE; PREDESTINATION.** EUGENE TESELLE

Onesimus, the slave mentioned in the letter of Paul to Philemon*. Traditionally viewed as a runaway slave from Philemon's house, who has met Paul* in prison and been baptized by him; alternatively viewed as a slave who has gone legally to Paul for intercession. It is not clear whether Paul intended that Philemon free Onesimus. Without questioning the institution of slavery*, Paul defined a new relationship between slave and master.

Ontological Argument, classic argument that begins with a definition or description of God and concludes from it that God exists. It can be formulated in various ways: that the proposition "God is" is self-evidently true; that God's essence includes God's existence; or that God is "necessary being," i.e. if God is possible, then God is necessary. The argument has been challenged for moving from thought to reality and for assuming that existence is a predicate included in a definition.

The classic expression of the argument is that by Anselm* (*Proslogion* 2–4). He begins with his characteristic theme of "faith* seeking understanding," praying that he might understand that God *is* as he *believes* God to be. While Chap. 2 seems to deduce God from a definition, Chap. 3 evokes a way of discovery, for when one understands that God "truly is" (i.e. is self-existent), it becomes evident that God "cannot not exist."

The ontological argument was challenged by Aquinas* and the Nominalists*, revived by Descartes* and Leibniz*, criticized by Kant*, and revived in an altered form by Hegel* (who saw it as thought's self-transcendence in Absolute Spirit) and by Hartshorne* (who interpreted it as a recognition that God must be both absolute and relative). A diminished form of the argument, championed by Barth*, is that it is simply an explication of the contents of belief based on revelation*. EUGENE TESELLE

Ontology, the part of philosophy that considers "being as being," viewing it comprehensively and asking about the cause or causes of all that is. Aristotle* discusses these questions in his work on "first philosophy," given the title of *Metaphysics* by its ancient editors (see Metaphysics and Christian Theology). Among the Greek philosophers, the Ionians first asked about *physis*, or "nature," and answered in terms of matter and its movements; Plato* and Aristotle asked about the definiteness of things, and answered in terms of the "forms" that shape matter. But Aristotle also went on to consider "being as being," and he generalized in terms of "potency" (what *can* be) and "act" ("actuality"; what *is*). His principle was that actualization, the change from potency to act, can occur only through the influence of something that is already "in act." Thus the motions of the heavenly bodies stimulate the changes in earthly matter; in turn, all finite being is moved by divine being, which is fully actual, "pure act," with no unactualized potentialities.

Subsequent thinkers developed this notion of God as "pure act." Finite things, they said, "receive" or "have" or "participate in" being, while God "is" being, Being Itself. Boethius* and Avicenna* took the additional step of differentiating, with respect to every finite thing, *what* it is (its definiteness or essence) from that *by which* it is (its existence). Finite things come into existence and pass away, and their being, on this view, is actualized not by themselves but by God. This ontology based on the "real distinction" of essence and existence in all finite beings, and on God as Being Itself through whom all other things are actualized, was developed most completely by Thomas Aquinas*.

This ontology was criticized as indemonstrable in the later Middle Ages by the Nominalists*. A different approach was taken by the founder of modern philosophy, Descartes*, who gave primacy to thought rather than being; he started with the syllogism "I think, therefore I am," then moved to God, and was able to connect thought with the external world only through God. Many see this emphasis on thought as the downfall of modern philosophy, although there were many attempts to connect thought with being, especially by Hegel* and Whitehead*. Another kind of criticism is found in Heidegger* and Derrida*, for whom the chief error is "ontotheology," supposing that God can be known as the source of all other beings; the "différance" between beings and their being is affirmed, but the "being of beings" is concealed and is disclosed through interaction with human beings, with no transcendent source.

EUGENE TESELLE

Open Communion, celebration of Communion in which all who have faith in Christ are invited to take part in the Eucharist* (because it is an invitation from the Lord, and not from a given church). It is contrasted with the practice in certain churches of limiting Communion to their own members* or (in the Reformed* tradition) of fencing* the table to exclude those who have not made formal repentance*.

Ophites (from Gk for "serpent"; also Naasenes, from Heb for "serpent"), members of a Gnostic* movement that gave a special role to the serpent (Gen 3), on the grounds that creation* was imprisonment of humanity by a lesser deity; through the serpent, a higher deity led Adam* and Eve* to eat from the tree of true knowledge (Gen 3).

Oppression, Oppressed. Oppression is an important biblical theological concept, although traditionally it has not been considered to be such. However, in view of the numerous times oppression is mentioned in the HB, expressed by a great variety of Hebrew words, and its centrality in Israel's faith creed (Deut 26:5–9), some biblical scholars and theologians concluded that it is an important theological concept. In the NT, from the outset the gospel proclaims itself to be good news to the poor and oppressed (Luke 4:18; Matt 11:5). In the Bible, manifestations of oppression are most frequently mentioned in the economic* sphere, in which the victims are poor*, impoverished because of other people's sin* of greed. However, theologically we can extend the concept of oppression to all degrading experiences inflicted on humans, including sexism*, racism*, and heterosexism (see Sexuality Cluster), and to the devastation of the environment (see Ecology and Christianity Cluster). The concept of oppression refers to the social manifestations of evil*, revealing that people ignore or reject God.

Oppression is tied to liberation*; both situations occur throughout the Scriptures, from the birth of the people of Israel, who were liberated from slavery* in Egypt; to the prophets* who denounce oppression as an offense against God; to the Psalms that cry out to God because of oppression; to Jesus' programmatic platform, "good news to the poor"; and finally to Revelation*, which, in the midst of the great repression of God's people (Jews or Christians), addressed the needs of the oppressed, encouraging them not to be overwhelmed, because God is present.

Oppression, when recognized as a theological experience, helps us recognize the historicity of salvation*. Oppression is related to sin* and exposes sin; the fact that there is oppression demonstrates that, in some way, someone harms someone else or some group harms other groups. Oppression, together with disease and other afflictions, are negations of God's Reign (or Kingdom*); therefore, the presence of oppressed people or refugees* is always a call to act; for Christians, struggling against oppression is giving witness to their calling as sons and daughters of God (Rom 8:23). The presence of oppression is thus a context that calls Christians to interpret the nature of this oppression and to demonstrate their faith in God. Situations of extreme poverty are privileged locations to better understand the message of salvation*.

ELSA TAMEZ (translated by Gloria Kinsler)

Optatus of Milevis (Numidia, now Algeria), bishop (365–85), author of a work against the Donatists*, *The Donatist Schism*, first written c367 and revised with an additional book c385. Augustine* later drew on Optatus's critique of the Donatists' claim to represent the one holy church and on his readiness to receive Donatists back into the Roman Catholic Church without rebaptism.

Option for the Poor. See PREFERENTIAL OPTION FOR THE POOR.

Opus Dei, an organization primarily of laypeople within the Roman Catholic Church that is similar to, though not identical with, a religious* order. It was founded by Josemaria Escrivá de Balaguer (1902–75, canonized 2002) as an informal association, originally of men studying at the university. They lived in a residence in Madrid purchased by Escrivá; a women's section was added shortly afterward. This nascent organization was disrupted by the Spanish civil war, during which Escrivá fled to France; he returned to Burgos, within the territory controlled by the Nationalist troops of General Franco. Opus Dei – the name means "the work of God," and it is commonly referred to by its members as "the Work" (Opus) – flourished in the aftermath of the civil war, largely through its involvement in Spanish higher education. To the lay organization was added (1943) the Sacerdotal Society of the Holy Cross, a branch constituted by priests to look after the members' spiritual needs. Meanwhile, Escrivá moved from Burgos to Madrid, where his society gained recognition as a "pious union" from the bishop of Madrid.

Escrivá sent his second-in-command, Alvaro del Portillo (who eventually succeeded him at the head of Opus Dei), to Rome (1945), where a new headquarters was opened. Opus Dei became a secular* institute (1947), but gradually outgrew this constraining status. It was granted the rank of "personal prelature" (1982), a form of diocese without geographic boundaries, the only one of its kind (as of 2007). From Rome, Opus Dei spread to Portugal (1945), England (1946), France and Ireland (1947), and Mexico and the USA (1948). Its more than 80,000 members are now widely scattered across the world.

Its spirituality is based on the writings of its founder, particularly on *Camino*, a small book of 999 maxims. Beyond promoting the sanctification* of its members in their daily, ordinary life, Opus Dei has no specific apostolate, although its members appear to be heavily involved in higher education* and communications. There are various types of membership. Some live celibate lives in communities, while others marry and remain with their families. Theologically and socially conservative, the organization has been criticized for its secrecy and what seemed to some rather questionable methods of recruitment. In December 1981, the cardinal archbishop of Westminster at the time, Basil Hume, issued a series of "guidelines" for the behavior of Opus in his diocese, which focused on these issues. MICHAEL J. WALSH

Orange, Second Council of (529), regional council held in Southern Gaul under the presidency of Caesarius of Arles. Pelagian* and semi-Pelagian* views are condemned in Canons 1–8; these are followed by propositions taken from the writings of Augustine* by Prosper* of Aquitaine a hundred years earlier; the conclusion affirms universally "prevenient" (anticipatory) grace* while condemning the view that God predestines* anyone to evil and damnation. Although the decrees were confirmed by Pope Boniface II (531), they were overlooked from the 10th to the 16th c., not being included in the collections of canons. They were rediscovered and published in 1538, influencing both the Reformation* and the Council of Trent*.

Orans, Orant (Lat "one praying"), artistic representation of a person praying with hands and arms upstretched, the usual posture for prayer in the ancient world.

Oratorio, musical work, usually on a biblical theme, sung by solo voices and chorus; similar to opera but without dramatic action. **See also PASSION.**

Oratory, place of worship other than a parish church, usually for a specific community or group. **See also CHAPEL.**

Orders, Holy Orders, ordination* as a sacrament* in the Roman Catholic Church; also a sacrament* (mystery) in the Orthodox churches. **See also RELIGIOUS ORDERS, ROMAN CATHOLIC, CLUSTER.**

Ordinal, liturgical book, especially in the Anglican Communion, containing the forms to be used for ordaining deacons* and priests* and consecrating bishops*.

Ordinances, Baptist designation for baptism and the Lord's Supper, to underscore the belief that these are not sacraments productive of grace, but mere symbols.

Ordinary, in canon* law, the bishop* or other official with permanent jurisdiction over a diocese* or other territory. In liturgy, the unvarying portions of a worship service (e.g. the Mass*), contrasted with the "proper*" portions.

Ordination (Lat *ordinatio*) designates a rite of initiation into a sacred *ordo* (rank, order, office, authority). In ancient Rome, *ordinatio* was used for appointments to civil office; for Latin Christians, *ordinatio* assumed the same meaning as the Greek, *cheirotonia*, an initiation into a sacred liturgical order by the laying* on of hands (cf. Jerome, *Comm. in Isaiam* 16.58.10).

In the OT, there were "ordinations" by anointing with oil for priests (Lev 8:10–36, 21:10) and kings (1 Sam 10:1, 16:13–14; 1 Kgs 19:16) and the laying on of hands for the Levites (Num 8:10–13) and Joshua, Moses' successor (Deut 34:9; Num 27:15–23). In later Judaism, rabbis were "ordained" by the imposition of hands.

In the NT, Jesus selects the Twelve* by personally calling them (Mark 3:13–19; Matt 10:1–4; Luke 6:12–16). Subsequent Roman Catholic tradition specifies Jesus' command, "Do this in remembrance of me" (Luke 22:19), as the primordial priestly ordination (cf. Council of Trent, *Doctrina de ss. Missae sacrificio*, can. 2; Denz.-Hün, *1752).

In Acts 6:6; 1 Tim 4:14; 1 Tim 5:22; and 2 Tim 1:6, the imposition of hands provides the paradigm for the ordination rite. By the time of Ignatius* of Antioch (c35–107), the three orders of bishop (*episkopos*), presbyter (*presbyteros*), and deacon (*diakonos*) (mentioned in Phil 1:1; 1 Tim 3:1–13; and Titus 1:5–9) are clearly distinguished from each other (cf. *Smyr.* 8:2). The minor orders (e.g. subdeacon and reader) developed later.

Ordination by prayer and the laying on of hands is found in the early church (cf. Hippolytus*, the Apostolic* Tradition; c3rd c.), and most Christian denominations continue to ordain in this way. Roman Catholics, Orthodox, and most Anglicans believe that only bishops* have the authority to ordain. Other denominations see ordination more as an installation into a public ecclesial function than as an initiation into a sacramental* order by bishops (see Orders, Holy Orders). Catholics and Orthodox reserve episcopal, priestly, and diaconal ordination for men. Accordingly, they generally regard the deaconesses of the early church as consecrated laywomen rather than as members of the ordained clergy (cf. Nicaea* I, Can. 19). **See also WOMEN'S ORDINATION CLUSTER.**

ROBERT FASTIGGI

Ordo Salutis (Lat "order of salvation"), a topic that originated among Lutheran theologians in the 17th and 18th c., stimulated by the growth of Pietism* and vigorously debated with Reformed and Catholic opponents. Paul seems to have suggested (Rom 8:29–30) a causal or temporal sequence in God's acts of salvation: foreknowledge*, predestination*, calling or vocation*, justification*, and glorification. Other stages were added in an attempt to clarify the process. Several areas of controversy arose: (1) Does predestination follow God's foreknowledge of human acts? (2) Is justification based on human decision (and thus will*) or on irresistible grace*? (3) If justification is through faith* alone, how is it supplemented by other divine gifts? (4) Is a mystical union* with God in Christ to be the culmination of the process? This way of thinking is generally criticized for its excessive claims of precision, both theological and psychological.

Organ, instrument with pipes sounded by compressed air, used during worship in Western* churches since the Middle Ages, especially in cathedrals; the use of organs in parish churches grew during the 19th c.

Orientation, positioning of a church so that the worshippers face the sunrise, symbolic of revelation* and of Christ's return in glory.

Origen (c185–c254), biblical scholar, theologian, spiritual writer. Born in Alexandria, he was a catechist and teacher in Alexandria (205–32) and Caesarea (234–50). He journeyed to Rome (c212), where he heard Hippolytus*; to Arabia (c213–c228) at the invitation of the governor; to Jerusalem and Caesarea (c231); to Antioch (c232–33) at the invitation of Julia Mammaea, mother of the emperor; to Greece (c232, c238–44); and to Arabia (c244–49), where he prosecuted the bishops Beryllus and Heraclides before church councils. During the Decian* persecutions (249–51), Origen was imprisoned and tortured; by living a few more years, he was denied the status of a martyr*.

In Alexandria Origen was in close contact with Platonist* philosophers, Gnostics* (especially Valentinians*), and Marcionites*, debating the relation of God to the world, the origin of evil*, and the compatibility of justice* and mercy* in God. The Nag* Hammadi library contains a number of Gnostic works known to have been debated somewhat later by Plotinus*, who began his career in Alexandria. Origen's theological system responds to the concerns of these various movements, refuting them with references to the Bible, which Origen interpreted allegorically*, in a framework that was influenced by the movements themselves. Toward the end of his life, he was in contact with the young Porphyry*, the Neoplatonist* philosopher who would later write against the Christians, viewing Christianity as un-Hellenic and doomed to failure.

In Palestine, Origen was ordained a presbyter and was permitted to preach, but his chief function was the less formal one of a teacher, or *didaskalos*. He permitted his homilies to be recorded after he reached the age of 60 (c245). His lifetime work on the text of the Bible led to the compilation of the Hexapla*. In Caesarea he also became more fully acquainted with Jewish scholars and their interpretations of the Bible.

Origen's theological "system," while it peeks through his exegetical works, is made explicit in *On First Principles* (229–30). He thinks of the Trinity* as coming forth when the Father wills to create; this activity is everlasting, because God could never have been unwilling or unable. The original creation* is of finite minds or spirits, created equal since God cannot be the source of inequality, and united with God through the light of the Word* and the fire of the Spirit*. Through *koros* (satiation, weariness, carelessness, self-centeredness) their fall* occurs. The mind named "Christ" is the only one who remains united with God; Satan* is the one who rebels most radically; others drift away to various degrees.

Because of the fall*, God designs a succession of worlds with pedagogical intent, leading fallen spirits back to their original unity with God through both suffering and persuasion, in ways that speak to the needs of each spirit at its stage of development. The various ranks of angels*, e.g., are spirits doing penance by moving the heavenly bodies and ministering to human beings. Following the Stoics*, Origen thought of the soul* as self-moving but influenced by external stimuli and internal inclinations; God's pedagogy, then, works through stimuli in ways that preserve free choice (see Moral Influence). Origen speculates that all spirits, even Satan, might eventually be led back to God. The hardening of Pharaoh's heart (Exod 4:21) is interpreted pedagogically, and the drowning of Pharaoh's army (Exod 14:21–29) is described by language reminiscent of that of baptism. This pedagogical process goes through many successive worlds; in one place (*On Prayer* 27.16), Origen suggests (if we are to take him literally!) that the worlds are numbered by weeks, months, and years of ages, and by sabbatical and jubilee years, at least 50 × 365 epochs.

The present world is the one in which Christ becomes incarnate* in human flesh. (Origen also mentions the possibility that Christ made himself present to angelic powers in other ages.) Christ mediates divine truth and on the cross ransoms* human beings from bondage to Satan (see Atonement). The gospel is proclaimed by the Christian Church, with its sacraments and its ordained clergy, but Origen felt that these externals symbolize a more internal and charismatic* authority exercised by spiritual persons like himself, who gain deeper insights into the truth and whose authority is not necessarily reflected in outward office.

The allegorical* method, earlier applied by Greek grammarians to their classics and by Philo* of Alexandria to the Septuagint*, was applied by Origen to the entire Bible, including the NT. In approaching a text, the grammarians differentiated between history (what actually occurred), fiction (what could have occurred but did not), and myth (what could not have occurred as narrated). These "stumbling blocks" in the text are a clue that it has a higher, nonliteral meaning; indeed, even "history," when properly understood, reflects higher levels of meaning. Origen sometimes speaks of three levels of meaning: body (the letter of the text), soul (its moral overtones), and spirit (its intimations of transcendent realities). Thus the creation narrative (Gen 1) becomes fully intelligible when "heaven" means the spiritual "heaven above heaven" and "earth" means matter in all its forms; the land of promise is the "pure land" of spirits united with God. The exodus from Egypt and the wandering in the wilderness are an allegory of ascent to God; the Book of Joshua (= Jesus) is an allegory of the conquest of desire* under the guidance of Christ.

Although Origen aroused controversy, his work was also valued for its exegetical insights and spiritual ardor. Origenism* was both attacked and defended for several centuries; Origen's works survived largely through Latin translations, often under others' names. Many of his interpretations and teachings were later abandoned. Yet it can be argued that his perspective was at core a biblical one, examining the complex relationships between God and finite spirits under all possible circumstances and finding them resolved through divine initiative and free creaturely response.

His major works include a lost autobiographical letter cited by Eusebius* (233); *Hexapla* (215–45); *On First Principles* (229–30); commentaries on Ps 1–25 and Lamentations (c225), Genesis (230–34), John (231–48), Pauline Epistles, Isaiah, and Ezekiel (243–45), Canticles (245–47), Ps 1–72 and 118 (245–47), Matthew and Luke (249); homilies on many biblical books (239–42); *On Prayer* (234); *Exhortation to Martyrdom* (235); and an apologetic work, *Against Celsus* (249). EUGENE TESELLE

Origenist Controversy (the) erupted in the last years of the 4th c. over varying interpretations of the works of the 3rd-c. Origen, especially his speculative treatise *On First Principles* (see Origen). Origen was the most prominent pre-Nicene* Greek-writing theologian, and a "tamed" version of his theology had influenced such 4th-c. figures as Gregory* of Nyssa, Basil* of Caesarea, and Ambrose*. Although serious theological issues were at stake – centering on the relation of the members of the Godhead, a cosmic vision of creation* and final end, the origin of the soul*, humans' possession of the "image* of God," the status of the body*, ascetic* spirituality, evil*, and the justice* of God – the controversy was heightened by enmity between the circles of Jerome* and of Rufinus* of Aquileia, with various aristocrats, monks, and bishops from Palestine, Egypt, and Italy choosing sides. Jerome had earlier translated a number of Origen's less speculative writings, yet when Rufinus brought out *On First Principles* in Latin (397–98), Jerome charged that Rufinus had deliberately masked heterodox elements in Origen's theology; the controversy thus also involved debates over proper principles of translation. Both Rufinus and Jerome defended their positions at length, Jerome being pressed to respond to Rufinus's allegation that his writings advocating a stringent asceticism and his *Commentary on Ephesians* were tainted by Origenist ideas. Even after Bishop Anastasius* of Rome in 400 (apparently) condemned Origen's writings, the controversy continued. Some issues (e.g. whether a human can live without sin*) spilled over into the Pelagian* controversy in the second decade of the 5th c. Until that time, Jerome seemed unaware that Rufinus and his partisans knew a stronger, more speculative form of Origenism through their association with the 4th-c. monk and theologian Evagrius* Ponticus.

It was largely an Evagrian adaptation of Origenist theology centered on Christology* that spurred the second outbreak of controversy over Origenism among monks in 6th-c. Palestine: Would or would not, in the "restoration of all things," believers be made equal to Christ? At the Council of Constantinople* (553), propositions linked to Origenism were condemned; and in the Syriac* Church, Origenism became deeply embedded in disputes between Monophysites*/Miaphysites* and Nestorians*. In the West, the condemnation of both Origenism and Pelagianism* left the field open to the development of Augustinian* theology, which stressed human sinfulness and divine determination, not human potential and freedom*. **See also MONASTICISM CLUSTER: IN THE SYRIAC TRADITION.** ELIZABETH A. CLARK

Original Righteousness, creation of human beings in a state of rectitude before the Fall*. Debates continue as to whether this righteousness was natural or the result of grace*, actual or merely potential.

Original Sin, the doctrine, primarily in Western* churches, that the sin of Adam* and Eve* was somehow transmitted to their offspring. It was used to explain the practice of infant baptism "for the remission of sins" (from the Apostles' Creed), an explanation not needed in the East, where churches emphasized infant baptism as an initiation into the Kingdom* of God (see Baptism Cluster; Orthodox Churches, Eastern, Cluster).

The doctrine was justified by reference to several passages in Paul (e.g. Rom 5:12–15; 1 Cor 15:45–50) and the statement about being conceived in sin (Ps 51:5). The latter reinforced the association of original sin with concupiscence* and sexuality* (even in marriage*) and the emphasis on the virginity of Mary* as the only way in which Jesus could be without original sin.

The first explicit attack on the doctrine came from the Pelagians* (who emphasized freedom* of choice and were repeatedly condemned, 418–31). The doctrine of original sin was shaped by Augustine's* anti-Pelagian writings. For him original sin was not genetic, not a change in the "seed," but a privation or a dysfunction in human life. Peter* Lombard's later statement that original sin is "a wounding of nature and a deprivation of grace*" may be an appropriate summary. Original sin does not abolish individual responsibility; Augustine tended to treat it as the *penalty* of sin, which then becomes *sin* when a person "voluntarily" fails to resist it.

During the Protestant Reformation, Luther* emphasized original sin, and his follower Flacius* located it in the "substance" of the soul*. Calvin* and his followers called it accident rather than substance, but with their doctrine of "total depravity" they insisted that it affects all aspects of human life, not merely with a lack of orientation toward good but with an inclination toward evil*.

Enlightenment* writers often attacked the doctrine for its pessimism and negativity (see Kierkegaard, Søren Aabye). But Kant* revived it on a different basis, looking not to the origins of the human race but to the structure of human willing*, operating with a kind of moral inevitability: because of a natural inclination toward lesser values, actual willing falls short of the moral law that is apprehended by practical reason; by the time we come to full moral awareness, Kant argues, we are already guilty. Thus human history is from the first a history of sin and redemption*. Kant's approach has been adopted, with important differences of detail, by almost all subsequent German theologians.

In contemporary (Liberation*) theology, another way of interpreting original sin is to emphasize "structural* evil" (or systemic evil*): the oppression* that arises from inequalities of class, race, sex, and other conditions. These are types of evil that are larger than, and prior to, the individual, enveloping all, both the oppressor and the oppressed, in a web of guilt and powerlessness. EUGENE TESELLE

ORTHODOX CHURCHES, EASTERN, CLUSTER

1) *Introductory Entries*

2) *A Sampling of Eastern Orthodox Churches in Context*

1) Introductory Entries

Orthodox Churches, Eastern. Eastern Orthodox churches (also known as the Greek* Orthodox Church) are a worldwide communion of autonomous (autocephalous*) churches constituting a major branch of Christianity. The body of Orthodox Christians identifies itself as the "one, holy, catholic, and apostolic church" of the Nicene* Creed, emphasizing its spiritual unity despite the administrative independence of the churches. "Orthodox" means both "correct worship" and "correct belief"; with this name, Orthodox Christianity highlights its profound care for apostolic purity in worship and dogma.

The mother churches of Orthodoxy are the sees* of apostolic foundation in Constantinople*, Alexandria*, Antioch*, and Jerusalem*. The Orthodox Church today includes these patriarchates* and their dependencies along with the churches of Russia*, Serbia*, Romania*, Bulgaria*, Georgia*, Cyprus*, Greece*, Poland*, Albania*, the Czech* Republic, and Slovakia*. Estimates of worldwide Orthodox Church membership range between 225 and 250 million. The Church has active mission* efforts in every inhabited continent.

In Orthodoxy each local church is presided over by one bishop* assisted by presbyters* and deacons*. Each is regarded as manifesting the catholicity of the one Orthodox Church. Orthodox men may be married before being ordained as priests* but not thereafter; bishops are selected from the celibate or widowed clergy. The clerical ranks are not open to women; however, the role of deaconess* once existed and is being revived in certain places. All bishops are of equal authority, but in every synod one bishop is granted the place of "first among equals" for administrative purposes and given the title of metropolitan*, archbishop*, or patriarch*. The patriarch of Constantinople has carried the title of ecumenical* patriarch since the 5th c., has the primacy of honor among all hierarchs, functions as coordinator among the Orthodox churches, and presides over all inter-Orthodox meetings. He does not exercise supreme administrative authority like the pope of Rome.

Unity and continuity are at the heart of the Orthodox Christian ethos. Embracing the Pauline dictum that "there is one body and one Spirit," Orthodoxy insists that the Holy* Spirit guides the Church into a single, unchanging understanding of truth* across all times and cultures. The Orthodox Church regards itself as the sole authentic successor of apostolic Christianity, as expressed in its Scriptures, Holy Tradition, forms of worship, and canonical succession of bishops (see Apostolicity and Apostolic Succession).

Divine truth is manifested in the life of the Church* through "conciliarity," i.e. the consensus of the whole body of Orthodox believers, both clergy and laity. The highest authority in the Orthodox Church is an ecumenical council, a worldwide gathering of representatives that unanimously proclaims the mind of the Church on disputed matters. The Orthodox Church recognizes the inspired and infallible authority of the seven ecumenical councils: Nicaea* I (325), Constantinople* I (381), Ephesus* (431), Chalcedon* (451), Constantinople* II (553), Constantinople* III (680–81), and Nicaea* II (787). (The Quinisext* Council of 692 in Constantinople is seen as the completion of the fifth and sixth councils and is therefore implicitly included in the seven.) Adherence to the principle of conciliarity led the four Eastern Patriarchates to reject papal claims of Roman supremacy and the *Filioque**, resulting in the Great* Schism of 1054.

The Orthodox Church identifies itself as the continuation of the church of the martyrs*. In Orthodox spirituality, martyrdom remains the paradigmatic path to holiness, and the Church continues to venerate martyrs from even the earliest decades of Christianity. Relics of martyrs are a sine qua non for the consecration of new churches. In the past three centuries, when large parts of the Orthodox homelands have been under the persecution* of totalitarian regimes, the Orthodox Church has offered up countless new martyrs for Christ.

The Orthodox Church identifies itself as the continuation of the church of the fathers (see Patristics), whose writings are still used for liturgy and catechesis. Particularly important are the saints Basil* the Great, Gregory* the Theologian, John* Chrysostom, Athanasius*, and Cyril* of Alexandria, Maximus* the Confessor, John* of Damascus, and Gregory* of Nyssa. The patristic age remains open-ended, and such late figures as the saints Photius* the Great, Gregory* Palamas, and Mark* of Ephesus are considered fathers. Two other writers not counted as fathers have exerted an incalculable influence on Orthodox theology: Origen* of Alexandria and Dionysius* the Pseudo-Areopagite. Patristic* modes of thought and exegesis remain paradigmatic for Orthodoxy; the idea of the development of doctrine is accepted to a limited degree.

The ascetic* ethos of early Christianity exerts a strong influence on Orthodox piety. The disciplines of prayer, fasting, and almsgiving are emphasized for all Christians and especially for those with monastic vocations. Orthodox monasteries are largely independent of one another, although for the past millennium Mount Athos* in Greece has acted as the spiritual center of Orthodox monasticism* and its tradition of hesychasm*. Orthodoxy does not have different monastic orders as in the West.

The spirit of Orthodox theology is epitomized by the maxim "The theologian is the one who prays, and the one who prays is a theologian." Orthodox theology is experiential and doxological in character, drawing from and leading to the personal encounter of love between God and humankind. Orthodoxy disfavors speculative or scholastic approaches to theology, reserving the title "theologian" for those who have been enlightened by personal experience of God.

Orthodox theology is markedly apophatic* in character, starting from the premise that human words and concepts are inadequate for speaking of God, who in essence is unknowable. The idea of a *mysterion* (mystery*) is quintessentially Orthodox: the Trinity*, the Incarnation*, and the Church* and its sacraments* are all referred to as "mysteries" – those things that cannot be grasped intellectually and yet may be known through personal participation. Humanity can experience God in God's uncreated energies, attributes of divinity in which humans participate by the cooperation of their free will. God is known always as *philanthropos* (loving humankind). Responding fully to divine love leads a person to union with God, known as theosis*.

"Ousia*" and "hypostasis*," "being, nature*," and "person*" are key concepts in Orthodox thought. The unity of the Trinity derives not from some abstract common substance, but from the one Father who is the unique cause of all being, begetting the Son and giving procession to the Spirit as coequal divine persons. The Western *Filioque* is rejected as blurring the distinction between persons* and as without basis in Scripture or Holy Tradition. In the Incarnation, the person of the Son was fully united to human nature. All of Orthodox ecclesiology and spirituality grows organically out of these dogmas of the Trinity and the Incarnation.

The Orthodox understanding of the human condition differs markedly from Western conceptions (including the Western emphasis on atonement* and justification*). The salvific effects of the Incarnation extend not just to fallen humanity, but to the entire cosmos. Original* sin is not understood as a sharing of the guilt of Adam's fall* but as the inheritance of his corrupted mortal nature. Humans are seen more as victims of the devil's* deception than as criminals to be condemned by divine justice. Death* is understood not as God's curse on creation, but as God's enemy and the inevitable consequence of separation from life with God. Sin* is viewed more in terms of a disease of the soul than as individual acts of lawbreaking. The human person is regarded as a psychosomatic unity that sin afflicts in its entirety, leading to all the suffering of soul and body of this present life.

Salvation* is defined not merely as forgiveness*, but even more as liberation* of the human mind from delusion and the renewal of human nature by union with the God-man Christ, whose healing presence is experienced through the Orthodox Church and its sacramental mysteries. These include baptism*, chrismation*, Communion*, confession*, unction*, matrimony*, and ordination*. The Divine* Liturgy is the high point of sacramental life. The church year is developed around the Resurrection*, called Pascha*.

Orthodoxy attaches a special devotion to the Virgin Mary*, called the Theotokos*, "birth-giver of God." She is venerated as the paragon of fallen humanity renewed by voluntary cooperation with divine grace*. She is regarded as *Panagia* (All-Holy) and *Aeiparthenos* (Ever-Virgin) but not as co-redemptrix or as the product of an immaculate* conception. The Orthodox believe that after her death, she was given a place of unique prominence in heaven, where she acts as an intercessor for Christians. Orthodox Christians venerate icons* of Christ, the Theotokos, the martyrs, and the saints as a means of expressing their honor to God and the saints. **See also FLOROVSKY, GEORGES; LOSSKY, VLADIMIR; STANILOAE, DUMITRU.**

ARCHBISHOP DEMETRIOS [TRAKATELLIS]

Orthodox Churches, Eastern: Greek Orthodox Church and Its Theology. The expression "Greek Orthodox Church" has two meanings. In the broad sense, it refers to the entire body of Orthodox (Chalcedonian) Christianity, sometimes also called "Eastern Orthodox," "Greek Catholic," or generally "the Greek Church," because the mother communities of Orthodoxy were all located in the Greek-speaking portion of the ancient Roman Empire.

The Orthodox Church as a whole is aptly described as Greek in its common preference for the Byzantine* rites of worship and its adherence to the ethos of Christianized Hellenism developed by the Greek-speaking fathers of the early church. Despite its name, the Greek Orthodox Patriarchate of Antioch is, ethnically and linguistically, mostly Arabic.

In a narrow sense, the expression "Greek Orthodox Church" refers to any of several independent churches within the worldwide communion of Orthodox Christianity that retain the use of the Greek language in formal ecclesiastical settings. In this sense, "Greek Orthodox" can be distinguished from "Russian Orthodox" or "Serbian Orthodox," the difference between churches being linguistic only, not theological or liturgical.

In the latter sense, the following Orthodox churches are properly called Greek Orthodox: the Ecumenical* Patriarchate of Constantinople and its dependencies in Europe, Asia, North, Central, and South America, and Australia and on Mount Athos* in Greece; the Patriarchate of Alexandria; the Patriarchate of Jerusalem*; the Church of Greece*; and the Church of Cyprus*. In both the broad and narrow senses of the term, the Greek Orthodox Church has always been ethnically diverse; phyletism* and nationalism are anathema to Orthodox ecclesiology. The Greek Orthodox Archdiocese of America, with headquarters in New York City, comprises the largest Orthodox ecclesiastical jurisdiction in the USA.

The theology of the Greek Orthodox Church is identical to that of all Eastern Orthodox* churches, which taken together are understood in Orthodox ecclesiology to constitute the one undivided body of Christ. Among the Orthodox churches, there are minor variations in liturgical expression, clerical dress, and ecclesiastical custom.

Greek Orthodox Christianity is characterized by great joyfulness in the presence of God, who is ever *philanthropos*, "who ever loves humankind," and who inspires a spontaneous, exuberant love* among people. The eucharistic service, called the Divine* Liturgy, is conducted by clergy and laity in a majestic and celebratory manner, as are baptisms and weddings. Even occasions of mourning, such as services of Christian burial, Lenten contrition, or Good* Friday, are conducted with a characteristic "joyous sadness," or *charmolupe*, to use the coinage of St. John* Climacus. This sense of joy* among the Greek Orthodox pervades their daily life and culture as well as their liturgical expressions: the customary street greeting in the Paschal season is *Christós Anésti*! – "Christ is risen!"

In the modern era, Greek Orthodoxy has been significantly affected by its subjugation to Muslim rule in many places. Under the Tourkokrateia, the period of Ottoman domination, Orthodox bishops were forced to become not only spiritual leaders but also ethnarchs, leaders of the ethnic community and advocates of Hellenic culture in the face of official repression (see *Millet*). Religious persecution in this era resulted in the recognition of many *neomartyres* (new martyrs*). The repressions of the Tourkokrateia sparked several waves of emigration to the New World, Africa, and Australia, giving rise to large communities in what is often referred to as the diaspora. Most of Greek Orthodoxy in the diaspora follows the Gregorian calendar* for liturgical purposes; however, the date of Pascha* (Orthodox Easter) is always calculated to ensure a common celebration among all the Orthodox, including those who follow the Julian calendar*.

Greek Orthodox Christianity is especially conscious of the influence of Hellenistic thought and culture in the development of early Christianity. In the diaspora, the Church has made special efforts to support the study of Greek language and Hellenic culture among its people. While all Orthodox churches follow the same festal calendar, emphasis is given by Greek Orthodoxy to the Annunciation* on March 25, celebrated simultaneously with the day of Greek independence from Turkish rule. Likewise, the Feast of the Holy Protection on October 28 is celebrated as OCHI day, commemorating Greece's refusal in 1940 to accede to Fascist demands for capitulation. The Feast of the Three Hierarchs (Basil* the Great, John* Chrysostom, Gregory* Nazianzen the Theologian) on January 30 is also a celebration of Greek literacy and learning.

Greek Orthodoxy is characterized by a deep devotion to the saints* of the early church, especially the Virgin Mary*. Great affection is also shown for ancient martyrs like St. George and St. Demetrios, beloved hierarchs like St. Nicholas and St. Spyridon, and St. Constantine* and St. Helen*. Particular devotion is shown for St. Nektarios of Pentapolis (1846–1920), the "saint of our time," a monastic who served as a hierarch and teacher in Alexandria, Athens, and the Greek island of Aegina, and whose life epitomizes the love, joy, humility, and miraculous existence of Greek Orthodox Christianity.

ARCHBISHOP DEMETRIOS [TRAKATELLIS]

---

2) A Sampling of Eastern Orthodox Churches in Context

Orthodox Church, Eastern: In Georgia. The Apostolic Autocephalous* Orthodox Church of Georgia is one of the most ancient Christian churches. It originated, according to tradition, with the apostle Andrew's 1st-c. mission and was established as a state religion (for the Eastern part of present-day Georgia) when through the ministry of a young Cappadocian woman, Nino*, the royal family converted to Christianity (early 4th c.) in Mtskheta. First under the jurisdiction of the See* of Antioch*, it became autocephalous* (self-governing, led by a catholicos*) from the 480s but was still linked with the "mother church" of Antioch until the 740s, when it started confirming a locally elected catholicos. The full separation from Antioch took place in the 11th c. Catholicos Melkisedek I (1010–33) was made the first patriarch of all Georgia. In 1811 autocephaly was abolished as a result of the annexation of Georgia by Russia. It was restored in 1917 but gradual recognition came in 1943 (by the Russian* Orthodox Church) and in 1990 (by the Ecumenical* Patriarchate).

The Orthodox Church of Georgia, having adhered to the Chalcedonian Christology, is one of the Eastern Orthodox* churches and shares their liturgy and theology. Yet traditional liturgical Eastern Orthodox chant, architecture, wall paintings, and icons* have distinctive characteristics, despite a significant Byzantine influence.

Many biblical, liturgical, and patristic texts were translated before the 8th c. from Armenian, Syriac, and Greek but later were corrected according to the Greek. The Church kept close ties with the Palestinian Church until the 8th–9th c., but then stayed closer to Byzantine tradition. Georgians were present in monasteries* outside of Georgia as early as the 5th c., in the Holy Land; among the many notable Georgian monasteries are Iviron on Mount Athos* (10th–11th c.) and Holy Cross in Jerusalem (11th c.).

Original Georgian hagiography described the lives and martyrdom of local saints, including Shushaniki (5th c.), Eustatius of Mtskheta (6th c.), Abo of Tbilisi (8th c.), Gregory of Khandzta (10th c.), Euthymius (10th–11th c.), and George the Athonites (11th c.). Theologian Ephrem Mtsire (the Minor; 11th c.) translated and commented on works by church fathers such as Gregory* of Nazianzus. Philosopher Ioane Petritsi translated and commented on *Elements of Theology* by Proclus (12th c.) and initiated Neoplatonic studies at the Gelati Academy in West Georgia.

As a result of wars, successive occupations by Ottoman, Persian, and Russian troops, and ensuing dire economic situations, the Church suffered a great deal from the 16th to the 20th c. Restoration of autocephaly (1917) offered a moment of relief, but was soon overshadowed by Communist rule in Georgia. From 1977 (enthronement of Catholicos-Patriarch Ilya II), the Church went through a complex process of renewal and struggle with some aspects of the newly established democratic society, such as nationalism and fundamentalism*. In the early 21st c., the Church had 36 bishops, c570 monasteries, and c900 ordained priests. It also had two newspapers, a journal, and a television channel. The church actively participates in the life of the country but is not closely associated with the state. TAMARA GRDZELIDZE

Orthodox Church, Eastern: In Greece.

The modern history of the Orthodox Church of Greece begins with the declaration of Greek independence from Ottoman rule (1821). Early postrevolutionary Greek governments were supportive of the Church, although political leaders educated in the West were critical of its backwardness and the isolation of its leadership. Western powers appointed Otho, a Bavarian prince, to head the kingdom of Greece. Bavarian advisers drew up the blueprint for the organization of the Church of Greece and its relationship to the state. The Ecclesiastical Constitution of 1833 defined the church as a department of the new state and declared the Church of Greece independent from the Ecumenical* Patriarchate of Constantinople, under whose ecclesiastical jurisdiction most of Greece had been for many centuries. The Church was to be governed by a permanent synod consisting of a president and two to four additional members, all appointed by the king. In 1850 Constantinople recognized the autocephaly* of the Church of Greece. State control of the church progressively decreased over the following decades, although national politics, especially the republican–royalist controversy (first quarter of the 20th c.) and the military junta (1967–74), often adversely affected the Church.

The jurisdictional boundaries of the Church of Greece expanded as the Greek nation claimed additional territories. The Church of Crete is semiautonomous under the jurisdiction of the Patriarchate of Constantinople, while the Dodecanese Islands are organized with five metropolises, each directly under Constantinople. The Church of Greece is governed by two synods, both presided over by the archbishop of Athens: a permanent synod consisting of 12 metropolitans reconstituted yearly and a larger synod consisting of all metropolitans (currently about 80).

The Orthodox Church of Greece plays an important role in the political, cultural, and economic life of the country. Clerical salaries are paid by the state, and members of the theological faculties of the universities of Athens and Thessaloniki are, like those of other university faculties, employees of the state. Religious instruction is mandatory for Greek Orthodox students attending primary and secondary public schools. Lay theologians and brotherhoods contributed greatly to the spiritual and educational life of the church in the 20th c., in particular the Church's own Apostoliki Diakonia and the lay brotherhoods of Zoe and Soter (the former since the early 20th c.). The late-20th-c. monastic revival (especially that of Mount Athos*) has had a significant impact as well. **See also GREECE.**
JAMES C. SKEDROS

Orthodox Churches, Eastern: In Mexico. The Antiochian Orthodox Church and the Greek Orthodox Church arrived with immigrants from the Ottoman Empire and Greece (1875). The Archdiocese of North America of the Patriarchate of Antioch provided pastoral care for Orthodox believers in Mexico. A diocese of Mexico, Central America, Venezuela, and the Caribbean was established in 1966 and was elevated to an archdiocese in 1995. In Mexico there are about 570 Orthodox families of Syrian-Lebanese origin, which belong to the Antiochian community. There were also 150 families of Greek origin, but they withdrew (1969) from the Antiochian Orthodox Church when Bishop Pablo de Ballester built a cathedral and named it Santa Sofía (Hagia Sophia), the name of the venerated Greek Orthodox Church. The Antiochian Orthodox Church is in communion with the Ecumenical* Patriarchate of Constantinople. In 1972 the Holy Synod established the Exarchate of Mexico at the request of the community of Peñón de los Baños (Mexico City), which had belonged to the Mexican Apostolic Catholic Church, and its 10,000 members became Orthodox.

MONICA URIBE

Orthodox Church, Eastern: In Romania. The Eastern Orthodox Church in Romania (Biserica Ortodoxă Română) is an autocephalous* Eastern Orthodox* Church, in full communion with the other Eastern Orthodox churches.

It is the only Eastern Orthodox Church using a Romance language. The majority of people in Romania (18.8 million, or 86.8% of the population; 2002 census) belong to it, as do some 0.7 million Romanians from the Republic of Moldova* and other important diaspora communities. The Romanian Orthodox Church is often viewed as the second largest after the Russian Orthodox Church.

After the Great* Schism (1054), the people of Romania remained in communion with the Eastern Orthodox churches. With the creation of Romanian principalities during the Middle Ages, the first Metropolitanate of Ungro-Vlachia was founded in 1359 in Curtea de Argeş. The Metropolitanate of Moldavia was founded in 1401 in Suceava. The Metropolitanate of Transylvania (founded in the 15th c.) has its center in Alba Iulia. All these metropolitanates were under the jurisdiction of the patriarch of Constantinople.

During the following centuries, the Orthodox Church flourished mainly in Wallachia and Moldavia. Many well-known churches and monasteries erected at that time (e.g. Cozia, Voronet, Putna, Sucevita) are still among the glories of the Romanian people.

The Romanians first adopted Church Slavonic as the language of their liturgy (early 9th c.). Until the 16th c., many religious texts were only transcribed in Church Slavonic. However, important Romanian language translations circulated, including, e.g., the Codicele Voroneţean (the Codex of Voronet). Later (16th–18th c.), Slavonic was abandoned in favor of Romanian. Thus for the past few centuries, Romanians (unlike the inhabitants of other major Orthodox nations) have had no sacred language other than their own spoken language.

In 1859 the Romanian principalities of Moldovia and Wallachia formed the modern state of Romania. Since the Orthodox Church organization tends to follow the structure of the state, in 1872 the Orthodox Metropolitanates of Ungro-Vlachia and of Moldovia were united to form the Romanian Orthodox Church, which became autocephalous* (1885) and was raised to the rank of patriarchate (1925).

After World War II, the Orthodox Church as an institution was more or less tolerated by the atheist regime, although it was severely controlled and excluded from the public sphere. Persecution was always present, in many and varied ways. The Communist authority initiated mass purges that decimated the Orthodox hierarchy. By January 1953, about 500 Orthodox priests were in prison. As a result of measures passed in 1947–48, most Orthodox universities and high schools were closed. A new persecution campaign struck the Church in 1958–62, when more than half of its remaining monasteries were closed, more than 2,000 monks forced to take secular jobs, and about 1,500 clergy and lay activists arrested (out of a total of up to 6,000 in the 1946–64 period).

During the timid liberalization period (from 1962), the Romanian Orthodox Church, under the wise leadership of Patriarch Justinian, recovered dramatically. Its diocesan clergy numbered about 12,000 in 1975, and by then it was already publishing eight high-quality theological reviews, including *Ortodoxia* and *Studii teologice*.

Since the 1989 Romanian Revolution and the advent of democracy, the Church lives a clear renewal in different sectors of its life.

The Romanian Orthodox Church has jurisdiction over a minority of believers in Moldova*, who belong to the Metropolitanate of Bessarabia. About 2 million Romanians in the Republic of Moldova have resisted Russification for 192 years (after the annexation of Bessarabia by the Russian Empire in 1812). Romanian is their principal language, as well as their liturgical language. With the creation of greater Romania after World War I, Orthodox Christians in Moldavia became part of the Church of Romania. After Stalin's annexation of this region (1944), the Church there was again brought under the authority of the Russian Orthodox Church. After the fall of Communism, Moldova's government refused to allow the Romanian Church to exercise any authority in Moldova. Yet the European Court ruling of 2001 declared the Metropolitanate of Bessarabia to be a part of the Church of Romania and permitted its operation in Moldova.

The Orthodox Church of Romania is organized as a patriarchate, its highest hierarchical and canonical authority being the Holy Synod, under the presidency of the patriarch. The primate of the Church (in 2007, His Beatitude Daniel [Ciobotea]) is archbishop of Bucharest, metropolitan of Ungro-Vlachia, and patriarch of Romania, *locum tenens* of Caesarea in Cappadocia. There are six metropolitanates and ten archdioceses in Romania, with more than 14,000 priests and deacons. There are also more than 630 monasteries, with more than 8,500 monks and nuns; three metropolitanates; and seven dioceses of the Orthodox Church of Romania. There are more than 15,000 existing church buildings, and many others are in the process of being built or rebuilt.

There are in Romania 15 theological universities where more than 10,000 students (some of them from Bessarabia, Bukovina, and Serbia) currently study for bachelor's, master, or doctoral degrees in theology. Among the renowned Romanian theologians are Fr. Dumitru Staniloae* (1903–93), an Orthodox theologian with far-reaching influence. Father Ilie Cleopa (1912–98) from the Sihastria Monastery can appropriately be viewed as representative of the many "spiritual fathers" of contemporary Orthodox monastic* spirituality. VASILE MIHOC

Orthodox Church, Eastern: In Russia. Orthodox Christianity came to Russia in 988–89, when Vladimir*, grand prince of Kiev, like his grandmother, Olga*, was baptized and chose the religion of Byzantium as the state religion. The Mongol invasion (1237) prompted the Orthodox metropolitan to relocate from Kiev to the city of Vladimir and then to Moscow. This move mirrored other changes in Russian church culture. The northeast, less devastated than the southwest, partly owing to such saint-princes as Alexander Nevsky, could spread Orthodoxy to the indigenous peoples of Siberia through missionaries, including Stephen of Perm. The southwest, by contrast, was absorbed by Poland* and Lithuania*. There, the Russian Orthodox Church encountered Roman Catholics and Jews* on a regular basis and learned to articulate and defend their faith in multiconfessional and minority conditions.

Paradoxically, the 14th- to 15th-c. Mongol occupation of the northeast in many ways strengthened the Orthodox Church. Sergius* of Radonezh created the Trinity-Sergius Monastery. Theophanes the Greek and Andrei Rublev created unsurpassed iconography*. Orthodox metropolitans supported Moscow's consolidation of rival principalities and its struggle against the Mongols, enabling it to becoming the political center (mid-15th c.).

If Russia was baptized by the Byzantines*, it was catechized by the Bulgarians*, who provided a ready-made Slavic language and Orthodox culture through the missionary efforts of Cyril* and Methodius. A second wave of translations, largely of a monastic nature, came from the same lands (14th c.).

The theological characteristics of this early period of Russian Orthodoxy are found primarily in the fabric of the Church's life and in its self-conception, rather than in explicitly theological treatises. The early historical narratives tell of the adoption of Byzantine Orthodoxy as the providence of God, placing Russia within the greater narrative of biblical history. The 1071 canonization of St. Boris* and St. Gleb as martyrs (they died in self-sacrificing humility, though not explicitly for their faith) testifies to the beginnings of what the 20th-c. historian George Fedotov identifies as a characteristically Russian "kenoticism" (from *kenosis**, or "self-emptying"). This model of humility* can be traced through the monasticism* pioneered by Theodosius of the Kiev Caves (d1074), Sergius* of Radonezh (d1392), and Nil* Sorsky (d1508). The flourishing of monasticism (from the 14th c.) may also have been influenced by the rise of hesychasm* in Byzantium and especially on Mount Athos*. Kenosis and asceticism* also took a striking form in the enduring Russian hagiographic (and literary) tradition of the holy* fool.

Theology also finds expression in the musical, liturgical, and perhaps especially iconographic output of this era. Later Russian thinkers (including Evgenii Trubetskoy) link the explosion of Russian spiritual aesthetics of this period with the terrible suffering arising from its material and political turmoil under the Mongols.

At the same time, the plight of Orthodox peoples outside Russia strengthened the global significance of Muscovite Orthodoxy. The fall of Constantinople to the Ottomans (1453) meant that Moscow became the world's only sovereign Orthodox nation. Some monks elaborated the "Third Rome" theory (Rome and the "New Rome," Constantinople, had fallen; Moscow was now the world center of the true faith). Others believed that the end of the world was at hand. Ultimately, Muscovites concluded that, as only ritual and language distinguished them from their beleaguered Orthodox neighbors, they had to take particular care to preserve those forms. This concern with ritual would manifest itself in numerous church councils, including the "Stoglav" (1550–51).

Orthodoxy in Russia faced a number of crises echoing those in Europe, including the "Judaizing" heresy* in Novgorod, according to which Christ was an OT prophet (and which thus shunned all formal elements of the Church), and the "Non-Possessors" conflict (over whether monks should be poor, as Nil* Sorky argued, or use material power for social work, as Joseph of Volokolamsk emphasized).

Russia attained full ecclesiastical autonomy in 1589, with the election of the first patriarch of Moscow. This change in status would prove important in 1596, when part of the Orthodox clergy in Poland-Lithuania agreed to union with Rome (see Brest-Litovsk, Union of). Muscovy could defend the interests of fellow Orthodox Christians, the primary reason that a Cossack-led Ukrainian independence movement pledged allegiance to the Orthodox czar (1654). The resulting inflow of Ukrainian and Belarusian clergy educated at the Kiev Academy (founded by Petr Mohyla, 1632) served as Russia's hierarchs for more than a century and brought their multiconfessional experience with them.

This era involved some of the earliest high-level exchange with the Christian West, with mixed results. After the ecumenical patriarch Cyril Lucaris* published a confession of faith that was more Calvinist than Orthodox, Petr Mohyla produced one that relied on Roman Catholic catechisms and required significant revisions before the Council of Jassy could ratify it (1642).

Ironically, it was contact with other Orthodox churches that led to Russia's first serious church–state crisis (1650s), when Patriarch Nikon* introduced changes in liturgical rituals and texts based on contemporary Greek and Ukrainian practices. Full-scale religious rebellion erupted, including a power struggle with Czar Aleksei Mihailovich. A church council (1666–67) both deposed Nikon and condemned the Old* Believers, who vehemently opposed his reforms.

Church–state relations took a new turn in 1721. Peter I eliminated the office of patriarch and replaced it with a church governing body, the Holy Synod. While the church retained much autonomy, the state now enlisted it to help modernize and "enlighten" society and its administration. But educated hierarchs also helped rebuild the Optina hermitage, which, through Paisii Velichkovskii (1722–94) and his disciples, revitalized the Greek tradition of spiritual elders (*startsy*) and produced a spiritual and ascetical* literature drawn from hesychast* sources, notably the *Philokalia**, which Velichkovskii translated into Russian. Seraphim of Sarov exemplified these mystical* ideals. In the 19th c., Optina Monastery and its line of *startsy* would attract such religious writers as Ivan Kireevsky, Nikolai Gogol, Fedor Dostoevsky*, Lev Tolstoy*, and Konstantin Leontiev.

Catherine II continued Peter I's policy of undermining the Church's autonomy by strictly limiting the number of monks and nuns and secularizing* church lands (1764). Women wishing to pursue the religious life responded by organizing separate communities. Bishop Feofan the Recluse (1815–94) helped foster diocesan schools for girls and establish new convents.

The 19th c. saw continued growth in church construction and missionary activity as far as Alaska and Japan, in theological academies, and in religious education and publication. Metropolitan Filaret (Drozdov, 1782–1867) sponsored the Biblical Society and the translation of the Bible into Russian (previously available only in Church Slavonic). The great reforms of Alexander II spurred the astronomical growth of convents and such charismatic, socially active priests as Ioann of Kronstadt.

The Revolution of 1905 prompted many within the clergy to call for changes in church government, most notably in the form of a church council and the election of a patriarch. Paradoxically, this opportunity arose from the February Revolution and the installation of the provisional government in 1917. The First All-Russian Council (Sobor) began its sessions in August 1917. The patriarchate was restored, with Metropolitan Tikhon (Bellavin) being elected. Liberal reforms included an emphasis on preaching (including lay preaching), monastic autonomy, and a new emphasis on the role of women in church life (among the issues on the agenda was the restoration of the order of deaconesses).

But these reforms had little chance of being implemented. After the October Revolution, the Church lost the right to own real estate and its legal status. In an encyclical (January 1918), Tikhon* admonished the Soviet government for its anti-Church actions, persecution, and terror, and excommunicated those who took part in those activities.

The patriarch refused to take sides in the civil war. But "Red priests," also known as Renovationists or "the Living Church," formed an alliance with the Bolsheviks and separated from the Russian Orthodox Church, trying to force parishes to use the vernacular, accept married bishops, and adopt the Gregorian* calendar. The mass of the people rejected these changes, and Renovationism vanished.

The hierarchy leading the millions who left Russia after the civil war found itself in an unprecedented position. In 1920 Tikhon issued a decree that allowed the "higher church administration in exile" to continue until the Russian Church could freely administer itself. Several splits ensued in the Church over differing interpretations of this decree; different groups were led by Metropolitan Antony (Khrapovitsky) and Metropolitan Evlogy (Georgievsky). Yet for decades, Russian Church practice and publications survived in the diaspora in ways that were impossible in Russia.

In Soviet Russia, the situation of the Church deteriorated rapidly. The League of the Militant Godless, launched in 1925, sought to organize antireligious campaigns. On July 20, 1927, attempting to win the favor of the authorities, Metropolitan Sergii issued his controversial declaration of loyalty to the Soviet government. The Church in Russia and abroad split three ways on the basis of people's attitudes toward Sergii's declaration.

Arrests of the clergy and forced liquidation of churches reached catastrophic proportions. In 1939, in most regions of the USSR, only one church was functioning. Attempts to reorganize monasteries as "workers' collectives" failed. According to the most conservative estimates, by the end of the 1930s at least 40,000 clergy, a similar number of monastics, and unknown millions of lay believers had died for their faith.

The German invasion in 1941 brought an abrupt halt to the terror. Stalin's appointment of Sergei as patriarch in 1943 marked official recognition of the Church in Soviet society. Over the following two decades, the Soviet government showed little overt hostility toward organized Orthodox activity. This changed in 1961, when the 22nd Congress of the Communist Party adopted a program of renewed antireligious propaganda that guided Soviet policy for the next quarter-century: thousands more churches and monasteries were closed. Nevertheless, such dedicated priests as Dmitry Dudko and the spiritual-intellectual Alexander Men* found ways to preach the Orthodox faith, and an underground network of duplication and distribution of religious literature arose.

During the decades of Communist oppression, Russian Orthodox theology flourished abroad. Émigré theologians, first in Paris and later in the USA, found themselves in an environment conducive to fresh theological reflection, not least because of their contact with Western Christian intellectuals and secular philosophers. Their thought in turn influenced Western Christianity, as could be seen, e.g., at Vatican* II. They often drew on the theological creativity of the late 19th c., such as that of the "Slavophile" Alexei Khomiakov or the "Westernizers" Vladimir Soloviev* and Pavel Florensky. Sergei Bulgakov*, Nicolas Afanasiev, Paul Evdokimov, and Elisabeth Behr-Sigel were prolific authors of fresh and often challenging theology; Vladimir Lossky* and Georges Florovsky* produced a more conservative (but still creative) "neopatristic synthesis." All of these thinkers, together with other colleagues of the St. Serge Institute in Paris, figured in the work of Alexander Schmemann (who spearheaded a liturgical renewal within Orthodoxy concomitant with that in the West) and patristic scholar John Meyendorff, both of whom moved to the USA in the 1950s.

There, schools such as St. Vladimir's Seminary and Holy Trinity Seminary play a vital role in theological education and publication. Orthodoxy in Western Europe and North America is enriched by Russian ecclesiastical culture through iconography (e.g. Leonid Ouspensky, Gregory Kroug), monastic life (Jordanville, St. Tikhon's), popular writers and preachers (Alexander Elchaninov, Metropolitan Anthony Bloom), and holiness (Archbishop John Maximovich).

In 1988, the millennium anniversary of Christianity in Russia, policies toward religion reversed thanks partly to glasnost. Thousands of churches opened, millions of people were baptized, new and old monasteries, convents, and seminaries received new members, a flood of religious publications appeared, and religious feasts became legal holidays. The Church attained a prominent, privileged position. Patriarch Aleksey II (enthroned in 1990) became a highly visible national figure.

But the impact of 80 years of atheist rule persists. Church attendance is low. Debates over the 1997 federal law "On Freedom of Conscience and Religious Associations" showed the chasm between the Church's conservatives and nationalists, who sought guarantees protecting the Russian Orthodox Church, and liberals and democrats, who sought freedom of conscience for all denominations. The Moscow Patriarchate chose to support the former. Membership in the World* Council of Churches is another divisive issue.

Yet with newly thriving theological schools such as St. Tikhon Orthodox Humanities University and St. Andrew Biblical Theological Institute, and the rise of many young theological scholars studying in Russia and abroad, signs of theological life continue. Serious theological reflection undergirds documents on the Church's social concept and on relations with non-Orthodox produced by the Jubilee Bishops' Council of 2000.

Orthodox Christianity in Russia has a great and varied tradition, born of the Byzantine legacy, enriched by its cultural particularity, and steeped in incalculable suffering. Alternately grandiose and humble, brilliantly creative and staunchly conservative, it is deeply rooted yet still sprouting rapid new growth, in directions that are difficult to predict.

PETER C. BOUTENEFF and NADIESZDA KIZENKO

Orthodox Church, Eastern: In Ukraine. Orthodox Christianity, the main religious tradition of Ukraine, shaped Ukrainian cultural identity throughout its turbulent history. According to the tradition, Christianity came to the territory of contemporary Ukraine in the 1st–2nd c. on the Crimean Peninsula (then a part of the Eastern Roman Empire, later Byzantium*). Yet Christianity was not accepted into the entire territory of Ukraine until the 10th c., when Prince Volodymyr (Vladimir*) the Great established Christianity in its Eastern Christian (Byzantine*) form as the state religion (988 or 989).

In the 11th–13th c., the Metropolitanate of Kiev included 16 dioceses in territories that are presently part of Ukraine and Belarus* and European parts of Russia*. Appointed by patriarchs of Constantinople, the metropolitans of Kiev were ethnic Greeks. After the Great* Schism (1054) between the Roman Catholic and Orthodox churches, clergy of medieval Rus remained in communion with the Orthodox churches. The Kiev-Pechersky Monastery* (later called Lavra*), established in the 11th c., became the main center of the Orthodox monastic tradition among the Rus principalities.

The Mongol invaders (1238–42) disrupted the political and religious life of the Rus principalities; the metropolitans of Kiev moved their see from ruined Kiev to Vladimir (later called Moscow). As the Ukrainian and Belorussian territories became parts of Lithuania* (14th c.), princes of Lithuania campaigned for independent Ukrainian and Belorussian metropolitanates, against the wishes of Moscow. Because of a conflict between the patriarch of Constantinople and the Russian Church over the Council of Florence* (1438–45), the Orthodox Metropolitanates of Ukraine and of Russia were divided. In 1448 Russian bishops elected their own metropolitan and proclaimed the independence of the Moscow Metropolitanate from Constantinople. As a consequence, the Metropolitanate of Kiev (encompassing Ukrainian and Belorussian territories) became once again a part of the Patriarchate of Constantinople and was independent of Moscow.

Following the alliance between Lithuania and Catholic Poland* (1385), the Orthodox Church in Lithuania lost state support. The Roman Catholic Church became much more powerful in Ukraine, especially after 1569, when Lithuania and Poland were united and Ukrainian territories became Polish. The 1596 Brest*-Litovsk Union created Uniatism*, "Greek Catholicism"; all Orthodox bishops in Ukraine recognized the authority of the pope, although the Ukrainian Church kept its Eastern Christian liturgical tradition (see Divine Liturgy). It was illegal for the Orthodox clergy not to recognize the Union; the Ukrainian aristocracy started to convert to Roman Catholicism.

Thus the Ukrainian Orthodox Church became illegal. But as such, it became one of the bastions of national identity for Ukrainians under Polish occupation. The Brest-Litovsk Union prompted a wave of Ukrainian polemical literature that defended Orthodoxy; Orthodox movements supported by the Ukrainian elite established Orthodox educational institutions. Most important, the Ukrainian Cossack military took the side of the Orthodox Church and supported the consecrations of a metropolitan of Kiev and of five bishops by the patriarch of Jerusalem (1620); an Orthodox hierarchy in Ukraine had thus been reestablished. In 1632 the metropolitan of Kiev, Peter Mohila*,

 Orthodox Church, Eastern: In Ukraine

founded the Kievan Collegium (later called the Kiev-Mohila Academy), which was for a long time the sole higher educational institution for Orthodox Slavic peoples. In exchange, the Orthodox Church supported the rebellion of the Cossack Bohdan Khmelnytsky against the Poles in his victorious war of liberation, which established the Cossack elite in power in Ukraine.

The Pereyaslav Treaty (1654) gave control of most of the Ukrainian territory to the Moscow czar (as a protection against the Poles). Russian authorities tried to incorporate the Metropolitanate of Kiev (a part of the Constantinople Church) into the Russian* Orthodox Church, forcing the newly elected metropolitan of Kiev to swear allegiance to the patriarch of Moscow. Soon this act was condemned by a council of Constantinople bishops, and the Orthodox dioceses in Ukrainian territories under Polish control joined the Uniate Church.

As a part of the Russian Orthodox Church (18th c.), the Metropolitanate of Kiev lost its autonomy, becoming an ordinary diocese. Ukrainian Church rules and traditions were made to conform to Russian patterns. However, educated Church leaders from Ukraine received important positions in the Russian Church and its educational institutions. In 1786 Russian authorities secularized Church lands and in exchange financially supported the Orthodox clergy. The dubious results were that monasteries that did not get state support were closed and that the Orthodox clergy became alienated from ordinary believers, since they did not need financial support from them.

Meanwhile, in Western Ukraine, the Uniate Church had taken root in the population, while all of the Church's properties remained under (Catholic and Uniate) Church authority.

After the partition of Polish territories among Russia, Prussia, and Austria, most of the Ukrainian territories became part of the Russian Empire, opening Western Ukraine to an attempted restoration of the Orthodox Church. The well-known monastery Pochayiv Lavra was returned to Orthodoxy (1833). The Uniate Synod of Polotsk (1839) repudiated the Brest*-Litovsk Union; all remaining Uniate Church property in the territory of the Russian Empire was returned to the Russian Orthodox Church. In the late 18th c., after the conquest of Crimea by the Russian Empire (Crimea had previously been under the Ottoman Empire), the colonization of these lands by Orthodox people, particularly Ukrainians and Russians, was encouraged; new Orthodox parishes were created in Southern Ukraine.

The collapse of the czarist regime in the Russian Empire (1917) promoted national and church life in Ukraine. The independent Ukrainian People's Republic was proclaimed (1918). There were movements in favor of an autocephalous* or at least an autonomous Ukrainian Orthodox Church within the Russian Orthodox Church; this second movement was supported by the All-Ukrainian Church Council (1918). But the Ukrainian independent state was defeated in its liberation war (1917–20) by the Russian Bolsheviks; Ukraine became one of the Soviet Socialist Republics of the USSR. During that war thousands of Orthodox clergy and believers were cruelly killed.

Some of the Orthodox parishes in Ukraine proclaimed the Ukrainian Autocephalous Orthodox Church. But this Church was short lived: no bishop joined it; it was not recognized by world Orthodox churches, and the Bolsheviks liquidated it during a campaign of repression.

In the 1920s and 1930s, the Orthodox Church in Ukraine suffered from severe persecution by Communist powers; in 1926 thousands of clergy were imprisoned and killed (formally recognized as holy martyrs in 2000). Orthodox Church buildings were ruined or confiscated. Church properties were expropriated. Christian missionary activity became a state crime; Church educational fellowships were forbidden. The collaboration of Church authorities with the Communist regime split Orthodox believers. Some of the clergy and believers refused to recognize the authority of the official Church hierarchy and created "catacomb" groups.

After World War I, Orthodox parishes in Western Ukraine were part of the new Polish state. In 1924 the patriarch of

Constantinople recognized the autocephaly of the Orthodox Church of Poland (mainly Ukrainian parishes). However, Western Ukraine was conquered by the Soviet Union, becoming a part of the USSR (1939). During World War II and the German occupation (1941–44), Ukrainian bishops consecrated in the Polish Orthodox Church declared the creation of a second Ukrainian Autocephalous Orthodox Church, in addition to the Ukrainian Autonomous Orthodox Church (a part of the Russian Orthodox Church). With the restoration of Soviet control over Ukraine (1944) the second Ukrainian Autocephalous Orthodox Church became illegal; its hierarchs emigrated to North America and Western Europe and continue to serve Ukrainians of the diaspora under the jurisdiction of the Patriarchate of Constantinople.

From the 1940s through the 1980s, the Ukrainian Autonomous Orthodox Church (as a part of the Russian Orthodox Church) survived despite severe limitations on its missionary activity and religious education and despite pressing state atheist propaganda. It was only during the period of democratization ("perestroika") in the Soviet Union (1980s) that state control over the Church abated. Hundreds of Orthodox parishes opened in 1988, the year when the 1,000 years of Christianization was celebrated.

The rebirth of the Orthodox Church brought conflicts with the Ukrainian Greek Catholic Church (the Uniate Church in Western Ukraine), which had been forced to join the Russian Orthodox Church in 1946, while all its buildings and properties were given to the Orthodox Church. During the restoration of the Ukrainian Greek Catholic Church (1980s–1990s) believers of that Church reappropriated hundreds of Church buildings in Western Ukraine (which had belonged to the Orthodox Church for about 40 years).

In 1990 the patriarch of Moscow granted to the Ukrainian Orthodox Church an autonomous status within the Russian Orthodox Church, while a number of parishes of the Russian Orthodox Church in Western Ukraine declared the restoration of the Ukrainian Autocephalous Orthodox Church (its third form), which resulted in the inter-Orthodox conflicts in Ukraine (from the 1990s).

In 1991, when Ukraine became an independent state, the head of the Ukrainian Orthodox Church, Philaret, the metropolitan of Kiev, tried to gain autocephaly for the Ukrainian Orthodox Church from Moscow. Following the rejection by the Moscow Patriarchate (1992), Metropolitan Philaret left the Ukrainian Orthodox Church and proclaimed the creation of the Ukrainian Orthodox Church of the Kiev Patriarchate, which included some of the bishops of the Ukrainian Autocephalous Orthodox Church. However, not all its believers and clergy recognized this union and continued their independent existence.

Among these Orthodox denominations, the world Orthodox churches recognize and are exclusively in communion only with the Ukrainian Orthodox Church (c17,000 parishes in 2008; still a part of the Russian Orthodox Church). The independent Orthodox denominations – the Ukrainian Orthodox Church of the Kiev Patriarchate (c4,000 parishes) and the Ukrainian Autocephalous Orthodox Church (c1,200 parishes) – do not "have the grace of church sacraments," because their clergy were consecrated by bishops forbidden by the Church to serve.

In the early 21st c., efforts to resolve these complex issues were in process. The Ukrainian state repeatedly declared its interest in a union of all three Orthodox denominations in one independent church. The Patriarchate of Constantinople and the Russian Orthodox Church continue to engage in negotiations on the status of the Ukrainian churches.

DMYTRO BONDARENKO

Orthodox Churches, Eastern: In the United States. The Orthodox Church in the USA was established through mission in Alaska in the late 18th and 19th c. and then through immigration in the late 19th and early 20th c.

Missionaries from the Church of Russia* (among them the monk Herman, 1760–1837; and Innocent John Veniaminov, 1797–1879, bishop of Alaska, 1840–52)

 Orthodox Churches, Eastern: United States

established a mission in Alaska (1794) and translated the Scriptures and liturgical texts into local languages, while supporting indigenous cultures. The mission, serving about 10,000 faithful, continued after the sale of Alaska to the USA (1867). Yet Protestant missionaries proselytized among the native Orthodox. Although the Orthodox Church maintained a presence in the Alaskan territory, the office of the bishop moved to San Francisco (1872).

Numerous Orthodox immigrants arrived in the USA during the late 19th and early 20th c. from Greece*, Asia Minor, Russia*, the Balkans*, and the Middle East. Early parishes often began as pan-Orthodox communities, serving immigrants from many ethnic backgrounds, in, e.g., New Orleans (1864), San Francisco (1867), and New York City (1870). As the number of Orthodox immigrants increased, parishes served particular ethnic communities.

The Greeks, the largest group of Orthodox immigrants (c200,000 in 1920), were organized into about 138 parishes, initially maintaining a connection with the Greek Orthodox* Church of Greece or with the Ecumenical* Patriarchate of Constantinople (claiming responsibility for all Orthodox in the "diaspora"). Because the Patriarchate was not in a position to adequately exercise its ministry in the USA, Orthodox Church life developed with little hierarchical supervision. Yet in 1922, the Patriarchate established the Greek Orthodox Archdiocese of North and South America led (1931–48) by Archbishop Athenagoras Spirou (1886–1972; who became patriarch of Constantinople).

Most parishes serving Slavic immigrants became associated with the Russian Orthodox Diocese (located in San Francisco). With the rapid increase of Slavic immigrants in the Eastern USA (including 150,000 Carpatho–Russian immigrants), the diocesan center moved to New York (1905) under Archbishop Tikhon Bellavin (1865–1925; later patriarch of Moscow); about 50 formerly Eastern Catholic Carpatho-Russian parishes entered the Russian Orthodox Diocese.

By 1933 three major Russian Orthodox jurisdictions opposed each other over the Bolshevik Revolution (1917). (1) The Russian Orthodox Greek Catholic Church, or Metropolia, the largest, declared itself temporarily independent of the Church of Russia (1924). (2) A diocese of the Russian Orthodox Church Abroad, serving Russian immigrants with royalist sympathies, refused after 1925 to acknowledge the authority of the Church of Russia. (3) The Church of Russia established an exarchate (1933).

Other autocephalous* Orthodox churches – the churches of Serbia (1921), Antioch (1924), Romania (1930), Albania (1932), and Bulgaria (1938) – established dioceses in the USA, while the Ecumenical Patriarchate established dioceses for the Ukrainians (1937) and the Carpatho-Russians (1938). These "ethnic" (rather than territorial) dioceses served the immigrants' short-term needs but sacrificed canonical order and the unity of the episcopacy; a polity of congregationalism and an attitude of phyletism* and parochialism pervaded church life.

After World War II, having lost their immigrant character, many parishes adapted themselves in order to serve parishioners who were born and educated in the USA and often married beyond their ethnic communities. English gradually became an acceptable liturgical language. Clergy were educated at Holy Cross Greek Orthodox School of Theology (Boston) or St. Vladimir's Orthodox Theological School (New York). People from other religious traditions became members of the Orthodox Church. Pan-Orthodox cooperation for retreats, charitable outreach, religious education, and campus ministry increased.

The Standing Conference of Canonical Orthodox Bishops in America – from 1960 under the leadership of Archbishop Iakovos Coucousis (1911–2005) of the Greek Orthodox Archdiocese – brought together most of the primates, coordinated pan-Orthodox activities, including religious education and campus ministry, and established bilateral theological dialogues with the Episcopal Church (1962), the Roman Catholic Church (1966), the Lutheran Church (1968), and the Reformed churches (1968).

The Patriarchate of Moscow granted autocephaly to the Russian Orthodox Metropolia, which became the Orthodox Church in America (1970), regularizing the formal relationship with the Church of Russia lost in 1924. Yet the autocephalous status of the Orthodox Church in America was not recognized by the Ecumenical Patriarchate and most other autocephalous churches. Tensions among the jurisdictions in the USA increased. In 1975 the Patriarchate of Antioch unified its two diocesan jurisdictions in the new Antiochian Orthodox Christian Archdiocese.

The Orthodox churches around the world engaged in renewed conciliarity*. The Ecumenical Patriarchate organized conferences (early 1970s) on themes relevant to the entire church. Pan-Orthodox conferences (1990, 1993) examined the issues related to the "diaspora." All Orthodox bishops in the USA met (1994, 2000) and confirmed the need for greater administrative unity. The Standing Conference continued to serve Orthodox cooperation and unity under the leadership of Archbishop Demetrios [Trakatellis] (1928–), the exarch of the Ecumenical Patriarchate and primate of the Greek Orthodox Archdiocese. The c5 million Orthodox Christians in the USA (2007) are gathered in more than 1,500 parishes, with about 20 monasteries, 3 graduate schools of theology, and a college. THOMAS E. FITZGERALD

ORTHODOX CHURCHES, ORIENTAL, CLUSTER

1) *Introductory Entry*

Orthodox Churches, Oriental (Non-Chalcedonian): Their Theologies and Liturgies

2) *A Sampling of Oriental Orthodox Churches in Context*

Orthodox Churches, Oriental: Armenian Apostolic Church

Orthodox Churches, Oriental: Coptic Orthodox Church

Orthodox Churches, Oriental: Ethiopian Orthodox Tewahedo Church

Orthodox Churches, Oriental: Malankara Orthodox Syrian Church

Orthodox Churches, Oriental: Syriac Orthodox Church, Universal

---

1) Introductory Entry

Orthodox Churches, Oriental (Non-Chalcedonian) Churches: Their Theologies and Liturgies. The ancient churches in the East that decided not to adhere to the dogmatic formulation of the Council of Chalcedon*, usually known as "Oriental Orthodox churches," number six: the Armenian Apostolic Church, Syriac Orthodox Church Universal, Coptic Orthodox Church, Ethiopian Orthodox Tewahedo Church, Malankara Orthodox Syrian Church of India, and Eritrean Orthodox Church. During the 20th c., owing to various historical circumstances, especially foreign oppression, these churches were scattered all over the world, establishing their jurisdictions in Europe, North America, and Australia.

Historically these churches have remained closely associated. Their relationships became more active after 1965, when the heads of the churches met in Addis Ababa to confirm their unity in faith and tried to coordinate their ecumenical activities as one church family. They are connected through their traditions and teachings. The Coptic Orthodox Church is the mother church of the Ethiopian and Eritrean churches. The Indian Malankara Orthodox Church is closely related to the Syriac Orthodox Church. The Armenian Church has two jurisdictions: the Armenian Apostolic Church, Mother See of Holy Etchmiadzin; and the Catholicosate of the Great House of Cilicia. Etchmiadzin enjoys the honor of primacy.

These churches accept the dogmatic decisions of the first three ecumenical councils: Nicaea* (325), Constantinople* (381), and Ephesus* (431). Their Christology is based on the formulation of Cyril* of Alexandria (see Miaphysite). All of them accept seven sacraments*. Although they are not in communion with the Byzantine Church (Eastern Orthodox* Church), they have a common heritage.

Remaining faithful to the tradition of the early church, the Oriental Orthodox churches have a hierarchical system of church administration, including the threefold* office of ministry (deacons*, priests*, bishops*), implemented according to the general trends in the entire Orthodox family.

In the Oriental Orthodox churches, only male believers can be ordained. Women can become deaconesses, especially in the Armenian Church. The clergy are both celibate and married. The married clergy are not allowed to take high offices in the Church. Canonically marriage is allowed only before ordination for the diaconate.

These churches have rich liturgical traditions. The influence of monasticism* is strong (see Monasticism Cluster: Monasticism; Monasticism Cluster: In the Syriac Tradition), especially on their liturgies for the Divine* Office (see Eucharist Cluster: In Oriental Orthodox [Non-Chalcedonian] Churches). Although they share core liturgical principles, the liturgical tradition is different from one church to another, depending on region and culture. Their church calendars* are based on the old Jerusalem tradition but reflect local particularities. The hymnal systems are also different.

The Armenians have one Divine Liturgy, mainly that of St. Basil* the Great with prayers from the liturgies of St. John Chrysostom*, Athanasius* the Great, and Gregory of Narek. During the 12–13th c., the Armenian Liturgy was influenced by the Roman Mass*. Unleavened bread and pure wine are used. The Armenian Church celebrates the Nativity and Epiphany on the same day, January 6.

The Divine Liturgy of the Syriac Church belongs to the original version of the Antiochene liturgy, with some slight changes. This liturgy is ascribed to James* the Apostle (see James, Liturgy of St.). Originally, it was written in Greek, then translated into Syriac in the 5th c. before the Council of Chalcedon. In the liturgy, leavened bread is used with salt and oil.

The liturgy of the Coptic Orthodox Church takes the form of a dialogue between people and priest. During the whole year, the Coptic Orthodox Church celebrates the Liturgy of St. Basil* the Great (as edited in the 12th c.) every day except for Christmas, Epiphany, and Easter. During these feasts, the liturgies of St. Gregory* the Theologian and of St. Mark* are celebrated. Leavened bread and wine made of grapes are used.

Almost all the forms of the Divine Office of the Ethiopian Orthodox Church, except some local particularities, correspond to the liturgies of the Coptic Orthodox Church. Yet the Ethiopian Orthodox stipulates that, for celebrating liturgy, there must be at least two priests and three deacons. The Ethiopian Liturgy comprises 15 anaphoras*, including the Anaphoras of the St. Apostles, of St. John the Evangelist, of St. Athanasius the Great, of St. Gregory of Nazianzus, and of St. Gregory the Armenian. Each of these anaphoras has a special emphasis either on the incarnation of our Lord Jesus Christ or on the Last Supper and Resurrection.

The liturgies of the Malankara Orthodox Syrian Church and Syriac Orthodox Church are alike. The Malankara Indians have 16 anaphoras for liturgy, although they celebrate mainly the Liturgy of St. James, as well as the liturgies of St. Matthew and St. Mark, St. Ignatius of Antioch, St. Cyril of Rome, St. Basil the Great, and St. John Chrysostom.

These churches have strong monastic* traditions regulated by the rules of desert fathers in Egypt and Cappadocia, although local elements have been inculturated.

BISHOP YEZNIK PETROSSIAN

---

2) A Sampling of Oriental Orthodox Churches in Context

Orthodox Churches, Oriental: Armenian Apostolic Church. One of the Oriental Orthodox (non-Chalcedonian) churches, the Armenian Apostolic Church is the national church of the Armenian people, in Armenia and beyond (especially in Georgia*, Russia*, and Iran*; c5.6 million members worldwide). Its spiritual center is the Holy See of Etchmiadzin, headed by the catholicos* of all Armenians, the supreme spiritual and hierarchical authority. In addition there are three hierarchical sees: the Catholicosate of the Great House of Cilicia (since 1446), the Armenian Patriarchate of Jerusalem (since the 7th c.), and the Armenian Patriarchate of Constantinople (since 1464).

The Armenian Church is called "apostolic" because tradition says that it was founded by two apostles of Jesus Christ, Thaddeus* and Bartholomew*, the "first illuminators of Armenia", who were martyred there (1st c.). The preaching of Christianity among different groups of people, among them the members of the royal family, the martyrdom of the first Christians, the establishment of Christian communities, and the construction of churches, monasteries, and chapels all created favorable conditions for Gregory* the Illuminator, the first catholicos* of the Armenian Church, to proclaim Christianity in the country, to struggle against paganism, to found dioceses, and to organize the Armenian Church. During the reign of King Tiridates, c314 (301, according to some), Christianity was proclaimed the state religion in Armenia.

The theology and dogma of the Armenian Apostolic Church are based on the Holy Bible, sacred tradition*, canons, and teachings of great 4th- and 5th-c. church fathers, especially Athanasius* of Alexandria (d370), Basil* the Great (d379), Gregory* the Theologian (d390), Gregory* of Nyssa (d394), and Cyril* of Alexandria (d444), as well as on the dogmas adopted by the ecumenical councils of Nicaea* (325), Constantinople* (381), and Ephesus* (431).

Except for the christological* issue regarding the two natures of Christ, divine and human, the doctrine of the Armenian Church is identical with that of the Eastern Orthodox* churches. The decisions of the fourth ecumenical council, Chalcedon* (451), created division and estrangement between the Armenian and Byzantine churches, which previously had cooperated with each other and maintained close relations. In the 6th c., the Armenian Church officially rejected the decisions of Chalcedon.

The Divine* Liturgy of the Armenian Church is based on the missals of St. Basil* of Caesarea and St. Gregory* the Theologian. In the course of time, the Divine Liturgy underwent changes: it was celebrated in the Armenian language; it incorporated special rites and original Armenian chants; and it assumed a national character. During the Divine Liturgy, unleavened bread and pure wine are used. Communion is given to the faithful in the form of consecrated bread steeped in the wine. For each liturgy, only one consecrated loaf of bread is used. Only one liturgy can be celebrated each day on the same altar, and only one priest can celebrate the Divine Liturgy, for there is no concelebration* in the liturgy of the Armenian Church (see Eucharist Cluster: In Oriental [Non-Chalcedonian] Orthodox Churches).

Those who do not receive the sacrament partake in the Divine Liturgy through prayer and especially unceasing remembrance of our Lord Jesus Christ. At the end of the liturgy (*patarag*), portions of blessed thin unleavened bread, *mas*, are distributed to those who have not received the sacrament. *Mas* is distributed in remembrance of the agape*, which used to take place after the Divine Liturgy, in order that the faithful who have not received the sacrament might not be deprived of the blessing and might share in the divine feast.

BISHOP YEZNIK PETROSSIAN

Orthodox Churches, Oriental: Coptic Orthodox Church. One of the Oriental Orthodox (non-Chalcedonian) churches, the Coptic Orthodox Church is the main Christian church in predominantly Muslim Egypt*, although it is also present in other countries, with c9.5 million members worldwide. The name "Coptic" is derived from the Arabic *qibt*, "Egyptian." (Arabic is the language commonly used by Church members since the 10th c.). The Coptic language is derived from ancient Egyptian, written in an alphabet derived from Greek. The central parts of the liturgy continue to be said in Bohairic, one of the Coptic dialects.

The pope of Alexandria heads the Coptic Orthodox Church's clergy, which includes bishops who oversee the priests ordained in more than 60 dioceses in Egypt, Jerusalem, and other parts of the world. Both the pope and the bishops must be monks; they regularly meet as the Coptic Orthodox Holy Synod to oversee matters of faith and pastoral care. The pope of the Coptic Church, although highly regarded, is not viewed as infallible*. Priests are married.

The theology of the Coptic Church was influenced by a strong monastic tradition (see Monasticism Cluster: Monasticism) and has its foundation in the school of Alexandria*, which included Clement* of Alexandria and Origen*, who, with the Church in Egypt, played an important role in the theological debates of the time in a quest for a catholic (universal) church. Athanasius* of Alexandria was a key theologian in combating Arianism* and defending the Council of Nicaea* (325). His successor, Cyril*, played a similar role in combating Nestorianism* at the First Council of Ephesus* (431). The Coptic Orthodox Church emerged as one of the Oriental Orthodox* churches (falsely) accused of Monophysitism* (the belief that Christ as the Son of God has "only one nature," *monophysis*). The Coptic Church denies that it is Monophysite. But rather than affirming the christological* formulations of the Council of Chalcedon* (451; Christ is one person* or hypostasis*, "known in two natures without division or separation, confusion, or change"), the Coptic Church accepted the formulation of Cyril, who wrote of "one incarnate nature of the divine Word" (the Greek phrase begins with *Mia physis*). Hence the Coptic Church is "Miaphysite*." For Copts, the Lord's perfect divinity and perfect humanity are united in one nature called "the nature of the incarnate Word." Among the great 6th-c. theologians, Severus* of Antioch wrote many theological treatises refuting both Nestorian* Dyophysitism (two natures in Christ) and Eutychian* Monophysitism.

The beginnings of the Coptic Liturgy are obscure; it is difficult to trace its origin before the 4th c. Yet as in the Eastern Orthodox churches, for which "the theologian is the one who prays, and the one who prays is a theologian" (see Orthodox Churches, Eastern, Cluster: Introductory Entries), these theological debates about Christologies were intense because they reflected and affected the life of prayer in the Coptic Church. In addition, the liturgy is informed by the Scriptures, the Apostolic* Tradition attributed to Hippolytus* of Rome (c215; which survived only in Arabic), the *Didascalia* apostolorum* (written in Syria, 3rd c.), the Apostolic* Constitutions (4th c.), the *Euchologion** of Sarapion of Thmuis (4th c.), and the description of the liturgy of Jerusalem by Egeria*.

After the Arab conquest of Egypt (7th c.), and especially from the 10th c., scholars and ecclesiastical authorities of the Coptic Church started to write in Arabic rather than Greek. Yet the Coptic Church adopted the Bohairic dialect (of Lower Egypt) as its liturgical language; the service books now include Bohairic and Arabic translations in parallel columns, but the actual use of Arabic is limited to the lessons of the Bible and certain hymns.

The Coptic *Euchologion* (liturgical book) contains the evening and the morning offerings of incense* and, since Pope Gabriel Ibn Turaik (1131–45), three liturgies: those of St. Basil*, St. Gregory* of Nazianzus, and St. Cyril* (also known as the Liturgy of St. Mark).

From monastic spirituality, the Coptic Church inherited the *Horologion* (Book of Hours), which contains the "seven hours" (worship services), each including 12 psalms, a reading from the gospel, hymns (*troparia*), and an absolution.

The Coptic Church trains its clergy in several theological colleges and laypeople in Sunday schools. There are around 30 monasteries of men and women. In the past, the Coptic Church contributed to the evangelization of Nubia and Ethiopia* and now conducts missions in Kenya, South Africa, Congo, and Latin America under the leadership of several bishops. The Coptic Church engages in ecumenical theological dialogue* as a member of the World* Council Churches, Middle East Council of

Churches, and the All African Conference of Churches. **See also** EGYPT.

YOUHANNA NESSIM YOUSSEF

Orthodox Churches, Oriental: Ethiopian Orthodox Tewahedo Church. One of the Oriental Orthodox (non-Chalcedonian) churches, the Ethiopian Tewahedo Church was the national church of Ethiopia (the second "Christian nation," after Armenia*) from the 4th c. until 1974 (the fall of Emperor Haile Selassie). It remains the church of the majority of Ethiopians (in Ethiopia and abroad), with a total membership of about 40 million (in Ethiopia c38 million; 35,000 parishes, nearly 500,000 priests and monks). Throughout its history, the Ethiopian Orthodox Tewahedo Church was an instrument of cultural integration, assimilation, and unity in traditional Ethiopia. It was under the authority of the Coptic pope of Alexandria from the 4th c. until it became autocephalous* (1959) with the crowning of Abuna Baslios, the first patriarch of Ethiopia.

The appellation "Tewahedo" (from the Ge'ez verb meaning "to be of more than one by unity") emphasizes its belief in the existence, in Christ, of humanity and divinity in unity. Jesus Christ is one person, the Word incarnate, with one will. He is perfect man and perfect God. According to the Ethiopian Orthodox Tewahedo Church, both Eutyches* and Nestorius* are heretics* – Eutyches for denying the existence of humanity in Christ, and Nestorius for denying divinity in Christ united with his humanity.

Ethiopian cultural and religious identity has its roots in the OT, which narrates the journey of the queen of Sheba to the palace of King Solomon* in Jerusalem (1 Kgs 10:1–9). According to traditions recorded in *Kebra Nagast* (Book of the glory of kings), the (legitimate) Ethiopian emperors were descendants of the son of King Solomon and the queen of Sheba, Menelik, who with his companions stealthily brought to Ethiopia the Ark (*Tabot*) of the Covenant, which became an important symbol* for the Ethiopian Orthodox Tewahedo Church.

The Church (with a bishop and all the sacraments) was established in the 4th c. when Athanasius*, the patriarch of Alexandria, appointed Frumentius* the first bishop of Ethiopia. It became and remains the center of Christianity in the Horn of Africa. The Ethiopian Orthodox Tewahedo Church as an apostolic, autocephalous, and ecumenical church, led by its patriarch, is in full communion with the other Oriental Orthodox churches, a founding member of the World* Council Churches, and a member of the All African Conference of Churches.

Five Pillars of Mystery. The Ethiopian Orthodox Tewahedo Church rests on five "pillars of mystery," grounded in Scripture: the mysteries* of the Trinity*, the Incarnation*, baptism*, Holy Communion*/Eucharist*, and the resurrection* of the dead.

1. The Holy Trinity is three in name, in person (*akal*), and in deed and one in essence, in divinity, in eternity, and in will. The Father is himself heart, and is the heart for the Son and the Holy Spirit. The Son is himself Word, and is the Word of the Father and of the Holy Spirit. The Holy Spirit is himself life (breath), and is the life (breath) of the Father and the Son.
2. The Incarnation is the mystery of God the Son, one of the Trinity, having descended from heaven and taken up flesh and rational soul from the Holy Virgin Mary*; it is the mystery of God becoming human and of human becoming God (John 1:14). The Divinity with the flesh and the flesh with the Divinity become one person and one nature in perfect union without change, without confusion, without separation, and without division. As the liturgy expresses, "He [Christ] is one before and after His Incarnation" (see Miaphysite).
3. Baptism, a sacrament, is a mystery in the sense that, when the priest recites the prayer over the water and blesses it, the water becomes "water of life" (which flowed from the side of Christ; John 19:34–35) and one receives the invisible grace* and is adopted as a

child of God. In Church practice, a boy is circumcised at the age of 8 days and baptized on his 40th day, and a girl is baptized on her 8th day. (Circumcision of girls was once the norm but is now proscribed by civil law.)

4. Holy Communion is a supreme act of life through which believers can hold intimate communion with God and that which makes them one with God. It is a mystery because, when the priest blesses the bread and the wine with the liturgical prayer, the bread and the wine are changed into the real Flesh and Blood of the Son of God.
5. Resurrection is the mystery of life after death. All those who have departed will arise in the union of body* and soul* (the souls being united with their bodies) on the day of resurrection, when Christ will come in his glory to judge the living and the dead.

The Ethiopian Orthodox Tewahedo Church also observes the sacraments of confirmation* (or holy myron; see Chrismation), holy orders (see Ordination), matrimony*, penance*, and unction* of the sick, as do other churches (Orthodox, Roman Catholic, Anglican).

Holy Scriptures. With Cyril of Alexandria, the Ethiopian Orthodox Tewahedo Church affirms that "holy books are the breath of God," the absolute truth; nothing can be added or removed from them. In addition to the books of the Protestant Bible and the OT Apocrypha (see Bible, Canon of the), the Ethiopian Bible includes Joseph Ben Gurion (or Josippon, a popular chronicle of Jewish history from Adam to Titus), Jubilees*; Enoch*; the Testament* of Our Lord; Apostolic* Church Order, Apostolic* Constitutions (or Apostolic Canons), and the Didascalia* of the Apostles.

Church Buildings. A church building is the abode of God and, irrespective of one's age, race, or gender, a place of education where the gospel is taught; a place for prayer, intercession, and forgiveness of sin; a place of worship where Holy Communion and baptism are conducted; and the final resting place of Christians. The church is different from other buildings because it has been consecrated by bishops and anointed with myron/chrism, and is the place where sacraments are conducted and where the Ark of the Covenant is kept (see Ethiopia).

According to the Ethiopian Orthodox Tewahedo Church rites and tradition, the church building has three parts (divided by partitions): the outer ambulatory (*qene mahlet*), where the choir leads worship and chant hymns; the surrounding ambulatory (*kidest*), where the faithful receive Holy Communion; and the sanctuary (Holy of Holies, *Mekdes*, reserved for ordained men), where the liturgy is conducted and which houses the throne for the Ark of the Covenant.

The Ark of the Covenant (*Tabot*) is the repository of the tablet (*tsilat*) on which the Ten Commandments are written as given to Moses by God on Mount Sinai. In a church, the tablet represents and thus is called the Ark. The reason for bowing and praying in front of the Ark is that, when the Israelites were in penance and begging God for forgiveness, God revealed himself through the Ark, which is a means of mercy and salvation (Exod 25:20–25) (see Symbolism).

The Ark of the Covenant did not disappear after OT times; it was brought to Ethiopia long before Christianity arrived. The Ethiopian Orthodox Tewahedo Church has accepted and preserved the OT and the rites contained therein, following Christ's teaching in Matt 5:17–19. It honors the Ark of the Covenant and bears witness publicly and openly to it as a cornerstone of its doctrine. The *Tabot* placed in each church building is made in the names of the Trinity, the Virgin Mary, the saints, prophets, apostles, and martyrs.

The Holy Virgin Mary is revered in the Ethiopian Orthodox Tewahedo Church as the abode of the Holy Spirit, the Mother of God (see Mary, the Virgin, Cluster: Theotokos), the Eternal Virgin, the Holy of Holies. According to the Liturgy/Anaphora of Jacob* of Serug (Syria, 5th c.), since the Word of God graced her by being born of her, the Church honors, thanks, and implores God through her.

Prophets, Apostles, and Martyrs are given the honor and title of "holy" and "saint," for they gave their lives for the sake of God, bore witness in his name, and served God with all their energies and capacities. The Church honors, thanks, and implores not only the Holy Virgin Mary, but also angels (created on the first Sunday, according to Jubilees, 2:6–8) and the saints (holy ones, made from fire and wind, 3 Macc 2:10–11). Angels are always praising God (Rev 4:8–11), "ascending and descending" between God and humans (John 1:51; Heb 1:14). Angels and/or saints present human prayers, alms, and offerings to God; bring God's mercy and gifts to humans (Dan 9:20–22; Luke 1:13; Acts 10:3–5); bring souls before God after death (Luke 16:22); guard every creature (Matt 18:10); bring solace and help in times of suffering and hardship (Acts 2:7–11; Ps 89:7); and are sent to separate sinners from the righteous at the end of time (Matt 24:31; Rev 7:1–4). Thus the Ethiopian Orthodox Tewahedo Church honors the relics of saints who departed after serving God in word and deed; their relics, kept in church buildings, continue to perform miracles.

Praying, Fasting, and Observing Feasts. These observances follow both Scripture and tradition. Fasting* does not merely entail abstinence from food. There is true fast when the eye is kept from seeing evil, the mouth from speaking evil, and the ear from hearing evil (Matt 15:10–20). There are seven fasting periods: Lent (the great fast), Wednesdays and Fridays, Nineveh (commemorating the prophet Jonah), the eves of Christmas and Epiphany, Advent, the feasts of the apostles, and the assumption of the Holy Virgin Mary.

Prayers, said seven times a day (from morning to midnight), are of three kinds: private, family, and public. Public prayers conducted by priests, including the Holy Liturgy, include hymns, often *qenes* composed in honor of a saint, including those composed by Yared (6th c.). The Ethiopian Orthodox Tewahedo Church uses 14 anaphoras (liturgies) to celebrate Holy Communion, including the Anaphoras of St. Mary, St. Athanasius*, St. Basil*, St. Gregory*, St. Epiphanius*, St. John* Chrysostom, St. Cyril*, and St. Jacob* of Serug.

Alms (giving one's bread to the hungry, bringing the homeless poor into one's house) are among the most important religious deeds and are always associated with worship.

Icons* are important for all Orthodox churches. The difference is that for the Ethiopian Orthodox Tewahedo Church, icons and the making of icons and other sacred objects are associated with the making of Arks (of the Covenant). Thus the making of icons is understood in terms of biblical texts about the building of the Ark of the Covenant. Exodus 31:1–6, especially, underscores the idea that God selects artists to design the tabernacle, the holy vestments, the Ark, the cherub, and the paintings that, once consecrated and blessed, become means of blessing. They are venerated and God blesses all who venerate them as "godly art," in contrast with images that should not be worshipped. As the Church understood when books were not readily available (as in catacombs), sacred images, sacred arts and buildings, sacred objects, relics, and sacred gestures, including the sign of the cross, are necessary means to teach the faithful and to express one's faith.

The Ethiopian Orthodox Tewahedo Church has played an important role in education in Ethiopia. It developed the Ethiopian script and literature. It established an education system for the clergy. Before the advent of modern education, the Church trained all the government functionaries, including judges, officials of the imperial court, and civil servants. Churches and monasteries were virtually the country's only "libraries." Every parish had its own school, although as a result of recent political events, only about 43% have their own schools (in 2005 there were only c125,000 students). Because of a lack of teaching materials, lessons are largely oral and learned by rote memory, and educational programs are consequently lengthy. The Church struggles to introduce modern teaching methods and teaching materials.

BISHOP ABBA SAMUEL WOLDE TEKESTEBIRHAN

Orthodox Churches, Oriental: Malankara Orthodox Syrian Church (Indian Orthodox Church). The Malankara Orthodox Syrian Church is an autocephalous* Oriental* Orthodox Church deeply rooted in Indian social culture and spirituality, with about 2 million faithful headed by a supreme catholicos* (in Kottayam, Kerala). It traces its origin to the apostle Thomas*, who, according tradition, arrived on the Malabar coast (present-day Kerala, South India) in 52.

Since the 16th c., the history of the Malankara Orthodox Syrian Church has been deeply marked by bitter struggles, first with the Portuguese* Roman Catholic colonizers, then with the British missionaries and other ecclesiastical authorities who wanted either to proselytize or to wield power over the ancient Christians of India. These foreign "missionary" efforts eventually divided the one Christian community into several bodies. Because of the Malankara Orthodox Syrian Church's spiritual and liturgical connections with Syriac-using Persian and Middle Eastern Christian communities (see present cluster: Syriac Orthodox Church, Universal), the British rulers labeled the native Indian Christians of St. Thomas "Syrian Christians."

The Malankara Orthodox Syrian Church fully shares its faith and eucharistic Communion with the other churches in the Oriental Orthodox family. Rooted in the mystery* of the Holy Trinity* and the incarnation* of God in Jesus Christ, the Church centers its liturgical life on the Holy Eucharist and practices the other sacraments of baptism*, chrismation*, ordination*, marriage*, confession*, and the anointing* of the sick. Holy Scripture* is widely used both in public liturgical celebrations and in personal and family devotional life. The Malankara Orthodox Syrian Church upholds the faith of three of the seven ecumenical councils (Nicaea*, 325; Constantinople*, 381; Ephesus*, 431) and practices with other Orthodox churches the intercession of the Holy Virgin Mary* and the saints*, and prayers for the departed.

A founding member of the World* Council of Churches and an active participant in the fruitful 20th-c. theological dialogue* between the Oriental Orthodox and the Eastern Orthodox churches, the Malankara Orthodox Syrian Church also maintains theological dialogues with the Roman Catholic Church and the churches of the Reformation.

The Malankara Orthodox Syrian Church has active social and teaching ministries, two thriving theological faculties, and a dynamic Sunday school and student movement. Its 1,500 parishes are governed by elected parish councils. The priests can choose to be married or celibate, while bishops are elected from among celibate clergy by the representative church assembly with two-thirds laypeople. The Malankara Orthodox Syrian Church is one of the few Orthodox churches that still practice the direct election of bishops and head of the church by the people and clergy. Its Holy Synod, the supreme body in matters of faith and discipline, has 25 member bishops.

KONDOTHRA M. GEORGE

Orthodox Churches, Oriental: Syriac Orthodox Church, Universal. According to tradition, Peter established his Holy See in Antioch (37), presiding over the church in Antioch (the capital of the Roman province of Syria) and consecrating Evodius and Ignatius Noorono as bishops, before leaving for missionary work. Thereafter, there was a succession of bishops or "patriarchs of Antioch and all the East," until Patriarch Ignatius Zakka I Iwas (consecrated 1980). The seat of the Patriarchate is now Damascus, the capital of present-day Syria.

The 1st-c. Syriac Orthodox Church flourished in the eastern part of the Roman Empire and soon beyond, in the Persian Empire, Iraq*, Mongolia, India*, and China*. Jacob* Baradai (c500–78) revived the spiritual life of the Church in Syria, Armenia*, Egypt*, Persia, and Cyprus*.

In the early 7th c., the Syriac Orthodox Church had c20,000 parishes and hundreds of monasteries and convents. The Syriac Orthodox Church survived dominion by Arabs (for whom Syrian monks and scholars translated the Greek philosophers into Arabic) and Mongols. Yet the Church suffered greatly during the Mongol invasions (14th c.). A separate uniate Patriarchate of Antioch (Syriac Catholics) was established (late 18th c.). Yet from the mid-20th c., the Syriac Orthodox Church began to flourish again, as it did in India (see the present cluster: Malankara Orthodox Syrian Church).

Theology and Liturgy. The Syriac Orthodox Church recognizes only three ecumenical councils (Nicaea, 325; Constantinople, 381; Ephesus, 431), rejecting the decisions of the Council of Chalcedon (451) about the person of Christ, which made too many concessions to the Nestorians*. The Syriac Orthodox Church believes in the Holy Trinity* – Father, Son, and Holy Spirit – the one true God, and in the Lord Jesus Christ as God in whom divinity and humanity are united in a real, perfect, indivisible, and inseparable way, and all their properties are present and active. The doctrinal position of the Syriac Orthodox Church is similar to that of the Coptic*, Armenian*, and Ethiopian* Orthodox churches. Veneration of the saints* and prayers for the dead are essential elements of the Church's tradition. The Church recognizes the seven traditional sacraments*. The liturgical language of the Church is Syriac (vernacular languages are used alongside Syriac); the usual anaphora* is that of St. James*. Famous schools of theology were established in Antioch*, Nisibis*, and Edessa*; Ephrem* the Syrian and Jacob* of Edessa graduated from these schools.

20th–21st Centuries. The Syriac Orthodox Church, now spread all over the world, has been an active member since 1960 of the World* Council of Churches (one of its presidents has been Patriarch Ignatius Zakka I Iwas, since 1998). It takes part in ecumenical and theological dialogues around the world. The Syriac Orthodox Church maintains a number of monasteries, an integral part of its spiritual and cultural heritage. There are three minor seminaries and two major seminaries (one in Syria and one in India) for training clergy. The Church includes about 4 million adherents (the major part in India) in 36 dioceses and 1 catholicos, 37 archbishops, and 1 bishop under the Syriac Orthodox patriarch.

METROPOLITAN ATHANASIOS GEEVARGIS

Orthodox Worship. See DIVINE LITURGY OF THE ORTHODOX CHURCHES; EUCHARIST CLUSTER: IN ORIENTAL ORTHODOX (NON-CHALCEDONIAN) CHURCHES.

Orthodoxy (Gk "correct belief") in Western Christianity emphasizes adherence to the accepted dogmas, viewed as revealed understandings or teachings, usually confirmed by an authority: Scriptures*; councils*, synods*, and other church assemblies; creeds*; or a prelate (pope, patriarch, bishop). Having an orthodox faith* is to believe in such authoritative teachings. Orthodoxy is opposed to heterodoxy ("alien teaching") and heresy*. In Eastern Christianity, "Orthodoxy" refers to the worship, belief, theology, and practices of the Eastern Orthodox* churches or Oriental Orthodox* churches. **See also ORTHOPRAXY.**

Orthodoxy, Festival of, first Sunday in Lent, first observed in 843 after the defeat of Iconoclasm* and the restoration of icons*.

Orthopraxy (Gk "correct practice") in Christianity emphasizes "lived faith*" rather than "faith" as "correct belief" (see Orthodoxy). Although the term is often used to characterize Judaism* because of its emphasis on action rather than belief, orthopraxy is also found throughout church history: for various groups (e.g. religious* orders, the Social* Gospel Movement, Liberation* theologians), the Christian faith* is not limited to a proper understanding of God, but is a matter of experiencing God's reality by entering and sharing in God's very life in a "praxis according to God" (G. Gutiérrez); as is written in Micah 6:8: "What does the Lord require of you but to do justice, and to love kindness, and to walk humbly with your God?"

Otto of Freising (c1115–58), bishop of Freising, historian. Born in Austria* of noble ancestry, he studied in Paris*, probably under Hugo* of St. Victor. He became a monk and abbot in a Cistercian* abbey in Champaign, then was appointed bishop of Freising (1138). He took part in the Second Crusade* (1147–48), introduced Aristotle* in Germany, and wrote both an interpretative *History of the Two Cities* and a narrative of Barbarossa's early reign.

Ousia (Gk "essence"), term used by the Cappadocians* to designate the divine "essence," which is the same in the Father, Son, and Holy Sprit, in the doctrine of the Trinity* (in contrast to the term *hypostasis**, "person"). **See also HOMOOUSIANS, HOMOIOUSIANS, HOMOIANS, ANOMOIANS.**

Oxford Group. Founded by Buchman* (1921), it was originally called "First Century Christian Fellowship." Nicknamed the "Oxford Group," it was subsequently called "Moral* Re-armament" (1938) and was finally (2001) given the name "Initiatives of Change." Known for its concern for personal and social transformation, it was criticized for moral absolutism, anti-Communist fervor, obsession with sex, exaggerated claims, and cultlike personal guidance. First organized in England, it entered the USA in 1939 and is now active in many countries, seeking interreligious cooperation. The conference center on Mackinac Island (Michigan, 1942–66) was superseded by the one in Caux, Switzerland (established in 1946).

Oxford Movement, religious revival* in the Church of England. In its initial stage (1833–45), it was known for its publication of *Tracts for the Times* (1833–41), the translation of major works by early church fathers, a series of writings by classic Anglo-Catholic theologians, as well as a rigorous campaign to oppose theological liberalism* and secular interference in religious life and to enliven Anglicanism's Catholic roots: its episcopal, sacramental, and creedal identity. Its major leaders included John Henry Newman*, Edward Bouverie Pusey*, and John Keble*. Despite Newman's "Tract 90" (1841), in which he argued that the Thirty*-nine Articles of the Anglican tradition could be interpreted in a Catholic sense, his conversion to Roman Catholicism (1845), and a crisis over the Gorham case (1850, when a secular court ruled on a theological matter), which led to the conversion of others to Roman Catholicism, the movement continued to exert a strong influence on the Anglican Church. Although its primary focus came to an end with Pusey's death (1882), it continued in other forms: the ongoing Anglican Old High Church Movement (which had begun before it), late Victorian ritualism, and the much different liberal Catholicism of Charles Gore (1853–1932) and *Lux mundi: A Series of Studies in the Religion of the Incarnation* (1889).

PETER C. ERB

P

Pacem in Terris, encyclical letter (1963) of Pope John* XXIII, calling for peace on earth though truth, justice, charity, and liberty, which should be based on the "divinely established order" of creation that grants rights and freedoms to all peoples. **See also SOCIAL ENCYCLICALS.**

Pachomius (c292–346), early Egyptian monastic leader; inaccurately described as "the founder of cenobitic* monasticism." Raised in a pagan family, he became a Christian after leaving the Roman army (313) and became a monk (c316). After settling in Tabennesi, Upper Egypt, he gradually organized and led a confederation of large monasteries, known as the Koinonia (Gk "fellowship"), and composed the first known monastic* rule. He was celebrated in several biographies (composed c390s), which were preserved in Greek and in dialects of Coptic. Scholars have discovered letters and catecheses attributed to Pachomius and his successors, Theodore and Horsiesius.

J. WILLIAM HARMLESS, SJ

Pacific, South, and Australia. See HISTORY OF CHRISTIANITY CLUSTER: IN THE SOUTH PACIFIC AND AUSTRALIA.

Pacifism and Christianity. History is replete with varieties of Christian pacifists. A single definition will not suffice. The word "pacifism" (from Lat *pacem facere,* "to make peace") reflects Jesus' teaching in Matt 5:9, "Blessed are the peacemakers, for they will be called children of God." It has a *proactive* meaning: a commitment to engage actively in practices of peacemaking. It has an *avoidance* meaning: a commitment to avoid practices of violence and war. It has a *Christ-is-Lord* meaning: a commitment to follow the way of Jesus Christ as revelation of God and God's will. Different Christian pacifists emphasize one or more of these three meanings and thus are not easily classified.

The Christ-is-Lord meaning is seen in the high Christologies* of John 1, Heb 1, Col 1, Phil 2, and Rev 5. We practice "preaching peace by Jesus Christ – he is Lord of all" (Acts 10:36). The Sermon* on the Mount, the most widely quoted portion of Scripture in the early church, became a manual for living this life as a reconciling community. Jesus' nonviolence is evident in his welcoming of outcasts and rejection of the temptation to achieve rule by violent revolution as the Maccabees* and revolutionaries in his time had tried to do. Jesus accepted his atoning* death on a Roman cross, eschewing violent resistance. Despite the view that the Book of Revelation supports violence, in it followers of the Beasts do violence, while followers of the Lamb do not; they perform the deeds that Jesus taught, as is repeatedly emphasized.

Pacifism was the practice of the church during the first centuries. In the Didache* and the writings of all the church fathers through Origen, participation in the violence and idolatrous culture of Caesar's wars was rejected. But with the "Constantinian shift," Christianity became the enforced religion of the Roman Empire, and the emperor's wars became "Christian" (see Constantine). Ambrose* and Augustine* introduced the ethic of just war*, although it has never been officially decreed as the ethic of the Roman Catholic Church.

In the Constantinian context, pledges to live by the Sermon on the Mount and vows of nonviolence were taken by priests, monks, and nuns, from the Desert* Fathers/Mothers and the Benedictine* communities to Patrick* of Ireland, Francis* of Assisi, and the noncrusading Celtic* Christian missionaries throughout Western Europe. But usually vows of nonviolence were not taken by laypersons.

Holy Spirit–minded and Bible-reading "sectarians" throughout the medieval period reclaimed Jesus' nonviolence for their own lives but were usually pessimistic about the political order. Among these were Peter Valdes* and the Waldenses*; John Wyclif* and the Lollards*; Petr Chelcicky and the Czech Brethren; the "*imitatio* Christi*" movement; and the Brethren* of the Common Life. The Radical Reformation of the 16th-c. Anabaptists* (Swiss Brethren, Dutch Mennonites*, Hutterites*, and later Amish* and Brethren in Christ) became the "historic peace church" movement of Protestantism; they were subsequently joined by the Quakers* (17th c.), the Church of the Brethren (18th c.), the Disciples of Christ/Christian* Churches (19th c.), and the Pentecostal* Movement (20th c.). Although most Disciples of Christ and Pentecostals gave up the normative peace position of their founders – not unlike the Roman Catholic Church itself – some are recovering it, and the United* Church of Christ has named itself a peace church.

A line of 19th-c. pacifist thought running from Tolstoy* and Thoreau (see Transcendentalism) to 20th-c. practitioners like Gandhi* and Martin Luther King*, Jr., has profoundly transformed the modern world, as seen in Indian independence, the US civil* rights struggle, Eastern European revolutions against Soviet Communism, "people power" in the Philippines*, the battle against apartheid in South* Africa, and lesser-known groups like the "Abejas" in Chiapas, Mexico*, and the Palestinian* Liberation Christian Movement dedicated to nonviolence. A long line of nonviolent warriors for justice preceded King (David Walker, Sojourner* Truth, Harriet Tubman*) and worked alongside him (James Farmer and the Fellowship of Reconciliation [Chicago, 1942], Bayard Rustin, Rosa Parks, Ella Baker*, Fanny Lou Hamer). South* African Christians (including Bishop Tutu and the martyred Stephen Biko) also testify to this African-rooted tradition of nonviolent challenge to injustice (see Reconciliation as a Christian Praxis). In the context of democracy, all of these warriors urged governments – not only churches – to adopt nonviolence: Christ is Lord of all of life.

Roman Catholic modern-day prophets follow in the footsteps of Dorothy Day* (founder of the Catholic* Worker Movement) and Thomas Merton*. The Fellowship of Reconciliation, American Friends Service Committee, Pax Christi, and Mennonite Central Committee have innovated new practices of peace and justice for healing a broken world. The Protestant trajectory of peace-minded radical Christians includes German radical Pietists* (e.g. Christoff Blumhardt*), Swiss Reformed (Leonhard Ragaz, Karl Barth*); German Lutherans (Dietrich Bonhoeffer*) and Hutterites (Eberhard Arnold); French Reformed (e.g. André Trocmé, Jacques Ellul); and North American pacifists (William Stringfellow, Clarence Jordan, John Howard Yoder, Brethren James McClendon). Dale Brown writes, "Pacifism – peacemaking – should not merely be a compliance with law but a joyful response to and participation in the kingdom* coming." **See also CONSCIENTIOUS OBJECTION; MILITARISM; PEACE MOVEMENTS; PEACE AND PEACEMAKING.**

KENT DAVIS SENSENIG and GLEN H. STASSEN

Padroado. See PATRONATO, PADROADO.

Paedobaptism, also Pedobaptism. See INFANT BAPTISM.

Pagan, Paganism, term used by Christians to refer to all religions outside the biblical tradition. The Latin *paganus* originally referred to people from the countryside, to civilians (when used by soldiers), and to any persons outside, and inferior to, one's group. Tertullian* compared Christians, with their disciplined life, to soldiers; thus all others were pagans, "civilians" or outsiders, in God's eyes. This Christian use became widespread (4th c.), although *gentilis*, "Gentile*," was still preferred. "Pagan" entered the language of imperial law (late 4th c.) as a term of derision. The terms "Gentile," "ethnic," and "non-Christian" are less contemptuous when one cannot designate groups by their proper names.

Pakistan, one of the largest Islamic countries with Islam* as the state religion, includes a significant Christian community, although it remains a small minority (2.5% of the population).

Thomas* the Apostle is said to have brought Christianity to Northern India, present-day Pakistan, in the 1st c. – a tradition now supported by archaeological discoveries in Taxila (coins of the reign of King Gundaphorus, before whom, according to the tradition, Thomas was brought) and the Taxila cross (2nd c.; used as a symbol of Christianity by the Church of Pakistan). But these first Christian communities soon disappeared.

The second wave of Christianity arrived with Jesuits* in the 1590s, then with Augustinians* and Carmelites* in the 17th c., leading to the establishment of a few churches, which also disappeared.

The third wave of Christianity came in the 19th c., when the Indian subcontinent was ruled by the British Empire; a few garrison churches were established, and the arrival of missionaries was facilitated. The United Presbyterian Church of North America sent its first missionary, Andrew Gordon, his family, and his sister (1854) to Sialkot, Punjab (East Pakistan); they were joined by Ifrahim H. Steven and A. R. Hall (1856) and by Scotch Presbyterian missionaries. The Church Missionary Society of England established a church in Karachi (1850) and an Anglican diocese in Lahore, Punjab (1877). Methodist and other Presbyterian churches also sent missionaries. Christianity flourished primarily among Hindu outcastes (Dalits*) in Punjab and is still growing despite difficulties. The Roman Catholic Church is also primarily in Punjab (in Lahore; vicariate, 1880) and Karachi (archdiocese, 1950).

The mainline churches now serving in Pakistan are the Roman Catholic Church and Protestant churches, including the Church of Pakistan (uniting Anglicans, Methodists, Lutherans, and Scotch Presbyterians) and the Presbyterian Church of Pakistan, the Associate Reformed Church, and the Salvation* Army. A large number of independent denominations (Baptists, Brethrens*, Pentecostals*/Charismatics*) and parachurch organizations and movements (e.g. YMCA*, YWCA*, Scripture Union, Serving in Mission [SIM], Inter Serve, Youth with a Mission, Pakistan Fellowship of Evangelical Students [PFES]) are also working in Pakistan.

Christianity, a tiny minority without official recognition, does not have much direct impact on Pakistan's political life. But Christian churches have played an important role as pioneers in education*, health*, and social programs. Many churches have opened schools and educated hundreds of thousand of people, making no distinction based on race, sex, or religion and thus training many people who held or hold positions of leadership in society. Unfortunately, schools and colleges were nationalized between 1972 and 1998, when the government denationalized these schools and one college (Forman Christian College in Lahore); the churches are busy mending the educational network, creating new schools, even in homes of Christians. Similarly, the churches and their programs make a significant contribution to adult literacy, welfare, and the protection of life. Struggling to eliminate poverty*, illiteracy, and injustice, and extending Christian love to the needy and to domestic, factory, and agriculture workers, are salient features of life for Christians in Pakistan. Church-sponsored clinics, dispensaries, and hospitals also help hundreds of thousands of people at low or nominal charges.

Since the early 1990s, Muslim militancy, fundamentalism, and extremism have put the Christian Church in a different situation. Hatred and enmity between Christian and Muslim communities have intensified. Some Christians have been killed; others have been accused of blasphemy in legal cases (under *shari'a*). Most Christians live in fear, even as they continue worshipping, holding evangelistic and healing Charismatic meetings, and carrying out their regular work, while the government protects them from terrorist attacks. **See also ISLAM AND CHRISTIANITY CLUSTER.**

Statistics: Population (2000): 156 million (M). Muslims, 150 M, 96%; Christians, 3.9 M, 2.5% (1970, 1.2 M, 1.8%) (Protestants, 1.8 M; Roman Catholics, 1.2 M; independents, 0.85 M); Hindus, 1.9 M, 1.2%. (Based on *World Christian Encyclopedia*, 2001.)

ARTHUR JAMES

Palafox y Mendoza, Juan de (1600–59), born and died in Spain*; bishop of La Puebla de los Angeles (1640–49), inspector general of New Spain (1642), acting viceroy (1642). With Pope Innocent X's support, he secularized the Roman Catholic Church (taking away the authority of the religious orders, Augustinians*, and Franciscans*), destroyed idols* of indigenous peoples, and confronted the Jesuits'* practices and doctrines. His many writings include *Nature and Virtues of the Indian*.

MARÍA ALICIA PUENTE LUTTEROTH and ELIZABETH JUDD

Palestinian Liberation Theology. Ever since their *nakba* (catastrophe) in 1948, Palestinian Christians – clergy and lay – have reflected on the reality of their lives in light of their Christian faith, even though this was not called a "Palestinian theology of liberation" until the late 1980s. In 2006 the Palestinian Christian community is less than 2% of the population, and the number of trained theologians is very small. Most theological reflection is done by parish priests and pastors. People's personal experiences and stories of their lives under the Israeli occupation provided the context of theology, as is clear in their writings. Thus besides the formal name "Palestinian theology of liberation," Palestinian theologians (e.g. Jeries Khoury, Mitri Raheb) use terms like "local" or "contextual* theology" in a similar sense.

At the heart of this theological reflection is the political injustice against Palestinians. One of the main instruments used to oppress the Palestinians has been the Bible. An exclusive reading of the biblical text by Jewish and Christian Zionists has provided the basis for the liberation of Israel, even as it has been used to condone the oppression* of Palestinians. Palestinian Liberation theology has sought to develop a theology that grants physical and spiritual liberation inclusively, to all people. Such a theology seeks to inspire people to work for justice*, peace*, and reconciliation*. An inclusive theology of God, people* (of God), and land* (including "promised* land") derived especially from the OT has been crucial for promoting the sharing of the land between Israelis and Palestinians (Lev 25:23; Ezek 47:21–23; Jonah). The prophetic material has been helpful in emphasizing God's demand for justice and mercy (Mic 6:8, Amos 5:24).

In Palestinian Liberation theology, Jesus is the paradigm of faith and life. He was born and lived under occupation, and was killed by occupation forces. For Palestinian Christians, Jesus Christ is the only hermeneutical key to biblical interpretation. He inspires Palestinian Christians to follow him in the way of nonviolence* and peacemaking (Matthew 5:9), emphasizing the importance of resisting evil* without resorting to evil methods.

Practically, Palestinian Liberation theology expresses itself through ecumenical programs for Christians, locally and internationally, in Christian–Muslim relations, and in the work of justice and peace, on the basis of nonviolence, in partnership with others, including Muslim and Jewish peace activists. **See also ISLAM AND CHRISTIANITY CLUSTER; JUDAISM AND CHRISTIANITY CLUSTER; PACIFISM AND CHRISTIANITY.** NAIM STIFAN ATEEK

Palestrina (Prenestino), Giovanni Pierluigi da (c1525–94), Italian composer. From 1551 he held appointments in Rome at the Capella Giulia, San Giovanni Laterano, Santa Maria Maggiore, San Pietro, and the Sistine Chapel. His oeuvre is regarded as the ideal implementation of the Council of Trent's* guidelines for liturgical music, emphasizing textual clarity. His reputation as *the* Roman Catholic composer led to the formulation of a "Palestrina style," which remained the paradigm of sacred music until the 19th c. His sacred works include at least 104 Masses*, 323 motets*, 72 hymns*, 68 offertories*, 35 *Magnificat** settings, 11 litanies*, and 55 sacred madrigals. TASSILO ERHARDT

Paley, William (1743–1805), British theologian and moral philosopher, whose coherent system of thought greatly influenced 19th-c. elites in Britain. His *Natural Theology* (1802) provided a clear and comprehensive statement of the argument from design*, which found in nature overwhelming empirical evidence of God's creative purposes. *The Principles of Moral and Political Philosophy* (1785) advocated a form of utilitarian ethics* that meshed traditional Christian theology with the rational pursuit of pleasure and the prudent avoidance of pain. Paley taught as a young man at Cambridge University, where his lucid, well-organized books became a required part of the curriculum. D. L. LEMAHIEU

Palladius (c364–420/30), writer on early monasticism, especially *Lausiac History* (c419) on monks, including Olympias*. Fearing an adulterous relationship with a woman in Constantinople, he went to Egypt and became associated with Evagrius* of Pontus. He served as a bishop in Bithynia (400), but as a friend of John* Chrysostom, whose biography he wrote, he was exiled (406).

Palladius (5th c.), first recorded bishop of the Irish, sent to Ireland* (431) by Pope Celestine I; probably worked in the southeastern part of the country because of contacts with Wales and Cornwall. His relationship to Patrick* is uncertain.

Pallium (Lat "cloak"), originally a rectangular cloak, often worn by philosophers, ascetics*, and clergy*. Later a narrow band worn over the shoulders and hanging down in front and back, conferred on archbishops* or patriarchs* by the pope* as a sign of legitimacy.

Palmer, Phoebe (1807–74), North American Methodist writer, theologian, and evangelist, central figure in 19th-c. Evangelicalism*.

Born to a prosperous family in New York City, she married Dr. Walter Palmer (1826). The death of three children led her to desire sanctification*, which she experienced in 1837. In a time when holiness teaching was becoming popular among US Evangelicals, Palmer promoted holiness among the well-educated middle class.

Her reformulation of John Wesley's* doctrine of entire sanctification influenced Wesleyan and Reformed branches of the Holiness* Movement and Pentecostalism*. Like Wesley, Palmer believed that Christians could experience "entire sanctification" – a state in which the presence of the Holy* Spirit eradicates the desire to sin*. In addition she emphasized the instantaneous manner of entire sanctification, "a second baptism of the Holy Spirit." For her, Christians became sanctified when they consecrated themselves to God and believed in God's promise to make them holy (*The Way of Holiness,* 1851). Palmer began Tuesday Meetings for the Promotion of Holiness (1840), edited the periodical *Guide to Holiness* (1862–74), and publicized her teachings through extensive travel in the USA and England. Although she never sought ordination, her 1859 book, *Promise of the Father,* defended women's right to preach. **See also** **WOMEN'S ORDINATION CLUSTER.**

SARAH JOHNSON

Palm Sunday, Sunday before Easter*, at the beginning of Holy* Week, celebrating Jesus' triumphal entry into Jerusalem (Mark 11:1–11, par.). In Jerusalem in the 4th c., worship on this day included a procession, and this practice spread throughout the Western Church during the Middle Ages.

Pammachius (c340–410), Roman senator, friend of Jerome*, who dedicated several works to him. After the death of his wife (the daughter of Paula*), he became a monk and established a hostel for pilgrims. He tried to mute the fury of Jerome's attacks on Jovinian* and on Rufinus* of Aquileia. He died during the Goths'* occupation of Rome.

Pamphilus (c240–310), champion of Origen*. After studying in Alexandria, he taught in the school in Caesarea that had been made famous by Origen and made use of its library. His *Apology for Origen,* written in collaboration with Eusebius* of Caesarea, carried on his tradition after his martyrdom during the Diocletian* persecutions.

Panama. The Christianization of Panama began when Panama was still a part of Colombia* during the colonial period. Strategically situated along a transoceanic route, it was quickly occupied by Spaniards (early 16th c.). The indigenous populations were decimated (now 6% of the population). The first bishop on the continent was sent to Panama (1513). Franciscans'* early evangelization was greatly hindered by the recurring violence of pirate raids and colonial oppression. After the independence movement, the Roman Catholic Church was granted governmental favors and concessions by the Concordat with Colombia (1887).

When Panama seceded from Colombia, assisted by the USA in a hegemonic and neocolonial role, the Constitution of 1904 established freedom of religion and civic control of public life. Constitutional modifications (1972) granted religious freedom and recognized Roman Catholicism as the dominant faith, but prevented clergy from holding public office. Although weakened by a lack of leadership, a hybrid religiosity, and Protestant proselytism*, the Roman Catholic Church was paradoxically revitalized by a renewed emphasis on evangelization, the Charismatic renewal, and the struggle for justice* to the marginalized that brought state persecution (1960s–1970s). Despite the scarcity of clergy (since colonial times), most of whom are from foreign countries, Roman Catholics (many of them closely associated with folk religionists) constitute more than 75% of the multiethnic population (with a majority of mestizos*, 70%; African Americans, 14%; whites and Asians, 10%; and Native Americans, 6%).

The work of Protestant missions began in the midst of international conflict over the building of a canal across the isthmus. Tens of thousands of mostly Caribbean black immigrants came to construct the trans-isthmus railroad, then to participate in French attempts to build a canal (1878–79) and to construct highways. Many of these workers and their families were members of Protestant (Methodist and Baptist) churches. The digging of the Panama Canal by the USA (1904–14) brought a wave of Protestant missionaries. The Methodists were the first to initiate significant work with the Latinos/as (1905), but until the mid-20th c. the growth of the Protestant Church was slower than that of the population. Yet Adventists* made notable progress among African Americans, and from 1929 Pentecostals* (the Quadrangular Pentecostal Church) grew most rapidly in number.

Since the mid-20th c., the Assemblies* of God and Charismatic* groups have spread like wildfire. Poverty, anomie, marginalization, lack of hope, a sense of impotence, unemployment, and forced migration were the lot of the multitudes. The search for the transcendent, a hope for better times to come, empowerment by the fire of the Holy* Spirit, the promise of healing* for the body and mind, and the assurance that God cares for them as persons have given them new purpose and meaning. Now Charismatics/ Pentecostals* constitute the largest Evangelical group (70–80% of Protestants).

Statistics: Population (2000): 2.8 million (M). Christians, 2.5 M, 88.2% (Roman Catholics, 77%; Protestants, 11%); Muslims, 4.4%; nonreligious, 3%; Baha'is, 1.2%; Buddhists, 1%; native religionists, 1.3%. (Based on *World Christian Encyclopedia,* 2001.)

SIDNEY ROOY

Panama Conference (1916). At the World Missionary Conference in Edinburgh (1910), US representatives were eager to describe Latin America as "missionary territory," but British and German representatives opposed this on the grounds that the continent was already

Christian. Nevertheless, in 1913 a conference on missions in Latin America was held in New York (1913), with the participation of many North American mission societies; it established the Committee on Cooperation in Latin America. While Europe was preoccupied with World War I, a major conference was held in Panama (1916) on mission activities in Latin America, followed by regional conferences including those in Montevideo (1925) and Havana (1929).

Panentheism, view that the world, while not identical with God (see Pantheism), exists "in God." This view is based on Acts 17:28 and the theological tradition (including Process* theology), which says that God "holds all things together."

Pantheism, philosophical and religious view that the world is identical with God: God is everything and everything is God. While the world and God may be differentiated as the All and the Whole, or the world may be viewed as the "expression" of God, God is thought not to have any being or life independent of the world. Another tenet of pantheism is that everything in existence is part of one Being, which highlights the unity of all things.

Papacy. See POPES, ROMAN CATHOLIC, AND THE PAPACY.

Papias (c60–130), bishop of Hierapolis in Asia Minor. Irenaeus* says that he was a disciple of John* and an associate of Polycarp*. His work on the "sayings of the Lord" – especially his statement about two of the Gospels: that Mark*, the interpreter of Peter, set down what he remembered and that Matthew* wrote down the "sayings" in Hebrew – is known only from quotations by Irenaeus* and Eusebius.*

Papua New Guinea. Christianity plays an important role in modern Papua New Guinea (taken here as an example of Melanesia, including New Caledonia, Solomon Islands, and Vanuatu; see also Fiji). In 2000, 96% of Papua New Guinea's 5.1 million people claimed to be Christian. The Preamble to the 1975 Constitution, drafted by a committee with a Roman Catholic priest as deputy chair, explicitly invokes "Christian principles."

Christianity was introduced by Loyalty Islands teachers of the London Missionary Society (LMS) from Australia across the Torres Strait (1871) and in New Britain by Fijian and Samoan teachers of the Methodist Church (1875). Papua New Guinea's rugged terrain and the difficulty of communication shaped the development of geographic missionary zones. In British New Guinea (Papua), a government-endorsed committee allotted separate regions to the LMS, Methodist, and Anglican missions (1890). The Roman Catholic mission led by Sacred Heart missionaries refused to subscribe to an agreement restricting its activities, and so was forced to work inland from the Gulf of Papua. In effect, the committee created virtual missionary "states within a state." The geographic isolation of each mission helped to avoid religious conflict. In each case, the Christianity planted by the missionaries was therefore strongly denominational, rooted in the soil of particular European and Pacific Islands churches.

Missionary attitudes toward indigenous culture differed widely. Anglicans belonging to the Anglo-Catholic school stressed continuity with the Melanesian past; conservative Evangelicals in the Kwato and Seventh-day Adventists* sought to create a new cultural environment to help their converts make a "clean break" with the past. Methodists tended to stand midway between these extremes. The Lutheran pioneer Christian Keysser, in the colony of German New Guinea (since 1899), sought integration between culture and Christianity and waited until a whole community was ready before baptizing anyone.

In pre-contact Papua New Guinea, myths and ritual acts represented people's understanding of the nature of the cosmos and of the way in which it could be controlled to human advantage by religious rituals. For all but a few, conversion to a new religion did not entail any loss of faith in the invisible world of spirits or the efficacy of rituals. In the first generations of contact, the knowledge system for obtaining material wealth and gaining control over life was barely affected. The widespread flourishing of Millennial* or prophetic "cargo" cults, predicting material equality between Papua New Guineans and Europeans in a blissful social order free of trouble, was an expression of the traditional Melanesian way of thinking during the period of upheaval.

The Christian missions differed widely in their response to the Japanese invasion of Papua New Guinea (1942). Many missionaries returned to Europe and Australia in the panic of the invasion, some believing they had been ordered out by the colonial government. Some who remained with their flocks were captured. Altogether 330 Christian missionaries and mission workers perished during the Pacific War. Many of them are honored by their respective churches as modern martyrs.

Since the 1960s, the dominance of the original mission churches has been challenged by the arrival of Jehovah's* Witnesses and, especially, Pentecostal churches, particularly the Four Square Gospel and Assemblies* of God. Few churches have sought to combine Christianity with traditional Melanesian religious beliefs. The only example of organic union has been the 1968 merging of the LMS and Methodist churches to form the United Church of Papua New Guinea and the Solomon* Islands.

After Papua New Guinea's independence (1975), the prominence of Christian leaders was evident in the Bougainville secessionist movement. Among the protagonists on both sides of the conflict were prominent Roman Catholics, including a priest-politician, a former seminarian who had become the provincial premier of Bougainville, and the bishop of Bougainville. In many areas, the churches continue to be responsible for maintaining basic health and education services. In the running of its day-to-day affairs, Papua New Guinea resembles the neighboring Solomon Islands in being permeated by strong Christian influences.

Statistics: Population (2000): 5.1 million (M). Christians, 4.4 M (Protestants, 2.6 M; Roman Catholics, 1.4 M; Anglicans, 0.3 M; independents, 0.3 M); native religionists, 0.2 M. (Based on *World Christian Encyclopedia*, 2001.)

DAVID WETHERELL

Parabalani, health care workers supervised by Alexandria's bishop; after they killed the Neoplatonist* Hypatia* (415), several imperial edicts restricted their numbers and activities.

Parable (Gk *parabole*; Heb *mashal*), as a literary genre, a short narrative fiction used by rabbis and Jesus as an illustration. In the Synoptic* Gospels and the Gospel of Thomas*, several parables are introduced by a formula: "The Kingdom* of God [or Heaven, or the Father] is like" (Mark 4:30–31 [13:34]; Matt 13:31–53, 20:1, 25:1; Luke 13:18–21; Thomas 20, 57, 76, 96–98, 107, 109). Most of Jesus' parables are "parables of the Kingdom," the core of Jesus' teaching; they do not have meaning in themselves but create it "by being laid beside the kingdom of God" (Bernard Scott).

Jesus' parables have been diversely interpreted according to the interpreters' views of the Kingdom (see Kingdom of God, Concept, Cluster).

1. Parables are read as wisdom* teachings or example stories when the Kingdom as reign is envisioned as a community of believers who submit to God's authority as king. Thus Luke and his followers throughout history tend to read the parables as wisdom teachings (Luke 4:23, 5:36, 6;13) and example stories (Luke 10:25–37 [the good Samaritan], 12:15–21, 16:19–31 18:9–14 [also the introduction of parables, 13:5, 14:7, 15:2–3, 18:1, 19:11]).
2. Parables are read as apocalyptic allegories that describe in figurative ways the coming of the Kingdom as the impending Judgment* when the Kingdom is envisioned as the eschatological, just empire ruled by God that will bring to an end the present evil, demonic empires. Matthew and his followers tend to read the parables in this apocalyptic* way. The secret of the Kingdom is the impending Judgment* of all that impedes the establishment of God's empire (Matt 13). This allegorical interpretation, sometimes subtly expressed (e.g. by a slight twist alluding to the Judgment; 15:13), is most often explicit when parables are presented as eschatological warnings, e.g., about the coming separation of "the sheep and the goats" (25:31–46; see also 18:1–35, 20:1–16, 21.28–22.14, 25:1–30).
3. Parables are read as mysterious symbols* of the Kingdom when the Kingdom is envisioned as the mystery* of God's kingly activity – a mystery (not a secret that could be unveiled) that by definition is beyond understanding (Mark 4:11) but can be glimpsed through parables. Thus for Mark and Thomas and their followers, parables do not "refer" to anything in particular. They are corrective lenses that enable believers to recognize the mysterious, ongoing activity of God. For Thomas parables focus believers' sight on a mysterious reality "within them" and within others (e.g. Thomas 3, 24, 70, 83). For Mark this mysterious reality is "among them," in mysterious interventions of God in life. For example, Mark offers an "allegorical/symbolic" interpretation of the parable of the sower (4:1–20) without taking the parable to be an example story (Luke) or an allegorical warning about the Judgment

(Matthew); the mysterious parable points to a mysterious reality in human experience: there are people with hard hearts who hear the word and fail to bear fruit; and there are people who bear fruit because mysteriously they are good ground, rather than paths, rocks, or thistles (the decision is not theirs).

Saying that each of the Synoptic Gospels *tends* to present the parables in one way or another is not saying that it necessarily and always views the parables in this way. These three views of the parables can be found in each of the Gospels.

Contemporary biblical scholars (following Perrin, Funk, Crossan) underscore that reading parables as symbols of the Kingdom (#3) is closer to the teaching of the historical Jesus*. Yet through the centuries, as well as today, the apocalyptic interpretation (#2) has been very popular and receives much scholarly attention (Weiss, Schweitzer, Dodd, Jeremias, and later "political" studies of Matthew, Mark, and the historical Jesus*), but the wisdom/moral interpretation (#1) is not ignored by scholars (from Jülicher to those who engaged in a different quest for the historical* Jesus). **See also DISCIPLESHIP; JESUS, QUEST FOR THE HISTORICAL; KINGDOM OF GOD, CONCEPT OF, CLUSTER; SYMBOLISM.** DANIEL PATTE

Parachurch Organizations, "parallel to, outside the church," i.e. without direct control by bishops or governing bodies, and led by either clergy or laity. Some examples include monastic communities, which are largely self-governing; confraternities* and sodalities* for laity during the Middle Ages; SPCK* (Society for Promoting Christian Knowledge,1698) and the SPG (Society for the Propagation of the Gospel, 1701); voluntary societies for mission and service within the Church of England; 18th-c. Methodist and Baptist missionary societies; voluntary societies in Congregational New England churches after 1800, which were formative in Midwestern states; and 19th-c. women's* missionary societies. Parachurch organizations without denominational ties are a major factor in foreign missions and youth ministries generally oriented toward individual conversion. Parachurches have become a worldwide phenomenon, as nondenominational and independent* churches multiply. Ecumenical efforts may run counter to parachurch mission organizations. **See also CHARISMATIC AND PENTECOSTAL MOVEMENTS CLUSTER; PROTESTANTISM CLUSTER: IN BRAZIL: PARACHURCH ASSOCIATIONS.**

Paraclete (Gk "advocate"), term in Johannine writings for the Holy* Spirit (John 14:16, 26; 15:26; 16:7) and Christ (1 John 2:1).

Paradise (from a Persian word for an enclosed garden), term used in the Septuagint* for the Garden of Eden (Gen 2–3) and later for heaven* (Luke 23:43; 1 Cor 12:4; Rev 2:7).

Paradox (from Gk), an event contrary to expectation (in the LXX*, Philo*, Josephus*); in philosophy, a crisis in logic. Twenty-six hundred years ago, the Greeks discovered the "liar's paradox": if a sentence like "I always lie" is true, then it is false; if it is false, then it is true. For atheists, claims about God are meaningless, not paradoxical. For Christians, paradoxes abound; they are the very stuff of faith*. Although rare in the NT, the word "paradox" designates Jesus' healings and words of forgiveness (Luke 5:26). For Barth* (about Rom 1:1), "The call to be an apostle is a paradoxical occurrence, lying always beyond one's personal self-identity." **See also METAPHOR; MYSTERY.** VOLNEY P. GAY

Paraguay. Christianity arrived in the 16th c., with the European conquest. The territory was occupied by peoples of different ethnic groups, especially the agrarian Guarani. The Roman Catholic Church and its religious orders, especially the Jesuits*, evangelized the natives and established an original system of reductions*.

During the colonial period, church and state were associated through the patronage system (see Patronato, Padroado), which superimposed religious and civil powers and subordinated the native population in quasi-slavery for forced labor. The native peoples instigated several unsuccessful rebellions, which often took religious forms, proclaiming the arrival of a liberating messiah.

After the period of colonization and a bloody war against Argentina*, Brazil*, and Uruguay* (1865–70) that decimated the local population, the Paraguayan state first organized itself independently of the Church. The Liberal governments promulgated laws establishing civil marriage and secular education (1903) and instigated an openness toward modernizing currents. During the late 19th c., Protestantism arrived with European immigrants; the Methodist Church (1886) and Lutheran Church (1893) were the first Protestants established in Paraguay.

Christianity in Paraguay, primarily Roman Catholic, was not highly institutionalized. It was only after 1940 that the Roman Catholic Church developed a larger clergy, founded Catholic* Action (1932), and established the Episcopal Conference (1955), Caritas (1958), and a Catholic university (1960). Following the Second Vatican* Council and the church renewal, headed in Paraguay by Bishop Bogarín Araña, conflicts with the government began. The Church defended human* rights and liberties, and resisted the dictatorship of Alfredo Stroessner (1954–89). The problem of the land* (colonization having deprived most people of access to the land that they needed to feed their families) is at the center of the reflection and practice of the churches, led by groups of lay Catholics who support the agricultural associations, which the dictatorship violently repressed (1976). At present, 300 religious institutions are registered with the Paraguayan state, yet the population remains primarily Roman Catholic.

Statistics: Population (2000): 5.5 million (M). Christians, 5.3 M, 97.7% (Roman Catholics, 4.9 M, 89%; Protestants, 0.2 M, 4%; independents [including Pentecostals/Charismatics], 0.1 M, 2%); nonreligious, 1.3%; native religionists, 0.6%. (Based on *World Christian Encyclopedia*, 2001.)

VERÓNICA GIMÉNEZ BELIVEAU and DAMIÁN SETTON

Parham, Charles F. See ASSEMBLIES OF GOD.

Parish (Gk *paroikia*), since the 5th c., a geographic subdivision of a diocese*, served by at least one priest*. The parish became a focus of community life, a repository of records of baptisms, marriages, and funerals; it had a role in civil government and assumed pastoral responsibility for all persons living in the area. Roman Catholic, Eastern Orthodox, Anglican, and European Protestant churches continue to be organized by geographic parishes. Even in these areas, this mode of organization is being replaced by congregations as "voluntary associations," which are typical of North American Protestantism (see Church, Concepts and Life, Cluster: In North America) and, globally, of independent* churches. One attends the congregation that seems most compatible with one's needs and inclinations.

Parousia (Gk "presence," "arrival"), Christ's return in glory to judge the living and the dead (1 Thess 2:19, 3:13, 4:13–5:23; 1 Cor 15:23; Matt 24:3, 27–39).

Particular Baptists, members of an early Baptist movement (see Baptist Churches Cluster) formed in the 1630s in London under the leadership of John Spilsbury with a commitment to Calvinist* theology centered on total depravity, election*, predestination*, and Christ's atoning death for the elect alone – hence the name "Particular" Baptists. Following revivals (18th c.) initiated in England by Andrew Fuller, Robert Hall, and William Carey, they founded the English Baptist Missionary Society (1792). Particular Baptists joined New Connection General Baptists to form the Baptist Union of Great Britain and Ireland (1891); their position was adopted by mainstream Baptist movements (contrast with Free Will Baptists).

Pascal, Blaise (1623–62), French mathematician, scientist, religious polemicist, apologist; most celebrated as the author of the *Provincial Letters* (January 1656–June 1657) and the *Pensées* (published posthumously, 1670). He was converted (1646) by two Jansenist* brothers who were tending to the broken hip of his father, Étienne. Three years after his sister, Jacqueline, entered the Port-Royal* convent, he underwent a definitive "second conversion," on November 23, 1654, which he recorded in a document known as the "Memorial," which he kept sewn into his clothing for the remainder of his life.

Through the *Provincial Letters*, a series of pamphlets, he defended the leading Jansenist* theologian, Antoine Arnauld*, based at Port Royal*, against the accusations of the Jesuits*. Pascal's vivid style, satirical depiction of the Jesuits, and clarification (or indeed simplification) of complex theological issues, such as sufficient and efficacious grace*, opened the debate to a wider secular public, which followed the increasingly bitter conflict with interest.

During the final years of his short life, Pascal drew on his earlier experience in worldly and scientific circles by writing a defense of the need for the Christian religion addressed to various skeptics and nonbelievers: the text, comprising a series of short fragments and longer passages and left in a disorderly state at his death, is now known as the *Pensées*. Perhaps the most well known and influential passage is that commonly called "Pascal's Wager," in which the reader is engaged in a debate on the odds of winning or losing if one wagers on the existence of God. In its analysis of free* will* and commitment, the "Wager" is perceived by many to foreshadow 20th c. existentialist* thought.

Strongly influenced by Augustine*, Pascal's portrait of the human condition in a world without God uncovers the absurdities of a life led without spiritual purpose. In key passages such as that known as the "Disproportion of Man," he draws on recent scientific discoveries (like the invention of the telescope and microscope) to demonstrate the inconstant and fluctuating state of humanity in the wider universe. Two thinkers who played a large part in Pascal's writing are Michel de Montaigne and René Descartes*. While Pascal made positive use of Montaigne's skepticism by placing uncertainty and doubt* at the core of his attempts to persuade a skeptical reader, he reacted against Descartes's belief in the primacy of reason to comprehend God. For Pascal, although reason signals human greatness, the heart (or intuition) must play the central role in matters of faith. **See also** APOPHATICISM; HETERONOMY; MYSTICISM, MYSTICS.

NICHOLAS HAMMOND

Pasch (Gk and Lat *pascha*; from Heb *pesach*), Jewish Passover* and Christian Easter* (cf. French, *Pâque*; Spanish, *Pascua*).

Paschal Candle, candle lit during the paschal vigil and remaining lit until the day of the Ascension* or the eve* of Pentecost*.

Paschal Controversies. See CALENDARS; EASTER.

Paschal Vigil, principal early church Easter* observance, celebrating Christ's dying and rising, from Saturday night to Sunday morning, when baptisms were administered.

Paschasius Radbertus (c790–c860), Carolingian* theologian, author of the treatise *On the Body and Blood of Christ* (831/33, revised 844), asserted the real presence* of Christ's flesh and blood in the Eucharist*, although he also called it a spiritual presence.

Passion (Lat "suffering"), the suffering* of Christ in Gethsemane, his trial*, suffering and death on the cross*, viewed as atonement* for human sin*.

Passion Play, a mystery* play traditionally performed during Lent that dramatically depicts the Passion*. First performed during the Middle Ages, especially in Roman Catholic Western Europe (the most famous being the Oberammergau Passion Play in Bavaria), Passion plays are still regularly performed all over the world in "Roman Catholic countries," including the Philippines* and Brazil*. There are movie versions of the Passion, e.g. Mel Gibson's *The Passion of the Christ* (2004). Unfortunately, Passion plays commonly convey anti*-Jewish messages and are often associated with anti*-Semitism.

Passions (Music). Passion narratives were at first chanted in a monotone with simple inflections by the single voice of the deacon* during Holy Week. Later chant forms distinguished the speech of different people by different pitches: the evangelist, tenor range; Jesus, bass range; and other "speakers," higher "discant" (or "descant") range. By the 15th c., these different pitches were assigned to different singers. From the 16th c., both Roman Catholic and Lutheran composers developed the Passion into a distinctive musical form of vocal, choral, and instrumental elements for Holy Week worship, culminating in J. S. Bach's* *St. John Passion* and *St. Matthew Passion*. Later, the Passion took the form of oratorios* performed outside of worship, though often within church buildings.

ROBIN A. LEAVER

Passover (= Pasch), Jewish spring festival celebrating the Exodus*, liberation* from bondage in Egypt, indirectly associated with the covenant*. The same term was applied to Christ's death and resurrection (cf. 1 Cor 5:7), which according to the Gospels occurred during the period of Passover (although the Synoptic* Gospels and John* presuppose slightly different calendars), and to the annual observance of these events (see Easter). **See also** LEAVEN.

Pastor (Lat "shepherd"). Leaders in the early church were often called shepherds (Acts 20:28; Eph 4:11; 1 Pet 5:2; Rev 2:27, 7:17, 12:5, 19:15). "Pastor" came to be a title emphasizing the watching, guiding, and healing role of bishops, priests, and ministers – their care* of souls. The pastoral role ideally follows the model of Jesus, the good shepherd (John 10:1–18), yet it can become authoritarian and patriarchal*. "Pastor" is the title commonly used in many parts of the world to designate Protestant clergy, as distinguished from Roman Catholic priests.

Pastoral Care refers to practices of guiding, healing, reconciling, sustaining, and liberating (Lartey's categories). While the God in whose name these practices are performed is confessed as one, the practices themselves are many.

1. Guiding. A thread running through the many practices of guidance is the leading of persons to righteousness* before God and within the church and the world. In all churches, this pastoral function has been closely linked to practices of the ordained office (e.g. the counsel of the *staretz* for Orthodox Christians; the office of *Seelsorger* [carer of souls] in Lutheranism). However, laity have provided these kinds of pastoral care. For example, several saints* and theologians whose sayings and writings guide Orthodox Christians were laypersons. Among Christians throughout much of West and Central Africa, the advice of nonordained elders* is frequently sought after. The pastoral formation that Susanna Wesley* gave to her son, John, exemplifies how one family member can guide another.

2. Healing. From the casting out of demons by disciples and the placing of hands on the sick by early church elders to today's medical ministries and charismatic* expulsion of illness and demons, the church has engaged in a great, and sometimes bewildering, variety of healing* practices. These practices are invariably shaped by context and culture; e.g. some Korean Christians have incorporated Shamanistic* practices into their ministries for the mentally ill; some South African churches have blended local and Christian practices of healing; Orthodox Christians have sought spiritual healing through secular physicians who as devoted Christians performed pastoral roles, such as St. Pantelemion. In many churches, these practices are linked to sacramental functions such as anointing* the sick among Roman Catholics, liturgies for healing among many Protestant and Orthodox communities, and revival preaching (e.g. that of the German Pietist Johann C. Blumhardt*).

3. Reconciling. Reconciliation* involves the setting right of broken relationships with God, other believers, and creation. Reconciling practices have involved various kinds of discipline* for and penance* by those adjudged responsible for those breaks. Adherence in various denominations to prescribed practices such as those detailed in early medieval manuals of penance have been matched by the careful use by many denominations of the Gospel of Matthew* as an authoritative penitential manual. In some churches, reconciliation is practiced as a sacrament* with individual and corporate rites. Throughout history certain disciplinary practices have taken on demonic* form and, consequently, have been rejected by later practitioners (e.g. the detailed prescriptions for the torture of suspected witches* in the 1486 *Malleus Maleficarum* [Witches' hammer]; Luther's* letters calling for the persecution of German Jews as a "severe mercy" to drive some of them to convert).

4. Sustaining. These practices aim to console and strengthen the spirits of those beset by turmoil within and misfortunes without. In their letters of consolation to those facing illness and death, Ambrose* and Chrysostom* provided literary templates that have been adopted and adapted throughout history. Sermons to persecuted congregations (e.g. by Martin Luther King*, Jr., and Desmond Tutu) have enabled them to endure, while sermons addressed to grieving congregations (e.g. by Jeremy Taylor [1613–67] and Richard Baxter* [1615–91]) have enabled them to hope*. Sacramental practices of Communion*, penance, and the anointing of the sick proffer solace, while commonplace ministries of both priests* and the priesthood* of all believers provide life-giving sustenance. Nevertheless, some of these practices have served as tools for political oppressors to dissuade the faithful from taking action against external misfortunes (cf. Liston Pope, *Millhands and Preachers*, 1942; W. E. B. DuBois, *The Souls of Black Folk*, 1903).

5. Liberating. Setting captives free from addictions within and oppression* without has been a prominent pastoral practice. In many churches, the pastoral teachings of the ordained have informed these practices (e.g. Roman Catholic social* encyclicals influenced many social ministries such as that of the Catholic Worker Movement in the 1900s). Furthermore, many routine pastoral practices, such as healing rituals within African Charismatic/Pentecostal churches, aim to liberate believers from oppressive political forces. Liberating practices have frequently placed their practitioners at odds with secular and even ecclesial authorities, as evidenced by the struggles of Bartolomé de las* Casas (1484–1566) to defend the rights of indigenous Americans. Nevertheless, prophetic pastoral practices have often endured opposition by those authorities and sometimes crossed confessional boundaries, as exhibited by the inspiration that the ministry of Las Casas provided to Ann Davison (1783–1871) before the US Civil War for her dissent from prevailing Southern Reformed pro-slavery theologians and church leaders.

Many finite, and therefore fallible, practices are the means by which the faithful seek to care for other Christians and the world. While any one of them may, in fact, fail to provide care, many of them may be acknowledged to represent the care of the one God for the faithful and the world. **See also DISABILITY AND CHRISTIANITY.** LEONARD M. HUMMEL

Pastoral Epistles, 1 and 2 Timothy and Titus, Deutero-Pauline letters, written c100 in Asia Minor, that emphasize the patriarchal household*, the danger of heresies*, and ecclesiastical authority. Traditionally, and in contemporary fundamentalist* readings, they were and still are used to marginalize women and discredit those who think differently from those in authority, without considering socioeconomic, cultural, or internal problems in Christian communities. The Pastoral Epistles were directed to churches in Asia Minor undergoing internal conflicts of class (1 Tim 2:9, 6:10, 17) and gender (1 Tim 2:9–15; 5:3–16; 2 Tim. 3:6–7), theological disputes (1 Tim 1:3, 4; 4:1–4; 2 Tim 2:14–26; Titus 1:10–14; 2:1–3), and power struggles (1 Tim 5:17–25). The author considered rich women, benefactors who taught in the churches, to be domineering women (1 Tim 2:9b–12) who imposed themselves on the congregation, were attracted by Gnostic*-leaning Judeo-Hellenistic teachings (1 Tim 6:20), and deprecated marriage* (1 Tim 4:3). Their teachings were considered dangerous because, by undermining the importance of marriage, they freed women and slaves (1 Tim 6:1–2; Titus 2:9–10) from conforming to household norms very similar to those upheld by the governing and aristocratic class throughout the Roman Empire. The author combated primarily the influence that his opponents' theology had on behavior, especially on that of women and slaves, but in the process presented (e.g. in 1 Tim 2:15; 4:16) a soteriology* contradicting what Paul* said about grace* in his own letters. The author worried that the free behavior of women and slaves exacerbated the hostility of Roman society and hindered the church's mission. To resolve the conflicts, the author's theology tied salvation* to moral instruction, affirmed the Aristotelian domestic codes (see Household codes), and imposed them on the church and its members (1 Tim 3:4–5, 15). The requirements for church leadership (1 Tim 3:1–13; Titus 1:5–9) reflect a move toward a rigid authoritarian church structure. These Pastoral Epistles reflect the church struggles of their time and propose solutions that must be carefully assessed before being applied to other times and contexts. ELSA TAMEZ

Pastoral Theology, branch of theology concerned with, and informed by, the care of God's people. "Pastoral" refers to the biblical image of shepherding. Pastoral theology focuses on the human condition and the shaping of a Christian response to human living and human suffering*. It has several overlapping meanings:

1. In its most general, and earliest, sense (also called "practical" theology; still understood as such in Roman Catholic and some Anglican contexts), the study of texts and methods underpinning the practice of ministry, beginning with patristic* treatises on the "cure of souls" and continuing through the 19th c.
2. The 20th-c. fields of psychology* and religion, as well as pastoral counseling/psychotherapy. Anton Boisen's refocusing of pastoral theology from the study of texts to "living human documents" coincided with an understanding of human suffering* through modern psychology and innovations in clinical and therapeutic methods. North Americans Seward Hiltner, William Clebsch, and Charles Jaekle articulated the "traditional functions of pastoral* care" as "healing, sustaining, guiding, and reconciling*," to which Carroll Watkins Ali recently added "nurturing, liberating*, and empowering." German writers integrated client-centered psychology with theology, except for neo-orthodox* pastoral theologians, who retained primacy for proclamation. British writers alternately integrated object-relations theory with Anglican sacramental theology or invoked premodern spiritual sources such as ascetical* theology and the practice of spiritual direction. While the degree to which 20th-c. pastoral theology engaged in biblical and theological reflection has varied, it is defined by its interaction with psychological theory and practice. This trajectory continues in the exploration of pastoral care and neuroscience.
3. In response to a critique that the pastoral discipline had neglected its authoritative theological voice in favor of secular psychological paradigms, pastoral theology in the 21st c. represents a movement to reengage in constructive theological work. Adopting "correlational" approaches beginning with Paul Tillich*, and revaluing experience as the ground of theology from Feminist*, Womanist*, Mujerista*, and

Black* theology, as well as Third World or global contextual* theologies, contemporary pastoral theologians affirm that *all* theology must begin with the human situation. Don Browning advocated reclaiming the authority of ethical* norms in pastoral and practical theology. Feminist proposals such as Bonnie Miller-McLemore's "living human web," Emmanuel Lartey's community-based intercultural models, and other writings at the intersection of pastoral and public theology, exemplify the shift of pastoral theology from individualistic to communal, justice*-oriented, and global approaches. Engagements with postmodernism* and social constructivism represent further avenues for pastoral theology as a constructive, interdisciplinary enterprise. PAMELA COOPER-WHITE

Patriarch, in Roman Catholicism, the title of a bishop who has the authority to ordain metropolitans*; in the Eastern Orthodox* Church, the title of the head of an autocephalous* church. **See also** ECUMENICAL PATRIARCHATE OF CONSTANTINOPLE.

Patriarchy and Christianity. Patriarchy refers to a legal, social, economic, cultural, and political system that validates and enforces the sovereignty of male heads of families over dependent persons in the household: wives, unmarried daughters, and dependent sons and slaves, male and female. In Roman law, the term *familia* referred to all persons and things ruled by the *paterfamilias,* including animals and land. Patriarchy as a social system has been found in classical societies around the world.

The status of women in patriarchal societies has many nuances, depending on how their physical protection and property deriving from their families of origin are related to their position in their husband's family. Although one cannot define a single social pattern true of all patriarchal societies at all times, there are general characteristics common to most patriarchal systems. Women's status under patriarchy is one of subjugation; they have no legal status in their own right. The lineage of children is passed down through the father. Male children are preferred to female children. The bodies, sexuality, and reproductive capacity of wives belong to their husbands. The sovereignty of the husband over the wife includes the right to beat her, to confine her physically, and sometimes to sell her into bondage. Women are excluded from public leadership roles in politics and culture. Their education is limited to household skills and minimal literacy. Their right to inherit as daughters or widows is restricted; what property they do inherit is usually administered by a male relative or guardian.

These patterns of patriarchy were reconfirmed in early modern European law codes and continued to define women in Europe and the Americas until the Feminist Movement of the late 19th and first half of the 20th c. The Feminist Movement in various societies has succeeded in winning for women the legal status of citizens, with the rights to vote, hold political office, make property transactions in their own name, and have access to higher education, professional credentials, and employment. Many remnants of patriarchy remain, however, in modern societies. Women are still seen as the primary household workers and child raisers. Cultural norms and legal restrictions continue to limit women's economic, political, and social equality and to ratify the view that women are subordinate to men as a gender group, a subordination interconnected with class and racial inferiority.

Christianity, like other classical religions, has been deeply influenced by patriarchy and has also functioned to ratify it as normal, natural, and the will of God. Religious validation of patriarchy is expressed on both the symbolic and the structural levels. The churches have traditionally been organized along patriarchal lines, with an exclusively male clergy as the ruling class. A hierarchy of patriarch or pope, bishops, priests, and laymen rules the church from the top, with laywomen and children as the most subordinate group. Women are excluded from ordination, public preaching, and public teaching; teaching is allowed only in private or with children. In Western cultures, this pattern gradually began to change in the 20th c. with the ordination of women (see Women's Ordination Cluster), but the Orthodox, Roman Catholic, and conservative Protestant churches still cling to it.

On a symbolic level, God is pictured as a patriarchal father and lord, ruling over humanity and creation. The patriarchal hierarchies of male over female, father over children, and lord over slaves* is reduplicated symbolically in the relation of God and Christ to the church as Father to Son, lord to servants, and husband to wife. The idea of Christ as head of the church as his body (Eph 4:15–16, 5:23–30; Col 1:18, 3:15–22) reduplicates the legal view of the wife's lack of autonomy* and her belonging, as a body*, to her

husband. **See also** **ANDROCENTRISM; KYRIARCHY; SEXISM AND CHRISTIANITY.**
ROSEMARY RADFORD RUETHER

Patrick (5th c.), British missionary, bishop, patron saint of Ireland; dates unknown (perhaps died 493). Born to a British landowning family and enslaved by Irish raiders at the age of 16, he escaped back to Britain after six years. He then returned to Ireland as a missionary, rising eventually to the rank of bishop. Some conflation of Patrick and Palladius* (sent from Rome in 431) has arguably occurred. Patrick's "Confession" and "Letter to Coroticus" survive but are difficult to interpret, although both suggest a highly controversial figure. The later hagiographical works on Patrick by Muirchu and Tirechan developed the legend and cult. NICHOLAS J. HIGHAM

Patripassianism, a form of Monarchianism*, also known as Sabellianism*, which held that the Trinity is only different modes of divine action, so that the Father also suffered as the Son.

Patristics, study of the "fathers," now also "mothers," of the church, after the "apostolic age." The period beginning in the 2nd c. was devoted to interpreting the apostolic message in the midst of Greco-Roman culture*, a culture originally hostile to Christianity that nevertheless contributed many of the concepts used in doctrine and canon law and that, during the 4th c., came to be dominated by Christianity (see Inculturation Cluster: Of Christianity in the Greco-Roman World). The "patristic era" includes the apostolic* fathers, the Apologists*, the debates over the doctrines of the Trinity* and Christology*, and the Pelagian* controversy. It is often viewed as the *formative* period for Christian doctrine, worship, and institutions, viewed as authoritative by later times.

When does it end? Possibly with the Islamic Conquest (634–41). For the Miaphysite*, Oriental Orthodox* churches, it ends with the third ecumenical* council at Ephesus* (431) and the separation from the Eastern Orthodox churches (451). For the Eastern Orthodox churches, the formative period is that of the seven ecumenical* councils (the last of which was in 787). For many Protestants, it ends with the Council of Chalcedon* (451). In the Western churches, in which the predominance of Greco-Roman culture is taken as its defining characteristic, it ends with the decline of vernacular Latin (6th c.). EUGENE TESELLE

Patristic Thought. Traditionally the term refers primarily to the contribution of the authoritative church leaders, the "church fathers" (Lat *patres*), to the development of Christian doctrine. More broadly, patristic thought embraces the entire literary output of Christian theological writers of the first millennium, including apologetic, exegetical, doctrinal, polemical, moral, ascetical, pastoral, homiletic, epistolary, and historical works.

Before the Edict of Milan (313), Christians in the Roman Empire were often persecuted by the state. The Apologists*, such as Aristides, Justin*, Tatian*, Athenagoras, Theophilus*, Minucius Felix, Tertullian*, Clement*, and Origen* of Alexandria, challenged the pagan worldview and defended Christianity against popular misconceptions and philosophical objections. The polemic against Judaism*, the struggle of orthodoxy* against heresy*, and the protection of church unity against schism all contributed to the formation of Christian identity and the development of doctrine. During this period, liturgical* practice and theology*, biblical canon* and methods of biblical exegesis*, as well as early creeds* began to take shape.

Under the patronage of Emperor Constantine* (d337), Christianity underwent considerable sociopolitical transformation. From the religion of a persecuted minority, Christianity was transformed into a religion of political establishment; worship acquired more public character; the social standing of the clergy increased significantly; and mass conversions became common. Local and ecumenical church councils* became major vehicles for dealing with controversial doctrinal and practical issues. The Council of Nicaea* (325) addressed the Arian* crisis by promulgating the creed stating that the Son of God was equal, or "of the same essence" (*homoousios**), with God the Father. The second ecumenical council endorsed the teaching of the Cappadocian* Fathers (Basil* of Caesarea, Gregory* of Nazianzus, Gregory* of Nyssa) regarding the Trinity* and affirmed the Son's full humanity. The Council of Ephesus (431) was summoned in response to the Nestorian* controversy and acknowledged Mary* as the God-bearer (Theotokos*). Faced with the Miaphysite*/Monophysite* controversy, the fathers of the council of Chalcedon* (451) issued a definition affirming that Christ was one person in two natures. The fifth ecumenical council (Constantinople* II, 553) returned to the emphasis of Ephesus on the unity of Christ's person. The sixth ecumenical council (Constantinople* III, 680–81), following Chalcedon, emphasized the distinction of two natures in

Christ by affirming the doctrine of two wills*. The seventh ecumenical council (Nicaea* II, 787) upheld the theological legitimacy of the veneration of religious images (icons*).

PAVEL L. GAVRILYUK

Patristic Thought in Orthodox Christianity is explicated in the writings of Athanasius*, John* Chrysostom, Basil* of Caesarea, Gregory* of Nazianzus, and Gregory* of Nyssa in response to the Arian* and Eunomian* controversies.

"It is not for all to theologize," says Gregory* of Nazianzus, but only for the pure of heart who are masters of meditation and prayer. Personal experience of the Triune God is the basis for theology, but only within the context of the church and its traditions of dogma and worship.

Holy Scripture*, the divinely inspired guide to the spiritual life, is authoritative in all its details but is revelation "through a glass darkly." Unable to describe God's essence, it reveals the divine energies. The deeper teachings of Scripture are sometimes beneath the mere letter, which in its plainest sense can at times be unworthy of God (e.g. allusions to God's "wrath*" or "repentance"). Rationalistic speculations about God are an impiety; still, in pagan culture and philosophy, discerning Christians can find some spiritual profit (see God, Christian Views of, Cluster: Introductory Entries).

In Orthodox patristic thought, Truth is ultimately not an idea but the person of the incarnate* Word*. Christology* and soteriology* are inextricably connected. The church, as an outgrowth of the Incarnation, communicates Truth to all creation. Its teachings, mysteries*, canons, and liturgy are viewed chiefly in therapeutic terms: salvation* is the healing of fallen humanity, the restoration* of God's likeness through union with the divine energies. **See also** BIBLE INTERPRETATION CLUSTER: IN EASTERN ORTHODOXY; FLOROVSKY, GEORGES.

B. MARK SIETSEMA

Patronage, the authority to nominate or "present" persons for ecclesiastical office. This authority of feudal* lords was questioned during the investiture* controversy. After the Reformation, when ministers were to be called by congregations in an egalitarian way, patronage (pejoratively called "intrusion") was exercised by rich landowners (the chief source of financial support for ministers) who imposed ministers on congregations. In Scotland, patronage disputes led to the Disruption* of 1843, a schism from the Church of Scotland. **See also** ADVOWSON.

Patronato, Padroado. Through the policy of royal patronage – Patronato Real (Spanish) or Padroado Régio (Portuguese) – the Roman Catholic Church granted sovereignty over newly discovered lands to the Roman Catholic monarchs of Portugal* and Spain*. A series of papal bulls (15th–16th c.) authorized Iberian kings and queens to conquer lands not already under Christian rule, charged them with evangelizing the inhabitants of these newly conquered territories, and ultimately ceded to the monarchs administrative control over the colonial Church. The unprecedented intermingling of papal authority and secular, royal power institutionalized in the Patronato formed the basis for the Iberian colonial project in Africa, Asia, and Latin America (see Portuguese Explorations, Conquests, and Missions; Spanish Explorations, Conquests, and Missions).

The rights and responsibilities encompassed by the system of royal patronage were extended gradually and incrementally, first to the Portuguese in the mid-15th c. as a result of their exploration of the coast of Africa. After Columbus's discovery (1492), Spain pushed for and won rights to the Indies, granted by the papal bull *Inter Caetera* (1493), which ceded to Spain the greater part of the Americas. The Treaty of Tordesillas (1494) created a line of demarcation affirming Portugal's right to lands to the east of the dividing line (i.e. Africa and India) and effectively extending to them a large portion of the east coast of South America (later Brazil).

The Spanish monarchs had achieved almost complete authority over the local Church in the New World when Rome, daunted by the task of evangelization and colonial administration, issued another series of bulls (early 16th c.). These relinquished Church tithes to the crown, granted the monarchs the right to build and fund churches and cathedrals, and, finally, allowed the king and queen to nominate bishops and archbishops. The Patronato was administered by the Council of the Indies in Spain and by the *audiencia* judicial system in the Americas.

JENNIFER S. HUGHES

Patron Saint, saint who is considered the special protector or advocate of a person, place, ethnic group, nation, or occupation.

Paul, Acts of. See APOCRYPHA CLUSTER: APOCRYPHAL ACTS OF APOSTLES.

Paula (347–404). As a widow*, she was guided in celibacy* by Jerome* and founded monasteries* in Bethlehem (386), where she died.

Born in Rome to a noble family, Paula married and had five children. After her husband's death, she devoted her life to asceticism* under the direction of the famed ascetic Jerome. As part of a group of Roman noblewomen, Paula studied Scripture with Jerome, excelling especially in Hebrew. With her daughter Eustochium*, Paula followed Jerome to Palestine, where she toured the holy sites, then visited Egyptian monks. She settled in Bethlehem, where she founded two monasteries – one for men and another for women – and built a hospice for pilgrims.

According to Jerome (*Epistle* 108), Paula was the perfect model of female asceticism. She spent her fortune to support ascetics, bishops, and the poor. She lived a humble and disciplined life, adopting simple clothing, practicing rigorous fasting, studying Scripture*, and lamenting the slightest sin with voluminous tears. She was praised for her ascetic leadership, guiding the women in her monastery in equally strict lifestyles until her death.

KRISTI UPSON-SAIA

Paul the Apostle, a highly influential figure in 1st-c. Christianity and throughout church history, and a bold missionary who opened the church to the "nations," Paul has been criticized by some as a dangerous innovator (cf. 2 Pet 3:15–16) and a divisive church leader, evoking passionate opposition but also, for many, deep-seated loyalty. This ambivalence derives from the fact that there were at least five distinct "Pauls." While there are fundamental disagreements about what Paul taught, there is a general agreement regarding his life.

Paul's Life. Paul was a Jew of the tribe of Benjamin (Phil 3:5), a Pharisee raised in Tarsus (Acts 21:39) with a solid Hellenistic and Jewish education, who zealously persecuted the church (Gal 1:13–14; Phil 3:5–6). Paul was "converted" c33/34 (Gal 1:15–16; Phil 3:7–9; 1 Cor 9:1, 15:8–11). "After fourteen years" (Gal 2:1) of mission work with Barnabas in Syria and Cilicia (Gal 1:21) and independently in Macedonia and Achaia (Corinth) (c39–c51, when he wrote 1 Thessalonians*), Paul went to the "Jerusalem conference" (c51), where he agreed with James, Cephas/Peter, and John (Gal 2:1–10 = Acts 18:22) that the mission could have two thrusts: one to the Jews/Judeans (led by Peter) and one to the nations/Gentiles* (led by Paul and Barnabas), and that the churches from the nations would support the "poor of Jerusalem." Should Gentile Christians become Jews and practice circumcision and eat kosher? This undecided issue came to a head in Antioch, where Paul confronted Peter about his ambivalent attitude (Gal 2:11–14). Barnabas and other Jewish Christians separated from Paul, who nevertheless remained confident that Gentile* and Jewish Christians could work together. Accordingly, during his subsequent missions in Asia Minor and Greece (c51–c56, when he wrote the rest of his letters), Paul gathered a collection for the church in Jerusalem that he brought to Jerusalem (c56/57; Rom 15:25–28), where he was arrested; he was then imprisoned in Caesarea (c57–59; Acts 23–24) and Rome (c61; Acts 28:16). Later traditions (Clement* of Rome, Ignatius* of Antioch, Acts* of Paul) suggest that he died a martyr in Rome (c62).

The positive and negative responses to Paul reflect different interpretations and assessments of his bold views regarding (1) the "gospel* of Jesus Christ" (instead of "the gospel of the Kingdom*" that Jesus proclaimed); (2) the human predicament addressed by God according to this good news; (3) the church* and the place of Jews and Gentiles/nations in it. One should distinguish the distinctive portrayals of Paul by Luke* and "Paul's school" (in the Deutero-Pauline* letters), as they sought to defend him against early opponents, from the self-portrayal of Paul in the undisputed letters, although biblical scholars propose three different "historical Pauls."

Paul and His Early Interpreters

Paul 1: The hero of the Acts of Apostles, according to Luke. Against those who distrusted Paul's gospel and apostleship, Luke portrayed Paul as an apostle* (14:1–4), a witness (22:15, 26:16), a "chosen instrument" (9:15; Jer 1:5), and "light of the Gentiles" (13:47; like Jesus, Luke 2:32; cf. Isa 49:6). For Luke the predicament addressed by the gospel was that Gentiles were unduly excluded from the people of God by "the Jews." Through Paul's gospel, they were now included. Luke emphasized Paul's "road to Damascus experience," presenting it three times. In Acts 9:1–31 this event can be viewed as a "conversion from Judaism" (and thus as a rupture with Judaism posited as an erroneous religion); in Acts 22:6–21 and 26:1–32 it is not the case. Luke presents this event as a *prophetic call* to go "for the sake of the hope of Israel" (28:20) and preach to Gentiles (22:21, 26:17–18) the fulfillment of Jewish messianic and resurrection expectations (22:3–4, 23:6, 24:14–21, 26:4–11).

Paul seeks to include "the Jews" in the church, but with limited success. He consistently begins his mission in local synagogues, turning to Gentiles after "the Jews" reject his inclusive proclamation (Acts describes Paul in conflict with "the Jews" some 70 times).

Paul 2: The orthodox teacher according to his school. Followers of Paul wrote the Deutero-Pauline letters in the name of their teacher (an appropriate practice in the culture): Ephesians*, Colossians*, the Pastoral* Epistles (1 and 2 Timothy, Titus) (and possibly 2 Thessalonians*). They present Paul's gospel as an "orthodoxy" by emphasizing adherence to the proper doctrine (Eph 1:3–14; Col 1:15–23) revealed by God through Christ. Erroneous beliefs, including deviant teachings of heretics* (e.g. Eph 4:25; Col 2:16–23; 1 Tim 1:3–11, 4:1–5, 6:3–10), are the predicament. Church members are those who hold orthodox beliefs; life in Christ involves rejecting pagan ways of life (e.g. Eph 5:3–20), but also conforming to the order of life in Roman imperial society reflected in the household* codes (Eph 5:21–6:9; Col 3.18–4:1; 1 Tim 2:8–3:13; Titus 2:1–10), which normalize the submission of women to men and of slaves to their masters as integral parts of the Christian way of life.

Paul and His Modern Interpreters. In their quest for the "historical Paul," modern scholars focused on the undisputed letters – Romans*, 1 and 2 Corinthians*, Galatians*, Philippians*, 1 Thessalonians*, and Philemon*. This quest yielded three different "Pauls," which can be called "Paul the Theologian" (with variants of it found, at least since Augustine*, in the Roman Catholic Church, Luther*, and Protestantism*), "the pastoral Paul" (with similarities with the Paul of Acts), and "the apocalyptic/messianic Paul" (variants found in the Greek fathers, Orthodox* and Charismatic* churches, and Liberation* theology), each with distinctive views of the gospel, the predicament it addresses, and the church and the place of Jews and Gentiles in it.

Paul 3: The theologian proclaiming justification through faith. Here Paul's gospel is understood to address theological problems arising in different church contexts, by providing the proper theological understanding that characterizes the true faith (see Faith #3; Augustine's* *fides quae creditur*). This first "historical Paul" is elucidated through philological* studies of the theological arguments of Paul's letters. The gospel addresses the question: How are sinners (all humans) saved from God's just condemnation? Pharisaic Judaism answered incorrectly: through "work righteousness" (justification* by works of the Law, e.g. Gal 2:21, a view which, for many scholars, shows that Paul had a distorted view of Pharisaism – a distortion that gave rise to anti-Judaism). Paul's gospel answers: through faith in Jesus Christ (justification through faith, e.g. Gal 3:8); one is graciously "justified" (forgiven) by faith in God's intervention in Christ's death and resurrection (see Atonement #2). Thus the road to Damascus event is a "conversion" from Pharisaic Judaism; without faith in Jesus Christ, Jews remain under God's condemnation.

Paul 4: The pastor with a ministry to the Gentiles. For the scholars of the "new perspective," Paul's gospel is the good news that through Jesus Christ's faithfulness (death and resurrection), Gentiles are "justified," i.e. "set in a covenantal relation with God" similar to that of the Jews, participating in the covenant* through a faith/faithfulness (see Faith #1) comparable to that of Jesus (see Atonement #3). Paul's letters address a pastoral problem, the tense relationships between Jewish and Gentile Christians, and help the latter assume their responsibilities as part of the people of God. This "new perspective" on the "historical Paul" is elucidated through rhetorical* and socio-historical studies of the letters as discourses through which Paul seeks to convince his readers to change their behavior toward each other. The predicament addressed by Paul's gospel is the exclusion (inflicted by others or self-exclusion) of people (especially Gentiles) from the covenantal relationship with God. Through Christ, believers are reconciled with God and each other and are called to participate in the ministry of the people of God (Jews and Gentiles), namely to bring all peoples to God. The road to Damascus event is a "prophetic call" from God. Jews as Jews remain a part of the people of God (God's call is irrevocable; Rom 11:29), in which they are now joined by Gentiles.

Paul 5: The apocalyptic/messianic apostle. Here the gospel as "power of God for salvation*" (Rom 1:16) is the good news that God's promises have been fulfilled in Jesus the Messiah *and* that the resurrected Lord (and the Spirit) continues to fulfill God's promises in the present; believers, through faith (see Faith #5), can recognize these new powerful interventions of God in their experience. From this third historical perspective, Paul's letters seek to convey this faith to the readers through a religious, apocalyptic* symbolism that scholars elucidate by a combination of history* of religion and ideological and rhetorical* studies of the letters, with close attention to the power relations. The predicament that necessitates these ongoing divine interventions is sin*, a power that keeps all humans (the nations as well as the Jews) and the entire creation in bondage to idols* and powers that enslave them. Through the resurrected Lord's interventions, believers are freed from these powers, redeemed (see Atonement #1; Redemption), and enabled to serve and glorify God. The road to Damascus event is the redemption of Paul from his overzealous Judaism and a "prophetic call" from God to become in turn a Christ-like agent of redemption for others, as in turn all believers are called to be through their own redemption, by remaining where they were, among Jews if they were Jews and among the nations if they were Gentiles.

Each of these views of Paul and his teaching is historically plausible (according to which textual features one selects as most significant). As their appropriations through history show, each has been chosen as the scriptural teaching proclaimed by different theologians, movements, and churches as a Word to live by, for religious and contextual reasons. Yet interpreters have to assume responsibility for their choices of interpretations and how they affect others (see Scriptural Criticism). **See also HELLENISTIC RELIGIOUS TRADITIONS AND CHRISTIANITY'S SELF-DEFINITION; INCULTURATION CLUSTER: OF CHRISTIANITY IN THE GRECO-ROMAN WORLD; MARCION.**

DANIEL PATTE

Paulicians, members of a Christian movement founded by Constantine of Mananalis (Constantine Silvanus) in Kibossa, Armenia* (mid-7th c.), who were severely persecuted by Constantine III, Justinian II, and later emperors. The group suffered from internal strife and schisms over succession throughout most of its history. Under the leadership of Sergius Tychicus (early 9th c.), the Paulicians expanded into Cilicia and Asia Minor; their numbers and influence were greatest until 872, when an expedition sent by Basil I broke their military resistance. Many Paulicians were then forcibly settled in Thrace, where their religion survived until at least the late 11th c. and influenced the Bogomils'* ideas and practices.

The Paulicians' fundamental doctrine – concerning two principles, an evil god who created and rules the present world and a good god who rules the one to come – may have been partly inspired by the dualism* of Marcionism* and Manichaeism*. Yet they based their doctrines and practices on the Gospels, especially Luke, and Paul's epistles, rejecting the epistles of Peter and the OT. They rejected rituals and the sacrament* of the Eucharist* (and, to some extent, baptism*); they refused to worship Mary and did not accept the divinity of Jesus. They emphasized spiritual communion in "prayer houses" and were opposed to traditional church hierarchy.

GUNNER BJERG MIKKELSEN

Pauline Privilege, Paul's concession (1 Cor 7:15) that a married person, upon becoming Christian, might separate from a non-Christian partner (see Divorce).

Paulinus of Nola (355–431), poet, letter writer, bishop; renounced great wealth to adopt an ascetic* life with his wife, Therasia. He was born and educated in Southern France, served as governor of Campania, was ordained in Barcelona, and moved to Nola near Naples, where he founded a monastery at the tomb of St. Felix (395). Committed to the ideal of Christian spiritual friendship*, he was a friend of Martin* of Tours, Ambrose*, Augustine*, Jerome*, Melania* the Elder, and Melania* the Younger, maintaining many friendships by letter, of which about 50 are extant. He also wrote a series of poems, the so-called *Natalicia* (dedicated to Felix), biblical paraphrases, and poems to friends.

CAROLINNE WHITE

Paul of Samosata (3rd c.). Elected bishop of Antioch when Queen Zenobia of Palmyra controlled the city (c260), he also held a governmental position. A letter from six bishops (264) raised questions about his orthodoxy, and a synod (268) deposed him, issuing an encyclical* letter that condemned Paul's mode of life and doctrine. It asserts that Paul denied that the Son of God came down from heaven, making him merely human. The *acta*, the minutes of the synod (held by some to be a 4th-c. forgery), quoted in later christological* controversies, suggest that he was not an Adoptionist*. He asserted that the Word came forth before the ages, in connection with creation, and was even to be called God's "offspring." Yet he avoided using the word "Son" for the preexistent Word, not wanting to speak of "two Sons."

When the synod appointed a new bishop, Paul refused to yield the church properties. After Zenobia's defeat (272), the new bishop appealed to the (pagan) emperor Gallienus, who decreed that the "house of the church" should be given to the group in communion with the bishops of Italy and Rome. This was the church's first appeal to the emperor, and the political overtones, including the appeal to Roman patriotism, are significant. EUGENE TESELLE

Paul VI, Pope (1963–78), born Giovanni Battista Montini (1897) in Concessio, educated at home, ordained (1920); he went to Rome, entered the secretariat of state, and for a few months served in the Warsaw nunciature. He was appointed archbishop* of Milan (1954), a role he filled energetically. The obvious candidate for the papacy in 1958, he was passed over because he was not a cardinal, which John* XXIII rectified almost immediately. Initially suspicious of the Second Vatican* Council, he committed himself to implementing its decrees. He was especially eager for Christian unity – receiving the archbishop of Canterbury (1966) and visiting the patriarch of Constantinople – and made an impassioned plea for peace (1965) before the UN. His important encyclicals* include *Populoroum Progressio* (1967) and *Humanae* Vitae* (1968), his (in)famous decision to ban artificial contraception*.

MICHAEL J. WALSH

Payne, Daniel Alexander (1811–93), bishop of the American Methodist Episcopal Church, educator, historian. The son of free blacks in South Carolina, he opened a school for African American children. When this school was declared illegal, he studied at the Lutheran Theological Seminary (Gettysburg, Pennsylvania) and was ordained in the Lutheran Church (his ordination oration was entitled "Slavery Brutalizes Man," 1839). He joined the African Methodist Episcopal Church (1841), became a bishop (1852), and then the first African American to head a college, as president of Wilberforce University, Ohio (1863–76), where he dedicated himself to the education of African Americans. A historian, he wrote *The History of the A.M.E. Church*. **See also AFRICAN METHODIST EPISCOPAL (AME) CHURCH.** DENNIS C. DICKERSON

Peace Churches. The term has been used to characterize the Church of the Brethren*, the Society of Friends* (Quakers), and the Mennonite* churches, which share a witness against war. In 1935 in a conference in Newton, Kansas, they shared their witness with other Christian bodies and with the US government. Since that time, the group of peace churches has broadened and have met with European churches. **See also PACIFISM AND CHRISTIANITY.**

Peace Movements. Throughout Christian history, there have been three basic views of war*. War as a crusade* or *holy war* was fought under the assumption that it was led by God. The *just war* doctrine (developed 2nd–3rd c.) acknowledged that war was wrong, but that under certain circumstances it could be justified morally; it provided the primary Christian theological justification for war over the centuries (see War, Christian Attitudes toward). In sharp contrast, *Christian pacifism* contends that war is not justifiable by Jesus' teachings or other NT writings; long a part of the monastic tradition, it has been embraced by various Christian peace movements within both Protestant and Catholic churches.

Christian peace theologians emphasize the ethical authority of the NT over the war stories in the OT. Peace advocates argue that Jesus' teaching in the Sermon* on the Mount to love one's enemies, to refrain from retaliation, and to do good to one's opponents is a clear ethical statement that forms the heart of the Christian gospel. They also argue that Jesus' life and nonviolent response to torture on the cross are models for peacemaking. Many Christian pacifists argue that an ethic of nonviolence is the core teaching of the Christian gospel.

Christian peace movements vary considerably in their understanding and expression of pacifism. Some groups, such as the Amish* and Old Order Mennonites*, emphasize a quiet nonresistance and refuse to join the military or to use force in daily life. Catholic and Protestant peace groups support active protests against government policies that endorse violence; some groups engage in civil* disobedience in the name of Christian faith. Christian peace groups typically emphasize the importance of nonviolence in all arenas of life, including family relations, employment, civic life, and entertainment and media, as well as international affairs. They often associate peacemaking with social justice*, arguing that peace is impossible if injustice prevails.

In 1935 three churches, those of the Mennonites, Brethren*, and Quakers*, were recognized as historic peace* churches because of their sustained opposition to war. The Church of the Brethren declared that "all war is sin." At the outset of World War II, the US government recognized the official status of conscientious* objectors and permitted them to serve in alternative service projects that benefited the national good, in lieu of military service. During the Vietnam War, the nuclear arms race of the 1970s and 1980s, the Gulf War of the 1990s, and the Iraq War, numerous Christian peace movements and coalitions have contested Christian support of and participation in war.

DONALD KRAYBILL

Peace and Peacemaking. Throughout history, Roman Catholic, Eastern Orthodox, and Protestant traditions have described peace as a dynamic force of holistic flourishing that inaugurates and sustains harmonious relationships between individuals, communities, and creation, as envisaged by YHWH's covenant* with Israel (e.g. Isa 54:10; Ezek 34:35, 37:26) and later proclaimed in Jesus' announcement of the Reign (Kingdom*) of God (Matt 5). Peace is not a narrowly circumscribed sense of individual equanimity or the mere absence of conflict.

This understanding of peace derives from the Bible, where references to *shalom* in the Psalms (85:7–11) and prophets (Isa 48:18, 60:17), as well as *eirene* in the Gospels (Luke 7:50) and Pauline Epistles (Rom 14:17–19) consistently evince a reciprocal relationship between peace as an aspect of salvation* and peace as requiring a just socioeconomic and political order.

Accordingly, the churches' wider deliberations about the nature and scope of peacemaking included preserving and edifying a greater sense of the common good. Nevertheless, differing approaches to peacemaking have developed. Beginning with Constantine's* conversion to Christianity and the subsequent "Christianization" of the Roman Empire and "Constantinianization" of the church (early 4th c.), churches have often been influenced by ideologies* of crusade*, right of state, and nationalism*. Yet reflection on peacemaking has predominantly focused on pacifism* and the just war* traditions. Both usually contend that peacemaking must include a set of practices to ameliorate and rectify oppressive* societal injustices that create violence*. Furthermore, both acknowledge that violence is a fundamental violation of the holistic flourishing that peace prescribes. However, contrasting hermeneutical strategies (conceptions of eschatology* and of political* responsibility) led pacifists and just war advocates to diverging conclusions on whether it is morally permissible to engage in violence to make peace. Pacifists claim that it is not, while just war traditionalists assert that it is, provided that the prosecution of violence abides by the criteria stipulated in the principles of just war.

More recently the churches' thinking on peacemaking has been influenced by thinkers responding to the threat of nuclear war and of post–cold war crises like global terrorism, intrastate ethnic conflict, mass displacement, and genocide. Christian ethicists (including Yoder, Stassen, Thistlethwaite) have advocated that the church needs a new paradigm to help focus public discussion on *proactive practices* that work for justice* and peacemaking, without supplanting pacifism's and just war's different paradigms regarding the legitimacy of waging war.

As a result, a third paradigm, *just peacemaking*, does not debate whether war is legitimate (its advocates are both pacifists and proponents of just war). Rather, it focuses on proactive practices effective in preventing many wars, with biblical grounding in the passages cited earlier, and also in gospel and Pauline texts where Jesus and Paul articulate transforming initiatives whose moral thrust is proactively to deliver individuals and communities from destructive cycles of hostility and violence.

Just peacemaking translates these biblical transforming initiatives into concrete peacemaking practices: (1) supporting nonviolent direct action; (2) taking independent initiatives to reduce the threat of war*; (3) using cooperative conflict resolution or transformation; (4) publicly acknowledging moral responsibility for injustice and seeking repentance* and forgiveness*; (5) advancing human* rights, religious liberty, and democracy*; (6) fostering just and sustainable economic development; (7) working with cooperative forces in the international system; (8) strengthening the UN and other international political bodies that promote cooperation and human rights; (9) reducing the number of offensive weapons and the international trade of weapons; and (10) encouraging grassroots peacemaking groups and associations.

Just peacemaking seeks to integrate these practices into one multilevel paradigm. Various Christians work on one or more of these, sometimes publicly discussing whether their government, which claims to be seeking peace, is actually doing so. **See also PACIFISM AND CHRISTIANITY; PEACE MOVEMENTS.**

NICHOLAS CANFIELD READ BROWN

Peasants' War (1524–26), German peasants' rebellion. The peasants resisted by two means: localized, spontaneous, and popular revolts appealing to traditional rights and customs; and more organized but far from popular supraregional conspiracies, appealing to "divine law" (*göttliches Recht*). The series of revolts, called the German Peasants' War, resulted from a combustible combination of religious, social, economic, and political factors. The Reformation provided a broader basis to appeal to "divine law." Encouraged by the Reformation doctrine of the priesthood* of all believers, which was interpreted to mean increased social equality, and by Thomas Müntzer's* apocalyptic* visions, the peasants rebelled against the authorities by looting and burning castles and monasteries. About one-third of the German territory, especially Swabia and Thuringia, was affected by mixed groups of serfs, farmers, townspeople, and minor clergy who dictated their grievances in the "Twelve Articles" (Memmingen, March 1525). Among the peasants' demands were the right to appoint their own pastors*; control over tithes*; abolition of serfdom (see Feudal System); rights in matters of fishing, game, and woodcutting; just conditions of work and rent; justice* in the courts; and abolition of *Todfall* ("death duty," a heavy tax on the estate of a serf collected by the lord). The military forces of the Swabian League of Protestant Princes defeated the rebels and ended the movement.

Many of the Reformers were initially sympathetic to the demands of the peasants. But Martin Luther* as well as Melanchthon*, Bucer*, and Zwingli*, declared their allegiance to the civil authorities. Nonetheless, Christoph Schappeler, pastor in Memmingen, helped compose the written demands of the peasants of his area, and he certainly was not the only priest or pastor who, although under Luther's influence, supported the peasants. Meanwhile, Johann Brenz* and Johann Eberlin wrote against pastors in their areas who were urging the peasants to revolt. ESTHER CHUNG-KIM

Pecock, Reginald (c1390–1461), Welsh bishop of St. Asaph and a theologian who trained at Chichester, Oxford, argued that the church should combat heterodoxy with reason, not force. Using Aquinas* and Scotus*, he constructed a vernacular program of Christian education to refute the bibliolatry* of the Lollard* Movement. Because his arguments downplayed ecclesiastical authority in favor of reason, he was forced to recant (1457) and was confined until his death. His *Repressor of Overmuch Blaming of the Clergy* argued that God inscribes the "moral lawe of kinde" in human hearts as a truth more fundamental than Scripture. STEPHEN E. LAHEY

Pectoral Cross, cross with precious metals, worn on the breast, suspended on a chain around the neck.

Pelagius, Pelagianism, Pelagian Controversy. Pelagius (c355–c425), born in Britain, went to Rome c380. He was an ascetic* in active contact with the world, manifesting the zeal of a reformer. His chief concern was Christian practice and its basis in free choice.

For Pelagius the issue of free choice was rooted in his basic convictions regarding human nature and sin*. Adam's* sin did not affect the abilities of later human beings, who become like Adam through imitation, not through generation. Thus believers have free choice in the practice of their Christian life. Others, including Rufinus* the Syrian, Caelestius*, and Julian* of Eclaṇum, took a more speculative position, asserting that death is not a consequence of Adam's sin.

Pelagius reacted angrily in the presence of a bishop (probably Paulinus* of Nola) to a passage in Augustine's *Confessions* that spoke of the need for grace*; this may have been the occasion for Pelagius's writing *On Nature*, arguing that Augustine had departed from his own earlier position on the freedom* of the will*. Shortly afterward (c405–9), Pelagius wrote his commentary on Paul's epistles, dealing cautiously with the disputed issues (e.g. he merely reported the questions raised by Rufinus and Caelestius about original* sin, without affirming their position). His own emphasis was that human nature has a permanent capability for sinlessness; wrong decisions cannot alter human nature. This capability, because it is natural and a gift of creation, endures, although he concedes that it must be burnished by the file of the law*, the hammer of Christ's example and teaching, and the fire of the Holy* Spirit.

When Alaric and the Goths* approached Rome (409), Pelagius and Caelestius went first to Sicily, where they gained new adherents, and then to Africa. Controversy focused not on Pelagius, with his emphasis on freedom, since he soon left for Palestine, but on Caelestius, who questioned original sin. He was accused of heresy* by Paulinus of Milan, without Augustine's participation, at a local council in Carthage (411), which reasserted the African tradition of original sin. Augustine seemed reluctant to attack Pelagius; his tone intensified after controversies led by Jerome* in Palestine.

Concern arose in Sicily over the radical social views of at least some members of the Pelagian movement. Quite in keeping with their perfectionism* and reforming zeal, they emphasized good works, stressed discipleship* in an almost Franciscan* fashion, and criticized the corruption of government and society. Because of these writings, the imperial court in Ravenna condemned Pelagius and Caelestius as heretics and a danger to the public peace. The pope, Zosimus, followed suit in an encyclical letter sent throughout the East (418).

The theological and political controversy was resolved in a few years (415–18). Julian* of Eclanum became the leader of the opposition, asking that a council* be convened to discuss the issues on their merits. Questions continued to be raised in Gaul over so-called Semi-Pelagianism* (the view that "the beginning of faith" comes from the human being); they were resolved only at the Second Council of Orange* (529), and there continued to be differences of interpretation even among those who followed the Augustinian position. Yet Pelagianism survived in many forms through the centuries, whenever the doctrine of original* sin was contested or ignored (see Anthropology Cluster).

In the Eastern Church, i.e. in areas not influenced by the African doctrine of original sin or by Augustine's approach to grace* and free will*, the entire dispute, including the condemnation of Pelagius, was and is questionable and beside the point. EUGENE TESELLE

Penance and Forgiveness. Penance is the Christian practice through which Christians who sin are forgiven, i.e. are reconciled with God and reunited with the church*. The emphasis on penance and forgiveness presupposes a juridical view of atonement (see Atonement #2), a central concern for the Western churches. From this perspective, one may ask the following questions: Is the church a "club for saints" or a "refuge for sinners"? Is the church the "body of Christ" that manifests God's presence in the world or the sanctuary where sinners are saved from God's wrath? (see Anger or Wrath of God). The relative weight given to these alternatives has varied throughout the history of Christianity.

What Does the NT Say? The church was given the "power of binding and loosing" (Matt 16:18, 18:18), and Christians were told to forgive sins against each other "seventy times seven" (Matt 18:22; cf. Luke 17:6). Yet in a countertradition, the purity of the church is essential: members who sinned were excluded (Mark 3:29; 1 John 5:16; Heb 6:4–8, 10:26–31), "delivered to Satan" (1 Tim 1:20; 1 Cor 5:5), with perhaps the hope that they would be saved "as through fire" (1 Cor 3:15).

Public Repentance after Baptism. The opportunity for a single repentance of major sins after baptism* was presented by Hermas* as a new revelation; this, not the NT, shaped the church's practice for several centuries. There came to be a technical distinction between "remission" (*aphesis*) of sins committed before baptism and "repentance" (*metanoia*) for those committed after baptism. Those guilty of apostasy, murder, or fornication were excommunicated*, confessed publicly, performed acts of humiliation, and eventually were received back into the church, but only for that one time. Even this one occasion for repentance was opposed by the Montanists*, but the church at large defended it. The procedures for penance were tested and gained new definitiveness when it became necessary to deal with the lapsed* during the 3rd-c. persecutions (see Cyprian of Carthage), and they remained intact until the 6th c. The purpose of public penance was to maintain the church's purity so that it might fulfill its role as the body of Christ in the world.

Private Penance. This originated in monasticism*. The monastic life was regarded as itself a penance and always included provisions for private confession and spiritual direction. In Celtic* Christianity, this monastic practice was gradually extended to all Christians. Contrition and deeds of "satisfaction" led to eventual reconciliation with the church as a sanctuary where sinners were saved from God's wrath. The Celtic "penitentials*" prescribed periods of penance for various sins.

In the Eastern Church, there was a parallel tendency to seek spiritual direction from monks, but the transition to private penance was easier because of an emphasis on reconciliation with the church as the body of Christ manifesting God's presence in the world.

With Columbanus* the Celtic practice was brought to the Continent; in England, Theodore* of Tarsus blended the Celtic system with that of the Eastern Church. The Celtic system of private penance made its strongest advance during the time of Charlemagne*, probably through the influence of Alcuin*, and was reinforced by the appearance of a French penitential (c830). In Italy the older system of exclusion and readmission was retained until the Fourth Lateran Council (1215), which, following the 12th-c. Scholastic view of penance as a sacrament, required confession to a priest at least once a year and imposed on the priest the seal* of secrecy.

Penance as a Sacrament. The earlier sequence of contrition, satisfaction, and reconciliation was replaced by the new sequence of contrition, confession and absolution, and satisfaction. With respect to satisfaction, it was increasingly possible to substitute penances such as prayer, saying psalms, fasting, going on a pilgrimage, going on a crusade*, or furnishing equipment for another crusader.

A new view of confession and absolution made penance a sacrament*: since these acts are an outward sign that grace is imparted, there is no need to wait for reconciliation until satisfaction has been completed; "eternal penalty" (damnation*) is canceled, and "temporal penalty" (purgatory*) may be relaxed through penances and through indulgences* offered by the church. Genuine contrition* ("filial fear" of God) became central, since it was sufficient for absolution, although a place was made for "attrition"* ("servile fear," fear of punishment). In Scholastic* theology, the development of moral* theology was stimulated by the need for priestly discernment during the penitential process.

The Protestant Debt to Roman Catholicism. This medieval development was crucial not only for Catholicism but for Protestantism, which adopted the framework of confession and forgiveness but transformed it with the doctrine of justification by faith (see Justification, Theological Views and Practices, Cluster: A Central Doctrine for Western Christianity). The development of Evangelicalism* and revivalism* builds on the same assumptions.

The Problem of "Cheap Grace." Private penance encourages constant self-examination, with the expectation that one will constantly find within oneself struggle, failure, and hope for transformation. Yet both the Roman Catholic and the Protestant traditions can be criticized for opening the way to "cheap grace," offering forgiveness too easily and placing confession and penance behind the veil of confidentiality, quite in contrast to the early church (see Forgiveness, Christian Discourses of). Now, under conditions quite different from those that prevailed during the era of Christendom*, we must ask how both forgiveness and justice* are to be played out in the private life of Christians and in the life of the church, whether it is viewed as a "refuge of sinners" who seek forgiveness and struggle for justice, or as the "body of Christ," which manifests both God's forgiveness and justice in the world. EUGENE TESELLE

Penitential Books, Penitentials include directions for confessors and penances for various sins. The use of penitentials began in the Celtic* Church and spread to the Continent in the early Middle Ages.

Penitential Psalms, Ps 6, 32, 38, 51, 102, 130, 143. **See also PENANCE AND FORGIVENESS.**

Penitentiary, a place for confining penitents in special areas for the punishment of their sins. Such confinement began within monasteries, and entered secular law in Florence (c1300), perhaps because in an increasingly commercial society, depriving someone of the ability to work was a severe form of punishment. It was subsequently championed by 18th-c. reformers in Italy, England, Western Europe, and the USA. A spirit of vengeance often overrides the intended penitential, corrective, or restorative function.

Penn, William (1644–1718), Quaker minister and founder of Pennsylvania. Son of a naval admiral; studied at Oxford and Paris; committed Friend* from about 1667; twice married. He wrote prolifically in defense of George Fox* and the Quakers* and was imprisoned in the Tower of London for blasphemy after the publication of *Sandy Foundation Shaken* (1668). His most well known work, *No Cross, No Crown*, published in 1669 and written in the London Tower, espoused the submission of one's life to God.

In 1680 Penn received a grant of land in the New World from the British king for a debt owed his father. He attempted to create a "holy experiment" in this colony.

One of the Quaker leaders, Penn helped guide the Society of Friends through its period of prosecution, and was himself tried in the well-known Bushell case (1670) for violating the Conventicle Act. He made a great effort to win respectability for Friends. He wrote an introduction to Fox's* *Journal* (1694), in which he envisioned Quakers championing a return to primitive Christianity, a position he stressed four years later in *Primitive Christianity Revived*: "the light of Christ within man," he wrote, was what fundamentally distinguished Quakers from other Christians and empowered God's servants to live in obedience. H. LARRY INGLE

Pentateuch (Gk *pentateuchos*), the name in the LXX* (and commonly used today by scholars)

for the "five books" ("the Five Books of Moses") that form the first section of the Bible, called Torah* in Hebrew: the books of Genesis*, Exodus*, Leviticus*, Numbers*, and Deuteronomy*. It combines prose, poetry, and law in the framework of a narrative that can be subdivided into six parts (Friedman): the primeval history (Gen 1–11), the patriarchs (Gen 12–50), the liberation from Egypt (Exod 1–16), the stay in Sinai/Horeb (Exod 17–40; Leviticus), the journey (Numbers), and Moses' farewell (Deuteronomy).

Pentecost (Gk "50th day"), Feast of Weeks, 50 days after Passover*; day the Holy* Spirit descended on the apostles (Acts 2:1). **See also** LITURGICAL YEAR.

Pentecostal Movement. Classical Pentecostalism is numerically the smallest of the three major groups of the Charismatic Movement (c65 million Pentecostals in 2000). Sometimes Pentecostals are categorized as the "first wave," in contrast to the "second wave," or Charismatics in the historic mainline churches, and the "third wave," or independent Charismatics, who gather in indigenous, nondenominational congregations that they call "peoples of the Spirit*" (see Charismatic and Pentecostal Movements Cluster).

Most historians of the Pentecostal renewal consider it to have originated on January 1, 1901, at Charles Fox Parham's Topeka Bible School, USA. Parham asked his students to study the Bible for evidence of Spirit baptism*. After reading Acts 2, the account of the day of Pentecost, they concluded that glossolalia*, speaking in tongues*, was the confirmation of Spirit baptism. In the revival that followed, Pentecostalism spread to Kansas, Missouri, Texas, and Arkansas.

In 1906 the second phase of North American Pentecostalism was ushered in at Azusa Street, Los Angeles. William Seymour*, Parham's student, carried the message of Pentecost to Los Angeles, where he began a revival among ethnic minorities in one of the poorest sections of the city. Blacks, whites, and Hispanics worshipped together. Men and women shared leadership responsibilities. The barrier between clergy and laity vanished, because it was assumed that endowment with spiritual power in order to practice ministry was intended to be received by all, not just pastors.

The racial harmony of Azusa Street waned within a few months, with the result that Pentecostalism remains racially divided, and very little progress has been made toward reconciliation. Women's freedom to participate actively in ministry also faded, with few exceptions. In addition, theological issues divided the movement. Questions involving the nature of sanctification*, the gift of tongues, and the Trinity* generated tensions that have remained.

From Azusa Street, the revival spread throughout the USA. Pentecostals ranged from Wesleyan-Holiness, to Reformed*, and Unitarian*. Holiness leaders from the already existing Church of God in Christ (Memphis, Tennessee), the Church of God (Cleveland, Tennessee), and the Pentecostal Holiness Church (Georgia and the Carolinas) were present at Azusa and carried its message back to their churches (see Holiness Movement). Pentecostalism soon spread beyond the Holiness Movement. Most notable was the Assemblies* of God, formed in 1914 in Hot Springs, Arizona, to serve those with a Baptist background. The Assemblies, which always had a strong distrust of organization, had a nationwide base and grew rapidly to become the largest classical Pentecostal body in the world.

In 1916 the young Assemblies of God (AG) organization was torn by a disagreement over the Godhead known at that time as the "New Issue." Adherents of the "Jesus Name" group baptized in the name of Jesus "alone" (following Acts 2:38), rather than in the name of the Father, the Son, and the Holy Spirit. Those who left the AG formed "Oneness" denominations, later known as the United Pentecostal Church and the Pentecostal Assemblies of the World, among others.

Another "new wave on the shore," the so-called Latter Rain Movement, ignited controversy in the Pentecostal ranks. Originating in Canada and the Northern USA, this bore a distinct resemblance to the Azusa Street revival, with which certain of the classical Pentecostal churches no longer claimed as strong a common identity.

From its beginnings, North American Pentecostalism placed an emphasis on evangelism and missions. Pentecostal missionaries were sent throughout the world from Azusa, soon reaching Canada, England, Scandinavia, Germany, India, China, Africa, and South America. While opposition was often severe and expansion was slow between the world wars, Pentecostalism experienced rapid growth in the postwar period.

The period after 1945 also saw the beginnings of Pentecostal ecumenism. In 1928 Pentecostals were "disfellowshiped" by organized fundamentalism*. At the same time, relations improved with the more moderate Evangelicals, who also distanced themselves from the fundamentalists. By 1942 the Pentecostals were admitted as charter members of the National* Association of Evangelicals, and the Pentecostal Thomas F. Zimmerman, general superintendent of the Assemblies of God, was elected its president in 1960.

In 1948 North American Pentecostals formed the Pentecostal Fellowship of North America. Black Pentecostals did not join, and Oneness Pentecostals were excluded. In 1994 the Fellowship was disbanded in favor of a new, racially integrated organization known as the Pentecostal/Charismatic Churches of North America. Most North American groups also were involved with the Pentecostal World Conferences, first convened in 1947.

Pentecostalism is growing far more rapidly outside than inside Europe and North America, yet in most instances it takes the form of independent Charismatic* churches, rather than that of classical Pentecostalism. Megachurches* have been built in the non-Western world, in, among other places, Korea* (the largest megachurch is David Paul Yonggi Cho's Yoido Full Gospel Church in Seoul, with nearly a million members), Africa, and Latin America. At present, Brazil has the largest number of self-described "Pentecostals" (c24 million in 2000, yet many of these are best designated as Charismatics*; see Charismatic and Pentecostal Movements Cluster: In Latin America: Brazil), with the USA a distant second (c5 million in 2000).

STANLEY M. BURGESS

Pentecostal Worship tends to proceed in a less linear fashion, appearing to be less programmed and more spontaneous, than most Christian liturgies. Yet it is ritually structured. "Worship in song," "the Word" (a pastoral message), and "altar response" are foundational rites that form a flexible framework for a rich variety of "microrites," e.g. testimonies, charismatic* words, congregational glossolalia*, anointing and prayers for healing*, raising hands, clapping, dancing, and falling under the Spirit.

The ethos of Pentecostal worship greatly depends on the sensibilities – embodied attitudes and affections – that enliven and give a sense of purpose to acts of worship. For example, the altar response may have a repentant or celebratory mode, or an efficacious mode (orienting prayers for healing), or it may involve ecstasy (with Spirit* baptism). The same diverse types of sensibility (repentance, celebration, efficacy, and ecstasy and, beyond these, contemplation, improvisation, and ceremony) are also found in "worship in song" and "the Word."

For Pentecostals, worship in the Spirit must be rooted in and dependent on "the Word." Scripture* both grounds and arbitrates their worship. The belief that God "still speaks today" frames the doctrine that all Scripture is inspired and profitable, although the Book of Acts and Pauline teachings concerning the Holy* Spirit, Spirit* baptism, and the charismata* are most important.

Pentecostal worship is highly participatory. Liturgical leadership and liturgical roles can be shared by many because the true leader is God's Spirit. Furthermore, the belief that God is present as both leader and object of worship arouses expectations of manifestations of the supernatural, provides a context for encountering the Holy, and calls for an attentive receptivity to God.

Pentecostal worship contextualizes and sensitizes worshippers to the concrete needs of believers and nonbelievers alike. For worshippers the Spirit seeks to sanctify, to provide gifts, and to empower believers so that they might minister to others. This ministering can take the form of healing prayers (which is commonly the case) or of evangelism* – being God's witnesses, through the worship service as a whole and through testimonies and evangelistic messages. What begins in church unfolds into the world, as believers also deal with people's concrete needs.

Pentecostal worship cuts across cultural boundaries. It flourishes both in North Atlantic cultures and in very diverse cultures around the world, readily taking diverse inculturated* forms, because of its adaptable, mobile, and oral nature. For Pentecostals these inculturated forms of worship are the work of the Holy Spirit both in worship and in the world.

DANIEL E. ALBRECHT

People of God, generic description of Israel* and the church*. Hebrew Scriptures refer to "people of YHWH" (e.g. Exod 3:12; Num 11:29); "Holy [to YHWH]" (Jer 2:3; 1 Pet 2:9); the "chosen people" (Deut 4:37; Amos 3:2; Isa 45:4; Acts 13:17); and saved by God (Hab 3:13). No other nation is like Israel (Deut 4:7; 2 Sam 7:23; Ps 147:20). In the NT, *laos* sometimes designates Israel (Acts 4:10, 5:34) or the Jewish Christians (Acts 18:10). The covenant* with Israel is eternal (Rom 9–11). The church is a "chosen race" (1 Pet 2:9; Tit 2:14; cf. Rom 8:29–30), already in the Kingdom (Matt 13:38, 43), as a fulfillment of promise (Gen 12:2–3; Isa 19:24–25), for Christ is "with them always" (Matt 28:20). In keeping with these various citations, the NT sometimes describes the church as the renewed Israel (Gal 6:16; Rom 9:6; Jas 1:1; 1 Pet 1:1; Heb 4:9, 11:1–39, 13:12–14), at other times as a new people superseding and replacing the old (Mark 12:9, par.; Matt 27:25). This supersessionist*, and thus anti-Jewish, view of the people of God was incorporated in the view of "manifest destiny" of certain Christian nations (including the USA; see Racism and Christianity Cluster). Vatican* II used "people of God" as the basic image for its doctrine of the Roman Catholic Church. **See also ISRAEL, PEOPLE OF; NATIONALISM AND CHRISTIANITY.** ANDRÉ LACOCQUE

Pépin, Pippin. (1) Pippin of Héristal (d714), "mayor of the palace" of the French kings, father of Charles Martel. (2) Pippin the Short (714–68), son of Charles Martel and father of Charlemagne*, declared king (751) by the pope, with the support of Boniface*.

Perfection. In ancient Israel, to be perfect (Heb *tamim*; also *shalom*) was to be complete, to be unblemished, or to have integrity; the Greek term (*teleios*) used to translate the Hebrew terms in the LXX* meant "being undivided" in one's relation to God and neighbors, a meaning retained in the NT. Jesus calls on his followers to be perfect as God is perfect (Matt 5:48), but Luke substitutes "merciful" (Luke 6:36), emphasizing undivided relations with others. Perfection belongs first to God, and it is to be received with gratitude and trust; the human response is best characterized by love for God and neighbor (Mark 12:28–34, par.; Rom 13:9; Gal 5:14; Jas 2:8; 1 John 4:7–21).

The "counsels* of perfection" were important to the monastic* movement; its emphasis on celibacy* or singleness was interpreted to mean singleness of mind, free from the concerns of marriage and life in the world. In Protestantism*, the doctrine of justification* by faith diminished the striving for perfection, but sanctification* remained an expectation for the Christian life; assurance* of salvation through election* and grace* took the place of perfection. In the Wesleyan* Movement (Methodism*), it was expected that at some time after conversion, one might receive the conviction that sin* had been rooted out and one had been restored to the original image* of God, feeling nothing but love.

Perfectionist Ethics is an approach to ethics that emphasizes the formation of the self as moral agent. Noting the remoteness of (deontological*) moral principles from concrete situations and the difficulty of achieving the goals of consequentialist* ethics, perfectionist ethics underscores the need for moral discernment or "practical wisdom" (Aristotle) as one applies moral principles. A moral agent needs "virtues" – the know-how to address moral issues in concrete situations – which one acquires by learning "practical wisdom" through imitation of a teacher. For example, a disciple is formed through *imitatio Christi*. **See also CONSEQUENTIALIST ETHICS; DEONTIC, DEONTOLOGICAL ETHICS.**

Performatory Language. Often speaking is itself an action. When we say, "I promise," the saying is the doing; when it is not said, it is not done. The speaker "stands behind" the words, is self-involved, and enacts a new relationship. Much biblical and traditional language is performatory: promise or threat, command or encouragement, or prayer. The sacraments* usually contain performatory language that accompanies physical actions: in a wedding, the joining of hands and the saying of the vows; in baptism*, the use of water and the declaration, "I baptize you ..."; and in the Eucharist*, the physical action characterized by the statements "This is my Body," "This is my Blood." Like the beatitudes ("Blessed are ...") and curses ("Woe to you ...") (Matt 5; Luke 6), a priest's or pastor's blessing ("May the peace of God be with you") is performatory, conveying or calling forth a new reality. For Protestants, at least in intent, preaching is performatory language, speaking on God's behalf.

Pergamum, city near Asia Minor's western coast, famous for its altar to Zeus, temple to Athena, and shrine of Asclepius; one of the seven churches addressed in Rev 1:11, 2:12–17.

Perkins, William (1558–1602). Internationally recognized Calvinist* theologian of the Church of England*, fellow of Christ's College, Cambridge (1584–95), and popular preacher, he represented the Reformed* piety and theology prevalent in late Elizabethan England. His *Golden Chaine* (Latin, 1590; English, 1591) described the process of salvation* and the covenants* of works and grace*. He defended the doctrine of predestination* and employed the new Ramist* logic. His theology was practical: it was focused on conversion*, sanctification*, and the search for assurance of salvation*, encouraging systematic though warmhearted introspective piety. His influence on Puritan* preaching, theology, and pastoral care was important and extended to later Evangelicalism*.

DEWEY D. WALLACE, JR.

Perpetua and Felicitas, North African women (Perpetua, c180–203; Felicitas, d203) martyred in the Roman amphitheater in Carthage (March 7, 203). *The Passion of Perpetua and Felicitas,* a 3rd-c. Latin text with a debatably Montanist* slant, details their experiences. The section devoted to Perpetua's imprisonment reportedly comes from her own diary, making it the earliest writing attributed to a Christian woman; she describes a series of visions, her anxiety over her disapproving father and her infant son, and her efforts as an intercessor for both her deceased brother and fellow prisoners. *The Passion* also depicts the slave Felicitas prematurely giving birth in prison moments before her martyrdom*.

PAMELA MULLINS REAVES

Persecutions

Persecutions by the Roman Empire. Christians were condemned and sentenced by officials of the Roman Empire from the 1st to the 4th c. The reasons for the persecutions and their basis in Roman law remain controversial.

Jesus had been executed by a Roman procurator using a Roman means of execution, probably as a revolutionary, mockingly described in the inscription on the cross as "the king of the Jews." The term "Christian*" has a Latin suffix, suggesting that the movement in its early years was suspected of being a political faction. The Romans repeatedly reassured themselves, however, that the movement was not an overt political threat. Yet the opposition between *Kyrios Christos* and *Kyrios Kaisar* (and the imperial cult) emerged, possibly as early as Paul's* letters and the Gospel of Mark*.

On what legal basis were the Christians persecuted? The procedure was known as *cognitio*: governors heard complaints, made judgments, and ordered appropriate action after hearing individual accusations by private persons. Jesus' followers were accused and prosecuted "as Christians" (1 Pet 4:14–16). The very name or identity, the *nomen christianum*, was prohibited, probably not by statute but by precedent, and in trials followers of Jesus were urged to abandon it. Why? Because of the Christians' perceived crimes, immoralities, and "atheism*." Yet it was clear that the *nomen* itself was outlawed. When Christians renounced their identity, they were not held liable for these past offenses; the crime was *being* a Christian, not *having been* one (as Geoffrey de Ste. Croix says).

For the Romans, the jurisdiction of the state extended to religious affairs. The Christians shifted religious authority from the state to the individual conscience. In an era when the concept of religious freedom was largely unknown, Christians created it by deciding which obligations to accept or reject. The persecutions were sporadic, based on the emperors' temperament or the crises of the time (famine, plague, or invasion) that stimulated the quest for scapegoats. After the persecution under Nero* (64–68), we next hear of one under Domitian* (c95). Scattered hearings continued, as we know from Pliny's letter and from the case of Ignatius* (c110–15). The first widespread persecution came during Marcus Aurelius's reign (161–80), partly because of his sense of tradition, partly because of plague and invasion. Victims included Justin*, Polycarp*, and the martyrs of Lyon and Vienne.

Under Decius*, who required all persons to sacrifice to the traditional deities and obtain certificates (249 or 250), persecutions were for the first time empire-wide. The Decian persecutions created a major dispute within the church, centered on Cyprian*, concerning what to do about the lapsed*. However, there was also popular revulsion against the persecutions. Under Valerian (257–58), all public meetings were prohibited and all clergy were required to make sacrifices. Following his defeat and captivity in Persia (260), there was another period of peace.

When Diocletian* became emperor (284), he maintained the tacit toleration of Christianity, although he remained loyal to Roman traditions. However, under pressure from intellectuals loyal to Greek traditions (possibly including Porphyry*), Diocletian issued four edicts, with increasing severity. After his abdication, persecutions stopped in the West (Constantius was never a persecutor; Maxentius made peace with Christians in 306). But persecutions continued in the East, where Christians were much more numerous, under Galerius and Maximinus. Sacrifice was ordered (306, 308); resisters were sent to the mines with one eye blinded and the tendons of one foot severed (a number of these "confessors" would come in this condition to the Council of Nicaea*, 325). Maximinus's defeat by Licinius (313), following Maxentius's defeat in the West by Constantine* (312), was the setting for the Edict of Milan*.

After 320, in the East Licinius turned against the Christians, but Constantine defeated him, becoming sole emperor (324). His encyclical letter to the provinces of the East, a new edict of toleration, still gave "equal privileges" to all religions on the principle that adherence to the Christian faith should be voluntary.

Persecution of Christians Outside the Roman World up to the Middle Ages. While Roman persecution of Christians ended in the 4th c., there were moves against Christians in other areas.

In Persia, persecution was triggered by Constantine, who took it upon himself to protect Christians everywhere and shortly before his death (337) indicated that he planned to conquer Persia. In 339 Shapur imposed a double tax on Christians, destroyed churches, and required, in Zoroastrian style, veneration of the sun, with refusal punished by death; martyrs numbered in the thousands or tens of thousands. When Julian the Apostate invaded Persia (363), losing his life, there were new pressures against Christians, and many of them, including Ephrem*, fled to Edessa* in Roman territory.

Christianity was tolerated in Persia in 409, and as time went on, it became clear that the Church* of the East (commonly known as the Nestorian* Church, a misnomer) held a different view of Christ than the churches within Roman territory, making them seem less like a Roman "fifth column."

When Christianity spread to the north, through traders and Christian captives, and especially because of Ulfila* (the "apostle to the Goths", c311–83), the Goths* adopted Christianity in its Arian* form, which was at odds with the Christianity of the Roman Empire. There was relatively little persecution, because it was assumed that Latin speakers would remain Catholic and that Teutonic speakers would remain Arian.

The Islamic conquests in the Middle East had mixed results. They ended persecution of Monophysites*/Miaphysites* and of Nestorians* by the Byzantine Empire, and of Christians by Zoroastrians in Persia; they gave Christians the cohesiveness of a *millet**, a recognized and self-controlled Christian community responsible to the ruler; and Christians were often sought out by the Islamic rulers as traders, physicians, scholars, and architects. But Christians were forbidden to seek converts, ring bells, or display crosses in public; and all men had to pay a special tax. From time to time, there were attacks on Christians as a result of local factors.

See also HISTORY OF CHRISTIANITY CLUSTER. EUGENE TESELLE

Person, the Trinity, and the Self. *Prosopon* (Gk) and *persona* (Lat) originally applied to the actor's "mask." These terms came to mean the role played, the character depicted; hence it could also be asked whether one was acting in one's own or another's "person." In the ancient world, "person" did not mean a personal center of consciousness – as it later came to be viewed – although it could mean the "presented self" (as in the modern psychological term "persona"). But the ancient view of person should not be ignored today, especially as we become aware of the cultural character of this concept.

Tertullian* was the first to speak of the Trinity* as three persons, meaning three modes or expressions of the one Divinity; in the East, the Trinity was more often called three hypostases*, although three "persons" was sometimes used. In Christology* the notion of "two sons" (divine and human) was generally condemned. The Antiochenes* also insisted, however, that each nature has its *prosopon* (person, in the sense of activity). They went on to say that these different modes of activity are harmonized, by a conjunction of wills, in a single *prosopon* (person, in the sense of manifestation) with neither division nor confusion.

After the Council of Chalcedon*, it became a commonplace to say that God is one nature in three persons or hypostases, while Christ is of two natures in one person or hypostasis; in the Trinity, then, there is a difference of persons but not of natures, while in Christ there is a difference of natures but not of persons. All of these reflections led to the definition proposed by Boethius*: a person is "an individual substance [i.e. hypostasis] of a rational nature."

The "turn to the subject" associated with Augustine* and especially Descartes* encouraged a new emphasis on consciousness and freedom in understanding personhood. If God was to be understood as "personal" in this sense, did it mean that God is one "personality" in the three modes of immediacy, self-concept, and will (as in Augustine), or is God three personalities in a social unity (which tended to be the view of the Cappadocians*)? Disagreement over this continues into the present. The ancient meaning of "person" was not entirely lost, however, for Western philosophers and theologians; Hobbes and Spinoza* denied that God is a "person" in the sense of a delimited form and visage, and Tillich* later took a similar position.

New issues were raised by Locke* and Hume* when they pointed out that subjective activities and experiences do not necessarily imply an underlying "substance." Process* thought sees the "self" as an ongoing series of events whose consistency results from inheritance and reenactment, not substantial continuity. Social theories of selfhood and also community-centered culture suggest that personhood is shaped by interactions with other selves (in the community). **See also** AUTONOMY; HETERONOMY; RELATIONALITY. EUGENE TESELLE

Personalism, Christian. See BERDYAEV, NIKOLAI ALEKSANDROVICH; MARCEL, GABRIEL.

Peru lies at the heart of the Andes and was the home of the Inca Empire; it was also the center of Spanish power in South America until the 18th c. Christianity in Peru reflects the country's multiethnicity (white, 15%; mestizo, 37%; Quechua, Aymara, and other indigenous peoples, 45%; black and Asiatic, 3%), multilinguistic nature (Spanish, Quechua, Aymara, 12 major languages in the Amazon region), and geographic extremes. The Andes mountain range divides the country in half. To the southeast a vast, barren *altiplano*, with Lake Titicaca in the middle, connects Peru to Bolivia*. The capital, Lima, is located midway along a dry coastal desert that runs from Chile to Ecuador, and a huge tropical rain forest covering half the country extends in the east from the Andes to Brazil. Although Christianity and Christian symbols confer on Peru a definite cultural unity, differing religious practices and customs also reflect this great cultural and geographic variety.

Roman Catholic Christianity arrived with the Spanish Conquest in 1532. The first religious – Franciscans*, Augustinians*, and Dominicans* – practiced mass baptisms, and at least on a superficial level, the native populations accepted Christianity. In 1572 Viceroy Francisco Toledo accelerated the evangelization process by ordering all indigenous people to live in "reductions*" (Christian towns), under the supervision of a royal official. For the next 300 years, the inhabitants of these towns attended Sunday Mass and memorized catechism lessons. Although ordinary native people did not read or write, and the Bible was not accessible, the residents of the reductions put on biblical and morality plays to represent the great biblical truths. The most widespread ritual that survives from that time is the Passion* of Christ, which is reenacted every Holy Week in countless towns throughout the Andes. The Jesuits*, who arrived with Toledo, were entrusted with the education of the sons of native chiefs.

By the middle of the 17th c., most of the major devotions* that make up popular* Roman Catholicism in Peru had emerged. These devotions reflected the new cultural patterns and realities that had arisen since the Conquest. The strong appeal of these devotions is attested by the fact that most of them were very much alive in the 21st c. Colonial Lima had a distinct Spanish-Creole (a Creole being a white born in the New World) identity, although it also had a large native and black population. Two of the most popular saints today are St. Rose* of Lima and St. Martin of Porres. St. Martin, a mulatto Dominican, endeared himself to the people by his works of charity and is especially popular among black Roman Catholics. The major devotion remains the Lord of Miracles procession*, which takes place three times during the month of October. The origins of the procession can be traced to the survival during an earthquake in 1655 of an image of the crucified Christ painted on a wall by an anonymous slave (1651). The first procession was held in 1687. Over time it grew until it became one of the largest processions in the entire Catholic world. Thousands of devotees, many dressed in purple as a sign of penance*, accompany the image through the streets of Lima. The confraternity of the Lord of Miracles is made up mainly of Afro- and mestizo-Peruvians. The devotion has spread to other Peruvian cities, and Peruvians in New York, Chicago, and Los Angeles annually hold their own, smaller Lord of the Miracles processions.

In the southern Andes, pre-Conquest rituals were incorporated into Roman Catholic feasts and ceremonies. In Cuzco the main feasts are Corpus Christi and the Lord of Tremors. Although the image of Christ is Spanish, these processions attract Peruvians of all races and social classes. One hundred miles to the east, a much more Andean devotion has increasingly attracted attention: the Lord of Qollur Rit'i ("snow star" or "bright snow"), which began around 1780. Each year thousands of pilgrims (50,000 in 2002), wearing brightly colored clothes, dance and sing as they walk up to a mountain valley 16,000 feet above sea level. There, under the shadow of Ausangate, one of the highest peaks in the Andes, they pay homage to an image of Christ painted on a rock. Dancing is accompanied by songs of praise in Quechua. Men dressed as mountain bears bring ice from the mountain to the main plaza of

Cuzco, a gift of the Lord of Qollur Rit'i to the city.

Another deeply revered figure is the Virgin Mary*. In many Andean towns, she replaced, or became the Christian manifestation of, the Pachamama, the mother earth, a pre-Conquest cult still very much alive. The Virgin of the Candle Stick (la Candelaria) is venerated in Puno and throughout the *altiplano*, along with Our Lady of Carmel. In Arequipa, a city located between the *altiplano* and the coast, there is strong devotion to Our Lady of Chapi.

In 1780 Tupac Amaru led the greatest rebellion of indigenous peoples in the history of South America. The native leader, a graduate of the Jesuit school for Inca nobility in Cuzco, cited the Bible to justify the rebellion. His movement was crushed in 1781. Many Creole priests supported the cause of independence, which was won in 1821. But in the 19th c., the Peruvian Church became increasingly conservative. It also experienced a sharp decline in the number of vocations.

After Vatican* II, Roman Catholicism in Peru experienced major changes. Under Cardinal Juan Landázuri, the Church became one of the most progressive in Latin America. Gustavo Gutiérrez (1928–) became one of the main founders of Liberation* theology. Born in Lima, he studied medicine, pursued studies for the priesthood in Santiago (ordination, 1960), then at Louvain, and received his doctorate from the Université Catholique in Lyon. Subsequently, he served as moderator of the Union of Catholic University Students. His book, *A Theology of Liberation* (1971), and many later works, had a major impact on Christian thought. Although subjected to questioning by Rome, he always remained loyal to the Church and entered the Dominican* order in 2000. Because of Gutiérrez's conciliatory style, Liberation theology had a major impact on Christians in university circles, in the *pueblos jóvenes* (shantytowns) surrounding the cities, and throughout the Andes and in the jungle. During the Shining Path years (1980–92), Liberation theology inspired thousands of poor who were victims of terrorism and government forces to stand together in defense of their communities.

Contemporary Roman Catholicism in Peru is multifaceted. Churches in the center of the cities tend to be traditional, with little lay participation in the liturgy. But participation in modern middle-class parishes is noticeably greater. In the poor districts surrounding the cities, there is a blending of traditional customs and Liberation theology. Yet under Pope John Paul II, the episcopate has become increasingly conservative. Opus* Dei is very influential among the upper classes (8 of 46 bishops are members), and the archbishop of Lima, Juan Luis Cipriani, is the only Opus Dei cardinal in the world. Sodalitium* Vitae Christianae, another conservative movement, founded in Lima in 1971, attracts many middle-class youth. The Catholic Charismatic* Movement, founded in the 1970s, reached a peak and has stabilized. But Charismatic healing Masses, including those celebrated by Father Manuel Rodríguez in Lima at the beginning of the 21st c., are very popular. Although Liberation theology no longer has the appeal it once did, progressive Catholics are still influential at the Catholic University, in human rights groups, and in parishes among the poor.

The few Protestants in Peru after independence (1821) were Anglicans, mostly diplomats or merchants. Diego (James) Thomson, a representative of the British Bible Society, visited Peru after independence and was well received by the liberal clergy of the period. But the Roman Catholic Church grew increasingly conservative and opposed religious toleration. In 1890 Francisco Penzotti, a Methodist and representative of the American Bible Society, was imprisoned for public proselytizing. Following many protests, he was freed. Finally, freedom of religion was granted in 1915. Two groups made noticeable inroads: the Methodists*, who founded several schools in Lima and Callao, and the Adventists*, who founded many schools and clinics for indigenous peoples in the *altiplano* bordering Lake Titicaca. Two important figures of this period were John Mackay*, a missionary of the Free Church of Scotland, and John Ritchie, a Scottish Baptist, who founded the Evangelical Church of Peru (1922), a confederation of several denominations (with c15,000 members in 1930). In 1940 the principal Protestant churches in Peru founded CONEP, the National Protestant Council of Peru.

Since the 1960s, churches with Pentecostal or Charismatic* orientation have grown rapidly. Currently, among the four largest Protestant denominations – the Evangelical Church of Peru, the Assemblies of God, the Church of God, and the Pentecostal Church of Peru – only the first is not Pentecostal or Charismatic. The Adventist* Church (now part of CONEP) is the second-largest non-Catholic denomination. The humanitarian and educational work of the Adventists in the *altiplano* drew praise from intellectuals and native rights advocates.

An important figure in early Adventist history was Ferdinand Stahl (1874–1950), who founded schools and clinics.

An organization that has drawn much attention is the Evangelical Association of the Israelite Mission of the New Universal Pact, or simply, the Israelites of the New Universal Pact, founded in the 1960s by Ezequiel Ataucusi (1918–2000), a Quechua-speaking peasant who was influenced by Adventists. The Israelites combine Andean mountain elements with the OT. Now constituting a significant movement (more than 200,000 members in 2002), the Israelites have adopted OT customs: beards for men, veils for women, and animal sacrifices.

In the 1990s, some Protestant churches and the Israelites entered politics, a sign of their growing influence. Relations between Protestants and Roman Catholics have improved considerably since Vatican* II, but are still very limited. Fundamentalist* groups continue to harbor anti-Catholic sentiments. **See also ROMAN CATHOLICISM CLUSTER: IN LATIN AMERICA: PERU.**

Statistics: Population (2007): 29 million (M). Christians, 28.1 M, 97% (Roman Catholics, 23 M; Protestants, 2.7 M; Baptists, 0.3 M; Assemblies of God, 1.3 M; Adventists, 0.5 M; Israelites of the New Universal Pact, 0.2 M; Jehovah's Witnesses, 0.08 M; Mormons, 0.05 M); nonreligious, 1.4%. It is estimated that only 10% of Roman Catholics regularly attend Mass. (*Source*: 2007 census.)

JEFFREY KLAIBER, SJ

Pesher (plural, Pesharim), Hebrew term used to refer to a distinctive kind of "interpretation" in commentaries on biblical prophetic texts (including Psalms) found among the Dead* Sea Scrolls. Pesharim (e.g. the Habakkuk Pesher) stressed the fulfillment of the prophecies; through the Holy* Spirit, God revealed to the interpreter the "secret mysteries" of the words of the prophets, namely God's role in the events surrounding the Qumran* community. Their use of Scripture* is similar to that of Matthew* and Paul*.

Peshitta (Syriac, "simple," "straightforward"), the name for the translation of the Bible into Syriac (Late Eastern Aramaic), probably composed by Jews (who possibly converted to Christianity) in Edessa* (second half of the 2nd c.). The OT Peshitta, a translation of a Hebrew text (though some books show the influence of the LXX* and the Targum*), was the biblical version known to early Syriac authors such as Ephrem* and Aphrahat*. For biblical scholars today, it offers a window into the state of the 2nd-c. Hebrew text. More important, the Peshitta preserves an interpretation of the HB, such as in 2 Sam 15:32 and 16:1, where it presents David as a person of prayer. A critical edition is available and an English translation (*The Bible of Edessa*) is forthcoming. The Peshitta NT, the standard Syriac NT, is an early-5th-c. revision of an older Syriac version that brings the Syriac translation into closer line with the Greek text; it lacks 2–3 John, 2 Peter, Jude, and Revelation. The book series *Das Neue Testament in syrischer Überlieferung* provides an interlinear edition of the Peshitta and the later Harklean Syriac versions for the Pauline and Catholic letters. Today, the Peshitta is the authoritative text for the Syriac* churches.

CRAIG E. MORRISON, O. Carm.

Peter (c10–c64), Simon, son of John, Galilean fisherman and prominent disciple of Jesus* of Nazareth, reestablished the Jesus movement in Jerusalem after the Crucifixion; he later traveled as a missionary and was martyred in Rome under Nero*.

Jesus nicknamed Simon "Cephas" (Aramaic, "stone," "rock"), which when translated into Greek became "Peter." Although he denied being a disciple after Jesus' arrest, Peter was one of the first to have a vision of the risen Jesus. The leader of the Jerusalem community (Acts*), where Paul* later met him (Galatians*), Peter subsequently shared leadership there with James* and John* and engaged in negotiations with Paul and Antioch Christians over the status of non-Jewish believers. Nothing is known of his travels or eventual arrival in Rome, where he was martyred. A monument in an ancient necropolis under St. Peter's Basilica has been venerated as his burial place (since the 2nd c.).

Matthew 16:17–19 interprets the name "Peter" as Jesus' promise that Simon Peter will be the foundation stone of his community. The keys entrusted to Peter (and to the community; Matt 18:18) represent the authority to decide how Jesus' teaching will be applied. The debates over the status of non-Jewish believers (Gal 2; Acts 15) show that Peter did not have sole authority. He acted in consultation with other apostles. John 21:15–19 reflects another tradition, in which the risen Jesus rebukes Peter for his betrayal, entrusts him with care of Jesus' flock, and predicts Peter's martyrdom.

Two letters in Peter's name evoke his role as a shepherd (pastor*) and authoritative teacher:

1 Peter*, sent from Rome to suffering believers in Asia Minor, and 2 Peter*, written to shore up waning belief in Jesus' second coming. By the 2nd c., the Gospel of Mark* was thought to preserve Peter's teaching about Jesus to Christians in Rome. An apocryphal Gospel of Peter (2nd c.) expanded on the Passion and Resurrection stories (see Peter, Gospel of). An apocryphal* Acts of Peter described his abilities as a missionary and miracle worker, his defense of Christianity against the false prophet/magician Simon Magus (Acts 8), and the story about his insistence on being crucified head down. For Jewish Christians, Peter was the heroic opponent of Paul. Although some Gnostic* Christians cast him as their unenlightened opponent, others composed apocalypses and acts in which Peter conveys Gnostic teaching. Considered the founding bishop of the Roman See*, Peter became the guarantor of both governing and teaching authority for the Roman Catholic popes* during the Middle Ages and especially after the Reformation. PHEME PERKINS

Peter, Acts of. See APOCRYPHA CLUSTER: APOCRYPHAL ACTS OF APOSTLES.

Peter, Apocalypse of, short pseudonymous Christian Gnostic* document written when the distinction between orthodox and heretic*/Gnostic was clearly drawn (3rd c.) and found in the Nag* Hammadi library. Following the apocalyptic literary genre, it is organized around three visions explained by the Savior. It posits a radically dualistic worldview contrasting the material, mortal, and counterfeit with the spiritual, immortal, and true. Interpretations of the three visions – visions of the "blind ones," priests and people ready to kill Jesus and Peter; of the crucifixion of Jesus, "glad and laughing on the tree"; and of the living Savior (filled "with a Holy Spirit") – oppose immortal souls (the Gnostics) and mortal souls (false teachers, non-Gnostics, presumably the nascent orthodox church, as well as other Gnostic groups). The Apocalypse of Peter is a good example of docetic* Christology, which emphasizes that Jesus is the manifestation of a preexistent* divine being and that his humanity was merely apparent.

DANIEL PATTE

Peter, Gospel of, lengthy but fragmentary story of Jesus' Passion and Resurrection told by Peter* in the first-person singular ("I, Simon Peter") and plural ("we, the twelve disciples"). The text in a parchment codex was discovered in 1886/87 in a monk's tomb in Upper Egypt.

Most scholars accept that it is the Gospel of Peter that Serapion, bishop of Antioch (190–209), knew, classifying some of its passages as docetic* (Jesus' humanity was simply apparent). The relationship of the Gospel of Peter with the NT Passion stories, especially with Matthew's special material, is self-evident. The attempt to distill from the Gospel of Peter the oldest, independent stratum of these traditions does not withstand close scrutiny. The arguments that the Gospel of Peter is a later stage of tradition-history are overwhelming: e.g. Jesus is consistently called "the Lord"; Jewish customs are ignored; and responsibility for Jesus' death is transferred from Pilate to Herod and the Jews.

A driving goal of the narrative is the intensification of apologetic* motifs; eyewitnesses of the Resurrection (among the Jews and the Roman soldiers) are produced. The miraculous elements are equally emphasized, with enormous angelic beings and a cross that speaks. The evidence for docetism is not so clear, although the crucifixion scene itself is open to a docetic reading. **See also APOCRYPHA CLUSTER: APOCRYPHAL GOSPELS.** HANS-JOSEF KLAUCK

Peter, 1 and 2 Epistles of. While both "letters" claim Petrine authorship, most scholars agree that 2 Peter is pseudonymous* (written by Peter's followers c90–125 in Rome, Asia Minor, or Egypt), and many also debate the authorship of 1 Peter (written either c62 if by Peter or c73–92 if by his followers, probably in Rome, called "Babylon").

1 Peter addressed five Asia Minor communities that were experiencing persecution*. Called "exiles," "a chosen race, royal priesthood, holy nation," and "aliens and strangers," they were admonished to honor government officials, "do good," withstand suffering (a "fiery ordeal"), and follow a household* code within their communities. 1 Peter 3:19, Jesus' "proclamation to the spirits in prison," is the basis for the creeds' affirmation of Jesus' "descent into hell" (see Descent into Hell; Hell).

2 Peter includes a list of virtues, the author's claim to be the last of the apostolic witnesses, and a mention of Paul's* letters as "writings" (Scripture*). 1 Peter appears to draw on sermonic, baptismal, and/or catechetical material, including quotations of hymns and Scripture. 2 Peter, a "farewell testament," is heavily dependent on Jude* (cf. 2:1–18, 3:1–3) and is similar in style and vocabulary to 1 Clement* and Shepherd of Hermas*.

1 Peter seeks to establish continuity with, yet supersession* over, the promises and Scriptures of Israel, and portrays Christ's sufferings as worth emulating. 2 Peter is concerned with false teachers who twist the words of Paul and others and with the eschatological Judgment*. 1 and 2 Peter, rarely a part of lectionary readings, attest to the importance of Peter and his tradition. 1 Peter's "royal priesthood" became the basis for Luther's* "priesthood* of all believers." Attributing Christ-likeness to suffering both encouraged those in abusive situations and led to the belief that suffering* should be passively accepted, which has done much harm over the centuries.

JENNIFER BIRD

Peter, Preaching of (*Kerygma Petrou*), an early (late 2nd c.?) Apologetic document (see Apologists). According to the only extant fragments quoted by Clement* of Alexandria, it depicted Peter as an authoritative Christian missionary preaching on monotheism, on the dangers of paganism and of Judaism, and apparently on Christology, using OT passages to defend the Christian interpretation of Jesus' death and resurrection. Origen* does not view it as part of the legitimate Christian writings. Eusebius* listed it among the noncanonical writings.

Peter of Callinicus (c540–91), theologian, patriarch. Born in Callinicus, present-day al-Raqqah (Northern Syria); ordained patriarch of Antioch (581). Versed in both Greek and Syriac, he is credited with having written numerous theological works (mainly on the doctrine of the Trinity*), treatises, and letters. Involved in a stormy controversy (c586) with his patron, Damian*, patriarch of Alexandria (578–605), he wrote his magnum opus, *Adversus Damianum*. Peter rebuts Damian's thesis (developed against the tritheists) that the characteristic properties of the divine persons, i.e. fatherhood, sonship, and procession, are the hypostases* themselves. Peter's argument concentrates on the Trinity, the single substance, and the three hypostases, explicitly condemning Sabellianism* and tritheism*, especially the views of its prominent advocate, John Philoponus (c490–575).

RIFAAT EBIED

Peter Damiani (1007–72), Italian reformer. A monk at Fonte Avellana near Gubbio, he became prior because of his ascetic discipline. A member of the reforming party around Hildebrand (later Gregory* VII), he denounced immorality among the clergy, and his *Liber Gomorrhianus* was a dramatic attack on homosexuality*. In the debates over simony*, he opposed the rigorist and nearly Donatist* position of Cardinal Humbert, defending the validity of sacraments administered by simoniacal priests.

Peter the Fuller (d488), patriarch of Antioch. A monk in the Sleepless Monastery in Constantinople sympathetic to Nestorianism*, he was expelled for his Monophysite*/Miaphysite* tendencies. With the emperor Zeno's support, he became bishop of Antioch (470), then was deposed and reinstated several times. In the history of liturgy, he is significant for adding the "theopaschite* supplement," "crucified for us," to the *Trisagion** and for instituting the recitation of the Niceno*-Constantinopolitan Creed during the Eucharist*.

Peter Lombard (c1100–60), author of the standard textbook of systematic theology used in the later Middle Ages, the *Sentences* (1155–58). Born in Lombardy, he studied in Italy, Reims, and Paris, where he was a master who taught in the cathedral school from c1143. He became bishop of Paris in 1159.

In the 1140s, Peter Lombard lectured on the Bible. His commentaries on the Psalms (before 1148) and the Pauline Epistles (after 1148) survive. At the trial of Gilbert, bishop of Poitiers, for heresy about the Trinity* (Council of Reims, 1148), he was one of Gilbert's opponents. He was himself a subject of criticism. Walter of St. Victor accused him of heretical teaching on the Trinity in a treatise *The Four Labyrinths of France*.

He was first and foremost an organizer of material. In the *Sentences*, he brought together systematically the opinions of (mainly Western) patristic authors under topic headings in four sections: Trinity*; creation* and the Fall*; Incarnation* and the living of a good life; and sacraments* and the end of the world.

He became caught up in two contemporary controversies over the Trinity. Joachim*, the controversial abbot of Fiore, attacked one of the views Peter Lombard had listed; an attempt was made to get Peter Lombard condemned at the Fourth Lateran Council. In the event, it was Joachim who was condemned, and once the *Sentences* had the Council's approval, this very useful book began to be adopted widely in theology courses.

At a time when theology was beginning to take shape as an academic discipline, Peter Lombard was concerned chiefly with providing students with materials for discussion, rather than putting forward pioneering theological arguments of his own. His *Sentences* were commented on by the majority of theologians during the next few centuries, with the emphasis shifting as different issues became topical. It was not generally superseded by the *Summa Theologiae* of Thomas Aquinas until the 16th c.

GILLIAN R. EVANS

Peter the Venerable (1092/94–1156), abbot of Cluny*. His promotion of study in the Cluniac monasteries led to controversy regarding the role of possessions, including servants and land, with his friend Bernard* of Clairvaux, who wanted the monastic life to be one of prayer and manual labor. He also gave shelter to Abelard* while the latter was under attack by Bernard. He sponsored the first translation of the Qur'an* into Latin and wrote against both Islam and Judaism.

Petrarch, Francesco (1304–74), along with Dante* and Boccaccio, a founding figure of the Christian humanism of the Italian Renaissance*. His Christian allegorical interpretation of his ascent of Mount Ventoux near Avignon (1336; in *Rerum familiarium*) as a metaphor of the *vita beata* (blessed life) is particularly suggestive of the religious and specifically Augustinian orientation of his thinking. His *Secretum* is written as an intimate dialogue with Augustine* that develops the discovery of the interiority of the subject (a dimension of interior transcendence explored by Augustine in the *Confessions*, originally through his dialogue with God). At the same time, Petrarch secularizes the Christian outlook by interpreting this transcendence in a subjective and worldly register of thought and feeling, most powerfully in his lyric poetry (*Il canzoniere*). His poetry of love for Laura is replete with religious motifs translated into terms of a profane love pivoting on the affirmation of an autonomous (and ultimately empty) human self.

Petrarch was deeply affected by his brother Gherardo's entry into a Carthusian* monastery. His Latin humanist writings (notably *De vita religiosa*, *De otio religioso*, and *De vita solitaria*) probe the question of how to live in order to become happy and blessed, and are strongly tinged with a Christian ascetic* sensibility.

WILLIAM FRANKE

Petre, Maude Dominica (1863–1942), laywoman, author of 14 books and more than 90 articles, member of the Society of the Daughters of Mary (1890–1908), participant in an informal network of people concerned with renewal in the Roman Catholic Church, including George Tyrrell*, Friedrich von* Hügel, and Alfred Loisy*. The movement known as Modernism* was condemned by Pope Pius X (1907). When Tyrrell died (1909), Petre, his literary executor, edited and published a number of his works, including *Christianity at the Crossroads* (1909) and a two-volume *Autobiography and Life of George Tyrrell* (1912). One of the first to write a history of Modernism (1918), she refused to take the anti-Modernist oath; ecclesiastical censure deprived her of the sacraments in her home diocese. In her autobiographical *My Way of Faith* (1937), she described Modernism as "a movement of genuine Catholic believers . . . who held to their religious faith, and were endeavoring to answer their own difficulties as well as those of others." Her life and writings reflect a critical approach to authority*, an insistence on spiritual independence, and respect for pluralism*.

ELLEN M. LEONARD

Pew, fixed wooden bench that seats a number of worshippers in a church. The use of pews began during the Middle Ages and increased after the Reformation, owing to the emphasis on preaching.

Pharisees (2nd c. BCE–1ST c. CE), a group of Jews known for their meticulous observance of the Torah* according to the interpretive traditions received from their ancestors. This observance emphasized the proper sanctifying of the Sabbath*, full tithing*, and the application of the priestly laws of ritual purity to the preparation and consumption of the ordinary food that they ate each day apart from the Temple. The latter two concerns were reflected in the exclusiveness of their communal table fellowship. Many of their legal interpretations differed substantially from those of the Sadducees* and from the often more stringent ones of the Qumran Essenes*. The Pharisees did not separate themselves from society, but sought to reform society to conform to their understanding of divine law. Although the NT Gospels share some beliefs (including resurrection*) with the Pharisees, they mount some vehement polemics against what they portray as the Pharisees' self-righteousness and hypocrisy (e.g. Matt 23). These invectives, however, are tendentious reflections of 1st-c. tensions between sectors of the emerging church and Pharisaic Judaism, and should not be read as accurate generic descriptions of Pharisaic religion.

GEORGE W. E. NICKELSBURG

Phenomenology and Christianity were first connected through Hegel* (who popularized the term). Yet phenomenology is associated primarily with Edmund Husserl and Martin Heidegger*. Phenomenology is the science (*logos*) of phenomena (what is manifest or visible, from Gk *phaino*); it tries to ground all knowledge in what appears. Such an experiential foundation requires a "reduction" (Husserl), i.e. a turning off of our natural beliefs in an external world independent of experience and in all that we consider to be transcendent to our experience, including God. Phenomenology as a kind of atheism* echoes Nietzsche*, but it is consistent with Christianity's belief in a God who is able to die.

Since phenomenology brackets out the transcendent, it is a philosophy of immanence*. But immanence is not alien to Christianity. The Incarnation* means that the transcendent God becomes a human who exists *within* ("immanent" to) our experience. Thus phenomenologists (especially Heidegger) attempt to speak of the divine within experience. But the divine always exceeds any experience of it and is therefore un-presentable, what we are not able to make appear. Similarly, when Husserl described the experience of the other, he recognized: I can never intuit the internal life of another; my access to it is always mediated. Yet Husserl recognized that experience consists in intentions determined in language; "meaning intentions" can be fulfilled with an intuition, which would make the meaning intention true. "Meaning fulfillment" has a temporal sense: the fulfillment is to come just as the returning Savior is to come; truth is promised in the future. Therefore, phenomenology can always be associated with the messianism that defines Christianity (and Judaism, as well as strains of Islam).

Messianism always implies waiting (see Messiah). Because we are not able to make God be present, we find ourselves always waiting. The image of Jesus returning "like a thief in the night" implies (as Heidegger noted) that we must be prepared; he may come at any moment, in the place called "home." Taking up the idea of place, more recent phenomenologists (or "post-phenomenologists") like Derrida and Levinas* have spoken of hospitality*. This is perhaps the most crucial intersection between phenomenology and Christianity. Beyond Husserl's (and Merleau-Ponty's) description of intuition as passive capacities, Derrida and Levinas tried to find ways to make these passive capacities active. That we *must* receive sensations is a sign of our *weakness*; we have no choice but to "turn the other cheek." Yet this weakness is a capacity; we have the power to open the door as wide as possible; (passive) waiting becomes (active) welcoming. Welcoming is to be prepared for the coming of the Messiah*. LEONARD LAWLOR

Philemon, Epistle to, shortest and most personal Pauline letter, whose authenticity has never been doubted. Written to a Christian assembly (*ekklesia*) in the house of Philemon, Apphia, and Archippos, the letter is placed (by references in it) in the Lycus valley, near Colossae, mid-50s.

Since antiquity, the traditional interpretation has been that Onesimus is a slave* who has run away from Philemon's house, has met Paul* in prison, and has been baptized by him (9–10). A more recent interpretation by Lampe suggests that he is not a runaway, but has gone legally to Paul for intercession. Another interpretation by Callahan is that Onesimus is not the slave but the abused brother of Philemon (16). Whatever the case, Onesimus comes from the household of Philemon, all is not well between the two men, everyone else in the assembly knows about the situation, and Paul intervenes to bring about reconciliation.

The letter is a masterpiece of deliberative rhetoric that gives a glimpse of real relationships and problems in a 1st-c. house* church. The institution of slavery continued to be accepted by Christians but was modified by insistence on just treatment and relationships. Paul probably intended that Philemon manumit (free) Onesimus, yet slavery remained part of the Christian household (Col 3:33–4:1; Eph 6:5–9). CAROLYN OSIEK

Philip. (1) Name of one of the apostles (listed among the Twelve*, Mark 13:18, par.); Philip the Apostle, like Andrew* and Peter*, was from Bethsaida (John 1:43). (2) One of seven deacons* chosen to minister to the Hellenists* (Acts 6:5). He is often called "the Evangelist" because he visited Samaria* (Acts 8:4–8), baptized the Ethiopian* eunuch (Acts 8), and had four prophet* daughters (Acts 21).

Philip, Acts of (c4th c.). Composed of 15 numbered "acts" and a martyrdom story, written in Greek, it probably originated near Hierapolis, Phrygia. This text was familiar to the ascetic* movements of Asia Minor condemned by the Cappadocian* Fathers and the Synod of Gangra (mid-4th c).

The majority of the text has been condemned for violating the orthodoxy of the time; however, the last part, the martyrdom story, has been detached, revised, and used as a liturgical document for the Feast of Saint Philip (November 14).

In this text, Philip* the Evangelist (Acts 6:5, 8:4–40, 21:8) and Philip* the Apostle (Matt 10:3, par.; Acts 1:13) are merged into one figure. Acts of Philip 1–7 are concerned with activities recalling the evangelist, which are presented in several cycles of stories of miracles and conversions. Acts of Philip 8–15 and the martyrdom story deal with the apostle's destiny, forming a single, long travel narrative from Christ's commission through Philip's martyrdom in "Ophyoryme," most likely Hierapolis, Phrygia. During this missionary trip, Philip is accompanied by his sister Mariamne, who is probably Mary* Magdalene, and, as in the synoptic list of disciples, by Bartholomew. Symbols* ("signs") of eschatological reconciliation, such as a leopard and the kid of a goat, both having been converted to the good news, accompany the apostolic procession.

This text is important for what it promotes: a spiritual type of encratism* (through purity one can see God); the idea that women can preach and baptize (with Mariamne/Mary Magdalene as the model); the offer of salvation to wild animals; and archaic forms of prayer (see Acts of Philip 1, reusing the hymn of Christ of the Acts of John). FRANÇOIS BOVON

Philip, Gospel of, third treatise in the second Nag* Hammadi codex called the "Gospel of Philip," presumably because Philip is the only male apostle mentioned. Epiphanius* quotes from a Gnostic Gospel of Philip in Greek. The Coptic text shows affinities to Valentinian* Gnosticism* and may have been composed (c200) in Syria (some etymologies make sense only in Syriac). The Gospel of Philip, based on NT material, including John and Paul, seems to be a collection of excerpts or notes, progressively becoming longer. Nevertheless, some compositional threads run throughout the text. The opening paragraphs describe a way of conversion that leads from being a Gentile to a proselyte to a Hebrew to a true (Gnostic) Christian believer. A fine example of the reuse of canonical episodes is the figure of Mary* Magdalene, seen as the beloved* disciple and the true *syzygos* (spiritual twin?) of Jesus. Of interest is the sacramental* theology of the Gospel of Philip, which tries to find a middle course between the rejection of all material things and a ritual praxis that cannot do without them. Notable concepts include baptism* (cf. the metaphor* of God and Jesus as "dyers"), anointing* (who has received it "is no longer a Christian but a Christ"), and "the bridal chamber," possibly connected to the Eucharist* by the wedding feast metaphor.

HANS-JOSEF KLAUCK

Philippians, Paul's Letter to the, written during one of Paul's several imprisonments (1:12–14; 2 Cor 11:23), sometime in the 50s. Paul expresses appreciation for the financial support of the assembly he established in the Roman colony of Philippi, Macedonia (4:10–20). Although others question Paul's ministry (1:15–18), the Philippians remained loyal. Paul exhorts them to remain unified despite opposition (1:27–30). He cites himself as an example of someone who experiences joy despite difficulty (1:12–26, 2:17), as well as the examples of Timothy, his close colleague (2:19–24), and Epaphroditus, who has become seriously ill while visiting Paul on the Philippians' behalf (2:25–30).

Yet Paul depicts Jesus as the prime exemplar, using a striking early Christian hymn (2:5–11). Jesus abandoned heavenly glory and "humbled himself" on behalf of humanity, but has been exalted as the Christ. With this "Christ hymn," Paul encourages the Philippians; although suffering is the believer's lot (1:29), ultimate vindication is imminent. Thus Paul invokes eschatological traditions about the return of Christ. These traditions have a hortatory role, but also exemplify Paul's anti-imperial stance. Jesus is exalted as Lord (*kurios*) and Savior (*soter*), terms associated with the Roman emperor. In a context in which local authorities sought to placate their Roman overseers through the imperial cult, belief in Jesus as Lord and Savior caused conflict for Paul's followers. Paul calls these opponents of the faith "dogs" (3:2) and urges his followers to seek out a "heavenly citizenship" over against the coveted Roman citizenship (3:20).

The letter promotes a high Christology* to unify a conflicted community. Local leaders like the women Euodia and Syntyche are called to model that unity and heal personal rifts (4:2–3). All believers are called to a spirit of joy and excellence in moral virtue (4:4–9).

Traditional readings of this letter often focus on the Christ hymn as its central theological contribution, but the context of imperial domination has been highlighted more recently to show Paul's anti-imperial ethic.

EFRAIN AGOSTO

Philippine Independent Church, now called the Iglesia Filipina Independiente, prides itself on being a nationalist church and considers itself the only one that can teach Filipinos love of country. It is romantically viewed by its members as the "remaining tangible result of the Philippine Revolution" (1898), because its first leader was Gregorio Aglipay, a hero of the Revolution. In fact, the Church was instituted on August 3, 1902, by Isabelo de los Reyes, Sr., at a meeting of the Union Obrera Democratica, the first labor federation in the Philippines.

At first prominent laypeople and priests denied their involvement in the Church, but peasants, laborers, fishers, women, local elites, journalists, Protestants, and expatriates soon joined it. Gregorio Aglipay declined to participate in the Church leadership until October 1, 1902, when he signed the Temporary Constitution and Canons, becoming the first *obispo maximo* (supreme bishop). The Doctrinas y Reglas Constitucionales was adopted a year later (1903), stating that the Church was "Catholic as it considered all men [*sic*] equally children of God, but in that said universality, it accepts servility to no one." Shortly thereafter, at least 25% of the Filipino population had joined the Philippine Independent Church. Yet many refused to follow the Supreme Court's order (1906) to return church properties to their legal owner, the Roman Catholic Church, because many members of the Philippine Independent Church wanted to continue worshipping in what they viewed as their own sanctuaries. After Church membership declined to 14% of the population in 1918 and continued to decline until the 1960s, in part because of lack of trained clergy, it is once again rapidly growing; the Church claimed to have more than 4 million members in 2000.

Many of its songs and prayers implore the Almighty to allow the "rising of the joyful day of national freedom, independence and abundant life." The official liturgical book, the *Oficio Divino* (1906), was complemented by the *Misang Parangal sa mga Bayani ng Himagsikan* (Mass in honor of the heroes of the Revolution, 1910) and the *Pagsisiyam sa Virgen ng Balintawak* (Novena for the Virgin of Balintawak, 1926). Gregorio Aglipay later leaned toward Unitarianism*, but many bishops rebuffed him. Under the leadership of Isabelo de los Reyes, Jr., the Church returned to mainstream Christianity when it adopted the Declaration of Faith and Articles of Religion in 1947, entering into relations with the Episcopal Church of the USA, and other churches in the Anglican Communion; this was the beginning of many other ecumenical endeavors. The priests of the Iglesia Filipina Independiente are now trained at St. Andrew's Theological Seminary, an Episcopal seminary, even as the Church maintains and recaptures its nationalist heritage. **See also ANGLICANISM CLUSTER: IN ASIA: EPISCOPAL CHURCH IN THE PHILIPPINES.**

APOLONIO M. RANCHE

Philippines. Christianity arrived with Ferdinand Magellan's expedition (1521; which included priests) and with Spanish colonization, which took place in earnest from 1565 until 1898 on this archipelago of 7,107 islands in Southeast Asia. In 1565 Augustinian* missionaries arrived, followed by Jesuits* (opening their first college in 1595, the Colegio de Manila) and Dominicans* (who established the Colegio de Santo Tomas [University of St. Thomas], 1611). From these beginnings, Roman Catholicism spread throughout the Philippines (with the exception of Mindanao, which remained primarily Muslim). Filipino Catholicism had a Spanish character even though, in periods of resistance, revolt, and ultimately revolution (1896) against the Spanish colonial power, there were moves to "Filipinize" the Roman Catholic Church. The Iglesia Filipina Independiente (Philippine* Independent Church) was created before the multiplication of churches that took place with the arrival of Protestant missionaries in association with US colonization (and neocolonization after World War II). These Protestant missionary churches would together form the United Church of Christ in the Philippines (UCCP). Subsequently, other churches were established: Filipino independent churches, including the Iglesia ni Christo (Church of Christ, since 1914) and, after World War II, many Charismatic* churches.

The Filipino Geographical and Historical Context. The Philippines is an archipelago of 7,107 islands in four groups, from north to south: (1) the large island of Luzon, where the capital, Manila, is located; (2) the central Visayan Islands; (3) the large island of Mindanao; and (4) the Sulu Archipelago. The islands were under Spain for three and a half centuries

(1565–1898) and then the USA (1899–1946); they became an independent republic in 1946. Japan invaded the islands in 1941 and imposed a harsh occupation, which ended in 1945 with a bloody campaign of liberation by US troops, which resulted in the massive destruction of Manila and other cities. Democratic government was suspended in 1972 when President Ferdinand Marcos imposed a dictatorship under martial law, but he was ousted by a bloodless "people power" revolution in 1986.

The population (c88 million in 2007), mainly from the Indo-Malay stock, includes a small semi-nomadic tribe called the Aetas, considered aboriginal, and a mestizo* populace evolving from trade relations with and colonization by Chinese, Japanese, Arabs, Spanish, and North Americans. While Filipino (mainly Tagalog) and English are the official languages, about 8 languages and more than 100 dialects are spoken.

Christian Origins and Development in the Philippines. The Philippines are now predominantly Christian. But when Christianity arrived with the Spaniards, it encountered both animistic people and Muslims (primarily in Mindanao).

Most precolonial Filipinos were animistic*. Their belief system included a world filled with spirits and supernatural beings. Ancestor* worship (or veneration) was practiced in many of the tribes, with the belief that the spirits of the dead continue to coexist with the living, albeit in another dimension. In some areas and among some tribes, specific supreme deities, such as "Bathala" among the Tagalogs, "Kabunian" among some Cordillera tribes, and "Magbabaya" in Bukidnon, were worshipped. Both women and men exercised spiritual leadership. Women priestesses and shamans*, known as *babaylans*, were especially popular in the Visayan Islands. Some have theorized that the strong attachment to the Virgin Mary* in the Philippines is a latent evocation of the regard for the *babaylans*, who were consulted by political leaders (chieftains and monarchs known as *datus* and *rajahs*).

Islam* predated Christianity in the Philippines. It first arrived with Arab and Malay traders and merchants (c1380) in the Sulu Archipelago. The first Muslim sultanate was established in Sulu (1450); later, other sultanates were established on the larger Mindanao Island (c1475). In the 16th c., a Muslim sultanate was already in existence in the Manila area under Rajahs Sulayman, Lakandula, and Matanda, when the Spanish conquistadores arrived. Spanish wars against the Moros (Philippine Muslims) progressively pushed them back, so that they became a minority in Mindanao itself (see Islam and Christianity Cluster: In Asia: The Philippines).

Ferdinand Magellan, a Portuguese navigator serving under the king of Spain, claimed the Philippine Islands for Spain*. The king of Spain was a devout Roman Catholic who recognized the leadership of the Roman pope in spiritual matters; hence evangelization was one of the justifications for colonizing the islands (see Spanish Explorations, Conquests, and Missions). But it was only after 1565 (Legazpi expedition) that the spread of Christianity really began.

The different religious orders were assigned to different parts of the country for the purposes of evangelization. (The same strategy would be adopted three centuries later by North Americans in spreading the Protestant faith in the Philippines, following what is known as the "comity* principle.")

The Spanish friars were not only missionaries and evangelizers; they also played an active role in the Spanish pacification process. This gave rise to the saying commonly repeated at that time: "In every friar, the Spanish king had a captain and an army" (see Mission Cluster: Thematic Issues: Imperialism).

Despite the role of exceptional Spanish administrators and local priests, the Spanish response to the growing Filipino nationalism and religious consciousness came to be more oppressive and repressive.

The legacy of the Spaniards in the "Christianization" of the Philippines has been appropriately summed up by John England, Jose Kuttianimattathil, John Mansford Prior, and Lily A. Quintos (*Asian Christian Theologies*, Vol. 2). That legacy was primarily religious syncretism* (or inculturation*). Under Spanish colonial rule, Filipinos in most islands "had experienced rapid 'Christianization,' along with widespread oppression and destruction of their culture." But despite the widespread destruction of indigenous culture and religious practices (including native scripts and literature), "many Catholic practices blended well with indigenous myth, ritual and art-forms" that became vehicles for Christian practices. Conversely, "the best of Spain's traditions in law and scholarship, in the arts and in devotion would continue to be valuable sources for Philippine society and church."

Thus as several authors (England, Kuttianimattathil, Prior, Quintos) emphasize, the Roman Catholic theology that evolved in the Philippines in the Spanish period was "a Catholicism that had come to blend elements of native animistic religion with the teachings of catechism." They further observe that "the introduction of the Catholic cult of the saints*, many of the roles and functions of spirits still recognized in nature were transferred to the saints, while in 'folk Catholicism' the indigenous belief in a spirit world remained basically intact."

Secularization Movement and Nationalism. Filipino nationalism grew together with religious consciousness. Consequently, the Spanish response to the growing Filipino nationalism, a response that came to be more oppressive and repressive, deeply affected the Roman Catholic Church.

In the 19th c., as there were more secular* priests (i.e. priests who did not belong to religious orders), including more Filipinos, there was a movement demanding that these priests rather than the friars (i.e. regular* priests who belonged to an order and came from Spain) be assigned to the parishes. This secularization movement came at a time of growing unrest over Spanish rule and a growth of national consciousness. Three Filipino priests, all graduates of the University of St. Thomas, Fr. Mariano Gomez, Fr. Jose Apolonio Burgos, and Fr. Jacinto Zamora, headed the secularization movement, which also called for more liberal laws. In addition, Gomez, a parish priest in Bacoor, Cavite, founded a newspaper, *La verdad* (The truth), which described the deplorable conditions of the country and printed the liberal articles by Burgos. All these activities were viewed as hostile by the Spaniards, who called Gomez, Burgos, and Zamora *Filibusteros* and executed them by garroting (1872). José Rizal dedicated his second novel to them (*El filibusterismo*, 1891), and the martyrdom of Gomburza (an acronym of their three names) became a cause célèbre of the rising underground revolutionary movement, the Katipunan (from 1892). Another catalyst for the revolution was the execution (1896) of José Rizal, a leader of this revolutionary movement and a Philippine national hero, well known for his writings (including his first novel, *Noli me tangere*, 1887) advocating social reform.

On June 12, 1898, the Republic of the Philippines was born. It was a short-lived republic, however, for the USA, using the Spanish–American War as a pretext, took over the Philippines as its colony in 1898.

In the meantime, with the outbreak of the Philippine Revolution of 1896, there was a move to "Filipinize" the Roman Catholic Church. Upon the suggestion of Apolonario Mabini, the "brains" of the Katipunan, that an independent national church be formed, Isabelo de los Reyes, Sr., the leader of the first labor union of the Philippines (Union Obrera Democratica), initiated the creation of the Iglesia Filipina Independiente (1902; see Philippine Independent Church) and named Monsignor Gregorio Aglipay the supreme bishop. Aglipay, though reluctant at first, eventually accepted the leadership of the new church. Within a short time, the Philippine Independent Church constituted at least 25% of the Filipino population. The percentage declined until the 1960s, when it once again began to increase rapidly; the Church claimed to have more than 4 million members in 2000 (although the census identifies slightly fewer than 2 million), making it the third-largest church in the Philippines (after the Roman Catholic Church and the Iglesia ni Cristo [Church of Christ]).

In 1898, North American Protestants began arriving. It was clear that they supported the annexation of the Philippines by the USA and saw it as God-sent opportunity to evangelize.

Nationalism and the leadership of churches by Filipinos became thorny issues in the relationship between North American missionaries and Filipino converts. There were several schisms, which resulted in the formation of churches such as the Iglesia Metodista en las Islas Filipinos, a number of local churches that separated from the missionary-led churches, eventually forming the Iglesia Unida de Cristo and the Iglesia Evangelica Cristiana Independiente.

Iglesia ni Cristo (Church of Christ) is another national church, with exclusively Filipino leadership. Established in 1914 by Felix Manalo, it is known as a non-trinitarian church. Felix Manalo was baptized a Roman Catholic, joined the Methodist Episcopal Church, transferred to the Christian and Missionary Alliance, and became a Seventh-day Adventist. Felix Manalo is believed by Iglesia ni Cristo adherents to be a messenger sent by God to reestablish the Church of Christ. While not adhering to the divinity of Christ, Eraño Manalo (who succeeded his father as the head of the Church) underscored in the *Fundamental Beliefs of the Iglesia ni Cristo* that the Church affirms Christ as the Son of God, a mediator, and the Savior who will return; his second coming will be "the great day when the Church of Christ will receive the reward promised by God – the everlasting home for God's chosen people." Thus the Church of Christ, which defines itself in contradistinction to the Roman Catholic Church, claims that there is no salvation* outside the Church of Christ, which demands strict discipline from its members – a "new life" requiring regular attendance at worship services and giving "thanksgiving offerings" to support the needs of the Church. To fulfill these obligations, "and to love one another as true brothers and sisters," is to lay "a good foundation for the attainment of eternal life." In addition to these fundamental beliefs is the conviction that each member should do missionary work, calling people to enter the Church of Christ, a social order parallel to that of the world. This explains its rapid growth, which is apparent from the proliferation of its distinctive church buildings (with narrow, pointed spires): it has an estimated 2–3 million members, according to the 2000 census (the Church does not publish statistics; other estimates vary from 3 to 10 million worldwide). The church owns and operates near Manila the New Era University, the New Era Hospital, and many other institutions; it publishes two magazines, *Pasugo* and *God's Message*, and has its own radio and television stations. It is a powerful political force in the Philippines because of the "bloc voting" of all members in Philippine elections, following instructions from the leadership of the Church.

In culture, society, and religion, evidence of the "syncretism" that is a legacy of US colonization remains. Many aspects of Filipino culture and identity "further decline[d] in the decades of US control, despite positive advances in education, livelihood, and social welfare for sections of the Filipino people. Economic exploitation and cultural domination . . . also continue[d]" (England, Kuttianimattathil, Prior, and Quintos).

Ecumenical Movement among Non-Catholic Churches. The history of the ecumenical movement in the Philippines parallels and is linked with the history of the United Church of Christ in the Philippines (see United Church of Christ in the Philippines). The Evangelical Union formed by the missionaries in 1901 agreed to move toward the establishment of one, and only one, evangelical church in the Philippines. The formation of the United Church of Christ in the Philippines (as well as, earlier, the United Evangelical Church in the Philippines and even the Evangelical Church of the Philippines foisted on Christians by the Japanese) is a testimony to this ecumenical effort. But since not all of the Evangelical/Protestant churches joined the organic union, and many newer mission groups, which began arriving after World War II, did not adhere to or respect the comity* principle, a newer form of unity was sought that did not make organic union one of its main aims. There was also an attempt to attract the Iglesia Filipina Independiente (Philippine Independent Church) and the Philippine Episcopal Church into the ecumenical movement. This conciliar movement eventually formed the National Council of Churches in the Philippines (1963). The Council is the result of earlier attempts at unity, including the Evangelical Union (1901), followed by the National Christian Council (1929), the Philippine Federation of Evangelical Churches (1938), the Federation of Evangelical Churches in the Philippines (1942, wartime Japanese-sponsored federation), and the Philippine Federation of Christian Churches (1949).

Filipino Religious Psychological Makeup. Fr. Gerry Bulatao, SJ, writing in the 1960s, called the religious consciousness of Filipinos "split-level Christianity," in that there seems to be one kind of behavior that Filipinos adopt for "Christian occasions" – e.g. attendance at Sunday Mass and celebration of religious holidays (for patron saints, Holy Week, Christmas) – and another kind of behavior for the rest of life (business dealings, politics, relationships with others); this is a way of living in two harshly conflicting worlds. "Split-level" can be defined as the coexistence of two thought and behavior systems within the same person or even within the same culture, without guilt, even though these two systems are inconsistent with each other. So while the Philippines prides itself on being the only Christian nation in Southeast Asia, it also is one of the most corrupt societies.

It is also because of this "split-level" mentality that Filipinos can be Christian and yet continue to practice customs and tradition that are steeped in animistic or ancestor* worship practices and belief systems; e.g., they can do a novena for a dead relative and, at the same time, set aside a meal and offer it in front of a picture of this relative.

Leonardo N. Mercado, SVD, writing on Filipino theology and Filipino religious psychology, observes that the sacred and profane are intertwined. God and spirits are often inseparable from planting and harvesting. Religious ceremonies are integral to agriculture, fishing, hunting, and everyday life. These are so blended, he observes, that anthropologists do not know how to draw the line between the social and the religious. He also noted that Philippine languages have no original or non-loaned world for "religion" or "sacred." For him this means that Filipinos do not stress the distinction between the sacred and the profane, between grace and nature. **See also ANGLICANISM CLUSTER: IN ASIA: EPISCOPAL CHURCH IN THE PHILIPPINES; HUMAN RIGHTS CLUSTER: AND THE CHURCHES IN ASIA: THE PHILIPPINES; ROMAN CATHOLICISM IN THE PHILIPPINES.**

Statistics: Population (2007): 88 million. Christians, 92.5% (Roman Catholics, 80.9%; members of Iglesia ni Cristo, 2.3%; members of Iglesia Filipina Independiente, 2%, members of United Church of Christ, 1.2%; Evangelical, Charismatic, and other Christians, 6.1%); Muslims, 5%; others, 2.5%. (Based on 2000 Philippine National Statistics Office Census.)

REUEL NORMAN MARIGZA

Philip II (1527–98), king of Spain and supporter of the Catholic* Renewal. Son of Holy Roman Emperor Charles V and Isabella of Portugal; married (1543) Maria of Portugal, who died two years later while giving birth to their son, Charles; remarried (1554) Mary I of England. He reigned as king of Spain after the abdication of his father, Charles (1556). He inherited a powerful empire, including Spain, the Spanish Netherlands, Naples, and the Americas, which he attempted to expand through marriage and military campaigns. Roman Catholicism became an important tool in maintaining order in such a vast territory. He organized the Holy League (1560) – an alliance of Spain, Venice, Genoa, the Papal States, and other countries – to counter the threat of the Ottoman advance, culminating in victory at the Battle of Lepanto (1571) and stabilization of the Mediterranean region. His ongoing influence over the increasingly militant Roman Catholic Church in Spain is evidenced by his support of the reform of religious orders* throughout Spain; his attendance at public *autos* de fé* of the Spanish Inquisition* (1559); his support of enforcing the decrees of the Council of Trent* in Spain; and his support of ongoing missionary efforts in the Americas. **See also SPAIN; SPANISH EXPLORATIONS, CONQUESTS, AND MISSIONS.**

GILLIAN T. W. AHLGREN

Philo of Alexandria (c20 BCE–c50 CE) is the most significant witness to the exegetical traditions and practices of the Diaspora* in Second Temple Judaism*. A member of an eminent family of the Alexandrian Jewish community, Philo had received both a good education in his ancestral traditions (either at home or in a school attached to a house of prayer) and a full Hellenistic education (gymnasium and ephebate and beyond, for advanced training in rhetoric and philosophy). He made at least one pilgrimage to the Temple in Jerusalem. He may have operated a private school of exegesis where he taught and wrote. He led the first Jewish delegation to Caligula following the pogrom that broke out during Agrippa I's visit in 38 CE (*Embassy* 370; Josephus, *Ant.* 18.257–60).

A prolific author, Philo wrote more than 70 treatises (about two-thirds have survived in some form). Philo wrote three series of commentaries on the Pentateuch. (1) The *Questions and Answers* works through the texts of Gen 2.4–28:9 and Exod 6:2–30:10. (2) The *Allegorical Commentary* is a series of consecutive treatises that emphasize the allegory of the soul in the interpretation of Gen 2.1–41.24. (3) The *Exposition of the Law* is a thematic commentary on the law that spans the entire Pentateuch. His two-volume *Life of Moses* was probably an introduction to the Pentateuch. He also wrote philosophical treatises (an arithmology, *Numbers*; two dialogues, *Animals* and *Providence*; a thesis, *Eternity*; and a discourse, *Good Person*) and apologetic treatises in the aftermath of the pogrom (*Contemplative Life, Hypothetica, Flaccus,* and *Embassy*).

Philo was not a systematic thinker but an exegete*. He read Moses largely through Middle Platonism*, although he incorporated Stoic* and Neopythagorean concepts as well. He used allegory* as a hermeneutic* to read his ancestral Scriptures* in terms of Hellenistic philosophy. He believed that both Moses* and Plato saw the same realities, but that Moses saw them more fully and clearly (*Virtues* 65). He represents the apex of the rich exegetical tradition of the Alexandrian Jewish community that began in the 3rd c. BCE and continued until the destruction of the community (115–17 CE). At some point before the destruction of the Alexandrian Jewish community, his works made their way into Christian hands. Christians not only preserved them, but later gave Philo a posthumous baptism and, in some circles, even thought of him as a bishop. His work was particularly important for Alexandrian* Christianity and those influenced by it.

GREGORY E. STERLING

Philokalia (Gk "Love of the Beautiful"), a collection of ascetic* and spiritual writings (between the 4th and 15th c.; compiled and published in the late 18th c.) by masters (including Gregory* Palamas) of the Eastern Orthodox* hesychast* tradition centered on Mount Athos*.

Philology, study of the way in which language* is used in literature through historical comparisons with earlier texts. Philology is applied to biblical studies mainly as a means of establishing the specific theological meaning of biblical terms.

Philosophy and Christian Theology. Literally "the love for wisdom," philosophy is the discipline that deals with the most general characteristics and principles of things, also asking how these can be known and put into words. The use of human reason* and experience is authorized in the wisdom* writings in the OT and Apocrypha, and by a number of passages in the NT (Rom 1:19–20, 2:14–15; Phil 4:8; Acts 17:27–28), although these texts also suggest that human wisdom is based on and completed by divine wisdom. Many kinds of philosophy take their departure from religious myths, symbols, or doctrines, attempting to understand them in connection with more generally accessible human experience and reason. Still, philosophy is usually more careful in its methods and more cautious in drawing conclusions than the doctrine* and theology* of Christianity or other religious traditions.

In the Christian tradition, philosophy influenced theology in several distinct episodes.

1. Patristic Theology was influenced by Platonism*, often with the addition of Stoic* motifs. Justin* Martyr and the Logos* theology thought of God as the "Father and Maker" (Plato's *Timaeus* 31b, 50d) who created the world by uttering the Word, identified with Plato's "intelligible world." This theme was important in the development of the doctrine of the Trinity*, along with determinative elements drawn from the Bible. Platonism also placed great importance on the human soul*, its quest for wisdom, and its need for divine illumination; these concerns are reflected in Christian thinkers like Origen*, Gregory* of Nyssa, and Augustine*. The Platonist heritage continued to be the primary one into the Middle Ages. This philosophical influence is assessed in different ways (see Patristic Thought; Patristic Thought in Orthodox Christianity; Platonism and Christianity).

2. During the Middle Ages the thought of Aristotle* became more influential. The simpler writings on logic (the so-called old logic) were supplemented by the "new logic," more complex works dealing with syllogisms (early 11th c.), and then by the "physical books," works that dealt with the nature of the world and its divine cause in a rational way, with little religious concern and without dependence on religious traditions (see Metaphysics and Christian Theology). Aristotle's philosophy was the 12th- and 13th-c. "secular humanism," a way of thinking independent of biblical revelation that had been introduced in Christian Europe through Arabic translations, interpreted by Muslim thinkers. The rediscovery of Aristotle stimulated both "natural philosophy" and "natural* theology."

3. In the Early 17th Century a new approach to philosophy began with the natural science of Copernicus* and Galileo* (which questioned many features of Aristotelian physics) and the philosophy of Descartes*, which encouraged methodological doubt*, moving from the self to God to the physical world. While several 17th-c. theologians, both Roman Catholic and Protestant, were self-proclaimed Cartesians, Descartes's approach tended to direct attention away from revelation toward rational* theology. British empiricists like Locke* and Hume* probed the extent of human knowledge, and Kant* argued that our understanding of the world is finally determined not by experience but by our own concepts, making it impossible to know God through the natural world.

4. Hegel (1770–1831) bridged the chasm between consciousness and the world that had been created in one way by Descartes and in another way by Kant. Hegel* asserted that the real is the rational, such that knowledge is being's returning to itself. Hegel himself thought in terms of a pantheistic* development through which Spirit finally comes to itself in human art, religion, and philosophy. Theologians suggested a more orthodox approach in the doctrine of the Trinity*, for which God is always self-related and acts freely in creation* and reconciliation*. The priority of consciousness, both human and divine, was asserted in various kinds of "Personalist" philosophies (see Berdyaev, Nikolai; Marcel, Gabriel).

5. In the 20th Century there was a shift of attention away from metaphysics and toward human experience in phenomenology* and existentialism (see Bultmann, Rudolf; Kierkegaard, Søren Aabye), hermeneutics* (see Ricoeur, Paul), and linguistic philosophy (especially under the manifold influence of Wittgenstein*). These trends made a place once again for the role of belief and doctrinal traditions* in attempts to gain a comprehensive understanding of the human situation. Yet they were challenged by the more "deconstructive" analyses of language and experience linked with Michel Foucault and Jacques Derrida. Process* thought was also influential, especially in the USA. Taking seriously the evolutionary* understanding of the world, it thought of God as acting through "persuasion" rather than control, and it placed a new emphasis on God's receptivity and sympathy as well as active influence on the world (see Process Theology). EUGENE TESELLE

Philosophy of Religion. While theologians seek to clarify and defend religious convictions* (beliefs that are self-evidently true for believers), contemporary *philosophers of religion* seek to determine through critical analysis the extent to which these religious beliefs can justifiably be considered true.

For this purpose, philosophy of religion examines such issues as religious experience, religious ethics*, religion and science*, arguments for God's* existence, divine attributes, personal immortality*, and world religions*. It also ponders specific topics, including the problems of evil* and theodicy*. How is it possible to justify the affirmation of a belief in the existence of an all-powerful, all-knowing, perfectly good God given the nature and amount of horrendous evil we experience in a world allegedly created and controlled by God? Religious diversity is another problem that has received increasing attention. Seemingly sincere, knowledgeable individuals continue to differ on almost every significant theological issue. But if this is so (not all grant that it is), under what conditions can proponents of a given perspective continue to justify their belief that their perspective is the correct one?

Philosophers of religion who start from Western Christian premises pay particular attention to two of God's attributes: power and knowledge. Regarding God's power, *theological determinists* (e.g. Leibniz, Piper) claim that God unilaterally controls all. By contrast, *free will* theists* (e.g. Wesley*, Hick*) claim that while God could unilaterally control all, God voluntarily gives up control when granting us true freedom*. Yet for *Process* theists* (e.g. Hartshorne*), who step out of these traditional Western concerns, it is inappropriate to conceive of God as possessing the capacity for unilateral control; while God contributes to the becoming of each event, God does so interactively, never coercively.

Regarding God's knowledge, also starting from Western Christian premises, some (following Origen*, Augustine*, and the Jesuits* Molina*, Bellarmine*, and Suarez*) claim that God knows not only all that has occurred, is occurring, and will occur but even (with "middle* knowledge") all that would happen, including what we would freely do, in every conceivable set of circumstances. Others (e.g. traditional Thomists*) deny that God possesses middle knowledge, although they do maintain that God knows all that will actually occur in the future, including what all humans will freely do. *Open theists* (e.g. Pinnock) deny that God knows infallibly what will occur in those future contexts involving free choice. Still others (e.g. Boethius*) are uncomfortable with any attempt to conceive of God's knowledge in terms of our temporal understanding of past, present, and future. They hold that God's knowledge, whatever its extent, is best understood as "timeless" (outside of time).

Historically, many Western Christian philosophers believed that such questions could often be settled conclusively by careful consideration of the relevant evidence (e.g. Aquinas*, Anselm*). But the majority of contemporary Western philosophers of religion now accept that there exist no neutral, non-question-begging criteria in relation to which competing belief claims on most, if not all, religious issues can be settled with certainty. Accordingly, among philosophers starting with Western premises, most current discussions of competing perspectives on religious issues center on what is necessary for justified belief. One group of contemporary Western philosophers of religion, *reformed epistemologists* (e.g. Plantinga), deny that positive evidence of any sort is necessary for a justified religious belief; a successful defense against negative evidence is sufficient. However, *critical rationalists* (e.g. Alston, Quinn), the majority of contemporary philosophers of religion, acknowledge that the continuing affirmation of one of these competing perspectives can be considered rational or justified, even in the absence of positive evidence convincing to all. But they also hold that, since what can seem true changes over time and since our beliefs have practical consequences, the relevant evidence for or against the relative value of a religious belief should always be critically assessed. DAVID BASINGER

Philostorgius (c368–c439), Arian* historian, follower of Eunomius* who lived most of his life in Constantinople. His *Church History* deals with the period 300–430 from the Arian perspective and describes several of the leading Arians.

Phoebe, woman commended by Paul in Rom 16:1–2 to the letter's recipients; she was probably the bearer of Paul's letter to Rome and therefore its interpreter with full authority from Paul. He called her *diakonos* (servant, minister, agent) and *prostatis* (benefactor, patron). The term *diakonos* was also used figuratively in early Christian circles for ministers of the gospel (2 Cor 5:18) and was not gender specific. (*Diakonia* came to designate a more specific ministry in Acts 6:1, 2, 4.) As *diakonos* of a particular local church (Cenchrae, near Corinth), Phoebe was probably its representative; she is the only person in the NT named as deacon of a particular church. As a *prostatis* to Paul and many others, she was a provider of hospitality*, financial support, and networking. **See also DEACON, DIACONATE; DEACONESS.** CAROLYN OSIEK

Phos Hilaron (Gk "Gladsome Light"), evening hymn sung in the Eastern Church, at least since the 4th c.

Photios (c810/20–c892/95), patriarch of Constantinople*. One of the most learned persons of his time, and a teacher at the university in Constantinople, the emperor made him patriarch while he was still a layperson (858). He compiled a (second) version of the *Nomocanon** (combining both canons* of the church and imperial laws, affirming the close relationship between church* and state in the Eastern Orthodox Church). He was removed from office (867), reinstated (877), and once again forced to resign (886). He is remembered chiefly for his controversies with Rome and the equally strong minded pope Nicholas I. Photios challenged Rome's jurisdiction in Bulgaria*, denied the pope's right to approve the election of the patriarch, and condemned several Latin practices and beliefs (especially the *Filioque**). The controversies of his time were revived with the schism between East and West (1054) and the failed attempts at reunion (1274, 1439).

Phyletism, the division of Christians into separate churches along lines of nation, race, or ethnicity. Condemned by the 1872 Orthodox Constantinople Synod. B. MARK SIETSEMA

Pietà (Italian, "pity," "piety"), a representation, often sculptured, of Mary* holding Christ's dead body. The most famous is Michelangelo's in St. Peter's, Rome.

Pietism. Pietism is best known as a movement of spiritual and theological renewal within the Lutheran Church of Germany during the post-Reformation Era. It was chiefly represented by Philipp Jakob Spener* (1635–1705), pastor in Frankfurt am Main and later preacher at the court of Brandenburg/Prussia, Prussia in Berlin. This school of Pietism developed a comprehensive and massive program of education*, philanthropy, and world evangelization* under the leadership of August Hermann Francke* (1663–1727), theological professor at the University of Halle. Founded under the auspices of the emerging Prussian nation, Hallensian Pietism offered a revivalist*, spiritually transformative ethos* that would counter the influence of the Prussians' political adversaries. These were German nobles who, intent on preserving their traditional privileges, were allied to an intellectualized and socially stratified form of post-Reformation religious culture known as Protestant Orthodoxy. Francke's evangelistic, philanthropic, and educational program had a pervasive impact on all strata of Prussian society. It involved the education of youth from all social classes and genders, the deployment of the converted in massive Bible distribution, care for orphans, and the beginning of evangelistic missions* to populations beyond Europe. Funding came from the entrepreneurial efforts of converted Prussian laypersons. Both Spener and Francke had been influenced by the classic work of Lutheran devotional thought, the *True Christanity* of Johann Arndt* (1555–1621), pastor and superintendent at Braunschweig, who interfaced motifs from medieval German mystical texts with those from Lutheran doctrine.

Lutheran Pietism traces its inception to Spener's *Pia Desideria* (1675), which called for conventicles intent on personal spiritual renewal (the *collegia pietatis*). Influenced by his encounter in Geneva with the separatistic conventicles of the erstwhile Huguenot Labadie*, Spener believed that pastors could not effectively implement the Lutheran "priesthood of all believers" without enlisting the aid of consecrated laypersons. His work included a diagnosis of the corrupt conditions he perceived within the ecclesial and civil "estates," as well as the demoralized state of the general laity*. This critique was followed by proposals for correcting these conditions, including affective biblical preaching and relating sacraments to the "new birth" in Christ rather than administering them by rote, *ex opere operato*. Spener balanced justification* with sanctification*, understood to be the renewal of the image of God in the pardoned sinner*, effected by Christ through the indwelling Holy* Spirit.

Francke placed more emphasis on the active role of the human will* in effecting conversion* through heartfelt repentance*. Conversion must occur through human discernment and appropriation of God-given "hours of grace*." One of his Halle students, Count Nicholas von Zinzendorf* (1700–60), developed an extensive missional focus based on adoration of the crucified Lamb of God. He transformed his inherited estate, within the territory of a Lutheran parish, into the Moravian* community of Herrnhut, of which he became a bishop, in the line of the venerable "Unitas Fratrum." An authoritarian leader, he structured his community into "choirs" and instituted a rich tradition of hymnody and liturgy. Zinzendorf sought dialogue with disparate church traditions, although others tended to view the count's intentions with suspicion. That became apparent in his abortive effort to unify the disparate Pennsylvania German sectarians into a "congregation of God in the Spirit." Zinzendorf saw his missionaries, sent forth from Herrnhut under an intercessory prayer watch, as the seed of the gospel to be dispersed throughout the world. Their influence on the young John Wesley* was instrumental in that evangelist's conversion, hymnody, and shaping of the class structures of Primitive Methodism*.

In Württemberg the focus on biblical theology reached its zenith in the commentaries of Albrecht Bengel* at Tübingen.

Parallels to Pietism can be traced among the Dutch and German Reformed, including the work of "precisianists" (William Ames, 1576–1633, and Jodocus van Londenstein, 1620–77) and federal theologians (Johannes Cocceius*, 1603–69, and Friedrich A. Lampe, 1683–1729), who replaced Aristotelian philosophy with logical reasoning based on scriptural premises ("Ramist* logic") and the theology of the covenant. Underlying Pietism in the Reformed Church was the irenic impulse of the Heidelberg* Catechism (1563). Herborn Academy (established in 1584) was the center of Pietism in the Reformed Church in Germany.

Radical Pietists include the church historian Gottfried Arnold, author of an "unpartisan history of the church," in which Arnold stated his preference for the legacy of uncoerced Christian mystics* over the Constantinian church tradition. Linked to the speculative theosophy* of Jacob Boehme*, including his desire to recover a lost androgynous humanity, radical groups proliferated (c1690–1750); among these were Millennialist* societies (Philadelphians) and sectarians (e.g. Dunkers, Ephrata* cloister) in the German Rhineland (especially the Wittgenstein region) and in Pennsylvania.

As a whole, Pietism, developing alongside the Enlightenment*, gave birth to awakenings*, world mission* and ecumenical* efforts, new denominations, and modern Protestant theology. J. STEVEN O'MALLEY

Pietism in Scandinavia. With emphasis on conversion*, personal piety, Bible reading, and a committed life, Pietism* gained a foothold in Scandinavia, where it met and merged with domestic and Anglo-Saxon revivalism* and influenced churches and society from the 1680s to the present.

The way for Pietism in Scandinavia was prepared by earlier spirituality and books (Thomas* à Kempis, Arndt*). The influence of Spener* and Francke* came through direct and indirect contacts with Pietists in Germany (travels, letter writing, literature) and, after the Great Northern War (1700–21), through prisoners of war returning to Sweden-Finland from Siberia, where many had become Pietists. This moderate Lutheran Pietism won adherents among both nobility and clergy. The first missionaries from Scandinavia were Halle-trained Pietists sent from Denmark to the Danish colony in India. Moravian Brethren*, influenced by von Zinzendorf's* evangelical Pietism, were sent to Lapland and Greenland. Pietists also promoted Scandinavian missionary* societies for both foreign and domestic mission and created social-work and educational institutions welcoming both men and women.

Because it questioned religious formalism and ritualism, Pietism became a target of state censorship. Though forbidden in both Sweden-Finland (1726) and Denmark-Norway (1741), characteristic Pietist conventicles continued. Separatist groups, opposed to the state church and emanating from early contacts with radical spiritual Pietism (Arnold, Dippel), were expelled from Sweden-Finland in the 1730s and 1740s. Egalitarian and individualistic, uniting "believers" regardless of gender or social class, and stressing individual piety and lay activity, Pietism was an early advocate of freedom of religion and ecumenical* approaches. As a result of domestic revival movements (in Norway*, Haugeanism; in Denmark*, the Inner Mission; in Sweden*, Conservative Pietism, Schartauanism, Rosenian Evangelical Pietism, and certain free churches; in Finland*, Old Pietism, Evangelism, Laestadianism, and neo-Pietism, all within the Folk* Church), Pietism has been and is a complex spiritual, sociological, and political force, theologically conservative, but sometimes politically radical. RUTH FRANZÉN

Pietism and Women. Laywomen and laymen played an active role alongside prominent theologians at the beginning of the Pietism Movement. There were so many women involved in the 17th c. that some supporters of Pietism saw them as a sign of divine grace expressing God's favor for this reform movement, while opponents of Pietism, fearing disorder in the church and public life, saw them as a sign of decline. During the 18th c., the role of laywomen and laymen declined but remained significant.

Laywomen and laymen justified their involvement in Pietism mainly on the basis of the biblical and Reformation notion of the priesthood* of all believers. With this understanding of the Christian vocation*, differences in gender, social status, education, and profession lost their importance; all Christians were equal. Some Pietist groups simply combined traditional church structures and a renewed spiritual priesthood, so as to tamper as little as possible with the hierarchical order of priestly office and congregation. Spener* and Franke* belonged to this group. Others advocated a more radical version of spiritual priesthood (1 Pet 2:5–9) by connecting it with texts such as Joel 3:1, Gal 3:28, and 1 Thess 5:19. In line with the biblical and early Christian traditions, they insisted that there should be no restriction of women because of their gender at the ecclesiastical and social level. Gottfried Arnold was one of the prominent advocates of this position. This model, however, could also be considered to serve the interests of a new elite marked by a divine call rather than by gender, social status, or office. Johanna Eleonora Petersen advocated such an interpretation, seeing herself as someone directly called by God to bring God's messages to her contemporaries.

The egalitarian beginnings of Pietism are apparent in the so-called *collegia pietatis*, typical Pietistic groups that discussed the Bible and the members' faith experiences. In these meetings, mutual exchange was most important and was fostered through the Pietistic culture of letter writing and friendship*. In circles influenced by Spener, hierarchical structures were preserved even in such communication networks, whereas other groups experimented with new forms of friendship and living that partially overcame barriers of gender and social status.

Pietism spread in the period following the destruction of the Thirty* Years' War (1618–48). The lower nobility, in particular women, who were receptive to this reform movement, had lost its economic and political influence. Of the women active in the early period of Pietism, the number of those who belonged to the lower nobility is striking (although we have very little information about women and men of the lower classes). Johanna E. Petersen, née von Merlau, is a good example of such a woman. Pietism stressed that education was required for a proper understanding of the Bible. Thus several Pietistic women acquired broad theological knowledge. Although the greater part of Pietistic literature was produced by men, women were also active. Besides spiritual lyric poetry and autobiographic texts, they composed theological works. In a time when scholarship was not yet considered to be the province of those with a university education, women who published poems and songs might also be thought of as scholars. This stress on the equality of all before God, on spiritual equality beyond boundaries determined by gender and social status, and the original impulse for reform were lost to a great extent with the consolidation of the Pietism Movement, which became theologically and socially conservative.
RUTH ALBRECHT

Pilate, Acts of, an extended account based on the canonical Gospels' narrative about the trial, crucifixion, and resurrection of Jesus. It owes its name to the initial episode, in which the intriguing figure of Pontius Pilate* and his activities are elaborated on, as are those of Nicodemus* (thus it is sometimes called the Gospel of Nicodemus). Although Justin* Martyr and Tertullian* mentioned (but did not quote) such a work, the text we know from 12th-c. manuscripts (in two versions) apparently was written in the 3rd c. (Eusebius* mentioned a "forgery" of the Acts of Pilate) or later. By presenting Pilate in a more positive light than the canonical Gospels do, the Acts of Pilates attributes to the Jews greater responsibility for Jesus' death. **See also ANTI-SEMITISM.** DANIEL PATTE

Pilate, Pontius, appointed by Rome to govern Judea in 26 CE. Pilate maintained order with the 3,000 Roman soldiers whom he commanded, as well as with the help of the high priest who, as the official representative the people of Israel, cooperated with him as a prudent political strategy for the sake of the people. The Gospels are often read as absolving Pilate of guilt for ordering Jesus' execution. Scholars debate the issue, however, and it seems clear that in the period of the patristic writings directed against the Jews (the *adversus Judaeos* literature), early interpretations would have exaggerated any such tendencies in the Gospels. Both Josephus* and Philo* remember Pilate as an exceptionally cruel and provocative Roman official. **See also ANTI-SEMITISM.** NICOLE WILKINSON DURAN

Pilgrim, Pilgrimage (from Lat *peregrinus*; French *pèlerin*). The original meaning of "pilgrim" in the Greco-Roman world was "sojourner*," describing the status of Christians as citizens of the heavenly Jerusalem* (Gal 4:26; 2 Cor 5:6–7; Phil 3:20), not fully at home in the world, like Abraham before them (Gen 12:1–8; Heb 11:8–12). This meaning was preserved among Celtic* monks, for whom wandering for Christ was a way of self-denial, detachment, and reliance on God's guidance. The sense of not fully belonging has been revived in our own time, as indicated by the use of the term "sojourners."

After Constantine* and Helena*, pilgrimage came to mean journeying to holy places, first to Jerusalem (see Egeria*) and later to the tombs of martyrs, most notably those of Peter* and Paul* in Rome. Pilgrimage in this sense grew steadily during the Middle Ages, when Compostela (Spain) became a major destination; many Italian, French, and English cathedrals became pilgrimage sites because they contained famous relics*. Pilgrimage was one means of making satisfaction for sins in the sacrament of penance*.

The term also has broader connotations. In the framework of cultural anthropology, "pilgrimage" often has the character of liminality, separation from the ordinary and the achievement of a new degree of community and spiritual integration. Pilgrimage is often a metaphor for the inward journey toward God and eternal* life.

The Crusades* began as a form of armed pilgrimage to the Holy Land. The Age of Exploration was a secularized kind of sojourning or pilgrimage, justified by its professed goal of converting peoples to Christianity.

Both Erasmus* and the Reformation* criticized the abuses and superstitions* connected with pilgrimage. In modern times, pilgrimage is practiced mostly by Roman Catholics and Eastern Orthodox. Well-known destinations include Loreto (Italy), Lourdes*, and, in the New World, Guadalupe* Hidalgo; among the Orthodox, they include monasteries such as Mount Athos*.

In the contemporary world, mass pilgrimages function as acts of national penance, public testimony, or group identity. **See also POPULAR CHRISTIAN PRACTICES CLUSTER.** EUGENE TESELLE

Pilgrims (North American). See PLYMOUTH BRETHREN; PURITANS, PURITANISM.

Pillars (Dutch, *zuilen*), in the Netherlands*, four subcultures (Liberal, Socialist, Protestant, Roman Catholic) that have their own clubs, news media, and political parties. Their cohesiveness began to decline in the 1960s.

Pisa, Council of (1409). The cardinals who had elected two rival popes called this council in order to end the Great* Schism (in the West). It deposed both popes and elected a new pope. The council failed to end the schism – there were now three popes – and its validity was questioned by many because it had not been convened by a pope. But it prepared the way for the Council of Constance* (1414–18), which resolved the crisis.

Pistis Sophia, a 3rd-c. Gnostic* "revelation dialogue" between Jesus, the risen Savior, and his disciples, which is preserved in a single manuscript, Codex Askewianus. The text, consisting of four books, seems to be a compilation of Gnostic teachings. Books 1 and 2 concern the repentance of the fallen Sophia and the deliverance of Pistis Sophia; Book 3 addresses how authentic knowledge is preached to the world and to whom the forgiveness of sins and access to the light are granted. Included later, Book 4 has a different dialogue setting; it reveals the punishments of evil archons and the divine mysteries by which the disciples can escape judgment*. In all of the books, Mary* Magdalene has a dominant role in the dialogues between Jesus and his disciples. This causes tension between her and some of the male disciples, especially Peter. ANTTI MARJANEN

Pius IX, Pope (1846–78), born Giovanni Maria Mastai Ferretti (1792) in Senigallia. He served as nuncio* in Chile*, ran an orphanage in Rome, was appointed bishop of Spoleto (1827), then of Imola (1832), and made a cardinal (1840). Although he was seen as having liberal sympathies and supporting Italian nationalism, his refusal to help drive Austria out of Italy (1849) turned Rome against him. When Rome fell to the forces of the new Kingdom of Italy, Pius became "the prisoner of the Vatican." He oversaw the First Vatican* Council (1869–70), expanded Roman Catholic missions, and increased the centralization of the Church's administration. His conservatism was displayed in the Syllabus* of Errors (1864). He was beatified* in 2000. MICHAEL J. WALSH

Pius X, Pope (1903–14), born Giuseppe Melchior Sarto (1835) in Riese. The son of a village postman, he studied for the priesthood (Padua), served in the cathedral of Treviso, and was made bishop of Mantua (1885) and patriarch of Venice (1893). His insistence on the rights of the church against the state (see Church and State Relations Cluster) led to a breakdown of relations with several countries. He backed a campaign against those accused of "Modernism*" within the Roman Catholic Church and focused on a renewal of the liturgical and spiritual life of the Church (e.g. allowing children of the age of reason [usually age seven] to receive Communion*). He began the codification of canon* law (completed in 1918). Pope Pius* XII declared him a saint. MICHAEL J. WALSH

Pius XI, Pope (1922–39), born Ambrogio Damiano Achille Ratti (1857) in Desio. He studied in Milan and Rome, and after ordination (1879) taught at Padua's seminary. He was appointed librarian to Milan's Ambriosian Library and to the Vatican Library (1911). He was named a prefect in 1914, and shortly thereafter was made a cardinal archbishop in Milan. As pope, he entered negotiations with the Kingdom of Italy over the Vatican (Lateran* Pacts, 1929), establishing the Vatican city-state. His encyclical* *Quadragesimo Anno* further developed Leo* XIII's social doctrine, and his encyclical *Mit brennender Sorge* (1937), condemning Nazi atrocities, was smuggled into Germany. He was preparing an encyclical condemning the persecution of the Jews when he died. MICHAEL J. WALSH

Pius XII, Pope (1939–58), born Eugenio Maria Giuseppe Giovanni Pacelli (1876) in Rome into a family with a long tradition of papal service, chiefly as lawyers. Pacelli was ordained (1899), assisted in the codification of canon* law, was named nuncio* to Munich (1917) and the Weimar Republic (1920), and was made a cardinal (1929) and secretary of state (1930). He was involved in negotiating the concordat* with Germany (1933). As pope, he maintained careful neutrality during World War II, leading to his being accused of keeping silence in the face of the Jews' persecution. His encyclical *Divino Afflante Spiritu* (1943) encourages the scientific study of Scripture, although his *Humani* Generis* (1950) expresses alarm at current theological trends; he encouraged discussions between Roman Catholics and other Christians on theological matters. MICHAEL J. WALSH

Plainsong, or plain chant, unison vocal music, especially as developed in the Western or Roman Catholic Church. Changes of pitch are gradual, without large intervals; rhythms are free, followings the texts (the Mass*, psalms*, canticles*, and short traditional verses). This style of singing had Jewish roots and was influenced by the early Greek-speaking church. In the West, several different styles developed, with the Gregorian most widely used. The style was revived (19th c.) by the Benedictine* monks of Solesmes.

Plato. See NEOPLATONISM AND CHRISTIANITY; PLATONISM AND CHRISTIANITY.

Platonism and Christianity. Christianity, as a social and intellectual phenomenon, began to impress itself on the surrounding environment in the late 1st c., largely as a result of Paul's missionary travels. Yet it did not come to the notice of Platonist philosophers until much later.

The first philosophical influences on Christianity seem to be Stoic* rather than Platonist; in matters of ethics at least, Paul* seems to have been somewhat influenced by the flourishing Stoic school of Tarsus. Even the Logos* doctrine of the Gospel of John* is primarily Stoic, although it might have been influenced by a Stoicizing Platonism emanating from Antiochus of Ascalon (1st c. BCE) and mediated through the Platonizing Jewish philosopher Philo* of Alexandria (c20 BCE–45 CE). John's Logos is, after all, the world-immanent representative of a transcendent God, which is not the case with Stoicism, where God is also immanent in the world and material (pure fire).

Only with the 2nd-c. Christian Apologists*, such as Justin* (c100–65), is some degree of engagement with Platonism discernible. Justin, a Hellenic intellectual, claimed in *Dialogue with*

Trypho to have tried out all the philosophical schools, culminating in Platonism, before converting to Christianity. His ethical position remained primarily Stoic, advocating the extirpation of the passions, but that was also a position adopted by some Platonists (e.g. his contemporary Atticus) and maintained by Philo as the correct position for a wise person. In metaphysics*, Justin, again like Philo, adopted the originally Stoic (but now Platonized) doctrine of the Logos of God as a means of characterizing the role of Christ, while he adopted the originally Aristotelian (now also Platonist) view of God as Unmoved Mover, "remaining in his own place" above the universe.

Yet Justin was no crypto-Platonist. In *Dialogue* (Chaps. 3–6), he allows the Old Man to criticize both Platonic intellectualism (the view that only through intellectual activity can one attain knowledge of the truth and of God) and the doctrine of the eternity* and reincarnation of souls*. He also advances a consoling theory (first propounded by Philo and later taken up by the Alexandrian theologians Clement* and Origen*) that all Greek wisdom is derived from Moses; specifically, Pythagoras studied for some time with followers of Moses on Mount Carmel and passed on what he had learned, ultimately, to Plato, Aristotle, and the Stoics. This theory motivates Philo's bold allegorizing* of the Pentateuch, and Christian thinkers' allegorizing of the Prophets and the NT, especially the Gospel of John and the Pauline Epistles.

After Justin's martyrdom (Rome, 165), his positions were taken up and greatly elaborated in Alexandria, by Clement* (c150–215) and Origen* (185–254). Clement exhibited a wide knowledge of Greek philosophy and adopted a good deal of Platonism in his many writings, on the same lines as Justin: a belief in the Platonic tripartite soul*, the extirpation of the passions, and the Christ as the Logos of God. But above all, there emerged in Clement the idea that Christianity is itself a philosophy, to be argued for rationally, and not simply accepted on the basis of faith.

This position was carried further by Origen* (who, unlike the previous two thinkers, was a Christian by birth, his father Leonidas having been martyred in 205). Of his many works, his commentaries on Matthew and on John are showcases of his allegorical method, while his treatise *On First Principles* is arguably the foundation of Christian philosophy. There he deals comprehensively with the natures of God*, Christ (as the Logos, and firstborn of the Father), and the Holy* Spirit, angelology, the soul*, and fate, providence, and free will*, presenting in all cases a doctrinal position deeply influenced by Platonism (including the Pythagoreanizing version of Platonism earlier propounded by Numenius of Apamea), but buttressed at every stage by proof-texts from the Bible.

Origen subsequently fell foul of the ecclesiastical authorities precisely because of certain of these Platonist influences. Specifically, he was condemned for subordinating Christ to God the Father as the "firstborn of all creation" (influenced by Numenius's doctrine of the Demiurge as a secondary deity) and for holding not only that the human soul preexisted embodiment and might undergo a series of incarnations in order to work its way back to total purification, but even that the devil* himself would ultimately be saved, since the doctrine of eternal punishment seemed to him to derogate from God's infinite goodness and power. For him, the Pauline tag "Christ will be all in all" signified the ultimate reassumption of all creation into the Divinity.

Platonism provided early Christianity with a strong philosophical underpinning, enabling it to commend itself to the wider intellectual world of late antiquity, but it also held within itself certain threats to faith*, which emerged in due course as heresies*. **See also NEOPLATONISM AND CHRISTIANITY.** JOHN M. DILLON

Plotinus (204–69 CE). See NEOPLATONISM AND CHRISTIANITY.

Pluralism, Religious, and Christian Theology.

For most of Christian history, religious pluralism was not an issue. Early Christians understood their own religion to have superseded* Judaism* and surpassed pagan* religions. Those who did not share the Christian faith, or even a particular version of the Christian faith, were generally deemed to be outside God's favor, despite some ambivalence regarding pagans such as Plato*, whom Augustine* called "almost Christian." Cyprian's* 2nd-c. dictum, "outside the church there is no salvation," was the dominant Christian view, with several notable exceptions.

In 1076 Pope Gregory* VII stated that Christians and Muslims worshipped the same God in different ways, and in Dante's* *Divine Comedy* (13th c.), virtuous pagans are given a place in Limbo*, just outside the gates of hell*. Mystic* forms of Christianity, e.g. Nicholas* of Cusa's *The Peace Between Different Forms of Faith* (15th c.), envisaged reason* as a unifying basis of all religions, a theme also found in Enlightenment* figures. Gotthold Lessing's *Nathan the Wise* (18th c.) portrays Judaism, Christianity, and Islam as valid before God, each in its own right.

In the 19th c., history* displaced reason as the unifying force underlying religions. Hegel* developed an evolutionary theory according to which the various world religions are stepping stones of the Spirit to subsequent, more complete revelations, culminating in Christianity. Troeltsch* proposed a more fully developed historical view. Every religion, including Christianity, is molded by its context of place and time; every religion, including Christianity, tends toward forms of its own absoluteness. Troeltsch wrestled with the notion of Christian superiority, finding it in some sense through the personalism he identified with Christianity, but ultimately even this fell to the historical relativity by which each religion tends to see its own forms as superior and to use its own norms to evaluate the norms of others. Troeltsch, like Hegel, finally saw a transcendent God at work in all religions, but unlike Hegel, he could not view these religions as stepping stones to the one final religion. Each religion is final to its own adherents.

World wars and the rise of Barth's* neo-orthodoxy overshadowed Troeltsch's work. For Barth, Christianity in its deepest sense is not a religion; it is the revelation of God and thus stands outside all comparison with religions per se. But after World War II, theologians again raised the question of Christianity's place among world religions, usually in ways that made Christianity the norm by which all religions were judged. The most notable example was Rahner's* notion of "the anonymous* Christian" (1961). God, as the transcendent horizon of being, is present to every person, calling that person to righteousness. When persons respond to this call, the response is itself a yearning toward God that constitutes a "baptism by desire," making the person a Christian within the depths of his or her being, albeit unknowingly.

John Hick's *God and the Universe of Faiths* (1971) marks a universalism that decenters Christianity by positing a transcendent "The Real" to which all religions point and that some religions name God. Paul Knitter's *No Other Name? A Critical Survey of Christian Attitudes toward the World Religions* (1985) sparked a major interest in the issue, which moved it to a more central place in theological studies. Knitter gives a typology of three Christian approaches to religious pluralism: (1) *exclusivism*: asserting that other religions are not ways of salvation; (2) *inclusivism*: embracing other religions under the normative superiority of Christianity; and (3) *pluralism*: like Troeltsch, recognizing the historical nature of religions and the validity of each within its context. **See also AFRICAN RELIGION AND CHRISTIANITY CLUSTER; CONFUCIANISM AND CHRISTIANITY CLUSTER; DAOISM AND CHRISTIANITY CLUSTER; HINDUISM AND CHRISTIANITY CLUSTER; ISLAM AND CHRISTIANITY CLUSTER; JUDAISM AND CHRISTIANITY CLUSTER; SHINTO AND CHRISTIANITY; SIKHISM AND CHRISTIANITY CLUSTER.**

MARJORIE HEWITT SUCHOCKI

Plymouth Brethren, movement originating in early-19th-c. England and Ireland in reaction against the established church. In the 1830s, groups of Brethren gathered to restore the primitive practices and teachings of the NT church that they believed the Anglican Church neglected, including simplicity of worship and leadership based on spiritual experience rather than clerical title or education. Beginning in the 1840s, the movement divided into "Open" and "Exclusive" factions over membership standards and whether those outside the movement could receive Communion, which was offered weekly. Theologically, the Brethren emphasized biblical prophecy. A founder and leader was former Anglican minister John Nelson Darby*, whose Dispensationalist* interpretation of Scripture shaped Evangelical and fundamentalist* movements and influenced various writings from the *Scofield Reference Bible* (1909) to the popular *Left Behind* novels (1990s–2000s). Through devout missionary work, Brethren spread from the United* Kingdom to various European countries, in addition to Africa and India. In 2003, there were 86,000 Open Brethren living in the USA. JAMES P. BYRD

Pneumatology, doctrine and discussion of the Holy* Spirit in relation to God, human history, and salvation.

Pneumatomachi (Gk "Spirit fighters"), those who denied (4th c.) the divinity of the Holy* Spirit. This question had been left unanswered by the Council of Nicaea*, and it was not explicitly debated until Eustathius* of Sebaste supported the position of the Pneumatomachi (373). The argument advanced by Didymus* the Blind for the divinity of the Holy Spirit was that the holiness of the church and of individuals must be grounded in divine reality. While the Council of Constantinople* (381) condemned the Pneumatomachi, it claimed only that the Spirit is "worshipped and glorified" with the Father and Son, not that it is "of the same essence."

Pogrom (Yiddish, from Russian), organized violence against helpless people, especially Jews; a violent attack involving the destruction of property, murder, and rape perpetrated by local non-Jewish, often Christian, populations on Jews in the Russian Empire and in other countries. **See also ANTI-SEMITISM; HOLOCAUST, JEWISH (OR SHOAH).**

Poland. The distinctive features of contemporary Polish Roman Catholicism include its ability to resist laicization*, secularization*, and postmodern liberalism*. This became clear in the 1970s, a turning point in the relations between church* and state, when the totalitarian Communist regime in Poland started to decline.

1. Early Christianization (9th–14th Centuries). Christianity arrived in the territories that constitute contemporary Poland in two ways. First, Methodius* (c815–85), the apostle to the Slavic people, converted the powerful prince of Wislica (Upper Vistula). The Slavonic liturgical language and the Methodian Rite survived in this region until the 11th c., but failed to influence nearby people and disappeared after the fall of the Moravian Empire (906).

Christianity next arrived among the Polany ethnic group ruled by the Piast dynasty, which ruled the Polish lands from the 9th to the 14th c. The population worshipped gods symbolizing forces of nature (e.g. Swarozyc, the sun, giver of life and material goods; Swietowid, related to war and fertility). Because the Polany territory was crisscrossed by trade routes, the first contacts with Christianity were missionaries who traveled with merchants. To strengthen his state, Prince Mieszko achieved political union with the Czechs by marrying the Czech princess Dabrowka, who arrived in Poland (965) "with a large retinue of clergy and laypeople." She had a decisive influence on Prince Mieszko's decision to accept Christianity from Rome; he and his court in Poznan were christened in 966. Thus Poland entered into the family of Christian nations, gaining military assistance from the West in its struggles against both non-Christian princes and the (German) Holy* Roman Empire, which was seeking to absorb Poland under the pretext of spreading Christianity. In the process, Poland was shaped largely by the Western, feudal* style of sacred princely power. Christianity eliminated polygamy*, forbade the killing of wives during husbands' funerals (a common practice until then), and implemented as norms of social life the principles of the Ten Commandments.

The first known bishops, Jordan (968) and Unger, found it difficult to convince Polany people "to till the Lord's vineyard." They were missionary bishops with a see in Poznan under direct papal care (officially after c990). Through this direct connection with Rome, Prince Mieszko protected his nation against raids by neighboring Christian rulers and obtained permission to create a Polish archdiocese (independent of German dioceses).

The archdiocese was actually created in 1000 by Mieszko's successor, Boleslaw Chrobry (the Brave) (992–1025), with the help of Adalbert (Wojchiech, 956–97), a martyred missionary bishop and friend of Emperor Otto III. In 1000 Otto, together with papal legates, cardinals, numerous dignitaries, and rulers, made a pilgrimage to the grave of St. Adalbert, located in Gniezno (Central Western Poland). There the papal delegates announced the establishment of the Polish Archdiocese of Gniezno. The first archbishop, Adalbert's brother Gaudenty-Razim, had three dioceses: Krakow, Wroclaw, and Kolobrzeg. During the meeting in Gniezno, Otto III placed on Boleslaw Chrobry's head an imperial diadem, acknowledging him as an ally of the Holy Roman Empire and of the Papal State. A number of years later, Prince Boleslaw's official coronation as king was a significant recognition by the Holy See.

King Boleslaw Chrobry valued the Western Church and did not spare any efforts to solidify the new faith in his lands and disseminate it beyond the borders of his kingdom. Monks were the primary propagators of the gospel. Three Benedictine* convents were established, in Trzemeszno, Tum, and Wislica (10th–11th c.). The Cameldolese brothers from Italy settled in Miedzyrzecze and led missions in Southwest Poland, ultimately successfully, after five of the brothers (including two Poles) were murdered. Their suffering was described by Bruno of Kwerfurt (Querfurt), who conducted missions among the Jacwingi (a Baltic ethnic group). He too paid for his activities with his life.

After King Boleslaw Chrobry's death, Poland went through a political crisis, which led to a religious breakdown. Rivalry among potential successors was also a struggle between non-Christians (inside and outside the kingdom) and Christians (supported by the clergy). The clergy was almost completely wiped out. The Czechs invaded Poland (1039), destroying churches, including the cathedrals of St. Adalbert (in Gniezno) and St. Peter (in Poznan). The situation was finally brought under control by Prince Casimir (Kazimierz) (1038–58), who restored the nation and the Catholic Church. He reintroduced the population to Catholicism with the help of numerous clergy sent by his uncle Herman, archbishop of Cologne. Bishop Aron settled in the undisturbed diocese in Krakow, which, with a considerable library, became the center of cultural and intellectual life.

Casimir's efforts were continued by his son, Boleslaw Smialy (1058–79), who led the Polish Church to participate in Pope Gregory* VII's reforms. By helping to install pro-papal kings on the Hungarian throne, Boleslaw Smialy gained numerous concessions from Rome, including a royal crown (1076), the reestablishment of the Archdiocese of Gniezno, and the creation of a diocese in Plock. But the murder of the bishop of Krakow (1079) ordered by the king abruptly severed the good relations with Rome. During the reign of Boleslaw Smialy's successor, Wladyslaw Herman (1079–1102), Poland and its church found itself in the German camp, enemy of Gregory VII's reforms, although they were finally brought into conformity by Herman's successor, Boleslaw Krzywousty (1102–38), and by the archbishop of Gniezno Henryk Kietlicz (1199–1219). The Polish Church was reborn through the efforts of German clergy, including, from the early 13th c., clergy emerging from the German settlers flowing into Poland. As a result, the Polish Church started to lose its Polish character. Except for the Dominicans, convents and monastic orders became so Germanized that Poles were not allowed to become members. Similarly the parish priests were Germans who did not know the language of their flocks. The archbishop of Gniezno, Jakub Swinka, corrected the situation, requiring at least a minimum knowledge of the Polish language by the clergy.

2. Christianity in the Commonwealth of Poland and Religious Tolerance (14th–17th Centuries). With the territorial expansion of Poland along the Russo-Polish and Lithuanian–Polish borders (including Ruthenia), many changes occurred, especially during the reign of Casimir the Great (1333–70). A Roman Catholic diocese was established in the borderlands of Przemysl (1340). Catholic missionaries, mostly from the mendicant* orders (Dominicans* and Franciscans*), flowed into Ruthenia, leading to the establishment of new dioceses in Wlodzimierz, Lvov, and Chelm and an archdiocese in Halych (1375), which was later transferred to Lvov (1412).

The king granted to Ruthenia freedom of religion for the Eastern Orthodox* (1351), appointing a metropolitan in Halych, with four Orthodox dioceses. The king also granted permission to establish a diocese to two groups of Armenian Miaphysites* in Lvov and Kamieniec Podolski, whose most visible monument was the Armenian cathedral in Lvov. The three groups of Christians coexisted with Jews – a freedom of religion that so far had been exclusively reserved for Catholics in Western Christianity. This was the beginning of "Polish religious tolerance," thanks to which Poland never experienced heretics'* pyres or inquisitions*. This religious freedom was not caused by a lack of religious fervor; all of the faiths, particularly that of the Roman Catholics (who were socially and politically privileged), sought to increase their ranks.

Poland's great achievement in spreading Christianity was the conversion of Lithuania. The Piast dynasty ended with the death of King Casimir the Great (1370). Following much international intrigue, Jadwiga (Hedvig, in her native Hungarian), Casimir's 10-year-old relative, became "king of Poland" (1384) and married the ruler of Lithuania (and the lands of former Kievian Rus), Wladyslaw Jagiello. Following Jagiello's christening and marriage to Jadwiga, Polish missionaries started the systematic conversion of the peoples of Lithuania, beginning with the controversial campaigns of Teutonic* Knights from the 1230s. During her brief life, Queen Jadwiga was devoted to Christianizing Lithuania, founding churches, and promoting religious practices. After her early death (1399), King Jagiello created two dioceses in Lithuania, in Wilno (or Vilnius) and Miedniki. In the Polish–Lithuanian commonwealth, the distinctive Polish policy of religious freedom continued and applied not only to Roman Catholic and Orthodox Christians but also to Jews and Muslims (Tatars).

Church work was carried out through a network of parishes. The number of parishes in Poland grew from c800 in the 12th c. to more than 3,000 in the early 15th c., and to almost twice as many by the 16th c. This growth was interrupted by the Reformation, but starting again in the 17th and 18th c. Similarly, a well-developed network of Orthodox parishes continued to increase in the East; by the end of the 18th c., there were more than 9,000 Orthodox parishes in the eight dioceses of the Kiev Metropolitanate (see Ukraine).

The Roman Catholic Church also developed elementary schools in the parishes. At the end of the 16th c., more than 90% of parishes had schools; by the 17th and 18th c., education was widespread in urban as well as rural parishes. For a long time, teachers for these schools were educated at Krakow University (founded by Casimir the Great, 1364); education deteriorated after Casimir's death (1370), but was revived by Queen Jadwiga and her husband, Jagiello (1400). Later four additional institutions of higher education were established: the Academy of Poznan (1519), the Academy of Wilno, or Vilnius (1579), the Zamojsky Academy (1594), and the Academy in Lvov (1661).

The Reformation was slow to take hold in Poland because of people's respect for King Sigismund I. After his death (1548), a majority of the nobility and upper classes in the cities, mostly of German descent, joined the Reformation, although the Polish townsfolk and peasants remained faithful to the Catholic Church. The nobility preferred Calvinism* and its democratic structure, which was similar to the Polish parliamentary monarchy (there were more than 500 Calvinist congregations in Poland), to Lutheranism* (there were merely 140 Lutheran congregations, all of them in Wielkopolska, most conducting worship services in German).

Other Reformers arrived in Transylvania and Poland from Italy, fleeing the Inquisition* because of their anti-trinitarian views. With powerful Polish protectors, the Italians Francesco Stancaro (arriving in 1558) and Faustus Socinus* (settling in Krakow, 1579) rejected the dogma of the Trinity*, affirming that there was only one God and that Christ was the "son of God," not by nature but because God shared his divine power with him. Along with their sympathizers among the poorer Calvinist nobles, they became an independent Socinian movement, later called Unitarian*. The definitive break with the Calvinist Reformation occurred in 1562, as a result of both the Socinians' theological views and their social radicalism calling for the abolition of the death* penalty, pacifism*, and the rejection of private wealth*.

Another group of lay Christians and clergy led by Cardinal Jakub Uchanski proposed the creation of a national church, which King Sigismund II Augustus (reigned 1548–72) finally rejected.

The Roman Catholic Church in Poland was reinforced when the conclusions of the Council of Trent* were accepted by the king (1564), posing a threat to the other churches. After the king's death (1572), the Sejm (parliament) included in the oath taken by every elected king a provision that guaranteed permanent peace between the various churches. In this way, freedom of religion was extended to new religious groups. Yet in 1658 the Socinian Movement was refused protection under this law and expelled from Poland for betrayal of the state because it had sided with Sweden during the 1655–56 war. With this exception, during the 16th–17th c., Poland was a nation of religious tolerance, a nation without pyres.

3. The Catholicization of the Polish Commonwealth (Late 16th–Late 18th Centuries). In East Prussian towns (then part of the Polish kingdom), the majority of the population was Lutheran (in contrast to the rest of Poland, which was heavily Roman Catholic). In one of these Prussian towns, Torun, the sons of the local nobility were educated at a Jesuit college. A mob attacked the college, destroying the interior and desecrating its religious objects (1724). Local authorities (the Lutheran mayor and nine citizens) were condemned to death for not ensuring the safety of the Jesuit college. After their execution, the Prussian and Russian courts proclaimed that they guaranteed religious freedom (for Protestants and Orthodox, respectively) in Poland. Russian troops entered Poland under this pretext in 1725.

The Catholic* Renewal in Poland, starting with the king's acceptance of the Council of Trent, was promoted by the influx of new religious orders, particularly the Jesuits, who gained control of middle schools where children of the nobility were educated (including [former] Protestants). Intelligent and religious bishops who were more pastors than politicians exerted a great influence by encouraging the clergy and their parishes through theological writings, pastoral letters, and regular visits. By contrast, the churches of the Reformation declined and almost disappeared, except for the Lutheran churches in Wielkoposka and Prussian cities.

In the eastern portion of the Polish Commonwealth (Lithuania and Ukraine), the Orthodox churches were first placed under the control of Moscow. The fall of Constantinople to the

Ottomans (1453) made Russia the world's only sovereign Orthodox nation. Russia had attained full ecclesiastical autonomy in 1589, with the election of the first patriarch of Moscow. But the Orthodox Church in Poland lagged far behind the Roman Catholic Church in the education of its clergy and in vitality. In this situation, encouraged by King Sigismund III, Catholic theologians (the Jesuits Skarga and Warszewski, as well as Frycz Modrzewski and Orzechowski) and bishops (Bernard Maciejowski, among others) advocated the unification of the Polish Orthodox Church with Rome. This was ratified in the Union of Brest*-Litovsk (1596) and accepted by both the metropolitan of Kiev, Michael Ragoza, and Pope Clement VIII, former papal legate to Poland, despite resistance in parts of Ukraine: two of the nine dioceses of Kiev (Lvov and Przemysl) did not accept the Union until 1693 and 1700, respectively.

A similar union between the Roman Catholic Church and the Polish Armenians, again encouraged by the king, was resisted by Armenian clergy and elders but resulted in a Unitate Armenian Church in Poland, Moldavia, and Walachia, officially established in 1686.

In the late 17th and 18th c., Polish Catholic religious orders, the Jesuits (especially), Dominicans, and Franciscans (including Reformed Franciscans and Capuchins), developed rapidly. The Jesuits gained almost complete control of middle and higher education, and the mendicant orders contributed to parish work (especially in eastern regions).

4. Christianity in Partitioned Poland (1772–1918). The Enlightenment*, cultivated by the royal court and many bishops, led to the downfall of the nation, which was partitioned (1772–95) among Prussia, Russia, and Austria until 1918. Under pressure from the liberal European courts, Pope Clement XIV suppressed the Jesuits (1773–1815). In Poland their colleges were transferred to the Ministry of National Education, reformed in the spirit of the Enlightenment. But because of their educational function in the annexed Polish territories, neither Russia nor Prussia accepted the banishment of the Jesuits (although in 1820 Jesuits were expelled from Russia).

After the partition, Poles recognized that Roman Catholicism and the Polish language were the keystones of their national identity. The Roman Catholic Church was the only institution where the Polish language was used – in the liturgy, sermons, catechism, songs, customs, and religious rituals. Similarly, the cult of Mary* ("the Queen of Poland"), with its pilgrimages* in many locations throughout Poland helped retain Polish identity, as did the celebrations at different churches and sanctuaries associated with martyrs.

The national uprising against Russian occupation (1830–31), supported by most bishops, ended with Czar Nicolas I placing the Catholic Church under the control of the state, creating the Roman Catholic Ecclesiastical Collegium, leaving bishop positions vacant, curtailing contact with Rome, and, most significantly, liquidating the Uniate Church in Lithuania and Belorus by reintegrating 1.5 million believers into the Russian Orthodox Church (1830–38).

In the part of Poland under Prussian control, German bishops were rapidly installed in Polish territories. Yet some (such as the archbishop of Gniezno-Poznan, Leon Przyluski, 1845–65) resisted this Germanization of the Church by maintaining the use of the Polish language in the Mass. Recognizing the bond between Roman Catholicism and Polish nationalism, the Prussians imprisoned or banished such church leaders.

In response to the Russian efforts to suppress the Polish desire for political independence, Poles initiated the "moral revolution," i.e. massive participation in religious and patriotic observances during national anniversaries in Poland, Lithuania, and Belorus. Similarly, funeral services, such as that of the archbishop of Warsaw, Antoni Fijalkowski (1856–61), became religious and patriotic manifestations, resulting in this case in the imposition of martial law. With Poland under Russian control, this period was marked by the execution of clergy and their deportation to Siberia; the closing of monasteries; the interdiction of processions and pilgrimages; police surveillance of preaching and even of confessionals; the annulment of the relations with the Holy See; the interdiction to the bishops to attend the First Vatican* Council; and the abolition of all remaining Uniate churches in Poland (1871–75), despite the resistance of believers.

With the deep economic and social changes of the late 19th c. in Western Europe, a new group of extremely exploited people emerged – the workers in large industries. Pope Leo XIII's social* encyclical *Rerum Novarum* (1891) affirmed the workers' right to form Catholic labor organizations. At that time, Polish workers in Warsaw and Lodz followed what became the Polish Socialist Party (PPS, founded 1892) calling for the "equality of all citizens" and Polish independence. Rather than struggling against Christianity, the PPS included clergy, e.g. Fr. Jerzy Matulewich (beatified in 1987), theoretician of Christian labor organizations, and Fr. Marcel Godlewski, organizer of secret labor groups, *Straz* (Guards), and the above-ground Association of Christian Labor. Fr. Waclaw Blizinski organized a similar rural social movement.

In territories under Prussian control, Cardinal Przyluski encouraged resistance to Germanization (*Kulturkampf**) through the preservation of Polish and Roman Catholic possessions, and the application of *Rerum Novarum* to rural areas, also resulting in an economic awakening of the Wielkopolska region. This was achieved in part through the Organization of For-Profit Cooperatives* (Zwiazek Spolek Zarobkowych, initiated by the clergy, especially August Szamarzewski, Piotr Wawrzyniak, and Kazimierz Zimmermman) and the journal *Ruch Chrzescijansko-Spoleczny* (Christian Social Movement). Archbishops Edward Likowski and Florian Stablewski also promoted the development of Christian social organizations in parishes. Similarly, in Galicia (under Austrian control), the priests developed education along with charitable work as an effort to prevent impoverishment, although the bishops of Galicia did not understand the importance of social action.

5. Christianity in Reunited Poland (20th Century). On November 11, 1918, Poland regained its independence. Although its territory was smaller, it expanded in the wake of uprisings and local wars (1920). In 1921 the population of Poland was 27.8 million, with 17.3 million Roman Catholics (62.2%), 3.3 million Greek Catholics (Uniate) (11.9%), 3 million Orthodox (11%), 1 million Lutherans (3.5%), and 2.9 million (10%) Jews. The Roman Catholic Church had three archdioceses: Warsaw, Gniezno-Poznan, and Lvov. The Greek Catholic Church (associated with the Ukrainian Greek Catholic Church) had a metropolitan in Lvov. The Orthodox Church, emancipated from Moscow in 1922, joined the Warsaw–Wolyn metropolitan. The Protestants were organized into three churches: the Augsburg Lutheran, United Evangelical, and Reformed churches. In 1921 the Polish Sejm (parliament) guaranteed freedom of religion for all, although the Roman Catholic Church was "first among equals" and the relations between the Roman Catholic Church and the state were regulated separately by a concordat with Rome (1925).

Cardinal August Hlond, son of a miner, affirmed in a pastoral letter (1932) following Pope Pius XI's encyclical *Quadragesimo Anno* that "the nation is for the citizens" and not the citizens for the nation. This criticism of totalitarian regimes was a basis for the call to social action to counteract poverty*. Cardinal Hlond promoted the development of Catholic* Action (legalized in Poland in 1934) to encourage the implementation of moral and religious principles in social life without regard for political parties. The bishops established the Social Council, which sought to delineate new directions for social action by the Polish Roman Catholic Church.

In 1939 two totalitarian nations, Germany and Russia, attacked Poland, occupying it for six years. The Catholic Church played a significant role in helping the nation endure, engaging in various forms of resistance by providing shelter, material assistance, as well as spiritual aid. Convents and parish churches either hid, or organized hiding places for, thousands of Poles and Jews, many clergy paying for these activities with their lives in Nazi extermination camps and Russian camps. Approximately 2,000 priests died at the hands of the Nazis (861 in Dachau). More than 500 priests were killed by the Soviets, and many priests and monks were forced to abandon their parishes and monasteries. The martyr of Auschwitz, St. Maksimilian Kolbe, a Franciscan from Niepokalanow, became the symbol of Christian love opposing totalitarian hatred. All of this took place in the midst of the unthinkable extermination of the entire Jewish population of Poland and of million of Jews from other nations, Gypsies*, and other pariahs, as well as millions of Polish Christians (see Holocaust, Jewish [or Shoah]).

At the end of the war, Communist rule was established and enforced in Poland by the Red Army. Communists sought to legitimize themselves with the aid of clergy, although they severed the concordat with the Holy See (1945). They also sought to weaken the church from the inside-out, by instituting "patriot priests" and breaking up the solidarity among the clergy in the national church. The Communist rulers also sought to weaken the Roman Catholic Church by confiscating Church property (1950); establishing a state commissar as leader of Caritas, the Church's charitable organization with 900 preschools, hundreds of orphanages, shelters, and walk-in clinics, supported primarily by donations from North America; closing seminaries and monasteries; banning religious orders; and characterizing Pope Pius XII as a Nazi sympathizer and the bishops as the backbone of the underground resistance against Communism. Cardinal Stefan Wyszynski's efforts to regulate the relations between the Roman Catholic Church and the Communist state led to an "accord" (1950) allowing the Roman Catholic Church to run the Catholic University in Lublin and seminaries; to have monasteries; to have chaplains in the army, hospitals, and prisons; and to teach religion in schools with "respect for the laws and authority of the state" (thus with many restrictions).

In the meantime, Stalin compelled the remaining Greek Catholic Church in Poland (and Ukraine) to become part of the Russian Orthodox Church (1946). Within the framework of the "repatriation" (1945–46), thousands of believers from the Przemysl Diocese were resettled in the USSR or the "Recovered Territories" (1947). Estates left behind were confiscated. Similarly, the Orthodox Church in Poland was put under the control of the Moscow patriarch (1951) and became a compliant tool for the domination of Poland by the Soviets.

The Catholic bishops protested the ongoing breach of the "accord" by issuing a letter of protest (*Non Possumus*, 1953), emphasizing their own compliance with the "accord." A month later, Cardinal Wyszynski declared in a sermon, "Give to Caesar what is Caesar's and to God what is God's; but when Caesar sits on the altar we simply say: Forbidden!" The cardinal and several bishops were imprisoned. From prison (until 1956), Cardinal Wyszynski developed a program for a religious rebirth of the nation under totalitarian conditions. The cardinal walked out of prison as a national hero; through his actions, he prevented the useless loss of blood.

After a brief thaw, the Communists found two new areas of conflict with the Roman Catholic Church: the celebration of the 1,000-year anniversary of Christianity in Poland (1966), which the state wanted to be secular; and the proclamation by Polish bishops to the Germans, which concluded with the words "We forgive and beg for forgiveness," with the hope of improving relations between Poland and Germany. The state initiated a media campaign against this proclamation. During that time, the archbishop of Krakow, Karol Wojtyla, stood alongside Cardinal Wyszynski for 14 years. Karol Wojtyla became Pope John* Paul II (1978), changing the Vatican's political stance toward the East and contributing to the collapse of the Communist system.

The union between Poland and the Roman Catholic Church over a span of 1,000 years (except for some of the periods noted) has been very powerful, during times of glory and downfall. The Church was especially close to the Polish people in times of crisis, when Poles could feel free to be Poles only in the churches. Conversely, the Polish people stood with the Church when it was threatened, attacked, or persecuted. Thus the Church emerged from such crises empowered and in solidarity with the Polish faithful.

Statistics: Population (2000): 38.8 million (M). Christians, 37.7 M; 97.4% (Roman Catholics, 35.7 M; Orthodox, 1 M; independents, 330,000; marginal Christians, 200,000; Protestants, 195,000); nonreligious, 1 M, 3%; Jews, 6,000. (Based on *World Christian Encyclopedia*, 2001.)

TEOFIL WOJCIECHOWSKI

Political Studies of Christianity, identification and interpretation of the relationships between Christianity and political ideas or actions; study of influences of Christian ideas and institutions on political life; study of relationships between religious and political values. Originating in early social scientific studies of religion, political studies of Christianity have increasingly dealt with political norms as well as political behavior.

In the early 20th c., Max Weber* and Ernst Troeltsch* pioneered studies that showed the influence of religious ideas on the sociology of religious organizations and the economic* life of society. Rejecting Karl Marx's* claim that religious ideas merely reflect material causes, Weber and Troeltsch insisted that religious ideas have political and economic consequences, although these consequences are often unintended. Troeltsch connected his "ideal types" of Christian community, which he identified as the church*, the sect*, and the mystic* types, to the political and economic actions of their members.

H. Richard Niebuhr* used this typological method to study the social effects of Christian belief, both in the USA and throughout Christian history. Reinhold Niebuhr* applied a less definite method, but was similarly concerned with the effects of religious ideas on political actions and was sharply critical of those who sought political implications of Christianity in utopian* visions of social transformation or idealized, nonhistorical accounts of Jesus' ethics*.

These political studies consider not only the effects of Christianity on political behavior, but the effects of Christian ideas on the normative ideas of political philosophers and political leaders. Like interpretative methods in sociology, political studies of Christianity attempt to identify connections between Christian beliefs and widely accepted cultural norms and values.

Recent political studies of Christianity by Glenn Tinder and Jean Bethke Elshtain have drawn on Augustine* and Martin Luther* to develop theoretical accounts of the limits of politics. Robert Bellah has identified key Christian ideas that play a normative role in US civil* religion, and he distinguishes its ideas of community from the predominant US individualism. Alongside these studies of normative political ideas, the emergence of politically conservative religious movements gives new impetus to empirical studies of how Christian beliefs influence voting patterns in the USA. Political studies of Christianity in the future will most likely make use of increasingly detailed methods of social and historical analysis to focus attention on particular local connections as well as the broad historical influences of Christianity on politics. **See also CHURCH AND STATE RELATIONS CLUSTER; DEMOCRACY AND CHRISTIANITY; MARXISM AND CHRISTIANITY.**

ROBIN W. LOVIN

Political Theology, theological interpretation of the source, meaning, and purposes of political society. All political theology begins with the absolute claims that the modern state makes for its role in human life. Conservative political theology supports the claims of the state against other historic powers and movements, while critical political theology rejects those claims in favor of a human solidarity that crosses all boundaries between states, social classes, ethnic groups, and other divisions.

After the religious unity of Western Europe ended with the Reformation*, modern states became the organizing centers of loyalty and identity. National churches, especially in Protestant countries, united faith and nationality, and many observers thought that the stability of this new order required religious authority* for the ruler, as well as secular power. Niccolò Machiavelli suggested that princes might make use of religious authority to secure their own positions. Thomas Hobbes developed an account of political power that made the sovereign the sole source of both religious and political authority, the arbiter of doctrine, as well as law. In its earliest forms, then, political theology took the religious authority that a united church once claimed over the divided realms of European princes and transferred it, not to the divided churches that ministered to increasingly privatized religious needs, but to an all-powerful state that claimed authority over every aspect of public life. Religious authority is not merely instrumental to the power of the state. It is a constitutive part of that power.

Philosophers speculated about political theology, but European states rarely practiced it. Most maintained a close relationship between church and state, such as the Prussian "union of throne and altar." Other countries, like the USA, experimented with an unprecedented separation of church and state or developed a civil* religion like those of postrevolutionary France or newly modernized Japan. Only in the early 20th c. did it become possible for conservative thinkers in Western Europe to propose political theology as an alternative to workers' revolutionary movements. Political theology affirmed the nation above the rights of individuals and the interests of social classes, so that service to the state became a religious act and not merely an obligation of citizenship. While political theology was not directly involved in the creation of National Socialism in Germany, it offered a way of thinking that readily supported Hitler's power (see German Christians).

Contemporary political theology takes approaches diametrically opposed to those earlier, conservative forms. Critical political theology probes the connections between political power and class interests, suggesting that the state is no more than an instrument of the wealthy* and powerful segment of the population. Jürgen Moltmann and Johann Baptist Metz make use of Marxist thought in this social analysis, so that their political theologies have more in common with socialism than with the anti-socialist affirmation of the state in previous political theology (see Marxism and Christianity). Critical political theology, however, is not an economic program. Its aim is to understand the actual political functioning of all institutions and movements, including churches, so that no partial, limited interest can present itself as ultimate, eternal, and necessary (see Idol, Idolatry).

Eschatological* political theology likewise opposes the absolute claims of political authority, but with theological, rather than social, criticism. Oliver O'Donovan argues that Christians must view the state in light of the decisive setting aside of all human authority that had already begun with Jesus' messianic proclamation. Notwithstanding the weakness and division of the church in the modern world, political power must be understood theologically to be responsible merely for creating the conditions under which the church can fulfill its mission, rather than a bearer of religious authority in its own right. **See also CHURCH AND STATE RELATIONS CLUSTER; DEMOCRACY AND CHRISTIANITY; LIBERATION THEOLOGIES CLUSTER.** ROBIN W. LOVIN

Polity, form of church government, varying greatly from one church or denomination to another, depending on their answers to several important questions.

Who Governs? The NT supports various polities: congregational* (Matt 18:17; 1 Cor 14:23), presbyterian (Acts 20:28; 1 Tim 3:5; 1 Pet 5:1–3), and episcopal* (Acts 20:28; Phil 1:1). By the late 2nd c., most churches had a threefold office: a single bishop* (see Monepiscopate, Monarchical Episcopate), assisted by presbyters and deacons*.

How Are Controversies Resolved? Disagreements between local churches were resolved through mutual consultation (Acts 15), and it became customary to call regional councils* or synods* of bishops to decide issues of doctrine* or discipline*. Councils often adopted canons* specifying beliefs, procedures, and penalties.

Is Authority "Structured"? The consecration of a new bishop required the presence of the metropolitan* and other nearby bishops. In addition, the bishops of churches founded by apostles* (traditionally Antioch, Alexandria, and Rome, then Constantinople as the "New Rome") gained special authority in their regions. As the role of the pope* in the West increased, there was a countervailing emphasis on the authority of councils, with or without the pope (see Conciliarism).

What Is the Role of the State in Church Government? The first ecumenical* council, at Nicaea*, was called by Emperor Constantine* (325), and its decrees were enforced by him. The role of the emperor was similar for all seven ecumenical councils of the undivided church and was enshrined in the Justinian* Code, which became part of civil law in the West as well as the East. While this role was increasingly contested by the medieval popes, those who did not wish the pope to have sole supremacy in the church kept the role of secular rulers alive (see Erastianism; Gallicanism; Henry VIII; Marsilius [or Marsiglio] of Padua). During the Reformation*, German princes, Swiss cities, and English monarchs played a key role. But when Protestant churches were persecuted by Roman Catholic governments, they had to develop forms of governance totally independent of the state (see France; Scotland). Worldly power found a different role in the practice of patronage*: donors, landowners, and rulers expected to have a part in naming pastors and especially bishops.

What Role Do the Members Have? Administrative authority was vested increasingly in bishops, popes, and patriarchs. A more participatory style of governance developed in the monastic* communities and in the Lay* Piety Movement. During the Reformation*, these impulses bore fruit, sometimes within the congregation alone, sometimes in representative bodies that included laity* as well as ministers. The principle of the Reformed* churches was that no minister has authority over another except through election, usually for a fixed term of office (see Presbyterian Churches). This representative, or "synodal," form of governance spread to the Lutheran, Anglican, and, with modifications, Roman Catholic churches.

Is Polity a Matter of Divine or Human Law? Debate within the Church of England (16th and 17th c.) raised the question of whether the office of bishop belongs to the "essence" of the Church or merely to its "well-being," or perhaps is not necessary at all. This continues to divide Catholics (including Anglo-Catholics), who insist on episcopacy as commanded by God, from most Protestants, who take a more functional or pragmatic view of ministry and especially of polity, adapting it to the needs of the times. **See also APOSTOLICITY AND APOSTOLIC SUCCESSION; CHURCH, CONCEPTS AND LIFE, CLUSTER: TYPES OF ECCLESIASTICAL STRUCTURES.** EUGENE TESELLE

Polycarp (c70–c155/72), bishop of Smyrna; a leading figure in Asia Minor, acquainted in his youth with the mysterious John* and remembered in the next generation by Irenaeus*. He visited Ignatius*, who was on his way to martyrdom in Rome (c106–13), and received a letter from him. His own letter to the church in Philippi may actually be two letters, one accompanying a collection of Ignatius's letters (c110) and one warning against Marcionism* (c135). He visited Rome (c155–60) to defend the Quartodeciman* observance of Easter. Not long after his return, he was tried and executed; the account of his martyrdom is one of the first to survive and the first to mention the veneration of a martyr's relics*.

Polygamy and Christianity. In the African religiocultural tradition, polygamy was an accepted institution of marriage among patriarchal* societies, while Christianity considers monogamy the only valid and recognized form of Christian marriage. Although the Anglican Church withheld baptism from polygamous households starting in 1888, inspired by pastoral concerns it reversed its stand; now baptism is open to members of polygamous households, although under conditions inspired by the monogamous ideal (Nasimiyu-Wasike).

"Polygamy" commonly means the simultaneous marriage of one man and several women, what anthropologists would call "polygyny." In patriarchal traditional Africa, polygamy fulfilled various social purposes. First, as Mbiti shows, it was (as it still is) every man's ideal to increase the number of his wives (and children) in order to gain and expand "immortality*" for that family. Children were the glory of marriage; a childless marriage was considered meaningless and pushed the man into polygamy (Nasimiyu-Wasike). Second, the purpose of polygamy was (and still is) to produce male progeny. In patriarchal societies, male children were much more highly valued than female children. Third, in both agrarian and pastoral cultures, production depended on the number of hands available to help; several wives and many children were necessary to work the fields, tend the cattle, and increase the wealth of the man of the homestead. Fourth, strict gender division of labor was maintained by taboos; thus the first wife asked her husband to marry more women to assist her with the workload. Fifth, in some societies women outnumbered men; polygamy ensured that all women would be under the protection and guidance of men: as daughters under their fathers, as wives under their husbands, and as old and widowed women under their sons. Unmarried or childless women were considered incomplete.

Although polygamy is still practiced throughout Africa, the factors on which traditional polygamy was based have drastically changed as a result of the economic transformation of small farms to large machine-operated farms, and of nomadic pastoral life to life in irrigated settlements; it has also changed because of urbanization and industrialization and the greater number of poor and homeless people. Polygamy has always been the privilege of rich men who can afford bride-wealth, but their number is decreasing.

Some Christian ethicists seek to justify polygamy by emphasizing its socioeconomic dimensions. But its religious dimensions cannot be ignored. The institution of polygamy favors men and reduces women to subservient and inferior status, contrary to God's will. Christian marriage* by definition is monogamous and indissoluble. The Bible, particularly the OT, contains stories of polygamy. But rather than interpreting these stories as normative (as certain African* Instituted Churches do), they may read them as warnings and criticism (Gen 16 and 21; 29:30–31; 37; 2 Sam 14; Judg 9:5; Kgs 11:1–4). Furthermore, the metaphor* of marriage that runs through the Scriptures is one of monogamy. For instance, in Hosea, Israel is implored to be faithful to the marriage covenant* with her husband, God; in the NT, Jesus Christ is the bridegroom and the church his bride (Rev 18–22). Thus, against polygamy, most Christians affirm monogamous marriage as the ideal, indeed as a divine gift requiring those who receive it to form a lasting union (Mbula). If a polygamous man sought Christian baptism, he was advised to put aside all his wives but one. This is still the practice among many Christian denominations, including the Roman Catholic Church. Yet, as stated earlier, the Anglican Church has a different approach, as do many African* Instituted Churches. **See also FAMILY, CHRISTIAN VIEWS OF, CLUSTER; MARRIAGE, THEOLOGY AND PRACTICE OF, CLUSTER.**

ANNE NASIMIYU WASIKE

Polyglot Bibles, Bibles in which the text is written in several languages, in parallel columns. Origen's* Hexapla, with the Hebrew and several Greek translations, is the earliest example. Bibles with Greek and Latin, Greek and Coptic, and Latin and Gothic survive from antiquity. The most famous such Bible was the Complutensian Polyglot, prepared under Cardinal Ximenes*, with the OT in Hebrew, Greek, and Latin, and the NT in Greek and Latin. Others were subsequently published in Antwerp, Paris, and London.

Polytheism, belief in or worship of more than one deity, widespread throughout the world, perhaps reflecting the multiple powers that influence human life and nature. It was practiced by Israelites, although it is condemned by biblical writings, e.g. the first of the Ten*

Commandments (Exod 20:3) and many statements by the prophets. Although Judaism and Christianity are monotheistic* religions, the belief in angels* and demons*, and the veneration of saints*, may be remnants of, or replacements for, polytheism*. The Christian belief in the Trinity* has also been perceived to be polytheistic.

Pontifical, relating to a pope. **See also POPES, ROMAN CATHOLIC, AND THE PAPACY.**

Pontifical Biblical Commission, body of Roman Catholic scholars appointed by the pope, created by Leo XIII (1902) and reorganized by Paul VI (1971). Until 1971 members were cardinals* with 40 consultants. Until 1933 the decrees confronting Modernism* favored traditional exegesis* over scientific approaches; in 1955 these were declared superseded. Indeed, after 1934 the commission was constructive and gave much freedom to biblical scholars. Starting in 1941, it published documents favorable to historical criticism, including one on the historical truth of the Gospels (1964), which encouraged "form-criticism" (see Bultmann, Rudolf). Since 1971 the Commission has consisted of 20 scholars, with the prefect of the former Holy* Office as president; it issued five documents, including a well-received statement on the practice of interpretation of the Bible in the context of the Roman Catholic Church (1993). **See also BIBLE INTERPRETATION CLUSTER: HISTORY OF.** MAURICE GILBERT

Pontificals, liturgical books in the Western Church containing texts for the ceremonies used by bishops (e.g. confirmation*, ordination*, consecration of churches).

Poor. See POVERTY CLUSTER; PREFERENTIAL OPTION FOR THE POOR.

Poor Clares, the Second Order of Franciscans, authorized by Francis* of Assisi with Clare* of Assisi as first abbess (1215) in Italy. Clare's Rule, approved in 1253, focused on the necessity of poverty*, as did the 15th-c. French Colettine reform. Devotion to the Passion and imitation of Mary* as the compassionate mother* were key to the Clarissan vocation from the beginning. Authors addressing communities of Poor Clares, such as Bonaventure*, recommended a spiritual life focused on humility, obedience, and contemplation of Christ's humanity. Medieval Clarissan authors Battista da Varano and Catherine of Bologna described spiritual lives nourished by visions and focused on elevating God and distrusting the self. The relative importance of enclosure versus a Franciscan ideal of absolute poverty was contested by Pope Gregory IX, Urban IV, and the male Franciscans who oversaw the new convents. The 16th c. led to greater control of the convents by male Franciscans and a return to the Urbanist Rule. Although monasteries and convents were closed down in England during the Reformation, the Poor Clares saw a revival in the 19th-c. Anglican Church. The Roman Catholic version was transplanted to North America after its suppression in Italy (late 19th c.). JESSICA A. BOON

Popes, Roman Catholic, and the Papacy. "Pope" (Gk "father") is a title applied to the bishop of Rome, particularly with respect to his role as the center of communion of the Roman Catholic Church. The term was regularly used for bishops throughout the early Christian world from the 3rd c. When Greek ceased to be a common language of Christianity, "pope" was increasingly applied only to the bishop of Rome; Gregory* VII (11th c.) instructed that it be limited to him. It is, however, still also used for the Coptic patriarch of Alexandria.

It was early acknowledged that the Roman Christian community played a special role in the Catholic Church. However, it is difficult to demonstrate that there was a single presiding bishop in the capital of the Roman Empire until the mid-2nd c. Clement* of Rome, anachronistically called bishop of Rome, wrote a letter (c96) to the Corinthian Christians regarding a dispute, but he did so as if he were the secretary presenting the advice proffered by the whole Roman community. Clement could intervene in the affairs of the Corinthian community because of the special position that the Roman community had within Christianity, owing to its two apostle* martyrs*, Peter* and Paul*. While neither founded the church in Rome – Paul's letter to the Roman Christians was written to a church he did not personally know – the presence of the apostles provided an all-important direct contact with the preaching of Christ, similarly claimed by the major churches of Jerusalem, Alexandria, and Antioch. Of the two, Peter was more important for the subsequent claims of the bishopric of Rome, because he was chief or "prince" (*princeps*) of the apostles (a term that apparently came into use in the late 4th c.). Christ commanded Peter to strengthen the faith of the brethren (Luke 22:32) and said to him, after the Resurrection, "Feed my sheep" (John 21:16–18). Most significant for papal claims were Christ's words to Peter *(Petros-petras*, "rock") at Caesarea Philippi, "You are Peter and upon this rock I will build my church" (Matt 16:18). Pope Stephen I (254–7) fell back on this verse in an acrimonious letter to Cyprian* of Carthage.

Rome was the Apostolic See* – a term apparently first used by Pope Liberius (352–66) – *par excellence*. Since the late 4th c., the title "vicar of St. Peter" has been applied to Rome's bishop. Liberius's successor, Pope Damasus (366–84), therefore objected when Canon 3 of the Council of Constantinople* (381) declared, "Because [Constantinople] is the new Rome, the bishop of Constantinople is to enjoy the privileges of honor after the bishop of Rome." Similarly Pope Leo* I (440–61) rejected Canon 28 of the Council of Chalcedon* – a council that otherwise reflected papal views – because it made Constantinople's point even more explicitly: "We issue the same decree and resolution concerning the prerogatives of the most holy Church of the same Constantinople, new Rome. The fathers rightly accorded prerogatives to the see of older Rome, since that is an imperial city; and moved by the same purpose the 150 most devout bishops [at the Council of Constantinople] apportioned equal prerogatives to the most holy see of the new Rome."

This contradicted the papal ideology* that presented the Roman bishop as the heir to Peter. For example, Irenaeus* of Lyons (c140–c202) put Peter and Paul at the head of his succession list of Roman bishops. Conveniently, he named 12 bishops between Peter and the current pope, recalling the 12 apostles. The sixth one was suspiciously called Sixtus. This papal ideology was backed by liturgical celebration. By the early 4th c., there were two feasts of Peter; June 29, for Peter and Paul, apparently entered the Roman calendar just after the time of Pope Stephen I; February 22 celebrated the "Chair of Peter." This odd title, a term used by Cyprian, evokes the role of teacher.

Some who challenged this ideology denied that Peter was ever in Rome and that the papal claims therefore rested on a historical fiction; this claim was initially presented during the 16th-c. Reformation and has since been frequently repeated. It is true that there is no direct literary evidence of Peter's presence in Rome, although 1 Peter* sends greetings from "Your sister church in Babylon" (1 Pet 5:13), where "Babylon" can only be Rome. But not only do early Christian writers, such as Clement (late 1st c.), take it for granted that Peter was martyred in Rome, the archaeological evidence seems conclusive: Peter was buried under what became (in the 4th c.) St. Peter's basilica. The cupola, which bears the words, "You are Peter and upon this rock I will build my church," is immediately over the saint's grave, located beneath the papal altar.

It is one thing to claim special prerogatives, but quite another to persuade others to accept them. As the clash between Pope Stephen I and Cyprian of Carthage demonstrated, other bishops, especially in the West, thought it proper to refer to the bishop of Rome controversial issues, such as the rebaptism of those baptized by heretics, which Cyprian favored and Stephen opposed. The case of Pope Siricius* (384–99) is particularly illuminating. The bishop of Tarragona submitted to Siricius's predecessor a number of questions on canonical matters. Siricius responded by drawing attention to his role as the heir to Peter and then gave his rulings. In doing so, he requested that the bishop pass on his decisions to neighboring provinces* of the church. These decisions were couched in authoritative language, like decrees issued by imperial administration. The Pope was legislating for the whole church, or at least for the church in the West.

It would be impracticable to attempt to document the gradual extension of papal authority fully. For much of the 10th c., for instance, the office was in serious decline until it was rescued by the German emperors. Papal authority was much advanced by the imposing figure of Innocent* III (1198–1216), who laid claim to the *plenitudo potestatis* (fullness of power) over the "whole Church", which he encapsulated in the use of the title "vicar* of Christ" rather than the traditional "vicar of Peter." Perhaps papal authority might be said to have reached its apogee under Boniface* VIII (1294–1303), who claimed in the bull* *Unam* sanctam* (1302) that no one could be saved unless subject to the papacy (see Salvation).

Meanwhile the papacy had become not just a spiritual power, but a temporal one as well, controlling a great swath of land across the middle of Italy and elsewhere, specifically the Comtat Venaissin surrounding Avignon. Successive popes resided at Avignon rather than in Rome (1309–76). When Urban VI was chosen (1378), the election was disputed and an antipope was elected who went back to live in Avignon, thus beginning what came to be known as the Great* Western Schism. From 1378 there were two popes claiming authority over the Church, and from 1409 there were three (the third was appointed by a council in Pisa). The schism was resolved by the Council of Constance (1414–18), where Martin V (1417–31) was elected by a conclave* of cardinals* and representatives of the five "nations," or language groups, present at Constance. Constance also produced decrees asserting the authority of councils over popes (*Haec sancta*) and demanding regular councils of the Roman Catholic Church to govern ecclesiastical affairs (*Frequens*).

The Conciliarist* Movement, represented by these two decrees, presented perhaps the greatest theoretical challenge to its authority the papacy had ever faced. There would be further councils, but summoned by reluctant popes and under pressure from the emperor. It was fear of Conciliarism* that contributed to the papacy's hesitation to summon a council to address both Church reform and those doctrinal matters in dispute with the Protestant Reformers. The Council of Trent*, meeting spasmodically from 1545 to 1563, finally addressed both topics, and the papacy emerged with its authority enhanced and with a far better structure for governing the Church. The cardinals – who in the Middle Ages had often thought of themselves, if not as an alternative authority to the pope, at least as co-governors with him – were divided among various congregations. These congregations were to, and still do, consider various aspects of the Church's life – e.g. the liturgy and the preservation of doctrine – but the cardinals henceforward were not to meet as a "college" (although the label "sacred college" is still applied to them) except on the most formal occasions. Their only significant role as a college now is to elect a new pontiff, although individual cardinals play an important role in the administration of the Roman Catholic Church worldwide.

During all this time, the Papal States had survived. Although temporarily overrun during the Napoleonic Wars, they were restored – with the exception of Avignon – at the Congress of Vienna. During the mid-19th c., however, papal territories were gradually eroded as the Kingdom of Italy came into being. Rome, the capital of the Papal States, fell in 1870. As the pope's temporal authority declined, his spiritual authority increased, in part through the developing concept of the *magisterium* (teaching authority). Earlier, this term had been used for the teaching of theologians, but in the 19th c. it was applied to bishops and, particularly, to the bishop of Rome. More recently, it has tended to be reserved for papal teaching authority, usually exercised through encyclicals*. Papal authority was given more systematic expression at the First Vatican* Council (1869–70), which defined the pope's infallibility*, in formal teaching concerning faith or morals, and his primacy over the whole Roman Catholic Church. In a sense, these doctrines were not new. As already pointed out, Rome had had a certain primacy since the Church's beginning, and even infallibility had been discussed since the late Middle Ages. But in the context of the pontificate of Pius* IX (1846–78), and the extremely conservative set of propositions in his Syllabus* of Errors (1864–80), the last of which claimed that it was anathema to believe the pope should or could accommodate himself to modern civilization, the definitions of Vatican I, including its declaration of papal infallibility*, aroused considerable opposition within and outside the Roman Catholic Church. To be fair to Vatican I, the fall of Rome brought the Council to an abrupt conclusion. It could be argued that its teaching was not completed until Vatican* II (1962–65), whose perspective was that papal authority was to be monitored by all bishops for the well-being of the Church.

Nonetheless, in the meantime, papal authority had expanded greatly, aided not least by the increasing speed of travel and communication since the mid-19th c., by the expansion of Roman Catholic missionary activity, and by the Vatican's almost total control over the appointment to bishoprics around the world.

MICHAEL J. WALSH

POPULAR CHRISTIAN PRACTICES CLUSTER

1) *Introductory Entries*

Popular Christian Practices
Popular Christian Practices in Eastern Orthodoxy

2) *A Sampling of Contextual Views and Practices*

Popular Christian Practices in Africa
Popular Christian Practices in Asia
Popular Christian Practices in Asia: China
Popular Christian Practices in Australian Aboriginal Contexts
Popular Christian Practices in Latin America: Brazil

Popular Christian Practices in Latin American: Mexico

Popular Christian Practices in Latin America: Native Traditions in Mexico

Popular Christian Practices in North America

Popular Christian Practices in Western Europe

See also INCULTURATION CLUSTER

1) Introductory Entries

Popular Christian Practices. Expressions of popular Christianity are present in abundance in virtually every context. Some are visible as dimensions of popular media, while others function among devotees, within families, or as personal manifestations of faith. What makes such expressions "popular" is less the demographics than the initiative and energy; they come from "ordinary people" who are not employed by or working on behalf of ecclesiastical institutions or bodies. Studies of popular religion often highlight polarities: clergy–laity*, official–unofficial, ecclesiastical–extraecclesiastical, elite–marginalized*, and formal–informal, the second term in each case indentifying what is "popular." But if the initiative for a particular religious perspective or practice comes from outside ecclesiastical structures and significantly influences the members, it is clear that popular religion can arise inside faith communities as well as outside. Popular Christianity was often what survived in countries where official expressions of Christianity were forbidden or persecuted. Historical investigation shows the richness, complexity, and multiplicity of religious expressions, as well as the ways in which religious perspectives are shaped by competition among forms of Christianity. Popular Christianity is often related to a specific locale (e.g. a rural or urban area; house* churches; base* communities), is resistant to change (antimodern) or embraces change (countercultural), is experiential rather than doctrinal, is syncretistic* or involves self-help strategies, is attentive to the role of the supernatural in one's personal life (e.g. miracles* or apparitions), is focused more on activity than on theology (ritual practices, festivals, pilgrimages*), is anticlerical regarding religious authority*, and thus readily embraces dissent. **See also** ANCESTOR VENERATION AND CHRISTIANITY CLUSTER; BLACK MADONNA; FÁTIMA; LOURDES; MARY, THE VIRGIN, CLUSTER; SYNCRETISM. DALE A. JOHNSON

Popular Christian Practices in Eastern Orthodoxy. Orthodoxy is an incarnate faith. The doctrinal and ethical teachings, the canonical discipline, and the liturgy of the Orthodox Church have penetrated the practical, everyday things of life, its activities, enterprises, and relationships. Daily prayer and an ordered system of fasting are essential expressions of Orthodox life, as are quiet acts of charity, since nothing and no one must escape the concern of the Church and its members.

The *Euchologion**, the Church's official service book, contains, in addition to the sacramental rites and other sacred services, prayers for every need and circumstance, including blessings for women in childbirth and for newborn infants; for the sick, the frail, and the dying; for sowing and harvesting; and for the protection of persons and communities from the devastation of fires, floods, earthquakes, civil strife, foreign invasion, epidemics, and all manner of calamities. The Church embraces everything and everyone, in order to bring all things within the realm of salvation*. Blessed water (see Holy Water) is sprinkled over persons, animals, and things as a sign of God's transforming power and the ultimate transfiguration of the world. Special services are used for blessing new homes, the start of a new school year, and the establishment of new enterprises. Blessings are bestowed on new cars, tractors, plows, fishing boats, airplanes, ships, spacecraft, and every other kind of vehicle or instrument that serves the needs and occupations of people. Making the sign* of the cross over things and over one's own body is an act of silent prayer and a confession of faith.

Homes have a designated prayer space where Scriptures* are read, cherished icons* are kept, a vigil lamp burns, and incense* is offered to accompany personal and family prayers. Wedding bands are worn on the right hand, and marriage crowns are kept in an honored place in the home. Newborn infants and their mothers are "churched" (see Churching of Women) on the 40th day after birth. Name days are faithfully observed and families regularly submit to their priest the names of family members, living and deceased, for prayers on their behalf, accompanied usually by an offering of bread, wine, oil, or flowers for use in the divine services. Although attending divine services in casual dress is unthinkable, an air of intimacy characterizes the assembly. The church calendar with its cycle of feasts and fasts, and especially the Sunday liturgy, the solemnities of Holy Week, and the splendor of the paschal feast, permeates the social and cultural fabric of personal and communal life.

ALKIVIADIS CALIVAS

2) A Sampling of Contextual Views and Practices

Popular Christian Practices in Africa. See AFRICAN INSTITUTED CHURCHES CLUSTER; AFRICAN RELIGION AND CHRISTIANITY CLUSTER.

Popular Christian Practices in Asia. The Roman Catholic and Protestant churches in Asia inherited Western Christian practices, and Eastern and Oriental Orthodoxy in Asia was guided by the practices of Eastern and Oriental churches. However, as the Christian faith took root in Asian cultural contexts, these received practices were altered and/or replaced by local cultural practices, although Protestants have been more cautious and slow to adopt local cultural practices. Folk practices in Asian Christianity offer, as elsewhere, a dynamic of difference in the definition of Christian identity. Certain practices are rejected to highlight the difference between Christians and other religionists, while others are adopted to signal the difference between Asian Christians and other Christians in the global context. A few examples from India illustrate these points.

Folk Practices Linked to Rites of Passage. In certain parts of India, girls go through a series of traditional rites of passage, which are observed and blessed by the churches. Thus the celebration of puberty with local rituals is combined for Christians with a visit by the pastor and a prayer service at home. Weddings incorporate several rituals related to local cultures, e.g. the wearing of the *thaali* (wedding chain) by the bride, and the wearing and exchanging of garlands. The arranging of marriages also has a local cultural flavor. Endogamy (marrying within one's subcaste) is observed by many Christians in India. Some follow rules concerning auspicious times during which weddings are to be held. Christian funerals carry many local cultural customs and practices, e.g. a festive meal with the local community at the end of 16 days of mourning, thus giving a central role to community relationships.

Liturgical Practices that come from the former religious traditions of the converts are incorporated into church liturgy. The Church of South India includes, in its wedding liturgy, the ritual of the couple's taking seven steps toward the altar during the singing of Ps 128, reflecting a local practice among Hindu couples to symbolize their seven vows.

Various Festivals of the surrounding culture are observed by Asian Christians, even as new Christian festivals are created to prevent converts from reverting to their former religion; e.g. church anniversary celebrations in South India resemble similar festivals in local Hindu* shrines.

The appropriation of folk practices both raises serious theological issues regarding the relation between Christianity and local culture* and provides a fresh understanding of the catholicity of the church.

M. THOMAS THANGARAJ

Popular Christian Practices in Asia: China. When missionaries approached the Chinese people, they encountered a culture with rich and varied religious traditions, beliefs, practices, and organizations. Charismatic* Christians in China (commonly called "Pentecostals"), in particular, have many practices and beliefs that are surprisingly similar to those of Chinese folk religions.

The influence of Chinese folk religions on Chinese Christianity was limited until 1949, when the Chinese Church was isolated from world Christianity, and Chinese Christianity survived totally on its own. In this unfavorable atmosphere, the Christian theological education of preachers was totally disrupted, most preachers receiving no theological training at all; thus Christians understood Christianity with the resources they had, namely from the perspective of Chinese folk religions. When Christianity experienced enormous development following reform and an open door policy, the theological education of clergy fell far behind. As a result, while Christianity filled the spiritual gaps left by ancient folk religions, it was itself deeply influenced by folk religion traditions. "Folk Christianity" arose. Its followers include primarily poorly educated farmers who believe in God but regard God as one who has the direct power of karma, exorcises* evil spirits, and intervenes in answer to prayers* in proportion to a believer's offering. The concept of reciprocity is strongly held. A phrase commonly used to praise a Chinese god is *youqiu biying*, "infallibly granting requests for favors." Almost identical terms are used in the Christian environment of the church. Healing*, or more accurately the widespread belief in it, is one of the most important factors in the spread of Christianity in the 1980s. Calling on spiritual beings for healing and exorcism* has long been a core feature of Chinese religious life. Its Christian version requires a new orientation of believers, but is not a radical innovation. Folk Christians believe particularly in miracles* and treat the Bible as the sacred book on which their faith relies, although most of them cannot read it (see Scripture). They further indigenize Christian ethics* by worshipping God in church while often venerating their ancestors* at home and closely associating their belief in Christianity with their holistic hope* for the family's happiness, health, and longevity. Their religious ritual includes joyfully singing spirit songs, performing spirit dancing, and praying aloud. Folk Christianity can be viewed as marked by superstition*, yet it accounts for the large number of inculturated* Christians in rural areas of China. TAO FEIYA

Popular Christian Practices in Australian Aboriginal Contexts. See ANTHROPOLOGY CLUSTER: AUSTRALIAN ABORIGINAL THEOLOGICAL ISSUES.

Popular Christian Practices in Latin America: Brazil. Popular Christian practices originated in the medieval Catholicism brought from Portugal* in the midst of the colonial enterprise. Because of this origin, Brazilian Catholicism came to have a primarily lay* and social character. Owing to the scarcity of priests, lay brothers and friars predominated, and still do. Because of the need for social ties among widely dispersed residents, popular devotions have a social function; as collective devotions, they encourage the development of social ties (which are otherwise missing), both during festivals (Christmas, patron saint festivals, June folk festivals) and during the "path of penitence" (Holy Week) (see Roman Catholicism Cluster: In Brazil: Colonial Period).

The Centrality of the Cults of Saints. The central element of each of these popular devotions is the cult of a saint*, which is not limited to saints canonized by the Roman Catholic Church. The saint is always a protector, worshipped through his or her icon*, which for the devotee is not a mere representation, but an embodiment of the very presence of the saint. It is to the icon that the faithful bring presents and decorations, ask for blessings, and make vows. Sometimes devotees inflict punishment on themselves when they fail to fulfill their vows. The saint is kept in the oratory of a chapel, which devotees visit.

The Leading Shrines in Brazil. These include the shrines of Our Lady of Aparecida of the north, with her majestic basilica in homage of the patron saint of Brazil, of Good Jesus of Lapa in Bahia, and of the Divine Eternal Father in Goiás and in Ceará, the pilgrimage* center in Juazeiro devoted to Fr. Cicero (Cicero

 Popular Christian Practices in Latin America

Romão Batista, 1844–1934), the most popular saint in the country (about 2 million pilgrims visit the center each year).

In these centers, worship is characterized by a devotional relationship with the saint in the form of petitions and the fulfilling of vows, such as the vow to ascend the steps of the sanctuary on one's knees. Each shrine has a "miracle room," where devotees leave ex*-votos (objects, photos, or sculptures of feet, hands, arms, heads, representing the parts of the body that have been cured) as a testimony to the grace granted by the saint.

The administration of these shrines is in the hands of the hierarchy of the Roman Catholic Church, even though in most instances these saints are not officially canonized. Consequently, at times conflicts erupt between the Church and common devotees, when the clergy seeks to discourage what it considers to be manifestations of fanaticism and superstition* in popular devotions.

The People's Saints. The people choose saints among persons in whom they perceive virtues associated with Christ himself, such as sacrifice, intense suffering, and dedication to the next life. A saint is in heaven with God and therefore has supernatural powers. The people's saints may be priests or nuns, or humble people, thieves, prostitutes, slaves, pious women, children, and at times imaginary people. Many are worshipped at their tombs, and are therefore known as "cemetery saints," but also through statues and cards in people's homes and copies of prayers that are kept in wallets and purses.

Notable among these popular saints are Fr. Cicero, Br. Damian, Sr. Dulce, the slaves Antoninho and Anastácia, the simple woman Nhá Chica, the girl Odetinha, the prostitute Jandira, the bandit Jararaca, and the legendary Negrinho of Pastoreio. **See also BRAZIL.**

MARCELO AYRES CAMURÇA

Popular Christian Practices in Latin America: Mexico. Popular Christian practices vary with the contexts in which they take place. Depending on the kind of devotional group, popular Christianity involves person-to-person relations and social and religious ties (friendship*) or person(s)-to-community commitments to communal service related to religious icons and shrines (stewardship). Examples of such devotional organizations include groups devoted to St. Jude Thaddeus, to various local icons, statues, or shrines of the Holy Child, Christ, or the Virgin.

The locations of shrines, church buildings, or cathedrals are frequently associated with pre-Columbian sacred places. For instance, the Virgin of Guadalupe* Tepeyac (whose shrine is in the hills near Mexico City), the Virgin of San Juan de los Lagos, the Virgin of Zapopan, the Virgin of Juquila, the Christ of Chalma (near Cuernavaca), the Christ of Cubilete, the Holy Child of Atocha in Fresnillo, Zacatecas, and the Santo Niño Doctor in Tepeaca, Puebla, are all located at or near pre-Columbian sacred places. Yet other patterns exist, especially in the Xochimilco region, where there are no definite shrines. The several statues or icons of the Holy Child (Niñopan, Niño de Belem, Niño Dormidito, Niño de San Juan) and of the Pietà* (Vírgen de Dolores) are moved from home to home, each household assuming in turn responsibilities for the devotion.

Fixed or mobile feasts are peak moments of popular religiosity, whether they are national or local, related to the liturgical calendar or not. The feasts of Wise Men's Day (January 6), *la Candelaria* (Candlemas, the presentation of Jesus at the Temple; February 2), Ash Wednesday and Holy Week (variable dates), Children's Day (April 30), the Holy Cross (May 3), Corpus Christi (variable), Santiago Apóstol (July 25), St. Jude Thaddeus (October 28), All Saints and the Day of the Dead (November 1 and 2), Virgin of Guadalupe (December 12), *las Posadas* (celebrating Mary and Joseph's quest for lodging; December 16–24), and Christmas (December 25). What is celebrated on these feast days varies. The Day of the Dead (*el Día de los Muertos*) deserves special mention; it preserves magical-religious traditions of pre-Columbian origin, including giving food, beverages, and flowers to the souls* of the deceased, who come back to enjoy these gifts. The first day of this two-day celebration is for deceased children and lonely souls (who have no descendants to give them gifts); the second day is for deceased adults.

Rituals are performed to establish or fulfill commitments made before religious icons, including "petitions" to express what one needs, oaths as formal commitments to set aside time for devotion, and offering to do certain things commensurate with the favor asked in the petition. Expressions of gratitude for receiving the favor requested in the petition might include offering a *milagrito* (a small brass figure) or making a votive offering (a painting or figurine) that reflects the favor received (see Ex-voto), decorating the shrine, or welcoming the icon into one's home and offering food, toys, or flowers to it and its visitors.

AURORA ZLOTNIK

Popular Christian Practices in Latin America: Native Traditions in Mexico. How should the interactions of popular Christian practices and native traditions be understood? As a form of superstitious* syncretism* or as a form of inculturation* of Christianity called for by the Incarnation* (see Mission Cluster; the current cluster: In Eastern Orthodoxy). These questions call for a closer look at the specific native traditions involved.

Regarding Central American religions in Mexico, the first step is to recognize how rich and complex they were when Christianity arrived in the area. They had matured through a 1,000-year-old process in response to geographic demands and to the high civilizations and cultures in which they developed. Unfortunately, these religious traditions were seen through the lenses of a Christian ideology that prompted the "conquerors" to justify their invasion and oppression* of the peoples of the Latin American continent.

Central American cultures* and religions have the same basic orientation and sense of the transcendent, and thus constitute a macroculture. The language and the representations used to express these traditions are symbolic* and mythical*. At first these traditions emphasized respect for and devotion to natural forces. Later they unified the natural forces in a theological conception of life that kept in balance and harmony the earthly and the cosmic. Subsequently they perceived that the Divine is best understood in its relation to humans and history. They finally reached an extremely abstract conception of God. Various Nahuatl and Maya documents show the monotheistic perspective of these traditions. Nezahualcóyotl (1402–72) writes that the Nahuan people "have only one God, and they worship only One God, whose name is Quetzalcóatl." The Maya had various names for this one God, including Hun-oh-pú, a name that literally means "One-God-Is."

One might be surprised to find that, having become monotheists, the Nahuatl and Maya peoples abandoned neither the polytheistic language and religious representations of nature as a pantheon (a temple of all the gods) nor the references to divine manifestations in human affairs. One explanation is that any society comprises a diversity of people with different beliefs. Furthermore, one can say that all the diverse religious practices are held together in the broader, monotheistic conception. Thus according to the Myth* of the Fifth Sun (*Quinto Sol*), "Quetzalcóatl transformed the other gods into springs, others into fertile soil." The one and only God is present and acts in everything that exists, and God's presence, not God's representations, is worshipped.

The gospel and Christianity were proclaimed by means of categories, symbols, and a cultural worldview completely foreign to Central American peoples. Through the missionaries' first evangelization efforts, native peoples perceived the fundamental message of the gospel; but because the gospel was presented in a foreign religious and cultural code, they could not fully assimilate it. In order to adopt the gospel, they had to bring it into contact with the heart and the root of their own religious and cultural experiences, developing popular Christian practices, as well as popular Native religious practices. Thus current religious celebrations on sacred mountains, in sacred caves, and at other sacred places incorporate Christian practices – and thus can be viewed as popular Christian practices – even though they preserve ancient Central American religious practices and theology.

CLODOMIRO SILLER and
FERNANDO MATAMOROS PONCE

Popular Christian Practices in North America. The diffusion of religion in the late 20th c. greatly increased the number and range of expressions of popular Christianity in North America. In media* such as music, television, and film, in popular religious magazines such as *Guideposts,* and in the large greeting card business, these might more appropriately be called religious dimensions of popular culture (e.g. generalized appeals to the supernatural) than popular Christianity itself, yet they often influence Christian expressions within the culture as well. On the other hand, ethnic identities formed partly in response to persecution or violence (especially Native* American and African* American) have strongly shaped expressions of Christianity within these communities. On one end of a spectrum of religious perspectives are persons for whom individuality is of particular importance: seekers, New Agers, and devotees of meditation or nature, whose Christianity may be mixed with other influences or religious strands. At the other end are those who emphasize mission and whose religious activity is connected with one or more of the hundreds of Evangelical* parachurch* organizations that exist outside of denominational structures (e.g. Youth for Christ, Promise Keepers, Women's Aglow, the Gideons*). Roman Catholic and Orthodox expressions of popular Christianity often incline toward visual images (statues or icons of the Virgin Mary* and the saints*, crucifixes, home altars, sacred sites). Warner Sallman's *Head of Christ* (1940) was reproduced more than 500 million times and significantly influenced Protestant popular religion. Protestant expressions often incline toward inspirational or apocalyptic* religious literature (e.g. in the past century, *In His Steps; The Man Nobody Knows; The Power of Positive Thinking; The Late, Great Planet Earth;* and the *Left Behind* series). These books have been attractive not just because they are accessible to a wide audience, but also because they communicate the message that reliance on God's power can solve human problems. Various forms of music began as expressions of popular Christianity (evangelical hymnody, the Sacred Harp singing tradition, African American gospel, and Christian rock) and continue to attract followers. Advances in communications technology in the late 20th c., notably cable television and the Internet, have made connections to popular Christianity far beyond the local into a global phenomenon in a postmodern world. Its many forms include continuities with the past as well as newer variants dependent on contemporary cultural expressions. DALE A. JOHNSON

Popular Christian Practices in Western Europe. See BLACK MADONNA; FÁTIMA; LOURDES; MARY, THE VIRGIN, CLUSTER.

Porete, Marguerite, a wandering Beguine*, most likely from Hainault (Belgium); a speculative mystic*, author of *The Mirror of Simple Annihilated Souls and Those Who Only Remain in Will and Desire of Love* (in Old French, c1290), an allegory* dependent on chivalric motifs. She was declared a relapsed heretic* on the basis of 15 propositions extracted from her writings and executed (1310); this was the first *auto* da fé* for mystical* heresy* in Western Europe.

Porete's work is an example of medieval women's vernacular* theology, which both challenged and complemented traditional scholastic* and monastic* theology. She provoked church authorities by making antinomian ideas accessible to other lay Christians and by claiming authority* from God rather than an earthly power.

Her anticlerical, antidevotional, and speculative treatise anticipates some issues prominent in 16th-c. reforms, yet the text is generally considered an anomaly in medieval mysticism. Porete's mystical speculation never became mainstream church doctrine, but her work directly influenced Jan van Ruusbroec* and Meister Eckhart*.

Porete employed ideas from Neoplatonic* cosmology* and the negative* theology of

Dionysius* the Pseudo-Areopagite to posit two paths of return to God. Souls*, as descended from Adam* (created) and from the Trinity* (eternal), can pass through the church-mediated cycle of fall*, redemption*, and return to God after a virtuous life. Yet certain noble souls can embrace their wretchedness and abandon virtue, returning to their true nature: the state of not-willing, not-knowing, and not-having, which Porete calls annihilation. For her, certain human beings can become "what God is" during bodily life, without the mediation of the church, through a seven-stage path of increasing detachment. JOANNE MAGUIRE ROBINSON

Porphyry (c232–c303), Neoplatonist* philosopher. Of pagan background, he was acquainted with Origen*, gained a detailed knowledge of the Bible and Christian thought, but disliked Christianity's exclusive claims and thought that Origen misused both Platonism* and the Greek method of allegory*. He studied in Athens, then sought out Plotinus* in Rome (c262–70). While greatly influenced by Plotinus, arranging his treatises into *Enneads* (six groups of nine) and writing a life of Plotinus, he was an independent thinker, taking, e.g, a nontraditional view of the three divine hypostases*. In *Against the Christians* (c270–c295), he was one of the first biblical critics, noting the inconsistencies among the Gospels* and showing that Daniel* must have been written at the time of the Maccabees*. Late in his life, he was probably one of the philosophers who persuaded Diocletian* to resume persecution* of the Christians. In his *Philosophy from Oracles*, he held Jesus to be a sincere teacher, though not divine, attacked the apostles for superstition and magic, and condemned Christians' resistance to civil* religion. His work on Aristotle's *Categories* was later translated by Boethius* and was widely used during the Middle Ages.

Portiuncula, small chapel in the plain below Assisi; the center of the activities of Francis* of Assisi, where he received his vocation (1208), commissioned Clare (1212), and died (1226). In the 16th c., it was enclosed by a church.

Port-Royal, Cistercian* convent of nuns, southwest of Paris, that became a center of Jansenism*. It was moved to Paris (1625–26) while Jacqueline Marie Angélique Arnauld* was abbess.

Portugal is and always has been a predominantly Roman Catholic country since its emergence as a nation (12th c.). Christianity came to the area under Roman rule (2nd c.) and, despite outbreaks of Arianism* and Priscillianism*, maintained its Roman Catholic orthodoxy under Suevic rulers (converted in the 5th c.). The territory was overrun from 713 by Muslim invaders, who were driven out in 1249.

Under Christian rule, Jews and the few remaining Muslims had very limited autonomy. In 1496–97, most of them preferred expulsion to conversion. Those remaining, known as New Christians, suffered popular hostility. From the 1540s, the Inquisition* enforced orthodoxy, and the Jesuits* dominated and expanded education. The Protestant Reformation left Portugal unaffected. In the 18th c., the crown asserted its power when the despotic royal minister, the marquess of Pombal (1699–1782), expelled the Jesuits (1759) and converted the Inquisition into a royal court (1774). Enlightenment ideas began to circulate among the elite around the time of the French invasions (1807–11), to which the clergy led the resistance. In the politically turbulent 19th c., the liberal elite distanced itself from militant Roman Catholicism. The Inquisition was abolished (1821), and when the clergy supported the anti-liberal cause in the civil war of 1832–34, the victors abolished the religious orders, nationalized their property, dethroned bishops, and broke with the Vatican. Normal relations were restored by the Concordat of 1848, after which the clergy became dependent on the state for its income. Religious orders began to reestablish themselves in the late 19th c. By 1900 religion was again a political issue: battle was joined between a more militant Roman Catholicism, including Jesuits, and the militant anticlericalism of the republican movement. In 1910 the monarchy was overthrown and the Republic dissolved all religious orders. Church and state were separated by decree (1911), ecclesiastical property was confiscated, divorce was permitted, and freedom of religion was proclaimed while an attempt was made to subordinate Catholic clergy to the secular power. Relations with the Vatican were severed (1913–18) and bishops exiled from their dioceses. It was in this state of tension that the Virgin appeared to three children near Fátima*, in central Portugal, in 1917. After the military coup of 1926, the religious situation changed, and in 1933 the new state was installed with the Catholic militant António de Oliveira Salazar (1889–1970) as head of government (1932–68). His student friend, Manuel Gonçalves Cerejeira (1888–1977), was cardinal-patriarch of Lisbon

(1929–71), but the Concordat* of 1940 maintained the regime of separation, and church property was not returned. The Concordat was modified in 1971 when the Law of Religious Freedom, in accordance with Vatican* II, officially recognized non-Catholic denominations and in 1975, after the fall of the authoritarian regime, when divorce was again permitted. In 2001 a new law of religious freedom gave equality of treatment to non-Catholic denominations and enabled taxpayers to donate 0.5% of their tax payments to their religion. The Concordat of 2004 generally reflected this law, with the Roman Catholic Church able to appoint bishops freely.

In 1826 foreign non-Catholics were permitted to worship in private. From 1867 religious denominations were allowed to form associations, one of the first being the Lusitanian Church, set up by Old* Catholics in 1880, which joined the Anglican Communion in 1980. Other Protestant denominations followed, with Pentecostalists flourishing from the 1970s. **See also** **BRAZIL; ROMAN CATHOLICISM CLUSTER: IN LATIN AMERICA: BRAZIL** and **IN EUROPE: PORTUGAL.**

Statistics: Population (2007): 10.6 (million) M. Christians, 10.1 M, 95% (Roman Catholics, 9.5 M, 89%; Protestants, including Pentecostalists/Charismatics, 0.4 M, 4.2%; Eastern Orthodox immigrants, 0.2 M, 2.2%; Jehovah's Witnesses, 48,000; Mormons, 35,000); Muslims, 37,000; Hindus, 7,000; Jews, fewer than 1,000. (Source: Instituto Nacional de Estatística, 2007; % of Christians in each group, 2003, and Mormons, 1999; many Christians are secularized*.)

RICHARD A. H. ROBINSON

Portuguese Explorations, Conquests, and Missions. The Portuguese seaborne empire was constituted by an expansive system of strategically located, fortified coastal trading posts linking three continents: Africa, Asia, and the easternmost region of Latin America (contemporary Brazil*). The Treaty of Tordesillas (1494) ensured Portugal's exclusive right to these territories. Portugal's early activity in the islands off the West African coast (early 15th c.) represented the earliest European colonial experiment, including slavery*, settlement, and single-crop agriculture (sugarcane). With King João II's mandate to chart a trade route to India via the southern coast of Africa, Bartholomeu Dias rounded the Cape of Good Hope (1487). Vasco de Gama arrived in Calicut, India, via the East African coast (1498). Pedro Alvares Cabral inadvertently "discovered" Brazil (1500), when winds blew his India-bound ship off course.

At first the purpose of Portuguese colonialism* was not settlement but rather the establishment of a commercial trading empire. Even into the 17th c., settlement was primarily a means to fortify small trading colonies. Nonetheless, Padroado* Real granted the Portuguese rights to the missionary church in all of Asia, Africa, and Brazil. The first preachers and missionaries arrived on commercial ships.

The Jesuits* were the primary agents of mission and evangelization in the Portuguese Empire. Their arrival in Goa (1542) was the turning point for Roman Catholic mission to Asia; the Diocese of Goa became the administrative center for mission to India*, China*, and Japan*.

The Jesuit mission to Brazil was launched (1549) under the leadership of Manoel da Nóbrega (1517–70), who founded a string of coastal missions (mid-16th c.). The Portuguese crown employed Jesuits as administrators of "Indian" labor, which often set them at odds with settlers. When the order's attentions turned to evangelization of the indigenous and African populations in Brazil, their role as administrators of sugar plantations and as owners of African slaves (17th c. especially) compromised their efforts. The Portuguese Jesuit and missionary to the Amazon, António Vieira (1608–97), preached against slavery and argued for a unified model of mission that transcended the divide between colony and empire. The Jesuit mission in indigenous Brazil was organized in *aldeias* (reductions*), which sought to bring European regimentation and ordering to indigenous communities. The Jesuits saw a decline in their influence in Brazil beginning with the crisis in the sugar industry (1680s). This decline culminated in their expulsion from Brazil (1758). **See also COLONIALISM AND IMPERIALISM AND CHRISTIAN THEOLOGY; MISSION CLUSTER.** JENNIFER S. HUGHES

Portuguese Literature and Christianity. The emergence of Portuguese literature is commonly dated from the late 12th c. Some of the best-known Portuguese poetry, the *Cantigas de Santa Maria*, comprising 430 short songs in praise of the Virgin Mary*, was composed and set to music (mid-13th c.) by King Afonso X ("the Wise"). Portuguese medieval prose includes the anonymous doctrinal/devotional Christian essays *Orto do espôso, Boosco deleitoso,* and *Livro da côrte imperial,* promoting solitary life and defending Christian doctrines against Judaic and Muslim attack.

Bilingual playwright Gil Vicente (c1465–c1537) offers among his copious dramatic productions numerous *autos* (mystery* plays), including the most frequently staged *Auto da Índia,* the trilogy of the *Barcas* ("Inferno," "Purgatory," "Glory"), *Auto da alma* (on the "pilgrim*" theme), and *Auto da feira* (critique of a commercialized Roman Church).

King João III's Renaissance court (1521–57) brought simultaneously Erasmian* Christian humanism, the Dominican-administered Inquisition*, and the Jesuits* as members of the intellectual vanguard and most favored mission arm of Portugal* and its far-flung empire. Portuguese Christian humanists included essayist João de Barros, who produced historiographic and travel works and several dialogues on moral education (e.g. *Rhopica pnefma*); and Damião de Góis, who chronicled the Portuguese monarchy, militated for Christian ecumenism, and was temporary imprisoned by the Inquisition on charges of "Lutheranism." Renaissance poets included Luiz de Camões, whose 10-canto epic poem, *Os Lusíadas,* peppered by biblical references, sings the glories of Christian Portuguese colonial expansion and mourns the gradual loss of the national epic spirit to crass materialism and greed. Camões gives full voice to his Christian devotion in his numerous love sonnets (e.g. "Seven years the shepherd Jacob labored") and the stately elegiac poem *Super flumina* (based on Ps 137).

The baroque period (17th c.), a time of general Portuguese malaise, is typified by solemn clerical writing. Preacher-essayists such as Fr. António Vieira, SJ, and Oratorian Fr. Manuel Bernardes address in sermons and letters issues related to the dissolution of public and personal morality, ethical errors of secular governance, and Portugal's faltering position vis-à-vis newer Protestant colonial powers (notably Holland). In an age when intellectual and poetic female voices sought freedom in convents, Sr. Violante do Céu's sonnets progressively evolve from themes of physical love to a spiritualized passion for Christ, while Sr. Mariana Alcoforado's love letters (*Cartas portuguesas*) pour forth the frustration of a novice's unrequited attraction to a secular love.

The romantic period (beginning c1825) brought a vigorous new wave of Christian devotion and emotion to Portuguese letters. Strongly nationalistic in tone, the historical novels and stories of Almeida Garrett (*O Arco de Santana*) and Alexandre Herculano (*Eurico, o Presbítero*) interpret medieval and Renaissance figures – both clerical and secular – as exemplifying devotion, loyalty, and other Christian virtues. Garrett's play, *Frei Luis de Sousa,* re-creates the tense, lugubrious atmosphere of early-17th-c. Portugal and the internal drama of men and women facing uncontrollable circumstances. The prolific novelist Camilo Castelo Branco shows in his best-known novels the agonized religious polarization of his own life: *Onde está a felicidade?, O Romance de um homem rico, Amor de Perdição, Amor de Salvação, A Queda dum anjo.* His series of 10 novelettes, *Novelas do Minho,* reflects Roman Catholic devotional piety and folk superstition* in Portugal's mountainous northernmost province.

The advent of literary realism (1860s) replaced religious emotion with a more analytical view of religion. The official and popular practices of the Roman Catholic Church were scrutinized by the academic "Generation of '65," especially Eça de Queiroz, whose novels and hagiographic stories convey an implicit or explicit critique of church and monarchy, while defending the Christian Socialism of the primitive church. His *O crime do Padre Amaro* depicts traditional seminary education that deprives young men of natural contact with women, predisposing them toward (sometimes tragic) future excesses with female parishioners, and *A relíquia* re-creates in a humorous vein the lucrative 19th-c. traffic in counterfeit relics from the Holy Land. In another spiritual mode, Antero de Quental reflects his tragic personal struggles with faith* in deistic and transcendentalist sonnets.

Except for Antônio Nobre's symbolist poetry and Fernando Pessoa's ontological modernist verses, 20th-c. Portuguese letters – especially fictional works (e.g. the short stories of Miguel Torga) – tend toward neorealistic depictions of rural life, with its traditional popular* Catholicism, although with occasional forays into more existential novels such as *Aparição* (Vergílio Ferreira) and *A paixão* (Almeida Faria). Nobel laureate José Saramago returns in his 1991 novel, *O evangelho segundo Jesus Cristo,* to a critique of Christianity reminiscent of Eça de Queiroz.

MARY L. DANIEL

Porvoo Declaration is a part of the "Porvoo Common Statement" (1994–95), the theological foundation of church unity between (1) British and Irish Anglican* churches and (2) Nordic and Baltic Lutheran* churches of Norway, Sweden, Finland, Estonia, and Lithuania. The churches acknowledged each other's doctrinal basis and ordained ministries and created a fellowship, an Anglican–Lutheran communion. Similar agreements in the USA (Called to Common Mission, 1999) and Canada (Waterloo, 1999) and new Anglican positions concerning episcopacy and the ordination of women* offer possibilities for enlarging the Anglican–Lutheran communion. However, the status of women bishops and the compatibility of the Porvoo agreement with other ecumenical agreements remain unclear. RISTO SAARINEN

Positive Theology, Positive Law, Positivism. Something is called positive because it is factual, given, or "posited," in contrast to that which is rationally self-evident or deduced. It may be "posited" in several different ways, and saying that something is "posited" may be viewed favorably or not.

Positing may occur in the context of legislation. "Positive law" is that which is posited by lawgivers, as contrasted with claims about natural* law or rational theories of justice* and the good. Ever since the Stoics*, there has been a tendency to regard positive law as less worthy than natural law. Legal positivism is the position taken by many interpreters of the development of US law; it was also the position of Carl Schmitt, one of the theorists who reinforced the Nazi Movement in Germany.

Positing may occur in the context of tradition. "Positive theology" deals with the doctrines that have come from Scripture*, tradition, and the councils and "doctors of the church," without first asking critical questions about historical or rational justifications. Several "positive theologians" were appointed to the faculty of the University of Berlin in the late 19th c. to counteract the liberalism* of Adolf Harnack*.

Positing may occur in the context of experience. "Positivism" is the designation for several types of philosophy that deal only with observable facts and processes. Comte's Positivism tried to overcome the illusions of both theology and philosophy with a scientific approach, which, he thought, supported an optimistic theory of progress.

Historical positivism places emphasis on the data derived from the historical record and on the historical development of all ideas and theories, and thus is skeptical about general theories of history* and of hermeneutics*.

The "logical positivism" of the Vienna circle asserted that meaning must be based on either sense experience or logical coherence. Coherent concepts, while meaningful, are merely formal or tautologous until they are combined with sense experience. Assertions about the world are meaningful only if they are "verifiable" or, at a minimum, "falsifiable" through experience.

EUGENE TESELLE

Post-Christian Thought. In the secular* world of Western Europe, there are many (perhaps mostly women) who retain a marked spirituality*. During the 1980s and 1990s, a period during which women's groups on the periphery of the church and the Feminist Movement flourished, the term "post-Christian" was widely employed, in Britain and beyond, to designate those who, having moved beyond and outside Christianity, adhered to a spirituality that bore the marks of the tradition from which they had come.

With the Enlightenment*, central assertions made by Christianity became unthinkable: there could be no resurrection or miracles, since by definition they are supposed to be singular events, contrary to the interrelatedness that characterizes nature and history in which any event necessarily belongs to a larger class ("resurrections"); there could be no person whose relation to God was qualitatively different from that of all others. Furthermore, Christian belief in a transcendent God* implies a heteronomy* that, in modernity, came to be viewed as morally unacceptable. A long tradition, extending through Kant*, Hegel*, Feuerbach*, and Marx* to Freud*, concluded that Christianity was a mythical* projection, the product of human immaturity. In the face of such a critique, some thinkers struggled to reformulate that which could still be considered both ethically enlightening and believable from the Christian past.

More recently feminists have added a twist to the analysis, contending that Christian dogma is by no means benign, but rather is an ideology* that has both reflected and in turn served to legitimize patriarchy*. As such it is a form of fascism, if that term connotes an ideology that makes it appear only natural that one part of humanity (in this case, men) is normative, these people having the power to designate what is the essence and "place" of others (women). Given the 20th-c. recognition, arising in particular out of French thought, that we are embedded in language and culture, the attempt to escape such a mindset must be particularly challenging, if also a prerequisite for human equality. In this respect, many intellectual women have read the work of Luce Irigaray.

Mary Daly employed the term "postchristian," but soon abandoned it, commenting on the inappropriateness of naming oneself by that which one has divorced. In Britain the term is in particular associated with those who are convinced that there is a dimension to reality that has hitherto been hypostasized, anthropomorphized, and projected as an "other" called God (Hampson). Such a critique suggests how one might conceptualize what is the case in terms that are both epistemologically viable and ethically acceptable. But there has never been a post-Christian movement; those who designate themselves as post-Christians have held a variety of views. What is of significance is that many continue to count themselves spiritual, not simply ethical, persons. They may meditate, attend Quaker meetings, join some alternative group, or simply share a post-Christian outlook with their friends.

In the widest sense of the term, "post-Christian" could surely indicate a whole trajectory of thought, extending from Schleiermacher's* "second" speech on the nature of religion, through Otto's* phenomenological depiction of the sense of the holy*, to Iris Murdoch's philosophical writing. In Britain Don Cupitt's books gave rise to the Sea of Faith Movement, also strong in Australia and New Zealand, which provides a home and forum for debate for many of unorthodox belief. Research carried out by the "Religious Experience Research Unit" (based originally in Oxford) has shown how prevalent in Britain is the conviction of persons that they have had a religious experience, whether they call it of "God" or not (30–40%). Compare this with the results of one poll showing that less than 3% of the population attend any form of Christian worship at Christmas.

The question that presents itself is how, in the midst of what may be the first great experiment in secularity in modern Europe (this being also true of formerly Roman Catholic countries), we may retain a spirituality and sense of God; for it may be (to employ Kantian vocabulary) that the positive, historical religions that we have known have indeed been "vehicles," which we may think to have carried, if also distorted, human awareness of a certain dimension of reality. Those who think this (but have rejected Christian dogma) may rightly be named post-Christian. The fact that modern science* tells us that there is no "outside" or "before" suggests that the paradigms that theology has formerly employed must be discarded. In this situation, it is vital that we recast what we would say, for human beings need some kind of concrete articulation, in words or imagery, of that which they believe to be the case. Lacking this we should be left with a wholly amorphous spirituality, or indeed a purely material transcendental against which the human spirit rebels.

DAPHNE HAMPSON

Postcolonialism and Christian Theology. Christian theology has engaged postcolonialism both as a historical phenomenon and as a theory. In both cases, "postcolonial" usually refers to the 20th-c. period following the rule by European powers over colonies in Africa and Asia, beginning with India's independence (1947) and extending through the decolonization of the 1970s and 1980s in Asia and Africa. Yet this time frame can be misleading, for two reasons. First, European (and US) imperial and neocolonial policies still constrain Asian and African polities. Thus the "post" in "postcolonial" is often used also to mean a "continual pushing against and beyond" still powerful colonial legacies. Second, the time frame overlooks the longer period of decolonization during the 19th c. in Latin America and its ongoing "postcolonial" struggle with subsequent imperial policies of Europe and the USA.

As a historical phenomenon, postcolonialism has been engaged in various ways by Christian theology. Theology, when not complicit in reinforcing colonial structures (as it usually was throughout Asia, African, and Latin America), could articulate anticolonial discontent, sometimes fusing into inculturated* (or syncretistic*) revivalist* movements in the colonies or emerging, at other times, as politicized missionary* support for decolonizing struggle.

It is as a theory, though, that postcolonialism has been engaged by Christian theologians most intentionally, producing "postcolonial theology" in the 21st c. Most influential have been the theorists Edward Said, Homi Bhabha, and Gayatri Chakravorty Spivak, whose works parse postcolonial themes with poststructuralist theory. These three focus mainly on concerns of Asia, but they have been joined by African theorists, such as Achille Mbembe, and Latin America ones (often highly critical of postcolonial theory), such as Walter Mignolo.

Theology's turn to postcolonial theory began mainly in biblical studies of the 1990s, when some scholars found the terms of imperialism*, colonialism*, and neocolonialism, to be valuable for analysis of the Bible and of biblical hermeneutics. More recently, constructive or systematic theologians have begun to engage postcolonial theories of difference, hybridity, mimicry, diaspora, border thinking, empire, and neocolonialism. These notions are revising the context and content of theological method, especially in Feminist, Liberation, and political theologies throughout the world. The central problematic that emerges amid these revisions focuses on how complex affirmations of difference modulate colonized peoples' liberating resistance and well-being. Even though this problematic is also shaping reconstructive reflection on traditional doctrines of Western theology (God*, Christ*, Spirit*, church*), there are at this writing very few doctrinal works emerging from conversations with postcolonial theory. **See also COLONIALISM AND IMPERIALISM AND CHRISTIAN THEOLOGY; DECOLONIZING THEOLOGY.** MARK LEWIS TAYLOR

Postdenominationalism. See INDEPENDENT OR FREE CHURCHES.

Postmillennialism, the belief that Christ will return after the millennium* (Rev 20), a period of righteousness and peace that fulfills the church's proclamation and action. It became widespread in Protestantism, e.g. in the writings of John Foxe* and Jonathan Edwards*. It inspired reform-minded North American Christians to work for justice* and peace* to prepare for Christ's millennial reign. **See also DISPENSATIONALISM; MILLENNIALISM CLUSTER.**

Postmodernism and Liberation Theologies are tied to overarching transformations in society. Liberation* theologies emerged in the context of liberation movements – the US civil rights struggles and Latin American movements of the poor who personally experienced the failure of economic policies. Independently of each other, Frederick Herzog, a white theologian in North Carolina, James Cone, an African American theologian in New York, and Gustavo Gutiérrez, a Peruvian priest, published the first "theologies of liberation" (1970–71), at the same time that the first strands of Feminist* theology, by Rosemary Radford Ruether and others, were being developed. These different "academic" Liberation theologies interacted with particular liberation struggles and encountered each other only later on, not without tensions and disagreements. They share a new encounter with marginalized* people (along the lines of race, class, and gender) who gradually became the subjects (rather than objects) of theological reflection. This theological practice initiated significant and lasting shifts that challenge the academy.

Postmodernism is a new way of thinking (since the 1970s and 1980s) that is also closely tied to a context involving broad socioeconomic and cultural changes. Developments in communications and media* blurred the line between reality and virtual reality. Even the production of wealth* is located more in virtual reality (e.g. finance capital, stock market, label) than in "hard" reality (e.g. industrial production). Postmodernist ways of thought, including poststructuralism and deconstruction, challenge modern ways of thought (which presuppose hard notions of reality), such as scientific positivism*, philosophical foundationalism, and structuralism. Postmodernism is mirrored in cultural phenomena like multiculturalism and increased acceptance of cultural differences; affirmations of identity (based on a fixed referent in reality) are replaced by affirmations of difference.

Postmodern thought appears to challenge key concerns of Liberation theologies. If difference is broadly acknowledged and accepted and if hard facts are challenged, can we still speak of oppression along the lines of race, class, and gender? Are differences no longer oppressive*? Is the preferential* option for the poor and marginalized that is promoted by Liberation theologies the special interest of limited groups? Nevertheless, in postmodern times, pressure on the margins has become worse as the gap between rich and poor continues to grow and as tensions along the lines of race and gender continue, although they may be less visible, having been pushed underground. Contemporary Liberation theologians, taking into account the changes brought by postmodernity, carry on their work in light of these ongoing tensions. Yet postmodernism opens the possibility of new related projects, such as postcolonial* theology and subaltern studies, by providing insights on the oppressive impact of colonialism on all areas of life, including the realm of ideas. **See also FEMINIST THEOLOGY CLUSTER; LIBERATION THEOLOGIES CLUSTER.** JOERG RIEGER

Postmodernism and Theology. It is widely assumed that an epochal shift occurred in the last decades of the 20th c. that took the Western industrialized world, at least, beyond the modernity ushered in by the Enlightenment*. The precise nature of the shift is not described consistently in the same terms, perhaps demonstrating the slipperiness of epochal designations, especially when made in close temporal proximity to events. Within theological circles, however, a certain version of "postmodernism" seems to hold sway, one to which François Lyotard's *The Postmodern Condition: A Report on Knowledge* provides a helpful index. Lyotard identifies the "post" with "an incredulity toward metanarratives" (xxiv), particularly those inherited from the Enlightenment*. These include metanarratives of progress, whether epistemological (scientific* or philosophical*), political* (democratic or socialist), or economic* (Marxist or capitalist), and of representation (linguistic or artistic). The decline of confidence in these meta-narratives calls into question their underlying standards of truth* and justice*. In the wake of the unanimity of perspective comes social and epistemological fragmentation.

Though Lyotard was published in France in 1979, well before the advent of the World Wide Web, the Web helpfully illustrates the postmodern condition as he describes it. Both in infrastructure and in content, the Web embodies a radically decentralized version of authority* and authorization. As a conduit for commerce and information, the Web enables the circulation of various forms of capital – virtual and real, economic and social – through a global network that both requires and transcends material structures (e.g. computer hardware, bricks-and-mortar stores). It makes possible new forms of social alliance (virtual and real) that can either buttress or transgress the topographies of nation-states and taxonomies of race, class, sex, and religion. Thus like the World Wide Web, "postmodernity" both draws on and transcends features of the "modern."

Postmodernism's consequences for religion are ambivalent. On the one hand, as metanarratives, religions are vulnerable to fragmentation and dispersal. The decline of mainline Protestantism* (a modern phenomenon) and the rise of nondenominational independent* churches and parachurch* movements evince such vulnerability. On the other hand, others argue that, just as modernity's pursuit of the purely rational displaced religious authorities, so rationality's displacement allows for a return of the religious (see Rationalism and Christian Theology). Doubtless, this putative return (where did religion go, exactly?) takes many benign, even banal forms, but those that grab headlines seek to reassert traditional (and authoritarian) religiosities. Among the parachurch movements that have emerged in recent decades in the USA are the Moral* Majority and Focus on the Family. And the events of September 11, 2001, acquainted the world with forms of Islam that, while structurally decentralized and fragmentary, are able to marshal lethal force in service of their political agenda. Clearly, then, religion, like every other aspect of culture, finds itself caught in the crosscurrents of the postmodern condition.

Theological assessments of postmodernism follow the lines of ambivalence just described. While some argue that postmodernity confronts theology with new and distinctive challenges (Lakeland and Davaney), certain theologies with modern roots continue to assert their relevance. Heirs of the radical theology (or Death* of God) movement of the 1980s see postmodernity as carrying forward the triumph of the secular* over the religious, though not without residue (Crockett). Process* theology has found new life by staking a claim to postmodern terrain (Griffin, Keller, and Daniell). Advocates of various Liberation* theologies argue that modernity's dissolution, while posing challenges to liberative projects, need not block and can even bolster the pursuit of social justice* (Min and Rieger). Some read modernity's demise as an opportunity for a reprise of more traditional forms of Christianity. Post-liberal theology is sometimes put forward as an antidote to postmodernity's vertigo or malaise (Webster and Schner). From England comes "radical orthodoxy." While its claims to radicality and to orthodoxy of interpretation have not gone unchallenged (Ruether and Grau), its affiliates advocate premodern Christian theologies as newly resonant and politically progressive responses to postmodern challenges (Milbank). Finally, the return of religion is illustrated by its newly found cachet as a scholarly topic among philosophers and cultural critics (e.g. Agamben, Badiou, Bloechl, Caputo, Zizek, and Keller and Daniell).

One finds echoes of these various responses in a new form of Evangelicalism*, the Emerging Church Movement (see Independent or Free Churches). Theologians writing for this movement (and thus in a more popular vein; see Smith) embrace postmodernism as a breath of fresh air for Christianity. Its advocates argue for abandoning the emphasis on right belief characteristic of Evangelicalism* (itself a product of modernity) in favor of an emphasis on communal practices that cultivate spiritual development and/or social justice. That engagements with postmodernism can produce such widely differing theological projects is an interesting feature of this current in contemporary Christianity. **See also RATIONALISM AND CHRISTIAN THEOLOGY; REASON.**

ELLEN T. ARMOUR

POVERTY CLUSTER

1) *Introductory Entries*

1) Introductory Entries

Poverty and the Eastern Orthodox Church. Theological and ethical considerations of the Eastern Orthodox* Church concerning poverty have been determined by the teachings of the *hiera* (Holy Scriptures*) and the *thyrathen* (natural* theology, Greek philosophy) sources. Even though an appreciation for and use of Greek ideas and principles are found as early as the NT (John 1:1; Acts 16:28, 26:24; Rom 2:14, 7:15; 1 Cor 3:22; see also Hellenistic Religious Traditions and Christianity's Self-Definition; Inculturation Cluster: Of Christianity in the Greco-Roman World), it was after the 4th c. that church fathers emphasized the importance of Greek thought for theology and practice in teachings used for effective missionary work among the Greek-speaking world.

From antiquity, some attributed the existence of poverty to God, others to human nature: "The Lord makes the poor and makes the rich" (1 Sam 2:7); "Poverty and wealth come from the Lord" (Sirach 11:14; cf. Eccl. 4:1; 6:8). In the NT, poverty is a given: "You always have the poor with you," Jesus said to his disciples (Matt 26:11; cf. Deut 15:11); helping the poor would be rewarded by God (Matt 25:31–46).

By contrast, Greek philosophy did not consider poverty a fixed, divinely ordained condition. For Plato* "there must be no place for poverty in any section of the population." Aristotle* added that poverty was an impediment to peace and a civilized life, and "the only way to prevent social conflicts and civil wars is to banish poverty." Helping the poor has its own inner satisfaction. Givers help fellow human beings like themselves. The teachings of Plato and Aristotle, Zeno and the Stoics*, who emphasized the practical application of ethics*, were familiar to Christian theologians of the Greek-speaking world. The church fathers viewed the philosophers' teachings as "preparation for the gospel."

Early Christianity was greatly influenced by the Greek language and culture, in which it grew and prospered. Thus "there are neither rich nor poor, because for all God has created nothing unnecessarily and has omitted nothing that is necessary," said Basil* of Caesarea (329–79), one of the most influential writers on Orthodox theology, ethics, and monasticism. He advocated balance and harmony in social relationships, encouraging monks to be active in social and cultural issues. Basil* of Caesarea advised students to study not only philosophers, but also the Greek poets. He wrote, "Read Homer because what he writes is about virtue*."

The belief that the human being is "an image* of God" (Bible) or "a spark of divinity" (Greek philosophy) played a major role in the formation and application of theology and ethics in the Orthodox Church. "Receive a poor person as an unknown God" (Greek) and "Receive a poor person as a brother or sister in Christ" (Christian) are mottoes that have never been forgotten. Christian Orthodoxy follows a traditional and consistent theology, including an ethics of poverty and the poor. Historically, the reaction to poverty was the practice of philanthropy, individually as well as through *ptocheia* or *ptochotropheia,* institutions established and usually maintained by the Orthodox Church to care for the needs of the poor (those unable to work).

Poverty was considered a virtue for monks (along with celibacy* and obedience); before joining a monastery, they would distribute their possessions to the poor or to philanthropic institutions. But monks who were poor as individuals might be collectively wealthy in a monastery, because of donations by the faithful (cf. the Poverty* Movement in Western churches).

Eastern Orthodoxy today does not condone poverty, which it sees as the result of human sinfulness, greed, exploitation, and selfishness. The restoration of human being to its pristine goodness, the practice of love*, and the establishment of institutionalized philanthropy are means by which poverty will be mitigated if not eliminated.

DEMETRIOS J. CONSTANTELOS

Poverty and Protestant Churches. The Reformation held to the traditional ascetic* notion of "spiritual poverty" as a virtue, but Protestantism increasingly spiritualized and internalized it. Of the NT's two quotations from Deuteronomy 15:4–11 – "There will be no poor [needy] among you" (Acts 4:34) and "There will always be poor among you" (Mark 14:7 = Matt 26:11; John 12:8) – Protestant churches have tended more readily to accept the latter, thereby settling for a narrow, spiritual view of salvation*. For Luther* and Calvin*, being justified by God should lead to good works on behalf of the poor neighbor. But the mark of salvation as participation in a transformed beloved community with the poor, as in earlier strands of the history of the church, has appeared only occasionally in Protestantism.

The tendency has been to identify poverty with material poverty, thus downplaying the political, cultural, natural, and spiritual dimensions of poverty. At worst Protestants have contributed to systematic poverty by succumbing to Aristotle's view that the poor are destined to be poor (and ignoring other teachings of Aristotle about poverty; see the present cluster: And the Eastern Orthodox Church). The poor have only themselves to blame owing to laziness, lack of faith, or ignorance, or because they are suffering God's punishment for wrongdoing.

But where Protestant churches have viewed poverty as unjust or unacceptable because it is involuntary or because it diminishes human community or because in Jesus Christ God identifies with the poor and works for the salvation of all through the salvation of the poor, they have sought ways to struggle against poverty. Generally these Protestant Church movements have sprung from the left wing of the Reformation, Lutheran Pietism*, Arminian* Calvinism, Evangelical* revivals*, the Holiness* Movement, Christian Socialism, the Social* Gospel emphasis of mainline Protestant churches, and Protestant forms of Liberation* and postcolonial* theology. One pervasive theme is reordering the church to minister to the poor.

The most effective Protestant measures have come from the conviction that life with and ministry to the poor is constitutive of the experience of salvation. The great experiment of the Lutheran Pietist Francke* in Halle provided a model for *diakonia** to the poor that is effective even today. John Wesley's* revival was focused on the poor. By offering universally available salvation, these movements seek to change the hearts, habits, and conditions of the destitute and working poor.

The low point of Protestantism's relation to poverty came in the 18th to early 19th c. when the "enclosure" of farmland and common land caused rural depopulation and unemployment, creating a labor market for the burgeoning industrial revolution, and the old Poor Laws and parish* protection of the poor succumbed to new legislation in 1834. The resulting horrendous suffering of the poor led in the mid-19th c. to a new social and structural view of poverty in Marx*, nascent sociology*, and literature (e.g. Dickens). A new form of Protestant theology of poverty ensued that related the identity and justice* of God to the unjust social and political systems in which poverty thrives.

Various forms of 19th-c. Christian Socialism (F. D. Maurice in England; the Blumhardts* and Leonhard Ragaz on the Continent) had a lasting effect on William Temple, Tillich*, and Barth*, all socialists. In the USA (early 20th c.), the Social* Gospel, led by Washington Gladden and Rauschenbusch*, directed Protestants to the structurally complex life of the working poor. The Social Gospel was Postmillennialist* but not limited to simple prophetic denunciations of poverty; it sought to address poverty by radically changing systems of education*, health* care, hygiene, slums, infrastructure, housing codes, labor protection, voting rights, rights of women, racial tensions, and militarization. The Methodist "Social Principles" (1908), adopted the same year by the Federal* Council of Churches, represents a good example of the ecumenical effort. In the New Deal, this Protestant heritage joined with Roman Catholic social teachings, the Jewish tradition, and secular movements to bring about a "welfare state."

The legal and political gains on behalf of the poor were soon jeopardized by a resurgence of an unregulated market and the second modern globalization beginning in the 1960s. A plethora of new Protestant theologies dealing with poverty arose following the "political* theology" of Jürgen Moltmann and J. B. Metz in Germany and "Liberation* theology" in Latin America (led by Gustavo Gutiérrez) and later Africa and Asia. Frederick Herzog broke new theological ground in relating God and the poor in North America. Gradually Black* theology, initiated by James Cone, Feminist* and Womanist* theology, peace* theology, and ecological* theology began to see that racism*, sexism*, the degradation of nature, and permanent warfare are all inexorably related to poverty. More recent theologians (e.g. Milbank, Tanner, Meeks, Long) – address poverty by means of an even deeper theological criticism of the assumptions behind the global market economy. M. DOUGLAS MEEKS

Poverty and the Roman Catholic Church. The centrality of the Roman Catholic Church's concern for the poor flows directly from Jesus' mission of salvation* and his preference for the poor. Solidarity with the poor, as John Paul II stated, is "a proof of [the Church's] fidelity to Christ, so that she can truly be the 'church of the poor'" (*Laborem Exercens*, 8). The Church's view of "poverty" is twofold. It encourages poverty of spirit, which heightens one's openness to the needy, and it adopts the alleviation and prevention of poverty as a central part of its earthly mission. Voluntary poverty, as Thomas Aquinas* tells us, "is praiseworthy according as it frees [one] from the vices in which some are involved through riches [see Poverty Movement]. . . . However, insofar as poverty takes away the food which results from riches, . . . it is purely an evil" (*Summa contra Gentiles*, Chap. 133).

Poverty, often defined as a state of material insufficiency, contrasts with God's promise of abundance (Isa 60–65) and is the result of our propensity to sin*. From a Christian perspective, individual poverty is caused by social exclusion. Many of the church fathers saw the greed of the rich as the primary mode of exclusion, emphasizing, as had the OT prophets, that wealth* is often created at the expense of the poor (Clark). They also cited the obligation to use one's surplus for the benefit of the poor. As John* Chrysostom stated, the only safe place to store wealth is in "the stomachs of the poor."

Poverty is more than an economic phenomenon, and the Church is equally concerned with social and spiritual poverty, which are also caused by exclusion – from participation in one's community in the case of social poverty; and from communion with God and God's people in the case of spiritual poverty. Exclusion is usually caused by both individual actions and social structures. Thus the Roman Catholic Church promotes inclusion, both in the choices individuals make and in the social order. The Church emphasizes that all wealth* comes from God, and it is a sin* to exclude without cause some from God's gift to all.

This principle of the universal destination of goods, a key principle in the Roman Catholic social thought tradition, highlights the importance of "participation" for the authentic development of the human person. Poverty caused by exclusion both denies and prevents human development and is thus contrary to the dignity of the human person, made in the image* and likeness of God (*imago Dei*). Charity* (care for the poor) is tied to both love* of God and love of neighbor (Benedict XVI, *Deus Caritas Est*). The Church's approach to care for the poor, then, is grounded in efforts to achieve authentic human development (Paul VI, *Populorum Progressio*) and not continued dependency or exclusion.

The Roman Catholic Church's institutional commitment to serving the poor started with the first Christians. The apostles (Acts 6) appointed seven men (probably the first deacons*) to minister to the material needs of the poor. Fundraising for the poor ("the saints") was part of Paul's* mission. By the time of Pope Gregory* I (540–604), the Church had institutionalized the practice of devoting one-quarter of Church revenues to care for the poor. By the Middle Ages, assistance for the poor was institutionalized in canon* law as a duty. It was carried out in thousands of institutions administered by bishops, parishes, monasteries, religious orders, and lay groups. Each era of Church history witnessed new efforts to "include" the poor. The work of Vincent* de Paul (c1580–1660) is especially noteworthy, as it continues to inspire successive generations, religious and lay, to work with the poor, for the poor. The 19th- to 20th-c. rise of industrialism and urbanism brought forth a series of new forms of economic, social, and spiritual exclusion. The numerous papal social* encyclicals of the past 120 years, under the influence of social sciences in the modern era, have focused particularly on social, political, and economic structures that create exclusion and thus create poverty. Many of these injustices stem from the "worship of wealth," which creates material poverty for the poor and spiritual poverty for the affluent.

These "structures of sin*" (as they are referred to in *Sollicitudo Rei Socialis*) cannot be adequately addressed by change in individual behavior alone, although that is necessary. Through its teaching mission, the Church seeks first to bring about a "change in heart," a turning toward God. But it recognizes the need to promote social justice* in public policy, the economy*, social structures, and international institutions if material poverty is to be lessened. Being the "Church of the poor" requires a "preferential* option for the poor," which will effect the elimination of exclusionary structures, the promotion of participation by the poor, and sharing by all in the world's goods, God's wealth. **See also PREFERENTIAL OPTION FOR THE POOR.**

CHARLES M. A. CLARK.

2) A Sampling of Contextual Views and Practices

Poverty, Theology, and Ethics: African Views. Although the continent of Africa is endowed with abundant natural resources, its people continue to suffer from abject poverty, because human resources and economic infrastructures are underdeveloped and controlled by people from other continents.

To understand this situation, it is enough to remember that poverty can be defined as an ensemble of conditions that prevent human beings from flourishing and attaining fulfillment. The conditions of poverty – unemployment, illiteracy, ethnocentrism, civil war, famine, disease, and marginalization – make realization of human dignity and human* rights impossible and form an interlocking web that is difficult to unlock all at once. It is perpetuated largely by ill-founded development theories, erroneous assumptions, and misguided development programs designed to eradicate poverty.

Poverty also is a deprivation of capabilities, empowerment, and basic freedoms. Thus, as can be observed in Africa, prolonged poverty produces in the oppressed a pattern of internalized oppression* that manifests itself as fatalism, dependence, and hopelessness, which perpetuate the cycle of poverty. The lack of abundant wealth production and control of it and the lack of self-confidence and visionary leadership have ultimately resulted in the loss of survival mechanisms among the present generation of Africans.

Because poverty is conditioned by the dynamics of political organizations, socioeconomic infrastructures, and trade systems, by value systems and patterns of social organizations and relationships, and by religiocultural traditions, eradicating poverty cannot be achieved immediately. The notion that poverty could be instantly overcome with the help of international financial institutions and foreign aid alone is erroneous and misleading, because it ignores the dynamics of value systems and contextual social realities. A change at the level of value systems occurs slowly because each group of people has its own understanding of the good life and conceptualizes its setting differently.

Thus development programs that propose to eradicate poverty seem artificial, ineffective, and problematic. International financial institutions, donor agencies, and governments have offered an array of solutions, ranging from the control of population growth to structural adjustment programs, from debt relief to direct aid, but none of these has succeeded in bringing significant relief. Instead of reducing poverty, these "solutions" have helped perpetuate it. To eradicate poverty, there must be a localized initiative, linking all dimensions of human experience with the spirit of survival, that advocates transformation of the patterns of social relationships by a process of conscientization* and of mobilization of the poor. **See also THE PRESENT CLUSTER: POVERTY, THEOLOGY, AND ETHICS: AFRICAN AMERICAN VIEWS.** AQUILINE TARIMO, SJ

Poverty, Theology and Ethics: African American Views. African Americans and African Canadians cannot envision poverty apart from their inheritance of an African worldview according to which the unity of body* and soul* implies a similar unity between the material and spiritual realms of life commonly expressed in human practice and thought. Since the unity of body and soul and of material and spiritual realms is grounded in God*, the source of all reality, any rupture in that unity constitutes a theological problem, because God is part of the relationship.

The resulting disharmony from the rupture penetrates the entire social order. Poverty is one of the major forms of that imbalance. Its vivid signs are seen in the deficit of the necessary conditions for life, e.g. the loss of food, land*, water*, and/or shelter; disease; physical pain and suffering*; captivity; and death*. Most important, the loss of communal relationships – in both life and death – constitutes the greatest of all evils. It alone evidences the full-blown state of poverty. Thus African Americans may not view themselves as poor simply because they lack material resources. If their family* and communal relationships are intact they are not in a state of poverty regardless of their needs. For this reason, African* American churches have always striven to be surrogate families and support systems for their members. In fact, mutual aid societies constituted one of the earliest forms of such communal helpfulness (see Prosperity Gospel Cluster: And Economic Empowerment Gospel and African American Churches).

Whenever the spirit of African peoples was broken by the conditions of the slave* trade, colonialism*, racial segregation, and discrimination (see Racism and Christianity Cluster: In Africa), their fundamental ontological unity was disrupted and, consequently, all dimensions of their common life were threatened. The resulting discord affected the psyches of individual persons, families, and neighborhoods everywhere. A residue of their African communal spirit enabled them to hold on to the ancestral germ of sympathy, empathy, and support for one another. Broken but not destroyed, they were able to endure as a people. While praying for deliverance, they kept alive the faith and hope that their suffering would be overcome one day.

Thus the African American view of poverty has always been correlated with the injustice inflicted on them by the external forces of racism* and oppression*. Yet because they viewed their societal condition as a theological problem primarily, they always knew that deliverance necessitated the habitual performance of prescribed religious rituals in order to restore the ontological balance that had been disrupted by the power of evil forces. Invariably, such a ritual performance implied subtle forms of resistance to their social condition as well as acts of compensation for God's displeasure. Most important, it implied a willing partnership with the God of creation in effecting the desired political, ethical, and theological resolution. (Contrast this perspective with the theoretical and limited view of the unity of body and soul held by Christians in cultures influenced by Greek thought; see Soul.)

PETER PARIS

Poverty, Theology, and Ethics: Asian Views. Poverty, perhaps the most daunting problem in many countries in Asia, is a central topic of most consultations and conferences on mission*, service, or development held by the church in Asia.

Economically understood, poverty is the deprivation of basic necessities of life – chiefly food, shelter, and clothing – and the lack of a minimum level of economic security, i.e. the lack of a reasonable assurance that the basic necessities of life will continue to be met.

Beyond purely economic factors, poverty is linked with unjust structures and faulty economic systems that favor the rich. Most disturbing is the persistence of mass poverty and the increasing gap between the rich and the poor despite planned development.

Thus poverty is clearly is an ethical problem, concerning development and justice*. Development is not simply about economic growth; it is also a participation in the process toward a more just society by the powerless, who need to acquire power in order to participate with dignity in decisions affecting their lives. Christian ethical responsibility involves "advocating a strategy of developing people's power as the only safeguard of justice in any political system" (Thomas).

For the Asian Conference on Church and Society (1999), economic witness demands that specific attention be given to "the challenge of globalization and its consequence on peoples and societies in Asia." "An uncritical attitude and unquestioned acceptance of globalization is morally unethical, economically unwise and socially undesirable."

Theology can perform a critical role here. Like the prophets* of old, theologians of today can challenge those who wield power (by covertly using ideologies* to further their own interests) to take more seriously their responsibilities toward the defenseless. Beyond this important critical role, theology has a more positive role to play. In creative dialogue with each specific situation, theology can articulate and clarify the vision and aspirations that sustain the people in their struggle by confronting them with the ever widening horizon of God's liberative acts. "A theology that does not stimulate Christians to commit themselves to the liberation of the exploited and oppressed* has nothing to say to them. Theologizing would be futile toil if it does not contribute to the radical social change of peoples and institutions in our semi-feudal and semi-colonial society" (1975 Statement on Theological Reflection in the Philippines). **See also GLOBALIZATION: CHRISTIAN RESPONSES.**

K. C. ABRAHAM

Poverty, Theology, and Ethics: Caribbean Views. The scarcity of resources in the Caribbean Islands has made it difficult for Caribbean people to press for structural changes in the areas of economics*, health* care, and politics*. One alternative has been to respond to symptoms without addressing root causes, particularly in relationship to poverty, racism*, and the cycle of dependency – an approach that makes poverty seem intractable.

The culture of resistance of the Caribbean Christian Church has provided over the centuries a key that unlocked the doors of freedom in many island states. Thus in some ways, Caribbean people have begun to break the back of oppression* and to fashion a language opening up a new future for them. This language of a culture of resistance provides a way of dealing with issues of identity and of discrimination on the basis of gender, class, race, and sexual orientation. Could it help take on poverty as well, even though poverty seems intractable?

Thus, out of this culture of resistance, Caribbean theologians begin to ask self-critical and systemic questions such as: Why is power concentrated in the hands of a few, while the majority are "poor," i.e. are powerless to determine their own destinies? How can the church take responsibility for issues of stewardship while it is the largest landowner in the Caribbean? How can the church stand with the poor so as to speak to issues of homelessness and scarcity of resources? How can the church become the site of resistance against all forms of poverty that afflict Caribbean people? How can the church speak from the cross, from the hurt and despair of Caribbean people, identifying itself with the least of these and thus letting itself be broken for the sake of the marginalized* and abused*?

Quite often in the Caribbean, the real misery and pain of the people are hidden behind forms of partial liberation, including behind preaching that advocates the salvation* of the soul* without making a connection with the real life situations that confront people's bodies*. For too long, the church's fear of losing faith* has made it protective and defensive, while it ignores structures of oppression and fails to be proactive in its commitment to transform life in the Caribbean as it affirms its faith.

NOEL LEO ERSKINE

Poverty, Theology, and Ethics: Latin American Views. See PREFERENTIAL OPTION FOR THE POOR.

Poverty, Theology, and Ethics: North American Feminist Views. Feminist views on poverty, Christian theology, and ethics are varied but share a methodological principle to take seriously women's experience in all its complexity (the interstructuring of gender, race/ethnicity, class, sexual orientation, and nationality) and an ethical commitment to the well-being of women, their families, and communities.

The majority of the world's poor are women. Feminists understand poverty to mean not just a lack of material possessions but also social powerlessness. Women's economic vulnerability is shaped by their female physicality and socially constructed gender identities and relations. It is exacerbated by neoliberal economic globalization, which exploits women's paid and unpaid labor and commodifies women's bodies.

Feminists' views on poverty range from liberal to radical. Liberal feminists advocate changes within capitalism, such as equal employment opportunity, to overcome poverty and sexual inequality. Radical feminists doubt that these can be overcome within capitalism, with its gendered and racialized systems of domination and exploitation. They advocate participatory forms of economic democracy in which women have equal social and economic power (see Democracy and Christianity). Ecofeminists* link the oppression of women and the earth. They prioritize sustainability and care for the earth and all its inhabitants.

Feminists charge that both economics and ethics are androcentric. Women's reproductive and domestic labor is not perceived as an economic contribution or domain involving moral agency and decision making. Androcentrism is manifested in economics in the privileging of market exchange as the basis of all value. In liberal and Protestant thought, it is manifested in the public–private split. The public sphere is the realm of justice*, the private the realm of love*. This results in a romanticization of the family* and expectations that women sacrifice their own well-being for their families. This is also a problem in Roman Catholic thought. Some feminists advocate that caring and care work be made visible, valued, and shared equitably by women and men.

Roman Catholic social* teaching and various Liberation* theologies are strands of Christian tradition many feminists find relevant to understanding poverty.

However, the usefulness of these traditions is limited by their justification of gender hierarchies (patriarchy*) and the inequality of women on grounds of natural* law or orders of creation*. Feminist theologies* offer more useful theological anthropologies* for understanding gender identities and relations.

Feminists envision just, sustainable, caring economies that uphold life. Human rights are upheld, and meeting the basic needs of all is a priority. This vision resonates with biblical notions of shalom and the kin-dom of God (see Feminist Theology Cluster: In North America: Mujerista; Kingdom of God, the Concept of, Cluster: In the New Testament).

PAMELA K. BRUBAKER

Poverty, Theology, and Ethics: North American Latino/a Views. Contemporary Latino/a theological reflection has focused on the poverty that results from an unjust social system. Latino/a theologians denounce capitalism because, while it is efficient in increasing material production and trade, it remains incapable of including all people. It creates wealth* for the few and misery for the many. Latino/a theologians suspect that the process of globalization*, based on capitalist forms of production, will result in more extreme forms of social exclusion, environmental degradation, social strife, and civil wars, all of which contribute to the phenomenon of socioeconomic marginalization*, political repression, massive migration, refugees*, and massive human poverty on a global scale.

As they read Scripture*, Latino/a theologians note that few issues receive as much attention as poverty does. Scripture speaks positively of the poor in spirit (Matt 5:3), as those who have God's purposes at the center of their lives. They acknowledge their dependence on God and are even willing to sacrifice their life plans and goals to be faithful servants of God, as the prophets and Jesus have been. Rather than "being" for the sake of "having," the poor in spirit are those who "have" in order "to be" (committed to the love and justice* at the heart of God's purpose).

Latino/a theologians also note that Scripture denounces the poverty that results from exploitation and domination and dehumanizes. Wealth* gained at the expense of the poor is tantamount to idolatry* in that it gives the illusion that we are self-sufficient or independent from God and/or from poor brothers and sisters whose needs cry for social justice.

Latino/a theologians claim the centrality of the biblical image of God's preferential* option for the poor. The community of faith, in obedience to God, is to love the poor in a preferential way through acts of social justice. Christians are to advocate for the poor, responsibly sharing their resources, but most importantly struggling with them so they, too, become moral and political agents who can forge a new and more inclusive and caring society.

ISMAEL GARCÍA

Poverty Movement. In the 11th and 12th c., with the rise of a money economy, there was increasing anxiety about money and wealth; wandering reformers advocated poverty in its various forms. Pope Urban II encouraged the laity* to adopt the "religious life" (1091). The notion of three orders for clerics, professed women, and laypersons was formalized (1201) when Innocent* III approved the Humiliati and other lay reform groups. The Poverty Movement culminated in the founding of the mendicant*, or begging, orders (especially the Franciscans* and Dominicans*, early 13th c.). **See also PROPERTY; VOWS; WEALTH.**

Practical Syllogism, type of reasoning developed in the Reformed* tradition as a way of gaining assurance* of salvation*. Faith* itself was regarded as sufficient assurance, but Calvin* also sought confirmation in sanctification* and good works*, not as *cause* but as *evidence* of salvation. The following "practical syllogism" was formulated by the Puritan* theologian William Perkins* at Cambridge and promoted by Teelinck in the Netherlands: "Whoever experiences the gift of sanctification is justified; I feel this by the grace of God; therefore I am justified." In popular Protestantism, hard work, thrift, and the accumulation of wealth* came to be viewed as the signs of election (see Protestant Ethic).

Praedestinatus, a work produced in Rome (c430–40) that sought a middle position in the

Pelagian* controversy, denouncing Caelestius's* views (condemned in 418 and 431) but opposing the heresy of "predestinarianism*" as a corruption of the teaching of Augustine*.

Pragmatism and Christian Theologies. A central tenet of pragmatic theologies is that Christian theologies reflect particular situations of distinct times and places and are to be ethically assessed in terms of their practical consequences. North American philosophical pragmatism is generally identified with three main figures: Charles Sanders Peirce, William James, and John Dewey*. It is sometimes called classical pragmatism to differentiate it from the contemporary neopragmatism of W. V. Quine, Nelson Goodman, Wilfrid Sellars, Donald Davidson, Hilary Putnam, Thomas Kuhn, and most notably Richard Rorty. Eclipsed by Anglo-American analytic philosophy, classical pragmatism's influence on Christian thought was relatively short (1898–1940). Many North American students of Christian thought turned from pragmatist accounts of religious experience to either Alfred North Whitehead's* metaphysical philosophy or the history* of religion and comparative religion schools. During its height, pragmatism was most influential on North American philosophy* of religion.

Four themes mark the pragmatist movement: (1) naturalism: there is no knowledge outside of human experience; (2) instrumentalism: all forms of inquiry are tools that satisfy basic human purposes; (3) fallibilism: all knowledge claims are fragments and hence fallible; and (4) ameliorism: knowledge contributes to social equilibrium or betterment.

The greatest impact of pragmatism on Christian thought was the Chicago School of Theology's *Guide to the Study of the Christian Religion* (1916), D. C. Macintosh's *Religious Realism* (1931), and humanistic naturalism at Columbia University in the *Humanist Manifesto* (1933). The central tenets of these projects are (1) contextual: Christian theologies are historical responses to the particular situations of distinct times and places; (2) ethical: the meaning of Christian doctrine is ethical, expressing and clarifying Christian moral values; (3) process*: God is interpreted as natural processes, patterns, and powers operating in human experience; and (4) humanism: pragmatic theologies seek human and planetary flourishing as their ultimate goal. By the 1940s and 1950s, these pragmatic theologies were eclipsed by neo-orthodox theology, Christian Realism, and post-Holocaust theologies. Renewed interest in pragmatism and Christian thought surfaced in the 1980s and 1990s as such thinkers as William Dean, Nancy Frankenberry, Shelia Davaney, and Robert Corrington confronted neopragmatism. What emerged were pragmatic naturalism (nothing outside of natural processes for theological interpretation) and pragmatic historicism (no appeal outside of history for interpreting theology). Both pragmatic theologies are supported by the Highlands Institute for the Study of American Religious Thought, through which pragmatism in Christian thought has become international, interreligious, and a means of critically assessing Christian thought. VICTOR ANDERSON

Praise, in worship, expression of admiration for and thanks to God through prayer, song, or gesture.

Praise and Worship denotes a style of contemporary hymnody, a style of Charismatic* worship, and a commercial product within the contemporary Christian/gospel music industry. Growing out of two and a half centuries of revival* culture in England and North America, the Praise and Worship Movement began in house* churches and independent* Evangelical congregations as the convergence of a popular* culture-oriented renaissance in worship arts and the experience and theology of Spirit*-filled Evangelicalism*.

Music is the primary medium through which the Praise and Worship Movement renews* Christian worship through fresh and intensified expressions of praise*. Praise and worship is embodied, participatory worship in which music and religion become coextensive. For worshippers participation in musical worship is often the activity wherein they realize God's reality and presence most profoundly. Praise and worship liturgy is more fluid than the liturgies in mainline churches, both because of its Spirit-led performance of worship and because of its ties to trend-driven consumer culture*. The role of the worship leader is one of spiritual authority* and leadership. Women often function as worship leaders. Praise and worship songs are spiritualized popular songs. Like the mainstream pop music whose sounds it emulates, praise and worship is a stylistically diverse genre that includes soft pop, folk rock, soul, classic rock, alternative rock, hardcore punk, rap, bluegrass, jazz, and electronica. While most of these styles are not the typical fare of Sunday morning worship services, they have a place at youth group meetings, music festivals, and other extraecclesial gatherings.

Praise and worship music is one product of a burgeoning worship industry. The commodification of Evangelical worship music began as early as John and Charles Wesley's* production of hymnbooks. However, the music of worship is no longer a niche product marketed to churchgoers, but one promoted, via cable TV and other media, in the general marketplace. Worship music now functions beyond the church as a mode of alternative entertainment.

Critics allege that praise and worship music is theologically shallow and that its popularity and trendiness pose a threat to traditional liturgies and hymnody. Advocates say that praise and worship music revitalizes worship by facilitating intimacy with God and that it can be blended into and renew traditional liturgies (see Liturgies, History of). Others argue that the malleable theology of praise and worship music is the characteristic that allows it to be used in a variety of liturgical locations, where it takes on a meaning relative to each local ethos. With its affinity to pop music forms and its use of technology* in the context of worship, praise and worship music bridges worship and popular culture. **See also** CHARISMATIC AND PENTECOSTAL MOVEMENTS CLUSTER; EVANGELICALS/EVANGELICAL CLUSTER; GOSPEL MUSIC; MEDIA AND CHRISTIANITY; MEGACHURCHES REMAKING RELIGIOUS TRADITION IN NORTH AMERICA; PENTECOSTAL WORSHIP. DAVID HORACE PERKINS

Praxis (Gk "doing"), application of faith* in action, as contrasted with mere thought, although it implies reflective action. **See also** ORTHOPRAXY.

Prayer, for Christians, as for practitioners of other religions, is as essential for the health of the human spirit as breathing is for the body. Prayer is a universal language; some form of prayer is found in every religion and in every century of recorded history. Basically, in Christianity and many other religions, prayer is communication between human beings and a deity.

Prayer can be both an individual activity and a group activity. Individuals may pray silently, voice their prayers, chant or sing their prayers, or write their prayers on paper or cloth and put them in sacred places (such as the Western Wall in Jerusalem) or a prayer wheel (as in Tibet), or they may simply remain in contemplation ("abiding").

Group prayers are voiced by families and groups of friends; in churches, synagogues, temples, and mosques; in the natural world; and in gatherings of persons dedicated to working for peace and social justice and the meeting of urgent human needs.

Forms of prayer include *praise* of God** (by whatever name the deity is called); *confession**, expressions of sorrow for wrongdoings, by individuals or groups – even by a whole nation – by both omission and commission; *intercession**, requests for help, for healing, for guidance and blessings, for individuals, groups, or nations; *thanksgiving** for blessings received; and *contemplation* (see Contemplation, Contemplative Prayer and Life; Prayer of the Heart).

Prayer is a major practice of monks and nuns in monasteries of various faiths, including Buddhism* and Christianity (see Monasticism Cluster). So as to devote themselves totally to prayer, some orders, such as the Trappists (Cistercians*), maintain silence except to communicate something essential and to participate in several worship services each day.

In the early centuries of the Christian era, a number of monks – among whom were the desert fathers – lived in solitude in the wilderness and spent the major part of their time in prayer and meditation or contemplation (see Monasticism Cluster).

The sacred scriptures* of various religions contain teachings about prayer and collections of prayers, often used in worship services. The Bible contains both the Psalms* (widely read and sung in both Jewish and Christian worship services; see Worship Cluster: In Ancient Israel) and teachings about prayer and prayers themselves (such as the Lord's Prayer, taught by Jesus Christ to his disciples; Matt 6:9–13).

A longtime effort to strengthen a sense of spiritual oneness in the human family is the World Day of Prayer, observed by many Christian denominations. **See also** LITURGY; WORSHIP CLUSTER. FRED CLOUD

Prayer Breakfast, in the USA, a meeting for businesspeople or legislators, featuring prayer and usually a short address by a religious or political leader. The custom was originated by Abraham Vereide, a Norwegian immigrant and Methodist pastor, who began the breakfasts to counter the influence of socialism in Seattle (1935). The National Prayer Breakfast, addressed by the US president, has been held since 1953. It is criticized for seeking out powerful leaders, including some dictators, for taking a "top-down" approach to politics, and for compromising the separation between church* and state.

Prayer of the Heart, a nondiscursive, affective intuition of the presence of God that touches the will*, resulting in the perfecting of love* and other virtues*, in joy and repose. The prayer of the heart is also known as active contemplation or centering prayer. In Roman Catholic teaching, this form of prayer is considered to be "acquired" through an active contemplation preceded by the mental disciplines of spiritual meditation. It is therefore not "infused" (mystic or passive) and is thus distinct from mystic* contemplation and union with the Divine.

Prayer of the heart was called "active recollection" or the "prayer of simplicity" in Carmelite* spirituality as taught and practiced by Teresa* of Ávila and John* of the Cross. Prayer of the heart was also part of the spirituality of Francis* de Sales (17th c.) and was popularized in Western Europe, especially by Quietists* such as François Malaval (1627–1718; *An Easy Practice to Elevate the Soul to Contemplation*) and Jeanne Guyon* (1648–1717; *Short and Easy Method of Prayer*), who viewed this form of prayer as open to all. Their treatises were condemned in part for diminishing the role of meditation as a preparation for contemplation and for blurring the distinction between acquired and mystic contemplation. Yet the active prayer of the heart remained a constant emphasis within Western spirituality*, even among German Pietists* (e.g. *A Short, Easy, and Comprehensive Method of Prayer*, attributed to Johann Kelpius, 1673–1708), who were influenced by Quietist spirituality. In the late 20th c., Thomas Keating of the Cistercian* Trappist tradition popularized "centering prayer" in North American ecumenical contexts. **See also CONTEMPLATION, CONTEMPLATIVE PRAYER AND LIFE.**

PATRICIA A. WARD

Preaching, talking of God, is as ancient as human speech. Before there were preachers, there were Hebrew storytellers, prophets, and sages. Storytellers gave us the great myths of creation* in Gen 1–11, as well as stories of God's covenant* promises to patriarchs. But prophets*, called by God, were more obvious precursors of preachers, for they spoke a public "Word of God" to people. Later, there were sages who instructed people (as in Proverbs*) to lead prudent lives for God.

Israel also contributed a "theology of the Word." According to Genesis, God spoke and the world was created. Again God spoke, "Let my people go," and Israel passed through the sea, free of enslavement. God's words are never idle; they accomplish what God intends (see Performatory Language).

Scattered Jewish communities, separated during the Exile from the Jerusalem Temple, founded local places for prayer and learning. The word "synagogue*" means "place of assembly." After the destruction of the Second Temple, synagogues became central to Jewish life. Synagogue worship featured a sermon usually based on readings from the Torah, but also referring to the Prophets and wisdom writings, and thus continued to shape Israel's identity.

Jesus was a Jewish preacher. He spoke of a coming realm (kingdom*) of God, urging people to live in God's new social order in preparation for God's new social order. In God's realm, the poor would be raised up, the hungry fed, the powerless empowered, and the oppressed set free. Jesus gathered disciples to share the task of preaching his message of liberation. Evidently he welcomed followers to meals, perhaps celebrating the eschatological banquet on Mount Zion, anticipating the actual end of time. After staging a prophetic protest in the Temple during Passover week, Jesus was arrested and publicly crucified* by Roman authority. Cruel death seemed to discredit his message, and the Jesus movement scattered. But disciples came together again to testify to his resurrection*, a divine endorsement of Jesus' gospel message. Christianity began with a message.

As a Jewish sectarian movement, Christianity inherited in-house patterns of worship from the Jewish synagogue, including the biblical sermon. But as ties with Judaism became strained, Christianity began to expand in a Gentile world with evangelical preaching. Although the sample sermons in Acts* are probably products of Luke's rhetoric, early missionary preaching may well have been a kind of storied recital. From the start and through the centuries, there were both preaching to spread the message and in-house preaching from scriptural texts.

Gradually, preaching practices were learned. Origen* (d254) urged interpreters to discern different senses of Scripture: literal, moral, and mystical. The Cappadocians* and John* Chrysostom (347–407) in the East, and Augustine* (354–430) in the West, set preaching styles that prevailed for centuries. Augustine wrote *De doctrina christiana*, the first Christian homiletic guide.

Although preaching languished during the Middle Ages, Charlemagne* in the 8th c. encouraged the education of clergy and required sermons to be preached in the language of the people every Sunday and holy day. Much preaching was catechetical. As for the training of preachers, there were 12th-c. guides, including Alan of Lille's (1128–1202) significant *The Art of Preaching*. Preaching revived in the 13th and 14th c. when Franciscan* and Dominican* friars produced collections of sermons as well as homiletic guidebooks.

With the Renaissance and Reformation, there was a huge renewal of preaching. In the Roman Catholic tradition, Erasmus* wrote his formidable rhetoric. And Protestant Reformers, Luther*, Zwingli*, and Calvin*, inaugurated influential patterns of preaching. Reformers often preached sermons in which they interpreted books of the Bible from beginning to end, *lectio continua,* day after day. To Reformers, preaching was the Word of God and thus bound to be effective. Luther and Calvin preached thousands of sermons but did not write homiletic guides. Instead, Melanchthon*, Luther's colleague, wrote the first Protestant rhetoric for preachers.

The Catholic* Renewal, begun by Erasmus, was carried on with the founding of the Jesuit* order. In 1545 the Council of Trent* mandated preaching every Sunday and feast day, and provided for the homiletic training of priests.

In 1607 the Puritan* William Perkins* wrote his *Arte of Prophesying* urging a plain, but reasoned style of preaching. His work was influential. By contrast Continental Pietism* favored preaching to the heart, the style of which was both affective and personal. Pietists influenced John Wesley* in England and Jonathan Edwards* in the USA. With Evangelical preachers, such as George Whitefield*, a pattern of revival* preaching developed that was centered on "the conviction of sin" (a feeling of the dreadfulness of sin* that dishonors God and condemns the sinner), the acknowledgment of helplessness, and the announcement of the free unmerited mercy of God.

In the centuries that followed, one can trace alternating currents of rational plain-style preaching and the fervor of Evangelical sermons. In the 20th c., four movements have been significant:

1. *The rise of the Social Gospel.* Early in the century, Walter Rauschenbusch* wrote *A Theology for the Social Gospel* (1917) urging preachers to address social issues and thereby effect social change.
2. *The Biblical Theology Movement.* P. T. Forsyth led the way with his 1908 Beecher Lectures and Karl Barth* followed with *The Word of God and the Word of Man* (1928). They championed biblical preaching, rejecting addresses on topics or themes.
3. *A turn toward pastoral preaching.* In 1928 Harry Emerson Fosdick proposed "life situation" preaching, measuring the success of sermons by how many people requested pastoral counseling. Fosdick's methodology led to widespread therapeutic preaching.
4. *The Liturgical* Movement.* This movement prompted Vatican* II's insistence that a priest's first duty is the proclamation of the gospel. Thereafter Roman Catholic theology schools began employing full-time homiletic faculty members.

Other social factors influenced preaching: the rise of the Black churches in North America and the ordination of women* led to the publication of significant works on homiletics. Henry Mitchell's *Black Preaching* (1970) established an African American homiletic. Although women have preached for centuries, Christine Smith's *Weaving the Sermon* (1989) inaugurated a growing literature on women's homiletic. Since the 1970s, homiletic literature has multiplied, as have academic societies for the promotion of homiletic thought. **See also** RECEPTION STUDIES OF PREACHING. DAVID BUTTRICK

Predestination. Discussions of predestination are concerned with the extent to which God intentionally determines in advance what will occur. "General predestination" refers to God's predetermination of all that occurs. "Salvific predestination" refers to God's predetermination of who will spend eternity with God.

The differing perspectives on "general predestination" reflect diverging understandings of the extent to which God controls all of creation. For theological determinists (e.g. Luther*, Leibniz), since God controls even "free" human choice, while not every state of affairs is of inherent value, God's comprehensive decree predetermined on balance the "best of all possible creative options."

For most free will theists (e.g. Wesley*, Hicks*), God could be, but is not, all controlling. God has voluntarily granted us a type of freedom* (libertarian freedom) over which God does not exercise control; consequently, much of what occurs as the result of human choice was not predetermined. Some free will theists (following Origen*, Augustine*, Molina*, Bellarmine*, and Suarez*), however, believe that God possesses "middle* knowledge." God has always known what every person would freely do in every possible circumstance. Thus by planning and actualizing a world containing only those circumstances in which God knows we will freely do what God would have us do, a predetermined creative plan of God's choice was brought about. Thus we are predestined "for" some task; predestination is related to vocation*, ministry*, and mission*, to which people are called by God, as is the case when predestination is related to the doctrine of the church*, as for Calvin*.

The differing perspectives on "salvific predestination" (a concern of Western Christianity with an "honor and juridical satisfaction" perspective; see Atonement #2) center on the extent to which individuals are saved or damned apart from personal choice or action.

For "double predestinarians" (e.g. Gottschalk*, Calvin*), because all humans since the Fall have been "born in sin," all can justly be allowed by God to spend eternity in hell* (apart from God). However, God has predetermined that some will be "saved" by God's irresistible, unconditional grace*, while others will not be offered such grace. This predetermination is based neither on any decision or action by those individuals nor on God's foreknowledge of their actions.

For "conditional predestinarians" (e.g. Arminius*), God has offered saving grace to everyone; whether someone is saved is conditional on whether he or she accepts God's gift. God, with middle knowledge, saw from the beginning who would freely choose to accept his grace and predetermined to offer such grace to them.

For "conditional non-predestinarians" (e.g. "open theists" such as Clark Pinnock), God's grace is offered to everyone, but God does not foreknow who will accept this conditional offer. **See also** GRACE OF GOD CLUSTER: IN THE WESTERN TRADITION. DAVID BASINGER

Preexistence, the belief that Jesus Christ existed before his incarnation*. Paul calls Christ the power and wisdom of God (1 Cor 1:24), who was in the form of God yet took that of a human (Phil 2:6–8). Identifying Jesus with preexisting divinity is much stronger in Hebrews (Heb 1:1–4) and in John (especially 1:1–14).

Preferential Option for the Poor. Since its inception, Latin American Liberation* theology emphasized the preferential option for the poor as a positive affirmation of the faith commitment to live in solidarity with the poor, i.e. the vast majority of the population in Latin* America and the Caribbean* Islands. Actually, the preferential option for the poor is not "optional." It is at the core of the Christian faith and the major challenge of the gospel.

From the perspective of the Christian faith, the poverty* of the majority of Latin American people has a historical basis; it is the result of unjust conditions and thus is contrary to the will of the God of the Bible, who wants love*, life, and justice*. It is this historical condition of poverty that the Latin American Episcopal Conferences of Medellín* (1968) and of Puebla (1979) called "inhuman," "antievangelical," and a demonstration of "institutionalized violence."

As the Peruvian theologian Gustavo Gutiérrez has repeatedly said since 1971, the preferential option for the poor is a theocentric option: it is based on God. There is another valid reason for adopting this option: the injustice of poverty, as is demonstrated by economic and social analysis. Nonetheless, ultimately the preferential option for the poor is anchored in faith* in God. To adopt it in our own historical circumstances is to take the same option that God unconditionally took when siding with the impoverished and the oppressed*, saying, "I have witnessed the affliction of my people in Egypt and have heard their cry" (Exod 3:7; NAB). This is the God of the Psalms, who "cares for the lowly and knows the proud from afar" (Ps 138:6; cf. Ps 72:12–14); the God of the prophets, who denounces oppression as an offense against God; the God whom Jesus proclaimed in parables; the God of Lazarus; the God of the lepers. This is the God who, when the powerful and rich are indifferent and refuse the invitation in the parable of the Great Supper, gives the order, "Go out quickly into the streets and alleys of the town and bring in here the poor and the crippled, the blind and the lame" (Luke 14:21); this is the God of the song of Mary, who "has thrown down the rulers from their thrones but lifted up the lowly. The hungry he has filled with good things; the rich he has sent away empty" (Luke 1:52–53).

The preferential option for the poor is also clearly a Christocentric option: Jesus made the preferential option for the poor the key to his messianic praxis and his message. In deeds and words, Jesus proclaimed "the Kingdom* of God and God's justice" (Matt 6:33), which, for the benefit of the poor and of those who suffer, transform the unjust order that prevails in the world. In this way, Jesus proclaimed justice*, liberty, fulfillment, health, restoration, reconciliation, community life, and welfare – all granted by God.

Jesus was born in the world of the poor and lived in solidarity with the "little ones" and with the socially and religiously marginalized* – living a preferential option for the poor. In the synagogue of Nazareth, by reading the prophet Isaiah (Luke 4:16–20) Jesus defined his mission as bringing the good news of liberation to the poor, as the Jubilee* and an affirmation of the right to life.

The preferential option for the poor has two aspects: evangelical solidarity with the poor and the denunciation of poverty* as unjust and anti-life. Social analysis shows that poverty is caused by unjust socioeconomic structures and marginalization. Poverty is not just an economic phenomenon; it is also cultural and ethnic, and takes many forms. The preferential option for the poor demands a detailed knowledge and understanding of the multidimensionality of poverty.

Consequently, Latin American Liberation theology placed the preferential option for the poor at its very core. Liberation theology sees the poor and marginalized as in urgent need of liberation in a globalized world ruled by a market economy and a lack of solidarity, both of which ignore the pain and injustice suffered by humiliated and impoverished people. Liberation theology chose to speak of the "preferential option" because of the universality of God's love* that reaches every person without exception, but first the "little ones" and the vulnerable, those who live under unjust conditions characterized by exclusion and death, because they cannot meet their basic needs for work, food, dwelling, health care, and education.

For Latin American Liberation theology, believers are called to take on themselves with deep faith* and hope* the theocentric and Christocentric preferential option for the poor and to express it in gestures of love and solidarity with the poor and the excluded, the truly crucified ones, who struggle for the fundamental right to life. VICTORIO GUILLÉN ARAYA

Pregnancy. Scripture, medical knowledge, and cultural attitudes have influenced Christian views of pregnancy.

In Scripture pregnancy is portrayed as intrinsic to human nature, related to the Fall*, and a sign of God's favor. With the words "Be fruitful and multiply," Gen 1:28 links pregnancy to the fecundity and goodness of creation*; procreation is an intrinsic aspect of the order of the universe. In Gen 2, Eve's* defiance of God's command is tied to pain in childbearing. Pregnancy is also viewed as a sign of God's favor. For example, Noah*, Abraham*, Sarah*, and Hagar* are promised that they will be blessed with children and that their descendants will cover the earth; the angel Gabriel* views Mary's* status as the mother of Jesus as an indication that she has "found favor with God."

Medieval attitudes about the physiological process of pregnancy were influenced by Aristotle's medical view that the male "seed," or sperm, contained a *homunculus*, a tiny but completely formed human being that was deposited inside the female, who simply nourished the growing being. For Aristotle male children were the product of "good" seed, and the *anima* (soul*) entered the body 40 days after conception, while female children were the product of "weak" seed, and the soul did not enter the body until 90 days after conception. These attitudes reinforced a hierarchical understanding of gender relations that viewed women as inferior to men.

Pregnancy has historically been the domain of women. Western cultural convention through the 19th c. dictated that pregnancy be acknowledged when a woman announced she was pregnant or when her physical appearance showed it. Given the numerous causes of a lack of or irregular menstrual periods, many women could not confirm pregnancy until they detected fetal movement (between the 4th and 6th months). Furthermore, women's pregnancies and deliveries were managed largely by other women, often midwives, "wise women," or other female healers. Evidence suggests that many of these same women were persecuted as "witches*" and killed during the Inquisition*. In the mid-19th c., male physicians sought to increase their professionalization through guild membership, advanced degrees, and licensure. By 1850 women were sent to doctors to have their pregnancy confirmed by physical examination.

Ambiguous scriptural and cultural attitudes about procreation, sexual activity, pregnancy, infertility/barrenness, and motherhood have had and will continue to have a significant impact on attitudes toward women, their roles in society, and their capacity for leadership in the church. **See also BIRTH CONTROL AND CONTRACEPTION, CHRISTIAN VIEWS OF.**

REBECCA TODD PETERS

Prelate, a person holding a high ecclesiastical office, usually a bishop*, an archbishop*, a metropolitan*, a patriarch*, or an official in the Roman curia*.

Premillennialism. See DISPENSATIONALISM; MILLENNIALISM CLUSTER.

Preparatory Service, Reformed* service of confession* and repentance* before the Lord's* Supper; admittance traditionally required a Communion* token (see Fencing the Table). Camp* meetings on the US frontier may have originated in the Scotch and Irish preparatory service.

Presanctified Liturgy, or "Liturgy of the Presanctified Gifts," is a Lent* service of the Orthodox* Church, which typically takes place on Wednesdays and Fridays and during Holy Week. It is a great vespers* fused with rites for the distribution of Holy Communion (from gifts consecrated on the preceding Sunday).

B. MARK SIETSEMA

Presbyter (from Gk for "elder"), title for a leader in the early church, at first identical with "bishop"* (Acts 20:18; Titus 1:5–7) but later applied to the clergy* under the bishop. This title is equivalent to the French *prêtre* and the English "priest," terms derived from "presbyter" (and not derived from the Greek and Latin words now translated "priest*"). **See also PRIESTHOOD.**

Presbyterian Churches. Presbyterianism is named for its basic principle of governance: rule by elected elders (presbyters). Presbyterian churches and their theology emerged from the 16th-c. Protestant Reformation*, with a Reformed* theology inspired by John Calvin*. John Knox* studied with Calvin and brought Reformed theology to his native Scotland*. A systematic exposition of this theology, and its application in polity and worship, was developed in the Westminster* Confession of Faith, produced by 17th-c. English Puritans* with Scottish advisers. In 1706, seven ministers formed the first colonial American presbytery in Philadelphia.

Presbyterians hold in common with all Christians the mystery* of the Triune God (see Trinity in Eastern Orthodoxy; Trinity in the Western Tradition) and the belief that Jesus Christ is human and divine. Like all Protestants, Presbyterians believe in the authority of the Bible (see Scripture) and salvation* by God's grace*, accepted through faith*. In addition, Reformed and Presbyterian churches have characteristic theological emphases: the sovereignty and providence* of God*, the election* of people to salvation and service (vocation*), the covenant* life of the church, stewardship of God's creation*, the sin* of idolatry, and a commitment to transform the world in obedience to the Word of God.

Presbyterian history in the USA reflects the effort to balance unity in essentials with diversity in nonessentials. For Presbyterians, doctrinal discussion has often been combined with theological debate about issues in the larger society. For 320 years, the Westminster Standards – the Westminster Confession of Faith, the Larger Catechism*, and the Shorter Catechism – were the sole confessional documents of British and North American Presbyterianism. Nonetheless, differences over what were essentials led to divisions. There was a division from 1741 to 1758 between the New Side, which favored revivalism*, and the Old Side, which advocated formal creedal agreement. Later, in 1837, the New School, which supported cooperation with Congregationalists*, was ejected by the Old School, which insisted on remaining separate. The underlying cause was slavery*; the New School favored abolitionism*, whereas the Old School held that slavery was biblically justified. New and Old School factions consolidated in the North in 1869. In the South, both sides also reunited after the Civil War. From 1893 to 1927, the modernists, who embraced contemporary science*, quarreled with the fundamentalists*, who promoted five essential and necessary doctrines based on an inerrant* Bible. In this case, the underlying issue was evolution*, which the modernists accepted and the fundamentalists rejected. This conflict was resolved in 1927 when the right to interpret the confessional standards was returned to the presbytery.

Changes in the Presbyterian confessional stance took place in the 20th c. The Westminster Confession was revised in 1903 to balance the doctrine of God's decrees with an affirmation of God's love. In 1958, with the union of the United Presbyterian Church of North America and the Presbyterian Church in the USA, a committee was created to draft a contemporary statement of faith. The theme of the resulting Confession of 1967 was "reconciliation*," focused on conflicts over race*, war*, poverty*, and "anarchy in sexual* relations."

Early in its process, the committee received permission to publish the *Book of Confessions* to broaden Presbyterian understanding of its

Reformed roots. Adopted in 1967 by the United Presbyterian Church in the USA, the book included the Nicene* Creed, Apostles'* Creed, Scots Confession* (1560), Heidelberg* Catechism (1563), Second Helvetic Confession (1566), Westminster Confession of Faith and Shorter Catechism, Theological Declaration of Barmen* (1934), and Confession of 1967.

When, for some, the balance between essentials and nonessentials was upset, other, smaller Presbyterian bodies came into being: the Orthodox Presbyterian Church in 1939, the Presbyterian Church in America in 1973, and the Evangelical Presbyterian Church in 1981. These new denominations, objecting to changes in social mores and what they perceived to be changes in church doctrine, returned to the Westminster Confession as their theological standard.

In 1983 the United Presbyterian Church in the USA reunited with the (Southern) Presbyterian Church in the United States to form the Presbyterian Church (USA). The first moderator of the reunited church was charged to appoint a committee to compose a brief statement of the Reformed faith for possible inclusion in the *Book of Confessions*. Adopted in 1991, "A Brief Statement of Faith: Presbyterian Church (USA)," summarized the Christian, Protestant, and Reformed faith in contemporary language. It also enlarged the Reformed tradition by including an account of Jesus' life and ministry; proclaiming the equality of all people, both men and women; and asserting that the Spirit calls women and men to all the ministries of the church. JACK B. ROGERS

Presence, Divine. See MYSTICISM.

Presence of Christ. Several NT passages state that, after his resurrection and exaltation, Jesus in his humanity "is not here but has risen" (Matt 28:6; cf. Acts 1:9–11). This is often interpreted to mean that his resurrected body is located in heaven, beyond human experience. The problem for Christian piety is, How can Jesus become/remain present? Four kinds of answer are given.

1. Christ is present in his divinity; his human presence is no longer needed (based on verses like "Do not touch me, for I have not yet ascended to the Father" [John 20:17] and Paul's statement that he no longer knows Christ in a human way [2 Cor 5:16]).
2. Popular piety often assumes a human presence of Jesus, as in the hymn "And he walks with me and he talks with me," theologically grounded in the Miaphysite* emphasis on the inseparable unity of the divine and human in Christ and in the Lutheran doctrine that Christ's humanity acquires the attributes of his divinity, including omnipresence.
3. Jesus' humanity is present in the Eucharist*. For the Roman Catholic Church and (in a slightly different way) the Eastern Orthodox Church, the bread and cup are transformed into the Body and Blood of Christ; this doctrine is usually termed "real presence." Thomas Aquinas argued, however, that the body and blood are present *substantially* but not *locally*. Sacramental presence is not the same as local presence.

   Calvin* abandoned any notion of substantial presence; according to his eucharistic doctrine, believers' hearts are lifted up to the ascended Jesus by faith, he is truly exhibited by the bread and wine, and he is made present by the power of the Holy Spirit. This is a "virtual presence" or a "spiritual real presence" (J. W. Nevin*).

   Others in the Reformed tradition emphasized the *sign* character of the Eucharist, making Christ present not substantially but in the *event* of proclaiming the Word and "showing forth" his death in the Eucharist.
4. Christ is present in others, either in a Christian gathering, "where two or three are gathered together in my name, there am I in the midst of them" (Matt 18:20), or among the disciples in mission (Matt 28:20); or in "the least of these" (when the parable of the sheep and goats in Matt 25 is interpreted as gospel).

See also PREFERENTIAL OPTION FOR THE POOR. EUGENE TESELLE

Presentation, Feast of (also Candlemas*), liturgical celebration of Jesus' presentation in the Temple and the purification of his mother, 40 days after his birth (Luke 2:22–39; cf. Lev 12:1–4), February 2 in the West.

Prester John ("Presbyter" John), legendary Christian ruler variously thought to have been in Asia, India, or Ethiopia. The first vague mention of Prester John was made by a traveler from India in Rome (1122). In the crusader* kingdoms of Palestine, the story was told (1145) about this Christian ruler and priest in his empire beyond the territory ruled by Islam.

The legend could be based on garbled traditions concerning an Assyrian Christian ruler (belonging to the Church* of the East, often unduly called Nestorian) among the Mongols or the Christian emperor of Ethiopia*. It stimulated the hope that he would appear to rescue the crusaders in their fight against the Muslims.

Priesthood. From a cross-cultural perspective, priesthood refers to the office of a priest; one empowered or authorized to perform sacred rituals*, especially sacrifices*. In some traditions, priesthood is largely hereditary (as in ancient Mesopotamia); in other cases, priesthood is received through ordination* (as among Roman Catholic, Orthodox, and Anglican Christians).

The Hebrew biblical term for priest, *kohen*, was translated into Greek as *hiereus* and Latin as *sacerdos*. The English word "priest" comes from the French *prêtre*, derived from the Greek *presbyteros* (elder), the comparative of *presbys* (old man). In Roman Catholic ecclesiastical Latin, *presbyter* and *sacerdos* are equivalent terms for "priest."

In ancient Israel, the construction of the Temple in Jerusalem led to the centralization of the priesthood, linked variously to the family of Aaron (Exod 28:1; Lev 8:1–9:22) and the tribe of Levi (Num 3:6–9). The high (or anointed) priest was responsible for the sin offering (Lev 4) and the sacrifice for the Day of the Atonement (Lev 16).

The NT presents Jesus as the "great high priest" (Heb 4:14) linked to "the order of Mechizedek," the king of Salem, who brought out bread and wine and blessed Abraham (Gen 14:18–20; Heb 5:6, 10; 7:1). By offering himself as the sacrifice "once for all" (Heb 10:10), Jesus superseded the need for the Jewish priesthood (Heb 5:7–10) and established his followers as a "holy priesthood" (1 Pet 2:5) (see Priesthood of All Believers).

The Greek NT does not use "priest" (*hiereus*) in reference to Christian ministers. In the First Epistle of Clement* (c96), presbyters and bishops are described as merely analogous to the priests of ancient Israel (1 Clem 41), but gradually the term itself was adopted, just as the Communion table became an altar* and the Eucharist* a sacrifice. By the time of Tertullian* (c160–221), Hippolytus* of Rome (c170–235), and Cyprian* of Carthage (c200–58), the term "priest" (*sacerdos/hiereus*) can be found in reference to bishops and presbyters, but not deacons (cf. Tertullian, *Exhort.* 7; Hippolytus, *Trad. Ap.* 3; Cyprian, *Ep.* 61.3.1).

Roman Catholics, Orthodox, and many Anglicans believe Jesus instituted the Christian priesthood at the Last Supper when he authorized his disciples to offer the eucharistic* memorial of his sacrifice (Luke 22:14–20). Reformed and Protestant Christians, however, reserve the title "priest" for Christ and the priesthood shared by all believers. "Presbyters" are elders, pastors, or ministers, not members of a separate "priesthood." ROBERT FASTIGGI

Priesthood of All Believers, doctrine that all Christians are truly "priests," based on several NT passages, especially 1 Pet 2:5–9 and Rev 1:6, 5:10, 20:6. The early church called its leaders presbyters* (elders*) and bishops* (overseers), and "priests" only after the 3rd–4th c., by analogy with the priests of Israel. The term "priest" acquired a quite different meaning when the term "presbyter" was contracted into "priest." The Protestant Reformation* reasserted the priesthood of all believers; the Roman Catholic Church acknowledges that all believers are priests through baptism*, continuing to think of presbyters as priests in this distinctive sense.

Primate, bishop who holds first place in a province* or, more recently, in a region or state.

Prior, Prioress, person with second place after the abbot or abbess in a monastery, or the superior of a priory subordinate to an abbey.

Prisca (Priscilla). Prisca is mentioned by Paul, along with her husband, Aquila, as one of his very active "co-workers" (Rom 16:3; see also 1 Cor 16:19; 2 Tim 4:19; Acts 18, using the diminutive Priscilla) and hosting a house church (first in Rome, then in Corinth, Ephesus, and again in Rome). There is no evidence that she was the martyr whose grave was venerated in the Roman catacomb* of Priscilla.

Priscillianism, movement in the 4th c. that originated with Priscillian (d386), a Spanish layman of high rank who promoted an ascetic* mode of life. This aroused suspicion about private meetings and confusion of gender roles (cf. Eustathius* of Sebaste), which were condemned by a synod of 10 bishops in Saragossa (380). Accused of Manichaeism*, Priscillian defended his orthodoxy in several writings and sought approval from Ambrose* in Milan and Damasus* in Rome, without success. On his return to Spain, he became bishop of Ávila (381). When a synod of bishops in Bordeaux condemned his views, he appealed to the new emperor in the

West, the "usurper" Maximus, under whom he was beheaded (386). This first execution of an accused Christian by a Christian ruler – though on grounds of sorcery, not heresy – was opposed by Martin* of Tours, Ambrose of Milan, and Siricius of Rome as secular interference in church matters. The stereotyping of "Priscillianism" as a movement came at the council of Toledo (400) after Priscillian's death, and in the writings of several heresiologists, including Jerome* and Orosius. He was widely regarded as a martyr in Spain, and the shrine at Compostela* may be located at his burial place.

EUGENE TESELLE

Private Judgment, in Protestant churches, the responsibility of each person to base judgments on Scripture*, not on human (including ecclesial) authority*.

Proaño, Leonidas (1910–88), "the Bishop of the Indians." Born in San Antonio of Ibarra, Ecuador; founded the first popular radiophonic schools of Ecuador. As bishop of Riobamba (1954), he dedicated 33 years to defending the rights and dignity of native people throughout Ecuador*. He was the subject of misunderstanding, slander, and unfair persecution by dictatorships, economic groups, and the Roman Catholic Church hierarchy. He was nominated for the Nobel Peace Prize (1986).

LUIS MARÍA GAVILANES DEL CASTILLO

Procession, orderly movement of a body of persons on a solemn liturgical occasion, either festal* or penitential* in function.

Process Theology affirms that biblical thinking is supported by the philosophical idea that the world is composed of events each of which is a synthesis of relations to other events. This applies to electrons and human experiences, and even to God, who, far from being immutable, is constantly enriched by new occurrences. People, instead of being self-contained, are constituted by their relations in community.

Process theology arose at the Chicago Divinity School in the 1930s. Its antecedent was the sociohistorical school, whose leaders wanted to end the controversy between science and theology by integrating them. They found hope in new developments in science* that broke with its reductionism.

They were impressed by Alfred North Whitehead, the English mathematical physicist whose cosmology of events was both more responsive to new scientific knowledge and more hospitable to religion. Every event is a subject as it occurs. Hence, the incorporation of human beings by evolutionary theory did not deny the role of emotion, reason, or purpose. God also is a subject interacting with creature.

Whitehead's thought was taught in Chicago by a radical empiricist, Henry Nelson Wieman, and a rationalistic metaphysician, Charles Hartshorne*. Wieman thought that faith* requires full confidence in God, whom he described in a fully empirical way. Those who came to be called Process theologians followed Hartshorne and Whitehead in affirming God as a subject. They rejected creation* out of nothing and God's total control. While God contributes to the becoming of each event, these create themselves by integrating their past with new, God-given possibilities. An interactive God who influences everything but fully controls nothing seems more compatible both with the Bible and with the reality of evil*.

This philosophical approach separated Chicago from mainstream theology. This changed when Schubert Ogden integrated Hartshorne's theism with Rudolf Bultmann's* existentialism*. Daniel Day Williams wrote a Whiteheadian systematic theology. Since then much similar work has been done. Diverse doctrines and emphases have been formulated in process terms. For example, different process Christologies* have focused on incarnation*, revelation*, and salvation*. Some emphasize Jesus' similarity to us; others, his difference.

Process theology's nondualism* and nonanthropocentrism prepared it for the ecological challenge and close alliance with ecofeminists*. Its nonsupernaturalism opened it to the wisdom not only of Christian faith but also of other communities. It works supportively with Liberation theologies. It continues to seek the integration of science and theology by reformulating both in processive terms.

JOHN B. COBB, JR.

Proclus (c390–446), patriarch of Constantinople. A celebrated preacher, he delivered (429/30) a renowned homily on Mary* as Theotokos* (Mother of God), triggering a controversy with Nestorius*, who asserted that Mary could be the mother only of Jesus' humanity. Proclus's homily was given special honor at the Council of Ephesus* (431), which condemned Nestorius. His "Tome to the Armenians*" (433) persuaded many of them to abandon the Nestorian* position. Proclus differentiated between hypostasis* and nature*, mediating between the Cyrillian insistence on one hypostasis and the Nestorian on two natures. His formulation became an important source of the doctrine of the Council of Chalcedon* (451).

Profession, declaration, promise, or vow on entering the religious* life, usually to follow the three counsels* of perfection (poverty, chastity, obedience). In Reformed traditions, a (weekly) profession of faith, a declaration of faith (usually by the recitation of a creed*).

Programme for Theology and Cultures in Asia (PTCA; since 1983; C. S. Song, first dean) is not an institution but a theological movement committed to implementing living theologies with Asian resources, seriously engaging local, regional, and global issues (see Contextual Theologies). Gathering existing theological associations from all over Asia at its national, regional, and theological seminar-workshops and consultations, PTCA has, as attested to by its list of publications, promoted cross-generational Christian theologizing in Asian ways that engages issues concerning Asian people's movements; Asian religions*, cultures*, symbols*, and images; Asian festivals and customs; Asian Spirit movements (see Charismatic and Pentecostal Movements Cluster: In Asia); women*; religious fundamentalism*; globalization*; mission* in Asia; and naming God* in Asia.

SIMON SHUI-MAN KWAN

Prohibited Degrees of Marriage, relationships of blood or family that make it unlawful (on the basis of biblical, Roman, or Germanic criteria) for two persons to marry. **See also MARRIAGE, THEOLOGY AND PRACTICE OF, CLUSTER.**

Pro Juárez, Miguel Agustín (1891–1927), Mexican Jesuit* priest who, despite the anticlerical restrictions of the 1917 Constitution and the resistance that culminated in the 1926 armed uprising of the "Cristeros", devoted his ministry to workers and the poor*. Detained as a suspect in an assassination attempt against the president-elect Álvaro Obregón, without judicial process, he and his brother Humberto were executed (1927). He was beatified by John* Paul II (1988). **See also MEXICO.**

MARÍA ALICIA PUENTE LUTTEROTH and ELIZABETH JUDD

Prologues (to Biblical Books)

Marcionite Prologues are brief introductions to the letters of Paul, contained in most Latin manuscripts of the Bible, including the Vulgate*. The oldest are the prologues to Galatians, 1 Corinthians, Romans, 1 Thessalonians, Ephesians, Colossians (with Philemon), and Philippians. Originally written in the form of a connected introduction to the Pauline corpus, these prologues set the letters in "chronological" order before the inclusion of the Pastorals*. Since Marcion* assumed this sequence, the prologues have been attributed to him; but the same order is found elsewhere, the content is not Marcionite, and the prologues were widely used in the Western Church.

Monarchian Prologues are short introductions to each of the four Gospels in many manuscripts of the Vulgate*. Today they are generally attributed to Priscillian* or his followers, since the Monarchian* teachings are similar to his.

Anti-Marcionite Prologues are short introductions to the Gospels of Mark, Luke, and John in many manuscripts of the Vulgate*. They were originally composed in Greek, but only the prologue to Luke (probably the earliest, perhaps from the late 2nd c.) survives in that language. The others are from the late 4th c.. Their anti-Marcionite character is generally doubted.

Promised Land. The Bible displays a strong "land mystique," from the patriarchal sagas with their central promise of the land, through the postexilic restoration. The conquest of Canaan* (13th c. BCE) is a watershed. The pre-conquest is a time of the promise, followed by a time of covenantal* relationship of Israel as a nation with God as its king. Subsequently, the land is almost completely lost but is reclaimed in some fashion until 135 CE.

The land is the concrete embodiment of Israel's faith*, hope*, and love* and of the covenant* with God, preventing the revelation* from being a disincarnate set of ideas. The covenant is way of life in time and space (land).

God's own property, the land is "inherited" by Israel through conquest (see Canaan). Any nation that invades the land is dispossessing God and will be punished, said the prophets. When the land's dispossession was completed by the Romans (70–135 CE), the land was "spiritualized" both by Jews (e.g. Rabban Yohanan ben Zakkai, 1st c. CE) and by early Christians. While some insist that the land has become obsolete for the church, others see a displacement of the biblical land to Rome, Constantinople, or Moscow. Certain fundamentalists* hail the modern Jews' emigration to the ancestral land as a process leading eventually to their conversion* to Christianity.

Throughout, the land remains, paradoxically, a *promised* land. The promise at the beginning of salvation* history stands valid until the end. The land can never be claimed by anyone but God. The land of "Palestine" is a microcosm for the creation, God's "garden." The inhabitants of the "land" anywhere in the creation are only guests or "renters" (Lev 25:23; 1 Chr 29:15; Heb 11:9; 1 Pet 2:11). **See also LAND, THEOLOGICAL PERSPECTIVES AND PRAXIS, CLUSTER.**

ANDRÉ LACOCQUE

Propaganda Fide, Congregatio de, office of the papal administration (curia) concerned with mission activities and the administration of areas without an indigenous hierarchy. It was formally established (1622) in order to consolidate Roman Catholic gains in Germany during the Thirty* Years' War; its responsibilities soon became global. It was renamed the Congregation for the Evangelization of Peoples (1967). **See also CATHOLIC RENEWAL.**

Proper, any portion of the liturgy* (e.g. prayers, readings, hymns) that is specific to a particular day in the church year.

Property (from Lat for "one's own"), that which is gained, possessed, owned, and controlled to the exclusion of others. Hunter-gatherer and pastoral societies generally assumed that all members had access to resources: ownership, and thus "property," was communal. In agrarian and urban societies, under feudalism*, and in colonialist* and neocolonialist situations, sole access to and control of property confer both advantages that lead to class differentiation and obligations to superiors and inferiors that readily authorize economic exploitation or slavery*. Under capitalism, property is held "in fee simple" and can be "alienated," or sold. Ownership is never absolute; it may be restricted by contracts, deeds, or wills* and/or regulated by public authority for the common good or to protect human* rights.

Major changes from shared access to private property, with disruptive social consequences, include the "enclosures" of common woods and pastures in Germany at the time of the Reformation* (one of the causes of the Peasants'* War) and in England and Scotland during the 18th c.; seizure of lands in colonial settings for the benefit of European owners; and changes in the Mexican Constitution (1992), commodifying all land.

In Christian history, ethical concern for the use of property may be compatible with, and critical of, any of these ways of understanding of property. Thomas* Aquinas's general theory of property finds a place for each understanding: (1) the earth as a whole is given to the whole human race, (2) private property is not absolute, although it is advisable on pragmatic grounds, but (3) private property is still held as a trust conferring obligations toward others. In extreme cases, the poor are allowed to "take" what they need, and this is not theft.

In the NT, Jesus had harsh words about wealth* and urged giving without expecting a return. The early church in Jerusalem held all things in common and distributed to those in need (Acts 2:44–45, 4:32–35). Paul (Gal 2:10) calls the Jerusalem Church "the poor" (Heb *ebionim*), possibly its self-designation (Ebionites*). In the Gentile mission, Paul and Luke replaced community of goods with almsgiving*, thus viewing property as a trust held on behalf of the poor. Similarly, in the patristic period, many early bishops, especially John* Chrysostom, reproached persons of great wealth for stealing from the poor and urged almsgiving as a means of salvation for the wealthy (cf. Matt 19:16–26; Luke 12:33, 18:18–27, 16:19–31).

"Community of use" has come to be a widespread approach to issues of property. The Council of Antioch* (341) stated that church properties belong first to the poor, then to the bishop, the clergy, and their dependents. Rome and the West acknowledged four equal claims: the bishop and his household, the clergy, the poor, and repair of church buildings. In the East, it was expected that a third of one's property would be given to the church; in the West, bequests took the place of an additional child (see Will).

Each monastery owned its property in common, on the model of the Jerusalem Church (see Monasticism Cluster). But the Franciscans* championed poverty*, following Jesus' instructions (Matt 10:9–10). While *using* "property" (houses, furnishings, books), they *owned* nothing, either personally or as an order; ownership was placed in the hands of the cardinal protector. This practice, called "poor use," was mandated by Francis* and Bonaventura*, and was later called "dominion" (Gen 1:26, 2:15), i.e. stewardship* without ownership. There was controversy, however, over this Franciscan tradition. Nicholas III in *Exiit** (1279) acknowledged the difference between ownership and use, but affirmed "right of use," calling it a kind of ownership, which John XXII reaffirmed, declaring it heretical to claim that Christ owned nothing (1323).

Other religious* orders followed Paul's practice of "working with one's own hands" (1 Thess 2:9, 4:11–12); this ideal of the 4th-c. monastic movement was lost in the West, until the Beguines*.

During the Renaissance, new attitudes toward property developed when Erasmus* and his Catholic and Protestant followers criticized almsgiving* as a means of encouraging dependency, and instead championed poor* relief. The Reformation* revived and reinterpreted the NT notion of vocation*, making daily work a "calling" in which one could exercise discipleship to the glory of God. Property was needed for most callings, and its use was to be guided by a sense of stewardship*. The Protestant* ethic enhanced the importance of private property as one basis for assurance* of salvation. **See also ECONOMY AND CHRISTIANITY CLUSTER: ECONOMIC ETHICS AND CHRISTIAN THEOLOGY; POVERTY CLUSTER; PROSPERITY GOSPEL CLUSTER; WEALTH AND CHRISTIANITY.** EUGENE TESELLE

Prophecy and Prophets. The earliest recorded human mediation of the divine will to others comes from Mari (early 2nd millennium BCE). A similar phenomenon existed in Nineveh (early 1st millennium), when a third prophetic movement, biblical prophecy, was flourishing. Affinities among these three movements – particularly those entailing the language employed to designate prophets as divine messengers and seers and formulaic expressions (e.g. "Fear not"; "The god has sent me;" "Thus shall you say") – suggest some kind of relationship.

Just as prophets in Mari and Nineveh included ecstatic messengers to kings and diviners who responded to inquiries by ordinary citizens, so biblical prophets filled a wide spectrum of roles, from peripheral critics of royalty to central officials in the royal cult. The usual title for a biblical prophet (*nabi*) is etymologically tied to the Akkadian word for one who is either summoned by a deity or who proclaims a divine word. Other designations indicate a capacity to divine things hidden from normal individuals, often by technical means; an ability to see into the immediate future; and special intimacy with the deity and the spirit. Ecstatic conduct and clairvoyance are found in only a single example of prophecy (from Syria, transmitted through an Egyptian narrative). Above all, prophets directed their words to kings, often assuring them of a god's protection but also demanding specific actions on their part. Because their message occasionally fomented social revolt, administrators devised methods for punishing dangerous prophets. Biblical prophecy presented a vexing problem, for no adequate criteria for determining authenticity were devised. The failure was not for lack of effort; prophets who advocated contrasting messages in the name of the same deity made the quest an urgent one. In Israel, the iconic David complicated matters, for prophets held opposite views about the claim that the biblical God had established the Davidic kingdom for perpetuity. Those who accepted this disputed theological affirmation developed messianic* hopes* pertaining to the future.

As in the Bible, prophets in Mari normally delivered their words orally, and letters summarizing the oracles were transmitted to distant rulers. Standing before a statue of a god, a prophet functioned as spokesperson for that deity. The ranks of prophets included both men and women; they delivered messages for deities of both sexes. The most prominent goddess was Ishtar of Arbela. The only named prophetess in the Bible was Huldah, but frequent references to female prophets indicate that divine intermediation was open to all, and Joel* envisioned a day when prophecy would break all social barriers. The designation of Abraham*, Moses*, and Deborah* as prophets is probably anachronistic.

Israelite prophecy can be defined by three stages: preclassical, classical, and postclassical. The temporal marker for the transition to the ethical monotheism* of classical prophecy was the 8th c. BCE, the time of Amos*, Isaiah*, Hosea*, and Micah*. Seventh-century prophecy took on priestly elements with Ezekiel* and to some extent Jeremiah*. The shift to postclassical prophecy occurred in the late 6th c. when prophets began either to reflect on earlier prophetic oracles or to incorporate elements of apocalyptic* thinking into their words.

Zechariah 13:2–6 represents the low point of biblical prophecy, but the promise in Deut 18:15 kept the hope* alive into NT times that in every generation, or at some future time, a prophet like Moses would arise and command obedience by the people.

Biblical prophecy gave voice to the people by boldly criticizing kings, nobles, and priests for oppressing* the poor*. This championing of widows, orphans, and the needy in the name of their maker was often costly, for those in authority were reluctant to surrender power. Prophets spoke on behalf of the deity, but they did not surrender their individuality. Jeremiah even struggled with his commissioner, personally resisting the message entrusted to him.

JAMES L. CRENSHAW

Prophets, the, biblical books that constitute the concluding part of the OT: Isaiah*, Jeremiah*, Lamentations*, Ezekiel*, Daniel*, Hosea*, Joel*, Amos*, Obadiah*, Jonah*, Micah*, Nahum*, Habakkuk*, Zephaniah*, Haggai*, Zechariah*, and Malachi*. For Jews, the list of books that constitute the second part of Tanakh*, the Prophets, is similar but not identical; it adds Joshua*, Judges*, 1 and 2 Samuel*; 1 and 2 Kings* but excludes Lamentations and Daniel (which are included in the Writings*).

Propitiation, action performed to render another person propitious or favorable, specifically to appease the anger* of God after a sin* has been committed. It is often contrasted with expiation*, where the emphasis is on making up for, or erasing, a sin. **See also ATONEMENT #2.**

Proselytism (Gk "newcomer"). In Judaism and the NT, a proselyte was one who had been circumcised and "come into" the Jewish community. In modern times, the term "proselyte" is applied to a convert to any group. "Proselytism" has acquired negative connotations. Since the 17th c., it has been applied to overzealous, coercive, or manipulative attempts to convert other Christians to one's own Christian church or movement. One aspect of colonialism* (or imperialism*) was its sponsorship of proselytizing among many peoples; e.g. the Berlin* Conference gave missionaries rights of access throughout Africa. With the growth of religious freedom in Eastern Europe, the hegemony of Western culture, and the financial resources (as well as zeal) of missionary organizations, proselytism has become an issue in many countries. Proselytizing of other Christians has been outlawed in Greece since 1911, and it has been opposed in contemporary Russia*. Proselytizing of non-Christians is outlawed in several states in India* and in many Islamic* countries. **See also MISSION CLUSTER.**

Prosper of Aquitaine (c390–c463), advocate of Augustinian theology. Probably a monk in Marseilles, he was disturbed by the opposition to Augustine's views among John Cassian's* followers. While not denying grace*, they wanted to ensure a role for free* will, specifically at the "beginning of faith" (see Semi-Pelagianism). Prompted by correspondence from Prosper (c428), Augustine* wrote his last two treatises, *On the Predestination of Saints* and *On the Gift of Perseverance*. In 431 Prosper went to Rome to defend Augustine's position, published several works against his critics, and was a close adviser to Pope Leo* (440–61). The canons of the Council of Orange* (529) are based partly on Prosper's excerpts from Augustine.

PROSPERITY GOSPEL CLUSTER

Prosperity Gospel in Africa
Prosperity Gospel and Economic Empowerment Gospel in African American Churches
Prosperity Gospel and Liberation Theology
Prosperity Gospel and the Word-Faith Movement

Prosperity Gospel in Africa. Prosperity theology came to Africa from the USA through the Pentecostal* churches, and especially through the Charismatic* Movement that radiated through a multiplicity of African-led Christian communities – the "revivalist*" churches of an "African Great* Awakening."

This theology is grounded in a particular vision of God* as the lord of all wealth*, following the prophet Haggai 2:8: "The silver is mine, and the gold is mine, says the LORD of hosts." This God is proclaimed to be the one who blesses his children by showering on them material treasures and success in all that they undertake. Visible prosperity and success are unmistakable signs of divine blessing and of believers' faithfulness. Jesus said, "I came that they may have life, and have it abundantly" (John 10:10). A Christian community demonstrates that it truly is a church that God loves and supports by its ostensible financial abundance. Yet such churches are shown to be truly blessed only insofar as their pastors are themselves rich, indeed very rich, thanks to believers' bountiful gifts. This wealth must be imposing: luxury cars, huge, lavish houses, and magnificent church buildings.

The pastors have to be successful in recruiting new members through acts of wonder and miracles* (including spiritual healings*), which demonstrate that the pastors' power comes from God and the Holy* Spirit. Spiritual power is the second pillar of Prosperity theology (after wealth); it provides a lens through which pastors' material wealth is justified and validates their preaching, which makes it a duty for all God's servants to be most generous, and even extravagantly so, in giving to others.

From the perspective of other churches in Africa and the concern for ethical responsibility in preaching, this teaching is misleading and highly dangerous. The entire message of the theology of prosperity is colored by the atmosphere and language of "a delirious mysticism." It appears to be designed primarily to manipulate Christian believers to give a lot of money to the leaders of their communities. In the present situation in Africa, what is needed instead is a message that will open believers' eyes to the political, economic, cultural, and social problems that crucify Africa on the cross of underdevelopment and despair. From this perspective, in Africa the Prosperity Gospel seems to be a big but shallow enterprise of psychological manipulation of believers by a few skillful preachers, rather than a deep and powerful movement of transformation of the African continent into a fertile space of shared happiness. KÄ MANA

Prosperity Gospel and Economic Empowerment Gospel in African American Churches. The Prosperity Gospel, an increasingly popular though theologically problematic ecclesial orientation, has had a profound impact on African American Christian practices in the post–civil rights era. Its popularity can be attributed, in part, to the late-20th-c. Evangelical* and Charismatic* revivals* and the Word*-Faith Movement. A renewed emphasis on personal encounters with the divine made evident via Spirit baptism (baptism* in the Holy* Spirit), physical healing*, and the promise of material wealth* helped to shift the terrain of North American Protestantism from traditional mainline to more Pentecostal-informed, Charismatic* religious expressions. Such an orientation may be related to the Black Church's long-standing emphasis on God as an "ever present help in the time of trouble" (see African American Cluster).

Mutual aid societies (since the late 18th c.) were part and parcel of independent black congregations. When Richard Allen* adopted the slogan "To Seek for Ourselves" for the newly organized Free African Society and subsequent African* Methodist Episcopal Church, members pooled economic resources to provide health* care coverage, unemployment compensation, and death benefits for members. This overt economic agenda found a new mode of expression amid the Great Migration Era (1900–50). As more than 3 million blacks moved from the southern region of the USA, they looked to the Black Church as their social service provider. African American megachurches in cities like New York, Chicago, and Detroit acted as welfare agencies, retail centers, employment bureaus, and real estate investors in order to mitigate the callous conditions of urban life that befell Southern migrants. Congregations such as the Abyssinian Baptist Church in Harlem and the Concord Missionary Baptist Church in Brooklyn continue this legacy by establishing community development corporations and job training centers, and by investing in and providing affordable housing.

This historical emphasis on economic empowerment explains why many interpret Word*-Faith teachings as an extension of this tradition. On the surface, such a connection appears plausible. Financial stability and upward mobility, central tenets of Word-Faith practices, are staples of the progressive Black Church's mission. But theologians and progressive-oriented clergy have criticized the Prosperity Gospel as little more than the sanctification of North American capitalism used to justify individual economic gain rather than promoting the social good and economic empowerment of the community. Therefore, many African American clergy seek to distinguish the Prosperity teachings of Rev. Ike (1970s) and Word-Faith teachers (since then) from the Black Church tradition of economic empowerment embodied in the progressive wing of civil* rights activism.

See also POVERTY CLUSTER: POVERTY, THEOLOGY AND ETHICS: AFRICAN AMERICAN VIEWS. JONATHAN L. WALTON

Prosperity Gospel and Liberation Theology. Efforts to incorporate concepts of prosperity, retribution, self-improvement, and individualism into North American Protestantism began as early as the first settlements in North America, at Jamestown and Massachusetts Bay, and continued through the Enlightenment* and the industrial revolution. These are the roots of what is known as Prosperity theology or Prosperity Gospel.

Many of the diatribes against Prosperity theology focus solely on the more extreme manifestations of this perspective. These extreme manifestations do exist (see the present cluster: In Africa). However, like Liberation theology, which is more properly referred to as Liberation* theolog*ies*, Prosperity theology is a complex phenomenon with many incarnations. The basic tenets that Prosperity theologies hold in common are (1) the idea that God desires prosperity for all of God's children, (2) a biblical grounding of prosperity ideals as an extension of the Abrahamic covenant* to include Christians after the death and resurrection of Christ, (3) the practice of "positive confession" or "name it and claim it" as the means of obtaining the material blessings associated with health* and wealth*, and (4) the concept of "seed faith" as giving in faith* more than one can reasonably afford in order to reap better returns. These various aspects are emphasized to greater or lesser degrees in different Prosperity teachings.

The concept of prosperity encompasses spiritual, mental, and physical, as well as financial, benefits. Furthermore, from the more moderate perspectives, financial prosperity is not given to believers to make it possible for them to live in luxury, but rather to enable them to address the issue of global poverty*. Thus financial security, in contexts of deprivation, can be a form of liberation. According to Kenneth Copeland, the good news for the poor is that God does not want the poor to be poor anymore.

It is this message in particular that has popularized Prosperity theologies as a significant theological export, evidenced by the exponential growth of Prosperity churches recorded in Latin America, Africa, and Asia in the later part of the 20th c. Prosperity theologies are often deemed inimical to Liberation theologies. Upon further exploration, however, some surprising convergences emerge.

Both Liberation and Prosperity theologies recognize poverty as an evil (see Poverty Cluster). Both can agree that God does not want the poor to be poor and that God wishes to rectify their suffering in this life, not the next. Both argue for a holistic view of salvation* as a matter of spiritual, physical, social, and psychological well-being. The spiritual aspects of salvation are not denied, but in both cases the physical aspects are emphasized in reaction to a perceived deemphasis of these very aspects in many Christian traditions.

Both Liberation and Prosperity theologies make selective use of biblical texts. Liberation and prosperity are both key biblical themes, and interpretation of the biblical text does not definitively support either perspective. Furthermore, both theologies assume a certain level of direct correspondence and relevance between biblical and contemporary issues, whether these are liberation struggles or questions of health and wealth.

Both Liberation and Prosperity theologies are interested in resistance to domination and oppression*. Prosperity theology views domination primarily as a spiritual issue, one that can be addressed through faith* and positive affirmations; Liberation theology views domination as a systemic social issue, which can be resolved through active religious and political resistance. Both perspectives evince and could be united around a spirit of resistance. Both offer resources of empowerment that can be utilized politically. The challenge, particularly in communities that preach prosperity, is activating those resources.

The similarities between these two perspectives extend far beyond these points. The differences between the two theologies should not be minimized. Nevertheless, Prosperity and Liberation theologies may have more to learn from each other than proponents of either perspective have been willing to consider. **See also MEGACHURCHES IN EL SALVADOR; THE PRESENT CLUSTER: IN AFRICA.**

ALISSA JONES NELSON

Prosperity Gospel and the Word-Faith Movement. See WORD-FAITH MOVEMENT AND ITS WORSHIP.

Protestant Ethic, so named by Weber*, a pattern of habitual, disciplined work and self-control that shuns luxury and pleasure and values thrift and accumulation. It developed in late medieval and early modern times (in monasteries), and was often associated with the Lay* Piety Movement (c11th–13th c.). The link with Calvinism* and Protestantism*, and their view of labor as an expression of thanks to God for one's election, was not made until the 17th c. **See also LABOR, THEOLOGIES OF.**

PROTESTANTISM CLUSTER

1) *Introductory Entry*

Protestantism

2) *A Sampling of Contextual Views and Practices*

Protestantism in Africa: Southern Africa
Protestantism in Africa: Western Africa
Protestantism in Asia: China
Protestantism in Europe: France
Protestantism in Europe: Germany
Protestantism in Europe: The Nordic Countries
Protestantism in Europe: Russia
Protestantism in Latin America
Protestantism in Latin America: Argentina
Protestantism in Latin America: Brazil: Churches of Immigrants
Protestantism in Latin America: Brazil: Churches of Resident Aliens
Protestantism in Latin America: Brazil: Colonial Period
Protestantism in Latin America: Brazil: Mission Protestantism
Protestantism in Latin America: Brazil: Parachurch Associations
Protestantism in Latin America: Central America
Protestantism in Latin America: Colombia
Protestantism in Latin America: Mexico
Protestantism in North America: Canada
Protestantism in North America: United States
Protestantism in the South Pacific and Australia

---

1) Introductory Entry

Protestantism. The term "Protestantism" denotes a family of Christian religious trends that originated in the 16th c. as a consequence of the European Reformation*. The variegated historical, cultural, and intellectual origins of Protestantism meant that, from the outset, it was a complex phenomenon. The term "Protestant" dates from the late 1520s and came to be applied to the movement at a relatively late stage. In its earlier stages, the Protestant Movement tended to define itself in terms of its "Evangelical*" identity. In actuality, "Evangelicals" is the general term used to designate Protestants in Latin America and other parts of the world (in contrast to North America, where the term "Evangelicals" designates exclusively conservative Protestants, as distinguished from mainline Protestants; see Evangelicals/Evangelicalism Cluster: And Evangelical Theologies).

Four significant constituencies can be identified in the first era of Protestantism. First, a group crystallized around Martin Luther* (1483–1546), whose reforming activity centered on the university town of Wittenberg in Northeastern Germany. Although Luther was reluctant to use the term "Lutheranism*," this epithet rapidly came into general usage to designate this movement.

Second, an essentially independent reform movement developed in Switzerland. Initially, this movement was particularly linked to the city of Zurich and its Reformer, Huldrych Zwingli* (1484–1531). During the 1540s, the center of intellectual and political power in the movement gradually shifted toward the free city of Geneva, and its leading Reformer, John Calvin* (1509–64). Although often referred to as "Calvinism*," this term is probably best reserved for Calvin's own views or those of his close followers; the epithet "Reformed*" is preferred.

Third, a more radical wing of the Reformation emerged in both Germany and Switzerland, which held that Luther's and Zwingli's reforms had not been sweeping enough. The term "Anabaptist" (literally, "rebaptizers") was initially used to refer to this movement because of its tendency to insist on adult baptism. In recent years, the term "Radical Reformation" has come to be preferred (see Radical Reformation).

Fourth, a distinctive style of Protestantism emerged in England during the period 1535–70, when the themes of the Reformation on the Continent were adapted to the English situation.

Early Protestantism derived its distinct identity from its emphasis on returning to the Bible as the supreme authority* of Christian life and thought. This principle is often expressed in the Latin phrase *sola scriptura* (by Scripture* alone). It paralleled, though was not identical with, a characteristic theme of Renaissance humanism: the importance of returning *ad fontes*, to the fountainhead of cultural norms in antiquity. This emphasis has remained characteristic of Protestantism, although it is interpreted in different ways. For example, for most Lutheran and Reformed Protestants, this emphasis on the Bible does not rule out the relevance of patristic or certain medieval writers. In marked contrast, more radical Protestant writers tend to regard patristic* and medieval theology and spirituality as corrupt or inauthentic.

This emphasis on the authority of the Bible had a further consequence for Protestantism: the rejection of papal* authority. Although Protestantism went on to develop a wide variety of church polities and ministries, the movement maintained its original criticism of the concentration of theological and institutional authority in the person of the pope. There is no equivalent of the papacy in Protestantism. The absence of a central authority is often seen as a cause of the movement's subsequent fragmentation.

Many Protestants regarded the doctrine of justification* by faith alone (Lat *sola fide*) as being of critical importance. According to this distinctive doctrine, associated primarily with Martin Luther, humanity is unable to enter into a relationship with God under terms of its own choosing. A right relationship with God is a matter of grace*, not of works*; it is to be seen as the result of divine graciousness, not human achievement. This aspect of the Reformation was generally seen (e.g. by Philipp Melanchthon*) as an extension of Augustine's* anti-Pelagian* agenda to the late medieval church. Although it was widely regarded as an integral aspect of early Protestant identity, radical Protestant writers tended to regard this teaching with suspicion, believing that it undermined Christian morality and discipleship.

These emphases have remained a part of Protestant identity since the 16th c. As the movement has expanded and developed, the interaction of these elements has shifted. The first two distinctive features remain substantially intact: most Protestant thinkers and denominations remain committed to the primacy of Scripture (though differences of interpretation must be noted; see Scripture) and a rejection of any formal institutional, theological, or spiritual authority of the pope (though many recognize the personal gifts and authority of individual popes, particularly the late John Paul II). Although most Protestants continue to consider the doctrine of justification by faith important to Protestant self-identity, there are indications that some no longer see it as definitive. In part, this reflects continuing concerns among some Protestants over the biblical foundations of the doctrine or its moral and spiritual implications; it also reflects the rise of ecumenism*, which has led many Protestants to reexamine the history of early Protestantism and offer revisionist accounts of the role of this doctrine. **SEE ALSO JUSTIFICATION, THEOLOGICAL VIEWS AND PRACTICES,**

CLUSTER: A CENTRAL DOCTRINE FOR WESTERN CHRISTIANITY.

ALISTER E. MCGRATH

2) A Sampling of Contextual Views and Practices

Protestantism in Africa: Southern Africa. Protestantism arrived in Southern African (South* Africa, Lesotho*, Swaziland*, Mozambique*, Zimbabwe*, Botswana*, Namibia*) with colonizers from Portugal (Mozambique), Holland (South Africa), Britain (South Africa, Lesotho, Swaziland, Zimbabwe, Botswana), and Germany (Namibia). The earliest Protestant Church was probably established in 1652 by Dutch settlers: the Dutch Reformed Church (Nederduitse Gereformeerde Kerk).

The second half of the 20th c. was a period of rapid change. Countries in Southern Africa attained independence. Protestantism played a major role in the transitions from colonialism to self-rule. Change continues as the region seeks to define itself amid threats of globalization*, poverty*, HIV/AIDS, and political instability (e.g. in Zimbabwe*).

Protestants constitute a relatively large percentage of the population in South Africa (30.7%) and Namibia (47%); they constitute a smaller percentage (between 8 and 14%) in the other countries. As elsewhere Protestants are distinctive for their emphasis on the supreme authority of the Bible, liberty* of conscience, the individual's right to interpret Scripture*, and commitment to a just social order. As elsewhere there is a struggle between conservative and liberal theologies.

Although Protestants were seldom allied with colonial governments, they did not mount an effective opposition to colonial regimes. Nevertheless, they trained some who became leaders in liberation movements. In Mozambique*, FRELIMO (Front for Liberation of Mozambique) had leaders trained in Protestant schools. Many of these, including 31 African Presbyterian leaders, were arrested in 1972, among them Zedequias Manganhela and Jose Sidumo (who died in Machava prison).

Apartheid* in South Africa crumbled under the pressure of critics that included Anglican Bishop Desmond Tutu, Presbyterian Alan Boesak, and the Christian Institute of South Africa, with its influential *Journal of Theology in Southern Africa.* In Namibia the United Evangelical Church of South West Africa (uniting two Lutheran churches; 37% of the population in 1995) played an important role in the struggle for independence in 1971 when its African leaders published a pastoral letter condemning the politics of apartheid.

Protestants help set trajectories of stability, development, and hope* in the face of challenges posed by post-9/11 anxieties, a shrinking globe, phenomenal advances in science and technology, and the concentration of wealth* among elites. In South Africa, the Truth* and Reconciliation Commission headed by Bishop Tutu helped former bitter enemies to envision a future together. In the face of HIV/AIDS and a life expectancy that has plummeted to less than 40 years, Protestant campaigns have emphasized abstinence, faithfulness to one's partner(s), and the use of condoms.

HENRY MUGABE and ISAAC M. T. MWASE

Protestantism in Africa: Western Africa. Formal planting of Protestantism in Western Africa dates to 1618. Until then all Christian activities in the region were undertaken by Roman Catholics. Various European merchants established themselves along the coast by building forts for commercial purposes; these merchants were accompanied by chaplains who played the dual role of providing spiritual welfare for the Europeans and preparing the ground for later organized missions in Western Africa.

Following the 18th-c. Evangelical revival* in Europe, Protestant missionary societies, such as the Church Missionary Society, Wesleyan Missionary Society, Basel Missionary Society, and North German Missionary Society, successfully planted various Protestant churches, including Presbyterian, Methodist, and Anglican churches in Western Africa during the 19th c.

Protestant missionary activities had both positive and negative results. They contributed immensely to the development of the region in terms of social infrastructure, formal classroom education*, and the stimulation of African mother tongues (see Bible Translations Cluster: Present-Day Translations in Africa). However, the missionary endeavor failed to sympathize with and constructively relate to the indigenous spiritual beliefs that underpin the traditional worldview in West African cultures (see African Religion and Christianity Cluster). The resultant Protestant churches directly inherited both the gains and the deficiencies of the missionary efforts.

The responses to Protestant Christianity in Western Africa have been so varied that they could be placed on a spectrum ranging from total rejection through partial acceptance to total acceptance. The churches have been contending with pressing issues, such as church* and state relations, the quest for a new form of spirituality, liturgical renewal, indigenization, selfhood and aid, relationships between Western African churches and European churches, and church unity. The Protestant churches spearhead social action, particularly through schools and hospitals.

A major response to the gospel in Western Africa has been the emergence of African* Instituted Churches, which marked a new era in the contextualization* of Christianity on African soil. Making good use of the Bible translated into West African languages, the African Instituted Churches, as well as Pentecostal* and other Charismatic* churches, have arguably made headway in appropriating biblical resources in the West African context, helping Protestant churches to discover ways of being the church in Africa by ceasing to be a Western church. Contemporary African Protestantism seeks to engage the interior of the indigenous worldview and to reclaim it for Christ. As such it is a manifestation of the existence of an identifiable contemporary African Christianity. **See also** **AFRICAN INSTITUTED CHURCHES CLUSTER: IN WEST AFRICA; CHARISMATIC AND PENTECOSTAL MOVEMENTS CLUSTER: IN AFRICA: WESTERN AFRICA.**

CEPHAS N. OMENYO

Protestantism in Asia: China. Protestant Christianity, introduced in China (1807) by British missionary Robert Morrison (1782–1843), remained alien to a majority of the Chinese people for more than 150 years. Early missionaries were too closely involved, politically and militarily, with Western foreign powers to understand the need for and significance of indigenization and inculturation*. After the Opium Wars (1840, 1860), a long series of incidents involving missionaries, culminating in the Boxer Uprising (1900), set the scene for the Centennial Missionary Conference (Shanghai, 1907). The ensuing rethinking and readjustments of mission policy led to more successful developments in the early 20th c., when churches rapidly developed educational, medical, literary, and philanthropic services. In the meantime, important developments – political and social unrest following the downfall of the Manchurian imperial regime (1911), and the introduction of democratic thinking, Western scientific knowledge, and Marxist revolutionary theory among students and intellectuals – gave rise to the May Fourth New Culture Movement (1915) and to the Anti-Religion and Anti-Christianity movements (1919–26). In response to these, two important reformist movements marked a new era of change (1920s–1930s): the Independent Church Movement (pioneered in 1906 by Rev. Yu Guozhen) extended and demanded the separation of the churches from foreign missionary societies in financial, personnel, and organizational matters; similarly, the Indigenization Movement stressed sinicization (assimilation into Chinese culture) in theology and liturgy (heralded by Dr. T. C. Chao and others). These movements culminated in the Declaration of Churches by the General Conference of Chinese Protestant Churches in Shanghai (1922), which affirmed the "three-self" principle of self-government, self-support, and self-propagation that would later become a formal movement.

The war against the Japanese (1937–45) and the liberation civil war (1946–49) plunged the country into disorder, which was conducive to the spread of fundamentalism*, Millennialism*, and spiritual revivalism*. By midcentury there were about 700,000 Protestant Christians organized into denominational churches affiliated with foreign missionary associations and independent indigenous churches (e.g. the Little Flock, the True Jesus Church, and the Jesus Family). In a country of more than 600 million people, these constituted only a tiny minority of less than 1% of the population, culturally marginalized and dissociated from the broad masses of people.

With the founding of the People's Republic (1949), the church entered a new phase in which all relationships with foreign missions were severed. Under the leadership of Wu Yaozung (Y. T. Wu), the Three-Self Patriotic Movement was formally launched, purporting to build the Christian Church anew as a truly Chinese church. After the Cultural Revolution (1966–76), the church emerged as "postdenominational," organized around the Three-Self Patriotic Committees and Christian Councils on the national, provincial, and local levels, respectively. Since then, Protestant Christianity has witnessed unprecedented growth and development. It is estimated that at present there are more than 16 million Protestants worshipping in more than 60,000 Three-Self churches and "assembly points," with 25,000 "clergy" or "church workers." In 2004 a Bible printing press in Nanjing celebrated the printing of 40 million copies of the Bible in Chinese and ethnic minority languages. A network of some 20 theological seminaries and hundreds of short-term theological schools are preparing thousands of young preachers and ministers to serve the ever growing and developing churches. The theology of the local churches, generally speaking, is rather conservative, following the Evangelical* tradition. But currently under the leadership of Ding Guangxun (Bishop K. H. Ting), a campaign of "reconstruction of theological thought" is being launched among urban church leaders and theological seminaries, with more open, humanistic, and socialist leanings, stressing contextualization and accommodation within the contemporary social and cultural milieu.

In the meantime, there have arisen outside the established Three-Self churches an increasing number of "house* churches," the numerical strength of which has been variously estimated as comparable to or higher than that of the Three-Self churches. Although Protestant, they try to remain at a distance from the Three-Self churches, but not necessarily because of hostility. They are nondenominational and independent of each other, without centralized regional or national organization; they are not registered with the Bureau of Religious Affairs and usually stand aloof from social or political involvement. Their theology is either fundamentalist or Evangelical (see Chinese Contemporary Independent and House Churches).

Another phenomenon since the late 1990s worth noting is the emergence of "cultural Christians" and an increasing interest in Christianity among intellectuals, in stark contrast to the antireligious and anti-Christian attitude of previous decades. Many university departments and institutions specializing in Christian studies have been set up, and theological books, either translated or written by Chinese scholars, have been published, attracting many sympathetic readers. Most scholars involved may not be confessed Christians, but the general tone of discussion is appreciative and positive about the gospel. This seems to point to a bright future for the development of Christianity in China, but the Protestant churches, whether established or house churches, do not appear to be prepared to meet the challenge of academia. **See also CHINA; NORTH INDIA, CHURCH OF; SOUTH INDIA, CHURCH OF; THREE-SELF PRINCIPLE AND PATRIOTIC MOVEMENT IN CHINA; UNITED CHURCH OF CHRIST IN THE PHILIPPINES.** CHEN ZEMIN

Protestantism in Europe: France. French Protestantism (which developed on the basis of its Huguenot* heritage) broadly supported the process of laicization* that eventually led to the 1905 law establishing a strict separation of church* and state (1905). This support reflected the complex interactions and tensions (since the mid-19th c.) between Protestant churches and the revival* movement, and among the Protestant movements of mission, evangelization, social action, and education. This dynamics also strongly contributed to the creation of the French Protestant Federation (1907), composed of Protestant churches and charitable institutions. The Federation was needed to assuage the tensions resulting from heated debates on secularism* and from the division between Evangelical and liberal groups. Under the strong leadership of Marc Boegner during the difficult period from 1930 to 1964, it fostered union among Protestants and the safeguard of freedom of public worship. By 2000 most Protestant churches in France (Reformed, Lutheran, Baptist, Evangelical, several Pentecostal-Charismatic* church unions), social work institutions (including CIMADE*), and mission societies were participating in the French Protestant Federation (900,000 members) and were in constant contact with the Evangelical Federation of France and the National Union of Assemblies of God. Each member church maintains its own identity and distinctive qualities. Though the churches disagree about many issues (e.g. baptism, social ethics), they remain committed both to a cordial yet demanding dialogue* on local and national levels and to a common witness and social service. Representing Protestantism in conversation with the French government and the media, the Protestant Federation emphasizes Protestant unity beyond its diversity. In this way, with the help of remarkable leaders such as Suzanne de Dietrich and Madeleine Barrot*, as well as scholars such as Roger Mehl, Georges Casalis, André Dumas, Jacques Ellul, and Paul Ricoeur*, French Protestantism makes a distinctive contribution to the practice of secularism* in a nation with strict separation of church and state. JACQUES STEWART

Protestantism in Europe: Germany. The Reformed* tradition in Germany was influenced by several factors. The Reformed churches in Switzerland* established relationships with Reformers in Strasbourg and other south German cities before the death of Zwingli* (1530), and Calvin's* years in Strasbourg (1538–41) strengthened the relationship. The elector of the Palatinate invited Reformed theologians to draw up the Heidelberg* Catechism (1563); other German princes, especially in Anhalt and on the lower Rhine, also inclined toward Reformed rather than Lutheran doctrines and practices. While this tradition was not acknowledged by the Peace of Augsburg* (1555), the Reformed were often tolerated as moderate Lutherans in the tradition of Melanchthon*, and they gained further legitimacy at the Reichstag of 1566.

The fortunes of the Reformed tradition in Germany were closely linked with the house of Hohenzollern. The elector John Sigismund of Brandenburg converted to the Reformed faith (1613), guaranteeing freedom of conscience for his Lutheran subjects. He became duke of Jülich-Cleve-Mark-Berg on the lower Rhine, which was already Reformed (1614), and duke of Prussia (1618), where most people were Lutherans.

Reformed pastors served in either the court or the army. The Prussian rulers supported religious tolerance and encouraged both the Enlightenment* and Pietism* in their realms, giving special support to Zinzendorf* and the Moravians*.

Maintaining this inclusive spirit, and inspired by the model of the Church of England (see Anglicanism Cluster: Anglican Communion and Its Theology), Friedrich Wilhelm III promoted the Prussian* Union between the Lutheran and Reformed churches in his territories (announced in 1817 in connection with the 300th anniversary of the Reformation). While the Union was opposed by most Lutherans, and Schleiermacher*, its most important defender, objected to many details, the Prussian Union persisted and was gradually adopted in other territories. Following classic Protestant principles, a representative "synodal" government was adopted, especially after the revolution of 1848. The major liberal theologians of the 19th c. (Schleiermacher*, Rothe, Ritschl*, Harnack*) were either Reformed or Unionist. Many Lutherans continued to take positions that were more "conservative" or "confessional," even as they became affiliated with the comprehensive Evangelical Church in Germany. **See also GERMANY; LUTHERANISM CLUSTER: IN GERMANY; ROMAN CATHOLICISM CLUSTER: IN EUROPE: GERMANY AND LUTHERANISM; REFORMED CHURCHES.**

EUGENE TESELLE

Protestantism in Europe: The Nordic Countries. See LUTHERANISM CLUSTER: IN NORDIC COUNTRIES.

Protestantism in Europe: Russia. Protestants appeared in Moscow in the first half of the 16th c. Unlike Roman Catholics, Protestants were treated with tolerance in Russia, because they neither interfered with politics nor made any attempts to spread their doctrines among the Orthodox Russians. Peter the Great granted freedom of faith to foreigners in 1702. Catherine II invited German colonists (Lutherans, Reformed, Mennonites) to settle along the Volga River and in the south of Russia. In 1763 she issued a manifesto granting them religious freedom. However, Protestantism in Russia had very little influence on the Slavic population until the mid-19th c. In the 1860s, the first Slavic Protestant groups emerged in the south of Russia. So-called Evangelical Christians established themselves in St. Petersburg. Seventh-day Adventists began to attract Russians in the 1880s; the Pentecostal Movement had reached Russia by 1911–13. It was only in 1905 that Russian Protestants were recognized by the state through the imperial edict "On Strengthening the Beginnings of the Religious Tolerance."

Having declared freedom* of conscience, the Bolsheviks were comparatively tolerant of Russian Protestants in the first decade after the 1917 revolution. Yet in 1929 they banned all religious and missionary activities other than worship services. Protestant theological schools and periodicals were shut down, many prayer houses were confiscated, and ministers were arrested.

The postwar years (1945–1950s) witnessed the revival of Protestant churches, although the restricted registration and suspicion toward authorities kept many communities underground for many decades. The revival of religious life in the 1990s, fervent missionary activity, and international contacts produced a rapid growth of Protestants confessions, including new denominations such as Charismatics* and Quakers. Gradually, Protestants have been able to integrate themselves into modern society by overcoming their social circumspection and isolation. They often cooperate with evangelism across denominational lines and emphasize individual conversion*, personal piety, Bible reading, a role for the laity* in worship, evangelism, and teaching.

In many contemporary Protestant congregations (especially Baptist), worship includes hymns* and spirited "choruses," the use of various musical instruments, but with only some traditional Christian symbolism. Although Protestantism's impact in Russia is growing, Protestants constituted only a little more than 1% of the population in 2000. ALEXANDER NEGROV and TATYANA NIKOLSKAYA

Protestantism in Latin America. Since the early 1900s, all Protestants in Latin America have been called *evangélicos*, "evangelicals" (accentuating "evangel," good news, gospel, as in Germany), but in a different sense than in England and the USA.

The Protestant (Evangelical) Movement was banned by the Spanish rulers during colonial times (except in small areas controlled by Protestant nations, e.g. Jamaica and the Guianas). After independence (early 19th c.), small beachheads were established in the Roman Catholic nations through immigration, Bible societies, and mission efforts. By the early 20th c., more than 40 missionary societies were collaborating in a changing social and political scene. With the secularizing spirit of liberalism, Protestants/Evangelicals joined with liberal Catholics in gradually achieving religious liberty*, in limiting ecclesiastical control of civic functions (civil registers of births, weddings, and deaths), and the development of municipal cemeteries, public education, and state-run health services.

By 1950 Protestant churches had slowly gained adherents, then began to mushroom, owing mainly to cooperative evangelism* and the growing Pentecostal*/Charismatic* movements. Mainline churches, which tended to maintain their imported languages and liturgies (e.g. see the present cluster: In Latin America: Brazil), continued to experience slow growth, mostly through immigration. The more conservative churches underwent moderate growth, despite a spectacular increase in missionaries (a 680% growth between 1930 and 1960). However, without significant missionary and foreign financial support, in the tumultuous 1950–90 period the independent Charismatic Movement experienced phenomenal spontaneous growth, coming to comprise 70–75% of Protestants in Latin America.

Many reasons are given for this rapid Evangelical growth: deteriorating social conditions, the rise of dictatorships and internal wars, forced migrations, the spread of indigenous and Catholic folk religions, the blending of native and gospel mysticism*, and resistance to Western secularism*. Religious workers tend to accentuate spiritual factors: persistent evangelism*, the use of religious media* (there are more than 1,000 Evangelical radio stations and 100 television channels), mass revivals*, and more participatory worship than in the liturgical Roman Catholic tradition. However, in the 1990s, growth began to level off, as many second- and third-generation youth started to become disaffected with the churches.

Some estimate that, by 2000, 12% of Latin Americans were Protestants, although the percentages varied widely among nations: Guatemala*, 25%; Brazil*, 15%; Chile*, 15%; Uruguay*, 4%; and Mexico*, 6%. More progressive Protestants engage in an active dialogue with some Roman Catholics, whereas conservative Protestants maintain a defensive and critical attitude. This tension is reflected in the existence of two continental church councils, neither of which, however, has much influence because the majority of Protestants do not participate in them. Diversity with some anti–North American overtones characterizes Latin American Protestantism/Evangelicalism.

SIDNEY ROOY

Protestantism in Latin America: Argentina. The first Protestant churches manifested the relationship between religion and nationality of origin. English, German, Swiss, and Danish immigrants established ethnic communities around their churches as they sought to avoid assimilation into Argentine society. Thus the Evangelical Church of Río de la Plata originated as the German Evangelical Synod of Río de la Plata; it was initially related to the protection of German culture and linked to Nazism*. The word "German" was removed from its name during its reorganization in the 1970s.

But Protestantism does not remain insular; Methodist, Baptist, Seventh*-Day Adventist, and Lutheran churches, the Hermanos Libres Church, the Salvation* Army, and the Mennonite* Mission proselytize* or evangelize* (depending on one's perspective). For instance, William Morris (1864–1932), associated with the North American Methodist Episcopal Church and later with the (Anglican) South American Missionary Society, led a mission aimed at bringing education* and Christian teaching to working-class children, especially street children, and created many schools.

In the 1980s, the Pentecostal* and neo-Pentecostal (Charismatic*) churches expanded. The ministries of pastors Cabrera (Visión de Futuro), Giménez (Ondas de Amor y Paz), and Anacondia (Mensaje de Salvación) appealed to a great number of believers. **See also ARGENTINA.**

DAMIÁN SETTON

Protestantism in Latin America: Brazil: Churches of Immigrants. As an independent nation (1824), Brazil began to receive immigrants from Central Europe. Around 300,000 Germans, 60% of them Lutherans, settled in Southern Brazil between 1824 and 1942. Their first pastors were hired either by the Brazilian Empire or by private settlement companies. The religious life of these immigrants was centered on the Bible, their hymnbook, and catechism; they organized schools, "temples*," and cemeteries. Lacking pastors, they entrusted the laity* with pastoral duties. After 1860 Prussia helped Lutherans to found the German Evangelical Synod of the Province of Rio Grande do Sul (1868) to defend their interests against the Empire and Roman Catholicism (the official religion until 1889). A messianic movement, the "Mucker Movement," emerged in reaction to both the clericalization represented by the Synod and the influence of the Enlightenment* among German intellectuals; it was crushed by the Brazilian army.

After the failure of the first synod, new ones were founded: the Synod of Rio Grande do Sul (1886), the Evangelical Lutheran Synod of Santa Catarina, Paraná, and Other States (1905), the Synod of the Evangelical Congregations of Santa Catarina and Paraná (1911), and the Evangelical Synod of Central Brazil (1912). Pastors from the USA founded the Brazilian District of the German Lutheran Missouri Synod (1900). The two Lutheran churches in Brazil today, the Evangelical Church of the Lutheran Confession in Brazil and the Evangelical Lutheran Church of Brazil, grew out of these five synods.

German influences left deep marks on the immigrants' churches. The Lutherans' integration into Brazilian life was painful. Since they were immigrants and not Roman Catholics, they did not have the right to vote or to be elected. Their marriages* were viewed as concubinage until 1869; mixed marriages were prohibited (even after 1869); their dead could not be buried in public cemeteries; their "temples" could not resemble churches. Their legal isolation was exacerbated by geographic, ethnic, and linguistic isolation. In this situation, the pan-Germanic policy of the German Third Reich found fertile soil, especially when nationalizing measures implemented by the Brazilian government (1930–45) harshly affected Lutherans. Many Lutherans were attracted to Nazi/Fascist ideology. But Brazil's participation in World War II progressively led Lutheran churches to abandon the German language, to have pastors raised and educated in Brazil, and to become involved in issues concerning Brazilian national life.

MARTIN N. DREHER

Protestantism in Latin America: Brazil: Churches of Resident Aliens. Little is known about the many Protestant foreigners who stayed for short times in Brazil: sailors, merchants, soldiers, adventurers, and scientists. In colonial times, their presence was viewed with suspicion; Protestants were considered undesirable.

With the arrival of the Portuguese royal family (1808) escorted by a British (Protestant) fleet headed by Sir Sidney Smith, and the subsequent support of the British ambassador Lord Strangford, the 1810 Trade and Shipping Treaty included a clause giving British Protestants freedom to worship in Brazil using their language.

The main Brazilian harbors soon had Protestant (Evangelical) communities, the first church being built by the Anglicans in Rio de Janeiro (1819). Chaplains and priests settled down and, in their absence, consuls performed religious duties. For instance, in 1821 Maria Graham attended a worship service in the Salvador Chapel in Bahia and noted that the preacher gave thanks to God for King João VI of Portugal, who permitted them to worship according to their faith.

Brazilians welcomed such Protestants, but the boundaries between the two groups remained clear. Nevertheless, the presence of these churches of resident aliens opened the doors for the establishment of Protestant churches with Brazilians' participation.

EDUARDO GUZMÃO QUADROS

Protestantism in Latin America: Brazil: Colonial Period. During the colonial period, religious dissidents were exiled from the country. The few Flemish, German, French, and English Protestant colonizers soon became Roman Catholic through marriage or for economic reasons (only Roman Catholics could own land).

At São Vicente (1532), one of the first colonizers was the Flemish Erasmus Schetz. Several of his employees were Protestants, and his son Gaspar had contact with Melanchthon* and Helius Eobanus Hessus, the first rector of the University of Marburg, whose grandson, Heliodorus, settled in São Vicente. The English Protestant John Whithall also settled there (1578), but became Catholic when he married the daughter of an Italian and adopted the name João Leitão. The cannoneer Hans Staden, a shipwrecked Lutheran, left an important report about 16th-c. Brazil.

As Jean de Lery reported, in 1555 a French expedition under the command of Admiral Villegaignon established France Antarctique at the Guanabara Bay as a settlement for 300 Huguenots*. On March 30, 1557, the first Calvinist congregation in Latin America (Peter Richer and Guillaume Chartier, pastors) was constituted. But these Calvinists were expelled in 1567 by the Portuguese Inquisition* (in Brazil since 1557).

The Dutch conquered a considerable portion of Northeastern Brazil. In the Dutch colony (1637–44), 15 Calvinist temples, a synagogue, and the first Talmudic school of the Americas were built. But when the Dutch were expelled, the Calvinist preachers left Brazil and the remaining Protestants were progressively assimilated.

In subsequent years, only the subjects of the Portuguese crown could enter Brazil. Nonetheless, soldiers from the German Lutheran territory of Hesse and German Protestant officials at the service of the Portuguese crown came to the colony, particularly after 1761. The Protestants who wanted to occupy public positions converted to Roman Catholicism; among them were Daniel Pedro Müller (1779–1842), the son of the Lutheran pastor of Lisbon, and Carlos Augusto de Oeynhausen (1778), a cousin of the Count of Lippe, who reorganized the Portuguese army.

The coming of the Portuguese royal family to Brazil (1808) and the 1810 Trade and Shipping Treaty (giving British Protestants freedom of worship), as well as the arrival of Leopoldina of Hapsburg, put an end to the prohibition of entry by Protestants. Some Lutherans also came to Brazil at that time: Baron Wilhelm von Eschwege (1777–1855), the father of Brazilian mineralogy, the botanist Karl Friedrich Phillip von Martius, and the mineral engineer Friedrich Ludwig Wilhelm Varnhagen (1783–1842).

MARTIN N. DREHER

Protestantism in Latin America: Brazil: Mission Protestantism. The term "Mission Protestantism" refers to the establishment of Protestant (Evangelical) churches in Brazil by North American missionaries. This designation is helpful to distinguish this branch of Protestantism – including Presbyterian, Methodist, Baptist, Congregationalist*, and Adventist* churches – from independent Charismatics*/Pentecostalists* (see Charismatic and Pentecostal Movements Cluster: In Latin America: Brazil) and from churches of immigrants (see the present cluster: In Brazil: Churches of Immigrants). This type of Protestantism established itself in Brazil through the distribution of the Bible and religious edification literature, its emphasis on family devotionals, its schools for secular education* and theological* formation, and its permanent polemic against Roman Catholicism. Its followers were poor peasants, who encountered these new religious beliefs through family networks. With the intense migration from rural areas to the cities in the late 20th c., this Protestantism became increasingly identified with the urban middle class.

Mission Protestantism was founded on the central theological affirmations of the Protestant Reformation*: the exclusive authority of the Bible in questions of faith (Scripture* principle); salvation* as the exclusive work of God's grace*; the priesthood* of all believers; and the rational explanation of faith, ethical rigor as public witness. Mission Protestantism was dominated by pastoral practices inspired by the Wesleyan Methodist* tradition, with emphasis on conversion*, charity, and sanctification*. Local congregations were relatively autonomous, although they were organized by regional federative systems (e.g. as regions, districts, according to the denominations) and under the jurisdiction of a supreme council. Although not always a harmonious meeting ground for different theological perspectives and religious experiences, Mission Protestantism provided a vanguard articulation of ecumenical* relations and actions focused on the social responsibility of churches, especially after the 1916 Panama* Conference.

Compared with Roman Catholicism, Mission Protestantism can be viewed either as a foreign body, not well adapted to the cultural context of Brazil (especially because it functions as an ideological legitimation of the US economic and political penetration), or as an integral part of the modernization of the continent, confronting its colonial* traditionalism and conservative authority. Yet neither view takes into account the classical typology of Brazilian Protestantism that focuses on differences in dogma, rite, and religious experience. LAURI EMÍLIO WIRTH

Protestantism in Latin America: Brazil: Parachurch Associations. Parachurch* associations are formed by peoples or institutions outside particular ecclesiastical structures. They are interconfessional and financially independent. There are four main types: Bible societies, youth organizations, ecumenical organizations, and educational associations.

The history of parachurch associations in Brazil begins in Europe, when the British* and Foreign Bible Society published the NT in the Portuguese language (1809). Copies of this NT and, later, Bibles from the American* Bible Society were sold at Brazilian harbors. After independence (1822), foreign and national colporteurs* traveling throughout the countryside distributed these "Protestant Bibles", along with religious literature, and explained their doctrine. The Sociedade Bíblica do Brasil (1948) conformed to the same interdenominational patterns.

A parachurch organization aimed at youth was the YMCA*, founded between 1891 and 1893 in Rio de Janeiro by the missionary Myron J. Clarck, who promoted sports and recreational activities to attract youth; it had a book-lending library. That model spread to other cities. In 1940 the Brazilian Student Christian Federation (a branch of the World* Student Christian Federation) and in 1957 the International Fellowship of Evangelical Students were founded with the intention of promoting alternatives to the fundamentalist* theology dominating the main Protestant churches.

Other parachurch organizations aimed at promoting ecumenism among the churches. The Confederação Evangélica Brasileira (Brazilian Evangelical Confederation, from 1934 to 1964, when it disbanded after the military coup) became the main link between global ecumenical activities and the national churches after the foundation of the World* Council of Churches (1948). In 1982 a less representative and less effective Conselho Nacional de Igrejas Cristãs (National Council of Christian Churches) emerged.

Some educational parachurch organizations, such as the Aliança Pró-Evangelização de Crianças (Pro-children Evangelization Alliance, since 1940), support children's education; others, such as the Associação dos Seminários Teológicos Evangélicos (Evangelical Theology Seminaries Association, since 1961), support higher education. The Igreja e Sociedade na América Latina (Latin American Church and Society, since 1961) and the Fraternidade Teológica Latino-americana (Latin American Theology Fraternity, since 1970) also play an important role in theological education; relying on active Brazilian participation, they influenced theological thought during the troubled dictatorial period.

EDUARDO GUZMÃO QUADROS

Protestantism in Latin America: Central America. After Columbus's arrival on the coast of Central America (1502) and during the Spanish colonial period, the Roman Catholic Inquisition closed the doors to Protestantism. John Martin, an Irish Anglican, was the first protestant martyr: he was taken prisoner in Guatemala* (1574), hanged, and publicly burned by the Inquisition in Mexico*. In 1655 English pirates took the island of

Jamaica*, from which they banned Roman Catholicism, establishing the Anglican Church. English settlements along the coast and British Honduras* (Belize) became Protestant enclaves.

In 1821 the independence of Central America from Spain was declared. Commercial treaties facilitated the immigration of European Protestant colonists and merchants, including William Le Lacheur, an Englishman who transported coffee to England and sold Bibles in Costa* Rica (1843). Yet the persecution of Protestants still existed; Juana Mendia, a young Guatemalan native, became the first native Protestant martyr of Central America; she died following a ferocious beating (1843). The late 19th c. saw confrontations between political conservatives and liberals and the alliance of liberals with Freemasons and Protestants. In 1871 in Guatemala*, the general Rufino Barrios promulgated anticlerical laws, expelled the Jesuits, and introduced the Presbyterian Church.

The construction and appropriation of the Panama* Canal by the USA (1904–14) established US economic control over Central America, while the Panama* Conference (1916) prompted the establishment of North American Protestant missions on the continent, through organizations such as the Latin American Mission (launched in 1921 by Harry Strachan and Susan Beamish).

The organization of unions of native people, rural workers, women, and factory workers and of student movements, as well as the guerrilla warfare unleashed in El* Salvador, Guatemala*, and Nicaragua* against military states supported by the USA (from the 1960s), culminated in the triumph of the Sandinista revolution (Nicaragua, 1979). An example of a Protestant committed to this struggle is the Baptist Luz Marina Torres, who abandoned his studies to join the insurrection against Somoza's dictatorship in Nicaragua. Both Roman Catholic and Protestant theologians, poets, martyrs, prophets, and prophetesses disseminated Liberation theology.

In 1960 Protestants were merely 3.9% of the mostly Catholic population. In 1995 Protestants constituted 18.3% of the population (5.9 million out of a total of 32.4 million). The growth of Protestantism is due both to the appeal of the Protestant ethic, which theologically legitimizes the work of the middle class and the development of business, and to the expansion (from the 1970s) in rural and urban areas of the Pentecostalist*/Charismatic* movements, which are considered to be expressions of individual liberty and of rebellion against centralized authority. The theology of the Holy* Spirit – with its healing, glossolalia*, new* creation, and diverse ecstatic experiences – provides a way for the poor* and mestizos* to combine popular* Christian traditions and Charismatic experiences with the myths of ancient religions of the Maya, Emberá, Wounan, and Guaymies, as well as with the spirituality of the descendents of African slaves, such as the Garífunas, and of the Miskitos and Antilleans, who immigrated to Central America. **See also** **COSTA RICA; EL SALVADOR; GUATEMALA; HONDURAS; NICARAGUA.**

JAIME ADRÍAN PRIETO VALLADARES

Protestantism in Latin America: Colombia. Protestantism arrived in Colombia in the 1820s, although it had been in San Andres Island since colonial times. Although the Colombian Biblical Society was founded in 1825, the first missions targeted the foreign populations in Colombia. Yet the Liberal government, seeking to break the Roman Catholic Church's monopoly (second half of the 19th c.), called the Presbyterian US mission to establish an indigenous Protestant church. Following the failure of Liberal governments to remain in power, politicians reestablished the Roman Catholic Church as the official church (the 1886 Constitution). The Protestants' situation worsened during the civil war in the 1940s; Protestant public worship was prohibited, as was private Protestant worship in "Catholic missionary territories" (75% of Colombia); 116 Protestants were killed. In 1949 Protestants founded the Colombian Evangelical Confederation, which promoted the freedom of religion (established in 1991).

Protestants have several education centers in Colombia, but their membership remains low. Mennonite* organizations work for economic and social development and for peace, especially in regions of conflict. But Protestants involved in humanitarian activities have been victimized.

Since the 1960s, the Pentecostal* and Charismatic* movements (c7% of the population) have diversified the Colombian religious landscape. They lack a unified theology, but share some practices e.g. glossolalia*, spiritual healings*, and demonology*, as well as involvement in sociopolitical affairs. Since 1991 they have joined to form their own political parties.

SANDRA RIOS

Protestantism in Latin America: Mexico. Since its origins in the 16th c., Protestantism has been a diversified series of movements of "dissenters" from the Roman Catholic Church, arising in a great diversity of theological, cultural, political, and geographical contexts, and thus taking a great variety of expressions and ecclesial forms. Consequently in Mexico there are (1) diverse historic Protestant churches with European origins; (2) Evangelical and Holiness* movements, which originated in the USA; and (3) Pentecostal and Charismatic* movements (see Charismatic and Pentecostal Movements Cluster: In Latin America: Mexico) rooted in the Charismatic renewals in both historical and Evangelical churches; these renewals resulted in part from the activities of North American missions but are now growing mainly out of movements originating in Mexico.

1. Historic Protestantism. The first Protestant incursion into Mexico took the form of the distribution of Bibles (e.g. sent by the British Bible Society, 1828–42) with the support of José María Luis Mora (1795–1856; priest, writer, lawyer, reformist Mexican statesman). Santiago Hickey arrived in Matamoros (1860) with a shipment of Bibles, as a colporteur of the American Bible Society.

Organized Protestantism arrived in 1859, when apparently the first public Protestant worship service in Mexico was celebrated in Zacatecas by Julio Provost and José Llaguno. The first Baptist Church and the first Presbyterian Church (organized by Melinda Rankin) were established in Monterrey (1864). Methodist work began in 1872 with missions from two Methodist* Episcopal churches in the USA, together with the Religious Society of Friends* (Quakers, 1871), Congregationalists* (1872), Reformed* (1878), Disciples* of Christ (1890), Seventh-day Adventists* (1893), Nazarenes* (1908), Lutherans* (1950), Mennonites* and Anabaptists* (1955), among others.

Another form of Protestant work in Mexico was that of education* and health* care. Methodist, Presbyterian, Baptist, and Quaker schools had a certain amount of success, especially between 1880 and 1920, because they provided a liberal "laic" (i.e. non–Roman Catholic) education. Protestant health care work included the implementation of local health care programs and the establishment of health care centers, clinics, and hospitals in the main cities and rural areas.

The main doctrines and principles of these Protestant churches include the Bible as the supreme standard for faith and life; the Trinity as the hermeneutical criterion in theology; commitment to mission*; freedom* of conscience and religion; the priesthood* of all believers; and the separation of church* and state. Three forms of church government – episcopal, presbyterian and congregational – are represented (see Church, Concepts and Life, Cluster: Types of Ecclesiastical Structure). Each denomination has publications, including *El faro* (1885, Presbyterian), *Abogado cristiano ilustrado* (1876–1930, Methodist), *La luz bautista* (1903, Baptist), *Luminar* (1937–51), *La Biblia en América Latina* (1967–87), and three journals related to theological education: *Cristianismo y sociedad* (1963; published in Mexico, 1983–91), *Taller de teología* (1976–84), which became *Oikodomein* (1994), and *El apóstol* (1977, Baptist).

2. Evangelical Movements. Although the name "Evangelical" designates all Protestant churches in Mexico, it more specifically refers to the Evangelical Protestantism that arose from the work of North American missionaries (since 1840) as a continuation in Mexico c1916 of the North American "Second Great* Awakening" (revivalism*). The latter was characterized by individual religious experience, soteriological Christology (see Atonement #2), and emphasis on sanctification*.

After World War II, missionaries of a different kind arrived. They were part of the Holiness* Movement, with Millennialist* and fundamentalist* interpretations, and preached a faith that appeared to be a reaction to the threats posed by the progression of secularism*, science*, and communism*. (The "mother churches" – Methodist, Presbyterian and Baptist – were themselves strongly influenced by this movement.) It involved a dualistic perspective, emphasizing the Holy* Spirit and teaching an ethics of separation from the world, accompanied by a legalistic inflexibility. It held on to the Protestant tradition that considers the Bible to be the only source of faith and conduct, yet their reading of the Bible was now very literal*, and they emphasized individual conversion*, being born again, and missionary zeal.

From this radicalization of the Evangelical ethos*, and in the context of the cold war, Evangelical communities themselves (especially in institutions of theological* education) developed an alternative ecumenical position associated with Christians' social and political commitments. The Conference of Oaxtepec (1979) and the magazine *Cristianismo y sociedad* marked a shift in the conception of Evangelical mission in Latin America, which is now committed to the overall transformation of society. The Fraternidad Teológica Latinoamericana (Latin American Theological Fraternity, 1970) similarly retrieved the Evangelical tradition of the 16th- to 17th-c. Anabaptist Movement, rereading the Bible with a commitment to a well-balanced and complete mission of the church. **See also CHARISMATIC AND PENTECOSTAL MOVEMENTS CLUSTER: IN LATIN AMERICA: MEXICO; MEXICO.**

JAVIER ULLOA and
REBECA MONTEMAYOR

Protestantism in North America: Canada. See CANADA.

Protestantism in North America: United States. See UNITED STATES.

Protestantism in the South Pacific and Australia. Mission activities were predominantly British, with French and German influences in their respective colonies. As elsewhere Protestants stress the supreme authority of the Bible, liberty of conscience, the right of private judgment, and commitment to the rule of law. Yet there were marked divisions among established churches in Australia.

Protestant churches of the South Pacific, notably in Tonga, were comfortable with a Polynesian version of partnership, and therefore with communal churches that included different Protestant denominations. Everywhere in the region, commitment to missionary outreach, philanthropy, community service, and vocational integrity transcended separatism and modified divisive individualism. Many Protestants were attracted by liberal theological and political views, although confessional convictions remained strong among small Protestant churches.

In Australia some three-quarters of the population was Protestant during the 19th c. State aid was given to all the major denominations (including Roman Catholics) until the 1870s; by the end of the 20th c., new forms of aid had emerged. The Commonwealth Constitution prohibited the establishment of any religion as the state religion. Protestant political parties were unsuccessful, although the Orange and Masonic Lodges had an informal political influence.

Protestants constituted a majority on most Pacific Islands, with the exception of New Caledonia. By the mid-20th c., many Protestant denominations were engaged in ecumenical dialogue*. The United Church of Papua* New Guinea and the Solomon* Islands and the Uniting Church were the only major reunions of churches. Other forms of cooperation grew steadily, especially among Evangelicals and Pentecostals. The Second Vatican* Council forced many Protestants to reconsider their identity, as did the major cultural changes of the later 20th c., such as feminism, sexual liberation, postmodernism, changes in family life, and migration. The erosion of traditional Protestantism was slower in villages of the South Pacific than in the cities. Political problems, including civil wars in Fiji, Papua New Guinea, and the Solomon Islands, have shown how difficult it has been for churches to transcend ethnic rivalries.

In Australia, Protestantism's impact on those under 50 has steadily diminished. Some 25% of the population no longer claims any religious allegiance. The future of historic Protestantism looks problematic except among the smaller confessional churches, the Anglican Diocese of Sydney, and Pentecostals, who have established Family First (2004), the only Protestant group so far to obtain representation in the federal Parliament. IAN BREWARD

Protestant Principle, for Tillich*, the insistence that God is not to be identified with any manifestation (without denying God's presence in these manifestations); thus it is "the prophetic judgment against religious pride, ecclesiastical arrogance and secular self – sufficiency and their destructive consequences." It can be viewed as analogous to the "negative Scripture* principle." **See also** ICONOCLASM AS A THEOLOGICAL CONCEPT.

Proverbs, Book of, one of the Kethubim* (Writings), this anthology comprises nine collections, seven with superscriptions (1:1–9, 10:1–22:16, 22:17–24:22, 24:23–34, 25–29, 30:1–14, 31:1–9). A prologue (1–9) and an epilogue (31:10–31) provide a theological perspective for the entire book, which emphasizes the fear of the Lord as the first principle/beginning of knowledge and lauds a feminine embodiment of wisdom.

The sayings were composed over several centuries, starting during the monarchy and extending to the Hellenistic period. At first located within the family in small villages and subsequently the domain of a scribal elite, probably in Jerusalem, the proverbial sayings lack any reference to Israel's sacred traditions and represent insights available to everyone. Indeed, even a few sayings from the Egyptian *Instruction of Amen-emopet* are preserved in the biblical context, along with one saying from the *Aramaic Ahikar*. Two of the nine collections just listed are said to come from foreign instructors, Agur and the mother of Prince Lemuel.

The primary goal of sages was to teach youth how to cope with daily existence by acquiring the virtues of timing, eloquence, restraint, and integrity. Those who did so were promised the blessings of society: long life, progeny, wealth, and honor. Initially, the instruction came from parents, but the artistic structure of the sayings and the theological agenda in the introductory collection indicate professional expertise and interests. The poetic structure of the sayings utilizes parallel lines, usually two or three, in relationships that are synonymous, antithetic, or ascending. The poetry highlights two themes above all: the tree of life and the path (or way) of wisdom.

The sayings acknowledge a threat to boys posed by a foreign woman and imagine that they can receive assistance from her rival, personified wisdom*. Historians of religion have accented the similarities between this female figure and the goddesses Ma'at and Isis, especially the fact that the Egyptian Ma'at is depicted with the ankh, the symbol of life, in one hand and justice in the other, and Isis praises herself in the same manner that Wisdom does in Prov 1–9. Christians and Jews have gleaned insights from this book on various aspects of daily life, particularly the formation of character. Some early church fathers drew christological implications from personified wisdom, who is described as present at creation and bringing delight to the creator and life to humans (Chaps. 1 and 8), language applied to Jesus in the NT.

JAMES L. CRENSHAW

Providence. See GOD, CHRISTIAN VIEWS OF, CLUSTER.

Province, group of dioceses*, originally equivalent to a province of the Roman Empire. The metropolitan* or archbishop* is the chief city's bishop.

Prussian Union, union of the Lutheran and Reformed churches in Prussia. Friedrich Wilhelm III suggested the formation of the United Evangelical Church (1817). Schleiermacher* presided over the first united synod in Berlin, and on Reformation Day in 1817 he, representing the Reformed, and Philip Marheineke, representing the Lutherans, led a celebration of the Eucharist, with 93 ministers in attendance. But many Lutherans opposed the Union. Two crises soon surfaced. (1) While Schleiermacher wanted to leave room for both traditions, the king promoted a new prayer book, which both groups found objectionable; (2) while Schleiermacher championed government of the church by synod, the king wanted to function as "lay bishop." Synodal government ultimately prevailed; it was enshrined in law after the 1848 revolutions, decreed by Bismarck after 1871, and reinforced by the Weimar Republic.

Psalms, Book of, is Israel's normative collection of songs of praise* and prayer*. It contains materials borrowed from the ancient Near Eastern religious milieu as well as poems and songs that are "homegrown," or based on Israel's faith traditions. The Book of Psalms is constituted by a collage of smaller collections, some of which have been assembled by groups of temple singers such as the Levites* and the groups named after Asaph and Korah.

The two dominant themes of the collection, announced respectively in Ps 1 and 2, are the Torah* as the path to life and Davidic kingship as an expression of the rule of YHWH. The accent on Torah articulates an ordered life of obedience and promises of well-being for Torah keepers, and becomes a basis for prayers of complaint when the guarantees for Torah keepers do not materialize in life. The accent on kingship in the Psalms celebrates the centrality of the monarch to the right ordering of life and presents human kingship as a way in which Israel can survive in a dangerous world.

The Psalms have two primary functions. Some are essentially instructional, inculcating in the community a way of life as understood in Israelite faith. By contrast Psalms of cultic celebration are performative* and generate the liturgical reality of which they speak, especially the assertion of YHWH's kingship.

The primary genres of the Psalms are hymns* and laments. The hymns exuberantly affirm and "magnify" YHWH in acts of praise that are acts of self-abandon by Israel to the wonder of YHWH. Conversely, laments and complaints are prayers that voice Israel's legitimate entitlement to good treatment from YHWH. The interaction of hymn and lament gives the Psalter an existential tension that has been definitional for Jewish and Christian pastoral* care.

The several collections have been ordered into a final canonical form of five books. These are intended to be an imitation of the "Five Books of Moses" and provide a normative attestation to YHWH as the God of Israel and creator of the world. The imaginative poetry of the Psalter has continued to fuel the imagination of Jews and Christians who are preoccupied with the defining reality of YHWH.

WALTER BRUEGGEMANN

Psalter, a biblical book of Psalms*, or a book containing them, which in the Reformed* churches may take the form of metrical* Psalms.

Pseudepigrapha of the Old Testament. The phrase "Old Testament Pseudepigrapha" designates a varied body of Jewish and Christian literature. These writings contain stories about, and speeches ascribed to, figures known from the OT. They are not included in the Jewish or Christian canons* of Scripture*, but depend on biblical literature and on oral tradition. These writings vary immensely in their provenance (geographical and chronological), manner of transmission and preservation, size, form, style, subject matter, message, and purpose. Their authors are unknown, either because the writings were anonymous or because they were pseudonymous, i.e. bearing the name of the biblical figure with which they were mainly concerned (hence "Pseudepigrapha"). They have been transmitted almost exclusively by Christian groups, although a number are of Jewish origin. The best-known Pseudepigrapha include the Testament of Abraham*, the Assumption* of Moses, the Syriac Apocalypse of Baruch*, the Ethiopic Book of Enoch*, Fourth Ezra*, the Ascension of Isaiah, the Book of Jubilees*, the Life of Adam and Eve, Pseudo-Philo's Book of Biblical Antiquities, the Sibylline* Oracles, the Odes* of Solomon, the Psalms* of Solomon, and the Testaments* of the Twelve Patriarchs.

The collection of OT Pseudepigrapha is first and foremost a scholarly construct. NT scholars have been especially interested in these writings; they have regarded them as reflecting the cultural and religious background of the historical Jesus* and the Jesus movement. From these scholars' perspective, "Pseudepigrapha" stands for a specific corpus of literature: those anonymous, arguably Jewish writings not found in the Septuagint* that can be dated to no later than the 1st or 2nd c. CE. Taken together, they are regarded as a more or less coherent reservoir of parallels to the early Christian texts that are their principal object of study. This impression may have been strengthened by the collections of translations of Pseudepigrapha into modern languages (English: Charles, 1913; Charlesworth, 1983–1985; Sparks, 1984). These collections are helpful because the Pseudepigrapha were transmitted in such a wide variety of languages that no scholar could be expected to master them all. However, even a quick comparison of the various collections immediately reveals that in NT times the Pseudepigrapha were not compiled into a corpus as biblical books were. Modern editors and publishers decided which writings to include or not to include in collections of Pseudepigrapha. Nonetheless, many scholars include "the" Pseudepigrapha in their discussions of certain subjects as if they comprised a corpus distinct from, e.g., the Qumran* literature and later Jewish haggadic and Christian hagiographic traditions.

Modern collections of OT Pseudepigrapha are also potentially misleading because of their tidy arrangement in printed volumes. This easily gives a false impression of textual stability, whereas in reality many of these writings exist in a bewildering variety of versions and recensions without clear interrelations. Furthermore, the continuous change in form and content that occurred during their transmission has rendered the context and meaning of many passages obscure. If the reconstruction of the archetype of a particular writing proves possible, its text can usually be dated to no earlier than the 8th–9th c. in the Byzantine period. Occasionally, patristic references or quotations, or, very exceptionally, the finding of fragments among the Dead* Sea Scrolls, make it possible to date the *writing* of some pseudepigraphal texts to a much earlier period; one cannot presuppose that the medieval text is consistent with the original, since evidence shows that copyists took many liberties with such texts (in contrast, see Bible, Texts and Manuscripts).

These observations suggest that the interest of Christians in these writings was not merely antiquarian. Copyists tended to act as redactors, creatively adapting the writing they were dealing with to their own and their audiences' specific needs with an eye to admonishing or comforting their audiences through the lives and teachings of OT figures. This activity reflects a Christian interest in the OT and its main figures that contradicts the notion that the church was solely preoccupied with the figure of Christ. For these copyists/redactors, the lessons to be learned from the patriarchs and prophets were not subordinate and inferior to specifically Christian teachings. Thus much of the subject matter of the OT Pseudepigrapha concerns questions of an existential, cosmological, or ethical nature, e.g. the origin of death*, the number of heavens*, the orders of the angels*, the location of hell*, and how to be a good human being. These issues are commonly assumed to be relevant, although they are not specifically Christian.

Thus the aim of outlining the religious and cultural background of Jesus and the Jesus movement by establishing a corpus of Pseudepigrapha has failed. This scholarly project has uncovered a jumble of medieval Christian texts, instead of the clear and transparent picture of 1st-c. Judaism that was expected. In a more positive vein, the Pseudepigrapha of the OT are evidence of a continuing interest in the lives and teachings of OT figures, both in the Christian Church and in earlier and contemporary Jewish milieus. Paradoxically, the dynamic nature of the traditions concerning OT figures (as opposed to the fixed textual transmission of the Bible itself) demonstrates both that the writings which recorded them (adding, omitting, altering) did not claim authority for the letter of their texts, and that the issues addressed were central to their transmitters' worldview. Whereas the static text of the sacred writings may have enjoyed high respect and veneration, the dynamic texts of the Pseudepigrapha reflect the ways in which the people of old actually functioned in the context of everyday Jewish and Christian religion. JOHANNES TROMP

Pseudo-Clementine Literature. See CLEMENTINE LITERATURE.

Pseudo-Isidorean Decretals. See DECRETALS, FALSE (PSEUDO-ISIDOREAN).

Pseudonymity. A pseudonymous document is not written by the person whose name it bears, but is either written after the supposed author's death or during the supposed author's lifetime by someone not commissioned to do so. However, a work written with the help of an amanuensis (secretary) or one penned by a co-worker for a writer's later approval is not pseudonymous. A text written after the supposed author's death but incorporating his material (or the supposed author's views, as conceived of by the writer, a common school practice in the Hellenistic world) would be pseudonymous, unless the writer were fulfilling a request to prepare existing material for later circulation.

TERRY L. WILDER

Pseudo-Philo's Book of Biblical Antiquities, summary of biblical history from creation to Saul, enriched with apocryphal material, much of which it shares with Jewish haggadic tradition. Although it is often dated to the

1st c. CE, a much later date cannot be ruled out. Preserved only in the Western Christian Church, it is a prime example of the medieval continuity of Jewish and Christian narrative tradition. The ascription to Philo is secondary. **See also PSEUDEPIGRAPHA.** JOHANNES TROMP

Psychology and Theology. The relationship between theology and psychology depends on their respective definitions. An antireligious psychological paradigm (e.g. Sigmund Freud's or Albert Ellis's) necessarily conflicts with a neo-orthodox* theology (e.g. Barth's* or Reinhold Niebuhr's*). But a proto-theological psychological system (e.g. Carl Jung's or William James's) can readily engage in dialogue with a theology of mediation (e.g. Tillich's* or Schleiermacher's*). Or conflict can be muted and synthesis prevented if one follows the linguistic turn of analytic philosophy (Wittgenstein*) whereby theology and psychology are viewed as incommensurate and self-referential "language games" that share no terms or concepts.

Psychology and theology intersect through certain themes and issues.

1. Diagnoses of the Human Condition. For both psychology and theology, there is something not right about ordinary human life: it falls short, misses the mark, is estranged from its full nature. For most theologies, such estrangement is a part of the human condition. For most psychologies, it is contingent (on social conditioning, bad parenting, genetic malfunctioning), a disease to be treated. Freudians insist that human life is intrinsically conflicted: internally by incompatible wishes and fears, externally by the tension between desire and social constraint. Thus despite the fact that they have entirely different bases, Freud's view of human nature is close to an Augustinian* doctrine of original* sin*. By contrast humanistic psychologies (e.g. Carl Rogers's and Abraham Maslow's) affirmed the essential perfectibility of human nature; even their arch-antagonist, B. F. Skinner, concurred that human nature could be conditioned into perfection by rewards and punishments. Christian theologies could be organized along a similar continuum.

2. Norms. As a discipline closely associated with modernity, psychology proposes norms of health and sickness, maturity and immaturity that originally shared modernity's valuation of autonomy* and self-realization, and eschewed or minimized dependency. Thus those schools most indebted to modernity (both Freudian psychoanalysis and its humanistic antagonists) are strongly suspicious of dependency. Most theologies insist that we are dependent on a divine source or reality outside of ourselves (see Heteronomy), a vertical dimension foreign to psychology.

3. The Nature of Religious Language. A literalistic* interpretation of Christian speech tends to preclude a constructive engagement with psychology, whereas symbolic* and analogical* models of theological language, for which language works on many different levels, facilitate such engagement.

Historically, when the discipline of psychology began at the height of modern rationalism* and scientism* (late 19th–early 20th c.), psychologists tended to regard theological beliefs as pathological and emotionally immature – a reductionist attitude that treated theological beliefs exclusively as psychological processes.

After World War II, a more open dialogue between theologians and psychologists (including Rollo May, Paul Tillich, and Erich Fromm) developed, using existentialism* as a common language. The psychology involved in discussions with theology was clinically oriented, primarily post-Freudian psychoanalytic psychology and secondarily Jungian depth psychology, but not experimental psychology.

This postwar, very academic dialogue eventually petered out. Psychologists and theologians treated theological claims primarily as cognitive constructs to be debated and affirmed or denied, and psychology as a system of propositions about human nature. This proved to be a dead end. Terms were clarified and issues seen differently, but eventually people agreed, disagreed, or agreed to disagree.

Three new trends have emerged. (1) A dialogue has developed among those who see both psychology and Christianity (and other religions) as sets of practices rather than as propositional systems. (2) Clinical psychoanalysis has moved from the exclusive individualism of the Freudian, Jungian, and humanistic paradigms to embrace a more relational model with obvious resonances with the relational theological models of Schleiermacher, Buber*, Tillich, and Process* and Feminist* theologies*. Here dependency, even on a divine source, is not necessarily problematic. (3) New subdisciplines of psychology, rooted in the experimental traditions (e.g. cognitive neuroscience and evolutional psychology) have tended once again to approach theological material with reductionist attitudes.

A dialogue with psychology requires a theology which insists that religious truth is mediated through human psychological, neurological, social, cultural, and historical processes. Theologies, like neo-orthodoxy, that eschew such mediation and insist on transcendental truths inevitably find little in common with psychology. For psychology, discussions with theology require the epistemic* humility to recognize that a psychological account of religious phenomena, however complete *on its own terms*, is not a complete account.

Psychoanalytic psychology suggests that theological beliefs are not purely cognitive but rather involve potent affects, strongly held sensibilities about self and world, deeply felt wishes and fears. Beliefs are carriers of profound, early experiences and developmental processes. To fully understand them involves comprehending more than their cognitive content. Attempts to inculcate or transform a person's beliefs by purely conscious means (preaching, theological lecturing, reading, or debating) seem slightly naive.

Psychology is not simply relevant to the praxis of pastoral* care. It shares common concerns with theology and illuminates connections between theological positions and theologians' individual histories and personalities.

James William Jones

Puerto Rico. Christianity arrived in Boriquén (one of the three Great Antilles in the Caribbean*, east of Cuba* and the Dominican* Republic) when Christopher Columbus claimed it with his sword for the Roman Catholic sovereigns of Spain during his second voyage (1493). During the Spanish colonial period, the Roman Catholic Church, as the state church, was led by poorly trained priests. Consequently, Catholicism took form as a popular* religion among peasants, slaves*, and free slaves working on sugar plantations – most of the population – even as the Church framed the formal Hispanic culture of the island, especially among the upper classes. An intellectual and political elite was influenced by the Enlightenment* and liberalism during the 19th c., and antagonism between the Catholic Church and liberals developed. The Holy See* condemned the liberal principles and institutions; liberals were alienated from the Church.

Three hundred years after Columbus's arrival, the USA, a Protestant nation, invaded the island during the Cuban–Spanish–American War (1898). After the war, the Catholic Church was reorganized according to Roman Catholic models in the USA: many Spanish priests returned to Spain; the Catholic bishops and the religious orders (in charge of the Catholic parochial schools) came from the USA. Meanwhile, the pope granted independence to the dioceses so that they might join the Latin American synods. After the US invasion, the Protestant missions (Adventist*, Baptist, Christian* Church, Congregationalist*, Episcopalian*, Methodist, Lutheran) soon established churches in every town, and were followed by Pentecostals* (1916) and many other groups (including Charismatics*). By 2008 the overall Protestant membership (including that of all independent churches, among which are the Charismatic churches) is said to have reached 35% of the population (with only 50% remaining Roman Catholics), taking into account both the Puerto Ricans living on the island (c4 million) and those living in the USA (about the same number; frequently commuting, as US citizens, although the island is not a state of the USA).

For the first 30 years (1899–1930), the US Catholic bishops and Protestant missionaries participated in the North Americanization of Puerto Rico. But with the economic crisis of the 1930s, nationalist groups often seeking independence emerged and strongly challenged Americanization. In this vein, Catholic and Protestant theologians sought to demythologize* the "providentialist" understanding of the US political presence as they developed theologies affirming the Puerto Rican national identity and taking into account the interests of Puerto Ricans. Following a decade of US political repression against the nationalists, a new class of moderate but populist professionals and intellectuals organized a coalition of rural and urban workers that were in control of political power from 1940 to 1968. The resulting modernization of the island encouraged the development of a large network of Roman Catholic private schools and fostered the social mobility of Protestants from the rural and lower classes into the new middle classes.

During the 1960s, problems associated with the growing urbanization and young people's political resentment against the USA and the US military presence in Puerto Rico (as they were drafted to fight during the Vietnam War) led Roman Catholic and Protestant youth to join the political manifestations against all forms of imperialism. Catholics were motivated by Vatican* II and by the Medellín* conference of

Latin American bishops (CELAM*), and Protestants were influenced by the theology of social responsibility of the World* Student Christian Federation, the Latin American approach of the Unión Latinoamericana de Juventudes Evangélicas, and the ecumenical theology of the World* Council of Churches. The radicalization of Christian students, seminarians, priests, and young pastors led to serious conflicts with the older generations and church authorities in both Catholic and Protestant churches. While the proposals and actions of the radical young generation were strongly repressed, their contribution to the life of the churches had and continues to have a lasting influence. After 1970 the Pentecostal* and Charismatic* churches multiplied and influenced the mainline Protestant churches. In the early 21st c., these last two movements constituted the main focus of theological reflection and pastoral attention, led especially by Liberation* theologians and biblical scholars, such as Luis Rivera-Pagán.

SAMUEL SILVA-GOTAY

Pulcheria (399–453), Eastern empress (450–53). Older sister of Theodosius II and a powerful figure in Constantinople, she supported the condemnation of Nestorius* (428) and the restoration of John* Chrysostom's bones (438), and opposed Eutyches* (449). When Theodosius died (450), she chose his successor, Marcian, whom she married. She encouraged the convening of the Council of Chalcedon* (451), which reversed the actions of the Second Council of Ephesus* (449).

Punishment. See ATONEMENT; DAMNATION; HELL; JUDGMENT; PURGATORY.

Purgatory, in Roman Catholicism, the place where, in the interim between an individual's death* and the general resurrection*, the soul* of a person to be saved expiates venial* sins* or mortal* sins* after contrition* and confession* (but not satisfaction). Purgatory was considered to be a place only from c1170 and was dogmatically defined only in 1254. References to "purgatorial fire" in "the punishments" or the "places of punishment" appear in vision literature, where frightening landscapes present some eternal and some temporary punishments. Believers perform actions called suffrages (prayers, masses, alms), entreating saints to intercede for suffering* souls* and so accelerate expiation. The granting of indulgences* and papal declarations occasioned a quantification and even a monetization of progress through purgatory. The bull *Unigenitus* (1343) posited an infinite "treasury of merits" that Christ* had "invested" and that popes could "expend" for the dead. The most venal excesses provoked widespread protest, culminating in Luther's* "95 Theses Against Indulgences" (1517). The sale of indulgences helped shape Protestant opposition to "works theology." Defenders of purgatory claim to find legitimation in Matt 12:31–32 (forgiveness in the world to come), 1 Cor 3:11–15 ("purified as if by fire"), and 2 Macc 12:41–46 (prayers to absolve dead soldiers of sin*). **See also DAMNATION; HELL; JUDGMENT.**

ALAN E. BERNSTEIN

Purification of Mary, feast on February 2 that is also known as the Presentation* of Christ and Candlemas*.

Puritans, Puritanism, militant movement to further reform the Protestant Church of England (see Anglicanism Cluster: Anglican Communion and Its Theology) and to shape a model church and society in New England. Named "Puritans" by opponents because of their extreme efforts to "purify" the church, by the later 1600s they took pride in the name. Dubbed by modern historians "the hotter sort of Protestants" and by themselves "the godly," Puritans sought to promote an ardent Christian piety and a Calvinist* or Reformed* theology.

In England Puritanism began as nonconformity in matters of ritual and ceremony during the reign of Elizabeth* I (1558–1603), focused on preaching and pastoral work during the reign of James* I (1603–25), became more oppositional after 1625 when Charles I and Archbishop William Laud* promoted anti-Calvinism and sacramental ceremony, and came to power during Oliver Cromwell's* rule (1649–58). After the restoration of the monarchy in 1660, many Puritan clergy were ejected from the Church of England. Thereafter, they were also called "Dissenters*," and their presbyterian and congregationalist* (independent) meetings were illegal until the Toleration* Act (1689). Many Puritans, led by William Bradford, John Winthrop, Thomas Hooker, and John Cotton, went to New England (1620s and 1630s) to found churches consonant with their ideals. But tensions over Anne Hutchinson's* supposed antinomianism*, baptism* (the "half-way covenant"), and toleration were disruptive. Later Cotton Mather bemoaned the declension from their original ideals.

Believing that the Bible should be the authority for church practice (see Scripture) and attuned to the pattern of the Reformed* churches on the Continent (e.g. Geneva*, where some later Puritan leaders were exiles during the reign of Roman Catholic Queen Mary), Puritans wanted to simplify worship by purging the church of surviving aspects of medieval Catholic ritual and ceremony such as eucharistic vestments*. Many, following Thomas Cartwright, rejected the government of the church by bishops, preferring a presbyterian system with authority vested in the parochial clergy or a congregational system stressing the fellowship and self-determination of local congregations. Congregationalism* prevailed briefly during Cromwell's rule in England and throughout the history of colonial New England (where it was codified in the Cambridge Platform of 1648). A few congregationalist Puritans known as Separatists thought the Church of England so unreformed that they formed illegal congregations outside of it, some migrating to the Netherlands, such as the congregation led by Robert Browne, author of *Reformation without Tarrying for Any* (1582). The settlers of Plymouth in New England were Separatist in inspiration; Roger Williams* was a thoroughgoing Separatist who denounced the union of church and state.

The heart of Puritanism was a piety and theology of God's grace* and of holiness of life. Puritans emphasized preaching, spiritual counsel, restriction of the Sabbath* (for them, Sunday) to religious exercises, a scrupulous morality, and an introspective piety concerned with assurance of salvation*, producing notable devotional writing from such authors and preachers as Richard Greenham, Richard Sibbes, Richard Baxter*, and Joseph Alleine. Puritan theologians such as William Perkins*, William Ames*, and John Owen developed a theology of grace* that stressed predestination*, outlined the steps of salvation* and the Christian life, and expressed these teachings in the biblical framework of covenant*. Puritan piety also entailed a concern for the Christianization of society.

Puritanism's impact has extended to the present. It helped shape such British Protestant denominations as Baptist*, Congregationalist*, and Presbyterian*; influenced thinking about the spiritual life in Protestantism in Europe; bequeathed its understanding of the conversion* experience to later Evangelicalism*; produced classics of Christian literature, including John Milton's* *Paradise Lost* and John Bunyan's* *Pilgrim's Progress*; legitimated the right to resist tyrannical government; and left a reformist and revolutionary spirit to posterity. **See also** **UNITED KINGDOM; UNITED STATES.**

DEWEY D. WALLACE, JR.

Pusey, Edward Boverie (1800–82), educated at Christ Church, Oxford, elected a fellow of Oriel (1823), appointed Regius Professor of Hebrew at Christ Church (1828) just as he published his defense of the new German theology and historical critical studies. Pusey, the acknowledged leader of the Oxford* Movement even before Newman's* reception as a Roman Catholic (1845), played an important role in the *Library of the Fathers* series (translations of major patristic authors, from 1838), made significant contributions to *Tracts for the Times* on fasting* (1831) and baptism* (1836), and supported the foundation of Anglican sisterhoods. His sermon on the Holy Eucharist*, defending the doctrine of the real presence* (1843), was condemned by the university. He preached in support of private confession and priestly absolution (1846), and helped to rally opposition to the Gorham decision by the Privy Council (by which a priest, condemned by his bishop for holding a heretical view on baptismal regeneration, won on appeal; 1850) and to the liberal historical and theological positions enunciated by Anglican liberal priests in *Essays and Reviews* (1860). His *Eirenicon* (1864) initiated a published conversation with Newman and others on various contended aspects of Roman Catholic doctrine and the possibility of the Anglican Church union with Rome. PETER C. ERB

Q

Q, a Collection of Sayings Ascribed to Jesus, identified in 1838 as the second "source" (German, *Quelle*; hence the nickname "Q") that Matthew and Luke used in addition to Mark in their redaction* of their respective gospels (see Synoptic Gospels). This source consisted of sayings of Jesus (with some narratives). Yet no copy of this source has ever been found. Scholars reconstructed it on the basis of the sayings that are found in both Matthew and Luke but not in Mark. Q has come to be a widely accepted explanation by modern scholarship for the parallel sayings in Matthew and Luke that are not found in Mark; alternative hypotheses have not gained widespread acceptance.

The sayings in Q – e.g. those found both in the Sermon on the Mount (Matt 5–7) and in parallel passages in Luke – could not have been derived from Mark (since they are not in Mark), but are found in Matthew and Luke in much the same order and wording. This observation leads to the conclusion that Q was written in Greek. What were the actual sayings of Jesus in Q? This needs to be established since the wordings in Matthew and Luke often differ. This is done in two steps. First, the distinctive grammar, vocabulary, style, and theology of Matthew and Luke can be established from their way of editing materials taken from the Gospel of Mark. Second, it then becomes possible to reconstruct the original wording of Q by choosing the formulation that does not include the distinctive "fingerprints" of one or the other gospel writer – the original formulation being found at times in Matthew and at other times in Luke. There might have been sayings in Q cited in only one of these Gospels, because either Matthew or Luke omitted them; yet it is difficult to discern whether or not sayings found in only one of the Gospels were actual parts of Q. Thus proposals for including such sayings in the reconstructed Q have not gained wide support. The discovery in 1945 of the Gospel of Thomas*, a collection of 114 sayings ascribed to Jesus, has led to the recognition that Q was a "saying Gospel," like Thomas, in contrast to the "narrative Gospels," such as Matthew, Mark, Luke, and John.

The primary importance of Q is that it contains the most reliable collection of sayings that go back to Jesus himself (see Jesus, Quest for the Historical). There are later accretions in Q, as there are in the Gospels, such as woes pronounced on the Jewish leadership, reflecting the lack of success of the Jewish Christian mission with which Q was associated, in contrast to the Gentile Christian mission of Paul. A reference to the fall of Jerusalem in Q (Luke 13:34–35) puts the date of the final redaction around 70 CE.

JAMES M. ROBINSON

Quadragesimo Anno. See SOCIAL ENCYCLICALS; SUBSIDIARITY, PRINCIPLE OF.

Quadrilateral. See LAMBETH QUADRILATERAL; WESLEYAN QUADRILATERAL.

Quakers. See FRIENDS, RELIGIOUS SOCIETY OF.

Quaker Worship. From its origins in mid-17th-c. revolutionary England, Quaker worship consisted of a respectful silent waiting for the leadings of the Holy* Spirit, without ritual, sacrament, program, or human leadership. This "unprogrammed" approach remained dominant until the last half of the 19th c.

Rooted in the assumption that "Christ has come to teach his people himself," Quakers believed that during silent worship God's Spirit would descend on his people and lead them to minister in a meeting where all, children, men, and women, were equal. Gradually, through a collective agreement of the meeting, some men and women were recorded as ministers*, but they required no special training or education; the only expectation was that those so designated were favored and would often preach or pray. There was no pulpit or rostrum, only a raised area, or "gallery," where the ministers sat. Others, designated "elders*," were responsible for general oversight of the ministry and had regular joint meetings with the ministers. Sometimes, meetings might go for years in total silence, while at other times, the Spirit might lead others to minister often. The women sat on one side of the plain, unadorned meeting room, the men on the other. There were no sacraments or formal religious education.

By the late 1860s, in the Midwestern USA, traditional Quaker worship was being influenced by the spread of revivalism*, and a pattern of evangelical preaching emerged, with mourner's benches, altar calls, and gospel songs. By the 1890s, pastors were employed by these meetings, with a few allowing or encouraging baptism or the "Supper." Some meetings included the use of hymnals and musical instruments, as well as choirs, in their formally organized services. Sometimes, there were periods of "waiting" during these services, which offered worshippers a chance to testify. Distinctive Quaker practices, such as wearing plain clothing, virtually disappeared. Sunday schools became a part of the meetings, making them all but indistinguishable from Methodist or Baptist churches. Pastors often co-pastored with their wives; less frequently women held pastorates, and by the end of the 20th c., some theological training was expected, if not required; two or three Quaker seminaries were built in the USA.

Thanks to missionary activities, the pastoral approach predominates in the world today; yet unprogrammed meetings also exist, primarily in Europe and parts of the USA and Canada.

H. LARRY INGLE

Quartodecimans, early Christians who observed Easter* as the Christian Passover* on the 14th day of the moon, in the month of Nisan. While the Church of Rome celebrated Easter on the following Sunday, this older tradition continued in Asia Minor, and it was defended by Polycarp*, who claimed that it had been handed down from John* the Apostle, and by Irenaeus*. While most churches eventually adopted the Roman practice, a separate church that maintained the older tradition continued into the 5th c.

Quebec. The brand of Roman Catholicism that took root along the banks of the St. Lawrence River, the birthplace of French settlement in North America (the first priest arrived in 1608) was similar to that found in contemporary France: a religion operating under state regulation but animated by the ideals of the Council of Trent* (1545–63). The first bishop of Quebec, François de Laval; the mystic and teacher Marie de l'Incarnation (Marie Guyard*); the nursing sister Catherine de Saint Augustin; the Jesuit* fathers, both missionaries and explorers; the founders of Montreal (Maisonneuve, Jeanne Mance, Marguerite Bourgeois): all these prominent figures of the colony were deeply committed to the 17th-c. Catholic* Renewal. All were looking for a new world where they could live in harmony with their convictions. Well ensconced by the time of the British Conquest (1759), this Catholicism was Ultramontane*, even though the secular elites were both royalist and Gallican. Somewhat paradoxically, this characteristic expedited the transition to English rule. Pragmatic despite their staunchly anti-papist stance, the new masters of the French colony feared not so much the faraway pope as the French and American Revolutions and thus granted the Roman Catholic Church liberties that would have been impossible in England.

Early in the 19th c., the Church became impoverished as the French aristocrats and merchants returned to France. It was now serving a dispersed population with a small and poorly educated Canadian clergy. By the mid-19th c., however, a Catholic revival once again took hold, with an exploding demand for European religious*, nuns, and brothers. Catholic organizations developed a network of educational and health institutions. Given the sustained growth of the Church, which still sought direction from Rome rather than from any other center of power, the Province of Quebec earned a strong reputation for being a Catholic civilization, if not the "priest-ridden province" mocked by Anglo-Protestant satirists of the day. For almost a century, the Catholic Church challenged the English bourgeoisie and, later, the Canadian elite who held the reins of industry and commerce. It was the only organization capable of providing a framework for the identity of the French-speaking people under English domination. Thus the Church became a real political actor, controlling community life and addressing the population's quests for meaning.

The years following World War II greatly changed the situation. A relatively new urban middle class, produced by Roman Catholic institutions, was now in a position to demand its autonomy, both from English Canada and from the Church. It adopted the ideals and the myths of modernity that characterize the North American way of life. In the 1960s, the "quiet revolution" successfully challenged the traditional place occupied by Catholicism and transformed the question of identity into a political one that no longer needed to be justified on the basis of religion. In fewer than 40 years, Quebec French culture became one of the most secularized* in the Western world; rates of church attendance fell to less than 10% in the cities, and the new generations became less and less familiar with the tradition.

One may now properly speak of a post-Catholic society in Quebec. In fact, participation in Church activities, knowledge of the creeds, and commitment to moral issues seem to be less prevalent among the French-speaking Catholic population of Quebec than among other groups in Canadian society, including Catholics who speak other languages and French-speaking citizens of other parts of Canada, where confessional identification is still tied up with the memory of a cultural history or ethnic origin.

Traditionally, Roman Catholics and Protestants were as estranged from one another as were the dominant cultural groups, separated by language, way of life, and contrasting visions of the world. Now, ecumenism*, at the level of church leadership at least, has developed new and original opportunities for dialogue. Despite a decline in power, the Christian churches have demonstrated new modes of vitality since the last decades of the 20th c. Pastoral* and social* projects have been created, sometimes in cooperation with other vital forces within society, that challenge dominant social policies. The Catholic Church and other Christian denominations no longer hold sway in contemporary culture and have become deeply concerned with the question of modes of admissibility and creativity of Christianity in the secular world. Perhaps more radically than anywhere else, Christianity in Quebec is now confronting one of the most fundamental challenges of the modern contemporary world: how can Christianity become meaningful in a society that claims to have no need of its traditional ideals, morals, and comprehensive system of meaning? **See also POST-CHRISTIAN THOUGHT; SCIENCE AND CHRISTIAN THEOLOGY; SECULARISM AND SECULARIZATION; SECULARIZATION AND DESECULARIZATION IN EUROPE AND NORTH AMERICA.**

RAYMOND LEMIEUX

Queer, a word sometimes used pejoratively for persons known to engage, or suspected of engaging, in homosexual practice. Now the word functions primarily as a rallying point for those who affirm and defend such practice or contest the assumed normativity of heterosexuality. Queer interpretation challenges the assumption that biblical texts must be read in ways that conform to certain normative views about sex, gender, and sexuality*. **See also BIBLE INTERPRETATION CLUSTER: IN NORTH AMERICA AND WESTERN EUROPE: QUEER.**

Quietism, a form of religious devotion emphasizing passive contemplation and withdrawal from thought, will, and the senses. It advocates contemplative* prayer, abnegation of the self, union with the divine will, inner repose, acceptance of suffering and persecution, and disinterested or pure love*. In its orthodox form, Quietism was part of the mystic* tradition (e.g. that of John* of the Cross). In the context of the Catholic* Renewal (Counter Reformation) and Jesuit–Jansenist* controversies, Quietism in its popular form was accused of neglecting external disciplines of devotion and acts of charity. **See also FÉNELON, FRANÇOIS DE SALIGNAC DE LA MOTHE; GUYON, JEANNE BOUVIER DE LA MOTHE; MOLINOS, MIGUEL DE.**

PATRICIA A. WARD

Quinisext Council (or Trullan Synod) of Eastern bishops (692) met in the domed *trullus* of the imperial palace (thus "Trullan") to complete the disciplinary canons of the fifth (553) and sixth (680–81) ecumenical* councils (thus "Quinisext" [fifth–sixth]). Its decisions about clerical marriage, matrimony, ecclesiastical dress and ordination, and other issues are authoritative in the Eastern Church but were recognized only indirectly by Pope Hadrian I (772–95).

Quiroga, Vasco de (Tata Vasco) (1470?–1565), Dominican priest born in Spain, visitor (inspector) of New Spain (Mexico*), pacificator of the Chichimecs of Michoacán, one of the five judges (*oidores*) in the "Audencia" that governed New Spain (1531–35), the first bishop of Michoacán (1538–65). Inspired by Thomas More's* *Utopia* and its idealistic vision of a tolerant society, he founded the self-governing San Nicolas School in Pátzcuaro and created towns where Chichimecs, Purépecha, and other native peoples lived in security, were taught religion, developed arts and crafts industries, and practiced self-government.

MARÍA ALICIA PUENTE LUTTEROTH and ELIZABETH JUDD

Qumran, site near the northwest shore of the Dead Sea, noteworthy for its substantial archeological remains and the hundreds of fragmentary manuscripts, the Dead* Sea Scrolls, found in caves in nearby cliffs. Although the Qumran ruins were first described as the remains of a fortress or a villa, the contents of major scrolls and the dating of the pottery in the caves, which parallels that of pottery in the ruins, indicate that Qumran housed a community of Essenes* between c100 BCE and 68 CE, when the army of Titus destroyed it during the First Jewish Revolt.

GEORGE W. E. NICKELSBURG

Qur'an and Christianity. The Qur'an has many Jewish elements, as well as numerous outspoken references to the Christian tradition. The latter can be divided into the critical appropriation of stories about Jesus, his mother, Mary (the only woman to be mentioned by name in the Qur'an), and his disciples, and statements about the condition of contemporary Christians.

Of the nearly 6,500 verses in the Qur'an, some 100 deal with the story of Jesus. Two longer and partly overlapping episodes tell the story of the Annunciation, the virgin birth, and the early years of Jesus. Jesus is characterized as a prophet* who reinforced the Torah but also relaxed some regulations. His preaching evoked protest and unbelief among the Jews, who tried to kill him on the cross. That was their plan, but God had another plan: Jesus was not crucified (another man who looked like him was), but was raised by God to heaven to be with God (Qur'an 4:157–58). The followers of Jesus are called "Nasara," a term used by Jews in the Talmud* but also in Mesopotamia/Iraq* (East Syrian) by outsiders. The term "people of the Book" refers in the Qur'an to Jews and Christians.

Some passages in the Qur'an show a preference for Christians over Jews. The best known is Qur'an 5:82: "Of all men you will find the Jews and those who associate others with Allah in His divinity to be the most hostile to those who believe; and you will surely find that of all people they who say: We are Christians, are closest to feel affection for those who believe. This is because there are worshipful priests and monks among them, and because they are not arrogant." Qur'an 9:31–4, however, blames rabbis and monks equally because they are taken as "Lords beside Allah" and "they wrongfully devour men's possessions and hinder people from the way of Allah." Qur'an 57:27 refers to the monastic* life characteristic of Christians in a mildly critical way: "And monasticism they invented – We did not prescribe it for them – only seeking the good pleasure of God; but they observed it not as it should be observed." Christians are blamed for saying that Jesus is the Son* of God and for referring to God as "Three" (see Trinity*) instead of one (4:171) – the "Three" being interpreted as Allah, Jesus, and Mary (5:116). Christians are often blamed for conflicts and differences of opinion. They are seen as proselytizers: "Neither the Jews nor the Christians will be pleased with you unless you follow their religion" (2:120). Believing Muslims are commanded not to take Jews or Christians as their associates or friends (5:51).

According to Qur'an 61:6, Jesus predicted the coming of a successor: "Jesus son of Mary said: Children of Israel, I am indeed the messenger of God to you, confirming the Torah that is before me, and giving good tidings of a messenger who shall come after me, whose name shall be Ahmad. Then, when he brought them the clear signs, they said: This is a manifest sorcery."

The oldest evidence of the text of the Qur'an can be found in the mosaic inscriptions of the Dome of the Rock (constructed 692, 60 years after Muhammad's death). Some of these inscriptions are taken from Qur'an 19:33–36. They praise Jesus, son of Mary. But they also warn believers that "[i]t is not for God to take a son unto him." It is this mixture of admiration for and warning about Jesus and Christians that is consistently found in the Qur'an.

Karel Steenbrink

R

Rabanus Maurus (c780–856), German scholar and theologian, "preceptor of Germany." A child oblate* in Fulda*, he studied under Alcuin* and then became a teacher (818–24) and abbot (824–42) of Fulda, writing treatises on the arts, canon* law, and the clergy, and commentaries on Scripture. When his activities were disrupted by dynastic struggles after the death of Louis* the Pious, he retired to write an encyclopedic work on the world, human life, and Christian faith. As archbishop of Mainz (847–56), he was closely involved in the condemnation of Gottschalk*, ironically a child oblate like himself.

Rabbi, Rabboni (Heb "my teacher," "my highest teacher," respectively), forms of direct address to Jewish teachers, especially in the Pharisaic* tradition; later these became third-person titles. Jesus is addressed as "rabbi" (Mark 9:5, 11:21, 14:45, par.) and "rabboni" (Mark 10:51; John. 20:16).

Rabbula (c350–35), bishop of Edessa (412–35), metropolitan of Osrhoene. After the Council of Ephesus* (431), he became a leading opponent of Nestorianism* and Theodore* of Mopsuestia, allying himself with Cyril* of Alexandria, whose works he translated into Syriac. He opposed the Antiochene christological* position. His opponent, Ibas*, succeeded him.

Rachel, younger daughter of Laban, with whom Jacob fell in love at the well near Haran. Through deception Jacob was married first to the older daughter Leah* and was able to marry Rachel only after seven years. Rachel was the mother of Joseph* and Benjamin*; she died while giving birth to the latter (Gen 35:16–20). Allegorically*, Rachel is considered the higher wisdom, Leah the lower.

---

1) Introductory Entry

Racism and Christianity: Ethnocentrism. Generally understood, the term "racism" designates prejudice, bias, discrimination, violence*, and terror directed at persons or groups solely on the basis of what are perceived to be inferior traits, characteristics, manners, customs, or other cultural markers such as language, dress, or skin color.

Ethnocentrism mobilizes the "racial superiority" of a dominant hegemonic group and turns it against a distinct ethnic group perceived as inferior, even within the same geographic region, as in, e.g., the European conquerors' treatment of Native Americans, Nazi Germany's "final solution" (see Holocaust, Jewish [or Shoah]), and the Rwandan* and Kosovo genocides.

In Western culture, racism takes the form of white supremacy over people of color, of bifurcating race relations between "white" and "black." Racism as the ideology* of white supremacy has historically defined relationships between Europeans and Africans and their descendants since the time of their initial contact and the conquest of Africans, and it has been supported by the mobilization of Christian missionary activities against African people in European colonization and imperialism (see Colonialism and Imperialism and Christian Theology). Perhaps in no greater geographic area has this type of racism been more insidiously sedimented and mobilized in race relationships than in the USA through the transatlantic slave trade, chattel slavery*, Jim Crow legislation, lynching, the Ku Klux Klan organizations, and the use of juridical and penal systems to regulate and subjugate black bodies. The effects of these acts of white supremacy continue to structurally influence forms of prejudice, bias, discrimination, and physical, institutional, and psychological violence and terror among people of African descent in the USA.

Racism, whether that of white supremacy or ethnocentrism, not only manifests itself in the personal attitudes and personalities of individuals. It is also systematic and institutional, permeating the structures of groups, communities, nations, and societies throughout the world. Moreover, racism does not always manifest itself in overt patterns and practices of violence and terror by judicial, penal, governmental, military, educational, and Christian churches. It may also manifest itself as a banality of evil* in the form of demeaning and denigrating epithets, slurs, wit, and jokes directed at or referring to African Americans. It is so deeply entrenched, preserved, cultivated, and enacted in the everyday practices of people and groups that no social institutions, not even the Christian churches in the USA, are free of its power to distort interhuman encounters.

Whether as ethnocentrism or white supremacy, racism is idolatry*. In the USA, it raises white power and privilege to the status of the divine, which determines the worth, value, and dignity of all who fall under its power. Many believed that racism could be eliminated through progressive liberal reforms, propagation of the Social* Gospel, and the marshaling of religious forces in the fight for civil* rights and the efforts of the Civil Rights Movement to overhaul social systems that by law protected the lynching of blacks and racial discrimination against blacks in work, housing, and all other social spheres – as if racism were only an ideology. Many believed that racism could be eliminated by people of goodwill, black and white – as if racism were only a matter of personal attitudes and individual personalities. Yet racism as idolatry exhibits a permanency that makes it the cultural logic of race relations in the USA.

The Christian churches must accept their share of responsibility for the endurance of racism. Christians are called everywhere to make their greatest efforts to expose the violence and terror spawned by racism and its demonic* power to distort interhuman relations. Where racism is masked as white supremacy or ethnocentrism, people of goodwill are called to discipline themselves personally and as communities in order to be ever on the alert for the manifestations and operations of power of this idolatry in their own lives.

VICTOR ANDERSON

---

2) A Sampling of Contextual Views and Responses

Racism and Christianity in Africa. The ideology* of racism that shaped the policy of apartheid ("separate development") was formulated and justified theologically by the Dutch Reformed Church of South Africa. It was the official doctrine on race relations in South Africa until apartheid was legally abolished (1994). At this time, the democratic Republic of South* Africa was established after a long struggle for liberation supported by campaigners both within and outside the country. According to the doctrine of apartheid, the people of African descent were cursed and condemned to be "hewers of wood and drawers of water" in the service of the people of European descent. This doctrine was biblically defended by reference to the "curse" of Ham (Noah's third son) by his father in Gen 9:24–27.

The World* Alliance of Reformed Churches in the declaration by its General Council (Ottawa, Canada, 1982) proclaimed that this abuse of the Bible to justify racial oppression was a heresy*. This declaration reads in part, "The gospel

Racism and Christianity in Africa

confronts racism, which is in its very essence a form of idolatry*. Racism fosters a false sense of supremacy, it denies the common humanity of believers, and it denies Christ's reconciling, humanizing work. It systematizes oppression, domination and injustice. As such the struggle against racism, wherever it is found, in overt and covert forms, is a responsibility laid upon the church by the gospel of Jesus Christ in every country and society."

The World* Council of Churches, following a mandate of the Fourth Assembly (1968, Uppsala, Sweden), established the Programme to Combat Racism (1970), which organized a consultation (1975) entitled "Racism in Theology and Theology Against Racism." This report outlines the contexts in which racism thrives, indicating that racism is present whenever:

- Persons, even before they are born, because of their race, are assigned to a group severely limited in their freedom of movement, their choice of work, their places of residence and so on.
- Groups of people, because of their race, are denied effective participation in the political process, and so are compelled (often by force) to obey the edicts of governments which they were allowed to have no part in choosing.
- Racial groups within a nation are excluded from the normal channels for gaining economic power, through denial of educational opportunities and entry into occupational groups.
- The policies of a nation-state ensure benefits for that nation from the labor of racial groups (migrant or otherwise), while at the same time denying to such groups commensurate participation in the affairs of the nation-state.
- The identity of persons is denigrated through stereotyping of racial and ethnic groups in textbooks, cinema, mass media, interpersonal relations, and other ways.
- People are denied equal protection of the law, because of race, and when constituted authorities of the state use their powers to protect the interests of the dominant group at the expense of the powerless.
- Groups or nations continue to profit from regional and global structures that are historically related to racist presuppositions and actions.

Racism in Africa has been justified through the selective and literalist reading of specific Bible texts to suit the interests of the perpetrators. In particular, Christian descendants of the people who invaded Africa and the Americas from Europe used selected Bible texts to justify their conquest and oppression of the peoples they had conquered. The doctrine of "chosen* people" as narrated in the OT was interpreted to refer to the invading conquerors. Racism ignores and negates the doctrine that all human beings are created in the image* of God. Furthermore, racism portrays Jesus* as a Caucasian (see Christologies Cluster), particularly in the indoctrination of the oppressed, and in the art, drama, and music used for the purposes of subjugation. Racism has been further entrenched by means of individualistic expressions of Christianity (see Autonomy), which inhibit social mobilization and resistance by racially oppressed Christians. Martin Luther King*, Jr., and Archbishop Desmond Tutu are two of the most renowned church leaders who rose to prominence because of their campaigns against racism in the USA and South Africa, respectively.

It is worthwhile heeding the challenge articulated by the WCC report cited earlier: "Discovering the sin* of racism with all its implications and choosing the risky road of repentance-action, these are two aspects of one and the same process. It is a process which involves individuals and groups in the whole of their life and challenges their entire pattern of behavior. But it is also a process which involves and challenges the Church of Christ in a pre-eminent way since there the message of forgiveness is spelt out and articulated as explicitly as possible. In this process we are driven to rethink our ideas as to the nature of the Church* and to recover the meaning and implications of its original mission."

JESSE NDWIGA KANYUA MUGAMBI

Racism and Christianity in Asia. Asia is a continent in which multitudes of racial, ethnic, and cultural groups exist, frequently in tension. Pride in their racial heritage is characteristic of Asian people. Often this pride breeds contempt and hatred toward people outside their own group. These negative feelings are reflected in the social and political spheres and affect the economic process as well.

A definition of racism proposed by the Uppsala Assembly of World Council of Churches (1968) is helpful for understanding the role of racism in Asia: "By racism we mean ethnocentric pride in one's own racial group and preference for the distinctive characteristics of that group; belief that these characteristics are fundamentally biological in nature and are thus transmitted to succeeding generations; strong negative feelings towards other groups who do not share these characteristics, coupled with the thrust to discriminate against and exclude the out-groups from full participation in the life of the community." From this perspective, many conflicts in Asia can be characterized as racial.

Many countries in Asia experienced white supremacy during periods of subjugation under colonial* rule: Pandit Jawaharlal Nehru, the first prime minister of independent India*, articulated this forcefully: "We in India have known racialism in all its forms even since the commencement of British Rule. The idea of a master race is inherent in imperialism – India is a nation and Indians as individuals were subjected to insult, humiliation, and contemptuous treatment. The English were an imperial race, we were told, with a God given right to govern us and keep us in subjection; if we protested we were reminded of the tiger qualities of an imperial race."

However, a variety of ethnic conflicts can be found in different countries in Asia. Often parallels are drawn between the heinous caste* system in India and racism. Some scholars even argue that casteism is nothing but a subtle form of racism. The atrocities committed against the Dalits* (untouchables) have a parallel only in the racial genocide of Native Americans and the racial slavery* of blacks in the USA and other countries. But most scholars agree that notwithstanding the similarity between casteism and racism, they are not the same; casteism involves social, economic, and religious features that cannot be reduced to racial issues.

The discrimination and misery experienced by ethnic minorities in Japan*, particularly Buraku*, Korean, and Okinawan people, are widely known. Japan itself is a country where some racial groups gained prominence over others socially and culturally.

In almost all Asian countries, indigenous "tribes" (see Tribalism and Christianity) are subjected to discrimination, humiliation, and exclusion. Racial tension prevails in Hong* Kong, Singapore*, and Malaysia*, which influences the economic and political processes in these areas. In other countries in Asia, especially Vietnam*, Cambodia, and Pakistan*, ethnic conflicts, which sometimes exist below the surface, negatively affect the life of the people. In short, the pernicious evil of racism is rampant in Asia.

K. C. ABRAHAM

Racism and Christianity in the Caribbean. Racism in the Caribbean (as in many other places in Latin America) constitutes the systemic and systematic exclusion, exploitation, and marginalization of anyone who is not of European descent. A combination of European power and prejudice, racial attitudes were historically used to justify violent oppression* and colonization in the name of Christianity. The expansion of the Spanish Empire in the Caribbean starting in the 15th c., then of the British, French, and Dutch Empires (17th and 18th c.), was synonymous with the massacre of indigenous peoples, the evangelization of African slaves*, and the exploitation of Asian laborers in the 19th c. Christianity and the law worked together to subjugate and exploit African slaves and indentured laborers.

During the period of slavery, colonizers created laws that banned miscegenation ("race mixing"; marriage between spouses of different racially defined groups); these laws prohibited African religious, cultural, and social practices and limited the movement of slaves. They established hierarchies according to skin color that maintained white power and justified the inferiority of slaves and of later indentured laborers. Miscegenation between white planters and African slaves occurred nonetheless, and their offspring, "mulattos" or "colored," were seen as inferior to their white counterparts and had little if any economic, social, or political power. Simultaneously, colonizers used their religion, Christianity, to "save" African slaves, whom they deemed to be "heathens" and to reacculturate them in ways that reinforced their assumed inferiority to Europeans. For example, the Anglican Church maintained social and ethnic differences within worship services by prohibiting slaves from taking Communion from the same cups as their European counterparts. Moreover, all African religious practices were illegal and punishable by law.

Although racism was officially dismantled with the emancipation of slaves and the termination of colonization, people of African descent continued to experience economic, political, and social restrictions in their own countries. The emancipation process actually consisted of monetary "compensation" to the planters (slave owners) for the loss of their labor force, but there was no real economic redress for the African slaves who had suffered centuries of violent exploitation. Indeed, emancipation did not dismantle the political and social hierarchies of colonialism. African workers were further exploited through the establishment of "apprenticeship" (akin to indenture) in most of the British Caribbean. Once African Caribbean people obtained full freedom, white planters brought Chinese and Indians to the region by means of indenture schemes. The result was the creation of a cheap labor class and hence a decline in the price of wage labor in the Caribbean. Indenture pitted the African Caribbean population and Asian population against each other and worked as a buffer between whites and people of African descent (especially in Trinidad, Tobago, and Guyana).

In the 20th c., resistance and liberation movements emerged against the continued discrimination of both African and Asian Caribbean people. Perhaps the most popular are the African-based religious movements, such as Rastafarianism* and the Back to Africa Movement.

When many of the white planters left and "people of color" gained control of political and legal institutions, on some islands racism evolved into "colorism", i.e. the building of an economic, political, and social hierarchy according to skin color. Dark-skinned people continued to experience discrimination. Thus while racism no longer exists as a legal system, prejudice among people in the Caribbean remains.

Even after the emergence of a black middle class in Caribbean territories, a social hierarchy based on skin color persists. As an economic force, "benign" racism in the Caribbean merely preserves inherited advantages. Imaging in the media – whereby African people are portrayed as people of dubious character who are indifferent to social responsibility – reinforces self-contempt and self-doubt among African Caribbean persons. The saddest manifestation of this internalized racism is apparent in the desire of many African Caribbean youth (particularly in Jamaica*) to "de-pigmentize" themselves with bleaching cream. In sum, racism remains a serious problem for the churches in the Caribbean, especially because in many ways they have themselves internalized racism. GARNETT ROPER

Racism and Christianity in North America: Feminist Theology and Systemic Racism. In the 1980s and 1990s, Womanist*, Mujerista*, and Asian American Feminist theologians (see Feminist Theology Cluster: In Asia) exposed as false the claim by Feminist theology (developed mostly by white women theologians) to speak for all women. Around the same time, historical studies of the emergence of whiteness as a racial identity and sociological studies of the effects of whiteness on white women's perceptions of race began to appear.

In response, white Feminist theologians began to acknowledge and address the effects of systemic racism on the field. The centrifugal force at work in systemic racism is white privilege. Whiteness is not perceived and identified as a "race," but occupies the ostensibly neutral center. It constitutes the normative gaze by which racialized minorities are recognized, evaluated, and assigned their "proper" places. The system is asymmetrical; non-whites who more closely conform to the standards that govern that gaze are more easily assimilated than others.

Systemic racism is one of many contextual forces that affect all of us regardless of our best intentions. White Feminist theologians have found a variety of theoretical resources helpful in exposing and combating systemic racism, even as they recognize that the battle is ongoing. In addition to those already mentioned, among the resources used to expose systemic racism are critical race theory in legal and literary studies, as well as poststructuralist* and postmodernist* thought and the analytical tools they provide. ELLEN T. ARMOUR

Racism and Christianity in North America: White Racism as a Theological Issue in White Churches. In European and USA-based societies, white racism refers less to prejudices of individuals than to routinized outcomes of beliefs and practices that sustain hierarchical social structures, based on privileging "white" essentialized physical features over "black" ones. This anti-black racism is also projected on most non-white communities, compounding white racist practices against other peoples of color: indigenous, African, Asian, Latino/a-Hispanic, Asian, and Arab. White racism has been reinforced by such practices as slavery*, massacre, housing and job discrimination, land theft, lynching, disenfranchisement, marginality, imprisonment, war, and poverty.

Theologians from communities of color often challenged white racism, but it remains an oft-neglected theme among white theologians. Five theological questions are key: (1) How have Christian beliefs helped create and sustain white racist systems? (2) How might theologians name the central event of Christian faith to facilitate antiracist work? As reconciliation*? Liberation*? Emancipation? Redemption*? (3) How are theologies of racism related to theologies that address other modes of oppression? (4) How have recent portrayals of Jesus* as "black," "yellow," or "brown" contributed to the antiracist struggle? (5) What is the meaning of Jesus' execution on the cross for the suffering and death of peoples of color by lynching, imprisonment, and capital punishment? MARK LEWIS TAYLOR

Racism and Christianity in the South Pacific and Australia. Christianity came to Oceania in colonial* wrappings, inevitably creating tensions over racial definitions – the basis for racism. In localized settlements characterized by diverse forms of interaction among ethnicity, colonial resource exploitation, and Christian presence, Christianity had three types of roles in racial definition:

1. Christianity fused with a dominant group, which monopolized Christian ideology* to legitimize its racist dominance over a minority. Thus in Fiji*, missionary success created a society that fused Methodist holiness* with Fijian tribal authority. The colonial imposition of a labor system on indigenous people (1879–1916) and a "chosen people*" theology fused with national identity to create an "other" (a "racial minority"). Because both Christian ideology and Fijian ethnicity dominate the national constitution (reinforced since the 1987 election by a series of military coups), Fijian racism is public, religious, and constitutional.
2. Christianity functioned as a bystander to the enforcement of homogeneity through migration control in secular societies in which questions about the relation of religion and culture were resolved and religious legitimization

was unnecessary. In Australia, imported forms of Christianity were denominational rather than missionary, and plantation economies (with indentured labor) were restricted to the north. Consequently, the racism that emerged was largely detached from the increasingly urban Christian praxis. (The exception was on the "frontier," where a minority Calvinist election* theology played a role in legitimizing the clash between dispossessed Scottish Gaels and dispossessed Aborigines.) Thus Australian racism has been largely secular, operating through the churches' politics of neglect – the indentured labor "problem" being "solved" by the White Australia Policy and national unification (1901). However, when Australia's first indigenous international Christian mission, the South Seas Evangelical Mission, emerged among the indentured population as an Australian Pentecostal*/Charismatic* movement, it was active in antiracist causes and worked against the oppression of Aborigines.

3. The churches actively contributed to the struggle against racism by helping contractual identities to emerge. The prime example of this role of Christianity was the Treaty of Waitangi, a national settlement in New Zealand establishing the rights of Maori people. It was won by Maori resistance but articulated and supported by Christian leaders, the indigenous Ratana Church Movement, and, from the 1980s, the Councils of Churches.

Only the emergence of pluralist, globally open economies after World War II challenged the tie between race and religion in Oceania. Yet the contemporary rise of religion as a reintegrating force in various national constituencies is an ironic result of the success of colonial secularism.

MARK HUTCHINSON

Racism and Christianity in Western Europe. The origin of racism lies in the construction of hegemonic conceptions of culture in European and Northern American societies that began in the early modern period. Modern racism emerged in the context of 19th- and 20th-c. colonialism* and imperialism, and was directly linked to the establishment of nation-states and nationalism*.

Starting in the second half of the 19th c., racist claims of superiority over other – mostly minority – ethnic groups and their oppression* were legitimized by (pseudo-) science, especially "social Darwinism*." Racist ideologists had, however, pre-Darwinist forerunners who posited a genealogical racism in the 16th c. In the Christian context, this type of racism was found not least in discourses of racial superiority by missionaries involved in the Christianization of indigenous people and the legitimization of slave* trade (see Mission Cluster: And Race). Theological arguments, including "chosen people*" discourses, legitimized white ethnocentrism and oppression* of indigenous people (e.g. the theory that they were "Hamites," descendants of the cursed Ham; Gen 9:20–27). In the late 18th c., often in connection with the missionary movement (see Mission Cluster: Thematic Issues: Anti-slavery), anti-slavery movements arose, which justified their positions by the perceived biblical mission to make all people their followers. In the early 20th c., Protestant World' Missionary Conferences directed their attention to the problem of racism. Although opposed to it, they still participated in the discourse of white paternalism that declared "races" to be part of the divine order.

The declarations by Protestant German delegates at the World Missionary Conferences in Jerusalem in 1928 and Oxford in 1937 were openly racist. Their theological discourses drew on modern racist and anti-Semitic* conceptions developed by Huston Stewart Chamberlain, Wilhelm Marr, Paul de Lagarde, and others.

The political use of racist theories culminated in the *Weltanschauung* (see Ideology) of diverse Fascist movements in Europe and particularly in German National Socialism. The latter based its ideology primarily on the myth of "Aryan" superiority, hence justifying the genocide of the Jews (see Holocaust, Jewish [or Shoah]). The most extreme representative of National Socialism in the Christian spectrum, the Protestant movement of the German* Christians (Deutsche Christen), intended to insert Christianity into Aryan racism in order to obliterate the Jewish roots of Christianity. (Similarly radical was the fundamentalist Protestant Ku Klux Klan in the USA.)

Racist ideas and anti-Semitic codes were propagated beyond right-wing movements into the wider Christian population. Discourses going back to stock anti-Semitic commonplaces – the so-called deicide *topos* (Matt 27:22–25: "The people as a whole answered, "His blood be on us and on our children!") and that of the perennial Jewish collective guilt – had been the basis of anti-Judaism since early Christianity. In addition, 19th- and 20th-c. modern anti-Semitism consisted of two basic orientations: biologically based racial anti-Semitism and sociocultural anti-Semitism. Christians readily linked sociocultural anti-Semitism to traditional Christian anti-Judaism. Whereas Protestant anti-Semites tended to include racist ideas in their argumentation, the majority of Roman Catholics rejected the biological essentialism of racial anti-Semitism, emphasizing the primacy of religion over "race"; they nonetheless endorsed sociocultural anti-Semitism. In his encyclical *Mit brennender Sorge* (With burning concern; 1937), Pope Pius* XI spoke out against the absolutizing of "race" and "nation," yet he did not broach the issue of anti-Semitism.

Although the end of World War II was an ideological turning point, anti-Semitism and racism persisted, even among Christian circles, during the second half of the 20th c. Outside of Europe, during this period racism was particularly apparent in racial discrimination in the USA and apartheid in South* Africa. In Europe, especially in Germany, debates on racism strove to deal with Germany's racist and anti-Semitic past. In the Christian churches, the debates over racism that began in the 1950s and 1960s culminated in the 1980s and 1990s. The Second Vatican* Council lamented the hatred of Jews by Christians in the declaration *Nostra Aetate* (1965). The Vatican published the document "We Remember: A Reflection on the Shoah" (1998), expressing its deep regret over the "errors and failures of those sons and daughters of the Church," yet denouncing only individual Christians for their responsibility for the Shoah, and not the responsibility of the Church itself.

At the same time that these European debates over the Holocaust were taking place, the ecumenical movement focused on the thematization of and reaction against racism on a global scale. In 1954 the World* Council of Churches declared segregation based on race to be incompatible with a Christian worldview, and then addressed apartheid in South Africa (e.g. through the Program to Combat Racism, 1970). During the same period, the US Civil Rights Movement was led by churches with roots in Protestant revivalism*, and Roman Catholic Liberation* theology was directed in large part against racist oppression*. After World War II, the Christian churches initially condemned racism as a sin* and heresy*, e.g. in proclamations by the Lutheran World Federation (1977), the World* Alliance of Reformed Churches (1981), and the papal commission *Justitia et Pax* (1989). In the 1990s, a shift toward an interpretation of racism as a societal phenomenon could be detected (e.g. WCC's reports of 1991 and 1995).

URS ALTERMATT and
FRANZISKA METZGER

Racovian Catechism (1605), the confession of faith for the Minor Reformed Church (antitrinitarian "Polish Brethren") in Poland*, considered to be the most influential document in Unitarian* history. It was named for Rakow, Poland, where many persecuted Polish Brethren migrated (1569) in order to create a New Jerusalem. For 60 years Polish Brethren published c500 tractates and books, which were sent to Transylvania, Germany, and England.

The Racovian Catechism, largely the work of Faustus Socinus*, was published, after his death, by four ministers, with Peter Statorius as the principal editor. It summarized church beliefs in question-and-answer format, strongly emphasizing Jesus' ethical teachings and the Ten* Commandments, as well as social relations within the state, including a stance against the death* penalty and in favor of pacifism*. According to the Catechism, there is no knowledge of God and Christ without biblical revelation*; God's nature is one, not three; Jesus Christ, a real man with only a human nature, is God's son by his utter obedience, resurrection, and ascension; there is only one sacrament, the Eucharist*; and humans have free will*, so there is no original* sin.

After the Brethren fled Poland (1658), the Racovian Catechism, in many editions (including Latin, Polish, English, Dutch, and German), remained an influential statement of Unitarianism*. MARK W. HARRIS

Radical Orthodoxy, theological movement originating in the 1990s in Anglican Catholic circles at Cambridge University. It urges the recovery of a premodern ontological vision associated with catholic liturgical* practice and the Christian doctrines of the trinity* and *creatio* ex nihilo*, in the service of a critique of the metaphysical assumptions, social relations, and cultural practices characteristic of modernity*. A quasi-Heideggerian* narrative traces the violence*, anomic, and exploitative technophilia of secular* societies back to impoverished philosophical notions of being as sheer givenness without inherent order, meaning, or beauty, unwittingly abetted by deficient theologies that solidify dualistic relationships between reason* and faith*, nature*, and grace*.

PAUL DEHART

Radical Reformation, a diversified movement that emerged in the wake of the 16th-c. Protestant Reformation. The leading Protestant Reformers, including Luther, Zwingli, and Calvin, breaking with centuries of Roman Catholic tradition, questioned many aspects of Christian faith, including the views of Scripture*, the Holy* Spirit, baptism* and other sacraments*, and the relationship between church* and state. In response to some of the doctrinal formulations of leading Reformers, alternative groups arose, including the Anabaptists*, Spiritual* Reformers, and Evangelical Rationalists. These Radical Reformers challenged the subjugation of religion to territorial princes and civic officials (still accepted by the leading Reformers). They found their most lasting institutional forms in the Society of Friends* (Quakers), Pietism*, the Moravian* tradition, and Methodism*. DONALD KRAYBILL

Radio. See MEDIA AND CHRISTIANITY; MEDIA AND CHRISTIAN WORSHIP.

Rahner, Karl (1904–84). Born in Germany, Karl Rahner entered the Society of Jesus in 1922 and, after undertaking philosophical and theological studies, was ordained as a priest in 1932. His doctoral studies in philosophy at the University of Freiburg (1934–36) included several courses with Martin Heidegger* and a dissertation on the metaphysics of knowledge in Thomas Aquinas* under Martin Honecker. Rahner's thesis was rejected for being insufficiently Thomistic*. He obtained a doctorate in theology from the University of Innsbruck, Austria (his dissertation was on patristic interpretations of John 19:34). Appointed professor of theology, he taught at Innsbruck (1936–64), then at the Universities of Munich (1964–67) and Münster (1967–71).

A Sapiential Theology. One should not be deceived by Rahner's self-description as an "amateur theologian." Because of his enormous philosophical and theological output – some 4,000 items – Rahner is widely regarded as one of the most influential Roman Catholic theologians of the 20th c. What is true, however, about Rahner's self-deprecation is that his overriding concern was always "pastoral" and not academic. His goal was to help Christians of his time make sense of their faith in the face of contemporary questions and challenges and to grow spiritually. Rahner's theology is sapiential or even mystical, deeply rooted in faith and worship; it aims at fostering an experience of God by ordinary Christians in their everyday life. It is an initiation into a personal experience of God. While influenced by philosophers such as Kant*, Hegel*, Pierre Rousselot, Joseph Maréchal, and Heidegger, especially in his two philosophical works, *Spirit in the World* (1939) and *Hearers of the Word* (1941), Rahner was most indebted to the spiritual writings of the fathers (especially Origen*), Bonaventure*, Thomas* Aquinas, Teresa* of Ávila, and, above all, Ignatius* of Loyola (*Spiritual Exercises*). Indeed, the most fruitful way to approach Rahner's theology is through his popular writings on prayer and spirituality and his interviews. Yet one cannot ignore his more difficult works: his 23-volume *Theological Investigations* (translation of the 16-volume *Schriften zur Theologie*) and *Foundations of the Christian Faith* (1976).

God as Mystery. In his early philosophical works, Rahner attempts to show that in every act of knowing and loving, humans necessarily, though implicitly, "reach out in anticipation" (*vorgreiffen*) toward the infinite horizon of being and goodness (God, the Mystery), without being able to grasp it. Using the Kantian* transcendental method, Rahner argues that such reaching-out-toward-without-ever-grasping the horizon of being and goodness (the "transcendental experience") is the condition of possibility for every act of knowing and loving a particular object (the "categorial experience"). The goal of theology* is to help everyone come to an explicit awareness of this orientation toward God, which defines what being human means.

God as Self-Giving Holy Mystery. For Rahner the conviction that this distant Mystery has, freely and out of love, come near us is central to the Christian faith. God has given God's own *self* to humans. This divine self-communication is trinitarian in structure. God the Father is self-communicated in two distinct and related modes: as origin, history, invitation, and knowledge (in the Son*); and as future, transcendence, acceptance, and love (in the Spirit*).

Humans as "Supernatural Existential." Using Heidegger's terminology, Rahner calls grace* an "existential." However, he adds the adjective "supernatural" to highlight the gratuitous character of God's self-communication. Thus the natural capacity (*potentia obedientialis*) by which humans open themselves to God and desire beatific* vision has been in fact fulfilled by God's self-gift and transformed into the "supernatural existential," which humans are enabled to live out concretely.

Jesus Christ as the "Absolute Savior." Faithful to his pastoral and spiritual intention, Rahner develops a Christology that responds to the contemporary challenges of science* and religious pluralism. The Chalcedonian* dogma is not the end but the beginning of a search for a deeper understanding of who Christ is. In the evolutionary context, Rahner sees the Incarnation* as the meeting point between two movements, one by the Spirit (God) "coming down" to matter ("descending Christology"), the other by matter "moving up" or actively self-transcending toward the Spirit ("ascending Christology"). The person in whom this meeting occurs is the "Absolute Savior," identified by Christian revelation as Jesus of Nazareth.

"Anonymous Christians." With regard to religious pluralism, Rahner argues on the basis of God's universal salvific will (1 Tim 2:4), the unity between love* of God and love of neighbor (Matt 25:40), and the role of Jesus as the Absolute Savior that anyone who lives out the supernatural existential concretely can be called an "anonymous Christian." While one cannot *affirm* with certainty that all will be saved, one must *hope* and *act* as if it will be so. The church's mission* remains; it still consists in being the sacrament* of God's salvation*. **See also MISSION CLUSTER: MISSION, THEOLOGIES OF, AND WESTERN AND ASIAN CHURCHES; PLURALISM, RELIGIOUS, AND CHRISTIAN THEOLOGY.** PETER C. PHAN

Ramist Logic. An alternative to Aristotelian* logic, Ramist logic divides and subdivides any topic into a series of dichotomies. Developed by Petrus Ramus (1515–72), it was influential among Reformed* thinkers, particularly in Cambridge.

Ransom. Many in the early church interpreted Christ's ministry, his death on the cross, and/or his resurrection (e.g. 1 Pet 1:18; Rev 5:9; Matt 20:28 // Mark 10:45; 1 Tim 2:5) as "ransoming" humanity from captivity to Satan or to the "powers" (1 Cor 2:8; Col 2:13–15). **See also ATONEMENT #1; REDEMPTION.**

Rapture (Lat *raptus*, "being carried away"), in mystical language, the ecstatic experience of being carried out of oneself through awareness of God, and thus losing self-awareness. For Dispensationalists* and other Millennialists*, "rapture" refers to Paul's statement (1 Thess 4:17), in speaking of Christ's return, that believers living on earth will be caught up to meet him in the air.

Rastafari Movement. This movement originated in Jamaica* (early 1930s) and is widespread throughout the Caribbean* region, where it interacts with Christianity. It became internationally known through the Jamaican-born Reggae singer Bob Marley. It takes its name from Emperor Haile Selassie of Ethiopia* before his coronation, *Ras* being his title of nobility and *Tafari* his family name. For the Rastafaris, Haile Selassie is the black Messiah*. This movement proclaims that God* is black and that the black people are the true people* of God, marching toward the new Zion*, which is "Ethiopia," where they will no longer be oppressed*. "Babylon" refers to the present situation of racism* and exploitation of the poor*.

The theological and philosophical foundations of Rastafari were laid by Marcus Mosiah Garvey* (born in Jamaica, 1887), the founder of the Back to Africa Movement: black people, like the people of Israel before them, are exiles in the land of the whites, and it is God's will that they should be set free. This reflects a cultural rather than a geographic problem. Thus Rastafaris have issued a call for the Africanization of the Caribbean.

ARMANDO LAMPE

Rationalism and Christian Theology. Christianity is rooted in faith*. For Augustine*, faith is not only an act of believing that there is a God, but also an act of believing what God says, because one believes in (i.e. trusts) God. Faith so defined is construed according to a model of personal relations, and it has never been thought to be intellectually blind. Like Judaism, Christianity claims that faith results in wisdom* and that through faith one receives other gifts of God's Spirit such as understanding, counsel, and knowledge. Reason*, therefore, ought to benefit from faith; Augustine claimed that "unless you believe you will not understand." Reason has also been used to articulate, teach, and clarify faith. Christianity has thus always engaged in theology*, a reasoned exposition of its teaching and narratives, and a critical reflection of its beliefs. Faith is thus exercised in a reasonable way; Augustine also claimed it is "thinking with assent." Still, the precise relation between faith and reason in theology has always been debated (in part because faith is understood in different ways; see Faith).

In the early church, philosophers such as Justin* and Athenagoras were attracted to Christianity because of the truth they saw there. Conversely, the teachings of the ancient philosophical schools found their way into Christian theology and made it a discipline. Platonism*, which acknowledged not only a creator but also a transcendent good and a mystery* that remained beyond all attempts to fully understand it, had a particularly strong influence on early Christian theology. Its insistence on a link between morals and thought was also amenable to Christian thinkers. Alexandrian theologians such as Clement* and Origen* owed much to Platonism and transmitted it to later theology. There were also limits. Thinkers such as Irenaeus*, Hippolytus*, Tertullian*, and the Cappadocians* blamed heresy* and speculative excess on an overreliance on reason and the use of pagan philosophy. Reason dwelled within the limits of a developing relation with a transcendent God.

Christian theology's use and understanding of reason stayed largely within Augustinian and Platonist horizons through the Middle Ages, yielding a spiritually oriented theology. When the writings of Aristotle* reappeared, there was a period of tension between his secular, scientific claims and the Augustinian–Platonist tradition. Ultimately Aristotle was subsumed within the larger framework, as thinkers such as Aquinas* argued that natural reason did not give direct access to the mind of God but could deal with God's effects in creation and, by analogy*, say something about God. This approach allowed theology to become an academic discipline, just when the university, and not the monastery, became the chief place where it was exercised.

The role of reason in theology changed significantly in the modern period, as reason came to be defined in terms that owed more to mathematics and physics than to interpersonal knowledge. For example, John Locke* insisted that strength of belief be in direct proportion to the degree of evidence for what is believed. This upset the balance between intellect and other elements of the Christian life; neutral, objective evidence became the fulcrum on which all aspects of faith were balanced. For many thinkers, evidence became the sole criterion for accepting or rejecting theological claims. No longer an active search for wisdom, theology came to resemble a natural science, based on publicly defensible first principles systematically worked out and tied to foundations in secular knowledge. In some cases, this led to a strictly "rational theology," such as Deism*, which said no more than could be built out of reason and public, empirical evidence. Other theologians attempted to make the best public case for central traditional doctrines, but also trimmed them accordingly. Others, such as Karl Barth*, rejected all such attempts, insisting that theology as the knowledge of God exists only within the space set out by the activity of God's own Word. Nonetheless, Barth assumes that reason is what modern philosophy says it is.

Much recent philosophy and theology has been extremely critical of the view of reason that reigned from the time of the Enlightenment* to the 20th c., recognizing that its strict insistence on objectivity, neutral reason, method, and certainty has been unrealistic and unworkable even in the natural sciences. Seeking out Christianity's own internal logic has therefore been an important quest for some theologians (see Conviction; Metaphor; Symbolism), as has been an attempt to recover ancient spiritual sources. Other theologians, however, have kept alive an appeal to the secular world, seeking to find a neutral, public reason and to strike a balance between its demands and those of maintaining the internal integrity of Christian faith. **See also POSTMODERNISM AND LIBERATION THEOLOGIES; POSTMODERNISM AND THEOLOGY; REASON; REVELATION.**

ERIC O. SPRINGSTED

Ratramnus (9th c.), Carolingian* theologian. A fellow monk of Paschasius* Radbertus in Corbie, he wrote a treatise (843) in opposition to the latter's realistic* view of the Eucharist*, emphasizing a more symbolic understanding. Through consecration the bread and wine of the Eucharist become mystic symbols commemorative of Christ's body and blood; in the bread and wine, which retain their outward appearance, resides a power perceived only by the faith* that makes them effective. There was little controversy at the time, but in the 11th c. Retramnus's position, along with that of Berengarius*, was condemned under Pope Leo IX at the Synod of Vercelli (1050). His treatise attracted serious attention during the eucharistic disputes of the Reformation* when his position appeared to be akin to Calvin's; i.e. the substance of the body of Christ is made present through the bread and wine received by faith.

Rauschenbusch, Walter (1861–1918), US clergyman, professor, author, who became a leader in the Social* Gospel Movement (early 1900s). Ordained in 1886, he became pastor of the Second German Baptist Church in New York City, a congregation of needy working-class immigrants. Awakened by their poverty and unjust treatment, he worked with area pastors to help meet their needs.

In 1902 Rauschenbusch was appointed professor of church history at Rochester Theological Seminary, where he had graduated. By then he was also working with Washington Gladden and other leaders of the emerging Social Gospel Movement and was active in the social ministries of the new Federal Council of Churches of Christ in America. The Federal Council adopted the Social Creed of the Churches (1908), which member denominations also approved. These actions were the origin of Social Gospel ministry. Rauschenbusch was among its leaders throughout his life, writing several influential books. Three of them indicate his evolving thoughts and concerns for economic and social justice informed by Christianity: *Christianity and the Social Crisis* (1907), *Christianizing the Social Order* (1912), and *A Theology for the Social Gospel* (1918). **See also SOCIAL GOSPEL MOVEMENT.**

DONALD K. GORRELL

Realism. Today the term connotes either dependence on facts rather than myth* or speculation, or the philosophical position that knowledge is based on the world and not primarily on consciousness. Earlier it referred to the doctrine that universals* have a reality independent of consciousness. Sacramental realism is the view that Christ's body and blood are "really" present in the Eucharist. **See also UNIVERSALS.**

Reason. In classical usage, reason applied first to counting, computing, or calculating; then to other activities of reasoning; then to the principles that govern a process of reasoning; and finally to the human capacity for thinking, the "eye of the mind." In medieval thought, "reason" tends to mean the process of reasoning, while "understanding" is the insight at the beginning or end of such a process. Reason was said to be presupposed by, and preparatory to, revelation*. Reason was associated with knowledge of God through the natural world generally available to human beings (Rom 1:19–20; Acts 17:23–29), but it needed to be perfected through revelation, for only then would it lead to insights that were otherwise impossible to reach. This way of relating reason and revelation* is not uncontested, however. The Enlightenment* favored reason over revelation, because it was more generally accessible and did not make claims to special insight or authority; if revelation had a role, it was merely as the vehicle by which the truths of reason first came to be discovered. Others disputed the claims of natural theology and reason and relied exclusively on revelation (Kierkegaard*, Ritschl*, Barth*).

What is the relation between will* and reason, i.e. between willing and deliberation about good and evil, better and worse choices? The Greek philosophers tended to assume that willing follows the judgment of reason, while the biblical tradition emphasized divine willing and human obedience or disobedience (Deut 26:16–19; Josh 24:15). Ultimately the question is whether an act is good because a legislator – God, or society, or the state – wills it (see Positive Theology, Positive Law, Positivism; Voluntarism), or whether it is legislated because it is good or natural or reasonable (see Rationalism and Christian Theology). **See also LOCKE, JOHN.**

EUGENE TESELLE

Rebecca, Rebekah, daughter of Bethuel, sister of Laban, wife of Isaac*, mother of Esau* and Jacob*. She helped Jacob deceive Isaac and obtain his blessing (Gen 27:1–28:5).

Rebirth, Spiritual. See EVANGELICALS/EVANGELISM CLUSTER.

Rebmann, Johannes (1820–76), a German, went to the East African coast as a missionary sponsored by the Church Missionary Society (founded 1799). He joined Dr. Ludwig Krapf* in Rabai near Mombasa (1846) and lived there until his death (1876). Krapf and Rebmann were not interested in vocational training as a means of evangelization. Rather, they were preoccupied with anthropological, linguistic, and geographic documentation. For more than three decades, they made very few converts to Christianity, but their documentation paved the way for the European occupation of Eastern Africa. Rebmann was most well known for being the first European, guided by the local people, to see the snow-covered peak of Mount Kilimanjaro, the highest mountain in Africa. His reports to England and Germany about high, snow-capped mountains within the tropics were received with much skepticism, but they also aroused curiosity and encouraged more European (especially British and German) adventurers and explorers to come to East Africa.

Recapitulation (Gk *anakephalaiosis*, "summing up"), term used in the NT for love as the summation of the Ten* Commandments (Rom 13:9). For Irenaeus* (following Eph 1:10), Christ sums up all things; as a recapitulation of Adam*, reversing Adam's disobedience with his own obedience, Christ recapitulates humanity, leading it back to the beginning, i.e. the divine Word*.

Reccared (d601). King of the Visigoths in Spain (586–601), he converted from Arianism* to Roman Catholicism (587), publicly announcing his conversion at the Council of Toledo (589). Despite resistance from some of the Goths*, he achieved a new unity between Christians of Roman and of Gothic descent.

Receptionism, the position that, in the Eucharist*, the Body and Blood of Christ are received not physically but through faith, and thus are not received by unbelievers.

Reception Studies of Preaching investigate the processes and practices involved in receiving and using sermons, and promote awareness of common reception patterns, as well as issues of social location and identity. What difference do race, ethnicity, and social location make in the reception of sermons? What are the key factors that affect sermon reception? What makes a sermon more effective? What do listeners do with sermons? What are the roles of psychology, perception, and memory in the reception of sermons? What are the purposes of sermons in the lives of listeners (see Preaching)?

Empirical studies of reception* have increased, especially in late-20th-c. North American and German contexts. For example, the "Listening to Listeners Project" (2000–3), led by Ronald Allen and funded by the Lilly Foundation, was based on in-depth interviews with individuals and focus groups, involving 263 laypersons and 32 preachers in 28 Midwestern congregations in the USA. The published analyses of these interviews elucidate listeners' perceptions of content, feeling, the preacher, and embodiment. Intensified awareness of issues of reception brought about a "turn to the listener" in homiletic* theory starting in the late 1970s, first in inductive sermon methods (Craddock; Meyers) and in experientially grounded narrative and imaginative approaches to preaching (Lowry; Steimle, Niedenthal, Rice). These theories assumed a humanist* theory of subjectivity and made use of existentialist* philosophies and theologies grounded in ideas of "common human experience." They somewhat mirrored the rhetoric of Kenneth Burke, who advocated "identification" with one's interlocutor as the key to rhetoric effectiveness and encouraged a shift from "persuasion" to "consubstantiality" as the goal for rhetoric. It was assumed that preachers could and should identify with those listening to sermons, and speak from and for listeners when speaking from the pulpit.

Postmodern* and hermeneutical* philosophies, postcolonial* theories, cultural* studies, critical race* theories, and feminist* and womanist* theories provided strong critiques of ideas regarding sameness or interchangeability with respect to human subjectivity. With an awareness of these critiques and through reception studies, homiletic theories have incorporated the awareness of the differences and otherness of listeners in four homiletic models: (1) perspectival, "targeted-audience" models; (2) ethnographic homiletics, wedded to congregational study (Tisdale); (3) conversational and collaborative homiletics; and (4) testimonial homiletics. JOHN S. MCCLURE

Reception Studies of Scripture (German, *Wirkungsgeschichte*) investigate the ways readers, including Christian believers, have been affected by particular biblical texts throughout history. With this knowledge, present readers of Scripture are able to acknowledge both "the otherness of the other" (Gadamer*) and the contextual character of their own interpretations, including "detached" scholarly exegeses*.

This critical approach emerged in the 1980s in biblical commentaries (Luz), and later in collective studies and compilations in the series Ancient Christian Commentary on Scripture. Reception studies became feasible because of the methodological effervescence of the 1970s–1980s. Literary, structural, semiotic*, rhetorical, feminist*, liberationist*, ideological*, and sociocultural* critical approaches were introduced in biblical studies to complement historiographic* and philological* methods. These studies demonstrated the legitimacy of a diversity of interpretations of the same biblical texts. These practical exegetical results affirmed the polysemic nature of any discourse or text by specialists of hermeneutics*, semiotics*, and communication theories, according to whom interpreters necessarily read a text from the perspective of their "pre-understandings."

While this hermeneutical circle may result in a problematic "reading into the text," it also is a necessary interpretive process, especially when believers read biblical texts as Scripture* in their quest for a Word-to-live-by in a particular sociocultural and religious context. To make sense of a text, readers necessarily choose certain textual features as most significant. These textual choices – made by scholars using the aforementioned methods or by believers throughout history – reflect the readers' contextual, cultural, and religious stances and concerns. One can no longer affirm that the textual features underscored by modern* Western methods are the only significant ones and that interpretations based on other textual features are illegitimate until proved otherwise. Rather one can view biblical interpretations developed in different sociocultural and historical contexts, including those by ordinary believers, as legitimate until proved otherwise and as sources of insight into the richness of biblical texts.

Interpretation of the Bible in African*, American*, Chinese*, English*, French*, German*, Indian*, Italian*, Japanese*, Portuguese*, Russia*, Scandinavian*, and Spanish* literature and the differences in biblical interpretation in various contemporary cultural contexts (see Bible Interpretation Cluster) are all reminders of "the otherness of the other" and of the contextual character of each biblical interpretation. **See also SCRIPTURAL CRITICISM.** DANIEL PATTE

Recluse, person enclosed in a cell, out of contact with the world, for purposes of spiritual meditation.

Reconciliation, process of restoring right relationships when harm or injury has come between two or more persons, through a process or ceremony to mark the resolution of difficulties.

The classic Christian concept of reconciliation begins with an understanding of sin* as a disruption of the relationship between God and humankind, viewed by Western* churches as the responsibility of believers who are guilty of sin, or viewed by Eastern Orthodox* churches as the result of sin understood as a disease from which humans need to be cured. In either case, by their sin, humans become alienated from God and are unable to mend the torn fabric through their own efforts. This broken relationship can be restored only by God's initiative. "Be reconciled to God," the Scriptures urge (2 Cor 5:20), and this appropriate attitude is understood as a response to God, "who reconciled us to himself through Christ" (2 Cor 5:18), i.e. who healed humans so that union with God would once again be possible (in Eastern traditions) or who made peace with alienated humanity (in Western traditions). Western traditions emphasize that in ancient Israel reconciliation was built on the concept of atoning* sacrifice*. The symbolic offering is a price paid for restoring relationships. Making things right after harm has been inflicted is accomplished by payment of damages or costs of restitution, symbolized by the sacrificial lamb.

Traditional Western understandings assumed the need for a rough parity between the extent of harm and the price of reconciliation. Justice* depends on restoring balance; the wrongs require some effort to put things right. Most difficult is the irreparable harm incurred when life itself is lost. How can life be restored? What is the price for its restitution? Even when such payment cannot possibly undo the harm, rather than resorting to retaliation, symbolic means are employed to represent the process of making things right. The classic example is Jesus on the cross saying, "Father, forgive them for they do not know what they are doing" (Luke 23:34).

In traditional Roman Catholicism, reconciliation is understood in the sacrament of penance, whereby a believer is restored to right relationship with God after committing sin. In confession to a priest (understood to be God's authorized representative), the person identifies the offense, bears witness to its gravity, and shows a spirit of contrition. The priest then pronounces forgiveness, releasing the individual from the burden of guilt (see Penance and Forgiveness).

In recent decades, Christians have taken Paul's mandate for "the ministry of reconciliation" to new levels of service in conflict resolution. Consistent with Eastern traditions of reconciliation as "healing" (rather than justice), the mediation of disputes and skills and techniques for peace building and healing of traumas are applied to major arenas of recovery from warfare and widespread social conflict, as is done in the Truth* and Reconciliation Commissions in South Africa. **See also RECONCILIATION AS A CHRISTIAN PRAXIS.** N. GERALD SHENK

Reconciliation as a Christian Praxis. To work for reconciliation is to want to realize God's dream for humanity – when we will know that we are indeed members of one family, bound together in a delicate network of interdependence. True forgiveness deals with the past, all of the past, to make the future possible. That is what makes a community a community or a people a people.

Most of human history is a quest for that harmony, friendship*, and peace* for which we appear to have been created. The Bible depicts it all as a God-directed campaign to recover that primordial harmony when the lion will again lie with the lamb and they will learn war no more. Now and again, we catch a glimpse of the better thing for which we are meant, e.g. when we work together to counter the effects of a natural disaster, when for a little while we are bound together by bonds of a caring humanity, a universal sense of *ubuntu*. Then we experience fleetingly that we are made for togetherness, for friendship, for community, for family*, that we are created to live in a delicate network of interdependence.

It is crucial, when a relationship has been damaged, that the perpetrator acknowledge the truth and be ready and willing to apologize. It is never easy. In almost every language, the most difficult words are "I am sorry." Thus it is not at all surprising that those accused of horrendous deeds adopt the denial mode, asserting that such and such has not happened. The Germans claimed they had not known what the Nazis were up to. White South Africans have also tried to find refuge in claims of ignorance; they had not wanted to know (see Racism and Christianity Cluster).

In forgiving, people are not being asked to forget. It is important to remember, so that we do not let such atrocities happen again. Forgiveness does not mean condoning what has been done. It means taking what happened seriously and not minimizing it, drawing out the sting in the memory that threatens to poison our entire existence. Forgiving means abandoning your right to pay back the perpetrator in his own coin, but it is a loss that liberates the victim. In the act of forgiveness, we are declaring our faith in the future of a relationship and in the capacity of the wrongdoer to make a new beginning on a course that will be different from the one that caused us the wrong. We are saying that here is a chance to make a new beginning. It is an act of faith* that the wrongdoer can change. **See also JUSTICE, THEOLOGICAL VIEWS AND PRACTICES, CLUSTER: IN AFRICA.**

ARCHBISHOP DESMOND TUTU

Reconstruction, African Theologies of. Theologies of reconstruction arose in Africa from a critical reflection on the theologies of liberation* and inculturation*. The liberation paradigm had dominated progressive theological thinking in Africa since the 1960s. The theologies of liberation have been premised on the Exodus narratives, Isa 61:1–2 and Luke 4: 16–22, emphasizing that God liberates the oppressed* from all domination by their oppressors. All theologies of liberation are dialectical – the oppressed against the oppressor, and the oppressor against the oppressed. Furthermore, theologies of liberation provide justification for the oppressed to engage in struggles for their own liberation, with God as their ultimate source of power in their resistance. All theologies of liberation are preoccupied with the suffering, which the theologians reject, and with the oppressors, whom they oppose. Theologies of liberation are essential conceptual tools for resistance to oppression, domination, and exploitation.

New conceptual tools are necessary for facilitating reflection on the new society that must be rebuilt on the ruins of the old, oppressed, and divided society. Theologies of reconstruction provide such conceptual tools in anticipation of the new society that results from successful struggles for liberation. Since the struggle for liberation is a process, it necessarily overlaps with social reconstruction. The new society is anticipated at the same time as the old society is dismantled. Theologies of liberation and theologies of reconstruction are sequentially related, but spatially and temporally integrated. The main features of African theologies of reconstruction can be outlined as follows (summarizing the main points in Mugambi, *From Liberation to Reconstruction*, 33–51).

It was assumed by most African secular and religious leaders that the withdrawal of the colonial administrations would automatically lead to new social structures. Of course, this was not the case. Thus since the 1990s African Christian theologians have recognized the urgent need of theologies of reconstruction as systematic articulations of human response to revelation in their particular African situations and contexts. These theologies will be effective in 21st-c. Africa if, and only if, the social and physical reality of the continent and its peoples is accurately and comprehensively understood and reinterpreted. Developing African theologies of reconstruction involves discerning alternative social structures, symbols, rituals, myths, and interpretations of Africa's social reality by Africans themselves – as European theologies did in periods of reconstruction, e.g. after World War II in Germany (as Hans Dieter Betz noted in his response to Mugambi's 1999 presentation of African theologies of reconstruction).

African theologies of reconstruction strive to clarify the relationship between gospel and culture (see Culture Cluster: And Christianity). While Christian theologians commonly engage either the discontinuity or the continuity between gospel and culture, African theologians of reconstruction underscore that the gospel is a challenge to every culture. This means that no person has any reason to posit his or her culture as superior to others. Each culture has its strengths and weaknesses, but qualitative comparisons have no ethical justification. Thus the portrayal of African culture as a deficient vehicle for expressing the Christian faith – a long-standing practice by missionaries in Africa – must be set aside. Theologies of reconstruction advocate the amplification of the ongoing cultural stabilization of African Christianity through a characteristically African outlook in rituals, symbols, vestments, music, liturgy, architecture, metaphors, and theological emphases. No church can survive the challenges of history unless the gospel is effectively appropriated to the cultural and religious heritage of its members – as is the case with the Coptic* Church and the Ethiopian* Orthodox Church, which are distinctly African and trace their history to the patristic period. Theologies of reconstruction have the task of helping African Christians assert their own cultural heritage, just as Christians of other cultures have done. The Christian faith has many forms of inculturation, none of which is perfect. African Christians need their own (see Inculturation Cluster).

Regarding social life, the gospel has reached many people in Africa as very bad news. In colonial* Africa, the Christian community tended to be identified with the ruling elite, a social profile that defined in each country the relationship between church* and state in the postcolonial era. The challenge of reconstruction is for the churches to enhance the reconciliatory roles of secular organizations, a process that also calls for overcoming the squabbles among denominations and Christians in order to promote social harmony and cohesion.

Similarly, African theologies of reconstruction have to rethink the relationship between African* Religion and Christianity (see African Religion and Christianity Cluster). The missionary enterprise in Africa was conducted as if it intended to secularize the African outlook. If Africans are notoriously religious, why is it necessary to convert them from their religiosity? Thus another challenge for theologies of reconstruction is to discern the connection between secularization* and the process of evangelization*.

At the beginning of the 21st c., although Africa was in a pitiable condition, the possibility remained that it would emerge as an influential continent. But this would require the determination to utilize the available and potential resources for the welfare of the people. African theologians challenge the churches to assume the responsibility to prepare the people for this immense task and to proclaim with faith, hope, and love that God makes possible what to human beings appears an impossibility.

Theologies of reconstruction are needed beyond Africa. At the end of the 20th c. – the most violent and destructive in history, with two world wars that annihilated millions of people and subjugated millions more – a truce closed the "cold war," and transnational interactions, "globalization," emerged. Upon these ruins, following African theologies of reconstruction, theologians have to provide a critique that transcends globalization, affirming the particularities of peoples and cultures while appreciating the blessings of humanity and of the ecology* of the earth as a whole. Theologies of reconstruction have an essential role in this process of building new relationships and structures and rebuilding a new social consciousness.

JESSE NDWIGA KANYUA MUGAMBI

Recusants, Roman Catholics who refused to attend the services of the Church of England, especially after the excommunication of Elizabeth (1570), for which they were deprived of civil privileges by penal laws and subject to high taxes. **See also ROMAN CATHOLICISM CLUSTER: IN EUROPE: UNITED KINGDOM.**

Redaction Criticism (German, *Redaktionsgeschichte*), a historical*-critical method in biblical studies that views biblical texts as edited ("redacted") versions of earlier sources and traditions and seeks to elucidate the theological stance of the author/redactor. It is particularly important in the study of the Synoptic* Gospels.

Redemption. Christians have always believed that, because of sin*, death*, and other forms of evil*, all human beings need to be redeemed. Paul maintained, "All have sinned and are deprived of the glory of God" (Rom 3: 23). Self-redemption is not a possibility; human beings cannot set themselves free. Without Christ the Redeemer, they will not be delivered from the dominion of evil.

From the beginning, Christians understood that the dying and rising of Jesus effected a new exodus from bondage (see Atonement #1). Christian liturgies incorporated the songs with which Moses* and Miriam* led the people in praising God for their victorious liberation from slavery (Exod 15:1–21). The divine rescue of the Israelites gave a specifically Jewish meaning to the language of redemption used by Paul. Christians also interpreted redemption in the light of the return from exile in Babylon (Isa 40–55). The manumission of slaves and/or the ransoming of prisoners of war also helped to shape the way some early Christian communities proclaimed Christ as redeeming or liberating* them.

Unlike the doctrine of incarnation*, redemption did not provoke debates and official teaching from general councils during the church's early centuries. It was taken for granted that it was only through Christ that human beings could be redeemed. The NT told of Christ "buying" us "at price" (e.g. 1 Cor 6: 20, 7: 23) or "giving his life as ransom for many" (Mark 10:45). The NT had in mind what redemption "cost" Christ (his life) and never spoke of a ransom being paid to someone or something. But in the patristic period and later, some Christians expanded the metaphor to describe a transaction and even a specific price paid to God, to the Law*, or even to the devil*. Frequently, redemption has been associated with Christ's work of expiating* sins, a work explained by Anselm* (d1109) as "satisfaction," with Christ setting right a moral order disturbed by sin (see Atonement #2). Later, in the Western Church, some took this to mean that Christ was burdened with human sin, punished in our place, and so propitiated* an angry God. Yet the Orthodox churches (see Orthodox Churches, Eastern, Cluster: Introductory Entries) – like many Charismatic* churches and Liberation* theologians – conceive of redemption as liberation from bondage to evil powers (e.g. demonic powers or systemic evil) or as healing from sin as a disease (see Atonement #1). Much contemporary theology stresses that Christ redeemed humanity not only by his death, but also by what came before (his incarnation* and ministry) and after (his resurrection*, gift of the Holy* Spirit, and second* coming), and that the redemption concerns the whole of creation (Rom 8:18–23). Not only humanity but also the whole universe needs redemption. **See also ATONEMENT; CROSS AND CRUCIFIXION; LIBERATION THEOLOGIES CLUSTER; RECONCILIATION; RECONCILIATION AS A CHRISTIAN PRAXIS; SACRIFICE; SALVATION.**

GERALD O'COLLINS, SJ

Reductions (Spanish, *reducciones*; Portuguese, *aldeias*), settlements founded by Spanish or Portuguese colonizers for the purpose of assimilating South American native populations into European culture and religion. The reductions were related to the *encomienda** system. In "exchange" for the "privilege" of living as Christians in the reduction, natives provided forced labor for the colonizers, which was akin to slavery. By contrast the Jesuits* developed an egalitarian form of reductions, "Jesuit reductions," where numerous natives lived with Jesuit clergy, all of them following similar strict rules of Christian life. For instance, after landing in South America in 1550 (in a region that encompassed the northwest areas of present-day Argentina*, Paraguay*, and Brazil*), the Jesuits promised the Spanish monarch generous rewards, in the form of tributes, in exchange for exempting the Tupi and Guarani in their reductions from hard labor. In certain countries, e.g. Mexico*, reductions were called "congregations" (Spanish, *congregaciones*).

In Western Africa (see Nigeria), 19th-c. missionaries established "Christian villages" (Roman Catholics) and "mission villages" (Protestants) where Christians lived together apart from the African culture (a practice later discontinued). **See also** ***ENCOMENDEROS, ENCOMIENDA*****; PORTUGUESE EXPLORATIONS, CONQUESTS, AND MISSIONS; SPANISH EXPLORATIONS, CONQUESTS, AND MISSIONS.** DANIEL PATTE

Reformation. The term refers to several types of "reformation," but especially "magisterial reformation" led by academics (*magistri*) and supported by magistrates: the Anglican*, Lutheran*, and Calvinist* Reformations; the "Radical* Reformation" by dissidents and Anabaptists*; and the "Catholic Reformation" or "Catholic* Renewal." There would not have been a Reformation without Reformers driven by Luther's* question, "What makes a person a Christian?"

Answers were found through the recovery of biblical preaching* and pastoral* theology that addressed fundamental issues of religious life: personal anxiety, God's acceptance, and ethical guidance. Humanists such as Lefèvre* d'Etaples (c1460–1536) and Erasmus* (c1469–1536) aided the Reformers. Lefèvre d'Etaples promoted biblical study by means of commentaries, sermons, and a French lectionary. Erasmus promoted biblical understanding with his edition of the Greek NT (1516). Preachers became translators and translators became preachers. Their conviction that theology serves proclamation is expressed in Erasmus's rendering of the opening of the Gospel of John: "In the beginning was the speech, i.e., the *sermon*."

The Reformation in Germany. Luther's (1483–1546) biblical studies led him to believe that righteousness* before God is not a human achievement but a free gift from God. Convinced that salvation* is not the goal of life but the foundation of life, Luther reversed medieval piety: good works do not make the sinner acceptable to God; rather, God's acceptance of the sinner prompts good works. Faith* active in love* energized innovative approaches to social welfare, public education*, and political* authority. Rejection of mandatory clerical celibacy* enabled clergy to become citizens with homes, families*, and civic responsibilities.

Dissension among Reformers began early and escalated as Thomas Müntzer* (c1490–1525) joined the Peasants'* War (1524–25), claiming "the godless have no right to live." Medieval apocalypticism*, oppressive social and economic conditions, Reformation calls to "Christian freedom*," and critiques of canon* law and papal authority fueled peasants' social and religious expectations but misfired with their defeat.

Emperor Charles* V's foreign preoccupations impeded the elimination of Reformation movements in his realm. Protestant princes presented an irenic confession of their faith to the emperor at the 1530 Diet of Augsburg. Composed by Luther's colleague, Melanchthon* (1497–1560), the Augsburg* Confession became foundational for Lutheran churches and remains so today. By 1555 Protestant movements had gained sufficient strength to gain official toleration in the Peace of Augsburg* (see Germany).

Other Reformation Movements. Reformation movements throughout Europe shared the watchwords "Scripture* alone," "grace* alone," and "faith* alone," but their contexts varied. Zwingli* (1484–1531) and Calvin (1509–64) in Switzerland* lacked princely protection and had to implement their movements through town councils. Conflicts arose with Anabaptism*, initially led by Conrad Grebel (1498–1526). Anabaptists understood baptism* to depend on a confession of faith rather than to be a sacrament* administered to infants who neither understood nor evidenced Christian life. Their Schleitheim Confession (1527) also rejected what their contemporaries assumed were normal obligations of citizenship: oaths, tithes, and military service. Zwingli fought with Luther over whether the Lord's* Supper is primarily an act of thanksgiving for the gospel (Zwingli's memorial view) or a concrete offer of the gospel (Luther's sacramental emphasis).

In Geneva, Calvin and French exiles directed evangelization toward France. The first national synod of the Reformed Church in France met in Paris (1559) and accepted Calvin's draft of the Gallican Confession (modified at the Synod of La Rochelle, 1571; the Confession of La Rochelle continues to inform Protestantism* in France). However, the French tradition of "one king, one law, one faith" moved the Roman Catholic crown to try to root out Protestantism.

In England, Henry* VIII's break with Rome over his divorce informs the traditional view of the English Reformation as an act of state. Royal imposition of ecclesiology continued with his heirs: Protestantism with Edward VI, Roman Catholicism with Mary* Tudor, and Protestantism with Elizabeth* I. The English Reformation benefited from residual anticlericalism and the spread of ideas by scholars, merchants, pamphlets, Bible translations, and Protestant refugees fleeing Continental persecution. During Elizabeth I's reign, Marian exiles (Calvinists who fled during Mary Tudor's reign) returning from Protestant centers in Frankfurt and Geneva radicalized reform in the direction of Puritanism*.

In Scandinavia and Eastern Europe, Lutheran influences were present in the 1520s. Christian III established the Lutheran Reformation in Denmark* (1537). Luther's theology arrived in Sweden*-Finland* via students from Wittenberg. The Swedish king Gustavus Vasa established the Reformation there (1527). In Eastern Europe, the Reformation was established in Prussia and Livonia but remained a minority movement in other areas.

The Catholic Renewal (reform) stemmed from medieval devotional movements and Conciliarism* (14th c.), which called for reform of the church "in head and members." Ignatius* Loyola (1491–1556), founder of the Society of Jesus (Jesuits*), continued medieval monastic reforms and promoted pastoral and mission work. However, papal antipathy toward reform impeded calls for a council. When a council finally met, a generation of strife had hardened positions. The Council of Trent* (1545–63) focused on Catholic* renewal and the refutation of Protestantism. **See also CREEDS, SYMBOLS, AND CONFESSIONS OF FAITH.**

CARTER LINDBERG

Reformation, Catholic. See CATHOLIC RENEWAL.

Reformed Churches. The term "Reformed churches" usually refers to those Reformation* churches whose theological self-understanding, worship practices, and forms of church organization and discipline originated in the 16th-c. Swiss (rather than German Lutheran) Reformation.

While the German and Swiss Reformations agreed on the need to renew the Roman Catholic Church by the biblical message that God graciously* saves sinners in Jesus the Christ through faith* alone conferred by the Holy Spirit, the Swiss Reformation focused on God's glory and obedience to God and hence on the application of the biblical authoritative teaching to all aspects of ecclesial, individual, and public life, thus excluding any customs (e.g. vestments, hymns, church art) not warranted by Scripture.

Therefore, the Reformed churches understand themselves to be shaped by the concern to discern the Word of God, again and again, in order to witness to God's will within changing historical situations. They are hermeneutical* communities of obedience to Christ in each new context.

Led initially by Zwingli* in Zurich and animated especially by Calvin* in Geneva, the "Reformed" wing of the Reformation spread through the south of France and the Upper Rhineland (the western part of Germany*), reached Scotland*, England, the Netherlands*, Poland*, and Hungary*, Bohemia, and Transylvania. Earlier Reformation movements – those of the Hussites* and Waldensians* – later recognized themselves in the Reformed tradition.

From England and Scotland, the Reformed Movement reached North America. Following European emigration and colonial and missionary expansion – especially during the 19th c. – Reformed churches were established in Africa, Asia, Latin America, and the Caribbean. Today most members of the World* Alliance of Reformed Churches are religious minorities living and witnessing in the Southern Hemisphere.

The historical development of the Reformed churches took place under diverse and often adverse circumstances. As a result, the Reformed family of churches is marked by differences in theology and church government, which are visible in the different names by which these churches identify themselves.

One of these names is "Presbyterian*," used by Reformed churches with roots in the Swiss but also in the Scottish and Puritan* wings of the English Reformation. Presbyterian churches often recognize in the 1647 Westminster* Confession a major expression of their traditional theology. They have a form of church government by elders* elected by a local congregation that, in association with elders elected by other congregations in the same area, constitute – together with the ministers of Word and sacraments – the presbytery, whose governing powers distinguish this form of church polity*.

Another name is "Congregational*," used by churches that look to the 1658 Savoy* Declaration for their traditional theology. They hold in particular that Christ is the only head of the local gathering of the saints. As a result, they emphasize the autonomy of the local church – the congregation – and adopt a "congregational" form of church government. Other churches simply call themselves "Reformed" churches. These are in general located in Western Europe or are related to European emigration or mission in the Southern Hemisphere. Their traditional theology finds expression in such texts as the 1566 Second Helvetic* Confession, the 1563 Heidelberg* Catechism, and the 1561 Belgic* Confession.

Still other churches, with historical and theological ties with the revival* movement, bear the name "Evangelical*" in order to emphasize their core message and the evangelistic imperative, in opposition to what they see as "liberal" Protestantism. In the context of the 20th-c. ecumenical movement, several Reformed churches, often encouraged by the World* Alliance of Reformed Churches, have become "united" churches, "uniting" churches, or simply "Protestant" churches following intraconfessional or transconfessional unions or reunions.

This significant diversity raises the question of what the Reformed churches hold as theologically distinctive. Their answers once again differ. For some, their uniqueness lies in church government and structure. Others point to a constellation of theological themes that emerge from Reformed past and contemporary confessions, such as God's sovereignty, God's covenant* with humanity in Christ, and the way the authority of God's Law in the OT is construed in church life. Others hold that there are "essential tenets" that constitute Reformed identity, but the ones most commonly quoted – the Trinity*, Incarnation*, the ancient christological* affirmations, the Protestant* principle, and election* – are also shared by "non-Reformed" denominations. During the first 50 years of its history, the World Alliance of Reformed Churches tried to establish harmony among the different Reformed confessions or to formulate a confession of faith that its member churches would recognize and receive, but abandoned this project c1925, following Karl Barth's* advice.

As they feel called to relate what the Bible says to what needs to be said in today's world, Reformed churches make evident that they understand themselves to be reformed in the sense that they are always being reformed by the Word* of God. As a result, they feel at times the need to restate their faith as part of their call to proclaim the gospel. The following are three examples:

1. Against the risk represented by the influence of National Socialist ideology on the so-called German* Christians, the 1934 Barmen* Theological Declaration states that Jesus Christ is the one Word of God, that this Word is at the same time God's pledge of forgiveness* of sins and God's claim on our whole life. Consequently, the church can have only one master, and the state cannot embody the total order of human life.
2. Against the sin of the racist* ideology of apartheid* and the "heresy*" of its theological legitimation, the 1982–86 Belhar Confession affirms that the church gathered by God's Word cannot be divided by human prejudices and therefore holds together Christian unity, human reconciliation*, and the search for justice*.
3. Against the neoliberal economic* ideology and its idolatrous claim that outside the market there is no salvation, Reformed Christians from all over the world gathered in Ghana* in 2004 and adopted the Accra Confession, which seeks to correct the modern anthropocentric understanding of Christian stewardship* often associated with the domination of nature and the colonial domination of other peoples.

ODAIR PEDROSO MATEUS

Reformed Ecumenical Council, a council of 41 Reformed* churches in 25 countries, formed in 1946, with offices in Grand Rapids, Michigan. While it has been more conservative than the World* Alliance of Reformed Churches (WARC), a majority of its member churches have become members of the WARC as well. The two organizations agreed (2008) to merge in 2010.

Reformed Worship is an expression of Reformed theology: We worship God because of who God is and what God has done, believing humanity's "chief end is to glorify God" (Westminster Catechism). Reformed worship is initiated by God, who calls us to worship, and not by our religious inclinations. The essential substance of Reformed worship is gratitude to God.

Reformed worship was shaped by Zwingli* in Zurich and by Calvin* in Geneva, who drew on practices of Bucer's* Strasbourg congregation. The Reformers kept the basic Word and sacrament structure of Roman Catholic liturgy, but they worshipped in the vernacular, moved the center of worship from chancel to nave, replacing the altar with a table, and introduced the singing of psalms and hymns by the congregation. This was a shift from ritual to full congregational participation.

Practices were different in Zurich and Geneva. Zwingli merely modified the medieval "prone," a simple service of Scripture, preaching, and bidding prayers that often preceded the Mass. He celebrated the Lord's* Supper only quarterly, the congregation receiving bread and wine as symbols for remembering Jesus' supper with his disciples. But in Calvin's Geneva, the order for worship was derived from the traditional ante-Communion and included a call to worship, followed by a confession of sin, a declaration of pardon, and a reading or singing of the Ten* Commandments interspersed with *kyries**. Then Scripture was read and a sermon preached, after which there was an offering, prayers of intercession with the Lord's Prayer, the Apostles' Creed, a psalm, and a final blessing. Metrical Psalms were sung throughout the service. When the Supper was celebrated, the words of institution were read from 1 Cor 11, followed by a theological exhortation. Then the *Sursum Corda* (the call to "lift up your hearts") preceded the distribution of bread and wine. The worship concluded with a brief prayer of thanksgiving, the *Nunc Dimittis* (the Song of Simeon, Luke 2:29–32, beginning with "now you are dismissing your servant in peace"), and the Aaronic blessing (Num 6:24). Calvin urged a weekly observance of the Supper, but his proposal was rejected. His congregation instead welcomed Zwingli's quarterly practice.

If there was "real presence," for Zwingli it was within the collective faith of the people. But Calvin set forth a higher doctrine: the congregation was a royal priesthood*, and although Calvin practiced no consecration of elements, he affirmed a real presence through the total enactment of the Eucharist. DAVID BUTTRICK

Reformers, term commonly used to designate the leaders of the 16th c. Protestant Reformation. **See also BUCER, MARTIN; BULLINGER, HEINRICH; CALVIN, JEAN; CRANMER, THOMAS; FAREL, GUILLAUME; FLACIUS, MATTHIAS ILLYRICUS; KNOX, JOHN; LUTHER, MARTIN: MELANCHTHON, PHILIP; TYNDALE, WILLIAM; ZWINGLI, HULDRYCH (ULRICH).**

Refugees as a Theological Concept and an Ethical Issue. The OT term *ger* (stranger, alien) designates both foreign migrants and refugees who depend on the protection of the country, town, or sanctuary willing to welcome them. The Pentateuch* underlines the duty of offering hospitality and solidarity to such strangers: "When an alien resides with you in your land, you shall not oppress the alien. The alien who resides with you shall be to you as the citizen among you; you shall love the alien as yourself, for you were aliens in the land of Egypt: I am the LORD your God" (Lev 19:33, 34). The migrants remind Israel of its own history: captivity in Egypt; being welcomed in a land that belonged to God alone; later exile in Babylon, accompanied by the liberating faithfulness of God. Strangers should find empathy and solidarity in Israel, which can readily identify with those who have had to leave everything behind. Similarly, in the gospel, a stranger, a Samaritan, a neighbor that one should love as oneself, is in turn called to fulfill the commandment of love (Luke 10:25–37). For believers this is a reminder that it is always from an Other/other that one receives life and that it is with an Other/other that one builds the future.

Many forced population movements brought about by religious persecutions have marked world history. For instance, in 17th-c. France, the revocation of the Edict of Nantes*, which resulted in the banning of Protestant religious practices, forced 300,000 French Huguenots* from all social spheres to leave their country and go to Switzerland, the Netherlands, Germany, or Britain, and even to the Americas and South Africa. They were generally well received, as they brought with them knowledge and techniques that contributed to economic growth in their adopted countries. Yet established churches in these countries extended only a cautious welcome to the Huguenots, for they continued their religious service and teaching in French, making an effort to maintain their cultural practices (understood by some exiles to be a preparation for their return home). "Refuge" – whatever haven where their ancestors were welcomed and protected – still has an important place in the memory of European Protestants. This memory inspired the support given in the 20th c. by churches and Protestant institutions to programs designed to welcome and protect people fleeing from totalitarian regimes and anti-Semitism (e.g. the Cimade* in France). According to the United Nations High Commission for Refugees, in 2006 there were 9.5 million refugees in the world, immigrants who had crossed their national borders. In addition, at least 20 million uprooted people were displaced within their own countries due to insecurity and penury resulting from civil wars. This huge number of refugees is a real challenge to the international community and to ecumenical solidarity with churches and religious communities in such countries, often among the poorest in the world. The official status of "refugee," as defined by the Geneva Convention, has recently been subject to severe restrictions in certain countries that, after having been "host countries" for many years, now practice strict forms of selective immigration.

In Europe, church councils and numerous Christian associations and other organizations have jointly denounced the growing political tendency to close borders, to suspect systematically those who seek political asylum of being "false refugees," and to force refugees to return to their countries of origin. These organizations also oppose policies of assimilation whereby refugees or immigrants are forced to adopt as rapidly and as completely as possible the culture of the host country, even though this usually means integration into a pluricultural society. **See also** CIMADE. JACQUES STEWART

Regula Fidei (Rule of Faith), term used since the 2nd c. to designate the basic tenets of faith; a phrase often used with reference to the Apostles'* Creed as a summary of the kerygmatic* tradition, or to Scripture* as the Word of God.

Regula Magistri early Western monastic rule with 95 chapters, written anonymously in Latin. Certain scholars (since the 1930s) have argued that it was written in the early 6th c. in Southern Italy and was a major source of the Rule of Benedict*. Recent research suggests that the *Regula Magistri* was developed on the basis of Benedict's Rule in Bobbio after Columbanus's* death and that it is related to the 7th-c. "mixed" monastic rules. Nearly four times as long as Benedict's Rule, it is detailed and verbose and presents its teaching as the Word of God speaking through a "Master." Deploring monastic instability, it gives the abbot extensive powers.
MARILYN DUNN

Regular. In the Roman Catholic Church, the term refers to members of religious* orders, both women and men, bound by vows* and living in community, following a rule (*regula*).

Regular Clergy, in the Roman Catholic Church, priests bound by vows* and living in community, following a rule (*regula*), in contrast to secular* clergy.

Reign of God. See KINGDOM OF GOD, THE CONCEPT OF, CLUSTER.

Relationality, as a mode of existence in relation with others, is either a primary or a secondary dimension of human existence, according to theologians' understanding of God.

1. In Western churches, relationality is commonly viewed as secondary, because theologies tend to emphasize the autonomy* and sovereignty of God* as a person, known to humans as Father, Son, and Holy Spirit, but the relationality of the Trinity* is fundamentally hidden from humans. Thus individuals are ideally autonomous, as God is.
2. The Cappadocian* theologians emphasized the relationality of God's self as the Triune God (Trinity*). This tradition dominated the Eastern churches, which affirm the basic relational character of human existence.
3. By resisting the Enlightenment* and the modern one-sided affirmation of autonomy, relational views of God and humans have been brought to the fore in contemporary theology following Buber*. Bonhoeffer* emphasized the "sociality of humanity" from a christological-ecclesiological perspective. Barth* and Rahner* mark the return to trinitarian relational theology. The relational character of existence has been elaborated in feminist ethics* of care and extended to all existing things in Process* theology and ecotheology*.
4. Feminist* and postcolonial* critics pointed out the risks involved in affirming relationality at the expense of autonomy. Some, like Elizabeth A. Johnson, have affirmed a middle position of "relational autonomy."

Relationality balances the two other modes of existence, autonomy* and heteronomy*. Giving undue preference to relationality might hide an oppressive* tendency, as individuals' autonomy risks being abandoned and giving way to an oppressive form of heteronomy*.
CRISTINA GRENHOLM

Relics, remains of martyrs* and other saints* after their death, or objects that have been in contact with their bodies. The earliest evidence for the veneration of relics is the *Martyrdom of Polycarp**, which describes his body as being preserved and honored so that others can share in the power of his life and death. While there was some continuity with the Greek veneration of heroes, polytheists generally expressed repugnance toward this Christian practice, Julian* the Apostate being perhaps the most vocal. Christians viewed the body as the temple of the Holy Spirit (1 Cor 6:19); the martyr's body, furthermore, was associated with a faithful life, an often gruesome death, and the future resurrection*. Shrines and then basilicas* were built over the tombs of saints; meals were eaten at these tombs, and people would sleep near them (see Incubation) to receive visions or healing. While Ambrose* opposed eating meals at these tombs, he himself may have initiated the practice of placing saints' remains under the altar (cf. Rev 6:9).

Roman tradition forbade moving or disturbing a body. Consequently in Roman culture, "relics" were usually a cloth that had been lowered into the saint's grave, or oil, or a flower from the altar (which contained the saint's remains). But in the East and in Germanic territory, saints' bodies were more freely transferred and divided into parts. The Second Council of Nicaea* required saints' relics to be placed in every consecrated church. The veneration of relics was debated along with the veneration of icons*, and definitive approval came in the 11th c. in both the East and the West (see Saints, Devotion to, in the Orthodox Tradition; Saints, Devotion to, in the Roman Catholic Tradition). After the Islamic conquests, relics, usually stolen, were transferred to the West (e.g. relics of St. Mark from Alexandria to Venice [828] and of St. Nicholas from Myra to Bari [1087]); many relics in Constantinople were looted during the Fourth Crusade (1204). There was an extensive trade in relics, often of doubtful authenticity. During the Middle Ages these were displayed in reliquaries*, and miracles* were attributed to them. The sites of famous relics became destinations of pilgrimage*.

The veneration of relics, criticized by Erasmus* and the Reformation*, was defended by the Council of Trent*, although it tried to eliminate superstition* and commercialization. The practice of distributing relics as gifts helps to legitimate the Roman Catholic Church as a worldwide community. Popular* Christianity, Protestant as well as Catholic and Orthodox, continues to treasure the remains or mementos of holy persons, because they make sanctity more tangible and more approachable, offering both patronage and protection.

EUGENE TESELLE

Religion as a Concept and Christianity.

What Kind of Category Is "Religion"? The concept of "religion" has functioned as a crucial category in defining the nature and identity of Christianity and its relationship to other cultural traditions, philosophies, and communities. Rarely, however, does one pause to consider the precise nature, complex history, and changing uses of this category. Recent scholarship within religious studies, building on the pioneering work of Wilfred Cantwell Smith (1962, *The Meaning and End of Religion*), has drawn attention to the changing pattern of usage of this term from classical antiquity to the post-Enlightenment* period.

The Chicago historian of religion Jonathan Z. Smith has argued, e.g, that religion is in fact an "imagined" category in the sense that it exists as an intellectual or scholarly tool for analyzing complex data, but does not exist "outside the academy." Neither "religion" nor reified entities known as "the religions" exist "out there" in the world; rather, complex traditions, belief systems, and patterns of ritual behavior are labeled "religions" (while others are not). Moreover, Smith argues, the modern usage of the term, developed in the context of the late-19th-c. emergence of a comparative "science of religion," modeled itself on the biological sciences in seeing "religion" as a genus with a number of identifiable members. Defining what counts as a religion and what does not, however, has proved a difficult task, not least because of a misunderstanding of the "imagined" nature of the category.

In sum, the term "religion" is a social construction with a specific history that one can plot. Since the work of W. Cantwell Smith and Jonathan Z. Smith, a number of scholars have argued that the modern concept of religion carries with it a strongly Eurocentric (and Christocentric) imprint that has played a significant role not only in the classification of "other cultures" according to a broadly Eurocentric rubric, but also in the furthering of the European colonial project (as Asad, Balagangadhara, Chidester, Dubuisson, Fitzgerald, and King have argued).

The History of the Category. In a pre-Christian context, Cicero explained that the Latin term *religio* derives from *re-legere*, "to retrace" or "reread." For him, *religio* involves the practice of retracing the "lore of the ritual" of one's ancestors (*De natura Deorum* II.72). Thus the Romans, the Thracians, and the Jews, among others, had their own *religio*. The Christian writer Lactantius* (c250–c325) offered a rival etymology, deriving *religio* from *religare*, "to bind together" or "link" (*Institutiones divinae* IV.28). This shifted the focus to one's relationship to the divine and also allowed the emerging Christian movements to circumvent an understanding of *religio* that emphasized ancestral tradition. This new etymological definition, therefore, became crucial in legitimating the separation of Christianity from the more ancient Hebrew ancestral traditions and also in allowing for the Christian message to be seen not as grounded in ancestral practices and laws, but as a message to be passed on to Jews and Gentiles alike.

One consequence of Lactantius's rendition is the explicit polarization of *religio* vs. *superstitio*: *religio* as grounded in historical truth vs. *superstitio* as the myths and legends of the various "pagan" traditions. This characterization of *religio* in terms of "true vs. false religion" would become a powerful ideological* marker in later Christian centuries.

In the medieval period, the *religiones* generally referred to the various monastic* orders and those who undertook "the religious life," a life governed by monastic vows. This usage has survived into the modern period in the adverb "religiously," which denotes a particularly zealous or committed approach to a specific activity (as in "He reads the newspaper religiously every morning").

After the Protestant Reformation, religion increasingly came to be understood in Northern Europe in terms of the notion of personal "faith" and "piety," and the term began to appear in the vernacular languages of Europe. By the 17th c., the association of "religion" with an internal faith and piety within the individual believer was becoming firmly established.

However, much of our modern understanding of "religion" and "the religions" derives from the Enlightenment, where the terms came to denote historical systems of beliefs and practices followed by people of faith. Theologians such as Schleiermacher* also developed the Protestant emphasis on religion as an inner "creaturely feeling," and "religion" increasingly came to be understood as a substantive noun with a specific essence shared by the various historical "religions" (as in Feuerbach's* 1851 *Lectures on the Essence of Religion*). This was a necessary conceptual step in the birth of various secular philosophies during the Enlightenment period that sought to treat Christianity and the "other religions" as discrete cultural phenomena, to be located increasingly in the realm of private choice rather than in the realm of public politics. In this way, in the emerging nation-states of Northern Europe and the USA, "religion" came to be seen as a private phenomenon, a matter of personal choice, which was an extension of earlier Protestant notions of "private faith" but in a secularist* and, to an increasingly significant extent (through increased global migration patterns), a pluralistic* setting.

Although the term was coined much earlier, it was not until the late 19th and early 20th c. that the concept of "world religion" grew in prominence. This idea became popular as a means of classifying Christianity and the other major traditions of the world (Hinduism*, Buddhism*, Judaism*, Islam*) under a single pluralistic rubric (Masuzawa). Although this reflected a movement away from an older, more exclusivist attitude (according to which either Christianity was the "only" real religion as opposed to superstitions* and heresies*, or Christianity as the "true" religion was contrasted with the various false religions), the world-religions paradigm tends to locate all other traditions according to a broadly Christian prototypical model of what a "religion" is (Masuzawa). Nevertheless, one of the consequences of rendering "Christianity" as one of a number of "world religions" has been to throw into relief its historical and cultural embeddedness as one of a number of culturally embedded "cosmographic formations" (to use Daniel Dubuisson's preferred alternative to the concept of "religion"). **See also** INCULTURATION CLUSTER; RELIGIONS AND CHRISTIANITY.

RICHARD KING

RELIGIONS AND CHRISTIANITY

See AFRICAN RELIGION AND CHRISTIANITY CLUSTER; ANCESTOR VENERATION AND CHRISTIANITY CLUSTER; AUSTRALIAN ABORIGINAL TRADITIONS AND CHRISTIANITY; BAHA'I FAITH AND CHRISTIANITY CLUSTER; BUDDHISM AND CHRISTIANITY CLUSTER; CIVIL RELIGION; CONFUCIANISM AND CHRISTIANITY CLUSTER; DAOISM AND CHRISTIANITY CLUSTER; FREEMASONRY AND CHRISTIANITY; HELLENISTIC RELIGIOUS TRADITIONS AND CHRISTIANITY'S SELF-DEFINITION; HINDUISM AND CHRISTIANITY CLUSTER; ISLAM AND CHRISTIANITY CLUSTER; JUDAISM AND CHRISTIANITY CLUSTER; MITHRAISM AND CHRISTIANITY; MYSTERY RELIGIONS AND CHRISTIANITY; NATIVE AMERICAN TRADITIONS AND CHRISTIANITY; NEW AGE SPIRITUALITY AND CHRISTIANITY; SHAMANISM AND CHRISTIANITY; SHINTO AND CHRISTIANITY; SIKHISM AND CHRISTIANITY CLUSTER; VODOU AND CHRISTIANITY

Religiosity, a term that has maintained its Latin connotations of scrupulousness, sometimes to excess or superstition*.

Religious Experience. See CHARISMATIC* AND PENTECOSTAL MOVEMENTS CLUSTER; EVANGELICALS/EVANGELICALISM CLUSTER; MYSTICISM, MYSTICS; ORTHODOX CHURCHES, EASTERN, CLUSTER.

RELIGIOUS ORDERS, ROMAN CATHOLIC, CLUSTER

1) Introductory Entries

Religious Orders, Roman Catholic. There are many ways to live one's faith in God, ranging from educating children to leading a contemplative life. Believers make a choice according to their aptitudes and personality.

The origin of the monastic lifestyle is commonly linked with asceticism* based on the eschatological character of faith in the eternal God. Yet in a transitory creation, there are also divinely given norms for life that reflect God's twofold relations to the world: God for the world, and the world for God. Both must be respected. Religious life, therefore, reflects the "incarnational*" character of Christian faith. Each person cannot embrace all aspects of faith. One can serve God in many ways, although the goal remains the same: the Reign (Kingdom*) of God. One must choose between a certain detachment from the world and a strong connection with it. Unfortunately, the term "asceticism" often has negative connotations: rejection of the world, flight from reality, hostility toward the body* and enjoyment. Asceticism, however, is never an end in itself. Through it one applies oneself to a higher good. The ascetic elements concretized in vows* are the external form of a religious life driven by the inner aspiration to cultivate a personal relationship with God. Jesus' life is full of ascetic elements. Traveling around in the service of his prophetic-religious task entailed his refusing to amass possessions, abandoning his own family, and not having a home of his own. He gave no thought to a customary trade or profession and accepted the risk of being despised, persecuted, and rejected by the established order. His message reflects his lifestyle: he accepted being baptized by John, called the masses to repent, proclaimed the priority of the Reign of God, insisted that a believer cannot serve two lords, and invited his followers to abandon all.

Antony and Egyptian Monasticism. Religious life, an indirect outgrowth of the lifestyle of the peripatetic preachers, is first explicitly found in the life of Antony*, who (c275) left his village in Egypt and lived in the nearby desert as the disciple of an older hermit*. Antony was not the first monk, but the first to belong to the group called "hermitic anchorites," hermits who "withdraw from public life" (Gk *anachorein*). Their way of live did not entail complete isolation. Humans cannot exist without a minimum of contact. Antony the hermit lived in a cell alone, and the older monk was his spiritual father. Once a week they celebrated the Eucharist; they devoted themselves to manual labor.

About 320, cenobitism* with a highly organized common life appeared in the Egyptian desert. Pachomius* founded a community of brothers who wanted to reach salvation* together and convened much more frequently than the semi-anchorites. They ate together, dressed in the same way, and shared manual labor, prayer, the Eucharist, and acceptance of the authority of the leader. For such groups a rule* became indispensable. They considered communal living to be of value in itself. Their goal was to build a community after the model of the first Christians in Jerusalem (Acts 4:32–35). Pachomius also founded communities of women.

Egyptian monasticism started to decline in the 5th c., because the original inspiration faded away, a common occurrence in monastic communities. Nevertheless, monasticism survived in Palestine, Syria, and Asia Minor (see Monasticism Cluster: In the Byzantine Empire; Monasticism Cluster: In the Syriac Tradition). The history of religious life is characterized by growth and decline, by ups and downs; it fades away and rises again. Crises arose because of external events, such as wars, plagues, and political repression, or because of internal factors, such as the slackening of discipline and of commitment to the ideal of monastic life. Numerous reform movements gave rise to new orders or communities, which were not actually completely new, but rather old forms coming to new life, as in the cases of the Carthusians* and Cistercians*.

Western Monasticism (c370–1050) was at first influenced by Egyptian monasticism. Augustine* speaks of monasteries in Treves, Milan, and Rome. The Augustinian* Rule, the oldest monastic rule of the West, is somewhat in the Pachomian tradition: the religious community seeks to signify a new society in this world. In Augustine's interpretation, "monk" no longer means someone who stays alone, but someone who forms a unit with others.

A difference between the Augustine and Benedict* Rules is that the Augustinian Rule was intended for a small group with common ideals, whereas the Rule of Benedict sought to exert a pronounced influence on the whole of social life. The great abbeys cared for schools, hospitals, courts, hospices, and services for the poor.

Reformation of the Church. From 1050 to 1300, the goal of monastic life became the reformation of the church. By 1050 the strict monastic orders had been founded and one could speak of "religious life" as a broader movement. Many mixed forms of religious life came into existence as a result of new social situations. The Roman Catholic Church began to participate actively in the expansion of society as a great political whole. In this context, there was a role for military* orders (Templars* and Hospitallers*, who intended to liberate the Holy Land). Still more influential was the movement of the canons* regular* at the time of the Gregorian reformation (see Gregory VII, Pope), where monastic elements and official priesthood were brought together. The clergy, unified in communal living around the bishop, started to live under a rule as canons, very much as monks did in a monastery. Norbert* (early 11th c.) wanted the canons regular to be open to (rather than separated from) the world through preaching and missionary work. The canon regular Dominic* initiated groups of itinerant Friar-Preachers, the Dominicans*.

During this period, the life of the mendicant* orders became the most typical form of religious life, following Francis*. At first Francis lived as a hermit but eventually became a homeless worker and preacher. Francis's and the mendicant orders' radical material poverty* was a protest against the wealth of the emerging European cities, where capitalism originated, and their mentality of "power through wealth." Those committed to a life of poverty believed that one should not be ashamed to live as a beggar. Furthermore, a mendicant monk was not bound to one house. The role of group father or mother was replaced by more democratic forms of government.

The success of the mendicant orders can be explained in part by the decline of the pastoral and spiritual life of the Roman Catholic Church at a time when new institutions, the universities, surpassed the teaching of the old monastic schools. The needs of the Church were so great that hermits from Palestine (Carmelites*) and Italy (Augustinians) could no longer live in isolation. In the late Middle Ages, the Devotio* Moderna called for greater interiority and personalization of the act of faith; and the observant movements (to which

Luther* belonged) called for renewal and reformation.

Religious Life as Apostolic Service to the Church. This was initiated by Ignatius* (1539), who wanted to free himself from the old and decaying structures of the Church. A religious community ceased to be an entity in its own right. Ignatius continued to call for the individual's experience of God (Devotio Moderna) and affirmed centralized authority in the religious community, but he required neither habit nor choral prayer, a reflection of the development of personalism in Western culture. The community became the matrix of apostolic work, a support for the pastoral commitment of individual members. In the same period, congregations for women devoted themselves to social work, especially among girls (Angela Merici*). Belonging to the Church involved working together; thus obedience became essential, and religious life contributed to the edification of the church.

In the late Middle Ages, objections arose to religious life: it was asserted that neither Holy Scripture nor Jesus Christ supported life in religious orders and that it was a form of "Pharisaism" because members of religious communities considered themselves better than other Christians.

Expansion of Religious Orders. The 16th and 17th c. were times of expansion of religious orders. In the great abbeys, certain monks specialized in and published scientific works. Thus, e.g., the Maurists* preserved much of the ancient cultures (both Christian and non-Christian cultures); seminaries and vocational schools flourished. Many religious communities sought their identity in secondary elements of Christian faith, e.g. the adoration of the Eucharist.

General Secularization. In the 18th and early 19th c., secularization* went further than a separation between state and religion. The saying was: only what is useful is valid; and in modern society, religious orders and their life were not considered useful. Hence many orders and congregations were abolished. Even prominent theologians thought that religious orders and their life were dead. But in the 19th c., there was an astonishing growth of religious establishments and religious groups of all sizes. Nearly all modern congregations devoted themselves to an active goal: caring for the sick, teaching, providing schools for everyone, creating presses, caring for the poor, housing the homeless, caring for unwed mothers, helping juvenile delinquents, and carrying out missionary work in foreign countries. The Redemptorists*, the Montfortans, and the Fathers of the Holy Spirit were founded to address the need for pastoral services among the lowest classes. This disinterested commitment to the needy is characteristic of modern congregations and reflects the devotional and individual spirituality of that age. While Ignatius's spirituality placed Jesus at the center, many modern congregations adopted particular saints, such as Mary, Joseph, and Barbara.

Cultural Crisis. Between 1960 and 1970, especially in Europe, there was a sharp decline in the number of religious, there were no new vocations, and young people did not seem interested in the way of life of a religious order. Secularization took on a new significance, the autonomous human person became the judge and the end of all things. Only what can be observed in human experience is true; thus the existence of a transcendental reality is denied. Yet even in this situation, there are signs of a new beginning. For members of religious orders and other Christians, the goal of religious life remains the same: contributing to the realization of the Reign* of God. New forms of communal life with more specialized activities are emerging, emphasizing interpersonal relationships in smaller groups. In countless groups, abandoning the world takes the form of being socially critical in the name of the Christian faith. Is this a sign of revival of religious life?

T. J. VAN BAVEL, OSA

Religious Orders, Roman Catholic: Forms of Religious Life. Religious life has taken many forms. It arose within 60 years of the Crucifixion in response to Jesus' resurrection. Some Christians, predominantly women, convinced of the active presence of the risen Jesus in their lives, and liberated by faith in the resurrection from the fear of personal or social extinction through death, felt personally called to express the totality and exclusiveness of their relationship to Christ by lifelong consecrated virginity*, characteristically interpreted as espousal to him. The first virgins usually lived in their own homes, participated as specially honored members in the life of the local church, and devoted themselves especially to a life of prayer. Virgins were a prime target of Roman persecution*, both because as Christians they refused to participate in the cult of the emperor and because virginity itself constituted a withholding of their reproductive capacities from the service of the Empire. Some, e.g. Agnes, appear in the calendar of Christian saints as "virgins and martyrs," highlighting virginity as a chosen way of life.

A parallel phenomenon was the institution of consecrated widowhood*, to which 1 Tim 5:3–16 testifies. These widows, who chose not to remarry, were recognized as a special order in the church that carried out caritative ministries, catechized* new converts, and prayed unceasingly for the church.

When the church, freed from persecution, became increasingly involved in the life of the Roman Empire (3rd c.), some Christians fled to the deserts of Egypt and Arabia, seeking refuge from the secularization of the institutional church. Desert monasticism* retained the original features of religious life, namely virginity or celibacy as a form of total consecration to Christ, ecclesial recognition, dedication to prayer, and service to the neighbor. In addition, there was an emphasis on rejection of the "world," which was understood to be the sinful secular order, and rigorous asceticism* of mind and body in quest of an ideal of contemplation*. Antony* (c250–350) remained the prototype of the desert hermit, while Pachomius* (d346) founded the first monastery in Egypt. Cenobitic* monastic life (in community) was codified in the Rule of Basil* (c330–379) in the East and the Rule of Benedict* (c480–c534) in the West.

As the church spread into diverse geographic and cultural contexts in Europe and eventually the New World, religious life diversified. During the medieval period, monasticism remained the dominant form among both men and women. But from the 12th c. to the Reformation (which suppressed religious orders among Protestants), the mendicant* religious life, typified by the Franciscans* and Dominicans*, modified classical monasticism. The apostolic energy of this new form of religious life eventually fueled the emergence of nonmonastic male clerical orders like the Jesuits* and lay male orders like the Christian Brothers, which were devoted to the work of evangelization at home and abroad. Efforts to found apostolic women's congregations such as the Ursulines (see Angela of Foligno; Merici, Angela; Religious Women's Orders Cluster: In Europe and North America) were repeatedly suppressed by ecclesiastical authorities in their attempts to enforce cloister. Finally, in 1900 Pope Leo XIII recognized what the people who had been served for centuries by committed religious women providing health, educational, and social service had long known, namely that these members of the "congregations of simple vows," like members of traditional cloistered orders, were indeed religious. During the 1800s and early 1900s, the number of women religious increased to the hundreds of thousands, and women religious outnumbered their male counterparts three to one.

The Second Vatican* Council called religious to renew their life according to the gospel and their founding charisms* and to modernize their lives and ministries. This renewal effort precipitated 30 years of turbulence from which religious life is slowly emerging. Contemporary religious life is no longer seen, by its members or others, as an elite or superior form of Christian life but as a distinct life form in the church characterized by the total commitment of its members to Christ in prayer and ministry expressed in the perpetual profession of vows of consecrated celibacy, voluntary poverty*, and obedience, lived in community. SANDRA M. SCHNEIDERS, IHM

2) A Sampling of Contextual Views and Practices

Religious Orders, Roman Catholic, in Africa. Religious life has its origins with the desert fathers and hermits* in North Africa, where they lived solitary, ascetic*, and prayerful lives. Religious life in communities began with monasticism*, often said to have originated with Antony* of Egypt* (250–356). Later developments in Western monasticism introduced religious as "contemplatives in action" (not cloistered and with a missionary thrust). On the African continent, cloistered contemplatives* exist in a few communities of Carmelites*, Poor* Clares, and Benedictines*; however, there are more "contemplatives in action." Men and women religious are more numerous in Tanzania*, the Democratic Republic of Congo*, Nigeria*, Kenya*, and Madagascar*.

Consecrated life in Africa came with colonization and evangelization. Missionary bishops initially founded "local orders" in their dioceses for pastoral needs. Much later, missionaries from main orders like the Jesuits*, Dominicans*, Franciscans*, Carmelites*, Comboni, and Missionary Oblates (OMI) recruited locals into international orders. Religious were compartmentalized into teaching and nursing orders according to the founding charism* of each. Their schools and hospitals offer high-quality education* and health* care. Men and women religious promote the Roman Catholic ethos and values of the founder/foundress (e.g. Jesuit, Dominican, Mary Ward* values in education).

Vatican II urged religious groups to go back to their founding charism* and to adapt to the "signs of the times." The response in Africa was a diversification of apostolates, as well as local and national collaboration in ministry among different religious orders, a sharing of resources and expertise (including, at different stages of formation, candidacy, noviceship, juniorate, and tertianship). Decrees by general congregations of the different orders have affirmed the preferential* option for the poor and marginalized of society (women, children, and people affected and infected by the HIV/AIDS pandemic). Today new ministries locate religious in pastoral care and in working for social justice and peace. Women religious are gradually engaging in theology, spiritual direction, and lecturing at seminaries and theological faculties.

Evangelical vows*, key to the religious life, are not totally strange to African cultures*. African cultures place a high value on simple and social communal living (poverty*), virginity* (chastity), and obedience to authority. However, celibacy* seems to be a contradiction of Africans' love for family* life and children. Poverty is also problematic in the African context of material poverty. By virtue of their education and skills, religious cannot be considered materially poor. But they live out poverty by sharing their goods (through charitable work) and living a simple life style.

FRANCISCA H. CHIMHANDA

Religious Orders, Roman Catholic, in Latin America: Brazil. The concept of religious order (*status religionis*) in the Roman Catholic Church is essentially based on vows* of obedience, chastity*, and poverty* of a member of a religious community, which bind him or herself to the rules of a certain order canonically admitted. Religious orders are basically divided into two clerical groups: regular* and secular*. The regular orders comprise clergy/priests and nuns who live according to a rule (*regula*), whereas the secular clergy (who serve "in time" or in the world) comprise clergy/priests and members of the Roman Catholic Church who respond to the needs of ordinary people. Both kinds of clergy had a decisive role in Brazilian history.

There are roughly five phases in the history of religious orders in Brazil. The first (1500–1759) was characterized by missionary and catechizing activities in the new land, mainly with regard to indigenous groups. Their conversion led to the spread of the Roman Catholic Church throughout the overseas territories of the Portuguese Empire. The process of evangelization was not divorced from the colonization process, in which the state used the spiritual work of the Church for its own ends through the system of royal patronage (Padroado* Régio), a juridical institution by which the crown could interfere with ecclesiastical matters and subject the colonial Church to its authority. This period saw the establishment of convents and monasteries, as well as colleges and missionary schools. Six religious orders had a conspicuous role during this phase: the Jesuits* (1549), the Carmelites* (1580/84), the Benedictines* (1581), the Franciscans* (1585), the Capuchins (1612), and the Mercedarians (1639).

The second phase (1759–1822) was marked by two kinds of conflicts initially provoked by the expulsion of the Jesuit order from Brazil (1767). First, there were conflicts between religious orders and secular clergy regarding the strategy for conducting missions*; religious orders established "reductions*" (Spanish, *reducciones*; Portuguese, *aldeias*), Christian settlements where people lived with the regular clergy, primarily Jesuits, following strict rules, whereas the secular clergy preferred to establish parishes. The expulsion of the Jesuits signaled the Portuguese crown's fear of the autonomy of the religious orders. Second, there was the beginning of the struggle between crown and church. This struggle was exacerbated not only by the very controlled enlargement and multiplication of dioceses and prelacies and their submission to the colonial state, but also by the reinforcement of the Padroado (see Church and State Relations Cluster: In Latin America).

The third phase (1830–1930) witnessed the reorganization of the religious orders under the authority of the Roman Catholic Church and, simultaneously, an alleviation of the influence of the Iberian metropolis, Portugal*, on its colony; the movement of independence coincided with, and was stimulated by, these changes. This was also a period of intensified political crisis, which culminated in the so-called Religious Question (1872–75), when two clergy (D. Macedo Costa and Friar Vital Maria) were punished by the emperor of Brazil, Pedro II (1825–1891), for their opposition to Freemasonry*, with which the emperor himself was affiliated.

The fourth phase (1930–60) saw the rise of a growing number of other religious orders (e.g. Theatines, Marists, Laterans, Ursulines, Salesians), which established new hospitals and educational institutions.

The last phase (since 1960) has witnessed a split among the religious orders. The dictatorial governments that simultaneously sprang up throughout Latin America sharpened the division between, on the one side, contemplative orders, like the Augustinians* (since 1889) and Benedictines*, and, on the other side, socially engaged orders, such as the Dominicans* (after 1882) and Franciscans*. Yet on both sides, in the early 21st c. there were conservative and progressive trends, making it difficult to say which trend will prevail in the future. **See also BRAZIL; WOMEN'S RELIGIOUS ORDERS CLUSTER: IN LATIN AMERICA: BRAZIL.**

MARCOS CALDAS

Religious Orders, Roman Catholic, in Latin America: Mexico. Although Friar Bartolomé de Olmedo, a Mercedarian friar, arrived with Hernán Cortés in 1519, religious orders began to appear in Mexico with the first Franciscan* mission (1524). The orders (including several small orders founded in Spain) arrived successively: Dominicans* (1526), Augustinians* (1533), Jesuits* (1572), Discalced (barefoot) Carmelites* (1585), Mercedarios ("Knights of Mercy," 1589), Conceptionist sisters (1530), Dominican sisters (1567), Poor* Clares (1570), and Jerónimites (1585), followed by Juaninos (1604) and Oratorians (1659). During the colonial period, the life of the Roman Catholic Church was marked by rivalry between Spanish and native members, by the different areas of competence and charisms* of the orders, and by constant conflict with the diocesan hierarchy, given the special status of the regulars*. The religious orders in New Spain were extremely active, as demonstrated by the large number of vocations they gave rise to and by their contribution to the economic, cultural, and social life of Mexico. But after the expulsion of the Jesuits (1767), the number of regulars dwindled; the decline was intensified during the time of national independence and continued in the 19th c. The Laws of Reform (1856–60) were especially difficult for regulars: in 1863 the only legally admitted order was that of the Sisters of Charity. When the conflict with the government subsided (c1873), church members asked that the regulars and their ministries be reinstated; the first male Mexican congregation, the Missionaries of San José of Mexico, and its female branch, the Sisters Josefinas, were established (1873). Gradually new religious orders arrived in Mexico: Claretians (1872), Salesians (1892), Marists Brothers (1899), Lasallians (1903), Benedictines (1903), Capuchins* (1907), Redemptorists (1908), Escolapians (1913), and the Sisters of the Sacred Heart, the Sisters of San José, and the Sisters of Good Shepherd (c1914–16). The second Mexican congregation, the Missionaries of the Holy Spirit, was created in 1914. Owing to legal intolerance and subsequent governmental religious persecutions, the period from 1917 to 1938 was difficult for the regulars. After a *modus vivendi* was worked out (see Mexico), several additional congregations were founded, including the Legion of Christ (1941). The number of male orders, including new native orders, increased from 25 in 1914 to 67 in 1990 (along with an additional 7 lay, apostolic, or contemplative orders), and the number of female orders, including 89 new national orders, increased from 97 in 1914 to 231 in 1990 (along with an additional 27 apostolic or contemplative orders). By 2000 there were 313 orders performing their respective ministries, coordinated by the Conferencia de Superiores Mayores de México (CIRM). **See also WOMEN'S RELIGIOUS ORDERS CLUSTER.**

MONICA URIBE

Reliquary, small container for relics*, usually decorated with precious materials. Initially portable, sometimes in the shape of the cross, the gabled shrine originated in the Middle Ages.

Remnant, the portion that remains after the removal of all else; a concept (expressed by various biblical terms) applied to those who remained after many in Israel were destroyed or exiled (Ezra 9:8; Zech 14:2) or to those who would return from exile among the nations to constitute a new Israel. In the Prophets, the reference to "remnant" is often threatening; only a few, a faithful remnant, will remain (Amos 5). Whether and how Paul* used this concept in Rom 9–11 is debated. In the Synoptic Gospels, passages about the Last Judgment* often allude to a remnant that alone will be saved (e.g. Matt 3:7–10, 7:13–14, 13:10–17, par.).

Remonstrance, statement composed by Jan Uytenbogaert (1610) that outlined the views of the followers of the Dutch theologian Jacobus Arminius, known as the Remonstrants or Arminians*. The Remonstrants challenged the Calvinist doctrine of divine grace* and argued for the convocation of a synod to reconsider the Belgic* Confession and the Heidelberg* Catechism. The Remonstrance included five articles: grace is universally prevenient (anticipatory); election* is conditional on faith*; the atonement* provided by Jesus' death was intended to be unlimited and universal; God's grace can be resisted; and perseverance in faith is not certain and thus it is possible for believers to fall from grace. Condemned by the Counter-Remonstrance, the theological dispute that followed soon took on political overtones and led to the division of the states of Holland. The Remonstrance was condemned by the Synod of Dort* (Dordt, Dordrecht) (1618), which prohibited Remonstrant church services and exiled church leaders unwilling to renounce their beliefs. Remonstrant exiles reunited in Antwerp (1619) and returned to Holland (1631) to form the Remonstrant Reformed Church (finally formally recognized in 1795). Many congregations joined the Netherland* Reformed Church and continue to exist.

RENÉE JEFFERY

Renaissance (French, "rebirth"). Jacob Burckhardt's influential *Civilization of the Renaissance in Italy* (1860) made famous the notion that the Renaissance represented the birth of the self-conscious, "modern" individual. But during the 20th c., we learned that Renaissance men and women belonged more to their own time than they did to a future one. There was a rebirth during the Renaissance, in two senses: (1) a recovery of the artifacts (objects and texts) of classical Greek and Roman civilizations and (2) the rise of innovative practices, texts, works of art and architecture, and politics that grew out of this recovery.

Humanists rediscovered Latin texts in monasteries and other archives that had been forgotten for centuries, expanding knowledge of classical literature to its present limits. Only one major text has been discovered (19th c.) since: Cicero's *De republica* (see Erasmus, Desiderius; Humanism and Renaissance). The rediscovery extended to artifacts – the remains of buildings, sculpture, and a few paintings. These led to transformations in painting (linear perspective, use of color; during the 1400s), sculpture (freestanding statues, Donatello; early 1400s), and architecture (culminating in Palladian style; 1500s); music (polyphony, wedding of words and notes; 1500s); cosmology (sun-centered, Copernicus*; 1543); and medicine (empirical attitude toward the body, which led to knowledge of the circulation of blood; 1600s). These innovations were powered by a mercantile capitalist economy that generated great wealth for a few and thriving urban centers.

Most people who lived during the Renaissance, however, were unaware of it and did not share in it. Social historical studies of this much larger population, especially since the early 1970s, has led many to see greater continuity than fundamental change during the Renaissance, and these studies have led to an academic quarrel over terminology –"Renaissance" describing a higher culture, "early modern" the continuity of social history before, during, and after the Renaissance.

Religion represents a special case in this debate, inasmuch as the Reformation* was at once a high culture (scholarly) movement and a mass movement, mobilizing large populations and leading to fundamental shifts in ways of thinking about a host of issues close to most people: the relation of men and women (see Marriage, Theology and Practice of, Cluster; Women's Christian Practice and Theologies Cluster), the purposes and extent of education*, and the sources of authority and its justification. By 1648, when the wars of religion finally ended, Europe had been transformed; the Renaissance and the Reformation were the engines that powered the transformation.

ALBERT RABIL, JR.

Renunciation of the Devil, formal renunciation of Satan and all his company; part of baptism* at least since the 3rd c. and still found in several traditions. It was linked not only with the rejection of idolatry* but with the view of the Crucifixion as a ransom* from captivity to the devil*. **See also ATONEMENT.**

Reordination. Should ordination* be repeated? In light of the controversies related to Cyprian*, the Donatists*, and simony* (11th c.), the Western Church concluded that ordinations need not be repeated if performed in the right form and with the right intention.

Repentance (verb roots: Heb *shuv*; Gk *metanoeo*), sorrow over and confession of one's sins, "turning away from" evil, along with a turning toward God. True contrition* is motivated by love for God, whereas attrition* is motivated by fear of punishment. In contrast, conversion* emphasizes the "turning toward" God. **See also PENANCE AND FORGIVENESS.**

Reprobation. See ATONEMENT; DAMNATION; HELL; JUDGMENT; PURGATORY.

Requiem Mass, normally celebrated as a Funeral Mass, includes the rite of final commendation of the deceased, followed by the rite of Christian burial when there is no cremation. In broader terms, a Requiem Mass can refer to other Masses celebrated for the deceased such as on All Souls' Day (November 2) and on anniversaries of death. **See also MASS, ROMAN CATHOLIC.**

KEITH F. PECKLERS, SJ

Rerum Novarum. See SOCIAL ENCYCLICALS.

Responsorial Psalms, Psalms sung by a solo cantor or choir, with the congregation responding by singing a repeated verse. The practice originated with Joseph Gelineau, SJ, was further developed in the Taizé* community, and was adapted from the Roman Catholic liturgical reading of the Psalms that used certain verses as a refrain during the recitation of an entire Psalm (a practice found before and after the Council of Trent*).

Restoration Movement, the 1830s union in the USA of followers of Barton Stone* and Alexander Campbell* (also known as the Stone–Campbell Movement). It sought Christian unity through the restoration of what were believed to be NT practices, including the confession of Christ (not creeds*), weekly Lord's Supper*, and believer's baptism*. The movement spread to Great Britain and has become worldwide. Changing social contexts led to several branches: Christian Church (Disciples of Christ), Churches of Christ, and Christian Churches and Churches of Christ. Each witnesses in distinctive ways to Christian unity through faithfulness to Jesus Christ. **See also CHRISTIAN CHURCH (DISCIPLES OF CHRIST).** D. NEWELL WILLIAMS

Resurrection of the Body in Western Christianity refers to two related resurrections: the resurrection* of Jesus on the third day after his death and the general resurrection of all humans in the last days. While bodily resurrection is at the heart of NT teachings, it was not self-evident that a decayed body could become whole again: "How are the dead raised? With what kind of body do they come?" (1 Cor 15:35). These questions became a subject of theological inquiry and debate, leading to a plurality of understandings about the resurrection of the body.

Authors used a number of metaphors* grounded in the Bible, each with its own assumptions and consequences.

1. *Body as seed.* This metaphor was used by Paul (1 Cor 15:36–54) to explain the resurrection of the body after burial. "Seed" connotes both continuity and transformation. The seed and the sprout are the same entity, but the sprout differs from the seed, suggesting that the post-resurrection individual differs from his or her former self.
2. *Body as reassembled pieces.* In the patristic period, authors such as Tertullian* of Carthage and Augustine* of Hippo preferred the metaphor of a mended pot or statue, which emphasized the material continuity of the individual body (i.e. the continuity of its particles and members). Reassemblage metaphors remained popular through the 17th c., as did ideas about the survival in the afterlife of physical markers such as sex or personal appearance.
3. *Love between body and soul.* In the late Middle Ages, art, hagiography, poetry, and theology emphasized the theme of desire*, making parallels between the body*–soul* connection and romantic love*. Many other metaphors existed (e.g. the reassemblage of ships, the donning of new clothes, the smelting of ore, the hatching of an egg).

No matter which metaphor was preferred, resurrection theology led to a host of concerns: Would aborted* fetuses be resurrected? Would physical deformities persist in heaven? At what age would bodies be resurrected? Theologians addressed these in various ways.

Western Christianity consistently identified the physical body as an inherent part of the self. This position made necessary the doctrine of bodily resurrection, since the soul could not ultimately be rewarded or punished without the body. The paradox* of resurrection is that the body is understood to be both subject to decay and incorruptible. Premodern theologians were for the most part willing to accept this paradox to preserve the material and structural continuity of the self in the afterlife. LEAH DEVUN

Resurrection of the Dead in Eastern Orthodoxy. Orthodox Christians derive their beliefs about the bodily resurrection of the dead from the Nicene Creed, in which the faithful profess, "I expect the resurrection of the dead and the life of ages to come." The resurrection and transfiguration*, heralded by the life of Jesus Christ, mark the beginning of a "new* creation," after which the final Judgment* will occur. The transformation is understood to be a natural, biological event rather than a magical or mechanical one.

Eastern Orthodoxy maintains that many details concerning death* and the resurrection of the dead have not been revealed by God; therefore, theologians offer nondoctrinal teachings based in Holy Tradition, called *theologoumena*. For example, for theologian Metropolitian Maximos*, partial judgment follows physical death and ushers the righteous into an intermediate stage of partial blessedness during which the fate of the deceased may be influenced by intercessory prayer.

Orthodox liturgical practices reflect these beliefs through hymns of gratitude to God and traditional Byzantine chants designed to convey the range of human emotions experienced at death. The burning of incense signifies prayers carried upward to Christ, and candles symbolize liberation from darkness as the departed embark on a path to Light. **See also DYING, CARE OF THE, AN EASTERN ORTHODOX PERSPECTIVE.** JOHN T. CHIRBAN

Resurrection of Jesus, proclaimed in Matt 28:1–15, Mark 16:1–8, Luke 24:1–49, John 20:1–29, and 1 Cor 15:1–58, has been debated by Western theologians and historians since the Enlightenment*.

Historiography* effectively precluded any affirmative judgment concerning the historicity of Jesus' resurrection (Troeltsch*, 1865–1923). Hermann Reimarus (1694–1768), influenced by Deism*, insisted that Jesus' disciples stole his body. Strauss* (1808–74), influenced by Hegel*, pioneered an understanding of the Gospels and

Jesus' resurrection as myth*. William Wrede (1859–1906) saw both the Resurrection and the messianic secret in Mark* as creations of Jesus' disciples. For Wilhelm Bousset (1865–1920; history* of religion school), the early church grafted Greek and Hellenistic ideas onto Christianity and thus deified Jesus. For Martin Kähler (1835–1912), historical research is always limited and provisional; one should thus not assess the claims of Scripture historically.

Theologians struggled with these issues. Barth's* (1886–1968) dialectical* theology rejected both liberal* and natural* theologies, emphasized revelation*, and thus downplayed historical affirmations of Jesus' resurrection because they placed human assertions above God's Word*. Bultmann* (1884–1976) shifted the focus from Jesus to the early church with form criticism; he demythologized* NT miracle* and resurrection stories; influenced by Heidegger*, he emphasized the existential significance of these stories for believers. Wolfhart Pannenberg (1928–) rejects Barth's view as indistinguishable from "self-delusion" and Bultmann's as "pure myth" in order to come back to a historical affirmation (Jesus actually rose from the dead) as the most plausible explanation of the Christology of Jesus' followers. In their natural theologies, the analytic philosophers Stephen Davis, Richard Swinburne, and Gary Habermas reach similar conclusions.

N. T. Wright, John Dominic Crossan, and Gerd Lüdemann seek to explain the rise of resurrection belief. For Crossan, influenced by literary criticism and cross-cultural anthropology, resurrection language is about ecclesiastical authority* (rather than life after death), arising from a sense of Jesus' presence* in the church. From Lüdemann's psychological perspective, the resurrection stories reflect the experience of Jesus' loving presence by the deeply grieving Peter and the guilt-driven Paul. According to Wright's worldview analysis, the natural meaning of resurrection in 1st-c. Judaism was bodily and corporate. As a mutation of Jewish belief (Jesus is raised *prior to* the general resurrection), early Christian belief in Jesus' resurrection and empty tomb and the reports of his appearance are most easily understood if Jesus was in fact raised bodily from the dead. For Wright (like Crossan), resurrection is also about God establishing justice* in the world.

Presuppositions concerning miracles*, historical* method, Scripture*, hermeneutics*, and faith* are involved in any understanding of Jesus' resurrection. ROBERT B. STEWART

Retreat, withdrawal or seclusion for religious meditation and devotion, first institutionalized by the Jesuits*, Francis* de Sales, and Vincent* de Paul.

Revelation (Gk *apokalypsis,* Lat. *revelatio,* translating Heb *glh,* "unveiling" or "disclosure" of what was hidden). Expanding on the visual metaphor of unveiling, the term was applied sometimes to a dramatic act of God, sometimes to a theophany*, and sometimes to the genre known as apocalyptic* (Book of Revelation*). An alternative to the visual metaphor was the auditory mode of disclosure – "the Word* of God" and Scripture* as inspired*.

In Christianity, revelation means primarily God's encounter with those to whom God wishes to communicate God's own being, promise, and will. This God, "the God of Abraham, the God of Isaac, and the God of Jacob," the "God not of the dead but of the living" (Matt 22:32), "who raised Jesus our Lord from the dead" (Rom 4:24), reveals God's self – not something or someone else, not even something about God, but God's own self.

This divine communication may happen in diverse ways, through, e.g., stories, the created world, and events. Revelation is differentiated from knowledge of God given through the natural world (Rom 1:19–20; Acts 17:23–29). Revelation happens. It is *not* a form of knowledge that would result from such encounters with the divine and that would need to be conserved and held. Yet revelation is to be retold in the form of stories of these encounters and thus communicated to others (see, e.g., Julian of Norwich).

The story of the prophet Elijah's encounter with God presents the revelation of God's self in "sheer silence," in contrast to the "shaking elements" of nature such as earthquakes, thunderstorms, and fire (1 Kgs 19:11–12). This silence causes Elijah to cover himself. Within this haunting silence, God shows him the path he is to follow in the midst of a world full of confusion and directs him to the inconspicuous community of believers. God's revelation tells people what they cannot tell themselves. The Bible bears witness to this revelation, made known in Christ's proclamation. What is disclosed in this way illuminates human history and makes possible the reading and understanding of other testimonies to this history in its light (see Typology).

Revelation is the event in and through which God discloses who God is, how God is acting, and what God's intentions are. Since this divine self-revelation also reveals the situation and condition of those to whom God communicates, it is often painful to be exposed to this revealing process. It causes fear and trembling. At the same time, God's communication gives believers a clarity about themselves that liberates them from self-centeredness, opening them to God's communication, which transforms them into beings capable of being drawn into participation in God's work. God's revelation unveils what humans want to conceal and suppress, yet this unveiling is only the obverse of the nearness of a God who is closer to humans than they are to themselves. Such revealed nearness transforms the whole context of believers' life (see Heteronomy; Mysticism, Mystics).

One can glimpse the mystery* of both God's gracious nearness and the hiddenness of God's presence (see Apophaticism), perceive the utter otherness of the ground of faith (see Faith #5), and also be overwhelmed by joy at the abundance of God's love*. Each revelatory event makes one surprisingly aware that one's perception of God's acting is always provisional and partial, not only because of the limitations of human knowledge (see Reason), but also, and even more so, because God reserves further action for the future so that one perceives God's faithfulness only through hope* and confidence in the divine promises.

A very different understanding of revelation is suggested by the last book of the Bible, "Revelation*," which belongs to the apocalyptic genre. Its title has often caused misunderstanding, because the book describes visions of future dramatic events, seemingly known only in advance through God's revealing their secret developments to elected persons. In this case, revelation would be defined as the uncovering of secrets rather than the encountering of a mystery. Furthermore, at times the Book of Revelation has been understood to be a blueprint of God's acting in history, or even as a divine timetable by which we may plot our present position and distance from the end of all things.

A more appropriate reading of this apocalyptic book underscores that Rev 1:1 speaks of "the revelation of Jesus Christ." He is the crucified victor who destroys the powers of hell*. In Christ's ongoing story, his people's future is decided and contained. Christ is the coming one who personifies God's truthfulness in the midst of all the pain and passion of a tortured world. His revelation is given to encourage hope, endurance, and confidence. The whole scope of the story of Christ is revealed and will be consummated in the coming of God, who will dwell with his people and will make all things new (Rev 21: 3–5).

A third conception identifies revelation with "the word of God" and Jesus Christ as the incarnate Word of God. This view was developed by thinking of the Logos* (the Word; John 1:1–18), the second person of the Trinity*, not only as the revealer of God's decisions and purposes for the world, but also as the gestalt of God's gracious will, the manifestation of God to human beings. Whatever awareness humans have of God and God's purposes has its origin in God's own self-disclosure, the Logos.

Finally, revelation is associated with the Holy* Spirit, which reminds one of, testifies to, and extends Jesus' proclamation and mission (John 16:7–15) and inspires Scripture* (2 Tim 3:16). To affirm the revealed origin of Scripture is not to say that revelation is contained in the Bible. It is rather to claim that these texts have a revelatory role; through the Scriptures, revelation takes place (see Scripture).

Revelation has been contrasted through history with reason* and the knowledge (of God) gained through reason and through observation of the natural world (see Science and Christian Theology). While in medieval times and beyond, revelation was viewed as nurturing reason and going beyond its reach (see Locke, John), the Enlightenment* favored reason over revelation, because it did not make claims to special insight or authority (see Rationalism and Christian Theology). In turn, certain theologians, including Kierkegaard* and Barth*, disputed the claims of natural* theology and relied exclusively on revelation. GERHARD SAUTER

Revelation, Book of. The vision John records in Revelation (1:1) includes Christ and heaven (1:9–20; 4, 5), Christ's messages to seven local churches (2, 3), partial destruction of the earth (e.g. 6:1–16; 8:6–9:21; 16:1–21), mythical creatures (13; 17:1–18:19; 19:11–20:15), and God's establishment of the New Jerusalem (21:1–22:5). The authorship of the book has been disputed since the 2nd c. For some the author was John*, son of Zebedee, a disciple of Jesus. Most modern scholars, denying this identification, argue that this "John" is the author of neither the Gospel of John nor the Epistles of John*.

Through symbolic language, Revelation points to the dominance of the Roman Empire, both economically (e.g. 13:16–17; 17:4; 18:11–19) and politically (13:1–2; 17:18). It addresses problems experienced by early Christians, including persecution* (2:10, 13; 13:7, 15; 17:6), whether to participate in Roman religious customs (2:14, 20; 13:6, 12), and a lack of fervor by adherents (2:4; 3:16).

The author understands his work to be "prophecy" (1:3; 22:18–19). His imagery draws heavily on Jewish Scripture, especially prophetic literature (e.g. Rev 4:1–11; cf. Isa 6:1–9; Ezek 1:4–28). The use of familiar OT imagery lends authority to the author's vision: what John sees is similar to what prophets before him have seen. Imagery from the OT also lends meaning to the vision, as when God's domination of Egypt during the plagues (Exod 7–12) recurs in a new context (Rev 16) (see Typology). As prophecy, Revelation speaks words of exhortation and comfort to the author's situation.

Revelation also uses conventions of apocalyptic literature – such as a heavenly journey (Rev 4:1) interpreted by an angel (21:9–10) and visions of beasts (Rev 13; cf. Dan 7:1–8) – to communicate a divine perspective rather than a worldly one.

In a context in which the Roman Empire appeared to be all powerful, Revelation emphasizes the dominion of God. Christians experiencing persecution are comforted by the promise of God's triumph over evil (Rev 19–22); Christians tempted to participate in Roman religious or economic practices are reminded that the power of these is illusory and that their own inheritance of God's promises requires faithfulness to God in the present (2–3; 21–22).

Christians have disputed the authority of Revelation since the 2nd c. In many traditions, it is infrequently read during worship. Other traditions rely heavily on Revelation to support expectations of Christ's immediate return. A wide variety of artistic renderings of scenes from Revelation have shaped readers' imaginations throughout Christian history. **See also APOCALYPTICISM CLUSTER; MILLENNIALISM CLUSTER.** SUSAN E. HYLEN

Revival, Revivalism, terms that refer to a phenomenon among Protestant Evangelicals* in which, through extraordinary community experiences, a large number of people find themselves experiencing a greater desire for fervent devotion to Christianity.

Early manifestations of revivalism took place in Europe, notably the 17th- to 18th-c. Pietist* Movement led by Phillip Spener* and August Francke*, and the Moravian* revival (1727) led by Count Ludwig Zinzendorf*. Moravians inspired the Methodist John Wesley* and his friend George Whitefield* in their leadership of the transatlantic Great* Awakening, the first and archetypal revival movement of the English-speaking world. The work of a movement of theologically sympathetic Evangelicals, the Great Awakening revivals began in the 1730s, rapidly spreading fervor for conversion and personal experience of God throughout England, Europe, and the American colonies. The Great Awakening can be interpreted as the formative event of modern Evangelicalism*.

In the early 19th c., the Second Great* Awakening spread across the USA on a platform of personal piety, social reform and, most significantly, a major international mission movement, which exported US revivalist Evangelicalism worldwide.

The first major global revival movement began with the rise of Pentecostalism* via the Azusa Street revival (Los Angeles, 1906). Today, Pentecostalism and the Charismatic* Movement together comprise the second-largest Christian movement in the world.

While revivalists are not theologically unified, some features are generally common to all forms of revivalism. (1) Revivalism involves a desire for individuals to experience conversion* to Christianity through a direct, immediate connection to God the Holy* Spirit, an experience typically accompanied by a strong conviction of personal sin* and distance from God. In the conversion experience, God is seen to be demonstrably overcoming that estrangement. (2) Revivalism is usually accompanied by dramatic, exhortatory preaching in which preachers call listeners to repentance and conversion. (3) Much revivalism strongly emphasizes an ongoing experience of the mysterious* reality of God. Thus revivals are also for converted Christians who often pursue revival to experience more of God's supernatural presence and work in their lives. Thus phenomena like visions, prophecy*, healing*, and other physical manifestations often accompany revivals. (4) For the participants, revivals are exciting, life-defining events in which heaven seems to come to earth, concretizing and validating the intellectual and theological components of faith. Such experiences often provoke widespread evangelism* and missionary activity. Revival spreads.

Revivalism strongly influenced Evangelicals*, shaping innumerable popular expressions of Christianity around the globe, and continues to do so, e.g. in the African revival (see Charismatic and Pentecostal Movements Cluster). In addition, the term "revival," combining religious and secular connotations, refers to a key characteristic of the nationalism of certain Christian nations (see Nationalism and Christianity).

CALEB J. D. MASKELL

Ricci, Matteo (1552–1610), Italian missionary in China, known for his missionary method of "accommodation." He changed an initial policy of accommodation to the Buddhist* way of life into an adaptation to the lifestyle and etiquette of the Confucian* elite. He opted for openness and tolerance toward Chinese values; he believed that the Confucian social doctrine should be complemented by the metaphysical ideas of Christianity. He also adopted a tolerant attitude toward certain Confucian rites, such as ancestral* worship and the veneration* of Confucius, which he declared to be "civil rites." This policy determined the Jesuits'* basic attitudes during the 17th and 18th c. but was denounced by the Dominicans*. The "Chinese* rites controversy" had a great influence on missionary methods (see Mission Cluster).

Ricci's most significant Chinese writing, *Tianzhu shiyi* (The solid meaning of the Lord of Heaven, 1603), is a typical example of the use of Christian natural* theology to approach Chinese literati. As part of his argumentation, Ricci quotes the Chinese classics to show that in ancient times the Chinese had a natural knowledge of God. His journal, originally written in Italian, became known in the 1615 Latin translation by Nicolas Trigault, *De Christiana Expeditione apud Sinas*. **See also CHINA.**

NICOLAS STANDAERT

Richard of St. Victor (d1173), Victorine* theologian. Born in Scotland, he spent his life in the Abbey of St. Victor and became the successor of Hugo* of St. Victor as an interpreter of Scripture, combining themes from Dionysius* and Augustine*. His *Benjamin Minor* and *Benjamin Major* delineated, respectively, the preparation for and the grace* of mystical* contemplation*. He also wrote a speculative work on the Trinity*, arguing from the nature of love*.

Ricoeur, Paul (1913–2004), one of the most influential European philosophers of the 20th c. His work ranged from existentialism* and phenomenology* to political* theory and hermeneutics*. His first two books, written after World War II, dealt with the religious existentialism of Gabriel Marcel* and Karl Jaspers*. But he is most celebrated for his radical contribution to philosophical hermeneutics, following Schleiermacher*, Dilthey, Heidegger*, and Gadamer*, through his innovative applications of contemporary hermeneutics to questions of religion, theology, and biblical study.

Ricoeur's first major contribution to the hermeneutics of religion, *The Symbolism of Evil* (1960; English 1967), was followed by anthologies of essays on religious and theological subjects, including *The Conflict of Interpretations* (1969; English 1974), *Essays in Biblical Interpretation* (1980), *Figuring the Sacred* (1995), and *Thinking Biblically* (co-written with André LaCocque, 1998). In these Ricoeur seeks to relate key concepts of semantic innovation, ontological surplus, and critical interpretation to notions of divinity and eschatology*. Though a liberal French Protestant, Ricoeur was always open to dialogue with Jewish, Catholic, and other faith traditions. From *Symbolism of Evil*, Ricoeur extended his range of reference to include nonmonotheistic as well as monotheistic traditions. This amplified ecumenical and exegetical scope was influenced by his collegial friendship with Mircea Eliade (the phenomenologist of comparative religion in Chicago), which modified the earlier influence of thinkers like Bultmann* and Barth*.

Despite his major contributions to a hermeneutics of religion, Ricoeur went to considerable lengths to maintain a formal division between his philosophical and theological writings, thus he withheld the explicitly "religious" Gifford Lectures when it came to the publication of the philosophical *Oneself as Another* (1992). In his later years, however, Ricoeur had some reservations about this dual-track separation of philosophy and theology, his "methodological asceticism," in part because of the deep influence of the French Enlightenment and Republican culture of education.

Ricoeur's contribution to the philosophy of religion might best be summed up in terms of his distinction between a "hermeneutics* of suspicion" and "hermeneutics of affirmation." While the hermeneutics of suspicion exposed the symbols*, myths*, and messages of revelation* to "masters of suspicion" such as Freud*, Marx*, and Nietzsche*, the hermeneutics of affirmation offered interpretations informed by charity*, compassion*, and hope* – "in spite of all" (*en dépit de tout*). The smashing of idols* lets symbols speak. There is no affirmation without a prior negation. By squarely facing the critiques of religion* offered by psychoanalysis, Marxism, and structuralism, Ricoeur helped to keep open the study of religion to the critical debates of his times. Eschatology* was, he claimed, his "secret passion," as summed up in his sentiment that if, like Moses, he would never possess the Promised Land, he could still glimpse it – patiently and passionately – from afar.

RICHARD KEARNEY

Righteousness (Old English, rightwise; cf. Lat *rectitudo* and *justitia*), right orientation or uprightness, usually equivalent to justice*. When the Hebrew term *tsedaqa* designates God's righteousness/justice (e.g. in the Psalms and Isa 40–66), it refers to God's saving action, directed to the *shalom* (well-being, prosperity) of the people. Righteousness/justice as the comportment of the community or individuals is to be consistent with God's righteousness/justice. In the NT, in addition to these connotations, one finds the concern regarding "being made righteous," i.e. justification, and being justified. **See also JUSTICE, CHRISTIAN THEOLOGICAL VIEWS AND PRACTICES, CLUSTER; JUSTIFICATION, CHRISTIAN THEOLOGICAL VIEWS AND PRACTICES, CLUSTER.**

Rings. Christians adopted the Roman use of engagement rings. The bishop's ring, sign of betrothal to the church, came into use during the early Middle Ages.

Rite, term used to describe all customary acts of worship or the written instructions for them.

Ritschl, Albrecht (1822–89), German Protestant exegete, historian, and dogmatic theologian, professor at Bonn (1846–64) and Göttingen (1864–89).

His many writings, principally *Der christliche Lehre von der Rechtfertigung und Versöhnung* (3 vols., 1870–74), *Unterricht in der christlichen Religion* (1875), and *Geschichte des Pietismus* (3 vols., 1880–86), gained him international repute and led to the formation of a highly influential "Ritschlian school," whose leading members included Wilhelm Herrmann*, Adolf von Harnack*, and (for a time) Ernst Troeltsch*.

Ritschl judged that the 16th-c. Protestant Reformers had indeed renewed the Christian religion but had failed (along with their successors) to reconstruct Christian doctrine on the basis of their guiding ideas. Hence he aimed to bring this "unfinished Reformation*" to completion in his own holistic system of theology, centered on the themes of justification* (unconditional pardon) by God, reconciliation* (unconstrained fellowship) with God, Christian freedom from the world's oppressive burdens through a lively trust in God's providence (see Faith #2), and freedom for the world's compelling needs through a love*-prompted action that advances the Kingdom* of God. Partly in response to this last Ritschlian theme, NT scholars began to give heightened attention to the specific role of "kingdom" in the teachings of Jesus.

DAVID W. LOTZ

Rogation Days (Lat *rogare*, "to ask"), Western Church days of prayer, including intercession, and fasting (April 25 and the three days before Ascension* Day).

Roman Catechism is the popular name for the manual of Roman Catholic doctrine composed by order of the Council of Trent* (1545–1563). Its full title is *Catechismus ex Decreto SS. Concilii Tridentini ad Parochos PII V. Pont. Max. Jussu Editus* (Catechism of the Council of Trent for parish priests issued by order of Pius V, the Supreme Pontiff).

At Trent a plan emerged for a catechism designed for parish priests to be used in the instruction of the faithful. A committee of theologians composed the manual under the supervision of Charles Borromeo, the archbishop of Milan. Pope Pius V promulgated the text in 1566.

The Roman Catechism follows the four-part division of some late medieval catechisms: (1) the Apostles'* Creed, (2) the sacraments*, (3) the Decalogue, and (4) the Lord's* Prayer. The *Small Catechism* and *Large Catechism* of Luther* also follow this four-part structure, although in a slightly different order.

The Roman Catechism incorporates the doctrines of Trent and prior councils and follows a theology that is largely Augustinian* and Thomistic*. Translated into numerous vernacular languages, the Catechism continued to exert substantial influence until superseded by the *Catechism of the Catholic Church* in 1992.

ROBERT FASTIGGI

ROMAN CATHOLICISM CLUSTER

1) *Introductory Entry*

Roman Catholicism: The Roman Catholic Church and Its Theology

2) *A Sampling of Contextual Views and Practices*

Roman Catholicism in Africa: Southern Africa

---

1) Introductory Entry

Roman Catholicism: The Roman Catholic Church and Its Theology. The largest Christian* institution, the Roman Catholic Church has more than a billion baptized members, who are led by local bishops* and are in communion with the pope*, or bishop of Rome. The overwhelming majority of Catholics belong to the Western Church, or "Roman Rite" – generally speaking the church that used Latin for Mass* and the administration of the sacraments* but that now (since the Second Vatican* Council, 1962–65) largely uses vernacular languages for its public worship. There are also 21 Eastern churches in union with Rome (sometimes inappropriately called "Uniate* churches"), which have followed somewhat different traditions for their religious ceremonies and enjoyed a variety of eucharistic* prayers or anaphoras* for the Mass*, unlike the Roman Rite (which until Vatican II used only one eucharistic prayer, the Roman Canon). The Armenian*, Byzantine*, Coptic*, and other major Eastern rites for centuries used Syriac and other ancient languages for worship, but in recent times often switched to Arabic, English, Malayalam, and other contemporary languages.

What characterizes the Roman Catholic Church is not necessarily unique to it. It shares with the vast majority of Christians respect for the Bible* as the inspired* and authoritative Word* of God, the practice of baptism* and the Eucharist*, and the Niceno*-Constantinopolitan Creed of 381. Along with Eastern Orthodox* Christians, as well as some Anglicans*, it accepts and practices seven sacraments*: baptism*, confirmation*, Eucharist, penance*, the anointing* of the sick, holy orders*, and matrimony*. The Roman Catholic Church recognizes 21 general councils* of the Church (though not necessarily giving the same authority to all): from Nicaea* I (325) to Vatican II. Eastern Orthodox* churches recognize only the seven councils, from Nicaea I to Nicaea* II (787); and the Oriental Orthodox* (non-Chalcedonian) churches recognize only three (Nicaea I; Constantinople, 381; Ephesus, 431).

Even before the time of Benedict* of Nursia and his sister Scholastica* in the 6th c., some Christian men and women joined communities, followed the same spiritual rule, and lived celibate, poor, and obedient lives under a superior.

Later orders, such as the Carmelites*, Dominicans*, Franciscans* and Jesuits*, and other religious institutes flourished and have become a distinctive feature of the Roman Catholic Church (see Religious Orders, Roman Catholic, Cluster). Such consecrated life in monasteries* and other religious communities originated among Eastern Orthodox Christians and continued among them, and emerged in modern times in the Anglican Communion and among some Protestants.

Key characteristics of Roman Catholicism include a deep love for Christ, fostered through the regular celebration of the Eucharist, and a sense that all human reality and the whole material cosmos have been blessed and changed by "the Word becoming flesh" (John 1:14). It is also typically Catholic to embrace "both/and" and hold together things that some Christians view as standing in opposition to each other (see Paradox). Hence Catholics, like Orthodox, do not acknowledge an "either/or" in the case of Jesus and his mother. Many Protestant Reformers and their followers hold that honoring Mary* (and other saints*) somehow blurs the unique role of Christ as Savior. But Catholics and Orthodox do not admit a choice here; they honor Jesus *and* his mother.

Roman Catholics accept both divine grace* and human freedom*, rejecting, on the one hand, a Pelagian*-style "do it yourself" salvation* and, on the other hand, any overemphasis on divine predestination* that would turn salvation in a puppet show arranged by an omnipotent* God*. Debates flared over late works by Augustine* of Hippo that pushed too far God's predestining will and over some Reformers' views on the destruction of human freedom by sin. Yet the interaction of God's sovereign grace with the human will* remains mysterious. The need to endorse both grace and freedom is expressed by the admonition to "pray as if everything depended on God, and work as if everything depended on yourself." Dante* Alighieri (d1321) knew that human salvation is due to God's grace, yet he called free will "the greatest gift God made to his creatures" (*Paradiso* 5, 19–22).

Another Roman Catholic "both/and," one shared by other Christians, concerns the love of God and love of neighbor. Catholics want to devote time to God in prayer, but they also want to care for their neighbors in need. Catholics, at their best, have combined satisfying the spirit's hunger for God through prayer with feeding the hungry of this world. Another "both/and" is seen in the existence of both contemplative* and active religious institutes. Groups of men and women who follow the Benedictine*, Camaldolese, Carmelite*, Carthusian*, Cistercian*, and other monastic lives of prayer and silence, as well as those who live as solitary hermits, support spiritually the works of consecrated men and women who serve the world through schools, colleges, hospitals, and other social "ministries*."

Education* entails another Roman Catholic "both/and," both faith* and reason* (see Rationalism and Theology). Roman Catholicism has never embraced the opposition between Athens (standing for reason) and Jerusalem (standing for faith) that Tertullian* championed. From the patristic* period, through Thomas* Aquinas (d1274), and down to the 1998 encyclical of John* Paul II, *Fides et Ratio* (Faith and reason), Catholic Christianity has never accepted any separation between God's gift of faith* and the cultivation of human reason. By leading a renewal in theological learning and recovering the philosophy of Aristotle*, Thomas Aquinas expressed for all time a harmony between faith and reason. Following his lead, Dante* blended human learning and divine revelation in the *Comedy*. His two companions in that masterpiece were Virgil and Beatrice, the former symbolizing true humanism and the latter divine wisdom. Sometimes, above all with the growth of the natural sciences*, tensions emerged between the truths* of revelation* and worldly learning. Certain tensions arose from rational claims to interpret autonomously all reality. At other times, Catholics, in particular Church officials, were to blame, as in the condemnation of Galileo Galilei* (d1642), whose observations that the earth moved around the sun were wrongly taken to challenge the Church's authority to interpret the Scriptures*. Nowadays advances in the life sciences and biotechnology make a full and honest dialogue between faith and scientific reason more urgent than ever (see Science and Christian Theology).

Some additional "both/ands" that typify Roman Catholicism are both married and celibate priests (the first being typical in Eastern Catholicism and the second in Western Catholicism); both the (very many) lay members and the (comparatively few) ordained ministers; both saints and sinners belonging to the Catholic Church; both institutional structures (essentially the pastoral government of bishops in communion with the bishop of Rome) and fresh, charismatic* initiatives; both permanent beliefs and developments in doctrine and practice. Examples of the former include faith in Christ* as truly divine and fully human, his personal resurrection* from the dead, and such moral positions as rejection of abortion* and euthanasia*. Developments include, for instance, changes in public worship, in the way popes* understand and exercise their authority as successors of Peter, and in attitudes toward the institution of slavery*. After centuries of tolerating that institution, Vatican II and John Paul II rejected it as "intrinsically evil."

The present Roman Catholic Church needs a better balance between the centralized power of Rome and the decisions of local churches and national conferences of bishops. Genuine "collegiality*" or authoritative guidance for the whole Church shared by the bishops with Peter's successor, the bishop of Rome, was a principle endorsed by Vatican II in 1963 but it still needs to be fully implemented. A far wider role for laymen and laywomen in the life of the Roman Catholic Church is another development that many Catholics want. Under the leadership of John* XXIII (d1963) and through the work of Vatican II (which he convoked) and of his successors in the papacy, huge strides have been made in relations with other Christians, Jews*, and adherents of other religions. But much more remains to be done in carrying forward a prayerful and practical dialogue at every level.

From the very beginning of Roman Catholic Christianity, theologians proved an indispensable resource for the church and wider society. They have drawn on the data of God's self-revelation, available inseparably through the inspired Scriptures* and the living tradition* guided by the Holy* Spirit. Vatican II understood Scripture and tradition to be intimately connected in their past origin, present function, and future goal (*Dei Verbum*, The constitution on divine revelation, 9). Vatican II wanted the study of Scripture to be "the soul of all theology" (ibid., 24).

Western Roman Catholic theology has characteristically engaged in an intellectual pursuit of truth ("faith seeking understanding") making use of terminology and schemes of thought originating with Aristotle*, Plato* and other great philosophers*. Eastern Catholic theologians, like their more numerous counterparts among the Orthodox, have persistently looked to liturgical texts and the infinitely beautiful God in the spirit of "faith seeking worship." Recent Liberation* theology privileges the voices of the poor* and oppressed* and takes a very practical approach as "faith seeking justice." Roman Catholic theology is enriched whenever these approaches are allowed to complement each other. Contexts and audiences that vary around the world will affect the application of these three approaches.

GERALD O'COLLINS, SJ

---

2) A Sampling of Contextual Views and Practices

Roman Catholicism in Africa: Southern Africa. Roman Catholicism in Southern Africa varies in size and character as a result of different historical dynamics. In Botswana*, Roman Catholics constitute 5% of the population; in Lesotho*, 70%; in Namibia*, 17%; in South* Africa, 6.5%; and in Swaziland*, 5%. Roman Catholicism is culturally more homogeneous in Botswana, Lesotho, and Swaziland, but culturally and racially more diverse in Namibia and South Africa. These five countries (participating in one economic bloc, the Southern African Customs Union) have been under the oversight of one apostolic nuncio from the Vatican since 2000, with three distinct bishop conferences: the South African (South Africa, Botswana, Swaziland), the Namibian, and the Lesotho.

With more than 3 million members, the Roman Catholic Church in South Africa is the largest in the region. Yet it is relatively small compared with the many Protestant churches, owing to its historical marginalization during the period of Dutch colonization (1652–1804) and in the decades of Afrikaner nationalism (1851–1903). Despite the conquest by the British (1806), it was not until 1837 that a Roman Catholic bishop could take residence. This minority status did not prevent it from carrying out its prophetic mission. In fact, some of its clerics, including Archbishop Dennis Hurley (Durban) and Fr. Smangaliso Mhkatshwa, became most strident opponents of apartheid, advocating freedom and the respect of human dignity.

New challenges emerged after 1994 (when South Africa attained freedom), including poverty, crime, and HIV/AIDS. Inculturation* is also a great challenge, aiming both at making the Roman Catholic faith a part of the life of the faithful and at eradicating disturbing forms of syncretism* or relapse into "paganism*." For example, Archbishop Buti Tlhagale searched for an authentic way of integrating the ritual of offering blood libations to ancestors within the Mass*, while resisting the growing practice among African Catholics, both lay and clergy, to resort in times of crisis to "the intervention of ancestral spirits, the engagement of spirit mediums, spirit possession, consulting diviners, . . . magical practices" (2006; see Ancestor Veneration and Christianity Cluster).

The erosion of family* values that has resulted from long-standing migrant labor and the ravages of industrialization in African communities is another challenge for all the countries in this region.

In Lesotho, Catholicism has been historically the dominant religion, in part because of its unwavering commitment to education*, at both the primary and secondary levels. It was instrumental in the founding of the Basotho National Party (1959), which ruled Lesotho from 1966 to 1985.

PAUL H. GUNDANI

Roman Catholicism in Africa: Western Africa. The history of Roman Catholicism in Western Africa began along the Atlantic coast in the context of disruptive colonial incursions (18th and 19th c.). (Earlier missionaries, Portuguese Capuchins* [15th c.], did not have a lasting impact.) Modern Roman Catholicism gradually evolved from the missions to Western Africa pioneered by Sisters of St. Joseph of Cluny, under the leadership of Anne-Marie Javouhey (1779–1851); the Congregation of the Holy Ghost, under the inspiration of François Libermann (1802–52); and the Society of African Missions, founded by Melchior de Marion Brésillac (1813–58). Since then the number of Roman Catholics has steadily grown (in 2000, c36 million out of 269 million West Africans).

The colonial* legacy endures in the linguistic divide between two regional umbrella bodies: the Association of Episcopal Conferences of Anglophone West Africa and the Episcopal Conferences of French-Speaking West Africa. Phenomenal growth continues in the recruitment of ministers, with some seminaries training more than 500 seminarians (e.g. in Nigeria). Since the late 20th c., indigenous bishops, priests, and nuns have assumed leadership of the Church. As elsewhere in Africa, Catholic religious* orders operate hospitals, schools, and social centers. The increasingly public profile of Catholicism in Western Africa can be attributed to the active roles played by prominent Church leaders in the political sphere.

Two key issues have shaped the character of Roman Catholicism in Western Africa: the challenge of Islam* and the struggle to adapt and integrate indigenous religious traditions. The tense relation with Islam often results in violent confrontations, especially where Muslims constitute the majority, as in Senegal*, Nigeria*, and Burkina* Faso. On the contrary, the encounter with African* Religion has generated various forms of inculturated* theology and worship in countries like Ghana* and Nigeria. This positive view departs from erstwhile attempts to suppress the beliefs and practices of indigenous religions.

Indicators of a vibrant Roman Catholicism in Western Africa include the recent beatification* of the Nigerian Cyprian Michael Iwene Tansi (1903–64) and the development of an active missionary vocation. Many of its priests and nuns serve in churches in the Western Hemisphere. A pivotal example is the Missionary Society of St. Paul founded in 1977 by the Catholic Bishops Conference of Nigeria for the sole purpose of sending priests on mission to other parts of Africa as well as to the First World and elsewhere, which is a confirmation of the maturity of Roman Catholicism in Western Africa.

AGBONKHIANMEGHE E. OROBATOR, SJ.

Roman Catholicism in Asia: China. After centuries of missionary labor, the Holy See* elevated the China Mission (see Mission in Asia: Catholic Mission in China, 16th–18th Centuries) to the rank of local church (1946). All dioceses were gradually placed under Chinese leadership, bringing about a profound and ongoing transformation of the Chinese Catholic Church.

Shortly after Mao Zedong founded the People's Republic of China (October 1, 1949), the Communist government began to accuse Church leaders of being spies and counterrevolutionaries. In 1951 it expelled the Holy See's nuncio*, and by 1956 it had driven out most foreign missionaries. The regime also fostered a political organization to monitor and direct all Church activities, the Catholic Patriotic Association (CPA, set up in 1957). Local clergies began to choose "patriotic" priests to fill episcopal vacancies following the departure of foreign bishops, but Rome refused to approve these elections. After the first consecrations without his approval (1958), Pope Pius XII rejected the CPA and reaffirmed his sole authority in making episcopal appointments. The Chinese government retaliated by forbidding Church authorities to have further contact with the Vatican and by making sweeping arrests of those bishops and priests who opposed the CPA and the illicit ordinations (1955–59). During the Cultural Revolution (1966–76), all public religious activities were suspended and Church properties confiscated. During this period of great violence, Christians suffered persecution, sisters had to return to secular life, and all religious ministers were sent to labor camps to join those arrested during the preceding decade.

After the 10-year nightmare of the Cultural Revolution, the country began to open to the outside world, and the clergy were allowed to resume ministry. Since 1982 a new constitution has guaranteed freedom of religious belief. The view that religion was the opium of the people is no longer popular and has been replaced by the position that religious believers make good citizens. Most confiscated properties have been returned, and churches are full on Sundays. Since 1989 the government has recognized the pope's spiritual leadership over Roman Catholics.

After the clergy returned to their dioceses, some refused to register their churches with the government Religious Affairs Bureaus and to accept the supervision of the CPA. They carry out their religious ministry for the most part in private and attract a great number of "followers." These "underground" Catholics are often harassed and arrested. Other priests and bishops have chosen to perform their sacramental ministry openly and to submit their churches to CPA control. Although some have compromised themselves in collaborating with the government, the majority give only lip service to the CPA. Following years of mistrust, the two groups have mostly reconciled. Rome has legitimized most of the "patriotic" bishops, and no new bishop accepts consecration without prior papal consent. Thus both the "underground Church" and the "patriotic Church" are faithful to Rome, each in its own way. The Chinese Catholic Church exists in two main forms but remains only one church in communion with the worldwide Roman Catholic Church. A more accurate way of describing the situation in the early

2000s is to speak of registered and unregistered churches. Registered churches are allowed to engage in religious activities under government supervision. Unregistered churches are deemed illegal, and their members are often forced to pay fines and imprisoned.

In 2005 it was estimated that 12 million Roman Catholics worshipped in more than 6,000 churches. There were 110 dioceses with 114 active bishops and 22 inactive bishops. The number of priests exceeded 3,000, and there were more than 5,000 sisters. Informal talks between the Vatican and the People's Republic of China about reestablishing diplomatic relations have taken place periodically since the late 1980s. JEAN-PAUL WIEST

Roman Catholicism in Asia: Philippines. The first Roman Catholic priests came with Magellan's "discovery" of the islands (1521). But systematic Christianization started only after 1565 when Spanish colonization began. Five religious orders of missionaries came from Spain, four of them orders of friars* (Augustinians*, Dominicans*, Franciscans*, Augustinian Recollects). The fifth order, the Jesuits*, were regular* clergy.

By the time Spanish rule ended in 1898, the vast majority of the population was Catholic. The census of 1903 listed the total population as 7,635,426, and 6,987,686 (91.52%) were Christians – almost entirely Roman Catholics. The Protestant missionaries who started arriving from the USA in 1900 had not yet gained a following, and the Aglipayan Movement, whose members rebelled against the Spanish friars, had not yet seceded from the Roman Catholic Church (see Philippine Independent Church). Tribal groups (animists) remained in the mountains, and Muslims inhabited the Sulu Archipelago and parts of Southern Mindanao.

Organization. The first bishop of Manila arrived in 1581. In 1595 Manila was raised to an archbishopric, with three suffragan* bishoprics. A fifth episcopal see was added in 1865. These five were the only episcopal sees until 1910, when new bishoprics began to be created. The centrality of the Roman Catholic Church in Philippine life and society was symbolized by the organization of the towns around the church and central plaza. Manila was a city of churches. So was Cebu City.

Education and Charities. Under Spanish rule, education* and charitable services were entirely under Church initiative and administration. Mission schools (elementary) were organized from the start. There were two institutions of higher learning (with degree programs in philosophy, theology, and canon law) during the first two centuries of the Spanish regime: the (Jesuit) Colegio de Manila (1595) and the (Dominican) Colegio de Santo Tomas (1611).

In 1768 with the expulsion of the Jesuits, Santo Tomas University (Dominican) alone remained, with law and medicine added in the late 19th c. Secondary education (the European baccalaureate) was provided by colleges in the various episcopal sees*. In Manila the leading institutions were the Dominican Colegio de San Juan de Letran (1620) and the Ateneo de Manila, opened by the Jesuits upon their return in 1859. Parochial schools provided elementary education. Yet the inadequacies of the Philippine educational system were exposed by the national hero José Rizal in his two novels, *Noli me tangere* and *El filibusterismo*.

Hospitals maintained by religious orders have been established, the two oldest being San Lazaro (Franciscans) and San Juan de Dios (by brothers of an order of that name, San Juan de Dios). Christian burial for the poor was provided in Manila by the Confraternity of Mercy.

Catholicism in the Philippines during the Spanish regime was beset with problems. One was recurring Muslim raids, during which the coastal settlements were destroyed and much of the population was carried off and sold into slavery. Another was the lack of priests and the long delay in developing a native clergy. A more basic problem, however, was the Patronato* Real (royal patronage), which

 Roman Catholicism in Asia: Philippines

gave the Spanish monarch the duty to support the Church but also a right to dictate Church policies. While government support was helpful in the early stages of Christianization, long-distance governance from Madrid became a hindrance in the long run. Another basic problem was the latent animism* among the less educated classes, which tinged their Catholic faith with a tendency toward superstition*.

Philippine Roman Catholicism in the 20th Century. The change of sovereignty from Spanish to North American (1898) put an end to the Patronato Real. It freed the Church from government control and established direct communication between the Philippine Roman Catholic Church and the Holy See in Rome. On the other hand, the withdrawal of government support left the Church in financial straits, and the people had not yet been trained to support the Church and its educational and charitable institutions. Moreover, the US principle of separation of church* and state (an excellent principle in itself) was often misinterpreted to mean hostility by officials toward the Roman Catholic Church (see Anticlericalism). There was also much anti-Catholic propaganda in schools and in the press.

The Aglipayan Movement (1902), which led to the establishment of the Philippine* Independent Church (now officially called Iglesia Filipina Independiente), gained a large following (at least 25% of Catholics in 1903), which progressively declined to 6% in 1960, before rapidly growing once again to 15% in 2000.

Gradually a revival took place in Roman Catholicism, aided largely by the arrival of new missionary groups of various nationalities. Catholic schools were greatly improved and more schools opened, and greater impetus was given to the development of a native clergy. Catholic newspapers in English and the native languages and a popular radio program helped the revival. The result became evident in the International Eucharistic Congress held in Manila (1937), attended by more than a million people, the largest crowd in Philippine history.

Further Developments. World War II (1941–45) and the Japanese occupation, with their attendant tragedies, dangers, and privations, aroused a deeper piety and brought clergy and people closer together. Since the end of the war (1945), there has been a rapid increase in the population, particularly in Mindanao as a result of massive migration from Luzon and the Visayas. According to the 2000 census, the total population is 76,332,470 and the number of Catholics is 61.8 million, representing 81.04% of the total. This rapid increase in population, together with an increase in the number of priests, has resulted in the creation of new bishoprics. In 1910 there were only 5 episcopal jurisdictions (1 archbishopric, 4 bishoprics). By 2005 there were 16 archbishoprics and 70 bishoprics. In addition to this numerical increase, there has been an intensification of church life, stimulated by the Second Vatican* Council (1962–65). That vitality was given spectacular expression during Pope John Paul II's second visit to Manila when, on January 19, 1995, an estimated 5 million people joined the pope at Mass, the largest gathering of people anywhere in the world.

The numerical strength and the increased vitality of the Church have had political repercussions. Before 1920 no one in government or the press would have paid attention to a bishop who had raised his voice on a national issue. Today, people listen when the bishops speak. In certain national crises, notably in the ousting of the dictatorship in 1986 (see Human Rights Cluster. And the Churches in Asia: The Philippines), the bishops' intervention was crucial. Nonetheless, the Church faces serious problems, including massive poverty* and widespread social problems. The number of priests is totally inadequate to serve the large population, both urban and rural. There is also a lack of religious instruction among the poorer classes. But the principal problems of the past no longer exist. Instead, there is a friendly spirit among all Christian groups and a desire to cooperate in projects for the common good. **See also PHILIPPINES.**

FR. MIGUEL A. BERNAD

Roman Catholicism in Europe: France.

Church–State Relations: From Conflict to Appeasement. At the end of the 19th c., wary of the Roman Catholic Church, the Third Republic secularized* hospitals (1879) and teacher training (1880), required seminarians to do military service (1889), and under the leadership of Jules Ferry, created an obligatory, free, secular public school system (1879–82) removed from Catholic influence. Delayed by the "Ralliement" of Catholics to the Republic recommended by Leo XIII (1892), the struggle between church and state culminated in the dissolution of religious congregations (1903), the termination of the Concordat* of 1801, the rupture of diplomatic relations with Rome (1904), and especially the strict law of separation of church and state (1905): "The Republic does not recognize, employ, or subsidize any religion."

After the "sacred union" during World War I (25,000 priests were drafted for wartime service), church–state relations became less conflicted with the canonization of Joan* of Arc (1920), the resumption of diplomatic relations with the Holy See* (1921), the return of the exiled religious orders, and the preservation of the 1801 Concordat in Alsace-Lorraine. According to the 1905 laws, the municipal governments owned the local churches, while the national government owned the cathedrals. The separation of church and state thus turned out to be financially helpful for the Catholic Church, as public funds covered the upkeep of churches built before 1905. In 1940 religious orders returned to teaching, and laws passed in 1951, 1959, and 1977 granted public subsidies to Catholic education. In 1984, under pressure from public opinion, the Socialist government of François Mitterand abandoned plans to nationalize Catholic schools, which have since attained parity with public schools and currently educate 20% of France's students. Catholics such as Robert Schuman were active in politics, and the calmer political climate allowed the Church to invest more energy in pastoral activities and theology.

Vitality Despite Hardship. During the years of intense conflict (late 19th–early 20th c.), the Catholic Church of France proved to be very creative in maintaining relations with the French members of religious orders in exile. Dominican priest M. J. Lagrange (1855–1938) founded the École Biblique et Archéologique de Jérusalem and the *Revue biblique*. Both provided important support for biblical studies from the start of the Modernist* crisis. Ambroise Gardeil (1859–1931) earned, with his *Revue des sciences philosophiques et théologiques* (1907), recognition for the Saulchoir, Dominican Pontifical Faculties, Belgium, which included other influential theologians, such as Marie-Dominique Chenu (1904–90), who restored a historical dimension to Thomism, and Yves Congar (1904–95), who revitalized ecclesiology (*Unam Sanctam* series) and was a pioneer of Catholic ecumenism. During their exile in England or Belgium, the Jesuits founded the *Recherches de sciences religieuses* (1910, Léonce de Grandmaison, first editor). Two diocesan priests, Alfred Vacant and Eugène Mangenot, had launched in 1903 the *Dictionnaire de théologie catholique*. At the same time, a philosophical and literary renewal flourished with the involvement of such lay Catholic intellectuals as Charles Péguy, Paul Claudel, Blondel*, Maritain*, Étienne Gilson, François Mauriac, Georges Bernanos, and Emmanuel Mounier (founder of the review *Esprit*), while Henri Bremond made classical spirituality accessible to a wider public.

Creativity and the Second Vatican Council (1940–70). The defeat of France during World War II reinitiated renewal within the Roman Catholic Church. Louis Joseph Lebret, OP, started (1940) the society Économie et Humanisme. The Jesuits Henri de Lubac and Jean Daniélou established (1942) the *Sources chrétiennes* series (more than 500 volumes) at the Dominican publishing house, Le Cerf; this series was an expression of the renewal of patristic theology. The creation (1943) of the Centre de Pastorale Liturgique formalized liturgical renewal, while two Dominican priests, Pie-Raymond Regamey and Marie-Alain Couturier, directed the review

Roman Catholicism in Europe: France

Art sacré, and artists and architects began working for the Church again. Two priests, Henry Godin and Yvan Daniel, published *France pays de mission?* (1943), a work that inspired the Worker*–Priest Movement. After the Liberation, the ecumenical group Les Dombes, founded (1937) by Abbé Couturier, went public and took up the same ministry as the Dominican center Istina (established in 1925, publishing the journal *Istina* since 1954). Important spiritual currents included those of Thérèse* de Lisieux, Charles de* Foucauld, and Teilhard* de Chardin, SJ. The Jesuits supervised the publication of the *Dictionnaire de spiritualité*, and the worldwide influence of Lourdes* continued.

In the 1950 encyclical *Humani Generis*, Rome expressed concern about the "nouvelle théologie" that seemed to have abandoned neo-Thomism. Jesuit representatives (Fourvière School) and later Dominicans (in 1954, during the worker–priest crisis) were banned from teaching. John* XXIII did, however, restore their reputations by naming them experts at Vatican* II, where the cardinals Daniélou, de Lubac, and Congar were influential. In 1964 Paul* VI publicly honored French theology, stating that it "bakes the intellectual bread of Christendom."

The post–Vatican II era was difficult. Following the encyclicals *Sacerdotalis Caelibatus* (1967), which reaffirmed celibacy for priests, and *Humanae Vitae* (1968), which prohibited the use of artificial contraception*, many young people drifted away from ministry and religious practice. The public saw these decisions as regressive in light of Vatican II. A small minority of Catholics led by Msgr. Lefebvre, former apostolic delegate in Dakar, refused to accept the Vatican II reforms, resulting in a schism.

The Pontificate of John Paul II: Grappling with Cultural Change. The late 20th c. was characterized by an unprecedented desertion of institutionalized forms of Catholic life. Lay movements (Action Catholique) were in decline after 1970. From 1975 to 2000, the number of Catholic religious marriages diminished by half (now only 32.5% of the marriages in France) and the number of Catholic baptisms diminished by a third (now only 39.5% of children are baptized, although the number of adult baptisms is growing). In a country where 80% of the population is nominally Catholic, only 50% of children attend catechism classes (in Paris, from 1990 to 2001, the number dropped from 34 to 28%). Attendance at Sunday Mass fell to an average of 8%. The clergy and religious orders can no longer fill their ranks. In 1970 there were 92,000 religious sisters active as "feminine clergy" in daily life (parishes, schools, hospitals, and catechesis). In 2000 only 3,000 of them were less than 50 years old. During the same period, the number of priests decreased by half, and their average age was 70. For the past 20 years, on average, one priest has been ordained per diocese per year (five or six in Paris; one for every 10,000 Catholics). The number of Dominicans decreased by 50% in 50 years, while that of Jesuits decreased by 80%. Some religious orders are, however, actively engaged in publishing books (Dominicans) and journals and newspapers (Assumptionists).

The decline has led to some reforms: reorganization of parishes; promotion of the permanent diaconate and lay ministry (often feminine); development of synods; modest growth of Charismatic groups; and new religious communities. Yet creative innovations that can stand up to the serious cultural challenges are still lacking. Theological work informed by ecumenism and concerned about interreligious dialogue continues. Cardinal Lustiger (1926–2007) brought Jews and Christians closer together. Although the dialogue between theology and the humanities (sociology, psychoanalysis, linguistics) continues, the most recent trends are concerned with phenomenology and hermeneutics (*Dictionnaire de théologie critique*, 2002).

Academic theology rarely reaches the Catholic faithful. The teaching they receive seems either too attached to the past (e.g. the Catholic teaching about "woman") or too far from the gospel (e.g. regarding divorced and remarried Catholics or the obligation of priestly celibacy). Church teaching also seems unable to take medical progress into account in the areas of reproduction (contraception and assisted reproductive technology) and the end of life, as if biological laws were the immediate expression of the will of God the Creator. The Catholic Church's suspicion of legislators who work in this domain has led the faithful to hope for a more sophisticated articulation of the gospel, ethics, and civil law.

The Catholic Church is searching for new forms of inculturation* of Christian belief in daily life. Without it, secularization* will continue to advance, and a sociologist (Hervieu-Léger, 2003) has already diagnosed an "exculturation" of Catholicism. The long pontificate of John* Paul II did not or could not slow down the process of secularization, despite reinforced Roman centralization and eight visits to a country where he appointed all of the bishops. The media's interest in this pope did not prevent 70% of the French people polled during his 1996 visit from expressing doubt that he had the right answers to today's questions. His refusal to compromise with contemporary culture did, however, gain him some support. In the early 21st c., the Catholic Church in France shared the common lot of Western European churches. Whether they were Catholic, Protestant, Anglican, supported or not by governments, centralized or nationally autonomous, prescriptive or liberal, all were having difficulty evangelizing. At a time when opinion polls indicated that the youngest generations have more interest in religiosity than previous ones, the Catholic bishops' pastoral letter, *Proposer la foi dans la société actuelle* (1999), presented the new image that the traditional Church has of this country's future. **See also FRANCE; SECULARISM AND SECULARIZATION.** HERVÉ LEGRAND

Roman Catholicism in Europe: Germany and Lutheranism. The papal bull *Decet Romanum Pontificem* (1521), which excommunicated Martin Luther* and his followers, marked the breakup of unity within the Western Church and gave rise to denominationalism: the Roman Catholic, Lutheran, Anglican, and Reformed churches, and the Radical* Reformation churches/communities. However, in Germany, the Roman Catholic and Lutheran Churches remained dominant.

The Roman Catholic Church did not accept the serious theological criticism of the late medieval church voiced by the Wittenberg Reformers. Following the humanists' "back to the sources" program, the Reformers rediscovered the importance of Scripture*, the Word of God, as the only *regula* fidei* of the church; they honored the dogmatic and ecclesial traditions of the ancient church as true interpretations of Scripture and rejected the medieval additions regarding salvation as superfluous and harmful. The central idea of Luther's theology is a new but biblical understanding of justification* by faith alone and its implications for understanding the sacraments*, the church*, and its constitution. Luther's opponents, especially Johann Eck and Johannes Cochlaeus, defended the inherited organization of the Roman Catholic Church with its late medieval features (e.g. purgatory*, indulgences*, veneration of the saints*, vows*, pilgrimages*). Often with a mixture of misunderstanding and hatred, they rejected Luther's theological convictions, precluding any agreement between Reformers and the Catholic Church, although it could have been achieved at the Diet of Augsburg (1530) or at Hagenau, Worms, and Regensburg (1540–41).

The first biography of Luther, written by Cochlaeus (1549), presented a distorted image of Luther and his theology that deeply influenced the Roman Catholic Church and its theology for more than 400 years (as Herte shows). Ignaz von Döllinger (1799–1890), the most famous Catholic theologian of his time, exemplified this attitude, although he achieved a more positive understanding of Luther after his own excommunication (1872). Heinrich Denifle and Hartmut Grisar (early 20th c.) still followed Cochlaeus's judgment – Denifle, in attacking Luther's understanding of justification as the source of all evil in modern times; Grisar, in making psychological-pathological statements against Luther.

The church historian Sebastian Merkle laid the foundations for serious Catholic research on Luther by seeking to exercise justice in historical research, without prejudice. A breakthrough came with Joseph Lortz's historical and theological research regarding justification (1939–40). For him "Luther fought against a Catholic thinking that was not Catholic." Followed by his students, Erwin Iserloh and Peter Manns, Lortz strove to distinguish the "Catholic" from "the (heretical) Protestant" in Luther's theology. After Vatican* II, Heinrich Fries's school (Otto Hermann Pesch, Johannes Brosseder, and, in the USA, Harry McSorley) abandoned this approach; for them Luther's theology as a whole was a challenge to the Roman Catholic Church and its theology. Thus for Pesch, Luther's theology was new (and remains new for the Catholic Church so long as it does not address the questions raised by Luther), but not so new that a Catholic theologian would not be able to follow Luther's thinking. Nevertheless (in the 1960s–1980s), some (Paul Hacker, Theobald Beer, Remigius Bäumer) continued to adhere to Cochlaeus's prejudices.

After World War II and Vatican II, Catholic and Lutheran theologians in Germany (the "Jäger-Stählin Kreis," now the "Ökumenischer Arbeitskreis") began a serious ecumenical dialogue leading to a remarkable consensus about formerly controversial subjects. The German Bishops' Conference and the Bishops of the United Lutheran Church in Germany founded a bilateral working group and published two important documents (*Kirchengemeinschaft in Wort und Sakrament*, 1984; *Sanctorum Communio*, 2000). Another ecumenical document (1986) asks, "The Condemnations of the Reformation Era: Do They Still divide?" The answer was and is: no longer. Indeed, the Catholic Church and Lutheran churches worldwide signed the Joint Declaration on Justification (Augsburg, 1999), the first official document since the Reformation signed by both.

JOHANNES BROSSEDER

Roman Catholicism in Europe: Italy. The history of the Roman Catholic Church in Italy* since the beginning of the Christian Era is almost identical with the history of Christianity in the peninsula south of the Alps (see Italy). But one should not necessarily call this church "Italian."

After the early evangelization, marked by the martyrdom in Rome of the apostles Peter* and Paul*, the conquest of Rome by the Visigoths of Alaric (410; see Goths) constituted a turning point. Rome became the center of Latin culture and assumed for the Christian faith a normative role analogous to the earlier role of Jerusalem. In contrast to the Christian Arian* Visigoths (viewed as "barbarian" invaders), the "true" Christian Church represented and defended the Roman–Latin cultural and social order.

By the 5th c., the evangelization of the countryside led to the establishment of numerous Christian communities, yet without any sense of church unity in a region without national unity. For example, the Episcopal Sees of Milan, Aquileia, and Ravenna had to contend not only with the Episcopal See of Rome but also with the political authority dominating their respective regions. Conversely, events in the Italian Church often had a significance that was more "universal" than "Italian" – e.g. the pastoral experience of Ambrose* of Milan (c338–97) and of Charles Borromeo* (1538–84), the monastic* movement originating with Benedict* of Nursia (c480–c555), and the evangelical witness of Francis* of Assisi (c1182–1226).

The accumulation of landholdings that became a territorial dominion of the Roman Church and its bishop from the 8th c. had a considerable impact on the Italian Church. The actions and programmatic decisions of the Roman Church closely reflected the concern to preserve and expand the temporal power of the Church. The solemn imperial coronation of Charlemagne* (800) revived the ecclesiastic authorities' demand that civil and political authorities be more subordinated to the power of the Sovereign (God, represented by the Church).

In feudal* medieval Italy, dioceses and monasteries constituted the framework of society. In each city, the highest authority

 Roman Catholicism in Europe: Italy

was the bishop, who often had the function and title of prince-bishop. The importance of episcopal authority was matched by that of the cathedral chapters*, which claimed for themselves the authority to elect the bishops. This fragmentation of the Italian Church included the founding of "private churches" by important families that established monasteries or churches and retained perpetual control over them.

During the Middle Ages, the bishops were recruited from aristocratic ranks, while the numerous clergy struggled to find minimal living resources and often had very limited education. The central problems of the Italian churches were related to the clergy's simony* and concubinage*. The reform, promoted by monks, emphasized the distinction between laity and clergy. Italian Christianity gave rise to the Lay* Piety Movement – including religious revivals (e.g. the Alleluia movement, 1233) and the Flagellants of Northern Italy (who from 1260 called the populace to repent) – the reverberations of which were felt way beyond the peninsula, as were those of the *Concordantia discordantium canonum* (by Gratian*, in Bologna, 12th c.), the nucleus of canon* law, and the Franciscan* movement. Likewise, the Italian bishops had a decisive role at the Council of Trent* (1545–63), which had a similar universal impact.

It is only with the second millennium and the end of the Byzantine presence in the peninsula that Rome and its church progressively gained a major role in all the Italian dioceses. In the 13th c., Italian replaced Latin as the common language of the Italian churches, although the liturgy remained in Latin until Vatican* II. Anti-intellectualism and anticlericalism, based on a biblical literalism and an active concern with poverty*, were the main features of the movements (including that of the Waldenses*) that the Italian Church condemned as heretical*. But Lutheranism and Protestantism did not have a significant impact on the Italian Roman Catholic Church.

With the political unity of the peninsula, the Italian Church began to move toward independence, a process of unification complicated by the great number of its dioceses (about 300). Its primary distinctive feature remained, at least until Vatican* II, its relation to the Roman papacy. The Italian Church's vocation was to defend the papacy. This vocation was amplified by Pius IX's decision (1874) that Italian Catholics should abstain from participation in Italian political life as a protest against the government's "conquest" of Rome. Romolo Murri's (1870–1944) attempt to bridge the separation of Catholics from Italian political, economic, and social life (a movement that led to the creation of "Christian Democracy") was met by reaction and repression by the Vatican and resulted in a climate of suspicion within the Italian Church, owing to the constant fear of being denounced. This political conflict engendered the 1871 state law that abolished the faculties of theology in Italian public universities, which had the positive effect of facilitating the development of seminaries for the education of the clergy. Yet these seminaries were under the control of the Holy See, since the Italian Conference of Bishops did not yet exist.

Because of its fear of communism, the Church adopted a positive attitude toward fascism (1922–45) and in the process obtained recognition of the State of the Vatican (1929). After the end of the fascist dictatorship (1945), the Church supported the Christian Democratic Party.

The convocation of the Second Vatican* Council (1959) challenged the views of the large majority of the clergy and the Italian bishops' passive dependence on Rome. Contact with other churches highlighted the limitations of many features of the life of the Italian Church, while the liturgical reforms – above all, the use of the vernacular – became an occasion for involving all the "people of God" (the laity*) in the life of the Roman Catholic Church.

The election of a non-Italian pope (1978) (the first in four centuries) opened a new phase in the history of the Italian Church. With a pope much less involved in Italian affairs, Italian "movements" (the Focolare*, Communion and Liberation, Sant' Egidio) played a positive role. The fact that diocesan synods were held in every region demonstrated the revival that

Vatican II had introduced in the Italian Church. The recently created Italian Conference of Bishops (Conferenza Episcopale Italiana), presided over by a bishop named by the pope rather than by a bishop elected by the Conference, can focus its attention on the problems the Italian Roman Catholic Church faces in a secularized* Italy. **See also ITALY.**

GIUSEPPE ALBERIGO

Roman Catholicism in Europe: Portugal. Ecclesiastical administration is based on 20 dioceses organized into 3 archdioceses (Braga, Évora, and Lisbon, the latter made a patriarchate in the 18th c.). The Portuguese Episcopal Conference was set up (1967) in the wake of Vatican* II. Chaplains to the armed and security forces have their own bishop, and Opus* Dei has eight centers. As of 2003, there were 4,358 parishes served by 3,029 diocesan clergy. The number of those attending seminaries is declining (to 471 in 2003), with the deaths of every two priests matched by only one ordination. The number of those baptized and married in the Church has also declined. Although 91.5% of the population was nominally Roman Catholic in 2003, a church census in 2001 found that only 18.7% were observant. Religious practice has been and is stronger in the north and the islands (Azores and Madeira) than the south and among women than men. In 2004 there were 1,375 resident male religious and 5,919 female religious. In the same year, there were 39,161 pupils in independent Catholic schools. The vast majority of religion and morality classes in state schools are provided by Catholics. The multicampus Portuguese Catholic University (UCP) was created in 1967. *Misericórdias* (lay charitable brotherhoods, from 1498) still play a role in health and social services, caring particularly for the young and the aged. About 75% of religious time on television is allocated to the Catholic Church, which owns the popular Rádio Renascença, broadcasting since 1936, and briefly owned a television channel in the 1990s. Seven of the 16 national holidays are Catholic holy days. Well over 1,000 traditional local festivals, processions, and pilgrimages* are still celebrated; among the most prominent is St. Antony's Eve in Lisbon. These events reflect a mixture of unorthodox and traditional influences.

Sameiro, near Braga in the north, was overtaken as the prime national pilgrimage center in the 1930s by Fátima*, in central Portugal, where the Virgin is said to have appeared to three children in 1917 on six occasions. Fátima soon became an international pilgrimage destination, with hundreds of thousands visiting each year. During the cold war, the anti-Communist significance of the veneration of Our Lady of Fátima was enhanced, and the site was visited by Pope Paul VI and notably by Pope John Paul II, who had a particular affection for Our Lady of Fátima. While the Catholic Church remains an influence in Portuguese national life, its opposition to legislation on abortion* since the 1980s has been unsuccessful. **See also PORTUGAL.**

RICHARD A. H. ROBINSON

Roman Catholicism in Europe: Spain. Ecclesiastical administration is based on 14 archdioceses and 51 dioceses. In 2000, parishes numbered 22,964, although nearly one-half lacked a resident parish priest. The number of diocesan priests, 19,825, is less impressive than it would appear to be because 41% were retired. The number of male religious was 8,700; the number of nuns, 58,406. Approximately 1,300,000 students were enrolled in 5,197 Roman Catholic schools. The number of Catholic associations, which were engaged in a wide range of activities, was 11,887.

Until the dramatic changes that followed the end of the Franco dictatorship (1975), Catholicism was the state religion. The Church received official financial support and enjoyed other privileges. The democratic Constitution of 1978 declared that the state had no official religion, but according to the terms of four diplomatic agreements with the Vatican between 1976 and 1979, the government continued to provide limited financial support for clerical salaries. It also subsidized the Church's schools. These arrangements were accepted later by successive Socialist governments, although with certain modifications.

The Church's gradual disengagement from the Franco regime between 1960 and 1975 proved divisive and controversial. The apparent consensus that once had supported the interdependence of church and state began to disintegrate. The directives of the Second Vatican* Council (1962–65) on religious liberty and the right of political communities to determine their own future sent shock waves through the Spanish Church. During the 1960s and early 1970s, a wave of protest swept through the clerical ranks. Some priests were motivated by support for regional autonomy (Catalonia and the Basque Provinces), others by a sense of social justice*, and still others by a concern with human* rights.

From a religious perspective, Vatican II stimulated, perhaps unintentionally, a surge in theological debate. Liberation* theology arrived from Latin America. The ideas of liberal European Catholic theologians, such as Hans Küng, received an enthusiastic reception in a rapidly growing number of theological faculties (in universities) that had reached 39 by 1980. The intensity of theological studies should be kept in perspective, for it corresponded to a crisis within the ranks of the clergy that produced a significant decline in the number of priests and seminarians.

In the decade following Vatican II, a "parallel church" made its appearance among Roman Catholics. It did not form a coherent or unified movement, but offered alternatives to traditional models of evangelization. The Popular Christian Communities followed the model of Liberation theology. Christians for Socialism (since 1973) caused controversy by asserting that socialism and Christianity were fully compatible. The "Neocatechumens" (since 1966) attempted to follow the example of the early church in evangelizing campaigns, and the Popular Charismatic* Communities (since 1973) offered a Roman Catholic version of Pentecostalism*. The activities of these groups often distressed the hierarchy. But it is important to note that the "parallel church" enlisted only a small minority of the faithful, an estimated 200,000 members in 1982.

The age of religious effervescence and optimism characteristic of the 10 or 15 years that followed Vatican II could not be sustained. There were clear signs by the early 1980s that it had runs its course. Diocesan bishops, many of whom were less than enthusiastic about what they saw as excessive theological restlessness and the bold criticism of some in the "parallel church," began to assert firmer control over expressions of dissent. Pope John Paul II, elected in 1978, appointed bishops who could be relied on to maintain effective control over clergy and laity* (see Opus Dei). Voices of dissent have not disappeared by any means, but they have become less influential among the faithful.

WILLIAM J. CALLAHAN

Roman Catholicism in Europe: United Kingdom. From the 16th to the 18th c., following the Reformation, Roman Catholics became a small minority, known as recusants*, who were deprived of civil privileges by penal laws, sometimes actively persecuted and suspected of treachery. Nevertheless, significant communities survived, especially in areas where Catholic noble families gave some protection, notably in the remote parts of the north of England and in the highlands and islands of Scotland. The Roman Catholic Church was led by vicars apostolic, holding episcopal status but without territorial sees.

In the late 18th c., the penal laws began to be relaxed; in 1829 the Catholic Emancipation conceded the right of Catholics to sit in Parliament. By this time, the number of Catholics was growing steadily: in England from c80,000 in 1770 to c750,000 in 1850; in Scotland from c30,000 in 1760 to c325,000 in 1878. The increase was attributable largely to immigration from Ireland*, especially during the famine years of the 1840s, but there was also significant growth in the indigenous English and Scottish Catholic communities. The restoration of episcopal hierarchies – England, 1850; Scotland, 1878 – gave the Roman Catholic Church in Britain a formal institutional identity, which was strengthened by the building of cathedrals and the expansion of monasteries and nunneries.

The Catholic population continued to grow substantially in the late 19th and early 20th c., and by 1950 amounted to an estimated 2.75 million in England and Wales and 745,000 in Scotland. It remained somewhat insulated from the mainstream of national life. The Church was run by a conservative hierarchy, and a strong commitment to education secured its influence on successive generations. It was exposed to continuing Protestant antagonism, especially in Scotland and Lancashire.

After 1962 the changes brought by the Second Vatican* Council were enthusiastically embraced, although in 1968 Pope Paul* VI's condemnation of artificial contraception* dismayed many British Catholics. The spiritual and sexual transitions in the English Catholic Church of the 1950s and 1960s were brilliantly evoked by David Lodge in his novel *How Far Can You Go?* (1980). Although the visit of Pope John* Paul II (1982) gave a short-term boost to morale, the last quarter of the century saw a serious decline in Catholic observance. Paradoxically, though, as the Church's grassroots situation weakened, it secured greater integration into the mainstream of British Christianity and increased social and cultural acceptability.

JOHN WOLFFE

Roman Catholicism in Latin America: Argentina. The largest church in Argentina, the Roman Catholic Church has 68 ecclesiastical districts organized in archdioceses, dioceses, and other prelatures. From the 1930s, Catholicism adopted an Integrist* perspective, with various anti-Modernist* stances and an active presence in the public domain with the goal of Christianizing society and the state. Catholic* Action (established in 1931) was a decisive factor in the growth of the Catholic Movement and its social advance.

The growth of the Catholic Church also reflected the establishment of powerful ties with the Holy See. The Church's quest for autonomy from the state did not interfere with the development of a Rome-centered church that provided internal cohesion and discipline. Thus the Catholic Church in Argentina is one of the most "Italianized" churches in the Americas.

The establishment of religious* orders was an essential part of the "Romanization" process. Among them, the Salesian order is preeminent. Since their arrival in the country (c1875), the Salesians, working closely with the government and the army, have succeeded in establishing many schools, hospitals, and presses.

"Romanization" included a struggle against liberalism and communism in an Argentine context where the state promoted a vision of laicism* (in the sense of anticlericalism), economic and social progress, and reason (associated with the development of an intellectual middle class). Until 1930 Catholicism was on the defensive, seeking accommodation with the liberal state. But since the 1930s, the Integrist* model of Argentine Catholicism was consolidated through close relations between the Church and the army. Catholicism began to act as the provider of national identity.

Urbanization following the crisis of 1930 reinforced the importance of the presence of the newcomers in Buenos Aires. Institutionalized Catholicism was ready to receive them and to help them become integrated in the life of the city. Catholicism occupied the public domain; thus it could gather more than 1 million persons for the International Eucharistic Congress in Buenos Aires (1934).

Then the Church sought to "re-Catholicize" the state and society by establishing ties with the different military governments, as well as with the popular Peronist Movement. Mandatory religious teaching was restored in public schools (1943); social rights were emphasized; and the state controlled non-Catholic religious groups.

Under the influence of the Second Vatican* Council and as a result of political events in the country, reforms were initiated (mid-1960s), including sociocultural, liturgical, and political renewals in large segments of Argentine Catholicism. The rise of the Movement of Priests for the Third World contributed to tensions and conflicts both within and between ecclesiastical and political spheres. The expulsion of 40 priests by the bishop of Rosario, because they disagreed with the Integrist episcopal authority, illustrates the tensions within the Church. Examples of the changing relations and tensions between the Church and state include the Church's fight against the law permitting divorce during the government of Raúl Alfonsín (1983–89), the Church's cooperation with the government of Carlos Menem (1989–99) in defense of the "rights of the unborn" and on sociopolitical issues, and the Church's distance from the government of Néstor Carlos Kirchner (2003–7).

Central Catholic practices include massive annual pilgrimages* to the shrines of the Virgin of Lujan, the Virgin of San Nicolas, and the Virgin of San Cayetano in Buenos Aires, where the unemployed pray for work. Popular* religiosity of this kind is very important for Catholics in Argentina. Social work organized by Caritas and nongovernmental organizations related to the Catholic Church includes the distribution of food and a large number of social programs for the poor*. **See also ARGENTINA; CHURCH AND STATE RELATIONS: IN LATIN AMERICA: ARGENTINA.**

DAMIÁN SETTON

Roman Catholicism in Latin America: Brazil: Colonial Period (1500–1822). Brazilian colonial Roman Catholicism started taking shape during the 16th and 17th c. through the activities of missionaries and Catholic settlers in the context of the system of royal patronage (Padroado* Régio). Brazilian Catholicism became well defined in the 18th c. when the Brazilian colony underwent a massive geographic transformation in its central southern region, with the discovery of gold in the present-day states of Minas Gerais, Goiás, and Mato Grosso. Gold-mining towns, with strong economic, social, and religious characteristics, were the setting of highly visible confraternities typical of the 18th and 19th c. There was also a territorial expansion of the colony in Northern Pará. Within this context, two movements defined Catholicism: one linked to the Church as an institution and another reflecting lay religious practices.

The institutional movement was marked by the reaffirmation of the Church as an institution that defined and demanded the implementation of a code of standards, known as the First Constitutions of the Archdiocese of Bahia (1707; first printed in 1720). The Constitutions were designed to normalize the sacramental and canonical practices of the Church according to the Council of Trent*. This institutional movement was evident in the creation of new dioceses (Mariana and São Paulo) and parishes and in the establishment of control mechanisms, including pastoral visits, as a reaction to the changes taking place in the colony. Yet a shortage of priests made these pastoral visits relatively rare in many places, and thus the effect of Trent on most lay Catholics was often minimal.

The second movement, popular* Catholicism (see Popular Christian Practices Cluster: In Latin America: Brazil), was distinguished by the religious practices of laypeople, including illiterate people and slaves*, in the everyday life of the colonial Church. These laypeople were in charge of organizing, funding, and often leading the processions and festivities in honor of Our Lady and the patron saints*. Laypeople were also responsible for the construction of chapels, churches, and sanctuaries, over which they kept control. Hermits, members of brotherhoods, and sextons acted as respected religious leaders in many towns, in the absence of clergy and regardless of the presence of members of the Church hierarchy. This lay movement introduced many popular Catholic practices (processions, devotions to the Virgin Mary*), including the reaffirmation of popular devotions of Portuguese origin, such as those of Bom Jesus (Good Jesus) and Our Lady, which incorporated Brazilian popular features, especially during local festivals such as those of Nossa Senhora de Aparecida (who became the patronness of Brazil), Bom Jesus da Lapa, and Círio de Nazaré.

FERNANDO TORRES-LONDOÑO

Roman Catholicism in Latin America: Brazil: Imperial Period (1822–89). This was a time of consolidation of the Roman Catholic Church throughout Brazilian society. After the political emancipation (1822) and the accession to the throne of a sovereign of Portuguese origin, the royal patronage (Padroado* Régio) continued. Conversely, a clerical elite was actively engaged in the politics of the First Empire (1822–31) and the Regency (1831–40) in the sphere of religious affairs and also occupied high political positions; e.g. Fr. Diogo Antônio Feijó (1784–1843) was regent of the Empire (1835–37) during the minority of Emperor Pedro II.

Around 1840 the Ultramontanist* Catholic tradition (emphasizing the centralization of the Church, giving preeminence to Rome) gained political importance. Ultramontanists followed the Council of Trent*, zealously training the clergy, evangelizing the faithful, and reforming religious practices as directed by the Holy See in Rome. They "Romanized" the Brazilian Church; e.g. Romualdo de Sousa Coelho, bishop of Pará (1819–41), and Romualdo Antônio de Seixas, bishop of Bahia (1827–60), were deeply committed to training priests and sent them to study in Europe. Leaders of Ultramontane theological thought, such as bishops Antônio Ferreira Viçoso (Mariana, 1844–75) and Antônio Joaquim de Melo (São Paulo, 1851–61), reformed the clergy (confining their activity to the realm of religious affairs) and supported the union of church and state. At the same time, they affirmed the autonomy of the clergy regarding religious affairs and the absolute authority of the pope, and promoted devotions to the saints* as Church practices (resisting the excessive role of lay fraternities in such devotions). Ultramontanists were supported by Lazarist priests (founded by Vincent* de Paul to champion the Catholic* Renewal) dedicated to the education of clergy and laypeople.

Following the anti-liberal movement launched by the encyclical *Quanta Cura* and the Syllabus* of Errors (1864), which rejected Modernist* ideologies such as rationalism and naturalism, and especially the foundations of liberalism (e.g. freedom of worship, secularized education, church–state separation, civil marriage), the Ultramontanists criticized imperial authorities for their lukewarm support of the training of priests and of religious education, and especially for their lax attitude toward lay fraternities. This led to a direct clash regarding the "religious issue" (1872–75), which involved the imprisonment of two bishops, Antônio de Macedo Costa (of Pará) and Vital Maria Gonçalves de Oliveira (of Olinda), who, following Vatican directives, imposed canonical penalties on members of lay brotherhoods and Third* Orders who participated in Masonic lodges, although the emperor himself was a Freemason*. Despite its distancing from the declining Empire, amplified by other factors such as the abolition of slavery* (1888), the Brazilian Roman Catholic Church continued to support and legitimize the established order. **See also CHURCH AND STATE RELATIONS CLUSTER: IN LATIN AMERICA: BRAZIL.**

CÉSAR AUGUSTO ORNELLAS RAMOS

Roman Catholicism in Latin America: Brazil: Period of the Republic (from 1889). When the Republic was proclaimed (1889), the interim government established the separation of church* and state and ended the Padroado* Régio (system of royal patronage). The Brazilian bishops reacted by publishing the 1890 collective "Pastoral Letter." Nevertheless, the republican Constitution of 1891 ended the privileges historically granted to the Roman Catholic Church, and the laicization* of institutions (including education*) began. Yet the Church maintained a policy of collaboration with the republican government, seeking rapprochement. In order to strengthen its religious influence on society, especially after 1920, the Catholic Church maintained a strong presence in the press, with Catholic intellectuals intervening regularly in public questions; held large faith demonstrations (eucharistic* congresses); proclaimed Our Lady of Aparecida the patron saint* of Brazil (1930); and inaugurated the statue of *Cristo Redentor* (Christ the Redeemer) in Rio de Janeiro (1931).

These and many other interventions were led by Sebastião Leme* Cintra, archbishop of Rio de Janeiro; Alceu Amoroso Lima*, an intellectual layman; and the laypeople involved in the Brazilian Catholic* Action.

The 1929 crisis followed by the 1930 civil and military coup that brought Getúlio Vargas to the presidency created an unstable atmosphere. To achieve legitimation and stability, the state approached the Church for help in maintaining order. The Catholic hierarchy used the situation to push the Church's agenda. An implicit alliance between the Church and the state was established (and lasted until 1945) in the "new state" led by the president-dictator Vargas and Archbishop Leme.

With redemocratization in post-Vargas Brazil (1945–64), the Church changed course. The National Conference of Bishops of Brazil (CNBB, created in 1952; see the present cluster: In Latin America: Brazil: Two Pastoral Initiatives of the National Conference of Brazilian Bishops) initiated a pastoral action focused on social and political problems. During the governments of Juscelino Kubitschek (1956–61), Jânio Quadros, and João Goulart (1961–64), the CNBB led the Church to cooperate with the government by mobilizing people to support Brazilian social reform projects, such as the Movement of Basic Education. Workers, peasants, and students were mobilized to address injustices in their respective spheres of society.

But when a military coup installed an authoritarian government (1964), the Church hierarchy was divided. More conservative members of the CNBB, fearing the progress of Communism in the country, sided with the government; others were concerned by the dangers represented by an anti-democratic regime and did not want to give up the social reform process they had launched. The government violently repressed any opposition, imprisoning and torturing both clergy and laity. After the 1968 promulgation of a law reinforcing military dictatorial powers, the Church withdrew its support of the government. Several bishops (including Candido Padim, Hélder Câmara*, Paulo Evaristo Arns*, and Waldir Calheiros) and many laypeople defended human* rights and the poor*, even as social-political organizations were forbidden, and assumed the prophetic role of being the "voice of those who had no voice" and of actively participating in the struggle for the redemocratization of the country. The Base* Ecclesial Communities (Comunidades Eclesiais de Base) became the privileged space for the Church's pastoral actions in pursuit of social justice* in urban and rural areas.

Since the restoration of democracy (1988), changes in the directives from the Roman Curia and in the leadership of the CNBB have shifted the attention of the Brazilian Church toward ecclesial issues. **See also BRAZIL.** BEATRIZ DE VASCONCELLOS DIAS

Roman Catholicism in Latin America: Brazil: Two Pastoral Initiatives of the National Conference of Bishops of Brazil (CNBB). The CNBB, founded in 1952 in Rio de Janeiro, was viewed by Dom Helder Câmara*, one of its foremost protagonists, as necessary for facilitating communication among Brazilian bishops, overcoming their individualistic behavior, and creating a holistic structure for pastoral services beyond parishes.

In the prophetic* tradition of the Bible, of Jesus' ministry and his proclamation of the Kingdom* of God, and of the Church, the CNBB was created in response to the bishops' deep concern with social issues in Northeast Brazil and to a national Catholic lay organization, the Catholic* Action, which promoted the people's engagement in the struggle for social reforms. The strong support of these two movements by priests, members of religious* orders, and laypeople, together with the new openness of the Church brought about by the Second Vatican* Council, prepared the way for the work of the CNBB. Even though from 1964 the leadership of CNBB was assumed by conservative bishops unwilling to overtly oppose the military coup, in the 1970s changes within the CNBB and growing repression by the military government led the CNBB to take publicly the side of the various sectors of the Brazilian society that were struggling against the regime in the pursuit of human* rights. During the 1960s and 1970s, the CNBB pursued two pastoral initiatives:

1. The Campaign of Fraternity sought to raise the political consciousness of the entire Brazilian population (and not merely of Catholics) through a series of widely publicized activities focused on annual topics chosen by the CNBB following recommendations by regional representatives of the Church. The actions of the Campaign of Fraternity were initially driven (1964–72) by a quest for the internal renovation of the Church and its individual members; in 1973, however, the Campaign turned to social issues. With a prophetic undertone criticizing the social situation, it promoted a critical assessment by the entire population of the grave problems that plague contemporary Brazilian society.
2. Social pastoral ministries are another expression of the prophetic efforts of the Catholic Church in Brazil. They help the Catholic Church and its members to deal effectively with social problems by increasing their understanding of the structural causes of social problems and empowering them through the development of political consciousness.

See also **CHURCH AND STATE RELATIONS CLUSTER: IN LATIN AMERICA: BRAZIL; LIBERATION THEOLOGIES CLUSTER; PREFERENTIAL OPTION FOR THE POOR.** WAGNER LOPES SANCHEZ

Roman Catholicism in Latin America: Brazilian New Movements. Initiated in the second half of the 1980s following John* Paul II's project of "New Evangelization," these new Catholic movements are of three types.

The first type has opted for communitarian life, following a spirituality model concerned primarily with conversion* and the refounding of the Christian community. Laypersons predominate in the leadership and the organization of communities, which favor various forms of participatory liturgy and liturgical leadership, as transparent manifestations of the "communion* of saints." The religious authorities, who officially approve these communities, intervene as little as possible, if at all, in their administration. This is not because of tensions between communities and religious authorities. Rather than expecting guidance from authorities, laypeople work together to develop the communities by sharing a vision of what the communities should be. These groups can be defined as *ecclesiolae in ecclesia* (little churches within the Church). In Brazil, some examples of such Catholic communities are Canção Nova (New Song), Shalom Community, and Neocatechumenate.

The second type of movement follows an Integrist* model. It either advocates a return to medieval Christianity or conceives of Catholicism as a historical project aimed at total control of the Church community and society, a totalizing project viewed as an authentic and accurate expression of the gospel. This demands that Christians pledge themselves to obtaining, holding on to, and defending political power, ideally in the form of a monarchic regime, because such political power is an indispensable instrument for the realization of the gospel by bringing about the Kingdom* of God. The principal groups in this movement are University Front Lepanto, Tradition, Family and Property, and the Heralds of the Gospel.

The third, relatively recent type of movement can be called reformist. The reform of the world is its primary concern. It seeks to focus on the classical issues and concerns of both Integrism and social Catholicism. Its goal is to enlist, select, and shape the economic and political leadership (from intermediate social levels to the top of the political hierarchy) in all the societies where the movement can establish itself and gain recognition. Moreover, this reformist movement operates according to the organizational logic of "religion as a social-political enterprise" aimed at a Catholic reconquest of the secularized* world (Enzo Pace). Examples are Opus* Dei and the Legionnaires of Christ.

See also CHARISMATIC AND PENTECOSTAL MOVEMENTS CLUSTER: IN LATIN AMERICA: BRAZIL. SÉRGIO COUTINHO

Roman Catholicism in Latin America: Chile. The Roman Catholic Church arrived in Chile with the conquistador Pedro de Valdivia (1540), accompanied by the priest Rodrigo González Marmolejo, who became the first bishop of Santiago. From the beginning, the Church sought to evangelize the natives, even as it sought to come to their defense in the midst of colonization, especially through the work of religious orders: Mercedarians (1540), Franciscans* (1551), Dominicans* (1557), and Jesuits* (1593).

When Chile achieved independence, priests participated in the first national government (1810). Bernardo O'Higgins, head of the new country, although tolerant of other religions, sought to establish relations with the Holy See and helped formalize the Church hierarchy in Santiago and Concepción.

The Constitution of 1833 established a state–church union that excluded other denominations. Inspired by Pope Leo* XIII (1878–1903), social Catholicism replaced the conservatism that dominated the 19th c. Between 1940 and 1950, strong social Christian currents became characteristic of Chilean Catholicism. In the 1960s, the Second Vatican* Council had a great influence on the Church and the hierarchy, even to the point that the Church supported agrarian reforms. And the Church remained in dialogue with the Socialist government of Salvador Allende.

Confronted with the military state, the Chilean Church played an important role in the defense of human* rights. This prophetic role, along with the promotion of sociopolitical debates, mark this period of Church life in Chile, exemplified by Cardinal Silva Henríquez.

As democracy was reestablished (1990s), the Church turned away from public affairs, focusing on family* values and individual morality, although continuing to pursue many initiatives regarding social issues. CRISTIÁN G. PARKER

Roman Catholicism in Latin America: Colombia. Roman Catholicism was introduced in Columbia with the Spanish* explorations, conquests, and colonization (early 16th c.). The mendicant* orders were directed to evangelize the conquered indigenous peoples through doctrinal instruction. Dominicans*, Franciscans*, Augustinians*, and Jesuits* struggled in this work, which was hampered by controversy and contradiction and combined conquest and evangelization – a "ministry" conceived by the Spanish crown, despite the protests of some missionaries.

As the ecclesiastical institutions were established with the help of colonialist authorities, in turn the ecclesiastical institutions, including male and female religious communities, came to support the colonial system. They propagated a baroque religiosity accepted by both the dominant and the dominated people. In the social sphere, the Spanish Creole elites and other sectors of society wove alliances through guilds, brotherhoods, and other corporations that became the spine of the regime. In the economic sphere, chapels helped clergy, as well as female and male religious, to acquire extensive properties for their financial support. The Church shaped education* and was in total control of the few high schools and universities (Universidad Santo Tomás, Colegio del Rosario, Colegio de San Bartolomé, Universidad Javeriana). Finally, ecclesiastical institutions attended to the poor, the sick, and the destitute, and even had responsibility for the distribution of water in villages and cities, in effect carrying out the responsibilities of the state.

The symbiosis between church* and state started to crumble when the Spanish Bourbon dynasty (18th c.) tried both to reform the clergy and to reduce its autonomy for the sake of administrative unification. This attempt to put the clergy under closer control by the crown did not succeed with the regular* clergy, as the expulsion of the Jesuits (1767) exemplifies.

However, the Bourbon reforms made possible the introduction of Enlightenment* ideas and their acceptance by the secular clergy, as well as some laypeople, such as Francisco Antonio

Moreno y Escandon (with his views of education) and José Celestino Mutis (with his botanical studies), which led to the reform of the educational system of New Granada. Using their intellectual skills and social influence, the clergy mobilized people and supported theologically both sides of the civil wars leading to independence (1810–19). Many priests participated in the fighting and even led troops, as Ignacio Mariño did. Popular religiosity also supported these causes.

After independence (1819), the new government, with a majority of liberal Catholics, continued the Patronato* system, the new government (replacing the Spanish crown) using the clergy to support its regime. In a cultural climate filled with a sense of "newness," liberal ideas from several origins were adopted by members of the clergy; many of them supported Freemasonry* and even promoted the foundation of a Protestant Biblical society. Meanwhile, a campaign was launched to discredit the regular clergy, the small convents were closed down, and the religious communities were beset by internal chaos (early 19th c.). This campaign against religious orders was driven, behind the scenes, by the government's desire to confiscate the many properties of the orders in order to supplement the income of the state's weak treasury.

A second and more radical generation of liberal leaders founded the Liberal Party, which took power in 1849. The Party undertook a number of reforms, which exacerbated the confrontation between the state and the clergy; among these reforms were the suppression of the tithe* and of ecclesiastical laws (*fueros*), the expulsion of the Jesuits, the total separation of church and state (1853), and ultimately the confiscation of ecclesiastical properties, a "cult tax" (a law requiring priests to acquire special licenses to preach), and the suppression of all religious communities (1861).

These events coincided with the beginning of the Romanization of the Church by the Vatican. Since 1863, and during the Olimpo Radical government (1863–82), the Colombian Church tried to reorganize under Roman rules and, with the support of the Conservative Party, to assume a confrontational attitude vis-à-vis the government and Liberalism. This attitude became more and more Integrist* and intransigent in the dispute between the parties, the religious issues becoming fuel for the civil wars that exploded during that epoch.

In 1886 the new regime adopted Catholicism as its ideological support, leading to a new period of partial symbiosis between the Church and the state. The Church controlled the educational system and was in charge of the social services through hospitals, orphanages, charity organizations, and lay programs related to the emerging Catholic* Action.

In 1930 the Liberals regained power; this gave rise to another period of confrontation between the government and the Conservative Party and its ally, the Church hierarchy. The intransigence of both sides led to a new period of uncontrolled violence in Colombia, especially in the rural and village areas (1940s–1950s). During those years, the Church attempted to engage in dialogue with the modern world through individual and collective initiatives, e.g. among workers (Jocists*, Catholic Union Movement) and students (Specialized Catholic* Action, testimony groups). Yet the Integrist* positions of the Church hierarchy and the intransigency of Conservative and Liberal politicians engendered a tense situation that led to a radicalization of the proposals, as in the case of Camilo Torres, the Golconda group, and several priests and women religious who ended up supporting or being part of the guerrilla movements.

The transformations called for by the Second Vatican* Council (1960s) took the Colombian Church hierarchy and most of the clergy by surprise. They generally interpreted its declarations in a superficial way. Pastoral initiatives like the Base* Ecclesial Communities collapsed as a result of internal contradictions, the opposition of the Church hierarchy led by Alfonso Lopez Trujillo, and the intensification of the military conflict among leftist guerrillas, the national army, and paramilitary groups. In the 1980s, the Colombian Church was perceived as having lost legitimacy and popularity.

After Lopez Trujillo's departure to Rome (1991), the Colombian episcopacy became more committed to helping resolve the conflict. It initiated negotiations among the parties, supported economic development, and struggled to reduce violence, intervening especially through laypeople and members of the female and male religious orders.

The Roman Catholic Church of the early 21st c. had gained institutional strength and a broader presence in society. Yet the maturation and growth of Pentecostalism*, the Charismatic* Movement, and other religious organizations was challenging it.

WILLIAM ELVIS PLATA

Roman Catholicism in Latin America: Mexico. See CHURCH AND STATE RELATIONS CLUSTER: IN LATIN AMERICA: MEXICO; MARY, THE VIRGIN, CLUSTER: OF GUADALUPE; MEXICO; MISSION CLUSTER: IN LATIN AMERICA: CATHOLIC MISSION IN MEXICO; POPULAR CHRISTIAN PRACTICES CLUSTER: IN LATIN AMERICA: MEXICO; RELIGIOUS ORDERS, ROMAN CATHOLIC, CLUSTER: IN LATIN AMERICA: MEXICO.

Roman Catholicism in Latin America: Paraguay. The Roman Catholic Church is by far the largest church in the country, with an archdiocese and 11 dioceses. In 1992 the National Constitution discontinued the recognition of Catholicism as the state religion. This change of status is part of a cycle in which the Church and the state have experienced periods of close collaboration and periods of separation, if not conflict. From 1929, when the Archdiocese of Asunción was created, through the 1950s, the Church and the state collaborated. During Stroessner's dictatorship (1954–89), the Church opposed the government. The visit of Pope John* Paul II (1988) provided support and mobilized the Paraguayan Church, especially because the pope canonized the Jesuit Roque González de la Cruz.

At present the Paraguayan Episcopal Conference denounces the neoliberal economic system and seeks to deal with rural problems, fighting for a complete agrarian reform that would give land* to the poor farmers. Mass is conducted both in Spanish and in Guarani, as well as in Japará, which combines both languages. The main popular devotions include pilgrimages to the Virgin of Caacupé (December 8) and to San Blas, patron saint* of Paraguay (February 3). **See also PARAGUAY.**

DAMIÁN SETTON and
VERÓNICA GIMÉNEZ BELIVEAU

Roman Catholicism in Latin America: Peru. Roman Catholicism in Peru is highly centered on devotions, processions, sanctuaries, rituals, and images. Although 85% of Peruvians are nominally Catholics, only 10% actually follow all the practices prescribed by Roman Catholicism. Nevertheless, the vast majority practice some form of popular* Catholicism: participation in the great Lord of Miracles procession in Lima or in the many other processions held in honor of Mary*, St. Rose* of Lima, St. Martin de Porres, and other saints*. Homes and cars are typically adorned with rosaries* and images of saints. Some figures, such as Sarita Colonia, are very popular but have not been recognized by the Church. Committed churchgoing Catholics often belong to one of many lay organizations: the more traditional belong to a confraternity or the Legion of Mary; the more conservative belong to Opus* Dei or Sodalitium Vitae Christianae; and the more progressive belong to the Christian Life Communities of the Jesuits. Liberation theology, closely identified with Gustavo Gutiérrez, a Peruvian priest, had a major impact on progressive Catholics in university circles and among the poor. Although Rome questioned elements of Liberation theology, and the episcopate is now largely conservative, Father Gutiérrez continues to be perceived by many Christians, in Peru and beyond, as a symbol of the Church's commitment to the poor.

The official Church consists of 46 jurisdictions, administered by 7 archbishops, 18 bishops, and 19 prelates who are not bishops. Eight bishops belong to Opus* Dei. There are 2,599 priests: 1,488 diocesan and 1,111 religious. The Church has a missionary character: around 60% of the priests and half the bishops are foreign born. Women religious number more than 4,000. The Church administers hundreds of parishes, many parish schools, several seminaries, clinics, orphanages, and many retreat houses. There are several Catholic universities. Since 1980 the separation between church and state has been official. But Catholicism is still part and parcel of Peruvian culture. All national events, including presidential inaugurations and Independence Day, begin with a Mass or a ceremony in the cathedral. **See also** PERU.

JEFFREY KLAIBER, SJ

Roman Catholicism in Latin America: Uruguay. Since the mid-19th c., Roman Catholicism in Uruguay has been marked by the radical confrontation of church* and state; this has affected the role of the Church in education*, as well as the Church's understanding of all aspects of life in society, including family* and the place of women*.

The state that emerged in Uruguay in this period was a modern state driven by secularization* and led by rationalists, Freemasons*, and liberals. The church that reacted against what it viewed as an invasion of its traditional role by the secular, irreligious, irreverent, and skeptical state was (as in the rest of Latin America) a new Catholic Church in the process of both "Romanization" and reformation. Following an institutionalization of the church–state conflict (1859–85), and a period of adjustment to this new church–state relation (1885–1906), the constitutional separation of church and state (1906–19) opened a new phase in the history of the Uruguayan Catholic Church. The Church constructed itself as a "Catholic ghetto," a besieged Catholicism, a "private Christendom," "a Christian enclave in a laicized country" (Segundo and Rodé), framed by a fear of what was not Christian and resulting in the absence of the Church in vital parts of Uruguayan life. (Protestantism has a similar attitude, according to Julio de Santa Ana.)

Aware of this problem, in the 1960s – a time of economic, cultural, and political crisis that threatened the very existence of social order (Alberto Methol Ferré) – a number of priests and laypeople developed a network of Catholic groups that intervened in all domains of Uruguayan daily life: schools, recreational institutions for youth, health care, business, social works, political life, and media (including the press). Within this gigantic social network, Catholics lived as a majority in a Catholic "nation" that protected Catholic faith and practices against the laicized*, secularized*, and de-Christianized environment (Rodé). This change of attitude was triggered and supported by the Second Vatican* Council, which challenged the Uruguayan Church to adopt a renewed sense of mission* in the country; a response to this challenge was spearheaded by Archbishop Carlos Parteli, despite significant opposition. In the face of a global cultural crisis paired with society's insensitivity to the poor, exiled, and marginalized in the context of a growing political authoritarianism, the 1968 Socio Pastoral Archdiocesan Conference emphasized that the urgent mission of the Church was to foster a sense of social responsibility. The Church was not to do this by itself: instead of appealing to the "goodwill" of those in power, it was to contribute to an awakening of the people, so that they might participate in their own liberation and development.

During the dictatorship (1973–85), despite contradictory positions (some Catholics supporting the dictatorship, other resisting it), participation in the antidictatorial movement was prevalent. Parishes and Catholic schools served as refuges for professors and intellectuals pursued by the state; Church hierarchies adopted nonconformist positions against the government; many priests (like Luis Pérez Aguirre) and lay Catholics were militants in social organizations that defended human* rights, justice*, and peace, and supported political prisoners.

The Church's antidictatorial role renewed its social legitimacy during the democratic recovery period. Yet since 1985, the Church has been confronted by new phenomena, including the shift in the location of the "religious" in life from institutional life to individual life and independent groups, and a change of the relations between religion and politics. These new phenomena have deep roots in Uruguayan history but are also part of the process of globalization. **See also CHURCH AND STATE RELATIONS CLUSTER: IN LATIN AMERICA: URUGUAY.**

GERARDO CAETANO

Roman Catholicism in North America: Canada. See QUEBEC.

Roman Catholicism in North America: United States. Statistics published in the *Official Catholic Directory* (2007) state that there are almost 70 million Roman Catholics in the USA, although this figure is difficult to verify. It includes persons of varying commitment to Catholicism and does not imply that all are actually "practicing," however practice is measured. Among Catholics there are different levels of participation in the Church's liturgical and community programs. Some disagree with certain diocesan or papal directives regarding reception of the sacraments*, social obligations, and sexual* norms within marriage*. Among practicing US Catholics, tensions exist between "conservative traditionalists" and "progressive liberals."

Catholics in the USA, after those in Brazil and Mexico, constitute the third-largest Catholic population of a country worldwide. Catholics represent some 25% of the US population, although their distribution varies from one section of the country to another. Regions heavily populated by Catholics are found on the East Coast and in such major cities as Los Angeles, New York, Chicago, and Boston. There are some 195 dioceses (of which 146 are Latin Rite and 17 are Eastern Catholic). Latinos/as constitute 39% of the US Catholic population (2007): c25 million, i.e. 73% of the US Latino/a population (c35.3 million). Among African Americans (36 million in the USA) only some 2.5 million, or 7%, are Catholics; however, their voice, long neglected, is gradually being heard. With the arrival of immigrants, especially from Asian countries such as Vietnam and the Philippines, ethnic diversity among Catholics has grown, especially in some sections of the country.

Roman Catholicism originally came to what is today the USA even before the Reformation through Spanish explorers and settlers in present-day Florida (from 1513) and in various parts of the Southwest. The California missions, dating back to 1769, also introduced Catholicism to that area of the country. The English colonies in the East were largely Protestant, with the exception of the Maryland settlement, which after 1634 allowed religious toleration of Catholics. At the outbreak of the American Revolution (1776), US Catholics were less than 1% of the population within the 13 colonies. A large proportion of present-day American Catholics trace their origins to the massive immigrations in the 19th and early 20th c., especially from such countries as Ireland, Germany, Italy, Poland, and French Canada.

In general, because of the immigrant character of most US Catholics, it was difficult until the second half of the 20th c. to identify a vibrant intellectual life among them. Few of the bishops and priests had more than a seminary education, which was often constricted by measures taken by the Vatican to prevent the spread of Catholic Modernism*. Beginning in the 1960s and especially after the Second Vatican* Council (1962–65), a notable shift in theological training took place, with the emergence of laymen and laywomen scholars. Controversies over the conciliar reforms of the liturgy and divergent opinions about the force of certain papal teachings contributed to internal tensions in the US Church. Finally, toward the close of the 20th c., with the disclosure of sexual abuse of minors by some members of the clergy, as well as the perception that priestly predators had not been appropriately punished by bishops, a widespread malaise gripped the Church. Among the challenging issues facing the US Catholic Church today are the notable decline of ordinations to the priesthood and the financial viability of some dioceses in the wake of change and crises.

MICHAEL A. FAHEY, SJ

Roman Catholicism in the South Pacific and Australia. The Australian Roman Catholic Church was composed largely of Irish settlers until the coming of European (and later Asian) migrants after World War II. This influx strained Church resources, especially the voluntarily funded Church school system, until government aid was received in the 1960s. Catholicism was dependent on overseas members of religious orders who staffed schools, overseas clergy who provided pastoral care, and overseas Church personnel who maintained many charitable institutions. Organizing Church life in Australia has been beset by the "tyranny of distance," although most Australians now live in the large coastal cities. The 1960s provided a watershed for Australian Catholicism with the impact of the Second Vatican* Council and the increasing secularism* that eroded widely accepted Christian values. Leadership in the Australian Church was originally in the hands of English Benedictine* monks, although increasingly Irish bishops were appointed and were prominent in Church leadership until the death of Archbishop Daniel Mannix of Melbourne (1963). He featured largely in the turbulent relations between the Church and the Labour Party, which resulted in "the split" of 1955, diminishing Catholics' support for Labour and their move toward more conservative parties. However, a strong commitment to social and justice* issues remains a characteristic of Catholicism.

New Zealand Catholics also depended on overseas clergy and often supported the Labour Party and the country's advanced social services. With 13% of the population, the New Zealand Catholic Church has continued to be a vocal presence in the public discourse. Catholic bishops have often voiced strong liberal views in series of short, readable statements. The Irish tradition in Catholicism was tempered by French missionaries such as Bishop Jean-Baptiste Pompallier and the Marists. Catholics supported the resurgence of the Maori people in the early 20th c. and the appointment of the first Maori bishop in 1988.

Small island communities scattered over the vast distances of the southern Pacific Ocean offered major challenges to missionaries. Generally Catholics came later than Protestants and, like them, faced hostility, which resulted in the murder of missionaries, and tropical diseases, which decimated their ranks. Numerous languages, a lack of Christian literature in indigenous languages, and little appreciation for local cultures exacerbated the missionary challenge. The Marists, Missionaries of the Sacred Heart, and many orders of women served on these islands. Among these numerous islands, New Caledonia has the largest percentage of Catholics (60% of the population). AUSTIN COOPER, OMI

Roman Catholic Worship. See MASS.

Roman Curia (often referred to as "the Vatican" or "Rome") is the administrative apparatus of the Holy See* and, with the pope*, is the central governing body of the entire Roman Catholic Church. It includes the "Secretariat of State," nine Roman congregations (including the Congregation for the Doctrine of the Faith), tribunals, pontifical councils, the Synod of Bishops, and various other offices and pontifical commissions.

Romanesque Architecture, church building style (c1000–1150) characterized by round arches and heavy piers and columns. **See also HIEROTOPY, THE CREATION OF CHRISTIAN SACRED SPACES.**

Romania is a secular state, and is thus without a state church. Yet almost all the inhabitants of Romania are Christians, and the dominant religious body is the Romanian Orthodox* Church, an autocephalous church within the Eastern Orthodox* Church.

The territory now occupied by Romania in Southeastern Europe has a recorded history that encompasses the Dacian era, the Roman Empire, and the medieval era of principalities (*voivodats*) of Walachia, Moldavia, and Transylvania. According to tradition, Christianity first arrived in present-day Romanian territory with the apostle Andrew, who preached the gospel in Scythia Minor (modern Dobrogea). Dacia was conquered by the Romans under Emperor Trajan (106 CE) and heavily colonized by people who came primarily from Asia Minor, many of whom were Christians. During a relatively short period of Roman occupation, the inhabitants of this territory emerged as a major Romance people, with a powerful Christian Church, represented at the first ecumenical* councils, as the church fathers duly recorded. Historians appropriately say that the Romanian people were born as a Christian people. In any case, when the Romanians formed a nation, it is clear that they already had the Christian faith, as apparent not only from tradition but also from archeological and linguistic evidence. In either 271 or 275, the Roman army and administration left Dacia, which was invaded by the Goths*.

Yet the Romans and their successors were ruthless with the Christians, as is shown by the great number of martyrs. Bishop Ephrem, killed in 304 in Tomis, was followed by countless other martyrs. The 1971 archeological digs under the paleo-Christian basilica in Niculiţel (near ancient Noviodunum in Scythia Minor) excavated an old martyrion that contains the relics of Zoticos, Attalos, Kamasis, and Filippos, who suffered martyrdom under Diocletian (304–5), and, under the crypt, the relics of two earlier martyrs who died during the repressions of Emperor Decius (249–51).

The Orthodox Church in the Romanian principality of Wallachia (founded c1310), also known as Ungro-Vlachia (Hungary-Wallachia), north of the Danube, became in 1359 a metropolitanate, with Curtea de Arges as the first see*. Similarly the Church in the principality of Moldovia (founded c1352) became a metropolitanate in 1401, with its first see in Suceava. The Church in the principality of Transylvania (though part of the Hungarian kingdom between the 10th and 16th c.; officially a principality in 1711) became a metropolitanate in the 15th c., with its first see in Alba Iulia.

While Wallachia slowly fell under the suzerainty of the Ottomans during the 15th c., Moldovia reached its most glorious period under the rule of Stephen III the Great (1457–1504), a highly successful political and military leader. After his victory against the Ottomans in 1475, Pope Sixtus IV deemed him "true champion of the Christian faith." However, after his death, Moldovia also came under the suzerainty of the Ottoman Empire.

During the following centuries, the Orthodox Church flourished mainly in Wallachia and Moldavia. Many well-known churches and monasteries (e.g. Cozia, Voronet, Putna, Sucevita) were erected at that time. In 1859 the modern state of Romania was created by the union of Moldavia and Wallachia, becoming a kingdom in 1881. In 1872 the Orthodox Metropolitanates of Ungro-Vlachia and of Moldovia were united to form the Romanian Orthodox Church. This Church became autocephalous* (1885) and was raised to the rank of a patriarchate (1925).

In 1918, after World War I, Bessarabia, Northern Bukovina, and Transylvania became part of the Kingdom of Romania. With World War II, Bessarabia and Northern Bukovina were lost to the Soviets, who imposed their harsh rule. The monarchy was abolished in 1947. From 1947 to 1964, many people were arbitrarily imprisoned and even killed for political, religious, economic, or unknown reasons. After the retreat of Soviet troops in 1958, Romania started to pursue independent policies. But the dictatorial regime of Nicolas Ceausescu (from 1965) continued the oppression and exhausted the Romanian economy, leading to his overthrow and execution in a bloody revolution (1989).

The new democratic Romania joined NATO (2004) and the European Union (2004). With freedom of travel, 2–3 million Romanians emigrated, leading to the creation of many new Orthodox communities (and dioceses) in Western Europe, the USA, Canada, and Australia.

A first translation of the Bible into Gothic was completed by Bishop Ulfila* (4th c.) during the Goth occupation. However, given the complex relationship with the Byzantine Patriarchate and Bulgarian kingdoms, Romanians adopted Church Slavonic in the liturgy (from the early 9th c.). Yet this was never the language of the people, and the priests always preached in Romanian. More and more Bible texts and liturgical books were translated and later printed in Romanian. Consequently, since the 16th–18th c., Slavonic has been progressively abandoned in favor of Romanian as the liturgical language (in contrast, other major Orthodox nations do not use their own spoken language as a sacred language). The Bucharest Bible (*Biblia de la Bucureşti*) was the first complete Romanian translation of the Bible. Published in 1688, it is a mature and highly developed work that was founded on much previous translation work (as older manuscripts and early printed works show).

Although they remained for a long time under foreign suzerainty, Romanians characteristically kept their Orthodox faith, which proved to be an essential part of their national and ethnic identity. The Romanian Orthodox Church has since 1885 been an autocephalous* Orthodox church, with its own Holy Synod presided over by its own patriarch.

The oldest traces of Roman Catholic activities in present-day Romanian territory have been found in Transylvania, recorded in connection with the extension of Magyar (Hungarian) rule. The Roman Catholic Diocese of Alba Iulia was probably established in the 11th c. Other dioceses were created later in Cenad and Oradea. In 1304 Pope Boniface VIII sent Catholic missionaries over the Carpathian Mountains, where Eastern Orthodox churches and dioceses were already present. A Catholic diocese was created in this area.

In the 16th c., some of the Catholics in Transylvania embraced the Reformation*; most of the Saxons adhered to the Lutheran Reformation as early as 1547, and large groups of the Hungarian population converted to Calvinism* (Reformed* Church).

In 1698, under great pressure from the Austrian imperial authority, the metropolitan and a small number of Orthodox priests in Transylvania became Uniates*. This action was simply a political move designed to secure equality of rights with Catholics in the region. Powerfully sustained by the imperial authority that persecuted the resistant Orthodox, the "Greek Rite Roman Catholic" Church became part of Romanian life in Transylvania.

But in 1948, the Uniate Catholics joined the Orthodox Church, a union supported by the regime. Some of the Greek Catholic clerics who refused to make this move were jailed. The Greek Catholic Church regained legal status after the fall of Communism, but most of its former members chose to remain Orthodox. The Romanian Church United with Rome, the church of Greek Catholics, now has a separate jurisdiction, a number of bishops, and an archbishop. In May 1999 Romania was the first country with an Orthodox majority to be visited by Pope John* Paul II. But problems between Orthodox and Uniates continue, mostly with respect to the status of Greek Catholic properties.

The newer evangelical denominations (Pentecostal*, Baptist*, Seventh*-day Adventist) arrived in Romania mostly after World War I. The Pentecostals and Charismatics* are most numerous, followed by the Baptists.

Statistics: Population (2002): 22.3 million (M). Christians, 22 M, 99% (Orthodox, 18.9 M, 82.1%; Protestants, 1.41 M, 6.4%; Roman Catholics, 1.02 M, 4.7%; Pentecostals, 0.33 M, 1.5%; Greek Catholics, 0.19 M, 0.9%; Baptists, 0.13 M, 0.6%; Seventh-day Adventists, 0.08 M, 0.4%; Unitarians, 0.06 M, 0.3%); Muslim minority, mostly of Turkish ethnicity (c0.06 M); with the emigration of many Jews to Israel, a very small Jewish minority (6,200). (Based on the 2002 census.)

VASILE MIHOC

Romans, Epistle to the, Paul's* most influential letter, underscores central Christian doctrines, especially "justification* by faith*." The letter (c54–58) also addresses issues the house churches in Rome confront concerning the relations between Jews and Gentiles (1:16–11:36, 14:1–15:33) and between Christians and Roman imperial authorities (1:1–15, 12:1–13:14).

Paul was leaving Corinth* with some apprehension (15:25–31) to take the money collected from Gentile churches in Greece (Macedonia and Achaia) to the Jewish-Christian churches in Jerusalem*, before going to Rome, then Spain (15:23–24). Although he was not personally acquainted with the Romans (1:10–13, 15:18–22), he was aware of the tensions between Jewish and Gentile Christians and of the uncertainty regarding how Christians should relate to Roman authorities. Claudius's expulsion of the Jews from Rome in 49 and Nero's reversal of it might have generated these tensions because of the Jewish Christians' return to predominantly Gentile churches.

Paul addresses the issues by interpreting the gospel about Jesus' sacrificial* death (3:25) and resurrection* (1:4) in relation to traditions about imperial Roman authority and Jewish Scriptures (Moses' Law*, 2:12–3:31, 7:1–8:39; Abraham*, 4:1–25; Adam*, 5:12–21; Israel*, 9:1–11:36).

In an ironic challenge to Roman authority, Paul portrays the spreading of the gospel as an imperial conquest in the name of the Lord Jesus Christ, by servants who "put on" Christ as an armor of light (13:12–14) to bring everyone to the "obedience of faith" (1:5), just as the Roman legions brought everyone to "voluntary" obedience to the emperor. Thus the emperor is not the true Lord, but simply a "servant of God" (13:1–7); one should not conform to "this world" (12:2). "Obedience of faith" is righteousness*, justification, the right relation to God exemplified by Abraham and fulfilled in Christ's faithful death, which makes possible the justification of both Gentile and Jewish sinners (1:18–4:25). The Law is "holy, just, and good," but not sufficient, because it fuels sin* instead of overcoming it (7:1–24). When

God justifies Gentile sinners "through faith," even though most Jews did not join the Gentiles who believed (9:1–11:12), God remains just (1:17). Mysteriously God's covenant* with Israel remains irrevocable (11:29). Thus Gentile Christians should not boast (11:13–36, 15:31).

Romans and its powerful theological argument for Christians in Rome was appropriated by believers in many other contexts. Romans influenced, e.g., the Gnostics* and Origen's* understanding of evil* and salvation*; Augustine's* understanding of sin* and grace*, faith, the bondage* of the will*, predestination*, and church* and state; Luther* and the Reformers'* understanding of justification by faith; and certain Liberation* theologians' understanding of salvation as liberation from bondage. DANIEL PATTE

Romanticism and Christianity. Anglo-American romanticism, as distinct from Euro-Continental romanticism of either a French rationalist or a German idealist stripe, generated religious, as well as philosophical, language. This local habitation of the long Romantic Movement sensed, rather than deduced or intuited, "whatsoever things" were true, honest, just, pure, lovely, and "of good report" (Phil 4:8). Thus a radically immanent* Christianity hovered near romanticism. The empirical and experiential dimensions of Arminian* (free-will) Evangelical practice, as opposed to the antiexperiential aspect of Calvinist* theology, stiffened romantic Anglo-America's "spiritual sense." This romanticism proclaimed the imperatives "Trust in Experiment!" "Test Religion!"

The two pioneers of transatlantic revivalism, John Wesley* (1703–91) and Jonathan Edwards* (1703–58), absorbed and spiritualized the sensationalist epistemology of John Locke* (1632–1704) and, through the complex process of cultural osmosis, passed on to the 19th c. an empirical idiom of Evangelical expression. As a result, the British romantics William Blake*, William Wordsworth, Samuel Taylor Coleridge*, Percy Bysshe Shelley, and John Keats could conceive of the physical senses as portals to epiphany*, and not just as analogies of spiritual insight. Thomas Carlyle, Alfred, Lord Tennyson, and Ralph Waldo Emerson*, as an illustrative Anglo-American trio of late romantic writers, continued to blend "the language of the sense" (Wordsworth's phrase) with "poetic faith" (Coleridge). Even Emily Dickinson, herself as much (or more) of a late romantic poet as a Victorian American (anti-romantic) or premodern author, dwelled in the possibility of, and gravitated toward, the synthesis of scientific method with the varieties of religious experience. Like her precursors and coevals on the high to late romantic arc (the ark back and forth across the Atlantic), Dickinson proved more apt to expect truth, joy, and grace (after the manner of Locke, Wesley, and Edwards) than to suspect false consciousness (à la Karl Marx*, Friedrich Nietzsche*, or Sigmund Freud*).

Experience and faith emerged from the Anglo-American climate as "contraries" that produced "progression" (Blake's dialectical terms). Science* and religion, it is true, may seem to be "non-overlapping magisteria" (Stephen Jay Gould). Faith, moreover, scarcely moved mountains "so well / As she was fam'd to do, deceiving elf" (Keats, "Ode to a Nightingale," 1819). Nonetheless, Anglo-American romantics imagined that faith* in experience, for better or worse, would lead, through dust and heat, to an experience of faith. Thus instead of nihilistic unbelief, constructive skepticism informed all that the Anglo-American century from 1770 to 1870 found resonant in "the burden of the mystery" (Wordsworth's language).

RICHARD E. BRANTLEY

Rome, the location of Vatican* City, the pope*, and the Holy See*. The term "Rome" often refers to the Roman Curia located in it or to the pope, the bishop of Rome.

Romero, Oscar Arnulfo (1917–80), archbishop of El* Salvador (1977), assassinated by an ultra-Right death squad while saying Mass* in the chapel of the Divina Providencia Hospital. The "martyred bishop of the poor" lived in solidarity with the most impoverished in his country and the victims of human* rights violations perpetrated by security forces and other armed groups. His commitment was reinforced by the murder of Jesuit Priest Rutilio Grande (1977), and from that time he devoted himself to the struggle of the persecuted and the poor. While extremely critical of the army, he did not promote any political ideology; he also criticized popular organizations and leftist parties that gave priority to their organizations or political ideals over suffering people and their hopes. He denounced the attacks against peasants, workers, and religious leaders, the "disappearances," and the assassinations. The day before his own assassination, he said in his homily, "In the name of God, in the name of this suffering* people whose cries, every day more distraught, reach the heavens, I implore you,

I beg you, I order you in the name of God, stop the repression." "Monseñor Romero" or "San Romero of America" (his popular designations) became an international and interconfessional symbol of the struggle for human* rights. Procedures for his beatification are in process. **See also POVERTY CLUSTER; PREFERENTIAL OPTION FOR THE POOR.**

ELSA TAMEZ (translated by Gloria Kinsler)

Rosary, prayer involving the recitation of 15 sets of 10 Hail* Marys, each set of Hail Marys being preceded by the Lord's* Prayer and followed by the *Gloria* Patri*; thus the rosary beads with which one prays are divided into five groups of 10 to assist the recitation. Despite popular lore, this practice was introduced not by Dominic*, but rather after him, although similar practices existed earlier on at Cluny and elsewhere.

Rose, St., of Lima (1581–1617). Born Isabel Flores de Oliva, she is the patron saint* of Lima, the Americas, and the Philippines, the first saint of the New World to be canonized (1651), and a symbol of a new Creole identity. Born in Lima, called "Rose" because of her rosy cheeks, she became a member of the Third Order of St. Dominic (1606) and usually wore the Dominican* habit, although she was not formally a nun. She lived in her family's home, practiced severe penances*, and performed works of charity. St. Rose is the patroness of the police and unofficially of couples about to be married. **See also PERU.**

JEFFREY KLAIBER, SJ

Rouse, C. (Clara) Ruth (1872–1956), British Anglican evangelist, promoter of foreign mission and ecumenism, international pioneer among women students, and foremother of the modern ecumenical movement. She traveled, together with John R. Mott*, to five continents organizing Christian student unions among both women and men (1897–1924).

As a student at Cambridge she committed herself to the Student* Volunteer Movement (1894), became a missionary in India, and subsequently worked for the World* Student Christian Federation, visiting universities, evangelizing students, organizing unions, planning and implementing camps and conferences, and choosing and training future leaders for Christian work all over the world.

No hard-core feminist, she nevertheless was a resolute modern reformer. The World Student Christian Federation was for Western Protestant men only; she was instrumental in opening it up to women on equal terms (1905–20), to Orthodox and Catholic Christians (Constantinople, 1911; a reflection of her conscious ecumenical stance), and to non-Westerners (Tokyo Conference, 1907). She was secretary to the Missionary Council of the Church of England (1924–38); she later served as president of the World's YWCA* (1938–46). She devoted her last years to writing a history of the World Student Christian Federation (1948) and to editing a first history of the ecumenical movement (published, 1954).

RUTH FRANZÈN

Rufinus, Tyrannius (c345–411), monk, historian, translator. He studied in Rome, becoming Jerome's* friend. After some years in Egypt* (373–81), he and Melania* the Elder founded a double* monastery on the Mount of Olives* (381–82). His translations into Latin include Origen's* *On First Principles* (a translation made after Jerome attacked Origenism*) and Origen's commentary on Romans, the Clementine* *Recognitions*, works by Basil* of Caesarea and Gregory* Nazianzen, and Eusebius's* *Church History* (adding a narrative through the triumph of Theodosius*). His commentary on the Apostles'* Creed gives the earliest text of the form of the creed as used in Aquileia and Rome.

Rufinus the Syrian (d401), priest member of Jerome's* monastery in Bethlehem, who probably translated the Pauline Epistles in the Vulgate* and represented Jerome in Rome during the Origenist* dispute (399). He opposed the nascent doctrine of original* sin, saying that the soul is created with a mortal body, death is punishment for individual sins, and there were sinless persons before the advent of Christ.

Rule of Faith. See *REGULA FIDEI*.

Rules, Monastic. See AUGUSTINIAN RULE; BENEDICT, RULE OF; MONASTICISM CLUSTER: MONASTIC RULES.

Rupert of Deutz (c1075–1129), scriptural exegete, monastic theologian. From an early age a monk of St. Laurent, Liège, Rupert experienced periods of exile before becoming abbot of Deutz, Cologne (1120–29). He produced scripturally based treatises on the liturgy and on the Trinity* and its works, and innovative commentaries on many biblical books that emphasized historical* as well as allegorical* interpretation and the role of the Holy Spirit in history. A defender of monasticism* and ecclesiastical reform, he came into conflict with Scholastics* and faced accusations about his own orthodoxy. CONSTANT J. MEWS

Russell, Charles Taze (1852–1916), founded the movement that became known as the Jehovah's* Witnesses. He grew up in Pennsylvania and as a young man was strongly influenced by "Millerite*" teachings (see Adventism), which shaped his millennial* convictions and analytical approach to Scripture*. Russell sold his businesses while in his 20s to concentrate on religious work. He founded Zion's Watch Tower Tract Society to distribute religious tracts and Bibles. By using colporteurs (traveling booksellers), he established the missionary methods continued by Jehovah's Witnesses today. Russell wrote a number of books, including seven volumes entitled *Studies in the Scriptures*.

DAVID VOAS

Russia. Dominated by the Orthodox* Church, Christianity in Russia has developed somewhat separately from its Western European and Mediterranean counterparts. Though planted in Russia by Greeks, Christianity has grown and flowered in many and rare ways, ranging from Catholic influence along the western Russian frontier to homegrown mystical sects and traditionalist Old* Believers. Religious life in contemporary Russia is experiencing a period of rapid transition; Christianity seeks to return to its deep roots in Russia even as it struggles with the legacy of militant atheist policies of the Soviet period.

1. History of Christianity in Russia. The arrival of Christianity in Russia is dated to 988, when Prince Vladimir of Kiev baptized his subjects en masse (see Ukraine). According to tradition, Vladimir had sent emissaries to explore the major monotheistic religions. Each religion came up short except Orthodoxy. "We knew not," exclaimed the emissaries after experiencing the Orthodox liturgy, "whether we were on heaven or on earth!" While the story is certainly apocryphal, it does illustrate two major themes: the supremacy of Orthodoxy in Russia and an emphasis on the transformative power of Christianity.

Though he was revered, the admiration for Prince Vladimir cannot match the love traditionally shown for the first Russian saints*, Boris* and Gleb. These Christian princes chose to accept suffering and lay down their lives rather than fight their brother Sviatopolk for political dominance. In doing so, they created a particularly Russian form of saintliness* that still influences Russian Christianity. Their 11th-c. canonization as "passion bearers" (not martyrs) showed that human beings could act in a Christ-like way even in political or social situations. Although their deaths were political, their actions were quintessentially Christian.

As it spread northward and eastward from Kiev, Orthodoxy was layered over existing magical and animist beliefs. Soon Christianity outwardly replaced "pagan" religion, but many animist traditions (including the belief in forest sprites and other supernatural beings) were integrated into rural Christian traditions. Thus Russian Christianity can be seen as a mixture of high theology, monasticism*, parish life, and popular* culture.

Mongol occupation of Russian Lands (13th–14th centuries) influenced Orthodoxy, paradoxically strengthening it even as the Mongols stamped out political opposition. When Muscovy broke free of Mongol dominance, its religious traditions began to dominate Russian Christianity. Muscovite Orthodoxy tended to emphasize ritual, liturgical, and communal themes over those of personal piety. Still, the monastic tradition in Russia long struggled between the "Non-Possessor" and "Possessor" teachings. The Non-Possessors were spiritually led by Nil* Sorsky, who taught that monks ought to live in small hermitages, spend their days in prayer, and not accept worldly gifts (following the model of Sketic monasticism in Egypt). The Possessors, exemplified by Joseph of Volokolamsk, emphasized the creation of large monasteries with significant wealth and strictly hierarchal structures that would interact with the world. While the Muscovite Possessors became the dominant strand, the Non-Possessor spirit remained alive in hermitages, informal women's monastic communities, and "sketes," the smaller outgrowths of major monasteries (see Monasticism Cluster: In the Russian and Ukrainian Tradition.)

First peak of Muscovite Orthodoxy (1589). This peak was reached when Moscow's bishop received the status of patriarch*, which placed him on equal terms with the most senior Orthodox leaders worldwide. Russian Orthodoxy was now autocephalous*. In fact, the fall of Constantinople to the Ottomans (1453) convinced some theologians that Moscow was the "Third Rome" and thus the undisputed defender of Orthodox Christianity. Indeed, Moscow completely opposed an attempt at union with Rome (1596).

17th century. During this period, Russian Orthodoxy suffered its most important internal upheaval, known as the "*raskol*" (schism) of the Old Belief. A new patriarch, Nikon*, introduced (1650s) ritual changes to attune Russian Orthodoxy to its contemporary Greek counterparts. Aghast at the changes and their theological implications, many Orthodox refused to implement Nikon's reforms. He then used his considerable influence over Czar Alexei Mikhailovich (1645–76) to force acceptance, sometimes at gunpoint. The result was a religious rebellion rather than the centralization of control that Nikon pursued. Those Orthodox who refused to accept either ritual reform or centralized administration became known as Old* Believers (or Old Ritualists). Without a hierarchy, the Old Believers split into many groups called "concords," with various eschatological*, apocalyptic*, ideological, and political views. The Russian Orthodox Church condemned both Nikon and the Old Believers at a church council (1666–67). Unfortunately, during the schism, the Orthodox Church lost many of its most zealous adherents, and the Old Believers were pushed out of the religious mainstream. Some Old Believers lost their sacramental life as their priests died off, while others sought to "convert" priests from the state-sponsored church or imported bishops from other Orthodox jurisdictions. Old Believers suffered persecution until 1905.

Reign of Peter I (1682–1725). The symbolic power of Russian Orthodoxy was further eroded during the reign of Peter I ("the Great"), who abolished the throne of patriarch, replacing it with the Holy Synod – first known as the Spiritual College – to administer the Church. Many Old Believers viewed Peter I as the Antichrist* for his Westernizing tendencies, although as a pragmatist Peter let most Old Believer communities thrive. Western Christians were welcomed by Peter as part of his project to Westernize Russia.

The Russian Orthodox Church's financial independence next came under fire, when Emperor Peter III secularized Church land and property (1762). This freed up significant land for state use but effectively cut off much of the Church's source of independent income. Still, Orthodoxy commanded the loyalty of most Russian Christians, even though some quietly preferred the rituals and autonomy of the Old Belief.

Catherine II (1762–96) through Alexander I (1801–25). During the reigns of these monarchs, Russia became home to many non-Orthodox Christians. Catherine II invited German Mennonites into Russia to act as model farmers in Ukraine*. Concurrently, the expansion of Russian power into Europe led to the incorporation into the Russian Empire of millions of Polish Roman Catholics and Finnish Lutherans. The Eastern Rite Catholic Church (often known as "Uniate*") retained significant support, especially in Western Ukraine. Interaction among these groups fostered the growth of new Christian communities in the Empire, while expanding contacts with the West helped to develop some influence of Pietists*, Freemasons*, and even Jesuits* in Russian high society. The Russian Bible Society was first lauded and then suppressed in this period.

Orthodoxy responded to its many new neighbors by strengthening its own educational system and championing a quasi-scholastic view that deemphasized mystical elements of the faith while simultaneously rationalizing church administration. The priesthood remained split between monastic clergy ("black") and parish clergy ("white"). Church leadership came only from the ranks of monks, while married parish clergy tended to serve with poor pay, little real power, and even less prestige. The introduction of widespread seminary training helped, but very little, since the schools tended to train clergy in Latin and dogmatic theology rather than in the liturgical and pastoral duties that they would perform in the parishes. Each year some priests fled to the Old Believers, who promised better financial support and more autonomy at the parish level.

19th century. During this time, Russia experienced an explosion of new religious forms. Many homegrown groups protested against Orthodoxy's prayers to the saints*, its sacramental life, icons*, and allegedly poor moral development. Some of these, such as the Molokans, Dukhobors, and Shtundists (a movement that included many traditional Protestant groups), tended toward theological and community structures resembling those prevalent in Anabaptism*. The Russian Orthodox Church denigrated these as "rationalist sects." Other groups became increasingly radical; among these, which the Russian Orthodox Church denigrated as "mystical sects," were the Khlysts (Flagellants) and Skopts (Castrators), who participated in ecstatic group worship and sometimes even ritual castration, mutilation, and dismemberment. The Church and the state maintained a legal monitoring of these "schismatics" or "most pernicious sects," which tended to develop in or move toward the Russian borderlands in the Caucasus and Ukraine. By the late 19th c., Shtundist communities in Ukraine openly identified themselves as Baptists. Some embraced female leadership, which was less likely to exist in Russian Orthodox communities.

This foment also gave rise to a renewal of Russian Orthodoxy in the 19th c. The Slavophile Movement promoted the idea of "community" or "conciliarity*" (*sobornost'*) as a social and cultural agenda for Russian development, both supporting Orthodoxy and challenging the autocratic status quo. Likewise, Slavophile ideas helped to revive Orthodox philosophy, monasticism, and social activism. For instance, Fr. Zosima in Dostoevsky's* *Brothers Karamazov* was a composite character taken from the spiritual fathers of the Optina community, a center of Orthodox renewal.

Concurrently, academic ethnographers began to analyze the syncretism* of popular religion in the Russian countryside, deriding it as a "dual faith" that masked "pagan" belief with Christian themes. Yet the peasantry possessed not a dual faith so much as a view of Christianity which differed from that of academics or theologians. Indeed, for a Russian peasant, it was not odd to invoke Christ, Mary, or the saints when reciting a magical incantation in a bathhouse or at a crossroad, both of which had heightened religious importance in rural Russia. (For similar phenomena elsewhere, see Inculturation Cluster; Popular Christian Practices Cluster.)

For the majority of Russian Christians in the countryside, the liturgical calendar was inextricably tied to the agricultural year. The various summer holidays celebrating Christ's life (called "Christs," for short) also marked important days of harvest. Russian Christians would speak of the "Apple Christ," for example.

The emancipation of the serfs by Alexander II (1861) further strengthened public celebrations of Orthodoxy, as peasant pilgrimage* grew exponentially in the late 19th c. While some Orthodox believers traveled to the Holy Land, thousands more made pilgrimages to Russian holy sites, such as the famed monastery of Solovetskii near the Arctic Circle. Likewise, the greater mobility of peasants and workers strengthened both the Old Believers and non-Orthodox Christian communities. Women's religious communities, either official monasteries or unofficial groups, became more prominent as an alternative to parish life in the Orthodox Church.

20th century. This period dealt blow after blow to Russia, including its Christian population. Social and economic upheaval during the explosive industrialization of the late imperial period was exacerbated by the disastrous Russo-Japanese War, the revolution of 1905, World War I, and the ensuing revolutions of February and October 1917 (led by Alexander Kerensky and Vladimir Lenin, respectively). Millions of Russian Christians suffered, although denominations responded in different ways to the ravages of war and revolution.

Significantly, the period 1905–17 offered a window of opportunity for Christians outside of the state-sponsored Church. The Edict of Toleration of 1905 legalized all denominations within the Russian Empire. For the first time, all groups could build churches, publish openly, proselytize, and receive converts from Orthodoxy. The result was a short-lived golden era for groups ranging from Old Believers to Baptists, which saw their numbers rise very quickly. Significantly, during these years, many of these groups held regional and national meetings for the first time to develop a national presence in Russia.

Although the Bolshevik Revolution had an expressly atheist agenda, response to the revolution was quite varied. The Russian Orthodox Church, meeting in its first all-Russian council in centuries, roundly decried the revolution. Its newly elected patriarch, Tikhon*, allowed Church leaders to go into exile. Other groups, however, tentatively welcomed the change in power. Some Baptists, e.g., embraced revolutionary fervor as a way to revitalize and expand their faith throughout Russia.

The young Bolshevik state nationalized all religious property and regularly looted and burned buildings while martyring religious leaders and laity alike. The League of Militant Godless (from the mid-1920s to 1940) began an often unsuccessful campaign of atheist propaganda across the USSR. Although the official line against all forms of religion was unrelenting, the state sometimes tried to co-opt sectarian groups that had been persecuted by the imperial government. In addition, rank-and-file Communist Party members were often caught between the appeals of militant atheism* and their own (or their family's) Christian heritage. Parishes often tried to recast themselves according to new Soviet laws to avoid being liquidated. The situation on the ground was therefore considerably more complicated than propagandists on either side might portray.

Once Soviet power was well established, Christian groups had to discern how best to respond. The Russian Orthodox Church split along three lines: the Church in exile, the Church underground, and the patriarchal Church, which made peace with the Soviet government in 1927 under the leadership of Patriarch Sergii. The short-lived "Renovationist" or "Living Church," which sought to integrate itself into the Bolshevik agenda, died out during the 1920s.

Smaller denominations, especially Protestant ones, thrived for about 10 years. Their numbers swelled, especially as the government focused its attacks on the Russian Orthodox, which the Communists perceived as the most counterrevolutionary of all Christian churches. In fact, officials complained that the Baptist Youth Organization – Bapsomol – was sometimes more effective than its Communist counterpart, the Komsomol.

The cultural revolution of the late 1920s–1930s was tied to the extremes of the Five-Year Plans, collectivization, and the purges. The government redoubled its efforts to persecute the faithful by killing thousands, exiling even more to the Gulag camps, and liquidating churches. Priests and ministers were deemed to be social parasites and lost their rights to work and even their food rations. Together, these phenomena crushed much of the organized Christian activity in Russia.

Outward signs of Christian worship abruptly revived as the Soviet regime roused its people to defend Mother Russia against the Nazi invaders (1941). Churches reopened and priests even blessed tanks as they left for the front. While this was surely a cynical ploy to enlist the support of its citizens, the Soviet thaw did provide room for Christian churches to grow. Ironically, the government threw most of its support behind the Russian Orthodox Church, which it had recently condemned as an enemy of socialism.

After the 1945 victory, the relationship waxed and waned between Christian denominations and the state. Except for a short revival of militant atheism under Krushchev, Christians were less overtly persecuted than they had been a generation before. Yet throughout the Soviet period, the state retained the constitutional right of antireligious propaganda while simultaneously criminalizing all attempts of Christian propagation. Openly active Christians, though sent to jail less frequently than before World War II, were precluded from professional advancement or elite education; the exceptions were those few men who rose through the Russian Orthodox hierarchy with the support of the Soviet government.

As a result, those who attended church often seemed to be old women ("babushkas") who no longer had to worry about state interference. The Soviets used this as an example of the dying away of religion in the USSR, without taking into account that new generations of "babushkas" were taking the place of older ones as they died off. The rites of passage for Christians (e.g. baptism) were often kept secret. Marriage* became a civil act rather than a religious one.

The Soviet government also tried to control non-Orthodox denominations, especially those they feared as hotbeds of national resentment. The Soviet Ministry for Religious Affairs in the Baltic Republics of Latvia, Lithuania, and Estonia, e.g., considered Lutheranism and Roman Catholicism to be potentially anti-Soviet. Russian Old Believers in these countries, however, sometimes received good treatment from the state, which saw them as a bastion of Russian patriotism.

The year 1988 – the millennium anniversary of "Russia's baptism" (when Vladimir baptized his subjects en masse) – provided an opportunity for Christian groups to test the limits of Mikhail Gorbachev's policies of openness (glasnost) and restructuring (perestroika). Hence 1,000 years after its introduction, Christianity began to find a voice again. Scholars were allowed to publish actively on religious matters, churches were reopened or renovated, and the restive borderlands saw a resurgence of religious activity.

When the Soviet Union fell, Christianity exploded across Russia. The Russian Orthodox Church revived. Well-established Protestant groups renewed their presence in Russia, while Evangelical denominations found extremely fertile ground in Russia. Suddenly, instead of signs proclaiming Marxist slogans, subways were full of advertisements for Charismatic* preachers proclaiming their own brand of Christianity. Western groups sought to re-Christianize Russia, while Orthodoxy hoped to regain its own position of dominance in the country.

At the beginning of the third millennium, retrenchment of organized Russian Christianity paralleled that of the resurgence of state authority. In 1997 the law on religious associations gave privileged status to the traditional Christian churches found in Russia – Orthodox, Old Belief, Roman Catholic, Baptist, and some others. New denominations and Evangelical preachers have found it more difficult to open churches or attract members, since they are not listed among the accepted denominations. The Russian Orthodox Church, on the other hand, has tried to increase its public role, hoping to be the accepted moral arbiter during the post-Soviet period. A welcome sight for Christians across Russia is that of renovated church buildings, once closed by Soviet authorities and often turned into clubs, garages, or barns. These historic sites are increasingly being returned to use as parish churches and monasteries.

2. Distinctive Features of Christianity in Russia

Experiential, not rational, faith. In general terms, Russian Christianity places higher value on experiential faith than on intellectual faith. As Athanasius* wrote, "God became human so that human could become God." Without taking this statement literally, Russian Christianity has nevertheless developed in response to it. Salvation* for many Russians is a process rather than a state, a spiritual struggle (*podvig*) to be transformed into the image and likeness of God. While this is Orthodox theology, the emphasis on transformation through action has also influenced Protestants and other Christian communities in Russia.

A good marker of difference between the Russian Orthodox tradition and its Western counterparts can be found in the earliest years of life of its members. The Russian Orthodox Church baptizes children at a very young age, typically 40 days after birth. Immediately after baptism and chrismation* with oil, the child is a full member of the Church; he or she can take Communion immediately and does not have to be confirmed in the faith. The transformative power of baptism and the Eucharist, therefore, does not rely on rational understanding. These "mysteries" (as the Orthodox call sacraments*) are transforming agents no matter what the age or mental abilities of the believer.

The Divine Liturgy. For the Orthodox and Old Believers (which make up the large majority of Russian Christians), Christian life revolves around the Divine* Liturgy, which culminates, if possible, in the partaking of the Body and Blood of Christ. The process of worship in a liturgical setting asks a lot from those taking part: services are notoriously long and endlessly complex, involving the chanting or reading of Psalms and passages from the OT, canons, prayers, sermons, and NT readings. The most important parts of the liturgy for many Russians are not the words, however, but the associated actions: kissing icons*, singing, receiving blessings, bowing and prostrating, making the sign of the cross, and lighting candles. Worship in the Russian Church is the experiential opposite of Quaker* worship.

Liturgy and ritual can be understood as "theology in action" rather than as "theology of the mind." In some ways, this is well suited to a country with historically low literacy rates, since the Divine Liturgy does not require that people read the Bible by themselves. Yet the liturgy is not simpleminded; it often introduces complex ideas through its chants, prayers, and readings.

The liturgical cycle (fully carried out only in monasteries) confirms the authoritative texts of Orthodoxy: readings from the Psalms and OT; NT readings; teachings of the seven ecumenical* councils and others; recitation of canons and prayers that follow a lectionary year; and practices based on the generally accepted Holy Tradition, as well as on local religious traditions.

Icons. Icons* play an important role; touched, kissed, and revered, they are considered more than pictorial representations of heaven on earth. The people depicted on icons are in a symbolically transfigured state, identifiable but different because they have become the image and likeness of God. Put another way, salvation for Russian Christians might be defined as the change of a person from an earthly form to an iconic state, as portrayed by the holy images. Icons are therefore almost portals to a divine state of being. For that reason, they are often understood to have miraculous power that can help believers on their way to salvation.

The 17th-c. Old Believer schism highlights the importance of ritual. When Patriarch Nikon introduced ritual changes into Orthodoxy, he called into question the efficacy and truth of these rituals. For many Russians, this was tantamount to changing theology or creed. The most important ritual change had to do with how a person made the sign* of the cross on his or her body. When Nikon obliged Russian Orthodox to change the position of the hands (from a "two-fingered" gesture symbolizing the joined human and divine natures of Christ to a "three-fingered" gesture symbolizing the Trinity), they considered it equivalent to discounting the icons in their churches and the instructions in their psalmbooks, which explicitly showed the older Russian style of the sign of the cross. In fact, a century earlier, the Stoglav Council had condemned anything *but* the "two-fingered sign."

Emphasis on spiritual transformation in other Christian groups. As some Russian Christian groups broke away from the Orthodox tradition, they often retained its emphasis on transformation. The most extreme cases were those of the Dukhobors, the Khylsts, and especially the Skopts, who physically transformed themselves through ecstatic worship, flagellation, and sometimes self-mutilation. Even groups that developed a theology similar to Anabaptism occasionally retained Orthodox ritual actions, e.g. bowing, making the sign of the cross, and prostrating. The Baptist view, emphasizing individual salvation through adult baptism, was rare in Russian Christian history. Charismatic Christianity, however, through its emphasis on transformation (related to the Holiness* Movement), has undergone an explosive growth in the post-Soviet period.

For Russian Christianity, community practices have been particularly important, and individual practices have been deemphasized. The liturgical year, including holy days, periods of fasting, and personal or regional commemorations, is given strong emphasis. For the peasantry in most of Russian history, especially when serfdom prevailed, the large number of holidays provided a respite from work. Parishes generally took the name of a saint, holiday, or miraculous icon, and celebrated the appropriate day of the calendar. In the post-Soviet era, rural communities sometimes continue this tradition even though, as is often the case, the parish church building has been demolished.

Religious authority. For centuries the Russian Christian tradition has grappled with the question of authority*. Should it reside at the community level or should it have a centralized hierarchy? Traditionally, the Orthodox Church was considered complete when it had laity, clergy, and bishops. After the 17th-c. reforms of Patriarch Nikon, Russian Orthodoxy tended toward centralization of authority. The bishop's seat (with its administrative bureaucracy) increasingly became the locus of decision making. Today, Orthodox parishes are led by priests who have been appointed by a local bishop. Yet, historically, the huge geographic space of Russia has also played an important role in the community structure of Christian groups. In the far north and Siberia, for example, Orthodox communities could go for months or years without the services of a priest. The lack of a clergy member deprived these communities of a complete sacramental life and yet strengthened their independent spirit.

Old Believers prefer a less centralized structure. They are organized in parish-like "concords," some with bishops, but the control of the parish remains more clearly in local hands. Old Believers are joined together in a "textual community" (as Crummey has argued) through their shared liturgical traditions rather than through their organizational structures.

The small Roman Catholic presence in Russia is governed by the centralized Apostolic Administration for Latin Rite Catholics. Protestant and sectarian groups have tended toward even greater local autonomy than Old Believers.

The monasteries. The monastic tradition in Russia has been very rich. As in the West, medieval Russia depended on its monasteries for cultural and social cohesion in addition to their primary functions: prayer and work. In Russia, as in other Orthodox countries, there is no monastic order and not even a word for "nun." All monastic people wear similar clothing.

Monasticism waned during the 18th and early 19th c., although it saw some revival from 1860 to 1917, especially in female monasticism, both in unofficial hermitages and in sanctioned female monasteries. Many young women were educated at these institutions, and even some of the most elite aristocrats took the veil. The Soviet regime particularly targeted monastic communities during the Revolution and afterward, closing and destroying many monasteries and persecuting the monastic population.

The early years after the end of Communism saw a rise in the number of monks and nuns, a trend quite different from the rest of Europe. That phenomenon, perhaps in response to years of enforced public atheism, has since tapered off (see Monasticism Cluster: In the Russian and Ukrainian Tradition).

Women and Russian Orthodoxy. Although Russian monasticism* is in some ways gender neutral in its symbolism, the Russian Orthodox Church has generally retained conservative gender roles. Only men are consecrated into the priesthood and can be part of the hierarchy (see Women's Ordination Cluster: And the Orthodox Church); in fact, only men can serve at the altar. Women tend to take part in the liturgy by reading and singing and may take on traditionally male roles in the Church only in some circumstances, although they never serve as clergy. Russian priests may marry, however, and the *matiushka*, or "priest's wife," receives respect for her position.

As in many other countries, Russian Christianity has undergone a profound feminization at the parish level. Women are far more likely than men to attend church and to serve it in nonclerical positions. They are likely to be the practical leaders of the parish. Old Believer women have often taken on more public leadership roles than women in the rest of the Orthodox tradition. In some congregations without a priest, women have served in pastoral roles. In the Protestant and sectarian traditions, women have played a far greater official role than they are allowed in Orthodoxy, although in conservative Protestant churches, women are still less likely to take leadership positions than are men.

Lay Christians (and some monastics) may take part in all forms of legal economic and social activities and may serve in the military. The Social Gospel tradition is not emphasized in Orthodoxy. Charity and almsgiving tend to take the form of individual initiatives rather than the intervention of institutionalized organizations. Yet a system of unofficial mutual aid has been most prevalent among Old Believers, Protestants, and sectarian groups and among rural Russian villagers.

3. Russian Christianity after the Soviet Era. The Russian Orthodox Church has recently begun concelebrating with the Russian Orthodox Church Outside of Russia after years of fighting over the legacy of Communism. The Moscow Patriarchate maintains cordial relations with other Christian denominations through the World* Council of Churches and other ecumenical bodies, although Orthodoxy tends to embrace ecumenism far less actively than other Christian traditions.

The Roman Catholic Church and Protestant denominations have representatives in Russia, but in practice these tend to be somewhat separated from their Western European counterparts. Most of the Eastern Rite Catholic, Lutheran, and Roman Catholic believers in the former Soviet Union are now citizens of recently independent states in Central Europe.

If Russian Christianity has been dominated by Orthodoxy, its history during the past century has been overshadowed by Marxism*. All Christian faiths now struggle with the legacy of the official atheist policy and of a sometimes murderous regime. Hierarchal church structures were often infiltrated by the secret police: How should those men be treated now? Church attendance is low by historical Russian standards: Is it the fault of atheist education or of a broader secularization* of Russian society? Should the church that was most severely persecuted during the Soviet period – the Russian Orthodox – be restored to its status as state* church? Should "Christians" from outside Russia be allowed to "re-Christianize" Russia? Should there be an open marketplace for religion, or should some churches receive preference? Will Russian Christianity follow a separate path or will it come to resemble Christianity in Western Europe? All of these questions have yet to find long-term answers.

Statistics: Population (2000): 147 million (M). Christians, 84.3 M; 58% (Orthodox, 75.9 M; independents, 7.8 M; Protestants, 1.6 M; Roman Catholics, 1.5 M; marginal Christians, 0.2 M); Muslims, 11.2 M, 8%; Jews, 1 M, 0.7%; nonreligious, 48 M, 33%. (Based on *World Christian Encyclopedia*, 2001.)

ROY R. ROBSON

Russian Literature and Christianity. Until the 17th c., Russian literature was mostly religious, influenced by the Byzantine* Orthodox* tradition and the Bible and written in Church Slavonic, the alphabet invented by the Greek missionaries Cyril* and Methodius (9th c.).

The first notable text was Metropolitan Hilarion's *Sermon on Law and Grace* (c1050–51), which praised Grand Prince Vladimir, who converted his people to Christianity. Nestor wrote a life of the brothers Boris and Gleb, Russian princes canonized in 1072 as "passion bearers" (*strastoterpets*), because they suffered and died like Christ, not resisting when they were murdered. Russian hagiography developed its distinctive typology of sainthood (about 150 hagiographies by 1917).

The *Russian Primary Chronicle* (c1113) gives a Christian account of the history of Eastern Slavs (up to 1110). Many heroic epic tales and poems, like *Zadonshchina* (Battle beyond the Don, c1390), depict Russian princes as Christian warriors defending Holy Russia against the Tartar invasion (1237). Epiphanius the Wise wrote *Life of Sergius* of Radonezh* (1418), the national saint who encouraged resistance against the Tartars and developed kenotic* monasticism.

Starting in the 11th c., apocryphal stories from folklore were very popular (*Descent into Hell, King Solomon and Queen of Sheba, Tale of Babylon*). Literature in the 16th c. portrayed Russia as a powerful Christian empire. *Domostroy* (House order) emphasizes the fear of God, obedience in everyday life, and the proper way to revere icons*. The first theater (1672) staged many religious plays: Simeon of Polotsk's *Comedy of the Prodigal Son, Tragedy of Nebuchadnezzar,* and *Holofernes* and Dimitry of Rostov's *Christmas Drama* and *Repenting Sinner.*

After the 17th-c. Old* Believers schism (arising from resistance to revisions of the Russian Divine* Liturgy), a leader of the Old Believers, Avvakum*, wrote a polemical spiritual autobiography and several biblical commentaries, using the simple language of the peasantry. During the more secular 18th c., Russian classical writers, such as Gavriil Derzhavin, wrote religious odes, and the scholar Mikhail Lomonosov stated that Truth and Faith, daughters of the Almighty Parent, could never quarrel. Despite anticlericalism, 19th-c. poetry abounded in biblical themes: thus the romantic Vasily Zhukovsky wrote *Tale of the Handsome Joseph, Death of Jesus,* and *From Apocalypse* and composed the lyrics for the national anthem *God Save the Czar!*; Alexander Pushkin and Mikhail Lermontov developed the romantic idea of the poet as prophet*; and Alexander Griboedov wrote *David.* The theme of inexpressibility stemmed from the apophatic* tradition of Eastern Orthodoxy.

Two realist writers turned from writing fiction to preaching Christianity: Nikolay Gogol, in *Meditations on the Divine Liturgy,* and Leo Tolstoy,* in *The Kingdom of God is Within You.* Fyodor Dostoyevsky* addressed the problems of theodicy*, holiness*, and sin* and its consequences, e.g., in interpreting Christ's temptation ("the Grand Inquisitor" in *Brothers Karamazov*).

A religious renaissance began at the end of the 19th c. with Vladimir Soloviev's* philosophy, which influenced the "Silver Age" Symbolists with their reconsideration of the Bible and Orthodoxy and their view of literature as a new religion; among their works were Dmitry Merezhkovsky's *Unknown Jesus,* Leonid Andreev's *Judas Iskariot,* Alexander Kuprin's *Sulamif,* and Andrei Bely's *Symbolism.*

The 1917 revolution led to persecutions when religious literature was banned. Mikhail Bulgakov's novel *The Master and Margarita* portrays Moscow during the Great Terror with its "Godless" Five-Year Plans ruled by the Satan-like figure of Woland. In the 1980s, the Orthodox priest Alexander Men (murdered 1990) helped inspire a religious revival through his books on Christian faith and history of religion. With the 1988 celebration of the millennium of Christianity in Russia, most of formerly banned religious literature was republished. Many lives of martyrs of the Communist period were written; 1,154 martyrs were canonized at the 2001 church council.

ELENA VOLKOVA

Ruth, a book of the OT, narrates the story of Ruth, a foreign woman from Moab who journeys to Israel with her widowed mother-in-law, Naomi, where she meets her future husband, Boaz, and becomes the ancestress of the great King David.

Ruth was written either as an apology for the Moabite ancestry of David (c10th c. BCE) or during the time of Ezra and Nehemiah (5th c. BCE), when intermarriages between Judeans and the indigenous peoples of Yehud became a serious issue.

The book highlight Ruth's conversion from belief in the gods of Moab to the religion of her Israelite mother-in-law, Naomi. To support Naomi, Ruth gleans in the fields of Boaz, a kinsman of Naomi and a rich landowner. As Naomi's kinsman, Boaz is obligated to marry Ruth under the law of the levirate (Deut 25:5–10), in which the closest male relative must marry the widow of a man who dies childless. Boaz marries Ruth, and they produce a son named Obed, the father of Jesse, who is in turn the father of David.

Although often read as a tender love story between a man and woman, the book covers a greater range of social relationships: those of husband and wife; mother and son; mother-in-law and daughter-in-law; owner, overseer, and laborers; resident and foreigner; native and immigrant. How one reads Ruth depends on one's context and social location. For example, readings of the Book of Ruth in cultures such as China, where mother-in-law/daughter-in-law relations are conflicted, will be different than those in cultures where this relationship is more harmonious.

Ruth 1:16–17 ("Where you go, I will go . . .") is a favorite text in Christian marriage ceremonies. The original context, however, is that of a foreign woman pledging herself to her Israelite mother-in-law. **See also MEGILLOTH.**

GALE A. YEE

Ruthenian Churches. See UKRAINE.

Ruusbroec (Ruysbroeck), Jan van (1293–1381), Flemish mystical* writer who ministered as a priest in Brussels until the age of 50, then retired to a more solitary setting. While in Brussels, he completed 5 treatises, including his masterpiece, *The Spiritual Espousals,* and subsequently wrote 5 more, leaving an 11th unfinished at the time of his death. Jan van Ruusbroec was unequaled in his descriptions of all stages of the spiritual life, from the practice of the most basic virtues to the experience of intimate union with the triune God. A critical edition of his works, including English translations, was completed in 2006.

JAMES A. WISEMAN, OSB

Rwanda was first evangelized by the White* Fathers (Society of Missionaries of Africa, since 1868), led by Bishop Jean-Joseph Hirth, who arrived in 1900 from Uganda, where there had been intense religious wars. Impressed by the strong monarchy and the large population of Rwanda, the White Fathers met with King Musinga, who authorized their presence. In order to "conquer the country before the arrival of Protestants and Muslims," they created a network of stations around the country (1901–13).

Protestant missionaries (of the German Bethel Missions) arrived from Tanzania* (1907) and established a series of stations before being replaced by missionaries of the Society of Belgian Missions, which came from Congo (1916). Anglicans and Seventh-day Adventists from Uganda, Danish Baptists from Burundi, and Methodists and Swedish Pentecostals from Congo successively arrived (1920s–1940s). An alliance of Protestant churches of Rwanda and Burundi, created (1930) for the sake of cooperation in education* and to avoid cross-proselytism*, split when the two countries became independent (1962). In 1978 out of 7.8 million Rwandans, 65% identified themselves as Roman Catholics and 22% as Protestants.

Within the Catholic Church, mass conversion known as the "tornado" ended with the conversion of the ruling class (1930s). In 1931 King Musinga, accused of threatening evangelism, was deposed and replaced by his son, Mutara Rudahigwa, a Roman Catholic catechumen. Baptized together with the queen mother, the king offered Rwanda and its people to the Virgin and to Christ (1947).

The Protestant "East African revival" emerged from Gahini, an Anglican missionary station (1936), but needed to be revivified in the 1970s among the younger generation in missionary schools led by Peter Guillebaud (son of the first Bible translator in 1925). After the 1994 genocide, new religious groups emerged, including the Zion Temple and the Restoration Church, mainly among the refugees who returned but refused to join existing churches accused of being linked with the regime that caused their exile and even organized the 1994 genocide.

Church–State Relations. The overwhelming influence of the Roman Catholic Church up to the 1994 tragedy has been documented by many observers. It had the status of a state* church, which it maintained by defending the idea of the supremacy of the Tutsis – the idea of "Hamite supremacy," promoted by educating an elite among the Batutsi social group as colonial and missionary subordinates. However, following the independence movement in Africa (1950s), the Catholic Church shifted its alliance to sponsor the Bahutu (Hutus), who in the "1959 social revolution" took power and held it until 1994. This new control of power coincided with the exile of many former ruling elite (Tutsis) and their families. The Catholic Church had been headed by Europeans – Mgrs. Classe, Deprimoz, and Perraudin (1907–73); they were succeeded by a local bishop, Vicent Nsengiyumva (1974–94), who was also appointed a member of the central committee of the governing party, the MRND. Furthermore, the regime of the Hutu Habyarimana (1973–94) initiated new relations with Protestants. Catholic and Protestant church leaders were given political and diplomatic status. Then, when many human* rights abuses occurred (the murder of political prisoners during the Kayibanda regime, 1962–73; the repression of religious dissidents, 1986; the October 1990 war and the massacre of those involved in the rebellion; and ultimately the 1994 genocide), Church authorities were unable to condemn the regime.

Interaction with African Religion. Roman Catholicism assumed its dominant position to the detriment of African* Religion, as well as of Protestantism and Islam*, which had no political protection. Converting to Catholicism meant being open to progress; adherents of the traditional African Religion were considered old-fashioned followers of a demonic* religion* and were legally repressed. The Catholic Church had abundant material, economic, and cultural means (e.g. schools, hospitals) to impose its worldview. The new converts had to adopt Catholicism as the true religion of the true God.

Although no dialogue between the two religions was tolerated, some Catholic believers, like Father Bernardin Muzungu (author of *God of Our Fathers,* three volumes on African Religion), found issues of common interest. Yet

Catholicism was suspicious of a religion that was integral to the Rwandan civilization. The name "Imana" ("God" in the Rwandan language) was replaced by the Swahili name "Mungu." Any association with the practices of African Religion, such as consulting diviners (*kuraguza*), appeasing the spirits of ancestors* (*guterekera*), or participating in the cult of religious heroes (Lyangombe and Nyabingi), was considered sacrilege.

Ecumenism. Despite the ecumenical proposals of Vatican* II and the efforts of the World* Council of Churches to achieve unity, the likelihood of implementing ecumenism remained distant. For example, in 1968 and 1972 documents of the Conference of Roman Catholic Bishops of Rwanda and Burundi, only three categories of people were acknowledged: Roman Catholics, catechumens, and pagans. This was a reflection of a long anti-ecumenical history, fueled by the Protestants' lack of unity, their anti-Catholicism, and their lack of trained theologians to discuss the relevant issues with well-trained Catholic clergy. Nevertheless, a few common initiatives were undertaken, including the translation of the Bible into a revised Kinyarwanda language (1981); the establishment of Bufmar (Bureau des Formations Médicales Agrées du Rwanda), a church-affiliated health organization that interacts with the government regarding church-sponsored hospitals and clinics; the creation of the Committee of Contacts for Protestant and Catholic hierarchies amid the political turmoil of 1990, in order to minister to politicians and influence them; and joint but unsuccessful efforts to play a reconciling role in the 1993 crisis, which led to the April 1994 genocide during which more than a million people were killed.

Today, three entities – the Conference of Roman Catholic Bishops, the Council of Protestant Churches, and the new Alliance of Evangelical Churches – are competing to win over people by operating their own schools and universities, hospitals, rural projects, and programs in healing* and reconciliation*. Some churches, like the Presbyterian Church in Rwanda and the Council of Protestant Churches, confessed and repented for having failed to stand against the genocide. Others, including the Roman Catholic Church, still have to declare their position.

Statistics: Population (2000): 7.7 million (M). Christians, 6.4 M, 83% (Roman Catholics, 4 M; Protestants, 1.6 M; Anglicans, 0.6 M; members of African Instituted Churches, 0.17 M); African Religionists, 0.7 M, 9%; Muslims, 0.6 M, 8%. (Based on *World Christian Encyclopedia*, 2001.)

THARCISSE GATWA

Ryerson, Egerton (1803–82), born in Upper Canada*, had an Evangelical* conversion* experience, was ordained in the Methodist Church (1827). As an itinerant preacher, Egerton soon became the leading challenger of Strachan* and of Tory and Anglican privilege, publishing letters and articles, and editing (1829–39) the Methodist journal *The Christian Guardian*, which argued for the equality of religious denominations. Appointed school superintendent in Upper Canada (1844–76), Ryerson fashioned Ontario's dual public school system (highly centralized nondenominational schools, allowing public Roman Catholic schools for the Catholic minority). **See also CANADA.**

ROBERT CHOQUETTE

S

Sabbatarianism, emphasis on the observance of the Sabbath (Sunday) as a day of rest, found especially among English and Scottish Calvinists. More generally, a tendency toward a legalistic view of Christianity. **See also SPORTS, BOOK OF.**

Sabbath, in the Bible the seventh day of the week, a day of abstention from secular work to be observed as a day blessed and consecrated by God (Exod 20:10–11). It has religious, social, and humanitarian significance, as emphasized in Isa 58:13–14; Jer 17, 19–27; and Ezekiel. In the Gospels, Jesus worships on the Sabbath (e.g. Luke 4:16), although he also heals on that day. He declares himself Lord of the Sabbath in controversial debates, which some interpret to mean that Jesus abrogated the Sabbath and some that Jesus restored the Sabbath as a day of benefit for humankind. The Sabbath is observed in Judaism, by Seventh*-day Adventists, and by the Ethiopian* Church. Since the Reformation, "Sabbath" has also referred to Sunday as "the Lord's Day," a day of rest. **See also LABOR, THEOLOGIES OF.**

Sabellianism, the Monarchianist* views held by Sabellius, possibly a presbyter active in the debate over Modalism* in Rome (c217–20). **See also MONARCHIANS.**

Sabiniana, intrepid female deacon* of Antioch, aunt of John* Chrysostom. She followed him into exile in 404; although she was of advanced age and travel was difficult for her, she declared she would go anywhere with him, "young in her willingness and insensitive to her sufferings." John praises her in a letter to Olympias*. Palladius* was impressed when meeting her earlier in Antioch. As a deacon of the church in Antioch, she was active in ministry. **See also DEACONESS.** CAROLYN OSIEK

Sacramental, (1) as an adjective, *pertaining to* the sacraments, especially the Lord's* Supper; also, *like* the sacraments, as in "sacramental universe," manifesting God and mediating grace; (2) as a noun, a rite or observance like the sacraments but not included among them (e.g. anointing with oil).

Sacramental Theology in Eastern Orthodox Churches. The Byzantine theological tradition calls the sacraments "mysteries" because every sacramental celebration represents and actualizes, by the work of the Holy Spirit, the original and fundamental mystery*: the self-giving of Christ to the Father for the salvation* of the world. Every liturgical celebration of the Orthodox Church draws on and participates in this mystery through the symbols* of the bread*, wine*, and water* and the acts of the imposition of hands (see Laying on of Hands) and the blessing, and the text associated with them. On a personal and ecclesiastical level, the sacraments have a "mystical" function: the union of people with God and participation in the divine life. Because of this perspective, individual Eastern Orthodox churches have not felt the need to define an exact number of sacraments. Theodore* Studite (759–826), e.g., following Dionysius* the Pseudo-Areopagite, lists six "mysteries" (illumination, Eucharist, chrismation*, ordination, monastic profession, and funerals). At present the Eastern Orthodox Church has seven sacraments (as the Roman Catholic Church does), possibly by association with the sacred number seven or with the seven gifts of the Holy Spirit (as suggested by Symeon of Thessalonica; d1419).

Modern Greek theology underscores the dynamic character of the "mystery" and tends to reject the sevenfold medieval doctrine of the sacraments, reintroducing among them the monastic profession and funerals. Because of the doctrine of theosis* (divinization), it is pointless to specify which "particular grace" is attached to each sacrament.

The acknowledgment of the sacraments celebrated in the other Christian churches, baptism included, is a delicate issue. Two principles are in tension: (1) strict orthodoxy (*akribeia*), which denies any liturgical action of the Holy* Spirit outside of the Orthodox Communion – since recognizing the efficacy of another church's sacraments would mean acknowledging they are "Orthodox"; and (2) ecumenical openness (*oikonomia*), according to which, for the sake of the faithful, improper liturgical acts can be, case by case, "healed" or "filled with life." In the absence of a common declaration of the Orthodox churches on the efficacy of the sacraments celebrated outside of the Orthodox Church, there is no way to know, when Orthodox churches have recognized other churches' sacraments, whether they did so because of *oikonomia* or because of *akribeia*. The principle of *akribeia* has been applied against the Roman Catholic Church only since the 15th c. as a reaction to the "Decree of Union" of the Council of Florence*. **See also SACRAMENTS AS MYSTERIES IN EASTERN ORTHODOX CHURCHES.**

STEFANO PARENTI

Sacramental Theology in Western Churches. is the systematic study of those ritual ceremonies, especially baptism* and the Eucharist*, that the church traces back to Jesus' public ministry, his post-Resurrection appearances, or even to the Holy* Spirit's inspiration during the church's formative apostolic era. Reflecting on its firm belief in the incarnation* of the Son of God, the church recognized that matter, including the human body of Christ, can be a bearer or channel of grace*. Thus, in response to an instruction by Christ, the ritual of pouring water* on the head of a catechumen in order to initiate him or her into the church "in the name of the Father, and of the Son, and of the Holy Spirit" is believed to convey countless spiritual blessings and privileges on the recipient. Similarly, the bread* and wine* liturgically blessed, as Jesus blessed them during the Last Supper, is seen by faith to allow the believer to enter into sacramental communion with the body and blood of the Savior. These two rituals constitute the foundation of sacramental theology.

Along with baptism and the Eucharist, the first-millennium church recognized other rites as conveying God's blessings, healings, and covenantal* renewal through matter and a specifying prayer. Among these rites were anointing* with blessed oil or chrism* to designate the outpouring of the Holy* Spirit. (For Eastern Orthodoxy, see Sacramental Theology in Eastern Orthodox Churches; this anointing was part of the triple rite of initiation, whereas the Western Church came to separate the actions, reserving anointing for a later conferral by a bishop.) Public or private avowal of post-baptismal sin to a minister of the church, with the assignment of a penance*, was practiced in response to Jesus' instruction to the Twelve about "binding or loosing sins." Anointing of the sick* was another ritual that sought to remind those who suffered about Jesus' healing ministry and the responsibility of the believing community to provide care for those who were ill. The public designation of official church ministers was practiced by the "laying* on of hands," a ritual borrowed in part from Judaism. Eventually, even the church's blessing on the exchange of marriage vows came to be associated with liturgical celebration.

In addition to these principal rites, the undivided church practiced rituals that at first seemed to fit into the same category: Christian burial rites, consecration by anointing of Christian kings or queens, consecration of abbots and abbesses, distribution with blessed ashes, and the use of blessed water to sanctify. Eventually, to avoid confusion and discord, the Western Church adopted the teaching that there were, strictly speaking, only seven "sacraments*" and that the other rituals should be considered "sacramentals*" or legitimate devotional practices.

With the Reformation, Protestant theologians gave pride of place to baptism and the Eucharist (which could be clearly traced to the NT), but felt uneasy about designating the other rituals as sacraments. They preferred to see them as church ordinances with grounding in the tradition of the church. Thus Reformation churches teach that there are two sacraments.

When medieval theologians reflected on the similarities of the seven principal rituals, they began to draw on philosophical categories to systematize these acts of Christ and of the church. This medieval and post-Reformation sacramental theology was heavily influenced by the juridical considerations of canon* law and even moral theology. Much attention was given to the sacrament-celebrating ministers, the recipients' intention, the "matter" (e.g. water or oil), the "form" (the wording accompanying the ritual), the "effects," and the valid and licit nature of the rituals.

Although medieval Scholasticism brought order to the understanding of the chief ritual celebrations of the church, it has appeared in recent times that the decision to combine the sacraments into a single doctrinal treatise *de sacramentis in genere* has somewhat obscured the uniqueness of each rite. The differences among the sacraments are more notable than their commonalities. Consequently, modern ecumenical consensus statements, with rare exceptions, have explored, how, e.g., unity of Christians through baptism, complementary understandings of the eucharistic memorial, the meaning of ordination, and other rites illustrate the incarnational principle operative in Christian communities worldwide.

In modern Roman Catholic theology, what binds the sacramental actions together is the fact that each action, to a greater or lesser extent, illustrates what is meant by the "incarnational* principle," namely that material, human realities can be vehicles of divine grace*, not because of any intrinsic connection, but solely because God has so designated these acts to bestow divine favor on those who receive them with faith*. The rituals are not intended to be private, individualistic actions; each in its own way is a communal act of worship* praising God. **See also WORSHIP CLUSTER.**

MICHAEL A. FAHEY, SJ

Sacramentarian, Luther's* term for the position of those Protestants* (especially Zwingli* and Bucer*) who claimed that the Body and Blood of Christ were only "sacramentally," not physically, present in the Lord's* Supper. The term has been used more recently in the opposite sense of taking a "high" view of the sacrament and its efficacy.

Sacramentary, service book of the Western Church in use until the 13th c., containing the canon* of the Mass* and the proper* prayers to be recited on particular days of the church year, but not all readings and chants; replaced by the missal* and the pontifical*.

Sacraments as Mysteries in Eastern Orthodox Churches. Byzantine churches defined their sevenfold sacramental doctrine only in the 13th c. under the influence of Western theology and officially confirmed it in the Confession of Faith (1672) of Dositheos*, patriarch of Jerusalem. As in the Roman Catholic Church, the seven sacraments are baptism*, chrismation*, Eucharist*, orders, matrimony*, confession*, and anointing* of the sick*. Their celebration was definitely fixed in Greek liturgical books printed in Venice (late 16th c.; see Sacramental Theology in Eastern Orthodox Churches).

Until the late 13th c., every sacrament was either celebrated in connection (before or after) with the Divine* Liturgy or was followed by the Eucharist. This tie was weakened through the centuries because of the privatization of baptism, matrimony, and anointing of the sick. Also in the 13th c., the rite of the ordination of women to the diaconate disappeared from the liturgical books.

In the Eastern Orthodox* churches, baptism is administrated by the total immersion of the child or adult, and is always followed by chrismation and the Eucharist. Ordination to the diaconate and the presbyterate (priesthood) is conferred on married candidates (but if candidates are celibate when receiving ordination, they remain celibate). Regarding matrimony, the wedding is preceded by the betrothal (the couple exchanging rings) and performed by crowning the couple (sign of the glory bestowed on them by God and also of martyrdom*, i.e. self-sacrifice; see Marriage, Theology and Practice of, Cluster: In Eastern Orthodoxy). Confession is made not to the priest, but to Christ (the priest stands only as witness and guide); it can be personal, but also collective, without a specific identification of the sins. The anointing* of the sick is ideally performed by seven priests (but can be performed by fewer, and even by one) and may be performed over the healthy (usually before Communion). The sacramental formulas, when prescribed, are always in the passive tense (e.g. he/she is baptized, is crowned, is anointed) rather than the indicative (e.g. I baptize you), to indicate that it is God, and not the priest, who acts.

In the different Orthodox churches, there are no significant differences in the celebration of the sacraments, except that the churches of Russia and Ukraine adopted (late 17th c.) the indicative formula of absolution ("I absolve you" rather than "you are absolved" [by God]). In the Eastern Catholic churches (Uniates*), the Byzantine ritual has been abbreviated and partly modified in terms of the Roman Rite.

STEFANO PARENTI

Sacraments in Western Churches are ritual acts that are rooted in a firm belief in the Incarnation* (the human body of Christ as bearer of the divine) and in which matter, including the human body*, water*, bread*, wine*, and oil (chrism*), are bearers or channels of grace*, as well as divine presence and favor.

In continuity with the salvific actions of Jesus and his specific instructions to his disciples to baptize believers and to celebrate the Lord's* Supper "in remembrance of me," the early church faithfully continued these rituals and gradually structured them into liturgical formulas. There is evidence that the early church anointed with oil and prayed over the sick* and dying; there is also evidence that the church felt authorized to absolve believers from post-baptismal sin, and that the laying* on of hands was conferred on those who were to carry special responsibilities within the ecclesial community. Gradually these signs of grace and prayerful rituals came to be associated within a cluster of special rites entrusted to the church. Their number underwent some fluctuation, since actions such as funeral rites, distribution of blessed ashes, pilgrimages*, and the consecration of abbots and abbesses were seen as extensions of the established rituals. Pope Eugenius IV listed seven sacraments in his apostolic bull *Exsultate domine* (1439). This number was formally established by the Council of Trent*, which decreed, in opposition to the Protestant Reformers, that there were seven sacraments, no more, no less.

The Continental Protestant Reformers, such as Luther*, Calvin*, and Zwingli*, in reaction to what were seen as serious abuses in the sacramental practice of the Roman Catholic Church and a neglect of sacred Scripture, argued against the accepted sevenfold doctrine, identifying baptism and the Lord's Supper as the two authentic sacraments. Without necessarily denying the meaningfulness of the proper celebration of the other rituals, Protestants generally relegated these rituals to the rank of church ordinances.

Besides the conciliar and papal statements about the seven sacraments, a stunning altarpiece painted by Rogier van der Weyden (c1445–50) of the Netherlands depicts the seven sacraments. These sacraments were baptism*, confirmation* or chrismation*, the Eucharist*, penance* or confession*, anointing* of the sick*, holy orders*, and matrimony*. Medieval theology, partly by borrowing classical philosophical categories as well canonical notions, elaborated a vast systematic explanation of the sacraments (*de sacramentis in genere*), which focused on the matter and form of a sacrament, the minister and recipient of a sacrament, and other categories, such as one's intention as well as the valid and licit character of a sacrament. Baptism, confirmation, and holy orders were seen as conveying a permanent and indelible character or seal, so that they could not be repeated. To explain how it was possible for a sinful priest to administer an efficacious sacrament, the medieval Scholastics argued that the efficacy of a sacrament occurs *ex* opere operato* (by the very fact of its being administered). This expression, actually a shortened form of the phrase *ex opere operato Christi*, did not deny the importance of faith* in the recipient (*ex opere operantis*) or the desirability that the one administering the sacrament be a person of integrity and committed belief in Christian revelation (see Sacramental Theology in Western Churches).

At the Second Vatican* Council, the Roman Catholic Church initiated a general reform of the sacramental rituals to enhance their meaning as communal acts of worship and to enhance the symbolic or sign value of the rituals. By entering into ecumenical dialogue with other churches and by concentrating on individual sacraments, Catholics and Protestants have ascertained vast areas of consensus and agreement. These mutual understandings have highlighted the fact that Protestants and Catholics alike both appeal to "Word" and "sacrament." The Lord's Supper, e.g., is regarded as a preached Word intensified by a symbolic, ritual action. Sacred Scripture* prepares for, illuminates, and undergirds what the sacraments symbolize. Roman Catholic doctrine describes the Church itself, by its relationship with Christ, as a kind of sacrament or sign of intimate union with God and of the unity of all humankind.

MICHAEL A. FAHEY, SJ

Sacrifice refers to a group of practices in which offerings are made for religious purposes, ostensibly as gifts to deities. The offerings vary (grains, liquids, possessions) and sometimes include sacrificed animals or humans. Such rites in some form have characterized virtually all ancient human societies, although there is no agreement as to whether they have a common origin and purpose or what their roots might be. Some prominent theorists see sacrifice as the ritualizing of early human hunting activities; others consider it to be based on an economy* of reciprocity where gifts are offered to the gods in return for benefits (such as renewed agricultural or biological fertility). According to some theorists, sacrifice was focused on a communal meal or was part of a patriarchal attempt to reorder kinship ties. Others view it as having been patterned implicitly on the violence* associated with scapegoating, by which human groups resolved internal conflicts. Although what actions sacrifice entailed is clear, their meaning is not.

Historic Israel and Second Temple Judaism engaged in specific sacrificial practices that provided the background for the thinking and terminology of rabbinic Judaism and early Christianity. Animal sacrifice was central, but other types of sacrifice (e.g. involving grain offerings) were also common. Sacrifice figures prominently in Scripture: the sacrifices of Cain* and Abel*, the "sacrifice" of Isaac* (see Sacrifice of Isaac: The Aqedah), the use of blood in covenant* making, the sacrifice of the paschal lamb during each Passover*, and the system of rites centralized in the Jerusalem Temple. Sacrifice is a paradigmatic act of worship. Indeed, the monotheism* of Judaism – the refusal to worship gods other than the God of Israel – is concretely defined by the refusal to offer sacrifice in any other name. An "anti-sacrificial" theme is also found in the Bible: in the averted death of Isaac, in the Prophets (Amos 5:21–24; Hos 6:6), and in Jesus' critical attitude toward the Temple.

Sacrifice explicitly figures in Christian interpretations of Jesus' death and, more broadly, in understandings of the role that Christ plays in the life of believers. Jesus' death took place in the context of the Passover celebration with its lamb offerings. In the Gospel of John (19:14, 36), 1 Corinthians (5:7), Ephesians (5:2), and Hebrews (10:5–10), Christ is regarded as a sacrificial victim, an interpretation consistent with the words of Christ at the Last Supper about his death being offered for the sake of others, as presented in the Synoptic Gospels. The Eucharist* was called a sacrifice in the 2nd-c. church, based on its character as a representation of Jesus' death and as a functional substitute for sacrificial rites in other traditions. The concept of sacrifice has been central in later theological controversies among Christians about the nature of the Eucharist (see Priesthood).

It is not surprising that there are different theological interpretations of the sacrificial metaphors* related to Jesus' death, because (1) the key root term, "sacrifice," can be understood in different ways, (2) there is both positive and negative material in Scripture bearing on Israel's specific sacrificial practices, and (3) Jesus' death is presented in the Gospels as the result both of God's saving purpose and of human sin. Thus sacrifice can be regarded as having a positive quality, which the death of Jesus maximizes and fulfills. It can also be seen as essentially misguided and inadequate, abolished by the cross. Jesus' death can be emphasized as a divinely mandated sacrifice to atone for human sin or as a divine identification with the victims of human sacrificial impulses (see Atonement; Sin).

These various interpretations converge on the same conclusion: whatever reconciliation* between believers and God or among believers had been sought by means of sacrificial practices (and particularly by the blood of victims), this reconciliation is now realized through one's relation with Christ – hence the diversity of views of Christ's death on the cross as sacrifice, of the atonement (see Atonement), and of the Eucharist (see Eucharist Cluster). One of the reasons that early Christians were regarded as irreligious by their neighbors was precisely their belief that ethical behavior, spiritual worship, and communal life rooted in Christ fulfilled the essential role formerly held by sacrificial rituals. Thus they could think of the Eucharist as a sacrifice of praise and of the Christian life as a means of presenting their bodies before God as a living sacrifice. S. MARK HEIM

Sacrifice of Isaac: The Aqedah (Heb "binding"). Genesis 22:1–19 tells the story of God's testing of Abraham by commanding him to sacrifice his son; Abraham obediently binds Isaac, only to be stopped from carrying out the sacrifice at the last moment. The language, "fraught with background," leaves much to the imagination while introducing a poignant refrain, "The two of them walked together." Readers learn that Abraham's agonizing decision is only a test and that the deity is acutely aware of the patriarch's ordeal. Deuterocanonical references to this story (Sir 44:22; Dan 3:35 [LXX]; Jdt 8:26) add nothing new, but later Jewish fantasy soared.

In 2 Macc 7, the mother of seven martyrs* rhetorically chides Abraham with the words: "Yours were the trials, mine the performances." As if in response, a passive Isaac of biblical tradition becomes a volunteer who joyfully hurls himself on the altar (Josephus), making the incident a veritable sacrifice (Philo). The Book of Jubilees* links the story with the paschal sacrifice, and various Targums amplify this view (Neofiti Codex associates the sacrifice with a lamb bound for holocaust and has Isaac plead, "My father, bind me well so that I do not kick you in the way that your offering might be invalid"). Before the Christian interpretation of Gen 22 as prefiguring Christ, the Aqedah was probably understood to be a redemptive act, although the evidence is unclear.

Some theologians of the patristic period viewed Isaac as a perfect sacrifice and interpreted the story allegorically*, and mystery plays relate the story to suffering imposed on Jews. For many, Gen 22:19 opens the possibility that at one time the story ended with Isaac's death. Jewish tradition refers to a divine resuscitation in the Garden of Eden. Poets, artists, and philosophers have been fascinated with this text (Wiesel, Rembrandt, Chagall, Kant*, Kierkegaard*). JAMES L. CRENSHAW

Sadducees, Palestinian Jews, 2nd c. BCE to 1st c. CE, with conservative beliefs and practices. Although their name suggests a connection with the Zadokite priesthood, and a few known Sadducees had connections with the governing priestly aristocracy, the priestly and aristocratic status of all Sadducees cannot be demonstrated. In Jewish and NT sources, they are paired and contrasted with the Pharisees*, whose belief in resurrection* and angels* they denied and whose liberal interpretations of the Torah they opposed. Some of their conservative interpretations of biblical norms are paralleled in the (Zadokite) laws of the Qumran* community.

GEORGE W. E. NICKELSBURG

Sahagún, Bernardino de (1501–90), Franciscan* missionary and historian, director of the School of Santa Cruz de Tlatelolco in Mexico. In collaboration with students trilingual in Nahuatl, Spanish, and Latin, such as Antonio Valeriano, he produced the 12-volume *General History of the Things of New Spain* (*Historia general de las cosas de Nueva España*), the first, remarkable transcultural work. **See also MEXICO.**

MARÍA ALICIA PUENTE LUTTEROTH and ELIZABETH JUDD

Saints. Eastern Orthodoxy, Roman Catholicism, and Protestantism have various understandings of who the saints are and their role in the life of the church.

According to Eastern Orthodox, all are "called to be saints" (Rom 1:7; 1 Cor 1:2), i.e. called to be personally holy (1 Pet 1:13–17, 22–23). Generally speaking, the formally canonized saints are Christians who lived with such virtue, through real communion with Christ, that their lives radiated purity and sanctity* to an exceptional degree, and usually with a significant impact on many people. Their designation as saints in no way implies that they are the only Christians to have lived with such sanctity. Canonized saints often demonstrated extraordinary wisdom in helping others spiritually and otherwise. Often, miracles were worked through their prayers during their lives, and especially after their deaths; miracles are necessary in order to for someone to be acknowledged as a saint. Today, saints are acknowledged and proclaimed as such through a ceremony of glorification (or canonization), conducted by a regional or national church in response to popular acclaim. The first Christians popularly honored as saints were the martyrs*, who had demonstrated exceptional faith in Christ (see Rev 6:9–11). Gradually a more ordered canonization process developed for saintly Christians who did not die as martyrs, though this process is much less formal than that in the Roman Catholic Church.

The basic current Roman Catholic understanding of saints is close to that of the Orthodox. However, the saintly OT figures (Heb 11:1–12:1) are not included in the calendar of the Roman Church. Canonization is a very detailed, legal procedure carefully delineated in canon* law, including an intermediate stage called beatification*. It is the pope who makes the final declaration for the entire Church about the canonization of every saint.

The Protestant Reformers vigorously rejected the understanding of saints of the late medieval Roman Catholic Church, since these ideas had led to serious abuses, especially practices – like indulgences* – associated with "the treasury of merits." Despite some variations, Protestants consider all Christians to be "saints" (1 Cor 1:2; 2 Cor 1:1; Col 1:2), in that the righteousness of Christ is "imputed" to them (1 Cor 1:30; cf. Rom 4:3–11). Hence there is little or no recognition of canonized saints in Protestantism.

Special recognition of certain people exemplary for their great faith and personal holiness arose quite naturally very early on. Saints continue to be formally recognized in both the Eastern Orthodox and Roman Catholic churches.

DAVID FORD and MARY FORD

Saints, Devotion to, in the Orthodox Tradition. Saints are given veneration* (Gk *proskunesis*) (not worship [Gk *latreia*], which is given to God alone) by the faithful in many complementary ways.

Each saint is commemorated on the day of his or her death* (a practice dating from the mid-2nd c.). Hymns devoted to the saint are included in the regular liturgical services for that day, and a service dedicated to the saint (an "Akathist hymn") may also be held.

Icons* of saints are painted on boards of various sizes. Orthodox Christians usually have an "icon corner" in their homes where icons are kept and venerated. In the church, icons of saints are painted on the iconostasis (icon screen) and traditionally on the walls of the church; icons of the saints are also displayed for veneration on the day of their commemoration.

Relics* of saints are embedded in the altars of churches when the altars are consecrated. If a church has additional relics, they are displayed for public veneration at various times, especially on the day of a saint's commemoration.

During baptism each Orthodox Christian is given the name of a saint, who thus becomes his or her patron* saint. (The Serbian Orthodox have a patron saint for the entire family instead.) Through prayer, one can develop a special spiritual relationship with this saint, looking to the saint as a role model. Some cities and nations have patron saints, e.g. St. Demetrius for Thessaloníki and St. Sava for Serbia.

In the Orthodox Church, the prayers of the saints are considered especially effective because of the saints' exceptional closeness to the Lord and because many miraculous healings have occurred as a result of their prayers. Hence in public worship and in private devotions, the faithful frequently ask saints for their prayers and intercessions. Although not so systematically as in Roman Catholicism, some saints are associated with helping in particular situations, e.g. St. Nicholas in marriage* and St. Xenia of St. Petersburg for finding employment.

Biographies of saints and collections of their teachings are published to guide and inspire the faithful. Believers make pilgrimages* to the graves of saints, where their spiritual presence is often felt; many healings have taken place at these sites.

In the Orthodox Church, devotion to saints brings believers into meaningful fellowship with them, enriches their lives, and strengthens the bonds that link the church on earth with the church in heaven.

DAVID FORD and MARY FORD

Saints, Devotion to, in the Roman Catholic Tradition. The communion of saints is the great company of "friends of God and prophets" (Wis 7:27) in every generation of people who seek union with God. In this company, particular individuals embody certain values of their faith community in striking ways. Such individuals are customarily called "saints," although they are but a segment of the community, living and deceased, who support one another through memory and hope on their spiritual journeys.

Traditionally, the faithful express devotion to the saints by calling on them to act as benefactors for earthly petitioners. In this *patron*–saint model* of devotion, believers approach the saints as their intercessors before the throne of God. Saints rank higher than the living in the spiritual hierarchy and so can plead their causes and obtain blessings for them. Devotions based on this pattern include pilgrimages*, novenas*, veneration of relics*, and use of medals through which the faithful implore their heavenly patrons to intercede on their behalf with a distant God.

A more ancient pattern of relationship, that of *companionship*, emphasizes equality within the communion of saints. In this model, based on Scripture and early Christianity, the living and the dead are a community of the redeemed at different stages of their journey. They are related in mutuality across time and space and are drawn by the mystery* of love* that is poured out from Christ for the cosmos and its creatures. This model draws on devotional practices of memory* and hope*. Through icons*, lives* of the saints, and hymns of companionship, the graced community of the living have the memory of others' lives to spark their religious imagination and increase their hope. In prayers of praise*, the living proclaim gratitude for their past companions and confidence in God's ongoing providence*. The lives of those who have gone before provide inspiration and example and kindle a new fire of fidelity*, justice*, and love.

Liturgical celebrations like that of All* Saints celebrate this company of the redeemed, acknowledged and anonymous, living and dead, who are encircled in divine embrace and sustained by divine grace*. Such remembrances crystallize in the powerful litanies of the Easter vigil* and of particular faith communities. The rhythmic naming of ancestors* in faith makes present the empowering and subversive memory of lives that continually witness to the power of resurrection*. With the stirring response of the gathered community, such litanies create solidarity* in faith and hope across the expanses of time and space. **See also POPULAR CHRISTIAN PRACTICES CLUSTER.**

ELIZABETH A. JOHNSON and GLORIA L. SCHAAB

Salome was one of the women at the cross and the tomb (Mark 15:40, 16:1). Tradition has taken Josephus's* word that Herodias's daughter (not named in Mark 6:14–30 and parallels) was another Salome. This Salome has loomed large in Orientalist Western art and opera, portrayed as both seductive and lethal. By placing blame on the daughter's sexuality* for John the Baptist's execution, Christians tend to excuse Herod, although he appears to have blamed himself (Mark 6:16).

NICOLE WILKINSON DURAN

Salvation. For most Christians, the concept of salvation suggests spiritual and future salvation – salvation from what separates people from God (sin* and evil*) and from the disastrous consequences of this separation (especially death*). Biblical views are more diversified. Salvation generally refers to deliverance from this-worldly bondage, threats, danger, illness, or death – from whatever endangers the existence or identity of a people, of a community, or of individuals – although salvation also has spiritual and future dimensions. Since self-salvation is relatively rare in the Bible, three questions must be asked: (1) Who needs to be saved, and from what predicament? (2) By whom are they saved and how? (3) What is the state of "being saved"?

Salvation in the Old Testament

1. Saved from What? In the OT, the broad terminology of salvation refers to deliverance and rescue (Heb *nasal, malat, yasa*), bringing to safety (*palat*), and redemption* (Heb *gaal*, "ransoming," "setting free"; translated in the LXX as *sozo*, the main NT term). The paradigmatic salvation event is the deliverance of the people of Israel from bondage in Egypt (Exod 1–15). Other salvation events are found in the Genesis narratives (e.g. Joseph's family is saved from starvation by escaping to Egypt; Gen 37–50) and the many texts referring to the deliverance of Israel from other peoples (salvation from Canaanite oppression, Judg 4–5; salvation from exile) and from oppression and social* injustice – a salvation that other nations will also experience "in the last days" (Isa 2:1–4, 49:6–23, 60:1–14). The OT also includes many references to the salvation of individuals from threat, disease, or death (Ps 7, 12, 43, 86, 109) and from barrenness (Judg 13; 1 Sam 1–2).

2. Saved by Whom and How? All these instances of deliverance are credited to God as Savior, "God of salvation" (Ps 17–78). Yet the texts also underscore the role of human actors, such as Moses*, "judges" (e.g. Deborah*, Gideon, Samson), kings, including David* and his everlasting dynasty (2 Sam 7; Ps 89), as well as the "Servant" (Israel, or a representative individual) in the Servant Songs of Isaiah (42:1–4, 49:1–6, 50:4–11, 52:13–53:12). Nonetheless, God's role is always preeminent.

3. What Is the State of "Being Saved"? In the OT, there is a strong emphasis on this-worldly salvation as the restoration of the collective and individual good life. Yet this salvation also has a spiritual character: the overcoming of separation from God through the intervention of this God of grace* (*hesed*). The salvation from bondage in Egypt culminates in the Sinai covenant* and the giving of the Law; the salvation through the kings culminates in the building of Solomon's temple; the redemption* from exile and the restoration of Israel (Isa 43:14–44:6) is also a revelation of the redeemer God that Israel is called to worship* and serve (Ezek 36–48; Jer 31). Furthermore, in many passages of the Prophets, salvation concerns the future. It is not simply past or present. A future and more radical salvation is expected beyond the present state of Israel, through new divine interventions (Amos 7–8; Hos 2–3), with a new exodus (Isa 40), a new covenant (Jer 31), and a new Davidic king (Isa 9, 11). These expectations progressively gained an eschatological* dimension, already in Isaiah, but mainly in Joel, Zech 14, and Daniel.

Salvation in the New Testament

1. Saved from What? The terms for salvation (related to the Gk verbs *sozo*, "save" and *ruomai*, "rescue," and to "healing*," "exorcism*," and the "Kingdom* of God") frequently refer to deliverance from physical threat (drowning, Matt 8:25, par.; shipwreck, Acts 23, 27, 28), death (Mark 5:23, 15:30–31), illness (Mark 5:28, 34), and demonic or satanic* possession (Mark 1:34). Salvation is both healing (from sin as disease) and deliverance/redemption from bondage to the pervasive power of evil (Matt 6:13, in the Lord's Prayer) or of sin (Rom 2–7), which is directly related to death (1 Cor 15:56). Eschatological salvation is a "rescue from the wrath that is coming" (1 Thess 1:10). Since sin involves separation from God, salvation is also a reconciliation with God conceived of as redemption (from the bondage to sin), healing, or forgiveness (rather than condemnation, John 3:17, 12:47).

2. Saved by Whom and How? Although healing, deliverance, and redemption from the powers of evil and sin are at times credited to the faith* of the beneficiary ("your faith saved you"; Matt 8:13; Mark 5:34; 10:52; Luke 17:19), they are credited primarily to God and Jesus Christ. Such is the case of all the healings and exorcisms in the Gospels that are associated with the "Kingdom of God" as manifestations of God's powerful kingly activity (Mark 1:15), as well as the declarations that Jesus came to save the world (John 3:16–17) and that Christ died on the cross for our salvation (1 Cor 1:18). Thus salvation has three components: faith; the intervention of divine power to overcome evil powers (in healings and exorcisms); and the power of the cross, the paradoxical power of kenosis* (the embracing of human vulnerability by the divine) resulting in resurrection* and exaltation (Phil 2:6–11).

3. What Is the State of "Being Saved"? Although salvation is the restoration of the good life through healing, exorcism, or deliverance (as in the Gospels and Acts) and includes, for Jesus' followers, participating in this salvation by addressing the needs of the poor, the oppressed, and victims of injustice (Matt 25:31–46), in the NT salvation is primarily spiritual: an overcoming of the separation from God because, in Jesus, God is among us ("Emmanuel," Matt 1:23) and because, through Christ's death, humans are "reconciled to God" (Rom 5:7–11; 2 Cor 5:17–21). The Synoptic Gospels express this by presenting salvation as "entering" the "Kingdom of God" (Mark 10:23–26, par.), "accepting" it as a child would (Mark 10:15, par.), and as "sit[ting] at table in the Kingdom of God" (Luke 13:29, RSV). Yet the Kingdom is also present in Jesus' ministry (and beyond). Thus participation in the Kingdom is viewed as a deliverance at the Last Judgment* and as an eschatological entering into God's presence for eternal life (Rom 13:11; 1 Pet 1:5). But those who *will* be delivered are already delivered *in the present* (they "were saved" and thus "have salvation" [Rom 8:24]; they already have eternal life [John 5:24]). Now they are, at least partially, healed or freed from sin, guilt*, bondage* of the will, captivity to Satan*, and spiritual death (justification*), although the resurrected Christ is still in the process of "putting all his enemies under his feet" (1 Cor 15:24–25).

Throughout Christian history, the necessity for salvation has been attributed to the loss of proper relationship with God, which, for many, results from the Fall*, i.e. the beginning of human sin* and hence alienation from God. In the Western* tradition, Christ's death on the cross is the event through which guilt, the chief obstacle to salvation, is overcome (atonement as forgiveness and being saved from condemnation; see Atonement #2).

The Eastern Orthodox* tradition emphasizes salvation as healing from sin as a disease and underscores the positive effects of renewal through Christ: through the Incarnation*, divine presence transforms human life; salvation is not merely forgiveness*, but primarily liberation of the human mind from delusion and the renewal of human nature by union with the God-man Christ, whose healing presence is experienced through the church and its sacramental* mysteries*. Salvation is a process rather than a state, a spiritual struggle to be transformed into the image and likeness of God (see Theosis, Deification). Put another way, salvation for Orthodox Christians might be defined as the change of a person from an earthly form to an iconic state, as portrayed by holy images; the people depicted on icons* are in a symbolically transfigured state, identifiable but different because they have become the image and likeness of God.

The contemporary Charismatic* Movement puts much emphasis on salvation from evil powers now as well as for eternal life. For Liberation*, Feminist*, Womanist*, and other theologians and the large number of Christians who are marginalized and oppressed, the primary concern is with present-day salvation from oppression*, poverty*, and injustice; eschatological salvation is not a primary issue, though it remains important; for many the necessary salvation has been or will be met by Christ.

As already suggested, salvation is not an end in itself; humans are saved for a purpose. This teleology* becomes visible as one notes how salvation is related to such concepts as covenant*, election*, vocation*, justification*, and predestination*. **See also *ORDO SALUTIS*; REDEMPTION.** DANIEL PATTE

Salvation Army (the) developed out of English Methodism* (mid-19th c.). It was founded as the Christian Mission by William and Catherine Booth* (1865), before becoming the Salvation Army (1878). Concerned with ministering to the physical and spiritual needs of the growing population of working poor* in London, the Booths created a unique blend of a denomination and a service organization.

William and Catherine Booth intended to supplement the work of other churches among the poor, but formed their own organization when new converts were not comfortable within, or accepted by, traditional churches. They structured their mission along the lines of the military, with William Booth as the general, the ministers as officers, and the laity as soldiers in God's army. They developed their own flag and hymnody, and the local church was called a "corps." The "Articles of War" formed their statement of faith, and William and Catherine

Booth established a strong line of authority from the general down to the local corps, along with an efficient system for training leaders.

To become one of its officers, little formal education is required, but a commitment to serving the poor* and preaching the gospel is imperative. In many countries, people identify the Salvation Army exclusively with social* services. But the Army considers itself a church where members live out the Christian gospel in their daily lives. This dual emphasis allows the Army to adapt to local needs. When a Protestant presence is needed, the local corps functions mainly as a church. When strong churches are present, the Army, while maintaining a local corps, implements more service programs and becomes a major player in social welfare issues.

Although initially opposed to gender equality, William quickly accepted Catherine's assertion that women and men must be equal as officers and lay leaders. General Booth later noted that "some of the best men in the Army are women." Married couples who enter officer training are both ordained and share their social work and local corps duties. The Army has had two women generals. Evangeline Booth (1865–1950, youngest daughter of Catherine and William Booth) served as general from 1934 to 1939. She had begun to assume leadership roles in 1882; she then organized disaster relief after the 1906 San Francisco earthquake and the Army's famous canteens during World War I. Eva Burroughs (born in Australia, 1929) acted as general from 1986 to 1993 after serving in Zimbabwe, Great Britain, and Ireland.

The Salvation Army has corps in more than 100 countries. It operates evangelical centers, hospitals, schools, and social welfare agencies with about 15,000 officers and more than 1 million soldiers in more than 140 languages. With international headquarters in London, the Salvation Army remains committed to traditional Methodist theology while placing a strong emphasis on meeting people's physical and spiritual needs. ROSALIE BECK

Salvation History (German, *Heilsgeschichte*), a view of the biblical narrative based on the romantic* and Hegelian* assumptions that the divine is expressed in and through history. This view, which originated in 19th-c. Germany, enabled many Christians to accept historical studies of the Bible; it was often overconfident, however, about what could be read from the historical data. **See also** **HISTORIOGRAPHY OF EARLY CHRISTIANITY AS DEVELOPED IN THE 19TH AND 20TH CENTURIES.**

Salve Regina (Lat "Hail, Queen"), one of the oldest Western antiphons*, used since c1100, included in the canonical* hours and the Breviary*.

Samaria, Samaritans. Now nearly extinct, Samaritans, Jewish descendants of inhabitants of Samaria not deported by the Assyrians (722 BC), used their own version of the Pentateuch, remaining committed to the Law, keeping festivals, practicing circumcision, awaiting the Messiah, and worshipping on Mount Gerizim. Rejected by other Jews for their mixed Gentile ancestry, Samaritans were a focus of Jesus' ministry; he traveled through Samaria, spoke of the good Samaritan (Luke 10:25–37), and met with a Samaritan woman (John 4), an outrageous notion to righteous Jews. Early church fathers favored John 4, interpreting it from numerous allegorical* perspectives. Samaria welcomed the gospel (Acts 8:1b–28). JEFFRY C. DAVIS

Samaritan, Good, the man who lived out the great* commandment in the parable that Jesus told (Luke 10:30–37) in response to the question "Who is my neighbor?" A priest* and a Levite* passed by a traveler who had been robbed and beaten by brigands, but a Samaritan* took him to an inn and promised to pay for his care.

Samson, last of the "judges*" (Judg 13–16). A Nazirite (ascetic*), he did not drink wine or cut his hair. He used his miraculous strength to conquer the Philistines (Judg 13–15). He revealed to Delilah the secret of his strength, leading to his capture. Brought to the Philistine temple of Dagon, with a new burst of strength Samson razed the building, killing many, including himself (Judg 16).

Samuel, 1 and 2, Books of. Named for the key character, Samuel, a judge (1 Sam 1–7), prophet (1 Sam 8–28), and priest (1 Sam 3), these books are included in the "Former Prophets" as the 8th and 9th books of the Hebrew canon, while they belong to the historical books (part of the Deuteronomistic* History) as the 9th and 10th books of the Christian canon.

The end of the period of the judges is the setting of the opening chapters (1 Sam 1–7). The demand for a king and the conflicting sentiments about monarchy in Israel (1 Sam 8–11) set the stage for the two main cycles of tradition: the election and rejection of Saul* (1

Sam 13–31), followed by the rise and reign of David* (2 Sam 1–24). In these accounts, 1 and 2 Samuel wrestle with the legitimacy of kingship and eventually establish David as the deuteronomistic template against which all other kings shall be assessed.

Authorship and sources remain matters of debate. Duplicate narratives (e.g. Saul's rejection as king, 1 Sam 13, 17; David's sparing Saul's life, 1 Sam 24, 26; the death of Saul, 1 Sam 31, 2 Sam 1) have led some to try to trace pentateuchal* traditions J and E across these texts. However, the continuity of theme, language, and character development emblematic of these pentateuchal traditions are lacking here. Others have studied the doublets in conjunction with pro-monarchic vs. anti-monarchic sentiments with little success. Based on themes and stylistics, Leonard Rost proposed that 2 Sam 9–20 and 1 Kgs 1–2 constituted a succession narrative traceable to a composer close to the events. By contrast, Martin Noth argued that the books of Samuel along with the rest of the Deuteronomistic History were written much later during the exilic period. Abandoning compositional questions, recent studies explore the narrative dimensions of plot, themes, and characters of the final form of the text. Close readings expose the vast array of characters – including the audacious Abigail (1 Sam 25), the wise woman of Tekoa (2 Sam 14), and the maimed Mephibosheth (2 Sam 9) – that contribute to these rich and engaging stories. Socio-rhetorical studies reveal the personal struggles (Saul's jealousy of David, 1 Sam 18), individual aspirations to act virtuously (David's kindness to Mephibosheth, 2 Sam 9), and even personal sin (David's adulterous and murderous deeds, 2 Sam 11) that confronted the communities with exemplars of moral issues. GINA HENS-PIAZZA

Sanctification, process by which persons are purified and become holy. As God is holy, persons, times (e.g. the Sabbath), and things dedicated to God are called holy in the OT; the Christian life is described as holy (Rom 12:1); Christians as a community are called "saints"* (Phil 1:1, 1; Cor 6:2; Rom 8:27, 12:13, 15:25). The veneration of individuals as saints (first martyrs*, then ascetics* and other persons of unusual holiness) developed after the 2nd or 3rd c.

In the NT, sanctification is effected by Christ (1 Cor 1:30; Eph 5:25–26; John 17:19) and the Holy* Spirit (1 Thess 4:3–8; 1 Pet 1:2), is manifested through baptism (1 Cor 6:11), and becomes a human responsibility (Rom 6:19, 22). Good actions come from a "good tree" (Matt 7:17 = Luke 6:43), made so by God.

While Paul makes much of justification*, he says little about its relation to sanctification. Through the centuries, in the West he has been read as ambivalent – as assuming that all will be judged according to their actions (Rom 2:6; 1 Cor 3:8; 2 Cor 5:10) but mercifully justified by faith*; these actions are fruits of sanctification by God, as the passive forms "You were sanctified," "You were justified" express (1 Cor 6:11; 1 Thess 5:23).

Luther* differentiated between justification (God's imputation* of Christ's righteousness to sinners through faith*) and sanctification (God's transformation of their hearts through the Spirit), and based salvation* on the former alone. The Reformed* churches added sanctification as a factor in salvation, with the proviso that good character and actions, while far from sufficient, are considered holy on the basis of Christ's own holiness.

The Roman Catholic tradition links justification with sanctification more closely, affirming that pure motives and good works merit* salvation, but not in the strictest sense, as a reward, since they are the fruit of divine grace*.

The Eastern Orthodox* churches emphasize deification (theosis*), i.e. participation in the divine nature (2 Pet 1:4) through Christ and the Holy Spirit; because of the Incarnation*, not only the human world but the natural world is sanctified (purified of sin* as disease).

The Puritan* Movement looked for signs that a person was indeed predestined* to attain salvation. While faith in the grace* of Christ had been regarded as sufficient for the assurance of salvation, Puritans sought evidence of sanctification and found it in purity and holiness of life, in the renunciation of worldly pleasures (dancing, the theater), and in self-discipline and thrift, which gave rise to the "Protestant ethic."

Wesley* and his followers sought holiness of life, and their emphasis on "entire sanctification" or "Christian perfection*" gave rise to the theory of a "second blessing." Debates over its meaning led to several divisions within the Wesleyan Movement and gave rise to the Holiness* and Pentecostal* churches. EUGENE TESELLE

Sanctuary, a holy place, specifically the part of the church containing the altar*.

Sanctuary, Right of (cf. Gk *asylon*, "asylum," "free from harm"). By the 4th c., an offender who took refuge in a church could not be removed for a period of time. In the Middle Ages, this came to be 40 days after the taking of an oath of abjuration*, during which there was an opportunity to depart from the church. Secular rulers acknowledged the church's right of sanctuary and sometimes established their own procedures. After the Reformation*, the right was abolished in most countries, often in stages. In recent times, churches have offered sanctuary to conscientious* objectors to war, to undocumented refugees fleeing from violence, and to other people viewed as unjustly threatened by the law. **See also REFUGEES AS A THEOLOGICAL CONCEPT AND AN ETHICAL ISSUE.**

Sanctus (Lat "holy"), cherubim's* hymn in Isa 6:3: "Holy, holy, holy is the LORD of hosts; the whole earth is full of his glory"; also "Blessed is the one who comes in the name of the Lord" (Matt 21:9).

Sanhedrin (Heb form of Gk *synedrion*), highest Jewish "council" and court of justice in Jerusalem under Roman rule. In the rabbinic literature, the Sanhedrin had exclusively religious functions (as in the talmudic period). But it is more likely that, as both Josephus* and the NT say, the Sanhedrin also had civil functions, subject to the wishes of the Roman governor (Saldarini), and thus the power to sentence Jesus (Mark 14:53–15:1, par.), Stephen (Acts 6:12), and Paul (Acts 22:30). Because these accounts and their interpretations overlooked the fact that the Romans held Jewish leaders responsible for maintaining order in their own society, these biblical texts led to anti-Semitic views.

DANIEL PATTE

Sarah (or Sarai) first appears in the Bible as the barren and beautiful wife of Abraham. When they travel to Egypt, he endangers her, to save himself, by passing her off to the pharaoh as his sister. God protects her and eventually blesses her with a son, Isaac (Gen 11–23). Judaism recognizes Sarah as the matriarch of the people Israel (Isa 51:2). Christianity claims her as a symbol of the new covenant* (Gal 4:24–26) and as a model of an obedient wife (1 Pet 3:6). Islam recognizes her as a paragon of piety and purity, who shunned adulterous advances by appealing to Allah (Surah 11:69). PHYLLIS TRIBLE

Sarai (Heb "princess") was in Gen 12–25 the original name of Sarah* (also "princess"). The giving of a new name to the matriarch (Gen 17:15) as part of the covenant to Abram*/Abraham* confirmed that she was included in the covenantal promise; from this point in her story, she was no longer a barren woman.

Sarcophagus, stone coffin, often adorned with bas-relief carvings and inscriptions, used by Christians in late antiquity and into the Byzantine* period.

Satan (Heb "adversary"), in the OT, angelic being and tempter, prosecutor, or adversary of God; in the NT, tempter and chief of the demons. **See also DEVIL, SATAN, DEMONS, AND DEMONIC POWERS.**

Saturninus (2nd c.), Syrian Gnostic known only through Irenaeus*, said to be part of a tradition originating with Simon* Magus, who taught in Antioch. Saturnius was considered a heretic* for his doctrines concerning God as unknown to all and the creation of the world by angelic powers. **See also BASILIDES.**

Saudi Arabia. The Arabian Peninsula, which today is known for the near absence of indigenous Christianity, is one of the regions where Christianity was present as early as the 2nd c. In the 7th c., it became the heartland of the new religion of Islam*, which, although tolerant of Christianity in most of the countries it conquered, soon started to force Christians to leave its sacred center. Even today, Saudi Arabia requires its citizens to be Muslim, preferably of the purist Salafi type, which in the 18th c. was propagated by Muhammad ibn Abd al-Wahhab; other Islamic schools encounter government discrimination. Nonetheless, over the past decades, the country has seen the growth of a considerable Christian community, whose size is difficult to establish. These Christians are part of the large group of immigrant workers and foreign military service members that make up about 20% of the population. The Christians among them, such as Philippine* Catholics, Indian Syrian* Christians, Palestinian Greek Orthodox*, Eastern Rite Catholics, and Egyptian Copts*, reflect a wide variety of nationalities and denominations, In addition, Protestants and Evangelicals of all kinds, as well as Latin Rite Catholics, are found among US, European, and African expatriates. Roman Catholicism, represented not only by Western Catholics, but also by Philippine, Indian, and Middle Eastern Christians, forms the largest denomination, followed by various forms of Eastern Orthodoxy. The size of the Evangelical and Pentecostal groups can only be guessed at. Public worship of religions other than Islam, much less any attempt to convert Muslims, is not permitted; one may assume, however, that some groups of Christians do include local converts. Although officially private worship is allowed, all Christian gatherings, including those in private homes, are viewed with suspicion, and if they are discovered, members are usually expelled from the country. This results in styles of worship and community that are small-scale, lay-oriented, and often without formal affiliations.

Statistics: Population (2006): 27 million (20% resident foreigners: Indians, 25%; Bangladeshi, 18%; Filipinos, 17%; Pakistani, 11%; Egyptians, 13%; Westerners, 2%); Christians, 10–30% of this group, i.e. 2–6% of the total population.

HELEEN MURRE-VAN DEN BERG

Saul, first king of Israel*, chosen after Samuel*, guided by God, reluctantly consented to Israel's having a human king in addition to, or instead of, God (1 Sam 8: 4–22; see Theocracy). God rejected Saul after he committed several acts of disobedience (see David). His visit to the woman of Endor* to consult Samuel's spirit is a source of much controversy.

Saul of Tarsus, the name of Paul before his conversion, according to Acts 7–26. **See also PAUL THE APOSTLE.**

Savior, one who delivers others from evil*, originally from physical harm or captivity, then from moral* evil and punishment. God is often called Israel's deliverer, especially in 2 Isaiah*. In the OT, the term was applied to human beings (Judg 3:9; 2 Kgs 13:5; Neh 9:27). In Hellenistic culture, saviors included deities, mythic heroes, and rulers. In the NT, "savior" is used exclusively for God and Christ; 12 of the 24 instances of the title are found in the Pastoral* Epistles, suggesting that its use (augmenting "Christ" and "Lord") developed in the late 1st c. in order to venerate Christ rather than the Roman emperor, also hailed as "savior." **See also SALVATION.**

Savoy Conference, gathering called by Charles II to review the Book* of Common Prayer (1661), with equal numbers of Episcopalians and Presbyterians. The Presbyterians, led by Richard Baxter*, offered a revised service book and asked that ministers who had not been ordained by a bishop be recognized. Both the revised book and the request were rejected. The 1662 Book of Common Prayer was unacceptable to the Presbyterians, and the Act of Uniformity (1662) required episcopal ordination; more than 2,000 ministers were removed from their positions in the Church of England.

Savoy Declaration, statement of Congregationalist* principles (1658). Its Confession of Faith, an adaptation of the Westminster* Confession, claims to be only an expression of the faith shared at the time, allowing congregations to frame their own confessions. Its Platform of Discipline declares that all the powers of the church rest with the congregation; broader bodies were given only an advisory rather than a jurisdictional function.

Sayers, Dorothy Leigh (1893–1957), an advertising copywriter, poet, crime writer, and impeccably orthodox Church of England theologian, had an exceptional talent for communicating the importance of theological thinking. A pioneer of religious radio broadcasting, she tirelessly argued for theological reengagement with lay* dedication to the business of living, with creativity in the arts, and with work and politics, and fiercely criticized the secular and ecclesiastical devaluation of women*. World War II renewed her appreciation of Dante's* *Divine Comedy*, and her translations, theological introductions, notes, and commentary on *Hell* and *Purgatory* remain unsurpassed. ANN LOADES

Sayings of the Fathers. See *APOPHTHEGMATA PATRUM*.

Scandinavian Literature and Christianity. In her *Revelations*, Birgitta* (1303–73) of Sweden combines theology and politics in an earthy realism, branding the king, the pope, and the aristocracy in biblical visions.

The Swedish translation of the Bible (1541, revised 1703) provided a source of inspiration for novelists and poets until 1917. The hymnbooks (1695 onward) and Christian lyrics, e.g. by Haqvin Spegel (1645–1714), Jesper Svedberg (1653–1735), Israel Kolmodin (1643–1709), Peter Dass (1647–1707), Thomas Kingo (1634–1702), Hans Brorson (1694–1764), Nicolaus Grundtvig (1783–1872), and Johan-Olov Wallin (1779–1839), remain a living part of Scandinavian literature.

Anders Arrebo's (1587–1637), Haqvin Spegel's, and Henrik Wergeland's (1808–45) great epics on the creation* mark the end of an era when literature was closely related to the Bible. The romantic poets found inspiration in old Northern mythology, and scientific developments in the 19th c. led to biblical skepticism. However, a new interest in Christian themes emerged. Søren Kierkegaard's (1813–55) Pietist* and existentialist* philosophy and theology influenced the early plays of Henrik Ibsen (1828–1906) and August

Strindberg (1849–1912). After his "Inferno crisis," Strindberg also drew on the OT.

Pietism played an important part in 19th-c. religious life and indirectly in 20th-c. literature. Selma Lagerlöf's *Jerusalem* (1901–2) tells the story of a revivalist group's emigration to the Holy Land. Vilhelm Moberg's emigration epic (1949–59) deals with political and religious oppression and new life in the USA. The corresponding Norwegian story was told by Alfred Hauge (1961–65). The novelists Sara Lidman (1923–2004), Torgny Lindgren (b1938), and Per Olov Enquist (b1934) are stylistically and thematically influenced by their Pietist background.

Despite the prevalence of secularism* and anticlericalism in 20th-c. Scandinavian literature, many writers, e.g. Jacob Knudsen (1858–1917), Kaj Munk (1898–1944), and Pär Lagerkvist (1891–1974), were concerned with religious and sacred themes. Gnosticism* is noticeable in the novels of Lars Gyllensten (b1921) and Sven Delblanc (1931–92), while Lars Ahlin (1915–97) developed an aesthetic* that made him a Lutheran theologian in his own right. Birgitta Trotzig's (b1929) poetry and prose are influenced by mysticism* and Orthodox iconography*.

Biblical rhetoric is still frequently employed in Scandinavian literature, e.g. in Christine Falkenland's (b1967) and Hanne Ørstavik's (b1969) novels. ANDERS TYRBERG

Scapular, garment worn over the shoulders, hanging down in front and behind, a required part of the monastic* habit; in smaller dimensions, a sign of affiliation worn by tertiaries* and other persons living in the world.

Schaff, Philip. See MERCERSBURG THEOLOGY.

Schelling, Friedrich Wilhelm Joseph von (1775–1854), German idealist philosopher and speculative Christian thinker. Educated at Tübingen with Hegel* and Hölderlin; professor of philosophy at Jena, Würzburg, Munich, and finally Berlin. As a celebrated prodigy linked to German romanticism, he overshadowed Hegel, who later became his more famous rival. A Lutheran, he influenced Roman Catholic thinkers of the Tübingen school and Bavaria, especially Franz von Baader. His early writings include systematic philosophies of nature, of art, and of the absolute identity of subject and object knowable by intellectual intuition, and his *System of Transcendental Idealism*. Influenced by the theosophical speculation of Boehme*, he focused on issues of will* and evil* in *Of Human Freedom*. His voluntarist view of God as bipolar, as ultimate will, and as self-constituting, in *The Ages of the World*, contrasts with medieval and rationalist* doctrines of God, and influenced the thought of Tillich* and Berdyaev*. His ultimate "positive philosophy" embraces ancient mythologies and religions in a "philosophy of mythology and revelation" and sets Christianity at the apex of God's long process of self-realization and historical self-disclosure. The young Kierkegaard*, before attacking Hegelianism, attended Schelling's Berlin lectures on revelation*. ROBERT F. BROWN

Schism, a breaking of the unity of the visible church, or the consequent state of division, usually involving doctrinal differences or accusations of heresy*. **See also GREAT SCHISM.**

Schlatter, Adolf. See NEW TESTAMENT THEOLOGY.

Schleiermacher, Friedrich Daniel Ernst (1768–1834), father of modern theology; professor and four-time dean of the theological faculty of the University of Berlin from 1810 to 1834. His early education was provided by the Moravian* Brethren (Herrnhuter) of Southeastern Saxony, a strict Pietist* sect. Even as he reconceived the meaning of religion, Pietism remained an influence throughout his life.

Schleiermacher's "Copernican revolution in theology" sought to come to terms with Kant's revolutionary philosophy, the scientific world view, and the higher biblical criticism. Key to this revolution is the idea that the basic datum of Christian theology is not dogma, the letter of Scripture, or the rational understanding, but the feeling of absolute dependence as it has been awakened in and through the believer's relation to Christ. In *On Religion* (1799, 1806, 1821, 1831), Schleiermacher grounds religion in an original unity of consciousness preceding the subject–object dichotomy; in *The Christian Faith* (*CF*, 1821–22, 1830–31), the feeling of absolute dependence is grounded in the immediate self-consciousness (see Religion as a Concept and Christianity). In *The Christian Faith*, Christian doctrines are defined as "accounts of the Christian religious affections set forth in speech" (*CF*, §15). Rather than assume that pious feeling is the result of an individual's reaction to the *content* of a belief apprehended through cognitive capacities, Schleiermacher prioritizes religious experience. Kant's denial of the possibility of objective knowledge of supersensible objects played a role in the development of Schleiermacher's position. We have access to God only as

God stands in relation to us, as the *whence* of our active and receptive existence. Hence we know God only as God is *experienced* in the immediate self-consciousness. The original expressions of piety are the poetic and rhetorical, from which arise symbols pointing past themselves to the ground of all that is (*CF*, §§15, 16). Christian doctrines are second-order statements reflecting and systematizing these original expressions (*CF*, 79, §16.1). Sin* is the blocking of the God consciousness, i.e. "an arrestment of the determinative power of spirit, due to the independence of the sensuous functions" (*CF*, §66.2). Through our relation to Christ, the power of sin is broken and the God consciousness awakened. In the eternal divine decree, God ordained that human nature should achieve its completion in Christ* (*CF*, §95). Jesus Christ is the archetype of perfect human nature, which, *as perfect*, expresses the divine love completely (*CF*, §97.3); our own perfection is achieved through our incorporation into the divine life of Christ, through which "[h]is motive principle becomes ours" (*CF*, §104.3). Christ's saving work is his inauguration of the Kingdom* of God, a kingdom of divine love.

Regarding the Trinity*, Schleiermacher denied that the Christian experience of redemption implied original and eternal distinctions within the divine essence. Nevertheless, a proper understanding of the divine nature needs to show how the union of God with human nature in both Christ and the human community is possible. Such an understanding does not affirm eternal distinctions in God but is "capable of exhibiting in their truth both unions of the Essence with human nature" (*CF*, §172.2). In his influential *Brief Outline* (1811), Schleiermacher divided theology into three branches. Philosophical theology, the "root" of theology, identifies the essential features of Christian faith; historical theology explores its historical manifestations; and practical theology, the "crown" of theology, is the craft through which theological conclusions are implemented for the care of souls.

Schleiermacher played a foundational role in developing a general hermeneutic theory. He defined hermeneutics* as "the art of understanding ... the discourse of another correctly" (*Hermeneutik und Kritik*, 75) and identified two dimensions of interpretation. "Grammatical" interpretation concerns the meaning of utterances in relation to the givenness of language: the vocabulary, syntax, morphology, and phonetics of a language all preexist the subject. The "psychological" or "technical" dimension of interpretation concerns how the *subject* employs given structures and meanings already present within language for his or her own purposes. Both dimensions of interpretation are crucial if interpretation is to be complete. Schleiermacher's theory of interpretation developed as he struggled to interpret both Plato and NT texts. His translations of Plato's dialogues appeared from 1804 to 1828 and are still widely used today; his interpretation of Plato is considered a watershed in the history of Plato interpretation. Schleiermacher stood at the forefront of the development of higher criticism of the NT. His prioritizing of the experience of Christ over Scripture freed him to investigate NT documents just as one would any other historical text.

Schleiermacher's philosophical ethics are only now being recovered in the English-speaking world. His focus on the transcendental ground of character allowed him to develop a theory of the relation of ethics to religion that avoids heteronomy and to combine the advantages of virtue ethics with an ethic affirming the significance of duty. He also developed an understanding of the significance of culture for ethical relations.

JACQUELINE MARIÑA

Schmalkaldic Articles, confessional statement written by Martin Luther*, endorsed by Lutheran theologians in 1537 in Schmalkalden, Germany, and included in the *Book of Concord** (1580). The statement was requested by Elector John Frederick of Saxony in response to the call of Pope Paul III for a council. The Articles have three parts: (1) trinitarian* doctrine, which was not disputed; (2) Christ the only savior* (see Uniqueness of Christ) and justification* by faith alone, neither of which could be negotiated; (3) matters that could be discussed "with learned, reasonable people or among ourselves."

SCOTT H. HENDRIX

Scholarios, George. See GENNADIOS II (GEORGE SCHOLARIOS).

Scholasticism is a method of inquiry, influenced by Aristotle*, that developed in the schools and universities of the Latin West between the 12th and 15th c., in relation both to the liberal arts and to theology. Its foundations were laid by Boethius* (c475–c525) through his writings on logic and his brief essays on theology. In the early Middle Ages, however, there was only limited awareness of the peripatetic tradition, the dominant philosophical system being shaped by the Christian Neoplatonism* of Augustine*. Scholasticism started to assert itself as a dominant movement in the 12th-c. schools of Northern France (see Hugh of St. Victor). Monks viewed some Scholastics as promoting a way of teaching theology that emphasized logic and disputation rather than meditation and silent reflection. In fact, Scholastics developed a range of perspectives while adopting a common educational method, which emphasized both argument and the critical study of written authority, whether in the liberal arts or in theology.

Although certain early Scholastics, like Peter Abelard* and Gilbert* of Poitiers, provoked controversy for applying Aristotelian principles to theology, theologians like Anselm of Laon and Peter* Lombard (mid-12th c.) succeeded in making systematic and rational inquiry into theological questions a standard method in the Parisian schools. Even if there were serious differences of opinion between schools of thought (as documented in John of Salisbury's *Metalogicon*), the consensus was that questions should be debated rationally, by recourse to both authority and reason* (see also Rationalism and Christian Theology).

In the 13th c., growing awareness of Aristotle's scientific writing, initially mediated by translations from Arabic versions and commentaries, but subsequently by direct translations of the Greek (many by William of Moerbeke), both challenged and gradually transformed Latin Scholasticism. When statutes were drawn up for the University of Paris (1210, 1215), an ecclesiastical prohibition was placed on lecturing on the scientific writings of Aristotle, including the *Metaphysics*. After 1231, however, this prohibition gradually ceased to be enforced. This led to a significant growth of Scholastic inquiry into many philosophical areas, namely logic, ethics, natural science, and theology, leading to the enduring achievements of Albertus* Magnus and Thomas Aquinas*. The Scholastic method continued to shape European universities at least until the Renaissance, if not beyond.

CONSTANT J. MEWS

Schweitzer, Albert (1875–1965), philosopher, ethicist, theologian, musician, physician. Born in Alsace, he earned degrees in philosophy, theology, and medicine, and after an early career as a Lutheran minister and scholar, he turned to humanitarian work. He left for equatorial Africa (1913) with his wife, Hélène Bresslau, a nurse, to establish a hospital in Lambaréné, in present-day Gabon*. For the rest of his life, Schweitzer devoted himself to his work in Africa and was awarded the Nobel Peace Prize (1953). During his last years, he spoke out in opposition to nuclear weapons.

Schweitzer published studies of Kant* and Bach*, autobiographical accounts of his life (*Out of My Life and Thought; Memoirs of Childhood and Youth; On the Edge of the Primeval Forest; More from the Primeval Forest*), and several significant books on religion and ethics (*The Mystery of the Kingdom; The Quest of the Historical Jesus; The Mysticism of Paul; Indian Thought; The Philosophy of Civilization*). His contributions on Jesus, in the spirit of rational* thought combined with a mystical* sense, called into question previous scholarly efforts to understand the historical Jesus. He concluded that although Jesus was a 1st-c. apocalyptic* preacher and a stranger to our own world, he proclaimed a message of love (e.g. in the Sermon* on the Mount) that continues to resonate in the contemporary world. Schweitzer's approach to Jesus, with its emphasis on ethical mysticism, shaped scholarship on Jesus for decades. In ethics and philosophy, Schweitzer relied on the insights of Goethe, Nietzsche*, and Schopenhauer, and his ethic elaborates on themes found in Jesus and early Christianity, as well as Indian religions (see Hinduism and Christianity Cluster). He was committed to a life of service and to the articulation of an ethic of reverence for all forms of life, human, animal, and plant.

MARVIN MEYER

Schwenckfeld von Ossig, Caspar (1489–1561). A nobleman and irenic reformer, Schwenckfeld attempted to provide a "middle way" for Christian unity in the midst of 16th-c. religious division. He held that the Last* Supper celebration was properly understood as a daily "spiritual eating" by which faithful Christians are nourished on Christ's celestial flesh. He therefore called for a cessation of this ritual practice until all Christians once again lived together in peace. A mystical* spiritualist, he distinguished sharply between the written word and spiritual Word* of Scripture*, the visible and spiritual church, and emphasized the need for growth in Christian holiness (see Sanctification).

PETER C. ERB

Science and Christian Theology. The relationship between theology and the natural sciences depends on their respective definitions and on the worldview assumptions that underlie these definitions.

1. No-Contact Views. If one understands Christian theology to be an internal self-examination of the Christian faith* with reference to its distinctive views of God* and humanity, science is of no central importance for theology. No-contact views have been strong in 19th- to 20th-c. Protestant theologies. Schleiermacher*, the father of liberal* Protestantism, held that theology should elucidate the doctrine of creation* by excluding "every alien element," scientific or metaphysical (*The Christian Faith,* 1821–22). Likewise Barth*, the initiator of neo-orthodoxy, contended that theology should not submit itself to standards valid for other sciences, nor should scientific descriptions interfere with theological expositions of the Christian credo (*Church Dogmatics,* 1932). Similarly in Personalist* and existentialist* theologies, faith in the Word* of God entails an I–thou* relation distinct from the objective I–it relationships investigated by the sciences. In his program of demythologization*, Bultmann* argued that although faith is compatible with modern science, theology should explain Christian faith only with reference to constant features of human self-understanding. Within Wittgensteinian* programs of theology, Christian practices are likewise claimed to constitute specific "language games" that are distinct from scientific practices with their corresponding rules. Theology has one territory, the sciences another.

2. Contact Views. This territorial view is hard to maintain if God is the creator and sustainer of the world at large. Then inevitably the world of which theologians speak is also the object of scientific descriptions, although languages and perspectives may differ. Hence theology must accommodate nontheological descriptions of reality, including scientific theories prompted by the observation of data and subsequently tested by experiments (Wolfhart Pannenberg). In classical Roman Catholic theology, we find a hierarchical version of the contact view: God the Creator is the principle or universal cause (*causa prima*) of the universe, who then gives a certain independence to the workings of the secondary causes (*causae secundae*) within the created order. While these causes are investigated by the sciences, theology complements the scientific perspective with a teleological* one: God uses natural causality to implement divine intentions – hence the Thomistic* principle "Grace* does not abolish, but perfects nature*."

In modernity, however, theology is no longer the queen of the sciences. The order is reversed: Big Bang cosmology and Darwinian* evolution* (in their differing interpretations) provide the common foil for doctrines of creation and anthropology*. In the new dialogue* between theology and the sciences (initiated in the 1970s by Ian Barbour, Arthur Peacocke, John Polkinghorne, and others), critical realism* became the default position: there is but one world to which theology and the sciences can refer; no language can elucidate all aspects of reality in a one-to-one relation; yet both science and theology seek intimations of an endemically rich world. Critical realism exemplifies a contact view with ample space for mutual interactions between science and theology. Despite their similarities and differences in approach, science and theology both focus on the search for truth, or verisimilitude.

Other proponents of the dialogue are worried about critical realism's emphasis on reference and representation. The coherence model argues more modestly that science and religion meet horizontally rather than in putative objects "out there" (world or God). Both science and theology include hypotheses about reality, yet the only accessible criterion of truth lies in the respective integration of relevant data into a coherent whole. The goal of the dialogue is thus to reach the highest possible cognitive equilibrium between theological contents and established results of science.

This dialogue may take place at different levels: (1) data (e.g. fossil records), (2) theories (e.g. Darwinian evolution), (3) modes of thinking (e.g. relational thinking), (4) metaphors and bridging concepts (e.g. "field" or "law and contingency"), and (5) worldview assumptions (e.g. determinism vs. indeterminism; naturalism vs. theism). Science is expected to have epistemic priority on levels (1) and (2). Under the constraints of science, theology therefore has to accept serious revisions. For example, there would be no Adam* and Eve* 6,000 years ago, and hence no explanation of natural evil* on the basis human sinning* and no harmonious divine design of the world of biology. At levels (3)–(5), however, theology may become a more active partner in the dialogue. It may both adopt scientific modes of thinking (e.g. evolutionary thinking) and be critical of specific scientific worldview assumptions (e.g. a closed universe).

From this perspective, the task of theology is to offer re-descriptions of a world already described and (partially) explained by the sciences. According to the coherence model, however, theology cannot resort to authoritarian thinking; the dialogue requires philosophical mediation. For example, a core theological assumption is that God is the author of the laws of nature (not their competitor). How, then, should one conceive of continuous divine action throughout the history of the universe? Divine actions would be more coherent with science if laws of nature emerge in time (rather than being flatly eternal), if laws of nature describe the habits of nature (rather than being strictly prescriptive), and if the statistical laws of quantum mechanics imply a structural openness of physics (rather than a closed deterministic system). Then divine creativity can be maintained by presupposing laws of nature without violating them (rather than remaining in painful tension). Similarly, a theological anthropology is more plausible if the emergence of intelligent life builds on a general evolutionary propensity toward complexification and self-directed agency (rather than humanity being an accidental by product of evolution). Here a number of sciences become relevant to theology: not only the fundamental sciences of physics and (bio)chemistry, but also historical disciplines (e.g. geology, paleontology, paleoanthropology) and the sciences of complexity dealing with vast interconnected systems (e.g. astronomy, meteorology, ecology).

A third area of contact, apart from ontology and interpretation, is ethics*. Both science and religion are cultural forces that both interpret and transform the world. Concerns of research ethics, as well as of bioethics and ecological ethics, bring theology into dialogue with other sciences, such as medicine, applied genomics, ecology, and the many technical sciences. Alongside philosophy and the human sciences, theology is a source of information about ethical and practical issues.

3. Monistic Views. Apart from the independence and contact view, we find various monistic approaches. Some seek a synthesis of science and theology.

Teilhard* de Chardin's "Omega theory" of evolution exemplifies a theological synthesis encapsulated in a grand-scale religious interpretation of evolution; holistic religious approaches are similarly popular in New* Age circles. Followers of Whitehead's* process* philosophy exemplify a synthesis based on a philosophical metaphysics that includes a philosophical theology.

Scientific expansionists, by contrast, opt for a science-alone approach. Scientism entails the worldview that science is the only and self-sufficient source of reliable information about reality. Some representatives broaden the definition of science to include ethical and aesthetic* dimensions (e.g. E. O. Wilson's program of a "consilience" of knowledge). Other proponents claim that science is the only valid source of information about reality, while admitting that religion, like poetry, may have a legitimacy in the celebration of the natural wonders of nature (religious naturalism).

Finally, religious expansionists take a Christianity-alone view of reality, presupposing stark conflicts between science and religion, as normally defined. Examples are the young-earth creationism* of the Fundamentalist* Movement, which asserts the geological and historical inerrancy of the biblical creation stories or the more philosophically attuned Intelligent Design Movement.

NIELS HENRIK GREGERSEN

Scofield Reference Bible. See BIBLE TRANSLATIONS CLUSTER; DISPENSATIONALISM.

Scopes Trial, sometimes known as "the Monkey Trial," in Dayton, Tennessee (July 1925), the most famous court case occasioned by the teaching of evolution* in the USA. John T. Scopes was found guilty of violating a law (the Butler Act) that prohibited the teaching of Darwin's* theory in the public schools of Tennessee and fined $100. Scopes's conviction was, however, overturned on a technicality. The public prosecutors in Tennessee made no further effort to enforce the provisions of the Butler Act (repealed in 1967). Nevertheless, the court proceedings attracted national attention in part because two famous public figures – Clarence Darrow for the defense and William Jennings Bryan for the prosecution – took part in the trial. Bryan died five days after the trial and came to be seen by some fundamentalists* as a martyr in the crusade against evolution. Many educated North Americans, however, regarded the proceedings in Dayton as an atavistic embarrassment. For many the Scopes Trial highlighted the connections between fundamentalism and anti-intellectualism.

DAVID HARRINGTON WATT

Scotism. See DUNS SCOTUS, JOHN.

Scotland, Church of. The Church of Scotland, a Reformed* Church, is the largest denomination and faith group in Scotland (c500,000 professed members plus baptized children and nonprofessed adult adherents). Reformed by John Knox* and others in the Calvinist tradition (c1560), its polity* was further developed by Andrew Melville (c1590). The 17th c. was dominated by struggles over state control with the Anglican monarchy after the union of crowns (1603, King James* VI/I); the resistance was partly inspired by federal Calvinist thought, which led to the signing of the National* Covenant (1638) and the ensuing Wars of the Covenant. In the British colonial era, the Church was responsible for extensive evangelism and church planting throughout the British Empire. The modern solution to the problem of the church*–state relationship was enshrined in a 1921 constitutional document (the Articles Declaratory) recognized in civil law, providing a separate church jurisdiction for spiritual matters. In the 20th c. the Church of Scotland declined in strength in the context of British secularization* and increased Roman Catholic strength in Scotland.

The Church holds the Scriptures* of the OT and NT (but not the Apocrypha*) as the supreme rule of faith and life, and maintains the Westminster* Confession of Faith as its subordinate standard, but with great variation in adherence to its terms. The denomination has broad theological diversity within the Reformed tradition; only a minority of its most conservative ministers and members would adhere to a recognizably Calvinist or federal* theological tradition. The Church includes proponents of different approaches to scriptural interpretation, and debates on matters of personal, social*, and political ethics are often significant in its corporate life. The Church is a full member of the World* Council of Churches, the World* Alliance of Reformed Churches, and the Conference of European Churches, as well as of national ecumenical organizations.

Worship is mainly preaching*-based, with a variety of attitudes toward the proper frequency of Holy Communion*. Baptism* was historically administered to infants, and this remains the principal practice, although many adult members are now baptized at the point of profession of faith. Praise includes hymns and choruses, but most congregations continue a tradition of singing metrical Psalms. As a Reformed Church, it has no cult of place and no significant "Holiness*" tradition as found in other Protestant traditions.

With its view of itself as a national institution, the Church of Scotland engages national and international issues at an institutional level, although, locally, congregational activity is more likely to focus on the immediate parish community and on partnership between the congregation and projects abroad. The Church always had a strong focus on issues of its own governance and on the Reformed model of decision making by tiered courts consisting of ministers of Word and sacrament, professional deacons, and local elders, all of whom are ordained and any of whom, since the 1960s, can be women. In ascending order of superiority, the Kirk Session (congregation and parish authority), Presbytery (regional), and General Assembly (national) administer the law of the Church, comprising common law and legislation. There is constant debate about, and adjustment of, the jurisdictional extent of the Church's authority (subject to no control by civil law) in four traditional areas: worship, doctrine, discipline, and Church government.

The Church of Scotland remains a significant institution in the life of the Scottish nation, with extensive social capital in local community work and high visibility in national debate. It remains overwhelmingly the denomination providing the ordinances of religion to those who profess Christian adherence without Church membership. Its missionary activity leaves a legacy of Presbyterian churches throughout the English-speaking world, all now self-governing but recognizing their historical connection with their parent denomination. **See also UNITED KINGDOM.** MARJORY A. MACLEAN

Scotland, Free Church of. The Free Church of Scotland came into being on May 18, 1843, when some 400 ministers walked out of the General Assembly of the Church of Scotland* and hours later constituted themselves as the Church of Scotland *Free*.

The "freedom" was very specific: freedom from state control. The roots of the problem lay in the 1712 Patronage Act, in which the UK Parliament invested in local "heritors" (usually landowners) the right to choose parish ministers, even in defiance of the wishes of parishioners. The Patronage Act bred instant and lingering resentment, with serious opposition arising in the mid-19th c., when the Evangelical revival* prompted a movement for spiritual independence. During the "Ten Years' Conflict" (1833–43), it became clear that so long as the Church remained established, it would be subject to interference by the state. This was a price Evangelical leaders were no longer prepared to pay. The result was "the Disruption" of 1843:

not a disruption of the Church, but a disruption of the Church–state partnership.

The new Church, enjoying popular support, proceeded to build hundreds of churches, establish three fully staffed theological colleges, set up a nationwide network of schools, and plant mission churches in every continent. In 1863 union negotiations began between the Free Church and the United Presbyterian Church. To facilitate this union, the Free Church radically altered its relation to the Westminster* Confession. Instead of subscribing to "the whole doctrine," ordinands now subscribed only to "the substance of the faith." Union took place on these terms in 1900, creating a denomination of half a million members, the United Free Church of Scotland. However, 26 Free Church ministers and some 40,000 people refused to enter the union, arguing that the new terms of subscription opened the door to unlimited theological pluralism and created an entirely different church. Unfortunately, but inevitably, the union was followed by litigation. In 1904 the House of Lords found in favor of the minority and declared it to be the legal Free Church.

In 2000 the Free Church of Scotland had 180 congregations served by 125 ministers. It operated a youth program, maintained a theological college offering validated degrees, and supported international missions in South Africa, India, Colombia, and Peru.

Theologically, it adheres to the Westminster Confession; liturgically, it practices exclusive psalmody; ecumenically, it is linked to the International Conference of Reformed Churches; ideologically, it remains rigidly conservative on such issues as homosexuality* and women's* ordination. DONALD MACLEOD

Scotus, John Duns. See DUNS SCOTUS, JOHN.

Scribes, in the Hebrew tradition, interpreters of Torah whose teachings came to be transmitted orally in conjunction with the written text; later deemed authoritative among some Jewish sects (e.g. Pharisees*); eventually codified into Mishnah* and Talmud*. The NT frequently portrays scribes teaming with Pharisees in disputes against Jesus.

More generally, scribes manually reproduced personal or official documents, including sacred texts. Recent scholarship on the work of Christian scribes has shown that various social and historical influences, including early Christological controversies, anti-Judaic bias, and apologetic interests, appear to have led them to modify their exemplars (the manuscript from which they copied) and thus the transmitted NT text.

WAYNE C. KANNADAY

Scriptural Criticism, critical study of the Bible* as Scripture*, i.e. as read by believers for whom it is a Word-to-live-by. Reception* studies of Scripture (*Wirkungsgeschichte*) show that any scriptural interpretation has a threefold frame, reflecting three kinds of interpretive choices: (1) a textual choice of certain features of the text as most significant; (2) a hermeneutical* choice of a set of theological issues raised in dialogue with the biblical text, because of readers' positive or negative concerns arising from religious experiences and convictions; (3) a contextual choice of a set of pragmatic* issues raised in dialogue with the biblical text, because readers' life contexts must be ethically assessed in terms of their practical consequences.

The history of scholarship shows that, despite claims to the contrary, critical biblical scholars themselves always make these three interpretive choices. By choosing a method, they choose to view certain textual features as most significant; by striving (consciously or not) to demonstrate that believers' interpretations are biased and providing alternatives, they make hermeneutical and contextual choices: there is no exegesis* without preunderstanding. These interpretive choices are quite visible when one compares, e.g., the sharply distinct scholarly interpretations of Paul (see Paul the Apostle).

Most readers of the Bible are not aware they have made such interpretive choices. As a pedagogical tool, scriptural criticism helps these readers to recognize that there are alternative interpretive choices, putting them in a position to assume responsibility for their own choices of interpretation and how they affect others. For exegetes scriptural criticism brings the different kinds of "advocacy readings" (e.g. feminist* or postcolonialist* Bible* interpretations) on a par with other scholarly readings. It also highlights the close formal similarities between scholarly and religious interpretations and offers the possibility of scholarly clarity in the process of exegesis seen within this (inevitable) context. **See also BIBLE INTERPRETATION CLUSTER; SCRIPTURE; SEMIOTICS AND THE STUDY OF CHRISTIANITY.**

DANIEL PATTE and CRISTINA GRENHOLM

Scripture. By saying that the Bible is Scripture, Christians affirm that this collection of texts (see Canon) is the Word* of God, the rule of faith* (*regula* fidei*) and life, or more specifically a

"Word-to-live-by" that speaks to them as individuals and/or religious communities in specific domains of their lives, including their most intimate and private experiences, and their familial, liturgical, social, cultural, political, and universal life contexts.

Biblical texts are received as authoritative Words-to-live-by because they are viewed as having divine origin. Thus most Christians affirm that Scripture is "inspired" (originating from the Spirit*), written by persons "inspired" by God or the Spirit – prophets*, apostles*, sages, and teachers (e.g. 2 Tim 3:16; 2 Pet 1:21). For Jesus, according to the Gospels, Scripture is the Word of God (Matt 22:31), the Word of the Father (John 5:33–41), and inspired by the Spirit (Matt 22:43); the authority of Scripture is such that "not one letter, not one stroke of a letter, will pass from the law until all is accomplished" (Matt 5:18; see also Luke 24:44); it is "bread" with which believers should nourish themselves (Matt 4:3–11). Yet there have been disagreements regarding which books are "inspired" and thus are parts of the canon* of Scripture; whether Scripture has a unique authority* (for those following the Protestant Reformation) or an authority shared with the church and its councils and the pope (Roman Catholic Church) or shared with Holy Tradition* (Orthodox churches; see Patristic Thought in Orthodox Christianity); whether the Bible *is* the Word of God or contains or conveys it; whether the Bible is inspired and thus infallible* in all aspects (including scientific and historical statements) or only in matters affecting the human relationship with God; and whether the Bible as inspired should be understood as inspiring believers.

Christian views of the Bible as Scripture vary according to three equally important factors: (1) believers' convictions* about God's* role in human affairs and in these texts, (2) their reading/hearing of the biblical texts, and (3) their perception of those aspects of their lives that require a Word-to-live-by. Rather than being prescriptive (from an orthodox* doctrinal perspective or from that of an orthopraxy* regarding the way of relating Scripture and life), it is possible to make sense of the numerous debates about the authority of Scriptures by describing (using a phenomenological* approach) some of the roles that Scriptures play for believers, as summarized by common metaphors.

As *lamp to my feet* and *light for my path* (Ps 119:105), Scripture provides (individual) believers with knowledge of what is good and evil, a sense of direction for their lives, and thus also doctrinal instructions.

As *rule of the community* for assessing behavior, Scripture provides the community of believers with knowledge of God's will and shapes believers' moral life, so that the community/church might fulfill its mission.

Both of the preceding uses of Scripture are based on the position that believers search Scripture for inspired (moral and doctrinal) "knowledge"; the inspired, infallible Word is identified with the "content" of the text ("what the text says"). These roles of Scripture are most common in the North Atlantic world, so much so that they are often taken to be the only ones or "the" literal readings of biblical texts. But they are not.

As *good news* or as *warning* (as rule of the community can also be), Scripture motivates believers to do God's will in response either to the good news of God's love or to threats of punishment. Thus the inspired, infallible Word is the motivation "conveyed" by the text (rather than the knowledge of God's will).

As *book of the covenant* (testament), Scripture conveys to the community of believers a vision of their identity and vocation as members of God's people; by entering the story of God's people, believers participate in this story and gain a true sense of relationship to others, the world, and to God.

As *corrective lens* and *prophecy being fulfilled*, Scripture conveys to the community of believers a vision of God's interventions in their present life experiences; believers can recognize that the Scriptures are fulfilled (a role of Scripture strongly emphasized by the Gospels and Paul).

As *empowering Word*, Scripture is a performative* word through which powerless people are transformed and empowered to be agents of the Kingdom (as the poor are in the Beatitudes*).

As *Holy Bible*, Scripture is itself a divine manifestation; the encounter with the holy through Scripture iconoclastically* shatters believers' previous convictions. Scripture is sacramental* (e.g. as in mystical* readings and in the Orthodox tradition; see Bible Interpretation Cluster: In Eastern Orthodoxy).

Each time Christian believers read Scripture, they adopt one or another of these views of the role of Scripture to the exclusion of other views, although in other life contexts the same believers might make other choices. Disputes readily erupt over the authority of Scripture among believers – who accuse each other of neglecting or denying the authority of Scripture – when they do not recognize the diversity of roles that Scripture can play as a Word-to-live-by for believers in different life contexts.

DANIEL PATTE

Scripture Principle, the Protestant insistence that the Bible, or the Word* of God conveyed through Scripture*, is the supreme authority for faith* and practice (*sola scriptura*, "by Scripture alone"). While the historic creeds* and confessions* of the church are honored, they are regarded as interpretations of what is taught more authoritatively in Scripture. The Reformed* churches stemming from Zwingli* and Calvin* adopted what has been called the "negative Scripture principle": nothing is to be believed or done that is not explicitly taught in Scripture. Other Protestants tolerated devotional or liturgical* practices that were not found in Scripture so long as they did not contradict it. **See also PROTESTANT PRINCIPLE; TRADITION CLUSTER.**

Seal of Confession (the) prohibits, upon pain of automatic excommunication, a confessor from betraying a penitent in any way for any reason (1983 *Codex* Iuris Canonici* 983, 1388). Absolution need not have been conferred for the seal to apply; disclosure need not be express to qualify as betrayal. Can penitents release confessors from the seal? This is disputed. The safer, minority opinion is that they cannot. Others who might come into confessional knowledge are bound not to disclose such information, but their obligation is rooted in natural*, not divine, law. The seal of confession does not apply to other kinds of communications, but obligations of confidentiality might still arise.

EDWARD N. PETERS

Sebastian, St (d c288), martyr* said to have been killed during Diocletian's* persecutions*. Ambrose* mentioned in a sermon that he was from Milan and was venerated there as a saint*. Sebastian is commonly depicted in art and literature as having been shot with arrows.

Second Coming of Christ, term used for Christ's coming at the Parousia* (e.g. 1 Thess 2:19, 3:13). When the term "coming" (Lat *adventus*, "arrival,") was also applied to his incarnation*, the Parousia became the "Second Coming." The season of Advent* both celebrates the first coming and awaits the second. **See also ESCHATOLOGY CLUSTER; MILLENNIALISM CLUSTER.**

Sect (Lat *sequor*, "follow"; etymologically similar to "heresy*" in Gk), group of persons who adhere to definite beliefs and practices and form a distinct organization. The term can be used for any religious denomination*, but it has come to apply to zealous groups separated from major churches; the term "cult"* usually connotes a smaller group with more unusual beliefs. In sociology*, "sectarian" movements are those that, in a given historical context, adopt stricter ideals and ways of life than the mainline churches; many major movements and denominations started as sectarian movements in Christian history.

Secular Arm, medieval term in the West* for government. Unlike the church, it used coercive means, yet it was understood to be one part of the *corpus christianum*.

Secular Clergy. Unlike regular* clergy, members of religious* orders who live according to a rule*, secular clergy are priests who live according to the customs of the culture* of which they are a part.

Secular Institutes, Roman Catholic, since 1947, have given laypeople the opportunity to consecrate their secular way of life (in the world), under the three vows of poverty*, celibate* chastity*, and obedience, following a rule*, usually inspired by a religious* order.

Secularism and Secularization, terms in Western Europe and in the former colonies of France, Spain, and Portugal (where the term "laicization*" is also used) referring to movements, starting with Voltaire and the French Revolution, and laws that sought to implement anticlericalism* in social life through a strict separation of church and state, especially by transferring responsibilities for education* and other civic roles (e.g. registration of birth, marriage, death; burials) from the state* church (usually Roman Catholic) to the secular state, so as to avoid religious interference in social life. (For the cultural movement, see Secularization and Desecularization in Europe and North America.) **See also ANTICLERICALISM; LAICIZATION.**

Secularization and Desecularization in Europe and North America.

The Secularization Thesis. Max Weber* (1918) described modern society as a disenchanted world where the supernatural and mysteries* of transcendence have no meaningful place: as societies modernize, the social* significance of religion* diminishes. Since

Secularization and Desecularization

secularization theorists have focused their analysis largely on modern Western societies, particularly Europe, "religion" usually refers to Christianity and the institutional church. The "loss of social significance" is taken to mean both a decline in the power and influence religion has over social organization, and the decreasing salience, plausibility, and usefulness of traditional religious beliefs and practices for the majority of people in their daily lives.

Secularization theorists suggest that this uneasy relationship between religion and modernity results from a number of socio-historical factors, especially the processes of rationalization and the fragmentation of community. Rationalization is part of the progressive urge of modernization to harness and control the world so that life might become more predictable, productive, and efficient. Rationalization challenges tradition* to the extent that beliefs and practices are continually under review, judged according to their utility and effectiveness. This posed problems for the church, because much of its organization and authority* relied on tradition. As the processes of rationalization took hold in early modernity, particularly in the development of science* from the Enlightenment* onward, the church had to confront not only doubts* about specific teachings, but a change in how people thought about the world. It became possible first to query the religious worldview and then to explain the world* in its own terms, without any reference to a divine order. Although the Enlightenment was important for accelerating rationalization, secularization theorists have, ironically, argued that rationalization has been an inherent part of the history of Christianity itself, most notably in the Protestant Reformation. By stripping down ritual* to a minimum, Protestantism* took much of the mystery* out of religion. Moreover, by giving people more freedom to read and interpret Scripture* for themselves, Protestantism contributed to the individualization of beliefs and practices, which further attenuated the church's authority.

Rationalization forms a central theme in the Weberian analysis of secularization. A more Durkheimian* perspective highlights the significance of the fragmentation of social organization that arose as new technologies came into operation and society moved from small, close-knit, agricultural communities to large industrialized urban centers where economic production was divided into discrete functions and specialist institutions took over some of the social* responsibilities the church had previously fulfilled. More significantly, the church's role in integrating, celebrating, and marking communal life was undermined to some extent. Social differentiation left neighbors with less in common, and the maintenance of social order gradually moved away from reliance on shared faith* and common values to a shared recognition of mutual dependence and the operation of rational bureaucratic institutions and impersonal legal systems of the nation-state.

Secularization in Europe. Empirically there is little doubt that if Christianity and the church are taken as the focal point, there is a trend toward secularization in Europe. All the main indicators show that there is less interest and involvement in Christianity than there has been in past. Church membership and attendance have declined (particularly since the 1960s) and continue to do so. Fewer people hold traditional Christian beliefs, and for those who do such beliefs appear to make little impact on daily life. But Christian practices and, especially, beliefs are more robust than secularization theorists first predicted and are far from disappearing altogether, especially among the female population. The European Values Survey for 1999–2000 suggests that about a third of Western Europeans still attend church at least once a month, while a little more than three-quarters believe in God*, approximately half in heaven* and life after death*, and a third in hell*. The British sociologist Grace Davie characterizes the overall nature of religious belief and practice in Western Europe as "vicarious": most people like to know that the church is there and available to them should they need it, but otherwise are happy to let a minority maintain the tradition on their behalf. The fact that European culture is still steeped in its Christian past helps preserve the Christian memory*, and the significance of Christianity is further bolstered by the various links that have emerged between church* and state throughout European history. The secularization process in Europe is therefore far from complete. There are also considerable differences across the Continent.

In Western Europe, for example, the Protestant countries in the north tend to be less overtly religious than the Roman Catholic countries farther south. More precisely, while the Lutheran Church in the Nordic countries has benefited from close state ties, and religious identification remains high (and linked to national identity), church attendance is considerably lower than the European average. This contrasts with the Roman Catholic countries in Southern Europe (and the Republic of Ireland*), where levels of belief and practice remain reasonably high. Church attendance, however, is declining and there is a degree of anticlericalism that is not apparent in the north. An exception to countries with a relative endurance of faith among Roman Catholic populations is France*, where church attendance is particularly low. The French state is explicitly secular, and religion is not taught in state schools. This has meant the Christian memory is not easily passed from one generation to the next and consequently is atrophying at a fast rate. Though less severe elsewhere, the problem of transmitting faith from one generation to another is apparent throughout Europe.

In between the Protestant north and Catholic south are the countries where denominational affiliation is more equally balanced (notably the Netherlands* and Germany*). These countries display levels of belief and belonging midway between the northern and southern countries, but more people believe than actively belong.

In Eastern Europe, the secularization trend is complicated by the fact that, for a large part of the 20th c., many of these countries were influenced by the secular ideology* of communism*, which expressly sought to limit the church's potential for social significance. Church movements were therefore either marginalized or driven underground. The effects of this can be seen in the low levels of religiosity in, e.g., the former East German region and the Czech* Republic. A rather different reaction to this secularizing trajectory, however, can be found in Poland*, where the Roman Catholic Church played an important part in the eventual overthrow of the Communist regime (late 1980s). Catholic identity and Polish identity merged, each protecting the other. (For Eastern Europe, see Church and State Relations Cluster: In Europe: Orthodox Perspective; Gospel and Culture Cluster: In Eastern Europe; History of Christianity Cluster: In Europe: Eastern Europe.)

Secularization in North America. The USA is one of the world's most modern societies and yet, on all the standard measures, it turns out to be far more religious (Christian) than Europe, particularly in the southern and central "Bible Belt" (less so in the north and toward the coasts). Yet it is unclear exactly how much more religiously inclined North Americans are compared with Europeans; indeed, there is some evidence that secularization is also occurring in the USA, albeit at a slower rate than in Europe. (Canada lies somewhere between the two, although Quebec* is highly secularized.) Nevertheless, it is still regarded as a "good thing" for individuals to be seen as churchgoers in the USA, and while the state is essentially a secular institution, religious (Christian) language still features in political rhetoric, and vocal, religiously and politically conservative social movements (such as the New Christian Right) keep traditional Christian beliefs and values in the public domain.

The reason North America has maintained its Christian identity to a greater extent than Europe is a matter of debate. One important explanation draws on rational choice theory, according to which religion enables people to meet inherent psychological and emotional needs that cannot be met in any other way. Free of the constraints of a specific state*–church relationship, the USA allows for a greater degree of religious diversity by way of immigration and religious innovation, both of which have ensured that people have had enough religious choice to maintain their preferences of religious expression; hence religion remains relevant and its presence strong.

Desecularization. Rational choice theory is contested, but it raises interesting questions about the importance of religious diversity as a means of countering secularization. Furthermore, although traditional expressions of Christianity may be receding in the public sphere, it is becoming increasingly apparent in both the USA and Europe, that "new" or "renewed" forms of religious expression are developing. Some theorists have even argued that modernity has reached a point (sometimes called postmodernity*) where the conditions are set for a process of *desecularization*.

This changing face of religion in North America and Europe has three main facets. The first relates to an increase in the population of minority religious communities through natural growth and immigration. Islam in particular has a growing presence. Converts from Christianity, however, are still relatively rare. The second is a turn toward more conservative forms of religious expression within both Christianity and other world faiths. Sociological explanations for this include people's need for certainty in an increasingly uncertain world and the use of religion to articulate distinctive ethnic identities. Conservative religious groups tend to be more vocal than liberal ones and at the very least raise popular awareness of religion. Moreover, since 9/11 it has been clear that radical Islam potentially has considerable social significance for North America and Europe. In terms of the reestablishment of ethnic identity, the current interest in Orthodox* Christianity in parts of the former Soviet countries of Eastern Europe can also be noted. The third facet of religious diversification is a growing interest in personal spirituality* – a potential "spiritual revolution" (at least in Britain), according to sociologists Paul Heelas and Linda Woodhead. The continuing decline of traditional institutional Christianity appears to have made room for the rise of "new" forms of spiritual expression that focus primarily on the development of the inner self and healing and emphasize the experiential and emotional sides of spirituality over doctrinal "truths." An important characteristic of the spiritual revolution is that it eschews institutional organization. Individuals are the authors of their own spiritual identity and expression, free to choose from a range of spiritual traditions – in line with the modern consumer ethos. Spirituality becomes a matter of personal choice rather than of public obligation. Sources of spirituality in this sphere are diverse, ranging from Eastern religions and Western psychology to pre-Christian folk religions and cosmologies of ancient civilizations – yoga, reiki, crystology, astrology, Wicca, and paganism, to name but a few. Such practices are sometimes brought together under the broad heading of "New* Age" or Heelas and Woodhead's term, the "holistic milieu."

How socially significant are these new forms of spirituality? Do they constitute a desecularization of Europe and North America? It is uncertain. At present New Age is favored by a minority of middle-aged, middle-class women, many of whom were influenced by the 1960s–1970s counterculture. There is little evidence in either Europe or North America that New Age is of much interest to young people. That said, in the early 21st c. spirituality in its various forms has given rise to a growing and significant market in self-improvement books and magazines; it is in vogue in popular entertainment and the leisure industries; and the language of spirituality has appeared in mainstream health care (especially in the UK).Where does this leave us? Europe, to use Davie's phrase, seems to be an "exceptional case" in the extent of its secularization, at last in comparison with North America and the rest of the world. It is true that modernity appears to sit uneasily alongside certain forms of traditional religion, but that is by no means the whole story. Religions*, including Christianity, are flexible – they can and do evolve. Only time will tell what forms of Christianity will flourish in the rest of the 21st c. What shape will Christianity take in Western Europe and North America as Christian memory mutates into private forms of spirituality, and as the Charismatic* Movement and developing "independent*" churches diversely emphasize individual experience, emotion, healing, personal choice, and suspicion of institutional organization? (For examples, see France; Uruguay.)

SYLVIA COLLINS-MAYO

See (Holy See, Episcopal See, Patriarchal See) designates (1) the seat (Lat *sedes*) from which authoritative teaching is given; (2) the authority figure on the seat: the pope* (on the Holy See), patriarch*, archbishop, or bishop; (3) the location of the seat: and (4) the assisting bodies of the authority.

Seleucia, Council of. See ARIMINUM AND SELEUCEIA, COUNCILS OF.

Self-control (Gk *enkrateia*; Lat *continentia*). In Greek philosophy, control of the passions was highly desirable among public figures. Aristotle* thought that self-control, which involves an inward struggle, was inferior to habit*, by which one spontaneously does what is good. In the NT, the word and its cognates are sometimes used with philosophical generality (Acts 24:25; Tit 1:8; 2 Pet 1:6; Gal 5:23) and are sometimes used to refer to the control of desire (1 Cor 7:9). The latter became the usual meaning among Christians, for whom sexual discipline and asceticism* were of major importance. Christians whose ascetic practices seemed extreme were called "encratites*" (see Tatian).

Self-definition, Christian. See HELLENISTIC RELIGIOUS TRADITIONS AND CHRISTIANITY'S SELF-DEFINITION.

Semi-Arianism, a movement, named by Epiphanius*, that arose in opposition to Arianism*. Semi-Arianism, or more accurately "homoiousianism*," was developed by George* of Laodicea and Basil* of Ancyra (358–60): the Son is "like in being" to the Father. Its emphasis on God's threeness was harmonized with the Nicenes' emphasis on unity, producing the orthodox doctrine: God is one nature in three persons. **See also ARIANISM.**

Semiotics and the Study of Christianity. Semiotics (Gk *semeiotikos*, an interpreter of symptoms and signs), the study of *sign*-communication and of *sign*ification (the production of meaning) provides theoretical models for understanding (1) sacraments* and religious symbolism and (2) the ongoing inculturation* of Christianity in a plurality of social, cultural, and religious contexts.

1. Sacraments, Religious Symbolism, and Signs. Communication through signs and the relationship of signs to the world were already concerns of Plato* and Aristotle*. Augustine* wrote of *signum* as the universal means of communication and examined the relationship between natural signs (symptoms, e.g. in medicine) and human-made signs (language and other cultural artifacts). Augustine pondered consistent symbol* systems (which presume connections between individual, community, and ultimate reality) and sacraments* ("sacred signs") as ritual acts in which material signs (e.g. water, bread, wine, oil) are bearers of grace* and divine presence. As a metaphor* suggests that two unlike "things" are actually the same despite their strong incongruity, Augustine, following Aristotle, maintained the intrinsic relation between sign/symptom and the signified; although the material signs (words of different languages) vary, they refer to the same concept for all humans. This symbolic understanding of sign is most helpful for theology as a discourse about a mystery, God who transcends human language.

2. General Semiotic Theories and the Study of Christianity. General semiotic theories seek to account for the overall signification process, because a sign is always also part of a signification process, as Augustine emphasized: "A sign is something that shows itself to the senses and something other than itself to the mind." Augustine's triadic view of sign provided the framework for semiotic reflections and its implications in logic from Boethius* (5th–6th c.) to Anselm* of Canterbury and Abelard* (11th c.), later Scholastics*, Bacon*, John Duns* Scotus (13th c.), and, following them, Charles Sanders Peirce (1839–1914), who further explored the implications of this triadic definition of sign for logic, pragmatism, and communication.

Peirce and the linguist Ferdinand de Saussure (1857–1913) initiated modern semiotics. For Saussure, a sign is the *arbitrary* (not intrinsic) relation of a signifier (e.g. the four letters and uttered sounds in "tree" or five letters and sounds in *arbre*) and a signified (the similar but not identical mental concept of the reality "tree"). Thus Saussure challenged the universalist view of the signified (all humans have the same signified concept) posited from Aristotle and Augustine to the Enlightenment* (when cultural diversity was viewed as being transcended in an intelligible realm).

From Saussure's perspective, any theological discourse (creeds, sermons, church doctrine, set of personal beliefs) or Christian practice (liturgy, prayer, family life, community life, social and political involvement) is a semiotic system through which Christians make sense of their lives as Christian participants in a culture*, characterized by a series of semiotic systems, including specific languages. Thus an understanding of Christianity depends not only on abstract concepts and theories about the divine, but also and primarily on its concrete, everyday involvement at all levels of social interactions and communications and in concrete religious practices, including the use and reception* of symbols, rituals, and beliefs in the semiotic systems that shape its life. Thus traditional theological and biblical studies must be complemented by the study of the conflicted daily practices of the Christian masses throughout history and today in different cultural settings.

The question is: how does one proceed with such a study? Semiotics provides methodological tools by exploring further the implications of the triadic character of sign: a sign is always a sign *of* something *to* some mind. Beyond Peirce, for the linguist Charles W. Morris, this triad refers to three aspects of linguistic communication: syntax, semantics, and pragmatics. Saussure's followers, including Louis Hjelmslev, Roland Barthes, Umberto Eco, and A. J. Greimas, broadened the application of this triadic view of communication to any semiotic system.

Thus, for Greimas, any semiotic system is characterized by three kinds of structure. For instance, in a narrative as semiotic system one can distinguish (1) the "narrative syntax," the plot and the interactions of the characters in time and space; (2) the "narrative semantics," the convictional* value system that spontaneously distinguishes between what is euphoric and dysphoric, real and illusory (this value system frames the perception of the narrative syntax); and (3) the "discursive structure" through which the storyteller pragmatically addressing an audience (with a different perspective) seeks to "make realistic" for this audience the narrative plot and characters and to "make sensible" the value system posited by the narrative (by constructing through the analogical* imagination a symbolic system).

Beyond its complexity, this semiotic structure (found in all semiotic systems) provides a simple general model for the study of all aspects of Christianity – e.g. theological concepts, liturgical, community, and social* practices, Scriptures and traditions, figures, movements, and sacred spaces (hierotopy*). From a semiotic perspective, one can anticipate that there exist several understandings of any given theological concept (e.g. Christ*) throughout history and across cultures because, implicitly or explicitly, each of these understandings is the result of a hermeneutical process through which three variable components are interpreted in terms of each other: (1) a tradition viewed as authoritative by the interpreters (e.g. a biblical story, a teaching by Augustine; *narrative syntax*), (2) the interpreters' religious, theological, or ethical concerns (*narrative semantics*), and (3) the interpreters' pragmatic concerns for people's needs in specific cultures and life contexts (*discursive structure*). From a semiotic perspective, this plurality is not problematic; without this inculturation*, the given theological concept would be meaningless for Christian believers beyond the original context in which it was formulated. **See also SCRIPTURAL CRITICISM.**

DANIEL PATTE

Semi-Pelagianism, the name later given to the movement led by John Cassian* and Vincent* of Lérins. While they did not deny the role of grace* and condemned Pelagianism*, they insisted on a role for human freedom*, specifically at the "beginning of faith." Prosper* of Aquitaine reported their views to Augustine*, whose last treatises were directed against them. The position continued to be held in Gaul, especially by Faustus* of Riez (c472). It came under attack in the early 6th c. and was condemned at the Council of Orange* (529).

Senegal. This former West African French colony is known for its religious and political stability. In 1960 Léopold Sédar Senghor, a practicing Roman Catholic, was elected the first president by 90% of the Muslim community and the African* religionists (6.2%). More than 65% of Muslim students attended Catholic schools, and many Muslim elders were active members of groups called "Friends of the Christians." This stability continued well after Senghor's resignation in 1981.

Christianity was established as early as 1763. Modern Roman Catholic mission was pioneered by Mother Javouhey (Anne Mary Javouhey, 1779–1851; canonized, 1961), founder of the Congregation of St. Joseph of Cluny. She sent her first sisters to take charge of hospitals in St. Louis and Gorée (1819). She started a society dedicated to pastoral assistance among local people and to the formation of an indigenous clergy (1822). She believed that "civilization must go together with Christianity in the conversion of Africa." In 1840 six African priests were ordained in a seminary founded (1836) by Fr. Baradère, then apostolic prefect. A Carmelite convent was built (1953) beside the existing Grand Séminaire Libermann, then the Benedictine monastery Keur Moussa (1963).

Christians in Senegal are found among the Serer, Diola, and Wolof peoples. After the Second Vatican* Council, the liturgy was inculturated; it was practiced in the Serer, Diola, and Wolof languages using some of their symbols, ritual gestures, and musical instruments. Until 1970 the development of this Christian community was slow, as the Islamic presence (88%) left little room for evangelization. Since 1970 the number of Protestants and Charismatics* has rapidly increased. In recognition of the prominence of the Roman Catholic Church in Senegal, Pope Paul VI made Hyacinthe Thiandoum the archbishop of Dakar (since 1960) and a cardinal (1976). The archbishop was the president of the Regional Episcopal Conference of Francophone West Africa.

Statistics: Population (2000): 9.5 million (M). Christians, 523,000, 5.5% (Roman Catholics, 441,000; independents, 14,000; Protestants, 10,000); Muslims, 8.3 M, 88%; African Religionists, 592,000, 6.2%. (Based on *World Christian Encyclopedia*, 2001.)

VALENTIN DEDJI

Sentences, Books of, compilations of doctrinal statements by earlier teachers of the church, the most notable of which is that by Peter* Lombard (1155–58).

Septuagint (LXX), earliest and most influential Greek translation of the HB and the Apocrypha*, undertaken by Hellenistic Jews c250–100 BCE. According to Jewish tradition (Letter of Aristeas and Josephus*), Ptolemy Philadelphus, king of Egypt (285–46 BCE), initiated the translation on behalf of the Jewish diaspora in Alexandria; 72 translators working independently for 72 days (hence the name) found that their versions coincided, suggesting divine inspiration. The LXX was the Bible of the Hellenistic synagogue and subsequently the Greek-speaking church; it was quoted by the NT writers and became the basis for other versions of the OT (such as the Old Latin Version). It is still used in the Greek Church. **See also BIBLE TRANSLATIONS CLUSTER, EARLY TRANSLATIONS/VERSIONS.**

Seraphim, highest-ranking celestial beings (followed by the cherubim*), who declared God's glory (see *Sanctus*) and purified the prophet's lips (Isa 6:2–3, 6). **See also ANGELS.**

Serbia. See YUGOSLAVIA.

Sergius (d638), patriarch of Constantinople (610–38), champion of Monothelitism*. Hoping to effect a reconciliation with the Miaphysites*, Sergius taught two natures but one divine–human activity in Christ; he received the assent of Pope Honorius, and the doctrine was enforced by the emperor Heraclius in his *Ecthesis** (638), but it was condemned by the Third Council of Constantinople* (680–81).

Sergius of Radonezh, (c1314–1392), monk and founder of a monastery near Moscow, now called the Trinity-St. Sergius Lavra. Born to a high-ranking Muscovite family, Sergius became the father of Muscovite monastic life and is perhaps Russia's most beloved saint. His followers founded hundreds of monasteries across Russia based on his example of a simple communal life. Sergius blessed Prince Dmitrii Donskoi before his battle against the Tatars at Kulikovo Field. He was canonized in 1452. ROY R. ROBSON

Sermon on the Mount, the customary name, used as early as Augustine*, to designate Jesus' first programmatic discourse in Matt 5–7, summarizing his radical ethics of the Kingdom*. Comparison with Luke 6:20–40, "the Sermon on the Plain," shows that these two "sermons" are presenting alternative interpretations of similar traditions arising out of Jesus' teaching (see Jesus, Quest for the Historical) that apparently had already been compiled in the source "Q" (see Q, a Collection of Sayings Ascribed to Jesus). Throughout its history, the church read the Sermon on the Mount as conveying divergent teachings according to the church's ever-changing life contexts (see Reception Studies of Scripture). Contemporary biblical scholarship includes a similar diversity of interpretations (Betz) reflecting a diversity of critical approaches.

The Sermon on the Mount as a Perfectionist Ethics. "Be perfect, therefore, as your heavenly Father is perfect" (Matt 5:48): for minority church communities developing a way of life radically different from the dominant culture*, this was a kind of perfectionist* ethics. For such communities – e.g. early monastic* communities, Greek fathers (e.g. John* Chrysostom), Waldenses*, Franciscans*, Cathars*, Anabaptists*, Quakers*, early Methodists*, and various 20th- and 21st-c. Base* Ecclesial Communities and radical Evangelical communities – the Sermon provided a vision of the Christian community (a symbolic* worldview) that believers were called to enter and implement in a radical way of life marked by love* for others, voluntary poverty*, and nonviolence*. The ethical teaching of the Sermon could be fulfilled in this alternative society and functioned (along with the rest of Matthew) as a kind of "church* order."

Contemporary scholarship that analyzes Matt 5–7 as a religious discourse, through comparison and contrast with biblical discourses and later Jewish and Hellenistic religious discourses (using a history* of religion critical approach), as well as through close attention to its literary and figurative organization (e.g. Davies, Luz, Betz), generally supports this perfectionist reading of the Sermon on the Mount by emphasizing the vision of the Kingdom* and the fatherhood of God – a reading of the Sermon from the perspective of its center, the Lord's Prayer (6:9–13).

The Sermon on the Mount as a New Law. For the church, which was integrated into society and was often a majority group (since the conversion of Armenia*, 301; Constantine*, 312; and Georgia*, 330), the Sermon as a whole often remained a "perfectionist" teaching (as Augustine* and Thomas Aquinas* interpreted it), yet viewing the Sermon as a "new law" progressively led to a two-level ethics that appeared in the interpretations of individual commands. While some of these teachings are "precepts" or "commands" (*praecepta*) that can realistically be implemented in daily life, and thus are for every Christian, other teachings are "counsels" (*consilia*) for consecrated life, summed up in the monastic vows* (the three counsels of perfections) of poverty, chastity, and obedience taken in the Roman Catholic Church by members of religious* orders. The distinction between "precepts" and "counsels," first explicitly formulated by Rupert* of Deutz (c1075–1129), was systematized by Thomas Aquinas.

Similarly, certain contemporary scholars analyze Matt 5–7 as a series of discrete ethical teachings of Jesus (found in Q and oral traditions) "redacted" in a specific way by Matthew – e.g. transforming the beatitude "Blessed are you poor" (Luke 6:20) into an exhortation-like ethical teaching, "Blessed are the poor *in spirit*" (Matt 5:3) (Strecker; see Redaction Criticism). Thus, beyond the specificity of each command, one can recognize the basic ethical principles conveyed by the Sermon that readers are called to implement in various ways in their different life contexts (as in deontological* ethics).

The Sermon on the Mount as a Consequentialist Ethics. The Reformation churches, integrated into society while refusing a two-level ethics, struggled with the idea that, because of sin*, the teaching of the Sermon on the Mount could never be fulfilled. Thus for these churches, the Sermon reveals our sinfulness. But because in daily life one acts in relationality* (*in relatione,* Luther*), our acts affect our neighbors. For example, renouncing possessions, while good in and of itself, also affects one's family. The essential teaching of the Sermon is to help believers distinguish between consequences: "fruits" from thorns, or true prophets and blessed ones from false prophets (7:16–27, 5:3–12).

Similarly certain contemporary scholars analyze the diverse teachings of Matt 5–7 by setting them within the eschatological* and apocalyptic* framework of the Sermon (Matt 5:3–10, 7:16–27). This framework is the horizon of Jesus' proclamation of the Kingdom (Weiss, Schweitzer*), even if this horizon needs to be demythologized* in a secular* world (Bultmann*). From this perspective, the overall teaching of the Sermon is a radical call to decision and obedience, based on the discernment of the fruits (an implicit consequentialist* ethics, also sometimes called ethics of intention).

This brief review of the main types of interpretations of the Sermon on the Mount in various contexts of Western Church history and scholarship suggests that other types of interpretations are to be found in other sociocultural and religious contexts, as seen in the present-day diversity of ethics. **See also** ETHICS AND CHRISTIANITY CLUSTER. DANIEL PATTE

Service of Worship, or Worship Service, modern designation of acts of public worship that reflect the original meaning of "liturgy*" as a work of the people for God's sake, e.g. praising God or sanctifying* parts of human existence. **See also** LABOR, THEOLOGIES OF; LITURGIES, HISTORY OF; LITURGY; LITURGY OF THE HOURS; WORSHIP CLUSTER.

Seven Last Words of Christ on the Cross. Often read, or sung to music, on Good* Friday, they are, in traditional order: "Father, forgive them" (Luke 23:34); "This day you will be with me in Paradise" (Luke 23:43); "Woman, behold your son" (John 19:26–27); "My God, why have you forsaken me" (Mark 15:34); "I thirst" (John 19:28); "It is finished" (John 19:30); and "Into your hands, O Lord, I commend my spirit" (Luke 23:46).

Seven Saints, seven persons, possibly of Syrian origin, credited with the late-5th-c. restoration of the Ethiopian* Church.

Seventh-day Adventist Worship. Worship among Seventh-day Adventists* is typically Protestant in that it centers on the proclamation of the Word. The liturgy is quite uniform around the world. After a few brief experiments with Charismatic expression, early Seventh-day Adventists adopted the conventional Protestant style. In the 1980s, a more celebratory style emerged.

Sacred Time. The sacrality of the Sabbath* is demarcated by opening and closing rituals at home or at church: typically the singing of certain hymns, recitation of the Sabbath commandment, recitation of the Lord's* Prayer in unison, and the expression of wishes for a "happy Sabbath" (repeated three times in South America). Family members embrace each other; some light a "Sabbath candle."

Format. Instruction dominates in Sabbath school (attended by those of all ages), praise and exhortation in formal worship services. Early Adventist camp* meetings and "social meetings" (personal testimonies) produced a strong sense of community in marginality. This function is still served in many non-Christian cultural contexts by daylong worship, which maintains the sanctity of the Sabbath.

Hymnody. Millerite and early Adventist hymns were explicitly doctrinaire, unique in message, and lively in cadence. They were supplanted by the more conventional hymns of US Protestantism as Seventh-day Adventism moved into mainstream forms.

Architecture, Decor. In North America, early Seventh-day Adventist "meetinghouses" were austere, as they still tend to be in mission settings. The central pulpit reflects a focus on proclamation. The cross, once spurned as a symbol of "apostate Protestantism," is now standard in most countries. Symbolism may include a replica of the Ten Commandments. In Japan the central floral arrangement is taken as a silent sermon. Internal baptisteries are common in North America but are rare elsewhere.

Lord's Supper. Communion*, observed quarterly, is regularly preceded by foot*-washing, a ritual that is an affront to cultural sensibilities in some Asian contexts. With some exceptions in Europe, unfermented wine is used in the Seventh-day Adventist ritual. A common chalice is standard in Europe. The Communion service concludes without a benediction, echoing Mark 14:28.

Cultural Adaptation. In style, African American Seventh-day Adventist congregations have traditionally mediated between their European-American counterparts and more enthusiastic "black" expressions. In mission contexts, there were two stages: (1) Before the 1990s, vernacular hymnals were used; these were simply translations of North American hymnals, although a few compositions were in the local idiom. Outside of the Caribbean, there was little use of indigenous instruments. (2) Since the 1990s, there has been an increasing localization of style, instruments (such as the tabla and harmonium in Southern Asia), and composition.

Leadership. Women have historically exercised considerable leadership in Seventh-day Adventist worship, evangelism*, and church life in North America and Europe, especially Scandinavia. Today, women's leadership roles vary greatly by culture: women leaders are universally accepted in Sabbath school but are rejected as leaders in formal worship in Confucian*, Hispanic, and some African cultures. The Seventh-day Adventist polity* presently treats ordination* as a worldwide authorization, which effectively denies it to all women. On their own authority, congregations in North America are increasingly "ordaining" women to ministry, locally the functional equivalent of ordination of men.

Seventh-day Adventist worship ritually integrates personal holiness* with Sabbath sacrality. It connects the believer with the divine and with a worldwide movement by interpreting these vertical and horizontal axes as one cosmic reality. The Church's challenge is to retain this sense of larger community, while providing for increasingly contextualized expression. The church's theology of ordination, e.g., remains caught between these two imperatives. **See also ADVENTISM; WHITE, ELLEN GOULD.**

JOHN R. JONES

Severus, Patriarch of Antioch (512–18), anathematized Chalcedon*, the Tome* of Leo, Nestorius*, Eutyches*, Diodore*, and Theodore*. Expelled from Antioch under Emperor Justin (518), he fled to Egypt but returned to Constantinople (534) when summoned by Justinian*. Although he initially received support, the political tide (Western interests) turned against him. He was condemned (536), banished, and died in Egypt c538. His books were banned, but survived in Syriac translation.

Severus's controversial but important works have a common thread: he was a faithful disciple of Cyril* of Alexandria, from whom he inherited Miaphysite* language (affirming the unity of divine and human nature in Christ). A traditionalist, defensive thinker, not an innovator, he was equally hostile to Nestorian* Dyophysitism (two natures in Christ) and to Eutychian* Monophysitism* (only one nature in Christ), and attempted to walk between these two extremes, armed only with Cyrillian vocabulary.

Was Severus able to endow the Miaphysite vocabulary with sufficient elasticity to cope with the questions raised by the Theopaschite* and Monothelite* disputes? He did succeed in continuing to elaborate a dynamic view of the union of divine and human in Christ, as opposed to the Chalcedonians' static view. The most important Greek theologian between Cyril and Maximus*, Severus remains the major exemplar of the Oriental Orthodox churches. **See also ORTHODOX CHURCHES, ORIENTAL, CLUSTER.**

IAIN R. TORRANCE

Sexism and Christianity. Sexism is the attitude and belief that one gender is superior to the other. In Christian theology and churches, sexism links Christian status and worth to gender, usually conferring superior status and worth on men over women.

At a time when the assumption that gender identity consists of only two opposite categories – male and female – is increasingly contested in contemporary societies, sexism upholds the idea that characteristics associated with femaleness are inferior to those associated with maleness, regardless of whether they are attributed to women, men, or transgendered persons. Christian sexism is a systemic arrangement of power advantaging men and maleness through privileges, status, and control of church institutions, attitudes, and beliefs that generate norms in Christian faith. This arrangement has been supported by Christians regardless of their gender, although some have opposed it.

Christian sexism creates a rationale for devaluing women. Historical Christian doctrines, written predominantly by men from elite social sectors, have portrayed women as inferior to men in intellectual, emotional, and bodily makeup, and in their overall ability to reflect the image* of God. Repeated statements in Christian Scripture, produced in the patriarchal ancient eastern Mediterranean, affirm that women should not speak in church because they are subordinate to men and because Eve*, their progenitor, created after Adam*, was deceived and sinned* (1 Cor 14:34–35; 1 Tim 2:11–14). In influential European medieval and modern theology, claims about women's inferiority often focus on their blameworthiness, especially for tempting men to commit sexual sins. Yet from Christianity's earliest movements as reflected in Christian Scripture to the present, church women have resisted such bias.

Discriminatory church practices concretely express Christian beliefs about women's inferiority by limiting women's access to power and authority, especially in public forums, and by restricting or barring them from teaching, preaching, baptizing, consecrating sacraments, ordaining clergy, and/or selecting a pope. These limitations are official church policy in the Roman Catholic, the Orthodox, and some Protestant traditions; they are de facto institutional patterns in other traditions without such official policies. Feminist leaders across Christian traditions worked to dismantle these barriers and had some success, especially in the Protestant churches (late 20th c.).

Christian sexism is linked to the shaming* of women in the broader society and amplifies other forms of social devaluation. For example, it was by stigmatizing poor black and Latina single mothers, in ways that poor white women were not, that late-20th-c. US Christian political leaders advocated Christian moral standards in public policy. **See also ANDROCENTRISM; PATRIARCHY AND CHRISTIANITY; SEXUALITY, ISSUES OF, CLUSTER.** TRACI C. WEST

SEXUALITY, ISSUES OF, CLUSTER

---

1) Introductory Entry

Sexuality, Issues of. Sexuality refers to a human's deepest most fully embodied response to his or her world. Among Western Christians, sexuality is generally assumed to include genital sensation, activity, and fantasy. But should sexuality be understood much more broadly, to include its connections to the ways societies are structured economically and how we understand race and class? One of the most hotly contested issues in the early 21st c. among Christians in the West (and throughout the world in cultures whose understanding of sexuality is significantly shaped by Western Christianity), sexuality is therefore understood in different ways by Western Christians.

Sexuality as a Basis of Patriarchal Social Relations and Religion. Male dominance, patriarchy* understood as a spiritual good and religious necessity, undergirds major segments of Christianity. Accordingly, the male possesses both a natural ability and a supernatural* authority to exercise sexual power over the female, whose nature is submissive and cooperative. This concept of sexuality characterizes Roman Catholicism, Eastern Orthodoxy*, and much of conservative Protestantism*. Its historical roots lie in literal* readings of Scripture* and in many theological sources, including those of Augustine*, Aquinas*, and Luther*. It is the official position of the Vatican and churches such as the Southern* Baptist Convention, the self-proclaimed largest Protestant denomination in the USA. This attitude toward sexuality has resulted in the exclusion of women from ordained* ministry; mandatory celibacy* for Roman Catholic priests* and all nonmarried persons; the elevation of marriage* above all other human relationships, especially in Protestantism*; the rejection of feminism* as a social movement; the spurning of Feminist* theology as a creative resource for thinking about God; the denunciation of efforts to affirm gay, lesbian, bisexual, and transgender Christians; and general suspicion of movements that espouse the liberation of women and children from traditional marriage and family* structures. One of the most devastating consequences of this Christian view of sexuality is its implicit sanctioning of sexual violence* against women and children.

Sexuality as a Source of Complementary Gender and Sexual Relations. Here sexuality arguably is not so much an instrument of patriarchal power relations as a foundation for harmonious relations between men and women who are naturally and, religiously speaking, supernaturally endowed with unique powers that each brings to the dyadic relationship. Sexually, men, who are the more "masculine," are assertive; women, the more "feminine," are receptive. During the 20th c., much of Western Christianity was impacted by the social sciences, especially psychological* theories, including those of Sigmund Freud and of the more spiritually inclined Carl Jung and his followers. Under the influence of both psychology and feminism*, liberal Roman Catholics and Protestants developed (late 20th c.) this complementary understanding of sexuality. Theologically, this position presupposes a Western version of a "yin–yang" spiritual energy in the universe. This "masculine–feminine" sexual energy is embodied by men and women in accordance with their given (or assigned) biological identity as male or female. This theory has been challenged as the stability of male/female biological identity has become less certain and assumptions about gender, as a psychosocial construct, have become more fluid. Sometimes used by liberal, or progressive, Christians to discredit gay, lesbian, and other sexual liberation movements, the complementarity theory has served primarily as a way to soften, rather than seriously challenge, patriarchal social relations and religion.

Sexuality as a Spiritual Energy for Shaping Mutual Relations in the World. Feminist* Liberation theologies and some Womanist* theologies have seriously challenged both of the preceding interpretations by asserting that sexuality is a deeply embodied yearning for right, mutual relations in the world that include those persons closest to us, but extend to the larger realms of social* justice*. According to this view, one's sexual partners need not be of the "opposite" sex. "Opposite" is itself misleading for imagining right, mutual relations between men and women, just as "opposition" is a mistaken way to think of how people of different races*, tribes*, religions*, and cultures* are rightly related. Feminist and Womanist theologies, later joined by Queer* theologies, introduced in the late 20th c. passionate, intelligent voices to Roman Catholic, Orthodox, and Protestant Western traditions. In the USA, the Unitarian* Universalist Association and the United* Church of Christ have taken the Feminist theological critique of traditional sexual understanding most seriously in theory and practice. From this perspective, most of Christianity is held fast and more or less static by its patriarchal moorings. So long as this prevails, Christian discourse will not transcend its polarized understandings of human beings as either male or female, and as either heterosexual* or homosexual*, without any variation or spectrum of identities. Thus Feminist and Queer theologians argue that the church will remain mired in patriarchal power relations and sexual injustice until it begins to catch up with the best that science and other arenas of human culture and discovery have to offer by acknowledging sexuality as shaping mutual relations.

Western churches, and much of the rest of global Christianity, are likely to remain bitterly divided between those whose faith* is anchored in patriarchal or complementary understandings of sexuality and those who believe the Spirit* is leading them to an understanding of sexuality as a passion for mutual relations. **See also HETERONOMY; RELATIONALITY.**

CARTER HEYWARD

---

2) A Sampling of Contextual Views and Practices

Sexuality, Issues of, in Africa. Silence surrounds sexuality and all its difficulties in African Christian communities as well as in African society as a whole. Although sexuality is a central and intimate aspect of human life, probably it is the most misconstrued, misused, and violated, especially among women and children. In Africa, sexuality is experienced and expressed through rituals (female genital mutilation, puberty rituals, marriage), beliefs (about life under God and African cosmology), attitudes, thoughts, behaviors, roles, and relationships (in marriage*, family*, society), but these aspects remain largely unexplored. However, since the 1990s, in addition to the HIV/AIDS pandemic, two other items have forced Christians (and others) in Africa to study sexuality: the highly controversial issue of homosexuality* and the increased awareness of gender-based violence against women and children (see Abuse as Pastoral Care Issue; Patriarchy and Christianity; Sexism and Christianity; Violence Cluster). Most significant is the introduction of gender and theology courses in theological education and ministerial formation that is forcing future church leaders and theologians to explore issues related to sexuality, among them African masculinity and sexual violence. Yet these are strongly resisted. How can one teach students about sex and sexuality on the "holy" grounds of the seminary? Yet such teaching takes place in a growing number of seminaries. Another sign of hope is a renewed call for African theological and religious scholars to study African cosmology and African* Religion in their own light and as framing the understanding of sexuality in Africa. Yet much remains to be done, because there is a rich and wide diversity of African cultures, religions (including Christianity), and languages in terms of which sexuality must be understood.

NYAMBURA J. NJOROGE

Sexuality, Issues of, in Asia. Although Asia is a vast region with diverse and rich cultures, religions, and traditions, the expression of Asian sexuality can be characterized by three shared assumptions: sex is a cultural taboo; sex is usually restricted to procreation; and women's bodies are regarded as ritually unclean and inferior. Consequently, sexual pleasure becomes a privilege only for men.

With the importation of Christianity into Asia, accompanied by European colonialism* and imperialism, Western Christian sexual conventions in which sex is permitted only in a one-on-one heterosexual* marriage* relationship became a dominant legal practice in most Asian societies. However, in the past few decades, the impact of the global human* rights movement and of the Feminist* and Queer* movements has challenged such a narrow religious interpretation of sexual norms.

Today issues of sexuality discussed in Asian Christian communities include whether procreation and heterosexual marriage should be the only goal of human sexuality and how the Father God who comes to symbolize male dominance legitimizes the power of the church to subordinate women to male authorities. Regarding issues of sexual violence* in Asian societies as well as in Christian communities, many pressing concerns are being addressed, including domestic violence, sexual harassment. discrimination against people of sexual orientations that differ from what is considered the norm and against those with HIV/AIDS, double standards with respect to virginity* and its impact on women's sexuality, forced abortion* in China*, and the dowry system in India*. Furthermore, the borderless societies promoted by the global economy continue to exploit girls and women by selling them as "wives" or forcing them into prostitution. As many Asian Feminist theologians point out, in analyzing sexuality, we cannot focus on sex just as a personal moral issue. Rather, we must examine the unequal power structures and the social and religious constructions of gender, sexuality, class, and race that create systems that exploit the vulnerable, especially poor, young, and socially outcast women.

Throughout church history, the narrowly conceived authority of Scripture* and Christian doctrines has been used as the language of Christian imperialism, exclusivism, and domination. Bringing liberation to women and sexual minorities demands that we construct a Liberation* theology truly framed by a holistic understanding of sexuality that reflects the justice* and love* of God among all people, because sex is a gift from God. The criteria by which to measure any sexual relationship are based neither on gender nor on the form of sexual activity; rather, these criteria are whether there is any abuse of power, domination, and exclusion, or holistic justice* and love*. ROSE WU

Sexuality, Issues of, in Latin America. To understand the relationship between sexuality and Christianity in Latin America, one must start with the assumption that sexuality is not static, defined by essential aspects or biological identity. Rather, it is a social construct that varies according to sociocultural and historical contexts. Sexuality consists of activities and practices related to human bodies and their genital organs, as well as to the satisfaction of desires and the choices of relationships.

One must also make the assumption that Latin America is a collective unit. Despite the enormous differences among regions, whether on the Latin American continent or in the Caribbean, there are some shared characteristics that give a basic homogeneity to the region: increasing poverty* and domination by external economic powers; a history of colonization*, authoritarianism, fragile attempts at democracy, and machismo; cultural diversity influenced by African, indigenous, and European roots; and the political and religious predominance of the Roman Catholic Church. Thus in dealing with the relationship between sexuality and religion in Latin America, one must take into consideration the predominant Catholic sexual morality in the region.

In moral and sexual terms, Christian thought connected pleasure with sin*. Sex, seen as a tool for procreation (see Pregnancy), was relegated to the heterosexual* realm; premarital relations were prohibited. This approach, combined with the absolutization of the Christian family model (see Family, Christian Views of, Cluster) and female submissiveness, shaped the sense of what sexual practices were permitted and morally acceptable. In the area of legislation and public policies, the influence of the Catholic Church has also been perceptible, despite the formal separation of church* and state in most countries. For women, especially poor* women, the religious regulation of sexuality has meant strict control over their behavior and their possibilities for autonomy in this area, as well as in decisions regarding their reproductive capacity. Christian codes on virginity* and the indissolubility of marriage vows (see Marriage, Theology and Practice of, Cluster), along with the concept of women as "natural" mothers, served to maintain religious institutions' control over women's bodies.

But despite the persistence of Christian sexual morality in Latin America, there is an enormous distance between it and the real practices of the faithful, men and women alike. To adhere to a religion does not necessarily mean to obey its dicta. Moreover, different Christian churches vary in their thinking on sexual morality. Also in the public sphere, the dissemination of new ideas such as the inclusion of sexuality in the human* rights sphere has brought considerable changes in political agendas in the region. Recent years have been marked by intense feminist mobilizations, in which Christian women are included, in favor of liberalizing access to abortion*. Studies in different Latin American countries indicate growing popular support, especially among the more educated, for the idea that marriages can come to an end and new relationships can then be formed. The idea of homosexual* unions and other ways of expressing sexuality and affectivity is also gaining acceptance. Indices of approval for condom use and rejection of official Catholic doctrines on the subject (see Birth Control and Contraception, Christian Views of) are significant, even among Catholics. Further contributions to these divergent positions have been made by Feminist* theology, which takes into account the social reality of the lives of women, especially poor women. Such formulations approach sexuality in a positive way, affirming the religious validity of experiencing pleasure from sexuality.

MARIA JOSÉ FONTELAS ROSADO-NUNES

Sexual Violence. See ABUSE AS PASTORAL CARE ISSUE; PATRIARCHY AND CHRISTIANITY; SEXISM AND CHRISTIANITY; SEXUALITY, ISSUES OF, CLUSTER; VIOLENCE CLUSTER.

Seymour, William Joseph (1870–1922), early Pentecostal* leader, pastor of Apostolic Faith Mission on Azusa Street, Los Angeles; born to former slaves Simon and Phyllis Seymour (1870, Centerville, Louisiana). He traveled north to Indianapolis, Indiana (1895), for employment. Possibly converted in an African* Methodist Episcopal (AME) Church, he embraced the Holiness* theology of the Evening Light Saints and attended God's Bible School (1901–2). In Houston, Texas (1902–4), Seymour joined an African American church led by Lucy Farrow. He met the Pentecostal leader Charles F. Parham (1905) and accepted his teaching on Spirit baptism* with "biblical evidence" of glossolalia*. In Los Angeles (from February 1906), he was the pastor of a Holiness congregation. As a result of the Pentecostal revival* (from April 1906), the services moved to the former Stevens AME Church on Azusa Street. Under the leadership of Seymour and others, the "Azusa Street revival" (1906–9), the best known of the early formative Pentecostal revivals, was unique because of its interracial nature. Seymour and Clara Lum edited *Apostolic Faith* (1906–8), a newspaper providing worldwide coverage. Seymour's humility, belief in the restoration of charismatic* gifts*, concern for world evangelization*, and work toward reconciliation* in a segregated society continue to inspire many, including those living in contexts of oppression*.

GARY B. MCGEE

Shaker Theology reflects the experiences of Ann Lee* (1736–84), the English founder of the United Society of Believers in Christ's Second Appearing, and of her US followers in subsequent generations. Lee was a powerful charismatic visionary who emigrated to the New World in 1774. Many of the Believers, who called her "Mother Ann," regarded her as the beloved daughter of God, a second manifestation of the Christ spirit. The Shakers applied this theme of gender duality to the nature of God, identifying God as both father and mother. Shaker theological traditions progressively became more systematic, especially through the efforts of 19th-c. Believers. But Shaker theology has consistently involved ethical responsibilities linked to the practice of communal living. Shakers regard carnality and sexual relations as a major source of sin*. Therefore, they reject the institution of marriage* and require a commitment to celibacy*. The Shakers reconstitute family* life with all Believers, living in community as brothers and sisters under the leadership of elders and eldresses. They practice a community of goods and require a vigorous work ethic. They steadfastly pursue the Spirit* in their worship meetings, which through the centuries have been filled with song and dance, personal testimonies, ecstatic experiences, together with scriptural readings and reflections. The construction of Shaker communities (up to 6,000 members in the mid-19th c.) was a conscious effort to separate those intent on being part of the kingdom* of Christ from the sinful ways of the "world*." The pursuit of righteousness* also called for Believers in the Millennial* Church to practice peaceful ways and to live simple lives. In doing so, for more than 200 years down to the present, when only a few members remain, Shakers have offered a striking and distinctive expression of Christian faith and practice. **See also APOCALYPTICISM CLUSTER: PROLONGATION IN THE MODERN PERIOD; MILLENNIALISM CLUSTER: IN NORTH AMERICA.**

STEPHEN J. STEIN

Shakespeare and Christianity. The amount and range of Shakespeare's religious usage show him to be an unusually well informed Christian layperson during a period energized by repeated religious persecution and religious discourse. Among the many religious words, used with Reformation* overtones, in Shakespeare are *altar**, *beads, candle**, *charity**, *confession**, *controversy, cross** as object and gesture, *equivocation, grace**, *idolatry**, *justification**, *Mass**, *miracles**, *Pope**, *Puritan**, *sacrament**, *scripture**, and *zeal.* Words evoking religious commonplaces range from hundreds of references to some form of *God* (or *the gods*), *heaven**, *damn*, and *sin** to single uses of esoteric words like *pax, unanel'd*, and *unhousel'd*. Complex words like *angel**, *blessed, devil**, *grace, soul**, and *spirit** take on from three to six discernible meanings in Shakespeare. Some of his most informed and imaginative religious usage is figurative, like the metaphor of the *pilgrim** and the *saint** that informs the first exchange between Romeo and Juliet. *Religion** has five different meanings in Shakespeare, including the figurative. He names 33 saints and even more biblical characters.

Equally important, religious themes are often central to Shakespeare's plays. Examples include penance* and repentance* in *Hamlet, The Winter's Tale*, and *King Lear*; providence* in *Richard III, Measure for Measure*, and *Hamlet*; merit* vs. grace and Old Law* vs. New in *The Merchant of Venice*; the Last Judgment* in *Othello* and *Macbeth*; analogies between romantic and religious faith* and love* in *A Midsummer Night's Dream* and *Much Ado about Nothing*; and edifying humiliation and forgiveness* in *Lear, Hamlet*, and most of the comedies and romances. So numerous and profound are Shakespeare's biblical and liturgical allusions that scholars have even shown him alternating between the Bishops' and the Geneva Bibles* in his quotations or allusions. Shakespeare's works also refer to religious art, the mystery plays, religious lyrics, and religious festivals.

Some readers have tried to define Shakespeare's own positions on Reformation controversies through his persistent and informed religious usage. More reserve judgment on just what and how Shakespeare believed. The plays never clearly advocate sectarian positions; characters sometimes do, but their voices are not necessarily Shakespeare's. Documentary evidence shows that Shakespeare and his children were baptized in the Church of England; his will contains traditional if formulaic references to "God my Creator" and "Jesus Christ my Saviour," as well as his hope "to be made partaker of life everlasting." Aside from this, on the religious issues of his time his works are deeply informed, but he is profoundly silent.

R. CHRIS HASSEL, JR.

Shamanism and Christianity

Age-Old Shamanism. Shamanism is a holistic spirituality inseparably linked to shamans and their initiation rites, their indigenous cosmology and mythology, and the rituals that they perform, with accompanying signs and symbols. It is an age-old religiocultural institution, intact to various degrees, wherein beliefs and practices are communicated and sustained by practicing communities of the past and present. Beyond the communal shamanic beliefs and practices are the interrelated worlds of spirits and the supreme spirit-beings, including the spirits of ancestors*, of living or dead animals, and plants, whether they are bound to the earth, with its underworld, middle world, and upper world, or are extraterrestrial. Shamanism, as practiced today, remains ever subversive of the one-dimensional positivistic perception of the world and ever creative in imagining a sustainable livelihood in harmony with creation. Shamanism remains a web of relations ritually manipulated by shamans.

The arduous apprenticeship, under the aegis of a renowned shaman and/or a visiting spirit-guide, has contributed to the prominent centrality of shamans in practicing communities. On the strength of the filial bond and the mutuality of trust established with the local community, not a few of the reputable shamans confide the source of their power, the ethical codes they follow, and their ability to distinguish the moral intentions of fellow shamans. With their intimate knowledge and experience of the sources of shamanic power, they differentiate between shamans empowered by benevolent spirits and those empowered by malevolent spirits. Shamans of integrity are known to have overpowered wicked shamans through exorcism* that neutralized the evil effects the wicked shamans intended. With the consent of the inflicted persons, the evil* is turned back on the wicked initiator as an admonition. Unfortunately, such reversals have sometimes proved to be fatal because the originators were killed by the evil* they themselves had initiated.

The growing though uneven regional assertion that Shamanism is the living tradition of human civilization calls for a paradigm change that allows *shamanic realism*, a perspective beyond scientific rationality acknowledging realities that are knowable to the extent that they can be experienced.

The Relationship between Shamanism and Christianity can be approached in terms of the current hermeneutical critique by Christian theologians of the demonization* (1300–721 BCE) of ancient Near East spirituality, particularly of Canaan. In the light of ethnographic studies of Shamanism, this process of demonization can be attributed to a strategy of domination, characterized by the relentless pursuit of an ideology* of conquest when Yahwism became politicized under a fledgling monarchy in the Kingdom of Israel. This critique has created the discursive space to generate some refreshing biblical insights. The Genesis* account (1:1–2:3) affirms God as the creator of a creation* suffused with God's goodness (Gen 1:4, 10, 12, 18, 21, 25, 31). Such pervasive presence of divine goodness cannot be juxtaposed with evil, which is in no way connected with Gen 1. Evil appears with Gen 3. Evil already exists in the world (as the serpent), and humankind does not so much introduce evil as sustain the already-present evil through acts of immorality. In spite of the prevalence of evil, the creator God sustains creation and humankind by initiating the covenant* with Noah (Gen 9:8–17), Abraham and Isaac (Gen 17:4–22), and Israel (Exod 19–20). The Christ event definitively seals God's covenantal presence with creation through Jesus, the God-with-us who becomes the God-in-Spirit* whose creative power is mediated through the moral agency of integrity.

God's creative power has been mediated through healing* rituals that are shamanic in nature. Tobit applied a fish's gall to Tobias's eyes (Tob 11:5–17), and God healed the father's blindness. In Bethsaida a shamanic ritual of healing involved Jesus (John 9:1–7; Mark 8:22). He spat on the ground, mixed his saliva with mud, and applied it to the eyes of the blind and healed him. The Gospels (Matt 12:35; Luke 6:45) emphasize the store of goodness in the hearts of the moral agents whom Mark (9:40) and Luke (9:50) empathically foreground, even if they do not explicitly belong to the Christian community. The account of Jesus and Beelzebul (Matt 12:22–32) lends salvific importance to the shamanic practices of exorcism* by demonstrating that shamans, albeit not professed Christians, mediate God's creative and salvific power. The moral legitimacy of shamans, as alluded to in Matt 12:30, 32, rests in their implicit openness to God's saving powers through their trust in the Spirit. The mediation of the creative and salvific power of God by life-giving shamans with upright intentions aimed at the greater good of individuals and the overall well-being of communities constitutes the fundamental morality of Shamanism. **See also EXORCISM; HEALTH, HEALING, AND CHRISTIANITY CLUSTER: IN AFRICA: SPIRITUAL HEALING** and **IN NORTH AMERICAN AND EUROPEAN PENTECOSTAL/ CHARISMATIC MOVEMENTS;**

JOJO M. FUNG, SJ

Shame. See HONOR AND SHAME.

Shaw, Anna Howard (1847–1919), clergywoman, social reformer, suffrage leader, orator. Licensed to preach (1873) by the Methodist Episcopal Church, she earned degrees in theology (1878) and medicine (1885) at Boston University and was ordained by the Methodist Protestant Church (1880). She served as pastor in Massachusetts (1878–85), as national superintendent of franchise for the Woman's Christian Temperance* Union (1886–92), and as vice president (1892–1904) and president (1904–15) of the National American Woman Suffrage Association.

Shaw challenged Victorian cultural assumptions and practices that denied women equal opportunities with men, working closely with other leaders in the Suffrage Movement, especially Susan B. Anthony*, to win the vote for women. Forced to justify her calling as a woman to ministry, Shaw countered the theological arguments aligned against her with historical and biblical precedents, her own success in ministry, and a feminist* interpretation of Bible verses traditionally used to deny women equal privileges with men.

Using her exceptional oratorical skills, she promoted new ways of thinking about women's roles in society, politics, and the church, by emphasizing the authority of God over women and men and a progressive interpretation of the Bible. Her life story provides an authoritative model for Christian leadership in relationship to social reform.

WENDY J. DEICHMANN EDWARDS

Shekinah, in Judaism, the majestic presence or manifestation of God that has descended to "dwell" among humans, as in the Tabernacle or among the people of Israel (Exod 25:8, 29:45–46) and in Jerusalem (Zech 8:3; Ps. 135:21). Since the Shekinah is light, NT passages mentioning radiance and the glory of God (Gk *doxa*), as in Luke 2:9, and the Transfiguration* (Mark 9:2, par.) refer to the Shekinah and identify Jesus with a manifestation of the Shekinah.

Shema, confession of the Jewish faith, recited morning and evening, consisting of Deut 6:4, "Hear (Heb *shema*), O Israel: The LORD is our God, the LORD alone" or "The LORD our God, the LORD is one," followed by Deut 6:5–9, 10:13–21 and Num. 15:37–41, including Deut 6:5, "You shall love the LORD your God with all your heart, and with all your soul, and with all your might." Thus in giving the "first commandment," Jesus recites the Shema (Mark 12:29–30; only a part of it is in Matt 22:37).

Shenoute (348–465), leader of an Egyptian monastic federation; first great stylist of the Coptic language. A director of souls, not a theologian, Shenoute urged fear of Jesus' judgment* and the need for confession*, remorse, and good works. He was an active opponent of pagan religion and defender of the poor*. His monastic federation (near Sohag, Egypt), which was modeled on that of Pachomius*, provides our best documentation of cenobitic* monasticism* in late antiquity, including remains of monastic buildings, religious art, ecclesiastical architecture, two standing 5th-c. churches, monastic rules, and thousands of pages of his writings. The Coptic* Orthodox feast day of Shenoute is celebrated on July 1. BENTLEY LAYTON

Sheol, Hebrew for the place of the dead; translated in the LXX* as "Hades*," the term used in the NT and the Apostles'* Creed for the abode or state of the dead before the Last Judgment*, or before the resurrection*, sometimes a hell*-like place of punishment (Luke 16:19–31, Lazarus and the rich man).

Shepherd, one of the earliest occupations. Shepherds provided food, water, and protection for their flocks (1 Sam 17:34–35; Amos 3:2). The term is used as a metaphor* for a leader (2 Sam 7:7) or for one who offers spiritual care. Thus God is the ultimate shepherd (Gen 48:15; Ps 23). Jesus is the good shepherd (John 10:1–18, 25–30; cf. Mic 5:1–3; Heb 13:20; 1 Pet 5:4). Jesus commands Peter to feed his sheep (John 21:15–17), and others are told to care for their flock (Acts 20:28; 1 Pet 5:3). Ignatius* of Antioch and Clement* of Rome favored the shepherd metaphor, used today when ministers or priests are called "pastors." JEFFRY C. DAVIS

Shinto and Christianity. Shinto, the indigenous tradition of Japan, is translated as "the Way of the *Kami*/Deities." Being a non-membership-based tradition, Shinto pervades Japanese culture and, except for a brief period (late 19th–mid-20th c.), has been compatible with and noncontentious toward all religious traditions that it has encountered. Shinto turns on an axis of purity and impurity, rather than on concepts of good and evil. It focuses on concrete particulars here and now in a seamless worldview – seamless in the sense that no ontological distinctions are made between animate and inanimate. Without ontological distinctions, all natural phenomena, including rocks, people, and plants, can be recognized as *kami* (deities).

Shinto's ultimate point of reference – myriad deities animating the landscape and dynamics of the natural world – contrasts with the Christian concept of a transcendent deity. Christian missionaries during the Christian century (1549–1650) in Japan were challenged by this seamless ontological orientation, which did not include abstract concepts like omniscience*, omnipotence*, and absolute truth*. Hence exclusivity was an elusive concern. Although many Japanese became Christian after undergoing a profound conversion* experience, numerous others maintained a Shinto orientation to the world and saw the Christian god* as a kind of *kami*. Other points of contrast are that Shinto is nondogmatic* and does not have a scriptural tradition. A Shinto worldview focused on concrete phenomena excels at perfecting detailed forms in material and motion, and it does not engage in abstract philosophical analysis as is found in a Christian worldview.

Although concepts of self are based on different root assumptions, Christianity and Shinto share an understanding about responsibilities that hold people together in a relationship of mutual concern. The Sermon* on the Mount teaching to "love* your neighbor" resonates with the Shinto awareness that all things affect each other and should be respected. Placing stress on the quality of activity focuses attention on the present moment and direct interaction among people. Thus the Christian goal to love and the Shinto goal to live in harmonious respect are embodied. Central to both Shinto and Christianity is the impulse to express gratitude and respect through ritual offerings at their respective altars. Both raise a vessel of wine (Christian red and Shinto rice wine) toward God or *kami* in a ritualized mode that signals a similar concern to embody respect in explicit action. **See also JAPAN.** PAULA ARAI

Shoah (Heb "calamity," "devastation"), term for the Holocaust* preferred by many Jews, especially in Israel and parts of Europe (used in Poland in the 1940s), because of its origin in the Hebrew Bible (in contrast to the Greek origin of "Holocaust," with potentially problematic pagan connotations, although "Holocaust" is used in the LXX*). Holocaust has remained the most common name since the 1950s, in part because of its broader meaning. **See also HOLOCAUST, JEWISH (OR SHOAH).**

Shroud, white sheet in which a corpse is laid out for burial. The Shroud of Turin, known since 1578, bears the image of a human body with the stigmata* and is claimed to be the sheet in which Christ was wrapped for burial; debate continues over its authenticity and origin.

Sibylline Oracles, large collection of prophecies ascribed to Greco-Roman prophetesses, notably Sibyl, but partly of Jewish, though mainly Christian, origin. Book III is Jewish (praising Judaism as the perfect example of a proper, natural religion), as are Book IV and possibly parts of I and II as well. The rest of the 14 books are Christian, often containing prophecies that refer to Jesus Christ. **See also PSEUDEPIGRAPHA.** JOHANNES TROMP

Sick, Visitation and Anointing of. Christian care for the sick is rooted both in the 1st-c. cultural commonality of family and friendship and in the specificity of NT Christian teaching. Care for the sick was modeled on examples of Jesus responding to pleas for healing, and the early church saw prayer with the sick as a primary vehicle for continuing Christ's ministry. Incorporated within visitation to the sick was prayer, the laying* on of hands, and anointing* with olive oil (Mark 6:13; Jas 5:13–15). The developing Christian practices were seen to be expressions of faith in God, hope in the *eschaton**, and love for one's neighbor.

Blessing prayers, liturgical texts, letters, hagiographical* writings, and homilies* encouraging visitation by all indicate that, in the first Christian millennium, there were a variety of rituals for caring for the sick. From these sources, we can discern some commonality. First, the oil blessed by a bishop* (or passed through the grave of a martyr*; see Relics) carried an ecclesial* association different from the work of a charismatic* individual. Second, anointing in the context of prayer was related to the healing of all aspects of a person, physical, emotional, mental, and spiritual, with the important distinction that curing spiritual ills involved the forgiveness* of sins*. Third, geographic differentiation was most apparent in those who ministered to the sick. In some places, they were the simple faithful using blessed oil to anoint themselves and their family members when ill (such as in Gaul*); in other places, widows, deacons, and deaconesses* were ordained to pray for the sick and to visit and anoint the sick as extensions of the bishop's ministry (such as in Christian Egypt*).

In the second millennium, different emphases arose as ritual care for the sick was influenced by changes in views of reconciliation*, atonement*, and life after death. The growing emphasis on spiritual healing overshadowed physical healing, and the anointing of the sick became the last (extreme) anointing (unction*) before death, no longer a sacrament* for the living. Apart from this ritual of last rites, visitation to the sick continued, as did pilgrimages* to healing shrines and prayers to saints*.

Protestant Reformers uniformly rejected extreme unction as unscriptural, but encouraged prayer for and visitation to the sick, and some retained or restored anointing for physical healing. A 20th-c. return to broader pastoral and ritual practices in caring for the sick was seen in Roman Catholicism, in Anglicanism, and in many Protestant churches.

The theological and practical arguments of the present day focus on who may be anointed, who may anoint, what is healed, how charismatic* and ecclesial healing are related, and what is the Christian meaning of suffering*, sickness, and health. **See also HEALTH, HEALING, AND CHRISTIANITY CLUSTER.**

LIZETTE LARSON-MILLER

Sierra Leone represents (with Liberia*) a curious paradox in the history of African Christianity. Established as a Christian settlement for former African slaves* (1787) and home to the first modern church of tropical Africa, it presently has the lowest percentage of Christians of any non-Islamic country in West Africa. A partial explanation is that the small coastal region (which contains a fifth of the population and includes Freetown, the capital) became a British colony (1808) that was subsequently conjoined to the larger hinterland as a British protectorate (1896) and fully integrated when it achieved independence (1961).

In the early 19th c., the Sierra Leone colony was a successful Christian experiment owing to extensive missionary efforts by European missionaries and African American settlers, mass conversions among tens of thousands of slaves freed from slave ships captured by the British navy, and Protestant mission schools; Roman Catholics arrived in the late 19th c. The Fourah Bay Institution (now a university college) trained many African clergy, including Samuel Adjai Crowther* (c1806–99) – the slave boy who became the first Anglican African bishop – and produced a vigorous African missionary movement that took Christianity to Southern Nigeria.

This robust Christian growth took place in an interreligious environment that included Islam* and African* Religion. This dynamic ensured interpenetration and religious tolerance. The form of Christianity that emerged was outwardly Europeanized but well adapted to the indigenous culture. Today the Krios, descendants of early settlers and recaptured slaves, are the most highly Christianized group.

The spread of Islam limited Christian expansion beyond the costal region, despite missionary efforts (early 20th c.). African* Instituted Churches and Pentecostal*/Charismatic* movements (from the 1960s) gave rise to new missionary vigor. Despite chaotic political conditions, including a decade-long civil war that triggered massive migrations to Freetown, there has been a burgeoning of Christian ministries and major revivals*, although the long-term impact remains to be seen. But the influence of Christianity on public life and institutions in Sierra Leone remains substantial despite the small Christian presence.

Statistics: Population (2000): 4.8 million (M). Christians, 0.55 M, 11.5% (Protestants, 0.17 M; Roman Catholics, 0.17 M; members of African Instituted Churches, 0.17 M; Anglicans, 0.03 M); Muslims, 2.2 M, 46%; African Religionists, 2 M, 40.4%; nonreligious, 0.09 M, 2.0%. (Based on *World Christian Encyclopedia*, 2001.)

JEHU J. HANCILES

Siger of Brabant (c1240–c1284), Averroist philosopher. As a master of arts at the University of Paris, he commented on the works of Aristotle* with the aid of the commentaries of Avicenna* and Averroes*, pointing out that Aristotle seemed to teach the eternity of the world and the unity of the intellect in all persons (thus denying the immortality of individual souls*). He was accused of teaching "double truth," but this was also an expression used by Thomas Aquinas*. Some of his views were condemned by the bishop of Paris (1270, 1277), as were some of Aquinas's. Dante* puts him in Paradise, probably because of his defense of the role of reason*.

Sign of the Cross. As early as Tertullian*, Christians traced the cross on their foreheads for sanctification and protection against temptation. In the early Middle Ages, the sign began to be made by moving the hand from forehead to breast, then from shoulder to shoulder (left to right in the West, right to left in the East), either, in the West, with the open hand or, in the East, with the thumb, index, and middle finger brought to a point (symbolizing the Trinity) or, in the Russian* Orthodox Church before Patriarch Nikon's* reform (17th c.), with two fingers (symbolizing the human and divine natures of Christ).

Signs. See SEMIOTICS AND THE STUDY OF CHRISTIANITY.

SIKHISM AND CHRISTIANITY CLUSTER

Sikhism and Christianity: A Christian Perspective. In 1834 the North American Ludhiana Mission was established in the Sikh kingdom of Punjab, but Christian activity was limited until its British annexation in 1849. Christian missionary pressure and the work of the Hindu Arya Samaj Movement caused much consternation among the Sikhs, who responded by establishing several Khalsa Colleges and making their scripture, the *Guru Granth Sahib*, widely available in printed form. The British regarded the Sikhs as a martial people, and the studies they undertook tended to serve the administration's purpose of gaining their loyal support.

Sikhism is a monotheistic* and universalistic spiritual movement founded on the teachings of Guru Nanak and his successors, contained in the *Guru Granth Sahib* and *Dasam Granth*. These are the foci of all life and worship. Aspects of Christianity that might be of interest and concern to Sikhs are its evangelistic and hierarchical traditions; these are not present in Sikkhism, which believes that the Divine Light (*jot*) is to be found in everyone and thus that all human beings are equal. Consequently, Sikhism rejects caste* discrimination, the low status or impurity of women*, religious hierarchy and ministry, and the concept of God as male.

W. OWEN COLE

Sikhism and Christianity: A Sikh Perspective. The encounter with Christianity had both detrimental and beneficial effects on Sikhs (c20 million in 2000). The conversion to Christianity of the 14-year-old Maharaja Dalip (Duleep) Singh (1853) was hailed as "the first instance of the accession of an Indian prince to the communion of the church." The gift of a Bible inscribed, "You have gained a rich inheritance," after he was dispossessed of his kingdom and the Kohinoor diamond (at one time the largest in the world) seemed ironic. Such conversions jolted the Sikhs into vigorous restorative action through preaching by the Nirankari, Namdhari, and Singh Sabha movements, books for developing the Sikh identity by writers like Bhai Kahan Singh and Vir Singh, and the struggle to manage by themselves their *gurdwaras* (places of worship), which were often in Hindu hands. The observance of the Sikh Code of Conduct (Rehat Maryada) became a requirement for joining the British army.

In the Western diaspora, Sikhs responded to racism* with successful campaigns for the right to wear Sikh symbols. Christian influence is evident in the "King James English" used in translations of the Sikh scriptures, stained glass windows, Sunday worship services, seating in (some) *gurdwaras*, and young Sikhs' perception of their faith. With self-confidence Sikhs participate in interfaith activity and scripture studies.

CHARANJIT KAUR AJITSINGH

Sikh Scriptures and the Bible. There are two bodies of Sikh scripture: the *Guru Granth Sahib* and the *Dasam Granth*. The *Guru Granth Sahib* (1,430 printed pages) contains poetical compositions, similar to the biblical psalms, set to 31 musical forms by Guru Arjan, its original compiler in 1604 CE. Unlike the Bible, it contains very little biographical, historical, or specifically ethical material, although its message of spiritual liberation based on a God-centered life permeates the whole text. These compositions were revealed to 6 of the 10 gurus, to Hindu and Muslim poets, and to men like Kabir who rejected any sectarian allegiance.

The scriptures are written in the Gurmukhi script (used for everyday Punjabi), but their language varies from medieval Indian dialects to Persian. This is especially true of the *Dasam Granth*, a 1,428-page compilation of poems attributed to the 10th guru, Gobind Singh, and compiled some years after his death (1708 CE). Both collections are canonical but emphasis is placed, in practice, on the first, which is also the primary focus of worship and the authoritative basis of the Panth (Sikh community), no religious activity being valid that does not take place in its presence.

W. OWEN COLE

Sillon, Le, periodical founded (1894) by Marc Sangnier, a Roman Catholic legislator from Paris, to promote democracy, social* justice*, and the French Republic. It was condemned by Pope Pius* X (1910). *Action Française* represented the opposing tendency.

Simeon Stylites (c390–459), Syrian hermit*, most famous of the "pillar" saints. He began as a monk, then moved to pillars of increasing height. Widely admired, he was often consulted for his advice; he championed the doctrines of the Council of Chalcedon*. Imitators included Simeon Stylites the Younger (521–97), who was ordained a priest at the age of 35 and whose followers climbed a ladder to receive Communion from him.

Simon of Cyrene, a passerby, from Cyrene in present-day Libya, compelled to carry Jesus' cross to Golgotha*, the place of crucifixion (Mark 15:21, par.).

Simon Magus, "magician" in Samaria (Acts 8:9–24) who claimed to be the "Great Power" (i.e. God) and was rebuked by Peter for trying to buy the gift of the Holy* Spirit. Irenaeus* called him the father of Gnosticism*. He was said to have been accompanied by Helen, identified with the First Thought, whom he had redeemed from a brothel (this may be one source of the Faust legend). This tradition, and the authorship of the *Apophasis* ascribed to Simon, continue to be debated.

Simony, sale or purchase of spiritual offices, named from Simon* Magus's attempt to buy the Holy* Spirit. The sale of offices was prohibited by some early councils and popes, but it became a crucial issue in the age of feudalism*, when lay appointment to office and investiture* with the symbols of office was widespread. Humbert* (*Against the Simoniacs*, 1058) called simony a heresy*, an erroneous view of the Holy Spirit as being less than the Father and Son, subject to human control (see Trinity in Eastern Orthodoxy; Trinity in the Western Tradition). But other reformers, including Peter* Damiani, saw Humbert's position as Donatist* in claiming that sacraments administered by simoniacs were invalid. A Lateran synod (1060) ordered the removal of simoniacs but decreed that clergy ordained by simoniacs but not purchasing their office needed only the laying* on of hands.

Sin refers to any human activity or stance opposed to God and God's purposes, separating humans from God. It initiates a process of destruction ruinous for the human community, the natural world, and sinners themselves (see Violence Cluster). It is typically understood in Western churches as a moral evil involving individual guilt and responsibility (see Atonement #2), although early traditions (often Eastern) emphasized that satanic deception or disease-like manifestations were intrinsic to the nature of sin; similarly, contemporary interpretations often stress systemic sin related to environmental and structural factors (see Atonement #1).

The term "sin" comprises a vast biblical vocabulary (about 50 Hebrew words, more than a dozen Greek words), with themes of rebellion and disobedience prominent. "Sin" applies to acts ("sins") violating the divine law by commission or omission (1 John 3:4; Matt 25:31–46; Prov 24:11–12); to a moral state of being ("sin") in which human nature is fundamentally disordered or depraved (Matt 15:19; Jer 17.9), and sometimes, especially in Paul, to a seemingly active agent with power over humankind (Rom 5–7). Humans as slaves to sin (Rom 6:17) cannot free themselves but depend on the atoning (see Atonement #1) or redemptive* work of Christ.

The individually oriented understandings of major traditions differ somewhat among themselves. Roman Catholicism privileges the intellect: sin violates both God's law and right reason*, especially through inordinate sensual appetites; sin is by definition a voluntary act (see Will). Protestantism*, in line with the Reformation*, emphasizes pride and unbelief, seeing sin as corrupting humanity in all of its aspects, including motives (will), and thus views sin as radically limiting human freedom*. (Arminian* and Anabaptist* strands of Protestantism give a larger place to human freedom.)

Many contemporary feminists complain, however, that in Protestantism the signature sins of pride and self-assertiveness over against God represent typically male rather than female temptations: many women are prone to sin by self-abnegation and the refusal to take proper responsibility for their lives.

Eastern Orthodoxy*, with its less individual-centered anthropology, sees sin more in terms of error (being deceived by the devil*) and illness that need correction and healing. Sin afflicts the whole person, regarded as a psychosomatic unity.

Other contemporary interpretations (with roots in biblical and early tradition and influenced by the modern social sciences and socio-economic realities) tend to reduce the emphasis on individual responsibility. Some stress constraints on individuals, including finitude (is it possible, in a finite world, for creatures not to be at cross-purposes with one another?); the negative formative effects of environment; genetic predispositions and psychological weaknesses; and basic human immaturity and the need for growth. Such constraints suggest responses of compassion and attempts at healing or education rather than the judgment and repentance typical of classical Western paradigms. Others, including Liberation* theologians, emphasize structural or systemic sin: unjust economic and political structures produce larger and more pervasive evils than do individual sinners, and may leave individuals caught up in them with no good options. No moral probity at the individual level suffices to fix the faulty structure.

The way one fundamentally conceives of sin is critical to how one conceives of its proper remedy. Less individual-centered interpretations call attention to important aspects of the problem that have received too little attention, at least in Western traditions. However, any tendency to treat sin as a small matter, or merely as a normal part of an interesting character structure, denies the fundamental Christian affirmation that sin is not intrinsic to our humanity but radically defaces it (the church has confessed Jesus, the model of genuine humanity, to be sinless) and calls into question the meaning of the incarnation*, death, and resurrection of Christ, who came specifically to save us from our sins (Matt 1:21; Rom 8:3). **See also ANTI-SEMITISM; COLONIALISM**

AND IMPERIALISM AND CHRISTIAN THEOLOGY; PENANCE AND FORGIVENESS: POVERTY CLUSTER; RACISM AND CHRISTIANITY CLUSTER; VIOLENCE CLUSTER.

MARGUERITE SHUSTER

Singapore. For many young and well-educated women and men in Singapore, Christianity is modern, rational, and English-based, in comparison with their parents' religions, namely a combination of Buddhism*, Daoism*, and ancestor* worship, which they consider illogical and superstitious.

As a free port founded in 1819 by Thomas Stamford Raffles, a British Indies administrator, Singapore was opened to the London Missionary* Society, the Church* Missionary Society, and the Roman Catholic mission. Initially the missionary work proved to be difficult. However, mission schools become important evangelistic channels for the propagation of the Christian gospel and opportunities for female education*.

During the Japanese occupation (1941–45), interned missionaries and Western laypersons realized the importance of indigenous Christian leadership. Hence 1948 saw the birth of Trinity Theological College and the present National Council of Churches of Singapore.

From 1970 to 2000, the number of male and female Christians steadily increased; the majority tended to be Chinese, younger and better educated than the rest of the population, to attend English-speaking schools, and to have a higher socioeconomic status. The significant growth of the Charismatic* renewal movements is attributed in part to more expressive worship, emphasis on evangelistic zeal, more fundamentalist interpretation of the Bible, and demand for greater commitment to the church. Although the church leadership is male dominated, the role of female pastors and laity is gradually gaining recognition and acceptance.

The Religious Harmony Act (1991) seeks to maintain religious tolerance and to minimize religious interference in politics in multireligious Singapore.

Statistics: Population (2000): 3.6 million (M). Christians, 0.44 M, 12.3% (Roman Catholics, 0.14 M; Protestants, 0.13 M; independents, 0.09 M; Anglicans, 0.04 M); native religionists, 1.5 M, 42.7%; Muslims, 0.66 M, 18.4%; Buddhists, 0.52 M, 14.5%; Hindus, 0.18 M, 5.1%; nonreligious, 0.17 M, 4.7%. (Based on *World Christian Encyclopedia*, 2001.)

TAN YAK-HWEE

Singing in Worship. In Israel, praise for God was typically sung. The song of Miriam* (Exod 15:20–21) celebrates the passage through the Red Sea; the song of Hannah* (1 Sam 2:1–10), the birth of Samuel*. Mary's* *Magnificat**, Zechariah's* *Benedictus**, and Simon's* *Nunc Dimittis** (Luke 1:46–55, 68–79; 2:29–32) celebrate the coming of salvation. Temple* worship and the Passover* and other rituals involved singing psalms*. The early church sang "psalms, hymns, and spiritual songs" (Eph 5:19; Col 3:16–17). Hymns, composed through the centuries for the Eucharist* or the daily Divine* Office, were sung by priests*, monks*, and canons* in choir* (with boys or castrati* instead of women). Singing by the people took place mostly in settings outside formal worship.

The Reformation* encouraged the singing of hymns by the entire congregation, and this also entered Roman Catholic practice. In Germany, both Lutherans and Catholics encouraged singing by skilled choirs, accompanied by instruments. Reformed and Anglicans restricted singing to psalms and "canticles*." In Britain and the USA, congregational singing was enriched first by the Dissenters'* metrical* Psalms, then by the Wesleys'* many hymns, and translations of Greek and Latin hymns by participants in the Oxford* Movement.

In the USA, spirituals* were part of revivalism* and the African* American Church. Missionaries, after initial resistance, now encourage the use of indigenous music in worship, as independent churches always did. After the Second Vatican* Council, guitars, drums, and folk-style melodies became acceptable in Roman Catholic churches. EUGENE TESELLE

Siricius, Pope (384–99), born and died in Rome, venerated as a saint. A deacon under Pope Damasus, his choice as bishop was popular with the people of Rome and the emperor Valentinian II. Little is known of his pontificate except that, in the manner of the imperial court, he issued decrees that he regarded as binding on much of the Western Church, thus marking an important stage in the growth of papal authority. Although an opponent of Priscillianism*, he rebuked those who had Priscillian put to death.

MICHAEL J. WALSH

Skepticism, the doctrine that certain knowledge is unattainable, at least in some areas of concern; thus the term refers to doubt* about Christian beliefs.

Sketic Monasticism, in the area of Skete or Scetis (in the desert bordering the Nile valley in Egypt*), near other Anchorite* monastic centers (Nitria, Ta Kellia), emphasized withdrawal from the world for contemplation* and prayer in small communities or individually. It continued to be a vivid image among later monks who developed the method of hesychasm* and was especially influential in Russia*, particularly through Nil* Sorsky. Forsaking the large monasteries of the region around Moscow and reviving the monastic ideals of "non-possession" and working with one's own hands, Nil promoted a "third way" between cenobite* and eremite* monasticism in the forests north of the Volga. Suppressed by the czars, the movement continued within larger monasteries; *staretsi* were respected by the people and influenced many intellectuals (e.g. Dostoyevsky*, Tolstoy*, Soloviev*, Berdyaev*, Bulgakov*).

Slave in the Bible. See SLAVERY AND CHRISTIANITY CLUSTER: IN THE BIBLE: SLAVES AND SERVANTS.

SLAVERY AND CHRISTIANITY CLUSTER

1) *Introductory Entries*

1) Introductory Entries

Slavery and Christianity: In the Bible: Slaves and Servants. Both *doulos* (Gk) and *'ebed* (Heb) are ambivalent terms in the Bible (hence the double English translation, "slave"/ "servant").

In the Roman Empire, slavery was a common social institution. Slaves were owned by their masters and remained in bondage until they were redeemed. The slaves' brutalization and their shameful* status stood in contrast to that of "free" persons (Gal 3:28). In metaphorical phrases ("slave to Christ," "slave to sin"), the connotation of "bondage" often remained, along with that of "redemption*" as freedom from bondage.

Slaves as members of the household often carried out tasks with the authority of their master (as the "slaves of Caesar" did). Thus the NT term "servant" or "slave" may have this connotation, e.g. in the parables where slaves act in their masters' names; metaphorically, the designation "Paul, slave of Christ" (Rom 1:1) might carry the connotation of one who acts with the authority of Christ.

The NT term "servant" or "slave" may also evoke the metaphorical designation as "servant of God" of figures – e.g. Abraham, Moses, David, prophets, the "servant of YHWH" (Isa 49:1–8), the entire people of God – who *willingly* submit to the authority of God, e.g. as Christ did "taking the form of a servant" (Phil 2:7) (see Isaiah, Book of). These three meanings are potentially present in each use of the term in the NT.

DANIEL PATTE

Slavery and Christianity through the Centuries. Slavery existed throughout the ancient world in which the Christian churches originated and expanded. The early church consisted of both slaves and slave owners, and both were known to suffer martyrdom*. A reciprocal relationship existed in which slaves were urged to be obedient and industrious, and slaveholders were compelled to act with kindness, fairness, and respect. Paul addressed the issue in the Epistle to Philemon* in one way; the later pseudonymous Pauline literature (Eph 6:5–8; Col 3:22–4; Titus 2: 9–10; cf. 1 Pet 2:18–25) addressed it in another way (see Household Codes). Slavery had a great impact on the institutional life, teachings, and practices of the apostolic church.

During the early Middle Ages, Slavs in Eastern Europe were enslaved, often being sold in the Muslim world; the word for "slave" in all European languages is derived from "Slav." In the context of the feudal* system, the acceptance of slavery in the medieval churches and beyond was equally unquestioned; neither Roman Catholics nor Protestants condemned the standard definitions and values of human bondage. To various degrees, the same applied to the churches in all the countries in Latin America (see History of Christianity Cluster: In Latin America), the Caribbean* Islands, and North America, all of which embraced from the 17th to the 19th c. a system of slavery that targeted indigenous people and particularly African peoples. Missionaries were implicated in slave trade. For example, the Society for the Propagation of the Gospel (1701) inherited a slave plantation in Barbados, and its first missionary to Africa, Thomas Thompson, published a book in defense of the slave trade (1756). In the French Caribbean colonies (e.g. Guadeloupe*, Haiti*), Roman Catholic missionaries followed the 1685 Black Code, which made evangelization a fundamental part of the slavery system, until the official abolition of slavery in all French colonies (1848) (see Mission Cluster: Thematic Issues: Anti-slavery).

Anti-slavery sentiment did appear in various parts of the so-called New World. Even though few Christians questioned the legitimacy of slavery in the 16th c., some Spanish priests in the Americas (e.g. Bartolomé de las* Casas and, later, Jesuits*) urged that slaves be treated humanely. But it was only with the Enlightenment* (from the 18th c.) and its emphasis on the equality of all humans and their potential to become "civilized" that churches progressively embraced first the ideology that all Christians, including slaves, could improve by grace* and later became champions of slave emancipation (e.g. Protestant missionaries in the British Empire from 1833 to 1834). Yet these issues were highly contentious in political and economic life, as well as in the churches, as tragically exemplified by the Civil* War in the United States (1861–65) and, in the preceding decades, by the division of Methodists* (1844), Baptists* (1845), and Presbyterians* (1857) into Northern abolitionist and Southern pro-slavery churches. By that time the colonies of Sierra* Leone (1807) and Liberia* (1820) had been founded for freed slaves (both African and African American). The colonization movement was widely supported in the period before the Civil War, since many people in the USA could not envisage a society in which people of African descent would have full participation.

By the mid-19th c., the abolition of slavery was promoted by many churches and missionary societies – first by African* American churches (especially the African* Methodist Episcopal [AME] Church) and their leaders (e.g. Richard Allen*, Frederick Douglass*, Harriet Tubman*, Nat Turner*) and later by Adventists*, American* Baptists (the Baptist* Missionary Society secured the abolition of slavery in Jamaica*, 1833–34), Mennonites*, Quakers* (with leaders such as Sarah and Angelina Grimké*; Hicks*; Woolman*), Anglicans (e.g. Wilberforce*), and members of the Holiness* Movement and revivalism* (including Finney*; Phoebe Palmer*; Sojourner* Truth) and of the Salvation* Army (founded by Catherine and William Booth*). In the late 19th c., anti-slavery became a preoccupation of Roman Catholic missionaries, especially the White* Fathers (in central and Western Africa).

More than a century after the official abolition of slavery (although it still exists in various forms, often designated as "human trafficking"), lingering questions abound regarding the long history of slavery in Christian churches as a whole, the most pressing among which are the following: What exactly did Jesus say, if anything at all, about the benefits and/or evils of human bondage? How have the churches from apostolic times reconciled slavery with the gospel's message of love, charity, and human equality and community? To what extent did pro-slavery churches in the New World and elsewhere find precedent in the early and medieval churches? See also **RACISM AND CHRISTIANITY CLUSTER.** LEWIS V. BALDWIN

2) A Sampling of Contextual Views and Practices

Slavery and Christianity in Brazil

The Roman Catholic Church. The position taken on slavery by the Roman

Catholic Church in Brazil reflects the alliance agreed upon by the Holy See and the Portuguese crown and codified in the papal bulls *Dum Diversas* (1452) and *Romanus Pontifex* (1455). These and other bulls granted the Portuguese the power to either convert the "infidels" to the Catholic faith or enslave them and sell them. During colonial times, the just war* theory provided the theological basis for slavery; those who refused to accept Christianity could be enslaved.

The Roman Catholic Church was pro-slavery, and its concerns regarding black slaves were incidental and occasional. The First Constitutions of the Archdiocese of Bahia (1707) – the most important legal-canonical document of the Church in colonial times – deals exclusively with the salvation* of the souls* of black slaves and completely ignores their physical pain. Similarly, the document "A Brief Instruction on the Mysteries of Faith," for slaves, is concerned primarily with the compulsory and superficial conversion of blacks.

Conniving with slavery, the Roman Catholic Church benefited from the slave-holding system, a fact kept silent for many years and presently brought to light by historiography. Catholic priests and male and female members of religious orders (e.g. Benedictines*, Jesuits*, Carmelites*, Mercedarians, Franciscans*, Clarissas, Ursulines, Discalced Carmelites) owned male and female slaves, who worked in convents, farms, and mission colonies ("reductions*").

The structural link between the Church and slavery was so strong during colonial and imperial times that the Church not only refused to hear theologians' objections, but also reprimanded and punished the few priests who spoke up against it (e.g. the Jesuits were expelled in 1750), and never even questioned slavery. It was only in 1885 that it took a stand against "slave traffic," although without advocating the abolition of slavery.

Protestantism was regarded as a heresy* in the Portuguese colonies and a threat to the unity and integrity of Christianity. In 1630 the Dutch of the West Indies Company conquered the city of Recife and held it for 24 years. The Dutch reviewed the issue of replacing cheap and abundant slave labor. But they soon realized that slavery was necessary to accomplish the project of colonization. Thus they gradually abandoned the Calvinist ethic, which defended the dignity of labor*, and initiated mechanisms for slave trafficking.

Among Protestants the moral discussion regarding the legitimacy or immorality of slavery had been taking place since 1599, involving businessmen, politicians, theologians, and ministers. During the occupation years, approximately 50 ministers strove to build a Reformed Church in the Dutch colony. But the general government of Brazil, under pressure from economic interests, declared that Africans were indispensable to the colony. Furthermore, the Reformed Church benefited from slavery; even its ministers were slave masters. The Church was concerned with saving the souls* of slaves and tried to teach them the Christian religion. The religious tolerance granted by the Dutch to the Portuguese and indigenous people was not extended to blacks. They all had to be brought to the Reformed Church worship services, even if their masters were Catholic.

The path followed by Dutch merchants – from mere interceptors to regular slave traffickers – marred evangelization by Protestants in the colony. The anti-slavery reaction of Protestant churches appeared with the Pietists* toward the end of the 18th c.

The Golden Law, signed by Princess Isabel on May 13, 1888, put an end to slavery in Brazil. The signature was preceded by intensive action on the part of the Abolitionist Movement, with the support of both public opinion and many members of the Catholic and Protestant churches.

ÊNIO JOSÉ DA COSTA BRITO

Slavery and Christianity in North America. In the 17th–19th c., a close relationship existed between slavery and the Christian churches in British North America. From the very beginning of the African slave trade, the conversion* of slaves to Christianity had been the justification for the enslavement of African peoples. After European Christians and African captives arrived on the North American continent (early 17th c.), slavery developed among Anglicans* in the colony of Virginia as early as 1619. The acceptance of slavery was initially unquestioned by both the Church of England and the Roman Catholic Church, in which the institution was believed to be supported by natural* law and sanctioned by Scripture and tradition, and the practice of owning slaves also existed among Congregationalists*, Presbyterians*, Baptists*, Methodists*, and even Quakers* and Moravians*. Colonial statutes stipulated that baptism* did not alter the earthly status of slaves; churches were encouraged to convert and monitor the spiritual welfare of the enslaved, and slaveholders were told to exercise Christian charity in the treatment of slaves. Quaker involvement in the owning of slaves had essentially ended by the 18th c., as "the Friends" embraced quietistic forms of abolitionism, and Presbyterians, Baptists, and Methodists increasingly experienced sharp divisions over slavery. Such divisions were most evident in the aftermath of the American Revolution, as slavery faded in the North and became more deeply entrenched in the South, and as churches confronted the paradox of a new nation born in freedom while some 700,000 Africans languished in bondage.

The early 19th c. witnessed both increased missionary activity among slaves and the emergence of prominent pro-slavery and anti-slavery voices in the churches. Slaves were converted in greater numbers than in the colonial period, but the remnants of African* Religion in slave culture remained strong, even as the churches sought to discourage and eliminate them. Pro-slavery elements in the Protestant churches of the agrarian South defended slave missions and slavery on the basis of Scripture, tradition, and federalist social theory, thus fashioning an evangelical slaveholding ethic that highlighted the sense of Christian obligation and duty that slaves and slave owners should display toward each other. Slaves were admonished to be passive, obedient, and productive, and slaveholders were expected to meet the material and spiritual needs of the slaves. Roman Catholic Churches in the South had a similar perspective on the reciprocal relationship between slaves and their masters, and this tempered anti-Catholic bias and made the intermingling of the Church and Southern life and culture easier for them. In contrast, anti-slavery voices in the Northern churches, and especially African* American churches, denounced slavery as un-Christian, immoral, and an impediment to the physical, psychological, and spiritual well-being of slaves. African American churches were uniform in their opposition to human bondage, and militant abolitionists like David Walker and Henry Highland Garnet surfaced among those in the North. Disputes along regional lines resulted in schisms in the white churches. Northern and Southern Methodists (1844), Baptists (1845), and Presbyterians (1857) split from each other. Differences over slavery generally translated into divided loyalties during the Civil* War (1861–65), as Northern churches tended to support Union efforts and Southern churches the Confederate cause. LEWIS V. BALDWIN

Slovak Republic. The beginnings of church organization in this region are associated with the Byzantine mission of Cyril* and Methodius. But very little survived the fall of the Moravian Empire (906), and Christianity ultimately spread (in its Latin form) from the West as the region became part of medieval Hungary* (Upper Hungary) and was incorporated into its ecclesiastical structures (archbishopric of Esztergom, 1025–28).

The Reformation, especially Luther's teaching, found a favorable response, particularly among the (partly German speaking) population of mining towns. In the same period, the Ottoman Turks gained control over a substantial part of Hungary, and the seat of the Hungarian archbishopric moved from Esztergom to Trnava (1543–1822). Although most of Upper Hungary remained under Hapsburg control, the tense political situation prevented the Hapsburgs from implementing their re-Catholicization policy to the same extent as in the Western parts of their empire. The existence of three minority churches (Lutheran, Reformed, and Greek

Catholic) was ultimately legalized by the Act of Toleration (1781).

In the 19th c., the religious situation became increasingly complicated by national tension between the (dominant) Magyar- and Slovak-speaking populations. In 1918 Slovakia became part of Czechoslovakia; in 1939 Slovakia became an independent state under Hitler's tutelage. The role of the Roman Catholic Church, owing to its involvement in political life, is seen as highly controversial: a Roman Catholic priest who was president of the state, Jozef Tiso, was later executed as a war criminal.

Incorporated into Czechoslovakia again in 1945, Slovakia was exposed to a Communist regime (1948–89). Although less successful than in the Czech part of the country, the Communist antireligious campaign contributed to the secularization* of society. Present-day Slovakia (an independent state since 1993) experiences a situation common in other European countries: stagnation of membership in traditional churches. **See also CZECH REPUBLIC.**

Statistics: Population (2001): 5.4 million (M). Roman Catholics, 68.9%; Evangelicals, 6.9%; Greek Catholics, 4.1%; Reformed, 2%; others, 2.1%; without religious affiliation, 13%; unknown, 3%. (*Source*: 2001 census.)

MARTIN ELBEL

Slovenia. Slovenia became a nation state in 1991, the first of the six former Yugoslav republics to declare independence. Its population is largely homogeneous in ethnic and religious terms, with a large Roman Catholic majority. In 2006 a total of 41 religious groups and associations were officially registered with the state's Office for Religious Communities. Public opinion surveys, however, reveal a considerably lower percentage of regularly practicing believers (in surveys conducted in the 1990s, one-third of the population declared that they did not follow any religion). Thus some authors concluded that secularized* Catholics form the majority of the country's population.

The Roman Catholic Church championed the cultural and linguistic identity of the Slovenes in the 19th c. by endorsing the use of the Slovenian language in Church services. Although the first translation of the Bible was undertaken by Protestants (mid-16th c.), Protestantism was suppressed in the late 16th and early 17th c. In 1918 Slovenes were included in the Kingdom of Serbs, Croats, and Slovenes (renamed Yugoslavia*, 1929). During World War II, most of the Catholic clergy sided with the German and Italian occupiers and their collaborators, while in some areas it actively supported the anti-Fascist movement. In Tito's Yugoslavia, the Catholic Church was marginalized but not strongly oppressed and it gained prestige after the reestablishment of diplomatic relations with the Holy See (1970). After Slovenia achieved independence, the government signed agreements with the Catholic Bishops' Conference, which were followed by agreements with other denominations.

Social attitudes toward minority religions are generally tolerant. An issue of concern has been the absence of mosques for the country's Muslim population, a matter discussed for more than three decades. **See also HISTORY OF CHRISTIANITY CLUSTER: IN EUROPE: THE BALKANS; YUGOSLAVIA.**

Statistics: Population (2002): 2 million. Christians, 60.9% (Roman Catholics, 57.8%; Orthodox, 2.3%; Evangelicals, 0.8%); Muslims, 2.4%; other religionists, 3.5%; atheists, 10.1% (others did not specify). (*Source*: 2002 census.)

INA MERDJANOVA

Smith, Joseph (1805–44). An influential 19th-c. US religious figure, Joseph Smith was a 14-year-old boy living in New York when, by his own account, God the Father and Jesus Christ appeared to him, urging him not to join any organized religion. Three years later, he reported, the angel Moroni came to him and identified himself as a resurrected prophet and guardian of an ancient sacred record that was buried nearby. In 1827 Smith retrieved this record, which he said was inscribed on gold plates, and began to translate it "through the gift and power of God," making use of a "seer-stone" and an instrument called "interpreters." In March 1830, Smith published the resulting Book of Mormon*. Days later, Smith organized the Church of Jesus Christ of Latter-day Saints. A dynamic and charismatic leader with a prodigious talent for scriptural production, Smith was a locus of angelic visitations and heavenly revelations, claiming to restore ancient texts, doctrines, rituals, priesthood keys, and sealing powers.

He relocated converts to Kirtland, Ohio, and to areas in Missouri, and then founded the town of Nauvoo, Illinois. His teachings were centered on a fully restored church, modern-day prophets and apostles, premortal existence, eternal families, and the human potential for godhood.

Rumors of his practice of polygamy enraged opponents suspicious of his local and national political activity and a mob murdered him in 1844 in Carthage, Illinois. **See also** LATTER-DAY SAINTS; MORMON, BOOK OF; MORMON WORSHIP; YOUNG, BRIGHAM. TERRYL GIVENS

Social Darwinism. See DARWINISM.

Social Encyclicals. From 1891 to 1991, popes* of the Roman Catholic Church promulgated a series of 10 documents addressing issues of economic* justice*, political* relations within and between states, the proper ordering of cultural* values, and life in society. The purpose of these social teaching documents is not to propose detailed blueprints for how secular* society should organize its social and economic institutions, but rather to offer general moral guidance that can then be applied to specific local issues by those with the requisite expertise. Among the most prominent principles and concepts highlighted in social encyclicals are the following: the protection of human dignity, universal solidarity, the common good, the importance of family* life, the urgency of peacemaking and disarmament, the rights and responsibilities attached to property* ownership, the proper role of government, special protection for the poor*, and the full range of human* rights, including the right of workers to organize and the right of nations to sovereignty and self-determination.

Drawing on scriptural and theological sources, each encyclical attempts to interpret contemporary social realities in terms of Christian values, often praising certain courses of action (such as commitment to achieving living wages and the alleviation of poverty) and condemning others (such as environmental degradation and quick resort to wars* of aggression). Most of these documents devote considerable space to commenting on the dominant 20th-c. economic systems. Communism is consistently condemned for trampling on human freedom, while capitalism receives a mixture of praise for its virtues of free enterprise and efficiency, and criticism for its tendency to devolve into a system of overly materialistic competition in which market mechanisms are indifferent to dire poverty, severely inequitable concentrations of wealth*, unmitigated consumerism, and other inhumane outcomes.

The social encyclicals are supplemented by several other genres of related documents, such as pastoral letters of national or regional conferences of bishops, exhortations from synods of bishops, and other less authoritative papal writings and addresses concerned with social issues. The following are the "social encyclicals" (the documents can easily be found under their Latin titles):

Leo XIII	1891	*Rerum Novarum*
Pius XI	1931	*Quadragesimo Anno* (see Subsidiarity, Principle of)
John XXIII	1961	*Mater et Magistra*
John XXIII	1963	*Pacem in Terris*
Paul VI	1967	*Populorum Progressio*
Paul VI	1971	*Octogesima Adveniens*
Paul VI	1975	*Evangelii Nuntiandi*
John Paul II	1981	*Laborem Exercens*
John Paul II	1987	*Sollicitudo Rei Socialis*
John Paul II	1991	*Centesimus Annus*

See also CHRISTIAN SOCIALISM.

THOMAS MASSARO, SJ

Social Ethics entails normative reflection on society and its institutions in light of theological principles or shared moral commitments to justice* or human* rights. Emphasis may be placed on general Christian principles or on the issues that arise in a specific social context. In a modern, pluralistic society, Christian social ethics must strike a balance between a distinctive religious witness and relevance to wider social discussion.

Theologians have always thought that Christian ethics provides guidance for social, as well as individual, moral problems. The principles of natural law* articulated by Thomas Aquinas*, e.g., provide guidance for distinguishing between just and unjust laws. Calvin* derives general principles for the organization of society from the Ten* Commandments. In these traditions, social ethics consists primarily of reasoning from principles to social policy conclusions that share in the normative authority of the principles from which they are derived (see Deontological Ethics). More recent statements, however, emphasize the complex relationships between facts and principles that govern specific moral choices, so that conscientious Christians may disagree about how principles apply to cases.

Finding solutions to social problems often requires cooperation among different religious traditions and secular philosophies. To participate more effectively in these discussions, social ethics often seeks to formulate principles of justice* or statements of human* rights that can be widely affirmed, independently of the authority of the religious traditions involved. Sometimes called "middle axioms," these principles provide starting points from which all groups can move toward shared normative judgments about particular situations. North American Protestant churches have made extensive use of this type of social ethics. While reliance on generally shared principles risks losing distinctive elements of the Christian witness that fall outside of the consensus, many theologians regard participation in these public discussions that allow justice to be done for needy and marginalized people in the whole society as the distinctive task of Christian social ethics today.

Some recent critics question whether the consensus approach to social ethics relies too much on the expertise of educated elites. For Liberation* theologies, social ethics involves primarily the creation of alternative social communities, where people establish the conditions for justice and human dignity among themselves. Understood in this way, social ethics builds on the commitments and values that constitute a Christian community. It relies less on general principles than on specific, local experience, and it may result in resistance to the wider society rather than reform of it. **See also ECONOMY AND CHRISTIANITY CLUSTER: ECONOMIC ETHICS AND CHRISTIAN THEOLOGY; ETHICS AND CHRISTIANITY CLUSTER; LAW.** ROBIN W. LOVIN

Social Gospel Movement (the) took form in the USA from 1907 to 1920 to Christianize social, economic, political, and family life. With a growing conviction that the Kingdom* of God embraces all of human life, its advocates believed it was the church's duty to be the conscience and guide for "the Christian transfiguration of the social order," in the words of Walter Rauschenbusch*, pastor, professor, author, and one of its prominent leaders. Another leader was Washington Gladden, a nationally renowned preacher and orator, who was called "father of the Social Gospel."

Basic ideas and actions grounded in the OT prophets* and the social teachings of Jesus were not widespread until Protestant denominations created the Federal Council of Churches (December 1908). Social service programs were created by leaders of its new Church and Social Service Commission (1908–12). The Council also adopted the Social Creed of the Churches, based on a small-scale social creed first adopted by a Methodist General Conference, which Federal Council member denominations enlarged and approved, creating the Social Gospel Movement.

Social Gospel ideology was not accepted by all Protestants. Fundamentalists* during the 1920s attacked Federal Council assumptions that God's Kingdom could be attained on earth before the millennium* and that the church could be directly involved in politics*. Neo-orthodox* theologians attacked the Federal Council for its overly optimistic understanding of human nature and unrealistic ideas of social change. Reinhold Niebuhr's* *Moral Man and Immoral Society* (1932) convinced several denominations to abandon social pronouncements like the Social Creed of the Churches.

The economic depression of the 1930s, the impact of Hitler and Mussolini in Europe, and World War II overwhelmed Social Gospel optimism. The Federal Council responded by changing its Social Creed to Social Ideals, and was replaced by a new National Council of Churches in 1950. In the new organization, modified Social Gospel ideas continued to be implemented by four departments of its social service and social action, Division of Christian Life and Work. But the National Council abandoned the Social Ideals. Many denominations by then believed it was not possible for Christianity to transform the social order, but it could continue to be helpful in meeting human needs and offering social services. Christianizing the social order, as early advocates believed, was not feasible, but helping the needy has been a continuing ministry. **See also CHRISTIAN SOCIALISM.** DONALD K. GORRELL

Society of Jesus. See JESUITS.

Society for Promoting Christian Knowledge. See SPCK, SOCIETY FOR PROMOTING CHRISTIAN KNOWLEDGE.

Socinus, Faustus (1539–1604). Italian reformer, scholar. In *On Christ the Savior* (1578), he concluded from biblical studies that Christ was divine only by office, not by nature; Jesus was totally human, but God shared his divine power with him, making him an adopted deity who could be worshipped. Fearing accusations of heresy*, he settled in Krakow, Poland* (1579), where he was the prime inspiration for an anti-trinitarian movement. For him, reason* is the foremost authority in interpreting scripture; God's nature is one, not three; and humans have free will*. Many of his views were embodied in the Racovian* Catechism (1605). **See also UNITARIANISM.** MARK W. HARRIS

Sociological Studies of Christianity. Like sociology itself, the sociological study of Christianity began in the 19th c., as modernization called into question established social institutions. The key figures were Ernst Troeltsch* (1865–1921) and Max Weber* (1864–1920). Both related Christian life and teaching to its wider social contexts. This aim remains definitive of the sociological study of Christianity, a special field within the sociology of religion.

Rather than focusing on "the church*," and rather than invoking divine agency and individual human acts to explain its nature and development, sociological study views churches as social institutions that exist in relation to other institutions and structures. Like all sociology, there is a foundational commitment to the belief that "society" is a reality that shapes individuals, just as much as individuals shape society. Sociological studies of Christianity employ a range of methods. Troeltsch and Weber related general observations about premodern and modern societies to observations about the churches and Christianity. Subsequent sociologists have developed a range of more systematic and replicable methods for collecting and analyzing data. Quantitative methods (e.g. surveys) are used to collect information from a large number of sources (e.g. from a representative sample of the population). This makes them particularly suitable for testing theories and hypotheses. Qualitative methods include interviewing, participant observation, focus groups, and discourse analysis. These are useful in gathering in-depth information about social life and in generating new theories and hypotheses. Some significant studies of Christianity combine both approaches. There is a close relation and significant overlap between sociological and anthropological studies of religion. The latter are usually defined by their focus, through participant observation, on small-scale societies.

Sociological studies of Christianity differ in the scale of their social focus. Microlevel studies look at individual congregations (e.g. Ammerman). Mesolevel studies may investigate a denomination, network, or association (e.g. Griffith). Macrolevel studies consider topics like the growth of Pentecostalism* (e.g. Martin), the state of religion in the USA (e.g. Wuthnow), or the relations between Protestantism and capitalism (e.g. Weber).

Sociological studies of Christianity are undertaken both by committed Christians and by those who stand outside the tradition. There is a lively debate about the relative merits of "insider" versus "outsider" approaches. There is also an ongoing debate about the compatibility of theology and sociology. Sociological insights are sought by some Christians who seek to halt church decline and encourage church growth.

LINDA WOODHEAD

Sodality (Lat *sodalis,* "comrade"), a term used primarily in the Roman Catholic Church to designate religious organizations, Christian communities, or church groups defined by a specialized, task-oriented ministry, be it a devotional, missionary, or social ministry. Comparable to confraternities* in the Middle Ages, sodalities have similarities today to parachurch* organizations.

Sodom, portrayed as a place inhabited by wicked people (Gen 13:12–13), where Lot settled but from which he fled when God vowed to destroy it (Gen 19; cf. Amos 4:11; Isa 13:19; Jer 50:40). Condemned for sexual* perversion and violation of hospitality* (Gen 19:5) and neglect of the poor* (Ezek 16:48–50), Sodom is described as subject to eternal fire (Jude 7). Yet it will be more bearable for Sodom than for those towns that reject Jesus (Matt 10:15; 11:23–24; Luke 10:12), for as God destroyed Sodom, God will destroy the ungodly (2 Pet 2:6–8). Augustine* saw Sodom, like Babylon*, as the earthly city at the Last Judgment*, representing God's wrath.

JEFFRY C. DAVIS

Sojourner Truth (c1797–1883) was born into slavery* in New York as Isabella. She was sold several times, and while owned by the John Dumont family in Ulster County, she married Thomas, another of Dumont's slaves. They had five children. In 1827, New York law emancipated all slaves, but Isabella had already left her husband and run away with her youngest child. She went to work for the family of Isaac Van Wagenen in Ulster County.

In 1843 she took the name Sojourner Truth, believing this to be in accord with the instructions of the Holy* Spirit, and became a traveling preacher. She was a popular speaker with the Abolitionist Movement (late 1840s) and later began speaking on woman suffrage (1850). She delivered her most famous speech – "Ain't I a Woman?" – at a women's rights convention in Ohio (1851).

During the Civil* War, Sojourner Truth collected contributions of food and clothing for black regiments. She met Abraham Lincoln at the White House (1864), and while there she challenged the racial discrimination that condoned the segregation of streetcars.

After the Civil War, Sojourner Truth organized efforts to provide jobs for black refugees from the war, then continued speaking on women's rights and human* rights. **See also AFRICAN AMERICAN CLUSTER: HOLINESS; DOUGLASS, FREDERICK.**

MONYA A. STUBBS

Sola Scriptura (by Scripture alone). See SCRIPTURE PRINCIPLE.

Solemn League and Covenant, agreement between the Scottish and English Parliaments (1643) when the Scots, engaged in warfare with King Charles I, needed military assistance from the English. It pledged a "reformation of religion" in the three kingdoms of Scotland, England, and Ireland, outlawing both papacy and prelacy (bishops) in favor of the presbyterian form of church polity*. The work of the Westminster* Assembly was shaped by this political context, including the presence of the Scottish army in London. The Covenant pledged to "preserve and defend" the king's "person and authority"; this led to an alliance between the Scots and the king against Cromwell's army and Presbyterian opposition to the execution of the king (1649).

Solidarity, unity of interests and aspirations, sometimes through participation in a collective response to a concrete situation, sometimes through mutual commitment. **See also PREFERENTIAL OPTION FOR THE POOR.**

Solomon. The son of David* by Bathsheba*, Solomon succeeded to the throne of Israel* and ruled with magnificence and wisdom, according to 2 Samuel and 2 Chronicles. His 40-year reign is regarded as Israel's golden age of prosperity and peace. His theological importance is based on his role as the builder of the Temple* in Jerusalem*, whose physical plan and sacrificial rituals represent the actualization of the Israelite faith. Solomon's reputation for wisdom* gave rise to later traditions of his exorcistic* powers and mystical* knowledge, elaborated in the apocryphal Wisdom* of Solomon. The authorship of the Song* of Songs as well as Proverbs* was traditionally attributed to him. In the deuteronomistic perspective of 2 Samuel, Solomon succumbs to apostasy late in his reign, bringing about the gradual disintegration of the united Kingdom of Israel. In the NT, Solomon is rarely mentioned directly, but the identification of Jesus as "the son of David" (Mark 10:46–52) in connection with healing may refer indirectly to Solomon. The church fathers, particularly Augustine*, regarded the biblical traditions connected with Solomon as theological allegories*. The Song of Songs was seen as an allegorical expression of God's love for the church.

NEIL SILBERMAN

Solomon, Odes of, collection of 42 Christian hymns transmitted together with the Psalms of Solomon in the 2nd c. CE. Themes include gratitude for deliverance, purity and holiness*, and the love between God and believers. The alleged authorship of Solomon is not suggested by the manuscripts or the content of the Odes, and the reference to Solomon in the title may be secondary. **See also PSEUDEPIGRAPHA.**

JOHANNES TROMP

Solomon, Psalms of, 18 Jewish poems, written in Judea in the 1st c. BCE, in the tradition of the biblical psalms and representing an unpretentious piety of holiness. A number of them seem to reflect the political circumstances of their age. Psalm 17 gives an elaborate description of the coming of the awaited Davidic Messiah. Psalm 18 is sometimes held to be a Christian addition. **See also PSEUDEPIGRAPHA.**

JOHANNES TROMP

Solomon Islands. Christianity has a strong, pervasive, and diversified presence in Solomon Islands. The churches play an important public role as the only institutions outside the government with the capacity to provide a moral basis for civil society.

Spanish explorers (16th c.) and subsequently French Roman Catholics (1840s) made the first, unsuccessful attempts to introduce Christianity to Solomon Islands. The Melanesian Mission of the Anglican Church, based in New* Zealand, arrived in the 1850s. Its first bishop, J. C. Patteson, was killed (1871) and is regarded as a martyr. The British protectorate (1893) opened the door to Roman Catholic, Methodist, South Sea Evangelical, and Seventh*-day Adventist missions, which generally had a comfortable relationship with the colonial government. They provided basic medical services and education (one of the main attractions of Christianity was its association with literacy and Western education). The Pacific War (1942–45) brought severe disruption. In 1961 the Christian Fellowship Church, an indigenous religious movement, separated from the Methodist mission. The Anglican and Protestant missions became self-governing churches with local leadership (1960s and 1970s). By the time Solomon Islands had become an independent state within the

British Commonwealth (1978), the great majority of the population had adopted Christianity.

Since the 1950s, the historic churches have been challenged by new religious movements: Jehovah's* Witnesses, Baha'i*, and numerous Evangelical*, especially Pentecostal*/ Charismatic*, bodies; the latter gained a strong following in expanding urban areas. Starting in 1999, ethnic conflicts and a breakdown in effective government pushed Solomon Islands almost to civil war. Some within the older churches played important roles as mediators, encouraging disarmament. Seven members of the Melanesian Brotherhood, an indigenous Anglican religious community, were killed (2003) while doing this peacemaking work.

Statistics: Population (1999): 0.40 million (M). Christians, 97.5% (Anglicans, 0.13 M; Roman Catholics, 0.08 M; members of South Sea Evangelical Church, 0.07 M; Seventh-day Adventists, 0.05 M; members of United Church [formerly Methodist], 0.04 M; members of Christian Fellowship Church, 0.01 M; other Christians, 0.02M); traditional religionists, 0.8%; other religionists (including Muslims), 1.2%. (*Source*: 1999 census.)

DAVID HILLIARD

Soloviev, Vladimir Sergeevich (1853–1900), philosopher, poet, Orthodox lay theologian. Born and educated in Moscow; briefly a university lecturer; thereafter an independent scholar and writer. He was a pioneer of ecumenism and interfaith dialogue, and a collaborator in Russia's first professional philosophy journal, *Questions of Philosophy and Psychology*.

The historical context of Soloviev's work was the bitter debate about whether Russia* should become a European liberal society or promote the religious and communal values of Orthodox* Christianity. Soloviev believed Russia could do both. He envisioned the reconciliation of Russia and the West, Orthodoxy and Western Christianity, Christendom and Judaism*, the gospel and the secular* world.

The theological core of Soloviev's thought is the concept of *bogochelovechestvo*, translated as "Godmanhood," "theandry," "divine humanity," or "humanity of God." The concept thematizes the Incarnation* as the foundation for universal reconciliation. Soloviev promoted human* rights and called the Orthodox Church to philanthropic service in the world. He also renovated the notion of Sophia, or Wisdom* of God, describing his encounters with Sophia in a small but important body of lyric poetry.

The epitome of a lay Christian intellectual, Soloviev had an influence extending far beyond philosophy and theology to law, politics, and literature. **See also BERDYAEV, NIKOLAI ALEKSANDROVICH; BULGAKOV, SERGEI NIKOLAEVICH.**

PAUL VALLIERE

Song of Songs (Song of Solomon), a poetic biblical book, dated as late as the 3rd c. BCE, is strikingly secular. It does not allude to God or the sacred, and refers only in an uncommitted manner to some biblical names like Jerusalem and Solomon. In the form of a dialogue between two lovers (not spouses), the praises that each sings of the other's handsomeness are exquisite, although surprising metaphors signal that the poem's topic is not purely aesthetic (see 4:4). Historically, the Song has been allegorically* interpreted in both the synagogue and the church: "he" represents God (or Christ) and "she" Israel or the church or the individual soul. Such interpretations may have been instrumental in the canonization of the poem (Rabbi Aqiba [2nd c. CE]: "All Scripture will pass, but not the Song").

Today, by scholarly consensus, the poem is read literally: it is about carnal, embodied love, and the latter is glorified as the most precious human sentiment. To detect a magnificent gift of God behind this hymn of praise to eros is not illegitimate. But love here is subversive (see 3:3–4, 5:7); the female author shuns customs and conventions. Love is not dictated (by external authority) or made commonplace by being institutionalized. In this way, the Song is challenging all power that be. It ends as it started, with the lover escaping and jumping "upon the mountains of spices." For "love is strong as death, passion fierce as the grave" (8:6); no one can domesticate it (8:7). **See also BODY; LOVE; SEXUALITY, ISSUES OF, CLUSTER.**

ANDRÉ LACOCQUE

Song of the Three Children, a section of 68 verses in the Septuagint* and Vulgate* versions of the Book of Daniel* but not found in the Aramaic–Hebrew text. Since it has little connection with the story of Daniel, it appears to have been written for another occasion, then inserted into Daniel (between 3:23 and 3:24). It includes the prayer of Azarias and the canticle of the three young men, used in both Eastern and Western liturgies and called the *Benedicite*.

Son of God in the New Testament has different connotations in the Synoptic* Gospels, Paul's letters, the Gospel of John, Hebrews, and other texts. Later Christologies* and debates about the Trinity* are based on these NT texts, each emphasizing one set of NT texts or another, but without exhausting their meaning.

1. "Son of God" refers to the divine nature of Jesus Christ when understood in light of the NT texts about the incarnation* of a preexistent* divine being (e.g. John 1:1–14), which was identified with the "Logos" and the wisdom* of God (1 Cor 1:24), was with God at the creation (Heb 1:1–4), and was in the form of God yet took that of a human (Phil 2:6–8). The divine nature of the Son was much debated in the controversies over Christologies and the Trinity* that arose from the ecumenical* councils and, later, in both the Western* and the Eastern* churches.
2. "Son of God" refers to a father–son relationship with God and the specific role that Christ has because of this relationship, when the NT texts (especially the Synoptic Gospels, including about the virginal conception in Matthew and Luke, and Pauline texts) are read in terms of the OT. Jesus as the Christ/Messiah*, like his followers (who pray "our Father in Heaven" or "Abba") as the people of God (see Children of God), is in a father–son relationship with God, just as were the kings in Israel-Judah (especially David and his descendants, 2 Sam 7; Ps 2) and the people of God (Israel; e.g. Exod 4:22–23; cf. Matt 2:15). Because of this special relationship, Christ has divine authority and speaks in God's name, manifesting the divine Wisdom (as in Matthew), just as the kings reigned in the name of God and as the people represented God among the nations (e.g. Exod 19:4–6).
3. "Son of God" refers to Jesus as filled with divine power (e.g. Mark 1:11; Rom 1:3–4) or with God's Spirit (e.g. Luke 4:1, 14, 18) or as empowered by God to free people from bondage (to evil powers/diseases and to sin; Mark 2:1–12). This meaning is found when the NT texts are read in terms of Jewish apocalyptic texts, and in terms of the Hellenistic traditions about miracle workers (*theios aner*), and when one takes into account the dual designation of Jesus as the Son of God and the Son* of man. **See also CHRISTOLOGIES CLUSTER; TRINITY IN EASTERN ORTHODOXY; TRINITY IN THE WESTERN TRADITION.**

DANIEL PATTE

Son of Man (also translated "Son of humanity"), a self-designation of Jesus in the canonical Gospels, is understood in two ways: (1) "Son of man" as a Semitic expression referring to a specific human being is popularly and dogmatically taken to be an affirmation of Jesus' humanity ("Son of God" refers to his divinity). While this interpretation is plausible in many passages (referring to the lowliness of Jesus; e.g. Matt 8:20) and can be grounded in the use of this Semitic phrase in the OT, especially to designate the prophet in Ezekiel*, it is unlikely in most passages of the Gospels. (2) "Son of man" as a reference to Jesus as an apocalyptic figure, namely the judge and supernatural deliverer of the end-time, is quite common in the Gospels. "You will see the Son of Man seated at the right hand of Power and coming on the clouds of heaven" (Mark 14:62, par.) is a quasi-quotation of Dan 7:13–14, apparently interpreted as in 1 Enoch* 37–71, Wis 1–6, and 4 Ezra 11–13 to refer to Jesus as God's anointed one, the eschatological judge and deliverer, who will come back as the exalted Jesus as judge (at the Parousia*); but in Jesus and his ministry, the Son of man already had an earthly existence and was persecuted because he initiated the end-time.

DANIEL PATTE

Sons of God. See CHILDREN OF GOD.

Sophia. See WISDOM.

Sophia ("Second Phoebe") was a deacon* of the Jerusalem* Church, according to an elegant funerary inscription of the Byzantine period found incomplete and broken into five pieces on the Mount of Olives, Jerusalem (1903), perhaps from a cemetery of one of the many monasteries built on the west side of the mount facing Jerusalem. The inscription, now in the museum of the White* Fathers, Church of St. Anne, Jerusalem, reads, "Here lies the slave and bride of Christ, Sophia, deacon, the second Phoebe, who slept in peace the twenty-first of the month of March in the eleventh Indiction . . . the Lord God . . ."

"Slave*" or "servant" of Christ or God is a common early Christian term (cf. Rom 1:1). The comparison is to Phoebe* (Rom 16:1–2) as deacon* but probably also as benefactor. A female deacon of Jerusalem would have had an important role in the care of pilgrims*, instruction and assistance at baptism*, and liturgical leadership of women in the choir. The titles "deacon" and "deaconess*" seem to have been interchangeable for women. Benefaction of prominent women included adorning churches, supporting clergy and hospices, and giving direct assistance to the poor* and needy.

CAROLYN OSIEK

Soteriology (Gk *soteria*), aspect of Christian theology that deals with salvation through Christ, redemption*, atonement*, and grace*, and indirectly with sin*, the Fall*, and eschatology*. **See also SALVATION.**

Soul, in the Bible and Christian tradition, was usually *not* defined as a spiritual substance chained in the prison of the body*, as many Christians view it and as it was viewed in some ancient Greek (Orphism) and Indian traditions that influenced Platonism* and Neoplatonism*. The HB uses the word *nephesh,* often translated "soul," which refers to the visible living creature and not to soul as distinct from body. In the NT, *psyche,* often translated "soul," means the life principle or even living thing; although it can indicate soul as opposed to body, it also indicates the moral self. Similarly, despite the Gnostic* interpretations, the opposition of flesh (*sarx*) and spirit (*pneuma*) in Paul is not a contrast of body and soul but a contrast of human selfishness and God's grace. *Sarx, pneuma,* and *psyche* each refer to the whole human being.

In Greek thought, a variety of views emerged. With Plato's attempt to account for rationality, soul was described as the *incorporeal* seat of reason* (*nous*), passion (*thumos*), and desire (*epithumia*). Platonism thought of the soul as immortal*, or undying, not only surviving the body but preexisting it (see Immortality). For Aristotle* (in his classic *On the Soul* [Gk *Peri psyche;* Lat *De anima*]), there is *not* a "soul" using a body, as a captain uses a ship; rather, the soul is the actuality or form of a living body, that which makes the body alive. Hence form and matter are principles of an individual living organism, not two separate substances (Aristotle is not a dualist).

The Christian tradition beginning with Irenaeus*, Origen*, Gregory* of Nyssa, and especially Nemesius* of Emesa introduced the distinctive notion of a human as a soul–body unit, although for Origen soul was a spiritual being that had become a soul. Augustine*, influenced by Neoplatonism, held that the soul is a spiritual substance that uses the body, yet later emphasized the unity of the human being. Aristotle's position was renewed by Thomas Aquinas* (13th c.); soul and body are principles of an individual living organism, not two separate substances. This complex but unitary account of soul, whether Augustinian or Thomist, was rejected in early modern times by Descartes*.

Attempting to offer a new proof of the immortality of soul (in opposition to Renaissance materialist accounts), Descartes ends up destroying the notion of a unified human being: in any human being, there are two substances, one spiritual (studied by philosophy), the other material (studied by the science of mechanics). Locke* uses the word "soul" but rejects the notion of a spiritual substance.

For Kant* the picture changes; proofs of the immortality of the soul lead to "paralogisms"; one cannot give a valid rational proof of the immortality of the soul, yet the word "soul" can be used as a moral postulate. In later modern philosophy, words such as "*Ich,*" "Will," "Absolute Subject," and "Will-to-Power" replace "soul." Hegel rejects the notion of a substantial soul and replaces it with "Subject." In some modern approaches, "person*" replaces the word "soul."

JEREMIAH M. HACKETT

South Africa. The presence of Christianity in South Africa dates back to 1501, when a small chapel was built in Mossel Bay (between present-day Cape Town and Port Elizabeth) by Portuguese Roman Catholics, possibly explorers (Bartolomeu Dias and Vasco da Gama) and traders. But there is no record of any church activity beyond the building of this chapel until the arrival of Dutch settlers under Jan Van Riebeeck (1652). The newly established Dutch Reformed Church was to receive its first minister to serve their religious needs in 1665.

Although the Synod of Dordrecht, Holland, had decided in 1618 that the "heathen" were not to be baptized, the Church experienced in 1661 the conversion* of the first Khoi ("Hottentot," in colonial parlance; the Khoi people together with the San people, so-called "Bushmen," were the earliest inhabitants of the Cape and Kgalagadi areas of South Africa). But the Dutch Reformed Church did not engage in missionary activity in the country for more than two centuries. Given the different stages in which various churches arrived and manifested themselves in South Africa, it is possible to categorize them as follows: the settler churches, the missionary churches, the African Instituted Churches, and the witnessing mission churches.

The Settler Churches. The earliest settler church in South Africa was the Dutch Reformed Church. Originally this church was intended to minister purely to the spiritual needs of the settlers. It is clear, however, that even so, it did not exclude the participation of the local people – hence the first native conversion referred to earlier. By 1829, however, some members of the Church began clamoring for segregated Communion* services for settlers and native Christians. Although the Church's initial response was to reject such appeals, it finally yielded to the pressure in 1857. This was the beginning of a segregated Dutch Reformed Church.

The Church broke into different settler churches, the first that of the Nederduitse Herformde Kerk (1853). It was followed by the formation of the Gereformeerde Kerk (Reformed Church) (1859) and later by the Apostolic Faith Mission (1910). All these churches adopted segregationist policies, basing them on the Bible. The Gereformeerde Kerk, in addition, was deeply Calvinistic, following the teachings of Dutch theologian Abraham Kuyper*.

The Missionary Church. The Dutch Reformed Church officially began to engage in mission work in 1857, and this was a mission limited to the "coloured" people (i.e. African people of mixed race) in the Cape. The leading figure in this effort was Andrew Murray, Jr., son of a Scottish Presbyterian missionary, who had been invited by the British Cape authorities to minister to the Dutch Reformed Church in preference to a missionary of Dutch origin. The Dutch Reformed Church established its first "coloured church" in 1881. The other white reformed churches engaged in mission still later; the Gereformeerde Kerk ordained its first missionary in 1910, and the Nederduitse Herformde Kerk commissioned its first missionary in 1916. But by the time the white reformed churches officially ventured into the mission field, their unofficial missionary work in South Africa had been going on for more than a century.

The first missionary pioneer to arrive in South Africa was the Moravian George Schmidt. He began mission work among the Khoi people in Genadendal, Cape, in 1737 but returned to Germany in 1744 with a sense of frustration and failure. The Dutch Reformed Church ministers and settlers were apparently suspicious of his motives. In 1792 the Genadendal mission station was reopened by his successors, and mission work gradually spread among the Khoi people.

The Moravians were followed in 1799 by London Missionary Society (LMS) missionary Johannes van der Kemp. After experiencing initial failure in working among the AmaXhosa people (1799–1800) in the Eastern Cape, he established a mission station for the Khoi people in Bethelsdorp, near Port Elizabeth. Van der Kemp integrated into the Khoi community and married a Khoi woman. Several LMS missionaries succeeded him, working in different areas of the country. They included Robert Moffat, who was later joined by David Livingstone* in Kuruman in 1841, and John Philip, who became Cape superintendent of the LMS in the years 1819–51 (see also Colenso, John William).

Protestant missions in general began to expand in the country after the British occupation of the Cape in 1806 and the coming of the British settlers in 1820. Lutherans and Roman Catholics were not allowed to establish churches in South Africa until 1778 and 1804, respectively. The Catholics were expelled by the British only two years later, but returned in 1852 in the form of the religious* order of the Oblates of Mary Immaculate (OMI); they did not settle successfully, however, until after the arrival of the Australian Order of Trappists (1882), who founded the Marianhill Mission and its institutions near Durban in 1884.

A trail of missionary societies and denominations followed the lead of the LMS and spread throughout the country. They included the Rhenish Mission Society (1829), representing the Lutheran, Reformed, and United Churches of Germany; the Paris Missionary Society (1829); the Berlin Mission (1834); the American Board of Commissioners (1834); and the Glasgow Missionary Society, which established itself in the Eastern Cape and later helped to found the well-known Lovedale Institute (1841–1950), which provided education on the basis of complete equality (although not without features of a segregated vocational model) and would eventually comprise a primary school, a high school, a technical school, a teacher training college, a theological college, and the first hospital to train African women as nurses, before being closed by the Bantu Education Act of 1953 (which enforced separation of races in all educational institutions). By 1860 various missionary societies were active in the Cape, Natal, Namibia*, Botswana*, and Lesotho*.

One of the significant presences in the Eastern Cape following the British settlers in 1820 was that of Methodist missionaries, including Rev. William Shaw (who founded a chain of mission stations from the Eastern Cape to Natal), John Ayliffe (credited with bringing the gospel to the Mfengu, one group among the Nguni people, Eastern Cape, often identified as part of the

Xhosa), and J. W. Appleyard (who, with the help of African assistants, translated into Xhosa the NT, 1846, then the whole Bible, 1859). By 1827 Methodists had also established a presence in the Transkei. They established the Kilnerton Institute, the first African teachers' college in the Transvaal in 1883–4. The Presbyterians and the Anglicans followed the Methodists into the Eastern Cape mission fields.

Missionary strategy varied between the "civilizing" approach of converting natives to Western culture and the "indigenizing" approach, which sought to establish native leadership and to Christianize the African way of life. Consequently, it was not always the settlers alone who advocated separation between settler churches and mission churches; it was also the missionaries. Some scholars have observed that, whatever their shortcomings, missionaries are to be credited for their pioneering efforts in black education through the establishment of institutions such as Lovedale, Kilnerton, Marianhill, Healdtown, and St. Matthews.

African Instituted Churches. Missionaries in South Africa were agents not only of conversion* but also of transformation through education* and other forms of social* development. One of the common problems of earlier evangelization, however, was the missionaries' tendency to equate Christianity with Western civilization, thus not allowing the Christian message to be integrated into the culture of the people.

Some missionaries had a very low regard for the natives and almost seemed to doubt their humanity. This kind of attitude was prominent among members of the clergy, which created resentment and led some of the early African clergy to leave the missionary church. A variety of reasons were given for these secessions, including the clash of cultures* over religion, the missionaries' association of Christianity with Western culture, the discriminatory attitudes of some missionaries and of white Christians in general, white authoritarianism and domination, racial* discrimination and paternalism, and the denial of leadership and initiative to native African Christians. African leaders perceived that they could overcome these ills only by leaving the missionary churches and founding their own, where they would not only preach the gospel by word of mouth but also live it in practice.

By 1884, therefore, the missionary churches were to experience their first breakaway and the establishment of the first African* Instituted Church (AIC). Other AICs followed:

Founder	Date	From	Name of new church
Rev. Nehemiah Tile	1884	Methodist Church	Thembu National Church
	1889	Berlin Mission	Lutheran Bapedi Church
Mangena* Mokone	1892	Methodist Church	Ethiopian Church
James Dwane*	c1900	Methodist Church, then the Anglican Church	Order of Ethiopia
	1892	American Board of Mission	Zulu Congregational Church
Gardiner Mvuyana	1917	Congregational Church	African Congregational Church
P. J. Mzimba	1893	Free Church of Scotland	Presbyterian Church of Africa
Mdlelwa Hlongwane	1932	Methodist Church	Bantu Methodist Church

The AICs represent one aspect of the struggle of the Christian Church in South Africa, namely the struggle for freedom. After these early breakaways, there were to be other secessions, including those from among the AICs themselves, and initiatives that resulted in the formation of thousands of smaller churches as well as large, interprovincial and international churches, such as the Zion Christian Church, Amanazaretha, St. John's Church, and a significant number of Pentecostal* and Charismatic* churches. Today the South African scene is replete with AICs and Pentecostal/Charismatic movements, which are increasing in number and many of which numerically rival the traditional "mission churches."

The Witnessing Mission Churches. The racial and discriminatory problems that led to the original secessions from the mission churches and the establishment of the AICs were part and parcel of the Christian Church in South Africa from the very beginning. These discriminatory problems within the churches were a reflection of the larger society, in which segregation was practiced in most aspects of life. It is not surprising, therefore, that there was almost no reaction in the church to discriminatory legislation against the African people. The church's witness against segregatory practices thus began only in 1948, when the National Party won the country's national elections with the promise of fully implementing segregation through its policy of apartheid*.

Even though the churches had tried to struggle against apartheid since 1948, their own internal practices in matters of race were often contradictory. Yet the churches had seen the need to establish a Christian council (1936), which later became the South African Council of Churches (1968; including all the major mission churches but not the AICs), in order to address the social ills that even before 1948 bedeviled the country. The Council was responsible for organizing a number of conferences that challenged the government's policy of apartheid in various ways and the government's interference with church practices. They included the Rosettenville Conference (1949) and the Cottesloe Consultation (1960), both in Johannesburg. The resolutions of the Cottesloe Consultation were severely reprimanded by Prime Minister Hendrik Verwoerd, leading to a retraction by the participating Dutch Reformed churches. Those Dutch Reformed Church delegates who resisted were ostracized by their congregations, which created an opportunity for the establishment of the Christian Institute (1963) by one of the leaders, the Rev. Dr. Beyers Naude. The Christian Institute was later investigated by the government, subsequently declared an "affected organization" (i.e. an organization that could continue its operations but was proscribed from raising or receiving funds from sources outside the country), and finally became the only white-led organization to be banned along with 19 black organizations and newspapers in the aftermath of the 1976 student uprising.

In 1968 the South African Council of Churches was brought to prominence by its publication of a document entitled "A Message to the People of South Africa." Like the Cottesloe Consultation documents, the "Message" provoked the ire of Verwoerd's successor, John Vorster, by suggesting that the apartheid policy was in conflict with the Christian faith.

The incipient "radicalization" of the South African Council of Churches began with its first lay Methodist general secretary, John Rees, who was succeeded by then-Bishop Desmond Tutu as its first black general secretary in 1978. During Tutu's leadership, the Council increasingly became "provocative" enough to be investigated by a government commission, ostensibly with respect to the finances of the Council and its many social projects; Tutu's passport was withheld for a time. On the eve of the democratic national elections in South Africa, two last conferences were organized by the churches through the South African Council of Churches. One, in Rustenburg (1990), published a document known as the Rustenburg Declaration, envisaging a future society, church, and state. The second conference, in Cape Town, was organized in collaboration with the World* Council of Churches. The fact that it lacked the momentum of the first conference raised questions about the real strength and appeal of the mission churches in the country.

Since the dawn of democracy in 1994, there has been a certain degree of rapprochement between black and white segments of the missionary churches in South Africa. Although old attitudes have not completely died out, black people now have more say in the affairs of their churches, they are more assertive, and the number of church leaders has grown. Because of the new law of the land, all the churches have done away with their segregationist policies, at least in theory. Although black leadership is now firmly established in most missionary churches, the question remains open regarding the extent to which these leaders have full control in steering their congregations as members of the single body of Christ.

Statistics: Population (2000): 40.4 million (M). Christians, 33.6 M, 83% (members of African Instituted Churches and other independents, 19 M; Protestants, 12.4 M; Roman Catholics, 3.4 M; Anglicans, 2.6 M); African Religionists, 3.4 M; Hindus, 1 M; Muslims, 1 M; nonreligious, 1 M. (Based on *World Christian Encyclopedia*, 2001.)

MOKGETHI MOTLHABI

Southern Baptist Convention. With an estimated 16 million members in affiliated congregations in all 50 states, the Southern Baptist Convention (SBC) is the largest Protestant denomination in the USA. Southerners formed the SBC in 1845 at a meeting in Augusta, Georgia, when it became clear that the two primary Baptist mission societies, the Triennial Convention and the American Baptist Home Mission Society, would not appoint slaveholding missionaries (see Baptist Churches Cluster:

In North America). The SBC adopted the convention model, which put both home and foreign mission agencies under the auspices of one ongoing denominational entity.

Any Baptist Church in "friendly cooperation with the Convention" is considered a Southern Baptist Church. "Friendly cooperation" usually means financial support for SBC enterprises. Congregations are autonomous and usually aligned with their local associations and state conventions as well as the SBC. All such affiliations are voluntary, and the only SBC mechanism for disciplining congregations is to deny seats to messengers (delegates) at the annual meeting or to return funds sent to the denomination's agencies and institutions. Congregations are free to appoint and dismiss their pastors and dispense with their property as they wish.

From 1979 to 1995, the SBC experienced a tumultuous schism between "moderates," who had controlled the Convention's agencies and seminaries, and "conservatives," who claimed that moderate leaders were too liberal. The conservative battle cry was the "inerrancy* of Scripture," but a variety of other theological and cultural issues played a role in the split as well. The SBC controversy, as it was called, resulted in conservatives taking the reins of power in all SBC agencies and all six Southern Baptist seminaries. Moderates formed their own missionary agency, several seminaries, and a quasi-denomination called the Cooperative Baptist Fellowship. The vast majority of congregations, however, continue to support the SBC.

BARRY HANKINS

Southern Christian Leadership Conference (SCLC), an interdenominational organization formed by Martin Luther King*, Jr., and other church and civil* rights leaders at the Ebenezer Baptist Church, Atlanta, Georgia (1957), to expand the Montgomery Improvement Association that led the bus boycott in Montgomery (1955–56). King served as its first president until his death (1968). Designed to "serve as a channel through which local protest organizations in the South could coordinate their activities" and "to give the total struggle a sense of Christian and disciplined direction," the SCLC has been called "a church," "a faith operation," "the social action arm of the Black Church," "the Black Church writ large," and "the dynamic center of a cluster of organizations that made up the Civil* Rights Movement." Committed to nonviolent direct action and civil disobedience, the organization's first action (1957) was a prayer pilgrimage to Washington, D.C., led by King and supported by some 25,000. Afterward, the SCLC led mass marches and provided moral and financial support for sit-ins, freedom rides, and other protest activities aimed at eliminating segregation and achieving voting rights and economic justice in the US South. It figured prominently in mass protest movements in Albany, Georgia (1961–62), Birmingham, Alabama (1963), Washington, D.C. (1963), St. Augustine, Florida (1964), Selma, Alabama (1965), Chicago, Illinois (1966–67), and Memphis, Tennessee (1968), and spearheaded the Poor People's Campaign (1967–68). After King received the Nobel Peace Prize (1964), the organization paid more attention to global affairs, including the war in Vietnam, South African apartheid, and poverty and economic injustice in Asia, Africa, and Latin America. After King's death, the organization gradually declined in visibility and influence, despite the efforts of its other presidents, Ralph Abernathy, Joseph E. Lowery, Martin Luther King, III, Fred D. Shuttlesworth, and Charles Steele.

LEWIS V. BALDWIN

South India, Church of (CSI), formed in 1947 as the union of Anglican, Methodist, Presbyterian, and Congregationalist denominations in South India. CSI (with c2.9 million members in 2000) was formed in response to the rise of Indian national consciousness, as its founding leaders declared: "The Church of South India desires, conserving all that is of spiritual value in its Indian heritage, to express under Indian conditions and in Indian forms, the spirit, the thought and the life of the church Universal." The Church pledges to be mindful of its missionary calling for the evangelization* of South India and other parts of the world. This was initially understood to be direct evangelization, but after the first synod it came to be seen in a broader framework.

CSI accepts the threefold* ministry but distinctively emphasizes that the primary focus and function of ministry should be pastoral, and not administrative or ritual, and thus uses the title "presbyter" rather than "priest." Similarly, although it incorporates non-episcopal churches, CSI accepts the historic episcopacy, but without accepting the doctrine of apostolic* succession, thus affirming that churches without episcopacy are true churches. A bishop is a chief pastor, feeding the flock of God, with the conviction that all members are called to participate in the ministry of building up the Church. Ordained and specialized ministries are envisioned from this perspective.

Just after the union, some churches, especially in urban areas, tried to maintain their earlier identities, particularly regarding worship. But actual union was soon aided by the uniformity of worship. The CSI liturgy carefully incorporates elements from the worship services of all traditions and includes more participation for the laity, free liturgical movements, and contemporary concerns in prayer. Furthermore, the bishops are agents of unity, because each diocese includes congregations from different traditions. However, another issue of disunity continues to plague the Church, namely the divisions of caste*, language, and region. **See also** INDIA. K. C. ABRAHAM

Spain. Few nations in Western Europe have so closely identified Roman Catholicism with the state than Spain. The Second Republic (1931–39) separated church and state for the first time in the nation's history. The defeat of the Republic and the dictatorship of General Francisco Franco restored the Church's official status through generous financial support and privileges, especially in the field of education. The country's small Protestant minority lost the religious liberty it had enjoyed under the Republic, until 1966, when the government, following the exhortations of the Second Vatican* Council (1962–65), passed the Law on Religious Liberty, which removed most restrictions on religious minorities. The emergence of democratic institutions following the death of Franco (1975) led to the introduction of full religious liberty in the Constitution of 1978. As a result, membership in the Protestant churches has increased, although a majority of the population identifies itself as Roman Catholic. The challenge to Catholicism has come primarily from secularizing* currents, which by the early 20th c. had led to the de-Christianization of certain social groups, especially industrial workers and the landless day laborers employed on the estates of Andalusia and Extremadura. The accelerated modernization of the economy and society occurring since 1960 following a West European model was accompanied by a significant decline in religious practice and the Church's influence over public moral standards.

Early History. Christianity was introduced among the diverse peoples inhabiting Roman Spain during the later 2nd and 3rd c. Although subject to periodic waves of persecution, especially during the reign of Emperor Diocletian* (284–305), the Christian population survived and grew during the 5th c. The disintegration of the Roman Empire and the incursion of Goth* Germanic tribes (5th c.), Arian Christians, led to the establishment of the Visigothic monarchy and a long period of tension with Latin Christianity (Roman Catholicism). The Spanish Church became an Arian Christian Church (415–587), which viewed itself as the "Catholic Church." The conversion (587) of King Reccared* from Arianism* to Latin Christianity (Roman Catholicism) initiated a period of closer cooperation between church and monarchy that produced a flourishing religious culture.

The stability of the Visigothic monarchy was compromised by chronic civil conflicts that left it exposed to the invasion (711) of a Muslim army of Arabs and Berbers. By 719, they had swept through the Iberian Peninsula and reached the Pyrenees. Of Visigothic Spain there remained only a few small Christian principalities in the northern mountains along the Cantabrian coast. The establishment of Islamic rule over most of the Iberian Peninsula was fundamental to the history of Christianity for centuries to come.

The struggle of the medieval Christian kingdoms to recover the lands under Muslim rule lasted until the conquest of the Moorish kingdom of Granada in 1492 by Ferdinand and Isabella. The conflict between the Islamic states of Iberia and its several Christian kingdoms was far from being a straightforward battle between two opposing religions. The fabled *reconquista* enshrined in Spanish national historiography took the form less of uninterrupted warfare than of episodic conflict between periods of political, economic, and cultural interchange between Islamic and Christian Spain, although from the 13th c. onward the most important Christian kingdoms, Castile and Aragon, became more aggressive toward Islam.

Toward Religious Uniformity. Christian and Islamic Spain each faced the problem of dealing with religious minorities. Following the triumph of Islam (7th c.), much of the Christian population converted to Islam*. A Christian minority and an institutional church survived in spite of episodic persecution. But, in general, Muslim rulers allowed their Christian and Jewish subjects to practice their religion subject to certain limitations. As Christian Spain expanded southward, the Muslim population was displaced either to North Africa or to the surviving Islamic territories in the south. Muslims remaining in the Peninsula following the triumph of Christian arms were forced to convert to Christianity, but the newly converted (*moriscos**) continued to hold tenaciously to their old faith through the 16th c. Between 1609 and 1611, the entire *morisco* population was expelled (see Islam and Christianity Cluster). The survival of the Jewish population depended on the sufferance of rulers, aristocrats, and Christian society itself. Toward the end of the 14th c., popular riots, often encouraged by the clergy, were directed against the Jews in an increasingly hostile atmosphere that caused some Jews to convert to Christianity. The situation of converted Jews (*conversos*) improved dramatically with the removal of certain civil disabilities imposed on the Jews. *Conversos* came to occupy important positions in church and state. As the 14th c. progressed, hostility toward these "New Christians" increased among sectors of the clergy and the populace (see Judaism and Christianity Cluster).

The establishment of the Royal and Supreme Council of the Inquisition* by Ferdinand and Isabella (1478) was motivated in part by hostility toward the *conversos*. The Inquisition directed its energies, almost exclusively during its first three decades, against *conversos* accused of secretly observing their Jewish faith. The Inquisition went about its task implacably and ordered the execution during this period of more individuals, largely *conversos*, than at any other time in its 300-year history. The Inquisition's authority extended only to baptized Christians. Unconverted Jews remained beyond its reach. In 1492 Ferdinand and Isabella ordered the expulsion of Jews from the Hispanic kingdoms.

16th-Century Revival. The religious uniformity achieved between 1492 and 1611 remained a characteristic of Spanish society until recent times. It is ironic that during the 16th c. the movement toward uniformity and intolerance corresponded to an era of ecclesiastical reform and spiritual revival. A sustained effort to improve the quality of bishops and clergy, begun by Queen Isabella*, intensified following the Council of Trent* (1545–63) with the creation of diocesan seminaries. Under the influence of Renaissance* biblical humanism, study of the Scriptures intensified through the work of eminent scholars gathered in the University of Alcala (founded in 1508). The Spanish Church produced a series of extraordinary figures in Ignatius* Loyola (1491–1556), founder of the Jesuits*, and the great mystics Teresa* of Ávila (1510–82) and John* of the Cross (1542–91). During the 1520s, the works of Erasmus* of Rotterdam, emphasizing an interior faith rather than reliance on the external devotions associated with popular religion, attracted a wide readership among the educated. At the same time, religious life at the grass roots was manifested in a luxuriant array of pious devotions, shrines, and vows, often criticized by admirers of Erasmus. Scholars have shown that this world of popular religion, intensely local and intimately linked to the earthy concerns of peasants and town dwellers alike, contributed to the vitality of religious life in cities, towns, and villages throughout the monarchy. Moreover, the intensification of religious instruction following the Council of Trent inculcated a basic knowledge of the faith among the general population.

This surge in religious vitality subsided into a religion of routine, what one historian has called "a religion of habit." From the mid-16th c. onward, the Inquisition stamped out any deviation from its conception of orthodoxy*, while the spirited debates of theologians and philosophers, such as Melchor Cano (1509–60), Domingo de Soto (1495–1560), Francisco de Vitoria (1492–1548), and Francisco Suarez* (1548–1617), gradually yielded to a narrow scholasticism*. The 18th c., under the Bourbons, witnessed a revival of sorts. Some bishops and priests embraced reforming ideas characteristic of "enlightened Catholicism" elsewhere in Roman Catholic Europe. Efforts were undertaken to improve clerical education, reestablish scholarly biblical studies, and moderate the excesses of popular* religion. But the Church and monarchy alike entered a period of crisis before the impact of the French Revolution and the Napoleonic intervention in Spain beginning in 1807.

The Crisis of the 19th Century. In 1808 the emperor Napoleon deposed the Bourbon dynasty and placed his brother on the Spanish throne. In 1810 opponents of the Napoleonic monarchy came together in Cadiz in the country's first modern parliamentary assembly. It endowed the country with its first written constitution (1812) and imposed limits on the sovereign's power. The liberal majority in Parliament abolished the Inquisition (January 1813) but refused any concession in the direction of religious liberty. Liberals also planned a thorough internal reform of the Church. Although they made little progress, they set a precedent imitated by later governments that believed the state held primary responsibility for carrying out ecclesiastical reform even in the realm of pastoral activity. The liberal cause triumphed definitively in 1834. In the following decade, the male religious orders were suppressed and their property sold for the benefit of the treasury; the tithe, bedrock of ecclesiastical finances for centuries, was abolished, while in periods when the more radical elements of liberalism ruled, bishops were exiled and the parish clergy harassed by the authorities. The endowments of the diocesan clergy were sold in 1841.

In 1851 a government of the Moderate Party agreed to a concordat* with the papacy that would govern civil–ecclesiastical relations until 1931. The government agreed to pay the salaries of the diocesan clergy, authorized a limited reintroduction of the male religious orders, and recognized Roman Catholicism as the religion of the state. After 1834 Protestants established a foothold in the country. They numbered 10,000 in 1860 but faced sporadic harassment by the authorities. The democratic 1869 Constitution permitted limited religious liberty, but the more conservative charter of 1876 allowed only the private practice of religion by dissenters.

No government in the history of the liberal constitutional monarchy (1834–1923) ever considered the separation of church and state. But the dissolution of the male religious* orders and the turbulent political conditions of the 1830s and early 1840s compromised the Church's pastoral activities. By 1840 only 11 of the country's bishops occupied their dioceses, while in regions affected by the civil war between the government and supporters of absolutism (Carlism), parish life suffered to the point that nearly half of the parishes in the Archdiocese of Tarragona lacked parochial clergy.

The Catholic Revival. After 1843 the Church experienced an episodic organizational and religious recovery. The career of Antonio Claret (1807–70), a distinctly modern religious propagandist (during the 1840s) before his appointment as archbishop of Santiago de Cuba (1851) and confessor to Queen Isabella II (1857), provides an example of the Church's ability to adapt its pastoral strategy to the individualist emphasis of liberal society. Claret undertook an ambitious campaign of popular missions and oversaw an extensive publishing program designed to reach the masses. In 1843 he published what would become the most widely published work in the history of Spanish devotional writing. It emphasized individual acts of piety and reflected the social values of the new society.

The Roman Catholic revival developed more fully during the Restoration (1874–1923), when a conservative constitutional monarchy sought an accommodation with the Church. The Catholic revival of the late 19th and early 20th c. had many sides. Catholic devotional associations devoted to the cults of the Sacred* Heart and the Virgin Mary* attracted thousands of members. Popular* piety was stimulated through the mass production of inexpensive statues, religious objects, and popular books and tracts. The old, intensely local world of devotions associated with shrines and vows survived, but yielded increasingly to a more highly organized piety, national in scope and individualist in emphasis, such as the cult of Our Lady of Lourdes*.

By the late 19th c., the influence of Pope Leo XIII's social* encyclical, *Rerum Novarum* (1891), moved the Church for the first time into the realm of social action with the appearance of workers' circles during the 1890s and, later, of Catholic trade unions and agricultural syndicates. The expansion of these organizations received the support of an influential figure in early-20th-c. Spanish Catholicism, Angel Herrera Oria (1886–1968). Educated as a lawyer, he became editor of the newspaper *El Debate* (1911) and soon established it as the country's leading journal of Catholic opinion. Herrera wished to use modern techniques of organization and propaganda to create a Catholic political party of the masses, an objective partially achieved in 1933 with the foundation of the CEDA party. Herrera also served as president of the governing committee of Catholic* Action (1933–35), which organized the laity under the hierarchy's direction in a variety of initiatives. Under the Restoration, the Church also significantly expanded its role in education*; 5,000 schools had come into existence by 1910. Clerical support for these initiatives was possible because of a massive increase in the membership of the religious orders authorized by successive Restoration governments.

The Catholic revival produced benefits for the Church. But it failed to halt the advance of formidable opposition among some liberals, intellectuals, and new radical groups, such as the socialists and anarchists, who saw the Church as a conservative bloc opposed to political and social progress. This struggle continued under the Second Republic, which attempted to create a thoroughly lay state. A majority of the clergy and committed Catholics supported the rising of the generals against the Republic in July 1936. At no time in its modern history did the Church suffer more than during the civil war (1936–39), when nearly 7,000 priests and religious were assassinated in Republican Spain and religious practice disappeared. Bishops, priests, and the faithful, with a few exceptions, saw Franco as the providential figure who would deliver Roman Catholicism and the Church from its enemies.

It fell to Cardinal lsidro Goma y Tomas (1869–1940), archbishop of Toledo, primate of Spain, and president of the Committee of Metropolitans, to provide leadership during the war. Goma supported Franco and justified the rising against the Republic in his controversial *Collective Letter* (1937) to the Roman Catholic bishops of the world. But he was apprehensive about the totalitarian aspects of the regime, particularly its decision to abolish Catholic trade unions and teachers' associations in favor of a state syndicate system under the influence of the quasi-fascist Falange Party.

These concerns gradually diminished following the war's end as the regime bestowed numerous benefits on the Church. The alliance of the Church and the state, often known as "national Catholicism," endured for two decades, but began to weaken during the 1960s, especially as a result of the teachings of the Second Vatican* Council. The process through which the Church disengaged itself from the regime was long, difficult, and controversial. Vicente Enrique y Tarancon (1907–94), who became archbishop of Madrid and president of the Spanish Episcopal Conference in 1971, played a key role by steering the hierarchy through the political minefield of Franco's last years to acceptance of democratic change.

Statistics: Population (2005): 43.9 million (M). Roman Catholics, 34 M, 79.3%; Protestants, 0.4 M, 1%; Jews, 0.04 M, 0.1%; agnostics, atheists, 7 M, 16% (Muslims, c1 M, possibly more, not included). A 2005 survey shows that 47.1% of Catholics never attend Mass. (*Source*: *Department of State, Religious Freedom Report,* 2005.)

WILLIAM J. CALLAHAN

Spanish Explorations, Conquests, and Missions. Spanish exploration of the Americas began with Columbus's now legendary arrival (1492) in Hispaniola (Dominican* Republic and Haiti*). Francisco Hernández de Córdoba (1516) and Juan de Grijalva (1517) led explorations of the Caribbean* coast of Central America and Mexico*. Hernán Cortés' unlikely 1521 victory in the Aztec capital, Tenochtitlán, with just several hundred soldiers, effectively completed the military conquest of Mexico. The Incan Empire in the Andes fell to the Spanish conqueror Francisco Pizzarro (1532–36). A military expedition launched from Mexico brought the Philippines into the territory of New Spain (1565).

Although priests and friars arrived with each voyage from Spain and were present during every major military expedition, for the first two decades the Roman Catholic Church's presence in the New World remained negligible and focused primarily on ministry to colonists. Responsibility for Christianization fell to the conquistadors themselves and subsequently to the *encomenderos**, colonists to whom the Spanish crown granted communities of indigenous people in trust as a source of compulsory labor and tribute. Deliberate attempts at Christian conversion of the indigenous populations did not begin until the Spanish crown finally secured royal patronage* (see Patronato, Padroado) from Rome, which effectively granted the Spanish monarchs administrative control over the Church in the New World. The crown designated the three mendicant* religious orders as the primary agents of evangelization. The 1524 arrival of 12 Franciscan missionaries in newly conquered Mexico City marked the symbolic beginning of Christian mission in the New World. Hernán Cortés personally welcomed them upon their arrival; the military subjugation of the people of Mexico* paved the way for their so-called spiritual conquest. The Dominican friar Bartolomé de las* Casas contested this method of evangelization, deploring "the destruction of the Indies" and arguing for more peaceful forms of persuasion.

Franciscans, Dominicans, and Augustinians arrived in New Spain in rapid succession; later the Jesuits came to Lima (1568). The first generations of friars believed they were building a religious utopia: an "Indian"–Christian millennial kingdom. Employing a panoply of methods, including extirpation, debate, catechesis, physical discipline, and exhortation, the friars labored to bring about a new faith for a New World. The key institutions of mission were the *convento,* monastery complex, the *doctrina,* rural parish church, and the forced settlements of indigenous people known as *reducciones* (reductions*).

According to the Laws of the Indies, once native people were fully Christianized, they were to be released to the care of secular clergy and thus "secularized." This turning over of the missions to diocesan governance began in the 17th c., and, except for the missions of Alta California (secularized in 1835), was largely completed in the 18th c. JENNIFER S. HUGHES

Spanish Literature and Christianity. Spanish literature is strongly informed by religious piety, controversies, and polemics. Despite a policy of militant Catholicism against the forces of Islam, Christians lived in relative harmony with Muslims and Jews during much of the Reconquest (718–1492). A high point was the scholarly activity and sharing of knowledge among the three faiths during the reign of Alfonso X ("the Wise") of Castile and León (1252–84). The first Castilian poet whose identity is known, Gonzalo de Berceo, wrote *Miracles of Our Lady* and several hagiographical works (first half of the 13th c.). The earliest extant theatrical pieces drew from biblical and liturgical themes. The influential Cardinal Francisco Ximénez* de Cisneros (1436–1517) assembled scholars at the University of Alcalá de Henares to produce the original polyglot* Bible, called the Complutensian*. Among the most important writers of devotional material are Ignatius* of Loyola (1491–1556), founder of the Jesuit* order and author of *Spiritual* Exercises*; Luis de Granada (1504–88), author of *The Book of Prayer and Meditation* and *Guide for Sinners*; Luis de León (1527–91), poet and author of *On the Names of Christ* and *The Perfect Wife*, in prose; and Pedro Malón de Chaide (1530–89), author of *The Conversion of the Magdalen*. Popular and high art abound in Christian imagery and symbolism. Literature on sacred themes finds its greatest intensification in the mystic* tradition, which recounts the spiritual journey of the soul* to its union with God and which is best exemplified by the prose of Teresa* of Ávila (1515–82) and the poetry of John* of the Cross (1542–91).

The early modern period in Spain, the "Golden Age," witnessed the political and religious unity established by Ferdinand and Isabella*. Those Muslims and Jews who did not convert to Catholicism were forced into exile, and Spanish society was divided into urban and rural sectors, the rich and the poor, and, based on blood purity, Old and New Christians. The presence of the Inquisition* is felt in the literature of the time, and censorship was a fact of life for writers. Picaresque narrative, which begins in the mid-16th c. with *Lazarillo de Tormes*, is an anti-idealistic genre that depicts the tensions produced by doubt and suspicion. Erasmian humanism, vitalized by its battle against Scholasticism*, attracted many adherents while dismaying others, including some inquisitors. The Protestant Reformation* initiated a new holy war. The Council of Trent* (1545–60) sought ways of using literature to promote Roman Catholicism, thus denouncing those works that had little or no didactic value. The canon from Toledo in the first part of Cervantes's *Don Quixote* (1605) reflects this position in his condemnation of the romances of chivalry. Golden Age theater, notably the works of Tirso de Molina and Pedro Calderón de la Barca, both of whom were priests, frequently dramatizes theological issues. The most honored play of early modern Spain, Calderón's *Life Is a Dream* (1635), builds on the metaphor of the title to explore the question of determinism versus free will*, among other topics. Religious drama includes the *autos sacramentales*, short allegorical plays originally associated with the Feast of Corpus* Christi; *The Great Theater of the World*, by Calderón, is a key example. The major baroque poets, including Luis de Góngora, Lope de Vega, and Francisco de Quevedo, wrote on spiritual as well as secular topics. Matters of religion and faith have been mainstays of Spanish literature and culture. Perhaps the most notable modern writer in this category was Miguel de Unamuno (1864–1936) – philosopher, novelist, essayist, playwright, poet, and academician – whose works include *The Tragic Sense of Life* and *The Agony of Christianity*.

EDWARD H. FRIEDMAN

SPCK, Society for Promoting Christian Knowledge. Founded in 1698, the Society institutionalized the work already begun by Thomas Bray* (1656–1730) in the American colony of Maryland. Emphasizing education and publishing, it printed tracts and pamphlets, constructed schools, libraries, and church buildings, and supplied chaplains in England, North America, India, and other British colonies. It supported missions* through the Society for the Propagation of the Gospel (SPG). In the spirit of 18th-c. ecumenism, the SPCK supported many German and Danish Lutheran missionaries in India, mostly students from Halle. The SPCK press, one of the oldest in Britain, continues to publish a variety of materials.

Spener, Philip Jacob (1635–1705), born an Alsatian, completed his studies for the Lutheran ministry at Strasbourg, where he earned a doctorate in the NT, and became the senior of the Lutheran clergy at Frankfurt am Main. His interest in authorizing laypersons to assist in parish renewal led him to institute private meetings of consecrated laypersons, the *collegia pietatis*, featuring discussion of the Sunday homily, prayer, and the devotional reading of Scripture and edificatory literature.

In his *Pia Desideria* (1675), Spener outlined his case for reactivating Luther's* doctrine of the priesthood* of all believers by facilitating the ministry of the laity through these means. This seminal work of Lutheran Pietism* included an indictment of the "corrupt" conditions of European Christendom, including its stratified civil and spiritual classes, as well as those of the common people. It also included a catalog of proposals for correcting these conditions, such as deploying the Bible in preaching and teaching to effect spiritual regeneration, reforming schools to integrate spiritual and intellectual development, and acting charitably during doctrinal controversy. Spener held prominent Lutheran posts in Dresden and Berlin, where his literary record documents his importance as a Pietist theologian. **See also PIETISM.**

J. STEVE O'MALLEY

Spinoza, Baruch (1632–77), argued that God is substance underlying the attribute of thought; God is a necessarily existing substance, which corresponds to a descriptively exhaustive, explanatorily complete psychology. Nature is substance underlying the attribute of extension, which corresponds to a similar physics. Only substance and its modes (states) exist. The modes necessarily follow from substance, which is conceivable underlying an infinite number of attributes (fundamental properties), only two of which are accessible to us.

The structure of psychology and physics can be fully described using such metaphysical* terms as "substance," "attribute," "mode," and "cause." God is not creator, providence, or agent, has no chosen people, forgives no sins, and answers no prayers. For Judaism or Christianity, this is atheism*. Substance necessarily exists. Every truth is necessarily true. Falsehood is merely confusion. One is "free" only in the sense of one's properties not being caused by another or their being caused by states of oneself that are conceptually clear. The mind, under the attribute of thought, is the idea of the body, underlying the attribute of extension. There is no possibility of revelation* or resurrection*. That one might survive the death of one's body is logically impossible. Spinoza replaces Judaism by a philosophy that has no room for theology.

KEITH E. YANDELL

Spirit (in many languages, "breath" or "wind"), applying generically to any immaterial and intelligent beings, including God*, angels*, human souls*, and human attitudes; the animating principle of God (cf. Eccl 8:8, 12:7) and of human beings (their mind*, affection). Holy Spirit (the third person of the Trinity) is the divine Spirit that inspires and empowers believers to bear the fruit* of the Spirit (Gal 5:22–23) and provides believers with "gifts" (graces* or charisms*) to be used in the service of others (1 Cor 12:4–11). Yet people can also be inspired and empowered by evil spirits (usually plural, equivalent to demons*) that mislead believers. So throughout church history, spiritual* exercises emphasized the importance of testing and discerning (Rom 12:2; 1 Thess 5:21) the spirits. **See also DEVIL, SATAN, DEMONS, AND DEMONIC POWER; HOLY SPIRIT CLUSTER; TRINITY IN EASTERN ORTHODOXY; TRINITY IN THE WESTERN TRADITION.**

Spirit Baptism. See BAPTISM CLUSTER: IN THE HOLY SPIRIT.

Spiritism, beliefs and practices related to communication with the spirits of the dead. Generally, any movement that believes that spirit entities exist and that human beings can engage in spirit communication, usually through mediums. More specifically, a 19th-c. Western European movement (popular in France and England).

***Spiritual Exercises*, of Ignatius of Loyola.** Although spiritual exercises had existed since the desert fathers, Ignatius (early 16th c.) gave them a specific direction following his spiritual experience at Manresa (1522). Almost everything in Ignatius's *Spiritual Exercises* is found in earlier similar works, especially the *Vita Christi* of Ludolphe the Carthusian* and the *Exercitatorio* by the Abbot of Montserrat, Garcia of Cisneros, which Ignatius used at the time of his conversion.

The originality of Ignatius's *Spiritual Exercises* lies in its goal and pedagogy. As he wrote, "spiritual exercises are means to prepare and entice the soul to separate itself from disorderly desires and then to seek and find God's will for one's life." The election* (by God) for a state of life, or one's choice of one state of life, is at the heart of the four-week quest that, beyond conversion, leads retreatants in the contemplation* of life, of the Passion* of Christ, and of his resurrection*.

Pedagogically, Ignatius's spiritual exercises are a personal quest. The spiritual director and the retreatant submit themselves together to the Holy* Spirit and to spiritual discernment regarding the movements, consolations, and desolation that arise in the soul* of the retreatant so as to recognize among them those which are signs of the good spirit rather than of the evil spirit.

Having noticed that certain practices that had helped him were also helpful to others, Ignatius wrote *Spiritual Exercises* by progressively expanding upon his meditations on the Kingdom* of God and on the two standards (of Christ and Satan*). In Paris he directed the spiritual exercises of Francis Xavier, Peter Favre, and his other companions, founders with him of the Society of Jesus (1541). The Latin text of the *Exercises* (a translation from the Spanish original) was approved by the pope in 1548. From then on, the book was broadly diffused and used as much for personal spiritual exercises as for collective retreats, in monasteries and religious communities and among laypeople and clergy. Vincent Huby founded the first retreat center in Vannes (France; 1663). *Spiritual Exercises* was applied to the pedagogy of the Jesuit* "colleges" (high schools) in the famous *Ordo Studiorum*. Today there is a renewed emphasis on personally guided exercises and broader adaptations of Ignatius's spiritual exercises in parish life and spiritual formation.

Contemporary culture's emphasis on the autonomy* of the person, individual freedom*, and decision making, and on the emotional life of the individual, demonstrates the current relevance of *Spiritual Exercises*. CLAUDE FLIPO SJ

Spiritual Franciscans. See FRANCISCANS.

SPIRITUALITY CLUSTER

1) *Introductory Entry*

Spirituality, Christian Forms of

2) *A Sampling of Contextual Views and Practices*

Spirituality, Christian Forms of, Denominational View: African Instituted Churches

Spirituality, Christian Forms of, Denominational View: Eastern Orthodox

Spirituality, Christian Forms of, Denominational View: Protestant

Spirituality, Christian Forms of, Denominational View: Roman Catholic

Spirituality, Christian Forms of, Denominational View: Roman Catholic Mystical

Spirituality, Christian Forms of: In Africa

Spirituality, Christian Forms of: In Asia

Spirituality, Christian Forms of: In North America

Spirituality, Christian Forms of: In North America: African American

Spirituality, Christian Forms of: In the South Pacific and Australia

---

1) Introductory Entry

Spirituality, Christian Forms of. In contemporary usage, "spirituality" commonly refers to the human experience in daily life of that which is perceived to have ultimate meaning and value. The stress on immediacy and experience is sometimes used to distinguish "spirituality" from "religion," with its more formalized doctrinal and institutional structures, but most people acknowledge that spirituality can be found both within and outside the boundaries of religious traditions. Spirituality is human engagement with reality at its most fundamental level, whether that reality is identified as divinity or the cosmos or the deepest dimensions of the self. Spirituality connects belief with practice, feeling with commitment, and the personal with the political. Thus spirituality may be understood as the human experience of – and response to – all that is perceived to be good, beautiful, and true (see Heteronomy; Mysticism, Mystics).

Since human beings live in groups with distinct cultures, it is possible to identify particular schools or traditions of spirituality that exhibit characteristic attitudes, values, and practices. Christianity as a whole is one such great tradition, but within it are many subtraditions associated with diverse historical periods, religiocultural groups, and sociopolitical contexts.

Christian forms of spirituality generally have many common features, such as acknowledgement of one supreme God* who created the universe as a positive good, devotion to Jesus* of Nazareth as God's agent of self-revelation, interpretation of the Bible* (both OT and NT) as a sacred text (see Scripture), participation in the church* as a community of believers in which God's Spirit* is actively present, practices of prayer* and worship both private and communal, and compassionate service to those in need. However, the various forms also display notable differences. No typology could ever encompass the wide range of Christian forms of spirituality, but it is possible to identify some significant points of tension:

Immanentist/Transcendentalist. Some Christian forms of spirituality emphasize God's involvement with humanity here and now (see Incarnation Cluster), with a focus on encountering God in the present world (immanentist*). Others stress the awesomeness of a God beyond human comprehension, who is to be sought in heaven* above or in a future age (transcendentalist*; see Eschatology Cluster).

Contemplative/Active. The biblical sisters Martha and Mary (Luke 11:38–42) have often been taken as indicative of two styles of spirituality: Martha with her hospitality and service represents the active life, while Mary, who sits attentively at the Lord's feet, has chosen the "better part" of the contemplative* life. Some forms of spirituality conclude that contemplation is to be valued over action, but others see them as complementary or alternating modes.

Apophatic/Cataphatic. Stressing the impossibility of knowing or saying anything definitive about God or one's experience of God, negative or apophatic* (imageless) forms of spirituality find God in the "luminous darkness" of paradox* and mystery*. Affirmative or cataphatic (imaginative) forms of spirituality acknowledge the limitations of all human language and symbols but nevertheless employ them in a positive fashion to engage the senses and the mind in the quest for God.

Corporate/Individual. In some forms of Christian spirituality, the primary human subject is the church (local congregation, denomination, national church, or mystical body). In others the communal dimension may be recognized, but in practice the focus is on the individual Christian living in solitude (e.g. the hermit* ideal) or as the recipient of spiritual gifts (e.g. Charismatics*).

Knowledge/Love. All forms of Christian spirituality affirm that God is to be both known and loved. However, some stress the primacy of the intellect and identify the vision of God as the goal of the spiritual journey, while others hold to the primacy of the affections ("heart" or "will") and point toward loving union as the proper end of the Christian life.

Against Culture/Of Culture. An influential typology has been drawn from H. Richard Niebuhr's *Christ and Culture* (1951). Niebuhr noted two relatively deficient types of spirituality in which the Christian life is either opposed to the surrounding culture* ("Christ against culture") or virtually identified with it ("Christ of culture"). Three mediating types see the Christian life as building on but transcending culture ("Christ above culture"), or in more-or-less creative tension with culture ("Christ and culture in paradox"), or engaged with culture in a way that changes it for the better ("Christ transforming culture") (see Culture Cluster: And Christianity). This typology can be used to analyze the attitude and practice of a particular form of spirituality toward various aspects of human culture, including politics and the state, the arts and sciences, and the particular identities of national or ethnic groups.

In each pair of contrasting emphases, the two positions should be understood not as opposites demanding a simple choice but as points of tension between which every form of Christian spirituality must find its way. Most forms will aim to respect both sides of each pair, negotiating some balance between the two. Moreover, all of these typologies can be only heuristic, inviting further study of Christian spirituality in its variety and ever-changing vitality. ARTHUR HOLDER

2) A Sampling of Contextual Views and Practices

Spirituality, Christian Forms of, Denominational View: African Instituted Churches. Spirituality in African* Instituted Churches (AICs) is biblical and African traditional in texture and orientation (see African Religion Cluster). It is grounded in the sovereignty of God over life, holistic appropriation of the salvific mission of Christ, an intense experience of God through the Holy* Spirit, a search for holiness*, and a strong evangelistic* zeal. AICs are engaged in creating a synthesis of the apostolic *kerygma** and authentic African insights derived from the vernacular Scriptures.

Spirituality is expressed and experienced through exuberant liturgics, symbolism, healing rituals, vestments, colors, prayers, song and dance, prophecy, glossolalia*, and fasting. The spirituality of AICs reflects a holistic worldview that links secular and sacred dimensions of life. The world is an arena for the contest between good and evil* forces. AIC spirituality seeks deliverance from evil, protection, and transformation of one's terrestrial condition.

Although AIC spirituality addresses pragmatic life concerns such as healing* illness, being successful in life, and overcoming satanic attacks, its overt spiritualization of evil, literalist interpretation of the Scriptures, and uncritical dependence on the powers of the charismatic prophet may be detrimental to personal salvation, healing, and individual spirituality.

PHILOMENA N. MWAURA

Spirituality, Christian Forms of, Denominational View: Eastern Orthodox. Eastern Orthodox spirituality is the result of the merger of five streams:

1. The incarnation* was viewed as the embodiment of the divine Logos* as Jesus of Nazareth, simultaneously fully human and fully divine. In Orthodox thought, materiality (the human nature of the God-man), while remaining integral and intact, does not remain simply what it was before the Incarnation. The humanity of Christ is "new humanity," not Adam's* old humanity, as Paul would say. Without mediation, Christ's very physicality is charged with divine power.

   Patristic theologians emphasized that the Incarnation was a paradigm for the world. All human nature was caught up into the Logos in the Incarnation. "[The Logos] became what we are, in order that we might become what He is" (Athanasius*, *De Incarnatione*). According to this doctrine of deification (theosis*), what Christ was by nature, humans could become by grace*. This process of transfiguration* drives most Orthodox spiritual reflection.
2. The view that approaching God is an experience of purifying light was shared by many theologians and mystics. Gregory* of Nyssa, Evagrius*, Dionysius*, and others preferred the image of a deepening obscurity, wherein material conceptions and experiences were increasingly recognized as defectively partial. Both schools emphasized the Christian life as a path toward enlightenment.
3. Training and purifying the physical drives (*pathemata*) and mental obsessions (*phantasmata*) was stressed throughout the monastic* movement, so that a clearer sense of self merging with the risen Christ could be established. Such an ascetic* quest for the "true self" was closely related to ethical fidelity and devotion to prayer.
4. Opening the "eye of the heart" to see Christ by affective and intuitive paths, rather than through uncommitted intellectualist constructs, was emphasized by many, especially the Byzantine–Syrian fathers.
5. All of these intellectual and ascetic traditions are subordinated to specific forms of prayer and worship. Orthodoxy moves within a profoundly liturgical matrix: long services, as well as eucharistic* and other sacramental mysteries*. In addition, ancient "monologistic" prayer (the repetition of simple phrases or biblical verses) is

used to quiet the mind and focus the heart; the best known is the "Jesus* Prayer": "Lord Jesus Christ, Son of God, have mercy on me." The long repetition of this slow invocation is often used in private prayer to illuminate and focus the central hope of Orthodox spirituality: looking constantly to the risen Christ to make his presence felt transfiguratively in the Church and in the life of society.

JOHN A. MCGUCKIN

Spirituality, Christian Forms of, Denominational View: Protestant. Historically, Protestant spirituality has been informed by a theology of grace* offered freely through Jesus Christ, devotion to Scripture*, and imitation* of Christ. Today, "spiritual formation" names traditional understandings of classical piety or devotional discipleship*. Among many contemporary developments, the globalization of Protestantism has been critical. Indeed, more Quakers* reside in Kenya* than in the rest of the world combined. Spiritually, this decentralization has enlivened horizons of worship and prayer, such as the Korean corporate practice of *tongsung kido* (praying aloud and in unison). Yet this shift, along with movements in Liberation* theology, has asked hard questions of a largely Eurocentric and North Americanized spirituality, one tied to the Enlightenment* and wealth, white privilege and power. Another key development relates to Vatican* II, which significantly furthered ecumenical dialogue between Roman Catholics and Protestants, enabling Protestants to drink from the contemplative wells of a Catholic monastic* and mystical* tradition. The Centering Prayer Movement, e.g., has been ecumenical in purpose and popularity. Another development is based on wide-ranging sociocultural factors. While mainline Protestants have witnessed a decline in numbers in Europe and North America, they have also witnessed innovation in women's roles in leadership as well as spiritual growth among laity. The "new monasticism" of Christian communities and solitaries is one such movement. Contemporary Protestant spiritual leaders have included Dietrich Bonhoeffer*, C. S. Lewis*, Howard Thurman*, Martin Luther King*, Jr., and Evelyn Underhill*.

STEPHANIE A. FORD

Spirituality, Christian Forms of, Denominational View: Roman Catholic. The sheer size of the Roman Catholic Church, its global and historical diversity, and its capacity to be catholic, i.e. to accommodate variety, means that, unlike Protestant churches, which tend to splinter when differences occur, Roman Catholicism makes room for diversity. While Catholics remain united in their central sacramental* practices and within the doctrinal perimeters of the Nicene* Creed, there are many spiritual schools and a large number of variant spiritual practices within the Catholic fold. In all of them, the Christic* pattern of death and resurrection – dying and rising – is foundational. They all share a sense that the human person cooperates with divine grace* through the practices of an intentional Christian life. A major strain of Catholic spirituality has strong roots in the ascetic*, monastic* tradition with its emphasis on silence and solitude punctuated by the rhythm of the liturgy* of the hours. Monastic-inspired practices of *lectio divina* (sacred reading), the daily Divine Office*, and contemplative* prayer have similarly shaped clerical and lay spirituality. Active religious communities are another influence, especially the Jesuits* with their spiritual* exercises of daily examination of conscience and imaginative meditation on Scripture. These exercises aid in the art of "finding God in all things" and aligning one's life with the mission of the Church in the world. An additional strain of Catholic spirituality emphasizes participative devotion*. The rosary*, stations* of the cross, novenas*, pilgrimages* to sacred sites, and veneration* of the saints* and the Virgin Mary* are widely practiced.

WENDY M. WRIGHT

Spirituality, Christian Forms of, Denominational View: Roman Catholic Mystical. The Western Roman Catholic mystical tradition is apophatic*, emphasizing contemplation of and union with God, who is always beyond what can be said about God. It can be traced back to the translations of the mystical theological treatises attributed to Dionysius* the Pseudo-Areopagite. The first translation was given to the Frankish king Louis* the Pious by the Byzantine emperor Michael the Stammerer (827); subsequent translations were made by John* Scotus Eriugena (9th c.) and by Scholastics* (12th–13th c.). In essence the Dionysian corpus gave rise to apophaticism, or "negative theology," which restated the simple theological position that anything that could be said or envisaged about God could not be God. Commentaries on Dionysius in the High Middle Ages abound, most notably those by great mystics such as Thomas Gallus, the anonymous author of *The Cloud* of Unknowing*, the Victorines, Beguines*, Thomas Aquinas*, and Meister Eckhart*. Declaring "God free me from God," Meister Eckhart took the mystical tradition to its extremes and was consequently investigated by Church authorities. With the Reformation, interest in Dionysius waned in the non-Catholic West, although scholarship and commentary continued in the Catholic West, most notably with writers such as John* of the Cross, Miguel de Molinos* and Jean Pierre de Caussade.

PETER TYLER

Spirituality, Christian Forms of: In Africa. Spirituality in Africa is, as elsewhere, a lived experience of being connected, challenged, inspired, and embraced by God's compassionate and gracious Holy* Spirit based on the saving work of Jesus Christ (Tapia). Weaving together the strands of doctrine, discipline, liturgy, and life illuminates the particular African understandings of spirituality, often identified with denominations.

Everywhere spirituality is inculturated*. Likewise, African Christianity includes a variety of indigenous forms of spirituality, associated with the three "mainline" forms of Christian spirituality: Roman Catholic, Coptic Orthodox, and Protestant.

Among Protestants and African Instituted Churches (AICs) there are different levels of inculturation: classical-mainline Protestantism maintains a largely Western form of spirituality; postclassical Protestantism and Pentecostalism embrace African conceptions of the Holy* Spirit and of deliverance from witchcraft*; Charismatic churches overtly spiritualize evil*; and AICs thoroughly structure spirituality in an African way. For example, Ethiopian AICs (Providence Industrial Mission, African Blackman's Church) are usually politically shaped by the principle "Africa for Africans"; Zionist AICs (Bapostoli, Chalitchi cha Zioni) were started by prophet-healers using indigenous knowledge systems of sickness and healing* (cure, deliverance, exorcism*) and prophecy; and women's embodied spirituality (Bishop Ayami, Mai Mpondeni, NyaJere) thoroughly incorporates an African view of the Holy* Spirit. **See also** AFRICAN INSTITUTED CHURCHES CLUSTER; CHARISMATIC AND PENTECOSTAL MOVEMENTS CLUSTER: IN AFRICA; PRESENT CLUSTER: DENOMINATIONAL VIEW: AFRICAN INSTITUTED CHURCHES.

FULATA MOYO

Spirituality, Christian Forms of: In Asia. Asia is rich with many religions and forms of spirituality. Christianity, a latecomer, has left its marks on the already crowded religious landscape and the fertile spiritual soil of Asia.

Christian spirituality has stood apart from other forms of religious spirituality, refusing to merge into the spiritual stream of Asia. By contrast, Buddhism, Daoism, and Confucianism, while maintaining their distinctiveness, blend into one another to create what is perceived as "Asian spirituality." At the beginning of the 21st c., this situation was changing.

The roots of human spirituality found in the depth of the human heart, soul*, and spirit* make religions possible and necessary, and also call religions to task when they corrupt and abuse the human spirit. Beyond differences in external religious expressions, spirituality is the quest for the meaning of life and the power to live, the attainment of the serenity with which to face death*, and the longing for a life beyond life. Both a Zen story and a Christian story explain these points.

The Zen story is as follows: A samurai came to Hakuin, a Zen master, and asked: "Do heaven and hell really exist?" "Who are you?" inquired the master. "I am a samurai," the warrior replied. "You, a samurai?" exclaimed Hakuin. "You have the face of a beggar!" The samurai became so angry that he reached for his sword and drew it. Hakuin looked right at him and exclaimed, "*That* is hell!" Sheathing his sword, the samurai bowed with great humility and respect. "And *this*," Hakuin announced, "is heaven." A powerful spirituality welled out of the depths of the Zen master and touched the depths of the samurai to create heaven out of hell! (abbreviated from Kapleau, *The Wheel of Death*).

The Christian story is Jesus' proclamation of the Kingdom* of God to a crowd, as expressed in Luke's version (Luke 6:20–21; cf. Matt 5:3–10):

> Blessed are you who are poor, for yours is the Kingdom of God.
> Blessed are you who are hungry now, for you will be filled.
> Blessed are you who weep now, for you will laugh.

This proclamation is an expression of Jesus' spirituality. Far from a luxury for the rich and powerful, Jesus' spirituality empowers the oppressed*, the poor*, and the distressed, and this is also so in Asia. This Christian spirituality can readily interact with the spiritualities of Asian people of different religions. Practice, according to Jesus, is the test of one's spirituality, whether one is Asian or not.

CHOAN-SENG (C. S.) SONG

Spirituality, Christian Forms of: In North America. The narrative of Christian spirituality in contemporary North America is complicated, for it is embedded in the story of early European discovery and conquest, as well as the "understories" of Native* American peoples and later immigrants. Nevertheless, certain themes become apparent. Ralph Waldo Emerson's* self-reliant "seeker" of early-19th-c. Transcendentalism* continues in the contemporary "New* Age" movement. The Emersonian-styled seeker has tended toward a hybrid Christian universalism with Eastern influences, searching for unity among sacred texts, meditative practices, and positivism*. At the opposite end have been fundamentalists* and Evangelicals*, who have sought to keep the message pure by endorsing scriptural inerrancy* and missionary conversion*. More recently, Black* Liberation and Feminist* forms of spirituality have challenged the white male hegemony, by furthering new images of God*, discipleship*, and community. With changing urban and rural scenes, phenomena like interdenominational megachurches* and, negatively, cultish aberrations like Jonestown have developed. The growing Latino/a population has brought a stronger family*-based spirituality, rich in symbol and ritual, as opposed to European American individualistic spiritual practice (see Feminist Theology Cluster: In North America: Latina; In North America: Mujerista). The Eastern Orthodox* Church has an increasing number of followers who long for traditional roots, while Roman Catholics have ministered within a creative spectrum. In the aftermath of 9/11, North American Christians face new interfaith concerns. Understanding Muslims in one's own society has become urgent. Notable contemporary figures include Thomas Merton*, Henri Nouwen, and Billy Graham.

STEPHANIE A. FORD

Spirituality, Christian Forms of: In North America: African American. The spirituality of African Americans is deeply rooted in and emerges from their historical experiences in the USA and their ancestral origins in Africa. The people of West and Central Africa – a people of deep religious faith and traditions, both indigenous and influenced by Christian and Muslim sources – were brought to the Americas in chains yet were able, in many ways, to retain and even strengthen their religious traditions, especially in Roman Catholic colonies. The result was a spirituality that fostered their survival as a people and a community of faith, by inculturating* European Christianity into "African retentions" (forms of Africanism). Theirs is a spirituality of struggle, survival, and liberation* embodied in a deep and abiding faith in and personal relationship with a God actively involved in their lives. This same God, who is black as they are, and his son, Jesus, also black, promised a salvation* that was both physical and spiritual. Jesus, they believe, suffered as they suffered but was not overcome as they have not been overcome. In Jesus they see the Divine living and acting within their own experience and empowering them to overcome obstacles of race*, class, and gender that persist in the USA and the African American community itself. DIANA L. HAYES

Spirituality, Christian Forms of: In the South Pacific and Australia. Indigenous peoples of the South Pacific and Australia possessed rich religions and mythologies explaining the origins of the universe and its sustenance. Generally Christian missionaries showed little appreciation of these, believing that indigenous people should be "civilized" and Christianized. The Spanish Benedictine monk Rosendo Salvado in Western Australia was a significant exception, who sought to discern how indigenous beliefs could serve as an introduction to the gospel. In an epoch-making statement in Alice Springs in 1986, Pope John* Paul II told Aborigines* that their beliefs were "your own way of touching the mystery* of God's Spirit." This affirmation typifies recent, more positive approaches to indigenous religious experience, especially regarding the sacredness of the land*. It reaches back to an older tradition attested to by the desert fathers, Bonaventure*, the English poet Thomas Traherne, Teilhard* de Chardin, and others: the world is a revelation of God (see Rom 1:20); Christian spirituality involves appreciating and caring for it.

Interest in the great classics of Christian spirituality is growing, thanks to reliable and readable translations, as well as to institutes such as the Centre for Christian Spirituality in Sydney. This resurgence of an older and more liberal approach to contemplative* prayer blends well with indigenous peoples' appreciation of silence, contemplation*, and sense of mystery* in life.

Another type of spirituality is represented by the plethora of imported and adapted spirituality movements – Charismatic*, Focolari*, Cursillo, Marriage Encounter, Antioch, Alpha, and various other study and prayer groups both within denominations and within independent churches. Among the many imported and local initiatives that bring together spirituality and charitable works, the St. Vincent* de Paul Society is best known. Conversely many traditional Western devotional practices, imported earlier by the missionaries, are fading, including Catholic devotions such as the rosary* and benediction* of the sacrament.

The contemporary Liturgical* Movement, especially in the Anglican and Roman Catholic churches, involves various efforts at inculturation* by incorporating popular devotional practices such as folk hymns and music, the symbolic ritual entailing the solemn entry of the sacred Scriptures into the church, and the formal offering of gifts on celebratory occasions in many island communities. These efforts reflect a belated effort to respect cultures that have almost been lost. The pivotal role of Word and sacrament in the liturgy reinforces the belief that all Christian spirituality is centered on the Savior. And this encounter with the Lord involves service and witness, to "gossip the Gospel," as Archbishop Runcie told Anglican laypeople in Australia. AUSTIN COOPER, OMI

Spiritual Reformers, Spirituals, Spiritualists. The mystical* tendency within Christianity, and specifically its claim to experience God without the mediation of Scripture*, sacraments*, or clergy*, was emphasized by some members of "the left wing" of the Reformation* (e.g. Caspar Schwenkfeld, Valentin Weigel, Sebastian Franck, Dirck Coornheert). It found its most lasting institutional form in the Society of Friends*, but it also became one aspect of Pietism*, the Moravian* tradition, and Methodism*. From the 16th c. onward, its advocates have championed religious toleration and human rights.

Spirituals, religious or sacred folksongs that grew out of the artistic genius of African American slaves* in the 19th c. Spirituals were a product of the combined influences of African musical forms, the characters and stories of the Bible, evangelical sermons, hymns of revivals* and camp* meetings, and the experiences of the enslaved in slave* quarters and "hush harbor" meetings. Spirituals, created and disseminated spontaneously or in the fashion of popular* Christianity, gave expression to an indestructible hope* for both freedom in this world (liberation*) and salvation* in the next. The personal God, the suffering of Jesus, faith*, love*, community, the experience of rebirth*, salvation, and reunion in the afterlife are among the major themes expressed, thus revealing the religious intent of spirituals. Images of "freedom," "the chosen people," "the Promised* Land," "Canaan land," and "Egyptian bondage" all captured the slaves' longing for physical freedom. This dual focus, the "double meanings," the vivid biblical imagery, the pervasive sense of identification with the children of Israel, and the dramatization of stories of the HB in explicating the unfolding history of the enslaved: all of these distinguished the spirituals of the slaves from those of their white counterparts. Affirming the interrelationship between this-worldly and otherworldly concerns, spirituals survived slavery and were repopularized (late 19th–early 20th c.) by the Fisk Jubilee Singers, Roland Hayes, James Weldon Johnson, Paul Robeson, and others, who shared them, often in a denatured form, with different cultures worldwide. Displaced by gospel* songs after the 1930s as the dominant body of African American sacred music, spirituals still figure prominently in the performative and celebrative character of African American ecclesiastical and liturgical life. **See also GOSPEL MUSIC; MEDIA AND CHRISTIANITY; MEDIA AND CHRISTIAN WORSHIP; MEGACHURCHES REMAKING RELIGIOUS TRADITION IN NORTH AMERICA; PENTECOSTAL WORSHIP; PRAISE AND WORSHIP.** LEWIS V. BALDWIN

Sports, Book of, a royal document that provided an alternative to the Sabbatarian* approach of the Puritans* in the Church of England*; it permitted archery and dancing on Sunday. Issued by James* I for Lancastershire (1617), then for all of England (1618), it was reissued by Charles* I (1633). It was ordered burned by the Puritan Parliament (1643).

Sri Lanka (Ceylon before 1972). A Christian community was first established by Christian merchants from Persia (c5th c.), according to trading documents whose authenticity was confirmed by the archeological discovery (early 20th c.) at the site of the ancient capital, Anuradhapura, of a "Nestorian cross" of the period (i.e. a cross of the Church* of the East, presently the symbol of the [Episcopal] Church of Ceylon).

Portuguese (1505–1668) brought the Roman Catholic Church, the first church to take root in Ceylon, with Franciscan* missionaries, followed by Jesuits* (including Francis Xavier*, c1544), Dominicans*, Augustinians*, and secular* clergy, who learned the language, translated books, and established parishes (Franciscans), schools (Jesuits), monasteries, and a seminary (Jesuits; 1605). When the Portuguese left (1658), strong Roman Catholic communities withstood persecutions (early 18th c.) during the Dutch occupation and negligence during the British period, remaining today the largest Christian Church in Sri Lanka.

During the Dutch colonization (1658–1796), the Dutch Reformed Church was established (emphasizing education*) with clergy from Holland and South India, and later with Ceylonese (lay and clergy) trained in local seminaries (in Jaffna since 1690; in Colombo since 1696). The Church set up the first printing presses in Ceylon, printing translations of the NT in Sinhala and Tamil, as well as Portuguese. Duplicating the Reformation/Counter Reformation conflict in Europe, the Dutch persecuted Catholics. Since the Dutch had exclusive control of the coast, Catholics moved to the center of the island (the Kandyan Kingdom), with Fr. Joseph Vaz (in the process of being canonized) as one of the rare priests. When the Dutch left (1796), the Dutch Reformed Church was not strong, and today its members are a very small minority.

The British colonization period (1796–1948) saw the arrival of the Church of England through the London Missionary Society (1806–18), followed and replaced by the Baptist (since 1812) and Wesleyan (since 1814) Missionary Societies, the Congregational American Board of Foreign Missions (since 1816), and the Church Missionary Society (Church of England), each mission working in distinct areas (following the principle of comity*). Eventually, the Ceylon churches united (as in India), forming the Jaffna Diocese of the Church of South* India (1947) and cooperating through the National Christian Council (NCC) of Ceylon. During this period, the first Ceylonese Roman Catholic bishop (1940) and the first Ceylonese Anglican bishop (1945) were ordained.

After Ceylon achieved independence (1948), the established "missionary" churches further developed. The Roman Catholic Church was organized in different dioceses, and the first Ceylonese cardinal (Thomas Cardinal Cooray) was named by Pope John* XXIII. The Church of England in Ceylon (Church of Ceylon) became two dioceses (1950). The Methodist Church in Ceylon became an independent conference (1964). Catholic* Action organized workers, peasants, and students, while the Student* Christian Movement was active. This period also saw the arrival of Pentecostal* churches and the Charismatic* Movement, which worked within existing churches.

Despite being a small minority (less than 7%), Christians are heavily involved in state affairs. They joined the struggle for independence and took part in the peace process. Along with Buddhists, Hindus, and Muslims, they are a significant force in the multireligious ethos.

Statistics: Population (2000). 21.3 million (M); Christians, 1.3 M 6.2% (Roman Catholics, 1 M; independents, 0.2 M; Protestants, 0.1 M); Buddhists, 69.1%; Muslims, 7.6%; Hindus, 7.1%; nonspecified, 10%. (Based on 2001 census.)

SYDNEY KNIGHT

Stalls, seats in the choirs* of cathedrals or large churches, elaborately carved and often covered with canopies.

Staniloae, Dumitru (1903–93), priest theologian of the Romanian* Orthodox Church. Studied in Cernauţi, Athens (doctorate), as well as Germany and France (postdoctorate); wrote a book on Gregory* Palamas; taught in Sibiu, then Bucharest from 1949 to 1973, except for a period of six years, during which he lived in a prison camp.

Throughout the early years of the newly formed Romanian* state and the Communist rule, Staniloae sought as a journalist to interpret the times from an Orthodox perspective. He gained national stature and was known internationally as an articulate Orthodox voice in the ecumenical* movement with a good knowledge of Western theology.

Theologically, Staniloae represented the "neopatristic synthesis," which he explored much more thoroughly than Lossky* or Florovsky* through an extensive work of translation: an expanded *Philokalia**, with theological commentary, and translations of other fathers, especially Maximos* the Confessor, with whom he had a particular affinity.

His mature theology is summed up in two works: *Orthodox Dogmatic Theology*, entitled in English *The Experience of God*, and *Orthodox Spirituality*. The traditional style of theological textbooks sometimes disguises their radical nature. Staniloae's theology, with its Palamite emphasis on a living experience of God, its profound sense of creation* as already grace*, through which we encounter Christ as revealed "in the cross," and his constant recourse to his patristic learning, does not fit well into traditional structures. *Orthodox Spirituality* reveals Staniloae's deep sympathy for the creative philosophical movements, associated with thinkers such as Blondel*, that he encountered in Paris. The later volumes of the *Dogmatic Theology* make creative use of liturgical sources, thus keeping his theology close to everyday Christian experience, and to the devout old ladies who, Staniloae used to claim, were his real mentors in theology.

ANDREW LOUTH

Stanton, Elizabeth Cady (1815–1902), US suffragist, abolitionist, freethinker, author, compiler of *The Woman's Bible* (1895, 1898); born in Johnstown, New York. Raised in the Presbyterian Church, as a young girl she befriended the local minister, Simon Hosack, who taught her Greek. According to her autobiography, Stanton tried but failed to undergo an experience of conversion to Evangelical* Christianity during the revivals* of the Second Great* Awakening. She contended that her true conversion* was to rationalism*. As a young woman, she was deeply influenced by the Unitarian* Theodore Parker and later by the writings of Auguste Comte on the religion of humanity. She ultimately became a lifelong advocate of free thought.

At the margins of liberal Christianity and increasingly investigating the 19th-c. "new" religions, Stanton nevertheless maintained a Protestant orientation. To her mind, Protestantism's most salient contribution was its emphasis on the primacy of individual conscience; she put great stock in individuals' ability to read and interpret biblical texts for themselves.

Stanton was particularly motivated by what she perceived to be the androcentric* nature of Christianity. Her mission throughout her 50-year reform career centered on liberating women from religious superstition*. She drew on the insights of 19th-c. higher biblical criticism and argued that its findings held the potential to alter the traditional interpretations of women's status in the Bible. For example, Stanton pointed to the multiple authorship of the books of the Pentateuch* to challenge the authority of biblical accounts rendering Eve* as the primary author of the Fall*. Biblical texts were not unassailable; they were created within historical contexts. The divine wisdom* found in the Bible had to be freed from the prejudices of its authors, translators, and historical circumstances. These beliefs led Stanton to organize, compile, and serve as the primary author of *The Woman's Bible*. This two-volume text attempted to offer readers an array of women's commentaries on biblical texts concerning women. Stanton had hoped to form a revising committee of women of diverse political and religious views to offer interpretations. But because of the controversial nature of the project, she was unable to lure conservative Evangelical women to join her. The book was lauded in some liberal circles but was routinely condemned by conservative clergy and mainstream reformers, including the National American Woman Suffrage Association, for which Stanton had served as president.

While Stanton and her *Woman's Bible* were considered highly controversial in the 19th c., both she and her "bible" emerged as an inspiration for second-wave feminists* in the 1970s. **See also ANTHONY, SUSAN B.; BIBLE INTERPRETATION CLUSTER: WORLDWIDE: FEMINIST.** KATHI LYNN KERN

Star of Bethlehem (the) guided the wise men from the East to Jesus' birthplace in Bethlehem (Matt 2:1–12); the narrative alludes to the star prophecy in Num 24:17 (cf. Rev 22:16). Ignatius* of Antioch, Justin* Martyr, Clement*, and Tertullian* commented on the star. Two common interpretations exist. Origen* represents the natural view, calling the star "something of another order," a comet, heralding the fulfillment of messianic prophecy. John* Chrysostom epitomizes the miraculous view, according to which it is doubtful that a star could lead men to a particular physical place without divine direction. Ultimately, the star symbolizes new life and the hope* Christ brings from heaven*. JEFFRY C. DAVIS

State Churches, churches officially recognized and supported by governments. Often bishops* and other ecclesiastical leaders are appointed or approved by the government. There are at least three types: (1) national churches (e.g. the Churches of England*, Scotland*, Denmark*, Sweden*); (2) universal churches (e.g. Roman Catholic Church) recognized through concordats* with individual governments; and (3) multiple churches supported by the state and its tax revenues (e.g. in Germany*, the Netherlands*). **See also CULTURE CHRISTIANITY; FOLK CHURCHES IN THE NORDIC COUNTRIES.**

States of the Church, portion of central Italy, stretching north and south from Rome to Ravenna, controlled by the pope from the 8th to the 19th c. **See also DONATION OF CONSTANTINE.**

Stational Liturgy (from Lat *statio*, "guard post"), worship conducted by the bishop of a city at changing locations, depending on saints' days or times of the year. The term eventually came to be used for processions from one site to another.

Stations of the Cross, a series of depictions of 14 stages of Christ's Passion*, from Pilate's house to the cross, arranged around the walls of a church, which faithful visit in sequence for prayer and meditation. This practice probably originated in Jerusalem (4th c.) and spread to Europe in the Middle Ages.

Status Confessionis (Lat "situation of confession"), doctrine developed by the Gnesio-Lutheran Flacius* in opposing the 1548 Augsburg Interim* of Charles V. It states that there is a need for "confession" (a denunciation) when the response to a given situation gives rise to an erroneous view of the gospel. The doctrine originally denounced the state's interference with the gospel; since then it has been used primarily to denounce the church's failures. Thus the Barmen* Declaration accused the German* Christians of betraying the source, extent, form, ministry, relation to the state, and purpose of Christian proclamation – a *status confessionis*. The 1967 Confession of the United Presbyterian Church in the USA declares that the church betrays its calling when it is associated with racism*, nationalism, enslaving poverty, or lack of compassion. The Lutheran World Federation (1977) and the World Alliance of Reformed Churches (1982) declared apartheid* a *status confessionis*. During the 1980s and 1990s, there were calls to declare nuclear warfare and the gross differences of wealth and power in the world a *status confessionis*.

Stephanas, Paul's first convert in Corinth*, baptized by Paul himself; he later brought aid to

Paul and was with him when he wrote to the church in Corinth (1 Cor 1:16, 16:15–17).

Stephen (d32–35), proto-martyr*; a "Hellenist*" (Acts 6:1–7) who angered many Jews by his address in Jerusalem about the Temple and the Law of Moses (Act 7:2–53). He was stoned without a formal trial; Saul, the future Paul* the Apostle, was involved (Acts 7:58–8:1). Relics* (dust) from his alleged tomb near Jerusalem (415) were brought to the West by Orosius; Augustine* publicized the miracles they had wrought. Melania* the Younger gained possession of the site; Empress Eudoxia built the shrine (439). The "new birth" of this first martyr is observed on December 26 in the West, December 27 in the East.

Stewardship, management of property* by a servant on behalf of the owner; a metaphor for fidelity to God's call (Luke 12:42) and for administration of the gospel and the gifts of grace* (1 Cor 4:1; 1 Pet 4:10). In churches supported by voluntary gifts (especially since the late 19th c.; in the Economy and Christianity Cluster: see Economic Studies of Christianity and Studies of the History of Christianity in the United States), stewardship meant responsibility to God in the management of property and financial resources, since all wealth* belongs to God. Today one also refers to stewardship of natural resources.

Stigmata, marks like those on the crucified body of Christ that appear on the bodies of some devout persons, e.g. Francis* of Assisi.

Stoicism, Greek school of philosophy that grew out of Cynicism* but took more interest in issues of physics, logic, and ethics. Founded by Zeno (c300 BCE) and his pupil Cleanthes, it was set down in a classic way by Chrysippus (280–207 BCE). The emphasis was on natural* law in both the cosmos and human thought. This natural law was identified with the divine Logos* or cosmic reason. Stoic philosophical theology influenced by the Cynic Antisthenes (c445–365 BCE) assumed that the universal status of a reasoned theo*logical* explanation (grounded in Logos) was philosophically and religiously superior to common religious convictions – "so-called" knowledge about God, assertions without proof. Paul discusses the "real/so-called" distinction regarding the knowledge of God (1 Cor 8:1, 5), a distinction reminiscent of the Stoic differentiation between God and common convictions about the gods of the cosmos. Similarly, in ethics, natural law was the criterion against which custom and human law must be tested. According to the Stoics' view of nature, events occur with inevitability, and freedom consists in willing whatever occurs. Stoic themes are found in Philo* and, beyond Paul*, in most early Christian thinkers.

Stole, narrow liturgical vestment worn by priests and ministers around the neck and hanging down in front, or by a deacon over the left shoulder.

Stone, Barton (1772–1844), preacher, editor, leader of a unity movement. Raised in Maryland and Virginia, Stone studied in North Carolina, was ordained by Presbyterians* in Kentucky (1798), and moved to Illinois (1834). Committed to Christian unity and social* justice*, Stone hosted the Cane Ridge camp* meeting with Methodists* (1801). Separated from Presbyterians over his refusal to preach predestination* (1803), Stone founded the Christian Church as a unity movement (1804), which became the Christian* Church (Disciples of Christ) after union with the followers of Alexander Campbell* (1832). As many others did, he supported both colonization (1826–34) and immediate abolition of slavery (1835). Disillusioned by politics and the US failure to end slavery*, Stone advised Christians to withdraw from civil government (1842). D. NEWELL WILLIAMS

Stowe, Harriet Beecher (1811–96), daughter of Lyman Beecher*, sister of Catharine Beecher*. A prolific writer of poems, travel books, biographies, and children's books, she is best known for *Uncle Tom's Cabin* (1852), a novel documenting the evils of slavery*, which was read widely in the USA and abroad and influenced public opinion in the years leading up to the Civil* War.

Strachan, John (1778–1867), born in Scotland, moved (1799) to Upper Canada* to teach boys to become British patriots and Christian gentlemen; ordained in the Church of England (1803). As a rector (1812) in York (Toronto), he displayed courageous conduct during two US invasions (1813). He was a member of the colony's executive council (1817–36) and the colony's legislative council (1820–41). He helped draft the colony's Common School Act (1816), obtained a royal university charter in Toronto (King's College, Trinity College), and fended off political reformers who sought to diminish the rights and privileges of the crown and the Church of England in the colony. As the founding bishop of the Anglican Diocese of York

(1839–67), he stood for Tory adherence to the High Church, even when it went out of fashion. **See also CANADA.** ROBERT CHOQUETTE

Strangers. See REFUGEES AS A THEOLOGICAL CONCEPT AND AN ETHICAL ISSUE.

Structural Evil, evil or oppression* that arises from social, economic, and political structures or from basic cultural assumptions; often viewed as a version of, or substitute for, original* sin. Inequalities of class, race*, gender, and sexual* orientation are types of evil* that are larger than, and prior to, the individual; they envelop the oppressor and the oppressed in a web of guilt and powerlessness, and require structural solutions. Concern about such a "kingdom of evil" was expressed by Kant*, Schleiermacher*, Ritschl*, and Rauschenbusch* and continues to be addressed by Liberation* theology.

Structural Studies of Christianity. See SEMIOTICS AND THE STUDY OF CHRISTIANITY.

Student Christian Movement, organization that grew out of YMCA* and YWCA* activities on college campuses in the USA and Great Britain, uniting Christians across (Protestant) denominational lines and promoting missions. More specifically, the British branch of this federation that gave rise to the influential SCM Press. **See also WORLD STUDENT CHRISTIAN FEDERATION.**

Student Volunteer Movement for Foreign Missions grew out of a YMCA* conference (1886) with the slogan "the evangelization of the world in this generation" (1888). In the USA, its base was the YMCA and YWCA*; in Great Britain, the Student Volunteer Missionary Union was an arm of the Student* Christian Movement. Thousands of college-educated students became missionaries throughout the world on an interdenominational* basis, especially before World War I.

Studios Monastery, the monastery of St. John the Baptist in Constantinople, named for the senator on whose land it was built (late 5th c.). Following the practice of Acoemetae*, the Sleepless Monastery, its monks ceaselessly praised God. Because of their defense of the decrees of Chalcedon*, they were driven out by Miaphysite* patriarchs and emperors. The monastery was reorganized under Theodore* of Studios after 799 with a rule based on that of Basil*, which became widely used in monasteries of the Eastern Church. The monks of Studios were the foremost champions of icons* during the Iconoclastic* controversy.

Stylite, Stylitism. A stylite is a monk living alone on the top of a pillar. Stylitism as a practice (5th–10th c.) was modeled on Simeon* Stylites.

Suárez, Francisco (1548–1617), Spanish Jesuit, philosopher, theologian; prominent representative of the "Silver Age of Scholasticism*" (c1525–c1625), which sought to address the difficult questions arising from the colonization* and Christianization of the New World, humanism*, and the Reformation*. Born in Granada, starting at the age of 14 Suárez studied canon* law, then philosophy and theology in Salamanca; he joined the Jesuit* order in 1564. From 1571 he taught at several of the most distinguished academic centers of his time: Ávila, Segovia, Valladolid, Rome, Alcalá, Salamanca, and Coimbra. He subsequently served as a consultant on moral and canonical matters in Lisbon.

Suárez's 28 large volumes on metaphysics*, theology, and law* discuss with extraordinary erudition the ancient Greek, patristic, Arabic, and Scholastic intellectual traditions on their own terms. Occasionally misunderstood as "eclectic," his method leads to an original position that synthesizes elements from the Thomistic*, Scotistic (see Duns Scotus, John) and Ockhamistic* schools in a sophisticated way. The essential features of this synthesis and its role in the history of ideas are under debate and require further exploration.

Suárez's most important philosophical contribution, a comprehensive exposition of "first philosophy," the *Disputationes Metaphysicae* (1597; 20 editions), became a standard textbook, even in 17th-c. Protestant universities. Descartes*, Leibniz, Berkeley, Wolff, Schopenhauer, F. Brentano, and Heidegger* acknowledged their indebtedness to it.

Suárez's theological contributions range from fundamental issues about the Trinity* to questions pertaining to spiritual life. His *De Legibus* (1612) was most influential in the field of law. With his doctrine on the law of peoples (*ius gentium*), Suárez (and De Vitoria) founded modern international law. His doctrine concerning the sovereignty of the people contributed to colonial emancipation following its reception by Hispano-American universities. In *De Gratia* (1619), he systematized Molina's* ideas on grace* (as appropriate inducement, rather than as intrinsically efficacious) in the formula *gratia congruens*, which became canonical for the Jesuits. ROLF DARGE

Subintroductae. See AGAPETAI.

Sublimus Dei, Pope Paul III's bull (1537) declaring that "the said Indians and all other people who may later be discovered by Christians, are by no means to be deprived of their liberty or the possession of their property, even though they be outside the faith of Jesus Christ; and that they may and should, freely and legitimately, enjoy their liberty and the possession of their property; nor should they be in any way enslaved." This reversed Pope Nicholas V's bull, *Dum Diversas* (1452), which encouraged the enslavement of "pagans." **See also** ***ENCOMENDEROS, ENCOMIENDA;*** **LAS CASAS, BARTOLOMÉ DE; PATRONATO, PADROADO; REDUCTIONS; SLAVERY AND CHRISTIANITY CLUSTER.**

Subordinationism, any view that the second person of the Trinity* is "less than" the Father. Logos* theology in the 2nd–3rd c. assumed that the Word is not eternal but uttered for the sake of creation* and providence, and thus less than the Father in order to interact with the created world. Arius* said that the Son was created out of nothing and thus was radically different from God. Subordinationism was justified by scriptural passages about divine Wisdom as "created" by God (Prov 8:22) and about Jesus as sent by the Father and doing the Father's will (John 5:19, 7.16, 8.42, 14:28). **See also TRINITY IN EASTERN ORTHODOXY; TRINITY IN THE WESTERN TRADITION.**

Subscription. In Protestantism, when ministers are ordained*, they are often expected to subscribe to (i.e. state their agreement with) the creeds* or confessions of their churches. Since the 16th c., this was debated (especially in the Church of Scotland and Church of England) on the grounds that confessions were subordinate to Scripture*, that all persons have the responsibility to interpret Scripture for themselves, and that "God alone is the Lord of the conscience." "Strict subscription" was commonly set aside by legitimating a broader interpretation of the confessions and insisting only on the "substance" or "essentials" of the faith.

Subsidiarity, Principle of, concerning political and economic relationships. First enunciated in *Quadragesimo Anno* (1931), the social* encyclical of Pope Pius* XI, it states (Para. 79) that what can be performed by local bodies should not be transferred to central authorities, whose role is to be an "aid," a *subsidium*, to local bodies, rather than destroy or absorb them. The central body nevertheless has the task of "directing, watching, stimulating, and restraining, as circumstances suggest or necessity demands" (Para. 80). Thus the principle of subsidiarity not only blocks interference but calls for intervention whenever local authorities do not carry out their tasks adequately. John* XXIII in *Mater et Magistra* (1961) and the Second Vatican* Council (in "The Church in the Modern World") reaffirmed it.

The principle entered European law in the Maastricht Treaty (1992, Article 3B): the European Community will intervene *only if* and *insofar as* the intended objectives can be better achieved by it rather than by the member states. **See also DEMOCRACY AND CHRISTIANITY; SOCIAL ENCYCLICALS.**

Succession (Gk *diadoche*), term used in reference to the three rulers who succeeded Alexander the Great; also used in reference to the heads of Greek philosophical schools and, in Judaism, to both high priests and leading rabbis. Among Christians, Gnostic* groups claimed succession from Paul or other apostles, and Hegesippus* drew up the first succession lists of bishops*. While it was not the sole basis of authority, succession was an important guarantee of continuity and legitimation. Many historians judge the lack of agreed-upon rules of succession to be a major cause of the crises of the Roman Empire. **See also APOSTOLICITY AND APOSTOLIC SUCCESSION.**

Sudan. In the northern part of present-day Sudan, there were once three Christian kingdoms. Christianity was introduced as early as c350, flourished, and became the state religion in 580, following the pattern of the Byzantine Empire, from which the missionaries originated. These Nubian kingdoms were, from north to south along the Nile River, Nobatia (Nobatae; Miaphysite*), Makuria (Maqurrah; Miaphysite), and Alwa (Alodia; Chalcedonian*) (see History of Christianity Cluster: In Africa). Their rulers were priest-kings, vested with both ecclesiastical and secular powers. So intertwined were the church and the state that the two were nearly indistinguishable.

Christianity withstood the challenge of Islam until the 15th c. Initially, Islam did not come to the Christian Nubian kingdoms through invasion but through Arab nomads and itinerant teachers. Some of these intermarried with local people, settling to teach Islam and trade in the area. After gaining access to royal courts, they established good relations with the royals. Thus Islam spread in peaceful ways. But the Arabization and Islamization of Northern Sudan gained impetus with the Mamluk dynasty in Egypt (from 1250). Although Christianity survived for a time, the more militant Arab nomads from Egypt had freer access to the Nubian kingdoms. Once settled in the area, they established themselves quickly in the Nile Valley and adjacent plains. In 1504 Christianity as a state religion was replaced by the Islamic sultanate of Funj.

In the south, beyond the Nubian kingdoms, African* Religion dominated. A combination of fierce resistance by the local people, natural barriers (e.g. the vast swamps of the Sudd and associated diseases), and, later, colonial policies made it difficult for Christian missionaries to reach the south of present-day Sudan. Thus it was only in the early 20th c. that Christianity arrived in the south, mainly in urban centers. Much of rural Southern Sudan remained untouched by the gospel until the outbreak of the civil war (1983), when the church experienced persecution and growth.

Christianity has become the faith of the majority in Southern Sudan, as Islam is in the north. The largest church is the Roman Catholic Church, followed by the Anglican Church. Others are Presbyterian, Church of Christ, and African Inland. The Pentecostal and Charismatic* churches are the fastest growing in Sudan. The church has experienced persecution and oppression – including the expulsion of missionaries (as in 1964) and elimination of church leaders – inflicted by the Islamic authorities, for whom Christianity is a "foreign religion" in Sudan. The Sudan Council of Churches (SCC), which operates in Northern and Southern Sudan, and the New Sudan Council of Churches (established when the war between the north and south from 1983 to 2005 made it difficult for the SCC to serve the needs of people in the south) are widely representative; both councils include Catholics, Orthodox, and Protestants, and work cooperatively under incredibly difficult conditions to build a grassroots movement for peace, as they have done in Darfur (in Western Sudan), a distinct site of conflict and genocide.

Statistics: Population (2000): 29.5 million (M). Christians, 4.9 M, 16.7% (Roman Catholics, 3.1 M; Anglicans, 2.3 M; Protestants, 0.8 M; Orthodox, 0.16 M; members of African Instituted Churches, 0.15 M); Muslims, 20.7 M, 70.3%; African Religionists, 3.4 M, 13%. (Based on *World Christian Encyclopedia*, 2001.)

ISAIAH DAU

Suffering. Christianity accounts for the omnipresence of suffering through the myth* of creation* and the Fall* (Gen 1–3). A benevolent God created the world so that humanity could enjoy intimacy with the divine and harmonious relations with the world. Humanity fell from this paradise* and thus suffers alienation from the divine, disharmony, pain, and death. The incarnation* and Passion* of Christ reconcile the divine and human but do not alter the conditions of the Fall. The faithful can only look forward to an eschatological* existence without tears and death (Rev 21:4). The metaphor* of the Fall captures the paradox* of suffering as universal and yet alien to what humanity was intended to be.

Suffering as Punishment. For Augustine* and the Reformers*, suffering and death are punishment for the prideful disobedience that led to the Fall. God becomes incarnate in Christ, whose atoning death absorbs the guilt of humanity (see Atonement #2). Participation in the church makes available the means of salvation* through which those predestined for salvation will be delivered from suffering in heaven*.

Standard in Western churches, this narrative, which interprets suffering as penalty, appeals to the psychological need to find meaning in suffering. Cosmic principles of justice* are maintained by an omnipotent* God, who punishes wrongdoers, yet Christians can look forward to a condition in which suffering is ended. But when suffering is conflated with punishment, guilt exacerbates suffering. Imagining God* as an angry father/king can make the divine terrifying and distant rather than consoling. This interpretation supports the institutional power of the church, which alone controls the means of salvation* that free humanity from suffering.

Suffering as an Inevitable Aspect of the Created Order. This fundamentally different view of the causes and cures of suffering is found throughout Christian history. According to this interpretation, suffering is an inevitable aspect of the created order, which is under the power of evil forces (or is diseased), a situation worsened by human cruelty. Consequently, the cure of suffering, the manifestation of God's love, is a manifestation of divine power. Christ's Passion reveals divine compassion* for suffering humanity and promises that God will overcome suffering and the powers of evil (or disease) that cause it (see Atonement #1).

Among those who held this view were the Gnostics*, who thought that the Savior freed the faithful from the deceptions and violence of the current order by awakening them to their divine identity. Medieval contemplatives (e.g. Beguines*) meditated on Christ's Passion so that their own suffering would be transformed into healing for humanity. Schleiermacher* argued that the stability of God consciousness enables Christians to endure suffering without despair or guilt. Without the same countercultural attitude, Eastern Orthodox* meditate on the Incarnation* as a renewal of human nature; through (sacramental) union with Christ, Christians' suffering becomes a healing presence for humanity (see Culture and Christianity Cluster: In Eastern Orthodoxy). Similarly, most Charismatic* churches and many African* Instituted Churches envision their ministries as forms of spiritual warfare against diverse evil powers that cause suffering. Both God and Christians alleviate suffering through compassion* and powerful interventions.

Suffering and Systemic Evil. The Holocaust* and late-20th-c. liberation* movements emphasized the social, political, and economic causes of suffering. Attention was turned to those who suffer from evils such as poverty*, patriarchy*, racism*, and anti-Semitism*. Justice* meant not punishment of sinners but humane social systems. The parable of the good Samaritan and Matt 25:31–46 emphasize Christianity's responsibility to mediate divine compassion to humanity by correcting injustices to alleviate suffering.

Christianity struggles to understand the anguish and ubiquity of suffering in light of the goodness of God (see Theodicy). The church has often been concerned more with its own power than with the pain of humanity. But the revelation of divine love* in Christ continues to bring healing and comfort to the afflicted.

WENDY FARLEY

Suffragan Bishop, traditionally a bishop who assists his metropolitan* by voting at a synod; now also an assistant bishop.

Sunday School Movement (the) originated in the late 18th c. in Great Britain and soon spread to the USA and other parts of the world. Sunday school and its basic structure and purpose have been incorporated into the patterns and norms of some Christian churches, significantly shaping their mission.

The Sunday School Movement was motivated by both biblical teaching and social circumstances. The Bible teaches the urgency of teaching both children and adults the beliefs and practices of faith*. In Torah the following commandment is given Mosaic authority: "These commandments that I give you today are to be upon your hearts. Impress them on your children. Talk about them when you sit at home and when you walk along the road, when you lie down and when you get up" (Deut 6:6–7). In the Gospels, Jesus is called rabbi (teacher); in Acts, the first generation of Christians met to study the teachings (*didache);* and in Matthew, Jesus commands the new community "to teach them everything I have commanded you" (Matt 28:19–20).

Robert Raikes (1735–1811), influential in the origin and development of Sunday school, was an Anglican layperson born in Gloucester, England. Committed to issues of social* justice* (especially penal reform), he was concerned about the plight of the poor children of his city and believed that Sunday school would improve their condition. He offered a program (from 1780) in Gloucester for working-class children and soon the Sunday School Movement was present in London.

With a similar motivation, a comparable program was begun in Accomack County, Virginia, by William Elliot (1785), and the "First Day School Society" was established in Philadelphia (1791). The movement, rooted in Evangelical Protestant denominations (Baptist, Congregationalist, Low Church Episcopalian, Methodist, Presbyterian), joined forces to found the American Sunday School Union. Conventions were held in Philadelphia (1832, 1833). The movement became an integral part of church life.

In the late 19th and 20th c., the movement increased in influence and adopted sophisticated educational strategies. Professional Christian educators with primary responsibility for Sunday schools became a part of the educational mission of the church and part of the staff of larger congregations. Seminary training for pastors included courses in Christian education. Currently, the Sunday School Movement for both children and adults is grounded in contemporary theology, current educational theory, teaching training, and excellent printed and electronic materials.

DUNCAN S. FERGUSON

Sung Shang-Jie John (1901–44), a Chinese revivalist*, grew up in Fujian, China*, during Sun Yat-sen's revolution. Son of a Methodist pastor, Sung first assisted his father. After studying in the USA (1920–26; doctorate in chemistry; briefly a student at Union Theological Seminary), he served as a minister in Fujian (1927–1930), then traveled, preaching throughout North China with Andrew Gih's Bethel Worldwide Evangelistic Band (1931–33). Through wars and poverty, Sung also preached in Southeast Asian countries (the Philippines*, Indonesia*, Singapore*, Malaysia*) and Taiwan* (1934–40). Renowned for prophetic preaching, vision, and healing, Sung emphasized prayer, discipleship modeled on Christ's suffering on the cross, repentance*, sanctification*, evangelism*, and self-sufficiency of the Chinese Church.

MENGHUN GOH

Supernatural, that which is beyond the human realm or nature: God* and the grace* by which human beings are brought into communion with God.

Supersessionism, view according to which Christianity supersedes or replaces Judaism*, since Christ is the complete and final revelation that not only fulfilled but ended the purpose of the Law*. It stands in contrast to the affirmation of a continuity between Judaism and Christianity, an alternative position that is often linked with the conviction that Christ* presages other revelatory manifestations (including transforming manifestations of the Spirit*). **See also ANTI-JEWISH, ANTI-JUDAISM; NEW COVENANT; TYPOLOGY; UNIQUENESS OF CHRIST.**

Superstition, excessive or irrational fear of divine or demonic powers, resulting in overscrupulous activities. Superstition has usually been considered less serious than either magic or heresy*, probably because it is more naive than purposeful. The difference between religion and superstition lies in the judgment of the beholder: beliefs and practices with which one disagrees are often labeled superstitions. In "traditionally Christian" countries, many folkways were considered superstitious in comparison with orthodoxy, but were usually tolerated as harmless "local customs" until reform movements (e.g. Renaissance*, Reformation*) called them into question and sought to abolish or transform them. The Enlightenment* rejected many aspects of Christianity and other religions as irrational superstitions; (scientific)* rationality renders religious views and practices irrelevant. Romanticism* and postmodernism* rehabilitated them as unconsciously carrying profound meaning for human life and questioning the Enlightenment's premises.

Supralapsarianism, view that God's predestination* of the elect was decided before God's foreknowledge of human sin*, thus "prior" to God's knowing and willing (cf. Infralapsarianism).

Supremacy, Acts of, two acts of the English Parliament. The first (1534) made Henry* VIII the "supreme head" of the Church of England; the second (1559) made Elizabeth* I the "supreme governor" of spiritual and temporal affairs.

Surplice, a loose vestment of white linen, with wide sleeves, worn over a cassock by priests, acolytes, and choristers.

Susanna, Book of, one of the additions to the book of Daniel*, exclusively preserved in Greek translations of the OT (in LXX*, after Dan 12, and in Theodotion*, before Dan 1). It tells the story of Susanna, a "religious and God-fearing woman," who refused the advances of two "elders," was accused by them of adultery, but was saved by Daniel, who cross-examined the two elders and discredited their testimony. This book is part of the Roman Catholic and Orthodox Bibles (as Dan 13), but not the Jewish Tanakh* (HB) and Protestant Bibles. **See also BIBLE, CANON OF.**

Swaziland, a homogeneous society ruled by an absolute monarch, where Christians coexist with practitioners of Swazi Traditional Religion (STR), which is thoroughly enmeshed in the Swazi culture and way of life. Despite constitutional provisions for the freedom of religion, public holidays are Christian holidays and the monarch participates in all significant Christian activities to reiterate his support of Christianity. Other religions (e.g. Baha'i*, Islam*) have few followers.

The story of Christianity in Swaziland began in 1836 when King Somhlolo, a stalwart of the STR, dreamed of strange people (whites) emerging from the sea, carrying *umculu* (a scroll) and *indilinga* (a coin). A voice cautioned the king that the nation should accept the scroll (the Bible) and reject the coin (money). After relating the dream, the king died. Subsequently, his successor, King Mswati I, sent emissaries to South Africa to invite Methodist missionaries to Swaziland. The enthusiastic welcome of the first missionaries (1844) opened doors for many others, including Nazarenes*, Anglicans*, Lutherans*, Roman Catholics, and Evangelicals*. As they preached the gospel, they made invaluable contributions to the welfare of the Swazi by building schools and hospitals.

Later, the Swazi realized that their culture had been repressed by European settlers (including missionaries) and that they had been robbed of their land through the Partition Proclamation of 1907. Consequently, some Swazi Christians seceded from mission churches to institute indigenous churches (African* Instituted Churches), including "Ethiopian churches," "Zionist churches," and the fast-growing "Ministries." These churches have lively charismatic* worship, view life as a daily spiritual struggle with demonic powers, originated with charismatic* prophets and healers, and emphasize healing*, revelations, visions by the Holy Spirit, and prophecies.

Most churches are affiliated with the Conference of Churches, the Council of Churches, or the League of Churches. The League, the umbrella organization of all the indigenous churches (except for "Ministries"), includes about 40% of the population.

Statistics: Population (2007): 1.1 million. Christians, 85% (members of African Instituted Churches, 45%; unaffiliated [Charismatics and others], 16%; Protestants, 15%; Roman Catholics, 5%; Anglicans, 4%); Swazi Traditional Religionists, 12%; others, 3%. (Based on *World Christian Encyclopedia*, 2001, and governmental statistics.)

SONENE NYAWO

Sweden. The developments of Christianity in Sweden and of the Swedish nation were closely connected. Following the church's establishment, originally influenced by both Denmark and England, Sweden became a church province (1164), with strong ties to Rome during the Middle Ages. Holy orders were established. Birgitta* (1303–73, now the patron saint of Europe) played a critical role in Sweden's relationship with Rome and in political issues.

Following the Reformation (de facto adopted in 1536; officially confirmed in 1593), the Church of Sweden kept many of the Catholic liturgical practices. However, Lutheran orthodoxy, with strongholds at the universities, unified the country by emphasizing church discipline in preaching. The Enlightenment* drastically changed the theological climate. Several scientists were also theologians, including the botanist Carl Linnaeus (1707–78) and Emanuel Swedenborg* (1688–1772).

Sweden resisted the revivalist* movements until 1860, when Baptists and Methodists gradually established small denominations alongside the Missionary Covenant Church, a Pietist* group within the Church of Sweden. In the early 20th c., the Pentecostal* Movement developed rapidly, publishing a daily newspaper and forming a political party. These conservative movements did not become major denominations, have significantly decreased in the past few generations, and do not have a clear voice in society.

Until 2000 the Church of Sweden was formally a state* church. Nowadays, in a state considered religiously neutral, it is still constitutionally a privileged church, rules its own affairs, and continues to be strongly dedicated to the ecumenical* movement.

The decline in Sunday service attendance might suggest that Sweden has become post-Christian. Yet Christianity provides the dominant view of life for many who describe themselves as "Christian in their own way" (see Culture Christianity). In line with this increasing privatization of religion, public rituals are limited to holidays, rites of passage, burial in graveyards as sacred space, and times of crisis. Yet these still tie the population to the churches. In addition, alternative spiritual (and Charismatic) practices have emerged.

The Bible and Luther's *Small Catechism* have had the greatest influence on Swedish culture. Theological education (in the universities), strong since the 15th c., has recently been broadened to include religious studies programs at decentralized higher education institutions and revivalist colleges. In public schools, Christianity is taught alongside other religions and ideologies. Christianity has influenced strong social movements, including the women's*, workers', and environmental movements (which are often integrated into church activities). Swedish Christians have a general acquaintance with other religions and ideologies, yet dialogue with members of other religions and their integration into society need improvement.

Statistics: Population (2000): 8.91 million (M). Christians, 7.56 M, 85% (members of Church of Sweden, 7.26 M; Orthodox, 0.12 M; Roman Catholics, 0.17 M); Muslims, 0.2 M, 2.3%; atheists and nonreligious, also within churches,

2.6 M, 29.4%. (*Source*: Church of Sweden and governmental statistics.)

CRISTINA GRENHOLM

Swedenborg, Emanuel (1688–1772), Swedish scientist and civil servant; founder of a new Christian church. Swedenborg's father was a prominent bishop, but he himself became fascinated by modern science and technology. He published the first scientific journal in Sweden* (1716–18) and was appointed assessor in the College of Mines. Starting from a Cartesian point of view, he presented a theory of the origin of inorganic nature (1734); during the next decade, he studied human anatomy and physiology, aiming at a unification of science and Christian theology. This attempt resulted in a religious crisis (1743–44), following which a divine call made him abandon all scientific activities. Instead, he wrote (in Latin) a number of books in which he interpreted biblical texts and reported on his meetings with angels and spirits. His idea was to restore Christianity to its original purity before Nicaea*, as made clear by the title of his last work, *Vera Christiana Religio* (True Christianity, 1771). Swedenborg never acted as a missionary but relied on the effect of his books for the establishment of a new church. The first Swedenborgian congregations were founded in England (in the 1780s). Today the Swedish 18th-c. visionary still has followers in many parts of the world. INGE JONSSON

Switzerland was shaped as a country by Christianity, which arrived with the Romans (early 4th c.) and was substantially reinforced under Burgundian rule (6th c.). Dioceses were established with bishop sees in Augusta Raurica, Chur, Martigny, Geneva, Lausanne, and Constance. Monasteries*, centers of monastic* culture, were founded in, e.g., Saint-Maurice (Valais) (6th c.), Saint-Gall (under Irish influence, 7th c.), and Einsiedeln (934). Both popular* religious practices (cult of saints*, pilgrimages*) and mysticism* (notably, that of the 15th-c. politician and hermit Klaus von Flüe, sanctified in 1947) developed in late medieval times.

In the 16th c., Basel became a center of debates on church reform among humanists*, including Erasmus*. Zwingli* in Zurich and Farel* and Calvin* in Geneva were leaders of the Reformation* in Switzerland. After two religious wars (1529, 1531), as the momentum of the Protestant Reformation faltered, the First Helvetic* Confession (1536) became the first common creed of the German-speaking parts of the Swiss Confederation (Eidgenossenschaft), and the Second Helvetic* Confession (1566) drafted by Bullinger* was adopted by all Reformed* churches of German-speaking Switzerland (except Basel) and by the French, Scottish, Polish, and Hungarian Reformed churches. In addition, Calvinist and Zwinglian Protestantism established a common creed, the *Consensus Tigurinus* (1549), initiating a rapprochement between the Reformed confessions.

The Catholic* Renewal (from the late 16th c.) – promoted by Borromeo* (archbishop of Milan), Francesco Bonhomini (nuncio in Lucerne), Jesuits* (e.g. Petrus Canisius, Fribourg), and Capuchins* – revitalized clergy and religious institutions. Jesuit colleges (e.g. Lucerne, 1577; Fribourg, 1581; Solothurn, 1646) were founded.

In the 16th–17th c., the Swiss Confederation generated a model of religious coexistence, the principle of territoriality (*cuius regio eius religio*, "a region's government determines the faith of its population") guaranteeing confessional homogeneity within regions. Yet two additional confessional wars took place (1656, 1712). In the 18th c., the Enlightenment* and Pietism* marked Protestantism (with Bern, Zurich, Saint-Gall, and Schaffhausen as centers). In Roman Catholicism, Enlightenment ideas centered on issues of pastoral and liturgical reform.

In the 19th c., religion was one of the most important forces in conceptualizing the Swiss nation. The percentage of Protestants (59.2–57.8%) and Roman Catholics (40.6–41.6%) remained stable. When Liberals were eager to subjugate the Catholic Church to state power (1830s), a civil war erupted (1847), leading to the foundation of the federal state (1848). Politicization of religion and confessionalization of politics continued in the *Kulturkampf* * (1870s–1880s), intensified by anti-Jesuit articles in the federal Constitution of 1874, by the increasingly Ultramontane* character of Catholicism, and by the social and political mobilization of Catholics. Starting in 1891, the Catholic Conservative party was continuously represented in the national government. The Catholic subculture (Altermatt) had its organizational heyday between 1900 and 1950. The centralization of Church authority (cf. the 1870 dogmatization of papal infallibility) was resisted by "liberal" Catholics who founded the Old* Catholic Church (also Christ Catholic Church), which remained a small minority church in Switzerland.

A Protestant revivalist movement (early 19th c.), in reaction to liberal theology, led to the establishment of Evangelical churches (centered in Basel and Geneva), in addition to the cantonal *Landeskirchen* and the *Schweizerische reformierte Kirchenkonferenz.* Revivalism* gave rise to a number of religious, welfare, and missionary societies (e.g. the Basel* Mission).

Since 1945, and especially since 1960, all churches have been affected by "deconfessionalization" – not so much a secularization* as a transformation of religion into a plurality of religious movements and civil* religion. Yet ideological solidarities (as seen, e.g., in the mainly Catholic Christian Democratic Party, supported by some Protestant and secular people) remain a factor of the Swiss party system.

Statistics: Population (2000): 7.4 million. Roman Catholic, 41.8%; Protestant, 35.3%; Orthodox, 1.8%; other Christians, 0.4%; Muslims, 4.3%; other religionists, 1%; nonreligious (and unspecified), 15.4%. (Based on 2000 census.)

URS ALTERMATT and FRANZISKA METZGER

Syllabus of Errors, collection of 80 theses that had already been condemned in earlier documents, issued as an appendix to the encyclical *Quanta Cura* by Pope Pius* IX (1864). There were 10 sections. The concluding condemned thesis reads as follows: "The Roman Pontiff can and ought to reconcile and adjust himself with progress, liberalism, and modern civilization." Protestants reacted with alarm; moderate Roman Catholics tried to soften its interpretation; and the Ultramontanists* and other conservative Catholics considered it their charter. Since the Syllabus was in fact a classified index to previous statements, there is no agreement on the question of whether each thesis condemned in the Syllabus was "infallibly* false" or whether the Syllabus's condemnations of errors should be interpreted in terms of the situations to which they had been addressed. For many, Vatican* II, and especially *Gaudium et Spes* (the pastoral constitution on the Roman Catholic Church in the modern world promulgated by Pope Paul* VI in 1965), are viewed as "an attempt to officially reconcile the Church with the [modern] world," and thus as a "counter-syllabus" (as Cardinal Ratzinger [later Pope Benedict XVI] wrote, in variously interpreted words).

Symbolism, system of symbols representing the connections between individual, community, and ultimate* reality ("symbol" from Grk *syn* [together]-*bole* [a throw], "to throw together," "to connect"). Christian symbolism begins in Scripture. "In the beginning was the Word." Augustine* explains in *On Christian Doctrine* that symbols require interpretation (see Semiotics and the Study of Christianity). Outside of mysticism*, the divine is not immediately experienced. Rather, images such as icons* of Jesus* or Mary*, words such as "Father*" or "love*," and actions such as genuflection before the altar or caring for the sick mediate believers' experience of the divine. Believers use symbols to orient themselves in space and time, in nature and history, toward the good and God. Interpreting symbols is a way toward communion both with the Christian community and with Christ. The Christian symbolic order must be understood in the context of liturgy*, sacrament*, prayer*, architecture (see Hierotopy, the Creation of Christian Sacred Spaces), art*, and music* and in the context of Christians' relation to non-Christians, e.g. apologetically or inquisitorially, as missionaries* or as crusaders*. The resulting rich variety of Christian symbolism reflects the diverse ways of life of Christians over the globe since Jesus preached. Christians, whether Orthodox, Roman Catholic, Protestant, or "independent," whether viewed as heretical, heterodox, lapsed, or recovering, also use symbolism to mark conflicts between (and within) groups and individuals.

Critics of Christianity understand Christian symbols to have material rather than transcendent referents. By these accounts, God* is a "mere" (dead) metaphor*, a figure of speech, expressing nothing but the deluded believer's best wishes or unspoken resentments. Sociology* interprets religious symbols as reflecting a social order in which God serves one side in social conflicts (see Ideology). Psychology* identifies symbolic orders within the unconscious, representing repressed desires, and so God becomes a fantasy of omniscience* and omnipotence*. These types of radical skepticism risk stripping religious symbols of all reference to the divine or ultimate reality, explaining them away as empty signs or symptoms. But such hermeneutics* of suspicion can also help save believers from bad faith or sentimental credulity.

Among believers, religious symbols presume a connection to ultimate reality. Symbolic systems may be rationally systematic and aesthetically coherent. They can also be transgressive; e.g. the cross as a symbol of Christ's incarnation and crucifixion is, in Paul's words, a "stumbling block" to systematic rationalism or utilitarian calculation. The cross reveals symbolically the believer's dependence on God's grace*. Just so, Christian symbols order a life of faith. **See also APOPHATICISM; CONVICTION; METAPHOR; MYSTICISM, MYSTICS.**

CHRISTIAN SHEPPARD

Symeon, the "New Theologian" (c949–1022); abbot of the monastery of St. Mamas in Constantinople. Reacting against the influences on monastic* life of liturgical formality, scholastic theology, and wealth, in his *Chapters, Catecheses, Hymns,* and *Treatises,* Symeon affirmed intense spiritual prayer* as the fundamental vocation of monks and affirmed the charismatic power of holy monks to forgive sins. An apophatic*, mystical* theologian, Symeon stressed the divine mercy, powerful love of the living Christ, and a second baptism* in the Holy* Spirit accessible through repentance*, prayer, and asceticism*, and experienced as light and fire transforming the entire body and leading to union with the Trinity. Symeon provides a link between patristic and orthodox spirituality* with modern Pentecostal* and Charismatic* themes. KATHLEEN E. MCVEY

Synagogue (Gk "gathering together"), the Jewish gathering for worship and instruction, and thus also the place of gathering. The synagogue may have originated in the Diaspora*; it was part of Jewish life at the time of Jesus and the early Christians.

Syncletica of Palestine (6th c.?). Daughter of a Constantinopolitan aristocrat, she fled an arranged marriage to become a hermit* in the Palestinian desert, exemplifying a common typological and hagiographical theme in the early monastic literary tradition. But her story as narrated by Silas, a monk, appears to be plausible and, at least in part, historical. Syncletica stands firmly within the tradition of the widows* and virgins* in the first four centuries of Christianity: as a female ascetic*, she detached herself from the world and its values and strengthened her attachment to God through seclusion and the study of Scripture. TIM VIVIAN

Syncretism (etymologically, "to act as the Cretans," a Hellenistic way [Plutarch's] of referring to the inclusion of foreign gods in one's own pantheon) is the complex phenomenon by which two religious systems enter into contact with each other without becoming a complete synthesis and without being merely juxtaposed. According to the accepted understanding, syncretism involves the formation of a religious system out of the dialectic interactions of two religious systems, often in a situation of colonialism*.

Marzal (2002) identifies three types of syncretism: when Christian rituals are given an indigenous meaning; when indigenous rituals are given a Christian meaning; and when Christian rituals are accepted but new meanings are added to their original meaning. In Christian theology and pastoral practices, syncretism has traditionally been viewed as an "impure" and inappropriate expression of the Christian faith. But these negative connotations have been set aside in contemporary theologies of inculturation*. It is helpful to distinguish the process of syncretism from "syncretistic religions" and popular syncretistic practices.

The process of religious syncretism is intrinsic to the history of religions; through their constant intersections, religions are not simply fused with, or identified, with each other; rather, religions reinterpret themselves in terms of each other. Syncretism is primarily a cultural process combining symbols*, myths*, rituals, and embodiments (songs, dances, healing rituals).

Syncretism viewed as a creative synthesis or as a stigmatized contamination is in fact an indigenous phenomenon that is a part of local actors' discourses and practices as they struggle for symbolic legitimacy (André Mary). Symbols, rituals, and signifying structures follow a logic different from that of Western rationalism and dualism. Symbolism evolves through "bricolage" (Lévi-Strauss), a popular do-it-yourself transformation of available symbols and rituals, quite different from the rational production of theology.

In Roman Catholicism, syncretism is very common in the different popular and local forms of Catholicism around the world. For example, in Latin America syncretism is different in Central America, Andean regions, and Afro-American communities.

In the Eastern Orthodox* tradition and in the Anglican Communion, one finds religious phenomena with syncretistic features in popular or colonial local settings (e.g. Russian popular* religions; religions in the Caribbean Islands). In Evangelical traditions, especially in Charismatic*/ Pentecostal* movements (which often claim to reject syncretism), one finds many syncretistic expressions most explicit in local syncretistic churches, such as the African* Instituted Churches, or in many local Charismatic/Pentecostal Latin American churches (see Charismatic and Pentecostal Movements Cluster).

Syncretism, a phenomenon found throughout the history of Christianity, is alive today. New forms of religious syncretism in the Two-thirds World and in highly modern contexts (e.g. in the form of New* Age Christianity) constantly generate new hybrid features. **See also INCULTURATION CLUSTER; POPULAR CHRISTIAN PRACTICES CLUSTER; RELIGIONS AND CHRISTIANITY.** CRISTIÁN G. PARKER

Synod. See COUNCIL, SYNOD.

Synodikon of Orthodoxy, liturgical declaration of the Eastern Orthodox* faith, initiated after the triumph* of Orthodoxy ending the Iconoclastic* controversy. Recited each year on the first Sunday of Lent*, it condemns heretical positions and their advocates (added to as new controversies arise).

Synod of Jerusalem (1672). Convened by Dositheos*, patriarch of Jerusalem, this synod addressed in the name of traditional Orthodoxy the "Calvinist" Confession of 1629 attributed to Cyril Lucaris*. Lucaris, patriarch of Constantinople (1620–37), had responded to intense missionary efforts by the Roman Catholic Church by exploring Protestant–Orthodox rapprochement, including the endorsement of a modern Greek version of the NT. In the decrees of the Synod, Lucaris's authorship of the "Calvinist" Confession is refuted, and Orthodox doctrine is stated in the "Confession of Dositheos," which affirms real presence in the Eucharist*, the theology of icons*, the seven (rather than two) sacraments*, and the infallibility* of the Orthodox Church, and rejects predestination*, salvation* by faith* alone, as well as the *Filioque**. Modern scholarship has been unable to resolve the question of Lucaris's beliefs, but it is clear that this synod and its decisions marked the beginning of an anti-Protestant tendency in modern Orthodoxy. KATHLEEN E. MCVEY

Synoptic Gospels, the Gospels of Matthew*, Mark*, and Luke*, so called because they can be viewed side by side ("syn-optically") in a three-column book called a "synopsis" for easy comparison, and because they have much material in common and often present it in the same order. When the three Synoptic Gospels are compared with the very different Gospel of John*, their close similarities cannot be accidental or explained by oral tradition. There is a literary connection between them. The problem is: Which one was the source on which the others are based? Which other source(s) do they have in common? A few scholars claim that Matthew came first, and that Luke used Matthew, and Mark came third as an abbreviation of Matthew and Luke (the "Griesbach theory"). But most contemporary scholars are convinced that the "two-source theory" provides the most probable explanation: Mark was written first and was used as a source for both Matthew and Luke; in addition Matthew and Luke used a common source – a collection of Jesus' sayings, which scholars designated as the "Q* source", that can be reconstructed by gathering all the passages that Matthew and Luke have in common and that are not found in Mark. Moreover, Matthew and Luke have used independent sources. **See also LUKE, GOSPEL OF; MARK, GOSPEL OF; MATTHEW, THE GOSPEL OF; Q, A COLLECTION OF SAYINGS ASCRIBED TO JESUS.**

DANIEL PATTE

Syria. Because Syria is halfway between East and West, Syrian Christianity was greatly influenced by both Greek and Semitic cultures. Syria's proximity to Palestine placed it at the forefront of the Christian movement. Paul was converted near Damascus (Acts 9); Eusebius claims that Peter was the bishop of Antioch. It was in Antioch that the followers of Jesus were first called "Christians*" (Acts 11.26) and that Ignatius* of Antioch (early 2nd c.) gave instructions concerning church administration, theology, and spirituality.

The school of Antioch* (from the 4th c.) began to formulate its own theology, following a literal and historical interpretation of the Bible and concentrating on the human aspect of Jesus, while the school of Alexandria followed allegorical exegesis and highlighted the divine aspect of Jesus. The two approaches led to conflicting Christologies*, Nestorianism* and Miaphysitism*, both subsequently condemned at the Council of Ephesus* (431) and the Council of Chalcedon* (451). The early 6th c. witnessed the rise and fall of Miaphysitism (rejected as Monophysitism*), followed by the imposition of the Chalcedonian doctrine, both through imperial interference. Two communities rose up: the Melkite* ("follower of the emperor") and the Syriac* Orthodox (later given the polemical nickname "Jacobite," after the 6th-c. Miaphysite* bishop Jacob* Baradai).

With obscure roots in the 2nd and 3rd c., an ascetic* movement marked by extremism was in evidence as early as the 4th c. A monasticism* that incorporated (and moderated) this extremism, along with Greek monastic models, emerged (late 4th c.) and has played essential roles at the ecclesiastical and community levels to this day. Stylitism*, introduced by Simeon* Stylites (386–459) near Aleppo, was practiced for several centuries in Syria and beyond. Ascetics were not secluded and involved themselves in the social and religious life of the church. Women among them actively participated in the public and individual lives of the Christian communities.

During the first centuries of Islam* (see Islam and Christianity Cluster: In the Middle East), Christians remained publicly prominent despite sporadic persecutions and forced conversions. They worked as administrators, translators, educators, and builders. As a sign of assimilation into Arabic society, Christian Arabic literature began to emerge with the work of Theodore Abu Qurra (8th c.); the Arabic translation of the Melkite liturgy was initiated as early as the 12th c.

During the Ottoman period (1516–1918), church hierarchies were integrated into the Empire's *millet** system. Increasing contact with Christian Europe gave rise to Catholic branches of both Melkite and Syriac Orthodox churches, and the old and new churches became entangled in political relations between the Ottoman Empire and European states. Educated Syrian Christians launched a 19th-c. Arabic literary *nahda* ("renaissance") to forge a new, cross-confessional Arab national identity in the context of the modern state. These identities and their political implications remain significant to this day.

Statistics: Population (2000): 16.1 million (M). Christians, 1.3 M, 8% (various Orthodox, 0.8 M; various Roman Catholics, 0.32 M; independents, 0.1 M); Muslims (mostly Sunnis), 14.4 M, 89%; nonreligious, 0.47 M, 3%. (Based on *World Christian Encyclopedia*, 2001.)

AMIR HARRAK

Syriac Catholic Church. In communion with Rome, the Syriac Catholic Church shares its basic theology with the Roman Catholic Church. Yet it also shares a linguistic, spiritual, and liturgical heritage with the Syriac* Orthodox Church, from which it emerged (18th c.).

The Syriac Catholic Church, like other Syriac churches, considers abstract theology irrelevant if it is not lived by the faithful. Thus its ancient and magnificent liturgy invites the phrase "living theology." The history* of salvation, from the annunciation* of the angel to Mary through every step in the life of Jesus to his ascension* to heaven, where he is seated at the right side of the Father, is solemnly celebrated in cyclical feasts, festivals, and commemorations throughout the year. The liturgical cycle culminates in the cornerstone of faith, the resurrection* of Jesus. The Holy Trinity is confessed in agreement with the Nicene* Creed, and the Son of God is called Lord and Savior, the greatest of all titles given to him. The "Mother of God" (see Mary, the Virgin, Cluster: Theotokos) plays a major role in the history of salvation*, and thus is venerated in the liturgy and in numerous churches and shrines dedicated to her. Under the influence of the Syriac Church, Muslims revere *Mariam Ana*, Turkish for "Mother Mary," and some, especially in Iraq*, participate in the liturgy of the Assumption* (August 15).

Christian theological beliefs are conveyed to the faithful in the Church's rich liturgy in Syriac, which has been partially translated into Arabic for those who no longer understand Syriac. The liturgy consists of assigned readings from the Bible, recited commentaries (*sedro*, "orders"), and poetic hymns and melodies, which are lyrical, didactic, and always chanted. Most of these poems, written by Ephrem* the Syrian (306–73), contain theological information and warn the faithful of heresies*. Other poems were written by Jacob* of Sarug (451–521) and Balai (mid-5th c.). Additional liturgical elements derive from the ancient liturgies of Jerusalem and Antioch.

The faithful hold the liturgy in esteem and celebrate it publicly and collectively. Although the clergy presides over the liturgical prayers, the lay community is typically represented by large choirs of subdeacons, readers, psalmodists, and nonordained participants of all ages. The entire liturgy, including the reading of the gospel, is sung, and the religious music follows the same conventions as Syrian secular music. Incense, musical instruments (cymbals and flabella), abstract art, and monumental Syriac inscriptions inside the church invite all participants to pray while learning theology.

AMIR HARRAK

Syriac Christianity, History of. See HISTORY OF CHRISTIANITY CLUSTER: IN THE MIDDLE EAST: SYRIAC CHRISTIANITY.

Syriac Orthodox Church, Universal. See ORTHODOX CHURCHES, ORIENTAL CLUSTER: SYRIAC ORTHODOX CHURCH, UNIVERSAL.

T

Tabernacle, temporary dwelling. In ancient Israel, the "Tent of Meeting" (Exod 25–31, 35–40), the place of communication between the Deity and Moses, the visible sign of the Deity's presence among the people of Israel, the shrine that houses the Ark of the Covenant erected at Shiloh, then at Gibeon, before its placement inside the Temple* of Solomon. In Roman Catholic, Orthodox, and Anglican churches, an ornamented receptacle for the consecrated bread (host) and wine. Among Baptist and Charismatic churches, especially in Latin America, "Tabernacle" is often part of the name of a congregation.

Taché, Alexandre (1823–94). Born in Quebec into a Roman Catholic family, studied for the priesthood, joined (1844) the Missionary Oblates* of Mary Immaculate newly arrived from France. Taché undertook a 2,300-kilometer canoe journey to Red River (Canada's Northwest, 1845), a wild territory. The young missionary became bishop (1853) of the Diocese of Saint-Boniface (today's provinces of Manitoba, Saskatchewan, Alberta, and the Yukon and Northwest Territories), organizing the arrival of Oblate missionaries, recruiting religious brothers and sisters, founding missions, schools, colleges, hospitals, and services for the poor, and playing a key role in political events in Canada's Northwest. **See also CANADA.**

ROBERT CHOQUETTE

Taiwan. During occupations by the Dutch (1624–61) and Spanish (1626–42), Dutch Reformed and Spanish Roman Catholics came to the island; they left when the colonists were expelled by Chinese forces (1662). English Presbyterians (1865) and Spanish Dominicans (1859) established the current Presbyterian and Catholic churches in Taiwan. With the defeat of the Kuomintang (Chinese Nationalist Party) by the Communist Party in China (1949), refugees coming to Taiwan with the Nationalist government of China introduced other Christian denominations.

The Presbyterian Church in Taiwan, the main and oldest Protestant Church, illustrates the development of Christianity on the island.

1. During the "receiving period" (1865–1950), Taiwan was a "mission land"; the church was governed by Western missionary societies and related to Taiwanese people mainly through pastoral care and material provision.
2. The formative period (1951–70) formally began when the two synods of the Presbyterian Church in Taiwan formed the General Assembly (1951), officially bypassing the missionary societies (from Britain in the south; from Canada in the north) that governed the synods. Yet the Taiwanese Church had already assumed full responsibility for its mission, especially among indigenous (non-Chinese) people, since 1942, when foreign missionaries were expelled by the Japanese military government. By 1970 all 10 mountain peoples were heavily Presbyterian.
3. The social witness awakening period (1971–85) started with a "statement on our national fate" issued by the Presbyterian Church in response to martial law (1971, when the UN seat of the Republic of China [Taiwan] was given to the People's Republic of China), which was followed by other social witness declarations, including one on human* rights, especially those of indigenous (non Chinese) people. These statements advocating political self-determination extended the Church's mission programs to include social witness and concerns, while calling attention to Taiwan's internal and international problems.
4. The confessing faith period (since 1985) began with the first contextual confession of faith issued by the Presbyterian Church in Taiwan as a theological reflection on the relation of mission to social and political struggles (see Mission Cluster).

This contextualization of the Christian faith has not been fully shared either by those churches that emerged after 1949 (with different historical experiences) or by the independent churches that have arisen since the late 20th c. (whose members include "tribal people"). Most of the "mission churches" share the theological traditions of Western mainstream churches. Yet as social witness lost its momentum after the democratization of society (1990s), the Charismatic* Movement gained strength in many local churches.

Despite political and theological tensions, many denominations participate in the Taiwanese National Council of Churches (including the Roman Catholic Church), although many denominations keep their distance for theological and ideological reasons.

Statistics: Population (2001): 22.4 million (M). Christians, 0.57 M, 2.6% [or 1.4 M, 6.3%] (independents, 0.01 M [or 0.4 M]; Protestants (mostly Presbyterians), 0.37 M [or 0.4 M]; Roman Catholics 0.18 M [or 0.3 M]; Daoists, 0.8 M [or 2.2 M]; Buddhists, 0.2 M [or 4.7 M]; Muslims, 0.07 M [or 0.9 M]; Chinese folk religionists, the rest of the population, a majority. (*Sources*: Primary statistics: Department of Statistics, MOI, Taiwan, 2003 [focused on official membership in churches and religion]. Statistics in brackets: *World Christian Encyclopedia*, 2001.)

HUANG PO HO

Taizé Community, founded (1940) by Roger Schutz (1915–2005) in Taizé, France. Here Protestant and Roman Catholic brothers (more than 100 brothers from many nations, as well as members of the Orthodox* Church on a semipermanent basis) endeavor daily to realize peace and reconciliation*.

Born in Switzerland, Roger, the son of a Protestant pastor, was particularly influenced by his maternal grandmother, who harbored refugees during World War I and who, while remaining faithful to her Protestant origins, attended Mass* and received Communion in the Roman Catholic Church, thus effecting inner reconciliation. Convinced of the need for a form of traditional monasticism* in which Protestants could participate, Roger began (1940) a life of gospel simplicity in Taizé, centered on thrice daily prayer, the Beatitudes, and the injunction "Be one . . . that the world may believe" (John 17:21). In 1949 the first seven brothers took their monastic vows.

In the vanguard of the ecumenical movement, Brother Roger established close relations with several popes, notably John* XXIII, who invited him to the Second Vatican* Council. When the Council's ecumenical promise remained unfulfilled, Roger put increasing trust in his grandmother's way of inner reconciliation.

Seeking to be close to the poor*, he took in Jewish refugees (1940s), then German prisoners of war, and subsequently others in need. Since the 1970s, small fraternities of brothers have shared the lives of the poor in different parts of the world.

For Roger and the Taizé community, God remains a mystery*, but what they grasp of the gospel must be tangibly expressed. The church is the presence of the resurrected Christ in the lives of humans, creating a communion, both hidden and visible. Reconciliation meant bringing together the separated members of this invisible and visible suffering body.

Taizé is a parable* of communion. Young people of all denominations flock there and to meetings held on every continent. John* Paul II described Taizé as a spiritual spring from which people may drink. They are then encouraged to become the "leaven of communion" in their own church communities. Taizé songs, in the tradition of the prayer* of repetition, sung in various languages to simple music and repeated until they lead to silence, are used in worship worldwide.

KATHRYN SPINK

Tall Brothers, four Egyptian monks who defended Origenism* against Theophilus* of Alexandria and were sheltered by John* Chrysostom of Constantinople.

Tamar (Gen 38). The story of Tamar is a good example of how the intensely patrilineal framework at times demands from its female characters an unexpected agency. The rather intricate narrative involving levirate marriage vindicates Tamar's unorthodox and risky plot to steal from Judah what the law demands he give her – a child. Tamar is credited with having been Boaz's ancestress, as well as David's* (Ruth 4:12, 18–22), and the Gospel of Matthew* even includes her in Jesus' genealogy.

NICOLE WILKINSON DURAN

Tamar (2 Sam 13). Within the walls of David's house, Tamar is raped by her half-brother, Amnon. Initially lovesick for her, he despises her after the rape, and her most prominent characteristic from then on becomes shame. Tamar's full brother, Absalom, avenges the rape by killing Amnon, but by then Tamar has been eclipsed in the narrative by the development of Absalom's character. Compare the rape of Dinah in Gen 34, which also features brotherly revenge and a passive father.

NICOLE WILKINSON DURAN

Tanakh, Jewish abbreviation that refers to the Jewish Scriptures, formed from the initial letters of its three parts: Torah (Law), Nebiim (Prophets), and Ketubim (Writings). Tanakh forms the part of Christian Scriptures called the Old* Testament.

Tanzania. Christians comprise the largest religious faith community (c44% of Tanzania's population), followed by Muslims (c34%), African* Religionists (c20%), and members of smaller faith groups (mainly Eastern religions). Because of its large membership and its history, Christianity has considerable influence on the legal, social, and political structures and attitudes of Tanzanian society.

Economic, political, and religious factors contributed to the introduction of Christianity in Tanzania. When the Portuguese merchant Vasco da Gama arrived (1499) in Zanzibar (the island that, in 1964, joined Tanganyika to form the United Republic of Tanzania), he brought with him Portuguese Roman Catholic priests who tried to introduce Christianity. But because Zanzibar was predominantly Muslim, they failed. Moreover, trade, not conversion, was the primary aim of the Portuguese.

The mid-19th c. saw the direct introduction of Christianity into Tanzania. Protestant missionaries Johann L. Krapf* (1844) and later Johann Rebmann* (1847), under the aegis of the British Church Missionary Society, arrived in the Mombasa region, and Krapf visited Zanzibar (1844). Subsequently, Krapf became the first (1844–46) to translate the NT into Kiswahili – the *lingua franca* of Tanzania, which originated in the 13th c. through contact between coastal peoples and Arab traders and has since incorporated many new words from ethnic groups, English, and the world of science and technology. Krapf returned to Europe (1853), but Rebmann later visited the Kilimanjaro area in Northern Tanzania. Refused permission by the local authorities to travel farther inland, he returned north to the region of the Giriama (Mombasa) and concentrated on writing.

Roman Catholic missionaries soon followed. Holy Ghost Fathers settled in Zanzibar (1863) and Bagamoyo (1868). White* Fathers went to work around Lake Tanganyika and Lake Victoria (1878). Benedictine monks established missions in Dar es Salaam (1887) and moved southward to Peramiho and Ndanda, toward the Ruvuma River.

German and British imperial ambitions (late 19th–early 20th c.) constituted another factor in the development of Christianity in Tanzania. The Berlin* Conference (1884–85) conceded Tanganyika (now mainland Tanzania) to Germany as part of German East Africa. After Germany's defeat during World War I, the League of Nations transferred Tanganyika to British administration (1918). There is a historical link between Christianity and colonialism in Tanzania. Colonial administrations facilitated missionary work, granting missionaries (especially German and later British missionaries) freedom of movement and teaching, and helping them with moral and material support. Missionaries in turn collaborated with colonialists in pacifying often rebellious populations by their religious teaching. This made it difficult for many Tanzanians to distinguish between colonial and missionary intentions, often considering them one.

Later in the 20th c., there was a proliferation of African* Instituted Churches (AICs) and movements throughout the country, but especially in the regions around lakes Victoria, Tanganyika, and Nyasa. Most AICs are Christian communities that have features of African* Religion, and in some these are predominant.

Nondenominational Pentecostal* or Charismatic* assemblies are also increasing, mostly in urban centers. They attract many followers, mainly from the mainline churches. Most Pentecostal/Charismatic groups seem to be transitory, holding occasional large, open-air prayer sessions for faith healing* and then moving on to a new locale, because their goal is to bring about a revival* in existing churches rather than to establish new churches. Among those that have become institutionalized, many are inspired and aided by foreign groups, although they often have local leadership.

AICs have always used indigenous symbols* in their teaching and worship. However, inculturation* as a deliberate process of expressing Christianity in African religious language and content is new in the mainstream churches and is often resisted by older generations of leaders and laity who prefer earlier missionary models of the church.

After independence (mainland, 1961; Zanzibar, 1963), church leadership gradually became indigenous. The politics of African socialism, or Ujamaa (a moral and ethical system derived from African cultural and humanist values aimed at bringing about justice* and equality), was suspected by Christian leaders of being Marxist. Yet Tanzania's founding father, Julius K. Nyerere, forced the churches to include economic self-reliance in their pastoral policies, resulting in an emphasis (in Roman Catholicism) on Small Christian Communities.

Mainline Christian churches provide social services. From the beginning, missionaries built education* and health* facilities at or near places of worship. Some churches currently own and run several universities. Among the medical facilities most important are the Lutheran Kilimanjaro Christian Medical Centre (Moshi) and the Catholic Bugando referral hospital (Mwanza). Attached to both are medical university colleges.

Many AICs are "dissident" groups, separated from the mainline churches or from one another, often because of disputes involving leadership or doctrine. Others are original creations, claiming to be based on direct divine inspiration or intervention. Some are very small, while others are large. Most are Bible based and interpret Scripture* "literally*" (in a fundamentalist* way, according to their critics) or (more descriptively) "contextually": they read the Bible in the context of local African cultures, circumstances, and experiences. Thus in contrast to the mission churches, they are in the forefront of inculturation*. All Christian churches in Tanzania accept the authority of the Bible, although they interpret it differently and their teachings differ. In Roman Catholicism, the authority to interpret the Bible and to teach is concentrated in the bishops. Protestantism and AICs allow individuals to interpret the Bible in ways that help their faith (see Bible Interpretation Cluster: In Africa).

Since the 1980s, because of the worldwide growth of fundamentalism*, relations between Christians and Muslims in Tanzania's urban centers have been tense, where previously there was harmony. There is a growing perception among Muslims that Tanzanian administrations since independence have defended Christian religious interests at the expense of Muslims' religious, political, and social rights (see Islam and Christianity Cluster: In Africa).

Politically, the Christian churches have suspected the Ujamaa socialist ideology, whose proponents have governed Tanzania since 1967, of being atheistic and communist. Christianity has thus unwittingly contributed to the failure of Ujamaa and facilitated the process of globalization (which Ujamaa resisted) even as it has decried some of its effects.

Occasionally, Christian church leaders gather to pray together or Christians and Muslims meet for discussions, but serious ecumenical* and interreligious dialogue*, contact, and practical cooperation among them are minimal. Mainstream churches do not as yet acknowledge AICs as "full churches," because they lack the material resources, recognized leadership, and theological education that their counterparts enjoy and provide.

Inculturation and ecumenism are two important theological and pastoral issues for Christianity in Tanzania: How can Christian unity be achieved and peace maintained between religions? How can Christianity in Tanzania become truly Tanzanian in character and identity? Corruption and HIV/AIDS are serious ethical issues. AIDS kills numerous people in Tanzania. It raises the question of prophylactics: Is the use of condoms moral in certain circumstances? Roman Catholicism, for example, completely rules it out. Efforts to eliminate corruption, so detrimental to justice* and human* rights but so endemic in Tanzanian society, have so far not succeeded.

Statistics: Population (2002): 35 million (rural, 76.9%; urban, 23.1%). Census by religious affiliation is not permitted in Tanzania. Estimates (2000): Christians, 44% (Roman Catholics, 24%; Protestants, 16%; Anglicans, 6%; members of African Instituted Churches, 2%; doubly affiliated, 4%); Muslims, 35%; African Religionists, 20%; others, 1%. (Estimate based on *World Christian Encyclopedia*, 2001, and local churches' reports.)

LAURENTI MAGESA

Taoism and Christianity. See DAOISM AND CHRISTIANITY CLUSTER.

Targum (Heb "translation"). Rabbinic translation of the HB into Aramaic originated in synagogue services where the biblical texts were first read in Hebrew and then, as a prelude to the homily, translated, clarified, and explained for the congregations in Aramaic – the vernacular in the ancient Near East from the postexilic period (Ezra*) to the early Middle Ages. Such translations were recorded and exist for almost all the books of the HB. They are an important source of early Jewish interpretations of the Bible, often comparable to Midrash*.

Tatian (2nd c.), Christian Apologist*. Born in Syria, he studied Greek rhetoric and philosophy, was a student of Justin* Martyr in Rome, and returned to Syria (c170). He was the founder of the ascetic* movement of the Encratites*, as well as the author of an apology that fiercely attacked Greek culture* and noted the achievements of the Syrian region. He also compiled the Diatessaron*, a harmony of the four Gospels, long used in the Syriac* Church.

Tauler, Johannes (c1300–61), German Dominican mystic*. He was influenced by Eckhart* and the Neoplatonism* of the followers of Albertus* Magnus in the Rhineland. When Strasbourg was under interdict, he went to Basel (1338–39), where he was associated with the Friends of God, a movement in the tradition of Eckhart. A noted preacher, his sermons were so widely circulated that many spurious works were attributed to him. He had a major influence on German spirituality, Protestant as well as Roman Catholic, and on Spanish writers through a Latin translation of his sermons.

Tausen, Hans (1494–1561), prominent theologian of the Danish Reformation, Lutheran bishop of Ribe (1541). Initially belonging to the order of St. John, he completed studies of theology at the universities of Rostock, Copenhagen, Leuwen, and Wittenberg (1516–24). Highly influenced by the new Lutheran theology, he was known as a skilled preacher and later became one of the first Lutheran ministers in Denmark (1526). As a minister, royal chaplain, and professor, he argued fiercely against the Roman Catholic Church, publishing extensively on the Lutheran* faith, especially regarding pastoral matters. He was ordained bishop of Ribe by Johannes Bugenhagen.

CARSTEN SELCH JENSEN

Teaching Authority. See AUTHORITY IN/OF THE CHURCH.

Teaching as Christian Practice. See EDUCATIONAL PRACTICES AS CHRISTIAN SERVICE CLUSTER; THEOLOGICAL EDUCATION CLUSTER.

Technology and Christianity. From philosophy – including the work of Heidegger*, who pointed out that the matter of technology is not merely technological – to sociology, since the early 20th c. no field of inquiry has been broached without some reference to the so-called technological revolution and its impact on life, including the origin and goal of life.

Technology's relation to religion* has been largely ignored, but there have been notable exceptions. Long ago Emerson* dared to speak of a concordance between the machine and Transcendentalism*. The mid-20th c. cardinal Daniélou defiantly stated that nothing was more biblical than technology. Indeed, technology has contributed to many a religious paradigm and calls for a new type of religiosity. Envisioning the church* in a technological civilization demands that we ponder technology.

Role of Technology in Cultural Revolutions. While no one ever spoke of a "natural" civilization, today we commonly speak of a "technological" civilization, regardless of whether it is hailed or decried. In the past, cultural* revolutions were triggered by religion*. The technological revolution seems to have overtaken that role and overshadows many aspects, ethical or spiritual, of our heritage, cultural as well as religious. Who am I when someone else's heart beats in me?

Human Fragility. The Bible affirms the original goodness of creation*. Whether that goodness is extended to nature is a moot question. "Natural human" is by and large consonant with "sinful* human." Technology does not make us less sinful, and never was meant to. Yet technology does make us more aware of either the fragility of nature or the ambiguities of human nature, as Hans Jonas poignantly pointed out and as Karl Jaspers* also said, though less obsessively.

Technology: Religious Phenomenon or Religiously Neutral? Technology is a method – "the totality of methods rationally arrived at and having absolute efficiency . . . in every field of human activity" (Ellul). Somewhat ominously this definition rests on the distinction between "efficiency" and "efficacy," technical efficiency replacing the efficacy of grace* proclaimed by Christianity. But this distinction is questionable. A proper understanding of technology and its assessment require concepts quite different from those of the very science* that in part brought it about (Prigogine and Stengers). Technology expands the human capacity for expressing the inexpressible (see Apophaticism) and for self-expression as well, yet without assigning any particular end, much less helping the human being to be human. An ensemble of means, technology can offer only means. Not unlike nature, technology is neutral, as Tillich* wisely, though not consistently, admits (while Heidegger refrains from saying it and Ellul strongly denies it).

Humanization of What Is Foreign to the Human. Technology is a tool, though not a mere tool. It is a machine, but not merely a machine. It is a system in quest of an instrument for its own eventual implementation. It exposes us to further choices between life and death*, imposing neither. A tool extends the human being. A machine, although it estranges the human being from what it means to be human, also calls for the overcoming of this estrangement if only because it does not necessarily alienate *from* humanness. Technology neither dehumanizes society nor depersonalizes human beings. It humanizes that which is still foreign to the human. Rather than growing wings or a shell, human beings build airplanes or houses.

In humanizing that which is alien to being human, technology is also a tool to humanize the human being. When lips move to form words, there may be a shift from tool to cybernetics and artificial intelligence (as when an oral command is recognized by a phone or a computer) – from tool to *techne* (way of life, mode of being) as the technique through which the human being can become human, can be that which the human is not yet, and can humanize that which is not yet humanized. Then, indeed, nothing is more biblical than technology.

Centuries ago Aristotle* was already defining the hand as an instrument of instruments. The human being – body* and soul*, flesh and spirit – is itself the instrument of technology, shaped by and shaping technology. In triggering cultural revolutions, technology has contributed to many a religious paradigm. Technological civilization does not mark the end of religion but calls for a new type of religiosity. **See also DEATH OF GOD THEOLOGY; SECULARISM AND SECULARIZATION.**

GABRIEL VAHANIAN

Te Deum, Latin hymn praising God the Father and Christ the King of Glory, sometimes called the Ambrosian Hymn, now the chief hymn of rejoicing and thanksgiving in the Roman Catholic Church.

Teilhard de Chardin, Pierre (1881–1955), Jesuit*, priest, scientist (geology, paleontology, anthropology), theologian, philosopher, spiritual writer, futurist. His writings were collected in 10 scientific volumes, 13 philosophical/religious volumes, and 15 volumes of letters.

Born in central France, Teilhard entered the Jesuit order in 1899. Anticlerical laws forced the Jesuits and other religious to leave France (1901). The papal condemnation of Modernism* (rejecting "the subjecting of everything to the laws of evolution*" and the new biblical* criticism) set the tone for Roman Catholic theology during the whole of Teilhard's life. Teilhard was ordained a Roman Catholic priest in England (1911). His studies in geology and human fossils with Marcellin Boule in Paris were interrupted by service in World War I, during which he developed his basic religious ideas.

After completing his doctorate, he went to China (1923), where he and another Jesuit were the first to find traces of prehistoric humans. He was the geologist for the group that found the Peking Man fossils; he spoke at many international conferences and worked on other scientific projects until he left China (1946). He visited South Africa (1951, 1953) and did much to bring world opinion to recognize that the human race originated in Africa, not Asia. Because of the originality of his religious ideas, Church authorities did not allow Teilhard to publish his theological writings (his scientific works were not restricted). Following his death (New York City, 1955), friends arranged for the publication of his religious/philosophical works. These quickly gave him a large popular following.

Teilhard saw that the radical changes in cosmology (e.g. evolution*, relativity, the age and size of the universe) that occurred in his lifetime called for a new theology. He was very much a scientist and personally devout. He told of two stars that once pulled him in opposite directions: one was the world of matter known through science, the other was the Christian God known through revelation*. With his scientific understanding of evolution, he demonstrated that matter rose through the levels of life into the human sphere, where matter became spirit. His theological study of the Pauline letters (especially Colossians* and Ephesians*) showed him that Christ* is the one in whom all things hold together. Ephesians speaks of Christ descending into the lower parts of the earth so that, rising from there, he might fill all things (Col 1:17; Eph 4:9–10). Because of such passages, Teilhard would speak of the cosmic body of Christ. Thus for him, the two stars converged with Christ, uniting and filling all things much as the human soul* unites with and fills the human body.

Teilhard saw evolution as the process by which the world is becoming a suitable body for the divine Soul. Our ordinary human actions can lead to building the infrastructure of the body of Christ. Developing these ideas while active in World War I, he was also aware of the failure, suffering*, and death that are part of life and evolution. He followed Jean-Pierre de Caussade, SJ, who saw all things (weal and woe) coming to us from the "Hand of God," and was also influenced by Henri Bergson*, John Henry

Newman*, Maurice Blondel*, and Edouard Le Roy.

Roman Catholic authorities had difficulties with his claims that the story of Adam* and Eve* is a parable* of the human condition and not a historical event, and that humans did not descend from a single couple – both points now fairly common in Roman Catholic theology. Some Catholic critics considered his thought pantheistic*; others were concerned about the minimal place he accorded to sin* and redemption*. Yet all recognized his personal devotion. His statements calling for the development of the secular* world did much to reorient Catholic thought.

Many have noted his influence at the Second Vatican* Council, especially in the document "The Church and the Modern World." John* Paul II and Cardinal Ratzinger (now Benedict XVI) quoted him with approval. Several Liberation* theologians appealed to him. In the 1960s–1970s, he was much discussed in popular culture. U Thant, then secretary general of the UN, sponsored several UN conferences on his thought. His ideas on globalization* and politics were picked up by Marshall McLuhan, Kenneth Boulding, Michel Camdessous, and Sargent Shriver.

In *The Phenomenon of Man* (or *The Human Phenomenon*), Teilhard reflects on the stages of evolution to show that many souls* increasingly become (more like) one soul, and thus the world is increasingly animated by a single Soul; the Epilogue suggests that this Soul is Christ. In *The Divine Milieu*, a spiritual guide for such a world, he presents both a spirituality of growth and one of diminishment or death. In his most popular essay, "The Mass* on the World" (collected in *The Heart of Matter*), Teilhard proposes that the bread* symbolizes growth and the wine* symbolizes diminishment; when these are consecrated, they lead to a recognition that each moment in our life is a moment of Communion*. **See also KINGDOM OF GOD, CONCEPT OF, CLUSTER: IN THE EASTERN ORTHODOX TRADITION: KINGDOM AND WILDERNESS; SCIENCE AND CHRISTIAN THEOLOGY.**

THOMAS M. KING, SJ

Teleology, Teleological Argument. Aristotle* is the classic exponent of the view that all things, physical and biological, act for an "end" (Gk *telos*). His general principle was that each kind of thing acts when "form" (natural or mental) gives rise to the appropriate inclinations and actions. Thomas Aquinas* made the "teleological argument" the fifth and final argument for God's existence: if all things act for an end, they must have their source in some intellect that acts purposively and is implicitly the end toward which all things move. The classic Aristotelian–Thomist argument emphasizes "internal teleology," which is also emphasized by Process* theology. During the 18th c., there were many "arguments from design," emphasizing an "external teleology," focusing on interrelationships – the adaptation of things to each other and their environment. Teleology is also an important, though frequently overlooked, component of covenant*, election*, vocation*, justification*, predestination,* and salvation*.

Televangelism and Western Culture. Evangelicals* in the USA developed "TV evangelism" during the 1950s–1980s. Using commercial and religious TV channels, satellites, cable, and local broadcast stations, they further distributed programs in Europe, Africa, Asia, and Latin America.

Televangelism's success in the USA required Evangelicals to adapt their presentations to existing TV genres. While other Christian traditions feared secular cooptation – such as Christian fare that was mere entertainment, self-help teaching, or disguised political propaganda – Evangelicals tried everything from religious soap operas and talk shows to musical extravaganzas and evangelistic worship services (see Media and Christian Worship) patterned after 18th- to 19th-c. revivals*.

Nevertheless, these programs converted relatively few viewers while attracting overwhelmingly Evangelical audiences. They also came under fire from other Christian groups and from nonreligious viewers, who claimed that TV evangelists were self-promoting hucksters and right-wing ideologues. Some of the most popular televangelists formed political movements; M. G. "Pat" Robertson ran unsuccessfully as a Republican for president of the USA. Even after a series of major sexual and financial scandals involving televangelists, many Evangelicals remained hopeful about using TV to convert the world.

As Evangelical TV ministries exported their programming to other countries, indigenous groups and national governments complained that the shows had a stronger US flavor than a Christian one. Canada and some European governments banned religious broadcasting, but the privatization of formerly publicly owned broadcast systems in many parts of the Western world opened up opportunities for foreign Evangelicals to purchase airtime. Latin American broadcasters, in particular, welcomed North American program revenues, which eventually contributed to the Protestantization and perhaps the politicization of parts of Central and South America.

Televangelism is a distinctly US form of mass evangelism that adapts Christianity to popular culture (see Popular Christian Practices Cluster), seems to be more successful religiously where Western culture is predominant, and regularly comes under fire for moral and political if not theological abuse of Christianity. **See also MEDIA AND CHRISTIANITY.**

QUENTIN J. SCHULTZE

Temperance Movement (1784–1933), organized efforts to moderate or eliminate the consumption of alcoholic beverages. Such attempts have existed sporadically in history but became widespread in North America and the UK in the 19th–early 20th c. The start of the modern movement is associated with Dr. Benjamin Rush's study (1784) that linked excessive use of alcohol with health problems, and with the Second Great* Awakening (early 1800s). Numerous organizations were founded to promote the cause, including the American Temperance Society (1826), the Order of Good Templars (1851), the Woman's Christian Temperance Union (1874), and the Anti-Saloon League (1895). Some temperance advocates favored moderation; others promoted total abstinence. Strategies varied, ranging from an emphasis on moral suasion in the early years, to research and education, and finally to governmental prohibition and enforcement. The movement crested with the Eighteenth Amendment (1920) to the U.S. Constitution, which outlawed the manufacture, transport, and sale of alcoholic beverages, and ended with the Twenty-first Amendment (1933), which repealed the earlier prohibition.

By the 1840s and 1850s, increasing emphasis was placed on political and legislative action, making it more difficult for women to participate without the right to vote. In the "Woman's Crusade" of 1873–74, women marched into saloons to pray and exhort owners to stop selling alcohol. From this point on, women claimed a dominant role in the Temperance Movement and increasingly associated temperance reform with woman suffrage. The movement was especially popular among Protestant Evangelicals*, who regarded intemperance as a matter of personal sin*, a barrier to the development of a Christian nation and to the success of the Kingdom* of God on earth. Advocates of temperance were frequently ridiculed as self-righteous, hypocritical, and ideologically naive. Women who participated in these efforts were accused of inappropriate or "unwomanly" behavior beyond their proper sphere. Temperance leaders, especially Frances Willard*, countered that the work was appropriate to woman's role as moral guardian of the home and family*. Greatly influenced by the leadership of Willard, Susan B. Anthony*, and Carry A. Nation, the movement was catalytic in enlarging white, middle-class women's public involvement in US society.

The achievements of the Temperance Movement demonstrate the potential for social and legislative change as a result of concerted grassroots efforts. Although it clashed with the values of some social, religious, and ethnic communities, the movement raised international awareness about the causes, effects, prevention, and treatment of alcoholism. **See also ALCOHOLICS ANONYMOUS (AA).**

WENDY J. DEICHMANN EDWARDS

Temple, an enclosed space dedicated to the worship of a deity and containing holy objects for such worship. In the ancient Near East and the Greco-Roman world, nearly all religions had temples for sacrificial worship. Israel's worship in the wilderness took place at the "Tent of Meeting" (or Tabernacle*), until the Temple was built in Jerusalem on Mount Zion* by Solomon*; under Josiah* it became the only place of sacrifice. It was destroyed by the Babylonians (586 BCE), rebuilt under the Persians (from 520 BCE), and then built on a grander scale under Herod (the "Second Temple," c20 BCE).

As the dwelling place of God on earth, the Temple made God accessible (1 Kgs 8:27–53). At the center of Solomon's empire, the Temple had an important religious symbolic role as the place where heaven and earth converge and from which God controls the universe (as Psalms of the Temple and Zion celebrate). The sacredness of the Temple, which was centered on the Holy of Holies, the altar*, sacrifice*, and the priesthood, conveyed the sense of divine nearness and was associated with both physical and moral purity. The Temple also had a political function, giving legitimacy to the monarchy and its rule, and an economic function. With its treasuries, it was a kind of national bank that held, besides precious cultic objects, the tributes of people conquered and taxes; as a sacred space off-limits to most people, it offered the best security. Thus the destruction of the Temple was also the loss of political and economic autonomy; the reconstructions (c520, c20 BCE) were efforts to reverse this loss in the contexts of Persian and Roman rule as well as to reestablish the religious symbolism.

While Jesus and the earliest Christians continued to worship in the Temple, there was an undercurrent of criticism of the "Temple made with hands" (Mark 14:58; Heb 9:11, 24). Parallel themes are found in the Qumran* community's view that the holy community was itself the true Temple (also Eph 2:21–22) and in the suggestion of Philo* and the Hellenists* in the early church that the Tent of Meeting was an image of the heavenly "pattern" seen by Moses (Acts 7:44; cf. Exod 25:9, 40). For several centuries, all Christian groups avoided the language of altars and priests*; subsequently, these terms gained a new Christian meaning. Similarly, these groups spoke of the building used for worship as the "house of the church," only occasionally speaking of it as a temple.

Curiously, the term "temple" came to be used in French, Italian, Hungarian, and Brazilian Portuguese for Protestants' houses of worship, while "church" was used for Roman Catholic buildings. It seems that Protestants used it on the grounds that God can be worshipped anywhere "in spirit and in truth" (John 4:23) or that the true temple is the community of the faithful. **See also HIEROTOPY, THE CREATION OF CHRISTIAN SACRED SPACES.**

EUGENE TESELLE and DANIEL PATTE

Temptation (from Heb, Gk, and Lat words for "testing" or "trying"). Usually understood as "enticement to sin*," temptation can also call one to prove one's resistance to sin. God is often said to test persons' fidelity; Satan* has the function of testing, then of accusing. But it is improper to test God (Deut 6:16; cf. Matt 4:7 = Luke 4:12). Adam*, who was tested and failed (Gen 3), is contrasted with Christ, who was tested in the wilderness (Mark 1:13, par.), in Gethsemane* (Mark 14:32–42, par.), and on the cross* (Matt 27:40–44; cf. Matt 4:3) but did not yield. In common Christian terminology, "temptation" usually leads to a negative result; "testing" (e.g. testing of martyrs*) to a positive result.

Ten Commandments, Decalogue (Gk), also referred to as the Ten Words (Jewish usage). The central commandments of the Torah*, revealed to Moses* on Mount Sinai (Exod 20:1–17; Deut 5:6–21). In Exodus the listing includes the neighbor's wife among the neighbor's property; thus the "second table" of obligations to human beings includes six commandments and the "first table" of obligations to God includes four. This listing was followed by the Calvinist tradition and is the most common today. The version in Deuteronomy, adopted by Augustine, the Roman Catholic Church, and Luther, distinguishes between the neighbor's wife and the neighbor's property; thus the "second table" includes seven commandments, and the "first table" three.

Frequent references to individual commandments confirm the centrality of this fluid moral code in Jesus' preaching according to the Gospels. Jesus' readiness to reinterpret precepts like the Sabbath empowered subsequent Christian modifications, emphasizing love* as the supreme expression of human morality in faith*-motivated ethics (Paul) and catechetical instruction. Pliny* observed (c100 CE) a baptismal oath that called on believers not to commit theft, robbery, adultery, or perjury or betray trust, thus reiterating the Decalogue's last five commandments.

To graft the Decalogue onto the life of Christians, theologians synthesized, allegorized, and rephrased the commandments in terms of Jesus' sayings. Thus for Irenaeus*, the essence of Christian life is living not according to the verbosity of the Law* but rather according to the brevity of faith that teaches love of God and neighbors. For Clement* of Alexandria, the Ten Words symbolized Jesus; honoring father meant honoring God; adultery meant abandoning the true knowledge of Christianity. Origen* associated the 10 plagues of Egypt with the Ten Commandments since the law of Law, like the plagues, reproves and corrects the world. Thus the Decalogue emerged as an ongoing revelation* of moral concerns affecting one's relations with God and other Christians. HAGITH SIVAN

Terce, Sext, None, third, sixth, and ninth hours, respectively, as distinct parts of the Divine* Office, observed in the early church, especially in the monastic* movement.

Teresa of Ávila (1515–82), monastic* reformer, mystic*, theologian, doctor of the Roman Catholic Church. One of history's most beloved mystics, Teresa of Ávila's life spanned the Golden Age of Spain* and the intensity of the Roman Catholic Counter* Reformation period. Author of numerous books, including the classic mystical text *The Interior Castle*, Teresa was a creative force to be reckoned with in an era that was not entirely hospitable to spirituality.

Born in Ávila to a merchant class family of *conversos** (her grandfather Juan Sanchez was prosecuted in Toledo as a "judaizer"), Teresa received an education at the Augustinian* convent of Santa María de la Gracia. She joined the Carmelite* order (1535) but left the Convent of the Incarnation several times because of illness. On her sickbed, she began to read spiritual classics and engage in prayer more deeply. She experienced a spiritual conversion (c1554) and sought a structure that would support her desire for contemplative* prayer, a discipline that would, in turn, support the apostolic life of the Church. Teresa initiated the reform of the Discalced* Carmelites by founding the Convent of San José (1562), which exemplified the cloistered life of women recognized by the decrees of the Council of Trent* (promulgated in Spain in 1564). She wrote *The Book of Her Life* (1562, 1565), an account of her prayer practice, and *The Way of Perfection* (1565, 1568) to encourage women in their practice of contemplative prayer. She consulted numerous spiritual directors, including Francis Borgia (1555), Peter of Alcántara (1560), and John* of Ávila (1568), all of whom encouraged her to pursue her way of prayer.

Teresa recruited John* of the Cross to join the Discalced reform (1568); he began a male wing of the order and eventually became the spiritual director of the Carmelite nuns at the Incarnation. As John nurtured the spiritual growth of these nuns, Teresa began placing them in Discalced convents she founded throughout Spain. Thus the two of them accomplished a major spiritual renewal in Spain, a revivification of the medieval mystical tradition despite deep contemporary suspicion of mental prayer. Inquisitional review of *The Book of Her Life*, which had been circulating quietly in manuscript form, resulted in its confiscation by the Spanish Inquisition* (1575); it was never returned to Teresa. However, subsequent investigation by the Spanish Inquisition of the charge of *alumbradismo* ("illuminism," or false mysticism) (1575–76) and her exoneration led Teresa to believe that she had an experiential wisdom to share with others, especially women who lacked a theological vocabulary to defend the authenticity of their experiences of God. Immediately afterward, she wrote a definitive description of the mystical life, *The Interior Castle* (1577), widely recognized as a unique subjective account of mystical union but also increasingly appreciated as a theological work in its own right.

Teresa oversaw the foundation of 17 Discalced Carmelite convents before her death; colorful accounts of this massive endeavor, as well as insights into her shrewd administrative capacity, are contained in her *Book of the Foundations* and her prolific correspondence. Her works were collected and edited by Luis de Leon, published (1588), and became an influential source of spiritual wisdom, leading to her canonization (1622) and declaration as the "Doctor of Prayer" (1970), one of three female doctors of the Roman Catholic Church. In an age preoccupied with a catechetical approach to Christianity, Teresa invited her contemporaries to enter into the reality of God through prayer and thereby to experience theological truth. Because she was so deeply committed to the sacramental* life of the Church and a strict monastic life of prayer, she was able to speak authoritatively from her own experience, literally opening up her inner life as a guidebook for other spiritual seekers (see Prayer of the Heart). The frankness and familiarity of her writing style, which reflects a committed mystical discipline, make her a timeless spiritual teacher. But her writings also convey deep theological insights – insights into the Incarnation*, the hypostatic union, and the inner life of the Trinity* – all of which she makes real by speaking with an intimate knowledge of God. The authority of her experience rings true even today; she is a consummate teacher of the Christian mystical tradition.

GILLIAN T. W. AHLGREN

Teresa of Calcutta (1910–97), founder of the Roman Catholic congregation of the Missionaries of Charity (MC); "Mother" of the poor*; acclaimed a living saint*; Nobel Peace Prize laureate (1979); beatified 2003. Born Agnes Gonxha Bojaxhiu in Skopje, Macedonia, of Albanian parents; Loreto sister and teacher in India (1928–48). Called to serve God among the poorest of the poor (1946), she successively founded the MC Sisters in Calcutta (1951), the MC Brothers (1967), MC contemplative branches (1976, 1978), MC Fathers (1984), Lay MCs (1984), and the ecumenical Association of Co-workers (1969).

Her congregation, founded in the wake of the atrocities of the partition of India, is characterized by rigorous poverty and discipline. Her Roman Catholicism reflected her Eastern Bloc origins, and she welcomed Vatican* II's renewal of the Church but not individual laxity. Contact with the materially rich West led her to see spiritual poverty as more problematic than physical deprivation, and she used her growing international influence and attention in the media not only to intercede for peace* but also to uphold family* life and voice conservative objections shared with Pope John Paul II to abortion*, the ordination* of women, and feminism*.

She took literally Matt 25:35–40. Christ "thirsted" in the broken bodies of the poor and simultaneously offered himself as spiritual sustenance in the Eucharist so that this thirst might be satiated. Because in tending to the dying, leprous, or abandoned she was touching Christ, love* was of primary importance. Like Thérèse* of Lisieux, she advocated doing small things with great love. With Francis* of Assisi, she sought to be a channel of God's peace.

Her mission, despite her orthodoxy, reflected supreme tolerance and respect for God's presence in every human. The worldwide response to her mission showed faith* to be at its most articulate in action. Revealed only after her death, her inner life was nonetheless marked by a sense of separation from God and an increasing longing for God's love. Through this "darkness," she was led to deeper union with God, participating in Jesus' thirst, his longing for love, and sharing the desolation of the poor. Posthumously she offered hope for the doubtful.

KATHRYN SPINK

Tertiary. See THIRD ORDER AND TERTIARY.

Tertullian, Quintus Septimius Florens (c150/60–c225/30), African theologian. The son of a centurion and raised as a pagan, he was well educated, and some have identified him with the Tertullian known in Roman law. After becoming a Christian (before 197), he wrote apologetic works, including *Ad nationes* (To the nations) and *Apologeticum*, and was one of the first to write a polemic *adversus Judaeos* (against the Jews). He was probably the author of *The Passion of Perpetua* and Felicitas*, and he may have been involved in the translation of Irenaeus* into Latin and of the Old* Latin version of the Bible from the Septuagint*. His *Prescription against Heretics* follows Irenaeus* in arguing that the apostolic churches alone have the right to interpret Scripture*. In several works, he attacked Marcion*, the Gnostics*, and others whose work he regarded as heresies*. His work *Against Praxeas* shaped the doctrine of the Trinity* in the West, arguing against modalism* and using the language of "one substance" and "three persons." Several writings on the Christian mode of life urge separation from pagan society, and his position became more rigorist after he joined the Montanist* Movement. His Latin style is vigorous, complex, and rhetorically effective, although he is often unfair to his opponents. He became the "father of Latin theology," admired by Cyprian* and influential among later theologians even when they took different positions; something of his temperament may be reflected in the Donatists* and in the North African doctrine of original* sin.

EUGENE TESELLE

Testament, formal declaration of what a person wishes to be done after his or her death or departure on a long journey (e.g. Paul's address to the Ephesian elders in Acts 20). While the NT term *diatheke* can mean both "testament" and "covenant," the former sense is unilateral, the latter mutual; thus in discussing predestination*, theologians in the Reformed* tradition sometimes differentiated between a unilateral testament and a mutual covenant. In NT texts, *diatheke* is usually understood as "covenant" ("my blood of the covenant," Mark 14:24 = Matt. 26:28; "the new covenant in my blood," Luke 22:20; cf. 1 Cor 11:25; 2 Cor 3:6). Thus Old and New "Testaments" refer to the old and new "covenants" (although Calvin*, Barth*, and possibly Augustine* envision one covenant in two dispensations or testaments). Yet Jesus' parting words (e.g. John 14–17; Acts 1:7–8) are sometimes called his testament. The Deutero-Pauline Pastoral* Epistles have the character of a testament, laying down "Paul's" expectations for doctrine, church order, and morality in epistles that represented him as being in danger of death (2 Tim 4:16–18); the same can be said of the letters of Ignatius*, which he wrote while on his way to trial and death in Rome. The testament of Francis* of Assisi, written shortly before his death, reaffirmed his original ideal of poverty and gave support to the Spirituals* as against the Conventual Franciscans* in coming decades. **See also** COVENANT.

Testaments of the Twelve Patriarchs, OT pseudepigraphon that presents the patriarchs of the tribes of Israel delivering their last words on their deathbeds. Moral lessons are drawn from history, and the "future" (from the perspective of the patriarchs) is predicted, including the salvific work of a messiah, i.e. Jesus Christ. In their present form, the Testaments are Christian; a Jewish pre-Christian stage has been surmised but is difficult to prove. **See also** PSEUDEPIGRAPHA.

JOHANNES TROMP

Tetragrammaton, four-letter Hebrew name of God* (YHWH), pronounced "Yahweh." Some time after the Exile, the divine name ceased to be pronounced; its four consonants continued to be written, but the term *Adonai* (my Lord) was substituted in reading. The Massoretes* added the vowel points for *Adonai* under the consonants *YHWH*. During the Reformation, Calvin* and others, taking these literally, inaccurately pronounced the divine name "Jehovah." Today, given that any pronunciation of the divine name is offensive to Jews, most Christian Bibles translate the tetragrammaton "the Lord," often in full capital letters, instead of using "Yahweh," and scholarly literature uses "YHWH" without translation. **See also GOD, CHRISTIAN VIEWS OF: NAMES FOR GOD IN THE BIBLE AND CHURCH TRADITIONS; YHWH.**

Teutonic Knights. The Hospital of St. Mary of the Teutons, commonly known as the Teutonic Knights, is a military*-religious order originally founded as a field hospital during the Third Crusade* (1189–92). It was soon converted to a military order that served God by defending Christians and Christian territory in battle, while still operating hospices for the care of the sick, its central activity today.

From the 1230s, the Teutonic Knights sought new opportunities to defend Latin Christians on the frontiers against the non-Christian peoples of Eastern Europe, by conquering and converting the peoples of Prussia, Livonia (Latvia* and Estonia*), and Lithuania*. In 1309 they moved their headquarters to Prussia. After their great defeat at Tannenberg/Grunwald (1410) by the forces of Poland*-Lithuania, the Knights' territorial power dwindled. They continued to engage in military activity while serving the German emperors, initially against the Ottoman Turks and later against the Christian enemies of Germany and Austria.

As a military*-religious order, the Teutonic Knights believed that they served God by fighting the enemies of Christendom and if necessary dying in that service. The members of the order originally included knights, other warriors and servants, priests, and sisters; today there are only priests and sisters. Since the medieval period, the sisters have usually lived in separate communities and are involved in the care of the sick.

The Teutonic Knights' involvement in the Christianization and Westernization of the Baltic region of Europe (they never entered Russia) is highly controversial; it was undertaken at a great cost of human lives and local culture. **See also MILITARY ORDERS.**

HELEN J. NICHOLSON

Thaddaeus the Apostle. One of the 12 apostles (Mark 3:18; Matt. 10:3), often identified with "Jude*" (literally "Judas of James*," i.e. either the son or brother of James) mentioned in the comparable list in Luke 6:16 and Acts 1:13 (where Thaddaeus is not mentioned). **See also TWELVE APOSTLES.**

Thaddeus (Addai* in Syriac) was, according to Syrian* and Armenian* traditions, one of the 70 apostles (Luke 10:1, 17); as a disciple of the apostle Thomas*, Thaddeus served as a missionary in Edessa*.

Thailand. Christianity is a minority religion (together with Islam, in the south) in this Buddhist country with the motto "To be a Thai is to be a Buddhist." This motto makes Thai Christian identity somewhat problematic and shapes the church's understanding of its presence and mission.

Christianity was introduced in Thailand by two Dominican* missionaries, Friar Jeronimo da Cruz and Sabastião da Canto (who arrived in 1567, in the capital of the kingdom, Ayudhaya), followed by Franciscan* and Jesuit* missionaries. Royal support (especially from King Narai, mid-17th c.) enabled the missionaries to make progress, gaining converts and building hospitals and a seminary. During the reign of the subsequent king, the Roman Catholic Church suffered periods of repression. Yet during the reign of King Rama I of the Chakri (Bangkok) dynasty (late 18th c.), the Catholic mission was renewed, following the same pattern: evangelization*, education*, and health* care. Catholic mission expanded in Northern Thailand (early 19th c.) and remains influential there today. The number of Roman Catholics has grown to approximately 300,000 members (in 2000).

The efforts of Protestant missionaries initially failed (mid-19th c.) owing to resistance from the king and a lack of responsiveness by Thais, as well as illness and death among the missionaries, and language and cultural barriers. Jesse Caswell and Dan Beach Bradley established their mission in Bangkok and the north. Bradley's son-in-law, Daniel McGilvary, established a Presbyterian mission in the north. Protestant mission focused on evangelicalism and education; Edna Cole and Sarah Bradley started modern schools for Thai girls. During the 20th c.,

Protestant Christians grew in number, developing partnerships among Presbyterians, Baptists, Lutherans, and Disciples of Christ, and founding the Church of Christ in Thailand (1934), an ecumenical body that facilitates the work of mainline Protestant denominations. In the early 21st c., although influenced by Presbyterian missionaries, the Church of Christ in Thailand was under Thai leadership; although male dominated, the Church increasingly recognizes women's participation. Its members (c100,000) include, in addition to traditional lowland Thais, "hill people" (e.g. Lahu people), who comprise about half of its total membership.

The Evangelical Fellowship of Thailand, another church organization representing Evangelical* and Pentecostal* groups, has gained popularity among Thai Christians and became an important part of Thai Christianity. It emphasizes a literal* interpretation of the Bible, proselytizing, prayers, strict moral codes, and a separation of church and state politics.

Through the centuries, Christian churches have made important contributions to Thai society. Church-related schools, universities, seminaries, hospitals, and other community outreach organizations continue to serve their existing communities and beyond. Yet the Christians' minority status and their lack of active engagement and collaboration with other religions – namely Buddhism* and Islam* – prevent the churches from providing solutions to major social issues facing Thai society, i.e. sex tourism, AIDS, poverty, and political turmoil.

Statistics: Population (2000): 61.4 million (M). Christians 1.4 M; 2.2% (independents, 0.79 M; Protestants, 0.3 M; Roman Catholics, 0.25 M); Buddhists, 52.4 M, 85.3%; Muslims, 4.2 M, 6.8%; native religionists, 1.8 M, 3%; nonreligious, 1.3 M, 2.1%. (Based on *World Christian Encyclopedia*, 2001.)

NANTAWAN BOONPRASAT LEWIS

Thecla, legendary Christian virgin, known only through the "Acts of Paul and Thecla" (a part of the Acts of Paul, c180). Converted by Paul*, she was condemned to death but miraculously escaped and baptized herself. According to tradition, she was martyred in Seleuceia in Asia Minor, where a large basilica was built over her supposed tomb (4th c.). Macrina*, one of the Cappadocians*, was secretly named Thecla and took her as a model in setting up a monastic community. **See also APOCRYPHA CLUSTER: APOCRYPHAL ACTS OF APOSTLES; VIRGIN MARTYR TRADITION.**

Theism, belief in a transcendent and personal God (as contrasted with atheism*, pantheism*, and deism*).

Theocracy, a form of government in which God directly rules and God's revealed laws become the law of the realm, often administered by priests, prophets, or teachers. The term was coined by Josephus* to characterize the government of Israel before the institution of kingship. In 1 Sam 8:4–22, the establishment of kingship was regarded as an abandonment of theocracy, which was restored after the Exile, when Judah was governed directly by priests, although they were subordinate to the Persian rulers. Islam* is theocratic in character, especially where *shari'a* is made the law of the state. Theocracy has also been seen in the claims of medieval popes like Gregory* VII and Boniface* VIII, the restriction of government to the saints by Wyclif* and Hus*, the Geneva* of Calvin*, the Münster of Thomas Münzer and Jan van Leyden, the New England of the Puritans*, and the English Commonwealth under Cromwell*. It is explicit in the Scottish Covenanters*, especially the Cameronians* and Reformed Presbyterians, and in the Mormon* state of Deseret. Theocratic norms have been enunciated by contemporary groups such as the Unification* Church, the Moral Majority (in the USA), and (Protestant) Christian Reconstructionists.

Theodicy. First coined by the rationalist Leibniz* (1710), the word "theodicy" juxtaposes the Greek words for God and justice*. Leibniz attempted to answer a question long asked (e.g. by Plato*): how can God be just if God is omnipotent* and totally good and yet allows humankind, whom God has created in God's image, to suffer? Leibniz answered: all things considered, the present world is the best of all possible worlds – a vague position widely attacked, notably by Voltaire. More generally, "theodicy" refers to the way any religion deals with suffering (as proposed by the sociologist Max Weber*).

Suffering in the Christian tradition has always been closely associated with sin* and evil. Evil can be seen to be an interpretation of suffering, an empirical phenomenon. For theologians theodicy raises many issues regarding creation*, heaven* and hell*, the Fall*, free will*, redemption*, and atonement*.

The problem that Job* faced in the OT was similar to that of Leibniz. Job had to square God's transcendence with his own extreme suffering. His answer (like Leibniz's) was vague: things have to be accepted as they are. Paul's* position was similar (Rom 11:33–35); he fell back on the mystery* of God's will, which humans cannot understand. Origen* explained all misfortunes as the result of free choices by created spirits and regarded misfortunes as pedagogical, as means by which God leads them back to their primal communion with God. Augustine* placed emphasis on the Fall*; evil is like the shadows that emphasize the harmony of the whole. Thomas Aquinas*, like Tillich*, pointed to the intrinsic limitations in a spatiotemporal world. Because God acts in a consistent way, something that is "logically possible" will be "circumstantially impossible."

When considered from theological perspectives less influenced by Plato and his heirs, theodicy changes. Process* theology abandons conventional notions of omnipotence and emphasizes God's goodness, luring the world toward greater complexity, intensity, and harmony. Following Irenaeus*, Hick's approach is evolutionary and eschatological*, visualizing the world and its sufferings as a backdrop for soul making. Bonhoeffer* found comfort in the thought that God shares human suffering and rejection. Liberation* theology emphasizes God's identification with the oppressed*. As in the Psalms, God has a preferential* option for the poor. Nonphilosophically minded Christians who bypass the enigma set by theodicy and deal with their sufferings by relating them to those of the crucified Christ often implicitly adopt one of the previously mentioned answers. **See also EVIL, THE PROBLEM OF; GOD, CHRISTIAN VIEWS OF, CLUSTER; SUFFERING.**

EUGENE TESELLE and
WILLIAM S. F. PICKERING

Theodora (c500–48), wife of Justinian*. An actress and dancing girl, she married Justinian (523) and on his accession was crowned joint ruler (527). His equal in political acumen, she ended the Nika sedition (532) by encouraging Belisarius to kill 30,000 rioters. She sympathized with the Miaphysites*, following a different policy than Justinian, possibly with his collusion; she also encouraged him to compromise with the Miaphysites, especially during the Three* Chapters controversy.

Theodora the Iconodule (c810–62), empress (842–55). Born in Paphlagonia with an iconodule* background, she married the emperor Theophilus, who was strongly Iconoclastic*. After his death, she became regent for their son (842–67); with this authority, she replaced the Iconoclast patriarch*, restored icons*, and on February 19–20, 843, after an all-night vigil*, a procession entered Hagia* Sophia for a formal restoration of the icons. In commemoration of this event, the Orthodox* Church celebrates the Festival of Orthodoxy on the first Sunday in Lent*. After a conflict with her son and her brother, she was banished to a convent, her property was seized, and all honors were rescinded.

Theodore of Mopsuestia (c350–428), Antiochene* exegete and theologian, a major figure in the Church* of the East, which called him "the Commentator." With his friend John* Chrysostom, he studied in the monastery school in Antioch and adopted its method of literal* interpretation of the Bible (e.g. viewing Song* of Songs as a marriage poem; opposing a messianic interpretation of the Psalms). His Christology*, like that of Nestorius*, affirmed a union of human and divine wills that developed progressively, until Jesus' exaltation. In his view humans have a permanent capability for sinlessness, through Christ and the Spirit; wrong decisions cannot alter human nature. Because his view of sin* was similar to the Pelagian* view held by Julian* of Eclanum, Theodore protected him after his condemnation (418). This stance helped reinforce an alliance between Rome and the opponents of Nestorius at the Council of Ephesus* (431), although he was not condemned until the next century (see Three Chapters).

Theodore of Studios, or Theodore Studite (759–826), monastic reformer. A monk and abbot, he was banished after opposing the adulterous marriage of Emperor Constantine VI (796), but after the overthrow of the emperor, he was recalled by Irene* (797). He and his followers took over the nearly empty old monastery of Studios*. He reformed it according to the Rule of Basil*, making the monastic life within it the model for later Eastern monasticism*. When Leo V renewed the Iconoclastic* policies of the preceding century, Theodore became his most vocal opponent and was exiled again (809); even after the policies were relaxed, he refused out of conscience to return to Constantinople.

Theodore of Tarsus (c602–90), archbishop of Canterbury. Born in Tarsus, he studied in Antioch and Constantinople, traveled to Edessa, and entered a monastery in Rome. He participated in the Monothelite controversy along with Maximus* the Confessor and was involved in the Lateran* Council (649) that defied the emperor. Appointed archbishop of Canterbury (668), he held several synods of the English Church. His surviving writings include commentaries in the Greek tradition. His work and his attitude toward learning prepared the way for Bede* and Alcuin*.

Theodoret of Cyrrhus (c393–c460), Syrian theologian. Friend of Nestorius* and a monk in Apamea, he was made bishop of Cyrrhus against his will (423). He defended Nestorius and attacked Cyril's* position; he drafted the Formulary* of Reunion (433), agreed to by both parties. Deposed by the Second Council of Ephesus* (449), he was reinstated by the Council of Chalcedon* (451) after reluctantly anathematizing Nestorius. His commentaries on Scripture exemplify the Antiochene* approach; his *Church History* continues that of Eusebius* (up to 428); other writings are valuable sources about popular Christianity in Syria*. During the Three* Chapters controversy, his views were condemned.

Theodosian Code. Issued by Theodosius II (438), it systematizes the many laws promulgated since Constantine, arranging them by topics (Book 16 deals with religious matters). It continued to be used in the West even after being superseded by the Code of Justinian*.

Theodosius (c346–95), emperor of the East (379–95) and the West (392–95). After the Arian* emperor Valens was killed by the Arian Goths* (378), Gratian chose Theodosius to rule the East, where he persuaded the Goths to settle in a designated area. Baptized (380), he issued the decree *Cunctos populos* enforcing the Nicene* position on the Trinity*. In the West, there were usurpations by Maximus (383–88) and by Arbogast, with Eugenius as figurehead emperor (392–94), who continued Constantine's tradition of religious toleration. In 394 Theodosius's armies met those of Maximus in Aquileia. The battle was staged by Theodosius as a contest against paganism. Theodosius was the victor, pagan morale collapsed, and Theodosius and his sons issued new decrees outlawing pagan worship.

Theodotion (late 2nd c.), translator of a Greek version of the OT and Apocrypha, included in Origen's* Hexapla*.

Theodotus the Cobbler (2nd c.). A leather merchant from Byzantium, he was condemned in Rome by Victor (189–98) for teaching that Jesus was a man who became the Christ by being anointed with the Holy Spirit at his baptism. **See also CHRISTOLOGIES CLUSTER: IN WESTERN CHURCH HISTORY.**

THEOLOGICAL EDUCATION CLUSTER

1) *Introductory Entries*

2) *A Sampling of Contextual Views and Practices*

1) Introductory Entries

Theological Education: Concepts of. Theological education in the broadest sense is the education of people in religious faith. The term is most often used by Christians to describe both a pattern of study that prepares clergy and other religious professionals and the institutions in which such studies take place. The pattern of study that dominates today has deep roots in catechesis*, the instruction of early Christian converts before baptism*. The pattern took form in medieval universities and has evolved into a fourfold framework including biblical studies,

Theological Education: Concepts of

theology, history of the church, and practical studies. Over the centuries, these areas of study have incorporated a wide variety of modern intellectual developments, including historical, literary, and social scientific methods of inquiry and contemporary philosophical approaches. Numerous subspecialties have developed within the segments, including ethics*, religious education, women's* studies, ethnic studies, liturgy*, preaching*, pastoral* care, social and cultural analysis, and administration and leadership.

With some slight variations in nomenclature, the fourfold framework and its subdivisions pervade theological education in all Christian traditions. Programs vary, however, by their guiding goals and purposes. They also vary in format in different cultural contexts.

Programs can be divided into three major types by purpose or goal: religious formation, philosophical and historical reasoning, and ministerial practice.

1. The pattern of religious-formation-focused theological education is most highly developed in Roman Catholic theological schools but is also dominant in some Protestant ones. The aim is to shape candidates for the priesthood or ministry intellectually, spiritually, pastorally, and as human beings. The theological school does this according to the *Program of Priestly Formation* of the U.S. Conference of Catholic Bishops, by creating "a formational community responding to a call to continuing conversion of mind and heart." Religious practices are significant features of the overall educational process. The spirit of this kind of theological education is the ancient Greek *paideia*, which, according to David Kelsey in *Between Athens and Berlin: The Theological Education Debate*, sought to cultivate the excellence of the soul "in knowledge of the 'Good' itself" and which requires "inward and religious transformation."
2. Rationally focused theological education seeks to cultivate theological habits of mind. This kind of education emphasizes critical thinking, analysis, and reasoned reflection. It involves the kind of inquiry that is, according to David Kelsey, "*critical* in that it begins by requiring justification of all alleged authorities or bases of truth." Critical and rational approaches result in a theological wisdom that depends not on the unquestioned appropriation of religious authority but on a reasoned religious understanding. Education in a number of Protestant institutions falls into this category.
3. Practice-focused theological education, another common pattern in Protestant seminaries, emphasizes the professional dimensions of educating clergy and other church leaders. Because much of the work of religious professionals involves skilled activities, the educational strategies of this type focus on obtaining the knowledge base to develop the requisite skills. The study of religious texts and traditions is oriented to their utility in the leadership of communities of faith. The goal is graduates who are effective preachers and worship leaders, teachers and administrators, counselors and group leaders, and congregational and public leaders.

Few theological schools reflect a "pure" version of these three kinds of educational practice; most include elements of all three. Almost always, however, a single goal dominates not only the curriculum but also the ethos of a particular school. Although all three patterns involve, for the most part, the study of the same subject areas, topics are approached in different ways toward different educational ends.

The format of theological schooling and the structure of the institutions in which it is carried out tend to follow dominant educational patterns in the cultures in which the institutions are located.

1. In Western Europe, North America, and much of North Asia, theological education is organized in programs leading to a degree at the college level or higher. These programs may be offered in a Bible college, a church-related college, a public university

with an affiliated faculty of theology, or theological seminary. In Western Europe the majority of degree-based theological education is at the bachelor's degree level (following a slightly longer "high school" program), while in the USA and Canada, the majority of theological schools offer graduate, professional degrees, although the training of religious leaders in undergraduate Bible colleges is not uncommon. Theological education also takes place in thousands of nondegree pastoral training institutes offering both basic and continuing training for religious leaders.

2. In Africa, much of Latin America, and South Asia, theological education is typically offered in seminaries, training institutes, Bible colleges, and some denominationally funded colleges that may or may not offer degrees. These range from the secondary level to the college level; a few offer graduate-level programs.
3. Regardless of the level of education at which theological education is offered, it tends to encompass a similar range of subjects. Many theological schools are operated by or closely affiliated with denominations, churches, or religious movements, although some are religiously independent. Some are closely associated with a university or other higher education institution; others are freestanding.

See also EDUCATIONAL PRACTICES AS CHRISTIAN SERVICE CLUSTER.

DANIEL O. ALESHIRE and BARBARA G. WHEELER

Theological Education: Its Practice in the Roman Catholic Tradition: Contemporary Challenges in the Western World. Before the Second Vatican* Council (1962–65), most Roman Catholic theological education took place in seminaries and was intended to prepare future priests for their pastoral ministries. There were some exceptions. A few schools – including the Gregorian University, Rome; the University of Tübingen; the Institut Catholique, Paris; and the Catholic University of America – offered graduate degrees in theology open to laymen, but primarily to priests who wished to teach in seminaries. St. Mary's School of Theology (1943–63) in South Bend, Indiana, and Regina Mundi (1954–2006) in Rome also offered graduate degrees to women, lay as well as religious, who wished to teach theology in colleges and convents.

After the Council, Catholic theological education developed not only in seminaries but also in colleges and universities. Vatican II's Decree on Priestly Formation (1965) laid out general directions for the revision of theological education, calling for more focus on the study of Scripture (the "heart of theology"), dialogue with modern patterns of philosophy and science, and serious study of Protestant and Jewish thought that had influenced the modern world. The Decree and subsequent directives from Rome put into motion a revision of the seminary curriculum that continued into the 21st c.

The primary locus of post-conciliar theological education shifted toward the Catholic colleges and universities. Major doctoral programs in theology emerged at some of the universities (e.g. Marquette, Fordham, Notre Dame, Boston College, St. Louis). Theology in the universities differed from seminary theology in its aim, methods, and audience. University theology aimed to prepare college and university theological researchers and teachers; was much more focused than seminary theology on engaging in dialogue with the other disciplines in the universities and colleges; and was offered to laymen and laywomen (the vast majority by the mid-1970s), as well as clergy and women religious.

PATRICK W. CAREY

2) A Sampling of Contextual Views and Practices

Theological Education in Africa: Issues It Faces. The long-term sustainability of Christian churches depends greatly on the effectiveness of pastoral (and lay leader) training. The problem faced by theological education in tropical Africa is apparent as soon as one notes that most pastoral training has been conducted by missionaries, the majority of whom know little or nothing about the inner dynamics of the African cultural and religious heritage. This situation persists because of the high cost of residential pastoral formation and the lack of contextualization* of the training curriculum. To cut costs, African bishops and churches invite foreign missionary instructors to conduct training in their pastoral institutes. As long as the syllabi of African theological colleges and seminaries are imported from elsewhere, pastoral training will continue to be out of tune with the cultural and religious dynamics of African societies among whom the trainees are expected to work after graduation.

Urgent transformation of the curriculum in theological education in tropical Africa is needed. Curriculum development is a professional undertaking, which must begin from the context of the learners and proceed to discern the texts that can provide relevant knowledge, skills, and experience appropriate for each context (Jesus' pedagogy is exemplary in this regard). Two issues that confront African Christianity in the early 21st c. ought to be taken seriously in any effective African curriculum of theological education. How can we prepare African pastors, priests, and lay leaders without contributing to their alienation from their culture? How can we prepare them to cope with the present split between Christian identity and practice that characterizes African Christianity?

1. Cultural Identity. Inevitably, every Christian mission agency from outside Africa has introduced into the continent the cultural and religious values of the home country of that agency. This cultural flooding of tropical Africa with North Atlantic culture is particularly marked as a result of schooling and indoctrination. The curricula in schools, colleges, seminaries, and universities have been overloaded with cultural values from Europe and North America at the expense of the African cultural and religious heritage. Christian instruction and the use of foreign languages as the medium of instruction have reinforced this alienation of African students from their culture. How can one envision a theological education that would be academically sound and yet avoid this shortcoming?

2. Doctrinal Identity and Daily Practice among African Christians. There is nothing specifically African in the doctrines recited by African branches of various denominations, e.g. Anglican, Roman Catholic, Lutheran, Moravian, Presbyterian, Methodist, Baptist, Congregationalist, Mennonite, and Quaker. Yet *in practice* African Christians in these denominations remain rooted in their respective African cultural traditions. For them Christianity remains largely a Sunday affair, with little or no direct impact on the political, economic, ethical, or aesthetic norms of the wider society. This inconsistency between doctrinal identity and actual life conduct among African Christians brings into question the significance of the rapid numerical increase in church membership in tropical Africa, which has no direct impact on the actual life of people in a continent burdened with civil strife, administrative inefficiency, and economic failure. Apparently many Africans turn to the church for refuge, hoping that through the church they might survive the collapse of social institutions (which fail to serve them) and the postcolonial political crises in predominantly "Christian" countries (e.g. in Angola*; Burundi*; Congo*, Democratic Republic [DRC]; Congo*, Republic [Congo-Brazzaville]; Ghana*; Kenya*; Mozambique*; Nigeria*; Rwanda*; South* Africa; Zimbabwe*).

This lack of social engagement of African Christians reflects the fact that in most instances the Christianity that has been introduced to the continent is a religion aimed at securing eternal life* for believers after their death (see Salvation). What believers do now is insurance for the life to come, leading to an abdication of social responsibility with regard to political and economic affairs. Most priests, pastors, and lay leaders fail to provide any relevant guidance for their life as Christians during social and political crises. Instead, churches are often the focal points for fomenting social strife. African churches, especially those that are extensions of foreign denominations, remain largely detached from the daily social concerns of the nations to which their members belong. This is a problem with the training and continuing education of priests, pastors, and lay leaders.

3. Toward a Theological Education with Contextual Relevance. The dissonance between theological education training and contextual relevance leads to a pastoral workforce that cannot deliver relevant contextual service to the congregations in both rural and urban areas in tropical Africa. An African theological education curriculum that addresses these issues must be an African ecumenical undertaking (overcoming the denominational splits brought by the missions) that rethinks its relationship with a North Atlantic Christianity with reverse problems.

Whereas tropical Africa has numerous churches without enough adequately trained theologians, churches in the North Atlantic countries have an excess of trained theologians without enough Christians to serve. How could these theologians help support and train African theologians ready to address the above-mentioned needs in African theological education? The question will not be easily answered, because cultural presuppositions and power relations (including those between rich North Atlantic churches and pauperized tropical African churches) tend to overshadow any chances of unanimity in matters of doctrine, institutional structure, pastoral care, and conceptual clarity. But an Africanization of theological education in Africa is necessary and urgent in view of the strong demographic shift of Christianity from the North Atlantic to tropical Africa.

JESSE NDWIGA KANYUA MUGAMBI

Theological Education in Asia. The question of theological education in Asia did not arise until the advent of indigenous church movements and the development of a spirit of national independence. During the previous centuries, missionaries taught the different Western models they had learned when trained in the Western theological centers; the Roman Catholic seminaries followed the scholastic theological tradition; the Protestant seminaries reproduced their inherited Reformation tradition.

With the advent of indigenous churches in independent nations, there were pioneering attempts to impart theological education that would reflect the spirit, ethos, and thought patterns of Asian peoples and their civilizations. The movement of Contextual* theology called for a theological education sensitive to the social* and political* conditions of Asia. Consequently, in many centers of theological education, analysis of the society and exposure to the realities of poverty* and suffering* became an integral part of the training. The method of theological learning shifted from the concept of "banking" to that of critical study and reflection aimed at transformation. This has led to appropriating within theological education the sapiential Asian tradition, emphasizing the aspect of experience and deemphasizing theology as a system of thought. This approach received fresh impetus from the Asian ecumenical* movement and interchurch theological linkages in trying to meet the new challenges posed by the postcolonial Asian situation. Since the 1960s, the number of seminaries and Bible schools has greatly increased all over Asia. At the same time, efforts were made to group them, bringing them under some general umbrella, such as the Association of Theological Education in South East Asia, formed in 1981. It has a membership of 92 theological schools in 14 different countries and supervises the theological education of about 9,000 students. In India many Protestant and Orthodox centers of theological education are members of the Senate of Serampore College, which also became an affiliating institution.

Four new developments in the field of theological education in Asia can be identified: (1) Theological education is being extended to laymen and laywomen. (2) There is a remarkable growth in the quality of theological education. Thus many schools are now offering degrees not only at the bachelor's and master's levels but also at the doctoral level. (3) An emerging trend is the training of theology teachers in Asia, instead of Europe and the USA, and the use of Asian resources (including about 200 Asian theological journals) for doing theology and theological education. (4) More and more highly qualified women are theological educators and have begun to contribute to the reshaping of traditional theological education.

At the institutional level, theological education has acquired a new dimension with the establishment of Christian studies departments or chairs in some of the state or public universities. The secular and interreligious context in which Christian history and theology are studied and researched has led to a reconsideration of the method of theological education as a process of continuous dialogue* with the larger realities of society, including the plurality of religions and cultures, in an interdisciplinary manner. Two examples of institutions that are headed in this new direction are the Chung Chi College of Chinese University of Hong Kong and the Department of Christian Studies, University of Madras, India, which pursue interdisciplinary and dialogical approaches in theological education. FELIX WILFRED

Theological Education in Latin America. Theological education came to Latin America as an essential component of the European and North American missionary movements, first Roman Catholic and later Protestant, but often failed to adapt to the realities and opportunities of the New World.

Guatemala is a microcosm of these realities. Roman Catholic seminaries have offered a classical formation for the priesthood, but after 450 years the Catholic Church is still largely dependent on imported clergy. Similarly, Protestant seminaries and Bible institutes as residential institutions for the training of pastors and evangelists (for c70 years) demonstrate the inadequacy of the traditional understanding of ministry as a profession of highly schooled, ordained, and salaried clergy, which relatively few local churches can support.

A notable alternative (incorporating Ivan Illich's radical critique of education as schooling and Paulo Freire's insight into education as liberation in *Pedagogy of the Oppressed*) has been the development since the 1960s of decentralized Protestant and Pentecostal training programs (first in Guatemala). This approach offers widespread access to and training for diverse ministries (lay and ordained, men and women, mestizo and indigenous [Mayan], old and young, poor and non-poor) and the possibility of incorporating in much greater numbers indigenous leaders, whatever their geographic, cultural, economic, or educational location, into both social and ecclesial ministries.

The Central American Center for Pastoral Studies in Guatemala, e.g., offers theological and pastoral courses each year to some 300 Protestant, Pentecostal, and Catholic students at two academic levels. It also offers a women's pastoral program of holistic training to confront the challenges of daily life, to contribute to the development of the participants' families and churches and communities, to eradicate violence, and to promote justice and equality, through basic courses, workshops, and celebrations that reach out each year to 3,000 women in Central America.

ROSS KINSLER

Theological Education in North America. Christian theological education in North America is conducted primarily in the c250 seminaries, divinity schools, and schools of theology that offer graduate-level professional education for clergy and other religious professionals. The primary degree for Christian clergy is the master of divinity (M.Div.), a three-year, post-college program that includes the study of religious texts, theological ideas, historical traditions, social issues, and professional skills. Attention is also given to personal and spiritual formation. Other programs, including various master's and doctoral degrees, are offered by some schools. Professors in North American seminaries are highly trained and generally hold a Ph.D. in a theological subject. Most theological schools are financed by a combination of gifts, grants from denominations, and endowment, but students bear a substantial portion of the cost of theological training; some borrow heavily to pay for their education. Theological schools in North America are generally respected by churches, although they sometimes become embroiled in theological conflicts in their denominations.

Other training for Christian ministers, lay and ordained, is offered at the undergraduate level in Bible colleges and denominationally related or Christian colleges, and at the non-degree level in urban ministry training programs and institutes.

DANIEL O. ALESHIRE and BARBARA G. WHEELER

Theological Education in the Orthodox World of Eastern Europe. Schools of higher theological education were sparse for centuries in the Orthodox world, the result in large part of Ottoman rule. Nevertheless, before the 19th c. well-known theological institutions existed, especially in the Romanian* countries, Ukraine*, and later Russia*. Highly educated scholars in theology played important roles in the Eastern Orthodox Church (as hierarchs, professors) and in their nations (as state ministers). These theological scholars ensured not only the preservation of the Orthodox culture in difficult times, but also achieved major accomplishments, such as the translation of the Bible into different languages. During that period, the candidates for priesthood were trained mostly in monastery* schools, where they learned the basics of the Orthodox doctrine and the practice of Church music and worship.

During the 19th c., modern theological schools, both Church-based seminaries and university-based theological schools, were founded in each Orthodox country. The primary goal of these theological institutions and of their generally highly educated faculty was to train future clergy and schoolteachers. Their pioneering scholars produced an important corpus of theological literature and included the "Slavophile" Alexei Khomiakov and the "Westernizer" Vladimir Soloviev*. But this trend was dramatically interrupted by the Bolshevik Revolution in Russia (1917) and later by the imposition of Communist regimes in other Orthodox countries. The positive consequence was the foundation by Russian emigrants of important theological schools in the West: St. Sergius Institute in Paris (1925), St. Tikhon's Seminary in South Canaan, Pennsylvania (1937), and St. Vladimir's Seminary in Crestwood, New York (1938). Among the great theologians who taught in these schools were Vladimir Lossky* and Georges Florovsky*, as well as Sergei Bulgakov*, Nicolas Afanasiev, Paul Evdokimov, Elisabeth Behr-Sigel, Alexander Schmemann (emphasizing a liturgical renewal within Orthodoxy), and patristic scholar John Meyendorff. These seminaries and their scholars played a unique role in making Orthodoxy and Orthodox theology known in the Western world. They also had a significant influence on the renewed development of theological education in Eastern Europe after 1989.

During the 20th c in Eastern Europe, theological education continued. Greece was part of the free world, and its theological schools flourished after World War II. Theological education continued to exist in the Communist countries as well, even though most theological schools were closed and the regime imposed drastic reductions in the number of students. The remaining theological schools continued to train future clergy and to do theological research, with scholars such as Dumitru Staniloae* (in Romania).

After the fall of Communism, many new theological schools, both seminaries and university-based theological schools (theological faculties), were founded. In Romania, e.g., whereas before 1989 there were 5 seminaries and 2 theological university institutes, in 2008 there were 45 seminaries and 15 university-based theological schools. Russia had seen a similarly large increase in the number of its theological schools and the students being trained for the priesthood. Generally speaking, there is no shortage of vocations for the priesthood in the Orthodox churches. **See also BIBLE INTERPRETATION CLUSTER: IN EASTERN ORTHODOXY.**

VASILE MIHOC

Theological Education in Western Europe: Germany. Theological education in German is university based. For medieval priests, university study was an exception. The Reformers, however, made university attendance obligatory for all future pastors. After the Council of Trent*, the Roman Catholic Church intensified the training of priests, although university training of priests has been required only since the *Kulturkampf** (1871–87). After two main ecclesiastical examinations (following guidelines from Rome as implemented by the German Bishops' Conference in consultation with the theological faculties of state universities), the diploma in Catholic theology is awarded. For all but two semesters, students preparing for the priesthood live in seminaries, where they also receive practical pastoral training. In addition, theological education serves as preparation for ordination as a deacon or priest.

Protestant ministerial studies take place at state faculties or church colleges. Upon the completion of these studies, students receive a diploma or take the first ecclesiastical examination. The subsequent vicariate offers experience in pastoral practice and, with intermittent attendance at preaching seminars, leads to the second ecclesiastical examination, which precedes ordination and appointment. The faculties draw up plans of study and examination in consultation with the churches. Protestant pastors, as a rule, are married. The free churches train their officials entirely in their own educational institutions.

The content of the training of priests and pastors is a matter of ongoing discussion at Protestant and Catholic theological faculty conferences. The future of the Christian churches depends in large measure on the quality of the training of their priests and pastors.

INGE MAGER

Theological Education in Western Europe: Nonconformity in England. See NONCONFORMITY AND THEOLOGICAL EDUCATION.

THEOLOGIES

See ANCESTOR VENERATION AND CHRISTIANITY CLUSTER; ANTHROPOLOGY CLUSTER; APOCALYPTICISM CLUSTER; BAPTISM CLUSTER; CHRISTOLOGIES CLUSTER; CHURCH, CONCEPTS AND LIFE, CLUSTER; DEATH, CHRISTIAN VIEWS OF, CLUSTER; ESCHATOLOGY CLUSTER; ETHICS AND CHRISTIANITY CLUSTER; EUCHARIST CLUSTER; FAMILY, CHRISTIAN VIEWS OF, CLUSTER; GOD, CHRISTIAN VIEWS OF CLUSTER; GOSPEL AND CULTURE CLUSTER; GRACE OF GOD CLUSTER; HOLY SPIRIT CLUSTER; HUMAN RIGHTS CLUSTER; INCARNATION CLUSTER; INCULTURATION CLUSTER; JESUS, IMAGES OF, CLUSTER; JUSTICE, CHRISTIAN THEOLOGICAL VIEWS AND PRACTICES, CLUSTER; JUSTIFICATION, THEOLOGICAL VIEWS AND PRACTICES, CLUSTER; KINGDOM OF GOD, THE CONCEPT OF, CLUSTER; LAND, THEOLOGICAL PERSPECTIVES AND PRAXIS, CLUSTER; MARRIAGE, THEOLOGY AND PRACTICE OF, CLUSTER; MILLENNIALISM CLUSTER; MISSION CLUSTER; POVERTY CLUSTER; RACISM AND CHRISTIANITY CLUSTER; SEXUALITY, ISSUES OF, CLUSTER.

Theology as Human Practice. See CONTEXTUAL THEOLOGIES.

THEOLOGY AS HUMAN UNDERTAKING CLUSTER

Theology as Human Undertaking: African Women Theologians Doing Theology by Making Connections

Theology as Human Undertaking: North Atlantic Theologians Doing Theology: A Dialogue between Text and Context

See also AESTHETICS AND THEOLOGY; ARTS AND THEOLOGY; CULTURE CLUSTER: CULTURE AND CHRISTIAN THEOLOGY; DEATH OF GOD THEOLOGY; ECOLOGY AND CHRISTIANITY CLUSTER: ECOFEMINIST THEOLOGY; ECOLOGY AND

Theology as Human Undertaking

CHRISTIANITY CLUSTER: ECOTHEOLOGY; ESOTERIC THEOLOGY; FUNDAMENTAL THEOLOGY; LABOR, THEOLOGIES OF; LAITY CLUSTER: THEOLOGY OF; LIBERAL THEOLOGY; LIBERATION THEOLOGIES CLUSTER; MEDIATING THEOLOGY; MERCERSBURG THEOLOGY; NATURAL THEOLOGY; NEW HAVEN THEOLOGY; PASTORAL THEOLOGY; POLITICAL THEOLOGY; POSITIVE THEOLOGY, POSITIVE LAW, POSITIVISM; RATIONALISM AND CHRISTIAN THEOLOGY; SACRAMENTAL THEOLOGY IN EASTERN ORTHODOX CHURCHES; SACRAMENTAL THEOLOGY IN WESTERN CHURCHES

Theology as Human Undertaking: African Women Theologians Doing Theology by Making Connections. A way of doing theology, essential in Africa, especially for African women, is to tell stories, and in particular one's story and the story of a community. The story of the Circle* of Concerned African Women Theologians ("the Circle") began, like all circles, with a single point, which then disappeared. A solitary person does not make a community; a circle is about community. So when one lone woman went into the theological field and found herself alone among men, she had no choice but to seek other sisters to join her so that together they might brave the challenges of being a woman theologian in one's own faith community. For African women theologians, doing theology is a matter of making connections. The story has been told by others; this is an attempt to get behind the story to what doing theology as African women theologians entails.

Working with the World* Council of Churches and meeting people from all walks of life was a privilege that opened my eyes to the need for Africans to work out their own salvation (a view reflecting the nationalism and Pan-Africanism of Kwam Nkruma of Ghana). We could not forget we were African women and Christians who are blessed to be a blessing to others.

My move to Nigeria following my marriage expanded my view of African women's lives and the need to have religion play a positive role in women's development – not subordinating them under patriarchy*, but enabling them to distinguishing humanizing cultural norms from norms that are obstacles to women's flourishing. An immersion in interreligious living in Africa (as a teacher) reinforced my acceptance of religious pluralism as an African reality.

As members of the Ecumenical* Association of Third World Theologians (EATWOT), a few African women and I began to envision the Circle as enabling African women to craft theologies that would be liberative for African women. A community of women was needed to pursue this line of study. Akan wisdom says, "Dua Kor gye Mframa a obu" – "A single tree standing against a storm will fall." This storm imagery speaks of inclusivity, participation, and community. It motivates us to initiate a multireligious Circle that embodies a dialogical lifestyle, which brings with it the challenge of defining who is a theologian and the challenges related to religious pluralism*, linguistic pluralism, racism*, and our Africanness.

Who Is a Theologian? The Circle envisioned a community of women theologians that research, write, and publish liberative theological literature to empower women and challenge the patriarchal and androcentric* practices of society and especially of faith-based organizations. For us, theologians are women whose praxis is anchored in religion, be they researchers and writers trained in seminaries and universities or women who communicate their experiences through drama, storytelling, and other media. The tension between these two types of women theologians remains a challenge but it does not split the community. The Circle enjoys unity in diversity with respect for member's charisma and skills.

Religious Pluralism. The Circle is a multireligious community of women sharing the empowering aspects of their faith. Doing theology as African women calls for religious pluralism. But can members representing the various strands of Christianity present in Africa, Muslims (see Islam and Christianity Cluster: In Africa), and

Theology as Human Undertaking

practitioners of African* Religion worship together? Open joint devotional exercises, conducted with respect for each woman's pieties, are welcomed by many as enriching, but they scandalize others.

Language. For our Pan-African community, language was a first challenge. Different accents in our uses of colonial languages, and the French–English divide on ways of reasoning out issues, had to be overcome, although until recently most of our publications have been in English. Besides using a local African language (e.g. Swahili), it was also important that our meetings be accessible to a large local audience. Doing theology as African women calls for cross-linguistic, and thus cross-cultural, dialogue.

Racism. Apartheid in South Africa was a challenge for the nationals, who at first attempted two Circles along racial* lines. Should African culture be viewed as including the cultures of the white and colored women of South* Africa? The rest of us very openly said, "Women, black, colored, or white, are welcome," and soon discovered that our women's experiences in different churches are not dissimilar – and a multiracial Circle emerged in Cape Town.

Our Africanness. The challenge before the Circle was to devise cultural hermeneutics* at once critical and affirming, so as to uphold our Africanness, including our religious and cultural heritage. We needed a language that would not allow the West to continue its calumnies of Africa but that would allow us to explore, expose, and work for the transformation of what prevents women in African cultures from experiencing the fullness of life. In the process, we had to challenge partners, such as Western women theologians, to shed their racist and patronizing approaches to African women's issues. We are not "objects" of their academic pursuit or collaborators in the projects they designed. Indeed, many Western women friends of the Circle have joined us in our quest for mutual respect and a liberative interdependence, respecting the uniqueness of our quest in the context of the global women's movements.

The rhetoric of working with and not for people, and of opening doors for participation in decision making is agreed upon by all the women associated with the Circle. Yet an Akan proverb says, "It is one person who hunts down an elephant to feed the whole village." Indeed, active participation by women theologians involves overcoming many obstacles: difficult communication; low financial income; nonsupportive or antagonistic spouses; responsibilities for the care of young children and old people; objections of church leaders to women doing their own thinking; and publishing houses and foundations who presume to determine what constitutes African women's issues. Yet all women of the Circle are initiators and growers.

This collectively lived story has taught us the necessity of staying open to change. To be of service to real life, we need to be relevant to changing contexts. Flexibility is a strength, not a weakness. From a vision of an elite group of academic theologians, we became a broadly based group of women doing theology. The sharply defined objectives of African women doing theology are a prism through which new social, cultural, and religious issues can be viewed, e.g. women's health arising from research into cultural practices that has metamorphosed into a full-blown focus on HIV and AIDS.

We have also learned that, in an interdependent world, reciprocity is not just offering the other exactly what the other offers you or complementing what the other has. Reciprocity is what is done in a way that honors, respects, and enhances the humanity of the other. The question "What is in it for me?" is a real one. When the community flourishes, we as individuals will flourish; but to achieve this community enhancement, we must insist that our individuality and humanity and gifts be accepted and respected, as we in turn accept those of others.

MERCY AMBA ODUYOYE

Theology as Human Undertaking: North Atlantic Theologians Doing Theology: A Dialogue between Text and Context. Theology, whatever else may be said of it, is an undertaking of *human beings*. Theologians hope to be "inspired" by revelatory truth transcending their grasp, but by the same token they may not claim for their own work ultimate veracity. As finite (and sinful*) creatures, theologians "see through a glass darkly" (1Cor 13:12), and the lens through which they look at reality is shaped by concrete factors in their own personal and societal situations. They contemplate the meaning of the Christian faith as persons who live at particular moments in history and specific geopolitical situations and who bring to this vocation assumptions, values, and concerns they have acquired as persons of those times and places.

This does not mean that theological work is determined solely by the circumstances in which it is undertaken; for it is of the essence of this calling in its authentic expressions that it implies a highly critical dimension. That is, far from merely reflecting the context in which it occurs and that it wishes to address, theology understood in the Christian mode intends to engage its context from a perspective that it does not derive directly from the context as such. That perspective it gains from what it may call "the gospel*" or "the Christian message" or *kerygma**, as this "good news" is transmitted to the faithful (transmitted "from faith to faith,*" as Paul says; Rom 1:17) through the Scriptures*, traditions*, and present witness of the Christian community under the impact of the divine Spirit.

Theology is thus an ongoing dialogue between "text" and "context." The "text" (which includes but is not exhausted by the scriptural text) constitutes the revelatory source of the theologian's witness and illumines his or her discernment of the "context"; the context, in turn, conditions the theologian's reception or "reading" of the text and determines the emphases and general disposition of his or her articulation of the faith*.

While this dialectic (text/context) has always been covertly present in Christian theology, it is only within the past few decades that it has become conspicuous and (for many Christian thinkers) intentional. Partly as a consequence of post-Enlightenment* historical consciousness and partly as a result of the movement of Christianity beyond its traditional Eurocentric base, the contextual character of all theological-ethical reflection has been seen to be decisive in a new way. A faith that intends to engage its "world" cannot and must not be everywhere and at all times the same, for our "worlds" are diverse. Times differ: what perceptive theologians (e.g. Karl Barth*) had to say *after* World War II was significantly different from their messages before the war. But places also differ: what is "gospel" for the possessing peoples of the earth is not necessarily gospel for the dispossessed! Too often in the past, what was advanced as eternal and unchanging Christian truth served to obscure the vested interests of the powerful who proclaimed it and to perpetuate the status quo of the less powerful who heard it.

This recognition of the fact that contexts play a decisive role in theological work has meant a new openness on the part of thoughtful Christians everywhere to the development of theologies emerging quite explicitly out of a variety of sociocultural contexts, especially contexts (whether geographic or identity based) that heretofore have seemed content to be guided by theological trends emanating from the old Euro-American flagship of Christendom. An observer of "theological *Existenz*" today would have to speak not about Christian "theology" but about Christian *theologies*. In a real sense, "theology" has become an abstract term. What actually exists are various theologies, accounts of the meaning and direction of Christian faith and life emanating from the spiritual crises and yearnings of identifiable groups within the global church.

Serious Christians ought to welcome this development, for it is a consequence of the realization that the Christian message can be "good news" only if it is appropriated by human beings in their always-specific times and places. Theological "absolutes" have always implied the imposition on others of the alleged truths of the most dominant groups in Christendom. At the same time, the obvious danger of the rampant proliferation of theologies that are answerable to no core of meaning or authority* means that all Christians are obliged today to wrestle the more seriously with "the text" and – perhaps even more important – to pursue a vital ecumenical* discourse that ensures the dialogue of differing theologies with one another.

DOUGLAS JOHN HALL

Theopaschitism, the view that Christ, as divine, suffered and was crucified, and thus that God suffered on the cross. It arose from the Miaphysite* emphasis that the Incarnation* brought a real and permanent union between human and divine ("one incarnate nature of the divine Word"). Against Theopaschitism the Second Council of Constantinople* (553) affirmed that Christ was "crucified *in the flesh,*" but his divinity was free of suffering.

Theophany (Gk "appearance of God"). The OT speaks of God appearing to the patriarchs and matriarchs (e.g. Abraham and Sarah, Gen 17–18; Hagar, Gen 16:7), Moses (e.g. Exod 19), and the people of Israel (e.g. Ps 48) in visible form. Such passages were interpreted in the early church as temporary manifestations of the Logos*, which later becomes incarnate*. For the Eastern Orthodox* Church, the Feast of Theophany celebrating the divine manifestation in Jesus' baptism corresponds to the Epiphany* in Western churches. **See also REVELATION.**

Theophilus (Gk "loved by God"), addressee of the Gospel of Luke* (Luke 1:3) and the Acts* of the Apostles (Acts 1:1).

Theophilus of Alexandria (d412), patriarch of Alexandria (385–412). He took an active role in suppressing paganism, encouraging the destruction of the Serapeum (391). In the controversy over anthropomorphism*, he opposed the Origenist* position that God does not have human form. When the Tall* Brothers found refuge with John* Chrysostom, Theophilus used his influence to have him deposed at the Synod of the Oak*. His nephew Cyril* succeeded him and was similarly effective in asserting the power of Alexandria against Constantinople.

Theophilus of Antioch (late 2nd c.). His sole surviving work is the apology addressed to Autolycus, arguing for creation through the Logos*. He first stated the view (soon adopted by Irenaeus* and later by Augustine*) that Adam* and Eve* were created with the capacity for either mortality or immortality, depending on their response to God's command.

Theosis, Deification, "participation in the divine nature" (2 Pet 1:4), through immediate relationship to God, making the knower like the known. Irenaeus* wrote, "The glory of God is humanity fully alive; the life of human beings is the vision of God" (*Adv. haer.* 4.20.7). Athanasius* wrote, "God became human that human might become God." "Theosis" refers to the transforming effect of grace* (having a God-like life) emphasized by Greek patristic writers, Eastern Orthodox* theology, and the Oxford* Movement. What Christ was by nature through the Incarnation* humans can become by grace*, when they are thoroughly united in body and soul with the will and energies of God. **See also ETHICS AND CHRISTIANITY CLUSTER: IN EASTERN ORTHODOXY.**

B. MARK SIETSEMA

Theosophy (Gk "wisdom about divine things"). The term, found in Greek magical papyri (verbal formulas used to compel deities to perform certain actions), was adopted by the Neoplatonists* and their Christian followers. It was also applied to speculations like those of Boehme* about the generation of all things from God.

Theotokos (Gk God-bearer), the title given to Mary in the Eastern Orthodox* (Chalcedonian) and Oriental Orthodox* (non-Chalcedonian) churches since the christological* controversies of the 5th c. over the Incarnation*. **See also MARY, THE VIRGIN, CLUSTER: THEOTOKOS.**

Therapeutae, Jewish monastic community near Alexandria, possibly a branch of the Essenes*, reported by Philo* in *De vita contemplativa* (1st c. CE). Eusebius* thought that Philo must have been describing the early Christian Church in Egypt*. In fact the community is an indication that monasticism* had pre-Christian roots.

Thérèse of Lisieux (1873–97), Carmelite* nun, spiritual author, canonized (1925). The youngest of nine children of a prosperous family in Normandy, Thérèse had a happy early childhood until her mother's death (1877), which initiated for her a period of weariness and religious obsession, a "winter of trial." The family moved to Lisieux (1881). As a student in the Benedictine Abbey school, Thérèse was seriously ill (1883); she was healed and believed her cure was miraculous. On Christmas 1886, she experienced "conversion." Henceforth, she had an intense interest in the apostolate, desiring to suffer for God, and planned to enter the Carmelite convent in Lisieux, where her two older sisters were already nuns. Because she was too young, Thérèse and her father made a pilgrimage to Rome, where she was presented to Leo XIII, who assured her she would enter the convent if it was God's will. She did (1888), with the name Thérèse de l'Enfant Jésus et de la Sainte Face. Intensely faithful to the rule of the order, she concentrated on her prayer life. Appointed mistress of novices (1893), she articulated her "Little Way," "feeling and acting under the discipline of virtue as a child feels and acts by nature" (Pius XI). She became ill with tuberculosis (1896), and in her last months, realizing she had a mission to teach others her "Little Way," she asked her sister to collect and edit her writings: *History of a Soul*, which became an immediate success. YVES KRUMENACKER

Thessalonians, 1 and 2 Epistles to. 1 Thessalonians, Paul's* first extant letter (c50), encourages an assembly (*ekklesia*, church) confronted with believers' deaths (4:13–18) and persecutions by other Thessalonians (2:14–16). Subsequently, 2 Thessalonians (uncertain date; written by Paul or a successor) reaffirms the teaching of the first letter and challenges enthusiastic apocalypticism*, which engenders community alarm (2:1–2) and social disorder (3:6–12).

In Thessalonica, the capital of the Roman province of Macedonia where most Thessalonians cultivated the beneficence of Roman patrons, Paul's gospel about a commitment to an exclusive patron (God) met with "great opposition" (2:2–12). After leaving Thessalonica, a painful separation for Paul, and after Timothy's visit (2:17–3:5), Paul exhorts the Thessalonians to maintain exclusive commitment to their new "patron," despite opposition (2:14–16) and death (4:13).

Their negative experiences are redefined in light of apocalyptic* traditions of resistance; the present time is a counterconventional eschatological* era; believers await the Parousia*; benefits (including resurrection*, 1 Thess 4:13–17, 5:9–10) accrue to believers, not from local and Roman imperial cults, but from exclusive devotion to God, their new patron (1 Thess 1:9–10; 5:3). An ethic of solidarity, shared values, and moral transformation (1 Thess 4:1–8; 4:18; 5:11, 12–22) – including independence from conventional, pro-Roman networks of power (1 Thess 4:9–12) – connect believers to an international countercultural network of *ekklesiai* (1 Thess 1:7, 2:14, 4:10).

2 Thessalonians presupposes the earlier opposition and affirms the interpretation of the assembly's persecution in the light of apocalyptic traditions (1:5–10), but counters alarmist and enthusiastic interpretations that could mitigate the effectiveness of Paul's earlier teachings (2:1–12, 3:6–15).

Augustine*, Thomas Aquinas*, and Calvin* drew from 1 Thessalonians ideas about the Parousia, the resurrection of believers, and the immortality of the soul*. Darby* and conservative Christians based beliefs in Millennialism* and in a "rapture" on 1 Thess 4:17. References in 2 Thess 2:3–4 to a "man of sin" (2:3–4, 6–10) led to speculation about the "Antichrist*" from Irenaeus* to Ambrosiaster*, Jerome*, John* Chrysostom, Theodore* of Mopsuestia, Augustine, and medieval, Reformation*, and modern leaders. ABRAHAM SMITH

Third Orders and Tertiary. Religious organizations affiliated with one of the mendicant* orders. The first order is for men under vows, the second for women under vows; the third order, which grew out of the Lay* Piety Movement, was for laypeople living in the world, usually with distinctive dress. The Beguines* survived the condemnations at the Council of Vienne* (1312) by becoming Third Order Dominicans* or Franciscans*. Today the Dominican and Franciscan sisters who are not cloistered but engage in service and education are either third order regulars* (under vows) or secular tertiaries (not under vows).

Thirty-nine Articles of Religion. During Elizabeth I's reign, an edited form of the Forty*-two became Thirty-eight in 1562, by omitting the last four Articles (dealing largely with Anabaptist and Millennialist* "heresies*"). Though adopted by the Convocations*, these had not yet been approved by the queen when the pope excommunicated her (1570). She then authorized the Articles, and a new Article 29 ("Of the Wicked which eat not the Body of Christ in the use of the Lord's Supper") was added, reinforcing the "receptionist*" doctrine of the sacraments*. This collection became the Thirty-nine Articles of 1571.

The Articles were taken as an authoritative confession of faith (see Creeds, Symbols, and Confessions of Faith) and a measure of orthodoxy* in the Elizabethan and Stuart reigns. Subscription to them was required by the Canons* of 1604. The relevant canons were revised in 1865, although the form of subscription to the Articles remained rigorous. In England the new Declaration of Assent (1975) relocated the Articles as a historic "witness" to the faith of the Church of England, rather than as expressing the personal faith of the individuals. The Articles had meanwhile gone to the far ends of the earth and had been incorporated with differing requirements of assent into the constitutions of many Anglican provinces. **See also ANGLICANISM CLUSTER.**

BISHOP COLIN O. BUCHANAN

Thirty Years' War (1618–48), a destructive war that involved most of the European powers. In many ways a confrontation between Protestants and Roman Catholics, it was directed chiefly against the Hapsburgs in Germany*, Austria*, the Netherlands*, and Spain*, and Catholic France* was allied with Protestant powers. It began with a rebellion in Bohemia, but the attempt to replace a Catholic by a Protestant ruler was crushed (James I of England refused to aid his son-in-law); Protestantism was extirpated in Bohemia, and the Palatinate was invaded by French and German forces (1622–23). Denmark* then entered the conflict and was defeated. When the emperor (of the Holy* Roman Empire) decreed a return to the religious situation before the Peace of Augsburg* (1555), Protestantism was threatened, and Sweden* intervened, securing Northern Germany (1630–32). Although a peace that satisfied most German princes was agreed upon (1635), France renewed the war in order to weaken the Hapsburgs; fighting spread to most of Europe, and much of Germany was devastated. Peace negotiations over a period of eight years finally led to the Peace of Westphalia* (1648), which had a lasting impact on European diplomacy, strengthening the territorial state and reducing the role of religion in international affairs.

Thomas, disciple and apostle, mentioned in all four Gospels; also called Didymus (John 11:16, 20:24, 21:2), which, like Thomas, means "Twin." He is depicted as doubting and then confessing (John 20:24–29), a feature that also appears in apocryphal accounts of the bodily assumption of Mary (*De Obitu S. Dominae, De Transitu Virginis*). Tradition linked him with Edessa, Parthia, and India, where the church claims him as its founder. At his legendary place of martyrdom in Mylapur (India), there is a stone cross (6th–8th c.).

Thomas, Acts of. This Apocryphal* Acts is the only one preserved in its entirety. Although its original text, probably in Syriac, has been lost, a Greek translation and a Syriac rewriting for Orthodox service remain.

This work most likely originated from several legend narratives but seeks to present a unified work focused on one character, Thomas*, Jesus' twin brother, his life, ministry, and martyrdom. It was probably written in the 3rd c. CE in eastern Syria, perhaps in Edessa, the location of Egeria*'s (*Pilgrimage*, 17.1, 19.2) visit to Thomas's tomb a century later. The Acts of Thomas was appreciated by the Manichaeans* and despised by Orthodox Christians. The Manichaean Psalter* of the early 4th c. CE is the earliest reference to the Acts of Thomas. Soon after, Christian adversaries of the Apocryphal Acts of Apostles, figures such as Epiphanius* of Salamis, Augustine* of Hippo, Philastrius of Brescia, and Turribius of Astorga, mention and condemn the book.

The work is composed of three main parts. Acts 1–2 present as an introduction the legend of the apostle, who was sold as a slave to a merchant and eventually became an architect for the king Gundaphor of India*. Acts 3–8 unfurl two parallel series of miracles, and finally Acts 9–14 tell the story of the apostle's martyrdom.

The Acts of Thomas depicts an ascetic* form of Christianity present in eastern Syria. It contains important liturgical material that contributes to an understanding of the baptismal rite in that part of the ancient world. Other typical expressions of early Syriac* Christianity are demonstrated in the text's "Hymn to the Bride" and the "Hymn of the Pearl."

FRANÇOIS BOVON

Thomas, Gospel of, one of the Coptic Gospels (the second treatise in the second codex of Nag* Hammadi), divided by modern scholars into 114 "sayings of Jesus." There are a few dialogical elements but virtually no narrative framing. Its composition is attributed to the apostle "Didymus Judas Thomas," i.e. "Judas the twin" (brother of Jesus; see Mark 6:3).

The Coptic text, discovered in 1945, is a translation produced in Egypt (c300). Some patristic writers mention and quote a Gospel of Thomas. The papyri *Logia Iesou* in Greek (published 1897) are fragments of the Gospel of Thomas: POxy 654 corresponds to Thomas 1–7; POxy 1 (from c200) to Thomas 26–60, 77b, 31–33; and POxy 655 to Thomas 24, 36–39. The Greek version reflects an older stage of the tradition-history. According to cautious scholars, an early form of the Gospel of Thomas was written in Syria c120–140; some scholars argue for a much earlier date, c50–70.

The Gospel of Thomas includes sapiential, prophetic, and "I"-sayings of Jesus; metaphors* and parables*; beatitudes*; cries of lamentation; proverbs; words of law; and community ordinances. Roughly 50% of the sayings have parallels in the Synoptic* Gospels but also in John (cf. Thomas 77 and John 8:12; 1:3) and Paul (cf. Thomas 17 and 1 Cor 2:9). The question of dependence is controversial and has to be decided on a case-by-case basis. Sometimes Thomas adopts typical features of one of the Synoptic Gospels, thus indicating that the writer is familiar with them. But there are also independent sayings (including some parables [cf. Thomas 97–98]), as well as sayings with an unmistakable Gnostic* flavor (cf. 28, 50).

These traditions are often cast in a provocatively enigmatic style (Thomas 7). The reader, privy to esoteric knowledge, is meant to detect the hidden meaning of these sayings and thus find true (spiritual) life (1). Thomas is clearly established as the real leader of the apostles (13). The role of the individual believer is emphasized, while that of the community is diminished (cf POxy 1, 23–27 and Matt 18:29). Ritual praxis is viewed with skepticism (Thomas 6, 104).

Sayings about the inner presence of the Kingdom* of God in Thomas 3 and 113 frame the Gospel of Thomas and form a recurrent theme. The much-discussed saying 114 about "making Mary* [Magdalene] male" intends to reestablish a primordial unity (22) that includes resurrection* and salvation*. The Gospel of Thomas clearly propagates an alternative vision of Christian life; thus its later Coptic form was most likely preserved among monastic* circles in Egypt.

HANS-JOSEF KLAUCK

Thomas, Infancy Gospel of, late-2nd-c. narrative with episodes from the life of Jesus between the ages of 5 and 12 (often called *paidika* in manuscripts). The work exists in three different Greek recensions and in translations (some with additional material, such as the Slavonic version). The attribution to the apostle Thomas* is probably an interpolation.

The Infancy Gospel of Thomas quotes the nucleus from which the whole work grew: the story about the 12-year-old Jesus in the Temple (Luke 2:41–52). New material fills the gap from Jesus' birth. The NT supplies expressions and personal names, patterns of speech, and narrative motifs. Some stories imitate the accounts of healing and raising of the dead in the canonical Gospels and Acts. The repeated emphasis on the efficacy of Jesus' words and a repetition of motifs (e.g. Jesus outdoing a total of three teachers in disputations) structure the loosely connected individual scenes. The vivid style is sometimes interrupted by Jesus' profound words (e.g. his "trinitarian" exegesis of the letter "A"). These tales of an "arrogant divine child" (Cullmann's phrase) meet certain cultural expectations. Biographies in antiquity tended to see their heroes' future deeds presaged in their youth. Thus the boy Jesus is shown as a great wonderworker and superior teacher: God is already recognized in the child. **See also APOCRYPHAL GOSPELS.**

HANS-JOSEF KLAUCK

Thomas, Madathilparampil Mammen (M. M.) (1916–96), a layperson from Kerala, India, along with Paul Devanandan and D. T. Niles*, was seminal in shaping the ecumenical* movement and the theological conversation in South Asia. A self-educated theologian, Thomas shaped global theology by paying close attention to the interplay of theology and his local context of India*.

Thomas, a contextual* theologian, believed Jesus Christ was the hermeneutical* key to helping Christians understand and relate to the issues of their world. The two critical interrelated issues of India and elsewhere in Thomas's time were nation building and religious pluralism*. In such a context, it was important for Christians to bring their unique vision into conversation with persons of other faiths in order to create a vision of the nations that was for the betterment of all.

Thomas articulated his vision through the ecumenical movement. He was a strong influence in the World Student Christian Federation (as secretary and later vice chairmen, 1947–53). He contributed to the formation of the Department of Church and Society of the World* Council of Churches and was a member of it (1961–68); and he was the moderator of the Council's Central Committee (1968–75).

DAMAYANTHI M. A. NILES

Thomas Aquinas. See AQUINAS, THOMAS.

Thomas Christians, members of a Christian community in Kerala, on the Malabar coast in Southwest India*. They claim to have been founded by the apostle Thomas*. **See also MALABAR CHRISTIANS.**

Thomas à Kempis, Thomas Hemerken (c1380–1471), spiritual writer. Born in Kempen and educated at Deventer by the Brethren* of the Common Life, he joined the Augustinian* canons (1399) and was ordained a priest (c1409). He was well known both as a copyist and as an author; *The Imitation* of Christ,* which bears his name, may be based on writings by Geert Groote*, edited and translated into Latin by Thomas.

Thomas Mass, a Holy Communion service celebrated on Sunday evenings in Helsinki (where it originated in 1988), throughout Finland*, other parts of Scandinavia*, and Germany*. It is at once a service for doubters and unaffiliated people, a form of evangelization*, and sacramental* worship centered on a festal eucharistic celebration. The liturgy incorporates old liturgical traditions, the spirit of ecumenism, an emphasis on lay activity, and contemporary popular music. With this variety of spiritual traditions, Thomas Mass addresses the needs of very different people. It is an urban form of worship in an atmosphere of pluralism* and religious uncertainty.

HEIKKI KOTILA

Thomism. Thomas Aquinas completed his second three-year appointment at the University of Paris in 1272, returned to Naples to teach Scripture to junior Dominican* friars, but died in March 1274. Thomism, the theological movement based on his work and expanding it, slowly emerged.

Soon after his death, his secretary, Reginald of Piperno, "completed" the *Summa Theologiae* on which he was working, by incorporating much earlier material. Perhaps surprisingly, Aquinas left no "disciples," no "school." On the contrary, as early as 1270, proscription by the bishop of Paris of 13 problematic theses allegedly taught in the arts faculty cast an unfavorable light on the use of Aristotle* that Aquinas more than anyone was responsible for introducing into theological discourse. In 1277 more extensive lists of supposedly Aristotelian positions were proscribed, in Paris but also at Oxford, with the authority of the archbishop of Canterbury, himself a Dominican friar.

By 1286, however, the Dominicans* seem to have felt obliged to defend their confrere in an atmosphere of misgivings and suspicions about his ideas. The Franciscans* in particular contended that certain Aristotelian ideas undermined the legacy of theological orthodoxy inherited especially from Augustine*. Their worries revolved round Aquinas's claim that, since the doctrine of creation* has to do with the world's total dependence on God, the world might have existed from eternity and yet be created; Aquinas's insistence on the role of the senses in the acquisition of knowledge (ruling out direct divine illumination); and his characterization of the soul* as the one and only substantial form of the body (hylomorphism, against the traditional conception of the plurality of forms in the human person, e.g. corporeal, vegetative, intellectual). A handful of theologians began to defend Aquinas's doctrine of the superiority of reason* over will*. They reacted against the dominant Franciscan doctrine of the self-determination of the will* (voluntarism) in John Duns* Scotus and then William* Ockham. This reaction eventually settled down into an identifiably "Thomistic" philosophical anthropology* and, by extension, an anti-voluntaristic doctrine of God*.

In Italy, by the mid-15th c., a humanistic Christian moral theology, clearly indebted to Aquinas's integration of Aristotle's *Ethics,* was being developed by Dominicans (Antoninus of Florence, 1379–1459). In Germany the Neoplatonist* elements in Aquinas were incorporated into the apophatic* theology of Meister Eckhart* (d1328). By 1409 the Dominican John Capreolus (1380–1444) had inaugurated the first comprehensive presentation of Thomist theology. The *Summa Theologiae* became the standard textbook for professors of theology, especially in universities where Dominicans taught. A school of Northern Italian Thomists, again mostly Dominicans, contributed significantly to the development of 16th-c. Renaissance humanism.

Erasmus* disparaged Aquinas's theology on the grounds that it was composed at a time when theologians were generally ignorant of Greek and Hebrew. On the other hand, Thomas de Vio Cajetan, an Italian Dominican, composed an exposition of the *Summa Theologiae,* which would be included at the foot of each page in the critical edition commissioned by Pope Leo* XIII (late 19th c.). During the deliberations of the Council of Trent*, Aquinas's theology was treated as a benchmark, especially with regard to the distinction between nature* and grace*; the doctrine of justification*; the conception of the human person as a true secondary cause, with no room for alleged competition between human and divine freedom; the sacraments* as instrumental causes that effect what they signify *ex opere operato* (and thus are not dependent on human will); the doctrine of transubstantiation* at the eucharistic consecration (neither annihilation of the bread and wine nor merely symbolic presence of Christ's body and blood); the doctrine of eternal life as consisting in seeing God face to face; and much else. While it is not true that the *Summa Theologiae* was placed side by side with the Bible on the altar at the Council of Trent, nevertheless in 1567, Pope Pius V, himself a Dominican, ranked Aquinas among the four major doctors of the church, which gave theology "according to the mind of Saint Thomas," *secundum mentem Sancti Thomae*, quasi-official status in the Roman Catholic Church. In the 17th c., especially on the Spanish peninsula, Thomists composed commentaries on Aquinas's treatment of the gifts of the Holy* Spirit, while others elaborated on Aquinas's positions on natural justice* to allow for properly humane and Christian treatment of the indigenous peoples whom Europeans found in Central and Latin America. In the mid-19th c., in response to what was perceived to be an abandonment of respect for reason, Aquinas's arguments for the existence of God and his conception of the natural moral law gave rise to a widely taught natural* theology and natural law ethics, which, for better or worse, began to dissipate in the second half of the 20th c., freeing Aquinas (as many would think) from the burden of being studied through any form of Thomism. **See also AQUINAS, THOMAS.** FERGUS KERR

Thomson, James (1788–1854), British colporteur who distributed the Bible in Mexico*, where he arrived in 1827 from Argentina*; he was sponsored by the British and Foreign Bible Society.

MARÍA ALICIA PUENTE LUTTEROTH and ELIZABETH JUDD

Thou. See I–THOU RELATION.

Three Chapters ("three headings") include (1) Theodore* of Mopsuestia's writings, (2) Theodoret's* writings against Cyril, and (3) Ibas's* letter to Maris. These pro-Chalcedonian writings were at the center of a 6th-c. attempt to find middle ground in the controversy between "Diphysites"* (Chalcedonians)*, who affirmed two natures in Christ, and "Miaphysites,"* who, following Cyril*, affirmed one nature. Ibas and Theodoret had been condemned at the Second Council of Ephesus* (449) but vindicated at Chalcedon (451); Justinian* moved closer to Cyril's language, while claiming to remain faithful to Chalcedon. Justinian condemned the Three Chapters (544), as did the Second Council of Constantinople* (551). Pope Vigilius*, under pressure, twice affirmed these condemnations (547, 553). Large portions of the Western* Church in Africa, Spain, and Northern Italy broke communion with Rome and Constantinople, buttressing their argument with Latin translations of many crucial sections of the Three Chapters, influencing later Western thought about the person of Christ. **See also FACUNDUS OF HERMIANE.**

Threefold Office of the Church. See POLITY.

Three-Self Principle and Patriotic Movement in China. The three goals of self-government, self-support, and self-propagation were initially implemented through the development of independent Chinese churches in the late 19th c. The "three-self principle" was officially endorsed by the General Conference of Chinese Protestant Churches in Shanghai (1922) and the National Christian Council of China (1922). After the establishment of the People's Republic of China, the "Three-Self Patriotic Movement" was founded (1950) to assure the government of the churches' patriotism and became a governmental agency functioning as a tool for governmental supervision of the churches. To avoid this supervision, many house churches do not register with it. **See also CHINA; CHINESE CONTEMPORARY INDEPENDENT AND HOUSE CHURCHES.**

Thurman, Howard (1900–81), was born in Daytona Beach, Florida, reared in a nurturing home, attended the Black Church, and was spiritually enlivened by the beauty of nature. A graduate of Morehouse College and recipient of a Ph.D. from Boston University, Thurman was professor of theology and dean of Rankin Chapel at Howard University (1932–44). He gained world recognition as the dean of Marsh Chapel at Boston University (1953–65). Thurman did not fit easily into any academic specialization. He cultivated a spirituality that many regarded as an "activistic" mysticism*. Fundamental to his Christian spirituality was the concept of encounter. The human–divine relation is always an encounter mediated by personality, a direct subject-to-subject relation. The principle of personality is universal. As cofounder of the Church for the Fellowship of All People, Thurman embodied this principle in his commitment to race* relations, ecumenism*, and interreligious reconciliation*. Among his enduring works are *Jesus and the Disinherited* (1949), *The*

Creative Encounter (1954), *The Luminous Darkness* (1965), *The Search for Common Ground* (1971), and *For the Inward Journey* (1984).

VICTOR ANDERSON

Tiara, originally a Persian raised headdress or Phrygian cap, adopted by the pope (8th c.); three crowns were successively added (14th c.).

Tikhon, Patriarch (Vasily Ivanovich Bellavin, 1865–1925), monk, priest, bishop, patriarch (1917) of the Russian Orthodox Church. Tikhon's election as patriarch was the pinnacle of an illustrious career in the Russian Church. He was the first to hold the patriarchy since it had been disbanded by Peter I in 1700. Tikhon, however, presided over the Church during a period of great upheaval – the 1917 Bolshevik Revolution. He was imprisoned and constantly harassed for alleged anti-Soviet activity until his death. He was canonized as a saint in 1989.

ROY R. ROBSON

Tillich, Paul (1886–1965), theologian, born and educated in Germany, ordained Lutheran minister (1912), chaplain during World War I. He taught in Germany (1918–33) until dismissed because he opposed the Nazi regime, then at Union Theological Seminary (New York), Harvard University, and the University of Chicago (1933–65).

"A man on the boundary" was Tillich's definition of himself – on the boundary between essence and existence, church and world, memory and hope*, transcendence and immanence, or "Catholic substance" and "Protestant* principle." One of the most prolific theologians of his time, he invented a new way of doing theology: by "outsourcing" it (a term he did not use). He talked about religion* and culture*, each outsourcing itself in the other: as the ultimate concern, religion is the substance of culture and culture gives form to religion. The realm to which both religion and culture belong is the symbol*, each of its two parts outsourcing itself in the other. No outsourcing, no symbol – and no ultimate concern. There is no way, either, of correlating symbol and that which is symbolized, no method by which to test theology and its relevance – as Tillich made plain by writing *Systematic Theology* (3 vols., 1951–63), which was organized around this correlation.

In a century whose every field of inquiry underwent a radical mutation, Tillich spearheaded the long overdue scrubbing of theological language. Combining antiquity and modernity, myth* and technology*, secularization* and the death* of God, Tillich's method of correlation sharpened the focus of his quest for a new religious paradigm fit for a world characterized by the porosity of religious and cultural traditions.

On the boundary, Tillich was torn between his Lutheran heritage and the still predominantly Calvinistic* orientation of his US refuge. Torn between Catholic substance and Protestant principle (*Protestant Era,* 1948), the aesthetic* and the ethical* (*Morality and Beyond,* 1963), being and speaking, he was both irresistibly beckoned by one prong and fascinated by the other. The traditional coupling of religion (sacred) and culture (profane) is subverted by the iconoclastic* dialectic of the holy* and the not-yet-holy, i.e. of the religious and the secular* (*Theology of Culture,* 1959). Whatever might be the language in which one dwells, Tillich switched the symbol of this language from its traditional housing in (sacred) music to (secular) architecture: there is no church in the New Jerusalem (*On Art and Architecture,* 1987). The universalism proclaimed by today's world religion, East or West, is henceforth subject to what is common to them all – not the religious, but the secular (*Christianity and the Encounter of the World Religions,* 1963).

This inference shows that the method of correlation is so construed that the symbolic demythologization*, or ethical desacralization, or metaphysical deconstruction hanging on one prong affects the other, theology. Theology, obligated to "the eternal truth of its foundation," must speak to "the temporal [secular] situation in which its truth is received." Having no language of its own, theology is apologetic* more than kerygmatic*; it deals no less with penultimate concerns than with the ultimate concern to which they point. Holding that human beings ask questions to which they have no answer, Tillich also holds that being has primacy over speaking. The ultimate concern – faith* (*Dynamics of Faith,* 1957) – is not properly framed unless the substance of the answer is independent, though the form itself is not, nor need be, independent of the question. The Unconditioned (God) has no condition other than a human condition.

A figure of that condition is Jesus as the Christ. "Christ" is an eschatological* designation, and Tillich never forgets that the quest of the Kingdom* need result neither in "religious devaluation of nature" nor in "naturalistic devaluation of religion." No "enemy of salvation," nature partakes of history, even of salvation* and its symbolics, although Tillich admits he thought of calling for a moratorium on the idea of salvation. Instead, nature being involved in human fall, Tillich's substitute for a sacrificial* Christology is sketched in his scheme of a nature-friendly Christology of which salvation* is and remains the matrix. Through the Incarnation*, God participates in what is estranged from God, yet God remains God.

God* is "being-itself." This only nonsymbolic statement means that, although the fundamental symbol of our ultimate concern is God, God is not merely a symbol, nor is God the only symbol. God is not this or that kind of highest being, but the ground of being and no less personal for not being a particular person. Beyond the contrast of essential and existential being, God is the power of being, i.e. of the "at-onement*" of the divine and the human. God's quest, which is essential to human beings in quest of being human, becomes historical in Jesus as the Christ. The human on the boundary is the New Being in Christ, the being for whom the boundary is what, always, lies ahead.

GABRIEL VAHANIAN

Time. Events occur and then perish; future events are awaited, occur, and perish. All that is "real" is the fleeting present. Yet past events can continue to have an influence through their effects, or through the memory of those who have participated, or through writings that recount them. Future events can influence the present through hope* or fear. Augustine* (*Confessions*, 11th book) notes both the transitoriness of events and the "presence" of the past through memory, the "presence" of the future through anticipation. He knows that the passage of time can be measured by the movement of the heavenly bodies or by clocks (primitive as they were in his day compared with the mechanical clocks of the late Middle Ages or digital clocks). What chiefly interests Augustine, however, is our *awareness* of time through memory and anticipation; he calls it a "distention" or stretching of the mind, the persistence of consciousness through many fleeting moments. In addition to this subjective awareness of time, however, there is also the *pathos* of time: not only do we know that events are constantly passing, but we have specific regrets about, or fond memories of, the past and fears, sometimes vague and sometimes precise, about the future. In Greek, *chronos*, measured time, was differentiated from *kairos*, the time of temptation, opportunity, or fulfillment.

All peoples have tried to impose order on the passage of time through the repetition of ceremonies during the cycles of the day, the year*, or the seven-day week, so that new events will not be totally unexpected but can be interpreted, perhaps even ritually influenced, by what is familiar from the past. Ancient Israel not only looked to decisive events in the past (especially the Exodus* and Sinai*) but anticipated future events, e.g. "the day of the Lord" (Amos 5:18–20), "the year of God's favor" (Isa 61:2), and eventually a definitive judgment* and fulfillment (see Eschatology Cluster). When there is hope for life and fulfillment after death – often called "eternal life" – this is understood to be an overcoming of the hazards of temporality, an enjoyment of God without fear of loss, without vulnerability.

The early Christian message added an "already" to this "not yet," avowing that the time of fulfillment had already come, that "now is the day of salvation" (2 Cor 6:2), the time of the "new* creation" (Isa 43:19, 65:17; 2 Cor 5:17; Gal 6:15), that one's response to Christ would affect one's entire destiny (see Justification, Theological Views and Practice, Cluster). While the early church thought of itself as still living in the "old age" and anticipating the "age to come," increasingly it thought of itself as living in the time of fulfillment and eventually began dating events "before" and "after" Christ (Dionysius* Exiguus, c470–c544, invented the *anno Domini* era).

In the Bible, there is an awareness not only that God does not change as the world changes (Ps 90:2; Isa 40:6–8), but that God's purposes extend from the past into the future (since God is the everlasting God; Gen 21:33; Isa 40:28) and are sovereign over the events in the world.

As lord over time, God brings into transitory time the divine promise of salvation*, redemption*, righteousness*, and covenant* (Isa 40:8; 45:17; 51:6, 8; 55:3), which transcends time. Christ's eucharistic* presence (however understood) is associated with both past and future: the present moment is constituted by both the memory and the anticipation of the church.

Then how should one understand eternity*? What does it mean to say that God is "eternal"? Originally it seems to have meant that God is everlasting, without beginning or end. Increasingly, it came to mean that God is timeless, atemporal, beholding all moments of time in a single eternal "now." Boethius* gave the classic definition of eternity as "the total, simultaneous, and perfect possession of an unlimited life."

Modern theologians have tended to move away from this notion on the grounds that it makes God's purposes static rather than living; God's experience, they suggest, may be temporal, but without the vulnerabilities of finite beings. Yet with Kierkegaard*, they often emphasize the Christian paradox* that the infinite God has become a finite human. Latin American Liberation* theologians go further in their affirmation of the Incarnation* as God assuming both temporality and vulnerability. Process* theology has affirmed the positive aspects of seeing God as related to, and thus affected by, events in the world rather than aloof from them.

Theologians from non-European cultures (including Native* American theologians) have noted that under the influence of Western European cultures, Christian theologies give a central role to temporality and history*, leading to a clash (rather than an inculturated* dialogue*) with cultures that give a central role to spatiality. EUGENE TESELLE

Timor-Leste. The Portuguese colonized the island of Timor in the mid-16th c. After a military clash, Portugal surrendered West Timor to the Dutch (1859). The Portuguese ruled East Timor ("Timor-Leste") until 1975 (except from 1942 to 1945, the period of Japanese occupation). Most East Timorese were not forced to convert to Christianity and held onto their traditional animist beliefs. Local leaders, however, were encouraged to embrace Roman Catholicism and sent their children to Catholic schools. By 1974 only 30% of the population had joined the Roman Catholic Church.

The invasion of East Timor by the Indonesian army (1975) enhanced the role of the Catholic Church; it provided moral support, general assistance, and a communication network for suffering East Timorese, as well as sanctuaries for those who escaped from the repression. Furthermore, the Indonesian rulers brought with them the *pancasila*, the five state principles (see Indonesia) to which every Indonesian was supposed to adhere. Since the first of these principles is "belief in one God," and since the traditional Timorese beliefs were not considered part of an official religion, many East Timorese adopted the Catholic faith.

Pope John* Paul II's visit to East Timor in October 1989 was a major boost for the Church and gave East Timorese a sense of identity. By 1996 the number of Catholics had increased significantly to around 80% of the population.

The Catholic Church and its spiritual leader, Bishop Carlos Filipe Ximenes Belo, SDB, gained more influence among the people after the 1999 referendum. The overwhelming vote for independence from Indonesia led not to an easy transition but to a traumatic struggle that included a terror campaign by pro-Indonesian militias. After a brief period under the UN transitional administration in East Timor, East Timor gained its independence (2002) as the Democratic Republic of Timor-Leste, or Republika Demokratika Timor Lorosa'e (in the Tetun language).

However, the result of the referendum left deep divisions within families, within communities, and within (and between) churches in a nation plagued by continuing unrest and violence. Nevertheless, the Catholic Church, along with the minority Igrejas Protestantes de Timor Lorosa'e (East Timor Protestant Churches) and Pentecostal churches, remains central to the life of the community.

Statistics: Population (2008 estimate): between 0.8 and 1.1 million; Christians, 99% (Roman Catholics, 98%; Protestants, 1%); Muslims, 1%. (*Source*: *World Christian Encyclopedia*, 2001; updated with 2005 census and *The CIA World Factbook*, 2008.)

DAUD SOESILO

Timothy, Paul's companion, assistant, emissary (1 Cor 4:17; Rom 16:21; Phil 2:19–23). Because he is called Paul's "child in the Lord" (1 Cor 4:17), he was probably converted by Paul. In order not to offend the Jews, he was circumcised (Acts 16:1–3). The epistles to Timothy represent him as a guardian of the apostolic tradition against heresy* and immorality.

Timothy, 1 and 2 Epistles to. See PASTORAL EPISTLES, 1 AND 2 TIMOTHY AND TITUS.

Timothy II Aelurus (d477), theologian; 26th patriarch of Alexandria (457–77, though mostly in exile). He was labeled "the great" by Zacharias Rhetor, but "Aelurus" (implying "weasel") by his opponents because of his austere, lean physique. He supported the doctrinal position of Dioscorus (d454) during the Chalcedonian controversies. By standing up against Rome, he began a new era in the history of the church and of the politics of the Middle East. Timothy vigorously rebutted the Tome* of Leo and refuted the Definition of the

Council of Chalcedon*. Opposed to Chalcedon because it was "Nestorian*," he equally opposed Eutychianism*, which he considered a mirror image of Nestorianism. For him (as is evident in his Syriac letters) a simple assertion of a real and true incarnation* by the truly divine Word of God was sufficient. Divinity and flesh had but one immutable nature in the person of Christ. **See also MIAPHYSITE; ORTHODOX CHURCHES, ORIENTAL, CLUSTER: COPTIC ORTHODOX CHURCH.** RIFAAT EBIED

Tithe, in ancient Israel, one-tenth of all grain and fruit, herds and flocks, due to God for the support of the priests and Levites, as well as the poor (Lev 27:30–32; Deut 14:22–30). For convenience the tithe could be given as money. The early church was supported by voluntary gifts, but from the 4th c. the tithe steadily became the normal expectation for the support of the church ministries. Originally voluntary, during the Middle Ages in Europe it became a land tax (beginning between the late 6th and late 8th c. in France, Spain, Italy, Germany, and Anglo-Saxon England). At first, the tithe was paid in agricultural produce and livestock for use by the parishes and stored in tithe barns near church buildings for the benefit of the church ministries. It was divided among the local churches (to meet, among other things, the needs of clergy and monasteries), the poor, and the bishops. After the Reformation, in several European countries (e.g. Germany, Scandinavia, Switzerland), the state began collecting the tithe for the (state-)church as a "church tax," before being progressively abolished (from the late 18th c. to the mid-20th c.). In the USA, with its total separation of church and state, after the Civil War the "tithe" as a voluntary gift of 10% of one's income was claimed to be a divine command by church leaders. **See also ECONOMY AND CHRISTIANITY CLUSTER: ECONOMIC STUDIES OF THE HISTORY OF CHRISTIANITY IN THE UNITED STATES.**

Titus, companion of Paul, born of Gentile parents (Gal 2:3); a member of the delegation from Antioch accompanying Paul and Barnabas* to the meeting in Jerusalem even though he was not circumcised (Gal 2:1–5); Paul's emissary to Corinth (2 Cor 8:16–24). In the Epistle to Titus*, he is portrayed as supervising Cretan* churches and giving instructions to bishops* and male and female presbyters*.

Titus, Epistle to. See PASTORAL EPISTLES, 1 AND 2 TIMOTHY AND TITUS.

Tobit, an apocryphal* (or deuterocanonical*) Greek book, is a tale of two main characters, a pious Jew, Tobit, and a pious Jewess, Sarah, in Nineveh, capital of the Assyrian Empire, one of the places to which Jews were exiled (late 8th–7th c. BCE). Scholars agree that this tale is fictitious, as historical inaccuracies show. Tobit among the exiles observed fervently the Law of Moses, yet in return suffered blindness. Sarah married seven times, but each of her husbands died before the consummation of the marriage, killed by the demon Asmodeus. Both Tobit and Sarah prayed for death. God heard their respective prayers, delivered them from their pain, and restored their faith and dignity through the act of Tobias, son of Tobit (who married Sarah), with the help of the angel Raphael disguised as Azarias. The fact that there is no suspense in the storytelling – the resolution of the crisis is revealed in early chapters (3:16–17, 6:6–8) – increases the opportunity for irony. Because this is the story of ordinary people (rather than heroic figures such as Daniel*, Esther*, or Judith*), some scholars considered it a romance weaving together biblical themes (especially from Job, Genesis, Jonah, Amos) and variants of secular folktales such as "The Grateful Dead" (Tobit buries the dead), "The Bride of the Monster" (Sarah is a "Dangerous Bride," another name for this folktale), and "Ahiqar" (the story of an Aramaic wise man).

Tobit was probably written during the 3rd or 2nd c. BCE in either Hebrew or Aramaic (fragments were found in Cave 4 of Qumran*); the book is best known in three Greek recensions. The edifying moral and pious Jewish teachings are clear throughout the book.

PHILIP CHIA PHIN YIN

Togo. Togo was occupied by the Germans from 1884 to 1920. German Togoland was partitioned between the British and the French (1920–60); after independence, the British portion became part of Ghana*, while the French portion became the Togolese Republic, or Togo.

Christians (42.6%) have the largest religious presence in the south, although there are many African Religionists (38%); Muslims (19%) exercise the dominant religious influence in the north. African* Instituted Churches (3%) and Charismatics* are quite visible.

In 1886 Fr. Jerry Moran and his companions in the Society of African Missions built a medical mission in Atakpame. After Fr. Moran's sudden death, they were replaced by German Divine Word missionaries (in Lomé, 1890), who developed an education* system and built the twin-towered Gothic cathedral that still dominates the skyline in Lomé. During the French occupation, vocations to sisterhood were high (first Togolese congregation, Soeurs de Notre Dame de l'Église, founded in 1952). When Togo became independent (1960), the first president, Sylvanus Olympio, was Roman Catholic, as were two-thirds of parliamentarians under his successors. In 1965 the majority of bishops in Togo were native born. A Benedictine monastery was established at Dzogbegan (1967), where it is also serve as a cultural center.

Although the Methodist Church of Togo was the first Protestant Church founded in Togo (mid-1800s), the Evangelical Presbyterian Church (Église Évangélique Presbytérienne du Togo), established by the Bremen Missionary Society (late 1800s) and later supported by the Paris Missionary Society (since 1922), is much larger and has focused on evangelizing North Togo and administering schools and catechists' training. The Assemblies of God also have a large following.

The Roman Catholic Church and the (Protestant) Christian Council of Togo (since 1983) played a role in the social transformation of Togo by initiating social and rural projects, educating local elites, building hospitals and dispensaries, and sponsoring active women organizations. The major challenge remains the lack of democracy and the cooperation of some church leaders with corrupt political structures.

Statistics: Population (2000): 4.6 million (M). Christians, 1.98 M, 42.6% (Roman Catholics, 1.1 M; Protestants, 0.5 M; members of African Instituted Churches, 0.14 M); African Religionists, 1.7 M, 38%; Muslims, 0.9 M, 19%. (Based on *World Christian Encyclopedia*, 2001.)

VALENTIN DEDJI

Toleration is a political term referring to a particular governmental attitude: allowing the presence of what is not officially approved, rather than persecuting or eradicating it. The term was used in the Act of Toleration (1689), by which Dissenters* in England were allowed to worship under certain conditions, and Locke* defended it in his *Letters on Toleration* (1689–92). Toleration is weaker and more begrudging than religious liberty* (see Church and State Relations Cluster), being granted on pragmatic grounds (usually to avoid public disorder), while religious liberty is a matter of principle.

Two milestones in toleration were the Peace of Augsburg* (1555) in Germany and, more decisively, the Peace of Westphalia* (1648), which allowed princes to adhere to either the Roman Catholic or the Protestant faith. The Edict of Nantes* (1598) granted certain privileges to French Protestants, although the official religion was Catholicism. Religious toleration could be granted when a ruler of one faith inherited a region that was of another faith (e.g. the Hohenzollerns in Prussia). It was also granted to diplomats or traders in a territory with another official religion (e.g. Catholics and Protestants in Turkish territory or Protestants in Latin American countries where Catholicism remained the only approved religion).

Tolstoy, Leo Nikolayevich (1828–1910), influential Russian writer, religious thinker, moral philosopher, social reformer, pacifist. He was particularly noted for his masterpieces of realistic fiction, *War and Peace* and *Anna Karenina*, although he thought that his novel *Resurrection* better expressed his religious ideas.

Following his conversion (c1878), this rich landlord reexamined Christian theology (*A Critique of Dogmatic Theology*, 1880–83) and described his spiritual development in *Confession* and *What I Believe In*, emphasizing that one should find one's own way to God and live according to Christ's teaching, instead of blindly performing church rituals. In 1901 the Russian Synod denounced Tolstoy's teaching as anti-Christian because he denied Christ's* divine nature, the doctrine of the Trinity*, and the virginity of the Mother of God (see Mary, the Virgin, Cluster: Theotokos), and rejected all the sacraments*. For him, true Christianity is based on the Gospels, which he translated, having taught himself Greek (*A Harmony and Translation of the Four Gospels*, 1880–91).

Tolstoy preached nonresistance to evil, love* for one's enemy, peace*, meekness*, repentance*, forgiveness*, chastity*, charity*, and asceticism*. He felt that Christ's moral teaching was incompatible with wars*, law courts, aristocratic luxury and idleness, adultery, and a state supported by brutal force. In his *Diaries*, he confessed his sins* and analyzed their origin, looking for moral improvement. Inspired by Rousseau and Thoreau, he contrasted nature and civilization, was a vegetarian, and tried to adopt a peasant's lifestyle – wearing simple clothes, working the land, and making shoes. Opposed to private property, he resisted accepting money for his books.

As a religious and social reformer, Tolstoy was renowned among peasants for his generosity, had many followers in Russia, particularly among anarchists and pacifists, and strongly influenced Mahatma Gandhi's nonviolent* resistance. ELENA VOLKOVA

Tomb of Jesus. In the Gospels, Jesus' tomb is notable for what is not there, i.e. Jesus himself. All four Gospels use the tomb as a backdrop for Jesus' resurrection*. Because preparation for burial was women's work in 1st-c. Palestine, the Gospels tell of female followers finding the tomb empty and being the first to confront Jesus' resurrection. While scholars and Christians generally content themselves with the literary tomb, there have been searches for the archaeological remains of the burial, on the one hand, and denials that Jesus was ever properly buried, on the other. NICOLE WILKINSON DURAN

Tome of Leo, letter sent by Pope Leo to Flavian of Constantinople (449), which argued against Eutyches'* position. Ignored by the Second Council of Ephesus* (449), it was officially recognized by the Council of Chalcedon* (451) as one important source of its doctrinal statement that Christ is "one person in two natures."

Tongues, or Glossolalia, shorthand referring to "speaking in tongues" under the inspiration of the Holy* Spirit (1 Cor 14), emphasized in the Pentecostal* and Charismatic* movements. One of the gifts* of the Spirit.

Tonsure, haircut with religious significance, in which all or part (top or front half) of the head is shaved; commonplace by the 4th–5th c. in the monastic* movement and later extended to the priesthood (6th–7th c.). The early practice ("tonsure of St. Paul") was to shave the entire head; the Roman practice ("tonsure of St. Peter") was to shave the top of the head, leaving a ring or crown of hair; the Celtic practice ("tonsure of St. John") was to shave the front half of the head.

Torah (Heb "instruction"), term used in Judaism to designate (1) the first part of Tanakh* (the Pentateuch*; a mixture of foundational narrative and Law*), (2) the entirety of the HB (though Tanakh is the preferred term); or (3) "Oral Torah," the halakhah* ("the way to walk"), the authoritative tradition* derived from, and going beyond, the HB. The halakhah, which envisioned how to carry out the covenantal* vocation* in particular contexts, remained oral for centuries before being written in Mishnah, then Talmud. In the LXX and NT, the Gk *nomos*, "law," is usually the translation of "Torah." One should not overlook the fact that, in the NT, *nomos* has the diversified connotations of Torah (rather than the narrow sense of "law"). **See also** LAW.

Tractarian Movement. See OXFORD MOVEMENT.

Trading. See ALTERNATIVE TRADING.

Traditionalism, 19th-c. school of thought, associated with Lamennais*, that opposed individualistic rationalism* and looked to the collective tradition* of the human race, manifested most accurately in the Roman Catholic Church. It was condemned at the First Vatican* Council (1870).

TRADITION CLUSTER

1) *Introductory Entry*

Tradition

2) A Sampling of Views and Practices

Tradition in the NT and the Early Church
Tradition and the Reformation's Scripture Principle
Tradition: A Roman Catholic Post–Vatican II Perspective

---

1) Introductory Entry

Tradition (Lat *traditio;* Gk *paradosis*), literally, "something delivered or handed down," is a verbal noun referring both to what is handed down (the tradition-content) and how it is handed over (the tradition-process). Tradition played an important role in the NT and early church, even though in the history of the church its relation to Scripture* was debated, especially in the controversy between the Reformation's* "Scripture* principle" (*sola scriptura,* "by Scripture* alone") and the Roman Catholic Church's emphasis on tradition (at the Councils of Trent* and Vatican* II). **See also** BIBLE INTERPRETATION CLUSTER: IN EASTERN ORTHODOXY.

---

2) A Sampling of Views and Practices

Tradition in the NT and the Early Church. When the Synoptic* Gospels were written during the second Christian generation, the church already possessed a normative standard called "tradition" (tradition-content), which Paul said he "received" from the Lord and "delivered" (*paradidomi*) to his readers, who in turn received it (tradition-process; 1 Cor 11:2, 23; 15:3; 2 Thess 2:15). Paul zealously followed the "traditions of [his] fathers" (Gal 1.4), in which he had been trained. While preserving the essential Jewish principle of "tradition" (associated with the concept of "Oral Torah*"), he made it the vehicle of the gospel*, wherein Jesus Christ became both its content and the principle of its origin (authority). For example, Paul argued that believers are freed from slavery to sin* as a result of "wholeheartedly obey[ing] the form [or pattern] of teaching to which [they] were entrusted" (or "delivered," Rom 6:17). The *paradosis* (tradition-content and tradition-process) of Jesus functioned as a dialectic between a pattern of belief and a pattern of conduct that identified believers as disciples of Christ.

The church's "tradition" in the NT, which, along with Scripture, provided a point of unity for the churches, included kerygmatic (or proclaimed), ecclesial, and ethical traditions, even though such subdivisions were not self-consciously present during the church's growth.

Kerygmatic Tradition is foundational; it summarizes the Christian message focused on Christ's death and resurrection. The tradition-process is exemplified in 1 Cor 15:1–3, where Paul reminds the Corinthians of the gospel, which he had received and "delivered" to them (15:3) through preaching, which they received and "in which [they] stand" firmly (15:1). The content of this "kerygmatic tradition" is Christ's death and resurrection "in accordance with the Scriptures" (15:3–4) and a list of resurrection appearances (15:5–7). This content – later called "the faith," or "rule*" (of faith; *regula* fidei*), or "the tradition" – is presented and explained by 1st- and 2nd-c. authors concerned with precisely defining or defending the Christian position.

Ecclesial or Liturgical Tradition is exemplified by Paul's admonitions about the Lord's Supper (1 Cor 11:17–34). Before citing Jesus' words, he states, "I received from the Lord that which I also delivered to you" (11:23), implying that while the ultimate authority for the tradition is the Lord, the words of this institution had become the common property of the believing church (his formulation suggests a previous liturgical usage).

Ethical Tradition is also exemplified by Paul's frequent use of the language of tradition for corporate and personal Christian practices, e.g. when he proposes that his ministry is a model for the life of believers, who by imitating Paul and the Lord become in turn a model (type) for others (1 Thess 1.5–7; 1 Cor 4:16; 11:1; Eph 4:20–21; Phil 2:5; 4:9). Similarly, Col 2:6 states, "Just as you have received (*paralambano*) Christ Jesus as Lord, continue to live in him," rather than following "human traditions" (2.8; see also 2 Thess 3:6). The writer of 1 Clement* used a similar tactic, exhorting schismatics to give up futile concerns concerning rivalry over leadership and "turn to the glorious and holy rule of our tradition" (7.2). This "ethical tradition" is also exemplified by the "two ways" tradition of the Didache* (late 1st–early 2nd c.).

In the next three centuries, the course of defining the church's tradition became increasingly more complex because of the need for increased theological precision about God as Trinity*, Christology* (the divinity and humanity of Christ), and liturgical* procedures. Baptismal formulas became qualified, though not replaced, by the rule(s)* of faith (as found in Irenaeus*, Tertullian*, and Origen*), by catechetical statements (e.g. in the Apostolic* Tradition or Cyril* of Jerusalem), and later by conciliar and non-conciliar creeds* (such as the Nicene* Creed and the Apostles'* Creed, respectively). DANIEL H. WILLIAMS

Tradition and the Reformation's Scripture Principle. The 16th-c. Reformers* valued the tradition expressed in patristic literature, especially Augustine, as a means of interpreting Scripture* and of developing a truly biblical theology; this is what Reformers such as Luther* and Melanchthon* were doing in following Augustine's injunction to "seek [God's] will in the holy scriptures" (*On Christian Teaching* III. 1). Their point was not to make Scripture autonomous, liberated from its ecclesiastical shackles, in a Gnostic*-like fashion. Rather, Scripture was supposed to be free in order to stand in judgment of all traditions and practices.

The assertion that the Reformers rejected the concept of tradition and the authority of the fathers and councils in their bid for "Scripture alone" (see Scripture Principle) is a misconstrual of the 16th-c. conflict as one of Scripture vs. tradition. Scripture could not be properly understood apart from the foundational tradition of the church, even when certain institutions of the church were being opposed. The Reformation was concerned to reclaim the ancient tradition – the "catholic" Tradition – against distortions of that Tradition in the Roman Catholicism of the time; this was ultimately a conflict of Tradition versus traditions. **See also** AUTHORITY IN/OF THE CHURCH.

DANIEL H. WILLIAMS

Tradition: A Roman Catholic Post–Vatican II Perspective. After an opening chapter on divine revelation*, the Second Vatican* Council's 1965 Constitution on Divine Revelation (*Dei Verbum*, §2) treats tradition, understood both as the process of "handing on" (tradition as process) and as the living heritage that is handed on (tradition as content). Through the Holy* Spirit, the invisible bearer of tradition, the whole visible Church*, and not simply its authoritative leaders, has been empowered to transmit its memory*, experience, and expression of the foundational self-revelation of God that was completed with Christ and the NT community. Thus tradition involves the present "Church in her doctrine, life and worship" handing on to every generation "all that she is, all that she believes" (*Dei Verbum*, §8).

Tradition both as process and as content was challenged by the Reformation's* principle of "Scripture* alone" (*sola scriptura*). In reaction the Council of Trent* in its fourth session (1546) taught that "the gospel" (here roughly equivalent to revelation) is "the source of all saving truth and rule of conduct" and is "contained" not only in "the written books" but also in "the unwritten traditions which have come down to us." Even though the Council spoke of only *one source*, its language about the gospel being "contained" in "written books" and "unwritten traditions" led many Roman Catholics to develop the "two-source theory," according to which some revealed truths were contained in tradition and not in Scripture.

In effect Vatican II and *Dei Verbum* ruled out this theory by interpreting revelation as *primarily* the living self-communication of God (§1) rather than as a body of revealed propositions contained in the Bible* or other sources. Moreover, in highlighting the process of tradition (singular) rather than individual traditions (or particular teachings and practices), *Dei Verbum* (§9) insists that tradition and Scripture are united in their origin (revelation*), function (clarifying and actualizing revelation), and goal (the final, face-to-face revelation of God). Hence they may not be treated as two separate sources.

Two other Vatican II documents (on ecumenism* and the Eastern* churches) express the way Tradition (uppercase), or the patrimony as a whole, is passed on through particular traditions (lowercase). While the inspired* Scriptures (as the Word of God) have a unique power to reform particular traditions, the Tradition of the whole Church is the essential setting for understanding divine revelation and appropriating the message of the Bible. GERALD O'COLLINS, SJ

Traditio-Redditio Symboli, the teaching of the Apostles'* Creed (*traditio*) and its recital (*redditio*) before the bishop, one of the last stages before baptism* in the early church.

Traducianism, theory that the soul*, like the body*, is generated by the parents, championed by Tertullian*, Apollinaris, and Gregory* of Nyssa; for Augustine*, this is the view which is the most compatible with original* sin. The alternatives, preexistence* and creatianism*

(each soul is created by God), are not as compatible with original sin. Traducianism is widely held in the Eastern Orthodox* Church and among Lutherans*. **See also SOUL.**

Transcendent, that which is "beyond": God's utter difference from the world; also the ability of human thought to rise reflectively above its immediate circumstances.

Transcendentalism, a New England religious movement that challenged conventional ideas of revelation*, the church*, and religious authority*. Among its key figures were Ralph Waldo Emerson*, Henry David Thoreau, Margaret Fuller, and Theodore Parker. Transcendentalism emerged in the 1830s from the liberal wing of the New England Congregational churches, Unitarianism*, which had displaced Calvinism with a conception of religion as the cultivation of a "likeness to God" (as William Ellery Channing said). Best remembered now as a literary movement, Transcendentalism also challenged what Emerson called "historical Christianity" and was shaped by concerns for social* justice*, such as Fuller's advocacy of women's* rights, Thoreau's concern for nature (see Ecology and Christianity Cluster) and advocacy of civil disobedience (see Conscientious Objection), and the anti-slavery preaching of Parker (see Slavery and Christianity Cluster). The Transcendentalists emphasized personal spiritual experience and ethical judgment over church, tradition*, or scriptural* authority. It was one of the earliest examples of the convergence of religious reform with artistic innovation and progressive political reform in the USA. DAVID M. ROBINSON

Transcendentals, in Scholasticism* those concepts that apply to all entities (e.g. being, one, truth, good).

Transept, transverse arms of a cross-shaped church (usually called "north" and "south" transepts because of the orientation* of the church).

Transfiguration. The story of Jesus' transfiguration (*metamorphosis*) in Mark 9:1–8 is set in the context of death and rejection (8:31–38) and of suffering and humble service (9:9–37). The narrative is based on a midrashic* retelling of the Sinai epiphany* (Exod 19–20, 34). The cloud (the divine *Shekinah**, Exod 24:16), the presence of Moses* (radiant in glory; see Exod 24:16–18, 34:35; 2 Cor 3:12–18), and the three chosen to go up the mountain (Exod 24:9; Mark 9:2) allude to Sinai. Following Bultmann* several scholars have approached this narrative of Jesus' glorification as a misplaced "resurrection* narrative." While significant, this approach risks reducing to a one-dimensional notion the multidimensional notion of Jesus' glorification that includes the Resurrection*, Ascension*, Transfiguration, and Exaltation (Phil 2:9). Mark has clearly edited the story he received in depicting Peter as obtuse and uncomprehending (Peter is less so in Matthew* and the other Gospels). This might be Mark's attempt to scale down Peter's pretensions to claim global authority* over the Jesus movement after the Lord's heavenly exaltation. Just as Moses had been exalted, and his authority was passed on to Aaron and those who ascended with him, so the exalted Jesus, the New Moses, intended his authority to be continued on earth by Cephas/Peter, James, and John (the Jerusalem "pillars"; Gal 2:9), whom he left behind. As a response to this claim, Mark underscores that the true glory of Jesus is his humble service (Mark 10:45). The divine voice that commands the apostles not to judge on the basis of appearances but to "listen" (Mark 9:8) explicitly refers them to Jesus' teaching on abnegation, which Peter does not accept, leading to Jesus' rebuke (Mark 8:31–33).

Long after these early power struggles, another feature of the story became prominent. The early fathers recognized that the story also reflects Jewish traditions of angelic metamorphosis (Moses and Elijah* were believed to have been lifted into heavenly glory when their earthly lives ended). From this perspective, Byzantine spirituality viewed the Transfiguration as the uncovering of the "natural" state of Jesus, as the God-man, which he normally obscured but allowed the apostles and later saints to glimpse in a uniquely graced mystical* perception. Developing this theme, patristic and Byzantine writers presented the Transfiguration as an overall symbol* of redemption* – when all natural life would be caught up into a graced deification* (theosis*) because of the risen Lord's glory radiating through the new world of his kingdom*. JOHN A. MCGUCKIN

Translation of the Bible. See BIBLE TRANSLATIONS CLUSTER.

Transubstantiation, the conversion of bread* and wine* into the Body and Blood of Christ in the Eucharist*, declared a dogma of the Roman Catholic Church at the Fourth Lateran* Council (1215).

Tree of Life. Adam* and Eve* are evicted from Eden after eating the fruit of the tree of knowledge to prevent them from eating the fruit of the tree of life and thus from attaining immortality (Gen 3:22). The image of the tree of life recurs as a symbol* of wisdom* in the Hebrew Scriptures; in Revelation* it symbolizes the eternal, perfect life in the New Jerusalem. Medieval Christian theologians connected the cross* (of death) with the tree of life, using the latter image to express the life-giving power of Jesus' death. Sometimes envisioned as an inverted tree, with its roots in God, the tree of life also symbolizes Jesus' power to form a bridge from the human (earth/soil/roots) to divine (heaven/sky/branches) realm.

NICOLE WILKINSON DURAN

Trent, Council of, convoked by three popes (Paul III, Julius III, Pius IV), met in 25 sessions over three periods (1545–48, 1551–52, 1562–63), mostly in Trent, an Italian city on the frontier of the Holy* Roman Empire. It had three aims: the eradication of the religious schism caused by the Protestant Reformation*; the reform of the Roman Catholic Church and the restoration of peace in Christendom; and the reclamation of the holy sites in Palestine for Christians. Its work was divided into "doctrine" and "reform," the former to delineate the boundaries between orthodoxy* and heresy*, the latter to address the abuses within the Catholic Church. For the papacy, the first aim was crucial, and it privileged discussion of doctrine over that of reform, leaving the question of the reform of the head of the Church to the Roman Curia* itself.

The first two periods of the Council focused on the Protestant heresy in Germany, while the third concentrated on the new Calvinist heresy in France. In spite of the attendance of German Protestants at the Council during the second period, which was forced by the temporary military defeat of Protestant princes by the Catholic emperor Charles V, the divisions of Christendom were sealed by the proclamations on doctrine that affirmed the Catholic interpretations of the sacraments*, the authority of the Vulgate* Bible, and the supremacy of the pope*, and by the condemnations of key Protestant doctrines, such as "justification* by faith alone." Other important doctrinal work included tightening the requirements for marriage* in order to avoid the problems caused by union between young people without parental consent. In the area of reform, the Council passed decrees that touched on all aspects of clerical life: the strengthening of episcopal authority (see Bishop) over chapters* and colleges; restrictions on appeals to Rome; regular episcopal visitations of dioceses; reform of all religious* orders, including the enforcement of strict closure for female convents; the stipulation that seminaries be established in every diocese; and the definition of the bishop's duty to reside in his diocese. Subjected both to the tugging demands of the papal court and the bishops and to the political considerations of the Holy Roman Empire, Spain*, and France, the decrees of the Council were not universally accepted. Rejected by Protestants, the Council was criticized in some Catholic areas, notably Venice and France, while its authority won quick acceptance in Spain, Portugal*, Italy*, and the Spanish Low Countries. It remained definitive for the Roman Catholic Church until the Vatican* councils of the 19th and 20th c. **See also** CATHOLIC RENEWAL.

RONNIE PO-CHIA HSIA

Trial of Jesus. Jesus' trial before Pilate has drawn historians' attention since the beginning of biblical scholarship, for what transpired there seems to define the relationship of Jesus to the Roman Empire and, by extension, to prescribe the relationship of Christianity to politics* and power. Indisputable historical facts about the trial are, however, few and hard won. Ultimately what we know best according to historical criteria is the result of the trial – that Jesus was sentenced to be crucified. Accounts of Pilate's* interrogation of Jesus in the canonical Gospels vary, and since in every version Jesus' followers have fled, our story of the trial seems to be based on no eyewitness reports. The fact that all the canonical Gospels report Jewish crowds calling for Jesus' death has lent support to anti-Semitic* interpretations in scholarship and in the church, making the Jews collectively responsible and mysteriously exonerating the very Romans who, according to the Gospels themselves, ordered and performed the execution. **See also** BIBLICAL INTERPRETATION CLUSTER.

NICOLE WILKINSON DURAN

Tribalism and Christianity. From an anthropological perspective, tribalism refers to both traditions and identity politics of "tribes" – defined in the broad sense of cultural, socioeconomic, and ethnic entities. These cultural and political dimensions of tribalism converge when contemporary "tribes" strive for identity and recognition for their ways of life within dominant and larger political entities. Conversely, the larger political entities marginalize* segments of society by designating them as "tribes" or "tribal," in a colonialist* manner. The impact of Christianity on the emerging identity and political aspirations of "tribes" and on their struggles for preserving their cultural traditions has been both positive and negative. The Christian missionary enterprise has diluted tribal traditions, sometimes to the point of extinction, but has also provided a global platform for political aspirations through identification with Christian denominations associated with North Atlantic cultures. Missionaries were widespread in the 19th c., and most indigenous people throughout Asia were under the influence of Christianity by the early 20th c. There was an uneasy relationship between missionaries and colonial administrations, which were interested in conversion* only so long as it favored their administrative policies. The evolutionism* of the 19th c. (social Darwinism*) fueled missionary zeal by its apparent relegation of many indigenous societies to the bottom of the scale of progress and the presumption that all societies would eventually attain the highest stage of monotheism*.

Proponents of the anthropological concept of cultural relativism were critical of the missionary zeal to convert, and more broadly, the gendered and postcolonial critique (launched in the last half of the 20th c.) took particular aim at the replacement of values, such as sharing, cooperation, liberal sexual norms, and the high position of women in indigenous societies, by Christian or Western values, such as patriarchy*, private property*, and puritanical* views. In particular, Christianity had problematic relationships with matrilineal norms, communal living, polygamy*, and lack of control of women's sexuality.

Conversely, anthropological fieldworkers often found that the conversion* process translated Christian views and practices into native values and meaning systems, as it had done in the Hellenistic world and later in Europe (see Inculturation Cluster: Of Christianity in the Greco-Roman World). Thus the Ten Commandments meant something specific to the Papuans (Engas, Medlpas, Chimbus) of Papua* New Guinea, who emphasized kinship relations and the sexual purity of women. The Modekngei religion of the Palauans of Micronesia preached that their local god was reincarnated as Jesus Christ. The local practices were not always given up, and sometimes traditional elements were hidden from sight and practiced in secret or adapted to fit in with the new religion. The acceptance of Christianity by indigenous people in the early mission period was often rooted in their traditional religion. They assumed that the gods of the missionaries were more powerful than their own and could give them all that they had given to the colonialists. In many traditional religions, there was a supreme and benevolent god figure that could easily be translated into the God of the Christians.

The egalitarian and humanistic values propagated by Christianity were often analogous to those held by indigenous peoples. However, traditional views of the environment (often seen as positive in modern times) were transformed by missionaries into views of nature as passive and inanimate. Thus some environmental activists have called for a return to pre-Christian values in order to maintain a sustainable relationship with the environment. Judeo-Christian theology makes a clear distinction between humanity and nature, giving a privileged position to humanity that has led to an exploitative attitude toward nature by Europeans and North Americans. Such distinctions between humanity and nature often do not exist in traditional societies, where nature is seen as both animate and in close kinship to humans. Feminists have also likened the exploitation of nature to the exploitation of women, pointing out that both are a feature of patriarchal religions such as Christianity. The conversion process is blamed both for the emergence of patriarchy in indigenous societies and for the loss of respect for nature (see Ecology and Christianity Cluster: Ecofeminist Theology).

At the political level, Christianity often encourages indigenous people to push for their own agenda as a unified body. Consequently, fragmented indigenous communities are often united under the umbrella of Christianity, which has frequently provided the needed transition to modernity. The emergence of a unified Naga identity in Northeastern India is a case in point. The experience of ethnic communities within largely Western and Christian nations like the USA and Mexico is again different from that of "original dwellers of the land" (Adivasis*) in non-Christian nations like India* and Myanmar*. In the latter cases, being Christian gives indigenous people a higher status in society where they would otherwise be relegated to the bottom. Thus in the caste* society of India, converted Adivasis enjoy a higher social standing than those who have not been converted and have been able to push for greater recognition within the larger state. The stigma associated with "tribal customs" that are considered savage continues to exist, and only "converted tribes" are recognized as modern.

Although the term "tribalism" has universal connotations, the experience of various ethnic communities in different parts of the world is not uniform. The colonial as well as the missionary impact has taken multifarious forms owing, e.g., to the particular Christian denomination that has taken a lead in proselytism*. However, the missionaries' interest in imparting formal education* and making preliterate indigenous people literate has been universal. In middle India, missionaries devised a script for the local language of the Santals and wrote books on the traditional culture of the people. Many ethnic communities have become completely assimilated into the global culture through this Western education. In some places, local languages have been favored and in some cases the language of the dominant group, like English, has been imparted. The retention or rejection of local customs often parallels the treatment of the native language.

Exposure to the value systems of dominant cultures created aspirations in colonized peoples that included the desire for modern occupations and Western or urban lifestyles, and in many cases fanned indigenous sentiments of self-assertion, calling for a distinct identity. Christianity was one of the vehicles that linked ethnic communities to the larger world and created in them needs based on Western lifestyles. In the process, some of the old practices were condemned as backward and embarrassing. In most parts of the world, Christianity was equated with modernity and development, specifically as based on a Eurocentric model.

More recently, the changes brought about by two or more generations of Western education and exposure to the world through the adoption of dominant languages like English have created a backlash: in a search for their roots and identity, ethnic communities are going back to their traditions and in some cases even rejecting Christianity or modifying it to conform to their own idiom.

The political sentiments of "tribalism" were a major force in global politics in the early 21st c. Christianity played a dual role in helping to create identity consciousness as well as a non-Christian ethnic identity fostered by this very consciousness. Criticism of a Western model of development and Western ways of life has been politically connected to issues of global racism*, which have forced Christianity to project itself as a global and not a Western religion, adapting to local customs and values. In the last analysis, one can say that tribalism has had an effect on the nature of Christianity.

SUBHADRA MITRA CHANNA

Trinidad and Tobago. Together, these islands have formed the Independent Republic of Trinidad and Tobago since 1962. Africans (40.8%) and East Indians (from India, 40.7%) constitute the majority of its unusual population.

Roman Catholic mission, first established by Dominicans in 1513 during Spanish rule and then by Belgian Benedictines* and Jesuits*, became the Archdiocese of Port of Spain (1850). In the late 20th c., the Roman Catholic Church succeeded in creating a native clergy, which is exceptional for the Caribbean Islands; this success was due to the dynamic presence of the Catholic seminary at Mount St. Benedict. The Charismatic* Movement now plays an important role in the Catholic Church, making a solid contribution to the liturgical renewal and religious music.

Under British rule (from 1797), the centrality of the Roman Catholic Church did not change. The Anglican Church was at first a class church of the English plutocracy. The competition of Nonconformist* missionaries effected a change; thus before and after emancipation (1834), many Africans became members of the Anglican Church. Moravians (from 1783), Methodists* (from 1795), Baptists, Disciples of Christ, and Presbyterians, all influenced by the Evangelical Movement, helped to Christianize the African population, while the Presbyterians established a church among East Indian workers. Inculturation* and syncretism* played a role in this process and gave birth to African-Christian groups like the Shango in Trinidad, where the African element is predominant. The Pentecostal* and Charismatic* churches are very influential, especially among the poor. But the most impressive characteristic of Trinidad is the peaceful coexistence of Hindus*, Muslims (see Islam and Christianity Cluster), and Christians.

Statistics: Population (2000): 1.3 million (M). Christians, 0.8 M, 64% (Roman Catholics, 0.4 M; Protestants, 0.18 M; Anglicans, 0.15 M; independents, 0.04 M); Hindus, 0.3 M, 22%; Muslims, 0.09 M, 7%; native religionists, 0.02 M, 1.9%; nonreligious, 0.03 M, 2.2%. (*Source*: A. Lampe, ed., *Christianity in the Caribbean*, Kingston 2001.)

ARMANDO LAMPE

Trinity in Eastern Orthodoxy. The doctrine of the Trinity in Eastern Orthodoxy* is rooted in the apostolic affirmation of Jesus as the Messiah*. Early Christian thought, however, was defined in part by a debate over the person of Christ. There was general agreement among early Christians that Jesus as the Christ was divine, but there was debate over the degree of his divinity, i.e. whether Jesus as the Christ was of the same divinity as God the Father.

This debate came to a head in the 4th c. when Athanasius* of Alexandria asserted the full divinity of the Logos* against Arius* and against various forms of Arianism* that claimed the less than full divinity of the Logos. Notwithstanding the diversity, what unified Arian-like thought was the assertion that the full divinity of the Logos threatens monotheism* and leads to polytheism*. Athanasius, however, affirmed the full divinity of the Logos on the basis of the axiom that the created cannot save the created; only the uncreated can save the created. Humans ultimately need salvation* from death* and corruption, and only the union of the divine and human in Christ (see Incarnation Cluster: In the Orthodox Tradition) can accomplish this salvation. Athanasius' logic has two particularly significant implications: (1) God as Trinity rests on what Christians affirm about the divinity of Christ. Insofar as God as Trinity is the coexistence of the full divinity of the Father, Son, and Holy Spirit, an affirmation about Jesus that involves less than full divinity cannot lead to an understanding of God as Trinity. Trinity is thus more than a way of understanding God's relation to the world (cf. Modalism). (2) The basis for affirming the full divinity of the Son for Athanasius is the creation's need for divine–human communion. The doctrine of the Trinity is then not simply the affirmation of God as one and three, but the conceptualization of God as free to relate to the world so as to allow for a communion between God and the world through the Logos by the Holy Spirit. Athanasius was not disputing monotheism*, but asserting the need to think of a monotheism that can conceptualize a communion between God and the world; anything less, for Athanasius, would leave no hope* for the world.

The Cappadocians*, Basil* the Great, Gregory* the Theologian, and Gregory* of Nyssa were instrumental in providing the language for expressing the sameness and particularity of God's being as Trinity. *Ousia**, "essence," expresses what is the same in the Father, Son, and Holy Sprit, while *hypostasis** signifies that which is particular and irreducible in the Father, Son and, Holy Spirit. The 9th c. saw the emergence of the debate between Eastern and Western Christians over the *Filioque**, which is the statement inserted in the Niceno-Constantinopolitan Creed in the West that the Son proceeds from the Father "and the Son." The classic defense against the *Filioque* in the East is given by Photius* the Great (820–91), who argues that if the Spirit proceeds from the Father and the Son, there is no way of distinguishing the Son from the Father.

After the fall of Constantinople (1453), the Orthodox tradition did not witness any discernible creative thinking about the Trinity until the sophiology (theological reflection on wisdom*) of 19th- and early-20th-c. Russia. Vladimir Sergeevich Soloviev* (1853–1900) is considered the father of Russian sophiology, but among the followers of Soloviev, Sergei Nikolaeivich Bulgakov* (1871–1944) advanced the most developed and coherent theology of the Trinity. There are two central concepts in Russian sophiology: the humanity of God (*bogochelovechestvo*) and Sophia. The Incarnation reveals the humanity of God, which means that God exists as eternally free to create what is not God, i.e. the world. Although Russian sophiology does not affirm a creation eternally existing with God, insofar as God is the one who is always free to create, God's essence is such that God is eternally relating to creation. The essence of God understood in this way is what sophiologists identify as Sophia. *Hypostasis* for Bulgakov means much more than identifying what is particular in God; the relations between the persons of the Trinity are best understood in terms of kenosis's* movement of self-giving and self-receiving that has the capacity to overflow and reflect itself in the creation of the world.

Vladimir Lossky* (1903–58), a Russian émigré theologian, faulted Russian sophiology and the trinitarian theology of Bulgakov for attempting to provide a philosophical justification for that which lies beyond philosophical reasoning. For Lossky, God as Trinity is a revealed "fact" of revelation*, the adequate expression of which requires an antinomic approach to theology, i.e. the nonopposition of opposites. *Ousia* and *hypostasis* in their deconceptualized form are adequate categories for expressing the Trinity because they convey the simultaneity of the sameness and particularity in God without leaning too heavily to one side. An apophatic* and antinomic approach to theology is necessary, for Lossky, so that theology can guide one to true knowledge of God made possible by the Incarnation, which is mystical* union with God. Lossky also developed a trinitarian theology of personhood in terms of uniqueness and freedom that would become influential in contemporary Orthodox theology.

John Zizioulas (b1931) was indirectly influenced by Lossky's theology of personhood via the thought of his contemporary, Christos Yannaras. Zizioulas also developed a theology of trinitarian personhood in terms of uniqueness and freedom, which is decisively non-apophatic and emphasizes more the category of relation: a person is constituted as a free and unique being in relations of loving communion. This understanding of person is grounded in Zizioulas's understanding of the experience of the divine through incorporation into the hypostasis of Christ in the Eucharist*. According to Zizioulas, it was the experience of divine–human communion in the Eucharist that formed the basis for the Christian affirmation of the full divinity of Christ and thus the Trinity. This divine–human communion in Christ in the Eucharist reveals an ontology that is distinct from those prevalent in ancient Greek philosophies and that the Cappadocians attempted to express by uniting the categories of *hypostasis* and *prosopon*. This "ontological revolution" is such that, for the first time in the history of Western philosophy, being is identified with otherness, communion, particularity, freedom, and uniqueness. Insofar as the Eucharist is an event of divine–human communion that frees creation from the tragedy of death and corruption, it reveals God's life to be such that God is free from the necessity of nature, since God gives what God *is*. God's life as Trinity is constituted in freedom, which is the meaning of the patristic assertion of the monarchy of the Father. Zizioulas's trinitarian understanding of person as a free and unique being in relations of loving communion is evident in other aspects of this theology, including his theology of ministry, his ecclesiology*, and his theology of the environment.

ARISTOTLE PAPANIKOLAOU

Trinity Sunday, Sunday after Pentecost*, observed since the middle ages; popularized by its association with Thomas Becket's* consecration on that Sunday (1162).

Trinity in the Western Tradition (Lat *Trinitas*; Gk *Trias*). The doctrine of the Trinity affirms that God is three, reflecting the Christian experience of God as Father, Son, and Holy Spirit. Historically, the chief point of controversy was in what sense God is also one and thus "triune."

The NT speaks of God as Father, Son, and Holy Spirit (Matt 28:20) or as God, Christ, and Holy Spirit (2 Cor 13:14; cf. 1 Cor 8:6; Gal 1:3; Phil 1:2; 1 Thess 1:2). Passages in the HB seem to imply some kind of plurality, differentiating, e.g., between God and God's Wisdom (Prov 8:22–31; Wis 7:22–8:1), Word (Isa 55:11), and God's Spirit (Gen 1:2; Exod 31:3; Num 11:25; Deut 34:9; 1 Sam 10:6, 19:23; Isa 42:1). Some NT passages seem to imply that the Son, or Word, is inferior to the Father (Prov 8:22; Mark 13:32, 17:18; 1 Cor 15:28; John 14:28); others imply equality (John 5:26, 10:30, 14:9–11; 17:3, 10).

The Trinity and Hellenistic Culture. The development of the doctrine of the Trinity between the 2nd and 4th c. cannot be isolated from philosophical speculation, especially in Middle Platonism*, and from Near Eastern religions and Gnosticism*. The 2nd-c. Apologists*, relating this biblical tradition with Hellenistic culture, thought of God as uttering the Word as the instrument of creation (see Logos), in a position that was both derivative and subordinate (see Subordinationism). Other patristic writers, to avoid a plurality that seemed to imply polytheism*, asserted that "Father," "Son," and "Spirit" are names for different modes of activity by one and the same God, first in creation, then in redemption then in sanctification (see Modalism; Monarchians).

This suggests to some that the doctrine of the Trinity is nothing more than a part of a more general cultural trend, limited to its time and place. To the patristic writers, however, the reflections of the philosophers were proof that the truth* could be glimpsed, at least to some degree, outside the sphere of Christian revelation*, which then brought it to perfect formulation. Philosophical speculation could help to interpret the Bible, in two distinct ways. Cosmologically, the theory of a second and often a third divine principle seemed to resolve the question of how an unchanging God could be related to a changing world. Epistemologically, the divine Word could be viewed as the source of human knowledge of abstract intelligibles, for very few in the ancient world thought of these as coming solely from abstraction by the individual human mind.

Arius's Subordinationism and the Nicene Response. The ambiguities of the inherited doctrine were exhibited when Arius* asserted that

Trinity in the Western Tradition

the Father, being ungenerated, is alone God, in the proper sense; the only begotten Son is the "God" and creator of everything else, but was himself "created out of nothing" by the Father's will and is thus "unlike" the Father in essence. Against Arius, the Council of Nicaea* in 325 decreed that the Son is *homoousios** with (of the same essence as) the Father. The Council, however, did not explain how the Father and the Son are distinct, and in fact it anathematized those who said that the Son was in any way different from the Father.

Four Understandings of the Father–Son Relation. Many in the East were convinced that their doctrinal tradition did not require the stark alternative of either the Nicene or the Arian positions. Starting with the Council of Antioch* (341), the Eastern bishops, without denying the Nicene doctrine, produced other creeds that seemed more satisfactory to them. Eventually four distinct positions developed concerning the relation of the Son to the Father, and these took explicit form in the 350s: the Homoousians*, or Nicenes, asserted "of the same essence"; the Homoiousians*, or "Semi-Arians," "of similar essence"; the Homoians*, or moderate Arians, "similar"; and the Anomoians*, "dissimilar," the extreme Arian position.

Arianism in its more moderate Homoian form gained approval after Constantius became sole emperor in 353, with a series of councils culminating in the Council of Constantinople* in 360. In protest against these developments, a new movement coalesced in the East, that of the Homoiousians*, or "Semi-Arians," who kept the Eastern emphasis on threeness but were willing to say that the three were "like in essence."

The death of Constantius (361) and the rise of Emperor Julian* the Apostate, who removed all doctrinal sanctions, made a resolution possible. At the Council of Alexandria in 362, presided over by Athanasius*, the Nicene party made peace with the Semi-Arians; thus the "orthodox" doctrine of the Trinity owes something to both traditions. The Council of Constantinople* in 381 likewise reached a compromise between the Nicenes and the Pneumatomachians*, stating that the Holy Spirit is "honored together with the Father" but not using the term *homoousios*.

Monotheism and Monarchy. The unification of the Mediterranean world by the Roman Empire was accompanied by a growth of monotheism: one ruler on earth suggested one ruler in heaven, too. In this sense, the official adoption of Christianity during the 4th c., begun under Constantine* (ruled 306–37) and completed under Theodosius* (ruled 379–95), can be seen as the completion of a process long in the making. While political and religious unity has its advantages, it is often accompanied by intolerance and repression, and in this respect monotheism is vulnerable to criticism. While Constantius and the Arians identified God with the Father alone, the Nicene doctrine of three equally divine persons* supported a more social and perhaps even more democratic view of the state; perhaps it even undermined totalitarianism, as E. Peterson, H. Berkhof, C. Cochrane, and G. H. Williams argued independently during the Hitler era. In a more psychological vein, the Arians' subordinationist theory that the Son is "less than" the Father, perhaps even the product of the Father's will, seems to have a resonance with the arbitrary role of the father in Roman society. The Nicene doctrine that the Father and the Son are of the same essence might be interpreted as a more benign relation between the generations, with the offspring possessing the same attributes as the parent.

The Definitive Role of the Cappadocians. A more definitive understanding of the Trinity came not from councils but from the work of individual theologians, termed "doctors of the church." The Cappadocians* differentiated between *ousia* (essence) and *hypostasis* (particular substance, reality, person), applying the former to the unity, the latter to the threeness in God. The crucial insight of the Cappadocians is that the words "Father" and "Son" are used not because God is sexual or the Son grows like a human embryo, but solely because these are relational terms (one is a parent only by having an offspring, and vice versa). Thus they emphasize the relational terms "unbegotten," "begotten," and "proceeding," which alone differentiate the three persons*. The persons are distinct "modes of subsistence or relation" (Amphilochius* of Iconium) of the one divine essence, which is identical in all three persons and is fully present in each.

Augustine's "Psychological" Doctrine of the Trinity. In keeping with this insight, Augustine* understood the Trinity in terms of an analogy with the human mind, which, while remaining one, relates to itself in three ways: memory (immediate self-awareness), understanding (explicit self-concept), and will (self-love or self-affirmation). What is said "relatively" refers to the three persons; what is said "simply" or "directly" refers to the divine essence. While the East thought of the Father as the "source of the entire deity," the West emphasized relation, according to which the Father is Father by begetting the Son.

Two Interpretations of the Holy Spirit. After the doctrine of the Trinity had been resolved on these terms, a new dispute emerged: Does the Holy* Spirit proceed from the Father alone or also from the Son? The East held to the former, the West to the latter, asserting that the Spirit proceeds from the Father *and* the Son (Lat *Filioque**). The *Filioque* was a major point of controversy between East and West during the tensions of the 800s and after the schism of 1054, and it remains so today. Recently this issue has been raised in a more symbolic way. For some Feminist* and Liberation* theologians, the Western view implies that the Spirit is "tied to" or "controlled" by the Word and thus by the church and its offices. If, on the other hand, the Spirit comes directly from the Father, this seems to suggest that the Spirit is "free," not bound by earthly means and ministries, more readily authorizing a role for women* and the poor*.

Is the Trinity Biblical? The Reformation, with its demand that doctrine be based on Scripture, posed a new set of questions. The mainstream Reformers retained the classic doctrine, affirming that the teachers of the early church were reliable interpreters of Scripture. Others, however, were convinced that the doctrine of the Trinity was *not* taught in Scripture but that God is one (Socinianism*, Unitarianism*); still others, who emphasized inward experience, speculated in new ways about the immediate presence of the Word and the Spirit in each human being.

Can the Trinity Be Proved? While most patristic and medieval thinkers regarded the doctrine of the Trinity to be at least partially demonstrable by reason, the position of the Thomists*, Scotists*, and Nominalists* was that it is a mystery* of faith, disclosed by revelation* alone. Thus during the Enlightenment*, the doctrine came into question among those who emphasized what could be known about God through reason. Schleiermacher* affirmed the Trinity but only in a modalist way, arguing that Christian experience involves absolute dependence on God in three modes: the unactualized potentialities of human life, redemption through Christ, and the community of the church.

Reaffirming and Reconceptualizing the Trinity. It was unusual, then, when Hegel* made the Christian doctrines of Trinity and incarnation the basis of an entire speculative system. In his interpretation, the Trinity unfolds through the world process, reaching completion in art, religion, and the pure concepts of philosophy; incarnation is the implicit presence of concepts in sensory experience, resurrection, their becoming explicit. Hegel influenced many modern theologians in taking a more dynamic view of the Trinity as developing through the process of creation and redemption. While these motifs are most evident among German theologians, they also influenced Process* theology.

The "Social" Understanding of the Trinity. Traditionally the three divine persons were viewed as mutually indwelling, and this seems to reinforce the intuition that mutuality is better and more fulfilling than solitariness. Beyond this rather obvious point, serious questions arise. Does God become "more complete," more "actualized," as a result of the trinitarian relations? Plotinus* and Porphyry* in the ancient world, and Hegel in the modern, responded positively to this suggestion. But most Christian thinkers denied it. For them the Trinity is like the overflowing of an already perfect divinity, first in the Father (the "source of the entire deity"), then through mutual relatedness in the Son and the Spirit.

The Trinity and Gender. Traditional language includes the terms "Father" and "Son." Feminists point out that this privileges men as being more like God than are women, even perhaps to the exclusion of women. They note other, more emotive overtones of the traditional language: women who have been abused by their fathers may have difficulty calling God "Father," and the language of "Son," when accompanied by views of the atonement as a satisfaction of the wrath of the Father (see Atonement #2), can look like "divine child abuse."

In the doctrinal tradition, God has rarely been thought of as in any sense gendered. Many theologians, therefore, are willing to substitute inclusive terms like "Parent" and "Offspring" for gendered terms, following the precedent of several 2nd-c. texts that address Christ as God's "child" (Gk *pais*). There are others, however, who insist on keeping the inspired and authoritative language of the Bible and the creeds, understanding the terms "Father" and "Son" to be metaphorical, without gendered connotations.

The question of gendered language becomes most intense – pastorally, liturgically, and canonically – in the ritual of baptism*. In all churches that claim to be part of the universal church, baptism is "in the name of the Father, the Son, and the Holy Spirit." Some ministers and priests, to avoid gendered language, have substituted the words "Creator, Redeemer, and Sustainer." These terms, however, apply to divine activity in relation to the world and thus imply a modalist* understanding of the Trinity, inappropriate to any baptism whose motive is to act with and for the universal church. Use of the terms "Parent" and "Offspring" would seem to overcome this difficulty. The NT formula "God, Christ, and Spirit" is also free of modalist overtones. EUGENE TESELLE

Trisagion ("three times holy"), hymn based on the seraphim's praise of God (Isa 6:3); it became the focus of controversy when the so-called theopaschite* supplement added that one of the Trinity was "crucified for us." Eventually it was agreed that this notion should be qualified by the phrase *"in the flesh,"* maintaining the difference between Christ's human and divine natures.

Tritheism. This scarcely Christian designation derives from opponents of the doctrine of three substances in the Trinity*, who view this doctrine as an implicit affirmation of three Gods. Tritheists maintain that the divine unity is not an objective reality, but purely intellectual. Tritheism came into existence c557 through the activity of a certain John, a Syrian of the Syriac Orthodox Church (polemically nicknamed "Jacobite") and a native of Apamea (named differently by contemporary and later authors, including Bar* Hebraeus). Drawing its inspiration from a philosophical system that it applies to the Trinity, tritheism is a rationalistic approach that seeks to explain the Divine by concepts and principles derived from the created order. **See also NOMINALISM.**

RIFAAT EBIED

Troeltsch, Ernst (1865–1923), was one of the leading representatives of German liberal* theology. After studying at Erlangen, he moved to Göttingen, where, under the influence of Albrecht Ritschl*, he became a member of the so-called history* of religion school (*Religionsgeschichtliche Schule*). After a brief spell at Bonn, he became professor of systematic theology at Heidelberg (1895). In 1915, having "outgrown" the theological faculty, he moved to the Berlin Philosophy Faculty.

Troeltsch's work is often unsystematic and touches on many different disciplines, from ethics to intellectual history. Accepting the inevitability of the Enlightenment* with its liberation of the individual, Troeltsch sought to root such freedom in something higher. His main project was to work out the implications of modernity for any practical expression of Christianity. To this end, he sought to liberate theology from its dependence on what he called the "dogmatic" or supernatural method and pioneered an alternative "historical" method, which he outlined in his 1901 book, *The Absoluteness of Christianity*. Unlike many of his contemporaries, including Wilhelm Herrmann, he did not believe that theology and religion could have their own special methods. At Heidelberg his interests expanded into historical studies of Christian social teaching, and in dialogue with the sociologist Max Weber*, with whom he shared a house, he analyzed Christian social formation in his large-scale work, *The Social Teaching of Christian Churches and Groups* (*Die Soziallehren*, 1912). He saw this book as providing the basis for a reconstruction of Christian ethics compatible with the modern world.

He spent much of World War I trying to understand Germany's role in relation to the other powers and was also engaged in the philosophical analysis of history, which led to his unfinished work, *Der Historismus und seine Probleme*, in which he sought to forge a unified worldview from what he called the "melting pot of historicism." After the war, he campaigned for the establishment of democracy in Germany, playing an active part in Weimar politics. His posthumously published lectures, intended for delivery in Britain in 1923, present a view of history in which there are only "relative victories."

While he has often been dubbed a "Culture Protestant" (see Culture Christianity) Troeltsch always maintained a critical distance from his society. Nevertheless, his call for a unified vision of religion and society, his acceptance of the Enlightenment, his espousal of relativism, and his interdisciplinary method made him one of the least favored theologians of the so-called dialectical theologians of the 1920s. **See also HISTORIOGRAPHY OF EARLY CHRISTIANITY AS DEVELOPED IN THE 19TH AND 20TH CENTURIES; HISTORY, CONCEPTS OF; HISTORY OF RELIGION SCHOOL; RELIGION AND CHRISTIANITY; SOCIOLOGICAL STUDIES OF CHRISTIANITY.** MARK D. CHAPMAN

Truce of God (Lat *treuga*), bishops' declaration limiting personal feuds, insisting on the protection of innocent bystanders and their possessions. It forbade warfare on Sundays and during Advent* and Lent*. The Crusades*, ironically, were carried out under the auspices of the peace and truce of God.

Trullan Synod. See QUINISEXT COUNCIL (OR TRULLAN SYNOD).

Truth. The most common meaning of truth is "saying what is." There can be numerous contexts. "Telling the truth" may mean that one's words agree with one's experiences, valuations, intentions, or promises. In the OT, truth is faithfulness or reliability on the part of those who make promises and those who trust them (see Faith). Shakespeare* urged, "To thine own self be true." A "true statement" is one that agrees with the actual state of affairs, and one can verify or falsify the statement by examining the evidence. Art is "true to life," although not always by stating facts, for fiction can be more effective in evoking the texture of human life. A carpenter "trues up a board" by making it fit a plan drawn on paper or in the imagination; similarly, traditional theology speaks of the world as being "true to" the ideas* in God's mind. Truth can also "spring forth": God's truth is expressed in and understood through the things that are made (Rom 1:20, 23); God's Word* is truth in the sense of revelation* (John 8:32, 14:6, 16:13, 18:37–38). In the doctrine of the Trinity*, the Word is often understood to be God's self-expression and self-knowledge. Heidegger*, exploiting the Greek word *aletheia* (that which does not escape notice, is not hidden), speaks of *being* as disclosing itself, at least to those who are not distracted and forgetful. In the case of human beings, however, truth is not merely given; it is also a task to be carried out, self-critically, and it may not be achieved.

If truth involves "agreement" or "relationship" of many kinds, this comes close to the so-called correspondence theory of truth. That theory has often been criticized, usually on limited grounds. It is not as simple as a "picturing" theory of truth, for the sentences we utter are not isomorphic with the things we talk about; they are different from and far more complex than pictures. It does not deny that our statements are "constructed" by human language; culture and thought are deeply influenced, as postmodernists point out, by our participation in communities of discourse (see Hermeneutics; Hermeneutics of Suspicion; Postmodernism and Theology; Semiotics and the Study of Christianity).

Even in the best of cases, our access to the world is patched together from subject and predicate terms, and we gain access to reality through an act of *judgment*, the conviction or conclusion that we have now said our best about the subject matter. Much that goes by the name of truth is conventional belief or scientific hypothesis, "confirmed" by our experiences or not yet "falsified," and we have the privilege of saying what would count for or against those statements.

Religious belief is quite different from natural science in that, if it is verifiable at all, it is so by its comprehensiveness in giving meaning to our entire range of experience or indicating a way of life that is fulfilling. **See also SCIENCE AND CHRISTIAN THEOLOGY.** EUGENE TESELLE

Truth, Sojourner. See SOJOURNER TRUTH.

Truth and Reconciliation Commissions are official, temporary bodies set up to investigate and report on a pattern of past human* rights violations. Truth commissions can provide official acknowledgment of abuses that may have long been denied or hidden from view. Truth commissions typically take testimony from thousands of victims, investigate key events, and sometimes hold public hearings for select cases.

The Truth and Reconciliation Commission of South* Africa was the most well known. Under the leadership of Archbishop Desmond Tutu, it projected a strong emphasis on reconciliation and often suggested a religious, and explicitly Christian, foundation. Religious leaders, both Christian and Muslim, have been appointed to serve on other truth commissions, as in Argentina*, Ghana*, Liberia*, Peru*, and Sierra* Leone. Their discourse has sometimes imparted a religious tone to a commission's public profile. This has given rise to a perception that truth commissions are generally religious in nature. However, most of the more than 30 truth commissions that have existed to date have been largely or entirely secular, strongly focused on their core task: clear fact-finding and the making of recommendations for policy or institutional reforms so that human rights are protected in the future. **See also RECONCILIATION AS A CHRISTIAN PRAXIS.** PRISCILLA HAYNER

Tubman, Harriet (1820–1913), was born into the chattel slave system of the USA in Bucktown near Cambridge (eastern shore of Maryland), 1 of 11 children of Harriet and Benjamin Ross. At 25 she ran away, escaping through the Underground Railroad to the North. Tubman's escape was inspired and sustained by a deep theological conviction that the institution of slavery* denied her the dignity warranted by her humanness. Tubman concluded, "I had reasoned it out in my mind, there was one or two things I had a right to – freedom or death. If I could not have the one, I would have the other, but no man would take me alive. I would fight for my freedom as long as my breath lasted, and when the time came for me to go, the Lord would let them take me." After carefully reflecting on the condition she shared with her enslaved cohorts, Tubman became convinced that slavery stood outside the will of God. As a response to this conviction, she seized her own freedom by escaping from the South and then returned repeatedly, leading more than 300 enslaved people to the metaphoric "promised land." **See also SLAVERY AND CHRISTIANITY CLUSTER: IN NORTH AMERICA.** MONYA A. STUBBS

Turkey. In the modern secular state of Turkey, Christians form a tiny minority (0.6%) of a mostly Muslim diversified population that includes Nursis, Nakshibendis, Bektashis, Alevis, as well as secularists and Islamists. Turkey's Christian history goes back to the first centuries of Christianity, symbolized by cities such as Antakya (Antioch*), Urfa (Edessa*), and Istanbul (Constantinople*). Turkey comprises large portions of the former homelands of Armenian*, Greek Orthodox*, Syriac* Orthodox, and Assyrian (Church* of the East) Christians. These communities still constitute the majority of the Christian population, alongside small communities of Roman Catholics, Protestants, and Evangelicals.

Christianity experienced a strong decline during and after World War I, when political, military, and ethnic factors caused the murder, expulsion, and flight of a large part of the Christian population (see Armenian Genocide). This remains a sensitive issue, and it is often difficult for members of the Armenian and Syriac Orthodox communities to refer to this aspect of Turkey's history in public. Although interest in Turkey's Christian past is growing, and freedom of religion is officially a basic aspect of Turkey's secular outlook, strong Turkish-ethnic consciousness and the connection between religion and ethnicities that are not Turkish complicate the efforts of Armenian, Greek, and Syrian Orthodox communities to educate their members and clergy about their own cultural contexts. Turkey's rapprochement with the European Union has encouraged significant legal and practical changes. Conversion* to Christianity by those with Muslim backgrounds commonly meets with disapproval. Open evangelistic activities by Evangelicals and Pentecostals/Charismatics and the establishment of new churches are distrusted and face substantial legal obstacles. Despite such hindrances, ethnic Turkish churches, including the local Roman Catholic Church, have experienced some modest growth, whereas the membership of older churches continues to shrink as a result of emigration.

Statistics: Population (2000): 66.6 million. Muslims, 97.2%; atheists and nonreligious, 2.1%; Christians, 0.6% (Orthodox, 0.3%, most belonging to the Armenian* Apostolic Church; Protestants, 0.1%; Roman Catholics, 0.1%; independents, 0.1%.) (Based on *World Christian Encyclopedia*, 2001.)

HELEEN MURRE-VAN DEN BERG

Turner, Nat (1800–31), Baptist preacher, slave revolutionary, subject of *The Confessions of Nat Turner* (1831). Born into slavery* in Southampton County, Virginia, he taught himself to read and write, and was respected by fellow slaves as a man of unusual intelligence and one whose future would be linked to a special destiny for his people. Given to dreams and visions, and known as "the Prophet," Turner led the most famous slave revolt in the antebellum South in August 1831, a bloody uprising that resulted in the deaths of some 60 slave owners. He was inspired by African traditions and a radical reading of the NT, especially as it related to the life of Jesus Christ. Turner was hanged in 1831 but became an inspiration to generations of black Christian and Islamic nationalists, from Henry H. Garnet to Malcolm X. LEWIS V. BALDWIN

Twelve Apostles, a particular group of disciples* to whom the resurrected Christ appeared (1 Cor 15:5). According to the Gospels, Jesus chose among the disciples* 12 apostles*, sending them (Gk *apostoloi*, "sent") in mission (Mark 3:16–19; Matt 10:1–4; Luke 6:13–16; also John 6:67–71): Simon Peter*; James* and John, sons of Zebedee; Andrew; Philip; Bartholomew; Matthew; Thomas*; James, son of Alphaeus; Thaddaeus* (replaced by Judas, son of James, in Luke); Simon the Cananaean (or the Zealot); and Judas Iscariot the Betrayer. These slight variations regarding Thaddaeus and Simon (there could have been 13 or 14 close companions of Jesus) and, after Judas Iscariot's betrayal (when there were only 11 apostles left), the quest for a replacement (Matthias; Acts 1:13–26) show that the number 12 is symbolic, possibly reflecting the number of tribes of Israel, itself a symbolic number.

DANIEL PATTE

Two Kingdoms, Two Realms. The twofold Reign of God in Lutheran doctrine expresses the notion that that God acts through both the Word and the sword, i.e. through love and persuasion in the church, through force in civil government. Both have the task, each in its own way, of opposing the kingdom of Satan*, the outward and inward reign of evil* in the world. Luther's doctrine had varied influence. Used during the Hitler era to attack the Barmen* Declaration, it anticipates the modern separation of church* and state. Conservatives and "realists" cite it in their criticism that Christian principles are too closely identified with political causes or that Christian "sentimentalism" overlooks the need for coercion in the political life of the earthly city.

Two Swords, medieval interpretation of Peter's statement (Luke 22:38) "Here are two swords." First articulated by Peter* Damiani, it was popularized by Bernard* of Clairvaux: both the spiritual and the temporal swords are in the hands of Peter (and thus the pope*), but he gives the temporal sword to the secular* arm and has the authority to say how it will be used.

Tyconius (d c400), Donatist* layman, excommunicated by the Donatist Church because of his belief that the true church is universal and contains a mixture of good and bad. His *Book of Rules* for the interpretation of Scripture* influenced Augustine*, especially in its finding of continuities between the OT and the NT and its emphasis on tensions within history. A commentary on Revelation, now lost, was used by several writers in the early Middle Ages.

Tyndale, William (c1494–1536), the scholar to whom is attributed the first Bible in English translation (1526–34) fully based on the original languages and the first to take advantage of a new medium, the printing press. Tyndale's translation was superseded by the Geneva* Bible (1560) and the King James Version (1611). Tyndale drew primarily on the NT of Erasmus (1516, Greek) and Luther* (1522, German). Although it was not acceptable in England to print Scripture in English during this period, Tyndale rendered the text brilliantly and in a style of English that excited and inspired readers; he illustrated it with woodcuts to further engage the reader and illuminate the texts. In 1535 Tyndale was arrested, jailed in a castle outside Brussels, tried for heresy*, and burned at the stake. **See also BIBLE TRANSLATIONS CLUSTER: ENGLISH TRANSLATIONS.**

Typology, a method of interpreting Scripture* in which it is assumed that events, institutions, and persons in the OT ("type") foreshadow events, institutions, and persons in the NT, and/or such features of both the OT and the NT foreshadow events, institutions, and persons in the time of the interpreter. Then believers discern God's interventions in their present context (see Faith #5). Allegory*, by contrast, looks for the spiritual meaning of these events. **See also SEMIOTICS AND THE STUDY OF CHRISTIANITY; SYMBOLISM.**

Typos, the decree of the emperor Constans (647/48), superseding the *Ecthesis** of Heraclius. It forbade all discussion of the issues that arose during the Monothelite* controversy, limiting doctrine to that of the first five ecumenical* councils. Pope Martin I refused to sign it, a refusal that led to his deposition.

Tyrrell, George (1861–1909), Jesuit* priest, spiritual director, apologist, major figure in the Roman Catholic Modernism* Movement (1890–1907). His writings, including *Lex Credendi* (1906), *Lex Orandi* (1907), *Through Scylla and Charybdis* (1907), and *Christianity at the Crossroads* (1909), were courageous efforts to reconcile the Roman Catholic Church's traditional teaching both with the needs of the spiritual life and with modern scientific and historical research. With like-minded Catholic scholars, Tyrrell was a sharp critic of the reigning Roman Catholic scholastic* theology. From 1899 many of his works were prohibited; he was expelled from the Jesuit order and was refused a Catholic burial.

JAMES C. LIVINGSTON

U

Ubertino da Casale (1259–c1330), leader of the Spiritual Franciscans*. Although he studied for nine years in Paris, he took a negative view of such intellectual pursuits. His activity was centered in Italy, where he was influenced by John of Parma and Peter John Olivi*. He twice defended the Spirituals' view of poverty* at the papal court in Avignon (1310, 1322) but later had to flee (1325). He was admired by Dante* and later by the Fraticelli*.

Ubiquity, Lutheran doctrine that Christ's human nature acquires the divine attribute of omnipresence* and thus is literally received in the Eucharist*.

Uganda. Christianity in Uganda has been dominated by Anglicanism and Roman Catholicism. Until 1986 other Christian denominations and African* Instituted Churches had a limited presence. Uganda is the only African country that virtually became a Christian nation in the 19th c., before colonial rule by the British.

Late 19th Century. Ethnic, autonomous monarchies and chiefdoms made up the region of present-day Uganda. Buganda, the biggest kingdom, was the stage on which Christianity had its first impact. Kabaka (King) Mutesa I was open to outside influences; he first converted to Islam* (the first foreign religion in the territory), then expressed interest in Christianity when he met the British explorer Henry Stanley. Impressed by Mutesa, Stanley wrote to the *London Daily Telegraph* (1875) appealing to missionaries to evangelize the country. Anglicans of the Church Missionary Society arrived (1877), followed by the Roman Catholic French White* Fathers (1879). Both groups settled around the king's palace, attracting the youth. Mutesa played off British, French, and Arab interests, using them as political pawns to prevent any of them from gaining control over his territory. His erratic son, Mwanga, who succeeded him, quickly turned against the Christians, killing hundreds – including the Anglican missionary Bishop Hannington, who had just arrived, and Joseph Mukasa, a leading Catholic, who protested against the killing at the court. Mwanga massacred many Muslims as well. Fifteen Anglicans and 22 Catholics are officially recognized as the Uganda martyrs. The Catholics were canonized as saints by Pope Paul VI (1964).

1894–1914. The killing of Christians and Muslims was later followed by religious wars among all groups. Uganda became a British protectorate (1894) as a result of the collaboration of notable chiefs and the arrival of the Imperial British East African Company, led by Captain Lugard, who fought alongside the Anglicans during the religious wars, thus ensuring British control over Uganda. The Anglican mission became a dominant force, while Catholics and Muslims lost their political significance.

This period of turmoil was followed by the spread of Christianity throughout Uganda. Ugandan Anglican and Catholic evangelists were instrumental in the process, disseminating the gospel to all parts of Uganda and beyond, often ahead of the European evangelists that they had originally accompanied, because European missionaries had to flee for their lives on several occasions. Prominent among these pioneer missionaries were the Anglican Apolo Kivebulaya (the first missionary to the pygmies of Eastern Congo) and the Catholic Yohana Kitagana (an apostle in Southwest Uganda).

1914–50. This rapid growth of Christianity continued between the two world wars. Being a Christian was synonymous with being literate; Christians were known as the "readers" (*abasomi*), because they had been taught to read and write. The translation of the Bible into local languages became an important part of mission (see Bible Translations Cluster: Present-Day Translations in Africa). Anglican and Catholic missionaries opened schools and hospitals, sometimes in fierce competition with each other. It was not until 1950 that the British administration set up its own schools and health services. The Anglican "Mothers' Union" promoted the active participation of women in the Anglican Church. Catholics founded local congregations of women religious who worked tirelessly for the promotion of women.

Both Anglicans and Catholics opened seminaries to train local clergy. The first Ugandan Catholic priest of modern times, Victor Mukasa, was ordained in 1913 and the first bishop, Joseph Kiwanuka, was named in 1939. Similarly Bishop Tucker College was opened to educate Anglican clergy. A revival movement of the Balokole (the Saved), which was started by Ugandan Anglicans in Rwanda*, spread through Uganda and put new life into the rather dry spirituality of the time. Malaki Musjjakawa founded (1914) the Malakite Church, a revivalist church that rejected Western medicine and was soon banned by the British administration. Being Anglican or Catholic was so important for one's identity that African Instituted Churches did not thrive in Uganda. In 1929 Spartas Rueben Mukasa broke away from the Anglican Church to form an African Orthodox Church, later affiliated with the Greek Patriarchate.

1950–65. Christianity continued to play a major role in politics; the two main parties were the Democratic Party (mainly Roman Catholic) and the Uganda People's Congress (mainly Anglican). Tension between these parties were reflected in the churches as Uganda achieved independence (1962) under the premiership of Milton Obote.

After 1966. Obote abolished monarchies and political parties, then turned to Marxism. The advent of Idi Amin Dada, who ousted Obote with British help (1971), was disastrous to Christianity: there were years of persecution, missionaries were deported, clergy and prominent Christian politicians were killed, and Uganda was proclaimed an Islamic state (although Muslims were only 5% of the population). During this difficult period, individuals who spoke out, such as the Anglican Archbishop Janan Luwum, were brutally murdered. There was more unity between Catholics and Anglicans. Instability continued after Amin until 1986, when Yoweri Museveni came to power (1986), although his regime faced resistance organized by the Christian "Lord's Resistance Army," followers of Alice Lakwena's Holy Spirit Movement in the north (a war that has been going on for more than 20 years). Since 1986 new, especially Charismatic*, churches, have proliferated as a result of both local initiatives and the arrival of evangelical missionaries, especially from North America. Many of these churches preach personal salvation* and a prosperity* gospel. Muslims have tended to decline in number, as adherents of African* Traditional Religion have also diminished. Women's leadership has always been a key feature of Christianity in Uganda. The Anglican Church has ordained women priests since 1980. The Roman Catholic Church has a great number of dynamic and well-trained women* religious, a major force in education and social work. However, patriarchal structures are still in place in most churches.

Sexual ethics have dominated the political and theological debate in recent years. In the face of HIV/AIDS, an urgent issue in the 1980s and 1990s, churches have responded in different ways. Pentecostal and Charismatic churches have offered faith healing* sessions. Some churches have discouraged the use of condoms. Yet the main churches have supported the government's openness to the problem; as a result, Uganda is seen internationally as a success story in the fight against AIDS.

Ritual practices in most of the churches include charismatic and exuberant worship that is an occasion for socializing and building a sense of community. Music and drama play an important part. Traditional instruments together with Western ones provide lively accompaniment. Pilgrimages to shrines of the martyrs are important among Catholics and Anglicans, while the Charismatic churches often hold healing sessions with all-night vigils and the celebration of baptism* (by immersion).

Important theological issues include inculturation*, liberation*, reconciliation*, social* justice, human* rights, and economic development. Most churches have been involved in social* and economic development projects. Individual Christians have defended human rights, although church leaders have sometimes been slow to denounce abuses. Mainline churches have founded universities to promote the Christian ethos. Uganda's turbulent history has been characterized by ethnic tensions in all parts of the country. Church leaders occasionally perpetuate divisions and conflicts, even as they work for reconciliation.

Statistics: Population (2000): 22 million (M). Christians, 19.3 M, 89% (Roman Catholics, 9.2 M; Anglicans, 8.6 M; members of African Instituted Churches, 0.8 M; Protestants, 0.6 M); Muslims, 1.1 M, 5%; African Religionists, 1 M, 4.4%. (Based on *World Christian Encyclopedia*, 2001.)

ROBERT KAGGWA

Ukraine. Ukraine, whose cultural identity was forged under the influence of Christianity, has been a meeting place of Western and Eastern Christian traditions, which has led both to historic clashes and to growing pluralism. Many Ukrainians integrate symbols, customs, and fragments of historical memory from both traditions, even while the formal institutions of Eastern Orthodoxy and Roman Catholicism, along with several later movements, serve as conflicting centers of ethnic, cultural, and political mobilization.

Starting in the 9th c., Christianity began to influence the nobles and military elite of the Kievan Rus state (mid-9th–mid-13th c.). The first Christian bishop was sent to Kiev (Kyiv) from Constantinople* in 866 or 867. Despite the dominance of non-Christian religions, by the mid-10th c. there was already a Christian community in Kiev led by Byzantine priests. Princess Olga* was the first ruler of Kievan Rus to convert to Christianity (955 or 957). Her grandson Prince Volodymyr (Vladimir*) the Great accepted Christianity in its Byzantine form and established it as the state religion (988).

Situated at the convergence of two great trade routes, the Varangian (Viking) Road (from north to south) and the Silk Road (from east to west), Kiev developed into a formidable Christian state. The coming of the Mongol hordes (13th c.) interrupted the life of both state and church. The metropolitan see was moved from ruined Kiev to Vladymyr-Suzdal' (1299). The princes in Western Ukraine obtained Constantinople's authorization to create their own metropolitanate for a time (1303–47).

In the late 14th c., Ukraine was partitioned between Poland* and Lithuania*, with the Tatar Golden Horde ruling parts of the southern steppes. Partition caused the division of the Kiev Metropolitanate into the Ruthenian Church (with Polish links) and Muscovite Church (with Lithuanian ties), and two distinctive patterns of Eastern Orthodox religious culture developed.

Throughout the 15th and early 16th c., Polish and Lithuanian rulers introduced legislation that favored Roman Catholics to the detriment of Orthodox clergy and believers. The Orthodox Church was challenged by Western political and intellectual superiority and by deepening inner crises.

Toward the end of the 16th c., the search for a solution led Orthodox bishops toward union with the Holy* See. The Council of Brest*-Litovsk (1596) established a church united with Rome, known as the Uniate* or Greek Catholic Church. Yet some hierarchs and members of the Kiev Metropolitanate were dissatisfied with the Roman vision of unity and insisted on maintaining canonical dependence on the Patriarchate of Constantinople. They successfully demanded a parallel hierarchy (1620) and official recognition by the Polish-Lithuanian Commonwealth (1632). The confessional division of the Kiev Church into Eastern Orthodox and Eastern Catholic churches led to bitter polemics between supporters and opponents of the Union of Brest that have continued to the present.

The war of liberation from Poland led by the Cossack hetman (commander) Bohdan Kmelnytskyi (Chmielnitsky; 1648–54) improved the position of the Orthodox Church and seriously endangered the Uniates. The war for the protection of the "native Orthodox faith" and the "Cossack Church," carried out under these religious slogans in opposition to Roman Catholic expansion, became an important feature of the Ukrainian national myth. During this war, practically the whole of Ukraine fell under Cossack control. Yet a lack of resources led Khmelnytskyi to sign the Pereyaslav Treaty (1654), swearing loyalty to the Moscow czar in exchange for protection from the Poles. In 1667 Ukraine was partitioned along the Dnipro (Dnieper) River, with the western side under Polish control and the eastern side an autonomous hetman state under Russian protection.

In 1686 the Kiev Metropolitanate was transferred from the jurisdiction of the patriarch of Constantinople to that of Moscow. Educated, Westernized Ukrainians had an immense influence on Russian Orthodoxy and the early Russian Empire. The first president of the Holy* Synod (1700) was the Ukrainian Stefan Yavorsky (1658–1722); the Ukrainian Teofan Procopovich (1681–1736) was one of the main ideologues of Peter's religious "enlightenment." About 70% of the upper-level hierarchs were from Ukraine or Belarus in the first half of the 18th c. Ukrainian clerics created an image of the Rus past that transcended political boundaries. Through their compilations of varied and often contradictory opinions from Ukrainian, Polish, and Russian writings, they were able to link Ukraine and Moscow through religion, dynasty, land, and ethnicity.

In the 19th c., Russian policy eroded the organizational and architectural uniqueness and, more broadly, the general character of Ukrainian religious culture. Paradoxically, however, the Ukrainian Orthodox Church was neither completely absorbed into the Russian Church nor set against it as an alien body.

When the Western Ukraine, after the partitions of Poland (1772, 1793, 1795), was annexed by the Hapsburg Empire, the Greek

Catholic Church flourished under relatively liberal Austrian rule. The civil authorities encouraged the formation of an ecclesiastical administrative structure for the Greek Catholics. The educational reforms of the Hapsburg rulers Maria-Teresa and Joseph II gave Ukrainian youth access to education in their native language. Greek Catholics were given legal status equal to that of adherents of the Latin Rite, and their spiritual leaders were given at least minimal material subsistence. This led to the close integration of the Greek Catholic Church with the national political structure and social life, and the active participation of the clergy in the Ukrainian national movement.

In 1860 the Evangelical* Movement spread through Southern Ukraine. Baptist doctrine was welcome among educated workers and peasants with high moral standards who disliked the formalism of the established Church. Ukrainian Baptists*, Evangelicals, and later Pentecostals* saw Evangelicalism not as a "foreign" doctrine brought from the West but as an autochthonous spiritual phenomenon, the natural result of God-seeking activity among the common people.

The collapse of the czarist government (1917) led to the formation of a Ukrainian government and temporary independence that occurred simultaneously with the movement for independence of the Orthodox Church in Ukraine. The Ukrainian Autocephalous Orthodox Church was formed in 1921 but lacked recognition by the Orthodox community. Soviet authorities perceived in this church and the various Evangelical groups a counterbalance to the Russian Orthodox Church, and thus provided them with limited and short-lived support. In 1929 the Soviet regime unleashed war against all churches and denominations. Mass arrest of the hierarchy and clergy culminated in the liquidation of the churches in the 1930s.

Forced agricultural collectivization and the 1932–33 "Famine Genocide" were followed by religious persecution, the demolition of sacred buildings, and repression of the clergy. By the beginning of World War II, only 3% of the pre-revolutionary parishes in Ukraine remained open to the public.

World War II brought a dramatic Christian revival and a "concordat*" between Stalin and the Russian Orthodox Church. This did not mean the cessation of mass persecution of Christians in Ukraine. In early 1945, the Greek Catholic Church was accused of supporting Nazi and Ukrainian partisans; its metropolitan, Yosyf Slipyi, and all prominent priests were arrested and sentenced to long prison terms. In March 1945, this church was forcibly united with the Russian Orthodox Church and officially liquidated, after which it maintained only a clandestine existence.

In the years of Khrushchev's antireligious campaign (1953–64), almost half of all Orthodox churches in Ukraine were closed, including the well-known Cave Monastery in Kiev (1961). During the next 20 years, however, Christianity in Ukraine was viewed by the thinking public as an alternative system of values that was able to withstand the official ideology*, whose untenability became more and more obvious. Noticing the increase in adult baptisms, the obsession of the intelligentsia with religious literature, the growing popularity of religious broadcasts from foreign radio stations, and the outspoken neglect of atheistic propaganda, Communist Party officials expressed anxiety over anti-Communist trends. Secret reports submitted by Party officials revealed that in 1985, the first year of Gorbachev's reforms, 26% of newborns in Ukraine were baptized, contrary to official statements about "the country of mass atheism." Nearly 3% consecrated their marriages in a church, and more than 40% were buried with the church's assistance.

Beginning in mid-1988, the Kremlin's "new way of thinking" finally affected church–state relations. During Gorbachev's first years in power, legal and secret restrictions on religious practices were somewhat relaxed; by 1989 all religious prisoners and deportees, including a number of Uniate priests and defenders of religious freedom, were allowed to return home. From 1988 to 1991, there was a mass opening of formerly closed churches, monasteries, and ecclesiastical schools. The number of religious communities increased an average of 30% every year during that period. At the same time, the fall of Communism revived old controversies and pent-up conflicts. Beginning in 1989, hundreds of Russian Orthodox parishes (mostly in Western Ukraine) declared themselves to belong to the Ukrainian Autocephalous Orthodox Church. Challenged by this church, the Ukrainian exarchate of the Russian Orthodox Church asked the Moscow Patriarchate to transform it into a semiautonomous Ukrainian Orthodox Church and later (1991) to grant it autocephalous* status. The Moscow Patriarchate refused to do so, suspending the head of the Ukrainian Orthodox Church, Metropolitan Philaret, who managed to organize (1992) the Ukrainian Orthodox Church of the Kiev

Patriarchate. Consequently, three Orthodox churches were constituted in Ukraine: the Ukrainian Orthodox Church (more than two-thirds of all Orthodox parishes), the Ukrainian Orthodox Church of the Kiev Patriarchate (one-fourth of all Orthodox parishes), and the Ukrainian Autocephalous Orthodox Church (7% of all Orthodox parishes). The Ecumenical Patriarchate and other Orthodox churches now recognize only the Ukrainian Orthodox Church under the Moscow jurisdiction and reject the other two as "heretical schismatics."

All Ukrainian Orthodox churches recognize the canons of the seven ecumenical* councils as normative for doctrine, canon* law, and church life. They share the common Eastern Orthodox liturgical practices, sacraments, holy days, and fasts. The conflict among these churches is rooted in their differing attitudes toward the Moscow Patriarchate. While some Orthodox believers reject the latter's authority and regard subordination to Moscow as offensive, others accept it. The post-1991 evolution of Ukrainian Orthodoxy vividly mirrors its ambivalent nature as both contributing to the creation of Russian imperial identity and guarding "native Ukrainian" identity. More generally, the split within the Orthodox Church in Ukraine is an accurate reflection of the political and cultural contradictions in Ukrainian society and the conflicting patterns of historical memory.

The legalization of the Ukrainian Greek Catholic Church after more than 40 years of prohibition and humiliation has also created an explosive nexus of contradiction. The very existence of this church, with 3.5 million adherents, was doubted by the Orthodox hierarchy, while its years in the catacombs have sparked feelings of triumph and even a desire for revenge from the Greek Catholic side. As a result, a severe struggle between Orthodox and Greek Catholic factions arose in Western Ukraine over which church would gain the loyalty of believers and achieve the dominant position in the parceling of church buildings and property. This struggle, accompanied by physical frays between adherents of the conflicting churches (early 1990s), was far from being fully resolved in the early 2000s.

Roman Catholics (Latin* Rite), having made tremendous gains since Soviet times (from about 100 communities in 1985 to 870 in 2006), have a distinctly ethnic character. Two-thirds of them are centered in the regions where most Ukrainian Poles live; a number of Hungarians and Slovaks also have traditionally belonged to Roman Catholic communities. By the beginning of the 21st c., Ukraine had become the country with the largest Baptist, Pentecostal, and Charismatic communities in Central and Eastern Europe. Their evolution after the fall of Communism has further increased religious diversity and given rise to attempts by these groups to gain a more noticeable place on the religious map of the country.

Orthodox hierarchs sharply criticize the activity of the Roman Catholic Church in Ukraine, accusing it of proselytism* and expansionism toward the east. Even though the Catholic community in Ukraine (Latin and Eastern Rites together) is the largest of those in the countries of the former Soviet Union, the Orthodox hierarchs under the Moscow Patriarchate tried to block both the visit of Pope John* Paul II to Ukraine (2001) and the move of the administrative center of the Ukrainian Greek Catholic Church from the western city of Lviv to the Ukrainian capital of Kiev (2005). At the same time, both the Orthodox and Greek Catholic churches demonstrate a hostile attitude toward foreign Evangelical missions and new religious movements. Halting or eliminating these rivals became one of the chief goals of the churches' leadership. Their hierarchs appeal constantly to the public, to local authorities, and to the Ukrainian government for protection against foreign missionaries and so-called cults* and sects*.

The fact of religious pluralism, with multiple centers of religious power, prevents any one of these centers from repressing its rivals. Each addresses its own sector of public opinion and its own circles among the political elite. This balance of power prevents the establishment of a religious institution that can dominate others and be identified with the Ukrainian nation.

Almost all Christian churches deny ordination to women, insisting on alternative ways for them to exercise leadership (as parish deans, Sunday school teachers, members of seminary faculties, theological lecturers, church hospital executives, cantors). The issue of additional leadership roles for women is still contested despite the work of theologians and women's organizations.

Christian leaders are one in claiming a greater presence in various social spheres, first of all in schools and in the military, where social service might be accompanied by apostolic service. There is a growing unity among Christian activists in criticizing the moral situation in Ukraine, especially abortion* and youth crime. Sometimes secular circles interpret these criticisms as a campaign for clerical domination of the society.

Ukrainian Christians are searching for an appropriate theological response to the challenges of the post-Communist situation. Will the churches support the anomalies of this situation, remaining silent about social stratification, corruption, and official irresponsibility? What is the role of Ukrainian Christians in East–West Christian reconciliation? How can one harmonize the individual's right to hold any belief, change his or her religion or belief, and manifest that religion, with the collective right to defend one's traditional religious identity? How can the Christian motifs in the Ukrainian tradition be developed while avoiding chauvinism and aggressive nationalist feelings?

The "Orange Revolution" (2004) powerfully challenged Ukrainian Christians by raising questions about the churches' participation in politics (during political clashes, Christians were on different sides of the barricades) and about the admissible forms of defending truth and justice* and resisting evil.

Statistics: Population (2001): 48.4 million (M). Christians (2000), 39.3 M, 81.2% (Orthodox, 34 M; Catholics, 4.3 M [Roman Catholics, 0.8 M; Greek Catholics, 3.5 M]; Protestants, 1.M); Muslims, 0.9 M; Jews, 0.1 M; nonreligious, 7.5 M. (*Source*: Plokhy and Sysyn, *Religion and Nation in Modern Ukraine, 2003*).

VICTOR YELENSKY

Ulfila (c311–83), "apostle to the Goths*." Born of Cappadocian parents captured by the Goths, he spent some time in Constantinople, converted to Christianity, and was ordained (341) by the city's Arian* bishop. Returning to the Goths, he translated the liturgy and most of the Bible (except for the warlike Books of Kings) into their language, using an alphabet of his own devising. He was present at the Homoian* Council of Constantinople* (360). The Goths championed this moderate form of Arianism* for several centuries, partly to maintain their cohesion through contrast with the Latin-speaking Catholics.

Ultramontanism (Lat *ultra*, "beyond," *montanes*, "the mountains," i.e. the Alps). This term designates a 19th-c. movement within the Roman Catholic Church supporting the centralization of ecclesiastical jurisdiction in Rome, the pope, and the papal administration (the Curia). It stood in opposition to nationally oriented movements such as Gallicanism* in France and was characterized by a clear opposition to liberalism (as in Pius* IX's Syllabus* of Errors, 1864). It reached its zenith with the promulgation of the doctrine of papal infallibility* at the First Vatican* Council (1870) (opposed by Old* Catholics in German-speaking Europe).

PETER C. ERB

Unam Sanctam ("One Holy [Church]"), bull* issued by Boniface* VIII (1302) during the quarrel with Philip the Fair of France, establishing the high point of papal claims: that there is no salvation* outside the Roman Catholic Church, that the pope has supreme authority in the Church, and that the two* swords remain within the authority of the pope.

Unction, anointing* at baptism* and confirmation*, and especially the anointing of the sick (a sacrament* for Roman Catholic, Orthodox, and Anglican churches).

Underhill, Evelyn (1875–1941), independent lay scholar, religious writer, spiritual guide, retreat director. Underhill published 39 books and more than 150 articles. *Mysticism: A Study in the Nature and Development of Man's Spiritual Consciousness* (1911) became a classic, interpreting mysticism* for ordinary people. Although baptized and confirmed in the Church of England, Underhill was nonpracticing. She was attracted to Roman Catholicism, but the condemnation of Roman Catholic Modernism* discouraged her. In 1920 she returned to the Church of England. She credited Friedrich von* Hügel, her spiritual director (1921–25), with leading her from a disembodied mysticism to a more integrated spirituality. ELLEN M. LEONARD, CSJ

Uniate Churches, common designation (but a name that neither these churches nor the Roman Catholic Church use) for churches that separated from Eastern or Oriental Orthodox churches (which in most instances still exist independently), retaining their traditional language, liturgy, and canon* law but acknowledging the primacy of the pope*. They are thus in union with Rome (hence the term "Uniate") and are properly known as Eastern Catholic or Greek Catholic churches.

The first such unions were with the Maronite* Church (1182) and the Armenians* of Cilicia (1198). The Council of Florence* approved unions with the Greek* Orthodox and Armenian* churches (1439), as well as with the Syriac* Orthodox (polemically nicknamed "Jacobites*"), Copts*, and Ethiopians* (1442). The largest union was with the Ukrainian* Orthodox Church in the Polish realm, concluded in the Treaty of Brest*-Litovsk (1596). After much of this territory became part of the Russian Empire, Czar Nicholas I required the Uniate churches to return to the Russian* Orthodox Church (1828–38); the Uniate Church (often called Ruthenian) continued in territories ruled by the Hungarian, Austrian, and Ottoman empires, as well as among emigrants in the USA and other countries. Stalin compelled the remaining Uniates in Poland and Ukraine to become part of the Russian Orthodox Church (1946). In 1989 Uniate churches once again became legal throughout the former Soviet Union and now compete with two Russian Orthodox churches.

Unification Church. The Unification Church is the familiar name given Rev. Sun Myung Moon's first organization, the Holy Spirit Association for the Unification of World Christianity, founded (1954) as a Christian ecumenical organization and replaced (1996) by the Family Federation for World Peace and Unification, a multi-faith association.

Sun Myung Moon was born in 1920 in Pyongyang (now North Korea) to a traditional Confucian* family that converted to Christianity in 1930. Moon reports that the risen Lord Jesus Christ appeared to him on Easter Sunday morning, 1935, on a Korean mountainside and called him to take up Jesus' original mission to establish the Kingdom* of God on earth. Moon spent nine years seeking the divine truth necessary to fulfill this mission, studying the Bible, and the natural and spiritual worlds, and presenting each discovery to God for confirmation or rejection. This became the "Divine Principle," the primary study text for Unificationists, which teaches the principles of creation*, the origin of evil* (human "fall*"), and the principles and providence* of restoration (salvation* history) hidden in the Bible, as well as in Christian and world history. Moon's sermons fill more than 230 major volumes.

Reverend and Mrs. Moon are known to Unificationists as "true parents" and "the king and queen of peace." The designation "true parents" means that they fulfilled their respective responsibilities to embody God's life, love, and lineage and now stand as original human ancestors*, true parents who "bless" couples that form "blessed families." These families inherit and transmit God's life, love, and lineage, expanding to become the foundation of the Kingdom of God on earth and in heaven, the original purpose of creation and the destiny of all human beings.

Marriage blessing and the "Divine Principle" teaching inform all Unification activity. The foundational piety for Unificationists is to realize a godly nature by living with a parental and sacrificial heart for the sake of others.

FRANK KAUFMANN

Union, Mystical. The NT speaks of believers being united with each other in the same Spirit (1 Cor 12:4–11). But "mystical" union is something more, as perhaps implied in Paul's rapture to the "third heaven" (2 Cor 12:2). Mystical union shares similarities with the Platonist* tradition, which argued that true happiness is found only in the immediate contemplation of God (see Beatific Vision). 2 Peter 1:4 speaks of being "participants in the divine nature," and deification (theosis*) was a frequent theme in patristic* thought, such as that of Irenaeus*, Origen*, and the Cappadocians*. Contrasted with deification, which focuses on the change within humans arising from love and knowledge of God, mystical union is the means by which such love and knowledge are imparted. **See also HETERONOMY; MYSTICISM, MYSTICS.**

Uniqueness of Christ. This phrase affirms that Jesus Christ is the only savior* of all humankind. "There is salvation* in no one else" (as Peter says in Acts 4:12). A related affirmation is that this salvation of all is mediated by the church*; "There is no salvation outside the church," Boniface* VIII said in the bull* *Unam* Sanctam* (1302). From this perspective, although individuals may be saved in spite of their adherence to other religions, they are always saved by Christ and are related in some mysterious way to the church.

Historically, Christ's universal salvific outreach was explained in two ways. The Greek tradition (and the Eastern Orthodox Church) said that the Word* becoming incarnate* united itself with the whole of humanity, which continuously participates in his saving paschal mystery*; As Athanasius* said, "God became human that human might become God" (see Atonement #1; Theosis, Deification). The Latin tradition (and the Western Roman Catholic and Protestant churches) held that Jesus suffered and died for every one; he once and for all took on himself the sins* of the world and redeemed humanity (see Atonement #2). Salvation* happens independently of humans, although they have to appropriate it by explicit or implicit faith* in

Christ. Those who have only implicit faith can be considered "anonymous* Christians" (Karl Rahner*).

In the postcolonial* period, the world is no longer monolithic. There has been a reassertion of other world religions, and they have become factors of social and political identity. Hinduism*, Buddhism*, and Islam* claim to offer unique ways to attain humankind's ultimate goal. After World War II and the Holocaust*, some Christians are less confident that their religion is the only way. Europe has become increasingly secular* and religion privatized. With Christians' growing appreciation of other religions, people are said to be saved not only in spite of their religions, but in and through them. This may be justified a priori: if God wishes to reach out to people, God has to do so in bodily, human, and social ways, namely through religions*. The a posteriori argument is based on the "fruits* of the Spirit" found in the believers of other religions. John* Paul II's encyclical, "The Mission of the Redeemer" (1990) affirms that the Spirit of God is present and active in all the world's cultures* and religions. Christ is unique, but Christianity is not (see Mission Cluster: Theologies of, and Western and Asian Churches).

Such an appreciation of other religions raises questions regarding the uniqueness of Christ as Savior. Some simply deny it, saying that all religions are salvific and each religion has its savior. Others argue from a Kantian* philosophical perspective. The Ultimate Reality is unknowable. Religions are limited and unsuccessful human efforts, influenced by the local cultural context, to reach out to this Ultimate (see Inculturation Cluster). At this level, all religions are similar, formally equal. Most believers find such pluralism unpalatable. Religions lose their specific identity, and no religion is taken seriously. By contrast, many think that their own religion is perfect, while other religions, although they contain some truth and goodness, will find their fulfillment in it. In that case, they do not take other religions seriously.

Others raise different issues. Religions* do not save; only God does. Religions only facilitate divine–human encounter, which is salvific. This is true also of the church. God may save even nonreligious people if they love God in others, especially the poor and the needy (Matt 25:31–46). So religions can be transcended. Divine–human encounter is mediated by the Word* and the Holy* Spirit (emphasized in the Charismatic* Movement and the Eastern Orthodox churches). In this encounter, we have to respect the freedom* of God who calls and the freedom of the humans who respond. This twofold freedom gives rise to a pluralism of encounters.

Christian theologians in contexts marked by religious pluralism (such as India*) emphasize that God's salvific will and action are unique and universal. They also point out that since the Christian God is trinitarian*, the Word and the Spirit participate in the salvific act of God. Embracing the whole universe and the totality of cosmic and human history, God manifests God-self through many sages and prophets. At the appropriate time, God enters history bodily, the Word becoming incarnate* in Jesus. In Jesus the "last times" have started when God gathers all things to God-self (Eph 1:3–10) so that God will be "all in all" (1 Cor 15:28). Recognizing Jesus as Savior, believers also experience him as divine. These theologians emphasize, however, that one should not think that Jesus replaces other divine manifestations; Jesus works with and coordinates them. The true enemies are not other religions, but Satan* and Mammon*. Thus for these theologians, it is appropriate for Christians to believe that Jesus Christ plays a central, indispensable, and historic role in this plan; but they should not assume that Jesus' role is an exclusive one. He is the real symbol* and servant* of the salvific action of God in the world. The church is also the symbol and servant of this mystery. It is God's mystery that is unique and universal. Christ as the Word participates in it, but this divine mystery is also manifested in other ways than through Jesus. These theologians affirm that the salvific mystery is one, that Christians know it in Jesus and experience it as Christic. Yet other believers may experience this mystery and give it other names.

MICHAEL AMALADOSS, SJ

Unitarianism. The beginnings of Unitarianism are often traced to Arius* (d336), who taught that Christ, the only begotten Son, the "God" and creator of everything else, was himself "created out of nothing" by the Father's will. Arius's followers were outvoted at the Council of Nicaea (325), when Arius's view of Christ was declared a heresy* and the Nicene Creed was affirmed.

The organized beginnings of Unitarianism date from the Renaissance* to the establishment of congregations after the Reformation. Erasmus* had shown that the doctrine of the Trinity* did not appear in the oldest NT manuscripts. Italian reformers began to question the Trinity and had to flee the Inquisition*. Some organization of anti-trinitarians took place in Switzerland* and, primarily after the Reformation, in Poland* and Transylvania. In Poland the Socinians, followers of Faustus Socinus*, rejected Arius's view that Jesus was divine and preexistent, believing instead that Jesus was a human being with a special mission.

The word "Unitarian" was first used in Transylvania and in 1638 became the commonly accepted name for the anti-trinitarians when the Diet of Dees affirmed a new creed, instructing Unitarians to worship Christ, but not as God. After the suppression of the Socinian Movement in Poland (1658–60), its views were imported to the Netherlands and then to England, where scattered liberals preached and wrote, leading to the establishment of the first official (mostly Socinian) Unitarian congregation in London (1774) by Theophilus Lindsay, a disaffected Anglican.

Joseph Priestley and other English Socinians brought their views to North America, but most US Unitarians initially were Arian and preferred to be called "liberal Christians." Mainstream Unitarianism developed out of Congregational and Puritan churches in Massachusetts, by those who rejected the Puritan doctrines concerning original sin and predestination. This liberal group further defined itself after the Great* Awakening by opposing revival* tactics and advocating a reasoned educational approach to faith*; it formed the American Unitarian Association (1825) with William Ellery Channing as its leader.

Unitarianism drifted away from its Christian center under the influence of Ralph Waldo Emerson* and the Transcendentalists*. The centrality of biblical revelation* and miracles* was rejected in favor of natural* religion and human experience. Unitarianism became an ethical faith that was quick to affirm science* while emphasizing Jesus' ethical teachings rather than a revealed mission of salvation*. When the Unitarians consolidated with the Universalists (1961), the Christian emphasis was further diminished in favor of a pluralistic* approach to faith. MARK W. HARRIS

Unitas Fratrum. See BOHEMIAN BRETHREN; MORAVIAN CHURCH.

United Church of Christ in the Philippines

(UCCP) was a union (1948) of three churches: the United Evangelical Church of the Philippines, the Evangelical Church in the Philippines, and the Philippine Methodist Church (separated since 1933 from the Methodist Episcopal Church). The United Church of Christ arose from five faith heritages: Presbyterian, Congregationalist, Church of Christ (Disciples), Philippine Methodist, and the Evangelical United Brethren.

The coordinated effort to bring Filipinos to the Protestant faith began (1898) with US missionaries and was pursued through the Evangelical Union (1901) and agreements on (1) territorial division among the different missions (see Comity Principle), (2) a common name for newly organized churches, (3) a plan to produce one national church, and (4) cooperation in schools, press, newspapers, and other media*. The goal was to bring about "a spirit of comity, unity and cooperation that will eliminate competition and effect harmony for the common task."

The United Church of Manila was formed (1924) to "demonstrate the possibility and practicability of Filipino church union." Its membership came from the United Brethren, Congregationalists, and Baptists. Next, the United Evangelical Church in the Philippine Islands gathered together (1929) Presbyterians, Congregationalists, United Brethren, and the United Church of Manila. During World War II, the Japanese army pressured Protestants to unite into the broader Evangelical Church of the Philippines (1942), which also included the Church of Christ (Disciples), Iglesia Evangelica Unida de Cristo, Iglesia Evangelica Cristiana Independiente, the Salvation* Army, a segment of the Philippine Methodist Church, congregations of Iglesia Metodista en las Islas Filipinas, Iglesia Evangelica National, and more than 20 smaller churches. After the Philippines gained its political independence from the USA (1946), the United Church of Christ was founded (1948).

The United Church of Christ in the Philippines is at the forefront in addressing social* and political* issues. For example, it issued the Statement of Social Concern (1960) "as a guide for Christian thinking and action in meeting the present problems of Philippine society." This statement signaled the shift toward a posture of critical engagement. In response to martial law (1972), the United Church of Christ expressed concern (1974) and later called (1978) for the "immediate dismantling of the machinery of Martial Law in the country."

In 2006 the United Church of Christ in the Philippines, with nearly 1 million members in 1699 parishes and 181 house fellowships led by 743 ordained clergy (including women), is divided into 6 jurisdictions, headed by bishops, and 45 conferences, headed by conference ministers. The General Assembly, the highest policy-making body, meets quadrennially. The National Council, the ad interim body, meets annually. REUEL NORMAN MARIGZA

United Church of Christ (UCC) (in the United States) is part of a worldwide movement toward united and uniting churches in 20th-c. Protestant Christianity. It was formed in 1957 as a union of the Evangelical and Reformed Church and most of the members of the Congregational Christian Churches, themselves complex unions of other traditions.

The Evangelical and Reformed Church (since 1934) was itself a union of the Reformed Church in the U.S. (during the colonial period, the German Reformed Church) and the Evangelical Synod of North America (founded in the early 19th c. by German immigrants to the Midwest arriving with a united church tradition; see Prussian Union) with a group of Hungarian Reformed churches.

The Congregational Christian Churches (since 1932) united the Congregational churches (including numerous ethnic minority congregations, especially the black Congregational churches in the South related to the work of the American Missionary Association) with the General Convention of Christian Churches and the Afro-Christian Convention (both originating in the early national period) and smaller congregationally organized bodies.

The United Church of Christ is a Protestant denomination claiming the Bible as its basic authority (see Scripture) and celebrating two sacraments, baptism* and the Lord's* Supper. Because of its ecumenical vocation and spirit as a united and uniting church, the United Church of Christ claims a complex diversity of theological and doctrinal traditions rather than a single theological stance or position. Nonetheless, it is broadly in the Reformed* tradition of the Protestant Reformation and theologically liberal.

The United Church of Christ's ecumenical* impetus arose from the ecumenical idealism of early-20th-c. mainline Protestantism. More specifically the ecumenism of the United Church of Christ was grounded in the ideal of Christian unity espoused by the Congregational Christian Churches and in the Evangelical Synod's practical experience (Lutheran and Reformed union) that led them to advocate unity as a vehicle for social* justice* and unity – a point expressed by their important theologians, especially Reinhold and Richard Niebuhr*. Similarly, the 19th-c. Mercersburg* Movement in the German Reformed Church (with Philip Schaff and John Nevin) influenced the ecumenical movement.

Ecumenical commitments create tensions in the United Church of Christ between a broad liberal emphasis on inclusivity – embracing ethnic and racial minorities, women, gays and lesbians, and the new theological issues they raise for Christianity – and a more conservative sense of responsibility to the common Christian commitment to ancient ecumenical creeds and traditional practices of faith and life. People in the United Church of Christ seek to keep a balance between assuming a liberal position on social and theological issues – being open to ideas from many sources – and remaining decisively Christian in commitment.

The United Church of Christ has addressed a constellation of social issues related to racial justice, equal rights for women, the acceptance of people of minority sexual orientations, and concerns about war, urban violence, environmental degradation, economic justice, and the general well-being of people in the world. The 1.2 million members (2007) do not all agree on these issues; local and regional/national interpretations and commitments often are in tension. In addition, the cultural diversity of the church has increased significantly since the 1960s, bringing with it changes in the denominational culture and in the understanding of the nature and purpose of the church.

The United Church of Christ is not marked by a specific theological confession, pattern of worship, or unique organizational structure. It is characterized by a commitment to human community, especially in Christian congregations, in order to express more fully the churches' oneness in Christ and make a more effective common witness to Jesus Christ.

RANDI JONES WALKER

United Kingdom. Christianity in the UK exists in the face of increasingly pervasive secularism* and pluralism*. It is characterized by enormous internal diversity and by residual ties between church, state, and national identity. While in the past the religious histories of the component nations of the UK – England, Scotland, Wales, and Ireland (until 1921) / Northern Ireland (since 1921) – have shown marked divergences, at the turn of the millennium UK-wide trends were becoming more apparent.

First Millennium. There is evidence of a Christian presence in Britain in the later Roman Empire, but it almost completely disappeared in the early Anglo-Saxon period. However, Christianity survived in the western regions and in Ireland*, where it had been established by Patrick* (5th c.). Its reintroduction to Britain in the late 6th and 7th c. was the work of both (Celtic*) monks from Ireland, led by Columba* (521–97), and missionaries from Rome, competing traditions that have had an enduring legacy. The conversion of England was commemorated in Bede's* *Ecclesiastical History* (731). Christianity was maintained in the face of pagan invasions from Scandinavia during the reign (871–99) of Alfred the Great. In succeeding centuries, the medieval church came to enjoy enormous power and wealth, to which the surviving great cathedrals and abbeys bear enduring testimony. Among its greatest figures were the philosopher Anselm*, archbishop of Canterbury (1093–1109), and Thomas Becket*, archbishop of Canterbury (1162–70), whose defiance of King Henry II led to his dramatic murder in his own cathedral (1170).

Reformation. During the later Middle Ages, the church encountered significant criticism, notably from John Wyclif* (c1330–84), but the immediate catalyst for the English Reformation was the marital and dynastic problems facing King Henry* VIII, who defied the pope by divorcing Queen Catherine of Aragon (1533) and marrying Anne Boleyn. Henry subsequently dissolved the monasteries*, but it was only during the short reign (1547–53) of his son, Edward VI, that the government sought to impose a distinctively Protestant religious settlement. Mary* I (reigned 1553–58) attempted to restore Roman Catholicism, but Elizabeth* I (reigned 1558–1603) stabilized the Church of England as a moderate religious compromise, adopting a Protestant theology and ritual but retaining a hierarchy of bishops (see Anglicanism Cluster). Meanwhile the Scottish Reformation followed a more radical Calvinist course, from which the Church of Scotland* emerged with a Presbyterian* organization. In England more radical Protestants dissented* from the Anglican settlement and challenged it effectively during the period of the civil war and subsequent interregnum (1640–60). When Anglican order was restored in 1662, ministers who refused to comply were expelled from the Church, leading to the development of Baptist, Congregational, and Presbyterian denominations* in England. The Society of Friends* (Quakers) led by George Fox* (1624–91) also emerged (mid-17th c.). From the late 16th c. to the early 18th c., Roman Catholics were seen as a significant political threat. Hence they suffered legal disabilities and became a small minority of the population, except in Ireland*.

18th Century. This period saw a cooling of earlier conflicts, but the emergence from the 1730s of a new dynamic force: the Evangelical revival* led by John Wesley* (1703–91), George Whitefield* (1714–70), and, in Wales, Howell Harris (1714–73). Evangelicals established the Methodist* Movement and also had a profound influence on other Protestant denominations, including the Church of England, with their conversion zeal and intense biblicism.

19th Century. Until late 18th c., British Christianity was dominated by the state churches, Anglican in England and Wales, and Presbyterian in Scotland. The (Anglican) Church of Ireland was always relatively weak in the face of the numerical dominance of Roman Catholicism over much of the island and of the strength of Presbyterianism in Northeast Ulster. With industrialization, however, Nonconformists* (including Baptists, Congregationalists, numerous groups of Methodists, and the Salvation* Army in the last quarter of the century) gathered momentum, coming to rival Anglicans in number in England and substantially exceeding them in Wales. The Church of Scotland split in 1843 (see Disruption of 1843). Roman Catholics, strengthened by immigration from Ireland, were also an increasingly substantial minority, especially in Northwest England and Western Scotland. Meanwhile, from the 1830s, the Oxford* Movement asserted a Catholic understanding of Anglicanism. While some of its adherents, led by John Henry Newman* (1801–90), eventually converted to Roman Catholicism, others remained in the Church of England in uneasy coexistence with both Evangelical and liberal wings. Such growing pluralism within Christianity led to adjustments in the relationships between church* and state, with many of the educational, fiscal, and legal privileges of the Church of England gradually reduced and disestablishment of the Church of Ireland (1870) and the Church in Wales (1921). Nevertheless, the Church of England retained a privileged constitutional status. Overall the Victorian Era (1837–1901) was characterized by a high degree of public Christian religiosity, determined evangelism, and substantial but by no means universal churchgoing.

20th Century to 1960. By the outbreak of World War I (1914), Christian observance in Britain was on a plateau or even beginning to decline, and the war itself had a significant disruptive impact on conventional patterns of worship and belief. It was also the backdrop of the division of Ireland (1921), with the predominantly Roman Catholic south forming a separate state. Six counties in the north remained in the UK, forming the Protestant-dominated province of Northern Ireland with an alienated and oppressed Roman Catholic minority. The interwar period saw mixed trends for the Christian churches. The Church of England suffered internal tensions arising from Modernist* theology and from conflicts between Protestant and Catholic interpretations of Anglican identity that reached a climax in parliamentary rejection of a proposed revised Book of Common* Prayer (1928). Disestablishment initially gave a new lease on life to the Church in Wales, and reunion among Methodists (1932) and Scottish Presbyterians (1929) was seen as heralding a new confidence in witness, but such promise was not sustained. Roman Catholics grew in strength, but the Nonconformist (or Free) churches lost vision and momentum. World War II was followed by a period of stability and even recovery in Christian influence during the austerity of the 1940s and 1950s.

After 1960. From the 1960s onward, there was a serious and sustained decline in active Christian observance, a trend that has been dubbed "the death of Christian Britain." All denominations were affected, although Roman Catholicism was initially relatively resilient, and in Northern Ireland decline occurred later and was less pronounced than in other parts of the UK. The causes of this recession in Christian practice are much debated, but important factors include changing sexual mores, shifting attitudes among women (who made up a large share of earlier 20th-c. congregations), weakening links between the churches and community and national identities, competing leisure activities, and the secularization of Sunday, which became for the majority of the population a day for shopping and sport rather than for churchgoing. The reduction in the number of active Christians also has to be seen in the context of the growth during the same period of other world faiths, especially Islam, Hinduism, and Sikhism, mainly through immigration but partly through the conversion of British people. It should be noted, however, that the presence of religions other than Christianity was greater in England than in the smaller nations of the UK and remained tiny in Northern Ireland.

Statistics. The raw figures can be misleading. Only very superficially did Christianity still look dominant in 2000. It is true that, in the 2001 census, 72% of the population of England and Wales and 86% of the population of Northern Ireland identified themselves as Christian. In Scotland 65% of the population identified their "current religion" as Christianity, and 73% saw it as their "religion of upbringing." But many of these are "culture* Christians" (see Secularism and Secularization). In 2000 only 12% of the population of the UK were church members and church attendance amounted to only 7.9% of the population of Great Britain. If allowance is made for occasional and erratic attendance, a rather larger proportion may be judged to have some degree of church connection, but it is clear that the great majority of self-identified Christians do not practice their faith in any active way.

The denominational makeup of the dwindling community of active Christians was also changing. Sunday attendance for the Church of England fell from 1,370,000 (1980) to 960,000 (2000) and 850,000 (2006); and for the Roman Catholic Church, it fell from 2,064,000 (1980) to 1,394,000 (2000) and 860,000 (2006). However, from 1980 to 2000, the number of Baptists and Pentecostals declined only slightly – respectively, from 286,000 to 280,000 and from 221,000 to 216,000. Meanwhile the movement of new, independent* house* and community churches grew substantially, from 75,000 people attending in 1980 to 248,000 in 2000. Overall, therefore, there was an especially steep decline in liberal and Catholic forms of Christianity, while more conservative Protestant, Charismatic*, and Pentecostal* churches held their own or even grew. Indeed, within the Church of England, numerical strength shifted toward the Evangelical and Charismatic parishes. A further underlying factor has been the relatively high percentage of Afro*-Caribbean Christians who are practicing their faith – a fact that hides the sharp decline in Christian practice in the rest of the population (see Afro-Caribbean Christianity in the United Kingdom).

Worship. The later 20th c. saw substantial innovation in forms of worship. Change was driven partly by the aspiration to address decline by greater cultural responsiveness, but it also stemmed from the influence of the Charismatic* Movement, which, claiming direct inspiration from the Holy* Spirit, stimulated churches to seek greater spontaneity and less structure in worship. In the Roman Catholic Church, the traditional Latin Mass was entirely abandoned in favor of liturgies in English. In the Church of England, although the 17th-c. Book of Common* Prayer retained official status, it was superseded in practice in the majority of parishes by more contemporary liturgies collected in the Alternative Service Book (1980) and Common Worship (2000). The Church of Scotland Book* of Common Order has been similarly subject to ongoing revision.

Leadership and Ministry. In past centuries, Britain gave the Christian world leaders such as Boniface*, Wyclif, Cranmer*, Bunyan*, Wesley, Wilberforce*, Livingstone*, and Newman*. Although in recent generations, British Christianity has not produced any such seminal figures, there have been numerous distinguished and courageous endeavors to respond effectively to the challenges of a predominantly secular society. The most radical such attempt was made by John Robinson, the Anglican bishop of Woolwich, in his book *Honest to God* (1963), in which he argued that a traditional image of God* needed to be discarded in the modern world. Leaders such as Robert Runcie, archbishop of Canterbury (1980–91), were more cautious but pursued a strategy of constructive engagement with wider cultural and social forces and endeavored to maintain and extend unity within the Christian community. Similarly, Basil Hume, cardinal archbishop of Westminster (1976–99), ensured the continuing implementation in England of the reforms of the Second Vatican Council and held in check the more conservative and authoritarian tendencies in the Roman Catholic Church. Both men, however, presided over a continuing serious decline in service attendance in their respective churches, which they seemed powerless to control, let alone reverse.

Influential conservative voices have included Martyn Lloyd-Jones, minister of Westminster Chapel, London (1943–68); John Stott, central to the resurgence of Evangelicalism in the Church of England after World War II; and David Watson, who played a key role in promoting the Charismatic renewal (1960s and 1970s). The leaders of new independent churches in Britain include Bryn Jones of Covenant Ministries and Terry Virgo of New Frontiers, while in Northern Ireland, Ian Paisley's Free Presbyterian Church became a dynamic neoconservative force. International visitors have also played a significant role, notably Billy Graham, whose rallies have been seen as a significant factor in maintaining Christian strength in the 1950s. Graham returned to Britain in the 1980s, and other influential visitors in the more recent past include Pope John* Paul II (1982), the Argentinean evangelist Luis Palau, and John Wimber, whose California-based Vineyard Churches have established a presence in the UK.

Historically, the clergy of the Church of England and the Church of Scotland were an integral part of the social order, although varying enormously in wealth and influence. They were normally graduates of the ancient English or Scottish universities. Ministerial formation in the mainstream churches remains predominantly academic. In Scotland prospective ministers continue to be educated at the universities, and although in England ordinands attend separate theological colleges, they, too, often take university degrees.

The most significant trend during recent decades has been the gradual opening up of ordained ministry to women. From the 7th-c. abbess Hilda of Whitby to 19th-c. Methodist and Salvation* Army preachers, and in Quakerism throughout its history, women have exercised significant informal leadership roles in British Christianity. However, the first recorded formal ordination of a woman was that of the Congregationalist Constance Coltman (1917). Other Protestant denominations followed suit only in the second half of the 20th c.: the Church of Scotland in 1968 and the Methodists in 1974. The Church of England did not begin to ordain women as deacons until 1987 and as priests until 1994, but now women make up a rapidly increasing proportion of the clergy. Although significant opposition and objection remain, women are moving into senior positions as archdeacons and cathedral deans, and the Church of England is currently considering consecrating them as bishops (see Women's Christian Practices and Theologies Cluster: In Western Europe: United Kingdom).

Christianity and Society. In past centuries, Christianity had a profoundly formative role in British social development. During the 20th c., its impact became more limited and ambivalent, but it remained significant, notably through the numerous schools controlled by the Church of

England and the Roman Catholic Church. In the late 20th c., the tide of legislative change moved against "traditional" Christian morality and customs with, e.g., the legalization of abortion and homosexual practice (1960s) and of Sunday shopping in large stores (1990s). While associated with conservative personal morality, Christianity also showed a socially radical tendency, not only in the socialism of the veteran Methodist preacher Donald Soper (1903–98), but also in the Church of England report "Faith in the City" (1985), which was perceived as an attack on the policies of the government of Margaret Thatcher.

The 2001 census indicated that Christianity remains an acknowledged strand in the identity of the majority of British people, and its role in national identity is symbolized by the public religiosity of the monarchy and the state. In Northern Ireland, despite the peace process, sectarian religious identities remain deeply entrenched and potentially divisive. Elsewhere in the UK, the growth of religious pluralism has led to experimentation with multi-faith and secular forms of public religion and made the maintenance of historic Christian claims to unquestioned ascendancy increasingly contentious. **See also ANGLICANISM CLUSTER; EVANGELICALS/EVANGELICALISM CLUSTER: IN THE UNITED KINGDOM; METHODISM CLUSTER: IN THE UNITED KINGDOM; ROMAN CATHOLICISM CLUSTER: IN EUROPE: UNITED KINGDOM; SCOTLAND, CHURCH OF; SCOTLAND, FREE CHURCH OF.**

Statistics: *England and Wales*: Population (2001): 52 million (M). Christians, 37.4 M, 72%; Muslims, 1.5 M, 3%; Hindus; 0.55 M, 1.06%; Sikhs, 0.33 M, 0.63%; Jews, 0.26 M, 0.5%; others, 0.15 M (0.3%); nonreligious, 7.7 M, 15%; religion not stated, 4 M.

Scotland: Population (2001): 5.1 M. Members of Church of Scotland, 2.1 M, 42%; Roman Catholics, 0.8 M, 16%; other Christians, 0.34 M, 7%; Muslims, 0.04 M, 0.8%; others, 0.05 M, 1%; nonreligious, 1.4 M, 28%; religion not stated, 0.28 M.

Northern Ireland: Population (2001): 1.7 M; Roman Catholics, 0.68 M, 40%; members of Presbyterian Church in Ireland, 0.34 M, 21%; members of Church of Ireland, 0.26 M, 15%; other Christians, 0.16 M, 10%; others, 0.005 M, 0.3%; nonreligious or religion not stated, 0.24 M, 14%. (Based on 2001 census.)

JOHN WOLFFE

United States. Christianity in the USA is characterized by both unifying religious impulses and perpetual religious diversity, by both a blurring of the boundaries between the sacred and the secular and a clear distinction between church* and state.

The USA is widely regarded as a highly religious nation. Most US citizens profess to believe in God; presidential speeches and political ceremonies often proclaim national commitments in religious terms, portraying the USA as a nation with religious roots in the past and a righteous mission for the future – "one nation, under God," with a mandate to spread democracy* and justice* throughout the world. Yet religion exerts its great influence in the USA in a variety of ways through a vast diversity of communities and traditions, by no means limited to Christianity. Even before the arrival of Christian explorers and missionaries, Native Americans engaged in a multiplicity of religious practices in disparate communities. Religious diversity, therefore, is not a modern phenomenon but a perennial component.

Alongside religious diversity, a central religious "unity" developed that powerfully influenced American society. Mainstream Protestantism shaped the contours of this religious "center," beginning with the large number of British – mostly Protestant – immigrants who populated 13 colonies and founded a new nation. Much of the story of Christianity in the USA, therefore, concerns the interactions between "the one and the many": the Protestant mainstream repeatedly encountered religious diversity, beginning with Native* American traditions and continuing through interactions with other Christian traditions (Spanish and French Catholicism, and later Russian Orthodoxy), the religions of African* American slaves, mounting waves of Jewish and Catholic immigrants in the 19th c., and the explosion of Asian and Latin American immigration in the 20th and 21st c.

16th and 17th Centuries: Exploration and Colonization. When Christians first arrived in America, they encountered religions practiced by a variety of peoples, including Huron, Iroquois, Narragansett, Cherokee, Pueblo, Sioux, and Aleut. Despite the so-called European "conquest," the religious systems of native peoples were not annihilated. Native Americans who converted to Christianity rarely abandoned their indigenous beliefs. More often, they incorporated their beliefs and practices into European

Christianity to create new religious systems. It was less a Christian conquest than an exchange between Christianity and indigenous American religions (see Native American Traditions and Christianity).

If "conquest" does not describe the reality, it does describe the attitudes of many European explorers toward indigenous peoples, their cultures, and religions. Europeans believed that Christianity was an essential component of "civilized" European culture and that converting the "Indians" to Christianity was essential to replacing "savage" cultures with civilized societies.

Moreover, while explorers interacted with Native Americans, they also competed among themselves. For Spanish*, French*, and British* explorers, America was a prize to be won, a bountiful land rich with opportunity for profit, colonization, and Christianization; they therefore competed to implant the "right" kind of Christianity. Much like the crusaders* before him, and the Portuguese* in Africa and the Indian Ocean, Christopher Columbus in 1492 conducted his explorations on behalf of his nation and his religion, seeking territory for Spain and converts for Spanish Catholicism. Roman Catholic nations, Spain and France, preceded England's Protestant settlements.

Spanish and French Catholic Exploration and Mission. Spanish explorers moved quickly to claim the New World for Spain and the pope. In the early 16th c., Ponce de León and Vásquez de Allón named and explored Florida while conquistadores such as Hernán Cortés moved into Mexico, overpowering native populations with little regard for indigenous souls or cultures. The agendas of Spanish conquest and Roman Catholic conversion often clashed, with missionaries such as Dominican* Bartholomé de las* Casas insisting that indigenous people were human beings who deserved humane treatment. Las Casas and other missionaries were heard in Rome, resulting in Pope Paul III's papal bull, *Sublimus Dei* (1537), which decreed that European explorers and missionaries should seek to convert Native Americans while respecting their humanity, freedom, and property. But the inhumane treatment continued (see Spanish Explorations, Conquests, and Missions).

Tensions between conquest and mission also had an impact on French explorations of territories that are now part of Eastern Canada and the Midwestern USA. Unlike most Spanish missionaries, however, French Jesuits* such as Jean de Brébeuf achieved some success because they ignored the idea that Native Americans needed to adopt European culture to become Christian. In his work with the Hurons, Brébeuf lived among them, learned their language, ate their food, and incorporated Christianity into their culture. Brébeuf's immersion in Huron society eventually cost him his life; he was captured, tortured, and killed by the Hurons' enemies, the Iroquois, who nevertheless admired his courage. Brébeuf's missionary activity demonstrated a zeal for the gospel and a sensitivity to native cultures that earned the respect of Europeans and Native Americans alike.

While Spanish and French Catholics staked the first claims to what became the USA and Canada, their efforts were soon eclipsed by England's Protestant colonization, which indelibly marked the religious nature of North America (see Mission Cluster: In North America: Mission as Emigration-Colonization).

British Protestant Exploration and Mission: The Puritans. British migration to the New World reflected the tumultuous impact of religious reform in the homeland. Unlike Spain and France, England's church shifted from Roman Catholicism to Protestantism* in the 16th c., but the British people widely disagreed over how Protestant their church should be – whether it could retain many of the rites and traditions of its past or whether it should reject all remnants of Roman Catholicism. Henry* VIII's motivations for seizing control of the English Church from Rome were personal: the pope's refusal of his divorce from Catherine of Aragon. Thus, while rejecting papal authority, Henry retained much Catholic doctrine and liturgy. His heirs did not exercise a steady influence on the English Church. Edward VI endorsed a Protestant church; Mary* Tudor ("bloody Mary") violently returned the church to Catholicism, executing Protestant sympathizers; Elizabeth* I erected a moderately Protestant church that avoided liturgical extremes on either side. But her policies dissatisfied radical Protestants, who were often called Puritans* because they wanted to "purify" the church of any Catholic remnants and reform the liturgy according to strictly biblical precepts. When Elizabeth's successors, James* I and Charles, moved the English Church toward Catholicism and adopted anti-Puritan policies, Puritans looked beyond England, hoping to locate a place where they could practice their faith without the interference of the crown. This quest led some to Holland and many more to America (see Puritans, Puritanism).

The estimated 20,000 Puritans who migrated to America during the years 1620–40 created a "New England" society modeled on a particular religious vision. All Puritans agreed that the English Church was corrupt, although they disagreed on the extent of the corruption. More radical Puritans separated themselves from the Anglican* Church because they believed it was corrupt beyond the possibility of reform. Among "Separatist" Puritans were the founders of Plymouth* Colony led by William Bradford and remembered as "Pilgrims" in US popular history. The majority of Puritans, however, populated the Massachusetts Bay Colony, centered in Boston. These Puritans were not Separatists; they believed that the Anglican Church was corrupt but could be reformed with a return to the Bible and a rejection of "popish" liturgical practices. In New England, Puritans created a church without the "errors" imposed by Catholic tradition. Puritans used a simple worship style shorn of the liturgical trappings of Anglicanism, displaced the Eucharist from the center of worship and replaced it with the sermon, and preached in a "plain style" that focused on scriptural exposition rather than the Anglican penchant for quotations from church fathers and ornate arrangements.

The Puritan devotion to the Bible above all authorities (see Scripture) led to an emphasis on education*. Convinced that everyone needed to be able to read and understand God's Word, Puritans required that all children be taught to read and founded Harvard College early in the settlement process (1636). To the Puritans, the Bible was a book of covenants† between God and humanity, beginning with Adam* and continuing with Abraham* and, finally, Christ. Puritans constructed their society around covenants; salvation* was based on a covenant of grace; the church was organized through a covenant, as were the family and the commonwealth itself. In each covenant, people were bound by its terms, just as God agreed to honor the peoples' faithfulness to the covenants and to punish their violations. When the Massachusetts Bay Colony experienced struggles – in the form of wars with Native Americans, drought, dissent, and witchcraft* – Puritans viewed these crises as signs that God was punishing them for unfaithfulness to the covenant. In response, preachers called for the people to "return" (repent and return to the true faith) and to renew their commitments to God. These sermons, now called "jeremiads," communicated the divine commission that Puritans believed guided their society. This Puritan vision of a divinely commissioned society influenced later Protestant zeal to create a Christian America and contributed to the persistent idea that the USA was a special nation, chosen by God for a righteous purpose in the world (see Civil Religion).

Despite their efforts to create a uniform movement for church reform and godly society, Puritans engendered dissent and controversy. The first crises came from within their own ranks, with challenges from Roger Williams* and Anne Hutchinson*. Williams was a respected, educated Puritan clergyman who surprised Puritan leaders by adopting radical views, especially that church* and state should be separate and citizens should be allowed freedom to believe as they chose, without fear of reprisal by the state. After four years of controversy, the Massachusetts Bay Colony banished Williams in 1635 for threatening the foundation of Puritan society and the Puritans' attempt to establish a holy commonwealth. In addition, Williams denied the Puritans' right to New England territories since they had not been purchased from Native Americans, the rightful owners. After his banishment, Williams fled south, eventually establishing relations with Narragansetts, founding Providence as a colony based on religious freedom, and cofounding the first Baptist Church in the USA.

Soon after the Williams controversy, Anne Hutchinson, a woman with sharp theological sensitivities, questioned the orthodoxy of the Puritan ministry. Hutchinson, a follower of Puritan minister John Cotton, claimed that most of the clergy based their godly commonwealth on a doctrine of salvation by works, not grace*. Puritan society depended on obedience to the covenant and an outwardly righteous life. Hutchinson argued that this emphasis on godly works implicitly neglected salvation by grace, which should be the central focus of Christian life. Partly because of her ideas and partly because of her gender, Hutchinson was labeled a radical and banished from the Colony. But together with Williams, she demonstrated that the Puritans' zeal for a righteous society was not without flaws; it required the combined efforts of a biblical church and a sovereign state that had the authority to punish religious dissenters.

While influential, the Puritan story does not represent the entirety of British Protestantism in colonial America. Unlike the Puritans, most Anglican colonists were not as interested in reforming the Church as they were in establishing it in America. Eventually Anglicanism* became the official religion in most of the South, including Virginia, the Carolinas, Georgia, and Maryland. Yet the vast territories were a challenge for Anglicanism; because ministers had to cover much larger parishes in America than they had in England, they could not maintain the same degree of control over parishioners. Many colonial Anglicans also questioned the quality of their clergy, who may have moved to America after being rejected at home. In addition, the Anglican Church lacked the leadership of a bishop in America. The Anglican Church was not without good leadership, however. James Blair led the Church in Virginia and founded the College of William and Mary in 1693. Even broader support came from Thomas Bray* of Maryland, who created influential societies to promote religious literature (SPCK*, Society for Promoting Christian Knowledge) and clerical support (Society for the Propagation of the Gospel) in America.

Along with Anglicans and Puritans, more radical religious imports flowed from England to the colonies, including the Society of Friends* (Quakers). This society, much like the Puritan Movement, reflected the religious controversy in 17th-c. England. George Fox*, the founder of the movement, grew weary of religious divisiveness, much of which seemed focused on external rites that did not plumb what he believed were the spiritual depths of the faith. Fox, therefore, emphasized Christ's revelatory presence in the heart and deemphasized all other religious practices, including Bible reading, which was sacred to Puritans (see Quaker Worship). Because the Society of Friends insisted on pacifism* and rejected hierarchical class structure, the first Quakers to land in Boston received harsh treatment from Puritans; several were even executed. But Quakers thrived outside of Puritan jurisdiction. Many found refuge in Rhode Island, but the greatest support for Quakers came through the leadership of William Penn*, whose Quaker faith shaped his policy of religious liberty in Pennsylvania.

Puritans, Anglicans, and Quakers exemplified the great diversity of Protestant colonists from England alone. This diversity was increased by other immigrants from the British Isles and the European continent, including Scottish Presbyterians*, who settled throughout the colonies, beginning with the first congregation in Maryland, founded by Francis Makemie in 1684. Makemie was the primary catalyst for Presbyterianism in the colonies as he promoted Presbyterian unity in the Presbytery of Philadelphia organized in 1706. Other expressions of the Reformed* tradition included Dutch and German Reformed congregations, which clustered in New Amsterdam (later New York), Pennsylvania, and New Jersey. Many of these congregations were influenced by Pietism*, an international movement influenced by Puritanism that reacted against sectarian controversy and theological scholasticism by emphasizing individual spirituality and practical discipline. This movement, which can be traced to German Lutheran Philip Spener*, had a broad influence in America, especially through the Moravians*, and initiated revivalist preaching and later the Great* Awakening.

18th Century. In the 18th c., the distinctive character of Christianity in America began to take shape. Europeans and Africans continued to arrive (the latter shackled in slavery*); revivalism* erupted among Protestants; and the colonists won a war for independence and founded a republic that would have no officially established church. These and other factors helped to transform European strands of Christianity into uniquely North American forms.

Regional revivals in the 1740s later became known as the Great* Awakening. While historians debate the unity, extent, and political impact of the Awakening, there is no question that revivals broke out in various places among Christian groups. One of the strongest ties that bound the scattered revivals into a unified movement was the preaching of George Whitefield*, an Oxford-educated Anglican who toured the colonies five times. Whitefield's dramatic preaching style drew huge audiences from all levels of society, impressing even Benjamin Franklin*, despite his Deist sensibilities. Whitefield and other traveling preachers created a furor among some clergy, such as Charles Chauncy of Boston, who saw the itinerants encroaching on their territory and implored the people to resist the fanatical "enthusiasm" of the revivals in which passions ruled the intellect and made a mockery of respectable society and true religion.

The nature of "true religion*" was very much open to debate. In opposition to Chauncy, revivalists had an eloquent, articulate defender in Jonathan Edwards*, a Congregational pastor in Northampton and the greatest colonial theologian. Edwards argued that the revivals did not negate true religion; indeed, while some revivalist piety was illegitimate, much of it expressed the essence of authentic faith. Edwards, a revivalist preacher himself, located true religion not in the emotions, as Chauncy accused, but in the "affections," which included the intellect, inclinations, and will. In true religious faith, the entire person is oriented toward God's love and will, and this submission to God provides the foundation for all virtue and morality.

The revivals changed the nature of Christianity in America, dividing clergy, contributing to the rise of Baptist churches, and finally convincing people that religion was a matter of choice and that they had the freedom to make on their own. Although the clergy still led the churches, parishioners became religious consumers.

If the Great Awakening encouraged Christians to question religious authority*, the political revolution later in the century encouraged citizens to embrace similar liberties in political revolt against England. Were the two "revolutions" – religious and political – related? Historians debate this question. But it is clear that the American Revolution divided the churches as much as it did colonists. Christians were on all sides of the struggle; some, particularly Anglicans, were loyalists; many were patriots; others were pacifists, particularly Quakers, Mennonites*, and Moravians*. Patriot Christians understood Christianity and republicanism to be complementary. For them, republicanism was the most Christian form of government because it recognized that all people were sinners, even the best monarchs, and therefore no ruler should have too much power. In government there should thus be a separation of powers and the voice of citizens should be a shaping force. Both Christianity and republicanism were centered on freedom – from sin and oppressive rulers – and advocated revolution against tyrannical rule wherever it appeared, whether in Satan's vile grip on the soul or in King George's tyrannical hold on the colonies (see Democracy and Christianity).

While many patriots argued for revolution on Christian grounds, others were influenced more by Enlightenment* thought, which had a religious perspective of its own. Several of the nation's "founders," including Washington*, Franklin*, Madison, and Jefferson*, advocated a deistic* faith in a universal God who ruled through natural laws and was revealed in morality and reason, not revelation.

The Enlightenment-inspired convictions of the founders led them to determine that the government should not favor one religion over another. This principle was stated in the First Amendment to the Constitution (1791), which said that "Congress shall make no law respecting an establishment of religion, or prohibiting the free exercise thereof." The founders realized that the religious diversity of the new nation was incompatible with any attempt to establish a "national" church. The founders were also wary of ways in which religious controversy erupted in political turbulence in 17th-c. England and Europe. While the First Amendment provoked many questions, it challenged the traditional assumption that churches deserved governmental support. Although individual states continued to endorse established churches as late as 1831, eventually they all followed the First Amendment in abandoning civil endorsements of churches.

The heightened rhetoric of liberty and freedom inspired by revival, Enlightenment, and revolution reverberated through a slaveholding nation. The slaves* forced from Africa to the USA brought their religious practices with them, thereby adding to the country's religious diversity. Just as the European Christians were separated from Native Americans by cultural differences, African American slaves inhabited religious worlds that stood in stark contrast to the Christianity of their masters. The slaves first encountered Christianity as an enslaving religion, the ideological justification for their oppression, which hardly made Christianity attractive to them. Often, masters resisted Christianizing their slaves because Christianity implied full humanity and citizenship, and therefore conversion would undermine the slave system. Nevertheless, Christianity was received by many slaves, with their own creative adaptation of the faith. While masters preached a Christianity that enforced the slave system and encouraged obedience to authority, slaves fashioned a Christianity that centered on the freedom of the Exodus, human equality, and the redemptive freedom in Christ and that incorporated religious practices indigenous to the slaves' African cultures. This new form of Christianity provided the foundation for present-day flourishing African American churches (see African Religion and Christianity Cluster).

As in the periods of exploration and colonization, Christianity in the 18th c. – and later on, during the addition of territory as a result of the Louisiana Purchase (1803), the Mexican War (1846–48), and the Alaska Purchase (1868) – encountered other religions and cultures, adapted to US patterns of settlement and leadership, and continued to negotiate the boundaries of sacred and secular, church and state. At the close of the 18th c., Christianity in the new nation was in an intriguing position. While religious observance was predominantly Christian, Christianity no longer enjoyed the support of the state. How would Christianity survive under these new circumstances? Would some varieties of Christianity thrive while others faltered? And, finally, what would determine success?

19th Century. The language of liberty that empowered the American Revolution dramatically influenced Christianity in the 19th c. With the First Amendment's rejection of governmental support for religion, churches lost the power of the state and had to compete for the allegiance of the people. The people, therefore, had more power than ever to shape their religious lives and to determine the viability of the churches. Following the lead of the new nation, much of Christianity became "democratized," and revivalism was a pivotal force.

The early 19th c., therefore, experienced a Second Great* Awakening, with revivals* breaking out in various locations, including the frontier and upstate New York. Unlike the first Great Awakening, which stressed that only God's predestined "elect" could be saved, the 19th-c. revivals refuted predestination* and emphasized that all people had the power to choose salvation. This denial of election in favor of individual freedom was consistent with the rhetoric of liberty in a new nation with an expanding frontier. The primary institution of frontier revival was the "camp* meeting." The most famous one, in Cane Ridge, Kentucky, in 1801, led by Presbyterian preacher Barton Stone*, lasted several days and attracted thousands of people; many experienced strange bodily symptoms of the Spirit's presence, including jerking and fainting. In upstate New York, Charles Finney* viewed religious revival as a science and crafted "new measures" that outlined detailed methods for success. In both the camp meetings and Finney's carefully planned revivals, the message emphasized democratic freedom: all sinners have the power to respond to grace, turn to God, and be saved.

Baptists and Methodists benefited most from the democratic turn in religion, because of their polities and leadership styles. Baptists had no ecclesial hierarchy: each church controlled its own affairs and chose its own ministers without enforcing stringent ordination* requirements. Many Baptist ministers were bivocational "farmer-preachers," similar in educational and social background to their parishioners. While Methodists had an ecclesial hierarchy that controlled the churches, they made extensive use of "circuit rider" preachers who traveled countless miles to take the faith to every corner of the frontier. Bishop Francis Asbury* set the sacrificial example for Methodist ministers by traveling thousands of miles to preach and create churches. Primarily because of these democratic structures and practices, Baptists and Methodists became the most numerous religious groups in the USA by 1850.

While revivalism propelled Baptists and Methodists into the mainstream, new religious groups took their place on the margins of Christianity. Several strands of the Restoration* Movement sought to restore the NT church and its unity in the hope of ending the denominational competition that raged in the 19th c. These groups, led by Barton Stone, Alexander Campbell*, and others, eventually merged, calling themselves both the Christian* Church and Disciples* of Christ, ironically creating an additional strand of denominations. Subsequent divisions underscored the point that, in the USA, denominationalism* was a pattern that was not easily avoided.

While the Restoration Movement looked to the biblical past for guidance, other new groups were oriented toward the future, specifically the biblically inspired anticipation of the second* coming of Christ. Among these groups were Millerites*, Adventists*, and the Church of Jesus Christ of Latter-day* Saints. The last group, also known as Mormons*, began in upstate New York with Joseph Smith's* publication of the Book of Mormon* (1830), a new scripture that Smith claimed to have translated from golden plates revealed to him by the angel Moroni. While Mormons shared much with their Evangelical neighbors, there were also significant differences, including polygamy*, for which Mormons were persecuted. As the Mormons moved west, Smith and others were lynched for their beliefs, although the movement continued to thrive, soon settling in present-day Utah (1846). In the 20th c., Mormonism abandoned polygamy and entered the religious mainstream, promoting family values and conservative politics alongside Protestant Evangelicals.

Not only did 19th-c. revivals transform the churches, they empowered the churches to reshape society. Inspired by revival, Christians joined a variety of voluntary societies for social reform. The spirit of reform was enhanced by the theology of perfectionism* as taught by Finney and Methodist revivalist Phoebe Palmer*. According to perfectionism, Christians can cleanse themselves of sin and achieve entire sanctification*. Furthermore, perfection is not limited to individuals; society itself can be perfected if Christians devote themselves to the effort. Many Christians did just that, supporting societies for abolitionism, temperance*, and other efforts to preach the gospel through social activism.

The most controversial Christian reform movement was the effort to abolish slavery* – an issue that separated Christians along regional lines. The three major denominations – Presbyterian, Methodist, and Baptist – experienced regional division in the decades before the Civil War (1861–65). This division among the churches set the stage for the rupture of the nation. The religious split reinforced regional differences, which were increasingly reflected in opposing political parties.

Christian reform movements were substantially women's movements. While women were traditionally barred from ordination in most denominations, they constituted the majority of parishioners and empowered various efforts for social reform. Women were particularly influential in the anti-slavery effort. Among them were sisters Angelina and Sarah Grimké*, Quaker abolitionists who also advocated women's rights. Possibly the most influential was the daughter of prominent revivalist Lyman Beecher*, Harriet Beecher Stowe*, whose best-selling novel, *Uncle Tom's Cabin* (1852), vividly depicted the atrocities of slavery and divided the nation to such an extent that Abraham Lincoln later referred to her as "the little lady who started the big war." Following the Civil War, women's suffrage became a crucial issue. Christian reformers argued that granting women the right to vote would result in a more Christian society, and a more righteous society, because mothers were moral leaders. Although women were not granted the right to vote until 1920, 19th-c. Protestants prepared the way. Women's* missionary societies and women's activities on the mission field offered new opportunities for leadership positions.

In the second half of the 19th c., millions of European immigrants (including German, Irish, and Polish Catholics) flooded the USA and transformed it into a more urban and more ethnically diverse society. Although the nation had no officially established religion, immigrants soon discovered that Protestantism had substantial public presence and political power. Partially in self-defense, most immigrants gravitated to the cities and gathered in communities that shared their religious and ethnic identities. Religion provided immigrants with a familiar way of life in an unfamiliar nation. Tensions developed as Polish, German, and Italian Catholics encountered a US Catholic Church dominated by Irish clergy. Therefore, some Polish Catholics formed the Polish National Catholic Church, and some Ukrainian Catholics gravitated toward the Orthodox Church.

Many Eastern European immigrants were Jews fleeing persecution in Russia*; relishing the opportunity to live as orthodox Jews without fear of reprisal, they gathered in cities and created synagogues. These Jews had a very different attitude toward US culture than the more Americanized Reform Jewish position represented by Rabbi Isaac Mayer Wise. Later, Conservative Judaism developed a "middle" position, attempting to maintain a tension between adaptation to US culture and faithfulness to Jewish traditions.

Just as immigrant Roman Catholics and Jews struggled with the question of how "American" they wanted to be, culturally dominant Protestants struggled with the question of whether the immigrants could be "American" at all. Though nativism was not new in the USA, anti-Catholic polemics led to the rise of groups that opposed the perceived religious and cultural threats that immigrants posed to Anglo-Saxon America.

The millions of immigrants often lived in deplorable conditions, brought on by the rise of the cities and the industrial revolution. Poverty*, sweatshops, and child labor were effects of the new manufacturing economy* in an urbanized nation. Protestant reformers saw these developments as threats to their "Christian America" and sought avenues for ameliorating these unjust conditions. Liberal Protestant efforts for reform became known as the Social* Gospel Movement. Unlike conservative groups such as the Salvation* Army, advocates of the Social Gospel argued that sin* infected social structures, not just individuals, and thus a Social Gospel was needed to combat unjust structures of society. Leaders of the Social Gospel Movement included Congregationalist minister Washington Gladden, economist Richard T. Ely, and theologian Walter Rauschenbusch*, who wrote *Christianity and the Social Crisis* and *A Theology for the Social Gospel*.

The same force that compelled mainstream Protestants to reform the homeland motivated them to spread the gospel throughout the world. This impulse toward world mission* also had political ramifications, as the drive to preach the gospel was tightly woven with the simultaneous effort to expand the influence of the USA through war and colonization. These efforts for mission and empire combined in the Spanish–American War (1898), during which US Protestants stoked the fires of conflict against what they perceived as Spain's oppressive Roman Catholic regime in Cuba*. The decisive victory over Spain also brought the Philippines* under US political and religious control. Many Protestants interpreted the victory as the triumph of God's nation against injustice, giving them a religious responsibility to shed Protestant light on the Filipinos, who had endured the oppression of Spanish rule and its Catholic faith.

The drive toward a US empire in the world merged with missionary zeal to inaugurate a new stage in the nation's Christianity. Throughout the 20th c., US involvement with international conflicts continued to be propelled by the rhetoric of a righteous empire with a divine mandate (see Mission Cluster: And Imperialism).

20th Century. At the beginning of the 20th c., the USA was a new world power and Protestantism was its most pervasive religious presence. Protestants increasingly defined what it meant to be American. This Protestant achievement met challenges, however, from the ongoing Jewish and Roman Catholic immigration. Protestants had to adjust to a more diverse ethnic and religious society; Jews and Catholics had to determine the extent to which they would accommodate themselves to Protestant America. Catholic adaptation to Protestant America intensified into controversy, with leaders such as Archbishop John Ireland* emphasizing that US ideas of democracy* and liberty were consistent with Catholicism; by contrast, other Roman Catholic leaders followed Rome's stance against adapting Catholicism to liberal, democratic societies.

Fissures also appeared within the Protestant world itself, as mainline churches divided over the new science* and its evolutionary* theories of life and radical Protestant groups emerged to challenge the mainstream faith. Liberals* like Shailer Mathews and Harry Fosdick* attempted to preserve the faith by updating traditional doctrines to make them consistent with evolution and other emerging scientific theories; fundamentalists* advocated faithfulness to an inerrant* Bible and traditional doctrines. While liberal viewpoints evolved among many leaders in the mainline denominations, fundamentalists withdrew to create a religious subculture that would nurture their convictions through separate institutions and publications. Conservative Evangelicalism* would reemerge later in the century to once again take an active role in public life.

The victories of "moderates," with tolerant attitudes, over fundamentalists made perfect sense in the optimistic 1920s as science, technology*, and economic* advancement offered great promise for solving humanity's problems. Adaptations of traditional pessimistic doctrines such as original* sin and the need for Christ's sacrificial atonement* seemed necessary if Christianity was to maintain its relevance. The situation changed dramatically in the 1930s: economic prosperity gave way to the Great Depression, and the world found itself dealing once again with the devastation of world war. Amid these ominous crises, neo-orthodoxy* emerged as a theological perspective that rejected the simplistic optimism of liberalism and called for a reassessment of traditional Christianity's teachings on human depravity. This theological reassessment was influenced by European theologians, chiefly Karl Barth*, but the US movement was led by Reinhold Niebuhr*, a former theological liberal and pacifist who came to advocate a form of "realism" whereby Christians recognized the threats of evil in the world and argued that force was sometimes the only viable opposition.

Meanwhile, Evangelical groups interpreted years of economic crisis and war through their Premillennialist and Dispensationalist* reading of the Bible. By focusing on apocalyptic scriptures, particularly Daniel and Revelation, these Christians became convinced that history was regressing, not progressing, and that Jesus would soon return to gather the faithful and inaugurate his millennial rule. This Premillennialist theology influenced many groups, including Jehovah's* Witnesses, but the Pentecostal* Movement was most prominent.

"Pentecostalism" is a general term for a variety of denominations that witness to a post-conversion baptism of Holy* Spirit, confirmed by speaking in tongues. This vast, multiracial, multinational movement began in 1901 with the preaching of Charles F. Parham at a Kansas Bible school and spread through Parham's influence on others, including William Joseph Seymour*, an African American preacher whose leadership in the Azusa* Street revival in 1906 greatly influenced Pentecostalism's expansion.

The growing vitality of Pentecostalism and other Evangelical movements through the mid-20th c. demonstrated that conservative Protestantism flourished despite losing status in mainline denominations. In the postwar years, evangelist Billy Graham led Evangelicalism's resurgence in popular culture, garnering the national spotlight and the respect of political leaders. The 1950s also evidenced a civil* religion that drew on Jewish–Christian traditions but transcended them in symbols and practices. This civil religion supported the American way of life – a sentiment expressed by President Eisenhower's statement that "our form of government has no sense unless it is grounded in a deeply felt religious faith, and I don't care what it is."

America's optimistic civil religion encountered formidable obstacles in the turbulent, countercultural revolutions of the 1960s. From the Civil Rights Movement, to the countercultural movement (e.g. Woodstock), and to protests against the Vietnam War, the resounding theme was the disillusionment of youth with the USA and its supporting institutions. Traditional religion was attacked as passé, US civil religion was lambasted as hypocritical, and many saw the ironies of injustice and racism* in a nation that championed freedom and equality.

Christianity was on both sides of the cultural divide – both a supporter of the status quo and a critical element in revolution. The cry for justice came principally from the African American Church, led by Martin Luther King*, Jr., an academically trained theologian and Baptist minister whose eclectic influences included the Black Church tradition, the Social Gospel Movement, the theology of Reinhold Niebuhr, and the pacifism of Mahatma Gandhi. The success of the Civil Rights Movement resulted primarily from King's religious sensibilities, substantial oratory skills, and willingness to advocate nonviolent* protest against racism.

Another attack on the US status quo came from the Feminist* Movement, which advocated women's liberation from confinement in the patriarchal* structures of US society. As Feminist theologians recognized, patriarchal structures pervaded the churches, their theologies, and their practices. Most visible was the denial to women of a place in ordained ministry, even though the majority of church members were women. The Feminist Movement served as a catalyst for a progressive change in this pattern. The Methodist Church began ordaining women in 1939, followed by the Presbyterian Church in the USA in 1956. The American Lutheran Church and the Lutheran Church in America followed in 1970, and the Episcopal Church ordained women priests in 1976. Resistance remains in Orthodox and Roman Catholic churches and conservative Protestant denominations such as the Southern Baptist Convention.

The tremors of change in the 1960s also affected Roman Catholicism. Vatican* II (1962–65), called by John* XXIII, inaugurated a new era in Catholicism's attitude toward modernity and the USA. Jesuit John Courtney Murray – along with French Catholics – facilitated the passage of the "Declaration on Religious Liberty," also known as the "American document," which modernized Church attitudes toward religious coercion in a modern world. The council also approved liturgical changes, replacing Latin with vernacular languages, mandated a more congenial attitude toward other Christians, and issued statements against anti-Semitism*. While Vatican II did not resolve all the issues between traditional doctrine and the modern world, it dramatically altered the Church's direction and at least engaged these issues.

Ironically, the radicalism of the 1960s is largely responsible for the resurgence of conservative Evangelicalism in more recent years. Politically charged movements such as the Moral Majority flourished as conservatives responded to what they perceived to be the downfall of the USA by attempting to restore the nation to its Christian roots. Ronald Reagan won the presidential election in 1980 with the support of the Evangelical Religious Right and other conservatives.

Others responded to 1960s radicalism and the counterculture by adopting Jesus as a symbol of their revolt against authority, including the mainstream church. This countercultural Jesus movement was centered in California and moved eastward with institutions that combined Pentecostalism with progressive views on worship. Communities such as Calvary Chapel rejected formal Protestant worship styles and adopted contemporary music, encouraged informal dress, and generally attempted to relate Christianity to popular culture. The result was church that did not look and feel like church. The proliferation of independent community churches of many kinds, coupled with the decline of mainline Protestantism, provided one of many examples of Evangelicalism's appeal to the world through traditional theologies and untraditional forms such as contemporary worship styles, music, and Christian novels. The beginning of the 21st c. witnessed a complex blend of religious vitality in such independent Evangelical groups and steady decline in membership in mainstream Protestant denominations.

Mainstream Roman Catholicism also faced turmoil and decline. Nearly 40 years after Vatican II, tensions remained between Catholics and many Americans who criticized the Church's opposition to birth* control, abortion*, and women's ordination. In addition, scandal plagued US Catholicism when many priests were accused of sexually abusing minors or of conspiring to cover up the crimes of abusive priests.

With the approach of the year 2000, anticipation of the promise of a new millennium was perhaps overshadowed by anxieties. While most Evangelicals refrained from making specific forecasts of Christ's return in the year 2000, the expectation was revitalized and the *Left Behind* series of novels about the second coming of Jesus and the rise of Antichrist outsold most secular titles. This religious reaction to millennial anxieties reflects a keen interest in religion that set the nation apart from other Western societies.

A new phenomenon emerged in the late 20th to early 21st c.: the multiplication of megachurches*, from 50 in 1970 to 1,300 in 2008.

At the end of the 20th c., more than 90% of Americans professed to believe in either God or a higher power, and this religious interest expanded beyond diverse religious groups to encapsulate US attitudes toward the nation itself. This US civil religion, which held that the nation had a special mission in the world, continued into the 21st c. and became a prominent theme in political speeches and policies. While political rhetoric always had religious overtones – with the common conclusion "God bless America" – political religious language dramatically increased after the terrorist attacks on the World Trade Center and the Pentagon on September 11, 2001. Three days after the attacks, President George W. Bush spoke at the National Cathedral on a "National Day of Prayer and Remembrance." His speech reverberated with images of America's devotion to God and mission "to answer these attacks and rid the world of evil." As Bush's rhetoric affirmed, many Americans still thought of the USA in religious terms, as a righteous empire that preached the gospel of democracy in a hostile world. The perseverance of this idea was one indication that, despite the general secularizing influences, for better or worse, religion remained a vital element of US public life, even in a time when the loss of a Protestant majority seems imminent.

Statistics: Population (2000): 278.4 million (M). Christians, 235 M, 84.7% (independents, 78.6 M; mainline Protestants, 64.6 M; Roman Catholics, 58 M; Orthodox, 5.8 M; Anglicans, 2.4 M; marginal Christians, 10.1 M; all have declined as a percentage of the population since 1970, except for independents [almost doubled], marginal Christians, and Orthodox); nonreligious and atheists, 26 M; Jews, 5.6 M; Muslims, 4.1 M; Buddhists, 2.5 M; Hindus, 1 M. (Based on *World Christian Encyclopedia*, 2001.)

JAMES P. BYRD

Unity. In reference to God or the church, unity can mean uniqueness*, unification of discrete things, the reunion of what had been divided, or the fecundity that produces similar things. The unity of the church, furthermore, can be visible and institutional (the Roman Catholic approach), or it can be a spiritual unity (as in Eastern Orthodoxy).

Universalism, the belief that all receive salvation* and go to heaven*, in contrast to "double issue," according to which some go to heaven, some to hell*. Two considerations have been involved:

1. If God's grace overcomes sin*, should not one believe that it might overcome the sin of everyone, whatever that sin might be? Origen* and Gregory* of Nyssa were confident that grace and providence would bring all created spirits, even the devil*, back to unity with God, but this position was condemned under Justinian* (543), with the endorsement of the Western Church. In modern times, universalism has reasserted itself, especially in the Universalist* Church in England and the USA, as well as in F. D. Maurice. A different kind of universalism was set forth by Schleiermacher*, Karl Barth*, and many others; for them, the meaning of predestination* changes from that of "double issue" to God's sequential dealings with the human race: all are first condemned so that they will take sin seriously, and then all are offered salvation*.
2. The alternative of either eternal salvation or damnation* seems to be too stark for the majority of human beings, who may not see themselves as clearly destined for one

or the other. Belief in purgatory* is a more moderate approach, allowing this middle group, those who are neither dramatically good or dramatically evil, to become sufficiently pure of heart to behold God. An analogous notion that all human beings are offered salvation after death was put forward by C. A. Briggs and more recently by John Hick.

The debate over universalism presupposes specific views of atonement (see Atonement #2, as honor and juridical satisfaction), of salvation* (from condemnation), of sin* (as a moral evil involving individual guilt and responsibility), and related theological concepts – views prevalent in Western* churches. For the many other Christian traditions (including those of the Eastern* churches, as well as many churches outside the North Atlantic world) that do not share these views, a more important debate concerns the uniqueness* of Christ (see, e.g., Colenso, John William).

EUGENE TESELLE and DANIEL PATTE

Universals. The debate over universals between nominalists* and realists* framed discussions regarding Christology* and the Trinity* (from the 4th and 5th c.), as well as Scholasticism* (late Middle Ages). In different guises, it also played a significant role in theological developments in the late 20th to early 21st c.

Experience shows that discrete things may have identical characteristics, making them instantly recognizable; they may also have the power to reproduce themselves (fire spreads, and living things reproduce offspring). These "samenesses" are called universals because they are exemplified in all instances.

Plato* thought that universals subsist independently and that they are the source of both the definiteness of things and of human knowledge. Plato's position is traditionally called "realism*," in the sense that universals are realities. An important modification in Middle Platonism* was that universals are ideas* in God's mind, the exemplars by which the world is created.

Aristotle* agreed that universals give form to things, but he denied that they are self-subsisting; instead they are present in things as their "forms," and they are known not in a separate realm of ideas but through abstraction from sense experience. Plato's error, he said, was in supposing that because universals exist in the mind they must also exist in reality. Aristotle's position is usually called "moderate realism," since it affirms universals but gives them reality only as they are in things and, in a different mode, in the mind. This position presupposes an orderly world and the ability of the mind to discover, understand, and speak about that order.

Others argued that universals are nothing more than human words (hence "nominalism*" or "terminism") or at best human concepts (hence "conceptualism"), with no status outside language or mind. Porphyry's* *Isagoge* (Introduction to Aristotle's Categories; its translation by Boethius* introduced the problem of universals to the Middle Ages) raised three questions: Are kinds in reality or only in thought? If kinds are real, are they bodies or incorporeal? Are they separated from sensible things or are they in them?

During the 4th- to 5th-c. discussions of Christology*, some thinkers, positing that "kinds are real," affirmed that the Word* assumed "humanity" rather than "a man" (a specific human being), often in the sense that the saving power of the Incarnation* extended, at least potentially, to all humans. Regarding the Trinity*, Gregory* of Nyssa had already compared the Trinity to three human beings sharing a common nature. A realist like Gilbert* de la Porrée was criticized for making too strong a differentiation between the divine essence (a reality) and the three persons (as three realities), in effect postulating a "quaternity" instead of the Trinity. By contrast a nominalist like Johannes Roscellinus (Abelard's* teacher) was accused of tritheism*, because he affirmed three persons but denied any real unity in the divine essence.

Scholasticism* was ultimately called into question when nominalism became dominant in the later Middle Ages. Nominalists of that period (beginning with William of Ockham*) were critical of the attempts of theology to make inferences from a given assertion, since there may be no basis in reality. Therefore, nominalists found incoherence in a large number of the theological arguments; the only resolution to many problems, they said, was revelation* alone. In one sense, their subtle arguments represented the fulfillment of Scholasticism, but the end result was to call Scholastic argumentation into question.

Scientific developments in the 17th c. introduced the new element of mathematics, which refocused the question of universals. Looking not at the intrinsic forms of things but at their interactions, scientists found striking regularities in the natural world. Yet confidence in the orderliness of the world was modified by 20th-c. physics with the principle of indeterminacy and the increased reliance on probability rather than exact prediction. This change of approach had alternative outcomes, ranging from skepticism* and pragmatism* to a new form of realism in Whitehead*, for whom universals ("eternal objects") are the multiple "forms of definiteness" in both the mental and the physical poles of all actual occasions, recombining in many ways as the world process moves ahead.

The biological sciences have come to recognize that each living entity has a unique genetic code (the exceptions are plants that spread through propagation or grafting and animals that are duplicated through cloning). In this respect, the nominalists' ontology seems to be confirmed. At the same time, a species is defined as an interbreeding "population" of organisms, usually incapable of genetic combination with members of other species, or if there is successful hybridization, the offspring are often sterile. In this respect, "moderate realism" seems to be confirmed.

Reflecting on the work of biologists and other scientists, in the philosophy of science "realists" assume that the regularities formulated in scientific laws correspond with those in the natural world, while conceptualists or nominalists emphasize the creative role of human thought and discourse, and even the influence of cultural* assumptions, in formulating the concepts and propositions used in science; if these propositions are deemed to be true, it is only because they are "confirmed," without exceptions, by experiments or careful measurements (see Science and Christian Theology).

Another contemporary equivalent of the debate over universals is the accusation of essentialism*, e.g. by feminist* scholars who attack facile assumptions that women always have the same inclinations and needs, regardless of social and cultural factors. Many Liberation* theologians have a similar argument. Essentialism in this context is the cognitive assumption that what one knows about women or about human culture in one's own situation will be true of them universally; its ontological assumption is that there is an "essence" of the feminine in all women or an essence of the human in all people in other cultures and social situations (a realist perspective). The alternative to essentialism is a nominalist perspective that reasserts the need to consider individual persons in their specific social and cultural settings, which is found in different guises in postmodern, postcolonial, and Liberation theologies (see Liberation Theologies Cluster; Postcolonialism and Christian Theology; Postmodernism and Liberation Theologies; Postmodernism and Theology), as well as in contemporary cultural studies of Christianity (see Culture Cluster: And Christianity). **See also NOMINALISM; REALISM.**

EUGENE TESELLE

Universities (derived from Lat *universitas*, a term used to refer to the "totality" of teachers and students). Some features of modern universities can be traced to the schools of Athens and Alexandria, with their attention to texts and philosophical and theological problems. Universities can be traced even more directly to the Miaphysite* schools in Antioch*, Nisibis*, and Edessa*, where Syriac* Christians translated Aristotle and mediated other aspects of Greek culture, and the monasteries* and cathedral schools of the early Middle Ages, which preserved texts and interpreted Greek and Latin traditions under the adverse circumstances of the Arian* Goth invasions. In the West, intellectual inquiry was necessitated by apparent conflicts in theology, biblical* interpretation, and canon* law (see *Glossa Ordinaria*; Gratian; Peter Lombard); by the rediscovery of civil law (see Justinian); and by new translations of works of Aristotle*, works that were based on autonomous reason* and lacked the explicitly religious overtones of Platonism* that influenced earlier theology.

The first universities were established in Bologna, Paris, and Oxford (late 12th c.; formalized early 13th c.). Supported by city governments and national rulers (because of the potential income, travel, trade, and prestige they could generate) they were defended by organized bodies of teachers and students (the initial meaning of "university"), as well as by the papacy, which permitted universities to accept students from anywhere in Europe and to confer on graduates the authority to teach anywhere, thus reinforcing an international community of scholars. The University of Naples, founded by Frederick* II (1224), was the first state university.

Paris and Oxford became centers of theology, and their best-known theologians were members of the mendicant* orders (including Alexander* of Hales, Roger Bacon*, Bonaventura*, Thomas Aquinas*, Duns* Scotus, and William of Ockham*). The universities played a major role in late medieval life, training officials of both church and state, as well as theologians, many of whom became bishops, cardinals, and popes. The leaders of the universities tried to maintain a balance between the church hierarchy and political rulers (see Babylonian Captivity; Conciliarism).

Although they did not initiate the Renaissance*, universities engaged in the study of the classics in Latin, Greek, Hebrew, and Arabic, which had been newly edited and printed, usually by individual scholars. With the Age of Exploration, universities spread to other parts of the world; those in Lima (1551), Mexico City (1551), and Manila (1595 and 1611) were founded before Harvard (1636).

Movements for reform often began in the universities. Wyclif*, Hus*, and Luther* were professors. Battles between Roman Catholic and Protestant, Jesuit* and Dominican*, Anglican* and Puritan* theology were fought either in the universities or using the modes of argumentation learned in them. Opposing groups influenced each other, even in heated debate: they read each other's editions of the classics and engaged in a common task of historical investigation, steadily overcoming partisan tendencies – hence the gradual rise of the modern university, with its increasingly comprehensive studies and variety of disciplines.

Colleges and universities in the European and American colonies had varied origins. Some were founded by governments, some by missionary churches, and some by citizens. As a result of their diverse origins, universities were under potentially conflicting influences, both before and after the colonies' independence. Some universities emphasized traditional culture and religion; some adapted to Western commerce, technology, culture, and religion; some adopted a nationalist approach.

Women had traditionally received an education through informal learning, through private tutoring in the case of the wealthy, or by joining a religious order. But in the 19th c. they began to be admitted to colleges and universities. For example, in the USA, Oberlin College was founded (1833) without restrictions of either gender or race; Mount Holyoke was the first women's college (1837). Many state and private colleges and universities followed these two models, namely coeducation and gender-differentiated education. Racial desegregation came more slowly in the USA (finally required by law in the 1960s).

The relationships of universities to religion are varied. In Germany*, universities are under the control of the state, which in turn sanctions church control of theological faculties. In Great Britain, the links between the state and the Church of England were gradually loosened (19th c.). In the meantime, Dissenters* established their own colleges and seminaries, some of which are now affiliated with Oxford and Cambridge. In France after the Revolution, universities were placed under state control, but independent Roman Catholic universities were established. In the USA, there has been a mixture of church, state, and private control. State universities "teach about religion" (in an academic way), in contrast to church-related seminaries and universities that "teach religion" and train students for religious vocations in a particular church setting. Many universities in Africa are like state universities; they offer a varied set of courses in Roman Catholicism, Protestantism*, Islam*, and African* Traditional Religion. **See also** THEOLOGICAL EDUCATION CLUSTER. EUGENE TESELLE

Upper Room, second-story room built in the Greco-Roman world for privacy, for entertaining guests, or to provide comfort during hot seasons. Place where Jesus and his disciples had their last Passover meal together (Mark 14:15, par.) and which became the meeting place for the disciples after Jesus' death and resurrection (Acts 1:13).

Urban II, Pope (c1042–99), prior of the monastery of Cluny, cardinal, and bishop of Ostia before his election (1088). Having inherited a tenuous position – his predecessors, Gregory VII and Victor III, had faced strong imperial opposition – Urban held a number of local synods aimed at strengthening his authority. In Piacenza (1095), the probable presence of an imperial envoy may have turned his attention to the plight of the Byzantine Empire in its struggle against the Turks. Urban summoned the Council of Clermont (November 1095), which, while continuing the agenda of the reform papacy, called for support to liberate the Eastern churches and Jerusalem from the control of Muslims. During the First Crusade*, as it came to be called, large parts of Asia Minor were conquered and Latin rule was established in the Holy Land. JAMES M. POWELL

Ursulines. See MERICI, ANGELA; WOMEN'S RELIGIOUS ORDERS CLUSTER: IN EUROPE AND NORTH AMERICA.

Uruguay. Among Latin American countries, Uruguay is by far the most secularized. Thus Christianity has a unique form: the Roman

Catholic Church, marginalized by a strong European-style secularization*, does not dominate the culture and society, yet Christianity remains highly influential in the paradoxical form of a civil* religion.

Because the region was sparsely populated by a few thousand Charrua, there was no sustained effort to develop an "Indian Christianity." The reductions* established by Jesuits* and Franciscans* (from 1616) and their inhabitants disappeared after the expulsion of the Jesuits (1767). Spanish colonization was slow and weak in this region, which lacked gold or silver, and was settled by people of European (today 94%) and African descent (from slaves that escaped from Brazil*). In this context, a rather liberal and enlightened Catholicism, more Franciscan than Jesuit, supported independence from Spain* (1811) and later from Argentina* and Brazil (1828). The long series of wars leading to independence prevented the institution of a Christian state. A process of secularization, from c1860 to c1919, pitted the state against the Catholic Church. The state (led at decisive moments by an anticlerical liberal elite) developed and occupied key "social spaces" in the new nation (e.g. education, health care) before the Catholic Church could.

Besides the predominant Roman Catholicism, Uruguay traditionally had two basic forms of Protestantism: missionary churches (e.g. Methodist*) and "ethnic churches of immigrants" (e.g. Anglicans*, Waldenses*, Swiss Reformed*), which sustained the identity of their immigrant communities. The relations between Protestants and Catholics oscillated: Protestants tended to side with the liberal state during periods of secularization* and anticlericalism* (preventing Catholicism from assuming hegemonic power), but distanced themselves from the state when secularization became "antireligious." During the 1960s political crisis and the dictatorship of 1973–85, Catholics and Protestants joined in a struggle for social* justice*, human* rights, and democratization*.

Despite Uruguay's reputation as a secularized and laicized* country, Christianity continues to have a great influence on the moral and social spheres, although often in the form of a civil* religion. The latter has replaced the churches in public and private life, promoting itself in the social imagination by the use of key Christian phrases, symbols, and rituals, even as it practices an antireligious and often anti-Christian discourse. "Batllism" (the liberal politics, from the early to middle 20th c., of President José Batlle and later his nephew President Luis Batlle), a pragmatic mixture of elements of the welfare state and anticlericalism – including the banning of crucifixes from hospitals and the replacement of Christmas by a national family holiday – exemplifies the recent history of Christianity in Uruguay.

Early in the 21st c., after the deinstitutionalization of Christianity, in Uruguay as elsewhere (especially Western Europe) religion became more individualistic and doctrinally flexible. Yet the ongoing secularization, considered an inevitable expansion of the "modern" and "progressive" liberalism of the 19th c., seemed to have collapsed. What emerged in its place is not easy to describe, as it includes multiple and often contradictory features: the rise of new religious movements and practices; the influence of "the religious" throughout society; "mystical-esoteric" themes expressing, and appealing to, a highly individualistic "religion à la carte"; the growth of extremist, integrist*, and fundamentalist* movements; and the transformation of the relation between religion and politics. Evidence that the traditional perception of Uruguay as a secularized country is eroding includes the expansion of international religious movements, including the Charismatic* Movement, which often ignores social issues and introduces unexpected practices and doctrines.

Many recent events are indicative of this erosion of secularization. For example, there was a proposal to make permanent a cross that had been erected near a public highway (a secular place) for a liturgical ceremony during the visit of Pope John Paul II (1987). Other religious monuments have been erected in public spaces. Proselytizing religious programs are common in the mass media*. For traditional Christian feasts as well as for new celebrations of diverse religious origins, there are large religious gatherings and popular ceremonies. Religious and political authorities interact more readily than they did in the past.

Public opinion surveys in the early 21st c. seem to indicate a considerable growth in personal religious quests, to which religious institutions have responded in different ways. The archbishop of Montevideo, Nicolás Cotugno, brought attention to and defended the emerging "neo-Christianity" – a controversial stance within both the Uruguayan Catholic Church and the society. The "New Age" Movement (often linked with Eastern religions) has spread. The Pentecostal* and Charismatic* movements are economically powerful and omnipresent in the mass media. These are only a few of the many signs of the strong religious momentum, with significant social and political consequences, that challenges the continued "laicized" and antireligious trend in secular and secularized Uruguayan society. **See also ROMAN CATHOLICISM CLUSTER: IN LATIN AMERICA: URUGUAY; SECULARISM AND SECULARIZATION.**

Statistics: Population (2006): 3.4 million. Roman Catholics, 47.1%; "non-Catholic Christians" (various Protestants, presumably including some Charismatics), 11.1%; "believers in God without confession" (presumably including members of independent churches, including Charismatics), 23.2%; "atheistic or agnostic," 17.2%. (*Source*: 2006 Survey of Encuesta Nacional de Hogares.)

GERARDO CAETANO

Usury, charging of interest on loans, forbidden in the OT (Exod 22:25; Deut 23:19–21) and by several early councils; formally condemned in the Middle Ages, although permitted among Jews*.

Usus Pauper, "poor use," doctrine of the Franciscans* (approved by Pope Nicholas III, 1279) that they owned nothing and that they merely used things that were owned on their behalf by others, although this use was to be minimal. **See also PROPERTY.**

Utilitarianism. See CONSEQUENTIALIST ETHICS.

Utraquism, Hussite* practice (promulgated by Jacob of Mies, 1414) stipulating that both the bread and wine should be given to all communicants during the Eucharist* (Lat *utraque specie,* "in both kinds"), in contrast to the Roman Catholic practice of giving the bread alone.

V

Valdes, Peter (flourished 1173–1205; also known as Waldo or Valdesius), wealthy merchant of Lyon who converted to a life of poverty (c1173). After making provisions for his wife and daughter, he lived on alms and preached poverty with his followers, the "Poor Men of Lyon." Although initially approved by the Roman Catholic Church (Pope Alexander III and the Third Lateran Council, 1179), the Poor Men were later excommunicated, and the Council of Verona (1184) condemned them. Valdes's followers became lay preachers and formed groups found from Languedoc to Northern Italy and Austria. **See also WALDENSES.**

Valentinians (followers of Valentinus*) were members of what was probably the largest and most influential of the Gnostic* movements; according to Irenaeus*, they participated in the life of the church but had their own secret teachings. They divided human beings into three groups, but how this was determined has been disputed among scholars: was it by predestination*, by nature, by their attitude toward the three components of human life (matter, soul, and spirit), or the degree of their transformation? In any case, the three human groups are clear: the "hylics" (dominated by matter), who cannot be saved; the "psychics" (cf. 1 Cor 2:14, 15:46), who are saved by faith and good works; and the "pneumatics," who return to the fullness of spiritual life. **See also GNOSTICISM; SALVATION.** EUGENE TESELLE

Valentinus (d c165), Gnostic* theologian. Born in Egypt, he claimed to have been taught by Theudas, a disciple of Paul*. He went to Rome (c136), and after a period in Cyprus* returned to Rome. His works were known chiefly through Irenaeus*, Clement* of Alexandria, and Hippolytus* until the publication of the Nag* Hammadi library, which included several writings of his school, including the Gospel* of Truth.

Validity of Sacraments. Against Cyprian's* and the Donatists'* claim that only pure persons can administer the sacraments effectively, Augustine* argued that the sacraments do not depend on the minister's worthiness. Being signs instituted by Christ, they are valid if administered by an ordained* person using the correct words and with the intention to perform a sacrament. Validity does not guarantee "efficacy" (which depends on grace*).

Valladolid Debate (1550). Juan Ginés de Sepúlveda, Bartolomé de las* Casas, and Francisco de Vitoria debated, in one of the most remarkable events in the history of Western political, theological, and missiological traditions, the justification for conquering and evangelizing the Amerindians in the New World. After the violent encounter between Cortés and the urban and socially ordered Aztec Empire, the Spanish crown could no longer justify the *encomienda** system as it did with Caribbean* Amerindians. The debate centered, among other things, on who is a human being and what are the religious and political rights to the newly "discovered other." **See also MISSION CLUSTER: IN THE CARIBBEAN ISLANDS.**

CARLOS F. CARDOZA-ORLANDI

Vandals, a Germanic people who were converted to Arian* Christianity (as were the Goths*) before invading and ruling Spain* and (Southern) Gaul (409–15), and primarily North Africa (429–534). Arian Vandal authorities persecuted Roman Christians, most of whose bishops were deposed or expelled. Many faithful were killed or tortured. As the churches became Arian, many Roman church leaders took refuge in Europe, while others were deported. When the Byzantines destroyed the Vandal kingdom (534), Rome once again ruled North Africa and restored the churches to the Roman Church. **See also ARIANISM; HISTORY OF CHRISTIANITY CLUSTER: IN AFRICA: NORTH AFRICA.**

van der Kemp, Johannes, Dutch missionary of the London Missionary Society in South* Africa. He arrived in 1799 and, after a failed mission to the AmaXhosa of the Eastern Cape, settled among the Khoi people of Bethelsdorp, Cape. He integrated himself with the Khoi, adopted their way of life, and married a Khoi woman. **See also SOUTH AFRICA.**

MOKGETHI MOTLHABI

Vanity, emptiness, futility, worthlessness, instability, mere show, deception, vainglory; a theme in Ecclesiastes (1:2, 3:19, 11:8, 12:8) and Romans (8:29). Vanity can be associated with misdirected human values and desires, with idolatry*, or with the human condition, which is not only finite but subject to change and corruption.

Vatican, the city-state in Rome where the pope* resides and the Holy See* is located. The term "the Vatican" often refers to the Roman Curia located within it or to the pope.

Vatican Council I, or First Vatican Council (Vatican I) (1869–70), 20th general council of the Western, Latin Church, held in Rome, best known and often misunderstood for its teaching on papal infallibility*. As modern constitutional republics advanced, Pius IX* (1846–78) was determined to stave off attacks on his authority*. There were two small groups of bishops, one in support of infallibility and the other opposed to this doctrine, while a substantial number generally backed the idea but saw its promulgation as inopportune: the Roman Catholic Church had long survived without such an explicit statement, which would be another barrier to unity with non–Roman Catholic Christians. After several months of debate, a compromise was legislated in *Pastor Aeternus*. Instead of declaring the infallibility of the person of the pope in all matters, the statement asserts the infallibility of the teaching authority of the pope when he speaks *ex cathedra* (as universal shepherd sitting on the chair of St. Peter*, which no other bishop holds) on a matter of faith and morals. Such statements are irreformable and do not require the consent of a general council. The related discussion of how papal and episcopal authorities operate in tandem was not taken up until the Second Vatican* Council (1962–65).

CHRISTOPHER M. BELLITTO

Vatican Council II, or Second Vatican Council (Vatican II) (1962–65). When he called the Second Vatican Council, Pope John* XXIII wanted it to renew Roman Catholic spirituality*, heal divisions within Christianity, and alter the Roman Catholic* Church's reactionary attitude to the world. He presided over more than 2,500 bishops when the first session of the Council opened in 1962 and died in June 1963 before the Council met for its next session. Pope Paul* VI saw the Council through the second, third, and fourth sessions, and closed it on December 8, 1965. He then led the implementation of Vatican II's general policies (e.g. regarding justice* and peace*) and particular decisions (e.g. about celebrating the Mass* and other sacraments in the vernacular languages) until his death in August 1978. When he was elected pope* in 1978, John* Paul II pledged to continue implementing the Council's teaching. Benedict XVI made the same pledge when he became pope in 2005.

Vatican II produced 16 documents, which amount to 30% of the written texts from all 21 general councils recognized by Roman Catholics. The first document ("The Constitution on the Sacred Liturgy*," approved in 1963) aimed at revitalizing worship*. The final document ("The Pastoral Constitution on the Church in the Modern World," approved on the last working day of the Council) aimed at promoting the ultimate well-being of the whole human community. The central document was "The Dogmatic Constitution on the Church" (approved in November 1964), which acted as an umbrella for such documents as "The Decree on Ecumenism*" and "The Declaration on the Relation of the Church to Non-Christian Religions*." Vatican II gave rise to subsequent texts that applied the Council's new "Code of Canon* Law" (1983), its "Code of Canons of the Oriental Churches" (1990) (see Orthodox Churches, Eastern, Cluster; Orthodox Churches, Oriental, Cluster), and its "Catechism* of the Catholic Church" (1992).

Vatican II reshaped many institutions and created new ones. In Rome the Pontifical Council for Promoting Christian Unity, e.g., was founded in 1960 to help prepare for the Council. It has guided relations with non-Catholic Christian churches and communities, as well as with Judaism*. Around the world, new institutions were formed, such as the Federation of the Asian Bishops' Conferences (1974). Since 1971, a total of 17 Synods* of Bishops have been held in Rome to continue the work of Vatican II in such areas as evangelization* (1974), the Christian family* (1980), and the formation of priests* (1990).

GERALD O'COLLINS, SJ

Veil, the most important part of the habit* of women who enter the religious* life, connoting spiritual marriage with Christ.

Velázquez, Pedro (1913–68), priest, director of the Mexican Social Department (1941–68). He initiated in Mexico the national network of credit unions (Movimiento Nacional de Cajas Populares) and cooperatives for housing, agriculture, and artisanship, adapting them from

European models (see Cooperative). His books include *Dimensión social de la caridad* and *Miseria de México*. **See also MEXICO.**

MARÍA ALICIA PUENTE LUTTEROTH and ELIZABETH JUDD

Veneration (Gk *douleia*; Lat *dulia**), offered to saints* and holy things, in contrast to worship*, *latreia* (Gk; Lat *latria**), offered only to God. Veneration often takes the form of devotions* – acts of veneration associated with a shrine, an icon, or a sacred place of pilgrimage dedicated to a saint or the Virgin Mary*. Yet such veneration is not (or should not be) an end in itself; it leads to worship of God because, as Basil* of Caesarea said referring to icons*, "The honor rendered to the image rises to the prototype." **See also ANCESTOR VENERATION AND CHRISTIANITY CLUSTER; NICAEA, SECOND COUNCIL OF.**

Venezuela. Christopher Columbus* arrived in Venezuela during his third journey to the New World (1498). The country was named "Venezuela," which means "small Venice," because the natives' houses were built on stilts in the water. Hundreds of different indigenous peoples (referred to as "Indians") inhabited the territory.

After establishing themselves, the Spanish conquerors, began to convert the native people, planting the Roman Catholic Church, and eventually also converted the black slaves* they had brought from Africa. As elsewhere in Latin America, the arrival of Christianity in Venezuela resulted in a demographic disaster for the Chibcha, Arawak, Carib, and other native peoples – currently a statistically small percentage of the population, located primarily in the western part of the country – and in the rise of a racially mixed population (*pardos*) – now nearly half of the population, including mestizos* (European/Amerindian), mulattos (European/black African), and *zambos* (Amerindian/Black African), the rest of the population being either white Europeans (in addition to Spaniards, immigrants from many countries) and Africans. After independence other churches were established in Venezuela. Today a large majority of the population claims to be Roman Catholic (c81%, although the percentage of those who attend Mass* is much lower). A small Protestant and Orthodox population (in a great diversity of churches) is quite active; starting in the late 20th c., following the rise of the Pentecostal churches, the Charismatic* Movement emerged in the historic churches and in many independent churches (c10%, including indigenous churches).

When the Spanish arrived, several indigenous nations inhabited the country, the majority belonging to the Chibcha, Arawak, and Carib (Mariche) linguistic families. Dominican* and Franciscans* priests arrived in the northeastern part of the country (1513), and later Andalusian monks settled in other regions. The newly baptized Indians were exploited without mercy by the *encomenderos** (colonists, including the religious* orders themselves, to whom the Spanish crown "entrusted" the indoctrination of the natives in exchange for services and tax revenues), who were seeking slave labor for their cocoa, coffee, and sugar plantations. The indigenous slaves, who were progressively replaced by African slaves, were used for tending cattle (introduced in the Llanos grasslands, Western Venezuela, and Eastern Colombia, areas served by Andalusian monks).

The biological and cultural "mestization" process set the stage for syncretism*/inculturation* in the religious field. The temples where the cults of traditional gods were performed were destroyed. But now saints* are celebrated in chapels built on the very sites of these temples; the old gods have been "baptized" as saints. For example, the Maria Lionza indigenous devotion associates Maria Lionza (a chief's daughter, born c1502) with both the goddess of water and vegetation and the Virgin Mary*, and in addition its followers venerate two saints murdered by colonists: Guaicaipuro, an Indian chief, and Negro Felipe, a black slave. Many Roman Catholics participate in this devotion, which combines elements of indigenous and African religions with Roman Catholicism.

By the time Venezuela declared independence from Spain (1811), the Catholic Church was the only church established in the country. During the war for independence (1811–23), a significant number of British soldiers came to Venezuela to support the war against Spain led by Simón Bolívar, who incorporated Venezuela into Gran Colombia*. Since many British soldiers were Anglicans, the Anglican Church was introduced (1830). Yet after Venezuela's independence from Gran Colombia (1830), the law of patronage (see Patronato, Padroado), ratified in 1830, extended to the republican regime privileges that the Holy See* had originally granted to the Spanish crown. In return the government granted to the Roman Catholic Church legal status in Venezuela, although it was always somewhat precarious during the periods of political turmoil and dictatorial rule that characterized the rest of 19th and much of the 20th c.

The life of Juan Bautista Castro (1846–1915) illustrates the vicissitudes of the Roman Catholic Church during this period. He attended the seminary in Caracas and was ordained a priest (1870) in Barcelona (Eastern Venezuela). At that time, the government of Antonio Guzman Blanco (three terms as president, from 1870 to 1887) was persecuting the Catholic Church, exiling bishops and priests, closing seminaries, monasteries, and convents, banning religious orders, and expropriating buildings and other property of the Church. In 1882 Fr. Castro was appointed rector of the Episcopal School in Caracas, which concealed a seminary that prepared future priests while other seminaries were closed. At the same time, he was given charge of a church in the center of Caracas, called "Santa Capilla" (named after the Sainte-Chapelle of Paris), dedicated to the adoration of the Holy Sacrament, a devotion* which Fr. Castro disseminated by founding newspapers and a religious congregation, "Siervas del Santísimo Sacramento" (Servants of the Holy Sacrament, 1896), ultimately leading to the official consecration of the Republic to the Holy Sacrament (1899). Appointed coadjutor archbishop of Caracas, Fr. Castro was consecrated a bishop (1904). After surviving an attempted murder (1906) when poisoned wine was given him during Mass, he presided over the International Eucharistic Congress in Caracas (1907), the first of its kind convened in Latin America, helping the Roman Catholic Church in Venezuela to regain the ground it had lost during the persecution (see Eucharistic Congresses).

In addition to the Siervas del Santísimo Sacramento, five religious congregations were founded between 1889 and 1909, in response to the persecution of the Church: the Sisters of the Poor of Maiquetía (1889), the Franciscan Sisters of the Sacred Heart of Jesus (1890), the Augustine Recollect Sisters of the Heart of Jesus in Venezuela (1901), and the Catechist Sisters of Our Lady of Lourdes (1909). The founding of these congregations is epitomized by the founding of the Carmelite Sisters of Mother Candelaria (1906) by Susana Paz Castillo-Ramírez (1863–1941). In Altagracia de Orituco, a village in the Llanos where she was born and raised, the "Revolution of Liberation" (1901) left thousands of wounded. Susana took care of many of them at her home. A priest, Sixto Sosa, founded a hospital for the sick and the wounded, asking Susana to assist the doctors (1903); she and other young women began to live and work together in the hospital. The Sisters of Mother Candelaria (with Susana, now Mother Candelaria, as its head), soon worked in other hospitals: Upata (1917), Porlamar (1917), Barcelona (1921), and Cumaná (1921). In 1925 this congregation was officially incorporated into the Carmelite order.

During the 19th and much of the 20th c., many immigrants came from Spain, Portugal, Italy, Syria, Lebanon, Greece, Russia, Ukraine, Romania, Serbia, Germany, England, and the Caribbean Islands (particularly those belonging to the British Empire). For this reason, some Eastern rites within the Catholic Church are present in Venezuela, e.g. the Greek Melkite* and the Maronite* Rites. Several Oriental and Eastern Orthodox churches, such as the Armenian* Apostolic Church and the Antiochian Orthodox, Greek Orthodox, Romanian Orthodox, Russian Orthodox, Serbian Orthodox, and Ukrainian Orthodox churches (see Orthodox Churches, Eastern, Cluster) established sizable congregations, although they are relatively small compared with the Roman Catholic Church. Some churches of the Reformation are also represented: the Lutheran and Presbyterian churches, as well as other Evangelical* churches (a generic term referring to most Protestant churches). By the late 20th c., the largest percentage of non-Catholic Christians were Pentecostals*, Charismatics* (c10% of the population, often in independent churches or as members of other churches), and Seventh-day Adventists*. Jehovah's* Witnesses make up the largest non-Catholic church.

Frequent meetings of the representatives of the churches, during the Week of Prayer for Christian Unity and throughout the year, led to the establishment of the Council of Historic Churches of Caracas (2001). Immigrants to Venezuela during the 19th and 20th c. included a significant number of Jews and Muslims. The Committee for Relations between Churches and Synagogues (since 1970) fosters good relations between Christians and Jews by promoting a dialogue not only about theological questions, but also about social and political issues of interest to the country. The relationship between Christians and Muslims has been improving since 2000.

The relations between church and state have been subject to constant change and tension. In 1964 the Bilateral Agreement (which replaced the law of patronage) was jointly signed by the state and the Roman Catholic Church. This *modus vivendi* recognized that the Catholic Church had legal status and guaranteed its right to conduct religious and social* work (including education*) and acknowledged the rights of Catholic lay associations. The state pledged financial assistance to the Church hierarchy for the maintenance of church buildings as well as for Catholic education (universities, high schools, and elementary schools). Conversely, the agreement made the Catholic Church somewhat dependent on the state; e.g. the appointment of bishops can be vetoed by the government, bishops must be Venezulan nationals, and foreign ecclesiastical personnel must have special visas. Despite this agreement, Catholic education, which was supposed to be supported by the state, often suffered harassment at the hands of changing governments, so that the future of Catholic education is always uncertain. Bishops, priests, sisters, and laypeople feel threatened by political change.

The Constitution of the Bolivarian Republic of Venezuela, approved by the National Assembly in 1998, declares religious freedom. As a result, the presence of other churches and religions is now respected. Yet, although most of the population is Christian, in the early 21st c. the government was still trying to undermine the churches and the Christian faith, and to impose its socialist ideology.

Statistics: Population (2008): 28 million. Christians, 94.4% (Roman Catholics, 81.1%; Orthodox, 1.1%; Protestants, 0.5%; independent Pentecostals/Charismatics, 10.2%; marginal Christians, 1.5%; doubly affiliated, 3.1%); Jews, 0, 4%; Muslims, 1.7%; ethnoreligionists and Spiritists, 3.3%; nonreligious, 2.3%; others, 1.0%. (*Source*: CEHILA [Comisión de Estudios de Historia de la Iglesia en Latinoamérica] and González-Oropeza's *Iglesia y Estado en Venezuela.*)

RAMÓN VINKE

Veni Creator, hymn to the Holy* Spirit, written in 9th-c. France; attributed to Rabanus* Maurus.

Venial Sin, a sin that is not so serious as to deprive the soul* of sanctifying grace*, because it is a transgression of God's law without complete commitment to the evil end; in contrast to mortal* sin. **See also SIN.**

Veracruz, Alonso de la (Alonso Gutiérrez) (1504–84). Upon his arrival in Veracruz, Mexico, he entered the Augustinian* order and changed his name. He performed important functions in the Augustinian* order, in the Diocese of Michoacán, and at the Universidad Real y Pontificia (the Royal and Papal University) and was a steady advocate of indigenous people and their rights. **See also MEXICO.**

Vernacular, Use of. The vernacular is the language used in everyday speech. The earliest followers of Jesus spoke Aramaic; soon Greek speakers joined the community (Act 6). Both languages continued to be used, but the earliest-surviving writings (NT) are in Greek. Just as Jews had translated the HB into Greek (Septuagint*) and Aramaic (Targums*), early Christians assumed that the Bible and worship should be in the vernacular. Coptic and Syriac (2nd c.), and slightly later Latin (in North Africa), came into use; but Greek remained the language of the Roman Church until the 4th c.

Missionary activity encouraged the use of other vernaculars. Ulfila* devised a Gothic* alphabet (c340–50) and translated the Bible and the liturgy into the Gothic language, which was used by Germanic nations for several centuries (see Arianism); Ethiopic became a church language soon afterward in Ethiopia*; and an Armenian alphabet was invented (c405) by Mesrop Mashtots* in Armenia*.

Cyril* and Methodius developed an alphabet for their mission to the Slavs (c863) and translated the Bible and the liturgy into the dialect spoken in the region of Thessalonica; Old Church Slavonic continues to be the language of the Russian*, Ukrainian*, and Serbian* churches. Farther east, Syriac-speaking Christians traveled to China* and produced Christian writings in Chinese.

The British Isles were a notable exception, in that vernacular languages (Irish, Welch, Anglo-Saxon) were used in popular Christian poetry and devotion but Latin was used for the Bible and worship. Similarly, in Germany and Scandinavia, Latin was the language of worship, although vernacular epics like the *Heliand** (c830) based their depictions of Christ on the model of the Germanic hero.

The missionary impulse associated with Francis* (c1182–1226) and Dominic* (1170–1221) stimulated the fresh study of languages, especially Arabic, in European schools. The Age of Exploration (first down the coast of Africa, then to the Indies and the Americas) brought a greater awareness of the world's many peoples and languages. Although missionaries learned indigenous languages for evangelization and popular devotions, the Mass* was said in Latin.

There had already been translations of the Vulgate* Bible into many European languages in the late Middle Ages (see Bible Translations

Cluster). During the Protestant Reformation*, the Bible was translated directly from Hebrew and Greek and, with the help of the newly invented printing press, became accessible to many believers. Literacy was encouraged. Translations of the Bible helped to standardize many European and other languages (see Bible Translations Cluster; also, e.g., Indian Literature, the Bible, and Christianity).

The Roman Catholic Church officially changed its stance at the Second Vatican* Council, declaring that the Mass and other sacraments should be recited in the language of the people. Latin has been retained, however, and at times its use has even been encouraged because of its antiquity and its worldwide uniformity.

EUGENE TESELLE

Vespers, the ancient evening prayer of the church; its use in Roman Catholic parishes* was encouraged at the Council of Trent* (1545–63) and Vatican* II (1962–65). Anglican evensong* is based on this liturgy.

KEITH F. PECKLERS, SJ

Vestiges (Lat "footprints"), traces of God in the natural world, as contrasted with the image* of God in humans.

Vestments or Vesture, garments worn by the clergy during worship. In the early church, there was no distinctive liturgical garb. But when laypersons abandoned long tunics and cloaks during the 4th–9th c., these garments became a priestly costume. Today they vary significantly among denominations.

Viaticum, Communion given to those facing death*, to strengthen them for their journey.

Vicar (Lat *vicarius*), anyone acting "in the person of" a superior; in the Roman Catholic Church, the representative of any ecclesiastic; a "second-level" bishop (Russian Orthodox Church) or priest (Anglican Church).

Vicar of Christ, in Roman Catholicism, a title used since the early Middle Ages by bishops and rulers to indicate that they were Christ's representatives; limited to the pope since the 13th c.

Victorinus, Marius (4th c.). Born in Africa, he became a noted rhetorician in Rome. His conversion to Christianity aroused public comment and made him a role model for Augustine*. His works on the Trinity* attack Arianism* and make use of difficult Neoplatonic* concepts, drawn especially from Porphyry*; while Augustine adopted some of them, he followed his own course of reflection.

Vienna Circle, group of philosophers of science* (from 1907) that issued a manifesto (1929), published a series of papers, and was dispersed after the Nazi annexation (*Anschluss*) of Austria (1938). **See also POSITIVE THEOLOGY, POSITIVE LAW, POSITIVISM; WITTGENSTEIN, LUDWIG.**

Vietnam. Tradition has it that the first Christian missionary was a certain I-Ni-Khu (Ignatius), who preached the gospel in coastal villages of Northern Vietnam in 1533. The systematic establishment of missions began in 1615, mostly (until 1659) by Jesuits*, including Alexandre de Rhodes (1593–1660). De Rhodes proposed (1645) that Rome appoint bishops as vicars apostolic, directly responsible to the Congregation of the Propagation of the Faith. He also asked the Vatican to nominate bishops and priests and to create local dioceses and parishes for the 300,000 Vietnamese Roman Catholics, because the original Portuguese missionaries and the Portuguese Padroado* could no longer provide for such a large number of believers. Two French priests were appointed bishops, François Pallu (Tonkin, Northern Vietnam) and Pierre Lambert de la Motte (Cochin China, Southern Vietnam).

This action freed Catholic missions from the interference of Portugal and led to the introduction into Asia of new missionaries, the Missions Étrangères de Paris, Dominicans*, and Franciscans*, who opposed the Jesuits'* accommodationist policies.

From the beginning the Vietnamese Catholic Church suffered heavy persecution (17th–18th c., 30,000 killed; 19th c., 100,000 killed, especially during the Van Than Movement, 1864–85). Of these martyrs, 117 were canonized by Pope John* Paul II (1988). Politically, Catholics were regarded as collaborators with France, which used the persecution of French missionaries as an excuse to invade (1859) and colonize Vietnam. Christianity was branded by Vietnamese the *ta dao* (false religion) because its prohibition of ancestor* worship undermined the moral and religious foundation of the Vietnamese society.

In 1954 French colonial rule ended; Vietnam was divided into the northern Democratic Republic of Vietnam (Communist) and the southern Republic of Vietnam. During the war between the two regions, some 700,000 Catholics emigrated from north to south. In the north, the Communist regime severely curtailed church activities. In the south, the Roman Catholic Church expanded rapidly, thanks to the Vatican* II reforms. The so-called Vietnam war ended with the Communists' victory (1975), and several hundred thousand South Vietnamese, mostly Catholic, sought refuge in the West.

The Protestant/Evangelical Church of Vietnam, "Tin Lanh" (Good News), emerged mainly from the Christian and Missionary Alliance (since 1911), with 4,000 members by 1927. After World War II, the Protestant Church reached out to "original dwellers of the land" (especially Raday and Koho), and by 1974 there were 45,000 Raday and Koho Protestants. In the rest of Vietnam, by 1975 there were 510 Protestant churches (including US Protestant denominations), with 54,000 members. After the Communist takeover, the Protestant Church suffered grievously; most churches were shut down and 100 pastors sent to "reeducation camps."

The Roman Catholic Church under the Socialist Republic of Vietnam also suffered great losses. Its educational and social institutions were confiscated and all its religious organizations disbanded. Hundreds of priests were sent to reeducation camps. Pastoral activities were strictly regulated. In 1988 the Communist government officially guaranteed freedom of religion, allowing the opening of six major seminaries and other public church activities. Yet religious persecutions still occur. In 2005 the Catholic Church had 25 dioceses and 5,500,000 members (6.7% of the population); there were about 600,000 Protestants and as many "independent" Christians.

Statistics: Population (2005): 82 million (million). Christians, 6.7 M, 8.2% (Roman Catholics, 5.5 M, 6.7%; Protestants, 0.6 M, 0.7%; independent Pentecostals/Charismatics, 0.6 M, 0.7%); Buddhists, 40.1 M, 49%; nonreligious, 16.4 M, 20%; new religionists, 9.2 M, 11.3%; ethnoreligionists, 7.4 M, 9%. (Based on *World Christian Encyclopedia*, 2001, and church statistics.)

PETER C. PHAN

Vigil, eve of a festival or holy day, and thus a devotional "watching" during a worship service. In the early church, the paschal* vigil went through the night, when baptism was administered, ending with the Eucharist at dawn.

Vigilius, Pope (537–55). A Roman, he gained Justinian's* and Theodora's* support as an official in Constantinople; he became pope in 537. Involved in the Three* Chapters controversy, he eventually affirmed Justinian's position, endorsing the decrees of the Second Council of Constantinople* (553) just before his death. His vacillating behavior is often cited to refute papal infallibility*.

Vincentian Canon, test of Catholic tradition enunciated in the early-4th-c. *Commonitorium* of Vincent of Lérins: "what has been believed everywhere, always, and by all." Vincent's purpose was probably to attack Augustine's* views on grace* and predestination* as incompatible with the tradition* of the Catholic Church. **See also VINCENT OF LÉRINS.**

Vincent of Lérins (early 4th c.), monk on the island of Lérins; probably one of the Semi-Pelagians* opposed by Prosper* of Aquitaine. His *Commonitorium* enunciates the well-known Vincentian* canon. The Athanasian* Creed may go back to him.

Vincent de Paul (c1580–1660), priest, central figure in the Roman Catholic Counter* Reformation (Catholic* Renewal) in France. With his organizational skills, nourished by a life of intense prayer, he helped to focus the charitable activities of others, rich and poor alike, on the indwelling person of Jesus, the "evangelizer of the poor." His interest in missions of parish renewal, especially in rural areas, resulted in the founding of Confraternities of Charity. He founded the Congregation of the Mission (priests and lay brothers) to preach and aid in the formation of clergy (1625) and, with Louise de* Marillac, the Daughters of Charity (1633) and the *Ladies of Charity* (1634). He was canonized in 1737. JOHN E. RYBOLT

Vine, Vineyard. Grapevines cultivated in vineyards are often mentioned in the Bible (from Gen 9:20). "Vineyard" is sometimes a metaphor for Israel (Isa 3:14; 5:1–7; Jer 12:10), as is "vine" (Hos 10:1; Ps 80:8, 14). "Vine" is also a symbol of safety (Israelites sitting under their vines; 1 Kgs 4:25; Mic 4:4) or associated with judgment* (Ezek 15:1–8; Jer 2:21; 6:9). Jesus used vineyard imagery in his parables (Matt 20:1–16, 21:28–46; Mark 12:1–12; Luke 13:6–9) and identified himself as the true vine (John 15:1–17). Drinking the "fruit of the vine" is associated with both the Last Supper and the Kingdom* (Mark 14:25; Matt 26:29; Luke 22:18). JEFFRY C. DAVIS

Violence Cluster

Violence and the Bible
Violence and Christianity throughout History
Violence and Pastoral Care

Violence and the Bible. One of the oldest hymns in the HB proclaims that "YHWH is a warrior" (Exod 15:3). The biblical story of the people of Israel is grounded not only in the miraculous escape from slavery in Egypt but also in the violent conquest of Canaan. The Israelites are commanded to "utterly destroy" the inhabitants of the land, and the Book of Joshua* claims that at least in some cases they did so. Scholars now doubt the historicity of the conquest narratives, but violent conquest is presented as an ideal in the biblical text, typified by the example of Phinehas, who showed his zeal by killing an Israelite and a Midianite woman (Num 25). The biblical story has often been invoked as a paradigm, e.g. by the Puritans* in Ireland and North America, the Boers in South Africa, and right-wing Zionists in modern Israel.

Stories of actual violence, whether historical or fictional, are found primarily in the early books of the HB (but see Maccabees*). The prophets and apocalyptic* writers typically do not call for violent human action, but they predict violent intervention by God to destroy their enemies. The Psalms* include many prayers for violent retribution. Post-biblical texts such as the Dead* Sea Scrolls often predict the coming of a messiah* who would kill the wicked. These expectations played a part in the Jewish revolts against Rome, e.g. that of Bar Kokhba (132–35 CE).

Jesus repudiates violence in the Sermon on the Mount (Matt 5:38–39). Much of the NT, however, is animated by apocalyptic hope* for the final Judgment* when the wicked will be violently destroyed. The classic expression is found in the Book of Revelation, where Christ is expected to come with a sharp sword in a robe dipped in blood (Rev 19). Revelation calls for patient endurance, not violent action. In the history of Christianity, however, as well as of Judaism, people animated by apocalyptic hopes have often taken it upon themselves to "force the end" by violent revolution (e.g. the Puritans). Despite the words of Jesus, Christians have only occasionally embraced pacifism*.

Scholars and religious leaders rightly point out that the biblical commands are restricted to specific occasions and that apocalyptic violence is the prerogative of God. Nonetheless, there is no doubt that the violence of biblical imagery has often been conducive to violence on the part of zealots. JOHN J. COLLINS

Violence and Christianity throughout History. Violence* can be defined as any imposition or use of force, including religious indoctrination. Christianity, like most religions, readily accepts a narrowed definition restricting violence to coercion producing mental or physical harm.

Although the Bible demands personal and collective commitment to peace*, it also accepts divinely sanctioned violence for the sake of justice* or sanctification* (see the present cluster: Violence and the Bible). The gospel presupposes violence inflicted on Christ, and persecution* of the church motivated apostolic* teachings on perseverance and heavenly reward.

Despite moral condemnation of coercion, Christianity supported violence in specific political and historical contexts. Whereas the early church practiced pacifism*, Augustine* allowed for war* in extreme cases, guided by justice*, and supported coercive practices against the Donatists*. Constantine's* endorsement of Christianity established a formal church*–state relationship that permeated European history. This occasionally led to complicity between Christianity and state-sponsored violence, e.g. Charlemagne's* forced conversions, European conquest of the Americas, and Britain's colonizing* in Africa, China*, and India*. Connections between Christian practice and violence were justified by a combination of theological, political, and economic agendas, as in the Crusades*, the Spanish Inquisition*, and the British and US slave* trades. Theological tensions among religious factions led to religious wars during the European Middle Ages and the 16th–17th c. (after the Reformation*) and to anti-Semitic* pogroms, culminating in the silence of many Protestant and Roman Catholic* churches during the Holocaust*. Because of the global spread of Christianity as an indigenous cultural* movement, Christian allegiances were accompanied by ethnic or national tensions, such as in Northern Ireland*, Sudan*, the Balkans*, and Rwanda*, adding a religious element to violence, sometimes involving ethnic cleansing. Western missionaries* occasionally have crossed the line from persuasion to cultural coercion.

Most contemporary theologians denounce Christian-sponsored violence, distinguishing authentic Christianity from its corrupted inculturation*. Some reject or reinterpret scriptural accounts celebrating violence (e.g. juridical atonement*, conquest of Canaan). A few support violence to resist unjust authority, as in cases of racial separation (e.g. apartheid in South* Africa) or economic oppression* (e.g. in Nicaragua). A full ethical assessment sets Christian-sponsored violence in balance with the benefits of Christianity to most populations, including, e.g., literacy and health care. For some apologists, the ethical indictment of Christian-sponsored violence may ironically depend on the Christian exhortation to love victims. Christians agree that peace with God directs believers to seek peace with others, but Christians disagree over which, if any, cultural and political concerns should alter this pursuit.

KENNETH R. CHASE

Violence and Pastoral Care. Violence, the use of threatening human behavior to exercise power and control over persons, creates perpetrators, injured and/or killed victims, and bystanders. Pastoral care involves expressing God's love* and justice* by providing resources for healing* for victims, for holding perpetrators accountable, and for helping bystanders to assume their responsibility.

In Christian theology, violence is a special topic of reflection; violence is central in Jesus' arrest, torture, and crucifixion ritualized in the Eucharist*. Christian faith exposes human violence (including that toward God) and teaches that violence, sin*, and death are overcome by God in Jesus' resurrection*.

Most churches distinguished legal and justified violence (e.g. self-defense, just war*) from illegal and sinful violence (e.g. most interpersonal violence, including assault, rape, and domestic violence). Unclear ethical areas include corporal punishment of children, the subjection of subordinate adults to the enforcement of family* rules by heads of households, and political revolt against corrupt political authority.

A minority of Christians argue that Jesus was nonviolent and Christians should be pacifists*. Most Christians believe that violence, one of the most egregious human sins*, must be carefully circumscribed and controlled, e.g. as postulated by the just war* theory. War and violence must (1) be the last resort; (2) be waged by a legitimate authority; (3) be justified by the evil done; (4) be proportional to the injury; and (5) distinguish between combatants and noncombatants. An adequate theology regarding gender violence against women and other oppressed groups deprived of full participation in family, church, and society has yet to be developed.

Pastoral care focuses primarily on Christian responsibility toward the victims of violence, e.g. by providing care for refugees*, for victims of crimes (including robbery, assault, and rape), and (more recently) for children abused by parents and women victims of domestic battery. Such programs seek to provide safety (ensuring that a person is no longer subject to violence), healing (from the trauma of violence), and reconnection (so that a person can create a new life and future).

Programs for perpetrators have not yet been fully developed. The churches' active involvement in truth* and reconciliation* commissions provides a model. Perpetrators of violence were encouraged to follow the biblical formula of confession* (telling the truth about perpetrated violence), repentance*, restitution, and sanctification*. Such restorative justice* focuses on the restoration of community relationships after incidents of violence.

JAMES NEWTON POLING

Virginity, Theology of. Early Christians interpreted NT verses to mean that commitment to a life of sexual abstinence was more advantageous and praiseworthy than marriage*. Jesus' implied criticism of family* commitments (Matt 10:35–37; Luke 14:26; Mark 3:31–35), his praise for those who become "eunuchs for the sake of the Kingdom of Heaven" (Matt 19:10–12), and his claim that "in the resurrection they neither marry nor are given in marriage, but are like angels in heaven" (Matt 22: 30) encouraged celibacy* among his followers, who expected the imminent arrival of the Kingdom* of God. Paul* in 1 Cor 7 claimed that celibate Christians both avoid the distractions of married life and are "holy in body and spirit." Since marital intercourse might interfere with prayer (1 Cor 7:5), it seemed tainted – a notion reinforced by the belief that Jesus' mother had conceived him without engaging in sexual relations (Matt 1:18; Luke 1:34).

From the 2nd c. onward, Christian writers praised commitment to lifelong virginity. By the 4th c., treatises and letters (especially those directed to women, and in contrast to traditional praise for reproduction) encouraged virginal commitment by practical as well as theological arguments: virgins avoided the dangers of pregnancy*, household duties, marital subjection, and anxiety over spouses and children*. To "reproduce and multiply" (Gen 1:28) was a teaching of the Old Law, now surpassed by that of Jesus and Paul.

Early Christian writers such as Jerome*, Gregory* of Nyssa, and John* Chrysostom taught that the heavenly afterlife became more certain if one opted for virginity. The 100-fold harvest of the parable of the sower (according to which the harvest is "yielding thirty- and sixty- and a hundredfold," Mark 4:1–9) was interpreted as referring to virgins (the 60-fold represents widows; the 30-fold, the married). Biblical imagery representing Jesus as a bridegroom was appropriated to argue that virgins would become his spouse in heaven. Virginity was the "natural" condition of original humankind to be recaptured here and now: Had not Adam* and Eve* been virgins in Eden*, reproducing only after their sin* and subsequent expulsion (Gen 4:1)? As is commonly recognized, the Genesis story teaches that the first sin led to death. Yet does it not also say that virginity stayed the force of death? Following this additional teaching, virgins chose not to contribute to the number of new humans, who were in any case doomed to die. So prominent was the exalted evaluation of virginity that even writers who wished to praise marriage, such as Clement* of Alexandria and Augustine*, conceded that virginity was a "higher" and holier state of life than marriage; those who questioned its superior status could be deemed "heretics*." This evaluation of virginity was not seriously challenged by Christian theologians until the Protestant Reformation*.

ELIZABETH A. CLARK

Virgin Martyr Tradition. Virgin martyrs have been popular subjects of devotion* since early Christian times. Narratives concerning the martyrdom* of beautiful young women, ending with spiritual triumph over bodily tribulation, tend to be conventional in form: the young woman is desired by a pagan, rebuffs him for the sake of Christ, is tortured, and finally beheaded. Her body is imagined to be a pure receptacle for the Holy* Spirit. One early exception to the association between virginity and death is the life of Thecla* (2nd c.), who survived two martyrdoms. Later virgin martyrs include Lucy, Agnes, Margaret, and Catherine. There is little or no evidence for the existence of most virgin martyrs, and many of their cults were purged from the Roman calendar in 1969.

Regardless of their dubious historicity, the stories of virgin martyrs played an important cultural role in the Middle Ages and later, often inspiring women. Hildegard* of Bingen was devoted to St. Ursula; Joan* of Arc, a virgin martyr herself, was devoted to St. Catherine and St. Margaret. The canonization (1950) of Maria Goretti (1890–1902), a victim of attempted rape, became a subject of continuing controversy. The example of the virgin martyr remains powerfully ambivalent, in some instances empowering of women and in others deeply misogynistic.

MAUD BURNETT MCINERNEY

Virgin Mary. See MARY, THE VIRGIN, CLUSTER.

Virtues, Cardinal and Theological. "Virtue" is the term applied to a power or capability for action (usually a "good" or "honored" action), on the principle that any act presupposes the agent's capability to act. Aristotle* suggested that virtues can be developed through practice (as by an apprentice), as well as exhortation and education. At best they are "habits" that come into play spontaneously on the appropriate occasion, although Aristotle was also aware of inward conflict and the need for self-control. The classic virtues, starting with Plato* and Aristotle, were prudence (wisdom*), courage (endurance), temperance (self-control*), and justice*. In medieval Christian thought, they were called the "cardinal virtues" and were deemed to be achievable in principle by all human beings, although sin* made them difficult to actualize. The corrective was grace*, motivating and purifying the human subject.

The theological virtues are faith*, hope*, and love* (1 Cor 13). From the perspective of medieval Christian thought, faith, hope, and love are human acts based on "virtues" or capabilities inspired or infused by God and oriented toward God, transforming a person and all of his or her actions. According to the NT, and especially Paul, faith, hope, and love do not have to be based on the cardinal virtues; they are fruits produced by the Holy* Spirit (Gal 5:22–23), indeed the greatest gifts (graces*) of the Holy* Spirit (1 Cor 12:31).

Visigoths. See GOTHS.

Visions, Vision of God. See MYSTICISM, MYSTICS.

Visitation, Episcopal, bishop's periodic inspection to ensure that all the affairs of a diocese*, especially in the parishes*, are being carried out properly.

Vladimir (c958–1015; Old Norse, Valdamarr; christened Basil, after his brother-in-law, the Byzantine emperor), ruler of Kiev, celebrated for his conversion, together with that of the population of Kiev, to Byzantine Christianity (987/88, according to the *Primary Chronicle*). He married a Byzantine princess and established the Metropolitan See of Kiev under the authority of the Constantinople Patriarchate. Canonized (13th c.), designated "equal to the apostles," for Russians he remains, along with his grandmother Olga*, the founder of Russian* Christianity. **See also UKRAINE.** PETRE GURAN

Vocation (from Lat *vocare*, what one is "called" to do) is a basic theological pattern relating divine call and human response. In view of its different interpretations, vocation is best understood as a process.

Vocation connects theological views of God*, revelation*, anthropology*, biblical texts, and scriptural* authority with specific contextual conditions. The Gospels interpret vocation through the lens of discipleship*. The Epistles do so in terms of the community of Christians and later the church (see Church, Concepts and Life, Cluster: Types of Ecclesiastical Structures). For the early church, vocation – be it that of Christ, individual believers, or the church – called for loyalty, faithfulness*, and obedience.

The Roman Catholic tradition emphasized spirituality* and related vocation to priesthood* and religious* orders and to the work and mission of the Church. Martin Luther* reinterpreted vocation by emphasizing that ordinary duties of life, such as work and parenthood, are holy callings and commitments, ways of obediently serving God. Luther's reinterpretation was received either as a trivialization of the holy or as a sanctification* of ordinary life. Jean Calvin* related the idea of vocation to the concept of predestination*: being predestined is being called to a particular service. In Protestant theology, vocation became closely associated with the work ethic (see Protestant Ethic).

How useful is the concept of vocation for interpreting work situations in modern societies characterized by industrialization, urbanization, unemployment, and globalization? This is debated. Yet the concept of vocation certainly shaped the self-perceptions of women and men. Vocation can be criticized for being too often understood as defining a person's identity in a static way, becoming normative even in new situations, and for being applied differently to women and men as a means of subordinating women. But as the history of this concept shows, vocation is open to constant reinterpretation, according to the way one conceives of the relation between the divine address and human response, and according to the specific life contexts of believers.

As a process, the reinterpretation of vocation begins with questions of "how": How are theological views, biblical interpretations, and contextual reflections interrelated in the formulation of one's vocation? How does one conceive of the divine address? How does a particular view of vocation affect one's views of gender, class, ethnicity, and other religious groups? Raising such questions makes possible a view of vocation that respects the process to which this concept refers and that assumes responsibility for the relations between genders, classes, ethnicities, and the religions that it promotes.

CECILIA NAHNFELDT

Vodou and Christianity. The relations between Vodou and Christianity in Haiti are deeply sullied by the violence* of slavery*. The first missionaries refused to acknowledge that the slaves had any religion; they considered their ritual practices to be nothing but magic and sorcery. Before embarking on the slave boats, they were usually baptized, yet they still needed to be evangelized. Thus throughout the long history of the institution of slavery, the Roman Catholic Church saw that its mission was to evangelize the slaves. For this they followed the "Black Code" (*Code Noir*, promulgated by Louis XIV, 1685), which in French colonies regulated all aspects of the slaves' relations to their masters and strictly forbade all forms of African worship. Thus it was in secret that the slaves elaborated their own religious system. Vodou (Voudoun), originally from Africa, especially from the Fon (Benin*) and Yoruba (Nigeria* and Benin) peoples, together with the religious heritage of many Bantu people, was reinterpreted by the slaves as they sought to link it to the worship of Catholic saints* and to the liturgical calendar that the missionaries forced on them.

The slaves revitalized their religious heritage in "chestnut camps" (*marronnages*), i.e. in remote areas in the mountains where they took refuge to escape the hardships of the slavery system, be it on plantations, in sugar mills, or in their masters' houses. The goal of the colonialist administration was the production of a vast amount of sugar to be exported to European capitals. The administration wanted slaves to suffer from cultural amnesia, without ancestors* and without descendants, as pieces of furniture and tools at the service of their masters. In response, the slaves used the Catholic ceremonies as opportunities for gathering and transmitting messages of revolt, and then for reappropriating their beliefs in African divinities through the cult of saints. The Virgin Mary* is the goddess of love, called Ezili Freda; St. James is Ogou Feray, the god of war; and St. Peter is Legba, the god who is the intermediary between the present world and the invisible world. Thus Vodou gave to slaves a symbolic world that allowed them to stay connected to their roots, to have a system of mutual recognition, and to share a culture that united them in the fight for freedom. In times of revolt, Vodou priests and priestesses encouraged slaves to use poison as a weapon. The fear of poison and spells was ever present among masters (late 18th c.). Furthermore, it was during Vodou ceremonies that the decision was made to launch the insurrection of August 22, 1791, which resulted in general freedom and soon after independence for Haiti (1804).

Vodou was not recognized by the new political authorities, who adopted Roman Catholicism as the official state religion. Yet during the first decades after independence, the clergy were tolerant of Vodou, so much so that one still hears today that it is necessary to be Catholic to practice Vodou. But after the concordat* between Haiti and the Vatican (1860), the Catholic Church, with the support of the state, repeatedly persecuted practitioners of Vodou: in 1864, 1896, and 1915–34 (during the occupation of Haiti by the USA, for whom Vodou was cannibalism and sorcery). In 1941 a national "anti-superstition" campaign was launched to eradicate once and for all Vodou beliefs and practices. All Catholics were required to take an oath of renunciation: "I renounce Satan, all his pomps, and all his works," because Vodou was viewed as devil* worship. Similarly, Freemasonry* and Protestantism* were not tolerated, because the clergy viewed Catholicism as alone able to provide national identity. However, Vodou continued to be practiced by poor people.

In the 1930s and 1940s, intellectuals influenced by the *indigeniste* literary movement began to recognize Vodou as an element of the national culture and a distinctive religion. Jean Price Mars, instigator of this movement, showed that Vodou had temples (*ounfo*), priests and priestesses (*oungan* and *manbo*), initiates (*ounsi*), rites of initiation, and a rich pantheon of divinities (*lwa* or *mysteries*). The divinities are called to intervene among the faithful – a ritual possession that takes place during dances driven by the rhythm of the drum, the main instrument in worship services. Today, many people who convert to Protestantism, Pentecostalism*, and the Catholic Charismatic* Movement demonize* belief in Vodou divinities, even as they incorporate many elements of the same beliefs, including dreams and visions, trances, and possession by the Holy* Spirit. LAËNNEC HURBON

Voluntarism, the position that will* is more basic (in human action or in shaping the universe) than nature or reason* (see Rationalism and Christian Theology). Dunns* Scotus asserted this with respect to both God and humans. Descartes* thought that even the rules of mathematics came from God's will. Less contested are voluntarist positions emphasizing faith* as obedience (Rom 1:5, 16:26) and the priority of love* in Christian life (1 Cor 13:8–13).

Voluntarist Church Community has a fellowship that is determined not by geographic parish* but by the decision of the individual members. See Congregationalism.

von Balthasar, Hans Urs (1905–1988), Swiss Roman Catholic theologian, famous for his

15-volume theological trilogy, *The Glory of the Lord, Theo-Drama,* and *Theo-Logic.* Each part attempts to transpose the entirety of Christian theology into one of the three "Platonic transcendentals," the beautiful, the good, and the true (these "transcend" the particularities of each being; if something exists, it is simultaneously beautiful, good, and true). Balthasar held that, because of habits inherited from Descartes* and Kant* (whose concerns were first epistemological, and only secondarily ethical and aesthetic), most theology started with questions of truth* (e.g. apologetics, justification for theological truth claims). Then the ethical obligations incumbent on the Christian were set forth (see Ethics and Christianity Cluster), with *aesthetics* treated (if at all) as a mere embellishment (see Aesthetics and Theology). According to Balthasar, this approach proved sterile; today's rampant secularization* is one indication of modernity's* habit of looking at things through the wrong end of the telescope. Rather, he said, one must first *perceive* Christian revelation* as beautiful; only then would the soul be prompted to assent to follow Christ in a dramatic life of Christian discipleship; finally, only inside that life of obedience to Christ would one come to see how and why Christianity is true.

EDWARD T. OAKES, SJ

von Hügel, Baron Friedrich (1852–1925), leader and spiritual guide in the movement known as Roman Catholic Modernism*; friend of Tyrrell*, Loisy*, and Petre*. As a financially independent lay scholar of religion with an aristocratic background, he had access to the Western European ecclesiastical and scholarly world. His philosophy of religion, *The Mystical Element of Religion as Studied in St. Catherine of Genoa and Her Friends* (1908, 2 vols.), distinguishes three elements of religion: "the authoritative, historical, institutional; the critical, speculative, philosophical; [and] the intuitive, vocational, mystical" (cf., respectively, Relationality; Autonomy; Heteronomy). Von Hügel strove to keep these elements in creative tension before and after the condemnation of Modernism. He escaped ecclesiastical censure and remained a loyal but critical Roman Catholic. ELLEN M. LEONARD, CSJ

Voodoo, anglicized form of the term "Vodou*," used by outsiders who view Vodou as superstition*.

Votive Mass, optional liturgical formulary that may be used on any day when there is no assigned feast or obligatory memorial on the liturgical calendar. Votive Masses in the current Roman Missal celebrate mysteries of the life of Christ, the Holy* Trinity, the Blessed Virgin Mary*, angels*, and saints. Their purpose is to promote piety and devotion*.

KEITH F. PECKLERS, SJ

Vows, solemn promises voluntarily made to God, specifically to follow the three counsels* of perfection (poverty, chastity, obedience); also the promises given by partners in a wedding ceremony.

Vulgate (Lat *vulgatus,* "common," "commonly known"; a designation from the Middle Ages), official Latin translation of the Bible that Pope Damasus requested of Jerome*; started in 382. Jerome revised the Gospels and all of the OT, with three versions of the Psalms. Others revised the rest of the NT; the Apocrypha* was revised by Jerome and others. These translations gradually replaced the Old* Latin version. The first book printed by Gutenberg was the Vulgate (1454–56). The Council of Trent* made the Vulgate text authoritative; corrected texts were issued in 1590, 1592, and in the 20th c. **See also BIBLE TRANSLATIONS CLUSTER: EARLY TRANSLATIONS/VERSIONS.**

Wake, vigil* on the eve of a church festival; also the watch or vigil beside a dead body or the feasting and remembrance following the funeral.

Waldenses. The name "Waldenses" refers to the members of a movement of "heretical*" dissent from the medieval Roman Catholic Church. In the 16th c., Waldensian communities joined the Reformed Church in Italy as the Chiesa Evangelica Valdese.

A wealthy lay citizen of Lyon, Valdesius (Valdes*), underwent a conversion experience c1173. Like Francis*, he wished to lead a life of poverty and of spreading the gospel. The archbishop of Lyon, the Cistercian* Guichard de Pontigny, protected Valdes against accusations of irregular actions and beliefs, but after a dispute with Guichard's successor, Valdes and his followers were expelled from Lyon. The first Waldensians were lay preachers. The doctrinal content of their proclamation was conventional, especially where the Waldenses opposed the Cathars* in Languedoc and Northern Italy. Innocent III reconciled some "Lyonnais" and "Lombard" Waldenses to the Roman Catholic Church (1208–10).

By c1250 Waldensian groups were identified from Gascony and the Languedoc to the Danube valley in Austria. They were accused of questioning the ministries of sinful priests (see Donatism) and denying the Church's power to assist souls* in purgatory*, as well as the legitimacy of its consecrations. They formed tight-knit endogamous groups, heard sermons from celibate, traveling pastors of the movement, and confessed their sins to them.

Medieval inquisitions* based in Toulouse (early 14th c.), Prague (1330s–1350s), and Brandenburg (late 14th c.) recorded many investigations of Waldenses. In the Alps, between the Dauphiné and the Duchy of Savoy, they formed tenacious defensive groups: those of the Dauphiné endured a vicious and corrupt "crusade" against them (1487–88). A Waldensian literary corpus of c1500 includes poems, sermons, and translations or paraphrases from Catholic moralistic literature mixed with extracts from late Hussite* theology derived from the Bohemian* Brethren.

From c1530 the Waldenses of the southwestern Alps and their colonies in Provence made contact with the Reformers of the Vaud and Neuchâtel region. Initially Reformed ideas on justification* by faith and spiritual worship clashed with the Waldensian stress on ethics and purity. Protestant influence grew during the French occupation of Piedmont (1536–59). After 1555 the Waldensian communities received Protestant ministers trained in Geneva and adopted (1560) a confession of faith modeled on the French Reformed Church's *Confessio Gallicana*. Following a short war (1560–61), the Waldensian communities in Savoy were given limited rights to worship within an enclave. Those of Provence and the Dauphiné were subsumed within the French Reformed Church.

From 1561 to 1848, the Waldensian Church, an outpost of the Geneva tradition, was often attacked (e.g. 1655 and 1686) but never eliminated. Given civil rights in Piedmont-Savoy in 1848, the Waldenses established their own theological college and traditions. The Facoltà Valdese di Teologia, founded 1855 (in Rome since 1922), appropriated the message of liberal Protestantism early and remains in the vanguard of progressive religious thought in Italy.

EUAN K. CAMERON

War, Christian Attitudes toward. The Christian tradition has manifested a spectrum of responses to questions of conflict and war, ranging from the violent zeal of the medieval crusaders* to the thoroughgoing pacifism* of the Amish*. Cultural differences, political and technological developments, and the complexity of the Bible have all helped produce this diversity of views. Depending on their respective commitments regarding the necessity of combating injustice, the morality of violence*, and the need for limitations on the justified use of force, Christians have historically adopted stances endorsing nonresistance, nonviolent* resistance, just war, and holy war.

Each of these positions can claim scriptural roots. In the OT, the Decalogue establishes a prohibition against killing (Exod 20:13), and a world is foretold in which swords will be beaten into plowshares and war shall be learned no more (Isa 2:4), yet God is elsewhere portrayed as underwriting various sorts of wars against Israel's foes, including the ban (*herem*), a war of total extermination (Deut 20:16–18). In the NT, while Paul insists that the governing authority does not bear the sword in vain (Rom 13:4), Jesus enjoins his followers to love their enemies and not to resist evildoers (Matt 5:39, 44).

The early Christian community appears to have lived out an ethos* of sacrificial forgiveness* and nonresistance, rooted in the Sermon* on the Mount, which was held (at least until 170) to be incompatible with military service. In subsequent centuries, this attitude of strict nonresistance was sustained at the margins of Christian life: in monastic* orders, in countercultural communities such as that of the Waldenses*, and in the Anabaptist* Movement that emerged from the Radical* Reformation and gave rise to present-day "peace churches," such as the Mennonite* Church and the Church of the Brethren*.

The epochal shift marked by Constantine's* marriage of church* and state gradually led Christian authorities, such as Ambrose*, to accept a qualified rationale for the use of force that ultimately became known as the "just war tradition." Rooted in the notion that, in a sinful world, Christian neighbor-love sometimes requires the reluctant and limited use of force to restrain grievous injustice, the just war idea developed over time into a two-part theory joining criteria for when the resort to armed force is justified (*jus ad bellum*) with standards defining how war may justly be fought (*jus in bello*).

Much of the *jus ad bellum* was adapted from Roman practice, including the provisions that war have a just cause; that it be declared by a proper political authority; and that it be waged only when it is a last resort, its hoped-for goods remain in proportion to its foreseeable evils, and peace is the desired outcome. Augustine*, who upheld the possibility of just war even while condemning the use of violence in individual self-defense, contributed the stipulation that war could be pursued only with a right intention characterized by a dispassionate spirit of service. Thomas Aquinas* shifted the theory's theological footing from love to natural justice* and, reflecting the shifting political sensibilities of his own age, included a qualified right to rebellion. The definitive 16th-c. formulation of the just war theory by Francisco de Vitoria added the criterion of relative justice, a distinctively modern principle of humility and restraint regarding claims of absolute justice in war.

In the wake of the traumatic religious wars accompanying the transition to modernity*, the just war idea gradually eclipsed the "Christian holy war tradition," which, as evidenced in the Crusades* and the Puritan* Revolution, typically envisaged war as an enterprise to be conducted under God's auspices, unsparingly, in the pursuit of religious ends. Over time, the *jus ad bellum* notion of just cause, which early on included the conversion of non-Christians and the punishment of heresy*, became largely restricted to defense against unjust aggression. The emergence in the 20th c. of the techniques of total war and mass destruction, meanwhile, raised the stature of the two central *jus in bello* requirements mandating proportionality in the use of force and, in particular, the preservation of noncombatant immunity.

At the same time, Gandhi's practice of *satyagraha*, the US civil* rights campaign, and the peaceful revolutions that swept the world in the 1980s prompted a resurgence of nonviolent action as a viable alternative to both war and nonresistance in Christian thought. Christians who have historically held that discipleship requires nonviolent activity to promote the justice* of the Kingdom* of God, including the Quakers* and pacifists within mainline denominations, have found their view reinforced by the example of Martin Luther King*, Jr., and by a burgeoning emphasis in Roman Catholic teaching on nonviolence* and forgiveness*.

As Christians consider how to respond to contemporary problems of war, such as nuclear proliferation, humanitarian intervention, and terrorism, it is the conceptions of nonviolent resistance and just war that largely define the debate. **See also RECONCILIATION AS A CHRISTIAN PRAXIS; VIOLENCE CLUSTER: AND PASTORAL CARE.** WILLIAM A. BARBIERI

Ward, Mary (1585–1645), founder of the unenclosed apostolic religious* life for women. Born into a Roman Catholic family in Yorkshire during a time of religious persecution, she fled to St. Omer in Flanders. There she sought to fulfill her religious vocation by entering a cloistered order. It was revealed to her that "some other thing" was required of her. With a group of companions, she spent the rest of her life experimenting with the unenclosed apostolic life, founding communities in continental

Europe and England. As a woman, she drew disapproval from the Roman Catholic Church; her attempts to adopt the Constitutions of the Society* of Jesus were thwarted at every turn.

LAVINIA BYRNE

Washington, Booker T. (1856–1915), established the Tuskegee Normal and Industrial Institute in 1881, a school dedicated to inculcating business values and basic literacy among formerly enslaved African Americans in the antebellum South. Reflecting on his memories of childhood under slavery*, he said that although plantation hymns had often contained references to "freedom of the body in this world," slave religion had been excessively otherworldly and emotional. He therefore attempted to reform Black religion as an instrument for developing a body of yeoman farmers, a class of skilled craftsmen, and a vanguard of small capitalists. Decades before Max Weber* published *The Protestant Ethic and the Theory of Capitalism*, Washington had seen a practical tie between religion and economics*. Thus he regularly preached a gospel of industry and commercialism during Sunday evening talks in the Tuskegee chapel. **See also PROTESTANT ETHIC.**

WILSON J. MOSES

Washington, George (1732–99), planter, military officer, politician, commander of the Continental Army (1775–83), first president of the USA (1789–96). Baptized as an infant, Washington remained a member of the Anglican Church in Virginia all his life and was an active vestryman in his parish. He firmly believed in a benevolent and active Providence, and incorporated Judeo-Christian language, themes, and symbols into his military leadership as well as his presidential inaugurations and communications. Throughout his public career, Washington insisted that religion was among the firmest props of a republican government, promoted religious liberty, and occasionally commended Christianity for its political benefits.

JEFFRY H. MORRISON

Water. "Water, source of life," has become an international catchphrase. It impels us to reflect on the multiple values of water: water as a public good, as the inherited property of all living beings, and as a fundamental right of each human being. It serves as a denunciation of the privatist and mercantilist politics of water embedded in the discourse of the "international oligarchy of the water," a small group of international companies, supported by multilateral corporations and local governments. Today the ecumenical* struggle for the recognition of water as a human* right is global; it has become a central issue for the World* Council of Churches and other church organizations. **See also LAND, THEOLOGICAL PERSPECTIVES AND PRAXIS, CLUSTER.**

NANCY CARDOSO PEREIRA

Water, an African Perspective. In the countries of the developing world, like Africa, water is scarce. Access to clean water is a privilege that few can lay claim to, because it has been commercialized. Upholding the dignity of men and women created in God's image involves ensuring that all have safe and clean water.

Water, whether a blessing or a nightmare, is everybody's business. In the Bible, water is a multivalent natural symbol. For instance, it connotes instability and incompleteness in the "deep" over which the Spirit hovers (Gen 1:2); punishment in the Flood* (Gen 7); protection in the crossing of the Red Sea (Exod 14); God's life-sustaining gift in the wilderness (Exod 17:5–8) and Jesus' encounter with the Samaritan woman (John 4:13–14); and purification in baptism*.

The water is blessed during the baptismal ceremony. In addition, holy* water is used for blessings, dedications, healings*, and exorcisms* (as is the case in many African* Instituted Churches); for ceremonial cleansing on entering a church; and for the *asperges* (based on Ps 51, "Cleanse me, O Lord") at the beginning of the Mass* on Sundays.

Christians live in a world blessed with oceans, lakes, rivers, and streams; water makes the world beautiful. Yet for many, water is nightmarish. Today, as in biblical times, tsunamis, hurricanes, and floods are destructive. Even more disastrous, millions of people lack clean water. Water has become an essential commodity, for which many people in Africa and elsewhere have to queue every day.

Without water there is no life: "water is life." God provided water so as to sustain all life; hence this precious gift should be appreciated and respected. Water should not be wasted but preserved wisely, at all costs. Every drop counts. Saving water is saving life.

MULAMBYA PEGGY KABONDE

Wealth and Christianity. Being wealthy means having more than one needs to survive the day and, for Christians, more than one needs to fulfill one's calling as the "image* of God" or disciple* of Christ. Wealth in itself is not evil*; in the Scriptures, images of wealth are used to depict salvation*. But in life "before God" (*coram Deo*), wealth becomes deadly when one is much wealthier than others, because it leads to inequality, separation from God and neighbor, and lack of solidarity*; when one's wealth becomes an idol*, an object of loyalty and devotion; or when wealth becomes a means of oppressing others.

Wealth's potential for destruction derives from the power it gives one to control the labor of others or to exclude others from what it takes to be human. Contemporary Christian studies of wealth, following human development theory, expand the conception of wealth to include well-being, capability, freedom, human relations, social capital, and belonging. But this good wealth can readily turn into a poisonous self-obsession.

The NT presents three kinds of teaching on wealth: (1) the command to relinquish wealth in order to be free to serve the reign* of God's righteousness; (2) the spiritual and moral peril of wealth as idol (see Mammon), resulting in separation from God; and (3) the right use of wealth to love God and neighbor (being "rich toward God"; e.g. Mark 10:17–31; Luke 12:22–34; 2 Cor 8:1–15; Jas 5:16). "You cannot serve God and mammon [wealth]" (Matt 6:24) sums up these teachings.

The church fathers underscore, with the Scriptures*, that all wealth belongs to God. Luxury is condemned. What is strictly needed for one's life or for the service of others is a legitimate possession. What is beyond this belongs to the poor. "The superfluous things of the wealthy are the necessities of the poor" (Augustine*). Justice* is administering what belongs to God according to God's will. Wealth can be used rightly. "Goods are called goods because they do good"; the right use of wealth "ministers to righteousness" (Clement* of Alexandria).

The Christian tradition has typically sought to moderate the acquisition of wealth and limit its allocation, disposition, and inheritance through almsgiving*, household* codes, common* goods, reciprocity, and redistribution. The Franciscans* rejected wealth and undertook a life of voluntary begging to demonstrate the power of Christ's poverty*. Other mendicant* religious orders (Dominicans*, Carmelites*, Augustinians*) also forbade wealth; yet their community of common goods often produced significant wealth. Various projects in "Christian Socialism" have generally failed but kept open the concern for the right use of property.

Vast changes in the Christian conception of wealth took place in modernity. The rise of the market, it was claimed, meant a "farewell to alms*." Accumulated wealth came to be seen as a possible sign of one's election*. Locke's* labor* theory of property justified wealth as inherently and exclusively one's own. Christians now consider wealth a form of property* that they own, but one that they must use as good stewards. Contemporary theology and ethics restate the best of the Christian tradition of stewardship*. Our possessions and capabilities are God's, not our own. The use of every resource of nature, time, and capability is wholly accountable before God. Because one creates wealth by controlling the combination of materials, labor*, land*, and technology*, justice* that serves the life of human beings and nature demands an inclusive property claim by all and thus a regulated market. **See also ECONOMY AND CHRISTIANITY CLUSTER; POVERTY CLUSTER; PROSPERITY GOSPEL CLUSTER.** M. DOUGLAS MEEKS

Weber, Max (1864–1920), German professor of economics* (first at Freiburg, then Heidelberg), social* theorist, a principal architect of modern social science. Weber did not consider the emergence of a capitalist economy to be self-evident. Besides favorable political conditions, a particular ethos* was necessary. Impending capitalism needed the support of an internal power, because it first had to bring down "traditionalism." "A person does not 'by nature' want to make more and more money, but simply to live – to live in the manner in which he is accustomed to live, and to earn as much as is necessary for this" (as Weber wrote in his *Protestant Ethic,* 1905). This resistance to capitalism was broken by Puritanism*, since that religion required from believers a methodical pattern of working and abstention from consumption.

In carrying on this perspective, Weber investigated the relationship of the world religions to economic* ethics*. During this research, he discovered that in the West a process of "rationalization" dissolved magical notions and increasingly "disenchanted" the world. Disenchantment, understood to be the development of a world in which the gods lost their natural and historical roots, became a central element of Weber's concept of modernity (see Secularization and Desecularization in Europe and North America). In order to introduce religious history into his analysis, Weber distinguished an actor's "motives" (an ethic of responsibility) from the "meaning" according to which this person acts (an ethic of conviction*). The more a religion of salvation* evolved and became systematized as an ethic of commitment and conviction (in contrast to an ethic of compliance with laws and responsibility), the more its adherents experienced "tensions" with the world. The same religious ethics that engendered the awareness that social orders were ruled by hostile rational forces generated new kinds of religiosity.

Regarding the spheres of sexuality and art, Weber observed a development of subjective practices that entailed a re-enchantment of the world through the cultivation of eroticism and art as means of escaping cold rationality. In the "disenchanted" world, the gods acquire a peculiar new life and take the form of impersonal values that "strive to gain power over our lives" (Gerth, Mills). HANS G. KIPPENBERG

Weil, Simone (1909–43), French activist, philosopher, mystic*; one of the first women graduates of the École Normale Supérieure. Her early writings were concerned with work and social* justice*. In 1934, seeking a concrete experience of the object of her reflections, she spent a year working in several Paris factories, hoping to find a way of organizing work so that it always lent dignity to human beings. Instead she discovered what she called "affliction" (*malheur*), the destruction of a human's social being. Deeply wounded by this experience, in subsequent years she had three mystical experiences, effecting a conversion from Judaism to Christianity, although she refused baptism until shortly before her death. Realizing that God could be present in evil* and suffering*, she wrote from here on chiefly about religious topics and moral philosophy. Heavily influenced by Plato* and the ancient Greeks, she sought to show the universality of grace*. Her works are also rooted in a distinctive reading of Christ's kenosis* and affliction on the cross, in which she sees genuine human spirituality participating. She even considers the creation* kenotic, for God creates, she claims, by withdrawing; Christ's sacrifice on the altar of the whole of time and space gives life to the world. In her last year, while working for the Free French in London, she united religious interests with social ones, writing a number of profound works on moral philosophy and social life, such as *The Need for Roots*. She argued there that obligations toward human beings are eternal and that they, not rights, are the basis of social good; societies are crucial intermediaries that form and feed the human soul. Weil died in London of tuberculosis; she is remembered for her refusal during this time to eat more food than she thought her compatriots in occupied France were getting.

ERIC O. SPRINGSTED

Wells, Ida B. (1862–1931), a regal and complex woman, whose crusades advocating African Americans' civil* rights, women's rights, and justice often jeopardized her safety. As a creative social researcher, critic, journalist, and activist, Wells viewed life through her moral compass of Christian leadership, truth, and duty. Born and educated in Mississippi, the eldest of eight, she assumed responsibility for her siblings when her parents died. She protested against lynching and the notion of white female purity. She and her husband, Ferdinand Barnett, had five children. She ran unsuccessfully for the Illinois Senate. Wells was one of the first to connect the oppression* and exploitation of blacks to white economic opportunities.

CHERYL A. KIRK-DUGGAN

Wesley, Charles (1707–88), Anglican priest (ordained 1735), poet, hymn writer, who, with his elder brother John, started the Methodist Movement. He journeyed to the American colony of Georgia with his brother (1735–37). Like John, he was influenced by the Moravians* and had a spiritual experience (finding himself "at peace with God"; May 21, 1738). He became an eloquent preacher and wrote more than 5,000 hymns (George Frederic Handel* wrote the music for some of them). But Charles progressively withdrew from active leadership of the Methodist societies, ending his itinerant preaching in 1756, remaining more attached to the Church of England, and disapproving of John's ordaining of preachers. **See also METHODISM CLUSTER: METHODIST WORSHIP.**

Wesley, John (1701–91), Anglican clergy, chief founder of Methodism. The 15th child born to Susanna Wesley and her husband, Samuel, who was at that time rector of Epworth, England. John attended Charterhouse School (London, from 1714), then Oxford University, matriculating at Christ Church in 1720 (B.A., 1724, M.A., 1727). He was ordained a deacon in the Church of England (1725) and a priest (1728). While a fellow and tutor at Lincoln College (from 1727), he followed a disciplined regimen of study, devotion, prison visitation, and social service that others viewed as fanatical and earned him and his small group of followers, including his brother Charles, a variety of names, including the "Oxford Methodists," which was also the title of a pamphlet (1733) written by a sympathetic observer of the controversy. Some 50 years later, Wesley would refer to the beginnings of this group as "the first rise of Methodism."

The Wesley brothers ventured to the new colony of Georgia (1735) at the behest of James Oglethorpe and the Society for the Propagation of the Gospel (see SPCK, Society for Promoting Christian Knowledge). John, who had volunteered as a missionary, soon received an appointment as the priest in Savannah. Their stay was short (especially Charles's); the Wesleys were often at odds with the colonial administrators. But the nearby fortress village of Frederica did witness the implementation of the religious patterns from Oxford in what Wesley later called "the second rise of Methodism" (1736). John's resolute exercise of his priestly office and his unfortunate entanglement with a young woman, Sophey Hopkey (niece of the chief magistrate), resulted in legal pressures that led him to leave this remote colony (1737).

Back in England, Wesley helped establish the "Fetter Lane Society" in London (May 1738), which he later designated as "the third rise of Methodism." This group was organized by Peter Boehler, a German Pietist* (Moravian*) who had become Wesley's spiritual mentor. The Pietist influence, heightened by the Wesleys' long-standing search for assurance* of salvation*, resulted in an important religious experience for each of the brothers. Charles felt a special sense of Christ's presence on Pentecost Sunday, accompanied by "a strange palpitation of heart." Three days later (May 24, 1738), John felt his heart "strangely warmed" at a religious society meeting in the region of Aldersgate Street, and he "received an assurance that Christ had died for [him]." The fact that this experience did not result in constant and continuing love*, peace*, and joy in the Holy* Spirit (and an absence of fear, doubt*, and sin*), which the Moravians had taught him to expect, led John Wesley to continue refining the theological positions that unfolded with his ongoing spiritual journey.

Wesley's stance was basically grounded in an Anglican appreciation for a mediating position that included both faith and works, evangelism* and sacramentalism*, knowledge and vital piety, preaching and praying. He eventually broke with the Moravians (early 1740s) because they leaned too much toward a theology that emphasized faith at the expense of works of piety and mercy, which Wesley understood to be important means of grace* or channels of God's presence and power. The "grand doctrines" of Methodism – repentance*, faith*, and holiness* – were Wesley's focus grounded in the soteriology* of the Church of England, of which he remained a priest. The movement became notable for its lay preaching, vibrant singing, and programs of social outreach, which characterized its concern for "practical divinity" (the practice of Christian living). Besides building preaching houses throughout the rural areas of the British Isles, Wesley began medical clinics, schools, orphan houses, loan funds, and subsidized housing programs, largely in the growing urban areas.

The Wesleyan revival* was spread through a combination of field preaching (in extra-ecclesiastical locations, including marketplaces), careful organization of local societies, a vast publications program, and the amalgamation of other regional revivals into the national Wesleyan fold. The Methodist message was carried on the wings of hymns published by the Wesley brothers, written primarily by Charles. After 1744 the preachers were both encouraged and disciplined by an annual conference and the circulation of the minutes of these meetings, which provided guidance as well as records for the movement. Although the Methodists soon developed both a public and a self-conscious identity, Wesley was adamant that they not separate from the Church of England. Although opposed by many Anglican clergy, Wesley maintained a good relationship with many bishops of the Anglican* Church. In Wesley's lifetime, Methodists were a tiny proportion of the population and experienced relatively slow growth.

In his later years, the earlier prejudices against Wesley melted into a more benign appreciation of his active concern for the good of the country, especially its most disadvantaged citizens. At the time of his death, he was generally acknowledged as a man of genuine piety who actively pursued altruistic endeavors throughout his life. One obituary referred to him as "one of the most extraordinary characters this or any other age ever produced." He was buried behind the Methodist Chapel on City Road, London. **See also METHODISM CLUSTER: METHODIST CHURCHES AND THEIR THEOLOGY.** RICHARD P. HEITZENRATER

Wesleyan Quadrilateral, a 20th-c. summary of John Wesley's* four sources of true worship: Scripture*, tradition*, reason*, and religious experience.

Western Churches, in contrast to the term "Eastern* churches," a designation for all churches in the Latin-speaking area of the ancient world, which became the western part of the Roman Empire; it later referred to the churches loyal to the bishop of Rome and the Roman Catholic Church, as well as subsequently to the Protestant churches originating during the Reformation*.

Westminster Catechisms and Confession. When the Westminster Assembly convened (1643), it had no intention of compiling a new creed. The Thirty-nine* Articles satisfied even ardent Puritans*. But when Parliament sought military assistance from the Scots, the Scots demanded in return the promotion of religious uniformity throughout the British Isles. The Westminster Confession would provide the doctrinal foundation for that uniformity.

The dream never materialized, but in 1647 the Westminster Confession replaced the Scots Confession as the official creed of the Church of Scotland*; it was later adopted by Presbyterian* churches worldwide and, with relevant modifications, by Congregational* churches (1658) and the Calvinistic Baptists (1689).

The Westminster Confession represents the mature theology of the Reformation*, affirming Scripture* as the only rule of faith, proclaiming Luther's doctrine of justification*, and taking for granted the Augustinian doctrine of predestination*.

The same theology is set forth in the Larger and Shorter Catechisms, the latter becoming the most influential of all the Assembly's documents. It focused on Christian essentials, covering successively "what we are to believe concerning God," the Ten Commandments, and the Lord's Prayer. Still used in conservative Presbyterian churches, it is best remembered for its opening statement: "Man's chief end is to glorify God and to enjoy [God] for ever."

DONALD MACLEOD

Westphalia, Peace of (1648), treaties between the German Empire and France in Münster, and between Sweden and the Protestant powers in Osnabrück, that ended the Thirty* Years' War. It revived the provisions of the Peace of Augsburg* (1555), adding protections for certain religious minorities and explicitly recognizing Reformed* churches. It symbolized the end of religious wars during this period and the beginning of toleration (but not full religious rights) and secular politics.

White, Ellen Gould (1827–1915), North American visionary religious speaker and writer whose "messages" were formative in the emergence and the doctrinal and organizational development of the Seventh-day Adventist* denomination. Ellen Gould Harmon and her twin sister, Elizabeth, were the youngest of eight children in a middle-class Methodist family in Portland, Maine. Ellen's formal education was effectively ended when she was nine years old by a severe concussion and facial injury. In 1843 she and her family were "disfellowshipped" from their Methodist congregation for harboring Millerite expectations of Jesus' return. After the "Great Disappointment" (December 1844), she had the first of her 2,500 visionary experiences, the source of her guidance of the Seventh-day Adventist Church. She married James White in 1846. She worked in Europe (1885–87), as well as Australia and New Zealand (1891–1900), writing 4,600 articles for church journals and some 50 books, including *The Great Controversy* (1888), *Christian Education* (1894), *Steps to Christ* (1898), *The Desire of Ages* (1898), *The Ministry of Healing* (1905). She insisted, however, that her writings always be subordinated to the Bible. Her devotional writings have exerted influence beyond the denomination.

White's fundamental conception was that of a cosmic "great controversy" between good and evil, in which every human being participates, which was soon to conclude in an apocalyptic* climax. Her complementary holistic view of the human condition led to this-worldly activism. She affirmed Christ's divinity, salvation* by grace* through faith*, observance of the seventh-day Sabbath*, and Jesus' special high-priestly ministry. She worked to improve the lot of women and influenced the establishment of Oakwood College for African Americans (1895), as well as other educational and medical institutions.

Recent discoveries that certain of White's writings (e.g. *The Great Controversy*) are highly dependent on unacknowledged sources have shaken some Seventh-day Adventists' confidence in her. Yet her overall spiritual values and principles remain credible for many. White's modeling of spiritual leadership affirms the equal contribution of men and women to church life. She challenges today's Christians through her refusal to isolate the spiritual from other aspects of human experience, her strong social* conscience, her rejection of "verbal-dictation" views of the Bible's inspiration, her lifelong warning against centralized "kingly power" in church administration, and her repeated calls for humble openness to the Spirit's leading into new doctrinal light. **See also** ADVENTISM; SEVENTH-DAY ADVENTIST WORSHIP. JOHN R. JONES

White Fathers, priests and brothers of the Roman Catholic Society of Missionaries of Africa who "live in communities at the service of the people of Africa" and practice evangelization through assimilation. Founded (1868) by the archbishop of Algiers, Charles-Martial-Allemand Lavigerie, to evangelize Algeria, they wear a religious habit resembling traditional North African clothing: a white tunic and a hooded cape (burnoose). As a result of Archbishop Lavigerie's preoccupation with slavery*, a few years after their founding the White Fathers entered the East African lakes region (now Rwanda*, Uganda*, Burundi*) and West Africa. **See also** MISSION CLUSTER: THEMATIC ISSUES: ANTI-SLAVERY.

Whitefield, George (1714–70), great revivalist*, transatlantic itinerant Anglican minister, Christian celebrity; archetypal preacher of the Great* Awakening. Born poor, Whitefield paid his way through Pembroke College, Oxford, by working as a servant of wealthier students. Befriending John and Charles Wesley*, Whitefield associated with early Methodists*, although he disputed the Wesleys' Arminianism*. He adopted an Anglican revivalist Calvinism, which held together perhaps because he was more preacher than theologian.

After a transatlantic voyage (1738), Whitefield preached wildly popular revivals until his death and was called "the Grand Itinerant." Criticized by anti-revivalists for being emotionally manipulative, he was heard by untold thousands who flocked to hear him preach, especially in the American colonies, where he was seen as an exponent of Christian liberty.

Whitefield had a lifelong love of the stage that he brought to the pulpit in a manner unlike any English-speaking preacher before him. His sermons were inspirational calls to conversion*, delivered with an extraordinary rhetorical power. Whitefield also employed sophisticated media* campaigns to further the impact of his ministry, sending a publicist ahead of him to distribute promotional literature, much of which was printed by his friend Benjamin Franklin*. CALEB J. D. MASKELL

Whitehead, Alfred North (1861–1947). Whitehead's writings on God and Christianity came late in his life, after he had accepted a position at Harvard. In a time when God was disappearing from philosophical consideration, he taught that God is a contributor to every event and that events also contribute to God. His vision of a world of interrelated events encouraged a new theological approach by Process theologians (cf. Incarnation Cluster: In the Orthodox Tradition).

In England he had developed elaborate theories of mathematics and of relativity. In his cosmology, he analyzed these events, both human and electronic, into "occasions of experience" each of which integrates the world. These require a realm of forms so ordered as to evoke value in the world. This "primordial nature of God" requires completion by a "consequent nature" in which the ephemeral events of the world acquire permanence.

Whitehead viewed Christianity, Buddhism, and science as the three greatest potential contributors to spiritual progress. The first two are in decline, partly because they are unwilling to grow through the kind of openness characteristic of science.

He complained that when Rome accepted Christianity, it turned God into a cosmic Caesar. Jesus offered an understanding of God, centered on love, on which Whitehead could build philosophically. **See also** GOD, CHRISTIAN VIEWS OF, CLUSTER; PROCESS THEOLOGY.

JOHN B. COBB, JR.

Wichern, Johann Hinrich (1808–81), father of the Inner Mission*, a precursor of Protestant social* service agencies in Europe and North America. After studying in Göttingen and Berlin, he returned to his native Hamburg to work with the city's poor. Repulsed by the inhumane conditions of the old psychiatric asylum system, Wichern adopted the cottage model with "house parents" and founded the Rough House (*Das Rauhe Haus*) for destitute children (1833). His historic speech at the Wittenberg Kirchentag* (1848) galvanized opinion in the church for an "inner mission" to complement "foreign mission" and serve the needs of those adversely affected by the industrial revolution. He established numerous other charitable works. He was influenced primarily by the church historian August Neander and by Martin Luther*. He was broadly ecumenical, emphasized the importance of community and the priesthood* of all believers, and became the foremost exponent in the German Awakening of the principle "faith active in love." He ranks with Hegel* and Schleiermacher* as a shaping force in

19th-c. Protestantism in Germany. He detested communism* and revolution, viewing these as results of moral decay, but he was among the best of his century in grasping social problems and human suffering. **See also GERMANY.**

DAVID CROWNER and GERALD CHRISTIANSON

Wiclif, John See WYCLIF (WYCLIFFE), JOHN.

Widow, a woman whose husband has died, leaving her socially and economically vulnerable. The care of widows was of special concern in the Torah and prophetic writings (cf. Exod 22:22; Deut 24:19–21; Isa 1:17; Jer 7:1). As a group of independent women, widows had a recognized status in the early church (Acts 6; 1 Tim 5:3–16), and their life was seen as an alternative to marriage. This view may have been considered subversive to the Roman order and possibly gave rise to some apocryphal* NT writings.

Wilberforce, William (1759 1833), educated at Cambridge, member of Parliament (1780–1825). From 1797 he was a prominent member of the Evangelical Anglican "Clapham Sect," named after the London area in which he lived. His *A practical View of the prevailing religious System of professed Christians, in the higher and middle Classes in this Country, contrasted with real Christianity* (1797) was popular in his lifetime and during the Victorian Era. Well known for his support of Christian charities and missions*, he devoted much of his later career to the movement to abolish slavery* in British territories.

PETER C. ERB

Wilderness. Described in the Bible as a desert (Exod 19:2; Deut 32:10), it proved unsuitable to the Israelites for long-term habitation. After fleeing Egypt, they wandered in the wilderness for 40 years (Num 14:33). The experience was "terrible" (Deut 1:19), but it was also providential (Ps 78:52), for God fed them (Exod 16:32) and made a covenant* with them (Exod 19:1–6). In the NT, John* the Baptist lived in the wilderness (Matt 3:1–6), and Jesus was tempted in the wilderness immediately after his baptism (Mark 1:12–13). Early Christians feared the wilderness, believing it was haunted by the devil* (Matt 4:3–11), a concept that influenced eremitic* monasticism*. **See also DESERT; KINGDOM OF GOD, THE CONCEPT OF, CLUSTER: IN THE EASTERN ORTHODOX TRADITION: KINGDOM AND WILDERNESS.** JEFFRY C. DAVIS

Will. In the Western* churches, Christian discussions of the will center on two questions: To what extent does our freedom (human will) affect God's control? To what extent are we spiritually free, given the Fall*, to choose good or evil?

Human Will and God's Control. Five answers are given:

1. *Theological determinists*: Since God controls all circumstances preceding human choice, God ultimately determines all we do. Some (e.g. Steven Houck) grant that this negates free will (voluntary choice).
2. *Compatibilists* (e.g. J. I. Packer and many theological determinists): We are free as long as we are not forced to act against our will (desires); this is always possible, because God acts in nonconstraining ways to ensure that we desire to do what God would have us do.
3. *Limited compatibilists* (e.g. John Feinberg): God may need at times to eradicate inappropriate desires to ensure that we do not make wrong choices; therefore, God may not always be able to control decisively our voluntary decision making.
4. *Free will theists* (e.g. William Hasker): Since God cannot both grant us freedom and control our choice, to the extent that God grants us freedom, God's ability to control our choices is self-limited.
5. *Process theists* (e.g. John Cobb): Since God does not intervene unilaterally in earthly affairs, God is never in a position to ensure that we act in accordance with the divine will, although interactively God influences everything.

Freedom to Choose Good or Evil. The debate over spiritual freedom of the will centers on the impact of original* sin:

1. *Pelagianism**: Human will is morally unaffected by the Fall. We remain free to choose either good or evil. While God's grace* assists us, we freely choose to accept or reject Christ.
2. *Semi-Pelagianism:* Human will is bent toward unrighteousness after the Fall. Thus God's grace is necessary for virtuous behavior. Unaided by divine grace, we seek God, who graciously completes the salvific process. Whether past or present Arminians* are Semi-Pelagianists remains a matter of significant debate.
3. *Augustinianism**: Post-Fall human will is totally unable to choose that which is spiritually good; free will is totally lost

(Luther*). For Augustine* and Calvin*, the bondage of the will is the consequence of free choice and is also a continued exercise of willing (freely choosing evil). Only after redemption by God are we free to do what is right. God alone determines who will be extended the irresistible grace to be saved. Contemporary Calvinists* are acknowledged Augustinians.

With 20th-c. atrocities and oppression, and the recognition of the role of systemic evil*, "bondage of the will" took on another connotation: as humans (involuntarily) contribute to systemic evil, their will is in bondage, because despite their will to do good they do the evil they do not want to do (cf. Rom 7:19). **See also MORAL INFLUENCE; POSITIVE THEOLOGY, POSITIVE LAW, POSITIVISM; REASON; VOLUNTARISM.** DAVID BASINGER

Willard, Frances E. (1839–98), educator, social reformer, temperance* leader, women's rights activist. A graduate of Northwest Female College (1859), she served as president of Evanston College for Ladies (1871–74), corresponding secretary of the Chicago Woman's Christian Temperance Union (WCTU; 1874–79), president of the National WCTU (1879–91) and the World WCTU (1891–98). Leader of the largest women's organization in the world, Willard broadened the focus of the WCTU to include woman suffrage and other reforms.

Willard argued for women's right to vote as a means to address rampant poverty*, alcoholism*, and other social crises. She used the Victorian view of women as guardians of moral virtue and a progressive interpretation of the Bible to argue for increasing women's leadership in society and the church (see Bible Interpretation Cluster: Worldwide: Feminist). She worked closely with other temperance, suffrage, and Social* Gospel leaders, including Mary Livermore, Susan B. Anthony*, Richard Ely, and Jane Addams*.

Willard, raised in a Methodist family in an era of historical optimism, shared the Social Gospel beliefs that God could redeem both souls and society; human hands, hearts, and minds are needed to transform the nation and world into the Kingdom* of God. Willard traveled extensively to educate, inspire, and engage others in this mission. Her lifework demonstrates the potential for achieving social progress when the Christian faith is applied to both personal and social salvation.

WENDY J. DEICHMANN EDWARDS

William of Ockham (or Occam). See OCKHAM (OCCAM), WILLIAM OF.

William of St.-Thierry (1075/80–1148), Cistercian* theologian. Born in Liège, he became a Benedictine* monk and was elected abbot* of St.-Thierry near Reims. After a long acquaintance with Bernard* of Clairvaux, he resigned as abbot and joined a Cistercian group establishing a new house in the Ardennes. Several works by William and by Bernard profited from their correspondence with each other, and they joined in opposing Abelard*. William read extensively, making use of some patristic works that have since been lost. Both he and Bernard developed a mysticism* of love*, often utilized by the Beguines* and by Ruusbroeck*.

Williams, Roger (1603–83), pioneer of religious liberty, founder of Rhode Island and the first Baptist* church in the USA, student of Native* American culture. Born in London and educated at Cambridge, Williams shared the Puritans'* intention to "purify" Anglicanism* of unbiblical elements. Williams joined the Puritan migration to New England, but Puritan leaders banished him from the Massachusetts Bay Colony for his claims that American territories rightly belonged to Native Americans, that the Anglican Church was corrupt beyond reform, and that civil officers had no jurisdiction in religious activities – against the Puritan mutual reinforcement of church and state. Williams fled south, lived with the Narragansetts, studied their culture, and purchased from them land for a settlement he called "Providence," with cofounder Anne Hutchinson*.

Williams despised forced "conversions" of Native Americans, the civil persecution of religious offenders, and religious wars. While maintaining Calvinist* beliefs, Williams eventually rejected all churches as unbiblical and insisted that Providence be the first colony to grant liberty to all religions. While conventional wisdom held that religious diversity promoted conflict, Williams argued that forced religious uniformity led to conflict, while liberty provided the only basis for peace.

Williams's views remain a relevant model for religious liberty, frequently cited in US Supreme Court decisions on church* and state and by Baptists regarding their advocacy of religious liberty. JAMES P. BYRD

Wills and Bequests. A will or testament* is a formal declaration, usually in writing, of the way a person's property is to be transferred after death. Up through the Middle Ages, bequeathing land or property to religious institutions was a common form of indulgence* (see Mortmain); suppression* of this practice was a major feature of the Reformation*. Memorial gifts continue to be an important part of the Western Christian ethos.

Wine, fermented juice, usually of grapes, is a mixed blessing: drunk in moderation, it gives rise to joy and festivity; in excess, it impairs judgment and endangers health. As old as civilization, wine is a daily table drink in many cultures.

Wine is a gift from God (Deut 7:13), brings joy and gladness (Ps 104:15), and is a sign of blessing (Prov 3:10b), as well as peace and prosperity (2 Kgs 18:31–32). One of the messianic promises (Amos 9:13–14; Jer 25:6, 31:12), it is a fare at the messianic banquet (Isa 55:1). When God withholds rain, poor harvest and a lack of wine are signs of divine judgment (Jer 51:7–9) (see Apocalypticism Cluster).

In the Gospel of John, Jesus inaugurated his public ministry by turning water into wine at the wedding feast of Cana (2:6–10) and ended his life ingesting wine on the cross (19:30 refers to the ordinary wine of common people, despite some translations). Furthermore, Jesus is considered the true vine who invites his followers to abide in him (15:1–5).

During the Eucharist, wine is changed into the Blood of Christ or understood to "symbolize" Christ's presence in the celebration of the Last Supper, fulfilling Jesus' command "Do this in remembrance of me" (Luke 22:19b).

JOYCE ANN ZIMMERMAN, CPPS

Winnowing or Threshing, throwing grain into the air so that the wind, or air from a fan, will carry away the chaff and the grain will drop into a container. Often used as a metaphor* for the separation of good from evil persons.

Wisdom. Divine Wisdom is an intriguing figure in the Hebrew Scriptures. A grammatically feminine term (Heb *hokmah*; Gk *sophia*; Lat *sapientia*), Wisdom is the personification of God's presence. Described in various ways as an aspect of God and as the feminine divinity, Wisdom is referred to as sister, mother, preacher, judge, and transcendent power that both animates the world and mediates between the heavenly and earthly spheres. Wisdom is also a vehicle of God's self-revelation, granting knowledge of God to those who pursue her.

In the Book of Job*, Wisdom appears as a hidden treasure known only to God and in Proverbs* as a prophet who calls aloud in the streets, raising her voice in the public square, and delivering her message at the city gate: "You ignorant people, how much longer will you cling to your ignorance?" (Prov 1:22). Later, Wisdom speaks in the singular, describing herself as the giver of life, as the source of knowledge and insight, and as existing before the beginning of the world: "The Lord created me at the beginning of his work, the first of his acts of old" (Prov 8:22).

The identity of Wisdom is most clearly developed in the Wisdom* of Solomon, where she is linked to the mystery* of God's omnipotence*, the mother of all things who mediates between the upper and lower worlds, and the source who guides humans back to God. Wisdom is the breath and power of God, a mirror of God, an image of divine goodness, a radiance of eternal light, and a pure emanation of divine glory (Wis 7:25–26).

One source of the Christian association of Wisdom with Jesus (1 Cor 1:24 and 2:1–7 are the earliest texts, as is John 1:1–14, though the association is more subtle) may be the personification of Wisdom in the Wisdom of Solomon and Philo*. This tension between the grammatical gender and usage of Wisdom in the Hebrew Scriptures and her co-optation by the demands of Christology (see Son of God in the New Testament) contributed to the suppression of Wisdom as a divine feminine personification in the patristic period. In associating Sophia with Jesus, the feminization of Jesus in male and female writers became a prominent feature of patristic and medieval theology. During the High Middle Ages, there was a resurgence of interest in the feminine divine, and the expression of Wisdom as a goddess figure or female deity witnessed an unprecedented development in Christian spiritual practices and texts. **See also BULGAKOV, SERGEI NIKOLAEVICH; FEMINIST THEOLOGY CLUSTER; SOLOVIEV, VLADIMIR SERGEEVICH; TRINITY IN EASTERN ORTHODOXY.**

BEVERLY J. LANZETTA

Wisdom of Ben Sira (or Sirach [Gk] or Ecclesiasticus). The author, Jesus Eleasar ben Sira, wrote his book c180 BCE, breaking precedent by providing his name and autobiographical information. Two things solidify the date: a prologue from c117 by his grandson and a hymn describing the high priest Simon II (d196). Ben Sira lived during the heyday of Hellenistic influence just before the Maccabean* revolt against Syrian persecution. The Wisdom of Ben Sira marks a transition from the earlier wisdom books of Proverbs*, Job*, and Ecclesiastes* to the incorporation of Israel's sacred history. Radical attacks from the latter two books made no impact on Ben Sira, who continues the tradition of Proverbs, although grouping thematic sayings into paragraphs. He also explores in greater depth the myth of personified Wisdom*, equating her with Torah*, while accepting teachings from Hellenism, such as the positive role of physicians, symposia, and Stoic philosophy of opposites in nature that assure divine justice*. These influences are muted by frequent references to biblical events and people, above all by a hymn to great *men*. In his admiration for priests, he exalts Aaron* over Moses* but inexplicably omits Ezra*. A conservatism led him to resist the new teaching about the resurrection* and to blame Eve* for all subsequent sin*.

JAMES L. CRENSHAW

Wisdom of Solomon, purportedly a book from the ancient past, but written in Greek by an unknown Hellenistic Jew, probably from Alexandria (c100 BCE), it exhorts its readers to consider wisdom*.

Chapters 1–5 commend wisdom as the way to immortality*. In Chaps. 6–9, the author takes on the role of Solomon*, urging the rulers of the earth to seek (personified) Wisdom and her virtues. Wisdom is viewed as saving Israel's forebears (10); the author then points out that Wisdom delivered Israel from Egypt as he contrasts God's dealings with Israel and Egypt during the time of the plagues (11–19).

The Wisdom of Solomon was recognized as authoritative Scripture by the compiler of the Muratorian* Canon (c200 CE), who recognized Wisdom (though possibly referring to Proverbs) as written by some to honor the ancient king of Israel. Similarly, Clement* of Alexandria, Tertullian*, Origen*, Hippolytus*, Cyprian*, and Lactantius* considered the book inspired and believed that Solomon* actually wrote it. The book, however, was not held to be authoritative by all in the early church. Today Roman Catholics and Orthodox Christians include Wisdom in their Bible*, although it is not part of the HB.

TERRY L. WILDER

Wise Men. See MAGI.

Witchcraft, Witches. On an anthropological level, belief in witchcraft is a universal phenomenon. Witches symbolize the inversion of moral values and serve as an embodiment of evil*, as well as a projection of social fears of terror and subversion, and cultural taboos like bestiality, incest, infanticide, and cannibalism. Witchcraft is often associated with darkness, sexual perversion, and demonic* conjuration, and it is enriched by fantasies of invisibility, shape-shifting, and flying. Lacking a concept of coincidence, many traditional societies believe that accidents, bad luck, illness, and death are caused by witchcraft. Most societies try to ward off witches by applying protective magic.

In its equation of "black" and "white magic," the Christian tradition is quite peculiar. According to Augustine* (354–430), any kind of magic was thought to rely on a contract between a human being and a demon, either explicitly or implicitly, since the practitioner expected an effect from a ceremony or an object that by itself could not be effective (*De doctrina christiana* II, 30–40). As offenders against the law*, biblical (Exod 22:18) as well as Roman, magicians and witches were to be killed. However, during the Middle Ages, theologians and judges considered witchcraft a minor offense. It was only during a period of severe hardship (from the 15th c.) that witch-hunting became prevalent in large parts of Europe, and about 50,000 victims were tried and killed as witches. Many witch trials were illegal, even by contemporary standards, and protest and disbelief in witchcraft increased (16th c.). The rise of rationalism* and an awareness of human* rights brought these killings to an end (17th c.).

Disbelief in witchcraft became a marker of European civilization. In the Americas, Australia, Asia, and Africa, this attitude caused discontent among indigenous peoples because it seemed that the colonial authorities were aiming to protect evildoers. Throughout the 19th c., illegal witch killings were conducted in Russia, and among indigenous peoples in Mexico and the USA. Throughout the 20th c., violent anti-witchcraft movements swept through tropical Africa, with about 10,000 victims in Tanzania* alone. Only recently has the "modernity of witchcraft" (Peter Geschiere) been emphasized and the adaptive capacities of witch beliefs been demonstrated in the midst of the challenges of a globalized world. Witch-hunts are no closed chapter in history, and belief in witchcraft will continue to haunt us in the future. **See also DEMONIZATION; DEVIL, SATAN, DEMONS, AND DEMONIC POWERS; EXORCISM.**

WOLFGANG BEHRINGER

Witchcraft Trials in North America took place mostly in New England (especially Massachusetts and Connecticut) from 1640 to 1700, many of them during the Salem crisis of 1692–93. Only a few such prosecutions were carried out elsewhere, with just one (in Virginia) documented after 1700. That pattern has caused speculation that the Puritan* branch of Protestantism was especially likely to give rise to charges of witchcraft. Yet regardless of religious belief, only in New England did colonists live in small communities with stable populations most prone to developing the long-term feuds that commonly preceded accusations of witchcraft.

Except in 1692–93, formal trials were relatively rare compared with the number of known accusations. Defamation suits brought by the accused or interventions by clergy (seeking spiritual solutions through prayer and fasting) deflected many potential criminal actions. Even when purported witches were tried, convictions were few and executions even fewer (again, except in 1692) because colonial magistrates tended to be skeptical of classic *maleficium* charges. The Salem trials differed in their reliance on spectral evidence and in their context – a prolonged war with Native* Americans that convinced many New Englanders they were facing simultaneous assaults from the devil* in the visible and invisible worlds.

MARY BETH NORTON

Witch Hunt, modern expression for overzealous searching for deviant beliefs or behavior, political as well as religious.

Witherspoon, John (1723–94), Scots-American clergyman, president of the College of New Jersey at Princeton (1768–94), politician, sole clerical signer of the US Declaration of Independence (1776), ratifier of the US Constitution (1787). Educated at Edinburgh, Witherspoon immigrated to North America (1768). In Scotland he had a thriving Presbyterian pastoral ministry that included preaching to more than a thousand persons daily. Siding with the theologically conservative and Evangelical Popular Party, he became a principal conduit of Evangelical* piety and the Scottish* philosophy into the American colonies, as well as a leading figure in the American Enlightenment*. At Princeton, President Witherspoon lectured on moral philosophy, divinity, and history, and trained many future religious and civic leaders, including James Madison. Committed to Evangelical Presbyterian* orthodoxy, he was apparently skeptical of revivalist* emotionalism and encouraged an ecumenical* spirit toward those outside the denomination. He was instrumental in the nationalization of the Presbyterian Church in the USA, drafted the Introduction to the Form of the Government (1788), and was appointed first moderator of the General Assembly. Witherspoon frowned on government establishment of any denomination and was an advocate for the rights of conscience while insisting that "true religion" was vital to public life.

JEFFRY H. MORRISON

Witness (Heb *edh*; Gk *martus*), evidence for an alleged fact, or the person or thing (Gen 31:46–52; Deut 4:26, 30:19) giving that evidence. It is needed because of uncertainty in a legal proceeding, in public opinion, or in persons' minds. The Bible takes much interest in the testimony given by witnesses in legal proceedings, and the Ten* Commandments prohibit false witness. Witnesses are also needed to tell about human acts (e.g. oaths and promises) or divine acts (e.g. acts of deliverance, moments of revelation*) to those who do not experience them directly. In the NT, the apostles* are called witnesses to Christ's life, acts, death, and resurrection; this function is continued by the gospel*, the apostolic writings, and martyrdom* (whose original meaning was "witness"). "Witnessing" in current parlance means telling others about Christ. In the Prophets*, witness often takes the negative form of denouncing sins or threatening disaster – thus the phrase "prophetic witness" against social injustices.

Wittenberg. See LUTHERANISM CLUSTER: LUTHER, MARTIN.

Wittgenstein, Ludwig (1889–1951), philosopher. Born in Vienna into a wealthy family; baptized and raised Roman Catholic. His education overlapped with that of Adolf Hitler, who attended the same school as Wittgenstein in Linz for at least one year. He studied mechanical engineering in Berlin and Manchester. Interest in applied mathematics drew him to Cambridge to study logic with Bertrand Russell (1911–13). He served in the Austrian army; he completed *Tractatus Logico-Philosophicus* (1918, published 1921) and gave up philosophy. Finding the *Tractatus* misread as logical positivism*, he returned to Cambridge to teach (1929–47).

The *Tractatus* contains the famous remarks "Not *how* the world is, is the mystical, but *that* it is" and "Whereof one cannot speak, thereof one must be silent" (see Apophaticism). His lifelong interest in religion* came out in *Remarks on Frazer's Golden Bough* ("We could almost say, man is a ceremonious animal") and *Culture and Value* ("Perhaps one may say: Only *love* can believe the Resurrection*"; "Theology that insists on *certain* words & phrases & prohibits others makes nothing clearer"). Many memorable remarks in *Philosophical Investigations* include "An 'inner process' stands in need of outward criteria" and "The human body* is the best picture of the human soul*."

FERGUS KERR, OP

Woman, Theological Views About. Christianity has no consistent body of theological teachings about women. Its history reflects shifting arguments variously vindicating the inferiority, complementarity, or equality of women with men. This ambiguity is rooted in the NT. Here we find a conflict between two ideals, liberation* and patriarchy*. On the liberationist side, many gospel stories suggest that redemption* in Christ will transform gender relations. Arrogant representatives of the male leadership class, Pharisees and rulers, and false teachers are set against women of despised groups, prostitutes, Samaritans and Canaanites, poor widows, and the physically infirm, who are praised for their true insight into Jesus' teachings. The women disciples* are the last to remain at the cross and the first to appear at the tomb, first witnesses* of the Resurrection, in contrast to the male disciples who run away. This liberationist vision is summarized in Gal 3:28: in Christ "there is neither Jew nor Greek, neither slave nor free, nor male and female."

However, fairly quickly other Christian leaders sought to blunt the social application of this theological vision. The household* codes reinforce patriarchal social hierarchy with the command to wives to obey their husbands, slaves* their masters, and children* their parents (Col 3; Eph 5–6; 1 Pet 2–3). 1 Timothy 2:15 insists that women were created second and sinned first, bringing about the fall of humanity into sin*. This view defined a double subordination of women, by nature and as punished for sin, justifying their removal from public leadership and teaching.

The patristic era (2nd–6th c.) saw a steady removal of women from ordained or public lay ministry. Whether women were created in the image* of God was debated by Ambrosiaster* and many others. Augustine* developed the normative view for Western Christianity: woman possesses the image of God spiritually and so is capable of redemption. But she was created subordinate in the original order of creation and was primarily culpable for the Fall*. Her subordination is to be enforced both as reestablishing her true nature and as punishment for her sin. Women who accept this subordination, even when abusive, and cultivate inner spiritual life will be saved, becoming equal in heaven according to their merits.

This general view of women was accentuated by Thomas Aquinas*, who adopted Aristotle's* view that women were biologically defective. Although Aquinas accepted women's capacity for redemption, their biological and moral defectiveness meant that they could not exercise leadership in the church or society. In order to reflect the full humanity, Christ had to be incarnated* as a male, and only males can represent Christ in the ordained* priesthood. This view continues to be echoed in Roman Catholicism's official opposition to women's* ordination, although it is based on a complementarian anthropology* rather than Aristotle's claim of women's defectiveness. The Reformation opened marriage* to the ordained male, but the traditional teaching that women were created second and sinned first continued to be used as a rationale for excluding women from public leadership and ordained ministry and preaching. Baptist* and Quaker* Christians in 17th-c. England cultivated an alternative view. The Pentecostal text "Your sons and your daughters shall prophesy" (Acts 2:17) was reclaimed to vindicate women's right to preach. Quakers argued that humans, male and female, were created equal. Subordination of women and other oppressed people came about "through the usurpation of power of some over others" that caused sin to come into the world. Thus the Quakers shifted the onus of blame for sin from women to ruling-class men. Modern Feminist theologies draw on this Quaker legacy to define patriarchy* as sin rather than the order of creation*.

From the 15th through the 18th c. in Europe, a *querelle des femmes* argued either for women's goodness and equality or for their evilness and need for subordination. Women increasingly spoke for themselves, discrediting the arguments against women and emphasizing scriptural and historical arguments in women's favor. The 19th and 20th c. saw the liberalization of laws in society regarding women, as well as an acceptance of women's equality in Christ and capacity for ordination in more and more protestant* churches. Other churches continue to argue either for male headship over women or for a masculine–feminine complementarity that both exalts women as "naturally" altruistic and self-sacrificing, and denigrates them as incapable of representing Christ in ordained ministry.

At the beginning of the 21st c., Christian churches around the world were deeply divided over women's status in the church and society. Liberal Christians drew on the teachings of equality in the image of God, restored in Christ, to argue that equality between men and women is part of both God's intended order of creation and the redemptive mission of the church, while Orthodox, Roman Catholic, and conservative Protestant churches revived the views of women as either subordinate or different by nature and so to be confined to roles separate from those of men. ROSEMARY RADFORD RUETHER

Womanist and African American Theologies. Womanist theologies emerged (mid-1980s) as a critical response to the failures of both Black*/African American and Feminist* theologies to address the concerns and needs of North American women of African descent. Although they are both women and black, African American women have shared the historical experiences of both racial and sexual oppression or exclusion. The Womanist Movement is global, but Womanist theology began with African American Christian women in the USA. It has developed beyond Christianity today to include the religious experiences of Buddhist, Muslim, and other women. Those doing Womanist theology are all women of African descent who share the experience of being oppressed as a result of their race, gender, class, and, often, sexual orientation.

The term "womanist" was coined by Alice Walker, who sought a way to speak of the experiences of women of color without simply adding a color or racial designation to the term "feminist." Most Womanist theologians moved far beyond Walker's definition, and many reject the word "feminist" as descriptive of what they are and seek to do, namely eliminate all forms of oppression wherever they exist. Thus the focus of Womanist theology is on survival, on quality of life, and, only after these have been achieved, on liberation.

Womanist theology is a part of Black/African American theology, which emerged in the late 1960s fueled by the Civil* Rights Movement as a theology of black Protestant men, with roots in Africa, its religious traditions, and the Middle Passage that brought millions of Africans from West and Central Africa to the Americas as slaves*. As Womanist theology grounds itself in the experience of black women, African American theology grounds itself in the experiences of North Americans of African descent and their centuries' long experience of racial oppression in the USA. A critique of mainstream theology's tendency to claim universality while ignoring the religious experiences of persons of African descent, it proclaims a black creator God and his son, Jesus, also black, who are in solidarity with the struggle of African Americans. Although the original emphasis on liberation from racial oppression alone overlooked the experiences of black women, black Catholics, and Afro-Latinos, today Black theologians, influenced by womanists and others, are moving to a more inclusive critique of class, racial, and gender oppression as well as a theological reflection on issues that affect persons of color today. **See also ANTHROPOLOGY CLUSTER: WOMANIST THEOLOGICAL ISSUES; CHRISTOLOGIES CLUSTER: FEMINIST AND WOMANIST; ETHICS AND CHRISTIANITY CLUSTER: ETHIC OF RISK AND WOMANIST ETHICS; JUSTICE, THEOLOGICAL VIEWS AND PRACTICES, CLUSTER: IN NORTH AMERICA: WOMANIST; LIBERATION THEOLOGIES CLUSTER: IN NORTH AMERICA: WOMANIST.**

DIANA L. HAYES

WOMEN'S CHRISTIAN PRACTICES AND THEOLOGIES CLUSTER

1) *Introductory Entry*

Women's Christian Practices and Theologies throughout History

2) *A Sampling of Contextual Views and Practices*

Women's Christian Practices and Theologies in Africa

Women's Christian Practices and Theologies in Africa: African Instituted Churches and Charismatic Churches

Women's Christian Practices and Theologies in Asia

Women's Christian Practices and Theologies in Australia

Women Christian Practices and Theologies in Europe: Germany

---

1) Introductory Entry

Women's Christian Practices and Theologies throughout History. Women have lived and pondered the Christian faith ever since its inception. But even if historically women have often made up the majority of those "in the pews," writing women (back) into the history of Christianity is a recent endeavor. The cultural contexts in which the Christian faith grew were marked both by the notional and legal inferiority of women and by myriad forms of marginalization. At the same time, women-specific power structures, networks, and sites of agency were never missing. The latter fact precludes seeing women merely as victims, i.e. as objects of patriarchal* oppression, in this faith tradition.

There is, of course, no unified history of Christian women. The category "women" is a variable rather than a constant, always inflected by other markers of difference, e.g. ethnicity, geographic location, and ecclesial affiliation. For much of the history of Christianity, the dominant marker of difference might be said to be ascribed status (combining gender and class) rather than gender alone. Writing women back into history is thus an attempt to account for the historical reality of women rather than to discern the theological concepts regarding gender differentiations and meanings associated with femininity and masculinity (see Woman, Theological Views About).

In the Bible, the witness to women's voices is uneven (e.g. only a small number of recorded words purport to be those of women; many women remain unnamed or are described simply as wives, mothers, and daughters of the leading male figures). This uneven biblical witness is apparent throughout the Christian tradition. There exist merely a handful of texts written by women in the first millennium of Christianity. What we know about women's faith thus is not only fragmentary but also mediated through male voices and male-dominated politics of documentation and interpretation. That said, Christianity from the very beginning had inclusive rites of initiation; women without question were baptized*, received the Holy* Spirit, and shared in the breaking of the bread. Glimpses of women's formative presence in Christianity also remain visible, e.g. the resurrected Christ appearing first to a woman, Mary* Magdalene (the "apostle to the apostles"); women's leadership in early house* churches (e.g. Prisca*, Phoebe*, Junia*); and women's roles as prophets*, patrons, widows*, martyrs*, exorcists*, healers, deacons*, and missionaries.

At the same time, there are clear indications (starting in the NT) of a struggle over women's roles and authority in the church. The presence of women at worship was policed by regulations concerning clothing, coiffure, and jewelry. Female prophecy, the administering of baptism, liturgical singing, teaching the faith, and other forms of ministry all became sites of conflict in the first few centuries. But women also found new avenues of ecclesial agency, from the Aristocratic women of the late Roman Empire who functioned as powerful patrons, and the newly emerging ascetic* communities of women, to women on pilgrimage* to sacred sites (Egeria*); moreover, the importance of devotion* to (women) saints was growing. Much of the domestic sphere, including raising children in the faith, was profoundly shaped by women's practices of piety and devotion.

With the Middle Ages, more texts by women themselves become available, most of them written by elite and educated women in religious communities. Despite manifold constraints (e.g. legal inferiority, lack of ordination, liturgical menstrual taboos), medieval women claimed ecclesial space based on mystic* encounters with the Divine or on simple communal life and service (Beguines*). How the vast majority of women, i.e. illiterate peasants or women of the emerging urban artisan class, lived their faith is much less visible. That women easily became marked as "other," deviant, and dangerous is clear both from women's pronounced presence in heterodox movements and from the women who lost their lives in witch* hunts.

Even if the 16th-c. (Radical, Protestant, and Roman Catholic) reformations did not lead to the upheaval in women's lives that theological claims suggest, these movements did initiate new developments. Women found novel spaces of ecclesial agency (e.g. as lay theologians, pastors' wives, or religious teachers in schools for girls, or through public works of charity), even as struggle over their ecclesial ministries continued. With modern times, a broadening of women's ministries took place (e.g. women preachers and missionaries in some churches). Cultural shifts also produced new narratives of women's leadership; e.g. the 19th-c. "cult of domesticity" found its echo in the notion of woman as the "priestess of the home."

Not until the 20th c., however, did major cultural shifts in women's lives profoundly reshape the churches' life. Women now gained unprecedented access to theological* education and leadership positions, and developed diverse Feminist* theological visions. Today, from Sunday worship to Feminist rituals, from convent liturgies* to Base* Ecclesial Communities, from Charismatic* healing services to Pentecostal/Charismatic revivals*, the more than 1 billion Christian women worldwide have become visible as never before. The future of Christianity is in their children's hands. TERESA BERGER

2) A Sampling of Contextual Views and Practices

Women's Christian Practices and Theologies in Africa. African women's experiences in contemporary African Churches are increasingly varied and engender distinctive theological expressions. Women's roles are different in the mission churches (churches established by foreign missionaries) and the African* Instituted Churches (AICs). For African women, participation in African theologies is an avenue to reclaim their erstwhile-lost voice. They garner support for their full liberation* and a more effective representation in both church and society. For them, Western Christianity has been biased by misogyny since the time of the early church fathers and has contributed little to their search for full humanity. Rather than discard Christian faith in its entirety, these African women embrace Christology* with vigor and utilize it as a basis for constructing a theology of liberation for African women. The Circle* of Concerned African Women Theologians is interested in the problems that African women face because of entrenched cultural construction of man and woman relationships, Christian traditions, and church practices. The quest for emancipation is a high priority for them, because African society is an overtly patriarchal one in which men usually lord it over women. Christology empowers women to decry the injustices meted against their personhood and the "web of oppression*" with which they are confronted. They contrast with the patriarchal figures of authority that oppress them Jesus crucified, whom they see as a savior, husband/lover, friend, father, redeemer, confidant, and, as such, a liberator.

Women's leadership roles, especially in New Generation churches, provide an impetus for an emerging "theology of dignity and self esteem" for the human woman who is created in the image* of God. Theologies of dignity such as the image of God have encouraged women to reread the Bible in liberative ways, propounding the biblical principles of equality. Furthermore, African women's experiences of poverty*, rape, and marginalization* as battered and underprivileged peoples ground an emerging "theology of vitality." Such a theology emerges from the ravages of wars, growing insecurity, and the HIV/AIDs pandemic. African women see themselves as "Mother Africa" because of the love*, care, and compassion they provide both to those living with the virus and to those orphaned or widowed by the pandemic. These contextual* theologies anchored in African women's experiences empower them to minister hope*, to grapple with and seek to untangle the web of oppression* against women, and to affirm God's presence in all contexts and cultures.

BOLAJI OLUKEMI BATEYE

Women's Christian Practices and Theologies in Africa: African Instituted Churches and Charismatic Churches. African Instituted Churches (AICs) originated as a protest against missionary Christianity and with a view to Africanizing Christianity. As this form of Christianity is rooted in African cultures* and an African-conscious reading of the OT, women's ministries in many of these churches are restricted. Generally, church leadership responsibilities, except where women are founders, is still in male hands. However, women in many AICs are relied on as prophetesses and healers*. Women's theologies are centered on themes such as unity among believers, the role of the Holy* Spirit, and God's revelation* through dreams*.

In comparison, women's ministerial roles in the newly formed Charismatic* churches (neo-Pentecostal and Charismatic) are not so restricted. There is an underlying perception that the salvation* ushered in by Jesus, and the gifts (charisms*) bestowed on an individual believer by the Holy Spirit, can be manifested through each believer, irrespective of gender. According to Owanikin, "In no other churches I know of are women more free to speak, teach, pray, shout and hold responsible positions than in Pentecostal or full Gospel assemblies". Women's theologies focus on such themes as individual salvation, holiness*, the ministries, and gifts of the Holy Spirit.

A disturbing trend that begs scrutiny, particularly by female adherents of these churches, is the new form of (US) missionary imperialism with its proclamation of the "Prosperity* Gospel." It will benefit the leaders of these churches not only to shun such problematic teachings, but also to protect their members from its wholesale consumption. **See also PROSPERITY GOSPEL CLUSTER: IN AFRICA.**

MADIPOANE MASENYA (NGWAN'A MPHAHLELE)

Women's Christian Practices and Theologies in Asia. Women in Asia face complex challenges in all spheres of their lives. There are issues of race*, caste*, class, language, ethnicity, gender, economic security, and sexual preference. Poverty*, unequal wages, discrimination, violence*, marginalization*, and trafficking in women are entrenched in systems, structures, cultures*, and family* values with deep historical roots. The perpetrators of these interconnected, pervasive, globalized acts of violence against women are many: "powers and principalities" in their societies, men and women in their lives, and even themselves.

In addressing these challenges, Asian Christian women speak with many voices, including those of women from minority communities: Dalit* (India*), Burakhumin (see Buraku Liberation in Japan), Tamil (Sri* Lanka), Korean in Japan, and indigenous (Taiwan*, Northeast India, Indonesia*). These voices plead, protest, and are aggressive, angry, shrill, wise, strong, and resourceful. They call for a "revolution" in expectations, accomplishments, self-realization, and relationships with men. Such a revolution promises not only to address the dire situations of many Asian women by bringing about profound changes in the lives of both women and men, but also to revitalize the church.

The Women's Movement in Asia is dedicated to building societies where women, men, and children are empowered to live full human lives. This entails transforming structures, institutions, relationships, and values in the economic, political, social, and cultural spheres of life. Women also need to be empowered in their individual self-understanding, identity, and sexuality*. This is what the Women's Movement does through issue-based initiatives, developing sustainable, gender-sensitive, and empowering strategies to rally against forces that have kept women poor* and powerless. These issue-based initiatives give women an increasing ability to take on issues that traditional culture and religion regard as unalterable, such as marriage*, divorce*, reproductive rights (see Birth Control and Contraception, Christian Views of), and sexuality*.

Christian women, the majority of church members, are deeply religious. Their faith* plays a key role in their lives and is a source of empowerment. Regular church attendance, reading, listening to, and studying Scripture*, prayer, fasting, worship, charity, and fund-raising are common practices. Yet because of their position in society, Christian women in Asia have been kept away from "religious ideological production." Since the late 20th c., however, women have been claiming space and authority for themselves in the theological fields by acknowledging the power of God's grace at work in and through them and their lives as sources of theological reflection aimed at bringing about wholeness and community life in the church and beyond, in the relationships among religions, classes, races, and castes.

The Christian Scriptures and traditional indigenous texts interpreted from the embodied experience of suffering* and marginalization* are the sources of their theology. Symbols, images, institutions, attitudes, and ideologies used to legitimize their subordination are unmasked; those that contribute to women's liberation are identified. Using formal critical methods (historical* critical, postcolonial*, cultural*) and informal ones (performance and storytelling, most effective in largely illiterate communities), women theologians offer a critique of women's cultural and religious subordination. Their theological reflections take both written (e.g. narrative, poetry, essay) and creative forms (e.g. dance, art).

God* – the source of life, sustainer of creation*, and fountain of hope* – identifies with women's suffering and pain and empowers them to reject and cope with death-dealing forces (see God, Christian Views of, Cluster: In Asia). The goddess traditions in Asia have also equipped women to envision God in feminine forms. Similarly, owing to the excessive violence against women, the female body* is recognized as the site of liberation (Dalit), which poses a challenge to the cultural and religious views of sexuality. Asian ecofeminists* ponder the relationship of the female body to nature.

Asian women's spirituality*, committed to enhancing life in its fullness, calls for a redefinition of what it means for the church to be a community of equals that transcends the barriers between family, class, caste, ethnicity, and race. This faith community is called to empower the multitudes of women who live in deplorable conditions under violent and oppressive systems. **See also CHRISTOLOGIES CLUSTER: IN ASIA: THE JESUS OF ASIAN WOMEN; FEMINIST THEOLOGY CLUSTER: IN ASIA.**

MONICA JYOTSNA MELANCHTHON

Women's Christian Practices and Theologies in Australia are shaped by the ancient traditions and practices of indigenous women, as well as by the appropriation of Christian traditions.

Indigenous Australian women have reclaimed their ancient spirituality*, their Dreaming (see Australian Aboriginal Traditions and Christianity), and those who are Christian have brought this into dialogue, which is at times critical, with the Christian tradition. White women are challenged by these women to be attentive to the racism* in their emerging theologies, their forms of spirituality, and their lifestyles. Women across traditional Christian denominations have embraced Feminist* theologies and supported movements toward the ordination* of women.

Tensions with male church leaders and a need for space for Christian women's spiritual development have led to women establishing spirituality centers: Sophia (Adelaide), the Grove (Melbourne), and Womenspace (Brisbane). Here women explore both Feminist theologies and traditions of divinity imaged as female, healing, and women's spiritual practices from ancient Europe and elsewhere. These various traditions nurture different forms of spirituality, shape rituals, and inform

Christian engagement in issues of justice* and ecology*. *Women-Church: An Australian Journal of Feminist Studies in Religion* is a key vehicle for women's theologies and practices of the Pacific region.

ELAINE M. WAINWRIGHT

Women's Christian Practices and Theologies in Europe: Germany. Women, burdened with the "original* sin" of their progenitor Eve*, were limited for a long time, in Germany, to the role of pious ascetics*, as cloistered nuns or mystics* inspired by the Holy* Spirit; this was their only option apart from marriage and having a family. With its almost complete abolition of monasticism* and its greater recognition of the value of marriage*, the Reformation reduced the options available to women. Furthermore, women fell victim to scapegoating during the waves of persecution of witches* (late 15th to mid-17th c.), supported by theologians of both Roman Catholic and Protestant churches. With the Enlightenment*, romanticism*, and idealism, a gradual shift in attitude toward women initiated the process of women's emancipation.

The early-19th-c. shortage of caregivers for the wounded in the wars of liberation and the working classes' deplorable situation required the service of widows and single women. Theodor Fliedner founded the Deaconess* Mother-Hospital in Kaiserswerth (1836), inaugurating church-recognized feminine vocational work (today only a few deaconesses still serve in the 72 Kaiserswerth hospitals). But the descendants of these pioneers largely lost the spiritual energy to live a celibate* life and to work for inadequate wages. At last women were permitted to take the high school graduation examination (*Abitur*; late 19th c.); starting in 1908, they were able to study at all German universities. The first women theologians, most with doctoral degrees, worked as teachers, later as pastoral assistants, and finally as consecrated vicars with limited authority. Yet the Nazi mythology of the mother once again drove women away from public life.

World War II forced a more affirmative attitude toward women, in the church as well as in society. The struggle for women's ordination* in Protestant churches continued until 1991, when women were given full pastoral authority in the last regional church of the Evangelische Kirche Deutschlands – a struggle greatly helped by the relentless work of the Women's Movement in the church and the development of Feminist* theology (with the support of North American feminism). Dorothee Sölle (1929–2003, Protestant) and Elisabeth Gössmann (b1928, Roman Catholic) sought a fundamental shift in thinking concerning the interrelationship of the sexes and exposed the discrimination, oppression*, and marginalization* of individuals and groups. In contributing to the life of the church, women are limited to filling roles at a level below the priesthood, e.g. as pastoral advisers. Yet from 1988 to 1997, a woman served as head of the Central Committee of German Catholics.

INGE MAGER

Women's Christian Practices and Theologies in Europe: United Kingdom. Although the term "feminism"* was not used before the late 19th c., it can be detected in the 16th-c. feminist voices within UK churches that advocated a greater participation of women in the life of the church, which usually attracted more women than men.

In the 16th c., Christianity remained ostensibly a patriarchal* religion, following the various biblical texts that assert male headship and female silence and submission. In Protestantism*, the male-headed "godly household*" limited women's roles, and the Catholic* Renewal enforced the enclosure of nuns. Yet Mary Ward* founded what became the Institute of the Blessed Virgin Mary*, in which women operated outside the normal authority structures. The order was suppressed and its members denounced in a 1631 papal bull, but on his 1982 visit to Britain Pope John Paul II recognized Ward as a pioneer ahead of her times.

In the 17th c., a more explicit feminism emerged in the radical sects of the English civil war. The Quaker* Margaret Fell's* *Women's Speaking Justified* (1666–67) is the first known plea for women to be permitted to preach. The High Anglican Mary Astell argued in the two volumes of her *Serious Call to the Ladies, for the Advancement of Their True and Greatest Interest* (1694, 1697) for a "Protestant nunnery" in which women could pursue independent intellectual and spiritual lives.

The 18th-c. Evangelical revival opened up new opportunities when John Wesley* allowed Mary Bosanquet and other women to preach, although his decision was overturned by the 1803 Methodist Conference. The 18th-c. Enlightenment* with its stress on human* rights and rationality opened up an opportunity for a more explicit feminism. Mary Wollstonecraft's *Vindication of the Rights of Woman* (1792) was rooted in the Enlightenment and in her somewhat idiosyncratic Christianity.

The domestic ideology* of the early 19th c. relegated women to the private sphere but also allowed them to engage in philanthropy. Members of Tractarian (High Church) sisterhoods in the Church of England (see Oxford Movement) ran orphanages and schools. The Salvation* Army allowed women to preach.

In the 20th c., the ordained ministry became the battleground for Christian feminists. First the Church League for Women's Suffrage was founded (1909). Then the Congregationalist* Constance Coltman became the first woman to be ordained to the Christian ministry (1917). Another Congregational minister, Elsie Chamberlain, enjoyed a distinguished broadcasting career. Other free churches also came to recognize women's ordained ministry. Catherine McConnachie became the first ordained minister in the Church of Scotland* (1969). However, the Anglican* Maude Royden found her call to ministry frustrated; the 1930 Lambeth* Conference stated that the Order of Deaconess* was the only one open to women. This issue came to dominate Anglican politics. In July 1979 the Movement for the Ordination of Women was founded. The 1992 General Synod authorized the ordination of woman priests, and on March 12, 1994, a total of 32 women were ordained in Bristol Cathedral. Women clergy are now accepted in most Anglican parishes, and the popular situation comedy, "The Vicar of Dibley", shows how they have become part of mainstream life in the UK.

However, the issue remains controversial. Pope John* Paul II's apostolic letter, *Ordinatio Sacerdotalis* (May 1994), stated that the Roman Catholic Church is not authorized to ordain women, despite a small Roman Catholic movement for women's ordination.

Those who campaign for ordination have always denied accusations that they surrender Christian principles to secular feminism. Nevertheless, the movement to ordain women began in a period when women gained the vote, entered the labor market, and through contraception* were able regulate the size of their families. As always, changes in the church reflected developments in the wider society.

ANNE STOTT

Women's Christian Practices and Theologies in Latin America: Brazil. Christianity in Brazil, as in many other places, is structured, organized, and led by men, but it is lived and experienced primarily by women. Thus speaking of Christian practices is to enter a women's world and to show the significance of women's presence in family*, community, and church life, even when this presence has been silenced and condemned to anonymity.

In Brazil, from the 1970s, the new winds of the Second Vatican* Council opened up a time when women's participation in theological studies and in the lives of Christian communities was not only permitted, but also recognized and affirmed. Women, who had always been involved in "daily-life theology" as catechists and teachers, began to risk themselves by daring, through academic inquiry, to develop a theology about the God* whom women experienced in their own lives.

The fact that women have entered theological schools and other institutions of higher education has made it possible for them to articulate and make public their own perspectives. The theology formulated by women displays a different mode of expression and a different vision of life with a God who creates and re-creates men and women in God's image*. The manner in which a woman has constructed her own identity in the midst of a patriarchal* and androcentric* world is reflected in the way she makes theology.

In this first phase, women's theological production in Brazil is necessarily located in academic centers of research and emphasizes themes related to women's situations and conflicts in society and the church, today and in history, as well as to women's difficulties and longings. At present, women theologians often lean on traditional theological themes, because they provide a safe space in which to engage in theological dialogue with men, but always from the perspective of a person marked by the potentiality of motherhood*: pregnancy*, harboring within herself a life that does not belong to her, giving birth, feeding, and nurturing.

While actual theological production by women in Brazil is not yet large, its quality is recognized, and an impressive number of women have obtained doctorates in theology or religion, contribute to research, and teach in colleges and universities, as well as provide professional counseling. The work by (Roman Catholic and Protestant) Brazilian women in biblical studies and biblical* theology is particularly significant and innovative (as published, e.g., in the journals *Estudos bíblicos* and *Revista de interpretação [bíblica] Latino-Americana, RIBLA* and, in English, in the *Global Bible Commentary*.

MARIA INÊZ DE CASTRO MILLEN

Women's Christian Practices and Theologies in Latin America: Mexico. In the 16th–17th c., women in religious orders followed a monastic* life that made possible mystical* and theological reflections, like those of Sr. Juana* Inés de la Cruz, Sr. Mariana de Jesús, and Catarina de San Juan (nicknamed China Poblana*)*. Beyond this devotion to the mystical and the theological, these monastic women had a life in religious community and devoted themselves to works of charity. Convent life opened up in the 18th c., when the Congregation of María (nuns devoted to teaching) arrived with permission to engage in social work.

Protestants (in the 19th c. and later) allowed for the active participation of women as colporteurs*, as teachers, and, in the medical field, mostly as nurses. Women founded congregations: Melinda Rankin, an apostolic church; Romana Carvajal, a Presbyterian church; and Anna Sanders, a congregation of the Assemblies of God. The Sociedades Mutualistas (mutual aid associations) and Protestant School for Women Teachers offered women a liberal education with political and social dimensions. Some anticlerical associations were led by Protestant women.

During the 20th c., Roman Catholic women's associations developed under the supervision of bishops and priests (Unión de Damas Católicas, 1913; Unión Femenina Católica Mexicana, 1930), as did associations for women students (Unión Femenina de Estudiantes Católicas, 1939) and for women as teachers and defenders of the faith and of the family*. Vatican* II and the Latin American Episcopal Conference (CELAM*) of Medellín* made it possible for Catholic women to establish autonomous women groups. Women religious of many congregations left their convents to integrate themselves into society, especially in communities with urgent social needs.

Christian feminists, in line with Liberation* theology, brought together the first Meeting of Latin American Theologians (Encuentro de Teólogas de América Latina, Oaxtepec, 1979). They also organized Women for Dialogue (1979), the first nongovernmental organization for reflection from a Christian/feminist perspective on social and political issues, including women's rights. Similarly, Catholics for the Right to Decide (Católicas por el Derecho a Decidir, 1993) actively participate in political debates over reproductive rights by reflecting on these issues from the perspective of the Christian faith. In Protestant circles, congresses of women theologians, La Mujer en la Sociedad y la Iglesia (Woman in Society and the Church), met in Edomex (1990) and Monterrey (1991) to analyze the situation and action of Protestant women.

At present women participate in church life at different levels. The Base* Ecclesial Communities in the 1970s were spaces of formation and transformation for women within the social, ecclesiastic, and personal dimensions of their lives. In Protestant and Charismatic* churches, male leadership still thrives, but women have ways of participating in church ministries – as deaconesses*, group leaders, preachers, and ministers – although often without the ordination that would allow them to administer the sacraments (baptism* and the Lord's* Supper). The Methodist, Anglican, Mennonite*, and Congregational* churches, as well as one Baptist church and some Pentecostal churches, have ordained women as ministers.

Women actively participate in higher theological education. A good number of women theologians teach in seminaries and colleges, where they have introduced gender studies into the existing curriculum. REBECA MONTEMAYOR

Women's Christian Practices in North America: United States. In many places throughout the USA, women gather in small communities, often in their homes, to shape their own alternative Christian practices. These rituals rely not on what has been handed down through patriarchal* traditions but rather on what emerges from particular experiences and yearnings of women. No one expects these rituals to be "nice" or "pretty" but rather to be real, gritty, honest, and encouraging, inextricably connected to everyday lives. They are organic ritual practices.

Female bodies, regular bleeding, breast milk, the joys and demands of sexual pleasure, varied physical shapes: all these are primary metaphors of God–human relationships. The emotional and physical demands of pregnancy* and giving birth are honored not as romantic notions, but as sources of fear, anxiety, weeping, and fretting, along with joy and happy anticipation. As with birth, so, too, with death*. Rather than heaven, the focus is on life in the face of death, on everyday loss, many moments of uncertainty, and many unanswered questions about faith*. Any certainty handed down in dogmas or prescriptions about death or an afterlife pales in relation to the complexity of living in the here and now. Abuse*, illness, and negativity are also pivotal in women's ritualizing.

While many church communities avoid the persistence and implications of sexual abuse, women break that silence by facing its terror, the absence of God in "saving us from it," and the need for healing. When there is fear, shame, and anger from the persistent pain of mental illness, women's rituals can create moments of relief, rest, comfort, and blessing. Where women are diminished through texts or images, there are alternative interpretations to be found. Christian women's rituals can evoke patterns that resist every kind of violence: verbal abuse, marginalization*, stereotyping, negative images (witch, crone, gossip), and the objectification of female bodies as if "for sale."

Women's Christian practices focus on ritual forms as well as content. Since planning, leadership, and participation are collaborative, no one structure is canonized. No elite speaks for all. The most memorable moments are the occasions when each person speaks about what she is feeling or thinking in response to ritual actions. Many different voices are solicited and heard. Everyone speaks; everyone blesses. JANET WALTON

Women's Christian Practices and Theologies in Western Europe and North America. Women, always central to the transmission and practice of the Christian life, have become explicit since the late 20th c. about how they see their lives in the light of the limitations of received Christian doctrine. Dorothy Sölle (1929–2003), e.g., became a shrewd critic of authoritarian, male-dominated theism and the academic, ecclesiastical, and political institutions that sustain it. Natalie Watson perceptively asks whether Christian churches truly grace and enhance women among the human family. Susan Ross raises painful questions about women's presence in and exclusion from "sacred" space. Tina Beattie argues from a reconfiguring of the

"Marian" tradition for a renewed understanding of women's salvation* and therefore for their ordination. Mary Grey articulated the connections between the degradation and suffering* of women, especially among the poor, and the misappropriation of the natural world. Ann Loades addressed difficult issues, such as abortion* and the sexual abuse* of children, and women's own complicity in the world's wrongs. Much, too, may be learned from those who live in women-only communities, living lives of "consecrated celibacy*," and their struggles in an arguably dysfunctional church, as Sandra Schneiders rightly maintains. Women thus insist on their full human dignity, seeking resources within their traditions for securing justice* for all.

ANN LOADES

Women's Missionary Societies developed in parallel with the modern mission* movement. In 1800 Mary Webb formed the first society in the USA when she led Baptist and Congregational women to organize the Boston Female Society for Missionary Purposes. Within five decades, more than 200 such societies marked the US religious scene. In time they became the primary financial source for the Protestant missionary enterprise.

Women had little training in leadership at this time. Yet their growing awareness of the spiritual needs of the world made the establishment of societies necessary. Concerned women, like Sarah Doremus, gathered others, usually across denominational lines, to learn about, gather funds for, and do missions. They believed they were fulfilling the Great* Commission.

The societies emphasized "woman's work to woman." They supported female missionaries who spread the gospel among women and children through primary medical care (see Health, Healing, and Christianity Cluster), education*, and the distribution of literature. They did not assert the right to preach to or teach men, but generally accepted the limitations placed on Christian Western women. Yet these societies helped women develop leadership and financial management skills. Even though most churches denied their women members the right to minister officially, the society members established an international network of capable women.

ROSALIE BECK

WOMEN'S ORDINATION CLUSTER

1) *Introductory Entries*

Women's Ordination: The Early Church
Women's Ordination and the Orthodox Church
Women's Ordination and the Roman Catholic Church

2) *A Sampling of Contextual Views and Practices*

Women's Ordination in Africa
Women's Ordination in Africa: African Instituted Churches and Charismatic Churches
Women's Ordination in Asia
Women's Ordination in North America
Women's Ordination in Western Europe

See also WOMEN'S CHRISTIAN PRACTICES AND THEOLOGIES CLUSTER

---

1) Introductory Entries

Women's Ordination: The Early Church. The preliminary question is: What is the earliest evidence for ordination as "a ritualized recognition of clerical orders"? Neither the NT nor the Didache* contains descriptions of actual ordination rituals. Prayer and laying on of hands, both elements of later ordination rituals, are present in the NT (see Ordination). Before the 3rd c., qualifications for church leadership included indwelling by the Holy* Spirit (divine selection), gifts of the Spirit (such as successful evangelizing), teaching competence, and communal selection and approval (social reputation, Christian ethics, patronage). Ordination was not always an expressed qualification for church leadership.

These qualifications were relatively gender inclusive, with the result that women occupied roles of ministry and governance alongside men as itinerant evangelists*, prophets*, stewards, patrons, teachers, house*-church leaders, healers, administrators, ritual celebrants, prayer leaders, and elders – as is shown by NT documents and many other early Christian sources (church orders, treatises, commentaries, letters, conciliar legislation, martyrologies, hagiographies, popular narratives, memorial and dedicatory inscriptions, art). There were chronological and regional variations (up to the 6th c.) in the meanings of key terms (e.g. ministry*, sacrament*, minister, bishop*, presbyter*, deacon*, teacher, prophet, widow*, virgin*, apostle*, steward). Contradictions between a growing number of legislative prescriptions against ordaining women and literary and epigraphic evidence show the persistence of women's ordained and nonordained ministries. Thus the question is not whether women were ordained but why ordination was increasingly prohibited among women from the 4th c. onward.

Detailed evidence for specific ordination rituals first appears in the Apostolic* Tradition (early 3rd c.), a church* order that systematically distinguishes clerical orders and rituals of ordination, reflecting the consolidation, definition, and elaboration of the previously amorphous ministerial and governance roles. The practice of organizing ecclesial leaders into ordained and nonordained clerical orders through episcopal authority is not gender exclusive (though not gender neutral), and women continue to fulfill ministerial and governance roles.

Four major ordained clerical orders receiving women can be identified from the early 3rd c.:

1. *Widows* constituted a clerical order of women prophets and penitential prayer leaders that was variously listed as an ordained or nonordained order.
2. *Ordained female deacons** (cf. deaconesses*) were a regular feature of clerical organization, although there were fewer in Western churches than in Eastern churches, and age of admission and exact functions were debated.
3. *Ordained women presbyters (priests)*, fewer than women deacons, were present in both Eastern and Western churches. Sporadic Western prohibitions against female priestly ordinands – unsuccessfully attempted by Pope Gelasius I (late 5th c.) – reveal that local bishops continued to ordain women priests.
4. *Ordained women bishops* were still fewer, but their presence is shown by the evidence that some Christian bishops in Spain and Asia Minor were called heretics by bishops in other regions because of their practice of ordaining women in clerical orders, including the order of bishops. The latest evidence for a female bishop is attested in a 9th-c. Roman church mosaic representing Bishop Theodora (whether the title *episcopa* is honorific or functional is debated).

Repeated 5th- and 6th-c. Western prohibitions against ordaining women into any clerical order (preferring a ritual blessing instead) testify to the ongoing resistance of local bishops to such prohibitions. These prohibitions articulated theological concerns for ritual purity in service of the altar, although other social and political factors were relevant. Nevertheless, these prohibitions indicate an awareness that women had been ordained in the past and were continuing to be ordained at the time of the councils. Indeed, the practice of ordaining women was confirmed as a papal prerogative by Gregory the Great (late 6th c.) and by Pope Benedict VIII (11th c.), who delegated to a Portuguese bishop the right of ordaining deaconesses.

KAREN JO TORJESEN and LESLIE HAYES

Women's Ordination and the Orthodox Church. Ordaining women to the presbyterate and episcopacy generally is not considered possible today by the Orthodox, although a small but growing number of theologians are requesting that they begin to study this issue in more depth. Contemporary discussions regarding the ordination of women in the Orthodox Church revolve mostly around the diaconate. Deacons*, male and female, are ordained to the "sacred" or "priestly ministry" (*hiera diakonia*) but are not allowed to preside at the Eucharist*, as are bishops and presbyters*. The historic Inter-Orthodox Conference (Rhodes, 1988), to which all of the autocephalous* Orthodox* churches were invited, called for the restoration of the order of deaconess*, stating:

> (32) The apostolic order of the deaconess should be revived. It was never altogether abandoned in the Orthodox Church.... There is ample evidence... that this order was held in high honor.... (34) Such a revival would represent a positive response to many of the needs and demands of the contemporary world in many spheres. This would be all the more true if the diaconate in general (male as well as female) were restored in all places in its original, manifold services (*diakoniai*), with extension in the social sphere, in the spirit of ancient tradition and in response to the increasing specific needs of our time. It should not be restricted to a purely liturgical role or considered to be a mere step on the way to higher "ranks" of clergy. (35) The revival of women deacons in the Orthodox Church would emphasize in a special way the dignity of woman and give recognition to her contribution to the work of the Church as a whole.

See also OLD BELIEVERS.

KYRIAKI KARIDOYANES FITZGERALD

Women's Ordination and the Roman Catholic Church. The nonordination of Roman Catholic women is a mixed blessing. Catholic women are engaged in multiple forms of ministry all over the world unfettered by the constraints of a hierarchical, male-dominated structure. Yet authorities of the Roman Catholic Church continue to discriminate against women by declaring (*Inter Insignores*, 1977) that women do not "image Christ" in a biologically male way and therefore cannot be ordained.

Many Catholic women, theologically trained with master's and doctoral degrees, receive preparation that is equal to (and at times well beyond) that of male priests. They minister in schools, parishes, prisons, and hospitals as laypeople (not clergy). When they work in Catholic institutions, they are barred from most decision making that clerics enjoy. Laypeople cannot licitly celebrate the Eucharist* or hear confessions, although anecdotal evidence reveals that many do *in extremis*. At the heart of the matter is power – who decides how to use the community's resources, from real estate to sacraments – assigned according to gender.

One creative response is the Women-Church Movement, a network of feminist Base* Ecclesial Communities striving to live a "discipleship of equals" (Elisabeth Schüssler Fiorenza). Many Catholic women participate in these house* churches, which function without hierarchical, ordained leadership. Some Catholic women are ordained in other Christian denominations and still consider themselves "Catholic" women in ministry. Still others in the Roman Catholic Womenpriests organization challenge exclusive practices by claiming to be ordained in a valid but not licit way by bishops who claim to be in apostolic* succession. Other people have left the Roman Catholic Church, scandalized by its treatment of women.

The nonordination of Roman Catholic women raises issues of gender justice and theology. A growing number of communities are concerned more with the quality of ministry than with the gender of the minister – a worldwide approach that will prevail in time. MARY E. HUNT

---

2) A Sampling of Contextual Views and Practices

Women's Ordination in Africa is a complex and contested domain. Africa is the home of very diverse Christian traditions: churches dating from early Christianity, Western missionary-founded churches, and African* Instituted Churches (AICs). Each tradition has its own biblically grounded theological arguments on the place of women in the church, their ordination, and their relation to ecclesiastical leadership. Most church structures are overwhelmingly patriarchal* and hierarchal and deny women's leadership because of deeply entrenched gender discrimination, a justice* issue. Regional and global Christian world communions, ecumenical organizations, global women's movements, and human* rights groups contribute their voices to the debate. Nevertheless, in many Christian traditions, the local African church, diocese, or synod has the last word. Fortunately, theologically trained and/or ordained women (present in several churches) and women who have founded churches (especially AICs) contribute most effectively to the battle against patriarchy*, sexism*, exclusion, and gender inequality in the church. However, they have a long way to go. There is a need for well-coordinated research to go beyond each Christian tradition's attitude toward women and their practical experiences in church ministry (ordained or not), in order to account for the socioculturally constructed perceptions of power relationships between women and men in the family*, society, and religious communities. NYAMBURA J. NJOROGE

Women's Ordination in Africa: African Instituted Churches and Charismatic Churches. See WOMEN'S CHRISTIAN PRACTICES AND THEOLOGIES CLUSTER: IN AFRICA: AFRICAN INSTITUTED CHURCHES AND CHARISMATIC CHURCHES.

Women's Ordination in Asia reflects the recognition by the church that, like men, women are called to the Christian ministry, following the way of Jesus the Christ by preaching; teaching; casting out evil; caring for the sick, weak, and poor; building up the community entrusted to their care; administering the sacraments* (Lord's Supper and baptism); and conducting marriage*. From the beginning, Christian women in Asia were included in the ministry, but without ordination. Thus they were prohibited from administering the sacraments. Their ordination came about only after a long struggle by women church workers, although the Roman Catholic Church has retained its age-old position that women have access neither to the priesthood nor to the diaconate. Although most Protestant denominations in Asia now ordain women, the process leading to women's ordination varies; given the patriarchal* cultures*, hierarchical church structures, and patriarchal reading of Scriptures*, the steps toward ordination for women are often not easy. In some denominations, the requirements for ordaining women are much stricter than those for ordaining men, demanding, e.g., that they pass virginity tests, prove their singlehood (and celibacy) throughout their life, or be postmenopausal. Asian Feminist* theologians have supported the struggle for women's ordination, although some have opted not to be ordained in protest against the inherently patriarchal and institutionalized notions of ordination and because of their vision of alternative models of leadership in an egalitarian community. HOPE S. ANTONE

Women's Ordination in North America. During the colonial period, Protestant and Roman Catholic women were actively engaged in North American church life as laity*. Their religious activities revolved around prayer, Bible reading, teaching children, and attending church. Formal church leadership, usually marked by a sacred service of ordination, remained a male privilege.

In colonial society (early 18th c.), Protestant women who participated in religious revivals* (the "Great* Awakenings") became active as informal religious leaders; in some sectarian groups, such as those of the Quakers* and Shakers*, women's leadership was recognized without formal ordination. In the Roman Catholic Church, nuns exercised significant leadership in educational and medical ministries.

After the Revolutionary War, a second wave of frontier revivals promoted more egalitarian thinking about Christian mission and social reform. Christians reexamined Scripture and embraced new thinking about race* and gender. Antoinette Brown* became the first woman ordained (1853) to Christian ministry in an established denomination (Congregationalist*). Brown's ordination caused little controversy, because Congregationalists make decisions about ordination in local congregations. Congregationally organized denominations (Universalist, Unitarian*, Disciples*, and some Baptist*) ordained women by the late 19th c. The more structured Protestant denominations – Presbyterian*, Methodist*, Lutheran*, and Episcopalian* – supported by new biblical scholarship, church mergers, and renewed feminist thinking, granted full ordained status to women from the 1950s to the 1970s.

Meanwhile openness to clergywomen slowed among conservative Christians in the 20th c. With growing concern about biblical inerrancy*, they argued that women's ministries should be limited to home and family*. By the 1980s, the Southern* Baptist Convention, the largest Protestant denomination in the country, declared that women's ordination was unscriptural.

The historic African* American denominations also resisted. They insisted that formal leadership "on the pulpit" was reserved for men, with women exercising complementary* power from the pew. Many black women who felt a call to preach switched denominations or simply started small independent storefront churches. Since 1853 more than 50% of ordained women in North America have been leaders of unaffiliated congregations or in racially mixed Holiness*, Pentecostal*, Evangelical*, and paramilitary denominations, such as the Salvation* Army.

US Roman Catholic women were hopeful that canon* laws against the ordination of women would change after the Second Vatican* Council (1960s). They enrolled in seminaries to prepare themselves. Vatican documents continued to insist, however, that only celibate male priests could "represent" Jesus Christ at the altar* (see the present cluster: Women's Ordination and the Roman Catholic Church).

Women's ordination is still debated. However, the issue is more than a question of women's leadership; it illustrates basic ways in which Christians struggle to define their faith in the context of modern culture. BARBARA BROWN ZIKMUND

Women's Ordination in Western Europe. Gender has always been a constitutive part of the conception of ecclesial ordination*, commonly providing a criterion for the division between laity* and clergy*. In Western European Protestant churches, theological and political claims for gender equality have led to the gradual acceptance of women's ordination to the offices of missionaries, deaconesses*, pastors and priests, and eventually bishops.

At times difference and complementarity* were stressed. Deaconesses remained within traditional women's roles and women pastors or priests were seen as a complement to male clergy. But sameness and equality were also affirmed; both female and male clergy are needed by the congregation.

While secular cultural motives played a role, theological motivation has recently been emphasized, based on the views that every human being is an image* of God and that baptism* and thus the priesthood* of all believers are gender inclusive. At minimum, gender has been regarded as neutral in relation to faith*. However, women's ordination is ultimately based on the conviction* that women are necessary for the fullness of the gospel to be preached and lived, and that women's subordination, although supported by strands of Christian tradition, must be clearly confronted. Female church leaders are important for reinforcing the trustworthiness of the church.

These theological perspectives have been contextually implemented in Western European Protestant churches following a pattern exemplified by Germany, France, and Scandinavia. A prelude was the 19th-c. revivalist* movement in these countries, where women-led congregations were legitimated by apocalyptic* expectations and charismatic* emphases. In Germany during World War II, because most male pastors and priests were drafted into the army, women stepped into the pulpits. Theologically trained women petitioned for ordination, which was finally granted (Prussia, 1942; Baden, 1944) as an "emergency" measure. They remained in their positions after the war, yet the ordination of other women did not occur until 1960 (fully established, 1978; women Lutheran bishops since 1992). Similarly, during World War II in France, women functioned as Lutheran priests (Alsace-Lorraine) and pastors of the Reformed Church, though without ordination. Elisabeth Schmidt, pastor in Sète during and after the war, was alone in being ordained (1949). Women's ordination in the Reformed Church of France was established in 1966. In Scandinavia, women's ordination as priests in the Lutheran churches began in Sweden in 1958 and reached Finland in 1986; in 2004 Denmark, Norway, and Sweden each had two women bishops. Women now constitute a substantial portion of the Protestant clergy all over Western Europe. Some women priests and pastors conform to their church tradition and others have taken it in feminist directions. **See also WOMEN'S CHRISTIAN PRACTICES AND THEOLOGIES CLUSTER: IN WESTERN EUROPE: UNITED KINGDOM.** CRISTINA GRENHOLM

WOMEN'S RELIGIOUS ORDERS CLUSTER

Women's Religious Orders in Africa
Women's Religious Orders in Asia
Women's Religious Orders in Europe and North America
Women's Religious Orders in Latin America
Women's Religious Orders in Latin America: Brazil

Women's Religious Orders in Africa. See RELIGIOUS ORDERS, ROMAN CATHOLIC, CLUSTER: IN AFRICA.

Women's Religious Orders in Asia. Roman Catholic women's religious orders made their appearance in Asia with the colonial expansion of the West in the 17th c. and are present in their Western form in the majority of Asian countries today. These orders or congregations include cloistered orders, religious institutes with active apostolates, and societies of apostolic life. According to their mode of consecration*, they voluntarily observe the evangelical counsels* and live life in common to fulfill the mission of Christ and his church*.

Part of the European colonial enterprise under Roman Catholic monarchs was to Christianize the "natives," and male religious* were sent with the colonizers. Gradually the help of women was deemed more practical in the evangelization of women and children. At that time, however, the only legitimate form of religious life for women was the cloister*, which precluded external works, as in the case of the Order of St. Clare founded in Manila in 1621 by a member from Spain.

The early native sisterhoods began with women responding to the call of the Holy* Spirit to lead holy lives, whether in seclusion or in small groups. In due time, they served the Church's purposes as well. The earliest native congregation, the Lovers of the Cross, originally a small band of celibate Vietnamese Catholic women doing pious works in the 1640s, was organized as a religious community in 1670 by the vicar apostolic of Cochin China. All subsequent indigenous congregations in Vietnam* trace their roots to this religious group. Having weathered several countrywide persecutions and suppression in North Vietnam, it now has more than 3,000 members in Asian countries as well as in Europe and the USA.

Likewise, some groups of *beatas* (women of exceptional piety) in 17th- and 18th-c. Philippines eventually formed religious institutes; similarly, "Christian Virgins" in mid-18th- and 19th-c. China became active in service to the Church, no longer solely in pursuit of personal perfection. Asian-based institutes are now established in many Asian countries, with the greatest number in India, where more than 200 sisterhoods have been founded, most of them in the 19th c.

By the 18th c., there was some leniency with women's orders, made official by a 1900 papal decree that allowed them some external apostolate. Hence European orders began responding to the call of Asian missions, followed by North American congregations in the 20th c. Whether foreign based or indigenous, women's congregations in Asia before Vatican* II were involved in education*, in medical, pastoral, and social* work, in training local sisters and catechists, and in other forms of evangelization*. After Vatican II, facing new needs, they opened retreat centers, taught in theological schools, participated in basic Christian communities, assisted drug and HIV/AIDS victims, fostered gender sensitivity and ecological* awareness, and sent members overseas. Following the Synod of Bishops' call for justice* in 1971, women's orders became more involved with workers and indigenous peoples, offering advocacy and other services.

While women's orders have their own governing bodies, in many Asian countries they have formed national conferences for intercongregational collaboration. Spurred by the 1971 Synod to make justice a priority in their lives, the Asia Meeting of Religious was created in 1972 as a continent-wide forum for conference members for sharing their hopes, concerns, and challenges. A challenge to the Church in Asia is to be truly Asian in its identity and mission* and to engage in authentic dialogue* with Asia's religions* and cultures* and its many poor*. Interreligious dialogue*, inculturation*, and integral liberation* are challenges facing women's orders in Asia as well. **See also** **RELIGIOUS ORDERS, ROMAN CATHOLIC, CLUSTER.** VIRGINIA FABELLA, MM

Women's Religious Orders in Europe and North America. Religious life for women flourished in Europe from the beginning of Christianity, first in the form of groups of virgins* and widows* living together as a vital part of the local church and later in monasteries following the Rule of Basil* in the East and the Rule of Benedict* in the West. Monastic* life offered the only education available for girls throughout the Middle Ages, enabling women like Hildegard* of Bingen and Mechtilde* of Magdeburg to achieve prominence as mystics*, scholars, and educators.

Clare* of Assisi and others led women into a new, evangelical expression of religious life based on the example of Francis* of Assisi and Dominic*. The daily life of Franciscan* and Dominican* women was more circumscribed by ideals of cloister than was that of the men, but both genders were inspired by the desire to spread the gospel through the example of radical poverty, preaching, and good works. Still other groups – Beguines* in the Low Countries and the Rhineland, *beatas* in Spain, and the French *dévotées* – lacked official Church recognition as religious but gave many women a way to live in community as consecrated virgins while practicing charitable works in their neighborhoods.

The requirement of cloister finally gave way, in practice if not in Church law, when many congregations of women were established to address social ills during the Counter* Reformation (Catholic* Renewal). These congregations included Angela Merici's* Ursulines, Mary Ward's* Institute of Mary, the Daughters of Charity, and the Visitandines led by Louise de* Marillac and Jane* Frances de Chantal, respectively, and the Sisters of St. Joseph. All of these, along with the older Benedictines*, Franciscans*, Dominicans*, and Carmelites* and 19th-c. foundations, including the Society of the Sacred Heart, the School Sisters of Notre Dame, and the Sisters of Mercy, were seeds for the growth of women's congregations in North America.

Religious life for women was brought to Canada* by Marie (Guyard*) de l'Incarnation, whose missionary zeal impelled her to cross the Atlantic (1639) to join a small group of colonists who had come from France to Quebec* just five years before. A member of a cloistered Ursuline community, she emigrated with that community's blessing and soon set what was to be the pattern for women religious in North America by opening the first school in the colony, for Native American and French girls.

Her initiatives were followed shortly after (1642) by Marguerite Bourgeoys. A devout member of a lay association while in France, she came to Canada, where she cofounded the settlement that became Montreal, established the first free school in North America, and founded a noncloistered teaching order, the Congregation of Notre Dame. For three decades, she directed the colony's only hospital and served as treasurer of Montreal.

A third outstanding colonist, Marguerite d'Youville, later founded the Gray Nuns to assist her in caring for the sick poor.

In the USA, Ursulines from France introduced religious life for women in New Orleans, Louisiana Territory, in 1727. Toward the end of the 1700s, several women brought the Carmelite life from Belgium to Baltimore. Growth began to accelerate when North American women, such as the widow and convert to Roman Catholicism Elizabeth Bayley Seton, founded congregations in which women could support one another in prayer and charitable works. Elizabeth Lange addressed the needs of current and former slaves* by founding the first congregation for African Americans, the Oblate Sisters of Providence. Philadelphia heiress Katherine Drexel, moved by the neglect of freed slaves and of Native Americans, founded the Sisters of the Blessed Sacrament to work among these populations.

Growth was further stimulated by the resurgence of religious life for women in postrevolutionary Europe coupled with anticlerical laws that banned congregations devoted solely to prayer and contemplation and constrained others from exercising their traditional roles in education. These factors, along with massive immigration from Ireland and parts of the Continent, led hundreds of European congregations to begin missions in the USA and, to a lesser extent, in Canada, where women religious ultimately established a presence in every province.

An estimated 220,000 women religious have served over the years in the USA, forming centers of prayer and social service in every region and establishing an extensive network of schools, universities, and hospitals. Sisters' service as nurses during the U.S. Civil War is credited with having disarmed anti-Catholic prejudice in the USA. A dynamic movement of lay association has characterized the post–Vatican II decades in North America, whereas the number of women religious has been in decline since their peak in the 1960s.

Women's congregations in North America are self-governing within the framework of their own constitutions and canon law. Voluntary federations and national conferences offer mutual support and facilitate common action in promoting the cause of the poor and disadvantaged in society. **See also RELIGIOUS ORDERS, ROMAN CATHOLIC, CUSTER.**

KAREN M. KENNELLY, CSJ

Women's Religious Orders in Latin America. When women's religious orders arrived in Latin America, they encountered cultures* that strongly emphasized the consecration of women and the worship of goddesses among indigenous communities in the lands called Abya-yala (the Continent of Life). Women's religious orders shared the three principal vows of the religious life (poverty, obedience, and chastity) through different paths: contemplative* life, active life, and service within secular* institutes. The cloister* had a central role during colonial times. Religious women of active life gained legitimacy during the 19th c. The secular institutes were born with the Second Vatican* Council; these institutes choose their vocation (it is not imposed by the hierarchy of the Roman Catholic Church).

When Liberals ruled most Latin American countries (late 19th–early 20th c.), there was a strict separation between church* and state. Under these circumstances, Catholics developed a social network including primary and secondary schools, universities, hospitals, and a mass communication system. Laypeople as well as religious, both men and women, were responsible for these social and apostolic tasks.

The Holy See* rapidly recognized that the sisters' work in the social and religious fields was important, but Church authorities imposed on them a monastic* discipline, in line with the First Vatican* Council (1869). All religious congregations were to move their central houses to Rome in order to work closely with the Vatican, which would control them. In 1917 a new canon* law was promulgated that oversaw everything in the life of the Catholic Church, including women's religious apostolic life. Consequently, all congregations shared similar approaches to formation, promotion of vocation, community life, and conception of how to live the three vows. These rules were followed regardless of national context; the canonical disposition was more important than the local social or cultural reality.

In most Latin American countries, Liberal governments tried to establish a public school system, but universal education was not possible. Women's education* was often provided by reestablished monastic orders that had initiated those tasks in colonial times and sometimes by European monastic orders that came to Latin America along with immigrants. After the 1930s economic crisis, welfare state systems were established in Latin America, with strong state involvement in the economy providing many social benefits for members of the working class and peasants. Because of its past experience, the Church, and especially women's religious congregations, knew how to mobilize people to fulfill these roles. As a result, a true church-and-state symbiosis developed. The state gave the Catholic Church's institutions – particularly, women's congregations – the facilities and economic means to accomplish this social* work. Social work was placed on the shoulders of regular* men (members of religious orders), secular* clergy (priests living "in the world"), but predominantly women religious.

	1912	1945	1950
Women religious	14,000	55,567	69,073
Regular men	4,578	11,389	13,282
Secular men	11,776	12,992	14,270

Despite the increase in the number of women religious, it was impossible to cope with the needs for social services of a population increasing even more rapidly, and the state never managed to resolve the situation.

The congregations' essential religious aspect was based on the principles of canon* law, and particularly on the three vows that governed the essence and meaning of cloistered lives. The central goal, a "state of perfection" (following the counsels*), was reachable only through life inside the cloister, where women could keep themselves safe from the world and its temptations. Despite their tremendous impact on the social, religious, and political realms, they saw social work merely as a part of their quest for piety and sanctity. Until the 1960s, the walls of cloisters and convents aroused people's curiosity because of the secrecy and mysterious aura that surrounded them. The mother superior ruled the life inside the convent and was considered God's representative. She reported to her major superior in the mother house (normally located in Europe, particularly in Rome), which in turn reported to the Vatican.

With Vatican* II, the sisters moved to a mission-centered life in society. Women religious who chose the process of "insertion" into society moved from a service through which the poor* were objectified as receivers of works of charity to a mission through which these women became agents of social and political transformation who empowered the poor to become themselves agents in their own life contexts. This process of insertion changed the way they lived their vows, as they returned to their roots and refounded their communities, rediscovering their founding charisms* and at the same time their feminine religious identity. The great majority of Latin American congregations went to live in small communities, leaving upper-class neighborhoods and comforts. For many of them, pastoral work among the poor signified a radical rupture with their social milieu and with their way of life and work.

In the early 21st c., beyond ecclesiastical confrontations, women religious continue to live and work among the poor while reflecting on their own experience of insertion into society and inculturation* in search of personal and social liberation*. In fact, as they redefine their feminine identity and develop a new theology – a Liberation* and Feminist* theology – they draw extensively on their new social consciousness. They have brought their experience with poor, indigenous, and black women to their feminist reading of the Bible and to their effort to bring about new social movements. **See also RELIGIOUS ORDERS, ROMAN CATHOLIC, CLUSTER.**

Ana María Bidegain

Women's Religious Orders in Latin America: Brazil. During the colonial period (1500–1822), it was not easy for women to enter the religious life because Portugal*, through the Padroado Régio (Royal Patronage; Spanish, Patronato*), restricted and controlled, for economic and political reasons, the foundation of female convents in Brazil. Yet women in the colony found ways of bypassing the prohibition by establishing *recolhimentos*, institutions where women of different stations in life (orphaned girls, middle-aged women, widows) gathered and lived, (unofficially) observing the rules of an order. Such *recolhimentos* included the "Recolhimento do Desterro" in Bahia and the "Convento da Ajuda" in Rio de Janeiro (which never was a canonical religious order). Following the creation of the *recolhimentos*, monasteries were also established in Brazil. The first were the Santa Clara do Desterro in Bahia (1677) and the Convento da Luz in São Paulo. Thus during the colonial period, noncanonic and canonic religious ways of life existed side by side and were often interconnected.

During the period of the Brazilian Empire (1822–89), women's congregations started to arrive from Europe, having been invited by reformer bishops who sought to implement the Catholic* Renewal initiated by the Council of Trent* (1545–63) through education, moral formation, and social work. These bishops needed the collaboration of women religious (often simply called "religious") in education, as well as in the moral formation of women and the development of social work in order to care for the sick, orphans, and elderly. These were women religious pursuing the "active life," religious life associated with some form of social* work. The first three women's congregations to arrive in Brazil were the Daughters of Charity of Saint Vincent* de Paul (1849), the Sisters of Saint Joseph of Chambéry (1858), and the Sisters of Saint Dorothy (1868). After 1891 the number of new congregations grew rapidly, most of them coming from France and Italy.

The Second Vatican* Council and, more important for Brazil, the Latin American Episcopal Conferences of Medellín*, Colombia (1968), and Puebla, Mexico (1979), introduced new ways of practicing the religious life. Structural changes were proposed for the internal reorganization of the congregations: a shift from the wearing of habits to simple street clothes and separation of the place of work from the living place. Major changes for larger communities included their dislocation into small groups; the democratization of internal structures, including the election of their superiors by the groups; and the emergence of a sense of individuality and a greater appreciation for each religious as a person. Most changes occurred out of the women's desire to live with others, to be free of a way of life so far apart from the world. **See also RELIGIOUS ORDERS, ROMAN CATHOLIC, CLUSTER.**

BEATRIZ DE VASCONCELLOS DIAS

Woolman, John (1720–72), Quaker* mystic*, known for his *Journal* and other writings on slavery* and wealth*. Born in Northampton, New Jersey, Woolman taught school, worked as a tailor, and traveled as an itinerate opponent of slavery and trading in slaves, with an active concern for Native Americans. A kindly man of utter simplicity, he dressed plainly, mostly in undyed linen clothing, spoke out against consumerism, horseback riding, and rum and tea drinking, and insisted that ordinary folk could achieve perfection*. Active in the affairs of the Philadelphia Yearly Meeting of the Religious Society of the Friends*, he was part of a reform movement within it. He married Sarah Ellis, a neighbor in Mt. Holly, New Jersey (1749). In 1772 Woolman sailed in steerage to England, where he was not well received by other Friends, partly because he insisted on walking around the country. He died and was buried in Yorkshire.

His oft-edited *Journal* (in print since 1774) amounts to a reflection on his experiences and his approach to life, and it continues to inspire. The simple prose of this minor classic suggests a man with strong principles yet broad sympathies, because he seldom alienated contemporaries.

H. LARRY INGLE

Word-Faith Movement and Its Worship. The Word-Faith (or Word of Faith) Movement is a primarily North American new religious movement best known for its stance that physical healing* and financial prosperity* represent the will of God for all believers and are readily available to anyone with sufficient faith*. Originating in the 1960s–1970s through the labors of Kenneth "Dad" Hagin (1917–2003), Kenneth Copeland, and Fred Price, the Word-Faith Movement has mushroomed into a network of independent nondenominational churches (many ranking as megachurches) located mostly in the USA (2,300–2,500 churches claiming as many as 4,800,000 worshippers) and rapidly spreading worldwide. Several Word-Faith leaders have made themselves culturally visible through their widespread use of media*, especially television, and popular books. Although Word-Faith churches style themselves as "Bible believing," leading to their common misclassification as simply "conservative" or "Evangelical," the novel meanings that they ascribe to traditional language reveal a vastly different theological background. The latest research indicates that the Word-Faith Movement's theological roots lie within the Nation of Islam and Mormonism*. However, the structure and praxis of Word-Faith worship stem directly from the Pentecostal*/Charismatic* tradition, making the movement a blend of diverse US religious modalities.

Three core beliefs undergird the writings and sermons of virtually all Word-Faith teachers. First, God* is a spirit, where "spirit" is construed as the agency producing the force of faith*. This identity between "God" and "spirit" entails that any other spirits that come into being will, by definition, be gods. Faith is understood to be the most elemental substance of all matter and thus the raw material out of which all physical objects are created. Moreover, words are the containers of faith and the instruments by which faith produces its material effects; therefore, by speaking faith-filled words, a god can create her or his own reality. Accordingly, God spoke the universe into being via words filled with faith, a notion that Word-Faith teachers support by a woodenly literalistic reading of Gen 1.

Second, the *imago Dei* is understood as the *imago Dei essentialis*, or comprising the same species of being as God, and not, as historically affirmed by Roman Catholic, Protestant, and Orthodox thought, the *imago Dei accidentalis*, or the imperfect and finite reflection of an ontologically superior creator. According to the Word-Faith equation of deity and spirituality, Adam* and Eve* were spirits and so "little gods," whom God gave two additional faculties for earthly survival, namely bodies for physical movement and souls for analytical thinking. During the 1980s–1990s, Word-Faith teachers frequently employed the language of "little gods," to the tune of sharp denunciation by Evangelicals. Consequently, most Word-Faith exponents have recast their anthropology in theological vocabulary acceptable to mainstream Christians. Such implicit terminology either logically or contextually necessitates that original humanity be of the same species of being as God; examples include "having the (very) nature of God," "the nature of Jesus," "the life of God," "the God-kind of life," and "the champion in you."

Third, the biblical notions of spiritual death and rebirth are construed literally as the death and revivification of the spirit, where the spirit lies dormant during the interim. With the Fall*, Word-Faith practitioners hold that Adam and Eve suffered spiritual death; they ceased to be divine and degenerated to mere body–soul humans, lacking the faculty to generate the force of faith. Hence in traducian* fashion, every human is born with all three components – body, soul, and spirit – but initially only the first two parts are alive, while the spirit is nonfunctional. By accepting Jesus as Lord and Savior, a person is "born again"; namely the spirit is reborn or brought back to life, thus restoring the person's divine status and corresponding power to speak words of faith and create material blessings, especially health*, wealth*, and prosperity. Proof texts for this position include John 10:34, Ps 82:6, and Paul's affirmations that believers are "sons and daughters of God" and "joint heirs with Jesus," which Word-Faith teachers interpret as natural lineage rather than adoption.

Word-Faith worship style encompasses praise songs (see Praise and Worship) designed for maximal physical involvement (e.g. lifting hands, dancing, glossolalia*) and "signs and wonders" (e.g. healings, "slaying in the Spirit," exorcisms*), and it largely mirrors Pentecostal/Charismatic worship. But unlike the Pentecostal/Charismatic conviction that God alone can perform miracles and inspire spiritual gifts, Word-Faith teachers insist that believers, as divine beings, are responsible for wielding the force of faith to personally effect healings and all other charismata. This "do-it-yourself" character of supernaturally creating one's own temporal advantages constitutes the thread running throughout all facets of the Word-Faith Movement, a thread reflecting the distinctly US emphases of self-empowerment and individualism. **See also PROSPERITY GOSPEL CLUSTER.**

KIRK R. MACGREGOR

Word-Flesh Christologies are characterized by the view that Jesus Christ is the divine Word incarnate, taking flesh but not a human mind or soul*, which would be superfluous. The Word takes flesh by a "natural union" analogous to the union of the rational soul with flesh in other human beings; thus Christ does not have human subjectivity. This was the predominant view after the condemnation of Paul* of Samosata, until Apollinaris* stated it in a blatant way and it was condemned.

Word of God. The expression is used in the OT for God's communication with Moses (Exod 20:1) and the prophets (in Jer, 50 times), and sometimes for creation itself (Gen 1; Ps 33:6). In the NT, it refers to Jesus' words and to the gospel that is preached by the apostles (Acts 4:31; 1 Thess 2:13; Rev 1:9). It is personified as the Word that becomes incarnate* in Jesus (John 1:1–3, 14), just as Wisdom* had been personified in the OT (Prov 8:22–31). This divine Word and Wisdom could also be linked with the cosmic Logos of the Stoics and the intelligible light of the Platonists, apprehended at least dimly by all human beings.

The last meaning became determinative in the development of the doctrine of the Trinity*, with the Word being identified with the Son, the second person of the Trinity. At first the Word was assumed to be uttered or generated when God decided to create the world; after the Council of Nicaea* (325), the Word was understood to be eternal, God's complete self-expression and self-concept, acting in the world through creation*, revelation, and redemption*.

The OT emphasis on the Word of God speaking through Moses and the prophets, augmented by the NT emphasis on God's speaking through a Son (Heb 1:1–2), led to the identification of Scripture with the Word of God, especially when Scripture was understood to have been inspired* by the Holy* Spirit. The Reformation*, with its criticism of tradition* and the authority* of the church, insisted especially on this identification; in many of the Reformed confessions* of faith, Scripture is the first topic discussed, as the source of all else that is asserted.

With the historical study of the Bible, it has become difficult to think of Scripture as identical with the Word of God; therefore, it is now more common to speak of the Bible as "containing" the Word of God or, more satisfactorily, to say that the Word of God "speaks through" the Bible. **See also LOGOS; REVELATION; SCRIPTURE.**

EUGENE TESELLE

Word-Man Christologies are characterized by the view that Jesus exists as a human being, united with the divine Word. This was the view held by Gregory* Nazianzen (after the condemnation of Apollinarianism*), the Antiochene* school, and Augustine*. Criticized as Adoptionist*, or as holding a "two Sons" doctrine, they emphasized that "the man" did not first exist and then become united with the Word, but was created by being assumed by the Word.

Worker-Priests. Some priests in France and Belgium decided (early 1940s) "to become workers among the workers" in order to overcome the gap between the Roman Catholic Church and the industrial working class. After 1945 some worker-priests joined combat organizations and Communist trade unions, leading to condemnation by the Vatican (1953–54). Thus bishops clamped down on the experiment that included about 100 priests. With the decree *Presbyterorum Ordinis* (1965), the Second Vatican* Council once again made room to connect the priestly life with the world of labor, yet under more stringent conditions. In 2000 approximately 1,000 worker-priests were active worldwide.

EMIEL LAMBERTS

World. Among the Greeks, the term *kosmos* had to do with ordering, and it could be applied both to the earth as a whole and to the broader cosmos, including the heavenly bodies. Thus the world could be viewed as God's good ordering, as the field of God's providence*, and as the basis of a natural* theology that discovers not only God's existence but also God's goodness.

The notion of "world" was sometimes limited, however, to the inhabited world, the *oikoumene*, and thus to its inhabitants and their "mundane" possessions and concerns. In the latter case, it could be associated with the negative aspects of the world, its ungodly inhabitants, and the demonic powers that rule the world (e.g. John 7:7, 14:17 and 27; 1 John 4:4–5; 1 Cor 1:21). The devil* is called the "god of this world" (2 Cor 4:4) or the "ruler of this world" (John 12:31, 14:30, 16:11).

Early Christians dealt with these negative aspects of the world in several ways. The predominant approach, shaped by the apocalyptic* tradition, anticipated that the present evil age would soon be superseded by a new age. In the meantime, God was understood to love this world, coming not to judge but to save it (John 3:16, 12:47). Paul spoke of the world as groaning in travail, awaiting transformation (Rom 8:22). For the Gnostics*, however, the world was the sinister cosmos, the result of a tragic fall from the divine realm or, as Marcion* saw it, the work of a God of rigid, unimaginative justice, so that redemption had to come from a different realm, taking the form of rescue from this world.

Early Christian spirituality*, perhaps seeing these alternative views of the world as expressions of human attitudes, tended to shift the focus inward: one can be captured by the world and its concerns, but one ought to be drawn by God's love* so that one loves God primarily and then loves everything else in relation to God (see Asceticism; Monasticism Cluster).

Christian ethics has also taken an interest in the external world, natural and social. Those who live "in the world" are concerned about the things that affect them, threaten them, and might be transformed through their actions. Christians are called to aid the victims of poverty* and disease and to end the conditions that exacerbate them. Thus there is a place for Christian "worldliness," expressed most notably in the "secular* Christianity" of Bonhoeffer* and of many thinkers in the 1960s. Worldly achievement was even given a noble face in the Protestant* ethic (developed in the 17th c.) and the Gospel of Prosperity* (20th c.). In all of this there is, of course, a temptation to succumb to human pride and self-centeredness, seeing the world as merely the theater for human activity and glorifying the achievements of human technology.

A positive evaluation of the world is found today in various types of "nature spirituality." This implication of the doctrine that God created all things good has been enhanced in the modern context by stimuli as diverse as pantheism*, increased understanding of ecosystems, and fear of ecological* disaster through nuclear war, pollution, or global warming and climate* change. Awareness of the many ways human life depends on the natural world, combined with evidence that human action might significantly endanger the planet, has led to a new sense of human responsibility for the health of the earth as a whole. Here the emphasis is not on the human race as the greatest of God's creations (one way of reading Gen 1) but on its task to "till and keep" the garden in which it has been placed by God (Gen 2:15). This "ethic of stewardship*" emphasizes responsibility before God and among human beings for the many species on earth and the ecosystems that support them. EUGENE TESELLE

World Alliance of Reformed Churches (Presbyterian and Congregational) includes 75 million Reformed Christians in more than 200 churches in about 100 countries. It consists of Reformed*, Congregational*, Presbyterian*, Waldensian*, United, and Uniting churches. It seeks to be a communion of churches joined together in Christ to promote the renewal and unity of the church and to participate in God's transformation of the world. Its member churches are rooted in the 16th-c. Reformation* of Calvin*, Zwingli*, and earlier Reformers, such as Valdes* and Hus*.

The Alliance of Reformed Churches throughout the World Holding the Presbyterian System (founded in 1875) merged in 1970 with the International Congregationalist Council (founded in 1891) to form the World Alliance of Reformed Churches, with its main office in Geneva, Switzerland.

The World Alliance of Reformed Churches has always been committed to being a platform on which its member churches can fulfill their mission as agents of transformation and justice* in society. For example, the 21st General Council (Ottawa, 1982) declared that apartheid* is a sin and its moral and theological justification a heresy*. The 22nd General Council (Seoul, 1989) affirmed the commitment to address injustices experienced by women in church and society.

The 23rd General Council (Debrecen, 1997) called on member churches to commit themselves to a process of confession concerning economic* injustice and ecological* destruction. The 24th General Council (Accra, 2004) adopted a confession stating that the integrity of believers' faith is at stake if they fail to resist the current system of neoliberal economic globalization.

The World Alliance of Reformed Churches seeks theological clarity that unites churches in their struggle for economic, ecological, and gender justice*. It has always been strongly interested in Christian unity, endorsing attempts to unite churches in particular countries and mission fields, and today engages in dialogue* with Roman Catholics, Pentecostals, Lutherans, Orthodox, and others. It has close ties with the Reformed Ecumenical Council.

In the early 2000s, its core callings included striving for justice in the economy and the earth; searching for spiritual renewal and renewal of Reformed worship; fostering communion within the Reformed family and unity of the church ecumenical; interpreting and reinterpreting the Reformed tradition and theology for contemporary witness; fostering mission in unity, mission renewal, and mission empowerment; promoting inclusivity and partnership in church and society; and enabling Reformed churches to witness for justice and peace.

In 2008 the World Alliance of Reformed Churches and the Reformed* Ecumenical Council agreed to merge (in 2010).

CLIFTON KIRKPATRICK

World Council of Churches (WCC), inaugurated in 1948 after a process of formation that began in 1938, is a fellowship of Christian churches dedicated to that unity in faith and action characteristic of the modern ecumenical movement. The WCC's inspiration is Jesus' prayer that Christians "may be one, that the world may believe" (John 17:21). Council membership includes more than 340 churches from Orthodox, Protestant, Anglican, Old Catholic, independent, and uniting traditions. The WCC cooperates with the Roman Catholic Church in various projects and through their Joint Working Group. The WCC's main offices are in Geneva, Switzerland.

The WCC traces its roots to student and lay movements of the 19th c., the 1910 Edinburgh World Missionary Conference, and a 1920 encyclical from the (Orthodox) Synod of Constantinople suggesting a "fellowship of churches" similar to the League of Nations. Predecessor bodies incorporated into the Council include international conferences on "Faith* and Order" (theology, sacraments, ordinances) and on "Life* and Work" (social ministries, international affairs, relief services), the International Missionary Council, and the Sunday* School Movement. Largely Protestant and Western in its earliest years, the WCC's profile and identity evolved during the 1960s with the influx of many Orthodox churches from the East and newly independent churches from formerly colonial regions in the South. The Second Vatican* Council improved relations between the WCC and Roman Catholics.

Two WCC projects were launched in 1946: the Ecumenical Institute for postgraduate study in Bossey, Switzerland, and the Churches' Commission on International Affairs. After World War II, the Council encouraged churches' development of ministries and continues this work among refugees*, migrants, and the poor*. During the cold war, the WCC provided a forum for East–West dialogue. The Program to Combat Racism*, although controversial, assisted in ending apartheid in Southern Africa. A landmark document, *Baptism, Eucharist, and Ministry* (1982), provided some consensus in the quest for full Christian unity.

Recent emphases of the WCC include initiatives in common prayer, mission, and evangelism; a spirituality of resistance to injustice; the solidarity of churches with women; the overcoming of violence; interfaith dialogue; advocacy concerning persons living with HIV/AIDS; the welcoming of youth leadership; and the broadening and deepening of ecumenical fellowship.

SAMUEL KOBIA

World Evangelical Alliance. See EVANGELICAL ALLIANCE.

World Evangelical Fellowship. See EVANGELICAL ALLIANCE.

World Missionary Conference (Edinburgh, 1910), precursor of the World* Council of Churches and other ecumenical endeavors, which convened 1,200 mostly Western delegates from Protestant and Anglican missionary societies. As a "field" conference led by John R. Mott* (president of the World* Student Christian Federation), it did not address doctrinal issues but the immediate problems facing missionary work. It affirmed reciprocal cooperation ("comity*") in Bible translation and in major enterprises, such as medical and educational infrastructures (hospitals, schools). The 17 Asian delegates consciously articulated, for the first time, the regional identities of Asian* Christians and resisted continuing control by their founding Western churches.

World Student Christian Federation, union of Christian student organizations founded in Vadstena, Sweden (1895), with the goals of evangelism*, deepened spiritual life, and extension of the Kingdom* of God. John Mott* became its first general secretary. Members of the Federation from the non-Western world played significant roles in the missionary conferences of Edinburgh (1910) and Jerusalem (1928). It has cooperated closely with the World* Council of Churches.

World Wide Web and Christian Theology. See POSTMODERNISM AND THEOLOGY.

Worms, Concordat of (1122), agreement between Pope Calixtus II and Emperor Henry V that resolved the investiture* controversy, setting a lasting pattern for church*–state relationships. The emperor gave up the right to invest bishops and abbots with spiritual office symbols and promised canonical elections, free of simony*. The pope gave the emperor the power to prevent the election of unacceptable candidates and to confer temporal powers on ecclesiastical representatives.

Worms, Edict of (1521), issued by the Holy Roman emperor Charles V, banned the writings of Luther* and labeled him a heretic* (he had challenged the absolute authority of the pope over the Roman Catholic Church) and enemy of the Holy* Roman Empire. Luther remained in seclusion at Wartburg castle for several years, continuing to write and translate the Bible into German; the Edict was never enforced.

WORSHIP CLUSTER

Worship
Worship in Ancient Israel
Worship in Early Christianity

See also ANGLICAN CLUSTER: ANGLICAN WORSHIP AND LITURGIES; BAPTIST CHURCHES CLUSTER: BAPTIST WORSHIP; DIVINE LITURGY OF THE ORTHODOX CHURCHES; EUCHARIST CLUSTER; LITURGIES, HISTORY OF; LORD'S SUPPER; LUTHERANISM CLUSTER: LUTHERAN WORSHIP; MASS, ROMAN CATHOLIC; MEDIA AND CHRISTIAN WORSHIP; MENNONITE WORSHIP; METHODISM CLUSTER: METHODIST WORSHIP; MORMON WORSHIP; MUSIC IN/AS WORSHIP; PENTECOSTAL WORSHIP; PRAISE AND WORSHIP; QUAKER WORSHIP; REFORMED WORSHIP; SEVENTH-DAY ADVENTIST WORSHIP

Worship. "Service of worship," a contemporary usage, preserves an ancient usage. The Hebrew *abodah Elohim* meant work or service directed to God. The Greek *latreia* means "service" (hired, thus voluntary; not slavery or servitude); *leitourgia,* "liturgy," was a Greek term for voluntary public service. The Latin *opus Dei,* coined by Benedict* of Nursia, refers to the worship of God, the "divine service." Some believe that humans are naturally inclined to worship that which powerfully affects them or is supremely valued as worthy of praise (see Holiness), which gives rise to conflicting motivations for worshipping. One's motivation is either negative, based on fear and the desire to placate powerful forces for one's benefit, or positive, based on admiration and inspiring a devotion that frames all actions. Reflecting aspects of both is motivation based on gratitude for salvation*.

Worship in Ancient Israel consisted of variegated complex practices of liturgical utterance and gesture. Much of that practice was borrowed from ancient Near Eastern culture*. Israel characteristically transposed such practices in a distinctive way to make them appropriate to the God of Israel. The purpose of such worship, in its many diverse expressions, was to create, sustain, and renew the covenant* between YHWH and Israel. The tension between generically appropriated practices and distinctive Yahwistic identity was resolved in various ways in different traditions of practice. Israel utilized praise*, prayer*, sacrifices*, festivals, and pilgrimages* that reinforced the connection between Israel and its God.

One source of that worship, known in the book of Deuteronomy*, was the regular reappropriation of the covenant of Sinai. The community heard the commands of Sinai and pledged loyalty to the God of covenant. The accent was on the distinctiveness of Israel as a people of obedience to the God of Sinai, especially obedience in the public and economic realms. This tradition culminated in the scribal movement associated with Ezra* (see Neh 8:1–8) and came to be articulated in the life of the synagogue*.

A second source of worship, known in the Book of Psalms*, was the Jerusalem Temple*, which was viewed as the epicenter of creation; there dwelled the Creator, who presided as king and judge over the affairs of the nations. This worship tradition incorporated the myth and ritual practices of the Near East, celebrated YHWH as king, and took the Davidic monarch as YHWH's regent on earth. This tradition generated the cosmic eschatological vision of both Jews and Christians.

Alongside these foundational traditions, it is plausible that worship was conducted in many settings of family* and clan; in these venues a more intimate God–people relationship was practiced.

The great prophets of Israel carried on a polemic against distorted worship (see Isa 1:12–15). That polemic was evoked when the God of the covenant was distorted in manipulative ways. Prophets and kings sought to reform worship and make it congruent with the God of the covenant. Worship of this God has been through the centuries a vigorous, subversive alternative to the dominant practices of nationalism and naturalism, for these are seen, in this tradition, to be idolatrous* and death producing. By contrast, worship of this God is known, in the tradition, to be life giving and hope* generating.

WALTER BRUEGGEMANN

Worship in Early Christianity. Liturgy* throughout the first few Christian centuries was dynamic and multifaceted, neither simple nor monolinear. Rather than a single prototype, there were multiple practices and traditions in different cultural contexts from the beginning.

There are numerous references to worship in the NT, but in many cases it is difficult to know whether a reference is merely literary or reflects actual ritual practice. Baptism* and Eucharist* are both clearly attested to, but practical details are sparse. There is a risk of anachronistically reading later practices back into the text, when the text itself provides no clear evidence of them. An example would be assuming the actual recitation in the liturgy of a Last Supper* institution* narrative or a trinitarian baptismal formula, when the texts themselves indicate no such recitation.

At first eucharistic practices varied both in the content of the meal and in prayer. Eucharistic prayers were originally orally improvised, according to various forms from Jewish meal practice. Written forms began to be set down in the 2nd c., and the subsequent addition of new elements led to differing anaphoral* structures. Similarly, it is possible that the earliest Christian communities used various initiation rites, and not always a water bath: anointing*, laying* on of hands, and foot*-washing are all noted in the NT and are found combined in later baptismal rites. The pre-Nicene period (before 325) saw two increasingly dominant models of baptismal practice and theology: a death and resurrection model (based on Rom 6) and a rebirth/baptism of Jesus model (based on John 3), centered on a prebaptismal Spirit anointing.

In the 4th c., the new relationship between church and society spurred liturgical development. Liturgy moved from a modified domestic setting into the public setting of basilicas. Stational* liturgy led to the incorporation of litanies*, processions*, and the greater use of ceremony. Prayer texts continued to be composed and redacted, often under the influence of doctrinal developments. In Christian initiation, the influx of many new members led to an expansion of the catechumenate*, both in the time it took and in the ritualization of the process. For a time, paschal* baptism became a norm in both East and West, until the later growth of normative infant* baptism. The major centers of Rome, Antioch, and Alexandria were joined by Jerusalem and Constantinople in influencing local practice elsewhere, as diverse local practices coalesced into classic liturgical families, or rites.

MAXWELL E. JOHNSON and CHRISTIAN MCCONNELL

Wrath of God. See ANGER OR WRATH OF GOD.

Wrede, William. See NEW TESTAMENT THEOLOGY.

Writings (Heb *ketubim*, "writings"; Gk *hagiographa*, "sacred writings"), third part of the Hebrew canon (Tanakh*), placed after Torah (the Law) and the Prophets. These books are Psalms*, Proverbs*, Job*, the five Megilloth* (Ruth*, Lamentations*, Song* of Songs, Ecclesiastes*, Esther*), Daniel*, 1 and 2 Chronicles*, Ezra*, and Nehemiah*.

Wyclif (Wycliffe), John (c1320–84), theologian, philosopher, priest, Oxford theologian whose reformative vision led to the first English translation of the Bible, the lay piety movement of Lollardy*, and the Hussite* Movement in Bohemia. He taught at Oxford (1350–73), served in the royal service (1371–81), and was the rector of Lutterworth, Leicestershire.

Late-14th-c. England saw tension between the crown and the Avignon papacy, the Peasants'

Rebellion in 1381, and dissatisfaction with ecclesiastical abuses. Wyclif advocated the analytical approach that made Oxford University a center for scientific and logical innovation in the period before the plague. For him Augustinian* metaphysics, while ontologically opposed to Ockham's*, involved a more thorough use of Ockhamist "modern" principles than Aquinas's* or Duns* Scotus's earlier approaches. At Oxford Wyclif wrote *Postilla*, an extensive Bible summary for student use, *De Logica*, and *Summa de Ente*.

Because of his conception of divine and human dominion, he argued that grace* determined just human dominion. Because property* ownership was caused by the Fall* and because early Christians practiced apostolic poverty*, Wyclif believed the king should divest the church of all property, ultimately supervising its material needs. While evocative of Olivi* and the Fraticelli*, Wyclif polemicized against them because of his dedication to scriptural preaching (see Scripture) and frustration with friars' abuses. His metaphysics led him to deny transubstantiation*, arguing for Christ's real presence in the sacrament without committing to the substantial change that orthodoxy demanded. His conviction that Scripture ought be available to all church members, the elect* in Augustine's strict sense, spurred him to supervise the translation of the Vulgate into Middle English.

His teachings, condemned as heresy at Constance in 1415, became the basis for the Lollard Movement and inspired Hus* and Jerome* of Prague. Wyclif's theology is more consonant with late medieval thought than with Protestantism*; it is best not to compare it to either Luther* or Anglicanism*.

STEPHEN E. LAHEY

Wycliffism. See LOLLARDY.

Xavier, Francis of (1506–52), founding member of the Society of Jesus and the first missionary to Japan. Born in the family castle of Xavier, Navarre, he studied in Paris (from 1525), where he met Ignatius* of Loyola (1529). They took vows of poverty* and celibacy* with five friends (1534), the origin of the Society of Jesus. Xavier visited Paul III in Rome (1537) to ask permission to be ordained and to make a pilgrimage to the Holy Land. He did not make the pilgrimage, but was ordained a priest in Venice. Then, commissioned by King John III of Portugal, Ignatius sent Xavier from Lisbon to the (East) Indies, where he began to evangelize (1542) in South India* and Ceylon (Sri* Lanka). When he visited Malacca (1547), he met a Japanese, Yajiro (Anjiro), and later baptized him in Goa. Accompanied by this first Japanese Christian, Xavier journeyed to Kagoshima, Japan, with Cosme de Torrès (1549).

The ruler (*daimo*) of Kagoshima and a southwestern region of Japan, Takahisa Shimazu, allowed Francis of Xavier to engage in mission work. Based at Fukushouji Temple, Kagoshima, Xavier enjoyed a good relationship with its Buddhist priest, Ninshitsu. To seek permission from the Japanese emperor and the shogun to undertake a more extensive evangelism, and to refute Buddhism at Enryakuji Temple, the stronghold of Buddhism, Xavier went to Kyoto (1551), only to find it politically and socially unstable. He went to Yamaguchi, the "Kyoto" of Western Japan, to evangelize under the aegis of the ruler, Yoshitaka Oouchi. Invited by the ruler Yoshishige Ootomo in the same year, Xavier moved back to Funai (Kyoto Province). Realizing the need to evangelize the Chinese, whose culture had long and deeply affected Japan, in order to convert the Japanese more effectively, he returned to India and from there left for China; on his way, however, he died of fever.

Xavier endeavored to adopt the language, customs, and culture* of the people among whom he worked, and this missionary method influenced subsequent missionaries (see Ricci, Matteo). He was beatified (1619) and canonized as a saint (1622, with Ignatius of Loyola) as the apostle of the Indies and of Japan, one of the greatest Roman Catholic missionaries to the East. His numerous letters have been published.

NOZOMU MIYAHIRA

Ximénez de Cisneros, Francisco (1436–1517), Spanish cardinal, archbishop of Toledo (1495–1517), who founded the University of Alcalá (1500, opened 1508) and sponsored the Complutensian* Polyglot Bible. After serving as vicar general to Cardinal Mendoza, he became an Observantine Franciscan*, subjecting himself to unusual austerities. Against his will, he was made confessor to Queen Isabella* (1492). Appointed provincial of the Franciscans (1494), he carried out a number of reforms. As archbishop of Toledo (1495), he acted as regent of Castile (1506–7), was made a cardinal and inquisitor* general (1507), and financed and led the Spanish conquest of Oran, North Africa (1509). Once again he became regent (1516), but when the successor, Charles* V, arrived from the Low Countries, Ximénez was dismissed from his position and died, possibly poisoned.

Year, Liturgical. See LITURGICAL YEAR.

Yeast. See LEAVEN.

YHWH, a transliteration of the Hebrew name of God revealed to Moses (Exod 3:14; variously translated "I am who I am," "I am that I am," "I will be what I will be") and used to designate God in many passages of the HB. According to Jewish tradition, this sacred name should not be pronounced; thus when one encounters it, one says "Adonai" (Heb for "the Lord," as one finds in many translations). Non-Jews pronounced it "Jehovah" and, more commonly today, "Yahweh." Out of respect for Jewish tradition, in which Christianity has its roots, scholars use the transliteration YHWH when no other designation for God is appropriate. **See also GOD, CHRISTIAN VIEWS OF, CLUSTER: NAMES FOR GOD IN THE BIBLE AND CHURCH TRADITIONS; TETRAGRAMMATON.**

YMCA (Young Men's Christian Association) is a worldwide Christian, ecumenical*, voluntary movement for women and men with special emphasis on, and the genuine involvement of, young people. The YMCA works for social* justice* for all people, irrespective of religion, race, gender, or cultural background. One of the largest and oldest youth movements in the world, it is present in 124 countries, with more than 45 million members.

The World Alliance of YMCAs, based in Geneva, Switzerland, represents YMCAs around the world. The first world conference (Paris, 1855) drew up the YMCA's mission statement, the "Paris Basis," making the World Alliance of YMCAs a pioneer of ecumenism*. A contemporary statement of mission, "Challenge 21" was adopted in 1998. The World Alliance has had "consultative status" with the Economic and Social Council of the United Nations since 1947.

YMCA work includes providing Christian leadership on social issues; supporting youth at risk; community empowerment; educational, recreational, and health and fitness programs; HIV/AIDS prevention and care; environmental protection; and co-coordinating disaster preparedness and response. MUSIMBI KANYORO

Young, Brigham (1801–77). Upon Joseph Smith's murder in 1844, Young, as president of the Quorum of the Twelve Apostles, was recognized as the new leader by most members of the Church of Jesus Christ of Latter-day Saints. He led the exodus of some 12,000 Mormons from Illinois to the Salt Lake valley, orchestrated the colonization of more than a hundred settlements throughout the US West, and publicly announced the doctrine of plural marriage in 1852. During his 30-year tenure, Young supervised a vast religious, political, and economic empire, coordinating the immigration of thousands of foreign converts. **See also LATTER-DAY SAINTS, CHURCH OF JESUS CHRIST OF; MORMON, BOOK OF; MORMON WORSHIP; SMITH, JOSEPH.** TERRYL GIVENS

Young Christian Workers (Jocists), Catholic Action movement for working young people, founded by Jozef Cardijn* (Brussels, 1924). It was originally an education* movement providing young workers with the tools for their social* and cultural* emancipation through an inductive, empirical method: "see–judge–act." From Belgium, the movement spread quickly, particularly after 1945, becoming a worldwide organization, the International Young Christian Workers (1957). Starting in 1960, it largely lost its social base in Europe. Internal tensions between those critical of the social structure and the more traditional wing ultimately led to a break within the organization (1986). In early 21st c., the global movement had roughly 3 million members in some 100 countries. EMIEL LAMBERTS

Yugoslavia. In the Kingdom of Serbs, Croats, and Slovenes (1918–41), renamed the Kingdom of Yugoslavia (1929), the intermingling of religious and national identities induced growing divisions between the Orthodox Serbs, Roman Catholic Croats, and Muslim Slavs. These politically manipulated ethnoreligious divisions proved to be a powerful source of rivalry and antagonism, which culminated in fratricidal interethnic and intraethnic strife during World War II. Tito's regime, which intended to create a new multinational state of South Slavs, succeeded in suppressing interethnic and interreligious conflicts without resolving them.

The initial hostility against religion and repression was gradually relaxed starting in the mid-1950s in favor of a cautious promotion of religious identities. The liberalization of official policy regarding the nationality question in Yugoslavia during the 1970s led to a heightened awareness of ethnic differences, which were de facto culturally and religiously based.

With the collapse of Communism (1990), the Yugoslav Federation broke down. Slovenia*, Croatia*, and Macedonia* declared independence (1991), and Bosnia* followed suit (1992). The remaining Serbia and Montenegro formed the "Federal Republic of Yugoslavia," renamed in 2002 "Confederate State Union of Serbia and Montenegro." The Union lasted until 2006, when Montenegro became an independent state.

In 2008 in Serbia and Montenegro, the Orthodox Church, although not a state church, enjoyed a considerable influence in the public sphere, particularly in Serbia, where it is commonly perceived as the national church. Yet the law on religion (2006) in Serbia singles out seven "traditional" religious communities: the Serbian Orthodox Church, the Roman Catholic Church, the Slovak Evangelical Church, the Reformed Christian Church, the Evangelical Christian Church, and the Islamic and the Jewish communities. The recognized groups enjoy certain privileges, like the right to teach religion in public schools; among smaller religious communities, this law imposes burdensome procedures for registration.

Interreligious relations have undergone considerable improvement since the end of the post-Communist wars, yet they are often tense. Intolerance toward minority religions and expressions of anti-Semitism* and anti-Islamic sentiments are not rare. Moreover, tensions between the Serbian Orthodox Church and the Montenegrin Orthodox Church have increased significantly since Montenegro declared independence.

After Kosovo's autonomy was abolished (1989), the Albanian Muslims (95% of the population of this province, with a small minority of Serbs) were under increasingly repressive control by the Serbs. As a consequence, the Kosovo Albanians established parallel institutions. In the aftermath of the 1998–99 war between the Albanians and Serbs, the UN Security Council placed Kosovo under transitional UN administration. In 2008 the Albanians declared Kosovo's independence from Serbia. The souring of interethnic relations had a negative impact on interreligious relations. Attacks against Orthodox religious sites have continued. The level of religious observance among Muslims in Kosovo is generally low; Orthodox Christianity and Islam are widely perceived as ethnic markers by the Serbs and Albanians, respectively.

Statistics: *Serbia*: Population (2008): 7.5 million (M). Christians, 90% (Orthodox, 84%; Roman Catholics, 4–5%; Protestants, 1–2%); Muslims, 5%.

Montenegro: Population (2008): 0.63 M. Christians, 79% (Orthodox, 74%; Roman Catholics, 4–5%; Protestants, 1–2%); Muslims, 18%.

Kosovo: Population (2008): 2 M. Muslims, 95%; Christians 4% (Roman Catholics, 3%; Protestants, 1%). (*Source*: *International Religious Freedom Report*, 2008.)

INA MERDJANOVA

YWCA (Young Women's Christian Association) began in London (1855), although the YWCA of Great Britain was actually formed in 1877 through the merger of two separate (a spiritual and a social) movements. In New York City, it was originally the Ladies Christian Association (1858). In 1894 the YWCA of England, Sweden, Norway, and the USA formed the World Young Women's Christian Association. Today the World YWCA is a global network of women and girls empowered to advocate for social* and economic* changes, peace*, justice*, human* rights, and the environment. For more than a century, the YWCA has been at the forefront in developing women's leadership in order to find local solutions to the global inequalities that women face. The YWCA is a volunteer membership movement, inclusive of women and girls from many faiths, backgrounds, and cultures. Its work is inspired by Christian principles and a commitment to women's full and equal participation in society. Each year it reaches more than 25 million women in 22,000 communities. YWCA programs provide immediate support (housing, child care, shelters, soup kitchens, day care for the elderly, home visits to AIDS patients) for people in vulnerable situations, but they also strive to change individual behavior as well as policies and laws that promote and enforce good practices. MUSIMBI KANYORO

Z

Zacchaeus, wealthy "chief tax collector" in Jericho (Luke 19:1–10). He climbed a tree to see Jesus*, who then dined at his house; during the meal, Zacchaeus promised restitution for his financial transgressions.

Zadok, descendant of Aaron*. Joint high priest with Abiathar (2 Sam 8:17), he accompanied David* and the Ark* in flight from Absalom*. During the struggle over succession (1 Kgs 1), Abiathar was discredited; Zadok anointed Solomon* and became sole high priest.

Zadokites, priests descending from Zadok. The Dead* Sea Scrolls suggest that they had an important role in the Qumran* Community.

Zairian or Congolese Rite. See CONGO, DEMOCRATIC REPUBLIC OF.

Zambia. The Christian presence in the territory of what is now Zambia dates back to 1880. David Livingstone*'s death (1873) had given a strong impetus to several missionary societies to begin evangelizing this subregion of Southern Africa. Livingstone had expressed his concern for Central Africa as a call to mission by writing (1857), "I know that in a few years I shall be cut off in that country [Africa], which is now open: do not let it be shut again! I go back to Africa to make an open path for commerce and Christianity." A Scottish missionary, Fredrick Arnot of the Plymouth* Brethren, who had been brought up alongside Livingstone's children, responded to Livingstone's challenge. Arnot worked with the Lunda of North Western province (1880) and established the Christian Mission in Many Lands. François Coillard, of the Paris Evangelical Missionary Society, similarly established the first permanent mission station in Western Zambia. The White* Fathers came to the northern part of the country (1891). Following the comity* principle, the London Missionary Society, the Primitive Methodist Church, the Dutch Reformed Church, Baptists, Pilgrim Weslyans, the Brethren in Christ, Seventh-day Adventists, and the Africa Evangelical Fellowship divided the country into mission fields. By the early 20th c., the missionaries were at work in almost all of Zambia. Pentecostals and Charismatics* became part of church life in the late 20th c. and their churches, together with the Roman Catholic Church, were the fastest growing in the country.

Evangelistic crusades, revival* meetings, and the media* have been used effectively by Pentecostal/Charismatic churches and evangelical ministries to proclaim the gospel. Catholics and mainline Protestants focus on developing social* outreach programs, although this does not mean that they fail to proclaim the gospel.

With the prevalence of HIV/AIDS, Roman Catholics have a particularly significant impact in most Zambian communities through their programs for widows, orphans, and youth. Another form of evangelism that has proved effective in Zambia is door-to-door witnessing, as practiced by Jehovah's Witnesses.

Christianity has also spread in Zambia through hospitals and schools set up by the early missions. People were attracted to Christianity through the services these institutions offered. One could say that the education* and health* care were not ends in themselves but rather avenues for spreading the gospel and gaining converts. But one could also say that these services are themselves expressions of the gospel, and as such had a lasting effect on the people who benefited from them.

The churches in Zambia have been shaped to meet the needs of a particular context, yet they remain ecumenically linked with churches from other parts of the world.

Statistics: Population (2000): 9.2 million (M). Christians, 7.5 M, 82.3% (Roman Catholics, 3 M, 33%; mainline Protestants, 2.7 M, 29%; independents and members of African Instituted Churches, 1.3 M, 14%; Seventh-day Adventists, 0.27 M, 3%; Jehovah's Witnesses, 0.27 M, 3%); African Religionists, 1.1 M, 13%; Bahai'is, 0.1 M, 1.2%; Muslims 0.09 M, 1%. (Based on *World Christian Encyclopedia*, 2001, and 2000 census.)

MULAMBYA PEGGY KABONDE

Zealots (Gk "zealous ones"; Heb *qanna'im*), designation, reported by the Jewish historian Josephus*, for a patriotic Jewish faction resisting Roman occupation, from the Maccabean revolt

(167–42 BCE) to the Jewish* revolt beginning in 66 CE and ending with the destruction of Jerusalem (70) and of Masada, the Zealot stronghold (73). The apostle Simon was called "the Zealot" (Luke 6:15; Acts 1:13; but in Matt 10:4 "the Cananaean"; cf. *qanna'im*) to distinguish him from Simon Peter*. Questions regarding the Zealots include: How were they related to apocalypticism*? In what sense did they understand themselves to be "zealous"?

Zebedee, fisherman, father of James* and John* (Mark 1:19–20, par.), possibly husband of Salome* (Matt 27:56; Mark 15:40). The "mother of the sons of Zebedee" asked that her sons sit at Jesus' right and left in his kingdom (Matt 20:20; Mark 10:35).

Zechariah, Book of, one of the Minor Prophets, encourages the acceptance of changes soon to take place, affirms the centrality of Jerusalem as a worship site for all people (1:12–16, 9:8–12), describes the cleansing and renewal of the community (5:1–11, 13:1–2), and proclaims the future arrival of a universal kingdom (8:20–23, 14:6–11).

Scholars agree that the book is arranged in two parts. Chapters 1–8 belong to the "Historical Zechariah" (a contemporary of the Book of Haggai*, although neither mentions the other) and are dated between 520 and 518 BCE, just before the Temple's dedication. Chapters 9–14, often referred to as Deutero-Zechariah, are a collection of anonymous prophecies from the early Hellenistic period, after the conquests of Alexander the Great (d323 BCE).

Zechariah exhibits a strong messianic current with apocalyptic* overtones, including night visions replete with symbols and images and an interpreting angel (1–6) and concern with the final revolution of history (9–14). Among the traditions emphasized are the crowning of a messianic ruler (6:9–15; the designation of the high priest Joshua, rather than a descendant of David, as "the branch" may reflect an increase in the importance of the priesthood after the monarchy ended), the establishment of Israel as a cultic theocracy (9–14), and the kingship of YHWH (14).

Zechariah's prophecy, especially Chaps. 9–14, was a favorite of early Christian writers. For example, Zech 9:9, with its identification of the Messiah with the poor, is prominently alluded to in Jude 9 and Matt 21:1–7. Both Jewish and Christian communities look to Zechariah to bolster their respective messianic hopes.

BETH GLAZIER-MCDONALD

Zephaniah, Book of, one of the Minor Prophets, notable for its sweeping pronouncement of doom. It opens (1:2–3) with a prediction of worldwide destruction, a poetic hyperbole. Then it details God's meting out of punishment on Judah, especially Jerusalem (1:4–2:3); the Philistines (2:4–7); Ammon and Moab (2:8–11); Ethiopia (2:12); and Nineveh/Assyria (2:13–15). It depicts once again the punishment and restitution of Jerusalem (3:1–13), then God's defense of Jerusalem in the future (3:14–20).

Zephaniah flourished during the reign of King Josiah (640–609 BCE), predicting the downfall of Nineveh (612), Assyria (605), and other nations surrounding Judah. His book also predicts the downfall of Judah and Jerusalem, which occurred in 597/86, and their restoration. At least 3:14–20 was added after the Exile had ended (539).

The book utilizes the concept of the Day of the Lord, the day when God's enemies (the surrounding peoples just mentioned) would be punished. The book also draws on the tradition of God's residing in the Temple* in Jerusalem.

The tension between these traditions is resolved by including Jerusalem/Judah among those whose sins* deserved God's wrath*, but then envisioning a new day when God would bring home exiles (3:20), dwell in their midst (3:17), and protect God's people (3:18–19).

The book inveighs against religious syncretism* (1:8), dishonest business practices (1:11), and complacency in the midst of human want (1:12–13). PAUL L. REDDITT

Zimbabwe. Zimbabwe's first contact with Christianity was the arrival of Gonçalo Da Silveira, a Jesuit* priest, at Negomo Mupunzagutu's court (1560). His easy access to the young emperor after his baptism and that of his mother threatened Muslim traders and Shona diviners, who spread rumors that Da Silveira was a spy for the Portuguese government, resulting in Da Silveira's death only a few months later. Halfhearted missionary efforts by fellow Jesuits and Dominicans* followed. No trace of Christian activity has been found in the Mutapa Empire and the Zambezia region after 1759, when the Duke of Pombal called off the missionary work of the Jesuit order in Portugal and its colonies.

During the second phase of Christian mission (late 19th c.), the London Missionary Society founded missions in the Ndebele kingdom (in Inyathi and Hope Fountain, among other places). The Dombodema mission, led by Thomas M. Thomas, who decided to work independently of the London Missionary Society, was more successful, registering the first 12 converts (and the first Christian marriage, 1882), before the Ndebele kingdom fell into the hands of the British South Africa Company (1893). Jesuit missionaries went back to Zimbabwe via South Africa, without any notable results between 1879 and 1899, when they left Zimbabwe (Fr. Peter Prestage was the last to leave). While this second phase of mission was largely a failure, it created a foundation for future mission in colonial Zimbabwe.

The third phase of Christian mission was linked with the colonization of Mashonaland (1890) by the British South African Company, viewed as a providential opportunity to evangelize the Shona peoples by many Protestant missionary societies and Roman Catholic religious orders. After the fall of King Lobengula in 1893, the Zimbabwean religious landscape became characterized by a concerted and unmitigated thrust toward Christianization. The Catholic Church divided the country among its religious orders – a division that has shaped the current diocesan structures. The scramble for Zimbabwe by Protestant mission societies – including Anglican, Methodist (British, US, and Free), the Salvation* Army, Presbyterian, Dutch Reformed, Lutheran, Congregational, United Church of Christ, and Baptist – was regulated through the comity* principle.

The Roman Catholic and Protestant churches have in most instances given birth to autonomous local churches that constitute mainstream Christianity in Zimbabwe – in contrast to the African Instituted Churches (AICs) and the more recent and often fractious Pentecostal* and Charismatic* churches.

The current state of affairs reflects the rapid growth in membership of AICs and Pentecostal and Charismatic churches, which far surpasses those of the "mainline" churches. Both Zionist and Ethiopian AICs have developed a less antagonistic approach to African* Religion and the African worldview. For instance, Pentecostal and Charismatic churches tend to focus more and more on assisting their members in transitioning from traditional society to a modern Western culture and ethos. Thus the AICs have been very successful among the poor, among uneducated, elderly urbanites, and within rural populations, while the Pentecostals and Charismatics have been equally successful among the educated elites and young urbanites.

The Christian churches have been at the forefront of the struggle to free the African people from myriad oppressive forces. Such forces range from ignorance, colonial and racial oppression, patriarchal domination, to postcolonial oppression. Through their schools, health services, social welfare institutions, and civic awareness, backed by a robust prophetic ministry, the Christian churches have to a large extent managed to establish an inculturated* gospel and its values in Zimbabwean society. Some of the Christian prophets include John White (Wesleyan Methodist), Arthur S. Cripps (Anglican), Bishop Ralph Dodge (United Methodist), Bishop Donal R. Lamont (Roman Catholic), and Archbishop Pius Ncube (Roman Catholic). There have also been martyrs, such as Bernard Mizeki, Modumeli Moleli, James Anta, and unsung "saintly souls" who inspired faith among many, including John Bradburne, Rev. Matthew Rusike, and Mrs. Elizabeth Musodzi Ayema. Yet despite their efforts, the churches were powerless to prevent the social* (including HIV/AIDS), economic*, and political* crisis that tragically reduced the life expectancy of Zimbabweans to about 40 years (2007 estimate).

Statistics: Population (2000): 11.67 million (M). Christians, 7.88 M, 68% (members of AICs and independent Pentecostals/Charismatics, 4.7 M; Protestants, 1.4 M; Roman Catholics, 1.1 M; Anglicans, 320,000); African Religionists, 3.5 M, 30%; nonreligious, 0.1 M; 1%. (Based on *World Christian Encyclopedia*, 2001.)

PAUL H. GUNDANI

Zinzendorf, Nicholas Ludwig Graf von (1700–60), theologian, hymn writer, renewer of the Moravian* Church. Influenced by Francke* and Spener*, Zinzendorf attempted to reconcile Pietism*, Lutheran orthodoxy, and Enlightenment* thought. His Christocentric "theology of the heart" emphasized religious experience in addition to doctrinal clarity. He welcomed refugee members of the Bohemian* Brethren (1722), who built the village of Herrnhut on his estate in Saxony, from which he sent them out as missionaries (1732) as he developed the concept of "the whole church in mission." He sought to organize the "Congregation of God in the Spirit" among German-speaking Protestants in Pennsylvania (1742), which despite its failure provided a vision of what an ecumenical movement could accomplish.

OTTO DREYDOPPEL, JR.

Zion, a name for parts of Jerusalem*, serves as a metaphor for God's people. Sometimes called the "city of David" (2 Sam 5:7; 1 Kgs 8:1), Zion is the place where God is enthroned (Ps 9:11), God's dwelling place (Ps 76:2; Isa 8:18), God's holy hill (Joel 3:17), and the place where God shines forth (Ps 50:2). Jesus' triumphant entry into Jerusalem fulfills OT prophecies, demonstrating that he is the Davidic king of Zion (Matt 21:1–11; John 12:12–19; cf. Zech 9:9). Like God (Mic 4:7; Isa 24:23), Christ will rule forever at Mount Zion, where the Lamb will stand with the 144,000 (Rev 14:1). Consequently, "Zion" is often included in the names of independent churches, e.g. the Zion Christian Church, a major African* Instituted Church.

JEFFRY C. DAVIS

Zipporah, Midianite wife of Moses and the daughter of a Midianite priest. Zipporah and her six sisters first encountered Moses when he defended their access to a well (Exod 2:16–22). She is best remembered for her spontaneous circumcision of their son, which mysteriously saved Moses from God's equally mysterious efforts to kill him (Exod 4:24–26).

NICOLE WILKINSON DURAN

Zumarraga, Juan de (1468–1548), Franciscan priest; first archbishop of Mexico (1546). He introduced the printing press in Mexico and was instrumental in founding schools, including Holy Cross de Tlatelolco and San Juan de Letran, and a university, Universidad Real y Pontificia. It was while he was a bishop that the tradition centered on the apparitions of the Guadalupe arose (1531; see Mary, the Virgin, of Guadalupe).

MARÍA ALICIA PUENTE LUTTEROTH and ELIZABETH JUDD

Zwingli, Huldrych (Ulrich) (1484–1531), Swiss humanist, theologian, founder of Reformed* Protestantism, Reformer of Zurich (1522–25). Studied at the universities of Vienna and Basel, was ordained a priest (1506), served as pastor in Zurich (1519 until his death), died in the battle of Kappel against Swiss Roman Catholics.

In 1520 Zwingli abandoned his Erasmian* view of the freedom* of the will* and embraced an evangelical understanding of human nature and the necessity of divine grace* for salvation*. Under his leadership, Zurich became a Reformed city when the government instituted the Reformed Eucharist* to replace the Mass* (1525).

Zwingli developed four doctrines that became emblematic of Reformed Protestantism. (1) His emphasis on salvation through faith in Christ was close to Luther's* doctrine. (2) His teaching that the Eucharist* is a memorial of Christ was contrary to Luther's doctrine of the real presence. The two Reformers could not make peace over the Eucharist even during a personal meeting in Marburg (1529). (3) Zwingli's teaching that the moral law* is the revelation of God's eternal will also ran counter to Luther's doctrine. (4) In opposition to the Anabaptists*, Zwingli taught that infant baptism* is the sacrament* of the new covenant. This was the genesis of Bullinger's* Reformed covenant* theology.

J. WAYNE BAKER